THE NEW CAMBRIDGE EDITION

A Revision of the Cambridge Edition
Edited by William Allan Neilson

The Complete Plays and Poems of

WILLIAM SHAKESPEARE

A NEW TEXT EDITED WITH
INTRODUCTION AND NOTES

BY

WILLIAM ALLAN NEILSON
LATE OF SMITH COLLEGE

AND CHARLES JARVIS HILL
PROFESSOR OF ENGLISH
SMITH COLLEGE

HOUGHTON MIFFLIN COMPANY
The Riverside Press Cambridge

The Riverside Press
CAMBRIDGE · MASSACHUSETTS
PRINTED IN THE U.S.A.

PREFACE

THE CONTENTS of the present volume are based on those of *The Complete Works of William Shakespeare* originally published in the series known as "The Cambridge Poets" in 1906; but both text and apparatus have undergone so thorough a revision as to constitute what is virtually a new book. The text has been collated anew with the early Quartos and the First Folio, the punctuation has been revised, notes both textual and explanatory have been placed at the foot of the page instead of being printed at the end of the volume in an appendix and glossary, and the Introductions, besides being brought into accord with the results of recent scholarship, have been considerably expanded by fuller critical discussion.

The fundamental principles and methods governing the treatment of the text have remained the same but have been applied more consistently, and many inadvertent lapses have been corrected. As before, the choice of the old text used as a basis has been dictated by the considerations relevant to each play, and in the special introductions the grounds for the choice between the Folio and a Quarto are set forth. Stage directions, if modern, are enclosed in [brackets]; when they are substantially those of editions not later than 1623, they are unbracketed, or are set aside by a single bracket only, or, when occurring within a line, are enclosed in (parentheses). In the dialogue, when the text of a play is based on, say, that of the First Folio, and passages absent from the Folio are supplied from a Quarto, such passages are also bracketed. Readings which are due to modern conjecture are similarly marked, and the displaced reading is recorded in the Notes.

Since the publication of the edition of 1906 certain scholars have argued that there can be found in the old editions evidences of a so-called "dramatic punctuation." This punctuation, if it exists, is subject to so many exceptions that the rule is hard to discern, and its reproduction in a modern edition would be hopelessly misleading. A study of the original editions makes it manifest that their punctuation is chiefly the work of the compositors of whom there were many, and these were consistent neither with themselves nor with one another. We have, therefore, repunctuated frankly throughout according to modern usage, gaining, it is hoped, a considerable advantage in clearness without any sacrifice of author-

ity. The use of the apostrophe has raised some difficult and interesting points, the
consideration of which has resulted in a decision of some importance.   In spite of
the comparative carelessness of the printing of the First Folio, it has been found
that there is clearly discernible a somewhat remarkable consistency in the insertion
or omission of the *e* of *ed* endings.   To the practice of the early editions in this regard, therefore, the same respect has been shown as in the case of the text in general; i.e., the original has been departed from only when it seemed fair to believe
that there was a mistake of the copyist or printer.   The result is that the *ed* is
printed, and was apparently sounded, much more frequently than we are accustomed to see and hear it.   In many cases where no new syllable is added to the
line, this preservation of the full ending points to a different elision from that usually made, *threat'ned*, for example, instead of *threaten'd*.   This often leads to a distinct gain in sonority, and sometimes to a marked change in rhythm.   The practice of the early editions is exceptional in the case of monosyllables in *ied*, being
on the whole against the use of the apostrophe; so in such cases we have preserved
the *e* even when not syllabic, representing, for example, the Folio *dyde* by *died* rather
than by the somewhat misleading *di'd*.   Attention has also been paid to the frequent elisions and contractions of the old texts, such as *th'* for *the*, *o'* for *on* or *of*, *t'*
for *to*, and *i'* for *in*, since these have often no inconsiderable effect on the rhythm.

In order to make easy the use of the present volume in connection with such
standard works of reference as Bartlett's *Concordance*, the line-numbering of the
Globe edition has been adhered to, with these differences, that the lines are num-
bered in fives instead of in tens, and the numbering is carried through the prose as
well as the verse.

Scholarly opinion on the dates of the dramas has now reached such a degree of
harmony as to suggest the arranging of the plays in chronological order, according
to the approximate date of composition.   The Folio division into Comedies, Histories, and Tragedies has, however, been preserved; the chronological order being
adopted in the case of the Comedies and Tragedies, while for obvious reasons the
Histories have been retained in their historical sequence.

The tasks of collation, annotation, and interpretation have been shared by the
two editors of the present revision, and for whatever merits or shortcomings it
may possess they are jointly responsible.

WILLIAM A. NEILSON

CHARLES J. HILL

NORTHAMPTON, MASSACHUSETTS

CONTENTS

Comedies

Histories

Tragedies

Poems

INTRODUCTION

I. LIFE OF SHAKESPEARE

THE NAME OF SHAKESPEARE was of wide and frequent occurrence in the midlands of England in the sixteenth and preceding centuries; and this fact, along with the scarcity of exact documentary evidence, makes even the immediate ancestry of the dramatist a matter of less than absolute certainty. But there is no reason to doubt that he was the son of one John Shakespeare, a glover and dealer in agricultural produce, who at the time of William's birth was a person of increasing importance in the town of Stratford-on-Avon in Warwickshire. John Shakespeare's wife was Mary Arden, the youngest daughter of Robert Arden, a substantial farmer and landowner of Wilmcote, near Stratford. Their first son and third child, William, was baptized on April 26, 1564, the exact date of his birth being unrecorded. The history of his childhood is purely a matter of inference. He would naturally enter, as Rowe says he did, the grammar school of his native town, since he was entitled to free education there; and from what is known of the usual curricula of such schools at that period it is to be supposed that his studies were chiefly in Latin grammar and literature. Four years after the poet's birth, John Shakespeare had reached the most honorable municipal office, that of High Bailiff; but after 1572 there are signs that his fortunes had begun to decline. He absented himself from the meetings of the town council, and was deprived of office; and the nature of his financial transactions indicates that he was sinking deeply into debt. He may have withdrawn his son from school to aid him in business; for Aubrey, who died in 1697, says of the poet, "I have been told heretofore by some of the neighbours that when he was a boy he exercised his father's trade," which, according to this antiquary, was that of a butcher. Aubrey adds the two often-quoted statements: "When he kill'd a calf, he would doe it in a high style and make a speech. There was at that time another butcher's son in this towne, that was held not at all inferior to him for a naturall witt, his acquaintance, and coetanean, but dyed young."

The only additional information we have regarding Shakespeare's early years in Stratford pertains to his marriage, which took place when he was in his nineteenth year. No record of the actual ceremony has been found, but the date is approximately fixed by a document in the registry of the diocese of Worcester, dated November 28, 1582, in which two Stratford farmers gave bonds to free the bishop of responsibility in case of the subsequent discovery of any impediment rendering invalid the prospective marriage of William Shakespeare to Anne Hathaway. This Anne Hathaway is usually identified with Agnes, daughter of Richard Hathaway, a farmer of Shottery, in the parish of Stratford; and from the inscription on her tombstone it appears that she was eight years older than her husband. On May 26, 1583, the Stratford Registers record the baptism of "Susanna, daughter to William Shakspere;" and in February, 1584, the baptism of "Hamnet and Judeth sonne and daughter to William Shakspere." These few facts comprise all that is certainly known about Shakespeare's life before his removal to London; but mention may be made of two interesting traditions. Aubrey reports, "Though as Ben Johnson sayes of him, that he had but little Latine and lesse Greek; He understood Latine pretty well: for he had been in his younger yeares a Schoolmaster in the Countrey." The other tradition is thus recorded by Rowe in 1709: "He had, by a misfortune common enough to young fellows, fallen into ill company; and amongst them, some that made a frequent practice of Deer-stealing engag'd him with them more than once in robbing a Park that belong'd to Sir *Thomas Lucy* of *Cherlecot*, near *Stratford*. For this he was prosecuted by that gentleman, as he thought, somewhat too severely; and in order to revenge that ill usage, he made a ballad upon him. And tho' this, probably the first essay of his Poetry, be lost, yet it is said to have been so very bitter, that it redoubled the prosecution against him to that degree, that he was oblig'd to leave his business and family in *Warwickshire*, for some time, and shelter himself in *London*." This exploit is recorded also by Archdeacon Davies of Saperton in Gloucestershire in the latter part of the seventeenth century, and corroboration of a different kind is found in the supposed allusion to Lucy and his coat of arms in the "dozen white luces" on Shallow's "old coat" in *The Merry*

Wives of Windsor, I.i.1–23. Unfortunately for the credibility of the legend, it now appears that Sir Thomas Lucy did not own a deer park, and that, if he had, the poaching of deer was an offence against the Crown, not the local landowner. Belief in a germ of truth in the tradition, moreover, does not carry with it the necessity of supposing that Shakespeare's migration to London was due to Lucy's persecution. Interest in the stage, with which he seems to have become connected soon after his arrival in the metropolis, may have begun before he left home. While he was still a small boy, the actors of the Queen's Company and of the Earl of Worcester's Company were officially received in Stratford by his father as High Bailiff; and four companies visited the town in 1587. Those who place his removal as late as 1587 do so chiefly in order to find in the visit of the theatrical companies in that year a possible motive and occasion for the change.

The circumstances and occupation of Shakespeare on his first arrival in London are as uncertain as the date and cause of his leaving Stratford. Various late traditions unite in assigning to him some humble office in connection with the theatre, that of his holding horses outside the door being first printed in 1753. It is known, however, that by 1592 he had achieved considerable reputation as an actor and had begun to write. The company of which he was early a member, and to which he belonged during the greater part, if not the whole, of his career, was that known successively as the Earl of Leicester's (–1588), Lord Strange's (1588–92), Lord Derby's (1592–94), the Lord Chamberlain's (1594–July, 1596), Lord Hunsdon's (July, 1596–March, 1597), the Lord Chamberlain's (1597–1603), and finally, His Majesty's (1603–). Of the two playhouses in London at the beginning of his career, The Theatre is the one in which his later associations make it probable that he first acted. Others in which this company performed were The Rose, Newington Butts, The Curtain, and, after 1599, The Globe. It is doubtful whether Shakespeare was often on the stage after his company began to occupy The Blackfriars about Christmas, 1609. To these must be added the scenes of the performances given in many provincial towns while the company was touring, from Dover to Bristol and from Richmond to Coventry. There is no satisfactory evidence that Shakespeare ever accompanied any of the English actors who performed in Scotland or on the Continent, or, indeed, that he was ever out of England at all. As to his skill as an actor, Chettle stated in 1592 that he was "exelent in the qualitie he professes," and a later report, recorded by Aubrey, says that he acted "exceedingly well." His name ranks high in the actors' lists of his time; he played in Jonson's *Every Man in his Humour* and *Sejanus*; and tradition associates his name with the parts of the Ghost in *Hamlet* and of Adam in *As You Like It*, neither character, it must be allowed, being one likely to be assigned to the leading performer. That he had thought deeply and wisely on the purpose and methods of theatrical art is proved by the speech of Hamlet to the players.

As early as 1592, Shakespeare's success in theatrical matters was sufficiently marked to call forth an envious attack from Robert Greene, who died in September of that year. Addressing his fellow playwrights, Greene speaks of the actors as "those Puppets ... that spake from our mouths; those Anticks garnisht in our colours. Is it not strange that I, to whom they all haue beene beholding: is it not like that you, to whome they all haue beene beholding, shall (were yee in that case as I am now) bee both at once of them forsaken? Yes trust them not: for there is an vpstart Crow, beautified with our feathers, that with his *Tygers hart wrapt in a Players hyde*, supposes he is as well able to bombast out a blanke verse as the best of you: and beeing an absolute *Iohannes fac totum*, is in his owne conceit the onely Shake-scene in a countrey.... Let those apes imitate your past excellence, and neuer more acquaint them with your admired inuentions; ... for it is pittie men of such rare wits should be subiect to the pleasures of such rude groomes." The words italicized are a parody on the line, "O tiger's heart wrapt in a woman's hide!" which occurs in both *The True Tragedie of Richard Duke of Yorke* and *3 Henry VI*, I.iv.137; and the wordplay in "Shake-scene" confirms the interpretation which finds in the passage a denunciation of Shakespeare, who had incurred Greene's special ill-will as a dramatist as well as an actor. *A Groats-worth of Witte bought with a Million of Repentance*, in which the passage occurs, was published after Greene's death by Henry Chettle, who in December of the same year issued an apology in the prefatory address to his own *Kind-Harts Dreame*. "I am as sory," he says, and he is understood to be speaking of Shakespeare, "as if the originall fault had beene my fault, because myselfe haue seene his demeanor no lesse ciuill than he excelent in the qualitie he professes: Besides, diuers of worship haue reported his vprightnes of dealing, which argues his honesty, and his facetious grace in writting, that aprooues his Art."

We thus find Shakespeare at the age of twenty-eight a person of some importance in theatrical circles, and recognized as a man to be reckoned with both as actor and as writer. In the two following years his versatility showed itself still farther in the publication of the highly popular *Venus and Adonis* and *Lucrece*; and the suggestion of good relations with men of rank contained in Chettle's phrase, "divers of worship," is made more definite by the terms of the dedications of these poems to the Earl of Southampton. The history of his next few years is mainly contained in the list of the dramas he produced; but there are other evidences of steady progress in fortune and repute. Already in 1594 he had been summoned to play before the Queen along with the most distinguished actors of the day; and from 1595 till long after his death, appeared a series of publications, poems as well as plays, with which he had nothing to do, but to which unscrupulous publishers attached his name or initials, thus testifying to the market-value of his reputation.

Meantime, in Stratford, his father's affairs were going from bad to worse, until in 1596 the stopping of all actions for debt suggests that the dramatist had returned and restored the family fortunes. In August of that year his only son Hamnet died. In that year, too, an attempt to increase the family prestige was made in the name of John Shakespeare, though probably on the initiative of the poet, by applying to the College of Heralds for the grant of a coat of arms. Two drafts of such a grant are extant dated 1596, assigning to John Shakespeare a shield described thus: "Gould on a Bend Sable a Speare of the first, steeled, argent; and for his creast or cognizaunce a falcon, his winges displayed Argent, standing on a wrethe of his coullors, supporting a Speare Gould steeled as aforesaid, sett vppon a healmett with mantelles and tasselles as hath ben accustomed." The grant does not seem to have been issued at this time; but three years later an application was made for an "exemplification" of the coat, the previous right to wear it being taken for granted. This application was successful, and the Shakespeares were henceforth regarded as entitled to the style of "gentlemen." A more substantial evidence of the improved status of the family was afforded in 1597, when the dramatist bought and repaired New Place, then the largest house in Stratford. He did not, however, take up his permanent residence there till several years later. Various other legal and financial transactions indicate that he had come to be regarded as a man of substance; and his profession was sufficiently remunerative easily to account for this. It has been reckoned that his income as an actor must have averaged before the end of the century about £130 a year, and to this must be added about £20 annually from his plays. After The Globe was built in 1599 he became a shareholder, and the profits from this source are likely to have more than doubled his income. Gifts from patrons were not uncommon, and there may be some ground for the tradition handed down by Rowe from D'Avenant,

that Shakespeare received from Southampton the gift of £1000, though the amount stated seems incredibly large. Money is usually reckoned to have had at that period from five to eight times its present purchasing power; but the difficulty of determining this with certainty, and the fragmentary and inconclusive nature of the bases of our information as to the financial side of the Elizabethan theatre, make it necessary to receive with caution the results of the calculations that have been made of Shakespeare's gains. There is no doubt, however, that he was an extremely successful man, that his affairs were conducted with much practical sense and shrewdness, and that he died rich. In his will he left £350 in money, with a considerable amount of real estate and other property. There is in his life, certainly, no evidence that he shared the alleged incapacity of men of imaginative genius for practical affairs.

Along with this material prosperity, Shakespeare gained steadily in literary reputation. As early as 1598, Francis Meres, in his *Palladis Tamia or Wit's Treasury*, wrote "A Comparative Discourse of our English Poets with Greek, Latin, and Italian Poets;" and here he awards the highest praise to Shakespeare as both poet and playwright. "As the soule of *Euphorbus* was thought to liue in *Pythagoras*: so the sweete wittie soule of *Ouid* liues in mellifluous and hony-tongued *Shakespeare*, witnes his *Venus and Adonis*, his *Lucrece*, his sugred Sonnets among his priuate friends, etc. As *Plautus* and *Seneca* are accounted the best for Comedy and Tragedy among the Latines: so *Shakespeare* among ye English is the most excellent in both kinds for the stage; for Comedy, witnes his *Gentlemen of Verona*, his *Errors*, his *Loue labors lost*, his *Loue labours wonne*, his *Midsummers night dreame*, and his *Merchant of Venice*; for tragedy, his *Richard the 2.*, *Richard the 3.*, *Henry the 4.*, *King Iohn*, *Titus Andronicus*, and his *Romeo and Iuliet*. As *Epius Stolo* said that the Muses would speake with *Plautus* tongue, if they would speake Latin, so I say that the Muses would speake with *Shakespeares* fine filed phrase, if they would speake English."

References by his literary contemporaries are fairly numerous, and are in general in this enthusiastic vein. Allusions to his personality reflect a kindly feeling in the speakers, and indicate a genial disposition in the poet, with a love of wit and good fellowship. Legendary gossip suggesting occasional extreme conviviality need not be taken too seriously, and probably implies nothing more than a fondness for making merry with his friends.

The documentary records of the later years of Shakespeare's life are concerned chiefly with lawsuits and the investment of money. They are of interest chiefly as showing in Shakespeare some of his father's tendency to litigiousness, and that carefulness of his pecuniary interests already referred to. His father died in 1601; his mother in 1608. He was not a shareholder in any of the London theatres at his death, and it is not known when he sold out; but it is conjectured that about 1611 he disposed of these interests and retired to Stratford to enjoy his means in leisure. On April 23, 1616, he died, and two days later was buried beneath the chancel of Stratford Church according to a right acquired as part-owner of the tithes. Within seven years of his death an elaborate monument to his memory was placed in the wall of the church, and in it a colored portrait bust, which has been more than once repainted. The only well-authenticated portrait is the engraving by Martin Droeshout prefixed to the Folio editions of the plays, and this is far from lifelike. It is supposed that Droeshout worked from a painting, but there is yet no general agreement as to which, if any, of the existing claimants was his original. Two seem to have stronger support than the others, that sometimes known as the "Flower Portrait," now hanging in the Memorial Picture Gallery at Stratford; and the "Ely Palace Portrait," now in the possession of the Birthplace Trustees. The former of these is reproduced as the frontispiece to the present volume. Pretended portraits have been fabricated without number, and even those to which no suspicion of fraud attaches, with the one exception of the Droeshout engraving, lack a sufficient pedigree.

Of Shakespeare's immediate family there survived him his wife, his two daughters, and one brother. Mrs. Shakespeare lived till August 6, 1623, dying three months before the publication of the great collected edition of her husband's works known as the First Folio. The elder daughter, Susanna, married Dr. John Hall, and died in 1649, leaving one child, Elizabeth. This Elizabeth Hall, later Mrs. Thomas Nash, and still later Lady Barnard, died in 1670 without issue. The younger daughter, who married Thomas Quiney of Stratford, died in 1662, having outlived her three sons. Lady Barnard was thus the last surviving descendant of the poet. Descendants of his sister Joan, who married William Hart, are still living in England, Australia, and the United States.

II. CHRONOLOGY

The chronology of the works of Shakespeare is, except in the case of the two long poems and a few plays, the result of inferences of varying degrees of certitude. Four main divisions are generally recognized, and each of them has a fairly distinctive content. The first stretches from the undated beginnings of his work as a dramatist till about 1594,

and it contains probably a greater variety of kinds of production than any other. It is no mere guess work to call this a period of experiment. Besides the poems, we find in it representatives of all three kinds of drama then in vogue, Comedy, History, and Tragedy. For whatever reason, he seems after these experiments to have laid aside Tragedy for a time except, perhaps, for the uncertainly dated *Romeo and Juliet*, to take it up again after he had mastered the more technical elements of his art, and had a larger experience of life on which to draw.

In History he may have begun with the revision of the work of others; and when he constructed plays for himself he was clearly under the influence of Marlowe. In *Richard III*, conception of theme and manipulation of character are alike Marlowesque; and both in that play and in *King John* the echo of the "mighty line" of Marlowe is clearly discernible in the versification.

In Comedy the lines of experiment are drawn with singular clearness. In *The Two Gentlemen of Verona* he shows already his interest in the problem of characterization, and in the contrasts of Proteus with Valentine and Julia with Silvia he employs a method of which he was to avail himself again and again. In *The Comedy of Errors* he is concerned mainly with the manipulation of plot and situation, finding his model in the Latin Comedy and contenting himself, as Plautus did, with a treatment of character typical rather than individual. *Love's Labour's Lost* is a playful burlesque upon current fashions, and it derives its interest mainly from its clever dialogue and ingenious playing with language, characterization and plot being alike slight. Of the plays of this period, *The Two Gentlemen* most clearly lays down the lines on which he was first to create masterpieces.

The period from 1595 to 1601 is mainly occupied with Comedy, and the Histories written in this period are more than leavened with Comedy. *Henry IV*, though its serious plot is filled with war and rebellion, owed its popularity to the comic elements centering in Falstaff, and constituting about half of the scenes. *Henry V* is free from any note of tragedy. From *A Midsummer-Night's Dream* to *Twelfth Night* we have a succession of plays of unexampled brilliance, surpassing in structure and dialogue anything that had hitherto been produced on the English stage, and in the creation of character still unrivalled. Touches of seriousness undoubtedly occur in these plays. Again and again, in the midst of the love-in-idleness with which they are chiefly occupied, we are reminded of the real business of life presently to be taken up; not infrequently the humor is mingled with pathos or grave reflection; sometimes the folly of Claudio or the fate of Shylock brings us perilously near the brink of tragedy. Yet all this does not invalidate the statement that the temper of the plays written in the last six years of the century is prevailingly that of Comedy.

Equally undeniable are the change of temper and change of theme after 1601. The intrusion of *Troilus and Cressida, Measure for Measure,* and *All's Well that Ends Well* among the great Tragedies cannot be regarded as an objection to the calling of this the tragic period, since their presence serves in no degree to lighten the gloom. It is clear that for eight or nine years Shakespeare's dominant artistic interest was tragic; that is, he was immersed in the problem of presenting dramatically the results of certain elements of weakness and vice in human character.

About 1610 the tone changes once more. In the so-called Dramatic Romances we continue to see pictured the suffering brought about by sin and weakness; but the colors used are less sombre, and in the end the evil men turn from their ways and live. The dominant characters are men of good will, and the motto of the group is Prospero's saying, "The rarer action is in virtue than in vengeance."

All this has often been summed up before; and it is done here once more partly to gather and make more significant the chronological details scattered through the special introductions, partly to make intelligible the standing discussion as to whether from this arrangement of Shakespeare's literary activity there can be drawn evidence as to his emotional and spiritual history. The meaning of the experimental period will hardly be disputed. The collaborated and revised plays show that Shakespeare at the beginning of his career was glad to take what work was given him to do; and the original plays show him trying his hand upon all the chief dramatic types in vogue. His *Venus and Adonis* and *Lucrece* are only further instances of this versatility and curiosity. Prevailing emotional mood of any distinctive kind in this first period there is none.

With the three later divisions the case is very different. Here the temptation is obvious to interpret them respectively as periods of sunshine, gloom, and placidity in the dramatist's life. Up to a certain point this interpretation need not be quarrelled with. There is an appropriateness to the prime of life in the creation of the buoyant personalities of the Comedies and in the triumphant extrication of them from all the tangle of opposing forces invented only to be foiled. The profundity of reflection and the brooding on the mystery of life, of which the Tragedies give abundant evidence, were only possible, in the degree in which we find them, to a man who had already lived and seen

much. It is hardly possible to refrain from associating the victories of good over evil in the Dramatic Romances with a mood natural to a sane spirit contemplating near the close of his career a world which had brought to him in large measure the things for which he had mainly striven. But it is easy to press this method too far. The succession of the various kinds of drama in Shakespeare's production bears a suggestive relation to what appears to have been the popular demand of the time; and if Tragedy was in vogue at a period when Shakespeare was ripe for writing it, then the world was fortunate in the coincidence. Yet the fact of this and similar coincidences should serve to guard us against supposing that the tone of the Tragedies is necessarily a reflection of gloom or pessimism in Shakespeare's soul. Great imaginative creation is, indeed, but rarely the outcome of experience immediately contemporary. Wordsworth's description of poetry as "emotion recollected in tranquillity," though not a universal formula, is most frequently a true account, and ought in itself to caution us against the dogmatism that is based on the assumption that in drama and sonnet alike "Shakespeare unlocked his heart" and left the door ajar for all the world to see. If we are to find in the poet's work a record, not perhaps of his experience, but of his attitude toward human life and human nature, it must be by methods more subtle and cautious than are implied in the kind of inference we are discussing.

III. SHAKESPEARE'S OPPORTUNITY

The height of Shakespeare's preëminence has frequently led to a manner of speaking which sets him apart from his kind as something abnormal and unaccountable. Without entering into a discussion of the natural history of genius, it is desirable to recount those factors in his age and environment which explain many of his characteristics, even if they do not account for the magnitude of his achievement. For that achievement is of a range and quality so stupendous that it required for its accomplishment the highest degree of coincidence between the hour and the man.

The hour was, indeed, the most propitious that had occurred in the history of England. After the long controversies of the Reformation the country was for the time enjoying a comparative truce among warring sects. This truce was partly induced by the necessity of the nation's presenting a united front against the hostility of Spain; and the period of peril had been succeeded by a mood of exhilaration that resulted naturally from the escape from a formidable danger, and the opening up of a national future of untold possibilities of expansion

APPROXIMATE DATES OF COMPOSITION OF SHAKESPEARE'S PLAYS

	Comedies	Histories	Tragedies
I	Comedy of Errors 1591–92 Two Gentlemen 1592 Love's Labour's Lost 1594	1 Henry VI ⎱ 2 Henry VI ⎰1590–92 3 Henry VI ⎰ Richard III 1593 King John 1594	Titus Andronicus 1591–92
II	Midsummer-Night's Dream 1595 Merchant of Venice 1596 Taming of the Shrew 1596 Much Ado 1598–99 As You Like It 1599–1600 Merry Wives 1599–1600 Twelfth Night 1600–01	Richard II 1595 1 Henry IV 1597 2 Henry IV 1598 Henry V 1599	Romeo and Juliet 1595 Julius Cæsar 1599
III	Troilus and Cressida 1602 All's Well 1602 Measure for Measure 1604 Pericles 1607–08		Hamlet 1601–02 Othello 1604 King Lear 1605–06 Macbeth 1606 Timon of Athens 1607 Antony and Cleopatra 1607 Coriolanus 1608–09
IV	Cymbeline 1610 Winter's Tale 1611 Tempest 1611	Henry VIII 1613	

and conquest. The compiling of chronicles and of endless narratives of travel and exploration in the Western Ocean expressed and symbolized the rising pride in England's past and England's future; and it supplied the basis for the most distinctively national part of the drama, that flourishing of Chronicle History which found its culmination in the martial rhetoric of *Henry V.*

No small part of the credit for all this belongs to the great Queen. Elizabeth was no lofty idealist, but she served England well. After the extremes in religion which had torn the country apart during the reigns of her two predecessors, Edward VI and Mary Tudor, she imposed on the country a church which was in important respects a compromise, but which was broad enough and tolerant enough to embrace the main body of her subjects. Though she dealt severely with extremists to both the right and left, she achieved a substantial degree of unity and peace.

Her foreign policy also was one of peace, and though the threat of the Great Armada called for a mustering of all the nation's forces, this was a defensive effort, and in general she sought to extend the power of England without impoverishing her by foreign wars. Under these circumstances the country enjoyed a long period of prosperity which

made possible, among much merely material luxury and ostentation, a notable flourishing of the arts.

From abroad there reached England at last the full impulse of the Renaissance. The more purely intellectual side of this movement had been delayed by the religious turmoil; but now that this was for the time assuaged, the stimulus to intellectual curiosity and the desire for imaginative entertainment had full scope. Men and books representing all the arts of the Continent poured into England, and hundreds of translations opened to those who could read no language but English the intellectual treasures of antiquity and of modern Italy, France, and Spain. A still less literate public were enabled to share the narrative element in this stream by the presentation of stories on the stage; and the plays based on Plutarch's *Lives* and French and Italian *novelle* represent respectively the classical and the contemporary elements in this contribution.

The drama in England had always largely represented what would have been the common reading matter of the people if the people had been able to read. Miracle plays, Moralities, and Interludes were each merely the translation into action and dialogue of the stories from Scripture and the Saints' Lives, of the characteristic medieval mode of allegory, of the bourgeois humorous and satirical anecdote, which the illiterate populace could receive only by the ear. With the Revival of Learning came a vast expansion in the amount and variety of reading matter, especially on the side of secular literature and, more specifically, of the literature of entertainment; and in the reign of Elizabeth the drama showed a responsive development. In the work of Shakespeare's immediate predecessors, Lyly, Marlowe, Peele, Greene, and Kyd, the three forms of Comedy, History, and Tragedy had, partly under the influence of foreign and classical models, taken fairly definite shape. But they were still primarily dramatic arrangements of narrative rather than drama; and to Shakespeare was offered the opportunity, of which he availed himself magnificently yet gradually, of framing and applying the conception of pure drama as a distinct form of art.

In considering his equipment for this momentous task two elements must be constantly kept in mind: that which he received as an actor and manager, and that which he had as a man well-read in the literature of his time. To the former must be credited a large part of his skill as a practical playwright, a factor that is at last receiving its due in the interpretation of his dramas, and which accounts for this among other facts, that so large a number of his plays are still capable of effective presentation upon the modern stage. As a student of literature, Shakespeare's range was large, but not extraordinary. Latin he had presumably learned at school, and with the works of some half-dozen Latin writers he had begun an acquaintance while a boy. But, in addition to the learned Jonson's ascription to him of "small Latine and lesse Greeke," we have the evidence of the plays themselves that he used translations when he could get them. French he seems to have known fairly well; Italian he may have mastered to the extent of being able to extract the plot of a novel, but this is less certain. There is no evidence that he knew Spanish or Greek. The wide and detailed knowledge of history and fiction and of many arts and trades, the evidences of which lie open on every page, is no greater and no more accurate than would be expected of a mind of the quality of his, of an observation so keen, of sympathies so catholic and so intense.

Some ten years before Shakespeare came to London an important event occurred in the building of The Theatre (1576), the first structure erected primarily for the purpose of acting in England. Up to this time, and for at least a quarter of a century longer, it was customary to use inn-yards for theatrical purposes. This was an improvement on the earlier practice of performing on an improvised platform in an open space; and as time went on some five inns in London had made more or less permanent arrangements for actors and audience. But the erection of The Theatre marks not only the provision of much more convenient facilities for performances and for the collecting of admission fees, but a growing recognition of acting as a profession. Later many more play-houses were erected — The Curtain (1577), The Rose (1587), The Swan (1595), The Globe (1599), The Fortune (1600), and others — and, as we have seen, Shakespeare himself found profit in part ownership.

Before the time of Elizabeth, professional actors were legally classed with vagabonds and had no recognized social status. The performance of stage plays was strongly disapproved by the growing Puritan element in the population on grounds of religion and morality, and the civic authorities were also opposed because of the disorderly crowds which gathered to see them, and because of the risks of spreading the plague. The hostility of the city government led to the building of the theaters in the suburbs, beyond its jurisdiction. Important for the improvement of the status of the players was the practice of enrolling their companies under the protection of powerful noblemen, and this culminated in the patronage of the Court. Indeed, it was the fact that the actors were employed to give plays before the Queen which more than any other prevented the opposition from suppressing them altogether. When James succeeded Elizabeth, he continued and extended the support and encouragement given by court performances, and the dramatic companies passed to the patronage of the different members of the royal family, the actors themselves receiving the status of "grooms of the chamber."

Of an importance only less than the intellectual temper of the time and the moment in the development of the drama was the state of the language and of versification. Along with the enthusiasm for the classics and the cultivation of pure Latinity which characterized the Renaissance there appeared a patriotic desire to refine and dignify the vernaculars of the various countries and, among them, of England. The pedantry of the group of men of letters known as the Areopagus, the Euphuism of Lyly, and the Arcadianism of Sidney were only exaggerated instances of the widespread interest in what could be done with the native speech; and, in spite of grotesque eccentricities, these fashions had served to expand the resources and supple the sinews of English. Writers went back to Chaucer and other older authors to recover words which had dropped out of use, and numbers of Romance words were introduced from French, Italian, and Spanish as well as direct from Latin. Traces of this interest in feats in the manipulation of words are apparent in Shakespeare in *Love's Labour's Lost* and elsewhere; but the more important consideration is that when he came to write his plays he had at hand a linguistic medium whose capacities both in vocabulary and structure had not yet become hardened under the dogmatism of the schools, and whose plasticity proved of inestimable value when wielded by a master. A century earlier the language was too poor in resources for such supreme literary achievement; a century later the settling down of convention had made such daring as Shakespeare showed in subduing it to his use all but impossible. Equal good fortune appears in the matter of prosody. Before Shakespeare began to write, drama in England had thrown off the shackles of stanza and rime which had hampered it for centuries, and had found in blank verse its appointed metre. With unerring instinct Shakespeare seized on this and played on it a variety of melodies such as had not hitherto been dreamed of.

Such are the more obvious factors in time and place which gave Shakespeare his opportunity. Peace and prosperity in the country at large; a rising national spirit, inspired and symbolized by a great Queen; the stimulus of Renaissance thought and imagination; a form of art developed to the precise point at which a great genius might carry it to heights never before reached; a language newly enriched and supplied by ingenious experiment, still plastic and fluent; a metre with possibilities proved by at least one great poet but really only tapped; a stage and a profession just emancipated from medieval crudity and waiting to be developed; a mass of material for plots — histories, romances, stories of the falls of princes — ready to the playwright's hand; these were all at Shakespeare's disposal. But they were also at the disposal of his colleagues of the theatre, and though some of these achieved high distinction, none reached and maintained Shakespeare's level. To understand his accomplishment we must turn to more personal matters.

IV. ACCOMPLISHMENT

In attempting to see what are some of the more important qualities that made it possible for Shakespeare to rise to his opportunity, it will be well to note first some of the negative elements in the case. It was not for sheer invention that Shakespeare was unique or even preëminent in his profession. Every form of drama that he touched he carried to a lofty pitch of perfection, but none of them did he create. In two or three cases he seems to have constructed the plot of a play, but such plots are slight and not distinguished by any striking originality. Whenever possible, he borrowed his stories; and the transformation he worked on them is due to a kind of imagination quite other, if much rarer, than is implied in inventive contrivance. Further, in the mechanics of his plays, he repeated himself freely.

When a device, a situation, a contrast of character, proved successful on the stage, he did not scruple to use it again and again, displaying in the variations he worked on it abundant cleverness, but at the same time an economy of invention, in striking contrast to his lavish prodigality in thought and imagery.

The element in his plays which, one is apt to think, must have struck the more thoughtful among his contemporaries as giving them marked distinction among the works of his predecessors and rivals, is his creation of character. In range, in individuality, above all in the illusion of life, there had been nothing in dramatic literature comparable to this endless procession of actual human beings. Here were no puppets labelled with a quality or a title, no mere walking gentlemen capable of being arranged in amusing situations. The persons of the Shakespearean drama, whenever drawn in detail and set in the foreground, are marked by idiosyncrasy that stops short of caricature, are humorous, pathetic, tender, cruel, profound, shallow, or any mixture of these, just as are the people one knows. In no respect does his genius more closely approach the supernatural than in this of the creation of men and women of a truly human complexity. Other qualities already referred to must also have appealed to the contemporary audience: the brilliance of phrase and sparkle of repartee; the consummate mastery of verse — now sweet and lyrical, now throbbing with passion, now echoing the tread of armies, now heavy with thought; — the ingenuity of the stage-craft; the variety of scene and atmosphere. But to the modern student there are deeper things to be found, which may or may not have been evident to his contemporaries, of some of which the poet himself may not have been explicitly conscious.

It has been frequently charged against Shakespeare that in contrast with poets like Dante and Goethe his work embodies no religion, no philosophy. Whatever of truth there may be in this, it is surely inaccurately phrased. Certain it is he was no fanatic, the propagandist of no sect; what philosophy he had is presented in no systematic scheme. If he had been or done these things, he could not have been the supreme dramatist. But the profoundest thought is not necessarily framed into a scheme; the most philosophical artist need not speak through allegory or abstractions. Philosophical ideas find abundant expression in both the dramas and the sonnets of Shakespeare; *obiter dicta* occur of immense suggestiveness and power; and it is hardly possible to read the plays as a whole without becoming conscious of a characteristic attitude toward human nature and the problems of human life. The expression of this attitude naturally varies with the period and the theme. In the Histories the dominant idea is that which one finds elsewhere in the early narratives of these sad stories of the death of kings. Among the strange paradoxes of the Middle Ages none is more remarkable than the persistence, among the Christian conceptions of the Catholic Church, of the pagan goddess of Fortune. So continually is she referred to as the determining force in the destinies of the great, so awed and reverential is the tone in which her caprices are alluded to, that one is forced to the conclusion that she was to the men of that age no mere figure of speech, but a deity who was always feared and often worshipped. The narratives on which Shakespeare based his Histories were pervaded by this conception, and it survives with impressive effect in the speeches of his characters. How far he personally shared it, it is hard to say; but he availed himself of it in a hundred instances of dramatic irony, and it underlies his melancholy insistence on the merely human limitations that assert themselves in the career of every king. With no lack of appreciation of the pomp of monarchy, he yet asserts in play after play that, whether coupled with the futile piety of Henry VI, the unscrupulous tenacity of Richard III, the policy of Henry IV, or the triumphant effectiveness of Henry V,

'Tis not the balm, the sceptre, and the ball,
The sword, the mace, the crown imperial,
The intertissued robe of gold and pearl,
The farced title running 'fore the King,
The throne he sits on, nor the tide of pomp
That beats upon the high shore of this world,

that can separate the king from the pathos of common humanity.

In the Comedies there is no such unity of idea; but generalized reflection is abundantly evident in the dwelling in successive plays on certain tendencies of human nature and their results in action and character; such tendencies as sentimentalism, cynicism, selfishness, and self-deception. The philosophical significance of these plays stops short, as a rule, of the fifth act. The marrying off, at the close, of all eligible youths and maidens is more a concession to the convention of the happy ending demanded by the particular type of drama than the logical outcome of the characters or their deeds. One is not convinced that Shakespeare believed that this was the way things happened in life; but a comedy must end so, and he provided accordingly a conventional dénouement, too often showing traces of the perfunctoriness of his interest in such an artificial adjustment.

Very different is his treatment of the conclusion of Tragedy. Here the crime or weakness which marks the tragic hero is shown bearing its inevitable fruit in suffering and disaster; and the great Tragedies form the crown of his achievement not only because they deal with the more serious problems of life, but because here are found all the elements of poetry, characterization, and construction, in each of which he had attained mastery in earlier plays, but which now are brought to their loftiest pitch and combined. Nowhere else are the two great dramatic elements of character and plot found in such perfect balance, in such complete interaction; nowhere else are they clothed in language so weighty with thought or so glorified by imagination. But it is in the determination of the catastrophes that the philosophical supremacy of the Tragedies most appears, as it is from these that critics who find evidence of pessimism in Shakespeare produce their proof. "Here," they say, pointing to the fifth act of *King Lear*, "here, at least, Shakespeare loses faith; here good and bad go down together in indiscriminate disaster." But so to observe is, surely, to lose sight of the most profound distinction running through these plays the distinction between the spiritual and the physical. From *Romeo and Juliet* to *Coriolanus* it is clear that Shakespeare hands over to natural and social law the bodies and temporal fortunes of good and bad alike, and such law is permitted its unrelenting sway. But it is equally clear that he regards the spiritual life of his creations as by no means submerged in this welter of suffering and death. Occasionally, as in *Macbeth*, the hero's spiritual career runs at the end parallel to his worldly fortune; more often, as in *Othello* or *Lear*, the moment of physical disaster witnesses a moral purgation, a spiritual triumph; always it is possible to discern two lines of interest, two kinds of value, two clearly distinguished spheres of existence.

For the lack of correspondence between these two lines of action, the absence in Tragedy of any control of worldly happiness in the interest of the good, he attempts no explanation. For he is not concerned to construct a philosophical system, to preach a gospel. Even the all-pervading distinction just set forth is not preached or argued. It is merely implied because no treatment of the greater issues of human life could be at once true and profound without this implication. Thus this limitation, as it has been regarded by those who would have the poet an explicit philosopher, is no limitation at all, but the mark of his allegiance to the true artistic ideal, the proof that he played his own game according to its own rules, and devoted himself with unparalleled disinterestedness, unparalleled range and profundity of insight, to the picturing of things as they are.

W. A. N.

INTRODUCTORY MATERIAL FROM
THE FIRST FOLIO EDITION OF 1623

INTRODUCTORY MATERIAL FROM
THE FIRST FOLIO EDITION OF 1623

To the Reader

This Figure, that thou here seest put,
    It was for gentle Shakespeare cut;
Wherein the Grauer had a strife
    with Nature, to out-doo the life:
O, could he but haue drawne his wit
    As well in brasse, as he hath hit
His face; the Print would then surpasse
    All, that vvas euer vvrit in brasse.
But, since he cannot, Reader, looke
    Not on his Picture, but his Booke.

B. I.

TO THE MOST NOBLE

AND

INCOMPARABLE PAIRE

OF BRETHREN.

WILLIAM

Earle of Pembroke, &c. Lord Chamberlaine to the
Kings most Excellent Maiesty.

AND

PHILIP

Earle of Montgomery, &c. Gentleman of his Maiesties
Bed-Chamber. Both Knights of the most Noble Order
of the Garter, and our singular good
LORDS.

Right Honourable,

Whilst we studie to be thankful in our particular, for the many fauors we haue receiued from your L. L. we are falne vpon the ill fortune, to mingle two the most diuerse things that can bee, feare, and rashnesse; rashnesse in the enterprize, and feare of the successe. For, when we valew the places your H. H. sustaine, we cannot but know their dignity greater, then to descend to the reading of these trifles: and, while we name them trifles, we haue depriu'd our selues of the defence of our Dedication. But since your L. L. haue beene pleas'd to thinke these trifles some-thing, heeretofore; and haue prosequuted both them, and their Authour liuing, with so much fauour: we hope, that (they out-liuing him, and he not hauing the fate, common with some, to be exequutor to his owne writings) you will vse the like indulgence toward them, you haue done vnto their parent. There is a great difference, whether any Booke choose his Patrones, or finde them: This hath done both. For, so much were your L. L. likings of the seuerall parts, when they were acted, as before they were published, the Volume ask'd to be yours. We haue but collected them, and done an office to the dead, to procure his Orphanes, Guardians; without ambition either of selfe-profit, or fame: onely to keepe the memory of so worthy a Friend, & Fellow aliue, as was our SHAKESPEARE, by humble offer of his playes, to your most noble patronage. Wherein, as we haue iustly obserued, no man to come neere your L. L. but with a kind of religious addresse; it hath bin the height of our care, who are the Presenters, to make the present worthy of your H. H. by the perfection. But, there we must also craue our abilities to be considerd, my Lords. We cannot go beyond our owne powers. Country hands reach foorth milke, creame, fruites, or what they haue: and many Nations (we haue heard) that had not gummes & incense, obtained their requests with a leauened Cake. It was no fault to approch their Gods, by what meanes they could: And the most, though meanest, of things are made more precious, when they are dedicated to Temples. In that name there-fore, we most humbly consecrate to your H. H. these remaines of your seruant SHAKESPEARE; that what delight is in them, may be euer your L. L. the reputation his, & the faults ours, if any be committed, by a payre so carefull to shew their gratitude both to the liuing, and the dead, as is

Your Lordshippes most bounden,

IOHN HEMINGE.

HENRY CONDELL.

TO THE GREAT VARIETY OF READERS

From the most able, to him that can but spell: There you are number'd. We had rather you were weighd. Especially, when the fate of all Bookes depends vpon your capacities: and not of your heads alone, but of your purses. Well! it is now publique, & you wil stand for your priuiledges wee know: to read, and censure. Do so, but buy it first. That doth best commend a Booke, the Stationer saies. Then, how odde soeuer your braines be, or your wisedomes, make your licence the same, and spare not. Iudge your sixe-pen'orth, your shillings worth, your fiue shillings worth at a time, or higher, so you rise to the iust rates, and welcome. But, what euer you do, Buy. Censure will not driue a Trade, or make the Iacke go. And though you be a Magistrate of wit, and sit on the Stage at *Black-Friers*, or the *Cock-pit*, to arraigne Playes dailie, know, these Playes haue had their triall alreadie, and stood out all Appeales; and do now come forth quitted rather by a Decree of Court, then any purchas'd Letters of commendation.

It had bene a thing, we confesse, worthie to haue bene wished, that the Author himselfe had liu'd to haue set forth, and ouerseen his owne writings; But since it hath bin ordain'd otherwise, and he by death departed from that right, we pray you do not envie his Friends, the office of their care, and paine, to haue collected & publish'd them; and so to haue published them, as where (before) you were abus'd with diuerse stolne, and surreptitious copies, maimed, and deformed by the frauds and stealthes of iniurious impostors, that expos'd them: euen those, are now offer'd to your view cur'd, and perfect of their limbes; and all the rest, absolute in their numbers, as he conceiued the. Who, as he was a happie imitator of Nature, was a most gentle expresser of it. His mind and hand went together: And what he thought, he vttered with that easinesse, that wee haue scarse receiued from him a blot in his papers. But it is not our prouince, who onely gather his works, and giue them you, to praise him. It is yours that reade him. And there we hope, to your diuers capacities, you will finde enough, both to draw, and hold you: for his wit can no more lie hid, then it could be lost. Reade him, therefore; and againe, and againe: And if then you doe not like him, surely you are in some manifest danger, not to vnderstand him. And so we leaue you to other of his Friends, whom if you need, can bee your guides: if you neede them not, you can leade your selues, and others. And such Readers we wish him.

IOHN HEMINGE.

HENRIE CONDELL.

TO THE MEMORY OF MY BELOUED,
THE AVTHOR

MR. WILLIAM SHAKESPEARE:

AND

what he hath left vs.

To draw no enuy (*Shakespeare*) on thy name,
   Am I thus ample to thy Booke, and Fame:
While I confesse thy writings to be such,
   As neither *Man*, nor *Muse*, can praise too much.
'Tis true, and all mens suffrage. But these wayes
   Were not the paths I meant vnto thy praise:
For seeliest Ignorance on these may light,
   Which, when it sounds at best, but eccho's right;
Or blinde Affection, which doth ne're aduance
   The truth, but gropes, and vrgeth all by chance;
Or crafty Malice, might pretend this praise,
   And thinke to ruine, where it seem'd to raise.
These are, as some infamous Baud, or Whore,
   Should praise a Matron. What could hurt her more?
But thou art proofe against them, and indeed
   Aboue th' ill fortune of them, or the need.
I, therefore will begin. Soule of the Age!
   The applause! delight! the wonder of our Stage !
My *Shakespeare*, rise; I will not lodge thee by
   Chaucer, or *Spenser*, or bid *Beaumont* lye
A little further, to make thee a roome:
   Thou art a Moniment, without a tombe,
And art aliue still, while thy Booke doth liue,
   And we haue wits to read, and praise to giue.
That I not mixe thee so, my braine excuses;
   I meane with great, but disproportion'd *Muses:*
For, if I thought my iudgement were of yeeres,
   I should commit thee surely with thy peeres,
And tell, how farre thou didstst our *Lily* out-shine,
   Or sporting *Kid*, or *Marlowes* mighty line.
And though thou hadst small *Latine*, and lesse *Greeke*,
   From thence to honour thee, I would not seeke
For names; but call forth thund'ring *Æschilus*,
   Euripides, and *Sophocles* to vs,
Paccuuius, Accius, him of *Cordoua* dead,
   To life againe, to heare thy Buskin tread,

And shake a Stage: Or, when thy Sockes were on,
  Leaue thee alone, for the comparison
Of all, that insolent *Greece*, or haughtie *Rome*
  sent forth, or since did from their ashes come.
Triúmph, my *Britaine*, thou hast one to showe,
  To whom all Scenes of *Europe* homage owe.
He was not of an age, but for all time!
  And all the *Muses* still were in their prime,
When like *Apollo* he came forth to warme
  Our eares, or like a *Mercury* to charme!
Nature her selfe was proud of his designes,
  And ioy'd to weare the dressing of his lines!
Which were so richly spun, and wouen so fit,
  As, since, she will vouchsafe no other Wit.
The merry *Greeke*, tart *Aristophanes*,
  Neat *Terence*, witty *Plautus*, now not please;
But antiquated, and deserted lye
  As they were not of Natures family.
Yet must I not giue Nature all: Thy Art,
  My gentle *Shakespeare*, must enioy a part.
For though the *Poets* matter, Nature be,
  His Art doth giue the fashion. And, that he,
Who casts to write a liuing line, must sweat,
  (such as thine are) and strike the second heat
Vpon the *Muses* anuile: turne the same,
  (And himselfe with it) that he thinkes to frame;
Or for the lawrell, he may gaine a scorne,
  For a good *Poet's* made, as well as borne.
And such wert thou.   Looke how the fathers face
  Liues in his issue, euen so, the race
Of *Shakespeares* minde, and manners brightly shines
  In his well torned, and true-filed lines:
In each of which, he seemes to shake a Lance,
  As brandish't at the eyes of Ignorance.
Sweet Swan of *Auon!* what a sight it were
  To see thee in our waters yet appeare,
And make those flights vpon the bankes of *Thames*,
  That so did take *Eliza*, and our *Iames!*
But stay, I see thee in the *Hemisphere*
  Aduanc'd, and made a Constellation there!
Shine forth, thou Starre of *Poets*, and with rage,
  Or influence, chide, or cheere the drooping Stage;
Which, since thy flight frō hence, hath mourn'd like night,
  And despaires day, but for thy Volumes light.

                              BEN: IONSON.

VPON THE LINES AND LIFE OF THE FAMOUS

Scenicke Poet, Master WILLIAM
SHAKESPEARE.

Those hands, which you so clapt, go now, and wring
You *Britaines* braue; for done are *Shakespeares* dayes:
His dayes are done, that made the dainty Playes,
Which made the Globe of heau'n and earth to ring.
Dry'de is that veine, dry'd is the *Thespian* Spring,
Turn'd all to teares, and *Phœbus* clouds his rayes:
That corp's, that coffin now besticke those bayes,
Which crown'd him *Poet* first, then *Poets* King.·
If *Tragedies* might any *Prologue* haue,
All those he made, would scarse make one to this:
Where *Fame*, now that he gone is to the graue
(Deaths publique tyring-house) the *Nuncius* is.
    For though his line of life went soone about,
    The life yet of his lines shall neuer out.

HVGH HOLLAND.

A CATALOGUE

OF THE SEVERALL COMEDIES, HISTORIES, AND TRAGEDIES CONTAINED IN THIS VOLUME.

[NOTE.— *The Tragedie of Troylus and Cressida,* though not catalogued, is printed immediately before *Coriolanus. Pericles* and the *Poems* were not included in the First Folio.]

TO THE MEMORIE
of the deceased Authour Maister
W. SHAKESPEARE.

Shake-speare, at length thy pious fellowes giue
The world thy Workes: thy Workes, by which, out-liue
Thy Tombe, thy name must: when that stone is rent,
And Time dissolues thy *Stratford* Moniment,
Here we aliue shall view thee still.   This Booke,
When Brasse and Marble fade, shall make thee looke
Fresh to all Ages: when Posteritie
Shall loath what's new, thinke all is prodegie
That is not *Shake-speares;* eu'ry Line, each Verse
Here shall reuiue, redeeme thee from thy Herse.
Nor Fire, nor cankring Age, as *Naso* said,
Of his, thy wit-fraught Booke shall once inuade.
Nor shall I e're beleeue, or thinke thee dead
(Though mist) vntill our bankrout Stage be sped
(Jmpossible) with some new straine t'out-do

Passions of *Iuliet*, and her *Romeo;*
Or till J heare a Scene more nobly take,
Then when thy half-Sword parlying *Romans* spake.
Till these, till any of thy Volumes rest
Shall with more fire, more feeling be exprest,
Be sure, our *Shake-speare*, thou canst neuer dye,
But crown'd with Lawrell, liue eternally.

L. DIGGES.

To the memorie of M. *W. Shake-speare.*

Wee wondred (*Shake-speare*) that thou went'st so soone
From the Worlds-Stage, to the Graues-Tyring-roome.
Wee thought thee dead, but this thy printed worth,
Tels thy Spectators, that thou went'st but forth
To enter with applause. An Actors Art,
Can dye, and liue, to acte a second part.
That's but an *Exit* of Mortalitie;
This, a Re-entrance to a Plaudite.

I. M.

THE WORKES OF WILLIAM SHAKESPEARE, CONTAINING ALL HIS COMEDIES, HISTORIES, AND TRAGEDIES: TRUELY SET FORTH, ACCORDING TO THEIR FIRST ORJGJNALL.

THE NAMES OF THE PRINCIPALL ACTORS
IN ALL THESE PLAYES.

WILLIAM SHAKESPEARE.	SAMUEL GILBURNE.
RICHARD BURBADGE.	ROBERT ARMIN.
JOHN HEMMINGS.	WILLIAM OSTLER.
AUGUSTINE PHILLIPS.	NATHAN FIELD.
WILLIAM KEMPT.	JOHN UNDERWOOD.
THOMAS POOPE.	NICHOLAS TOOLEY.
GEORGE BRYAN.	WILLIAM ECCLESTONE.
HENRY CONDELL.	JOSEPH TAYLOR.
WILLIAM SLYE.	ROBERT BENFIELD.
RICHARD COWLY.	ROBERT GOUGHE.
JOHN LOWINE.	RICHARD ROBINSON.
SAMUELL CROSSE.	IOHN SHANCKE.
AlEXANDER COOKE.	IOHN RICE.

The Complete Plays and Poems of

WILLIAM SHAKESPEARE

The Comedy of Errors

THERE HAS BEEN very general agreement in regarding *The Comedy of Errors* as one of the earliest of Shakespeare's productions. A play called *A Comedy of Errors* ("like to Plautus his Menaechmus") is stated in the *Gesta Grayorum* to have been acted by players at Gray's Inn as part of the Christmas revels on December 28, 1594, and there is no reason to doubt that this was the present play. Of internal evidences as to date the most pointed is the reference in III.ii.125–127 to France as "armed and reverted, making war against her heir," which is taken as an allusion to the contest between Henry of Navarre and the Catholic League (1589–1593). But Henry of Navarre was heir to the French throne before the death of Henry III in 1589, and had been at war with France as early as 1585. Thus there is nothing in the passage to prevent the dating of this comedy at the very beginning of Shakespeare's career. In *Four Letters Confuted* by Thomas Nashe, registered on January 12, 1593, there occur the words, "heart and good will, but never a ragge of money." The similarity to the lines of Dromio of Ephesus in IV.iv.88–89,

> Money by me? Heart and good will you might,
> But surely, master, not a rag of money,

suggests a borrowing which might have been either way, or from a common proverbial source. The reference in III.ii.141 to Spain's "whole armadoes of caracks" would have roused a quick response from English audiences for years after 1588; hence it offers little help towards a precise date. The large amount of verbal quibbling in the style of the play; the versification, which is marked by much rime both in couplets and alternates; the considerable amount of doggerel; the rarity of mid-line pauses, run-on lines, and weak or light endings; and the comparative scarcity of prose all point to an early date. The riming fourteen-syllabled lines in which the Dromios often speak belong to the tradition of the early drama, but are happily employed for their purpose. From all this it is a fair conjecture that the play was written about 1591 or 1592, but it may have been some years earlier or two years later.

It was first printed in the First Folio of 1623, and on this the present text is based. It is the shortest of Shakespeare's plays.

The main plot follows closely that of the *Menaechmi* of Plautus. The characters common to Plautus and Shakespeare are the two Antipholuses (Menaechmi), Dromio of Syracuse (Messenio), Adriana (Mulier), the Courtezan (Erotium), and Pinch (Medicus). Shakespeare preserves in the Dromio of Syracuse, whom he borrows, and bestows upon the Dromio of Ephesus, whom he invents, the stock characteristics of the witty slave of Plautus. The part of the Courtezan he conspicuously reduces. In Pinch's attempt to diagnose the madness of Antipholus, there is a strong reminiscence of the Medicus of Plautus. The character of Adriana Shakespeare has changed from the conventional shrew of Plautus into a jealous wife, jealous because devoted to her husband. Luciana, her appealing sister, is Shakespeare's happy invention. The Parasite who plays a large part in the Latin comedy, the cook and maid-servant of the Courtezan, and Senex, the father of Mulier, are all discarded by Shakespeare. Little of the detail is drawn from the Latin play, the most notable borrowings being the humorous treatment of the conjurer, the frequent thrashings of Dromio, and the reproof administered by the Abbess to Adriana, which resembles the remarks addressed to Mulier by Senex.

From the *Amphitruo*, another play by Plautus, are taken the scene (III.i.) in which Antipholus of Ephesus and his Dromio are shut out of their own home, and the notion of "doubling" the slaves as well as their masters. There is no reason for doubting that Shakespeare knew both the plays of Plautus in the original. The parallel passages which have been cited to show that he was indebted to the first English translation of the *Menaechmi*, that of W[illiam] W[arner] published in 1595, are not convincing. Furthermore, if he used this translation at all he must have had access to it in manuscript — a possibility but not a probability. Of the *Amphitruo* there was no English translation before the end of the seventeenth century.

The contention that *The Comedy of Errors* was a reworking of a lost play, *The History of Errors*, performed by the boys of St. Paul's at Hampton Court on January 1, 1577, is not acceptable. We know nothing about that play beyond what the title suggests, and the word "Error" need not have been used in the sense of mistaken identity as in the present play. There are, however, some indications that the text of the play as it has survived represents an abridgment of an earlier version which Shakespeare revised. Some broken lines and obscure passages may be due to cuts, but it is unlikely that the revision was drastic. The occasion for it may well enough have been that performance at Gray's Inn in 1594.

The most reluctant commentator cannot fail to give Shakespeare credit for originality in adding to his central plot the frame story of the separation and ultimate reunion of Ægeon and Æmilia, the parents of the twins. For this enveloping action Shakespeare found his inspiration in the long popular tale of Apollonius of Tyre, accessible to him both in the medieval version in Gower's *Confessio Amantis* and the one in Elizabethan prose by Laurence Twine (1576), and subsequently to be developed by him in his own *Pericles*. The tragic experience of this pair, with its happy ending, and the love of Antipholus of Syracuse for Luciana contribute a warmth and dignity to the play which stand athwart and relieve the artificiality and harshness of the dominant "errors." In the conversations of Luciana and the wandering Antipholus the poetry rises to its highest level, and in the personality of Æmilia is suggested a serene knowledge of the world.

Though one can hardly point out in *The Comedy of Errors* signal foreshadowings of the lyric and emotional richness of Shakespeare's mature comedies, one must recognize the theatrical competence and vitality which the play evinces. Though characterization is meager, a complicated plot is skillfully controlled and made to move swiftly. And the grave tone which the story of Ægeon and Æmilia introduces into the comedy would seem to anticipate the blending of the comic and the serious which was to become a distinctive feature of Shakespeare's later plays.

THE COMEDY OF ERRORS

[DRAMATIS PERSONÆ

SOLINUS, *duke of Ephesus.*
ÆGEON, *a merchant of Syracuse.*
ANTIPHOLUS of Ephesus, ⎱ *twin brothers, and*
ANTIPHOLUS of Syracuse, ⎰ *sons to Ægeon and*
⎱ *Æmilia.*
DROMIO of Ephesus, ⎱ *twin brothers, and attend-*
DROMIO of Syracuse, ⎰ *ants on the two Anti-*
⎱ *pholuses.*
BALTHAZAR, *a merchant.*
ANGELO, *a goldsmith.*

First Merchant, *friend to Antipholus of Syra-*
cuse.
Second Merchant, *to whom Angelo is a debtor.*
PINCH, *a schoolmaster.*

ÆMILIA, *wife to Ægeon, an abbess at Ephesus.*
ADRIANA, *wife to Antipholus of Ephesus.*
LUCIANA, *her sister.*
LUCE, *servant to Adriana.*
A Courtezan.

Gaoler, Officers, and other Attendants.

SCENE: *Ephesus.*]

ACT I

SCENE I. [*A hall in the Duke's palace.*]

Enter DUKE, ÆGEON, GAOLER, [Officers,]
and other Attendants.

Æge. Proceed, Solinus, to procure my fall,
And by the doom of death end woes and all.
Duke. Merchant of Syracusa, plead no more;
I am not partial to infringe our laws.
The enmity and discord which of late   5
Sprung from the rancorous outrage of your duke
To merchants, our well-dealing countrymen,
Who, wanting guilders to redeem their lives,
Have seal'd his rigorous statutes with their bloods,
Excludes all pity from our threat'ning looks.   10
For, since the mortal and intestine jars
'Twixt thy seditious countrymen and us,
It hath in solemn synods been decreed,
Both by the Syracusians and ourselves,
To admit no traffic to our adverse towns.   15
Nay, more: if any born at Ephesus
Be seen at any Syracusian marts and fairs;
Again, if any Syracusian born

Come to the bay of Ephesus, he dies,   20
His goods confiscate to the Duke's dispose,
Unless a thousand marks be levied,
To quit the penalty and to ransom him.
Thy substance, valu'd at the highest rate,
Cannot amount unto a hundred marks;   25
Therefore by law thou art condemn'd to die.
Æge. Yet this my comfort: when your words are
done,
My woes end likewise with the evening sun.
Duke. Well, Syracusian, say in brief the cause
Why thou departed'st from thy native home,   30
And for what cause thou cam'st to Ephesus.
Æge. A heavier task could not have been impos'd
Than I to speak my griefs unspeakable;
Yet, that the world may witness that my end
Was wrought by nature, not by vile offence,   35
I'll utter what my sorrow gives me leave.
In Syracusa was I born, and wed
Unto a woman, happy but for me,
And by me [too], had not our hap been bad.
With her I liv'd in joy; our wealth increas'd   40
By prosperous voyages I often made

Act I, sc. i, 4. **partial:** inclined. 8. **guilders:** Dutch silver coins worth about 1s.8d. English. 11. **intestine.** Properly
"civil"; here between Greeks. 22. **marks.** A mark was worth 13s.4d. 35. **nature:** natural affection. 39. [too] F2. Om.
F1.

To Epidamnum, till my factor's death
And the great care of goods at random left
Drew me from kind embracements of my spouse;
From whom my absence was not six months old   45
Before herself, almost at fainting under
The pleasing punishment that women bear,
Had made provision for her following me,
And soon and safe arrived where I was.
There had she not been long but she became   50
A joyful mother of two goodly sons;
And, which was strange, the one so like the other
As could not be distinguish'd but by names.
That very hour, and in the self-same inn,
A [meaner] woman was delivered   55
Of such a burden, male twins, both alike.
Those, for their parents were exceeding poor,
I bought and brought up to attend my sons.
My wife, not meanly proud of two such boys,
Made daily motions for our home return.   60
Unwilling I agreed. Alas! too soon
We came aboard.
A league from Epidamnum had we sail'd
Before the always wind-obeying deep
Gave any tragic instance of our harm.   65
But longer did we not retain much hope;
For what obscured light the heavens did grant
Did but convey unto our fearful minds
A doubtful warrant of immediate death;
Which though myself would gladly have embrac'd,
Yet the incessant weepings of my wife,   71
Weeping before for what she saw must come,
And piteous plainings of the pretty babes,
That mourn'd for fashion, ignorant what to fear,
Forc'd me to seek delays for them and me.   75
And this it was, for other means was none:
The sailors sought for safety by our boat,
And left the ship, then sinking-ripe, to us.
My wife, more careful for the latter born,
Had fast'ned him unto a small spare mast,   80
Such as seafaring men provide for storms;
To him one of the other twins was bound,
Whilst I had been like heedful of the other.
The children thus dispos'd, my wife and I,
Fixing our eyes on whom our care was fix'd,   85
Fast'ned ourselves at either end the mast;
And floating straight, obedient to the stream,
Was carried towards Corinth, as we thought.
At length the sun, gazing upon the earth,
Dispers'd those vapours that offended us;   90
And, by the benefit of his wished light,
The seas wax'd calm, and we discovered
Two ships from far making amain to us,
Of Corinth that, of Epidaurus this.

But ere they came, — O, let me say no more!   95
Gather the sequel by that went before.
    Duke. Nay, forward, old man; do not break off so;
For we may pity, though not pardon thee.
    Æge. O, had the gods done so, I had not now
Worthily term'd them merciless to us!   100
For, ere the ships could meet by twice five leagues,
We were encount'red by a mighty rock,
Which being violently borne [upon],
Our helpful ship was splitted in the midst;
So that, in this unjust divorce of us,   105
Fortune had left to both of us alike
What to delight in, what to sorrow for.
Her part, poor soul! seeming as burdened
With lesser weight but not with lesser woe,
Was carried with more speed before the wind;   110
And in our sight they three were taken up
By fishermen of Corinth, as we thought.
At length, another ship had seiz'd on us;
And, knowing whom it was their hap to save,
Gave healthful welcome to their shipwreck'd guests;
And would have reft the fishers of their prey,   116
Had not their [bark] been very slow of sail;
And therefore homeward did they bend their course.
Thus have you heard me sever'd from my bliss,
That by misfortunes was my life prolong'd   120
To tell sad stories of my own mishaps.
    Duke. And, for the sake of them thou sorrowest
        for,
Do me the favour to dilate at full
What [hath] befallen of them and [thee] till now.
    Æge. My youngest boy, and yet my eldest care,
At eighteen years became inquisitive   126
After his brother, and importun'd me
That his attendant — so his case was like,
Reft of his brother, but retain'd his name —
Might bear him company in the quest of him;   130
Whom whilst I labour'd of a love to see,
I hazarded the loss of whom I lov'd.
Five summers have I spent in farthest Greece,
Roaming clean through the bounds of Asia,
And, coasting homeward, came to Ephesus;   135
Hopeless to find, yet loath to leave unsought
Or that or any place that harbours men.
But here must end the story of my life;
And happy were I in my timely death,
Could all my travels warrant me they live.   140
    Duke. Hapless Ægeon, whom the fates have
        mark'd
To bear the extremity of dire mishap!
Now, trust me, were it not against our laws,
Against my crown, my oath, my dignity,
Which princes, would they, may not disannul,   145

---

42. **factor's**: agent's. 55. **[meaner]** (S. Walker) *meene* F₁; *poor meane* F₂. 60. **motions**: proposals. 62. Cunningham completes the line "and put to sea, but scarce." 65. **instance**: sign. 69. **doubtful**: uncertain but likely. 74. **for fashion**: in imitation. 103. **[upon]** (Pope). *up* F. 115. **healthful**: saving. 117. **[bark]** F₂. *backe* F₁. 123. **dilate**: relate. 124. **[hath]** ... **[thee]** F₂. *have* ... *they* F₁. 131. **of**: out of, from. 139. **timely**: speedy. 145. **disannul**: annul.

My soul should sue as advocate for thee.
But, though thou art adjudged to the death,
And passed sentence may not be recall'd
But to our honour's great disparagement,
Yet I will favour thee in what I can.   150
Therefore, merchant, I'll limit thee this day
To seek thy [life] by beneficial help.
Try all the friends thou hast in Ephesus;
Beg thou, or borrow, to make up the sum,
And live; if no, then thou art doom'd to die.   155
Gaol. I will, my lord.
Æge. Hopeless and helpless doth Ægeon wend,
But to procrastinate his lifeless end.   [*Exeunt.*

[SCENE II.   *The mart.*]

Enter ANTIPHOLUS of Syracuse, DROMIO of Syracuse,
and [FIRST] MERCHANT.

1. Mer. Therefore give out you are of Epidam-
num,
Lest that your goods too soon be confiscate.
This very day a Syracusian merchant
Is apprehended for arrival here;
And, not being able to buy out his life   5
According to the statute of the town,
Dies ere the weary sun set in the west.
There is your money that I had to keep.
Ant. S. Go bear it to the Centaur, where we host,
And stay there, Dromio, till I come to thee.   10
Within this hour it will be dinner-time;
Till that, I'll view the manners of the town,
Peruse the traders, gaze upon the buildings,
And then return and sleep within mine inn,
For with long travel I am stiff and weary.   15
Get thee away.
Dro. S. Many a man would take you at your
word,
And go, indeed, having so good a mean.   [*Exit.*
Ant. S. A trusty villain, sir, that very oft,
When I am dull with care and melancholy,   20
Lightens my humour with his merry jests.
What, will you walk with me about the town,
And then go to my inn and dine with me?
1. Mer. I am invited, sir, to certain merchants,
Of whom I hope to make much benefit;   25
I crave your pardon.   Soon at five o'clock,
Please you, I'll meet with you upon the mart
And afterward consort you till bed-time.
My present business calls me from you now.

Ant. S. Farewell till then.   I will go lose myself,
And wander up and down to view the city.   31
1. Mer. Sir, I commend you to your own content.
[*Exit.*
Ant. S. He that commends me to mine own
content
Commends me to the thing I cannot get.
I to the world am like a drop of water   35
That in the ocean seeks another drop,
Who, falling there to find his fellow forth,
Unseen, inquisitive, confounds himself.
So I, to find a mother and a brother,
In quest of them, unhappy, lose myself.   40

Enter DROMIO *of Ephesus.*

Here comes the almanac of my true date.
What now? How chance thou art return'd so soon?
Dro. E. Return'd so soon! rather approach'd
too late.
The capon burns, the pig falls from the spit,
The clock hath strucken twelve upon the bell;   45
My mistress made it one upon my cheek,
She is so hot because the meat is cold;
The meat is cold because you come not home;
You come not home because you have no stomach;
You have no stomach having broke your fast;   50
But we that know what 'tis to fast and pray
Are penitent for your default to-day.
Ant. S. Stop in your wind, sir; tell me this, I pray:
Where have you left the money that I gave you?
Dro. E. O, — sixpence, that I had o'Wednesday
last   55
To pay the saddler for my mistress' crupper?
The saddler had it, sir; I kept it not.
Ant. S. I am not in a sportive humour now.
Tell me, and dally not, where is the money?
We being strangers here, how dar'st thou trust   60
So great a charge from thine own custody?
Dro. E. I pray you, jest, sir, as you sit at dinner.
I from my mistress come to you in post;
If I return, I shall be post indeed,
For she will [score] your fault upon my pate.   65
Methinks your maw, like mine, should be your [clock]
And strike you home without a messenger.
Ant. S. Come, Dromio, come, these jests are
out of season;
Reserve them till a merrier hour than this.
Where is the gold I gave in charge to thee?   70
Dro. E. To me, sir? Why, you gave no gold to me.
Ant. S. Come on, sir knave, have done your
foolishness

152. [life] (Rowe).   *helpe* F.   Other conjectures are *store, sum, health.*
Sc. ii, S.D. ANTIPHOLUS of Syracuse.   *Antipholis Erotes* Ff.   9. host: lodge.   18. mean: means, sum of money.
19. villain.   Used good-naturedly as "fellow"; also bondman.   21. humour: a physiological term in Shakespeare's time,
here meaning "mood" or "disposition."   26. Soon at: about.   37. forth: out.   41. almanac... date. Because they were
born in the same hour, Antipholus can see his age in Dromio.   45. twelve. The Elizabethan dinner hour was 11:30.
49. stomach: appetite.   52. penitent: i.e., doing penance.   53. wind: talk.   63. post: haste.   64. post: post in a tavern
or shop on which reckonings were scored.   65. [score] (Rowe).   *scoure* F.   66. [clock] (Pope).   *cooke* F.

And tell me how thou hast dispos'd thy charge.
Dro. E. My charge was but to fetch you from
    the mart
Home to your house, the Phœnix, sir, to dinner. 75
My mistress and her sister stays for you.
Ant. S. Now, as I am a Christian, answer me
In what safe place you have bestow'd my money,
Or I shall break that merry sconce of yours
That stands on tricks when I am undispos'd. 80
Where is the thousand marks thou hadst of me?
Dro. E. I have some marks of yours upon my pate,
Some of my mistress' marks upon my shoulders,
But not a thousand marks between you both.
If I should pay your worship those again, 85
Perchance you will not bear them patiently.
Ant. S. Thy mistress' marks? What mistress,
    slave, hast thou?
Dro. E. Your worship's wife, my mistress at
    the Phœnix;
She that doth fast till you come home to dinner,
And prays that you will hie you home to dinner. 90
Ant. S. What, wilt thou flout me thus unto my face,
Being forbid? There, take you that, sir knave.
Dro. E. What mean you, sir? For [God's] sake,
    hold your hands!
Nay, an you will not, sir, I'll take my heels. [*Exit.*
Ant. S. Upon my life, by some device or other 95
The villain is [o'erraught] of all my money.
They say this town is full of cozenage,
As, nimble jugglers that deceive the eye,
Dark-working sorcerers that change the mind,
Soul-killing witches that deform the body, 100
Disguised cheaters, prating mountebanks,
And many such-like liberties of sin.
If it prove so, I will be gone the sooner.
I'll to the Centaur to go seek this slave;
I greatly fear my money is not safe. [*Exit.*] 105

ACT II

[SCENE I. *The house of Antipholus of Ephesus.*]

Enter ADRIANA *and* LUCIANA.

Adr. Neither my husband nor the slave return'd,
That in such haste I sent to seek his master!
Sure, Luciana, it is two o'clock.
Luc. Perhaps some merchant hath invited him
And from the mart he's somewhere gone to dinner. 5
Good sister, let us dine and never fret.
A man is master of his liberty.
Time is their master, and when they see time
They'll go or come; if so, be patient, sister. 9
Adr. Why should their liberty than ours be more?
Luc. Because their business still lies out [o' door].

Adr. Look, when I serve him so, he takes it [ill].
Luc. O, know he is the bridle of your will.
Adr. There's none but asses will be bridled so.
Luc. Why, headstrong liberty is lash'd with woe.
There's nothing situate under heaven's eye 16
But hath his bound; in earth, in sea, in sky,
The beasts, the fishes, and the winged fowls
Are their males' subjects and at their controls;
Man, more divine, the master of all these, 20
Lord of the wide world and wild watery seas,
Indu'd with intellectual sense and souls,
Of more preëminence than fish and fowls,
Are masters to their females, and their lords:
Then let your will attend on their accords. 25
Adr. This servitude makes you to keep unwed.
Luc. Not this, but troubles of the marriage-bed.
Adr. But, were you wedded, you would bear
    some sway.
Luc. Ere I learn love, I'll practise to obey.
Adr. How if your husband start some other-
    where? 30
Luc. Till he came home again, I would forbear.
Adr. Patience unmov'd! no marvel though she
    pause.
They can be meek that have no other cause.
A wretched soul, bruis'd with adversity,
We bid be quiet when we hear it cry; 35
But were we burd'ned with like weight of pain,
As much or more we should ourselves complain;
So thou, that hast no unkind mate to grieve thee,
With urging helpless patience would relieve me;
But, if thou live to see like right bereft, 40
This fool-begg'd patience in thee will be left.
Luc. Well, I will marry one day, but to try.
Here comes your man; now is your husband nigh.

Enter DROMIO *of Ephesus.*

Adr. Say, is your tardy master now at hand?
Dro. E. Nay, he's at two hands with me, and
that my two ears can witness. 46
Adr. Say, didst thou speak with him? Know'st
thou his mind?
Dro. E. Ay, ay, he told his mind upon mine ear.
Beshrew his hand, I scarce could understand it.
Luc. Spake he so doubtfully, thou couldst not
feel his meaning? 51
Dro. E. Nay, he struck so plainly, I could too
well feel his blows; and withal so doubtfully that
I could scarce understand them.
Adr. But say, I prithee, is he coming home? 55
It seems he hath great care to please his wife.
Dro. E. Why, mistress, sure my master is horn-
mad.

---

80. **stands on:** persists in. 93. **[God's]** (Hanmer). *God* F. 96. **[o'erraught]** (Hanmer). *ore-wrought* F. 97. **cozenage:** cheating. 102. **liberties:** licenses.

Act II, sc. i, 11. **[o' door]** (Capell). *adore* F. 12. **[ill]** F₂. *thus* F₁. 30. **start:** swerve aside. 39. **helpless:** unavailing. 41. **fool-begg'd:** idiotic. 49. **beshrew:** curse. **understand:** with a pun on "stand under." 57. **horn-mad:** mad as a beast.

Adr. Horn-mad, thou villain!
Dro. E.   I mean not cuckold-mad;
But, sure, he is stark mad.
When I desir'd him to come home to dinner,   60
He ask'd me for a [thousand] marks in gold.
"'Tis dinner-time," quoth I; "My gold," quoth he.
"Your meat doth burn," quoth I; "My gold!"
     quoth he.
"Will you come [home]?" quoth I; "My gold!"
     quoth he,
"Where is the thousand marks I gave thee, vil-
     lain?"   65
"The pig," quoth I, "is burn'd"; "My gold!"
     quoth he.
"My mistress, sir," quoth I; "Hang up thy mistress!
I know not thy mistress. Out on thy mistress!"
Luc. Quoth who?
Dro. E. Quoth my master.   70
"I know," quoth he, "no house, no wife, no mis-
     tress."
So that my [errand] due unto my tongue,
I thank him, I bare home upon my shoulders;
For, in conclusion, he did beat me there.
Adr. Go back again, thou slave, and fetch him
     home.   75
Dro. E. Go back again, and be new beaten home?
For God's sake, send some other messenger.
Adr. Back, slave, or I will break thy pate across.
Dro. E. And he will bless that cross with other
     beating.
Between you I shall have a holy head.   80
Adr. Hence, prating peasant! Fetch thy master
     home.
Dro. E. Am I so round with you as you with
     me,
That like a football you do spurn me thus?   83
You spurn me hence, and he will spurn me hither.
If I last in this service, you must case me in leather.
               [*Exit.*]
Luc. Fie, how impatience loureth in your face!
Adr. His company must do his minions grace,
Whilst I at home starve for a merry look.
Hath homely age the alluring beauty took
From my poor cheek? Then he hath wasted it.   90
Are my discourses dull? Barren my wit?
If voluble and sharp discourse be marr'd,
Unkindness blunts it more than marble hard.
Do their gay vestments his affections bait?
That's not my fault; he's master of my state.   95
What ruins are in me that can be found

By him not ruin'd? Then is he the ground
Of my defeatures. My decayed fair
A sunny look of his would soon repair.
But, too unruly deer, he breaks the pale   100
And feeds from home; poor I am but his stale.
Luc. Self-harming jealousy! fie, beat it hence!
Adr. Unfeeling fools can with such wrongs dis-
     pense.
I know his eye doth homage other-where,
Or else what lets it but he would be here?   105
Sister, you know he promis'd me a chain;
Would that [alone, alone] he would detain,
So he would keep fair quarter with his bed!
I see the jewel best enamelled
Will lose his beauty; [and tho'] gold bides still   110
That others touch, [yet] often touching will
[Wear] gold; and no man that hath a name
By falsehood and corruption doth it shame.
Since that my beauty cannot please his eye,
I'll weep what's left away, and weeping die.   115
Luc. How many fond fools serve mad jealousy?
               [*Exeunt.*

[Scene II. *A public place.*]

Enter ANTIPHOLUS *of Syracuse.*

Ant. S. The gold I gave to Dromio is laid up
Safe at the Centaur; and the heedful slave
Is wand'red forth, in care to seek me out.
By computation and mine host's report,
I could not speak with Dromio since at first   5
I sent him from the mart. See, here he comes.

Enter DROMIO *of Syracuse.*

How now, sir! is your merry humour alter'd?
As you love strokes, so jest with me again.
You know no Centaur? You receiv'd no gold?
Your mistress sent to have me home to dinner?   10
My house was at the Phœnix? Wast thou mad
That thus so madly thou didst answer me?
Dro. S. What answer, sir? When spake I such
     a word?
Ant. S. Even now, even here, not half an hour
     since.   14
Dro. S. I did not see you since you sent me hence,
Home to the Centaur, with the gold you gave me.
Ant. S. Villain, thou didst deny the gold's receipt
And told'st me of a mistress and a dinner;
For which, I hope, thou felt'st I was displeas'd.

61. [thousand] F4. *hundred* F1. *1000* F2,3. 64. [home] (Hanmer). Om. F. 72. [errand] F4. *arrant* F1–3. *due . . .
tongue:* which should have been given me to deliver in words. 80. **holy:** i.e., with pun on "full of holes." 82. **round:** (1)
spherical, (2) plain-spoken. 87. **minions:** favorites. 94. **bait:** lure. 98. **defeatures:** disfigurements. **fair:** beauty.
101. **stale:** laughing-stock, possibly stalking horse. 103. **dispense:** put up. 105. **lets:** prevents. 107. [alone, alone] F2.
alone, a love F1. **detain:** withhold. 108. **keep . . . with:** be true to. 110–111. [and tho'] . . . [yet] (Hanmer conj.) *yet . . .
and* F. 112. [Wear] (Theobald). *Where* F. The passage (109–113) is confused and very likely corrupt. The following paraphrase may give the meaning: "The best enamelled jewel tarnishes, but though handling does not destroy gold,
nevertheless it will impair it; and no man with a reputation risks shaming it by infidelity and debasement."

Dro. S. I am glad to see you in this merry vein. 20
What means this jest? I pray you, master, tell me.
  Ant. S. Yea, dost thou jeer and flout me in the
    teeth?
Think'st thou I jest? Hold, take thou that, and
    that.   *[Beats Dro.*
  Dro. S. Hold, sir, for God's sake! Now your
    jest is earnest.
Upon what bargain do you give it me?   25
  Ant. S. Because that I familiarly sometimes
Do use you for my fool and chat with you,
Your sauciness will jest upon my love
And make a common of my serious hours.
When the sun shines let foolish gnats make sport, 30
But creep in crannies when he hides his beams.
If you will jest with me, know my aspect
And fashion your demeanour to my looks,
Or I will beat this method in your sconce.   34
  Dro. S. Sconce call you it? So you would
leave battering, I had rather have it a head. An
you use these blows long, I must get a sconce for
my head and insconce it too, or else I shall seek my
wit in my shoulders. But, I pray, sir, why am
I beaten?   40
  Ant. S. Dost thou not know?
  Dro. S. Nothing, sir, but that I am beaten.
  Ant. S. Shall I tell you why?
  Dro. S. Ay, sir, and wherefore; for they say
every why hath a wherefore.   45
  Ant. S. Why, first, — for flouting me; and then,
    wherefore, —
For urging it the second time to me.
  Dro. S. Was there ever any man thus beaten
    out of season,
When in the why and the wherefore is neither
    rhyme nor reason?
Well, sir, I thank you.   50
  Ant. S. Thank me, sir! For what?
  Dro. S. Marry, sir, for this something that you
gave me for nothing.
  Ant. S. I'll make you amends next, to give you
nothing for something. But say, sir, is it dinnertime?
  Dro. S. No, sir. I think the meat wants that
    I have.   57
  Ant. S. In good time, sir; what's that?
  Dro. S. Basting.
  Ant. S. Well, sir, then 't will be dry.   60
  Dro. S. If it be, sir, I pray you, eat none of it.

  Ant. S. Your reason?
  Dro. S. Lest it make you choleric and purchase
me another dry basting.
  Ant. S. Well, sir, learn to jest in good time.
There's a time for all things.   66
  Dro. S. I durst have denied that, before you
were so choleric.
  Ant. S. By what rule, sir?
  Dro. S. Marry, sir, by a rule as plain as the plain
bald pate of father Time himself.   71
  Ant. S. Let's hear it.
  Dro. S. There's no time for a man to recover his
hair that grows bald by nature.
  Ant. S. May he not do it by fine and recovery? 75
  Dro. S. Yes, to pay a fine for a periwig and re-
cover the lost hair of another man.
  Ant. S. Why is Time such a niggard of hair,
being, as it is, so plentiful an excrement?   79
  Dro. S. Because it is a blessing that he bestows
on beasts; and what he hath scanted [men] in hair
he hath given them in wit.
  Ant. S. Why, but there's many a man hath
more hair than wit.
  Dro. S. Not a man of those but he hath the wit
to lose his hair.   86
  Ant. S. Why, thou didst conclude hairy men
plain dealers without wit.
  Dro. S. The plainer dealer, the sooner lost; yet
he loseth it in a kind of jollity.   90
  Ant. S. For what reason?
  Dro. S. For two; and sound [ones] too.
  Ant. S. Nay, not sound, I pray you.
  Dro. S. Sure ones, then.
  Ant. S. Nay, not sure, in a thing falsing.   95
  Dro. S. Certain ones, then.
  Ant. S. Name them.
  Dro. S. The one, to save the money that he
spends in [tiring]; the other, that at dinner they
should not drop in his porridge.   100
  Ant. S. You would all this time have prov'd
there is no time for all things.
  Dro. S. Marry, and did, sir; namely, no time
to recover hair lost by nature.
  Ant. S. But your reason was not substantial,
why there is no time to recover.   106
  Dro. S. Thus I mend it: Time himself is bald
and therefore to the world's end will have bald
followers.

Sc. ii, 22. **in the teeth:** to my face. 24. **earnest:** i.e., with a pun on "earnest-money," a sum laid down to bind a bargain. 29. **common:** public playground. 32. **aspect:** (1) expression, (2) disposition (malignant or benign) of planets, in the old astrology. 34. **sconce:** head (but *fort* in l. 35 and *helmet* in l. 37). 38. **insconce:** protect. 39. **seek...shoulders:** i.e., my head will be beaten into my shoulders. 58. **In good time:** forsooth. 63. **choleric.** Overdone meat was believed to make one irascible. 64. **dry basting:** severe beating. 75. **fine and recovery:** a legal procedure by which entailed estates could be transferred without entail from one owner to another. Antipholus seems to be punning on *heir* and *hair* (see l. 74). 79. **excrement:** outgrowth (of hair). 81. **[men]** (Theobald). *them* F. 86. **he...hair.** Reference to the diseases which produce loss of hair. 90. **jollity.** This word and *sound* (l. 93) and *falsing* (i.e., deceptive, l. 95) play upon the implications of l. 86 (see note). 92. **[ones]** F2. Om. F1. 99. **[tiring]** (Pope): dressing the hair. *trying* F. 103. **no time** F2. *in no time* F1.

Ant. S. I knew 't would be a bald conclusion. —
But, soft! who wafts us yonder?   111

Enter ADRIANA *and* LUCIANA.

Adr. Ay, ay, Antipholus, look strange and frown,
Some other mistress hath thy sweet aspects;
I am not Adriana, nor thy wife.
The time was once when thou unurg'd wouldst vow
That never words were music to thine ear,   116
That never object pleasing in thine eye,
That never touch well welcome to thy hand,
That never meat sweet-savour'd in thy taste,
Unless I spake, or look'd, or touch'd, or carv'd to
    thee.   120
How comes it now, my husband, O, how comes it,
That thou art then estranged from thyself?
Thyself I call it, being strange to me,
That, undividable, incorporate,
Am better than thy dear self's better part.   125
Ah, do not tear away thyself from me!
For know, my love, as easy mayst thou fall
A drop of water in the breaking gulf
And take unmingled thence that drop again,
Without addition or diminishing,   130
As take from me thyself and not me too.
How dearly would it touch thee to the quick
Shouldst thou but hear I were licentious,
And that this body, consecrate to thee,
By ruffian lust should be contaminate!   135
Wouldst thou not spit at me, and spurn at me,
And hurl the name of husband in my face,
And tear the stain'd skin off my harlot-brow,
And from my false hand cut the wedding-ring
And break it with a deep-divorcing vow?   140
I know thou canst; and therefore see thou do it.
I am possess'd with an adulterate blot;
My blood is mingled with the crime of lust;
For if we two be one and thou play false,
I do digest the poison of thy flesh,   145
Being strumpeted by thy contagion.
Keep then fair league and truce with thy true bed;
I live distain'd, thou undishonoured.

Ant. S. Plead you to me, fair dame? I know
    you not.
In Ephesus I am but two hours old,   150
As strange unto your town as to your talk;
Who, every word by all my wit being scann'd,
Wants wit in all one word to understand.

Luc. Fie, brother! how the world is chang'd
    with you!
When were you wont to use my sister thus?   155
She sent for you by Dromio home to dinner.

Ant. S. By Dromio?
Dro. S. By me?
Adr. By thee; and this thou didst return from
    him,
That he did buffet thee, and in his blows   160
Denied my house for his, me for his wife.

Ant. S. Did you converse, sir, with this gentle-
    woman?
What is the course and drift of your compact?

Dro. S. I, sir? I never saw her till this time.
Ant. S. Villain, thou liest; for even her very words
Didst thou deliver to me on the mart.   166

Dro. S. I never spake with her in all my life.
Ant. S. How can she thus then call us by our
    names,
Unless it be by inspiration?

Adr. How ill agrees it with your gravity   170
To counterfeit thus grossly with your slave,
Abetting him to thwart me in my mood!
Be it my wrong you are from me exempt,
But wrong not that wrong with a more contempt.
Come, I will fasten on this sleeve of thine.   175
Thou art an elm, my husband, I a vine,
Whose weakness married to thy [stronger] state
Makes me with thy strength to communicate.
If aught possess thee from me, it is dross,
Usurping ivy, brier, or idle moss;   180
Who, all for want of pruning, with intrusion
Infect thy sap and live on thy confusion.

Ant. S. To me she speaks; she moves me for her
    theme.
What, was I married to her in my dream?
Or sleep I now and think I hear all this?   185
What error drives our eyes and ears amiss?
Until I know this sure uncertainty,
I'll entertain the [offer'd] fallacy.

Luc. Dromio, go bid the servants spread for
    dinner.

Dro. S. O, for my beads! I cross me for a
    sinner.   190
This is the fairy land. O spite of spites!
We talk with goblins, owls, and sprites.
If we obey them not, this will ensue:
They'll suck our breath or pinch us black and blue.

Luc. Why prat'st thou to thyself and answer'st
    not?   195
Dromio, thou Dromio, thou snail, thou slug, thou
    sot!

Dro. S. I am transformed, master, am [not I]?
Ant. S. I think thou art in mind, and so am I.
Dro. S. Nay, master, both in mind and in my
    shape.   199

---

110. **bald:** senseless.   111. **wafts:** waves to, beckons.   113. **aspects:** glances.   125. **better part:** i.e., soul, spirit. 127. **fall:** let fall.   132. **dearly:** intimately, keenly.   148. **distain'd:** unstained.   Many editors read "unstained." 163. **compact:** plot.   172. **mood:** displeasure.   173. **exempt:** separated.   177. [**stronger**] F4.   *stranger* F1–3.   179. **possess:** take.   180. **idle:** barren, useless.   182. **confusion:** ruin.   183. **moves:** takes.   187. **know:** comprehend.   188. [**offer'd**] (Capell conj.) *free'd* F.   190. **beads:** rosary.   196. **sot:** fool.   197. [**not I**] (Theobald).   *I not* F.

Ant. S. Thou hast thine own form.

Dro. S. No, I am an ape.

Luc. If thou art chang'd to aught, 'tis to an ass.

Dro. S. 'Tis true; she rides me and I long for grass.

'Tis so, I am an ass; else it could never be

But I should know her as well as she knows me.

Adr. Come, come; no longer will I be a fool, 205

To put the finger in the eye and weep

Whilst man and master laughs my woes to scorn.

Come, sir, to dinner. Dromio, keep the gate.

Husband, I'll dine above with you to-day

And shrive you of a thousand idle pranks. 210

Sirrah, if any ask you for your master,

Say he dines forth and let no creature enter.

Come, sister. Dromio, play the porter well.

Ant. S. Am I in earth, in heaven, or in hell?

Sleeping or waking? Mad or well-advis'd? 215

Known unto these, and to myself disguis'd!

I'll say as they say and persever so,

And in this mist at all adventures go.

Dro. S. Master, shall I be porter at the gate?

Adr. Ay; and let none enter, lest I break your pate. 220

Luc. Come, come, Antipholus, we dine too late.

[*Exeunt.*

ACT III

SCENE I. [*Before the house of Antipholus of Ephesus.*]

Enter ANTIPHOLUS *of Ephesus,* DROMIO *of Ephesus,* ANGELO, *the goldsmith, and* BALTHAZAR, *the merchant.*

Ant. E. Good Signior Angelo, you must excuse us all;

My wife is shrewish when I keep not hours.

Say that I linger'd with you at your shop

To see the making of her carcanet,

And that to-morrow you will bring it home. 5

But here's a villain that would face me down

He met me on the mart, and that I beat him

And charg'd him with a thousand marks in gold,

And that I did deny my wife and house. 9

Thou drunkard, thou, what didst thou mean by this?

Dro. E. Say what you will, sir, but I know what I know.

That you beat me at the mart, I have your hand to show.

If the skin were parchment and the blows you gave were ink,

Your own handwriting would tell you what I think.

Ant. E. I think thou art an ass.

Dro. E. Marry, so it doth appear

By the wrongs I suffer and the blows I bear. 16

I should kick, being kick'd; and, being at that pass,

You would keep from my heels and beware of an ass.

Ant. E. You're sad, Signior Balthazar; pray God our cheer

May answer my good will and your good welcome here. 20

Bal. I hold your dainties cheap, sir, and your welcome dear.

Ant. E. O, Signior Balthazar, either at flesh or fish,

A table-full of welcome makes scarce one dainty dish.

Bal. Good meat, sir, is common; that every churl affords.

Ant. E. And welcome more common; for that's nothing but words. 25

Bal. Small cheer and great welcome makes a merry feast.

Ant. E. Ay, to a niggardly host and more sparing guest;

But though my cates be mean, take them in good part;

Better cheer may you have, but not with better heart.

But, soft! my door is lock'd. Go bid them let us in. 30

Dro. E. Maud, Bridget, Marian, Cicely, Gillian, Ginn!

Dro. S. [*Within.*] Mome, malt-horse, capon, coxcomb, idiot, patch!

Either get thee from the door or sit down at the hatch.

Dost thou conjure for wenches, that thou call'st for such store

When one is one too many? Go get thee from the door. 35

Dro. E. What patch is made our porter? My master stays in the street.

Dro. S. [*Within.*] Let him walk from whence he came, lest he catch cold on 's feet.

Ant. E. Who talks within there? Ho, open the door!

Dro. S. [*Within.*] Right, sir; I'll tell you when, an you'll tell me wherefore.

Ant. E. Wherefore? For my dinner. I have not din'd to-day. 40

Dro. S. [*Within.*] Nor to-day here you must not, come again when you may.

Ant. E. What art thou that keep'st me out from the house I owe?

---

210. **shrive:** to hear confession and give absolution. 212. **forth:** out. 215. **well-advis'd:** sane. 218. **at all adventures:** come what may.

Act III, sc. i, 4. **carcanet:** jeweled necklace. 8. **with:** i.e., with the possession of. 28. **cates:** refreshments, provisions. 32. **Mome:** blockhead. **malt-horse:** brewer's horse, hence a dullard. **patch:** fool. 33. **hatch:** a wicket or half-door. 42. **owe:** own.

Dro. S. [*Within.*] The porter for this time, sir,
   and my name is Dromio.
Dro. E. O villain! thou hast stolen both mine
   office and my name.
The one ne'er got me credit, the other mickle
   blame.   45
If thou hadst been Dromio to-day in my place,
Thou wouldst have chang'd thy face for a name,
   or thy name for an ass.

Enter LUCE [*within*].

Luce. [*Within.*] What a coil is there, Dromio?
   Who are those at the gate?
Dro. E. Let my master in, Luce.
Luce. [*Within.*] Faith, no; he comes too late;
And so tell your master.
Dro. E.   O Lord, I must laugh!
Have at you with a proverb — Shall I set in my
   staff?   51
Luce. [*Within.*] Have at you with another;
   that's — When? Can you tell?
Dro. S. [*Within.*] If thy name be called Luce, —
   Luce, thou hast answer'd him well.
Ant. E. Do you hear, you minion? You'll let
   us in, I hope?
Luce. [*Within.*] I thought to have ask'd you.
Dro. S.   [*Within.*] And you said no.
Dro. E. So, come, help: well struck! there was
   blow for blow.   56
Ant. E. Thou baggage, let me in.
Luce. [*Within.*] Can you tell for whose sake?
Dro. E. Master, knock the door hard.
Luce. [*Within.*] Let him knock till it ache.
Ant. E. You'll cry for this, minion, if I beat the
   door down.
Luce. [*Within.*] What needs all that, and a pair
   of stocks in the town?   60

Enter ADRIANA [*within*].

Adr. [*Within.*] Who is that at the door that
   keeps all this noise?
Dro. S. [*Within.*] By my troth, your town is
   troubled with unruly boys.
Ant. E. Are you there, wife? You might have
   come before.
Adr. [*Within.*] Your wife, sir knave! Go, get
   you from the door.
Dro. E. If you went in pain, master, this knave
   would go sore.   65
Ang. Here is neither cheer, sir, nor welcome; we
   would fain have either.

Bal. In debating which was best, we shall part
   with neither.
Dro. E. They stand at the door, master; bid
   them welcome hither.
Ant. E. There is something in the wind, that
   we cannot get in.
Dro. E. You would say so, master, if your
   garments were thin.   70
Your cake here is warm within; you stand here
   in the cold.
It would make a man mad as a buck, to be so
   bought and sold.
Ant. E. Go fetch me something; I'll break ope
   the gate.
Dro. S. [*Within.*] Break any breaking here, and
   I'll break your knave's pate.
Dro. E. A man may break a word with [you],
   sir, and words are but wind —   75
Ay, and break it in your face, so he break it not
   behind.
Dro. S. [*Within.*] It seems thou want'st breaking.
   Out upon thee, hind!
Dro. E. Here's too much "out upon thee!" I
   pray thee, let me in.
Dro. S. [*Within.*] Ay, when fowls have no feath-
   ers, and fish have no fin.   79
Ant. E. Well, I'll break in; go borrow me a crow.
Dro. E. A crow without feather? Master,
   mean you so?
For a fish without a fin, there's a fowl without a
   feather.
If a crow help us in, sirrah, we'll pluck a crow to-
   gether.
Ant. E. Go, get thee gone; fetch me an iron crow.
Bal. Have patience, sir; O, let it not be so! 85
Herein you war against your reputation
And draw within the compass of suspect
The unviolated honour of your wife.
Once this, — your long experience of [her] wisdom,
Her sober virtue, years, and modesty,   90
Plead on her part some cause to you unknown;
And doubt not, sir, but she will well excuse
Why at this time the doors are made against you.
Be rul'd by me; depart in patience,
And let us to the Tiger all to dinner;   95
And about evening come yourself alone
To know the reason of this strange restraint.
If by strong hand you offer to break in
Now in the stirring passage of the day,
A vulgar comment will be made of it,   100
And that supposed by the common rout
Against your yet ungalled estimation

45. **mickle:** much.   47. **face ... ass.** Not satisfactorily explained.   48. **coil:** fuss.   51. **set ... staff:** take up my abode.   52. **When ... tell?** An expression used to evade a question.   54. **minion:** hussy.   55–56. **I ... blow.** These lines seem pointless. Perhaps a line has dropped out, rhyming with *hope*.   65. **If ... sore.** Probably corrupt. 57. **part:** depart.   72. **bought and sold:** imposed upon.   75. **[you]** F₂   *your* F₁.   77. **hind:** slave.   80. **crow:** crowbar. 83. **pluck a crow:** pick a bone, settle accounts.   87. **suspect:** suspicion.   89. **Once this:** in short, briefly.   [her] (Rowe). *your* F.   93. **made:** fastened.   99. **stirring passage:** busy traffic.   100. **vulgar:** public.   102. **ungalled:** unblemished.

That may with foul intrusion enter in
And dwell upon your grave when you are dead;
For slander lives upon succession,   105
For ever hous'd where 't gets possession.
    Ant. E. You have prevail'd. I will depart in quiet,
And, in despite of mirth, mean to be merry.
I know a wench of excellent discourse,
Pretty and witty, wild, and yet, too, gentle.   110
There will we dine. This woman that I mean,
My wife — but, I protest, without desert —
Hath oftentimes upbraided me withal.
To her will we to dinner. [*To Ang.*] Get you home
And fetch the chain; by this I know 'tis made.   115
Bring it, I pray you, to the Porpentine;
For there's the house. That chain will I bestow —
Be it for nothing but to spite my wife —
Upon mine hostess there. Good sir, make haste.
Since mine own doors refuse to entertain me,   120
I'll knock elsewhere, to see if they'll disdain me.
    Ang. I'll meet you at that place some hour hence.
    Ant. E. Do so. This jest shall cost me some
     expense.   [*Exeunt.*

       [SCENE II. *The same.*]

Enter [LUCIANA] *and* ANTIPHOLUS *of Syracuse.*

[*Luc.*] And may it be that you have quite forgot
A husband's office? Shall, Antipholus,
Even in the spring of love, thy love-springs rot?
Shall love, in building, grow so [ruinous]?
If you did wed my sister for her wealth,   5
   Then for her wealth's sake use her with more
     kindness;
Or if you like elsewhere, do it by stealth;
   Muffle your false love with some show of blind-
     ness;
Let not my sister read it in your eye;
   Be not thy tongue thy own shame's orator;   10
Look sweet, speak fair, become disloyalty;
   Apparel vice like virtue's harbinger;
Bear a fair presence, though your heart be tainted;
   Teach sin the carriage of a holy saint;
Be secret-false. What need she be acquainted?   15
   What simple thief brags of his own [attaint]?
'Tis double wrong, to truant with your bed
   And let her read it in thy looks at board.
Shame hath a bastard fame, well managed;
   Ill deeds is doubled with an evil word.   20

Alas, poor women! make us [but] believe,
   Being compact of credit, that you love us;
Though others have the arm, show us the sleeve;
   We in your motion turn and you may move us.
Then, gentle brother, get you in again;   25
   Comfort my sister, cheer her, call her [wife].
'Tis holy sport to be a little vain,
   When the sweet breath of flattery conquers strife.
    Ant. S. Sweet mistress, — what your name is else,
     I know not,
Nor by what wonder you do hit of mine, —   30
Less in your knowledge and your grace you show not
   Than our earth's wonder, more than earth divine.
Teach me, dear creature, how to think and speak;
   Lay open to my earthy, gross conceit,
Smoth'red in errors, feeble, shallow, weak,   35
   The folded meaning of your words' deceit.
Against my soul's pure truth why labour you
   To make it wander in an unknown field?
Are you a god? Would you create me new?
   Transform me then, and to your power I'll yield.
But if that I am I, then well I know   41
   Your weeping sister is no wife of mine,
Nor to her bed no homage do I owe.
   Far more, far more to you do I decline.
O, train me not, sweet mermaid, with thy note,   45
   To drown me in thy sister's flood of tears.
Sing, siren, for thyself, and I will dote;
   Spread o'er the silver waves thy golden hairs,
And as a [bed] I'll take [them] and there lie,
   And in that glorious supposition think   50
He gains by death that hath such means to die.
   Let Love, being light, be drowned if she sink!
    Luc. What, are you mad, that you do reason so?
    Ant. S. Not mad, but mated; how, I do not know.
    Luc. It is a fault that springeth from your eye.   55
    Ant. S. For gazing on your beams, fair sun, being
     by.
    Luc. Gaze when you should, and that will clear
     your sight.
    Ant. S. As good to wink, sweet love, as look on
     night.
    Luc. Why call you me love? Call my sister so.
    Ant. S. Thy sister's sister.
    Luc.   That's my sister.
    Ant. S.   No;
It is thyself, mine own self's better part,   61
Mine eye's clear eye, my dear heart's dearer heart,

---

105. **slander...succession:** slander lives on after its victim is dead.   108. **in...mirth:** though I don't feel merry.
112. **desert:** my deserving it.   116. **Porpentine:** Porcupine (house-sign).
    Sc. ii, S.D. [LUCIANA] F2. *Iuliana* F1.   1. [*Luc.*] (Rowe). *Iulia* F.   3. **love-springs:** tender shoots of love.
4. [ruinous] (Capell). *ruinate* F.   11. **become disloyalty:** carry infidelity gracefully.   14. **carriage:** demeanor.   15. **What:**
why.   16. [attaint] (Rowe): dishonor, possibly conviction of crime. *attaine* F.   21. [but] (Theobald). Om. F.   22. **compact**
of credit: wholly credulous.   26. [wife] F2. *wise* F1.   27. **vain:** insincere.   30. **wonder:** miracle. **hit of:** guess.   32. **our**
earth's wonder. Probably a compliment to Queen Elizabeth.   34. **conceit:** understanding.   36. **folded:** concealed.
44. **decline:** incline.   45. **train:** lure. **note:** voice, music.   49. [bed] F2. *bud* F1. [them] (Edwards conj.) *thee* F.   52.
light: buoyant, aspiring. Cf. *V. A.* 149–150.   54. **mated:** amazed, with quibble on "matched with a wife."   56. **by:**
near you.   58. **wink:** close the eyes.

My food, my fortune, and my sweet hope's aim,
My sole earth's heaven, and my heaven's claim.
Luc. All this my sister is, or else should be.   65
Ant. S. Call thyself sister, sweet, for I am thee.
Thee will I love and with thee lead my life;
Thou hast no husband yet nor I no wife.
Give me thy hand.
Luc.   O, soft, sir! hold you still.
I'll fetch my sister, to get her good will. [*Exit.* 70

Enter DROMIO *of Syracuse.*

Ant. S. Why, how now, Dromio! Where runn'st
thou so fast?
Dro. S. Do you know me, sir? Am I Dromio?
Am I your man? Am I myself?   74
Ant. S. Thou art Dromio, thou art my man,
thou art thyself.
Dro. S. I am an ass, I am a woman's man, and
besides myself.
Ant. S. What woman's man, and how besides
thyself?   80
Dro. S. Marry, sir, besides myself, I am due to
a woman; one that claims me, one that haunts me,
one that will have me.
Ant. S. What claim lays she to thee?   84
Dro. S. Marry, sir, such claim as you would
lay to your horse; and she would have me as a
beast: not that, I being a beast, she would have me;
but that she, being a very beastly creature, lays
claim to me.
Ant. S. What is she?   90
Dro. S. A very reverend body; ay, such a one
as a man may not speak of without he say "Sir-
reverence." I have but lean luck in the match,
and yet is she a wondrous fat marriage.
Ant. S. How dost thou mean a fat marriage? 95
Dro. S. Marry, sir, she's the kitchen wench and
all grease; and I know not what use to put her to
but to make a lamp of her and run from her by her
own light. I warrant, her rags and the tallow in
them will burn a Poland winter. If she lives 100
till doomsday, she'll burn a week longer than the
whole world.
Ant. S. What complexion is she of?
Dro. S. Swart, like my shoe, but her face nothing
like so clean kept: for why, she sweats; a man 105
may go over shoes in the grime of it.
Ant. S. That's a fault that water will mend.
Dro. S. No, sir, 'tis in grain; Noah's flood could
not do it.
Ant. S. What's her name?   110

Dro. S. Nell, sir; but her name [and] three
quarters, that's an ell and three quarters, will not
measure her from hip to hip.
Ant. S. Then she bears some breadth?
Dro. S. No longer from head to foot than 115
from hip to hip. She is spherical, like a globe; I
could find out countries in her.
Ant. S. In what part of her body stands Ireland?
Dro. S. Marry, sir, in her buttocks; I found it
out by the bogs.   121
Ant. S. Where Scotland?
Dro. S. I found it by the barrenness; hard in the
palm of the hand.
Ant. S. Where France?   125
Dro. S. In her forehead; armed and reverted,
making war against her heir.
Ant. S. Where England?
Dro. S. I looked for the chalky cliffs, but I could
find no whiteness in them; but I guess it 130
stood in her chin, by the salt rheum that ran be-
tween France and it.
Ant. S. Where Spain?
Dro. S. Faith, I saw it not; but I felt it hot in
her breath.   135
Ant. S. Where America, the Indies?
Dro. S. Oh, sir, upon her nose, all o'er embel-
lished with rubies, carbuncles, sapphires, declining
their rich aspect to the hot breath of Spain; who
sent whole armadoes of caracks to be ballast at her
nose.   141
Ant. S. Where stood Belgia, the Netherlands?
Dro. S. Oh, sir, I did not look so low. To conclude, this drudge, or diviner, laid claim to me;
called me Dromio; swore I was assur'd to her; 145
told me what privy marks I had about me, as,
the mark of my shoulder, the mole in my neck,
the great wart on my left arm, that I, amaz'd,
ran from her as a witch.
And, I think, if my breast had not been made of
    faith and my heart of steel,   150
She had transform'd me to a curtal dog and made
    me turn i' the wheel.
Ant. S. Go, hie thee presently post to the road;
An if the wind blow any way from shore,
I will not harbour in this town to-night.
If any bark put forth, come to the mart,   155
Where I will walk till thou return to me.
If every one knows us and we know none,
'Tis time, I think, to trudge, pack, and be gone.
Dro. S. As from a bear a man would run for
    life,   159

64 **My ... claim:** My heaven on earth and my claim on heaven hereafter.   93. **Sir-reverence:** i.e., "save your reverence," an expression used as apology for a remark that might offend.   104. **Swart:** dark.   108. **in grain:** ineradicable.
111. **[and]** (Theobald). *is* F.   126. **armed ... heir.** See Introduction for reference to French civil wars. **armed:** also with
"eruptions" of the skin **reverted:** (1) revolted, (2) receding. **heir:** with a pun on *hair.* 130. **them:** the cliffs, presumably her teeth.   139. **declining:** bending.   140. **armadoes ... caracks:** fleets of galleons. See Introduction. 140. **ballast:**
loaded.   144. **diviner:** sorceress.   145. **assur'd:** betrothed.   151. **curtal dog:** a dog with a docked tail. **turn ... wheel:** i.e.,
turn the spit by running in a wheel.   152. **presently:** immediately. **road:** harbor, roadstead.

So fly I from her that would be my wife.   [*Exit.*
  Ant. S. There's none but witches do inhabit here;
And therefore 'tis high time that I were hence.
She that doth call me husband, even my soul
Doth for a wife abhor.   But her fair sister,
Possess'd with such a gentle sovereign grace,   165
Of such enchanting presence and discourse,
Hath almost made me traitor to myself.
But, lest myself be guilty to self-wrong,
I'll stop mine ears against the mermaid's song.

     Enter ANGELO *with the chain.*
  Ang. Master Antipholus —
  Ant. S.   Ay, that's my name.
  Ang. I know it well, sir; lo, here is the chain.   171
I thought to have ta'en you at the Porpentine;
The chain unfinish'd made me stay thus long.
  Ant. S. What is your will that I shall do with
    this?
  Ang. What please yourself, sir; I have made it
    for you.   175
  Ant. S. Made it for me, sir!   I bespoke it not.
  Ang. Not once, nor twice, but twenty times you
    have.
Go home with it and please your wife withal;
And soon at supper-time I'll visit you
And then receive my money for the chain.   180
  Ant. S. I pray you, sir, receive the money now,
For fear you ne'er see chain nor money more.
  Ang. You are a merry man, sir; fare you well.
                   [*Exit.*
  Ant. S. What I should think of this, I cannot tell;
But this I think, there's no man is so vain   185
That would refuse so fair an offer'd chain.
I see a man here needs not live by shifts
When in the streets he meets such golden gifts.
I'll to the mart and there for Dromio stay.   189
If any ship put out, then straight away.   [*Exit.*

ACT IV

SCENE I. [*A public place.*]

Enter SECOND MERCHANT, ANGELO, *and an* OFFICER

  2. Mer. You know since Pentecost the sum is due,
And since I have not much importun'd you;
Nor now I had not, but that I am bound
To Persia and want guilders for my voyage.
Therefore make present satisfaction,   5
Or I'll attach you by this officer.
  Ang. Even just the sum that I do owe to you
Is growing to me by Antipholus,
And in the instant that I met with you

He had of me a chain.   At five o'clock   10
I shall receive the money for the same.
Pleaseth you walk with me down to his house,
I will discharge my bond and thank you too.

    Enter ANTIPHOLUS of Ephesus *and* DROMIO of
      Ephesus *from the courtezan's.*
  Off. That labour may you save; see where he
    comes.
  Ant. E. While I go to the goldsmith's house, go
    thou   15
And buy a rope's end; that will I bestow
Among my wife and [her] confederates,
For locking me out of my doors by day.
But, soft! I see the goldsmith.   Get thee gone,
Buy thou a rope and bring it home to me.   20
  Dro. E. I buy a thousand pound a year! I buy a
    rope!   [*Exit.*
  Ant. E. A man is well holp up that trusts to you.
I promised your presence and the chain,
But neither chain nor goldsmith came to me.
Belike you thought our love would last too long   25
If it were chain'd together, and therefore came not.
  Ang. Saving your merry humour, here's the note
How much your chain weighs to the utmost [carat],
The fineness of the gold, and chargeful fashion,
Which doth amount to three odd ducats more   30
Than I stand debted to this gentleman.
I pray you, see him presently discharg'd,
For he is bound to sea and stays but for it.
  Ant. E. I am not furnish'd with the present
    money;
Besides, I have some business in the town.   35
Good signior, take the stranger to my house;
And with you take the chain, and bid my wife
Disburse the sum on the receipt thereof.
Perchance I will be there as soon as you.
  Ang. Then you will bring the chain to her your-
    self?   40
  Ant. E. No; bear it with you, lest I come not
    time enough.
  Ang. Well, sir, I will.   Have you the chain about
    you?
  Ant. E. An if I have not, sir, I hope you have,
Or else you may return without your money.
  Ang. Nay, come, I pray you, sir, give me the
    chain.   45
Both wind and tide stays for this gentleman,
And I, to blame, have held him here too long.
  Ant. E. Good Lord! you use this dalliance to
    excuse
Your breach of promise to the Porpentine.
I should have chid you for not bringing it,   50

  168. **to:** of.   185. **vain:** foolish.
  Act IV, sc. i, 6. **attach:** arrest.   8. **growing:** due, accruing.   16. **bestow:** employ.   17. **[her]** (Rowe).   *their* F.   21. **I...
year.** An obscure remark, but Dromio probably means, "What an idea, that *I* should be sent to buy that by which I shall
get a thousand pounds (thumps) a year!"   22. **holp:** helped.   28. **[carat]** (Pope).   *charect* F.

But, like a shrew, you first begin to brawl.
  2. Mer. The hour steals on; I pray you, sir, dis-
    patch.
  Ang. You hear how he importunes me; — the
    chain!
  Ant. E. Why, give it to my wife, and fetch your
    money.
  Ang. Come, come, you know I gave it you even
    now.   55
Either send the chain or send by me some token.
  Ant. E. Fie, now you run this humour out of
    breath.
Come, where's the chain? I pray you, let me see it.
  2. Mer. My business cannot brook this dalliance.
Good sir, say whe'r you'll answer me or no;   60
If not, I'll leave him to the officer.
  Ant. E. I answer you!   What should I answer
    you?
  Ang. The money that you owe me for the chain.
  Ant. E. I owe you none till I receive the chain.
  Ang. You know I gave it you half an hour since.
  Ant. E. You gave me none; you wrong me much
    to say so.   66
  Ang. You wrong me more, sir, in denying it.
Consider how it stands upon my credit.
  2. Mer. Well, officer, arrest him at my suit.
  Off. I do; and charge you in the Duke's name to
    obey me.   70
  Ang. This touches me in reputation.
Either consent to pay this sum for me
Or I attach you by this officer.
  Ant. E. Consent to pay thee that I never had!
Arrest me, foolish fellow, if thou dar'st.   75
  Ang. Here is thy fee; arrest him, officer.
I would not spare my brother in this case,
If he should scorn me so apparently.
  Off. I do arrest you, sir: you hear the suit.
  Ant. E. I do obey thee till I give thee bail.   80
But, sirrah, you shall buy this sport as dear
As all the metal in your shop will answer.
  Ang. Sir, sir, I shall have law in Ephesus,
To your notorious shame; I doubt it not.

Enter DROMIO *of Syracuse, from the bay.*

  Dro. S. Master, there is a bark of Epidamnum
That stays but till her owner comes aboard,   86
And then, sir, she bears away. Our fraughtage, sir,
I have convey'd aboard, and I have bought
The oil, the balsamum, and aqua-vitæ.
The ship is in her trim; the merry wind   90
Blows fair from land; they stay for nought at all
But for their owner, master, and yourself.

  Ant. E. How now! a madman! Why, thou peev-
    ish sheep,
What ship of Epidamnum stays for me?
  Dro. S. A ship you sent me to, to hire waftage.
  Ant. E. Thou drunken slave, I sent thee for a
    rope,   96
And told thee to what purpose and what end.
  Dro. S. You sent me for a rope's end as soon.
You sent me to the bay, sir, for a bark.
  Ant. E. I will debate this matter at more lei-
    sure,   100
And teach your ears to list me with more heed.
To Adriana, villain, hie thee straight;
Give her this key, and tell her, in the desk
That's cover'd o'er with Turkish tapestry
There is a purse of ducats; let her send it.   105
Tell her I am arrested in the street
And that shall bail me.   Hie thee, slave, be gone!
On, officer, to prison till it come.
        [*Exeunt [2. Merchant, Angelo, Officer, and
            Ant. E.*].
  Dro. S. To Adriana! That is where we din'd,
Where Dowsabel did claim me for her husband.
She is too big, I hope, for me to compass.   111
Thither I must, although against my will,
For servants must their masters' minds fulfil.
                                          [*Exit.*

[SCENE II. *The house of Antipholus of Ephesus.*]

        Enter ADRIANA *and* LUCIANA.

  Adr. Ah, Luciana, did he tempt thee so?
Mightst thou perceive austerely in his eye
That he did plead in earnest?   Yea or no?
Look'd he or red or pale, or sad or merrily?
What observation mad'st thou in this case   5
Of his heart's meteors tilting in his face?
  Luc. First he deni'd you had in him no right.
  Adr. He meant he did me none; the more my
    spite.
  Luc. Then swore he that he was a stranger here.
  Adr. And true he swore, though yet forsworn he
    were.   10
  Luc. Then pleaded I for you.
  Adr.   And what said he?
  Luc. That love I begg'd for you he begg'd of me.
  Adr. With what persuasion did he tempt thy
    love?
  Luc. With words that in an honest suit might
    move.
First he did praise my beauty, then my speech.   15
  Adr. Didst speak him fair?

---

60. **answer:** pay.   68. **stands upon:** concerns.   78. **apparently:** openly.   87. **fraughtage:** baggage.   89. **balsamum:**
balm.   **aqua-vitæ:** spirits.   90. **in ... trim:** rigged and ready to sail.   93. **peevish:** senseless.   95. **waftage:** passage.
98. **rope's end:** hangman's noose.   110. **Dowsabel:** derived from *douce et belle* and here applied ironically to Nell (see III.
ii.111).
  Sc. ii, 2. austerely: soberly.   6 **meteors:** changes of color and expression.   **tilting:** clashing (like the aurora borealis).
8. **spite:** grief.

Luc.   Have patience, I beseech.
Adr. I cannot, nor I will not, hold me still;
My tongue, though not my heart, shall have his will.
He is deformed, crooked, old, and sere,
Ill-fac'd, worse bodied, shapeless everywhere: 20
Vicious, ungentle, foolish, blunt, unkind,
Stigmatical in making, worse in mind.
Luc. Who would be jealous then of such a one?
No evil lost is wail'd when it is gone.
Adr. Ah, but I think him better than I say, 25
And yet would herein others' eyes were worse.
Far from her nest the lapwing cries away.
My heart prays for him, though my tongue do
    curse.

    Enter DROMIO *of Syracuse.*

Dro. S. Here! go; the desk, the purse! Sweet,
    now, make haste. 29
Luc. How hast thou lost thy breath?
Dro. S.   By running fast.
Adr. Where is thy master, Dromio? Is he well?
Dro. S. No, he's in Tartar limbo, worse than
    hell.
A devil in an everlasting garment hath him;
One whose hard heart is button'd up with steel;
A fiend, a fairy, pitiless and rough; 35
A wolf, nay, worse, a fellow all in buff;
A back-friend, a shoulder-clapper, one that counter-
    mands
The passages of alleys, creeks, and narrow lands;
A hound that runs counter and yet draws dry-foot
    well;
One that before the judgement carries poor souls to
    hell. 40
Adr. Why, man, what is the matter?
Dro. S. I do not know the matter; he is 'rested on
    the case.
Adr. What, is he arrested? Tell me at whose
    suit.
Dro. S. I know not at whose suit he is arrested
    well;
But he's in a suit of buff which 'rested him, that can
    I tell. 45
Will you send him, mistress, redemption, the money
    in his desk?
Adr. Go fetch it, sister. This I wonder at,
                  [*Exit Luciana.*
[That] he, unknown to me, should be in debt.

Tell me, was he arrested on a band?
Dro. S. Not on a band but on a stronger thing,
A chain, a chain! Do you not hear it ring? 51
Adr. What, the chain?
Dro. S. No, no, the bell; 'tis time that I were
    gone.
It was two ere I left him, and now the clock strikes
    one.
Adr. The hours come back! That did I never
    [hear]. 55
Dro. S. O, yes; if any hour meet a sergeant, 'a
    turns back for very fear.
Adr. As if Time were in debt! How fondly dost
    thou reason!
Dro. S. Time is a very bankrupt and owes more
    than he's worth to season.
Nay, he's a thief too; have you not heard men say,
That Time comes stealing on by night and day?
If ['a] be in debt and theft, and a sergeant in the
    way, 61
Hath he not reason to turn back an hour in a day?

    Re-enter LUCIANA.

Adr. Go, Dromio; there's the money, bear it
    straight,
And bring thy master home immediately.
Come, sister; I am press'd down with conceit— 65
Conceit, my comfort and my injury. [*Exeunt.*

    [SCENE III. *A public place.*]

    Enter ANTIPHOLUS *of Syracuse.*

Ant. S. There's not a man I meet but doth salute
    me
As if I were their well-acquainted friend;
And every one doth call me by my name.
Some tender money to me; some invite me;
Some other give me thanks for kindnesses; 5
Some offer me commodities to buy.
Even now a tailor call'd me in his shop
And show'd me silks that he had bought for me
And therewithal took measure of my body.
Sure, these are but imaginary wiles, 10
And Lapland sorcerers inhabit here.

    Enter DROMIO *of Syracuse.*

Dro. S. Master, here's the gold you sent me for.
What, have you got the picture of old Adam new-
    apparell'd?

18. **his:** its. 22. **Stigmatical:** crooked. **making:** form. 32. **Tartar limbo:** prison. *Limbo,* a region on the outskirts of hell, is qualified by *Tartar,* by which Dromio may have meant the classical Tartarus or the Asiatic people (or both). 33. **everlasting:** durable, i.e., made of *buff* (l. 36), a stout leather worn by police officers. 35. **fairy:** i.e., a *malevolent* sprite. 37. **back-friend:** a false friend; here the police officer who arrests by clapping on the back. **countermands:** forbids entrance into. 38. **creeks:** narrow, winding passages. 39. **counter:** in a direction opposite to that which the game has taken; with a pun on *counter,* a prison. **draws dry-foot:** tracks game by mere scent of the foot. 40. **judgement:** (1) a legal judgement, (2) the Day of Judgement. 42. **case:** legal term. 48. [that] F₂. *thus* F₁. 49. **band:** bond. 55. [hear] F₂. *here* F₁. 56. **'a:** he. 57. **fondly:** foolishly. 58. **season:** opportunity. 61. ['a] (Staunton). *I* F. 65. **conceit:** imagination.

Sc. iii, 11. Lapland. Lapland was traditionally famous for witchcraft and sorcery. 13-14. **picture ... new-apparell'd:** the sergeant. There seems to be a lost allusion here. Theobald inserted *rid of* after *got.*

Ant. S. What gold is this? What Adam dost
thou mean?   15
Dro. S. Not that Adam that kept the Paradise,
but that Adam that keeps the prison; he that goes
in the calf's skin that was kill'd for the Prodigal; he
that came behind you, sir, like an evil angel, and bid
you forsake your liberty.   20
Ant. S. I understand thee not.
Dro. S. No? Why, 'tis a plain case; he that went,
like a bass-viol, in a case of leather; the man, sir,
that, when gentlemen are tired, gives them a sob
and 'rests them; he, sir, that takes pity on de-   25
cayed men and gives them suits of durance; he that
sets up his rest to do more exploits with his mace
than a morris-pike.
Ant. S. What, thou mean'st an officer?
Dro. S. Ay, sir, the sergeant of the band; he   30
that brings any man to answer it that breaks his
band; one that thinks a man always going to bed
and says, "God give you good rest!"
Ant. S. Well, sir, there rest in your foolery. Is
there any [ship] puts forth to-night? May we be
gone?   36
Dro. S. Why, sir, I brought you word an hour
since that the bark Expedition put forth to-night;
and then were you hind'red by the sergeant, to
tarry for the hoy Delay. Here are the angels   40
that you sent for to deliver you.
Ant. S. The fellow is distract, and so am I;
And here we wander in illusions.
Some blessed power deliver us from hence!

Enter a COURTEZAN.

Cour. Well met, well met, Master Antipholus.
I see, sir, you have found the goldsmith now.   46
Is that the chain you promis'd me to-day?
Ant. S. Satan, avoid! I charge thee, tempt me
not.
Dro. S. Master, is this Mistress Satan?
Ant. S. It is the devil.   50
Dro. S. Nay, she is worse, she is the devil's
dam, and here she comes in the habit of a light
wench; and thereof comes that the wenches say,
"God damn me"; that's as much to say, God make
me a light wench. It is written, they appear to   55
men like angels of light; light is an effect of fire, and
fire will burn; *ergo*, light wenches will burn. Come
not near her.
Cour. Your man and you are marvellous merry,
sir.   59

Will you go with me? We'll mend our dinner here?
Dro. S. Master, if [you] do, expect spoon-meat;
or bespeak a long spoon.
Ant. S. Why, Dromio?
Dro. S. Marry, he must have a long spoon that
must eat with the devil.   65
Ant. S. Avoid [then], fiend! What tell'st thou
me of supping?
Thou art, as you are all, a sorceress.
I conjure thee to leave me and be gone.
Cour. Give me the ring of mine you had at
dinner,
Or, for my diamond, the chain you promis'd,   70
And I'll be gone, sir, and not trouble you.
Dro. S. Some devils ask but the parings of one's
nail,
A rush, a hair, a drop of blood, a pin,
A nut, a cherry-stone;
But she, more covetous, would have a chain.   75
Master, be wise; an if you give it her,
The devil will shake her chain and fright us with it.
Cour. I pray you, sir, my ring, or else the chain.
I hope you do not mean to cheat me so?
Ant. S. Avaunt, thou witch! Come, Dromio,
let us go.   80
Dro. S. Fly pride, says the peacock: mistress,
that you know.
                    [*Exeunt* [*Ant. S. and Dro. S.*].
Cour. Now, out of doubt Antipholus is mad,
Else would he never so demean himself.
A ring he hath of mine worth forty ducats,
And for the same he promis'd me a chain.   85
Both one and other he denies me now.
The reason that I gather he is mad,
Besides this present instance of his rage,
Is a mad tale he told to-day at dinner,
Of his own doors being shut against his entrance.   90
Belike his wife, acquainted with his fits,
On purpose shut the doors against his way.
My way is now to hie home to his house,
And tell his wife that, being lunatic,
He rush'd into my house and took perforce   95
My ring away. This course I fittest choose;
For forty ducats is too much to lose.   [*Exit.*]

[SCENE IV. *A street.*]

Enter ANTIPHOLUS *of Ephesus and* [*the* OFFICER].

Ant. E. Fear me not, man; I will not break away.
I'll give thee, ere I leave thee, so much money,

---

24. **sob**: "a rest given to a horse to recover its wind" (N.E.D.).   26. **durance**: durable cloth, as well as "prison."
27. **sets…rest**: stakes his all, with quibble upon "setting" a soldier's pike in "rest" for a charge.   **mace**: club carried by
a constable.   28. **morris-pike**: Moorish pike.   35. [ship] F$_2$. *ships* F$_1$.   40. **hoy**: small vessel.   **angels**: gold coins worth
about 10s. apiece.   48. **avoid**: away, avaunt.   57. **will burn**: i.e., are diseased.   60. **mend**: amend, supplement.
61. [you] F$_2$. Om. F$_1$.   **spoon-meat**: food for infants.   65. Proverbial.   66. [then] F$_4$. *thou* F$_{1-3}$.   81. **Fly…peacock.**
An accusation of dishonesty coming from a dishonest person is as out of place as a warning against pride would be from
the peacock.
Sc. iv, s.d. [*the* OFFICER] (Capell).   *a Jailor* F.

To warrant thee, as I am 'rested for.
My wife is in a wayward mood to-day,
And will not lightly trust the messenger.   5
That I should be attach'd in Ephesus,
I tell you, 'twill sound harshly in her ears.

Enter DROMIO of Ephesus *with a rope's-end.*

Here comes my man; I think he brings the money.
How now, sir! have you that I sent you for?
   Dro. E. Here's that, I warrant you, will pay
them all.   10
   Ant. E. But where's the money?
   Dro. E. Why, sir, I gave the money for the rope.
   Ant. E. Five hundred ducats, villain, for a rope?
   Dro. E. I'll serve you, sir, five hundred at the
rate.
   Ant. E. To what end did I bid thee hie thee
home?   15
   Dro. E. To a rope's end, sir; and to that end am
I return'd.
   Ant. E. And to that end, sir, I will welcome you.
                             [*Beating him.*]
   Off. Good sir, be patient.
   Dro. E. Nay, 'tis for me to be patient; I am in
adversity.   21
   Off. Good now, hold thy tongue.
   Dro. E. Nay, rather persuade him to hold his
hands.
   Ant. E. Thou whoreson, senseless villain!   25
   Dro. E. I would I were senseless, sir, that I might
not feel your blows.
   Ant. E. Thou art sensible in nothing but blows,
and so is an ass.
   Dro. E. I am an ass, indeed; you may prove   30
it by my long 'ears. I have served him from the
hour of my nativity to this instant, and have nothing at his hands for my service but blows. When I
am cold, he heats me with beating; when I am
warm, he cools me with beating. I am wak'd   35
with it when I sleep; rais'd with it when I sit; driven
out of doors with it when I go from home; welcom'd
home with it when I return; nay, I bear it on my
shoulders, as a beggar wont her brat; and, I think,
when he hath lam'd me, I shall beg with it from   40
door to door.

Enter ADRIANA, LUCIANA, *the* COURTEZAN, *and a*
Schoolmaster call'd PINCH.

   Ant. E. Come, go along; my wife is coming
yonder.
   Dro. E. Mistress, *respice finem*, respect your end;
or rather, [to] prophesy like the parrot, "beware
the rope's-end."   46

   Ant. E. Wilt thou still talk?   [*Beating him.*]
   Cour. How say you now? Is not your husband mad?
   Adr. His incivility confirms no less.
Good Doctor Pinch, you are a conjurer;   50
Establish him in his true sense again,
And I will please you what you will demand.
   Luc. Alas, how fiery and how sharp he looks!
   Cour. Mark how he trembles in his ecstasy!
   Pinch. Give me your hand and let me feel your
pulse.   55
   Ant. E. There is my hand, and let it feel your
ear.   [*Striking him.*]
   Pinch. I charge thee, Satan, hous'd within this
man,
To yield possession to my holy prayers
And to thy state of darkness hie thee straight.
I conjure thee by all the saints in heaven!   60
   Ant. E. Peace, doting wizard, peace! I am not
mad.
   Adr. O, that thou wert not, poor distressed soul!
   Ant. E. You minion, you, are these your cus-
tomers?
Did this companion with the saffron face
Revel and feast it at my house to-day,   65
Whilst upon me the guilty doors were shut
And I denied to enter in my house?
   Adr. O husband, God doth know you din'd at
home;
Where would you had remain'd until this time,
Free from these slanders and this open shame!   70
   Ant. E. Din'd at home! Thou villain, what
sayest thou?
   Dro. E. Sir, sooth to say, you did not dine at
home.
   Ant. E. Were not my doors lock'd up and I shut
out?
   Dro. E. Perdie, your doors were lock'd and you
shut out.   74
   Ant. E. And did not she herself revile me there?
   Dro. E. Sans fable, she herself revil'd you there.
   Ant. E. Did not her kitchen-maid rail, taunt,
and scorn me?
   Dro. E. Certes, she did; the kitchen-vestal scorn'd
you.
   Ant. E. And did not I in rage depart from thence?
   Dro. E. In verity you did; my bones bear witness,
That since have felt the vigour of his rage.   81
   Adr. Is't good to soothe him in these contraries?
   Pinch. It is no shame. The fellow finds his vein,
And, yielding to him, humours well his frenzy.
   Ant. E. Thou hast suborn'd the goldsmith to
arrest me.   85
   Adr. Alas, I sent you money to redeem you.

---

22. **Good now:** pray you. 28. **sensible:** sensitive. 39. **wont:** is accustomed to. 44. *respice finem. Respice funem.*
"heed the hangman's rope," was a popular quibble on this phrase. 45. **[to]** (Dvce). *the* F. 46. "beware the rope's
end": i.e., beware the hangman's noose; apparently a phrase taught to parrots. 50. **conjurer.** Being able to use Latin,
Pinch could exorcise evil spirits. 52. **please:** pay. 54. **ecstasy:** madness. 63. **minion:** darling. **customers:** guests
(both terms used contemptuously). 64. **companion:** fellow. **saffron:** yellow. 74. *Perdie:* certainly (corruption of *par*
Dieu). 76. *Sans:* without. 78. **kitchen-vestal:** i.e., Luce.

By Dromio here, who came in haste for it.
Dro. E. Money by me! Heart and good-will
    you might,
But surely, master, not a rag of money.
Ant. E. Went'st not thou to her for a purse of
    ducats?   90
Adr. He came to me and I deliver'd it.
Luc. And I am witness with her that she did.
Dro. E. God and the rope-maker bear me witness
That I was sent for nothing but a rope!
Pinch. Mistress, both man and master is pos-
    sess'd;   95
I know it by their pale and deadly looks.
They must be bound and laid in some dark room.
Ant. E. Say, wherefore didst thou lock me forth
    to-day?
And why dost thou deny the bag of gold?   99
Adr. I did not, gentle husband, lock thee forth.
Dro. E. And, gentle master, I receiv'd no gold;
But I confess, sir, that we were lock'd out.
Adr. Dissembling villain, thou speak'st false in
    both.
Ant. E. Dissembling harlot, thou art false in all
And art confederate with a damned pack   105
To make a loathsome abject scorn of me;
But with these nails I'll pluck out these false eyes
That would behold in me this shameful sport.

Enter three or four, and offer to bind him. He strives.

Adr. O, bind him, bind him! Let him not come
    near me.
Pinch. More company! The fiend is strong
    within him.   110
Luc. Ay me, poor man, how pale and wan he looks!
Ant. E. What, will you murder me? Thou
    gaoler, thou,
I am thy prisoner. Wilt thou suffer them
To make a rescue?
Off.   Masters, let him go.
He is my prisoner, and you shall not have him. 115
Pinch. Go bind this man, for he is frantic too.
    [*They offer to bind Dro. E.*]
Adr. What wilt thou do, thou peevish officer?
Hast thou delight to see a wretched man
Do outrage and displeasure to himself?
Off. He is my prisoner; if I let him go,   120
The debt he owes will be requir'd of me.
Adr. I will discharge thee e'er I go from thee.
Bear me forth unto his creditor
And, knowing how the debt grows, I will pay it.
Good master doctor, see him safe convey'd   125
Home to my house. O most unhappy day!
Ant. E. O most unhappy strumpet!
Dro. E. Master, I am here ent'red in bond for
    you.

Ant. E. Out on thee, villain! wherefore dost thou
    mad me?
Dro. E. Will you be bound for nothing? Be
mad, good master; cry "The devil!"   131
Luc. God help, poor souls, how idly do they talk!
Adr. Go bear him hence. Sister, go you with me.
Say now, whose suit is he arrested at?
    [*Exeunt all but Adriana, Luciana, Officer,*
        and Courtezan.

Off. One Angelo, a goldsmith. Do you know
    him?   135
Adr. I know the man. What is the sum he owes?
Off. Two hundred ducats.
Adr.   Say, how grows it due?
Off. Due for a chain your husband had of him.
Adr. He did bespeak a chain for me, but had it
    not.
Cour. When as your husband all in rage to-day
Came to my house and took away my ring —   141
The ring I saw upon his finger now —
Straight after did I meet him with a chain.
Adr. It may be so, but I did never see it.
Come, gaoler, bring me where the goldsmith is.
I long to know the truth hereof at large.   146

Enter ANTIPHOLUS *of Syracuse* with his rapier
    drawn, *and* DROMIO *of Syracuse.*

Luc. God, for thy mercy! they are loose again.
Adr. And come with naked swords.
Let's call more help to have them bound again.
Off. Away! they'll kill us.   150
    [*Exeunt all [but Ant. S. and Dro. S.]*
    as fast as may be, frighted.
Ant. S. I see these witches are afraid of swords.
Dro. S. She that would be your wife now ran
    from you.
Ant. S. Come to the Centaur; fetch our stuff
    from thence;
I long that we were safe and sound aboard.   154
Dro. S. Faith, stay here this night; they will
surely do us no harm. You saw they speak us fair,
give us gold; methinks they are such a gentle
nation that, but for the mountain of mad flesh that
claims marriage of me, I could find in my heart to
stay here still and turn witch.   160
Ant. S. I will not stay to-night for all the town;
Therefore away, to get our stuff aboard. [*Exeunt.*

ACT V

SCENE I. [*A street before a Priory.*]

Enter SECOND MERCHANT *and* ANGELO.

Ang. I am sorry, sir, that I have hind'red you;
But, I protest, he had the chain of me,

---

96. **deadly:** deathlike.   97. **bound...room.**   This was the regular treatment for lunatics in Shakespeare's day.
117. **peevish:** foolish.   147. **again.**   Here F reads *Runne all out.*

Though most dishonestly he doth deny it.
  2. Mer. How is the man esteem'd here in the
    city?
  Ang. Of very reverend reputation, sir,   5
Of credit infinite, highly belov'd,
Second to none that lives here in the city.
His word might bear my wealth at any time.
  2. Mer. Speak softly; yonder, as I think, he
    walks.

Enter ANTIPHOLUS *of Syracuse and* DROMIO *of
Syracuse.*

  Ang. 'Tis so; and that self chain about his neck
Which he forswore most monstrously to have.   11
Good sir, draw near to me, I'll speak to him.
Signior Antipholus, I wonder much
That you would put me to this shame and trouble;
And, not without some scandal to yourself,   15
With circumstance and oaths so to deny
This chain which now you wear so openly.
Beside the charge, the shame, imprisonment,
You have done wrong to this my honest friend,
Who, but for staying on our controversy,   20
Had hoisted sail and put to sea to-day.
This chain you had of me; can you deny it?
  Ant. S. I think I had; I never did deny it.
  2. Mer. Yes, that you did, sir, and forswore it too.
  Ant. S. Who heard me to deny it or forswear it?
  2. Mer. These ears of mine, thou know'st, did
    hear thee.   26
Fie on thee, wretch! 'Tis pity that thou liv'st
To walk where any honest men resort.
  Ant. S. Thou art a villain to impeach me thus.
I'll prove mine honour and mine honesty   30
Against thee presently, if thou dar'st stand.
  2. Mer. I dare, and do defy thee for a villain.
                                         [*They draw.*

Enter ADRIANA, LUCIANA, *the* COURTEZAN *and
others.*

  Adr. Hold, hurt him not, for [God's] sake!
    He is mad.
Some get within him; take his sword away.
Bind Dromio too, and bear them to my house.   35
  Dro. S. Run, master, run; for God's sake, take
    a house!
This is some priory. In, or we are spoil'd!
                     [*Exeunt Ant. S. and Dro. S. to the
                     Priory.*

Enter the LADY ABBESS.

  Abb. Be quiet, people. Wherefore throng you
    hither?
  Adr. To fetch my poor distracted husband hence.

Let us come in, that we may bind him fast   40
And bear him home for his recovery.
  Ang. I knew he was not in his perfect wits.
  2. Mer. I am sorry now that I did draw on him.
  Abb. How long hath this possession held the
    man?
  Adr. This week he hath been heavy, sour, sad,
And much different from the man he was;   46
But till this afternoon his passion
Ne'er brake into extremity of rage.
  Abb. Hath he not lost much wealth by wreck
    of sea?
Buried some dear friend? Hath not else his eye
Stray'd his affection in unlawful love?   51
A sin prevailing much in youthful men,
Who give their eyes the liberty of gazing.
Which of these sorrows is he subject to?   54
  Adr. To none of these, except it be the last;
Namely, some love that drew him oft from home.
  Abb. You should for that have reprehended him.
  Adr. Why, so I did.
  Abb.   Ay, but not rough enough.
  Adr. As roughly as my modesty would let me.
  Abb. Haply, in private.
  Adr.   And in assemblies too.
  Abb. Ay, but not enough.   61
  Adr. It was the copy of our conference.
In bed he slept not for my urging it;
At board he fed not for my urging it;
Alone, it was the subject of my theme;   65
In company I often glanced it;
Still did I tell him it was vile and bad.
  Abb. And thereof came it that the man was mad.
The venom clamours of a jealous woman
Poisons more deadly than a mad dog's tooth.   70
It seems his sleeps were hind'red by thy railing,
And thereof comes it that his head is light.
Thou say'st his meat was sauc'd with thy upbraid-
    ings;
Unquiet meals make ill digestions,
Thereof the raging fire of fever bred;   75
And what's a fever but a fit of madness?
Thou say'st his sports were hind'red by thy brawls:
Sweet recreation barr'd, what doth ensue
But moody and dull melancholy,
Kinsman to grim and comfortless despair,   80
And at her heels a huge infectious troop
Of pale distemperatures and foes to life?
In food, in sport, and life-preserving rest
To be disturb'd, would mad or man or beast.
The consequence is, then, thy jealous fits   85
Hath scar'd thy husband from the use of wits.
  Luc. She never reprehended him but mildly,
When he demean'd himself rough, rude, and wildly.

Act V, sc. i, 8. bear: claim.   **10. self:** self-same.   **11. forswore:** vehemently denied.   **16. circumstance:** details.
33. [God's] F₃.   *God* F₁.   **34. within him:** under his guard.   **36. take:** take to.   **49. of:** at.   **51. stray'd:** led astray.
62. copy: topic.   **conference:** conversation.   **66. glanced:** hinted at.   **82. distemperatures:** physical disorders.

Why bear you these rebukes and answer not?
Adr. She did betray me to my own reproof. 90
Good people, enter and lay hold on him.
Abb. No, not a creature enters in my house.
Adr. Then let your servants bring my husband
forth.
Abb. Neither. He took this place for sanctuary,
And it shall privilege him from your hands 95
Till I have brought him to his wits again,
Or lose my labour in assaying it.
Adr. I will attend my husband, be his nurse,
Diet his sickness, for it is my office,
And will have no attorney but myself; 100
And therefore let me have him home with me.
Abb. Be patient; for I will not let him stir
Till I have us'd the approved means I have,
With wholesome syrups, drugs, and holy prayers,
To make of him a formal man again. 105
It is a branch and parcel of mine oath,
A charitable duty of my order.
Therefore depart and leave him here with me.
Adr. I will not hence and leave my husband here;
And ill it doth beseem your holiness 110
To separate the husband and the wife.
Abb. Be quiet and depart; thou shalt not have
him.   [*Exit.*]
Luc. Complain unto the Duke of this indignity.
Adr. Come, go. I will fall prostrate at his feet
And never rise until my tears and prayers 115
Have won his Grace to come in person hither
And take perforce my husband from the abbess.
2. Mer. By this, I think, the dial points at five.
Anon, I'm sure, the Duke himself in person
Comes this way to the melancholy vale, 120
The place of [death] and sorry execution,
Behind the ditches of the abbey here.
Ang. Upon what cause?
2. Mer. To see a [reverend] Syracusian merchant
Who put unluckily into this bay 125
Against the laws and statutes of this town,
Beheaded publicly for his offence.
Ang. See where they come; we will behold his
death.
Luc. Kneel to the Duke before he pass the abbey.

Enter DUKE [*attended*], *and* ÆGEON *bareheaded,
with the* Headsman *and other* Officers.

Duke. Yet once again proclaim it publicly, 130
If any friend will pay the sum for him,
He shall not die; so much we tender him.
Adr. Justice, most sacred Duke, against the
abbess!
Duke. She is a virtuous and a reverend lady;

It cannot be that she hath done thee wrong. 135
Adr. May it please your Grace, Antipholus, my
husband,
Who I made lord of me and all I had
At your important letters, — this ill day
A most outrageous fit of madness took him;
That desperately he hurried through the street, —
With him his bondman, all as mad as he, — 141
Doing displeasure to the citizens
By rushing in their houses, bearing thence
Rings, jewels, any thing his rage did like.
Once did I get him bound and sent him home, 145
Whilst to take order for the wrongs I went
That here and there his fury had committed.
Anon, I wot not by what strong escape,
He broke from those that had the guard of him;
And with his mad attendant and himself, 150
Each one with ireful passion, with drawn swords,
Met us again and, madly bent on us,
Chas'd us away, till, raising of more aid,
We came again to bind them. Then they fled
Into this abbey, whither we pursu'd them; 155
And here the abbess shuts the gates on us,
And will not suffer us to fetch him out,
Nor send him forth that we may bear him hence.
Therefore, most gracious Duke, with thy command
Let him be brought forth and borne hence for help.
Duke. Long since thy husband serv'd me in
my wars, 161
And I to thee engag'd a prince's word,
When thou didst make him master of thy bed,
To do him all the grace and good I could.
Go, some of you, knock at the abbey-gate 165
And bid the lady abbess come to me.
I will determine this before I stir.

Enter a MESSENGER.

Mess. O mistress, mistress, shift and save
yourself!
My master and his man are both broke loose,
Beaten the maids a-row and bound the doctor, 170
Whose beard they have sing'd off with brands
of fire;
And ever, as it blaz'd, they threw on him
Great pails of puddled mire to quench the hair.
My master preaches patience to him and the while
His man with scissors nicks him like a fool, 175
And sure, unless you send some present help,
Between them they will kill the conjurer.
Adr. Peace, fool! thy master and his man are
here,
And that is false thou dost report to us.
Mess. Mistress, upon my life, I tell you true;

---

100. **attorney:** agent.   105. **formal:** normal.   106. **parcel:** portion.   121. **[death]** F₃   *depth* F₁,₂.   **sorry:** sad.   124.
[**reverend**] F₃.   *reverent* F₁,₂.   132. **so much:** i.e., so much leniency.   138. **important:** urgent. **letters.** Apparently
Adriana had been a ward of the Duke.   146. **take order:** make reparation.   148. **strong:** violent.   175. **nicks ..
fool:** cuts his hair fantastically like a professional jester's.

I have not breath'd almost since I did see it.   181
He cries for you, and vows, if he can take you,
To scorch your face and to disfigure you.
                       [*Cry within.*
Hark, hark! I hear him, mistress. Fly, be gone!
  Duke. Come, stand by me; fear nothing. Guard
     with halberds!   185
  Adr. Ay me, it is my husband! Witness you,
That he is borne about invisible.
Even now we hous'd him in the abbey here;
And now he's there, past thought of human reason.

      Enter ANTIPHOLUS *of* Ephesus *and* DROMIO *of*
                  Ephesus.

  Ant. E. Justice, most gracious Duke, O, grant
     me justice!   190
Even for the service that long since I did thee,
When I bestrid thee in the wars, and took
Deep scars to save thy life; even for the blood
That then I lost for thee, now grant me justice.
  [*Æge.*] Unless the fear of death doth make me
     dote,   195
I see my son Antipholus and Dromio.
  Ant. E. Justice, sweet prince, against that
     woman there!
She whom thou gav'st to me to be my wife,
That hath abused and dishonoured me
Even in the strength and height of injury!   200
Beyond imagination is the wrong
That she this day hath shameless thrown on me.
  Duke. Discover how, and thou shalt find me just.
  Ant. E. This day, great Duke, she shut the doors
     upon me,
While she with harlots feasted in my house.   205
  Duke. A grievous fault! Say, woman, didst
     thou so?
  Adr. No, my good lord. Myself, he, and my
     sister
To-day did dine together. So befall my soul
As this is false he burdens me withal!
  Luc. Ne'er may I look on day, nor sleep on night,
But she tells to your highness simple truth!   211
  Ang. O perjur'd woman! They are both for-
     sworn.
In this the madman justly chargeth them.
  Ant. E. My liege, I am advised what I say,
Neither disturbed with the effect of wine,   215
Nor heady-rash, provok'd with raging ire,
Albeit my wrongs might make one wiser mad.
This woman lock'd me out this day from dinner.
That goldsmith there, were he not pack'd with her,
Could witness it, for he was with me then;   220
Who parted with me to go fetch a chain,

Promising to bring it to the Porpentine,
Where Balthazar and I did dine together.
Our dinner done, and he not coming thither,
I went to seek him. In the street I met him   225
And in his company that gentleman.
There did this perjur'd goldsmith swear me down
That I this day of him receiv'd the chain,
Which, God he knows, I saw not; for the which
He did arrest me with an officer.   230
I did obey, and sent my peasant home
For certain ducats; he with none return'd.
Then fairly I bespoke the officer
To go in person with me to my house.
By the way we met   235
My wife, her sister, and a rabble more
Of vile confederates. Along with them
They brought one Pinch, a hungry lean-fac'd villain,
A mere anatomy, a mountebank,
A threadbare juggler and a fortune-teller,
A needy, hollow-ey'd, sharp-looking wretch,   240
A living dead man. This pernicious slave,
Forsooth, took on him as a conjurer,
And, gazing in mine eyes, feeling my pulse,
And with no face, as 't were, outfacing me,
Cries out, I was possess'd. Then all together   245
They fell upon me, bound me, bore me thence,
And in a dark and dankish vault at home
There left me and my man, both bound together;
Till, gnawing with my teeth my bonds in sunder,
I gain'd my freedom, and immediately   250
Ran hither to your Grace; whom I beseech
To give me ample satisfaction
For these deep shames and great indignities.
  Ang. My lord, in truth, thus far I witness with
     him,
That he din'd not at home, but was lock'd out.
  Duke. But had he such a chain of thee or no?
  Ang. He had, my lord; and when he ran in here,
These people saw the chain about his neck.
  2. Mer. Besides, I will be sworn these ears of
     mine
Heard you confess you had the chain of him   260
After you first forswore it on the mart;
And thereupon I drew my sword on you;
And then you fled into this abbey here,
From whence, I think, you are come by miracle.
  Ant. E. I never came within these abbey-walls,
Nor ever didst thou draw thy sword on me.   266
I never saw the chain, so help me heaven!
And this is false you burden me withal.
  Duke. Why, what an intricate impeach is this!
I think you all have drunk of Circe's cup.   270
If here you hous'd him, here he would have been.

---

183. **scorch:** score, slash.   195. [*Æge.*] *Mar. Fat.* F (i.e., Merchant Father).   203. **Discover:** relate.   205. **harlots:** lewd fellows, rascals.   209. **burdens:** charges.   214. **am advised:** know very well.   219. **pack'd:** conspiring.   231. **peasant:** servant.   238. **anatomy:** skeleton.   242. **took...as:** pretended to be.   269. **impeach:** accusation.   270. **Circe's cup:** the cup of poison which changed men into beasts.

If he were mad, he would not plead so coldly.
You say he din'd at home; the goldsmith here
Denies that saying. Sirrah, what say you?
  Dro. E. Sir, he din'd with her there, at the Por-
    pentine.   275
  Cour. He did, and from my finger snatch'd that
    ring.
  Ant. E. 'Tis true, my liege, this ring I had of her.
  Duke. Saw'st thou him enter at the abbey here?
  Cour. As sure, my liege, as I do see your grace.
  Duke. Why, this is strange. Go call the abbess
    hither.   280
I think you are all mated or stark mad.
                     [Exit one to the Abbess.
  Æge. Most mighty Duke, vouchsafe me speak a
    word.
Haply I see a friend will save my life
And pay the sum that may deliver me.   284
  Duke. Speak freely, Syracusian, what thou wilt.
  Æge. Is not your name, sir, call'd Antipholus?
And is not that your bondman, Dromio?
  Dro. E. Within this hour I was his bondman, sir,
But he, I thank him, gnaw'd in two my cords.
Now am I Dromio and his man unbound.   290
  Æge. I am sure you both of you remember me.
  Dro. E. Ourselves we do remember, sir, by you;
For lately we were bound, as you are now.
You are not Pinch's patient, are you, sir?
  Æge. Why look you strange on me? You know
    me well.   295
  Ant. E. I never saw you in my life till now.
  Æge. O, grief hath chang'd me since you saw me
    last,
And careful hours with time's deformed hand
Have written strange defeatures in my face.
But tell me yet, dost thou not know my voice?   300
  Ant. E. Neither.
  Æge. Dromio, nor thou?
  Dro. E.   No, trust me, sir, nor I.
  Æge. I am sure thou dost.
  Dro. E. Ay, sir, but I am sure I do not; and
whatsoever a man denies, you are now bound to
believe him.   306
  Æge. Not know my voice! O time's extremity,
Hast thou so crack'd and splitted my poor tongue
In seven short years, that here my only son
Knows not my feeble key of untun'd cares?   310
Though now this grained face of mine be hid
In sap-consuming winter's drizzled snow,
And all the conduits of my blood froze up,
Yet hath my night of life some memory,
My wasting lamps some fading glimmer left,   315

My dull deaf ears a little use to hear.
All these old witnesses — I cannot err —
Tell me thou art my son Antipholus.
  Ant. E. I never saw my father in my life.   319
  Æge. But seven years since, in Syracusa, boy,
Thou know'st we parted; but perhaps, my son,
Thou sham'st to acknowledge me in misery.
  Ant. E. The Duke and all that know me in the city
Can witness with me that it is not so.
I ne'er saw Syracusa in my life.   325
  Duke. I tell thee, Syracusian, twenty years
Have I been patron to Antipholus,
During which time he ne'er saw Syracusa.
I see thy age and dangers make thee dote.

Re-enter ABBESS, *with* ANTIPHOLUS of Syracuse
           and DROMIO of Syracuse.

  Abb. Most mighty Duke, behold a man much
    wrong'd.   *[All gather to see them.*   330
  Adr. I see two husbands, or mine eyes deceive me.
  Duke. One of these men is Genius to the other;
And so of these. Which is the natural man,
And which the spirit? Who deciphers them?
  Dro. S. I, sir, am Dromio; command him away.
  Dro. E. I, sir, am Dromio; pray, let me stay.   336
  Ant. S. Ægeon art thou not? or else his ghost?
  Dro. S. O, my old master! Who hath bound
    him here?
  Abb. Whoever bound him, I will loose his bonds
And gain a husband by his liberty.   340
Speak, old Ægeon, if thou be'st the man
That hadst a wife once call'd Æmilia
That bore thee at a burden two fair sons.
O, if thou be'st the same Ægeon, speak,
And speak unto the same Æmilia!   345
  Æge. If I dream not, thou art Æmilia.
If thou art she, tell me, where is that son
That floated with thee on the fatal raft?
  Abb. By men of Epidamnum he and I
And the twin Dromio all were taken up;   350
But by and by rude fishermen of Corinth
By force took Dromio and my son from them,
And me they left with those of Epidamnum.
What then became of them I cannot tell;
I to this fortune that you see me in.   355
  Duke. [Why, here begins his morning story right.
These two Antipholuses, these two so like,
And these two Dromios, one in semblance, —
Besides her urging of her wreck at sea, —
These are the parents to these children,   360
Which accidentally are met together.]
Antipholus, thou cam'st from Corinth first?

---

272. **coldly:** rationally, coolly.   281. **mated:** confused.   298. **careful:** full of care. **deformed:** deforming.   299. **de-**
features: disfigurements.   310. **my . . . cares:** my weak, discordant voice, that has been changed by sorrows.   311. **grained:**
furrowed.   315. **lamps:** eyes.   332. **Genius:** attendant spirit.   334. **deciphers:** distinguishes.   343. **burden:** birth.
356-61. In F these lines follow l. 345.   The rearrangement seems clearly necessary.   Perhaps a line has dropped out following 359.

Ant. S. No, sir, not I; I came from Syracuse.

Duke. Stay, stand apart; I know not which is which.

Ant. E. I came from Corinth, my most gracious lord, —   365

Dro. E. And I with him.

Ant. E. Brought to this town by that most famous warrior,

Duke Menaphon, your most renowned uncle.

Adr. Which of you two did dine with me to-day?

Ant. S. I, gentle mistress.

Adr.   And are not you my husband?

Ant. E. No; I say nay to that.   371

Ant. S. And so do I, yet did she call me so;

And this fair gentlewoman, her sister here,

Did call me brother. [*To Luc.*] What I told you then

I hope I shall have leisure to make good;   375

If this be not a dream I see and hear.

Ang. That is the chain, sir, which you had of me.

Ant. S. I think it be, sir; I deny it not.

Ant. E. And you, sir, for this chain arrested me.

Ang. I think I did, sir; I deny it not.   380

Adr. I sent you money, sir, to be your bail,

By Dromio; but I think he brought it not.

Dro. E. No, none by me.

Ant. S. This purse of ducats I receiv'd from you

And Dromio my man did bring them me.   385

I see we still did meet each other's man,

And I was ta'en for him, and he for me,

And thereupon these errors are arose.   388

Ant. E. These ducats pawn I for my father here.

Duke. It shall not need; thy father hath his life.

Cour. Sir, I must have that diamond from you.

Ant. E. There, take it; and much thanks for my good cheer.

Abb. Renowned Duke, vouchsafe to take the pains

To go with us into the abbey here

And hear at large discoursed all our fortunes;   395

And all that are assembled in this place

That by this sympathized one day's error

Have suffer'd wrong, go, keep us company,

And we shall make full satisfaction.

Thirty-three years have I but gone in travail   400

Of you, my sons; and till this present hour

My heavy burden [ne'er] delivered.

The Duke, my husband, and my children both,

And you the calendars of their nativity,

Go to a gossips' feast, and go with me;   405

After so long grief, such nativity!

Duke. With all my heart, I'll gossip at this feast.

[*Exeunt all but Ant. S., Ant. E., Dro. S., and Dro. E.*

Dro. S. Master, shall I go fetch your stuff from shipboard?

Ant. E. Dromio, what stuff of mine hast thou embark'd?

Dro. S. Your goods that lay at host, sir, in the Centaur.   410

Ant. S. He speaks to me. I am your master, Dromio.

Come, go with us; we'll look to that anon.

Embrace thy brother there; rejoice with him.

[*Exeunt [Ant. S. and Ant. E.].*

Dro. S. There is a fat friend at your master's house,

That kitchen'd me for you to-day at dinner;   415

She now shall be my sister, not my wife.

Dro. E. Methinks you are my glass, and not my brother.

I see by you I am a sweet-fac'd youth.

Will you walk in to see their gossiping?

Dro. S. Not I, sir; you are my elder.   420

Dro. E. That's a question: how shall we try it?

Dro. S. We'll draw cuts for the senior; till then lead thou first.

Dro. E. Nay, then, thus:

We came into the world like brother and brother;

And now let's go hand in hand, not one before another.   [*Exeunt.*   425

386. **still**: continually.   397. **sympathized**: suffered by all.   402. **[ne'er]** (Dyce). *are* F.   404. **calendars...nativity**: the Dromios. Cf. I.ii.41, note.   405. **gossips'**. A gossip is the sponsor in baptism to a child.   406. **grief**: labor.   407. **gossip**: make merry.   410. **lay at host**: were put up.   415. **kitchen'd**: entertained in the kitchen.

The Two Gentlemen of Verona

NO TEXT of this play exists earlier than that of the First Folio, which thus becomes the unquestioned basis for any edition. A signal bibliographical feature of this text is the absence of all stage directions and, with few exceptions, of entrances and exits within the scenes. At the head of each scene is printed a list of the characters appearing in it. This situation has led to the theory that the copy from which the play was set up was not the prompter's manuscript, which was supposedly lost, but was rather a copy which had been put together from the players' parts and the theatrical "plot," that is, the sheet posted in the playhouse, off-stage, for the use of actors, giving the sequence of scenes and naming the characters to appear in each. The theory has a certain plausibility, but is open to serious question. Not only would the process of assembling be exceedingly difficult, but it is hard to believe that the materials necessary would have been available. If the prompter's copy had been lost or destroyed (and the notion is purely hypothetical), one must wonder by what luck the players' parts and the "plot" survived, for one would expect that the company's librarian would file all the data governing any play in one place. Nevertheless, granting that the parts survived in the possession of various actors, they would presumably have been so widely dispersed by 1623 that collecting them would have been very hard, for most of Shakespeare's early confreres were dead; one would, in fact, have to assume that the parts had been transferred or bequeathed to successors in the company, a circumstance which itself involves considerable risk of loss. Furthermore, the suggested assembling is a business hazardous enough to make a false sequence of speeches somewhere at least very likely, yet the present text appears free of such errors. It is wisest to assume that Heminge and Condell found the manuscript of *The Two Gentlemen* in the company's archives or had it in their own possession. And if, indeed, the play were one but little acted, as the tradition that it was a failure on the stage might imply, the paucity of managerial directions in the text would at least become less surprising.

The most important source for the plot is the tale of Felix and Felismena in the Spanish pastoral romance, *Diana Enamorada*, by Jorge de Montemayor (1559/60). No printed English version of *Diana* appeared before that of Bartholomew Yonge in 1598, but this had existed in manuscript since about 1582. It is doubtful, however, that Shakespeare read this translation in manuscript. He could conceivably have read the translation into French by Nicolas Colin (1578, 1582, 1587). But it is quite probable, though impossible to prove, that a lost play called *Felix and Philiomena*, which was acted at Greenwich in 1584, told much the same story and provided Shakespeare with the basic structure and content of his play.

It is Julia's part of the plot that is found in the Spanish tale. Felismena in the romance corresponds to Shakespeare's Julia, and Felix to Proteus. The courtship of Felismena is much more minutely described in the novel, but its general character is retained by the dramatist. The scene in which Lucetta offers Proteus's letter to Julia follows closely the action of the corresponding scene in the original. The sending of Proteus to court, Julia's following him in disguise as a man, the scene in which she overhears the serenade to her rival, her taking service with Proteus as a page and being sent to Silvia as a messenger, her expressions of sympathy with her own case in her conversation with Proteus, her discussion of the awkwardness of her position when she is sent to plead with Silvia against her own interest, her report of her own beauty to her rival and Silvia's distrust of Proteus because of his unfaithfulness to his first love, are the main features in which the play follows the romance. On the other hand, the character of Valentine is completely absent in Montemayor, so that Proteus's treachery in friendship is no part of his character in the novel. Moreover, Celia, who corresponds to Shakespeare's Silvia, falls in love with the disguised Felismena (as Olivia does with Viola in *Twelfth Night*), and finding her love unreciprocated, voluntarily ends her life. The events by which Felix and Felismena are finally brought together bear no resemblance to the closing scenes of *The Two Gentlemen*.

It is, however, precisely in the divergence of Shakespeare's plot from Montemayor's story that influences from another quarter may be discernible. Correspondences between the plot of *The Two Gentlemen* and typical plots of Italian comedy have been remarked. Italian comedy, both of the literary and the popular kinds, is thoroughly stereotyped, repeating characters, situations, and devices constantly. Particularly interesting are details in *Flavio Tradito*, a play in Flaminio Scala's book of scenarios (published in 1611). There Oratio (Proteus) proves false to his sworn friend Flavio (Valentine) in making love to the latter's loved one, Isabella (Silvia). Thus the familiar struggle between love and friendship is provided. Flavio eventually learns of Oratio's perfidy, but delays taking action. Then one day Flavio, discovering his friend about to be slain in a duel, rushes in to save him. Oratio, overwhelmed with remorse, gives up Isabella to Flavio, and friendship is triumphant. This dénouement, though by no means identical with that in *The Two Gentlemen*, shows at least the same quixotism of friendship which has vexed so many of Shakespeare's critics. Without suggesting that Shakespeare was indebted to the *Flavio Tradito* itself, one may still lay stress on the fact that in the highly conventionalized brand of comedy of which it is an example, conflict between love and friendship was a common theme, and that in order to secure the victory of friendship over love and to provide the conventional happy ending with marriages, sudden wrenching of probability was a frequent feature. Thus the conclusion to *The Two Gentlemen* may be observed to be not without precedent and, wretched though it is, may be accepted as Shakespeare's with perhaps less anguish. Furthermore, in Italian comedy the girl

who, in pursuit of her lover, disguises herself as a page is a common feature. Typical also are the clowns, quick-witted and dull, like Speed and Launce; but though these clowns conform to widespread theatrical convention, it must be remembered that there were plenty of both sorts to be observed in Shakespeare's England.

The date of the play cannot be established with any certainty. Estimates have varied from 1591 to 1595. Internal evidence is ambiguous. Though the play contains less rhyme and less doggerel than *Love's Labour's Lost* and *The Comedy of Errors*, a certain crudity and inequality of workmanship point to an early date. There are inconsistencies in both geography and indications of time. On the other hand, affinities of the play with others indubitably later are many. To mention only the most prominent, Verona is the scene of the main action, as it is to be later in *Romeo and Juliet*; Silvia, like Juliet, has an unwanted suitor forced upon her by an inflexible father; Silvia's window and balcony prefigure Juliet's, as Valentine's rope-ladder anticipates Romeo's; and Valentine's expression of despair upon his banishment looks forward to Romeo's. Relations with *The Merchant of Venice* are equally explicit. Launce is the lineal forerunner of Launcelot Gobbo; Julia discusses her suitors with Lucetta in a manner to be vastly improved upon by Portia, who dissects hers with Nerissa; Julia goes travelling in man's clothes, as do Portia, Nerissa, and Jessica. Indeed, Julia's disguise as a page opens the way for more charming examples of Rosalind, Viola, and Imogen. Pointing resemblances of this kind is the most congenial office of the commentator upon this play; in fact *The Two Gentlemen* derives its chief interest as a vehicle of experiment and a forecast of finer things to come. Nevertheless, clearly a herald of the future though the play may be, the gap between its undeniable immaturity and the mastery exhibited in the later plays makes it injudicious to assign to it a date later than 1592.

THE TWO GENTLEMEN OF VERONA

[DRAMATIS PERSONÆ]

DUKE [OF MILAN], *father to Silvia.*
VALENTINE, } *the two Gentlemen.*
PROTEUS,
ANTONIO, *father to Proteus.*
THURIO, *a foolish rival to Valentine.*
EGLAMOUR, *agent for Silvia in her escape.*
HOST, *where Julia lodges.*
OUTLAWS, *with Valentine.*

SPEED, *a clownish servant to Valentine.*
LAUNCE, *the like to Proteus.*
PANTHINO, *servant to Antonio.*

JULIA, *beloved of Proteus.*
SILVIA, *beloved of Valentine.*
LUCETTA, *waiting woman to Julia.*

[Servants, Musicians.]

[SCENE: *Verona; Milan; and a forest between Milan and Mantua.*]

ACT I

SCENE I. [*Verona. An open place.*]

Enter VALENTINE *and* PROTEUS.

Val. Cease to persuade, my loving Proteus.
Home-keeping youth have ever homely wits.
Were't not affection chains thy tender days
To the sweet glances of thy honour'd love,
I rather would entreat thy company   5
To see the wonders of the world abroad
Than, living dully sluggardiz'd at home,
Wear out thy youth with shapeless idleness.
But since thou lov'st, love still and thrive therein,
Even as I would when I to love begin.   10
Pro. Wilt thou be gone? Sweet Valentine, adieu!
Think on thy Proteus, when thou haply seest
Some rare note-worthy object in thy travel.
Wish me partaker in thy happiness
When thou dost meet good hap; and in thy danger,
If ever danger do environ thee,   16
Commend thy grievance to my holy prayers,
For I will be thy beadsman, Valentine.
Val. And on a love-book pray for my success?
Pro. Upon some book I love I'll pray for thee.   20

Val. That's on some shallow story of deep love,
How young Leander cross'd the Hellespont.
Pro. That's a deep story of a deeper love,
For he was more than over shoes in love.
Val. 'Tis true; for you are over boots in love,   25
And yet you never swam the Hellespont.
Pro. Over the boots? Nay, give me not the
boots.
Val. No, I will not, for it boots thee not.
Pro.   What?
Val. To be in love, where scorn is bought with
groans;
Coy looks with heart-sore sighs; one fading mo-
ment's mirth   30
With twenty watchful, weary, tedious nights:
If haply won, perhaps a hapless gain;
If lost, why then a grievous labour won;
However, but a folly bought with wit,
Or else a wit by folly vanquished.   35
Pro. So, by your circumstance, you call me fool.
Val. So, by your circumstance, I fear you'll prove.
Pro. 'Tis love you cavil at; I am not Love.
Val. Love is your master, for he masters you;
And he that is so yoked by a fool,   40
Methinks, should not be chronicled for wise.

Act I, sc. i, 8. **shapeless:** aimless.   18. **beadsman:** one who prays (i.e., tells the beads of his rosary) for another.
19. **love-book:** a manual of love, or a romance.   27. **give...boots:** do not make sport of me.   28. **boots:** profits.   36. **cir-**
cumstance: argument.   37. **circumstance:** situation.

Pro. Yet writers say, as in the sweetest bud
The eating canker dwells, so eating love
Inhabits in the finest wits of all.

Val. And writers say, as the most forward bud
Is eaten by the canker ere it blow,   46
Even so by love the young and tender wit
Is turn'd to folly, blasting in the bud,
Losing his verdure even in the prime
And all the fair effects of future hopes.   50
But wherefore waste I time to counsel thee
That art a votary to fond desire?
Once more adieu! My father at the road
Expects my coming, there to see me shipp'd.

Pro. And thither will I bring thee, Valentine.   55

Val. Sweet Proteus, no; now let us take our leave.
To Milan let me hear from thee by letters
Of thy success in love, and what news else
Betideth here in absence of thy friend;
And I likewise will visit thee with mine.   60

Pro. All happiness bechance to thee in Milan!

Val. As much to you at home! and so fare-
        well.   [*Exit.*

Pro. He after honour hunts, I after love.
He leaves his friends to dignify them more;
I [leave] myself, my friends, and all, for love.   65
Thou, Julia, thou hast metamorphos'd me,
Made me neglect my studies, lose my time,
War with good counsel, set the world at nought;
Made wit with musing weak, heart sick with thought.

[*Enter* SPEED.]

Speed. Sir Proteus, save you! Saw you my
        master?   70

Pro. But now he parted hence, to embark for
Milan.

Speed. Twenty to one, then, he is shipp'd al-
        ready,
And I have play'd the sheep in losing him.

Pro. Indeed, a sheep doth very often stray,
An if the shepherd be a while away.   75

Speed. You conclude that my master is a shepherd, then, and I a sheep?

Pro. I do.

Speed. Why then, my horns are his horns,
whether I wake or sleep.   80

Pro. A silly answer, and fitting well a sheep.

Speed. This proves me still a sheep.

Pro. True; and thy master a shepherd.   84

Speed. Nay, that I can deny by a circumstance.

Pro. It shall go hard but I'll prove it by another.

Speed. The shepherd seeks the sheep, and not
the sheep the shepherd; but I seek my master,
and my master seeks not me: therefore I am no
sheep.   91

Pro. The sheep for fodder follow the shepherd;
the shepherd for food follows not the sheep: thou
for wages followest thy master; thy master for
wages follows not thee: therefore thou art a
sheep.   96

Speed. Such another proof will make me cry
"baa."

Pro. But, dost thou hear? gav'st thou my letter
to Julia?   100

Speed. Ay, sir; I, a lost mutton, gave your
letter to her, a lac'd mutton, and she, a lac'd
mutton, gave me, a lost mutton, nothing for my
labour.

Pro. Here's too small a pasture for such store of
muttons.   106

Speed. If the ground be overcharg'd, you were
best stick her.

Pro. Nay, in that you are astray; 'twere best
pound you.   110

Speed. Nay, sir, less than a pound shall serve me
for carrying your letter.

Pro. You mistake; I mean the pound, — a pinfold.

Speed. From a pound to a pin? Fold it over and
        over.   115
'Tis threefold too little for carrying a letter to your
        lover.

Pro. But what said she?

Speed. [*Nodding.*]   Ay.

Pro. Nod-ay; — why, that's noddy.

Speed. You mistook, sir. I say, she did nod;
and you ask me if she did nod, and I say, "Ay."

Pro. And that set together is noddy.   122

Speed. Now you have taken the pains to set it
together, take it for your pains.

Pro. No, no; you shall have it for bearing the
letter.   126

Speed. Well, I perceive I must be fain to bear
with you.

Pro. Why, sir, how do you bear with me?

Speed. Marry, sir, the letter, very orderly;
having nothing but the word "noddy" for my
pains.   131

43. **canker:** cankerworm.   49. **prime:** spring.   50. **effects:** fulfillments.   52. **fond:** foolish.   53. **road:** harbor.   54.
shipp'd: board ship. In this play Shakespeare's geography is manifestly confused. He obviously imagined Verona as a
port (cf. II.ii.14 and II.iv.187), but not a seaport (see II.iii.58). The river Adige, flowing by Verona, is not a tidal river.
There is no water route from Verona to Milan. Shakespeare was probably thinking of sailing from London. Cf. also
II.vii.8–10, 35.   55. **bring:** accompany.   58. **success:** fortune (good *or* bad).   65. [leave] (Pope).   *love* Ff.   69. **thought:**
brooding.   73. **sheep:** with a quibble on *ship*, and pronounced like it.   75. **An if:** if.   79. **horns.** Alluding also to the horns
of the *cuckold*, the husband whose wife is unfaithful.   85. **circumstance:** detailed proof.   102. **lac'd mutton:** a strumpet, perhaps as tight-laced or wearing lace.   108. **stick:** slaughter.   110. **pound:** impound, with a quibble on *beat*.   114. **pinfold:**
enclosure for stray animals.   122. **noddy:** simpleton.

Pro. Beshrew me, but you have a quick wit.

Speed. And yet it cannot overtake your slow purse.

Pro. Come, come, open the matter in brief. What said she?   136

Speed. Open your purse, that the money and the matter may be both at once delivered.

Pro. Well, sir, here is for your pains. What said she?   140

Speed. Truly, sir, I think you'll hardly win her.

Pro. Why, couldst thou perceive so much from her?

Speed. Sir, I could perceive nothing at all from her, no, not so much as a ducat for delivering   145 your letter; and being so hard to me that brought your mind, I fear she'll prove as hard to you in telling your mind.   Give her no token but stones, for she's as hard as steel.

Pro. What said she? Nothing?   150

Speed. No, not so much as "Take this for thy pains." To testify your bounty, I thank you, you have testern'd me; in requital whereof, henceforth carry your letters yourself: and so, sir, I'll commend you to my master.   155

Pro. Go, go, be gone, to save your ship from wreck,

Which cannot perish having thee aboard,

Being destin'd to a drier death on shore.

[Exit Speed.]

I must go send some better messenger.

I fear my Julia would not deign my lines,   160

Receiving them from such a worthless post.

[Exit.

SCENE II. [*The same.   Garden of Julia's house.*]

Enter JULIA *and* LUCETTA.

Jul. But say, Lucetta, now we are alone,

Wouldst thou then counsel me to fall in love?

Luc. Ay, madam, so you stumble not unheedfully.

Jul. Of all the fair resort of gentlemen

That every day with parle encounter me,   5

In thy opinion which is worthiest love?

Luc. Please you repeat their names, I'll show my mind

According to my shallow simple skill.

Jul. What think'st thou of the fair Sir Eglamour?

Luc. As of a knight well-spoken, neat, and fine;

But, were I you, he never should be mine.   11

Jul. What think'st thou of the rich Mercatio?

Luc. Well of his wealth; but of himself, so so.

Jul. What think'st thou of the gentle Proteus?

Luc. Lord, Lord! to see what folly reigns in us!   15

Jul. How now! what means this passion at his name?

Luc. Pardon, dear madam; 'tis a passing shame

That I, unworthy body as I am,

Should censure thus on lovely gentlemen.

Jul. Why not on Proteus, as of all the rest?   20

Luc. Then thus: of many good I think him best.

Jul. Your reason?

Luc. I have no other but a woman's reason:

I think him so because I think him so.

Jul. And wouldst thou have me cast my love on him?   25

Luc. Ay, if you thought your love not cast away.

Jul. Why he, of all the rest, hath never mov'd me.

Luc. Yet he, of all the rest, I think, best loves ye.

Jul. His little speaking shows his love but small.

Luc. Fire that's closest kept burns most of all.

Jul. They do not love that do not show their love.   31

Luc. O, they love least that let men know their love.

Jul. I would I knew his mind.

Luc. Peruse this paper, madam.

Jul. "To Julia." Say, from whom?   35

Luc. That the contents will show.

Jul. Say, say, who gave it thee?

Luc. Sir Valentine's page; and sent, I think, from Proteus.

He would have given it you; but I, being in the way,

Did in your name receive it.   Pardon the fault, I pray.   40

Jul. Now, by my modesty, a goodly broker!

Dare you presume to harbour wanton lines?

To whisper and conspire against my youth?

Now, trust me, 'tis an office of great worth

And you an officer fit for the place.   45

There, take the paper; see it be return'd,

Or else return no more into my sight.

Luc. To plead for love deserves more fee than hate.

Jul. Will ye be gone?

Luc.   That you may ruminate.

[Exit.

Jul. And yet I would I had o'erlook'd the letter: 50

It were a shame to call her back again

135. **open:** disclose.   144. **perceive:** receive.   148. **in telling:** when you tell her.   153. **testern'd:** tipped with a tester or sixpence.   158. **drier death:** i.e., hanging.   An echo of the proverb, "He that is born to be hanged shall never be drowned."   160. **deign:** accept graciously.   161. **post:** messenger, perhaps with quibble on sense of "log."

Sc. ii, 4. **resort:** company.   5. **parle:** talk.   9. **Sir Eglamour.** Not to be confused with the friend of Silvia, who appears later.   17. **passing:** surpassing.   19. **censure:** pass judgment.   27. **mov'd:** proposed to.   41. **broker:** go-between.   50. **o'erlook'd:** perused.

And pray her to a fault for which I chid her.
What ' fool is she, that knows I am a maid,
And would not force the letter to my view!
Since maids, in modesty, say "no" to that   55
Which they would have the profferer construe "ay."
Fie, fie, how wayward is this foolish love,
That, like a testy babe, will scratch the nurse
And presently, all humbled, kiss the rod!
How churlishly I chid Lucetta hence,   60
When willingly I would have had her here!
How angerly I taught my brow to frown,
When inward joy enforc'd my heart to smile!
My penance is to call Lucetta back
And ask remission for my folly past.   65
What ho! Lucetta!

[Re-enter LUCETTA.]

Luc.   What would your ladyship?
Jul. Is't near dinner-time?
Luc.   I would it were,
That you might kill your stomach on your meat,
And not upon your maid.
Jul. What is't that you took up so gingerly? 70
Luc. Nothing.
Jul. Why didst thou stoop, then?
Luc. To take a paper up that I let fall.
Jul. And is that paper nothing?
Luc. Nothing concerning me.   75
Jul. Then let it lie for those that it concerns.
Luc. Madam, it will not lie where it concerns
Unless it have a false interpreter.
Jul. Some love of yours hath writ to you in
    rhyme.
Luc. That I might sing it, madam, to a tune.   80
Give me a note; your ladyship can set.
Jul. As little by such toys as may be possible.
Best sing it to the tune of "Light o' love."
Luc. It is too heavy for so light a tune.
Jul. Heavy! belike it hath some burden then?
Luc. Ay, and melodious were it, would you sing
    it.   86
Jul. And why not you?
Luc.   I cannot reach so high.
Jul. Let's see your song. How now, minion!
Luc. Keep tune there still, so you will sing it out.
And yet methinks I do not like this tune.   90
Jul. You do not?
Luc.   No, madam; it is too sharp.

Jul. You, minion, are too saucy.
Luc. Nay, now you are too flat,
And mar the concord with too harsh a descant.
There wanteth but a mean to fill your song.   95
Jul. The mean is drown'd with your unruly bass.
Luc. Indeed, I bid the base for Proteus.
Jul. This babble shall not henceforth trouble me.
Here is a coil with protestation!
                              [Tears the letter.]
Go get you gone, and let the papers lie.   100
You would be fingering them, to anger me.
Luc. She makes it strange; but she would be best
    pleas'd
To be so ang'red with another letter.   *[Exit.]*
Jul. Nay, would I were so ang'red with the same!
O hateful hands, to tear such loving words!   105
Injurious wasps, to feed on such sweet honey
And kill the bees that yield it with your stings!
I'll kiss each several paper for amends.
Look, here is writ "kind Julia."   Unkind Julia!
As in revenge of thy ingratitude,   110
I throw thy name against the bruising stones,
Trampling contemptuously on thy disdain.
And here is writ "love-wounded Proteus."
Poor wounded name! my bosom as a bed
Shall lodge thee till thy wound be throughly heal'd;
And thus I search it with a sovereign kiss.   116
But twice or thrice was "Proteus" written down.
Be calm, good wind, blow not a word away
Till I have found each letter in the letter,
Except mine own name; that some whirlwind bear
Unto a ragged, fearful, hanging rock   121
And throw it thence into the raging sea!
Lo, here in one line is his name twice writ,
"Poor forlorn Proteus, passionate Proteus,
To the sweet Julia."   That I'll tear away;   125
And yet I will not, sith so prettily
He couples it to his complaining names.
Thus will I fold them one upon another.
Now kiss, embrace, contend, do what you will.

[Re-enter LUCETTA.]

Luc. Madam,   130
Dinner is ready, and your father stays.
Jul. Well, let us go.
Luc. What, shall these papers lie like telltales
    here?
Jul. If you respect them, best to take them up.

---

52. **to a fault:** to commit a fault.   53. **' fool:** a fool.   58. **testy:** fretful.   59. **presently:** straightway.   68. **kill:** allay.
stomach: a pun upon the two meanings, *anger* and *appetite*.   69. **maid.** Probably a quibble, *meat* (l. 68) being pronounced
like *mate*.   81. Here begins a series of interrelated quibbles. **note:** (1) i.e., of music, (2) a letter in reply to Proteus.   **set:**
(1) set to music, (2) write. Line 82 switches the sense of "set" to "set store by."   83. **"Light o' love":** a popular tune.
85. **burden:** (1) load, (2) refrain.   87. **I . . . high:** (1) it is too high for my voice, (2) Proteus is too high in rank for me.   89,
90. **tune:** (1) pitch, (2) mood.   91. **sharp:** (1) musical notation, (2) biting.   93. **flat:** (1) musical notation, (2) downright.
94. **descant:** variations upon an air.   95. **mean:** tenor (probably meaning Proteus).   97. **bid the base.** A phrase from
the game of prisoner's base.   Lucetta would "bid the base" by challenging Julia to pursue her, thus giving Proteus, the
prisoner at the base, opportunity to escape.   99. **coil . . . protestation:** fuss over protests of love.   102. **makes it strange:**
pretends indifference.   106. **injurious wasps:** i.e., her fingers.   115. **throughly:** thoroughly.   116. **search:** cleanse.
131. **stays:** waits.   134. **respect:** prize.

Luc. Nay, I was taken up for laying them down;
Yet here they shall not lie, for catching cold.   136
Jul. I see you have a month's mind to them.
Luc. Ay, madam, you may say what sights you
see;
I see things too, although you judge I wink.
Jul. Come, come; will't please you go?   140
[*Exeunt.*

SCENE III. [*The same. Antonio's house.*]

Enter ANTONIO *and* PANTHINO.

Ant. Tell me, Panthino, what sad talk was that
Wherewith my brother held you in the cloister?
Pan. 'Twas of his nephew Proteus, your son.
Ant. Why, what of him?
Pan.   He wond'red that your lordship
Would suffer him to spend his youth at home,   5
While other men, of slender reputation,
Put forth their sons to seek preferment out,
Some to the wars, to try their fortune there;
Some to discover islands far away;
Some to the studious universities.   10
For any or for all these exercises
He said that Proteus your son was meet,
And did request me to importune you
To let him spend his time no more at home,
Which would be great impeachment to his age,   15
In having known no travel in his youth.
Ant. Nor need'st thou much importune me to that
Whereon this month I have been hammering.
I have consider'd well his loss of time
And how he cannot be a perfect man,   20
Not being tried and tutor'd in the world.
Experience is by industry achiev'd,
And perfected by the swift course of time.
Then tell me, whither were I best to send him?
Pan. I think your lordship is not ignorant   25
How his companion, youthful Valentine,
Attends the Emperor in his royal court.
Ant. I know it well.
Pan. 'Twere good, I think, your lordship sent
him thither.
There shall he practise tilts and tournaments,   30
Hear sweet discourse, converse with noblemen,
And be in eye of every exercise
Worthy his youth and nobleness of birth.
Ant. I like thy counsel; well hast thou advis'd;
And that thou mayst perceive how well I like it   35
The execution of it shall make known.
Even with the speediest expedition
I will dispatch him to the Emperor's court.

Pan. To-morrow, may it please you, Don
Alphonso
With other gentlemen of good esteem   40
Are journeying to salute the Emperor,
And to commend their service to his will.
Ant. Good company; with them shall Proteus
go,

[*Enter* PROTEUS.]

And — In good time! Now will we break with him.
Pro. Sweet love! sweet lines! sweet life!   45
Here is her hand, the agent of her heart;
Here is her oath for love, her honour's pawn.
O, that our fathers would applaud our loves,
To seal our happiness with their consents!
O heavenly Julia!   50
Ant. How now! what letter are you reading
there?
Pro. May't please your lordship, 'tis a word or
two
Of commendations sent from Valentine,
Deliver'd by a friend that came from him.
Ant. Lend me the letter. Let me see what
news.   55
Pro. There is no news, my lord, but that he
writes
How happily he lives, how well belov'd
And daily graced by the Emperor;
Wishing me with him, partner of his fortune.
Ant. And how stand you affected to his wish?
Pro. As one relying on your lordship's will   61
And not depending on his friendly wish.
Ant. My will is something sorted with his wish.
Muse not that I thus suddenly proceed,
For what I will, I will, and there an end.   65
I am resolv'd that thou shalt spend some time
With Valentinus in the Emperor's court.
What maintenance he from his friends receives,
Like exhibition thou shalt have from me.
To-morrow be in readiness to go.   70
Excuse it not, for I am peremptory.
Pro. My lord, I cannot be so soon provided.
Please you, deliberate a day or two.
Ant. Look, what thou want'st shall be sent after
thee.
No more of stay! To-morrow thou must go.   75
Come on, Panthino, you shall be employ'd
To hasten on his expedition.
[*Exeunt Ant. and Pan.*]
Pro. Thus have I shunn'd the fire for fear of
burning,
And drench'd me in the sea, where I am drown'd.

135. **taken up:** rebuked. 136. **for:** for fear of. 137. **a month's mind:** strong desire. 139. **wink:** close [my] eyes.
Sc. iii, 1. **sad:** serious. 15. **impeachment:** reproach. 18. **hammering:** pondering. 27. **Emperor:** i.e., Duke. 32. **be in eye:** have opportunity of observing. 44. **break with:** disclose our purpose to. 47. **pawn:** pledge. 58. **graced:** honored. 63. **sorted with:** corresponding to. 69. **exhibition:** allowance (of money). 71. **Excuse it not:** don't make excuses. 72. **provided:** equipped.

I fear'd to show my father Julia's letter,   80
Lest he should take exceptions to my love;
And with the vantage of mine own excuse
Hath he excepted most against my love.
O, how this spring of love resembleth
   The uncertain glory of an April day,   85
Which now shows all the beauty of the sun,
   And by and by a cloud takes all away!

[*Re-enter* PANTHINO.]

Pan. Sir Proteus, your father calls for you.
   He is in haste; therefore, I pray you, go.
Pro. Why, this it is; my heart accords thereto,   90
And yet a thousand times it answers "no."
                     [*Exeunt.*

ACT II

SCENE I. [*Milan.   The Duke's palace.*]

Enter VALENTINE *and* SPEED.

Speed. Sir, your glove.
Val.   Not mine; my gloves are on.
Speed. Why, then, this may be yours, for this is
   but one.
Val. Ha! let me see; ay, give it me, it's mine.
Sweet ornament that decks a thing divine!
Ah, Silvia, Silvia!   5
Speed. Madam Silvia! Madam Silvia!
Val. How now, sirrah?
Speed. She is not within hearing, sir.
Val. Why, sir, who bade you call her?
Speed. Your worship, sir; or else I mistook.   10
Val. Well, you'll still be too forward.
Speed. And yet I was last chidden for being too
slow.
Val. Go to, sir.   Tell me, do you know Madam
Silvia?   15
Speed. She that your worship loves?
Val. Why, how know you that I am in love?
Speed. Marry, by these special marks: first, you
have learn'd, like Sir Proteus, to wreathe your arms
like a malcontent; to relish a love-song, like a   20
robin-redbreast; to walk alone, like one that had
the pestilence; to sigh, like a school-boy that had
lost his A B C; to weep, like a young wench that had
buried her grandam; to fast, like one that takes diet;
to watch, like one that fears robbing; to speak   25
puling, like a beggar at Hallowmas.   You were
wont, when you laugh'd, to crow like a cock; when

you walk'd, to walk like one of the lions; when you
fasted, it was presently after dinner; when you
look'd sadly, it was for want of money: and now   30
you are metamorphos'd with a mistress, that, when
I look on you, I can hardly think you my master.
Val. Are all these things perceiv'd in me?
Speed. They are all perceiv'd without ye.   35
Val. Without me?   They cannot.
Speed. Without you?   Nay, that's certain, for,
without you were so simple, none else would; but
you are so without these follies, that these follies are
within you and shine through you like the water   40
in an urinal, that not an eye that sees you but is a
physician to comment on your malady.
Val. But tell me, dost thou know my lady
Silvia?   45
Speed. She that you gaze on so as she sits at
supper?
Val. Hast thou observ'd that?   Even she, I
mean.
Speed. Why, sir, I know her not.   50
Val. Dost thou know her by my gazing on her,
and yet know'st her not?
Speed. Is she not hard-favour'd, sir?
Val. Not so fair, boy, as well-favour'd.
Speed. Sir, I know that well enough.   55
Val. What dost thou know?
Speed. That she is not so fair as, of you, well
favour'd.
Val. I mean that her beauty is exquisite, but her
favour infinite.   60
Speed. That's because the one is painted and the
other out of all count.
Val. How painted? and how out of count?
Speed. Marry, sir, so painted to make her fair,
that no man counts of her beauty.   65
Val. How esteem'st thou me?   I account of her
beauty.
Speed. You never saw her since she was de-
form'd.
Val. How long hath she been deform'd?   70
Speed. Ever since you lov'd her.
Val. I have lov'd her ever since I saw her, and
still I see her beautiful.
Speed. If you love her, you cannot see her.
Val. Why?   75
Speed. Because Love is blind.   O, that you had
mine eyes, or your own eyes had the lights they were
wont to have when you chid at Sir Proteus for
going ungarter'd!

83. **excepted ... against:** objected to.
   Act II, sc. i, 1–2. **on ... one.**   These words, commonly spelled alike and similarly pronounced in the sixteenth century,
admitted a pun.   19. **wreathe:** fold.   23. **A B C:** primer.   25. **watch:** lie awake.   26. **puling:** whining.   **Hallowmas:** All
Saints' Day, November 1, when beggars received special alms.   28. **lions:** possibly the lions in the Tower of London, or the
lions on a royal standard displayed in the theater.   38. **would:** i.e., would perceive them.   41. **urinal:** transparent tube for
testing urine.   53. **hard-favour'd:** ugly.   54. **Not ... well-favour'd.**   I.e., her beauty is surpassed by her graciousness, as
Valentine explains in l. 60.   60. **favour:** graciousness.   65. **counts of:** esteems.   69. **deform'd.**   Speed means that Love
falsifies the appearance of its object.   79. **going ungarter'd:** i.e., a symptom of love-sickness.

Val. What should I see then?   80

Speed. Your own present folly and her passing deformity; for he, being in love, could not see to garter his hose, and you, being in love, cannot see to put on your hose.

Val. Belike, boy, then, you are in love; for   85 last morning you could not see to wipe my shoes.

Speed. True, sir; I was in love with my bed. I thank you, you swing'd me for my love, which makes me the bolder to chide you for yours.

Val. In conclusion, I stand affected to her.   90

Speed. I would you were set, so your affection would cease.

Val. Last night she enjoin'd me to write some lines to one she loves.

Speed. And have you?   95

Val. I have.

Speed. Are they not lamely writ?

Val. No, boy, but as well as I can do them. Peace! here she comes.

Speed. [*Aside.*] O excellent motion! O ex-   100 ceeding puppet! Now will he interpret to her.

[*Enter* SILVIA.]

Val. Madam and mistress, a thousand good-morrows.

Speed. [*Aside.*] O, 'give ye good even! here's a million of manners.   105

Sil. Sir Valentine and servant, to you two thousand.

Speed. [*Aside.*] He should give her interest, and she gives it him.

Val. As you enjoin'd me, I have writ your letter   110
Unto the secret nameless friend of yours;
Which I was much unwilling to proceed in
But for my duty to your ladyship.

Sil. I thank you, gentle servant. 'Tis very clerkly done.

Val. Now trust me, madam, it came hardly off;
For being ignorant to whom it goes   116
I writ at random, very doubtfully.

Sil. Perchance you think too much of so much pains?

Val. No, madam; so it stead you, I will write,
Please you command, a thousand times as much;
And yet —   121

Sil. A pretty period! Well, I guess the sequel;
And yet I will not name it; and yet I care not;
And yet take this again; and yet I thank you,
Meaning henceforth to trouble you no more.   125

Speed. [*Aside.*] And yet you will; and yet an-other "yet."

Val. What means your ladyship? Do you not like it?

Sil. Yes, yes, the lines are very quaintly writ;
But since unwillingly, take them again.
Nay, take them.   130

Val. Madam, they are for you.

Sil. Ay, ay; you writ them, sir, at my request;
But I will none of them; they are for you.
I would have had them writ more movingly.

Val. Please you, I'll write your ladyship an-other.   135

Sil. And when it's writ, for my sake read it over,
And if it please you, so; if not, why, so.

Val. If it please me, madam, what then?

Sil. Why, if it please you, take it for your labour;
And so, good morrow, servant.   [*Exit.*   140

Speed. O jest unseen, inscrutable, invisible
As a nose on a man's face or a weathercock on a steeple!
My master sues to her, and she hath taught her suitor,
He being her pupil, to become her tutor.
O excellent device! was there ever heard a better,
That my master, being scribe, to himself should write the letter?   146

Val. How now, sir? What are you reasoning with yourself?

Speed. Nay, I was rhyming; 'tis you that have the reason.   150

Val. To do what?

Speed. To be a spokesman for Madam Silvia.

Val. To whom?

Speed. To yourself. Why, she wooes you by a figure.   155

Val. What figure?

Speed. By a letter, I should say.

Val. Why, she hath not writ to me.

Speed. What need she, when she hath made you write to yourself? Why, do you not perceive the jest?   160

Val. No, believe me.

Speed. No believing you, indeed, sir. But did you perceive her earnest?

Val. She gave me none, except an angry word.

Speed. Why, she hath given you a letter.   165

Val. That's the letter I writ to her friend.

Speed. And that letter hath she deliver'd, and there an end.

Val. I would it were no worse.

Speed. I'll warrant you, 'tis as well: 170
"For often have you writ to her; and she, in modesty,

---

88. **swing'd**: thrashed (as at III.i.392). 91. **set**: seated. 100–101. **motion ... interpret.** In a puppet-show ("motion") the manipulator of the puppets provided a discourse to "interpret" the action. 104. **'give**: God give. 106. **servant**: one whose lady accepts his attentions without committing herself because of them. 114. **clerkly**: in scholarly fashion. 119 **stead**: benefit. 128. **quaintly**: skillfully. 149. **reasoning**: arguing. 155. **by a figure**: i.e., indirectly. 163–64. **earnest ... none.** A pun upon "earnest" (serious) and "earnest" a sum paid to bind a bargain.

Or else for want of idle time, could not again reply;
Or fearing else some messenger that might her mind
     discover,
Herself hath taught her love himself to write unto
     her lover."
All this I speak in print, for in print I found it.
Why muse you, sir? 'Tis dinner time.   176

Val. I have din'd.

Speed. Ay, but hearken, sir; though the chameleon Love can feed on the air, I am one that
am nourish'd by my victuals and would fain have
meat. O, be not like your mistress; be moved, be
moved.   [*Exeunt.* 181

SCENE II. [*Verona. Julia's house.*]

Enter PROTEUS *and* JULIA.

Pro. Have patience, gentle Julia.

Jul. I must, where is no remedy.

Pro. When possibly I can, I will return.

Jul. If you turn not, you will return the sooner.
Keep this remembrance for thy Julia's sake.   5
                              [*Giving a ring.*]

Pro. Why, then, we'll make exchange. Here,
     take you this.

Jul. And seal the bargain with a holy kiss.

Pro. Here is my hand for my true constancy;
And when that hour o'erslips me in the day
Wherein I sigh not, Julia, for thy sake,   10
The next ensuing hour some foul mischance
Torment me for my love's forgetfulness!
My father stays my coming; answer not;
The tide is now: — nay, not thy tide of tears;
That tide will stay me longer than I should.   15
Julia, farewell!   [*Exit Julia.*]
               What, gone without a word?
Ay, so true love should do; it cannot speak;
For truth hath better deeds than words to grace it.

[*Enter* PANTHINO.]

Pan. Sir Proteus, you are stay'd for.

Pro. Go; I come, I come.   20
Alas! this parting strikes poor lovers dumb.
                              [*Exeunt.*

SCENE III. [*The same. A street.*]

Enter LAUNCE [*leading a dog*].

Launce. Nay, 'twill be this hour ere I have done
weeping; all the kind of the Launces have this very
fault. I have receiv'd my proportion, like the
prodigious son, and am going with Sir Proteus to
the Imperial's court. I think Crab my dog be   5

the sourest-natured dog that lives. My mother
weeping, my father wailing, my sister crying, our
maid howling, our cat wringing her hands, and all
our house in a great perplexity, yet did not this
cruel-hearted cur shed one tear. He is a stone,   10
a very pebble stone, and has no more pity in him
than a dog. A Jew would have wept to have seen
our parting; why, my grandam, having no eyes,
look you, wept herself blind at my parting. Nay,
I'll show you the manner of it. This shoe is my   15
father; no, this left shoe is my father; no, no, this
left shoe is my mother; nay, that cannot be so
neither; yes, it is so, it is so, it hath the worser sole.
This shoe, with the hole in it, is my mother, and
this my father; a vengeance on't! there 'tis.   20
Now, sir, this staff is my sister, for, look you, she
is as white as a lily and as small as a wand. This
hat is Nan, our maid. I am the dog; — no, the dog
is himself, and I am the dog, — O! the dog is
me, and I am myself; ay, so, so. Now come   25
I to my father: "Father, your blessing." Now
should not the shoe speak a word for weeping.
Now should I kiss my father; well, he weeps on.
Now come I to my mother. Oh, that she could
speak now like a wood woman! Well, I kiss   30
her; why, there 'tis; here's my mother's breath up
and down. Now come I to my sister; mark the
moan she makes. Now the dog all this while sheds
not a tear nor speaks a word; but see how I lay the
dust with my tears.   35

[*Enter* PANTHINO.]

Pan. Launce, away, away, aboard! Thy master
is shipp'd and thou art to post after with oars.
What's the matter? Why weep'st thou, man?
Away, ass! you'll lose the tide, if you tarry any
longer.   40

Launce. It is no matter if the [tied] were lost;
for it is the unkindest [tied] that ever any man tied.

Pan. What's the unkindest tide?

Launce. Why, he that's [tied] here, Crab, my
dog.   45

Pan. Tut, man, I mean thou'lt lose the flood,
and, in losing the flood, lose thy voyage, and, in
losing thy voyage, lose thy master, and, in losing
thy master, lose thy service, and, in losing thy
service, — Why dost thou stop my mouth?   51

Launce. For fear thou shouldst lose thy tongue.

Pan. Where should I lose my tongue?

Launce. In thy tale.

Pan. In thy tail!   55

Launce. Lose the tide, and the voyage, and

---

175. **speak in print:** speak precisely. The source of Speed's quotation is unknown.   177. **din'd:** i.e., on the beauty of
Silvia.
     Sc. ii, 4. **turn:** prove unfaithful.   15. **tide.** Cf. I.i.54 n.
     Sc. iii, 2. **kind:** kindred.   3–4. **proportion, prodigious:** malapropisms for *portion* and *prodigal.*   30. **wood:** mad.   32. **up
and down:** exactly.   41, 42, 44, 57. [tied] (Steevens).   *tide* Ff.

the master, and the service, and the [tied]! Why, man, if the river were dry, I am able to fill it with my tears; if the wind were down, I could drive the boat with my sighs.   60

Pan. Come, come away, man; I was sent to call thee.

Launce. Sir, call me what thou dar'st.

Pan. Wilt thou go?

Launce. Well, I will go.   [*Exeunt.*   65

SCENE IV. [*Milan.   The Duke's palace.*]

Enter SILVIA, VALENTINE, THURIO, *and* SPEED.

Sil. Servant!

Val. Mistress?

Speed. Master, Sir Thurio frowns on you.

Val. Ay, boy, it's for love.

Speed. Not of you.   5

Val. Of my mistress, then.

Speed. 'Twere good you knock'd him.   [*Exit.*]

Sil. Servant, you are sad.

Val. Indeed, madam, I seem so.

Thu. Seem you that you are not?   10

Val. Haply I do.

Thu. So do counterfeits.

Val. So do you.

Thu. What seem I that I am not?

Val. Wise.   15

Thu. What instance of the contrary?

Val. Your folly.

Thu. And how quote you my folly?

Val. I quote it in your jerkin.

Thu. My jerkin is a doublet.   20

Val. Well, then, I'll double your folly.

Thu. How?

Sil. What, angry, Sir Thurio! Do you change colour?

Val. Give him leave, madam; he is a kind of chameleon.   26

Thu. That hath more mind to feed on your blood than live in your air.

Val. You have said, sir.

Thu. Ay, sir, and done too, for this time.   30

Val. I know it well, sir; you always end ere you begin.

Sil. A fine volley of words, gentlemen, and quickly shot off.

Val. 'Tis indeed, madam; we thank the giver.   35

Sil. Who is that, servant?

Val. Yourself, sweet lady; for you gave the fire. Sir Thurio borrows his wit from your ladyship's looks, and spends what he borrows kindly in your company.   40

Thu. Sir, if you spend word for word with me, I shall make your wit bankrupt.

Val. I know it well, sir; you have an exchequer of words and, I think, no other treasure to give your followers, for it appears, by their bare liveries, that they live by your bare words.   46

Sil. No more, gentlemen, no more; here comes my father.

[*Enter* DUKE.]

Duke. Now, daughter Silvia, you are hard beset. Sir Valentine, your father 's in good health.   50
What say you to a letter from your friends
Of much good news?

Val.   My lord, I will be thankful
To any happy messenger from thence.

Duke. Know ye Don Antonio, your countryman?

Val. Ay, my good lord, I know the gentleman   55
To be of worth and worthy estimation,
And not without desert so well reputed.

Duke. Hath he not a son?

Val. Ay, my good lord; a son that well deserves
The honour and regard of such a father.   60

Duke. You know him well?

Val. I knew him as myself, for from our infancy
We have convers'd and spent our hours together;
And though myself have been an idle truant,
Omitting the sweet benefit of time   65
To clothe mine age with angel-like perfection,
Yet hath Sir Proteus (for that's his name)
Made use and fair advantage of his days;
His years but young, but his experience old;
His head unmellow'd, but his judgement ripe;   70
And, in a word (for far behind his worth
Comes all the praises that I now bestow)
He is complete in feature and in mind
With all good grace to grace a gentleman.

Duke. Beshrew me, sir, but if he make this good,
He is as worthy for an empress' love   76
As meet to be an emperor's counsellor.
Well, sir, this gentleman is come to me
With commendation from great potentates;
And here he means to spend his time awhile.   80
I think 'tis no unwelcome news to you.

Val. Should I have wish'd a thing, it had been he.

Duke. Welcome him then according to his worth.
Silvia, I speak to you, and you, Sir Thurio;
For Valentine, I need not cite him to it.   85
I will send him hither to you presently.   [*Exit.*]

Val. This is the gentleman I told your ladyship
Had come along with me, but that his mistress
Did hold his eyes lock'd in her crystal looks.

58. **river**: cf. I.i.54 n.
Sc. iv, 18. **quote**: observe. 20. **jerkin, doublet.** Both common Elizabethan upper garments. 28. **live ... air.** The chameleon was said to live on air. 53. **happy messenger**: bringer of good news. 65. **omitting**: letting slip. 70. **unmellow'd**: untinged with gray. 73. **feature**: outward form. 85. **cite**: urge.

Sil. Belike that now she hath enfranchis'd them
Upon some other pawn for fealty.   91
  Val. Nay, sure, I think she holds them prisoners
still.
  Sil. Nay, then he should be blind; and, being
blind,
How could he see his way to seek out you?   94
  Val. Why, lady, Love hath twenty pair of eyes.
  Thu. They say that Love hath not an eye at all.
  Val. To see such lovers, Thurio, as yourself.
Upon a homely object Love can wink.
  Sil. Have done, have done; here comes the gen-
tleman.   *[Exit Thurio.]*

[*Enter* PROTEUS.]

  Val. Welcome, dear Proteus! Mistress, I be-
seech you,   100
Confirm his welcome with some special favour.
  Sil. His worth is warrant for his welcome hither,
If this be he you oft have wish'd to hear from.
  Val. Mistress, it is. Sweet lady, entertain him
To be my fellow-servant to your ladyship.   105
  Sil. Too low a mistress for so high a servant.
  Pro. Not so, sweet lady; but too mean a servant
To have a look of such a worthy mistress.
  Val. Leave off discourse of disability.
Sweet lady, entertain him for your servant.   110
  Pro. My duty will I boast of, nothing else.
  Sil. And duty never yet did want his meed.
Servant, you are welcome to a worthless mistress.
  Pro. I'll die on him that says so but yourself.
  Sil. That you are welcome?
  Pro.   That you are worthless.

[*Re-enter* THURIO.]

  Thu. Madam, my lord your father would speak
with you.   116
  Sil. I wait upon his pleasure. Come, Sir Thurio,
Go with me. Once more, new servant, welcome.
I'll leave you to confer of home affairs;
When you have done, we look to hear from you.   120
  Pro. We'll both attend upon your ladyship.
        [Exeunt Silvia and Thurio.]
  Val. Now, tell me, how do all from whence you
came?
  Pro. Your friends are well and have them much
commended.
  Val. And how do yours?
  Pro.   I left them all in health.
  Val. How does your lady, and how thrives your
love?   125
  Pro. My tales of love were wont to weary you;
I know you joy not in a love-discourse.
  Val. Ay, Proteus, but that life is alter'd now.

I have done penance for contemning Love,
Whose high imperious thoughts have punish'd me
With bitter fasts, with penitential groans,   131
With nightly tears, and daily heart-sore sighs;
For in revenge of my contempt of love,
Love hath chas'd sleep from my enthralled eyes
And made them watchers of mine own heart's sorrow.
O gentle Proteus, Love's a mighty lord   136
And hath so humbled me as I confess
There is no woe to his correction,
Nor to his service no such joy on earth.
Now no discourse, except it be of love;   140
Now can I break my fast, dine, sup, and sleep,
Upon the very naked name of love.
  Pro. Enough; I read your fortune in your eye.
Was this the idol that you worship so?
  Val. Even she; and is she not a heavenly saint?
  Pro. No; but she is an earthly paragon.   146
  Val. Call her divine.
  Pro.   I will not flatter her.
  Val. O, flatter me; for love delights in praises.
  Pro. When I was sick, you gave me bitter pills,
And I must minister the like to you.   150
  Val. Then speak the truth by her; if not divine,
Yet let her be a principality,
Sovereign to all the creatures on the earth.
  Pro. Except my mistress.
  Val.   Sweet, except not any;
Except thou wilt except against my love.   155
  Pro. Have I not reason to prefer mine own?
  Val. And I will help thee to prefer her too.
She shall be dignified with this high honour —
To bear my lady's train, lest the base earth
Should from her vesture chance to steal a kiss,
And, of so great a favour growing proud,   161
Disdain to root the summer-swelling flower
And make rough winter everlastingly.
  Pro. Why, Valentine, what braggardism is this?
  Val. Pardon me, Proteus; all I can is nothing 165
To her, whose worth makes other worthies nothing.
She is alone.
  Pro.   Then let her alone.
  Val. Not for the world. Why, man, she is mine
own,
And I as rich in having such a jewel
As twenty seas, if all their sand were pearl,   170
The water nectar, and the rocks pure gold.
Forgive me that I do not dream on thee,
Because thou see'st me dote upon my love.
My foolish rival, that her father likes
Only for his possessions are so huge,   175
Is gone with her along, and I must after,
For love, thou know'st, is full of jealousy.
  Pro. But she loves you?

---

90. **Belike:** likely. 104. **entertain:** engage. 114. **die on:** die in fight with. 123. **them...commended:** sent kind remembrances. 138. **to:** comparable to. 152. **principality:** a celestial being ranking above archangels. 155. **Except...love:** unless you will leave my love out of the question altogether. 157. **prefer:** promote. 172. **dream.** Cf. IV.iv.86–87.

Val. Ay, and we are betroth'd: nay, more, our
    marriage-hour,
With all the cunning manner of our flight,   180
Determin'd of; how I must climb her window,
The ladder made of cords, and all the means
Plotted and 'greed on for my happiness.
Good Proteus, go with me to my chamber,
In these affairs to aid me with thy counsel.   185
    Pro. Go on before; I shall inquire you forth.
I must unto the road, to disembark
Some necessaries that I needs must use,
And then I'll presently attend you.
    Val. Will you make haste?   [*Exit.* 190
    Pro. I will.
Even as one heat another heat expels,
Or as one nail by strength drives out another,
So the remembrance of my former love
Is by a newer object quite forgotten.   195
[Is it mine eye, or Valentinus' praise],
Her true perfection, or my false transgression,
That makes me, reasonless, to reason thus?
She is fair; and so is Julia that I love —
That I did love, for now my love is thaw'd;   200
Which, like a waxen image 'gainst a fire,
Bears no impression of the thing it was.
Methinks my zeal to Valentine is cold,
And that I love him not as I was wont.
O, but I love his lady too too much!   205
And that's the reason I love him so little.
How shall I dote on her with more advice,
That thus without advice begin to love her!
'Tis but her picture I have yet beheld,
And that hath dazzled my reason's light;   210
But when I look on her perfections,
There is no reason but I shall be blind.
If I can check my erring love, I will;
If not, to compass her I'll use my skill.   [*Exit.*

SCENE V. [*The same. A street.*]

Enter SPEED *and* LAUNCE [*severally*].

Speed. Launce! By mine honesty, welcome to
[Milan]!
    Launce. Forswear not thyself, sweet youth, for
I am not welcome. I reckon this always, that a
man is never undone till he be hang'd, nor never   5
welcome to a place till some certain shot be paid
and the hostess say, "Welcome!"
    Speed. Come on, you madcap, I'll to the ale-
house with you presently; where, for one shot of
five pence, thou shalt have five thousand wel-   10
comes. But, sirrah, how did thy master part with
Madam Julia?
    Launce. Marry, after they clos'd in earnest, they
parted very fairly in jest.

Speed. But shall she marry him?   15
    Launce. No.
    Speed. How then? Shall he marry her?
    Launce. No, neither.
    Speed. What, are they broken?
    Launce. No, they are both as whole as a fish.   20
    Speed. Why, then, how stands the matter with
them?
    Launce. Marry, thus: when it stands well with
him, it stands well with her.
    Speed. What an ass art thou! I understand thee
not.   26
    Launce. What a block art thou, that thou canst
not! My staff understands me.
    Speed. What thou say'st?
    Launce. Ay, and what I do too. Look thee,   30
I'll but lean, and my staff understands me.
    Speed. It stands under thee, indeed.
    Launce. Why, stand-under and under-stand is
all one.
    Speed. But tell me true, will't be a match?   35
    Launce. Ask my dog. If he say ay, it will; if he
say, no, it will; if he shake his tail and say nothing,
it will.
    Speed. The conclusion is then that it will.
    Launce. Thou shalt never get such a secret   40
from me but by a parable.
    Speed. 'Tis well that I get it so. But, Launce,
how say'st thou, that my master is become a
notable lover?
    Launce. I never knew him otherwise.   45
    Speed. Than how?
    Launce. A notable lubber, as thou reportest him
to be.
    Speed. Why, thou whoreson ass, thou mistak'st
me.   50
    Launce. Why, fool, I meant not thee; I meant
thy master.
    Speed. I tell thee, my master is become a hot
lover.
    Launce. Why, I tell thee, I care not though   55
he burn himself in love. If thou wilt, go with me
to the alehouse; if not, thou art an Hebrew, a Jew,
and not worth the name of a Christian.
    Speed. Why?   59
    Launce. Because thou hast not so much char-
ity in thee as to go to the ale with a Christian. Wilt
thou go?
    Speed. At thy service.   [*Exeunt.*

SCENE VI. [*The same. The Duke's palace.*]

Enter PROTEUS.

    Pro. To leave my Julia, shall I be forsworn;
To love fair Silvia, shall I be forsworn;

---

186. **forth:** out.   188. **road:** harbor.   196. [Is ... praise] (Theobald). *It is mine, or Valentine's praise* F.   207-08
advice: deliberation.   209. **picture:** outer form.   212. **no ... but:** no doubt that.   214. **compass:** obtain.
    Sc. v, 2. [Milan] (Pope). *Padua* Ff.   6. **shot:** reckoning.   13. **clos'd:** (1) came to terms, (2) embraced.

To wrong my friend, I shall be much forsworn;
And even that power which gave me first my oath
Provokes me to this three fold perjury.   5
Love bade me swear and Love bids me forswear.
O sweet-suggesting Love, if thou hast sinn'd,
Teach me, thy tempted subject, to excuse it!
At first I did adore a twinkling star,
But now I worship a celestial sun.   10
Unheedful vows may heedfully be broken;
And he wants wit that wants resolved will
To learn his wit to exchange the bad for better.
Fie, fie, unreverend tongue! to call her bad,
Whose sovereignty so oft thou hast preferr'd   15
With twenty thousand soul-confirming oaths.
I cannot leave to love, and yet I do;
But there I leave to love where I should love.
Julia I lose, and Valentine I lose.
If I keep them, I needs must lose myself.   20
If I lose them, thus find I by their loss
For Valentine, myself; for Julia, Silvia.
I to myself am dearer than a friend,
For love is still most precious in itself;
And Silvia — witness Heaven, that made her
     fair! —   25
Shows Julia but a swarthy Ethiope.
I will forget that Julia is alive,
Rememb'ring that my love to her is dead;
And Valentine I'll hold an enemy,
Aiming at Silvia as a sweeter friend.   30
I cannot now prove constant to myself,
Without some treachery us'd to Valentine.
This night he meaneth with a corded ladder
To climb celestial Silvia's chamber-window,
Myself in counsel, his competitor.   35
Now presently I'll give her father notice
Of their disguising and pretended flight,
Who, all enrag'd, will banish Valentine.
For Thurio, he intends, shall wed his daughter;
But, Valentine being gone, I'll quickly cross   40
By some sly trick blunt Thurio's dull proceeding.
Love, lend me wings to make my purpose swift,
As thou hast lent me wit to plot this drift!
                                        [*Exit.*

SCENE VII. [*Verona. Julia's house.*]

Enter JULIA *and* LUCETTA.

Jul. Counsel, Lucetta; gentle girl, assist me;
And ev'n in kind love I do conjure thee,
Who art the table wherein all my thoughts
Are visibly character'd and engrav'd,
To lesson me and tell me some good mean   5
How, with my honour, I may undertake

A journey to my loving Proteus.
Luc. Alas, the way is wearisome and long!
Jul. A true-devoted pilgrim is not weary
To measure kingdoms with his feeble steps;   10
Much less shall she that hath Love's wings to fly,
And when the flight is made to one so dear,
Of such divine perfection, as Sir Proteus.
Luc. Better forbear till Proteus make return.
Jul. O, know'st thou not his looks are my soul's
     food?   15
Pity the dearth that I have pined in
By longing for that food so long a time.
Didst thou but know the inly touch of love,
Thou wouldst as soon go kindle fire with snow
As seek to quench the fire of love with words.   20
Luc. I do not seek to quench your love's hot fire,
But qualify the fire's extreme rage,
Lest it should burn above the bounds of reason.
Jul. The more thou damm'st it up, the more it
     burns.
The current that with gentle murmur glides,   25
Thou know'st, being stopp'd, impatiently doth rage;
But when his fair course is not hindered,
He makes sweet music with the enamell'd stones,
Giving a gentle kiss to every sedge
He overtaketh in his pilgrimage;   30
And so by many winding nooks he strays
With willing sport to the wild ocean.
Then let me go, and hinder not my course.
I'll be as patient as a gentle stream,
And make a pastime of each weary step,   35
Till the last step have brought me to my love;
And there I'll rest, as after much turmoil
A blessed soul doth in Elysium.
Luc. But in what habit will you go along?
Jul. Not like a woman; for I would prevent   40
The loose encounters of lascivious men.
Gentle Lucetta, fit me with such weeds
As may beseem some well-reputed page.
Luc. Why, then, your ladyship must cut your
     hair.
Jul. No, girl; I'll knit it up in silken strings   45
With twenty odd-conceited true-love knots.
To be fantastic may become a youth
Of greater time than I shall show to be.
Luc. What fashion, madam, shall I make your
     breeches?
Jul. That fits as well as, "Tell me, good my
     lord,   50
What compass will you wear your farthingale?"
Why even what fashion thou best likes, Lucetta.
Luc. You must needs have them with a codpiece,
     madam.

Sc. vi, 35. **competitor:** accomplice. 37. **pretended:** intended. 41. **blunt:** stupid. 43. **drift:** scheme.
Sc. vii, 3. **table:** tablet for memoranda. 4. **character'd:** inscribed. 18. **inly:** inward. 47. **fantastic:** fanciful. 48.
greater time: older years. 51. **farthingale:** hooped petticoat. 53. **codpiece:** a bagged appendage at the front of close-
fitting breeches.

Jul. Out, out, Lucetta! that will be ill-favour'd.
Luc. A round hose, madam, now's not worth a
pin,   55
Unless you have a codpiece to stick pins on.
Jul. Lucetta, as thou lov'st me, let me have
What thou think'st meet and is most mannerly.
But tell me, wench, how will the world repute me
For undertaking so unstaid a journey?   60
I fear me, it will make me scandaliz'd.
Luc. If you think so, then stay at home and go
not.
Jul. Nay, that I will not.
Luc. Then never dream on infamy, but go.
If Proteus like your journey when you come,   65
No matter who's displeas'd when you are gone:
I fear me, he will scarce be pleas'd withal.
Jul. That is the least, Lucetta, of my fear.
A thousand oaths, an ocean of his tears,
And instances of infinite of love   70
Warrant me welcome to my Proteus.
Luc. All these are servants to deceitful men.
Jul. Base men, that use them to so base effect!
But truer stars did govern Proteus' birth;
His words are bonds, his oaths are oracles,   75
His love sincere, his thoughts immaculate,
His tears pure messengers sent from his heart,
His heart as far from fraud as heaven from earth.
Luc. Pray heaven he prove so, when you come
to him!
Jul. Now, as thou lov'st me, do him not that
wrong   80
To bear a hard opinion of his truth:
Only deserve my love by loving him;
And presently go with me to my chamber,
To take a note of what I stand in need of,
To furnish me upon my longing journey.   85
All that is mine I leave at thy dispose,
My goods, my lands, my reputation;
Only, in lieu thereof, dispatch me hence.
Come, answer not, but to it presently!
I am impatient of my tarriance.   [*Exeunt.*   90

ACT III

Scene I. [*Milan. The Duke's palace.*]

Enter Duke, Thurio, *and* Proteus.

Duke. Sir Thurio, give us leave, I pray, awhile;
We have some secrets to confer about.
[*Exit Thu.*]
Now, tell me, Proteus, what's your will with me?
Pro. My gracious lord, that which I would dis-
cover

The law of friendship bids me to conceal;   5
But when I call to mind your gracious favours
Done to me, undeserving as I am,
My duty pricks me on to utter that
Which else no worldly good should draw from me.
Know, worthy prince, Sir Valentine, my friend,   10
This night intends to steal away your daughter.
Myself am one made privy to the plot.
I know you have determin'd to bestow her
On Thurio, whom your gentle daughter hates;
And should she thus be stolen away from you,   15
It would be much vexation to your age.
Thus, for my duty's sake, I rather chose
To cross my friend in his intended drift
Than, by concealing it, heap on your head
A pack of sorrows which would press you down,
Being unprevented, to your timeless grave.   21
Duke. Proteus, I thank thee for thine honest care;
Which to requite, command me while I live.
This love of theirs myself have often seen,
Haply when they have judg'd me fast asleep,   25
And oftentimes have purpos'd to forbid
Sir Valentine her company and my court;
But, fearing lest my jealous aim might err,
And so unworthily disgrace the man, —
A rashness that I ever yet have shunn'd, —   30
I gave him gentle looks, thereby to find
That which thyself hast now disclos'd to me.
And, that thou mayst perceive my fear of this,
Knowing that tender youth is soon suggested,
I nightly lodge her in an upper tower,   35
The key whereof myself have ever kept;
And thence she cannot be convey'd away.
Pro. Know, noble lord, they have devis'd a mean
How he her chamber-window will ascend
And with a corded ladder fetch her down;   40
For which the youthful lover now is gone,
And this way comes he with it presently,
Where, if it please you, you may intercept him.
But, good my lord, do it so cunningly
That my discovery be not aimed at;   45
For love of you, not hate unto my friend,
Hath made me publisher of this pretence.
Duke. Upon mine honour, he shall never know
That I had any light from thee of this.   49
Pro. Adieu, my lord; Sir Valentine is coming.
[*Exit.*]

[*Enter* Valentine.]

Duke. Sir Valentine, whither away so fast?
Val. Please it your grace, there is a messenger
That stays to bear my letters to my friends,
And I am going to deliver them.

55. **round hose:** hose bulging at the hips. 60. **unstaid:** unbecoming. 70. **infinite:** an infinity. 85. **longing:** prompted by longing. 86. **dispose:** disposal. 90. **tarriance:** delay.

Act III, sc. i, 4. **discover:** disclose (cf. I. 45). 21. **timeless:** untimely. 28. **jealous aim:** suspicious guess (cf. I. 45).
34. **suggested:** tempted 47. **pretence:** intention.

Duke. Be they of much import?   55
Val. The tenour of them doth but signify
My health and happy being at your court.
    Duke. Nay then, no matter; stay with me awhile;
I am to break with thee of some affairs
That touch me near, wherein thou must be secret.
'Tis not unknown to thee that I have sought   61
To match my friend Sir Thurio to my daughter.
    Val. I know it well, my lord; and, sure, the
    match
Were rich and honourable; besides, the gentleman
Is full of virtue, bounty, worth, and qualities   65
Beseeming such a wife as your fair daughter.
Cannot your Grace win her to fancy him?
    Duke. No, trust me; she is peevish, sullen, fro-
    ward.
Proud, disobedient, stubborn, lacking duty,
Neither regarding that she is my child   70
Nor fearing me as if I were her father;
And, may I say to thee, this pride of hers,
Upon advice, hath drawn my love from her;
And, where I thought the remnant of mine age
Should have been cherish'd by her child-like duty,
I now am full resolv'd to take a wife   76
And turn her out to who will take her in.
Then let her beauty be her wedding-dower,
For me and my possessions she esteems not.
    Val. What would your Grace have me to do in
    this?   80
    Duke. There is a lady of Verona here
Whom I affect; but she is nice and coy
And nought esteems my aged eloquence.
Now, therefore, would I have thee to my tutor —
For long agone I have forgot to court;   85
Besides, the fashion of the time is chang'd —
How and which way I may bestow myself
To be regarded in her sun-bright eye.
    Val. Win her with gifts, if she respect not words.
Dumb jewels often in their silent kind   90
More than quick words do move a woman's mind.
    Duke. But she did scorn a present that I sent her.
    Val. A woman sometimes scorns what best con-
    tents her.
Send her another; never give her o'er;
For scorn at first makes after-love the more.   95
If she do frown, 'tis not in hate of you,
But rather to beget more love in you.
If she do chide, 'tis not to have you gone;
For why, the fools are mad, if left alone.
Take no repulse, whatever she doth say;   100
For "get you gone," she doth not mean "away!"
Flatter and praise, commend, extol their graces;
Though ne'er so black, say they have angels' faces.

That man that hath a tongue, I say, is no man,
If with his tongue he cannot win a woman.   105
    Duke. But she I mean is promis'd by her friends
Unto a youthful gentleman of worth,
And kept severely from resort of men,
That no man hath access by day to her.
    Val. Why, then, I would resort to her by night.
    Duke. Ay, but the doors be lock'd and keys kept
    safe,   111
That no man hath recourse to her by night.
    Val. What lets but one may enter at her window?
    Duke. Her chamber is aloft, far from the ground,
And built so shelving that one cannot climb it 115
Without apparent hazard of his life.
    Val. Why then, a ladder, quaintly made of cords,
To cast up, with a pair of anchoring hooks,
Would serve to scale another Hero's tower,
So bold Leander would adventure it.   120
    Duke. Now, as thou art a gentleman of blood,
Advise me where I may have such a ladder.
    Val. When would you use it? Pray, sir, tell me
    that.
    Duke. This very night; for Love is like a child,
That longs for every thing that he can come by. 125
    Val. By seven o'clock I'll get you such a ladder.
    Duke. But, hark thee; I will go to her alone.
How shall I best convey the ladder thither?
    Val. It will be light, my lord, that you may bear
    it
Under a cloak that is of any length.   130
    Duke. A cloak as long as thine will serve the turn?
    Val. Ay, my good lord.
    Duke.   Then let me see thy cloak.
I'll get me one of such another length.
    Val. Why, any cloak will serve the turn, my lord.
    Duke. How shall I fashion me to wear a cloak? 135
I pray thee, let me feel thy cloak upon me.
What letter is this same? What's here? "To
    Silvia"!
And here an engine fit for my proceeding!
I'll be so bold to break the seal for once.   [*Reads.*]
"My thoughts do harbour with my Silvia nightly,
    And slaves they are to me that send them fly-
    ing: 141
O, could their master come and go as lightly,
    Himself would lodge where senseless they are
    lying!
My herald thoughts in thy pure bosom rest them,
    While I, their king, that hither them importune,
Do curse the grace that with such grace hath
    bless'd them,   146
    Because myself do want my servants' fortune.
I curse myself, for they are sent by me,

74. **where:** whereas. 81. **Verona:** mistake for *Milan.* 82. **nice:** fastidious. 87. **bestow:** conduct. 90. **kind:** nature. 91. **quick:** lively. 101. **For:** by. 103. **black:** dark-complexioned. 113. **lets:** prevents. 116. **apparent:** obvious. 121. **of blood:** well-born. 138. **engine:** instrument (the rope ladder). 143. **senseless:** insensible (of their privilege). 145. **importune:** command. 146. **grace:** favor.

That they should harbour where their lord would
be."
What's here?   150
"Silvia, this night I will enfranchise thee."
'Tis so; and here's the ladder for the purpose.
Why, Phaethon, — for thou art Merops' son, —
Wilt thou aspire to guide the heavenly car
And with thy daring folly burn the world?   155
Wilt thou reach stars, because they shine on thee?
Go, base intruder! overweening slave!
Bestow thy fawning smiles on equal mates,
And think my patience, more than thy desert,
Is privilege for thy departure hence.   160
Thank me for this more than for all the favours
Which (all too much) I have bestow'd on thee.
But if thou linger in my territories
Longer than swiftest expedition
Will give thee time to leave our royal court,   165
By heaven! my wrath shall far exceed the love
I ever bore my daughter or thyself.
Be gone! I will not hear thy vain excuse;
But, as thou lov'st thy life, make speed from hence.
                                    [Exit.]
Val. And why not death rather than living
    torment?   170
To die is to be banish'd from myself,
And Silvia is myself. Banish'd from her
Is self from self, a deadly banishment!
What light is light, if Silvia be not seen?
What joy is joy, if Silvia be not by?   175
Unless it be to think that she is by,
And feed upon the shadow of perfection.
Except I be by Silvia in the night,
There is no music in the nightingale;
Unless I look on Silvia in the day,   180
There is no day for me to look upon.
She is my essence, and I leave to be,
If I be not by her fair influence
Foster'd, illumin'd, cherish'd, kept alive.
I fly not death, to fly his deadly doom.   185
Tarry I here, I but attend on death;
But, fly I hence, I fly away from life.

[Enter PROTEUS and LAUNCE.]

Pro. Run, boy, run, run, and seek him out.
Launce. Soho, soho!
Pro. What seest thou?   190
Launce. Him we go to find. There's not a hair
on 's head but 'tis a Valentine.
Pro. Valentine?
Val. No.

Pro. Who then?   His spirit?   195
Val. Neither.
Pro. What then?
Val. Nothing.
Launce. Can nothing speak? Master, shall I
    strike?
Pro. Who wouldst thou strike?   200
Launce. Nothing.
Pro. Villain, forbear.
Launce. Why, sir, I'll strike nothing. I pray
    you, —
Pro. Sirrah, I say, forbear. Friend Valentine,
    a word.
Val. My ears are stopp'd and cannot hear good
    news,   205
So much of bad already hath possess'd them.
Pro. Then in dumb silence will I bury mine,
For they are harsh, untuneable, and bad.
Val. Is Silvia dead?
Pro. No, Valentine.   210
Val. No Valentine, indeed, for sacred Silvia.
Hath she forsworn me?
Pro. No, Valentine.
Val. No Valentine, if Silvia have forsworn me.
What is your news?   215
Launce. Sir, there is a proclamation that you are
    vanished.
Pro. That thou art banished — O, that's the
    news! —
From hence, from Silvia, and from me thy friend.
Val. O, I have fed upon this woe already,
And now excess of it will make me surfeit.   220
Doth Silvia know that I am banished?
Pro. Ay, ay; and she hath offered to the doom —
Which, unrevers'd, stands in effectual force —
A sea of melting pearl, which some call tears.
Those at her father's churlish feet she tender'd;
With them, upon her knees, her humble self,   226
Wringing her hands, whose whiteness so became
    them
As if but now they waxed pale for woe.
But neither bended knees, pure hands held up,
Sad sighs, deep groans, nor silver-shedding tears
Could penetrate her uncompassionate sire;   231
But Valentine, if he be ta'en, must die.
Besides, her intercession chaf'd him so,
When she for thy repeal was suppliant,
That to close prison he commanded her,   235
With many bitter threats of biding there.
Val. No more; unless the next word that thou
    speak'st

153. Phaethon...Merops' son. Phaethon, son of Apollo and Clymene (wife of Merops), obtained permission to drive
the chariot of the sun, but lost control and drove too near the earth, scorching a good part of it.   177. shadow: idea.   183.
influence: i.e., in the astrological sense. 186. attend on: wait for. 189. Soho. A cry used in hunting the hare (thus suggesting Launce's pun upon "hair" in l. 192). 192, 193. Valentine...Valentine? Punning upon the love-token and the
proper name. Cf. ll. 210-14. 216. proclamation. The issue of the proclamation, Silvia's interview with her father, and her
committal to prison would all appear to have occurred during Valentine's soliloquy (ll. 170 ff.).

Have some malignant power upon my life;
If so, I pray thee, breathe it in mine ear,
As ending anthem of my endless dolour.   240
    Pro. Cease to lament for that thou canst not help,
And study help for that which thou lament'st.
Time is the nurse and breeder of all good.
Here if thou stay, thou canst not see thy love;
Besides, thy staying will abridge thy life.   245
Hope is a lover's staff; walk hence with that
And manage it against despairing thoughts.
Thy letters may be here, though thou art hence;
Which, being writ to me, shall be deliver'd
Even in the milk-white bosom of thy love.   250
The time now serves not to expostulate.
Come, I'll convey thee through the city-gate;
And, ere I part with thee, confer at large
Of all that may concern thy love-affairs.
As thou lov'st Silvia, though not for thyself,   255
Regard thy danger, and along with me!
    Val. I pray thee, Launce, an if thou seest my boy,
Bid him make haste and meet me at the Northgate.
    Pro. Go, sirrah, find him out.   Come, Valentine.
    Val. O my dear Silvia! Hapless Valentine!   260
        [*Exeunt Val. and Pro.*]
    Launce. I am but a fool, look you, and yet I have
the wit to think my master is a kind of a knave; but
that's all one, if he be but one knave.   He lives not
now that knows me to be in love; yet I am in love;
but a team of horse shall not pluck that from   265
me; nor who 'tis I love; and yet 'tis a woman; but
what woman I will not tell myself; and yet 'tis a
milkmaid; yet 'tis not a maid, for she hath had gossips; yet 'tis a maid, for she is her master's maid,
and serves for wages.   She hath more quali-   270
ties than a water-spaniel, — which is much in a bare
Christian.   [*Pulling out a paper.*]   Here is the cate-
log of her condition.   "*Imprimis:* She can fetch and
carry."   Why, a horse can do no more; nay, a
horse cannot fetch, but only carry; therefore   275
is she better than a jade.   "*Item:* She can milk;"
look you, a sweet virtue in a maid with clean hands.

        [*Enter* Speed.]

    Speed. How now, Signior Launce! what news
with your mastership?   280
    Launce. With my master's ship?   Why, it is at
sea.
    Speed. Well, your old vice still; mistake the
word.   What news, then, in your paper?
    Launce. The blackest news that ever thou   285
heard'st.

    Speed. Why, man, how black?
    Launce. Why, as black as ink.
    Speed. Let me read them.
    Launce. Fie on thee, jolt-head!   Thou canst
not read.   291
    Speed. Thou liest; I can.
    Launce. I will try thee.   Tell me this: who begot
thee?
    Speed. Marry, the son of my grandfather.   295
    Launce. O illiterate loiterer! it was the son of
thy grandmother.   This proves that thou canst
not read.
    Speed. Come, fool, come; try me in thy paper.
    Launce. There; and Saint Nicholas be thy   300
speed!
    Speed. [*Reads.*]   "*Imprimis:* She can milk."
    Launce. Aye, that she can.
    Speed. "*Item:* She brews good ale."
    Launce. And thereof comes the proverb: 305
"Blessing of your heart, you brew good ale."
    Speed. "*Item:* She can sew."
    Launce. That's as much as to say, "Can she
so?"
    Speed. "*Item:* She can knit."   310
    Launce. What need a man care for a stock with a
wench, when she can knit him a stock?
    Speed. "*Item:* She can wash and scour."
    Launce. A special virtue; for then she need not
be wash'd and scour'd.   315
    Speed. "*Item:* She can spin."
    Launce. Then may I set the world on wheels,
when she can spin for her living.
    Speed. "*Item:* She hath many nameless vir-
tues."   320
    Launce. That's as much as to say bastard virtues,
that, indeed, know not their fathers and therefore
have no names.
    Speed. Here follow her vices.
    Launce. Close at the heels of her virtues.   325
    Speed. "*Item:* She is not to be [kiss'd] fasting,
in respect of her breath."
    Launce. Well, that fault may be mended with a
breakfast.   Read on.
    Speed. "*Item:* She hath a sweet mouth."   330
    Launce. That makes amends for her sour
breath.
    Speed. "*Item:* She doth talk in her sleep."
    Launce. It's no matter for that, so she sleep not
in her talk.   335
    Speed. "*Item:* She is slow in words."
    Launce. O villain, that set this down among her

---

247. **manage:** wield.   255. **though...thyself:** even though not for your own sake.   263. **that's...knave:** that's all right
if he is only slightly a knave.   268. **gossips:** sponsors for a child (of hers).   271. **bare:** mere.   273. **condition:** attributes.
Imprimis: in the first place.   276. **iade.** A pun upon "ill-conditioned horse" and "loose woman."   290. **jolt-head:** blockhead.   300. **Saint Nicholas:** the patron saint of scholars.   301. *Imprimis.* Speed should here read "*Item*" (see l. 276).
311, 312. **stock...stock:** dowry...stocking.   317. **set...wheels:** live at ease.   320. **nameless:** inexpressible.   330. **hath
...mouth:** i.e., is a wanton.   Launce takes it literally.

vices! To be slow in words is a woman's only virtue. I pray thee, out with't, and place it for her
chief virtue.   340

Speed. "*Item:* She is proud."

Launce. Out with that too; it was Eve's legacy,
and cannot be ta'en from her.

Speed. "*Item:* She hath no teeth."

Launce. I care not for that neither, because I
love crusts.   346

Speed. "*Item:* She is curst."

Launce. Well, the best is, she hath no teeth to
bite.

Speed. "*Item:* She will often praise her   350
liquor."

Launce. If her liquor be good, she shall; if she
will not, I will; for good things should be praised.

Speed. "*Item:* She is too liberal."   355

Launce. Of her tongue she cannot, for that's
writ down she is slow of, of her purse she shall not,
for that I'll keep shut. Now, of another thing she
may, and that cannot I help. Well, proceed.   360

Speed. "*Item:* She hath more hair than wit, and
more faults than hairs, and more wealth than
faults."

Launce. Stop there; I'll have her. She was mine
and not mine twice or thrice in that last article.
Rehearse that once more.   366

Speed. "*Item:* She hath more hair than
wit." —

Launce. More hair than wit? It may be; I'll
prove it. The cover of the salt hides the salt, and
therefore it is more than the salt; the hair   370
that covers the wit is more than the wit, for the
greater hides the less. What's next?

Speed. "And more faults than hairs," —

Launce. That's monstrous. O, that that were
out!   375

Speed. "And more wealth than faults."

Launce. Why, that word makes the faults
gracious. Well, I'll have her; and if it be a match,
as nothing is impossible, —

Speed. What then?   380

Launce. Why, then will I tell thee — that thy
master stays for thee at the North-gate.

Speed. For me?

Launce. For thee! Ay, who art thou? He hath
stay'd for a better man than thee.   385

Speed. And must I go to him?

Launce. Thou must run to him, for thou hast
stay'd so long that going will scarce serve the
turn.

Speed. Why didst not tell me sooner? Pox of
your love-letters!   [*Exit.*] 391

Launce. Now will he be swing'd for reading my

letter, — an unmannerly slave, that will thrust
himself into secrets! I'll after, to rejoice in the
boy's correction.   [*Exit.* 395

SCENE II. [*The same.   The Duke's palace.*]

Enter DUKE *and* THURIO.

Duke. Sir Thurio, fear not but that she will love
    you
Now Valentine is banish'd from her sight.

Thu. Since his exile she hath despis'd me most,
Forsworn my company, and rail'd at me,
That I am desperate of obtaining her.   5

Duke. This weak impress of love is as a figure
Trenched in ice, which with an hour's heat
Dissolves to water and doth lose his form.
A little time will melt her frozen thoughts
And worthless Valentine shall be forgot.   10

[*Enter* PROTEUS.]

How now, Sir Proteus! Is your countryman
According to our proclamation gone?

Pro. Gone, my good lord.

Duke. My daughter takes his going grievously.

Pro. A little time, my lord, will kill that grief.

Duke. So I believe; but Thurio thinks not so.   16
Proteus, the good conceit I hold of thee —
For thou hast shown some sign of good desert —
Makes me the better to confer with thee.

Pro. Longer than I prove loyal to your Grace
Let me not live to look upon your Grace.   21

Duke. Thou know'st how willingly I would effect
The match between Sir Thurio and my daughter.

Pro. I do, my lord.

Duke. And also, I think, thou art not ignorant
How she opposes her against my will.   26

Pro. She did, my lord, when Valentine was here.

Duke. Ay, and perversely she persevers so.
What might we do to make the girl forget
The love of Valentine, and love Sir Thurio?   30

Pro. The best way is to slander Valentine
With falsehood, cowardice, and poor descent,
Three things that women highly hold in hate.

Duke. Ay, but she'll think that it is spoke in hate.

Pro. Ay, if his enemy deliver it;   35
Therefore it must with circumstance be spoken
By one whom she esteemeth as his friend.

Duke. Then you must undertake to slander him.

Pro. And that, my lord, I shall be loath to do.
'Tis an ill office for a gentleman,   40
Especially against his very friend.

Duke. Where your good word cannot advantage
    him,
Your slander never can endamage him;

Therefore the office is indifferent,
Being entreated to it by your friend.   45
  Pro. You have prevail'd, my lord.   If I can do it
By aught that I can speak in his dispraise,
She shall not long continue love to him.
But say this weed her love from Valentine,
It follows not that she will love Sir Thurio.   50
  Thu. Therefore, as you unwind her love from him,
Lest it should ravel and be good to none,
You must provide to bottom it on me;
Which must be done by praising me as much
As you in worth dispraise Sir Valentine.   55
  Duke. And, Proteus, we dare trust you in this kind,
Because we know, on Valentine's report,
You are already Love's firm votary
And cannot soon revolt and change your mind.
Upon this warrant shall you have access   60
Where you with Silvia may confer at large, —
For she is lumpish, heavy, melancholy,
And, for your friend's sake, will be glad of you, —
Where you may temper her by your persuasion
To hate young Valentine and love my friend.   65
  Pro. As much as I can do, I will effect.
But you, Sir Thurio, are not sharp enough.
You must lay lime to tangle her desires
By wailful sonnets, whose composed rhymes
Should be full-fraught with serviceable vows.   70
  Duke. Ay,
Much is the force of heaven-bred poesy.
  Pro. Say that upon the altar of her beauty
You sacrifice your tears, your sighs, your heart;
Write till your ink be dry, and with your tears   75
Moist it again, and frame some feeling line
That may discover such integrity:
For Orpheus' lute was strung with poets' sinews,
Whose golden touch could soften steel and stones,
Make tigers tame, and huge leviathans   80
Forsake unsounded deeps to dance on sands.
After your dire-lamenting elegies,
Visit by night your lady's chamber-window
With some sweet consort; to their instruments   84
Tune a deploring dump.   The night's dead silence
Will well become such sweet-complaining grievance.
This, or else nothing, will inherit her.
  Duke. This discipline shows thou hast been in love.
  Thu. And thy advice this night I'll put in practice.
Therefore, sweet Proteus, my direction-giver,   90

Let us into the city presently
To sort some gentlemen well skill'd in music.
I have a sonnet that will serve the turn
To give the onset to thy good advice.
  Duke. About it, gentlemen!   95
  Pro. We'll wait upon your Grace till after supper,
And afterward determine our proceedings.
  Duke. Even now about it!   I will pardon you.
                               [*Exeunt.*

ACT IV

SCENE I. [*A forest between Milan and Mantua.*]

          Enter certain OUTLAWS.

  1. Out. Fellows, stand fast; I see a passenger.
  2. Out. If there be ten, shrink not, but down with 'em.

      [*Enter* VALENTINE *and* SPEED.]

  3. Out. Stand, sir, and throw us that you have about ye.
If not, we'll make you sit and rifle you.
  Speed. Sir, we are undone; these are the villains
That all the travellers do fear so much.   6
  Val. My friends, —
  1. Out. That's not so, sir; we are your enemies.
  2. Out. Peace! we'll hear him.
  3. Out. Ay, by my beard, will we, for he's a proper man.   10
  Val. Then know that I have little wealth to lose.
A man I am cross'd with adversity;
My riches are these poor habiliments,
Of which if you should here disfurnish me,
You take the sum and substance that I have.   15
  2. Out. Whither travel you?
  Val. To Verona.
  1. Out. Whence came you?
  Val. From Milan.
  3. Out. Have you long sojourn'd there?   20
  Val. Some sixteen months, and longer might have stay'd,
If crooked fortune had not thwarted me.
  1. Out. What, were you banish'd thence?
  Val. I was.
  2. Out. For what offence?   25
  Val. For that which now torments me to rehearse.
I kill'd a man, whose death I much repent;
But yet I slew him manfully in fight,
Without false vantage or base treachery.

---

44. **indifferent:** neither good nor bad.   45. **your friend:** i.e., the Duke.   53. **bottom it:** i.e., wind it as a skein of thread on a core of harder material.   62. **lumpish:** spiritless.   64. **temper:** mould (like wax).   68. **lime:** bird lime.   70. **serviceable:** service-pledging.   77. **discover...integrity:** reveal such true devotion.   78. **sinews:** nerves.   84. **consort:** company of musicians.   85. **dump:** mournful melody.   86. **grievance:** lamenting.   87. **inherit:** win.   88. **discipline:** instruction. 92. **sort:** select.   94. **give...to:** begin the following of.
  Act IV, sc. i, 10. **proper:** handsome.

1. Out. Why, ne'er repent it, if it were done so.
But were you banish'd for so small a fault?   31
Val. I was, and held me glad of such a doom.
2. Out. Have you the tongues?
Val. My youthful travel therein made me happy,
Or else I often had been miserable.   35
3. Out. By the bare scalp of Robin Hood's fat
    friar,
This fellow were a king for our wild faction!
1. Out. We'll have him.   Sirs, a word.
Speed. Master, be one of them; it's an honour-
able kind of thievery.   40
Val. Peace, villain!
2. Out. Tell us this: have you anything to take
    to?
Val. Nothing but my fortune.
3. Out. Know, then, that some of us are gentle-
    men,
Such as the fury of ungovern'd youth   45
Thrust from the company of awful men.
Myself was from Verona banished
For practising to steal away a lady,
An heir, and near allied unto the Duke.
2. Out. And I from Mantua, for a gentleman,   50
Who, in my mood, I stabb'd unto the heart.
1. Out. And I for such like petty crimes as these.
But to the purpose, — for we cite our faults
That they may hold excus'd our lawless lives;
And partly, seeing you are beautified   55
With goodly shape, and by your own report
A linguist and a man of such perfection
As we do in our quality much want, —
2. Out. Indeed, because you are a banish'd man,
Therefore, above the rest, we parley to you.   60
Are you content to be our general?
To make a virtue of necessity
And live, as we do, in this wilderness?
3. Out. What say'st thou?   Wilt thou be of our
    consort?
Say, ay, and be the captain of us all.   65
We ll do thee homage and be rul'd by thee,
Love thee as our commander and our king.
1. Out. But if thou scorn our courtesy, thou diest.
2. Out. Thou shalt not live to brag what we have
    offer'd.
Val. I take your offer and will live with you,   70
Provided that you do no outrages
On silly women or poor passengers.
3. Out. No, we detest such vile base practices.
Come, go with us, we ll bring thee to our crews,
And show thee all the treasure we have got;   75
Which, with ourselves, all rest at thy dispose.
                                    [*Exeunt.*

SCENE II. [*Milan.   Outside the Duke's palace,
    under Silvia's window.*]

Enter PROTEUS.

Pro. Already have I been false to Valentine
And now I must be as unjust to Thurio.
Under the colour of commending him,
I have access my own love to prefer.
But Silvia is too fair, too true, too holy,   5
To be corrupted with my worthless gifts.
When I protest true loyalty to her,
She twits me with my falsehood to my friend;
When to her beauty I commend my vows,
She bids me think how I have been forsworn   10
In breaking faith with Julia whom I loved;
And, notwithstanding all her sudden quips,
The least whereof would quell a lover's hope,
Yet, spaniel-like, the more she spurns my love,
The more it grows, and fawneth on her still.   15

[*Enter* THURIO *and* Musicians.]
But here comes Thurio.   Now must we to her
    window,
And give some evening music to her ear.
Thu. How now, Sir Proteus, are you crept before
    us?
Pro. Ay, gentle Thurio; for you know that love
Will creep in service where it cannot go.   20
Thu. Ay, but I hope, sir, that you love not
    here.
Pro. Sir, but I do; or else I would be hence.
Thu. Who?   Silvia?
Pro.   Ay, Silvia; for your sake.
Thu. I thank you for your own.   Now, gentle-
    men,
Let's tune, and to it lustily awhile.   25

[*Enter unobserved,* HOST, *and* JULIA *in boy's
    clothes.*]

Host. Now, my young guest, methinks you're
allycholly.   I pray you, why is it?
Jul. Marry, mine host, because I cannot be
merry.   29
Host. Come, we'll have you merry.   I'll bring
you where you shall hear music and see the gentle-
man that you ask'd for.
Jul. But shall I hear him speak?
Host. Ay, that you shall.
Jul. That will be music.   [*Music plays.*]   35
Host. Hark, hark!
Jul. Is he among these?
Host. Ay; but, peace! let's hear 'em.

32. **glad ... doom:** i.e., glad to get off so easily.   33. **the tongues:** foreign languages.   36. **friar:** Friar Tuck.   46. **awful:** commanding respect.   48. **practising:** plotting.   51. **mood:** anger.   58. **quality:** occupation.   60. **the rest:** any other reason. 64. **consort:** fellowship.   72. **silly:** helpless.
Sc. ii. 3. **colour:** pretence.   9. **commend** address.   20. **go:** walk.   27. **allycholly:** i.e., melancholy.

SONG.

Who is Silvia? What is she,
   That all our swains commend her?   40
Holy, fair, and wise is she;
   The heaven such grace did lend her,
That she might admired be.

Is she kind as she is fair?
   For beauty lives with kindness.   45
Love doth to her eyes repair
   To help him of his blindness,
And, being help'd, inhabits there.

Then to Silvia let us sing
   That Silvia is excelling;   50
She excels each mortal thing
   Upon the dull earth dwelling.
To her let us garlands bring.

Host. How now! are you sadder than you were
before? How do you, man? The music likes
you not.   56
Jul. You mistake; the musician likes me not.
Host. Why, my pretty youth?
Jul. He plays false, father.
Host. How? Out of tune on the strings?   60
Jul. Not so; but yet so false that he grieves my
very heart-strings.
Host. You have a quick ear.
Jul. Ay, I would I were deaf; it makes me have
a slow heart.   65
Host. I perceive you delight not in music.
Jul. Not a whit, when it jars so.
Host. Hark, what fine change is in the music!
Jul. Ay, that change is the spite.
Host. You would have them always play but
one thing?   71
Jul. I would always have one play but one thing.
But, host, doth this Sir Proteus that we talk on
Often resort unto this gentlewoman?
Host. I tell you what Launce, his man, told me:
he lov'd her out of all nick.   76
Jul. Where is Launce?
Host. Gone to seek his dog; which to-morrow,
by his master's command, he must carry for a
present to his lady.   80
Jul. Peace! stand aside; the company parts.
Pro. Sir Thurio, fear not you. I will so plead
That you shall say my cunning drift excels.
Thu. Where meet we?
Pro.   At Saint Gregory's well.
Thu.   Farewell.
   [*Exeunt Thu. and Musicians.*]

[*Enter* SILVIA *above.*]

Pro. Madam, good even to your ladyship.   85
Sil. I thank you for your music, gentlemen.
Who is that that spake?
Pro. One, lady, if you knew his pure heart's
   truth,
You would quickly learn to know him by his voice.
Sil. Sir Proteus, as I take it.   90
Pro. Sir Proteus, gentle lady, and your servant.
Sil. What's your will?
Pro.   That I may compass yours.
Sil. You have your wish. My will is even this,
That presently you hie you home to bed.
Thou subtle, perjur'd, false, disloyal man!   95
Think'st thou I am so shallow, so conceitless,
To be seduced by thy flattery,
That hast deceiv'd so many with thy vows?
Return, return, and make thy love amends.
For me, by this pale queen of night I swear,   100
I am so far from granting thy request
That I despise thee for thy wrongful suit;
And by and by intend to chide myself
Even for this time I spend in talking to thee.
Pro. I grant, sweet love, that I did love a lady;
But she is dead.   106
Jul. [*Aside.*] 'Twere false, if I should speak it;
For I am sure she is not buried.
Sil. Say that she be; yet Valentine thy friend
Survives, to whom, thyself art witness,   110
I am betroth'd; and art thou not asham'd
To wrong him with thy importunacy?
Pro. I likewise hear that Valentine is dead.
Sil. And so suppose am I; for in [his] grave
Assure thyself my love is buried.   115
Pro. Sweet lady, let me rake it from the earth.
Sil. Go to thy lady's grave and call hers thence;
Or, at the least, in hers sepulchre thine.
Jul. [*Aside.*] He heard not that.
Pro. Madam, if your heart be so obdurate,   120
Vouchsafe me yet your picture for my love,
The picture that is hanging in your chamber.
To that I'll speak, to that I'll sigh and weep;
For since the substance of your perfect self
Is else devoted, I am but a shadow;   125
And to your shadow will I make true love.
Jul. [*Aside.*] If 'twere a substance, you would,
   sure, deceive it,
And make it but a shadow, as I am.
Sil. I am very loath to be your idol, sir;
But since your falsehood shall become you well
To worship shadows and adore false shapes,   131
Send to me in the morning and I'll send it;
And so, good rest.
Pro.   As wretches have o'ernight

---

55. **likes**: pleases. 65. **slow**: heavy. 68. **change**: variation, modulation. 76. **out...nick**: beyond all reckoning. 95.
subtle: crafty. 96. **conceitless**: witless. 114. **[his]** F₂₋₄. *her* F₁. 125. **else**: elsewhere. **shadow**: mere nothing. 126.
shadow: portrait.

That wait for execution in the morn.
            [*Exeunt Pro. and Sil. severally.*]
Jul. Host, will you go?   135
Host. By my halidom, I was fast asleep.
Jul. Pray you, where lies Sir Proteus?
Host. Marry, at my house. Trust me, I think
'tis almost day.
Jul. Not so; but it hath been the longest night
That e'er I watch'd and the most heaviest.   141
                                    [*Exeunt.*]

SCENE III. [*The same.*]

Enter EGLAMOUR.

Egl. This is the hour that Madam Silvia
Entreated me to call and know her mind.
There's some great matter she'd employ me in.
Madam, madam!

[*Enter* SILVIA *above.*]

Sil.   Who calls?
Egl.   Your servant and your friend;
One that attends your ladyship's command.   5
Sil. Sir Eglamour, a thousand times good mor-
row.
Egl. As many, worthy lady, to yourself.
According to your ladyship's impose,
I am thus early come to know what service
It is your pleasure to command me in.   10
Sil. O Eglamour, thou art a gentleman, —
Think not I flatter, for I swear I do not, —
Valiant, wise, remorseful, well accomplish'd.
Thou art not ignorant what dear good will
I bear unto the banish'd Valentine,   15
Nor how my father would enforce me marry
Vain Thurio, whom my very soul abhors.
Thyself hast lov'd; and I have heard thee say
No grief did ever come so near thy heart
As when thy lady and thy true love died,   20
Upon whose grave thou vow'dst pure chastity.
Sir Eglamour, I would to Valentine,
To Mantua, where I hear he makes abode;
And, for the ways are dangerous to pass,
I do desire thy worthy company,   25
Upon whose faith and honour I repose.
Urge not my father's anger, Eglamour,
But think upon my grief, a lady's grief,
And on the justice of my flying hence,
To keep me from a most unholy match,   30
Which heaven and fortune still rewards with plagues.
I do desire thee, even from a heart
As full of sorrows as the sea of sands,
To bear me company and go with me;

If not, to hide what I have said to thee,   35
That I may venture to depart alone.
Egl. Madam, I pity much your grievances;
Which since I know they virtuously are plac'd,
I give consent to go along with you,
Recking as little what betideth me   40
As much I wish all good befortune you.
When will you go?
Sil.   This evening coming.
Egl. Where shall I meet you?
Sil.   At Friar Patrick's cell,
Where I intend holy confession.
Egl. I will not fail your ladyship. Good   45
morrow, gentle lady.
Sil. Good morrow, kind Sir Eglamour.
                            [*Exeunt* [*severally*].

SCENE IV. [*The same.*]

Enter LAUNCE [*with his Dog*].

Launce. When a man's servant shall play the
cur with him, look you, it goes hard: one that I
brought up of a puppy; one that I sav'd from
drowning, when three or four of his blind brothers
and sisters went to it. I have taught him, even   5
as one would say precisely, "Thus I would
teach a dog." I was sent to deliver him as a present
to Mistress Silvia from my master; and I came no
sooner into the dining-chamber but he steps me
to her trencher and steals her capon's leg. O,   10
'tis a foul thing when a cur cannot keep himself in
all companies! I would have, as one should say,
one that takes upon him to be a dog indeed, to
be, as it were, a dog at all things. If I had not
had more wit than he, to take a fault upon me   15
that he did, I think verily he had been hang'd for't;
sure as I live, he had suffer'd for't. You shall
judge. He thrusts me himself into the company
of three or four gentlemanlike dogs, under the
Duke's table. He had not been there — bless   20
the mark! — a pissing while, but all the chamber
smelt him. "Out with the dog!" says one. "What
cur is that?" says another. "Whip him out!"
says the third. "Hang him up!" says the Duke.
I, having been acquainted with the smell before,   25
knew it was Crab, and goes me to the fellow
that whips the dogs. "Friend," quoth I, "you
mean to whip the dog?" "Ay, marry, do I,"
quoth he. "You do him the more wrong," quoth
I; "'twas I did the thing you wot of." He makes   30
me no more ado, but whips me out of the
chamber. How many masters would do this for

136. **halidom:** holiness, all that one holds sacred. 141. **watch'd:** stayed awake.
Sc. iii, 8. **impose:** command. 13. **remorseful:** compassionate. 14. **dear:** affectionate, intense. 23. **Mantua.** Cf.
V.ii.47. 37. **grievances:** distresses. 41. **befortune:** befall.
Sc. iv, 3. **of:** from. 10. **trencher:** wooden plate. 11. **keep:** restrain. 14. **a dog at:** adept at. 20. **bless the mark.**
Originally a formula for averting evil omens, this phrase came to serve as an introduction for any obnoxious remark. 29.
wot: know.

his servant? Nay, I'll be sworn, I have sat in the
stocks for puddings he hath stolen, otherwise he
had been executed; I have stood on the pillory for
geese he hath kill'd, otherwise he had suffer'd 35
for't. Thou think'st not of this now. Nay, I remember the trick you serv'd me when I took my
leave of Madam Silvia. Did not I bid thee still
mark me and do as I do? When didst thou see
me heave up my leg and make water against a 40
gentlewoman's farthingale? Didst thou ever see
me do such a trick?

[*Enter* PROTEUS *and* JULIA.]

Pro. Sebastian is thy name? I like thee well
And will employ thee in some service presently.
Jul. In what you please. I'll do what I can. 46
Pro. I hope thou wilt. [*To Launce.*] How now,
    you whoreson peasant!
Where have you been these two days loitering?
Launce. Marry, sir, I carried Mistress Silvia
the dog you bade me.   50
Pro. And what says she to my little jewel?
Launce. Marry, she says your dog was a cur,
and tells you currish thanks is good enough for
such a present.
Pro. But she receiv'd my dog?   55
Launce. No, indeed, did she not; here have I
brought him back again.
Pro. What, didst thou offer her this from me?
Launce. Ay, sir; the other squirrel was stolen
from me by the [hangman] boys in the market- 60
place; and then I offer'd her mine own, who is
a dog as big as ten of yours, and therefore the gift
the greater.
Pro. Go get thee hence, and find my dog again,
Or ne'er return again into my sight.   65
Away, I say! stay'st thou to vex me here?
                                    [*Exit Launce.*]
A slave, that still an end turns me to shame!
Sebastian, I have entertained thee,
Partly that I have need of such a youth
That can with some discretion do my business, 70
For 'tis no trusting to yond foolish lout,
But chiefly for thy face and thy behaviour,
Which, if my augury deceive me not,
Witness good bringing up, fortune, and truth:
Therefore know thou, for this I entertain thee. 75
Go presently, and take this ring with thee,
Deliver it to Madam Silvia.
She lov'd me well deliver'd it to me.
  Jul. It seems you lov'd not her, to leave her
    token.
She is dead, belike?
  Pro.   Not so; I think she lives. 80

Jul. Alas!
Pro. Why dost thou cry "alas"?
Jul.   I cannot choose
But pity her.
  Pro.   Wherefore shouldst thou pity her?
Jul. Because methinks that she lov'd you as well
As you do love your lady Silvia.   85
She dreams on him that has forgot her love;
You dote on her that cares not for your love.
'Tis pity love should be so contrary;
And thinking on it makes me cry "alas!"   89
  Pro. Well, give her that ring and therewithal
This letter. That's her chamber. Tell my lady
I claim the promise for her heavenly picture.
Your message done, hie home unto my chamber,
Where thou shalt find me, sad and solitary.
                                    [*Exit.*]
Jul. How many women would do such a message?
Alas, poor Proteus! thou hast entertain'd 96
A fox to be the shepherd of thy lambs.
Alas, poor fool! why do I pity him
That with his very heart despiseth me?
Because he loves her, he despiseth me;   100
Because I love him, I must pity him.
This ring I gave him when he parted from me,
To bind him to remember my good will;
And now am I, unhappy messenger,
To plead for that which I would not obtain, 105
To carry that which I would have refus'd,
To praise his faith which I would have disprais'd.
I am my master's true-confirmed love;
But cannot be true servant to my master
Unless I prove false traitor to myself.   110
Yet will I woo for him, but yet so coldly
As, heaven it knows, I would not have him speed.

[*Enter* SILVIA, *attended.*]

Gentlewoman, good day! I pray you, be my mean
To bring me where to speak with Madam Silvia.
  Sil. What would you with her, if that I be she?
  Jul. If you be she, I do entreat your patience 116
To hear me speak the message I am sent on.
  Sil. For whom?
  Jul. From my master, Sir Proteus, madam.
  Sil. O, he sends you for a picture.   120
  Jul. Ay, madam.
  Sil. Ursula, bring my picture there.
Go give your master this. Tell him from me,
One Julia, that his changing thoughts forget, 124
Would better fit his chamber than this shadow.
  Jul. Madam, please you peruse this letter. —
Pardon me, madam; I have unadvis'd
Deliver'd you a paper that I should not.
This is the letter to your ladyship.

---

33. **puddings:** entrails.   47. **whoreson:** bastard, used in coarse playfulness.   60. **[hangman]** (Singer): fit for the hangman. *hangman's* Ff.   67. **still an end:** continually.   68. **entertained:** engaged.   78. **deliver'd:** who delivered.   79. **leave:** part with.   98. **poor fool:** i.e., herself.   112. **speed:** succeed.   127. **unadvis'd:** inadvertently.

Sil. I pray thee, let me look on that again. 130
Jul. It may not be; good madam, pardon me.
Sil. There, hold!
I will not look upon your master's lines.
I know they are stuff'd with protestations
And full of new-found oaths, which he will break
As easily as I do tear his paper. 136
Jul. Madam, he sends your ladyship this ring.
Sil. The more shame for him that he sends it me;
For I have heard him say a thousand times
His Julia gave it him at his departure. 140
Though his false finger have profan'd the ring,
Mine shall not do his Julia so much wrong.
Jul. She thanks you.
Sil. What say'st thou? 144
Jul. I thank you, madam, that you tender her.
Poor gentlewoman! my master wrongs her much.
Sil. Dost thou know her?
Jul. Almost as well as I do know myself.
To think upon her woes I do protest
That I have wept a hundred several times. 150
Sil. Belike she thinks that Proteus hath forsook
her?
Jul. I think she doth; and that's her cause of
sorrow.
Sil. Is she not passing fair?
Jul. She hath been fairer, madam, than she is.
When she did think my master lov'd her well, 155
She, in my judgement, was as fair as you;
But since she did neglect her looking-glass
And threw her sun-expelling mask away,
The air hath starv'd the roses in her cheeks
And pinch'd the lily-tincture of her face, 160
That now she is become as black as I.
Sil. How tall was she?
Jul. About my stature; for at Pentecost,
When all our pageants of delight were play'd,
Our youth got me to play the woman's part, 165
And I was trimm'd in Madam Julia's gown,
Which served me as fit, by all men's judgements,
As if the garment had been made for me;
Therefore I know she is about my height.
And at that time I made her weep agood, 170
For I did play a lamentable part.
Madam, 'twas Ariadne passioning
For Theseus' perjury and unjust flight;
Which I so lively acted with my tears
That my poor mistress, moved therewithal, 175
Wept bitterly; and would I might be dead
If I in thought felt not her very sorrow!
Sil. She is beholding to thee, gentle youth.
Alas, poor lady, desolate and left!

I weep myself to think upon thy words. 180
Here, youth, there is my purse; I give thee this
For thy sweet mistress' sake, because thou lov'st her.
Farewell. [*Exit Silvia, with attendants.*]
Jul. And she shall thank you for't, if e'er you
know her.
A virtuous gentlewoman, mild and beautiful! 185
I hope my master's suit will be but cold,
Since she respects my mistress' love so much.
Alas, how love can trifle with itself!
Here is her picture; let me see. I think,
If I had such a tire, this face of mine 190
Were full as lovely as is this of hers;
And yet the painter flatter'd her a little,
Unless I flatter with myself too much.
Her hair is auburn, mine is perfect yellow:
If that be all the difference in his love, 195
I'll get me such a colour'd periwig.
Her eyes are grey as glass, and so are mine.
Ay, but her forehead's low, and mine's as high.
What should it be that he respects in her
But I can make respective in myself, 200
If this fond Love were not a blinded god?
Come, shadow, come, and take this shadow up,
For 'tis thy rival. O thou senseless form,
Thou shalt be worshipp'd, kiss'd, lov'd, and ador'd!
And, were there sense in his idolatry, 205
My substance should be statue in thy stead.
I'll use thee kindly for thy mistress' sake,
That us'd me so; or else, by Jove I vow,
I should have scratch'd out your unseeing eyes,
To make my master out of love with thee! 210
[*Exit.*

ACT V

Scene I. [*Milan. An abbey.*]

Enter Eglamour.

Egl. The sun begins to gild the western sky,
And now it is about the very hour
That Silvia at Friar Patrick's cell should meet me.
She will not fail, for lovers break not hours,
Unless it be to come before their time, 5
So much they spur their expedition.
See where she comes.

[*Enter* Silvia.]
Lady, a happy evening!
Sil. Amen, amen! Go on, good Eglamour,
Out at the postern by the abbey-wall.
I fear I am attended by some spies. 10

145. **tender:** regard tenderly.   161. **black:** dark (i.e., from sunburn).   164. **pageants of delight:** delightful theatricals.
170. **agood:** in earnest.   172. **passioning:** lamenting.   173. **Theseus' perjury.** Ariadne, daughter of King Minos of Crete, having helped Theseus to slay the Minotaur, fled with him; but he abandoned her on the island of Naxos.   178. **beholding:** indebted.   186. **cold:** coldly received, ineffectual.   190. **tire:** headdress.   200. **respective:** worthy of respect.   202. **shadow ... shadow:** lifeless one ... portrait (cf. IV.ii.125–26 n.). **take ... up:** with pun on sense of "cope with."
Act V, sc. i. o. **postern:** small side door.

Egl Fear not; the forest is not three leagues off.
If we recover that, we are sure enough.   [*Exeunt.*

SCENE II. [*The same.   The Duke's palace.*]

Enter THURIO, PROTEUS, *and* JULIA *disguised.*

Thu. Sir Proteus, what says Silvia to my suit?
Pro. O, sir, I find her milder than she was;
And yet she takes exceptions at your person.
Thu. What, that my leg is too long?
Pro. No; that it is too little.   5
Thu. I'll wear a boot, to make it somewhat
    rounder.
[*Jul. Aside.*] But love will not be spurr'd to
    what it loathes.
Thu. What says she to my face?
Pro. She says it is a fair one
Thu. Nay, then the wanton lies; my face is
    black.   10
Pro. But pearls are fair; and the old saying is,
Black men are pearls in beauteous ladies' eyes.
[*Jul. Aside.*] 'Tis true; such pearls as put out
    ladies' eyes;
For I had rather wink than look on them.
Thu. How likes she my discourse?   15
Pro. Ill, when you talk of war.
Thu. But well, when I discourse of love and
    peace?
Jul. [*Aside.*] But better, indeed, when you hold
    your peace.
Thu. What says she to my valour?
Pro. O, sir, she makes no doubt of that.   20
Jul. [*Aside.*] She needs not, when she knows it
    cowardice.
Thu. What says she to my birth?
Pro. That you are well deriv'd.
Jul. [*Aside.*] True, from a gentleman to a fool.
Thu. Considers she my possessions?   25
Pro. O, ay; and pities them.
Thu. Wherefore?
Jul. [*Aside.*] That such an ass should owe them.
Pro. That they are out by lease.
Jul. Here comes the Duke.   30

[*Enter* DUKE.]

Duke. How now, Sir Proteus!   How now,
    Thurio!
Which of you saw Sir Eglamour of late?
Thu. Not I.
Pro.   Nor I.
Duke.   Saw you my daughter?
Pro.   Neither.
Duke. Why then,
She's fled unto that peasant Valentine,   35

And Eglamour is in her company.
'Tis true; for Friar Laurence met them both,
As he in penance wander'd through the forest.
Him he knew well, and guess'd that it was she,
But, being mask'd, he was not sure of it.   40
Besides, she did intend confession
At Patrick's cell this even; and there she was not.
These likelihoods confirm her flight from hence.
Therefore, I pray you, stand not to discourse,
But mount you presently and meet with me   45
Upon the rising of the mountain-foot
That leads toward Mantua, whither they are fled.
Dispatch, sweet gentlemen, and follow me.
    [*Exit.*]
Thu. Why, this it is to be a peevish girl,
That flies her fortune when it follows her.   50
I'll after, more to be reveng'd on Eglamour
Than for the love of reckless Silvia.   [*Exit.*]
Pro. And I will follow, more for Silvia's love
Than hate of Eglamour that goes with her.
    [*Exit.*]
Jul. And I will follow, more to cross that love
Than hate for Silvia that is gone for love.   56
    [*Exit.*

SCENE III. [*A Forest between Milan and Mantua.*]

Enter OUTLAWS *with* SILVIA.

1. Out. Come, come,
Be patient; we must bring you to our captain.
Sil. A thousand more mischances than this one
Have learn'd me how to brook this patiently.
2. Out. Come, bring her away.   5
1. Out. Where is the gentleman that was with
    her?
3. Out. Being nimble-footed, he hath outrun us,
But Moyses and Valerius follow him.
Go thou with her to the west end of the wood;
There is our captain.   We'll follow him that's fled.
The thicket is beset, he cannot 'scape.   11
1. Out. Come, I must bring you to our captain's
    cave.
Fear not; he bears an honourable mind,
And will not use a woman lawlessly.
Sil. O Valentine, this I endure for thee!   15
    [*Exeunt.*

SCENE IV. [*Another part of the forest.*]

Enter VALENTINE.

Val. How use doth breed a habit in a man!
This shadowy desert, unfrequented woods,
I better brook than flourishing peopled towns.
Here can I sit alone, unseen of any,

---

12. **recover:** reach. **sure:** safe.
Sc. ii, 9. **fair:** i.e., suggesting effeminacy. 13. **pearls:** cataracts. 28. **owe:** own. 29. **out by lease:** rented to others.
35. **peasant:** base fellow. 49. **peevish:** stubborn.

And to the nightingale's complaining notes   5
Tune my distresses and record my woes.
O thou that dost inhabit in my breast,
Leave not the mansion so long tenantless,
Lest, growing ruinous, the building fall
And leave no memory of what it was!   10
Repair me with thy presence, Silvia!
Thou gentle nymph, cherish thy forlorn swain!
What halloing and what stir is this to-day?
These are my mates, that make their wills their law,
Have some unhappy passenger in chase.   15
They love me well; yet I have much to do
To keep them from uncivil outrages.
Withdraw thee, Valentine: who's this comes here?

                                     [Steps aside.]

     [*Enter* PROTEUS, SILVIA, *and* JULIA.]

   Pro. Madam, this service I have done for you,
Though you respect not aught your servant doth,
To hazard life and rescue you from him   21
That would have forc'd your honour and your love.
Vouchsafe me, for my need, but one fair look;
A smaller boon than this I cannot beg
And less than this, I am sure, you cannot give.   25
   Val. [*Aside.*] How like a dream is this! I see
     and hear.
Love, lend me patience to forbear awhile.
   Sil. O miserable, unhappy that I am!
   Pro. Unhappy were you, madam, ere I came;
But by my coming I have made you happy.   30
   Sil. By thy approach thou mak'st me most
     unhappy.
   Jul. [*Aside.*] And me, when he approacheth to
     your presence.
   Sil. Had I been seized by a hungry lion,
I would have been a breakfast to the beast
Rather than have false Proteus rescue me.   35
O, Heaven be judge how I love Valentine,
Whose life's as tender to me as my soul!
And full as much, for more there cannot be,
I do detest false perjur'd Proteus.
Therefore be gone; solicit me no more.   40
   Pro. What dangerous action, stood it next to
     death,
Would I not undergo for one calm look!
O, 'tis the curse in love, and still approv'd,
When women cannot love where they're belov'd!
   Sil. When Proteus cannot love where he's be-
     lov'd.   45
Read over Julia's heart, thy first, best love,
For whose dear sake thou didst then rend thy faith
Into a thousand oaths; and all those oaths
Descended into perjury, to love me.
Thou hast no faith left now, unless thou'dst two,   50
And that's far worse than none. Better have none

Than plural faith, which is too much by one.
Thou counterfeit to thy true friend!
   Pro.   In love
Who respects friend?
   Sil.   All men but Proteus.
   Pro. Nay, if the gentle spirit of moving words
Can no way change you to a milder form,   56
I'll woo you like a soldier, at arms' end,
And love you 'gainst the nature of love, — force ye.
   Sil. O heaven!
   Pro.   I'll force thee yield to my desire.
   Val. Ruffian, let go that rude uncivil touch,   60
Thou friend of an ill fashion!
   Pro.   Valentine!
   Val. Thou common friend, that's without faith
     or love,
For such is a friend now! Treacherous man,
Thou hast beguil'd my hopes! Nought but mine
     eye   64
Could have persuaded me. Now I dare not say
I have one friend alive; thou wouldst disprove me.
Who should be trusted [now], when one's right hand
Is perjured to the bosom? Proteus,
I am sorry I must never trust thee more,
But count the world a stranger for thy sake.   70
The private wound is deepest. O time most accurst,
'Mongst all foes that a friend should be the worst!
   Pro. My shame and guilt confounds me.
Forgive me, Valentine; if hearty sorrow
Be a sufficient ransom for offence,   75
I tender 't here; I do as truly suffer
As e'er I did commit.
   Val.   Then I am paid;
And once again I do receive thee honest.
Who by repentance is not satisfied
Is nor of heaven nor earth, for these are pleas'd.   80
By penitence the Eternal's wrath's appeas'd;
And, that my love may appear plain and free,
All that was mine in Silvia I give thee.
   Jul. O me unhappy!   [*Swoons.*]
   Pro. Look to the boy.   85
   Val. Why, boy! why, wag! how now! what's the
matter? Look up; speak.
   Jul. O good sir, my master charg'd me to de-
liver a ring to Madam Silvia, which, out of my
neglect, was never done.   90
   Pro. Where is that ring, boy?
   Jul.   Here 'tis; this is it.
   Pro. How? let me see!
Why, this is the ring I gave to Julia.
   Jul. O, cry you mercy, sir, I have mistook;
This is the ring you sent to Silvia.   95
   Pro. But how cam'st thou by this ring? At my
     depart
I gave this unto Julia.

Jul. And Julia herself did give it me;
And Julia herself hath brought it hither.
   Pro. How! Julia!   100
   Jul. Behold her that gave aim to all thy oaths,
And entertain'd 'em deeply in her heart.
How oft hast thou with perjury cleft the root!
O Proteus, let this habit make thee blush!
Be thou asham'd that I have took upon me   105
Such an immodest raiment, if shame live
In a disguise of love.
It is the lesser blot, modesty finds,
Women to change their shapes than men their
    minds.
   Pro. Than men their minds! 'tis true. O heaven!
    were man   110
But constant, he were perfect. That one error
Fills him with faults; makes him run through all
    the sins.
Inconstancy falls off ere it begins.
What is in Silvia's face, but I may spy
More fresh in Julia's with a constant eye?   115
   Val. Come, come, a hand from either.
Let me be blest to make this happy close;
'Twere pity two such friends should be long foes.
   Pro. Bear witness, Heaven. I have my wish for
    ever.
   Jul. And I mine.   120

   [*Enter* OUTLAWS, *with* DUKE *and* THURIO.]
   Outlaws. A prize, a prize, a prize!
   Val. Forbear, forbear, I say! It is my lord the
    Duke.
Your Grace is welcome to a man disgrac'd,
Banished Valentine.
   Duke.   Sir Valentine!
   Thu. Yonder is Silvia; and Silvia's mine.   125
   Val. Thurio, give back, or else embrace thy
    death;
Come not within the measure of my wrath.
Do not name Silvia thine; if once again,
[Milano] shall not hold thee. Here she stands:
Take but possession of her with a touch, —   130
I dare thee but to breathe upon my love.
   Thu. Sir Valentine, I care not for her, I.
I hold him but a fool that will endanger

His body for a girl that loves him not.
I claim her not, and therefore she is thine.   135
   Duke. The more degenerate and base art thou
To make such means for her as thou hast done
And leave her on such slight conditions.
Now, by the honour of my ancestry,
I do applaud thy spirit, Valentine,   140
And think thee worthy of an empress' love.
Know then, I here forget all former griefs,
Cancel all grudge, repeal thee home again,
Plead a new state in thy unrival'd merit,
To which I thus subscribe: Sir Valentine,   145
Thou art a gentleman and well deriv'd;
Take thou thy Silvia, for thou hast deserv'd her.
   Val. I thank your Grace; the gift hath made me
    happy.
I now beseech you, for your daughter's sake,
To grant one boon that I shall ask of you.   150
   Duke. I grant it, for thine own, whate'er it be.
   Val. These banish'd men that I have kept withal
Are men endu'd with worthy qualities.
Forgive them what they have committed here
And let them be recall'd from their exile.   155
They are reformed, civil, full of good,
And fit for great employment, worthy lord.
   Duke. Thou hast prevail'd; I pardon them and
    thee;
Dispose of them as thou know'st their deserts.
Come, let us go; we will include all jars   160
With triumphs, mirth, and rare solemnity.
   Val. And, as we walk along, I dare be bold
With our discourse to make your Grace to smile.
What think you of this page, my lord?
   Duke. I think the boy hath grace in him; he
    blushes.   165
   Val. I warrant you, my lord, more grace than
    boy.
   Duke. What mean you by that saying?
   Val. Please you, I'll tell you as we pass along
That you will wonder what hath fortuned.
Come, Proteus; 'tis your penance but to hear   170
The story of your loves discovered;
That done, our day of marriage shall be yours;
One feast, one house, one mutual happiness.
                    [*Exeunt.*

101. **gave aim to:** was the subject of.   103. **root:** i.e., the bottom of her heart.   106-07. **if ... love:** if there is any shame in a disguise assumed for love.   113. **Inconstancy ... begins.** Perhaps meaning: "An inconstant man is unfaithful even before he begins to love."   117. **close:** conclusion.   126. **give back:** stand back.   127. **measure:** reach.   129. [**Milano**] (Theobald). *Verona* F.   137. **means:** efforts.   138. **on ... conditions:** so readily.   144. **Plead ... in:** take a new attitude towards.   152. **kept withal:** lived with.   160. **include:** conclude.   161. **solemnity:** festivity.   169. **That ... fortuned:** so that you will marvel at what has happened.

Love's Labour's Lost

THE FIRST EXTANT EDITION of *Love's Labour's Lost* is a Quarto of 1598, which is the direct source of the next printed text, that in the First Folio. The Folio text, though somewhat more carefully printed than that of the Quarto, has no independent authority, and adds nothing save the last line and the division into acts. The present text is, accordingly, based on the Quarto.

The Quarto professes on its title page to give the play "as it was presented before her Highnes this last Christmas. Newly corrected and augmented by W. Shakespere." If the Quarto was issued before March 25, 1598 (O.S.), "last Christmas" would mean Christmas of 1598; if after March 25, it would mean Christmas of 1597. Probability favors the latter case. The words "corrected and augmented" suggest an earlier form of the play and open fields of conjecture which have been fully exploited. A previous printing of the play, no trace of which has come down to us, is, of course, possible, and the belief that there was such a one can be supported by reference to the textual history of *Romeo and Juliet*. But even though an earlier printing of the present drama be assumed, it could conceivably have exhibited the text substantially as we know it. The theory that the received text represents a drastically revised version of a play composed much earlier remains to be proved. There are, nevertheless, at least two patent signs of reworking. The speech of Biron (IV.iii.289–365) and the conversation of Biron and Rosaline (V.ii.827–32, 846–80) contain obvious repetitions, and it is reasonable to think that Shakespeare had left those portions (which had, perhaps, been written in some haste) with signs for deletion which the printer did not heed. It is not, however, necessary to believe that these alterations were part of an extensive revision; they could equally well have been made during the period of original composition. Other textual peculiarities, typographical faults, and inconsistent use of generic and proper names in abbreviated speech headings, can be otherwise explained.

The date of the play cannot be precisely determined because all the evidence, beyond references by Meres in his *Palladis Tamia* (1598) and by Tofte in his *Alba or Month's Mind of a Melancholy Lover* (1598) is internal. Among the several topical allusions or pieces of incidental indebtedness which have been enlisted in attempts to solve this problem, the only one which seems at all helpful is the probable reference in the "conceit" of "piercing a hogshead" (IV.ii.85–91) to a passage in Gabriel Harvey's *Pierce's Supererogation* (1593), attacking Thomas Nashe, the author of *Pierce Pennilesse*, as follows: "She knew what she said that intituled Pierce the hogshead of wit Penniles, the tosspot of eloquence: and Nashe the very inventor of Asses." A date close to 1593 or 1594 is, however, strongly suggested by another kind of testimony. Although the stylistic features of the play, its diverse mixture of blank verse, couplets, and speeches rhyming alternately, and its prodigality in puns and conceits, may seem to indicate the exuberance of immaturity, yet the poetic tone and texture of many fine passages support belief that the performance stood nearer the end than the beginning of the dramatist's apprenticeship. Moreover, the introduction of sonnets may well point to a preoccupation with that form, and other matters render it highly probable that when Shakespeare was writing *Love's Labour's Lost* he had begun the composition of his Sonnets. Relationship between these poems and the play is reflected in thematic resemblances: in the many references within the play to eyes, and the stress upon Rosaline's dark beauty, which inevitably calls to mind the enigmatic "dark lady" of the Sonnets. Since the dating of the Sonnets is a controversial matter, the one certainty being that they were written over a period of years, the only point that can legitimately be argued from these parallels is that the composition of *Love's Labour's Lost* and of some of the Sonnets must be closely contemporaneous. The affinity of *Romeo and Juliet* with the Sonnets (sonnets are buried in the verse of that play also) is generally recognized. When everything has been taken into account, and despite the artificiality and linguistic virtuosity reminiscent of Lyly, 1594 emerges as a reasonable guess for *Love's Labour's Lost*.

No source for the plot has been discovered, and it is quite possible that the story was invented by

Shakespeare himself. Some hints, however, may have come from French history. In 1578 Queen Catherine de Medici and her daughter, Marguerite of Valois, journeyed with a bevy of ladies to the court of Henry of Navarre at Nerac for the purpose of establishing the sovereignty of Aquitaine and ending a quarrel over the payment of two hundred thousand crowns to Navarre by the King of France. The society enjoyed by the visiting ladies with Henry's courtiers, as described in Marguerite's *Memoires*, calls to mind the association of the female embassy with Navarre and his courtiers in the play. Shakespeare could not have seen the *Memoires*, but it is conceivable that he was given an account of what had gone on at Nerac by some English traveller. Coincidences in names are also interesting. Two of Navarre's trusted followers were the Maréchal Biron and the Duc de Longaville, and the Duc de Mayenne (Dumain) was one of his enemies. No Ferdinand was ever king of Navarre, yet it is hardly necessary to charge Shakespeare with ignorance; he may simply have preferred to avoid using Henry's name, perhaps to escape the risk of implying too much. The masque of the Muscovites (V.ii.158 ff.) may well have been inspired by a description in Holinshed of an entertainment given at Westminster for foreign ambassadors by Henry VIII.

Several characters in the play conform to conventionalized types of the Italian *commedia dell'arte*. Armado is the grandiloquent braggart, whose ancestor is the *miles gloriosus* of Plautus; Moth is the zany, who in the Italian comedy is always paired with the braggart; Holofernes is the pedant; Nathaniel, the parasite; Costard, the slow-witted rustic; Dull, the stupid magistrate. Nevertheless, despite the typical nature of these comic figures, ingenious scholarship has been unusually active in seeking in them a topical significance, of which it professes to find a great deal.

Holofernes has been identified with Florio, with Chapman, and with Gabriel Harvey; Chapman and Raleigh with Armado; and Nashe with Moth. It is evident that such theories tend to destroy one another. What may be admitted, however, is that the satire and wit flashing through the play are constantly suggestive of more than a general object and may hint at more than meets the eye. It may be true that in directing his satire at current literary fashions Shakespeare recalled various particular representatives, yet it does not follow that he used any one as model. In any event, the search for originals is a perilous and doubtfully rewarding enterprise. The general drift of the play is evident enough alike in the plot and the verbal parodies, namely, the exposure of the absurdity in departing from common sense, and the ability of Nature to assert herself to the discomfiture of those who foolishly attempt to organize society on artificial lines that run counter to the fundamental laws of our human constitution. Attempts to discover in Navarre's Academe a broad satire on a coterie headed by Raleigh and purporting to include Chapman, Marlowe, Thomas Harriot, and others interested in the new science, are not convincing. The theory stresses passages (e.g., I.i.88–93; I.ii.39–56; III.i.85–98; V.ii.487 ff.) which are construed as ridiculing astronomy and mathematics, and particularly the phrase, the "school of night" (IV.iii.254–55; see note), which has been taken, because of its resemblance to Chapman's *Shadow of Night* (1594), as alluding to the scientific group. But the reading *school* is probably wrong, and there is nothing to show that the epithet "school of night" was ever actually applied to the group.

The main point of *Love's Labour's Lost* for Shakespeare's contemporaries must have been in its pervading burlesque of current fads and affectations. The wit-combats of the lords and ladies, the affected diction of the sonneteering courtiers, the preposterous bombast of Armado, the Latinized English and pedantic alliteration of Holofernes, and the quips of Moth, are all parodies of the absurdities into which the prevailing interest in linguistic feats had led almost all classes of Elizabethan society. Euphuism is today the most familiar of these fashions, but Euphuism itself, in the strict sense, is not specifically attacked. There are, however, other indications of the influence of Lyly. The farcical scenes with Moth, Armado, and the clowns, the repartee between the ladies and the courtiers, the scene in which the lovers betray their broken vows, and the general method of representing courtly intercourse, are all foreshadowed in the work of Lyly. Nor need it be supposed that all the verbal affectation and quaintnesses in the play are due to a burlesque intention. Shakespeare himself, as all his early work goes to show, delighted in word-play.

Hazlitt declared that "if we were to part with any of the author's comedies, it would be this." If, however, modern readers were to imagine a sacrifice, it would probably not be of *Love's Labour's Lost*. It is too ample in its poetry, its irony, and its comic portraiture to be yielded up. In addition to these values, it manifests affinities with later plays greater than itself, which enhance its interest and its significance. To mention the most conspicuous foreshadowings, its histrionic Worthies look forward to Bottom and company in *A Midsummer-Night's Dream*; the witty sparring of Biron and Rosaline anticipates the superior duelling of Benedick and Beatrice; and the blood of Biron runs in the veins of Mercutio.

LOVE'S LABOUR'S LOST

[DRAMATIS PERSONÆ

FERDINAND, *king of Navarre.*
BIRON,
LONGAVILLE, } *lords attending on the King.*
DUMAIN,
BOYET, } Lords attending on the Princess of
MERCADE, } France.

DON ADRIANO DE ARMADO, *a fantastical Span-*
iard.
SIR NATHANIEL, *a curate.*
HOLOFERNES, *a schoolmaster.*

DULL, *a constable.*
COSTARD, *a clown.*
MOTH, *page to Armado.*
A Forester.

The PRINCESS *of France.*
ROSALINE,
MARIA, } *ladies attending on the Princess.*
KATHERINE,
JAQUENETTA, *a country wench.*

Lords, Attendants, etc.

SCENE: *Navarre, the King's palace, and the country near it.*]

ACT I

[SCENE I. *The king of Navarre's park.*]

Enter FERDINAND, *king of Navarre,* BIRON,
LONGAVILLE, *and* DUMAIN.

King. Let fame, that all hunt after in their lives,
Live regist'red upon our brazen tombs
And then grace us in the disgrace of death;
When, spite of cormorant, devouring Time,
Th' endeavour of this present breath may buy   5
That honour which shall bate his scythe's keen edge
And make us heirs of all eternity.
Therefore, brave conquerors, — for so you are,
That war against your own affections
And the huge army of the world's desires, —   10
Our late edict shall strongly stand in force.
Navarre shall be the wonder of the world:
Our court shall be a little Academe,
Still and contemplative in living art.
You three, Biron, Dumain, and Longaville,   15
Have sworn for three years' term to live with me
My fellow-scholars, and to keep those statutes

That are recorded in this schedule here.
Your oaths are pass'd; and now subscribe your
      names,
That his own hand may strike his honour down 20
That violates the smallest branch herein.
If you are arm'd to do as sworn to do,
Subscribe to your deep oaths, and keep it too.
     Long. I am resolv'd; 'tis but a three years' fast.
The mind shall banquet, though the body pine. 25
Fat paunches have lean pates, and dainty bits
Make rich the ribs, but bankrupt quite the wits.
     Dum. My loving lord, Dumain is mortified.
The grosser manner of these world's delights
He throws upon the gross world's baser slaves. 30
To love, to wealth, to pomp, I pine and die,
With all these living in philosophy.
     Bir. I can but say their protestation over.
So much, dear liege, I have already sworn,
That is, to live and study here three years.   35
But there are other strict observances;
As, not to see a woman in that term,
Which I hope well is not enrolled there.
And one day in a week to touch no food,

Act I, sc. i, 6. **bate:** blunt.   14. **living art:** the art of living, like the "ars vivendi" of the Stoics.   22. **arm'd:** prepared.
28. **mortified:** dead to worldly pleasures.

And but one meal on every day beside,   40
The which I hope is not enrolled there;
And then, to sleep but three hours in the night,
And not be seen to wink of all the day, —
When I was wont to think no harm all night
And make a dark night too of half the day, —   45
Which I hope well is not enrolled there.
O, these are barren tasks, too hard to keep,
Not to see ladies, study, fast, not sleep!
  King. Your oath is pass'd to pass away from
    these.
  Bir. Let me say no, my liege, an if you please.
I only swore to study with your grace   51
And stay here in your court for three years' space.
  Long. You swore to that, Biron, and to the rest.
  Bir. By yea and nay, sir, then I swore in jest.
What is the end of study? Let me know.   55
  King. Why, that to know which else we should
    not know.
  Bir. Things hid and barr'd, you mean, from
    common sense?
  King. Ay, that is study's god-like recompence.
  Bir. Come on, then; I will swear to study so,
To know the thing I am forbid to know;   60
As thus, — to study where I well may dine,
  When I to [feast] expressly am forbid;
Or study where to meet some mistress fine,
  When mistresses from common sense are hid;
Or, having sworn too hard a keeping oath,   65
Study to break it and not break my troth.
If study's gain be thus and this be so,
Study knows that which yet it doth not know.
Swear me to this, and I will ne'er say no.
  King. These be the stops that hinder study
    quite,   70
And train our intellects to vain delight.
  Bir. Why, all delights are vain, but that most
    vain,
Which, with pain purchas'd, doth inherit pain;
As, painfully to pore upon a book
To seek the light of truth; while truth the while
Doth falsely blind the eyesight of his look.   76
  Light seeking light doth light of light beguile;
So, ere you find where light in darkness lies,
Your light grows dark by losing of your eyes.
Study me how to please the eye indeed   80
  By fixing it upon a fairer eye,
Who dazzling so, that eye shall be his heed
  And give him light that it was blinded by.
Study is like the heaven's glorious sun
  That will not be deep-search'd with saucy looks.
Small have continual plodders ever won,   86

Save base authority from others' books.
These earthly godfathers of heaven's lights,
  That give a name to every fixed star,
Have no more profit of their shining nights   90
  Than those that walk and wot not what they are.
Too much to know is to know nought but fame;
And every godfather can give a name.
  King. How well he's read, to reason against
    reading!
  Dum. Proceeded well, to stop all good proceed-
    ing!   95
  Long. He weeds the corn and still lets grow the
    weeding.
  Bir. The spring is near when green geese are
    a-breeding.
  Dum. How follows that?
  Bir.   Fit in his place and time.
  Dum. In reason nothing.
  Bir.   Something then in rhyme.
  King. Biron is like an envious sneaping frost   100
That bites the first-born infants of the spring.
  Bir. Well, say I am; why should proud summer
    boast
Before the birds have any cause to sing?
Why should I joy in any abortive birth?
At Christmas I no more desire a rose   105
Than wish a snow in May's new-fangled shows;
But like of each thing that in season grows.
So you (to study now it is too late,)
Climb o'er the house to unlock the little gate.
  King. Well, sit you out. Go home, Biron, adieu.
  Bir. No, my good lord, I have sworn to stay with
    you;   111
And though I have for barbarism spoke more
Than for that angel, knowledge, you can say,
Yet, confident, I'll keep what I have sworn,
  And bide the penance of each three years' day.
Give me the paper; let me read the same;   116
And to the strictest decrees I'll write my name.
  King. How well this yielding rescues thee from
    shame!
  Bir. [*Reads.*] "*Item*, That no woman shall come
within a mile of my court" — Hath this been pro-
claimed?   121
  Long. Four days ago.
  Bir. Let's see the penalty. [*Reads.*] "On pain of
losing her tongue." Who devis'd this penalty?   125
  Long. Marry, that did I.
  Bir. Sweet lord, and why?
  Long. To fright them hence with that dread pen-
    alty.
  [*Bir.*] A dangerous law against gentility! [*Reads.*]

43. **wink of:** close the eyes during. 54. **By yea and nay:** most assuredly. 57. **common sense:** ordinary perception. 62. **[feast]** (Theobald). *fast* Q. 67–68. **If...know:** "If this is the profit of study, then study is merely getting to know what we are not supposed to know." 77. **beguile:** cheat. 80. **Study:** teach. 82–83. **Who...by.** This is loosely expressed. "Which fair (lady's) eye shall be the beacon of his dazzled eye and provide light to him whom it blinded." 92. **fame:** hearsay. 97. **green:** young. 100. **sneaping:** nipping. 101. **infants:** i.e., buds. 115. **three years' day:** day for three years. 129. **[Bir.]** (Theobald). Q continues to Longaville. 129. **gentility:** courtesy.

"*Item*, if any man be seen to talk with a   130
woman within the term of three years, he shall en-
dure such public shame as the rest of the court can
possibly devise."
This article, my liege, yourself must break;
    For well you know here comes in embassy   135
The French king's daughter with yourself to
        speak —
    A maid of grace and complete majesty —
About surrender up of Aquitaine
To her decrepit, sick, and bedrid father;
Therefore this article is made in vain,   140
    Or vainly comes the admir'd princess hither.
    King. What say you, lords? Why, this was quite
        forgot.
    Bir. So study evermore is overshot.
While it doth study to have what it would,
It doth forget to do the thing it should;   145
And when it hath the thing it hunteth most,
'Tis won as towns with fire, so won, so lost.
    King. We must of force dispense with this decree;
She must lie here on mere necessity.
    Bir. Necessity will make us all forsworn   150
    Three thousand times within this three years'
        space;
For every man with his affects is born,
    Not by might mast'red, but by special grace.
If I break faith, this word shall speak for me;
I am forsworn on "mere necessity."   155
So to the laws at large I write my name;
                                    [*Subscribes.*]
    And he that breaks them in the least degree
Stands in attainder of eternal shame.
    Suggestions are to other as to me;
But I believe, although I seem so loath,   160
I am the last that will last keep his oath.
But is there no quick recreation granted?
    King. Ay, that there is. Our court, you know,
        is haunted
With a refined traveller of Spain;
A man in all the world's new fashion planted,   165
    That hath a mint of phrases in his brain;
One who the music of his own vain tongue
    Doth ravish like enchanting harmony;
A man of complements, whom right and wrong
    Have chose as umpire of their mutiny.   170
This child of fancy, that Armado hight,
    For interim to our studies shall relate,
In high-born words, the worth of many a knight
From tawny Spain, lost in the world's debate.
How you delight, my lords, I know not, I;   175
But, I protest, I love to hear him lie,
And I will use him for my minstrelsy.

Bir. Armado is a most illustrious wight,
A man of fire-new words, fashion's own knight.
    Long. Costard the swain and he shall be our
        sport;   180
And, so to study, three years is but short.

Enter a Constable [DULL] *with a letter, and* COSTARD.
    Dull. Which is the Duke's own person?
    Bir. This, fellow. What wouldst?
    Dull. I myself reprehend his own person, for I am
his grace's tharborough; but I would see his own
person in flesh and blood.   186
    Bir. This is he.
    Dull. Signior Arme — Arme — commends you.
There's villany abroad. This letter will tell you
more.   190
    Cost. Sir, the contempts thereof are as touching
me.
    King. A letter from the magnificent Armado.
    Bir. How low soever the matter, I hope in God
for high words.   195
    Long. A high hope for a low heaven. God grant
us patience!
    Bir. To hear? or forbear hearing?
    Long. To hear meekly, sir, and to laugh moder-
ately; or to forbear both.   200
    Bir. Well, sir, be it as the style shall give us cause
to climb in the merriness.
    Cost. The matter is to me, sir, as concerning
Jaquenetta. The manner of it is, I was taken with
the manner.   205
    Bir. In what manner?
    Cost. In manner and form following, sir; all those
three: I was seen with her in the manorhouse, sitting with her upon the form, and taken following
her into the park; which, put together, is in   210
manner and form following. Now, sir, for the
manner, — it is the manner of a man to speak to a
woman; for the form, — in some form.
    Bir. For the following, sir?
    Cost. As it shall follow in my correction; and God
defend the right!   216
    King. Will you hear this letter with attention?
    Bir. As we would hear an oracle.
    Cost. Such is the simplicity of a man to hearken
after the flesh.   220
    King. [*Reads.*] "Great deputy, the welkin's
vicegerent, and sole dominator of Navarre, my
soul's earth's god, and body's fost'ring patron."
    Cost. Not a word of Costard yet.
    King. [*Reads.*] "So it is," —   225
    Cost. It may be so; but if he say it is so, he is, in
telling true, but so.

---

149. **lie:** lodge. **mere:** sheer. 152. **affects:** inclinations. 159. **Suggestions:** temptations. 162. **quick:** lively. 169.
complements: accomplishments. 174. **debate:** warfare. 182. **Duke's:** i.e., King's (as often). 184. **reprehend:** i.e., represent.
184. **tharborough:** thirdborough, constable. *Farborough* Q. 191. **contempts:** i.e., contents. 205. **with the manner:** in the
act. 209. **form:** bench. 215. **correction:** punishment.

King. Peace!

Cost. Be to me, and every man that dares not fight!   230

King. No words!

Cost. Of other men's secrets, I beseech you.

King. [*Reads.*] "So it is, besieged with sable-coloured melancholy, I did commend the black oppressing humour to the most wholesome physic of thy health-giving air; and, as I am a gentleman, 236 betook myself to walk The time when? About the sixth hour; when beasts most graze, birds best peck, and men sit down to that nourishment which is called supper; so much for the time when. 240 Now for the ground which; which, I mean, I walk'd upon: it is ycleped thy park. Then for the place where; where, I mean, I did encounter that obscene and most prepost'rous event, that draweth from my snow-white pen the ebon-coloured ink 245 which here thou viewest, beholdest, surveyest, or seest; but to the place where: it standeth north-north-east and by east from the west corner of thy curious-knotted garden. There did I see that low-spirited swain, that base minnow of thy mirth," —   251

Cost. Me?

King. [*Reads.*] "That unlettered small-knowing soul," —

Cost. Me?   255

King. [*Reads.*] "That shallow vassal," —

Cost. Still me?

King. [*Reads.*] "Which, as I remember, hight Costard," —

Cost. O, me!   260

King. [*Reads.*] "Sorted and consorted, contrary to thy established proclaimed edict and continent canon, which with — O, with — but with this I passion to say wherewith," —

Cost. With a wench.   265

King. [*Reads.*] "With a child of our grandmother Eve, a female; or, for thy more sweet understanding, a woman. Him I, as my ever-esteemed duty pricks me on, have sent to thee, to receive the meed of punishment, by thy sweet Grace's officer, An- 270 thony Dull; a man of good repute, carriage, bearing, and estimation."

Dull. Me, an't shall please you; I am Anthony Dull.

King. [*Reads.*] "For Jaquenetta, — so is the weaker vessel called which I apprehended with 276 the aforesaid swain, — I keep her as a vessel of thy law's fury; and shall, at the least of thy sweet notice, bring her to trial. Thine, in all compliments of devoted and heart-burning heat of duty, 280
DON ADRIANO DE ARMADO."

Biron. This is not so well as I looked for, but the best that ever I heard.

King. Ay, the best for the worst. But, sirrah, what say you to this?

Cost. Sir, I confess the wench.   285

King. Did you hear the proclamation?

Cost. I do confess much of the hearing it, but little of the marking of it.

King. It was proclaimed a year's imprisonment, to be taken with a wench.   290

Cost. I was taken with none, sir; I was taken with a damsel.

King. Well, it was proclaimed damsel.

Cost. This was no damsel neither, sir; she was a virgin.   295

King. It is so varied too; for it was proclaimed virgin.

Cost. If it were, I deny her virginity; I was taken with a maid.

King. This maid will not serve your turn, sir. 300

Cost. This maid will serve my turn, sir.

King. Sir, I will pronounce your sentence: you shall fast a week with bran and water.

Cost. I had rather pray a month with mutton and porridge.   305

King. And Don Armado shall be your keeper. My Lord Biron, see him deliver'd o'er; And go we, lords, to put in practice that Which each to other hath so strongly sworn.

                        [*Exeunt King, Longaville, and Dumain.*]

Bir. I'll lay my head to any good man's hat, 310 These oaths and laws will prove an idle scorn. Sirrah, come on.

Cost. I suffer for the truth, sir; for true it is, I was taken with Jaquenetta, and Jaquenetta is a true girl; and therefore welcome the sour cup of 315 prosperity! Affliction may one day smile again; and till then, sit thee down, sorrow!   [*Exeunt.*

[SCENE II. *The same.*]

Enter ARMADO *and* MOTH, *his page.*

Arm. Boy, what sign is it when a man of great spirit grows melancholy?

Moth. A great sign, sir, that he will look sad.

Arm. Why, sadness is one and the self-same thing, dear imp.   5

Moth. No, no; O Lord, sir, no.

Arm. How canst thou part sadness and melancholy, my tender juvenal?

Moth. By a familiar demonstration of the working, my tough senior.   10

Arm. Why tough senior? Why tough senior?

Moth. Why tender juvenal? Why tender juvenal?

---

242. **ycleped:** called.   262. **continent canon:** rule of chastity.   264. **passion:** grieve.   305. **mutton.** Possibly a pun on the sense, "loose woman."

Sc. ii, 5. **imp:** youngster.   9. **juvenal:** juvenile.

Arm. I spoke it, tender juvenal, as a congruent epitheton appertaining to thy young days, which we may nominate tender. 16

Moth. And I, tough senior, as an appertinent title to your old time, which we may name tough.

Arm. Pretty and apt.

Moth. How mean you, sir? I pretty, and 20 my saying apt? or I apt, and my saying pretty?

Arm. Thou pretty, because little.

Moth. Little pretty, because little. Wherefore apt?

Arm. And therefore apt, because quick. 25

Moth. Speak you this in my praise, master?

Arm. In thy condign praise.

Moth. I will praise an eel with the same praise.

Arm. What, that an eel is ingenious?

Moth. That an eel is quick. 30

Arm. I do say thou art quick in answers; thou heat'st my blood.

Moth. I am answer'd, sir.

Arm. I love not to be cross'd.

Moth. [*Aside.*] He speaks the mere contrary; crosses love not him. 36

Arm. I have promised to study three years with the Duke.

Moth. You may do it in an hour, sir.

Arm. Impossible. 40

Moth. How many is one thrice told?

Arm. I am ill at reck'ning; it fitteth the spirit of a tapster.

Moth. You are a gentleman and a gamester, sir? 45

Arm. I confess both; they are both the varnish of a complete man.

Moth. Then, I am sure, you know how much the gross sum of deuce-ace amounts to.

Arm. It doth amount to one more than two. 50

Moth. Which the base vulgar do call three.

Arm. True.

Moth. Why, sir, is this such a piece of study? Now here is three studied, ere ye'll thrice wink; and how easy it is to put "years" to the word "three," and study three years in two words, the dancing horse will tell you. 57

Arm. A most fine figure!

Moth. To prove you a cipher.

Arm. I will hereupon confess I am in love; 60 and as it is base for a soldier to love, so am I in love with a base wench. If drawing my sword against the humour of affection would deliver me from the reprobate thought of it, I would take Desire prisoner, and ransom him to any French courtier 65

for a new-devis'd courtesy. I think scorn to sigh; methinks I should outswear Cupid. Comfort me, boy: what great men have been in love?

Moth. Hercules, master.

Arm. Most sweet Hercules! More authority, dear boy, name more; and, sweet my child, let 71 them be men of good repute and carriage.

Moth. Samson, master. He was a man of good carriage, great carriage, for he carried the town gates on his back like a porter; and he was in 75 love.

Arm. O well-knit Samson! strong-jointed Samson! I do excel thee in my rapier as much as thou didst me in carrying gates. I am in love too. Who was Samson's love, my dear Moth? 80

Moth. A woman, master.

Arm. Of what complexion?

Moth. Of all the four, or the three, or the two, or one of the four.

Arm. Tell me precisely of what complexion. 85

Moth. Of the sea-water green, sir.

Arm. Is that one of the four complexions?

Moth. As I have read, sir; and the best of them too.

Arm. Green indeed is the colour of lovers; 90 but to have a love of that colour, methinks Samson had small reason for it. He surely affected her for her wit.

Moth. It was so, sir; for she had a green wit.

Arm. My love is most immaculate white and red. 96

Moth. Most maculate thoughts, master, are mask'd under such colours.

Arm. Define, define, well-educated infant.

Moth. My father's wit and my mother's 100 tongue, assist me!

Arm. Sweet invocation of a child; most pretty and pathetical!

Moth. If she be made of white and red,
  Her faults will ne'er be known, 105
For blushing cheeks by faults are bred
  And fears by pale white shown.
Then if she fear, or be to blame,
  By this you shall not know
For still her cheeks possess the same 110
  Which native she doth owe.
A dangerous rhyme, master, against the reason of white and red.

Arm. Is there not a ballad, boy, of the King and the Beggar? 115

Moth. The world was very guilty of such a ballad some three ages since, but I think now 'tis not to be

---

14. **congruent epitheton:** suitable epithet. 36. **crosses:** coins with crosses stamped on them. 49. **deuce-ace:** a low throw at dice, a two and a one. 57. **dancing horse:** a famous horse named Morocco, trained to count by tapping with his hoof. 87. **the four complexions.** According to medical theory current in Shakespeare's day a person's temperament ("complexion") was determined by the relative commixture in his body of the four "humours," *viz.,* blood, phlegm, choler or red bile, and melancholy or black bile. 92. **affected:** loved. **wit:** intelligence. 97. **maculate:** impure. 111. **native:** naturally. **owe:** possess. 114. **ballad.** The Ballad of King Cophetua and the Beggar-maid (cf. IV.i.65 ff.).

found; or, if it were, it would neither serve for the writing nor the tune. 119

Arm. I will have that subject newly writ o'er, that I may example my digression by some mighty precedent. Boy, I do love that country girl that I took in the park with the rational hind Costard. She deserves well.

Moth. [*Aside.*] To be whipp'd; and yet a 125 better love than my master.

Arm. Sing, boy; my spirit grows heavy in love.

Moth. And that's great marvel, loving a light wench.

Arm. I say, sing. 130

Moth. Forbear till this company be past.

Enter Clown [COSTARD], *Constable* [DULL], *and Wench* [JAQUENETTA].

Dull. Sir, the Duke's pleasure is, that you keep Costard safe; and you must suffer him to take no delight nor no penance, but 'a must fast three days a week. For this damsel, I must keep her at 135 the park; she is allow'd for the day-woman. Fare you well.

Arm. I do betray myself with blushing. Maid!

Jaq. Man?

Arm. I will visit thee at the lodge. 140

Jaq. That's hereby.

Arm. I know where it is situate.

Jaq. Lord, how wise you are!

Arm. I will tell thee wonders.

Jaq. With that face? 145

Arm. I love thee.

Jaq. So I heard you say.

Arm. And so, farewell.

Jaq. Fair weather after you!

[*Dull.*] Come, Jaquenetta, away! 150

[*Exeunt* [*Dull and Jaquenetta*].

Arm. Villain, thou shalt fast for thy offences ere thou be pardoned.

Cost. Well, sir, I hope when I do it I shall do it on a full stomach.

Arm. Thou shalt be heavily punished. 155

Cost. I am more bound to you than your fellows, for they are but lightly rewarded.

Arm. Take away this villain; shut him up.

Moth. Come, you transgressing slave; away!

Cost. Let me not be pent up, sir! I will fast, being loose. 161

Moth. No, sir; that were fast and loose. Thou shalt to prison.

Cost. Well, if ever I do see the merry days of desolation that I have seen, some shall see. 165

Moth. What shall some see?

Cost. Nay, nothing, Master Moth, but what they look upon. It is not for prisoners to be too silent in their words; and therefore I will say nothing. I thank God I have as little patience as another man, and therefore I can be quiet. 171

[*Exeunt* [*Moth and Costard*].

Arm. I do affect the very ground, which is base, where her shoe, which is baser, guided by her foot, which is basest, doth tread. I shall be forsworn, which is a great argument of falsehood, if I 175 love. And how can that be true love which is falsely attempted? Love is a familiar; Love is a devil; there is no evil angel but Love. Yet was Samson so tempted, and he had an excellent strength; yet was Solomon so seduced, and he 180 had a very good wit. Cupid's butt-shaft is too hard for Hercules' club; and therefore too much odds for a Spaniard's rapier. The first and second cause will not serve my turn; the passado he respects not, the duello he regards not: his disgrace is to be called 185 boy; but his glory is to subdue men. Adieu, valour! rust, rapier! be still, drum! for your manager is in love; yea, he loveth. Assist me, some extemporal god of rhyme, for I am sure I shall turn sonnet. Devise, wit! write, pen! for I am for whole volumes in folio. [*Exit.* 191

ACT II

[SCENE I. *The same.*]

Enter the PRINCESS OF FRANCE, *with three attending* LADIES, *and three* LORDS.

Boyet. Now, madam, summon up your dearest spirits;
Consider who the King your father sends,
To whom he sends, and what's his embassy:
Yourself, held precious in the world's esteem,
To parley with the sole inheritor 5
Of all perfections that a man may owe,
Matchless Navarre; the plea of no less weight
Than Aquitaine, a dowry for a queen.
Be now as prodigal of all dear grace
As Nature was in making graces dear, 10
When she did starve the general world beside
And prodigally gave them all to you.

Prin. Good Lord Boyet, my beauty, though but mean,
Needs not the painted flourish of your praise.
Beauty is bought by judgement of the eye, 15

118-19. **it ... tune**: i.e., neither words nor tune would suffice to express your case. 121. **example my digression**: vindicate my transgression. 123. **hind**: peasant. 136. **allow'd**: approved. **day-woman**: dairy woman. 162. **fast and loose**: a cheating game. 169. **words**. Possibly punning on *wards*. 175. **argument**: proof. 177. **familiar**: attendant spirit; demon. 183. **cause**: i.e., for a quarrel (in the jargon of dueling). 184. **passado**: a forward thrust with the sword. 185. **duello**: the code of dueling.
Act II, sc. i, 1. **dearest spirits**: best wits. 13. *Prin.* F₂. The speeches of the Princess are headed *Queene* in Q.

Not utt'red by base sale of chapmen's tongues.
I am less proud to hear you tell my worth
Than you much willing to be counted wise
In spending your wit in the praise of mine.
But now to task the tasker: good Boyet,   20
You are not ignorant, all-telling fame
Doth noise abroad, Navarre hath made a vow,
Till painful study shall outwear three years,
No woman may approach his silent court;
Therefore to 's seemeth it a needful course,   25
Before we enter his forbidden gates,
To know his pleasure; and in that behalf,
Bold of your worthiness, we single you
As our best-moving fair solicitor.
Tell him, the daughter of the King of France,   30
On serious business craving quick dispatch,
Importunes personal conference with his Grace.
Haste, signify so much; while we attend,
Like humble-visag'd suitors, his high will.
        Boyet. Proud of employment, willingly I go.   35
                                                      [*Exit.*
        Prin. All pride is willing pride, and yours is so.
Who are the votaries, my loving lords,
That are vow-fellows with this virtuous Duke?
        [1.] *Lord.* [Lord] Longaville is one.
        Prin.   Know you the man?
        [*Mar.*] I know him, madam; at a marriage-feast,
Between Lord Perigort and the beauteous heir   41
Of Jaques Falconbridge, solemnized
In Normandy, saw I this Longaville.
A man of sovereign [parts] he is esteem'd,
Well fitted in arts, glorious in arms;   45
Nothing becomes him ill that he would well.
The only soil of his fair virtue's gloss,
If virtue's gloss will stain with any soil,
Is a sharp wit match'd with too blunt a will;
Whose edge hath power to cut, whose will still wills
It should none spare that come within his power.   51
        Prin. Some merry mocking lord, belike; is't so?
        [*Mar.*] They say so most that most his humours
            know.
        Prin. Such short-liv'd wits do wither as they grow.
Who are the rest?   55
        [*Kath.*] The young Dumain, a well-accomplish'd
            youth,
Of all that virtue love for virtue lov'd;
Most power to do most harm, least knowing ill;
For he hath wit to make an ill shape good,
And shape to win grace though he had no wit.   60
I saw him at the Duke Alençon's once;
And much too little of that good I saw
Is my report to his great worthiness.
        [*Ros.*] Another of these students at that time

Was there with him, if I have heard a truth.   65
Biron they call him; but a merrier man,
Within the limit of becoming mirth,
I never spent an hour's talk withal.
His eye begets occasion for his wit,
For every object that the one doth catch   70
The other turns to a mirth-moving jest,
Which his fair tongue, conceit's expositor,
Delivers in such apt and gracious words
That aged ears play truant at his tales,
And younger hearings are quite ravished;   75
So sweet and voluble is his discourse.
        Prin. God bless my ladies! Are they all in love,
That every one her own hath garnished
With such bedecking ornaments of praise?
        [1.] *Lord.* Here comes Boyet.

                Re-enter BOYET.

        Prin.   Now, what admittance, lord?
        Boyet. Navarre had notice of your fair approach;
And he and his competitors in oath   82
Were all address'd to meet you, gentle lady,
Before I came. Marry, thus much I have learnt:
He rather means to lodge you in the field,   85
Like one that comes here to besiege his court,
Than seek a dispensation for his oath,
To let you enter his [unpeopled] house.

Enter KING, LONGAVILLE, DUMAIN, BIRON [*and*
                Attendants].

Here comes Navarre.   [*The ladies mask.*]
        King. Fair Princess, welcome to the court of
            Navarre.   90
        Prin. "Fair" I give you back again; and "wel-
come" I have not yet. The roof of this court is too
high to be yours, and welcome to the wide fields too
base to be mine.
        King. You shall be welcome, madam, to my
            court.   95
        Prin. I will be welcome, then. Conduct me
            thither.
        King. Hear me, dear lady; I have sworn an oath.
        Prin. Our Lady help my lord! He'll be forsworn.
        King. Not for the world, fair madam, by my will.
        Prin. Why, will shall break it; will, and nothing
            else.   100
        King. Your ladyship is ignorant what it is.
        Prin. Were my lord so, his ignorance were wise,
Where now his knowledge must prove ignorance.
I hear your grace hath sworn out house-keeping.
'Tis deadly sin to keep that oath, my lord,   105
And sin to break it.
But pardon me, I am too sudden-bold;

16. **utt'red:** sold. **chapmen's:** pedlars'. 28. **Bold:** confident. 29. **best-moving fair:** most persuasive and just. 39. **[1]** ...
[Lord] (Capell). Om. Q. 40. **[Mar.]** (Rowe). *I Lady* Q. 44. **[parts]** F. *peerelsse* Q. 46. **would:** would do. 50. **still:**
constantly. 53. **[Mar.]** (Rowe). *Lad.* Q. 56. **[Kath.]** (Rowe). *2 Lad.* Q. 57. **Of:** by. 63. **to:** on. 64. **[Ros.]** F. *3 Lad.* Q.
72. **conceit's:** fancy's. 82. **address'd:** prepared. 88. **[unpeopled]** F. *unpeeled* Q. 92. **roof of this court:** i.e., the sky.
104. **sworn out house-keeping:** renounced hospitality.

To teach a teacher ill beseemeth me.
Vouchsafe to read the purpose of my coming,
And suddenly resolve me in my suit.   110
          [*Hands a paper.*]
  King. Madam, I will, if suddenly I may.
  Prin. You will the sooner, that I were away;
For you'll prove perjur'd if you make me stay.
  Bir. Did not I dance with you in Brabant once?
  Kath. Did not I dance with you in Brabant
    once?   115
  Bir. I know you did.
  Kath. How needless was it then to ask the ques-
    tion!
  Bir. You must not be so quick.
  Kath. 'Tis long of you that spur me with such
    questions.
  Bir. Your wit's too hot, it speeds too fast, 'twill
    tire.   120
  Kath. Not till it leave the rider in the mire.
  Bir. What time o' day?
  Kath. The hour that fools should ask.
  Bir. Now fair befall your mask!
  Kath. Fair fall the face it covers!   125
  Bir. And send you many lovers!
  Kath. Amen, so you be none.
  Bir. Nay, then will I be gone.
  King. Madam, your father here doth intimate
The payment of a hundred thousand crowns;   130
Being but the one half of an entire sum
Disbursed by my father in his wars.
But say that he or we, as neither have,
Receiv'd that sum, yet there remains unpaid
A hundred thousand more; in surety of the which
One part of Aquitaine is bound to us,   136
Although not valued to the money's worth.
If then the King your father will restore
But that one half which is unsatisfied,
We will give up our right in Aquitaine,   140
And hold fair friendship with his majesty.
But that, it seems, he little purposeth,
For here he doth demand to have repaid
A hundred thousand crowns; and not demands,
On payment of a hundred thousand crowns,   145
To have his title live in Aquitaine;
Which we much rather had depart withal
And have the money by our father lent
Than Aquitaine, so gelded as it is.
Dear Princess, were not his request so far   150
From reason's yielding, your fair self should make
A yielding 'gainst some reason in my breast
And go well satisfi'd to France again.
  Prin. You do the King my father too much
    wrong,

And wrong the reputation of your name,   155
In so unseeming to confess receipt
Of that which hath so faithfully been paid.
  King. I do protest I never heard of it;
And, if you prove it, I'll repay it back
Or yield up Aquitaine.
  Prin.   We arrest your word.   160
Boyet, you can produce acquittances
For such a sum from special officers
Of Charles his father.
  King.   Satisfy me so.
  Boyet. So please your grace, the packet is not come
Where that and other specialties are bound.   165
To-morrow you shall have a sight of them.
  King. It shall suffice me; at which interview
All liberal reason I will yield unto.
Meantime receive such welcome at my hand
As honour without breach of honour may   170
Make tender of to thy true worthiness.
You may not come, fair Princess, in my gates;
But here without you shall be so receiv'd
As you shall deem yourself lodg'd in my heart,
Though so deni'd fair harbour in my house.   175
Your own good thoughts excuse me, and farewell.
To-morrow shall we visit you again.
  Prin. Sweet health and fair desires consort your
    Grace!
  King. Thy own wish wish I thee in every place!
                                              [*Exit.*
  Bir. Lady, I will commend you to mine own
    heart.   180
  Ros. Pray you, do my commendations; I would
be glad to see it.
  Bir. I would you heard it groan.
  Ros. Is the fool sick?
  Bir. Sick at the heart.   185
  Ros. Alack, let it blood.
  Bir. Would that do it good?
  Ros. My physic says "ay."
  Bir. Will you prick 't with your eye?
  Ros. No point, with my knife.   190
  Bir. Now, God save thy life!
  Ros. And yours from long living!
  Bir. I cannot stay thanksgiving.   [*Exit.*
  Dum. Sir, I pray you, a word. What lady is that
    same?   194
  Boyet. The heir of Alençon, [Katherine] her name.
  Dum. A gallant lady. Monsieur, fare you well.
                                              [*Exit.*]
  Long. I beseech you a word. What is she in the
    white?
  Boyet. A woman sometimes, an you saw her in
    the light.

---

110. **suddenly:** speedily. 115-127. **Kath.** Q₁. Given to Rosaline in Ff Q₂. 119. **long of:** because of. 147. **depart withal:** part with. 149. **gelded:** depreciated. 156. **unseeming to:** appearing not to. 160. **arrest:** accept. 190. **No point.** A pun on the English word "point" and the French "ne . . . point," "not at all." 195. **[Katherine]** (Capell conj.). *Rosalin* Qq Ff.

Long. Perchance light in the light. I desire her
    name.
Boyet. She hath but one for herself; to desire that
were a shame.   200
Long. Pray you, sir, whose daughter?
Boyet. Her mother's, I have heard.
Long. God's blessing on your beard!
Boyet. Good sir, be not offended.
She is an heir of Falconbridge.   205
Long. Nay, my choler is ended.
She is a most sweet lady.
Boyet. Not unlike, sir; that may be.
                          [Exit Long.

Re-enter BIRON.

Bir. What's her name in the cap?
Boyet. [Rosaline,] by good hap.   210
Bir. Is she wedded or no?
Boyet. To her will, sir, or so.
Bir. You are welcome, sir; adieu.
Boyet. Farewell to me, sir, and welcome to you.
                         [Exit Biron.
Mar. That last is Biron, the merry mad-cap
    lord.   215
Not a word with him but a jest.
Boyet.   And every jest but a word.
Prin. It was well done of you to take him at his
    word.
Boyet. I was as willing to grapple as he was to
    board.
Kath. Two hot sheeps, marry.
Boyet.   And wherefore not ships?
No sheep, sweet lamb, unless we feed on your lips.
Kath. You sheep, and I pasture: shall that finish
    the jest?   221
Boyet. So you grant pasture for me.
              [Offering to kiss her.]
Kath.   Not so, gentle beast.
My lips are no common, though several they be.
Boyet. Belonging to whom?
Kath.   To my fortunes and me.
Prin. Good wits will be jangling; but, gentles,
    agree.   225
This civil war of wits were much better used
On Navarre and his book-men; for here 'tis abused.
Boyet. If my observation, which very seldom lies,
By the heart's still rhetoric disclosed with eyes
Deceive me not now, Navarre is infected.   230
Prin. With what?
Boyet. With that which we lovers entitle af-
    fected.
Prin. Your reason?

Boyet. Why, all his behaviours did make their
    retire
To the court of his eye, peeping thorough desire;   235
His heart, like an agate, with your print impress'd,
Proud with his form, in his eye pride express'd;
His tongue, all impatient to speak and not see,
Did stumble with haste in his eyesight to be;
All senses to that sense did make their repair,   240
To feel only looking on fairest of fair:
Methought all his senses were lock'd in his eye,
As jewels in crystal for some prince to buy,
Who, tend'ring their own worth from where they
    were glass'd,   244
Did point you to buy them, along as you pass'd;
His face's own margent did [quote] such amazes
That all eyes saw his eyes enchanted with gazes.
I'll give you Aquitaine and all that is his,
An you give him for my sake but one loving kiss.
Prin. Come to our pavilion. Boyet is dispos'd—
Boyet. But to speak that in words which his eye
    hath disclos'd.   251
I only have made a mouth of his eye,
By adding a tongue which I know will not lie.
Ros. Thou art an old love-monger and speakest
    skilfully.
Mar. He is Cupid's grandfather, and learns news
    of him.   255
Kath. Then was Venus like her mother, for her
    father is but grim.
Boyet. Do you hear, my mad wenches?
Ros.   No.
Boyet.   What then, do you see?
Mar. Ay, our way to be gone.
Boyet.   You are too hard for me.
                   [Exeunt omnes.

ACT III

[SCENE I. *The same.*]

Enter Braggart [ARMADO] *and his Boy* [MOTH].
             Song.

Arm. Warble, child; make passionate my sense
of hearing.
Moth. Concolinel.
Arm. Sweet air! Go, tenderness of years, take
this key, give enlargement to the swain, bring   5
him festinately hither. I must employ him in a
letter to my love.
Moth. Master, will you win your love with a
French brawl?
Arm. How meanest thou? Brawling in French?

199. **light in the light:** wanton when known. 210. **[Rosaline]** (Brae conj.). *Katherin* Qq Ff. 223. **common:** common pasture. **several.** A pun on the three meanings "plural," "parted," and "inclosed pasture." 232. **affected:**
being in love. 238. **not see:** without seeing. 241. **looking:** through looking. 245. **point:** tell. 246. **margent:** margin of
a page containing a commentary. **[quote]** Q₂. *coate* Q₁. 250. **dispos'd:** i.e., to be mirthful.

Act III, sc. i, 2. **Concolinel.** Probably the title or the opening of Moth's song. 6. **festinately:** quickly. 8. **brawl:**
Fr. *branle*, an old type of figure dance.

Moth. No, my complete master; but to jig off   11
a tune at the tongue's end, canary to it with your
feet, humour it with turning up your eye-lids, sigh
a note and sing a note, sometime through the
throat, [as] if you swallowed love with singing love,
sometime through [the] nose, as if you snuff'd up   16
love by smelling love; with your hat penthouse-like
o'er the shop of your eyes; with your arms cross'd
on your thin-belly doublet like a rabbit on a spit; or
your hands in your pocket like a man after the   20
old painting; and keep not too long in one tune, but
a snip and away: these are complements, these
are humours; these betray nice wenches, that would
be betrayed without these; and make them men
of note — do you note? — men that most are   25
affected to these.

Arm. How hast thou purchased this experience?

Moth. By my penny of observation.

Arm. But O, but O, —

Moth. "The hobby-horse is forgot."   30

Arm. Callest thou my love "hobby-horse"?

Moth. No, master; the hobby-horse is but a colt,
and your love perhaps a hackney. But have you
forgot your love?

Arm. Almost I had.   35

Moth. Negligent student! learn her by heart.

Arm. By heart and in heart, boy.

Moth. And out of heart, master; all those three I
will prove.

Arm. What wilt thou prove?   40

Moth. A man, if I live; and this, by, in, and without, upon the instant. By heart you love her, because your heart cannot come by her; in heart you
love her, because your heart is in love with her; and
out of heart you love her, being out of heart that
you cannot enjoy her.   46

Arm. I am all these three.

Moth. And three times as much more, and yet
nothing at all.

Arm. Fetch hither the swain; he must carry me
a letter.   51

Moth. A message well sympathiz'd; a horse to
be ambassador for an ass.

Arm. Ha, ha! what sayest thou?

Moth. Marry, sir, you must send the ass upon
the horse, for he is very slow-gaited. But I go.   56

Arm. The way is but short; away!

Moth. As swift as lead, sir.

Arm. The meaning, pretty ingenious?
Is not lead a metal heavy, dull, and slow?   60

Moth. *Minime*, honest master; or rather, master,
no.

Arm. I say lead is slow.

Moth.   You are too swift, sir, to say so.
Is that lead slow which is fir'd from a gun?

Arm. Sweet smoke of rhetoric!   64
He reputes me a cannon; and the bullet, that's he;
I shoot thee at the swain.

Moth.   Thump then and I flee. [*Exit.*]

Arm. A most acute juvenal; voluble and free of
    grace!
By thy favour, sweet welkin, I must sigh in thy face.
Most rude melancholy, valour gives thee place.
My herald is return'd.   70

Re-enter Page [MOTH] *with Clown* [COSTARD].

Moth. A wonder, master! Here's a costard
    broken in a shin.

Arm. Some enigma, some riddle; come, thy
    l'envoy; begin.

Cost. No egma, no riddle, no l'envoy; no salve in
the mail, sir. O, sir, plantain, a plain plaintain!
No l'envoy, no l'envoy; no salve, sir, but a plantain!

Arm. By virtue, thou enforcest laughter; thy   76
silly thought my spleen; the heaving of my lungs
provokes me to ridiculous smiling. O, pardon me,
my stars! Doth the inconsiderate take salve for
l'envoy, and the word l'envoy for a salve?   80

Moth. Do the wise think them other? Is not
    l'envoy a salve?

Arm. No, page; it is an epilogue or discourse, to
    make plain
Some obscure precedence that hath tofore been sain.
I will example it:
    The fox, the ape, and the humble-bee,
    Were still at odds, being but three.   86
There's the moral. Now the l'envoy.

Moth. I will add the l'envoy. Say the moral
again.

Arm. The fox, the ape, and the humble-bee,   90
    Were still at odds, being but three.

Moth. Until the goose came out of door,
    And stay'd the odds by adding four.
Now will I begin your moral, and do you follow
with my l'envoy.   95
    The fox, the ape, and the humble-bee,
    Were still at odds, being but three.

Arm. Until the goose came out of door,
    Staying the odds by adding four.

Moth. A good l'envoy, ending in the goose; would
you desire more?   101

Cost. The boy hath sold him a bargain, a goose,
    that's flat.
Sir, your pennyworth is good, an your goose be fat.
To sell a bargain well is as cunning as fast and loose.
Let me see; a fat l'envoy; ay, that's a fat goose. 105

---

12. **canary:** dance (vb.). 15. **[as]** (Theobald). Om. Q. 15. **[the]** F₂. Om. Q. 23. **nice:** wanton. 30. "**The . . .
forgot.**" The refrain of a song. 33. **hackney:** i.e., a prostitute. 52. **well sympathized:** appropriately carried. 61.
Minime: by no means. 71. **costard:** head. 74. **plaintain:** a healing herb. 77. **spleen:** mirth. 81. **salve.** Pun on *salve*
(1) an ointment, (2) a salutation. 93. **adding:** i.e., making. 102. **hath . . . bargain:** has made a fool of him.

Arm. Come hither, come hither.   How did this argument begin?

Moth. By saying that a costard was broken in a shin.

Then call'd you for the l'envoy.

Cost. True, and I for a plantain; thus came your argument in;

Then the boy's fat l'envoy, the goose that you bought;   110

And he ended the market.

Arm. But tell me, how was there a costard broken in a shin?

Moth. I will tell you sensibly.

Cost. Thou hast no feeling of it, Moth.   I will speak that l'envoy: 116

I, Costard, running out, that was safely within, Fell over the threshold, and broke my shin.

Arm. We will talk no more of this matter.

Cost. Till there be more matter in the shin.

Arm. Sirrah Costard, I will enfranchise thee.   121

Cost. O, marry me to one Frances!   I smell some l'envoy, some goose, in this.

Arm. By my sweet soul, I mean setting thee at liberty, enfreedoming thy person.   Thou wert immured, restrained, captivated, bound.   126

Cost. True, true; and now you will be my purgation and let me loose.

Arm. I give thee thy liberty, set thee from durance; and, in lieu thereof, impose on thee nothing but this: bear this significant [*giving a letter*] to   130 the country maid Jaquenetta.   There is remuneration; for the best ward of mine honour is rewarding my dependents.   Moth, follow.   [*Exit.*]

Moth. Like the sequel, I.   Signior Costard, adieu.

[*Exit.*

Cost. My sweet ounce of man's flesh! my incony Jew!   136

Now will I look to his remuneration.   Remuneration!   O, that's the Latin word for three farthings: three farthings — remuneration. — "What's the price of this inkle?" — "One penny." — "No, I'll give you a remuneration:" why, it carries it.   140 Remuneration! why, it is a fairer name than French crown.   I will never buy and sell out of this word.

Enter BIRON.

Bir. O, my good knave Costard! exceedingly well met.   145

Cost. Pray you, sir, how much carnation ribbon may a man buy for a remuneration?

Bir. What is a remuneration?

Cost. Marry, sir, halfpenny farthing.   149

Bir. Why, then, three-farthing worth of silk.

Cost. I thank your worship; God be wi'you!

Bir. Stay, slave; I must employ thee.

As thou wilt win my favour, good my knave, Do one thing for me that I shall entreat.

Cost. When would you have it done, sir?   155

Bir. This afternoon.

Cost. Well, I will do it, sir; fare you well.

Bir. Thou knowest not what it is.

Cost. I shall know, sir, when I have done it.

Bir. Why, villain, thou must know first.   160

Cost. I will come to your worship to-morrow morning.

Bir. It must be done this afternoon.   Hark, slave, it is but this:

The Princess comes to hunt here in the park,   165 And in her train there is a gentle lady.

When tongues speak sweetly, then they name her name,

And Rosaline they call her.   Ask for her, And to her white hand see thou do commend   169 This seal'd-up counsel.   There's thy guerdon; go.

Cost. Gardon, O sweet gardon! better than remuneration, a 'leven-pence farthing better; most sweet gardon!   I will do it, sir, in print.   Gardon! Remuneration!   [*Exit.*

Bir. And I, forsooth, in love! I, that have   175 been love's whip;

A very beadle to a humorous sigh;

A critic, nay, a night-watch constable;

A domineering pedant o'er the boy,

Than whom no mortal so magnificent!   180

This wimpled, whining, purblind, wayward boy;

This senior-junior, giant-dwarf, Dan Cupid;

Regent of love-rhymes, lord of folded arms,

The anointed sovereign of sighs and groans,

Liege of all loiterers and malcontents,   185

Dread prince of plackets, king of codpieces,

Sole imperator and great general

Of trotting 'paritors; — O my little heart! —

And I to be a corporal of his field,

And wear his colours like a tumbler's hoop!   190

What! I love! I sue! I seek a wife!

A woman, that is like a German clock,

Still a-repairing, ever out of frame,

And never going aright, being a watch,

But being watch'd that it may still go right!   195

Nay, to be perjur'd, which is worst of all;

And, among three, to love the worst of all,

A whitely wanton with a velvet brow,

With two pitch-balls stuck in her face for eyes;

Ay, and, by heaven, one that will do the deed   200

Though Argus were her eunuch and her guard.

And I to sigh for her! to watch for her!

---

111. **ended the market.** Alluding to the proverb "three women and a goose make a market."   136. **incony:** fine.   139. **inkle:** tape.   140. **it carries it:** it's perfect.   177. **beadle:** a constable who whipped petty offenders.   186. **plackets:** petticoats.   188. **'paritors:** apparitors, officials of the ecclesiastical court.   189. **corporal:** a superior office of the army in the 16th century.   201. **Argus:** a monster with a hundred eyes.

To pray for her! Go to; it is a plague
That Cupid will impose for my neglect
Of his almighty dreadful little might.   205
Well, I will love, write, sigh, pray, sue, groan:
Some men must love my lady, and some Joan.
                                        [*Exit.*]

                    ACT IV

               [SCENE I. *The same.*]

Enter the PRINCESS, *a* FORESTER, *her* LADIES,
          and her LORDS.

Prin. Was that the King, that spurr'd his horse
          so hard
Against the steep uprising of the hill?
For. I know not, but I think it was not he.
Prin. Whoe'er 'a was, 'a show'd a mounting
          mind.
Well, lords, to-day we shall have our dispatch;   5
On Saturday we will return to France.
Then, forester, my friend, where is the bush
That we must stand and play the murderer in?
For. Hereby, upon the edge of yonder coppice;
A stand where you may make the fairest shoot.   10
Prin. I thank my beauty, I am fair that shoot,
And thereupon thou speak'st the fairest shoot.
For. Pardon me, madam, for I meant not so.
Prin. What, what? First praise me, and again
          say no?
O short-liv'd pride! Not fair? Alack for woe!   15
For. Yes, madam, fair.
Prin.   Nay, never paint me now;
Where fair is not, praise cannot mend the brow.
Here, good my glass, take this for telling true.
                                        [*Gives money.*]
Fair payment for foul words is more than due.
For. Nothing but fair is that which you in-
          herit.   20
Prin. See, see, my beauty will be sav'd by merit!
O heresy in fair, fit for these days!
A giving hand, though foul, shall have fair praise.
But come, the bow; now mercy goes to kill,
And shooting well is then accounted ill.   25
Thus will I save my credit in the shoot:
Not wounding, pity would not let me do't;
If wounding, then it was to show my skill,
That more for praise than purpose meant to kill.
And, out of question, so it is sometimes,   30
Glory grows guilty of detested crimes,
When, for fame's sake, for praise, an outward part,
We bend to that the working of the heart;
As I for praise alone now seek to spill

The poor deer's blood, that my heart means no
          ill.   35
Boyet. Do not curst wives hold that self-sov-
          ereignty
Only for praise' sake, when they strive to be
Lords o'er their lords?
Prin. Only for praise; and praise we may afford
To any lady that subdues a lord.   40

               Enter Clown [COSTARD].

Boyet. Here comes a member of the common-
          wealth.
Cost. God dig-you-den all! Pray you, which is
the head lady?
Prin. Thou shalt know her, fellow, by the rest
that have no heads.   45
Cost. Which is the greatest lady, the highest?
Prin. The thickest and the tallest.
Cost. The thickest and the tallest! It is so;
          truth is true.
An your waist, mistress, were as slender as my wit,
One o' these maids' girdles for your waist should be
          fit.   50
Are not you the chief woman? You are the thick-
          est here.
Prin. What's your will, sir? what's your will?
Cost. I have a letter from Monsieur Biron to one
          Lady Rosaline.
Prin. O, thy letter, thy letter! He's a good
          friend of mine.
Stand aside good bearer. Boyet, you can carve;   55
Break up this capon.
Boyet.   I am bound to serve.
This letter is mistook; it importeth none here.
It is writ to Jaquenetta.
Prin.   We will read it, I swear.
Break the neck of the wax, and every one give ear.
Boyet. [*Reads.*] "By heaven, that thou art fair,
is most infallible; true, that thou art beauteous;   61
truth itself, that thou art lovely. More fairer than
fair, beautiful than beauteous, truer than truth
itself, have commiseration on thy heroical vassal!
The magnanimous and most illustrate king Co-   65
phetua set eye upon the pernicious and indubitate
beggar Zenelophon; and he it was that might
rightly say, *Veni, vidi, vici;* which to annothanize in
the vulgar, — O base and obscure vulgar! — videlicet, He came, saw, and overcame: he came,   70
one; saw, two; overcame, three. Who came? The
king. Why did he come? To see. Why did he
see? To overcome. To whom came he? To the
beggar. What saw he? The beggar. Who overcame he? The beggar. The conclusion is victory;

---

207. **Joan:** stock name for a peasant wench.
Act IV, sc. i, 18. my glass: mirror.   22. **heresy in fair:** heresy with respect to beauty.   36. **curst:** shrewish.   42. **God
dig-you-den all:** God give you good evening.   56. **Break...capon:** open this billet-doux.   68. **annothanize:** anatomize,
interpret.

on whose side? The king's. The captive is 75
enrich'd; on whose side? The beggar's. The
catastrophe is a nuptial; on whose side? The
king's; no, on both in one, or one in both. I am the
king, for so stands the comparison; thou the 80
beggar, for so witnesseth thy lowliness. Shall I
command thy love? I may. Shall I enforce thy
love? I could. Shall I entreat thy love? I will.
What shalt thou exchange for rags? robes; for
tittles? titles; for thyself? me. Thus, expecting 85
thy reply, I profane my lips on thy foot, my eyes on
thy picture, and my heart on thy every part.
Thine, in the dearest design of industry,
        DON ADRIANO DE ARMADO.''
Thus dost thou hear the Nemean lion roar   90
'Gainst thee, thou lamb, that standest a his prey.
Submissive fall his princely feet before,
    And he from forage will incline to play.
But if thou strive, poor soul, what art thou then?
Food for his rage, repasture for his den.   95
    Prin. What plume of feathers is he that indited
        this letter?
What vane? What weathercock? Did you ever
    hear better?
    Boyet. I am much deceived but I remember the
        style.
    Prin. Else your memory is bad, going o'er it ere-
        while.
    Boyet. This Armado is a Spaniard, that keeps
        here in court;   100
A phantasime, a Monarcho, and one that makes
    sport
To the Prince and his bookmates.
    Prin.   Thou fellow, a word.
Who gave thee this letter?
    Cost.   I told you; my lord.
    Prin. To whom shouldst thou give it?
    Cost.   From my lord to my lady.
    Prin. From which lord to which lady?   105
    Cost. From my lord Biron, a good master of
        mine.
To a lady of France that he call'd Rosaline.
    Prin. Thou hast mistaken his letter. Come,
        lords, away.
[*To Ros.*] Here, sweet, put up this; 'twill be thine
    another day. [*Exeunt* [*Princess and train*].
    Boyet. Who is the shooter? Who is the shooter?
    Ros.   Shall I teach you to know? 110
    Boyet. Ay, my continent of beauty.

    Ros.   Why, she that bears the bow.
Finely put off!
    Boyet. My lady goes to kill horns; but, if thou
        marry,
Hang me by the neck if horns that year miscarry.
Finely put on!   115
    Ros. Well, then, I am the shooter.
    Boyet.   And who is your deer?
    Ros. If we choose by the horns, yourself; come
        not near.
Finely put on, indeed!
    Mar. You still wrangle with her, Boyet, and she
        strikes at the brow.
    Boyet. But she herself is hit lower. Have I hit
        her now?   120
    Ros. Shall I come upon thee with an old saying,
that was a man when King Pepin of France was a
little boy, as touching the hit it?
    Boyet. So I may answer thee with one as old, that
was a woman when Queen Guinever of Britain 125
was a little wench, as touching the hit it.
    Ros. Thou canst not hit it, hit it, hit it,
        Thou canst not hit it, my good man.
                                    [*Exit* [*Ros.*]
    Boyet. An I cannot, cannot, cannot,
        An I cannot, another can.   130
    Cost. By my troth, most pleasant. How both
        did fit it!
    Mar. A mark marvellous well shot, for they both
        did hit [it].
    Boyet. A mark! O, mark but that mark! A
        mark, says my lady!
Let the mark have a prick in't, to mete at, if it may
    be.
    Mar. Wide o' the bow hand! I'faith, your hand
        is out.   135
    Cost. Indeed, 'a must shoot nearer, or he'll ne'er
        hit the clout.
    Boyet. An if my hand be out, then belike your
        hand is in.
    Cost. Then will she get the upshoot by cleaving
        the [pin].
    Mar. Come, come, you talk greasily; your lips
        grow foul.
    Cost. She's too hard for you at pricks, sir; chal-
        lenge her to bowl.   140
    Boyet. I fear too much rubbing. Good night, my
        good owl.   [*Exeunt Boyet and Maria.*]
    Cost. By my soul, a swain! a most simple clown!

---

88. **industry:** zeal. 90. **Nemean lion:** the lion slain by Hercules. 95. **repasture:** repast. 98. **but I:** if I do not. 101.
phantasime: fantastic fellow. **Monarcho:** a crazy Italian who frequented Elizabeth's court a little before 1580 and was
subject to delusions of grandeur. 109. **shooter.** Farmer reads *suitor*, but the spelling "shooter" (Q), which renders
the Elizabethan pronunciation, points the pun. 112. **put off:** answered. 114. **miscarry:** are not plentiful. Boyet is jesting
about the horns of the cuckold, the husband whose wife is unfaithful. 119. **strikes at the brow:** takes careful aim. 122.
King Pepin: the father of Charlemagne. 123. **the hit it:** the proper execution of steps in dancing. 132. **[it]** F₄. Om. Q.
134. **prick:** peg in the center of the target. **mete:** aim. 135. **Wide ... hand:** too far to the left. 136. **clout:** mark. 138.
get ... [pin]: get the best shot by splitting the wooden peg in the center of the target. **[pin]** F₂ *is in* Q. 139. **greasily:**
indecently.

Lord, Lord, how the ladies and I have put him down!
O' my troth, most sweet jests! most incony vulgar
    wit!
When it comes so smoothly off, so obscenely, as it
    were, so fit.   145
Armado [o' th' one] side, — O, a most dainty man!
To see him walk before a lady and to bear her fan!
To see him kiss his hand! and how most sweetly 'a
    will swear!
And his page o' t'other side, that handful of wit!
Ah, heavens, it is a most pathetical nit!   150
Sola, sola!   [Exit [Costard]. Shout within.

[SCENE II. The same.]

Enter DULL, HOLOFERNES *the Pedant, and*
NATHANIEL.

Nath. Very reverend sport, truly, and done in the
testimony of a good conscience.
Hol. The deer was, as you know, *sanguis,* in
blood; ripe as the pomewater, who now hangeth
like a jewel in the ear of *caelo,* the sky, the wel- 5
kin, the heaven; and anon falleth like a crab on the
face of *terra,* the soil, the land, the earth.
Nath. Truly, Master Holofernes, the epithets are
sweetly varied, like a scholar at the least; but, sir,
I assure ye, it was a buck of the first head.   10
Hol. Sir Nathaniel, *haud credo.*
Dull. 'Twas not a haud credo; 'twas a pricket.
Hol. Most barbarous intimation! yet a kind of
insinuation, as it were, *in via,* in way, of explication;
facere, as it were, replication, or rather, *ostentare,* 15
to show, as it were, his inclination, after his undressed, unpolished, uneducated, unpruned, untrained, or rather, unlettered, or ratherest, unconfirmed fashion, to assert again my *haud credo* a
deer.   20
Dull. I said the deer was not a haud credo; 'twas
a pricket.
Hol. Twice-sod simplicity, *bis coctus!*
O thou monster Ignorance, how deformed dost thou
    look!
Nath. Sir, he hath never fed of the dainties that
    are bred in a book;   25
he hath not eat paper, as it were; he hath not drunk
ink; his intellect is not replenished; he is only an
animal, only sensible in the duller parts;
And such barren plants are set before us, that we
    thankful should be,
Which we of taste and feeling are, for those parts
    that do fructify in us more than he.   30

For as it would ill become me to be vain, indiscreet,
    or a fool,
So were there a patch set on learning, to see him in
    a school:
But *omne bene,* say I; being of an old father's mind,
Many can brook the weather that love not the wind.
Dull. You two are book-men; can you tell me by
    your wit   35
What was a month old at Cain's birth, that's not
    five weeks old as yet?
Hol. Dictynna, goodman Dull; Dictynna, good-
    man Dull.
Dull. What is Dictynna?
Nath. A title to Phœbe, to Luna, to the moon.
Hol. The moon was a month old when Adam was
    no more.   40
And raught not to five weeks when he came to five-
    score.
Th' allusion holds in the exchange.
Dull. 'Tis true indeed; the collusion holds in the
exchange.
Hol. God comfort thy capacity! I say, th' allu-
sion holds in the exchange.   46
Dull. And I say, the pollusion holds in the ex-
change, for the moon is never but a month old; and
I say beside that, 'twas a pricket that the Princess
killed.   50
Hol. Sir Nathaniel, will you hear an extemporal
epitaph on the death of the deer? And, to humour
the ignorant, [call I] the deer the Princess killed a
pricket.
Nath. Perge, good Master Holofernes, *perge;* so it
shall please you to abrogate scurrility.   56
Hol. I will something affect the letter, for it
argues facility.

"The preyful princess pierc'd and prick'd a pretty
    pleasing pricket;
Some say a sore; but not a sore, till now made sore
    with shooting.
The dogs did yell: put L to sore, then sorel jumps
    from thicket;   60
Or pricket, sore, or else sorel; the people fall
    a-hooting.
If sore be sore, then L to sore make fifty sores one sorel.
Of one sore I an hundred make by adding but one
    more L."

Nath. A rare talent!
Dull. [*Aside.*] If a talent be a claw, look how he
claws him with a talent.   66

146. [o' th' one] (Rowe) *atle toothen* Q. 150. **pathetical nit:** touching little chap ("nit": a young louse).
Sc. ii, 4. pomewater: a sweet apple. 10. **first head:** fifth year. 11. **haud credo:** I don't believe it. 12. **pricket:** buck of
the second year. 22. **bis coctus:** twice cooked. 30. **Which we:** we who. **than he:** than in him. 32. **patch:** blot. Some
prefer the meaning "fool." 33. **omne bene:** all's well. 41. **raught:** reached. 42. **allusion . . . exchange:** i.e., the riddle
remains the same when I alter the terms (cf. ll. 40-41 and l. 36). 53. **[call I]** (Camb. edd.). *call'd* Q. 55. **Perge:** proceed.
57. **affect the letter:** practise alliteration. 59. **sore:** a buck of the fourth year. 60. **sorel:** a deer of the third year. 62. **L:**
the Roman numeral for "fifty." 66. **talent:** talon. **claws:** scratches pleasantly, flatters.

[*Hol.*] This is a gift that I have, simple, simple; a foolish extravagant spirit, full of forms, figures, shapes, objects, ideas, apprehensions, motions, revolutions. These are begot in the ventricle of 70 memory, nourish'd in the womb of pia mater, and delivered upon the mellowing of occasion. But the gift is good in those in whom it is acute, and I am thankful for it.

[*Nath.*] Sir, I praise the Lord for you, and so 75 may my parishioners; for their sons are well tutor'd by you, and their daughters profit very greatly under you. You are a good member of the commonwealth.

[*Hol.*] *Mehercle*, if their sons be ingenious, 80 they shall want no instruction; if their daughters be capable, I will put it to them: but *vir sapit qui pauca loquitur;* a soul feminine saluteth us.

Enter JAQUENETTA *and the Clown* [COSTARD].

Jaq. God give you good morrow, master Parson.

[*Hol.*] Master Parson, *quasi* pers-on. An if 85 one should be pierc'd, which is the one?

Cost. Marry, master schoolmaster, he that is likest to a hogshead.

[*Hol.*] Of piercing a hogshead! a good lustre of conceit in a tuft of earth; fire enough for a flint, pearl enough for a swine; 'tis pretty; it is well. 90

Jaq. Good master Parson, be so good as read me this letter. It was given me by Costard, and sent me from Don Armado. I beseech you, read it.

[*Hol.*] *Fauste, precor gelida quando pecus omne sub umbra ruminat,* — and so forth. Ah, good 96 old Mantuan! I may speak of thee as the traveller doth of Venice:

Venetia, Venetia,
    Chi non ti vede non ti pretia. 100

Old Mantuan, old Mantuan! who understandeth thee not, loves thee not. *Ut, re, sol, la, mi, fa.* Under pardon, sir, what are the contents? or rather, as Horace says in his — What, my soul, verses? 105

[*Nath.*] Ay, sir, and very learned.

[*Hol.*] Let me hear a staff, a stanze, a verse; *lege, domine.*

Nath. [*Reads.*]
"If love make me forsworn, how shall I swear to love?

Ah, never faith could hold, if not to beauty vow'd! 110

Though to myself forsworn, to thee I'll faithful prove;

Those thoughts to me were oaks, to thee like osiers bow'd.

Study his bias leaves, and makes his book thine eyes,

Where all those pleasures live that art would comprehend.

If knowledge be the mark, to know thee shall suffice; 115

Well learned is that tongue that well can thee commend,

All ignorant that soul that sees thee without wonder;

Which is to me some praise that I thy parts admire.

Thy eye Jove's lightning bears, thy voice his dreadful thunder,

Which, not to anger bent, is music and sweet fire.

Celestial as thou art, O, pardon love this wrong, 121

That singes heaven's praise with such an earthly tongue."

[*Hol.*] You find not the apostrophas, and so miss the accent: let me supervise the canzonet. Here are only numbers ratified; but, for the elegancy, 125 facility, and golden cadence of poesy, *caret.* Ovidius Naso was the man; and why, indeed, Naso, but for smelling out the odoriferous flowers of fancy, the jerks of invention? *Imitari* is nothing: so doth the hound his master, the ape his keeper, the tired 130 horse his rider. But, damosella virgin, was this directed to you?

Jaq. Ay, sir, from one Monsieur Biron, one of the strange queen's lords.

[*Hol.*] I will overglance the superscript: "To 135 the snow-white hand of the most beauteous Lady Rosaline." I will look again on the intellect of the letter, for the nomination of the party writing to the person written unto: "Your ladyship's in all desired employment, BIRON." Sir [Nathaniel], 140 this Biron is one of the votaries with the King; and here he hath framed a letter to a sequent of the stranger queen's, which accidentally, or by the way of progression, hath miscarried. Trip and go, my sweet; deliver this paper into the royal hand of 145 the King; it may concern much. Stay not thy compliment; I forgive thy duty. Adieu.

Jaq. Good Costard, go with me. Sir, God save your life! 150

Cost. Have with thee, my girl.

[*Exeunt [Cost. and Jaq.*]

---

67. [*Hol.*] In Qq Ff ll. 67, 74, 80 are erroneously assigned to *Nath.*, *Hol.*, and *Nath.* respectively. Speeches at 85, 88, 94, 107, 123, and 135 are assigned to *Nath.* and those at 106, 152 to *Hol.* The generic speech headings, *Ped.* and *Per.*, used in Q became confused. 80. *Mehercle:* by Hercules. 83. *vir...loquitur:* "the man is wise who speaks little." 85–90. **Master Parson,** etc. See Introduction. 86. **pierc'd:** pronounced "perced." 94. *Fauste...ruminat:* "I pray thee, Faustus, when all the cattle ruminate 'neath the cool shade" (Mantuan's *Eclogues*). 98–99. *Venetia...pretia:* "Venice, Venice, he who has not seen thee does not prize thee" (Old Italian). 113. **Study...leaves:** i.e., the student leaves his favorite branch of study. 123. **find...apostrophas:** i.e., you miss the accent. An apostropha is the omission of a vowel from some portion of a word. But Holofernes doubtless means "diaeresis" here. I.e., in l. 122 Nathaniel read "sings" instead of "singes" as the meter demands. 124. **Here** (Theobald). *Nath. Heere* Q F. 125. **numbers ratified:** verses metrically correct. 126. *caret:* it is wanting. 137. **intellect:** signature. 140. **[Nathaniel]** (Capell). *Holofernes* Q. 141. **sequent:** follower. 146. **Stay... compliment:** do not stand on ceremony.

[*Nath.*] Sir, you have done this in the fear of God, very religiously; and, as a certain father saith, —

Hol. Sir, tell not me of the father; I do fear 155 colourable colours. But to return to the verses: did they please you, Sir Nathaniel?

Nath. Marvellous well for the pen.

Hol. I do dine to-day at the father's of a certain pupil of mine; where, if, before repast, it shall 160 please you to gratify the table with a grace, I will, on my privilege I have with the parents of the foresaid child or pupil, undertake your *ben venuto*; where I will prove those verses to be very unlearned, neither savouring of poetry, wit, nor invention. I be- 165 seech your society.

Nath. And thank you too; for society, saith the text, is the happiness of life.

Hol. And, certes, the text most infallibly concludes it. [*To Dull.*] Sir, I do invite you too; 170 you shall not say me nay: *pauca verba.* Away! the gentles are at their game, and we will to our recreation. [*Exeunt.*

[SCENE III. *The same.*]

Enter BIRON, *with a paper in his hand, alone.*

Bir. The King he is hunting the deer, I am coursing myself; they have pitch'd a toil, I am toiling in a pitch, — pitch that defiles; — defile! a foul word. Well, "set thee down, sorrow!" for so they say the fool said, and so say I, and I the fool: well proved, 5 wit! By the Lord, this love is as mad as Ajax. It kills sheep; it kills me, I a sheep: well proved again o' my side! I will not love; if I do, hang me; i'faith, I will not. O, but her eye, — by this light, but for her eye, I would not love her; yes, for her two 10 eyes. Well, I do nothing in the world but lie, and lie in my throat. By heaven, I do love; and it hath taught me to rhyme and to be melancholy; and here is part of my rhyme, and here my melancholy. Well, she hath one o' my sonnets already; the 16 clown bore it, the fool sent it, and the lady hath it: sweet clown, sweeter fool, sweetest lady! By the world, I would not care a pin, if the other three were in. Here comes one with a paper; God give him 20 grace to groan! [*He stands aside.*

Enter the KING [*with a paper*].

King. Ay me!

Bir. [*Aside.*] Shot, by heaven! Proceed, sweet Cupid; thou hast thump'd him with thy bird-bolt under the left pap. In faith, secrets! 25

King. [*Reads.*]
"So sweet a kiss the golden sun gives not
　To those fresh morning drops upon the rose,
As thy eye-beams, when their fresh rays have smote
　The [dew of night] that on my cheeks down flows;
Nor shines the silver moon one half so bright 30
　Through the transparent bosom of the deep,
As doth thy face through tears of mine give light.
　Thou shin'st in every tear that I do weep,
No drop but as a coach doth carry thee;
　So ridest thou triumphing in my woe. 35
Do but behold the tears that swell in me,
　And they thy glory through my grief will show.
But do not love thyself; then thou wilt keep
　My tears for glasses, and still make me weep.
O queen of queens! how far dost thou excel 40
No thought can think, nor tongue of mortal tell."

How shall she know my griefs? I'll drop the paper.
Sweet leaves, shade folly. Who is he comes here?
[*Steps aside.*

Enter LONGAVILLE [*with a paper*].
What, Longaville! and reading! Listen, ear.

Bir. Now, in thy likeness, one more fool appear!

Long. Ay me, I am forsworn! 46

Bir. Why, he comes in like a perjure, wearing papers.

King. In love, I hope; sweet fellowship in shame.

Bir. One drunkard loves another of the name. 50

Long. Am I the first that have been perjur'd so?

Bir. I could put thee in comfort. Not by two that I know.
Thou makest the triumviry, the corner-cap of society,
The shape of Love's Tyburn that hangs up simplicity.

Long. I fear those stubborn lines lack power to move. 55
O sweet Maria, empress of my love!
These numbers will I tear, and write in prose.

Bir. O, rhymes are guards on wanton Cupid's hose:
Disfigure not his [slop].

Long. 　　　　　This same shall go.
[*He reads the sonnet.*
"Did not the heavenly rhetoric of thine eye, 60
　'Gainst whom the world cannot hold argument,
Persuade my heart to this false perjury?
　Vows for thee broke deserve not punishment.
A woman I forswore; but I will prove,

---

156. **colourable colours:** specious excuses. 157. **for the pen:** in the composing. 163. *ben venuto:* welcome. 171. *pauca verba:* few words.
Sc. iii, 2. **pitched a toil:** set a net. 20. **in:** i.e., in love. 29. **[dew of night]** (Singer). I.e., the tears I shed at night. *night of dew* Q. 47. **perjure . . . papers.** A perjurer was punished by being shown in public with a paper on the head or breast announcing his offense. (Cf. IV.iii.125). 53. **corner-cap:** the cap with three (or four) corners worn by Catholic clergy and others. 54. **Tyburn:** a public place of execution in London. The gallows was sometimes triangular. 58. **guards:** trimmings. 59. **[slop]** (Theobald): loose breeches. *shop* Q.

Thou being a goddess, I forswore not thee.   65
My vow was earthly, thou a heavenly love;
  Thy grace being gain'd cures all disgrace in me.
Vows are but breath, and breath a vapour is;
  Then thou, fair sun, which on my earth dost
    shine,
Exhal'st this vapour-vow; in thee it is.   70
  If broken then, it is no fault of mine;
If by me broke, what fool is not so wise
To lose an oath to win a paradise?"
    Bir. This is the liver-vein, which makes flesh a
    deity,   74
A green goose a goddess; pure, pure idolatry.
God amend us, God amend! We are much out o'
  th' way.

        Enter DUMAIN [*with a paper*].

    Long. By whom shall I send this? — Company!
    stay.   [*Steps aside.*]
    Bir. "All hid, all hid;" an old infant play.
Like a demigod here sit I in the sky,   79
And wretched fools' secrets heedfully o'er-eye.
More sacks to the mill! O heavens, I have my wish!
Dumain transform'd! four woodcocks in a dish!
    Dum. O most divine Kate!
    Bir. O most profane coxcomb!   84
    Dum. By heaven, the wonder in a mortal eye!
    Bir. By earth, she is not, corporal; there you lie.
    Dum. Her amber hairs for foul hath amber
    quoted.
    Bir. An amber-colour'd raven was well noted.
    Dum. As upright as the cedar.
    Bir.   Stoop, I say;
Her shoulder is with child.
    Dum.   As fair as day.   90
    Bir. Ay, as some days; but then no sun must
    shine.
    Dum. O that I had my wish!
    Long.   And I had mine!
    King. And [I] mine too, good Lord!
    Bir. Amen, so I had mine. Is not that a good
    word?   94
    Dum. I would forget her; but, a fever, she
Reigns in my blood and will remem'bred be.
    Bir. A fever in your blood! why, then incision
Would let her out in saucers; sweet misprision!
    Dum. Once more I'll read the ode that I have
    writ.   99
    Bir. Once more I'll mark how love can vary wit.
    Dum. [*Reads.*]
      "On a day — alack the day! —
      Love, whose month is ever May,
      Spied a blossom passing fair

      Playing in the wanton air.
      Through the velvet leaves the wind,   105
      All unseen, can passage find;
      That the lover, sick to death,
      Wish himself the heaven's breath.
      Air, quoth he, thy cheeks may blow;
      Air, would I might triumph so!   110
      But, alack, my hand is sworn
      Ne'er to pluck thee from thy thorn;
      Vow, alack, for youth unmeet,
      Youth so apt to pluck a sweet!
      Do not call it sin in me,   115
      That I am forsworn for thee;
      Thou for whom Jove would swear
      Juno but an Ethiope were;
      And deny himself for Jove,
      Turning mortal for thy love."   120
This will I send and something else more plain
That shall express my true love's fasting pain.
O, would the King, Biron, and Longaville,
Were lovers too! Ill, to example ill,
Would from my forehead wipe a perjur'd note;
For none offend where all alike do dote.   126
    Long. [*Advancing.*] Dumain, thy love is far from
    charity,
That in love's grief desir'st society.
You may look pale, but I should blush, I know,
To be o'erheard and taken napping so.   130
    King. [*Advancing.*] Come, sir, you blush; as his
    your case is such;
You chide at him, offending twice as much.
You do not love Maria; Longaville
Did never sonnet for her sake compile,
Nor never lay his wreathed arms athwart   135
His loving bosom to keep down his heart.
I have been closely shrouded in this bush
And mark'd you both; and for you both did blush.
I heard your guilty rhymes, observ'd your fashion,
Saw sighs reek from you, noted well your passion.   140
"Ay me!" says one; "O Jove!" the other cries;
One, her hairs were gold, crystal the other's eyes:
[*To Long.*] You would for paradise break faith and
    troth;
[*To Dum.*] And Jove, for your love, would infringe
    an oath.
What will Biron say when that he shall hear   145
Faith infringed, which such zeal did swear?
How will he scorn! how will he spend his wit!
How will he triumph, leap, and laugh at it!
For all the wealth that ever I did see,
I would not have him know so much by me.   150
    Bir. Now step I forth to whip hypocrisy.
                    [*Advancing.*]

---

74. **liver-vein:** the style of a lover (the liver being the supposed "seat" of love).   78. **All hid:** i.e., as in the game of hide-and-seek.   82. **woodcocks:** proverbially silly birds.   87. **for . . . quoted:** made amber look ugly by contrast.   89. **Stoop, I say:** i.e., she stoops, rather.   93. **[I]** (Johnson). Om. Q.   98. **misprision:** mistake.   124. **example:** set a precedent for. 150. **by:** about.

Ah, good my liege, I pray thee, pardon me!
Good heart, what grace hast thou, thus to reprove
These worms for loving, that art most in love?
Your eyes do make no coaches; in your tears   155
There is no certain Princess that appears;
You'll not be perjur'd, 'tis a hateful thing;
Tush, none but minstrels like of sonneting!
But you are not asham'd? Nay, are you not,
All three of you, to be thus much o'ershot?   160
You found his mote; the King your mote did see;
But I a beam do find in each of three.
O, what a scene of fool'ry have I seen,
Of sighs, of groans, of sorrow, and of teen!
O me, with what strict patience have I sat,   165
To see a king transformed to a gnat!
To see great Hercules whipping a gig,
And profound Solomon to tune a jig,
And Nestor play at push-pin with the boys,
And critic Timon laugh at idle toys!   170
Where lies thy grief, O, tell me, good Dumain?
And, gentle Longaville, where lies thy pain?
And where my liege's? All about the breast!
A caudle, ho!
     King.   Too bitter is thy jest.
Are we betray'd thus to thy over-view?   175
     Bir. Not you to me, but I betray'd by you,
I, that am honest; I, that hold it sin
To break the vow I am engaged in;
I am betray'd by keeping company
With men like [you], men of inconstancy.   180
When shall you see me write a thing in rhyme,
Or groan for love, or spend a minute's time
In pruning me? When shall you hear that I
Will praise a hand, a foot, a face, an eye,
A gait, a state, a brow, a breast, a waist,   185
A leg, a limb?
     King.   Soft! whither away so fast?
A true man or a thief that gallops so?
     Bir. I post from love; good lover, let me go.

Enter JAQUENETTA *and Clown* [COSTARD.]

Jaq. God bless the King!
     King.   What present hast thou there?
Cost. Some certain treason.
     King.   What makes treason here?   190
Cost. Nay, it makes nothing, sir.
     King.   If it mar nothing neither,
The treason and you go in peace away together.
Jaq. I beseech your Grace, let this letter be read.
Our parson misdoubts it; 'twas treason, he said.
     King. Biron, read it over.   195
                    [*Biron reads the letter.*
Where hadst thou it?

Jaq. Of Costard.
     King. Where hadst thou it?
Cost. Of Dun Adramadio, Dun Adramadio.
                    [*Biron tears the letter.*]
     King. How now! what is in you? Why dost thou
     tear it?   200
     Bir. A toy, my liege, a toy; your Grace needs not
     fear it.
     Long. It did move him to passion, and therefore
     let's hear it.
     Dum. It is Biron's writing, and here is his name.
                    [*Gathering up the pieces.*]
     Bir. [*To Costard.*] Ah, you whoreson loggerhead!
     you were born to do me shame.
Guilty, my lord, guilty! I confess, I confess.   205
     King. What?
     Bir. That you three fools lack'd me fool to make
     up the mess.
He, he, and you, — and you, my liege, and I,
Are pick-purses in love, and we deserve to die.   209
O, dismiss this audience, and I shall tell you more.
     Dum. Now the number is even.
     Bir.   True, true; we are four.
Will these turtles be gone?
     King.   Hence, sirs; away!
     Cost. Walk aside the true folk, and let the
     traitors stay.
                    [*Exeunt Costard and Jaquenetta.*]
     Bir. Sweet lords, sweet lovers, O, let us embrace!
As true we are as flesh and blood can be.   215
The sea will ebb and flow, heaven show his face,
Young blood doth not obey an old decree.
We cannot cross the cause why we were born;
Therefore of all hands must we be forsworn.
     King. What, did these rent lines show some love
     of thine?   220
     Bir. Did they, quoth you? Who sees the heav-
     enly Rosaline,
That, like a rude and savage man of Inde,
At the first op'ning of the gorgeous east,
Bows not his vassal head and, strucken blind,
Kisses the base ground with obedient breast?
What peremptory eagle-sighted eye   226
Dares look upon the heaven of her brow,
That is not blinded by her majesty?
     King. What zeal, what fury hath inspir'd thee now?
My love, her mistress, is a gracious moon;   230
She an attending star, scarce seen a light.
     Bir. My eyes are then no eyes, nor I Biron.
O, but for my love, day would turn to night!
Of all complexions the cull'd sovereignty
Do meet, as at a fair, in her fair cheek,   235
Where several worthies make one dignity,

---

160. o'ershot: wide of the mark, in error.   161. You: i.e., Longaville. his: i.e., Dumain's. 164. teen: grief. 174. caudle: a warm spiced drink for the sick. candle Ff. 180. [you] (Walker conj.). Om. Q. 183. pruning: preening, adorning. 194. misdoubts: suspects. 207. mess: party of four. 212. turtles: turtle-doves, i.e., lovers. 219. of all hands: in any case. 236. Where...dignity. I.e., where several beauties make one superlative beauty (cf. l. 234).

Where nothing wants that want itself doth seek.
Lend me the flourish of all gentle tongues, —
　Fie, painted rhetoric! O, she needs it not.
To things of sale a seller's praise belongs,　240
　She passes praise; then praise too short doth blot.
A wither'd hermit, five-score winters worn,
　Might shake off fifty, looking in her eye.
Beauty doth varnish age, as if new-born,
　And gives the crutch the cradle's infancy.　245
O, 'tis the sun that maketh all things shine, —
　King. By heaven, thy love is black as ebony.
Bir. Is ebony like her? O wood divine!
A wife of such wood were felicity.
O, who can give an oath? Where is a book　250
　That I may swear beauty doth beauty lack
If that she learn not of her eye to look?
　No face is fair that is not full so black.
　King. O paradox! Black is the badge of hell,
The hue of dungeons and the [suit] of night;　255
And beauty's crest becomes the heavens well.
　Bir. Devils soonest tempt, resembling spirits of
　　light.
O, if in black my lady's brows be deck'd,
　It mourns that painting and usurping hair
Should ravish doters with a false aspect;　260
　And therefore is she born to make black fair.
Her favour turns the fashion of the days,
　For native blood is counted painting now;
And therefore red, that would avoid dispraise,
　Paints itself black, to imitate her brow.　265
Dum. To look like her are chimney-sweepers black.
　Long. And since her time are colliers counted
　　bright.
　King. And Ethiopes of their sweet complexion
　　crack.
Dum. Dark needs no candles now, for dark is
　light.
Bir. Your mistresses dare never come in rain,　270
　For fear their colours should be wash'd away.
King. 'Twere good, yours did; for sir, to tell you
　plain,
I'll find a fairer face not wash'd to-day.
Bir. I'll prove her fair, or talk till doomsday here.
　King. No devil will fright thee then so much as
　　she.　275
Dum. I never knew man hold vile stuff so dear.
　Long. Look, here's thy love; my foot and her
　　face see.
Bir. O, if the streets were paved with thine eyes,
　Her feet were much too dainty for such tread!

Dum. O vile! then, as she goes, what upward lies　280
　The street should see as she walk'd overhead.
King. But what of this? Are we not all in love?
　Bir. Nothing so sure; and thereby all forsworn.
King. Then leave this chat; and, good Biron, now
　prove
Our loving lawful, and our faith not torn.　285
Dum. Ay, marry there; some flattery for this evil.
　Long. O, some authority how to proceed;
Some tricks, some quillets, how to cheat the devil.
　Dum. Some salve for perjury.
　Bir.　　　'Tis more than need.
Have at you, then, affection's men at arms.　290
Consider what you first did swear unto,
To fast, to study, and to see no woman;
Flat treason 'gainst the kingly state of youth.
Say, can you fast? Your stomachs are too young;
And abstinence engenders maladies.　295
And where that you have vow'd to study, lords,
In that each of you have forsworn his book,
Can you still dream and pore and thereon look?
[For when would you, my lord, or you, or you,
Have found the ground of study's excellence　300
Without the beauty of a woman's face?
From women's eyes this doctrine I derive;
They are the ground, the books, the academes
From whence doth spring the true Promethean fire.]
Why, universal plodding poisons up　305
The nimble spirits in the arteries,
As motion and long-during action tires
The sinewy vigour of the traveller.
Now, for not looking on a woman's face,
You have in that forsworn the use of eyes　310
And study too, the causer of your vow.
For where is any author in the world
Teaches such beauty as a woman's eye?
Learning is but an adjunct to ourself,
And where we are our learning likewise is,　315
Then when ourselves we see in ladies' eyes,
Do we not likewise see our learning there?
O, we have made a vow to study, lords,
And in that vow we have forsworn our books.
For when would you, my liege, or you, or you,　320
In leaden contemplation have found out
Such fiery numbers as the prompting eyes
Of beauty's tutors have enrich'd you with?
Other slow arts entirely keep the brain;
And therefore, finding barren practisers,　325
Scarce show a harvest of their heavy toil;
But love, first learned in a lady's eyes,

238. flourish: eloquence. gentle: noble. 239. painted: artificial. 255. [suit] (Camb. edd. conj.). Schoole Qq Ff.
For pronunciation of suit cf. note on shooter, IV.1.109. See Introduction. 256. And . . . well. Navarre seems to be sar-
castic, saying in effect (see ll. 254–55), "Thus does your lady's beauty become the heavens." 262. favour: complexion.
263. native blood: natural complexion. 268. crack: boast. 275. then: i.e., at doomsday. 288. quillets: quibbles. 299–
304. [For . . . fire.] The substance of these lines is found elsewhere in this speech. The repetition is supposed to be due to
Shakespeare's revision having been misunderstood by the printer. 306. spirits: the "vital spirits" which were supposed to
convey life through the arteries to the whole body. 322. numbers: verses (referring to the poems he has read). 324. keep:
remain in.

Lives not alone immured in the brain;
But, with the motion of all elements,
Courses as swift as thought in every power,   330
And gives to every power a double power,
Above their functions and their offices.
It adds a precious seeing to the eye;
A lover's eyes will gaze an eagle blind;
A lover's ear will hear the lowest sound   335
When the suspicious head of theft is stopp'd;
Love's feeling is more soft and sensible
Than are the tender horns of cockled snails;
Love's tongue proves dainty Bacchus gross in taste.
For valour, is not Love a Hercules,   340
Still climbing trees in the Hesperides?
Subtle as Sphinx; as sweet and musical
As bright Apollo's lute, strung with his hair;
And when Love speaks, the voice of all the gods
Make heaven drowsy with the harmony.   345
Never durst poet touch a pen to write
Until his ink were temp'red with Love's sighs;
O, then his lines would ravish savage ears
And plant in tyrants mild humility.
From women's eyes this doctrine I derive: 350
They sparkle still the right Promethean fire;
They are the books, the arts, the academes,
That show, contain, and nourish all the world,
Else none at all in aught proves excellent.
Then fools you were these women to forswear,   355
Or keeping what is sworn, you will prove fools.
For wisdom's sake, a word that all men love,
Or for love's sake, a word that loves all men,
Or for men's sake, the authors of these women,
Or women's sake, by whom we men are men,   360
Let us once lose our oaths to find ourselves,
Or else we lose ourselves to keep our oaths.
It is religion to be thus forsworn,
For charity itself fulfils the law,
And who can sever love from charity?   365
    King. Saint Cupid, then! and, soldiers, to the field!
    Bir. Advance your standards, and upon them,
        lords;
Pell-mell, down with them! but be first advis'd,
In conflict that you get the sun of them.
    Long. Now to plain-dealing, lay these glozes by.
Shall we resolve to woo these girls of France?   371
    King. And win them too; therefore let us devise
Some entertainment for them in their tents.
    Bir. First, from the park let us conduct them
        thither;

Then homeward every man attach the hand   375
Of his fair mistress. In the afternoon
We will with some strange pastime solace them,
Such as the shortness of the time can shape;
For revels, dances, masks, and merry hours   379
Forerun fair Love, strewing her way with flowers.
    King. Away, away! no time shall be omitted
That will be time, and may by us be fitted.
    Bir. [*Allons! allons!*] Sow'd cockle reap'd no
        corn;
And justice always whirls in equal measure.
Light wenches may prove plagues to men forsworn;
If so, our copper buys no better treasure.   386
                                            [*Exeunt.*

ACT [V]

[SCENE I. *The same.*]

Enter the Pedant [HOLOFERNES], *the Curate*
[SIR NATHANIEL], *and* DULL.

Hol. Satis quod sufficit.
    Nath. I praise God for you, sir. Your reasons
at dinner have been sharp and sententious; pleasant
without scurrility, witty without affection, audacious without impudency, learned without opin-   5
ion, and strange without heresy. I did converse this
quondam day with a companion of the King's, who
is intituled, nominated, or called, Don Adriano de
Armado.
    Hol. Novi hominem tanquam te; his humor is   10
lofty, his discourse peremptory, his tongue filed, his
eye ambitious, his gait majestical, and his general
behaviour vain, ridiculous, and thrasonical. He
is too picked, too spruce, too affected, too odd, as
it were, too peregrinate, as I may call it.   16
    Nath. A most singular and choice epithet.
                            [*Draws out his table-book.*
    Hol. He draweth out the thread of his verbosity
finer than the staple of his argument. I abhor
such fanatical phantasimes, such insociable   20
and point-devise companions; such rackers of orthography, as to speak *dout*, fine, when he should
say *doubt; det,* when he should pronounce *debt,* —
d, e, b, t, not *d, e, t:* he clepeth a calf, *cauf;* half,
hauf; neighbour *vocatur nebour;* neigh abbrevi-   25
ated *ne.* This is abhominable, — which he would
call abbominable; it insinuateth me of [insanie];
ne intelligis, domine? to make frantic, lunatic.

336. **head of theft:** ear of a thief. 358. **loves:** is kind to (?). The sense of this jingle is not clear. 369. **get . . . them:**
get the sun in their eyes. 370. **glozes:** pretences. 383. [*Allons! allons!*] (Theobald). *Alone alone* Q. Sow'd . . . corn:
if one sows weeds, one reaps no corn.
    Act V, sc. i, 1. *Satis quod sufficit:* Enough is as good as a feast. 2. **reasons:** speeches. 3. **affection:** affectation. 5.
opinion: dogmatism. 10. *Novi . . . te:* I know the man as well as I know you. 11. **filed:** polished. 13. **thrasonical:** boastful
(from "Thraso," the braggart soldier in Terence's *Eunuchus*). 14. **picked:** fastidious. 16. **peregrinate:** foreign in manners.
18. **staple:** fiber. 21. **point-devise:** finical. 21. **fine:** fastidiously. 25. *vocatur:* is pronounced. Holofernes upholds the
pedantic theories of a contemporary group who wished to have the spelling and pronunciation of English words follow their
Latin originals. Thus, e.g., the M. E. *dout* was respelled *doubt*, restoring the b from the Latin *dubitum*. The new spellings
became established, but the new pronunciations did not. 28. [**insanie**] (Warburton conj.): insanity. *infamie* Q. **ne . . .
domine:** do you understand, sir?

Nath. Laus Deo, bone intelligo.   30
Hol. Bone? *bone* for *bene,* Priscian a little scratch'd, 'twill serve.

Enter Braggart [ARMADO], *Boy* [MOTH, *and* COSTARD].

Nath. Videsne quis venit?
Hol. Video, et gaudeo.
Arm. [*To Moth.*] Chirrah!   35
Hol. Quare chirrah, not sirrah?
Arm. Men of peace, well encount'red.
Hol. Most military sir, salutation.
Moth. [*Aside to Costard.*] They have been at a great feast of languages, and stol'n the scraps. 40
Cost. O, they have liv'd long on the almsbasket of words. I marvel thy master hath not eaten thee for a word, for thou art not so long by the head as *honorificabilitudinitatibus.* Thou art easier swallowed than a flap-dragon.   45
Moth. Peace! the peal begins.
Arm. [*To Hol.*] Monsieur, are you not lett'red?
Moth. Yes, yes; he teaches boys the hornbook. What is *a, b,* spelt backward, with the horn on his head?   51
Hol. Ba, pueritia, with a horn added.
Moth. Ba, most silly sheep with a horn. You hear his learning.
Hol. Quis, quis, thou consonant?   55
Moth. The [third] of the five vowels, if you repeat them; or the fifth, if I.
Hol. I will repeat them, — *a, e, i,* —
Moth. The sheep. The other two concludes it, — *o, u.*   60
Arm. Now, by the salt wave of the Mediterraneum, a sweet touch, a quick venue of wit! — snip, snap, quick and home! It rejoiceth my intellect. True wit!
Moth. Offer'd by a child to an old man; which is wit-old.   66
Hol. What is the figure? What is the figure?
Moth. Horns.
Hol. Thou disputes like an infant; go, whip thy gig.   70
Moth. Lend me your horn to make one, and I will whip about your infamy *unum cita,* — a gig of a cuckold's horn.
Cost. An I had but one penny in the world, thou shouldst have it to buy gingerbread. Hold, 75 there is the very remuneration I had of thy master, thou halfpenny purse of wit, thou pigeon-egg of discretion. O, an the heavens were so pleased that thou wert but my bastard, what a joyful father wouldst thou make me! Go to; thou hast it *ad dunghill,* at the fingers' ends, as they say. 83
Hol. O, I smell false Latin; *dunghill* for *unguem.*
Arm. Arts-man, preambulate, we will be 85 singuled from the barbarous. Do you not educate youth at the charge-house on the top of the mountain?
Hol. Or *mons,* the hill.
Arm. At your sweet pleasure, for the mountain.
Hol. I do, sans question.   91
Arm. Sir, it is the King's most sweet pleasure and affection to congratulate the Princess at her pavilion in the posteriors of this day, which the rude multitude call the afternoon.   95
Hol. The posterior of the day, most generous sir, is liable, congruent, and measurable for the afternoon. The word is well cull'd, chose, sweet, and apt, I do assure you, sir, I do assure.
Arm. Sir, the King is a noble gentleman, and my familiar, I do assure ye, very good friend; 101 for what is inward between us, let it pass; — I do beseech thee, remember thy courtesy; I beseech thee, apparel thy head; — and among other important and most serious designs, and of great import indeed, too, — but let that pass. For I must tell thee, it will please his Grace, by the 106 world, sometime to lean upon my poor shoulder, and with his royal finger, thus, dally with my excrement, with my mustachio; but, sweet heart, let that pass. By the world, I recount no fable: 111 some certain special honours it pleaseth his greatness to impart to Armado, a soldier, a man of travel, that hath seen the world; but let that pass. The very all of all is, — but, sweet heart, I do im- 115 plore secrecy, — that the King would have me present the Princess, sweet chuck, with some delightful ostentation, or show, or pageant, or antic, or firework. Now, understanding that the curate and your sweet self are good at such eruptions and 120 sudden breaking out of mirth, as it were, I have acquainted you withal, to the end to crave your assistance.

---

30. **Laus ... intelligo:** God be praised, I understand well.   31–32. **Priscian ... scratch'd:** i.e., your Latin is a bit faulty. Priscian wrote in the fifth century. 33. **Videsne quis venit:** Do you see who comes? 34. **Video, et gaudeo:** I see and rejoice. 36. **Quare:** why. 44. **honorificabilitudinitatibus:** the dative or ablative plural of a genuine medieval Latin word used by Dante, meaning "the state of being loaded with honors." It was famous as the longest word known. 45. **flap-dragon:** a raisin set on fire in liquor, to be swallowed flaming. 49. **hornbook:** a spelling primer, the paper of which was protected by a layer of horn. 52. **pueritia:** childishness. 52. **silly:** harmless, simple. 55. **quis:** who? 56. For [*third*] (Theobald) Qq Ff read *last,* which is the same as fifth and so has no point. If Holofernes repeats the vowels, the third gives him the answer, I: if Moth, the fifth gives him the same answer, U = You = Holofernes. 62. **venue:** thrust. 66. **wit-old:** i.e., wittol, cuckold. 70. **gig:** a whipping top. 72. **unum cita.** This is unintelligible. Of the proposed emendations, *circum circa* (Theobald) is most plausible. 85. **Arts-man:** professor. **preambulate:** go on before. 87. **charge-house:** schoolhouse. 96. **generous:** nobly born. 97. **liable:** fit. 102. **inward:** private. 118. **antic:** grotesque device.

Hol. Sir, you shall present before her the Nine Worthies. Sir [Nathaniel], as concerning some entertainment of time, some show in the posterior 125 of this day, to be render'd by our assistants, [at] the King's command, and this most gallant, illustrate, and learned gentleman, before the Princess, I say none so fit as to present the Nine Worthies. 130

Nath. Where will you find men worthy enough to present them?

Hol. Joshua, yourself; myself or this gallant gentleman, Judas Maccabæus; this swain, because of his great limb or joint, shall pass [as] Pom- 135 pey the Great; the page, Hercules, —

Arm. Pardon, sir; error. He is not quantity enough for that Worthy's thumb; he is not so big as the end of his club. 139

Hol. Shall I have audience? He shall present Hercules in minority; his enter and exit shall be strangling a snake; and I will have an apology for that purpose.

Moth. An excellent device! so, if any of the audience hiss, you may cry, "Well done, Her- 145 cules! now thou crushest the snake!" That is the way to make an offence gracious, though few have the grace to do it.

Arm. For the rest of the Worthies? —

Hol. I will play three myself. 150

Moth. Thrice-worthy gentleman!

Arm. Shall I tell you a thing?

Hol. We attend.

Arm. We will have, if this fadge not, an antic. I beseech you, follow. 155

Hol. *Via*, goodman Dull! thou hast spoken no word all this while.

Dull. Nor understood none neither, sir.

Hol. [*Allons!*] we will employ thee.

Dull. I'll make one in a dance, or so; or I will play 160
On the tabor to the Worthies, and let them dance the hay.

Hol. Most dull, honest Dull! To our sport, away!   [*Exeunt.*

[Scene II. *The same.*]

Enter the [Princess, *and*] Ladies.

Prin. Sweet hearts, we shall be rich ere we depart,
If fairings come thus plentifully in.

A lady wall'd about with diamonds!
Look you what I have from the loving King.   4
Ros. Madam, came nothing else along with that?
Prin. Nothing but this? Yes, as much love in rhyme
As would be cramm'd up in a sheet of paper,
Writ o' both sides the leaf, margent and all,
That he was fain to seal on Cupid's name.
Ros. That was the way to make his godhead wax,   10
For he hath been five thousand year a boy.
Kath. Ay, and a shrewd unhappy gallows too.
Ros. You'll ne'er be friends with him; 'a kill'd your sister.
Kath. He made her melancholy, sad, and heavy,
And so she died. Had she been light, like you, 15
Of such a merry, nimble, stirring spirit,
She might ha' been [a] grandam ere she died.
And so may you; for a light heart lives long.
Ros. What's your dark meaning, mouse, of this light word?
Kath. A light condition in a beauty dark.   20
Ros. We need more light to find your meaning out.
Kath. You'll mar the light by taking it in snuff;
Therefore I'll darkly end the argument.
Ros. Look, what you do, you do it still i' th' dark.   24
Kath. So do not you, for you are a light wench.
Ros. Indeed I weigh not you, and therefore light.
Kath. You weigh me not? O, that's you care not for me.
Ros. Great reason; for "past [cure] is still past [care]."
Prin. Well bandied both; a set of wit well play'd.
But, Rosaline, you have a favour too.   30
Who sent it? and what is it?
Ros.   I would you knew.
An if my face were but as fair as yours,
My favour were as great; be witness this.
Nay, I have verses too, I thank Biron;
The numbers true, and, were the numb'ring too, 35
I were the fairest goddess on the ground.
I am compar'd to twenty thousand fairs.
O, he hath drawn my picture in his letter!
Prin. Anything like?
Ros. Much in the letters; nothing in the praise. 40
Prin. Beauteous as ink; a good conclusion.

123. **Nine Worthies.** Traditionally they were Hector of Troy, Alexander, Julius Caesar, Joshua, David, Judas Maccabaeus, Arthur, Charlemagne, and Godfrey of Bouillon. Though the list varies with different writers, Hercules and Pompey are introduced only by Shakespeare, who probably included them for reasons of comedy. 124. [**Nathaniel**] (Capell). *Holofernes* Q. 126. [**at**] F₂. Om. Q. 135. [**as**] (Camb. edd. conj.) Om. Q. 141. **Hercules in minority.** The infant Hercules was reputed to have strangled in his bed two serpents which Juno sent to destroy him. 154. **fadge:** succeed. 156. *Via:* forward. 159. [*Allons!*] (Rowe). *Alone* Q. 161. **tabor: a** small drum. **hay:** a round dance.

Sc. ii, 2. **fairings:** gifts. 12. **shrewd . . . gallows:** cunning rogue. 17. [**a**] Om. Q. 22. **in snuff:** in anger — with pun on the snuff of a candle. 28. [**cure**] . . . [**care**] (Thirlby conj.). *care . . . cure* Q. 30. **favour:** gift. 33. **favour:** face. 35. **numbers:** meter. **numbering:** estimate.

Kath. Fair as a text B in a copy-book.

Ros. Ware pencils, [ho]! let me not die your debtor,

My red dominical, my golden letter;

O that your face were not so full of O's! 45

Prin. A pox of that jest! and I beshrew all shrews.

But, Katharine, what was sent to you from fair Dumain?

Kath. Madam, this glove.

Prin.   Did he not send you twain?

Kath. Yes, madam, and moreover

Some thousand verses of a faithful lover, 50

A huge translation of hypocrisy,

Vilely compil'd, profound simplicity.

Mar. This and these pearls to me sent Longaville.

The letter is too long by half a mile.

Prin. I think no less. Dost thou not wish in heart 55

The chain were longer and the letter short?

Mar. Ay, or I would these hands might never part.

Prin. We are wise girls to mock our lovers so.

Ros. They are worse fools to purchase mocking so.

That same Biron I'll torture ere I go. 60

O that I knew he were but in by th' week!

How I would make him fawn and beg and seek,

And wait the season and observe the times,

And spend his prodigal wits in bootless rhymes,

And shape his service wholly to my [hests], 65

And make him proud to make me proud that jests!

So pedant-like would I o'ersway his state

That he should be my fool and I his fate.

Prin. None are so surely caught, when they are catch'd, 70

As wit turn'd fool; folly, in wisdom hatch'd,

Hath wisdom's warrant and the help of school

And wit's own grace to grace a learned fool.

Ros. The blood of youth burns not with such excess

As gravity's revolt to [wantonness].

Mar. Folly in fools bears not so strong a note 75

As fool'ry in the wise, when wit doth dote;

Since all the power thereof it doth apply

To prove, by wit, worth in simplicity.

Enter BOYET.

Prin. Here comes Boyet, and mirth is in his face.

Boyet. O, I am [stabb'd] with laughter! Where's her Grace? 80

Prin. Thy news, Boyet?

Boyet.   Prepare, madam, prepare!

Arm, wenches, arm! Encounters mounted are

Against your peace. Love doth approach disguis'd,

Armed in arguments; you'll be surpris'd.

Muster your wits; stand in your own defence; 85

Or hide your heads like cowards, and fly hence.

Prin. Saint Denis to Saint Cupid! What are they

That charge their breath against us? Say, scout, say.

Boyet. Under the cool shade of a sycamore

I thought to close mine eyes some half an hour; 90

When, lo! to interrupt my purpos'd rest,

Toward that shade I might behold address'd

The King and his companions. Warily

I stole into a neighbour thicket by,

And overheard what you shall overhear, 95

That, by and by, disguis'd they will be here.

Their herald is a pretty knavish page,

That well by heart hath conn'd his embassage.

Action and accent did they teach him there;

"Thus must thou speak," and "thus thy body bear;" 100

And ever and anon they made a doubt

Presence majestical would put him out;

"For," quoth the King, "an angel shalt thou see;

Yet fear not thou, but speak audaciously."

The boy replied, "An angel is not evil; 105

I should have fear'd her had she been a devil."

With that, all laugh'd and clapp'd him on the shoulder,

Making the bold wag by their praises bolder.

One rubb'd his elbow thus, and fleer'd and swore

A better speech was never spoke before; 110

Another, with his finger and his thumb,

Cried, "*Via!* we will do't, come what will come;"

The third he caper'd, and cried, "All goes well;"

The fourth turn'd on the toe, and down he fell.

With that, they all did tumble on the ground, 115

With such a zealous laughter, so profound,

That in this spleen ridiculous appears,

To check their folly, passion's solemn tears.

Prin. But what, but what, come they to visit us?

Boyet. They do, they do; and are apparell'd thus 120

Like Muscovites or Russians, as I guess.

Their purpose is to parle, to court, and dance;

And every one his love-feat will advance

Unto his several mistress, which they'll know

By favours several which they did bestow. 125

---

42. **text B:** the letter B written elaborately and formally. 43. **Ware pencils:** beware this sketching of portraits. [ho] (Rowe). *how* Q. 44. **red dominical:** the red letter which marked Sundays in the old almanacs. Rosaline is jesting at Katherine's "amber" hair. 45. **O's:** marks left by the smallpox. 61. **in...week:** really caught. 65. **[hests]** (Walker conj.). *device* Q. 67. **[pedant-like]** (Theobald). *perttaunt-like* Q. Other suggested readings are "portent-like," "planet-like," etc. 74. **[wantonness]** F₃. *wantons be* Q. 79. **[stabb'd]** F. *stable* Q. 82. **Encounters:** assailants. 87. **Saint Denis:** patron saint of France. 101. **made a doubt:** expressed a fear. 109. **fleer'd:** grinned. 117. **spleen:** mirth. 124. **Several:** respective.

Prin. And will they so?   The gallants shall be
task'd,
For, ladies, we will every one be mask'd;
And not a man of them shall have the grace,
Despite of suit, to see a lady's face.
Hold, Rosaline, this favour thou shalt wear,   130
And then the King will court thee for his dear.
Hold, take thou this, my sweet, and give me thine,
So shall Biron take me for Rosaline.
And change you favours too; so shall your loves
Woo contrary, deceiv'd by these removes.   135
   Ros. Come on, then; wear the favours most in
sight.
   Kath. But in this changing what is your intent?
   Prin. The effect of my intent is to cross theirs.
They do it but in mocking merriment,
And mock for mock is only my intent.   140
Their several counsels they unbosom shall
To loves mistook, and so be mock'd withal
Upon the next occasion that we meet,
With visages display'd, to talk and greet.   144
   Ros. But shall we dance, if they desire us to't?
   Prin. No, to the death, we will not move a foot;
Nor to their penn'd speech render we no grace,
But while 'tis spoke each turn away her face.
   Boyet. Why, that contempt will kill the speaker's
heart,
And quite divorce his memory from his part.   150
   Prin. Therefore I do it; and I make no doubt
The rest will ne'er come in, if he be out.
There's no such sport as sport by sport o'erthrown,
To make theirs ours and ours none but our own;
So shall we stay, mocking intended game,   155
And they, well mock'd, depart away with shame.
                    [*Trumpet sounds* [*within*].
   Boyet. The trumpet sounds: be mask'd; the
maskers come.   [*The Ladies mask.*]

Enter Blackamoors *with music, the Boy* [MOTH]
with a speech, and the rest of the LORDS *disguised.*
   Moth. "All hail, the richest beauties on the
earth!" —
   [*Boyet*]. Beauties no richer than rich taffeta.
   Moth. "A holy parcel of the fairest dames   160
                    [*The Ladies turn their backs to him.*
That ever turn'd their — backs — to mortal views!"
   Bir. [*Aside to Moth.*] Their eyes, villain, their
eyes.
   Moth. "That ever turn'd their eyes to mortal
views! —
Out" —
   Boyet. True; out indeed.   165
   Moth. "Out of your favours, heavenly spirits,
vouchsafe
Not to behold" —

   Bir. [*Aside to Moth.*] Once to behold, rogue.
   Moth. "Once to behold with your sun-beamed
eyes,
—— with your sun-beamed eyes" —   169
   Boyet. They will not answer to that epithet;
You were best call it "daughter-beamed eyes."
   Moth. They do not mark me, and that brings me
out.
   Bir. Is this your perfectness?   Be gone, you
rogue!   [*Exit Moth.*]
   Ros. What would these strangers?   Know their
minds, Boyet.
If they do speak our language, 'tis our will   175
That some plain man recount their purposes.
Know what they would.
   Boyet. What would you with the Princess?
   Bir. Nothing but peace and gentle visitation.
   Ros. What would they, say they?   180
   Boyet. Nothing but peace and gentle visitation.
   Ros. Why, that they have; and bid them so be
gone.
   Boyet. She says, you have it, and you may be
gone.
   King. Say to her, we have measur'd many miles
To tread a measure with her on this grass.   185
   Boyet. They say, that they have measur'd many
a mile
To tread a measure with you on this grass.
   Ros. It is not so.   Ask them how many inches
Is in one mile: if they have measur'd many,
The measure then of one is easily told.   190
   Boyet. If to come hither you have measur'd
miles,
And many miles, the Princess bids you tell
How many inches doth fill up one mile.
   Bir. Tell her, we measure them by weary steps.
   Boyet. She hears herself.
   Ros.   How many weary steps
Of many weary miles you have o'ergone,   196
Are numb'red in the travel of one mile?
   Bir. We number nothing that we spend for you;
Our duty is so rich, so infinite,
That we may do it still without accompt.   200
Vouchsafe to show the sunshine of your face,
That we, like savages, may worship it.
   Ros. My face is but a moon, and clouded too.
   King. Blessed are clouds, to do as such clouds do!
Vouchsafe, bright moon, and these thy stars, to
shine,   205
Those clouds remov'd, upon our watery eyne.
   Ros. O vain petitioner! beg a greater matter;
Thou now requests but moonshine in the water.
   King. Then, in our measure do but vouchsafe
one change.   209
Thou bid'st me beg; this begging is not strange.

126. **task'd**: put to the test.   135. **removes**: exchanges.   159. [*Boyet*] (Theobald).   *Berow* Q.   185. **measure**: a stately
dance.   200. **accompt**: reckoning the cost.   209. **change**: i.e., round of dancing.   210. **begging**: request.

Ros. Play, music, then!   Nay, you must do it
   soon.   [*Music plays.*]
Not yet! no dance!   Thus change I like the moon.
King. Will you not dance?   How come you thus
   estranged?
Ros. You took the moon at full, but now she's
   changed.   214
King. Yet still she is the moon, and I the man.
The music plays; vouchsafe some motion to it.
Ros. Our ears vouchsafe it.
King.   But your legs should do it.
Ros. Since you are strangers and come here by
   chance,
We'll not be nice; take hands.   We will not dance.
King. Why take we hands, then?
Ros.   Only to part friends.   220
Curtsey, sweet hearts; and so the measure ends.
King. More measure of this measure; be not nice.
Ros. We can afford no more at such a price.
King. Price you yourselves; what buys your
   company?
Ros. Your absence only.
King.   That can never be.   225
Ros. Then cannot we be bought; and so, adieu;
Twice to your visor, and half once to you.
King. If you deny to dance, let's hold more chat.
Ros. In private, then.
King.   I am best pleas'd with that.
                                   [*They converse apart.*]
Bir. White-handed mistress, one sweet word with
   thee.   230
Prin. Honey, and milk, and sugar; there is three.
Bir. Nay then, two treys, an if you grow so nice,
Metheglin, wort, and malmsey; well run, dice!
There's half-a-dozen sweets.
Prin.   Seventh sweet, adieu.
Since you can cog, I'll play no more with you.   235
Bir. One word in secret.
Prin.   Let it not be sweet.
Bir. Thou griev'st my gall.
Prin.   Gall! bitter.
Bir.   Therefore meet.
                                   [*They converse apart.*]
Dum. Will you vouchsafe with me to change a
   word?
Mar. Name it.
Dum.   Fair lady —
Mar.   Say you so?   Fair lord, —
Take that for your fair lady.
Dum.   Please it you,   240

As much in private, and I'll bid adieu.
                                   [*They converse apart.*]
[*Kath.*] What, was your vizard made without a
   tongue?
Long. I know the reason, lady, why you ask.
[*Kath.*] O for your reason! quickly, sir; I long.
Long. You have a double tongue within your
   mask,   245
And would afford my speechless vizard half.
[*Kath.*] "Veal," quoth the Dutchman.   Is not
   veal a calf?
Long. A calf, fair lady!
[*Kath.*]   No, a fair lord calf.
Long. Let's part the word.
[*Kath.*]   No, I'll not be your half.
Take all, and wean it; it may prove an ox.   250
Long. Look, how you butt yourself in these
   sharp mocks!
Will you give horns, chaste lady?   Do not so.
[*Kath.*] Then die a calf, before your horns do
   grow.
Long. One word in private with you, ere I die.
[*Kath.*] Bleat softly then; the butcher hears you
   cry.   [*They converse apart.*]
Boyet. The tongues of mocking wenches are as
   keen   256
As is the razor's edge invisible,
Cutting a smaller hair than may be seen,
   Above the sense of sense; so sensible
Seemeth their conference; their conceits have wings
Fleeter than arrows, bullets, wind, thought, swifter
   things.   261
Ros. Not one word more, my maids; break off,
   break off.
Bir. By heaven, all dry-beaten with pure scoff!
King. Farewell, mad wenches; you have simple
   wits.
          [*Exeunt [King, Lords, and Blackamoors].*]
Prin. Twenty adieus, my frozen Muscovits.
Are these the breed of wits so wond'red at?   266
Boyet. Tapers they are, with your sweet breaths
   puff'd out.
Ros. Well-liking wits they have; gross, gross;
   fat, fat.
Prin. O poverty in wit, kingly-poor flout!
Will they not, think you, hang themselves tonight?
Or ever, but in vizards, show their faces?   271
This pert Biron was out of count'nance quite.
Ros. [O], they were all in lamentable cases!
The King was weeping-ripe for a good word.

215. **man:** i.e., man in the moon. 216. **The . . . it.** Given to Rosaline in Qq Ff.   Corrected by Theobald. 219. **nice:** coy.
222. **More measure.** The dance began with taking hands, curtsying, and kissing.   Probably the king is asking for a kiss.
232. **treys:** threes, a throw at dice. 233. **Metheglin:** a drink made from honey. **wort:** unfermented beer. **malmsey: a**
sweet wine. 235. **cog:** cheat. 237. **gall:** sore spot. 242, 244, 247, 248, 249, 253, 255. [*Kath.*] (Rowe).   *Maria, Mari,* or
Mar.   Qq Ff. 247. **"Veal."**   Not satisfactorily explained.   Guesses are foreigner's pronunciation of "well," or Englishman's of "veil." 249. **part:** divide. **half.** A pun, since "half" also means "wife." 259. **Above . . . sense:** beyond the
sense's power of perception. 263. **dry-beaten:** beaten without bloodshed. 268. **Well-liking:** plump. 269. **kingly-poor**
flout: a fling poor for a king. 273. **[O]** F₂.   Om. Q. 274. **weeping-ripe for:** ready to weep for want of.

Prin. Biron did swear himself out of all suit. 275

Mar. Dumain was at my service, and his sword.
"No point," quoth I; my servant straight was mute.

Kath. Lord Longaville said I came o'er his heart;
And trow you what he call'd me?

Prin.   Qualm, perhaps.

Kath. Yes, in good faith.

Prin.   Go, sickness as thou art!

Ros. Well, better wits have worn plain statute-
caps. 281
But will you hear? The King is my love sworn.

Prin. And quick Biron hath plighted faith to me.

Kath. And Longaville was for my service born.

Mar. Dumain is mine, as sure as bark on tree.

Boyet. Madam, and pretty mistresses, give ear:
Immediately they will again be here 287
In their own shapes; for it can never be
They will digest this harsh indignity.

Prin. Will they return?

Boyet.   They will, they will, God knows,
And leap for joy, though they are lame with
blows: 291
Therefore change favours; and, when they repair,
Blow like sweet roses in this summer air.

Prin. How blow? how blow? speak to be understood.

Boyet. Fair ladies mask'd are roses in their
bud; 295
Dismask'd, their damask sweet commixture shown,
Are angels vailing clouds, or roses blown.

Prin. Avaunt, perplexity! What shall we do,
If they return in their own shapes to woo?

Ros. Good madam, if by me you'll be advis'd, 300
Let's mock them still, as well known as disguis'd.
Let us complain to them what fools were here,
Disguis'd like Muscovites, in shapeless gear;
And wonder what they were, and to what end
Their shallow shows and prologue vilely penn'd
And their rough carriage so ridiculous 306
Should be presented at our tent to us.

Boyet. Ladies, withdraw; the gallants are at hand.

Prin. Whip to our tents, as roes [run o'er the]
land.   [*Exeunt [Princess and Ladies].*

Re-enter the KING, *and the rest [in their proper habits].*

King. Fair sir, God save you! Where's the
Princess? 310

Boyet. Gone to her tent. Please it your majesty
Command me any service to her thither?

King. That she vouchsafe me audience for one
word.

Boyet. I will; and so will she, I know, my lord.
       [*Exit.*

Bir. This fellow pecks up wit as pigeons pease,
And utters it again when God doth please. 316
He is wit's pedlar, and retails his wares
At wakes and wassails, meetings, markets, fairs:
And we that sell by gross, the Lord doth know,
Have not the grace to grace it with such show.
This gallant pins the wenches on his sleeve; 321
Had he been Adam, he had tempted Eve.
'A can carve too, and lisp; why, this is he
That kiss'd his hand away in courtesy;
This is the ape of form, monsieur the nice, 325
That, when he plays at tables, chides the dice
In honourable terms; nay, he can sing
A mean most meanly; and in ushering
Mend him who can. The ladies call him sweet;
The stairs, as he treads on them, kiss his feet. 330
This is the flow'r that smiles on every one,
To show his teeth as white as whalë's bone;
And consciences, that will not die in debt,
Pay him the due of honey-tongu'd Boyet.

King. A blister on his sweet tongue, with my
heart, 335
That put Armado's page out of his part!

Re-enter the [PRINCESS, *attended by* BOYET *and her*]
LADIES.

Bir. See where it comes! Behaviour, what wert
thou
Till this [man] show'd thee? And what art thou
now?

King. All hail, sweet madam, and fair time of
day!

Prin. "Fair" in "all hail" is foul, as I conceive. 340

King. Construe my speeches better, if you may.

Prin. Then wish me better; I will give you leave.

King. We came to visit you, and purpose now
To lead you to our court; vouchsafe it then.

Prin. This field shall hold me; and so hold your
vow: 345
Nor God, nor I, delights in perjur'd men.

King. Rebuke me not for that which you provoke.
The virtue of your eye must break my oath.

Prin. You nickname virtue; vice you should have
spoke,
For virtue's office never breaks men's troth. 350
Now by my maiden honour, yet as pure
As the unsullied lily, I protest,
A word of torments though I should endure,
I would not yield to be your house's guest;

279. **Qualm:** pronounced like "calm"; hence a pun.   281. **statute-caps:** woolen caps, as required by law to be worn by the London apprentices.   296. **commixture:** complexion.   297. **vailing:** letting fall. **blown:** full blown.   309. **[run o'er the]** F₄. *runs ore* Q.   323. **carve:** make amorous signals.   328. **mean:** tenor.   338. **[man]** (Theobald). *madman* Q.   349. **nickname:** miscall.

So much I hate a breaking cause to be 355
Of heavenly oaths, vow'd with integrity.
King. O, you have liv'd in desolation here,
 Unseen, unvisited, much to our shame.
Prin. Not so, my lord; it is not so, I swear;
 We have had pastimes here and pleasant game.
A mess of Russians left us but of late. 361
 King. How, madam! Russians!
 Prin.   Ay, in truth, my lord;
Trim gallants, full of courtship and of state.
 Ros. Madam, speak true. It is not so, my lord.
My lady, to the manner of the days, 365
In courtesy gives undeserving praise.
We four indeed confronted were with four
In Russian habit; here they stay'd an hour,
And talk'd apace; and in that hour, my lord,
They did not bless us with one happy word. 370
I dare not call them fools; but this I think,
When they are thirsty, fools would fain have drink.
 Bir. This jest is dry to me. [Fair] gentle sweet,
Your [wit makes] wise things foolish. When we greet,
With eyes best seeing, heaven's fiery eye, 375
By light we lose light; your capacity
Is of that nature that to your huge store
Wise things seem foolish and rich things but poor.
 Ros. This proves you wise and rich, for in my eye —
 Bir. I am a fool, and full of poverty. 380
 Ros. But that you take what doth to you belong,
It were a fault to snatch words from my tongue.
 Bir. O, I am yours, and all that I possess!
 Ros. All the fool mine?
 Bir.   I cannot give you less.
 Ros. Which of the vizards was it that you wore? 385
 Bir. Where? When? What vizard? Why demand you this?
 Ros. There, then, that vizard; that superfluous case
That hid the worse and show'd the better face.
 King. [*Aside.*] We were descried; they'll mock us now downright.
 Dum. Let us confess and turn it to a jest. 390
 Prin. Amaz'd, my lord? Why looks your highness sad?
 Ros. Help, hold his brows! he'll swoon! Why look you pale?
Sea-sick, I think, coming from Muscovy.
 Bir. Thus pour the stars down plagues for perjury.
Can any face of brass hold longer out? 395

Here stand I; lady, dart thy skill at me,
 Bruise me with scorn, confound me with a flout;
Thrust thy sharp wit quite through my ignorance;
 Cut me to pieces with thy keen conceit;
And I will wish thee never more to dance, 400
 Nor never more in Russian habit wait.
O, never will I trust to speeches penn'd,
 Nor to the motion of a schoolboy's tongue,
Nor never come in vizard to my friend,
 Nor woo in rhyme, like a blind harper's song! 405
Taffeta phrases, silken terms precise,
 Three-piled hyperboles, spruce [affectation],
Figures pedantical; these summer-flies
 Have blown me full of maggot ostentation.
I do forswear them, and I here protest, 410
 By this white glove, — how white the hand, God knows! —
Henceforth my wooing mind shall be express'd
 In russet yeas and honest kersey noes;
And, to begin, wench, — so God help me, la! —
 My love to thee is sound, sans crack or flaw. 415
 Ros. Sans sans, I pray you.
 Bir.   Yet I have a trick
Of the old rage. Bear with me, I am sick;
I'll leave it by degrees. Soft, let us see: —
Write "Lord have mercy on us" on those three.
They are infected; in their hearts it lies; 420
They have the plague, and caught it of your eyes.
These lords are visited; you are not free,
For the Lord's tokens on you do I see.
 Prin. No, they are free that gave these tokens to us.
 Bir. Our states are forfeit; seek not to undo us.
 Ros. It is not so; for how can this be true, 426
That you stand forfeit, being those that sue?
 Bir. Peace! for I will not have to do with you.
 Ros. Nor shall not, if I do as I intend.
 Bir. Speak for yourselves; my wit is at an end.
 King. Teach us, sweet madam, for our rude transgression 431
Some fair excuse.
 Prin.   The fairest is confession.
Were not you here but even now disguis'd?
 King. Madam, I was.
 Prin.   And were you well advis'd?
 King. I was, fair madam.
 Prin.   When you then were here,
What did you whisper in your lady's ear? 436
 King. That more than all the world I did respect her.
 Prin. When she shall challenge this, you will reject her.

---

365. **to the manner of:** after the fashion of. 373. [Fair] F₂. Om. Q. 374. [wit makes] F₂. *wits make* Q. 400. wish: invite. 407. [affectation] (Rowe). *affection* Q. 413. russet: homespun. kersey: coarse woolen, and so "plain" in contrast with the "silken terms" (l. 406). 419. "Lord . . . us": the sign put upon the door of a plague-stricken house. 422. visited: infected. 423. the Lord's tokens. A jesting reference to the plague spots on the body. Biron is speaking of the favors which the ladies are wearing. 427. forfeit . . . sue. A pun on the two meanings of *sue*: "prosecute" and "entreat." How can the prosecutor incur the penalty? 434. well advis'd: in your right mind.

King. Upon mine honour, no.

Prin.   Peace, peace! forbear.
Your oath once broke, you force not to forswear. 440
King. Despise me, when I break this oath of
    mine.
Prin. I will; and therefore keep it.   Rosaline,
What did the Russian whisper in your ear?
Ros. Madam, he swore that he did hold me dear
As precious eyesight, and did value me   445
Above this world; adding thereto, moreover,
That he would wed me, or else die my lover.
Prin. God give thee joy of him!   The noble lord
Most honourably doth uphold his word.
King. What mean you, madam?   By my life,
    my troth,   450
I never swore this lady such an oath.
Ros. By heaven, you did; and to confirm it plain,
You gave me this; but take it, sir, again.
King. My faith and this the Princess I did give.
I knew her by this jewel on her sleeve.   455
Prin. Pardon me, sir, this jewel did she wear;
And Lord Biron, I thank him, is my dear.
What, will you have me, or your pearl again?
Bir. Neither of either; I remit both twain.
I see the trick on't; here was a consent,   460
Knowing aforehand of our merriment,
To dash it like a Christmas comedy.
Some carry-tale, some please-man, some slight zany,
Some mumble-news, some trencher-knight, some
    Dick,
That smiles his cheek in years and knows the
    trick   465
To make my lady laugh when she's dispos'd,
Told our intents before; which once disclos'd,
The ladies did change favours; and then we,
Following the signs, woo'd but the sign of she.
Now, to our perjury to add more terror,   470
We are again forsworn, in will and error.
Much upon this [it is]; and might not you
                                [*To Boyet.*]
Forestall our sport, to make us thus untrue?
Do not you know my lady's foot by th' squire,
    And laugh upon the apple of her eye?   475
And stand between her back, sir, and the fire,
    Holding a trencher, jesting merrily?
You put our page out.   Go, you are allow'd;
Die when you will, a smock shall be your shroud.
You leer upon me, do you?   There's an eye   480
Wounds like a leaden sword.
Boyet.   Full merrily
Hath this brave [manage], this career, been run.

Bir. Lo, he is tilting straight!   Peace!   I have
    done.

Enter Clown [COSTARD].

Welcome, pure wit! thou partest a fair fray
Cost. O Lord, sir, they would know   485
Whether the three Worthies shall come in or no.
Bir. What, are there but three?
Cost.   No, sir; but it is vara fine,
For every one pursents three.
Bir.   And three times thrice is nine.
Cost. Not so, sir; under correction, sir; I hope it
    is not so.
You cannot beg us, sir, I can assure you, sir; we
    know what we know.   490
I hope, sir, three times thrice, sir, —
Bir. Is not nine.
Cost. Under correction, sir, we know whereuntil
it doth amount.
Bir. By Jove, I always took three threes for   495
nine.
Cost. O Lord, sir, it were pity you should get
your living by reck'ning, sir.
Bir. How much is it?
Cost. O Lord, sir, the parties themselves,   500
the actors, sir, will show whereuntil it doth amount.
For mine own part, I am, as they say, but to
parfect one man in one poor man, Pompion the
Great, sir.
Bir. Art thou one of the Worthies?   505
Cost. It pleased them to think me worthy of
Pompey the Great; for mine own part, I know
not the degree of the Worthy, but I am to stand
for him.
Bir. Go, bid them prepare.   510
Cost. We will turn it finely off, sir; we will take
    some care.   [*Exit.*
King. Biron, they will shame us; let them not
    approach.
Bir. We are shame-proof, my lord; and 'tis some
    policy
To have one show worse than the King's and his
    company.
King. I say they shall not come.   515
Prin. Nay, my good lord, let me o'errule you now;
That sport best pleases that doth [least] know how;
Where zeal strives to content, and the contents
Dies in the zeal of that which it presents.   519
Their form confounded makes most form in mirth,
When great things labouring perish in their birth.
Bir. A right description of our sport, my lord.

440. **force not**: find it easy.   460. **consent**: conspiracy.   462. **dash**: ridicule.   463. **zany**: clown.   464. **trencher-knight**: a parasite.   465. **in years**: i.e., into wrinkles.   472. **upon**: like.   **[it is]** F₂.   *tis* Q.   474. **know … squire**: know how to please my lady.   **squire**: square.   475. **laugh … eye**: i.e., jest intimately with her.   478. **allow'd**: privileged.   482. **[manage]** (Theobald): a swift course in the lists.   *nuage* Q.   490. **beg us**: prove us fools.   In the courts one "begged" (i.e., petitioned) for the guardianship of idiots.   503. **parfect**: present.   504. **Pompion**: pumpkin.   Costard gets the name right in his next speech.   517. **[least]** F.   *best* Q.   518. **contents**.   This may mean either the substance of the play or the pleasure it is meant to give.   522. **our sport**: i.e., the Muscovite masque.

Enter Braggart [ARMADO].

Arm. Anointed, I implore so much expense of
thy royal sweet breath as will utter a brace of
words.   525
    [*Converses apart with the King, and delivers
       him a paper.*]
Prin. Doth this man serve God?
Bir. Why ask you?
Prin. 'A speaks not like a man of God's making.
Arm. That is all one, my fair, sweet, honey   530
monarch; for, I protest, the schoolmaster is exceed-
ing fantastical; too too vain, too too vain: but we
will put it, as they say, to *fortuna de la guerra*.
I wish you the peace of mind, most royal couple-
ment!   [*Exit.* 535
King. Here is like to be a good presence of
Worthies. He presents Hector of Troy; the swain,
Pompey the Great; the parish curate, Alexander;
Armado's page, Hercules; the pedant, Judas Mac-
cabæus;   540
And if these four Worthies in their first show thrive,
These four will change habits, and present the
     other five.
Bir. There is five in the first show.
King. You are deceived; 'tis not so.
Bir. The pedant, the braggart, the hedge-   545
priest, the fool, and the boy:
Abate throw at Novum, and the whole world again
Cannot pick out five such, take each one in his vein.
King. The ship is under sail, and here she comes
     amain   549

Enter [COSTARD, *for*] *Pompey.*

Cost. "I Pompey am," —
Bir.   You lie, you are not he.
Cost. "I Pompey am," —
Boyet.   With libbard's head on knee.
Bir. Well said, old mocker. I must needs be
friends with thee.
Cost. "I Pompey am, Pompey surnam'd the
Big." —
Dum. The Great.
Cost. It is "Great," sir: —
         "Pompey surnam'd the Great;
That oft in field, with targe and shield, did make
     my foe to sweat;   556
And travelling along this coast, I here am come by
     chance,
And lay my arms before the legs of this sweet lass
     of France."
If your ladyship would say, "Thanks, Pompey,"
     I had done.

Prin. Great thanks, great Pompey.   560
Cost. 'Tis not so much worth; but I hope I was
perfect. I made a little fault in "Great."
Bir. My hat to a halfpenny, Pompey proves the
best Worthy.

Enter Curate [SIR NATHANIEL], *for Alexander.*

Nath. "When in the world I liv'd, I was the
     world's commander;   565
By east, west, north, and south, I spread my con-
     quering might.
My scutcheon plain declares that I am Alisan-
     der," —
Boyet. Your nose says, no, you are not; for it
     stands too right.
Bir. Your nose smells "no" in this, most tender-
     smelling knight.
Prin. The conqueror is dismay'd. Proceed,
     good Alexander.   570
Nath. "When in the world I liv'd, I was the
     world's commander," —
Boyet. Most true, 'tis right; you were so, Alisan-
     der.
Bir. Pompey the Great, —
Cost. Your servant, and Costard.
Bir. Take away the conqueror, take away   575
Alisander.
Cost. [*To Sir Nath.*] O, sir, you have overthrown
Alisander the conqueror! You will be scrap'd out
of the painted cloth for this. Your lion, that
holds his poll-axe sitting on a close-stool,   580
will be given to Ajax; he will be the ninth Worthy.
A conqueror. and afeard to speak! Run away for
shame, Alisander. [*Nath. retires.*] There, an't shall
please you, a foolish mild man, an honest man,
look you, and soon dash'd. He is a marvel-   585
lous good neighbour, faith, and a very good bowler;
but, for Alisander, — alas, you see how 'tis, — a
little o'erparted. But there are Worthies a-coming
will speak their mind in some other sort.   590
               [*Exit Curate.*
Prin. Stand aside, good Pompey.

Enter Pedant [HOLOFERNES], *for Judas, and
the Boy* [MOTH], *for Hercules.*

Hol. "Great Hercules is presented by this imp,
Whose club kill'd Cerberus, that three-headed
     canus;
And when he was a babe, a child, a shrimp,
     Thus did he strangle serpents in his *manus.* 595
Quoniam he seemeth in minority,
Ergo I come with this apology."

---

533. *fortuna de la guerra:* fortune of war.   545. **hedge-priest:** an illiterate priest.   547. **Abate . . . Novum:** i.e., except
for a rare throw of the dice.   551. **libbard's . . . knee:** i.e., the representation of a leopard's head sewed onto the knee of
the breeches. The point of the jest is now lost.   568. **right:** straight. Alexander's head was set awry.   579. **painted cloth.**
Painted cloths were hung for decoration upon the walls of Elizabethan houses, and the Nine Worthies were a common subject.   580. **lion.** The arms of Alexander bore a lion holding a battle-axe.   581. **Ajax.** A pun on *a jakes,* i.e., a privy.   589.
o'erparted: given too hard a part.   593. *canus:* dog (canis).   595. *manus:* hands.   596. *Quoniam:* since.   597. *Ergo:* therefore.

[*Aside.*] Keep some state in thy exit, and vanish.
                             [*Moth retires.*]

"Judas I am," —
Dum. A Judas!   600
Hol. Not Iscariot, sir.
"Judas I am, ycliped Maccabæus."
Dum. Judas Maccabæus clipt is plain Judas.
Bir. A kissing traitor. How art thou prov'd
    Judas?
Hol. "Judas I am," —   605
Dum. The more shame for you, Judas.
Hol. What mean you, sir?
Boyet. To make Judas hang himself.
Hol. Begin, sir; you are my elder.
Bir. Well follow'd: Judas was hang'd on an elder.
Hol. I will not be put out of countenance. 611
Bir. Because thou hast no face.
Hol. What is this?
Boyet. A cittern-head.
Dum. The head of a bodkin.   615
Bir. A Death's face in a ring.
Long. The face of an old Roman coin, scarce seen.
Boyet. The pommel of Cæsar's falchion.
Dum. The carv'd-bone face on a flask.
Bir. Saint George's half-cheek in a brooch. 620
Dum. Ay, and in a brooch of lead.
Bir. Ay, and worn in the cap of a tooth-drawer.
And now forward; for we have put thee in counte-
    nance.
Hol. You have put me out of countenance.
Bir. False; we have given thee faces.   625
Hol. But you have out-fac'd them all.
Bir. An thou wert a lion, we would do so.
Boyet. Therefore, as he is an ass, let him go.
And so adieu, sweet Jude! Nay, why dost thou
    stay?
Dum. For the latter end of his name.   630
Bir. For the ass to the Jude; give it him. Jud-as,
    away!
Hol. This is not generous, not gentle, not humble.
Boyet. A light for Monsieur Judas! It grows
    dark, he may stumble.   [*Hol. retires.*]
Prin. Alas, poor Maccabæus, how hath he been
    baited!

      Enter Braggart [ARMADO, *for Hector*].

Bir. Hide thy head, Achilles; here comes 635
Hector in arms.
Dum. Though my mocks come home by me, I
will now be merry.
King. Hector was but a Troyan in respect of
this.   640
Boyet. But is this Hector?

King. I think Hector was not so clean-timber'd.
Long. His leg is too big for Hector's.
Dum. More calf, certain.   645
Boyet. No; he is best indued in the small.
Bir. This cannot be Hector.
Dum. He's a god or a painter; for he makes faces.
Arm. "The armipotent Mars, of lances the al-
    mighty,   650
Gave Hector a gift," —
Dum. A gilt nutmeg.
Bir. A lemon.
Long. Stuck with cloves.
Dum. No, cloven.   655
Arm. Peace! —
"The armipotent Mars, of lances the almighty,
    Gave Hector a gift, the heir of Ilion;
A man so breathed, that certain he would fight,
    yea,
    From morn till night, out of his pavilion. 660
I am that flower," —
Dum.   That mint.
Long.   That columbine.
Arm. Sweet Lord Longaville, rein thy tongue.
Long. I must rather give it the rein, for it runs
against Hector.
Dum. Ay, and Hector's a greyhound.   665
Arm. The sweet war-man is dead and rotten;
sweet chucks, beat not the bones of the buried.
When he breathed, he was a man. But I will for-
ward with my device. [*To the Princess.*] Sweet
royalty, bestow on me the sense of hearing. 670
Prin. Speak, brave Hector; we are much de-
lighted.
Arm. I do adore thy sweet grace's slipper.
Boyet. Loves her by the foot.
Dum. He may not by the yard.   676
Arm. "This Hector far surmounted Hanni-
bal," —
Cost. The party is gone, fellow Hector, she is
gone; she is two months on her way.
Arm. What meanest thou?   680
Cost. Faith, unless you play the honest Troyan,
the poor wench is cast away. She's quick; the
child brags in her belly already. 'Tis yours.
Arm. Dost thou infamonize me among poten-
tates? Thou shalt die.   685
Cost. Then shall Hector be whipp'd for Jaque-
netta that is quick by him and hang'd for Pompey
that is dead by him.
Dum. Most rare Pompey!
Boyet. Renowned Pompey!   690
Bir. Greater than great, great, great, great
Pompey! Pompey the Huge!

614. **cittern:** cithern, guitar. 615. **bodkin:** dagger. 618. **falchion:** sword. 620. **half-cheek:** profile. 640. **Troyan:** Trojan, ordinary good fellow. 642. **clean-timber'd:** well built. 659. **breathed:** in good wind. 670. After *hearing* QFf insert *Berowne steppes forth* as a stage-direction. Some edd. add to this "and whispers to Costard," supposing that he suggests Costard's charge in l. 678. But seven lines hardly give time for so elaborate a communication. 678. **party:** i.e., Jacquenetta. In QFf *The . . . gone* is printed as a stage-direction. 684. **infamonize:** defame.

Dum. Hector trembles.

Bir. Pompey is moved.   More Ates, more Ates! stir them on! stir them on!   695

Dum. Hector will challenge him.

Bir. Ay, if 'a have no more man's blood in his belly than will sup a flea.

Arm. By the north pole, I do challenge thee.

Cost. I will not fight with a pole like a   700 northern man; I'll slash; I'll do it by the sword. I bepray you, let me borrow my arms again.

Dum. Room for the incensed Worthies!

Cost. I'll do it in my shirt.

Dum. Most resolute Pompey!   705

Moth. Master, let me take you a button-hole lower.   Do you not see Pompey is uncasing for the combat?   What mean you?   You will lose your reputation.

Arm. Gentlemen and soldiers, pardon me; I will not combat in my shirt.   711

Dum. You may not deny it; Pompey hath made the challenge.

Arm. Sweet bloods, I both may and will.

Bir. What reason have you for't?   715

Arm. The naked truth of it is, I have no shirt; I go woolward for penance.

Boyet. True, and it was enjoined him in Rome for want of linen; since when, I'll be sworn, he wore none but a dishclout of Jaquenetta's, and that 'a wears next his heart for a favour.   722

Enter a Messenger, Monsieur MERCADE.

Mer. God save you, madam!

Prin. Welcome, Mercade;
But that thou interruptest our merriment.   725

Mer. I am sorry, madam; for the news I bring Is heavy in my tongue.   The King, your father —

Prin. Dead, for my life!

Mer. Even so; my tale is told.   729

Bir. Worthies, away! The scene begins to cloud.

Arm. For mine own part, I breathe free breath. I have seen the day of wrong through the little hole of discretion, and I will right myself like a soldier.   [*Exeunt Worthies.* 735

King. How fares your majesty?

Prin. Boyet, prepare; I will away to-night.

King. Madam, not so; I do beseech you, stay.

Prin. Prepare, I say. I thank you, gracious lords,
For all your fair endeavours; and entreat,   740
Out of a new-sad soul, that you vouchsafe
In your rich wisdom to excuse or hide
The liberal opposition of our spirits,

If over-boldly we have borne ourselves
In the converse of breath.   Your gentleness   745
Was guilty of it.   Farewell, worthy lord!
A heavy heart bears not a humble tongue.
Excuse me so, coming too short of thanks
For my great suit so easily obtain'd.

King. The extreme parts of time extremely forms
All causes to the purpose of his speed,   751
And often, at his very loose, decides
That which long process could not arbitrate.
And though the mourning brow of progeny
Forbid the smiling courtesy of love   755
The holy suit which fain it would convince,
Yet, since love's argument was first on foot,
Let not the cloud of sorrow justle it
From what it purpos'd; since, to wail friends lost
Is not by much so wholesome-profitable   760
As to rejoice at friends but newly found.

Prin. I understand you not; my griefs are double.

Bir. Honest plain words best pierce the ear of
        grief;
And by these badges understand the King.
For your fair sakes have we neglected time,   765
Play'd foul play with our oaths.   Your beauty,
        ladies,
Hath much deform'd us, fashioning our humours
Even to the opposed end of our intents;
And what in us hath seem'd ridiculous, —
As love is full of unbefitting strains,   770
All wanton as a child, skipping, and vain,
Form'd by the eye and therefore, like the eye,
Full of [strange] shapes, of habits, and of forms,
Varying in subjects as the eye doth roll
To every varied object in his glance;   775
Which parti-coated presence of loose love
Put on by us, if, in your heavenly eyes,
Have misbecom'd our oaths and gravities,
Those heavenly eyes that look into these faults,
Suggested us to make.   Therefore, ladies,   780
Our love being yours, the error that love makes
Is likewise yours.   We to ourselves prove false,
By being once false for ever to be true
To those that make us both, — fair ladies, you;
And even that falsehood, in itself a sin,   785
Thus purifies itself and turns to grace.

Prin. We have receiv'd your letters full of love;
Your favours, the ambassadors of love,
And, in our maiden council, rated them
At courtship, pleasant jest, and courtesy,   790
As bombast and as lining to the time;
But more devout than this [in] our respects
Have we not been; and therefore met your loves

---

694. **Ates:** goddess of discord.   706. **take ... lower:** (1) help you to strip, (2) humiliate you.   716. **go woolward:** wear woolen next my skin.   743. **liberal:** too free.   745. **converse of breath:** conversation.   747. **humble.** Cf. l. 632, above. 750–51. **The ... speed.** The necessity for speedy decision settles everything speedily.   752. **at ... loose:** at the last moment. "Loose" literally means the discharge of an arrow.   754–56. **And ... convince.** Though a daughter's grief forbids love to press the suit it fain would win.   764. **badges:** tokens.   773. **[strange]** (Capell). *straying* Q.   780. **Suggested:** tempted.   791. **bombast:** padding.   792. **devout:** serious.   **[in]** (Hanmer). Om. Q.   **respects:** attitudes.

In their own fashion, like a merriment.
   Dum. Our letters, madam, show'd much more
       than jest.   795
   Long. So did our looks.
   Ros.   We did not quote them so.
   King. Now, at the latest minute of the hour,
Grant us your loves.
   Prin.   A time, methinks, too short
To make a world-without-end bargain in.
No, no, my lord, your Grace is perjur'd much, 800
Full of dear guiltiness; and therefore this:
If for my love, as there is no such cause,
You will do aught, this shall you do for me:
Your oath I will not trust; but go with speed
To some forlorn and naked hermitage,   805
Remote from all the pleasures of the world;
There stay until the twelve celestial signs
Have brought about the annual reckoning.
If this austere insociable life
Change not your offer made in heat of blood; 810
If frosts and fasts, hard lodging and thin weeds
Nip not the gaudy blossoms of your love
But that it bear this trial, and last love;
Then, at the expiration of the year,
Come challenge me, challenge me by these deserts,
And, by this virgin palm now kissing thine, 816
I will be thine; and till that instant shut
My woeful self up in a mourning house,
Raining the tears of lamentation
For the remembrance of my father's death.   820
If this thou do deny, let our hands part,
Neither intitled in the other's heart.
King. If this, or more than this, I would deny,
   To flatter up these powers of mine with rest,
The sudden hand of death close up mine eye! 825
   Hence [ever] then my heart is in thy breast.
   Bir. And what to me, my love? and what to me?
   Ros. You must be purged too, your sins are
      rack'd,
You are attaint with faults and perjury:
Therefore if you my favour mean to get,   830
A twelvemonth shall you spend, and never rest,
But seek the weary beds of people sick.
   Dum. But what to me, my love? but what to me?
A wife?
   Kath. A beard, fair health, and honesty;
With three-fold love I wish you all these three. 835
   Dum. O, shall I say, I thank you, gentle wife?
   Kath. Not so, my lord; a twelvemonth and a day
I'll mark no words that smooth-fac'd wooers say.
Come when the King doth to my lady come;
Then, if I have much love, I'll give you some. 840
   Dum. I'll serve thee true and faithfully till then.

   Kath. Yet swear not, lest ye be forsworn again.
   Long. What says Maria?
   Mar.   At the twelvemonth's end
I'll change my black gown for a faithful friend.
   Long. I'll stay with patience; but the time is
      long.   845
   Mar. The liker you; few taller are so young.
   Bir. Studies my lady? Mistress, look on me;
Behold the window of my heart, mine eye,
What humble suit attends thy answer there.
Impose some service on me for thy love.   850
   Ros. Oft have I heard of you, my Lord Biron,
Before I saw you; and the world's large tongue
Proclaims you for a man replete with mocks,
Full of comparisons and wounding flouts,
Which you on all estates will execute   855
That lie within the mercy of your wit.
To weed this wormwood from your fruitful brain,
And therewithal to win me, if you please,
Without the which I am not to be won,
You shall this twelvemonth term from day to day
Visit the speechless sick and still converse 86ı
With groaning wretches; and your task shall be,
With all the fierce endeavour of your wit
To enforce the pained impotent to smile.
   Bir. To move wild laughter in the throat of
      death?   865
It cannot be; it is impossible;
Mirth cannot move a soul in agony.
   Ros. Why, that's the way to choke a gibing spirit,
Whose influence is begot of that loose grace
Which shallow laughing hearers give to fools. 870
A jest's prosperity lies in the ear
Of him that hears it, never in the tongue
Of him that makes it; then, if sickly ears,
Deaf'd with the clamours of their own dear groans,
Will hear your idle scorns, continue then, 875
And I will have you and that fault withal;
But if they will not, throw away that spirit,
And I shall find you empty of that fault,
Right joyful of your reformation.
   Bir. A twelvemonth! Well, befall what will
      befall,   880
I'll jest a twelvemonth in a hospital.
   Prin. [*To the King.*] Ay, sweet my lord; and so
      I take my leave.
   King. No, madam; we will bring you on your
      way.
   Bir. Our wooing doth not end like an old play;
Jack hath not Jill. These ladies' courtesy 885
Might well have made our sport a comedy.
   King. Come, sir, it wants a twelvemonth and a
      day,

---

796. **quote:** interpret. 801. **dear:** kind. 813. **last:** continue. 822. **intitled:** having any title. 826. **[ever]** F. *herrite*
Q. 827-32. **And ... sick.** The substance of these lines is found later in this scene. (Cf. note on IV.iii.299-304). 828.
rack'd: stretched out. Rowe conjectures *rank.* 834. **A wife?** QFı give this to Kath. Corrected by Dyce. 852.
the ... tongue: the whole world. 855. **estates:** ranks. 874. **dear:** grievous, intense. 883. **bring:** escort.

And then 'twill end.
    Bir.   That's too long for a play.

          Re-enter Braggart [ARMADO].
    Arm. Sweet majesty, vouchsafe me, —
    Prin. Was not that Hector?
    Dum. The worthy knight of Troy.   890
    Arm. I will kiss thy royal finger, and take leave.
I am a votary; I have vow'd to Jaquenetta to hold
the plough for her sweet love three year. But,
most esteemed greatness, will you hear the dialogue that the two learned men have compiled 895
in praise of the owl and the cuckoo? It should
have followed in the end of our show.
    King. Call them forth quickly; we will do so.
    Arm. Holla! approach.   900

            Enter all.
This side is Hiems, Winter; this Ver, the Spring;
the one maintained by the owl, th' other by the
cuckoo. Ver, begin.

          THE SONG.
    Spring. When daisies pied and violets blue
      And lady-smocks all silver-white   905
And cuckoo-buds of yellow hue
      Do paint the meadows with delight,
The cuckoo then on every tree
Mocks married men; for thus sings he,
             "Cuckoo;   910
Cuckoo, cuckoo," — O word of fear,
Unpleasing to a married ear!

When shepherds pipe on oaten straws
    And merry larks are ploughmen's clocks,
When turtles tread, and rooks, and daws,   915
    And maidens bleach their summer smocks,
The cuckoo then on every tree
Mocks married men; for thus sings he,
           "Cuckoo;
Cuckoo, cuckoo," — O word of fear,   920
Unpleasing to a married ear!

Winter. When icicles hang by the wall
    And Dick the shepherd blows his nail
And Tom bears logs into the hall
    And milk comes frozen home in pail,   925
When blood is nipp'd and ways be [foul],
Then nightly sings the staring owl,
          "Tu-whit, tu-who!" —
A merry note,
While greasy Joan doth keel the pot.   930

When all aloud the wind doth blow
    And coughing drowns the parson's saw
And birds sit brooding in the snow
    And Marian's nose looks red and raw,
When roasted crabs hiss in the bowl,   935
Then nightly sings the staring owl,
          "Tu-whit, tu-who!" —
A merry note,
While greasy Joan doth keel the pot.

    Arm. The words of Mercury are harsh after 940
the songs of Apollo. [You that way: we this way.]
                         [*Exeunt.*

905–906. The order of these lines is reversed in Qq Ff. Corrected by Theobald. 915. **turtles:** turtle-doves. 926. [**foul**]
F. *full* Q. 930. **keel:** cool by stirring. 932. **saw:** maxim. 935. **crabs:** crab apples. 941. [**You ... way**] F. Om. Q.

A Midsummer-Night's Dream

THE FIRST QUARTO of this play appeared in 1600, printed by Thomas Fisher from what certain stage-directions would indicate was a prompter's play-house manuscript. A second Quarto, set up from Q_1 was printed by James Roberts in 1619, but dishonestly dated 1600. The text of the First Folio followed a copy of Roberts's Quarto which apparently had been collated anew with a theatrical prompt-book or had itself served in the play-house, for the Folio text carries more numerous stage-directions as well as divisions into acts and scenes. The present text is based on Q_1.

The date of the play, though not to be ascertained exactly, can at least be discussed in connection with certain definite things. That the play was first devised in celebration of some nobleman's wedding is suggested by the prominence of the marriage of Theseus in the setting, the general masque-like character of the whole, with its abundance of song and dance, and the virtual epithalamium with which it closes. The oblique flattery of Elizabeth in the praise of chastity (I.i.74–75), in the image of the "imperial votaress" in Oberon's vision (II.i.155–165), and in the sovereign courtesy of Theseus toward the faltering tributes of his well-meaning subjects (V.i.89–105) would point further to the actual presence of the Queen. A variety of occasions has been suggested, the most plausible of which is the marriage of the Earl of Derby to Elizabeth Vere at the Court in Greenwich on January 26, 1595. Elizabeth was in fact present at this wedding. Titania's description (II.i.88–114) of the abnormal weather caused by Oberon's brawls reflects in all probability the cold and stormy summer of 1594. Tenable but not wholly convincing is the notion that the fear of the "rude mechanicals" lest the lion affright the ladies (I.ii.76–80) refers to an actual occurrence at the Scottish Court on August 30, 1594, when at a banquet celebrating the baptism of Prince Henry a blackamoor was substituted for the lion which was to have drawn in a triumphal car. To seek an allusion to the death of a particular person in the mourning of the Muses for "the death

of Learning, late deceas'd in beggary" (V.i.52–55) is misguided. Shakespeare may have meant to imply no more than the decline of Learning in general. The matters already noted point to late 1594 or early 1595, and the impression one gains from the style, characterization, and construction of the play and the evidence from the meter fit this date. The lyric beauty and versatility, the crowning grace of this play, may well be the fine flowering of the poetic impulse which was released in Shakespeare by the success of his two poems dedicated to Southampton and the composition of his presumably early sonnets, and which imparted the lyric élan to *Richard II* and *Romeo and Juliet*, plays certainly close to *A Midsummer-Night's Dream* in date.

The text as it has survived carries three possible endings, any of which could be used without raising a question of completeness. The epithalamium and dance of the fairies would make a comely close for a private performance but would be less appropriate upon the public stage. Robin's epilogue, on the other hand, with its petition for applause, seems clearly composed for the general public. Theseus waived the epilogue of the "hempen homespuns," and the play could stop there, but Robin thrust one upon the audience in the theatre! This provision of alternative endings is a proof of adaptation. There is also evidence of revision. In the Quarto printing of V.i.1–84 there is some mislineation which suggests that Shakespeare had added material in the margin of his manuscript without dividing it into pentameter lines and that the compositor incorporated it as he found it. But the argument for extensive revision which has been advanced on the basis of inconsistency in speech-headings is not convincing. Throughout the Quarto some of Robin's speeches are headed *Puck*; some of Oberon's are headed *King*; some of Titania's, *Queen*; some of Bottom's, *Clown*; and in Act V the names of Theseus and Hippolyta give way to *Duke* and *Duch*. The most natural inference from this state of affairs is that Shakespeare, writing rapidly or at intervals and not concerned for consistency in his manuscript, set down in speech-headings whatever designation flashed to mind. But even if one postulates revision from this evidence, it seems odd to do so in the case of some of the alternative headings but not all; yet this is what has been done. Moreover, the texture of the verse assigned to the several characters seems perfectly uniform.

For his plot, which was original, Shakespeare drew upon a variety of sources. For the story of Theseus he had available Chaucer's *Knight's Tale* and Plutarch's *Life of Theseus* in North's translation (1579). From the former he might have got the idea of the marriage festivities of Theseus, the May-day observances, the hunting scene, the name of Philostrate, and some minor details. From the latter he might have taken a few proper names and allusions to the previous adventures of Theseus in love and war. The idea for the love charms he may have found in the *Diana* of Montemayor, whence he took details for the plot of *The Two Gentlemen of Verona*. The story of Pyramus and Thisbe was accessible in Ovid's *Metamorphoses* or in Golding's translation of the same, in Chaucer's *Legend of Good Women*, and in various later forms. The fairy-lore is based mainly on popular tradition, though Ovid applies the name Titania to both Diana and Circe. Oberon had appeared in the romance of *Huon of Bordeaux*, familiar in Shakespeare's time in Berners's translation, and he had already figured on the stage in Robert Greene's *James IV*. Robin Goodfellow, a beneficent goblin who assisted maids and farm hands but who loved mischief and making things "befall preposterously," was widely familiar in English folklore, and though Shakespeare could have read about him in books, he had his mind stored with fairy story in his Warwickshire boyhood.

Like Robin, Bottom and his company of "hempen homespuns" are pure English, even in their names, which derive from the common trades they ply. For example, Bottom the Weaver takes his name from the core or "bottom" of a skein of yarn; Quince is a spelling of "quines" or "quoins," wedges of wood, and thus applicable to a carpenter; Snout is the spout of a kettle, an article familiar enough to tinkers; Snug is a palpably fitting name for a joiner; Flute, the bellows-mender, would also be able to repair the "flutes" or pipes of an organ. The "tedious brief scene" which these "mechanicals" enact is such a one as a group of Elizabethan villagers might contribute to an entertainment in honor of their queen on one of her royal progresses. The awkwardness of their performance would undoubtedly have been in fact as natural, as expected, and as well tolerated as it is made to be in this play. In the play of the Nine Worthies performed by the clowns in *Love's Labour's Lost* Shakespeare had already had his fling at such "theatricals." It is possible that in "the most lamentable comedy" Shakespeare was burlesquing the exaggerated title-pages of the period, such as that of Thomas Preston's play, "A Lamentable Tragedie Mixed Full Of Pleasant Mirth, Containing The Life Of Cambises, King Of Percia," or that of one of his own Quartos, "The Most Excellent and lamentable Tragedie of Romeo and Juliet." That he intended Quince's play for a burlesque of *Romeo and Juliet* has been suggested.

The advance which *A Midsummer-Night's Dream* registers in Shakespeare's development as a dramatist is notable. The mastery of construction is consummate. The several plots are deftly interwoven; the result is organic unity, not merely geometric design. The handling of character shows Shakespeare's growth equally well. The Athenian aristocrats, the fairies, and Quince's crew all live and have their beings convincingly upon their several planes. To be sure, the four distracted lovers are not highly individual, but it must be clear that Shakespeare had no reason for making them so; it was situation, not personality, which concerned him in their case. Theseus, however, is eminently real; a ruler intelligent, energetic, benevolent, fond of sport, with the saving grace of humor, and withal in love. The supreme creation is, of course, Bottom. More real than any of the eccentrics in *Love's Labour's Lost*, he looks forward to Dogberry and Verges whose malapropisms he anticipates. Upon the fairy world Shakespeare worked a transformation into something all his own, and in so doing permanently modified this field of popular fancy. There is perhaps no one achievement of his genius which has had so pervasive an effect as his treatment of fairies in the present play and in Mercutio's speech on Queen Mab, in *Romeo and Juliet*.

A MIDSUMMER-NIGHT'S DREAM

ACT I

[SCENE I. *Athens. The palace of Theseus.*]

Enter THESEUS, HIPPOLYTA, [PHILOSTRATE,]
with others.

The. Now, fair Hippolyta, our nuptial hour
Draws on apace. Four happy days bring in
Another moon; but, O, methinks, how slow
This old moon wanes! She lingers my desires,
Like to a step-dame or a dowager   5
Long withering out a young man's revenue.
    Hip. Four days will quickly steep themselves
in night;
Four nights will quickly dream away the time;
And then the moon, like to a silver bow
New-bent in heaven, shall behold the night   10
Of our solemnities.
    The.   Go, Philostrate,
Stir up the Athenian youth to merriments;

Awake the pert and nimble spirit of mirth;
Turn melancholy forth to funerals:
The pale companion is not for our pomp.   15
                   [*Exit Philostrate.*]
Hippolyta, I woo'd thee with my sword,
And won thy love doing thee injuries;
But I will wed thee in another key,
With pomp, with triumph, and with revelling.

Enter EGEUS, HERMIA, LYSANDER, *and* DEME-
TRIUS.

    Ege. Happy be Theseus, our renowned Duke!
    The. Thanks, good Egeus; what's the news with
thee?   21
    Ege. Full of vexation come I, with complaint
Against my child, my daughter Hermia.
Stand forth, Demetrius. My noble lord,
This man hath my consent to marry her.   25
Stand forth, Lysander: and, my gracious Duke,
This man hath bewitch'd the bosom of my child.

Act I, sc. i, 5. **dowager**: widow with a dowry from an estate. 10. **New-bent** Qq. *Now bent* Ff. 13. **pert**: lively. 15. **companion**: fellow, referring to melancholy. 19. **triumph**: public festivity.

Thou, thou, Lysander, thou hast given her rhymes
And interchang'd love-tokens with my child.
Thou hast by moonlight at her window sung   30
With faining voice verses of faining love,
And stol'n the impression of her fantasy
With bracelets of thy hair, rings, gawds, conceits,
Knacks, trifles, nosegays, sweetmeats, — messengers
Of strong prevailment in unhard'ned youth.   35
With cunning hast thou filch'd my daughter's heart,
Turn'd her obedience, which is due to me,
To stubborn harshness; and, my gracious Duke,
Be it so she will not here before your Grace
Consent to marry with Demetrius,   40
I beg the ancient privilege of Athens,
As she is mine, I may dispose of her;
Which shall be either to this gentleman
Or to her death, according to our law
Immediately provided in that case.   45
   The. What say you, Hermia? Be advis'd, fair maid.
To you your father should be as a god,
One that compos'd your beauties, yea, and one
To whom you are but as a form in wax
By him imprinted, and within his power   50
To leave the figure or disfigure it.
Demetrius is a worthy gentleman.
   Her. So is Lysander.
   The.   In himself he is;
But in this kind, wanting your father's voice,
The other must be held the worthier.   55
   Her. I would my father look'd but with my eyes.
   The. Rather your eyes must with his judgement look.
   Her. I do entreat your Grace to pardon me.
I know not by what power I am made bold,
Nor how it may concern my modesty,   60
In such a presence here to plead my thoughts;
But I beseech your Grace that I may know
The worst that may befall me in this case,
If I refuse to wed Demetrius.
   The. Either to die the death or to abjure   65
For ever the society of men.
Therefore, fair Hermia, question your desires,
Know of your youth, examine well your blood,
Whether, if you yield not to your father's choice,
You can endure the livery of a nun,   70
For aye to be in shady cloister mew'd,
To live a barren sister all your life,
Chanting faint hymns to the cold fruitless moon.
Thrice-blessed they that master so their blood

To undergo such maiden pilgrimage;   75
But earthlier happy is the rose distill'd
Than that which withering on the virgin thorn
Grows, lives, and dies in single blessedness.
   Her. So will I grow, so live, so die, my lord,
Ere I will yield my virgin patent up   80
Unto his lordship, whose unwished yoke
My soul consents not to give sovereignty.
   The. Take time to pause; and, by the next new moon —
The sealing-day betwixt my love and me
For everlasting bond of fellowship —   85
Upon that day either prepare to die
For disobedience to your father's will,
Or else to wed Demetrius, as he would,
Or on Diana's altar to protest
For aye austerity and single life.   90
   Dem. Relent, sweet Hermia; and, Lysander, yield
Thy crazed title to my certain right.
   Lys. You have her father's love, Demetrius,
Let me have Hermia's; do you marry him.
   Ege. Scornful Lysander! true, he hath my love,
And what is mine my love shall render him.   96
And she is mine, and all my right of her
I do estate unto Demetrius.
   Lys. I am, my lord, as well deriv'd as he,
As well possess'd; my love is more than his;   100
My fortunes every way as fairly rank'd,
If not with vantage, as Demetrius';
And, which is more than all these boasts can be,
I am belov'd of beauteous Hermia.
Why should not I then prosecute my right?   105
Demetrius, I'll avouch it to his head,
Made love to Nedar's daughter, Helena,
And won her soul; and she, sweet lady, dotes,
Devoutly dotes, dotes in idolatry,
Upon this spotted and inconstant man.   110
   The. I must confess that I have heard so much,
And with Demetrius thought to have spoke thereof;
But, being over-full of self-affairs,
My mind did lose it. But, Demetrius, come;
And come, Egeus; you shall go with me;   115
I have some private schooling for you both.
For you, fair Hermia, look you arm yourself
To fit your fancies to your father's will;
Or else the law of Athens yields you up —
Which by no means we may extenuate —   120
To death, or to a vow of single life.
Come, my Hippolyta; what cheer, my love?
Demetrius and Egeus, go along.
I must employ you in some business

---

31. **faining:** longing.   32. **stol'n ... fantasy:** captured her fancy (by impressing it with gifts).   33. **gawds:** trinkets.
conceits: devices.   34. **knacks:** knickknacks.   39. **Be it so:** if.   45. **Immediately:** expressly.   51. **disfigure:** obliterate.
54. **in ... kind:** i.e., as a husband. **voice:** approval.   60. **concern:** beseem.   68. **blood:** passion.   69. **Whether.** One
syllable in pronunciation.   71. **mew'd:** shut up (a term from falconry).   80. **patent:** privilege, liberty.   89. **protest:** vow.
92. **crazed:** unsound.   98. **estate unto:** settle upon.   106. **head:** face.   120. **extenuate:** weaken.

Against our nuptial, and confer with you   125
Of something nearly that concerns yourselves.
Ege. With duty and desire we follow you.
        [Exeunt all but Lysander and Hermia.
Lys. How now, my love! why is your cheek so
  pale?
How chance the roses there do fade so fast?
Her. Belike for want of rain, which I could well
Beteem them from the tempest of my eyes.   131
Lys. Ay me! for aught that I could ever read,
Could ever hear by tale or history,
The course of true love never did run smooth;
But, either it was different in blood, —   135
Her. O cross! too high to be enthrall'd to [low].
Lys. Or else misgraffed in respect of years, —
Her. O spite! too old to be engag'd to young.
Lys. Or else it stood upon the choice of friends, —
Her. O hell! to choose love by another's eyes.   140
Lys. Or, if there were a sympathy in choice,
War, death, or sickness did lay siege to it,
Making it momentany as a sound,
Swift as a shadow, short as any dream,
Brief as the lightning in the collied night,   145
That, in a spleen, unfolds both heaven and earth,
And ere a man hath power to say "Behold!"
The jaws of darkness do devour it up:
So quick bright things come to confusion.
Her. If then true lovers have been ever cross'd,
It stands as an edict in destiny.   151
Then let us teach our trial patience,
Because it is a customary cross,
As due to love as thoughts and dreams and sighs,
Wishes and tears, poor Fancy's followers.   155
Lys. A good persuasion; therefore, hear me, Her-
  mia.
I have a widow aunt, a dowager
Of great revenue, and she hath no child.
From Athens is her house remote seven leagues;
And she respects me as her only son.   160
There, gentle Hermia, may I marry thee;
And to that place the sharp Athenian law
Cannot pursue us. If thou lov'st me then,
Steal forth thy father's house to-morrow night;
And in the wood, a league without the town,   165
Where I did meet thee once with Helena
To do observance to a morn of May,
There will I stay for thee.
Her.   My good Lysander!
I swear to thee, by Cupid's strongest bow,
By his best arrow with the golden head,   170
By the simplicity of Venus' doves,
By that which knitteth souls and prospers loves,

And by that fire which burn'd the Carthage queen
When the false Troyan under sail was seen,
By all the vows that ever men have broke,   175
In number more than ever women spoke,
In that same place thou hast appointed me
To-morrow truly will I meet with thee.
Lys. Keep promise, love. Look, here comes
  Helena.

       Enter HELENA.

Her. God speed fair Helena! Whither away? 180
Hel. Call you me fair? That fair again unsay.
Demetrius loves your fair, O happy fair!
Your eyes are lode-stars, and your tongue's sweet
  air
More tuneable than lark to shepherd's ear
When wheat is green, when hawthorn buds appear.
Sickness is catching; O, were favour so,   186
[Yours would] I catch, fair Hermia, ere I go;
My ear should catch your voice, my eye your eye,
My tongue should catch your tongue's sweet mel-
  ody.
Were the world mine, Demetrius being bated, 190
The rest I'll give to be to you translated.
O, teach me how you look, and with what art
You sway the motion of Demetrius' heart.
Her. I frown upon him, yet he loves me still.
Hel. O that your frowns would teach my smiles
  such skill!   195
Her. I give him curses, yet he gives me love.
Hel. O that my prayers could such affection
  move!
Her. The more I hate, the more he follows me.
Hel. The more I love, the more he hateth me.
Her. His folly, Helena, is no fault of mine.
Hel. None, but your beauty. Would that fault
  were mine!   201
Her. Take comfort; he no more shall see my
  face;
Lysander and myself will fly this place.
Before the time I did Lysander see,
Seem'd Athens as a paradise to me;   205
O, then, what graces in my love do dwell,
That he hath turn'd a heaven unto a hell!
Lys. Helen, to you our minds we will unfold.
To-morrow night, when Phœbe doth behold
Her silver visage in the wat'ry glass,   210
Decking with liquid pearl the bladed grass,
A time that lovers' flights doth still conceal,
Through Athens' gates have we devis'd to steal.
Her. And in the wood, where often you and I
Upon faint primrose-beds were wont to lie,   215

---

125. **against:** in anticipation of. 131. **Beteem:** allow. 136. **[low]** (Theobald). *love* Q. 137. **misgraffed:** mismatched.
143. **momentany:** momentary. 145. **collied:** blackened. 146. **spleen:** burst of passion. 150. **ever:** always. 155.
Fancy's: love's. 160. **respects:** regards. 171. **simplicity:** innocence. 173. **Carthage queen:** Dido, who killed herself after
the Trojan Aeneas had deserted her. 182. **fair:** beauty. 186. **favour:** beauty. 187. **[Yours would]** (Hanmer). *Your*
words Q. 190. **bated:** excepted. 191. **translated:** transformed. 209. **Phœbe:** Diana, the moon. 215. **faint:** pale.

Emptying our bosoms of their counsel [sweet].
There my Lysander and myself shall meet;
And thence from Athens turn away our eyes,
To seek new friends and [stranger companies].
Farewell, sweet playfellow! Pray thou for us;
And good luck grant thee thy Demetrius!   221
Keep word, Lysander; we must starve our sight
From lovers' food till morrow deep midnight.
 Lys. I will, my Hermia.   [*Exit Herm.*
       Helena, adieu:
As you on him, Demetrius dote on you!   225
          [*Exit.*
 Hel. How happy some o'er other some can be!
Through Athens I am thought as fair as she.
But what of that? Demetrius thinks not so;
He will not know what all but he do know;
And as he errs, doting on Hermia's eyes,   230
So I, admiring of his qualities.
Things base and vile, holding no quantity,
Love can transpose to form and dignity.
Love looks not with the eyes but with the mind,
And therefore is wing'd Cupid painted blind.   235
Nor hath Love's mind of any judgement taste;
Wings and no eyes figure unheedy haste;
And therefore is Love said to be a child,
Because in choice he is so oft beguil'd.
As waggish boys in game themselves forswear,   240
So the boy Love is perjur'd every where;
For ere Demetrius look'd on Hermia's eyne,
He hail'd down oaths that he was only mine;
And when this hail some heat from Hermia felt,
So he dissolv'd, and show'rs of oaths did melt.   245
I will go tell him of fair Hermia's flight;
Then to the wood will he to-morrow night
Pursue her; and for this intelligence
If I have thanks, it is a dear expense.
But herein mean I to enrich my pain,   250
To have his sight thither and back again.
          [*Exit.*

[SCENE II. *Athens. Quince's house.*]

Enter QUINCE, SNUG, BOTTOM, FLUTE, SNOUT, *and*
    STARVELING.

 Quin. Is all our company here?
 Bot. You were best to call them generally, man
by man, according to the scrip.
 Quin. Here is the scroll of every man's name,
which is thought fit, through all Athens, to play
in our interlude before the Duke and the Duchess, on his wedding-day at night.   7
 Bot. First, good Peter Quince, say what the play

treats on, then read the names of the actors, and so
grow to a point.   10
 Quin. Marry, our play is *The most lamentable
comedy, and most cruel death of Pyramus and
Thisby.*
 Bot. A very good piece of work, I assure you, and
a merry. Now, good Peter Quince, call forth   15
your actors by the scroll. Masters, spread yourselves.
 Quin. Answer as I call you. Nick Bottom, the
weaver.
 Bot. Ready. Name what part I am for, and
proceed.   21
 Quin. You, Nick Bottom, are set down for Pyramus.
 Bot. What is Pyramus? A lover, or a tyrant?
 Quin. A lover, that kills himself most gallant
for love.   26
 Bot. That will ask some tears in the true per-
forming of it. If I do it, let the audience look to
their eyes. I will move storms, I will condole in
some measure. To the rest. Yet my chief humour
is for a tyrant. I could play Ercles rarely, or a   31
part to tear a cat in, to make all split.
  "The raging rocks
   And shivering shocks
   Shall break the locks   35
    Of prison gates;
   And Phibbus' car
   Shall shine from far
   And make and mar
    The foolish Fates."   40
This was lofty! Now name the rest of the players.
This is Ercles' vein, a tyrant's vein; a lover is more
condoling.
 Quin. Francis Flute, the bellows-mender.
 Flu. Here, Peter Quince.   45
 Quin. Flute, you must take Thisby on you.
 Flu. What is Thisby? A wand'ring knight?
 Quin. It is the lady that Pyramus must love.
 Flu. Nay, faith, let not me play a woman; I have
a beard coming.   50
 Quin. That's all one; you shall play it in a mask,
and you may speak as small as you will.
 Bot. An I may hide my face, let me play Thisby
too. I'll speak in a monstrous little voice, "Thisne!
Thisne! Ah Pyramus, my lover dear! thy Thisby
dear, and lady dear!"   56
 Quin. No, no; you must play Pyramus; and,
Flute, you Thisby.
 Bot. Well, proceed.
 Quin. Robin Starveling, the tailor.   60
 Star. Here, Peter Quince.

216. **[sweet]** (Theobald). *sweld* Q. 219. **[stranger companies]** (Theobald). *strange companions* Q. 237. **figure:** symbolize
242. **eyne:** eyes. 248. **intelligence:** news. 249. **dear expense:** costly gain. 251. **his sight:** sight of him.
 Sc. ii, 2. generally: Bottom's error for *severally.* 3. **scrip:** written list. 10. **grow . . . point:** come to the point. 29.
condole: grieve. 31. **Ercles:** Hercules, a common ranting part in early drama. 31. **make all split,** i.e.. with passion. 37.
Phibbus': Phoebus'. 53. **An:** if.

Quin. Robin Starveling, you must play Thisby's mother. Tom Snout, the tinker.

Snout. Here, Peter Quince.

Quin. You, Pyramus' father; myself, Thisby's father; Snug, the joiner, you, the lion's part; 66 and, I hope, here is a play fitted.

Snug. Have you the lion's part written? Pray you, if it be, give it me, for I am slow of study.

Quin. You may do it extempore, for it is no- 70 thing but roaring.

Bot. Let me play the lion too. I will roar, that I will do any man's heart good to hear me. I will roar, that I will make the Duke say, "Let him roar again, let him roar again." 75

Quin. An you should do it too terribly, you would fright the Duchess and the ladies, that they would shriek; and that were enough to hang us all.

All. That would hang us, every mother's son. 80

Bot. I grant you, friends, if you should fright the ladies out of their wits, they would have no more discretion but to hang us; but I will aggravate my voice so that I will roar you as gently as any suck- ing dove; I will roar you an 'twere any night- 85 ingale.

Quin. You can play no part but Pyramus; for Pyramus is a sweet-fac'd man; a proper man, as one shall see in a summer's day; a most lovely gentle- man-like man: therefore you must needs play 90 Pyramus.

Bot. Well, I will undertake it. What beard were I best to play it in?

Quin. Why, what you will.

Bot. I will discharge it in either your straw- 95 colour beard, your orange-tawny beard, your pur- ple-in-grain beard, or your French-crown-colour beard, your perfect yellow.

Quin. Some of your French crowns have no hair at all, and then you will play barefac'd. But, 100 masters, here are your parts; and I am to entreat you, request you, and desire you, to con them by to- morrow night; and meet me in the palace wood, a mile without the town, by moonlight. There will we rehearse, for if we meet in the city, we shall be dogg'd with company, and our devices known. 106 In the meantime I will draw a bill of properties, such as our play wants. I pray you, fail me not.

Bot. We will meet; and there we may rehearse 110 most obscenely and courageously. Take pains; be perfect; adieu.

Quin. At the Duke's oak we meet.

Bot. Enough; hold or cut bow-strings.

[*Exeunt.*

ACT II

[SCENE I. *A wood near Athens.*]

Enter a FAIRY *at one door and* ROBIN GOODFELLOW *at another.*

Robin. How now, spirit! whither wander you?

Fai. Over hill, over dale,
　　Thorough bush, thorough brier,
　Over park, over pale,
　　Thorough flood, thorough fire, 5
I do wander every where,
Swifter than the moon's sphere;
And I serve the fairy Queen,
To dew her orbs upon the green.
The cowslips tall her pensioners be; 10
In their gold coats spots you see;
Those be rubies, fairy favours,
In those freckles live their savours.
I must go seek some dewdrops here
And hang a pearl in every cowslip's ear. 15
Farewell, thou lob of spirits; I'll be gone.
Our Queen and all her elves come here anon.

Robin. The King doth keep his revels here to-
　　night;
Take heed the Queen come not within his sight;
For Oberon is passing fell and wrath, 20
Because that she as her attendant hath
A lovely boy stolen from an Indian king.
She never had so sweet a changeling;
And jealous Oberon would have the child
Knight of his train, to trace the forests wild; 25
But she perforce withholds the loved boy,
Crowns him with flowers, and makes him all her joy:
And now they never meet in grove or green,
By fountain clear, or spangled starlight sheen,
But they do square, that all their elves for fear 30
Creep into acorn-cups and hide them there.

Fai. Either I mistake your shape and making
　　quite,
Or else you are that shrewd and knavish sprite
Call'd Robin Goodfellow. Are not you he
That frights the maidens of the villagery, 35
Skim milk, and sometimes labour in the quern,
And bootless make the breathless housewife churn,
And sometime make the drink to bear no barm,
Mislead night-wanderers, laughing at their harm?
Those that Hobgoblin call you, and sweet Puck, 40

---

83. **aggravate**: Bottom's mistake for *moderate.* 88. **proper**: handsome. 95–98. Bottom, the Weaver, refers glibly to several familiar dyes. 111. **obscenely**: Bottom's mistake for *obscurely.* 114. **hold ... bow-strings.** Apparently an archer's expression. Bottom probably means, "Keep your appointments or everything is off."

Act II, Sc. i, S.D. ROBIN GOODFELLOW. This character is described as a Puck, a name previously applied in English folklore to a minor order of evil spirits. Shakespeare recreates him as he does the fairies. 9. **orbs**: fairy rings. 10. **pensioners.** Elizabeth's bodyguards were called gentlemen pensioners. 13. **savours**: perfumes. 16. **lob**: lout. 20. **passing ... wrath**: exceedingly angry and wrathful. 23. **changeling**: a child exchanged by fairies. 30. **square**: quarrel. **that**: so that. 33. **shrewd**: mischievous. 36. **quern**: handmill. 38. **barm**: yeast.

You do their work, and they shall have good luck.
Are not you he?
    Robin.   Thou speakest aright;
I am that merry wanderer of the night.
I jest to Oberon and make him smile
When I a fat and bean-fed horse beguile,   45
Neighing in likeness of a filly foal;
And sometime lurk I in a gossip's bowl,
In very likeness of a roasted crab,
And when she drinks, against her lips I bob
And on her withered dewlap pour the ale.   50
The wisest aunt, telling the saddest tale,
Sometime for three-foot stool mistaketh me.
Then slip I from her bum, down topples she,
And "tailor" cries, and falls into a cough;
And then the whole quire hold their hips and laugh,
And waxen in their mirth, and neeze, and swear 56
A merrier hour was never wasted there.
But, room, fairy! here comes Oberon.
    Fai. And here my mistress.   Would that he were
        gone!

Enter the King of Fairies [OBERON] *at one door with
his train; and the Queen* [TITANIA] *at another with
hers.*

    Obe. Ill met by moonlight, proud Titania.   60
    Tita. What, jealous Oberon!   Fairies, skip hence:
I have forsworn his bed and company.
    Obe. Tarry, rash wanton!   Am not I thy lord?
    Tita. Then I must be thy lady; but I know
When thou hast stolen away from fairy land,   65
And in the shape of Corin sat all day,
Playing on pipes of corn and versing love
To amorous Phillida.   Why art thou here,
Come from the farthest steep of India?
But that, forsooth, the bouncing Amazon,   70
Your buskin'd mistress and your warrior love,
To Theseus must be wedded, and you come
To give their bed joy and prosperity.
    Obe. How canst thou thus for shame, Titania,
Glance at my credit with Hippolyta,   75
Knowing I know thy love to Theseus?
Didst thou not lead him through the glimmering
    night
From Perigenia, whom he ravished?
And make him with fair Ægle break his faith,
With Ariadne, and Antiopa?   80

    Tita. These are the forgeries of jealousy;
And never, since the middle summer's spring,
Met we on hill, in dale, forest or mead,
By paved fountain or by rushy brook,
Or in the beached margent of the sea,   85
To dance our ringlets to the whistling wind,
But with thy brawls thou hast disturb'd our sport.
Therefore the winds, piping to us in vain,
As in revenge, have suck'd up from the sea
Contagious fogs; which, falling in the land,   90
Hath every pelting river made so proud
That they have overborne their continents.
The ox hath therefore stretch'd his yoke in vain,
The ploughman lost his sweat, and the green corn
Hath rotted ere his youth attain'd a beard.   95
The fold stands empty in the drowned field,
And crows are fatted with the murrain flock,
The nine men's morris is fill'd up with mud,
And the quaint mazes in the wanton green
For lack of tread are undistinguishable.   100
The human mortals want their winter [cheer];
No night is now with hymn or carol blest.
Therefore the moon, the governess of floods,
Pale in her anger, washes all the air,
That rheumatic diseases do abound.   105
And thorough this distemperature we see
The seasons alter: hoary-headed frosts
Fall in the fresh lap of the crimson rose,
And on old Hiems' thin and icy crown
An odorous chaplet of sweet summer buds   110
Is, as in mockery, set; the spring, the summer,
The childing autumn, angry winter, change
Their wonted liveries; and the mazed world,
By their increase, now knows not which is which.
And this same progeny of evils comes   115
From our debate, from our dissension;
We are their parents and original.
    Obe. Do you amend it then; it lies in you.
Why should Titania cross her Oberon?
I do but beg a little changeling boy   120
To be my henchman.
    Tita.   Set your heart at rest;
The fairy land buys not the child of me.
His mother was a vot'ress of my order,
And, in the spiced Indian air, by night,
Full often hath she gossip'd by my side,   125
And sat with me on Neptune's yellow sands,

    47. **gossip's bowl:** christening-cup. Gossip is used here in the original sense of godmother. 48. **crab:** crab apple. 50. **dewlap:** loose skin on the neck. 51. **aunt:** old woman. **saddest:** soberest. 54. **"tailor" cries.** Meaning obscure. 56. **waxen:** increase. **neeze:** sneeze. 66–68. **Corin . . . Phillida:** names traditional in pastoral poetry. 71. **buskin'd:** wearing high boots. 75. **glance at:** cast reflections on. 79–80. **Ægle . . . Ariadne . . . Antiopa.** These names of women whom Theseus had loved Shakespeare found in North's *Plutarch.* Antiope is sometimes identified with Hippolyta, but in this speech they are treated as two. 82. **middle summer's spring:** beginning of midsummer. 85. **in:** on. **margent:** margin. 86. **ringlets:** circular dances. 87. **thy brawls.** See Introduction. 91. **pelting:** paltry. Ff read *petty.* 92. **continents:** banks. 97. **murrain:** diseased. 98. **nine men's morris:** a game played in squares marked out on the turf of the village green; something like hopscotch. 99. **mazes:** figures. **wanton:** luxuriant. 101. **[cheer]** (Theobald conj.). *heere* Q. 106. **distemperature:** disturbance. 109. **Hiems:** the god of winter. 112. **childing:** fruitful. 113. **mazed:** amazed. 117. **original:** origin. 121. **henchman:** page.

Marking th' embarked traders on the flood,
When we have laugh'd to see the sails conceive
And grow big-bellied with the wanton wind;
Which she with pretty and with swimming gait
Following, her womb then rich with my young
      squire,   131
Would imitate, and sail upon the land
To fetch me trifles, and return again,
As from a voyage, rich with merchandise.
But she, being mortal, of that boy did die;   135
And for her sake do I rear up her boy,
And for her sake I will not part with him.
    Obe. How long within this wood intend you stay?
    Tita. Perchance till after Theseus' wedding-day.
If you will patiently dance in our round   140
And see our moonlight revels, go with us;
If not, shun me, and I will spare your haunts.
    Obe. Give me that boy, and I will go with
thee.
    Tita. Not for thy fairy kingdom. Fairies, away!
We shall chide downright, if I longer stay.   145
                   [*Exit* [*Titania with her train*].
    Obe. Well, go thy way; thou shalt not from this
      grove
Till I torment thee for this injury.
My gentle Puck, come hither. Thou rememb'rest
Since once I sat upon a promontory,
And heard a mermaid on a dolphin's back   150
Uttering such dulcet and harmonious breath
That the rude sea grew civil at her song,
And certain stars shot madly from their spheres,
To hear the sea-maid's music?
    Robin.   I remember.
    Obe. That very time I saw, but thou couldst not,
Flying between the cold moon and the earth,   156
Cupid all arm'd. A certain aim he took
At a fair vestal throned by the west,
And loos'd his love-shaft smartly from his bow,
As it should pierce a hundred thousand hearts;
But I might see young Cupid's fiery shaft   161
Quench'd in the chaste beams of the wat'ry moon,
And the imperial vot'ress passed on,
In maiden meditation, fancy-free.
Yet mark'd I where the bolt of Cupid fell.   165
It fell upon a little western flower,
Before milk-white, now purple with love's wound,
And maidens call it love-in-idleness.
Fetch me that flower, the herb I shew'd thee once.
The juice of it on sleeping eye-lids laid   170
Will make or man or woman madly dote
Upon the next live creature that it sees.
Fetch me this herb; and be thou here again
Ere the leviathan can swim a league.

    Robin. I'll put a girdle round about the earth   175
In forty minutes.   [*Exit.*]
    Obe.   Having once this juice,
I'll watch Titania when she is asleep,
And drop the liquor of it in her eyes.
The next thing then she waking looks upon,
Be it on lion, bear, or wolf, or bull,   180
On meddling monkey, or on busy ape,
She shall pursue it with the soul of love;
And ere I take this charm from off her sight,
As I can take it with another herb,
I'll make her render up her page to me.   185
But who comes here? I am invisible;
And I will overhear their conference.

    Enter DEMETRIUS, HELENA *following him.*

    Dem. I love thee not, therefore pursue me not.
Where is Lysander and fair Hermia?
The one I'll stay, the other stayeth me.   190
Thou told'st me they were stol'n unto this wood;
And here am I, and wood within this wood
Because I cannot meet my Hermia.
Hence, get thee gone, and follow me no more.
    Hel. You draw me, you hard-hearted adamant;
But yet you draw not iron, for my heart   196
Is true as steel. Leave you your power to draw,
And I shall have no power to follow you.
    Dem. Do I entice you? Do I speak you fair?
Or, rather, do I not in plainest truth   200
Tell you, I do not nor I cannot love you?
    Hel. And even for that do I love you the more.
I am your spaniel, and, Demetrius,
The more you beat me, I will fawn on you.
Use me but as your spaniel, spurn me, strike me, 205
Neglect me, lose me; only give me leave,
Unworthy as I am, to follow you.
What worser place can I beg in your love,—
And yet a place of high respect with me,—
Than to be used as you use your dog?   210
    Dem. Tempt not too much the hatred of my
      spirit,
For I am sick when I do look on thee.
    Hel. And I am sick when I look not on you.
    Dem. You do impeach your modesty too much,
To leave the city and commit yourself   215
Into the hands of one that loves you not;
To trust the opportunity of night
And the ill counsel of a desert place
With the rich worth of your virginity.
    Hel. Your virtue is my privilege. For that   220
It is not night when I do see your face,
Therefore I think I am not in the night;
Nor doth this wood lack worlds of company,

148–168. See Introduction. 149. **Since:** when. 158. **vestal:** virgin. 168. **love-in-idleness:** pansy. 190. **stay . . . stayeth.** Thirlby's conjecture "slay . . . slayeth" has been followed by many editors. 192. **wood:** mad. 195. **adamant:** probably with both senses of "lode-stone" (magnet) and "hardest metal." 197. **Leave:** give up. 220. **privilege:** safeguard. **For that:** because.

For you in my respect are all the world.
Then how can it be said I am alone,   225
When all the world is here to look on me?

Dem. I'll run from thee and hide me in the brakes,
And leave thee to the mercy of wild beasts.

Hel. The wildest hath not such a heart as you.
Run when you will, the story shall be chang'd:
Apollo flies, and Daphne holds the chase;   231
The dove pursues the griffin; the mild hind
Makes speed to catch the tiger: bootless speed,
When cowardice pursues and valour flies.

Dem. I will not stay thy questions; let me go;   235
Or, if thou follow me, do not believe
But I shall do thee mischief in the wood.

Hel. Ay, in the temple, in the town, the field,
You do me mischief. Fie, Demetrius!
Your wrongs do set a scandal on my sex.   240
We cannot fight for love, as men may do.
We should be woo'd and were not made to woo.
[Exit Dem.]
I'll follow thee and make a heaven of hell,
To die upon the hand I love so well.   *[Exit.*

Obe. Fare thee well, nymph. Ere he do leave this grove,   245
Thou shalt fly him and he shall seek thy love.

Re-enter [ROBIN GOODFELLOW].

Hast thou the flower there? Welcome, wanderer.

Robin. Ay, there it is.

Obe.   I pray thee, give it me.
I know a bank where the wild thyme blows,
Where oxlips and the nodding violet grows,   250
Quite over-canopi'd with luscious woodbine,
With sweet musk-roses and with eglantine.
There sleeps Titania sometime of the night,
Lull'd in these flowers with dances and delight;
And there the snake throws her enamell'd skin,   255
Weed wide enough to wrap a fairy in;
And with the juice of this I'll streak her eyes,
And make her full of hateful fantasies.
Take thou some of it, and seek through this grove.
A sweet Athenian lady is in love   260
With a disdainful youth. Anoint his eyes,
But do it when the next thing he espies
May be the lady. Thou shalt know the man
By the Athenian garments he hath on.
Effect it with some care, that he may prove   265
More fond on her than she upon her love;
And look thou meet me ere the first cock crow.

Robin. Fear not, my lord, your servant shall do so.   *[Exeunt.*

[SCENE II. *Another part of the wood.*]

Enter TITANIA, *with her train.*

Tita. Come, now a roundel and a fairy song;
Then, for the third part of a minute, hence,
Some to kill cankers in the musk-rose buds,
Some war with rere-mice for their leathern wings   4
To make my small elves coats, and some keep back
The clamorous owl that nightly hoots and wonders
At our quaint spirits. Sing me now asleep;
Then to your offices and let me rest.

THE FAIRIES *sing.*

[1. *Fairy.*] "You spotted snakes with double tongue,
Thorny hedgehogs, be not seen;   10
Newts and blind-worms, do no wrong,
Come not near our fairy queen."

[*Cho.*] "Philomel, with melody
Sing in our sweet lullaby;
Lulla, lulla, lullaby; lulla, lulla, lullaby.   15
Never harm
Nor spell nor charm
Come our lovely lady nigh.
So, good night, with lullaby."

1. Fairy. "Weaving spiders, come not here;   20
Hence, you long-legg'd spinners, hence!
Beetles black, approach not near;
Worm nor snail, do no offence."

[*Cho.*] "Philomel, with melody," etc.

2. Fairy. Hence, away! now all is well.   25
One aloof stand sentinel.
[Exeunt Fairies.] Titania sleeps.

Enter OBERON [*and squeezes the flower on Titania's eyelids*].

Obe. What thou seest when thou dost wake,
Do it for thy true-love take,
Love and languish for his sake.
Be it ounce, or cat, or bear,   30
Pard, or boar with bristled hair,
In thy eye that shall appear
When thou wak'st, it is thy dear.
Wake when some vile thing is near.
[Exit.]

Enter LYSANDER *and* HERMIA.

Lys. Fair love, you faint with wand'ring in the wood;   35
And to speak troth, I have forgot our way.

---

224. **in my respect:** to me. 231. **Apollo ... chase.** According to the myth, Apollo pursued Daphne, but here the situation is reversed. 232. **griffin:** a monster having a lion's body and an eagle's head. **hind:** female of the red deer. 235. **questions:** arguments. 244. **upon:** by. 254. **dances and delight:** delightful dances. 256. **Weed:** garment. 257. **streak:** stroke.

Sc. ii, 1. **roundel:** circular dance. 3. **cankers:** cankerworms. 4. **rere-mice:** bats. 7. **quaint:** dainty. 11. **Newts:** water lizards. 13. **Philomel:** the nightingale. 30. **ounce:** lynx. **cat:** wildcat. 31. **Pard:** leopard.

We'll rest us, Hermia, if you think it good,
And tarry for the comfort of the day.
   Her. Be it so, Lysander. Find you out a bed;
For I upon this bank will rest my head.   40
   Lys. One turf shall serve as pillow for us both;
One heart, one bed, two bosoms and one troth.
   Her. Nay, good Lysander; for my sake, my dear,
Lie further off yet; do not lie so near.
   Lys. O, take the sense, sweet, of my innocence!
Love takes the meaning in love's conference.   46
I mean, that my heart unto yours is knit
So that but one heart we can make of it;
Two bosoms interchained with an oath,
So then two bosoms and a single troth.   50
Then by your side no bed-room me deny;
For lying so, Hermia, I do not lie.
   Her. Lysander riddles very prettily.
Now much beshrew my manners and my pride,
If Hermia meant to say Lysander lied.   55
But, gentle friend, for love and courtesy
Lie further off; in humane modesty,
Such separation as may well be said
Becomes a virtuous bachelor and a maid,
So far be distant; and, good night, sweet friend.   60
Thy love ne'er alter till thy sweet life end!
   Lys. Amen, amen, to that fair prayer, say I;
And then end life when I end loyalty!
Here is my bed; sleep give thee all his rest!
   Her. With half that wish the wisher's eyes be
     press'd!   *[They sleep.* 65

       Enter [ROBIN GOODFELLOW].

   Robin. Through the forest have I gone,
     But Athenian found I none,
     On whose eyes I might approve
     This flower's force in stirring love.
     Night and silence — Who is here?   70
     Weeds of Athens he doth wear!
     This is he, my master said,
     Despised the Athenian maid;
     And here the maiden, sleeping sound,
     On the dank and dirty ground.   75
     Pretty soul! she durst not lie
     Near this lack-love, this kill-courtesy.
     Churl, upon thy eyes I throw
     All the power this charm doth owe.
     When thou wak'st, let love forbid   80
     Sleep his seat on thy eyelid;
     So awake when I am gone,
     For I must now to Oberon.   *[Exit.*

     Enter DEMETRIUS *and* HELENA, *running*.

   Hel. Stay, though thou kill me, sweet Demetrius.
   Dem. I charge thee, hence, and do not haunt me
     thus.   85

   Hel. O, wilt thou darkling leave me? Do not so.
   Dem. Stay, on thy peril; I alone will go.
                                  [Exit.
   Hel. O, I am out of breath in this fond chase!
The more my prayer, the lesser is my grace.
Happy is Hermia, wheresoe'er she lies,   90
For she hath blessed and attractive eyes.
How came her eyes so bright? Not with salt tears;
If so, my eyes are oft'ner wash'd than hers.
No, no, I am as ugly as a bear,
For beasts that meet me run away for fear;   95
Therefore no marvel though Demetrius
Do, as a monster, fly my presence thus.
What wicked and dissembling glass of mine
Made me compare with Hermia's sphery eyne?
But who is here? Lysander! on the ground!   100
Dead? or asleep? I see no blood, no wound.
Lysander, if you live, good sir, awake.
   Lys. *[Awaking.]* And run through fire I will for
     thy sweet sake.
Transparent Helena! Nature shows art,
That through thy bosom makes me see thy heart.
Where is Demetrius? O, how fit a word   106
Is that vile name to perish on my sword!
   Hel. Do not say so, Lysander; say not so.
What though he love your Hermia? Lord, what
     though?
Yet Hermia still loves you; then be content.   110
   Lys. Content with Hermia! No; I do repent
The tedious minutes I with her have spent.
Not Hermia but Helena I love.
Who will not change a raven for a dove?
The will of man is by his reason sway'd;   **115**
And reason says you are the worthier maid.
Things growing are not ripe until their season,
So I, being young, till now ripe not to reason;
And touching now the point of human skill,
Reason becomes the marshal to my will   120
And leads me to your eyes, where I o'erlook
Love's stories written in Love's richest book.
   Hel. Wherefore was I to this keen mockery born?
When at your hands did I deserve this scorn?
Is't not enough, is't not enough, young man,   125
That I did never, no, nor never can,
Deserve a sweet look from Demetrius' eye,
But you must flout my insufficiency?
Good troth, you do me wrong, good sooth you do,
In such disdainful manner me to woo.   130
But fare you well; perforce I must confess
I thought you lord of more true gentleness.
O, that a lady, of one man refus'd,
Should of another therefore be abus'd!   *[Exit.*
   Lys. She sees not Hermia. Hermia, sleep thou
     there;   135
And never mayst thou come Lysander near!

---

46. **Love . . . conference**: Love gives lovers true understanding. 68. **approve**: test. 79. **owe**: own. 86. **darkling**: in the dark. 88. **fond**: foolish. 89. **my grace**: the favor I receive. 99. **sphery eyne**: starry eyes. 119. **point . . . skill**: summit of human discernment.

For as a surfeit of the sweetest things
The deepest loathing to the stomach brings,
Or as the heresies that men do leave
Are hated most of those they did deceive,   140
So thou, my surfeit and my heresy,
Of all be hated, but the most of me!
And, all my powers, address your love and might
To honour Helen and to be her knight.   [*Exit.*
    Her. [*Awaking.*] Help me, Lysander, help me! do
        thy best   145
To pluck this crawling serpent from my breast!
Ay me, for pity! what a dream was here!
Lysander, look how I do quake with fear.
Methought a serpent eat my heart away,
And you sat smiling at his cruel prey.   150
Lysander! what, remov'd? Lysander! lord!
What, out of hearing? Gone? No sound, no word?
Alack, where are you? Speak, an if you hear;
Speak, of all loves! I swoon almost with fear.
No? then I well perceive you are not nigh.   155
Either death or you I'll find immediately.   [*Exit.*

ACT III

[SCENE I. *The wood. Titania lying asleep.*]

Enter the Clowns [QUINCE, SNUG, BOTTOM, FLUTE,
    SNOUT, *and* STARVELING].

    Bot. Are we all met?
    Quin. Pat, pat; and here's a marvellous con-
venient place for our rehearsal. This green plot
shall be our stage, this hawthorn-brake our tiring-
house; and we will do it in action as we will do it before the Duke.   6
    Bot. Peter Quince!
    Quin. What say'st thou, bully Bottom?
    Bot. There are things in this comedy of Pyramus
and Thisby that will never please. First, Pyra- 10
mus must draw a sword to kill himself, which the
ladies cannot abide. How answer you that?
    Snout. By'r lakin, a parlous fear.
    Star. I believe we must leave the killing out,
when all is done.   16
    Bot. Not a whit! I have a device to make all
well. Write me a prologue; and let the prologue
seem to say, we will do no harm with our swords and
that Pyramus is not kill'd indeed; and, for the 20
more better assurance, tell them that I Pyramus am
not Pyramus, but Bottom the weaver. This will
put them out of fear.
    Quin. Well, we will have such a prologue; and it
shall be written in eight and six.   25

    Bot. No, make it two more; let it be written in
eight and eight.
    Snout. Will not the ladies be afeard of the lion?
    Star. I fear it, I promise you.
    Bot. Masters, you ought to consider with 30
yourselves. To bring in — God shield us! — a lion
among ladies, is a most dreadful thing; for there is
not a more fearful wild-fowl than your lion living;
and we ought to look to't.
    Snout. Therefore another prologue must tell he
is not a lion.   36
    Bot. Nay, you must name his name, and half his
face must be seen through the lion's neck; and he
himself must speak through, saying thus, or to the
same defect, "Ladies," or "Fair ladies, I would 40
wish you," or "I would request you," or "I would
entreat you, not to fear, not to tremble: my life for
yours. If you think I come hither as a lion, it were
pity of my life. No, I am no such thing; I am a man
as other men are;" and there indeed let him 45
name his name, and tell them plainly he is Snug the
joiner.
    Quin. Well, it shall be so. But there is two hard
things; that is, to bring the moonlight into a chamber; for, you know, Pyramus and Thisby meet by
moonlight.   51
    Snout. Doth the moon shine that night we play
our play?
    Bot. A calendar, a calendar! Look in the al-
manac! Find out moonshine, find out moonshine.
    Quin. Yes, it doth shine that night.   56
    Bot. Why, then may you leave a casement of the
great chamber window, where we play, open, and
the moon may shine in at the casement.
    Quin. Ay; or else one must come in with a 60
bush of thorns and a lantern, and say he comes to
disfigure, or to present, the person of Moonshine.
Then, there is another thing: we must have a wall
in the great chamber; for Pyramus and Thisby, says
the story, did talk through the chink of a wall. 66
    Snout. You can never bring in a wall. What say
you, Bottom?
    Bot. Some man or other must present Wall; and
let him have some plaster, or some loam, or some
rough-cast about him, to signify wall; or let him 71
hold his fingers thus, and through that cranny shal'
Pyramus and Thisby whisper.
    Quin. If that may be, then all is well. Come, sit
down, every mother's son, and rehearse your parts.
Pyramus, you begin. When you have spoken 76
your speech, enter into that brake. And so every
one according to his cue.

150. prey: preying.   154. of all loves: for love's sake.
    Act III, sc. i, 5. tiring-house: dressing room. 8. bully: "good old"; a term of friendship. 13. By'r lakin: by our ladykin.
i.e., the Virgin Mary. parlous: perilous. 25. eight and six: alternate lines of eight and six syllables, ballad meter. 32.
lion among ladies. See Introduction. 40. defect: error for *effect*. 62. disfigure: blunder for *prefigure*. 71. rough-cast:
plaster mixed with pebbles.

Enter ROBIN GOODFELLOW [*behind*].

Robin. What hempen home-spuns have we swag-
g'ring here,
So near the cradle of the fairy queen?   80
What, a play toward! I'll be an auditor;
An actor too perhaps, if I see cause.
Quin. Speak, Pyramus. Thisby, stand forth.
Bot. "Thisby, the flowers of odious savours
sweet," —
Quin. Odorous, odorous.   85
Bot. —— "odours savours sweet;
So hath thy breath, my dearest Thisby dear.
But hark, a voice! Stay thou but here awhile,
And by and by I will to thee appear." [*Exit.*
Robin. A stranger Pyramus than e'er play'd here.
[*Exit.*]
Flu. Must I speak now?   91
Quin. Ay, marry, must you; for you must under-
stand he goes but to see a noise that he heard, and is
to come again.
Flu. "Most radiant Pyramus, most lily-white
of hue,   95
Of colour like the red rose on triumphant brier,
Most brisky juvenal and eke most lovely Jew,
As true as truest horse that yet would never tire,
I'll meet thee, Pyramus, at Ninny's tomb."   99
Quin. "Ninus' tomb," man. Why, you must
not speak that yet; that you answer to Pyra-
mus. You speak all your part at once, cues and all.
Pyramus enter. Your cue is past; it is, "never tire."
Flu. O,—"As true as truest horse, that yet would
never tire."   105

[*Re-enter* ROBIN GOODFELLOW, *and* BOTTOM *with an
ass's head*.]

Bot. "If I were fair, Thisby, I were only thine."
Quin. O monstrous! O strange! we are haunted.
Pray, masters, fly, masters! Help!
[*Exeunt* [*Quince, Snug, Flute, Snout, and
Starveling*].
Robin. I'll follow you, I'll lead you about, a-
round,
Through bog, through bush, through brake,
through brier.   110
Sometime a horse I'll be, sometime a hound,
A hog, a headless bear, sometime a fire;
And neigh, and bark, and grunt, and roar, and burn,
Like horse, hound, hog, bear, fire, at every turn.
[*Exit.*
Bot. Why do they run away? This is a knavery
of them to make me afeard.   116

Re-enter SNOUT.

Snout. O Bottom, thou art chang'd! What do I
see on thee?
Bot. What do you see? You see an ass-head of
your own, do you?   [*Exit Snout.*] 120

Re-enter QUINCE.

Quin. Bless thee, Bottom! bless thee! thou art
translated.   [*Exit.*
Bot. I see their knavery; this is to make an ass of
me, to fright me, if they could. But I will not stir
from this place, do what they can. I will   125
walk up and down here, and I will sing, that they
shall hear I am not afraid.   [*Sings.*]
"The ousel cock so black of hue,
With orange-tawny bill,
The throstle with his note so true,   130
The wren with little quill," —
Tita. [*Awaking.*] What angel wakes me from my
flowery bed?
Bot. [*Sings.*]
"The finch, the sparrow, and the lark,
The plain-song cuckoo gray,
Whose note full many a man doth mark,   135
And dares not answer nay;" —
for, indeed, who would set his wit to so foolish a
bird? Who would give a bird the lie, though he
cry "cuckoo" never so?
Tita. I pray thee, gentle mortal, sing again.   140
Mine ear is much enamour'd of thy note;
So is mine eye enthralled to thy shape;
And thy fair virtue's force perforce doth move me
On the first view to say, to swear, I love thee.
Bot. Methinks, mistress, you should have   145
little reason for that; and yet, to say the truth,
reason and love keep little company together now-
a-days; the more the pity that some honest neigh-
bours will not make them friends. Nay, I can
gleek upon occasion.   150
Tita. Thou art as wise as thou art beautiful.
Bot. Not so, neither; but if I had wit enough to
get out of this wood, I have enough to serve mine
own turn.
Tita. Out of this wood do not desire to go;   155
Thou shalt remain here, whether thou wilt or no.
I am a spirit of no common rate;
The summer still doth tend upon my state;
And I do love thee; therefore, go with me.
I'll give thee fairies to attend on thee,   160
And they shall fetch thee jewels from the deep,
And sing while thou on pressed flowers dost sleep.
And I will purge thy mortal grossness so

81. **toward:** afoot. 97. **brisky juvenal:** lively youth. **Jew:** Probably a nonsensical repetition of the first syllable of *juvenal.* 100. **Ninus:** mythical founder of Babylon, the setting of the tale of Pyramus and Thisbe. 122. **translated:** transformed. 128. **ousel:** blackbird. Q₁ reads *woosel.* 131. **quill:** pipe. 134. **plain-song:** melody without variations. 135-136.
Whose ... nay. The note of the cuckoo sounded not unlike "cuckold," an unwelcome word to husbands. 150. **gleek:** jest
satirically. 158. **still:** always.

That thou shalt like an airy spirit go.
Peaseblossom! Cobweb! Moth! and Mustard-
    seed!   165

Enter four Fairies [PEASEBLOSSOM, COBWEB, MOTH,
    and MUSTARDSEED].

Peas. Ready.
Cob.   And I.
Moth.   And I.
Mus.   And I.
All.   Where shall we go?
Tita. Be kind and courteous to this gentleman.
Hop in his walks and gambol in his eyes;
Feed him with apricocks and dewberries,
With purple grapes, green figs, and mulberries; 170
The honey-bags steal from the humble-bees,
And for night-tapers crop their waxen thighs
And light them at the fiery glow-worm's eyes,
To have my love to bed and to arise;
And pluck the wings from painted butterflies 175
To fan the moonbeams from his sleeping eyes.
Nod to him, elves, and do him courtesies.
Peas. Hail, mortal!
Cob. Hail!
Moth. Hail!   180
Mus. Hail!
Bot. I cry your worships mercy, heartily. I be-
seech your worship's name.
Cob. Cobweb.
Bot. I shall desire you of more acquaintance, 185
good Master Cobweb. If I cut my finger, I shall
make bold with you. Your name, honest gentle-
man?
Peas. Peaseblossom.
Bot. I pray you commend me to Mistress 190
Squash, your mother, and to Master Peascod, your
father. Good Master Peaseblossom, I shall desire
you of more acquaintance too. Your name, I beseech you, sir?
Mus. Mustardseed.   195
Bot. Good Master Mustardseed, I know your
patience well. That same cowardly, giant-like ox-
beef hath devoured many a gentleman of your
house. I promise you your kindred hath made my
eyes water ere now. I desire you more acquaint-
ance, good Master Mustardseed.   201
Tita. Come, wait upon him; lead him to my
    bower.
The moon methinks looks with a wat'ry eye;
And when she weeps, weeps every little flower,
Lamenting some enforced chastity.   205
Tie up my [love's] tongue, bring him silently.
                                         [*Exeunt.*

[SCENE II. *Another part of the wood.*]

Enter OBERON.

Obe. I wonder if Titania be awak'd;
Then, what it was that next came in her eye,
Which she must dote on in extremity.

Enter ROBIN GOODFELLOW.

Here comes my messenger.
                              How now, mad spirit!
What night-rule now about this haunted grove? 5
Robin. My mistress with a monster is in love.
Near to her close and consecrated bower,
While she was in her dull and sleeping hour,
A crew of patches, rude mechanicals,
That work for bread upon Athenian stalls,   10
Were met together to rehearse a play
Intended for great Theseus' nuptial-day.
The shallowest thickskin of that barren sort,
Who Pyramus presented in their sport,
Forsook his scene and ent'red in a brake.   15
When I did him at this advantage take,
An ass's nole I fixed on his head.
Anon his Thisby must be answered,
And forth my mimic comes. When they him spy,
As wild geese that the creeping fowler eye,   20
Or russet-pated choughs, many in sort,
Rising and cawing at the gun's report,
Sever themselves and madly sweep the sky,
So, at his sight, away his fellows fly;
And, at our stamp, here o'er and o'er one fails; 25
He murder cries, and help from Athens calls.
Their sense thus weak, lost with their fears thus
    strong,
Made senseless things begin to do them wrong;
For briers and thorns at their apparel snatch;
Some sleeves, some hats, from yielders all things
    catch.   30
I led them on in this distracted fear,
And left sweet Pyramus translated there;
When in that moment, so it came to pass,
Titania wak'd and straightway lov'd an ass.
Obe. This falls out better than I could devise.
But hast thou yet latch'd the Athenian's eyes   36
With the love-juice, as I did bid thee do?
Robin. I took him sleeping, — that is finish'd
    too, —
And the Athenian woman by his side;
That, when he wak'd, of force she must be ey'd. 40

Enter DEMETRIUS *and* HERMIA.

Obe. Stand close; this is the same Athenian.
Robin. This is the woman, but not this the man.

191. **Squash:** unripe pea pod. 197. **patience:** suffering. 205. **enforced:** violated. 206. **[love's]** (Pope). *lovers* Q.
Sc. ii, 2. **next:** first. 3. **in extremity:** extremely. 5. **night-rule:** diversion planned for the night. 9. **patches:** yokels. **mechanicals:** artisans. 13. **barren sort:** dull crew. 17. **nole:** head. 19. **mimic:** buffoon, burlesque actor. 21. **choughs:** jackdaws. **in sort:** together. 24. **his sight:** sight of him. 36. **latch'd:** anointed. 40. **of force:** perforce.

Dem. O, why rebuke you him that loves you so?
Lay breath so bitter on your bitter foe.
　Her. Now I but chide; but I should use thee
　　worse,　　　　　　　　　　　　　　45
For thou, I fear, hast given me cause to curse.
If thou hast slain Lysander in his sleep,
Being o'er shoes in blood, plunge in knee-deep,
And kill me too.
The sun was not so true unto the day　　50
As he to me: would he have stolen away
From sleeping Hermia? I'll believe as soon
This whole earth may be bor'd and that the moon
May through the centre creep and so displease
Her brother's noontide with the Antipodes.　55
It cannot be but thou hast murd'red him;
So should a murderer look, so dread, so grim.
　Dem. So should the murd'red look, and so
　　should I,
Pierc'd through the heart with your stern cruelty;
Yet you, the murderer, look as bright, as clear,　60
As yonder Venus in her glimmering sphere.
　Her. What's this to my Lysander? Where is he?
Ah, good Demetrius, wilt thou give him me?
　Dem. I had rather give his carcass to my hounds.
　Her. Out, dog! out, cur! thou driv'st me past the
　　bounds　　　　　　　　　　　　65
Of maiden's patience. Hast thou slain him, then?
Henceforth be never numb'red among men!
O, once tell true, tell true, even for my sake!
Durst thou have look'd him being awake,
And hast thou kill'd him sleeping? O brave touch!
Could not a worm, an adder, do so much?　　71
An adder did it; for with doubler tongue
Than thine, thou serpent, never adder stung.
　Dem. You spend your passion on a mispris'd
　　mood.
I am not guilty of Lysander's blood;　　　75
Nor is he dead, for aught that I can tell.
　Her. I pray thee, tell me then that he is well.
　Dem. An if I could, what should I get therefore?
　Her. A privilege never to see me more.
And from thy hated presence part I so:　　80
See me no more, whether he be dead or no. [*Exit.*
　Dem. There is no following her in this fierce
　　vein;
Here therefore for a while I will remain.
So sorrow's heaviness doth heavier grow　84
For debt that bankrupt sleep doth sorrow owe;
Which now in some slight measure it will pay,
If for his tender here I make some stay.
　　　　　　[*Lies down [and sleeps].*
　Obe. What hast thou done? Thou hast mistaken
　　quite

And laid the love-juice on some true-love's sight.
Of thy misprision must perforce ensue　　90
Some true love turn'd and not a false turn'd true.
　Robin. Then fate o'er-rules, that, one man hold-
　　ing troth,
A million fail, confounding oath on oath.
　Obe. About the wood go swifter than the wind,
And Helena of Athens look thou find.　　95
All fancy-sick she is and pale of cheer
With sighs of love, that costs the fresh blood dear.
By some illusion see thou bring her here.
I'll charm his eyes against she do appear.
　Robin. I go, I go; look how I go,　　100
Swifter than arrow from the Tartar's bow. [*Exit.*
　Obe.　Flower of this purple dye,
　　　Hit with Cupid's archery,
　　　Sink in apple of his eye.
　　　When his love he doth espy,　　105
　　　Let her shine as gloriously
　　　As the Venus of the sky.
　　　When thou wak'st, if she be by,
　　　Beg of her for remedy.

　　　　Re-enter ROBIN GOODFELLOW.

　Robin.　Captain of our fairy band,　　110
　　　Helena is here at hand;
　　　And the youth, mistook by me,
　　　Pleading for a lover's fee.
　　　Shall we their fond pageant see?
　　　Lord, what fools these mortals be!　115
　Obe.　Stand aside. The noise they make
　　　Will cause Demetrius to awake.
　Robin.　Then will two at once woo one;
　　　That must needs be sport alone.
　　　And those things do best please me　120
　　　That befall preposterously.

　　　　Enter LYSANDER *and* HELENA.

　Lys. Why should you think that I should woo
　　in scorn?
Scorn and derision never come in tears.
Look, when I vow, I weep; and vows so born,
In their nativity all truth appears.　　125
How can these things in me seem scorn to you,
Bearing the badge of faith, to prove them true?
　Hel. You do advance your cunning more and
　　more.
When truth kills truth, O devilish-holy fray!
These vows are Hermia's; will you give her o'er?　130
　　Weigh oath with oath, and you will nothing
　　weigh.
Your vows to her and me, put in two scales,
Will even weigh, and both as light as tales.

Lys. I had no judgement when to her I swore.

Hel. Nor none, in my mind, now you give her
  o'er.   135

Lys. Demetrius loves her, and he loves not you.

Dem. [*Awaking.*] O Helen, goddess, nymph,
  perfect, divine!

To what, my love, shall I compare thine eyne?

Crystal is muddy.   O, how ripe in show   139

Thy lips, those kissing cherries, tempting grow!

That pure congealed white, high Taurus' snow,

Fann'd with the eastern wind, turns to a crow

When thou hold'st up thy hand.   O, let me kiss

This princess of pure white, this seal of bliss!

Hel. O spite!   O hell!   I see you all are bent

To set against me for your merriment.   146

If you were civil and knew courtesy,

You would not do me thus much injury.

Can you not hate me, as I know you do,

But you must join in souls to mock me too?   150

If you were men, as men you are in show,

You would not use a gentle lady so;

To vow, and swear, and superpraise my parts,

When I am sure you hate me with your hearts.

You both are rivals, and love Hermia;   155

And now both rivals, to mock Helena.

A trim exploit, a manly enterprise,

To conjure tears up in a poor maid's eyes

With your derision!   None of noble sort

Would so offend a virgin and extort   160

A poor soul's patience, all to make you sport.

Lys. You are unkind, Demetrius; be not so;

For you love Hermia; this you know I know.

And here, with all good will, with all my heart,

In Hermia's love I yield you up my part;   165

And yours of Helena to me bequeath,

Whom I do love and will do till my death.

Hel. Never did mockers waste more idle breath.

Dem. Lysander, keep thy Hermia; I will none.

If e'er I lov'd her, all that love is gone.   170

My heart to her but as guest-wise sojourn'd,

And now to Helen is it home return'd,

There to remain.

Lys.   Helen, it is not so.

Dem. Disparage not the faith thou dost not
  know,

Lest, to thy peril, thou aby it dear.   175

Look, where thy love comes; yonder is thy dear.

Re-enter HERMIA.

Her. Dark night, that from the eye his function
  takes,

The ear more quick of apprehension makes;

Wherein it doth impair the seeing sense,

It pays the hearing double recompense.   180

Thou art not by mine eye, Lysander, found;

Mine ear, I thank it, brought me to thy sound.

But why unkindly didst thou leave me so?

Lys. Why should he stay, whom love doth press
  to go?

Her. What love could press Lysander from my
  side?   185

Lys. Lysander's love, that would not let him bide,

Fair Helena, who more engilds the night

Than all yon fiery oes and eyes of light.

Why seek'st thou me?   Could not this make thee
  know,

The hate I bare thee made me leave thee so?   190

Her. You speak not as you think.   It cannot be.

Hel. Lo, she is one of this confederacy!

Now I perceive they have conjoin'd all three

To fashion this false sport, in spite of me.

Injurious Hermia! most ungrateful maid!   195

Have you conspir'd, have you with these contriv'd

To bait me with this foul derision?

Is all the counsel that we two have shar'd,

The sisters' vows, the hours that we have spent,

When we have chid the hasty-footed time   200

For parting us, — O, is all forgot?

All school-days' friendship, childhood innocence?

We, Hermia, like two artificial gods,

Have with our needles created both one flower,

Both on one sampler, sitting on one cushion,   205

Both warbling of one song, both in one key,

As if our hands, our sides, voices and minds

Had been incorporate.   So we grew together,

Like to a double cherry, seeming parted,

But yet an union in partition;   210

Two lovely berries moulded on one stem;

So, with two seeming bodies but one heart;

Two of the first, [like] coats in heraldry,

Due but to one and crowned with one crest.

And will you rend our ancient love asunder,   215

To join with men in scorning your poor friend?

It is not friendly, 'tis not maidenly.

Our sex, as well as I, may chide you for it,

Though I alone do feel the injury.

Her. I am amazed at your passionate words.

I scorn you not; it seems that you scorn me.   221

Hel. Have you not set Lysander, as in scorn,

To follow me and praise my eyes and face?

And made your other love, Demetrius,

Who even but now did spurn me with his foot,

To call me goddess, nymph, divine and rare,   226

Precious, celestial?   Wherefore speaks he this

---

141. **Taurus:** a mountain range in Asia Minor. 144. **seal:** pledge. 153. **parts:** qualities. 160. **extort:** wrest, torture.
169. **will none:** i.e., of her. 175. **aby:** pay for. 177. **his:** its. 188. **oes:** orbs, circles. 195. **Injurious:** insulting. 203. **artificial:**
skilled in art. 208. **incorporate:** joined in one body. 213. **Two of the first.**   Apparently a heraldic phrase used of two
coats of arms (such as those of husband and wife) arranged on either side of a vertical division of the shield, such division
being known as "the first" of several possible divisions.   **[like]** (Folks conj.).   *life* Q.

To her he hates?   And wherefore doth Lysander
Deny your love, so rich within his soul,
And tender me, forsooth, affection,   230
But by your setting on, by your consent?
What though I be not so in grace as you,
So hung upon with love, so fortunate,
But miserable most, to love unlov'd?
This you should pity rather than despise.   235
   Her. I understand not what you mean by this.
   Hel. Ay, do, persever, counterfeit sad looks,
Make mouths upon me when I turn my back,
Wink each at other, hold the sweet jest up;
This sport, well carried, shall be chronicled.   240
If you have any pity, grace, or manners,
You would not make me such an argument.
But fare ye well; 'tis partly my own fault,
Which death or absence soon shall remedy.
   Lys. Stay, gentle Helena; hear my excuse,   245
My love, my life, my soul, fair Helena!
   Hel. O excellent!
   Her.   Sweet, do not scorn her so.
   Dem. If she cannot entreat, I can compel.
   Lys. Thou canst compel no more than she entreat.
Thy threats have no more strength than her weak
   [prayers].   250
Helen, I love thee; by my life, I do!
I swear by that which I will lose for thee,
To prove him false that says I love thee not.
   Dem. I say I love thee more than he can do.   254
   Lys. If thou say so, withdraw, and prove it too.
   Dem. Quick, come!
   Her.   Lysander, whereto tends all this?
   Lys. Away, you Ethiope!
   Dem.   No, no; he'll [but]
Seem to break loose.   Take on as you would follow,
But yet come not.   You are a tame man, go!
   Lys. Hang off, thou cat, thou burr! Vile thing,
   let loose,   260
Or I will shake thee from me like a serpent!
   Her. Why are you grown so rude?   What change
   is this?
Sweet love, —
   Lys.   Thy love!   Out, tawny Tartar, out!
Out, loathed medicine!   O hated potion, hence!
   Her. Do you not jest?
   Hel.   Yes, sooth; and so do you. 265
   Lys. Demetrius, I will keep my word with thee.
   Dem. I would I had your bond, for I perceive
A weak bond holds you.   I'll not trust your word.
   Lys. What, should I hurt her, strike her, kill her
   dead?
Although I hate her, I'll not harm her so.   270
   Her. What, can you do me greater harm than
   hate?

Hate me! wherefore?   O me! what news, my love!
Am not I Hermia?   Are not you Lysander?
I am as fair now as I was erewhile.
Since night you lov'd me; yet since night you left
   me: 275
Why, then you left me — O, the gods forbid! —
In earnest, shall I say?
   Lys.   Ay, by my life;
And never did desire to see thee more.
Therefore be out of hope, of question, doubt;
Be certain, nothing truer; 'tis no jest   280
That I do hate thee and love Helena.
   Her. O me! you juggler! you canker-blossom!
You thief of love!   What, have you come by night
And stolen my love's heart from him?
   Hel.   Fine, i' faith!
Have you no modesty, no maiden shame,   285
No touch of bashfulness?   What, will you tear
Impatient answers from my gentle tongue?
Fie, fie! you counterfeit, you puppet, you!
   Her. "Puppet?"   Why so?   Ay, that way goes
   the game.
Now I perceive that she hath made compare   290
Between our statures; she hath urg'd her height;
And with her personage, her tall personage,
Her height, forsooth, she hath prevail'd with him.
And are you grown so high in his esteem,
Because I am so dwarfish and so low?   295
How low am I, thou painted maypole?   Speak,
How low am I?   I am not yet so low
But that my nails can reach unto thine eyes.
   Hel. I pray you, though you mock me, gentlemen,
Let her not hurt me.   I was never curst;   300
I have no gift at all in shrewishness;
I am a right maid for my cowardice.
Let her not strike me.   You perhaps may think,
Because she is something lower than myself,
That I can match her.
   Her.   "Lower!" hark, again. 305
   Hel. Good Hermia, do not be so bitter with me.
I evermore did love you, Hermia,
Did ever keep your counsels, never wrong'd you;
Save that, in love unto Demetrius,
I told him of your stealth unto this wood.   310
He followed you; for love I followed him;
But he hath chid me hence and threat'ned me
To strike me, spurn me, nay, to kill me too.
And now, so you will let me quiet go,
To Athens will I bear my folly back   315
And follow you no further.   Let me go.
You see how simple and how fond I am.
   Her. Why, get you gone; who is't that hinders
   you?
   Hel. A foolish heart, that I leave here behind.

---

237. **sad**: grave.   242. **argument**: subject for scorn.   250. **[prayers]** (Theobald).   *praise* Q.   257. **he'll [but]**. Nicolson conj. for the obviously corrupt *heele* of Q.   272. **what news?** what is the matter?   282. **canker-blossom**: worm that destroys a blossom.   300. **curst**: shrewish.   302. **right**: true.   310. **stealth**: stealing away.

Her. What, with Lysander?

Hel.   With Demetrius.   320

Lys. Be not afraid; she shall not harm thee, Helena.

Dem. No, sir, she shall not, though you take her part.

Hel. O, when she's angry, she is keen and shrewd! She was a vixen when she went to school; And though she be but little, she is fierce.   325

Her. "Little" again! Nothing but "low" and "little"! Why will you suffer her to flout me thus? Let me come to her.

Lys.   Get you gone, you dwarf, You minimus, of hind'ring knot-grass made; You bead, you acorn.

Dem.   You are too officious   330 In her behalf that scorns your services. Let her alone; speak not of Helena; Take not her part; for, if thou dost intend Never so little show of love to her, Thou shalt aby it.

Lys.   Now she holds me not.   335 Now follow, if thou dar'st, to try whose right, Of thine or mine, is most in Helena.

Dem. Follow! Nay, I'll go with thee, cheek by jowl.

            [*Exeunt Lysander and Demetrius.*

Her. You, mistress, all this coil is 'long of you. Nay, go not back.

Hel.   I will not trust you, I,   340 Nor longer stay in your curst company. Your hands than mine are quicker for a fray; My legs are longer though, to run away.   [*Exit.*]

Her. I am amaz'd, and know not what to say.

            [*Exit.*

Obe. This is thy negligence. Still thou mistak'st, Or else committ'st thy knaveries wilfully.   346

Robin. Believe me, king of shadows, I mistook. Did not you tell me I should know the man By the Athenian garments he had on? And so far blameless proves my enterprise,   350 That I have 'nointed an Athenian's eyes; And so far am I glad it so did sort, As this their jangling I esteem a sport.

Obe. Thou see'st these lovers seek a place to fight; Hie therefore, Robin, overcast the night.   355 The starry welkin cover thou anon With drooping fog as black as Acheron, And lead these testy rivals so astray As one come not within another's way. Like to Lysander sometime frame thy tongue,   360

Then stir Demetrius up with bitter wrong; And sometime rail thou like Demetrius; And from each other look thou lead them thus, Till o'er their brows death-counterfeiting sleep With leaden legs and batty wings doth creep.   365 Then crush this herb into Lysander's eye; Whose liquor hath this virtuous property, To take from thence all error with his might, And make his eyeballs roll with wonted sight. When they next wake, all this derision   370 Shall seem a dream and fruitless vision; And back to Athens shall the lovers wend With league whose date till death shall never end. Whiles I in this affair do thee employ, I'll to my queen and beg her Indian boy;   375 And then I will her charmed eye release From monster's view, and all things shall be peace.

Robin. My fairy lord, this must be done with haste, For Night's swift dragons cut the clouds full fast, And yonder shines Aurora's harbinger,   380 At whose approach, ghosts, wand'ring here and there, Troop home to churchyards. Damned spirits all, That in crossways and floods have burial, Already to their wormy beds are gone. For fear lest day should look their shames upon, They wilfully themselves exile from light   386 And must for aye consort with black-brow'd night.

Obe. But we are spirits of another sort. I with the Morning's love have oft made sport, And, like a forester, the groves may tread,   390 Even till the eastern gate, all fiery-red, Opening on Neptune with fair blessed beams Turns into yellow gold his salt green streams. But, notwithstanding, haste, make no delay; We may effect this business yet ere day.   [*Exit.*]

Robin. Up and down, up and down,   396 I will lead them up and down. I am fear'd in field and town. Goblin, lead them up and down. Here comes one.   400

            Re-enter LYSANDER.

Lys. Where art thou, proud Demetrius? Speak thou now.

Robin. Here, villain; drawn and ready. Where art thou?

Lys. I will be with thee straight.

Robin.   Follow me, then, To plainer ground.

            [*Exit Lysander, as following the voice.*]

323. **shrewd:** sharp-tongued. 329. **minimus:** dwarf. **knot-grass:** a weed supposed capable of stunting the growth. 333. **intend:** proffer. 339. **coil:** turmoil. **'long:** because. 352. **sort:** turn out. 357. **Acheron:** river of Hades. 361. **wrong:** taunts. 367. **virtuous:** powerful. 368. **his might:** its power. 379. **night's ... dragons:** the dragons drawing the car of Night. 380. **Aurora's harbinger:** star announcing the dawn. 383. **crossways ... burial.** Suicides were buried at crossroads, and like the ghosts of those who had drowned, having thus no proper burial, were believed condemned to cheerless wandering. 389. **Morning's love:** Cephalus, the youth loved by Aurora, or possibly Aurora herself.

Re-enter DEMETRIUS.

Dem. Lysander, speak again!
Thou runaway, thou coward, art thou fled? 405
Speak! In some bush? Where dost thou hide thy
head?
Robin. Thou coward, art thou bragging to the
stars,
Telling the bushes that thou look'st for wars,
And wilt not come? Come, recreant; come, thou
child,
I'll whip thee with a rod. He is defil'd 410
That draws a sword on thee.
Dem.   Yea, art thou there?
Robin. Follow my voice. We'll try no manhood
here. [*Exeunt.*

[*Re-enter* LYSANDER.]

Lys. He goes before me and still dares me on.
When I come where he calls, then he is gone.
The villain is much lighter-heel'd than I; 415
I followed fast, but faster he did fly,
That fallen am I in dark uneven way,
And here will rest me. Come, thou gentle day!
[*Lies down.*
For if but once thou show me thy grey light,
I'll find Demetrius and revenge this spite. 420
[*Sleeps.*]

Re-enter ROBIN GOODFELLOW *and* DEMETRIUS.

Robin. Ho, ho, ho! Coward, why com'st thou not?
Dem. Abide me, if thou dar'st; for well I wot
Thou runn'st before me, shifting every place,
And dar'st not stand, nor look me in the face.
Where art thou now?
Robin.   Come hither; I am here.
Dem. Nay, then, thou mock'st me. Thou shalt
buy this dear, 426
If ever I thy face by daylight see.
Now, go thy way. Faintness constraineth me
To measure out my length on this cold bed.
By day's approach look to be visited. 430
[*Lies down and sleeps.*

Re-enter HELENA.

Hel. O weary night, O long and tedious night,
Abate thy hours! Shine, comforts, from the east,
That I may back to Athens by daylight,
From these that my poor company detest.
And sleep, that sometimes shuts up sorrow's eye,
Steal me awhile from mine own company. 436
[*Lies down and*] *sleeps.*
Robin. Yet but three? Come one more;
Two of both kinds makes up four.

Re-enter HERMIA.

Here she comes, curst and sad.

Cupid is a knavish lad, 440
Thus to make poor females mad.
Her. Never so weary, never so in woe,
Bedabbled with the dew and torn with briers,
I can no further crawl, no further go;
My legs can keep no pace with my desires. 445
Here will I rest me till the break of day.
Heavens shield Lysander, if they mean a fray!
[*Lies down and sleeps.*]
Robin.   On the ground
Sleep sound.
I'll apply 450
To your eye,
Gentle lover, remedy.
[*Squeezing the juice on Lysander's eyes.*]
When thou wak'st,
Thou tak'st
True delight 455
In the sight
Of thy former lady's eye;
And the country proverb known,
That every man should take his own,
In your waking shall be shown. 460
Jack shall have Jill;
Nought shall go ill;
The man shall have his mare again, and all shall be
well. [*Exit.*]

ACT IV

[SCENE I. *The same.*]

[LYSANDER, DEMETRIUS, HELENA, *and* HERMIA,
lying asleep.]

Enter TITANIA *and Clown* [BOTTOM; PEASEBLOSSOM,
COBWEB, MOTH, MUSTARDSEED,] *and* [*other*]
Fairies [*attending*]; OBERON *behind* [*unseen*].

Tita. Come, sit thee down upon this flow'ry bed,
While I thy amiable cheeks do coy;
And stick musk-roses in thy sleek smooth head,
And kiss thy fair large ears, my gentle joy.
Bot. Where's Peaseblossom? 5
Peas. Ready.
Bot. Scratch my head, Peaseblossom. Where's
Mounsieur Cobweb?
Cob. Ready.
Bot. Mounsieur Cobweb, good mounsieur, get
you your weapons in your hand, and kill me a 11
red-hipp'd humble-bee on the top of a thistle; and,
good mounsieur, bring me the honey-bag. Do not
fret yourself too much in the action, mounsieur,
and, good mounsieur, have a care the honey-bag
break not; I would be loath to have you over- 16
flown with a honey-bag, signior. Where's Mounsieur Mustardseed?
Mus. Ready. 19

Act IV, sc. i, 2. coy: caress

Bot. Give me your neaf, Mounsieur Mustardseed.   Pray you, leave your courtesy, good mounsieur.

Mus. What's your will?

Bot. Nothing, good mounsieur, but to help
Cavalery Cobweb to scratch.   I must to the bar- 25
ber's, mounsieur; for methinks I am marvellous
hairy about the face; and I am such a tender ass, if
my hair do but tickle me, I must scratch.

Tita. What, wilt thou hear some music, my
sweet love?

Bot. I have a reasonable good ear in music. 30
Let's have the tongs and the bones.

     [Music. Tongs. Rural music.

Tita. Or say, sweet love, what thou desir'st to
eat.

Bot. Truly, a peck of provender; I could munch
your good dry oats.   Methinks I have a great desire to a bottle of hay.   Good hay, sweet hay,
hath no fellow. 36

Tita. I have a venturous fairy that shall seek
The squirrel's hoard, and fetch [for] thee new nuts.

Bot. I had rather have a handful or two of dried
peas.   But, I pray you, let none of your people 40
stir me; I have an exposition of sleep come upon me.

Tita. Sleep thou, and I will wind thee in my arms.
Fairies, be gone, and be always away.

     [Exeunt fairies.]

So doth the woodbine the sweet honeysuckle 45
Gently entwist; the female ivy so
Enrings the barky fingers of the elm.
O, how I love thee! how I dote on thee!

     [They sleep.]

Enter ROBIN GOODFELLOW.

Obe. [*Advancing.*] Welcome, good Robin.   See'st
 thou this sweet sight?
Her dotage now I do begin to pity; 50
For, meeting her of late behind the wood,
Seeking sweet favours for this hateful fool,
I did upbraid her and fall out with her.
For she his hairy temples then had rounded
With coronet of fresh and fragrant flowers; 55
And that same dew, which sometime on the buds
Was wont to swell like round and orient pearls,
Stood now within the pretty flowerets' eyes
Like tears that did their own disgrace bewail.
When I had at my pleasure taunted her 60
And she in mild terms begg'd my patience,
I then did ask of her her changeling child;
Which straight she gave me, and her fairy sent
To bear him to my bower in fairy land.

And, now I have the boy, I will undo 65
This hateful imperfection of her eyes;
And, gentle Puck, take this transformed scalp
From off the head of this Athenian swain,
That, he awaking when the other do,
May all to Athens back again repair, 70
And think no more of this night's accidents
But as the fierce vexation of a dream.
But first I will release the fairy queen.

     [Touching her eyes.]

 Be as thou wast wont to be;
 See as thou wast wont to see: 75
 Dian's bud o'er Cupid's flower
 Hath such force and blessed power.
Now, my Titania; wake you, my sweet queen.

Tita. My Oberon! what visions have I seen!
Methought I was enamour'd of an ass. 80

Obe. There lies your love.

Tita.   How came these things to pass?
O, how mine eyes do loathe his visage now!

Obe. Silence awhile.   Robin, take off this head.
Titania, music call; and strike more dead
Than common sleep of all these five the sense. 85

Tita. Music, ho! music, such as charmeth sleep!

     [Music, still.

Robin. Now, when thou wak'st, with thine own
 fool's eyes peep.

Obe. Sound, music!   Come, my queen, take
 hands with me, 89
And rock the ground whereon these sleepers be.
Now thou and I are new in amity
And will to-morrow midnight solemnly
Dance in Duke Theseus' house triumphantly
And bless it to all fair prosperity.
There shall the pairs of faithful lovers be 95
Wedded, with Theseus, all in jollity.

Robin. Fairy king, attend and mark;
 I do hear the morning lark.

Obe. Then, my queen, in silence sad
 Trip we after the night's shade. 100
 We the globe can compass soon,
 Swifter than the wand'ring moon.

Tita. Come, my lord, and in our flight
 Tell me how it came this night
 That I sleeping here was found 105
 With these mortals on the ground.

   [Exeunt.   Horns winded [within].

Enter THESEUS, HIPPOLYTA, EGEUS, *and all his*
train.

The. Go, one of you, find out the forester,
For now our observation is perform'd,

---

20. **neaf:** fist.   21. **leave your courtesy:** put on your hat.   24. **Cavalery:** cavaliero, gentleman.   **Cobweb.**   We should
expect *Peaseblossom* (cf. l. 7).   31. **tongs...bones:** rustic instruments of music.   35. **bottle:** bundle.   36. **fellow:** equal.
38. **[for]** (Collier conj.).   Om. Qq.   41. **exposition of.**   He means *disposition to.*   52. **favours:** i.e., flowers for love-tokens.
57. **orient:** eastern.   69. **other:** others.   76. **Dian's bud.**   The flower of the *agnus castus* or chaste tree was believed to
preserve chastity.   108. **observation:** observance, May-day rites (cf. I.i.167).

And since we have the vaward of the day,
My love shall hear the music of my hounds.   110
Uncouple in the western valley, let them go.
Despatch, I say, and find the forester.
                              [*Exit an attendant.*]
We will, fair queen, up to the mountain's top
And mark the musical confusion
Of hounds and echo in conjunction.   115
    Hip. I was with Hercules and Cadmus once,
When in a wood of Crete they bay'd the bear
With hounds of Sparta.   Never did I hear
Such gallant chiding; for, besides the groves,
The skies, the fountains, every region near   120
Seem'd all one mutual cry.   I never heard
So musical a discord, such sweet thunder.
    The. My hounds are bred out of the Spartan kind,
So flew'd, so sanded, and their heads are hung
With ears that sweep away the morning dew;   125
Crook-knee'd, and dew-lapp'd like Thessalian bulls;
Slow in pursuit, but match'd in mouth like bells,
Each under each.   A cry more tuneable
Was never holla'd to, nor cheer'd with horn,
In Crete, in Sparta, nor in Thessaly.   130
Judge when you hear.   But, soft! what nymphs are
    these?
    Ege. My lord, this is my daughter here asleep;
And this, Lysander; this Demetrius is;
This Helena, old Nedar's Helena.
I wonder of their being here together.   135
    The. No doubt they rose up early to observe
The rite of May, and, hearing our intent,
Came here in grace of our solemnity.
But speak, Egeus; is not this the day
That Hermia should give answer of her choice?
    Ege. It is, my lord.   141
    The. Go, bid the huntsmen wake them with their
    horns.
        [*Horns and shout within. Lys., Dem., Hel.,*
              and Her. wake and start up.
Good morrow, friends.   Saint Valentine is past;
Begin these wood-birds but to couple now?
    Lys. Pardon, my lord.
    The.   I pray you all, stand up.
I know you two are rival enemies;   146
How comes this gentle concord in the world,
That hatred is so far from jealousy
To sleep by hate and fear no enmity?
    Lys. My lord, I shall reply amazedly,   150
Half sleep, half waking; but as yet, I swear,
I cannot truly say how I came here.
But, as I think, — for truly would I speak,
And now I do bethink me, so it is, —

I came with Hermia hither.   Our intent   155
Was to be gone from Athens, where we might,
Without the peril of the Athenian law —
    Ege. Enough, enough, my lord; you have enough.
I beg the law, the law, upon his head.
They would have stol'n away; they would, De-
    metrius,   160
Thereby to have defeated you and me,
You of your wife, and me of my consent,
Of my consent that she should be your wife.
    Dem. My lord, fair Helen told me of their stealth,
Of this their purpose hither to this wood;   165
And I in fury hither follow'd them,
Fair Helena in fancy following me.
But, my good lord, I wot not by what power, —
But by some power it is, — my love to Hermia,
Melted as [is] the snow, seems to me now   170
As the remembrance of an idle gaud
Which in my childhood I did dote upon;
And all the faith, the virtue of my heart,
The object and the pleasure of mine eye,
Is only Helena.   To her, my lord,   175
Was I betroth'd ere I saw Hermia;
But like a sickness did I loathe this food;
But, as in health, come to my natural taste,
Now I do wish it, love it, long for it,
And will for evermore be true to it.   180
    The. Fair lovers, you are fortunately met;
Of this discourse we more will hear anon.
Egeus, I will overbear your will;
For in the temple, by and by, with us
These couples shall eternally be knit.   185
And, for the morning now is something worn,
Our purpos'd hunting shall be set aside.
Away with us to Athens; three and three,
We'll hold a feast in great solemnity.
Come, Hippolyta.   190
        [*Exeunt The., Hip., Ege., and train.*
    Dem. These things seem small and undistin-
    guishable,
Like far-off mountains turned into clouds.
    Her. Methinks I see these things with parted eye,
When every thing seems double.
    Hel.   So methinks;
And I have found Demetrius like a jewel,   195
Mine own, and not mine own.
    Dem.   [But] are you sure
That we are [now] awake?   It seems to me
That yet we sleep, we dream.   Do not you think
The Duke was here, and bid us follow him?
    Her. Yea; and my father.
    Hel.   And Hippolyta.   200

---

109. **vaward:** vanguard.   119. **chiding:** baying.   124. **flew'd:** with large chaps.   **sanded:** of sandy color.   128. **Each**
...each: with varied pitch.   Elizabethan huntsmen coveted packs of hounds whose cries would blend.   **cry:** pack.   138.
solemnity: marriage ceremony.   143. **Saint Valentine.**   Birds were popularly supposed to choose their mates on Valentine's day.   156. **where:** to a place where.   157. **Without:** beyond.   170. **[is]** (Steevens). Om. Qq. Ff.   193. **parted:** out of focus.
196–97. **[But]...awake?** (Steevens conj.).   *Are you sure that we are awake?* Qq. Om. Ff.

Lys. And he did bid us follow to the temple.

Dem. Why, then, we are awake. Let's follow him;

And by the way let us recount our dreams.

                            [Exeunt lovers.

Bot. (*Awaking.*) When my cue comes, call me, and I will answer. My next is, "Most fair Pyramus." Heigh-ho! Peter Quince! Flute, the bellows-mender! Snout, the tinker! Starveling! 207 God's my life, stolen hence, and left me asleep! I have had a most rare vision. I have had a dream, past the wit of man to say what dream it 210 was. Man is but an ass, if he go about to expound this dream. Methought I was — there is no man can tell what. Methought I was, — and methought I had, — but man is but a patch'd fool, if he will offer to say what methought I had. The eye of 215 man hath not heard, the ear of man hath not seen, man's hand is not able to taste, his tongue to conceive, nor his heart to report, what my dream was. I will get Peter Quince to write a ballad of this dream. It shall be called "Bottom's Dream," 220 because it hath no bottom; and I will sing it in the latter end of a play, before the Duke; peradventure, to make it the more gracious, I shall sing it at her death.   *[Exit.*

[SCENE II. *Athens. Quince's house.*]

Enter QUINCE, FLUTE, SNOUT, *and* STARVELING.

Quin. Have you sent to Bottom's house? Is he come home yet?

Star. He cannot be heard of. Out of doubt he is transported.

Flu. If he come not, then the play is marr'd. It goes not forward, doth it?   6

Quin. It is not possible. You have not a man in all Athens able to discharge Pyramus but he.

Flu. No, he hath simply the best wit of any handicraft man in Athens.   10

Snout. Yea, and the best person too; and he is a very paramour for a sweet voice.

Flu. You must say "paragon"; a paramour is, God bless us, a thing of naught.

Enter SNUG.

Snug. Masters, the Duke is coming from the 15 temple, and there is two or three lords and ladies more married. If our sport had gone forward, we had all been made men.

Flu. O sweet bully Bottom! Thus hath he lost sixpence a day during his life; he could not 20 have 'scaped sixpence a day. An the Duke had not given him sixpence a day for playing Pyramus, I'll be hang'd. He would have deserved it. Sixpence a day in Pyramus, or nothing.

Enter BOTTOM.

Bot. Where are these lads? Where are these hearts?   26

Quin. Bottom! O most courageous day! O most happy hour!

Bot. Masters, I am to discourse wonders, but ask me not what; for if I tell you, I am no true 30 Athenian. I will tell you everything, right as it fell out.

Quin. Let us hear, sweet Bottom.

Bot. Not a word of me. All that I will tell you is, that the Duke hath dined. Get your apparel 35 together, good strings to your beards, new ribbons to your pumps; meet presently at the palace; every man look o'er his part; for the short and the long is, our play is preferr'd. In any case, let Thisby have clean linen; and let not him that plays the 40 lion pare his nails, for they shall hang out for the lion's claws. And, most dear actors, eat no onions nor garlic, for we are to utter sweet breath; and I do not doubt but to hear them say, it is a sweet comedy. No more words; away! go, away!   46

                            [Exeunt.

ACT V

[SCENE I. *Athens. The palace of Theseus.*]

Enter THESEUS, HIPPOLYTA, PHILOSTRATE, Lords [*and* Attendants].

Hip. 'Tis strange, my Theseus, that these lovers speak of.

The. More strange than true; I never may believe

These antique fables, nor these fairy toys.

Lovers and madmen have such seething brains,

Such shaping fantasies, that apprehend   5

More than cool reason ever comprehends.

The lunatic, the lover, and the poet

Are of imagination all compact.

One sees more devils than vast hell can hold;

That is, the madman. The lover, all as frantic, 10

Sees Helen's beauty in a brow of Egypt.

The poet's eye, in a fine frenzy rolling,

Doth glance from heaven to earth, from earth to heaven;

And as imagination bodies forth

The forms of things unknown, the poet's pen   15

Turns them to shapes and gives to airy nothing

A local habitation and a name.

Such tricks hath strong imagination,

---

211. **go about:** attempt. 214. **patch'd:** wearing motley. 224. **at her death,** i.e., Thisbe's.

Sc. ii, 14. **thing of naught:** naughty thing. 20. **sixpence a day,** i.e., as royal pension. 39. **preferr'd:** chosen.

Act V, sc. i, 4–22. See Introduction. 8. **compact:** composed. 11. **Helen:** Helen of Troy. **brow of Egypt:** gypsy's face.

That, if it would but apprehend some joy,
It comprehends some bringer of that joy;   20
Or in the night, imagining some fear,
How easy is a bush suppos'd a bear!
Hip. But all the story of the night told over,
And all their minds transfigur'd so together,
More witnesseth than fancy's images,   25
And grows to something of great constancy;
But, howsoever, strange and admirable.

Enter lovers, LYSANDER, DEMETRIUS, HERMIA, *and*
HELENA.

The. Here come the lovers, full of joy and mirth.
Joy, gentle friends! joy and fresh days of love
Accompany your hearts!
Lys.   More than to us   30
Wait in your royal walks, your board, your bed!
The. Come now; what masques, what dances
    shall we have,
To wear away this long age of three hours
Between our after-supper and bed-time?
Where is our usual manager of mirth?   35
What revels are in hand? Is there no play
To ease the anguish of a torturing hour?
Call Philostrate.
    Phil.   Here, mighty Theseus.
    The. Say, what abridgement have you for this
        evening?
What masque? what music? How shall we be-
    guile   40
The lazy time, if not with some delight?
    Phil. There is a brief how many sports are ripe.
Make choice of which your Highness will see first.
                            [*Giving a paper.*]
    The. [*Reads.*] "The battle with the Centaurs,
        to be sung
By an Athenian eunuch to the harp."   45
We'll none of that: that have I told my love,
In glory of my kinsman Hercules.
"The riot of the tipsy Bacchanals,
Tearing the Thracian singer in their rage."
That is an old device; and it was play'd   50
When I from Thebes came last a conqueror.
"The thrice three Muses mourning for the death
Of Learning, late deceas'd in beggary."
That is some satire, keen and critical,
Not sorting with a nuptial ceremony.   55
"A tedious brief scene of young Pyramus
And his love Thisbe; very tragical mirth."
Merry and tragical! Tedious and brief!
That is, hot ice and wondrous strange snow.

How shall we find the concord of this discord?   60
    Phil. A play there is, my lord, some ten words
        long,
Which is as brief as I have known a play;
But by ten words, my lord, it is too long,
Which makes it tedious; for in all the play
There is not one word apt, one player fitted.   65
And tragical, my noble lord, it is;
For Pyramus therein doth kill himself.
Which, when I saw rehears'd, I must confess,
Made mine eyes water; but more merry tears
The passion of loud laughter never shed.   70
    The. What are they that do play it?
    Phil. Hard-handed men that work in Athens
        here,
Which never labour'd in their minds till now,
And now have toil'd their unbreath'd memories
With this same play, against your nuptial.   75
    The. And we will hear it.
    Phil.   No, my noble lord;
It is not for you. I have heard it over,
And it is nothing, nothing in the world;
Unless you can find sport in their intents,
Extremely stretch'd and conn'd with cruel pain, 80
To do you service.
    The.   I will hear that play;
For never anything can be amiss,
When simpleness and duty tender it.
Go, bring them in; and take your places, ladies.
                            [*Exit Philostrate.*]
    Hip. I love not to see wretchedness o'er-charged,
And duty in his service perishing.   86
    The. Why, gentle sweet, you shall see no such
        thing.
    Hip. He says they can do nothing in this kind.
    The. The kinder we, to give them thanks for
        nothing.
Our sport shall be to take what they mistake;   90
And what poor duty cannot do, noble respect
Takes it in might, not merit.
Where I have come, great clerks have purposed
To greet me with premeditated welcomes;
Where I have seen them shiver and look pale,   95
Make periods in the midst of sentences,
Throttle their practis'd accent in their fears,
And in conclusion dumbly have broke off,
Not paying me a welcome. Trust me, sweet,
Out of this silence yet I pick'd a welcome;   100
And in the modesty of fearful duty
I read as much as from the rattling tongue
Of saucy and audacious eloquence.

26. **constancy:** certainty. 39. **abridgement:** pastime. 42. **brief:** list, schedule. 44. **Centaurs.** The Centaurs and the
Lapithae fought at a wedding which Theseus would remember, since he had taken part on the side of the latter. 48-49.
The riot . . . rage. Orpheus, the poet-musician, was killed by the frenzied women followers of Bacchus. 52. **The thrice
three Muses.** A topical reference has been seen in these lines, but no explanation is satisfactory. 55. **sorting with:** befitting.
74. **unbreath'd:** unpractised. 80. **stretch'd:** strained. 85. **wretchedness o'ercharged:** weakness overburdened. 92.
takes . . . merit: takes the will for the deed. 93. **clerks:** scholars.

Love, therefore, and tongue-ti'd simplicity
In least speak most, to my capacity.   105

[Re-enter PHILOSTRATE.]

Phil. So please your Grace, the Prologue is address'd.
The. Let him approach.   [*Flourish of trumpets.*

Enter [QUINCE *for*] *the* Prologue.

Pro. If we offend, it is with our good will.
That you should think, we come not to offend,
But with good will. To show our simple skill,   110
That is the true beginning of our end.
Consider, then, we come, but in despite
We do not come, as minding to content you,
Our true intent is. All for your delight.
We are not here. That you should here repent
you,   115
The actors are at hand; and by their show
You shall know all that you are like to know.
The. This fellow doth not stand upon points.
Lys. He hath rid his prologue like a rough colt;
he knows not the stop.   A good moral, my lord: it is
not enough to speak, but to speak true.   121
Hip. Indeed he hath play'd on this prologue like
a child on a recorder; a sound, but not in government.
The. His speech was like a tangled chain;   125
nothing impaired, but all disordered.   Who is next?

Enter with a trumpet before them, PYRAMUS *and*
THISBE, WALL, MOONSHINE, *and* LION.

Pro. Gentles, perchance you wonder at this show;
But wonder on till truth make all things plain.
This man is Pyramus, if you would know;   130
This beauteous lady Thisby is certain.
This man, with lime and rough-cast, doth present
Wall, that vile Wall which did these lovers sunder;
And through Wall's chink, poor souls, they are content
To whisper.   At the which let no man wonder.   135
This man, with lantern, dog, and bush of thorn,
Presenteth Moonshine; for, if you will know,
By moonshine did these lovers think no scorn
To meet at Ninus' tomb, there, there to woo.
This grisly beast, which Lion hight by name,   140
The trusty Thisby, coming first by night,
Did scare away, or rather did affright;
And, as she fled, her mantle she did fall,
Which Lion vile with bloody mouth did stain.
Anon comes Pyramus, sweet youth and tall,   145

And finds his trusty Thisby's mantle slain;
Whereat, with blade, with bloody blameful blade,
He bravely broach'd his boiling bloody breast;
And Thisby, tarrying in mulberry shade,
His dagger drew, and died.   For all the rest,   150
Let Lion, Moonshine, Wall, and lovers twain
At large discourse, while here they do remain.
[*Exeunt Prologue, Thisbe, Lion, and Moonshine.*
The. I wonder if the lion be to speak.
Dem. No wonder, my lord; one lion may, when
many asses do.   155
Wall. In this same interlude it doth befall
That I, one Snout by name, present a wall;
And such a wall, as I would have you think,
That had in it a crannied hole or chink,
Through which the lovers, Pyramus and Thisby,   160
Did whisper often very secretly.
This loam, this rough-cast, and this stone doth show
That I am that same wall; the truth is so;
And this the cranny is, right and sinister,
Through which the fearful lovers are to whisper.   165
The. Would you desire lime and hair to speak
better?
Dem. It is the wittiest partition that ever I heard
discourse, my lord.   169

Enter PYRAMUS.

The. Pyramus draws near the wall.   Silence!
Pyr. O grim-look'd night!   O night with hue so
black!
O night, which ever art when day is not!
O night, O night! alack, alack, alack,
I fear my Thisby's promise is forgot!
And thou, O wall, O sweet, O lovely wall,   175
That stand'st between her father's ground and
mine!
Thou wall, O wall, O sweet and lovely wall,
Show me thy chink, to blink through with mine
eyne!   [*Wall holds up his fingers.*]
Thanks, courteous wall; Jove shield thee well for
this!
But what see I?   No Thisby do I see.   180
O wicked wall, through whom I see no bliss!
Curs'd be thy stones for thus deceiving me!
The. The wall, methinks, being sensible, should
curse again.
Pyr. No, in truth, sir, he should not.   "De-   185
ceiving me" is Thisby's cue.   She is to enter now,
and I am to spy her through the wall.   You shall
see it will fall pat as I told you.   Yonder she
comes.

105. **to my capacity:** in my opinion. In the sympathetic speech of Theseus a tribute was very likely intended to the graciousness of Queen Elizabeth, who may on some occasion have witnessed this play.   106. **address'd:** ready. 108 ff. The comic device of misconstruing punctuation had been used some sixty years before in *Ralph Roister Doister*. 118. **stand ... points.**   A quibble upon (1) "to be scrupulous" and (2) "heed punctuation."   123. **recorder:** an instrument like a flageolet.   124. **government:** control.   140. **hight:** is called.   148. **broach'd:** stabbed.   183. **sensible:** capable of feeling.

Enter THISBE.

This. O wall, full often hast thou heard my
    moans,
For parting my fair Pyramus and me!   191
My cherry lips have often kiss'd thy stones,
Thy stones with lime and hair knit up in thee.
Pyr. I see a voice! Now will I to the chink,
To spy an I can hear my Thisby's face.   195
Thisby!
    This. My love, thou art my love, I think.
    Pyr. Think what thou wilt, I am thy lover's
    grace;
And, like Limander, am I trusty still.
    This. And I like Helen, till the Fates me kill.   200
    Pyr. Not Shafalus to Procrus was so true.
    This. As Shafalus to Procrus, I to you.
    Pyr. O, kiss me through the hole of this vile wall!
    This. I kiss the wall's hole, not your lips at all.
    Pyr. Wilt thou at Ninny's tomb meet me
    straightway?   205
    This. 'Tide life, 'tide death, I come without de-
    lay.   [*Exeunt Pyramus and Thisbe.*]
    Wall. Thus have I, Wall, my part discharged so;
And, being done, thus Wall away doth go.   [*Exit.*
    The. Now is the moon used between the two
neighbours.
    Dem. No remedy, my lord, when walls are so
wilful to hear without warning.   211
    Hip. This is the silliest stuff that ever I heard.
    The. The best in this kind are but shadows; and
the worst are no worse, if imagination amend them.
    Hip. It must be your imagination then, and   216
not theirs.
    The. If we imagine no worse of them than they of
themselves, they may pass for excellent men. Here
come two noble beasts in, a man and a lion.   221

Enter LION *and* MOONSHINE.

Lion. You, ladies, you, whose gentle hearts do fear
The smallest monstrous mouse that creeps on
    floor,
May now perchance both quake and tremble here,
When lion rough in wildest rage doth roar.   225
Then know that I, as Snug the joiner, am
A lion fell, nor else no lion's dam;
For, if I should as lion come in strife
Into this place, 'twere pity on my life.
    The. A very gentle beast, and of a good   230
conscience.
    Dem. The very best at a beast, my lord, that e'er
I saw.
    Lys. This lion is a very fox for his valour.

    The. True; and a goose for his discretion.   235
    Dem. Not so, my lord; for his valour cannot carry
his discretion, and the fox carries the goose.
    The. His discretion, I am sure, cannot carry his
valour; for the goose carries not the fox. It is   240
well; leave it to his discretion, and let us hearken to
the moon.
    Moon. This lantern doth the horned moon
    present; —
    Dem. He should have worn the horns on his
head.   245
    The. He is no crescent, and his horns are invisible
within the circumference.
    Moon. This lantern doth the horned moon
    present;
Myself the man i' th' moon do seem to be.
    The. This is the greatest error of all the rest.
The man should be put into the lantern.   251
How is it else the man i' th' moon?
    Dem. He dares not come there for the candle; for,
you see, it is already in snuff.
    Hip. I am aweary of this moon. Would he would
change!   256
    The. It appears, by his small light of discretion,
that he is in the wane; but yet, in courtesy, in all
reason, we must stay the time.
    Lys. Proceed, Moon.   260
    Moon. All that I have to say, is, to tell you that
the lantern is the moon; I, the man i' th' moon;
this thorn-bush, my thorn-bush; and this dog, my
dog.
    Dem. Why, all these should be in the lantern;   265
for all these are in the moon. But, silence! here
comes Thisbe.

Re-enter THISBE.

    This. This is old Ninny's tomb. Where is my
    love?
    Lion. (*Roaring.*) Oh ——   [*Thisbe runs off.*
    Dem. Well roar'd, Lion.   270
    The. Well run, Thisbe.
    Hip. Well shone, Moon. Truly, the moon shines
with a good grace.
    [*The Lion shakes Thisbe's mantle and
    exit.*]
    The. Well mous'd, Lion.

Re-enter PYRAMUS.

    Dem. And then came Pyramus.
    Lys. And so the lion vanish'd.   275
    Pyr. Sweet Moon, I thank thee for thy sunny
    beams;

199–200. **Limander … Helen:** blunders for *Hero* and *Leander.*   201. **Shafalus to Procrus:** blunder for *Cephalus to Procris,*
also famous lovers.   206. **'Tide:** betide.   209. **moon used.** Qq. *morall downe* Ff. Pope's conj. *mural down* has been
generally followed. All are unsatisfactory.   221. **man.** Many edd. emend to *moon.*   226. **as.** Qq. *one* Ff.   244. **horns
… head.** The inescapable jest about the "horns" of the "cuckold."   254. **in snuff:** quibble on (1) "offended" and (2)
"in need of snuffing"

I thank thee, Moon, for shining now so bright;
For, by thy gracious, golden, glittering [gleams],
  I trust to take of truest Thisby sight.   280
    But stay, O spite!
    But mark, poor knight,
  What dreadful dole is here!
  Eyes, do you see?
  How can it be?   285
  O dainty duck! O dear!
    Thy mantle good,
  What, stain'd with blood!
  Approach, ye Furies fell!
  O Fates, come, come,   290
  Cut thread and thrum;
  Quail, crush, conclude, and quell!
The. This passion, and the death of a dear friend,
would go near to make a man look sad.
Hip. Beshrew my heart, but I pity the man. 295
Pyr. O wherefore, Nature, didst thou lions frame?
Since lion vile hath here deflow'r'd my dear;
Which is — no, no — which was the fairest dame
That liv'd, that lov'd, that lik'd, that look'd with
    cheer.
  Come, tears, confound;   300
  Out, sword, and wound
  The pap of Pyramus;
  Ay, that left pap,
  Where heart doth hop.   *[Stabs himself.]*
Thus die I, thus, thus, thus.   305
  Now am I dead,
  Now am I fled;
  My soul is in the sky.
  Tongue, lose thy light;   309
  Moon, take thy flight.   *[Exit Moonshine.]*
Now die, die, die, die, die.   *[Dies.]*
Dem. No die, but an ace, for him; for he is but one.
Lys. Less than an ace, man, for he is dead; he is
nothing.   315
The. With the help of a surgeon he might yet re-
cover, and yet prove an ass.
Hip. How chance Moonshine is gone before
Thisbe comes back and finds her lover?

Re-enter THISBE.

The. She will find him by starlight. Here 320
she comes; and her passion ends the play.
Hip. Methinks she should not use a long one for
such a Pyramus. I hope she will be brief.
Dem. A mote will turn the balance, which Pyramus, which Thisbe, is the better; he for a man, 325
God warrant us; she for a woman, God bless us.
Lys. She hath spied him already with those sweet
eyes.

Dem. And thus she moans, *videlicet:* —   330
This.   Asleep, my love?
  What, dead, my dove?
  O Pyramus, arise!
  Speak, speak! Quite dumb?
  Dead, dead? A tomb   335
Must cover thy sweet eyes.
  These lily lips,
  This cherry nose,
These yellow cowslip cheeks,
  Are gone, are gone!   340
  Lovers, make moan.
His eyes were green as leeks.
  O Sisters Three,
  Come, come to me,
With hands as pale as milk;   345
  Lay them in gore,
  Since you have shore
With shears his thread of silk.
  Tongue, not a word!
  Come, trusty sword;   350
Come, blade, my breast imbrue!
        [Stabs herself.]
  And, farewell, friends;
  Thus, Thisby ends.
  Adieu, adieu, adieu.   *[Dies.]*
The. Moonshine and Lion are left to bury 355
the dead.
Dem. Ay, and Wall too.
Bot. *[Starting up.]* No, I assure you; the wall is
down that parted their fathers. Will it please you
to see the epilogue, or to hear a Bergomask dance
between two of our company?   361
The. No epilogue, I pray you; for your play needs
no excuse. Never excuse; for when the players are
all dead, there need none to be blamed. Marry, if
he that writ it had played Pyramus and hang'd 365
himself in Thisbe's garter, it would have been a fine
tragedy; and so it is, truly; and very notably discharg'd. But, come, your Bergomask; let your
epilogue alone.   *[A dance.]*
The iron tongue of midnight hath told twelve. 370
Lovers, to bed; 'tis almost fairy time.
I fear we shall out-sleep the coming morn
As much as we this night have overwatch'd.
This palpable-gross play hath well beguil'd
The heavy gait of night. Sweet friends, to bed.
A fortnight hold we this solemnity   376
In nightly revels and new jollity.   *[Exeunt.*

Enter ROBIN GOODFELLOW.

Robin. Now the hungry lion roars,
  And the wolf [behowls] the moon;

---

279. **[gleams]** (Knight). *beames* Q.   283. **dole:** grief.   291. **thrum:** the loose threads at the end of the web.   292.
quail: overpower. **quell:** kill.   312. **ace:** the lowest cast of the dice.   330. **moans.** Qq. Ff. *means:* laments. **videlicet:**
as follows.   343. **Sisters three:** the Fates.   351. **imbrue:** stain with blood.   360. **Bergomask dance:** a rustic dance named
from Bergamo in Italy.   374. **palpable-gross:** palpably crude.   379. **[behowls]** (Warburton). *beholds* Q.

Whilst the heavy ploughman snores,   380
　All with weary task fordone.
Now the wasted brands do glow,
　Whilst the screech-owl, screeching loud,
Puts the wretch that lies in woe
　In remembrance of a shroud.   385
Now it is the time of night
　That the graves, all gaping wide,
Every one lets forth his sprite,
　In the church-way paths to glide.
And we fairies, that do run   390
　By the triple Hecate's team
From the presence of the sun,
　Following darkness like a dream,
Now are frolic. Not a mouse
Shall disturb this hallowed house.   395
I am sent with broom before,
To sweep the dust behind the door.

Enter OBERON *and* TITANIA *with their train.*

Obe. Through the house give glimmering light
　By the dead and drowsy fire,
Every elf and fairy sprite   400
　Hop as light as bird from brier;
And this ditty, after me,
　Sing, and dance it trippingly.
Tita. First, rehearse your song by rote,
　To each word a warbling note.   405
Hand in hand, with fairy grace,
　Will we sing, and bless this place.
　　　　　　　　　　　[*Song [and dance*].
Obe. Now, until the break of day,
　Through this house each fairy stray.
To the best bride-bed will we,   410
　Which by us shall blessed be;

And the issue there create
Ever shall be fortunate.
So shall all the couples three
Ever true in loving be;   415
And the blots of Nature's hand
Shall not in their issue stand;
Never mole, harelip, nor scar,
Nor mark prodigious, such as are
Despised in nativity,   420
Shall upon their children be.
With this field-dew consecrate,
Every fairy take his gait,
And each several chamber bless,
Through this palace, with sweet peace;   425
And the owner of it blest
Ever shall in safety rest.
Trip away; make no stay;
Meet me all by break of day.
　　　　　[*Exeunt [Oberon, Titania, and train*].
Robin. If we shadows have offended,   430
Think but this, and all is mended,
That you have but slumb'red here
While these visions did appear.
And this weak and idle theme,
No more yielding but a dream,   435
Gentles, do not reprehend.
If you pardon, we will mend.
And, as I am an honest Puck,
If we have unearned luck
Now to 'scape the serpent's tongue,   440
We will make amends ere long;
Else the Puck a liar call.
So, good night unto you all.
Give me your hands, if we be friends,
And Robin shall restore amends.   445
　　　　　　　　　　　[*Exit.*]

381. **fordone**: worn out.　391. **triple Hecate's.** Hecate ruled in three capacities: as Diana on earth, as Cynthia in heaven, and as Proserpine in hell.　394. **frolic**: merry.　397. **behind**: from behind.　419. **prodigious**: unnatural.　440. **serpent's tongue**: hissing.　444. **Give . . . hands**: applaud.

The Merchant of Venice

ON JULY 22, 1598, James Roberts entered *The Marchaunt of Venyce or otherwise called the Jewe of Venyce* in the Stationers' Register. The entry was presumably a "staying entry" to prevent piracy, for no Quarto appeared until 1600, when Roberts printed the play for Thomas Heyes, to whom he had, as witnessed by an entry of October 28, 1600, transferred his right. A second Quarto, purporting by its title page to have been printed by Roberts in 1600, has been proved to be one of the spuriously dated Quartos issued by Pavier in 1619. It has also been shown that this Quarto, formerly believed to be the earlier, and the text of the First Folio were each set up independently from the Heyes Quarto. Thus the Heyes Quarto now stands as the proper basis for any modern text.

As to the date of the play, there is not much to go upon. It is mentioned by Meres in his list of 1598, but it is undoubtedly earlier. In 1594 Dr. Roderigo Lopez, a prominent Jewish physician who had gained the distinction of serving the Queen herself, was hanged in London on a charge of treason and conspiracy to murder Elizabeth and the Portuguese pretender, Antonio Perez. It has been suggested that the present play was prepared about this time to take advantage of the popular excitement created by that affair. The notion gains support from the fact that rivals of Shakespeare's company were apparently making capital of it, for during the summer and fall of 1594 the Admiral's Men staged a highly successful revival of Marlowe's sensational *Jew of Malta*. Tenuous corroboration of the theory may be found in the occurrence of the name Antonio as that of the intended victim in both history and the drama, and in the possible though doubtful allusion to Lopez in Gratiano's abuse of Shylock in IV.i.133–38. The maturity exhibited in the workmanship of the play, however, has made scholars reluctant to accept a date earlier than 1596. Nevertheless, though the text probably was not earlier than 1596, the idea for the play may have originated in the events of 1594.

The main plot of the play is unquestionably derived from the story of Giannetto, the first novel of the fourth day in Ser Giovanni Fiorentino's *Il Pecorone* (written about 1378, though not printed until 1558), which combines the stories of the bond and the rings, sets the principal action in Venice, and names Belmont as the lady's residence. Suitors of the lady are to win her, however, not by a choice among caskets but by wooing her throughout a whole night, a consummation which the lady seeks to prevent by sleeping-potions administered in their drink. The one who ultimately gains her is successful only because the lady's maid-in-waiting kindly betrays the secret of the potion. The winning of Portia by the suitor who should choose correctly among caskets of gold, silver, and lead was probably suggested by a story in the *Gesta Romanorum*, a miscellaneous collection of tales dating from the Middle Ages, of which a popular translation had appeared in 1577. In the version in the *Gesta* the test is imposed by the Emperor of Rome upon a foreign princess to determine her worthiness to become his wife. No specific source has been discovered for Jessica's part in the play, but Shakespeare may have found the hint in the rôle of Abigail, the daughter of Marlowe's Jew of Malta, who also had a Christian lover. Mention should be made of a lost play called *The Jew*, of which the sole surviving record is a reference by Stephen Gosson in his *School of Abuse* (1579), describing it as "representing the greediness of worldly chusers, and bloody mindes of Usurers." From this description critics have inferred a play combining the story of the caskets with that of the pound of flesh. It is a likely conjecture, yet so long as the play remains undiscovered it is futile to speculate upon what it may have supplied to Shakespeare; and it is going far beyond the evidence to conjecture that *The Merchant of Venice* as we know it, is in fact *The Jew* adapted (after possible intermediate handlings) by Shakespeare in 1594 and further revised by him some time before 1600.

The two chief elements of the plot belong independently to old and widespread traditions. The story of the pound of flesh occurs in the medieval *Dolopathos* by Joannes de Alta Silva, the *Gesta Romanorum*, the Middle English *Cursor Mundi*, a ballad on the cruelty of "Gernutus the Jew," and *Histoires Tragiques*, a book of declamations by Alexandre Silvayn, of which an English translation, *The Orator*, appeared in 1596. The last named is of particular interest because it may be that the argument of a Jew before his judge supplied hints for some of Shylock's lines in the court scene. If the suggested indebtedness is real, it supports 1596 as the earliest possible date for the play. The story of the caskets appears, with different motivation, in the Greek romance of *Barlaam and Josaphat*, the *Speculum Historiale* (XV, 10) of Vincent of Beauvais, the *Legenda Aurea* (cap. 176), the *Decameron* (X, I) of Boccaccio, and the *Confessio Amantis* (V, 2273–2390) of John Gower.

The Merchant of Venice is unlike Shakespeare's other romantic comedies in not having love as the central interest. There are, to be sure, three pairs of lovers, but their affairs, though they bear upon the main plot significantly, are nevertheless subordinate issues. The protagonists are clearly Antonio and Shylock. Friendship, however, as exalted in the Renaissance conception over the love of man for woman, does constitute an important element in the main plot. Without demur Antonio equips Bassanio, already deep in his debt for like services, in his expedition to Belmont, and weeps, we are told, at his departure thither. Indeed, the melancholy from which Antonio is suffering when first we meet him seems to be owing to an intuition that something is about to deprive him of his friend. That some modern critics have found this devotion misplaced is nothing to the point. Antonio did not, and neither, certainly, did Shakespeare, who in his Sonnets celebrated friendship, making it superior to love. Antonio, however, receives his reward, for in his time of crisis Bassanio returns to him bearing twice the sum he owes the Jew. That the instigation as well as the bounty comes from Portia is perhaps little to Bassanio's credit, but this Antonio does not know, and he ultimately learns that in "losing" one friend he has gained another.

The question of anti-Semitism in this play has been widely discussed. There can be no doubt that Shakespeare intentionally endowed Shylock with traits which have fostered the traditional antipathy to his race. Shylock is an avaricious moneylender; he has a burning racial pride, with a con-

comitant scorn for his Gentile oppressors. He is despised by all the members of Antonio's circle, whose enmity would probably be shared by many of Shakespeare's contemporaries. But Shakespeare, with his rare creative gift for understanding and humanizing all sorts and conditions of men, did not find it possible to make of Shylock simply a conventional monster of avaricious cruelty. Rather he has made him at many points affectingly human. He has let him be eloquent upon the sufferings of his race and the common humanity of Jew and Gentile. And he has taken care to afford him comprehensible motivation for the relentlessness which the traditional story of the pound of flesh demanded. A judicious reading of the text shows that it was not primarily Antonio's forfeiture which made Shylock greedy to exact the literal penalty of the bond. Originally Shylock had said that the terms of the bond were named "in merry sport," and there is no real reason to accuse him of diabolical insincerity. The chances of Antonio's failing must have appeared as remote to him as to anyone else. The terms may well enough have been no more than awkward jesting after his offer, out of a protested desire to be friends with Antonio, to forgo his customary "usury." In any event, when Shylock is first informed of Antonio's losses, he hardly leaps to his chances as he should have done if from the beginning he had been thirsting for Antonio's ruin. At that moment his mind is racked by the discovery of his daughter's elopement; she, his own flesh and blood, has deceived and robbed him, running off with a Christian aided and abetted by Antonio's friends. That is what tortures him and goads him, once his opportunity has dawned upon him, into a fanatical desire for revenge. And in the initial frenzy of his grief, sympathy for Shylock cannot be denied. He is a father, terribly wronged.

In the end, however, Shylock is a defeated and a broken man. His lust for inexorable justice was evil, and the play is a comedy wherein the figure obstructing the happiness of those destined to be blest must be thwarted. The penalty that he renounce his religion appears to us today as a wanton cruelty, but to Shakespeare's contemporaries it probably did not seem so. Critics have, indeed, suggested that they would regard it as an act of charity to admit Shylock to the benefits of Christian sacraments. However that may be, it is impossible to accuse Shakespeare, who made of Shylock so intensely human a figure, of anti-Semitism.

THE MERCHANT OF VENICE

ACT I

[SCENE I. *Venice. A street.*]

Enter ANTONIO, SALARINO, *and* SALANIO.

Ant. In sooth, I know not why I am so sad.
It wearies me; you say it wearies you;
But how I caught it, found it, or came by it,
What stuff 'tis made of, whereof it is born,
I am to learn; 5
And such a want-wit sadness makes of me,
That I have much ado to know myself.

Salar. Your mind is tossing on the ocean,
There, where your argosies with portly sail,
Like signiors and rich burghers on the flood, 10
Or, as it were, the pageants of the sea,
Do overpeer the petty traffickers
That curtsy to them, do them reverence,
As they fly by them with their woven wings.

Salan. Believe me, sir, had I such venture forth,
The better part of my affections would 16
Be with my hopes abroad.   I should be still
Plucking the grass to know where sits the wind,
Peering in maps for ports and piers and roads;
And every object that might make me fear 20
Misfortune to my ventures, out of doubt
Would make me sad.

Salar.   My wind cooling my broth
Would blow me to an ague when I thought
What harm a wind too great might do at sea.
I should not see the sandy hour-glass run 25
But I should think of shallows and of flats,
And see my wealthy Andrew dock'd in sand,
Vailing her high-top lower than her ribs
To kiss her burial.   Should I go to church
And see the holy edifice of stone, 30
And not bethink me straight of dangerous rocks,
Which, touching but my gentle vessel's side,
Would scatter all her spices on the stream,
Enrobe the roaring waters with my silks,
And, in a word, but even now worth this, 35
And now worth nothing?   Shall I have the thought

Act I, sc. i, 5. **am to learn:** have not learned.   9. **argosies:** large merchant ships.   **portly:** billowing.   11. **pageants:** the wheeled stages of the Miracle Plays.   15. **venture forth:** investment at stake.   17. **still:** constantly.   19. **roads:** anchorages.   27. **Andrew:** name of a ship.   28. **Vailing:** lowering.   **high-top:** masthead.

To think on this, and shall I lack the thought
That such a thing bechanc'd would make me sad?
But tell not me; I know Antonio
Is sad to think upon his merchandise.   40
   Ant. Believe me, no. I thank my fortune for it,
My ventures are not in one bottom trusted,
Nor to one place; nor is my whole estate
Upon the fortune of this present year:
Therefore my merchandise makes me not sad.   45
   Salar. Why, then you are in love.
   Ant.   Fie, fie!
   Salar. Not in love neither? Then let us say you
    are sad
Because you are not merry; and 'twere as easy
For you to laugh and leap and say you are merry
Because you are not sad. Now, by two-headed
   Janus,   50
Nature hath fram'd strange fellows in her time;
Some that will evermore peep through their eyes
And laugh like parrots at a bag-piper,
And other of such vinegar aspect
That they'll not show their teeth in way of smile
Though Nestor swear the jest be laughable.   56

   Enter BASSANIO, LORENZO, *and* GRATIANO.

   Salan. Here comes Bassanio, your most noble
    kinsman,
Gratiano, and Lorenzo. Fare ye well;
We leave you now with better company.
   Salar. I would have stay'd till I had made you
    merry,   60
If worthier friends had not prevented me.
   Ant. Your worth is very dear in my regard.
I take it, your own business calls on you
And you embrace th' occasion to depart.
   Salar. Good morrow, my good lords.   65
   Bass. Good signiors both, when shall we laugh?
    Say, when?
You grow exceeding strange. Must it be so?
   Salar. We'll make our leisures to attend on yours.
       [*Exeunt Salarino and Salanio.*
   Lor. My Lord Bassanio, since you have found
    Antonio,
We two will leave you; but at dinner-time,   70
I pray you, have in mind where we must meet.
   Bass. I will not fail you.
   Gra. You look not well, Signior Antonio;
You have too much respect upon the world.
They lose it that do buy it with much care.   75
Believe me, you are marvellously chang'd.
   Ant. I hold the world but as the world, Gratiano,
A stage where every man must play a part,

And mine a sad one.
   Gra.   Let me play the fool!
With mirth and laughter let old wrinkles come,   80
And let my liver rather heat with wine
Than my heart cool with mortifying groans.
Why should a man, whose blood is warm within,
Sit like his grandsire cut in alabaster,
Sleep when he wakes, and creep into the jaundice   85
By being peevish? I tell thee what, Antonio —
I love thee, and it is my love that speaks —
There are a sort of men whose visages
Do cream and mantle like a standing pond,
And do a wilful stillness entertain,   90
With purpose to be dress'd in an opinion
Of wisdom, gravity, profound conceit,
As who should say, "I am Sir Oracle,
And when I ope my lips let no dog bark!"
O my Antonio, I do know of these   95
That therefore only are reputed wise
For saying nothing, when, I am very sure,
If they should speak, would almost damn those ears
Which, hearing them, would call their brothers
   fools.
I'll tell thee more of this another time;   100
But fish not with this melancholy bait
For this fool gudgeon, this opinion.
Come, good Lorenzo. Fare ye well awhile;
I'll end my exhortation after dinner.
   Lor. Well, we will leave you then till dinner-time.
I must be one of these same dumb wise men,   106
For Gratiano never lets me speak.
   Gra. Well, keep me company but two years moe,
Thou shalt not know the sound of thine own tongue.
   Ant. Farewell! I'll grow a talker for this gear.
   Gra. Thanks, i' faith, for silence is only com-
    mendable   111
In a neat's tongue dri'd and a maid not vendible.
       [*Exeunt [Gratiano and Lorenzo].*
   Ant. Is that any thing now?
   Bass. Gratiano speaks an infinite deal of nothing,
more than any man in all Venice. His reasons are
as two grains of wheat hid in two bushels of   116
chaff; you shall seek all day ere you find them, and
when you have them, they are not worth the search.
   Ant. Well, tell me now what lady is the same
To whom you swore a secret pilgrimage,   120
That you to-day promis'd to tell me of?
   Bass. 'Tis not unknown to you, Antonio,
How much I have disabled mine estate
By something showing a more swelling port   124
Than my faint means would grant continuance.
Nor do I now make moan to be abridg'd

---

42. **bottom:** ship. 50. **Janus:** a Roman god represented with two faces, one smiling, the other grave. 56. **Nestor:** a character of signal gravity in the *Iliad*. 61. **prevented:** anticipated. 67. **strange:** reserved, cold. 74. **have . . . upon:** give too much thought to. 82. **mortifying:** killing. 89. **mantle:** become covered with scum. 91. **opinion:** reputation. 92. **conceit:** thought. 98–99. **damn . . . fools.** An allusion to Matthew v.22: "Whosoever shall say to his brother . . . 'Thou fool,' shall be in danger of hell fire." 102. **gudgeon:** a small fish. 108. **moe:** more. 110. **for . . . gear:** because of this harangue. 112. **neat's:** ox's. **vendible:** marriageable.

From such a noble rate; but my chief care
Is to come fairly off from the great debts
Wherein my time something too prodigal
Hath left me gag'd. To you, Antonio,   130
I owe the most, in money and in love,
And from your love I have a warranty
To unburden all my plots and purposes
How to get clear of all the debts I owe.

Ant. I pray you, good Bassanio, let me know it;
And if it stand, as you yourself still do,   136
Within the eye of honour, be assur'd
My purse, my person, my extremest means,
Lie all unlock'd to your occasions.

Bass. In my school-days, when I had lost one
          shaft,   140
I shot his fellow of the self-same flight
The self-same way with more advised watch
To find the other forth, and by adventuring both
I oft found both. I urge this childhood proof,
Because what follows is pure innocence.   145
I owe you much, and, like a wilful youth,
That which I owe is lost; but if you please
To shoot another arrow that self way
Which you did shoot the first, I do not doubt,
As I will watch the aim, or to find both   150
Or bring your latter hazard back again
And thankfully rest debtor for the first.

Ant. You know me well, and herein spend but
          time
To wind about my love with circumstance;
And out of doubt you do me now more wrong   155
In making question of my uttermost
Than if you had made waste of all I have.
Then do but say to me what I should do
That in your knowledge may by me be done,
And I am prest unto it; therefore, speak.   160

Bass. In Belmont is a lady richly left;
And she is fair and, fairer than that word,
Of wondrous virtues. Sometimes from her eyes
I did receive fair speechless messages.
Her name is Portia, nothing undervalu'd   165
To Cato's daughter, Brutus' Portia.
Nor is the wide world ignorant of her worth,
For the four winds blow in from every coast
Renowned suitors; and her sunny locks
Hang on her temples like a golden fleece,   170
Which makes her seat of Belmont Colchis' strand,
And many Jasons come in quest of her.
O my Antonio, had I but the means
To hold a rival place with one of them,
I have a mind presages me such thrift,   175
That I should questionless be fortunate!

Ant. Thou know'st that all my fortunes are at sea;

Neither have I money nor commodity
To raise a present sum. Therefore go forth;
Try what my credit can in Venice do.   180
That shall be rack'd, even to the uttermost,
To furnish thee to Belmont, to fair Portia.
Go, presently inquire, and so will I,
Where money is; and I no question make
To have it of my trust or for my sake.   185

[*Exeunt.*

SCENE II. [*Belmont. A room in Portia's house.*]

Enter PORTIA *with her waiting-woman,* NERISSA.

Por. By my troth, Nerissa, my little body is
aweary of this great world.

Ner. You would be, sweet madam, if your miseries were in the same abundance as your good fortunes are; and yet, for aught I see, they are as   5
sick that surfeit with too much as they that starve
with nothing. It is no mean happiness, therefore,
to be seated in the mean. Superfluity comes sooner
by white hairs, but competency lives longer.   10

Por. Good sentences and well pronounc'd.

Ner. They would be better, if well followed.

Por. If to do were as easy as to know what were
good to do, chapels had been churches and poor
men's cottages princes' palaces. It is a good di-   15
vine that follows his own instructions; I can easier
teach twenty what were good to be done, than to be
one of the twenty to follow mine own teaching.
The brain may devise laws for the blood, but a hot
temper leaps o'er a cold decree; such a hare is   20
madness the youth, to skip o'er the meshes of good
counsel the cripple. But this reasoning is not in the
fashion to choose me a husband. O me, the word
choose! I may neither choose who I would nor refuse who I dislike; so is the will of a living   25
daughter curb'd by the will of a dead father. Is
it not hard, Nerissa, that I cannot choose one nor
refuse none?   29

Ner. Your father was ever virtuous, and holy
men at their death have good inspirations; therefore the lott'ry that he hath devised in these three
chests of gold, silver, and lead, whereof who chooses
his meaning chooses you, will, no doubt, never be
chosen by any rightly but one who you shall   35
rightly love. But what warmth is there in your
affection towards any of these princely suitors that
are already come?

Por. I pray thee, over-name them; and as thou
namest them, I will describe them; and, accord-   40
ing to my description, level at my affection.

Ner. First, there is the Neapolitan prince.

127. **rate**: style of living.   129. **time**: way of life.   130. **gag'd**: pledged.   143. **forth**: out.   144. **proof**: experience.   160.
prest: ready.   166. **Brutus' Portia.** See *Julius Caesar.*   172. **Jasons.** Jason obtained the famous golden fleece at Colchis.
175. **thrift**: success.   181. **rack'd**: stretched.   183. **presently**: at once.
    Sc. ii, 9. **comes ... by**: causes sooner.   11. **sentences**: maxims.   25-26. **will ... will**: desire ... testament.   41 **level at**:
aim at, judge of.

Por. Ay, that's a colt indeed, for he doth nothing but talk of his horse; and he makes it a great 45 appropriation to his own good parts, that he can shoe him himself. I am much afeard my lady his mother played false with a smith.

Ner. Then is there the County Palatine.

Por. He doth nothing but frown, as who 50 should say, "An you will not have me, choose." He hears merry tales and smiles not. I fear he will prove the weeping philosopher when he grows old, being so full of unmannerly sadness in his youth. I had rather be married to a death's- 55 head with a bone in his mouth than to either of these. God defend me from these two!

Ner. How say you by the French lord, Monsieur Le Bon? 59

Por. God made him, and therefore let him pass for a man. In truth, I know it is a sin to be a mocker; but, he! why, he hath a horse better than the Neapolitan's, a better bad habit of frowning than the Count Palatine. He is every man in no man. If a throstle sing, he falls straight a cap'r- 65 ing. He will fence with his own shadow. If I should marry him, I should marry twenty husbands. If he would despise me, I would forgive him, for if he love me to madness, I shall never requite him. 70

Ner. What say you, then, to Falconbridge, the young baron of England?

Por. You know I say nothing to him, for he understands not me, nor I him. He hath neither Latin, French, nor Italian, and you will come 75 into the court and swear that I have a poor penny-worth in the English. He is a proper man's picture, but, alas, who can converse with a dumb-show? How oddly he is suited! I think he bought his doublet in Italy, his round hose in France, his 80 bonnet in Germany, and his behaviour everywhere.

Ner. What think you of the Scottish lord, his neighbour?

Por. That he hath a neighbourly charity in 85 him, for he borrowed a box of the ear of the English-man and swore he would pay him again when he was able. I think the Frenchman became his surety and seal'd under for another.

Ner. How like you the young German, the Duke of Saxony's nephew? 91

Por. Very vilely in the morning, when he is sober, and most vilely in the afternoon, when he is drunk. When he is best, he is a little worse than a man, and when he is worst, he is little better than a beast. 95 An the worst fall that ever fell, I hope I shall make shift to go without him.

Ner. If he should offer to choose, and choose the right casket, you should refuse to perform your father's will if you should refuse to accept him. 102

Por. Therefore, for fear of the worst, I pray thee, set a deep glass of rhenish wine on the contrary casket, for if the devil be within and that tempta-tion without, I know he will choose it. I will do 106 anything, Nerissa, ere I will be married to a sponge.

Ner. You need not fear, lady, the having any of these lords. They have acquainted me with 110 their determinations; which is, indeed, to return to their home and to trouble you with no more suit, unless you may be won by some other sort than your father's imposition depending on the caskets. 115

Por. If I live to be as old as Sibylla, I will die as chaste as Diana, unless I be obtained by the man-ner of my father's will. I am glad this parcel of wooers are so reasonable, for there is not one among them but I dote on his very absence, and I pray 120 God grant them a fair departure.

Ner. Do you not remember, lady, in your father's time, a Venetian, a scholar and a soldier, that came hither in company of the Marquis of Montferrat?

Por. Yes, yes, it was Bassanio, — as I think, so was he call'd. 128

Ner. True, madam. He, of all the men that ever my foolish eyes look'd upon, was the best deserving a fair lady. 131

Por. I remember him well, and I remember him worthy of thy praise.

Enter a SERVING-MAN.

How now! what news?

Serv. The four strangers seek for you, madam, to take their leave; and there is a forerunner come 136 from a fifth, the Prince of Morocco, who brings word the Prince his master will be here tonight. 139

Por. If I could bid the fifth welcome with so good a heart as I can bid the other four farewell, I should be glad of his approach. If he have the condition of a saint and the complexion of a devil, I had rather he should shrive me than wive me. 145 Come, Nerissa. Sirrah, go before. While we shut the gates upon one wooer, another knocks at the door.   [*Exeunt.*

[SCENE III.   *Venice.   A public place.*]

Enter BASSANIO *and* SHYLOCK *the Jew.*

Shy. Three thousand ducats; well.

Bass. Ay, sir, for three months.

Shy. For three months; well.

---

51. **choose:** i.e., do what you please.   53. **weeping philosopher:** Heraclitus.   76. **proper:** handsome.   78. **suited:** dressed.   79. **round hose:** breeches.   81. **Scottish** Qq. F reads *other*, probably substituted in deference to King James. 88–89. **Frenchman … another:** i.e., the Frenchman pledged himself to pay the Englishman with another blow. An allusion to the old alliance between France and Scotland.   96. **fall … fell:** befall … befell.   115. **imposition:** conditions. 116. **Sibylla:** the Cumaean Sibyl, to whom Apollo granted as many years as there were grains in her handful of sand. 134. **four.** Nerissa has named six suitors.   143. **condition:** disposition.   145. **shrive me:** hear my confession.

Bass. For the which, as I told you, Antonio shall
be bound.   5
Shy. Antonio shall become bound; well.
Bass. May you stead me? Will you pleasure
me? Shall I know your answer?
Shy. Three thousand ducats for three months,
and Antonio bound.   10
Bass. Your answer to that.
Shy. Antonio is a good man.
Bass. Have you heard any imputation to the
contrary?
Shy. Ho, no, no, no, no! My meaning in   15
saying he is a good man is to have you understand
me that he is sufficient. Yet his means are in supposition: he hath an argosy bound to Tripolis, another to the Indies; I understand, moreover, upon
the Rialto, he hath a third at Mexico, a fourth   20
for England, and other ventures he hath, squand'red
abroad. But ships are but boards, sailors but men;
there be land-rats and water-rats, water-thieves and
land-thieves, I mean pirates, and then there is the
peril of waters, winds, and rocks. The man is,   25
notwithstanding, sufficient. Three thousand ducats:
I think I may take his bond.
Bass. Be assured you may.
Shy. I will be assured I may; and, that I may   30
be assured, I will bethink me. May I speak with
Antonio?
Bass. If it please you to dine with us.
Shy. Yes, to smell pork; to eat of the habitation
which your prophet the Nazarite conjured the   35
devil into. I will buy with you, sell with you, talk
with you, walk with you, and so following; but I
will not eat with you, drink with you, nor pray with
you. What news on the Rialto? Who is he comes
here?   40

Enter ANTONIO.

Bass. This is Signior Antonio.
Shy. [*Aside.*] How like a fawning publican he
looks!
I hate him for he is a Christian.
But more for that in low simplicity
He lends out money gratis, and brings down   45
The rate of usance here with us in Venice.
If I can catch him once upon the hip,
I will feed fat the ancient grudge I bear him.
He hates our sacred nation, and he rails,
Even there where merchants most do congregate,
On me, my bargains, and my well-won thrift,   51
Which he calls interest. Cursed be my tribe,

If I forgive him!
   Bass.   Shylock, do you hear?
   Shy. I am debating of my present store,
And, by the near guess of my memory,   55
I cannot instantly raise up the gross
Of full three thousand ducats. What of that?
Tubal, a wealthy Hebrew of my tribe,
Will furnish me. But soft! how many months
Do you desire? [*To Ant.*] Rest you fair, good
    signior;   60
Your worship was the last man in our mouths.
   Ant. Shylock, albeit I neither lend nor borrow
By taking nor by giving of excess,
Yet, to supply the ripe wants of my friend,
I'll break a custom. Is he yet possess'd   65
How much ye would?
   Shy.   Ay, ay, three thousand ducats.
   Ant. And for three months.
   Shy. I had forgot; three months; you told me so.
Well then, your bond; and let me see; — but hear
    you;
Methought you said you neither lend nor borrow   70
Upon advantage.
   Ant.   I do never use it.
   Shy. When Jacob graz'd his uncle Laban's
    sheep —
This Jacob from our holy Abram was,
As his wise mother wrought in his behalf,
The third possessor; ay, he was the third —   75
   Ant. And what of him? Did he take interest?
   Shy. No, not take int'rest, not, as you would say,
Directly int'rest. Mark what Jacob did.
When Laban and himself were compromis'd   79
That all the eanlings which were streak'd and pied
Should fall as Jacob's hire, the ewes, being rank,
In end of autumn turned to the rams,
And, when the work of generation was
Between these woolly breeders in the act,
The skilful shepherd pill'd me certain wands   85
And, in the doing of the deed of kind,
He stuck them up before the fulsome ewes,
Who then conceiving did in eaning time
Fall parti-colour'd lambs, and those were Jacob's.
This was a way to thrive, and he was blest;   90
And thrift is blessing, if men steal it not.
   Ant. This was a venture, sir, that Jacob serv'd
    for;
A thing not in his power to bring to pass,
But sway'd and fashion'd by the hand of Heaven.
Was this inserted to make interest good?   95
Or is your gold and silver ewes and rams?

Sc. iii, **7. stead:** help. **20. Rialto:** the mart of Venice. **35. Nazarite:** Nazarene. The reference is to Christ's driving
out devils from men into swine. (Luke vii.32–33.) **42. publican:** term of scorn. **46. usance:** interest. **47. catch ...
hip:** a wrestling term. **65–66. Is ... would.** Q₁. *Are you resolv'd, How much he would have* Q₂. **possess'd:** informed.
71. Upon advantage: for profit. **75. possessor:** i.e., of God's promise to Abraham. **78–89. Mark ... Jacob's.** See Genesis
xxx.35–43. **79. compromis'd:** agreed. **80. eanlings:** new-born lambs. **pied:** spotted. **85. pill'd:** peeled. **86. kind:**
nature. **89. Fall:** give birth to.

Shy. I cannot tell; I make it breed as fast.
But note me, signior.
  Ant.   Mark you this, Bassanio,
The devil can cite Scripture for his purpose.
An evil soul producing holy witness   100
Is like a villain with a smiling cheek,
A goodly apple rotten at the heart.
O, what a goodly outside falsehood hath!
  Shy. Three thousand ducats; 'tis a good round
   sum.
Three months from twelve; then, let me see; the
   rate —   105
  Ant. Well, Shylock, shall we be beholding to
   you?
  Shy. Signior Antonio, many a time and oft
In the Rialto you have rated me
About my moneys and my usances.
Still have I borne it with a patient shrug, 110
For suff'rance is the badge of all our tribe.
You call me misbeliever, cut-throat dog,
And spit upon my Jewish gaberdine,
And all for use of that which is mine own.
Well then, it now appears you need my help. 115
Go to, then! You come to me, and you say,
"Shylock, we would have moneys;" you say so —
You, that did void your rheum upon my beard
And foot me as you spurn a stranger cur
Over your threshold; moneys is your suit. 120
What should I say to you? Should I not say,
"Hath a dog money? Is it possible
A cur can lend three thousand ducats?" Or
Shall I bend low and in a bondman's key,
With bated breath and whisp'ring humbleness, 125
Say this:
"Fair sir, you spat on me on Wednesday last;
You spurn'd me such a day; another time
You call'd me dog; and for these courtesies
I'll lend you thus much moneys"?   130
  Ant. I am as like to call thee so again,
To spit on thee again, to spurn thee too.
If thou wilt lend this money, lend it not
As to thy friends; for when did friendship take
A breed for barren metal of his friend?   135
But lend it rather to thine enemy,
Who, if he break, thou mayst with better face
Exact the penalty.
  Shy.   Why, look you, how you storm!
I would be friends with you and have your love,
Forget the shames that you have stain'd me with,
Supply your present wants, and take no doit 141
Of usance for my moneys, and you'll not hear me.
This is kind I offer.
  Bass. This were kindness.
  Shy.   This kindness will I show.

Go with me to a notary, seal me there   145
Your single bond; and, in a merry sport,
If you repay me not on such a day,
In such a place, such sum or sums as are
Express'd in the condition, let the forfeit
Be nominated for an equal pound   150
Of your fair flesh, to be cut off and taken
In what part of your body pleaseth me.
  Ant. Content, i'faith, I'll seal to such a bond,
And say there is much kindness in the Jew.
  Bass. You shall not seal to such a bond for me;
I'll rather dwell in my necessity.   156
  Ant. Why, fear not, man; I will not forfeit it.
Within these two months, that's a month before
This bond expires, I do expect return
Of thrice three times the value of this bond. 160
  Shy. O father Abram, what these Christians are,
Whose own hard dealings teaches them suspect
The thoughts of others! Pray you, tell me this:
If he should break his day, what should I gain
By the exaction of the forfeiture?   165
A pound of man's flesh taken from a man
Is not so estimable, profitable neither,
As flesh of muttons, beefs, or goats. I say,
To buy his favour, I extend this friendship.
If he will take it, so; if not, adieu;   170
And, for my love, I pray you wrong me not.
  Ant. Yes, Shylock, I will seal unto this bond.
  Shy. Then meet me forthwith at the notary's;
Give him direction for this merry bond,
And I will go and purse the ducats straight, 175
See to my house, left in the fearful guard
Of an unthrifty knave, and presently
I will be with you.   *[Exit [Shylock].*
  Ant. Hie thee, gentle Jew.
The Hebrew will turn Christian: he grows kind.
  Bass. I like not fair terms and a villain's mind.
  Ant. Come on; in this there can be no dismay; 181
My ships come home a month before the day.
                [Exeunt.

ACT II

[SCENE I. *Belmont. A room in Portia's house.*]

Enter [the PRINCE OF] MOROCCO, *a tawny Moor, all
in white, and three or four followers accordingly,
with* PORTIA, NERISSA, *and their train. Flourish
of cornets.*

  Mor. Mislike me not for my complexion,
The shadowed livery of the burnish'd sun,
To whom I am a neighbour and near bred.
Bring me the fairest creature northward born,
Where Phœbus' fire scarce thaws the icicles, 5

---

108. **rated**: reviled. 113. **gaberdine**: cloak. 135. **breed**: increase, interest. 137. **Who**: from whom. **break**: fail. 141.
doit: a small Dutch coin; cf. a farthing. 146. **single**: without endorsement. 150. **equal**: exact. 176. **fearful**: precarious.
 Act II, sc. i, 2. **shadowed livery**: black uniform, as if Morocco were the "retainer" of the sun.

And let us make incision for your love,
To prove whose blood is reddest, his or mine.
I tell thee, lady, this aspect of mine
Hath fear'd the valiant. By my love I swear
The best-regarded virgins of our clime   10
Have lov'd it too. I would not change this hue,
Except to steal your thoughts, my gentle queen.
    Por. In terms of choice I am not solely led
By nice direction of a maiden's eyes;
Besides, the lott'ry of my destiny   15
Bars me the right of voluntary choosing.
But if my father had not scanted me
And hedg'd me by his wit, to yield myself
His wife who wins me by that means I told you,
Yourself, renowned Prince, then stood as fair   20
As any comer I have look'd on yet
For my affection.
    Mor.   Even for that I thank you;
Therefore, I pray you, lead me to the caskets
To try my fortune. By this scimitar
That slew the Sophy and a Persian prince   25
That won three fields of Sultan Solyman,
I would o'erstare the sternest eyes that look,
Outbrave the heart most daring on the earth,
Pluck the young sucking cubs from the she-bear,
Yea, mock the lion when he roars for prey,   30
To win thee, lady. But, alas the while!
If Hercules and Lichas play at dice
Which is the better man, the greater throw
May turn by fortune from the weaker hand.
So is Alcides beaten by his [page];   35
And so may I, blind fortune leading me,
Miss that which one unworthier may attain,
And die with grieving.
    Por.   You must take your chance,
And either not attempt to choose at all,
Or swear before you choose, if you choose wrong   40
Never to speak to lady afterward
In way of marriage; therefore be advis'd.
    Mor. Nor will not. Come, bring me unto my
        chance.
    Por. First, forward to the temple. After dinner
Your hazard shall be made.
    Mor.   Good fortune then! 45
To make me blest or cursed'st among men.
                        [*Cornets, and exeunt.*

[SCENE II. *Venice. A street.*]

Enter the Clown [LAUNCELOT] *alone.*

Laun. Certainly my conscience will serve me to

run from this Jew my master. The fiend is at mine
elbow and tempts me, saying to me, "Gobbo,
Launcelot Gobbo, good Launcelot," or "good
Gobbo," or "good Launcelot Gobbo, use your 5
legs, take the start, run away." My conscience
says, "No; take heed, honest Launcelot; take heed,
honest Gobbo," or, as aforesaid, "honest Launcelot
Gobbo; do not run; scorn running with thy heels."
Well, the most courageous fiend bids me pack. 10
"Via!" says the fiend; "away!" says the fiend;
"for the heavens, rouse up a brave mind," says the
fiend, "and run." Well, my conscience, hanging
about the neck of my heart, says very wisely to me,
"My honest friend Launcelot, being an honest 15
man's son," or rather an honest woman's son; for,
indeed, my father did something smack, something
grow to, he had a kind of taste, — well, my conscience says, "Launcelot, budge not." "Budge," says
the fiend. "Budge not," says my conscience. "Conscience," say I, "you counsel well;" "Fiend," 20
say I, "you counsel well." To be rul'd by my
conscience, I should stay with the Jew my master,
who, God bless the mark, is a kind of devil; and, to
run away from the Jew, I should be rul'd by the 26
fiend, who, saving your reverence, is the devil himself. Certainly the Jew is the very devil incarnation; and, in my conscience, my conscience is but a
kind of hard conscience, to offer to counsel me to
stay with the Jew. The fiend gives the more 31
friendly counsel. I will run, fiend; my heels are at
your commandment; I will run.

Enter Old GOBBO, *with a basket.*

    Gob. Master young man, you, I pray you, which
is the way to master Jew's?   35
    Laun. [*Aside.*] O heavens! this is my true-begot-
ten father, who, being more than sand-blind, high-
gravel blind, knows me not. I will try confusions
with him.
    Gob. Master young gentleman, I pray you, which
is the way to master Jew's?   41
    Laun. Turn up on your right hand at the next
turning, but at the next turning of all, on your left;
marry, at the very next turning, turn of no hand, but
turn down indirectly to the Jew's house.   46
    Gob. By God's sonties, 'twill be a hard way to
hit. Can you tell me whether one Launcelot, that
dwells with him, dwell with him or no?
    Laun. Talk you of young Master Launcelot?
[*Aside.*] Mark me now; now will I raise the 50
waters. — Talk you of young Master Launcelot?

13. **terms:** matters. 14. **nice:** fastidious. 17. **scanted:** restricted. 18. **wit:** wisdom, ingenuity. 25. **Sophy:** Shah of Persia. 26. **Solyman:** Turkish Sultan (1520-1566). 32. **Lichas:** servant of Hercules (Alcides). 35. **[page]** (Theobald). *rage* Qq. 44. **to the temple:** i.e., to take your oath.
Sc. ii, 10. **pack:** begone. 17-19. Launcelot means that his father was barely honest. 23. **well. To be** Q₁. *ill. To be* Q₂. 25. **God...mark:** a phrase of apology. 27. **incarnation** Q₁. *incarnall* Q₂. Incarnate. 33. **commandment** Q₁. *command* Q₂. 37. **high-gravel blind:** Launcelot's original term for something less than stone-blind and more than sand-blind. 38. **confusions** Q₁. *conclusions* Q₂. 47. **sonties:** diminutive of *sonts*, i.e., saints. 51. **waters:** tears.

Gob. No master, sir, but a poor man's son. His father, though I say't, is an honest exceeding poor man and, God be thanked, well to live.   55

Laun. Well, let his father be what 'a will, we talk of young Master Launcelot.

Gob. Your worship's friend and Launcelot, sir.

Laun. But I pray you, ergo, old man, ergo, I beseech you, talk you of young Master Launcelot.   60

Gob. Of Launcelot, an't please your mastership.

Laun. Ergo, Master Launcelot. Talk not of Master Launcelot, father; for the young gentleman, according to Fates and Destinies and such odd   65 sayings, the Sisters Three and such branches of learning, is indeed deceased, or, as you would say in plain terms, gone to heaven.

Gob. Marry, God forbid! The boy was the very staff of my age, my very prop.   70

Laun. [*Aside.*] Do I look like a cudgel or a hovel-post, a staff or a prop? — Do you know me, father?

Gob. Alack the day, I know you not, young gentleman; but I pray you, tell me, is my boy, God rest his soul, alive or dead?   75

Laun. Do you not know me, father?

Gob. Alack, sir, I am sand-blind; I know you not.

Laun. Nay, indeed, if you had your eyes, you might fail of the knowing me; it is a wise fa-   80 ther that knows his own child. Well, old man, I will tell you news of your son. Give me your blessing; truth will come to light; murder cannot be hid long; a man's son may, but in the end truth will out.   85

Gob. Pray you, sir, stand up. I am sure you are not Launcelot, my boy.

Laun. Pray you, let's have no more fooling about it, but give me your blessing. I am Launcelot, your boy that was, your son that is, your child that shall be.   91

Gob. I cannot think you are my son.

Laun. I know not what I shall think of that; but I am Launcelot, the Jew's man, and I am sure Margery your wife is my mother.   95

Gob. Her name is Margery, indeed. I'll be sworn, if thou be Launcelot, thou art mine own flesh and blood. Lord worshipp'd might he be! what a beard hast thou got! Thou has got more hair on thy chin than Dobbin my fill-horse has on his tail.   101

Laun. It should seem, then, that Dobbin's tail grows backward. I am sure he had more hair of his tail than I have of my face when I last saw him.   105

Gob. Lord, how art thou chang'd! How dost thou and thy master agree? I have brought him a present. How 'gree you now?

Laun. Well, well: but, for mine own part, as I

have set up my rest to run away, so I will not   110 rest till I have run some ground. My master's a very Jew. Give him a present! give him a halter. I am famish'd in his service; you may tell every finger I have with my ribs. Father, I am glad you are come; give me your present to one Master   115 Bassanio, who, indeed, gives rare new liveries. If I serve not him, I will run as far as God has any ground. O rare fortune! here comes the man. To him, father; for I am a Jew, if I serve the Jew any longer.   120

Enter BASSANIO, *with* [LEONARDO *and other*] *followers.*

Bass. You may do so; but let it be so hasted that supper be ready at the farthest by five of the clock. See these letters delivered; put the liveries to making, and desire Gratiano to come anon to my lodging.   [*Exit one of his men.* 125

Laun. To him, father.

Gob. God bless your worship!

Bass. Gramercy! wouldst thou aught with me?

Gob. Here's my son, sir, a poor boy, —   129

Laun. Not a poor boy, sir, but the rich Jew's man; that would, sir, as my father shall specify —

Gob. He hath a great infection, sir, as one would say, to serve —   134

Laun. Indeed, the short and the long is, I serve the Jew, and have a desire, as my father shall specify —

Gob. His master and he, saving your worship's reverence, are scarce cater-cousins —   139

Laun. To be brief, the very truth is that the Jew, having done me wrong, doth cause me, as my father, being, I hope, an old man, shall frutify unto you —

Gob. I have here a dish of doves that I would bestow upon your worship, and my suit is —   145

Laun. In very brief, the suit is impertinent to myself, as your worship shall know by this honest old man; and, though I say it, though old man, yet poor man, my father.

Bass. One speak for both. What would you? 150

Laun. Serve you, sir.

Gob. That is the very defect of the matter, sir.

Bass. I know thee well; thou hast obtain'd thy suit.

Shylock thy master spoke with me this day,
And hath preferr'd thee, if it be preferment   155
To leave a rich Jew's service, to become
The follower of so poor a gentleman.

Laun. The old proverb is very well parted between my master Shylock and you, sir: you have the grace of God, sir, and he hath enough.   160

---

55. **well to live:** well to do. 59. **ergo:** therefore (here meaningless). 71. **hovel-post:** support used for a shed. 85. **in the end** Q₁. *at the length* Q₂. 99. **beard.** Launcelot has kneeled with his back to his father. 101. **fill-horse:** shaft-horse. 110. **set ... rest:** resolved. 113. **tell:** count. 128. **Gramercy:** many thanks. 133. **infection:** blunder for *affection.* 139. **cater-cousins:** good friends. 143. **frutify:** blunder for *certify.* 152. **defect:** blunder for *effect* (heart). 158. **proverb:** "God's grace is gear enough."

Bass. Thou speak'st it well.   Go, father, with thy son.
Take leave of thy old master, and inquire
My lodging out.   Give him a livery
More guarded than his fellows'; see it done.   164
Laun. Father, in.   I cannot get a service, no;
I have ne'er a tongue in my head.   [*Looks on his palm.*]   Well, if any man in Italy have a fairer table, which doth offer to swear upon a book, I shall have good fortune.   Go to, here's a simple line of life!   Here's a small trifle of wives!   Alas, fifteen wives is nothing!   Eleven widows and nine   170 maids is a simple coming-in for one man.   And then to 'scape drowning thrice, and to be in peril of my life with the edge of a feather-bed; here are simple scapes.   Well, if Fortune be a woman, she's a good wench for this gear.   Father, come; I'll take my   175 leave of the Jew in the twinkling [of an eye].
    [*Exeunt Launcelot [and old Gobbo].*
Bass. I pray thee, good Leonardo, think on this:
These things being bought and orderly bestow'd,
Return in haste, for I do feast to-night   180
My best esteem'd acquaintance.   Hie thee, go.
Leon. My best endeavours shall be done herein.

Enter GRATIANO.

Gra. Where is your master?
Leon.   Yonder, sir, he walks.
                    [*Exit.*
Gra. Signior Bassanio!
Bass. Gratiano!   185
Gra. I have a suit to you.
Bass.   You have obtain'd it.
Gra. You must not deny me; I must go with you
to Belmont.
Bass. Why, then you must.   But hear thee, Gratiano;
Thou art too wild, too rude and bold of voice;   190
Parts that become thee happily enough
And in such eyes as ours appear not faults;
But where thou art not known, why, there they show
Something too liberal.   Pray thee, take pain
To allay with some cold drops of modesty   195
Thy skipping spirit, lest through thy wild behaviour
I be misconst'red in the place I go to,
And lose my hopes.
Gra.   Signior Bassanio, hear me:
If I do not put on a sober habit,
Talk with respect and swear but now and then,   200
Wear prayer-books in my pocket, look demurely,
Nay more, while grace is saying, hood mine eyes
Thus with my hat, and sigh and say Amen,

Use all the observance of civility,
Like one well studied in a sad ostent   205
To please his grandam, never trust me more.
Bass. Well, we shall see your bearing.
Gra. Nay, but I bar to-night; you shall not gauge me
By what we do to-night.
Bass.   No, that were pity.
I would entreat you rather to put on   210
Your boldest suit of mirth, for we have friends
That purpose merriment.   But fare you well!
I have some business.
Gra. And I must to Lorenzo and the rest;   214
But we will visit you at supper-time.   [*Exeunt.*

[SCENE III.   *The same.   A room in Shylock's house.*]

Enter JESSICA *and the Clown* [LAUNCELOT].

Jes. I am sorry thou wilt leave my father so.
Our house is hell, and thou, a merry devil,
Didst rob it of some taste of tediousness.
But fare thee well, there is a ducat for thee;
And, Launcelot, soon at supper shalt thou see   5
Lorenzo, who is thy new master's guest.
Give him this letter; do it secretly;
And so farewell.   I would not have my father
See me in talk with thee.   9
Laun. Adieu! tears exhibit my tongue.   Most beautiful pagan, most sweet Jew! if a Christian do not play the knave and get thee, I am much deceived.   But, adieu! these foolish drops do something drown my manly spirit.   Adieu!   [*Exit.*
Jes. Farewell, good Launcelot.   15
Alack, what heinous sin is it in me
To be asham'd to be my father's child!
But though I am a daughter to his blood,
I am not to his manners.   O Lorenzo,
If thou keep promise, I shall end this strife,   20
Become a Christian and thy loving wife.   [*Exit.*

[SCENE IV.   *The same.   A street.*]

Enter GRATIANO, LORENZO, SALARINO, *and* SALANIO.

Lor. Nay, we will slink away in supper-time,
Disguise us at my lodging and return,
All in an hour.
Gra. We have not made good preparation.   4
Salar. We have not spoke us yet of torch-bearers.
Salan. 'Tis vile, unless it may be quaintly order'd,
And better in my mind not undertook.

---

164. **guarded:** ornamented with braid.   168. **table:** palm.   169. **simple:** poor or small (ironical).   176. [**of an eye**] Q₂.
Om. Q₁.   194. **liberal:** free and easy.   199. **habit:** demeanor.   205. **sad ostent:** grave deportment.
Sc. iii, 10. **exhibit:** blunder for *inhibit*.
Sc. iv, 5. **spoke . . . of:** yet bespoken.   6. **quaintly:** elegantly.

Lor. 'Tis now but four o'clock; we have two hours
To furnish us.

Enter LAUNCELOT, *with a letter.*

Friend Launcelot, what's the news?
Laun. An it shall please you to break up this, it shall seem to signify.   11
Lor. I know the hand; in faith, 'tis a fair hand,
And whiter than the paper it writ on
Is the fair hand that writ.
Gra.   Love-news, in faith.
Laun. By your leave, sir.   15
Lor. Whither goest thou?
Laun. Marry, sir, to bid my old master the Jew, to sup to-night with my new master the Christian.
Lor. Hold, here, take this. Tell gentle Jessica   20
I will not fail her; speak it privately; go.
                              [*Exit Launcelot.*
Gentlemen,
Will you prepare you for this masque to-night?
I am provided of a torch-bearer.   24
Salar. Ay, marry, I'll be gone about it straight.
Salan. And so will I.
Lor.   Meet me and Gratiano
At Gratiano's lodging some hour hence.
Salar. 'Tis good we do so.
                         [*Exeunt [Salar. and Salan.].*
Gra. Was not that letter from fair Jessica?
Lor. I must needs tell thee all. She hath directed
How I shall take her from her father's house,   31
What gold and jewels she is furnish'd with,
What page's suit she hath in readiness.
If e'er the Jew her father come to heaven,
It will be for his gentle daughter's sake;   35
And never dare misfortune cross her foot,
Unless she do it under this excuse,
That she is issue to a faithless Jew.
Come, go with me; peruse this as thou goest.   39
Fair Jessica shall be my torch-bearer.   [*Exeunt.*

[SCENE V. *The same. Before Shylock's house.*]

Enter the Jew [SHYLOCK] *and* LAUNCELOT.

Shy. Well, thou shalt see, thy eyes shall be thy judge,
The difference of old Shylock and Bassanio. —
What, Jessica! — Thou shalt not gormandise,
As thou hast done with me, — What, Jessica! —
And sleep and snore, and rend apparel out; —   5
Why, Jessica, I say!
Laun.   Why, Jessica!

Shy. Who bids thee call? I do not bid thee call.
Laun. Your worship was wont to tell me I could do nothing without bidding.

Enter JESSICA.

Jes. Call you? What is your will?   10
Shy. I am bid forth to supper, Jessica.
There are my keys. But wherefore should I go?
I am not bid for love; they flatter me;
But yet I'll go in hate, to feed upon
The prodigal Christian. Jessica, my girl,   15
Look to my house. I am right loath to go.
There is some ill a-brewing towards my rest,
For I did dream of money-bags to-night.
Laun. I beseech you, sir, go. My young master
doth expect your reproach.   20
Shy. So do I his.
Laun. And they have conspired together. I will not say you shall see a masque; but if you do, then it was not for nothing that my nose fell a-bleeding on Black Monday last at six o'clock i' th' morn-   25
ing, falling out that year on Ash Wednesday was four year, in th' afternoon.
Shy. What, are there masques? Hear you me, Jessica.
Lock up my doors; and when you hear the drum
And the vile squealing of the wry-neck'd fife,   30
Clamber not you up to the casements then,
Nor thrust your head into the public street
To gaze on Christian fools with varnish'd faces,
But stop my house's ears, I mean my casements.
Let not the sound of shallow fopp'ry enter   35
My sober house. By Jacob's staff I swear
I have no mind of feasting forth to-night;
But I will go. Go you before me, sirrah;
Say I will come.
Laun. I will go before, sir. Mistress, look out at window, for all this;   41
            There will come a Christian by,
            Will be worth a Jewess' eye.   [*Exit.*]
Shy. What says that fool of Hagar's offspring, ha?
Jes. His words were "Farewell, Mistress!" nothing else.   45
Shy. The patch is kind enough, but a huge feeder;
Snail-slow in profit, and he sleeps by day
More than the wild-cat. Drones hive not with me;
Therefore I part with him, and part with him
To one that I would have him help to waste   50
His borrowed purse. Well, Jessica, go in.
Perhaps I will return immediately.
Do as I bid you, shut doors after you;
Fast bind, fast find;
A proverb never stale in thrifty mind.   [*Exit.* 55

10. **up:** open. 36. **dare:** i.e., will dare. **foot:** i.e., path. 38. **faithless:** unbelieving.
Sc. v, 18. **to-night:** last night. 20. **reproach:** blunder for *approach.* 30. **wry-neck'd fife:** fife-player holding his head awry. 33. **varnish'd faces:** painted faces or masks. 44 **fool of Hagar's offspring:** Ishmaelite, a term of reproach. 46. **patch:** fool.

Jes. Farewell; and if my fortune be not cross'd,
I have a father, you a daughter, lost.   [*Exit.*

[SCENE VI.   *The same.*]

Enter GRATIANO *and* SALARINO, *masked.*

Gra. This is the pent-house under which Lorenzo
Desir'd us to make stand.
Salar.   His hour is almost past.
Gra. And it is marvel he out-dwells his hour,
For lovers ever run before the clock.
Salar. O, ten times faster Venus' pigeons fly   5
To seal love's bonds new-made than they are wont
To keep obliged faith unforfeited!
Gra. That ever holds.   Who riseth from a feast
With that keen appetite that he sits down?
Where is the horse that doth untread again   10
His tedious measures with the unbated fire
That he did pace them first?   All things that are,
Are with more spirit chased than enjoy'd.
How like a younker or a prodigal
The scarfed bark puts from her native bay,   15
Hugg'd and embraced by the strumpet wind!
How like the prodigal doth she return,
With over-weather'd ribs and ragged sails,
Lean, rent, and beggar'd by the strumpet wind!
Salar. Here comes Lorenzo; more of this here-
after.   20

Enter LORENZO.

Lor. Sweet friends, your patience for my long
abode;
Not I, but my affairs, have made you wait.
When you shall please to play the thieves for wives,
I'll watch as long for you then.   Approach;
Here dwells my father Jew.   Ho! who's within?   25

Enter JESSICA, *above* [*in boy's clothes*].

Jes. Who are you?   Tell me for more certainty,
Albeit I'll swear that I do know your tongue.
Lor. Lorenzo, and thy love.
Jes. Lorenzo, certain, and my love indeed,
For who love I so much?   And now who knows
But you, Lorenzo, whether I am yours?   31
Lor. Heaven and thy thoughts are witness that
thou art.
Jes. Here, catch this casket; it is worth the pains.
I am glad 'tis night, you do not look on me,
For I am much asham'd of my exchange.   35
But love is blind and lovers cannot see
The pretty follies that themselves commit;
For if they could, Cupid himself would blush
To see me thus transformed to a boy.   39

Lor. Descend, for you must be my torchbearer.
Jes. What, must I hold a candle to my shames?
They in themselves, good sooth, are too too light.
Why, 'tis an office of discovery, love;
And I should be obscur'd.
Lor.   So are you, sweet,
Even in the lovely garnish of a boy.   45
But come at once;
For the close night doth play the runaway,
And we are stay'd for at Bassanio's feast.
Jes. I will make fast the doors, and gild myself
With some moe ducats, and be with you straight.
                                    [*Exit above.*]
Gra. Now, by my hood, a [Gentile] and no Jew.
Lor. Beshrew me but I love her heartily;   52
For she is wise, if I can judge of her,
And fair she is, if that mine eyes be true,
And true she is, as she hath prov'd herself,   55
And therefore, like herself, wise, fair, and true,
Shall she be placed in my constant soul.

Enter JESSICA [*below*].

What, art thou come?   On, gentlemen; away!
Our masquing mates by this time for us stay.
                        [*Exit* [*with Jessica and Salarino*].

Enter ANTONIO.

Ant. Who's there?   60
Gra. Signior Antonio!
Ant. Fie, fie, Gratiano! where are all the rest?
'Tis nine o'clock; our friends all stay for you.
No masque to-night; the wind is come about,
Bassanio presently will go aboard.   65
I have sent twenty out to seek for you.
Gra. I am glad on't.   I desire no more delight
Than to be under sail and gone to-night. [*Exeunt.*]

[SCENE VII.   *Belmont.   A room in Portia's house.*]
[*Flourish of cornets.*]   *Enter* PORTIA *with* [*the* PRINCE
OF] MOROCCO, *and their trains.*

Por. Go draw aside the curtains and discover
The several caskets to this noble prince.
Now make your choice.
Mor. The first, of gold, who this inscription bears,
"Who chooseth me shall gain what many men
desire;"   5
The second, silver, which this promise carries,
"Who chooseth me shall get as much as he deserves;"
This third, dull lead, with warning all as blunt,
"Who chooseth me must give and hazard all he
hath."
How shall I know if I do choose the right?   10

Sc. vi, 1. **pent-house:** projecting roof.   5. **Venus' pigeons:** the doves that drew Venus's chariot.   7. **obliged:** plighted.
10. **untread:** retrace.   14. **younker:** youngster.   15. **scarfed:** decked with flags.   42. **light:** wanton.   43. **office of dis-**
covery: i.e., the business of torches is to reveal.   45. **garnish:** garb.   47. **close:** dark, secret.   51. [**Gentile**] Q2.   *gentle* Q1.
In either case, there is a quibble.
Sc. vii, 1. **discover:** disclose.

Por. The one of them contains my picture, Prince:
If you choose that, then I am yours withal.
  Mor. Some god direct my judgement!   Let me
    see;
I will survey th' inscriptions back again.
What says this leaden casket?   15
"Who chooseth me must give and hazard all he
    hath."
Must give: for what?   For lead?   Hazard for
    lead?
This casket threatens.   Men that hazard all
Do it in hope of fair advantages;
A golden mind stoops not to shows of dross.   20
I'll then nor give nor hazard aught for lead.
What says the silver with her virgin hue?
"Who chooseth me shall get as much as he de-
    serves."
As much as he deserves!   Pause there, Morocco,
And weigh thy value with an even hand.   25
If thou be'st rated by thy estimation,
Thou dost deserve enough; and yet enough
May not extend so far as to the lady;
And yet to be afeard of my deserving
Were but a weak disabling of myself.   30
As much as I deserve!   Why, that's the lady.
I do in birth deserve her, and in fortunes,
In graces, and in qualities of breeding;
But more than these, in love I do deserve.
What if I stray'd no farther, but chose here?   35
Let's see once more this saying grav'd in gold:
"Who chooseth me shall gain what many men de-
    sire."
Why, that's the lady; all the world desires her.
From the four corners of the earth they come
To kiss this shrine, this mortal-breathing saint. 40
The Hyrcanian deserts and the vasty wilds
Of wide Arabia are as throughfares now
For princes to come view fair Portia.
The watery kingdom, whose ambitious head
Spits in the face of heaven, is no bar   45
To stop the foreign spirits, but they come
As o'er a brook to see fair Portia.
One of these three contains her heavenly picture.
Is't like that lead contains her?   'Twere damnation
To think so base a thought.   It were too gross   50
To rib her cerecloth in the obscure grave.
Or shall I think in silver she's immur'd,
Being ten times undervalu'd to tri'd gold?
O sinful thought!   Never so rich a gem
Was set in worse than gold.   They have in England
A coin that bears the figure of an angel   56
Stamped in gold, but that's insculp'd upon;
But here an angel in a golden bed
Lies all within.   Deliver me the key.
Here do I choose, and thrive I as I may!   60

Por. There, take it, Prince; and if my form lie
    there,
Then I am yours.   [*He unlocks the golden casket.*]
  Mor.   O hell! what have we here?
A carrion Death within whose empty eye
There is a written scroll!   I'll read the writing.
[*Reads.*] "All that glisters is not gold;   65
    Often have you heard that told.
    Many a man his life hath sold
    But my outside to behold.
    Gilded [tombs] do worms infold.
    Had you been as wise as bold,   70
    Young in limbs, in judgement old,
    Your answer had not been inscroll'd.
    Fare you well; your suit is cold."
  Cold, indeed; and labour lost:
  Then, farewell, heat, and welcome, frost!   75
Portia, adieu.   I have too griev'd a heart
To take a tedious leave; thus losers part.
                      [*Exit. Flourish of cornets.*
  Por. A gentle riddance.   Draw the curtains, go.
Let all of his complexion choose me so.   [*Exeunt.*

[SCENE VIII.   *Venice.   A street.*]

Enter SALARINO *and* SALANIO.

Salar. Why, man, I saw Bassanio under sail.
With him is Gratiano gone along,
And in their ship I'm sure Lorenzo is not.
  Salan. The villain Jew with outcries rais'd the
    Duke,
Who went with him to search Bassanio's ship.   5
  Salar. He came too late, the ship was under sail;
But there the Duke was given to understand
That in a gondola were seen together
Lorenzo and his amorous Jessica.
Besides, Antonio certified the Duke   10
They were not with Bassanio in his ship.
  Salan. I never heard a passion so confus'd,
So strange, outrageous, and so variable
As the dog Jew did utter in the streets.   14
"My daughter!   O my ducats!   O my daughter!
Fled with a Christian!   O my Christian ducats!
Justice! the law! my ducats, and my daughter!
A sealed bag, two sealed bags of ducats,
Of double ducats, stol'n from me by my daughter!
And jewels, two stones, two rich and precious stones,
Stol'n by my daughter!   Justice! find the girl;   21
She hath the stones upon her, and the ducats."
  Salar. Why, all the boys in Venice follow him,
Crying, his stones, his daughter, and his ducats.
  Salan. Let good Antonio look he keep his day,   25
Or he shall pay for this.
  Salar.   Marry, well remb'red.

30. **disabling:** undervaluing.   41. **Hyrcanian.** Hyrcania was a district in Asia.   51. **rib:** wrap, hold.   **cerecloth:** shroud.
63. **carrion Death:** death's head.   69. [tombs] (Johnson conj.).   *timber* Qq.

I reason'd with a Frenchman yesterday,
Who told me, in the narrow seas that part
The French and English, there miscarried
A vessel of our country richly fraught.   30
I thought upon Antonio when he told me;
And wish'd in silence that it were not his.
   Salan. You were best to tell Antonio what you
      hear;
Yet do not suddenly, for it may grieve him.
   Salar. A kinder gentleman treads not the earth.
I saw Bassanio and Antonio part;   36
Bassanio told him he would make some speed
Of his return; he answer'd, "Do not so;
Slubber not business for my sake, Bassanio,
But stay the very riping of the time;   40
And for the Jew's bond which he hath of me,
Let it not enter in your mind of love.
Be merry, and employ your chiefest thoughts
To courtship and such fair ostents of love
As shall conveniently become you there."   45
And even there, his eye being big with tears,
Turning his face, he put his hand behind him,
And with affection wondrous sensible
He wrung Bassanio's hand; and so they parted.
   Salan. I think he only loves the world for him. 50
I pray thee, let us go and find him out
And quicken his embraced heaviness
With some delight or other.
   Salar.   Do we so.   *[Exeunt.*

Scene IX. *Belmont. A room in Portia's house.]*

Enter Nerissa *with a* Servitor.

   Ner. Quick, quick, I pray thee; draw the curtain
straight.
The Prince of Arragon hath ta'en his oath,
And comes to his election presently.

Flourish of cornets. Enter the Prince of Arragon,
Portia, *and their trains.*

   Por. Behold, there stand the caskets, noble
      Prince.
If you choose that wherein I am contain'd,   5
Straight shall our nuptial rites be solemniz'd;
But if you fail, without more speech, my lord,
You must be gone from hence immediately.
   Ar. I am enjoin'd by oath to observe three things:
First, never to unfold to any one   10
Which casket 'twas I chose; next, if I fail
Of the right casket, never in my life
To woo a maid in way of marriage;
Lastly,
If I do fail in fortune of my choice,   15
Immediately to leave you and be gone.

   Por. To these injunctions every one doth swear
That comes to hazard for my worthless self.
   Ar. And so have I address'd me. Fortune now
To my heart's hope! Gold; silver; and base lead. 20
"Who chooseth me must give and hazard all he
      hath."
You shall look fairer, ere I give or hazard.
What says the golden chest? Ha! let me see:
"Who chooseth me shall gain what many men de-
      sire."
What many men desire! That many may be
      meant   25
By the fool multitude, that choose by show,
Not learning more than the fond eye doth teach;
Which pries not to th' interior, but, like the martlet,
Builds in the weather on the outward wall,
Even in the force and road of casualty.   30
I will not choose what many men desire,
Because I will not jump with common spirits
And rank me with the barbarous multitudes.
Why, then to thee, thou silver treasure-house;
Tell me once more what title thou dost bear: 35
"Who chooseth me shall get as much as he de-
      serves;"
And well said too; for who shall go about
To cozen fortune and be honourable
Without the stamp of merit? Let none presume
To wear an undeserved dignity.   40
O, that estates, degrees, and offices
Were not deriv'd corruptly, and that clear honour
Were purchas'd by the merit of the wearer!
How many then should cover that stand bare!
How many be commanded that command!   45
How much low peasantry would then be glean'd
From the true seed of honour! and how much honour
Pick'd from the chaff and ruin of the times
To be new-varnish'd! Well, but to my choice:
"Who chooseth me shall get as much as he deserves."
I will assume desert. Give me a key for this,   51
And instantly unlock my fortunes here.
              [He opens the silver casket.]
   Por. Too long a pause for that which you find
      there.
   Ar. What's here? The portrait of a blinking idiot,
Presenting me a schedule! I will read it.   55
How much unlike art thou to Portia!
How much unlike my hopes and my deservings!
"Who chooseth me shall have as much as he de-
      serves."
Did I deserve no more than a fool's head?
Is that my prize? Are my deserts no better?   60
   Por. To offend and judge are distinct offices
And of opposed natures.
   Ar.   What is here?

Sc. viii, **27. reason'd:** talked. **39. Slubber:** do slovenly. **44. ostents:** demonstrations. **48. sensible:** intense.
Sc. ix, **19. address'd:** prepared. **27. fond:** foolish. **28. martlet:** martin. **29. in:** exposed to. **30. casualty:** mischance.
32. jump: agree. **38. cozen:** cheat. **44. cover:** put on their hats. **46. glean'd:** picked out, i.e., separated. **47. seed of honour:** nobility. **61–62. To ... natures:** i.e., Having taken your chance, you are not entitled to quarrel with the outcome.

[Reads.] "The fire seven times tried this;
　　Seven times tried that judgement is,
　　That did never choose amiss.   65
　　Some there be that shadows kiss,
　　Such have but a shadow's bliss.
　　There be fools alive, iwis,
　　Silver'd o'er; and so was this.
　　Take what wife you will to bed,   70
　　I will ever be your head.
　　So be gone; you are sped."

　　Still more fool I shall appear
　　By the time I linger here.
　　With one fool's head I came to woo,   75
　　But I go away with two.
　　Sweet, adieu. I'll keep my oath,
　　Patiently to bear my wroth.
　　　　　　　[Exeunt Arragon and train.]
Por. Thus hath the candle sing'd the moth.
O, these deliberate fools! When they do choose, 80
They have the wisdom by their wit to lose.
Ner. The ancient saying is no heresy,
Hanging and wiving goes by destiny.
Por. Come, draw the curtain, Nerissa.

　　　　　Enter a MESSENGER.

Mess. Where is my lady?
Por.　　　　　Here; what would my lord? 85
Mess. Madam, there is alighted at your gate
A young Venetian, one that comes before
To signify th' approaching of his lord;
From whom he bringeth sensible regrets,
To wit, besides commends and courteous breath, 90
Gifts of rich value. Yet I have not seen
So likely an ambassador of love.
A day in April never came so sweet,
To show how costly summer was at hand,
As this fore-spurrer comes before his lord. 95
Por. No more, I pray thee. I am half afeard
Thou wilt say anon he is some kin to thee,
Thou spend'st such high-day wit in praising him.
Come, come, Nerissa, for I long to see
Quick Cupid's post that comes so mannerly. 100
Ner. Bassanio, lord Love, if thy will it be!
　　　　　　　[Exeunt.

ACT III

[SCENE I. *Venice. A street.*]

Enter SALANIO *and* SALARINO.

Salan. Now, what news on the Rialto?
Salar. Why, yet it lives there uncheck'd that Antonio hath a ship of rich lading wrack'd on the nar-

row seas; the Goodwins, I think they call the place;
a very dangerous flat, and fatal, where the carcases of many a tall ship lie buried, as they say, 5
if my gossip Report be an honest woman of her
word.
　　Salan. I would she were as lying a gossip in that
as ever knapp'd ginger or made her neighbours 10
believe she wept for the death of a third husband.
But it is true, without any slips of prolixity or crossing the plain highway of talk, that the good Antonio, the honest Antonio, — O that I had a title
good enough to keep his name company! — 16
　　Salar. Come, the full stop.
　　Salan. Ha! what sayest thou? Why, the end is,
he hath lost a ship.
　　Salar. I would it might prove the end of his
losses. 21
　　Salan. Let me say Amen betimes, lest the devil
cross my prayer, for here he comes in the likeness of
a Jew.

　　　　　Enter SHYLOCK.

How now, Shylock! what news among the mer-
chants? 26
　　Shy. You knew, none so well, none so well as you,
of my daughter's flight.
　　Salar. That's certain. I, for my part, knew the
tailor that made the wings she flew withal. 30
　　Salan. And Shylock, for his own part, knew the
bird was fledg'd; and then it is the complexion of
them all to leave the dam.
　　Shy. She is damn'd for it.
　　Salar. That's certain, if the devil may be her
judge. 36
　　Shy. My own flesh and blood to rebel!
　　Salan. Out upon it, old carrion! Rebels it at
these years?
　　Shy. I say, my daughter is my flesh and my
blood. 40
　　Salar. There is more difference between thy flesh
and hers than between jet and ivory; more between
your bloods than there is between red wine and
rhenish. But tell us, do you hear whether Antonio
have had any loss at sea or no? 45
　　Shy. There I have another bad match. A bankrupt, a prodigal, who dare scarce show his head on
the Rialto; a beggar, that was us'd to come so smug
upon the mart; let him look to his bond. He was
wont to call me usurer; let him look to his bond. 50
He was wont to lend money for a Christian courtesy; let him look to his bond.
　　Salar. Why, I am sure, if he forfeit, thou wilt not
take his flesh. What's that good for?

---

68. **iwis:** certainly.　78. **wroth:** chagrin.　89. **sensible regrets:** moving greetings.　94. **costly:** lavish.　98. **high-day:**
holiday, high-flown.
　　Act III, sc. i, 2. it ... uncheck'd: there is an unconfirmed report.　4. **Goodwins:** Goodwin Sands, off the mouth of the
Thames.　10. **knapp'd:** chewed.　32. **complexion:** instinct.　46. **match:** bargain.

Shy. To bait fish withal. If it will feed nothing else, it will feed my revenge. He hath disgrac'd 56 me, and hind'red me half a million; laugh'd at my losses, mock'd at my gains, scorn'd my nation, thwarted my bargains, cool'd my friends, heated mine enemies; and what's his reason? I am a 60 Jew. Hath not a Jew eyes? Hath not a Jew hands, organs, dimensions, senses, affections, passions; fed with the same food, hurt with the same weapons, subject to the same diseases, heal'd by the same means, warm'd and cool'd by the same winter 65 and summer, as a Christian is? If you prick us, do we not bleed? If you tickle us, do we not laugh? If you poison us, do we not die? And if you wrong us, shall we not revenge? If we are like you in the rest, we will resemble you in that. If a Jew 70 wrong a Christian, what is his humility? Revenge. If a Christian wrong a Jew, what should his sufferance be by Christian example? Why, revenge. The villainy you teach me, I will execute, and it shall go hard but I will better the instruction. 76

What about love, mercy, friendship

Enter a [SERVANT].

Serv. Gentlemen, my master Antonio is at his house and desires to speak with you both.

Salar. We have been up and down to seek him.

Enter TUBAL.

Salan. Here comes another of the tribe; a 80 third cannot be match'd, unless the devil himself turn Jew. [*Exeunt* [*Salan., Salar., and Servant*].

Shy. How now, Tubal! what news from Genoa? Hast thou found my daughter?

Tub. I often came where I did hear of her, but cannot find her. 86

Shy. Why, there, there, there, there! A diamond gone, cost me two thousand ducats in Frankfort! The curse never fell upon our nation till now. I never felt it till now. Two thousand ducats 90 in that; and other precious, precious jewels. I would my daughter were dead at my foot, and the jewels in her ear! Would she were hears'd at my foot, and the ducats in her coffin! No news of them? Why so? And I know not what's spent 95 in the search. Why, thou loss upon loss! the thief gone with so much, and so much to find the thief; and no satisfaction, no revenge, nor no ill luck stirring but what lights o' my shoulders, no sighs but o' my breathing, no tears but o' my 100 shedding.

Tub. Yes, other men have ill luck too. Antonio, as I heard in Genoa, —

Shy. What, what, what? Ill luck, ill luck?

Tub. Hath an argosy cast away, coming from Tripolis. 106

Shy. I thank God, I thank God. Is it true, is it true?

Tub. I spoke with some of the sailors that escaped the wreck. 110

Shy. I thank thee, good Tubal; good news, good news! Ha, ha! [Heard] in Genoa?

Tub. Your daughter spent in Genoa, as I heard, in one night fourscore ducats.

Shy. Thou stick'st a dagger in me. I shall 115 never see my gold again. Fourscore ducats at a sitting! Fourscore ducats!

Tub. There came divers of Antonio's creditors in my company to Venice, that swear he cannot choose but break. 120

Shy. I am very glad of it. I'll plague him; I'll torture him. I am glad of it.

Tub. One of them showed me a ring that he had of your daughter for a monkey.

Shy. Out upon her! Thou torturest me, 125 Tubal. It was my turquoise; I had it of Leah when I was a bachelor. I would not have given it for a wilderness of monkeys.

Tub. But Antonio is certainly undone.

Shy. Nay, that's true, that's very true. Go, 130 Tubal, fee me an officer; bespeak him a fortnight before. I will have the heart of him, if he forfeit; for, were he out of Venice, I can make what merchandise I will. Go, go, Tubal, and meet me at our synagogue; go, good Tubal; at our synagogue, 135 Tubal. [*Exeunt.*

[SCENE II. *Belmont. A room in Portia's house.*]

Enter BASSANIO, PORTIA, GRATIANO, [NERISSA,] *and all their train.*

Por. I pray you, tarry. Pause a day or two Before you hazard; for, in choosing wrong, I lose your company; therefore forbear awhile. There's something tells me, but it is not love, I would not lose you; and, you know yourself, 5 Hate counsels not in such a quality. But lest you should not understand me well, — And yet a maiden hath no tongue but thought, — I would detain you here some month or two Before you venture for me. I could teach you 10 How to choose right, but then I am forsworn. So will I never be; so may you miss me; But if you do, you'll make me wish a sin, That I had been forsworn. Beshrew your eyes, They have o'erlook'd me and divided me; 15 One half of me is yours, the other half yours, Mine own, I would say; but if mine, then yours,

71. **what ... humility:** how does a Christian show his humility?   72–73. **what ... be:** how should he bear it?   112. [Heard] Edd.   *Heere* Q₁.   Other editors emend to *Where.*
Sc. ii, 6. **Hate ... quality:** hate does not give this kind of counsel, i.e., to stay awhile.   15. **o'erlook'd:** bewitched.

And so all yours. O, these naughty times
Puts bars between the owners and their rights!
And so, though yours, not yours. Prove it so, 20
Let fortune go to hell for it, not I.
I speak too long; but 'tis to peize the time,
To eke it and to draw it out in length,
To stay you from election.
    Bass.   Let me choose;
For as I am, I live upon the rack. 25
    Por. Upon the rack, Bassanio! Then confess
What treason there is mingled with your love.
    Bass. None but that ugly treason of mistrust,
Which makes me fear th' enjoying of my love.
There may as well be amity and life 30
'Tween snow and fire, as treason and my love.
    Por. Ay, but I fear you speak upon the rack,
Where men enforced do speak anything.
    Bass. Promise me life, and I'll confess the truth.
    Por. Well then, confess and live.
    Bass.   "Confess and love"
Had been the very sum of my confession. 36
O happy torment, when my torturer
Doth teach me answers for deliverance!
But let me to my fortune and the caskets.
    Por. Away, then! I am lock'd in one of them;
If you do love me, you will find me out. 41
Nerissa and the rest, stand all aloof.
Let music sound while he doth make his choice;
Then, if he lose, he makes a swan-like end,
Fading in music. That the comparison 45
May stand more proper, my eye shall be the stream
And watery death-bed for him. He may win;
And what is music then? Then music is
Even as the flourish when true subjects bow
To a new-crowned monarch; such it is 50
As are those dulcet sounds in break of day
That creep into the dreaming bridegroom's ear
And summon him to marriage. Now he goes,
With no less presence but with much more love,
Than young Alcides, when he did redeem 55
The virgin tribute paid by howling Troy
To the sea-monster. I stand for sacrifice;
The rest aloof are the Dardanian wives,
With bleared visages, come forth to view
The issue of the exploit. Go, Hercules! 60
Live thou, I live. With much, much more dismay
I view the fight than thou that mak'st the fray.

    A song, the whilst BASSANIO *comments on the
caskets to himself.*

    Tell me where is fancy bred,
      Or in the heart or in the head?
    How begot, how nourished? 65
      Reply, reply.

    It is engend'red in the eyes,
      With gazing fed; and fancy dies
    In the cradle where it lies.
      Let us all ring fancy's knell; 70
      I'll begin it, — Ding, dong, bell.
    All. Ding, dong, bell.

    Bass. So may the outward shows be least them-
selves;
The world is still deceiv'd with ornament.
In law, what plea so tainted and corrupt 75
But, being season'd with a gracious voice,
Obscures the show of evil? In religion,
What damned error but some sober brow
Will bless it and approve it with a text,
Hiding the grossness with fair ornament? 80
There is no vice so simple but assumes
Some mark of virtue on his outward parts.
How many cowards, whose hearts are all as false
As stairs of sand, wear yet upon their chins
The beards of Hercules and frowning Mars, 85
Who, inward search'd, have livers white as milk;
And these assume but valour's excrement
To render them redoubted! Look on beauty,
And you shall see 'tis purchas'd by the weight;
Which therein works a miracle in nature, 90
Making them lightest that wear most of it.
So are those crisped snaky golden locks,
Which make such wanton gambols with the wind
Upon supposed fairness, often known
To be the dowry of a second head, 95
The skull that bred them in the sepulchre.
Thus ornament is but the guiled shore
To a most dangerous sea; the beauteous scarf
Veiling an Indian beauty; in a word,
The seeming truth which cunning times put on
T' entrap the wisest. Therefore, then, thou gaudy
    gold, 101
Hard food for Midas, I will none of thee;
Nor none of thee, thou pale and common drudge
'Tween man and man; but thou, thou meagre lead,
Which rather threat'nest than dost promise aught,
Thy plainness moves me more than eloquence; 106
And here choose I. Joy be the consequence!
    Por. [*Aside.*] How all the other passions fleet
    to air,
As doubtful thoughts, and rash-embrac'd despair,
And shudd'ring fear, and green-ey'd jealousy! 110
O love, be moderate; allay thy ecstasy;
In measure rein thy joy; scant this excess!
I feel too much thy blessing; make it less,
For fear I surfeit.
    Bass.   What find I here? 115
        [*Opening the leaden casket.*]

18 **naughty:** wicked. 22. **peize:** retard (by weighting down). 55. **Alcides:** i.e., Hercules, who rescued the Trojan princess Hesione. 58. **Dardanian:** Trojan. 63. **fancy:** love. 79. **approve:** confirm. 81. **simple:** unmixed. 87. **valour's excrement:** a brave man's beard. 88. **redoubted:** feared. 94. **supposed:** artificial. 97. **guiled:** treacherous. 102. **Midas:** the Phrygian king who turned whatever he touched to gold

Fair Portia's counterfeit! What demi-god
Hath come so near creation? Move these eyes?
Or whether, riding on the balls of mine,
Seem they in motion? Here are sever'd lips,
Parted with sugar breath; so sweet a bar   120
Should sunder such sweet friends. Here in her
       hairs
The painter plays the spider, and hath woven
A golden mesh t' entrap the hearts of men
Faster than gnats in cobwebs. But her eyes, —
How could he see to do them? Having made one,
Methinks it should have power to steal both his 126
And leave itself unfurnish'd. Yet look, how far
The substance of my praise doth wrong this shadow
In underprizing it, so far this shadow
Doth limp behind the substance. Here's the scroll,
The continent and summary of my fortune.   131
[*Reads.*] "You that choose not by the view,
       Chance as fair and choose as true!
       Since this fortune falls to you,
       Be content and seek no new.   135
       If you be well pleas'd with this
       And hold your fortune for your bliss,
       Turn you where your lady is
       And claim her with a loving kiss."
A gentle scroll. Fair lady, by your leave;   140
I come by note, to give and to receive.
Like one of two contending in a prize,
That thinks he hath done well in people's eyes,
Hearing applause and universal shout,
Giddy in spirit, still gazing in a doubt   145
Whether those peals of praise be his or no;
So, thrice-fair lady, stand I, even so,
As doubtful whether what I see be true,
Until confirm'd, sign'd, ratified by you.
  Por. You see me, Lord Bassanio, where I stand,
Such as I am. Though for myself alone   151
i would not be ambitious in my wish
To wish myself much better; yet, for you
I would be trebled twenty times myself,
A thousand times more fair, ten thousand times 155
More rich; that only to stand high in your account,
I might in virtues, beauties, livings, friends,
Exceed account. But the full sum of me
Is sum of — something, which, to term in gross, 160
Is an unlesson'd girl, unschool'd, unpractis'd;
Happy in this, she is not yet so old
But she may learn; happier than this,
She is not bred so dull but she can learn;
Happiest of all is that her gentle spirit   165
Commits itself to yours to be directed,
As from her lord, her governor, her king.
Myself and what is mine to you and yours
Is now converted. But now I was the lord

Of this fair mansion, master of my servants, 170
Queen o'er myself; and even now, but now,
This house, these servants, and this same myself
Are yours, my lord; I give them with this ring;
Which when you part from, lose, or give away,
Let it presage the ruin of your love   175
And be my vantage to exclaim on you.
  Bass. Madam, you have bereft me of all words,
Only my blood speaks to you in my veins;
And there is such confusion in my powers,
As, after some oration fairly spoke   180
By a beloved prince, there doth appear
Among the buzzing pleased multitude;
Where every something, being blent together,
Turns to a wild of nothing, save of joy   184
Express'd and not express'd. But when this ring
Parts from this finger, then parts life from hence;
O, then be bold to say Bassanio's dead!
  Ner. My lord and lady, it is now our time,
That have stood by and seen our wishes prosper,
To cry good joy. Good joy, my lord and lady!
  Gra. My Lord Bassanio and my gentle lady,
I wish you all the joy that you can wish,   192
For I am sure you can wish none from me;
And when your honours mean to solemnize
The bargain of your faith, I do beseech you, 195
Even at that time I may be married too.
  Bass. With all my heart, so thou canst get a wife.
  Gra. I thank your lordship, you have got me one.
My eyes, my lord, can look as swift as yours.
You saw the mistress, I beheld the maid;   200
You lov'd, I lov'd; for intermission
No more pertains to me, my lord, than you.
Your fortune stood upon the caskets there,
And so did mine too, as the matter falls;
For, wooing here until I sweat again,   205
And swearing till my very roof was dry
With oaths of love, at last, if promise last,
I got a promise of this fair one here
To have her love, provided that your fortune
Achiev'd her mistress.
  Por.   Is this true, Nerissa?   210
  Ner. Madam, it is, so you stand pleas'd withal.
  Bass. And do you, Gratiano, mean good faith?
  Gra. Yes, faith, my lord.
  Bass. Our feast shall be much honour'd in your
       marriage.   215
  Gra. We'll play with them the first boy for a
thousand ducats.
  Ner. What, and stake down?
  Gra. No; we shall ne'er win at that sport and
stake down.   220
But who comes here? Lorenzo and his infidel?
What, and my old Venetian friend Salerio?

116. **counterfeit:** portrait.   127. **unfurnish'd:** without its mate.   131. **continent:** container.   141. **note:** direction.   142.
prize: competition.   156. **account:** opinion.   159. **account:** reckoning.   176. **vantage:** opportunity.   **exclaim on:** reproach.   201. **intermission:** inactivity.   The punctuation is Theobald's (Qq read *lov'd for,*).   206. **roof:** i.e., of my mouth.

Enter LORENZO, JESSICA, *and* SALERIO, *a messenger from Venice.*

Bass. Lorenzo and Salerio, welcome hither,
If that the youth of my new interest here
Have power to bid you welcome. By your leave
I bid my very friends and countrymen,   226
Sweet Portia, welcome.
    Por.   So do I, my lord:
They are entirely welcome.
    Lor. I thank your honour. For my part, my lord,
My purpose was not to have seen you here;   230
But meeting with Salerio by the way,
He did intreat me, past all saying nay,
To come with him along.
    Saler.   I did, my lord;
And I have reason for it. Signior Antonio
Commends him to you.   [*Gives Bassanio a letter.*]
    Bass.   Ere I ope his letter,   235
I pray you, tell me how my good friend doth.
    Saler. Not sick, my lord, unless it be in mind,
Nor well, unless in mind. His letter there
Will show you his estate.   [*Bass. opens the letter.*]
    Gra. Nerissa, cheer yond stranger; bid her welcome.   240
Your hand, Salerio. What's the news from Venice?
How doth that royal merchant, good Antonio?
I know he will be glad of our success;
We are the Jasons, we have won the fleece.
    Saler. I would you had won the fleece that he
hath lost.   245
    Por. There are some shrewd contents in yon
same paper
That steals the colour from Bassanio's cheek.
Some dear friend dead; else nothing in the world
Could turn so much the constitution
Of any constant man. What, worse and worse!
With leave, Bassanio; I am half yourself,   251
And I must freely have the half of anything
That this same paper brings you.
    Bass.   O sweet Portia,
Here are a few of the unpleasant'st words
Than ever blotted paper! Gentle lady,   255
When I did first impart my love to you,
I freely told you all the wealth I had
Ran in my veins; I was a gentleman.
And then I told you true; and yet, dear lady,
Rating myself at nothing, you shall see   260
How much I was a braggart. When I told you
My state was nothing, I should then have told you
That I was worse than nothing; for, indeed,
I have engag'd myself to a dear friend,
Engag'd my friend to his mere enemy,   265
To feed my means. Here is a letter, lady;
The paper as the body of my friend,

And every word in it a gaping wound,
Issuing life-blood. But is it true, Salerio?
Hath all his ventures fail'd? What? Not one hit?
From Tripolis, from Mexico, and England,   271
From Lisbon, Barbary, and India?
And not one vessel scape the dreadful touch
Of merchant-marring rocks?
    Saler.   Not one, my lord.
Besides, it should appear, that if he had   275
The present money to discharge the Jew,
He would not take it. Never did I know
A creature that did bear the shape of man
So keen and greedy to confound a man.
He plies the Duke at morning and at night,   280
And doth impeach the freedom of the state,
If they deny him justice. Twenty merchants,
The Duke himself, and the magnificoes
Of greatest port, have all persuaded with him;
But none can drive him from the envious plea   285
Of forfeiture, of justice, and his bond.
    Jes. When I was with him I have heard him
swear
To Tubal and to Chus, his countrymen,
That he would rather have Antonio's flesh
Than twenty times the value of the sum   290
That he did owe him; and I know, my lord,
If law, authority, and power deny not,
It will go hard with poor Antonio.
    Por. Is it your dear friend that is thus in trouble?
    Bass. The dearest friend to me, the kindest man,
The best-condition'd and unwearied spirit   296
In doing courtesies, and one in whom
The ancient Roman honour more appears
Than any that draws breath in Italy.
    Por. What sum owes he the Jew?   300
    Bass. For me, three thousand ducats.
    Por.   What, no more?
Pay him six thousand, and deface the bond;
Double six thousand, and then treble that,
Before a friend of this description
Shall lose a hair through Bassanio's fault.   305
First go with me to church and call me wife,
And then away to Venice to your friend;
For never shall you lie by Portia's side
With an unquiet soul. You shall have gold
To pay the petty debt twenty times over.   310
When it is paid, bring your true friend along.
My maid Nerissa and myself meantime
Will live as maids and widows. Come, away!
For you shall hence upon your wedding-day.
Bid your friends welcome, show a merry cheer;   315
Since you are dear bought, I will love you dear.
But let me hear the letter of your friend.
    [*Bass. Reads.*] "Sweet Bassanio, my ships have

226. **very:** true. 239. **estate:** condition. 246. **shrewd:** evil, bitter. 249. **constitution:** state of mind. 250. **constant:** steady. 265. **mere:** absolute. 276. **present:** ready. 281. **impeach:** call in question. 283. **magnificoes:** grandees. 284. **port:** prestige. 285. **envious:** spiteful. 315. **cheer:** face.

all miscarried, my creditors grow cruel, my estate
is very low, my bond to the Jew is forfeit; and 320
since in paying it, it is impossible I should live, all
debts are cleared between you and I, if I might but
see you at my death. Notwithstanding, use your
pleasure; if your love do not persuade you to come,
let not my letter."   325
  Por. O love, dispatch all business, and be gone!
  Bass. Since I have your good leave to go away,
    I will make haste; but, till I come again,
No bed shall e'er be guilty of my stay,
    Nor rest be interposer 'twixt us twain.   330
                        [Exeunt.

[SCENE III. *Venice. A street.*]

Enter the Jew [SHYLOCK], [SALARINO], ANTONIO,
and Gaoler.

  Shy. Gaoler, look to him; tell not me of mercy.
This is the fool that lent out money gratis!
Gaoler, look to him.
  Ant.   Hear me yet, good Shylock.
  Shy. I'll have my bond; speak not against my
    bond.
I have sworn an oath that I will have my bond. 5
Thou call'dst me dog before thou hadst a cause;
But, since I am a dog, beware my fangs.
The Duke shall grant me justice. I do wonder,
Thou naughty gaoler, that thou art so fond
To come abroad with him at his request.   10
  Ant. I pray thee, hear me speak.
  Shy. I'll have my bond; I will not hear thee speak.
I'll have my bond; and therefore speak no more.
I'll not be made a soft and dull-ey'd fool
To shake the head, relent, and sigh, and yield 15
To Christian intercessors. Follow not;
I'll have no speaking; I will have my bond. *[Exit.*
  Sal[ar]. It is the most impenetrable cur
That ever kept with men.
  Ant.   Let him alone;
I'll follow him no more with bootless prayers. 20
He seeks my life; his reason well I know:
I oft deliver'd from his forfeitures
Many that have at times made moan to me;
Therefore he hates me.
  Sal[ar].   I am sure the Duke
Will never grant this forfeiture to hold.   25
  Ant. The Duke cannot deny the course of law;
For the commodity that strangers have
With us in Venice, if it be denied,
Will much impeach the justice of the state,
Since that the trade and profit of the city 30
Consisteth of all nations. Therefore, go.
These griefs and losses have so bated me,

That I shall hardly spare a pound of flesh
To-morrow to my bloody creditor.
Well, gaoler, on. Pray God, Bassanio come 35
To see me pay his debt, and then I care not!
                        [Exeunt.

[SCENE IV. *Belmont. A room in Portia's house.*]

Enter PORTIA, NERISSA, LORENZO, JESSICA, *and*
[BALTHASAR,] *a man of Portia's.*

  Lor. Madam, although I speak it in your pres-
    ence,
You have a noble and a true conceit
Of god-like amity, which appears most strongly
In bearing thus the absence of your lord.
But if you knew to whom you show this honour, 5
How true a gentleman you send relief,
How dear a lover of my lord your husband,
I know you would be prouder of the work
Than customary bounty can enforce you.
  Por. I never did repent for doing good,   10
Nor shall not now: for in companions
That do converse and waste the time together,
Whose souls do bear an egal yoke of love,
There must be needs a like proportion
Of lineaments, of manners, and of spirit; 15
Which makes me think that this Antonio,
Being the bosom lover of my lord,
Must needs be like my lord. If it be so,
How little is the cost I have bestow'd
In purchasing the semblance of my soul 20
From out the state of hellish cruelty!
This comes too near the praising of myself,
Therefore no more of it. Hear other things.
Lorenzo, I commit into your hands
The husbandry and manage of my house 25
Until my lord's return. For mine own part,
I have toward heaven breath'd a secret vow
To live in prayer and contemplation,
Only attended by Nerissa here,
Until her husband and my lord's return.   30
There is a monastery two miles off;
And there we will abide. I do desire you
Not to deny this imposition,
The which my love and some necessity
Now lays upon you.
  Lor.   Madam, with all my heart 35
I shall obey you in all fair commands.
  Por. My people do already know my mind,
And will acknowledge you and Jessica
In place of Lord Bassanio and myself.
So fare you well till we shall meet again.   40
  Lor. Fair thoughts and happy hours attend on
    you!

Sc. iii. S.D. [SALARINO] Q₂. *Salerio* Q₁. *Solanio* F₁. 19. **kept:** dwelt. 27. **commodity:** commercial privileges. 33.
bated: reduced.
Sc. iv, 2. **conceit:** conception. 9. **enforce you:** i.e., make you be. 13. **egal:** equal. 25. **husbandry:** economy.

Jes. I wish your ladyship all heart's content.

Por. I thank you for your wish, and am well pleas'd
To wish it back on you.   Fare you well, Jessica.

              [Exeunt [Jessica and Lorenzo].

Now, Balthasar,   45
As I have ever found thee honest-true,
So let me find thee still.   Take this same letter,
And use thou all th' endeavour of a man
In speed to [Padua].   See thou render this
Into my cousin's hands, Doctor Bellario;   50
And, look, what notes and garments he doth give
    thee,
Bring them, I pray thee, with imagin'd speed
Unto the [traject], to the common ferry
Which trades to Venice.   Waste no time in words,
But get thee gone.   I shall be there before thee.   55

Balth.   Madam, I go with all convenient speed.
              [Exit.

Por.   Come on, Nerissa; I have work in hand
That you yet know not of.   We'll see our husbands
Before they think of us.

Ner.   Shall they see us?

Por.   They shall, Nerissa; but in such a habit   60
That they shall think we are accomplished
With that we lack.   I'll hold thee any wager,
When we are both accoutred like young men,
I'll prove the prettier fellow of the two,
And wear my dagger with the braver grace,   65
And speak between the change of man and boy
With a reed voice, and turn two mincing steps
Into a manly stride, and speak of frays
Like a fine bragging youth, and tell quaint lies,
How honourable ladies sought my love,   70
Which I denying, they fell sick and died.
I could not do withal.   Then I'll repent,
And wish, for all that, that I had not kill'd them;
And twenty of these puny lies I'll tell,
That men shall swear I have discontinued school   75
Above a twelvemonth.   I have within my mind
A thousand raw tricks of these bragging Jacks,
Which I will practise.

Ner.   Why, shall we turn to men?

Por.   Fie, what a question's that,
If thou wert near a lewd interpreter!   80
But come, I'll tell thee all my whole device
When I am in my coach, which stays for us
At the park gate; and therefore haste away,
For we must measure twenty miles to-day.
            [Exeunt.

[SCENE V.   *The same.   A garden.*]

Enter Clown [LAUNCELOT] *and* JESSICA.

Laun.   Yes, truly; for, look you, the sins of the
father are to be laid upon the children; therefore, I
promise you, I fear you.   I was always plain with
you, and so now I speak my agitation of the matter;
therefore be o' good cheer, for truly I think you   5
are damn'd.   There is but one hope in it that can
do you any good; and that is but a kind of bastard
hope neither.

Jes.   And what hope is that, I pray thee?   10

Laun.   Marry, you may partly hope that your
father got you not, that you are not the Jew's
daughter.

Jes.   That were a kind of bastard hope, indeed.
So the sins of my mother should be visited upon me.

Laun.   Truly then I fear you are damn'd both   17
by father and mother; thus when I shun Scylla, your
father, I fall into Charybdis, your mother.   Well,
you are gone both ways.   20

Jes.   I shall be sav'd by my husband.   He hath
made me a Christian.

Laun.   Truly, the more to blame he; we were
Christians enow before; e'en as many as could well
live, one by another.   This making of Christians   25
will raise the price of hogs.   If we grow all to be
pork-eaters, we shall not shortly have a rasher on
the coals for money.

Enter LORENZO.

Jes.   I'll tell my husband, Launcelot, what you
say.   Here he comes.   30

Lor.   I shall grow jealous of you shortly, Launcelot, if you thus get my wife into corners.

Jes.   Nay, you need not fear us, Lorenzo; Launcelot and I are out.   He tells me flatly there is no
mercy for me in heaven because I am a Jew's   35
daughter; and he says, you are no good member of
the commonwealth, for in converting Jews to
Christians, you raise the price of pork.   39

Lor.   I shall answer that better to the commonwealth than you can the getting up of the negro's
belly.   The Moor is with child by you, Launcelot.

Laun.   It is much that the Moor should be
more than reason; but if she be less than an
honest woman, she is indeed more than I took   46
her for.

Lor.   How every fool can play upon the word!
I think the best grace of wit will shortly turn into
silence, and discourse grow commendable in   50
none only but parrots.   Go in, sirrah; bid them
prepare for dinner.

Laun.   That is done, sir; they have all stomachs.

Lor.   Goodly Lord, what a wit-snapper are you!
Then bid them prepare dinner.   56

Laun.   That is done too, sir; only cover is the
word.

49. **[Padua]** (Theobald conj.).   *Mantua* Qq. (Cf. iv.i.109.) Padua was famous for its law school.   52. **imagin'd speed:**
all imaginable speed.   53. **[traject]** (Rowe): crossing.   *tranect* Qq.   61. **accomplished:** provided.   72. **do withal:** help it.
Sc. v, 3. **fear you:** i.e., fear for you.   4. **agitation:** blunder for *cogitation.*   34. **are out:** have quarreled.   52. **stomachs:**
appetites, with a quibble.

Lor. Will you cover then, sir?

Laun. Not so, sir, neither; I know my duty.   59

Lor. Yet more quarrelling with occasion! Wilt thou show the whole wealth of thy wit in an instant? I pray thee, understand a plain man in his plain meaning: go to thy fellows; bid them cover the table, serve in the meat, and we will come in to dinner.   65

Laun. For the table, sir, it shall be serv'd in; for the meat, sir, it shall be cover'd; for your coming in to dinner, sir, why, let it be as humours and conceits shall govern.   [*Exit.*

Lor. O dear discretion, how his words are suited! The fool hath planted in his memory   71
An army of good words; and I do know
A many fools, that stand in better place,
Garnish'd like him, that for a tricksy word
Defy the matter. How cheer'st thou, Jessica?   75
And now, good sweet, say thy opinion,
How dost thou like the Lord Bassanio's wife?

Jes. Past all expressing. It is very meet
The Lord Bassanio live an upright life;
For, having such a blessing in his lady,   80
He finds the joys of heaven here on earth;
And if on earth he do not [merit them],
In reason he should never come to heaven.
Why, if two gods should play some heavenly match
And on the wager lay two earthly women,   85
And Portia one, there must be something else
Pawn'd with the other, for the poor rude world
Hath not her fellow.

Lor.   Even such a husband
Hast thou of me as she is for a wife.

Jes. Nay, but ask my opinion too of that.   90

Lor. I will anon; first, let us go to dinner.

Jes. Nay, let me praise you while I have a stomach.

Lor. No, pray thee, let it serve for table-talk;
Then, howsome'er thou speak'st, 'mong other things
I shall digest it.

Jes.   Well, I'll set you forth.   95
[*Exeunt.*

ACT IV

[Scene I. *Venice. A court of justice.*]

Enter the Duke, *the* Magnificoes, Antonio, Bassanio, Gratiano [Salerio, *and others*].

Duke. What, is Antonio here?

Ant. Ready, so please your Grace.

Duke. I am sorry for thee. Thou art come to answer
A stony adversary, an inhuman wretch
Uncapable of pity, void and empty   5
From any dram of mercy.

Ant.   I have heard
Your Grace hath ta'en great pains to qualify
His rigorous course; but since he stands obdurate
And that no lawful means can carry me
Out of his envy's reach, I do oppose   10
My patience to his fury, and am arm'd
To suffer, with a quietness of spirit,
The very tyranny and rage of his.

Duke. Go one, and call the Jew into the court.

Saler. He is ready at the door. He comes, my lord.   15

Enter Shylock.

Duke. Make room, and let him stand before our face.
Shylock, the world thinks, and I think so too,
That thou but lead'st this fashion of thy malice
To the last hour of act; and then 'tis thought
Thou'lt show thy mercy and remorse more strange
Than is thy strange apparent cruelty;   21
And where thou now exact'st the penalty,
Which is a pound of this poor merchant's flesh,
Thou wilt not only loose the forfeiture,
But, touch'd with humane gentleness and love,   25
Forgive a moiety of the principal;
Glancing an eye of pity on his losses,
That have of late so huddled on his back,
Enow to press a royal merchant down
And pluck commiseration of his state   30
From brassy bosoms and rough hearts of flint,
From stubborn Turks and Tartars, never train'd
To offices of tender courtesy.
We all expect a gentle answer, Jew.

Shy. I have possess'd your Grace of what I purpose;   35
And by our holy Sabbath have I sworn
To have the due and forfeit of my bond.
If you deny it, let the danger light
Upon your charter and your city's freedom.
You'll ask me why I rather choose to have   40
A weight of carrion flesh than to receive
Three thousand ducats. I'll never answer that;
But say it is my humour. Is it answer'd?
What if my house be troubled with a rat
And I be pleas'd to give ten thousand ducats   45
To have it ban'd? What, are you answer'd yet?

---

58. cover: (1) set the table, (2) put on your hat.   **60. quarrelling...occasion:** quibbling.   **70. suited:** dressed up, or adapted.   **74. Garnish'd:** equipped.   **tricksy:** fantastic.   **75. matter:** i.e., true sense.   **82. [merit them]** (Clar. conj.). *meane it, it* Q1.   *meane it, then* Q2.   If Q2 is followed, the sense would seem to be, "intend to live an upright life."   **87. Pawn'd:** staked.   **95. set you forth:** (1) extol, (2) serve up.

Act IV, sc. i, 7. qualify: moderate.   **18. fashion:** way of expressing.   **20. remorse:** pity.   **strange:** extraordinary.   **26. moiety:** part.   **29. enow:** enough.   **43. humour:** whim.   **46. ban'd:** poisoned.

Some men there are love not a gaping pig;
Some, that are mad if they behold a cat;
And others, when the bagpipe sings i' th' nose,
Cannot contain their urine: for affection,   50
Master of passion, sways it to the mood
Of what it likes or loathes. Now, for your answer:
As there is no firm reason to be rend'red
Why he cannot abide a gaping pig;
Why he, a harmless necessary cat;   55
Why he, a woollen bagpipe; but of force
Must yield to such inevitable shame
As to offend, himself being offended;
So can I give no reason, nor I will not,
More than a lodg'd hate and a certain loathing 60
I bear Antonio, that I follow thus
A losing suit against him. Are you answer'd?
  Bass. This is no answer, thou unfeeling man,
To excuse the current of thy cruelty.
  Shy. I am not bound to please thee with my an-
    swers.   65
  Bass. Do all men kill the things they do not love?
  Shy. Hates any man the thing he would not kill?
  Bass. Every offence is not a hate at first.
  Shy. What, wouldst thou have a serpent sting
    thee twice?
  Ant. I pray you, think, you question with the
    Jew.   70
You may as well go stand upon the beach
And bid the main flood bate his usual height;
You may as well use question with the wolf
Why he hath made the ewe bleat for the lamb;
You may as well forbid the mountain pines   75
To wag their high tops and to make no noise
When they are fretten with the gusts of heaven;
You may as well do any thing most hard,
As seek to soften that — than which what's
    harder? —
His Jewish heart. Therefore, I do beseech you, 80
Make no moe offers, use no farther means,
But with all brief and plain conveniency
Let me have judgement and the Jew his will.
  Bass. For thy three thousand ducats here is six.
  Shy. If every ducat in six thousand ducats 85
Were in six parts, and every part a ducat,
I would not draw them; I would have my bond.
  Duke. How shalt thou hope for mercy, rendering
    none?
  Shy. What judgement shall I dread, doing no
    wrong?
You have among you many a purchas'd slave, 90
Which, like your asses and your dogs and mules,
You use in abject and in slavish parts,
Because you bought them. Shall I say to you,
"Let them be free! Marry them to your heirs!
Why sweat they under burdens? Let their beds 95

Be made as soft as yours and let their palates
Be season'd with such viands"? You will answer,
"The slaves are ours." So do I answer you.
The pound of flesh, which I demand of him,
Is dearly bought; 'tis mine and I will have it. 100
If you deny me, fie upon your law!
There is no force in the decrees of Venice.
I stand for judgement! Answer: shall I have it?
  Duke. Upon my power I may dismiss this court,
Unless Bellario, a learned doctor,   105
Whom I have sent for to determine this,
Come here to-day.
  Saler.   My lord, here stays without
A messenger with letters from the doctor,
New come from Padua.
  Duke. Bring us the letters; call the messenger. 110
  Bass. Good cheer, Antonio! What, man, courage
    yet!
The Jew shall have my flesh, blood, bones, and all,
Ere thou shalt lose for me one drop of blood.
  Ant. I am a tainted wether of the flock,
Meetest for death. The weakest kind of fruit 115
Drops earliest to the ground, and so let me.
You cannot better be employ'd, Bassanio,
Than to live still and write mine epitaph.

  Enter NERISSA [*dressed like a lawyer's clerk*].
  Duke. Came you from Padua, from Bellario?
  Ner. From both, my lord. Bellario greets your
    Grace.   [*Presenting a letter.*]
  Bass. Why dost thou whet thy knife so ear-
    nestly?   121
  Shy. To cut the forfeiture from that bankrupt
    there.
  Gra. Not on thy sole, but on thy soul, harsh Jew,
Thou mak'st thy knife keen; but no metal can, 124
No, not the hangman's axe, bear half the keenness
Of thy sharp envy. Can no prayers pierce thee?
  Shy. No, none that thou hast wit enough to make.
  Gra. O, be thou damn'd, inexecrable dog!
And for thy life let justice be accus'd.
Thou almost mak'st me waver in my faith   130
To hold opinion with Pythagoras,
That souls of animals infuse themselves
Into the trunks of men. Thy currish spirit
Govern'd a wolf, who, hang'd for human slaughter,
Even from the gallows did his fell soul fleet, 135
And, whilst thou lay'st in thy unhallowed dam,
Infus'd itself in thee; for thy desires
Are wolvish, bloody, starv'd, and ravenous.
  Shy. Till thou canst rail the seal from off my
    bond,
Thou but offend'st thy lungs to speak so loud. 140
Repair thy wit, good youth, or it will fall
To cureless ruin. I stand here for law.

47. **gaping pig:** a pig roasted whole with its mouth open.   50. **affection:** natural inclination.   70. **question:** argue.
77. **fretten:** fretted.   87. **draw:** take.   92. **parts:** tasks.   140. **offend'st:** injurest.

Duke. This letter from Bellario doth commend
A young and learned doctor to our court.
Where is he?
 Ner.   He attendeth here hard by 145
To know your answer, whether you'll admit him.
 Duke. With all my heart. Some three or four of you
Go give him courteous conduct to this place.
Meantime the court shall hear Bellario's letter. 149
 [*Clerk. Reads.*] "Your Grace shall understand
that at the receipt of your letter I am very sick; but
in the instant that your messenger came, in loving
visitation was with me a young doctor of Rome.
His name is Balthazar. I acquainted him with the
cause in controversy between the Jew and 155
Antonio the merchant. We turned o'er many
books together. He is furnished with my opinion;
which, bett'red with his own learning, the greatness
whereof I cannot enough commend, comes with
him, at my importunity, to fill up your Grace's 160
request in my stead. I beseech you, let his lack of
years be no impediment to let him lack a reverend
estimation; for I never knew so young a body with
so old a head. I leave him to your gracious acceptance, whose trial shall better publish his commendation." 166

   Enter PORTIA *for* BALTHAZAR.

 Duke. You hear the learn'd Ballario, what he
  writes;
And here, I take it, is the doctor come.
Give me your hand. Come you from old Bellario?
 Por. I did, my lord.
 Duke.   You are welcome; take your place.
Are you acquainted with the difference 171
That holds this present question in the court?
 Por. I am informed throughly of the cause.
Which is the merchant here, and which the Jew?
 Duke. Antonio and old Shylock, both stand
  forth. 175
 Por. Is your name Shylock?
 Shy.   Shylock is my name.
 Por. Of a strange nature is the suit you follow;
Yet in such rule that the Venetian law
Cannot impugn you as you do proceed.
You stand within his danger, do you not? 180
 Ant. Ay, so he says.
 Por.   Do you confess the bond?
 Ant. I do.
 Por. Then must the Jew be merciful.
 Shy. On what compulsion must I? Tell me that.
 Por. The quality of mercy is not strain'd.
It droppeth as the gentle rain from heaven 185
Upon the place beneath. It is twice blest:
It blesseth him that gives and him that takes.

'Tis mightiest in the mightiest; it becomes
The throned monarch better than his crown.
His sceptre shows the force of temporal power, 190
The attribute to awe and majesty,
Wherein doth sit the dread and fear of kings;
But mercy is above the sceptred sway;
It is enthroned in the hearts of kings;
It is an attribute to God himself; 195
And earthly power doth then show likest God's
When mercy seasons justice. Therefore, Jew,
Though justice be thy plea, consider this,
That, in the course of justice, none of us
Should see salvation. We do pray for mercy, 200
And that same prayer doth teach us all to render
The deeds of mercy. I have spoke thus much
To mitigate the justice of thy plea,
Which if thou follow, this strict court of Venice
Must needs give sentence 'gainst the merchant
  there. 205
 Shy. My deeds upon my head! I crave the law,
The penalty and forfeit of my bond.
 Por. Is he not able to discharge the money?
 Bass. Yes, here I tender it for him in the court;
Yea, twice the sum. If that will not suffice, 210
I will be bound to pay it ten times o'er,
On forfeit of my hands, my head, my heart.
If this will not suffice, it must appear
That malice bears down truth. And I beseech you,
Wrest once the law to your authority; 215
To do a great right, do a little wrong,
And curb this cruel devil of his will.
 Por. It must not be; there is no power in Venice
Can alter a decree established.
'Twill be recorded for a precedent, 220
And many an error by the same example
Will rush into the state. It cannot be.
 Shy. A Daniel come to judgement! yea, a Daniel!
O wise young judge, how I do honour thee!
 Por. I pray you, let me look upon the bond. 225
 Shy. Here 'tis, most reverend doctor, here it is.
 Por. Shylock, there's thrice thy money off'red
  thee.
 Shy. An oath, an oath, I have an oath in heaven!
Shall I lay perjury upon my soul?
No, not for Venice.
 Por.   Why, this bond is forfeit; 230
And lawfully by this the Jew may claim
A pound of flesh, to be by him cut off
Nearest the merchant's heart. Be merciful;
Take thrice thy money; bid me tear the bond.
 Shy. When it is paid according to the tenour.
It doth appear you are a worthy judge; 236
You know the law, your exposition
Hath been most sound. I charge you by the law,
Whereof you are a well-deserving pillar,

---

171. **difference:** dispute.   184. **strain'd:** constrained, forced.   214. **truth:** honesty.   223. **Daniel.** In the Apocryphal
book of *Susannah*, Daniel is a judge.

Proceed to judgement. By my soul I swear 240
There is no power in the tongue of man
To alter me. I stay here on my bond.
   Ant. Most heartily I do beseech the court
To give the judgement.
   Por.   Why then, thus it is: 244
You must prepare your bosom for his knife, —
   Shy. O noble judge! O excellent young man!
   Por. For the intent and purpose of the law
Hath full relation to the penalty
Which here appeareth due upon the bond.
   Shy. 'Tis very true. O wise and upright judge!
How much more elder art thou than thy looks! 251
   Por. Therefore lay bare your bosom.
   Shy.   Ay, his breast;
So says the bond; doth it not, noble judge?
"Nearest his heart;" those are the very words.
   Por. It is so. Are there balance here to weigh
The flesh?
   Shy.   I have them ready. 256
   Por. Have by some surgeon, Shylock, on your
    charge,
To stop his wounds, lest he do bleed to death.
   Shy. Is it so nominated in the bond?
   Por. It is not so express'd; but what of that? 260
'Twere good you do so much for charity.
   Shy. I cannot find it; 'tis not in the bond.
   Por. You, merchant, have you anything to say?
   Ant. But little; I am arm'd and well prepar'd.
Give me your hand, Bassanio; fare you well! 265
Grieve not that I am fall'n to this for you;
For herein Fortune shows herself more kind
Than is her custom. It is still her use
To let the wretched man outlive his wealth,
To view with hollow eye and wrinkled brow 270
An age of poverty; from which ling'ring penance
Of such a misery doth she cut me off.
Commend me to your honourable wife.
Tell her the process of Antonio's end;
Say how I lov'd you, speak me fair in death, 275
And, when the tale is told, bid her be judge
Whether Bassanio had not once a love.
Repent but you that you shall lose your friend,
And he repents not that he pays your debt;
For if the Jew do cut but deep enough, 280
I'll pay it instantly with all my heart.
   Bass. Antonio, I am married to a wife
Which is as dear to me as life itself;
But life itself, my wife, and all the world,
Are not with me esteem'd above thy life. 285
I would lose all, ay, sacrifice them all
Here to this devil, to deliver you.
   Por. Your wife would give you little thanks for
    that,
If she were by, to hear you make the offer.

   Gra. I have a wife, who, I protest, I love; 290
I would she were in heaven, so she could
Entreat some power to change this currish Jew.
   Ner. 'Tis well you offer it behind her back.
The wish would make else an unquiet house.
   Shy. These be the Christian husbands. I have a
    daughter; 295
Would any of the stock of Barrabas
Had been her husband rather than a Christian!
                           [Aside.]
We trifle time. I pray thee, pursue sentence.
   Por. A pound of that same merchant's flesh is
    thine.
The court awards it, and the law doth give it. 300
   Shy. Most rightful judge!
   Por. And you must cut this flesh from off his
    breast.
The law allows it, and the court awards it.
   Shy. Most learned judge! A sentence! Come,
    prepare!
   Por. Tarry a little; there is something else. 305
This bond doth give thee here no jot of blood;
The words expressly are " a pound of flesh."
Take then thy bond, take thou thy pound of
    flesh;
But, in the cutting it, if thou dost shed
One drop of Christian blood, thy lands and goods
Are, by the laws of Venice, confiscate 311
Unto the state of Venice.
   Gra. O upright judge! Mark, Jew: O learned
    judge!
   Shy. Is that the law?
   Por.   Thyself shall see the act;
For, as thou urgest justice, be assur'd 315
Thou shalt have justice, more than thou desir'st.
   Gra. O learned judge! Mark, Jew: a learned
    judge!
   Shy. I take this offer, then; pay the bond thrice
And let the Christian go.
   Bass.   Here is the money.
   Por. Soft! 320
The Jew shall have all justice. Soft! no haste.
He shall have nothing but the penalty.
   Gra. O Jew! an upright judge, a learned judge!
   Por. Therefore prepare thee to cut off the flesh.
Shed thou no blood, nor cut thou less nor more 325
But just a pound of flesh. If thou tak'st more
Or less than a just pound, be it but so much
As makes it light or heavy in the substance
Or the division of the twentieth part
Of one poor scruple, nay, if the scale do turn 330
But in the estimation of a hair,
Thou diest and all thy goods are confiscate.
   Gra. A second Daniel! A Daniel, Jew!
Now, infidel, I have you on the hip.

---

248. **relation to:** bearing upon.   296. **Barrabas:** the thief freed by Pilate.   328–29. **in ... division:** by the whole or the fraction.   330. **scruple:** 20 grains.

Por. Why doth the Jew pause? Take thy for-
feiture.   335
Shy. Give me my principal, and let me go.
Bass. I have it ready for thee; here it is.
Por. He hath refus'd it in the open court.
He shall have merely justice and his bond.
Gra. A Daniel, still say I, a second Daniel!   340
I thank thee, Jew, for teaching me that word.
Shy. Shall I not have barely my principal?
Por. Thou shalt have nothing but the forfeiture,
To be so taken at thy peril, Jew.
Shy. Why, then the devil give him good of it!
I'll stay no longer question.
Por.   Tarry, Jew: 346
The law hath yet another hold on you.
It is enacted in the laws of Venice,
If it be prov'd against an alien
That by direct or indirect attempts   350
He seek the life of any citizen,
The party 'gainst the which he doth contrive
Shall seize one half his goods; the other half
Comes to the privy coffer of the state;
And the offender's life lies in the mercy   355
Of the Duke only, 'gainst all other voice:
In which predicament, I say, thou stand'st;
For it appears, by manifest proceeding,
That indirectly, and directly too,
Thou hast contriv'd against the very life   360
Of the defendant; and thou hast incurr'd
The danger formerly by me rehears'd.
Down therefore and beg mercy of the Duke.
Gra. Beg that thou mayst have leave to hang
thyself;
And yet, thy wealth being forfeit to the state, 365
Thou hast not left the value of a cord;
Therefore thou must be hang'd at the state's charge.
Duke. That thou shalt see the difference of our
spirit,
I pardon thee thy life before thou ask it.
For half thy wealth, it is Antonio's;   370
The other half comes to the general state,
Which humbleness may drive unto a fine.
Por. Ay, for the state, not for Antonio.
Shy. Nay, take my life and all; pardon not that.
You take my house when you do take the prop   375
That doth sustain my house; you take my life
When you do take the means whereby I live.
Por. What mercy can you render him, Antonio?
Gra. A halter gratis; nothing else, for God's sake.
Ant. So please my lord the Duke and all the court
To quit the fine for one half of his goods,   381
I am content; so he will let me have
The other half in use, to render it,
Upon his death, unto the gentleman
That lately stole his daughter: 385

Two things provided more, that, for this favour,
He presently become a Christian;
The other, that he do record a gift,
Here in the court, of all he dies possess'd,
Unto his son Lorenzo and his daughter.   390
Duke. He shall do this, or else I do recant
The pardon that I late pronounced here.
Por. Art thou contented, Jew? What dost thou
say?
Shy. I am content.
Por.   Clerk, draw a deed of gift.
Shy. I pray you, give me leave to go from hence.
I am not well. Send the deed after me,   396
And I will sign it.
Duke.   Get thee gone, but do it.
Gra. In christening shalt thou have two god-
fathers:
Had I been judge, thou shouldst have had ten more,
To bring thee to the gallows, not the font.   400
                            [*Exit* [*Shylock*].
Duke. Sir, I entreat you home with me to dinner.
Por. I humbly do desire your Grace of pardon.
I must away this night toward Padua,
And it is meet I presently set forth.
Duke. I am sorry that your leisure serves you not.
Antonio, gratify this gentleman;   406
For, in my mind, you are much bound to him.
                          [*Exeunt Duke and his train.*
Bass. Most worthy gentleman, I and my friend
Have by your wisdom been this day acquitted
Of grievous penalties; in lieu whereof   410
Three thousand ducats, due unto the Jew,
We freely cope your courteous pains withal.
Ant. And stand indebted, over and above,
In love and service to you evermore.
Por. He is well paid that is well satisfied;   415
And I, delivering you, am satisfied
And therein do account myself well paid.
My mind was never yet more mercenary.
I pray you, know me when we meet again.
I wish you well, and so I take my leave.   420
Bass. Dear sir, of force I must attempt you
further.
Take some remembrance of us, as a tribute,
Not as fee. Grant me two things, I pray you,
Not to deny me, and to pardon me.
Por. You press me far, and therefore I will yield.
[*To Ant.*] Give me your gloves, I'll wear them for
your sake;   426
[*To Bass.*] And, for your love, I'll take this ring
from you.
Do not draw back your hand; I'll take no more;
And you in love shall not deny me this.
Bass. This ring, good sir, alas, it is a trifle!   430
I will not shame myself to give you this.

372. **drive:** reduce. 381. **quit:** remit. 383. **use:** trust. 399. **ten more:** i.e., to make a jury of twelve. 406. **gratify:**
reward. 410. **lieu:** return. 412. **cope:** requite.

Por. I will have nothing else but only this;
And now methinks I have a mind to it.
   Bass. There's more depends on this than on the
    value.
The dearest ring in Venice will I give you,   435
And find it out by proclamation;
Only for this, I pray you, pardon me.
   Por. I see, sir, you are liberal in offers.
You taught me first to beg; and now methinks
You teach me how a beggar should be answer'd.   440
   Bass. Good sir, this ring was given me by my
    wife;
And when she put it on, she made me vow
That I should neither sell nor give nor lose it.
   Por. That 'scuse serves many men to save their
    gifts.
An if your wife be not a mad-woman,   445
And know how well I have deserv'd this ring,
She would not hold out enemy for ever,
For giving it to me.   Well, peace be with you!
          [Exeunt [Portia and Nerissa].
   Ant. My Lord Bassanio, let him have the ring.
Let his deservings and my love withal   450
Be valued 'gainst your wife's commandement.
   Bass. Go, Gratiano, run and overtake him;
Give him the ring, and bring him, if thou canst,
Unto Antonio's house.   Away! make haste.
          [Exit Gratiano.
Come, you and I will thither presently;   455
And in the morning early will we both
Fly toward Belmont. Come, Antonio.   *[Exeunt.*

       [SCENE II. *The same. A street.*]

     Enter PORTIA *and* NERISSA.

   Por. Inquire the Jew's house out, give him this
    deed
And let him sign it. We'll away to-night,
And be a day before our husbands home.
This deed will be well welcome to Lorenzo.

        Enter GRATIANO.

   Gra. Fair sir, you are well o'erta'en.   5
My Lord Bassanio upon more advice
Hath sent you here this ring, and doth entreat
Your company at dinner.
   Por.   That cannot be.
His ring I do accept most thankfully,
And so, I pray you, tell him; furthermore,   10
I pray you, show my youth old Shylock's house.
   Gra. That will I do.
   Ner.   Sir, I would speak with you.
[Aside to Por.] I'll see if I can get my husband's ring,

Which I did make him swear to keep for ever.
   Por. [*Aside to Ner.*] Thou mayst, I warrant.
We shall have old swearing   15
That they did give the rings away to men;
But we'll outface them, and outswear them too.
[*Aloud.*] Away! make haste. Thou know'st where
    I will tarry.
   Ner. Come, good sir, will you show me to this
    house?   *[Exeunt.*

ACT V

[SCENE I. *Belmont. Avenue to Portia's house.*]

     Enter LORENZO *and* JESSICA.

   Lor. The moon shines bright. In such a night as
    this,
When the sweet wind did gently kiss the trees
And they did make no noise, in such a night
Troilus methinks mounted the Troyan walls,
And sigh'd his soul toward the Grecian tents,   5
Where Cressid lay that night.
   Jes.   In such a night
Did Thisbe fearfully o'ertrip the dew,
And saw the lion's shadow ere himself
And ran dismay'd away.
   Lor.   In such a night
Stood Dido with a willow in her hand   10
Upon the wild sea banks, and waft her love
To come again to Carthage.
   Jes.   In such a night
Medea gathered the enchanted herbs
That did renew old Æson.
   Lor.   In such a night
Did Jessica steal from the wealthy Jew,   15
And with an unthrift love did run from Venice
As far as Belmont.
   Jes.   In such a night
Did young Lorenzo swear he lov'd her well,
Stealing her soul with many vows of faith
And ne'er a true one.
   Lor.   In such a night   20
Did pretty Jessica, like a little shrew,
Slander her love, and he forgave it her.
   Jes. I would out-night you, did no body come;
But, hark, I hear the footing of a man.

        Enter a MESSENGER.

   Lor. Who comes so fast in silence of the night? 25
   Mess. A friend.
   Lor. A friend! what friend? Your name, I pray
    you, friend?
   Mess. Stephano is my name; and I bring word
My mistress will before the break of day

---

434. depends...on Q₁. *then this depends upon* Q₂.
Sc. ii, 6. **advice:** consideration. 15. **old:** plentiful.
Act V, sc. i, 4-6. Reminiscent of Chaucer's *Troilus and Criseyde,* V.647-72. 10. **willow:** symbol of forsaken love.
11. **waft:** waved.

Be here at Belmont. She doth stray about   30
By holy crosses, where she kneels and prays
For happy wedlock hours.
    Lor.   Who comes with her?
    Mess. None but a holy hermit and her maid.
I pray you, is my master yet return'd?
    Lor. He is not, nor we have not heard from him.
But go we in, I pray thee, Jessica,   36
And ceremoniously let us prepare
Some welcome for the mistress of the house.

Enter Clown [LAUNCELOT].

    Laun. Sola, sola! wo ha, ho! sola, sola!
    Lor. Who calls?   40
    Laun. Sola! did you see Master Lorenzo and
[Mistress] Lorenzo? Sola, sola!
    Lor. Leave holloaing, man; here.
    Laun. Sola! where? where?
    Lor. Here.   45
    Laun. Tell him there's a post come from my mas-
ter, with his horn full of good news. My master will
be here ere morning.   [*Exit.*]
    Lor. Sweet soul, let's in, and there expect their
    coming.
And yet no matter; why should we go in?   50
My friend Stephano, signify, I pray you,
Within the house, your mistress is at hand;
And bring your music forth into the air.
                    [*Exit Mess.*]
How sweet the moonlight sleeps upon this bank!
Here will we sit and let the sounds of music   55
Creep in our ears. Soft stillness and the night
Become the touches of sweet harmony.
Sit, Jessica. Look how the floor of heaven
Is thick inlaid with patines of bright gold.
There's not the smallest orb which thou behold'st 60
But in his motion like an angel sings,
Still quiring to the young-ey'd cherubins.
Such harmony is in immortal souls;
But whilst this muddy vesture of decay
Doth grossly close it in, we cannot hear it.   65

[*Enter Musicians.*]

Come, ho! and wake Diana with a hymn;
With sweetest touches pierce your mistress' ear
And draw her home with music.   [*Play Music.*
    Jes. I am never merry when I hear sweet music.
    Lor. The reason is, your spirits are attentive;
For do but note a wild and wanton herd,   71
Or race of youthful and unhandled colts,
Fetching mad bounds, bellowing and neighing loud,
Which is the hot condition of their blood,
If they but hear perchance a trumpet sound,   75

Or any air of music touch their ears,
You shall perceive them make a mutual stand,
Their savage eyes turn'd to a modest gaze
By the sweet power of music; therefore the poet
Did feign that Orpheus drew trees, stones, and
    floods;   80
Since nought so stockish, hard, and full of rage,
But music for the time doth change his nature.
The man that hath no music in himself,
Nor is not mov'd with concord of sweet sounds,
Is fit for treasons, stratagems, and spoils.   85
The motions of his spirit are dull as night
And his affections dark as Erebus.
Let no such man be trusted. Mark the music.

Enter PORTIA *and* NERISSA.

    Por. That light we see is burning in my hall.
How far that little candle throws his beams!   90
So shines a good deed in a naughty world.
    Ner. When the moon shone, we did not see the
    candle.
    Por. So doth the greater glory dim the less.
A substitute shines brightly as a king
Until a king be by; and then his state   95
Empties itself, as doth an inland brook
Into the main of waters. Music! Hark!
    Ner. It is your music, madam, of the house.
    Por. Nothing is good, I see, without respect;
Methinks it sounds much sweeter than by day.   100
    Ner. Silence bestows that virtue on it, madam.
    Por. The crow doth sing as sweetly as the lark
When neither is attended, and I think
The nightingale, if she should sing by day,
When every goose is cackling, would be thought
No better a musician than the wren.   106
How many things by season season'd are
To their right praise and true perfection!
Peace, ho! the Moon sleeps with Endymion
And would not be awak'd.   [*Music ceases.*
    Lor.   That is the voice,
Or I am much deceiv'd, of Portia.   111
    Por. He knows me as the blind man knows the
    cuckoo,
By the bad voice.
    Lor.   Dear lady, welcome home!
    Por. We have been praying for our husbands'
    welfare,
Which speed, we hope, the better for our words.   115
Are they return'd?
    Lor.   Madam, they are not yet;
But there is come a messenger before,
To signify their coming.
    Por.   Go in, Nerissa;

---

39. **Sola:** perhaps imitation of a postman's horn.   41-42. **Master ... Lorenzo.** Q₁ reads *M. Lorenzo & M. Lorenzo.*
49. **expect:** await.   59. **patines:** disks.   77. **mutual:** simultaneous.   79. **the poet:** Ovid.   81. **stockish:** wooden, unfeeling.
87. **affections:** passions. **Erebus:** the hell of classical mythology.   91. **naughty:** wicked.   99. **respect:** reference to something.   103. **attended:** heeded.   109. **Endymion:** a shepherd loved by Diana.

Give order to my servants that they take
No note at all of our being absent hence;   120
Nor you, Lorenzo; Jessica, nor you.
                                        [*A tucket sounds.*
    Lor. Your husband is at hand; I hear his trumpet.
We are no tell-tales, madam; fear you not.
    Por. This night methinks is but the daylight sick;
It looks a little paler. 'Tis a day,   125
Such as the day is when the sun is hid.

    Enter BASSANIO, ANTONIO, GRATIANO, *and
                    their followers.*

    Bass. We should hold day with the Antipodes,
If you would walk in absence of the sun.
    Por. Let me give light, but let me not be light;
For a light wife doth make a heavy husband,   130
And never be Bassanio so for me.
But God sort all! You're welcome home, my lord.
    Bass. I thank you, madam. Give welcome to my
        friend.
This is the man, this is Antonio,
To whom I am so infinitely bound.   135
    Por. You should in all sense be much bound to
        him,
For, as I hear, he was much bound for you.
    Ant. No more than I am well acquitted of.
    Por. Sir, you are very welcome to our house.
It must appear in other ways than words,   140
Therefore I scant this breathing courtesy.
    Gra. [*To Ner.*] By yonder moon I swear you do
        me wrong;
In faith, I gave it to the judge's clerk.
Would he were gelt that had it, for my part,
Since you do take it, love, so much at heart.   145
    Por. A quarrel, ho, already! What's the matter?
    Gra. About a hoop of gold, a paltry ring
That she did give me, whose posy was
For all the world like cutler's poetry
Upon a knife, "Love me, and leave me not."   150
    Ner. What talk you of the posy or the value?
You swore to me, when I did give it you,
That you would wear it till your hour of death,
And that it should lie with you in your grave.   154
Though not for me, yet for your vehement oaths,
You should have been respective and have kept it.
Gave it a judge's clerk! No, God's my judge,
The clerk will ne'er wear hair on's face that had it.
    Gra. He will, an if he live to be a man.
    Ner. Ay, if a woman live to be a man.   160
    Gra. Now, by this hand, I gave it to a youth,
A kind of boy, a little scrubbed boy,
No higher than thyself, the judge's clerk,
A prating boy, that begg'd it as a fee.
I could not for my heart deny it him.   165

    Por. You were to blame, I must be plain with
        you,
To part so slightly with your wife's first gift;
A thing stuck on with oaths upon your finger
And so riveted with faith unto your flesh.
I gave my love a ring, and made him swear   170
Never to part with it; and here he stands.
I dare be sworn for him he would not leave it
Nor pluck it from his finger for the wealth
That the world masters. Now, in faith, Gratiano,
You give your wife too unkind a cause of grief.   175
An 'twere to me, I should be mad at it.
    Bass. [*Aside.*] Why, I were best to cut my left
        hand off
And swear I lost the ring defending it.
    Gra. My Lord Bassanio gave his ring away
Unto the judge that begg'd it, and indeed   180
Deserv'd it too; and then the boy, his clerk,
That took some pains in writing, he begg'd mine;
And neither man nor master would take aught
But the two rings.
    Por.   What ring gave you, my lord?
Not that, I hope, which you receiv'd of me.   185
    Bass. If I could add a lie unto a fault,
I would deny it; but you see my finger
Hath not the ring upon it; it is gone.
    Por. Even so void is your false heart of truth.
By heaven, I will ne'er come in your bed   190
Until I see the ring.
    Ner.   Nor I in yours
Till I again see mine.
    Bass.   Sweet Portia,
If you did know to whom I gave the ring,
If you did know for whom I gave the ring,
And would conceive for what I gave the ring,   195
And how unwillingly I left the ring,
When nought would be accepted but the ring,
You would abate the strength of your displeasure.
    Por. If you had known the virtue of the ring,
Or half her worthiness that gave the ring,   200
Or your own honour to contain the ring,
You would not then have parted with the ring.
What man is there so much unreasonable,
If you had pleas'd to have defended it
With any terms of zeal, wanted the modesty   205
To urge the thing held as a ceremony?
Nerissa teaches me what to believe:
I'll die for't but some woman had the ring.
    Bass. No, by my honour, madam, by my soul,
No woman had it, but a civil doctor,   210
Which did refuse three thousand ducats of me
And begg'd the ring; the which I did deny him
And suffer'd him to go displeas'd away;
Even he that had held up the very life

---

121. S.D. *tucket:* flourish on a trumpet.   132. **sort:** dispose.   141. **breathing courtesy:** courteous talk.   148. **posy:**
motto.   156. **respective:** careful, mindful.   162. **scrubbed:** stunted.   201. **contain:** retain.   206. **urge:** demand.   **cere-**
mony: something sacred.   210. **civil doctor:** doctor of civil law.

Of my dear friend.   What should I say, sweet lady?
I was enforc'd to send it after him;   216
I was beset with shame and courtesy;
My honour would not let ingratitude
So much besmear it.   Pardon me, good lady;
For, by these blessed candles of the night,   220
Had you been there, I think you would have begg'd
The ring of me to give the worthy doctor.

Por. Let not that doctor e'er come near my house.
Since he hath got the jewel that I lov'd,
And that which you did swear to keep for me,   225
I will become as liberal as you.
I'll not deny him any thing I have,
No, not my body nor my husband's bed.
Know him I shall, I am well sure of it.
Lie not a night from home.   Watch me like Argus.
If you do not, if I be left alone,   231
Now, by mine honour, which is yet mine own,
I'll have that doctor for my bedfellow.

Ner. And I his clerk; therefore be well advis'd
How you do leave me to mine own protection.   235

Gra. Well, do you so; let not me take him then;
For if I do, I'll mar the young clerk's pen.

Ant. I am th' unhappy subject of these quarrels.

Por. Sir, grieve not you; you are welcome notwithstanding.

Bass. Portia, forgive me this enforced wrong; 240
And in the hearing of these many friends
I swear to thee, even by thine own fair eyes,
Wherein I see myself —

Por.   Mark you but that!
In both my eyes he doubly sees himself,
In each eye, one.   Swear by your double self,   245
And there's an oath of credit.

Bass.   Nay, but hear me.
Pardon this fault, and by my soul I swear
I never more will break an oath with thee.

Ant. I once did lend my body for his wealth,
Which, but for him that had your husband's ring,
Had quite miscarried.   I dare be bound again,   251
My soul upon the forfeit, that your lord
Will never more break faith advisedly.

Por. Then you shall be his surety.   Give him this
And bid him keep it better than the other.   255

Ant. Here, Lord Bassanio; swear to keep this
ring.

Bass. By heaven, it is the same I gave the doctor!

Por. I had it of him.   Pardon me, Bassanio;
For, by this ring, the doctor lay with me.

Ner. And pardon me, my gentle Gratiano;   260
For that same scrubbed boy, the doctor's clerk,

In lieu of this last night did lie with me.

Gra. Why, this is like the mending of highways
In summer, where the ways are fair enough.
What, are we cuckolds ere we have deserv'd it? 265

Por. Speak not so grossly.   You are all amaz'd.
Here is a letter; read it at your leisure.
It comes from Padua, from Bellario.
There you shall find that Portia was the doctor,
Nerissa there her clerk.   Lorenzo here   270
Shall witness I set forth as soon as you
And even but now return'd; I have not yet
Ent'red my house.   Antonio, you are welcome;
And I have better news in store for you
Than you expect.   Unseal this letter soon;   275
There you shall find three of your argosies
Are richly come to harbour suddenly.
You shall not know by what strange accident
I chanced on this letter.

Ant.   I am dumb.   279

Bass. Were you the doctor and I knew you not?

Gra. Were you the clerk that is to make me
cuckold?

Ner. Ay, but the clerk that never means to do it,
Unless he live until he be a man.

Bass. Sweet doctor, you shall be my bedfellow.
When I am absent, then lie with my wife.   285

Ant. Sweet lady, you have given me life and liv-
ing;
For here I read for certain that my ships
Are safely come to road.

Por.   How now, Lorenzo!
My clerk hath some good comforts too for you.

Ner. Ay, and I'll give them him without a fee. 290
There do I give to you and Jessica,
From the rich Jew, a special deed of gift,
After his death, of all he dies possess'd of.

Lor. Fair ladies, you drop manna in the way
Of starved people.

Por.   It is almost morning,   295
And yet I am sure you are not satisfied
Of these events at full.   Let us go in;
And charge us there upon inter'gatories,
And we will answer all things faithfully.

Gra. Let it be so.   The first inter'gatory   300
That my Nerissa shall be sworn on is,
Whether till the next night she had rather stay,
Or go to bed now, being two hours to day.
But were the day come, I should wish it dark,
Till I were couching with the doctor's clerk.   305
Well, while I live I'll fear no other thing
So sore as keeping safe Nerissa's ring.   [*Exeunt.*

230. **like Argus:** i.e. with a hundred eyes. 245. **double:** deceitful. 249. **wealth:** weal, welfare. 298. **charge ... inter'-
gatories:** question us under oath. 306. **fear:** be anxious about.

The Taming of the Shrew

THE TAMING OF THE SHREW was first printed, so far as is known, in the First Folio. On this all subsequent texts have been based.

Evidence for the date of composition is purely internal; and this is notably weakened by the doubt as to the extent of Shakespeare's part in the authorship. Metrical tests are inconclusive. Similarities to other plays, such as the *Comedy of Errors* in the treatment of the servants, and *Hamlet* in the reception of the players, suggest any date from 1592 to 1602. The wit-contest between Katherine and Petruchio in II.i. associates it with plays like *Much Ado* and *As You Like It*, while the occurrence of lines in the dancing measure of the speeches of the Dromios would lead us to place it before these plays. A reasonable date is 1596.

The origin and workmanship of this play have been subjects of controversy. In 1594 was published a play of unknown authorship called *The Taming of A Shrew*. The close resemblance between this play and Shakespeare's establishes an intimate relationship, but the relationship has been variously construed. The conventional view is to regard *A Shrew* as the immediate source of *The Shrew*, but ingenious scholarship has argued that Shakespeare himself was in fact the author of *A Shrew* (which thus would be an honest printing of a Shakespearean play later completely rewritten by Shakespeare), and even that *A Shrew* was a "bad Quarto" of the play in the Folio. In addition to cogent arguments which may be brought against these latter suggestions individually, there is one which is equally destructive to them both, namely, that the nomenclature in the two plays is almost entirely different; thus one must explain why Shakespeare, reworking one of his own plays, should bother to change so many names, or why "pirates" should complicate their task of memory in the same way. The present editors adhere to the traditional conception of *A Shrew* as an earlier play by somebody else which Shakespeare reworked.

In the transforming of the earlier into the present play, phrases and very occasionally whole lines have been retained, but the dialogue is substantially new, greatly polished and invigorated. The essentials of both main plot and sub-plot are provided in *A Shrew*, but details of stagecraft have been improved throughout. The incidents in the Katherine-Petruchio plot remain fundamentally the same (the prototypes are Kate and Ferando). Some changes have been made in the Bianca plot. The older play gives Kate two younger sisters (Phylema and Emilia), each of whom has a lover (Aurelius and Polidor respectively); and the picture of their wooing, hindered only by the necessity of getting Kate married first, is uninspired. In *The Shrew*, on the other hand, there is but one younger sister (Bianca), whose rôle as foil to the shrewish Katherine is thus accented; and the suitors to the two sisters in the earlier play now become rivals (Lucentio and Hortensio) for the hand of Bianca. The interest of rival suitors is heightened by the addition of another, the dotard Gremio, and by having the disguised Tranio, Lucentio's servant, also do some courting. Gremio and the stratagem by which Lucentio and Tranio exchange characters were taken directly from George Gascoigne's *Supposes*, a translation of Ariosto's *I Suppositi* (1566; published 1573). In *Supposes* we have no shrew, but a plot turning on the wooing of a lady by two lovers. The author of *A Shrew* had earlier made use of *Supposes*, drawing from it the device, also employed in *The Shrew*, of introducing a casual stranger to personate a suitor's father and having the real father turn up later unexpectedly. In the handling of this device, however, *The Shrew* is closer to *Supposes* than is *A Shrew*, from which fact it would appear that at this point Shakespeare, though following *A Shrew*, turned again to *Supposes* at first hand. There would also seem to be a link with Gascoigne's play in the phrasing of the line (V.i.120), "While counterfeit *supposes* blear'd thine eyne." Hortensio's widow appears in neither of the earlier plays. The trick of the feigned instructors is elaborated from a scene in *A Shrew* in which Tranio's prototype attempts to give Kate a music lesson in order to afford his master and his friend an opportunity to court her sisters. The Latin lesson may have been suggested by a somewhat similar scene in Robert Wilson's *Three Lords and Three Ladies of London*, printed in 1590.

It is widely held that in the working over of *A Shrew* into the present play another hand than Shakespeare's is evident. The revised Induction and the scenes between Kate and Petruchio are usually assigned to Shakespeare, while the lines in the Bianca plot are thought not to show his style. This points either to an intermediate play, or to revision in collaboration. It has been tacitly assumed that the part of each author was confined to the scenes in which his style appears in the verse and diction. But it is clearly possible that a joint author might have a large share in planning the action of scenes which his partner wrote, and vice versa. In fact, the ingenious craftsmanship displayed in the interweaving of the two plots argues careful and intimate collaboration. Some critics, admiring the fine structure, and less impressed than others by the discrepancies in style and metre, uphold Shakespeare as the sole reviser.

The Induction is taken from *A Shrew*, but is marvellously transformed. The character of Christopher Sly, "old Sly's son of Burton Heath," drawing the free air of Warwickshire, is authentic Shakespeare. So also are the sportive lord and his retinue. A story similar to that of the drunken tinker is found in *The Arabian Nights*, and the trick played on him by the lord is said by Heuterus (*De Rebus Burgundicis*, 1584) to have been actually perpetrated upon a chance victim by Philip the Good. The story of the Duke's escapade was doubtless widely current in the sixteenth century, but none of the English books in which it is repeated appeared early enough to have served Shakespeare.

In *A Shrew* the characters of the Induction speak from time to time throughout the play, and at the close Sly again falls asleep and is transported by the lord's servants back to his ale-house door. There, roused by the Tapster, he asserts he has had the "bravest dream" about how to tame a shrew and departs forthwith inspired to subdue his own wife. This epilogue is absent from Shakespeare's play, to the great disappointment of his critics, most of whom feel that the failure to round off the frame plot is a blemish. Theoretically, it is; practically, perhaps not. Various explanations have been offered. A common view is that *The Shrew* did conclude with an Epilogue, but that this part of the manuscript was lost, perhaps having been kept as a loose sheet. Another, equally plausible, is that after a time the Epilogue came to be omitted in performance, because, however appropriate structurally it might be, it proved to be an anti-climax after the exhilaration of the central play; and therefore it was removed from the manuscript. One should remember, however, that *The Shrew* lacks not only the Epilogue but also the incidental comments which in the earlier play Sly makes upon the drama he is witnessing. The sacrifice of so much could hardly have been other than deliberate. Sly's remarks may of course have been included originally, only to be excised subsequently along with the Epilogue; or they may have been omitted from the beginning as inartistic interruptions. Perhaps that was the case. Sly speaks at only one point after the beginning of the play proper (I.i.254–59), pronouncing his verdict, "'Tis a very excellent piece of work, madam lady; would 'twere done!" After that he is supposed to "sit and mark"; but not, one must think, indefinitely. Drunk and somnolent (already his attention has been flagging), he could hardly stay awake for long, and the actor's business was, perhaps, soon to fall asleep and, at a convenient juncture thereafter, to be removed. It may be noted that the appearance of the Pedant at a window in V.i. necessitated the clearing of the gallery from which Sly had been viewing the play. The student of Shakespeare may regret the disappearance of Sly, but the Elizabethan theatre-goer perhaps missed him less, being plentifully absorbed in the lively farce of the taming. Sly is a superlative re-creation, but possibly Shakespeare decided that he sufficiently justified his existence by providing a fresh mode of introduction for a comedy of intrigue.

THE TAMING OF THE SHREW

[DRAMATIS PERSONÆ

A Lord.
CHRISTOPHER SLY, *a tinker.* ⎫ *Persons in the*
Hostess, Page, Players, Hunts- ⎬ *Induction.*
men, and Servants. ⎭

BAPTISTA, *a rich gentleman of Padua.*
VINCENTIO, *an old gentleman of Pisa.*
LUCENTIO, *son to Vincentio, in love with Bianca.*
PETRUCHIO, *a gentleman of Verona, a suitor to*
Katherina.
GREMIO, ⎫ *suitors to Bianca.*
HORTENSIO, ⎭

TRANIO, ⎫ *servants to Lucentio.*
BIONDELLO, ⎭
GRUMIO, ⎫ *servants to Petruchio.*
CURTIS, ⎭
A Pedant.

KATHERINA, *the shrew,* ⎫ *daughters to Baptista.*
BIANCA, ⎬
Widow.

Tailor, Haberdasher, and Servants attending on Baptista and Petruchio.

SCENE: *Padua, and Petruchio's country house.*]

[INDUCTION

SCENE I. *Before an alehouse on a heath.*]

Enter HOSTESS, *and beggar,* CHRISTOPHERO SLY.

Sly. I'll pheese you, in faith.
Host. A pair of stocks, you rogue!
Sly. Y' are a baggage; the Slys are no rogues.
Look in the chronicles; we came in with Richard
Conqueror. Therefore *paucas pallabris;* let the
world slide; sessa! 6
Host. You will not pay for the glasses you have
burst?
Sly. No, not a denier. Go by, Jeronimy! Go
to thy cold bed, and warm thee. 10
Host. I know my remedy; I must go fetch the
thirdborough. [*Exit.*]
Sly. Third, or fourth, or fifth borough, I'll an-

swer him by law. I'll not budge an inch, boy; let
him come, and kindly. [*Falls asleep.* 15

Wind horns. Enter a LORD *from hunting, with*
his train.

Lord. Huntsman, I charge thee, tender well my
hounds,
Brach Merriman, the poor cur, is emboss'd;
And couple Clowder with the deep-mouth'd brach.
Saw'st thou not, boy, how Silver made it good
At the hedge-corner, in the coldest fault? 20
I would not lose the dog for twenty pound.
1. Hun. Why, Belman is as good as he, my lord;
He cried upon it at the merest loss,
And twice to-day pick'd out the dullest scent.
Trust me, I take him for the better dog. 25
Lord. Thou art a fool; if Echo were as fleet,
I would esteem him worth a dozen such.

Induction, sc. i, 1. **pheese:** do for. Cf. modern slang "faze." 2. **A ... stocks:** i.e., I'll have you put in the stocks. 4. **Richard:** Sly's blunder for *William.* 5. *paucas pallabris:* a corruption of Sp. *pocas palabras,* few words. 6. **sessa!** Away! 9. **denier:** a small French coin. **Go by, Jeronimy.** A misquotation of "Hieronimo beware; go by, go by." This phrase from Kyd's *Spanish Tragedy* became a sort of byword to express impatience. 12. **thirdborough:** constable. 17. **Brach:** a hunting hound. **emboss'd:** foaming at the mouth. 20. **in ... fault:** when the scent was lost (cold) 23. **He ... loss:** i.e., he gave the cry when the scent was absolutely lost.

But sup them well and look unto them all;
To-morrow I intend to hunt again.
   1. Hun. I will, my lord.   30
   Lord. What's here? One dead, or drunk? See,
doth he breathe?
   2. Hun. He breathes, my lord. Were he not
warm'd with ale,
This were a bed but cold to sleep so soundly.
   Lord. O monstrous beast! how like a swine he
lies!
Grim death, how foul and loathsome is thine image!
Sirs, I will practise on this drunken man.   36
What think you, if he were convey'd to bed,
Wrapp'd in sweet clothes, rings put upon his fingers,
A most delicious banquet by his bed,
And brave attendants near him when he wakes,
Would not the beggar then forget himself?   41
   1. Hun. Believe me, lord, I think he cannot
choose.
   2. Hun. It would seem strange unto him when he
wak'd.
   Lord. Even as a flatt'ring dream or worthless
fancy.
Then take him up and manage well the jest.   45
Carry him gently to my fairest chamber,
And hang it round with all my wanton pictures.
Balm his foul head in warm distilled waters,
And burn sweet wood to make the lodging sweet.
Procure me music ready when he wakes,   50
To make a dulcet and a heavenly sound;
And if he chance to speak, be ready straight
And with a low submissive reverence
Say, "What is it your honour will command?"
Let one attend him with a silver basin   55
Full of rose-water and bestrew'd with flowers;
Another bear the ewer, the third a diaper,
And say, "Will 't please your lordship cool your
hands?"
Some one be ready with a costly suit
And ask him what apparel he will wear.   60
Another tell him of his hounds and horse,
And that his lady mourns at his disease.
Persuade him that he hath been lunatic;
And when he says he is, say that he dreams,
For he is nothing but a mighty lord.   65
This do and do it kindly, gentle sirs.
It will be pastime passing excellent,
If it be husbanded with modesty.
   1. Hun. My lord, I warrant you we will play our
part
As he shall think by our true diligence   70
He is no less than what we say he is.

   Lord. Take him up gently and to bed with him;
And each one to his office when he wakes.
       [Some bear out Sly.] Sound trumpets.
Sirrah, go see what trumpet 'tis that sounds.
                 [Exit Servingman.]
Belike, some noble gentleman that means,   75
Travelling some journey, to repose him here.

       Re-enter SERVINGMAN.

How now! who is it?
   Serv.   An 't please your honour, players
That offer service to your lordship.

       Enter PLAYERS.

   Lord. Bid them come near. Now, fellows, you
are welcome.
   Players. We thank your honour.   80
   Lord. Do you intend to stay with me tonight?
   [A] Player. So please your lordship to accept our
duty.
   Lord. With all my heart. This fellow I remember
Since once he play'd a farmer's eldest son.
'Twas where you woo'd the gentlewoman so well.
I have forgot your name; but, sure, that part   86
Was aptly fitted and naturally perform'd.
   [A Player.] I think 'twas Soto that your honour
means.
   Lord. 'Tis very true; thou didst it excellent.
Well, you are come to me in happy time,   90
The rather for I have some sport in hand
Wherein your coming can assist me much.
There is a lord will hear you play to-night;
But I am doubtful of your modesties,
Lest, over-eyeing of his odd behaviour, —   95
For yet his honour never heard a play, —
You break into some merry passion
And so offend him; for I tell you, sirs,
If you should smile he grows impatient.
   A Player. Fear not, my lord; we can contain
ourselves,   100
Were he the veriest antic in the world.
   Lord. Go, sirrah, take them to the buttery,
And give them friendly welcome every one.
Let them want nothing that my house affords.
           [Exit one with the Players.
Sirrah, go you to Barthol'mew my page,   105
And see him dress'd in all suits like a lady.
That done, conduct him to the drunkard's chamber;
And call him madam, do him obeisance.
Tell him from me, as he will win my love,
He bear himself with honourable action,   110

---

36. **practise:** play a trick.   40. **brave:** finely dressed.   57. **diaper:** towel.   64. **is:** is still.   66. **kindly:** naturally.
68. **husbanded with modesty:** managed with moderation.   82. *[A] Player.* (Camb. edd.).   *2 Player* F.   85. *[A Player.]*
(Camb. edd.).   *Sincklo* (the name of an actor) F.   **Soto:** a character in Fletcher's *Women Pleased* (1620). Ll. 83–89 must
have been inserted in the text after Shakespeare's death.   94. **modesties:** self-control. Cf. l. 68.   101. **antic:** buffoon.
102. **buttery:** room where liquors were kept.   106. **suits:** points.

Such as he hath observ'd in noble ladies
Unto their lords, by them accomplished;
Such duty to the drunkard let him do
With soft low tongue and lowly courtesy,
And say, "What is 't your honour will command,
Wherein your lady and your humble wife   116
May show her duty and make known her love?"
And then with kind embracements, tempting kisses,
And with declining head into his bosom,
Bid him shed tears, as being overjoy'd   120
To see her noble lord restor'd to health,
Who for this seven years hath esteemed him
No better than a poor and loathsome beggar.
And if the boy have not a woman's gift
To rain a shower of commanded tears,   125
An onion will do well for such a shift,
Which in a napkin being close convey'd
Shall in despite enforce a watery eye.
See this dispatch'd with all the haste thou canst;
Anon I'll give thee more instructions.   130

[Exit a Servingman.
I know the boy will well usurp the grace,
Voice, gait, and action of a gentlewoman.
I long to hear him call the drunkard husband;
And how my men will stay themselves from laugh-
ter
When they do homage to this simple peasant.
I'll in to counsel them; haply my presence   136
May well abate the over-merry spleen
Which otherwise would grow into extremes.

[Exeunt.]

[SCENE II. *A bedchamber in the Lord's house.*]

Enter aloft the drunkard [SLY, *richly dressed,*] *with* ATTENDANTS; *some with apparel, basin and ewer, and other appurtenances; and* LORD [*like a servant*].

Sly. For God's sake, a pot of small ale.

1. Serv. Will 't please your lordship drink a cup of sack?

2. Serv. Will 't please your honour taste of these conserves?

3. Serv. What raiment will your honour wear to-day?

Sly. I am Christophero Sly; call not me hon-   5
our nor lordship. I ne'er drank sack in my life;
and if you give me any conserves, give me conserves of beef. Ne'er ask me what raiment I'll
wear; for I have no more doublets than backs, no
more stockings than legs, nor no more shoes   10

than feet; nay, sometime more feet than shoes, or
such shoes as my toes look through the overleather.

Lord. Heaven cease this idle humour in your honour!
O, that a mighty man of such descent,   15
Of such possessions, and so high esteem,
Should be infused with so foul a spirit!

Sly. What, would you make me mad? Am not
I Christopher Sly, old Sly's son of Burton heath,
by birth a pedlar, by education a card-maker,   20
by transmutation a bear-herd, and now by present
profession a tinker? Ask Marian Hacket, the fat
ale-wife of Wincot, if she know me not. If she say
I am not fourteen pence on the score for sheer ale,
score me up for the lying'st knave in Christen-   25
dom. What! I am not bestraught. Here's —

3. Serv. O, this it is that makes your lady mourn!

2. Serv. O, this is it that makes your servants droop!

Lord. Hence comes it that your kindred shuns your house,   30
As beaten hence by your strange lunacy.
O noble lord, bethink thee of thy birth,
Call home thy ancient thoughts from banishment
And banish hence these abject lowly dreams.
Look how thy servants do attend on thee,   35
Each in his office ready at thy beck.
Wilt thou have music? Hark! Apollo plays,

[Music.
And twenty caged nightingales do sing.
Or wilt thou sleep? We'll have thee to a couch
Softer and sweeter than the lustful bed   40
On purpose trimm'd up for Semiramis.
Say thou wilt walk; we will bestrew the ground.
Or wilt thou ride? Thy horses shall be trapp'd,
Their harness studded all with gold and pearl.
Dost thou love hawking? Thou hast hawks will soar   45
Above the morning lark. Or wilt thou hunt?
Thy hounds shall make the welkin answer them
And fetch shrill echoes from the hollow earth.

1. Serv. Say thou wilt course; thy greyhounds are as swift
As breathed stags, ay, fleeter than the roe.   50

2. Serv. Dost thou love pictures? We will fetch thee straight
Adonis painted by a running brook,
And Cytherea all in sedges hid,
Which seem to move and wanton with her breath
Even as the waving sedges play with wind.   55

Lord. We'll show thee Io as she was a maid,

---

122. **him:** himself. 131. **usurp:** counterfeit. 137. **spleen:** laughter.

Induction, sc. ii, 2. **sack:** sherry. 14. **idle:** absurd. 19. **Burton heath:** Barton-on-the-heath; like Wincot (l. 23), a village near Stratford. 20. **card-maker:** i.e., of cards for combing wool. 21. **bear-herd:** leader of a tame bear. 24. **sheer ale:** ale alone. 26. **bestraught:** distraught. 41. **Semiramis:** a legendary Assyrian queen, notorious for her voluptuous living. 47. **welkin:** sky. 49. **course:** hunt. 50. **breathed:** in good wind. 53. **Cytherea:** Venus. 56. **Io:** a mortal, loved by Jupiter, who subsequently turned her into a cow to outwit the jealousy of Juno.

And how she was beguiled and surpris'd,
As lively painted as the deed was done.

3. Serv. Or Daphne roaming through a thorny
    wood,
Scratching her legs that one shall swear she bleeds,
And at that sight shall sad Apollo weep,   61
So workmanly the blood and tears are drawn.

Lord. Thou art a lord and nothing but a lord.
Thou hast a lady far more beautiful
Than any woman in this waning age.   65

1. Serv. And till the tears that she hath shed for
    thee
Like envious floods o'er-run her lovely face,
She was the fairest creature in the world;
And yet she is inferior to none.   69

Sly. Am I a lord? And have I such a lady?
Or do I dream? Or have I dream'd till now?
I do not sleep; I see, I hear, I speak,
I smell sweet savours, and I feel soft things.
Upon my life, I am a lord indeed
And not a tinker nor Christophero Sly.   75
Well, bring our lady hither to our sight;
And once again, a pot o' th' smallest ale.

2. Serv. Will 't please your mightiness to wash
    your hands?
O, how we joy to see your wit restor'd!
O, that once more you knew but what you are!   80
These fifteen years you have been in a dream;
Or when you wak'd, so wak'd as if you slept.

Sly. These fifteen years! by my fay, a goodly
    nap.
But did I never speak of all that time?

1. Serv. O, yes, my lord, but very idle words.   85
For though you lay here in this goodly chamber,
Yet would you say ye were beaten out of door,
And rail upon the hostess of the house,
And say you would present her at the leet
Because she brought stone jugs and no seal'd
    quarts.   90
Sometimes you would call out for Cicely Hacket.

Sly. Ay, the woman's maid of the house.

3. Serv. Why, sir, you know no house nor no such
    maid,
Nor no such men as you have reckon'd up,
As Stephen Sly, and old John Naps of Greece,
And Peter Turph, and Henry Pimpernell,   96
And twenty more such names and men as these
Which never were, nor no man ever saw.

Sly. Now Lord be thanked for my good amends!

All. Amen.   100

Enter [the PAGE *as a] lady, with attendants.*

Sly. I thank thee; thou shalt not lose by it.

Page. How fares my noble lord?

Sly. Marry, I fare well, for here is cheer enough.
Where is my wife?

Page. Here, noble lord; what is thy will with
    her?   105

Sly. Are you my wife and will not call me hus-
    band?
My men should call me "lord"; I am your good-
    man.

Page. My husband and my lord, my lord and
    husband,
I am your wife in all obedience.

Sly. I know it well. What must I call her?   110
Lord. Madam.

Sly. Al'ce madam, or Joan madam?

Lord. Madam, and nothing else: so lords call
    ladies.

Sly. Madam wife, they say that I have dream'd
And slept above some fifteen year or more.   115

Page. Ay, and the time seems thirty unto me,
Being all this time abandon'd from your bed.

Sly. 'Tis much. Servants, leave me and her
    alone.
Madam, undress you and come now to bed.

Page. Thrice-noble lord, let me entreat of you
To pardon me yet for a night or two,   121
Or, if not so, until the sun be set;
For your physicians have expressly charg'd,
In peril to incur your former malady,
That I should yet absent me from your bed.   125
I hope this reason stands for my excuse.

Sly. Ay, it stands so that I may hardly tarry so
long. But I would be loath to fall into my dreams
again. I will therefore tarry in despite of the flesh
and the blood.   130

Enter a MESSENGER.

Mess. Your honour's players, hearing your
    amendment,
Are come to play a pleasant comedy;
For so your doctors hold it very meet,
Seeing too much sadness hath congeal'd your blood,
And melancholy is the nurse of frenzy.   135
Therefore they thought it good you hear a play
And frame your mind to mirth and merriment,
Which bars a thousand harms and lengthens life.

Sly. Marry, I will; let them play it. Is not a
comonty a Christmas gambold, or a tumbling-   140
trick?

Page. No, my good lord; it is more pleasing stuff.

Sly. What, household stuff?

Page. It is a kind of history.   144

Sly. Well, we'll see 't. Come, madam wife, sit by
my side and let the world slip. We shall ne'er be
younger.   *[They all sit.] Flourish.*

---

59. **Daphne:** the nymph, pursued by Apollo. 65. **waning:** degenerate. 84. **of:** during. 89. **present:** accuse. **leet:** manor court. 90. **seal'd quarts:** quart measures officially stamped as a guarantee of just quantity. 95. **Greece.** Perhaps a misprint for *Greet,* a hamlet not far from Stratford. 140. **comonty:** Sly's blunder for *comedy.* **gambold:** gambol.

[ACT I

SCENE I. *Padua. A public place.*]

Enter LUCENTIO *and his man* TRANIO.

Luc. Tranio, since for the great desire I had
To see fair Padua, nursery of arts,
I am arriv'd for fruitful Lombardy,
The pleasant garden of great Italy;
And by my father's love and leave am arm'd   5
With his good will and thy good company,
My trusty servant, well approv'd in all.
Here let us breathe and haply institute
A course of learning and ingenious studies.
Pisa, renowned for grave citizens,   10
Gave me my being and my father first,
A merchant of great traffic through the world,
Vincentio, come of the Bentivolii.
Vincentio's son, brought up in Florence,
It shall become to serve all hopes conceiv'd,   15
To deck his fortune with his virtuous deeds;
And therefore, Tranio, for the time I study,
Virtue and that part of philosophy
Will I apply that treats of happiness
By virtue specially to be achiev'd.   20
Tell me thy mind; for I have Pisa left
And am to Padua come, as he that leaves
A shallow plash to plunge him in the deep
And with satiety seeks to quench his thirst.
    Tra. Mi *perdonato*, gentle master mine,   25
I am in all affected as yourself;
Glad that you thus continue your resolve
To suck the sweets of sweet philosophy.
Only, good master, while we do admire
This virtue and this moral discipline,   30
Let's be no Stoics nor no stocks, I pray,
Or so devote to Aristotle's checks
As Ovid be an outcast quite abjur'd.
Balk logic with acquaintance that you have,
And practise rhetoric in your common talk.   35
Music and poesy use to quicken you.
The mathematics and the metaphysics,
Fall to them as you find your stomach serves you;
No profit grows where is no pleasure ta'en.
In brief, sir, study what you most affect.   40
    Luc. Gramercies, Tranio, well dost thou advise.
If, Biondello, thou wert come ashore,
We could at once put us in readiness,
And take a lodging fit to entertain
Such friends as time in Padua shall beget.   45
But stay a while, what company is this?
    Tra. Master, some show to welcome us to town.

Enter BAPTISTA, KATHERINA, BIANCA, GREMIO, *a
pantaloon, and* HORTENSIO. LUCENTIO *and*
TRANIO *stand by.*

    Bap. Gentlemen, importune me no farther,
For how I firmly am resolv'd you know;
That is, not to bestow my youngest daughter   50
Before I have a husband for the elder.
If either of you both love Katherina,
Because I know you well and love you well,
Leave shall you have to court her at your pleasure.
    Gre. To cart her rather; she's too rough for me.
There, there, Hortensio, will you any wife?   56
    Kath. I pray you, sir, is it your will
To make a stale of me amongst these mates?
    Hor. Mates, maid! how mean you that? No
     mates for you,
Unless you were of gentler, milder mould.   60
    Kath. I' faith, sir, you shall never need to fear.
Iwis it is not half way to her heart;
But if it were, doubt not her care should be
To comb your noddle with a three-legg'd stool
And paint your face and use you like a fool.   65
    Hor. From all such devils, good Lord deliver us!
    Gre. And me too, good Lord!
    Tra. Hush, master! here's some good pastime
     toward.
That wench is stark mad or wonderful froward.
    Luc. But in the other's silence do I see   70
Maid's mild behaviour and sobriety.
Peace, Tranio!
    Tra. Well said, master; mum! and gaze your fill.
    Bap. Gentlemen, that I may soon make good
What I have said, Bianca, get you in;   75
And let it not displease thee, good Bianca,
For I will love thee ne'er the less, my girl.
    Kath. A pretty peat! it is best
Put finger in the eye, an she knew why.
    Bian. Sister, content you in my discontent.   80
Sir, to your pleasure humbly I subscribe.
My books and instruments shall be my company,
On them to look and practise by myself.
    Luc. Hark, Tranio! thou may'st hear Minerva
     speak.
    Hor. Signior Baptista, will you be so strange?
Sorry am I that our good will effects   86
Bianca's grief.
    Gre.   Why will you mew her up,
Signior Baptista, for this fiend of hell,
And make her bear the penance of her tongue?
    Bap. Gentlemen, content ye; I am resolv'd.
Go in, Bianca;   [*Exit Bianca.*]   91

Act I, sc. i, 3. **for:** in.   19. **apply:** pursue.   25. *Mi perdonato:* pardon me.   26. **affected:** disposed.   31. **stocks:** posts (with pun on *stoics*).   32. **checks:** restraints.   34. **Balk logic:** bandy arguments.   41. **Gramercies:** many thanks.   47. S.D. *pantaloon:* a foolish old man (a stock character in Italian comedy).   55. **cart.** Being driven publicly in a cart was a common punishment for female offenders.   58. **stale:** (1) laughing-stock, (2) harlot. **mates:** low fellows (with a pun on the stalemate in chess).   62. **Iwis:** certainly. **it:** i.e., marriage.   65. **paint your face:** i.e., with blood.   78. **peat:** pet. 79. **Put...eye:** i.e., to weep (cf. *Errors* II.ii.206).   87. **mew:** shut.

And for I know she taketh most delight
In music, instruments, and poetry,
Schoolmasters will I keep within my house,
Fit to instruct her youth.   If you, Hortensio,   95
Or Signior Gremio, you, know any such,
Prefer them hither; for to cunning men
I will be very kind, and liberal
To mine own children in good bringing up;
And so farewell.   Katherina, you may stay;   100
For I have more to commune with Bianca.   [*Exit.*
    Kath. Why, and I trust I may go too, may I not?
What, shall I be appointed hours, as though, be-
like,   104
I knew not what to take and what to leave?   Ha!
                                                              [*Exit.*
    Gre. You may go to the devil's dam; your gifts
are so good, here's none will hold you.   Their love
is not so great, Hortensio, but we may blow our
nails together, and fast it fairly out.   Our cake's
dough on both sides.   Farewell; yet, for the   110
love I bear my sweet Bianca, if I can by any means
light on a fit man to teach her that wherein she delights, I will wish him to her father.   114
    Hor. So will I, Signior Gremio.   But a word, I
pray.   Though the nature of our quarrel yet never
brook'd parle, know now, upon advice, it toucheth
us both, that we may yet again have access to our
fair mistress and be happy rivals in Bianca's love,
to labour and effect one thing specially.   121
    Gre. What's that, I pray?
    Hor. Marry, sir, to get a husband for her sister.
    Gre. A husband! a devil.   125
    Hor. I say, a husband.
    Gre. I say, a devil.   Think'st thou, Hortensio,
though her father be very rich, any man is so very
a fool to be married to hell?   129
    Hor. Tush, Gremio, though it pass your patience
and mine to endure her loud alarums, why, man,
there be good fellows in the world, an a man could
light on them, would take her with all faults, and
money enough.   134
    Gre. I cannot tell; but I had as lief take her
dowry with this condition, to be whipp'd at the
high cross every morning.
    Hor. Faith, as you say, there's small choice
in rotten apples.   But come; since this bar in law
makes us friends, it shall be so far forth friendly   140
maintain'd till by helping Baptista's eldest daughter
to a husband we set his youngest free for a husband,
and then have to't afresh.   Sweet Bianca!   Happy
man be his dole!   He that runs fastest gets the ring.
How say you, Signior Gremio?   146

    Gre. I am agreed; and would I had given him the
best horse in Padua to begin his wooing that would
thoroughly woo her, wed her and bed her, and rid
the house of her!   Come on.   150
                [*Exeunt Gremio and Hortensio.*
    Tra. I pray, sir, tell me, is it possible
That love should of a sudden take such hold?
    Luc. O Tranio, till I found it to be true,
I never thought it possible or likely.
But see, while idly I stood looking on,   155
I found the effect of love in idleness;
And now in plainness do confess to thee,
That art to me as secret and as dear
As Anna to the Queen of Carthage was,
Tranio, I burn, I pine, I perish, Tranio,   160
If I achieve not this young modest girl.
Counsel me, Tranio, for I know thou canst;
Assist me, Tranio, for I know thou wilt.
    Tra. Master, it is no time to chide you now;
Affection is not rated from the heart.   165
If love have touch'd you, naught remains but so,
"*Redime te captum quam queas minimo.*"
    Luc. Gramercies, lad, go forward; this contents.
The rest will comfort, for thy counsel's sound.
    Tra. Master, you look'd so longly on the maid,
Perhaps you mark'd not what's the pith of all.   171
    Luc. O yes, I saw sweet beauty in her face,
Such as the daughter of Agenor had,
That made great Jove to humble him to her hand,
When with his knees he kiss'd the Cretan strand.
    Tra. Saw you no more?   Mark'd you not how
        her sister   176
Began to scold and raise up such a storm
That mortal ears might hardly endure the din?
    Luc. Tranio, I saw her coral lips to move
And with her breath she did perfume the air.   180
Sacred and sweet was all I saw in her.
    Tra. Nay, then, 'tis time to stir him from his
        trance.
I pray, awake, sir.   If you love the maid,
Bend thoughts and wits to achieve her.   Thus it
        stands:
Her elder sister is so curst and shrewd   185
That till the father rid his hands of her,
Master, your love must live a maid at home;
And therefore has he closely mew'd her up,
Because she will not be annoy'd with suitors.
    Luc. Ah, Tranio, what a cruel father's he!   190
But art thou not advis'd, he took some care
To get her cunning schoolmasters to instruct her?
    Tra. Ay, marry, am I, sir; and now 'tis plotted.
    Luc. I have it, Tranio.

---

97. **Prefer:** recommend. **cunning:** skillful. 107. **Their love,** etc. Gremio's reasoning is hard to follow. 117. **parle:** discussion. 117. **advice:** reflection. 137. **high cross:** market cross. 139. **bar:** obstruction. 144. **Happy...dole:** happiness
be his lot. 165. **rated from:** scolded out of. 167. *Redime...minimo:* "Redeem yourself from captivity as cheaply as you
can."   A passage out of Terence (*Eunuchus* I.i.29) quoted from Lilly's *Latin Grammar.* 173. **daughter of Agenor:** Europa,
loved by Jupiter, who abducted her in the shape of a bull. 185. **curst:** bad-tempered. **shrewd:** shrewish.

Tra.   Master, for my hand,
Both our inventions meet and jump in one.   195
  Luc. Tell me thine first.
  Tra.   You will be schoolmaster
And undertake the teaching of the maid:
That's your device.
  Luc.   It is; may it be done?
  Tra. Not possible; for who shall bear your part,
And be in Padua here Vincentio's son,   200
Keep house and ply his book, welcome his friends,
Visit his countrymen and banquet them?
  Luc. Basta, content thee, for I have it full.
We have not yet been seen in any house,
Nor can we be distinguish'd by our faces   205
For man or master. Then it follows thus:
Thou shalt be master, Tranio, in my stead,
Keep house and port and servants, as I should.
I will some other be, some Florentine,
Some Neapolitan, or meaner man of Pisa.   210
'Tis hatch'd and shall be so. Tranio, at once
Uncase thee; take my colour'd hat and cloak.
When Biondello comes, he waits on thee;
But I will charm him first to keep his tongue.
  Tra. So had you need.   215
In brief, sir, sith it your pleasure is,
And I am tied to be obedient,—
For so your father charg'd me at our parting,
"Be serviceable to my son," quoth he,
Although I think 'twas in another sense,—   220
I am content to be Lucentio,
Because so well I love Lucentio.
  Luc. Tranio, be so, because Lucentio loves;
And let me be a slave, t' achieve that maid
Whose sudden sight hath thrall'd my wounded
      eye.   225

Enter BIONDELLO.

Here comes the rogue. Sirrah where have you
      been?
  Bion. Where have I been! Nay, how now!
where are you? Master, has my fellow Tranio
stol'n your clothes? or you stol'n his? or both?
Pray, what's the news?   230
  Luc. Sirrah, come hither; 'tis no time to jest,
And therefore frame your manners to the time.
Your fellow Tranio here, to save my life,
Puts my apparel and my count'nance on,
And I for my escape have put on his;   235
For in a quarrel since I came ashore
I kill'd a man and fear I was descried.
Wait you on him, I charge you, as becomes,
While I make way from hence to save my life.
You understand me?
  Bion.   I, sir! ne'er a whit.   240

  Luc. And not a jot of Tranio in your mouth.
Tranio is chang'd into Lucentio.
  Bion. The better for him; would I were so
    too!
  Tra. So could I, faith, boy, to have the next wish
    after,
That Lucentio indeed had Baptista's youngest
    daughter.   245
But, sirrah, not for my sake, but your master's, I
    advise
You use your manners discreetly in all kind of com-
    panies.
When I am alone, why, then I am Tranio;
But in all places else your master Lucentio.   249
  Luc. Tranio, let's go. One thing more rests, that
thyself execute to make one among these wooers.
If thou ask me why, sufficeth my reasons are both
good and weighty.   *[Exeunt.*

The presenters above speak.

  1. Serv. My lord, you nod; you do not mind the
    play.   254
  Sly. Yes, by Saint Anne, do I. A good matter,
surely; comes there any more of it?
  Page. My lord, 'tis but begun.
  Sly. 'Tis a very excellent piece of work, madam
lady; would 'twere done!   259
                   [They sit and mark.

[SCENE II. *Padua. Before Hortensio's house.*]

Enter PETRUCHIO *and his man* GRUMIO.

  Pet. Verona, for a while I take my leave
To see my friends in Padua, but of all
My best beloved and approved friend,
Hortensio; and I trow this is his house.
Here, sirrah Grumio; knock, I say.   5
  Gru. Knock, sir! whom should I knock? Is
there any man has rebus'd your worship?
  Pet. Villain, I say, knock me here soundly.
  Gru. Knock you here, sir! Why, sir, what am I,
sir, that I should knock you here, sir?   10
  Pet. Villain, I say, knock me at this gate
And rap me well, or I'll knock your knave's pate.
  Gru. My master is grown quarrelsome. I should
    knock you first,
And then I know after who comes by the worst.
  Pet. Will it not be?   15
Faith, sirrah, an you'll not knock, I'll ring it.
I'll try how you can *sol, fa*, and sing it.
              [He wrings him by the ears.
  Gru. Help, [masters], help! my master is mad.
  Pet. Now, knock when I bid you, sirrah villain!

---

  194. **for:** by. 195. **jump:** agree. 203. *Basta:* enough. **full:** fully. 208. **port:** state. 212. **Uncase:** undress. 234.
countenance: outer appearance. 250. **rests:** remains. 251. **execute:** take measures. 253. S.D. *presenters:* actors.
Sc. ii, 7. **rebus'd:** Grumio's blunder for *abused.* 8. **me:** i.e., for me. 18. **[masters]** (Theobald). *mistris* F.

Enter HORTENSIO.

Hor. How now! what's the matter? My old 20
friend Grumio! and my good friend Petruchio!
How do you all at Verona?

Pet. Signior Hortensio, come you to part the
fray?
Con tutto il cuore, ben trovato, may I say. 24

*Hor. Alla nostra casa ben venuto, molto honorato
signor mio Petruchio.*
Rise, Grumio, rise; we will compound this quarrel.

Gru. Nay, 'tis no matter, sir, what he 'leges in
Latin. If this be not a lawful cause for me to leave
his service, look you, sir. He bid me knock 30
him and rap him soundly, sir. Well, was it fit for
a servant to use his master so, being perhaps, for
aught I see, two and thirty, a pip out?
Whom would to God I had well knock'd at first,
Then had not Grumio come by the worst. 35

Pet. A senseless villain! Good Hortensio,
I bade the rascal knock upon your gate
And could not get him for my heart to do it.

Gru. Knock at the gate! O heavens! Spake
you not these words plain, "Sirrah, knock me 40
here, rap me here, knock me well, and knock me
soundly"? And come you now with, "knocking at
the gate"?

Pet. Sirrah, be gone, or talk not, I advise you.

Hor. Petruchio, patience; I am Grumio's pledge.
Why, this's a heavy chance 'twixt him and you, 46
Your ancient, trusty, pleasant servant Grumio.
And tell me now, sweet friend, what happy gale
Blows you to Padua here from old Verona?

Pet. Such wind as scatters young men through
the world 50
To seek their fortunes farther than at home
Where small experience grows. But in a few,
Signior Hortensio, thus it stands with me:
Antonio, my father, is deceas'd;
And I have thrust myself into this maze, 55
Happily to wive and thrive as best I may.
Crowns in my purse I have and goods at home,
And so am come abroad to see the world.

Hor. Petruchio, shall I then come roundly to thee
And wish thee to a shrewd ill-favour'd wife? 60
Thou'dst thank me but a little for my counsel;
And yet I'll promise thee she shall be rich
And very rich. But thou'rt too much my friend,
And I'll not wish thee to her.

Pet. Signior Hortensio, 'twixt such friends as we
Few words suffice; and therefore, if thou know 66
One rich enough to be Petruchio's wife,

As wealth is burden of my wooing dance,
Be she as foul as was Florentius' love,
As old as Sibyl, and as curst and shrewd 70
As Socrates' Xanthippe, or a worse,
She moves me not, or not removes, at least,
Affection's edge in me, were she as rough
As are the swelling Adriatic seas.
I come to wive it wealthily in Padua; 75
If wealthily, then happily in Padua.

Gru. Nay, look you, sir, he tells you flatly what
his mind is. Why, give him gold enough, and marry
him to a puppet or an aglet-baby, or an old trot with
ne'er a tooth in her head, though she have as 80
many diseases as two and fifty horses. Why,
nothing comes amiss, so money comes withal.

Hor. Petruchio, since we are stepp'd thus far in,
I will continue that I broach'd in jest.
I can, Petruchio, help thee to a wife 85
With wealth enough and young and beauteous,
Brought up as best becomes a gentlewoman.
Her only fault, and that is faults enough,
Is that she is intolerable curst
And shrewd and froward, so beyond all measure
That, were my state far worser than it is, 91
I would not wed her for a mine of gold.

Pet. Hortensio, peace! thou know'st not gold's
effect.
Tell me her father's name and 'tis enough;
For I will board her, though she chide as loud 95
As thunder when the clouds in autumn crack.

Hor. Her father is Baptista Minola,
An affable and courteous gentleman.
Her name is Katherina Minola,
Renown'd in Padua for her scolding tongue. 100

Pet. I know her father, though I know not her;
And he knew my deceased father well.
I will not sleep, Hortensio, till I see her;
And therefore let me be thus bold with you
To give you over at this first encounter, 105
Unless you will accompany me thither.

Gru. I pray you, sir, let him go while the humour
lasts. O' my word, an she knew him as well as I do,
she would think scolding would do little good upon
him. She may perhaps call him half a score 110
knaves or so,— why, that's nothing. An he begin
once, he'll rail in his rope-tricks. I'll tell you what,
sir, an she stand him but a little, he will throw a
figure in her face and so disfigure her with it that she
shall have no more eyes to see withal than a cat.
You know him not, sir. 116

Hor. Tarry, Petruchio, I must go with thee,

24. *Con ... trovato:* with all my heart, well met. 25. *Alla ... Petruchio:* welcome to our house, my much honored Signor
Petruchio. 33. **two ... out.** An allusion to a card game called "Thirty-one" and also a reference to Petruchio's age. **pip:**
spot on a card. 46. **heavy chance:** sad happening. 52. **in a few:** briefly. 59. **come roundly:** speak candidly. 68. **burden:** accompaniment. 69. **Florentius:** Florent, the hero of a tale in Gower's *Confessio Amantis.* 70. **Sibyl:** the Cumaean
prophetess to whom Apollo granted as many years as she could hold grains of sand in her hand. 79. **aglet-baby:** the figure
of a girl carved on an *aglet,* the point of a lace. 95. **board:** accost. 105. **give you over:** leave you. 112. **rope-tricks:** knavish
tricks. Bond thinks Grumio means "rhetoric," explaining *figure* in l. 114. 113. **stand:** oppose.

For in Baptista's keep my treasure is.
He hath the jewel of my life in hold,
His youngest daughter, beautiful Bianca,   120
And her withholds from me and other more,
Suitors to her and rivals in my love,
Supposing it a thing impossible,
For those defects I have before rehears'd,
That ever Katherina will be woo'd.   125
Therefore this order hath Baptista ta'en,
That none shall have access unto Bianca
Till Katherine the curst have got a husband.
    Gru. Katherine the curst!
A title for a maid of all titles the worst.   130
    Hor. Now shall my friend Petruchio do me grace,
And offer me disguis'd in sober robes
To old Baptista as a schoolmaster
Well seen in music, to instruct Bianca;
That so I may, by this device, at least   135
Have leave and leisure to make love to her
And unsuspected court her by herself.

Enter GREMIO, *and* LUCENTIO *disguised* [*as* CAMBIO].

    Gru. Here's no knavery! See, to beguile the old
folks, how the young folks lay their heads to-
gether!   140
Master, master, look about you! Who goes there, ha?
    Hor. Peace, Grumio! it is the rival of my love.
Petruchio, stand by a while.
    Gru. A proper stripling and an amorous!
    Gre. O, very well; I have perus'd the note.   145
Hark you, sir; I'll have them very fairly bound, —
All books of love, see that at any hand;
And see you read no other lectures to her.
You understand me? Over and beside
Signior Baptista's liberality,   150
I'll mend it with a largess. Take your paper too;
And let me have them very well perfum'd,
For she is sweeter than perfume itself
To whom they go to. What will you read to her?
    Luc. Whate'er I read to her, I'll plead for you
As for my patron, stand you so assur'd,   156
As firmly as yourself were still in place;
Yea, and perhaps with more successful words
Than you, unless you were a scholar, sir.
    Gre. O this learning, what a thing it is!   160
    Gru. O this woodcock, what an ass it is!
    Pet. Peace, sirrah!
    Hor. Grumio, mum! God save you, Signior
        Gremio.
    Gre. And you are well met, Signior Hortensio.
Trow you whither I am going?   To Baptista
        Minola.   165
I promis'd to inquire carefully

About a schoolmaster for the fair Bianca;
And by good fortune I have lighted well
On this young man, for learning and behaviour
Fit for her turn, well read in poetry   170
And other books, good ones, I warrant ye.
    Hor. 'Tis well; and I have met a gentleman
Hath promis'd me to help [me] to another,
A fine musician, to instruct our mistress;
So shall I no whit be behind in duty   175
To fair Bianca, so belov'd of me.
    Gre. Belov'd of me; and that my deeds shall
        prove.
    Gru. And that his bags shall prove.
    Hor. Gremio, 'tis now no time to vent our love.
Listen to me, and if you speak me fair,   180
I'll tell you news indifferent good for either.
Here is a gentleman whom by chance I met,
Upon agreement from us to his liking,
Will undertake to woo curst Katherine,
Yea, and to marry her, if her dowry please.   185
    Gre. So said, so done, is well.
Hortensio, have you told him all her faults?
    Pet. I know she is an irksome brawling scold.
If that be all, masters, I hear no harm.
    Gre. No, say'st me so, friend? What country-
        man?   190
    Pet. Born in Verona, old Antonio's son.
My father dead, my fortune lives for me;
And I do hope good days and long to see.
    Gre. O sir, such a life with such a wife, were
        strange!
But if you have a stomach, to't i' God's name;
You shall have me assisting you in all.   196
But will you woo this wild-cat?
    Pet.   Will I live?
    Gru. Will he woo her? Ay, or I'll hang her.
    Pet. Why came I hither but to that intent?
Think you a little din can daunt mine ears?   200
Have I not in my time heard lions roar?
Have I not heard the sea, puff'd up with winds,
Rage like an angry boar chafed with sweat?
Have I not heard great ordnance in the field,
And heaven's artillery thunder in the skies?   205
Have I not in a pitched battle heard
Loud 'larums, neighing steeds, and trumpets' clang?
And do you tell me of a woman's tongue,
That gives not half so great a blow to hear
As will a chestnut in a farmer's fire?   210
Tush, tush! fear boys with bugs.
    Gru.   For he fears none.
    Gre. Hortensio, hark.
This gentleman is happily arriv'd,
My mind presumes, for his own good and [ours].

131. **grace:** a favor. 134. **seen:** skilled. 144. **proper:** handsome. 147. **at any hand:** in any case. 151. **paper:** his testimonials, the *note* of l. 145. 152. **them:** the books. 161. **woodcock:** a proverbially stupid bird. 173. **help [me]** (Rowe). *helpe one* F. 178. **bags:** i.e., money-bags. 181. **indifferent:** equally. 211. **fear:** frighten. **bugs:** bogeys. 214. **[ours]** (Theobald). *yours* F.

Hor. I promis'd we would be contributors   215
And bear his charge of wooing, whatsoe'er.
Gre. And so we will, provided that he win her.
Gru. I would I were as sure of a good dinner.

Enter TRANIO *brave, and* BIONDELLO.

Tra. Gentlemen, God save you. If I may be
bold,
Tell me, I beseech you, which is the readiest way
To the house of Signior Baptista Minola?   221
Bion. He that has the two fair daughters? Is't
he you mean?
Tra. Even he, Biondello.
Gre. Hark you, sir; you mean not her to —
Tra. Perhaps, him and her, sir; what have you
to do?   226
Pet. Not her that chides, sir, at any hand, I
pray.
Tra. I love no chiders, sir. Biondello, let's away.
Luc. Well begun, Tranio.
Hor.   Sir, a word ere you go;
Are you a suitor to the maid you talk of, yea or
no?   230
Tra. And if I be, sir, is it any offence?
Gre. No; if without more words you will get you
hence.
Tra. Why, sir, I pray, are not the streets as free
For me as for you?
Gre.   But so is not she.   234
Tra. For what reason, I beseech you?
Gre.   For this reason, if you'll know,
That she's the choice love of Signior Gremio.
Hor. That she's the chosen of Signior Hortensio.
Tra. Softly, my masters! If you be gentlemen,
Do me this right: hear me with patience.
Baptista is a noble gentleman,   240
To whom my father is not all unknown;
And were his daughter fairer than she is,
She may more suitors have, and me for one.
Fair Leda's daughter had a thousand wooers;
Then well one more may fair Bianca have;   245
And so she shall. Lucentio shall make one,
Though Paris came in hope to speed alone.
Gre. What! this gentleman will out-talk us all.
Luc. Sir, give him head; I know he'll prove a
jade.
Pet. Hortensio, to what end are all these words?
Hor. Sir, let me be so bold as ask you,   251
Did you yet ever see Baptista's daughter?
Tra. No, sir; but hear I do that he hath two,
The one as famous for a scolding tongue
As is the other for beauteous modesty.   255
Pet. Sir, sir, the first's for me; let her go by.

Gre. Yea, leave that labour to great Hercules;
And let it be more than Alcides' twelve.
Pet. Sir, understand you this of me in sooth:
The youngest daughter, whom you hearken for,   260
Her father keeps from all access of suitors,
And will not promise her to any man
Until the elder sister first be wed.
The younger then is free and not before.
Tra. If it be so, sir, that you are the man   265
Must stead us all, and me amongst the rest,
And if you break the ice and do this [feat],
Achieve the elder, set the younger free
For our access, whose hap shall be to have her
Will not so graceless be to be ingrate.   270
Hor. Sir, you say well, and well you do conceive;
And since you do profess to be a suitor,
You must, as we do, gratify this gentleman,
To whom we all rest generally beholding.
Tra. Sir, I shall not be slack; in sign whereof,   275
Please ye we may contrive this afternoon
And quaff carouses to our mistress' health;
And do as adversaries do in law,
Strive mightily, but eat and drink as friends.
Gru. Bion. O excellent motion! Fellows, let's
be gone.   280
Hor. The motion's good indeed, and be it so.
Petruchio, I shall be your *ben venuto.*   [*Exeunt.*

[ACT II

SCENE I. *Padua. A room in Baptista's house.*]

Enter KATHERINA *and* BIANCA.

Bian. Good sister, wrong me not, nor wrong
yourself,
To make a bondmaid and a slave of me.
That I disdain; but for these other [gawds],
Unbind my hands, I'll pull them off myself,
Yea, all my raiment, to my petticoat;   5
Or what you will command me will I do,
So well I know my duty to my elders.
Kath. Of all thy suitors, here I charge [thee], tell
Whom thou lov'st best; see thou dissemble not.
Bian. Believe me, sister, of all the men alive   10
I never yet beheld that special face
Which I could fancy more than any other.
Kath. Minion, thou liest. Is't not Hortensio?
Bian. If you affect him, sister, here I swear
I'll plead for you myself, but you shall have him.   15
Kath. O then, belike, you fancy riches more.
You will have Gremio to keep you fair.
Bian. Is it for him you do envy me so?
Nay then you jest, and now I well perceive

---

216. **charge:** expenses.   244. **Leda's daughter:** Helen of Troy.   247. **speed:** succeed.   249. **jade:** a horse soon tired.
258. **Alcides:** Hercules.   260. **hearken:** lie in wait.   266. **stead:** help.   267. **[feat]** (Rowe).   *seeke* F.   269. **whose hap:** he
whose fortune.   273. **gratify:** recompense.   276. **contrive:** while away.   282. **I . . . venuto:** I shall be your host.
Act II, sc. i, 3. **[gawds]** (Theobald): ornaments.   *goods* F.   8. **[thee]** F₂.   Om. F₁.   18. **envy:** hate.

You have but jested with me all this while.   20
I prithee, sister Kate, untie my hands.
    Kath. If that be jest, then all the rest was so.
                          [Strikes her.

              Enter BAPTISTA.
    Bap. Why, how now, dame! whence grows this
    insolence?
Bianca, stand aside.   Poor girl! she weeps.
Go ply thy needle; meddle not with her.   25
For shame, thou hilding of a devilish spirit,
Why dost thou wrong her that did ne'er wrong thee?
When did she cross thee with a bitter word?
    Kath. Her silence flouts me, and I'll be reveng'd.
                   [Flies after Bianca.
    Bap. What, in my sight.   Bianca, get thee in.
                      [Exit Bianca.
    Kath. What, will you not suffer me?   Nay, now
    I see   31
She is your treasure, she must have a husband;
I must dance bare-foot on her wedding-day
And for your love to her lead apes in hell.
Talk not to me; I will go sit and weep   35
Till I can find occasion of revenge.   *[Exit.]*
    Bap. Was ever gentleman thus griev'd as I?
But who comes here?

Enter GREMIO, LUCENTIO *in the habit of a mean man;*
    PETRUCHIO *with* [HORTENSIO *as a musician; and*]
    TRANIO, *with his boy* [BIONDELLO] *bearing a lute*
    and books.
    Gre. Good morrow, neighbour Baptista.   39
    Bap. Good morrow, neighbour Gremio.   God
save you, gentlemen!
    Pet. And you, good sir!   Pray, have you not a
    daughter
Call'd Katherina, fair and virtuous?
    Bap. I have a daughter, sir, call'd Katherina.
    Gre. You are too blunt; go to it orderly.   45
    Pet. You wrong me, Signior Gremio; give me
    leave.
I am a gentleman of Verona, sir,
That, hearing of her beauty and her wit,
Her affability and bashful modesty,
Her wondrous qualities and mild behaviour,   50
Am bold to show myself a forward guest
Within your house, to make mine eye the witness
Of that report which I so oft have heard.
And, for an entrance to my entertainment,
I do present you with a man of mine,   55
                [Presenting Hortensio.]
Cunning in music and the mathematics,
To instruct her fully in those sciences,
Whereof I know she is not ignorant.

Accept of him, or else you do me wrong:
His name is Licio, born in Mantua.   60
    Bap. You're welcome, sir; and he, for your good
    sake.
But for my daughter Katherine, this I know,
She is not for your turn, the more my grief.
    Pet. I see you do not mean to part with her,
Or else you like not of my company.   65
    Bap. Mistake me not; I speak but as I find.
Whence are you, sir?   What may I call your name?
    Pet. Petruchio is my name; Antonio's son,
A man well known throughout all Italy.
    Bap. I know him well; you are welcome for his
    sake.   70
    Gre. Saving your tale, Petruchio, I pray,
Let us, that are poor petitioners, speak too.
Baccare! you are marvellous forward.
    Pet. O, pardon me, Signior Gremio; I would fain
    be doing.
    Gre. I doubt it not, sir; but you will curse your
    wooing.   75
Neighbour, this is a gift very grateful, I am sure of
it.   To express the like kindness, myself, that have
been more kindly beholding to you than any, freely
give unto you this young scholar [*presenting Lucen-*
tio], that hath been long studying at Rheims; as 80
cunning in Greek, Latin, and other languages, as
the other in music and mathematics.   His name is
Cambio; pray, accept his service.
    Bap. A thousand thanks, Signior Gremio. 85
Welcome, good Cambio.   [*To Tranio.*] But, gentle
sir, methinks you walk like a stranger.   May I
be so bold to know the cause of your coming?
    Tra. Pardon me, sir, the boldness is mine own,
That, being a stranger in this city here,   90
Do make myself a suitor to your daughter,
Unto Bianca, fair and virtuous.
Nor is your firm resolve unknown to me,
In the preferment of the eldest sister.
This liberty is all that I request,   95
That, upon knowledge of my parentage,
I may have welcome 'mongst the rest that woo,
And free access and favour as the rest;
And, toward the education of your daughters,
I here bestow a simple instrument,   100
And this small packet of Greek and Latin books.
If you accept them, then their worth is great.
    Bap. Lucentio is your name: of whence, I pray?
    Tra. Of Pisa, sir; son to Vincentio.
    Bap. A mighty man of Pisa; by report   105
I know him well.   You are very welcome, sir.
Take you the lute, and you the set of books.
You shall go see your pupils presently.
Holla, within!

26. **hilding:** menial wretch.   33. **dance bare-foot.**   According to the custom of elder unmarried sisters.   34. **lead...**
hell.   The proverbial fate of old maids.   63. **turn:** purpose.   71. **Saving:** no disrespect to.   73. **Baccare:** stand back
(origin unknown).

Enter a Servant.

Sirrah, lead these gentlemen
To my daughters; and tell them both,   110
These are their tutors.   Bid them use them well.
   [*Exit Servant, with Lucentio and Hortensio,
                Biondello following.*]
We will go walk a little in the orchard,
And then to dinner.   You are passing welcome,
And so I pray you all to think yourselves.
   Pet. Signior Baptista, my business asketh haste,
And every day I cannot come to woo.   116
You knew my father well, and in him me,
Left solely heir to all his lands and goods,
Which I have bettered rather than decreas'd.
Then tell me, if I get your daughter's love,   120
What dowry shall I have with her to wife?
   Bap. After my death the one half of my lands,
And in possession twenty thousand crowns.
   Pet. And, for that dowry, I'll assure her of
Her widowhood, be it that she survive me,   125
In all my lands and leases whatsoever.
Let specialties be therefore drawn between us,
That covenants may be kept on either hand.
   Bap. Ay, when the special thing is well obtain'd,
That is, her love; for that is all in all.   130
   Pet. Why, that is nothing; for I tell you, father,
I am as peremptory as she proud-minded;
And where two raging fires meet together
They do consume the thing that feeds their fury.
Though little fire grows great with little wind, 135
Yet extreme gusts will blow out fire and all;
So I to her, and so she yields to me,
For I am rough and woo not like a babe.
   Bap. Well mayst thou woo, and happy be thy
         speed!
But be thou arm'd for some unhappy words.   140
   Pet. Ay, to the proof; as mountains are for winds,
That shake not, though they blow perpetually.

Re-enter HORTENSIO, *with his head broke.*

   Bap. How now, my friend! why dost thou look
         so pale?
   Hor. For fear, I promise you, if I look pale.
   Bap. What, will my daughter prove a good
         musician?   145
   Hor. I think she'll sooner prove a soldier.
Iron may hold with her, but never lutes.
   Bap. Why, then thou canst not break her to
         the lute?
   Hor. Why, no; for she hath broke the lute to
         me.
I did but tell her she mistook her frets,   150
And bow'd her hand to teach her fingering;
When, with a most impatient devilish spirit,

"Frets, call you these?" quoth she; "I'll fume with
      them;"
And, with that word, she struck me on the head,
And through the instrument my pate made way;
And there I stood amazed for a while,   156
As on a pillory, looking through the lute;
While she did call me rascal fiddler
And twangling Jack, with twenty such vile terms,
As had she studied to misuse me so.   160
   Pet. Now, by the world, it is a lusty wench!
I love her ten times more than e'er I did.
O, how I long to have some chat with her!
   Bap. Well, go with me and be not so discomfited.
Proceed in practice with my younger daughter;
She's apt to learn and thankful for good turns.   166
Signior Petruchio, will you go with us,
Or shall I send my daughter Kate to you?
   Pet. I pray you do.   [*Exeunt all but Petruchio.*]
      I will attend her here,
And woo her with some spirit when she comes.   170
Say that she rail, why then I'll tell her plain
She sings as sweetly as a nightingale.
Say that she frown, I'll say she looks as clear
As morning roses newly wash'd with dew.
Say she be mute and will not speak a word,   175
Then I'll commend her volubility,
And say she uttereth piercing eloquence.
If she do bid me pack, I'll give her thanks,
As though she bid me stay by her a week.
If she deny to wed, I'll crave the day   180
When I shall ask the banns and when be married.
But here she comes; and now, Petruchio, speak.

Enter KATHERINA.

Good morrow, Kate; for that's your name, I hear.
   Kath. Well have you heard, but something hard
         of hearing.
They call me Katherine that do talk of me.   185
   Pet. You lie, in faith; for you are call'd plain
         Kate,
And bonny Kate, and sometimes Kate the curst;
But Kate, the prettiest Kate in Christendom,
Kate of Kate Hall, my super-dainty Kate,
For dainties are all Kates, and therefore, Kate,
Take this of me, Kate of my consolation;   191
Hearing thy mildness praised in every town,
Thy virtues spoke of, and thy beauty sounded,
Yet not so deeply as to thee belongs,
Myself am mov'd to woo thee for my wife.   195
   Kath. Mov'd! in good time.   Let him that mov'd
         you hither
Remove you hence.   I knew you at the first
You were a moveable.
   Pet.   Why, what's a moveable?

---

125. **widowhood:** estate as a widow.   127. **specialties:** contracts.   139. **speed:** fortune.   141. **to the proof:** in impenetrable armor.   147. **hold with her:** stand her usage.   150. **frets:** bars for fingering on a lute.   151. **bow'd:** bent. 190. **Kates:** with a quibble on *cates*, delicacies.   196. **in good time:** forsooth.   198. **moveable:** piece of furniture.

Kath. A join'd-stool.
Pet.   Thou hast hit it; come, sit on me.   199
Kath. Asses are made to bear, and so are you.
Pet. Women are made to bear, and so are you.
Kath. No such jade as you, if me you mean.
Pet. Alas! good Kate, I will not burden thee;
For, knowing thee to be but young and light —
Kath. Too light for such a swain as you to catch;
And yet as heavy as my weight should be.   206
Pet. Should be! should — buzz!
Kath.   Well ta'en, and like a buzzard.
Pet. O slow-wing'd turtle! shall a buzzard take
thee?
Kath. Ay, for a turtle, as he takes a buzzard.
Pet. Come, come, you wasp; i'faith, you are too
angry.   210
Kath. If I be waspish, best beware my sting.
Pet. My remedy is then, to pluck it out.
Kath. Ay, if the fool could find it where it lies.
Pet. Who knows not where a wasp does wear his
sting?
In his tail.   215
Kath. In his tongue.
Pet. Whose tongue?
Kath. Yours, if you talk of tales: and so farewell.
Pet. What, with my tongue in your tail?
Nay, come again,
Good Kate; I am a gentleman —
Kath.   That I'll try.
   [*She strikes him.*
Pet. I swear I'll cuff you, if you strike again.   221
Kath. So may you lose your arms.
If you strike me, you are no gentleman;
And if no gentleman, why then no arms.
Pet. A herald, Kate? O, put me in thy books!
Kath. What is your crest? A coxcomb?   226
Pet. A combless cock, so Kate will be my hen.
Kath. No cock of mine; you crow too like a
craven.
Pet. Nay, come, Kate, come; you must not look
so sour.
Kath. It is my fashion, when I see a crab.   230
Pet. Why, here's no crab; and therefore look not
sour.
Kath. There is, there is.
Pet. Then show it me.
Kath. Had I a glass, I would.
Pet. What, you mean my face?   235
Kath. Well aim'd of such a young one.
Pet. Now, by Saint George, I am too young for
you.

Kath. Yet you are wither'd.
Pet. 'Tis with cares.   240
Kath. I care not.
Pet. Nay, hear you, Kate. In sooth you scape
not so.
Kath. I chafe you, if I tarry. Let me go.
Pet. No, not a whit; I find you passing gentle.
'Twas told me you were rough and coy and sullen.
And now I find report a very liar;   246
For thou art pleasant, gamesome, passing courteous,
But slow in speech, yet sweet as spring-time
flowers.
Thou canst not frown, thou canst not look askance,
Nor bite the lip, as angry wenches will,   250
Nor hast thou pleasure to be cross in talk,
But thou with mildness entertain'st thy wooers,
With gentle conference, soft and affable.
Why does the world report that Kate doth limp?
O sland'rous world! Kate like the hazel-twig   255
Is straight and slender, and as brown in hue
As hazel nuts and sweeter than the kernels.
O, let me see thee walk. Thou dost not halt.
Kath. Go, fool, and whom thou keep'st com-
mand.
Pet. Did ever Dian so become a grove   260
As Kate this chamber with her princely gait?
O, be thou Dian, and let her be Kate;
And then let Kate be chaste and Dian sportful!
Kath. Where did you study all this goodly
speech?
Pet. It is extempore, from my mother-wit.   265
Kath. A witty mother! witless else her son.
Pet. Am I not wise?
Kath. Yes; keep you warm.
Pet. Marry, so I mean, sweet Katherine, in thy
bed;
And therefore, setting all this chat aside,   270
Thus in plain terms: your father hath consented
That you shall be my wife; your dowry 'greed on;
And, will you, nill you, I will marry you.
Now, Kate, I am a husband for your turn;
For, by this light whereby I see thy beauty,   275
Thy beauty, that doth make me like thee well,
Thou must be married to no man but me;

Re-enter BAPTISTA, GREMIO, *and* TRANIO.

For I am he am born to tame you Kate,
And bring you from a wild Kate to a Kate
Conformable as other household Kates.   280
Here comes your father. Never make denial;
I must and will have Katherine to my wife.

---

199. **join'd-stool:** a wooden stool made by a joiner.   204. **light:** wanton.   207. **be.** Suggesting *bee*, hence *buzz*.   **buz-zard:** blockhead.   208. **turtle:** turtle-dove.   **buzzard:** a kind of hawk.   209. **he:** the turtle.   **buzzard:** cockchafer.   222. **arms:** i.e., with a pun on the heraldic "coat of arms."   225. **books:** heraldic registers.   228. **craven:** a cock that is not "game."   230. **crab:** crab-apple.   236. **aim'd of:** guessed for.   249. **askance:** scornfully.   260. **Dian:** Diana, goddess of hunting and chastity.   268. **keep you warm:** watch out for yourself, echoing the proverb "wit enough to keep oneself warm."   279. **wild Kate.** Punning on *wild cat.*

Bap. Now, Signior Petruchio, how speed you
  with my daughter?
Pet. How but well, sir? How but well?
It were impossible I should speed amiss.   285
  Bap. Why, how now, daughter Katherine! In
  your dumps?
  Kath. Call you me daughter? Now I promise
  you
You have show'd a tender fatherly regard,
To wish me wed to one half lunatic;
A mad-cap ruffian and a swearing Jack,   290
That thinks with oaths to face the matter out.
  Pet. Father, 'tis thus: yourself and all the world,
That talk'd of her, have talk'd amiss of her.
If she be curst, it is for policy,
For she's not froward, but modest as the dove;
She is not hot, but temperate as the morn;   296
For patience she will prove a second Grissel,
And Roman Lucrece for her chastity;
And to conclude, we have 'greed so well together
That upon Sunday is the wedding-day.   300
  Kath. I'll see thee hang'd on Sunday first.
  Gre. Hark, Petruchio; she says she'll see thee
  hang'd first.
  Tra. Is this your speeding? Nay, then, good
  night our part!
  Pet. Be patient, gentlemen; I choose her for
  myself.
If she and I be pleas'd, what's that to you?   305
'Tis bargain'd 'twixt us twain, being alone,
That she shall still be curst in company.
I tell you, 'tis incredible to believe
How much she loves me. O, the kindest Kate!
She hung about my neck; and kiss on kiss   310
She vied so fast, protesting oath on oath,
That in a twink she won me to her love.
O, you are novices! 'Tis a world to see,
How tame, when men and women are alone,
A meacock wretch can make the curstest shrew. 315
Give me thy hand, Kate. I will unto Venice,
To buy apparel 'gainst the wedding-day.
Provide the feast, father, and bid the guests;
I will be sure my Katherine shall be fine.
  Bap. I know not what to say; but give me your
  hands.   320
God send you joy, Petruchio! 'Tis a match.
  Gre. Tra. Amen, say we. We will be witnesses.
  Pet. Father, and wife, and gentlemen, adieu.
I will to Venice; Sunday comes apace.
We will have rings and things and fine array; 325
And kiss me, Kate, "we will be married o' Sunday."
  [*Exeunt Petruchio and Katherina [severally].*

  Gre. Was ever match clapp'd up so suddenly?
  Bap. Faith, gentlemen, now I play a merchant's
  part,
And venture madly on a desperate mart.
  Tra. 'Twas a commodity lay fretting by you.
'Twill bring you gain, or perish on the seas.   331
  Bap. The gain I seek is, quiet in the match.
  Gre. No doubt but he hath got a quiet catch.
But now, Baptista, to your younger daughter.
Now is the day we long have looked for.   335
I am your neighbour, and was suitor first.
  Tra. And I am one that love Bianca more
Than words can witness, or your thoughts can guess.
  Gre. Youngling, thou canst not love so dear as I.
  Tra. Greybeard, thy love doth freeze.
  Gre.   But thine doth fry.
Skipper, stand back! 'Tis age that nourisheth. 341
  Tra. But youth in ladies' eyes that flourisheth.
  Bap. Content you, gentlemen; I will compound
  this strife.
'Tis deeds must win the prize; and he of both
That can assure my daughter greatest dower   345
Shall have my Bianca's love.
Say, Signior Gremio, what can you assure her?
  Gre. First, as you know, my house within the
  city
Is richly furnished with plate and gold,
Basins and ewers to lave her dainty hands;   350
My hangings all of Tyrian tapestry;
In ivory coffers I have stuff'd my crowns,
In cypress chests my arras counterpoints,
Costly apparel, tents, and canopies,
Fine linen, Turkey cushions boss'd with pearl,   355
Valance of Venice gold in needle-work,
Pewter and brass and all things that belongs
To house or housekeeping. Then, at my farm
I have a hundred milch-kine to the pail,
Six score fat oxen standing in my stalls,   360
And all things answerable to this portion.
Myself am struck in years, I must confess;
And if I die to-morrow, this is hers,
If whilst I live she will be only mine.
  Tra. That "only" came well in. Sir, list to me.
I am my father's heir and only son.   366
If I may have your daughter to my wife,
I'll leave her houses three or four as good,
Within rich Pisa walls, as any one
Old Signior Gremio has in Padua;   370
Besides two thousand ducats by the year
Of fruitful land, all which shall be her jointure.
What, have I pinch'd you, Signior Gremio?
  Gre. Two thousand ducats by the year of land!

---

297. **Grissel:** patient Griselda, heroine of Chaucer's *Clerk's Tale*. 298. **Lucrece.** See Shakespeare's poem, *The Rape of Lucrece.* 311. **vied:** i.e., in giving. 313. **world:** i.e., world's wonder. 315. **meacock:** milksop. 326. **"we ... Sunday."** A ballad refrain. 329. **mart:** bargain. 330. **fretting:** (1) irritable, (2) decaying. 341. **Skipper:** young, skipping fellow. 344. **he of both:** whichever of you. 353. **arras counterpoints:** tapestry counterpanes. 356. **Valance:** hanging (of a bed). 359. **milch-kine ... pail:** cows whose milk is not taken by the calves. 362. **struck:** advanced. 372. **jointure:** settlement.

(My land amounts not to so much in all,)   375
[*Aside*.]
That she shall have; besides an argosy
That now is lying in Marseilles' road.
What, have I chok'd you with an argosy?
    Tra. Gremio, 'tis known my father hath no less
Than three great argosies, besides two galliases 380
And twelve tight galleys.   These I will assure her,
And twice as much, whate'er thou off'rest next.
    Gre. Nay, I have off'red all, I have no more;
And she can have no more than all I have.
If you like me, she shall have me and mine.   385
    Tra. Why, then the maid is mine from all the
        world,
By your firm promise; Gremio is out-vied.
    Bap. I must confess your offer is the best;
And, let your father make her the assurance,
She is your own; else, you must pardon me,   390
If you should die before him, where's her dower?
    Tra. That's but a cavil.   He is old, I young.
    Gre. And may not young men die, as well as old?
    Bap. Well, gentlemen,
I am thus resolv'd: on Sunday next you know   395
My daughter Katherine is to be married.
Now, on the Sunday following, shall Bianca
Be bride to you, if you make this assurance;
If not, to Signior Gremio.
And so, I take my leave, and thank you both.
                                [*Exit*.
    Gre. Adieu, good neighbour.   Now I fear thee
        not.   401
Sirrah young gamester; your father were a fool
To give thee all, and in his waning age
Set foot under thy table.   Tut, a toy!
An old Italian fox is not so kind, my boy.   405
                                [*Exit*.
    Tra. A vengeance on your crafty withered hide!
Yet I have fac'd it with a card of ten.
'Tis in my head to do my master good.
I see no reason but suppos'd Lucentio
Must get a father, call'd "suppos'd Vincentio"; 410
And that's a wonder.   Fathers commonly
Do get their children; but in this case of wooing,
A child shall get a sire, if I fail not of my cunning.
                                [*Exit*.

ACT III

[SCENE I. *Padua.   Baptista's house*.]

Enter LUCENTIO, HORTENSIO, *and* BIANCA.

    Luc. Fiddler, forbear; you grow too forward, sir.
Have you so soon forgot the entertainment

Her sister Katherine welcom'd you withal?
    Hor. But, wrangling pedant, this is
The patroness of heavenly harmony.   5
Then give me leave to have prerogative;
And when in music we have spent an hour,
Your lecture shall have leisure for as much.
    Luc. Preposterous ass, that never read so far
To know the cause why music was ordain'd!   10
Was it not to refresh the mind of man
After his studies or his usual pain?
Then give me leave to read philosophy,
And while I pause, serve in your harmony.
    Hor. Sirrah, I will not bear these braves of
        thine.   15
    Bian. Why, gentlemen, you do me double wrong
To strive for that which resteth in my choice.
I am no breeching scholar in the schools.
I'll not be tied to hours nor 'pointed times,
But learn my lessons as I please myself.   20
And, to cut off all strife, here sit we down;
Take you your instrument, play you the whiles;
His lecture will be done ere you have tun'd.
    Hor. You'll leave his lecture when I am in tune?
    Luc. That will be never; tune your instrument.
    Bian. Where left we last?   26
    Luc. Here, madam:
        "*Hic ibat Simois; hic est Sigeia tellus;
        Hic steterat Priami regia celsa senis*."
    Bian. Construe them.   30
    Luc. "*Hic ibat*," as I told you before, "*Simois*,"
I am Lucentio, "*hic est*," son unto Vincentio of
Pisa, "*Sigeia tellus*," disguised thus to get your
love; "*Hic steterat*," and that Lucentio that comes
a-wooing, "*Priami*," is my man Tranio, "*regia*," 35
bearing my port, "*celsa senis*," that we might
beguile the old pantaloon.
    Hor. Madam, my instrument's in tune.
    Bian. Let's hear.   O fie! the treble jars.
    Luc. Spit in the hole, man, and tune again.
    Bian. Now let me see if I can construe it: 41
"*Hic ibat Simois*," I know you not, "*hic est Sigeia
tellus*," I trust you not; "*Hic steterat Priami*,"
take heed he hear us not, "*regia*," presume not,
"*celsa senis*," despair not.   45
    Hor. Madam, 'tis now in tune.
    Luc.   All but the base.
    Hor. The base is right; 'tis the base knave that
        jars.
[*Aside*.] How fiery and forward our pedant is!
Now, for my life, the knave doth court my love:
Pedascule, I'll watch you better yet.   50
    [*Bian*.] In time I may believe, yet I mistrust.

---

376. **argosy**: large merchant vessel.   377. **road**: harbor.   380. **galliases**: large galleys.   404. **toy**: fancy.   407. **fac'd** ...
ten: bluffed with a ten-spot.   412. **get**: beget.
    Act III, sc. i, 12. **pain**: toil.   18. **breeching**: liable to be whipped.   28–29. *Hic* ... *senis*.   "Here flowed the Simois;
here is the Sigeian land; here had stood the towering palace of old Priam." (Ovid's *Heroides*, i. 33–34.)   48. [*Aside*] (Capell).
Luc. F.   50. **Pedascule**: a coined word for *pedant* (contemptuously diminutive).   51. [*Bian*.] (Pope).   Cont. to *Luc*. F.

[*Luc.*] Mistrust it not; for, sure, Æacides
Was Ajax, call'd so from his grandfather.
   [*Bian.*] I must believe my master; else, I promise you,
I should be arguing still upon that doubt.
But let it rest. Now, Licio, to you. 55
Good master, take it not unkindly, pray,
That I have been thus pleasant with you both.
   Hor. [*to Luc.*] You may go walk, and give me leave a while.
My lessons make no music in three parts. 60
   Luc. Are you so formal, sir? Well, I must wait,
[*Aside.*] And watch withal; for, but I be deceiv'd,
Our fine musician groweth amorous.
   Hor. Madam, before you touch the instrument,
To learn the order of my fingering, 65
I must begin with rudiments of art;
To teach you gamut in a briefer sort,
More pleasant, pithy, and effectual,
Than hath been taught by any of my trade;
And there it is in writing, fairly drawn. 70
   Bian. Why, I am past my gamut long ago.
   Hor. Yet read the gamut of Hortensio.
   Bian. [*Reads.*]
"*Gamut* I am, the ground of all accord,
   A re, to plead Hortensio's passion.
B mi, Bianca, take him for thy lord, 75
   C fa ut, that loves with all affection.
D sol re, one clef, two notes have I.
   E la mi, show pity, or I die."
Call you this gamut? Tut, I like it not:
Old fashions please me best; I am not so nice, 80
To [change] true rules for [odd] inventions.

Enter a MESSENGER.

   Mess. Mistress, your father prays you leave your books
And help to dress your sister's chamber up.
You know to-morrow is the wedding-day.
   Bian. Farewell, sweet masters both; I must be gone. 85
      [*Exeunt Bianca and Messenger.*]
   Luc. Faith, mistress, then I have no cause to stay.
      [*Exit.*]
   Hor. But I have cause to pry into this pedant.
Methinks he looks as though he were in love;
Yet if thy thoughts, Bianca, be so humble
To cast thy wand'ring eyes on every stale, 90
Seize thee that list. If once I find thee ranging,
Hortensio will be quit with thee by changing.
      [*Exit.*

[SCENE II. *Padua. Before Baptista's house.*]

Enter BAPTISTA, GREMIO, TRANIO, KATHERINA,
  BIANCA, [LUCENTIO,] *and others, attendants.*

   Bap. [*To Tranio.*] Signior Lucentio, this is the 'pointed day,
That Katherine and Petruchio should be married,
And yet we hear not of our son-in-law.
What will be said? What mockery will it be,
To want the bridegroom when the priest attends 5
To speak the ceremonial rites of marriage!
What says Lucentio to this shame of ours?
   Kath. No shame but mine. I must, forsooth, be forc'd
To give my hand oppos'd against my heart
Unto a mad-brain rudesby full of spleen, 10
Who woo'd in haste and means to wed at leisure.
I told you, I, he was a frantic fool,
Hiding his bitter jests in blunt behaviour;
And, to be noted for a merry man, 14
He'll woo a thousand, 'point the day of marriage,
Make friends, invite, [yes,] and proclaim the banns,
Yet never means to wed where he hath woo'd.
Now must the world point at poor Katherine,
And say, "Lo, there is mad Petruchio's wife,
If it would please him come and marry her!" 20
   Tra. Patience, good Katherine, and Baptista too.
Upon my life, Petruchio means but well,
Whatever fortune stays him from his word.
Though he be blunt, I know him passing wise;
Though he be merry, yet withal he's honest. 25
   Kath. Would Katherine had never seen him though!
      [*Exit weeping* [*followed by Bianca and others*].
   Bap. Go, girl, I cannot blame thee now to weep;
For such an injury would vex a very saint,
Much more a shrew of thy impatient humour.

Enter BIONDELLO.

   Bion. Master, master! news, and such [old] news as you never heard of! 31
   Bap. Is it new and old too? How may that be?
   Bion. Why, is it not news to hear of Petruchio's coming?
   Bap. Is he come? 35
   Bion. Why, no, sir.
   Bap. What then?
   Bion. He is coming.
   Bap. When will he be here?
   Bion. When he stands where I am and sees you there. 41
   Tra. But say, what to thine old news?
   Bion. Why, Petruchio is coming in a new hat and

52. [*Luc.*] (Pope). *Bian.* F. 54. [*Bian.*] (Pope). *Hort.* F. 62. but: unless. 80. nice: whimsical. 81. [change] F₂. *charge* F₁. [odd] (Theobald). *old* F. 90. stale: decoy, lure. 91. Seize . . . list: let him take thee who will.
Sc. ii, 10. rudesby: rude fellow. spleen: sudden impulse, temper. 16. [yes] F₂₋₄. Om. F₁. 31. [old] (Collier). Om. F₁.

an old jerkin; a pair of old breeches thrice turn'd;
a pair of boots that have been candle-cases, one 45
buckled, another lac'd; an old rusty sword ta'en
out of the town-armoury, with a broken hilt, and
chapeless; with two broken points; his horse hipp'd
with an old mothy saddle and stirrups of no kindred, besides, possess'd with the glanders and 50
like to mose in the chine, troubled with the lampass,
infected with the fashions, full of windgalls, sped
with spavins, rayed with the yellows, past cure
of the fives, stark spoil'd with the staggers, be-
gnawn with the bots, sway'd in the back and 55
shoulder-shotten, nearlegg'd before, and with a
half-check'd bit and a head-stall of sheep's leather
which, being restrain'd to keep him from stumbling,
hath been often burst and now repaired with knots;
one girth six times piec'd, and a woman's crupper 60
of velure, which hath two letters for her name
fairly set down in studs, and here and there piec'd
with packthread.

Bap. Who comes with him? 65

Bion. O, sir, his lackey, for all the world caparison'd like the horse; with a linen stock on one
leg and a kersey boot-hose on the other, gart'red
with a red and blue list; an old hat and the humour
of forty fancies prick'd in't for a feather: a 70
monster, a very monster in apparel, and not like a
Christian footboy or a gentleman's lackey.

Tra. 'Tis some odd humour pricks him to this
fashion;
Yet oftentimes he goes but mean-apparell'd. 75

Bap. I am glad he's come, howsoe'er he comes.

Bion. Why, sir, he comes not.

Bap. Didst thou not say he comes?

Bion. Who? That Petruchio came?

Bap. Ay, that Petruchio came. 80

Bion. No, sir; I say his horse comes, with him
on his back.

Bap. Why, that's all one.

Bion. Nay, by Saint Jamy,
I hold you a penny, 85
A horse and a man
Is more than one,
And yet not many.

Enter PETRUCHIO *and* GRUMIO.

Pet. Come, where be these gallants? Who's
at home? 89

Bap. You are welcome, sir.

Pet.   And yet I come not well.

Bap. And yet you halt not.

Tra.   Not so well apparell'd
As I wish you were.

Pet. Were it better, I should rush in thus.
But where is Kate?   Where is my lovely bride?
How does my father?   Gentles, methinks you
frown, 95
And wherefore gaze this goodly company,
As if they saw some wondrous monument,
Some comet or unusual prodigy?

Bap. Why, sir, you know this is your wedding-
day.
First were we sad, fearing you would not come;
Now sadder, that you come so unprovided. 101
Fie, doff this habit, shame to your estate,
An eye-sore to our solemn festival!

Tra. And tell us, what occasion of import
Hath all so long detain'd you from your wife, 105
And sent you hither so unlike yourself?

Pet. Tedious it were to tell, and harsh to hear.
Sufficeth, I am come to keep my word,
Though in some part enforced to digress;
Which, at more leisure, I will so excuse 110
As you shall well be satisfied withal.
But where is Kate?   I stay too long from her.
The morning wears, 'tis time we were at church.

Tra. See not your bride in these unreverent
robes.
Go to my chamber; put on clothes of mine. 115

Pet. Not I, believe me; thus I'll visit her.

Bap. But thus, I trust, you will not marry her.

Pet. Good sooth, even thus; therefore ha' done
with words.
To me she's married, not unto my clothes.
Could I repair what she will wear in me, 120
As I can change these poor accoutrements,
'Twere well for Kate and better for myself.
But what a fool am I to chat with you,
When I should bid good morrow to my bride
And seal the title with a lovely kiss! 125

[*Exeunt* [*Petruchio and Grumio*].

Tra. He hath some meaning in his mad attire.
We will persuade him, be it possible,
To put on better ere he go to church.

Bap. I'll after him, and see the event of this.

[*Exeunt* [*Baptista, Gremio, and attendants*].

Tra. But [to her] love concerneth us to add 130
Her father's liking; which to bring to pass,
As [I] before imparted to your worship,
I am to get a man, — whate'er he be,
It skills not much, we'll fit him to our turn, —
And he shall be Vincentio of Pisa; 135
And make assurance here in Padua
Of greater sums than I have promised.
So shall you quietly enjoy your hope,
And marry sweet Bianca with consent.

45. **candle-cases**: receptacles for candle-ends.   48. **chapeless**: without chapes (metal plates on the scabbard).   **points:**
laces serving as buttons.   50. **glanders**, etc.   Biondello is an authority on diseases of horses.   58. **restrain'd**: pulled tight.
61. **velure**: velvet.   68. **kersey**: coarse woolen.   69. **list**: strip cut from the edge of a piece of cloth.   69. **humour ...**
fancies. Apparently some kind of fantastic ornament.   70. **prick'd**: pinned.   74. **pricks**: incites.   85. **hold**: bet.   120. **wear:**
wear out.   129. **event**: outcome.   130. **[to her] love** (Capell).   *sir, Love* F.   132. **[I]** (Pope).   Om. F.   134. **skills**: matters.

Luc. Were it not that my fellow-schoolmaster
Doth watch Bianca's steps so narrowly,   141
'Twere good, methinks, tc steal our marriage;
Which once perform'd, let all the world say no,
I'll keep mine own, despite of all the world.

Tra. That by degrees we mean to look into,   145
And watch our vantage in this business.
We'll over-reach the greybeard, Gremio,
The narrow prying father, Minola,
The quaint musician, amorous Licio,
All for my master's sake, Lucentio.   150

Re-enter GREMIO.

Signior Gremio, came you from the church?
Gre. As willingly as e'er I came from school.
Tra. And is the bride and bridegroom coming
home?
Gre. A bridegroom say you? 'Tis a groom in-
deed,   154
A grumbling groom, and that the girl shall find.
Tra. Curster than she? Why, 'tis impossible.
Gre. Why, he's a devil, a devil, a very fiend.
Tra. Why, she's a devil, a devil, the devil's dam.
Gre. Tut, she's a lamb, a dove, a fool to him!
I'll tell you, Sir Lucentio: when the priest   160
Should ask, if Katherine should be his wife,
"Ay, by gogs-wouns," quoth he; and swore so
loud,
That, all-amaz'd, the priest let fall the book;
And, as he stoop'd again to take it up,   164
The mad-brain'd bridegroom took him such a cuff
That down fell priest and book, and book and
priest.
"Now take them up," quoth he, "if any list."
Tra. What said the wench when he rose again?
Gre. Trembled and shook; for why, he stamp'd
and swore
As if the vicar meant to cozen him.   170
But after many ceremonies done,
He calls for wine. "A health!" quoth he, as if
He'd been aboard, carousing to his mates
After a storm; quaff'd off the muscadel,
And threw the sops all in the sexton's face,   175
Having no other reason
But that his beard grew thin and hungerly,
And seem'd to ask him sops as he was drinking.
This done, he took the bride about the neck
And kiss'd her lips with such a clamorous smack 180
That at the parting all the church did echo.
And I seeing this, came thence for very shame,
And after me, I know, the rout is coming.
Such a mad marriage never was before.
Hark, hark! I hear the minstrels play.   185
[*Music plays.*

Re-enter PETRUCHIO, KATHERINA, BIANCA, BAP-
TISTA, HORTENSIO [GRUMIO, *and Train*].

Pet. Gentlemen and friends, I thank you for
your pains.
I know you think to dine with me to-day,
And have prepar'd great store of wedding cheer;
But so it is, my haste doth call me hence,
And therefore here I mean to take my leave.   190
Bap. Is't possible you will away to-night?
Pet. I must away to-day, before night come.
Make it no wonder; if you knew my business,
You would entreat me rather go than stay.
And, honest company, I thank you all   195
That have beheld me give away myself
To this most patient, sweet, and virtuous wife.
Dine with my father, drink a health to me,
For I must hence; and farewell to you all.
Tra. Let us entreat you stay till after dinner. 200
Pet. It may not be.
Gre.   Let me entreat you.
Pet. It cannot be.
Kath.   Let me entreat you.
Pet. I am content.
Kath.   Are you content to stay?
Pet. I am content you shall entreat me stay;
But yet not stay, entreat me how you can.   205
Kath. Now, if you love me, stay.
Pet.   Grumio, my horse.
Gru. Ay, sir, they be ready; the oats have eaten
the horses.
Kath. Nay, then,
Do what thou canst, I will not go to-day;   210
No, nor to-morrow, not till I please myself.
The door is open, sir; there lies your way;
You may be jogging whiles your boots are green.
For me, I'll not be gone till I please myself.
'Tis like you'll prove a jolly surly groom,   215
That take it on you at the first so roundly.
Pet. O Kate, content thee; prithee, be not angry.
Kath. I will be angry. What hast thou to do?
Father, be quiet; he shall stay my leisure.
Gre. Ay, marry, sir, now it begins to work.   220
Kath. Gentlemen, forward to the bridal dinner.
I see a woman may be made a fool,
If she had not a spirit to resist.
Pet. They shall go forward, Kate, at thy com-
mand.
Obey the bride, you that attend on her.   225
Go to the feast, revel and domineer,
Carouse full measure to her maidenhead,
Be mad and merry, or go hang yourselves;
But for my bonny Kate, she must with me.
Nay, look not big, nor stamp, nor stare, nor fret;
I will be master of what is mine own.   231

---

149. **quaint:** elegant. 162. **gogs-wouns:** corruption of *God's wounds.* 170. **cozen:** cheat. 175. **sops:** cake soaked in wine
207. **oats...horses:** i.e., the horses are stuffed full of oats. 213. **green:** fresh. The whole line is a proverb wishing ⌐
speedy start for unwelcome guests. 226. **domineer:** swagger. 230. **big:** angry.

She is my goods, my chattels; she is my house,
My household stuff, my field, my barn,
My horse, my ox, my ass, my any thing;
And here she stands, touch her whoever dare,   235
I'll bring mine action on the proudest he
That stops my way in Padua.   Grumio,
Draw forth thy weapon, we are beset with thieves;
Rescue thy mistress, if thou be a man.
Fear not, sweet wench, they shall not touch thee,
    Kate;   240
I'll buckler thee against a million.

[Exeunt Petruchio, Katherina, [and Grumio].

Bap. Nay, let them go, a couple of quiet ones.
Gre. Went they not quickly, I should die with
laughing.
Tra. Of all mad matches never was the like.
Luc. Mistress, what's your opinion of your
sister?   245
Bian. That, being mad herself, she's madly
mated.
Gre. I warrant him, Petruchio is Kated.
Bap. Neighbours and friends, though bride and
bridegroom wants
For to supply the places at the table,
You know there wants no junkets at the feast.   250
Lucentio, you shall supply the bridegroom's place;
And let Bianca take her sister's room.
Tra. Shall sweet Bianca practise how to bride it?
Bap. She shall, Lucentio.   Come, gentlemen,
    let's go.   [*Exeunt.*

[ACT IV

SCENE I. *Petruchio's country house.*]

Enter GRUMIO.

Gru. Fie, fie on all tired jades, on all mad masters, and all foul ways! Was ever man so beaten?
Was ever man so ray'd? Was ever man so weary?
I am sent before to make a fire, and they are
coming after to warm them.   Now, were not I   5
a little pot and soon hot, my very lips might
freeze to my teeth, my tongue to the roof of my
mouth, my heart in my belly, ere I should come
by a fire to thaw me; but I, with blowing the fire,
shall warm myself; for, considering the weather,   10
a taller man than I will take cold.   Holla, ho!
Curtis.

Enter CURTIS.

Curt. Who is that calls so coldly?
Gru. A piece of ice. If thou doubt it, thou

mayst slide from my shoulder to my heel with
no greater a run but my head and my neck.   15
A fire, good Curtis.
Curt. Is my master and his wife coming, Grumio?
Gru. O, ay, Curtis, ay; and therefore fire,   20
fire; cast on no water.
Curt. Is she so hot a shrew as she's reported?
Gru. She was, good Curtis, before this frost;
but thou know'st, winter tames man, woman, and
beast; for it hath tam'd my old master and my
new mistress and myself, fellow Curtis.   26
Curt. Away, you three-inch fool! I am no beast.
Gru. Am I but three inches? Why, thy horn
is a foot; and so long am I at the least.   But   30
wilt thou make a fire, or shall I complain on thee
to our mistress, whose hand, she being now at
hand, thou shalt soon feel, to thy cold comfort,
for being slow in thy hot office?
Curt. I prithee, good Grumio, tell me, how goes
the world?   36
Gru. A cold world, Curtis, in every office but
thine; and therefore fire. Do thy duty and have
thy duty, for my master and mistress are almost
frozen to death.   40
Curt. There's fire ready; and therefore, good
Grumio, the news.
Gru. Why, "Jack, boy! ho! boy!" and as much
news as thou wilt.
Curt. Come, you are so full of cony-catching!   45
Gru. Why, therefore fire; for I have caught
extreme cold.   Where's the cook?   Is supper
ready, the house trimm'd, rushes strew'd, cobwebs swept; the servingmen in their new fustian,
the white stockings, and every officer his wed-   50
ding garment on?   Be the jacks fair within, the
gills fair without, the carpets laid, and every thing
in order?
Curt. All ready; and therefore, I pray thee,
news.   55
Gru. First, know, my horse is tired; my master
and mistress fall'n out.
Curt. How?
Gru. Out of their saddles into the dirt; and
thereby hangs a tale.   60
Curt. Let's ha't, good Grumio.
Gru. Lend thine ear.
Curt. Here.
Gru. There.   [*Strikes him.*] 64
Curt. This is to feel a tale, not to hear a tale.
Gru. And therefore 'tis call'd a sensible tale;
and this cuff was but to knock at your ear, and
beseech list'ning.   Now I begin: *Imprimis*, we

250. **junkets:** delicacies.
Act IV, sc. i, 3. **ray'd:** dirtied.   11. **taller:** stouter, with a pun on his stature (l. 5).   39. **duty:** due.   43. "**Jack...boy.**"
The beginning of a familiar song.   45. **cony-catching:** roguery.   49. **fustian:** coarse cloth.   51. **jacks:** drinking vessels
(used punningly).   51. **gills:** measuring vessels (used punningly).   **carpets:** table-covers.   66. **sensible:** (1) reasonable,
(2) moving.   68. *Imprimis:* first.

came down a foul hill, my master riding behind my
mistress, —   70
   Curt. Both of one horse?
   Gru. What's that to thee?
   Curt. Why, a horse.
   Gru. Tell thou the tale. But hadst thou not
cross'd me, thou shouldst have heard how   75
her horse fell and she under her horse; thou
shouldst have heard in how miry a place, how she
was bemoil'd, how he left her with the horse upon
her, how he beat me because her horse stumbled,
how she waded through the dirt to pluck him
off me, how he swore, how she pray'd that   80
never pray'd before, how I cried, how the horses
ran away, how her bridle was burst, how I lost
my crupper, with many things of worthy memory,
which now shall die in oblivion and thou return
unexperienc'd to thy grave.   86
   Curt. By this reck'ning he is more shrew than
she.
   Gru. Ay; and that thou and the proudest of
you all shall find when he comes home. But
what talk I of this? Call forth Nathaniel,   90
Joseph, Nicholas, Philip, Walter, Sugarsop and the
rest; let their heads be slickly comb'd, their blue
coats brush'd and their garters of an indifferent
knit; let them curtsy with their left legs and not
presume to touch a hair of my master's horse-   96
tail till they kiss their hands. Are they all ready?
   Curt. They are.
   Gru. Call them forth.   99
   Curt. Do you hear, ho? You must meet my
master to countenance my mistress.
   Gru. Why, she hath a face of her own.
   Curt. Who knows not that?
   Gru. Thou, it seems, that calls for company to
countenance her.   105
   Curt. I call them forth to credit her.

Enter four or five SERVINGMEN.

   Gru. Why, she comes to borrow nothing of them.
   Nath. Welcome home, Grumio!   110
   Phil. How now, Grumio!
   Jos. What, Grumio!
   Nich. Fellow Grumio.
   Nath. How now, old lad?
   Gru. Welcome, you; how now, you; what,
you; fellow, you; — and thus much for greeting.
Now, my spruce companions, is all ready, and   116
all things neat?
   Nath. All things is ready. How near is our
master?   119
   Gru. E'en at hand, alighted by this; and there-

fore be not — Cock's passion, silence! I hear my
master.

Enter PETRUCHIO *and* KATHERINA.

   Pet. Where be these knaves? What, no man
at door
To hold my stirrup nor to take my horse!
Where is Nathaniel, Gregory, Philip?   125
   All Serv. Here, here, sir; here, sir.
   Pet. Here, sir! here, sir! here, sir! here, sir!
You logger-headed and unpolish'd grooms!
What, no attendance? No regard? No duty?
Where is the foolish knave I sent before?   130
   Gru. Here, sir; as foolish as I was before.
   Pet. You peasant swain! You whoreson malt-
horse drudge!
Did I not bid thee meet me in the park,
And bring along these rascal knaves with thee? 134
   Gru. Nathaniel's coat, sir, was not fully made,
And Gabriel's pumps were all unpink'd i' th' heel;
There was no link to colour Peter's hat,
And Walter's dagger was not come from sheathing;
There were none fine but Adam, Ralph, and
   Gregory;
The rest were ragged, old, and beggarly;   140
Yet, as they are, here are they come to meet you.
   Pet. Go, rascals, go, and fetch my supper in.
                           [Exeunt Servants.
   [Singing.] "Where is the life that late I led" —
Where are those — Sit down, Kate, and welcome. —
Soud, soud, soud, soud!   145

Re-enter SERVANTS, *with supper.*

Why, when, I say? — Nay, good sweet Kate, be
   merry. —
Off with my boots, you rogues! You villains, when?
[Sings.] "It was the friar of orders grey,
   As he forth walked on his way:" —
Out, you rogue! you pluck my foot awry.   150
Take that, and mend the plucking off the other.
                           [Strikes him.]
Be merry, Kate. — Some water, here; what, ho!

Enter one with water.

Where's my spaniel Troilus? Sirrah, get you hence,
And bid my cousin Ferdinand come hither;
One, Kate, that you must kiss, and be acquainted
   with.   155
Where are my slippers? Shall I have some water?
Come, Kate, and wash, and welcome heartily.
You whoreson villain! Will you let it fall?
                           [Strikes him.]

---

78. **bemoil'd:** befouled. 94. **indifferent:** good enough. 101. **countenance:** honor (as "credit," l. 106). 121. **Cock's:**
a corruption of *God's.* 136. **unpink'd:** undecorated. 137. **link:** a torch of pitch, the soot of which was used as black-
ing. 143. **Where...led.** Fragment of a song (cf. *2 Hen. IV,* V.iii.146). 145. **Soud:** probably a mere expression of
impatience.

Kath. Patience, I pray you; 'twas a fault un-
        willing.   159
Pet. A whoreson beetle-headed, flap-ear'd knave!
Come, Kate, sit down; I know you have a stomach.
Will you give thanks, sweet Kate; or else shall I?
What's this?   Mutton?
1. Serv.   Ay.
Pet.   Who brought it?
Peter.   I.
Pet. 'Tis burnt; and so is all the meat.   164
What dogs are these.   Where is the rascal cook?
How durst you, villains, bring it from the dresser,
And serve it thus to me that love it not?
There, take it to you, trenchers, cups, and all.
                [*Throws the meat, etc., about the stage.*]
You heedless jolt heads and unmanner'd slaves!
What, do you grumble?   I'll be with you straight.
Kath. I pray you, husband, be not so disquiet. 171
The meat was well, if you were so contented.
Pet. I tell thee, Kate, 'twas burnt and dried away,
And I expressly am forbid to touch it,
For it engenders choler, planteth anger;   175
And better 'twere that both of us did fast,
Since, of ourselves, ourselves are choleric,
Than feed it with such over-roasted flesh.
Be patient; to-morrow't shall be mended,
And, for this night, we'll fast for company.   180
Come, I will bring thee to thy bridal chamber.
                                    [*Exeunt.*

            Re-enter SERVANTS *severally.*
Nath. Peter, didst ever see the like?
Peter. He kills her in her own humour.

            Re-enter CURTIS, *a servant.*
Gru. Where is he?
Curt. In her chamber, making a sermon of con-
tinency to her;   186
And rails, and swears, and rates, that she, poor soul,
Knows not which way to stand, to look, to speak,
And sits as one new-risen from a dream.
Away, away! for he is coming hither.   190
                                    [*Exeunt.*]

            Re-enter PETRUCHIO.
Pet. Thus have I politicly begun my reign,
And 'tis my hope to end successfully.
My falcon now is sharp and passing empty;
And till she stoop she must not be full-gorg'd,
For then she never looks upon her lure.   195
Another way I have to man my haggard,
To make her come and know her keeper's call,

That is, to watch her, as we watch these kites
That bate and beat and will not be obedient.
She eat no meat to-day, nor none shall eat;   200
Last night she slept not, nor to-night she shall not;
As with the meat, some undeserved fault
I'll find about the making of the bed;
And here I'll fling the pillow, there the bolster,
This way the coverlet, another way the sheets.
Ay, and amid this hurly I intend   206
That all is done in reverend care of her;
And in conclusion she shall watch all night;
And if she chance to nod I'll rail and brawl
And with the clamour keep her still awake   210
This is a way to kill a wife with kindness,
And thus I'll curb her mad and headstrong humour.
He that knows better how to tame a shrew,
Now let him speak; 'tis charity to show.   [*Exit.*

[SCENE II.   *Padua.   Before Baptista's house.*]

        Enter TRANIO [*as* LUCENTIO] *and* HORTENSIO
                    [*as* LICIO].

Tra. Is't possible, friend Licio, that Mistress
        Bianca
Doth fancy any other but Lucentio?
I tell you, sir, she bears me fair in hand.
[*Hor.*] Sir, to satisfy you in what I have said,
Stand by and mark the manner of his teaching. 5

        Enter BIANCA [*and* LUCENTIO *as* CAMBIO].
[*Luc.*] Now, mistress, profit you in what you
        read?
Bian. What, master, read you?   First resolve
        me that.
[*Luc.*] I read that I profess, the Art to Love.
Bian. And may you prove, sir, master of your
        art!
Luc. While you, sweet dear, prove mistress of
        my heart!   10
Hor. Quick proceeders, marry!   Now, tell me,
        I pray,
You that durst swear that your mistress Bianca
Lov'd none in the world so well as Lucentio.
Tra. O despiteful love!   Unconstant woman-
        kind!
I tell thee, Licio, this is wonderful.   15
Hor. Mistake no more; I am not Licio,
Nor a musician, as I seem to be;
But one that scorn to live in this disguise
For such a one as leaves a gentleman
And makes a god of such a cullion.   20
Know, sir, that I am call'd Hortensio.

161. **stomach:** (1) appetite, (2) temper. 183. **kills:** masters. 193. **sharp:** starved. 194-99. The terms from falconry
may be glossed together. **stoop:** fly to the lure; **lure:** decoy; **man my haggard:** tame my wild hawk; **watch:** keep awake;
bate and beat: flap and flutter the wings. 201. **Last night.** An oversight: No night has passed since the wedding. 206.
intend: pretend.
    Sc. ii, 8. **Art to Love:** i.e., Ovid's *Ars Amandi.* 20. **cullion:** base fellow.

Tra. Signior Hortensio, I have often heard
Of your entire affection to Bianca;
And since mine eyes are witness of her lightness,
I will with you, if you be so contented, 25
Forswear Bianca and her love for ever.

 Hor. See, how they kiss and court! Signior Lucentio,
Here is my hand, and here I firmly vow
Never to woo her more, but do forswear her,
As one unworthy all the former favours
That I have fondly flatter'd her withal. 30

 Tra. And here I take the like unfeigned oath,
Never to marry with her though she would entreat.
Fie on her! see, how beastly she doth court him!

 Hor. Would all the world but he had quite forsworn! 35
For me, that I may surely keep mine oath,
I will be married to a wealthy widow,
Ere three days pass, which hath as long lov'd me
As I have lov'd this proud disdainful haggard.
And so farewell, Signior Lucentio. 40
Kindness in women, not their beauteous looks,
Shall win my love; and so I take my leave,
In resolution as I swore before. [*Exit.*]

 Tra. Mistress Bianca, bless you with such grace
As 'longeth to a lover's blessed case! 45
Nay, I have ta'en you napping, gentle love,
And have forsworn you with Hortensio.

 Bian. Tranio, you jest; but have you both forsworn me?

 Tra. Mistress, we have.

 Luc. Then we are rid of Licio.

 Tra. I'faith, he'll have a lusty widow now, 50
That shall be woo'd and wedded in a day.

 Bian. God give him joy!

 Tra. Ay, and he'll tame her.

 Bian. He says so, Tranio.

 Tra. Faith, he is gone unto the taming-school.

 Bian. The taming-school! What, is there such a place? 55

 Tra. Ay, mistress, and Petruchio is the master;
That teacheth tricks eleven and twenty long,
To tame a shrew and charm her chattering tongue.

Enter BIONDELLO.

 Bion. O master, master, I have watch'd so long
That I am dog-weary; but at last I spied 60
An ancient angel coming down the hill,
Will serve the turn.

 Tra. What is he, Biondello?

 Bion. Master, a *mercatante*, or a pedant,
I know not what; but formal in apparel,
In gait and countenance surely like a father. 65

 Luc. And what of him, Tranio?

 Tra. If he be credulous and trust my tale,

I'll make him glad to seem Vincentio,
And give assurance to Baptista Minola,
As if he were the right Vincentio. 70
Take in your love, and then let me alone.

  [*Exeunt Lucentio and Bianca.*]

Enter a PEDANT.

 Ped. God save you, sir!

 Tra. And you, sir! you are welcome.
Travel you far on, or are you at the farthest?

 Ped. Sir, at the farthest for a week or two;
But then up farther, and as far as Rome; 75
And so to Tripoli, if God lend me life.

 Tra. What countryman, I pray?

 Ped. Of Mantua.

 Tra. Of Mantua, sir? Marry, God forbid!
And come to Padua, careless of your life?

 Ped. My life, sir! How, I pray? for that goes hard. 80

 Tra. 'Tis death for any one in Mantua
To come to Padua. Know you not the cause?
Your ships are stay'd at Venice, and the Duke,
For private quarrel 'twixt your Duke and him,
Hath publish'd and proclaim'd it openly. 85
'Tis marvel, but that you are but newly come,
You might have heard it else proclaim'd about.

 Ped. Alas! sir, it is worse for me than so;
For I have bills for money by exchange
From Florence, and must here deliver them. 90

 Tra. Well, sir, to do you courtesy,
This will I do, and this I will advise you.
First, tell me, have you ever been at Pisa?

 Ped. Ay, sir, in Pisa have I often been,
Pisa renowned for grave citizens. 95

 Tra. Among them know you one Vincentio?

 Ped. I know him not, but I have heard of him;
A merchant of incomparable wealth.

 Tra. He is my father, sir; and, sooth to say,
In count'nance somewhat doth resemble you. 100

 Bion. [*Aside.*] As much as an apple doth an oyster, and all one.

 Tra. To save your life in this extremity,
This favour will I do you for his sake;
And think it not the worst of all your fortunes
That you are like to Sir Vincentio. 105
His name and credit shall you undertake,
And in my house you shall be friendly lodg'd.
Look that you take upon you as you should;
You understand me, sir? So shall you stay
Till you have done your business in the city. 110
If this be court'sy, sir, accept of it.

 Ped. O sir, I do; and will repute you ever
The patron of my life and liberty.

 Tra. Then go with me to make the matter good.
This, by the way, I let you understand; 115

---

57. **tricks ... long.** Perhaps a reference to the card game "trentuno"; 11 + 20 = 31. Cf. I.ii.32. 63. *mercatante:* merchant. 106. **undertake:** assume. 108. **take upon you:** act your part.

My father is here look'd for every day,
To pass assurance of a dow'r in marriage
'Twixt me and one Baptista's daughter here.
In all these circumstances I'll instruct you.
Go with me to clothe you as becomes you.   120

[*Exeunt.*

SCENE [III. *A room in Petruchio's house*].

Enter KATHERINA *and* GRUMIO.

Gru. No, no, forsooth; I dare not for my life.
Kath. The more my wrong, the more his spite
    appears.
What, did he marry me to famish me?
Beggars, that come unto my father's door,
Upon entreaty have a present alms;   5
If not, elsewhere they meet with charity;
But I, who never knew how to entreat,
Nor never needed that I should entreat,
Am starv'd for meat, giddy for lack of sleep,   9
With oaths kept waking, and with brawling fed;
And that which spites me more than all these wants,
He does it under name of perfect love,
As who should say, if I should sleep or eat,
'Twere deadly sickness or else present death.
I prithee go and get me some repast;   15
I care not what, so it be wholesome food.
Gru. What say you to a neat's foot?
Kath. 'Tis passing good; I prithee let me have it.
Gru. I fear it is too choleric a meat.
How say you to a fat tripe finely broil'd?   20
Kath. I like it well; good Grumio, fetch it me.
Gru. I cannot tell; I fear 'tis choleric.
What say you to a piece of beef and mustard?
Kath. A dish that I do love to feed upon.
Gru. Ay, but the mustard is too hot a little.
Kath. Why then, the beef, and let the mustard
    rest.   26
Gru. Nay then, I will not; you shall have the
    mustard,
Or else you get no beef of Grumio.
Kath. Then both, or one, or any thing thou wilt.
Gru. Why then, the mustard without the beef.
Kath. Go, get thee gone, thou false deluding
    slave,   [*Beats him.* 31
That feed'st me with the very name of meat.
Sorrow on thee and all the pack of you,
That triumph thus upon my misery!
Go, get thee gone, I say.   35

Enter PETRUCHIO *and* HORTENSIO, *with meat.*

Pet. How fares my Kate? What, sweeting, all
    amort!

Hor. Mistress, what cheer?
Kath.   Faith, as cold as can be.
Pet. Pluck up thy spirits; look cheerfully upon
    me.
Here, love, thou see'st how diligent I am
To dress thy meat myself and bring it thee.   40
I am sure, sweet Kate, this kindness merits thanks.
What, not a word? Nay, then thou lov'st it not;
And all my pains is sorted to no proof.
Here, take away this dish.
Kath.   I pray you, let it stand.
Pet. The poorest service is repaid with thanks,
And so shall mine, before you touch the meat.   46
Kath. I thank you, sir.
Hor. Signior Petruchio, fie! you are to blame.
Come, Mistress Kate, I'll bear you company.
Pet. [*Aside.*] Eat it up all, Hortensio, if thou
    lovest me.   50
Much good do it unto thy gentle heart!
Kate, eat apace. And now, my honey love,
Will we return unto thy father's house
And revel it as bravely as the best,
With silken coats and caps and golden rings,   55
With ruffs and cuffs and farthingales and things,
With scarfs and fans and double change of brav'ry,
With amber bracelets, beads, and all this knav'ry.
What, hast thou din'd? The tailor stays thy
    leisure,
To deck thy body with his ruffling treasure.   60

Enter TAILOR.

Come, tailor, let us see these ornaments;
Lay forth the gown.

Enter HABERDASHER.

                What news with you, sir?
[*Hab.*] Here is the cap your worship did bespeak.
Pet. Why, this was moulded on a porringer;
A velvet dish. Fie, fie! 'tis lewd and filthy.   65
Why, 'tis a cockle or a walnut-shell,
A knack, a toy, a trick, a baby's cap.
Away with it! come, let me have a bigger.
Kath. I'll have no bigger; this doth fit the time,
And gentlewomen wear such caps as these.   70
Pet. When you are gentle, you shall have one
    too,
And not till then.
Hor. [*Aside.*]   That will not be in haste.
Kath. Why, sir, I trust I may have leave to
    speak;
And speak I will. I am no child, no babe.
Your betters have endur'd me say my mind,   75
And if you cannot, best you stop your ears.

117. **pass:** convey.
Sc. iii, 5. **present:** immediate. 17. **neat's:** ox's. 19. **choleric:** engendering anger. 36. **amort:** dejected. 43. **sorted ...**
proof: futile. 56. **farthingales:** hooped skirts. 57. **bravery:** finery. 60. **ruffling:** gaily ruffled. 63. [*Hab.*] (Rowe). *Fel.* F.
65. **lewd:** vile.

My tongue will tell the anger of my heart,
Or else my heart concealing it will break,
And rather than it shall, I will be free
Even to the uttermost, as I please, in words.   80
 Pet. Why, thou say'st true; it is a paltry cap,
A custard-coffin, a bauble, a silken pie.
I love thee well in that thou lik'st it not.
  Kath. Love me or love me not, I like the cap;
And it I will have, or I will have none.   85
               [Exit Haberdasher.]
  Pet. Thy gown? Why, ay. Come, tailor, let us
  see't.
O mercy, God! what masquing stuff is here?
What's this? A sleeve? 'Tis like a demi-cannon.
What, up and down, carv'd like an apple-tart?
Here's snip and nip and cut and slish and slash,   90
Like to a censer in a barber's shop.
Why, what, i' devil's name, tailor, call'st thou this?
  Hor. [*Aside.*] I see she's like to have neither cap
  nor gown.
  Tai. You bid me make it orderly and well,
According to the fashion and the time.   95
  Pet. Marry, and did; but if you be rememb'red,
I did not bid you mar it to the time.
Go, hop me over every kennel home,
For you shall hop without my custom, sir.
I'll none of it. Hence! make your best of it.   100
  Kath. I never saw a better-fashion'd gown,
More quaint, more pleasing, nor more commend-
able.
Belike you mean to make a puppet of me.
  Pet. Why, true; he means to make a puppet of
  thee.
  Tai. She says your worship means to make a
puppet of her.   106
  Pet. O monstrous arrogance! Thou liest, thou
thread, thou thimble,
Thou yard, three-quarters, half-yard, quarter, nail!
Thou flea, thou nit, thou winter-cricket thou!   110
Brav'd in mine own house with a skein of thread?
Away, thou rag, thou quantity, thou remnant,
Or I shall so be-mete thee with thy yard
As thou shalt think on prating whilst thou liv'st!
I tell thee, I, that thou hast marr'd her gown.
  Tai. Your worship is deceiv'd; the gown is made
Just as my master had direction.   117
Grumio gave order how it should be done.
  Gru. I gave him no order; I gave him the stuff.
  Tai. But how did you desire it should be made?
  Gru. Marry, sir, with needle and thread.   121
  Tai. But did you not request to have it cut?
  Gru. Thou hast fac'd many things.

  Tai. I have.   124
  Gru. Face not me; thou hast brav'd many men,
brave not me; I will neither be fac'd nor brav'd. I
say unto thee, I bid thy master cut out the gown;
but I did not bid him cut it to pieces; *ergo,* thou
liest.   129
  Tai. Why, here is the note of the fashion to
testify.
  Pet. Read it.
  Gru. The note lies in's throat, if he say I said so.
  Tai. [*Reads.*] "*Imprimis,* a loose-bodied
gown"—   135
  Gru. Master, if ever I said loose-bodied gown,
sew me in the skirts of it, and beat me to death with
a bottom of brown thread. I said a gown.
  Pet. Proceed.
  Tai. [*Reads.*] "With a small compass'd cape"—
  Gru. I confess the cape.   141
  Tai. [*Reads.*] "With a trunk sleeve"—
  Gru. I confess two sleeves.
  Tai. [*Reads.*] "The sleeves curiously cut."
  Pet. Ay, there's the villainy.   145
  Gru. Error i' th' bill, sir; error i' th' bill. I com-
manded the sleeves should be cut out and sew'd up
again; and that I'll prove upon thee, though thy
little finger be armed in a thimble.
  Tai. This is true that I say; an I had thee in
place where, thou shouldst know it.   151
  Gru. I am for thee straight. Take thou the bill,
give me thy mete-yard, and spare not me.
  Hor. God-a-mercy, Grumio! then he shall have
no odds.   155
  Pet. Well, sir, in brief, the gown is not for me.
  Gru. You are i' th' right, sir; 'tis for my mistress.
  Pet. Go, take it up unto thy master's use.
  Gru. Villain, not for thy life! Take up my mis-
tress' gown for thy master's use!   161
  Pet. Why, sir, what's your conceit in that?
  Gru. O, sir, the conceit is deeper than you think
  for.
Take up my mistress' gown to his master's use!
O, fie, fie, fie!   165
  Pet. [*Aside.*] Hortensio, say thou wilt see the
  tailor paid.—
Go take it hence; be gone, and say no more.
  Hor. Tailor, I'll pay thee for thy gown tomorrow;
Take no unkindness of his hasty words.
Away! I say; commend me to thy master.   170
                 [Exit Tailor.
  Pet. Well, come, my Kate; we will unto your
  father's
Even in these honest mean habiliments.

---

82. **custard-coffin:** pastry form of a custard.   87. **masquing:** fit (only) for a masquerade.   98. **kennel:** gutter.   102.
quaint: elegant.   109. **nail:** measure of 2¼ inches.   110. **nit:** egg of a louse.   112. **quantity:** fragment.   113. **be-mete:**
measure.   114. **think on prating:** remember thy prating.   123. **fac'd:** (1) trimmed, (2) defied.   125. **brav'd:** (1) made
fine, (2) defied.   128. **ergo:** therefore.   138. **bottom:** spool.   140. **compass'd:** rounded.   142. **trunk sleeve:** large puffed
sleeve.   152. **bill:** i.e., with a pun on *bill* (a weapon).   153. **mete-yard:** yardstick.   162. **conceit:** idea.

Our purses shall be proud, our garments poor,
For 'tis the mind that makes the body rich;
And as the sun breaks through the darkest clouds,
So honour peereth in the meanest habit.   176
What, is the jay more precious than the lark,
Because his feathers are more beautiful?
Or is the adder better than the eel,
Because his painted skin contents the eye?   180
O, no, good Kate; neither art thou the worse
For this poor furniture and mean array.
If thou account'st it shame, lay it on me;
And therefore frolic.   We will hence forthwith,
To feast and sport us at thy father's house.   185
Go, call my men, and let us straight to him,
And bring our horses unto Long-lane end.
There will we mount, and thither walk on foot.
Let's see; I think 'tis now some seven o'clock,
And well we may come there by dinner-time.   190
   Kath. I dare assure you, sir, 'tis almost two;
And 'twill be supper-time ere you come there.
   Pet. It shall be seven ere I go to horse.
Look, what I speak, or do, or think to do,
You are still crossing it.   Sirs, let't alone,   195
I will not go to-day, and ere I do,
It shall be what o'clock I say it is.
   Hor. [*Aside.*] Why, so this gallant will command
      the sun.   [*Exeunt.*]

[SCENE IV.   *Padua.   Before Baptista's house.*]

Enter TRANIO, *and the* PEDANT *dressed like* Vincentio.
   Tra. Sir, this is the house; please it you that I
      call?
   Ped. Ay, what else?   And, but I be deceived,
Signior Baptista may remember me,
Near twenty years ago, in Genoa,
Where we were lodgers at the Pegasus.   5
   Tra. 'Tis well; and hold your own, in any case,
With such austerity as 'longeth to a father.

Enter BIONDELLO.

   Ped. I warrant you.   But, sir, here comes your
      boy;
'Twere good he were school'd.
   Tra. Fear you not him.   Sirrah Biondello,   10
Now do your duty throughly, I advise you.
Imagine 'twere the right Vincentio.
   Bion. Tut, fear not me.
   Tra. But hast thou done thy errand to Baptista?
   Bion. I told him that your father was at Venice,
And that you look'd for him this day in Padua.   16
   Tra. Thou'art a tall fellow; hold thee that to
      drink.
Here comes Baptista; set your countenance, sir.

Enter BAPTISTA *and* LUCENTIO: PEDANT *booted and
      bare-headed.*

Signior Baptista, you are happily met.
[*To the Pedant.*] Sir, this is the gentleman I told
      you of.   20
I pray you, stand good father to me now,
Give me Bianca for my patrimony.
   Ped. Soft, son!
Sir, by your leave.   Having come to Padua
To gather in some debts, my son Lucentio   25
Made me acquainted with a weighty cause
Of love between your daughter and himself;
And, for the good report I hear of you,
And for the love he beareth to your daughter
And she to him, to stay him not too long,   30
I am content, in a good father's care,
To have him match'd; and if you please to like
No worse than I, upon some agreement
Me shall you find ready and willing
With one consent to have her so bestow'd;   35
For curious I cannot be with you,
Signior Baptista, of whom I hear so well.
   Bap. Sir, pardon me in what I have to say.
Your plainness and your shortness please me well.
Right true it is, your son Lucentio here   40
Doth love my daughter and she loveth him,
Or both dissemble deeply their affections;
And therefore, if you say no more than this,
That like a father you will deal with him
And pass my daughter a sufficient dower,   45
The match is made, and all is done.
Your son shall have my daughter with consent.
   Tra. I thank you, sir.   Where, then, do you
      know best
We be affied and such assurance ta'en
As shall with either part's agreement stand?   50
   Bap. Not in my house, Lucentio; for, you know,
Pitchers have ears, and I have many servants;
Besides, old Gremio is heark'ning still,
And happily we might be interrupted.
   Tra. Then at my lodging, an it like you.   55
There doth my father lie; and there, this night,
We'll pass the business privately and well.
Send for your daughter by your servant here;
My boy shall fetch the scrivener presently.
The worst is this, that, at so slender warning,   60
You are like to have a thin and slender pittance.
   Bap. It likes me well.   Cambio, hie you home,
And bid Bianca make her ready straight;
And, if you will, tell what hath happened:
Lucentio's father is arriv'd in Padua,   65
And how she's like to be Lucentio's wife.
      [*Exit Luc.*]
   Bion. I pray the gods she may with all my heart!

182. furniture: dress.
Sc. iv, 17. tall: clever.   36. curious: over-particular.   49. affied: affianced, betrothed.   54. happily: perchance.   56.
lie: lodge.   57. pass: transact.   61. pittance: hospitality.

Tra. Dally not with the gods, but get thee gone.
                                  [*Exit Bion.*]
Signior Baptista, shall I lead the way?
Welcome! one mess is like to be your cheer;   70
Come, sir; we will better it in Pisa.
    Bap. I follow you.   [*Exeunt [omnes]*.

       Re-enter LUCENTIO *and* BIONDELLO.
    Bion. Cambio!
    Luc. What say'st thou, Biondello?
    Bion. You saw my master wink and laugh upon
you?   76
    Luc. Biondello, what of that?
    Bion. Faith, nothing; but has left me here be-
hind, to expound the meaning or moral of his signs
and tokens.   80
    Luc. I pray thee, moralize them.
    Bion. Then thus. Baptista is safe, talking with
the deceiving father of a deceitful son.
    Luc. And what of him?
    Bion. His daughter is to be brought by you to
the supper.   86
    Luc. And then?
    Bion. The old priest of Saint Luke's church is at
your command at all hours.
    Luc. And what of all this?   90
    Bion. I cannot tell. Expect they are busied
about a counterfeit assurance; take you assurance
of her, "*cum privilegio ad imprimendum solum.*"
To th' church! Take the priest, clerk, and some
sufficient honest witnesses.   95
If this be not that you look for, I have no more to
    say,
But bid Bianca farewell for ever and a day.
    Luc. Hear'st thou, Biondello?
    Bion. I cannot tarry. I knew a wench married
in an afternoon as she went to the garden for   100
parsley to stuff a rabbit, and so may you, sir; and so,
adieu, sir. My master hath appointed me to go
to Saint Luke's, to bid the priest be ready to come
against you come with your appendix. [*Exit.* 104
    Luc. I may, and will, if she be so contented.
She will be pleased; then wherefore should I doubt?
Hap what hap may, I'll roundly go about her;
It shall go hard if Cambio go without her.   [*Exit.*

           [SCENE V. *A public road.*]

    Enter PETRUCHIO, KATHERINA, HORTENSIO
                  [*and* Servants].

    Pet. Come on, a God's name; once more toward
    our father's.
Good Lord, how bright and goodly shines the moon!

    Kath. The moon! the sun. It is not moonlight
    now.
    Pet. I say it is the moon that shines so bright.
    Kath. I know it is the sun that shines so bright.
    Pet. Now, by my mother's son, and that's my-
    self,   6
It shall be moon, or star, or what I list,
Or ere I journey to your father's house.—
Go on, and fetch our horses back again.—
Evermore cross'd and cross'd; nothing but cross'd!
    Hor. Say as he says, or we shall never go.   11
    Kath. Forward, I pray, since we have come so
    far,
And be it moon, or sun, or what you please.
An if you please to call it a rush-candle,
Henceforth I vow it shall be so for me.   15
    Pet. I say it is the moon.
    Kath.   I know it is the moon-
    Pet. Nay, then you lie; it is the blessed sun.
    Kath. Then, God be bless'd, it is the blessed sun;
But sun it is not, when you say it is not;
And the moon changes even as your mind.   20
What you will have it nam'd, even that it is;
And so it shall be so for Katherine.
    Hor. Petruchio, go thy ways; the field is won.
    Pet. Well, forward, forward! thus the bowl should
    run,
And not unluckily against the bias.   25
But, soft! company is coming here.

            Enter VINCENTIO.

[*To Vincentio.*] Good morrow, gentle mistress;
    where away?
Tell me, sweet Kate, and tell me truly too,
Hast thou beheld a fresher gentlewoman?
Such war of white and red within her cheeks!   30
What stars do spangle heaven with such beauty,
As those two eyes become that heavenly face?
Fair lovely maid, once more good day to thee.
Sweet Kate, embrace her for her beauty's sake.
    Hor. 'A will make the man mad, to make [a]
    woman of him.   36
    Kath. Young budding virgin, fair and fresh and
    sweet,
Whither away, or [where] is thy abode?
Happy the parents of so fair a child!
Happier the man, whom favourable stars   40
Allots thee for his lovely bed-fellow!
    Pet. Why, how now, Kate! I hope thou **art** not
    mad.
This is a man, old, wrinkled, faded, withered,
And not a maiden, as thou say'st he is.
    Kath. Pardon, old father, my mistaking eyes, 45
That have been so bedazzled with the sun

---

70. **mess:** dish.   93–4. *cum ... solum:* with the exclusive right of printing.   104. **appendix:** addition, i.e., wife.
     Sc. v, 25. **bias:** the lead in the side of a bowl which governs its direction.   35. [a] F2–4. *the* F1.   38. [where] F2–4.
whether F1.

That every thing I look on seemeth green.
Now I perceive thou art a reverend father.
Pardon, I pray thee, for my mad mistaking.
   Pet. Do, good old grandsire; and withal make
     known   50
Which way thou travellest. If along with us,
We shall be joyful of thy company.
   Vin. Fair sir, and you my merry mistress,
That with your strange encounter much amaz'd me,
My name is call'd Vincentio; my dwelling Pisa;
And bound I am to Padua, there to visit   56
A son of mine, which long I have not seen.
   Pet. What is his name?
   Vin.   Lucentio, gentle sir.
   Pet. Happily met; the happier for thy son.
And now by law, as well as reverend age,   60
I may entitle thee my loving father.
The sister to my wife, this gentlewoman,
Thy son by this hath married. Wonder not,
Nor be not griev'd; she is of good esteem,
Her dowry wealthy, and of worthy birth;   65
Beside, so qualified as may beseem
The spouse of any noble gentleman.
Let me embrace with old Vincentio,
And wander we to see thy honest son,
Who will of thy arrival be full joyous.   70
   Vin. But is this true, or is it else your pleasure,
Like pleasant travellers, to break a jest
Upon the company you overtake?
   Hor. I do assure thee, father, so it is.   74
   Pet. Come, go along, and see the truth hereof;
For our first merriment hath made thee jealous.
              [Exeunt [all but Hortensio].
   Hor. Well, Petruchio, this has put me in heart.
Have to my widow! and if she be froward,
Then hast thou taught Hortensio to be untoward.
                     [Exit.

[ACT V

SCENE I. *Padua. Before Lucentio's house.*]

Enter BIONDELLO, LUCENTIO, *and* BIANCA.
GREMIO *is out before.*

   Bion. Softly and swiftly, sir; for the priest is
ready.
   Luc. I fly, Biondello; but they may chance to
need thee at home, therefore leave us.
            [Exeunt [Lucentio and Bianca].
   Bion. Nay, faith, I'll see the church a your
back; and then come back to my [master's] as   6
soon as I can.   *[Exit.]*
   Gre. I marvel Cambio comes not all this while.

   Enter PETRUCHIO, KATHERINA, VINCENTIO,
       GRUMIO, *with* Attendants.

   Pet. Sir, here's the door, this is Lucentio's house.
My father's bears more toward the marketplace;
Thither must I, and here I leave you, sir.   11
   Vin. You shall not choose but drink before you
     go.
I think I shall command your welcome here,
And, by all likelihood, some cheer is toward.
                       [Knocks.
   Gre. They're busy within; you were best knock
louder.   16

     PEDANT *looks out of the window.*

   Ped. What's he that knocks as he would beat
down the gate?
   Vin. Is Signior Lucentio within, sir?
   Ped. He's within, sir, but not to be spoken
withal.   21
   Vin. What if a man bring him a hundred pound
or two, to make merry withal?
   Ped. Keep your hundred pounds to yourself; he
shall need none, so long as I live.   25
   Pet. Nay, I told you your son was well beloved
in Padua. Do you hear, sir? To leave frivolous
circumstances, I pray you, tell Signior Lucentio that
his father is come from Pisa and is here at the door
to speak with him.   30
   Ped. Thou liest. His father is come from Padua
and [is] here looking out at the window.
   Vin. Art thou his father?
   Ped. Ay, sir; so his mother says, if I may believe
her.   35
   Pet. [*To Vincentio.*] Why, how now, gentleman!
Why, this is flat knavery, to take upon you another
man's name.
   Ped. Lay hands on the villain. I believe 'a means
to cozen somebody in this city under my countenance.   41

     Re-enter BIONDELLO.

   Bion. I have seen them in the church together;
God send 'em good shipping! But who is here?
Mine old master Vincentio! Now we are undone
and brought to nothing.   45
   Vin. [*Seeing Biondello.*] Come hither, crack-
hemp.
   Bion. I hope I may choose, sir.
   Vin. Come hither, you rogue. What, have you
forgot me?   50
   Bion. Forgot you? No, sir; I could not forget
you, for I never saw you before in all my life.

---

66. **qualified**: having such qualities. 76. **jealous**: suspicious. 79. **untoward**: unyielding.
   Act V, sc. i, 4–5. **see ... back**: see you married. **[master's]** (Capell). *mistris* F. 10. **bears**: lies (nautical term).
32. **[is]** (Dyce). Om. F. 41. **countenance**: identity. 43. **shipping**: voyage, i.e., luck. 46. **crack-hemp**: gallows-bird.
47. **choose**: do as I choose.

Vin. What, you notorious villain, didst thou never see thy [master's] father, Vincentio?   55

Bion. What, my old worshipful old master? Yes, marry, sir; see where he looks out of the window.

Vin. Is't so, indeed?   [*Beats Biondello.*

Bion. Help, help, help! here's a madman will murder me.   [*Exit.* 61

Ped. Help, son! help, Signior Baptista!
[*Exit from above.*]

Pet. Prithee, Kate, let's stand aside and see the end of this controversy.   [*They retire.*]

Re-enter PEDANT [*below*], TRANIO, BAPTISTA,
and Servants.

Tra. Sir, what are you that offer to beat my servant?   66

Vin. What am I, sir! Nay, what are you, sir? O immortal gods! O fine villain! A silken doublet! a velvet hose! a scarlet cloak! and a copatain hat! O, I am undone! I am undone! While I play   70 the good husband at home, my son and my servant spend all at the university.

Tra. How now! what's the matter?

Bap. What, is the man lunatic?   74

Tra. Sir, you seem a sober ancient gentleman by your habit, but your words show you a madman. Why, sir, what 'cerns it you if I wear pearl and gold? I thank my good father, I am able to maintain it.

Vin. Thy father! O villain! he is a sailmaker in Bergamo.   81

Bap. You mistake, sir, you mistake, sir. Pray, what do you think is his name?

Vin. His name! as if I knew not his name! I have brought him up ever since he was three years old, and his name is Tranio.   86

Ped. Away, away, mad ass! his name is Lucentio; and he is mine only son, and heir to the lands of me, Signior Vincentio.   89

Vin. Lucentio! O, he hath murd'red his master! Lay hold on him, I charge you, in the Duke's name. O, my son, my son! Tell me, thou villain, where is my son Lucentio?

Tra. Call forth an officer.

[*Enter one with an officer.*]

Carry this mad knave to the gaol. Father Bap-   95 tista, I charge you see that he be forthcoming.

Vin. Carry me to the gaol!

Gre. Stay, officer; he shall not go to prison.

Bap. Talk not, Signior Gremio; I say he shall go to prison.   100

Gre. Take heed, Signior Baptista, lest you be

cony-catch'd in this business. I dare swear this is the right Vincentio.

Ped. Swear, if thou dar'st.

Gre. Nay, I dare not swear it.   105

Tra. Then thou wert best say that I am not Lucentio.

Gre. Yes, I know thee to be Signior Lucentio.

Bap. Away with the dotard! To the gaol with him!   110

Re-enter BIONDELLO, *with* LUCENTIO *and* BIANCA.

Vin. Thus strangers may be hal'd and abus'd. O monstrous villain!

Bion. O! we are spoil'd and — yonder he is. Deny him, forswear him, or else we are all undone.
[*Exeunt Biondello, Tranio, and Pedant, as fast as may be.*

Luc. (*Kneeling.*) Pardon, sweet father.

Vin.   Lives my sweet son?   115

Bian. Pardon, dear father.

Bap.   How hast thou offended? Where is Lucentio?

Luc.   Here's Lucentio,
Right son to the right Vincentio,
That have by marriage made thy daughter mine,
While counterfeit supposes blear'd thine eyne.   120

Gre. Here's packing, with a witness, to deceive us all!

Vin. Where is that damned villain Tranio,
That fac'd and brav'd me in this matter so?

Bap. Why, tell me, is not this my Cambio?   125

Bian. Cambio is chang'd into Lucentio.

Luc. Love wrought these miracles. Bianca's love
Made me exchange my state with Tranio,
While he did bear my countenance in the town;
And happily I have arriv'd at last   130
Unto the wished haven of my bliss.
What Tranio did, myself enforc'd him to;
Then pardon him, sweet father, for my sake.

Vin. I'll slit the villain's nose, that would have sent me to the gaol.   135

Bap. But do you hear, sir? Have you married my daughter without asking my good will?

Vin. Fear not, Baptista; we will content you, go to; but I will in to be reveng'd for this villainy.   140
[*Exit.*

Bap. And I, to sound the depth of this knavery.
[*Exit.*

Luc. Look not pale, Bianca; thy father will not frown.   [*Exeunt [Lucentio and Bianca].*

Gre. My cake is dough; but I'll in among the rest,   145
Out of hope of all but my share of the feast. [*Exit.*]

55. [master's] F₂₋₄. *Mistris* F₁. 69. copatain: high-crowned. 71. good husband: careful manager. 120. supposes: illusions (see Introduction). eyne: eyes. 121. packing: plotting. witness: vengeance. 130. arriv'd at last F₂₋₄. *arrived at the last* F₁.

Kath. Husband, let's follow, to see the end of this ado.

Pet. First kiss me, Kate, and we will.

Kath. What, in the midst of the street?

Pet. What, art thou asham'd of me?   150

Kath. No, sir, God forbid; but asham'd to kiss.

Pet. Why, then let's home again. Come, sirrah, let's away.

Kath. Nay, I will give thee a kiss; now pray thee, love, stay.

Pet. Is not this well? Come, my sweet Kate: Better once than never, for never too late.   155

[*Exeunt.*

SCENE [II. *Padua. Lucentio's house*].

Enter BAPTISTA, VINCENTIO, GREMIO, *the* PEDANT,
LUCENTIO, BIANCA [PETRUCHIO, KATHERINA,
HORTENSIO], *and* WIDOW, TRANIO, BIONDELLO,
and GRUMIO: *the Servingmen with Tranio bringing
in a banquet.*

Luc. At last, though long, our jarring notes agree;
And time it is, when raging war is [done],
To smile at scapes and perils overblown.
My fair Bianca, bid my father welcome,
While I with self-same kindness welcome thine.   5
Brother Petruchio, sister Katherina,
And thou, Hortensio, with thy loving widow,
Feast with the best, and welcome to my house.
My banquet is to close our stomachs up,
After our great good cheer. Pray you, sit down;
For now we sit to chat as well as eat.   11

Pet. Nothing but sit and sit, and eat and eat!

Bap. Padua affords this kindness, son Petruchio.

Pet. Padua affords nothing but what is kind.

Hor. For both our sakes, I would that word were true.   15

Pet. Now, for my life, Hortensio fears his widow.

Wid. Then never trust me, if I be afeard.

Pet. You are very sensible, and yet you miss my sense.

I mean, Hortensio is afeard of you.

Wid. He that is giddy thinks the world turns round.   20

Pet. Roundly replied.

Kath.   Mistress, how mean you that?

Wid. Thus I conceive by him.

Pet. Conceives by me! How likes Hortensio that?

Hor. My widow says, thus she conceives her tale.

Pet. Very well mended. Kiss him for that, good widow.   25

Kath. "He that is giddy thinks the world turns round:"

I pray you, tell me what you meant by that.

Wid. Your husband, being troubled with a shrew,

Measures my husband's sorrow by his woe:
And now you know my meaning.   30

Kath. A very mean meaning.

Wid.   Right, I mean you.

Kath. And I am mean indeed, respecting you.

Pet. To her, Kate!

Hor. To her, widow!

Pet. A hundred marks, my Kate does put her down.   35

Hor. That's my office.

Pet. Spoke like an officer. Ha' to thee, lad!

[*Drinks to Hortensio.*

Bap. How likes Gremio these quick-witted folks?

Gre. Believe me, sir, they butt together well.   39

Bian. Head, and butt! An hasty-witted body
Would say your head and butt were head and horn.

Vin. Ay, mistress bride, hath that awakened you?

Bian. Ay, but not frighted me; therefore I'll sleep again.

Pet. Nay, that you shall not; since you have begun,
Have at you for a [bitter] jest or two!   45

Bian. Am I your bird? I mean to shift my bush;
And then pursue me as you draw your bow.
You are welcome all.

[*Exeunt Bianca [Katherina, and Widow].*

Pet. She hath prevented me. Here, Signior Tranio,   49
This bird you aim'd at, though you hit her not;
Therefore a health to all that shot and miss'd.

Tra. O, sir, Lucentio slipp'd me like his greyhound,
Which runs himself and catches for his master.

Pet. A good swift simile, but something currish.

Tra. 'Tis well, sir, that you hunted for yourself;
'Tis thought your deer does hold you at a bay.   56

Bap. O ho, Petruchio! Tranio hits you now.

Luc. I thank thee for that gird, good Tranio.

Hor. Confess, confess, hath he not hit you here?

Pet. 'A has a little gall'd me, I confess;   60
And, as the jest did glance away from me,
'Tis ten to one it maim'd you two outright.

Bap. Now, in good sadness, son Petruchio,
I think thou hast the veriest shrew of all.

Pet. Well, I say no; and therefore [for] assurance
Let's each one send unto his wife,   66
And he whose wife is most obedient
To come at first when he doth send for her,
Shall win the wager which we will propose.

Hor. Content. What is the wager?

Luc.   Twenty crowns.

Pet. Twenty crowns!   71

Sc. ii, s.d. **banquet:** dessert. 2. **[done]** (Rowe). *come* F. 22. **conceive by:** understand. 23. **conceives by:** is pregnant by. 45. **[bitter]** (Theobald conj.). *better* F. 52. **slipp'd:** freed from the leash, set running. 58. **gird:** taunt. 63. **good sadness:** all seriousness. 65. **[for]** F₂-₄. *sir* F₁. **assurance:** proof.

I'll venture so much of my hawk or hound,
But twenty times so much upon my wife.
  Luc. A hundred then.
  Hor.   Content.
  Pet.   A match! 'tis done.
  Hor. Who shall begin?
  Luc.   That will I.   75
Go, Biondello, bid your mistress come to me.
  Bion. I go.   [*Exit.*
  Bap. Son, I'll be your half, Bianca comes.
  Luc. I'll have no halves; I'll bear it all myself.

Re-enter BIONDELLO.

How now! what news?
  Bion.   Sir, my mistress sends you word
That she is busy and she cannot come.   81
  Pet. How! she is busy and she cannot come!
Is that an answer?
  Gre.   Ay, and a kind one too.
Pray God, sir, your wife send you not a worse.
  Pet. I hope, better.   85
  Hor. Sirrah Biondello, go and entreat my wife
To come to me forthwith.   [*Exit Bion.*
  Pet.   O, ho! entreat her!
Nay, then she must needs come.
  Hor.   I am afraid, sir,
Do what you can, yours will not be entreated.

Re-enter BIONDELLO.

Now, where's my wife?   90
  Bion. She says you have some goodly jest in
    hand.
She will not come; she bids you come to her.
  Pet. Worse and worse; she will not come! O vile,
Intolerable, not to be endur'd!
Sirrah Grumio, go to your mistress;   95
Say, I command her come to me.   [*Exit Grumio.*
  Hor. I know her answer.
  Pet.   What?
  Hor.   She will not.
  Pet. The fouler fortune mine, and there an end.

Re-enter KATHERINA.

  Bap. Now, by my holidame, here comes Kath-
    erina!
  Kath. What is your will, sir, that you send for
    me?   100
  Pet. Where is your sister, and Hortensio's wife?
  Kath. They sit conferring by the parlour fire.
  Pet. Go, fetch them hither. If they deny to
    come,
Swinge me them soundly forth unto their husbands.
Away, I say, and bring them hither straight.   105
              [*Exit Katherina.*
  Luc. Here is a wonder, if you talk of a wonder.

  Hor. And so it is; I wonder what it bodes.
  Pet. Marry, peace it bodes, and love, and quiet
    life,
And awful rule, and right supremacy;
And, to be short, what not that's sweet and happy.
  Bap. Now, fair befall thee, good Petruchio!   111
The wager thou hast won; and I will add
Unto their losses twenty thousand crowns,
Another dowry to another daughter,
For she is chang'd, as she had never been.   115
  Pet. Nay, I will win my wager better yet
And show more sign of her obedience,
Her new-built virtue and obedience.

Re-enter KATHERINA, *with* BIANCA *and* WIDOW.

See where she comes and brings your froward wives
As prisoners to her womanly persuasion.   120
Katherine, that cap of yours becomes you not;
Off with that bauble, throw it under-foot.
         [*Kate throws down her cap.*]
  Wid. Lord, let me never have cause to sigh,
Till I be brought to such a silly pass!   124
  Bian. Fie! what a foolish duty call you this?
  Luc. I would your duty were as foolish too.
The wisdom of your duty, fair Bianca,
Hath cost me [a] hundred crowns since suppertime.
  Bian. The more fool you, for laying on my duty.
  Pet. Katherine, I charge thee, tell these head-
    strong women   130
What duty they do owe their lords and husbands.
  Wid. Come, come, you're mocking; we will have
    no telling.
  Pet. Come on, I say; and first begin with her.
  Wid. She shall not.
  Pet. I say she shall; and first begin with her.
  Kath. Fie, fie! unknit that threatening unkind
    brow,   136
And dart not scornful glances from those eyes,
To wound thy lord, thy king, thy governor.
It blots thy beauty as frosts do bite the meads,
Confounds thy fame as whirlwinds shake fair buds,
And in no sense is meet or amiable.   14[1]
A woman mov'd is like a fountain troubled,
Muddy, ill-seeming, thick, bereft of beauty;
And while it is so, none so dry or thirsty
Will deign to sip or touch one drop of it.   145
Thy husband is thy lord, thy life, thy keeper,
Thy head, thy sovereign; one that cares for thee,
And for thy maintenance commits his body
To painful labour both by sea and land,
To watch the night in storms, the day in cold,   150
Whilst thou liest warm at home, secure and safe;
And craves no other tribute at thy hands
But love, fair looks, and true obedience —
Too little payment for so great a debt.

78. **be your half:** share half your wager. 99. **holidame:** halidom, i.e., salvation. 104. **Swinge:** whip. 109. **awful:** commanding respect. 128. **[a]** (Hudson). *five* F. 129. **laying:** betting.

Such duty as the subject owes the prince   155
Even such a woman oweth to her husband;
And when she is froward, peevish, sullen, sour,
And not obedient to his honest will,
What is she but a foul contending rebel
And graceless traitor to her loving lord?   160
I am asham'd that women are so simple
To offer war where they should kneel for peace,
Or seek for rule, supremacy, and sway,
When they are bound to serve, love, and obey.
Why are our bodies soft and weak and smooth,
Unapt to toil and trouble in the world,   166
But that our soft conditions and our hearts
Should well agree with our external parts?
Come, come, you froward and unable worms!
My mind hath been as big as one of yours,   170
My heart as great, my reason haply more,
To bandy word for word and frown for frown;
But now I see our lances are but straws,
Our strength as weak, our weakness past compare,
That seeming to be most which we indeed least
     are.

Then vail your stomachs, for it is no boot,   176
And place your hands below your husband's foot;
In token of which duty, if he please,
My hand is ready; may it do him ease.
     Pet. Why, there's a wench!   Come on, and kiss
     me, Kate.   180
     Luc. Well, go thy ways, old lad; for thou shalt
     ha't.
     Vin. 'Tis a good hearing when children are to-
     ward.
     Luc. But a harsh hearing when women are fro-
     ward.
     Pet. Come, Kate, we'll to bed.
We three are married, but you two are sped.   185
[*To Luc.*] 'Twas I won the wager, though you hit
     the white;
And, being a winner, God give you good night!
          [*Exeunt Petruchio [and Katherina*].
     Hor. Now, go thy ways; thou hast tam'd a curst
     shrew.
     Luc. 'Tis a wonder, by your leave, she will be
     tam'd so.   [*Exeunt.*]

161. **simple:** silly.   167. **conditions:** qualities.   176. **vail your stomachs:** lower your pride.   **boot:** avail.   182. **toward:** docile.   185. **sped:** done for.   186. **hit the white:** white circle at the center of the target (with a pun on *Bianca*).

Much Ado About Nothing

MUCH ADO ABOUT NOTHING was entered in the Stationers' Register on August 4, 1600, as one of four plays "to be staied," but, for whatever reason, the prohibition was presently withdrawn and the normal pre-publication entry was made on August 24, a Quarto following before the end of the year. That the manuscript from which the Quarto was set up was the theatrical prompt-copy is established by the appearance in IV.ii. of the names of Kempe and Cowley, actors in Shakespeare's company, in certain speech-prefixes for Dogberry and Verges respectively. That the text in the Folio was printed from a copy of this Quarto which had eventually served in the playhouse is clear from certain changes in stage directions, in particular the insertion at II.iii.39 of the name of Jack Wilson, the actor playing Balthasar. The present text is based on the Quarto, which is the more accurately printed text.

The date of *Much Ado* can be established with gratifying accuracy. Its absence from the list of Meres (for it cannot be *Love's Labour's Won*) argues that it had not been performed at least until the very end of 1598, for so good an acting play could hardly have failed to win Meres's approbation. The title page of the Quarto, however, states that it had been "sundrie times publikely acted" by Shakespeare's company, and this fact, along with the apparent withdrawal of Kempe from the company early in 1599, fixes the date beyond reasonable doubt as some time in the winter of 1598–1599.

The story of Hero and Claudio is mainly derived from the twenty-second tale in a collection of Italian *Novelle* by Matteo Bandello (1554). No English translation of this has been found, but one in French by Belleforest appeared in 1582. As there is nothing in Shakespeare's rendering which could not have come equally well from either the French version or the Italian original, it is impossible to determine which one was actually used. In Bandello the scene is laid as in Shakespeare in Messina at the close of a successful war; Don Pedro of Arragon appears as King Piero d'Aragona, and Leonato as Lionato de' Lionati; and the thread of the story is the same as in Shakespeare with these main exceptions: the villain is a disappointed lover of Hero's (Fenicia's); there is no Margaret, the deceiving of the bridegroom, Timbreo, being accomplished merely by his being led to see a man enter a window in the heroine's home; the scene in the church, where Claudio casts off Hero, is lacking, the Italian lover sending a friend to announce the breaking off of the match; Timbreo repents of his own accord of his hasty inference; and the dénouement is brought about by the remorse of the villain. Thus it may be seen that in Shakespeare's main plot the character and motive of Don John are quite different, the deceiving of Claudio is made more plausible, and the humors of Dogberry and Verges are introduced to undo the tangle. The rôle of Margaret in this action and the scene at Hero's window appear to have been suggested to Shakespeare by the story of Ariodante and Ginevra in Book V of Ariosto's *Orlando Furioso* (translated into English by John Harrington in 1591), where Ariodante is persuaded that his lady is false after seeing her maid, dressed in the lady's clothes, receive another man at her window. A condensed and altered version appears in Spenser's *Faerie Queene*, II.iv.17.

A number of irregularities and discrepancies in the play have convinced some critics that the received text is Shakespeare's recasting of an earlier play now lost, but the evidence is not conclusive. Confused or redundant stage directions may be owing to no more than Shakespeare's carelessness. For example, at I.i.1 and II.i.1 Innogen, the mother of Hero, is introduced, though she utters not a word and nobody speaks to her in the whole play. This is undeniably odd, but Shakespeare perhaps intended originally to give Innogen a part, discovered, however, as he worked that he did not need her, and then neglected to revise his stage-directions; or Innogen may have been allowed to appear as a mute, as in fact Balthasar does, after an entrance at I.i.96. A kindred peculiarity occurs in the stage direction at II.i.218, where Don John, Borachio, and Conrade are given entrances, though they do not speak in that scene. Likewise Margaret is on the stage in V.iv., but does not speak. There are notable inconsistencies in speech headings; for the outstanding instances see the note on IV.ii.1. If such inconsistencies occurred in this play alone or only rarely in Shakespeare, it might be reasonable to take them as signs of revision, but they crop up in so many plays that one can regard them only as characteristic of Shakespeare's way in composition.

The sub-plot of Benedick and Beatrice and the parts of Dogberry and Verges are original with Shakespeare, and the skill with which he has fused these subordinate elements with his main plot deserves all the praise it has received. The characters of the main plot unite in a plan to make Benedick and Beatrice fall in love with each other, which ruse is carried out effectively in two parallel scenes, but it is the gross wrong to Hero, slandered by Claudio at the very altar, which precipitates the real understanding between them. Alone among the intimates of Hero, Benedick and Beatrice trust in her innocence, and it is Benedick who scents the villainy in Don John. To set the seal upon their affection, Beatrice demands that Benedick kill Claudio, but happily the injunction need go no further than a challenge, for at long last Dogberry and his comrades expose the crime and solve the problem. They were created, of course, to do just that; nevertheless, before they fulfill their office they provide not only diversion from the seriousness of the main plot, but, by their galling stupidities and delays, a fair degree of suspense and dramatic irony.

The villain of the piece is Don John, a "plain-dealing villain" so lacking in subtlety as to seem, in the study at least, almost funny; which is as much as to say, perhaps, that he is the proper kind of villain for a comedy. One cannot, even at the outset, believe that his evil designs are destined to prosper. The title of the play is never quite out of mind. Nevertheless, Shakespeare has given him a plausible human motive for his malignity. After some sort of sedition he has lately been reconciled to his brother (Don Pedro), but Claudio, who distinguished himself in the recent warfare, has been honored at his expense: "That young start-up hath all the glory of my overthrow." Thus Don John

has much the same reason for hating Claudio that Iago has for hating Cassio, whom Othello promoted over his head. But Iago is a villain of quite another order.

Despite the excellence in the structure of the play as a whole, the character and rôle of Margaret seem imperfectly realized. She is made the apparently innocent accomplice in Borachio's machination, though how she could have been so imposed upon, not being unintelligent, is hard to understand. Four important contexts are involved in the problem (II.ii.41–51; III.iii.153–175; IV.i.187–94; V.i. 236–51). Upon the cumulative evidence of these passages it is clear that the guileless Margaret had been induced to dress up in Hero's garments and to be called by Hero's name in a bit of play-acting, the implications of which she cannot have perceived. She should not have been so simple, but the fact remains that she was. There is a crux in Borachio's original outline of the villainy when he tells Don John that Claudio and Don Pedro will "hear me call Margaret Hero, hear Margaret term me Claudio" (II.ii.43–44). Some editors have substituted *Borachio* for *Claudio* in that line, but the change has not been generally adopted. It is idle to wonder why Margaret was not present to witness the repudiation of Hero in the church, or why, hearing of it later, as she could not avoid doing, she did not then explain everything. For Shakespeare had invented the watch to unravel the mystery, and that was that! Margaret is later exonerated in Borachio's confession, and although obviously "at some fault in this," suffers no loss of reputation. Though as a character she is less well developed than Emilia, she is no more consciously guilty in her error than is Iago's wife when she temporarily steals Othello's handkerchief to take a copy of it for her capricious husband.

Hero and Claudio, though the protagonists of the play, are relatively pale and ineffectual characters, by no means so interesting as Benedick and Beatrice, who completely capture one's imagination and affection. Scoffers at love, yet magnetized to each other, sparring at every turn, Benedick and Beatrice are the readiest victims for the Nemesis of Comedy. They are Biron and Rosaline of *Love's Labour's Lost* freed and perfected on a higher plane. Beatrice, though less warm and radiant than some of Shakespeare's women, is one of the most real and lovable of them all.

MUCH ADO ABOUT NOTHING

***

[DRAMATIS PERSONÆ

Don Pedro, *prince of Arragon.*
Don John, *his bastard brother.*
Claudio, *a young lord of Florence.*
Benedick, *a young lord of Padua.*
Leonato, *governor of Messina.*
Antonio, *his brother.*
Balthasar, *esquire to Don Pedro.*
Conrade, } *followers of Don John.*
Borachio, }
Friar Francis.

Dogberry, *a constable.*
Verges, *a headborough.*
A Sexton.
A Boy.

Hero, *daughter to Leonato.*
Beatrice, *niece to Leonato.*
Margaret, } *gentlewomen attending on Hero.*
Ursula, }

Messengers, Watch, Attendants, etc.

Scene: *Messina.*]

ACT I

Scene I. [*Before Leonato's house.*]

Enter Leonato, Hero, *and* Beatrice, *with a* Messenger.

Leon. I learn in this letter that Don Pedro of Arragon comes this night to Messina.

Mess. He is very near by this. He was not three leagues off when I left him.

Leon. How many gentlemen have you lost in 5 this action?

Mess. But few of any sort, and none of name.

Leon. A victory is twice itself when the achiever brings home full numbers. I find here that Don Pedro hath bestowed much honour on a young 10 Florentine called Claudio.

Mess. Much deserv'd on his part and equally rememb'red by Don Pedro. He hath borne himself beyond the promise of his age, doing, in the figure of a lamb, the feats of a lion. He hath indeed better bett'red expectation than you must expect of me to tell you how. 17

Leon. He hath an uncle here in Messina will be very much glad of it. 19

Mess. I have already delivered him letters, and there appears much joy in him; even so much that joy could not show itself modest enough without a badge of bitterness.

Leon. Did he break out into tears?

Mess. In great measure. 25

Leon. A kind overflow of kindness. There are no faces truer than those that are so wash'd. How much better is it to weep at joy than to joy at weeping!

Beat. I pray you, is Signior Mountanto return'd from the wars or no? 31

Mess. I know none of that name, lady. There was none such in the army of any sort.

Leon. What is he that you ask for, niece?

Hero. My cousin means Signior Benedick of 35 Padua.

Mess. O, he's return'd; and as pleasant as ever he was.

Beat. He set up his bills here in Messina and challeng'd Cupid at the flight; and my uncle's 40

***

Act I, sc. i. s.d. *Enter* Leonato. *Enter Leonato... Innogen his wife....* Q Ff. 1. Don Pedro. *Don Peter* Q. 7. sort: rank. name: reputation. 26. kind: natural. 30. Mountanto: an upward cut in fencing. 37. pleasant: facetious. 39. bills: placards. 40. flight: long-range shooting.

fool, reading the challenge, subscrib'd for Cupid, and challeng'd him at the bird-bolt. I pray you, how many hath he kill'd and eaten in these wars? But how many hath he kill'd? for indeed I promised to eat all of his killing.   45

Leon. Faith, niece, you tax Signior Benedick too much; but he'll be meet with you, I doubt it not.

Mess. He hath done good service, lady, in these wars.

Beat. You had musty victual, and he hath 50 holp to eat it. He is a very valiant trencherman; he hath an excellent stomach.

Mess. And a good soldier too, lady.

Beat. And a good soldier to a lady. But what is he to a lord?   55

Mess. A lord to a lord, a man to a man; stuff'd with all honourable virtues.

Beat. It is so, indeed; he is no less than a stuff'd man. But for the stuffing, — well, we are all mortal.   60

Leon. You must not, sir, mistake my niece. There is a kind of merry war betwixt Signior Benedick and her. They never meet but there's a skirmish of wit between them.   64

Beat. Alas! he gets nothing by that. In our last conflict four of his five wits went halting off, and now is the whole man govern'd with one; so that if he have wit enough to keep himself warm, let him bear it for a difference between himself and his horse; for it is all the wealth that he hath left to 70 be known a reasonable creature. Who is his companion now? He hath every month a new sworn brother.

Mess. Is't possible?   74

Beat. Very easily possible. He wears his faith but as the fashion of his hat; it ever changes with the next block.

Mess. I see, lady, the gentleman is not in your books.

Beat. No; an he were, I would burn my study. 80 But, I pray you, who is his companion? Is there no young squarer now that will make a voyage with him to the devil?

Mess. He is most in the company of the right noble Claudio.   85

Beat. O Lord, he will hang upon him like a disease. He is sooner caught than the pestilence, and the taker runs presently mad. God help the noble Claudio! If he have caught the Benedick, it will cost him a thousand pounds ere 'a be cur'd.   90

Mess. I will hold friends with you, lady.

Beat. Do, good friend.

Leon. You will never run mad, niece.

Beat. No, not till a hot January.

Mess. Don Pedro is approach'd.   95

Enter DON PEDRO, CLAUDIO, BENEDICK, BALTHASAR, *and* JOHN *the Bastard.*

D. Pedro. Good Signior Leonato, are you come to meet your trouble? The fashion of the world is to avoid cost, and you encounter it.

Leon. Never came trouble to my house in the likeness of your Grace, for trouble being gone, 100 comfort should remain; but when you depart from me, sorrow abides and happiness takes his leave.

D. Pedro. You embrace your charge too willingly. I think this is your daughter.   104

Leon. Her mother hath many times told me so.

Bene. Were you in doubt, sir, that you ask'd her?

Leon. Signior Benedick, no; for then were you a child.   109

D. Pedro. You have it full, Benedick. We may guess by this what you are, being a man. Truly, the lady fathers herself. Be happy, lady; for you are like an honourable father.

Bene. If Signior Leonato be her father, she would not have his head on her shoulders for all Messina, as like him as she is.   116

Beat. I wonder that you will still be talking, Signior Benedick. Nobody marks you.

Bene. What, my dear Lady Disdain! are you yet living?   120

Beat. Is it possible disdain should die while she hath such meet food to feed it as Signior Benedick? Courtesy itself must convert to disdain, if you come in her presence.   124

Bene. Then is courtesy a turncoat. But it is certain I am loved of all ladies, only you excepted; and I would I could find in my heart that I had not a hard heart, for, truly, I love none.

Beat. A dear happiness to women; they would else have been troubled with a pernicious suitor. I thank God and my cold blood, I am of your 131 humour for that. I had rather hear my dog bark at a crow than a man swear he loves me.

Bene. God keep your ladyship still in that mind! So some gentleman or other shall scape a predestinate scratch'd face.   136

Beat. Scratching could not make it worse, an 'twere such a face as yours were.

Bene. Well, you are a rare parrot-teacher.

Beat. A bird of my tongue is better than a beast of yours.   141

Bene. I would my horse had the speed of your tongue, and so good a continuer. But keep your way, i' God's name; I have done.

Beat. You always end with a jade's trick; I know you of old.   146

---

42. **bird-bolt:** blunt arrow. 47. **meet:** even, quits. 58. **stuff'd man:** dummy. 69. **difference:** a distinguishing symbol in heraldry. 77. **block:** design (hat-mould). 82. **squarer:** quarreler. 103. **charge:** burden. 129. **dear happiness:** great good luck. 145. **jade's trick,** such as slipping its head out of the halter. Evasion.

D. Pedro. That is the sum of all, Leonato. Signior Claudio and Signior Benedick, my dear friend Leonato hath invited you all. I tell him we shall stay here at the least a month; and he heartily prays some occasion may detain us longer. I 151 dare swear he is no hypocrite, but prays from his heart.

Leon. If you swear, my lord, you shall not be forsworn. [*To Don John.*] Let me bid you wel- 155 come, my lord. Being reconciled to the Prince your brother, I owe you all duty.

D. John. I thank you. I am not of many words, but I thank you.

Leon. Please it your Grace lead on? 160

D. Pedro. Your hand, Leonato; we will go together. [*Exeunt all except Benedick and Claudio.*

Claud. Benedick, didst thou note the daughter of Signior Leonato?

Bene. I noted her not; but I look'd on her. 165

Claud. Is she not a modest young lady?

Bene. Do you question me, as an honest man should do, for my simple true judgement; or would you have me speak after my custom, as being a professed tyrant to their sex? 170

Claud. No; I pray thee speak in sober judgement.

Bene. Why, i' faith, methinks she's too low for a high praise, too brown for a fair praise and too little for a great praise; only this commendation I can 175 afford her, that were she other than she is, she were unhandsome; and being no other but as she is, I do not like her.

Claud. Thou thinkest I am in sport. I pray thee tell me truly how thou lik'st her. 180

Bene. Would you buy her, that you inquire after her?

Claud. Can the world buy such a jewel?

Bene. Yea, and a case to put it into. But speak you this with a sad brow, or do you play the 185 flouting Jack, to tell us Cupid is a good hare-finder and Vulcan a rare carpenter? Come, in what key shall a man take you, to go in the song.

Claud. In mine eye she is the sweetest lady that ever I look'd on. 190

Bene. I can see yet without spectacles and I see no such matter. There's her cousin, an she were not possess'd with a fury, exceeds her as much in beauty as the first of May doth the last of December. But I hope you have no intent to turn husband, have you? 196

Claud. I would scarce trust myself, though I had sworn the contrary, if Hero would be my wife.

Bene. Is't come to this? In faith, hath not the

world one man but he will wear his cap with 200 suspicion? Shall I never see a bachelor of three-score again? Go to, i' faith, an thou wilt needs thrust thy neck into a yoke, wear the print of it, and sigh away Sundays. Look! Don Pedro is returned to seek you. 205

Re-enter DON PEDRO.

D. Pedro. What secret hath held you here, that you followed not to Leonato's?

Bene. I would your Grace would constrain me to tell.

D. Pedro. I charge thee on thy allegiance. 210

Bene. You hear, Count Claudio. I can be secret as a dumb man; I would have you think so; but, on my allegiance, mark you this, on my allegiance. He is in love. With who? Now that is your Grace's part. Mark how short his answer is: — With Hero, Leonato's short daughter. 216

Claud. If this were so, so were it utt'red.

Bene. Like the old tale, my lord: "It is not so, nor 'twas not so, but, indeed, God forbid it should be so." 220

Claud. If my passion change not shortly, God forbid it should be otherwise.

D. Pedro. Amen, if you love her; for the lady is very well worthy.

Claud. You speak this to fetch me in, my lord.

D. Pedro. By my troth, I [speak] my thought. 226

Claud. And, in faith, my lord, I spoke mine.

Bene. And, by my two faiths and troths, my lord, I spoke mine.

Claud. That I love her, I feel. 230

D. Pedro. That she is worthy, I know.

Bene. That I neither feel how she should be loved nor know how she should be worthy, is the opinion that fire cannot melt out of me. I will die in it at the stake. 235

D. Pedro. Thou wast ever an obstinate heretic in the despite of beauty.

Claud. And never could maintain his part but in the force of his will. 239

Bene. That a woman conceived me, I thank her; that she brought me up, I likewise give her most humble thanks; but that I will have a recheat winded in my forehead, or hang my bugle in an invisible baldrick, all women shall pardon me. Because I will not do them the wrong to mistrust 245 any, I will do myself the right to trust none; and the fine is, for the which I may go the finer, I will live a bachelor.

D. Pedro. I shall see thee, ere I die, look pale with love. 250

---

156. **Being:** i.e., since you are.   185. **sad:** serious.   186. **flouting Jack:** mocker.   186–87. **'Cupid ... carpenter.** Nonsense; for Cupid was blind and Vulcan was a blacksmith.   200. **wear ... suspicion:** i.e., be suspected of wearing his cap to hide his cuckold's horns.   204. **Sundays,** which one spends with one's wife.   206. s.d. *Re-enter* DON PEDRO. *Enter Don Pedro, John the bastard.* Q Ff.   226. **[speak]** F. *spoke* Q.   237. **despite:** contempt.   242. **recheat:** a call "winded" on a horn to recall the hounds.   244. **baldrick:** belt carrying the horn. The passage is another joke upon the imaginary horns of the cuckold.   247. **fine:** end.   **go the finer:** wear finer clothes.

Bene. With anger, with sickness, or with hunger, my lord, not with love. Prove that ever I lose more blood with love than I will get again with drinking, pick out mine eyes with a ballad-maker's pen and hang me up at the door of a brothel-house for the sign of blind Cupid.   256

D. Pedro. Well, if ever thou dost fall from this faith, thou wilt prove a notable argument.

Bene. If I do, hang me in a bottle like a cat and shoot at me; and he that hits me, let him be clapp'd on the shoulder, and called Adam.   261

D. Pedro. Well, as time shall try.
"In time the savage bull doth bear the yoke."

Bene. The savage bull may; but if ever the sensible Benedick bear it, pluck off the bull's horns 265 and set them in my forehead; and let me be vilely painted, and in such great letters as they write "Here is good horse to hire," let them signify under my sign, "Here you may see Benedick the married man."   270

Claud. If this should ever happen, thou wouldst be horn-mad.

D. Pedro. Nay, if Cupid have not spent all his quiver in Venice, thou wilt quake for this shortly.

Bene. I look for an earthquake too, then.   275

D. Pedro. Well, you will temporize with the hours. In the meantime, good Signior Benedick, repair to Leonato's; commend me to him, and tell him I will not fail him at supper; for indeed he hath made great preparation.   280

Bene. I have almost matter enough in me for such an embassage; and so I commit you —

Claud. To the tuition of God. From my house, if I had it, —

D. Pedro. The sixth of July. Your loving friend, Benedick.   286

Bene. Nay, mock not, mock not. The body of your discourse is sometime guarded with fragments, and the guards are but slightly basted on neither. Ere you flout old ends any further, examine your conscience; and so I leave you.   [*Exit.* 291

Claud. My liege, your Highness now may do me good.

D. Pedro. My love is thine to teach; teach it but how,
And thou shalt see how apt it is to learn
Any hard lesson that may do thee good.   295

Claud. Hath Leonato any son, my lord?

D. Pedro. No child but Hero; she's his only heir.
Dost thou affect her, Claudio?

Claud.   O, my lord,

When you went onward on this ended action,
I look'd upon her with a soldier's eye,   300
That lik'd, but had a rougher task in hand
Than to drive liking to the name of love.
But now I am return'd and that war-thoughts
Have left their places vacant, in their rooms
Come thronging soft and delicate desires,   305
All prompting me how fair young Hero is,
Saying, I lik'd her ere I went to wars.

D. Pedro. Thou wilt be like a lover presently
And tire the hearer with a book of words.
If thou dost love fair Hero, cherish it,   310
And I will break with her and with her father
And thou shalt have her. Was 't not to this end
That thou began'st to twist so fine a story?

Claud. How sweetly you do minister to love,
That know love's grief by his complexion!   315
But lest my liking might too sudden seem,
I would have salv'd it with a longer treatise.

D. Pedro. What need the bridge much broader than the flood?
The fairest grant is the necessity.
Look, what will serve is fit: 'tis once, thou lovest,
And I will fit thee with the remedy.   321
I know we shall have revelling to-night.
I will assume thy part in some disguise
And tell fair Hero I am Claudio.
And in her bosom I'll unclasp my heart   325
And take her hearing prisoner with the force
And strong encounter of my amorous tale;
Then after to her father will I break;
And the conclusion is, she shall be thine.
In practice let us put it presently.   [*Exeunt.* 330

[SCENE II. *A room in Leonato's house.*]

Enter LEONATO *and* ANTONIO, *meeting.*

Leon. How now, brother! Where is my cousin, your son? Hath he provided this music?

Ant. He is very busy about it. But, brother, I can tell you strange news that you yet dreamt not of.   5

Leon. Are they good?

Ant. As the event stamps them; but they have a good cover, they show well outward. The Prince and Count Claudio, walking in a thick-pleached alley in mine orchard, were thus much over- 10 heard by a man of mine. The Prince discovered to Claudio that he loved my niece your daughter and meant to acknowledge it this night in a dance; and if he found her accordant, he meant to take the

252–54. **I...drinking.** It was believed that every sigh cost the heart a drop of blood and that wine generated blood. 259. **bottle:** wicker basket. 261. **Adam:** Adam Bell, an archer celebrated in ballads. 263. **"In...yoke."** Quoted inaccurately from Kyd's *Spanish Tragedy* (II.i.3). 274. **Venice.** Then notorious for licentiousness. 276. **temporize... hours:** surrender eventually. 281. **matter:** sense. 283. **tuition:** protection. 288. **guarded:** trimmed. 298. **affect:** love. 311. **break:** open the subject. 319. **The...necessity.** The best gift is the one which is required. 320. **'tis once:** briefly. **Sc. ii.** S.D. *Enter Leonato and an old man brother to Leonato* Q. Q heads Antonio's speeches *Old.* 1. **cousin.** Used loosely for *relative.* 7. **event:** outcome. 9. **pleached:** with intertwined boughs. 14. **accordant:** agreeing.

present time by the top and instantly break with you of it.   16

Leon. Hath the fellow any wit that told you this?

Ant. A good sharp fellow. I will send for him; and question him yourself.   20

Leon. No, no; we will hold it as a dream till it appear itself; but I will acquaint my daughter withal, that she may be the better prepared for an answer, if peradventure this be true. Go you and tell her of it. [*Several persons cross the stage.*] Cousin, you know what you have to do. O, I cry 26 you mercy, friend; go you with me, and I will use your skill. Good cousin, have a care this busy time.

[*Exeunt.*

[SCENE III. *The same.*]

Enter JOHN *the Bastard and* CONRADE.

Con. What the good-year, my lord! Why are you thus out of measure sad?

D. John. There is no measure in the occasion that breeds; therefore the sadness is without limit.

Con. You should hear reason.   6

D. John. And when I have heard it, what blessing brings it?

Con. If not a present remedy, at least a patient sufferance.   10

D. John. I wonder that thou, being, as thou say'st thou art, born under Saturn, goest about to apply a moral medicine to a mortifying mischief. I cannot hide what I am. I must be sad when I have cause, and smile at no man's jests; eat 15 when I have stomach, and wait for no man's leisure; sleep when I am drowsy, and tend on no man's business; laugh when I am merry, and claw no man in his humour.   19

Con. Yea, but you must not make the full show of this till you may do it without controlment. You have of late stood out against your brother, and he hath ta'en you newly into his grace; where it is impossible you should take true root but by the fair weather that you make yourself. It is 25 needful that you frame the season for your own harvest.

D. John. I had rather be a canker in a hedge than a rose in his grace, and it better fits my blood to be disdain'd of all than to fashion a carriage 30 to rob love from any. In this, though I cannot be said to be a flattering honest man, it must not be denied but I am a plain-dealing villain. I am trusted with a muzzle and enfranchis'd with a clog; therefore I have decreed not to sing in my cage. 35

If I had my mouth, I would bite; if I had my liberty, I would do my liking. In the meantime let me be that I am and seek not to alter me.

Con. Can you make no use of your discontent?

D. John. I make all use of it, for I use it only. 41 Who comes here?

Enter BORACHIO.

What news, Borachio?

Bora. I came yonder from a great supper. The Prince your brother is royally entertain'd by Leonato; and I can give you intelligence of an intended marriage.   47

D. John. Will it serve for any model to build mischief on? What is he for a fool that betroths himself to unquietness?   50

Bora. Marry, it is your brother's right hand.

D. John. Who? The most exquisite Claudio?

Bora. Even he.

D. John. A proper squire! And who, and who? Which way looks he?   55

Bora. Marry, one Hero, the daughter and heir of Leonato.

D. John. A very forward March-chick! How came you to this?   59

Bora. Being entertain'd for a perfumer, as I was smoking a musty room, comes me the Prince and Claudio, hand in hand, in sad conference. I whipt me behind the arras, and there heard it agreed upon that the Prince should woo Hero for himself, and having obtain'd her, give her to Count 65 Claudio.

D. John. Come, come, let us thither; this may prove food to my displeasure. That young startup hath all the glory of my overthrow. If I can cross him any way, I bless myself every way. You are both sure, and will assist me?   71

Con. To the death, my lord.

D. John. Let us to the great supper; their cheer is the greater that I am subdued. Would the cook were o' my mind! Shall we go prove what's to be done?   76

Bora. We'll wait upon your lordship. [*Exeunt.*

ACT II

[SCENE I. *A hall in Leonato's house.*]

Enter LEONATO, ANTONIO, HERO, BEATRICE, *and a kinsman.*

Leon. Was not Count John here at supper?

Ant. I saw him not.

15. **top:** forelock. 26. **cry you mercy:** beg pardon.
Sc. iii, 1. **What the good-year.** An expletive. 12. **Saturn.** Nativity under the domination of the planet Saturn was supposed to give one a morose disposition. 13. **mortifying mischief:** deadly disease. 18. **claw:** flatter. 28. **canker:** dog-rose. 30. **carriage:** behavior. 54. **proper:** fine. 58. **March-chick:** chicken prematurely hatched. 60. **entertain'd for:** employed as. 61. **smoking:** fumigating. 70. **cross:** thwart (with quibbling reference to making the sign of the cross). 71. **sure:** trustworthy.
Act II, sc. i. S.D. Q and F read *Enter Leonato, his brother, his wife, Hero his daughter, and Beatrice his neece, and a kinsman.*

Beat. How tartly that gentleman looks! I never can see him but I am heart-burn'd an hour after. 5

Hero. He is of a very melancholy disposition.

Beat. He were an excellent man that were made just in the midway between him and Benedick. The one is too like an image and says nothing, and the other too like my lady's eldest son, evermore tattling. 11

Leon. Then half Signior Benedick's tongue in Count John's mouth and half Count John's melancholy in Signior Benedick's face, — 14

Beat. With a good leg and a good foot, uncle, and money enough in his purse, such a man would win any woman in the world, if 'a could get her good-will.

Leon. By my troth, niece, thou wilt never get thee a husband, if thou be so shrewd of thy tongue.

Ant. In faith, she's too curst. 22

Beat. Too curst is more than curst. I shall lessen God's sending that way; for it is said, "God sends a curst cow short horns;" but to a cow too curst he sends none. 26

Leon. So, by being too curst, God will send you no horns.

Beat. Just, if he send me no husband; for the which blessing I am at him upon my knees every morning and evening. Lord, I could not en- 30 dure a husband with a beard on his face! I had rather lie in the woollen.

Leon. You may light on a husband that hath no beard. 35

Beat. What should I do with him? Dress him in my apparel and make him my waiting-gentlewoman? He that hath a beard is more than a youth, and he that hath no beard is less than a man; and he that is more than a youth is not for me, 40 and he that is less than a man, I am not for him; therefore I will even take sixpence in earnest of the bear-'ard, and lead his apes into hell.

Leon. Well, then, go you into hell? 44

Beat. No, but to the gate; and there will the devil meet me, like an old cuckold, with horns on his head, and say, "Get you to heaven, Beatrice, get you to heaven; here's no place for you maids:" so deliver I up my apes, and away to Saint Peter for the heavens. He shows me where the bachelors sit, and there live we as merry as the day is long. 52

Ant. [*To Hero.*] Well, niece, I trust you will be rul'd by your father. 54

Beat. Yes, faith; it is my cousin's duty to make curtsy and say, "[Father], as it please you." But yet for all that, cousin, let him be a handsome fellow, or else make another curtsy and say, "Father, as it please me." 59

Leon. Well, niece, I hope to see you one day fitted with a husband.

Beat. Not till God make men of some other metal than earth. Would it not grieve a woman to be overmaster'd with a piece of valiant dust? to make an account of her life to a clod of way- 65 ward marl? No, uncle, I'll none. Adam's sons are my brethren; and, truly, I hold it a sin to match in my kindred.

Leon. Daughter, remember what I told you. If the Prince do solicit you in that kind, you know your answer. 71

Beat. The fault will be in the music, cousin, if you be not woo'd in good time. If the Prince be too important, tell him there is measure in every thing and so dance out the answer. For, hear me, 75 Hero: wooing, wedding, and repenting, is as a Scotch jig, a measure, and a cinque pace; the first suit is hot and hasty, like a Scotch jig, and full as fantastical; the wedding, mannerly-modest, as a measure, full of state and ancientry; and then 80 comes repentance and, with his bad legs, falls into the cinque pace faster and faster, till he sink into his grave.

Leon. Cousin, you apprehend passing shrewdly.

Beat. I have a good eye, uncle; I can see a church by daylight. 86

Leon. The revellers are ent'ring, brother; make good room. [*Antonio masks.*]

Enter Don Pedro, Claudio, Benedick, *and* Balthasar, [Borachio, Margaret, Ursula, *and others*], Don John *masked; with a drum.*

D. Pedro. Lady, will you walk about with your friend? 90

Hero. So you walk softly and look sweetly and say nothing, I am yours for the walk; and especially when I walk away.

D. Pedro. With me in your company?

Hero. I may say so when I please. 95

D. Pedro. And when please you to say so?

Hero. When I like your favour; for God defend the lute should be like the case!

D. Pedro. My visor is Philemon's roof; within the house is Jove. 100

Hero. Why, then, your visor should be thatch'd.

D. Pedro. Speak low, if you speak love.

[*Drawing her aside.*]

10. **eldest son:** a spoiled child. 21. **shrewd:** shrewish, sharp. 22. **curst:** ill-tempered. 32. **lie ... woollen:** sleep between blankets. 42. **earnest:** advance payment. 43. **lead ... hell.** The punishment for dying an old maid. 51. **bachelors:** the unmarried of both sexes. 56. **[Father]** (Theobald). Om. QF. 66. **marl:** clay. 74. **important:** importunate. 77. **measure:** slow dance. **cinque pace:** lively dance. 80. **ancientry:** antique style. 88. s.d. Q and F read *Enter Prince, Pedro, Claudio, and Benedicke, and Balthasar, or dumbe John;* F adds *Maskers with a drum.* 89. **about.** Some modern editors read *a bout.* 90. **friend:** lover. 97. **favour:** face. 99. **visor:** mask. **Philemon's roof.** Jupiter was once entertained *incognito* by the peasants, Baucis and Philemon.

[Balth.] Well, I would you did like me.

Marg. So would not I, for your own sake; 105
for I have many ill qualities.

[Balth.] Which is one?

Marg. I say my prayers aloud.

[Balth.] I love you the better; the hearers may
cry, Amen. 110

Marg. God match me with a good dancer!

[Balth.] Amen.

Marg. And God keep him out of my sight when
the dance is done! Answer, clerk.

Balth. No more words; the clerk is answered. 115

Urs. I know you well enough; you are Signior
Antonio.

Ant. At a word I am not.

Urs. I know you by the waggling of your head.

Ant. To tell you true, I counterfeit him. 121

Urs. You could never do him so ill-well, unless
you were the very man. Here's his dry hand up
and down. You are he, you are he.

Ant. At a word, I am not. 125

Urs. Come, come, do you think I do not know
you by your excellent wit? Can virtue hide itself? Go to, mum, you are he. Graces will appear,
and there's an end.

Beat. Will you not tell me who told you so? 130

Bene. No, you shall pardon me.

Beat. Nor will you not tell me who you are?

Bene. Not now.

Beat. That I was disdainful, and that I had my
good wit out of the "Hundred Merry Tales": —
well, this was Signior Benedick that said so. 136

Bene. What's he?

Beat. I am sure you know him well enough.

Bene. Not I, believe me.

Beat. Did he never make you laugh? 140

Bene. I pray you, what is he?

Beat. Why, he is the Prince's jester, a very dull
fool; only his gift is in devising impossible slanders.
None but libertines delight in him, and the commendation is not in his wit but in his villainy; 145
for he both pleases men and angers them, and then
they laugh at him and beat him. I am sure he is in
the fleet; I would he had boarded me.

Bene. When I know the gentleman, I'll tell him
what you say. 151

Beat. Do, do: he'll but break a comparison or
two on me; which, peradventure not mark'd or not
laugh'd at, strikes him into melancholy; and then
there's a partridge wing saved, for the fool will 155
eat no supper that night. *[Music.]* We must follow
the leaders.

Bene. In every good thing.

Beat. Nay, if they lead to any ill, I will leave
them at the next turning. 160

    [Dance. [Then] exeunt [all except Don John,
    Borachio, and Claudio].

D. John. Sure my brother is amorous on Hero
and hath withdrawn her father to break with him
about it. The ladies follow her and but one visor
remains.

Bora. And that is Claudio. I know him by his
bearing. 166

D. John. Are not you Signior Benedick?

Claud. You know me well; I am he.

D. John. Signior, you are very near my brother
in his love. He is enamour'd on Hero. I pray you,
dissuade him from her; she is no equal for his 171
birth. You may do the part of an honest man in it.

Claud. How know you he loves her?

D. John. I heard him swear his affection. 175

Bora. So did I too; and he swore he would marry
her to-night.

D. John. Come, let us to the banquet.

    [Exeunt Don John and Borachio.

Claud. Thus answer I in name of Benedick,
But hear these ill news with the ears of Claudio. 180
'Tis certain so; the Prince wooes for himself.
Friendship is constant in all other things
Save in the office and affairs of love;
Therefore all hearts in love use their own tongues.
Let every eye negotiate for itself 185
And trust no agent; for beauty is a witch
Against whose charms faith melteth into blood.
This is an accident of hourly proof,
Which I mistrusted not. Farewell, therefore, Hero!

    Re-enter BENEDICK.

Bene. Count Claudio? 190

Claud. Yea, the same.

Bene. Come, will you go with me?

Claud. Whither?

Bene. Even to the next willow, about your own
business, county. What fashion will you wear 195
the garland of? About your neck like an usurer's
chain, or under your arm like a lieutenant's scarf?
You must wear it one way, for the Prince hath got
your Hero.

Claud. I wish him joy of her. 200

Bene. Why, that's spoken like an honest drovier;
so they sell bullocks. But did you think the Prince
would have served you thus?

Claud. I pray you, leave me. 204

Bene. Ho! now you strike like the blind man.

104, 107, 109, 112. **[Balth.]** (Theobald). *Bene.* QFf. 114. **clerk.** The parish clerk read the responses in church. (Cf.
"Amen," ll. 110 and 112.) 122. **do...ill-well:** imitate his defects so well. 123. **dry hand.** A sign of age. 135.
"Hundred Merry Tales": a popular collection of coarse stories. 143. **only his gift:** his only talent. 148. **fleet:** i.e.,
company. **boarded:** accosted. 178. **banquet:** dessert. 187. **blood:** passion. 188. **accident:** happening. 194. **willow.**
Emblem of unrequited love.

'Twas the boy that stole your meat, and you'll beat the post.

Claud. If it will not be, I'll leave you.   [*Exit.*

Bene. Alas, poor hurt fowl! now will he creep into sedges. But that my Lady Beatrice should know me, and not know me! The Prince's 210 fool! Ha? It may be I go under that title because I am merry. Yea, but so I am apt to do myself wrong. I am not so reputed. It is the base (though bitter) disposition of Beatrice that puts the 215 world into her person, and so gives me out. Well, I'll be revenged as I may.

Re-enter DON PEDRO.

D. Pedro. Now, signior, where's the count? Did you see him?   219

Bene. Troth, my lord, I have played the part of Lady Fame. I found him here as melancholy as a lodge in a warren. I told him, and I think I told him true, that your Grace had got the good will of this young lady; and I off'red him my company to a willow-tree, either to make him a garland, as 225 being forsaken, or to bind him up a rod, as being worthy to be whipp'd.

D. Pedro. To be whipp'd! What's his fault?

Bene. The flat transgression of a school-boy, who, being overjoyed with finding a birds' nest, shows it his companion, and he steals it.   231

D. Pedro. Wilt thou make a trust a transgression? The transgression is in the stealer.

Bene. Yet it had not been amiss the rod had been made, and the garland too; for the garland he might have worn himself, and the rod he 236 might have bestowed on you, who, as I take it, have stol'n his birds' nest.

D. Pedro. I will but teach them to sing, and restore them to the owner.   240

Bene. If their singing answer your saying, by my faith, you say honestly.

D. Pedro. The Lady Beatrice hath a quarrel to you. The gentleman that danc'd with her told her she is much wrong'd by you.   245

Bene. O, she misus'd me past the endurance of a block! An oak but with one green leaf on it would have answered her. My very visor began to assume life and scold with her. She told me, not thinking I had been myself, that I was the 250 Prince's jester, that I was duller than a great thaw; huddling jest upon jest with such impossible conveyance upon me that I stood like a man at a mark, with a whole army shooting at me. She speaks poniards, and every word stabs. If her breath 255

were as terrible as her terminations, there were no living near her; she would infect to the north star. I would not marry her, though she were endowed with all that Adam had left him before he transgress'd. She would have made Hercules have 260 turn'd spit, yea, and have cleft his club to make the fire too. Come, talk not of her; you shall find her the infernal Ate in good apparel. I would to God some scholar would conjure her; for certainly while she is here, a man may live as quiet in hell as in 265 a sanctuary, and people sin upon purpose, because they would go thither; so, indeed, all disquiet, horror, and perturbation follows her.

Enter CLAUDIO, BEATRICE, HERO, *and* LEONATO.

D. Pedro. Look, here she comes.   270

Bene. Will your Grace command me any service to the world's end? I will go on the slightest errand now to the Antipodes that you can devise to send me on; I will fetch you a toothpicker now from the furthest inch of Asia, bring you the length of 275 Prester John's foot, fetch you a hair off the great Cham's beard, do you any embassage to the Pigmies, rather than hold three words' conference with this harpy. You have no employment for me?   280

D. Pedro. None, but to desire your good company.

Bene. O God, sir, here's a dish I love not. I cannot endure my Lady Tongue.   [*Exit.*

D. Pedro. Come, lady, come; you have lost the heart of Signior Benedick.   286

Beat. Indeed, my lord, he lent it me awhile; and I gave him use for it, a double heart for his single one. Marry, once before he won it of me with false dice, therefore your Grace may well say I have lost it.   291

D. Pedro. You have put him down, lady, you have put him down.

Beat. So I would not he should do me, my lord, lest I should prove the mother of fools. I have brought Count Claudio, whom you sent me to seek.   297

D. Pedro. Why, how now, count! wherefore are you sad?

Claud. Not sad, my lord.   300

D. Pedro. How then? Sick?

Claud. Neither, my lord.

Beat. The count is neither sad, nor sick, nor merry, nor well; but civil count, civil as an orange, and something of that jealous complexion.   306

D. Pedro. I' faith, lady, I think your blazon to be true; though, I'll be sworn, if he be so, his conceit

209. **sedges:** rushes.   213. **though.** Not satisfactorily explained.   221. **Fame:** Rumor.   222. **lodge in a warren:** keeper's house in a game preserve, presumably a solitary place.   252. **impossible conveyance:** incredible adroitness.   253. **mark:** target.   256. **terminations:** terms, words.   263. **Ate:** goddess of discord.   264. **conjure her:** i.e., conjure the evil spirit out of her.   276. **Prester John:** a mythical eastern king.   **the great Cham:** the Mongolian Khan.   288. **use:** interest.   304. **civil:** serious, with a pun on *Seville.*   306. **jealous complexion:** i.e., yellow, a conventional token of jealousy.   307. **blazon:** description.   308. **conceit:** idea.

is false. Here, Claudio, I have wooed in thy name, and fair Hero is won. I have broke with her father, and his good will obtained. Name the day of marriage, and God give thee joy!   312

Leon. Count, take of me my daughter, and with her my fortunes. His Grace hath made the match, and all grace say Amen to it.   315

Beat. Speak, Count, 'tis your cue.

Claud. Silence is the perfectest herald of joy; I were but little happy, if I could say how much. Lady, as you are mine, I am yours. I give away myself for you and dote upon the exchange.   320

Beat. Speak, cousin; or, if you cannot, stop his mouth with a kiss, and let not him speak neither.

D. Pedro. In faith, lady, you have a merry heart.   325

Beat. Yea, my lord; I thank it, poor fool, it keeps on the windy side of care. My cousin tells him in his ear that he is in her heart.

Claud. And so she doth, cousin.   329

Beat. Good Lord, for alliance! Thus goes every one to the world but I, and I am sunburnt. I may sit in a corner and cry "Heigh-ho for a husband!"

D. Pedro. Lady Beatrice, I will get you one.

Beat. I would rather have one of your father's getting. Hath your Grace ne'er a brother like   335 you? Your father got excellent husbands, if a maid could come by them.

D. Pedro. Will you have me, lady?

Beat. No, my lord, unless I might have an-   340 other for working-days. Your Grace is too costly to wear every day. But, I beseech your Grace, pardon me; I was born to speak all mirth and no matter.   344

D. Pedro. Your silence most offends me, and to be merry best becomes you; for, out o' question, you were born in a merry hour.

Beat. No, sure, my lord, my mother cried; but then there was a star danc'd, and under that was I born. Cousins, God give you joy!   350

Leon. Niece, will you look to those things I told you of?

Beat. I cry you mercy, uncle. By your Grace's pardon.   [*Exit.*

D. Pedro. By my troth, a pleasant-spirited lady.   356

Leon. There's little of the melancholy element in her, my lord. She is never sad but when she sleeps, and not ever sad then; for I have heard my daughter say, she hath often dreamt of unhappiness and wak'd herself with laughing.   361

D. Pedro. She cannot endure to hear tell of a husband.

Leon. O, by no means; she mocks all her wooers out of suit.   365

D. Pedro. She were an excellent wife for Benedick.

Leon. O Lord, my lord, if they were but a week married, they would talk themselves mad.

D. Pedro. County Claudio, when mean you to go to church?   371

Claud. To-morrow, my lord. Time goes on crutches till love have all his rites.

Leon. Not till Monday, my dear son, which is hence a just seven-night; and a time too brief, too, to have all things answer my mind.   376

D. Pedro. Come, you shake the head at so long a breathing; but, I warrant thee, Claudio, the time shall not go dully by us. I will in the interim undertake one of Hercules' labours; which is, to   380 bring Signior Benedick and the Lady Beatrice into a mountain of affection the one with the other. I would fain have it a match, and I doubt not but to fashion it, if you three will but minister such assistance as I shall give you direction.   386

Leon. My lord, I am for you, though it cost me ten nights' watchings.

Claud. And I, my lord.

D. Pedro. And you too, gentle Hero?

Hero. I will do any modest office, my lord, to help my cousin to a good husband.   391

D. Pedro. And Benedick is not the unhopefullest husband that I know. Thus far can I praise him: he is of a noble strain, of approved valour, and confirm'd honesty. I will teach you how to   395 humour your cousin, that she shall fall in love with Benedick; and I, with your two helps, will so practise on Benedick that, in despite of his quick wit and his queasy stomach, he shall fall in love with Beatrice. If we can do this, Cupid is no   400 longer an archer. His glory shall be ours, for we are the only love-gods. Go in with me, and I will tell you my drift.   [*Exeunt.*

[SCENE II.   *The same.*]

Enter [DON] JOHN *and* BORACHIO.

D. John. It is so; the Count Claudio shall marry the daughter of Leonato.

Bora. Yea, my lord; but I can cross it.

D. John. Any bar, any cross, any impediment will be med'cinable to me. I am sick in displeas-   5 ure to him, and whatsoever comes athwart his af-

---

327. **windy:** windward (i.e., safe). 330–31. **goes . . . world:** i.e., gets married. 331. **sunburnt:** i.e., unattractive. 332–33. "**Heigh-ho . . . husband.**" The title of a ballad. 359. **ever:** always. It has been suggested to emend to *even*. 378. **breathing:** waiting. 388. **watchings:** i.e., lying awake. 394. **strain:** lineage. **approved:** tested. 399. **queasy stomach:** squeamishness. 403. **drift:** scheme.

fection ranges evenly with mine. How canst thou cross this marriage?

Bora. Not honestly, my lord; but so covertly that no dishonesty shall appear in me.   10

D. John. Show me briefly how.

Bora. I think I told your lordship a year since, how much I am in the favour of Margaret, the waiting gentlewoman to Hero.

D. John. I remember.   15

Bora. I can, at any unseasonable instant of the night, appoint her to look out at her lady's chamber-window.

D. John. What life is in that, to be the death of this marriage?   20

Bora. The poison of that lies in you to temper. Go you to the Prince your brother; spare not to tell him that he hath wronged his honour in marrying the renowned Claudio — whose estimation do you mightily hold up — to a contaminated stale, such a one as Hero.   26

D. John. What proof shall I make of that?

Bora. Proof enough to misuse the Prince, to vex Claudio, to undo Hero, and kill Leonato. Look you for any other issue?   30

D. John. Only to despite them, I will endeavour anything.

Bora. Go, then; find me a meet hour to draw Don Pedro and the Count Claudio alone; tell them that you know that Hero loves me; intend a   35 kind of zeal both to the Prince and Claudio, as, — in love of your brother's honour, who hath made this match, and his friend's reputation, who is thus like to be cozen'd with the semblance of a maid, — that you have discover'd thus. They will   40 scarcely believe this without trial. Offer them instances; which shall bear no less likelihood than to see me at her chamber-window, hear me call Margaret Hero, hear Margaret term me Claudio; and bring them to see this the very night before   45 the intended wedding, — for in the meantime I will so fashion the matter that Hero shall be absent, — and there shall appear such seeming truth of Hero's disloyalty, that jealousy shall be call'd assurance and all the preparation overthrown.   51

D. John. Grow this to what adverse issue it can, I will put it in practice. Be cunning in the working this, and thy fee is a thousand ducats.

Bora. Be you constant in the accusation, and my cunning shall not shame me.   56

D. John. I will presently go learn their day of marriage.   [*Exeunt.*

[SCENE III. *Leonato's orchard.*]

Enter BENEDICK *alone.*

Bene. Boy!

[*Enter* BOY.]

Boy. Signior?

Bene. In my chamber-window lies a book; bring it hither to me in the orchard.

Boy. I am here already, sir.   [*Exit.* 5

Bene. I know that; but I would have thee hence, and here again. I do much wonder that one man, seeing how much another man is a fool when he dedicates his behaviours to love, will, after he hath laugh'd at such shallow follies in others, become   10 the argument of his own scorn by falling in love; and such a man is Claudio. I have known when there was no music with him but the drum and the fife; and now had he rather hear the tabor and the pipe. I have known when he would have   15 walk'd ten mile a-foot to see a good armour; and now will he lie ten nights awake, carving the fashion of a new doublet. He was wont to speak plain and to the purpose, like an honest man and a soldier; and now is he turn'd orthography; his   20 words are a very fantastical banquet, just so many strange dishes. May I be so converted and see with these eyes? I cannot tell; I think not. I will not be sworn but love may transform me to an oyster; but I'll take my oath on it, till he have   26 made an oyster of me, he shall never make me such a fool. One woman is fair, yet I am well; another is wise, yet I am well; another virtuous, yet I am well; but till all graces be in one woman, one   30 woman shall not come in my grace. Rich she shall be, that's certain; wise, or I'll none; virtuous, or I'll never cheapen her; fair, or I'll never look on her; mild, or come not near me; noble, or not I for an angel; of good discourse, an excellent mu-   35 sician, and her hair shall be of what colour it please God. Ha! the Prince and Monsieur Love! I will hide me in the arbour.   [*Withdraws.*

Enter DON PEDRO, CLAUDIO, *and* LEONATO. *Music [within].*

D. Pedro. Come, shall we hear this music?

Claud. Yea, my good lord. How still the evening is,   40 As hush'd on purpose to grace harmony!

D. Pedro. See you where Benedick hath hid himself?

Claud. O, very well, my lord. The music ended, We'll fit the kid-fox with a pennyworth.

Sc. ii, 21. **temper:** mix. 25. **stale:** harlot. 35. **intend:** pretend. 39. **cozen'd:** cheated. 41. **instances:** proofs. 44. **hear...Claudio.** See Introduction. Some edd. read *Borachio* for *Claudio.* 50. **jealousy:** suspicion.

Sc. iii, 14. **tabor:** small drum. 17. **carving:** planning. 20. **turn'd orthography:** i.e., become a faddist in language. 33. **cheapen:** ask the price of. 34-5. **noble...angel.** Both words, names of coins (worth 6s.8d. and 10s. respectively), are used punningly. 39. s.d. **Music [within].** *Musicke* Q; *and Iacke Wilson* Ff. See Introduction.

Enter BALTHASAR *with music.*

D. Pedro. Come, Balthasar, we'll hear that song
again.   45
Balth. O, good my lord, tax not so bad a voice
To slander music any more than once.
D. Pedro. It is the witness still of excellency
To put a strange face on his own perfection.
I pray thee, sing, and let me woo no more.   50
Balth. Because you talk of wooing, I will sing;
Since many a wooer doth commence his suit
To her he thinks not worthy, yet he wooes,
Yet will he swear he loves.
D. Pedro.   Now, pray thee, come;
Or, if thou wilt hold longer argument,   55
Do it in notes.
Balth.   Note this before my notes;
There's not a note of mine that's worth the noting.
D. Pedro. Why, these are very crotchets that he
speaks;
Note, notes, forsooth, and nothing.   [*Air.*]
Bene. Now, divine air! now is his soul rav- 60
ish'd! Is it not strange that sheeps' guts should
hale souls out of men's bodies? Well, a horn for
my money, when all's done.

THE SONG

[*Balth.*] Sigh no more, ladies, sigh no more,
    Men were deceivers ever,   65
One foot in sea and one on shore,
    To one thing constant never.
Then sigh not so, but let them go,
    And be you blithe and bonny,
Converting all your sounds of woe   70
    Into Hey nonny nonny.

Sing no more ditties, sing no moe,
    Of dumps so dull and heavy;
The fraud of men was ever so,
    Since summer first was leafy.   75
    Then sigh not so, etc.

D. Pedro. By my troth, a good song.
Balth. And an ill singer, my lord.
D. Pedro. Ha, no, no, faith; thou sing'st well
enough for a shift.   80
Bene. An he had been a dog that should have
howl'd thus, they would have hang'd him; and
I pray God his bad voice bode no mischief. I had
as lief have heard the night-raven, come what
plague could have come after it.   85
D. Pedro. Yea, marry; dost thou hear, Balthasar?
I pray thee, get us some excellent music; for to-
morrow night we would have it at the Lady Hero's
chamber-window.

Balth. The best I can, my lord.   90
                                    [*Exit Balthasar.*
D. Pedro. Do so; farewell. Come hither, Leonato. What was it you told me of to-day, that
your niece Beatrice was in love with Signior Benedick?
Claud. [*Aside.*] O, ay, stalk on, stalk on; the
fowl sits. — I did never think that lady would 95
have loved any man.
Leon. No, nor I neither; but most wonderful
that she should so dote on Signior Benedick, whom
she hath in all outward behaviours seemed ever
to abhor.   101
Bene. Is't possible? Sits the wind in that
corner?
Leon. By my troth, my lord, I cannot tell what
to think of it but that she loves him with an enraged affection. It is past the infinite of 105
thought.
D. Pedro. May be she doth but counterfeit.
Claud. Faith, like enough.
Leon. O God, counterfeit! There was never
counterfeit of passion came so near the life of passion as she discovers it.   111
D. Pedro. Why, what effects of passion shows
she?
Claud. [*Aside.*] Bait the hook well; this fish will
bite.
Leon. What effects, my lord? She will sit 115
you, — you heard my daughter tell you how.
Claud. She did, indeed.
D. Pedro. How, how, I pray you? You amaze
me; I would have thought her spirit had been in-
vincible against all assaults of affection.   120
Leon. I would have sworn it had, my lord; es-
pecially against Benedick.
Bene. I should think this a gull, but that the
white-bearded fellow speaks it. Knavery cannot,
sure, hide himself in such reverence.   125
Claud. [*Aside.*] He hath ta'en th' infection.
Hold it up.
D. Pedro. Hath she made her affection known to
Benedick?
Leon. No; and swears she never will. That's
her torment.   130
Claud. 'Tis true, indeed; so your daughter says.
"Shall I," says she, "that have so oft encount'red
him with scorn, write to him that I love him?"
Leon. This says she now when she is begin- 135
ning to write to him; for she'll be up twenty times a
night, and there will she sit in her smock till she
have writ a sheet of paper. My daughter tells us
all.   139
Claud. Now you talk of a sheet of paper, I re-
member a pretty jest your daughter told [us of].

58. **crotchets:** (1) whims, (2) musical notes. 59. **nothing:** i.e., with a pun on *noting* (l. 57). 80. **shift:** makeshift. 105.
enraged: violent. 111. **discovers:** shows. 123. **gull:** trick. 127. **Hold:** keep. 141. **[us of]** F. *of us* Q.

Leon. O, when she had writ it and was reading it over, she found Benedick and Beatrice between the sheet?

Claud. That.   145

Leon. O, she tore the letter into a thousand half-pence; railed at herself, that she should be so immodest to write to one that she knew would flout her. "I measure him," says she, "by my own spirit; for I should flout him, if he writ to me; yea, though I love him, I should."   151

Claud. Then down upon her knees she falls, weeps, sobs, beats her heart, tears her hair, prays, curses; "O sweet Benedick! God give me patience!"   155

Leon. She doth indeed, my daughter says so; and the ecstasy hath so much overborne her that my daughter is sometime afeard she will do a desperate outrage to herself. It is very true.

D. Pedro. It were good that Benedick knew of it by some other, if she will not discover it.   161

Claud. To what end? He would make but a sport of it and torment the poor lady worse.

D. Pedro. An he should, it were an alms to hang him. She's an excellent sweet lady; and, out of all suspicion, she is virtuous.   166

Claud. And she is exceeding wise.

D. Pedro. In every thing but in loving Benedick.

Leon. O, my lord, wisdom and blood com- 170 bating in so tender a body, we have ten proofs to one that blood hath the victory. I am sorry for her, as I have just cause, being her uncle and her guardian.   174

D. Pedro. I would she had bestowed this dotage on me; I would have daff'd all other respects and made her half myself. I pray you, tell Benedick of it, and hear what 'a will say.

Leon. Were it good, think you?   179

Claud. Hero thinks surely she will die; for she says she will die, if he love her not, and she will die, ere she make her love known, and she will die, if he woo her, rather than she will bate one breath of her accustomed crossness.   184

D. Pedro. She doth well. If she should make tender of her love, 'tis very possible he'll scorn it; for the man, as you know all, hath a contemptible spirit.

Claud. He is a very proper man.

D. Pedro. He hath indeed a good outward happiness.   191

Claud. Before God! and, in my mind, very wise.

D. Pedro. He doth indeed show some sparks that are like wit.

Claud. And I take him to be valiant.   195

D. Pedro. As Hector, I assure you; and in the managing of quarrels you may say he is wise, for either he avoids them with great discretion, or undertakes them with a most Christian-like fear. 200

Leon. If he do fear God, 'a must necessarily keep peace. If he break the peace, he ought to enter into a quarrel with fear and trembling.

D. Pedro. And so will he do; for the man doth fear God, howsoever it seems not in him by some large jests he will make. Well, I am sorry for 206 your niece. Shall we go seek Benedick, and tell him of her love?

Claud. Never tell him, my lord. Let her wear it out with good counsel.   210

Leon. Nay, that's impossible; she may wear her heart out first.

D. Pedro. Well, we will hear further of it by your daughter. Let it cool the while. I love Benedick well; and I could wish he would modestly 215 examine himself, to see how much he is unworthy so good a lady.

Leon. My lord, will you walk? Dinner is ready.

Claud. [*Aside.*] If he do not dote on her upon this, I will never trust my expectation.   220

D. Pedro. [*Aside.*] Let there be the same net spread for her; and that must your daughter and her gentlewomen carry. The sport will be, when they hold one an opinion of another's dotage, and no such matter; that's the scene that I would 225 see, which will be merely a dumb-show. Let us send her to call him in to dinner.

[*Exeunt* [*Don Pedro, Claudio, and Leonato*].

Bene. [*Coming forward.*] This can be no trick; the conference was sadly borne. They have the truth of this from Hero. They seem to 230 pity the lady; it seems her affections have their full bent. Love me! why, it must be requited. I hear how I am censur'd. They say I will bear myself proudly, if I perceive the love come from her; they say too that she will rather die than give any 235 sign of affection. I did never think to marry. I must not seem proud. Happy are they that hear their detractions and can put them to mending. They say the lady is fair; 'tis a truth, I can bear them witness; and virtuous; 'tis so, I cannot 240 reprove it; and wise, but for loving me; by my troth, it is no addition to her wit, nor no great argument of her folly, for I will be horribly in love with her. I may chance have some odd quirks and remnants of wit broken on me, because 245 I have rail'd so long against marriage; but doth not the appetite alter? A man loves the meat in his youth that he cannot endure in his age. Shall quips and sentences and these paper bullets of the brain awe a man from the career of his humour?

---

157. **ecstasy:** madness. 164. **an alms:** charity. 165. **out of:** beyond. 176. **daff'd:** waived. 186. **tender:** offer. 187. **contemptible:** contemptuous. 206. **large:** coarse. 225. **no such matter:** there's nothing in it. 229. **sadly borne:** gravely conducted. 241. **reprove:** disprove. 248. **sentences:** maxims. 249. **career...humour:** course of his inclination.

No, the world must be peopled.   When I said   250
I would die a bachelor, I did not think I should live
till I were married.   Here comes Beatrice.   By
this day! she's a fair lady.   I do spy some marks of
love in her.   255

Enter BEATRICE.

Beat. Against my will I am sent to bid you come
in to dinner.

Bene. Fair Beatrice, I thank you for your pains.

Beat. I took no more pains for those thanks
than you take pains to thank me.   If it had been
painful, I would not have come.   261

Bene. You take pleasure then in the message?

Beat. Yea, just so much as you may take upon
a knife's point and choke a daw withal.   You have
no stomach, signior?   Fare you well.   [*Exit.* 265

Bene. Ha!   "Against my will I am sent to bid
you come in to dinner;" there's a double meaning
in that.   "I took no more pains for those thanks
than you took pains to thank me;" that's as much
as to say, "Any pains that I take for you is as   270
easy as thanks."   If I do not take pity of her, I am
a villain; if I do not love her, I am a Jew.   I will
go get her picture.   [*Exit.*

ACT III

[SCENE I.   *Leonato's garden.*]

Enter HERO *and two Gentlewomen,* MARGARET *and*
URSULA.

Hero. Good Margaret, run thee to the parlour.
There shalt thou find my cousin Beatrice
Proposing with the Prince and Claudio.
Whisper her ear and tell her, I and Ursula
Walk in the orchard and our whole discourse   5
Is all of her.   Say that thou overheard'st us,
And bid her steal into the pleached bower,
Where honeysuckles, ripened by the sun,
Forbid the sun to enter, like favourites   9
Made proud by princes, that advance their pride
Against that power that bred it.   There will she
    hide her,
To listen our propose.   This is thy office;
Bear thee well in it and leave us alone.

Marg. I'll make her come, I warrant you, pres-
    ently.   [*Exit.*]

Hero. Now, Ursula, when Beatrice doth come,
As we do trace this alley up and down,   16
Our talk must only be of Benedick.
When I do name him, let it be thy part
To praise him more than ever man did merit.

My talk to thee must be how Benedick   20
Is sick in love with Beatrice.   Of this matter
Is little Cupid's crafty arrow made,
That only wounds by hearsay.   Now begin;

Enter BEATRICE [*behind*].

For look where Beatrice, like a lapwing, runs
Close by the ground, to hear our conference.   25

Urs. The pleasant'st angling is to see the fish
Cut with her golden oars the silver stream,
And greedily devour the treacherous bait.
So angle we for Beatrice, who even now
Is couched in the woodbine coverture.   30
Fear you not my part of the dialogue.

Hero. Then go we near her, that her ear lose
    nothing
Of the false sweet bait that we lay for it.
    [*Approaching the bower.*]
No, truly, Ursula, she is too disdainful.
I know her spirits are as coy and wild   35
As haggards of the rock.

Urs.   But are you sure
That Benedick loves Beatrice so entirely?

Hero. So says the Prince and my new-trothed
    lord.

Urs. And did they bid you tell her of it, madam?

Hero. They did entreat me to acquaint her of it;
But I persuaded them, if they lov'd Benedick,   41
To wish him wrestle with affection,
And never to let Beatrice know of it.

Urs. Why did you so?   Doth not the gentleman
Deserve as full as fortunate a bed
As ever Beatrice shall couch upon?   45

Hero. O god of love!   I know he doth deserve
As much as may be yielded to a man;
But Nature never fram'd a woman's heart
Of prouder stuff than that of Beatrice.   50
Disdain and scorn ride sparkling in her eyes,
Misprising what they look on, and her wit
Values itself so highly that to her
All matter else seems weak.   She cannot love,
Nor take no shape nor project of affection,   55
She is so self-endeared.

Urs.   Sure, I think so;
And therefore certainly it were not good
She knew his love, lest she'll make sport at it.

Hero. Why, you speak truth.   I never yet saw
    man,   59
How wise, how noble, young, how rarely featur'd,
But she would spell him backward.   If fair-fac'd,
She would swear the gentleman should be her sister;
If black, why, Nature, drawing of an antic,
Made a foul blot; if tall, a lance ill-headed;
If low, an agate very vilely cut;   65

Act III, sc. i, 3. **proposing:** conversing.   36. **haggards:** untamed female hawks.   52. **misprising:** undervaluing.   55. **project:** idea.   61. **spell him backward:** i.e., say the reverse of him.   63. **black:** dark.   **antic:** grotesque figure.   65. **agate:** tiny figure (cut in agate-stone).

If speaking, why, a vane blown with all winds;
If silent. why, a block moved with none.
So turns she every man the wrong side out,
And never gives to truth and virtue that
Which simpleness and merit purchaseth.   70
 Urs. Sure, sure, such carping is not commend-
able.
 Hero. No, not to be so odd and from all fashions
As Beatrice is, cannot be commendable.
But who dare tell her so? If I should speak,
She would mock me into air; O, she would laugh me
Out of myself, press me to death with wit.   76
Therefore let Benedick, like cover'd fire,
Consume away in sighs, waste inwardly.
It were a better death than die with mocks,
Which is as bad as die with tickling.   80
 Urs. Yet tell her of it; hear what she will say.
 Hero. No; rather I will go to Benedick
And counsel him to fight against his passion;
And, truly, I'll devise some honest slanders
To stain my cousin with. One doth not know   85
How much an ill word may empoison liking.
 Urs. O, do not do your cousin such a wrong.
She cannot be so much without true judgement —
Having so swift and excellent a wit
As she is priz'd to have — as to refuse   90
So rare a gentleman as Signior Benedick.
 Hero. He is the only man of Italy,
Always excepted my dear Claudio.
 Urs. I pray you, be not angry with me, madam,
Speaking my fancy; Signior Benedick,   95
For shape, for bearing, argument, and valour,
Goes foremost in report through Italy.
 Hero. Indeed, he hath an excellent good name.
 Urs. His excellence did earn it, ere he had it.
When are you married, madam?   100
 Hero. Why, every day, to-morrow. Come, go in;
I'll show thee some attires, and have thy counsel
Which is the best to furnish me to-morrow.
 Urs. [*Aside.*] She's lim'd, I warrant you. We've
caught her, madam.
 Hero. [*Aside.*] If it proves so, then loving goes
by haps.   105
Some Cupid kills with arrows, some with traps.
       [*Exeunt* [*Hero and Ursula*].
 Beat. [*Coming forward.*] What fire is in mine ears?
 Can this be true?
Stand I condemn'd for pride and scorn so much?
Contempt, farewell! and maiden pride, adieu!
No glory lives behind the back of such.   110
And, Benedick, love on; I will requite thee,
 Taming my wild heart to thy loving hand.
If thou dost love, my kindness shall incite thee
 To bind our loves up in a holy band;

For others say thou dost deserve, and I   115
Believe it better than reportingly.   [*Exit.*

  [SCENE II. *A room in Leonato's house.*]

 Enter DON PEDRO, CLAUDIO, BENEDICK, *and*
     LEONATO.

 D. Pedro. I do but stay till your marriage be
consummate, and then go I toward Arragon.
 Claud. I'll bring you thither, my lord, if you'll
vouchsafe me.
 D. Pedro. Nay, that would be as great a soil   5
in the new gloss of your marriage as to show a child
his new coat and forbid him to wear it. I will only
be bold with Benedick for his company; for, from
the crown of his head to the sole of his foot, he is all
mirth. He hath twice or thrice cut Cupid's   10
bowstring, and the little hangman dare not shoot
at him. He hath a heart as sound as a bell and his
tongue is the clapper, for what his heart thinks his
tongue speaks.
 Bene. Gallants, I am not as I have been.   15
 Leon. So say I; methinks you are sadder.
 Claud. I hope he be in love.
 D. Pedro. Hang him, truant! There's no true
drop of blood in him, to be truly touch'd with love.
If he be sad, he wants money.   20
 Bene. I have the toothache.
 D. Pedro. Draw it.
 Bene. Hang it!
 Claud. You must hang it first, and draw it after-
wards.   25
 D. Pedro. What! sigh for the toothache?
 Leon. Where is but a humour or a worm.
 Bene. Well, every one [can] master a grief but
he that has it.
 Claud. Yet say I, he is in love.   30
 D. Pedro. There is no appearance of fancy in
him, unless it be a fancy that he hath to strange
disguises; as, to be a Dutchman to-day, a Frenchman to-morrow, or in the shape of two countries
at once, as, a German from the waist downward,
all slops, and a Spaniard from the hip upward,   35
no doublet. Unless he have a fancy to this foolery,
as it appears he hath, he is no fool for fancy, as you
would have it appear he is.   39
 Claud. If he be not in love with some woman,
there is no believing old signs. 'A brushes his hat
o' mornings; what should that bode?
 D. Pedro. Hath any man seen him at the barber's?
 Claud. No, but the barber's man hath been   45
seen with him, and the old ornament of his cheek
hath already stuffed tennis-balls.

---

84. **honest**: harmless. 96. **argument**: intelligence. 104. **lim'd**: caught (as by bird-lime). 105. **haps**: chance. 110.
No ... such: i.e., such persons are not well spoken of when absent.
 Sc. ii, 28. [can] (Pope). *cannot* QF. 31. **fancy**: love. 35. **slops**: loose breeches.

Leon. Indeed, he looks younger than he did, by the loss of a beard.

D. Pedro. Nay, 'a rubs himself with civet. Can you smell him out by that?   51

Claud. That's as much as to say, the sweet youth 's in love.

[*D. Pedro.*] The greatest note of it is his melancholy.   55

Claud. And when was he wont to wash his face?

D. Pedro. Yea, or to paint himself? For the which, I hear what they say of him.   59

Claud. Nay, but his jesting spirit; which is now crept into a lute-string and now govern'd by stops.

D. Pedro. Indeed, that tells a heavy tale for him. Conclude, conclude he is in love.

Claud. Nay, but I know who loves him.   65

D. Pedro. That would I know too. I warrant, one that knows him not.

Claud. Yes, and his ill conditions; and, in despite of all, dies for him.

D. Pedro. She shall be buried with her face upwards.   71

Bene. Yet is this no charm for the toothache. Old signior, walk aside with me; I have studied eight or nine wise words to speak to you, which these hobby-horses must not hear.   75

[*Exeunt Benedick and Leonato.*]

D. Pedro. For my life, to break with him about Beatrice.

Claud. 'Tis even so. Hero and Margaret have by this played their parts with Beatrice; and then the two bears will not bite one another when they meet.   81

Enter JOHN *the Bastard.*

D. John. My lord and brother, God save you!

D. Pedro Good den, brother.

D. John. If your leisure serv'd, I would speak with you.   85

D. Pedro. In private?

D. John. If it please you; yet Count Claudio may hear, for what I would speak of concerns him.

D. Pedro. What's the matter?   90

D. John. [*To Claudio.*] Means your lordship to be married to-morrow?

D. Pedro. You know he does.

D. John. I know not that, when he knows what I know.   95

Claud. If there be any impediment, I pray you discover it.

D. John. You may think I love you not; let that appear hereafter, and aim better at me by that I

now will manifest. For my brother, I think he   100 holds you well, and in dearness of heart hath holp to effect your ensuing marriage; — surely suit ill spent and labour ill bestowed.

D. Pedro. Why, what's the matter?

D. John. I came hither to tell you; and, cir-   105 cumstances short'ned, for she has been too long a talking of, the lady is disloyal.

Claud. Who? Hero?

D. John. Even she; Leonato's Hero, your Hero, every man's Hero.   110

Claud. Disloyal?

D. John. The word is too good to paint out her wickedness. I could say she were worse; think you of a worse title, and I will fit her to it. Wonder not till further warrant. Go but with me to-night;   115 you shall see her chamber-window ent'red, even the night before her wedding-day. If you love her then, to-morrow wed her; but it would better fit your honour to change your mind.

Claud. May this be so?   120

D. Pedro. I will not think it.

D. John. If you dare not trust that you see, confess not that you know. If you will follow me, I will show you enough; and when you have seen more and heard more, proceed accordingly.   125

Claud. If I see anything to-night why I should not marry her to-morrow, in the congregation, where I should wed, there will I shame her.

D. Pedro. And, as I wooed for thee to obtain her, I will join with thee to disgrace her.   130

D. John. I will disparage her no farther till you are my witnesses. Bear it coldly but till midnight, and let the issue show itself.

D. Pedro. O day untowardly turned!

Claud. O mischief strangely thwarting!   135

D. John. O plague right well prevented! So will you say when you have seen the sequel.

[*Exeunt.*

[SCENE III. *A street.*]

Enter DOGBERRY *and his compartner* [VERGES] *with the* WATCH.

Dog. Are you good men and true?

Verg. Yea, or else it were pity but they should suffer salvation, body and soul.

Dog. Nay, that were a punishment too good for them, if they should have any allegiance in them, being chosen for the Prince's watch.   6

Verg. Well, give them their charge, neighbour Dogberry.

50. **civet:** perfume (from the civet cat).   54. [*Don Pedro*] F. *Bene.* Q.   61. **stops:** fingerings (of a stringed instrument).   68. **conditions:** qualities.   69–71. **dies . . . upwards.** I.e., Beatrice will die because of Benedick, not by taking her own life. Suicides were often buried face downwards.   75. **hobby-horses:** buffoons.   78. **Margaret.** Mistake for *Ursula.* 90. Some editors plausibly give this line to Claudio.   99. **aim . . . at:** judge better of.

Sc. iii, 3. **salvation:** blunder for *damnation,* the first of Dogberry's many malapropisms.

Dog. First, who think you the most desartless man to be constable?   10

1. Watch. Hugh Oatcake, sir, or George Seacole; for they can write and read.

Dog. Come hither, neighbour Seacole. God hath bless'd you with a good name. To be a well-favoured man is the gift of fortune, but to write and read comes by nature.   16

2. Watch. Both which, master constable, —

Dog. You have: I knew it would be your answer. Well, for your favour, sir, why, give God thanks, and make no boast of it; and for your writing 20 and reading, let that appear when there is no need of such vanity. You are thought here to be the most senseless and fit man for the constable of the watch; therefore bear you the lantern. This is your charge: you shall comprehend all vagrom men; you are 25 to bid any man stand, in the Prince's name.

2. Watch. How if 'a will not stand?

Dog. Why, then, take no note of him, but let him go; and presently call the rest of the watch together, and thank God you are rid of a knave.   31

Verg. If he will not stand when he is bidden, he is none of the Prince's subjects.

Dog. True, and they are to meddle with none but the Prince's subjects. You shall also make 35 no noise in the streets; for for the watch to babble and to talk is most tolerable and not to be endured.

[2.] Watch. We will rather sleep than talk; we know what belongs to a watch.   40

Dog. Why, you speak like an ancient and most quiet watchman, for I cannot see how sleeping should offend; only, have a care that your bills be not stol'n. Well, you are to call at all the ale-houses, and bid those that are drunk get them to bed.   46

[2.] Watch. How if they will not?

Dog. Why, then, let them alone till they are sober. If they make you not then the better answer, you may say they are not the men you took them for.   51

[2.] Watch. Well, sir.

Dog. If you meet a thief, you may suspect him, by virtue of your office, to be no true man; and, for such kind of men, the less you meddle or make with them, why, the more is for your honesty. 56

[2.] Watch. If we know him to be a thief, shall we not lay hands on him?

Dog. Truly, by your office, you may; but I think they that touch pitch will be defil'd. The 60 most peaceable way for you, if you do take a thief, is to let him show himself what he is and steal out of your company.

Verg. You have been always called a merciful man, partner.   65

Dog. Truly, I would not hang a dog by my will, much more a man who hath any honesty in him.

Verg. If you hear a child cry in the night, you must call to the nurse and bid her still it.   70

[2.] Watch. How if the nurse be asleep and will not hear us?

Dog. Why, then, depart in peace, and let the child wake her with crying; for the ewe that will not hear her lamb when it baes will never answer a calf when he bleats.   76

Verg. 'Tis very true.

Dog. This is the end of the charge: you, constable, are to present the Prince's own person. If you meet the Prince in the night, you may stay him. 81

Verg. Nay, by'r lady, that I think 'a cannot.

Dog. Five shillings to one on't, with any man that knows the [statues], he may stay him; marry, not without the Prince be willing; for, indeed, 86 the watch ought to offend no man, and it is an offence to stay a man against his will.

Verg. By'r lady, I think it be so.   89

Dog. Ha, ah ha! Well, masters, good night. An there be any matter of weight chances, call up me. Keep your fellows' counsels and your own, and good night. Come, neighbour.

[2.] Watch. Well, masters, we hear our charge. Let us go sit here upon the church-bench till two, and then all to bed.   96

Dog. One word more, honest neighbours. I pray you, watch about Signior Leonato's door; for the wedding being there to-morrow, there is a great coil to-night. Adieu! Be vigitant, I beseech you.

[Exeunt [Dogberry and Verges].

Enter BORACHIO *and* CONRADE.

Bora. What, Conrade!   102

[2.] Watch. *[Aside.]* Peace! stir not.

Bora. Conrade, I say!

Con. Here, man; I am at thy elbow.   105

Bora. Mass, and my elbow itch'd; I thought there would a scab follow.

Con. I will owe thee an answer for that; and now forward with thy tale.

Bora. Stand thee close, then, under this pent- 110 house, for it drizzles rain; and I will, like a true drunkard, utter all to thee.

[2.] Watch. *[Aside.]* Some treason, masters; yet stand close.

Bora. Therefore know I have earned of Don John a thousand ducats.   116

Con. Is it possible that any villainy should be so dear?

25. **comprehend:** for *apprehend*. **vagrom:** vagrant. 43. **bills:** halberds, i.e., pikes fixed to long poles. 54. **true:** honest. 84. **[statues]** F. *statutes* Q; but the error is undoubtedly Dogberry's. 100. **coil:** to-do. 107. **scab.** Also used contemptuously for *scurvy fellow*. 110. **pent-house:** projecting roof.

Bora. Thou shouldst rather ask if it were possible any villainy should be so rich; for when rich villains have need of poor ones, poor ones may make what price they will.   122

Con. I wonder at it.

Bora. That shows thou art unconfirm'd. Thou knowest that the fashion of a doublet, or a hat, or a cloak, is nothing to a man.   126

Con. Yes, it is apparel.

Bora. I mean, the fashion.

Con. Yes, the fashion is the fashion.   129

Bora. Tush! I may as well say the fool's the fool. But seest thou not what a deformed thief this fashion is?

[*2.*] *Watch.* [*Aside.*] I know that Deformed; 'a has been a vile thief this seven years. 'A goes up and down like a gentleman. I remember his name.   136

Bora. Didst thou not hear somebody?

Con. No; 'twas the vane on the house.

Bora. Seest thou not, I say, what a deformed thief this fashion is, how giddily 'a turns about all the hot bloods between fourteen and five-and-   141 thirty, sometimes fashioning them like Pharaoh's soldiers in the reechy painting, sometime like god Bel's priests in the old church-window, sometime like the shaven Hercules in the smirch'd worm-   145 eaten tapestry, where his codpiece seems as massy as his club?

Con. All this I see; and I see that the fashion wears out more apparel than the man. But art not thou thyself giddy with the fashion too, that thou hast shifted out of thy tale into telling me of the fashion?   152

Bora. Not so, neither; but know that I have to-night wooed Margaret, the Lady Hero's gentlewoman, by the name of Hero. She leans me   155 out at her mistress' chamber-window, bids me a thousand times good night, — I tell this tale vilely: — I should first tell thee how the Prince, Claudio, and my master, planted and placed and possessed by my master Don John, saw afar off in the orchard this amiable encounter.   161

Con. And thought they Margaret was Hero?

Bora. Two of them did, the Prince and Claudio; but the devil my master knew she was Mar-   165 garet; and partly by his oaths, which first possess'd them, partly by the dark night, which did deceive them, but chiefly by my villainy, which did confirm any slander that Don John had made, away went

Claudio enrag'd; swore he would meet her, as he   170 was appointed, next morning at the temple, and there, before the whole congregation, shame her with what he saw o'er night, and send her home again without a husband.   175

1. Watch. We charge you, in the Prince's name, stand!

2. Watch. Call up the right master constable. We have here recovered the most dangerous piece of lechery that ever was known in the common-wealth.   181

1. Watch. And one Deformed is one of them I know him; 'a wears a lock.

Con. Masters, masters, —

2. Watch. You'll be made bring Deformed forth, I warrant you.   186

Con. Masters, —

[*1. Watch.*] Never speak. We charge you let us obey you to go with us.

Bora. We are like to prove a goodly commodity, being taken up of these men's bills.   191

Con. A commodity in question, I warrant you. Come, we'll obey you.   [*Exeunt.*

[SCENE IV.   *Hero's apartment.*]

Enter HERO, MARGARET, *and* URSULA.

Hero. Good Ursula, wake my cousin Beatrice, and desire her to rise.

Urs. I will, lady.

Hero. And bid her come hither.

Urs. Well.   [*Exit.* 5

Marg. Troth, I think your other rabato were better.

Hero. No, pray thee, good Meg, I'll wear this.

Marg. By my troth, 's not so good; and I warrant your cousin will say so.   10

Hero. My cousin's a fool, and thou art another. I'll wear none but this.

Marg. I like the new tire within excellently, if the hair were a thought browner; and your gown's a most rare fashion, i' faith. I saw the Duchess of Milan's gown that they praise so.   16

Hero. O, that exceeds, they say.

Marg. By my troth, 's but a night-gown in respect of yours: cloth o' gold, and cuts, and lac'd with silver, set with pearls, down sleeves,   20 side sleeves, and skirts, round underborne with a bluish tinsel; but for a fine, quaint, graceful, and excellent fashion, yours is worth ten on't.

---

124. **unconfirm'd:** inexperienced.   126. **is . . . man:** i.e., does not make the man.   143. **reechy:** smoky, dirty. **god Bel's priests.** Alluding to Daniel's overthrow of the priests of Bel, as told in the apocryphal book of *Daniel.* 159. **possessed:** directed.   162. **they** Q. *thy* Ff.   183. **lock:** love-lock, a lock of hair hanging down on the left shoulder.   188. [*1. Watch*] (Theobald). QF print as part of Conrade's speech.   190–91. A punning speech. **commodity:** (1) goods, (2) bargain. **taken up:** (1) taken on credit, (2) arrested. **bills:** (1) bonds, (2) halberds.   192. **in question:** subject to legal trial

Sc. iv, 6. **rabato:** ruff.   13. **tire:** headdress.   **within:** i.e., in the inner room.   17. **exceeds:** excels.   18. **night-gown:** dressing-gown.   19. **cuts:** ornamental slashes showing fabric beneath.   20. **down sleeves:** i.e., the real sleeves.   21. **side sleeves:** ornamental sleeves hanging from the shoulder.   21. **round underborne:** lined around.

Hero. God give me joy to wear it! for my heart is exceeding heavy.   25

Marg. 'Twill be heavier soon by the weight of a man.

Hero. Fie upon thee! art not asham'd?

Marg. Of what, lady? Of speaking honourably? Is not marriage honourable in a beggar? Is not   30 your lord honourable without marriage? I think you would have me say, "saving your reverence, a husband." An bad thinking do not wrest true speaking, I'll offend nobody. Is there any harm in "the heavier for a husband"? None, I think, 35 an it be the right husband and the right wife; otherwise 'tis light, and not heavy. Ask my Lady Beatrice else; here she comes.

Enter BEATRICE.

Hero. Good morrow, coz.

Beat. Good morrow, sweet Hero.   40

Hero. Why, how now? Do you speak in the sick tune?

Beat. I am out of all other tune, methinks.

Marg. Clap's into "Light o' love"; that goes without a burden. Do you sing it, and I'll dance it.   46

Beat. Ye light o' love with your heels! Then, if your husband have stables enough, you'll see he shall lack no barns.

Marg. O illegitimate construction! I scorn that with my heels.   51

Beat. 'Tis almost five o'clock, cousin; 'tis time you were ready. By my troth, I am exceeding ill. Heigh-ho!

Marg. For a hawk, a horse, or a husband?   55

Beat. For the letter that begins them all, H.

Marg. Well, an you be not turn'd Turk, there's no more sailing by the star.

Beat. What means the fool, trow?

Marg. Nothing I; but God send every one their heart's desire!   61

Hero. These gloves the count sent me; they are an excellent perfume.

Beat. I am stuff'd, cousin; I cannot smell.

Marg. A maid, and stuff'd! There's goodly catching of cold.   66

Beat. O, God help me! God help me! How long have you profess'd apprehension?

Marg. Ever since you left it. Doth not my wit become me rarely?   70

Beat. It is not seen enough, you should wear it in your cap. By my troth, I am sick.

Marg. Get you some of this distill'd Carduus

Benedictus, and lay it to your heart. It is the only thing for a qualm.   75

Hero. There thou prick'st her with a thistle.

Beat. Benedictus! why Benedictus? You have some moral in this Benedictus.

Marg. Moral! no, by my troth, I have no moral meaning; I meant, plain holy-thistle. You 80 may think perchance that I think you are in love. Nay, by'r lady, I am not such a fool to think what I list, nor I list not to think what I can, nor indeed I cannot think, if I would think my heart out of thinking, that you are in love or that you will be 85 in love or that you can be in love. Yet Benedick was such another, and now is he become a man. He swore he would never marry, and yet now, in despite of his heart, he eats his meat without grudging; and how you may be converted I know 90 not, but methinks you look with your eyes as other women do.

Beat. What pace is this that thy tongue keeps?

Marg. Not a false gallop.   94

Re-enter URSULA.

Urs. Madam, withdraw; the Prince, the count, Signior Benedick, Don John, and all the gallants of the town, are come to fetch you to church.

Hero. Help to dress me, good coz, good Meg, good Ursula.   [*Exeunt.*]

[SCENE V. *Another room in Leonato's house.*]

Enter LEONATO, *with the Constable* [DOGBERRY] *and the Headborough* [VERGES].

Leon. What would you with me, honest neighbour?

Dog. Marry, sir, I would have some confidence with you that decerns you nearly.

Leon. Brief, I pray you; for you see it is a busy time with me.   6

Dog. Marry, this it is, sir.

Verg. Yes, in truth it is, sir.

Leon. What is it, my good friends?   9

Dog. Goodman Verges, sir, speaks a little off the matter; an old man, sir, and his wits are not so blunt as, God help, I would desire they were; but, in faith, honest as the skin between his brows.

Verg. Yes, I thank God I am as honest as 15 any man living that is an old man and no honester than I.

Dog. Comparisons are odorous. Palabras, neighbour Verges.

---

33. **wrest:** violate.   37. **light:** with pun on *wanton.*   44. **"Light o' love":** A popular song.   45. **burden:** bass part. 49. **barns:** with pun on *bairns*, children.   56. **H.**   Punning on *ache*, pronounced "aitch" in 16th cent.   57. **turn'd Turk.** Common expression for "entirely changed"; here "fallen in love."   64. **I am stuff'd:** I have a cold.   68. **apprehension:** wit. 73. **Carduus Benedictus:** the blessed thistle, a medicinal herb.   78. **moral:** hidden meaning.

Sc. v, S.D. *Headborough:* petty constable.   18. **odorous:** for *odious.*   **Palabras:** for *pocas palabras* (Span.), few words.

Leon. Neighbours, you are tedious.   20

Dog. It pleases your worship to say so, but we are the poor Duke's officers; but truly, for mine own part, if I were as tedious as a king, I could find in my heart to bestow it all of your worship.   25

Leon. All thy tediousness on me. ah?

Dog. Yea, an 'twere a thousand pound more than 'tis; for I hear as good exclamation on your worship as of any man in the city; and though I be but a poor man, I am glad to hear it.   30

Verg. And so am I.

Leon. I would fain know what you have to say.

Verg. Marry, sir, our watch to-night, excepting your worship's presence, ha' ta'en a couple of as arrant knaves as any in Messina.   35

Dog. A good old man, sir; he will be talking: as they say, When the age is in, the wit is out. God help us! It is a world to see. Well said, i' faith, neighbour Verges. Well, God's a good man; an two men ride of a horse, one must ride behind.   40 An honest soul, i' faith, sir; by my troth he is, as ever broke bread; but God is to be worshipp'd; all men are not alike; alas, good neighbour!

Leon. Indeed, neighbour, he comes too short of you.   46

Dog. Gifts that God gives.

Leon. I must leave you.

Dog. One word, sir. Our watch, sir, have indeed comprehended two aspicious persons, and we would have them this morning examined before your worship.   52

Leon. Take their examination yourself and bring it me. I am now in great haste, as it may appear unto you.   55

Dog. It shall be suffigance.

Leon. Drink some wine ere you go. Fare you well.

[*Enter a* MESSENGER.]

Mess. My lord, they stay for you to give your daughter to her husband.   60

Leon. I'll wait upon them; I am ready.

[*Exeunt Leonato and Messenger.*]

Dog. Go, good partner, go, get you to Francis Seacole; bid him bring his pen and inkhorn to the gaol. We are now to examination these men.

Verg. And we must do it wisely.   65

Dog. We will spare for no wit, I warrant you. Here's that shall drive some of them to a non-come; only get the learned writer to set down our excommunication, and meet me at the gaol.

[*Exeunt.*

ACT IV

[SCENE I. *A church.*]

Enter DON PEDRO, [JOHN *the*] *Bastard,* LEONATO, FRIAR FRANCIS, CLAUDIO, BENEDICK, HERO, BEATRICE [*and attendants*].

Leon. Come, Friar Francis, be brief; only to the plain form of marriage, and you shall recount their particular duties afterwards.

Friar. You come hither, my lord, to marry this lady.   5

Claud. No.

Leon. To be married to her. Friar, you come to marry her.

Friar. Lady, you come hither to be married to this count.   10

Hero. I do.

Friar. If either of you know any inward impediment why you should not be conjoined, I charge you, on your souls, to utter it.

Claud. Know you any, Hero?   15

Hero. None, my lord.

Friar. Know you any, count?

Leon. I dare make his answer, none.

Claud. O, what men dare do! What men may do! What men daily do, not knowing what they do!   21

Bene. How now! interjections? Why, then, some be of laughing, as, ah, ha, he!

Claud. Stand thee by, friar. Father, by your leave Will you with free and unconstrained soul   25 Give me this maid, your daughter?

Leon. As freely, son, as God did give her me.

Claud. And what have I to give you back, whose worth
May counterpoise this rich and precious gift?

D. Pedro. Nothing, unless you render her again.

Claud. Sweet Prince, you learn me noble thankfulness.   31
There, Leonato, take her back again.
Give not this rotten orange to your friend;
She's but the sign and semblance of her honour.
Behold how like a maid she blushes here!   35
O, what authority and show of truth
Can cunning sin cover itself withal!
Comes not that blood as modest evidence
To witness simple virtue? Would you not swear,
All you that see her, that she were a maid,   40
By these exterior shows? But she is none.
She knows the heat of a luxurious bed;
Her blush is guiltiness, not modesty.

Leon. What do you mean, my lord?

Claud.   Not to be married;

---

37. **When . . . out.** Corruption of the proverb, "When ale is in, wit is out." 38. **world:** wonder. 67. **non-come:** *non compos mentis.* 68. **excommunication:** for *examination.*

Act IV, sc. i, 22–23. interjections . . . he. Benedick is quoting from a grammar. 42. **luxurious:** lustful.

Not to knit my soul to an approved wanton.   45
   Leon. Dear my lord, if you, in your own proof,
Have vanquish'd the resistance of her youth,
And made defeat of her virginity,—
   Claud. I know what you would say. If I have
     known her,
You will say she did embrace me as a husband,   50
And so extenuate the 'forehand sin.
No, Leonato,
I never tempted her with word too large;
But, as a brother to his sister, show'd
Bashful sincerity and comely love.   55
   Hero. And seem'd I ever otherwise to you?
   Claud. Out on thee! Seeming! I will write
     against it:
You seem to me as Dian in her orb,
As chaste as is the bud ere it be blown;
But you are more intemperate in your blood   60
Than Venus, or those pamp'red animals
That rage in savage sensuality.
   Hero. Is my lord well, that he doth speak so
     wide?
   Leon. Sweet Prince, why speak not you?
   D. Pedro.   What should I speak?
I stand dishonour'd, that have gone about   65
To link my dear friend to a common stale.
   Leon. Are these things spoken, or do I but
     dream?
   D. John. Sir, they are spoken, and these things
     are true.
   Bene. This looks not like a nuptial.
   Hero.   True! O God!
   Claud. Leonato, stand I here?   70
Is this the Prince? Is this the Prince's brother?
Is this face Hero's? Are our eyes our own?
   Leon. All this is so; but what of this, my lord?
   Claud. Let me but move one question to your
     daughter.
And, by that fatherly and kindly power   75
That you have in her, bid her answer truly.
   Leon. I charge thee do so, as thou art my child.
   Hero. O, God defend me! how am I beset!
What kind of catechising call you this?   79
   Claud. To make you answer truly to your name.
   Hero. Is it not Hero? Who can blot that name
With any just reproach?
   Claud.   Marry, that can Hero;
Hero itself can blot out Hero's virtue.
What man was he talk'd with you yesternight
Out at your window betwixt twelve and one?   85
Now, if you are a maid, answer to this.
   Hero. I talk'd with no man at that hour, my lord.
   D. Pedro. Why, then are you no maiden.
     Leonato,
I am sorry you must hear. Upon mine honour,

Myself, my brother, and this grieved count   90
Did see her, hear her, at that hour last night
Talk with a ruffian at her chamber-window;
Who hath indeed, most like a liberal villain,
Confess'd the vile encounters they have had
A thousand times in secret.   95
   D. John. Fie, fie! they are not to be named, my
     lord,
Not to be spoke of;
There is not chastity enough in language
Without offence to utter them. Thus, pretty lady,
I am sorry for thy much misgovernment.   100
   Claud. O Hero, what a Hero hadst thou been,
If half thy outward graces had been plac'd
About thy thoughts and counsels of thy heart!
But fare the well, most foul, most fair! Farewell,
Thou pure impiety and impious purity!   105
For thee I'll lock up all the gates of love,
And on my eyelids shall conjecture hang,
To turn all beauty into thoughts of harm,
And never shall it more be gracious.
   Leon. Hath no man's dagger here a point for me?
                     [Hero swoons.]
   Beat. Why, how now, cousin! wherefore sink you
     down?   111
   D. John. Come, let us go. These things, come
     thus to light,
Smother her spirits up.
       *[Exeunt Don Pedro, Don John, and
         Claudio.]*
   Bene. How doth the lady?
   Beat.   Dead, I think. Help, uncle!
Hero! why, Hero! Uncle! Signior Benedick! Friar!
   Leon. O Fate! take not away thy heavy hand.
Death is the fairest cover for her shame   117
That may be wish'd for.
   Beat.   How now, cousin Hero!
   Friar. Have comfort, lady.
   Leon. Dost thou look up?   120
   Friar. Yea, wherefore should she not?
   Leon. Wherefore! Why, doth not every earthly
     thing
Cry shame upon her? Could she here deny
The story that is printed in her blood?
Do not live, Hero; do not ope thine eyes;   125
For, did I think thou wouldst not quickly die,
Thought I thy spirits were stronger than thy
     shames,
Myself would, on the rearward of reproaches,
Strike at thy life. Griev'd I, I had but one?
Chid I for that at frugal nature's frame?   130
O, one too much by thee! Why had I one?
Why ever wast thou lovely in my eyes?
Why had I not with charitable hand
Took up a beggar's issue at my gates,

---

46. **proof**: trial. 58. **Dian . . . orb.** Diana was goddess of chastity and of the moon. 63. **wide**: wide of the mark. 75. **kindly**:
natural. 93. **liberal**: gross, licentious. 107. **conjecture**: suspicion. 128. **on the rearward**: after. 130. **frame**: design.

parallels Titus and

Who smirched thus and mir'd with infamy, 135
I might have said "No part of it is mine.
This shame derives itself from unknown loins"?
But mine, and mine I lov'd, and mine I prais'd,
And mine that I was proud on, mine so much
That I myself was to myself not mine, 140
Valuing of her, — why, she, O, she is fall'n
Into a pit of ink, that the wide sea
Hath drops too few to wash her clean again,
And salt too little which may season give
To her foul-tainted flesh!

   Bene.   Sir, sir, be patient. 145
For my part, I am so attir'd in wonder,
I know not what to say.

   Beat. O, on my soul, my cousin is belied!

   Bene. Lady, were you her bedfellow last night?

   Beat. No, truly not; although, until last night,
I have this twelvemonth been her bedfellow. 151

   Leon. Confirm'd, confirm'd! O, that is stronger made
Which was before barr'd up with ribs of iron!
Would the two princes lie, and Claudio lie,
Who lov'd her so, that, speaking of her foulness,
Wash'd it with tears? Hence from her! Let her die. 156

   Friar. Hear me a little;
For I have only been silent so long
And given way unto this course of fortune,
By noting of the lady. I have mark'd 160
A thousand blushing apparitions
To start into her face, a thousand innocent shames
In angel whiteness beat away those blushes;
And in her eye there hath appear'd a fire
To burn the errors that these princes hold 165
Against her maiden truth. Call me a fool,
Trust not my reading nor my observations,
Which with experimental seal doth warrant
The tenour of my book; trust not my age,
My reverence, calling, nor divinity, 170
If this sweet lady lie not guiltless here
Under some biting error.

   Leon.   Friar, it cannot be.
Thou seest that all the grace that she hath left
Is that she will not add to her damnation
A sin of perjury; she not denies it. 175
Why seek'st thou then to cover with excuse
That which appears in proper nakedness?

   Friar. Lady, what man is he you are accus'd of?

   Hero. They know that do accuse me; I know none.
If I know more of any man alive 180
Than that which maiden modesty doth warrant,
Let all my sins lack mercy! O my father,

Prove you that any man with me convers'd
At hours unmeet, or that I yesternight
Maintain'd the change of words with any creature,
Refuse me, hate me, torture me to death! 186

   Friar. There is some strange misprision in the princes.

   Bene. Two of them have the very bent of honour;
And if their wisdoms be misled in this,
The practice of it lives in John the Bastard, 190
Whose spirits toil in frame of villainies.

   Leon. I know not. If they speak but truth of her,
These hands shall tear her; if they wrong her honour,
The proudest of them shall well hear of it.
Time hath not yet so dried this blood of mine, 195
Nor age so eat up my invention,
Nor fortune made such havoc of my means,
Nor my bad life reft me so much of friends,
But they shall find, awak'd in such a kind,
Both strength of limb and policy of mind, 200
Ability in means and choice of friends,
To quit me of them throughly.

   Friar.   Pause awhile,
And let my counsel sway you in this case.
Your daughter here the princes left for dead.
Let her awhile be secretly kept in, 205
And publish it that she is dead indeed.
Maintain a mourning ostentation
And on your family's old monument
Hang mournful epitaphs, and do all rites
That appertain unto a burial. 210

   Leon. What shall become of this? What will this do?

   Friar. Marry, this well carried shall on her behalf
Change slander to remorse; that is some good.
But not for that dream I on this strange course,
But on this travail look for greater birth. 215
She dying, as it must be so maintain'd,
Upon the instant that she was accus'd,
Shall be lamented, pitied, and excus'd
Of every hearer; for it so falls out
That what we have we prize not to the worth 220
Whiles we enjoy it, but being lack'd and lost,
Why, then we rack the value; then we find
The virtue that possession would not show us
Whiles it was ours. So will it fare with Claudio.
When he shall hear she died upon his words, 225
Th' idea of her life shall sweetly creep
Into his study of imagination,
And every lovely organ of her life
Shall come apparell'd in more precious habit,

140-41. **That... her:** that I was nothing to myself, so much I treasured her. 168-69. **Which... book:** which puts the seal of experience upon what I have learned by reading. 187. **misprision:** error. 188. **very bent:** true disposition. 190. **practice:** plotting. 199. **kind:** manner. 202. **quit me of:** avenge me on. 222. **rack:** strain, exaggerate. 227. **study of imagination:** musing. 228. **organ:** feature.

More moving-delicate and full of life, 230
Into the eye and prospect of his soul,
Than when she liv'd indeed.   Then shall he mourn,
If ever love had interest in his liver,
And wish he had not so accused her,
No, though he thought his accusation true. 235
Let this be so, and doubt not but success
Will fashion the event in better shape
Than I can lay it down in likelihood.
But if all aim but this be levell'd false,
The supposition of the lady's death 240
Will quench the wonder of her infamy.
And if it sort not well, you may conceal her,
As best befits her wounded reputation,
In some reclusive and religious life,
Out of all eyes, tongues, minds, and injuries. 245
  Bene. Signior Leonato, let the friar advise you;
And though you know my inwardness and love
Is very much unto the Prince and Claudio,
Yet, by mine honour, I will deal in this
As secretly and justly as your soul 250
Should with your body.
  Leon.   Being that I flow in grief,
The smallest twine may lead me.
  Friar. 'Tis well consented; presently away,
For to strange sores strangely they strain the cure.
Come, lady, die to live.   This wedding-day 255
Perhaps is but prolong'd; have patience and endure.
          [*Exeunt [all but Benedick and Beatrice].*
  Bene. Lady Beatrice, have you wept all this
while?
  Beat. Yea, and I will weep a while longer.
  Bene. I will not desire that.
  Beat. You have no reason; I do it freely. 260
  Bene. Surely I do believe your fair cousin is
wrong'd.
  Beat. Ah, how much might the man deserve of
me that would right her!
  Bene. Is there any way to show such friendship?
  Beat. A very even way, but no such friend. 265
  Bene. May a man do it?
  Beat. It is a man's office, but not yours.
  Bene. I do love nothing in the world so well as
you.   Is not that strange? 270
  Beat. As strange as the thing I know not.   It
were as possible for me to say I lov'd nothing so
well as you: but believe me not; and yet I lie not.
I confess nothing, nor I deny nothing.   I am sorry
for my cousin. 275
  Bene. By my sword, Beatrice, thou lov'st me.
  Beat. Do not swear, and eat it.
  Bene. I will swear by it that you love me; and I
will make him eat it that says I love not you.
  Beat. Will you not eat your word? 280

  Bene. With no sauce that can be devised to it.   I
protest I love thee.
  Beat. Why, then, God forgive me!
  Bene. What offence, sweet Beatrice?
  Beat. You have stayed me in a happy hour.   I
was about to protest I loved you. 286
  Bene. And do it with all thy heart.
  Beat. I love you with so much of my heart that
none is left to protest.
  Bene. Come, bid me do any thing for thee. 290
  Beat. Kill Claudio.
  Bene. Ha! not for the wide world.
  Beat. You kill me to deny it.   Farewell.
  Bene. Tarry, sweet Beatrice.
  Beat. I am gone, though I am here.   There is no
love in you.   Nay, I pray you, let me go. 296
  Bene. Beatrice,—
  Beat. In faith, I will go.
  Bene. We'll be friends first.
  Beat. You dare easier be friends with me than
fight with mine enemy. 301
  Bene. Is Claudio thine enemy?
  Beat. Is 'a not approved in the height a villain,
that hath slandered, scorned, dishonoured my
kinswoman?   O that I were a man!   What, bear
her in hand until they come to take hands; 305
and then, with public accusation, uncover'd slander,
unmitigated rancour, — O God, that I were a man!
I would eat his heart in the market-place.
  Bene. Hear me, Beatrice,— 310
  Beat. Talk with a man out at a window!   A
proper saying!
  Bene. Nay, but, Beatrice,—
  Beat. Sweet Hero!   She is wrong'd, she is
sland'red, she is undone. 315
  Bene. Beat —
  Beat. Princes and counties!   Surely, a princely
testimony, a goodly count, Count Comfect; a sweet
gallant, surely!   O that I were a man for his sake!
or that I had any friend would be a man for 320
my sake!   But manhood is melted into courtesies,
valour into compliment, and men are only turned
into tongue, and trim ones too.   He is now as
valiant as Hercules that only tells a lie and swears
it.   I cannot be a man with wishing, therefore I
will die a woman with grieving. 326
  Bene. Tarry, good Beatrice.   By this hand, I
love thee.
  Beat. Use it for my love some other way than
swearing by it. 330
  Bene. Think you in your soul the Count Claudio
hath wrong'd Hero?
  Beat. Yea, as sure as I have a thought or a soul.
  Bene. Enough, I am engag'd; I will challenge 335

233. **liver:** the supposed seat of passion. 239. **be ... false:** miscarry. 242. **sort:** turn out. 247. **inwardness:** intimacy. 256. **prolong'd:** postponed. 265. **even:** clear. 285. **in ... hour:** luckily. 295. **gone:** i.e., in spirit. 304. **bear
... hand:** delude with false hopes. 306. **uncover'd:** open. 318. **Comfect:** candy.

him. I will kiss your hand, and so I leave you. By
this hand, Claudio shall render me a dear account.
As you hear of me, so think of me. Go, comfort
your cousin. I must say she is dead; and so, farewell.   [*Exeunt.*] 340

[SCENE II. *A prison.*]

Enter the Constables [DOGBERRY, VERGES, *and*
SEXTON] *in gowns* [*and the* WATCH, *with* CONRADE]
and BORACHIO.

Dog. Is our whole dissembly appear'd?
Verg. O, a stool and a cushion for the sexton.
Sex. Which be the malefactors?
Dog. Marry, that am I and my partner.
Verg. Nay, that's certain; we have the exhibition
to examine.   6
Sex. But which are the offenders that are to be
examined? Let them come before master constable.
Dog. Yea, marry, let them come before me.
What is your name, friend?   11
Bora. Borachio.
Dog. Pray, write down, Borachio. Yours, sir-
rah?
Con. I am a gentleman, sir, and my name is
Conrade.   16
Dog. Write down, master gentleman Conrade.
Masters, do you serve God?
Con. ⎱
Bora. ⎰ Yea, sir, we hope.
Dog. Write down, that they hope they serve God;
and write God first; for God defend but God   21
should go before such villains! Masters, it is
proved already that you are little better than
false knaves; and it will go near to be thought so
shortly. How answer you for yourselves?   25
Con. Marry, sir, we say we are none.
Dog. A marvellous witty fellow, I assure you;
but I will go about with him. Come you hither,
sirrah; a word in your ear, sir. I say to you, it is
thought you are false knaves.   30
Bora. Sir, I say to you we are none.
Dog. Well, stand aside. 'Fore God, they are
both in a tale. Have you writ down, that they are
none?   34
Sex. Master constable, you go not the way to
examine. You must call forth the watch that are
their accusers.
Dog. Yea, marry, that's the eftest way. Let
the watch come forth. Masters, I charge you, in
the Prince's name, accuse these men.   40

1. Watch. This man said, sir, that Don John,
the Prince's brother, was a villain.
Dog. Write down Prince John a villain. Why,
this is flat perjury, to call a prince's brother
villain.
Bora. Master constable,—   45
Dog. Pray thee, fellow, peace. I do not like thy
look, I promise thee.
Sex. What heard you him say else?
2. Watch. Marry, that he had received a thousand ducats of Don John for accusing the Lady Hero
wrongfully.   51
Dog. Flat burglary as ever was committed.
Verg. Yea, by mass, that it is.
Sex. What else, fellow?
1. Watch. And that Count Claudio did   55
mean, upon his words, to disgrace Hero before the
whole assembly, and not marry her.
Dog. O villain! thou wilt be condemn'd into everlasting redemption for this.
Sex. What else?   60
1. Watch. This is all.
Sex. And this is more, masters, than you can
deny. Prince John is this morning secretly stol'n
away. Hero was in this manner accus'd, in this
very manner refus'd, and upon the grief of this   65
suddenly died. Master constable, let these men be
bound, and brought to Leonato's. I will go before
and show him their examination.   [*Exit.*]
Dog. Come, let them be opinion'd.
Verg. Let them be in the hands —   70
[*Con.*] Off, coxcomb!
Dog. God's my life, where's the sexton? Let
him write down the Prince's officer coxcomb.
Come, bind them. Thou naughty varlet!
Con. Away! you are an ass, you are an ass.   75
Dog. Dost thou not suspect my place? Dost
thou not suspect my years? O that he were here
to write me down an ass! But, masters, remember
that I am an ass; though it be not written down, yet
forget not that I am an ass. No, thou villain,   80
thou art full of piety, as shall be prov'd upon thee
by good witness. I am a wise fellow, and, which is
more, an officer, and, which is more, a householder,
and, which is more, as pretty a piece of flesh as any
is in Messina, and one that knows the law, go to;   85
and a rich fellow enough, go to; and a fellow that
hath had losses, and one that hath two gowns and
every thing handsome about him. Bring him
away. O that I had been writ down an ass!   90
                                    [*Exeunt.*

Sc. ii, 1. **Dog.** The speech-headings throughout this scene are jumbled. In Q Dogberry's speeches are headed *Keeper*
(l. 1), *Andrew* (l. 4), and *Kemp*, abbreviated variously (l. 10 up to l. 76, with the exception of l. 69 which is *Const.*). Verges's
speeches are headed *Cowley*, except at l. 53 where *Const.* appears. William Kempe and Richard Cowley were actors in
Shakespeare's company. *Keeper* (l. 1) may be the compositor's expansion of the abbreviation *Ke.; Andrew* (l. 4) may stand
for "Merry Andrew" or "clown," since Kempe regularly played comic parts. See Introduction. 28. **go about with:** get
the better of. 33. **are...tale:** tell the same story. 38. **eftest.** Apparently, easiest or quickest. 69. **opinion'd:** for
pinioned. 71. [Con.] **Off, coxcomb!** (Warburton). *of Coxcombe* Q. 81. **piety:** for *impiety.*

ACT V

[SCENE I. *Before Leonato's house.*]

Enter LEONATO *and* ANTONIO.

Ant. If you go on thus, you will kill yourself;
And 'tis not wisdom thus to second grief
Against yourself.

Leon.   I pray thee, cease thy counsel,
Which falls into mine ears as profitless
As water in a sieve.   Give not me counsel;   5
Nor let no comforter delight mine ear
But such a one whose wrongs do suit with mine.
Bring me a father that so lov'd his child,
Whose joy of her is overwhelm'd like mine,
And bid him speak of patience;   10
Measure his woe the length and breadth of mine,
And let it answer every strain for strain,
As thus for thus, and such a grief for such,
In every lineament, branch, shape, and form;
If such a one will smile and stroke his beard,   15
[Bid] sorrow wag, cry "hem!" when he should groan,
Patch grief with proverbs, make misfortune drunk
With candle-wasters, bring him yet to me,
And I of him will gather patience.
But there is no such man; for, brother, men   20
Can counsel and speak comfort to that grief
Which they themselves not feel; but, tasting it,
Their counsel turns to passion, which before
Would give preceptial medicine to rage,
Fetter strong madness in a silken thread,   25
Charm ache with air and agony with words.
No, no; 'tis all men's office to speak patience
To those that wring under the load of sorrow,
But no man's virtue nor sufficiency
To be so moral when he shall endure   30
The like himself.   Therefore give me no counsel;
My griefs cry louder than advertisement.

Ant. Therein do men from children nothing differ.

Leon. I pray thee, peace. I will be flesh and blood;
For there was never yet philosopher   35
That could endure the toothache patiently,
However they have writ the style of gods
And made a push at chance and sufferance.

Ant. Yet bend not all the harm upon yourself;
Make those that do offend you suffer too.   40

Leon. There thou speak'st reason.   Nay, I will
do so.
My soul doth tell me Hero is belied;
And that shall Claudio know; so shall the Prince
And all of them that thus dishonour her.   44

Enter DON PEDRO *and* CLAUDIO.

Ant. Here comes the Prince and Claudio hastily.

D. Pedro.   Good den, good den.

Claud.   Good day to both of you.

Leon. Hear you, my lords, —

D. Pedro.   We have some haste, Leonato.

Leon. Some haste, my lord!   Well, fare you well,
my lord.
Are you so hasty now?   Well, all is one.

D. Pedro. Nay, do not quarrel with us, good old
man.   50

Ant. If he could right himself with quarrelling,
Some of us would lie low.

Claud.   Who wrongs him?

Leon. Marry, thou dost wrong me; thou dis-
sembler, thou, —
Nay, never lay thy hand upon thy sword;
I fear thee not.

Claud.   Marry, beshrew my hand.   55
If it should give your age such cause of fear.
In faith, my hand meant nothing to my sword.

Leon. Tush, tush, man; never fleer and jest at me.
I speak not like a dotard nor a fool,
As under privilege of age to brag   60
What I have done being young, or what would do
Were I not old.   Know, Claudio, to thy head,
Thou hast so wrong'd mine innocent child and me
That I am forc'd to lay my reverence by
And, with grey hairs and bruise of many days,   65
Do challenge thee to trial of a man.
I say thou hast belied mine innocent child!
Thy slander hath gone through and through her
heart,
And she lies buried with her ancestors,
O, in a tomb where never scandal slept,   70
Save this of hers, fram'd by thy villainy!

Claud. My villainy?

Leon.   Thine, Claudio; thine, I say.

D. Pedro. You say not right, old man.

Leon.   My lord, my lord,
I'll prove it on his body, if he dare,
Despite his nice fence and his active practice,   75
His May of youth and bloom of lustihood.

Claud. Away! I will not have to do with you.

Leon. Canst thou so daff me?   Thou hast kill'd
my child.
If thou kill'st me, boy, thou shalt kill a man.

Ant. He shall kill two of us, and men indeed.
But that's no matter; let him kill one first.   81
Win me and wear me; let him answer me.
Come, follow me, boy; come, sir boy, come, follow me.
Sir boy, I'll whip you from your foining fence;
Nay, as I am a gentleman, I will.   85

Leon. Brother, —

Ant. Content yourself.   God knows I lov'd my
niece;

Act V, sc. i, 7. **suit:** match.   16. [Bid] (Dyce). *And* Q.   **wag:** go packing.   18. **candle-wasters:** revellers.   **yet:** then.
24. **preceptial:** made up of precepts.   30. **moral:** moralistic.   32. **advertisement:** advice.   37. **writ...gods:** taken a god-
like tone.   38. **made...at:** pooh-poohed.   55. **beshrew:** curse.   58. **fleer:** sneer.   75. **fence:** fencing.   78. **daff:** put off.
84. **foining:** thrusting.

And she is dead, slander'd to death by villains,
That dare as well answer a man indeed
As I dare take a serpent by the tongue.   90
Boys, apes, braggarts, Jacks, milksops!
 Leon.   Brother Antony,—
 Ant. Hold you content. What, man! I know
  them, yea,
And what they weigh, even to the utmost scruple, —
Scambling, out-facing, fashion-monging boys,
That lie and cog and flout, deprave and slander,   95
Go anticly and show outward hideousness,
And speak off half a dozen dang'rous words,
How they might hurt their enemies, if they durst;
And this is all.
 Leon. But, brother Antony, —
 Ant.   Come, 'tis no matter.
Do not you meddle; let me deal in this.   101
 D. Pedro. Gentlemen both, we will not wake your
  patience.
My heart is sorry for your daughter's death;
But, on my honour, she was charg'd with nothing
But what was true and very full of proof.   105
 Leon. My lord, my lord, —
 D. Pedro. I will not hear you.
 Leon. No? Come, brother, away! I will be
  heard.
 Ant. And shall, or some of us will smart for it.
     [*Exeunt Leonato and Antonio.*

    Enter BENEDICK.

 D. Pedro. See, see; here comes the man we went
  to seek.   110
 Claud. Now, signior, what news?
 Bene. Good day, my lord.
 D. Pedro. Welcome, signior. You are almost
come to part almost a fray.   114
 Claud. We had like to have had our two noses
snapp'd off with two old men without teeth.
 D. Pedro. Leonato and his brother. What
think'st thou? Had we fought, I doubt we should
have been too young for them.
 Bene. In a false quarrel there is no true valour.
I came to seek you both.   121
 Claud. We have been up and down to seek thee;
for we are high-proof melancholy and would fain
have it beaten away. Wilt thou use thy wit?
 Bene. It is in my scabbard; shall I draw it?   125
 D. Pedro. Dost thou wear thy wit by thy side?
 Claud. Never any did so, though very many have
been beside their wit. I will bid thee draw, as we
do the minstrels; draw, to pleasure us.
 D. Pedro. As I am an honest man, he looks pale.
Art thou sick, or angry?   131

 Claud. What, courage, man! What though care
kill'd a cat, thou hast mettle enough in thee to kill
care.
 Bene. Sir, I shall meet your wit in the career, an
you charge it against me. I pray you choose another subject.   137
 Claud. Nay, then, give him another staff. This
last was broke across.
 D. Pedro. By this light, he changes more and
more. I think he be angry indeed.   141
 Claud. If he be, he knows how to turn his girdle.
 Bene. Shall I speak a word in your ear?
 Claud. God bless me from a challenge!   144
 Bene. [*Aside to Claudio.*] You are a villain! I
jest not. I will make it good how you dare, with
what you dare, and when you dare. Do me right,
or I will protest your cowardice. You have kill'd
a sweet lady, and her death shall fall heavy on you.
Let me hear from you.   151
 Claud. Well, I will meet you, so I may have good
cheer.
 D. Pedro. What, a feast, a feast?   154
 Claud. I' faith, I thank him. He hath bid me to
a calf's head and a capon; the which if I do not
carve most curiously, say my knife's naught. Shall
I not find a woodcock too?
 Bene. Sir, your wit ambles well; it goes easily. 159
 D. Pedro. I'll tell thee how Beatrice prais'd thy
wit the other day. I said thou hadst a fine wit.
"True," said she, "a fine little one." "No," said I,
"a great wit." "Right," says she, "a great gross
one." "Nay," said I, "a good wit." "Just," said
she, "it hurts nobody." "Nay," said I, "the   165
gentleman is wise." "Certain," said she, "a wise
gentleman." "Nay," said I, "he hath the tongues."
"That I believe," said she, "for he swore a thing to
me on Monday night, which he forswore on Tuesday
morning. There's a double tongue; there's two   170
tongues." Thus did she, an hour together, trans-
shape thy particular virtues; yet at last she concluded with a sigh, thou wast the proper'st man in
Italy.
 Claud. For the which she wept heartily and said
she car'd not.   176
 D. Pedro. Yea, that she did; but yet, for all that,
an if she did not hate him deadly, she would love
him dearly. The old man's daughter told us all. 180
 Claud. All, all; and, moreover, God saw him when
he was hid in the garden.
 D. Pedro. But when shall we set the savage bull's
horns on the sensible Benedick's head?
 Claud. Yea, and text underneath, "Here dwells
Benedick the married man"?   186

---

94. **Scambling:** quarrelsome. **fashion-monging:** dandified. 95. **cog:** cheat. 96. **anticly:** like a buffoon. 102. **wake
your patience.** Not satisfactorily explained. It has been proposed to read *rack* for *wake* or *passions* for *patience.* 123.
high-proof: exceedingly. 135. **career:** onset. 136. **charge:** level. 138. **staff:** lance. 142. **turn his girdle:** i.e., so that he
can more quickly reach his dagger (a gesture of challenge). 148. **protest:** proclaim. 156–58. **calf's head, capon, woodcock.**
All figures of stupidity. 157. **curiously:** exquisitely. 167. **hath the tongues:** is a linguist. 171. **trans-shape:** distort.

Bene. Fare you well, boy; you know my mind. I will leave you now to your gossip-like humour. You break jests as braggarts do their blades, which, God be thanked, hurt not. My lord, for your many   190 courtesies I thank you. I must discontinue your company. Your brother the bastard is fled from Messina. You have among you kill'd a sweet and innocent lady. For my Lord Lackbeard there, he and I shall meet; and, till then, peace be with him.
                                                            [*Exit.*]

D. Pedro. He is in earnest.   197

Claud. In most profound earnest; and, I'll warrant you, for the love of Beatrice.

D. Pedro. And hath challeng'd thee?   200

Claud. Most sincerely.

D. Pedro. What a pretty thing man is when he goes in his doublet and hose and leaves off his wit!

Claud. He is then a giant to an ape; but then is an ape a doctor to such a man.   206

D. Pedro. But, soft you, let me be. Pluck up, my heart, and be sad. Did he not say, my brother was fled?   209

Enter Constables [DOGBERRY, VERGES, *and the* Watch, *with*] CONRADE *and* BORACHIO.

Dog. Come you, sir. If justice cannot tame you, she shall ne'er weigh more reasons in her balance. Nay, an you be a cursing hypocrite once, you must be look'd to.

D. Pedro. How now? Two of my brother's men, bound! Borachio one!   215

Claud. Hearken after their offence, my lord.

D. Pedro. Officers, what offence have these men done?   218

Dog. Marry, sir, they have committed false report; moreover, they have spoken untruths; secondarily, they are slanders; sixth and lastly, they have belied a lady; thirdly, they have verified unjust things; and, to conclude, they are lying knaves.

D. Pedro. First, I ask thee what they have   225 done; thirdly, I ask thee what's their offence; sixth and lastly, why they are committed; and, to conclude, what you lay to their charge.

Claud. Rightly reasoned, and in his own division; and, by my troth, there's one meaning well suited.

D. Pedro. Who have you offended, masters,   232 that you are thus bound to your answer? This learned constable is too cunning to be understood. What's your offence?   235

Bora. Sweet Prince, let me go no farther to mine answer. Do you hear me, and let this count kill me. I have deceived even your very eyes. What your wisdoms could not discover, these shallow fools have brought to light, who in the night   240

overheard me confessing to this man how Don John your brother incensed me to slander the Lady Hero, how you were brought into the orchard and saw me court Margaret in Hero's garments, how you disgrac'd her, when you should marry her. My   245 villainy they have upon record; which I had rather seal with my death than repeat over to my shame. The lady is dead upon mine and my master's false accusation; and, briefly, I desire nothing but the reward of a villain.   251

D. Pedro. Runs not this speech like iron through
     your blood?

Claud. I have drunk poison whiles he utter'd it.

D. Pedro. But did my brother set thee on to this?

Bora. Yea, and paid me richly for the practice of it.   256

D. Pedro. He is compos'd and fram'd of treachery. And fled he is upon this villainy.

Claud. Sweet Hero! now thy image doth appear In the rare semblance that I lov'd it first.   260

Dog. Come, bring away the plaintiffs. By this time our sexton hath reformed Signior Leonato of the matter; and, masters, do not forget to specify, when time and place shall serve, that I am an ass.

Verg. Here, here comes master Signior Leonato, and the sexton too.   267

Re-enter LEONATO *and* ANTONIO, *with the* Sexton.

Leon. Which is the villain? Let me see his eyes, That, when I note another man like him   270 I may avoid him. Which of these is he?

Bora. If you would know your wronger, look on
     me.

Leon. Art thou the slave that with thy breath
     hast kill'd
Mine innocent child?

Bora.   Yea, even I alone.

Leon. No, not so, villain; thou beliest thyself.   275
Here stand a pair of honourable men,
A third is fled, that had a hand in it.
I thank you, princes, for my daughter's death.
Record it with your high and worthy deeds.
'Twas bravely done, if you bethink you of it.   280

Claud. I know not how to pray your patience;
Yet I must speak. Choose your revenge yourself;
Impose me to what penance your invention
Can lay upon my sin; yet sinn'd I not
But in mistaking.

D. Pedro.   By my soul, nor I;   285
And yet, to satisfy this good old man,
I would bend under any heavy weight
That he'll enjoin me to.

Leon. I cannot bid you bid my daughter live,—
That were impossible; but, I pray you both,   290

205. **giant:** i.e., in stature. **to:** compared to. 206. **doctor:** scholar. 216. **Hearken after:** inquire into. 231. **one ... suited:** one idea dressed up in four different ways. 233. **bound ... answer:** arraigned. 242. **incensed:** instigated. 261. **plaintiffs:** for *defendants.*

Possess the people in Messina here
How innocent she died; and if your love
Can labour ought in sad invention,
Hang her an epitaph upon her tomb
And sing it to her bones, sing it to-night.   295
To-morrow morning come you to my house,
And since you could not be my son-in-law,
Be yet my nephew. My brother hath a daughter,
Almost the copy of my child that's dead,
And she alone is heir to both of us.   300
Give her the right you should have giv'n her cousin,
And so dies my revenge.
Claud.   O noble sir,
Your over-kindness doth wring tears from me!
I do embrace your offer; and dispose
For henceforth of poor Claudio.   305
Leon. To-morrow then I will expect your coming;
To-night I take my leave. This naughty man
Shall face to face be brought to Margaret,
Who I believe was pack'd in all this wrong,
Hir'd to it by your brother.
Bora.   No, by my soul, she was not,   310
Nor knew not what she did when she spoke to me,
But always hath been just and virtuous
In anything that I do know by her.
Dog. Moreover, sir, which indeed is not under
white and black, this plaintiff here, the offender, 315
did call me ass. I beseech you, let it be remem-
b'red in his punishment. And also, the watch heard
them talk of one Deformed. They say he wears a
key in his ear and a lock hanging by it, and borrows
money in God's name, the which he hath 320
used so long and never paid that now men grow
hard-hearted and will lend nothing for God's sake.
Pray you, examine him upon that point.
Leon. I thank thee for thy care and honest pains.
Dog. Your worship speaks like a most thankful and
[reverend] youth, and I praise God for you. 326
Leon. There's for thy pains.
Dog. God save the foundation!
Leon. Go, I discharge thee of thy prisoner, and I
thank thee.   330
Dog. I leave an arrant knave with your worship;
which I beseech your worship to correct yourself, for
the example of others. God keep your worship! I
wish your worship well. God restore you to health!
I humbly give you leave to depart; and if a merry
meeting may be wish'd, God prohibit it! Come, 336
neighbour.
                [Exeunt [Dogberry and Verges].
Leon. Until to-morrow morning, lords, farewell.
Ant. Farewell, my lords. We look for you to-
morrow.

D. Pedro. We will not fail.
Claud.   To-night I'll mourn with Hero.
Leon. [*To the Watch.*] Bring you these fellows on.
  We'll talk with Margaret,   341
How her acquaintance grew with this lewd fel-
low.
                  [Exeunt [severally].

[SCENE II. *Leonato's garden.*]

Enter BENEDICK *and* MARGARET [*meeting*].

Bene. Pray thee, sweet Mistress Margaret, deserve well at my hands by helping me to the speech
of Beatrice.
Marg. Will you then write me a sonnet in praise
of my beauty?   5
Bene. In so high a style, Margaret, that no man
living shall come over it; for, in most comely truth,
thou deservest it.
Marg. To have no man come over me! Why,
shall I always keep below stairs?   10
Bene. Thy wit is as quick as the greyhound's
mouth; it catches.
Marg. And yours as blunt as the fencer's foils,
which hit, but hurt not.   14
Bene. A most manly wit, Margaret; it will not
hurt a woman. And so, I pray thee, call Beatrice;
I give thee the bucklers.
Marg. Give us the swords; we have bucklers of
our own.   19
Bene. If you use them, Margaret, you must put
in the pikes with a vice; and they are dangerous
weapons for maids.
Marg. Well, I will call Beatrice to you, who I
think hath legs.   *[Exit Margaret.*
Bene. And therefore will come.   25
[*Sings.*]   The god of love,
          That sits above,
      And knows me, and knows me,
        How pitiful I deserve, —   29
I mean in singing; but in loving, Leander the good
swimmer, Troilus the first employer of panders,
and a whole bookful of these quondam carpet-
mongers, whose names yet run smoothly in the
even road of a blank verse, why, they were never
so truly turn'd over and over as my poor self in
love. Marry, I cannot show it in rhyme. I 35
have tried. I can find out no rhyme to "lady"
but "baby," an innocent rhyme; for "scorn,"
"horn," a hard rhyme; for "school," "fool," a
babbling rhyme; very ominous endings. No, I
was not born under a rhyming planet, nor I cannot
woo in festival terms.   41

291. possess: inform.   309. pack'd: leagued.   313. by: of.   326. [reverend] F. *reverent* Q.   328. God...foundation.
The usual formula upon receiving alms.   342. lewd: wicked.
Sc. ii, 6. style: with a pun on *stile*.   17. I...bucklers: I yield.   21. pikes: spikes (in the center of bucklers). vice:
screw.   32–33. quondam carpet-mongers: ancient carpet-knights.

Enter BEATRICE.

Sweet Beatrice, wouldst thou come when I call'd thee?

Beat. Yea, signior, and depart when you bid me.

  Bene. O, stay but till then!   45

  Beat. "Then" is spoken; fare you well now. And yet, ere I go, let me go with that I came for; which is, with knowing what hath pass'd between you and Claudio.

  Bene. Only foul words; and thereupon I will kiss thee.   51

  Beat. Foul words is but foul wind, and foul wind is but foul breath, and foul breath is noisome; therefore I will depart unkiss'd.   54

  Bene. Thou hast frighted the word out of his right sense, so forcible is thy wit. But I must tell thee plainly, Claudio undergoes my challenge; and either I must shortly hear from him, or I will subscribe him a coward. And, I pray thee now, tell me for which of my bad parts didst thou first fall in love with me?   61

  Beat. For them all together, which maintained so politic a state of evil that they will not admit any good part to intermingle with them. But for which of my good parts did you first suffer love for me?   66

  Bene. Suffer love! a good epithet! I do suffer love indeed, for I love thee against my will.

  Beat. In spite of your heart, I think; alas, poor heart! If you spite it for my sake, I will spite it for yours; for I will never love that which my friend hates.   72

  Bene. Thou and I are too wise to woo peaceably.

  Beat. It appears not in this confession. There's not one wise man among twenty that will praise himself.   77

  Bene. An old, an old instance, Beatrice, that liv'd in the time of good neighbours. If a man do not erect in this age his own tomb ere he dies, he shall live no longer in monument than the bell rings and the widow weeps.   82

  Beat. And how long is that, think you?

  Bene. Question. Why, an hour in clamour and a quarter in rheum; therefore is it most expedient for the wise, if Don Worm, his conscience, find 86 no impediment to the contrary, to be the trumpet of his own virtues, as I am to myself. So much for praising myself, who, I myself will bear witness, is praiseworthy. And now tell me, how doth your cousin?   91

  Beat. Very ill.

  Bene. And how do you?

  Beat. Very ill too.

  Bene. Serve God, love me, and mend. There will I leave you too, for here comes one in haste. 96

Enter URSULA.

  Urs. Madam, you must come to your uncle. Yonder's old coil at home. It is proved my Lady Hero hath been falsely accus'd, the Prince and Claudio mightily abus'd; and Don John is the author of all, who is fled and gone. Will you come presently?   102

  Beat. Will you go hear this news, signior?

  Bene. I will live in thy heart, die in thy lap, and be buried in thy eyes; and moreover I will go with thee to thy uncle's.   [*Exeunt.* 106

[SCENE III. *A church.*]

Enter DON PEDRO, CLAUDIO, *and three or four with tapers.*

  Claud. Is this the monument of Leonato?

  A Lord. It is, my lord.

  Claud. [*Reading out of a scroll.*]

EPITAPH.

"Done to death by slanderous tongues
  Was the Hero that here lies.
Death, in guerdon of her wrongs,   5
  Gives her fame which never dies.
So the life that died with shame
Lives in death with glorious fame."

Hang thou there upon the tomb,
  Praising her when I am [dumb].   10
Now, music, sound, and sing your solemn hymn.

SONG.

"Pardon, goddess of the night,
  Those that slew thy virgin knight;
For the which, with songs of woe,
  Round about her tomb they go.   15
   Midnight, assist our moan;
   Help us to sigh and groan,
    Heavily, heavily.
   Graves, yawn and yield your dead,
   Till death be uttered,   20
    Heavily, heavily."

[*Claud.*] Now, unto thy bones good night!
  Yearly will I do this rite.

  D. Pedro. Good morrow, masters; put your torches out.
The wolves have prey'd; and look, the gentle day,   25
Before the wheels of Phœbus, round about

---

 57. undergoes: has received. **79. time...neighbours:** good old times when neighbors were kindly. **85. rheum:** tears. **98. old coil:** great stir.

 Sc. iii, 10. [dumb] F. *dead* Q. **20. uttered:** cast out. **22.** [*Claud.*] (Rowe). *Lo.* Q.

Dapples the drowsy east with spots of grey.
Thanks to you all, and leave us.   Fare you well.
Claud. Good morrow, masters.   Each his several
    way.
D. Pedro. Come, let us hence, and put on other
    weeds;   30
And then to Leonato's we will go.
Claud. And Hymen now with luckier issue
    [speed's]
Than this for whom we rend'red up this woe.
                                    [Exeunt.

[SCENE IV. *A room in Leonato's house.*]

Enter LEONATO, *old man* [ANTONIO], BENEDICK,
[BEATRICE,] MARGARET, URSULA, FRIAR FRANCIS,
and HERO.

Friar. Did I not tell you she was innocent?
Leon. So are the Prince and Claudio, who
    accus'd her
Upon the error that you heard debated.
But Margaret was in some fault for this,
Although against her will, as it appears   5
In the true course of all the question.
Ant. Well, I am glad that all things sort so well.
Bene. And so am I, being else by faith enforc'd
To call young Claudio to a reckoning for it.   9
Leon. Well, daughter, and you gentlewomen all,
Withdraw into a chamber by yourselves,
And when I send for you, come hither mask'd.
The Prince and Claudio promis'd by this hour
To visit me.   You know your office, brother.
You must be father to your brother's daughter,   15
And give her to young Claudio.   *[Exeunt Ladies.*
Ant. Which I will do with confirm'd countenance.
Bene. Friar, I must entreat your pains, I think.
Friar. To do what, signior?
Bene. To bind me, or undo me; one of them. 20
Signior Leonato, truth it is, good signior,
Your niece regards me with an eye of favour.
Leon. That eye my daughter lent her; 'tis most
    true.
Bene. And I do with an eye of love requite her.
Leon. The sight whereof I think you had from
    me,   25
From Claudio, and the Prince.   But what's your
    will?
Bene. Your answer, sir, is enigmatical;
But, for my will, my will is your good will
May stand with ours, this day to be conjoin'd
In the state of honourable marriage;   30
In which, good friar, I shall desire your help.
Leon. My heart is with your liking.
Friar.   And my help.

Here comes the Prince and Claudio.

Enter DON PEDRO *and* CLAUDIO, *and two or
three other.*

D. Pedro. Good morrow to this fair assembly.
Leon. Good morrow, Prince; good morrow,
    Claudio;   35
We here attend you.   Are you yet determin'd
To-day to marry with my brother's daughter?
Claud. I'll hold my mind, were she an Ethiope.
Leon. Call her forth, brother; here's the friar
    ready.   *[Exit Antonio.]*
D. Pedro. Good morrow, Benedick.   Why, what's
    the matter,   40
That you have such a February face,
So full of frost, of storm and cloudiness?
Claud. I think he thinks upon the savage bull.
Tush, fear not, man; we'll tip thy horns with gold
And all Europa shall rejoice at thee,   45
As once Europa did at lusty Jove,
When he would play the noble beast in love.
Bene. Bull Jove, sir, had an amiable low;
And some such strange bull leap'd your father's cow,
And got a calf in that same noble feat   50
Much like to you, for you have just his bleat.

Re-enter ANTONIO, *with the* LADIES *[masked].*

Claud. For this I owe you: here comes other
    reck'nings.
Which is the lady I must seize upon?
[Ant.] This same is she, and I do give you her.
Claud. Why, then she's mine.   Sweet, let me
    see your face.   55
Leon. No, that you shall not, till you take her
    hand
Before this friar and swear to marry her.
Claud. Give me your hand.   Before this holy
    friar
I am your husband, if you like of me.   59
Hero. And when I liv'd, I was your other wife;
                         [Unmasking.]
And when you lov'd, you were my other husband.
Claud. Another Hero!
Hero.   Nothing certainer.
One Hero died defil'd, but I do live;
And surely as I live, I am a maid.   64
D Pedro. The former Hero! Hero that is dead!
Leon. She died, my lord, but whiles her slander
    liv'd.
Friar. All this amazement can I qualify,
When after that the holy rites are ended,
I'll tell you largely of fair Hero's death.
Meantime let wonder seem familiar,   70
And to the chapel let us presently.

32. [speed's] (Thirlby conj.): favor us. *speeds* QF.
Sc. iv, 6. question: investigation. 7. sort: turn out. 17. confirm'd: steady, grave. 43. Cf. I.i.263 ff. and V.i.183.
46. Europa. Jove, in the guise of a white bull, abducted the mortal Europa. 54. [Ant.] (Theobald). Leon. QF. 67.
qualify: moderate. 69. largely: in detail.

Bene. Soft and fair, friar.   Which is Beatrice?

Beat. [*Unmasking.*] I answer to that name. What is your will?

Bene. Do not you love me?

Beat.   Why, no; no more than reason.

Bene. Why, then your uncle and the Prince and Claudio   75
Have been deceived.   They swore you did.

Beat. Do not you love me?

Bene.   Troth, no; no more than reason.

Beat. Why, then my cousin, Margaret, and Ursula
Are much deceiv'd, for they did swear you did.

Bene. They swore that you were almost sick for me.   80

Beat. They swore that you were well-nigh dead for me.

Bene. 'Tis no such matter.   Then you do not love me?

Beat. No, truly, but in friendly recompense.

Leon. Come, cousin, I am sure you love the gentleman.

Claud. And I'll be sworn upon't that he loves her;   85
For here's a paper written in his hand,
A halting sonnet of his own pure brain,
Fashion'd to Beatrice.

Hero.   And here's another
Writ in my cousin's hand, stol'n from her pocket,
Containing her affection unto Benedick.   90

Bene. A miracle! here's our own hands against our hearts.   Come, I will have thee; but, by this light, I take thee for pity.

Beat. I would not deny you; but, by this good day, I yield upon great persuasion; and partly   95
to save your life, for I was told you were in a consumption.

[*Bene.*] Peace! I will stop your mouth.

[*Kissing her.*]

D. Pedro. How dost thou, Benedick, the married man?   100

Bene. I'll tell thee what, Prince; a college of wit-crackers cannot flout me out of my humour. Dost thou think I care for a satire or an epigram? No; if a man will be beaten with brains, 'a shall wear nothing handsome about him.   In brief, since I do purpose to marry, I will think   105
nothing to any purpose that the world can say against it; and therefore never flout at me for what I have said against it, for man is a giddy thing, and this is my conclusion.   For thy part, Claudio, I did think to have beaten thee; but   110
in that thou art like to be my kinsman, live unbruis'd and love my cousin.

Claud. I had well hop'd thou wouldst have denied Beatrice, that I might have cudgell'd thee out of thy single life, to make thee a double-   116
dealer; which, out of question, thou wilt be, if my cousin do not look exceeding narrowly to thee.

Bene. Come, come, we are friends.   Let's have a dance ere we are married, that we may lighten our own hearts and our wives' heels.   121

Leon. We'll have dancing afterward.

Bene. First, of my word; therefore play, music. Prince, thou art sad; get thee a wife, get thee a wife.   There is no staff more reverend than one tipp'd with horn.   126

Enter a MESSENGER.

Mess. My lord, your brother John is ta'en in flight, And brought with armed men back to Messina.

Bene. Think not on him till to-morrow.   I'll devise thee brave punishments for him.   Strike up, pipers.   [*Dance. [Exeunt.*]   131

98. [*Bene.*] (Theobald).   *Leon.* QF.   104. **beaten with brains:** ridiculed, satirized.   **wear...him:** i.e., to avoid ridicule.   116. **double-dealer:** (1) married man, (2) unfaithful husband.

As You Like It

UNDER THE DATE of August 4, 1600, *As You Like It* appears in the Stationers' Register, along with *Henry V*, *Much Ado*, and Jonson's *Everyman In His Humour*, as a play "to be staied." The entry was undoubtedly made to forestall piracy and in the case of this play was evidently successful, for no text of *As You Like It* appeared earlier than that of the First Folio. The history of the other Shakespearean plays is, however, otherwise. *Henry V* was printed in a sadly corrupt Quarto in 1600 (despite a formal entry eleven days later to Thomas Pavier), and a good Quarto of *Much Ado* appeared before the end of the year after a regular entry on August 23 to Andrew Wise and William Aspley. That *As You Like It* was not printed before 1623 would suggest that it remained sufficiently popular on the stage to afford Shakespeare's company no temptation to release it for the rewards of publication. The present text is that of the First Folio with some modifications taken from the later Folios and the emendations of modern editors.

The date of the play may be determined within close limits. Since it is not mentioned in the valuable list of Meres, it cannot be earlier than the end of 1598. The quotation from *Hero and Leander*, with the gentle reference to Marlowe as the "dead shepherd" (III.v.81–82), is also significant. That poem was first published in 1598, and though Shakespeare could conceivably have read it in manuscript before Marlowe's death on May 30, 1593, one must hold the printed work much more likely to have inspired the allusion in the play. In the light of the foregoing evidence, the preponderance of prose, and the generally high quality of the composition, 1599 or early 1600 may be taken as a safe date.

Certain discrepancies within the play have caused undue concern. The inconsistencies in connection with the relative statures of Rosalind and Celia (I.ii.284; I.iii.117; IV.iii.88–89), the length of the banished Duke's stay in Arden (I.i.120; I.iii.73; II.i.2), and the identities of the two Dukes are plainly the kind of inadvertence which is to be met with in a great many of Shakespeare's plays. In the Folio the speeches of Rosalind's father, the banished Duke, are headed *Duke* Senior; those of the usurping Duke, Celia's father, simply *Duke*. The former is nowhere called by any name, but from I.ii.246 and V.iv.160 it appears that the name of the latter was Frederick. Thus it seems somewhat odd when, in a line clearly addressed to Celia (I.ii.87), Touchstone calls her father, the *younger* Duke, "old Frederick." Such an inconsistency (if indeed it is one, for perhaps Touchstone is only speaking jocosely with a Clown's license) is not of great moment. It would never be noticed on the stage and it is hardly more disconcerting than Shakespeare's duplicating the conspicuous name of Jaques for the second son of Sir Rowland de Boys. The appearance of an appreciable number of blank verse rhythms in certain passages of prose has been held to indicate that those passages were originally in verse, and this factor, along with the other textual peculiarities already cited, has been taken as evidence of an earlier form of the play (1593) which Shakespeare was revising around 1598. But the occurrence of such "verse fossils" in prose no more calls for elaborate theorizing than do the other matters for which simple explanations are at hand. As has frequently been remarked, verse rhythms are by no means rare in English prose, certainly not in Shakespeare's. Indeed, there would be some reason for surprise if they did not occur in the prose of one who was a supreme master of verse, especially in a play which alternates prose and verse.

As You Like It is a straight dramatization of a pastoral tale in exuberant euphuistic prose called *Rosalynde, Euphues' Golden Legacie* (1590). Thomas Lodge, the author, had based his story upon an anonymous Middle English poem, *The Tale of Gamelyn*, which was at one time erroneously attributed to Chaucer because it is included in certain manuscripts of *The Canterbury Tales*. It does not, however, appear that Shakespeare knew this earlier work. From Lodge's tale he took the substance of his play, with omission and additions as he saw fit. The principal derivatives from Lodge are as follows: the themes of usurpation and banishment (in Lodge, Torismond, King of France, has usurped the throne of his brother Gerismond, the rightful king), the quarrel between Orlando and Oliver (Rosader and Saladyne), the wrestling match, the retreat into Arden, the affection of Rosalind and Celia (Rosalynde and Alinda, cousins as in the play), the wooing of the disguised Rosalind by Orlando (the pseudonym Ganymede also comes from Lodge), the eventual marriage of the remorseful Oliver and Celia, and the affair of Phebe and Silvius (Phoebe and Montanus). Shakespeare has compressed the time covered by the action and has eliminated some of the violent incidents which in the novel attend the quarrel between the hero and his persecuting brother. Oliver's reconciliation with Orlando is somewhat differently motivated in the novel. In the play it springs simply from his gratitude for Orlando's magnanimity in rescuing him from the lion; in the novel Saladyne has already repented of his cruelty to Rosader, owing to persecutions visited upon him by Torismond, and is seeking for his brother when this crisis occurs. Similarly, the marriage of Oliver and Celia is rendered more credible in the novel, because there, in an episode which Shakespeare omits, Saladyne rescues Alinda from a band of robbers who have abducted her. In *Rosalynde*, the restoration of the Duke is brought about by the overthrow and death of the usurper in battle, in contrast with the dramatist's milder device of conversion, which, however unplausible, suits better the mood of the play.

Shakespeare has created a number of new characters, of which Audrey, William, Amiens, Touchstone, and Jaques are the most interesting, the last two being, surely, immortal. Audrey and William, good Warwickshire rustics, add a touch of the true earth to the literary pastoralism of Silvius and Phebe inherited from Lodge. The rôle of Touchstone has something of novelty. Touchstone is the first of Shakespeare's court clowns and looks forward to Feste in *Twelfth Night* and the Fool in

Lear. To put down such a fellow in a pastoral setting was an innovation, but Touchstone, however incongruous in Arden, is merry there, and to good purpose. Often wiser than he is aware of, he breaks his wit over this thing and that with bracing and tonic effect. A genial provider of salutary comic remark, he is of the opposition party, but never with offense. He satirizes court life even while praising it; he ridicules the punctilios of professional quarrelling; he produces a fine "false gallop of verses" that puts Orlando's amorous jingle to shame; and by his grosser passion for Audrey he seems to burlesque, though this time doubtless unintentionally, the other love-making in the play. Jaques, like Touchstone, is a self-appointed critic, but his commentary has a different spirit. Where Touchstone is freely merry, Jaques is caustic. He has been disillusioned, because, one infers, he has been too much in the world. He is a malcontent, a Jonsonian humour character, though by the very distinction of his mind made individual, nursing his melancholy and taking his satisfaction in the contemplation and censure of human folly. His temperament has particular interest because it looks forward to Hamlet's. But whereas Hamlet's melancholy has profound tragic implications, that of Jaques remains a philosophic mood. Jaques, it may be noted, remains true to himself. When the other sojourners in Arden return to Court at the end of the play, he stays in the forest, retiring to the cell of the "convertite" Duke. Neither Touchstone nor Jaques is really necessary to the plot, yet they contribute immeasurably through the quality and the contrast of their personalities to the richness and vitality of the play.

Rosalind has ever enjoyed her due meed of praise. She is one of the most popular of Shakespeare's heroines. Her youth, her gaiety, her candor, and her courage have always captivated. She has, perhaps, the wit of Portia and Beatrice softened by the gentleness of Viola; but whatever the components of her charm, that charm is all her own.

AS YOU LIKE IT

[DRAMATIS PERSONÆ

DUKE, *living in banishment.*
FREDERICK, *his brother, and usurper of his dominions.*
AMIENS,
JAQUES,
} *lords attending on the banished Duke.*
LE BEAU, *a courtier attending upon Frederick.*
CHARLES, *wrestler to Frederick.*
OLIVER,
JAQUES,
ORLANDO,
} *sons of Sir Roland de Boys.*
ADAM,
DENNIS,
} *servants to Oliver.*

TOUCHSTONE, *a clown.*
SIR OLIVER MARTEXT, *a vicar.*
CORIN,
SILVIUS,
} *shepherds.*
WILLIAM, *a country fellow, in love with Audrey.*
A person representing Hymen.

ROSALIND, *daughter to the banished Duke.*
CELIA, *daughter to Frederick.*
PHEBE, *a shepherdess.*
AUDREY, *a country wench.*

Lords, pages, attendants, etc.

SCENE: *Oliver's house; Duke Frederick's court; and the Forest of Arden.*]

ACT I

SCENE I. [*Orchard of Oliver's house.*]

Enter ORLANDO *and* ADAM.

Orl. As I remember, Adam, it was upon this fashion: bequeathed me by will but poor a thousand crowns, and, as thou sayest, charged my brother, on his blessing, to breed me well; and there begins my sadness. My brother Jaques he keeps at 5 school, and report speaks goldenly of his profit. For my part, he keeps me rustically at home, or, to speak more properly, stays me here at home unkept; for call you that keeping for a gentleman of my birth, that differs not from the stalling of an 10 ox? His horses are bred better; for, besides that they are fair with their feeding, they are taught their manage, and to that end riders dearly hir'd; but I, his brother, gain nothing under him but growth; for the which his animals on his dung- 15 hills are as much bound to him as I. Besides this nothing that he so plentifully gives me, the some-thing that nature gave me his countenance seems to take from me. He lets me feed with his hinds, bars me the place of a brother, and, as much as 20 in him lies, mines my gentility with my education. This is it, Adam, that grieves me; and the spirit of my father, which I think is within me, begins to mutiny against this servitude. I will no longer endure it, though yet I know no wise remedy 25 how to avoid it.

Enter OLIVER.

Adam. Yonder comes my master, your brother.
Orl. Go apart, Adam, and thou shalt hear how he will shake me up. 30
Oli. Now, sir! what make you here?
Orl. Nothing. I am not taught to make any thing.
Oli. What mar you then, sir? 34
Orl. Marry, sir, I am helping you to mar that which God made, a poor unworthy brother of yours, with idleness.
Oli. Marry, sir, be better employed, and be naught awhile. 39

Act I, sc. i, 4. **on his blessing:** as a condition to his blessing. 6. **school:** university. 12-13. **taught ... manage:** given their training. 18. **countenance:** treatment. 19. **hinds:** menials. 21. **mines:** undermines. 39. **be naught awhile:** clear out.

Orl. Shall I keep your hogs and eat husks with them? What prodigal portion have I spent, that I should come to such penury?

Oli. Know you where you are, sir?

Orl. O, sir, very well; here in your orchard.

Oli. Know you before whom, sir?   45

Orl. Ay, better than him I am before knows me. I know you are my eldest brother; and, in the gentle condition of blood, you should so know me. The courtesy of nations allows you my better, in that you are the first-born; but the same tradi-   50 tion takes not away my blood, were there twenty brothers betwixt us. I have as much of my father in me as you; albeit, I confess, your coming before me is nearer to his reverence.

Oli. What, boy!   55

Orl. Come, come, elder brother, you are too young in this.

Oli. Wilt thou lay hands on me, villain?

Orl. I am no villain; I am the youngest son of Sir Roland de Boys. He was my father, and   60 he is thrice a villain that says such a father begot villains. Wert thou not my brother, I would not take this hand from thy throat till this other had pull'd out thy tongue for saying so. Thou hast rail'd on thyself.   65

Adam. Sweet masters, be patient; for your father's remembrance, be at accord.

Oli. Let me go, I say.

Orl. I will not, till I please. You shall hear me. My father charg'd you in his will to give me   70 good education. You have train'd me like a peasant, obscuring and hiding from me all gentleman-like qualities. The spirit of my father grows strong in me, and I will no longer endure it; therefore allow me such exercises as may become a gentle-   75 man, or give me the poor allottery my father left me by testament. With that I will go buy my fortunes.

Oli. And what wilt thou do? Beg, when that is spent? Well, sir, get you in. I will not long   80 be troubled with you; you shall have some part of your will. I pray you, leave me.

Orl. I will no further offend you than becomes me for my good.

Oli. Get you with him, you old dog.   85

Adam. Is "old dog" my reward? Most true, I have lost my teeth in your service. God be with my old master! He would not have spoke such a word.   89

[*Exeunt Orlando and Adam.*]

Oli. Is it even so? Begin you to grow upon me? I will physic your rankness, and yet give no thousand crowns neither. Holla, Dennis!

Enter DENNIS.

Den. Calls your worship?

Oli. Was not Charles, the Duke's wrestler, here to speak with me?   95

Den. So please you, he is here at the door and importunes access to you.

Oli. Call him in. [*Exit Dennis.*] 'Twill be a good way; and to-morrow the wrestling is.

Enter CHARLES.

Cha. Good morrow to your worship.   100

Oli. Good Monsieur Charles, what's the new news at the new court?

Cha. There's no news at the court, sir, but the old news: that is, the old Duke is banished by his younger brother the new Duke; and three or   105 four loving lords have put themselves into voluntary exile with him, whose lands and revenues enrich the new Duke; therefore he gives them good leave to wander.

Oli. Can you tell if Rosalind, the Duke's daughter, be banished with her father?   111

Cha. O, no; for the Duke's daughter, her cousin, so loves her, being ever from their cradles bred together, that [she] would have followed her exile, or have died to stay behind her. She is at the   115 court, and no less beloved of her uncle than his own daughter; and never two ladies loved as they do.

Oli. Where will the old Duke live?   119

Cha. They say he is already in the forest of Arden, and a many merry men with him; and there they live like the old Robin Hood of England. They say many young gentlemen flock to him every day, and fleet the time carelessly, as they did in the golden world.   125

Oli. What, you wrestle to-morrow before the new Duke?

Cha. Marry, do I, sir; and I came to acquaint you with a matter. I am given, sir, secretly to understand that your younger brother, Orlando,   130 hath a disposition to come in disguis'd against me to try a fall. To-morrow, sir, I wrestle for my credit; and he that escapes me without some broken limb shall acquit him well. Your brother is but young and tender; and, for your love, I   135 would be loath to foil him, as I must, for my own honour, if he come in; therefore, out of my love to you, I came hither to acquaint you withal, that either you might stay him from his intendment, or brook such disgrace well as he shall run into,   140 in that it is a thing of his own search, and altogether against my will.

Oli. Charles, I thank thee for thy love to me, which thou shalt find I will most kindly requite.

---

49. **courtesy of nations:** i.e., by virtue of the law of primogeniture.   54. **is ... reverence:** gives you better title to the respect due to him.   76. **allottery:** legacy.   90. **grow upon:** take liberties with.   91. **rankness:** exuberant growth, insolence. 114. **[she]** F₃.   *he* F₁.   125. **golden world:** the golden age.   134. **shall:** must.

I had myself notice of my brother's purpose 145 herein, and have by underhand means laboured to dissuade him from it, but he is resolute. I'll tell thee, Charles, it is the stubbornest young fellow of France; full of ambition, an envious emulator of every man's good parts, a secret and villainous 150 contriver against me his natural brother; therefore use thy discretion. I had as lief thou didst break his neck as his finger. And thou wert best look to't; for if thou dost him any slight disgrace, or if he do not mightily grace himself on thee, he 155 will practise against thee by poison, entrap thee by some treacherous device, and never leave thee till he hath ta'en thy life by some indirect means or other; for, I assure thee, and almost with tears I speak it, there is not one so young and so vil- 160 lainous this day living. I speak but brotherly of him; but should I anatomize him to thee as he is, I must blush and weep, and thou must look pale and wonder.   164

Cha. I am heartily glad I came hither to you. If he come to-morrow, I'll give him his payment. If ever he go alone again, I'll never wrestle for prize more. And so, God keep your worship!   [*Exit.*

Oli. Farewell, good Charles.   169 Now will I stir this gamester. I hope I shall see an end of him; for my soul — yet I know not why — hates nothing more than he. Yet he's gentle; never school'd, and yet learned; full of noble device; of all sorts enchantingly beloved; and indeed so much in the heart of the world, and espe- 175 cially of my own people, who best know him, that I am altogether misprised. But it shall not be so long; this wrestler shall clear all. Nothing remains but that I kindle the boy thither, which now I'll go about.   [*Exit.* 180

SCENE II.   [*Lawn before the Duke's palace.*]

Enter ROSALIND *and* CELIA.

Cel. I pray thee, Rosalind, sweet my coz, be merry.

Ros. Dear Celia, I show more mirth than I am mistress of; and would you yet [I] were merrier? Unless you could teach me to forget a banished 5 father, you must not learn me how to remember any extraordinary pleasure.

Cel. Herein I see thou lov'st me not with the full weight that I love thee. If my uncle, thy banished father, had banished thy uncle, the Duke my 10 father, so thou hadst been still with me, I could have taught my love to take thy father for mine.

So wouldst thou, if the truth of thy love to me were so righteously temper'd as mine is to thee.   15

Ros. Well, I will forget the condition of my estate, to rejoice in yours.

Cel. You know my father hath no child but I, nor none is like to have; and, truly, when he dies, thou shalt be his heir; for what he hath taken 20 away from thy father perforce, I will render thee again in affection. By mine honour, I will; and when I break that oath, let me turn monster. Therefore, my sweet Rose, my dear Rose, be merry.   25

Ros. From henceforth I will, coz, and devise sports. Let me see; what think you of falling in love?

Cel. Marry, I prithee, do, to make sport withal. But love no man in good earnest, nor no further 30 in sport neither than with safety of a pure blush thou mayst in honour come off again.

Ros. What shall be our sport, then?

Cel. Let us sit and mock the good housewife Fortune from her wheel, that her gifts may hence-forth be bestowed equally.   36

Ros. I would we could do so; for her benefits are mightily misplaced, and the bountiful blind woman doth most mistake in her gifts to women. 39

Cel. 'Tis true; for those that she makes fair she scarce makes honest, and those that she makes honest she makes very ill-favouredly.

Ros. Nay, now thou goest from Fortune's office to Nature's. Fortune reigns in gifts of the world, not in the lineaments of Nature.   45

Enter Clown [TOUCHSTONE].

Cel. No? When Nature hath made a fair creature, may she not by Fortune fall into the fire? Though Nature hath given us wit to flout at For-tune, hath not Fortune sent in this fool to cut off the argument?   50

Ros. Indeed, there is Fortune too hard for Nature, when Fortune makes Nature's natural the cutter-off of Nature's wit.

Cel. Peradventure this is not Fortune's work neither, but Nature's; who, [perceiving] our 55 natural wits too dull to reason of such goddesses, hath sent this natural for our whetstone; for al-ways the dulness of the fool is the whetstone of the wits. How now, wit! whither wander you?

Touch. Mistress, you must come away to your father.   61

Cel. Were you made the messenger?

Touch. No, by mine honour, but I was bid to come for you.

---

146. **underhand:** indirect.   151. **natural:** very own.   155. **grace ... thee:** win favor at your expense.   156. **practise:** plot.   167. **go alone:** walk without support.   170. **gamester:** would-be athlete.   173. **device:** aspiration.   174. **enchant-ingly:** as if by enchantment.   177. **misprised:** despised.   179. **kindle:** incite.

Sc. ii, 4. **[I]** (Rowe). Om. F.   11. **so:** so long as.   15. **righteously temper'd:** perfectly composed.   32. **come off:** escape.   41. **honest:** chaste.   42. **ill-favouredly:** ugly.   52. **natural:** idiot.   54. **[perceiving]** Ff₂₋₄.   *perceiveth* F₁.

Ros. Where learned you that oath, fool?   65

Touch. Of a certain knight that swore by his honour they were good pancakes, and swore by his honour the mustard was naught. Now I'll stand to it, the pancakes were naught and the mustard was good, and yet was not the knight forsworn.   71

Cel. How prove you that, in the great heap of your knowledge?

Ros. Ay, marry, now unmuzzle your wisdom.

Touch. Stand you both forth now. Stroke   75 your chins, and swear by your beards that I am a knave.

Cel. By our beards, if we had them, thou art.   79

Touch. By my knavery, if I had it, then I were. But if you swear by that that is not, you are not forsworn. No more was this knight, swearing by his honour, for he never had any; or if he had, he had sworn it away before ever he saw those pancakes or that mustard.   85

Cel. Prithee, who is't that thou meanest?

Touch. One that old Frederick, your father, loves.

[*Cel.*] My father's love is enough to honour him. Enough! speak no more of him. You'll be whipp'd for taxation one of these days.   91

Touch. The more pity, that fools may not speak wisely what wise men do foolishly.

Cel. By my troth, thou sayest true; for since the little wit that fools have was silenced, the little   95 foolery that wise men have makes a great show. Here comes Monsieur the Beau.

Enter LE BEAU.

Ros. With his mouth full of news.

Cel. Which he will put on us, as pigeons feed their young.   100

Ros. Then shall we be news-cramm'd.

Cel. All the better; we shall be the more marketable. *Bon jour,* Monsieur Le Beau. What's the news?

Le Beau. Fair princess, you have lost much good sport.   106

Cel. Sport! Of what colour?

Le Beau. What colour, madam? How shall I answer you?

Ros. As wit and fortune will.   110

Touch. Or as the Destinies decrees.

Cel. Well said. That was laid on with a trowel.

Touch. Nay, if I keep not my rank, —

Ros. Thou losest thy old smell.

Le Beau. You amaze me, ladies. I would   115 have told you of good wrestling, which you have lost the sight of.

Ros. Yet tell us the manner of the wrestling.

Le Beau. I will tell you the beginning; and, if it please your ladyships, you may see the end.   120 For the best is yet to do; and here, where you are, they are coming to perform it.

Cel. Well, the beginning, that is dead and buried.

Le Beau. There comes an old man and his three sons, —   126

Cel. I could match this beginning with an old tale.

Le Beau. Three proper young men, of excellent growth and presence.   130

Ros. With bills on their necks, "Be it known unto all men by these presents."

Le Beau. The eldest of the three wrestled with Charles, the Duke's wrestler; which Charles in a moment threw him, and broke three of his ribs,   135 that there is little hope of life in him. So he serv'd the second, and so the third. Yonder they lie; the poor old man, their father, making such pitiful dole over them that all the beholders take his part with weeping.   140

Ros. Alas!

Touch. But what is the sport, monsieur, that the ladies have lost?

Le Beau. Why, this that I speak of.

Touch. Thus men may grow wiser every day.   145 It is the first time that ever I heard breaking of ribs was sport for ladies.

Cel. Or I, I promise thee.

Ros. But is there any else longs to see this broken music in his sides? Is there yet another   150 dotes upon rib-breaking? Shall we see this wrestling, cousin?

Le Beau. You must, if you stay here; for here is the place appointed for the wrestling, and they are ready to perform it.   155

Cel. Yonder, sure, they are coming. Let us now stay and see it.

Flourish. Enter DUKE [FREDERICK], *Lords,* ORLANDO, CHARLES, *and* Attendants.

Duke F. Come on. Since the youth will not be entreated, his own peril on his forwardness.

Ros. Is yonder the man?   160

Le Beau. Even he, madam.

Cel. Alas, he is too young! Yet he looks successfully.

Duke F. How now, daughter and cousin! Are you crept hither to see the wrestling?   165

Ros. Ay, my liege, so please you give us leave.

Duke F. You will take little delight in it, I can tell you, there is such odds in the man. In pity of the challenger's youth I would fain dissuade   170 him, but he will not be entreated. Speak to him, ladies; see if you can move him.

---

68. **naught:** worthless.   89. **[*Cel.*]** (Theobald).   *Ros.* Ff.   91. **taxation:** satire.   107. **colour.** Le Beau had pronounced sport "spot," as it should probably be spelled in this line.   129. **proper:** handsome.   131. **bills:** proclamations.   138. **dole:** lament.   150. **broken music:** "part" music (for different instruments).

Cel. Call him hither, good Monsieur Le Beau.
Duke F. Do so; I'll not be by.   174
Le Beau. Monsieur the challenger, the princess
calls for you.
   Orl. I attend them with all respect and duty.
   Ros. Young man, have you challeng'd Charles
the wrestler?
   Orl. No, fair princess; he is the general chal- 180
lenger. I come but in, as others do, to try with him
the strength of my youth.
   Cel. Young gentleman, your spirits are too bold
for your years. You have seen cruel proof of this
man's strength. If you saw yourself with your 185
eyes, or knew yourself with your judgement, the
fear of your adventure would counsel you to a more
equal enterprise. We pray you, for your own sake,
to embrace your own safety, and give over this
attempt.   190
   Ros. Do, young sir; your reputation shall not
therefore be misprised. We will make it our suit
to the Duke that the wrestling might not go
forward.   194
   Orl. I beseech you, punish me not with your hard
thoughts, wherein I confess me much guilty to deny
so fair and excellent ladies any thing. But let your
fair eyes and gentle wishes go with me to my trial;
wherein if I be foil'd, there is but one sham'd that
was never gracious; if kill'd, but one dead that 200
is willing to be so. I shall do my friends no wrong,
for I have none to lament me; the world no injury,
for in it I have nothing. Only in the world I fill
up a place, which may be better supplied when I
have made it empty.   205
   Ros. The little strength that I have, I would it
were with you.
   Cel. And mine, to eke out hers.
   Ros. Fare you well! Pray heaven I be deceiv'd
in you!   210
   Cel. Your heart's desires be with you!
   Cha. Come, where is this young gallant that is so
desirous to lie with his mother earth?
   Orl. Ready, sir; but his will hath in it a more
modest working.   215
   Duke F. You shall try but one fall.
   Cha. No, I warrant your Grace, you shall not
entreat him to a second, that have so mightily per-
suaded him from a first.   219
   Orl. You mean to mock me after; you should not
have mock'd me before. But come your ways.
   Ros. Now Hercules be thy speed, young man!
   Cel. I would I were invisible, to catch the strong
fellow by the leg.   [*They wrestle.*
   Ros. O excellent young man!   225
   Cel. If I had a thunderbolt in mine eye I can tell

who should down.   [*Shout.* [*Charles is thrown.*]
   Duke F. No more, no more.
   Orl. Yes, I beseech your Grace. I am not yet
well breath'd.   230
   Duke F. How dost thou, Charles?
   Le Beau. He cannot speak, my lord.
   Duke F. Bear him away. What is thy name,
     young man?
   Orl. Orlando, my liege; the youngest son of Sir
Roland de Boys.   235
   Duke F. I would thou hadst been son to some
     man else.
The world esteem'd thy father honourable,
But I did find him still mine enemy.
Thou shouldst have better pleas'd me with this
     deed
Hadst thou descended from another house.   240
But fare thee well; thou art a gallant youth.
I would thou hadst told me of another father.
     [*Exeunt Duke* [*Fred., train, and Le Beau*].
   Cel. Were I my father, coz, would I do this?
   Orl. I am more proud to be Sir Roland's son,
His youngest son, — and would not change that
     calling,   245
To be adopted heir to Frederick.
   Ros. My father lov'd Sir Roland as his soul,
And all the world was of my father's mind.
Had I before known this young man his son,
I should have given him tears unto entreaties 250
Ere he should thus have ventur'd.
   Cel.   Gentle cousin,
Let us go thank him and encourage him.
My father's rough and envious disposition
Sticks me at heart. Sir, you have well deserv'd.
If you do keep your promises in love 255
But justly, as you have exceeded all promise,
Your mistress shall be happy.
   Ros.   Gentleman,
     [*Giving him a chain from her neck.*]
Wear this for me, one out of suits with Fortune,
That could give more, but that her hand lacks
     means.
Shall we go, coz?
   Cel.   Ay. Fare you well, fair gentleman.
   Orl. Can I not say, I thank you? My better
     parts   261
Are all thrown down, and that which here stands up
Is but a quintain, a mere lifeless block.
   Ros. He calls us back. My pride fell with my
     fortunes;
I'll ask him what he would. Did you call, sir? 265
Sir, you have wrestled well, and overthrown
More than your enemies.
   Cel.   Will you go, coz?

200. **gracious:** favored.   215. **working:** action.   222. **be thy speed:** favor you.   230. **breath'd:** put into good wind.
245. **calling:** name.   254. **sticks:** pierces.   258. **out...Fortune:** deprived of Fortune's livery, i.e., dismissed by her.   263.
quintain: a wooden dummy for tilting at.

Ros. Have with you. Fare you well.
                 [*Exeunt [Rosalind and Celia]*.
Orl. What passion hangs these weights upon my
    tongue?
I cannot speak to her, yet she urg'd conference. 270

Re-enter Le Beau.

O poor Orlando, thou art overthrown!
Or Charles or something weaker masters thee.
    Le Beau. Good sir, I do in friendship counsel you
To leave this place. Albeit you have deserv'd
High commendation, true applause, and love, 275
Yet such is now the Duke's condition
That he misconstrues all that you have done.
The Duke is humorous: — what he is, indeed,
More suits you to conceive than I to speak of.
    Orl. I thank you, sir; and, pray you, tell me
    this: 280
Which of the two was daughter of the Duke,
That here was at the wrestling?
    Le Beau. Neither his daughter, if we judge by
    manners;
But yet, indeed, the taller is his daughter.
The other is daughter to the banish'd Duke, 285
And here detain'd by her usurping uncle
To keep his daughter company; whose loves
Are dearer than the natural bond of sisters.
But I can tell you that of late this Duke
Hath ta'en displeasure 'gainst his gentle niece, 290
Grounded upon no other argument
But that the people praise her for her virtues,
And pity her for her good father's sake;
And, on my life, his malice 'gainst the lady
Will suddenly break forth. Sir, fare you well. 295
Hereafter, in a better world than this,
I shall desire more love and knowledge of you.
    Orl. I rest much bounden to you; fare you well.
                 [*Exit Le Beau*.]
Thus must I from the smoke into the smother,
From tyrant Duke unto a tyrant brother. 300
But heavenly Rosalind!   [*Exit.*

SCENE III. [*A room in the palace.*]

Enter CELIA *and* ROSALIND.

    Cel. Why, cousin! why, Rosalind! Cupid have
mercy! not a word?
    Ros. Not one to throw at a dog.
    Cel. No, thy words are too precious to be cast
away upon curs; throw some of them at me. Come,
lame me with reasons.   6
    Ros. Then there were two cousins laid up, when

the one should be lam'd with reasons and the other
mad without any.
    Cel. But is all this for your father?   10
    Ros. No, some of it is for my child's father. O,
how full of briers is this working-day world!
    Cel. They are but burs, cousin, thrown upon
thee in holiday foolery. If we walk not in the trodden paths, our very petticoats will catch them. 15
    Ros. I could shake them off my coat. These
burs are in my heart.
    Cel. Hem them away.
    Ros. I would try, if I could cry hem and have
him.   20
    Cel. Come, come, wrestle with thy affections.
    Ros. O, they take the part of a better wrestler
than myself!
    Cel. O, a good wish upon you! you will try in
time, in despite of a fall. But, turning these 25
jests out of service, let us talk in good earnest. Is
it possible, on such a sudden you should fall into so
strong a liking with old Sir Roland's youngest son?
    Ros. The Duke my father lov'd his father
dearly.   31
    Cel. Doth it therefore ensue that you should
love his son dearly? By this kind of chase, I should
hate him, for my father hated his father dearly;
yet I hate not Orlando.   35
    Ros. No, faith, hate him not, for my sake.
    Cel. Why should I not? Doth he not deserve
well?

Enter DUKE FREDERICK, *with* Lords.

    Ros. Let me love him for that, and do you love
him because I do. Look, here comes the Duke. 41
    Cel. With his eyes full of anger.
    Duke F. Mistress, dispatch you with your safest
    haste,
And get you from our court.
    Ros.   Me, uncle?
    Duke F.   You, cousin.
Within these ten days if that thou be'st found 45
So near our public court as twenty miles,
Thou diest for it.
    Ros.   I do beseech your Grace,
Let me the knowledge of my fault bear with me.
If with myself I hold intelligence,
Or have acquaintance with mine own desires; 50
If that I do not dream, or be not frantic, —
As I do trust I am not — then, dear uncle,
Never so much as in a thought unborn
Did I offend your Highness.
    Duke F.   Thus do all traitors.
If their purgation did consist in words, 55

276. **condition:** temper. 278. **humorous:** capricious. 284. **taller.** Inconsistent with other passages; e.g., I.iii.117,
IV.iii.88–89. 291. **argument:** reason. 299. **smoke ... smother:** frying-pan into the fire.
    Sc. iii, 6. **reasons:** talk. 18. **Hem:** cough. 37. **deserve well:** i.e., to be hated. 43. **safest haste:** i.e., all the speed your
safety requires. 55. **purgation:** acquittal.

They are as innocent as grace itself.
Let it suffice thee that I trust thee not.
   Ros. Yet your mistrust cannot make me a traitor.
Tell me whereon the likelihood depends.
   Duke F. Thou art thy father's daughter; there's
    enough.   60
   Ros. So was I when your Highness took his duke-
    dom.
So was I when your Highness banish'd him.
Treason is not inherited, my lord;
Or, if we did derive it from our friends,
What's that to me?   My father was no traitor.   65
Then, good my liege, mistake me not so much
To think my poverty is treacherous.
   Cel. Dear sovereign, hear me speak.
   Duke F. Ay, Celia; we stay'd her for your sake,
Else had she with her father rang'd along.   70
   Cel. I did not then entreat to have her stay;
It was your pleasure and your own remorse.
I was too young that time to value her,
But now I know her.   If she be a traitor,
Why so am I.   We still have slept together,   75
Rose at an instant, learn'd, play'd, eat together;
And wheresoe'er we went, like Juno's swans,
Still we went coupled and inseparable.
   Duke F. She is too subtle for thee; and her
    smoothness,
Her very silence, and her patience   80
Speak to the people, and they pity her.
Thou art a fool.   She robs thee of thy name,
And thou wilt show more bright and seem more
    virtuous
When she is gone.   Then open not thy lips.
Firm and irrevocable is my doom   85
Which I have pass'd upon her; she is banish'd.
   Cel. Pronounce that sentence then on me, my
    liege;
I cannot live out of her company.
   Duke F. You are a fool.   You, niece, provide
    yourself,
If you outstay the time, upon mine honour,   90
And in the greatness of my word, you die.
      [*Exeunt Duke Frederick and Lords.*
   Cel. O my poor Rosalind, whither wilt thou go?
Wilt thou change fathers?   I will give thee mine.
I charge thee, be not thou more griev'd than I am.
   Ros. I have more cause.
   Cel.   Thou hast not, cousin;   95
Prithee, be cheerful.   Know'st thou not, the Duke
Hath banish'd me, his daughter?
   Ros.   That he hath not.
   Cel. No, hath not?   Rosalind lacks then the love
Which teacheth thee that thou and I am one.
Shall we be sund'red?   Shall we part, sweet girl?   100
No; let my father seek another heir.

Therefore devise with me how we may fly,
Whither to go and what to bear with us;
And do not seek to take your [charge] upon you,
To bear your griefs yourself, and leave me out;   105
For, by this heaven, now at our sorrows pale,
Say what thou canst, I'll go along with thee.
   Ros. Why, whither shall we go?
   Cel. To seek my uncle in the forest of Arden.
   Ros. Alas, what danger will it be to us,   110
Maids as we are, to travel forth so far!
Beauty provoketh thieves sooner than gold.
   Cel. I'll put myself in poor and mean attire,
And with a kind of umber smirch my face.
The like do you.   So shall we pass along   115
And never stir assailants.
   Ros.   Were it not better,
Because that I am more than common tall,
That I did suit me all points like a man?
A gallant curtle-axe upon my thigh,
A boar-spear in my hand; and — in my heart   120
Lie there what hidden woman's fear there will —
We'll have a swashing and a martial outside,
As many other mannish cowards have
That do outface it with their semblances.
   Cel. What shall I call thee when thou art a
    man?   125
   Ros. I'll have no worse a name than Jove's own
    page,
And therefore look you call me Ganymede.
But what will you be call'd?
   Cel. Something that hath a reference to my state;
No longer Celia, but Aliena.   130
   Ros. But, cousin, what if we assay'd to steal
The clownish fool out of your father's court?
Would he not be a comfort to our travel?
   Cel. He'll go along o'er the wide world with me.
Leave me alone to woo him.   Let's away,   135
And get our jewels and our wealth together,
Devise the fittest time and safest way
To hide us from pursuit that will be made
After my flight.   Now go we in content
To liberty and not to banishment.   [*Exeunt.*   140

ACT II

SCENE I. [*The Forest of Arden.*]

Enter DUKE senior, AMIENS, *and two or three*
    LORDS, *like foresters.*

   Duke S. Now, my co-mates and brothers in
    exile,
Hath not old custom made this life more sweet
Than that of painted pomp?   Are not these woods
More free from peril than the envious court?

---

64. **friends:** kin.   72. **remorse:** compassion.   104. **[charge]** F₂: burden.   *change* F₁.   114. **umber:** brown pigment.
119. **curtle-axe:** cutlass.

Here feel we not the penalty of Adam,   5
The seasons' difference, as the icy fang
And churlish chiding of the winter's wind,
Which, when it bites and blows upon my body
Even till I shrink with cold, I smile and say,
"This is no flattery: these are counsellors   10
That feelingly persuade me what I am."
Sweet are the uses of adversity,
Which, like the toad, ugly and venomous,
Wears yet a precious jewel in his head;
And this our life, exempt from public haunt,   15
Finds tongues in trees, books in the running brooks,
Sermons in stones, and good in every thing.
   Ami. I would not change it.   Happy is your
     Grace,
That can translate the stubbornness of fortune
Into so quiet and so sweet a style.   20
   Duke S. Come, shall we go and kill us venison?
And yet it irks me the poor dappled fools,
Being native burghers of this desert city,
Should in their own confines with forked heads
Have their round haunches gor'd.
   1. Lord.   Indeed, my lord,
The melancholy Jaques grieves at that;   26
And, in that kind, swears you do more usurp
Than doth your brother that hath banish'd you.
To-day my Lord of Amiens and myself
Did steal behind him as he lay along   30
Under an oak whose antique root peeps out
Upon the brook that brawls along this wood;
To the which place a poor sequest'red stag,
That from the hunter's aim had ta'en a hurt,
Did come to languish; and indeed, my lord,   35
The wretched animal heav'd forth such groans
That their discharge did stretch his leathern coat
Almost to bursting, and the big round tears
Cours'd one another down his innocent nose
In piteous chase; and thus the hairy fool,   40
Much marked of the melancholy Jaques,
Stood on th' extremest verge of the swift brook,
Augmenting it with tears.
   Duke S.   But what said Jaques?
Did he not moralize this spectacle?
   1. Lord. O, yes, into a thousand similes.   45
First, for his weeping into the needless stream:
"Poor deer," quoth he, "thou mak'st a testament
As worldlings do, giving thy sum of more
To that which had too [much]."   Then, being there
     alone,
Left and abandoned of his velvet [friends],   50

"'Tis right," quoth he; "thus misery doth part
The flux of company."   Anon a careless herd,
Full of the pasture, jumps along by him
And never stays to greet him.   "Ay," quoth Jaques,
"Sweep on, you fat and greasy citizens.   55
'Tis just the fashion.   Wherefore do you look
Upon that poor and broken bankrupt there?"
Thus most invectively he pierceth through
The body of [the] country, city, court,
Yea, and of this our life; swearing that we   60
Are mere usurpers, tyrants, and what's worse,
To fright the animals and to kill them up
In their assign'd and native dwelling-place.
   Duke S. And did you leave him in this contempla-
     tion?
   2. Lord. We did, my lord, weeping and com-
     menting   65
Upon the sobbing deer.
   Duke S.   Show me the place.
I love to cope him in these sullen fits,
For then he's full of matter.
   1. Lord. I'll bring you to him straight. [*Exeunt.*

SCENE II.   [*A room in the palace.*]

Enter DUKE FREDERICK, *with* LORDS.

   Duke F. Can it be possible that no man saw
     them?
It cannot be.   Some villains of my court
Are of consent and sufferance in this.
   1. Lord. I cannot hear of any that did see her.
The ladies, her attendants of her chamber,   5
Saw her a-bed, and in the morning early
They found the bed untreasur'd of their mistress.
   2. Lord. My lord, the roynish clown, at whom
     so oft
Your Grace was wont to laugh, is also missing.
Hisperia, the princess' gentlewoman,   10
Confesses that she secretly o'erheard
Your daughter and her cousin much commend
The parts and graces of the wrestler
That did but lately foil the sinewy Charles;
And she believes, wherever they are gone,   15
That youth is surely in their company.
   Duke F. Send to his brother.   Fetch that gallant
     hither.
If he be absent, bring his brother to me;
I'll make him find him.   Do this suddenly,
And let not search and inquisition quail   20
To bring again these foolish runaways. [*Exeunt.*

SCENE III.   [*Before Oliver's house.*]

Enter ORLANDO *and* ADAM, *meeting.*

Orl. Who's there?

Adam. What, my young master?   O my gentle
    master!
O my sweet master!   O you memory
Of old Sir Roland!   Why, what make you here?
Why are you virtuous?   Why do people love you? 5
And wherefore are you gentle, strong, and valiant?
Why would you be so fond to overcome
The bonny priser of the humorous Duke?
Your praise is come too swiftly home before you.
Know you not, master, to [some] kind of men   10
Their graces serve them but as enemies?
No more do yours.   Your virtues, gentle master,
Are sanctified and holy traitors to you.
O, what a world is this, when what is comely
Envenoms him that bears it!   15

Orl. Why, what's the matter?

Adam.   O unhappy youth!
Come not within these doors!   Within this roof
The enemy of all your graces lives.
Your brother — no, no brother; yet the son —
Yet not the son, I will not call him son,   20
Of him I was about to call his father,—
Hath heard your praises, and this night he means
To burn the lodging where you use to lie
And you within it.   If he fail of that,
He will have other means to cut you off.   25
I overheard him and his practices.
This is no place; this house is but a butchery.
Abhor it, fear it, do not enter it.

Orl. Why, whither, Adam, wouldst thou have me
    go?

Adam. No matter whither, so you come not
    here.   30

Orl. What, wouldst thou have me go and beg my
    food?
Or with a base and boist'rous sword enforce
A thievish living on the common road?
This I must do, or know not what to do;
Yet this I will not do, do how I can.   35
I rather will subject me to the malice
Of a diverted blood and bloody brother.

Adam. But do not so.   I have five hundred
    crowns,
The thrifty hire I sav'd under your father,
Which I did store to be my foster-nurse   40
When service should in my old limbs lie lame,
And unregarded age in corners thrown.
Take that, and He that doth the ravens feed,
Yea, providently caters for the sparrow,

Be comfort to my age!   Here is the gold.   45
All this I give you.   Let me be your servant.
Though I look old, yet I am strong and lusty;
For in my youth I never did apply
Hot and rebellious liquors in my blood,
Nor did not with unbashful forehead woo   50
The means of weakness and debility;
Therefore my age is as a lusty winter,
Frosty, but kindly.   Let me go with you;
I'll do the service of a younger man
In all your business and necessities.   55

Orl. O good old man, how well in thee appears
The constant service of the antique world,
When service sweat for duty, not for meed!
Thou art not for the fashion of these times,
Where none will sweat but for promotion,   60
And having that do choke their service up
Even with the having.   It is not so with thee.
But, poor old man, thou prun'st a rotten tree,
That cannot so much as a blossom yield
In lieu of all thy pains and husbandry.   65
But come thy ways; we'll go along together,
And ere we have thy youthful wages spent,
We'll light upon some settled low content.

Adam. Master, go on, and I will follow thee
To the last gasp, with truth and loyalty.   70
From seventeen years till now almost fourscore
Here lived I, but now live here no more.
At seventeen years many their fortunes seek,
But at fourscore it is too late a week;
Yet fortune cannot recompense me better   75
Than to die well and not my master's debtor.
                                    [*Exeunt.*

SCENE IV.   [*The Forest of Arden.*]

Enter ROSALIND *for Ganymede,* CELIA *for
Aliena, and Clown, alias* TOUCHSTONE.

Ros. O Jupiter, how [weary] are my spirits!

Touch. I care not for my spirits, if my legs were
not weary.

Ros. I could find in my heart to disgrace my
man's apparel and to cry like a woman; but I   5
must comfort the weaker vessel, as doublet and hose
ought to show itself courageous to petticoat; therefore, courage, good Aliena.

Cel. I pray you, bear with me; I cannot go no
further.   10

Touch. For my part, I had rather bear with you
than bear you.   Yet I should bear no cross if I did
bear you, for I think you have no money in your
purse.

Ros. Well, this is the forest of Arden.   15

Sc. iii, 8. **bonny priser:** fine champion.   10. **[some]** Ff₂₋₄.   *seeme* F₁.   26. **practices:** plots.   27. **place:** i.e., for you.
37. **diverted blood:** perverted kinship.   39. **thrifty...saved:** wages I thriftily saved.   65. **lieu of:** return for.   68. **low**
content: lowly contentment.   74. **too...week:** much too late.

Sc. iv, 1. **[weary]** (Theobald).   *merry* Ff.   12. **cro⌠s:** silver coin with figure of a cross (with a pun).

Touch. Ay, now am I in Arden, the more fool I.
When I was at home, I was in a better place; but
travellers must be content.

Enter CORIN *and* SILVIUS.

Ros. Ay, be so, good Touchstone. Look you,
who comes here; a young man and an old in solemn
talk.   21
Cor. That is the way to make her scorn you still.
Sil. O Corin, that thou knew'st how I do love
her!
Cor. I partly guess; for I have lov'd ere now.
Sil. No, Corin, being old, thou canst not guess,
Though in thy youth thou wast as true a lover   26
As ever sigh'd upon a midnight pillow.
But if thy love were ever like to mine, —
As sure I think did never man love so —
How many actions most ridiculous   30
Hast thou been drawn to by thy fantasy?
Cor. Into a thousand that I have forgotten.
Sil. O, thou didst then ne'er love so heartily!
If thou rememb'rest not the slightest folly
That ever love did make thee run into,   35
Thou hast not lov'd;
Or if thou hast not sat as I do now,
Wearing thy hearer in thy mistress' praise,
Thou hast not lov'd;
Or if thou hast not broke from company   40
Abruptly, as my passion now makes me,
Thou hast not lov'd.
O Phebe, Phebe, Phebe!   [*Exit.*
Ros. Alas, poor shepherd! searching of [thy
wound],
I have by hard adventure found mine own.   45
Touch. And I mine. I remember, when I was
in love I broke my sword upon a stone, and bid him
take that for coming a-night to Jane Smile; and I
remember the kissing of her batler and the cow's
dugs that her pretty chopt hands had milk'd; 50
and I remember the wooing of a peascod instead of
her; from whom I took two cods and, giving her
them again, said with weeping tears, "Wear these
for my sake." We that are true lovers run into
strange capers; but as all is mortal in nature,   55
so is all nature in love mortal in folly.
Ros. Thou speak'st wiser than thou art ware of.
Touch. Nay, I shall ne'er be ware of mine own
wit till I break my shins against it.   60
Ros. Jove, Jove! this shepherd's passion
          Is much upon my fashion.
Touch. And mine; but it grows something stale
with me.

Cel. I pray you, one of you question yond man
If he for gold will give us any food.   65
I faint almost to death.
Touch.   Holla, you clown!
Ros. Peace, fool; he's not thy kinsman.
Cor.   Who calls?
Touch. Your betters, sir.
Cor.   Else are they very wretched.
Ros. Peace, I say. Good even to [you], friend.
Cor. And to you, gentle sir, and to you all.   70
Ros. I prithee, shepherd, if that love or gold
Can in this desert place buy entertainment,
Bring us where we may rest ourselves and feed.
Here's a young maid with travel much oppressed
And faints for succour.
Cor.   Fair sir, I pity her,   75
And wish, for her sake more than for mine own,
My fortunes were more able to relieve her;
But I am shepherd to another man,
And do not shear the fleeces that I graze.
My master is of churlish disposition,   80
And little recks to find the way to heaven
By doing deeds of hospitality.
Besides, his cote, his flocks, and bounds of feed
Are now on sale, and at our sheep-cote now,
By reason of his absence, there is nothing   85
That you will feed on; but what is, come see,
And in my voice most welcome shall you be.
Ros. What is he that shall buy his flock and pas-
ture?
Cor. That young swain that you saw here but
erewhile,
That little cares for buying any thing.   90
Ros. I pray thee, if it stand with honesty,
Buy thou the cottage, pasture, and the flock,
And thou shalt have to pay for it of us.
Cel. And we will mend thy wages. I like this
place,
And willingly could waste my time in it.   95
Cor. Assuredly the thing is to be sold.
Go with me. If you like upon report
The soil, the profit, and this kind of life,
I will your very faithful feeder be,
And buy it with your gold right suddenly.   100
                                                         [*Exeunt.*

SCENE V. [*The forest.*]

Enter AMIENS, JAQUES, *and others.*

SONG.

[*Ami.*] Under the greenwood tree
          Who loves to lie with me,

---

31. **fantasy:** love.   38. **Wearing.** F₁. *wearying* Ff₂₋₄. (Meanings identical.)   44. **searching:** probing. [thy wound]
(Rowe). *they would* F₁; *their wound* Ff₂₋₄.   49. **batler:** small club used by washerwomen. Ff₂₋₄ read *batlet*.   50. **chopt:**
chapped.   51. **peascod:** pea pod.   56. **mortal:** excessive.   62. **upon:** after.   69. [you] Ff₂₋₄. *your* F₁.   75. **for:** for want of.
80. **churlish:** miserly.   83. **cote:** cottage. **bounds of feed:** pasturage.   87. **in my voice:** as far as I have anything to say.
91. **stand:** is consistent.   99. **feeder:** shepherd.

And turn his merry note
Unto the sweet bird's throat,
Come hither, come hither, come hither!   5
    Here shall he see
    No enemy
But winter and rough weather.

Jaq. More, more, I prithee, more.
Ami. It will make you melancholy, Monsieur
Jaques.   11
Jaq. I thank it. More, I prithee, more. I can
suck melancholy out of a song, as a weasel sucks
eggs. More, I prithee, more.
Ami. My voice is ragged. I know I cannot
please you.   16
Jaq. I do not desire you to please me; I do desire
you to sing. Come, more; another stanzo. Call
you 'em stanzos?
Ami. What you will, Monsieur Jaques.   20
Jaq. Nay, I care not for their names; they owe
me nothing. Will you sing?
Ami. More at your request than to please myself.   24
Jaq. Well then, if ever I thank any man, I'll
thank you; but that they call compliment is like the
encounter of two dog-apes; and when a man thanks
me heartily, methinks I have given him a penny and
he renders me the beggarly thanks. Come, sing;
and you that will not, hold your tongues.   31
Ami. Well, I'll end the song. Sirs, cover the
while; the Duke will drink under this tree. He
hath been all this day to look you.
Jaq. And I have been all this day to avoid   35
him. He is too disputable for my company. I
think of as many matters as he; but I give heaven
thanks, and make no boast of them. Come,
warble, come.

SONG.   [*All together here.*

Who doth ambition shun,   40
And loves to live i' th' sun,
Seeking the food he eats,
And pleased with what he gets,
Come hither, come hither, come hither!
    Here shall he see   45
    No enemy
But winter and rough weather.

Jaq. I'll give you a verse to this note, that I made
yesterday in despite of my invention.
Ami. And I'll sing it.   50
Jaq. Thus it goes: —

If it do come to pass
That any man turn ass,
Leaving his wealth and ease
A stubborn will to please,   55
Ducdame, ducdame, ducdame!
    Here shall he see
    Gross fools as he,
An if he will come to me.

Ami. What's that "ducdame"?   60
Jaq. 'Tis a Greek invocation, to call fools into a
circle. I'll go sleep, if I can; if I cannot, I'll rail
against all the first-born of Egypt.
Ami. And I'll go seek the Duke; his banquet is
prepared.   [*Exeunt.* 65

SCENE VI. [*The forest.*]

Enter ORLANDO *and* ADAM.

Adam. Dear master, I can go no further. O, I
die for food! Here lie I down, and measure out my
grave. Farewell, kind master.
Orl. Why, how now, Adam! no greater heart in
thee? Live a little; comfort a little; cheer thy-   5
self a little. If this uncouth forest yield any thing
savage, I will either be food for it or bring it for
food to thee. Thy conceit is nearer death than
thy powers. For my sake be comfortable; hold
death awhile at the arm's end. I will here be   10
with thee presently; and if I bring thee not something to eat, I will give thee leave to die; but if thou
diest before I come, thou art a mocker of my labour.
Well said! thou look'st cheerly, and I'll be with thee
quickly. Yet thou liest in the bleak air. Come,   15
I will bear thee to some shelter; and thou shalt not
die for lack of a dinner if there live any thing in this
desert. Cheerly, good Adam!   [*Exeunt.*

SCENE VII. [*The forest.*]

[*A table set out.*] *Enter* DUKE senior, [AMIENS]
and LORDS, *like outlaws.*

Duke S. I think he be transform'd into a beast,
For I can no where find him like a man.
1. Lord. My lord, he is but even now gone hence.
Here was he merry, hearing of a song.
Duke S. If he, compact of jars, grow musical,   5
We shall have shortly discord in the spheres.
Go, seek him; tell him I would speak with him.

Enter JAQUES.

1. Lord. He saves my labour by his own approach.

Sc. v, 3. **turn:** attune.   21. **names:** i.e., as in lists of debtors.   27. **dog-apes:** dog-faced apes.   32. **cover the while:**
meanwhile set the table.   49. **in...invention:** though I have little imagination.   56. **Ducdame.** Probably mere jargon.
Sc. vi, 8. **conceit:** imagination.   14. **Well said:** well done.
Sc. vii, 5. **compact of jars:** composed of discords.   6. **spheres.** In the old Ptolemaic astronomy the spheres were thought
to make music in their turning.

Duke S. Why, how now, monsieur! what a life is this,
That your poor friends must woo your company?
What, you look merrily!   11
  Jaq. A fool, a fool! I met a fool i' th' forest,
A motley fool. A miserable world!
As I do live by food, I met a fool;
Who laid him down and bask'd him in the sun, 15
And rail'd on Lady Fortune in good terms,
In good set terms, and yet a motley fool.
"Good morrow, fool," quoth I. "No, sir," quoth he,
"Call me not fool till heaven hath sent me fortune."
And then he drew a dial from his poke,   20
And, looking on it with lack-lustre eye,
Says very wisely, "It is ten o'clock.
Thus we may see," quoth he, "how the world wags.
'Tis but an hour ago since it was nine;
And after one hour more 'twill be eleven;   25
And so, from hour to hour, we ripe and ripe,
And then, from hour to hour, we rot and rot;
And thereby hangs a tale." When I did hear
The motley fool thus moral on the time,
My lungs began to crow like chanticleer,   30
That fools should be so deep-contemplative;
And I did laugh sans intermission
An hour by his dial. O noble fool!
A worthy fool! Motley's the only wear.
  Duke S. What fool is this?   35
  Jaq. O worthy fool! One that hath been a courtier,
And says, if ladies be but young and fair,
They have the gift to know it; and in his brain,
Which is as dry as the remainder biscuit
After a voyage, he hath strange places cramm'd
With observation, the which he vents   41
In mangled forms. O that I were a fool!
I am ambitious for a motley coat.
  Duke S. Thou shalt have one.
  Jaq.   It is my only suit; —
Provided that you weed your better judgements
Of all opinion that grows rank in them   46
That I am wise. I must have liberty
Withal, as large a charter as the wind,
To blow on whom I please; for so fools have;
And they that are most galled with my folly,   50
They most must laugh. And why, sir, must they so?
The "why" is plain as way to parish church.
He that a fool doth very wisely hit
Doth very foolishly, although he smart,

[Not to] seem senseless of the bob; if not,   55
The wise man's folly is anatomiz'd
Even by the squand'ring glances of the fool.
Invest me in my motley. Give me leave
To speak my mind, and I will through and through
Cleanse the foul body of th' infected world,   60
If they will patiently receive my medicine.
  Duke S. Fie on thee! I can tell what thou wouldst do.
  Jaq. What, for a counter, would I do but good?
  Duke S. Most mischievous foul sin, in chiding sin.
For thou thyself hast been a libertine,   65
As sensual as the brutish sting itself;
And all th' embossed sores and headed evils
That thou with license of free foot hast caught,
Wouldst thou disgorge into the general world.
  Jaq. Why, who cries out on pride.   70
That can therein tax any private party?
Doth it not flow as hugely as the sea,
Till that the [wearer's] very means do ebb?
What woman in the city do I name,
When that I say the city-woman bears   75
The cost of princes on unworthy shoulders?
Who can come in and say that I mean her,
When such a one as she such is her neighbour?
Or what is he of basest function,
That says his bravery is not on my cost,   80
Thinking that I mean him, but therein suits
His folly to the mettle of my speech?
There then; how then? what then? Let me see wherein
My tongue hath wrong'd him. If it do him right,
Then he hath wrong'd himself. If he be free,   85
Why then my taxing like a wild-goose flies,
Unclaim'd of any man. But who comes here?

          Enter ORLANDO [*with his sword drawn*].

  Orl. Forbear, and eat no more.
  Jaq.   Why, I have eat none yet.
  Orl. Nor shalt not, till necessity be serv'd.
  Jaq. Of what kind should this cock come of? 90
  Duke S. Art thou thus bolden'd, man, by thy distress?
Or else a rude despiser of good manners,
That in civility thou seem'st so empty?
  Orl. You touch'd my vein at first. The thorny point
Of bare distress hath ta'en from me the show   95
Of smooth civility; yet am I inland bred
And know some nurture. But forbear, I say.

13. **motley:** wearing motley, i.e., a parti-colored costume. 20. **dial:** watch, or portable sun-dial. **poke:** pouch. 39. **dry.** According to Elizabethan physiology a "dry" brain was especially retentive. 40. **strange places:** odd corners. 44. **suit:** (1) costume, (2) request. 55. **[not to]** (Theobald). Om. Ff. **bob:** jibe. 57. **squand'ring glances:** random hits. 63. **counter:** valueless disk of metal used in counting. 66. **brutish sting:** carnal passion. 67. **embossed:** swollen. **headed evils:** sores come to a head. 71. **tax:** censure. 73. **[wearer's]** (Singer). *wearie* Ff. No satisfactory emendation has been proposed. 79. **function:** occupation. 80. **bravery:** finery. 84. **If ... right:** if the glove fits. 85. **free:** innocent. 93. **civility:** courtesy. 94. **You ... vein:** your first question explains my mood. 96. **inland bred:** i.e., near the centers of urbanity. (Cf. *outlandish.*) 97. **nurture:** breeding.

He dies that touches any of this fruit
Till I and my affairs are answered.
    Jaq. An you will not be answer'd with reason,
I must die.   101
    Duke S. What would you have? Your gentleness shall force,
More than your force move us to gentleness.
    Orl. I almost die for food; and let me have it.
    Duke S. Sit down and feed, and welcome to our
    table.   105
    Orl. Speak you so gently? Pardon me, I pray
    you.
I thought that all things had been savage here,
And therefore put I on the countenance
Of stern commandment. But whate'er you are   110
That in this desert inaccessible
Under the shade of melancholy boughs
Lose and neglect the creeping hours of time;
If ever you have look'd on better days,
If ever been where bells have knoll'd to church,
If ever sat at any good man's feast,   115
If ever from your eyelids wip'd a tear
And know what 'tis to pity and be pitied,
Let gentleness my strong enforcement be;
In the which hope I blush, and hide my sword.
    Duke S. True is it that we have seen better
    days,   120
And have with holy bell been knoll'd to church,
And sat at good men's feasts, and wip'd our eyes
Of drops that sacred pity hath engend'red;
And therefore sit you down in gentleness
And take upon command what help we have   125
That to your wanting may be minist'red.
    Orl. Then but forbear your food a little while,
Whiles, like a doe, I go to find my fawn
And give it food. There is an old poor man,
Who after me hath many a weary step   130
Limp'd in pure love. Till he be first suffic'd,
Oppress'd with two weak evils, age and hunger,
I will not touch a bit.
    Duke S.   Go find him out,
And we will nothing waste till you return.
    Orl. I thank ye; and be blest for your good com-
    fort!   [*Exit.*]   135
    Duke S. Thou seest we are not all alone un-
    happy.
This wide and universal theatre
Presents more woeful pageants than the scene
Wherein we play in.
    Jaq.   All the world's a stage,
And all the men and women merely players.   140
They have their exits and their entrances,
And one man in his time plays many parts,
His acts being seven ages. At first the infant,

Mewling and puking in the nurse's arms.
Then the whining school-boy, with his satchel   145
And shining morning face, creeping like snail
Unwillingly to school. And then the lover,
Sighing like furnace, with a woeful ballad
Made to his mistress' eyebrow. Then a soldier,
Full of strange oaths, and bearded like the pard,   150
Jealous in honour, sudden, and quick in quarrel,
Seeking the bubble reputation
Even in the cannon's mouth. And then the justice,
In fair round belly with good capon lin'd,
With eyes severe and beard of formal cut,   155
Full of wise saws and modern instances;
And so he plays his part. The sixth age shifts
Into the lean and slipper'd pantaloon,
With spectacles on nose and pouch on side,   159
His youthful hose, well sav'd, a world too wide
For his shrunk shank; and his big manly voice,
Turning again toward childish treble, pipes
And whistles in his sound. Last scene of all,
That ends this strange eventful history,
Is second childishness and mere oblivion,   165
Sans teeth, sans eyes, sans taste, sans every thing.

          Re-enter ORLANDO, *with* ADAM.

    Duke S. Welcome. Set down your venerable
    burden,
And let him feed.
    Orl. I thank you most for him.
    Adam.   So had you need;
I scarce can speak to thank you for myself.   170
    Duke S. Welcome; fall to. I will not trouble you
As yet, to question you about your fortunes.
Give us some music; and, good cousin, sing.

                SONG.

[*Ami.*] Blow, blow, thou winter wind,
        Thou art not so unkind   175
            As man's ingratitude;
        Thy tooth is not so keen,
        Because thou art not seen,
            Although thy breath be rude.
Heigh-ho! sing, heigh-ho! unto the green holly.   180
Most friendship is feigning, most loving mere folly.
        Then, heigh-ho, the holly!
        This life is most jolly.

        Freeze, freeze, thou bitter sky,
        That dost not bite so nigh   185
            As benefits forgot;
        Though thou the waters warp,
        Thy sting is not so sharp
            As friend rememb'red not.
Heigh-ho! sing, etc.   190

---

99. **answered:** satisfied.   118. **enforcement:** support.   125. **upon command:** at will.   144. **mewling:** whimpering.
150. **pard:** leopard.   154. **capon.** An allusion to the bribing of justices by gifts of poultry.   156. **saws:** maxims. **modern instances:** trite examples.   158. **pantaloon:** dotard.   175. **unkind:** unnatural.

Duke S. If that you were the good Sir Roland's
    son,
As you have whisper'd faithfully you were,
And as mine eye doth his effigies witness
Most truly limn'd and living in your face,
Be truly welcome hither.   I am the Duke   195
That lov'd your father.   The residue of your for-
    tune,
Go to my cave and tell me.   Good old man,
Thou art right welcome as thy master is.
Support him by the arm.   Give me your hand,
And let me all your fortunes understand.   200
                                    [Exeunt.

ACT III

SCENE I.   [*A room in the palace.*]

Enter DUKE [FREDERICK], OLIVER, *and* Lords.

Duke F. Not see him since?   Sir, sir, that cannot
    be.
But were I not the better part made mercy,
I should not seek an absent argument
Of my revenge, thou present.   But look to it.
Find out thy brother, wheresoe'er he is.   5
Seek him with candle!   Bring him dead or living
Within this twelvemonth, or turn thou no more
To seek a living in our territory.
Thy lands and all things that thou dost call thine
Worth seizure do we seize into our hands,   10
Till thou canst quit thee by thy brother's mouth
Of what we think against thee.
Oli. O that your Highness knew my heart in this!
I never lov'd my brother in my life.
Duke F. More villain thou.   Well, push him out
    of doors;   15
And let my officers of such a nature
Make an extent upon his house and lands.
Do this expediently and turn him going.   [*Exeunt.*

SCENE II.   [*The forest.*]

Enter ORLANDO [*with a paper*].

Orl. Hang there, my verse, in witness of my love;
    And thou, thrice-crowned queen of night, survey
With thy chaste eye, from thy pale sphere above,
    Thy huntress' name that my full life doth sway.
O Rosalind! these trees shall be my books,   5
    And in their barks my thoughts I'll character;
That every eye which in this forest looks
    Shall see thy virtue witness'd every where.

Run, run, Orlando; carve on every tree
The fair, the chaste, and unexpressive she.   10
                                    [Exit.

Enter CORIN *and Clown* [TOUCHSTONE].

Cor. And how like you this shepherd's life, Master Touchstone?
Touch. Truly, shepherd, in respect of itself, it is
a good life; but in respect that it is a shepherd's life,
it is naught.   In respect that it is solitary, I like   15
it very well; but in respect that it is private, it is a
very vile life.   Now, in respect it is in the fields, it
pleaseth me well; but in respect it is not in the
court, it is tedious.   As it is a spare life, look you,
it fits my humour well; but as there is no more   20
plenty in it, it goes much against my stomach.
Hath any philosophy in thee, shepherd?
Cor. No more but that I know the more one
sickens the worse at ease he is; and that he that   25
wants money, means, and content is without three
good friends; that the property of rain is to wet and
fire to burn; that good pasture makes fat sheep, and
that a great cause of the night is lack of the sun; that
he that hath learned no wit by nature nor art   30
may complain of good breeding or comes of a very
dull kindred.
Touch. Such a one is a natural philosopher.
Wast ever in court, shepherd?
Cor. No, truly.   35
Touch. Then thou art damn'd.
Cor. Nay, I hope.
Touch. Truly, thou art damn'd, like an ill-
roasted egg all on one side.
Cor. For not being at court?   Your reason.   40
Touch. Why, if thou never wast at court, thou
never saw'st good manners; if thou never saw'st
good manners, then thy manners must be wicked;
and wickedness is sin, and sin is damnation.   Thou
art in a parlous state, shepherd.   45
Cor. Not a whit, Touchstone.   Those that are
good manners at the court are as ridiculous in the
country as the behaviour of the country is most
mockable at the court.   You told me you salute
not at the court but you kiss your hands.   That   50
courtesy would be uncleanly if courtiers were shepherds.
Touch. Instance, briefly; come, instance.
Cor. Why, we are still handling our ewes, and
their fells, you know, are greasy.   55
Touch. Why, do not your courtier's hands sweat?
And is not the grease of a mutton as wholesome as

---

193. **effigies:** likeness.   194. **limn'd:** painted.

Act III, sc. i, 11. **quit:** acquit.   16. **of . . . nature:** whose business it is.   17. **extent:** seizure (legal term).   18. **expediently:**
expeditiously.

Sc. ii, 2. **thrice-crowned queen:** Diana.   She was a triple divinity: Cynthia or Luna in heaven; Diana on earth; Proserpine
or Hecate in the underworld.   6. **character:** inscribe.   10. **unexpressive:** inexpressible.   31. **of:** i.e., of lack of.   45. **parlous:**
perilous.   50. **but you kiss:** without kissing.   55. **fells:** fleeces.

the sweat of a man? Shallow, shallow. A better
instance, I say; come.

Cor. Besides, our hands are hard.   60

Touch. Your lips will feel them the sooner.
Shallow again. A more sounder instance, come.

Cor. And they are often tarr'd over with the
surgery of our sheep; and would you have us kiss
tar? The courtier's hands are perfum'd with
civet.   66

Touch. Most shallow man! thou worm's-meat,
in respect of a good piece of flesh indeed! Learn
of the wise, and perpend. Civet is of a baser birth
than tar, the very uncleanly flux of a cat. Mend
the instance, shepherd.   71

Cor. You have too courtly a wit for me. I'll
rest.

Touch. Wilt thou rest damn'd? God help thee,
shallow man! God make incision in thee! Thou
art raw.   76

Cor. Sir, I am a true labourer. I earn that I
eat, get that I wear, owe no man hate, envy no
man's happiness, glad of other men's good, content
with my harm, and the greatest of my pride is to
see my ewes graze and my lambs suck.   81

Touch. That is another simple sin in you, to
bring the ewes and the rams together, and to offer
to get your living by the copulation of cattle; to
be bawd to a bell-wether, and to betray a she-   85
lamb of a twelvemonth to a crooked-pated, old,
cuckoldly ram, out of all reasonable match. If
thou beest not damn'd for this, the devil himself
will have no shepherds. I cannot see else how thou
shouldst scape.   90

Cor. Here comes young Master Ganymede, my
new mistress's brother.

Enter ROSALIND [*with a paper, reading*].

Ros. From the east to western Ind,
     No jewel is like Rosalind.
Her worth, being mounted on the wind,
     Through all the world bears Rosalind.   96
All the pictures fairest lin'd
     Are but black to Rosalind.
Let no face be kept in mind
     But the fair of Rosalind.   100

Touch. I'll rhyme you so eight years together,
dinners and suppers and sleeping-hours excepted.
It is the right butter-women's rank to market.

Ros. Out, fool!   105

Touch. For a taste: —
     If a hart do lack a hind,
     Let him seek out Rosalind.

If the cat will after kind,
     So be sure will Rosalind.   110
Wint'red garments must be lin'd,
     So must slender Rosalind.
They that reap must sheaf and bind,
     Then to cart with Rosalind.
Sweetest nut hath sourest rind,   115
     Such a nut is Rosalind.
He that sweetest rose will find,
     Must find love's prick and Rosalind.
This is the very false gallop of verses. Why do you
infect yourself with them?   120

Ros. Peace, you dull fool! I found them on a
tree.

Touch. Truly, the tree yields bad fruit.

Ros. I'll graff it with you, and then I shall graff
it with a medlar. Then it will be the earliest 125
fruit i' th' country; for you'll be rotten ere you be
half ripe, and that's the right virtue of the medlar.

Touch. You have said; but whether wisely or no,
let the forest judge.   130

Enter CELIA, *with a writing.*

Ros. Peace!
Here comes my sister, reading; stand aside.

Cel. [*Reads.*] Why should this a desert be?
     For it is unpeopled? No!
Tongues I'll hang on every tree,   135
     That shall civil sayings show:
Some, how brief the life of man
     Runs his erring pilgrimage,
That the stretching of a span
     Buckles in his sum of age;   140
Some, of violated vows
     'Twixt the souls of friend and friend;
But upon the fairest boughs,
     Or at every sentence end,
Will I Rosalinda write,   145
     Teaching all that read to know
The quintessence of every sprite
     Heaven would in little show.
Therefore Heaven Nature charg'd
     That one body should be fill'd   150
With all graces wide-enlarg'd.
     Nature presently distill'd
Helen's cheek, but not her heart,
     Cleopatra's majesty,
Atalanta's better part,   155
     Sad Lucretia's modesty.
Thus Rosalind of many parts
     By heavenly synod was devis'd;
Of many faces, eyes, and hearts,

---

68. **in respect of:** compared with.   69. **perpend:** consider.   75. **make incision:** let blood.   76. **raw:** crude.   79. **content
... harm:** uncomplaining at misfortune.   97. **lin'd:** drawn.   100. **fair:** beauty.   103. **It ... market.** *i.e.,* the rhymes,
all alike, jog like a row of butter-women going to market.   119. **false gallop:** canter.   124. **graff:** graft.   125. **medlar:** (1)
meddler, (2) a fruit like an apple, not good to eat until it decays.   136. **civil sayings:** serious maxims.   140. **Buckles in:**
encompasses.   155. **better part:** *i.e.,* her swiftness.

To have the touches dearest priz'd   160
Heaven would that she these gifts should
     have,
And I to live and die her slave.

Ros. O most gentle [pulpiter]! what tedious homily of love have you wearied your parishioners withal, and never cri'd "Have patience, good people!"   166

Cel. How now! Back, friends! Shepherd, go off a little. Go with him, sirrah.

Touch. Come, shepherd, let us make an honourable retreat; though not with bag and baggage, yet with scrip and scrippage.   171

         [*Exeunt [Corin and Touchstone].*

Cel. Didst thou hear these verses?

Ros. O, yes, I heard them all, and more, too; for some of them had in them more feet than the verses would bear.   175

Cel. That's no matter. The feet might bear the verses.

Ros. Ay, but the feet were lame and could not bear themselves without the verse, and therefore stood lamely in the verse.   180

Cel. But didst thou hear without wondering how thy name should be hang'd and carved upon these trees?

Ros. I was seven of the nine days out of the wonder before you came; for look here what I found   185 on a palm tree. I was never so berhym'd since Pythagoras' time, that I was an Irish rat, which I can hardly remember.

Cel. Trow you who hath done this?

Ros. Is it a man?   190

Cel. And a chain, that you once wore, about his neck. Change you colour?

Ros. I prithee, who?

Cel. O Lord, Lord! it is a hard matter for friends to meet; but mountains may be removed with earthquakes and so encounter.   196

Ros. Nay, but who is it?

Cel. Is it possible?

Ros. Nay, I prithee now with most petitionary vehemence, tell me who it is.   200

Cel. O wonderful, wonderful, and most wonderful wonderful! and yet again wonderful, and after that, out of all whooping!

Ros. Good my complexion! dost thou think, though I am caparison'd like a man, I have a   205 doubtlet and hose in my disposition? One inch of delay more is a South-sea of discovery. I prithee,

tell me who is it quickly, and speak apace. I would thou couldst stammer, that thou might'st pour this conceal'd man out of thy mouth, as wine comes   210 out of a narrow-mouth'd bottle, either too much at once, or none at all. I prithee, take the cork out of thy mouth that I may drink thy tidings.

Cel. So you may put a man in your belly.   215

Ros. Is he of God's making? What manner of man? Is his head worth a hat or his chin worth a beard?

Cel. Nay, he hath but a little beard.   219

Ros. Why, God will send more, if the man will be thankful. Let me stay the growth of his beard, if thou delay me not the knowledge of his chin.

Cel. It is young Orlando, that tripp'd up the wrestler's heels and your heart both in an instant.   225

Ros. Nay, but the devil take mocking. Speak sad brow and true maid.

Cel. I' faith, coz, 'tis he.

Ros. Orlando?

Cel. Orlando.   230

Ros. Alas the day! what shall I do with my doublet and hose? What did he when thou saw'st him? What said he? How look'd he? Wherein went he? What makes he here? Did he ask for me? Where remains he? How parted he with   235 thee? And when shalt thou see him again? Answer me in one word.

Cel. You must borrow me Gargantua's mouth first. 'Tis a word too great for any mouth of this age's size. To say ay and no to these particulars is more than to answer in a catechism.   241

Ros. But doth he know that I am in this forest and in man's apparel? Looks he as freshly as he did the day he wrestled?

Cel. It is as easy to count atomies as to re-   245 solve the propositions of a lover. But take a taste of my finding him, and relish it with good observance. I found him under a tree, like a dropp'd acorn.

Ros. It may well be called Jove's tree, when it drops forth such fruit.   250

Cel. Give me audience, good madam.

Ros. Proceed.

Cel. There lay he, stretch'd along, like a wounded knight.

Ros. Though it be pity to see such a sight, it well becomes the ground.   256

Cel. Cry "holla" to [thy] tongue, I prithee; it

---

160. **touches**: traits.   163. **[pulpiter]** (Spedding). *Jupiter* Ff.   167. **Back, friends!** Addressed to Corin and Touchstone. 171. **scrip**: wallet.   186–87. **Pythagoras'...rat.** A double allusion: (1) to the theory of the transmigration of souls, advanced by the Greek philosopher, Pythagoras; (2) to the belief among Irish peasantry that rats could be killed by rhymed spells. 189. **Trow**: know.   199. **petitionary**: pleading.   204. **Good my complexion**: i.e., O my blushes! 206. **One...discovery.** I.e., the least delay is to me as long as a voyage of exploration.   221. **stay**: await.   226. **Speak...maid.** I.e., speak seriously and as an honest maid.   233. **Wherein went he**: what did he wear?   237. **Gargantua**: Rabelais' giant who once swallowed five pilgrims together.   245. **atomies**: motes.   **resolve**: solve.   247. **relish**: sauce (vb.).   247. **observance**: attention.   249. **Jove's tree**: the oak.   256. **ground.** With pun on *background*.   257. **"holla"**: halt. [thy] (Rowe). *the* Ff.

curvets unseasonably. He was furnish'd like a
hunter.

Ros. O, ominous! he comes to kill my heart. 260

Cel. I would sing my song without a burden.
Thou bring'st me out of tune.

Ros. Do you not know I am a woman? When
I think, I must speak. Sweet, say on.   264

Enter ORLANDO *and* JAQUES.

Cel. You bring me out. Soft! comes he not here?

Ros. 'Tis he. Slink by, and note him.

Jaq. I thank you for your company; but, good
faith, I had as lief have been myself alone.   270

Orl. And so had I; but yet, for fashion sake, I
thank you too for your society.

Jaq. God buy you; let's meet as little as we can.

Orl. I do desire we may be better strangers. 275

Jaq. I pray you, mar no more trees with writing
love-songs in their barks.

Orl. I pray you, mar no moe of my verses with
reading them ill-favouredly.

Jaq. Rosalind is your love's name?   280

Orl. Yes, just.

Jaq. I do not like her name.

Orl. There was no thought of pleasing you when
she was christen'd.

Jaq. What stature is she of?   285

Orl. Just as high as my heart.

Jaq. You are full of pretty answers. Have you
not been acquainted with goldsmiths' wives, and
conn'd them out of rings?   289

Orl. Not so; but I answer you right painted
cloth, from whence you have studied your questions.

Jaq. You have a nimble wit. I think 'twas made
of Atalanta's heels. Will you sit down with me?
and we two will rail against our mistress the world,
and all our misery.   296

Orl. I will chide no breather in the world but myself, against whom I know most faults.

Jaq. The worst fault you have is to be in love. 300

Orl. 'Tis a fault I will not change for your best
virtue. I am weary of you.

Jaq. By my troth, I was seeking for a fool when I
found you.

Orl. He is drown'd in the brook. Look but in,
and you shall see him.   306

Jaq. There I shall see mine own figure.

Orl. Which I take to be either a fool or a cipher.

Jaq. I'll tarry no longer with you. Farewell,
good Signior Love.   310

Orl. I am glad of your departure. Adieu, good
Monsieur Melancholy.   [*Exit Jaques.*]

Ros. [*Aside to Celia.*] I will speak to him like a
saucy lackey, and under that habit play the knave
with him.— Do you hear, forester?   315

Orl. Very well. What would you?

Ros. I pray you, what is't o'clock?

Orl. You should ask me what time o' day.
There's no clock in the forest.   319

Ros. Then there is no true lover in the forest;
else sighing every minute and groaning every hour
would detect the lazy foot of Time as well as a
clock.

Orl. And why not the swift foot of Time?
Had not that been as proper?   325

Ros. By no means, sir. Time travels in divers
paces with divers persons. I'll tell you who Time
ambles withal, who Time trots withal, who Time
gallops withal, and who he stands still withal.

Orl. I prithee, who doth he trot withal?   330

Ros. Marry, he trots hard with a young maid
between the contract of her marriage and the day
it is solemniz'd. If the interim be but a se'nnight,
Time's pace is so hard that it seems the length of
seven year.   335

Orl. Who ambles Time withal?

Ros. With a priest that lacks Latin, and a rich
man that hath not the gout; for the one sleeps easily
because he cannot study, and the other lives merrily because he feels no pain; the one lacking the 340
burden of lean and wasteful learning, the other
knowing no burden of heavy tedious penury.
These Time ambles withal.

Orl. Who doth he gallop withal?   344

Ros. With a thief to the gallows; for though he
go as softly as foot can fall, he thinks himself too
soon there.

Orl. Who stays it still withal?

Ros. With lawyers in the vacation; for they sleep
between term and term, and then they perceive not
how Time moves.   351

Orl. Where dwell you, pretty youth?

Ros. With this shepherdess, my sister; here in
the skirts of the forest, like fringe upon a petticoat.   355

Orl. Are you native of this place?

Ros. As the cony that you see dwell where she is
kindled.

Orl. Your accent is something finer than you
could purchase in so removed a dwelling.   360

Ros. I have been told so of many; but indeed an
old religious uncle of mine taught me to speak, who
was in his youth an inland man; one that knew
courtship too well, for there he fell in love. I have
heard him read many lectures against it, and I 365

---

258. **curvets:** prances.   261. **burden:** bass part.   265. **bring:** put.   273. **buy:** be with.   289. **out of rings:** i.e., from
verses carved in rings, which often have mottoes.   290. **painted cloth:** painted canvas wall-hangings.   331. **hard:** i.e.,
tediously.   357. **cony:** rabbit.   358. **kindled:** littered.   360. **purchase:** acquire. **removed:** remote.   363. **inland.** Cf.
II.vii.96 note.   364. **courtship:** (1) courtiership, (2) wooing.

thank God I am not a woman, to be touch'd with so many giddy offences as he hath generally tax'd their whole sex withal.

Orl. Can you remember any of the principal evils that he laid to the charge of women?   370

Ros. There were none principal; they were all like one another as half-pence are, every one fault seeming monstrous till his fellow-fault came to match it.

Orl. I prithee, recount some of them.   375

Ros. No, I will not cast away my physic but on those that are sick. There is a man haunts the forest, that abuses our young plants with carving Rosalind on their barks; hangs odes upon haw-thorns and elegies on brambles; all, forsooth,   380 deifying the name of Rosalind. If I could meet that fancy-monger, I would give him some good counsel, for he seems to have the quotidian of love upon him.   384

Orl. I am he that is so love-shak'd. I pray you, tell me your remedy.

Ros. There is none of my uncle's marks upon you. He taught me how to know a man in love, in which cage of rushes I am sure you are not prisoner.   390

Orl. What were his marks?

Ros. A lean cheek, which you have not; a blue eye and sunken, which you have not; an unquestion-able spirit, which you have not; a beard neglected, which you have not; but I pardon you for that,   395 for simply your having in beard is a younger broth-er's revenue. Then your hose should be ungarter'd, your bonnet unbanded, your sleeve unbutton'd, your shoe unti'd, and every thing about you dem-onstrating a careless desolation. But you are   400 no such man; you are rather point-device in your accoutrements, as loving yourself than seeming the lover of any other.

Orl. Fair youth, I would I could make thee be-lieve I love.   405

Ros. Me believe it! you may as soon make her that you love believe it; which, I warrant, she is apter to do than to confess she does. That is one of the points in the which women still give the lie to their consciences. But, in good sooth, are   410 you he that hangs the verses on the trees, wherein Rosalind is so admired?

Orl. I swear to thee, youth, by the white hand of Rosalind, I am that he, that unfortunate he.   415

Ros. But are you so much in love as your rhymes speak?

Orl. Neither rhyme nor reason can express how much.   419

Ros. Love is merely a madness, and, I tell you, deserves as well a dark house and a whip as madmen do; and the reason why they are not so punish'd and cured is, that the lunacy is so ordinary that the whippers are in love too. Yet I profess curing it by counsel.   425

Orl. Did you ever cure any so?

Ros. Yes, one, and in this manner. He was to imagine me his love, his mistress, and I set him every day to woo me; at which time would I, being but a moonish youth, grieve, be effeminate,   430 changeable, longing and liking, proud, fantastical, apish, shallow, inconstant, full of tears, full of smiles; for every passion something and for no pas-sion truly any thing, as boys and women are for the most part cattle of this colour; would now   435 like him, now loathe him; then entertain him, then forswear him; now weep for him, then spit at him; that I drave my suitor from his mad humour of love to a living humour of madness; which was, to forswear the full stream of the world and to live   440 in a nook, merely monastic. And thus I cur'd him; and this way will I take upon me to wash your liver as clean as a sound sheep's heart, that there shall not be one spot of love in't.   445

Orl. I would not be cured, youth.

Ros. I would cure you, if you would but call me Rosalind and come every day to my cote and woo me.

Orl. Now, by the faith of my love, I will. Tell me where it is.   451

Ros. Go with me to it and I'll show it you; and by the way you shall tell me where in the forest you live. Will you go?

Orl. With all my heart, good youth.   455

Ros. Nay, you must call me Rosalind. Come, sister, will you go?   [*Exeunt.*

SCENE III. [*The forest.*]

Enter Clown [TOUCHSTONE] *and* AUDREY;
JAQUES [*behind*].

Touch. Come apace, good Audrey. I will fetch up your goats, Audrey. And how, Audrey, am I the man yet? Doth my simple feature content you?

Aud. Your features! Lord warrant us! what features?   6

Touch. I am here with thee and thy goats, as the most capricious poet, honest Ovid, was among the Goths.

---

382. **fancy-monger:** dealer in love.   383. **quotidian:** daily fever (suggesting *love-shak'd*, l. 385).   392. **blue eye:** dark shadows under the eye.   393. **unquestionable:** averse to talk.   396. **having:** possession.   401. **point-device:** exact, fault-less.   430. **moonish:** changeable.   439. **living:** actual.   441. **merely:** entirely.   442. **liver:** the supposed seat of love.

Sc. iii, 3. **feature:** shape.   8. **capricious.** With a punning sense, *goat-like*, suggested by *caper* (goat), the Latin root of the word.   **Ovid...Goths.** Ovid was banished by the Emperor Augustus to the land of the Goths (another pun on *goats*).

Jaq. [*Aside.*] O knowledge ill-inhabited, worse than Jove in a thatch'd house!   11

Touch. When a man's verses cannot be understood, nor a man's good wit seconded with the forward child, understanding, it strikes a man more dead than a great reckoning in a little room. Truly, I would the gods had made thee poetical.   16

Aud. I do not know what "poetical" is. Is it honest in deed and word? Is it a true thing?

Touch. No, truly; for the truest poetry is the most feigning; and lovers are given to poetry,   20 and what they swear in poetry may be said as lovers they do feign.

Aud. Do you wish then that the gods had made me poetical?

Touch. I do, truly; for thou swearest to me   25 thou art honest. Now, if thou wert a poet, I might have some hope thou didst feign.

Aud. Would you not have me honest?

Touch. No, truly, unless thou wert hard-favour'd; for honesty coupled to beauty is to have honey a sauce to sugar.   31

Jaq. [*Aside.*] A material fool!

Aud. Well, I am not fair; and therefore I pray the gods make me honest.   34

Touch. Truly, and to cast away honesty upon a foul slut were to put good meat into an unclean dish.

Aud. I am not a slut, though I thank the gods I am foul.   39

Touch. Well, praised be the gods for thy foulness! Sluttishness may come hereafter. But be it as it may be, I will marry thee, and to that end I have been with Sir Oliver Martext, the vicar of the next village, who hath promis'd to meet me in this place of the forest and to couple us.   45

Jaq. [*Aside.*] I would fain see this meeting.

Aud. Well, the gods give us joy!

Touch. Amen. A man may, if he were of a fearful heart, stagger in this attempt; for here we have no temple but the wood, no assembly but horn-   50 beasts. But what though? Courage! As horns are odious, they are necessary. It is said, "Many a man knows no end of his goods." Right; many a man has good horns, and knows no end of them. Well, that is the dowry of his wife; 'tis none of   55 his own getting. Horns? — even so. Poor men alone? No, no; the noblest deer hath them as huge as the rascal. Is the single man therefore blessed? No: as a wall'd town is more worthier than a village, so is the forehead of a married   60 man more honourable than the bare brow of a bachelor; and by how much defence is better than no skill, by so much is a horn more precious than to want.

Enter SIR OLIVER MARTEXT.

Here comes Sir Oliver. Sir Oliver Martext, you are well met. Will you dispatch us here   65 under this tree, or shall we go with you to your chapel?

Sir Oli. Is there none here to give the woman?

Touch. I will not take her on gift of any man.

Sir Oli. Truly, she must be given, or the marriage is not lawful.   71

Jaq. Proceed, proceed. I'll give her.

Touch. Good even, good Master What-ye-call't; how do you, sir? You are very well met. God   75 'ild you for your last company. I am very glad to see you. Even a toy in hand here, sir. Nay, pray be cover'd.

Jaq. Will you be married, motley?   79

Touch. As the ox hath his bow, sir, the horse his curb, and the falcon her bells, so man hath his desires; and as pigeons bill, so wedlock would be nibbling.

Jaq. And will you, being a man of your breeding, be married under a bush like a beggar? Get   85 you to church, and have a good priest that can tell you what marriage is. This fellow will but join you together as they join wainscot; then one of you will prove a shrunk panel, and like green timber warp, warp.   90

Touch. [*Aside.*] I am not in the mind but I were better to be married of him than of another; for he is not like to marry me well; and not being well married, it will be a good excuse for me hereafter to leave my wife.   95

Jaq. Go thou with me, and let me counsel thee.

Touch. Come, sweet Audrey;
We must be married, or we must live in bawdry.
Farewell, good Master Oliver: not, —   100
            O sweet Oliver,
            O brave Oliver,
        Leave me not behind thee;
but, —
            Wind away,   105
            Begone, I say,
        I will not to wedding with thee.

[*Exeunt Jaques, Touchstone, and Audrey.*]

Sir Oli. 'Tis no matter. Ne'er a fantastical knave of them all shall flout me out of my calling.   [*Exit.* 109

---

10. **ill-inhabited:** inappropriately lodged. 11. **Jove...house.** Jupiter was entertained *incognito* by the peasants, Baucis and Philemon. 15. **great reckoning:** big bill. 20. **feigning:** (1) imaginative, (2) lying. 32. **material:** full of good sense. 49. **stagger:** falter. 52. **necessary:** inevitable. 54. **horns.** The inescapable quibble about the cuckold. 58. **rascal:** inferior deer. 62. **defence:** the ability to defend oneself. 64. **want:** lack one. 76. **'ild:** yield, reward. 77. **toy:** trifle. 78. **be cover'd:** put on your hat. 80. **bow:** yoke. 91. **I...mind:** I do not know.

SCENE IV. [*The forest.*]

Enter ROSALIND *and* CELIA.

Ros. Never talk to me; I will weep.

Cel. Do, I prithee; but yet have the grace to consider that tears do not become a man.

Ros. But have I not cause to weep?

Cel. As good cause as one would desire; there- fore weep.   6

Ros. His very hair is of the dissembling colour.

Cel. Something browner than Judas's. Marry, his kisses are Judas's own children.   10

Ros. I' faith, his hair is of a good colour.

Cel. An excellent colour. Your chestnut was ever the only colour.

Ros. And his kissing is as full of sanctity as the touch of holy bread.   15

Cel. He hath bought a pair of cast lips of Diana. A nun of winter's sisterhood kisses not more re- ligiously. The very ice of chastity is in them.

Ros. But why did he swear he would come this morning, and comes not?   21

Cel. Nay, certainly, there is no truth in him.

Ros. Do you think so?

Cel. Yes; I think he is not a pick-purse nor a horse-stealer; but for his verity in love, I do   25 think him as concave as a covered goblet or a worm- eaten nut.

Ros. Not true in love?

Cel. Yes, when he is in; but I think he is not in.   30

Ros. You have heard him swear downright he was.

Cel. "Was" is not "is." Besides, the oath of a lover is no stronger than the word of a tapster; they are both the confirmer of false reckonings.   35 He attends here in the forest on the Duke your father.

Ros. I met the Duke yesterday and had much question with him. He asked me of what parent- age I was. I told him, of as good as he; so he   40 laugh'd and let me go. But what talk we of fathers, when there is such a man as Orlando?

Cel. O, that's a brave man! He writes brave verses, speaks brave words, swears brave oaths and breaks them bravely, quite traverse, athwart   45 the heart of his lover, as a puisny tilter, that spurs his horse but on one side, breaks his staff like a noble goose. But all's brave that youth mounts and folly guides. Who comes here?

Enter CORIN.

Cor. Mistress and master, you have oft inquired

After the shepherd that complain'd of love,   51
Who you saw sitting by me on the turf,
Praising the proud disdainful shepherdess
That was his mistress.

Cel.   Well, and what of him?

Cor. If you will see a pageant truly play'd,   55
Between the pale complexion of true love
And the red glow of scorn and proud disdain,
Go hence a little and I shall conduct you,
If you will mark it.

Ros.   O, come, let us remove;
The sight of lovers feedeth those in love.   60
Bring us to this sight, and you shall say
I'll prove a busy actor in their play.   [*Exeunt.*

SCENE V. [*Another part of the forest.*]

Enter SILVIUS *and* PHEBE.

Sil. Sweet Phebe, do not scorn me; do not,
         Phebe.
Say that you love me not, but say not so
In bitterness. The common executioner,
Whose heart th' accustom'd sight of death makes
         hard,
Falls not the axe upon the humbled neck   5
But first begs pardon. Will you sterner be
Than he that dies and lives by bloody drops?

Enter ROSALIND, CELIA, *and* CORIN [*behind*].

Phe. I would not be thy executioner.
I fly thee, for I would not injure thee.
Thou tell'st me there is murder in mine eye: 10
'Tis pretty, sure, and very probable,
That eyes, that are the frail'st and softest things,
Who shut their coward gates on atomies,
Should be called tyrants, butchers, murderers!
Now I do frown on thee with all my heart;   15
And if mine eyes can wound, now let them kill thee.
Now counterfeit to swoon; why, now fall down;
Or if thou canst not, O, for shame, for shame,
Lie not, to say mine eyes are murderers!
Now show the wound mine eye hath made in thee.
Scratch thee but with a pin, and there remains   21
Some scar of it; lean [but] upon a rush,
The cicatrice and capable impressure
Thy palm some moment keeps; but now mine eyes,
Which I have darted at thee, hurt thee not,   25
Nor, I am sure, there is no force in eyes
That can do hurt.

Sil.   O dear Phebe,
If ever — as that ever may be near —
You meet in some fresh cheek the power of fancy,

Sc. iv, 9. **browner ... Judas's.** Judas was traditionally represented with red hair.   15. **holy bread:** sacramental wafer. 16. **cast:** cast-off.   45. **traverse:** across.   To break one's lance across an adversary's shield instead of by a direct blow was disgraceful.   46. **puisny:** inexperienced.

Sc. **v**, 5. **Falls:** lets fall.   7. **dies and lives:** makes his living.   22. [but] F₂. Om. F₁.   23. **cicatrice:** mark (strictly *scar*). **capable impressure:** perceptible imprint.

Then shall you know the wounds invisible   30
That love's keen arrows make.
    Phe.   But till that time
Come not thou near me; and when that time comes,
Afflict me with thy mocks, pity me not,
As till that time I shall not pity thee.
    Ros. [*Advancing.*] And why, I pray you?   Who
        might be your mother,   35
That you insult, exult, and all at once,
Over the wretched?   What though you have no
    beauty, —
As, by my faith, I see no more in you
Than without candle may go dark to bed —
Must you be therefore proud and pitiless?   40
Why, what means this?   Why do you look on me?
I see no more in you than in the ordinary
Of nature's sale-work.   'Od's my little life,
I think she means to tangle my eyes too!
No, faith, proud mistress, hope not after it.   45
'Tis not your inky brows, your black silk hair,
Your bugle eyeballs, nor your cheek of cream
That can entame my spirits to your worship.
You foolish shepherd, wherefore do you follow her,
Like foggy south, puffing with wind and rain?   50
You are a thousand times a properer man
Than she a woman.   'Tis such fools as you
That makes the world full of ill-favour'd children.
'Tis not her glass, but you, that flatters her;
And out of you she sees herself more proper   55
Than any of her lineaments can show her.
But, mistress, know yourself.   Down on your knees,
And thank heaven, fasting, for a good man's love;
For I must tell you friendly in your ear,
Sell when you can; you are not for all markets.   60
Cry the man mercy; love him; take his offer.
Foul is most foul, being foul to be a scoffer.
So take her to thee, shepherd.   Fare you well.
    Phe. Sweet youth, I pray you, chide a year to-
    gether.
I had rather hear you chide than this man woo.   65
    Ros. He's fall'n in love with your foulness, and
she'll fall in love with my anger.   If it be so, as
fast as she answers thee with frowning looks, I'll
sauce her with bitter words.   Why look you so
upon me?   70
    Phe. For no ill will I bear you.
    Ros. I pray you, do not fall in love with me,
For I am falser than vows made in wine.
Besides, I like you not.   If you will know my house,
'Tis at the tuft of olives here hard by.   75
Will you go, sister?   Shepherd, ply her hard.
Come, sister.   Shepherdess, look on him better,
And be not proud.   Though all the world could see,

None could be so abus'd in sight as he.
Come, to our flock.   80
        [*Exeunt* [*Rosalind, Celia, and Corin*].
    Phe. Dead shepherd, now I find thy saw of
    might,
"Who ever lov'd that lov'd not at first sight?"
    Sil. Sweet Phebe, —
    Phe.   Ha, what say'st thou, Silvius?
    Sil. Sweet Phebe, pity me.
    Phe. Why, I am sorry for thee, gentle Silvius.   85
    Sil. Wherever sorrow is, relief would be.
If you do sorrow at my grief in love,
By giving love, your sorrow and my grief
Were both extermin'd.
    Phe. Thou hast my love.   Is not that neigh-
    bourly?   90
    Sil. I would have you.
    Phe.   Why, that were covetousness.
Silvius, the time was that I hated thee,
And yet it is not that I bear thee love;
But since that thou canst talk of love so well,
Thy company, which erst was irksome to me,   95
I will endure, and I'll employ thee too.
But do not look for further recompense
Than thine own gladness that thou art employ'd.
    Sil. So holy and so perfect is my love,
And I in such a poverty of grace,   100
That I shall think it a most plenteous crop
To glean the broken ears after the man
That the main harvest reaps.   Loose now and then
A scatt'red smile, and that I'll live upon.
    Phe. Know'st thou the youth that spoke to me
    erewhile?   105
    Sil. Not very well, but I have met him oft;
And he hath bought the cottage and the bounds
That the old carlot once was master of.
    Phe. Think not I love him, though I ask for him;
'Tis but a peevish boy; yet he talks well.   110
But what care I for words?   Yet words do well
When he that speaks them pleases those that hear.
It is a pretty youth; not very pretty;
But, sure, he's proud, and yet his pride becomes
    him.
He'll make a proper man.   The best thing in him
Is his complexion; and faster than his tongue   116
Did make offence his eye did heal it up.
He is not very tall; yet for his years he's tall.
His leg is but so so; and yet 'tis well.
There was a pretty redness in his lip,   120
A little riper and more lusty red
Than that mix'd in his cheek; 'twas just the dif-
    ference
Betwixt the constant red and mingled damask.

---

37. **no.** Some edd. omit; others read *some.*   39. **without candle**: without anyone's wanting to see you.   43. **sale-work**: ready-made work.   47. **bugle**: black bead of glass.   79. **abus'd**: deceived.   81–82. Shakespeare's tribute to Christopher Marlowe, from whose poem *Hero and Leander* (I,176) line 82 is taken.   107. **bounds**: pasture.   108. **carlot**: peasant. 123. **constant**: uniform.   **mingled damask**: the blended red and white (pink) of the damask rose.

There be some women, Silvius, had they mark'd
     him
In parcels as I did, would have gone near   125
To fall in love with him; but, for my part,
I love him not nor hate him not; and yet
I have more cause to hate him than to love him,
For what had he to do to chide at me?
He said mine eyes were black and my hair black;
And, now I am rememb'red, scorn'd at me.   131
I marvel why I answer'd not again.
But that's all one; omittance is no quittance.
I'll write to him a very taunting letter,
And thou shalt bear it; wilt thou, Silvius?   135
   Sil. Phebe, with all my heart.
   Phe.   I'll write it straight;
The matter's in my head and in my heart.
I will be bitter with him and passing short.
Go with me, Silvius.   [*Exeunt.*

ACT IV

SCENE I. [*The forest.*]

Enter ROSALIND, CELIA, *and* JAQUES.

   Jaq. I prithee, pretty youth, let me [be] better
acquainted with thee.
   Ros. They say you are a melancholy fellow.
   Jaq. I am so; I do love it better than laughing.   4
   Ros. Those that are in extremity of either are
abominable fellows, and betray themselves to every
modern censure worse than drunkards.
   Jaq. Why, 'tis good to be sad and say nothing.
   Ros. Why then, 'tis good to be a post.   9
   Jaq. I have neither the scholar's melancholy,
which is emulation; nor the musician's, which is
fantastical; nor the courtier's, which is proud; nor
the soldier's, which is ambitious; nor the lawyer's,
which is politic; nor the lady's, which is nice; nor
the lover's, which is all these: but it is a melan-   15
choly of mine own, compounded of many simples,
extracted from many objects; and indeed the
sundry contemplation of my travels, in which [my]
often rumination wraps me in a most humorous
sadness —   20
   Ros. A traveller! By my faith, you have great
reason to be sad. I fear you have sold your own
lands to see other men's; then, to have seen much,
and to have nothing, is to have rich eyes and poor
hands.   25
   Jaq. Yes, I have gained my experience.

Enter ORLANDO.

   Ros. And your experience makes you sad. I

had rather have a fool to make me merry than experience to make me sad; and to travel for it too!
   Orl. Good-day and happiness, dear Rosalind!   30
   Jaq. Nay, then, God buy you, an you talk in
blank verse.   [*Exit.*
   Ros. Farewell, Monsieur Traveller. Look you
lisp and wear strange suits, disable all the benefits
of your own country, be out of love with your   35
nativity, and almost chide God for making you
that countenance you are, or I will scarce think
you have swam in a gondola. Why, how now,
Orlando! Where have you been all this while?
You a lover! An you serve me such another trick,
never come in my sight more.   41
   Orl. My fair Rosalind, I come within an hour of
my promise.
   Ros. Break an hour's promise in love! He that
will divide a minute into a thousand parts, and   45
break but a part of the thousandth part of a minute
in the affairs of love, it may be said of him that
Cupid hath clapp'd him o' th' shoulder but I'll
warrant him heart-whole.
   Orl. Pardon me, dear Rosalind.   50
   Ros. Nay, an you be so tardy, come no more in
my sight. I had as lief be woo'd of a snail.
   Orl. Of a snail?
   Ros. Ay, of a snail; for though he comes slowly,
he carries his house on his head; a better join-   55
ture, I think, than you make a woman. Besides,
he brings his destiny with him.
   Orl. What's that?
   Ros. Why, horns, which such as you are fain to
be beholding to your wives for. But he comes   60
armed in his fortune and prevents the slander of
his wife.
   Orl. Virtue is no horn-maker; and my Rosalind
is virtuous.
   Ros. And I am your Rosalind.   65
   Cel. It pleases him to call you so; but he hath a
Rosalind of a better leer than you.
   Ros. Come, woo me, woo me; for now I am in a
holiday humour and like enough to consent. What
would you say to me now, an I were your very very
Rosalind?   71
   Orl. I would kiss before I spoke.
   Ros. Nay, you were better speak first; and when
you were gravell'd for lack of matter, you might
take occasion to kiss. Very good orators,   75
when they are out, they will spit; and for lovers
lacking — God warn us! — matter, the cleanliest
shift is to kiss.
   Orl. How if the kiss be deni'd?

---

125. **In parcels:** piecemeal.
   Act IV, sc. i, 1. **[be].** Om. F.   7. **modern censure:** ordinary judgment.   14. **nice:** fastidious.   16. **simples:** ingredients.
18. **[my]** F₂.   *by* F₁.   19. **humorous:** whimsical.   34. **disable:** disparage.   38. **swam ... gondola:** i.e., been in Venice.
48. **clapp'd ... shoulder:** i.e., arrested.   55. **jointure:** marriage-settlement.   61. **prevents:** anticipates.   67. **leer:** face.
74. **gravell'd:** stuck.   76. **out:** at a loss.   77. **warn:** defend.   **cleanliest shift:** neatest trick.

Ros. Then she puts you to entreaty and there begins new matter.   81

Orl. Who could be out, being before his beloved mistress?

Ros. Marry, that should you if I were your mistress, or I should think my honesty ranker than my wit.   86

Orl. What, of my suit?

Ros. Not out of your apparel, and yet out of your suit. Am not I your Rosalind?

Orl. I take some joy to say you are, because I would be talking of her.   91

Ros. Well, in her person, I say I will not have you.

Orl. Then in mine own person I die.

Ros. No, faith, die by attorney. The poor world is almost six thousand years old, and in all this time there was not any man died in his 95 own person, *videlicet*, in a love-cause. Troilus had his brains dash'd out with a Grecian club; yet he did what he could to die before, and he is one of the patterns of love. Leander, he would have 100 liv'd many a fair year though Hero had turn'd nun, if it had not been for a hot mid-summer night; for, good youth, he went but forth to wash him in the Hellespont and being taken with the cramp was drown'd; and the foolish chroniclers of that age 105 found it was — Hero of Sestos. But these are all lies. Men have died from time to time and worms have eaten them, but not for love.

Orl. I would not have my right Rosalind of this mind; for, I protest, her frown might kill me. 110

Ros. By this hand, it will not kill a fly. But come, now I will be your Rosalind in a more coming-on disposition; and ask me what you will, I will grant it.

Orl. Then love me, Rosalind.   115

Ros. Yes, faith, will I, Fridays and Saturdays and all.

Orl. And wilt thou have me?

Ros. Ay, and twenty such.

Orl. What sayest thou?   120

Ros. Are you not good?

Orl. I hope so.

Ros. Why then, can one desire too much of a good thing? Come, sister, you shall be the priest and marry us. Give me your hand, Orlando. What do you say, sister?   126

Orl. Pray thee, marry us.

Cel. I cannot say the words.

Ros. You must begin, "Will you, Orlando," —

Cel. Go to. Will you, Orlando, have to wife this Rosalind?   131

Orl. I will.

Ros. Ay, but when?

Orl. Why now; as fast as she can marry us.

Ros. Then you must say, "I take thee, Rosalind, for wife."   136

Orl. I take thee, Rosalind, for wife.

Ros. I might ask you for your commission; but I do take thee, Orlando, for my husband. There's a girl goes before the priest; and certainly a woman's thought runs before her actions.   141

Orl. So do all thoughts; they are wing'd.

Ros. Now tell me how long you would have her after you have possess'd her.

Orl. For ever and a day.   145

Ros. Say "a day," without the "ever." No, no, Orlando. Men are April when they woo, December when they wed; maids are May when they are maids, but the sky changes when they are wives. I will be more jealous of thee than a 150 Barbary cock-pigeon over his hen, more clamorous than a parrot against rain, more new-fangled than an ape, more giddy in my desires than a monkey. I will weep for nothing, like Diana in the fountain, and I will do that when you are dispos'd to be 155 merry. I will laugh like a hyen, and that when thou art inclin'd to sleep.

Orl. But will my Rosalind do so?

Ros. By my life, she will do as I do.

Orl. O, but she is wise.   160

Ros. Or else she could not have the wit to do this. The wiser, the waywarder. Make the doors upon a woman's wit and it will out at the casement; shut that and 'twill out at the key-hole; stop that, 'twill fly with the smoke out at the chimney. 166

Orl. A man that had a wife with such a wit, he might say, "Wit, whither wilt?"

Ros. Nay, you might keep that check for it, till you met your wife's wit going to your neighbour's bed.   171

Orl. And what wit could wit have to excuse that?

Ros. Marry, to say she came to seek you there. You shall never take her without her answer, 175 unless you take her without her tongue. O, that woman that cannot make her fault her husband's occasion, let her never nurse her child herself, for she will breed it like a fool!

Orl. For these two hours, Rosalind, I will leave thee.   181

Ros. Alas, dear love, I cannot lack thee two hours!

Orl. I must attend the Duke at dinner. By two o'clock I will be with thee again.   185

Ros. Ay, go your ways, go your ways; I knew

---

85. **honesty ranker:** chastity greater. 96 ff. Troilus and Leander were types of faithful lovers, whose heroism Rosalind facetiously disparages. 138. **commission:** authority. 140. **goes before:** anticipates. 152. **new-fangled:** fond of novelty. 162. **Make:** shut. 168. **"Wit, whither wilt?"** An expression to stop a person talking. 177. **make ... occasion:** make out that her husband is to blame for her fault.

what you would prove. My friends told me as much, and I thought no less. That flattering tongue of yours won me. 'Tis but one cast away, and so, come, death! Two o'clock is your hour?   190

Orl. Ay, sweet Rosalind.

Ros. By my troth, and in good earnest, and so God mend me, and by all pretty oaths that are not dangerous, if you break one jot of your promise or come one minute behind your hour, I will think   195 you the most pathetical break-promise, and the most hollow lover, and the most unworthy of her you call Rosalind, that may be chosen out of the gross band of the unfaithful; therefore beware my censure and keep your promise.   200

Orl. With no less religion than if thou wert indeed my Rosalind; so adieu.

Ros. Well, Time is the old justice that examines all such offenders, and let Time try. Adieu.

[*Exit* [*Orlando*].

Cel. You have simply misus'd our sex in your   205 love-prate. We must have your doublet and hose pluck'd over your head, and show the world what the bird hath done to her own nest.

Ros. O coz, coz, coz, my pretty little coz, that thou didst know how many fathom deep I am   210 in love! But it cannot be sounded. My affection hath an unknown bottom, like the bay of Portugal.

Cel. Or rather, bottomless; that as fast as you pour affection in, it runs out.   215

Ros. No, that same wicked bastard of Venus that was begot of thought, conceiv'd of spleen, and born of madness, that blind rascally boy that abuses every one's eyes because his own are out, let him be judge how deep I am in love. I'll tell thee,   220 Aliena, I cannot be out of the sight of Orlando. I'll go find a shadow and sigh till he come.

Cel. And I'll sleep.   [*Exeunt.*

SCENE II. [*The forest.*]

Enter JAQUES, LORDS, *and* FORESTERS.

Jaq. Which is he that killed the deer?

A Lord. Sir, it was I.

Jaq. Let's present him to the Duke, like a Roman conqueror; and it would do well to set the deer's horns upon his head, for a branch of vic-   5 tory. Have you no song, forester, for this purpose?

[*1. For.*] Yes, sir.

Jaq. Sing it. 'Tis no matter how it be in tune, so it make noise enough.   10

SONG.   [*Music.*

[*1. For.*] What shall he have that killed the deer?
His leather skin and horns to wear.
Then sing him home.

[*The rest shall bear this burden.*
Take thou no scorn to wear the horn;
It was a crest ere thou wast born;   15
Thy father's father wore it,
And thy father bore it.
The horn, the horn, the lusty horn
Is not a thing to laugh to scorn.

[*Exeunt.*

SCENE III. [*The forest.*]

Enter ROSALIND *and* CELIA.

Ros. How say you now? Is it not past two o'clock? And here much Orlando!

Cel. I warrant you, with pure love and troubled brain, (*Enter* SILVIUS) he hath ta'en his bow and arrows and is gone forth — to sleep. Look, who comes here.   5

Sil. My errand is to you, fair youth;
My gentle Phebe bid me give you this.
I know not the contents; but, as I guess
By the stern brow and waspish action
Which she did use as she was writing of it,   10
It bears an angry tenour. Pardon me,
I am but as a guiltless messenger.

Ros. Patience herself would startle at this letter
And play the swaggerer. Bear this, bear all.
She says I am not fair, that I lack manners.   15
She calls me proud, and that she could not love me,
Were man as rare as phœnix. 'Od's my will!
Her love is not the hare that I do hunt.
Why writes she so to me? Well, shepherd, well,
This is a letter of your own device.   20

Sil. No, I protest, I know not the contents.
Phebe did write it.

Ros.   Come, come, you are a fool,
And turn'd into th' extremity of love.
I saw her hand; she has a leathern hand,
A freestone-colour'd hand. I verily did think   25
That her old gloves were on, but 'twas her hands;
She has a huswife's hand; but that's no matter.
I say she never did invent this letter.
This is a man's invention and his hand.

Sil. Sure, it is hers.   30

Ros. Why, 'tis a boisterous and a cruel style,
A style for challengers. Why, she defies me,
Like Turk to Christian. Women's gentle brain
Could not drop forth such giant-rude invention,

---

195. **pathetical:** pitiful. 201. **religion:** devotion. 205. **simply misus'd:** utterly abused. 217. **thought:** melancholy. **spleen:** impulsive passion.

Sc. ii, 7. [*1. For.*] *Lord* Ff.

Sc. iii, 7. **bid** F2. *did bid* F1. 17. **phœnix.** A fabulous bird, the only one of its kind, consumed by fire every five hundred years, and rising again from its own ashes. 23. **turn'd:** brought. 25. **freestone:** sandstone.

Such Ethiope words, blacker in their effect   35
Than in their countenance. Will you hear the
    letter?
  Sil. So please you, for I never heard it yet;
Yet heard too much of Phebe's cruelty.
  Ros. She Phebes me. Mark how the tyrant
    writes.
[*Reads.*]
    "Art thou god to shepherd turn'd,   40
    That a maiden's heart hath burn'd?"
Can a woman rail thus?
  Sil. Call you this railing?
  Ros. [*Reads.*]
    "Why, thy godhead laid apart,
    Warr'st thou with a woman's heart?"   45
Did you ever hear such railing?
    "Whiles the eye of man did woo me,
    That could do no vengeance to me."
Meaning me a beast.
    "If the scorn of your bright eyne   50
    Have power to raise such love in mine,
    Alack, in me what strange effect
    Would they work in mild aspect!
    Whiles you chid me, I did love;
    How then might your prayers move!   55
    He that brings this love to thee
    Little knows this love in me;
    And by him seal up thy mind,
    Whether that thy youth and kind
    Will the faithful offer take   60
    Of me and all that I can make;
    Or else by him my love deny,
    And then I'll study how to die."
  Sil. Call you this chiding?
  Cel. Alas, poor shepherd!   65
  Ros. Do you pity him? No, he deserves no pity.
Wilt thou love such a woman? What, to make
thee an instrument and play false strains upon thee!
Not to be endur'd! Well, go your way to her —
for I see love hath made thee a tame snake —   70
and say this to her: that if she love me, I charge her
to love thee; if she will not, I will never have her
unless thou entreat for her. If you be a true lover,
hence, and not a word; for here comes more company.   [*Exit Silvius.* 75

      Enter OLIVER.

  Oli. Good morrow, fair ones. Pray you, if you
    know,
Where in the purlieus of this forest stands
A sheep-cote fenc'd about with olive-trees?
  Cel. West of this place, down in the neighbour
    bottom.
The rank of osiers by the murmuring stream   80

Left on your right hand brings you to the place.
But at this hour the house doth keep itself;
There's none within.
  Oli. If that an eye may profit by a tongue,
Then should I know you by description;   85
Such garments and such years. "The boy is fair,
Of female favour, and bestows himself
Like a ripe sister; the woman low,
And browner than her brother." Are not you
The owner of the house I did enquire for?   90
  Cel. It is no boast, being ask'd, to say we are.
  Oli. Orlando doth commend him to you both,
And to that youth he calls his Rosalind
He sends this bloody napkin. Are you he?
  Ros. I am. What must we understand by
    this?   95
  Oli. Some of my shame, if you will know of me
What man I am, and how, and why, and where
This handkercher was stain'd.
  Cel.   I pray you, tell it.
  Oli. When last the young Orlando parted from
    you
He left a promise to return again   100
Within an hour; and pacing through the forest,
Chewing the food of sweet and bitter fancy,
Lo, what befell! He threw his eye aside,
And mark what object did present itself.
Under an oak, whose boughs were moss'd with
    age   105
And high top bald with dry antiquity,
A wretched ragged man, o'ergrown with hair,
Lay sleeping on his back. About his neck
A green and gilded snake had wreath'd itself,
Who with her head nimble in threats approach'd
The opening of his mouth; but suddenly,   111
Seeing Orlando, it unlink'd itself,
And with indented glides did slip away
Into a bush; under which bush's shade
A lioness, with udders all drawn dry,   115
Lay couching, head on ground, with catlike
    watch,
When that the sleeping man should stir; for 'tis
The royal disposition of that beast
To prey on nothing that doth seem as dead.
This seen, Orlando did approach the man   120
And found it was his brother, his elder brother.
  Cel. O, I have heard him speak of that same
    brother;
And he did render him the most unnatural
That liv'd amongst men.
  Oli.   And well he might so do,
For well I know he was unnatural.   125
  Ros. But, to Orlando. Did he leave him there,
Food to the suck'd and hungry lioness?

---

    35. **Ethiope:** i.e., black.   39. **Phebes me:** i.e., tries her scorn on me.   48. **vengeance:** mischief.   59. **youth and kind:**
youthful nature.   68. **instrument:** (1) tool, (2) musical instrument.   77. **purlieus:** borders.   79. **neighbour bottom:**
neighboring dell.   80. **rank of osiers:** row of willows.   87. **bestows:** carries.   88. **ripe:** mature.   105. **oak** (Pope). *old
oahe* Ff.   113. **indented:** zigzag.   123. **render:** describe.

Oli. Twice did he turn his back and purpos'd so;
But kindness, nobler ever than revenge,
And nature, stronger than his just occasion,   130
Made him give battle to the lioness,
Who quickly fell before him; in which hurtling
From miserable slumber I awaked.
    Cel. Are you his brother?
    Ros.   Was't you he rescu'd?
    Cel. Was't you that did so oft contrive to kill
        him?   135
    Oli. 'Twas I; but 'tis not I. I do not shame
To tell you what I was, since my conversion
So sweetly tastes, being the thing I am.
    Ros. But, for the bloody napkin?
    Oli.   By and by.
When from the first to last betwixt us two   140
Tears our recountments had most kindly bath'd,
As how I came into that desert place, —
In brief, he led me to the gentle Duke,
Who gave me fresh array and entertainment,
Committing me unto my brother's love;   145
Who led me instantly into his cave,
There stripp'd himself, and here upon his arm
The lioness had torn some flesh away,
Which all this while had bled; and now he fainted
And cri'd, in fainting, upon Rosalind.   150
Brief, I recover'd him, bound up his wound;
And, after some small space, being strong at heart,
He sent me hither, stranger as I am,
To tell this story, that you might excuse
His broken promise, and to give this napkin,   155
Dy'd in his blood, unto the shepherd youth
That he in sport doth call his Rosalind.
                                [*Rosalind swoons.*]
    Cel. Why, how now, Ganymede! sweet Gany-
        mede!
    Oli. Many will swoon when they do look on
        blood.
    Cel. There is more in it. Cousin Ganymede! 160
    Oli. Look, he recovers.
    Ros. I would I were at home.
    Cel.   We'll lead you thither.
I pray you, will you take him by the arm?
    Oli. Be of good cheer, youth. You a man!
You lack a man's heart.   165
    Ros. I do so, I confess it. Ah, sirrah, a body
would think this was well counterfeited! I pray
you, tell your brother how well I counterfeited.
Heigh-ho!   169
    Oli. This was not counterfeit. There is too
great testimony in your complexion that it was a
passion of earnest.
    Ros. Counterfeit, I assure you.
    Oli. Well then, take a good heart and counterfeit
to be a man.   175

    Ros. So I do. But, i' faith, I should have been a
woman by right.
    Cel. Come, you look paler and paler. Pray you,
draw homewards. Good sir, go with us.
    Oli. That will I, for I must bear answer back   180
How you excuse my brother, Rosalind.
    Ros. I shall devise something; but, I pray you,
commend my counterfeiting to him. Will you go?
                                            [*Exeunt.*

ACT V

SCENE I. [*The forest.*]

Enter Clown [TOUCHSTONE] *and* AUDREY.

    Touch. We shall find a time, Audrey; patience,
gentle Audrey.
    Aud. Faith, the priest was good enough, for all
the old gentleman's saying.   4
    Touch. A most wicked Sir Oliver, Audrey, a most
vile Martext. But, Audrey, there is a youth here
in the forest lays claim to you.
    Aud. Ay, I know who 'tis; he hath no interest
in me in the world. Here comes the man you
mean.   10

Enter WILLIAM

    Touch. It is meat and drink to me to see a clown.
By my troth, we that have good wits have much to
answer for; we shall be flouting; we cannot hold.
    Will. Good ev'n, Audrey.   15
    Aud. God ye good ev'n, William.
    Will. And good ev'n to you, sir,
    Touch. Good ev'n, gentle friend. Cover thy
head, cover thy head; nay, prithee, be cover'd.
How old are you, friend?   20
    Will. Five and twenty, sir.
    Touch. A ripe age. Is thy name William?
    Will. William, sir.
    Touch. A fair name. Was't born i' the forest
here?   25
    Will. Ay, sir, I thank God.
    Touch. "Thank God" — a good answer. Art
rich?
    Will. Faith, sir, so so.
    Touch. "So so" is good, very good, very excel-
lent good; and yet it is not; it is but so so. Art
thou wise?   31
    Will. Ay, sir, I have a pretty wit.
    Touch. Why, thou say'st well. I do now re-
member a saying, "The fool doth think he is wise,
but the wise man knows himself to be a fool."   35
The heathen philosopher, when he had a desire to
eat a grape, would open his lips when he put it
into his mouth; meaning thereby that grapes were

141. recountments: tales. 151. recover'd: revived.
Act V, sc. i, 11. clown: country fellow. Touchstone is a court jester. 14. shall...flouting: must have our jest.

made to eat and lips to open. You do love this
maid? 40
Will. I do, sir.
Touch. Give me your hand. Art thou learned?
Will. No, sir.
Touch. Then learn this of me: to have, is to have;
for it is a figure in rhetoric that drink, being 45
pour'd out of a cup into a glass, by filling the one
doth empty the other. For all your writers do
consent that *ipse* is he: now, you are not *ipse*, for
I am he.
Will. Which he, sir? 50
Touch. He, sir, that must marry this woman.
Therefore, you clown, abandon — which is in the
vulgar leave — the society — which in the boorish
is company — of this female — which in the common is woman; which together is, abandon the 55
society of this female; or, clown, thou perishest; or,
to thy better understanding, diest; or, to wit, I kill
thee, make thee away, translate thy life into death,
thy liberty into bondage. I will deal in poison with
thee, or in bastinado, or in steel. I will bandy 60
with thee in faction; I will o'er-run thee with
[policy]; I will kill thee a hundred and fifty ways:
therefore tremble, and depart.
Aud. Do, good William.
Will. God rest you merry, sir. [*Exit.* 65

      Enter CORIN.

Cor. Our master and mistress seeks you. Come,
away, away!
Touch. Trip, Audrey! trip, Audrey! I attend,
I attend. [*Exeunt.*

SCENE II. [*The forest.*]

    Enter ORLANDO *and* OLIVER.

Orl. Is't possible that on so little acquaintance
you should like her? That but seeing you should
love her? And loving woo? And, wooing, she
should grant? And will you persever to enjoy
her? 5
Oli. Neither call the giddiness of it in question,
the poverty of her, the small acquaintance, my
sudden wooing, nor [her] sudden consenting; but
say with me, I love Aliena; say with her that she
loves me; consent with both that we may enjoy
each other. It shall be to your good; for my 10
father's house and all the revenue that was old Sir
Roland's will I estate upon you, and here live and
die a shepherd. 14

      Enter ROSALIND.

Orl. You have my consent. Let your wedding

be to-morrow; thither will I invite the Duke and
all 's contented followers. Go you and prepare
Aliena; for look you, here comes my Rosalind.
Ros. God save you, brother. 20
Oli. And you, fair sister. [*Exit.*]
Ros. O, my dear Orlando, how it grieves me to
see thee wear thy heart in a scarf!
Orl. It is my arm.
Ros. I thought thy heart had been wounded with
the claws of a lion. 26
Orl. Wounded it is, but with the eyes of a lady.
Ros. Did your brother tell you how I counterfeited to swoon when he show'd me your handkercher? 30
Orl. Ay, and greater wonders than that.
Ros. O, I know where you are. Nay, 'tis true.
There was never any thing so sudden but the fight
of two rams, and Cæsar's thrasonical brag of "I
came, saw, and overcame." For your brother 35
and my sister no sooner met but they look'd;
no sooner look'd but they lov'd; no sooner lov'd
but they sigh'd; no sooner sigh'd but they ask'd one
another the reason; no sooner knew the reason but
they sought the remedy; and in these degrees 40
have they made a pair of stairs to marriage which
they will climb incontinent, or else be incontinent
before marriage. They are in the very wrath of
love and they will together. Clubs cannot part
them. 45
Orl. They shall be married to-morrow, and I
will bid the Duke to the nuptial. But, O, how
bitter a thing it is to look into happiness through
another man's eyes! By so much the more shall I
to-morrow be at the height of heart-heaviness, 50
by how much I shall think my brother happy in
having what he wishes for.
Ros. Why then, to-morrow I cannot serve your
turn for Rosalind?
Orl. I can live no longer by thinking. 55
Ros. I will weary you, then, no longer with idle
talking. Know of me, then, for now I speak to
some purpose, that I know you are a gentleman of
good conceit. I speak not this that you should bear
a good opinion of my knowledge, insomuch I 60
say I know you are; neither do I labour for a greater
esteem than may in some little measure draw a belief from you, to do yourself good and not to grace
me. Believe then, if you please, that I can do
strange things. I have, since I was three year 65
old, convers'd with a magician, most profound in
his art and yet not damnable. If you do love Rosalind so near the heart as your gesture cries it out,
when your brother marries Aliena, shall you marry

60. bastinado: cudgelling. 62. [policy] Ff₂₋₄: cunning. *police* F₁.
  Sc. ii, 8. [her] (Rowe). Om. Ff. 13. estate: settle. 33. thrasonical: boastful (like Thraso, the braggart in Terence's comedy, *Eunuchus*). 42. incontinent...incontinent: directly...unchaste. 43. wrath: passion. 59. conceit: intelligence. 66. convers'd: associated. 67. damnable. See note on l. 77. 68. gesture: behavior.

her. I know into what straits of fortune she is 70
driven; and it is not impossible to me, if it appear
not inconvenient to you, to set her before your
eyes to-morrow, human as she is, and without any
danger. 75

Orl. Speakest thou in sober meanings?

Ros. By my life, I do; which I tender dearly,
though I say I am a magician. Therefore, put you
in your best array; bid your friends; for if you will
be married to-morrow, you shall; and to Rosalind,
if you will. 81

Enter SILVIUS AND PHEBE.

Look, here comes a lover of mine and a lover of
hers.

Phe. Youth, you have done me much ungentle-
ness,
To show the letter that I writ to you.

Ros. I care not if I have. It is my study 85
To seem despiteful and ungentle to you.
You are there followed by a faithful shepherd;
Look upon him, love him. He worships you.

Phe. Good shepherd, tell this youth what 'tis to
love.

Sil. It is to be all made of sighs and tears; 90
And so am I for Phebe.

Phe. And I for Ganymede.

Orl. And I for Rosalind.

Ros. And I for no woman.

Sil. It is to be all made of faith and service; 95
And so am I for Phebe.

Phe. And I for Ganymede.

Orl. And I for Rosalind.

Ros. And I for no woman.

Sil. It is to be all made of fantasy. 100
All made of passion, and all made of wishes;
All adoration, duty, and observance,
All humbleness, all patience, and impatience,
All purity, all trial, all [obedience];
And so am I for Phebe. 105

Phe. And so am I for Ganymede.

Orl. And so am I for Rosalind.

Ros. And so am I for no woman.

Phe. If this be so, why blame you me to love
you? 110

Sil. If this be so, why blame you me to love you?

Orl. If this be so, why blame you me to love you?

Ros. Why do you speak too, "Why blame you
me to love you?" 116

Orl. To her that is not here, nor doth not hear.

Ros. Pray you, no more of this; 'tis like the howling of Irish wolves against the moon. [*To Sil.*] I
will help you, if I can. [*To Phe.*] I would love 120
you, if I could. To-morrow meet me all together.

[*To Phe.*] I will marry you, if ever I marry woman,
and I'll be married to-morrow. [*To Orl.*] I will
satisfy you, if ever I satisfi'd man, and you shall be
married to-morrow. [*To Sil.*] I will content 125
you, if what pleases you contents you, and you
shall be married to-morrow. [*To Orl.*] As you love
Rosalind, meet. [*To Sil.*] As you love Phebe,
meet. And as I love no woman, I'll meet. So, fare
you well. I have left you commands. 131

Sil. I'll not fail, if I live.

Phe. Nor I.

Orl. Nor I.   [*Exeunt.*

SCENE III. [*The forest.*]

Enter Clown [TOUCHSTONE] *and* AUDREY.

Touch. To-morrow is the joyful day, Audrey;
to-morrow will we be married.

Aud. I do desire it with all my heart; and I hope
it is no dishonest desire to desire to be a woman
of the world. Here come two of the banish'd
Duke's pages. 6

Enter two PAGES.

1. Page. Well met, honest gentlemen.

Touch. By my troth, well met. Come, sit, sit,
and a song.

2. Page. We are for you. Sit i' th' middle. 10

1. Page. Shall we clap into't roundly, without
hawking or spitting or saying we are hoarse, which
are the only prologues to a bad voice? 14

2. Page. I' faith, i' faith; and both in a tune, like
two gypsies on a horse.

SONG.

It was a lover and his lass,
  With a hey, and a ho, and a hey nonino,
That o'er the green corn-field did pass
  In the spring time, the only pretty ring time,
When birds do sing, hey ding a ding, ding; 21
Sweet lovers love the spring.

Between the acres of the rye,
  With a hey, and a ho, and a hey nonino,
These pretty country folks would lie, 25
  In spring time, &c.

This carol they began that hour,
  With a hey, and a ho, and a hey nonino,
How that a life was but a flower
  In spring time, &c. 30

And therefore take the present time,
  With a hey, and a ho, and a hey nonino;

77–78. **By ... magician.** Black magic was punishable by death. 104. **[obedience]** (Malone conj.) *observance* Ff.
Sc. iii, 4. **dishonest:** immodest. 4–5. **woman of the world:** married woman. 14. **the only:** only the. 15. **a:** one. 31–34.
F prints this as stanza 2. A version in Morley's *First Booke of Ayres* (1600) places it at the end, where it clearly belongs.

For love is crowned with the prime
In spring time, &c.   34

Touch. Truly, young gentlemen, though there
was no great matter in the ditty, yet the note was
very untuneable.

1. Page. You are deceiv'd, sir. We kept time,
we lost not our time.   39

Touch. By my troth, yes; I count it but time lost
to hear such a foolish song. God buy you — and
God mend your voices! Come, Audrey. [*Exeunt.*

SCENE IV. [*The forest.*]

Enter DUKE senior, AMIENS, JAQUES, OR-
LANDO, OLIVER, *and* CELIA.

Duke S. Dost thou believe, Orlando, that the boy
Can do all this that he hath promised?

Orl. I sometimes do believe, and sometimes do
not;
As those that fear they hope, and know they fear.

Enter ROSALIND, SILVIUS, *and* PHEBE.

Ros. Patience once more, whiles our compact
is urg'd.   5
You say, if I bring in your Rosalind,
You will bestow her on Orlando here?

Duke S. That would I, had I kingdoms to give
with her.

Ros. And you say, you will have her, when I
bring her.

Orl. That would I, were I of all kingdoms king.   10

Ros. You say, you'll marry me, if I be willing?

Phe. That will I, should I die the hour after.

Ros. But if you do refuse to marry me,
You'll give yourself to this most faithful shepherd?

Phe. So is the bargain.   15

Ros. You say, that you'll have Phebe, if she will?

Sil. Though to have her and death were both one
thing.

Ros. I have promis'd to make all this matter even.
Keep you your word, O Duke, to give your daugh-
ter;   20
You, yours, Orlando, to receive his daughter;
Keep your word, Phebe, that you'll marry me,
Or else, refusing me, to wed this shepherd;
Keep your word, Silvius, that you'll marry her,
If she refuse me; and from hence I go,
To make these doubts all even.   25

                   [*Exeunt Rosalind and Celia.*

Duke S. I do remember in this shepherd boy
Some lively touches of my daughter's favour.

Orl. My lord, the first time that I ever saw him
Methought he was a brother to your daughter.
But, my good lord, this boy is forest-born,   30
And hath been tutor'd in the rudiments
Of many desperate studies by his uncle,
Whom he reports to be a great magician,
Obscured in the circle of this forest.   34

Enter Clown [TOUCHSTONE] *and* AUDREY.

Jaq. There is, sure, another flood toward, and
these couples are coming to the ark. Here comes a
pair of very strange beasts, which in all tongues are
called fools.

Touch. Salutation and greeting to you all!   39

Jaq. Good my lord, bid him welcome. This is
the motley-minded gentleman that I have so often
met in the forest. He hath been a courtier, he
swears.

Touch. If any man doubt that, let him put me
to my purgation. I have trod a measure; I have   45
flatt'red a lady; I have been politic with my friend,
smooth with mine enemy; I have undone three
tailors; I have had four quarrels, and like to have
fought one.

Jaq. And how was that ta'en up?   50

Touch. Faith, we met, and found the quarrel was
upon the seventh cause.

Jaq. How seventh cause? Good my lord, like
this fellow.

Duke S. I like him very well.   55

Touch. God 'ild you, sir; I desire you of the
like. I press in here, sir, amongst the rest of the
country copulatives, to swear and to forswear,
according as marriage binds and blood breaks. A
poor virgin, sir, an ill-favour'd thing, sir, but   60
mine own. A poor humour of mine, sir, to take
that that no man else will. Rich honesty dwells
like a miser, sir, in a poor house, as your pearl in
your foul oyster.

Duke S. By my faith, he is very swift and sententious.   66

Touch. According to the fool's bolt, sir, and such
dulcet diseases.

Jaq. But, for the seventh cause, — how did you
find the quarrel on the seventh cause?   70

Touch. Upon a lie seven times removed, — bear
your body more seeming, Audrey, — as thus, sir.
I did dislike the cut of a certain courtier's beard.
He sent me word, if I said his beard was not cut
well, he was in the mind it was: this is call'd the   75
Retort Courteous. If I sent him word again "it
was not well cut," he would send me word, he cut

---

33. **prime:** spring. 36. **note:** music. 37. **untuneable:** discordant.
  Sc. iv, 4. **hope:** i.e., only hope. 19. **make . . . even:** clear up. 22. **your** (Rowe). *you your* Ff. 32. **desperate:** dangerous.
35. **toward:** coming. 45. **purgation:** proof. **measure:** stately dance. 50. **ta'en up:** made up. 58. **copulatives:** people
entering marriage. 59. **blood:** passion. 67. **fool's bolt.** Alluding to the proverb, "A fool's bolt is soon shot." 68. **dulcet
diseases.** Intentional nonsense. 72. **seeming:** seemly. 73. **dislike:** criticize.

it to please himself: this is call'd the Quip Modest. If again "it was not well cut," he disabled my judgement: this is called the Reply Churlish. If 80 again "it was not well cut," he would answer, I spake not true: this is called the Reproof Valiant. If again "it was not well cut," he would say, I lie: this is call'd the Countercheck Quarrelsome: and so to Lie Circumstantial and the Lie Direct.   86

Jaq. And how oft did you say his beard was not well cut?

Touch. I durst go no further than the Lie Circumstantial, nor he durst not give me the Lie 90 Direct; and so we measur'd swords and parted.

Jaq. Can you nominate in order now the degrees of the lie?

Touch. O sir, we quarrel in print, by the book, as you have books for good manners. I will 95 name you the degrees. The first, the Retort Courteous; the second, the Quip Modest; the third, the Reply Churlish; the fourth, the Reproof Valiant; the fifth, the Countercheck Quarrelsome; the sixth, the Lie with Circumstance; the 100 seventh, the Lie Direct. All these you may avoid but the Lie Direct; and you may avoid that too, with an If. I knew when seven justices could not take up a quarrel, but when the parties were met themselves, one of them thought but of an If, 105 as, "If you said so, then I said so"; and they shook hands and swore brothers. Your If is the only peace-maker; much virtue in If.

Jaq. Is not this a rare fellow, my lord? He's as good at any thing, and yet a fool.   110

Duke S. He uses his folly like a stalking-horse and under the presentation of that he shoots his wit.

Enter HYMEN, ROSALIND, *and* CELIA. [*Still Music.*

Hym. Then is there mirth in heaven,
        When earthly things made even   115
            Atone together.
    Good Duke, receive thy daughter.
    Hymen from heaven brought her,
        Yea, brought her hither,
    That thou mightst join her hand with his 120
    Whose heart within his bosom is.

Ros. [*To the Duke.*] To you I give myself, for I
    am yours.
[*To Orl.*] To you I give myself, for I am yours.

Duke S. If there be truth in sight, you are my
    daughter.

Orl. If there be truth in sight, you are my
    Rosalind.   125

Phe. If sight and shape be true,
    Why then, my love adieu!

Ros. I'll have no father, if you be not he;
I'll have no husband, if you be not he;
Nor ne'er wed woman, if you be not she.   130

Hym. Peace, ho! I bar confusion.
    'Tis I must make conclusion
    Of these most strange events.
    Here's eight that must take hands
    To join in Hymen's bands,   135
        If truth holds true contents.
    You and you no cross shall part;
    You and you are heart in heart;
    You to his love must accord,
    Or have a woman to your lord;   140
    You and you are sure together,
    As the winter to foul weather.
    Whiles a wedlock-hymn we sing,
    Feed yourselves with questioning;
    That reason wonder may diminish,   145
    How thus we met, and these things finish.

SONG.

    Wedding is great Juno's crown
        O blessed bond of board and bed!
    'Tis Hymen peoples every town;
        High wedlock then be honoured.   150
    Honour, high honour, and renown,
    To Hymen, god of every town!

Duke S. O my dear niece, welcome thou art to me!
Even daughter, welcome in no less degree.

Phe. I will not eat my word, now thou art mine;
Thy faith my fancy to thee doth combine.   156

Enter Second Brother [JAQUES DE BOYS].

Jaq. de B. Let me have audience for a word or
    two.
I am the second son of old Sir Roland,
That bring these tidings to this fair assembly.
Duke Frederick, hearing how that every day 160
Men of great worth resorted to this forest,
Address'd a mighty power, which were on foot,
In his own conduct, purposely to take
His brother here and put him to the sword;
And to the skirts of this wild wood he came, 165
Where meeting with an old religious man,
After some question with him, was converted
Both from his enterprise and from the world;
His crown bequeathing to his banish'd brother,
And all their lands restor'd to them again 170
That were with him exil'd. This to be true,
I do engage my life.

Duke S.   Welcome, young man;
Thou offer'st fairly to thy brothers' wedding:

78. **Quip:** jest.   94. **by the book.** Touchstone is satirizing the treatises on the etiquette of dueling and quarreling. 111. **stalking-horse:** a horse, real or artificial, underneath which a hunter moved closer to his game. 113. S.D. HYMEN: god of marriage. *Still Music:* soft music. 116. **Atone together:** are reconciled. 156. **combine:** bind. 162. **Address'd:** prepared. **power:** armed force. 166. **religious man:** hermit. 173. **offer'st fairly:** contributest handsomely.

To one his lands withheld; and to the other
A land itself at large, a potent dukedom.   175
First, in this forest let us do those ends
That here were well begun and well begot;
And after, every of this happy number,
That have endur'd shrewd days and nights with us,
Shall share the good of our returned fortune,   180
According to the measure of their states.
Meantime, forget this new-fall'n dignity,
And fall into our rustic revelry.
Play, music! And you, brides and bridegrooms all,
With measure heap'd in joy, to th' measures
      fall.   185
   Jaq. Sir, by your patience. If I heard you
      rightly,
The Duke hath put on a religious life
And thrown into neglect the pompous court?
   Jaq. de B. He hath.
   Jaq. To him will I. Out of these convertites   190
There is much matter to be heard and learn'd.
[*To Duke S.*] You to your former honour I be-
      queath;
Your patience and your virtue well deserves it:
[*To Orl.*] You to a love, that your true faith doth
      merit:
[*To Oli.*] You to your land, and love, and great
      allies: 195
[*To Sil.*] You to a long and well-deserved bed:
[*To Touch.*] And you to wrangling; for thy loving
      voyage
Is but for two months victuall'd. So, to your
      pleasures;
I am for other than for dancing measures.

   Duke S. Stay, Jaques, stay.   200
   Jaq. To see no pastime I. What you would have
I'll stay to know at your abandon'd cave. [*Exit.*
   Duke S. Proceed, proceed. We will begin these
      rites,
As we do trust they'll end, in true delights.
                    [*A dance.*] *Exeunt.*

[EPILOGUE]

   Ros. It is not the fashion to see the lady the
epilogue, but it is no more unhandsome than to
see the lord the prologue. If it be true that good
wine needs no bush, 'tis true that a good play needs
no epilogue; yet to good wine they do use good   5
bushes, and good plays prove the better by the help
of good epilogues. What a case am I in then, that
am neither a good epilogue, nor cannot insinuate
with you in the behalf of a good play! I am not
furnish'd like a beggar, therefore to beg will not 10
become me. My way is to conjure you, and I'll
begin with the women. I charge you, O women,
for the love you bear to men, to like as much of
this play as please you; and I charge you, O men,
for the love you bear to women,—as I perceive 15
by your simpering, none of you hates them — that
between you and the women the play may please.
If I were a woman I would kiss as many of you as
had beards that pleas'd me, complexions that lik'd
me, and breaths that I defi'd not; and, I am 20
sure, as many as have good beards or good faces or
sweet breaths will, for my kind offer, when I make
curtsy, bid me farewell.   [*Exit.*

179. **shrewd:** harsh. 181. **states:** ranks.
    Epilogue: 4. **good ... bush.** A bunch of evergreens hung over the door was the common sign of vintners; hence this phrase means "good wine needs no advertising." 8. **insinuate:** ingratiate myself. 18. **If ... woman.** Rosalind's part was, of course, played by a boy in woman's dress. 19. **lik'd:** pleased. 20. **defi'd:** disliked. 23. **bid me farewell:** i.e., with applause.

The Merry Wives of Windsor

THE EARLIEST KNOWN MENTION of *The Merry Wives of Windsor* is the entry of the play in the Stationers' Register for January 18, 1601/2. Later in 1602 appeared the First Quarto, with a much garbled text only a little more than half as long as the one in the Folio. A Second Quarto in 1619 was only a reprint of the First. The version in the First Folio alone has authority and is the basis of all modern texts.

Though it was once believed that the Quarto represented a first sketch of *The Merry Wives*, scholars are now generally agreed that the Quarto and the First Folio are related in being derived from essentially the same theatrical form of the play, the former being a sadly corrupt "pirated" version, the latter being a fairly good one, representing the play substantially as it was performed after becoming well established in the repertory of Shakespeare's company. The plot contains strands very imperfectly developed, notably the horse-stealing episode and the incident of Falstaff's deer-poaching; these defects may perhaps be owing to careless abbreviation of the play to meet demands of performance, but they may as probably have been the result of original haste, of which more will be said presently.

The text in the Folio, despite some peculiarities, may well have been set up from the playhouse manuscript. It exhibits the unusual bibliographical feature which has been noted in connection with the text of *The Two Gentlemen of Verona*; that is, throughout the play individual entrances and exits are unmarked, while at the beginning of each scene the characters who are to figure in it are listed in a blanket stage direction substantially in the order of their appearance, and a general exit is provided at the end of the scene. No satisfactory explanation of this oddity has been advanced. It has been shown that the "pirate" who reported the grossly mutilated text of the Quarto was probably an actor who had played the part of the Host, because his part and those of the characters who appear in scenes with him are rendered with more than usual fidelity to the text in the Folio, while speeches in scenes where he does not figure are paraphrased, sometimes in badly mangled fashion, and other scenes are omitted altogether.

The now fragmentary episode of the Host's stolen horses may conceivably have figured more prominently in Shakespeare's original conception of the play and have been cut down as the play was adapted to actual performance on the stage. The incident would seem to be the culmination of the resolve of Caius and Evans to be revenged upon mine Host for his frustration of their duel (III.i.118 ff.). One could wish, however, that the horse-stealing business had been more clearly and fully worked out, and perhaps originally it was. The Quarto version presents one variant in the climax (Sc. xvi) where Caius announces that the German Duke has actually come to Court, and Evans says, "there is three sorts of cosen garmombles, Is cosen all the Host of Maidenhead & Readings." This word "garmombles," associated with German horse-stealers, points to a topical allusion which most editors are inclined to credit.

In 1592 one Count Mömpelgart, who later became Duke of Württemberg, visited England. He was entertained by the Queen at Reading, August 17th to 19th. Thence he proceeded to Windsor where he stayed until the 21st, shooting deer, visiting Eton, and cutting his name in the highest tower in Windsor Castle. Later when visiting Oxford, he was sorely vexed at being unable to procure fresh post-horses, and he obtained from the Lord Admiral before leaving London to sail for home, a passport directing that he be provided post-horses and "shippage" free of charge. His conduct in England had been conspicuously pompous, and after his departure he did not allow himself to be forgotten. Having conceived a desire to be a Knight of the Garter, he pestered Elizabeth with requests until finally in 1597 she granted his election. But there was long delay in sending his insignia, and he was not invested until 1603, when James put an end to the matter by sending a mission to Stuttgart. Though the original visit of Mömpelgart to England had been in 1592, his ridiculous memory had been kept alive well enough to make a jest at his expense intelligible any time up to 1603. The "cosen garmombles" of the Quarto looks like a pun on his name, and any Knight of the Garter witnessing a performance of the play at Court would relish it. The absence from the Folio of any pun on Mömpelgart's name may indicate that eventually the allusion was toned down.

A tradition dating from the eighteenth century states that Shakespeare wrote *The Merry Wives* at the express command of Queen Elizabeth. The story is first recorded by John Dennis in his prefatory Epistle to *The Comicall Gallant* (1702), an adaptation of this very play. He says, "I knew very well, that it had pleas'd one of the greatest Queens that ever was in the World. . . . This Comedy was written at her Command, and by her direction, and she was so eager to see it Acted, that she commanded it to be finished in fourteen days." Rowe, in his *Life of Shakespeare* (1709), adds the reason for the Queen's request: she "was so well pleas'd with that admirable Character of *Falstaff*, in the two parts of *Henry the Fourth*, that she commanded him to continue it for one Play more, and to shew him in Love." The tradition, which seems credible enough, is generally accepted, and though the fortnight's allowance of time is probably not literally exact, the haste in which Shakespeare was obliged to prepare the play may account in large measure for the deficiencies in the development of the plot. The notion that for *The Merry Wives* Shakespeare reworked another play already in existence has never been convincingly demonstrated. The tradition confirms what would be inferred on other grounds, namely, that *Henry IV* had already been performed, and so fixes 1598 as the earliest possible date. The question whether it preceded or followed *Henry V* is more difficult. If Nym is, like the rest of Falstaff's followers, a revival, the play must be later than *Henry V*, the only other play in which he appears. The fact that Nym here bears his title of Corporal implies that he has seen military experience. The fact that in *Henry V* Falstaff dies and Pistol marries Mrs. Quickly does not really affect the question. If the tradition concerning the Queen's command is true, Shakespeare had to fulfill it even though it meant resurrecting Falstaff; moreover, the Queen may have remarked that in *Henry V* Shakespeare had not kept the promise made in the Epilogue to *2 Henry IV* to provide further merriment through Falstaff. A reference in the Folio text to "the wild prince" (III.ii.74) and another in the Quarto (Sc. xviii) to "the mad Prince of Wales" indicate that Shakespeare thought of the action of *The Merry Wives* as antedating the accession of Henry V. But none of the evidence is conclusive, and the wisest course is to assign the play to late 1599 or early 1600.

It would appear that alternative versions of the concluding scene of the play had been framed. At V.v.59-77 the fairies are commanded to bless Windsor Castle with their beneficent offices, and a pleasant tribute is paid to the Knights of the Garter. This matter is certainly appropriate for a performance at Court. At the corresponding point in the Quarto, however, there is none of this, but instead some unexpected stuff about pinching sergeants and proctors, which seems in some way designed for the common stage. The verse, moreover, is so poor as to be considered un-Shakespearean, and it may be that it was actually improvised by the pirate-Host whose memory failed him at this juncture. Where Elizabeth witnessed the play which she had ordered is nowhere recorded. The Garter passage and the title of the play point to an initial performance at Windsor, but that is all that one can say.

The corrupt Quarto seems to betray one interesting thing in the history of the play. In that version the name adopted by Ford with his disguise appears consistently as Brooke, and the relationship of meaning would indicate that Brooke was his original alias. But in the Folio the assumed name is everywhere Broome. This looks like cautious discretion, for Brooke was the family name of the Lord Cobham whose umbrage at Shakespeare's use of "Oldcastle," the name of a Cobham ancestor, had led to the substitution of "Falstaff" in *Henry IV*.

The most probable source for the main plot of *The Merry Wives* is *The Tale of the Two Lovers of Pisa* in Tarleton's *Newes out of Purgatorie* (1590). There a lady Margaret has her lover twice conveyed out of her house, once in a tub full of feathers, and later in an old chest full of documents. But the situation and the strategy are of a type widely current in Renaissance literature, especially Italian *novelle*. In the play the initial betrayal of Falstaff by Pistol and Nym, the disguise of Mother Prat, the pinching by the fairies, the underplot of the triple wooing of Anne Page, and all the characters save the commonplace of the jealous husband, seem to be original.

Despite its imperfections, *The Merry Wives* provides good fun in the theatre. Falstaff, though sadly deteriorated from the glorious creation of the *Henry IV* plays, is still entertaining in a limited fashion as a gullible ton of flesh. Evans and Caius, with their murdering of the King's English, are diverting. The two wives are as clean and honest as they are merry, and their husbands learn to rejoice in them, the jealous Ford being redeemed by his final good fellowship and his honest confession of his former folly. Slender is a figure in one dimension, but a welcome addition to Shakespeare's gallery of simpletons. Mistress Anne Page, "which is pretty virginity," appears only infrequently and is hardly more than a pastel figure, but she is lively and lovable for all that, and we are glad that she gets the man she wants. Her ejaculation, "Good Master Shallow, let him woo for himself," and her simple but heart-felt plea, "Good mother, do not marry me to yond fool," (III.iv.51,87) endear her to us forever.

THE MERRY WIVES OF WINDSOR

[DRAMATIS PERSONÆ

SIR JOHN FALSTAFF.	BARDOLPH, PISTOL, } *followers of Falstaff.* NYM,
FENTON, *a gentleman.*	
SHALLOW, *a country justice.*	
ABRAHAM SLENDER, *cousin to Shallow.*	ROBIN, *page to Falstaff.*
FORD, PAGE, } *gentlemen of Windsor.*	PETER SIMPLE, *servant to Slender.*
	JOHN RUGBY, *servant to Doctor Caius.*
WILLIAM PAGE, *a boy, son to Page.*	
SIR HUGH EVANS, *a Welsh parson.*	MISTRESS FORD.
DOCTOR CAIUS, *a French physician.*	MISTRESS PAGE.
HOST *of the Garter Inn.*	MISTRESS ANNE PAGE, *her daughter.*
	MISTRESS QUICKLY, *servant to Doctor Caius.*

Servants to Page, Ford, etc.

SCENE: *Windsor, and the neighbourhood.*]

ACT I

SCENE I. [*Windsor. Before Page's house.*]

Enter JUSTICE SHALLOW, SLENDER, *and* SIR HUGH EVANS.

Shal. Sir Hugh, persuade me not; I will make a Star Chamber matter of it. If he were twenty Sir John Falstaffs, he shall not abuse Robert Shallow, esquire.

Slen. In the county of Gloucester, justice of peace and "Coram." 6

Shal. Ay, cousin Slender, and "Custalorum."

Slen. Ay, and "Rato-lorum" too; and a gentleman born, master parson; who writes himself "Armigero," in any bill, warrant, quittance, or obligation, "Armigero." 11

Shal. Ay, that I do; and have done any time these three hundred years.

Slen. All his successors gone before him hath done't; and all his ancestors that come after him 15 may. They may give the dozen white luces in their coat.

Shal. It is an old coat.

Evans. The dozen white louses do become an old coat well; it agrees well, passant. It is a familiar beast to man, and signifies love. 21

Shal. The luce is the fresh fish; the salt fish is an old coat.

Slen. I may quarter, coz.

Shal. You may, by marrying. 25

Evans. It is marring indeed, if he quarter it.

Shal. Not a whit.

Evans. Yes, py'r lady. If he has a quarter of your coat, there is but three skirts for yourself, in my simple conjectures. But that is all one. If 30 Sir John Falstaff have committed disparagements unto you, I am of the church, and will be glad to

Act I, sc. i, 2. **Star Chamber:** a high court of justice. 6. **Coram:** a corruption of *quorum*, which word begins the official clause in the appointment of justices. 7. **Custalorum:** a blunder for *custos rotulorum*, keeper of the rolls. "Rato-lorum" (l. 8) is a similar blunder. 10. **Armigero:** i.e., esquire. 16. **give:** display. 16. **luces:** pikes (fish). It is generally agreed that Shakespeare is here glancing at Sir Thomas Lucy of Charlecote, whose arms were "three Luces Argent in a shield gules" (Camden). Tradition states that Shakespeare was taken up for poaching upon Lucy's land and, because of the ensuing trouble, left for London. 20. **passant:** walking (heraldic term). 24. **quarter:** add one coat of arms to another by placing it in one of the four divisions of a shield.

do my benevolence to make atonements and com-
premises between you.

Shal. The council shall hear it; it is a riot.   35

Evans. It is not meet the council hear a riot;
there is no fear of Got in a riot. The council, look
you, shall desire to hear the fear of Got, and not to
hear a riot. Take your vizaments in that.

Shal. Ha! O' my life, if I were young again, the
sword should end it.   41

Evans. It is petter that friends is the sword, and
end it; and there is also another device in my prain,
which peradventure prings goot discretions with it:
there is Anne Page, which is daughter to Master   45
[George] Page, which is pretty virginity.

Slen. Mistress Anne Page? She has brown hair,
and speaks small like a woman.

Evans. It is that fery person for all the orld,   50
as just as you will desire; and seven hundred pounds
of moneys, and gold and silver, is her grandsire upon
his death's-bed — Got deliver to a joyful resurrec-
tions! — give, when she is able to overtake seventeen years old. It were a goot motion if we   55
leave our pribbles and prabbles, and desire a marriage between Master Abraham and Mistress Anne
Page.

[*Shal.*] Did her grandsire leave her seven hundred
pound?   60

Evans. Ay, and her father is make her a petter
penny.

[*Shal.*] I know the young gentlewoman; she has
good gifts.

Evans. Seven hundred pounds and possibilities
is goot gifts.   66

Shal. Well, let us see honest Master Page. Is
Falstaff there?

Evans. Shall I tell you a lie? I do despise a liar as
I do despise one that is false, or as I despise one   70
that is not true. The knight, Sir John, is there; and,
I beseech you, be ruled by your well-willers. I will
peat the door for Master Page. [*Knocks.*] What,
hoa! Got pless your house here!

Page. [*Within.*] Who's there?   75

[*Enter* PAGE.]

Evans. Here is Got's plessing, and your friend,
and Justice Shallow; and here young Master
Slender, that peradventures shall tell you another
tale, if matters grow to your likings.

Page. I am glad to see your worships well.   80
ʟ thank you for my venison, Master Shallow.

Shal. Master Page, I am glad to see you. Much
good do it your good heart! I wish'd your venison better; it was ill kill'd. How doth good Mis-

tress Page? — and I thank you always with my
heart, la! with my heart.   86

Page. Sir, I thank you.

Shal. Sir, I thank you; by yea and no, I do.   89

Page. I am glad to see you, good Master Slender.

Slen. How does your fallow greyhound, sir? I
heard say he was outrun on Cotsall.

Page. It could not be judg'd, sir.

Slen. You'll not confess, you'll not confess.

Shal. That he will not. 'Tis your fault, 'tis your
fault; 'tis a good dog.   96

Page. A cur, sir.

Shal. Sir, he's a good dog, and a fair dog; can
there be more said? He is good and fair. Is Sir
John Falstaff here?   100

Page. Sir, he is within; and I would I could do a
good office between you.

Evans. It is spoke as a Christians ought to
speak.

Shal. He hath wrong'd me, Master Page.   105

Page. Sir, he doth in some sort confess it.

Shal. If it be confessed, it is not redressed. Is
not that so, Master Page? He hath wrong'd me;
indeed he hath; at a word, he hath. Believe me,
Robert Shallow, esquire, saith he is wrong'd.   110

Page. Here comes Sir John.

[*Enter* SIR JOHN FALSTAFF, BARDOLPH, NYM,
and PISTOL.]

Fal. Now, Master Shallow, you'll complain of
me to the King?

Shal. Knight, you have beaten my men, kill'd
my deer, and broke open my lodge.   115

Fal. But not kiss'd your keeper's daughter?

Shal. Tut, a pin! This shall be answer'd.

Fal. I will answer it straight; I have done all this.
That is now answer'd.

Shal. The Council shall know this.   120

Fal. 'Twere better for you if it were known in
counsel. You'll be laugh'd at.

Evans. *Pauca verba*, Sir John; goot worts.

Fal. Good worts! good cabbage. Slender, I
broke your head; what matter have you against
me?   126

Slen. Marry, sir, I have matter in my head
against you; and against your cony-catching rascals, Bardolph, Nym, and Pistol. [They carried
me to the tavern and made me drunk, and afterward picked my pocket.]

Bard. You Banbury cheese!   130

Slen. Ay, it is no matter.

Pist. How now, Mephostophilus!

Slen. Ay, it is no matter.

39. **vizaments:** advisements, counsels.   46. **[George]** (Theobald).   *Thomas* F.   55–56. **pribbles and prabbles:** quibbles
and quarrels.   59 and 63. **[Shal.]** (Capell).   *Slen.* F.   91. **fallow:** pale yellow.   92. **Cotsall:** the Cotswold Hills.   117.
pin: trifle.   **answer'd:** atoned for.   122. **counsel:** secret.   123. *Pauca verba:* few words.   128. **cony-catching:** swindling.
129–30. **[They...pocket]** Q. Om. F. Cf. l. 154.   130. **Banbury.** Banbury cheese being notably thin, this epithet ridicules
Slender's leanness.

Nym. Slice, I say! *Pauca, pauca.* Slice! that's
my humour.   135
Slen. Where's Simple, my man? Can you tell,
cousin?
Evans. Peace, I pray you. Now let us understand. There is three umpires in this matter, as I
understand; that is, Master Page, *fidelicet*   140
Master Page; and there is myself, *fidelicet* myself;
and the three party is, lastly and finally, mine host
of the Garter.
Page. We three to hear it and end it between
them.   145
Evans. Fery goot. I will make a prief of it in
my note-book, and we will afterwards ork upon the
cause with as great discreetly as we can.
Fal. Pistol!
Pist. He hears with ears.   150
Evans. The tevil and his tam! what phrase is
this, "He hears with ear"? Why, it is affectations.
Fal. Pistol, did you pick Master Slender's
purse?   155
Slen. Ay, by these gloves, did he, or I would I
might never come in mine own great chamber again
else, of seven groats in mill-sixpences, and two
Edward shovel-boards, that cost me two shilling
and two pence a-piece of Yead Miller, by these
gloves.   161
Fal. Is this true, Pistol?
Evans. No; it is false, if it is a pick-purse.
Pist. Ha, thou mountain-foreigner! Sir John
and master mine,
I combat challenge of this latten bilbo.   165
Word of denial in thy *labras* here!
Word of denial! Froth and scum, thou liest!
Slen. By these gloves, then, 'twas he.
Nym. Be avis'd, sir, and pass good humours.
I will say "marry trap" with you, if you run   170
the nuthook's humour on me. That is the very
note of it.
Slen. By this hat, then, he in the red face had it;
for though I cannot remember what I did when you
made me drunk, yet I am not altogether an ass.   176
Fal. What say you, Scarlet and John?
Bard. Why, sir, for my part, I say the gentle-
man had drunk himself out of his five sentences.   180
Evans. It is his five senses. Fie, what the ignorance is!
Bard. And being fap, sir, was, as they say,
cashier'd; and so conclusions pass'd the careers.   184

Slen. Ay, you spake in Latin then too. But
'tis no matter; I'll ne'er be drunk whilst I live again,
but in honest, civil, godly company, for this trick.
If I be drunk, I'll be drunk with those that have
the fear of God, and not with drunken knaves.   190
Evans. So Got udge me, that is a virtuous mind.
Fal. You hear all these matters deni'd, gentlemen; you hear it.

[*Enter* ANNE PAGE, *with wine;* MISTRESS FORD *and*
MISTRESS PAGE, *following.*]

Page. Nay, daughter, carry the wine in; we'll
drink within.   [*Exit Anne Page.*]   196
Slen. O heaven! this is Mistress Anne Page.
Page. How now, Mistress Ford!
Fal. Mistress Ford, by my troth, you are very
well met. By your leave, good mistress.   200
                                              [*Kisses her.*
Page. Wife, bid these gentlemen welcome.
Come, we have a hot venison pasty to dinner.
Come, gentlemen, I hope we shall drink down all
unkindness.
      [*Exeunt all except Shal., Slen., and Evans.*]
Slen. I had rather than forty shillings I had my
Book of Songs and Sonnets here.   206

[*Enter* SIMPLE.]

How now, Simple! where have you been? I must
wait on myself, must I? You have not the Book
of Riddles about you, have you?   209
Sim. Book of Riddles! Why, did you not lend
it to Alice Shortcake upon All-hallowmas last, a
fortnight afore Michaelmas?
Shal. Come, coz; come, coz; we stay for you. A
word with you, coz; marry, this, coz: there is, as
'twere, a tender, a kind of tender, made afar off
by Sir Hugh here. Do you understand me?   216
Slen. Ay, sir, you shall find me reasonable. If
it be so, I shall do that that is reason.
Shal. Nay, but understand me.
Slen. So I do, sir.   220
Evans. Give ear to his motions, Master Slender.
I will description the matter to you, if you be capac-
ity of it.
Slen. Nay, I will do as my cousin Shallow says.
I pray you, pardon me; he's a justice of peace in
his country, simple though I stand here.   226
Evans. But that is not the question: the question
is concerning your marriage.

134. **Slice.** Probably suggested by "cheese" (l. 130).   135. **humour:** mood.   139. *fidelicet:* i.e., *videlicet* = namely.
158. **groats:** coins worth fourpence.   **mill-sixpences:** coins with raised borders.   159. **Edward shovel-boards:** shillings
coined in the time of Edward VI, worn smooth and used in a game where coins were shoved along a board into holes at
the end.   160. **Yead:** dialect for Ed(ward).   165. **latten bilbo:** tin sword.   166. *labras:* lips (Spanish).   170. **"marry
trap."** Probably a term of insult.   171. **nuthook's humour.** A "nuthook" was a catchpoll, i.e., a constable.   177. **Scarlet
and John:** two of Robin Hood's men.   Falstaff is jesting at Bardolph's red face (cf. l. 173).   183. **fap:** drunk.   184.
cashier'd: robbed.   **conclusions ... careers.**   To "pass a career" was to run (a horse) a short gallop. Hence this phrase
probably means "the conclusion was swiftly reached."   191. **udge:** i.e., judge.   211. **All-hallowmas:** All Saints' Day,
Nov. 1.   212. **Michaelmas:** Sept. 29.   215. **tender:** offer.   **afar off:** indirectly.   226. **simple though:** as sure as.

Shal. Ay, there's the point, sir.

Evans. Marry, is it; the very point of it; to Mistress Anne Page. 231

Slen. Why, if it be so, I will marry her upon any reasonable demands.

Evans. But can you affection the 'oman? Let us command to know that of your mouth or of 235 your lips; for divers philosophers hold that the lips is parcel of the mouth. Therefore, precisely, can you carry your good will to the maid?

Shal. Cousin Abraham Slender, can you love her? 240

Slen. I hope, sir, I will do as it shall become one that would do reason.

Evans. Nay, Got's lords and his ladies! You must speak possitable, if you can carry her your desires towards her. 245

Shal. That you must. Will you, upon good dowry, marry her?

Slen. I will do a greater thing than that, upon your request, cousin, in any reason. 249

Shal. Nay, conceive me, conceive me, sweet coz; what I do is to pleasure you, coz. Can you love the maid?

Slen. I will marry her, sir, at your request; but if there be no great love in the beginning, yet heaven may decrease it upon better acquaintance, 255 when we are married and have more occasion to know one another. I hope, upon familiarity will grow more content. But if you say, "Marry her," I will marry her; that I am freely dissolved, and dissolutely. 260

Evans. It is a fery discretion answer, save the fall is in the ort "dissolutely." The ort is, according to our meaning, "resolutely." His meaning is good.

Shal. Ay, I think my cousin meant well. 265

Slen. Ay, or else I would I might be hang'd, la!

Shal. Here comes fair Mistress Anne.

[*Re-enter* ANNE PAGE.]

Would I were young for your sake, Mistress Anne!

Anne. The dinner is on the table. My father desires your worships' company. 271

Shal. I will wait on him, fair Mistress Anne.

Evans. Od's plessed will, I will not be absence at the grace. [*Exeunt Shallow and Evans.*]

Anne. Will't please your worship to come in, sir? 276

Slen. No, I thank you, forsooth, heartily; I am very well.

Anne. The dinner attends you, sir.

Slen. I am not a-hungry; I thank you, for- 280 sooth. Go, sirrah, for all you are my man, go wait upon my cousin Shallow. [*Exit Simple.*] A jus-

tice of peace sometime may be beholding to his friend for a man. I keep but three men and a boy yet, till my mother be dead. But what 285 though? Yet I live like a poor gentleman born.

Anne. I may not go in without your worship. They will not sit till you come.

Slen. I' faith, I'll eat nothing. I thank you as much as though I did. 291

Anne. I pray you, sir, walk in.

Slen. I had rather walk here, I thank you. I bruis'd my shin th' other day with playing at sword and dagger with a master of fence — three 295 veneys for a dish of stew'd prunes — and, by my troth, I cannot abide the smell of hot meat since. Why do your dogs bark so? Be there bears i' th' town?

Anne. I think there are, sir; I heard them talk'd of. 301

Slen. I love the sport well, but I shall as soon quarrel at it as any man in England. You are afraid, if you see the bear loose, are you not?

Anne. Ay, indeed, sir. 305

Slen. That's meat and drink to me, now. I have seen Sackerson loose twenty times, and have taken him by the chain; but, I warrant you, the women have so cri'd and shriek'd at it, that it pass'd. But women, indeed, cannot abide 'em; they are 310 very ill-favour'd rough things.

[*Re-enter* PAGE.]

Page. Come, gentle Master Slender, come; we stay for you.

Slen. I'll eat nothing, I thank you, sir. 315

Page. By cock and pie, you shall not choose, sir! Come, come.

Slen. Nay, pray you, lead the way.

Page. Come on, sir.

Slen. Mistress Anne, yourself shall go first. 320

Anne. Not I, sir; pray you, keep on.

Slen. Truly, I will not go first; truly, la! I will not do you that wrong.

Anne. I pray you, sir.

Slen. I'll rather be unmannerly than trouble-some. You do yourself wrong, indeed, la! 326

[*Exeunt.*

SCENE II. [*The same.*]

Enter SIR HUGH EVANS *and* SIMPLE.

Evans. Go your ways, and ask of Doctor Caius' house which is the way; and there dwells one Mistress Quickly, which is in the manner of his nurse, or his dry nurse, or his cook, or his laundry, his washer, and his wringer. 5

---

244. **possitable:** i.e., positively. 250. **conceive:** understand. 296. **veneys:** fencing bouts. 307. **Sackerson:** a famous bear exhibited at Paris garden on the Bankside. 316. **By cock and pie:** a common oath.

Sim. Well, sir.

Evans. Nay, it is petter yet. Give her this letter; for it is a 'oman that altogether's acquaintance with Mistress Anne Page; and the letter is, to desire and require her to solicit your master's desires 10 to Mistress Anne Page. I pray you, pegone. I will make an end of my dinner; there's pippins and cheese to come. [*Exeunt.*

SCENE III. [*A room in the Garter Inn.*]

Enter FALSTAFF, HOST, BARDOLPH, NYM, PISTOL, *and page* [ROBIN].

Fal. Mine host of the Garter!

Host. What says my bully-rook? Speak scholarly and wisely.

Fal. Truly, mine host, I must turn away some of my followers. 5

Host. Discard, bully Hercules; cashier. Let them wag. Trot, trot.

Fal. I sit at ten pounds a week.

Host. Thou'rt an emperor, Cæsar, Keisar, and Pheezar. I will entertain Bardolph; he shall 10 draw, he shall tap. Said I well, bully Hector?

Fal. Do so, good mine host.

Host. I have spoke; let him follow. [*To Bard.*] Let me see thee froth and [lime]. I am at a word; follow. [*Exit.*] 16

Fal. Bardolph, follow him. A tapster is a good trade. An old cloak makes a new jerkin; a wither'd serving-man a fresh tapster. Go; adieu. 20

Bard. It is a life that I have desir'd. I will thrive. [*Exit Bardolph.*]

Pist. O base Hungarian wight! wilt thou the spigot wield?

Nym. He was gotten in drink. Is not the humour conceited? 26

Fal. I am glad I am so acquit of this tinderbox; his thefts were too open. His filching was like an unskilful singer; he kept not time.

Nym. The good humour is to steal at a [minim's] rest. 31

Pist. "Convey," the wise it call. "Steal!" foh! A fico for the phrase!

Fal. Well, sirs, I am almost out at heels.

Pist. Why, then, let kibes ensue. 35

Fal. There is no remedy; I must cony-catch; I must shift.

Pist. Young ravens must have food.

Fal. Which of you know Ford of this town?

Pist. I ken the wight; he is of substance 40 good.

Fal. My honest lads, I will tell you what I am about.

Pist. Two yards, and more.

Fal. No quips now, Pistol! Indeed, I am in 45 the waist two yards about; but I am now about no waste, I am about thrift. Briefly, I do mean to make love to Ford's wife. I spy entertainment in her. She discourses, she carves, she gives the leer of invitation. I can construe the action of her 50 familiar style; and the hardest voice of her behaviour, to be English'd rightly, is, "I am Sir John Falstaff's."

Pist. He hath studied her [well], and translated her will out of honesty into English. 55

Nym. The anchor is deep. Will that humour pass?

Fal. Now, the report goes she has all the rule of her husband's purse. He hath a [legion] of angels. 60

Pist. As many devils entertain; and "To her, boy," say I.

Nym. The humour rises; it is good. Humour me the angels. 64

Fal. I have writ me here a letter to her; and here another to Page's wife, who even now gave me good eyes too, examin'd my parts with most judicious œillades; sometimes the beam of her view gilded my foot, sometimes my portly belly.

Pist. Then did the sun on dunghill shine. 70

Nym. I thank thee for that humour.

Fal. O, she did so course o'er my exteriors with such a greedy intention, that the appetite of her eye did seem to scorch me up like a burning-glass! Here's another letter to her. She bears the 75 purse too; she is a region in Guiana, all gold and bounty. I will be cheaters to them both, and they shall be exchequers to me. They shall be my East and West Indies, and I will trade to them both. Go bear thou this letter to Mistress Page; and thou 80 this to Mistress Ford. We will thrive, lads, we will thrive.

Pist. Shall I Sir Pandarus of Troy become, And by my side wear steel? Then, Lucifer take all!

Nym. I will run no base humour. Here, take 85 the humour-letter; I will keep the haviour of reputation.

Sc. iii, 2. **bully:** a term of endearment. The meaning of *rook* is not clear. 6. **cashier:** pay off. 7. **wag:** go on. 9. **Keisar:** another name for Caesar. 10. **Pheezar:** Vizier. 15. **froth:** i.e., draw beer with much froth (making the glass seem fuller than it is). **[lime]:** adulterate wine with lime to make it sweeter. *lyme* Q; *lyve* F. 25. **gotten:** begotten. 26. **conceited:** ingenious. 30. **[minim's]** (Langton conj.). *minute's* F Q. A minim-rest has the value of a half note in music. 33. **fico:** fig. 35. **kibes:** chilblains. 37. **shift:** contrive a trick. 49. **carves:** makes amorous gestures. 54. **[well]** Q. *will* F. 55. **honesty:** chastity. 56. **The . . . deep:** i.e., the scheme is deep and will hold fast. 59. **a [legion]** (Pope). *a legend* F; *legions* Q. 60. **angels:** gold coins worth about 10s. 68. **œillades:** amorous glances. 77. **cheaters:** (1) escheators, i.e., collectors of fines for the Exchequer, (2) sharpers. 82. **Pandarus:** the go-between in Chaucer's *Troilus and Criseyde.*

Fal. [*To Robin.*] Hold, sirrah, bear you these
    letters tightly;
Sail like my pinnace to these golden shores.
Rogues, hence, avaunt! Vanish like hailstones,
    go! 90
Trudge! Plod away o' th' hoof! Seek shelter!
    Pack!
Falstaff will learn the [humour] of the age,
French thrift, you rogues; myself and skirted page.
              [*Exeunt Falstaff and Robin.*

Pist. Let vultures gripe thy guts! for gourd and
    fullam holds,
And high and low beguiles the rich and poor. 95
Tester I'll have in pouch when thou shalt lack,
Base Phrygian Turk!

Nym. I have operations which be humours of
revenge.

Pist. Wilt thou revenge? 100

Nym. By welkin and her star!

Pist. With wit or steel?

Nym. With both the humours, I.
I will discuss the humour of this love to [Page].

Pist. And I to [Ford] shall eke unfold 105
    How Falstaff, varlet vile,
    His dove will prove, his gold will hold,
    And his soft couch defile.

Nym. My humour shall not cool. I will incense
[Page] to deal with poison; I will possess him 110
with yellowness, for the revolt of mine is dangerous.
That is my true humour.

Pist. Thou art the Mars of malcontents. I
second thee; troop on. [*Exeunt.*

SCENE IV. [*A room in Doctor Caius's house.*]

Enter MISTRESS QUICKLY, SIMPLE, *and* JOHN
RUGBY.

Quick. What, John Rugby! I pray thee, go to
the casement, and see if you can see my master,
Master Doctor Caius, coming. If he do, i' faith,
and find any body in the house, here will be an old
abusing of God's patience and the King's English. 6

Rug. I'll go watch.

Quick. Go; and we'll have a posset for 't soon at
night, in faith, at the latter end of a sea-coal fire.
[*Exit Rugby.*] An honest, willing, kind fellow 10
as ever servant shall come in house withal, and, I
warrant you, no tell-tale nor no breed-bate. His
worst fault is, that he is given to prayer. He is
something peevish that way; but nobody but has

his fault. But let that pass. Peter-Simple, you
say your name is? 16

Sim. Ay, for fault of a better.

Quick. And Master Slender's your master?

Sim. Ay, forsooth.

Quick. Does he not wear a great round beard,
like a glover's paring-knife? 21

Sim. No, forsooth; he hath but a little wee face,
with a little yellow beard, a Cain-colour'd beard.

Quick. A softly-sprighted man, is he not? 25

Sim. Ay, forsooth; but he is as tall a man of his
hands as any is between this and his head. He
hath fought with a warrener.

Quick. How say you? O, I should remember
him. Does he not hold up his head, as it were, and
strut in his gait? 31

Sim. Yes, indeed, does he.

Quick. Well, Heaven send Anne Page no worse
fortune! Tell Master Parson Evans I will do what
I can for your master. Anne is a good girl, and
I wish — 36

[*Re-enter* RUGBY.]

Rug. Out, alas! here comes my master.

Quick. We shall all be shent. Run in here, good
young man; go into this closet. He will not stay
long. [*Shuts Simple in the closet.*] What, John 40
Rugby! John! what, John, I say! Go, John, go
inquire for my master; I doubt he be not well, that
he comes not home.

[*Singing.*] And down, down, adown-a, etc.

[*Enter* DOCTOR CAIUS.]

Caius. Vat is you sing? I do not like dese 45
toys. Pray you, go and vetch me in my closet *une
boite en verde*, a box, a green-a box. Do intend vat
I speak? A green-a box.

Quick. Ay, forsooth; I'll fetch it you. [*Aside.*]
I am glad he went not in himself; if he had 50
found the young man, he would have been horn-mad.

Caius. Fe, fe, fe, fe! *ma foi, il fait fort chaud.
Je m'en vais à la cour, — la grande affaire.*

Quick. Is it this, sir? 55

Caius. Oui; mette le au mon pocket; dépêche,
quickly. Vere is dat knave Rugby?

Quick. What, John Rugby! John!

Rug. Here, sir! 59

Caius. You are John Rugby, and you are Jack
Rugby. Come, take-a your rapier, and come after
my heel to the court.

---

92. [humour] Q. *honour* F. 94. gourd and fullam: kinds of false dice (hollow or loaded). 95. high and low: throws of the
dice. 96. Tester: sixpence. 101. welkin: sky. 104-05. [Page] ... [Ford] Q. *Ford ... Page* F. 110. [Page] (Steevens).
Ford F Q. 111. yellowness: jealousy.

Sc. iv, 5. old: plentiful, great. 8. posset: a hot drink often made with milk and some liquor. 12. breed-bate: mischief
maker. 23. Cain-colour'd. Cain was traditionally represented with a yellowish-red beard. 25. softly-sprighted: gentle-
spirited. 26. tall: valiant. 28. warrener: gamekeeper. 38. shent: scolded. 46. toys: foolish things. 47. intend: hear,
understand. 51. horn-mad: stark mad. 52-54. *ma ... affaire:* Faith, it is very hot. I am going to the court — important
business. 56. *Oui ... dépêche:* Yes; put it in my pocket; hurry.

Rug. 'Tis ready, sir, here in the porch.

Caius. By my trot, I tarry too long. Od's me! *Qu'ai-j'oublié?* Dere is some simples in my 65 closet, dat I vill not for the varld I shall leave behind.

Quick. Ay me, he'll find the young man there, and be mad! 69

Caius. O diable, diable! vat is in my closet? Villainy! Laron! [*Pulling Simple out.*] Rugby, my rapier!

Quick. Good master, be content.

Caius. Wherefore shall I be content-a?

Quick. The young man is an honest man. 75

Caius. What shall de honest man do in my closet? Dere is no honest man dat shall come in my closet.

Quick. I beseech you, be not so phlegmatic. Hear the truth of it: he came of an errand to me from Parson Hugh. 81

Caius. Vell?

Sim. Ay, forsooth; to desire her to —

Quick. Peace, I pray you.

Caius. Peace-a your tongue. — Speak-a your tale. 86

Sim. To desire this honest gentlewoman, your maid, to speak a good word to Mistress Anne Page for my master in the way of marriage.

Quick. This is all, indeed, la! but I'll ne'er put my finger in the fire, and need not. 91

Caius. Sir Hugh send-a you? Rugby, [*baillez*] me some paper. Tarry you a little-a while.
[*Writes.*]

Quick. [*Aside to Simple.*] I am glad he is so quiet. If he had been thoroughly moved, you should 95 have heard him so loud and so melancholy. But notwithstanding, man, I'll do you your master what good I can; and the very yea and the no is, the French doctor, my master, — I may call him my master, look you, for I keep his house; and I 100 wash, wring, brew, bake, scour, dress meat and drink, make the beds, and do all myself, —

Sim. [*Aside to Quickly.*] 'Tis a great charge to come under one body's hand. 105

Quick. [*Aside to Simple.*] Are you avis'd o' that? You shall find it a great charge; and to be up early and down late; but notwithstanding, — to tell you in your ear; I would have no words of it, — my master himself is in love with Mistress Anne Page; 110 but notwithstanding that, I know Anne's mind, — that's neither here nor there.

Caius. You jack'nape, give-a this letter to Sir Hugh. By gar, it is a shallenge. I will cut his troat in de park; and I will teach a scurvy jack- 115 a-nape priest to meddle or make. You may be gone; it is not good you tarry here. By gar, I will cut all his two stones; by gar, he shall not have a stone to throw at his dog. [*Exit Simple.*]

Quick. Alas, he speaks but for his friend. 120

Caius. It is no matter-a ver dat. Do not you tell-a me dat I shall have Anne Page for myself? By gar, I vill kill de Jack priest; and I have appointed mine host of de Jarteer to measure our weapon. By gar, I will myself have Anne Page. 126

Quick. Sir, the maid loves you, and all shall be well. We must give folks leave to prate; what, the good-year!

Caius. Rugby, come to the court with me. 130 By gar, if I have not Anne Page, I shall turn your head out of my door. Follow my heels, Rugby.
[*Exeunt Caius and Rugby.*]

Quick. You shall have An —— fool's-head of your own. No, I know Anne's mind for that. Never a woman in Windsor knows more of 135 Anne's mind than I do; nor can do more than I do with her, I thank Heaven.

Fent. [*Within.*] Who's within there? ho!

Quick. Who's there, I trow! Come near the house, I pray you. 141

[*Enter* FENTON.]

Fent. How now, good woman! how dost thou?

Quick. The better that it pleases your good worship to ask. 145

Fent. What news? How does pretty Mistress Anne?

Quick. In truth, sir, and she is pretty, and honest, and gentle; and one that is your friend, I can tell you that by the way; I praise Heaven for it. 151

Fent. Shall I do any good, think'st thou? Shall I not lose my suit?

Quick. Troth, sir, all is in His hands above. But notwithstanding, Master Fenton, I'll be sworn 155 on a book, she loves you. Have not your worship a wart above your eye?

Fent. Yes, marry, have I; what of that?

Quick. Well, thereby hangs a tale. Good faith, it is such another Nan; but, I detest, an honest 160 maid as ever broke bread. We had an hour's talk of that wart. I shall never laugh but in that maid's company! But indeed she is given too much to allicholy and musing; but for you — well, go to. 165

Fent. Well, I shall see her to-day. Hold, there's money for thee; let me have thy voice in my behalf.

---

64. **trot:** i.e., troth. 65. **Qu'ai-j'oublié?** What have I forgotten? **simples:** medicinal herbs. 71. **Laron:** thief. 79. **phlegmatic.** Mistress Quickly's blunder for *choleric.* 92. [*baillez*] (Theobald): fetch. *ballow* F. 104. **charge:** burden. 123. **Jack:** a term of contempt. 128. **what...year.** A mild oath. 140. **trow:** wonder. 160. **another.** In this context "another" seems to have an endearing sense; i.e., "she is such a darling Nan." **detest:** blunder for *protest.* 165. **allicholy:** i.e., melancholy.

If thou seest her before me, commend me —   169

Quick. Will I? I' faith, that we will; and I will tell your worship more of the wart the next time we have confidence; and of other wooers.

Fent. Well, farewell; I am in great haste now. 175

Quick. Farewell to your worship.   [*Exit Fenton.*] Truly, an honest gentleman; but Anne loves him not; for I know Anne's mind as well as another does. Out upon't! what have I forgot?   [*Exit.* 180

ACT II

SCENE I. [*Before Page's house.*]

Enter MISTRESS PAGE [*with a letter*].

Mrs. Page. What, have I scap'd love-letters in the holiday-time of my beauty, and am I now a subject for them? Let me see. [*Reads.*]

"Ask me no reason why I love you; for though Love use Reason for his precisian, he admits him 5 not for his counsellor. You are not young, no more am I; go to then, there's sympathy. You are merry, so am I; ha, ha! then there's more sympathy. You love sack, and so do I; would you desire better sympathy? Let it suffice thee, 10 Mistress Page, — at the least, if the love of a soldier can suffice, — that I love thee. I will not say, pity me; 'tis not a soldier-like phrase; but I say, love me. By me,

> Thine own true knight,   15
> By day or night,
> Or any kind of light,
> With all his might
> For thee to fight,
>   JOHN FALSTAFF."

What a Herod of Jewry is this! O wicked, 20 wicked world! One that is well-nigh worn to pieces with age to show himself a young gallant! What an unweigh'd behaviour hath this Flemish drunkard pick'd — with the devil's name! — out of my conversation, that he dares in this manner 25 assay me? Why, he hath not been thrice in my company! What should I say to him? I was then frugal of my mirth. Heaven forgive me! Why, I'll exhibit a bill in the parliament for the putting down of men. How shall I be reveng'd 30 on him? for reveng'd I will be, as sure as his guts are made of puddings.

[*Enter* MISTRESS FORD.]

Mrs. Ford. Mistress Page! trust me, I was going to your house.   34

Mrs. Page. And, trust me, I was coming to you. You look very ill.

Mrs. Ford. Nay, I'll ne'er believe that; I have to show to the contrary.

Mrs. Page. Faith, but you do, in my mind.   39

Mrs. Ford. Well, I do then; yet I say I could show you to the contrary. O Mistress Page, give me some counsel!

Mrs. Page. What's the matter, woman?

Mrs. Ford. O woman, if it were not for one trifling respect, I could come to such honour! 45

Mrs. Page. Hang the trifle, woman! take the honour. What is it? Dispense with trifles. What is it?

Mrs. Ford. If I would but go to hell for an eternal moment or so, I could be knighted.   50

Mrs. Page. What? Thou liest! Sir Alice Ford! These knights will hack; and so thou shouldst not alter the article of thy gentry.

Mrs. Ford. We burn daylight. Here, read, read; perceive how I might be knighted. I shall think 55 the worse of fat men, as long as I have an eye to make difference of men's liking: and yet he would not swear; praised women's modesty; and gave such orderly and well-behaved reproof to all uncomeliness, that I would have sworn his disposition 60 would have gone to the truth of his words; but they do no more adhere and keep place together than the [Hundredth Psalm] to the tune of "Green Sleeves." What tempest, I trow, threw this whale, with so many tuns of oil in his belly, ashore at Windsor? 65 How shall I be revenged on him? I think the best way were to entertain him with hope, till the wicked fire of lust have melted him in his own grease. Did you ever hear the like?   70

Mrs. Page. Letter for letter, but that the name of Page and Ford differs! To thy great comfort in this mystery of ill opinions, here's the twin-brother of thy letter; but let thine inherit first, for, I protest, mine never shall. I warrant he hath a thou- 75 sand of these letters writ with blank space for different names, — sure, more, — and these are of the second edition. He will print them, out of doubt; for he cares not what he puts into the press, when he would put us two. I had rather be a 80 giantess, and lie under Mount Pelion. Well, I will find you twenty lascivious turtles ere one chaste man.

Mrs. Ford. Why, this is the very same; the very hand, the very words. What doth he think of us?   86

Mrs. Page. Nay, I know not. It makes me al-

Act II, sc. i, 5. **precisian:** spiritual adviser. **20–28. What...forgive me.** Verse in F. **23. unweigh'd:** unconsidered. **23–4. Flemish drunkard.** The Flemish were notorious drinkers. **25. conversation:** behavior. **52. hack.** Probably "grow degenerate." **53. article...gentry:** quality of your station. **54. burn daylight:** waste time. **57. make...of:** judge of. **liking:** looks. **60–61. disposition...words:** character would have accorded with his words. **62. adhere:** agree. **63. [Hundredth Psalm]** (Rowe). *hundred Psalms* F. **"Green Sleeves":** a popular tune, often sung with vulgar words (cf.V.v.21). **73. ill opinions:** i.e., the evil reputations we seem to have. **82. turtles:** turtle-doves (symbolic of fidelity in love).

most ready to wrangle with mine own honesty. I'll entertain myself like one that I am not acquainted withal; for, sure, unless he know some 90 strain in me that I know not myself, he would never have boarded me in this fury.

Mrs. Ford. "Boarding," call you it? I'll be sure to keep him above deck.   94

Mrs. Page. So will I. If he come under my hatches, I'll never to sea again. Let's be reveng'd on him. Let's appoint him a meeting, give him a show of comfort in his suit, and lead him on with a fine-baited delay, till he hath pawn'd his horses to mine host of the Garter.   100

Mrs. Ford. Nay, I will consent to act any villainy against him, that may not sully the chariness of our honesty. O, that my husband saw this letter! It would give eternal food to his jealousy.   105

Mrs. Page. Why, look where he comes; and my good man too. He's as far from jealousy as I am from giving him cause; and that I hope is an unmeasurable distance.

Mrs. Ford. You are the happier woman.   110

Mrs. Page. Let's consult together against this greasy knight. Come hither.   [*They retire.*

[*Enter* FORD *with* PISTOL, *and* PAGE *with* NYM.]

Ford. Well, I hope it be not so.

Pist. Hope is a curtal dog in some affairs. Sir John affects thy wife.   115

Ford. Why, sir, my wife is not young.

Pist. He woos both high and low, both rich and poor,
Both young and old, one with another, Ford.
He loves the gallimaufry. Ford, perpend.

Ford. Love my wife!   120

Pist. With liver burning hot. Prevent, or go thou,
Like Sir Actæon he, with Ringwood at thy heels,
O, odious is the name!

Ford. What name, sir?

Pist. The horn, I say. Farewell.   125
Take heed, have open eye, for thieves do foot by night.
Take heed, ere summer comes or cuckoo-birds do sing.
Away, Sir Corporal Nym!
Believe it, Page; he speaks sense.   [*Exit.*

Ford. [*Aside.*] I will be patient; I will find out this.   131

Nym. [*To Page.*] And this is true; I like not the humour of lying. He hath wronged me in some humours. I should have borne the humour'd letter to her; but I have a sword and it shall bite 135 upon my necessity. He loves your wife: there's the short and the long. My name is Corporal Nym; I speak and I avouch; 'tis true; my name is Nym and Falstaff loves your wife. Adieu. I love not the humour of bread and cheese [and there's the humour of it]. Adieu.   [*Exit.*]   141

Page. "The humour of it," quoth 'a! Here's a fellow frights English out of his wits.

Ford. I will seek out Falstaff.

Page. I never heard such a drawling, affecting rogue.   146

Ford. If I do find it! Well.

Page. I will not believe such a Cataian, though the priest o' the town commended him for a true man.   150

Ford. 'Twas a good sensible fellow. Well.

Page. How now, Meg! [*Mrs. Page and Mrs. Ford come forward.*]

Mrs. Page. Whither go you, George? Hark you.

Mrs. Ford. How now, sweet Frank! Why art thou melancholy?   156

Ford. I melancholy! I am not melancholy. Get you home, go.

Mrs. Ford. Faith, thou hast some crotchets in thy head now. Will you go, Mistress Page?   160

Mrs. Page. Have with you. You'll come to dinner, George. [*Aside to Mrs. Ford.*] Look who comes yonder. She shall be our messenger to this paltry knight.

Mrs. Ford. [*Aside to Mrs. Page.*] Trust me, I thought on her. She'll fit it.   166

[*Enter* MISTRESS QUICKLY.]

Mrs. Page. You are come to see my daughter Anne?

Quick. Ay, forsooth; and, I pray, how does good Mistress Anne?   170

Mrs. Page. Go in with us and see. We have an hour's talk with you.

[*Exeunt Mrs. Page, Mrs. Ford, and Mrs. Quickly.*

Page How now, Master Ford!

Ford. You heard what this knave told me, did you not?   175

Page. Yes; and you heard what the other told me?

Ford. Do you think there is truth in them?

Page. Hang 'em, slaves! I do not think the

89. **entertain**: conduct. 92. **boarded**: addressed. 99. **fine-baited**: subtly enticing. 102. **chariness**: scrupulousness. 114. **curtal dog**: a dog with a docked tail. 115. **affects**: loves. 117-19. **He ... perpend.** Prose in F. 119. **gallimaufry**: medley (i.e., all kinds of women). **perpend**: ponder. 121. **liver**: the supposed seat of love. 122. **Actæon.** Because he saw Diana bathing, Actæon was turned into a stag and killed by his own dogs. The horns which Actæon acquired as a stag become the horns of the cuckold in Pistol's suggestion. **Ringwood**: a common name for a hound. 127. **cuckoo-birds.** Again hinting at cuckold. 140-41. **[and ... it]** Q. Om. F. 143. **English** F. *humour* Q. 148. **Cataian**: Chinese (from Cataia, or Cathay). The Chinese were reputed liars. 161. **Have ... you**: I'll go with you.

knight would offer it; but these that accuse him   180
in his intent towards our wives are a yoke of his discarded men; very rogues, now they be out of service.

Ford. Were they his men?

Page. Marry, were they.   185

Ford. I like it never the better for that. Does
he lie at the Garter?

Page. Ay, marry, does he. If he should intend
this voyage towards my wife, I would turn her
loose to him; and what he gets more of her than
sharp words, let it lie on my head.   191

Ford. I do not misdoubt my wife; but I would be
loath to turn them together. A man may be too
confident. I would have nothing lie on my head.
I cannot be thus satisfied.   195

[Enter HOST.]

Page. Look where my ranting host of the Garter
comes. There is either liquor in his pate or money
in his purse when he looks so merrily.
How now, mine host!

Host. How now, bully-rook! thou'rt a gentleman.
Cavaleiro-justice, I say!   201

[Enter SHALLOW.]

Shal. I follow, mine host, I follow. Good even
and twenty, good Master Page! Master Page, will
you go with us? We have sport in hand.   205

Host. Tell him, cavaleiro-justice; tell him, bully-
rook.

Shal. Sir, there is a fray to be fought between Sir
Hugh the Welsh priest and Caius the French
doctor.   210

Ford. Good mine host o' th' Garter, a word with
you.
          [Drawing him aside.]

Host. What say'st thou, my bully-rook?

Shal. [*To Page.*] Will you go with us to behold
it? My merry host hath had the measuring of   215
their weapons, and, I think, hath appointed them
contrary places; for, believe me, I hear the parson
is no jester. Hark, I will tell you what our sport
shall be.   *[They draw aside.]*

Host. Hast thou no suit against my knight, my
guest-cavaleiro?   221

[*Ford.*] None, I protest; but I'll give you a pottle
of burnt sack to give me recourse to him and tell
him my name is [Brook]; only for a jest.

Host. My hand, bully; thou shalt have egress   225

and regress; — said I well? — and thy name shall
be [Brook]. It is a merry knight. Will you go,
[Mynheers]?

Shal. Have with you, mine host.

Page. I have heard the Frenchman hath good
skill in his rapier.   231

Shal. Tut, sir, I could have told you more. In
these times you stand on distance, your passes,
stoccadoes, and I know not what. 'Tis the heart,
Master Page; 'tis here, 'tis here. I have seen   235
the time, with my long sword I would have made
you four tall fellows skip like rats.

Host. Here, boys, here, here! shall we wag?

Page. Have with you. I had rather hear them
scold than fight.   240
          [Exeunt Host, Shal. [and Page.]

Ford. Though Page be a secure fool, and stands
so firmly on his wife's frailty, yet I cannot put off
my opinion so easily. She was in his company at
Page's house; and what they made there, I know
not. Well, I will look further into't; and I   245
have a disguise to sound Falstaff. If I find her
honest, I lose not my labour; if she be otherwise, 'tis
labour well bestowed.   *[Exit.*

SCENE II. [*A room in the Garter Inn.*]

Enter FALSTAFF *and* PISTOL.

Fal. I will not lend thee a penny.

Pist. Why, then the world's mine oyster,
Which I with sword will open.

Fal. Not a penny. I have been content, sir, you
should lay my countenance to pawn. I have   5
grated upon my good friends for three reprieves for
you and your coach-fellow Nym; or else you had
look'd through the grate, like a geminy of baboons.
I am damn'd in hell for swearing to gentlemen my
friends, you were good soldiers and tall fellows;   10
and when Mistress Bridget lost the handle of her
fan, I took't upon mine honour thou hadst it not.

Pist. Didst not thou share? Hadst thou not
fifteen pence?   14

Fal. Reason, you rogue, reason. Think'st
thou I'll endanger my soul gratis? At a word, hang
no more about me; I am no gibbet for you. Go. A
short knife and a throng! To your manor of Pickt-
hatch! Go. You'll not bear a letter for me, you
rogue! You stand upon your honour! Why,   20
thou unconfinable baseness, it is as much as I can

---

181. **yoke:** pair.   194. **nothing...head.** Another glance at cuckold's horns.   201. **Cavaleiro-justice.** Cavallero
(Span.) meant "gentleman."   203. **and twenty:** i.e., and twenty times "good evening."   217. **contrary:** different.   222.
[*Ford*] Q₃. *Shal.* F. **pottle:** tankard (a two quart measure).   224. [**Brook**] Q. *Broome* F (and so throughout the play).
227. [**Mynheers**] (Theobald): gentlemen. *An-heires* F.   233. **distance:** i.e., between fencers. **passes:** lunges.   234.
stoccadoes: thrusts.   237. **you:** i.e., for you.   241. **secure:** confident.

    Sc. ii, 2–3. **Why...open** F. *I will retort the sum in equipage* Q. *The line in Q, which sounds undoubtedly Shakespearean,*
has been added by many editors. ("in equipage" = in installments.)   5. **countenance:** surety.   6. **grated upon:** annoyed,
pestered.   8. **geminy:** pair.   18. **short knife:** i.e., for cutting purses.   18. **Pickt-hatch:** a disreputable district in London.

do to keep the terms of my honour precise. Ay, I myself sometimes, leaving the fear of [God] on the left hand and hiding mine honour in my necessity, am fain to shuffle, to hedge, and to lurch; and 25 yet you, rogue, will ensconce your rags, your cat-a-mountain looks, your red-lattice phrases, and your bold-beating oaths, under the shelter of your honour! You will not do it! You! 30

Pist. I do relent. What would thou more of man?

[Enter ROBIN.]

Rob. Sir, here's a woman would speak with you.
Fal. Let her approach.

Enter MISTRESS QUICKLY.

Quick. Give your worship good morrow.
Fal. Good morrow, good wife. 35
Quick. Not so, an't please your worship.
Fal. Good maid, then.
Quick. I'll be sworn,
As my mother was, the first hour I was born.
Fal. I do believe the swearer. What with me? 40
Quick. Shall I vouchsafe your worship a word or two?
Fal. Two thousand, fair woman; and I'll vouchsafe thee the hearing.
Quick. There is one Mistress Ford, sir; — I 45 pray, come a little nearer this ways; — I myself dwell with Master Doctor Caius, —
Fal. Well, on. Mistress Ford, you say, —
Quick. Your worship says very true. I pray your worship, come a little nearer this ways. 50
Fal. I warrant thee, nobody hears; mine own people, mine own people.
Quick. Are they so? [God] bless them and make them his servants!
Fal. Well, Mistress Ford; what of her? 55
Quick. Why, sir, she's a good creature. Lord, Lord! your worship's a wanton! Well, Heaven forgive you, and all of us, I pray!
Fal. Mistress Ford; come, Mistress Ford, —
Quick. Marry, this is the short and the long 60 of it: you have brought her into such a canaries as 'tis wonderful. The best courtier of them all, when the court lay at Windsor, could never have brought her to such a canary. Yet there has been knights, and lords, and gentlemen, with their 65 coaches; I warrant you, coach after coach, letter after letter, gift after gift; smelling so sweetly, all musk, and so rushling, I warrant you, in silk and gold; and in such alligant terms; and in such wine

and sugar of the best and the fairest, that would 70 have won any woman's heart; and, I warrant you, they could never get an eye-wink of her. I had myself twenty angels given me this morning; but I defy all angels, in any such sort, as they say, but in the way of honesty; and, I warrant you, they 75 could never get her so much as sip on a cup with the proudest of them all; and yet there has been earls, nay, which is more, pensioners; but, I warrant you, all is one with her. 80

Fal. But what says she to me? Be brief, my good she-Mercury.
Quick. Marry, she hath receiv'd your letter, for the which she thanks you a thousand times; and she gives you to notify that her husband will be 85 absence from his house between ten and eleven.
Fal. Ten and eleven?
Quick. Ay, forsooth; and then you may come and see the picture, she says, that you wot of. 90 Master Ford, her husband, will be from home. Alas! the sweet woman leads an ill life with him. He's a very jealousy man. She leads a very frampold life with him, good heart.
Fal. Ten and eleven. Woman, commend me to her; I will not fail her. 96
Quick. Why, you say well. But I have another messenger to your worship. Mistress Page hath her hearty commendations to you too; and let me tell you in your ear, she's as fartuous a civil 100 modest wife, and one, I tell you, that will not miss you morning nor evening prayer, as any is in Windsor, whoe'er be the other; and she bade me tell your worship that her husband is seldom from home, but she hopes there will come a time. 105 I never knew a woman so dote upon a man. Surely I think you have charms, la; yes, in truth.
Fal. Not I, I assure thee. Setting the attraction of my good parts aside I have no other charms. 111
Quick. Blessing on your heart for't!
Fal. But, I pray thee, tell me this: has Ford's wife and Page's wife acquainted each other how they love me? 115
Quick. That were a jest indeed! They have not so little grace, I hope. That were a trick indeed! But Mistress Page would desire you to send her your little page, of all loves. Her husband has a marvellous infection to the little page; and 120 truly Master Page is an honest man. Never a wife in Windsor leads a better life than she does: do what she will, say what she will, take all, pay all, go to bed when she list, rise when she list, all is as

22. **Ay, I.** I, I, I. F. 24. **[God]** Q. *heaven* F. This and similar changes may have been owing to the Jacobean law against profanity. 25. **hedge:** cheat (Q reads *filch*). **lurch:** pilfer. 26. **cat-a-mountain:** wildcat. 27. **red-lattice:** i.e., ale-house. 29. **bold-beating:** blustering, ranting. 61. **canaries.** Probably a blunder for "quandaries." 68. **rushling:** i.e., rustling. 69. **alligant:** i.e., elegant. 79. **pensioners:** members of the royal bodyguard. 82. **she-Mercury.** Mercury was the messenger of the gods. 93. **frampold:** worried. 100. **fartuous:** i.e., virtuous. 119. **of all loves:** for love's sake. 120. **infection:** i.e., affection.

she will; and truly she deserves it, for if there be 125
a kind woman in Windsor, she is one. You must
send her your page; no remedy.

Fal. Why, I will.

Quick. Nay, but do so, then; and, look you, he
may come and go between you both; and in 130
any case have a nay-word, that you may know one
another's mind, and the boy never need to understand any thing; for 'tis not good that children
should know any wickedness. Old folks, you
know, have discretion, as they say, and know the
world. 136

Fal. Fare thee well. Commend me to them
both. There's my purse; I am yet thy debtor.
Boy, go along with this woman. [*Exeunt Mistress
Quickly and Robin.*] This news distracts me! 140

Pist. This punk is one of Cupid's carriers.
Clap on more sails; pursue; up with your fights;
Give fire! She is my prize, or ocean whelm them
    all! [*Exit.*]

Fal. Say'st thou so, old Jack? Go thy ways.
I'll make more of thy old body than I have
done. Will they yet look after thee? Wilt 145
thou, after the expense of so much money, be now
a gainer? Good body, I thank thee. Let them
say 'tis grossly done; so it be fairly done, no
matter. 149

Enter BARDOLPH.

Bard. Sir John, there's one Master Brook below
would fain speak with you, and be acquainted with
you; and hath sent your worship a morning's
draught of sack.

Fal. Brook is his name?

Bard. Ay, sir. 155

Fal. Call him in. [*Exit Bardolph.*] Such Brooks
are welcome to me, that o'erflows such liquor. Ah,
ha! Mistress Ford and Mistress Page, have I encompass'd you? Go to; via!

Re-enter [BARDOLPH, *with*] FORD *disguised like
Brook.*

Ford. Bless you, sir! 160

Fal. And you, sir! Would you speak with
me?

Ford. I make bold to press with so little preparation upon you.

Fal. You're welcome. What's your will? Give
us leave, drawer. [*Exit Bardolph.*] 165

Ford. Sir, I am a gentleman that have spent
much. My name is Brook.

Fal. Good Master Brook, I desire more acquaintance of you. 169

Ford. Good Sir John, I sue for yours, — not to

charge you; for I must let you understand I think
myself in better plight for a lender than you are;
the which hath something embold'ned me to this
unseason'd intrusion; for they say, if money go
before, all ways do lie open. 175

Fal. Money is a good soldier, sir, and will
on.

Ford. Troth, and I have a bag of money here
troubles me. If you will help to bear it, Sir John,
take all, or half, for easing me of the carriage.

Fal. Sir, I know not how I may deserve to be
your porter. 181

Ford. I will tell you, sir, if you will give me the
hearing.

Fal. Speak, good Master Brook; I shall be glad
to be your servant. 185

Ford. Sir, I hear you are a scholar, — I will be
brief with you, — and you have been a man long
known to me, though I had never so good means as
desire to make myself acquainted with you. I shall
discover a thing to you, wherein I must very 190
much lay open mine own imperfection; but, good
Sir John, as you have one eye upon my follies, as
you hear them unfolded, turn another into the
register of your own, that I may pass with a reproof
the easier, sith you yourself know how easy it is to
be such an offender. 196

Fal. Very well, sir; proceed.

Ford. There is a gentlewoman in this town; her
husband's name is Ford.

Fal. Well, sir. 200

Ford. I have long lov'd her, and, I protest to you,
bestowed much on her; followed her with a doting
observance; engross'd opportunities to meet her;
fee'd every slight occasion that could but niggardly
give me sight of her; not only bought many 205
presents to give her, but have given largely to many
to know what she would have given; briefly, I have
pursu'd her as love hath pursued me; which hath
been on the wing of all occasions. But whatsoever I
have merited, either in my mind or in my 210
means, meed, I am sure, I have received none; unless experience be a jewel that I have purchased at
an infinite rate, and that hath taught me to say this:
"Love like a shadow flies when substance love
    pursues; 215
Pursuing that that flies, and flying what pur-
    sues."

Fal. Have you receiv'd no promise of satisfaction at her hands?

Ford. Never.

Fal. Have you importun'd her to such a purpose? 221

Ford. Never.

Fal. Of what quality was your love, then?

---

131. **nay-word**: password. 141. **punk**: strumpet. 142. **fights**: screens to protect sailors during a naval battle. 171.
charge: cause expense to. 174. **unseason'd**: unseasonable. 204. **fee'd**: i.e., paid for, employed.

Ford. Like a fair house built on another man's ground; so that I have lost my edifice by mistaking the place where I erected it.   226

Fal. To what purpose have you unfolded this to me?

Ford. When I have told you that, I have told you all. Some say that, though she appear honest to me, yet in other places she enlargeth   230 her mirth so far that there is shrewd construction made of her. Now, Sir John, here is the heart of my purpose: you are a gentleman of excellent breeding, admirable discourse, of great admittance, authentic in your place and person, generally   235 allow'd for your many war-like, court-like, and learned preparations.

Fal. O, sir!   239

Ford. Believe it, for you know it. There is money; spend it, spend it; spend more; spend all I have; only give me so much of your time in exchange of it, as to lay an amiable siege to the honesty of this Ford's wife. Use your art of wooing; win her to consent to you; if any man may, you may as soon as any.   246

Fal. Would it apply well to the vehemency of your affection, that I should win what you would enjoy? Methinks you prescribe to yourself very preposterously.   250

Ford. O, understand my drift. She dwells so securely on the excellency of her honour, that the folly of my soul dares not present itself. She is too bright to be look'd against. Now, could I come to her with any detection in my hand, my desires   255 had instance and argument to commend themselves. I could drive her then from the ward of her purity, her reputation, her marriage vow, and a thousand other her defences, which now are too too strongly embattled against me. What say you to't, Sir John?   261

Fal. Master Brook, I will first make bold with your money; next, give me your hand; and last, as I am a gentleman, you shall, if you will, enjoy Ford's wife.   265

Ford. O good sir!

Fal. I say you shall.

Ford. Want no money, Sir John; you shall want none.   269

Fal. Want no Mistress Ford, Master Brook; you shall want none. I shall be with her, I may tell you, by her own appointment; even as you came in to me, her assistant or go-between parted from me. I say I shall be with her between ten and eleven; for at that time the jealous rascally knave her   275

husband will be forth. Come you to me at night; you shall know how I speed.

Ford. I am blest in your acquaintance. Do you know Ford, sir?   280

Fal. Hang him, poor cuckoldly knave! I know him not. Yet I wrong him to call him poor. They say the jealous wittolly knave hath masses of money; for the which his wife seems to me well-favour'd. I will use her as the key of the   285 cuckoldly rogue's coffer; and there's my harvest-home.

Ford. I would you knew Ford, sir, that you might avoid him if you saw him.   289

Fal. Hang him, mechanical salt-butter rogue! I will stare him out of his wits; I will awe him with my cudgel; it shall hang like a meteor o'er the cuckold's horns. Master Brook, thou shalt know I will predominate over the peasant, and thou shalt lie with his wife. Come to me soon at night.   295 Ford's a knave, and I will aggravate his style; thou, Master Brook, shalt know him for knave and cuckold. Come to me soon at night.   299

[*Exit.*

Ford. What a damn'd Epicurean rascal is this! My heart is ready to crack with impatience. Who says this is improvident jealousy? My wife hath sent to him; the hour is fix'd; the match is made. Would any man have thought this? See the hell of having a false woman! My bed shall be abus'd,   305 my coffers ransack'd, my reputation gnawn at; and I shall not only receive this villanous wrong, but stand under the adoption of abominable terms, and by him that does me this wrong. Terms! Names! Amaimon sounds well; Lucifer, well;   310 Barbason, well; yet they are devils' additions, the names of fiends; but Cuckold! Wittol! — Cuckold! The devil himself hath not such a name. Page is an ass, a secure ass. He will trust his wife; he will   315 not be jealous. I will rather trust a Fleming with my butter, Parson Hugh the Welshman with my cheese, an Irishman with my aqua-vitæ bottle, or a thief to walk my ambling gelding, than my wife with herself. Then she plots, then she rumi-   320 nates, then she devises; and what they think in their hearts they may effect, they will break their hearts but they will effect. [God] be prais'd for my jealousy! Eleven o'clock the hour. I will prevent this, detect my wife, be reveng'd on Falstaff,   325 and laugh at Page. I will about it; better three hours too soon than a minute too late. Fie, fie, fie! cuckold! cuckold! cuckold!

[*Exit.*

231. **shrewd:** evil. 234. **admittance:** entrée, social prestige. 235. **authentic:** i.e., of guaranteed reputation. 236. **allow'd:** approved. 237. **preparations:** accomplishments. 256. **instance:** precedent. 257. **ward:** defence. 283. **wittolly:** cuckoldy. 284. **well-favour'd:** with a pun on the sense "good-looking." 290. **mechanical:** vulgar. **salt-butter:** rank. 296. **aggravate his style:** add to his title. 300. **Epicurean:** i.e., sensual. 311. **additions:** titles. 318. **aqua-vitæ:** whisky.

SCENE III. [*A field near Windsor.*]

Enter CAIUS *and* RUGBY.

Caius. Jack Rugby!

Rug. Sir?

Caius. Vat is [de] clock, Jack?

Rug. 'Tis past the hour, sir, that Sir Hugh promis'd to meet. 5

Caius. By gar, he has save his soul, dat he is no come; he has pray his Pible well, dat he is no come. By gar, Jack Rugby, he is dead already, if he be come.

Rug. He is wise, sir; he knew your worship would kill him, if he came. 11

Caius. By gar, de herring is no dead so as I vill kill him. Take your rapier, Jack; I vill tell you how I vill kill him.

Rug. Alas, sir, I cannot fence.

Caius. Villainy, take your rapier.

Rug. Forbear; here's company.

Enter HOST, SHALLOW, SLENDER, *and* PAGE.

Host. God bless thee, bully doctor!

Shal. God save you, Master Doctor Caius!

Page. Now, good Master Doctor! 20

Slen. Give you good morrow, sir.

Caius. Vat be all you, one, two, tree, four, come for?

Host. To see thee fight, to see thee foin, to see thee traverse; to see thee here, to see thee 25 there; to see thee pass thy punto, thy stock, thy reverse, thy distance, thy montant. Is he dead, my Ethiopian? Is he dead, my Francisco? Ha, bully! What says my Æsculapius? my Galen? my heart of elder? Ha! is he dead, bully stale? Is he dead? 31

Caius. By gar, he is de coward Jack priest of de vorld; he is not show his face.

Host. Thou art a Castalion-King-Urinal. Hector of Greece, my boy! 35

Caius. I pray you, bear witness that me have stay six or seven, two, tree hours for him, and he is no come.

Shal. He is the wiser man, Master Doctor. He is a curer of souls, and you a curer of bodies. 40 If you should fight, you go against the hair of your profession. Is it not true, Master Page?

Page. Master Shallow, you have yourself been a great fighter, though now a man of peace. 45

Shal. Bodykins, Master Page, though I now be old and of the peace, if I see a sword out, my finger itches to make one. Though we are justices and doctors and churchmen, Master Page, we have some salt of our youth in us; we are the sons of women, Master Page. 51

Page. 'Tis true, Master Shallow.

Shal. It will be found so, Master Page. Master Doctor Caius, I am come to fetch you home. I am sworn of the peace. You have show'd yourself 55 a wise physician, and Sir Hugh hath shown himself a wise and patient churchman. You must go with me, Master Doctor.

Host. Pardon, guest-justice. A [word], Mounseur Mockwater. 60

Caius. Mock-vater! Vat is dat?

Host. Mock-water, in our English tongue, is valour, bully.

Caius. By gar, den, I have as much mock-vater as de Englishman. Scurvy jack-dog priest! By gar, me vill cut his ears. 66

Host. He will clapper-claw thee tightly, bully.

Caius. Clapper-de-claw! Vat is dat?

Host. That is, he will make thee amends. 70

Caius. By gar, me do look he shall clapper-de-claw me; for, by gar, me vill have it.

Host. And I will provoke him to't, or let him wag.

Caius. Me tank you for dat. 75

Host. And, moreover, bully, — but first, master guest, and Master Page, and eke Cavaleiro Slender, go you through the town to Frogmore.

[*Aside to them.*]

Page. Sir Hugh is there, is he?

Host. He is there. See what humour he is in; 80 and I will bring the doctor about by the fields. Will it do well?

Shal. We will do it.

Page, Shal., and Slen. Adieu, good Master Doctor.   [*Exeunt Page, Shal., and Slen.* 85

Caius. By gar, me vill kill de priest; for he speak for a jack-an-ape to Anne Page.

Host. Let him die; [but first] sheathe thy impatience, throw cold water on thy choler, go about the fields with me through Frogmore. I will bring 90 thee where Mistress Anne Page is, at a farm-house a-feasting; and thou shalt woo her. Cried game! Said I well?

Caius. By gar, me dank you vor dat. By gar, I love you; and I shall procure-a you de good 95 guest, de earl, de knight, de lords, de gentlemen, my patients.

Sc. iii, 3. [de] F₃. the F₁,₂. 24. foin: thrust. 25. traverse: move back and forth. 26. punto: thrust with the point. stock: thrust. 27. reverse: a backhanded stroke. montant: an upward cut. 28. Francisco: i.e., Frenchman. 30. Æsculapius: god of medicine. Galen: a Greek physician (2d cent. A.D.) heart of elder: heart of pith, coward. 31. stale: i.e., physician. The epithet derives from the physician's examination of patients' urine (stale). 34. Castalion-King-Urinal. An epithet meaning in effect "monarch of doctors." The first two terms refer to the much hated Philip II of Spain; for the last see the preceding note. 46. Bodykins: God's little body. 48. make one: join in. 59. [word] Q. Om. F. 60. Mockwater. See l. 31 n. 67. clapper-claw: maul. 88. [but first] Q. Om. F. 92. Cried game. Perhaps "the game is on."

Host. For the which I will be thy adversary toward Anne Page. Said I well?

Caius. By gar, 'tis good; vell said.   100

Host. Let us wag, then.

Caius. Come at my heels, Jack Rugby. [*Exeunt.*

ACT III

SCENE I. [*A field near Frogmore.*]

Enter SIR HUGH EVANS *and* SIMPLE.

Evans. I pray you now, good Master Slender's serving-man, and friend Simple by your name, which way have you look'd for Master Caius, that calls himself Doctor of Physic?

Sim. Marry, sir, the pittie-ward, the park- 5 ward, every way; Old Windsor way, and every way but the town way.

Evans. I most fehemently desire you you will also look that way.

Sim. I will, sir.   [*Exit.*] 10

Evans. Pless my soul, how full of chollors I am, and trempling of mind! I shall be glad if he have deceived me. How melancholies I am! I will knog his urinals about his knave's costard when I have good opportunities for the ork. Pless my soul!   [*Sings.*] 16

> "To shallow rivers, to whose falls
>   Melodious birds sings madrigals;
> There will we make our peds of roses,
>   And a thousand fragrant posies.   20
> To shallow" —

Mercy on me! I have a great dispositions to cry.
                                             [*Sings.*]

> "Melodious birds sing madrigals" —
> "When as I sat in Pabylon" —
> "And a thousand vagram posies.   25
>   To shallow," etc.

[*Re-enter* SIMPLE.]

Sim. Yonder he is coming; this way, Sir Hugh.

Evans. He's welcome.   [*Sings.*]
> "To shallow rivers, to whose falls" —

Heaven prosper the right! What weapons is he? 30

Sim. No weapons, sir. There comes my master, Master Shallow, and another gentleman, from Frogmore, over the stile, this way.

Evans. Pray you, give me my gown; or else keep it in your arms.   35

Enter PAGE, SHALLOW, *and* SLENDER.

Shal. How now, Master Parson! Good morrow, good Sir Hugh. Keep a gamester from the

dice, and a good student from his book, and it is wonderful.

Slen. [*Aside.*] Ah, sweet Anne Page!   40

Page. Save you, good Sir Hugh!

Evans. Pless you from his mercy sake, all of you!

Shal. What, the sword and the word! Do you study them both, Master Parson?   45

Page. And youthful still! In your doublet and hose this raw rheumatic day!

Evans. There is reasons and causes for it.

Page. We are come to you to do a good office, Master Parson.   50

Evans. Fery well; what is it?

Page. Yonder is a most reverend gentleman, who, belike having received wrong by some person, is at most odds with his own gravity and patience that ever you saw.   55

Shal. I have lived fourscore years and upward; I never heard a man of his place, gravity, and learning, so wide of his own respect.

Evans. What is he?

Page. I think you know him; Master Doctor Caius, the renowned French physician.   61

Evans. Got's will, and his passion! Of my heart, I had as lief you would tell me of a mess of porridge.

Page. Why?   65

Evans. He has no more knowledge in Hibocrates and Galen — and he is a knave besides, a cowardly knave as you would desires to be acquainted withal.

Page. I warrant you, he's the man should fight with him.   71

Slen. [*Aside.*] O sweet Anne Page!

Enter HOST, CAIUS [*and* RUGBY].

Shal. It appears so by his weapons. Keep them asunder; here comes Doctor Caius.

Page. Nay, good Master Parson, keep in your weapon.   76

Shal. So do you, good Master Doctor.

Host. Disarm them, and let them question. Let them keep their limbs whole and hack our English.   80

Caius. I pray you, let-a me speak a word with your ear. Vherefore vill you not meet-a me?

Evans. [*Aside to Caius.*] Pray you, use your patience. In good time.

Caius. By gar, you are de coward, de Jack dog, John ape.   86

Evans. [*Aside to Caius.*] Pray you, let us not be laughing-stocks to other men's humours. I desire you in friendship, and I will one way or other make you amends. [*Aloud.*] I will knog your 90

Act III, sc. i, 5. pittie-ward. Presumably, a part of Windsor. 11. **chollors:** i.e., choler, anger. 14. **costard:** apple, i.c., head. 17–26. Muddled fragments from Marlowe's lyric, "The Passionate Shepherd to his Love." Line 24 is from Psalm 37. 25. **vagram:** i.e., fragrant. 58. **respect:** reputation. 66. **Hibocrates:** Hippocrates, Greek physician (5th cent. B.C.). 78. **question:** talk.

urinal about your knave's cogscomb [for missing your meetings and appointments].

Caius. Diable! Jack Rugby, — mine host de Jarteer, — have I not stay for him to kill him? Have I not, at de place I did appoint?   95

Evans. As I am a Christians soul, now look you, this is the place appointed. I'll be judgement by mine host of the Garter.

Host. Peace, I say, Gallia and Gaul, French and Welsh, soul-curer and body-curer!   100

Caius. Ay, dat is very good; excellent.

Host. Peace, I say! hear mine host of the Garter. Am I politic? Am I subtle? Am I a Machiavel? Shall I lose my doctor? No; he gives me the potions and the motions. Shall I lose my parson,   105 my priest, my Sir Hugh? No; he gives me the proverbs and the noverbs. [Give me thy hand, terrestrial; so.] Give me thy hand, celestial; so. Boys of art, I have deceiv'd you both; I have directed you to wrong places. Your hearts are   110 mighty, your skins are whole, and let burnt sack be the issue. Come, lay their swords to pawn. Follow me, [lads] of peace; follow, follow, follow.

                          [*Exit Host.*

Shal. Trust me, a mad host. Follow, gentlemen, follow.   116

Slen. [*Aside.*] O sweet Anne Page!

               [*Exeunt Shal., Slen., and Page.*]

Caius. Ha, do I perceive dat? Have you make-a de sot of us, ha, ha?

Evans. This is well; he has made us his vlout-   120 ing-stog. I desire you that we may be friends; and let us knog our prains together to be revenge on this same scall, scurvy, cogging companion, the host of the Garter.   124

Caius. By gar, with all my heart. He promise to bring me where is Anne Page; by gar, he deceive me too.

Evans. Well, I will smite his noddles. Pray you, follow.   [*Exeunt.*

SCENE II. [*A street.*]

Enter MISTRESS PAGE *and* ROBIN.

Mrs. Page. Nay, keep your way, little gallant; you were wont to be a follower, but now you are a leader. Whether had you rather lead mine eyes, or eye your master's heels?

Rob. I had rather, forsooth, go before you like a man than follow him like a dwarf.   6

Mrs. Page. O, you are a flattering boy. Now I see you'll be a courtier.

[*Enter* FORD.]

Ford. Well met, Mistress Page. Whither go you?   10

Mrs. Page. Truly, sir, to see your wife. Is she at home?

Ford. Ay; and as idle as she may hang together, for want of company. I think, if your husbands were dead, you two would marry.   15

Mrs. Page. Be sure of that, — two other husbands.

Ford. Where had you this pretty weathercock?

Mrs. Page. I cannot tell what the dickens his name is my husband had him of. What do you call your knight's name, sirrah!   21

Rob. Sir John Falstaff.

Ford. Sir John Falstaff!

Mrs. Page. He, he; I can never hit on's name. There is such a league between my good man and he! Is your wife at home indeed?   26

Ford. Indeed she is.

Mrs. Page. By your leave, sir. I am sick till I see her.   [*Exeunt Mrs. Page and Robin.*]

Ford. Has Page any brains? Hath he any   30 eyes? Hath he any thinking? Sure, they sleep; he hath no use of them. Why, this boy will carry a letter twenty mile, as easy as a cannon will shoot point-blank twelve score. He pieces out his wife's inclination; he gives her folly motion and ad-   35 vantage; and now she's going to my wife, and Falstaff's boy with her. A man may hear this shower sing in the wind. And Falstaff's boy with her! Good plots, they are laid; and our revolted wives share damnation together. Well; I will   40 take him, then torture my wife, pluck the borrowed veil of modesty from the so-seeming Mistress Page, divulge Page himself for a secure and wilful Actæon; and to these violent proceedings all my neighbours shall cry aim. [*Clock heard.*] The clock gives   45 me my cue, and my assurance bids me search. There I shall find Falstaff. I shall be rather prais'd for this than mock'd, for it is as positive as the earth is firm that Falstaff is there. I will go.   50

[*Enter* PAGE, SHALLOW, SLENDER, HOST, SIR
     HUGH EVANS, CAIUS, *and* RUGBY.]

Shal., Page, etc. Well met, Master Ford.

Ford. Trust me, a good knot. I have good cheer at home, and I pray you all go with me.

Shal. I must excuse myself, Master Ford.   54

Slen. And so must I, sir. We have appointed to dine with Mistress Anne, and I would not break with her for more money than I'll speak of.

91–92. [for ... appointments] Q.   Om. F.   99. **Gallia:** Wales.   107. [Give ... so] Q. Om. F.   109. **art:** learning. 112. **issue:** end.   113. [lads] Q.   *lad* F.   119. **sot:** fool.   120. **vlouting-stog:** i.e., laughing stock.   123. **scall:** scald, scabby.   **cogging companion:** cheating fellow.

     Sc. ii, 25. **league:** friendship.   34. **twelve score:** i.e., at twelve score paces.   **pieces out:** abets.   37–38. **A ... wind:** this matter is obvious.   45. **cry aim:** applaud.   52. **knot:** company.

Shal. We have linger'd about a match between Anne Page and my cousin Slender, and this day we shall have our answer.   60

Slen. I hope I have your good will, father Page.

Page. You have, Master Slender; I stand wholly for you: but my wife, Master Doctor, is for you altogether.

Caius. Ay, be-gar; and de maid is love-a me. My nursh-a Quickly tell me so mush.   66

Host. What say you to young Master Fenton? He capers, he dances, he has eyes of youth, he writes verses, he speaks holiday, he smells April and May. He will carry 't, he will carry 't; 'tis in his buttons; he will carry 't.   71

Page. Not by my consent, I promise you. The gentleman is of no having. He kept company with the wild Prince and Poins; he is of too high a region; he knows too much. No, he shall not knit a   75 knot in his fortunes with the finger of my substance. If he take her, let him take her simply. The wealth I have waits on my consent, and my consent goes not that way.

Ford. I beseech you heartily, some of you go   80 home with me to dinner. Besides your cheer, you shall have sport; I will show you a monster. Master Doctor, you shall go; so shall you, Master Page; and you, Sir Hugh.

Shal. Well, fare you well. We shall have the   85 freer wooing at Master Page's.

[Exeunt Shal. and Slen.

Caius. Go home, John Rugby; I come anon.

[Exit Rugby.]

Host. Farewell, my hearts. I will to my honest knight Falstaff, and drink canary with him.   89

[Exit.

Ford. [*Aside.*] I think I shall drink in pipe-wine first with him; I'll make him dance. Will you go gentles?

All. Have with you to see this monster.

[Exeunt.

SCENE III. [*A room in Ford's house.*]

Enter MISTRESS FORD *and* MISTRESS PAGE.

Mrs. Ford. What, John! What, Robert!

Mrs. Page. Quickly, quickly! Is the buck-basket —

Mrs. Ford. I warrant. What, Robin, I say!

[Enter Servants *with a basket.]*

Mrs. Page. Come, come, come.   5

Mrs. Ford. Here, set it down.

Mrs. Page. Give your men the charge; we must be brief.

Mrs. Ford. Marry, as I told you before, John and Robert, be ready here hard by in the brew-   10 house; and when I suddenly call you, come forth, and without any pause or staggering take this basket on your shoulders. That done, trudge with it in all haste, and carry it among the whitsters in Datchet-mead, and there empty it in the muddy   15 ditch close by the Thames side.

Mrs. Page. You will do it?

Mrs. Ford. I ha' told them over and over; they lack no direction. Be gone, and come when you are call'd.   *[Exeunt Servants.*   20

Mrs. Page. Here comes little Robin.

[Enter ROBIN.]*

Mrs. Ford. How now, my eyas-musket! what news with you?

Rob. My master, Sir John, is come in at your back-door, Mistress Ford, and requests your company.   26

Mrs. Page. You little Jack-a-Lent, have you been true to us?

Rob. Ay, I'll be sworn. My master knows not of your being here and hath threat'ned to put   30 me into everlasting liberty if I tell you of it; for he swears he'll turn me away.

Mrs. Page. Thou'rt a good boy. This secrecy of thine shall be a tailor to thee and shall make thee a new doublet and hose. I'll go hide me.   36

Mrs. Ford. Do so. Go tell thy master I am alone. *[Exit Robin.]* Mistress Page, remember you your cue.

Mrs. Page. I warrant thee; if I do not act it, hiss me.   *[Exit.]*   41

Mrs. Ford. Go to, then. We'll use this unwholesome humidity, this gross wat'ry pumpion. We'll teach him to know turtles from jays.

Enter FALSTAFF.

Fal. "Have I caught thee, my heavenly jewel?" Why, now let me die, for I have liv'd   45 long enough. This is the period of my ambition. O this blessed hour!

Mrs. Ford. O sweet Sir John!

Fal. Mistress Ford, I cannot cog, I cannot   50 prate, Mistress Ford. Now shall I sin in my wish: I would thy husband were dead. I'll speak it before the best lord; I would make thee my lady.

69. **holiday:** in fine phrases. 70. **carry 't:** win. 70–71. **'tis ... buttons:** i.e., he has it in him. 73. **having:** possessions. 77. **simply:** i.e., without dowry. 89. **canary:** a sweet wine. 90. **pipe-wine.** A double pun inspired by the Host's "canary" (l. 89). *Canary* is (1) a wine and (2) a lively dance; *pipe* is (1) a cask and (2) a musical instrument.

Sc. iii, 2. buck-basket: basket for soiled clothes. To "buck" clothes was to boil them in an alkaline lye as a step to bleaching. 4. **Robin.** Apparently the servant Robert is meant, not the page. 12. **staggering:** hesitating. 14. **whitsters:** bleachers. 15. **Datchet-mead.** Datchet was a village on the Thames near Windsor. 22. **eyas-musket:** young (male) sparrow-hawk, hence youngster. 27. **Jack-a-Lent:** a decorated puppet set up for boys to throw at in Lent. 43. **pumpion:** pumpkin. 44–45. **Have ... jewel.** A line from Sidney's *Astrophel and Stella* (1591). Q omits *thee*, which is not in Sidney's line. 46. **period:** end, final point. 50. **cog:** lie.

Mrs. Ford. I your lady, Sir John! Alas, I should be a pitiful lady!   56

Fal. Let the court of France show me such another. I see how thine eye would emulate the diamond. Thou hast the right arched beauty of the brow that becomes the ship-tire, the tire-valiant, or any tire of Venetian admittance.   61

Mrs. Ford. A plain kerchief, Sir John. My brows become nothing else; nor that well neither.

Fal. [By the Lord,] thou art a tyrant to say   65 so. Thou wouldst make an absolute courtier; and the firm fixture of thy foot would give an excellent motion to thy gait in a semi-circled farthingale. I see what thou wert, if Fortune thy foe were not, Nature thy friend. Come, thou canst not hide it.   71

Mrs. Ford. Believe me, there's no such thing in me.

Fal. What made me love thee? Let that persuade thee there's something extraordinary in   75 thee. Come, I cannot cog and say thou art this and that, like a many of these lisping hawthorn-buds, that come like women in men's apparel, and smell like Bucklersbury in simple time; I cannot; but I love thee, none but thee, and thou deserv'st it.   81

Mrs. Ford. Do not betray me, sir. I fear you love Mistress Page.

Fal. Thou mightst as well say I love to walk by the Counter-gate, which is as hateful to me as the reek of a lime-kiln.   86

Mrs. Ford. Well, heaven knows how I love you; and you shall one day find it.

Fal. Keep in that mind; I'll deserve it.

Mrs. Ford. Nay, I must tell you, so you do; or else I could not be in that mind.   91

[*Enter* ROBIN.]

Rob. Mistress Ford, Mistress Ford! here's Mistress Page at the door, sweating, and blowing, and looking wildly, and would needs speak with you presently.   95

Fal. She shall not see me. I will ensconce me behind the arras.

Mrs. Ford. Pray you, do so; she's a very tattling woman.   [*Falstaff stands behind the arras.*

[*Re-enter* MISTRESS PAGE.]

What's the matter? How now!   100

Mrs. Page. O Mistress Ford, what have you done? You're sham'd, you're overthrown, you're undone for ever!

Mrs. Ford. What's the matter, good Mistress Page?   105

Mrs. Page. O well-a-day, Mistress Ford! having an honest man to your husband, to give him such cause of suspicion!

Mrs. Ford. What cause of suspicion?

Mrs. Page. What cause of suspicion! Out upon you! How am I mistook in you!   111

Mrs. Ford. Why, alas, what's the matter?

Mrs. Page. Your husband's coming hither, woman, with all the officers in Windsor, to search for a gentleman that he says is here now in the   115 house by your consent, to take an ill advantage of his absence. You are undone.

Mrs. Ford. 'Tis not so, I hope.

Mrs. Page. Pray heaven it be not so, that you have such a man here, but 'tis most certain your   120 husband's coming, with half Windsor at his heels, to search for such a one. I come before to tell you. If you know yourself clear, why, I am glad of it; but if you have a friend here, convey, convey him out. Be not amaz'd, call all your senses to you,   125 defend your reputation, or bid farewell to your good life forever.

Mrs. Ford. What shall I do? There is a gentleman my dear friend; and I fear not mine own shame so much as his peril. I had rather than a thou-   130 sand pound he were out of the house.

Mrs. Page. For shame! never stand "you had rather" and "you had rather." Your husband's here at hand. Bethink you of some conveyance.   135 In the house you cannot hide him. O, how have you deceiv'd me! Look, here is a basket. If he be of any reasonable stature, he may creep in here; and throw foul linen upon him, as if it were going to bucking, or — it is whiting-time — send him by your two men to Datchet-mead.   141

Mrs. Ford. He's too big to go in there. What shall I do?

Fal. [*Coming forward.*] Let me see't, let me see't, O, let me see't! I'll in, I'll in. Follow your friend's counsel. I'll in.   146

Mrs. Page. What, Sir John Falstaff! Are these your letters, knight?

Fal. I love thee. Help me away. Let me creep in here. I'll never —   150
        [*Gets into the basket; they put clothes over him.*

Mrs. Page. Help to cover your master, boy. Call your men, Mistress Ford. You dissembling knight!

Mrs. Ford. What, John! Robert! John!
        [*Exit Robin.*

---

60. **ship-tire:** headdress shaped like a ship.   **tire-valiant:** a very fantastic headdress.   65. [**By the Lord**] Q. Om. F.   66. **absolute:** perfect.   68. **semi-circled farthingale:** a half-hooped skirt.   69–70. **if . . . friend.** I.e., if Fortune, thy foe, were thy friend as Nature is. "Fortune thy foe" is the name of a popular song, of which "Fortune my foe, why dost thou frown on me" is the first line.   77. **hawthorn-buds:** i.e., dandies.   79. **Bucklersbury:** a street in London where herbs (simples) were sold.   85. **Counter-gate:** gate of the debtor's prison, notorious for bad odors.   132. **stand:** lose time over.   140. **whiting-time:** bleaching-time.

[Re-enter SERVANTS.]
Go take up these clothes here quickly. Where's 155
the cowl-staff? Look, how you drumble! Carry
them to the laundress in Datchet-mead; quickly,
come.

[Enter FORD, PAGE, CAIUS, *and* SIR HUGH EVANS.]

Ford. Pray you, come near. If I suspect without cause, why then make sport at me; then 160
let me be your jest; I deserve it. How now! whither
bear you this?

Serv. To the laundress, forsooth.

Mrs. Ford. Why, what have you to do whither
they bear it? You were best meddle with buck-
washing.   166

Ford. Buck! I would I could wash myself of
the buck! Buck, buck, buck! Ay, buck; I warrant you, buck, and of the season too, it shall appear. *[Exeunt Servants with the basket.]* Gen- 170
tlemen, I have dream'd to-night; I'll tell you my
dream. Here, here, here be my keys. Ascend my
chambers, search, seek, find out. I'll warrant we'll
unkennel the fox. Let me stop this way first.
[Locking the door.] So, now uncape.   176

Page. Good Master Ford, be contented. You
wrong yourself too much.

Ford. True, Master Page. Up, gentlemen; you
shall see sport anon. Follow me, gentlemen. 180
                                                        [Exit.]

Evans. This is fery fantastical humours and
jealousies.

Caius. By gar, 'tis no the fashion of France; it
is not jealous in France.

Page. Nay, follow him, gentlemen; see the issue of
his search. *[Exeunt Page, Caius, and Evans.]* 186

Mrs. Page. Is there not a double excellency in
this?

Mrs. Ford. I know not which pleases me better,
that my husband is deceived, or Sir John. 190

Mrs. Page. What a taking was he in when your
husband ask'd who was in the basket!

Mrs. Ford. I am half afraid he will have need of
washing, so throwing him into the water will do
him a benefit.   195

Mrs. Page. Hang him, dishonest rascal! I
would all of the same strain were in the same distress.

Mrs. Ford. I think my husband hath some special suspicion of Falstaff's being here, for I 200
never saw him so gross in his jealousy till now.

Mrs. Page. I will lay a plot to try that; and we
will yet have more tricks with Falstaff. His dissolute disease will scarce obey this medicine. 204

Mrs. Ford. Shall we send that foolish carrion,
Mistress Quickly, to him, and excuse his throwing
into the water; and give him another hope, to betray him to another punishment?

Mrs. Page. We will do it. Let him be sent for
to-morrow, eight o'clock, to have amends. 210

[Re-enter FORD, PAGE, CAIUS, *and* SIR HUGH
EVANS.]

Ford. I cannot find him. May be the knave
bragg'd of that he could not compass.

Mrs. Page. *[Aside to Mrs. Ford.]* Heard you
that?

Mrs. Ford. You use me well, Master Ford, do
you?   216

Ford. Ay, I do so.

Mrs. Ford. Heaven make you better than your
thoughts!

Ford. Amen!   220

Mrs. Page. You do yourself mighty wrong,
Master Ford.

Ford. Ay, ay; I must bear it.

Evans. If there be any pody in the house, and in
the chambers, and in the coffers, and in the 225
presses, heaven forgive my sins at the day of judgement!

Caius. By gar, nor I too; there is no bodies.

Page. Fie, fie, Master Ford! are you not asham'd?
What spirit, what devil suggests this imagina- 230
tion? I would not ha' your distemper in this kind
for the wealth of Windsor Castle.

Ford. 'Tis my fault, Master Page. I suffer for
it.   234

Evans. You suffer for a pad conscience. Your
wife is as honest a 'omans as I will desires among
five thousand, and five hundred too.

Caius. By gar, I see 'tis an honest woman.

Ford. Well, I promis'd you a dinner. Come,
come, walk in the Park. I pray you, pardon me. 240
I will hereafter make known to you why I have done
this. Come, wife; come, Mistress Page. I pray
you, pardon me; pray heartily, pardon me.

Page. Let's go in, gentlemen; but, trust me, we'll
mock him. I do invite you to-morrow morn- 245
ing to my house to breakfast; after, we'll a-birding
together. I have a fine hawk for the bush. Shall
it be so?

Ford. Anything.

Evans. If there is one, I shall make two in the
company.   251

Caius. If dere be one or two, I shall make-a the
turd.

Ford. Pray you, go, Master Page.

---

156. **cowl-staff:** pole by which two persons could carry a basket, the pole passing through the handles.   **drumble:**
dawdle.   169. **of the season:** i.e., in prime condition.   171. **to-night:** last night.   176. **uncape:** uncover, disclose (i.e.,
what we have come to find).   191. **taking:** fright.   215–16. **You…you.** Q reads *I, I, peace* (which would be "aside" to
Mrs. Page).

Evans. I pray you now, remembrance to-morrow
on the lousy knave, mine host.   256
Caius. Dat is good; by gar, with all my heart!
Evans. A lousy knave, to have his gibes and his
mockeries!   [*Exeunt.* 260

SCENE IV. [*At Page's house.*]

Enter FENTON *and* ANNE PAGE.

Fent. I see I cannot get thy father's love,
Therefore no more turn me to him, sweet Nan.
Anne. Alas, how then?
Fent.   Why, thou must be thyself.
He doth object I am too great of birth;
And that, my state being gall'd with my expense,
I seek to heal it only by his wealth.   6
Besides these, other bars he lays before me,
My riots past, my wild societies;
And tells me 'tis a thing impossible
I should love thee but as a property.   10
Anne. May be he tells you true.
[*Fent.*] No, heaven so speed me in my time to
come!
Albeit I will confess thy father's wealth
Was the first motive that I woo'd thee, Anne;
Yet, wooing thee, I found thee of more value   15
Than stamps in gold or sums in sealed bags;
And 'tis the very riches of thyself
That now I aim at.
Anne.   Gentle Master Fenton,
Yet seek my father's love; still seek it, sir.
If opportunity and humblest suit   20
Cannot attain it, why, then, — hark you hither!
                       [*They converse apart.*]

[*Enter* SHALLOW, SLENDER, *and* MISTRESS
                QUICKLY.]

Shal. Break their talk, Mistress Quickly. My
kinsman shall speak for himself.
Slen. I'll make a shaft or a bolt on 't. 'Slid, 'tis
but venturing.   25
Shal. Be not dismay'd.
Slen. No, she shall not dismay me. I care not
for that, but that I am afeard.
Quick. Hark ye; Master Slender would speak a
word with you.   30
Anne. I come to him. [*Aside.*] This is my
         father's choice.
O, what a world of vile ill-favour'd faults
Looks handsome in three hundred pounds a-year!
Quick. And how does good Master Fenton?
Pray you, a word with you.   35
Shal. She's coming; to her, coz. O boy, thou
hadst a father!

Slen. I had a father, Mistress Anne; my uncle
can tell you good jests of him. Pray you, uncle,
tell Mistress Anne the jest how my father stole two
geese out of a pen, good uncle.   41
Shal. Mistress Anne, my cousin loves you.
Slen. Ay, that I do; as well as I love any woman
in Gloucestershire.   44
Shal. He will maintain you like a gentlewoman.
Slen. Ay, that I will, come cut and long-tail,
under the degree of a squire.
Shal. He will make you a hundred and fifty
pounds jointure.   50
Anne. Good Master Shallow, let him woo for
himself.
Shal. Marry, I thank you for it; I thank you for
that good comfort. She calls you, coz. I'll leave
you.   55
Anne. Now, Master Slender, —
Slen. Now, good Mistress Anne, —
Anne. What is your will?
Slen. My will! 'Od's heartlings, that's a pretty
jest indeed! I ne'er made my will yet, I thank   60
heaven. I am not such a sickly creature, I give
heaven praise.
Anne. I mean, Master Slender, what would you
with me.
Slen. Truly, for mine own part, I would little   65
or nothing with you. Your father and my uncle
hath made motions. If it be my luck, so; if not,
happy man be his dole! They can tell you how
things go better than I can. You may ask your
father; here he comes.   70

[*Enter* PAGE *and* MISTRESS PAGE.]

Page. Now, Master Slender. Love him, daugh-
         ter Anne.
Why, how now! What does Master Fenton here?
You wrong me, sir, thus still to haunt my house.
I told you, sir, my daughter is dispos'd of.
Fent. Nay, Master Page, be not impatient.   75
Mrs. Page. Good Master Fenton, come not to my
         child.
Page. She is no match for you.
Fent. Sir, will you hear me?
Page.   No, good Master Fenton
Come, Master Shallow; come, son Slender, in.
Knowing my mind, you wrong me, Master Fenton.
                    [*Exeunt Page, Shal., and Slen.*]
Quick. Speak to Mistress Page.   81
Fent. Good Mistress Page, for that I love your
         daughter
In such a righteous fashion as I do,
Perforce, against all checks, rebukes, and manners,
I must advance the colours of my love   85

Sc. iv, 5. **state**: estate. **gall'd**: squandered. 16. **stamps**: coins. 24. **make ... on 't**: i.e., do it one way or another.
'Slid: God's eyelid. 46. **cut and long-tail**: i.e., all kinds. 59. **'Od's heartlings**: God's little heart. 68. **happy ... dole**:
happiness be his (the lucky man's) portion (proverbial). 85. **colours**: banners, standards.

And not retire. Let me have your good will.
Anne. Good mother, do not marry me to yond
    fool.
Mrs. Page. I mean it not; I seek you a better
    husband.
Quick. That's my master, Master Doctor.
Anne. Alas, I had rather be set quick i' th'
    earth   90
And bowl'd to death with turnips!
Mrs. Page. Come, trouble not yourself. Good
    Master Fenton,
I will not be your friend nor enemy.
My daughter will I question how she loves you,
And as I find her, so am I affected.   95
Till then farewell, sir; she must needs go in.
Her father will be angry.
Fent. Farewell, gentle mistress; farewell, Nan.
                    [*Exeunt Mrs. Page and Anne.*]
Quick. This is my doing, now. "Nay," said I,
"will you cast away your child on a fool, and a   100
physician? Look on Master Fenton." This is my
doing.
Fent. I thank thee; and I pray thee, once to-
    night
Give my sweet Nan this ring. There's for thy
    pains.   104
Quick. Now heaven send thee good fortune!
[*Exit Fenton.*] A kind heart he hath. A woman
would run through fire and water for such a kind
heart. But yet I would my master had Mistress
Anne; or I would Master Slender had her; or, in
sooth, I would Master Fenton had her. I will   110
do what I can for them all three; for so I have
promis'd, and I'll be as good as my word; but
speciously for Master Fenton. Well, I must of
another errand to Sir John Falstaff from my two
mistresses. What a beast am I to slack it!   115
                                                    [*Exit.*

SCENE V. [*A room in the Garter Inn.*]

Enter FALSTAFF *and* BARDOLPH.

Fal. Bardolph, I say!
Bard. Here, sir.
Fal. Go fetch me a quart of sack. Put a toast
in 't. [*Exit Bard.*] Have I liv'd to be carried in a
basket like a barrow of butcher's offal and to   5
be thrown in the Thames? Well, if I be serv'd such
another trick, I'll have my brains ta'en out and
butter'd, and give them to a dog for a new-year's
gift. The rogues [slided] me into the river with as
little remorse as they would have drown'd a   10
blind bitch's puppies, fifteen i' th' litter; and you

may know by my size that I have a kind of alacrity
in sinking. If the bottom were as deep as hell, I
should down. I had been drown'd, but that the
shore was shelvy and shallow,—a death that I   15
abhor; for the water swells a man; and what a
thing should I have been when I had been swell'd!
I should have been a mountain of mummy.

[*Re-enter* BARDOLPH, *with sack.*]

Bard. Here's Mistress Quickly, sir, to speak with
you.   21
Fal. Come, let me pour in some sack to the
Thames water; for my belly's as cold as if I had
swallow'd snowballs for pills to cool the reins.
Call her in.   25
Bard. Come in, woman!

Enter MISTRESS QUICKLY.

Quick. By your leave; I cry you mercy. Give
your worship good morrow.
Fal. Take away these chalices. Go brew me a
pottle of sack finely.   30
Bard. With eggs, sir?
Fal. Simple of itself. I'll no pullet-sperm in my
brewage. [*Exit Bardolph.*] How now?
Quick. Marry, sir, I come to your worship from
Mistress Ford.   35
Fal. Mistress Ford! I have had ford enough. I
was thrown into the ford; I have my belly full of
ford.
Quick. Alas the day! Good heart, that was not
her fault. She does so take on with her men; they
mistook their erection.   41
Fal. So did I mine, to build upon a foolish woman's promise.
Quick. Well, she laments, sir, for it, that it would
yearn your heart to see it. Her husband goes   45
this morning a-birding. She desires you once more
to come to her between eight and nine. I must
carry her word quickly. She'll make you amends,
I warrant you.   49
Fal. Well, I will visit her. Tell her so; and bid
her think what a man is. Let her consider his
frailty, and then judge of my merit.
Quick. I will tell her.
Fal. Do so. Between nine and ten, say'st
thou?
Quick. Eight and nine, sir.   55
Fal. Well, be gone. I will not miss her.
Quick. Peace be with you, sir.   [*Exit.*
Fal. I marvel I hear not of Master Brook; he
sent me word to stay within. I like his money well.
O, here he comes.   60

90. **quick:** alive. 95. **affected:** inclined. 102. **once:** sometime. 113. **speciously:** especially. 115. **slack:** delay.
Sc. v, 9. [slided] Q. *slighted* F. 24. **reins:** kidneys. 27. **cry...mercy:** beg your pardon. 41. **erection:** i.e., direction.
45. **yearn:** grieve.

Enter FORD, *disguised.*

Ford. Bless you, sir!

Fal. Now, Master Brook, you come to know what hath pass'd between me and Ford's wife?

Ford. That, indeed, Sir John, is my business. 64

Fal. Master Brook, I will not lie to you. I was at her house the hour she appointed me.

Ford. And sped you, sir?

Fal. Very ill-favouredly, Master Brook.

Ford. How so, sir? Did she change her determination? 70

Fal. No, Master Brook; but the peaking cornuto her husband, Master Brook, dwelling in a continual 'larum of jealousy, comes me in the instant of our encounter, after we had embrac'd, kiss'd, protested, and, as it were, spoke the prologue of 75 our comedy; and at his heels a rabble of his companions, thither provoked and instigated by his distemper, and, forsooth, to search his house for his wife's love.

Ford. What, while you were there? 80

Fal. While I was there.

Ford. And did he search for you, and could not find you?

Fal. You shall hear. As good luck would have it, comes in one Mistress Page; gives intelligence 85 of Ford's approach; and, in her invention and Ford's wife's distraction, they convey'd me into a buck-basket.

Ford. A buck-basket! 89

Fal. [By the Lord,] a buck-basket! Ramm'd me in with foul shirts and smocks, socks, foul stockings, greasy napkins, that, Master Brook, there was the rankest compound of villanous smell that ever offended nostril.

Ford. And how long lay you there? 95

Fal. Nay, you shall hear, Master Brook, what I have suffer'd to bring this woman to evil for your good. Being thus cramm'd in the basket, a couple of Ford's knaves, his hinds, were call'd forth by their mistress to carry me in the name 100 of foul clothes to Datchet-lane. They took me on their shoulders; met the jealous knave their master in the door, who ask'd them once or twice what they had in their basket. I quak'd for fear, lest the lunatic knave would have search'd it; but fate, 105 ordaining he should be a cuckold, held his hand. Well, on went he for a search, and away went I for foul clothes. But mark the sequel, Master Brook. I suffered the pangs of three several deaths; first, an intolerable fright, to be de- 110 tected with a jealous rotten bell-wether; next, to be compass'd, like a good bilbo, in the circum-

ference of a peck, hilt to point, heel to head; and then, to be stopp'd in, like a strong distillation, with stinking clothes that fretted in their own 115 grease. Think of that,—a man of my kidney,— think of that,—that am as subject to heat as butter; a man of continual dissolution and thaw,— it was a miracle to scape suffocation. And in the height of this bath, when I was more than 120 half stew'd in grease, like a Dutch dish, to be thrown into the Thames, and cool'd, glowing hot, in that surge, like a horse-shoe; think of that,— hissing hot,—think of that, Master Brook. 124

Ford. In good sadness, sir, I am sorry that for my sake you have suffer'd all this. My suit then is desperate; you'll undertake her no more?

Fal. Master Brook, I will be thrown into Etna, as I have been into Thames, ere I will leave her thus. Her husband is this morning gone a- 130 birding. I have received from her another embassy of meeting. 'Twixt eight and nine is the hour, Master Brook.

Ford. 'Tis past eight already, sir.

Fal. Is it? I will then address me to my ap- 135 pointment. Come to me at your convenient leisure, and you shall know how I speed; and the conclusion shall be crowned with your enjoying her. Adieu. You shall have her, Master Brook. Master Brook, you shall cuckold Ford. [*Exit.* 140

Ford. Hum! ha! is this a vision? Is this a dream? Do I sleep? Master Ford, awake! awake, Master Ford! there's a hole made in your best coat, Master Ford. This 'tis to be married! This 'tis to have linen and buck-baskets! Well, I will 145 proclaim myself what I am. I will now take the lecher; he is at my house; he cannot scape me; 'tis impossible he should. He cannot creep into a halfpenny purse, nor into a pepper-box; but, lest the devil that guides him should aid him, I will 150 search impossible places. Though what I am I cannot avoid, yet to be what I would not shall not make me tame. If I have horns to make one mad, let the proverb go with me: I'll be horn mad. 155

[*Exit.*

ACT IV

SCENE I. [*A street.*]

Enter MISTRESS PAGE, MISTRESS QUICKLY, *and* WILLIAM.

Mrs. Page. Is he at Master Ford's already, think'st thou?

Quick. Sure he is by this, or will be presently. But, truly, he is very courageous mad about his

---

71. **peaking:** prying. **cornuto:** cuckold. 87. **distraction.** Hanmer and others read *direction.* 90. **[By the Lord]** Q. *yes* F. 99. **hinds:** servants. 111. **with:** by. **bell-wether:** old sheep, leader of the flock. 112. **bilbo:** sword blade (see I.i.165 n.). A perfectly tempered blade could be bent into a circle. 113. **peck:** i.e., a peck measure. 125. **sadness:** seriousness.

throwing into the water. Mistress Ford desires
you to come suddenly.   6
Mrs. Page. I'll be with her by and by; I'll but
bring my young man here to school.

[*Enter* SIR HUGH EVANS.]

Look, where his master comes; 'tis a playing-day,
I see. How now, Sir Hugh! no school to-day? 10
Evans. No; Master Slender is let the boys leave
to play.
Quick. Blessing of his heart!
Mrs. Page. Sir Hugh, my husband says my son
profits nothing in the world at his book. I 15
pray you, ask him some questions in his accidence.
Evans. Come hither, William; hold up your head;
come.
Mrs. Page. Come on, sirrah, hold up your head.
Answer your master; be not afraid.   20
Evans. William, how many numbers is in nouns?
Will. Two.
Quick. Truly, I thought there had been one num-
ber more, because they say, "'Od's nouns."   25
Evans. Peace your tattlings! What is "fair,"
William?
Will. Pulcher.
Quick. Polecats! There are fairer things than
polecats, sure.   30
Evans. You are a very simplicity 'oman. I
pray you, peace. What is *lapis*, William?
Will. A stone.
Evans. And what is "a stone," William?
Will. A pebble.   35
Evans. No, it is *lapis*. I pray you, remember
in your prain.
Will. Lapis.
Evans. That is a good William. What is he,
William, that does lend articles?   40
Will. Articles are borrowed of the pronoun, and
be thus declined, *Singulariter, nominativo, hic, hæc,
hoc.*
Evans. Nominativo, hig, hag, hog; pray you,
mark; *genitivo, hujus.* Well, what is your accusa-
tive case?   46
Will. Accusativo, hinc.
Evans. I pray you, have your remembrance,
child. *Accusativo, hing, hang, hog.*
Quick. "Hang-hog" is Latin for bacon, I war-
rant you.   51
Evans. Leave your prabbles, 'oman. What is
the focative case, William?
Will. O, — vocativo, O.
Evans. Remember, William; focative is *caret*. 55
Quick. And that's a good root.
Evans. 'Oman, forbear.

Mrs. Page. Peace!
Evans. What is your **genitive case plural**, Wil-
liam?   60
Will. Genitive case?
Evans. Ay.
Will. Genitive, *horum, harum, horum.*
Quick. Vengeance of Jenny's case! Fie on her!
Never name her, child, if she be a whore.   65
Evans. For shame, 'oman.
Quick. You do ill to teach the child such words.
He teaches him to hick and to hack, which they'll
do fast enough of themselves, and to call "horum,"
— fie upon you!   70
Evans. 'Oman, art thou lunatics? Hast thou
no understandings for thy cases and the numbers
of the genders? Thou art as foolish Christian crea-
tures as I would desires.
Mrs. Page. Prithee, hold thy peace.   75
Evans. Show me now, William, some declensions
of your pronouns.
Will. Forsooth, I have forgot.
Evans. It is *qui, quæ, quod*: if you forget your
quies, your *quæs*, and your *quods*, you must be 80
preeches. Go your ways and play; go.
Mrs. Page. He is a better scholar than I thought
he was.
Evans. He is a good sprag memory. Farewell,
Mistress Page.   85
Mrs. Page. Adieu, good Sir Hugh. [*Exit Sir
Hugh.*] Get you home, boy. Come, we stay too
long.   [*Exeunt.*

SCENE II. [*A room in Ford's house.*]

Enter FALSTAFF *and* MISTRESS FORD.

Fal. Mistress Ford, your sorrow hath eaten up
my sufferance. I see you are obsequious in your
love, and I profess requital to a hair's breadth; not
only, Mistress Ford, in the simple office of love,
but in all the accoutrement, complement, and 5
ceremony of it. But are you sure of your husband
now?
Mrs. Ford. He's a-birding, sweet Sir John.
Mrs. Page. [*Within.*] What, ho, gossip Ford!
What, ho!   10
Mrs. Ford. Step into th' chamber, Sir John.
                                       [*Exit Falstaff.*]

[*Enter* MISTRESS PAGE.]

Mrs. Page. How now, sweetheart! who's at home
besides yourself?
Mrs. Ford. Why, none but mine own people.
Mrs. Page. Indeed!   15

Act IV, sc. i, 6. **suddenly:** at once. 7. **by and by:** presently. 25. **'Od's nouns:** corruption of "God's wounds." 81.
preeches: i.e., breeched, flogged. 84. **sprag:** i.e., sprack, alert.
Sc. ii, 2. **sufferance:** suffering. **obsequious:** devoted. 9. **gossip:** friend.

Mrs. Ford. No, certainly. [*Aside to her.*] Speak louder.

Mrs. Page. Truly, I am so glad you have nobody here.

Mrs. Ford. Why?   20

Mrs. Page. Why, woman, your husband is in his old lines again. He so takes on yonder with my husband; so rails against all married mankind; so curses all Eve's daughters, of what complexion soever; and so buffets himself on the forehead,   25 crying, "Peer out, peer out!" that any madness I ever yet beheld seemed but tameness, civility, and patience, to this his distemper he is in now. I am glad the fat knight is not here.

Mrs. Ford. Why, does he talk of him?   30

Mrs. Page. Of none but him; and swears he was carried out, the last time he search'd for him, in a basket; protests to my husband he is now here, and hath drawn him and the rest of their company from their sport, to make another experiment of his   35 suspicion. But I am glad the knight is not here. Now he shall see his own foolery.

Mrs. Ford. How near is he, Mistress Page?

Mrs. Page. Hard by; at street end. He will be here anon.   41

Mrs. Ford. I am undone! The knight is here.

Mrs. Page. Why then you are utterly sham'd, and he's but a dead man. What a woman are you! — Away with him, away with him! Better shame than murder.   46

Mrs. Ford. Which way should he go? How should I bestow him? Shall I put him into the basket again?

[*Re-enter* FALSTAFF.]

Fal. No, I'll come no more i' the basket. May I not go out ere he come?   51

Mrs. Page. Alas, three of Master Ford's brothers watch the door with pistols, that none shall issue out; otherwise you might slip away ere he came. But what make you here?   55

Fal. What shall I do? I'll creep up into the chimney.

Mrs. Ford. There they always use to discharge their birding-pieces.

[*Mrs. Page.*] Creep into the kiln-hole.

Fal. Where is it?   60

Mrs. Ford. He will seek there, on my word. Neither press, coffer, chest, trunk, well, vault, but he hath an abstract for the remembrance of such places, and goes to them by his note. There is no hiding you in the house.   65

Fal. I'll go out then.

[*Mrs. Page.*] If you go out in your own semblance, you die, Sir John. Unless you go out disguis'd —

Mrs. Ford. How might we disguise him?   70

Mrs. Page. Alas the day, I know not! There is no woman's gown big enough for him; otherwise he might put on a hat, a muffler, and a kerchief, and so escape.

Fal. Good hearts, devise something. Any extremity rather than a mischief.   76

Mrs. Ford. My maid's aunt, the fat woman of Brainford, has a gown above.

Mrs. Page. On my word, it will serve him. She's as big as he is; and there's her thrumm'd hat   80 and her muffler too. Run up, Sir John.

Mrs. Ford. Go, go, sweet Sir John. Mistress Page and I will look some linen for your head.

Mrs. Page. Quick, quick! we'll come dress you straight. Put on the gown the while.   85

[*Exit Falstaff.*]

Mrs. Ford. I would my husband would meet him in this shape. He cannot abide the old woman of Brainford. He swears she's a witch; forbade her my house, and hath threat'ned to beat her.   89

Mrs. Page. Heaven guide him to thy husband's cudgel, and the devil guide his cudgel afterwards!

Mrs. Ford. But is my husband coming?

Mrs. Page. Ay, in good sadness, is he; and talks of the basket too, howsoever he hath had intelligence.   95

Mrs. Ford. We'll try that; for I'll appoint my men to carry the basket again, to meet him at the door with it, as they did last time.

Mrs. Page. Nay, but he'll be here presently. Let's go dress him like the witch of Brainford.   100

Mrs. Ford. I'll first direct my men what they shall do with the basket. Go up; I'll bring linen for him straight.   [*Exit.*]

Mrs. Page. Hang him, dishonest varlet! We cannot misuse him enough.   105
We'll leave a proof, by that which we will do,
Wives may be merry, and yet honest too.
We do not act that often jest and laugh;
'Tis old, but true: Still swine eats all the draff.
[*Exit.*]

[*Re-enter* MISTRESS FORD *with two* SERVANTS.]

Mrs. Ford. Go, sirs, take the basket again on   110 your shoulders. Your master is hard at door. If he bid you set it down, obey him. Quickly, dispatch.   [*Exit.*]

1. Serv. Come, come, take it up.

---

22. **lines** F. Q. reads *vaine*, i.e., *vein*, with the same meaning.   24. **complexion**: sort.   59. [*Mrs. Page*] (Malone conj.). F gives this sentence to Mrs. Ford, but the opening of Mrs. Ford's next speech shows F to be wrong.   63. **abstract**: list. 67. [*Mrs. Page*] (Malone) *Mist. Ford* F.   77–78. **woman of Brainford.** Q names her "Gillian." The "witch of Brainford" (Brentford) was an actual personage who kept a tavern.   80. **thrumm'd**: fringed. Thrums are the loose ends of the weaver's warp.   104. **dishonest**: unchaste.   109. **Still**: quiet. **draff**: swill.

2. Serv. Pray heaven it be not full of knight again.   116

1. Serv. I hope not; I had as lief bear so much lead.

Enter FORD, PAGE, SHALLOW, [CAIUS,] *and* SIR HUGH EVANS.

Ford. Ay, but if it prove true, Master Page, have you any way then to unfool me again?   Set   120 down the basket, villain!   Somebody call my wife. Youth in a basket!   O you panderly rascals! there's a knot, a [ging], a pack, a conspiracy against me.   Now shall the devil be sham'd.   What, wife, I say!   Come, come forth!   Behold what honest clothes you send forth to bleaching!   126

Page. Why, this passes, Master Ford.   You are not to go loose any longer; you must be pinion'd.

Evans. Why, this is lunatics!   This is mad as a mad dog!   131

Shal. Indeed, Master Ford, this is not well, indeed.

Ford. So say I too, sir.

[*Re-enter* MISTRESS FORD.]

Come hither, Mistress Ford; Mistress Ford,   135 the honest woman, the modest wife, the virtuous creature, that hath the jealous fool to her husband! I suspect without cause, mistress, do I?

Mrs. Ford. Heaven be my witness you do, if you suspect me in any dishonesty.   140

Ford. Well said, brazen-face! hold it out.   Come forth, sirrah!   [*Pulling clothes out of the basket.*]

Page. This passes!

Mrs. Ford. Are you not asham'd?   Let the clothes alone.   145

Ford. I shall find you anon.

Evans. 'Tis unreasonable!   Will you take up your wife's clothes?   Come away.

Ford. Empty the basket, I say!

Mrs. Ford. Why, man, why?   150

Ford. Master Page, as I am a man, there was one convey'd out of my house yesterday in this basket.   Why may not he be there again?   In my house I am sure he is.   My intelligence is true; my jealousy is reasonable.   Pluck me out all the linen.   156

Mrs. Ford. If you find a man there, he shall die a flea's death.

Page. Here's no man.

Shal. By my fidelity, this is not well, Master Ford; this wrongs you.   161

Evans. Master Ford, you must pray, and not follow the imaginations of your own heart.   This is jealousies.

Ford. Well, he's not here I seek for.   165

Page. No, nor nowhere else but in your brain.

Ford. Help to search my house this one time. If I find not what I seek, show no colour for my extremity, let me forever be your table-sport.   Let them say of me, "As jealous as Ford, that   170 search'd a hollow walnut for his wife's leman." Satisfy me once more; once more search with me.

Mrs. Ford. What, ho, Mistress Page! come you and the old woman down; my husband will come into the chamber.   176

Ford. Old woman!   What old woman's that?

Mrs. Ford. Why, it is my maid's aunt of Brainford.   179

Ford. A witch, a quean, an old cozening quean! Have I not forbid her my house?   She comes of errands, does she?   We are simple men; we do not know what's brought to pass under the profession of fortune-telling.   She works by charms, by spells, by th' figure; and such daub'ry as this is is be- 185 yond our element; we know nothing.   Come down, you witch, you hag, you; come down, I say!

Mrs. Ford. Nay, good, sweet husband!   Good gentlemen, let him [not] strike the old woman.   190

Re-enter FALSTAFF *disguised like an old woman, and* MISTRESS PAGE *with him.*

Mrs. Page. Come, Mother Prat; come, give me your hand.

Ford. I'll prat her.   Out of my door, you witch, you [hag], you baggage, you polecat, you ronyon! out, out!   I'll conjure you, I'll fortune-tell you!   195
        [*Ford beats him, and he runs away.*

Mrs. Page. Are you not asham'd?   I think you have kill'd the poor woman.

Mrs. Ford. Nay, he will do it.   'Tis a goodly credit for you.   200

Ford. Hang her, witch!

Evans. By [Jeshu], I think the 'oman is a witch indeed.   I like not when a 'oman has a great peard. I spy a great peard under his muffler.   205

Ford. Will you follow, gentlemen?   I beseech you, follow; see but the issue of my jealousy.   If I cry out thus upon no trail, never trust me when I open again.

Page. Let's obey his humour a little further. Come, gentlemen.   211
        [*Exeunt* [*Ford, Page, Shal., Caius, and Evans*].

Mrs. Page. Trust me, he beat him most pitifully.

Mrs. Ford. Nay, by th' mass, that he did not; he beat him most unpitifully, methought. 215

Mrs. Page. I'll have the cudgel hallow'd and hung o'er the altar. It hath done meritorious service.

Mrs. Ford. What think you? May we, with the warrant of womanhood and the witness of a 220 good conscience, pursue him with any further revenge?

Mrs. Page. The spirit of wantonness is, sure, scar'd out of him. If the devil have him not in fee-simple, with fine and recovery, he will never, I think, in the way of waste, attempt us again. 227

Mrs. Ford. Shall we tell our husbands how we have serv'd him? 229

Mrs. Page. Yes, by all means; if it be but to scrape the figures out of your husband's brains. If they can find in their hearts the poor unvirtuous fat knight shall be any further afflicted, we two will still be the ministers. 234

Mrs. Ford. I'll warrant they'll have him publicly sham'd; and methinks there would be no period to the jest, should he not be publicly sham'd.

Mrs. Page. Come, to the forge with it then; shape it. I would not have things cool. [*Exeunt.* 240

SCENE III. [*A room in the Garter Inn.*]

Enter HOST *and* BARDOLPH.

Bard. Sir, the [Germans desire] to have three of your horses. The Duke himself will be tomorrow at court, and they are going to meet him. 4

Host. What duke should that be comes so secretly? I hear not of him in the court. Let me speak with the gentlemen. They speak English?

Bard. Ay, sir; I'll call [them] to you. 9

Host. They shall have my horses; but I'll make them pay, I'll sauce them. They have had my houses a week at command. I have turn'd away my other guests. They must come off; I'll sauce them. Come. [*Exeunt.*

SCENE IV. [*A room in Ford's house.*]

Enter PAGE, FORD, MISTRESS PAGE, MISTRESS FORD, *and* SIR HUGH EVANS.

Evans. 'Tis one of the best discretions of a 'oman as ever I did look upon.

Page. And did he send you both these letters at an instant?

Mrs. Page. Within a quarter of an hour. 5

Ford. Pardon me, wife. Henceforth do what thou wilt.
I rather will suspect the sun with cold
Than thee with wantonness. Now doth thy honour stand,
In him that was of late an heretic,
As firm as faith.

Page. 'Tis well, 'tis well; no more. 10
Be not as extreme in submission
As in offence.
But let our plot go forward. Let our wives
Yet once again, to make us public sport,
Appoint a meeting with this old fat fellow, 15
Where we may take him and disgrace him for it.

Ford. There is no better way than that they spoke of.

Page. How? To send him word they'll meet him in the park at midnight? Fie, fie! he'll never come. 20

Evans. You say he has been thrown in the rivers and has been grievously peaten as an old 'oman. Methinks there should be terrors in him that he should not come; methinks his flesh is punish'd; he shall have no desires.

Page. So think I too. 25

Mrs. Ford. Devise but how you'll use him when he comes,
And let us two devise to bring him thither.

Mrs. Page. There is an old tale goes that Herne the hunter,
Sometime a keeper here in Windsor forest,
Doth all the winter-time, at still midnight, 30
Walk round about an oak, with great ragg'd horns;
And there he blasts the tree, and takes the cattle,
And makes milch-kine yield blood, and shakes a chain
In a most hideous and dreadful manner.
You have heard of such a spirit, and well you know
The superstitious idle-headed eld 36
Receiv'd and did deliver to our age
This tale of Herne the hunter for a truth.

Page. Why, yet there want not many that do fear
In deep of night to walk by this Herne's oak. 40
But what of this?

Mrs. Ford. Marry, this is our device;
That Falstaff at that oak shall meet with us
[Disguis'd like Herne, with huge horns on his head].

Page. Well, let it not be doubted but he'll come;
And in this shape when you have brought him thither, 44
What shall be done with him? What is your plot?

225. **fee-simple:** absolute possession (legal term). **fine and recovery:** the legal process by which a title in fee simple was established. 231. **figures:** fancies. 234. **ministers:** agents.

Sc. iii, 1. [Germans desire] (Capell). *Germane desires* F. 9. [them] Q. *him* F. 12. **at command:** reserved. 13. **come off:** pay up.

Sc. iv, 1. **best discretions:** most discreet. 32. **takes:** bewitches. 36. **eld:** folk of olden time. 43. [Disguis'd...head] Q. Om. F.

Mrs. Page. That likewise have we thought upon,
and thus:
Nan Page (my daughter) and my little son
And three or four more of their growth we'll dress
Like urchins, ouphes, and fairies, green and white,
With rounds of waxen tapers on their heads,   50
And rattles in their hands. Upon a sudden,
As Falstaff, she, and I are newly met,
Let them from forth a sawpit rush at once
With some diffused song. Upon their sight,
We two in great amazedness will fly.   55
Then let them all encircle him about
And, fairy-like, to pinch the unclean knight,
And ask him why, that hour of fairy revel,
In their so sacred paths he dares to tread
    shape profane.
    [*Mrs.*] *Ford.*   And till he tell the truth,   60
Let the supposed fairies pinch him sound
And burn him with their tapers.
    Mrs. Page.   The truth being known,
We'll all present ourselves, dis-horn the spirit,
And mock him home to Windsor.
    Ford.   The children must
Be practis'd well to this, or they'll ne'er do't.   65
    Evans. I will teach the children their behaviours;
and I will be like a jack-an-apes also, to burn the
knight with my taber.
    Ford. That will be excellent. I'll go and buy
them vizards.   70
    Mrs. Page. My Nan shall be the queen of all the
fairies,
Finely attired in a robe of white.
    Page. That silk will I go buy. [*Aside.*] And in
that time
Shall Master Slender steal my Nan away
And marry her at Eton. Go send to Falstaff
straight.   75
    Ford. Nay, I'll to him again in name of Brook.
He'll tell me all his purpose. Sure, he'll come.
    Mrs. Page. Fear not you that. Go get us prop-
erties
And tricking for our fairies.
    Evans. Let us about it. It is admirable pleasures
and fery honest knaveries.   81
        [*Exeunt Page, Ford, and Evans.*]
    Mrs. Page. Go, Mistress Ford,
Send [Quickly] to Sir John, to know his mind.
        [*Exit Mrs. Ford.*]
I'll to the doctor; he hath my good will,
And none but he, to marry with Nan Page.   85
That Slender, though well landed, is an idiot,

And he my husband best of all affects.
The doctor is well money'd, and his friends
Potent at court. He, none but he, shall have her,
Though twenty thousand worthier come to crave
    her.   [*Exit.*]   90

SCENE V. [*A room in the Garter Inn.*]

Enter HOST *and* SIMPLE.

    Host. What wouldst thou have, boor? What,
thick-skin? Speak, breathe, discuss; brief, short,
quick, snap.
    Sim. Marry, sir, I come to speak with Sir John
Falstaff from Master Slender.   5
    Host. There's his chamber, his house, his castle,
his standing-bed and truckle-bed; 'tis painted
about with the story of the Prodigal, fresh and new.
Go knock and call; he'll speak like an Anthropo-
phaginian unto thee. Knock, I say.   11
    Sim. There's an old woman, a fat woman, gone
up into his chamber. I'll be so bold as stay, sir,
till she come down. I come to speak with her,
indeed.   15
    Host. Ha! a fat woman? The knight may be
robb'd. I'll call. Bully knight! bully Sir John!
speak from thy lungs military. Art thou there?
It is thine host, thine Ephesian, calls.
    Fal. [*Above.*] How now, mine host?   20
    Host. Here's a Bohemian-Tartar tarries the com-
ing down of thy fat woman. Let her descend,
bully, let her descend; my chambers are honourable.
Fie! privacy? fie!

Enter FALSTAFF.

    Fal. There was, mine host, an old fat woman
even now with me; but she's gone.   26
    Sim. Pray you, sir, was't not the wise woman of
Brainford?
    Fal. Ay, marry, was it, mussel-shell. What
would you with her?   30
    Sim. My master, sir, my Master Slender, sent
to her, seeing her go thorough the streets, to know,
sir, whether one Nym, sir, that beguil'd him of a
chain, had the chain or no.
    Fal. I spake with the old woman about it.   35
    Sim. And what says she, I pray, sir?
    Fal. Marry, she says that the very same man
that beguil'd Master Slender of his chain cozen'd
him of it.   39
    Sim. I would I could have spoken with the

---

49. urchins: goblins (originally hedgehogs). ouphes: elves. 54. diffused: wild, disorderly. 60. [Mrs.] (Rowe). Om. F.
67. jack-an-apes. Correctly a monkey; but actually Evans appears later as a Satyr (see V.iv.1 S.D. and V.v.40 S.D.).
70. vizards: masks. 71-72. My...white. Prose in F. 73. time F. signe Q. Theobald emends to *tire* (attire).
79. tricking: adornment. 83. [Quickly] (Theobald). *quickly* F.
    Sc. v, 7. truckle-bed F. *trundle bed* Q. 10. Anthropophaginian: cannibal. 19. Ephesian: bully companion. 21.
Bohemian-Tartar: i.e., wild fellow. 29. mussel-shell: i.e., empty fellow, simpleton.

woman herself. I had other things to have spoken with her too from him.

Fal. What are they? Let us know.

Host. Ay, come; quick.

[*Sim.*] I may not conceal them, sir.   45

Host. Conceal them, or thou diest.

Sim. Why, sir, they were nothing but about Mistress Anne Page; to know if it were my master's fortune to have her or no.

Fal. 'Tis, 'tis his fortune.   50

Sim. What, sir?

Fal. To have her, or no. Go; say the woman told me so.

Sim. May I be bold to say so, sir?

Fal. Ay, sir; like who more bold?   55

Sim. I thank your worship. I shall make my master glad with these tidings.   [*Exit.*]

Host. Thou art clerkly, thou art clerkly, Sir John. Was there a wise woman with thee?   59

Fal. Ay, that there was, mine host; one that hath taught me more wit than ever I learn'd before in my life; and I paid nothing for it neither, but was paid for my learning.

Enter BARDOLPH.

Bard. Out, alas, sir! cozenage, mere cozenage.

Host. Where be my horses? Speak well of them, varletto.   66

Bard. Run away with the cozeners; for so soon as I came beyond Eton, they threw me off from behind one of them, in a slough of mire; and set spurs and away, like three German devils, three Doctor Faustuses.   71

Host. They are gone but to meet the Duke, villain; do not say they be fled. Germans are honest men.

Enter SIR HUGH EVANS.

Evans. Where is mine host?   75

Host. What is the matter, sir?

Evans. Have a care of your entertainments. There is a friend of mine come to town, tells me there is three cozen-germans that has cozen'd all the hosts of Readins, of Maidenhead, of Cole-   80 brook, of horses and money. I tell you for good will, look you. You are wise and full of gibes and vlouting-stocks, and 'tis not convenient you should be cozened. Fare you well.   [*Exit.*]

Enter DOCTOR CAIUS.

Caius. Vere is mine host de Jarteer?   85

Host. Here, Master Doctor, in perplexity and doubtful dilemma.

Caius. I cannot tell vat is dat; but it is tell-a me dat you make grand preparation for a duke de Jamany. By my trot, dere is no duke that de court is know to come. I tell you for good will; adieu.   [*Exit.*]   91

Host. Hue and cry, villain, go! Assist me, knight. I am undone! Fly, run, hue and cry, villain! I am undone!   [*Exeunt Host [and Bard.*]

Fal. I would all the world might be cozen'd;   95 for I have been cozen'd and beaten too. If it should come to the ear of the court, how I have been transformed and how my transformation hath been wash'd and cudgell'd, they would melt me out of my fat drop by drop, and liquor fishermen's   100 boots with me. I warrant they would whip me with their fine wits till I were as crestfall'n as a dri'd pear. I never prosper'd since I forswore myself at primero. Well, if my wind were but long enough [to say my prayers,] I would repent.   105

Enter MISTRESS QUICKLY.

Now, whence come you?

Quick. From the two parties, forsooth.

Fal. The devil take one party and his dam the other! and so they shall be both bestowed. I have suffer'd more for their sakes, more than the   110 villanous inconstancy of man's disposition is able to bear.

Quick. And have not they suffer'd? Yes, I warrant; speciously one of them. Mistress Ford, good heart, is beaten black and blue, that you cannot see a white spot about her.   116

Fal. What tellest thou me of black and blue? I was beaten myself into all the colours of the rainbow; and I was like to be apprehended for the witch of Brainford. But that my admirable   120 dexterity of wit, my counterfeiting the action of an old woman, deliver'd me, the knave constable had set me i' th' stocks, i' th' common stocks, for a witch.   124

Quick. Sir, let me speak with you in your chamber. You shall hear how things go, and, I warrant, to your content. Here is a letter will say somewhat. Good hearts, what ado here is to bring you together! Sure, one of you does not serve heaven well, that you are so cross'd.   130

Fal. Come up into my chamber.   [*Exeunt.*

SCENE VI. [*Another room in the Garter Inn.*]

Enter FENTON *and* HOST.

Host. Master Fenton, talk not to me; my mind is heavy. I will give over all.

---

45. [*Sim.*] (Rowe). *Fals.* F. 55. **like ... bold:** i.e., as bold as anybody. 58. **clerkly:** smart (properly "scholarly"). 64. **mere:** pure. 66. **varletto:** rascal. 79–81. **three ... money.** Q reads "three sorts of cosen garmombles, is cosen all the Host of Maidenhead and Readings." See Introduction. 104. **primero:** a card game. 105. **[to say my prayers]** Q. Om. F. 130. **cross'd:** thwarted.

Fent. Yet hear me speak.   Assist me in my pur-
          pose,
And, as I am a gentleman, I'll give thee
A hundred pound in gold more than your loss.   5
   Host. I will hear you, Master Fenton; and I will
at the least keep your counsel.
   Fent. From time to time I have acquainted you
With the dear love I bear to fair Anne Page;
Who mutually hath answer'd my affection,   10
So far forth as herself might be her chooser,
Even to my wish.   I have a letter from her
Of such contents as you will wonder at;
The mirth whereof so larded with my matter,
That neither singly can be manifested,   15
Without the show of both.   Fat Falstaff
Hath a great scene.   The image of the jest
I'll show you here at large.   Hark, good mine host.
To-night at Herne's oak, just 'twixt twelve and
          one,
Must my sweet Nan present the Fairy Queen;   20
The purpose why, is here; in which disguise,
While other jests are something rank on foot,
Her father hath commanded her to slip
Away with Slender and with him at Eton
Immediately to marry.   She hath consented.   25
Now, sir,
Her mother, ever strong against that match
And firm for Doctor Caius, hath appointed
That he shall likewise shuffle her away
While other sports are tasking of their minds,   30
And at the deanery, where a priest attends,
Straight marry her.   To this her mother's plot
She seemingly obedient likewise hath
Made promise to the doctor.   Now, thus it rests:
Her father means she shall be all in white,   35
And in that habit, when Slender sees his time
To take her by the hand and bid her go,
She shall go with him.   Her mother hath intended,
The better to denote her to the doctor,
For they must all be mask'd and vizarded,   40
That quaint in green she shall be loose enrob'd,
With ribands pendent, flaring 'bout her head;
And when the doctor spies his vantage ripe,
To pinch her by the hand, and, on that token,
The maid hath given consent to go with him.   45
   Host. Which means she to deceive, father or
          mother?
   Fent. Both, my good host, to go along with me.
And here it rests, that you'll procure the vicar
To stay for me at church 'twixt twelve and one,
And, in the lawful name of marrying,   50
To give our hearts united ceremony.
   Host. Well, husband your device; I'll to the vicar.
Bring you the maid, you shall not lack a priest.

   Fent. So shall I evermore be bound to thee;
Besides, I'll make a present recompense.   55
                                              [*Exeunt.*

ACT V

SCENE I.   [*A room in the Garter Inn.*]

Enter FALSTAFF *and* MISTRESS QUICKLY.

   Fal. Prithee, no more prattling; go.   I'll hold.
This is the third time; I hope good luck lies in odd
numbers.   Away! go.   They say there is divinity
in odd numbers, either in nativity, chance, or
death.   Away!   5
   Quick. I'll provide you a chain; and I'll do what
I can to get you a pair of horns.
   Fal. Away, I say; time wears.   Hold up your
head, and mince.   [*Exit Mrs. Quickly.*]

[*Enter* FORD, *disguised.*]

How now, Master Brook!   Master Brook, the   10
matter will be known to-night, or never.   Be you
in the park about midnight, at Herne's oak, and
you shall see wonders.
   Ford. Went you not to her yesterday, sir, as you
told me you had appointed?   15
   Fal. I went to her, Master Brook, as you see, like
a poor old man; but I came from her, Master Brook,
like a poor old woman.   That same knave Ford,
her husband, hath the finest mad devil of jealousy
in him, Master Brook, that ever govern'd   20
frenzy.   I will tell you.   He beat me grievously,
in the shape of a woman; for in the shape of man,
Master Brook, I fear not Goliath with a weaver's
beam; because I know also life is a shuttle.   I am in
haste; go along with me.   I'll tell you all, Master   25
Brook.   Since I pluck'd geese, play'd truant and
whipp'd top, I knew not what 'twas to be beaten
till lately.   Follow me.   I'll tell you strange things
of this knave Ford, on whom tonight I will be revenged, and I will deliver his wife into your   30
hand.   Follow.   Strange things in hand, Master
Brook!   Follow.

                                              [*Exeunt.*

SCENE II.   [*Windsor Park.*]

Enter PAGE, SHALLOW, *and* SLENDER.

   Page. Come, come; we'll couch i' th' castle-
ditch till we see the light of our fairies.   Remember,
son Slender, my daughter.
   Slen. Ay, forsooth; I have spoke with her and
we have a nay-word how to know one another.   5

Sc. vi, 14. **larded:** mingled.   22. **rank:** exuberantly.   41. **quaint:** elegantly.
   Act V, sc. i, 1. **hold:** i.e., keep the appointment.   9. **mince:** trip away.   23. **Goliath . . . beam.**   See 2 *Sam.* xxi.19
24. **life . . . shuttle.**   See *Job* vii.6.

I come to her in white, and cry "mum"; she cries "budget"; and by that we know one another.

Shal. That's good too; but what needs either your "mum" or her "budget"? The white will decipher her well enough. It hath struck ten o'clock.   10

Page. The night is dark; light and spirits will become it well. Heaven prosper our sport! No man means evil but the devil, and we shall know him by his horns. Let's away; follow me.   16

[*Exeunt.*

SCENE III. [*A street leading to the Park.*]

Enter MISTRESS PAGE, MISTRESS FORD, *and* DOCTOR CAIUS.

Mrs. Page. Master Doctor, my daughter is in green. When you see your time, take her by the hand, away with her to the deanery, and dispatch it quickly. Go before into the park; we two must go together.   5

Caius. I know vat I have to do. Adieu.

Mrs. Page. Fare you well, sir. [*Exit Caius.*] My husband will not rejoice so much at the abuse of Falstaff as he will chafe at the doctor's marrying my daughter. But 'tis no matter; better a little chiding than a great deal of heart-break.   11

Mrs. Ford. Where is Nan now and her troop of fairies, and the Welsh devil [Hugh]?

Mrs. Page. They are all couch'd in a pit hard by Herne's oak, with obscur'd lights; which, at the very instant of Falstaff's and our meeting, they will at once display to the night.   15

Mrs. Ford. That cannot choose but amaze him.

Mrs. Page. If he be not amaz'd, he will be mock'd; if he be amaz'd, he will every way be mock'd.   21

Mrs. Ford. We'll betray him finely.

Mrs. Page. Against such lewdsters and their lechery
Those that betray them do no treachery.

Mrs. Ford. The hour draws on. To the oak, to the oak!   [*Exeunt.* 26

SCENE IV. [*Windsor Park.*]

Enter SIR HUGH EVANS [*disguised*], *and* [*others as*] *Fairies.*

Evans. Trib, trib, fairies; come; and remember your parts. Be pold, I pray you. Follow me into the pit, and when I give the watch-'ords, do as I pid you. Come, come; trib, trib.   [*Exeunt.*

SCENE V. [*Another part of the Park.*]

Enter FALSTAFF *with a buck's head upon him.*

Fal. The Windsor bell hath struck twelve; the minute draws on. Now, the hot-blooded gods assist me! Remember, Jove, thou wast a bull for thy Europa; love set on thy horns. O powerful love! that, in some respects, makes a beast a   5 man, in some other, a man a beast. You were also, Jupiter, a swan for the love of Leda. O omnipotent Love! how near the god drew to the complexion of a goose! A fault done first in the form of a beast. O Jove, a beastly fault! And then another fault   10 in the semblance of a fowl; think on 't, Jove; a foul fault! When gods have hot backs, what shall poor men do? For me, I am here a Windsor stag; and the fattest, I think, i' th' forest. Send me a cool rut-time, Jove, or who can blame me to piss my tallow? Who comes here? My doe?   16

Enter MISTRESS FORD *and* MISTRESS PAGE.

Mrs. Ford. Sir John! art thou there, my deer? my male deer?   19

Fal. My doe with the black scut! Let the sky rain potatoes; let it thunder to the tune of "Green Sleeves," hail kissing-comfits, and snow eringoes; let there come a tempest of provocation. I will shelter me here.   24

Mrs. Ford. Mistress Page is come with me, sweetheart.

Fal. Divide me like a brib'd buck, each a haunch. I will keep my sides to myself, my shoulders for the fellow of this walk, and my horns I bequeath your husbands. Am I a woodman, ha? Speak I   30 like Herne the hunter? Why, now is Cupid a child of conscience; he makes restitution. As I am a true spirit, welcome!   [*Noise within.*]

Mrs. Page. Alas, what noise?

Mrs. Ford. Heaven forgive our sins!   35

Fal. What should this be?

Mrs. Ford. }
Mrs. Page. } Away, away!   [*They run off.*]

Fal. I think the devil will not have me damn'd, lest the oil that's in me should set hell on fire; he would never else cross me thus.   40

Enter SIR HUGH EVANS, *like a Satyr, and boys dressed like Fairies* [PISTOL, *as* Hobgoblin]; MISTRESS QUICKLY, *like the Queen of Fairies; they sing a song about him and afterward speak.*

Quick. Fairies, black, grey, green, and white, You moonshine revellers, and shades of night,

Sc. ii, 6–7. "mum" ... "budget." To play "mumbudget" was to pretend to be tongue-tied.
Sc. iii, 13. [Hugh] (Capell).   *Herne* F.
Sc. v, 20. scut: tail.   21. potatoes. Regarded as provocative to love.   22. kissing-comfits: perfumed sugar plums (used by women for sweetening the breath).   eringoes: candied sea-holly.   27. brib'd: stolen.   29. fellow: gamekeeper. walk: forest.   41. The speech-headings in this scene may mean only that those lines were spoken by the actors who had played Pistol and Quickly earlier.

You orphan heirs of fixed destiny,
Attend your office and your quality.
Crier Hobgoblin, make the fairy oyes.   45
  Pist. Elves, list your names. Silence, you airy
    toys!
Cricket, to Windsor chimneys shalt thou leap;
Where fires thou find'st unrak'd and hearths un-
    swept,
There pinch the maids as blue as bilberry;
Our radiant queen hates sluts and sluttery.   50
  Fal. They are fairies; he that speaks to them shall
    die.
I'll wink and couch; no man their works must eye.
    [*Lies down upon his face.*]
  Evans. Where's Bead? Go you, and where you
    find a maid
That, ere she sleep, has thrice her prayers said,
Raise up the organs of her fantasy,   55
Sleep she as sound as careless infancy.
But those as sleep and think not on their sins,
Pinch them, arms, legs, backs, shoulders, sides, and
    shins.
  Quick. About, about;
Search Windsor Castle, elves, within and out.   60
Strew good luck, ouphes, on every sacred room,
That it may stand till the perpetual doom
In state as wholesome as in state 'tis fit,
Worthy the owner, and the owner it.
The several chairs of order look you scour   65
With juice of balm and every precious flow'r.
Each fair instalment, coat, and sev'ral crest,
With loyal blazon, evermore be blest!
And nightly, meadow-fairies, look you sing,
Like to the Garter's compass, in a ring.   70
Th' expressure that it bears, green let it be,
More fertile-fresh than all the field to see;
And "*Honi soit qui mal y pense*" write
In em'rald tufts, flow'rs purple, blue, and white;
Like sapphire, pearl, and rich embroidery,   75
Buckled below fair knighthood's bending knee.
Fairies use flow'rs for their charactery.
Away; disperse! but till 'tis one o'clock,
Our dance of custom round about the oak
Of Herne the hunter, let us not forget.   80
  Evans. Pray you, lock hand in hand; yourselves
    in order set;
And twenty glow-worms shall our lanterns be,
To guide our measure round about the tree.
But, stay; I smell a man of middle-earth.

  Fal. Heavens defend me from that Welsh   85
fairy, lest he transform me to a piece of cheese!
  Pist. Vile worm, thou wast o'erlook'd even in
    thy birth.
  Quick. With trial-fire touch me his finger-end.
If he be chaste, the flame will back descend
And turn him to no pain; but if he start,   90
It is the flesh of a corrupted heart.
  Pist. A trial, come.
  Evans.   Come, will this wood take fire?
    [*They put the tapers to his fingers, and he
    starts.*
  Fal. Oh, Oh, Oh!
  Quick. Corrupt, corrupt, and tainted in desire!
About him, fairies; sing a scornful rhyme;   95
And, as you trip, still pinch him to your time.

THE SONG.

Fie on sinful fantasy!
Fie on lust and luxury!
Lust is but a bloody fire,
Kindled with unchaste desire,   100
Fed in heart, whose flames aspire
As thoughts do blow them, higher and higher.
Pinch him, fairies, mutually!
Pinch him for his villany!
Pinch him, and burn him, and turn him about,   105
Till candles and starlight and moonshine be out.

Here they pinch FALSTAFF *and sing about him.*
DOCTOR CAIUS *comes one way, and steals away
a boy in green;* SLENDER *another way, and takes
a boy in white; and* FENTON *comes, and steals*
ANNE PAGE. *A noise of hunting is made within.
All the Fairies run away.* FALSTAFF *pulls off
his buck's head, and rises up.*

Enter PAGE, FORD, MISTRESS PAGE, MISTRESS
    FORD, *and* SHALLOW.

  Page. Nay, do not fly; I think we have watch'd
    you now.
Will none but Herne the hunter serve your turn?
  Mrs. Page. I pray you, come, hold up the jest no
    higher.   109
Now, good Sir John, how like you Windsor wives?
See you these, husband? Do not these fair yokes
Become the forest better than the town?
  Ford. Now, sir, who's a cuckold now? Master
Brook, Falstaff's a knave, a cuckoldly knave; here

---

    43. orphan. Perhaps alluding to the common notion that fairies were of spontaneous birth and thus without parentage.
44. office: duty.   **quality:** profession.   **45. oyes:** oyez (Fr. for *hear*), the crier's call; here roll-call.   **49. bilberry:** blue-
berry.   **52. wink:** shut (my) eyes.   **65. chairs of order.** The Royal Chapel of Windsor still has stalls for the Knights of
the Garter, each with the individual's proper insignia. There is a pun on *Garter* in the "compass" (circle) of l. 70. *Honi
soit qui mal y pense* (l. 73) is the motto of the Order.   **66. juice . . . flow'r.** This cleansing, similar to old wedding rites, was
to hallow the precincts.   **67. instalment:** stall.   **68. blazon:** armorial bearings.   **71. expressure:** imprint.   **77. charactery:**
writing.   **84. man . . . earth:** mortal.   **87. o'erlook'd:** bewitched.   **98. luxury:** lasciviousness.   **99. bloody fire:** fire in the
blood.   **111. yokes:** i.e., the antlers Falstaff has been wearing, which suggest an ox yoke and also the cuckold's horns, the
"yoke" with which Ford had earlier been obsessed. The F spelling *yoakes* suggests a pun on *oaks*.

are his horns, Master Brook; and, Master 115
Brook, he hath enjoyed nothing of Ford's but his
buck-basket, his cudgel, and twenty pounds of
money, which must be paid to Master Brook. His
horses are arrested for it, Master Brook.   119

Mrs. Ford. Sir John, we have had ill luck; we
could never meet. I will never take you for my
love again; but I will always count you my deer.

Fal. I do begin to perceive that I am made an
ass.   125

Ford. Ay, and an ox too; both the proofs are
extant.

Fal. And these are not fairies? I was three or
four times in the thought they were not fairies; and
yet the guiltiness of my mind, the sudden sur- 130
prise of my powers, drove the grossness of the foppery into a receiv'd belief, in despite of the teeth of
all rhyme and reason, that they were fairies. See
now how wit may be made a Jack-a-Lent, when 'tis
upon ill employment!   135

Evans. Sir John Falstaff, serve Got, and leave
your desires, and fairies will not pinse you.

Ford. Well said, fairy Hugh.

Evans. And leave your jealousies too, I pray
you.   140

Ford. I will never mistrust my wife again, till
thou art able to woo her in good English.

Fal. Have I laid my brain in the sun and dri'd
it, that it wants matter to prevent so gross o'er-
reaching as this? Am I ridden with a Welsh 145
goat too? Shall I have a coxcomb of frieze? 'Tis
time I were chok'd with a piece of toasted cheese.

Evans. Seese is not good to give putter; your
belly is all putter.   149

Fal. "Seese" and "putter"! Have I liv'd to
stand at the taunt of one that makes fritters of
English? This is enough to be the decay of lust
and late-walking through the realm.

Mrs. Page. Why, Sir John, do you think, though
we would have thrust virtue out of our hearts 155
by the head and shoulders, and have given ourselves
without scruple to hell, that ever the devil could
have made you our delight?

Ford. What, a hodge-pudding? A bag of flax?

Mrs. Page. A puff'd man?   160

Page. Old, cold, wither'd, and of intolerable
entrails?

Ford. And one that is as slanderous as Satan?

Page. And as poor as Job?

Ford. And as wicked as his wife?   165

Evans. And given to fornications, and to taverns,
and sack, and wine, and metheglins, and to drink-
ings, and swearings and starings, pribbles and
prabbles?   169

Fal. Well, I am your theme; you have the start
of me. I am dejected; I am not able to answer the
Welsh flannel. Ignorance itself is a plummet o'er
me. Use me as you will.

Ford. Marry, sir, we'll bring you to Windsor,
to one Master Brook that you have cozen'd of 175
money, to whom you should have been a pander.
Over and above that you have suffer'd, I think to
repay that money will be a biting affliction.

Page. Yet be cheerful, knight. Thou shalt eat
a posset to-night at my house; where I will de- 180
sire thee to laugh at my wife, that now laughs at
thee. Tell her Master Slender hath married her
daughter.

Mrs. Page. [*Aside.*] Doctors doubt that. If
Anne Page be my daughter, she is, by this, Doctor
Caius' wife.   186

Enter SLENDER.

Slen. Whoa, ho! ho, father Page!

Page. Son, how now! how now, son! have you
dispatch'd?   189

Slen. Dispatch'd! I'll make the best in Gloucestershire know on't. Would I were hang'd, la,
else!

Page. Of what, son?

Slen. I cam yonder at Eton to marry Mistress
Anne Page, and she's a great lubberly boy. 195
If it had not been i' th' church, I would have
swing'd him, or he should have swing'd me. If I
did not think it had been Anne Page, would I might
never stir! — and 'tis a postmaster's boy.   199

Page. Upon my life, then, you took the wrong.

Slen. What need you tell me that? I think so,
when I took a boy for a girl. If I had been married
to him, for all he was in woman's apparel, I would
not have had him.   205

Page. Why, this is your own folly. Did not I
tell you how you should know my daughter by her
garments?

Slen. I went to her in [white] and cried "mum,"
and she cri'd "budget," as Anne and I had ap- 210
pointed; and yet it was not Anne, but a postmaster's
boy.

Mrs. Page. Good George, be not angry. I knew
of your purpose; turn'd my daughter into [green];
and, indeed, she is now with the Doctor at the
dean'ry, and there married.   216

Enter CAIUS.

Caius. Vere is Mistress Page? By gar, I am
cozened. I ha' married oon garsoon, a boy; oon
pesant, by gar, a boy; it is not Anne Page. By
gar, I am cozened.   220

---

131. **foppery:** fooling, deceit.   146. **coxcomb:** fool's cap.   **frieze:** woolen cloth made in Wales.   159. **hodge-pudding:** large sausage with various ingredients.   167. **metheglins:** fermented drink, with honey and spices.   168. **starings:**
swaggerings.   171. **dejected:** humbled.   197. **swing'd:** beaten.   199. **postmaster:** master of post horses.   209. [white]
(Pope).   *green* F.   214, 221. [green] (Pope).   *white* F.

Mrs. Page. Why, did you take her in [green]?

Caius. Ay, by gar, and 'tis a boy. By gar, I'll raise all Windsor. [*Exit.*

Ford. This is strange. Who hath got the right Anne?   225

Page. My heart misgives me. Here comes Master Fenton.

Enter FENTON *and* ANNE PAGE.

How now, Master Fenton!

Anne. Pardon, good father! good my mother, pardon!

Page. Now, mistress, how chance you went not with Master Slender?   231

Mrs. Page. Why went you not with Master Doctor, maid?

Fent. You do amaze her. Hear the truth of it. You would have married her most shamefully, Where there was no proportion held in love.   235 The truth is, she and I, long since contracted, Are now so sure that nothing can dissolve us. The offence is holy that she hath committed; And this deceit loses the name of craft, Of disobedience, or unduteous title,   240

Since therein she doth evitate and shun A thousand irreligious cursed hours Which forced marriage would have brought upon her.

Ford. Stand not amaz'd; here is no remedy. In love the heavens themselves do guide the state; Money buys lands, and wives are sold by fate.   246

Fal. I am glad, though you have ta'en a special stand to strike at me, that your arrow hath glanc'd.

Page. Well, what remedy? Fenton, heaven give thee joy!   250 What cannot be eschew'd must be embrac'd.

Fal. When night-dogs run, all sorts of deer are chas'd.

Mrs. Page. Well, I will muse no further. Master Fenton, Heaven give you many, many merry days! Good husband, let us every one go home,   255 And laugh this sport o'er by a country fire; Sir John and all.

Ford.   Let it be so. Sir John, To Master Brook you yet shall hold your word, For he to-night shall lie with Mistress Ford.

[*Exeunt*

241. **evitate**: avoid.   248. **stand**: hunter's post for shooting.   253. **muse**: complain.

Twelfth Night; or, What You Will

UNDER THE DATE of February 2, 1601/2, John Manningham, a student at the Middle Temple, wrote in his Diary: "At our feast wee had a play called Twelve Night, or What You Will, much like the Commedy of Errores, or Menechmi in Plautus, but most like and neere to that in Italian called *Inganni*." No one has doubted that the play he witnessed was Shakespeare's, and his record fixes a later limit for the date of composition. An earlier limit cannot be precisely established, but a variety of evidence suggests that the play was still fairly new. There is nothing to indicate either that Manningham was witnessing a first performance or that the play was written for production on Twelfth Night, that is Epiphany, the sixth of January just preceding, though the latter notion has a natural plausibility. The play is, however, despite obvious differences, akin to *As You Like It*, and the part of Feste, unquestionably written for Armin, the comic actor who succeeded Kemp in Shakespeare's company early in 1600, has affinity with that of Touchstone. Of the topical references within the play which have been stressed two may be noted, though they are debatable. The reference to "a pension of thousands to be paid from the Sophy" (II.v.197) may glance at Sir Robert Shirley, who in 1599 returned from a visit to the Shah of Persia laden with gifts of which he is said to have been boastful. Shirley's exploit received considerable publicity, and the likelihood of a topical reference here gains support from another allusion to the Sophy in III.iv.306. The "new map with the augmentation of the Indies" (III.ii.84) is almost certainly that published in England about 1599, giving a larger place to the Indies than any of its predecessors had done. It is barely possible that the name of Orsino was inspired by the visit of Orsino, Duke of Bracciano, to the English Court in 1600. All the available evidence confirms 1601, the generally accepted date, as the true one.

The printing of *Twelfth Night* in the Folio of 1623 was the first, and upon this the present text is based.

The problem of the source of the main plot becomes a study in the transmission of a story. Manningham noted the resemblance of the motivating idea of mistaken identity to that in *The Comedy of Errors* and its source in Plautus, and pointed to a nearer relation in an Italian play called *Inganni* (Cheats). Actually there were two Italian plays of that name, one by Nicolo Secchi (first acted in 1547 at Milan and printed at Florence in 1562) and another by Curzio Gonzaga (printed at Venice in 1592). In the latter the disguised sister takes the name of Cesare, which is provokingly like Viola's assumed name, Cesario. Aside from that fact neither of these plays has any importance, since neither contains the central situation of Olivia's love for Cesario. But a third Italian play, *Gl'Ingannati* (The Cheated), produced at Siena in 1531, does contain the substance of the plot of *Twelfth Night*, and may very likely have been the play which Manningham believed he was citing. *Gl'Ingannati* had a germinal influence, being widely translated and adapted. It was prepared for the French stage in 1549 and for the Spanish in 1556, and a version in Latin was acted at Queen's College, Cambridge, in 1590 and 1598. Its story was retold by Matteo Bandello in his *Novelle*, Part II, no. 36 (1554), and after him by Belleforest in *Histoires Tragiques* (1571). An English rendering, either from Bandello or Belleforest, was put forth by Barnabe Riche as the tale of *Apolonius and Silla*, the second "historie" in *Barnabe Riche, his Farewell to Militarie Profession* (1581). Shakespeare's plot is on the whole closer to this than to any of the others, and there is no reason to doubt that Riche's book came into his hands.

In Riche's story the love of the heroine for the Duke has a preliminary history which Shakespeare wisely ignores. Silla (Viola) had fallen in love with Duke Apolonius (Orsino) when he had been a guest at her father's court in Cyprus. She had made every effort to win him there, but he had returned home to Constantinople unimpressed. Still determined, Silla set out to follow him, taking with her a faithful servant Pedro, who posed as her brother. Her venture met with the shipwreck at which point Shakespeare's play opens. The omission of all these preliminaries not only makes the story more compact, but also permits a finer conception of the heroine. In the adventures of Viola after the shipwreck Shakespeare follows Riche's version, where Silla, in disguise and assuming the name of a brother (physically though not chronologically her twin) takes service with Apolonius, who is now, however, in love with a widow Julina. The relations of Julina (Olivia) and Silvio (Sebastian) are more delicately treated in the play than in the story, and the action is again compressed in the final scene. In Riche the brother, arriving at last in Constantinople after a wide search for his sister, is met and wooed by Julina, who mistakes him for Silla. He accepts her, but departs shortly to continue his search, leaving Julina pregnant. Soon after this, Apolonius, hearing gossip about Julina and Silla, has Silla thrown into a dungeon. Julina goes to him to plead for Silla, whom she supposes to be her husband; Silla is sent for, denies any love-compact with Julina, and under threat of death from the outraged Duke if she will not consent to marry Julina, reveals her identity. Julina departs in dismay and Apolonius promptly offers himself to Silla. The report of their marriage brings Silvio back to the city, where he is joyfully welcomed by his sister. Hearing from Apolonius about all that had transpired, Silvio confesses his former visit and hastens to Julina. They are joyfully reunited and in a few days they are married. This scattering conclusion is in strong contrast to the concentration of Shakespeare's dénouement.

The case for Shakespeare's dependence upon Riche's version of this widely popular story as his main source is further strengthened by his apparent indebtedness to another story in Riche's book for the suggestion of Malvolio's pretended lunacy. In the tale *Of Two Brethren and their Wives*, the younger brother, seeking to cure his wife of her shrewishness, shut her up in "a darke house ... with a greate chaine about her legge"; whereupon "callying his neibours about her, he would seeme with great sorrowe to lament his wives distresse, telling them that she was sodainly become lunatique." Her husband and the neighbors then prayed for her and sang the Miserere together outside the house, but "this did so spight and vexe her, that she never gave over her railyng and ragyng againste them all." Apart from this hint for the madness of Malvolio, the underplot, with its array of unforgettable characters, seems to be entirely original.

Indeed, Shakespeare's originality extends to the characterization of the main figures in the play, who are entirely recreated. The sentimentalism of the Duke, as well as the appealing union of wistfulness and arch humor which marks the charm of Viola, is altogether his conception. Orsino, in love with love, with a fondness "high fantastical," might easily have appeared only silly in his fancy, but Shakespeare keeps his sentiment from cloying, blending it with a larger grace and urbanity and giving it the complement of Viola's gentleness. Viola is one of Shakespeare's most lovable heroines. With her youthful freshness, her honesty, her innate refinement, her essential femininity, she has captivated all of Shakespeare's critics. Though her page's disguise and her situation in love are common themes in romance, it is to be noted that she has taken up her service with her master from the necessity of circumstance before she falls in love with him, and that all her conduct, both in his presence and on her missions to his flinty-hearted lady, is marked by a single-minded devotion. Her loyalty and purity are never compromised by so much as a hint; after one initial "aside" on the irony of her position (I.iv.40–42) she pleads her master's cause with genuine vigor and sincerity. Nowhere is Viola more clearly individualized than in her first scene with Olivia. Her address to Olivia is an adroit combination of rebuke and flattery, and she answers Maria, who would put her out, in her own saucy metaphor.

Of the minor characters several are distinguished creations. It is impossible not to associate Sir Toby with Falstaff, though his range of wit is narrower and he lacks entirely Falstaff's capacity for pathos. Sir Andrew Aguecheek is the most absolute fool in Shakespeare; he must be very close to the archetype of fatuity. Feste, the Clown, is the most jovial of Shakespeare's jesters. The character of Malvolio has been variously interpreted. The rather severe usage which he undergoes at the hands of those whom he has provoked, his vengeful resentment of it, and his mistress's pronouncement that he has been "most notoriously abus'd" tend to make a modern audience feel that he has suffered unjustly, but it is quite certain that Elizabethans found him deserving of all he got. He is perhaps more sinned against than sinning, but his utter lack of humor and his inordinate conceit qualify him for a pretty drastic taking down. After all, anyone as "sick of self-love" as Malvolio (and it is noteworthy that the accusation is made by Olivia herself well before his humiliation) is, either in Comedy or in real life, riding for a fall. And to make matters worse, Malvolio not only is a prig himself but obnoxiously sets out to be his brothers' keeper. Sir Toby stigmatizes this defect for all time: "Dost think because thou art virtuous, there shall be no more cakes and ale?"

TWELFTH NIGHT

OR

WHAT YOU WILL

[DRAMATIS PERSONÆ

ORSINO, *Duke of Illyria.*
SEBASTIAN, *brother to Viola.*
ANTONIO, *a sea captain, friend to Sebastian.*
A Sea Captain, *friend to Viola.*
VALENTINE, } *gentlemen attending on the Duke.*
CURIO,
SIR TOBY BELCH, *uncle to Olivia.*
SIR ANDREW AGUECHEEK.

MALVOLIO, *steward to Olivia.*
FABIAN, } *servants to Olivia.*
FESTE, *a clown,*

OLIVIA, *a rich countess.*
VIOLA.
MARIA, *Olivia's woman.*

Lords, Priests, Sailors, Officers, Musicians, and other Attendants.

SCENE: *A city in Illyria, and the sea-coast near it.*]

ACT I

SCENE I. [*A room in the Duke's palace.*]

Enter ORSINO, *Duke of Illyria,* CURIO, *and other
Lords* [*Musicians attending*].

Duke. If music be the food of love, play on!
Give me excess of it, that, surfeiting,
The appetite may sicken, and so die.
That strain again! It had a dying fall.
O, it came o'er my ear like the sweet sound   5
That breathes upon a bank of violets,
Stealing and giving odour. Enough! no more!
'Tis not so sweet now as it was before.
O spirit of love, how quick and fresh art thou,
That, notwithstanding thy capacity   10
Receiveth as the sea, nought enters there,
Of what validity and pitch soe'er,
But falls into abatement and low price
Even in a minute! So full of shapes is fancy
That it alone is high fantastical.   15

Cur. Will you go hunt, my lord?
Duke.   What, Curio?
Cur. The hart.
Duke. Why, so I do, the noblest that I have.
O, when mine eyes did see Olivia first,
Methought she purg'd the air of pestilence!   20
That instant was I turn'd into a hart;
And my desires, like fell and cruel hounds,
E'er since pursue me.

Enter VALENTINE.

                    How now! what news from her?
Val. So please my lord, I might not be admitted,
But from her handmaid do return this answer: 25
The element itself, till seven years' heat,
Shall not behold her face at ample view;
But, like a cloistress, she will veiled walk,
And water once a day her chamber round
With eye-offending brine: all this to season   30
A brother's dead love, which she would keep fresh
And lasting in her sad remembrance.

Act I, sc. i, 5. **sound** Ff. Pope's emendation, *south,* has been followed by many edd. 12. **validity:** value. **pitch:** height.
14. **fancy:** love. 15. **fantastical:** imaginative. 21–23. **That ... pursue me.** Allusion to Actæon, who, seeing Diana naked,
was changed into a hart and killed by his own dogs. 26. **element:** sky. **years' heat:** summers.

Duke. O, she that hath a heart of that fine frame
To pay this debt of love but to a brother,
How will she love when the rich golden shaft   35
Hath kill'd the flock of all affections else
That live in her; when liver, brain, and heart,
These sovereign thrones, are all suppli'd, and fill'd
Her sweet perfections with one self king!
Away before me to sweet beds of flowers;   40
Love-thoughts lie rich when canopi'd with bowers.
                   [*Exeunt.*

SCENE II.   [*The sea-coast.*]

Enter VIOLA, *a* CAPTAIN, *and Sailors.*

Vio. What country, friends, is this?
Cap. This is Illyria, lady.
Vio. And what should I do in Illyria?
My brother he is in Elysium.
Perchance he is not drown'd. What think you,
     sailors?   5
Cap. It is perchance that you yourself were
     saved.
Vio. O my poor brother! and so perchance may
     he be.
Cap. True, madam; and, to comfort you with
     chance,
Assure yourself, after our ship did split,
When you and those poor number sav'd with you
Hung on our driving boat, I saw your brother,   11
Most provident in peril, bind himself,
Courage and hope both teaching him the practice,
To a strong mast that liv'd upon the sea;
Where, like [Arion] on the dolphin's back,   15
I saw him hold acquaintance with the waves
So long as I could see.
Vio. For saying so, there's gold.
Mine own escape unfoldeth to my hope,
Whereto thy speech serves for authority,   20
The like of him. Know'st thou this country?
Cap. Ay, madam, well; for I was bred and born
Not three hours' travel from this very place.
Vio. Who governs here?
Cap. A noble duke, in nature as in name.   25
Vio. What is his name?
Cap. Orsino.
Vio. Orsino! I have heard my father name him.
He was a bachelor then.
Cap. And so is now, or was so very late;   30
For but a month ago I went from hence,
And then 'twas fresh in murmur — as, you know,
What great ones do the less will prattle of —
That he did seek the love of fair Olivia.

Vio. What's she?   35
Cap. A virtuous maid, the daughter of a count
That died some twelvemonth since, then leaving her
In the protection of his son, her brother,
Who shortly also died; for whose dear love,
They say, she hath abjur'd the [company   40
And sight] of men.
Vio.   O that I serv'd that lady,
And might not be delivered to the world,
Till I had made mine own occasion mellow,
What my estate is!
Cap.   That were hard to compass,
Because she will admit no kind of suit,   45
No, not the Duke's.
Vio. There is a fair behaviour in thee, captain;
And though that nature with a beauteous wall
Doth oft close in pollution, yet of thee
I will believe thou hast a mind that suits   50
With this thy fair and outward character.
I prithee, and I'll pay thee bounteously,
Conceal me what I am, and be my aid
For such disguise as haply shall become
The form of my intent. I'll serve this duke.   55
Thou shalt present me as an eunuch to him.
It may be worth thy pains, for I can sing
And speak to him in many sorts of music
That will allow me very worth his service.
What else may hap, to time I will commit,   60
Only shape thou thy silence to my wit.
Cap. Be you his eunuch, and your mute I'll be.
When my tongue blabs, then let mine eyes not see.
Vio. I thank thee. Lead me on.   [*Exeunt.*

SCENE III.   [*A room in Olivia's house.*]

Enter SIR TOBY BELCH *and* MARIA.

Sir To. What a plague means my niece, to take
the death of her brother thus? I am sure care's an
enemy to life.
Mar. By my troth, Sir Toby, you must come in
earlier o' nights. Your cousin, my lady, takes   5
great exceptions to your ill hours.
Sir To. Why, let her except before excepted.
Mar. Ay, but you must confine yourself within
the modest limits of order.   9
Sir To. Confine! I'll confine myself no finer than
I am. These clothes are good enough to drink in,
and so be these boots too; an they be not, let them
hang themselves in their own straps.   13
Mar. That quaffing and drinking will undo you.
I heard my lady talk of it yesterday, and of a fool-

---

35. **shaft:** i.e., Cupid's.   37. **liver ... heart.** The supposed seats of the passions.   39. **self:** sole.
Sc. ii, 15. **[Arion]** (Pope)   *Orion* F. Arion was a Greek poet, saved from drowning by dolphins who were so ravished by his lyre that they carried him to land.   40–41. **[company And sight]** (Hanmer).   *sight And company* F.   42–44. **And ... estate is.** I.e., And might not be delivered to the world.   59. **allow:** show, prove.   61. **wit:** design.
Sc. iii, 7. **except before excepted.** Quibble upon the legal phrase, *exceptis excipiendis,* "with the exceptions before named."

ish knight that you brought in one night here to be
her wooer.   17
  Sir To. Who? Sir Andrew Aguecheek?
  Mar. Ay, he.
  Sir To. He's as tall a man as any's in Illyria. 20
  Mar. What's that to th' purpose?
  Sir To. Why, he has three thousand ducats a
year.
  Mar. Ay, but he'll have but a year in all these
ducats. He's a very fool and a prodigal.   25
  Sir To. Fie, that you'll say so! He plays o' the
viol-de-gamboys, and speaks three or four languages
word for word without book, and hath all the good
gifts of nature.   29
  Mar. He hath indeed, almost natural; for besides
that he's a fool, he's a great quarreller; and but that
he hath the gift of a coward to allay the gust he hath
in quarrelling, 'tis thought among the prudent he
would quickly have the gift of a grave.   35
  Sir To. By this hand, they are scoundrels and
substractors that say so of him. Who are they?
  Mar. They that add, moreover, he's drunk
nightly in your company.   39
  Sir To. With drinking healths to my niece. I'll
drink to her as long as there is a passage in my
throat and drink in Illyria. He's a coward and a
coystrill that will not drink to my niece till his
brains turn o' th' toe like a parish-top. What,
wench! *Castiliano vulgo!* for here comes Sir Andrew
Agueface.   46

  Enter Sir Andrew Aguecheek.

  Sir And. Sir Toby Belch! How now, Sir Toby
Belch!
  Sir To. Sweet Sir Andrew!
  Sir And. Bless you, fair shrew.   50
  Mar. And you too, sir.
  Sir To. Accost, Sir Andrew, accost.
  Sir And. What's that?
  Sir To. My niece's chambermaid.
  Sir And. Good Mistress Accost, I desire better
acquaintance.   56
  Mar. My name is Mary, sir.
  Sir And. Good Mistress Mary Accost, —
  Sir To. You mistake, knight. "Accost" is front
her, board her, woo her, assail her.   60
  Sir And. By my troth, I would not undertake
her in this company. Is that the meaning of
"accost"?
  Mar. Fare you well, gentlemen.
  Sir To. An thou let part so, Sir Andrew, would
thou mightst never draw sword again.   66

  Sir And. An you part so, mistress, I would I
might never draw sword again. Fair lady, do you
think you have fools in hand?
  Mar. Sir, I have not you by th' hand.   70
  Sir And. Marry, but you shall have; and here's
my hand.
  Mar. Now, sir, "thought is free." I pray you,
bring your hand to th' butt'ry-bar and let it drink.
  Sir And. Wherefore, sweetheart? What's your
metaphor?   76
  Mar. It's dry, sir.
  Sir And. Why, I think so. I am not such an ass
but I can keep my hand dry. But what's your
jest?   80
  Mar. A dry jest, sir.
  Sir And. Are you full of them?
  Mar. Ay, sir, I have them at my fingers' ends.
Marry, now I let go your hand, I am barren. [*Exit.*
  Sir To. O knight, thou lack'st a cup of canary.
When did I see thee so put down?   86
  Sir And. Never in your life, I think, unless you
see canary put me down. Methinks sometimes I
have no more wit than a Christian or an ordinary
man has; but I am a great eater of beef and I believe
that does harm to my wit.   91
  Sir To. No question.
  Sir And. An I thought that, I'd forswear it. I'll
ride home to-morrow, Sir Toby.
  Sir To. *Pourquoi*, my dear knight?   95
  Sir And. What is "*pourquoi*"? Do or not do?
I would I had bestowed that time in the tongues
that I have in fencing, dancing, and bear-baiting.
O, had I but followed the arts!
  Sir To. Then hadst thou had an excellent head
of hair.   101
  Sir And. Why, would that have mended my
hair?
  Sir To. Past question; for thou seest it will not
[curl by] nature.   105
  Sir And. But it becomes me well enough, does't
not?
  Sir To. Excellent; it hangs like flax on a distaff,
and I hope to see a housewife take thee between her
legs, and spin it off.   110
  Sir And. Faith, I'll home to-morrow, Sir Toby.
Your niece will not be seen, or if she be, it's four to
one she'll none of me. The Count himself here
hard by wooes her.   114
  Sir To. She'll none o' th' Count. She'll not
match above her degree, neither in estate, years,
nor wit; I have heard her swear't. Tut, there's
life in't, man.

---

20. **tall:** fine. 27. **viol-de-gamboys:** bass viol. 30. **natural:** (1) naturally, (2) like an idiot. 33. **gust:** gusto, zest. 43. **coystrill:** knave. 45. *Castiliano vulgo.* Probably nonsense. 74. **buttery-bar.** Where drinks were served. 77. **It's dry.** Signifying lack of amorousness. 81. **dry jest:** dull jest. 85. **canary:** a sweet wine (from the Canary Islands). 100. **head of hair.** Sir Toby puns on *tongues* (l. 97) and (curling) tongs. 105. **[curl by]** (Theobald). *coole my* F. 118. **there's life in't:** there's still hope.

Sir And. I'll stay a month longer. I am a fellow o' the strangest mind i' th' world; I delight in masques and revels sometimes altogether.   121

Sir To. Art thou good at these kickshawses, knight?

Sir And. As any man in Illyria, whatsoever he be, under the degree of my betters; and yet I will not compare with an old man.   126

Sir To. What is thy excellence in a galliard, knight?

Sir And. Faith, I can cut a caper.

Sir To. And I can cut the mutton to't.   130

Sir And. And I think I have the back-trick simply as strong as any man in Illyria.

Sir To. Wherefore are these things hid? Wherefore have these gifts a curtain before 'em? Are they like to take dust, like Mistress Mall's   135 picture? Why dost thou not go to church in a galliard and come home in a coranto? My very walk should be a jig. I would not so much as make water but in a sink-a-pace. What dost thou mean? Is it a world to hide virtues in? I did think, by   140 the excellent constitution of thy leg, it was form'd under the star of a galliard.

Sir And. Ay, 'tis strong, and it does indifferent well in a damn'd colour'd stock. Shall we [set] about some revels?   145

Sir To. What shall we do else? Were we not born under Taurus?

Sir And. Taurus! That's sides and heart.

Sir To. No, sir, it is legs and thighs. Let me see thee caper. Ha! Higher! Ha, ha! Excellent!   [*Exeunt.*   151

SCENE IV.   [*A room in the Duke's palace.*]

Enter VALENTINE, *and* VIOLA *in man's attire.*

Val. If the Duke continue these favours towards you, Cesario, you are like to be much advanc'd. He hath known you but three days, and already you are no stranger.   4

Vio. You either fear his humour or my negligence, that you call in question the continuance of his love. Is he inconstant, sir, in his favours?

Val. No, believe me.

Enter DUKE, CURIO, *and Attendants.*

Vio. I thank you. Here comes the Count.

Duke. Who saw Cesario, ho?   10

Vio. On your attendance, my lord; here.

Duke. Stand you a while aloof. Cesario, Thou know'st no less but all. I have unclasp'd To thee the book even of my secret soul; Therefore, good youth, address thy gait unto her. Be not deni'd access, stand at her doors,   16 And tell them, there thy fixed foot shall grow Till thou have audience.

Vio.   Sure, my noble lord, If she be so abandon'd to her sorrow As it is spoke, she never will admit me.   20

Duke. Be clamorous and leap all civil bounds Rather than make unprofited return.

Vio. Say I do speak with her, my lord, what then?

Duke. O, then unfold the passion of my love, Surprise her with discourse of my dear faith.   25 It shall become thee well to act my woes. She will attend it better in thy youth Than in a nuncio's of more grave aspect.

Vio. I think not so, my lord.

Duke.   Dear lad, believe it; For they shall yet belie thy happy years,   30 That say thou art a man. Diana's lip Is not more smooth and rubious; thy small pipe Is as the maiden's organ, shrill and sound; And all is semblative a woman's part. I know thy constellation is right apt   35 For this affair. Some four or five attend him, — All, if you will; for I myself am best When least in company. Prosper well in this, And thou shalt live as freely as thy lord, To call his fortunes thine.

Vio.   I'll do my best   40 To woo your lady, — [*aside*] yet, a barful strife! Whoe'er I woo, myself would be his wife. [*Exeunt.*

SCENE V.   [*A room in Olivia's house.*]

Enter MARIA *and* CLOWN.

Mar. Nay, either tell me where thou hast been, or I will not open my lips so wide as a bristle may enter, in way of thy excuse. My lady will hang thee for thy absence.

Clo. Let her hang me! He that is well hang'd in this world needs to fear no colours.   6

Mar. Make that good.

Clo. He shall see none to fear.

Mar. A good lenten answer. I can tell thee where that saying was born, of "I fear no colours."

Clo. Where, good Mistress Mary?   11

122. **kickshawses:** trifles. 126. **old:** (possibly) experienced. 127. **galliard:** a lively dance. 130. Sir Toby puns: mutton is often served with *caper* sauce. 131. **back-trick:** i.e., the reverse step (in the galliard). 137. **coranto:** a fast dance. 139. **sink-a-pace:** (cinque pace) a five-step dance. 144. **damn'd colour'd.** Many editors amend to *flame-coloured.* **stock:** stocking. 144. **[set]** (Rowe). *sit* F. 147. **Taurus.** In the old medical astrology the constellation Taurus was held to control the neck and throat; so both Sir A. and Sir T. are wrong.
Sc. iv, 32. **rubious:** ruby-colored. 33. **sound:** clear. 34. **semblative:** like. 35. **constellation:** nature (which the stars determined). 41. **barful strife:** task full of obstacles.
Sc. v, 6. **colours:** flags (i.e., foes), with a pun on *collars* (the hangman's noose). 9. **lenten:** scanty.

Mar. In the wars; and that may you be bold to say in your foolery.

Clo. Well, God give them wisdom that have it; and those that are fools, let them use their talents.   16

Mar. Yet you will be hang'd for being so long absent; or, to be turn'd away, is not that as good as a hanging to you?

Clo. Many a good hanging prevents a bad 20 marriage; and, for turning away, let summer bear it out.

Mar. You are resolute, then?

Clo. Not so, neither; but I am resolv'd on two points.   25

Mar. That if one break, the other will hold; or, if both break, your gaskins fall.

Clo. Apt, in good faith; very apt. Well, go thy way. If Sir Toby would leave drinking, thou wert as witty a piece of Eve's flesh as any in Illyria. 31

Mar. Peace, you rogue, no more o' that. Here comes my lady. Make your excuse wisely, you were best.   [*Exit.*] 34

Enter LADY OLIVIA [*and retinue*] *with* MALVOLIO.

Clo. Wit, an't be thy will, put me into good fooling! Those wits, that think they have thee, do very oft prove fools; and I, that am sure I lack thee, may pass for a wise man; for what says Quinapalus? "Better a witty fool than a foolish wit." — 40 God bless thee, lady!

Oli. Take the fool away.

Clo. Do you not hear, fellows? Take away the lady.

Oli. Go to, you're a dry fool, I'll no more of you; besides, you grow dishonest.   46

Clo. Two faults, madonna, that drink and good counsel will amend; for give the dry fool drink, then is the fool not dry: bid the dishonest man mend himself; if he mend, he is no longer dishonest; 50 if he cannot, let the botcher mend him. Any thing that's mended is but patch'd; virtue that transgresses is but patch'd with sin, and sin that amends is but patch'd with virtue. If that this simple syllogism will serve, so; if it will not, what remedy? 55 As there is no true cuckold but calamity, so beauty's a flower. The lady bade take away the fool; therefore, I say again, take her away.

Oli. Sir, I bade them take away you.   60

Clo. Misprision in the highest degree! Lady, "*cucullus non facit monachum*"; that's as much to say as I wear not motley in my brain. Good madonna, give me leave to prove you a fool.

Oli. Can you do it?   65

Clo. Dexteriously, good madonna.

Oli. Make your proof.

Clo. I must catechise you for it, madonna. Good my mouse of virtue, answer me.

Oli. Well, sir, for want of other idleness, I'll bide your proof.   71

Clo. Good madonna, why mournest thou?

Oli. Good fool, for my brother's death.

Clo. I think his soul is in hell, madonna.

Oli. I know his soul is in heaven, fool.   75

Clo. The more fool, madonna, to mourn for your brother's soul being in heaven. Take away the fool, gentlemen.

Oli. What think you of this fool, Malvolio? Doth he not mend?   80

Mal. Yes, and shall do till the pangs of death shake him. Infirmity, that decays the wise, doth ever make the better fool.

Clo. God send you, sir, a speedy infirmity, for the better increasing your folly! Sir Toby will be sworn that I am no fox, but he will not pass 85 his word for twopence that you are no fool.

Oli. How say you to that, Malvolio?

Mal. I marvel your ladyship takes delight in such a barren rascal. I saw him put down the 90 other day with an ordinary fool that has no more brain than a stone. Look you now, he's out of his guard already. Unless you laugh and minister occasion to him, he is gagg'd. I protest, I take these wise men that crow so at these set kind of fools no better than the fools' zanies.   96

Oli. O, you are sick of self-love, Malvolio, and taste with a distemper'd appetite. To be generous, guiltless, and of free disposition, is to take those things for bird-bolts that you deem cannon- 100 bullets. There is no slander in an allow'd fool, though he do nothing but rail; nor no railing in a known discreet man, though he do nothing but reprove.

Clo. Now Mercury endue thee with leasing, for thou speak'st well of fools!   106

Re-enter MARIA.

Mar. Madam, there is at the gate a young gentleman much desires to speak with you.

Oli. From the Count Orsino, is it?

Mar. I know not, madam. 'Tis a fair young man, and well attended.   111

Oli. Who of my people hold him in delay?

Mar. Sir Toby, madam, your kinsman.

Oli. Fetch him off, I pray you. He speaks

---

25. **points:** (1) counts, (2) laces to hold up the *gaskins* or breeches. 39. **Quinapalus.** Feste's invention. 45. **dry:** dull. 51. **botcher:** mender of old clothes. 61. **Misprision:** mistake, with a possible reference to the literal sense, taking the wrong person. 62. *cucullus ... monachum:* the cowl does not make the monk. 63. **motley:** the parti-colored costume of jesters. 69. **mouse:** term of affection. **of virtue:** virtuous. 96. **zanies:** imitators. 100. **bird-bolts:** blunt arrows. 101. **allow'd:** licensed. 105. **leasing:** (gift of) lying. Mercury was the god of thieves and liars.

nothing but madman; fie on him! [*Exit* 115
Maria.] Go you, Malvolio; if it be a suit from the
Count, I am sick, or not at home, — what you
will, to dismiss it. (*Exit Malvolio*.) Now you see,
sir, how your fooling grows old, and people dislike it.

Clo. Thou hast spoke for us, madonna, as if 120
thy eldest son should be a fool; whose skull Jove
cram with brains! for — here he comes —

Enter Sir Toby.

one of thy kin has a most weak *pia mater*.

Oli. By mine honour, half drunk. What is he
at the gate, cousin?   125
Sir To. A gentleman.
Oli. A gentleman! What gentleman?
Sir To. 'Tis a gentleman here — a plague o'
these pickle-herring! How now, sot!
Clo. Good Sir Toby!   130
Oli. Cousin, cousin, how have you come so early
by this lethargy?
Sir To. Lechery! I defy lechery. There's one
at the gate.
Oli. Ay, marry, what is he?   135
Sir To. Let him be the devil, an he will, I care
not; give me faith, say I. Well, it's all one. [*Exit*.
Oli. What's a drunken man like, fool?
Clo. Like a drown'd man, a fool, and a madman.
One draught above heat makes him a fool, the 140
second mads him, and a third drowns him.
Oli. Go thou and seek the crowner and let him
sit o' my coz, for he's in the third degree of drink,
he's drown'd. Go, look after him.
Clo. He is but mad yet, madonna; and the fool
shall look to the madman.   [*Exit*. 146

Re-enter Malvolio.

Mal. Madam, yond young fellow swears he will
speak with you. I told him you were sick. He
takes on him to understand so much, and therefore
comes to speak with you. I told him you were 150
asleep. He seems to have a foreknowledge of
that too, and therefore comes to speak with you.
What is to be said to him, lady? He's fortified
against any denial.
Oli. Tell him he shall not speak with me. 155
Mal. Has been told so; and he says, he'll stand
at your door like a sheriff's post, and be the supporter to a bench, but he'll speak with you.
Oli. What kind o' man is he?
Mal. Why, of mankind.   160
Oli. What manner of man?
Mal. Of very ill manner. He'll speak with you,
will you or no.
Oli. Of what personage and years is he? 164

Mal. Not yet old enough for a man, nor young
enough for a boy; as a squash is before 'tis a peascod, or a codling when 'tis almost an apple. 'Tis
with him in standing water, between boy and man.
He is very well-favour'd and he speaks very shrewishly. One would think his mother's milk were
scarce out of him.   171
Oli. Let him approach. Call in my gentlewoman.
Mal. Gentlewoman, my lady calls.   [*Exit*.

Re-enter Maria.

Oli. Give me my veil. Come, throw it o'er my
face.   175
We'll once more hear Orsino's embassy.

Enter [Viola *and Attendants*].

Vio. The honourable lady of the house, which is
she?
Oli. Speak to me; I shall answer for her. Your
will?   180
Vio. Most radiant, exquisite, and unmatchable
beauty, — I pray you, tell me if this be the lady of
the house, for I never saw her. I would be loath
to cast away my speech, for besides that it is excellently well penn'd, I have taken great pains 185
to con it. Good beauties, let me sustain no scorn.
I am very comptible, even to the least sinister usage.
Oli. Whence came you, sir?   189
Vio. I can say little more than I have studied,
and that question's out of my part. Good gentle
one, give me modest assurance if you be the lady
of the house, that I may proceed in my speech.
Oli. Are you a comedian?   194
Vio. No, my profound heart; and yet, by the
very fangs of malice I swear, I am not that I play.
Are you the lady of the house?
Oli. If I do not usurp myself, I am.
Vio. Most certain, if you are she, you do usurp
yourself; for what is yours to bestow is not 200
yours to reserve. But this is from my commission.
I will on with my speech in your praise, and then
show you the heart of my message.
Oli. Come to what is important in't. I forgive
you the praise.   205
Vio. Alas, I took great pains to study it, and
'tis poetical.
Oli. It is the more like to be feigned. I pray
you, keep it in. I heard you were saucy at my
gates, and allow'd your approach rather to won- 210
der at you than to hear you. If you be not mad,
be gone. If you have reason, be brief. 'Tis not
that time of moon with me to make one in so skipping a dialogue.

---

123. *pia mater*: brain. 142. **crowner**: coroner. 157. **sheriff's post**: post before a sheriff's house for notices. 166. **squash**:
unripe pea pod. 167. **codling**: unripe apple. 168. **standing water**: at turn of the tide. 169. **shrewishly**: crossly. 177.
S.D. Viola. *Violenta* F. 186. **con**: memorize. 187. **comptible**: sensitive. 201. **from**: out of. 213. **skipping**: flighty.

Mar. Will you hoist sail, sir? Here lies your way.   216

Vio. No, good swabber, I am to hull here a little longer. Some mollification for your giant, sweet lady. Tell me your mind. I am a messenger. 220

Oli. Sure, you have some hideous matter to deliver, when the courtesy of it is so fearful. Speak your office.

Vio. It alone concerns your ear. I bring no overture of war, no taxation of homage. I hold 225 the olive in my hand. My words are as full of peace as matter.

Oli. Yet you began rudely. What are you? What would you?   229

Vio. The rudeness that hath appear'd in me have I learn'd from my entertainment. What I am, and what I would, are as secret as maidenhead; to your ears, divinity, to any other's, profanation.   234

Oli. Give us the place alone; we will hear this divinity. [*Exeunt Maria and Attendants.*] Now, sir, what is your text?

Vio. Most sweet lady, —

Oli. A comfortable doctrine, and much may be said of it. Where lies your text?   240

Vio. In Orsino's bosom.

Oli. In his bosom! In what chapter of his bosom?

Vio. To answer by the method, in the first of his heart.   245

Oli. O, I have read it; it is heresy. Have you no more to say?

Vio. Good madam, let me see your face.

Oli. Have you any commission from your lord to negotiate with my face? You are now out of 250 your text, but we will draw the curtain and show you the picture. Look you, sir, such a one I was — this present. Is't not well done? [*Unveiling.*]

Vio. Excellently done, if God did all.

Oli. 'Tis in grain, sir; 'twill endure wind and weather.   256

Vio. 'Tis beauty truly blent, whose red and white
Nature's own sweet and cunning hand laid on.
Lady, you are the cruell'st she alive
If you will lead these graces to the grave 260
And leave the world no copy.

Oli. O, sir, I will not be so hard-hearted; I will give out divers schedules of my beauty. It shall be inventoried, and every particle and utensil labell'd to my will: as, item, two lips, indifferent 265 red; item, two grey eyes, with lids to them; item,

one neck, one chin, and so forth. Were you sent hither to praise me?

Vio. I see you what you are, you are too proud;
But, if you were the devil, you are fair.   270
My lord and master loves you. O, such love
Could be but recompens'd, though you were crown'd
The nonpareil of beauty!

Oli.   How does he love me?

Vio. With adorations, [with] fertile tears,
With groans that thunder love, with sighs of fire.

Oli. Your lord does know my mind; I cannot love him.   276
Yet I suppose him virtuous, know him noble;
Of great estate, of fresh and stainless youth,
In voices well divulg'd, free, learn'd, and valiant,
And in dimension and the shape of nature 280
A gracious person. But yet I cannot love him.
He might have took his answer long ago.

Vio. If I did love you in my master's flame,
With such a suff'ring, such a deadly life,
In your denial I would find no sense.   285
I would not understand it.

Oli.   Why, what would you?

Vio. Make me a willow cabin at your gate,
And call upon my soul within the house;
Write loyal cantons of contemned love
And sing them loud even in the dead of night; 290
Halloo your name to the reverberate hills
And make the babbling gossip of the air
Cry out "Olivia!" O, you should not rest
Between the elements of air and earth,
But you should pity me!

Oli.   You might do much. 295
What is your parentage?

Vio. Above my fortunes, yet my state is well.
I am a gentleman.

Oli.   Get you to your lord.
I cannot love him. Let him send no more, —
Unless, perchance, you come to me again   300
To tell me how he takes it. Fare you well!
I thank you for your pains. Spend this for me.

Vio. I am no fee'd post, lady. Keep your purse.
My master, not myself, lacks recompense.
Love make his heart of flint that you shall love; 305
And let your fervour, like my master's, be
Plac'd in contempt! Farewell, fair cruelty. [*Exit.*

Oli. "What is your parentage?"
"Above my fortunes, yet my state is well.
I am a gentleman." I'll be sworn thou art.   310
Thy tongue, thy face, thy limbs, actions, and spirit

---

217. **swabber:** washer of decks — keeping up the nautical metaphor in "hoist sail." **hull:** float, drift. 218. **giant.** Ironical reference to Maria's small stature. 225. **taxation:** demand. 231. **my entertainment:** the way I have been received here. 253. **this present:** just now. 255. **in grain:** indelible, not painted. 265. **labell'd:** attached (as a codicil). 268. **praise:** appraise. 274. **[with]** (Pope). Om. F. 279. **In ... divulg'd:** of good repute. 283. **flame:** passion. 284. **deadly:** doomed to die. 289. **cantons:** cantos, songs. 303. **post:** messenger.

Do give thee five-fold blazon.　Not too fast!　Soft,
　　soft!
Unless the master were the man.　How now!
Even so quickly may one catch the plague?
Methinks I feel this youth's perfections　　315
With an invisible and subtle stealth
To creep in at mine eyes.　Well, let it be.
What ho, Malvolio!

Re-enter MALVOLIO.

　Mal.　　　　Here, madam, at your service.
　Oli.　Run after that same peevish messenger,
The County's man.　He left this ring behind him,
Would I or not.　Tell him I'll none of it.　　321
Desire him not to flatter with his lord,
Nor hold him up with hopes.　I'm not for him.
If that the youth will come this way to-morrow,
I'll give him reasons for't.　Hie thee, Malvolio.
　Mal.　Madam, I will.　　　　　[*Exit.*　326
　Oli.　I do I know not what, and fear to find
Mine eye too great a flatterer for my mind.
Fate, show thy force; ourselves we do not owe;
What is decreed must be, and be this so.　　330
　　　　　　　　　　　　　　　[*Exit.*]

ACT II

SCENE I.　[*The sea-coast.*]

Enter ANTONIO *and* SEBASTIAN.

　Ant.　Will you stay no longer?　Nor will you not
that I go with you?
　Seb.　By your patience, no.　My stars shine
darkly over me.　The malignancy of my fate might
perhaps distemper yours, therefore I shall crave　5
of you your leave that I may bear my evils alone.
It were a bad recompense for your love, to lay any
of them on you.
　Ant.　Let me yet know of you whither you are
bound.　　　　　　　　　　　　　　10
　Seb.　No, sooth, sir.　My determinate voyage
is mere extravagancy.　But I perceive in you so
excellent a touch of modesty, that you will not extort from me what I am willing to keep in; therefore it charges me in manners the rather to ex-　15
press myself.　You must know of me then, Antonio,
my name is Sebastian, which I call'd Roderigo.
My father was that Sebastian of Messaline, whom
I know you have heard of.　He left behind him
myself and a sister, both born in an hour.　If　20
the heavens had been pleas'd, would we had so
ended!　But you, sir, alter'd that; for some hour

before you took me from the breach of the sea was
my sister drown'd.
　Ant.　Alas the day!　　　　　　　25
　Seb.　A lady, sir, though it was said she much
resembled me, was yet of many accounted beautiful; but, though I could not with such estimable
wonder overfar believe that, yet thus far I will
boldly publish her: she bore a mind that envy　30
could not but call fair.　She is drown'd already,
sir, with salt water, though I seem to drown her
remembrance again with more.
　Ant.　Pardon me, sir, your bad entertainment.
　Seb.　O good Antonio, forgive me your trouble.　35
　Ant.　If you will not murder me for my love, let
me be your servant.
　Seb.　If you will not undo what you have done,
that is, kill him whom you have recover'd, desire it
not.　Fare ye well at once.　My bosom is full of　40
kindness, and I am yet so near the manners of my
mother, that upon the least occasion more mine
eyes will tell tales of me.　I am bound to the Count
Orsino's court.　Farewell.　　　　　[*Exit.*
　Ant.　The gentleness of all the gods go with
　　thee!　　　　　　　　　　　　45
I have many enemies in Orsino's court,
Else would I very shortly see thee there.
But, come what may, I do adore thee so
That danger shall seem sport, and I will go.　　49
　　　　　　　　　　　　　　　[*Exit.*

SCENE II.　[*A street.*]

Enter VIOLA *and* MALVOLIO, *at several doors.*

　Mal.　Were you not even now with the Countess
Olivia?
　Vio.　Even now, sir.　On a moderate pace I have
since arriv'd but hither.　　　　　　4
　Mal.　She returns this ring to you, sir.　You
might have saved me my pains, to have taken it
away yourself.　She adds, moreover, that you
should put your lord into a desperate assurance
she will none of him; and — one thing more — that
you be never so hardy to come again in his af-　10
fairs, unless it be to report your lord's taking of
this.　Receive it so.
　Vio.　She took the ring of me.　I'll none of it.
　Mal.　Come, sir, you peevishly threw it to her;
and her will is, it should be so return'd.　If it be　15
worth stooping for, there it lies in your eye; if not,
be it his that finds it.　　　　　　[*Exit.*
　Vio.　I left no ring with her.　What means this
　　lady?
Fortune forbid my outside have not charm'd her!

---

312. **blazon:** proof of nobility.　329. **owe:** own.
　Act II, sc. i, 5. **distemper:** disorder.　11–12. **My . . . extravagancy:** my destination is mere wandering.　15. **express:**
reveal.　23. **breach:** breakers, surf.　28. **estimable wonder:** admiring esteem.
　Sc. ii, 8. **desperate:** hopeless.

She made good view of me; indeed, so much   20
That [sure] methought her eyes had lost her tongue,
For she did speak in starts distractedly.
She loves me, sure.   The cunning of her passion
Invites me in this churlish messenger.
None of my lord's ring!   Why, he sent her none.   25
I am the man!   If it be so, as 'tis,
Poor lady, she were better love a dream.
Disguise, I see thou art a wickedness
Wherein the pregnant enemy does much.
How easy is it for the proper-false   30
In women's waxen hearts to set their forms!
Alas, [our] frailty is the cause, not we!
For such as we are made [of], such we be.
How will this fadge?   My master loves her dearly;
And I, poor monster, fond as much on him;   35
And she, mistaken, seems to dote on me.
What will become of this?   As I am man,
My state is desperate for my master's love;
As I am woman, — now alas the day! —
What thriftless sighs shall poor Olivia breathe!   40
O time! thou must untangle this, not I.
It is too hard a knot for me t' untie!   [*Exit.*]

SCENE III.   [*A room in Olivia's house.*]

Enter SIR TOBY *and* SIR ANDREW.

Sir To. Approach, Sir Andrew.   Not to be a-bed
after midnight is to be up betimes; and "*deliculo
surgere,*" thou know'st, —
Sir And. Nay, by my troth, I know not; but I
know, to be up late is to be up late.   5
Sir To. A false conclusion.   I hate it as an unfill'd can.   To be up after midnight and to go to
bed then, is early; so that to go to bed after midnight is to go to bed betimes.   Does not our lives
consist of the four elements?   10
Sir And. Faith, so they say; but I think it
rather consists of eating and drinking.
Sir To. Thou'rt a scholar; let us therefore eat
and drink.   Marian, I say! a stoup of wine!

Enter CLOWN.

Sir And. Here comes the fool, i' faith.   15
Clo. How now, my hearts!   Did you never see
the picture of "we three"?
Sir To. Welcome, ass.   Now let's have a catch.
Sir And. By my troth, the fool has an excellent
breast.   I had rather than forty shillings I had   20
such a leg, and so sweet a breath to sing, as the fool
has.   In sooth, thou wast in very gracious fooling

last night, when thou spok'st of Pigrogromitus, of
the Vapians passing the equinoctial of Queubus.
'Twas very good, i' faith.   I sent thee sixpence for
thy leman.   Hadst it?   26
Clo. I did impeticos thy gratillity; for Malvolio's
nose is no whipstock.   My lady has a white hand,
and the Mermidons are no bottle-ale houses.
Sir And. Excellent!   Why, this is the best
fooling, when all is done.   Now, a song.   31
Sir To. Come on; there is sixpence for you.
Let's have a song.
Sir And. There's a testril of me too.   If one
knight give a —   35
Clo. Would you have a love-song, or a song of
good life?
Sir To. A love-song, a love-song.
Sir And. Ay, ay.   I care not for good life.
Clo. (*Sings.*)
      O mistress mine, where are you roaming?   40
      O, stay and hear, your true love's coming,
         That can sing both high and low.
      Trip no further, pretty sweeting;
      Journeys end in lovers meeting,
         Every wise man's son doth know.   45

Sir And. Excellent good, i' faith.
Sir To. Good, good.
Clo. [*Sings.*]
      What is love?   'Tis not hereafter.
      Present mirth hath present laughter;
         What's to come is still unsure.   50
      In delay there lies no plenty;
      Then come kiss me, sweet and twenty,
         Youth's a stuff will not endure.

Sir And. A mellifluous voice, as I am true
knight.   55
Sir To. A contagious breath.
Sir And. Very sweet and contagious, i' faith.
Sir To. To hear by the nose, it is dulcet in con-
tagion.   But shall we make the welkin dance in-
deed?   Shall we rouse the night-owl in a catch   60
that will draw three souls out of one weaver?
Shall we do that?
Sir And. An you love me, let's do't.   I am dog
at a catch.
Clo. By'r lady, sir, and some dogs will catch
well.   65
Sir And. Most certain.   Let our catch be,
"Thou knave."
Clo. "Hold thy peace, thou knave," knight?

---

21. [sure] F₂.   Om. F₁.   lost: i.e., put at a loss.   29. pregnant: resourceful.   30. proper-false: handsome deceivers.   32.
[our] F₂.   O F₁.   33. made [of] (Tyrwhitt).   *made, if* F₁.   34. fadge: turn out.
Sc. iii, 3. *deliculo surgere* (*saluberrimum est*): to rise early is most healthful.   An extract from Lilly's *Latin Grammar.*
14. stoup: cup.   17. A picture of two asses or fools entitled "we three," the spectator making the third.   18. catch: round.
20. breast: voice.   23–24. Pigrogromitus . . . Queubus.   Mock learning.   26. leman: sweetheart.   27. impeticos thy
gratillity.   Nonsensical mode of saying "pocket thy gratuity."   28. whipstock: whip handle (i.e., Malvolio's nose is keen).
29. Mermidons: followers of Achilles.   34. testril: sixpence.   56. contagious breath: catchy song.   59. welkin: sky.

I shall be constrain'd in't to call thee knave, knight.   70

Sir And. 'Tis not the first time I have constrained one to call me knave. Begin, fool. It begins, "Hold thy peace."

Clo. I shall never begin if I hold my peace.

Sir And. Good, i' faith. Come, begin.   75

[*Catch sung.*

Enter MARIA.

Mar. What a caterwauling do you keep here! If my lady have not call'd up her steward Malvolio and bid him turn you out of doors, never trust me.   79

Sir To. My lady's a Cataian, we are politicians, Malvolio's a Peg-a-Ramsey, and "Three merry men be we." Am not I consanguineous? Am I not of her blood? Tilly-vally. Lady! [*Sings.*] "There dwelt a man in Babylon, lady, lady!" 84

Clo. Beshrew me, the knight's in admirable fooling.

Sir And. Ay, he does well enough if he be dispos'd, and so do I too. He does it with a better grace, but I do it more natural.   89

Sir To. [*Sings.*] "O, the twelfth day of December," —

Mar. For the love o' God, peace!   92

Enter MALVOLIO.

Mal. My masters, are you mad, or what are you? Have you no wit, manners, nor honesty, but to gabble like tinkers at this time of night? Do ye make an alehouse of my lady's house, that ye squeak out your coziers' catches without any mitigation or remorse of voice? Is there no respect of place, persons, nor time in you?   99

Sir To. We did keep time, sir, in our catches. Sneck up!

Mal. Sir Toby, I must be round with you. My lady bade me tell you that, though she harbours you as her kinsman, she's nothing alli'd to your disorders. If you can separate yourself and your 105 misdemeanours, you are welcome to the house; if not, an it would please you to take leave of her, she is very willing to bid you farewell.

Sir To. "Farewell, dear heart, since I must needs be gone."   110

Mar. Nay, good Sir Toby.

Clo. "His eyes do show his days are almost done."

Mal. Is't even so?

Sir To. "But I will never die."   115

Clo. Sir Toby, there you lie.

Mal. This is much credit to you.

Sir To. "Shall I bid him go?"

Clo. "What an if you do?"

Sir To. "Shall I bid him go, and spare not?"

Clo. "O no, no, no, no, you dare not."   121

Sir To. Out o' tune, sir! Ye lie. Art any more than a steward? Dost thou think, because thou art virtuous, there shall be no more cakes and ale?   125

Clo. Yes, by Saint Anne, and ginger shall be hot i' th' mouth too.

Sir To. Thou'rt i' th' right. Go, sir, rub your chain with crumbs. A stoup of wine, Maria!

Mal. Mistress Mary, if you priz'd my lady's 130 favour at anything more than contempt, you would not give means for this uncivil rule. She shall know of it, by this hand.   [*Exit.*

Mar. Go shake your ears.   134

Sir And. 'Twere as good a deed as to drink when a man's a-hungry, to challenge him the field, and then to break promise with him and make a fool of him.

Sir To. Do't, knight. I'll write thee a challenge, or I'll deliver thy indignation to him by word of mouth.   141

Mar. Sweet Sir Toby, be patient for to-night. Since the youth of the Count's was to-day with my lady, she is much out of quiet. For Monsieur Malvolio, let me alone with him. If I do not 145 gull him into a nayword, and make him a common recreation, do not think I have wit enough to lie straight in my bed. I know I can do it.

Sir To. Possess us, possess us. Tell us something of him.   150

Mar. Marry, sir, sometimes he is a kind of puritan.

Sir And. O, if I thought that, I'd beat him like a dog!

Sir To. What, for being a puritan? Thy exquisite reason, dear knight?   156

Sir And. I have no exquisite reason for't, but I have reason good enough.

Mar. The devil a puritan that he is, or anything constantly, but a time-pleaser; an affection'd 160 ass, that cons state without book and utters it by great swarths; the best persuaded of himself, so cramm'd, as he thinks, with excellencies, that it is his grounds of faith that all that look on him love him; and on that vice in him will my revenge find notable cause to work.   166

Sir To. What wilt thou do?

Mar. I will drop in his way some obscure epistles of love; wherein, by the colour of his beard,

---

80. **Catian:** Chinese, rascal.   81. **Peg-a-Ramsey:** a character in a ballad.   **Three merry men** (etc.). This and subsequent quotations are from popular songs.   97. **coziers':** cobblers'.   101. **Sneck up:** go hang.   128. **chain:** i.e., steward's badge.   145. **nayword:** byword.   149. **Possess:** inform.   160. **affection'd:** affected.   161. **cons...book:** memorizes courtly speeches.   162. **swarths:** swaths.

the shape of his leg, the manner of his gait, the   170
expressure of his eye, forehead, and complexion, he
shall find himself most feelingly personated. I can
write very like my lady your niece. On a forgotten
matter we can hardly make distinction of our
hands.   175
Sir To. Excellent! I smell a device.
Sir And. I have't in my nose too.
Sir To. He shall think, by the letters that thou
wilt drop, that they come from my niece, and that
she's in love with him.   180
Mar. My purpose is, indeed, a horse of that
colour.
Sir And. And your horse now would make him
an ass.
Mar. Ass, I doubt not.   185
Sir And. O, 'twill be admirable!
Mar. Sport royal, I warrant you. I know my
physic will work with him. I will plant you two,
and let the fool make a third, where he shall find
the letter. Observe his construction of it. For   190
this night, to bed, and dream on the event. Fare-
well.   [*Exit.*
Sir To. Good night, Penthesilea.
Sir And. Before me, she's a good wench.
Sir To. She's a beagle, true-bred, and one that
adores me. What o' that?   196
Sir And. I was ador'd once too.
Sir To. Let's to bed, knight. Thou hadst need
send for more money.
Sir And. If I cannot recover your niece, I am a
foul way out.   201
Sir To. Send for money, knight. If thou hast
her not i' the end, call me cut.
Sir And. If I do not, never trust me, take it how
you will.   205
Sir To. Come, come, I'll go burn some sack; 'tis
too late to go to bed now. Come, knight; come,
knight.   [*Exeunt.*

SCENE IV. [*A room in the Duke's palace.*]

Enter DUKE, VIOLA, CURIO, *and others.*

Duke. Give me some music. Now, — good
    morrow, friends, —
Now, good Cesario, but that piece of song,
That old and antique song we heard last night.
Methought it did relieve my passion much,
More than light airs and recollected terms   5
Of these most brisk and giddy-paced times.
Come, but one verse.
Cur. He is not here, so please your lordship, that
should sing it.

Duke. Who was it?   10
Cur. Feste, the jester, my lord; a fool that the
lady Olivia's father took much delight in. He is
about the house.
Duke. Seek him out, and play the tune the
    while.   [*Exit Curio.*] *Music plays.*
Come hither, boy. If ever thou shalt love,   15
In the sweet pangs of it remember me;
For such as I am all true lovers are,
Unstaid and skittish in all motions else,
Save in the constant image of the creature
That is belov'd. How dost thou like this tune?
Vio. It gives a very echo to the seat   21
Where Love is thron'd.
Duke.   Thou dost speak masterly.
My life upon't, young though thou art, thine eye
Hath stay'd upon some favour that it loves.   23
Hath it not, boy?
Vio.   A little, by your favour.
Duke. What kind of woman is't?
Vio.   Of your complexion.
Duke. She is not worth thee, then. What years,
    i' faith?
Vio. About your years, my lord.
Duke. Too old, by heaven. Let still the woman
    take   30
An elder than herself; so wears she to him,
So sways she level in her husband's heart.
For, boy, however we do praise ourselves,
Our fancies are more giddy and unfirm,
More longing, wavering, sooner lost and worn, 35
Than women's are.
Vio.   I think it well, my lord.
Duke. Then let thy love be younger than thy-
    self,
Or thy affection cannot hold the bent.
For women are as roses, whose fair flower
Being once display'd, doth fall that very hour. 40
Vio. And so they are; alas, that they are so!
To die, even when they to perfection grow!

Re-enter CURIO *and* CLOWN.

Duke. O, fellow, come, the song we had last
    night.
Mark it, Cesario, it is old and plain.
The spinsters and the knitters in the sun   45
And the free maids that weave their thread with
    bones
Do use to chant it. It is silly sooth,
And dallies with the innocence of love,
Like the old age.
Clo. Are you ready, sir?   50
Duke. Ay; prithee, sing.   [*Music.*

193. **Penthesilea:** Queen of the Amazons. 200. **recover:** win. 201. **out:** i.e., of money. 203. **cut:** horse with docked tail. 206. **burn:** heat and spice. **sack:** a Spanish wine.
  Sc. iv, 5. **recollected terms:** studied phrases. 18. **motions:** emotions. 25. **favour:** face. 38. **the bent:** its intensity 46. **free:** carefree. **bones:** bobbins (of bone). 47. **silly sooth:** simple truth. 49. **old age:** golden age.

SONG.

[*Clo.*] Come away, come away, death,
 And in sad cypress let me be laid.
Fly away, fly away, breath;
 I am slain by a fair cruel maid.   55
My shroud of white, stuck all with yew,
  O, prepare it!
My part of death, no one so true
  Did share it.

Not a flower, not a flower sweet,   60
 On my black coffin let there be strown.
Not a friend, not a friend greet
 My poor corpse, where my bones shall be thrown.
A thousand thousand sighs to save,
  Lay me, O, where   65
Sad true lover never find my grave,
  To weep there!

Duke. There's for thy pains.
Clo. No pains, sir; I take pleasure in singing,
sir.   70
Duke. I'll pay thy pleasure then.
Clo. Truly, sir, and pleasure will be paid, one
time or another.
Duke. Give me now leave to leave thee. 74
Clo. Now, the melancholy god protect thee, and
the tailor make thy doublet of changeable taffeta,
for thy mind is a very opal. I would have men of
such constancy put to sea, that their business might
be everything and their intent everywhere; for
that's it that always makes a good voyage of noth-
ing. Farewell.   [*Exit.* 81
Duke. Let all the rest give place.
    [*Curio and Attendants retire.*]
    Once more, Cesario,
Get thee to yond same sovereign cruelty.
Tell her, my love, more noble than the world,
Prizes not quantity of dirty lands.   85
The parts that fortune hath bestow'd upon her,
Tell her, I hold as giddily as fortune;
But 'tis that miracle and queen of gems
That nature pranks her in attracts my soul.
Vio. But if she cannot love you, sir? 90
Duke. [I] cannot be so answer'd.
Vio.   Sooth, but you must.
Say that some lady, as perhaps there is,
Hath for your love as great a pang of heart
As you have for Olivia. You cannot love her.
You tell her so. Must she not then be answer'd? 95
Duke. There is no woman's sides
Can bide the beating of so strong a passion

As love doth give my heart; no woman's heart
So big, to hold so much. They lack retention.
Alas, their love may be call'd appetite, 100
No motion of the liver, but the palate,
That suffer surfeit, cloyment, and revolt;
But mine is all as hungry as the sea,
And can digest as much. Make no compare
Between that love a woman can bear me 105
And that I owe Olivia.
Vio.   Ay, but I know —
Duke. What dost thou know?
Vio. Too well what love women to men may owe.
In faith, they are as true of heart as we.
My father had a daughter lov'd a man, 110
As it might be, perhaps, were I a woman,
I should your lordship.
Duke.   And what's her history?
Vio. A blank, my lord. She never told her love,
But let concealment, like a worm i' the bud,
Feed on her damask cheek. She pin'd in
  thought,   115
And with a green and yellow melancholy
She sat, like Patience on a monument,
Smiling at grief. Was not this love indeed?
We men may say more, swear more; but indeed
Our shows are more than will, for still we prove 120
Much in our vows, but little in our love.
Duke. But died thy sister of her love, my boy?
Vio. I am all the daughters of my father's house,
And all the brothers too; — and yet I know not.
Sir, shall I to this lady?
Duke.   Ay, that's the theme.
To her in haste. Give her this jewel. Say 126
My love can give no place, bide no denay.
        [*Exeunt.*

SCENE V. [*Olivia's garden.*]

Enter SIR TOBY, SIR ANDREW, *and* FABIAN.

Sir To. Come thy ways, Signior Fabian.
Fab. Nay, I'll come. If I lose a scruple of this
sport, let me be boil'd to death with melancholy. 4
Sir To. Wouldst thou not be glad to have the
niggardly rascally sheep-biter come by some notable
shame?
Fab. I would exult, man. You know, he brought
me out o' favour with my lady about a bear-baiting
here.   10
Sir To. To anger him we'll have the bear again,
and we will fool him black and blue. Shall we not,
Sir Andrew?
Sir And. An we do not, it is pity of our lives. 15

---

53. **cypress:** coffin of cypress wood. 58–59. **My ... share it:** i.e., No truer lover ever died than I. 76. **changeable taffeta:** shot silk. 87. **giddily:** carelessly. 89. **pranks:** adorns. 91. **[I]** (Hanmer). , *It* F. 99. **retention:** stability.
102. **cloyment:** satiety. **revolt:** revulsion. 115. **thought:** brooding. 116. **green and yellow,** signifying hope and jealousy.
117. **monument:** tomb.
 Sc. v, 6. **sheep-biter:** a vicious dog

Enter MARIA.

Sir To. Here comes the little villain. How now, my metal of India!

Mar. Get ye all three into the box-tree; Malvolio's coming down this walk. He has been yon- 20 der i' the sun practising behaviour to his own shadow this half hour. Observe him, for the love of mockery, for I know this letter will make a contemplative idiot of him. Close, in the name of jesting! Lie thou there [*throws down a letter*], for here comes the trout that must be caught with tickling.   [*Exit.* 26

Enter MALVOLIO.

Mal. 'Tis but fortune. All is fortune. Maria once told me she did affect me; and I have heard herself come thus near, that, should she fancy, it should be one of my complexion. Besides, she 30 uses me with a more exalted respect than any one else that follows her. What should I think on't?

Sir To. Here's an overweening rogue!   34

Fab. O, peace! Contemplation makes a rare turkey-cock of him. How he jets under his advanc'd plumes!

Sir And. 'S light, I could so beat the rogue!

Sir To. Peace, I say.

Mal. To be Count Malvolio!   40

Sir To. Ah, rogue!

Sir And. Pistol him, pistol him.

Sir To. Peace, peace!

Mal. There is example for't. The lady of the Strachy married the yeoman of the wardrobe. 45

Sir And. Fie on him, Jezebel!

Fab. O, peace! now he's deeply in. Look how imagination blows him.

Mal. Having been three months married to her, sitting in my state, —   50

Sir To. O, for a stone-bow, to hit him in the eye!

Mal. Calling my officers about me, in my branch'd velvet gown, having come from a day-bed, where I have left Olivia sleeping, —   55

Sir To. Fire and brimstone!

Fab. O, peace, peace!

Mal. And then to have the humour of state; and after a demure travel of regard, telling them I know my place as I would they should do theirs, to ask for my kinsman Toby, —   61

Sir To. Bolts and shackles!

Fab. O peace, peace, peace! Now, now.

Mal. Seven of my people, with an obedient start, make out for him. I frown the while, and per- 65 chance wind up my watch, or play with my — some

rich jewel. Toby approaches, curtsies there to me, —

Sir To. Shall this fellow live?

Fab. Though our silence be drawn from us with cars, yet peace.   71

Mal. I extend my hand to him thus, quenching my familiar smile with an austere regard of control, —

Sir To. And does not Toby take you a blow o' the lips then?   76

Mal. Saying, "Cousin Toby, my fortunes, having cast me on your niece, give me this prerogative of speech," —

Sir To. What, what?   80

Mal. "You must amend your drunkenness."

Sir To. Out, scab!

Fab. Nay, patience, or we break the sinews o. our plot.

Mal. "Besides, you waste the treasure of your time with a foolish knight," —   86

Sir And. That's me, I warrant you.

Mal. "One Sir Andrew," —

Sir And. I knew 'twas I; for many do call me fool.   90

Mal. What employment have we here?

[*Taking up the letter.*]

Fab. Now is the woodcock near the gin.

Sir To. O, peace, and the spirit of humours intimate reading aloud to him!   94

Mal. By my life, this is my lady's hand. These be her very C's, her U's, and her T's; and thus makes she her great P's. It is, in contempt of question, her hand.

Sir And. Her C's, her U's, and her T's: why that?   100

Mal. [*Reads.*] "To the unknown belov'd, this, and my good wishes": — her very phrases! By your leave, wax. Soft! And the impressure her Lucrece, with which she uses to seal. 'Tis my lady. To whom should this be?   105

Fab. This wins him, liver and all.

Mal. [*Reads.*]

"Jove knows I love;
    But who?
Lips, do not move;
No man must know."   110

"No man must know." What follows? The numbers alter'd! "No man must know!" If this should be thee, Malvolio?

Sir To. Marry, hang thee, brock!

Mal. [*Reads.*]

"I may command where I adore;   115

---

17. **metal of India:** gold.   22. **contemplative:** staring or self-regarding; cf. "Contemplation" (l. 35).   26. **tickling.** Trout can be caught by being stroked.   36. **jets:** struts.   45. **Strachy.** This lady, unidentified, obviously married below her station.   50. **state:** chair of state.   54. **branch'd:** flowered.   58. **humour of state:** mood of authority.   59. **demure ... regard:** grave look about (me).   73. **control:** authority.   92. **woodcock:** a bird noted for its stupidity. **gin:** snare. 97. **in contempt of:** beyond.   103. **By ... wax.** Spoken as he breaks the seal.   112. **numbers:** metre.   114. **brock:** badger.

But silence, like a Lucrece knife,
With bloodless stroke my heart doth gore.
M, O, A, I, doth sway my life."
Fab. A fustian riddle!
Sir To. Excellent wench, say I.   120
Mal. "M, O, A, I, doth sway my life." Nay,
but first, let me see, let me see, let me see.
Fab. What dish o' poison has she dress'd him!
Sir To. And with what wing the [staniel] checks
at it!   125
Mal. "I may command where I adore." Why,
she may command me. I serve her. She is my
lady. Why, this is evident to any formal capacity,
there is no obstruction in this. And the end, —
what should that alphabetical position portend? 130
If I could make that resemble something in me! —
Softly! M, O, A, I, —
Sir To. O, ay, make up that. He is now at a
cold scent.
Fab. Sowter will cry upon't for all this, though
it be as rank as a fox.   136
Mal. M, — Malvolio; M, — why, that begins
my name.
Fab. Did not I say he would work it out? The
cur is excellent at faults.   140
Mal. M, — but then there is no consonancy in
the sequel. That suffers under probation. A
should follow, but O does.
Fab. And O shall end, I hope.
Sir To. Ay, or I'll cudgel him, and make him
cry O!   146
Mal. And then I comes behind.
Fab. Ay, an you had any eye behind you, you
might see more detraction at your heels than fortunes before you.   150
Mal. M, O, A, I; this simulation is not as the
former. And yet, to crush this a little, it would
bow to me, for every one of these letters are in my
name. Soft! here follows prose.   154
[*Reads.*] "If this fall into thy hand, revolve. In
my stars I am above thee, but be not afraid of
greatness. Some are [born] great, some achieve
greatness, and some have greatness thrust upon 'em.
Thy Fates open their hands, let thy blood and spirit
embrace them; and, to inure thyself to what   160
thou art like to be, cast thy humble slough and
appear fresh. Be opposite with a kinsman, surly
with servants; let thy tongue tang arguments of
state; put thyself into the trick of singularity: she
thus advises thee that sighs for thee. Remem- 165
ber who commended thy yellow stockings, and

wish'd to see thee ever cross-garter'd. I say, remember. Go to, thou art made if thou desir'st to
be so; if not, let me see thee a steward still, the fellow of servants, and not worthy to touch For- 170
tune's fingers. Farewell. She that would alter
services with thee,

                    THE FORTUNATE UNHAPPY."

Daylight and champaign discovers not more.
This is open. I will be proud, I will read politic 175
authors, I will baffle Sir Toby, I will wash off gross
acquaintance, I will be point-device the very man.
I do not now fool myself, to let imagination jade me;
for every reason excites to this, that my lady loves
me. She did commend my yellow stockings of 180
late, she did praise my leg being cross-garter'd; and
in this she manifests herself to my love, and with a
kind of injunction drives me to these habits of her
liking. I thank my stars I am happy. I will be
strange, stout, in yellow stockings, and cross- 185
garter'd, even with the swiftness of putting on.
Jove and my stars be praised! Here is yet a postscript.
[*Reads.*] "Thou canst not choose but know who
I am. If thou entertain'st my love, let it appear 190
in thy smiling. Thy smiles become thee well;
therefore in my presence still smile, dear my sweet,
I prithee."
Jove, I thank thee. I will smile; I will do everything that thou wilt have me.   [*Exit.* 195
Fab. I will not give my part of this sport for a
pension of thousands to be paid from the Sophy.
Sir To. I could marry this wench for this
device —   200
Sir And. So could I too.
Sir To. And ask no other dowry with her but
such another jest.

Re-enter MARIA.

Sir And. Nor I neither.
Fab. Here comes my noble gull-catcher.   205
Sir To. Wilt thou set thy foot o' my neck?
Sir And. Or o' mine either?
Sir To. Shall I play my freedom at tray-trip,
and become thy bond-slave?
Sir And. I' faith, or I either?   210
Sir To. Why, thou hast put him in such a dream,
that when the image of it leaves him he must run
mad.
Mar. Nay, but say true. Does it work upon
him?   215
Sir To. Like aqua-vitæ with a midwife.

119. fustian: ridiculous. 124. [staniel] (Hanmer): untrained falcon. *stallion* F. checks at it: turns aside (as to
inferior prey). Cf. III.i.71. 128. formal: normal. 135-36. Sowter...fox. I.e., Even Sowter (a stupid hound) will
catch this scent though, in fact, it is as strong as a fox's. Cf. *Shrew*, Ind. i.23. 140. faults: failure of the scent. 141.
consonancy: agreement. 142. probation: testing. 151. simulation: suggestion. 152. crush: force (the meaning). 155.
revolve: consider. 157. [born] (Rowe). *become* F. Cf. III.iv.45 and V.i.378. 161. slough: skin (of a snake). 162.
opposite: contradictory. 174. champaign: open country. 175. politic: i.e., who treat state affairs. 177. point-device:
precisely. 178. jade: trick. 185. stout: haughty. 198. Sophy: Shah of Persia. 208. tray-trip: a game with dice.

Mar. If you will then see the fruits of the sport, mark his first approach before my lady. He will come to her in yellow stockings, and 'tis a colour she abhors, and cross-garter'd, a fashion she de- 220 tests; and he will smile upon her, which will now be so unsuitable to her disposition, being addicted to a melancholy as she is, that it cannot but turn him into a notable contempt. If you will see it, follow me.   225

Sir To. To the gates of Tartar, thou most excellent devil of wit!

Sir And. I'll make one too.   [*Exeunt.*

ACT III

Scene I. [*Olivia's garden.*]

Enter VIOLA *and* CLOWN [*with a tabor*].

Vio. Save thee, friend, and thy music! Dost thou live by thy tabor?

Clo. No, sir, I live by the church.

Vio. Art thou a churchman?   4

Clo. No such matter, sir. I do live by the church; for I do live at my house, and my house doth stand by the church.

Vio. So thou mayst say, the king lies by a beggar, if a beggar dwells near him; or, the church stands by thy tabor, if thy tabor stand by the church.   11

Clo. You have said, sir. To see this age! A sentence is but a chev'ril glove to a good wit. How quickly the wrong side may be turn'd outward! 15

Vio. Nay, that's certain. They that dally nicely with words may quickly make them wanton.

Clo. I would, therefore, my sister had had no name, sir.   20

Vio. Why, man?

Clo. Why, sir, her name's a word, and to dally with that word might make my sister wanton. But, indeed, words are very rascals since bonds disgrac'd them.   25

Vio. Thy reason, man?

Clo. Troth, sir, I can yield you none without words; and words are grown so false, I am loath to prove reason with them.   29

Vio. I warrant thou art a merry fellow and car'st for nothing.

Clo. Not so, sir, I do care for something; but in my conscience, sir, I do not care for you. If that be to care for nothing, sir, I would it would make you invisible.   35

Vio. Art not thou the Lady Olivia's fool?

Clo. No, indeed, sir; the Lady Olivia has no folly. She will keep no fool, sir, till she be married; and fools are as like husbands as pilchards are to herrings, the husband's the bigger. I am indeed not her fool, but her corrupter of words.   41

Vio. I saw thee late at the Count Orsino's.

Clo. Foolery, sir, does walk about the orb like the sun, it shines everywhere. I would be sorry, sir, but the fool should be as oft with your master as with my mistress. I think I saw your wisdom there.   47

Vio. Nay, an thou pass upon me, I'll no more with thee. Hold, there's expenses for thee.

Clo. Now Jove, in his next commodity of hair, send thee a beard!   51

Vio. By my troth, I'll tell thee, I am almost sick for one, — [*aside*] though I would not have it grow on my chin. Is thy lady within?

Clo. Would not a pair of these have bred, sir? 55

Vio. Yes, being kept together and put to use.

Clo. I would play Lord Pandarus of Phrygia, sir, to bring a Cressida to this Troilus.

Vio. I understand you, sir. 'Tis well begg'd.   60

Clo. The matter, I hope, is not great, sir, begging but a beggar. Cressida was a beggar. My lady is within, sir. I will construe to them whence you come. Who you are and what you would are out of my welkin — I might say "element," but the word is overworn.   [*Exit.* 66

Vio. This fellow is wise enough to play the fool, And to do that well craves a kind of wit. He must observe their mood on whom he jests, The quality of persons, and the time,   70 And, like the haggard, check at every feather That comes before his eye. This is a practice As full of labour as a wise man's art; For folly that he wisely shows is fit, But wise men, folly-fall'n, quite taint their wit. 75

Enter SIR TOBY *and* SIR ANDREW.

Sir To. Save you, gentleman.

Vio. And you, sir.

Sir And. Dieu vous garde, monsieur.

Vio. Et vous aussi; votre serviteur.

Sir And. I hope, sir, you are; and I am yours. 81

Sir To. Will you encounter the house? My niece is desirous you should enter, if your trade be to her.

Vio. I am bound to your niece, sir; I mean, she is the list of my voyage.   86

226. **Tartar:** Tartarus (Hell).
Act III, sc. i, 2. **tabor:** small drum. 13. **chev'ril:** kid. 18. **wanton:** equivocal (*unchaste*, l. 23). 24. **disgrac'd them:** i.e., became necessary to bind them. 39. **pilchards:** fish like herring. 48. **pass upon:** jest at. 50. **commodity:** consignment. 55. **these:** i.e., coins (see l. 49). 56. **use:** interest. 57. **Pandarus:** uncle to Cressida, who brought her and Troilus together. 62. **Cressida...beggar.** In Henryson's *Testament of Cresseid*, Cressida became a leper and begged by the roadside. 71. **haggard:** untrained hawk. 75. **folly-fall'n:** acting like fools. 79-80. *Dieu...serviteur:* God keep you, sir. And you, too; I am your servant. 86. **list:** goal.

Sir To. Taste your legs, sir; put them to motion.

Vio. My legs do better understand me, sir, than I understand what you mean by bidding me taste my legs.   91

Sir To. I mean, to go, sir, to enter.

Vio. I will answer you with [gait] and entrance. But we are prevented.

Enter OLIVIA *and Gentlewoman.*

Most excellent accomplish'd lady, the heavens rain odours on you!   96

Sir And. That youth's a rare courtier. "Rain odours;" well.

Vio. My matter hath no voice, lady, but to your own most pregnant and vouchsafed ear.   100

Sir And. "Odours," "pregnant," and "vouchsafed"; I'll get 'em all three all ready.

Oli. Let the garden door be shut, and leave me to hearing. [*Exeunt all but Olivia and Viola.*] Give me your hand, sir.   105

Vio. My duty, madam, and most humble service.

Oli. What is your name?

Vio. Cesario is your servant's name, fair princess.

Oli. My servant, sir! 'Twas never merry world Since lowly feigning was call'd compliment.   110 You're servant to the Count Orsino, youth.

Vio. And he is yours, and his must needs be yours. Your servant's servant is your servant, madam.

Oli. For him, I think not on him.   For his thoughts, Would they were blanks, rather than fill'd with me!   115

Vio. Madam, I come to whet your gentle thoughts On his behalf.

Oli.   O, by your leave, I pray you, I bade you never speak again of him; But, would you undertake another suit, I had rather hear you to solicit that   120 Than music from the spheres.

Vio.   Dear lady,—

Oli. Give me leave, beseech you. I did send, After the last enchantment you did here, A ring in chase of you; so did I abuse Myself, my servant, and, I fear me, you.   125 Under your hard construction must I sit, To force that on you, in a shameful cunning, Which you knew none of yours. What might you think? Have you not set mine honour at the stake And baited it with all th' unmuzzled thoughts 130

That tyrannous heart can think?   To one of your receiving Enough is shown. A cypress, not a bosom, Hides my heart. So, let me hear you speak.

Vio. I pity you.

Oli.   That's a degree to love.

Vio. No, not a grize; for 'tis a vulgar proof, 135 That very oft we pity enemies.

Oli. Why, then, methinks 'tis time to smile again. O world, how apt the poor are to be proud! If one should be a prey, how much the better To fall before the lion than the wolf!   140
                                   [*Clock strikes.*
The clock upbraids me with the waste of time. Be not afraid, good youth, I will not have you; And yet, when wit and youth is come to harvest, Your wife is like to reap a proper man. There lies your way, due west.   145

Vio. Then westward-ho!   Grace and good disposition Attend your ladyship! You'll nothing, madam, to my lord by me?

Oli. Stay! I prithee, tell me what thou think'st of me.   150

Vio. That you do think you are not what you are.

Oli. If I think so, I think the same of you.

Vio. Then think you right. I am not what I am.

Oli. I would you were as I would have you be!

Vio. Would it be better, madam, than I am? I wish it might, for now I am your fool.   156

Oli. O, what a deal of scorn looks beautiful In the contempt and anger of his lip! A murd'rous guilt shows not itself more soon Than love that would seem hid. Love's night is noon.   160 Cesario, by the roses of the spring, By maidhood, honour, truth, and everything, I love thee so, that, maugre all thy pride, Nor wit nor reason can my passion hide. Do not extort thy reasons from this clause,   165 For that I woo, thou therefore hast no cause; But rather reason thus with reason fetter, Love sought is good, but given unsought is better.

Vio. By innocence I swear, and by my youth, I have one heart, one bosom, and one truth,   170 And that no woman has; nor never none Shall mistress be of it, save I alone. And so adieu, good madam; nevermore Will I my master's tears to you deplore.

Oli. Yet come again; for thou perhaps mayst move   175 That heart, which now abhors, to like his love.
                                             [*Exeunt.*

---

93. **[gait]** (Johnson). *gate* F. A pun on the two words. 94. **prevented:** anticipated. 100. **pregnant:** ready. 127. **to force:** for forcing. 129–30. **Have...thoughts.** The figure of speech comes from bear-baiting. 131. **receiving:** intelligence. 132. **cypress:** thin crepe. 134. **degree:** step. 135. **grize:** step. **vulgar proof:** common experience. 163. **maugre:** in spite of. 166. **no cause:** i.e., to woo.

SCENE II. [*A room in Olivia's house.*]

Enter SIR TOBY, SIR ANDREW, *and* FABIAN.

Sir And. No, faith, I'll not stay a jot longer.

Sir To. Thy reason, dear venom, give thy reason.

Fab. You must needs yield your reason, Sir Andrew.   5

Sir And. Marry, I saw your niece do more favours to the Count's serving-man than ever she bestow'd upon me. I saw't i' th' orchard.

Sir To. Did she see thee the while, old boy? Tell me that.   10

Sir And. As plain as I see you now.

Fab. This was a great argument of love in her toward you.

Sir And. 'Slight, will you make an ass o' me?

Fab. I will prove it legitimate, sir, upon the oaths of judgement and reason.   16

Sir To. And they have been grand-jurymen since before Noah was a sailor.

Fab. She did show favour to the youth in your sight only to exasperate you, to awake your   20 dormouse valour, to put fire in your heart, and brimstone in your liver. You should then have accosted her; and with some excellent jests, fire-new from the mint, you should have bang'd the youth into dumbness. This was look'd for at   25 your hand, and this was balk'd. The double gilt of this opportunity you let time wash off, and you are now sailed into the north of my lady's opinion, where you will hang like an icicle on a Dutchman's beard, unless you do redeem it by some laudable attempt either of valour or policy.   31

Sir And. An't be any way, it must be with valour; for policy I hate. I had as lief be a Brownist as a politician.   34

Sir To. Why, then, build me thy fortunes upon the basis of valour. Challenge me the Count's youth to fight with him; hurt him in eleven places; my niece shall take note of it; and assure thyself, there is no love-broker in the world can more prevail in man's commendation with woman than report of valour.   41

Fab. There is no way but this, Sir Andrew.

Sir And. Will either of you bear me a challenge to him?

Sir To. Go, write it in a martial hand. Be   45 curst and brief. It is no matter how witty, so it be eloquent and full of invention. Taunt him with the license of ink. If thou thou'st him some thrice, it shall not be amiss; and as many lies as will lie in thy sheet of paper, although the sheet were big   50

enough for the bed of Ware in England, set 'em down. Go about it. Let there be gall enough in thy ink. Though thou write with a goose-pen, no matter. About it.

Sir And. Where shall I find you?   55

Sir To. We'll call thee at the cubiculo. Go.

[*Exit Sir Andrew.*

Fab. This is a dear manikin to you, Sir Toby.

Sir To. I have been dear to him, lad, some two thousand strong, or so.

Fab. We shall have a rare letter from him. But you'll not deliver't?   61

Sir To. Never trust me, then; and by all means stir on the youth to an answer. I think oxen and wainropes cannot hale them together. For Andrew, if he were open'd and you find so much blood in his liver as will clog the foot of a flea, I'll eat the rest of the anatomy.   67

Fab. And his opposite, the youth, bears in his visage no great presage of cruelty.

Enter MARIA.

Sir To. Look, where the youngest wren of mine comes.   71

Mar. If you desire the spleen, and will laugh yourselves into stitches, follow me. Yond gull Malvolio is turned heathen, a very renegado; for there is no Christian that means to be saved by   75 believing rightly can ever believe such impossible passages of grossness. He's in yellow stockings.

Sir To. And cross-garter'd?   79

Mar. Most villanously; like a pedant that keeps a school i' th' church. I have dogg'd him like his murderer. He does obey every point of the letter that I dropp'd to betray him. He does smile his face into more lines than is in the new map with the augmentation of the Indies. You have   85 not seen such a thing as 'tis. I can hardly forbear hurling things at him. I know my lady will strike him. If she do, he'll smile and take't for a great favour.

Sir To. Come, bring us, bring us where he is.   90

[*Exeunt.*

SCENE III. [*A street.*]

Enter SEBASTIAN *and* ANTONIO.

Seb. I would not by my will have troubled you; But, since you make your pleasure of your pains, I will no further chide you.

Ant. I could not stay behind you. My desire, More sharp than filed steel, did spur me forth,   5

Sc. ii, 14. **'Slight:** by God's light.   31. **policy:** tact (Sir Andrew interprets as *intrigue*).   33. **Brownist:** member of the sect of Independents, founded by Robert Brown.   46. **curst:** surly.   48. **thou'st:** use "thou" as to an inferior.   51. **bed of Ware:** a famous bed (nearly twelve feet square) in an inn at Ware in Hertfordshire.   56. **cubiculo:** i.e., Sir Andrew's apartment.   64. **wainropes:** cart-ropes.   68. **opposite:** opponent.   70. **mine** Ff. *nine* (Theobald).   72. **spleen:** fit of laughter.   77. **impossible ... grossness:** incredible acts of stupidity.   84. **new ... Indies.** Probably a map published about 1599 by Emerie Molyneux, giving more of the East Indies than any earlier one. See Introduction, p. 279.

And not all love to see you, though so much
As might have drawn one to a longer voyage,
But jealousy what might befall your travel,
Being skilless in these parts; which to a stranger,
Unguided and unfriended, often prove   10
Rough and unhospitable. My willing love,
The rather by these arguments of fear,
Set forth in your pursuit.
   Seb.   My kind Antonio,
I can no other answer make but thanks,
And thanks, and ever [thanks. Too] oft good turns   15
Are shuffl'd off with such uncurrent pay;
But, were my worth as is my conscience firm,
You should find better dealing. What's to do?
Shall we go see the reliques of this town?
   Ant. To-morrow, sir. Best first go see your
    lodging.   20
   Seb. I am not weary, and 'tis long to night.
I pray you, let us satisfy our eyes
With the memorials and the things of fame
That do renown this city.
   Ant.   Would you'd pardon me.
I do not without danger walk these streets.   25
Once, in a sea-fight, 'gainst the Count his galleys
I did some service; of such note indeed,
That were I ta'en here it would scarce be answer'd.
   Seb. Belike you slew great number of his people?
   Ant. Th' offence is not of such a bloody nature,
Albeit the quality of the time and quarrel   31
Might well have given us bloody argument.
It might have since been answer'd in repaying
What we took from them, which, for traffic's sake,
Most of our city did; only myself stood out,   35
For which, if I be lapsed in this place,
I shall pay dear.
   Seb.   Do not then walk too open.
   Ant. It doth not fit me. Hold, sir, here's my
    purse.
In the south suburbs, at the Elephant
Is best to lodge. I will bespeak our diet,   40
Whiles you beguile the time and feed your knowl-
    edge
With viewing of the town. There shall you have me.
   Seb. Why I your purse?
   Ant. Haply your eye shall light upon some toy
You have desire to purchase; and your store,   45
I think, is not for idle markets, sir.
   Seb. I'll be your purse-bearer and leave you
For an hour.
   Ant.   To th' Elephant.
   Seb.   I do remember.
                               [*Exeunt.*

SCENE IV. [*Olivia's garden.*]

Enter OLIVIA *and* MARIA.

   Oli. [*Aside.*] I have sent after him; he says he'll
    come.
How shall I feast him? What bestow of him?
For youth is bought more oft than begg'd or bor-
    row'd.
I speak too loud. —
Where is Malvolio? He is sad and civil,   5
And suits well for a servant with my fortunes.
Where is Malvolio?
   Mar. He's coming, madam, but in very strange
manner. He is, sure, possess'd, madam.
   Oli. Why, what's the matter? Does he rave? 10
   Mar. No, madam, he does nothing but smile.
Your ladyship were best to have some guard about
you, if he come; for, sure, the man is tainted in's
wits.
   Oli. Go call him hither.

Enter MALVOLIO.

                  I am as mad as he, 15
If sad and merry madness equal be.
How now, Malvolio!
   Mal. Sweet lady, ho, ho.
   Oli. Smil'st thou?
I sent for thee upon a sad occasion.   20
   Mal. Sad, lady? I could be sad. This does
make some obstruction in the blood, this cross-
gartering; but what of that? If it please the eye
of one, it is with me as the very true sonnet is,
"Please one, and please all."   25
   [*Oli.*] Why, how dost thou, man? What is the
matter with thee?
   Mal. Not black in my mind, though yellow in
my legs. It did come to his hands, and commands
shall be executed. I think we do know the sweet
Roman hand.   31
   Oli. Wilt thou go to bed, Malvolio?
   Mal. To bed! Ay, sweet heart, and I'll come to
thee.
   Oli. God comfort thee! Why dost thou smile
so and kiss thy hand so oft?   36
   Mar. How do you, Malvolio?
   Mal. At your request! Yes. Nightingales
answer daws.
   Mar. Why appear you with this ridiculous bold-
ness before my lady?   41
   Mal. "Be not afraid of greatness:" 'twas well
writ.
   Oli. What mean'st thou by that, Malvolio?
   Mal. "Some are born great," —   45

   Sc. iii, 8. **jealousy:** suspicion. 9. **skilless:** unacquainted. 15. **And thanks ... oft** (Seymour). *And thankes; and ever oft* F. 16. **uncurrent:** worthless. 17. **worth:** wealth. 28. **answer'd:** atoned for. 31. **quality:** nature. 36. **lapsed:** caught.
46. **idle markets:** frivolous purchases.
   Sc. iv, 5. **sad:** grave. 24. **sonnet:** ballad, of which the quotation is the refrain. 26–27. [*Oli.*] F2. *Mal.* F1.

Oli. Ha!

Mal. "Some achieve greatness," —

Oli. What say'st thou?

Mal. "And some have greatness thrust upon them."   50

Oli. Heaven restore thee!

Mal. "Remember who commended thy yellow stockings," —

Oli. Thy yellow stockings!

Mal. "And wish'd to see thee cross-garter'd."

Oli. Cross-garter'd!   56

Mal. "Go to, thou art made, if thou desir'st to be so;" —

Oli. Am I made?   59

Mal. "If not, let me see thee a servant still."

Oli. Why, this is very midsummer madness.

Enter SERVANT.

Ser. Madam, the young gentleman of the Count Orsino's is return'd. I could hardly entreat him back. He attends your ladyship's pleasure.   65

Oli. I'll come to him. [*Exit Servant.*] Good Maria, let this fellow be look'd to. Where's my cousin Toby? Let some of my people have a special care of him. I would not have him miscarry for the half of my dowry.   70

[*Exeunt [Olivia and Maria].*

Mal. O, ho! do you come near me now? No worse man than Sir Toby to look to me! This concurs directly with the letter. She sends him on purpose, that I may appear stubborn to him, for she incites me to that in the letter. "Cast thy   75 humble slough," says she; "be opposite with a kinsman, surly with servants; let thy tongue tang with arguments of state; put thyself into the trick of singularity;" and consequently sets down the manner how; as, a sad face, a reverend carriage, a   80 slow tongue, in the habit of some sir of note, and so forth. I have lim'd her; but it is Jove's doing, and Jove make me thankful! And when she went away now, "Let this fellow be looked to"; "fellow!" not Malvolio, nor after my degree, but "fel-   85 low." Why, everything adheres together, that no dram of a scruple, no scruple of a scruple, no obstacle, no incredulous or unsafe circumstance — What can be said? Nothing that can be can come between me and the full prospect of my hopes.   90 Well, Jove, not I, is the doer of this, and he is to be thanked.

Re-enter MARIA, *with* SIR TOBY *and* FABIAN.

Sir To. Which way is he, in the name of sanctity?

If all the devils of hell be drawn in little, and Legion himself possess'd him, yet I'll speak to him.   96

Fab. Here he is, here he is. How is't with you, sir? How is't with you, man?

Mal. Go off; I discard you. Let me enjoy my private. Go off.   100

Mar. Lo, how hollow the fiend speaks within him! Did not I tell you? Sir Toby, my lady prays you to have a care of him.

Mal. Ah, ha! Does she so?   104

Sir To. Go to, go to; peace, peace. We must deal gently with him. Let me alone. How do you, Malvolio? How is't with you? What, man, defy the devil! Consider, he's an enemy to mankind.

Mal. Do you know what you say?   110

Mar. La you, an you speak ill of the devil, how he takes it at heart! Pray God he be not bewitch'd!

Fab. Carry his water to the wise woman.   114

Mar. Marry, and it shall be done to-morrow morning if I live. My lady would not lose him for more than I'll say.

Mal. How now, mistress!

Mar. O Lord!   118

Sir To. Prithee, hold thy peace; this is not the way. Do you not see you move him? Let me alone with him.

Fab. No way but gentleness; gently, gently. The fiend is rough, and will not be roughly us'd.

Sir To. Why, how now, my bawcock! How dost thou, chuck?   126

Mal. Sir!

Sir To. Ay, "Biddy, come with me." What, man, 'tis not for gravity to play at cherry-pit with Satan. Hang him, foul collier!   130

Mar. Get him to say his prayers, good Sir Toby, get him to pray.

Mal. My prayers, minx!

Mar. No, I warrant you, he will not hear of godliness.   135

Mal. Go, hang yourselves all! You are idle shallow things; I am not of your element. You shall know more hereafter.   [*Exit.*

Sir To. Is't possible?

Fab. If this were played upon a stage now, I could condemn it as an improbable fiction.   141

Sir To. His very genius hath taken the infection of the device, man.

Mar. Nay, pursue him now, lest the device take air and taint.   145

Fab. Why, we shall make him mad indeed.

Mar. The house will be the quieter.

---

69. **miscarry:** suffer harm.   71. **come near:** begin to understand.   79. **consequently:** thereupon.   82. **lim'd:** caught.
84. **fellow:** originally *companion*, and so taken by Malvolio.   88. **incredulous:** incredible.   95. **little:** miniature. **Legion.**
See *Mark* v.9.   124. **rough:** violent.   125. **bawcock:** fine fellow.   129. **cherry-pit:** child's game of throwing cherry stones
into a hole.   137. **element:** sphere.   144. **take...taint:** become known and spoiled.

Sir To. Come, we'll have him in a dark room and bound. My niece is already in the belief that he's mad. We may carry it thus, for our pleasure 150 and his penance, till our very pastime, tired out of breath, prompt us to have mercy on him; at which time we will bring the device to the bar and crown thee for a finder of madmen. But see, but see. 155

Enter SIR ANDREW.

Fab. More matter for a May morning.
Sir And. Here's the challenge, read it. I warrant there's vinegar and pepper in't.
Fab. Is't so saucy? 159
Sir And. Ay, is't, I warrant him. Do but read.
Sir To. Give me. [*Reads.*] "Youth, whatsoever thou art, thou art but a scurvy fellow."
Fab. Good, and valiant. 164
Sir To. [*Reads.*] "Wonder not, nor admire not in thy mind, why I do call thee so, for I will show thee no reason for't."
Fab. A good note. That keeps you from the blow of the law. 169
Sir To. [*Reads.*] "Thou com'st to the lady Olivia, and in my sight she uses thee kindly. But thou liest in thy throat; that is not the matter I challenge thee for."
Fab. Very brief, and to exceeding good sense — less. 175
Sir To. [*Reads.*] "I will waylay thee going home; where if it be thy chance to kill me," —
Fab. Good.
Sir To. [*Reads.*] "Thou kill'st me like a rogue and a villain." 180
Fab. Still you keep o' th' windy side of the law; good.
Sir To. [*Reads.*] "Fare thee well, and God have mercy upon one of our souls! He may have mercy upon mine; but my hope is better, and so look 185 to thyself. Thy friend, as thou usest him, and thy sworn enemy,
                    ANDREW AGUECHEEK."
If this letter move him not, his legs cannot. I'll give't him. 189
Mar. You may have very fit occasion for't. He is now in some commerce with my lady, and will by and by depart.
Sir To. Go, Sir Andrew, scout me for him at the corner of the orchard like a bum-baily. So soon as ever thou seest him, draw; and, as thou 195 draw'st, swear horrible; for it comes to pass oft that a terrible oath, with a swaggering accent sharply twang'd off, gives manhood more approbation than ever proof itself would have earn'd him. Away!

Sir And. Nay, let me alone for swearing. 201
                                        [*Exit.*
Sir To. Now will not I deliver his letter; for the behaviour of the young gentleman gives him out to be of good capacity and breeding; his employment between his lord and my niece confirms no 205 less; therefore this letter, being so excellently ignorant, will breed no terror in the youth; he will find it comes from a clodpole. But, sir, I will deliver his challenge by word of mouth, set upon Aguecheek a notable report of valour, and drive the gentle- 210 man, as I know his youth will aptly receive it, into a most hideous opinion of his rage, skill, fury, and impetuosity. This will so fright them both that they will kill one another by the look, like cockatrices. 215

Re-enter OLIVIA *with* VIOLA.

Fab. Here he comes with your niece. Give them way till he take leave, and presently after him.
Sir To. I will meditate the while upon some horrid message for a challenge. 220
              [*Exeunt Sir Toby, Fabian, and Maria.*]
Oli. I have said too much unto a heart of stone,
And laid mine honour too unchary on't.
There's something in me that reproves my fault;
But such a headstrong potent fault it is
That it but mocks reproof. 225
Vio. With the same 'haviour that your passion bears
Goes on my master's grief.
Oli. Here, wear this jewel for me; 'tis my picture.
Refuse it not; it hath no tongue to vex you;
And I beseech you come again to-morrow. 230
What shall you ask of me that I'll deny,
That honour sav'd may upon asking give?
Vio. Nothing but this, — your true love for my master.
Oli. How with mine honour may I give him that
Which I have given to you?
Vio.   I will acquit you. 235
Oli. Well, come again to-morrow. Fare thee well!
A fiend like thee might bear my soul to hell.
                                        [*Exit.*]

Re-enter SIR TOBY *and* FABIAN.

Sir To. Gentleman, God save thee!
Vio. And you, sir. 239
Sir To. That defence thou hast, betake thee to't. Of what nature the wrongs are thou hast done him, I know not; but thy intercepter, full of despite, bloody as the hunter, attends thee at the orchard-end. Dismount thy tuck, be yare in thy

preparation, for thy assailant is quick, skilful, and deadly.   246

Vio. You mistake, sir, I am sure. No man hath any quarrel to me. My remembrance is very free and clear from any image of offence done to any man.   250

Sir To. You'll find it otherwise, I assure you; therefore, if you hold your life at any price, betake you to your guard; for your opposite hath in him what youth, strength, skill, and wrath can furnish man withal.   255

Vio. I pray you, sir, what is he?

Sir To. He is knight, dubb'd with unhatch'd rapier and on carpet consideration; but he is a devil in private brawl. Souls and bodies hath he divorc'd three; and his incensement at this mo- 260
ment is so implacable, that satisfaction can be none but by pangs of death and sepulchre. Hob, nob, is his word; give't or take't.

Vio. I will return again into the house and desire some conduct of the lady. I am no fighter. 265
I have heard of some kind of men that put quarrels purposely on others, to taste their valour. Belike this is a man of that quirk.

Sir To. Sir, no; his indignation derives itself out of a very competent injury; therefore, get you   270
on and give him his desire. Back you shall not to the house, unless you undertake that with me which with as much safety you might answer him; there-fore, on, or strip your sword stark naked; for med-dle you must, that's certain, or forswear to wear iron about you.   276

Vio. This is as uncivil as strange. I beseech you, do me this courteous office, as to know of the knight what my offence to him is. It is something of my negligence, nothing of my purpose.   280

Sir To. I will do so. Signor Fabian, stay you by this gentleman till my return.   [*Exit.*

Vio. Pray you, sir, do you know of this matter?

Fab. I know the knight is incens'd against   285
you, even to a mortal arbitrement, but nothing of the circumstance more.

Vio. I beseech you, what manner of man is he?

Fab. Nothing of that wonderful promise, to   290
read him by his form, as you are like to find him in the proof of his valour. He is, indeed, sir, the most skilful, bloody, and fatal opposite that you could possibly have found in any part of Illyria. Will you walk towards him? I will make your peace with him if I can.   296

Vio. I shall be much bound to you for't. I am one that had rather go with sir priest than sir

knight. I care not who knows so much of my mettle.   [*Exeunt.* 300

Re-enter SIR TOBY, *with* SIR ANDREW.

Sir To. Why, man, he's a very devil; I have not seen such a firago. I had a pass with him, rapier, scabbard, and all, and he gives me the stuck in with such a mortal motion, that it is inevitable; and on the answer, he pays you as surely as your feet 305
hits the ground they step on. They say he has been fencer to the Sophy.

Sir And. Pox on't, I'll not meddle with him.

Sir To. Ay, but he will not now be pacified. Fabian can scarce hold him yonder.   310

Sir And. Plague on't, an I thought he had been valiant and so cunning in fence, I'd have seen him damn'd ere I'd have challeng'd him. Let him let the matter slip, and I'll give him my horse, grey Capilet.   315

Sir To. I'll make the motion. Stand here; make a good show on't. This shall end without the per-dition of souls. [*Aside.*] Marry, I'll ride your horse as well as I ride you.   319

Re-enter FABIAN *and* VIOLA.

[*To Fab.*] I have his horse to take up the quarrel. I have persuaded him the youth's a devil.

Fab. He is as horribly conceited of him; and pants and looks pale, as if a bear were at his heels. 324

Sir To. [*To Vio.*] There's no remedy, sir; he will fight with you for's oath sake. Marry, he hath better bethought him of his quarrel, and he finds that now scarce to be worth talking of; therefore draw, for the supportance of his vow. He pro-tests he will not hurt you.   330

Vio. [*Aside.*] Pray God defend me! A little thing would make me tell them how much I lack of a man.

Fab. Give ground, if you see him furious.   334

Sir To. Come, Sir Andrew, there's no remedy; the gentleman will, for his honour's sake, have one bout with you. He cannot by the duello avoid it; but he has promised me, as he is a gentleman and a soldier, he will not hurt you. Come on; to't.   340

Sir And. Pray God, he keep his oath!

Enter ANTONIO.

Vio. I do assure you, 'tis against my will.
                                     [*They draw.*

Ant. Put up your sword. If this young gentle-man
Have done offence, I take the fault on me;

---

257. **unhatch'd:** unhacked.   258. **carpet consideration.** A "carpet knight" was one who had been dubbed not on the battlefield for valor, but on a carpet for money paid to the king.   265. **conduct:** escort.   268. **quirk:** humor.   274. **meddle:** fight.   286. **arbitrement:** trial.   302. **firago:** virago.   303. **stuck in:** thrust.   305. **on the answer:** on the return.   **pays you:** does for you.   320. **take up:** settle.   323. **is ... conceited:** has as horrible a conception.   337. **duello:** code of duel-ing.

If you offend him, I for him defy you.   345
Sir To. You, sir! Why, what are you?
Ant. One, sir, that for his love dares yet do more
Than you have heard him brag to you he will.
Sir To. Nay, if you be an undertaker, I am for
you.   [*They draw.* 350

Enter OFFICERS.

Fab. O good Sir Toby, hold! Here come the
officers.
Sir To. I'll be with you anon.
Vio. Pray, sir, put your sword up, if you please.
Sir And. Marry, will I, sir; and, for that I   356
promis'd you, I'll be as good as my word. He will
bear you easily and reins well.
1. Off. This is the man; do thy office.
2. Off. Antonio, I arrest thee at the suit of Count
Orsino.   361
Ant. You do mistake me, sir.
1. Off. No, sir, no jot. I know your favour well,
Though now you have no sea-cap on your head.
Take him away; he knows I know him well.   365
Ant. I must obey. [*To Vio.*] This comes with
seeking you.
But there's no remedy; I shall answer it.
What will you do, now my necessity
Makes me to ask you for my purse? It grieves me
Much more for what I cannot do for you   370
Than what befalls myself. You stand amaz'd,
But be of comfort.
2. Off. Come, sir, away.
Ant. I must entreat of you some of that money.
Vio. What money, sir?   375
For the fair kindness you have show'd me here,
And, part, being prompted by your present trouble,
Out of my lean and low ability
I'll lend you something. My having is not much.
I'll make division of my present with you.   380
Hold, there's half my coffer.
Ant.   Will you deny me now?
Is't possible that my deserts to you
Can lack persuasion? Do not tempt my misery,
Lest that it make me so unsound a man
As to upbraid you with those kindnesses   385
That I have done for you.
Vio.   I know of none,
Nor know I you by voice or any feature.
I hate ingratitude more in a man
Than lying, vainness, babbling, drunkenness,
Or any taint of vice whose strong corruption   390
Inhabits our frail blood.
Ant.   O heavens themselves!
2. Off. Come, sir, I pray you, go.
Ant. Let me speak a little. This youth that you
see here

I snatch'd one half out of the jaws of death,
Reliev'd him with such sanctity of love,   395
And to his image, which methought did promise
Most venerable worth, did I devotion.
1. Off. What's that to us? The time goes by;
away!
Ant. But, O, how vile an idol proves this god!
Thou hast, Sebastian, done good feature shame.
In nature there's no blemish but the mind;   401
None can be call'd deform'd but the unkind.
Virtue is beauty, but the beauteous evil
Are empty trunks o'erflourish'd by the devil.
1. Off. The man grows mad; away with him!
Come, come, sir.   405
Ant. Lead me on.   [*Exit [with Officers].*
Vio. Methinks his words do from such passion
fly
That he believes himself; so do not I.
Prove true, imagination, O, prove true,
That I, dear brother, be now ta'en for you!   410
Sir To. Come hither, knight; come hither, Fa-
bian; we'll whisper o'er a couplet or two of most
sage saws.
Vio. He nam'd Sebastian. I my brother know
Yet living in my glass; even such and so   415
In favour was my brother, and he went
Still in this fashion, colour, ornament,
For him I imitate. O, if it prove,
Tempests are kind and salt waves fresh in love.
[*Exit.*]
Sir To. A very dishonest paltry boy, and   420
more a coward than a hare. His dishonesty ap-
pears in leaving his friend here in necessity and
denying him; and, for his cowardship, ask Fabian.
Fab. A coward, a most devout coward, religious
in it.   425
Sir And. 'Slid, I'll after him again and beat him.
Sir To. Do; cuff him soundly, but never draw
thy sword.
Sir And. An I do not,—   430
Fab. Come, let's see the event.
Sir To. I dare lay any money 'twill be nothing
yet.   [*Exeunt.*

ACT IV

SCENE I. [*Before Olivia's house.*]

Enter SEBASTIAN *and* CLOWN.

Clo. Will you make me believe that I am not
sent for you?
Seb. Go to, go to, thou art a foolish fellow; let
me be clear of thee.
Clo. Well held out, i' faith! No, I do not   5
know you; nor I am not sent to you by my lady, to

349. **undertaker:** meddler. 380. **present:** present means. 402. **unkind:** unnatural. 404. **o'erflourish'd:** ornamented.
414-15. **I...glass:** I know I look like my brother. 418. **prove:** i.e., prove true. 426. **'Slid:** by God's eyelid.

bid you come speak with her; nor your name is not Master Cesario; nor this is not my nose neither. Nothing that is so is so.

Seb. I prithee, vent thy folly somewhere else. Thou know'st not me. 11

Clo. Vent my folly! He has heard that word of some great man and now applies it to a fool. Vent my folly! I am afraid this great lubber, the world, will prove a cockney. I prithee now, ungird thy strangeness and tell me what I shall vent to my lady. Shall I vent to her that thou art coming? 18

Seb. I prithee, foolish Greek, depart from me. There's money for thee. If you tarry longer, 20 I shall give worse payment.

Clo. By my troth, thou hast an open hand. These wise men that give fools money get themselves a good report — after fourteen years' purchase. 25

Enter SIR ANDREW, SIR TOBY, *and* FABIAN.

Sir And. Now, sir, have I met you again? There's for you.

Seb. Why, there's for thee, and there, and there. Are all the people mad?

Sir To. Hold, sir, or I'll throw your dagger o'er the house. 31

Clo. This will I tell my lady straight. I would not be in some of your coats for two pence.

[*Exit.*]

Sir To. Come on, sir. Hold! 34

Sir And. Nay, let him alone. I'll go another way to work with him. I'll have an action of battery against him, if there be any law in Illyria. Though I struck him first, yet it's no matter for that.

Seb. Let go thy hand. 40

Sir To. Come, sir, I will not let you go. Come, my young soldier, put up your iron; you are well flesh'd. Come on.

Seb. I will be free from thee. What wouldst thou now? 44

If thou dar'st tempt me further, draw thy sword.

Sir To. What, what? Nay, then I must have an ounce or two of this malapert blood from you.

Enter OLIVIA.

Oli. Hold, Toby! On thy life I charge thee, hold!

Sir To. Madam — 50

Oli. Will it be ever thus? Ungracious wretch, Fit for the mountains and the barbarous caves,

Where manners ne'er were preach'd! Out of my sight!

Be not offended, dear Cesario.

Rudesby, be gone!

[*Exeunt Sir Toby, Sir Andrew, and Fabian.*]
              I prithee, gentle friend,

Let thy fair wisdom, not thy passion, sway 56

In this uncivil and unjust extent

Against thy peace. Go with me to my house,

And hear thou there how many fruitless pranks

This ruffian hath botch'd up, that thou thereby 60

Mayst smile at this. Thou shalt not choose but go.

Do not deny. Beshrew his soul for me,

He started one poor heart of mine in thee.

Seb. What relish is in this? How runs the stream?

Or I am mad, or else this is a dream. 65

Let fancy still my sense in Lethe steep.

If it be thus to dream, still let me sleep!

Oli. Nay, come, I prithee. Would thou'dst be rul'd by me!

Seb. Madam, I will.

Oli.   O, say so, and so be!

[*Exeunt.*

SCENE II. [*Olivia's house.*]

Enter MARIA *and* CLOWN.

Mar. Nay, I prithee, put on this gown and this beard. Make him believe thou art Sir Topas the curate. Do it quickly; I'll call Sir Toby the whilst. [*Exit.*] 4

Clo. Well, I'll put it on, and I will dissemble myself in't; and I would I were the first that ever dissembled in such a gown. I am not tall enough to become the function well, nor lean enough to be thought a good student; but to be said an honest man and a good housekeeper goes as fairly as to 10 say a careful man and a great scholar. The competitors enter.

Enter SIR TOBY [*and* MARIA].

Sir To. Jove bless thee, master Parson.

Clo. *Bonos dies,* Sir Toby: for, as the old hermit of Prague, that never saw pen and ink, very 16 wittily said to a niece of King Gorboduc, "That that is is"; so I, being master Parson, am master Parson; for, what is "that" but "that," and "is" but "is"?

Sir To. To him, Sir Topas. 20

Clo. What, ho, I say! Peace in this prison!

Act IV, sc. i, 15. **cockney:** fop. 19. **Greek:** jester. 24–25. **after … purchase:** i.e., at a high price. The value of land was figured in terms of its annual rental. 43. **flesh'd:** initiated in bloodshed. 47. **malapert:** saucy. 55. **Rudesby:** ruffian. 57. **extent:** attack. 60. **botch'd up:** crudely contrived. 63. **started:** roused. **heart:** with pun on *hart.* 64. **relish:** meaning. 66. **Lethe:** river of forgetfulness.

Sc. ii, 10. **housekeeper:** host. 11. **competitors:** confederates. 15. **hermit of Prague.** Invented by Feste. 17. **Gorboduc:** mythical British king.

Sir To. The knave counterfeits well; a good knave.

Mal. (*Within.*) Who calls there?

Clo. Sir Topas the curate, who comes to visit Malvolio the lunatic.   26

Mal. Sir Topas, Sir Topas, good Sir Topas, go to my lady.

Clo. Out, hyperbolical fiend! How vexest thou this man! Talkest thou nothing but of ladies?   30

Sir To. Well said, master Parson.

Mal. Sir Topas, never was man thus wronged. Good Sir Topas, do not think I am mad. They have laid me here in hideous darkness.   34

Clo. Fie, thou dishonest Satan! I call thee by the most modest terms, for I am one of those gentle ones that will use the devil himself with courtesy. Say'st thou that house is dark?

Mal. As hell, Sir Topas.   39

Clo. Why, it hath bay windows transparent as barricadoes, and the clerestories toward the south north are as lustrous as ebony; and yet complainest thou of obstruction?

Mal. I am not mad, Sir Topas. I say to you, this house is dark.   45

Clo. Madman, thou errest. I say, there is no darkness but ignorance, in which thou art more puzzl'd than the Egyptians in their fog.

Mal. I say, this house is dark as ignorance, though ignorance were as dark as hell; and I   50 say, there was never man thus abus'd. I am no more mad than you are. Make the trial of it in any constant question.

Clo. What is the opinion of Pythagoras concerning wild fowl?   55

Mal. That the soul of our grandam might haply inhabit a bird.

Clo. What think'st thou of his opinion?

Mal. I think nobly of the soul, and no way approve his opinion.   60

Clo. Fare thee well. Remain thou still in darkness. Thou shalt hold th' opinion of Pythagoras ere I will allow of thy wits, and fear to kill a woodcock lest thou dispossess the soul of thy grandam. Fare thee well.   65

Mal. Sir Topas, Sir Topas!

Sir To. My most exquisite Sir Topas!

Clo. Nay, I am for all waters.

Mar. Thou mightst have done this without thy beard and gown. He sees thee not.   70

Sir To. To him in thine own voice, and bring me word how thou find'st him. I would we were well rid of this knavery. If he may be conveniently deliver'd, I would he were, for I am now so far in offence with my niece that I cannot pursue with   75 any safety this sport to the upshot. Come by and by to my chamber.   [*Exit* [*with Maria*].

Clo. [*Singing.*] "Hey, Robin, jolly Robin,
        Tell me how thy lady does."

Mal. Fool!   80

Clo. "My lady is unkind, perdy."

Mal. Fool!

Clo. "Alas, why is she so?"

Mal. Fool, I say!

Clo. "She loves another" — Who calls, ha?   85

Mal. Good fool, as ever thou wilt deserve well at my hand, help me to a candle, and pen, ink, and paper. As I am a gentleman, I will live to be thankful to thee for't.

Clo. Master Malvolio?   90

Mal. Ay, good fool.

Clo. Alas, sir, how fell you besides your five wits?

Mal. Fool, there was never man so notoriously abus'd. I am as well in my wits, fool, as thou art.   96

Clo. But as well? Then you are mad indeed, if you be no better in your wits than a fool.

Mal. They have here propertied me, keep me in darkness, send ministers to me, asses, and do all they can to face me out of my wits.   101

Clo. Advise you what you say; the minister is here. Malvolio, Malvolio, thy wits the heavens restore! Endeavour thyself to sleep, and leave thy vain bibble babble.   105

Mal. Sir Topas!

Clo. Maintain no words with him, good fellow. Who, I, sir? Not I, sir. God buy you, good Sir Topas. Marry, amen. I will, sir, I will.

Mal. Fool, fool, fool, I say!   110

Clo. Alas, sir, be patient. What say you, sir? I am shent for speaking to you.

Mal. Good fool, help me to some light and some paper. I tell thee, I am as well in my wits as any man in Illyria.   115

Clo. Well-a-day that you were, sir!

Mal. By this hand, I am. Good fool, some ink, paper, and light; and convey what I will set down to my lady. It shall advantage thee more than ever the bearing of letter did.   120

Clo. I will help you to't. But tell me true, are you not mad indeed, or do you but counterfeit?

Mal. Believe me, I am not. I tell thee true.

Clo. Nay, I'll ne'er believe a madman till I see his brains. I will fetch you light and paper and ink.   127

---

29. **hyperbolical:** extravagant.   41. **clerestories:** windows high up in the wall.   48. **Egyptians... fog.** See *Exodus* x.21. 53. **constant:** logical, rational.   68. **I... waters:** I can assume any rôle.   92. **wits.** Five by analogy with the five senses; they were common wit, imagination, fantasy, estimation, and memory.   99. **propertied:** treated as a tool.   102. **Advise you:** take care. From this point through l. 109 Feste alternates speaking as Sir Topas and in his own voice.   108. **buy:** be with. 112. **shent:** reproved.

Mal. Fool, I'll requite it in the highest degree.
I prithee, be gone.

  Clo. [*Singing.*] I am gone, sir,   130
    And anon, sir,
    I'll be with you again,
    In a trice,
    Like to the old Vice,
    Your need to sustain;   135

    Who, with dagger of lath,
    In his rage and his wrath,
     Cries, ah, ha! to the devil,
    Like a mad lad.
    Pare thy nails, dad.   140
    Adieu, goodman devil. [*Exit.*

SCENE III. [*Olivia's garden.*]

Enter SEBASTIAN.

Seb. This is the air, that is the glorious sun,
This pearl she gave me, I do feel't and see't;
And though 'tis wonder that enwraps me thus,
Yet 'tis not madness. Where's Antonio, then?
I could not find him at the Elephant; 5
Yet there he was, and there I found this credit,
That he did range the town to seek me out.
His counsel now might do me golden service;
For though my soul disputes well with my sense,
That this may be some error, but no madness, 10
Yet doth this accident and flood of fortune
So far exceed all instance, all discourse,
That I am ready to distrust mine eyes
And wrangle with my reason that persuades me
To any other trust but that I am mad 15
Or else the lady's mad; yet, if 'twere so,
She could not sway her house, command her fol-
  lowers,
Take and give back affairs and their dispatch
With such a smooth, discreet, and stable bearing
As I perceive she does. There's something in't 20
That is deceivable. But here the lady comes.

Enter OLIVIA *and* Priest.

Oli. Blame not this haste of mine. If you mean
  well,
Now go with me and with this holy man
Into the chantry by; there, before him,
And underneath that consecrated roof, 25
Plight me the full assurance of your faith,
That my most jealous and too doubtful soul
May live at peace. He shall conceal it
Whiles you are willing it shall come to note,

What time we will our celebration keep 30
According to my birth. What do you say?

  Seb. I'll follow this good man, and go with you;
And, having sworn truth, ever will be true.

  Oli. Then lead the way, good father; and heavens
  so shine
That they may fairly note this act of mine! 35
           [*Exeunt.*

ACT V

SCENE I. [*Before Olivia's house.*]

Enter CLOWN *and* FABIAN.

Fab. Now, as thou lov'st me, let me see his letter.

Clo. Good Master Fabian, grant me another request.

Fab. Anything.   5

Clo. Do not desire to see this letter.

Fab. This is to give a dog and in recompense
desire my dog again.

Enter DUKE, VIOLA, CURIO, *and* Lords.

Duke. Belong you to the Lady Olivia, friends?

Clo. Ay, sir! we are some of her trappings. 10

Duke. I know thee well; how dost thou, my good
fellow?

Clo. Truly, sir, the better for my foes and the
worse for my friends.

Duke. Just the contrary; the better for thy
friends.   16

Clo. No, sir, the worse.

Duke. How can that be?

Clo. Marry, sir, they praise me and make an ass
of me. Now my foes tell me plainly I am an 20
ass; so that by my foes, sir, I profit in the knowledge
of myself, and by my friends I am abused; so that,
conclusions to be as kisses, if your four negatives
make your two affirmatives, why then, the worse for
my friends and the better for my foes. 26

Duke. Why, this is excellent.

Clo. By my troth, sir, no; though it please you to
be one of my friends.

Duke. Thou shalt not be the worse for me.
There's gold.   31

Clo. But that it would be double-dealing, sir,
I would you could make it another.

Duke. O, you give me ill counsel.

Clo. Put your grace in your pocket, sir, for this
once, and let your flesh and blood obey it. 36

Duke. Well, I will be so much a sinner, to be a
double-dealer. There's another.

---

134. **the old Vice,** the Fool of the Moralities and Interludes, carried a wooden dagger with which he would attempt to
pare the Devil's nails.
 Sc. iii, 6. was: had been. **credit:** belief. 12. **instance:** example, precedent. **discourse:** reason. 15. **trust:** belief.
18. **Take ... dispatch:** undertake and discharge affairs. 21. **deceivable:** deceptive. 24. **chantry:** private chapel. 29.
Whiles: until. 30. **What:** at which.
 Act V, sc. i, 1. **his:** Malvolio's. 22. **abused:** deceived.

Clo. Primo, secundo, tertio, is a good play; and
the old saying is, the third pays for all. The 40
triplex, sir, is a good tripping measure; or the bells of
Saint Bennet, sir, may put you in mind; one, two,
three.

Duke. You can fool no more money out of me at
this throw. If you will let your lady know I am 45
here to speak with her, and bring her along with
you, it may awake my bounty further.

Clo. Marry, sir, lullaby to your bounty till I
come again. I go, sir, but I would not have you to
think that my desire of having is the sin of 50
covetousness; but, as you say, sir, let your bounty
take a nap, I will awake it anon.   [*Exit.*

Enter ANTONIO *and* OFFICERS.

Vio. Here comes the man, sir, that did rescue me.

Duke. That face of his I do remember well,
Yet, when I saw it last, it was besmear'd 55
As black as Vulcan in the smoke of war.
A bawbling vessel was he captain of,
For shallow draught and bulk unprizable,
With which such scatheful grapple did he make
With the most noble bottom of our fleet, 60
That very envy and the tongue of loss
Cri'd fame and honour on him. What's the matter?

1. Off. Orsino, this is that Antonio
That took the *Phœnix* and her fraught from Candy,
And this is he that did the *Tiger* board, 65
When your young nephew Titus lost his leg.
Here in the streets, desperate of shame and state,
In private brabble did we apprehend him.

Vio. He did me kindness, sir, drew on my side,
But in conclusion put strange speech upon me. 70
I know not what 'twas but distraction.

Duke. Notable pirate! Thou salt-water thief!
What foolish boldness brought thee to their mercies
Whom thou, in terms so bloody and so dear,
Hast made thine enemies?

Ant.   Orsino, noble sir, 75
Be pleas'd that I shake off these names you give me.
Antonio never yet was thief or pirate,
Though I confess, on base and ground enough,
Orsino's enemy. A witchcraft drew me hither.
That most ingrateful boy there by your side, 80
From the rude sea's enrag'd and foamy mouth
Did I redeem. A wreck past hope he was.
His life I gave him, and did thereto add
My love, without retention or restraint,
All his in dedication. For his sake 85
Did I expose myself, pure for his love,
Into the danger of this adverse town;

Drew to defend him when he was beset;
Where being apprehended, his false cunning,
Not meaning to partake with me in danger, 90
Taught him to face me out of his acquaintance,
And grew a twenty years removed thing
While one would wink; deni'd me mine own purse,
Which I had recommended to his use
Not half an hour before.

Vio.   How can this be? 95

Duke. When came he to this town?

Ant. To-day, my lord; and for three months
before,
No int'rim, not a minute's vacancy,
Both day and night did we keep company.

Enter OLIVIA *and Attendants.*

Duke. Here comes the countess; now heaven
walks on earth. 100
But for thee, fellow; fellow, thy words are madness.
Three months this youth hath tended upon me;
But more of that anon. Take him aside.

Oli. What would my lord, but that he may not
have,
Wherein Olivia may seem serviceable? 105
Cesario, you do not keep promise with me.

Vio. Madam!

Duke. Gracious Olivia, —

Oli. What do you say, Cesario? Good my
lord, — 109

Vio. My lord would speak; my duty hushes me.

Oli. If it be aught to the old tune, my lord,
It is as fat and fulsome to mine ear
As howling after music.

Duke.   Still so cruel!

Oli. Still so constant, lord.

Duke. What, to perverseness? You uncivil lady,
To whose ingrate and unauspicious altars 116
My soul the faithfull'st off'rings have breath'd out
That e'er devotion tender'd! What shall I do?

Oli. Even what it please my lord, that shall
become him.

Duke. Why should I not, had I the heart to do it,
Like to th' Egyptian thief at point of death, 121
Kill what I love? — a savage jealousy
That sometime savours nobly. But hear me this:
Since you to non-regardance cast my faith,
And that I partly know the instrument 125
That screws me from my true place in your favour,
Live you the marble-breasted tyrant still;
But this your minion, whom I know you love,
And whom, by heaven I swear, I tender dearly,
Him will I tear out of that cruel eye, 130

39. **Primo ... tertio:** possibly alluding to throws at dice. 41. **triplex:** triple time in music. 42. **Saint Bennet:** the church of St. Benedict in London. 57. **bawbling:** trifling. 58. **unprizable:** worthless. 59. **scatheful:** damaging. 64. **Candy:** Candia, Crete. 68. **brabble:** brawl. 71. **distraction:** madness. 74. **dear:** dangerous. 112. **fat and fulsome:** i.e., repulsive. 121. **Egyptian thief.** The *Ethiopica* of Heliodorus tells how a robber tried to kill his mistress rather than let her fall into the hands of his enemies. 128. **minion:** favorite.

Where he sits crowned in his master's spite.
Come, boy, with me; my thoughts are ripe in
　　mischief.
I'll sacrifice the lamb that I do love,
To spite a raven's heart within a dove.
　Vio. And I, most jocund, apt, and willingly, 135
To do you rest, a thousand deaths would die.
　Oli. Where goes Cesario?
　Vio.　　　　　　　After him I love
More than I love these eyes, more than my life,
More, by all mores, than e'er I shall love wife.
If I do feign, you witnesses above　　　140
Punish my life for tainting of my love!
　Oli. Ay me, detested! How am I beguil'd!
　Vio. Who does beguile you? Who does do you
　　wrong?
　Oli. Hast thou forgot thyself? Is it so long?
Call forth the holy father.
　Duke.　　　　　　Come, away!　145
　Oli. Whither, my lord? Cesario, husband, stay.
　Duke. Husband!
　Oli.　　　　Ay, husband! Can he that deny?
　Duke. Her husband, sirrah!
　Vio.　　　　　　No, my lord, not I.
　Oli. Alas, it is the baseness of thy fear
That makes thee strangle thy propriety.　150
Fear not, Cesario; take thy fortunes up.
Be that thou know'st thou art, and then thou art
As great as that thou fear'st.

Enter PRIEST.

　　　　　　　　　O, welcome, father!
Father, I charge thee by thy reverence
Here to unfold, though lately we intended　155
To keep in darkness what occasion now
Reveals before 'tis ripe, what thou dost know
Hath newly pass'd between this youth and me.
　Priest. A contract of eternal bond of love,
Confirm'd by mutual joinder of your hands, 160
Attested by the holy close of lips,
Strength'ned by interchangement of your rings;
And all the ceremony of this compact
Seal'd in my function, by my testimony;
Since when, my watch hath told me, toward my
　　grave　　　　　165
I have travell'd but two hours.
　Duke. O thou dissembling cub! What wilt
　　thou be
When time hath sow'd a grizzle on thy case?
Or will not else thy craft so quickly grow,
That thine own trip shall be thine overthrow? 170
Farewell, and take her; but direct thy feet
Where thou and I henceforth may never meet.

　Vio. My lord, I do protest —
　Oli.　　　　　　O, do not swear!
Hold little faith, though thou hast too much fear.

Enter SIR ANDREW.

　Sir And. For the love of God, a surgeon! 175
Send one presently to Sir Toby.
　Oli. What's the matter?
　Sir And. Has broke my head across and has
given Sir Toby a bloody coxcomb too. For the
love of God, your help! I had rather than forty
pound I were at home.　　　181
　Oli. Who has done this, Sir Andrew?
　Sir And. The Count's gentleman, one Cesario.
We took him for a coward, but he's the very devil
incardinate.　　　　　185
　Duke. My gentleman, Cesario?
　Sir And. 'Od's lifelings, here he is! You broke
my head for nothing; and that that I did, I was set
on to do't by Sir Toby.
　Vio. Why do you speak to me? I never hurt
　　you.　　　　　　　190
You drew your sword upon me without cause;
But I bespake you fair, and hurt you not.

Enter SIR TOBY *and* CLOWN.

　Sir And. If a bloody coxcomb be a hurt, you
have hurt me. I think you set nothing by a bloody
coxcomb. Here comes Sir Toby halting. You 195
shall hear more; but if he had not been in drink, he
would have tickl'd you othergates than he did.
　Duke. How now, gentleman! How is't with
　　you?　　　　　　　200
　Sir To. That's all one. Has hurt me, and there's
th' end on't. Sot, didst see Dick surgeon, sot?
　Clo. O, he's drunk, Sir Toby, an hour agone.
His eyes were set at eight i' th' morning.　205
　Sir To. Then he's a rogue, and a passy measures
[pavin]. I hate a drunken rogue.
　Oli. Away with him! Who hath made this havoc
with them?
　Sir And. I'll help you, Sir Toby, because we'll
be dress'd together.　　　211
　Sir To. Will you help? — an ass-head and a cox-
comb and a knave, a thin-fac'd knave, a gull!
　Oli. Get him to bed, and let his hurt be look'd
to.　　　　　　　215
　　*[Exeunt Clown, Fabian, Sir Toby, and Sir
　　　Andrew.]*

Enter SEBASTIAN.

　Seb. I am sorry, madam, I have hurt your
　　kinsman;

---

150. **strangle thy propriety:** deny thyself. 164. **function:** official capacity. 168. **grizzle:** gray hair. **case:** skin. 170. **trip:** i.e., as in wrestling. 179. **coxcomb:** head. 185. **incardinate:** incarnate. 197. **othergates:** otherwise. 207. **[pavin]** (Malone). *panyn* F. "Passy measures pavin" is an English form of the Italian "Passamezzo pavana," a measured dance with strains of eight bars each. Toby's outburst is inspired by "set at eight" (l. 205).

But, had it been the brother of my blood,
I must have done no less with wit and safety.
You throw a strange regard upon me, and by that
I do perceive it hath offended you.   220
Pardon me, sweet one, even for the vows
We made each other but so late ago.

   Duke. One face, one voice, one habit, and two
     persons,
A natural perspective, that is and is not!

   Seb. Antonio, O my dear Antonio!   225
How have the hours rack'd and tortur'd me,
Since I have lost thee!

   Ant.   Sebastian are you?

   Seb.   Fear'st thou that, Antonio?

   Ant. How have you made division of yourself?
An apple, cleft in two, is not more twin   230
Than these two creatures. Which is Sebastian?

   Oli. Most wonderful!

   Seb. Do I stand there? I never had a brother,
Nor can there be that deity in my nature,
Of here and everywhere. I had a sister,   235
Whom the blind waves and surges have devour'd.
Of charity, what kin are you to me?
What countryman? What name? What parent-
   age?

   Vio. Of Messaline; Sebastian was my father;
Such a Sebastian was my brother too;   240
So went he suited to his watery tomb.
If spirits can assume both form and suit
You come to fright us.

   Seb.   A spirit I am indeed;
But am in that dimension grossly clad
Which from the womb I did participate.   245
Were you a woman, as the rest goes even,
I should my tears let fall upon your cheek,
And say, "Thrice welcome, drowned Viola!"

   Vio. My father had a mole upon his brow.

   Seb. And so had mine.   250

   Vio. And died that day when Viola from her
     birth
Had numb'red thirteen years.

   Seb. O, that record is lively in my soul!
He finished indeed his mortal act
That day that made my sister thirteen years.   255

   Vio. If nothing lets to make us happy both
But this my masculine usurp'd attire,
Do not embrace me till each circumstance
Of place, time, fortune, do cohere and jump
That I am Viola; which to confirm,   260
I'll bring you to a captain in this town,
Where lie my maiden weeds; by whose gentle help

I was preserv'd to serve this noble count.
All the occurrence of my fortune since
Hath been between this lady and this lord.   265

   Seb. [*To Olivia.*] So comes it, lady, you have been
     mistook;
But nature to her bias drew in that.
You would have been contracted to a maid;
Nor are you therein, by my life, deceiv'd,
You are betroth'd both to a maid and man.   270

   Duke. Be not amaz'd, right noble is his blood.
If this be so, as yet the glass seems true,
I shall have share in this most happy wreck.
[*To Viola.*] Boy, thou hast said to me a thousand
     times
Thou never shouldst love woman like to me.   275

   Vio. And all those sayings will I over-swear;
And all those swearings keep as true in soul
As doth that orbed continent the fire
That severs day from night.

   Duke.   Give me thy hand,
And let me see thee in thy woman's weeds.   280

   Vio. The captain that did bring me first on shore
Hath my maid's garments. He upon some action
Is now in durance, at Malvolio's suit,
A gentleman, and follower of my lady's.

   Oli. He shall enlarge him; fetch Malvolio hither.
And yet, alas, now I remember me,   286
They say, poor gentleman, he's much distract.

   Re-enter CLOWN *with a letter, and* FABIAN.

A most extracting frenzy of mine own
From my remembrance clearly banish'd his.
How does he, sirrah?   290

   Clo. Truly, madam, he holds Belzebub at the
stave's end as well as a man in his case may
do. Has here writ a letter to you. I should have
given 't you to-day morning, but as a madman's
epistles are no gospels, so it skills not much when
they are deliver'd.   296

   Oli. Open 't and read it.

   Clo. Look then to be well edified when the fool
delivers the madman. [*Shouts.*] "By the Lord,
madam," —   300

   Oli. How now, art thou mad?

   Clo. No, madam, I do but read madness. An
your ladyship will have it as it ought to be, you
must allow Vox.

   Oli. Prithee, read i' thy right wits.   305

   Clo. So I do, madonna; but to read his right wits
is to read thus; therefore perpend, my princess, and
give ear.

---

   223. habit: dress.   **224. natural perspective:** an optical illusion produced by nature.   **228. Fear'st:** doubtest.   **234–35.
Nor ... everywhere:** nor can I, God-like, be everywhere.   **241. suited:** clothed.   **244. in ... clad:** clothed in that material
form.   **245. Which ... participate:** which I have possessed since birth.   **246. goes even:** agrees.   **256. lets:** prevents.
259. jump: agree.   **264. occurrence:** course.   **267. nature ... drew:** i.e., nature followed her own inclination.   **272. glass.**
Probably an allusion to the "perspective" of l. 224.   **278. orbed continent:** the sphere of the sun (according to the Ptolemaic
cosmology).   **283. in durance:** under arrest.   **288. extracting:** distracting.   **292. at ... end:** at staff's length.   **295. skills:**
matters.   **304. Vox:** i.e., the appropriate (loud) voice.   **307. perpend:** consider.

Oli. Read it you, sirrah.   *[To Fabian.]* 309
Fab. (Reads.) "By the Lord, madam, you wrong
me, and the world shall know it. Though you
have put me into darkness and given your drunken
cousin rule over me, yet have I the benefit of my
senses as well as your ladyship. I have your own
letter that induced me to the semblance I put
on; with the which I doubt not but to do my- 315
self much right, or you much shame. Think of
me as you please. I leave my duty a little un-
thought of and speak out of my injury.
THE MADLY-US'D MALVOLIO."
Oli. Did he write this?   320
Clo. Ay, madam.
Duke. This savours not much of distraction.
Oli. See him deliver'd, Fabian; bring him hither.
                             [Exit Fabian.]
My lord, so please you, these things further thought
    on,
To think me as well a sister as a wife,   325
One day shall crown th' alliance on't, so please
    you,
Here at my house and at my proper cost.
Duke. Madam, I am most apt t' embrace your
    offer.
[To Viola.] Your master quits you; and for your
    service done him,
So much against the mettle of your sex,   330
So far beneath your soft and tender breeding,
And since you call'd me master for so long,
Here is my hand. You shall from this time be
Your master's mistress.
Oli.   A sister! You are she.

Enter MALVOLIO [*and* FABIAN].

Duke. Is this the madman?
Oli.   Ay, my lord, this same. 335
How now, Malvolio!
Mal.   Madam, you have done me wrong,
Notorious wrong.
Oli.   Have I, Malvolio? No.
Mal. Lady, you have. Pray you, peruse that
    letter;
You must not now deny it is your hand.
Write from it, if you can, in hand or phrase; 340
Or say 'tis not your seal, not your invention.
You can say none of this. Well, grant it then
And tell me, in the modesty of honour,
Why you have given me such clear lights of favour,
Bade me come smiling and cross-garter'd to you,
To put on yellow stockings and to frown   346
Upon Sir Toby and the lighter people;
And, acting this in an obedient hope,
Why have you suffer'd me to be imprison'd,

Kept in a dark house, visited by the priest, 350
And made the most notorious geck and gull
That e'er invention play'd on? Tell me why.
Oli. Alas, Malvolio, this is not my writing,
Though, I confess, much like the character;
But out of question 'tis Maria's hand.   355
And now I do bethink me, it was she
First told me thou wast mad. Then cam'st in
    smiling,
And in such forms which here were presuppos'd
Upon thee in the letter. Prithee, be content. 359
This practice hath most shrewdly pass'd upon
    thee;
But when we know the grounds and authors of
    it,
Thou shalt be both the plaintiff and the judge
Of thine own cause.
Fab.   Good madam, hear me speak,
And let no quarrel nor no brawl to come
Taint the condition of this present hour,   365
Which I have wond'red at. In hope it shall not
Most freely I confess, myself and Toby
Set this device against Malvolio here,
Upon some stubborn and uncourteous parts
We had conceiv'd against him. Maria writ 370
The letter at Sir Toby's great importance,
In recompense whereof he hath married her.
How with a sportful malice it was follow'd
May rather pluck on laughter than revenge,
If that the injuries be justly weigh'd   375
That have on both sides pass'd.
Oli.   Alas, poor fool, how have they baffl'd
    thee!
Clo. Why, "some are born great, some achieve
greatness, and some have greatness thrown upon
them." I was one, sir, in this interlude; one Sir 380
Topas, sir; but that's all one. "By the Lord, fool,
I am not mad." But do you remember? "Madam,
why laugh you at such a barren rascal? An you
smile not, he's gagg'd." And thus the whirligig of
time brings in his revenges.   385
Mal. I'll be reveng'd on the whole pack of you.
                               [Exit.]
Oli. He hath been most notoriously abus'd.
Duke. Pursue him, and entreat him to a peace;
He hath not told us of the captain yet. 390
When that is known and golden time convents,
A solemn combination shall be made
Of our dear souls. Meantime, sweet sister,
We will not part from hence. Cesario, come;
For so you shall be, while you are a man; 395
But when in other habits you are seen,
Orsino's mistress and his fancy's queen.
                    [Exeunt [all, except Clown].

---

327. **proper:** own. 328. **apt:** ready. 329. **quits:** releases. 330. **mettle:** character. 340. **from:** i.e., differently from.
347. **lighter:** lesser. 351. **geck and gull:** fool and dupe. 358. **presuppos'd:** suggested. 360. **practice:** trick. **pass'd:**
imposed. 369. **parts:** qualities. 371. **importance:** importunity. 374. **pluck on:** excite. 391. **convents:** suits.

Clo. (Sings.)
When that I was and a little tiny boy,
  With hey, ho, the wind and the rain,
A foolish thing was but a toy,
  For the rain it raineth every day.   400

But when I came to man's estate,
  With hey, ho, &c.
'Gainst knaves and thieves men shut their gate,
  For the rain, &c.   405

But when I came, alas! to wive,
  With hey, ho, &c.

By swaggering could I never thrive,
  For the rain, &c.

But when I came unto my beds,   410
  With hey, ho, &c.
With toss-pots still had drunken heads,
  For the rain, &c.

A great while ago the world begun,
  With hey, ho, &c.   415
But that's all one, our play is done,
  And we'll strive to please you every day.

                                [*Exit.*]

400. toy: trifle.   **412. toss-pots:** drunkards.

Troilus and Cressida

THE COMPOSITION of the present play can be assigned with reasonable certainty to the year 1602, for under the date of February 7, 1602/3 the Stationers' Register carries the following record in the interest of James Roberts: "Entred for his copie in full Court holden this day to print when he hath gotten sufficient authority for yt, The booke of Troilus and Cresseda as yt is acted by my lord Chamberlens Men." This dating is confirmed by lines in the Prologue (23–25) which are generally regarded as a palpable allusion to the "armed Prologue" in Ben Jonson's *Poetaster* (1601).

Troilus and Cressida was not printed until 1609. In that year two Quartos appeared, with differing title pages but identical text, both published for Richard Bonian and Henry Walley, to whom a covering entry in the Register for January 20 indicates the rights had been transferred. The title page of the earlier Quarto states that the play had been acted by the King's Majesty's Servants (earlier the Lord Chamberlain's) at the Globe, thus corroborating the Roberts entry of 1602; but the later Quarto (whose title page omits any reference to performance) carries a preface, absent from the first, declaring that the play was new, "never stal'd with the Stage, never clapper-clawd with the palmes of the vulger." The best explanation of this apparent contradiction is that Bonian and Walley were trying to boost the sale of a play which had been unsuccessful on the stage by telling readers that it was brilliant fare for the intelligentsia but above the appreciation of the vulgar. For the language of the preface seems not to indicate that the play had never been acted, but to proclaim that the play has not grown stale on the stage (through many performances) and has not been sullied with the applause of the ground-lings. The preface is a publisher's subterfuge, but it is hardly fraudulent. What in all probability happened was that just as *Troilus and Cressida* was to be brought upon the public stage in 1608 or 1609, Bonian and Walley prepared a printed text with announcement of performance on the title page. Then the play proved a failure at the Globe because of its intellectual and reflective content, and the publishers found themselves stuck. Accordingly they hastily printed a new title page, and added a preface in which, with a fanfare of rhetoric, they strove to make a virtue of the reason for the failure of the play in the theatre.

The relation of the text in the Folio to that in the Quarto is difficult to determine. The verbal differences between them, though often minute, are very numerous, and each text carries a few important passages which the other lacks. Since at IV.v.96 the Folio intrudes words ("they call him Troilus") which recur in line 108, and again at V.iii.113–15 prints three lines which are repeated at V.x.32–34, it would appear that the Folio text was set up from the author's manuscript (see notes on these passages); and since the Quarto prints these passages only at the latter points in both instances, it seems likely that the Quarto was printed from a transcript. The present text is based upon the Folio.

There is no reason for doubting the genuineness of the Prologue, and not much more for believing that V.iv–x are by another hand. Those scenes are certainly very inferior both in metre and in style, but they may have been written by an unusually careless Shakespeare, who was not above scamping the ending of a play. One would gladly exonerate Shakespeare of Pandarus's wretched epilogue. It appears to be wholly gratuitous, for Pandarus has been dismissed at the close of V.iii, and one would hardly expect him to appear again suddenly upon the battlefield. Moreover, the final words of Troilus (V.x.30–31) constitute the natural ending for the play. It is quite conceivable, if the original performance was at the Inns of Court, that this fusty stuff was added to call forth some final deep chest-laughs from the revelling barristers.

On account of the extraordinary vogue of the story of Troy in literature, the versions from which Shakespeare may have drawn hints are innumerable. The main sources, however, are well known. The love-story is adapted from Chaucer's *Troilus and Criseyde;* the camp scenes derive from Caxton's *Recuyell of the Historyes of Troye* and from Homer in Chapman's translation, eight books (I, II, VII–XI, XVIII) of which had appeared in 1598. Details not to be accounted for in these sources it would be hard to allocate.

Interpretation of the play has called forth a wide range of controversial opinion. The general tone and temper are dark and unpleasant; the atmosphere suggests corruption, disintegration; the war muddles along in its futile course as the Greek chieftains dissipate their energies in petty dissensions; and over all is cast the filthy, flaying commentary of Thersites.

To one reading the play for the first time it may seem strange that the title-plot does not achieve a larger prominence. Upon consideration, however, this becomes less surprising, for throughout its literary development the love-story had been placed in a setting where a drama of epic proportions and of greater literary prestige was being enacted. It may well be that Shakespeare, who had already won great success with chronicle-history plays, began with the story of the lovers, but found himself quickly and increasingly engrossed with the martial plot.

What Shakespeare does with the latter business it is interesting to see. We do not get much martial action; rather, a great deal of debate, harangue, and colloquy. The war is at a stalemate, and this is viewed from different angles in the opposing camps. In the Greek camp it is perceived that insubordination and lack of discipline are undermining the army, and the great speech of Ulysses (I.iii.75–137) on the chaos which ensues in any sphere of life when due authority has been neglected, gives the key to the whole situation in terms of a current social and political philosophy in which Shakespeare quite certainly believed. On the Trojan side, there is an early debate among the princes on the merits of the cause they are fighting for (II.ii). It is sufficiently obvious that the chief, if not the sole, interest in all this speech-making is the reflective and critical content.

Shakespeare's treatment of the love-story, which is naturally disturbing to lovers of Chaucer's poem, was conditioned by the conception of the heroine which had evolved in the two centuries following Chaucer. In the *Testament of Cresseid*, an extension of Chaucer's story by the Scottish poet Robert Henryson which was commonly printed in sixteenth-century editions of Chaucer, Cressida suffers a severe retribution; she is deserted by Diomed and on the recoil of this misfortune becomes a "daughter of the game." She curses Venus and Cupid, and for this sin is smitten with leprosy.

Later, when she is begging by the roadside, Troilus passes by and, pitying her condition, gives her money without recognizing her. Shortly afterwards she dies of a broken heart. In spite of a sympathetic element in Henryson's account, the degeneration of Cressida into a byword for a strumpet was rapid. That this idea of Cressida dominated in the Elizabethan period there is ample witness, and other plays of Shakespeare contain unflattering allusions to her story, the strongest of which is Pistol's reference to Doll as a "lazar kite of Cressid's kind" (*Henry V*, II.i.80). When, therefore, Shakespeare came to dramatize the tale of Troilus, the potent authority of tradition stood against the heroine; to attempt to redeem her in men's eyes would have meant a kind of revolution Shakespeare was not in the habit of making. Yet his portrayal of her is not wholly unsympathetic; and, moreover, something of what is unpleasant in the situation of Cressida is owing to the continual presence of Pandarus, who serves as a kind of lecherous Chorus in this part of the action. Cressida treats him lightly, even banters him, but she does not incite him. Pandarus, a congenial character in Chaucer, had become degraded by Shakespeare's time into the archetype of male procurer, and Shakespeare did nothing to raise him. Troilus is kindly treated by Shakespeare. He is an honorable, chivalrous young man, deeply emotional and sensual, who, having loved and lost an unworthy woman whom he has idealized, suffers profoundly and is left to his suffering at the end of the play.

The inconclusive ending of the play, with justice unfulfilled in either plot, has seemed to many critics a great theatrical mistake and the consummation of futility. But the consummation of futility would seem to be precisely the impression Shakespeare desired to leave. Troilus is left to expiate in misery the error of having loved unwisely and too well a woman like Cressida. Cressida is left exactly where Chaucer left her, at the beginning of her liaison with Diomed. Justice is left for the future to enact, and everybody was free to remember what the future held for Cressida according to Henryson. The same thing holds true with respect to the martial plot. The war at Troy is being fought over a woman who merits nothing of the sacrifice. Hector knows in his heart that the Trojan cause is wrong, and Diomed utters (IV.i. 51–74) what many a disillusioned comrade, and very possibly Shakespeare himself, thought of the Greek cause. The intrigue of the Greek generals to bring Achilles back to his senses and his honor fails completely, and although Achilles is selfishly roused by the death of Patroclus to win a base victory over Hector, the stalemate of the war continues. Everything concludes in futility without honor.

TROILUS AND CRESSIDA

PRIAM, *King of Troy.*
HECTOR, ⎫
TROILUS,   ⎪
PARIS,   ⎬ *his sons.*
DEIPHOBUS, ⎪
HELENUS,   ⎭
MARGARELON, *a bastard son of Priam.*
ÆNEAS,   ⎫
ANTENOR, ⎬ *Trojan commanders.*
CALCHAS. *a Trojan priest, taking part with the Greeks.*
PANDARUS, *uncle to Cressida.*
ALEXANDER, *servant to Cressida.*
Servant to Troilus.
Servant to Paris.

AGAMEMNON, *the Greek general.*
MENELAUS, *his brother.*
NESTOR,   ⎫
ULYSSES,   ⎪
ACHILLES, ⎬ *Greek commanders.*
AJAX,   ⎪
DIOMEDES, ⎪
PATROCLUS, ⎭
THERSITES, *a deformed and scurrilous Greek.*
Servant to Diomedes.

HELEN, *wife to Menelaus.*
ANDROMACHE, *wife to Hector.*
CASSANDRA, *daughter to Priam, a prophetess.*
CRESSIDA, *daughter to Calchas.*

Trojan and Greek Soldiers, and Attendants.

SCENE: *Troy, and the Greek camp before it.*]

THE PROLOGUE

IN Troy, there lies the scene. From isles of
  Greece
The princes orgillous, their high blood chaf'd,
Have to the port of Athens sent their ships,
Fraught with the ministers and instruments
Of cruel war. Sixty and nine, that wore   5
Their crownets regal, from th' Athenian bay
Put forth toward Phrygia; and their vow is made
To ransack Troy, within whose strong immures
The ravish'd Helen, Menelaus' queen,
With wanton Paris sleeps; and that's the quarrel.
To Tenedos they come,   11
And the deep-drawing barks do there disgorge
Their warlike fraughtage. Now on Dardan plains
The fresh and yet unbruised Greeks do pitch
Their brave pavilions. Priam's six-gated city, 15
Dardan, and Timbria, Helias, Chetas, Troien,
And Antenorides, with massy staples
And corresponsive and fulfilling bolts
[Spar] up the sons of Troy.
Now expectation, tickling skittish spirits,   20
On one and other side, Troyan and Greek,
Sets all on hazard; and hither am I come
A prologue arm'd, but not in confidence
Of author's pen or actor's voice, but suited
In like conditions as our argument,   25
To tell you, fair beholders, that our play
Leaps o'er the vaunt and firstlings of those broils,
Beginning in the middle, starting thence away
To what may be digested in a play.
Like or find fault; do as your pleasures are; 30
Now good or bad, 'tis but the chance of war.

Prol., 2. **orgillous:** proud. 6. **crownets:** coronets. 8. **immures:** walls. 13. **fraughtage:** cargo. **Dardan:** Trojan. 15. **brave:** splendid. 19. **[Spar]** (Theobald): shut. *Stirre* F. 24. **suited:** clad. 25. **argument:** theme. 27. **vaunt:** van, beginning.

ACT I

Scene I. [*Troy. Before Priam's palace.*]

Enter Troilus [*armed*] *and* Pandarus.

Tro. Call here my varlet; I'll unarm again.
Why should I war without the walls of Troy,
That find such cruel battle here within?
Each Troyan that is master of his heart,
Let him to field; Troilus, alas! hath none.   5
    Pan. Will this gear ne'er be mended?
    Tro. The Greeks are strong, and skilful to their
        strength,
Fierce to their skill, and to their fierceness valiant;
But I am weaker than a woman's tear,
Tamer than sleep, fonder than ignorance,   10
Less valiant than the virgin in the night,
And skilless as unpractis'd infancy.
    Pan. Well, I have told you enough of this. For
my part, I'll not meddle nor make no further. He
that will have a cake out of the wheat must needs
tarry the grinding.   16
    Tro. Have I not tarried?
    Pan. Ay, the grinding; but you must tarry the
bolting.
    Tro. Have I not tarried?
    Pan. Ay, the bolting; but you must tarry the
leavening.   20
    Tro. Still have I tarried.
    Pan. Ay, to the leavening; but here's yet in the
word "hereafter" the kneading, the making of the
cake, the heating of the oven, and the baking; nay,
you must stay the cooling too, or you may chance
to burn your lips.   26
    Tro. Patience herself, what goddess e'er she be,
Doth lesser blench at suff'rance than I do.
At Priam's royal table do I sit,
And when fair Cressid comes into my thoughts, —
So, traitor, then she comes, when she is thence — 31
    Pan. Well, she look'd yesternight fairer than
ever I saw her look, or any woman else.
    Tro. I was about to tell thee: — when my heart,
As wedged with a sigh, would rive in twain,   35
Lest Hector or my father should perceive me,
I have, as when the sun doth light a [storm],
Buried this sigh in wrinkle of a smile.
But sorrow that is couch'd in seeming gladness
Is like that mirth fate turns to sudden sadness.   40
    Pan. An her hair were not somewhat darker than
Helen's — well, go to! — there were no more com-
parison between the women. But, for my part, she
is my kinswoman; I would not, as they term it,

praise her, but I would somebody had heard her   45
talk yesterday, as I did. I will not dispraise your
sister Cassandra's wit, but —
    Tro. O Pandarus! I tell thee, Pandarus, —
When I do tell thee, there my hopes lie drown'd,
Reply not in how many fathoms deep   50
They lie indrench'd. I tell thee I am mad
In Cressid's love; thou answer'st she is fair;
Pour'st in the open ulcer of my heart
Her eyes, her hair, her cheek, her gait, her voice;
Handlest in thy discourse, O, that her hand,   55
In whose comparison all whites are ink
Writing their own reproach, to whose soft seizure
The cygnet's down is harsh and spirit of sense
Hard as the palm of ploughman. This thou tell'st
        me,
As true thou tell'st me, when I say I love her;   60
But, saying thus, instead of oil and balm,
Thou lay'st in every gash that love hath given me
The knife that made it.
    Pan. I speak no more than truth.
    Tro. Thou dost not speak so much.   65
    Pan. Faith, I'll not meddle in't. Let her be as
she is. If she be fair, 'tis the better for her; and she
be not, she has the mends in her own hands.
    Tro. Good Pandarus! How now, Pandarus?   69
    Pan. I have had my labour for my travail; ill-
thought on of her and ill-thought on of you; gone
between and between, but small thanks for my
labour.
    Tro. What, art thou angry, Pandarus? What,
with me?   75
    Pan. Because she's kin to me, therefore she's
not so fair as Helen. An she were not kin to me, she
would be as fair on Friday as Helen is on Sunday.
But what care I? I care not an she were a blackamoor; 'tis all one to me.   80
    Tro. Say I she is not fair?
    Pan. I do not care whether you do or no. She's
a fool to stay behind her father; let her to the
Greeks; and so I'll tell her the next time I see her.
For my part, I'll meddle nor make no more i' th'
matter.   86
    Tro. Pandarus, —
    Pan. Not I.
    Tro. Sweet Pandarus, —
    Pan. Pray you, speak no more to me. I will
leave all as I found it, and there an end.   91
            [*Exit Pandarus. Sound alarum.*
    Tro. Peace, you ungracious clamours! Peace,
        rude sounds!
Fools on both sides! Helen must needs be fair,

Act I, sc. i, 1. **varlet:** servant. 6. **gear:** business. 10. **fonder:** more foolish. 18. **bolting:** sifting. 31. **traitor.** Troilus
rebukes himself for admitting that Cressida is ever out of his thoughts. 35. **rive:** split. 37. **[storm]** (Rowe). *scorne* QF.
55. **that her hand:** that hand of hers. 57. **to:** compared to. **seizure:** grasp. 58. **cygnet's:** young swan's. **sense:** sensi-
bility. 68. **mends:** remedies. 78. **as ... Sunday:** i.e., as beautiful in her weekday dress as is Helen in her Sunday best.
79. **blackamoor:** Negro. 83. **stay ... father.** Calchas had deserted to the Greeks, having been told by the oracle of Apollo
at Delphi that the Trojans were to be defeated.

When with your blood you daily paint her thus.
I cannot fight upon this argument;   95
It is too starv'd a subject for my sword.
But Pandarus, — O gods, how do you plague me!
I cannot come to Cressid but by Pandar,
And he's as tetchy to be woo'd to woo,
As she is stubborn-chaste against all suit.   100
Tell me, Apollo, for thy Daphne's love,
What Cressid is, what Pandar, and what we.
Her bed is India; there she lies, a pearl;
Between our Ilium and where she resides,
Let it be call'd the wild and wand'ring flood,   105
Ourself the merchant, and this sailing Pandar
Our doubtful hope, our convoy, and our bark.

Alarum. Enter ÆNEAS.

Æne. How now, Prince Troilus! wherefore not
afield?
Tro. Because not there. This woman's answer
sorts,
For womanish it is to be from thence.   110
What news, Æneas, from the field to-day?
Æne. That Paris is returned home and hurt.
Tro. By whom, Æneas?
Æne.   Troilus, by Menelaus.
Tro. Let Paris bleed; 'tis but a scar to scorn;
Paris is gor'd with Menelaus' horn. [*Alarum.* 115
Æne. Hark, what good sport is out of town to-
day!
Tro. Better at home, if "would I might" were
"may."
But to the sport abroad. Are you bound thither?
Æne. In all swift haste.
Tro.   Come, go we then together.
                                            [*Exeunt.*

[SCENE II. *The same. A street.*]

Enter CRESSIDA *and her man* [ALEXANDER].

Cres. Who were those went by?
Alex.   Queen Hecuba and Helen.
Cres. And whither go they?
Alex.   Up to the eastern tower,
Whose height commands as subject all the vale,
To see the battle. Hector, whose patience
Is as a virtue fix'd, to-day was mov'd.   5
He chid Andromache and struck his armorer,
And, like as there were husbandry in war,
Before the sun rose he was harness'd light,
And to the field goes he, where every flower
Did, as a prophet, weep what it foresaw   10
In Hector's wrath.
Cres.   What was his cause of anger?

Alex. The noise goes, this: there is among the
Greeks
A lord of Troyan blood, nephew to Hector;
They call him Ajax.
Cres.   Good; and what of him?
Alex. They say he is a very man *per se*,   15
And stands alone.
Cres. So do all men, unless they are drunk, sick,
or have no legs.
Alex. This man, lady, hath robb'd many beasts
of their particular additions: he is as valiant as 20
the lion, churlish as the bear, slow as the elephant;
a man into whom nature hath so crowded humours
that his valour is crush'd into folly, his folly sauced
with discretion. There is no man hath a virtue that
he hath not a glimpse of, nor any man an attaint 25
but he carries some stain of it. He is melancholy
without cause, and merry against the hair. He
hath the joints of everything, but everything so out
of joint that he is a gouty Briareus, many hands and
no use, or [purblind] Argus, all eyes and no sight. 31
Cres. But how should this man, that makes me
smile, make Hector angry?
Alex. They say he yesterday cop'd Hector in
the battle and struck him down, the disdain 35
and shame whereof hath ever since kept Hector
fasting and waking.

Enter PANDARUS.

Cres. Who comes here?
Alex. Madam, your uncle Pandarus.
Cres. Hector's a gallant man.   40
Alex. As may be in the world, lady.
Pan. What's that? What's that?
Cres. Good morrow, uncle Pandarus.
Pan. Good morrow, cousin Cressid. What do
you talk of? Good morrow, Alexander. How do
you, cousin? When were you at Ilium?   46
Cres. This morning, uncle.
Pan. What were you talking of when I came?
Was Hector arm'd and gone ere ye came to Ilium?
Helen was not up, was she?   50
Cres. Hector was gone, but Helen was not up.
Pan. Even so. Hector was stirring early.
Cres. That were we talking of, and of his anger.
Pan. Was he angry?   55
Cres. So he says here.
Pan. True, he was so. I know the cause too.
He'll lay about him to-day, I can tell them that;
and there's Troilus will not come far behind him.
Let them take heed of Troilus, I can tell them
that too.   61
Cres. What, is he angry too?

Pan. Who? Troilus? Troilus is the better man of the two.

Cres. O Jupiter! there's no comparison.   65

Pan. What, not between Troilus and Hector? Do you know a man if you see him?

Cres. Ay, if I ever saw him before and knew him.

Pan. Well, I say Troilus is Troilus.   70

Cres. Then you say as I say, for I am sure he is not Hector.

Pan. No, nor Hector is not Troilus in some degrees.

Cres. 'Tis just to each of them; he is himself.   76

Pan. Himself! Alas, poor Troilus! I would he were —

Cres. So he is.

Pan. Condition I had gone barefoot to India.

Cres. He is not Hector.   81

Pan. Himself! No, he's not himself. Would 'a were himself! Well, the gods are above; time must friend or end. Well, Troilus, well; I would my heart were in her body. No, Hector is not a better man than Troilus.   86

Cres. Excuse me.

Pan. He is elder.

Cres. Pardon me, pardon me.   89

Pan. Th' other's not come to't. You shall tell me another tale, when th' other's come to't. Hector shall not have his [wit] this year.

Cres. He shall not need it, if he have his own.

Pan. Nor his qualities.

Cres. No matter.   95

Pan. Nor his beauty.

Cres. 'Twould not become him; his own's better.

Pan. You have no judgement, niece. Helen herself swore th' other day that Troilus, for a brown favour — for so 'tis, I must confess, — not brown neither, —   102

Cres. No, but brown.

Pan. 'Faith, to say truth, brown and not brown.   105

Cres. To say the truth, true and not true.

Pan. She prais'd his complexion above Paris.

Cres. Why, Paris hath colour enough.

Pan. So he has.   109

Cres. Then Troilus should have too much. If she prais'd him above, his complexion is higher than his. He having colour enough, and the other higher, is too flaming a praise for a good complexion. I had as lief Helen's golden tongue had commended Troilus for a copper nose.   115

Pan. I swear to you, I think Helen loves him better than Paris.

Cres. Then she's a merry Greek indeed.   118

Pan. Nay, I am sure she does. She came to him th' other day into the compass'd window, — and, you know, he has not past three or four hairs on his chin, —

Cres. Indeed, a tapster's arithmetic may soon bring his particulars therein to a total.   124

Pan. Why, he is very young; and yet will he, within three pound, lift as much as his brother Hector.

Cres. Is he so young a man and so old a lifter?

Pan. But to prove to you that Helen loves   130 him: she came and puts me her white hand to his cloven chin —

Cres. Juno have mercy! how came it cloven?

Pan. Why, you know, 'tis dimpled. I think his smiling becomes him better than any man in all Phrygia.   136

Cres. O, he smiles valiantly.

Pan. Does he not?

Cres. O yes, an 'twere a cloud in autumn.

Pan. Why, go to, then. But to prove to you that Helen loves Troilus, —   141

Cres. Troilus will stand to the proof, if you'll prove it so.

Pan. Troilus! Why, he esteems her no more than I esteem an addle egg.   145

Cres. If you love an addle egg as well as you love an idle head, you would eat chickens i' th' shell.

Pan. I cannot choose but laugh, to think how she tickled his chin. Indeed, she has a [marvellous] white hand, I must needs confess, —   151

Cres. Without the rack.

Pan. And she takes upon her to spy a white hair on his chin.

Cres. Alas, poor chin! many a wart is richer.   155

Pan. But there was such laughing! Queen Hecuba laugh'd that her eyes ran o'er.

Cres. With mill-stones.

Pan. And Cassandra laugh'd.

Cres. But there was more temperate fire under the pot of her eyes. Did her eyes run o'er too?   161

Pan. And Hector laugh'd.

Cres. At what was all this laughing?

Pan. Marry, at the white hair that Helen spied on Troilus' chin.   165

Cres. An 't had been a green hair, I should have laugh'd too.

Pan. They laugh'd not so much at the hair as at his pretty answer.

Cres. What was his answer?   170

---

73. **in some:** by many. 80. **Condition . . . India.** Pandarus continues his last speech: "Would he were himself even on the condition that I had to go barefoot to India to make him so." 90. **come to't:** i.e., reached maturity. 92. **his:** i.e., Troilus'. **[wit]** (Rowe). *will* QF. 101. **favour:** complexion. 118. **merry Greek:** i.e., with a pun on the phrase as meaning *roisterer.* 120. **compass'd:** bay. 129. **lifter:** thief. 150. **[marvellous]** (Pope). *marvels* QF. 158. **With mill-stones.** Satiric way of saying no tears were shed.

Pan. Quoth she, "Here's but two and fifty hairs on your chin, and one of them is white."

Cres. This is her question.

Pan. That's true; make no question of that. "Two and fifty hairs," quoth he, "and one white. That white hair is my father, and all 175 the rest are his sons." "Jupiter!" quoth she, "which of these hairs is Paris my husband?" "The forked one," quoth he, "pluck 't out, and give it him." But there was such laughing! and Helen so blush'd, and Paris so chaf'd, and all the rest so 180 laugh'd, that it pass'd.

Cres. So let it now; for it has been a great while going by.

Pan. Well, cousin, I told you a thing yesterday; think on 't. 186

Cres. So I do.

Pan. I'll be sworn 'tis true; he will weep you, an 'twere a man born in April. [*Sound a retreat.*

Cres. And I'll spring up in his tears, an 'twere a nettle against May. 191

Pan. Hark! They are coming from the field. Shall we stand up here, and see them as they pass toward Ilium? Good niece, do, sweet niece Cressida. 195

Cres. At your pleasure.

Pan. Here, here, here's an excellent place; here we may see most bravely. I'll tell you them all by their names as they pass by; but mark Troilus above the rest. 200

Æneas [*passes*].

Cres. Speak not so loud.

Pan. That's Æneas; is not that a brave man? He's one of the flowers of Troy, I can tell you. But mark Troilus; you shall see anon.

Cres. Who's that? 205

Antenor [*passes*].

Pan. That's Antenor. He has a shrewd wit, I can tell you, and he's a man good enough. He's one o' th' soundest judgement in Troy, whosoever, and a proper man of person. When comes Troilus? I'll show you Troilus anon. If he sees me, you shall see him nod at me. 211

Cres. Will he give you the nod?

Pan. You shall see.

Cres. If he do, the rich shall have more.

Hector [*passes*].

Pan. That's Hector, that, that, look you, 215 that; there's a fellow! Go thy way, Hector! There's a brave man, niece. O brave Hector!

Look how he looks! There's a countenance! Is't not a brave man?

Cres. O, a brave man! 220

Pan. Is 'a not? It does a man's heart good. Look you what hacks are on his helmet! Look you yonder, do you see? Look you there; there's no jesting; [there's] laying on, take't off who will, as they say. There he hacks! 225

Cres. Be those with swords?

Paris [*passes*].

Pan. Swords! anything, he cares not; an the devil come to him, it's all one. By God's lid, it does one's heart good. Yonder comes Paris, yonder comes Paris. Look ye yonder, niece; is't not a 230 gallant man too, is't not? Why, this is brave now. Who said he came hurt home to-day? He's not hurt. Why, this will do Helen's heart good now, ha! Would I could see Troilus now! You shall see Troilus anon. 236

Cres. Who's that?

Helenus [*passes*].

Pan. That's Helenus. I marvel where Troilus is. That's Helenus. I think he went not forth to-day. That's Helenus. 240

Cres. Can Helenus fight, uncle?

Pan. Helenus? no. Yes, he'll fight indifferent well. I marvel where Troilus is. Hark! do you not hear the people cry "Troilus"? Helenus is a priest. 245

Cres. What sneaking fellow comes yonder?

Troilus [*passes*].

Pan. Where? Yonder? That's Deiphobus. 'Tis Troilus! There's a man, niece! Hem! Brave Troilus! the prince of chivalry!

Cres. Peace, for shame, peace! 250

Pan. Mark him; note him. O brave Troilus! Look well upon him, niece. Look you how his sword is bloodied, and his helm more hack'd than Hector's, and how he looks, and how he goes! O admirable youth! he ne'er saw three and twenty. Go thy way, Troilus, go thy way! Had I a 256 sister were a grace, or a daughter a goddess, he should take his choice. O admirable man! Paris? Paris is dirt to him; and, I warrant, Helen, to change, would give money to boot. 260

Common Soldiers *pass*.

Cres. Here come more.

Pan. Asses, fools, dolts! chaff and bran, chaff and bran! porridge after meat! I could live and die i' th' eyes of Troilus. Ne'er look, ne'er look;

---

174. **Two and fifty.** Tradition gave Priam fifty sons. 178. **forked one.** Another reference to the cuckold's horns. 191. **against:** anticipating. 198. **bravely:** excellently. 209. **proper:** handsome. 224. **[there's]** Q. Om. F. **laying on:** i.e., signs of heavy fighting. **take't off:** disparage it. 260. **money** F. *an eye* Q. 264. **eyes:** i.e., sight.

the eagles are gone; crows and daws, crows and 265
daws! I had rather be such a man as Troilus than
Agamemnon and all Greece.

Cres. There is among the Greeks Achilles, a
better man than Troilus.   269

Pan. Achilles! a drayman, a porter, a very camel.

Cres. Well, well.

Pan. "Well, well!" Why, have you any discretion? Have you any eyes? Do you know what
a man is? Is not birth, beauty, good shape, 275
discourse, manhood, learning, gentleness, virtue,
youth, liberality, and so forth, the spice and salt
that season a man?

Cres. Ay, a minc'd man; and then to be bak'd
with no date in the pie, for then the man's date's
out.   281

Pan. You are such another woman! One knows
not at what ward you lie.

Cres. Upon my back, to defend my belly; upon
my wit, to defend my wiles; upon my secrecy, 285
to defend mine honesty; my mask, to defend my
beauty; and you, to defend all these; and at all
these wards I lie, at a thousand watches.

Pan. Say one of your watches.   290

Cres. Nay, I'll watch you for that; and that's
one of the chiefest of them too. If I cannot ward
what I would not have hit, I can watch you for telling how I took the blow; unless it swell past hiding,
and then it's past watching.   295

Enter [Troilus's] Boy.

Pan. You are such another!

Boy. Sir, my lord would instantly speak with you.

Pan. Where?   299

Boy. At your own house; [there he unarms him.]

Pan. Good boy, tell him I come. [*Exit Boy.*]
I doubt he be hurt. Fare ye well, good niece.

Cres. Adieu, uncle.

Pan. I'll be with you, niece, by and by.

Cres. To bring, uncle?   305

Pan. Ay, a token from Troilus.

Cres. By the same token, you are a bawd.
                                    [*Exit Pandarus.*
Words, vows, gifts, tears, and love's full sacrifice,
He offers in another's enterprise;
But more in Troilus thousandfold I see   310
Than in the glass of Pandar's praise may be;
Yet hold I off. Women are angels, wooing.

Things won are done, joy's soul lies in the doing.
That she belov'd knows nought that knows not this:
Men prize the thing ungain'd more than it is. 315
That she was never yet that ever knew
Love got so sweet as when desire did sue.
Therefore this maxim out of love I teach:
Achievement is command; ungain'd, beseech.
Then though my heart's [content] firm love doth
     bear,   320
Nothing of that shall from mine eyes appear.
                                         [*Exeunt.*

[SCENE III. *The Greek camp. Before Agamemnon's tent.*]

Sennet. Enter AGAMEMNON, NESTOR, ULYSSES,
     DIOMEDES, MENELAUS, *with others.*

Agam. Princes,
What grief hath set the jaundice on your cheeks?
The ample proposition that hope makes
In all designs begun on earth below
Fails in the promis'd largeness. Checks and dis-
     asters   5
Grow in the veins of actions highest rear'd,
As knots, by the conflux of meeting sap,
Infect the sound pine and [divert] his grain
Tortive and errant from his course of growth.
Nor, princes, is it matter new to us   10
That we come short of our suppose so far
That after seven years' siege yet Troy walls stand;
Sith every action that hath gone before,
Whereof we have record, trial did draw
Bias and thwart, not answering the aim   15
And that unbodied figure of the thought
That gave't surmised shape. Why then, you
     princes,
Do you with cheeks abash'd behold our works,
And think them shame? which are indeed nought
     else
But the protractive trials of great Jove   20
To find persistive constancy in men;
The fineness of which metal is not found
In fortune's love; for then the bold and coward,
The wise and fool, the artist and unread,
The hard and soft, seem all affin'd and kin.   25
But, in the wind and tempest of her frown,
Distinction, with a loud and powerful fan,
Puffing at all, winnows the light away;

279. **minc'd:** affected (with pun on usual sense). 280. **date.** Dates were used to season pastry. 282. **You ... woman!** What a woman you are! 283. **what ... lie:** what position of defense you take (a fencing term); i.e., how to take you. 286. **honesty:** chastity. 289-90. **watches:** (1) vigilance, (2) lying awake. 293-94. **watch ... telling:** guard against your telling. 300. **[there ... him]** Q. Om. F. 302. **doubt:** fear. 305. **bring:** get even. The full expression is "I'll be with you to bring" (see l. 304). 312. **wooing:** being wooed. 315. **it is:** i.e., it is worth. 318. **out of:** taught by. 319. **Achievement ... beseech:** when men have achieved what they want, they command; when they are striving for it, they entreat. 320. **[content]** Q. *contents* F.

Sc. iii, S.D. *Sennet:* set of notes on a trumpet. 3. **proposition:** promise. 8. **[divert]** (Rowe). *diverts* QF. 9. **Tortive:** twisted. **errant:** wandering. 11. **suppose:** expectation. 15. **Bias ... thwart:** off course and awry. 24. **artist:** scholar. 25. **affin'd:** related. 27. **loud** F. *broad* Q.

And what hath mass or matter, by itself
Lies rich in virtue and unmingled.   30
    Nest. With due observance of thy [godlike] seat,
Great Agamemnon, Nestor shall apply
Thy latest words. In the reproof of chance
Lies the true proof of men. The sea being smooth,
How many shallow bauble boats dare sail   35
Upon her patient breast, making their way
With those of nobler bulk!
But let the ruffian Boreas once enrage
The gentle Thetis, and anon behold
The strong-ribb'd bark through liquid mountains
    cut,   40
Bounding between the two moist elements,
Like Perseus' horse; where's then the saucy boat
Whose weak untimber'd sides but even now
Co-rivall'd greatness? Either to harbour fled,
Or made a toast for Neptune. Even so   45
Doth valour's show and valour's worth divide
In storms of fortune; for in her ray and brightness
The herd hath more annoyance by the breese
Than by the tiger; but when the splitting wind
Makes flexible the knees of knotted oaks,   50
And flies fled under shade, why, then the thing of
    courage,
As rous'd with rage, with rage doth sympathize,
And with an accent tun'd in selfsame key
[Retorts] to chiding fortune.
    Ulyss.   Agamemnon,
Thou great commander, nerve and bone of Greece,
Heart of our numbers, soul and only spirit,   56
In whom the tempers and the minds of all
Should be shut up, hear what Ulysses speaks.
Besides th' applause and approbation
The which, [*To Agamemnon*] most mighty for thy
    place and sway,   60
[*To Nestor*] And thou most reverend for thy
    stretch'd-out life,
I give to both your speeches, which were such
As Agamemnon and the hand of Greece
Should hold up high in brass, and such again
As venerable Nestor, hatch'd in silver,   65
Should with a bond of air (strong as the axle-tree
On which the heavens ride) knit all Greek ears
To his experienc'd tongue, yet let it please both,
Thou great, and wise, to hear Ulysses speak.
    Agam. Speak, Prince of Ithaca; and be't of less
    expect   70
That matter needless, of importless burden,

Divide thy lips, than we are confident,
When rank Thersites opes his mastic jaws,
We shall hear music, wit, and oracle.   74
    Ulyss. Troy, yet upon his basis, had been down,
And the great Hector's sword had lack'd a master,
But for these instances:
The specialty of rule hath been neglected;
And, look, how many Grecian tents do stand
Hollow upon this plain, so many hollow factions. 80
When that the general is not like the hive
To whom the foragers shall all repair,
What honey is expected? Degree being vizarded,
The unworthiest shows as fairly in the mask.
The heavens themselves, the planets, and this
    centre   85
Observe degree, priority, and place,
Insisture, course, proportion, season, form,
Office, and custom, in all line of order;
And therefore is the glorious planet Sol
In noble eminence enthron'd and spher'd   90
Amidst the other; whose med'cinable eye
Corrects the ill aspects of planets evil,
And posts, like the commandment of a king,
Sans check, to good and bad. But when the
    planets
In evil mixture to disorder wander,   95
What plagues and what portents! what mutiny!
What raging of the sea! shaking of earth!
Commotion in the winds! Frights, changes, hor-
    rors,
Divert and crack, rend and deracinate
The unity and married calm of states   100
Quite from their fixture! O, when degree is shak'd,
Which is the ladder to all high designs,
Then enterprise is sick! How could communities,
Degrees in schools, and brotherhoods in cities,
Peaceful commerce from dividable shores,   105
The primogenitive and due of birth,
Prerogative of age, crowns, sceptres, laurels,
But by degree, stand in authentic place?
Take but degree away, untune that string,
And, hark, what discord follows! Each thing
    meets   110
In mere oppugnancy. The bounded waters
Should lift their bosoms higher than the shores
And make a sop of all this solid globe.
Strength should be lord of imbecility,
And the rude son should strike his father dead. 115
Force should be right; or rather, right and wrong,

---

30. **unmingled:** unalloyed. 31. **[godlike]** Q. *godly* F. 32. **apply:** moralize upon. 33. **reproof:** scorning. 38. **Boreas:** the north wind. 39. **Thetis:** i.e., the sea. Thetis, a sea nymph, the mother of Achilles, is here confused with Tethys, the wife of Oceanus. 48. **breese:** gadfly. 51. **fled:** have fled. 54. **[Retorts]** (Dyce). *Retyres* QF. 55. **nerve:** sinew. 58. **shut up:** engrossed. 62–68. **speeches ... tongue.** The general sense is clear, but a satisfactory paraphrase is hopeless on account of a corrupt text. 65. **hatch'd in silver:** silver-haired (**hatch'd:** engraved in fine lines). 73. **rank:** gross. **mastic.** Unexplained. 77. **instances:** reasons. 78. **specialty of rule:** prerogative of authority. 83. **Degree:** rank. **vizarded:** hidden. 84. **mask:** masquerade. 85. **centre:** earth. 87. **Insisture:** regularity. 88. **all ... order:** due order. 91. **other:** others. 93. **posts:** speeds. 99. **deracinate:** uproot. 106. **primogenitive:** primogeniture, the right of succession vested in the first-born son. 111. **mere oppugnancy:** absolute antagonism. 113. **sop:** pulp.

Between whose endless jar justice resides,
Should lose their names, and so should justice too.
Then everything includes itself in power,
Power into will, will into appetite;   120
And appetite, an universal wolf,
So doubly seconded with will and power,
Must make perforce an universal prey,
And last eat up himself.   Great Agamemnon,
This chaos, when degree is suffocate,   125
Follows the choking.
And this neglection of degree is it
That by a pace goes backward, in a purpose
It hath to climb.   The general's disdain'd
By him one step below, he by the next,   130
That next by him beneath; so every step,
Exampled by the first pace that is sick
Of his superior, grows to an envious fever
Of pale and bloodless emulation;
And 'tis this fever that keeps Troy on foot,   135
Not her own sinews.   To end a tale of length,
Troy in our weakness [stands] not in her strength.
    Nest. Most wisely hath Ulysses here discover'd
The fever whereof all our power is sick.
    Agam. The nature of the sickness found, Ulysses,
What is the remedy?   141
    Ulyss. The great Achilles, whom opinion crowns
The sinew and the forehand of our host,
Having his ear full of his airy fame,
Grows dainty of his worth, and in his tent   145
Lies mocking our designs.   With him Patroclus
Upon a lazy bed the livelong day
Breaks scurril jests,
And with ridiculous and awkward action
(Which, slanderer, he imitation calls)   150
He pageants us.   Sometime, great Agamemnon,
Thy topless deputation he puts on,
And, like a strutting player, whose conceit
Lies in his hamstring, and doth think it rich
To hear the wooden dialogue and sound   155
'Twixt his stretch'd footing and the scaffoldage, —
Such to-be-pitied and o'er-wrested seeming
He acts thy greatness in; and when he speaks,
'Tis like a chime a-mending, with terms unsquar'd,
Which, from the tongue of roaring Typhon dropp'd,
Would seem hyperboles.   At this fusty stuff   161
The large Achilles, on his press'd bed lolling,
From his deep chest laughs out a loud applause;
Cries, "Excellent!   'Tis Agamemnon just.

Now play me Nestor; hem, and stroke thy beard,
As he being drest to some oration."   166
That's done, as near as the extremest ends
Of parallels, as like as Vulcan and his wife;
Yet god Achilles still cries, "Excellent!
'Tis Nestor right.   Now play him me, Patroclus,
Arming to answer in a night alarm."   171
And then, forsooth, the faint defects of age
Must be the scene of mirth; to cough and spit,
And, with a palsy fumbling on his gorget,
Shake in and out the rivet; and at this sport   **175**
Sir Valour dies; cries, "O, enough, Patroclus;
Or give me ribs of steel!   I shall split all
In pleasure of my spleen."   And in this fashion,
All our abilities, gifts, natures, shapes,
Severals and generals of grace exact,   180
Achievements, plots, orders, preventions,
Excitements to the field, or speech for truce,
Success or loss, what is or is not, serves
As stuff for these two to make paradoxes.
    Nest. And in the imitation of these twain —   185
Who, as Ulysses says, opinion crowns
With an imperial voice — many are infect.
Ajax is grown self-will'd, and bears his head
In such a rein, in full as proud a place
As broad Achilles; keeps his tent like him;   190
Makes factious feasts; rails on our state of war,
Bold as an oracle, and sets Thersites.
A slave whose gall coins slanders like a mint,
To match us in comparisons with dirt,
To weaken and discredit our exposure,   195
How rank soever rounded in with danger.
    Ulyss. They tax our policy, and call it cowardice,
Count wisdom as no member of the war,
Forestall prescience, and esteem no act
But that of hand.   The still and mental parts,   200
That do contrive how many hands shall strike
When fitness calls them on, and know by measure
Of their observant toil the enemies' weight, —
Why, this hath not a finger's dignity.
They call this bed-work, mapp'ry, closet-war;   205
So that the ram that batters down the wall,
For the great swing and rudeness of his poise,
They place before his hand that made the engine,
Or those that with the fineness of their souls
By reason guide his execution.   210
    Nest. Let this be granted, and Achilles' horse
Makes many Thetis' sons.   [*A tucket.*

119. includes ... in: resolves itself into.   128–29. That ... climb: that forces men backward, step by step, when they mean
to climb.   132–33. the first ... superior: the man who takes the first step in disdaining his superior.   137. [stands] Q.   *lives* F.
138. discover'd: uncovered.   145. dainty of: over-nice about, too proud of.   151. pageants: mimics.   152. topless deputation: supreme authority.   153. conceit: understanding.   154. hamstring: a tendon behind the knee.   156. stretch'd
footing: pompous tread.   scaffoldage: stage.   157. o'er-wrested: strained.   159. unsquar'd: unsuitable.   160. Typhon:
a giant.   166. drest to: ready for.   168. his wife: Venus.   170. right: exactly.   171. answer in: respond to.   174. gorget:
armor for the neck.   178. spleen: fit of laughter.   180. Severals ... exact: individual and common excellencies.   184.
paradoxes: absurdities.   187. voice: acclaim.   189. In ... rein: so haughtily.   196. rank: excessively.   197. tax: censure.
199. Forestall: depreciate.   202. fitness: fit moment.   205. mapp'ry: map-making, i.e., bookishness.   211–12. Let ...
sons: If this conception of things be admitted, then Achilles' horsemen become each as valuable as Achilles himself.   S.D.
tucket: a trumpet call.

Agam. What trumpet? Look, Menelaus.
Men. From Troy.

Enter ÆNEAS.

Agam. What would you 'fore our tent?   215
Æne. Is this great Agamemnon's tent, I pray
you?
Agam. Even this.
Æne. May one that is a herald and a prince
Do a fair message to his kingly ears?   219
Agam. With surety stronger than Achilles' arm,
'Fore all the Greekish heads, which with one voice
Call Agamemnon head and general.
Æne. Fair leave and large security. How may
A stranger to those most imperial looks
Know them from eyes of other mortals?
Agam.   How?
Æne. Ay.   226
I ask, that I might waken reverence,
And [bid] the cheek be ready with a blush
Modest as Morning when she coldly eyes
The youthful Phœbus.   230
Which is that god in office, guiding men?
Which is the high and mighty Agamemnon?
Agam. This Troyan scorns us; or the men of Troy
Are ceremonious courtiers.
Æne. Courtiers as free, as debonair, unarm'd,
As bending angels; that's their fame in peace. 236
But when they would seem soldiers, they have galls,
Good arms, strong joints, true swords; and, Jove's
accord,
Nothing so full of heart. But peace, Æneas,
Peace, Troyan; lay thy finger on thy lips!   240
The worthiness of praise distains his worth,
If that the prais'd himself bring the praise forth;
But what the repining enemy commends,
That breath fame blows; that praise, sole pure,
transcends.
Agam. Sir, you of Troy, call you yourself Æneas?
Æne. Ay, Greek, that is my name.   246
Agam. What's your affair, I pray you?
Æne. Sir, pardon; 'tis for Agamemnon's ears.
Agam. He hears nought privately that comes
from Troy.
Æne. Nor I from Troy come not to whisper him.
I bring a trumpet to awake his ear,   251
To set his sense on the attentive bent,
And then to speak.
Agam.   Speak frankly as the wind;
It is not Agamemnon's sleeping hour.
That thou shalt know, Troyan, he is awake,   255
He tells thee so himself.
Æne.   Trumpet, blow loud,
Send thy brass voice through all these lazy tents,

And every Greek of mettle, let him know,
What Troy means fairly shall be spoke aloud.
                    [*The trumpets sound.*
We have, great Agamemnon, here in Troy   260
A prince call'd Hector, — Priam is his father —
Who in this dull and long-continu'd truce
Is rusty grown; he bade me take a trumpet,
And to this purpose speak. Kings, princes, lords!
If there be one amongst the fair'st of Greece   265
That holds his honour higher than his ease,
That seeks his praise more than he fears his peril,
That knows his valour, and knows not his fear,
That loves his mistress more than in confession
With truant vows to her own lips he loves,   270
And dare avow her beauty and her worth
In other arms than hers, — to him this challenge.
Hector, in view of Troyans and of Greeks,
Shall make it good, or do his best to do it,
He hath a lady, wiser, fairer, truer,   275
Than ever Greek did compass in his arms,
And will to-morrow with his trumpet call
Midway between your tents and walls of Troy,
To rouse a Grecian that is true in love.
If any come, Hector shall honour him;   280
If none, he'll say in Troy when he retires,
The Grecian dames are sunburnt and not worth
The splinter of a lance. Even so much.
Agam. This shall be told our lovers, Lord Æneas.
If none of them have soul in such a kind,   285
We left them all at home. But we are soldiers;
And may that soldier a mere recreant prove,
That means not, hath not, or is not in love!
If then one is, or hath, or means to be,
That one meets Hector; if none else, I am he. 290
Nest. Tell him of Nestor, one that was a man
When Hector's grandsire suck'd: he is old now;
But if there be not in our Grecian mould
One noble man that hath one spark of fire
To answer for his love, tell him from me   295
I'll hide my silver beard in a gold beaver
And in my vantbrace put this wither'd brawn,
And, meeting him, will tell him that my lady
Was fairer than his grandam, and as chaste
As may be in the world. His youth is flood,   300
I'll [prove] this truth with my three drops of blood.
Æne. Now heavens forbid such scarcity of youth!
Ulyss. Amen.
Agam. Fair Lord Æneas, let me touch your hand;
To our pavilion shall I lead you first.   305
Achilles shall have word of this intent;
So shall each lord of Greece, from tent to tent.
Yourself shall feast with us before you go
And find the welcome of a noble foe.
                    [*Exeunt all but Ulysses and Nestor.*

---

221. **heads:** chiefs. 228. **[bid]** Q. *on* F. 237. **galls:** fierce passions. 238. **Jove's accord:** Jove granting favor.
239. **heart:** courage. 252. **set...bent:** rouse him to attention. 270. **truant:** faithless. 282. **sunburnt:** swarthy.
293. **mould** F. *host* Q. 296. **beaver:** vizor (of helmet). 297. **vantbrace:** armor for forearm. 301. **[prove]** Q. *pawne* F.

Ulyss. Nestor!   310
Nest. What says Ulysses?
Ulyss. I have a young conception in my brain;
Be you my time to bring it to some shape.
Nest. What is't?
Ulyss. This 'tis: 315
Blunt wedges rive hard knots. The seeded pride
That hath to this maturity blown up
In rank Achilles must or now be cropp'd
Or, shedding, breed a nursery of like evil,
To overbulk us all.
Nest.   Well, and how?   320
Ulyss. This challenge that the gallant Hector
sends,
However it is spread in general name,
Relates in purpose only to Achilles.
Nest. The purpose is perspicuous even as sub-
stance,
Whose grossness little characters sum up;   325
And, in the publication, make no strain
But that Achilles, were his brain as barren
As banks of Libya, — though, Apollo knows,
'Tis dry enough, — will, with great speed of judge-
ment,
Ay, with celerity, find Hector's purpose   330
Pointing on him.
Ulyss. And wake him to the answer, think you?
Nest. Yes, 'tis most meet. Who may you else
oppose
That can from Hector bring his honour off,
If not Achilles? Though't be a sportful combat,
Yet in this trial much opinion dwells;   336
For here the Troyans taste our dear'st repute
With their fin'st palate; and trust to me, Ulysses,
Our imputation shall be oddly pois'd
In this wild action; for the success,   340
Although particular, shall give a scantling
Of good or bad unto the general;
And in such indexes, although small pricks
To their subsequent volumes, there is seen
The baby figure of the giant mass   345
Of things to come at large. It is suppos'd
He that meets Hector issues from our choice;
And choice, being mutual act of all our souls,
Makes merit her election, and doth boil,
As 'twere from forth us all, a man distill'd   350
Out of our virtues; who miscarrying,
What heart from hence receives the conquering part
To steel a strong opinion to themselves?

Which entertain'd, limbs are his instruments,
In no less working than are swords and bows   355
Directive by the limbs.
Ulyss. Give pardon to my speech:
Therefore 'tis meet Achilles meet not Hector.
Let us, like merchants, show our foulest wares,
And think, perchance, they'll sell; if not,   360
The lustre of the better yet to show,
Shall show the better. Do not consent
That ever Hector and Achilles meet;
For both our honour and our shame in this
Are dogg'd with two strange followers.   365
Nest. I see them not with my old eyes. What
are they?
Ulyss. What glory our Achilles shares from
Hector,
Were he not proud, we all should wear with him.
But he already is too insolent;
And we were better parch in Afric sun   370
Than in the pride and salt scorn of his eyes,
Should he scape Hector fair. If he were foil'd,
Why then, we did our main opinion crush
In taint of our best man. No, make a lott'ry;
And, by device, let blockish Ajax draw   375
The sort to fight with Hector; among ourselves
Give him allowance as the worthier man;
For that will physic the great Myrmidon
Who broils in loud applause, and make him fall
His crest that prouder than blue Iris bends.   380
If the dull brainless Ajax come safe off,
We'll dress him up in voices. If he fail,
Yet go we under our opinion still
That we have better men. But, hit or miss,
Our project's life this shape of sense assumes: 385
Ajax employ'd plucks down Achilles' plumes.
Nest. Now, Ulysses, I begin to relish thy advice;
And I will give a taste of it forthwith
To Agamemnon. Go we to him straight.   390
Two curs shall tame each other; pride alone
Must tarre the mastiffs on, as 'twere their bone.
[*Exeunt.*

a contrast to last scene

[ACT II

SCENE I. *A part of the Greek camp.*]

Enter AJAX *and* THERSITES.

Ajax. Thersites!
Ther. Agamemnon, how if he had boils — full,
all over, generally?

312. **young conception:** fresh plan. 313. **time:** maturing influence. 319. **shedding:** i.e., scattering its seeds. 325. **Whose ... up:** whose weighty amount is expressed in little figures. 326. **strain:** difficulty in understanding. 336. **opinion dwells:** reputation is at stake. 339. **imputation:** repute. **oddly pois'd:** unequally balanced. 340–42. **for ... general:** for the outcome, though (primarily affecting an) individual, will prove a sample of good or bad touching the army in general. 344. **To:** compared to. 349. **election:** basis of selection. 351. **who miscarrying:** if that man fails. 354–56. **Which ... limbs:** if this opinion is held it will guide the limbs of those who hold it, just as their limbs direct their weapons. 365. **followers:** consequences. 371. **salt:** bitter. 373. **main opinion:** general reputation. 375. **device:** trick. 376. **sort:** lot. 378. **Myrmidon:** Achilles, chief of the Myrmidons (his Thessalian followers). 379. **broils:** i.e., cooks or suns himself. **fall:** lower. 380. **Iris:** the rainbow. 382. **voices:** praises. 392. **tarre:** incite (to fight).

Ajax. Thersites!   4
Ther. And those boils did run? Say so: did not the general run then? Were not that a botchy core?

Ajax. Dog!

Ther. Then there would come some matter from him. I see none now.   10

Ajax. Thou bitch-wolf's son, canst thou not hear? Feel, then.   [*Strikes him.*

Ther. The plague of Greece upon thee, thou mongrel beef-witted lord!

Ajax. Speak then, thou [unsalted] leaven, speak. I will beat thee into handsomeness.   16

Ther. I shall sooner rail thee into wit and holiness; but I think thy horse will sooner con an oration than thou learn a prayer without book. Thou canst strike, canst thou? A red murrain o' thy jade's tricks!   21

Ajax. Toadstool, learn me the proclamation.

Ther. Dost thou think I have no sense, thou strik'st me thus?

Ajax. The proclamation!   25

Ther. Thou art proclaim'd a fool, I think.

Ajax. Do not, porpentine, do not; my fingers itch.

Ther. I would thou didst itch from head to foot and I had the scratching of thee. I would   30 make thee the loathsom'st scab in Greece. [When thou art forth in the incursions, thou strik'st as slow as another.]

Ajax. I say, the proclamation!   34

Ther. Thou grumblest and railest every hour on Achilles, and thou art as full of envy at his greatness as Cerberus is at Proserpina's beauty, ay, that thou bark'st at him.

Ajax. Mistress Thersites!

Ther. Thou shouldst strike him.   40

Ajax. Cobloaf!

Ther. He would pun thee into shivers with his fist, as a sailor breaks a biscuit.

Ajax. [*Beating him.*] You whoreson cur!

Ther. Do, do.   45

Ajax. Thou stool for a witch!

Ther. Ay, do, do; thou sodden-witted lord! Thou hast no more brain than I have in mine elbows; an asinico may tutor thee. Thou scurvy valiant ass! thou art here but to thrash Troyans;   50 and thou art bought and sold among those of any wit, like a barbarian slave. If thou use to beat me, I will begin at thy heel, and tell what thou art by inches, thou thing of no bowels, thou!

Ajax. You dog!   55

Ther. You scurvy lord!

Ajax. [*Beating him.*] You cur!

Ther. Mars his idiot! Do, rudeness; do, camel; do, do.   59

Enter ACHILLES *and* PATROCLUS.

Achil. Why, how now, Ajax! wherefore do you this? How now, Thersites! what's the matter, man?

Ther. You see him there, do you?

Achil. Ay; what's the matter?

Ther. Nay, look upon him.   65

Achil. So I do. What's the matter?

Ther. Nay, but regard him well.

Achil. Well! why, I do so.

Ther. But yet you look not well upon him; for, whosomever you take him to be, he is Ajax.   70

Achil. I know that, fool.

Ther. Ay, but that fool knows not himself.

Ajax. Therefore I beat thee.   73

Ther. Lo, lo, lo, lo, what modicums of wit he utters! His evasions have ears thus long. I have bobb'd his brain more than he has beat my bones. I will buy nine sparrows for a penny, and his *pia mater* is not worth the ninth part of a sparrow. This lord, Achilles, Ajax, who wears his wit in his belly and his guts in his head, I'll tell you what I say of him.   81

Achil. What?

Ther. I say, this Ajax —

[*Ajax offers to beat him.*]

Achil. Nay, good Ajax.

Ther. Has not so much wit —   85

Achil. Nay, I must hold you.

Ther. As will stop the eye of Helen's needle, for whom he comes to fight.

Achil. Peace, fool!   89

Ther. I would have peace and quietness, but the fool will not, — he there, that he! Look you there.

Ajax. O thou damn'd cur! I shall —

Achil. Will you set your wit to a fool's?   94

Ther. No, I warrant you; for a fool's will shame it.

Patr. Good words, Thersites.

Achil. What's the quarrel?

Ajax. I bade the vile owl go learn me the tenour of the proclamation, and he rails upon me.   100

Ther. I serve thee not.

Ajax. Well, go to, go to.

Ther. I serve here voluntary.   103

Act II, sc. i, 6. **botchy:** broken out. 9. **matter:** (1) sense, (2) pus. 14. **mongrel.** Ajax was the son of the Greek Telamon and the Trojan woman, Hesione. See II.ii.77–80 and note. 15. **[unsalted]** Q. *whinid'st* F. 19. **without book:** by heart. 20. **murrain:** plague. 21. **jade's tricks:** tricks of a vicious horse. 23. **sense:** feeling. 27. **porpentine:** porcupine. 31–33. **[When ... another]** Q. Om. F. 41. **Cobloaf:** bun. 42. **pun:** pound. 49. **asinico:** little ass. 51. **bought and sold:** made fun of (proverbial). 54. **bowels:** pity. 75. **His ... long:** i.e., his quibbles are those of an ass. 76. **bobb'd:** thumped 78. *pia mater:* brain.

Achil. Your last service was suff'rance, 'twas not voluntary; no man is beaten voluntary. Ajax was here the voluntary, and you as under an impress.   107

Ther. E'en so. A great deal of your wit, too, lies in your sinews, or else there be liars. Hector shall have a great catch, if he knock out either of your brains. He were as good crack a fusty nut with no kernel.   112

Achil. What, with me too, Thersites?

Ther. There's Ulysses and old Nestor, whose wit was mouldy ere [your] grandsires had nails on their toes, yoke you like draught-oxen and make you plough up the war.   117

Achil. What, what?

Ther. Yes, good sooth. To Achilles, to Ajax, to —   120

Ajax. I shall cut out your tongue.

Ther. 'Tis no matter; I shall speak as much as thou afterwards.

Patr. No more words, Thersites; [peace!]

Ther. I will hold my peace when Achilles' [brach] bids me, shall I?   126

Achil. There's for you, Patroclus.

Ther. I will see you hang'd like clodpoles ere I come any more to your tents. I will keep where there is wit stirring and leave the faction of fools.   131

[*Exit.*

Patr. A good riddance.

Achil. Marry, this, sir, is proclaim'd through all our host:
That Hector, by the fifth hour of the sun,
Will with a trumpet 'twixt our tents and Troy   135
To-morrow morning call some knight to arms
That hath a stomach; and such a one that dare
Maintain — I know not what; 'tis trash. Farewell.

Ajax. Farewell. Who shall answer him?

Achil. I know not; 'tis put to lott'ry. Otherwise,
He knew his man.   141

Ajax. O, meaning you. I will go learn more of it.   [*Exeunt.*

[SCENE II. *Troy. A room in Priam's palace.*]

Enter PRIAM, HECTOR, TROILUS, PARIS, *and*
HELENUS.

Pri. After so many hours, lives, speeches spent,
Thus once again says Nestor from the Greeks:
"Deliver Helen, and all damage else —
As honour, loss of time, travail, expense,

Wounds, friends, and what else dear that is con-
    sum'd   5
In hot digestion of this cormorant war —
Shall be struck off." Hector, what say you to't?

Hect. Though no man lesser fears the Greeks
    than I
As far as touches my particular,
Yet, dread Priam,   10
There is no lady of more softer bowels,
More spongy to suck in the sense of fear,
More ready to cry out, "Who knows what follows?"
Than Hector is. The wound of peace is surety,
Surety secure; but modest doubt is call'd   15
The beacon of the wise, the tent that searches
To th' bottom of the worst. Let Helen go.
Since the first sword was drawn about this question,
Every tithe soul, 'mongst many thousand dismes,
Hath been as dear as Helen; I mean, of ours.   20
If we have lost so many tenths of ours,
To guard a thing not ours nor worth to us,
Had it our name, the value of one ten,
What merit's in that reason which denies
The yielding of her up?

Tro.   Fie, fie, my brother!   25
Weigh you the worth and honour of a king
So great as our dread father in a scale
Of common ounces? Will you with counters sum
The past proportion of his infinite,
And buckle in a waist most fathomless   30
With spans and inches so diminutive
As fears and reasons? Fie, for godly shame!

Hel. No marvel though you bite so sharp at rea-
    sons,
You are so empty of them. Should not our father
Bear the great sway of his affairs with reasons,   35
Because your speech hath none that tells him so?

Tro. You are for dreams and slumbers, brother
    priest;
You fur your gloves with reason. Here are your
    reasons:
You know an enemy intends you harm;
You know a sword employ'd is perilous,   40
And reason flies the object of all harm.
Who marvels then, when Helenus beholds
A Grecian and his sword, if he do set
The very wings of reason to his heels
And fly like chidden Mercury from Jove,   45
Or like a star disorb'd? Nay, if we talk of reason,
Let's shut our gates and sleep. Manhood and honour
Should have [hare] hearts, would they but fat their
    thoughts

---

106. **impress:** enforced service.   115. **[your]** (Theobald).   *their* QF.   124. **[peace]** Q. Om. F.   126. **[brach]** (Rowe):
hound.   *brooch* QF.   128. **clodpoles:** blockheads.   137. **stomach:** appetite, i.e., courage.
Sc. ii, 6. **cormorant:** ravenous.   9. **my particular:** me personally.   14. **surety:** over-confidence.   16. **tent:** probe (for
wounds).   19. **Every...dismes:** i.e., every soul the war has taken as tithe, amongst tens of thousands (both *tithe* and
disme mean *tenth*).   28. **counters:** valueless discs used in counting.   29. **past...infinite:** his infinite, immeasurable greatness.   38. **You...reason:** you trim your speech with reasons as your gloves with fur.   45-46. **And...reason.** So Q.
F prints these lines in reverse order.   **disorb'd:** shot from its sphere.   48. **[hare]** Q.   *hard* F.   **would...fat:** if they fed.

With this cramm'd reason. Reason and respect
Makes livers pale and lustihood deject.   50
  Hect. Brother, she is not worth what she doth
    cost
The holding.
  Tro.   What is aught, but as 'tis valu'd?
  Hect. But value dwells not in particular will;
It holds his estimate and dignity
As well wherein 'tis precious of itself   55
As in the prizer. 'Tis [mad] idolatry
To make the service greater than the god;
And the will dotes that is inclineable
To what infectiously itself affects,
Without some image of th' affected merit.   60
  Tro. I take to-day a wife, and my election
Is led on in the conduct of my will,
My will enkindled by mine eyes and ears,
Two traded pilots 'twixt the dangerous shores
Of will and judgement: how may I avoid,   65
Although my will distaste what it elected,
The wife I chose? There can be no evasion
To blench from this and to stand firm by honour.
We turn not back the silks upon the merchant,
When we have spoil'd them, nor the remainder
    viands   70
We do not throw in unrespective [sieve],
Because we now are full. It was thought meet
Paris should do some vengeance on the Greeks.
Your breath of full consent bellied his sails;
The seas and winds, old wranglers, took a truce   75
And did him service; he touch'd the ports desir'd,
And for an old aunt whom the Greeks held captive,
He brought a Grecian queen, whose youth and
    freshness
Wrinkles Apollo's, and makes stale the morning.
Why keep we her? The Grecians keep our aunt. 80
Is she worth keeping? Why, she is a pearl,
Whose price hath launch'd above a thousand ships,
And turn'd crown'd kings to merchants.
If you'll avouch 'twas wisdom Paris went —
As you must needs, for you all cried "Go, go," — 85
If you'll confess he brought home noble prize —
As you must needs, for you all clapp'd your hands,
And cried "Inestimable!" — why do you now
The issue of your proper wisdoms rate,
And do a deed that Fortune never did,   90
Beggar the estimation which you priz'd
Richer than sea and land? O theft most base,
That we have stol'n what we do fear to keep!

But thieves, unworthy of a thing so stol'n
That in their country did them that disgrace   95
We fear to warrant in our native place!
  Cas. [*Within.*] Cry, Troyans, cry!
  Pri.   What noise, what shriek is this?
  Tro. 'Tis our mad sister, I do know her voice.
  Cas. [*Within.*] Cry, Troyans!
  Hect. It is Cassandra.   100

Enter CASSANDRA [*raving*] *with her hair about her
ears.*

  Cas. Cry, Troyans, cry! Lend me ten thousand
    eyes,
And I will fill them with prophetic tears.
  Hect. Peace, sister, peace!
  Cas. Virgins and boys, mid-age and wrinkled
    [eld],
Soft infancy, that nothing can but cry,   105
Add to my clamour! Let us pay betimes
A moiety of that mass of moan to come.
Cry, Troyans, cry! Practise your eyes with tears!
Troy must not be, nor goodly Ilion stand.
Our firebrand brother, Paris, burns us all.   110
Cry, Troyans, cry! A Helen and a woe!
Cry, cry! Troy burns, or else let Helen go. [*Exit.*
  Hect. Now, youthful Troilus, do not these high
    strains
Of divination in our sister work
Some touches of remorse? Or is your blood   115
So madly hot that no discourse of reason,
Nor fear of bad success in a bad cause,
Can qualify the same?
  Tro.   Why, brother Hector,
We may not think the justness of each act
Such and no other than event doth form it,   120
Nor once deject the courage of our minds,
Because Cassandra's mad. Her brain-sick raptures
Cannot distaste the goodness of a quarrel
Which hath our several honours all engag'd
To make it gracious. For my private part,   125
I am no more touch'd than all Priam's sons;
And Jove forbid there should be done amongst us
Such things as might offend the weakest spleen
To fight for and maintain!
  Par. Else might the world convince of levity
As well my undertakings as your counsels;   131
But I attest the gods, your full consent
Gave wings to my propension and cut off
All fears attending on so dire a project.

---

49. **respect:** caution.   53. **particular will:** the esteem of an individual.   56. **prizer:** appraiser.   [**mad**] Q. *made* F. 58–60. **that ... merit:** which desires the thing it unwholesomely craves if it has no conception of the quality desired. 64. **traded:** practiced. 67–68. **evasion ... blench:** subterfuge by which I may shrink. 70. **spoil'd** F. *soil'd* Q. 71. **unrespective:** undiscriminating. [**sieve**] Q. *same* F 74. **bellied:** swelled. 77. **aunt:** Hesione, sister of Priam, carried off from Troy by Telamon, father of Ajax. 79. **stale** F. *pale* Q. 89. **proper:** own. **rate:** condemn. 90. **do ... did:** i.e., show greater inconstancy than ever Fortune showed. 91. **estimation:** thing esteemed. 93. **That:** in that. 95. **their:** the Greeks'. 96. **We ... warrant:** which we are afraid to defend. 104. [**eld**] (Theobald conj.). *elders* Q; *old* F. 107. **moiety:** part. 118. **qualify:** moderate. 120. **event:** outcome. 123. **distaste:** make distasteful. 128. **spleen:** temper. 130. **convince:** convict. 133. **propension:** inclination.

For what, alas, can these my single arms?   135
What propugnation is in one man's valour
To stand the push and enmity of those
This quarrel would excite?   Yet, I protest,
Were I alone to pass the difficulties
And had as ample power as I have will,   140
Paris should ne'er retract what he hath done,
Nor faint in the pursuit.

    Pri.   Paris, you speak
Like one besotted on your sweet delights.
You have the honey still, but these the gall;
So to be valiant is no praise at all.   145

    Par.   Sir, I propose not merely to myself
The pleasures such a beauty brings with it;
But I would have the soil of her fair rape
Wip'd off, in honourable keeping her.
What treason were it to the ransack'd queen,   150
Disgrace to your great worths and shame to me,
Now to deliver her possession up
On terms of base compulsion!   Can it be
That so degenerate a strain as this
Should once set footing in your generous bosoms?
There's not the meanest spirit on our party   156
Without a heart to dare or sword to draw
When Helen is defended, nor none so noble
Whose life were ill bestow'd or death unfam'd
Where Helen is the subject.   Then, I say,   160
Well may we fight for her whom, we know well,
The world's large spaces cannot parallel.

    Hect.   Paris and Troilus, you have both said well,
And on the cause and question now in hand
Have gloz'd, but superficially; not much   165
Unlike young men, whom Aristotle thought
Unfit to hear moral philosophy.
The reasons you allege do more conduce
To the hot passion of distemp'red blood
Than to make up a free determination   170
'Twixt right and wrong, for pleasure and revenge
Have ears more deaf than adders to the voice
Of any true decision.   Nature craves
All dues be rend'red to their owners: now,
What nearer debt in all humanity   175
Than wife is to the husband?   If this law
Of nature be corrupted through affection,
And that great minds, of partial indulgence
To their benumbed wills, resist the same,
There is a law in each well-ord'red nation   180
To curb those raging appetites that are
Most disobedient and refractory.
If Helen then be wife to Sparta's king,
As it is known she is, these moral laws
Of nature and of nations speak aloud   185

To have her back return'd.   Thus to persist
In doing wrong extenuates not wrong,
But makes it much more heavy.   Hector's opinion
Is this in way of truth; yet ne'ertheless,
My spritely brethren, I propend to you   190
In resolution to keep Helen still,
For 'tis a cause that hath no mean dependence
Upon our joint and several dignities.

    Tro.   Why, there you touch'd the life of our de-
      sign.
Were it not glory that we more affected   195
Than the performance of our heaving spleens,
I would not wish a drop of Troyan blood
Spent more in her defence.   But, worthy Hector,
She is a theme of honour and renown,
A spur to valiant and magnanimous deeds   200
Whose present courage may beat down our foes,
And fame in time to come canonize us;
For, I presume, brave Hector would not lose
So rich advantage of a promis'd glory
As smiles upon the forehead of this action   205
For the wide world's revenue.

    Hect.   I am yours,
You valiant offspring of great Priamus.
I have a roisting challenge sent amongst
The dull and factious nobles of the Greeks
Will strike amazement to their drowsy spirits.   210
I was advertis'd their great general slept,
Whilst emulation in the army crept.
This, I presume, will wake him.   [*Exeunt.*

[SCENE III.   *The Greek camp.   Before Achilles's*
tent.]

Enter THERSITES, *solus.*

    Ther.   How now, Thersites!   What, lost in the
labyrinth of thy fury!   Shall the elephant Ajax
carry it thus?   He beats me, and I rail at him.   O,
worthy satisfaction! would it were otherwise; that
I could beat him, whilst he rail'd at me.   'S foot,   5
I'll learn to conjure and raise devils, but I'll see
some issue of my spiteful execrations.   Then there's
Achilles, a rare engineer!   If Troy be not taken till
these two undermine it, the walls will stand till
they fall of themselves.   O thou great thunder-   10
darter of Olympus, forget that thou art Jove, the
king of gods, and, Mercury, lose all the serpentine
craft of thy caduceus, if ye take not that little little
less than little wit from them that they have, which
short-arm'd ignorance itself knows is so abun-   15
dant scarce, it will not in circumvention deliver a fly
from a spider, without drawing their massy irons

---

136. **propugnation:** power of defense.   139. **pass:** undergo.   148. **rape:** abduction.   155. **generous:** noble.   165. **gloz'd:**
commented.   167. **moral.**   It was *political* philosophy of which Aristotle spoke, but which was regarded as a branch of
moral philosophy.   177. **affection:** appetite.   178. **of:** out of.   190. **spritely:** high-spirited.   **propend:** incline.   196. **heav-**
ing spleens: restless passions.   208. **roisting:** rousing.   211. **advertis'd:** informed.
    Sc. iii, 5. **'S foot:** God's foot.   6. **but I'll see:** rather than not see.   13. **caduceus:** Mercury's rod.

and cutting the web! After this, the vengeance
on the whole camp! or rather, the [Neapolitan]
bone-ache! for that, methinks, is the curse de-   20
pendent on those that war for a placket. I have
said my prayers, and devil Envy say Amen. What
ho! my Lord Achilles!

Enter PATROCLUS.

Patr. Who's there? Thersites! Good Thersites,
come in and rail.   26
Ther. If I could have rememb'red a gilt counterfeit, thou wouldst not have slipp'd out of my contemplation. But it is no matter; thyself upon
thyself! The common curse of mankind, folly   30
and ignorance, be thine in great revenue! Heaven
bless thee from a tutor, and discipline come not
near thee! Let thy blood be thy direction till thy
death, then if she that lays thee out says thou art
a fair corse, I'll be sworn and sworn upon't she   35
never shrouded any but lazars. Amen. Where's
Achilles?
Patr. What, art thou devout? Wast thou in
prayer?
Ther. Ay; the heavens hear me!   40
[*Patr.* Amen.]

Enter ACHILLES.

Achil. Who's there?
Patr. Thersites, my lord.
Achil. Where, where? Art thou come? Why,
my cheese, my digestion, why hast thou not serv'd
thyself in to my table so many meals? Come,
what's Agamemnon?   46
Ther. Thy commander, Achilles. Then tell me,
Patroclus, what's Achilles?
Patr. Thy lord, Thersites. Then tell me, I pray
thee, what's thyself?   50
Ther. Thy knower, Patroclus. Then tell me,
Patroclus, what art thou?
Patr. Thou mayst tell that know'st.
Achil. O, tell, tell.   54
Ther. I'll decline the whole question. Agamem-
non commands Achilles; Achilles is my lord; I am
Patroclus' knower; and Patroclus is a fool.
Patr. You rascal!
Ther. Peace, fool! I have not done.   60
Achil. He is a privileg'd man. Proceed, Ther-
sites.
Ther. Agamemnon is a fool; Achilles is a fool;
Thersites is a fool; and, as aforesaid, Patroclus is
a fool.   65
Achil. Derive this; come.

Ther. Agamemnon is a fool to offer to command
Achilles; Achilles is a fool to be commanded of
Agamemnon; Thersites is a fool to serve such a
fool; and Patroclus is a fool positive.   70
Patr. Why am I a fool?

Enter AGAMEMNON, ULYSSES, NESTOR, DIOMEDES,
AJAX, *and* CALCHAS.

Ther. Make that demand of the Creator; it suf-
fices me thou art. Look you, who comes here?
Achil. Patroclus, I'll speak with nobody. Come
in with me, Thersites.   [*Exit.*   76
Ther. Here is such patchery, such juggling, and
such knavery! All the argument is a cuckold and
a whore; a good quarrel to draw emulous factions
and bleed to death upon. Now, the dry serpigo on
the subject, and war and lechery confound all!   82
[*Exit.*]
Agam. Where is Achilles?
Patr. Within his tent; but ill dispos'd, my lord.
Agam. Let it be known to him that we are here.
He [shent] our messengers, and we lay by   86
Our appertainments, visiting of him.
Let him be told [so, lest] perchance he think
We dare not move the question of our place,   89
Or know not what we are.
Patr.   I shall so say to him.
[*Exit.*]
Ulyss. We saw him at the opening of his tent:
He is not sick.   92
Ajax. Yes, lion-sick, sick of proud heart. You
may call it melancholy, if you will favour the man,
but, by my head, it is pride; but why, why? Let
him show us the cause. A word, my lord.   97
[*Takes Agamemnon aside.*]
Nest. What moves Ajax thus to bay at him?
Ulyss. Achilles hath inveigled his fool from him.
Nest. Who, Thersites?   101
Ulyss. He.
Nest. Then will Ajax lack matter, if he have lost
his argument.
Ulyss. No, you see, he is his argument that has
his argument, Achilles.   106
Nest. All the better; their fraction is more our
wish than their faction. But it was a strong [com-
posure] a fool could disunite.
Ulyss. The amity that wisdom knits not, folly
may easily untie.

Re-enter PATROCLUS.

Here comes Patroclus.   III
Nest. No Achilles with him.

---

19. [Neapolitan] Q. Om. F.   21. placket: petticoat, i.e., woman.   28. slipp'd. A pun on *slip*, a counterfeit coin.
32. bless: save.   33. blood: passion.   36. lazars: lepers.   41. [Patr. Amen.] Q. Om. F.   55. decline: go through (as
in grammar).   77. patchery: roguery.   81. serpigo: eruption of the skin.   86. [shent] (Theobald): scolded. *sate* Q; *sent* F.
87. appertainments: rights, dignities.   88. [so, lest] Q. *of, so* F.   89. move: raise.   place: authority.   104. argument:
object for railing.   107. fraction: rupture.   109. [composure] Q: union. *counsell that* F.

Ulyss. The elephant hath joints, but none for
courtesy. His legs are legs for necessity, not for
[flexure]. 115
  Patr. Achilles bids me say, he is much sorry
If anything more than your sport and pleasure
Did move your greatness and this noble state
To call upon him. He hopes it is no other
But for your health and your digestion sake, 120
An after-dinner's breath.
  Agam.   Hear you, Patroclus.
We are too well acquainted with these answers;
But his evasion, wing'd thus swift with scorn,
Cannot outfly our apprehensions.
Much attribute he hath, and much the reason 125
Why we ascribe it to him; yet all his virtues,
Not virtuously of his own part beheld,
Do in our eyes begin to lose their gloss,
Yea, like fair fruit in an unwholesome dish,
Are like to rot untasted. Go and tell him 130
We came to speak with him; and you shall not sin
If you do say we think him over-proud
And under-honest, in self-assumption greater
Than in the note of judgement; and worthier than
    himself
Here tend the savage strangeness he puts on, 135
Disguise the holy strength of their command,
And underwrite in an observing kind
His humorous predominance; yea, watch
His pettish lines, his ebbs, his flows, as if
The passage and whole carriage of this action 140
Rode on his tide. Go tell him this, and add,
That if he overhold his price so much,
We'll none of him; but let him, like an engine
Not portable, lie under this report:
"Bring action hither, this cannot go to war." 145
A stirring dwarf we do allowance give
Before a sleeping giant. Tell him so.
  Patr. I shall; and bring his answer presently.
                        [Exit.]
  Agam. In second voice we'll not be satisfied;
We come to speak with him. Ulysses, enter you.
                      [Exit Ulysses.
  Ajax. What is he more than another? 151
  Agam. No more than what he thinks he is.
  Ajax. Is he so much? Do you not think he
thinks himself a better man than I am?
  Agam. No question. 155
  Ajax. Will you subscribe his thought, and say
he is?
  Agam. No, noble Ajax; you are as strong, as

valiant, as wise, no less noble, much more gentle,
and altogether more tractable. 160
  Ajax. Why should a man be proud? How doth
pride grow? I know not what it is.
  Agam. Your mind is the clearer, Ajax, and your
virtues the fairer. He that is proud eats up himself.
Pride is his own glass, his own trumpet, his own 165
chronicle; and whatever praises itself but in the
deed, devours the deed in the praise.

Re-enter ULYSSES.

  Ajax. I do hate a proud man, as I hate the en-
gendering of toads. 170
  Nest. *[Aside.]* Yet he loves himself. Is't not
strange?
  Ulyss. Achilles will not to the field to-morrow.
  Agam. What's his excuse?
  Ulyss.   He doth rely on none,
But carries on the stream of his dispose
Without observance or respect of any, 175
In will peculiar and in self-admission.
  Agam. Why will he not upon our fair request
Untent his person and share the air with us?
  Ulyss. Things small as nothing, for request's
    sake only,
He makes important. Possess'd he is with great-
    ness, 180
And speaks not to himself but with a pride
That quarrels at self-breath. Imagin'd [worth]
Holds in his blood such swoln and hot discourse
That 'twixt his mental and his active parts
Kingdom'd Achilles in commotion rages 185
And batters [down himself]. What should I say?
He is so plaguy proud that the death-tokens of it
Cry "No recovery."
  Agam.   Let Ajax go to him.
Dear lord, go you and greet him in his tent.
'Tis said he holds you well, and will be led 190
At your request a little from himself.
  Ulyss. O Agamemnon, let it not be so!
We'll consecrate the steps that Ajax makes
When they go from Achilles. Shall the proud lord
That bastes his arrogance with his own seam 195
And never suffers matter of the world
Enter his thoughts, save such as do revolve
And ruminate himself, shall he be worshipp'd
Of that we hold an idol more than he?
No, this thrice worthy and right valiant lord 200
Must not so stale his palm, nobly acquir'd;
Nor, by my will, assubjugate his merit,

---

115. **[flexure]** Q: bending. *flight* F. 118. **state:** retinue. 121. **breath:** exercise. 124. **apprehensions:** understandings. 127. **virtuously:** in proportion. 134. **note:** distinction. 135. **tend...strangeness:** wait upon the rude aloofness.
137. **underwrite...kind:** submit to in a respectful way. 138. **humorous predominance:** capricious superiority. 139. **lines:**
courses (of action). Hanmer reads *lunes*, mad freaks. 142. **overhold:** overestimate. 146. **allowance:** approval. 165. **glass:**
mirror. 176. **self-admission:** self-approval. 179. **for...only:** only because they are requested. 182. **at self-breath:** with
what it utters. **[worth]** Q; *wrath* F. 186. **[down himself]** Q. *'gainst itselfe* F. 187. **death-tokens:** plague spots.
195. **seam:** grease. 199. **Of:** by. 201. **stale his palm:** sully his glory. 202. **assubjugate:** debase.

As amply titled as Achilles' is,
By going to Achilles.
That were to enlard his fat-already pride   205
And add more coals to Cancer when he burns
With entertaining great Hyperion.
This lord go to him! Jupiter forbid,
And say in thunder, "Achilles go to him."
  Nest. [*Aside to Dio.*] O, this is well. He rubs
    the vein of him.   210
  Dio. [*Aside to Nest.*] And how his silence drinks
    up this applause!
  Ajax. If I go to him, with my armed fist
I'll pash him o'er the face.
  Agam. O, no, you shall not go.
  Ajax. An 'a be proud with me, I'll pheese his
    pride.   215
Let me go to him.
  Ulyss. Not for the worth that hangs upon our
    quarrel.
  Ajax. A paltry, insolent fellow!
  Nest. How he describes himself!
  Ajax. Can he not be sociable?   220
  Ulyss. The raven chides blackness.
  Ajax. I'll let his humours blood.
  Agam. He will be the physician that should be
the patient.
  Ajax. An all men were o' my mind, —   225
  Ulyss. Wit would be out of fashion.
  Ajax. 'A should not bear it so, 'a should eat
swords first. Shall pride carry it?
  Nest. An 'twould, you'd carry half.
  Ulyss. 'A would have ten shares.   230
  Ajax. I will knead him; I'll make him supple.
  Nest. He's not yet through warm. Force him
with praises; pour in, pour in; his ambition is dry.
  Ulyss. [*To Agam.*] My lord, you feed too much
on this dislike.   236
  Nest. Our noble general, do not do so.
  Dio. You must prepare to fight without Achilles.
  Ulyss. Why, 'tis this naming of him doth him
    harm.
Here is a man — but 'tis before his face;   240
I will be silent.
  Nest.   Wherefore should you so?
He is not emulous, as Achilles is.
  Ulyss. Know the whole world, he is as valiant.
  Ajax. A whoreson dog, that shall palter thus with
    us!
Would he were a Troyan!   245
  Nest. What a vice were it in Ajax now, —
  Ulyss. If he were proud, —

  Dio. Or covetous of praise, —
  Ulyss. Ay, or surly borne, —
  Dio. Or strange, or self-affected!   250
  Ulyss. Thank the heavens, lord, thou art of
    sweet composure.
Praise him that got thee, she that gave thee suck;
Fam'd be thy tutor, and thy parts of nature
Thrice fam'd, beyond all erudition;
But he that disciplin'd thy arms to fight,   255
Let Mars divide eternity in twain,
And give him half; and, for thy vigour,
Bull-bearing Milo his addition yield
To sinewy Ajax. I will not praise thy wisdom,
Which, like a bourn, a pale, a shore, confines   260
Thy spacious and dilated parts. Here's Nestor;
Instructed by the antiquary times,
He must, he is, he cannot but be wise.
But pardon, father Nestor, were your days
As green as Ajax' and your brain so temper'd,   265
You should not have the eminence of him,
But be as Ajax.
  Ajax.   Shall I call you father?
  Ulyss. Ay, my good son.
  Dio.   Be rul'd by him, Lord Ajax.
  Ulyss. There is no tarrying here; the hart Achilles
Keeps thicket. Please it our great general   270
To call together all his state of war.
Fresh kings are come to Troy; to-morrow
We must with all our main of power stand fast;
And here's a lord, — come knights from east to
    west,
And cull their flower, Ajax shall cope the best. 275
  Agam. Go we to council. Let Achilles sleep:
Light boats sail swift, though greater [hulks] draw
    deep.   [*Exeunt.*

[ACT III

Scene I. *Troy. Priam's palace.*]

Music sounds within. Enter Pandarus *and a*
Servant.

  Pan. Friend, you! pray you, a word. Do not
you follow the young Lord Paris?
  Serv. Ay, sir, when he goes before me.
  Pan. You depend upon him, I mean?
  Serv. Sir, I do depend upon the lord.   5
  Pan. You depend upon a noble gentleman; I
must needs praise him.
  Serv. The lord be praised!
  Pan. You know me, do you not?

206–207. **add . . . Hyperion**: add heat to summer (when the sun enters the zodiacal sign of Cancer). 210. **vein**: mood.
215. **pheese**: beat. 232. **He's . . . warm.** So Theobald. F continues to Ajax. Q gives ll. 230–32 (*'A would . . . warm*) to
Ulysses. **through**: thoroughly. **Force**: stuff. 250. **strange**: haughty. 254. **all erudition**: what could be learned. 258.
Milo. Milo of Crotona carried a bull on his shoulders at the Olympic games. **addition**: title. 260. **bourn**: boundary.
pale: fence. 262. **antiquary**: olden. 265. **green**: youthful. 273. **all . . . power**: our full force. 277. **sail** Q. *may sail* F.
[hulks] Q. *bulkes* F.

Serv. Faith, sir, superficially.   10
Pan. Friend, know me better; I am the Lord Pandarus.
Serv. I hope I shall know your honour better.
Pan. I do desire it.
Serv. You are in the state of grace.   15
Pan. Grace! No so, friend. Honour and lordship are my [titles]. What music is this?
Serv. I do but partly know, sir. It is music in parts.   20
Pan. Know you the musicians?
Serv. Wholly, sir.
Pan. Who play they to?
Serv. To the hearers, sir.
Pan. At whose pleasure, friend?   25
Serv. At mine, sir, and theirs that love music.
Pan. Command, I mean, friend.
Serv. Who shall I command, sir?
Pan. Friend, we understand not one another. I am too courtly and thou art too cunning. At whose request do these men play?   31
Serv. That's to't indeed, sir. Marry, sir, at the request of Paris my lord, who's there in person; with him, the mortal Venus, the heartblood of beauty, love's invisible soul.   35
Pan. Who? My cousin Cressida?
Serv. No, sir, Helen. Could you not find out that by her attributes?   38
Pan. It should seem, fellow, that thou hast not seen the Lady Cressida. I come to speak with Paris from the Prince Troilus. I will make a complimental assault upon him, for my business seethes.
Serv. Sodden business! There's a stew'd phrase indeed!   45

Enter PARIS *and* HELEN [*attended*].

Pan. Fair be to you, my lord, and to all this fair company! Fair desires, in all fair measure, fairly guide them, especially to you, fair queen! Fair thoughts be your fair pillow!   49
Helen. Dear lord, you are full of fair words.
Pan. You speak your fair pleasure, sweet queen. Fair prince, here is good broken music.   52
Par. You have broke it, cousin, and, by my life, you shall make it whole again; you shall piece it out with a piece of your performance. Nell, he is full of harmony.   56
Pan. Truly, lady, no.
Helen. O, sir, —
Pan. Rude, in sooth; in good sooth, very rude. 60
Par. Well said, my lord! Well, you say so in fits.
Pan. I have business to my lord, dear queen. My lord, will you vouchsafe me a word?

Helen. Nay, this shall not hedge us out. We'll hear you sing, certainly.   66
Pan. Well, sweet queen, you are pleasant with me. But, marry, thus, my lord: my dear lord and most esteemed friend, your brother Troilus, —   70
Helen. My Lord Pandarus, honey-sweet lord, —
Pan. Go to, sweet queen, go to: — commends himself most affectionately to you, —   74
Helen. You shall not bob us out of our melody. If you do, our melancholy upon your head!
Pan. Sweet queen, sweet queen! That's a sweet queen, i' faith.
Helen. And to make a sweet lady sad is a sour offence.   80
Pan. Nay, that shall not serve your turn; that shall it not, in truth, la. Nay, I care not for such words; no, no. And, my lord, he desires you, that if the King call for him at supper, you will make his excuse.   85
Helen. My Lord Pandarus, —
Pan. What says my sweet queen, my very very sweet queen?
Par. What exploit's in hand? Where sups he to-night?   90
Helen. Nay, but, my lord, —
Pan. What says my sweet queen? My cousin will fall out with you.
Helen. You must not know where he sups.   94
Par. [I'll lay my life,] with my disposer Cressida.
Pan. No, no; no such matter; you are wide. Come, your disposer is sick.
Par. Well, I'll make excuse.
Pan. Ay, good my lord. Why should you say Cressida? No, your poor disposer's sick.   101
Par. I spy.
Pan. You spy! what do you spy? Come, give me an instrument. Now, sweet queen.
Helen. Why, this is kindly done.   105
Pan. My niece is [horribly] in love with a thing you have, sweet queen.
Helen. She shall have it, my lord, if it be not my Lord Paris.
Pan. He! no, she'll none of him. They two are twain.   111
Helen. Falling in, after falling out, may make them three.
Pan. Come, come, I'll hear no more of this; I'll sing you a song now.   115
Helen. Ay, ay, prithee now. By my troth, sweet lord, thou hast a fine forehead.
Pan. Ay, you may, you may.
Helen. Let thy song be love. This love will undo us all. O Cupid, Cupid, Cupid!   120

Act III, sc. i, 17. **[titles]** Q. *title* F. 43. **seethes:** is urgent. 44. **stew'd phrase.** A quibbling allusion to *stews* (brothel). 52. **broken music:** part music (for different instruments). 61. **fits:** divisions of a song. 95. **[I'll ... life]** Q. Om. F. **disposer:** she who knows how to manage me. 96. **wide:** i.e., of the mark. 106. **[horribly]** Q. *horrible* F. 111. **twain:** at odds. 118. **you may:** i.e., have your joke.

Pan. Love! ay, that it shall, i' faith.

Par. Ay, good now, love, love, nothing but love.

Pan. In good troth, it begins so.　　　[*Sings.*]

Love, love, nothing but love, still more!　125
For, O, love's bow
Shoots buck and doe.
The shaft confounds
Not that it wounds,
But tickles still the sore.　130
These lovers cry Oh! ho! they die!
Yet that which seems the wound to kill,
Doth turn oh! ho! to ha! ha! he!
So, dying, love lives still.
Oh! ho! a while, but ha! ha! ha!　135
Oh! ho! groans out for ha! ha! ha!

Heigh-ho!

Helen. In love, i' faith, to the very tip of the nose.　139

Par. He eats nothing but doves, love, and that breeds hot blood, and hot blood begets hot thoughts, and hot thoughts beget hot deeds, and hot deeds is love.　143

Pan. Is this the generation of love, — hot blood, hot thoughts, and hot deeds? Why, they are vipers. Is love a generation of vipers? Sweet lord, who's a-field to-day?　147

Par. Hector, Deiphobus, Helenus, Antenor, and all the gallantry of Troy. I would fain have arm'd to-day, but my Nell would not have it so. How chance my brother Troilus went not?　151

Helen. He hangs the lip at something. You know all, Lord Pandarus.

Pan. Not I, honey-sweet queen. I long to hear how they sped to-day. You'll remember your brother's excuse?　156

Par. To a hair.

Pan. Farewell, sweet queen.

Helen. Commend me to your niece.

Pan. I will, sweet queen.　160
　　　[*Exit.*] *Sound a retreat.*

Par. They're come from field. Let us to Priam's hall
To greet the warriors. Sweet Helen, I must woo you
To help unarm our Hector. His stubborn buckles,
With these your white enchanting fingers touch'd,
Shall more obey than to the edge of steel　165
Or force of Greekish sinews. You shall do more
Than all the island kings, — disarm great Hector.

Helen. 'Twill make us proud to be his servant, Paris;

Yea, what he shall receive of us in duty
Gives us more palm in beauty than we have,　170
Yea, overshines ourself.
　　　[*Par.*] Sweet, above thought I love thee.
　　　　　　　　　　　　　　[*Exeunt.*

[SCENE II.　*The same.　Pandarus's orchard.*]

Enter PANDARUS *and Troilus's* BOY [*meeting*].

Pan. How now! where's thy master? At my cousin Cressida's?

Boy. No, sir; he stays for you to conduct him thither.

Enter TROILUS.

Pan. O, here he comes. How now, how now!　5

Tro. Sirrah, walk off.　　　[*Exit Boy.*]

Pan. Have you seen my cousin?

Tro. No, Pandarus. I stalk about her door,
Like a strange soul upon the Stygian banks　10
Staying for waftage. O, be thou my Charon,
And give me swift transportance to those fields
Where I may wallow in the lily-beds
Propos'd for the deserver! O gentle Pandarus,
From Cupid's shoulder pluck his painted wings,　15
And fly with me to Cressid!

Pan. Walk here i' th' orchard, I'll bring her straight.　　　[*Exit.*

Tro. I am giddy; expectation whirls me round.
Th' imaginary relish is so sweet　20
That it enchants my sense; what will it be,
When that the wat'ry palates taste indeed
Love's thrice [repured] nectar? Death, I fear me,
Swooning destruction, or some joy too fine,
Too subtle, potent, [tun'd] too sharp in sweetness　25
For the capacity of my ruder powers.
I fear it much; and I do fear besides
That I shall lose distinction in my joys,
As doth a battle, when they charge on heaps
The enemy flying.　30

Re-enter PANDARUS.

Pan. She's making her ready, she'll come straight. You must be witty now. She does so blush, and fetches her wind so short, as if she were frayed with a sprite. I'll fetch her. It is the prettiest villain; she fetches her breath so short as a new-ta'en sparrow.　　　[*Exit.*　36

Tro. Even such a passion doth embrace my bosom.
My heart beats thicker than a feverous pulse,
And all my powers do their bestowing lose,
Like vassalage at unawares encountering　40
The eye of majesty.

---

130. **sore:** (1) wound, (2) four-year-old buck.　167. **island:** i.e., Greek.　172. [*Par.*] Q. F continues to Helen.
Sc. ii, 11. **waftage:** passage.　**Charon:** ferryman of souls across the Styx.　14. **Propos'd:** promised.　17. **orchard:** garden.
22. **wat'ry:** watering.　23. [**repured**] Q. *reputed* F.　25. [**tun'd**] Q. *and* F.　28. **distinction:** power of distinguishing.
32. **be witty:** keep your wits.　34. **frayed:** frightened.　**sprite:** ghost.　35. **villain:** rogue.　39. **bestowing:** function.　40. **vassalage:** vassals.

Re-enter PANDARUS *with* CRESSIDA.

Pan. Come, come, what need you blush?
Shame's a baby. Here she is now; swear the oaths
now to her that you have sworn to me. [*Cressida
draws backward.*] What, are you gone again? You
must be watch'd ere you be made tame, must   45
you? Come your ways, come your ways; an you
draw backward, we'll put you i' th' fills. Why do
you not speak to her? Come, draw this curtain
and let's see your picture. Alas the day, how loath
you are to offend daylight! An 'twere dark,   50
you'd close sooner. So, so; rub on, and kiss the
mistress. How now! a kiss in fee-farm! Build
there, carpenter; the air is sweet. Nay, you shall
fight your hearts out ere I part you. The falcon as
the tercel, for all the ducks i' th' river. Go to, go
to.   56
Tro. You have bereft me of all words, lady.
Pan. Words pay no debts, give her deeds; but
she'll bereave you o' th' deeds too, if she call your
activity in question. What, billing again?   60
Here's "In witness whereof the parties interchangeably" — Come in, come in. I'll go get a fire.
                                                    [*Exit.*]
Cres. Will you walk in, my lord?
Tro. O Cressida, how often have I wish'd me
thus!   66
Cres. Wish'd, my lord! The gods grant, — O
my lord!
Tro. What should they grant? What makes
this pretty abruption? What too curious dreg
espies my sweet lady in the fountain of our love?   71
Cres. More dregs than water, if my [fears] have
eyes.
Tro. Fears make devils of cherubins; they never
see truly.   75
Cres. Blind fear, that seeing reason leads, finds
safer footing than blind reason stumbling without
fear. To fear the worst oft cures the worse.   79
Tro. O, let my lady apprehend no fear. In all
Cupid's pageant there is presented no monster.
Cres. Nor nothing monstrous neither?
Tro. Nothing but our undertakings when we
vow to weep seas, live in fire, eat rocks, tame tigers;
thinking it harder for our mistress to devise im-   85
position enough than for us to undergo any difficulty imposed. This is the monstruosity in love,
lady, that the will is infinite and the execution
confin'd, that the desire is boundless and the act a
slave to limit.   90
Cres. They say all lovers swear more performance

than they are able, and yet reserve an ability that
they never perform, vowing more than the perfection of ten, and discharging less than the tenth part
of one. They that have the voice of lions and the
act of hares, are they not monsters?   96
Tro. Are there such? Such are not we. Praise
us as we are tasted, allow us as we prove. Our head
shall go bare till merit crown it. No perfection in
reversion shall have a praise in present; we will   100
not name desert before his birth, and, being born,
his addition shall be humble. Few words to fair
faith. Troilus shall be such to Cressid as what
envy can say worst shall be a mock for his truth,
and what truth can speak truest not truer than
Troilus.   106
Cres. Will you walk in, my lord?

Re-enter PANDARUS.

Pan. What, blushing still? Have you not done
talking yet?
Cres. Well, uncle, what folly I commit, I dedicate to you.   111
Pan. I thank you for that; if my lord get a boy
of you, you'll give him me. Be true to my lord; if
he flinch, chide me for it.
Tro. You know now your hostages: your uncle's
word and my firm faith.   116
Pan. Nay, I'll give my word for her too. Our
kindred, though they be long ere they are wooed,
they are constant being won. They are burs, I can
tell you; they'll stick where they are thrown.   120
Cres. Boldness comes to me now, and brings me
   heart.
Prince Troilus, I have lov'd you night and day
For many weary months.
Tro. Why was my Cressid then so hard to win?
Cres. Hard to seem won; but I was won, my
   lord,   125
With the first glance that ever — pardon me —
If I confess much, you will play the tyrant.
I love you now; but not, till now, so much
But I might master it. In faith, I lie;
My thoughts were like unbridled children, grown   130
Too headstrong for their mother. See, we fools!
Why have I blabb'd? Who shall be true to us,
When we are so unsecret to ourselves?
But, though I lov'd you well, I woo'd you not;
And yet, good faith, I wish'd myself a man,   135
Or that we women had men's privilege
Of speaking first. Sweet, bid me hold my tongue,
For in this rapture I shall surely speak

45. **watch'd:** kept awake (hawks were so tamed). 47. **fills:** shafts. 48. **this curtain:** your veil. 51-52. **rub ... mistress.**
From the game of bowls, in which the object-ball was the *mistress* and to *rub* was to meet obstacles on the green. 52. **in
fee-farm:** in perpetuity. 54-55. **falcon ... river.** The female and male (tercel) falcon were used in duck hunting. Pandarus
means he will back Cressida as the equal of Troilus in love. 61-62. **"In ... interchangeably."** The opening of a legal
formula completed by the words, "have set their hands and seals." 70. **abruption:** breaking off. 72. **[fears]** F₃. *tears*
QF₁,₂. 98. **tasted:** tested. **allow:** approve. 100. **reversion:** future possession. 103-04. **as ... truth:** that the worst
which malice can say will be (only) a jibe at his constancy.

The thing I shall repent. See, see, your silence,
[Cunning] in dumbness, from my weakness draws
My soul of counsel from me! Stop my mouth. 141
   Tro. And shall, albeit sweet music issues thence.
   Pan. Pretty, i' faith.
   Cres. My lord, I do beseech you, pardon me;
'Twas not my purpose thus to beg a kiss. 145
I am asham'd. O heavens! what have I done?
For this time will I take my leave, my lord.
   Tro. Your leave, sweet Cressid!
   Pan. Leave! An you take leave till to-morrow
morning, — 150
   Cres. Pray you, content you.
   Tro. What offends you, lady?
   Cres. Sir, mine own company.
   Tro. You cannot shun yourself.
   Cres. Let me go and try.
I have a kind of self resides with you; 155
But an unkind self, that itself will leave
To be another's fool. Where is my wit?
I would be gone. I speak I know not what.
   Tro. Well know they what they speak that speak
      so wisely.
   Cres. Perchance, my lord, I shew more craft
      than love, 160
And fell so roundly to a large confession,
To angle for your thoughts. But you are wise,
Or else you love not, for to be wise and love
Exceeds man's might; that dwells with gods above.
   Tro. O that I thought it could be in a woman —
As, if it can, I will presume in you — 166
To feed for aye her lamp and flames of love,
To keep her constancy in plight and youth,
Outliving beauties outward, with a mind
That doth renew swifter than blood decays! 170
Or that persuasion could but thus convince me
That my integrity and truth to you
Might be affronted with the match and weight
Of such a winnow'd purity in love!
How were I then uplifted! But, alas! 175
I am as true as truth's simplicity,
And simpler than the infancy of truth.
   Cres. In that I'll war with you.
   Tro.   O virtuous fight,
When right with right wars who shall be most right!
True swains in love shall in the world to come
Approve their truths by Troilus. When their
      rhymes, 181
Full of protest, of oath and big compare,
Want similes, truth tir'd with iteration,
As true as steel, as plantage to the moon,

As sun to day, as turtle to her mate, 185
As iron to adamant, as earth to th' centre,
Yet, after all comparisons of truth,
As truth's authentic author to be cited,
"As true as Troilus" shall crown up the verse,
And sanctify the numbers.
   Cres.   Prophet may you be!
If I be false, or swerve a hair from truth, 191
When time is old and hath forgot itself,
When waterdrops have worn the stones of Troy
And blind oblivion swallow'd cities up,
And mighty states characterless are grated 195
To dusty nothing, yet let memory,
From false to false, among false maids in love,
Upbraid my falsehood! When they've said as false
As air, as water, as wind, as sandy earth,
As fox to lamb, as wolf to heifer's calf, 200
Pard to the hind, or stepdame to her son,
Yea, let them say, to stick the heart of falsehood,
"As false as Cressid." 203
   Pan. Go to, a bargain made; seal it, seal it, I'll be
the witness. Here I hold your hand, here my
cousin's. If ever you prove false one to another,
since I have taken such pains to bring you together,
let all pitiful goers-between be called to the world's
end after my name; call them all Pandars. Let 210
all constant men be Troiluses, all false women Cres-
sids, and all brokers-between Pandars! Say, amen.
   Tro. Amen.
   Cres. Amen. 214
   Pan. Amen. Whereupon I will show you a
chamber, [whose] bed, because it shall not speak of
your pretty encounters, press it to death. Away!
And Cupid grant all tongue-tied maidens here
Bed, chamber, Pandar to provide this gear! 220
                           [Exeunt.

[SCENE III. *The Greek camp. Before the tent
of Achilles.*]

Enter AGAMEMNON, ULYSSES, DIOMEDES, NESTOR,
[AJAX,] MENELAUS, *and* CALCHAS. *Flourish.*

   Cal. Now, princes, for the service I have done
      you,
Th' advantage of the time prompts me aloud
To call for recompense. Appear it to your mind
That, through the sight I bear in things to [come],
I have abandon'd Troy, left my possession, 5
Incurr'd a traitor's name, expos'd myself
From certain and possess'd conveniences
To doubtful fortunes, sequestering from me all

---

140. [Cunning] (Pope). *Comming* QF. 141. soul of counsel: inmost secret. 161. roundly: plainly. large: free.
162–63. But...not. Cressida's logic seems to break down here. 166. presume. Craig reads *presume't.* 168. in...youth:
i.e., true and fresh. 173. affronted: met. 181. Approve: attest. 184. plantage: vegetation. 185. turtle: turtle dove.
186. adamant: loadstone. 190. numbers: verses. 195. characterless: unrecorded. [201. Pard: leopard. 202. stick:
stab. 216. [whose] (Dyce conj.). *which* QF. because: so that.
    Sc. iii, 4. [come] F4. *love* QF1,2,3.

That time, acquaintance, custom, and condition
Made tame and most familiar to my nature;   10
And here, to do you service, am become
As new into the world, strange, unacquainted.
I do beseech you, as in way of taste,
To give me now a little benefit
Out of those many regist'red in promise,   15
Which, you say, live to come in my behalf.

Agam. What wouldst thou of us, Troyan?
Make demand.

Cal. You have a Troyan prisoner, call'd Antenor,
Yesterday took; Troy holds him very dear.
Oft have you — often have you thanks therefore —
Desir'd my Cressid in right great exchange,   21
Whom Troy hath still deni'd; but this Antenor,
I know, is such a wrest in their affairs
That their negotiations all must slack,
Wanting his manage; and they will almost   25
Give us a prince of blood, a son of Priam,
In change of him. Let him be sent, great princes,
And he shall buy my daughter; and her presence
Shall quite strike off all service I have done,
In most accepted pain.

Agam.   Let Diomedes bear him,
And bring us Cressid hither; Calchas shall have   31
What he requests of us. Good Diomed,
Furnish you fairly for this interchange;
Withal bring word if Hector will to-morrow
Be answer'd in his challenge: Ajax is ready.   35

Dio. This shall I undertake; and 'tis a burden
Which I am proud to bear.

[*Exeunt Diomedes [and Calchas].*

Enter ACHILLES *and* PATROCLUS, *and stand in
[the door of] their tent.*

Ulyss. Achilles stands i' th' entrance of his
tent.
Please it our general to pass strangely by him,
As if he were forgot; and, princes all,   40
Lay negligent and loose regard upon him.
I will come last. 'Tis like he'll question me
Why such unplausive eyes are bent, why turn'd on
him.
If so, I have derision med'cinable
To use between your strangeness and his pride,   45
Which his own will shall have desire to drink.
It may do good; pride hath no other glass
To show itself but pride, for supple knees
Feed arrogance and are the proud man's fees.

Agam. We'll execute your purpose, and put on   50
A form of strangeness as we pass along.
So do each lord, and either greet him not,
Or else disdainfully, which shall shake him more
Than if not look'd on. I will lead the way.

Achil. What comes the general to speak with
me?   55
You know my mind, I'll fight no more 'gainst Troy.

Agam. What says Achilles? Would he aught
with us?

Nest. Would you, my lord, aught with the general?

Achil. No.

Nest. Nothing, my lord.   60

Agam. The better.

[*Exeunt Agamemnon and Nestor.*]

Achil. Good day, good day.

Men. How do you? How do you?   [*Exit.*]

Achil. What, does the cuckold scorn me?

Ajax. How now, Patroclus!   65

Achil. Good morrow, Ajax.

Ajax. Ha?

Achil. Good morrow.

Ajax. Ay, and good next day too.   [*Exit.*]

Achil. What mean these fellows? Know they
not Achilles?   70

Patr. They pass by strangely. They were us'd
to bend,
To send their smiles before them to Achilles,
To come as humbly as they us'd to creep
To holy altars.

Achil.   What, am I poor of late?
'Tis certain, greatness, once fall'n out with for-
tune,   75
Must fall out with men too. What the declin'd is
He shall as soon read in the eyes of others
As feel in his own fall; for men, like butterflies,
Show not their mealy wings but to the summer;
And not a man, for being simply man,   80
Hath any honour, but honour'd for those honours
That are without him, as place, riches, and fa-
vour, —
Prizes of accident as oft as merit;
Which when they fall, as being slippery standers,
(The love that lean'd on them as slippery too)   85
Doth one pluck down another and together
Die in the fall. But 'tis not so with me;
Fortune and I are friends. I do enjoy
At ample point all that I did possess,
Save these men's looks; who do, methinks, find
out   90
Something not worth in me such rich beholding
As they have often given. Here is Ulysses;
I'll interrupt his reading.
How now, Ulysses!

Ulyss.   Now, great Thetis' son!

Achil. What are you reading?

Ulyss.   A strange fellow here   95
Writes me: "That man, how dearly ever parted,

---

13. **taste:** foretaste.   21. **right...exchange:** exchange for important prisoners.   23. **wrest:** tuning-key, harmonizing influence.   30. **accepted:** acceptable (on Calchas' part).   43. **unplausive:** unflattering.   48. **show:** reflect.   89. **At...point:** in full measure.   96. **how...parted:** however richly endowed.

How much in having, or without or in,
Cannot make boast to have that which he hath,
Nor feels not what he owes, but by reflection;
As when his virtues shining upon others   100
Heat them and they retort that heat again
To the first giver."
   Achil.   This is not strange, Ulysses.
The beauty that is borne here in the face
The bearer knows not, but commends itself
[To others' eyes; nor doth the eye itself.   105
That most pure spirit of sense, behold itself,]
Not going from itself; but eye to eye oppos'd
Salutes each other with each other's form;
For speculation turns not to itself,
Till it hath travell'd and is [mirror'd] there   110
Where it may see itself. This is not strange at all.
   Ulyss. I do not strain at the position, —
It is familiar, — but at the author's drift;
Who, in his circumstance, expressly proves
That no man is the lord of anything,   115
(Though in and of him there is much consisting,)
Till he communicate his parts to others;
Nor doth he of himself know them for aught
Till he behold them formed in th' applause
Where they're extended; who, like an arch, rever-
     b'rate   120
The voice again, or, like a gate of steel
Fronting the sun, receives and renders back
His figure and his heat. I was much wrapt in this;
And apprehended here immediately
The unknown Ajax.   125
Heavens, what a man is there! A very horse,
That has he knows not what. Nature, what things
     there are
Most abject in regard and dear in use!
What things again most dear in the esteem
And poor in worth! Now shall we see to-mor-
     row —   130
An act that very chance doth throw upon him —
Ajax renown'd. O heavens, what some men do,
While some men leave to do!
How some men creep in skittish Fortune's hall,
Whiles others play the idiots in her eyes!   135
How one man eats into another's pride,
While pride is [fasting] in his wantonness!
To see these Grecian lords! — why, even already
They clap the lubber Ajax on the shoulder,
As if his foot were on brave Hector's breast   140
And great Troy [shrieking].
   Achil. I do believe it; for they pass'd by me

As misers do by beggars, neither gave to me
Good word nor look. What, are my deeds forgot?
   Ulyss. Time hath, my lord, a wallet at his back,
Wherein he puts alms for Oblivion,   146
A great-siz'd monster of ingratitudes.
Those scraps are good deeds past, which are de-
     vour'd
As fast as they are made, forgot as soon
As done. Perseverance, dear my lord,   150
Keeps honour bright; to have done is to hang
Quite out of fashion, like a rusty mail
In monumental mock'ry. Take the instant way;
For honour travels in a strait so narrow,
Where one but goes abreast. Keep then the
     path;   155
For emulation hath a thousand sons
That one by one pursue. If you give way,
Or hedge aside from the direct forthright,
Like to an ent'red tide, they all rush by
And leave you hindmost;   160
Or, like a gallant horse fall'n in first rank,
Lie there for pavement to the abject [rear],
O'er-run and trampled on. Then what they do in
     present,
Though less than yours in past, must o'ertop yours;
For Time is like a fashionable host   165
That slightly shakes his parting guest by th' hand,
And with his arms outstretch'd as he would fly
Grasps in the comer. Welcome ever smiles,
And [Farewell] goes out sighing. O, let not vir-
     tue seek
Remuneration for the thing it was;   170
For beauty, wit,
High birth, vigour of bone, desert in service,
Love, friendship, charity, are subjects all
To envious and calumniating Time.
One touch of nature makes the whole world kin,   175
That all, with one consent, praise new-born gawds,
Though they are made and moulded of things past,
And [give] to dust that is a little gilt
More laud than gilt o'er-dusted.
The present eye praises the present object.   180
Then marvel not, thou great and complete man,
That all the Greeks begin to worship Ajax;
Since things in motion [sooner] catch the eye
Than what not stirs. The cry went [once] on thee,
And still it might, and yet it may again,   185
If thou wouldst not entomb thyself alive
And case thy reputation in thy tent;
Whose glorious deeds, but in these fields of late,

---

97. **having:** possession.   99. **owes:** owns.   105-06. [To...itself] Q. Om. F.   109. **speculation:** power of sight.
110. [**mirror'd**] (Coll. MS.). *married* QF.   112. **position:** theory.   114. **circumstance:** detailed exposition.   117. **parts:**
qualities.   120. **extended:** broadcast.   128. **regard:** estimation.   134. **in:** into.   137. [**fasting**] Q. *feasting* F. **wantonness:**
whims.   141. [**shrieking**] Q. *shrinking* F.   152. **mail:** suit of armor.   153. **instant:** immediate.   162. [**rear**] (Hanmer).
neere F.   168. **Welcome** (Pope). *The welcome* QF.   169. [**Farewell**] Q. *farewels* F.   175. **touch:** trait (viz., love of novelty).
This line, a familiar quotation, is usually misapplied.   176. **gawds:** gewgaws.   178. [**give**] (Thirlby *conj.*). *goe* QF.
183. [**sooner**] Q. *begin to* F.   184. **cry:** acclaim.   [**once**] Q. *out* F.

Made emulous missions 'mongst the gods them-
selves   189
And drave great Mars to faction.
Achil.   Of this my privacy
I have strong reasons.
Ulyss.   But 'gainst your privacy
The reasons are more potent and heroical.
'Tis known, Achilles, that you are in love
With one of Priam's daughters.
Achil.   Ha! known!
Ulyss. Is that a wonder?   195
The providence that's in a watchful state
Knows almost every grain of [Plutus'] gold,
Finds bottom in th' uncomprehensive deeps,
Keeps place with thought and almost, like the gods,
[Does] thoughts unveil in their dumb cradles. 200
There is a mystery — with whom relation
Durst never meddle — in the soul of state;
Which hath an operation more divine
Than breath or pen can give expressure to.
All the commerce that you have had with Troy   205
As perfectly is ours as yours, my lord;
And better would it fit Achilles much
To throw down Hector than Polyxena.
But it must grieve young Pyrrhus now at home
When Fame shall in [our] island sound her
trump,   210
And all the Greekish girls shall tripping sing,
"Great Hector's sister did Achilles win,
But our great Ajax bravely beat down him."
Farewell, my lord; I as your lover speak.   214
The fool slides o'er the ice that you should break.
[*Exit.*]
Patr. To this effect, Achilles, have I mov'd you.
A woman impudent and mannish grown
Is not more loath'd than an effeminate man
In time of action. I stand condemn'd for this.
They think my little stomach to the war   220
And your great love to me restrains you thus.
Sweet, rouse yourself; and the weak wanton Cupid
Shall from your neck unloose his amorous fold,
And, like a dew-drop from the lion's mane,
Be shook to [air].
Achil.   Shall Ajax fight with Hector?
Patr. Ay, and perhaps receive much honour by
him.   226
Achil. I see my reputation is at stake;
My fame is shrewdly gor'd.
Patr.   O, then, beware!
Those wounds heal ill that men do give themselves.
Omission to do what is necessary   230
Seals a commission to a blank of danger;

And danger, like an ague, subtly taints
Even then when we sit idly in the sun.
Achil. Go call Thersites hither, sweet Patroclus.
I'll send the fool to Ajax and desire him   235
T' invite the Troyan lords after the combat
To see us here, unarm'd. I have a woman's longing,
An appetite that I am sick withal,
To see great Hector in his weeds of peace,

Enter THERSITES.

To talk with him and to behold his visage,   240
Even to my full of view. — A labour sav'd!
Ther. A wonder!
Achil. What?
Ther. Ajax goes up and down the field, asking
for himself.   245
Achil. How so?
Ther. He must fight singly to-morrow with
Hector, and is so prophetically proud of an heroical
cudgelling that he raves in saying nothing.
Achil. How can that be?   250
Ther. Why, he stalks up and down like a peacock,
— a stride and a stand; ruminates like an hostess
that hath no arithmetic but her brain to set down
her reckoning; bites his lip with a politic regard, as
who should say there were wit in his head, an 255
'twould out; and so there is, but it lies as coldly in
him as fire in a flint, which will not show without
knocking. The man's undone for ever; for if
Hector break not his neck i' th' combat, he'll break
't himself in vain-glory. He knows not me. I 260
said, "Good morrow, Ajax;" and he replies,
"Thanks, Agamemnon." What think you of this
man that takes me for the general? He's grown a
very land-fish, languageless, a monster. A plague
of opinion! A man may wear it on both sides, like
a leather jerkin.   266
Achil. Thou must be my ambassador to him,
Thersites.
Ther. Who, I? Why, he'll answer nobody; he
professes not answering. Speaking is for beggars;
he wears his tongue in's arms. I will put on his
presence; let Patroclus make his demands to me,
you shall see the pageant of Ajax.   273
Achil. To him, Patroclus. Tell him I humbly
desire the valiant Ajax to invite the most valorous
Hector to come unarm'd to my tent, and to procure
safe-conduct for his person of the magnanimous
and most illustrious six-or-seven-times-honour'd
captain-general of the Grecian army, Agamemnon,
et cetera. Do this.   280
Patr. Jove bless great Ajax!

---

194. one...daughters: Polyxena. 196. providence: foresight. 197. [Plutus'] (Steevens conj.). *Plutoes* F. Plutus, god
of wealth, was frequently confused with Pluto, monarch of Hades. 198. uncomprehensive: limitless. 199. place. Hanmer
reads *pace*. 200. [Does] F₂. *Do* QF₁. 201. relation: report. 210. [our] Q. *her* F. 225. [air] Q. *ayrie ayre* F.
228. shrewdly gor'd: severely wounded. The figure is from bear baiting (cf. *at stake*, l. 227). 231. Seals...danger: commits one to undefined dangers. 245. himself. A quibble is implied on (1) *Ajax* and (2) *a jakes* (privy). 254. politic regard:
wise look. 271. put on: imitate.

Ther. Hum!

Patr. I come from the worthy Achilles, —

Ther. Ha!

Patr. Who most humbly desires you to invite
Hector to his tent, —   286

Ther. Hum!

Patr. And to procure safe-conduct from Agamemnon.

Ther. Agamemnon?   290

Patr. Ay, my lord.

Ther. Ha!

Patr. What say you to't?

Ther. God buy you, with all my heart.

Patr. Your answer, sir.   295

Ther. If to-morrow be a fair day, by eleven
o'clock it will go one way or other. Howsoever, he
shall pay for me ere he has me.

Patr. Your answer, sir.

Ther. Fare you well, with all my heart.   300

Achil. Why, but he is not in this tune, is he?

Ther. No, but he's out o' tune thus. What
music will be in him when Hector has knock'd
out his brains, I know not; but, I am sure, none,
unless the fiddler Apollo get his sinews to make
catlings on.   306

Achil. Come, thou shalt bear a letter to him
straight.

Ther. Let me carry another to his horse; for
that's the more capable creature.   310

Achil. My mind is troubled, like a fountain
stirr'd;
And I myself see not the bottom of it.

                    [*Exeunt Achilles and Patroclus.*]

Ther. Would the fountain of your mind were
clear again, that I might water an ass at it! I had
rather be a tick in a sheep than such a valiant
ignorance.   [*Exit.*] 316

[ACT IV

Scene I. *Troy. A street.*]

Enter, at one door, Æneas, with a torch; at another,
Paris, Deiphobus, Antenor, Diomedes *the*
Grecian [*and others*], *with torches.*

Par. See, ho! who is that there?

Dei. It is the Lord Æneas.

Æne. Is the prince there in person?
Had I so good occasion to lie long
As you, Prince Paris, nothing but heavenly business
Should rob my bed-mate of my company.   5

Dio. That's my mind too. Good morrow, Lord
Æneas.

Par. A valiant Greek, Æneas, — take his hand —

Witness the process of your speech, wherein
You told how Diomed, a whole week by days,
Did haunt you in the field.

Æne.   Health to you, valiant sir,   10
During all question of the gentle truce;
But when I meet you arm'd, as black defiance
As heart can think or courage execute.

Dio. The one and other Diomed embraces.
Our bloods are now in calm; and, so long, health! 15
But when contention and occasion meets,
By Jove, I'll play the hunter for thy life
With all my force, pursuit, and policy.

Æne. And thou shalt hunt a lion that will fly
With his face backward. In humane gentleness,   20
Welcome to Troy! now, by Anchises' life,
Welcome, indeed! By Venus' hand I swear,
No man alive can love in such a sort
The thing he means to kill more excellently.

Dio. We sympathize. Jove, let Æneas live,   25
If to my sword his fate be not the glory,
A thousand complete courses of the sun!
But in mine emulous honour let him die,
With every joint a wound, and that to-morrow!

Æne. We know each other well.   30

Dio. We do; and long to know each other worse.

Par. This is the most despiteful'st gentle greet-
ing,
The noblest hateful love, that e'er I heard of.
What business, lord, so early?

Æne. I was sent for to the King; but why, I know
not.   35

Par. His purpose meets you; 'twas to bring this
Greek
To Calchas' house, and there to render him,
For the enfreed Antenor, the fair Cressid.
Let's have your company, or, if you please,
Haste there before us. I constantly do think —   40
Or rather, call my thought a certain knowledge —
My brother Troilus lodges there to-night.
Rouse him and give him note of our approach,
With the whole quality whereof. I fear   44
We shall be much unwelcome.

Æne.   That I assure you.
Troilus had rather Troy were borne to Greece
Than Cressid borne from Troy.

Par.   There is no help.
The bitter disposition of the time
Will have it so. On, lord; we'll follow you.

Æne. Good morrow, all.   [*Exit.* 50

Par. And tell me, noble Diomed — faith, tell me
true,
Even in the soul of sound good-fellowship —
Who, in your thoughts, merits fair Helen most,
Myself or Menelaus?

---

294. **buy:** be with.   306. **catlings:** catgut (strings).   310. **capable:** intelligent.
Act IV, sc. i, 9. **a** Q. *in a* F.   11. **question of:** converse permitted by.   16. **occasion:** opportunity.   21. **Anchises'**
... **Venus:** father and mother of Æneas.   40. **constantly:** firmly.   44. **quality:** significance.   **whereof** F. *wherefore* Q.

Dio. Both alike.
He merits well to have her that doth seek her,   55
Not making any scruple of her soilure,
With such a hell of pain and world of charge;
And you as well to keep her, that defend her,
Not palating the taste of her dishonour,
With such a costly loss of wealth and friends.   60
He, like a puling cuckold, would drink up
The lees and dregs of a flat tamed piece;
You, like a lecher, out of whorish loins
Are pleased to breed out your inheritors.
Both merits pois'd, each weighs no less nor more; 65
But he as he, which heavier for a whore.
   Par. You are too bitter to your country-woman.
   Dio. She's bitter to her country. Hear me,
      Paris:
For every false drop in her bawdy veins
A Grecian's life hath sunk; for every scruple 70
Of her contaminated carrion weight,
A Troyan hath been slain. Since she could speak,
She hath not given so many good words breath
As for her Greeks and Troyans suff'red death.
   Par. Fair Diomed, you do as chapmen do, 75
Dispraise the thing that you desire to buy;
But we in silence hold this virtue well, —
We'll not commend what we intend to sell.
Here lies our way.

[*Exeunt.*

[SCENE II. *The same. Court of Pandarus's house.*]

Enter TROILUS *and* CRESSIDA.

   Tro. Dear, trouble not yourself; the morn is cold.
   Cres. Then, sweet my lord, I'll call mine uncle
      down;
He shall unbolt the gates.
   Tro. Trouble him not;
To bed, to bed. Sleep kill those pretty eyes,
And give as soft attachment to thy senses 5
As infants' empty of all thought!
   Cres. Good morrow, then.
   Tro. I prithee now, to bed.
   Cres. Are you a-weary of me?
   Tro. O Cressida! but that the busy day,
Wak'd by the lark, hath rous'd the ribald crows,
And dreaming night will hide our [joys] no longer, 10
I would not from thee.
   Cres. Night hath been too brief.
   Tro. Beshrew the witch! with venomous wights
      she stays
As [tediously] as hell, but flies the grasps of love

With wings more momentary-swift than thought.
You will catch cold, and curse me.
   Cres. Prithee, tarry;
You men will never tarry. 16
O foolish Cressid! I might have still held off,
And then you would have tarried. Hark! there's
      one up.
   Pan. (Within.) What, 's all the doors open here?
   Tro. It is your uncle. 20

Enter PANDARUS.

   Cres. A pestilence on him! now will he be mock-
      ing.
I shall have such a life!
   Pan. How now, how now! how go maidenheads?
Here, you maid! where's my cousin Cressid? 25
   Cres. Go hang yourself, you naughty mocking
      uncle!
You bring me to do — and then you flout me too.
   Pan. To do what? to do what? Let her say
what. What have I brought you to do?
   Cres. Come, come, beshrew your heart! You'll
      ne'er be good, 30
Nor suffer others.
   Pan. Ha, ha! Alas, poor wretch! a poor [capoc-
chia]! hast not slept to-night? Would he not, a
naughty man, let it sleep? A bugbear take him!
      [*One knocks.*
   Cres. Did not I tell you? Would he were knock'd
      i' th' head! 35
Who's that at door? Good uncle, go and see.
My lord, come you again into my chamber.
You smile and mock me, as if I meant naughtily.
   Tro. Ha, ha!
   Cres. Come, you are deceiv'd, I think of no such
      thing. [*Knock.* 40
How earnestly they knock! Pray you, come in.
I would not for half Troy have you seen here.
      [*Exeunt Troilus and Cressida.*
   Pan. Who's there? What's the matter? Will
you beat down the door? How now! what's the
matter? 45

[*Enter* ÆNEAS.]

   Æne. Good morrow, lord, good morrow.
   Pan. Who's there? My Lord Æneas! By my
      troth,
I knew you not. What news with you so early?
   Æne. Is not Prince Troilus here?
   Pan. Here! What should he do here? 50
   Æne. Come, he is here, my lord; do not deny him.
It doth import him much to speak with me.

---

57. **charge**: cost. 62. **tamed piece**: (1) a cask, long open, whose wine has grown flat, (2) a woman who has lost her charm. 65. **pois'd**: weighed. 66. **which** F. *the* Q. Johnson's conj. *each* gives better sense. 75. **chapmen**: merchants. 78. **We'll . . . sell**: we are modest about our wares. The line does not seem logical.
Sc. ii, 4. **kill**: subdue. 5. **attachment**: seizure. 10. **[joys]** Q. *eyes* F. 13. **[tediously]** Q. *hidiously* F. 32. **[capocchia]** (Theobald conj.): simpleton. *chipochia* QF. 52. **import**: concern.

Pan. Is he here, say you? 'Tis more than I know, I'll be sworn. For my own part, I came in late. What should he do here?   55

Æne. Who! — nay, then. Come, come, you'll do him wrong ere you're ware. You'll be so true to him, to be false to him. Do not you know of him, but yet go fetch him hither; go.   [*Exit Pan.*]

Re-enter TROILUS.

Tro. How now! what's the matter?   60

Æne. My lord, I scarce have leisure to salute you, My matter is so rash. There is at hand Paris your brother, and Deiphobus, The Grecian Diomed, and our Antenor Deliver'd to us; and for him forthwith,   65 Ere the first sacrifice, within this hour, We must give up to Diomedes' hand The Lady Cressida.

Tro.   Is it concluded so?

Æne. By Priam and the general state of Troy. They are at hand and ready to effect it.   70

Tro. How my achievements mock me! I will go meet them; and, my Lord Æneas, We met by chance; you did not find me here.

Æne. Good, good, my lord; the secrets of nature Have not more gift in taciturnity.   75   [*Exeunt* [*Troilus and Æneas*].

Re-enter PANDARUS AND CRESSIDA.

Pan. Is't possible? No sooner got but lost? The devil take Antenor! the young prince will go mad. A plague upon Antenor! I would they had broke 's neck!

Cres. How now! what's the matter? Who was here?   81

Pan. Ah, ah!

Cres. Why sigh you so profoundly? Where's my lord? Gone! Tell me, sweet uncle, what's the matter?   85

Pan. Would I were as deep under the earth as I am above!

Cres. O the gods! what's the matter?   88

Pan. Prithee, get thee in. Would thou hadst ne'er been born! I knew thou wouldst be his death. O, poor gentleman! A plague upon Antenor!

Cres. Good uncle, I beseech you, on my knees I beseech you, what's the matter?   94

Pan. Thou must be gone, wench, thou must be gone; thou art chang'd for Antenor. Thou must to thy father, and be gone from Troilus. 'Twill be his death; 'twill be his bane; he cannot bear it. 99

Cres. O you immortal gods! I will not go.

Pan. Thou must.

Cres. I will not, uncle. I have forgot my father; I know no touch of consanguinity; No kin, no love, no blood, no soul so near me As the sweet Troilus. O you gods divine,   105 Make Cressid's name the very crown of falsehood, If ever she leave Troilus! Time, force, and death, Do to this body what [extremes] you can; But the strong base and building of my love Is as the very centre of the earth,   110 Drawing all things to it. I'll go in and weep.

Pan. Do, do.

Cres. Tear my bright hair and scratch my praised cheeks, Crack my clear voice with sobs and break my heart With sounding Troilus. I will not go from Troy. 115   [*Exeunt.*

[SCENE III. *The same. Street before Pandarus's house.*]

Enter PARIS, TROILUS, ÆNEAS, DEIPHOBUS, ANTENOR, *and* DIOMEDES.

Par. It is great morning, and the hour prefix'd Of her delivery to this valiant Greek Comes fast upon. Good my brother Troilus, Tell you the lady what she is to do, And haste her to the purpose.

Tro.   Walk into her house. I'll bring her to the Grecian presently;   6 And to his hand when I deliver her, Think it an altar, and thy brother Troilus A priest there off'ring to it his [own] heart. [*Exit.*]

Par. I know what 'tis to love;   10 And would, as I shall pity, I could help! Please you walk in, my lords.   [*Exeunt.*

[SCENE IV. *The same. Pandarus's house.*]

Enter PANDARUS *and* CRESSIDA.

Pan. Be moderate, be moderate.

Cres. Why tell you me of moderation? The grief is fine, full, perfect, that I taste, And [violenteth] in a sense as strong As that which causeth it. How can I moderate it?   5 If I could temporize with my affection Or brew it to a weak and colder palate, The like allayment could I give my grief. My love admits no qualifying [dross];

Enter TROILUS.

No more my grief, in such a precious loss.   10

Pan. Here, here, here he comes. Ah, sweet ducks!

---

62. **rash:** urgent.   99. **bane:** death.   108. **[extremes]** Q.   *extremetie* F.
Sc. iii, 9. **[own]** Q. Om. F.
Sc. iv, 4. **[violenteth]** Q: rages. *no lesse* F.   9. **[dross]** Q. *crosse* F.

Cres. O Troilus! Troilus!   [*Embracing him.*]
Pan. What a pair of spectacles is here! Let me
embrace too. "O heart," as the goodly saying is, 16
"— O heart, heavy heart,
    Why sigh'st thou without breaking?"
where he answers again,
    "Because thou canst not ease thy smart   20
    By friendship nor by speaking."
There was never a truer rhyme. Let us cast away
nothing, for we may live to have need of such a
verse. We see it, we see it. How now, lambs? 25
Tro. Cressid, I love thee in so [strain'd] a purity
That the bless'd gods, as angry with my fancy,
More bright in zeal than the devotion which
Cold lips blow to their deities, take thee from me.
Cres. Have the gods envy?   30
Pan. Ay, ay, ay, ay; 'tis too plain a case.
Cres. And is it true that I must go from Troy?
Tro. A hateful truth.
Cres.   What, and from Troilus, too?
Tro. From Troy and Troilus.
Cres.   Is it possible?
Tro. And suddenly, where injury of chance   35
Puts back leave-taking, justles roughly by
All time of pause, rudely beguiles our lips
Of all rejoindure, forcibly prevents
Our lock'd embrasures, strangles our dear vows
Even in the birth of our own labouring breath.   40
We two, that with so many thousand sighs
Did buy each other, must poorly sell ourselves
With the rude brevity and discharge of one.
Injurious Time now with a robber's haste
Crams his rich thievery up, he knows not how.   45
As many farewells as be stars in heaven,
With distinct breath and consign'd kisses to them,
He fumbles up into a loose adieu,
And scants us with a single famish'd kiss,
[Distasted] with the salt of broken tears.   50
Æne. (*Within.*) My lord, is the lady ready?
Tro. Hark! you are call'd. Some say the Genius so
Cries "come" to him that instantly must die.
— Bid them have patience; she shall come anon.
Pan. Where are my tears? Rain, to lay this
wind, or my heart will be blown up by the root. 56
                    [*Exit.*]
Cres. I must then to the Grecians?
Tro.   No remedy.
Cres. A woeful Cressid 'mongst the merry
    Greeks!
When shall we see again?

Tro. Hear me, my love. Be thou but true of
    heart, —   60
Cres. I true! How now! what wicked deem is
    this?
Tro. Nay, we must use expostulation kindly,
For it is parting from us.
I speak not "be thou true," as fearing thee,
For I will throw my glove to Death himself   65
That there's no maculation in thy heart;
But "be thou true," say I, to fashion in
My sequent protestation; be thou true,
And I will see thee.
Cres. O, you shall be expos'd, my lord, to
    dangers   70
As infinite as imminent! But I'll be true.
Tro. And I'll grow friend with danger. Wear
    this sleeve.
Cres. And you this glove. When shall I see you?
Tro. I will corrupt the Grecian sentinels,
To give thee nightly visitation.   75
But yet be true.
Cres.   O heavens! "be true" again!
Tro. Hear why I speak it, love.
The Grecian youths are full of quality;
They're loving, well compos'd, with gifts of nature,
Flowing and swelling o'er with arts and exercise. 80
How novelties may move, and parts with person,
Alas, a kind of godly jealousy —
Which, I beseech you, call a virtuous sin —
Makes me afraid.
Cres.   O heavens! you love me not.
Tro. Die I a villain, then!   85
In this I do not call your faith in question
So mainly as my merit. I cannot sing,
Nor heel the high lavolt, nor sweeten talk,
Nor play at subtle games — fair virtues all,
To which the Grecians are most prompt and preg-
    nant —   90
But I can tell that in each grace of these
There lurks a still and dumb-discoursive devil
That tempts most cunningly; but be not tempted.
Cres. Do you think I will?
Tro. No.   95
But something may be done that we will not;
And sometimes we are devils to ourselves,
When we will tempt the frailty of our powers,
Presuming on their changeful potency.
Æne. (*Within.*) Nay, good my lord, —
Tro.   Come, kiss; and let us part. 100
Par. (*Within.*) Brother Troilus!

14. **spectacles:** (1) glasses, (2) sights. 26. **[strain'd]** Q. *strange* F. 27. **fancy:** love. 35. **injury of chance:** ill usage by Fortune. 45. **he ... how:** carelessly. 47. **With ... them:** each one a separate sigh and with a separate kiss. 50. **[Distasted]** Q. *Distasting* F. 52. **Genius:** a man's attendant spirit. 59. **When ... again.** So Q. Given to Troilus in F. 61. **deem:** thought. 63. **it ... us:** i.e., we are actually saying farewell. 65. **throw my glove:** challenge. 66. **maculation:** stain. 67–68. **to ... protestation:** as pattern for my own avowal. 78. **full of quality:** rightly gifted. 80. **arts and exercise:** theories and practical skill. 81. **parts:** accomplishments. **person:** personal charm. 88. **lavolt:** a lively dance. 90. **pregnant:** ready. 92. **dumb-discoursive:** speaking silently. 99. **Presuming ... potency:** trusting too far their strength, which is subject to change.

Tro.   Good brother, come you hither;
And bring Æneas and the Grecian with you.
Cres. My lord, will you be true?
Tro. Who? I? Alas, it is my vice, my fault.
Whiles others fish with craft for great opinion,
I with great truth catch mere simplicity;   106
Whilst some with cunning gild their copper crowns,
With truth and plainness I do wear mine bare.

Enter [ÆNEAS, PARIS, ANTENOR, DEIPHOBUS,
          and DIOMEDES].

Fear not my truth. The moral of my wit
Is "plain and true"; there's all the reach of it.   110
Welcome, Sir Diomed! Here is the lady
Which for Antenor we deliver you.
At the port, lord, I'll give her to thy hand,
And by the way possess thee what she is.
Entreat her fair; and, by my soul, fair Greek,
If e'er thou stand at mercy of my sword,   116
Name Cressid, and thy life shall be as safe
As Priam is in Ilion.
Dio.   Fair Lady Cressid,
So please you, save the thanks this prince expects.
The lustre in your eye, heaven in your cheek,   120
Pleads your fair usage; and to Diomed
You shall be mistress, and command him wholly.
Tro. Grecian, thou dost not use me courteously,
To shame the [zeal] of my petition [to thee
In] praising her. I tell thee, lord of Greece,   125
She is as far high-soaring o'er thy praises
As thou unworthy to be call'd her servant.
I charge thee use her well, even for my charge;
For, by the dreadful Pluto, if thou dost not,
Though the great bulk Achilles be thy guard,   130
I'll cut thy throat.
Dio.   O, be not mov'd, Prince Troilus.
Let me be privileg'd by my place and message,
To be a speaker free. When I am hence,
I'll answer to my lust; and know, my lord,
I'll nothing do on charge. To her own worth   135
She shall be priz'd; but that you say "Be't so,"
I'll speak it in my spirit and honour, "No."
Tro. Come, to the port. I'll tell thee, Diomed,
This brave shall oft make thee to hide thy head.
Lady, give me your hand, and, as we walk,   140
To our own selves bend we our needful talk.
          [*Exeunt Troilus, Cressida, and Diomedes.*]
          Sound trumpet.
Par. Hark! Hector's trumpet.
Æne.   How have we spent this morning!
The Prince must think me tardy and remiss,
That swore to ride before him in the field.

Par. 'Tis Troilus' fault. Come, come, to field
          with him.   [*Exit.* 145
[*Dei.*] Let us make ready straight.
Æne. Yea, with a bridegroom's fresh alacrity
Let us address to tend on Hector's heels.
The glory of our Troy doth this day lie
On his fair worth and single chivalry.   150
          [*Exeunt.*]

[SCENE V. *The Greek camp. Lists set out.*]

Enter AJAX, *armed;* AGAMEMNON, ACHILLES, PATRO-
          CLUS, MENELAUS, ULYSSES, NESTOR, *etc.*

Agam. Here art thou in appointment fresh and
          fair,
Anticipating time with starting courage.
Give with thy trumpet a loud note to Troy,
Thou dreadful Ajax, that the appalled air
May pierce the head of the great combatant   5
And hale him hither.
Ajax.   Thou, trumpet, there's my purse.
Now crack thy lungs, and split thy brazen pipe.
Blow, villain, till thy sphered bias cheek
Outswell the colic of puff'd Aquilon.
Come, stretch thy chest, and let thy eyes spout
          blood;   10
Thou blow'st for Hector.   [*Trumpet sounds.*]
Ulyss. No trumpet answers.
Achil.   'Tis but early days.
Agam. Is not [yond] Diomed, with Calchas'
          daughter?
Ulyss. 'Tis he, I ken the manner of his gait;
He rises on the toe. That spirit of his   15
In aspiration lifts him from the earth.

          [*Enter* DIOMEDES, *with* CRESSIDA.]

Agam. Is this the Lady Cressid?
Dio.   Even she.
Agam. Most dearly welcome to the Greeks, sweet
          lady.
Nest. Our general doth salute you with a kiss.
Ulyss. Yet is the kindness but particular.   20
'Twere better she were kiss'd in general.
Nest. And very courtly counsel. I'll begin.
So much for Nestor.
Achil. I'll take that winter from your lips, fair
          lady.
Achilles bids you welcome.   25
Men. I had good argument for kissing once.
Patr. But that's no argument for kissing now;
For thus popp'd Paris in his hardiment,
[And parted thus you and your argument.]

109. **moral:** motto.   113. **port:** gate.   114. **possess:** inform.   115. **Entreat:** treat.   124. [**zeal**] (Warburton).   *seale* QF.
124-25. [**to thee In**] Q.   *towards, I* F.   128. **even ... charge:** merely because I ask it.   134. **I'll ... lust:** I'll do as I please.
139. **brave:** vaunt.   146. [**Dei.**] (Ritson conj.).   *Dio.* F.   Q om. ll. 146-50.
Sc. v, S.D. QF add *Calcas.*   But see l. 53 below.   1. **appointment:** equipment.   2. **starting:** active.   6. **trumpet:** trumpeter.   8. **bias:** puffed out.   9. **Aquilon:** the north wind.   11. **for:** i.e., to rouse.   12. **days:** in the day.   13. [**yond**] Q.   *yong*
F.   28. **hardiment:** boldness.   29. [**And ... argument**] Q.   Om. F.

Ulyss. O deadly gall, and theme of all our
   scorns,   30
For which we lose our heads to gild his horns!
  Patr. The first was Menelaus' kiss; this, mine.
Patroclus kisses you.
  Men.   O, this is trim!
  Patr. Paris and I kiss evermore for him.
  Men. I'll have my kiss, sir. Lady, by your
   leave.   35
  Cres. In kissing, do you render or receive?
  Patr. Both take and give.
  Cres.   I'll make my match to live,
The kiss you take is better than you give;
Therefore no kiss.   39
  Men. I'll give you boot, I'll give you three for one.
  Cres. You're an odd man; give even, or give none.
  Men. An odd man, lady? Every man is odd.
  Cres. No, Paris is not; for you know 'tis true
That you are odd, and he is even with you.
  Men. You fillip me o' th' head.
  Cres.   No, I'll be sworn.
  Ulyss. It were no match, your nail against his
  horn.   46
May I, sweet lady, beg a kiss of you?
  Cres. You may.
  Ulyss.   I do desire it.
  Cres.   Why, beg, then.
  Ulyss. Why then for Venus' sake, give me a kiss.
When Helen is a maid again, and his —   50
  Cres. I am your debtor, claim it when 'tis due.
  Ulyss. Never's my day, and then a kiss of you.
  Dio. Lady, a word. I'll bring you to your
  father.   *[Exit with Cressida.]*
  Nest. A woman of quick sense.
  Ulyss.   Fie, fie upon her!
There's language in her eye, her cheek, her lip, 55
Nay, her foot speaks; her wanton spirits look out
At every joint and motive of her body.
O, these encounterers, so glib of tongue,
That give [accosting] welcome ere it comes,
And wide unclasp the tables of their thoughts 60
To every tickling reader! set them down
For sluttish spoils of opportunity
And daughters of the game.

Enter all of Troy, HECTOR *[armed;]* PARIS, ÆNEAS,
  HELENUS, *[*TROILUS, *and other* Trojans]* with
  Attendants. Flourish.

  All. The Troyans' trumpet.
  Agam.   Yonder comes the troop.
  Æne. Hail, all you state of Greece! What shall
  be done   65

To him that victory commands? or do you purpose
A victor shall be known? Will you the knights
Shall to the edge of all extremity
Pursue each other, or shall be divided
By any voice or order of the field?   70
Hector bade ask.
  Agam.   Which way would Hector have it?
  Æne. He cares not; he'll obey conditions.
  Achil. 'Tis done like Hector, but securely done;
A little proudly, and great deal disprizing
The knight oppos'd.
  Æne.   If not Achilles, sir,   75
What is your name?
  Achil.   If not Achilles, nothing.
  Æne. Therefore Achilles; but, whate'er, know
  this:
In the extremity of great and little,
Valour and pride excel themselves in Hector;
The one almost as infinite as all,   80
The other blank as nothing. Weigh him well,
And that which looks like pride is courtesy.
This Ajax is half made of Hector's blood;
In love whereof, half Hector stays at home;
Half heart, half hand, half Hector comes to seek 85
This blended knight, half Troyan and half Greek.
  Achil. A maiden battle, then? O, I perceive you.

[Re-enter DIOMEDES.*]*

  Agam. Here is Sir Diomed. Go, gentle knight,
Stand by our Ajax. As you and Lord Æneas
Consent upon the order of their fight,   90
So be it; either to the uttermost,
Or else a [breath]. The combatants being kin
Half stints their strife before their strokes begin.
          [Ajax and Hector enter the lists.]
  Ulyss. They are oppos'd already.
  Agam. What Troyan is that same that looks so
  heavy?   95
  Ulyss. The youngest son of Priam, a true knight,
Not yet mature, yet matchless, firm of word,
Speaking in deeds, and deedless in his tongue;
Not soon provok'd, nor being provok'd soon calm'd;
His heart and hand both open and both free; 100
For what he has he gives, what thinks he shows;
Yet gives he not till judgement guide his bounty,
Nor dignifies an impair thought with breath;
Manly as Hector, but more dangerous;
For Hector in his blaze of wrath subscribes 105
To tender objects, but he in heat of action
Is more vindicative than jealous love.
They call him Troilus, and on him erect
A second hope, as fairly built as Hector.

---

37. **make...live:** wager my life. 40. **boot:** odds. 45. **fillip:** tap. 57. **motive:** limb. 59. **[accosting]** (Theobald).
a coasting QF. 61. **tickling:** wanton. 62. **sluttish...opportunity:** loose women who yield to every occasion. 73. **securely:**
over-confidently. 87. **maiden:** bloodless. 90. **Consent:** agree. 92. **[breath]** Q: a spell of exercise. *breach* F. 95. **heavy:**
sorrowful, woeful. 96. **knight** Q. *knight; they call him Troylus* F. See l. 108. 98. **deedless...tongue:** not boastful.
100. **free:** generous. 103. **impair:** unsuitable. 105-06. **subscribes...objects:** is merciful to the weak.

Thus says Æneas; one that knows the youth   110
Even to his inches, and with private soul
Did in great Ilion thus translate him to me.
        [*Alarum*. [*Hector and Ajax fight.*]
Agam. They are in action.
Nest. Now, Ajax, hold thine own!
Tro.   Hector, thou sleep'st;
Awake thee!   115
Agam. His blows are well dispos'd. There,
  Ajax!
Dio. You must no more.   [*Trumpets cease*.
Æne.   Princes, enough, so please you.
Ajax. I am not warm yet; let us fight again.
Dio. As Hector pleases.
Hect.   Why, then will I no more.
Thou art, great lord, my father's sister's son,   120
A cousin-german to great Priam's seed.
The obligation of our blood forbids
A gory emulation 'twixt us twain.
Were thy commixtion Greek and Troyan so
That thou couldst say, "This hand is Grecian
  all,   125
And this is Troyan; the sinews of this leg
All Greek, and this all Troy; my mother's blood
Runs on the dexter cheek, and this sinister
Bounds in my father's;" by Jove multipotent,
Thou shouldst not bear from me a Greekish member   131
Wherein my sword had not impressure made
Of our rank feud; but the just gods gainsay
That any drop thou borrow'dst from thy mother,
My sacred aunt, should by my mortal sword
Be drained! Let me embrace thee, Ajax.   135
By him that thunders, thou hast lusty arms!
Hector would have them fall upon him thus.
Cousin, all honour to thee!
Ajax.   I thank thee, Hector.
Thou art too gentle and too free a man.
I came to kill thee, cousin, and bear hence   140
A great addition earned in thy death.
Hect. Not Neoptolemus so mirable,
On whose bright crest Fame with her loud'st Oyes
Cries, "This is he," could promise to himself
A thought of added honour torn from Hector.   145
Æne. There is expectance here from both the
  sides,
What further you will do.
Hect.   We'll answer it:
The issue is embracement. Ajax, farewell.
Ajax. If I might in entreaties find success —
As seld I have the chance — I would desire   150
My famous cousin to our Grecian tents.

Dio. 'Tis Agamemnon's wish, and great Achilles
Doth long to see unarm'd the valiant Hector.
Hect. Æneas, call my brother Troilus to me,
And signify this loving interview   155
To the expecters of our Troyan part.
Desire them home. Give me thy hand, my cousin.
I will go eat with thee and see your knights.

    AGAMEMNON *and the rest* [*come forward*].

Ajax. Great Agamemnon comes to meet us here.
Hect. The worthiest of them tell me name by
  name;   160
But for Achilles, mine own searching eyes
Shall find him by his large and portly size.
Agam. Worthy of arms! as welcome as to one
That would be rid of such an enemy.   164
But that's no welcome. Understand more clear,
What's past and what's to come is strew'd with
  husks
And formless ruin of oblivion;
But in this extant moment, faith and troth,
Strain'd purely from all hollow bias-drawing,
Bids thee, with most divine integrity,   170
From heart of very heart, great Hector, welcome.
Hect. I thank thee, most imperious Agamemnon.
Agam. [*To Troilus*.] My well-fam'd lord of Troy,
  no less to you.
Men. Let me confirm my princely brother's
  greeting.   174
You brace of warlike brothers, welcome hither.
Hect. Who must we answer?
Æne.   The noble Menelaus.
Hect. O, you, my lord? By Mars his gauntlet,
  thanks!
Mock not that I affect th' untraded oath,
Your quondam wife swears still by Venus' glove.
She's well, but bade me not commend her to
  you.   180
Men. Name her not now, sir; she's a deadly
  theme.
Hect. O, pardon; I offend.
Nest. I have, thou gallant Troyan, seen thee oft,
Labouring for destiny, make cruel way
Through ranks of Greekish youth, and I have seen
  thee,   185
As hot as Perseus, spur thy Phrygian steed,
And seen thee scorning forfeits and subduements,
When thou hast hung thy advanced sword i' th' air,
Not letting it decline on the declined,
That I have said unto my standers by   190
"Lo, Jupiter is yonder, dealing life!"

---

111. **Even ... inches:** from top to toe. **with ... soul:** confidentially. 128. **dexter:** right. **sinister:** left. 129. **multipotent:** almighty. 142. **Neoptolemus:** son of Achilles. Some edd. believe Achilles is meant. **mirable:** wonderful. 143. **Oyes.** Heralds cried *Oyez* (Hear ye!) to gain attention . 148. **issue:** outcome. 150. **seld:** seldom. 156. **expecters ... part:** the Trojans who await news. 168. **extant:** present. 169. **bias-drawing:** untruth. 178. **untraded:** uncurrent. 184. **Labouring for destiny:** i.e., as agent of Fate. 187. **forfeits and subduements:** the vanquished whose lives are forfeit. 188. **hung:** checked. 191. **dealing life:** i.e., by sparing it.

And I have seen thee pause and take thy breath,
When that a ring of Greeks have hemm'd thee in,
Like an Olympian wrestling. This have I seen;
But this thy countenance, still lock'd in steel,   195
I never saw till now. I knew thy grandsire,
And once fought with him. He was a soldier good;
But, by great Mars, the captain of us all,
Never like thee. Let an old man embrace thee;
And, worthy warrior, welcome to our tents.   200
    Æne. 'Tis the old Nestor.
    Hect. Let me embrace thee, good old chronicle,
That hast so long walk'd hand in hand with Time.
Most reverend Nestor, I am glad to clasp thee.
    Nest. I would my arms could match thee in con-
      tention,   205
As they contend with thee in courtesy.
    Hect. I would they could.
    Nest. Ha!
By this white beard, I'd fight with thee to-morrow.
Well, welcome, welcome! — I have seen the
      time.   210
    Ulyss. I wonder now how yonder city stands
When we have here her base and pillar by us.
    Hect. I know your favour, Lord Ulysses, well.
Ah, sir, there's many a Greek and Troyan dead
Since first I saw yourself and Diomed   215
In Ilion, on your Greekish embassy.
    Ulyss. Sir, I foretold you then what would ensue.
My prophecy is but half his journey yet,
For yonder walls, that pertly front your town,
Yond towers, whose wanton tops do buss the
      clouds,   220
Must kiss their own feet.
    Hect.   I must not believe you.
There they stand yet, and modestly I think
The fall of every Phrygian stone will cost
A drop of Grecian blood. The end crowns all,
And that old common arbitrator, Time,   225
Will one day end it.
    Ulyss.   So to him we leave it.
Most gentle and most valiant Hector, welcome!
After the general, I beseech you next
To feast with me and see me at my tent.
    Achil. I shall forestall thee, Lord Ulysses, thou!
Now, Hector, I have fed mine eyes on thee;   231
I have with exact view perus'd thee, Hector,
And quoted joint by joint.
    Hect.   Is this Achilles?
    Achil. I am Achilles.
    Hect. Stand fair, I prithee; let me look on
      thee.   235
    Achil. Behold thy fill.
    Hect.   Nay, I have done already.
    Achil. Thou art too brief. I will the second time,

As I would buy thee, view thee limb by limb.
    Hect. O, like a book of sport thou'lt read me
      o'er;   239
But there's more in me than thou understand'st.
Why dost thou so oppress me with thine eye?
    Achil. Tell me, you heavens, in which part of his
      body
Shall I destroy him, whether there, or there, or
      there?
That I may give the local wound a name
And make distinct the very breach whereout   245
Hector's great spirit flew. Answer me, heavens!
    Hect. It would discredit the blest gods, proud
      man,
To answer such a question. Stand again.
Think'st thou to catch my life so pleasantly
As to prenominate in nice conjecture   250
Where thou wilt hit me dead?
    Achil.   I tell thee, yea.
    Hect. Wert thou the oracle to tell me so,
I'd not believe thee. Henceforth guard thee well;
For I'll not kill thee there, nor there, nor there;
But, by the forge that stithied Mars his helm,   255
I'll kill thee everywhere, yea, o'er and o'er.
You wisest Grecians, pardon me this brag.
His insolence draws folly from my lips;
But I'll endeavour deeds to match these words,
Or may I never —
    Ajax.   Do not chafe thee, cousin;   260
And you, Achilles, let these threats alone
Till accident or purpose bring you to't.
You may have every day enough of Hector,
If you have stomach. The general state, I fear,
Can scarce entreat you to be odd with him.   265
    Hect. I pray you, let us see you in the field.
We have had pelting wars, since you refus'd
The Grecians' cause.
    Achil.   Dost thou entreat me, Hector?
To-morrow do I meet thee, fell as death;
To-night all friends.
    Hect.   Thy hand upon that match.
    Agam. First, all you peers of Greece, go to my
      tent;   271
There in the full convive you. Afterwards,
As Hector's leisure and your bounties shall
Concur together, severally entreat him.
Beat loud the tabourines, let the trumpets blow,   275
That this great soldier may his welcome know.
      [*Exeunt [all except Troilus and Ulysses].*
    Tro. My Lord Ulysses; tell me, I beseech you,
In what place of the field doth Calchas keep?
    Ulyss. At Menelaus' tent, most princely Troilus.
There Diomed doth feast with him to-night,   280
Who neither looks on heaven nor on earth,

---

195. **still:** ever.   196. **grandsire:** Laomedon.   220. **buss:** kiss.   233. **quoted:** noted.   249. **pleasantly:** merrily.
250. **prenominate:** name in advance.   **nice:** fine.   255. **stithied:** forged.   264. **state:** situation.   265. **entreat:** call for.
odd: at odds.   267. **pelting:** paltry.   269. **fell:** fierce, cruel.   272. **convive:** feast.   274. **severally:** individually.

But gives all gaze and bent of amorous view
On the fair Cressid.

Tro. Shall I, sweet lord, be bound to thee so much,
After we part from Agamemnon's tent,   285
To bring me thither?

Ulyss.   You shall command me, sir.
As gentle tell me, of what honour was
This Cressida in Troy? Had she no lover there
That wails her absence?

Tro. O, sir, to such as boasting show their scars
A mock is due. Will you walk on, my lord?   291
She was belov'd, she lov'd; she is, and doth:
But still sweet love is food for Fortune's tooth.

[*Exeunt.*

[ACT V

SCENE I. *The Greek camp.   Before the tent of
Achilles.*]

Enter ACHILLES *and* PATROCLUS.

Achil. I'll heat his blood with Greekish wine to-
night,
Which with my scimitar I'll cool to-morrow.
Patroclus, let us feast him to the height.

Patr. Here comes Thersites.

Enter THERSITES.

Achil.   How now, thou core of envy!
Thou crusty batch of nature, what's the news?   5

Ther. Why, thou picture of what thou seem'st,
and idol of idiot-worshippers, here's a letter for thee.

Achil. From whence, fragment?

Ther. Why, thou full dish of fool, from Troy.

Patr. Who keeps the tent now?   11

Ther. The surgeon's box, or the patient's wound.

Patr. Well said, adversity! and what need these
tricks?   15

Ther. Prithee, be silent, boy; I profit not by thy
talk. Thou art thought to be Achilles' male varlet.

Patr. Male varlet, you rogue! What's that?   19

Ther. Why, his masculine whore. Now, the
rotten diseases of the south, guts-griping, ruptures,
catarrhs, loads o' gravel i' th' back, lethargies, cold
palsies, [raw eyes, dirt-rotten livers, wheezing lungs,
)bladders full of imposthume, sciaticas, limekilns i'
th' palm, incurable bone-ache, and the rivelled   25
fee-simple of the tetter,] take and take again such
preposterous discoveries!

Patr. Why, thou damnable box of envy, thou,
what mean'st thou to curse thus?   30

Ther. Do I curse thee?

Patr. Why, no, you ruinous butt, you whoreson
indistinguishable cur, [no].

Ther. No! why art thou then exasperate, thou
idle immaterial skein of [sleave]-silk, thou green   35
sarcenet flap for a sore eye, thou tassel of a prodigal's purse, thou? Ah, how the poor world is
pest'red with such waterflies, diminutives of nature!

Patr. Out, gall!   40

Ther. Finch-egg!

Achil. My sweet Patroclus, I am thwarted quite
From my great purpose in to-morrow's battle.
Here is a letter from Queen Hecuba.
A token from her daughter, my fair love,   45
Both taxing me and gaging me to keep
An oath that I have sworn. I will not break it.
Fall Greeks; fail fame; honour or go or stay;
My major vow lies here, this I'll obey.
Come, come, Thersites, help to trim my tent;   50
This night in banqueting must all be spent.
Away, Patroclus!

[*Exeunt Achilles and Patroclus*].

Ther. With too much blood and too little brain,
these two may run mad; but, if with too much
brain and too little blood they do, I'll be a curer   55
of madmen. Here's Agamemnon, an honest fellow
enough, and one that loves quails; but he has not
so much brain as ear-wax: and the goodly transformation of Jupiter there, his brother the bull, the
primitive statue and oblique memorial of cuck-   60
olds; a thrifty shoeing-horn in a chain, hanging at
his brother's leg, — to what form but that he is
should wit larded with malice and malice forced
with wit turn him to? To an ass, were nothing; he
is both ass and ox: to an ox, were nothing; he is   65
both ox and ass. To be a dog, a mule, a cat, a
fitchew, a toad, a lizard, an owl, a puttock, or a
herring without a roe, I would not care; but to be
Menelaus! I would conspire against destiny.
Ask me not what I would be if I were not Ther-   70
sites; for I care not to be the louse of a lazar, so I
were not Menelaus. Hoy-day! spirits and fires!

Enter HECTOR, [TROILUS,] AJAX, AGAMEMNON,
ULYSSES, NESTOR, [MENELAUS,] *and* DIOMEDES,
with lights.

Agam. We go wrong, we go wrong.

Ajax.   No, yonder 'tis;
There, where we see the light.

Hect.   I trouble you,   75

Ajax. No, not a whit.

Act V, sc. i, 5. batch: bread made at one baking. **11. Who ... now?** A thrust at Achilles for no longer keeping to his tent. Line 12 involves a pun on *tent* as a *probe for wounds*. **22. back**: i.e., kidney. **lethargies**: apoplexies. **23–26. [raw ... tetter]** Q. Om. F. **24. imposthume**: abscess. **limekilns**: i.e., burnings. **25–26. rivelled ... tetter**: absolute rash or scurvy. **32. ruinous butt**: dilapidated hogshead. **33. indistinguishable**: lumpish, shapeless. **[no]** Q. Om. F. **35. [sleave]** Q: floss. *sleyd* F. **36. sarcenet**: silk. **46. taxing**: reproaching. **57. quails**: loose women. **59. Jupiter.** Changed himself into a bull when he abducted Europa. **61. thrifty**: niggardly. **67. fitchew**: polecat. **puttock**: kite. **71. care ... be**: don't mind being.

Re-enter ACHILLES.

Ulyss.　　　　Here comes himself to guide you.
Achil. Welcome, brave Hector; welcome, Princes all.
Agam. So now, fair Prince of Troy, I bid good night.
Ajax commands the guard to tend on you.
Hect. Thanks and good night to the Greeks' general.　　　　　　　　　　　　　80
Men. Good night, my lord.
Hect.　　　　Good night, sweet Lord Menelaus.
Ther. Sweet draught! "Sweet" quoth 'a! Sweet sink, sweet [sewer].
Achil. Good night and welcome, both at once, to those
That go or tarry.　　　　　　　　　　　85
Agam. Good night.
　　　　　[Exeunt Agamemnon and Menelaus.]
Achil. Old Nestor tarries, and you too, Diomed,
Keep Hector company an hour or two.
Dio. I cannot, lord; I have important business,
The tide whereof is now.　Good night, great Hector.　　　　　　　　　　　90
Hect. Give me your hand.
Ulyss. [Aside to Troilus.] Follow his torch; he goes to Calchas' tent.
I'll keep you company.
Tro.　　　　Sweet sir, you honour me.
Hect. And so, good night.
　　　　　[Exit Diomedes; Ulysses and Troilus following.]
Achil.　　Come, come, enter my tent.　94
　　　　　[Exeunt [Achilles, Hector, Ajax, and Nestor].
Ther. That same Diomed's a false-hearted rogue, a most unjust knave. I will no more trust him when he leers than I will a serpent when he hisses. He will spend his mouth, and promise, like Brabbler the hound; but when he performs, astronomers foretell it; it is prodigious, there will come some 100 change. The sun borrows of the moon when Diomed keeps his word. I will rather leave to see Hector than not to dog him. They say he keeps a Troyan drab, and uses the traitor Calchas his tent. I'll after. Nothing but lechery! All incontinent varlets!　　　　　　　　　　*[Exit.* 106

[SCENE II. *The same.　Before Calchas's tent.]*

Enter DIOMEDES.

Dio. What, are you up here, ho?　Speak.
Cal. [Within.] Who calls?
Dio. Diomed.　Calchas, I think.　Where's your daughter?
Cal. [Within.] She comes to you.

Enter TROILUS *and* ULYSSES [*at a distance;
after them,* THERSITES].

Ulyss. Stand where the torch may not discover us.　　　　　　　　　　　5

Enter CRESSIDA.

Tro. Cressid comes forth to him.
Dio.　　　　　How now, my charge!
Cres. Now, my sweet guardian!　Hark, a word with you.　　　　　*[Whispers.]*
Tro. Yea, so familiar!
Ulyss. She will sing any man at first sight.
Ther. And any man may [sing] her, if he can take her [cliff].　She's noted.　　　11
Dio. Will you remember?
Cres. Remember! yes.
Dio. Nay, but do, then;
And let your mind be coupled with your words. 15
Tro. What should she remember?
Ulyss. List.
Cres. Sweet honey Greek, tempt me no more to folly.
Ther. Roguery!
Dio. Nay, then, —　　　　　　　　　　20
Cres. I'll tell you what, —
Dio. Foh, foh! come, tell a pin.　You are a forsworn —
Cres. In faith, I cannot.　What would you have me do?
Ther. A juggling trick, — to be secretly open.
Dio. What did you swear you would bestow on me?　　　　　　　　　　25
Cres. I prithee, do not hold me to mine oath.
Bid me do anything but that, sweet Greek.
Dio. Good night.
Tro. Hold, patience!
Ulyss. How now, Troyan!　　　　　　　30
Cres. Diomed, —
Dio. No, no, good night.　I'll be your fool no more.
Tro. Thy better must.
Cres. Hark, one word in your ear.
Tro. O plague and madness!　　　　　35
Ulyss. You are moved, Prince.　Let us depart, I pray you,
Lest your displeasure should enlarge itself
To wrathful terms.　This place is dangerous;
The time right deadly.　I beseech you, go.　39
Tro. Behold, I pray you!
Ulyss.　　　　Nay, good my lord, go off;
You flow to great distraction.　Come, my lord.
Tro. I pray thee, stay.
Ulyss.　　　　You have not patience; come.
Tro. I pray you, stay.　By hell and [all hell's] torments,

82. **draught:** privy.　[sewer] (Rowe).　*sure* QF.　102. **leave:** omit.
Sc. ii, 10–11. [sing] . . . [cliff] Q.　*finde . . . life* F.　**Cliff:** clef, musical symbol; **noted** involves a pun.　43. [all hell's] Q.　*hell* F.

I will not speak a word!
Dio.   And so, good night.
Cres. Nay, but you part in anger.
Tro.   Doth that grieve thee?   45
O withered truth!
Ulyss.   Why, how now, lord!
Tro.   By Jove,
I will be patient.
Cres.   Guardian! Why, Greek!
Dio. Foh, foh! adieu; you palter.
Cres. In faith, I do not. Come hither once again.
Ulyss. You shake, my lord, at something. Will
    you go?   50
You will break out.
Tro.   She strokes his cheek!
Ulyss.   Come, come.
Tro. Nay, stay; by Jove, I will not speak a word.
There is between my will and all offences
A guard of patience. Stay a little while.   54
Ther. How the devil Luxury, with his fat rump
and potato-finger, tickles these together! Fry,
lechery, fry!
Dio. But will you, then?
Cres. In faith, I will, la; never trust me else.
Dio. Give me some token for the surety of it. 60
Cres. I'll fetch you one.   [*Exit.*
Ulyss. You have sworn patience.
Tro.   Fear me not, sweet lord.
I will not be myself, nor have cognition
Of what I feel. I am all patience.

Re-enter CRESSIDA.

Ther. Now the pledge; now, now, now!   65
Cres. Here, Diomed, keep this sleeve.
Tro. O beauty! where is thy faith?
Ulyss.   My lord, —
Tro. I will be patient; outwardly I will.
Cres. You look upon that sleeve; behold it well.
He lov'd me — O false wench! — Give't me again.
Dio. Whose was't?   71
Cres. It is no matter, now I have't again.
I will not meet with you to-morrow night.
I prithee, Diomed, visit me no more.   74
Ther. Now she sharpens. Well said, whetstone!
Dio. I shall have it.
Cres.   What, this?
Dio.   Ay, that.
Cres. O, all you gods! O pretty, pretty pledge!
Thy master now lies thinking in his bed
Of thee and me, and sighs, and takes my glove,
And gives memorial dainty kisses to it,   80
As I kiss thee. Nay, do not snatch it from me.
He that takes that [doth take] my heart withal.

Dio. I had your heart before, this follows it.
Tro. I did swear patience.
Cres. You shall not have it, Diomed; faith, you
    shall not.   85
I'll give you something else.
Dio. I will have this. Whose was it?
Cres.   It is no matter.
Dio. Come, tell me whose it was.
Cres. 'Twas one's that lov'd me better than you
    will.
But, now you have it, take it.
Dio.   Whose was it?   90
Cres. By all Diana's waiting-women yond,
And by herself, I will not tell you whose.
Dio. To-morrow will I wear it on my helm,
And grieve his spirit that dares not challenge it.
Tro. Wert thou the devil, and wor'st it on thy
    horn,   95
It should be challeng'd.
Cres. Well, well, 'tis done, 'tis past. And yet it
    is not;
I will not keep my word.
Dio.   Why, then, farewell;
Thou never shalt mock Diomed again.
Cres. You shall not go. One cannot speak a
    word,   100
But it straight starts you.
Dio.   I do not like this fooling.
Ther. Nor I, by Pluto; but that that likes not
[you] pleases me best.
Dio. What, shall I come? The hour?
Cres. Ay, come: — O Jove! — do come. — I
    shall be plagu'd.   105
Dio. Farewell till then.   [*Exit Diomedes.*
Cres.   Good night. I prithee, come.
Troilus, farewell! one eye yet looks on thee,
But with my heart the other eye doth see.
Ah, poor our sex! this fault in us I find,
The error of our eye directs our mind.   110
What error leads must err; O, then conclude
Minds sway'd by eyes are full of turpitude. [*Exit.*
Ther. A proof of strength she could not publish
    more,
Unless she say, My mind is now turn'd whore.
Ulyss. All's done, my lord.
Tro.   It is.
Ulyss.   Why stay we, then?
Tro. To make a recordation to my soul   116
Of every syllable that here was spoke.
But if I tell how these two did co-act,
Shall I not lie in publishing a truth?
Sith yet there is a credence in my heart,   120
An esperance so obstinately strong,

---

55. **Luxury**: lust. 56. **potato-finger**. The potato was held to excite lust. 75. **sharpens**: i.e., his desire. 81. **Nay . . . me**.
To *Dio.* in QF. 82. **[doth take]** Q. *rakes* F. 91. **Diana's waiting-women**: the stars. 102. **likes**: pleases. 103. **[you]** Q.
me F. 105. **plagu'd**: punished. 110. **error**: wandering. 111. **What**: whatever. 113. **proof of strength**: strong proof.
121. **esperance**: hope.

That doth invert th' attest of eyes and ears,
As if those organs had deceptious functions,
Created only to calumniate.
Was Cressid here?
   Ulyss.   I cannot conjure, Troyan.   125
   Tro. She was not, sure.
   Ulyss.   Most sure she was.
   Tro. Why, my negation hath no taste of madness.
   Ulyss. Nor mine, my lord. Cressid was here
      but now.
   Tro. Let it not be believ'd for womanhood!
Think, we had mothers; do not give advantage
To stubborn critics, apt, without a theme   131
For depravation, to square the general sex
By Cressid's rule. Rather think this not Cressid.
   Ulyss. What hath she done, Prince, that can
      soil our mothers?
   Tro. Nothing at all, unless that this were she.   135
   Ther. Will he swagger himself out on's own eyes?
   Tro. This she? no, this is Diomed's Cressida.
If beauty have a soul, this is not she.
If souls guide vows, if vows are sanctimony,
If sanctimony be the gods' delight,   140
If there be rule in unity itself,
This is not she. O madness of discourse,
That cause sets up with and against thyself,
[Bi-fold] authority, where reason can revolt
Without perdition, and loss assume all reason
Without revolt: this is, and is not, Cressid.   146
Within my soul there doth conduce a fight
Of this strange nature, that a thing inseparate
Divides more wider than the sky and earth,
And yet the spacious breadth of this division   150
Admits no orifex for a point as subtle
As Ariachne's broken woof to enter.
Instance, O instance! strong as Pluto's gates;
Cressid is mine, tied with the bonds of heaven.
Instance, O instance! strong as heaven itself;
The bonds of heaven are slipp'd, dissolv'd, and
     loos'd;   156
And with another knot, five-finger-tied,
The fractions of her faith, orts of her love,
The fragments, scraps, the bits and greasy relics
Of her o'er-eaten faith, are bound to Diomed.   160
   Ulyss. May worthy Troilus be half attached
With that which here his passion doth express?
   Tro. Ay, Greek; and that shall be divulged well
In characters as red as Mars his heart

Inflam'd with Venus. Never did young man fancy
With so eternal and so fix'd a soul.   166
Hark, Greek: as much as I do Cressid love,
So much by weight hate I her Diomed.
That sleeve is mine that he'll bear [on] his helm.
Were it a casque compos'd by Vulcan's skill,   170
My sword should bite it. Not the dreadful spout
Which shipmen do the hurricano call,
Constring'd in mass by the almighty [sun],
Shall dizzy with more clamour Neptune's ear
In his descent than shall my prompted sword   175
Falling on Diomed.
   Ther. He'll tickle it for his concupy.
   Tro. O Cressid! O false Cressid! false, false,
     false!
Let all untruths stand by thy stained name,
And they'll seem glorious.
   Ulyss.   O, contain yourself;
Your passion draws ears hither.   181

Enter ÆNEAS.

   Æne. I have been seeking you this hour, my lord.
Hector, by this, is arming him in Troy;
Ajax, your guard, stays to conduct you home.
   Tro. Have with you, Prince. My courteous lord,
     adieu.   185
Farewell, revolted fair! and, Diomed,
Stand fast, and wear a castle on thy head!
   Ulyss. I'll bring you to the gates.
   Tro. Accept distracted thanks.   189
      [*Exeunt Troilus, Æneas, and Ulysses.*
   Ther. Would I could meet that rogue Diomed!
I would croak like a raven; I would bode, I would
bode. Patroclus will give me anything for the
intelligence of this whore. The parrot will not do
more for an almond than he for a commodious drab.
Lechery, lechery; still wars and lechery; nothing
else holds fashion. A burning devil take them!   197
                      [*Exit.*]

[SCENE III. *Troy.*   *Before Priam's palace.*]

Enter HECTOR *and* ANDROMACHE.

   And. When was my lord so much ungently
     temper'd
To stop his ears against admonishment?
Unarm, unarm, and do not fight to-day.

---

122. **invert:** reverse. **attest:** witness. 125. **conjure:** raise spirits; i.e., she *was* here. 129. **for:** i.e., for the sake of.
132–33. **square ... rule:** measure the sex in general by Cressida's standard. 136. **swagger ... eyes:** brazenly defy his own
eyes. 139. **sanctimony:** a sacred thing. 141. **If ... itself:** if it is a law that a person can be only one. 142. **discourse:**
reason. 143. **cause:** trial, suit. 144–46. [Bi-fold] ... revolt: double authority, by which reason can now rebel against
itself without being destroyed, and now be completely destroyed without rebelling. [Bi-fold] Q. *By foule* F. 147. **conduce:**
come into being. 148. **inseparate:** indivisible (referring to Cressida's personality). 151. **orifex:** orifice, opening.
152. **Ariachne's ... woof:** the thread of a spider's web. Arachne a mortal skilled in weaving, was changed into a spider.
153. **Instance:** evidence. 158. **orts:** scraps. 160. **o'er-eaten:** much-mouthed. 161. **half attached:** half as much affected.
169. **[on]** Q. *in* F. 173. **Constring'd:** drawn together. [sun] Q. *Fenne* F. 177. **concupy.** Thersites' coinage for *con-
cupiscence.* 185. **Have ... you:** come along. 191. **bode:** portend (like a bird of ill omen).

Hect. You train me to offend you; get you gone.
By [all] the everlasting gods, I'll go!   5
And. My dreams will, sure, prove ominous to
the day.
Hect. No more, I say.

Enter CASSANDRA.

Cas.   Where is my brother Hector?
And. Here, sister; arm'd, and bloody in intent.
Consort with me in loud and dear petition,
Pursue we him on knees; for I have dream'd   10
Of bloody turbulence, and this whole night
Hath nothing been but shapes and forms of
slaughter.
Cas. O, 'tis true.
Hect.   Ho! bid my trumpet sound!
Cas. No notes of sally, for the heavens, sweet
brother.
Hect. Be gone, I say; the gods have heard me
swear.   15
Cas. The gods are deaf to hot and peevish vows.
They are polluted off'rings, more abhorr'd
Than spotted livers in the sacrifice.
And. O, be persuaded! do not count it holy
To hurt by being just. It is as lawful,   20
For we would [give much, to use] violent thefts
And rob in the behalf of charity.
Cas. It is the purpose that makes strong the vow,
But vows to every purpose must not hold,
Unarm, sweet Hector.
Hect.   Hold you still, I say;   25
Mine honour keeps the weather of my fate.
Life every man holds dear; but the [brave] man
Holds honour far more precious-dear than life.

Enter TROILUS.

How now, young man! mean'st thou to fight to-day?
And. Cassandra, call my father to persuade.   30
                              [*Exit Cassandra.*
Hect. No, faith, young Troilus; doff thy harness,
youth;
I am to-day i' th' vein of chivalry.
Let grow thy sinews till their knots be strong,
And tempt not yet the brushes of the war.
Unarm thee, go, and doubt thou not, brave boy,
I'll stand to-day for thee and me and Troy.   36
Tro. Brother, you have a vice of mercy in you,
Which better fits a lion than a man.
Hect. What vice is that, good Troilus? Chide
me for it.
Tro. When many times the captive Grecian falls,
Even in the fan and wind of your fair sword,   41
You bid them rise, and live.

Hect. O, 'tis fair play.
Tro.   Fool's play, by heaven, Hector.
Hect. How now! how now!
Tro.   For th' love of all the gods,
Let's leave the hermit Pity with our mothers,   45
And when we have our armours buckled on,
The venom'd vengeance ride upon our swords,
Spur them to ruthful work, rein them from ruth.
Hect. Fie, savage, fie!
Tro.   Hector, then 'tis wars.
Hect. Troilus, I would not have you fight to-day.
Tro. Who should withhold me?   51
Not fate, obedience, nor the hand of Mars
Beck'ning with fiery truncheon my retire;
Not Priamus and Hecuba on knees,
Their eyes o'ergalled with recourse of tears;   55
Nor you, my brother, with your true sword drawn,
Oppos'd to hinder me, should stop my way,
But by my ruin.

Re-enter CASSANDRA, *with* PRIAM.

Cas. Lay hold upon him, Priam, hold him fast;
He is thy crutch. Now if thou lose thy stay,   60
Thou on him leaning, and all Troy on thee,
Fall all together.
Pri.   Come, Hector, come, go back.
Thy wife hath dream'd; thy mother hath had
visions;
Cassandra doth foresee; and I myself
Am like a prophet suddenly enrapt   65
To tell thee that this day is ominous:
Therefore, come back.
Hect.   Æneas is a-field;
And I do stand engag'd to many Greeks,
Even in the faith of valour, to appear
This morning to them.
Pri.   Ay, but thou shalt not go.
Hect. I must not break my faith.   71
You know me dutiful; therefore, dear sir,
Let me not shame respect; but give me leave
To take that course by your consent and voice,
Which you do here forbid me, royal Priam.   75
Cas. O Priam, yield not to him!
And.   Do not, dear father.
Hect. Andromache, I am offended with you.
Upon the love you bear me, get you in.
                              [*Exit Andromache.*
Tro. This foolish, dreaming, superstitious girl
Makes all these bodements.
Cas.   O, farewell, dear Hector!
Look, how thou diest! look, how thy eye turns
pale!   81
Look, how thy wounds doth bleed at many vents!

Sc. iii, 4. train: incite. 5. [all] Q. Om. F. 16. peevish: headstrong. 21. [give ... use] (Tyrwhitt conj.). *count give much to* as F. Q om. ll. 20-22. 26. the weather: to windward (the position of vantage). 27. [brave] (Pope). *deere* QF. 34. brushes: encounters. 48. ruthful: piteous. ruth: pity. 49. then ... wars: i.e., war is serious business. 55. o'er-galled: inflamed. 60. stay: support, prop. 69. in ... valour: by the honor of a brave man.

Hark, how Troy roars! how Hecuba cries out!
How poor Andromache shrills her dolour forth!
Behold, distraction, frenzy, and amazement,   85
Like witless antics, one another meet,
And all cry, Hector! Hector's dead! O Hector!
    Tro. Away! away!
    Cas. Farewell; [yet], soft! Hector, I take my
        leave.
Thou dost thyself and all our Troy deceive.   90
                                                  [*Exit.*
    Hect. You are amaz'd, my liege, at her exclaim.
Go in and cheer the town. We'll forth and fight,
Do deeds of praise and tell you them at night.
    Pri. Farewell! The gods with safety stand
        about thee!
        [*Exeunt severally Priam and Hector.*]
            Alarum.
    Tro. They are at it, hark! Proud Diomed,
        believe,   95
I come to lose my arm, or win my sleeve.

            Enter PANDARUS.

    Pan. Do you hear, my lord? Do you hear?
    Tro. What now?
    Pan. Here's a letter come from yond poor girl.
    Tro. Let me read.   100
    Pan. A whoreson tisick, a whoreson rascally
tisick so troubles me, and the foolish fortune of
this girl; and what one thing, what another, that
I shall leave you one o' these days; and I have a
rheum in mine eyes too, and such an ache in my
bones that, unless a man were curs'd, I cannot tell
what to think on't. What says she there?   107
    Tro. Words, words, mere words, no matter from
        the heart;
Th' effect doth operate another way.
            [*Tearing the letter.*]
Go, wind, to wind, there turn and change together.
My love with words and errors still she feeds,   111
But edifies another with her deeds.
    Pan. Why, but hear you!
    Tro. Hence, [broker]! lackey! Ignomy and shame
Pursue thy life, and live aye with thy name!   115
            [*Exeunt [severally].*

        [SCENE IV. *Plains between Troy and the Greek
            camp.*]

    Alarum. Enter THERSITES *in excursion.*

    Ther. Now they are clapper-clawing one another;
I'll go look on. That dissembling abominable
varlet, Diomed, has got that same scurvy doting
foolish young knave's sleeve of Troy there in his

helm. I would fain see them meet, that that   5
same young Troyan ass, that loves the whore
there, might send that Greekish whoremasterly
villain with the sleeve back to the dissembling
luxurious drab, of a sleeveless errand. O' th'
t'other side, the policy of those crafty swearing 10
rascals, that stale old mouse-eaten dry cheese,
Nestor, and that same dog-fox, Ulysses, is not
prov'd worth a blackberry. They set me up, in
policy, that mongrel cur, Ajax, against that dog of
as bad a kind, Achilles; and now is the cur   15
Ajax prouder than the cur Achilles, and will not
arm to-day; whereupon the Grecians begin to proclaim barbarism, and policy grows into an ill
opinion.

    Enter DIOMEDES, TROILUS [*following*].
Soft! here comes sleeve, and th' other.
    Tro. Fly not; for shouldst thou take the river
        Styx,   20
I would swim after.
    Dio.   Thou dost miscall retire.
I do not fly, but advantageous care
Withdrew me from the odds of multitude.
Have at thee!   24
    Ther. Hold thy whore, Grecian! — now for thy
whore, Troyan! — now the sleeve, now the sleeve!
        [*Exeunt Troilus and Diomedes fighting.*]

            Enter HECTOR.

    Hect. What art thou, Greek? Art thou for
        Hector's match?
Art thou of blood and honour?   29
    Ther. No, no, I am a rascal; a scurvy railing
knave; a very filthy rogue.
    Hect. I do believe thee; live.   [*Exit.*] 32
    Ther. God-a-mercy, that thou wilt believe me;
but a plague break thy neck for frighting me!
What's become of the wenching rogues? I think
they have swallowed one another. I would laugh
at that miracle; yet, in a sort, lechery eats itself.
I'll seek them.   [*Exit.* 38

        [SCENE V. *Another part of the plains.*]

        Enter DIOMEDES *and a* SERVANT.

    Dio. Go, go, my servant, take thou Troilus' horse;
Present the fair steed to my lady Cressid.
Fellow, commend my service to her beauty;
Tell her I have chastis'd the amorous Troyan,
And am her knight by proof.
    Serv.   I go, my lord.   5
                                                  [*Exit.*]

---

86. antics: lunatics.   89. [yet] Q.   *yes* F.   101. tisick: cough.   113–15. **Why...name.** These lines appear at V.x.32–34
in Q, at which point they are repeated by F.   [broker] Sc. x.334.   *brother* F.
    Sc. iv, 9. sleeveless: fruitless.   18. proclaim barbarism: adhere to ignorant force.   20. take: take to.

Enter AGAMEMNON.

Agam. Renew, renew!   The fierce Polydamas
Hath beat down Menon; bastard Margarelon
Hath Doreus prisoner,
And stands Colossus-wise, waving his beam,
Upon the pashed corses of the kings   10
Epistrophus and Cedius; Polyxenes is slain,
Amphimachus and Thoas deadly hurt,
Patroclus ta'en or slain, and Palamedes
Sore hurt and bruised.   The dreadful Sagittary
Appals our numbers.   Haste we, Diomed,   15
To reinforcement, or we perish all.

Enter NESTOR.

Nest. Go, bear Patroclus' body to Achilles;
And bid the snail-pac'd Ajax arm for shame.
There is a thousand Hectors in the field.
Now here he fights on Galathe his horse   20
And there lacks work; anon he's there afoot
And there they fly or die, like scaled schools
Before the belching whale; then is he yonder,
And there the [strawy] Greeks, ripe for his edge,
Fall down before him like the mower's swath.   25
Here, there, and everywhere, he leaves and takes,
Dexterity so obeying appetite
That what he will he does, and does so much
That proof is call'd impossibility.

Enter ULYSSES.

Ulyss. O, courage, courage, Princes!   Great
    Achilles   30
Is arming, weeping, cursing, vowing vengeance.
Patroclus' wounds have rous'd his drowsy blood,
Together with his mangled Myrmidons,
That noseless, handless, hack'd and chipp'd, come
    to him,
Crying on Hector.   Ajax hath lost a friend   35
And foams at mouth, and he is arm'd and at it,
Roaring for Troilus, who hath done to-day
Mad and fantastic execution,
Engaging and redeeming of himself
With such a careless force and forceless care   40
As if that luck, in very spite of cunning,
Bade him win all.

Enter AJAX.

Ajax. Troilus! thou coward Troilus!   [*Exit.*
Dio.   Ay, there, there.
Nest. So, so, we draw together.   [*Exit.*

Enter ACHILLES.

Achil.   Where is this Hector?
Come, come, thou boy-queller, show thy face;

Know what it is to meet Achilles angry.   46
Hector! where's Hector?   I will none but Hector.
                                        [*Exeunt.*

[SCENE VI. *Another part of the plains.*]

Enter AJAX.

Ajax. Troilus, thou coward Troilus, show thy
    head!

Enter DIOMEDES.

Dio. Troilus, I say! where's Troilus?
Ajax.   What wouldst thou?
Dio. I would correct him.
Ajax. Were I the general, thou shouldst have
    my office
Ere that correction.   Troilus, I say! what, Troilus!   4

Enter TROILUS.

Tro. O traitor Diomed! turn thy false face, thou
    traitor,
And pay thy life thou ow'st me for my horse!
Dio. Ha, art thou there?
Ajax. I'll fight with him alone.   Stand, Diomed.
Dio. He is my prize; I will not look upon.   10
Tro. Come, both you cogging Greeks; have at
    you both!   [*Exeunt* [*fighting*].

Enter HECTOR.

Hect. Yea, Troilus?   O, well fought, my youngest
    brother!

Enter ACHILLES.

Achil. Now do I see thee.   Have at thee,
    Hector!
Hect. Pause, if thou wilt.
Achil. I do disdain thy courtesy, proud Troyan.
Be happy that my arms are out of use;   16
My rest and negligence befriends thee now,
But thou anon shalt hear of me again;
Till when, go seek thy fortune.   [*Exit.*
Hect.   Fare thee well:
I would have been much more a fresher man,   20
Had I expected thee.   How now, my brother!

Re-enter TROILUS.

Tro. Ajax hath ta'en Æneas!   Shall it be?
No, by the flame of yonder glorious heaven,
He shall not carry him; I'll ta'en too,
Or bring him off.   Fate, hear me what I say!   25
I reck not though thou end my life to-day.   [*Exit.*

Enter one in [*sumptuous*] *armour.*

Hect. Stand, stand, thou Greek; thou art a goodly
    mark.

No? Wilt thou not? I like thy armour well;
I'll frush it and unlock the rivets all,
But I'll be master of it. Wilt thou not, beast,
    abide?   30
Why, then fly on, I'll hunt thee for thy hide.
                            [*Exeunt.*

[SCENE VII. *Another part of the plains.*]

Enter ACHILLES, *with* Myrmidons.

Achil. Come here about me, you my Myrmidons:
Mark what I say. Attend me where I wheel;
Strike not a stroke, but keep yourselves in breath;
And when I have the bloody Hector found,
Empale him with your weapons round about,   5
In fellest manner execute your [aims].
Follow me, sirs, and my proceedings eye;
It is decreed Hector the great must die.   [*Exeunt.*

Enter MENELAUS *and* PARIS [*fighting: then*]
        THERSITES.

Ther. The cuckold and the cuckold-maker are   9
at it. Now, bull! now, dog! 'Loo, Paris, 'loo!
Now my double-henn'd sparrow! 'Loo, Paris, 'loo!
The bull has the game; ware horns, ho!   12
               [*Exeunt Paris and Menelaus.*

Enter Bastard [MARGARELON].

Mar. Turn, slave, and fight.
Ther. What are thou?
Mar. A bastard son of Priam's.   15
Ther. I am a bastard too; I love bastards. I
am a bastard begot, bastard instructed, bastard in
mind, bastard in valour, in everything illegitimate.
One bear will not bite another, and wherefore should
one bastard? Take heed, the quarrel's most 20
ominous to us. If the son of a whore fight for a
whore, he tempts judgement. Farewell, bastard.
Mar. The devil take thee, coward!   [*Exeunt.*

[SCENE VIII. *Another part of the plains.*]

Enter HECTOR.

Hect. Most putrefied core, so fair without,
Thy goodly armour thus hath cost thy life.
Now is my day's work done; I'll take good breath.
Rest, sword; thou hast thy fill of blood and death.
    [*Puts off his helmet and hangs his shield
    behind him.*]

Enter ACHILLES *and* Myrmidons.

 Achil. Look, Hector, how the sun begins to set,   5
How ugly night comes breathing at his heels.

Even with the vail and darking of the sun,
To close the day up, Hector's life is done.
   Hect. I am unarm'd; forego this vantage, Greek.
   Achil. Strike, fellows, strike; this is the man
    I seek.   [*Hector falls.*]   10
So, Ilion, fall thou! Now, Troy, sink down!
Here lies thy heart, thy sinews, and thy bone.
On, Myrmidons, and cry you all amain,
"Achilles hath the mighty Hector slain!"
              [*A retreat [sounded*].
Hark! a retreat upon our Grecian part.   15
   Myr. The Troyan trumpets sound the like, my
    lord.
   Achil. The dragon wing of night o'erspreads the
    earth,
And, stickler-like, the armies separates.
My half-supp'd sword, that frankly would have
    fed,
Pleas'd with this dainty [bait], thus goes to bed.
              [*Sheathes his sword.*]
Come, tie his body to my horse's tail;   21
Along the field I will the Troyan trail.   [*Exeunt.*

[SCENE IX. *Another part of the plains.*]
Sound retreat. Shout.

Enter AGAMEMNON, AJAX, MENELAUS, NESTOR,
   DIOMEDES, *and the rest, marching.*

 Agam. Hark! hark! what shout is that?
 Nest. Peace, drums!
 Soldiers. (*Within.*) Achilles! Achilles! Hector's
   slain! Achilles!
 Dio. The bruit is, Hector's slain, and by Achilles.
 Ajax. If it be so, yet bragless let it be;   5
Great Hector was a man as good as he.
 Agam. March patiently along; let one be sent
To pray Achilles see us at our tent.
If in his death the gods have us befriended,
Great Troy is ours, and our sharp wars are ended.   10
                       [*Exeunt.*

[SCENE X. *Another part of the plains.*]

Enter ÆNEAS, PARIS, ANTENOR, *and* DEIPHOBUS.

 Æne. Stand, ho! yet are we masters of the
   field.
Never go home; here starve we out the night.

Enter TROILUS.

 Tro. Hector is slain.
 All.   Hector! the gods forbid!

---

29. **frush:** smash.
  Sc. vii, 5. **Empale:** hedge in. 6. **[aims]** (Capell). *armes* Q; *arme* F. 11. **double-henn'd:** having two wives. Inappro-
priate for Paris, but Helen was doubly a wife.
  Sc. viii, 7. **vail:** setting. 18. **stickler-like:** like the umpire of a duel. 19. **frankly:** freely. 20. **[bait]** Q. *bed* F.
  Sc. ix, 4. **bruit:** rumor.

Tro. He's dead; and at the murderer's horse's
    tail,   4
In beastly sort, dragg'd through the shameful
    field.
Frown on, you heavens, effect your rage with
    speed!
Sit, gods, upon your thrones, and smile at Troy!
I say, at once let your brief plagues be mercy,
And linger not our sure destructions on!   9
   Æne. My lord, you do discomfort all the host.
   Tro. You understand me not that tell me so.
I do not speak of flight, of fear, of death,
But dare all imminence that gods and men
Address their dangers in.   Hector is gone.
Who shall tell Priam so, or Hecuba?   15
Let him that will a screech-owl aye be call'd
Go in to Troy and say there, "Hector's dead!"
There is a word will Priam turn to stone,
Make wells and Niobes of the maids and wives,
Cold statues of the youth, and, in a word,   20
Scare Troy out of itself.   But, march away.
Hector is dead; there is no more to say.
Stay yet.   You vile abominable tents,
Thus proudly pight upon our Phrygian plains,
Let Titan rise as early as he dare.   25
I'll through and through you! and, thou great-siz'd
    coward,
No space of earth shall sunder our two hates.
I'll haunt thee like a wicked conscience still,
That mouldeth goblins swift as frenzy's thoughts.
Strike a free march to Troy.   With comfort go;   30
Hope of revenge shall hide our inward woe.
                    [Exeunt Æneas and Trojans.]

      [As TROILUS *is going out]* enter *[from the other
             side]* PANDARUS.

   Pan. But hear you, hear you!
   Tro. Hence, broker! lackey! Ignomy and shame
Pursue thy life, and live aye with thy name!   34
                                  [Exit.
   Pan. A goodly med'cine for mine aching bones!
O world! world! world! thus is the poor agent
despis'd! O [traders] and bawds, how earnestly
are you set a-work, and how ill requited! Why
should our endeavour be so desir'd and the performance so loath'd? What verse for it? What
instance for it? Let me see: 41

"Full merrily the humble-bee doth sing,
   Till he hath lost his honey and his sting;
And being once subdu'd in armed tail,
   Sweet honey and sweet notes together fail."   45

Good traders in the flesh, set this in your painted
cloths:
   As many as be here of Pandar's hall,
   Your eyes, half out, weep out at Pandar's fall;
   Or if you cannot weep, yet give some groans,   50
   Though not for me, yet for your aching bones.
   Brethren and sisters of the hold-door trade,
   Some two months hence my will shall here be
      made.
It should be now, but that my fear is this,
Some galled goose of Winchester would hiss.   55
Till then I'll sweat and seek about for eases,
And at that time bequeath you my diseases.
                                  [Exit.

   Sc. x, 13–14. **all...in:** any imminent dangers that gods and men prepare. 19. **Niobes.** Niobe, weeping for her slain children, was turned to stone, yet still wept. 24. **pight:** pitched. 37. **[traders]** (Craig conj.). *traitors* QF. 46. **painted cloths:** tapestries. 55. **galled goose:** irritated prostitute. Prior to the Reformation, the brothels in Southwark were licensed by the Bishops of Winchester.

All's Well That Ends Well

FOR THE TEXT of this play one must rely upon the First Folio. The lack of an early Quarto is the more to be regretted, since the corruptions of the existing text are unusually frequent and baffling.

There is no certain external evidence of date. Critics have suggested various allusions and associations, but none is convincing. "John Drum's entertainment," which is prophesied for Parolles (III.vi.40), is more likely a proverbial expression for a beating than a glance at Marston's *Jack Drum's Entertainment* (1600). Lafeu's comment, "*Lustig*, as the Dutchman says" (II.iii.47), may echo the repeated expletive of Jacob van Smelt in *The Weakest Goeth to the Wall* (1600), though the reference may be general. In Meres's famous list is mentioned a play called *Love's Labour's Won*, which is not identified and which may have been the present play or an earlier version of it. This identification would place the date of *All's Well* before 1598.

The internal evidence is elusive and treacherous. To be sure, the title of the phantom play fits *All's Well* better than it fits any other, the only serious rival being *The Taming of the Shrew*, in which, though Petruchio wins Katherine as the result of his labors, the labors are hardly to be called love's (unless, perhaps, ironically). Moreover, Helena's words (V.iii.315), "Will you be mine, now you are doubly won?" may echo the old title, just as those of the King (V.iii.333, 336), "All yet seems well; and if it end so meet," and "All is well ended, if this suit be won," may suggest that the title was originally a double one. Yet if *All's Well* is *Love's Labour's Won*, one would expect more suggestive correspondences with *Love's Labour's Lost* than are to be found.

Quite apart from the matter of *Love's Labour's Won*, critics have seen in *All's Well* evidence of early work. The large number of rimed couplets (e.g., I.i.231–44; II.i.133–213; II.iii.78–110 and 132–51) has been taken by many to indicate an early version which Shakespeare sometime re-

worked. Yet upon scrutiny these couplets, with the facility and variety of pauses which they exhibit, do not sort so ill with the compact, pregnant blank verse of the play's best passages, or argue a hand so little practiced, as some scholars have believed. Why Shakespeare chose to employ the couplet so extensively is another matter; to accent a particular sentiment or mood, perhaps. In any event, the rimed passages by themselves hardly warrant assuming an earlier form of the play. There is, however, some bibliographical evidence more compelling. The Folio text contains telltale signs of patchwork, the most palpable of which appears at I.i.179, where occurs a broken line followed by a passage of verse which bears no relation to the preceding discourse. At V.iii.158 the Folio gives Parolles an entrance along with the Widow and Diana, though he is not supposed to be present until line 231, where his arrival is properly noted. Similarly at V.iii.199–201 Diana is credited with a statement she has not made. In the stage direction at III.v a character named Violenta is given an entrance, though she appears nowhere else and does not say a word. The Folio text shows considerable variation in speech headings. The amount of this technical evidence makes it likely that the surviving text of *All's Well* represents a recasting by Shakespeare, probably around 1602, of a play written considerably earlier. The earlier version may possibly have had *Love's Labour's Won* as title or sub-title.

Shakespeare's source for the main plot of *All's Well* is the story of Giletta of Narbon, a translation in William Painter's *Palace of Pleasure* (1566) of the ninth Novel of the third day in Boccaccio's *Decameron*. In this story, Giletta (Helena) is rich, is living with her own kinsfolk following her father's death, and has declined many husbands of their choosing. When, after she has cured the King, Giletta chooses Beltramo (Bertram) for her husband, he is not present, but has to be summoned and told. Cast off by Beltramo, Giletta, assuming her privilege as his lawful wife, goes back to Rossiglione, where she is "received of all his subjectes for their ladie." She wins their devotion by her careful repair of Beltramo's estate, which is grossly run down, and then, since Beltramo does not return, sends to him, saying that if he is staying away because of her, she, "to doe hym pleasure," will depart. It is in reply to this message that Beltramo writes the "churlish" letter which in the play he despatches on his own initiative. Giletta takes formal leave of her people, telling them that "she was lothe the counte for her sake should dwell in perpetuall exile: therefore she determined to spend the rest of her tyme in pilgrimages and devocion, for preservacion of her soul." In the story, the original of Diana (who is not named) disappears from the action after assisting Giletta to become the "mistress" of Beltramo. Giletta remains in Florence until she has borne twin boys. In the dénouement at Rossiglione, Giletta appears before Beltramo when he is giving a great banquet, entering "in her pilgrim's weeds ... with her twoo soones in her arms." Beltramo, amazed, "knewe the rynge and the children also, thei were so like hym." The King is not present; there has been no suggestion of a second marriage, nor is there anything about a second ring. The Countess, Lafeu, Parolles, and the clown are all added by Shakespeare.

In judging a play like *All's Well* it is particularly important to try to see, as far as possible, how it would affect Elizabethans, who would view it in the light of traditions and conceptions quite different from ours. It has been shown that the stratagem of Helena for winning the love of Bertram, which is now generally found to be repellent, is a central device in a plot widespread in popular literature. In these tales a wife is deserted by a capricious husband, who places upon her, perhaps among other tasks, the necessity of getting a child by him before he will consent to return to her; the lady, by some clever ruse, succeeds in fulfilling the condition imposed. Always the woman's action is set forth as honorable, and she wins back her husband by impressing him with this proof of her courage and her love. Thus it appears that Shakespeare's contemporaries would never have regarded the action of Helena as anything but an admirable proof of her perfect integrity and fidelity.

The man of Helena's choice is not a pleasant fellow, and Helena's taste has been impugned for desiring him. The best thing that can be said for him is that Helena does desire him. It is true that at first some sympathy may be due him, but it is quickly wiped out. If one forget one's feeling for Helena, for whom affection is enlisted from the outset, one can understand Bertram's irritation at having thrust upon him a woman whom he does not care for, even though he has known her from childhood, and who is his social inferior, just when an opportunity to realize his ambition to distinguish himself as a courtier and a soldier lies before him. Almost immediately, however, his cynical acquiescence even while he resolves to have none of her repels us, just as his heartless ultimatum soon to follow does even more. To be sure, the husbands in the traditional versions just discussed were cruel, but Bertram, though true to type, when vitalized by a Shakespeare becomes peculiarly disagreeable. It would seem, indeed, that Shakespeare deliberately sought to make Bertram as unsympathetic as possible. He appears to be only a vain, obstinate, mean, and blindly wilful boy. His false scale of values and his stubborn pride in his own judgment are further enhanced by his intimacy with Parolles, whom everyone except Bertram sees for the humbug he is. But generally when Shakespeare depreciates a hero, he subtly recovers at least some of our respect for him before the end. In the case of Bertram, however, he does not; Bertram remains a cad till the very last, boggling and putting off Diana and the King with lies, until Helena is brought in to resolve all difficulties. In partial extenuation it may be argued that Shakespeare was sacrificing everything in the final scene for the sake of a complicated dénouement. In saying this, one does not forget the happy ending necessitated by the traditional story and the type of comedy; the point is simply that Shakespeare renders it less plausible, or acceptable, than with his genius for transmuting traditional material he is accustomed to do. By his deliberate degradation of Bertram in order to throw our sympathy fully upon Helena, he comes perilously near to overshooting the mark.

ALL'S WELL THAT ENDS WELL

ACT I

SCENE I. [*Rousillon. The Count's palace.*]

Enter young BERTRAM, *Count of Rousillon, his mother* [*the* COUNTESS OF ROUSILLON], HELENA, *and* LORD LAFEU, *all in black.*

Count. In delivering my son from me, I bury a second husband.

Ber. And I in going, madam, weep o'er my father's death anew; but I must attend his Majesty's command, to whom I am now in ward, evermore in subjection.   6

Laf. You shall find of the King a husband, madam; you, sir, a father. He that so generally is at all times good must of necessity hold his virtue to you, whose worthiness would stir it up where it wanted rather than lack it where there is such abundance.   12

Count. What hope is there of his Majesty's amendment?

Laf. He hath abandon'd his physicians, madam, under whose practices he hath persecuted time with hope, and finds no other advantage in the process but only the losing of hope by time.   18

Count. This young gentlewoman had a father,—

O, that "had"! how sad a passage 'tis! — whose skill was almost as great as his honesty; had it stretch'd so far, would have made nature immortal, and death should have play for lack of work. Would, for the King's sake, he were living! I think it would be the death of the King's disease.   26

Laf. How call'd you the man you speak of, madam?

Count. He was famous, sir, in his profession, and it was his great right to be so,—Gerard de Narbon.

Laf. He was excellent indeed, madam. The   32 King very lately spoke of him admiringly and mourningly. He was skilful enough to have liv'd still, if knowledge could be set up against mortality.   36

Ber. What is it, my good lord, the King languishes of?

Laf. A fistula, my lord.

Ber. I heard not of it before.   40

Laf. I would it were not notorious. Was this gentlewoman the daughter of Gerard de Narbon?

Count. His sole child, my lord, and bequeathed to my overlooking. I have those hopes of her   45 good that her education promises. Her dispositions she inherits, which makes fair gifts fairer; for where an unclean mind carries virtuous quali-

Act I, sc. i, 9. **hold:** continue. 11. **wanted:** was lacking. 16. **persecuted...hope:** persisted in hoping. 20. **passage:** past tense. 23. **play:** playtime. 39. **fistula:** ulcer. 48. **virtuous qualities:** abilities.

ties, there commendations go with pity: they are virtues and traitors too. In her they are the 50 better for their simpleness: she derives her honesty and achieves her goodness.

Laf. Your commendations, madam, get from her tears. 54

Count. 'Tis the best brine a maiden can season her praise in. The remembrance of her father never approaches her heart but the tyranny of her sorrows takes all livelihood from her cheek. No more of this, Helena; go to, no more, lest it be rather thought you affect a sorrow than to have — 61

Hel. I do affect a sorrow indeed, but I have it too.

Laf. Moderate lamentation is the right of the dead, excessive grief the enemy to the living. 65

Count. If the living be enemy to the grief, the excess makes it soon mortal.

Ber. Madam, I desire your holy wishes.

Laf. How understand we that?

Count. Be thou blest, Bertram, and succeed thy father 70 In manners, as in shape! Thy blood and virtue Contend for empire in thee, and thy goodness Share with thy birthright! Love all, trust a few, Do wrong to none. Be able for thine enemy Rather in power than use, and keep thy friend 75 Under thy own life's key. Be check'd for silence, But never tax'd for speech. What Heaven more will That thee may furnish and my prayers pluck down Fall on thy head! Farewell! My lord, 'Tis an unseason'd courtier; good my lord, 80 Advise him.

Laf.   He cannot want the best That shall attend his love.

Count. Heaven bless him! Farewell, Bertram.

Ber. The best wishes that can be forg'd in your thoughts be servants to you! [*Exit Countess.*] [*To Helena.*] Be comfortable to my mother, your mistress, and make much of her. 87

Laf. Farewell, pretty lady. You must hold the credit of your father. [*Exeunt Bertram and Lafeu.*]

Hel. O, were that all! I think not on my father, And these great tears grace his remembrance more Than those I shed for him. What was he like? 92 I have forgot him. My imagination Carries no favour in't but Bertram's. I am undone! There is no living, none, 95

If Bertram be away. 'Twere all one That I should love a bright particular star And think to wed it, he is so above me. In his bright radiance and collateral light Must I be comforted, not in his sphere. 100 Th' ambition in my love thus plagues itself. The hind that would be mated by the lion Must die for love. 'Twas pretty, though a plague, To see him every hour; to sit and draw His arched brows, his hawking eye, his curls, 105 In our heart's table; heart too capable Of every line and trick of his sweet favour. But now he's gone, and my idolatrous fancy Must sanctify his reliques. Who comes here?

Enter PAROLLES.

[*Aside.*] One that goes with him. I love him for his sake; 110 And yet I know him a notorious liar, Think him a great way fool, solely a coward; Yet these fix'd evils sit so fit in him, That they take place when virtue's steely bones Looks bleak i' th' cold wind. Withal, full oft we see 115 Cold wisdom waiting on superfluous folly.

Par. Save you, fair queen!

Hel. And you, monarch!

Par. No.

Hel. And no. 120

Par. Are you meditating on virginity?

Hel. Ay. You have some stain of soldier in you; let me ask you a question. Man is enemy to virginity; how may we barricado it against him?

Par. Keep him out. 125

Hel. But he assails; and our virginity, though valiant, in the defence yet is weak. Unfold to us some warlike resistance.

Par. There is none. Man, setting down before you, will undermine you and blow you up. 130

Hel. Bless our poor virginity from underminers and blowers up! Is there no military policy, how virgins might blow up men?

Par. Virginity being blown down, man will quicklier be blown up. Marry, in blowing him 135 down again, with the breach yourselves made, you lose your city. It is not politic in the commonwealth of nature to preserve virginity. Loss of virginity is rational increase, and there was never virgin [got] till virginity was first lost. That 140

---

62. **I ... too.** Helena means that she assumes sorrow for her father, but feels a real sorrow at Bertram's departure. 66–67. **If ... mortal:** i.e., if a person honestly strives against grief, grief will wear itself out. 69. **How ... that?** Lafeu's question is probably inspired not by what Bertram says but by the preceding speech of the Countess, which, perhaps, it ought to follow. 71. **blood:** inheritance. 73. **Share with:** be equal to. 74. **Be able for:** be a match for. 75. **use:** practice. 75–76. **keep ... key:** guard thy friend with thy life. 76. **check'd:** reproved. 77. **tax'd:** blamed. 81–82. **He ... love:** he cannot lack the best (advice) because of the love people bear him. 85. **be ... you:** i.e., be fulfilled. 94. **favour:** image, countenance. 99. **collateral:** from another sphere than her own. 106. **table:** tablet, record. **capable Of:** susceptible to. 112. **solely:** entirely. 114. **place:** precedence. 116. **Cold:** i.e., bare. **superfluous:** luxurious. 122. **stain:** tincture, touch. 129. **setting down:** sitting down, laying siege. 140. [got] F2. *goe* F1.

you were made of is metal to make virgins. Virginity by being once lost may be ten times found; by being ever kept, it is ever lost. 'Tis too cold a companion; away with't!

Hel. I will stand for't a little, though therefore I die a virgin.   146

Par. There's little can be said in't; 'tis against the rule of nature. To speak on the part of virginity is to accuse your mothers, which is most infallible disobedience. He that hangs himself is 150 a virgin. Virginity murders itself, and should be buried in highways out of all sanctified limit, as a desperate offendress against nature. Virginity breeds mites, much like a cheese; consumes itself to the very paring, and so dies with feeding his 155 own stomach. Besides, virginity is peevish, proud, idle, made of self-love, which is the most inhibited sin in the canon. Keep it not; you cannot choose but lose by't. Out with't! Within [the] year it will make itself two, which is a goodly increase, 160 and the principal itself not much the worse. Away with't!

Hel. How might one do, sir, to lose it to her own liking?   164

Par. Let me see. Marry, ill, to like him that ne'er it likes. 'Tis a commodity will lose the gloss with lying; the longer kept, the less worth. Off with't while't is vendible; answer the time of request. Virginity, like an old courtier, wears her cap out of fashion; richly suited, but unsuit- 170 able, — just like the brooch and the tooth-pick, which wear not now. Your date is better in your pie and your porridge than in your cheek; and your virginity, your old virginity, is like one of our French wither'd pears, it looks ill, it eats drily; 175 marry, 'tis a wither'd pear; it was formerly better; marry, yet 'tis a wither'd pear. Will you anything with it?

Hel. Not my virginity yet . . .
There shall your master have a thousand loves,
A mother and a mistress and a friend,   181
A phœnix, captain, and an enemy,
A guide, a goddess, and a sovereign,
A counsellor, a traitress, and a dear:
His humble ambition, proud humility,   185
His jarring concord, and his discord dulcet,
His faith, his sweet disaster; with a world

Of pretty, fond, adoptious christendoms,
That blinking Cupid gossips. Now shall he —
I know not what he shall. God send him well! 190
The court's a learning place, and he is one —

Par. What one, i' faith?

Hel. That I wish well. 'Tis pity —

Par. What's pity?

Hel. That wishing well had not a body in't, 195
Which might be felt; that we, the poorer born,
Whose baser stars do shut us up in wishes,
Might with effects of them follow our friends,
And show what we alone must think, which never
Returns us thanks.   200

Enter PAGE.

Page. Monsieur Parolles, my lord calls for you.
     [*Exit.*]

Par. Little Helen, farewell. If I can remember thee, I will think of thee at court.

Hel. Monsieur Parolles, you were born under a charitable star.   205

Par. Under Mars, I.

Hel. I especially think, under Mars.

Par. Why under Mars?

Hel. The wars hath so kept you under that you must needs be born under Mars.   210

Par. When he was predominant.

Hel. When he was retrograde, I think, rather.

Par. Why think you so?

Hel. You go so much backward when you fight.

Par. That's for advantage.   215

Hel. So is running away, when fear proposes the safety. But the composition that your valour and fear makes in you is a virtue of a good wing, and I like the wear well.   219

Par. I am so full of businesses, I cannot answer thee acutely. I will return perfect courtier; in the which, my instruction shall serve to naturalize thee, so thou wilt be capable of a courtier's counsel and understand what advice shall thrust upon thee; else thou diest in thine unthankfulness, and 225 thine ignorance makes thee away. Farewell! When thou hast leisure, say thy prayers; when thou hast none, remember thy friends. Get thee a good husband, and use him as he uses thee. So, farewell. 230
     [*Exit.*]

Hel. Our remedies oft in ourselves do lie,

152. **sanctified limit:** consecrated ground, in which suicides could not be buried.   157. **inhibited:** forbidden.   159. **[the]** Edd.   *two* F.   165. **that . . . likes:** who cares not for it (virginity).   170. **suited:** ornamented.   172. **wear not:** are not fashionable.   172. **date.** A pun on (1) the fruit, (2) time of life.   179. **not:** i.e., not with.   179–80. **yet . . . There.** The obvious break indicates a loss here, very likely of several lines.   "There" refers to the court, as l. 191 finally reveals. In ll. 181–89 Helena is enumerating the epithets by which Bertram will address sweethearts at court.   188. **adoptious christendoms:** adopted names.   189. **gossips:** is godfather to.   197. **shut . . . wishes:** confine us to mere wishes.   198–99. **Might . . . think:** could realize our wishes for our friends and perform what we can only think.   211. **predominant:** in the ascendant and thus influential (astrological).   212. **retrograde:** descending.   218. **of . . . wing:** capable of long flight (a term from falconry, with punning reference to cowardly flight).   219. **wear:** fashion.   222. **naturalize:** familiarize.   226. **makes . . . away:** destroys thee.   227–28. **when . . . friends.** Parolles speaks cynically, alluding to courtiers who remember their friends only when they are too busy to help them.

Which we ascribe to heaven. The fated sky
Gives us free scope, only doth backward pull
Our slow designs when we ourselves are dull.
What power is it which mounts my love so high, 235
That makes me see, and cannot feed mine eye?
The mightiest space in fortune nature brings
To join like likes and kiss like native things.
Impossible be strange attempts to those 239
That weigh their pains in sense and do suppose
What hath been cannot be. Who ever strove
To show her merit, that did miss her love?
The King's disease — my project may deceive me,
But my intents are fix'd and will not leave me.

[Exit.

[SCENE II. *Paris. The King's palace.*]

Flourish of cornets. Enter the KING OF FRANCE,
with letters [LORDS] *and divers attendants.*

King. The Florentines and Senoys are by th'
ears,
Have fought with equal fortune, and continue
A braving war.
    1. Lord.   So 'tis reported, sir.
King. Nay, 'tis most credible. We here receive it
A certainty, vouch'd from our cousin Austria, 5
With caution that the Florentine will move us
For speedy aid; wherein our dearest friend
Prejudicates the business, and would seem
To have us make denial.
    1. Lord.   His love and wisdom,
Approv'd so to your Majesty, may plead 10
For amplest credence.
    King.   He hath arm'd our answer,
And Florence is denied before he comes.
Yet, for our gentlemen that mean to see
The Tuscan service, freely have they leave
To stand on either part.
    2. Lord.   It well may serve 15
A nursery to our gentry, who are sick
For breathing and exploit.
    King.   What's he comes here?

Enter BERTRAM, LAFEU, *and* PAROLLES.

    1. Lord. It is the Count [Rousillon], my good
lord,
Young Bertram.

King. Youth, thou bear'st thy father's face.
Frank nature, rather curious than in haste, 20
Hath well compos'd thee. Thy father's moral parts
Mayst thou inherit too! Welcome to Paris.
    Ber. My thanks and duty are your Majesty's.
    King. I would I had that corporal soundness now
As when thy father and myself in friendship 25
First tried our soldiership! He did look far
Into the service of the time, and was
Discipled of the bravest. He lasted long;
But on us both did haggish age steal on
And wore us out of act. It much repairs me 30
To talk of your good father. In his youth
He had the wit which I can well observe
To-day in our young lords; but they may jest
Till their own scorn return to them unnoted
Ere they can hide their levity in honour 35
So like a courtier. Contempt nor bitterness
Were in his pride or sharpness; if they were,
His equal had awak'd them, and his honour,
Clock to itself, knew the true minute when
Exception bid him speak, and at this time 40
His tongue obey'd his hand. Who were below him
He us'd as creatures of another place,
And bow'd his eminent top to their low ranks,
Making them proud of his humility,
In their poor praise he humbled. Such a man 45
Might be a copy to these younger times;
Which, followed well, would demonstrate them now
But goers backward.
    Ber.   His good remembrance, sir,
Lies richer in your thoughts than on his tomb.
So in approof lives not his epitaph 50
As in your royal speech.
    King. Would I were with him! He would always
    say —
Methinks I hear him now! His plausive words
He scatter'd not in ears, but grafted them,
To grow there and to bear, — "Let me not live," —
[Thus] his good melancholy oft began, 56
On the catastrophe and heel of pastime,
When it was out, — "Let me not live," quoth he,
"After my flame lacks oil, to be the snuff
Of younger spirits, whose apprehensive senses 60
All but new things disdain; whose judgements are
Mere fathers of their garments; whose constancies
Expire before their fashions." This he wish'd;

I after him do after him wish too,
Since I nor wax nor honey can bring home,   65
I quickly were dissolved from my hive,
To give some labourers room.
    2. Lord.   You're loved, sir;
They that least lend it you shall lack you first.
    King. I fill a place, I know't. How long is't,
        Count,
Since the physician at your father's died?   70
He was much fam'd.
    Ber.   Some six months since, my lord.
    King. If he were living, I would try him yet.
Lend me an arm; the rest have worn me out
With several applications. Nature and sickness
Debate it at their leisure. Welcome, Count;   75
My son's no dearer.
    Ber.   Thank your Majesty.
                      [*Exeunt. Flourish.*

   [SCENE III. *Rousillon. The Count's palace.*]

    Enter COUNTESS, STEWARD, *and* CLOWN.

    Count. I will now hear. What say you of this
gentlewoman?
    Stew. Madam, the care I have had to even your
content, I wish might be found in the calendar of
my past endeavours; for then we wound our modesty and make foul the clearness of our deservings,
when of ourselves we publish them.   7
    Count. What does this knave here? Get you
gone, sirrah. The complaints I have heard of you
I do not all believe. 'Tis my slowness that I do
not, for I know you lack not folly to commit them,
and have ability enough to make such knaveries
yours.   13
    Clo. 'Tis not unknown to you, madam, I am a
poor fellow.
    Count. Well, sir.   16
    Clo. No, madam, 'tis not so well that I am poor,
though many of the rich are damn'd; but, if I may
have your ladyship's good will to go to the world,
Isbel the woman and [I] will do as we may.   21
    Count. Wilt thou needs be a beggar?
    Clo. I do beg your good will in this case.
    Count. In what case?   24
    Clo. In Isbel's case and mine own. Service is
no heritage; and I think I shall never have the
blessing of God till I have issue o' my body; for
they say barnes are blessings.
    Count. Tell me thy reason why thou wilt marry.
    Clo. My poor body, madam, requires it. I   30

am driven on by the flesh; and he must needs go
that the devil drives.
    Count. Is this all your worship's reason?
    Clo. Faith, madam, I have other holy reasons,
such as they are.   35
    Count. May the world know them?
    Clo. I have been, madam, a wicked creature, as
you and all flesh and blood are; and, indeed, I do
marry that I may repent.
    Count. Thy marriage, sooner than thy wicked-
ness.   41
    Clo. I am out o' friends, madam; and I hope to
have friends for my wife's sake.
    Count. Such friends are thine enemies, knave.   44
    Clo. Y'are shallow, madam, in great friends;
for the knaves come to do that for me which I am
aweary of. He that ears my land spares my team
and gives me leave to in the crop. If I be his cuckold, he's my drudge. He that comforts my wife is
the cherisher of my flesh and blood; he that   50
cherishes my flesh and blood loves my flesh and
blood; he that loves my flesh and blood is my friend;
ergo, he that kisses my wife is my friend. If men
could be contented to be what they are, there were
no fear in marriage; for young Charbon the   55
puritan and old Poysam the papist, howsome'er
their hearts are sever'd in religion, their heads are
both one; they may joul horns together, like any
deer i' th' herd.
    Count. Wilt thou ever be a foul-mouth'd and
calumnious knave?   61
    Clo. A prophet I, madam; and I speak the truth
the next way:

    "For I the ballad will repeat,
        Which men full true shall find: 65
    Your marriage comes by destiny,
        Your cuckoo sings by kind."

    Count. Get you gone, sir; I'll talk with you
more anon.
    Stew. May it please you, madam, that he bid
Helen come to you. Of her I am to speak.   71
    Count. Sirrah, tell my gentlewoman I would
speak with her; Helen, I mean.
    Clo. [*Sings.*]

    "Was this fair face the cause, quoth she,
        Why the Grecians sacked Troy?   75
    Fond done, done fond, . . .
        Was this King Priam's joy?

---

66. **dissolved:** freed. 68. **lend it you:** i.e., give you love. 74. **several applications:** various treatments.
    Sc. iii, 3. **even . . . content:** meet your desires. 4. **calendar:** record. 20. **go . . . world:** marry. 21. **and [I] will** F₂. *and
w will* F₁. 26. **is no heritage:** i.e., brings no blessing. 28. **barnes:** children (bairns). 45. **Y'are shallow:** you don't know
much. **in:** about. 47. **ears:** plows. 48. **in:** gather. 55–56. **Charbon . . . Poysam.** These names are perhaps corrupt
versions of *Chairbonne* (good flesh) and *Poisson* (fish) respectively, the latter suggesting the Papist's fasting and the former,
the Puritan's scorn for such discipline. 58. **joul:** knock. A reference to the horns of the cuckold. 63. **next:** nearest.
67. **kind:** nature. 76–77. **Fond . . . joy.** One line in F. A few words are clearly lacking.

With that she sighed as she stood,
With that she sighed as she stood,
   And gave this sentence then;   80
Among nine bad if one be good,
Among nine bad if one be good,
   There's yet one good in ten."

Count. What, one good in ten? You corrupt
the song, sirrah.   85
Clo. One good woman in ten, madam; which is
a purifying o' th' song. Would God would serve
the world so all the year! We'd find no fault
with the tithe-woman, if I were the parson. One
in ten, quoth 'a! An we might have a good 90
woman born but [or] every blazing star or at an
earthquake, 'twould mend the lottery well; a man
may draw his heart out, ere 'a pluck one.
Count. You'll be gone, sir knave, and do as I
command you.   95
Clo. That man should be at woman's command,
and yet no hurt done! Though honesty be no
puritan, yet it will do no hurt; it will wear the surplice of humility over the black gown of a big heart.
I am going, forsooth. The business is for Helen to
come hither.   [*Exit.* 101
Count. Well, now.
Stew. I know, madam, you love your gentlewoman entirely.   104
Count. Faith, I do. Her father bequeath'd her
to me; and she herself, without other advantage,
may lawfully make title to as much love as she
finds. There is more owing her than is paid, and
more shall be paid her than she'll demand.   109
Stew. Madam, I was very late more near her
than I think she wish'd me. Alone she was, and
did communicate to herself her own words to her
own ears: she thought, I dare vow for her, they
touch'd not any stranger sense. Her matter was,
she lov'd your son. Fortune, she said, was no 115
goddess, that had put such difference betwixt their
two estates; Love no god, that would not extend
his might, only where qualities were level; [Dian
no] queen of virgins, that would suffer her poor
knight surpris'd, without rescue in the first 120
assault or ransom afterward. This she deliver'd
in the most bitter touch of sorrow that e'er I heard
virgin exclaim in; which I held my duty speedily to
acquaint you withal, sithence, in the loss that may
happen, it concerns you something to know it. 126
Count. You have discharg'd this honestly; keep
it to yourself. Many likelihoods inform'd me of

this before, which hung so tottering in the balance
that I could neither believe nor misdoubt. Pray
you, leave me. Stall this in your bosom; and I
thank you for your honest care. I will speak with
you further anon.   [*Exit Steward.* 133

Enter HELENA.
Even so it was with me when I was young.
  If ever we are nature's, these are ours. This
thorn   135
Doth to our rose of youth rightly belong;
  Our blood to us, this to our blood is born.
It is the show and seal of nature's truth,
Where love's strong passion is impress'd in youth.
By our remembrances of days foregone, 140
Such were our faults, or then we thought them
    none.
Her eye is sick on't; I observe her now.
  Hel. What is your pleasure, madam?
  Count.   You know, Helen,
I am a mother to you.
  Hel. Mine honourable mistress.
  Count.   Nay, a mother. 145
Why not a mother? When I said "a mother,"
Methought you saw a serpent. What's in
    "mother,"
That you start at it? I say, I am your mother;
And put you in the catalogue of those
That were enwombed mine. 'Tis often seen 150
Adoption strives with nature, and choice breeds
A native slip to us from foreign seeds.
You ne'er oppress'd me with a mother's groan,
Yet I express to you a mother's care.
God's mercy, maiden! does it curd thy blood 155
To say I am thy mother? What's the matter,
That this distempered messenger of wet,
The many-colour'd Iris, rounds thine eye?
Why? That you are my daughter?
  Hel.   That I am not.
  Count. I say, I am your mother.
  Hel.   Pardon, madam;
The Count Rousillon cannot be my brother. 161
I am from humble, he from honoured name;
No note upon my parents, his all noble.
My master, my dear lord he is; and I
His servant live, and will his vassal die. 165
He must not be my brother.
  Count.   Nor I your mother?
  Hel. You are my mother, madam; would you
    were, —
So that my lord your son were not my brother, —

91. [or] (Capell): before. *ore* F. blazing star: comet. 93. pluck: draw (as in a lottery). 97. honesty: chastity. 99.
surplice ... heart. The puritan clergy detested the surplice as an article of popery, preferring the black gown of Genevan
Calvinists. But since the law required the use of the surplice, they compromised by wearing it over the gown. big:
proud. 114. sense: i.e., ear. 118. qualities ... level: ranks were equal. [Dian no] (Theobald). Om. F. 120. surpris'd: to be caught unawares. 135. these: i.e., these passions. 142. on't: because of it. 152. slip: branch. The idea in
ll. 150–52 is that parents may love adopted children as dearly as their own. 158. Iris: rainbow. rounds: surrounds.
163. note: distinction. 168. So: provided.

Indeed my mother! Or were you both our mothers,
I care no more for than I do for heaven,   170
So I were not his sister. Can't no other,
But, I your daughter, he must be my brother?
   Count. Yes, Helen, you might be my daughter-
    in-law.
God shield you mean it not! daughter and mother
So strive upon your pulse. What, pale again? 175
My fear hath catch'd your fondness. Now I see
The myst'ry of your [loneliness], and find
Your salt tears' head. Now to all sense 'tis gross
You love my son. Invention is asham'd,
Against the proclamation of thy passion,   180
To say thou dost not: therefore tell me truly;
But tell me then, 'tis so; for, look, thy cheeks
Confess it, [th' one] to th' other; and thine eyes
See it so grossly shown in thy behaviours
That in their kind they speak it. Only sin   185
And hellish obstinacy tie thy tongue,
That truth should be suspected. Speak, is't so?
If it be so, you have wound a goodly clew;
If it be not, forswear't. Howe'er, I charge thee,
As heaven shall work in me for thine avail, 190
To tell me truly.
   Hel.   Good madam, pardon me!
   Count. Do you love my son?
   Hel.   Your pardon, noble mistress!
   Count. Love you my son?
   Hel.   Do not you love him, madam?
   Count. Go not about; my love hath in't a bond,
Whereof the world takes note. Come, come, dis-
    close   195
The state of your affection; for your passions
Have to the full appeach'd.
   Hel.   Then, I confess,
Here on my knee, before high heaven and you,
That before you, and next unto high heaven,
I love your son.   200
My friends were poor, but honest; so's my love.
Be not offended; for it hurts not him
That he is lov'd of me. I follow him not
By any token of presumptuous suit;
Nor would I have him till I do deserve him; 205
Yet never know how that desert should be.
I know I love in vain, strive against hope;
Yet in this captious and intenible sieve
I still pour in the waters of my love
And lack not to [lose] still. Thus, Indian-like, 210

Religious in mine error, I adore
The sun, that looks upon his worshipper,
But knows of him no more. My dearest madam,
Let not your hate encounter with my love
For loving where you do; but if yourself,   215
Whose aged honour cites a virtuous youth,
Did ever in so true a flame of liking
Wish chastely and love dearly, that your Dian
Was both herself and Love, O, then, give pity
To her, whose state is such that cannot choose 220
But lend and give where she is sure to lose;
That seeks not to find that her search implies,
But riddle-like lives sweetly where she dies!
   Count. Had you not lately an intent, — speak
    truly, —   224
To go to Paris?
   Hel.   Madam, I had.
   Count.   Wherefore? Tell true.
   Hel. I will tell truth; by grace itself I swear.
You know my father left me some prescriptions
Of rare and prov'd effects, such as his reading
And manifest experience had collected
For general sovereignty; and that he will'd me
In heedfull'st reservation to bestow them, 231
As [cures] whose faculties inclusive were
More than they were in note. Amongst the rest,
There is a remedy approv'd set down
To cure the desperate languishings whereof 235
The King is render'd lost.
   Count.   This was your motive
For Paris, was it? Speak.
   Hel. My lord your son made me to think of
    this,
Else Paris and the medicine and the King
Had from the conversation of my thoughts 240
Haply been absent then.
   Count.   But think you, Helen,
If you should tender your supposed aid,
He would receive it? He and his physicians
Are of a mind; he, that they cannot help him,
They, that they cannot help. How shall they credit
A poor unlearned virgin, when the schools, 246
Embowell'd of their doctrine, have left off
The danger to itself?
   Hel.   There's something in't
More than my father's skill, which was the greatest
Of his profession, that his good receipt 250
Shall for my legacy be sanctified

169–70. **Or . . . heaven.** Probably corrupt. No satisfactory emendation or explanation has been proposed. Cf. l. 199.
171. **Can't no other:** can't it be otherwise. 175. **strive upon:** affect. 177. **[loneliness]** (Theobald). *loveliness* F. 178.
head: source. **gross:** palpable. 179. **Invention is asham'd:** you are ashamed to lie. 183. **[th' one]** (Knight). *'ton tooth* F.
188. **clew:** tangle. 194. **Go not about:** don't evade the point. 197. **appeach'd:** informed against you. 208. **captious:**
capacious (ready to take). **intenible:** incapable of retaining. 210. **lack not:** have plenty, or, perhaps, cease not. **[lose]** F4.
loose F1. 218–19. **your . . . Love:** Diana and Venus were the same. 223. **riddle-like:** paradoxically. 229. **manifest:** well-
known. Perhaps we should read *manifold*. 230. **general sovereignty:** universal efficacy. 231. **heedfull'st reservation:**
utmost care. **bestow:** keep. 232. **[cures]** (Gould conj.). *notes* F. 233. **they . . . note:** was recognized. 236. **render'd:**
judged. 240–41. **Had . . . then:** had probably never entered my thoughts. 247. **Embowell'd:** exhausted. **doctrine:**
learning.

By th' luckiest stars in heaven; and, would your
  honour
But give me leave to try success, I'd venture
The well-lost life of mine on his Grace's cure
By such a day and hour.
  Count.   Dost thou believe't?
  Hel. Ay, madam, knowingly.   256
  Count. Why, Helen, thou shalt have my leave
  and love,
Means and attendants, and my loving greetings
To those of mine in court.   I'll stay at home
And pray God's blessing into thy attempt.   260
Be gone to-morrow; and be sure of this,
What I can help thee to thou shalt not miss.
                        [*Exeunt.*

ACT II

[SCENE I. *Paris. The King's palace.*]

Flourish of cornets. Enter the KING, *with divers
young* LORDS *taking leave for the Florentine war;*
BERTRAM *and* PAROLLES.

  King. Farewell, young lords! these warlike
  principles
Do not throw from you; and you, my lords, fare-
  well!
Share the advice betwixt you.   If both gain all,
The gift doth stretch itself as 'tis receiv'd,
And is enough for both.
  1. Lord.   'Tis our hope, sir,   5
After well ent'red soldiers, to return
And find your Grace in health.
  King. No, no, it cannot be; and yet my heart
Will not confess he owes the malady
That doth my life besiege.   Farewell, young lords!
Whether I live or die, be you the sons   11
Of worthy Frenchmen.   Let higher Italy, —
Those bated that inherit but the fall
Of the last monarchy, — see that you come
Not to woo honour, but to wed it.   When   15
The bravest questant shrinks, find what you seek,
That fame may cry you loud.   I say, farewell.
  2. Lord. Health, at your bidding, serve your
  Majesty!
  King. Those girls of Italy, take heed of them.
They say our French lack language to deny   20
If they demand.   Beware of being captives
Before you serve.
  Both.   Our hearts receive your warnings.
  King. Farewell.   Come hither to me.
                      [*Exit, attended.*]

  1. Lord. O my sweet lord, that you will stay
  behind us!
  Par. 'Tis not his fault, the spark.
  2. Lord.   O, 'tis brave wars! 25
  Par. Most admirable!   I have seen those wars.
  Ber. I am commanded here, and kept a coil with
"Too young" and "the next year" and "'tis too
  early."
  Par. An thy mind stand to't, boy, steal away
  bravely.
  Ber. I shall stay here the forehorse to a smock,
Creaking my shoes on the plain masonry,   31
Till honour be bought up and no sword worn
But one to dance with!   By heaven, I'll steal away.
  1. Lord. There's honour in the theft.
  Par.   Commit it, Count.
  2. Lord. I am your accessary; and so farewell. 35
  Ber. I grow to you, and our parting is a tortur'd
body.
  1. Lord. Farewell, captain.
  2. Lord. Sweet Monsieur Parolles!   39
  Par. Noble heroes, my sword and yours are kin.
Good sparks and lustrous, a word, good metals: you
shall find in the regiment of the Spinii one Captain
Spurio, [with his cicatrice, an] emblem of war, here
on his sinister cheek, — it was this very sword en-
trench'd it; — say to him, I live; and observe his
reports for me.   46
  1. Lord. We shall, noble captain.
                      [*Exeunt Lords.*]
  Par. Mars dote on you for his novices!   What
will ye do?

[*Re-enter the* KING.]

  Ber. Stay, the King!   50
  Par. [*To Ber.*] Use a more spacious ceremony to
the noble lords; you have restrain'd yourself within
the list of too cold an adieu.   Be more expressive
to them; for they wear themselves in the cap of the
time, there do muster true gait, eat, speak, and   55
move under the influence of the most receiv'd star;
and though the devil lead the measure, such are to
be followed.   After them, and take a more dilated
farewell.
  Ber. And I will do so.   60
  Par. Worthy fellows; and like to prove most
sinewy swordmen.
        [*Exeunt* [*Bertram and Parolles*].

Enter LAFEU.

  Laf. [*Kneeling.*] Pardon, my lord, for me and
  for my tidings.

Act II, sc. i, 6. **After . . . soldiers:** after being well initiated as soldiers.   9. **he owes:** it owns.   12. **higher Italy:** Italian
nobles, or Upper Italy.   13. **bated:** excepted.   16. **questant:** seeker.   27. **kept a coil:** fussed over.   30. **forehorse . . .
smock:** i.e., usher to a lady.   35. **accessary:** accomplice.   36. **a tortur'd body:** i.e., like dismemberment.   43. **[with . . . an]**
(Theobald).   *his sicatrice, with an* F.   **cicatrice:** scar.   44. **sinister:** left.   53. **list:** bounds.   54–55. **wear . . . time:** are
in the height of fashion.   55. **muster true gait:** show correct deportment.   56. **receiv'd star:** popular fashion.

King. I'll [fee] thee to stand up.

Laf. Then here's a man stands that has brought
    his pardon.   65
I would you had kneel'd, my lord, to ask me mercy,
And that at my bidding you could so stand up.

King. I would I had, so I had broke thy pate,
And ask'd thee mercy for't.

Laf. Good faith, across. But, my good lord,
    'tis thus: 70
Will you be cur'd of your infirmity?

King. No.

Laf. O, will you eat no grapes, my royal fox?
Yes, but you will my noble grapes, an if
My royal fox could reach them. I have seen a
    medicine   75
That's able to breathe life into a stone,
Quicken a rock, and make you dance canary
With spritely fire and motion; whose simple touch
Is powerful to araise King Pepin, nay,
To give great Charlemain a pen in's hand   80
And write to her a love-line.

King.   What her is this?

Laf. Why, Doctor She! My lord, there's one
    arriv'd,
If you will see her. Now, by my faith and honour,
If seriously I may convey my thoughts
In this my light deliverance, I have spoke   85
With one that, in her sex, her years, profession,
Wisdom, and constancy, hath amaz'd me more
Than I dare blame my weakness. Will you see
    her, —
For that is her demand, — and know her business?
That done, laugh well at me.

King.   Now, good Lafeu,
Bring in the admiration, that we with thee   91
May spend our wonder too, or take off thine
By wondering how thou took'st it.

Laf.   Nay, I'll fit you,
And not be all day neither.   [*Exit.*]

King. Thus he his special nothing ever pro-
    logues.   95

[*Re-enter* LAFEU.]

Laf. Nay, come your ways.

Enter HELENA.

King.   This haste hath wings indeed.

Laf. Nay, come your ways.
This is his Majesty; say your mind to him.
A traitor you do look like, but such traitors   99
His Majesty seldom fears. I am Cressid's uncle,

That dare leave two together; fare you well.
                        [*Exit.*

King. Now, fair one, does your business follow
    us?

Hel. Ay, my good lord.
Gerard de Narbon was my father;
In what he did profess, well found.

King.   I knew him.

Hel. The rather will I spare my praises towards
    him;   106
Knowing him is enough. On's bed of death
Many receipts he gave me; chiefly one,
Which, as the dearest issue of his practice,
And of his old experience th' only darling,   110
He bade me store up, as a triple eye,
Safer than mine own two, more dear. I have so;
And, hearing your high Majesty is touch'd
With that malignant cause wherein the honour
Of my dear father's gift stands chief in power,
I come to tender it and my appliance   116
With all bound humbleness.

King.   We thank you, maiden;
But may not be so credulous of cure,
When our most learned doctors leave us, and
The congregated college have concluded   120
That labouring art can never ransom Nature
From her inaidable estate; I say we must not
So stain our judgement or corrupt our hope,
To prostitute our past-cure malady
To empirics, or to dissever so   125
Our great self and our credit, to esteem
A senseless help when help past sense we deem.

Hel. My duty then shall pay me for my pains.
I will no more enforce mine office on you;
Humbly entreating from your royal thoughts   130
A modest one, to bear me back again.

King. I cannot give thee less, to be call'd grate-
    ful.
Thou thought'st to help me, and such thanks I give
As one near death to those that wish him live.
But what at full I know, thou know'st no part,
I knowing all my peril, thou no art.   136

Hel. What I can do can do no hurt to try,
Since you set up your rest 'gainst remedy.
He that of greatest works is finisher
Oft does them by the weakest minister: 140
So holy writ in babes hath judgement shown,
When judges have been babes; great floods have
    flown
From simple sources, and great seas have dried
When miracles have by the greatest been denied.
Oft expectation fails, and most oft there   145

64. [fee] (Theobald). *see* F. 70. across: i.e., a clumsy stroke (retort). 75. medicine: physician. 77. canary: a lively dance. 79. Pepin: father of Charlemagne (l. 80). 85. deliverance: speech. 88. blame...weakness: i.e., impute to my natural susceptibility. 91. admiration: marvel. 92. take off: banish. 93. took'st: didst get. fit: satisfy. 100. Cressid's uncle: Pandarus, who brought Troilus and Cressida together as lovers. 102. follow: concern. 105. found: versed. 111. triple: third. 114. cause: disease. 117. bound: dutiful. 125. empirics: quacks. 138. set...rest: make up your mind.

Where most it promises; and oft it hits
Where hope is coldest and despair most [fits].
  King. I must not hear thee; fare thee well, kind
    maid!
Thy pains not us'd must by thyself be paid.   149
Proffers not took reap thanks for their reward.
  Hel. Inspired merit so by breath is barr'd.
It is not so with Him that all things knows
As 'tis with us that square our guess by shows;
But most it is presumption in us when
The help of Heaven we count the act of men.   155
Dear sir, to my endeavours give consent;
Of Heaven, not me, make an experiment.
I am not an impostor that proclaim
Myself against the level of mine aim;
But know I think and think I know most sure
My art is not past power nor you past cure.   161
  King. Art thou so confident?   Within what space
Hop'st thou my cure?
  Hel.   The great'st grace lending grace,
Ere twice the horses of the sun shall bring
Their fiery torcher his diurnal ring,   165
Ere twice in murk and occidental damp
Moist Hesperus hath quench'd her sleepy lamp,
Or four and twenty times the pilot's glass
Hath told the thievish minutes how they pass,
What is infirm from your sound parts shall fly,
Health shall live free and sickness freely die.   171
  King. Upon thy certainty and confidence
What dar'st thou venture?
  Hel.   Tax of impudence,
A strumpet's boldness, a divulged shame,
Traduc'd by odious ballads, my maiden's name   175
Sear'd otherwise; [nay,] worse of worst extended,
With vilest torture let my life be ended.
  King. Methinks in thee some blessed spirit doth
    speak
His powerful sound within an organ weak;
And what impossibility would slay   180
In common sense, sense saves another way.
Thy life is dear; for all that life can rate
Worth name of life in thee hath estimate, —
Youth, beauty, wisdom, courage, all
That happiness and prime can happy call: 185
Thou this to hazard needs must intimate
Skill infinite or monstrous desperate.
Sweet practiser, thy physic I will try,
That ministers thine own death if I die.
  Hel. If I break time, or flinch in property   190
Of what I spoke, unpitied let me die,

And well deserv'd.   Not helping, death's my fee,
But, if I help, what do you promise me?
  King. Make thy demand.
  Hel.   But will you make it even?
  King. Ay, by my sceptre and my hopes of
    [heaven].   195
  Hel. Then shalt thou give me with thy kingly
    hand
What husband in thy power I will command,
Exempted be from me the arrogance
To choose from forth the royal blood of France,
My low and humble name to propagate   200
With any branch or image of thy state;
But such a one, thy vassal, whom I know
Is free for me to ask, thee to bestow.
  King. Here is my hand; the premises observ'd,
Thy will by my performance shall be serv'd.   205
So make the choice of thy own time, for I,
Thy resolv'd patient, on thee still rely.
More should I question thee, and more I must, —
Though more to know could not be more to trust, —
From whence thou cam'st, how tended on; but
    rest   210
Unquestion'd welcome and undoubted blest.
Give me some help here, ho!   If thou proceed
As high as word, my deed shall match thy deed.
    [*Flourish.   Exeunt.*

[SCENE II.   *Rousillon.   The Count's palace.*]

Enter COUNTESS *and* CLOWN.

  Count. Come on, sir; I shall now put you to the
height of your breeding.
  Clo. I will show myself highly fed and lowly
taught.   I know my business is but to the court.   4
  Count. To the court!   Why, what place make
you special, when you put off that with such contempt?   But to the court!
  Clo. Truly, madam, if God have lent a man any
manners, he may easily put it off at court.   He that
cannot make a leg, put off's cap, kiss his hand   10
and say nothing, has neither leg, hands, lip, nor
cap; and indeed such a fellow, to say precisely, were
not for the court.   But for me, I have an answer
will serve all men.
  Count. Marry, that's a bountiful answer that
fits all questions.   16
  Clo. It is like a barber's chair that fits all buttocks, the pin-buttock, the quatch-buttock, the
brawn buttock, or any buttock.

147. [fits] (Theobald conj.).   *shifts* F.   151. breath: talk.   153. square ... shows: conjecture by appearances.   158–59.
proclaim ... aim: i.e., exalt my powers beyond what I believe I can perform.   163. The ... grace: i.e., God willing.   173.
Tax: charge.   176–77. [nay] ... torture (Singer).   F reads *ne worse of worst extended With vilest torture.*   180–81. And ...
way: i.e., What common sense would hold impossible reason still finds a way to justify.   183. in ... estimate: i.e., are to be
reckoned thine.   185. prime: youth.   186. Thou ... hazard: your risking this.   190–91. flinch ... spoke: fall short in anything I have promised.   194. make it even: fulfil it.   195. [heaven] (Thirlby conj.).   *helpe* F.   198. Exempted: excepted.   201. image: member.
Sc. ii, 5–6. make you special: i.e., do you favor.   6. put off: spurn.   9. put it off: i.e., get by.   10. leg: bow.   18. pin:
thin.   quatch: fat.

Count. Will your answer serve fit to all questions? 21

Clo. As fit as ten groats is for the hand of an attorney, as your French crown for your taffeta punk, as Tib's rush for Tom's forefinger, as a pancake for Shrove Tuesday, a morris for Mayday, as the 25 nail to his hole, the cuckold to his horn, as a scolding quean to a wrangling knave, as the nun's lip to the friar's mouth, nay, as the pudding to his skin.

Count. Have you, I say, an answer of such fitness for all questions? 31

Clo. From below your duke to beneath your constable, it will fit any question.

Count. It must be an answer of most monstrous size that must fit all demands. 35

Clo. But a trifle neither, in good faith, if the learned should speak truth of it. Here it is, and all that belongs to't. Ask me if I am a courtier: it shall do you no harm to learn. 39

Count. To be young again, if we could, I will be a fool in question, hoping to be the wiser by your answer. I pray you, sir, are you a courtier?

Clo. O Lord, sir! — There's a simple putting off. More, more, a hundred of them. 44

Count. Sir, I am a poor friend of yours, that loves you.

Clo. O Lord, sir! — Thick, thick, spare not me.

Count. I think, sir, you can eat none of this homely meat. 49

Clo. O Lord, sir! — Nay, put me to't, I warrant you.

Count. You were lately whipp'd, sir, as I think.

Clo. O Lord, sir! — Spare not me. 53

Count. Do you cry, "O Lord, sir!" at your whipping, and "Spare not me"? Indeed your "O Lord, sir!" is very sequent to your whipping; you would answer very well to a whipping, if you were but bound to't. 58

Clo. I ne'er had worse luck in my life in my "O Lord, sir!" I see things may serve long, but not serve ever.

Count. I play the noble housewife with the time, To entertain't so merrily with a fool. 63

Clo. O Lord, sir! — Why, there't serves well again.

Count. An end, sir. To your business! Give Helen this, And urge her to a present answer back. Commend me to my kinsmen and my son. This is not much.

Clo. Not much commendation to them. 70

Count. Not much employment for you. You understand me?

Clo. Most fruitfully; I am there before my legs.

Count. Haste you again.   *[Exeunt [severally].*

[SCENE III. *Paris. The King's palace.*]

Enter BERTRAM, LAFEU, *and* PAROLLES.

Laf. They say miracles are past; and we have our philosophical persons, to make modern and familiar, things supernatural and causeless. Hence is it that we make trifles of terrors, ensconcing ourselves into seeming knowledge, when we should submit ourselves to an unknown fear. 6

Par. Why, 'tis the rarest argument of wonder that hath shot out in our latter times.

Ber. And so 'tis.

Laf. To be relinquish'd of the artists, — 10

Par. So I say; both of Galen and Paracelsus.

Laf. Of all the learned and authentic fellows, —

Par. Right; so I say. 15

Laf. That gave him out incurable, —

Par. Why, there 'tis; so say I too.

Laf. Not to be help'd, —

Par. Right; as 'twere a man assured of a —

Laf. Uncertain life, and sure death. 20

Par. Just, you say well; so would I have said.

Laf. I may truly say it is a novelty to the world.

Par. It is, indeed; if you will have it in showing, you shall read it in — what do ye call there? 26

Laf. A showing of a heavenly effect in an earthly actor.

Par. That's it; I would have said the very same.

Laf. Why, your Dauphin is not lustier. 'Fore me, I speak in respect — 32

Par. Nay, 'tis strange, 'tis very strange, that is the brief and the tedious of it; and he's of a most facinerious spirit that will not acknowledge it to be the —

Laf. Very hand of Heaven.

Par. Ay, so I say. 38

Laf. In a most weak —

Par. And debile minister, great power, great transcendence; which should, indeed, give us a further use to be made than alone the recov'ry of the King, as to be —

Laf. Generally thankful. 43

Enter KING, HELENA, *and Attendants.*

Par. I would have said it; you say well. Here comes the King.

---

23. **French crown:** bald head. **punk:** strumpet. 24. **rush.** A rush ring was sometimes used in rustic marriages. 25. **morris:** morris-dance. 27. **quean:** hussy. 28. **pudding:** sausage. 56. **very ... to:** a true follower of. 62. **I ... time:** I am generous of my time.

Sc. iii, 2. **modern:** common. 7. **argument:** topic. 10. **relinquish'd ... artists:** given up by the doctors. 11. **of:** i.e., the followers of. Galen (2nd cent.) and Paracelsus (16th cent.) were the leaders of rival schools. 12. **authentic:** authoritative. 35. **facinerious:** infamous. 40. **debile:** weak.

Laf. *Lustig*, as the Dutchman says. I'll like a maid the better, whilst I have a tooth in my head. Why, he's able to lead her a coranto.
Par. *Mort du vinaigre!* is not this Helen?   50
Laf. 'Fore God, I think so.
King. Go, call before me all the lords in court. Sit, my preserver, by thy patient's side; And with this healthful hand, whose banish'd sense Thou hast repeal'd, a second time receive   55 The confirmation of my promis'd gift, Which but attends thy naming.

Enter three or four LORDS.

Fair maid, send forth thine eye. This youthful parcel
Of noble bachelors stand at my bestowing,
O'er whom both sovereign power and father's voice
I have to use. Thy frank election make;   61
Thou hast power to choose, and they none to forsake.
Hel. To each of you one fair and virtuous mistress
Fall, when Love please! Marry, to each but one!
Laf. I'd give bay Curtal and his furniture,   65
My mouth no more were broken than these boys',
And writ as little beard.
King.   Peruse them well.
Not one of those but had a noble father.
Hel. Gentlemen,
Heaven hath through me restor'd the King to health.   70
All. We understand it, and thank Heaven for you.
Hel. I am a simple maid, and therein wealthiest
That I protest I simply am a maid.
Please it your Majesty, I have done already,
The blushes in my cheeks thus whisper me,   75
"We blush that thou shouldst choose; but, be refus'd,
Let the white death sit on thy cheek for ever,
We'll ne'er come there again."
King.   Make choice and see,
Who shuns thy love shuns all his love in me.
Hel. Now, Dian, from thy altar do I fly,   80
And to imperial Love, that god most high,
Do my sighs stream. Sir, will you hear my suit?
1. Lord. And grant it.
Hel.   Thanks, sir; all the rest is mute.
Laf. I had rather be in this choice than throw ames-ace for my life.   85
Hel. The honour, sir, that flames in your fair eyes,
Before I speak, too threat'ningly replies.

Love make your fortunes twenty times above
Her that so wishes and her humble love!
2. Lord. No better, if you please.
Hel.   My wish receive,
Which great Love grant! and so, I take my leave.   91
Laf. Do all they deny her? An they were sons of mine, I'd have them whipp'd; or I would send them to th' Turk, to make eunuchs of.
Hel. Be not afraid that I your hand should take;
I'll never do you wrong for your own sake.   96
Blessing upon your vows! and in your bed
Find fairer fortune, if you ever wed!
Laf. These boys are boys of ice, they'll none have her. Sure, they are bastards to the English; the French ne'er got 'em.   101
Hel. You are too young, too happy, and too good,
To make yourself a son out of my blood.
4. Lord. Fair one, I think not so.   104
Laf. There's one grape yet; I am sure thy father drunk wine: — but if thou be'st not an ass, I am a youth of fourteen. I have known thee already.
Hel. [*To Bertram.*] I dare not say I take you; but I give
Me and my service, ever whilst I live,   110
Into your guiding power. This is the man.
King. Why, then, young Bertram, take her; she's thy wife.
Ber. My wife, my liege! I shall beseech your Highness,
In such a business give me leave to use
The help of mine own eyes.
King.   Know'st thou not, Bertram,   115
What she has done for me?
Ber.   Yes, my good lord;
But never hope to know why I should marry her.
King. Thou know'st she has rais'd me from my sickly bed.
Ber. But follows it, my lord, to bring me down
Must answer for your raising? I know her well;   120
She had her breeding at my father's charge.
A poor physician's daughter my wife! Disdain
Rather corrupt me ever!
King. 'Tis only title thou disdain'st in her, the which
I can build up. Strange is it that our bloods,   125
Of colour, weight, and heat, pour'd all together,
Would quite confound distinction, yet [stand] off
In differences so mighty. If she be
All that is virtuous, save what thou dislik'st,
A poor physician's daughter, thou dislik'st   130
Of virtue for the name. But do not so.
From lowest place [when] virtuous things proceed,

46. *Lustig:* brisk. 49. **coranto:** a lively dance. 50. *Mort du vinaigre.* A meaningless oath. Parolles, wishing to swear in French, makes nonsense. 55. **repeal'd:** restored. 62. **forsake:** deny. 65. **Curtal:** horse with a docked tail. **furniture:** trappings. 66. **broken:** lacking teeth. 68. After *father* F inserts s.d., "She addresses her to a Lord." 83. **all . . . mute:** i.e., that's all I have to say to you. 85. **ames-ace:** double ace, the lowest possible throw of the dice. Jocose. 124. **title:** i.e., lack of title. 127. **distinction:** i.e., of "colour," etc. (l. 126). **[stand]** (Rowe). *stands* F. 132. **[when]** (Thirlby conj.). *whence* F.

The place is dignified by th' doer's deed.
Where great additions swell's, and virtue none,
It is a dropsied honour.   Good alone   135
Is good without a name.   Vileness is so;
The property by what it is should go,
Not by the title.   She is young, wise, fair;
In these to nature she's immediate heir,
And these breed honour.   That is honour's scorn,
Which challenges itself as honour's born   141
And is not like the sire.   Honours thrive,
When rather from our acts we them derive
Than our foregoers.   The mere word's a slave
Debauch'd on every tomb, on every grave   145
A lying trophy, and as oft is dumb
Where dust and damn'd oblivion is the tomb
Of honour'd bones indeed.   What should be said?
If thou canst like this creature as a maid,
I can create the rest.   Virtue and she   150
Is her own dower; honour and wealth from me.
    Ber. I cannot love her, nor will strive to do't.
    King. Thou wrong'st thyself, if thou shouldst
        strive to choose.
    Hel. That you are well restor'd, my lord, I'm
        glad.
Let the rest go.   155
    King. My honour's at the stake; which to defeat,
I must produce my power.   Here, take her hand,
Proud scornful boy, unworthy this good gift;
That dost in vile misprision shackle up
My love and her desert; that canst not dream   160
We, poising us in her defective scale,
Shall weigh thee to the beam; that wilt not know
It is in us to plant thine honour where
We please to have it grow.   Check thy contempt;
Obey our will, which travails in thy good;   165
Believe not thy disdain, but presently
Do thine own fortunes that obedient right
Which both thy duty owes and our power claims;
Or I will throw thee from my care for ever
Into the staggers and the careless lapse   170
Of youth and ignorance; both my revenge and hate
Loosing upon thee, in the name of justice,
Without all terms of pity.   Speak; thine answer.
    Ber. Pardon, my gracious lord; for I submit
My fancy to your eyes.   When I consider   175
What great creation and what dole of honour
Flies where you bid it, I find that she, which late
Was in my nobler thoughts most base, is now
The praised of the King; who, so ennobled,
Is as 'twere born so.
    King.   Take her by the hand,   180
And tell her she is thine; to whom I promise
A counterpoise, if not to thy estate

A balance more replete.
    Ber.   I take her hand.
    King. Good fortune and the favour of the King
Smile upon this contract, whose ceremony   185
Shall seem expedient on the now-born brief,
And be perform'd to-night.   The solemn feast
Shall more attend upon the coming space,
Expecting absent friends.   As thou lov'st her,
Thy love's to me religious; else, does err.   190
    [*Exeunt all but Lafeu and Parolles, who
        stay behind, commenting of this wedding.*
    Laf. Do you hear, monsieur?   A word with you.
    Par. Your pleasure, sir?
    Laf. Your lord and master did well to make his
recantation.   195
    Par. Recantation!   My lord!   My master!
    Laf. Ay; is it not a language I speak?
    Par. A most harsh one, and not to be under-
stood without bloody succeeding.   My master!   199
    Laf. Are you companion to the Count Rousillon?
    Par. To any count, to all counts, to what is
man.
    Laf. To what is count's man.   Count's master
is of another style.   205
    Par. You are too old, sir; let it satisfy you, you
are too old.
    Laf. I must tell thee, sirrah, I write man; to
which title age cannot bring thee.   209
    Par. What I dare too well do, I dare not do.
    Laf. I did think thee, for two ordinaries, to be a
pretty wise fellow.   Thou didst make tolerable
vent of thy travel; it might pass: yet the scarfs and
the bannerets about thee did manifoldly dissuade
me from believing thee a vessel of too great a   215
burden.   I have now found thee.   When I lose thee
again, I care not; yet art thou good for nothing but
taking up, and that thou'rt scarce worth.
    Par. Hadst thou not the privilege of antiquity
upon thee, —   221
    Laf. Do not plunge thyself too far in anger, lest
thou hasten thy trial; which if — Lord have mercy
on thee for a hen!   So, my good window of lattice,
fare thee well!   Thy casement I need not open, for
I look through thee.   Give me thy hand.   227
    Par. My lord, you give me most egregious in-
dignity.
    Laf. Ay, with all my heart; and thou art worthy
of it.   231
    Par. I have not, my lord, deserv'd it.
    Laf. Yes, good faith, ev'ry dram of it; and I
will not bate thee a scruple.
    Par. Well, I shall be wiser.   235
    Laf. Ev'n as soon as thou canst, for thou hast to

---

134. **additions swell's:** titles puff us up.   **none:** i.e., absent.   141. **challenges:** proclaims.   156. **which:** i.e., the threat
to which.   159. **misprision:** contempt.   161. **poising us:** adding our weight.   170. **staggers:** giddiness.   **lapse:** ruin.   186.
Shall...brief: i.e., shall follow promptly upon this fresh covenant.   199. **succeeding:** consequence.   203. **man:** servant.
211. **two ordinaries:** the space of two meals.   218. **taking up:** calling to account.   224. **hen:** i.e., coward.

pull at a smack o' th' contrary. If ever thou be'st
bound in thy scarf and beaten, thou shalt find what
it is to be proud of thy bondage. I have a desire to
hold my acquaintance with thee, or rather my
knowledge, that I may say in the default, "He is a
man I know."   242
Par. My lord, you do me most insupportable
vexation.
Laf. I would it were hell-pains for thy sake, and
my poor doing eternal; for doing I am past, as I will
by thee, in what motion age will give me leave.   248
                                                 [*Exit.*
Par. Well, thou hast a son shall take this disgrace off me, scurvy, old, filthy, scurvy lord! Well,
I must be patient; there is no fettering of authority.
I'll beat him, by my life, if I can meet him with any
convenience, an he were double and double a lord.
I'll have no more pity of his age than I would have
of — I'll beat him, an if I could but meet him   255
again.

Re-enter LAFEU.

Laf. Sirrah, your lord and master's married;
there's news for you. You have a new mistress.
Par. I most unfeignedly beseech your lordship
to make some reservation of your wrongs. He is
my good lord; whom I serve above is my master.
Laf. Who? God?   262
Par. Ay, sir.
Laf. The devil it is that's thy master. Why dost
thou garter up thy arms o' this fashion? Dost 265
make hose of thy sleeves? Do other servants so?
Thou wert best set thy lower part where thy nose
stands. By mine honour, if I were but two hours
younger, I'd beat thee. Methinks, thou art a general offence, and every man should beat thee. I
think thou wast created for men to breathe themselves upon thee.   272
Par. This is hard and undeserved measure, my
lord.
Laf. Go to, sir; you were beaten in Italy for 275
picking a kernel out of a pomegranate. You are a
vagabond and no true traveller. You are more
saucy with lords and honourable personages than
the commission of your birth and virtue gives you
heraldry. You are not worth another word, else
I'd call you knave. I leave you.   [*Exit.* 281

Re-enter BERTRAM.

Par. Good, very good; it is so then. Good, very
good; let it be conceal'd awhile.
Ber. Undone, and forfeited to cares forever!

Par. What's the matter, sweetheart?   285
Ber. Although before the solemn priest I have
     sworn,
I will not bed her.
Par. What, what, sweetheart?
Ber. O my Parolles, they have married me! I'll
to the Tuscan wars, and never bed her.   290
Par. France is a dog-hole, and it no more merits
The tread of a man's foot. To th' wars!
Ber. There's letters from my mother; what th'
import is, I know not yet.
Par. Ay, that would be known. To th' wars,
     my boy, to the wars!   295
He wears his honour in a box unseen,
That hugs his kicky-wicky here at home,
Spending his manly marrow in her arms,
Which should sustain the bound and high curvet
Of Mars's fiery steed. To other regions!   300
France is a stable, we that dwell in't jades,
Therefore, to th' war!
Ber. It shall be so. I'll send her to my house,
Acquaint my mother with my hate to her,
And wherefore I am fled; write to the King   305
That which I durst not speak. His present gift
Shall furnish me to those Italian fields
Where noble fellows strike. [War] is no strife
To the dark house and the [detested] wife.
Par. Will this *capriccio* hold in thee? Art sure?
Ber. Go with me to my chamber, and advise me.
I'll send her straight away. To-morrow   312
I'll to the wars, she to her single sorrow.
Par. Why, these balls bound; there's noise in it.
'Tis hard!
A young man married is a man that's marr'd; 315
Therefore away, and leave her bravely; go.
The King has done you wrong; but, hush, 'tis so.
                                             [*Exeunt.*

[SCENE IV. *Paris. The King's palace.*]

Enter HELENA *and* CLOWN.

Hel. My mother greets me kindly. Is she
well?
Clo. She is not well, but yet she has her health.
She's very merry, but yet she is not well; but thanks
be given, she's very well and wants nothing i' th'
world; but yet she is not well.   5
Hel. If she be very well, what does she ail that
she's not very well?
Clo. Truly, she's very well indeed, but for two
things.
Hel. What two things?   10

---

237. **pull ... contrary:** quaff a bit of the opposite (i.e., folly).   241. **in the default:** i.e., when you fail.   247. **will:** i.e.,
will pass (punning on *past*).   248. **motion:** pace.   260. **make ... wrongs:** check your insults.   271. **breathe:** exercise.   280.
heraldry: title (to).   299. **curvet:** leap.   301. **jades:** old nags.   308. **[War]** F₂. *Warres* F₁.   309. **To:** compared to.   **dark
house:** i.e., madness. In Shakespeare's day lunatics were confined in darkness.   **[detested]** (Rowe). *detected* F.   310.
capriccio: whim.

Clo. One, that she's not in heaven, whither God send her quickly! the other, that she's in earth, from whence God send her quickly!

Enter PAROLLES.

Par. Bless you, sir, my fortunate lady!

Hel. I hope, sir, I have your good will to have mine own good [fortunes]. 16

Par. You had my prayers to lead them on; and to keep them on, have them still. O, my knave, how does my old lady?

Clo. So that you had her wrinkles and I her money, I would she did as you say. 21

Par. Why, I say nothing.

Clo. Marry, you are the wiser man; for many a man's tongue shakes out his master's undoing. To say nothing, to do nothing, to know nothing, and to have nothing, is to be a great part of your title; which is within a very little of nothing. 27

Par. Away! thou'rt a knave.

Clo. You should have said, sir, "Before a knave thou'rt a knave"; that's, before me thou'rt a knave. This had been truth, sir. 31

Par. Go to, thou art a witty fool; I have found thee.

Clo. Did you find me in yourself, sir, or were you taught to find me? The search, sir, was profit- 35 able; and much fool may you find in you, even to the world's pleasure and the increase of laughter.

Par. A good knave, i' faith, and well fed. Madam, my lord will go away to-night; 40 A very serious business calls on him. The great prerogative and rite of love, Which, as your due, time claims, he does acknowl- edge, But puts it off to a compell'd restraint; Whose want, and whose delay, is strew'd with sweets, 45 Which they distil now in the curbed time, To make the coming hour o'erflow with joy And pleasure drown the brim.

Hel. What's his will else?

Par. That you will take your instant leave o' th' King,
And make this haste as your own good proceeding, Strength'ned with what apology you think 51 May make it probable need.

Hel. What more commands he?

Par. That, having this obtain'd, you presently Attend his further pleasure.

Hel. In everything I wait upon his will. 55

Par. I shall report it so. [*Exit Parolles.*

Hel. I pray you.
Come, sirrah. [*Exeunt.*

[SCENE V. *Paris. The King's palace.*]

Enter LAFEU *and* BERTRAM.

Laf. But I hope your lordship thinks not him a soldier.

Ber. Yes, my lord, and of very valiant approof.

Laf. You have it from his own deliverance.

Ber. And by other warranted testimony. 5

Laf. Then my dial goes not true. I took this lark for a bunting.

Ber. I do assure you, my lord, he is very great in knowledge and accordingly valiant. 9

Laf. I have then sinn'd against his experience and transgress'd against his valour; and my state that way is dangerous, since I cannot yet find in my heart to repent. Here he comes. I pray you, make us friends; I will pursue the amity. 15

Enter PAROLLES.

Par. [*To Bertram.*] These things shall be done, sir.

Laf. Pray you, sir, who's his tailor?

Par. Sir?

Laf. O, I know him well, I, sir; he, sir, 's a good workman, a very good tailor. 21

Ber. [*Aside to Par.*] Is she gone to the King?

Par. She is.

Ber. Will she away to-night?

Par. As you'll have her. 25

Ber. I have writ my letters, casketed my treasure, Given order for our horses; and to-night, When I should take possession of the bride, [End] ere I do begin. 29

Laf. A good traveller is something at the latter end of a dinner; but [one] that lies three thirds and uses a known truth to pass a thousand nothings with, should be once heard and thrice beaten. God save you, captain. 34

Ber. Is there any unkindness between my lord and you, monsieur?

Par. I know not how I have deserved to run into my lord's displeasure. 38

Laf. You have made shift to run into't, boots and spurs and all, like him that leap'd into the cus- tard; and out of it you'll run again, rather than suffer question for your residence.

Ber. It may be you have mistaken him, my lord. 44

Laf. And shall do so ever, though I took him at's prayers. Fare you well, my lord; and believe this of me, there can be no kernel in this light nut: the soul of this man is his clothes. Trust him not in matter of heavy consequence; I have kept of them

Sc. iv: 16. [fortunes] (Capell). *fortune* F. 27. title: worth. 33. in: by. 44. to...restraint: through forced necessity. 46. curbed time: i.e., time of waiting. 50. as...proceeding: appear your own desire. 52. probable: plausible.
Sc. v, 7. bunting: a bird like a lark, but almost songless. 9. accordingly: equally. 29. [End] (Collier). *and* F. 30-31. at...dinner: i.e., for telling stories. [one] (Rowe). *on* F. 42. residence: staying.

tame, and know their natures. Farewell, mon- 50
sieur! I have spoken better of you than you have
or will to deserve at my hand; but we must do good
against evil.   [*Exit.*]
 Par. An idle lord, I swear.
 Ber. I think so.   55
 Par. Why, do you not know him?
 Ber. Yes, I do know him well, and common
  speech
Gives him a worthy pass. Here comes my clog.

    Enter HELENA.

 Hel. I have, sir, as I was commanded from you,
Spoke with the King and have procur'd his leave 60
For present parting; only he desires
Some private speech with you.
 Ber.   I shall obey his will.
You must not marvel, Helen, at my course,
Which holds not colour with the time, nor does
The ministration and required office   65
On my particular. Prepar'd I was not
For such a business; therefore am I found
So much unsettled. This drives me to entreat you
That presently you take your way for home,
And rather muse than ask why I entreat you;   70
For my respects are better than they seem,
And my appointments have in them a need
Greater than shows itself at the first view
To you that know them not. This to my mother:
       [*Giving a letter.*]
'Twill be two days ere I shall see you, so   75
I leave you to your wisdom.
 Hel.   Sir, I can nothing say,
But that I am your most obedient servant, —
 Ber. Come, come, no more of that.
 Hel.   And ever shall
With true observance seek to eke out that
Wherein toward me my homely stars have fail'd 80
To equal my great fortune.
 Ber.   Let that go.
My haste is very great. Farewell; hie home.
 Hel. Pray, sir, your pardon.
 Ber.   Well, what would you say?
 Hel. I am not worthy of the wealth I owe,
Nor dare I say 'tis mine, and yet it is;   85
But, like a timorous thief, most fain would steal
What law does vouch mine own.
 Ber.   What would you have?
 Hel. Something; and scarce so much. Nothing,
  indeed.
I would not tell you what I would, my lord.
Faith, yes!   90
Strangers and foes do sunder, and not kiss.

 Ber. I pray you, stay not, but in haste to horse.
 Hel. I shall not break your bidding, good my
  lord.
 Ber. Where are my other men?
 Hel.   Monsieur, farewell! [*Exit.* 94
 Ber. Go thou toward home, where I will never
  come
Whilst I can shake my sword or hear the drum.
Away, and for our flight.
 Par.   Bravely, *coragio!*
        [*Exeunt.*]

      ACT III

[SCENE I. *Florence. The Duke's palace.*]

Flourish. Enter the DUKE OF FLORENCE, *the two
 French* LORDS, *with a troop of soldiers.*

 Duke. So that from point to point now have you
  heard
The fundamental reasons of this war,
Whose great decision hath much blood let forth
And more thirsts after.
 1. Lord.   Holy seems the quarrel
Upon your Grace's part; black and fearful   5
On the opposer.
 Duke. Therefore we marvel much our cousin
  France
Would in so just a business shut his bosom
Against our borrowing prayers.
 2. Lord.   Good my lord,
The reasons of our state I cannot yield   10
But like a common and an outward man
That the great figure of a council frames
By self-unable motion; therefore dare not
Say what I think of it, since I have found
Myself in my incertain grounds to fail   15
As often as I guess'd.
 Duke.   Be it his pleasure.
 2. Lord. But I am sure the younger of our nature,
That surfeit on their ease, will day by day
Come here for physic.
 Duke.   Welcome shall they be;
And all the honours that can fly from us   20
Shall on them settle. — You know your places well;
When better fall, for your avails they fell.
To-morrow to th' field.   [*Flourish.* [*Exeunt.*]

[SCENE II. *Rousillon. The Count's palace.*]

   Enter COUNTESS *and* CLOWN.

 Count. It hath happen'd all as I would have
had it, save that he comes not along with her.

54. **idle:** silly. 58. **pass:** i.e., name. 64. **holds not colour:** is not suitable. 66. **particular:** part. 70. **muse:** wonder.
71. **respects:** reasons. 72. **appointments:** commands. 84. **owe:** own. 94. **Where … men.** Cont. by F to Helena.
Corrected by Theobald.
 Act III, sc. i, 10. **yield:** tell. 11–13. **But … motion:** except as a common outsider who estimates the policy of a great
council by his own weak intelligence. 22. **better:** men of higher rank.

Clo. By my troth, I take my young lord to be a very melancholy man.

Count. By what observance, I pray you?   5

Clo. Why, he will look upon his boot and sing; mend the ruff and sing; ask questions and sing; pick his teeth and sing. I know a man that had this trick of melancholy [sold] a goodly manor for a song.   10

Count. Let me see what he writes, and when he means to come.   *[Opening a letter.]*

Clo. I have no mind to Isbel since I was at court. Our old [ling] and our Isbels o' th' country are nothing like your old ling and your Isbels o' th'   15 court. The brains of my Cupid's knock'd out, and I begin to love, as an old man loves money, with no stomach.

Count. What have we here?

Clo. [E'en] that you have there.   *[Exit.*   20
[Count. Reads] a letter. "I have sent you a daughter-in-law; she hath recovered the King, and undone me. I have wedded her, not bedded her; and sworn to make the 'not' eternal. You shall hear I am run away: know it before the report   25 come. If there be breadth enough in the world, I will hold a long distance. My duty to you.

Your unfortunate son,

BERTRAM."

This is not well, rash and unbridled boy,   30
To fly the favours of so good a king,
To pluck his indignation on thy head
By the misprising of a maid too virtuous
For the contempt of empire.

Re-enter CLOWN.

Clo. O madam, yonder is heavy news within between two soldiers and my young lady!   36

Count. What is the matter?

Clo. Nay, there is some comfort in the news, some comfort. Your son will not be kill'd so soon as I thought he would.

Count. Why should he be kill'd?   41

Clo. So say I, madam, if he run away, as I hear he does. The danger is in standing to't. That's the loss of men, though it be the getting of children. Here they come will tell you more; for my part, I only hear your son was run away.   *[Exit.]*   46

Enter HELENA *and the two French* LORDS.

2. Lord. Save you, good madam.

Hel. Madam, my lord is gone, for ever gone.

1. Lord. Do not say so.

Count. Think upon patience, pray you. Gentlemen,   50

I have felt so many quirks of joy and grief
That the first face of neither, on the start,
Can woman me unto't. Where is my son, I pray you?

1. Lord. Madam, he's gone to serve the Duke of Florence.
We met him thitherward; for thence we came,
And, after some dispatch in hand at court,   56
Thither we bend again.

Hel. Look on his letter, madam; here's my passport.

[Reads.] "When thou canst get the ring upon my finger which never shall come off, and show me   60 a child begotten of thy body that I am father to, then call me husband; but in such a 'then' I write a 'never.'"
This is a dreadful sentence.

Count. Brought you this letter, gentlemen?

1. Lord.   Ay, madam;
And for the contents' sake are sorry for our pains.

Count. I prithee, lady, have a better cheer;   67
If thou engrossest all the griefs are thine,
Thou robb'st me of a moiety. He was my son;
But I do wash his name out of my blood,   70
And thou art all my child. Towards Florence is he?

1. Lord. Ay, madam.

Count.   And to be a soldier?

1. Lord. Such is his noble purpose; and, believe't,
The Duke will lay upon him all the honour
That good convenience claims.

Count.   Return you thither?

2. Lord. Ay, madam, with the swiftest wing of speed.   76

Hel. [*Reads.*] "Till I have no wife, I have nothing in France."
'Tis bitter.

Count. Find you that there?

Hel.   Ay, madam.

2. Lord. 'Tis but the boldness of his hand, haply, which his heart was not consenting to.   80

Count. Nothing in France, until he have no wife!
There's nothing here that is too good for him
But only she; and she deserves a lord
That twenty such rude boys might tend upon
And call her hourly mistress. Who was with him?

2. Lord. A servant only, and a gentleman   86
Which I have sometime known.

Count.   Parolles, was it not?

2. Lord. Ay, my good lady, he.

Count. A very tainted fellow, and full of wickedness.
My son corrupts a well-derived nature   90
With his inducement.

2. Lord.   Indeed, good lady,

Sc. ii, 9. [sold] F₃. *hold* F₁,₂. **14.** [ling] F₂. *lings* F. A ling is a kind of cod. Probably corrupt. **20.** [E'en] (Theobald). *In* F. **33. misprising:** spurning. **34. For . . . empire:** for an emperor to despise. **53. woman me unto't:** make me weep. **68. engrossest . . . thine:** i.e., keep all your griefs to yourself. **69. moiety:** half, share. **91. inducement:** instigation.

The fellow has a deal of that too much
Which holds him much to have.
   Count. You're welcome, gentlemen.
I will entreat you, when you see my son,   95
To tell him that his sword can never win
The honour that he loses. More I'll entreat you
Written to bear along.
   1. Lord.   We serve you, madam,
In that and all your worthiest affairs.
   Count. Not so, but as we change our courtesies.
Will you draw near?   101
             [Exeunt [Countess and Lords].
   Hel. "Till I have no wife, I have nothing in
France."
Nothing in France, until he has no wife!
Thou shalt have none, Rousillon, none in France;
Then hast thou all again. Poor lord! is't I   105
That chase thee from thy country and expose
Those tender limbs of thine to the event
Of the none-sparing war? And is it I
That drive thee from the sportive court, where thou
Wast shot at with fair eyes, to be the mark   110
Of smoky muskets? O you leaden messengers,
That ride upon the violent speed of fire,
Fly with false aim; move the still-peering air,
That sings with piercing; do not touch my lord.
Whoever shoots at him, I set him there;   115
Whoever charges on his forward breast,
I am the caitiff that do hold him to't;
And, though I kill him not, I am the cause
His death was so effected. Better 'twere
I met the ravin lion when he roar'd   120
With sharp constraint of hunger; better 'twere
That all the miseries which nature owes
Were mine at once. No, come thou home, Rou-
    sillon,
Whence honour but of danger wins a scar,
As oft it loses all. I will be gone.   125
My being here it is that holds thee hence.
Shall I stay here to do't? No, no, although
The air of paradise did fan the house
And angels offic'd all. I will be gone,
That pitiful rumour may report my flight,   130
To consolate thine ear. Come, night; end, day!
For with the dark, poor thief, I'll steal away.
                        [Exit.

[SCENE III.   *Florence. Before the Duke's palace.*]

Flourish. Enter the DUKE OF FLORENCE, BER-
TRAM, PAROLLES, *Soldiers, drum and trumpets.*

   Duke. The general of our horse thou art; and we,

Great in our hope, lay our best love and credence
Upon thy promising fortune.
   Ber.   Sir, it is
A charge too heavy for my strength, but yet
We'll strive to bear it for your worthy sake   5
To th' extreme edge of hazard.
   Duke.   Then go thou forth;
And fortune play upon thy prosperous helm,
As thy auspicious mistress!
   Ber.   This very day,
Great Mars, I put myself into thy file.
Make me but like my thoughts, and I shall prove 10
A lover of thy drum, hater of love.
                       [Exeunt omnes.

[SCENE IV.   *Rousillon. The Count's palace.*]

      Enter COUNTESS *and* STEWARD.

   Count. Alas! and would you take the letter of
    her?
Might you not know she would do as she has done
By sending me a letter? Read it again.
   [Stew. Reads] letter.
"I am Saint Jaques' pilgrim, thither gone.
   Ambitious love hath in me so offended   5
That barefoot plod I the cold ground upon,
   With sainted vow my faults to have amended.
Write, write, that from the bloody course of war
   My dearest master, your dear son, may hie.
Bless him at home in peace, whilst I from far   10
   His name with zealous fervour sanctify.
His taken labours bid him me forgive.
   I, his despiteful Juno, sent him forth
From courtly friends, with camping foes to live,
   Where death and danger dogs the heels of worth.
He is too good and fair for Death and me,   16
   Whom I myself embrace, to set him free."
   [Count.] Ah, what sharp stings are in her mildest
    words!
Rinaldo, you did never lack advice so much
As letting her pass so. Had I spoke with her,   20
I could have well diverted her intents,
Which thus she hath prevented.
   Stew.   Pardon me, madam;
If I had given you this at over-night,
She might have been o'erta'en; and yet she writes,
Pursuit would be but vain.
   Count.   What angel shall   25
Bless this unworthy husband? He cannot thrive,
Unless her prayers, whom Heaven delights to hear
And loves to grant, reprieve him from the wrath
Of greatest justice. Write, write, Rinaldo,

92–93. **The … have:** i.e., He has a lot of that excess of "inducement" which it is so important for him to possess. 100.
but … change: except as we exchange. 107. **event:** outcome. 113. **still-peering.** Perhaps an error for *still-piecing*
(Steevens). 120. **ravin:** ravenous. 129. **offic'd all:** did all the duties. 130. **pitiful:** compassionate.
   Sc. iv, 12. **taken:** i.e., undertaken. 13. **Juno.** Alluding to the labors of Hercules, incurred through the enmity of Juno
17. **Whom.** The antecedent is *Death.* 19 **advice:** judgment. 23. **at over-night:** last evening.

To this unworthy husband of his wife. 30
Let every word weigh heavy of her worth
That he does weigh too light. My greatest grief,
Though little he do feel it, set down sharply.
Dispatch the most convenient messenger.
When haply he shall hear that she is gone, 35
He will return; and hope I may that she,
Hearing so much, will speed her foot again,
Led hither by pure love. Which of them both
Is dearest to me, I have no skill in sense
To make distinction. Provide this messenger. 40
My heart is heavy and mine age is weak;
Grief would have tears, and sorrow bids me speak.
                        [*Exeunt.*

[SCENE V. *Florence. Without the walls.*] *A tucket afar off.*

Enter an old WIDOW *of Florence, her daughter* [DIANA], VIOLENTA, *and* MARIANA, *with other Citizens.*

Wid. Nay, come; for if they do approach the city, we shall lose all the sight.

Dia. They say the French count has done most honourable service. 4

Wid. It is reported that he has taken their great'st commander, and that with his own hand he slew the Duke's brother. [*Tucket.*] We have lost our labour; they are gone a contrary way. Hark! you may know by their trumpets. 9

Mar. Come, let's return again and suffice ourselves with the report of it. Well, Diana, take heed of this French earl. The honour of a maid is her name, and no legacy is so rich as honesty. 14

Wid. I have told my neighbour how you have been solicited by a gentleman his companion.

Mar. I know that knave, hang him! one Parolles; a filthy officer he is in those suggestions for the young earl. Beware of them, Diana; their promises, enticements, oaths, tokens, and all these engines 20 of lust, are not the things they go under. Many a maid hath been seduced by them; and the misery is, example, that so terrible shows in the wreck of maidenhood, cannot for all that dissuade succession, but that they are limed with the twigs that 25 threatens them. I hope I need not to advise you further; but I hope your own grace will keep you where you are, though there were no further danger known but the modesty which is so lost. 30

Dia. You shall not need to fear me.

Enter HELENA [*disguised like a Pilgrim*].

Wid. I hope so. Look, here comes a pilgrim. I

know she will lie at my house; thither they send one another. I'll question her. God save you, pilgrim! whither are you bound? 36

Hel. To Saint Jaques le Grand.
Where do the palmers lodge, I do beseech you?

Wid. At the Saint Francis here beside the port.

Hel. Is this the way?   [*A march afar.* 40

Wid. Ay, marry, is't. Hark you! they come this way.
If you will tarry, holy pilgrim,
But till the troops come by,
I will conduct you where you shall be lodg'd;
The rather, for I think I know your hostess 45
As ample as myself.

Hel.   Is it yourself?

Wid. If you shall please so, pilgrim.

Hel. I thank you, and will stay upon your leisure.

Wid. You came, I think, from France?

Hel.   I did so.

Wid. Here you shall see a countryman of yours
That has done worthy service.

Hel.   His name, I pray you.

Dia. The Count Rousillon. Know you such a one? 52

Hel. But by the ear, that hears most nobly of him.
His face I know not.

Dia.   Whatsome'er he is,
He's bravely taken here. He stole from France, 55
As 'tis reported, for the King had married him
Against his liking. Think you it is so?

Hel. Ay, surely, mere the truth. I know his lady.

Dia. There is a gentleman that serves the Count
Reports but coarsely of her.

Hel.   What's his name? 60

Dia. Monsieur Parolles.

Hel.   O, I believe with him.
In argument of praise, or to the worth
Of the great Count himself, she is too mean
To have her name repeated. All her deserving
Is a reserved honesty, and that 65
I have not heard examin'd.

Dia.   Alas, poor lady!
'Tis a hard bondage to become the wife
Of a detesting lord.

Wid. [Ay, right!] Good creature, wheresoe'er she is,
Her heart weighs sadly. This young maid might do her 70
A shrewd turn, if she pleas'd.

Hel.   How do you mean?
May be the amorous Count solicits her

Sc. v. s.d. *tucket:* a flourish on a trumpet. VIOLENTA. See Introduction. 14. **honesty:** chastity. 18. **suggestions:** temptations. 20. **engines:** devices. 21. **go under:** pretend to be. 24. **succession:** i.e., other girls from the same course. 25. **limed:** ensnared. 31. **fear:** i.e., fear for. 39. **port:** gate. 46. **ample:** well. 55. **bravely taken:** taken for a brave fellow. 58. **mere:** plain. 65. **reserved:** well-guarded. 69. **[Ay, right]** (Capell). *I write* F₁; *I right* F₂₋₄.

In the unlawful purpose.
Wid.   He does indeed;
And brokes with all that can in such a suit
Corrupt the tender honour of a maid.   75
But she is arm'd for him and keeps her guard
In honestest defence.

Drum and colours. Enter BERTRAM, PAROLLES,
and the whole army.

Mar.   The gods forbid else!
Wid. So, now they come.
That is Antonio, the Duke's eldest son;
That, Escalus.
Hel.   Which is the Frenchman?
Dia.   He,   80
That with the plume; 'tis a most gallant fellow.
I would he lov'd his wife.   If he were honester
He were much goodlier.   Is't not a handsome gen-
        tleman?
Hel. I like him well.
Dia. 'Tis pity he is not honest.   Yond's that
        same knave   85
That leads him to these places.   Were I his lady,
I would poison that vile rascal.
Hel.   Which is he?
Dia. That jack-an-apes with scarfs.   Why is he
melancholy?
Hel. Perchance he's hurt i' th' battle.   90
Par. Lose our drum!   Well.
Mar. He's shrewdly vex'd at something.   Look,
he has spied us.
Wid. Marry, hang you!
Mar. And your courtesy, for a ring-carrier!   95
        [*Exeunt* [*Bertram, Parolles, and army*].
Wid. The troop is past.   Come, pilgrim, I will
        bring you
Where you shall host.   Of enjoin'd penitents
There's four or five, to great Saint Jaques bound,
Already at my house.
Hel.   I humbly thank you.
Please it this matron and this gentle maid   100
To eat with us to-night, the charge and thanking
Shall be for me; and, to requite you further,
I will bestow some precepts of this virgin
Worthy the note.
Both.   We'll take your offer kindly.
                                        [*Exeunt.*

[SCENE VI.   *Camp before Florence.*]

Enter BERTRAM *and the French* LORDS, *as at first.*

2. Lord. Nay, good my lord, put him to't; let him
have his way.

1. Lord. If your lordship find him not a hilding,
hold me no more in your respect.
2. Lord. On my life, my lord, a bubble.
Ber. Do you think I am so far deceived in him?   7
2. Lord. Believe it, my lord, in mine own direct
knowledge, without any malice, but to speak of him
as my kinsman, he's a most notable coward, an   10
infinite and endless liar, an hourly promise-breaker,
the owner of no one good quality worthy your
lordship's entertainment.   13
1. Lord. It were fit you knew him, lest, reposing
too far in his virtue, which he hath not, he might at
some great and trusty business in a main danger
fail you.
Ber. I would I knew in what particular action to
try him.   19
1. Lord. None better than to let him fetch off
his drum, which you hear him so confidently undertake to do.
2. Lord. I, with a troop of Florentines, will suddenly surprise him; such I will have, whom I am
sure he knows not from the enemy.   We will   25
bind and hoodwink him so that he shall suppose no
other but that he is carried into the leaguer of the
adversaries, when we bring him to our own tents.
Be but your lordship present at his examination;
if he do not, for the promise of his life and in the   30
highest compulsion of base fear, offer to betray you
and deliver all the intelligence in his power against
you, and that with the divine forfeit of his soul
upon oath, never trust my judgment in anything.   35
1. Lord. O, for the love of laughter, let him fetch
his drum; he says he has a stratagem for't.   When
your lordship sees the bottom of [his] success in't,
and to what metal this counterfeit lump of [ore]
will be melted, if you give him not John Drum's
entertainment, your inclining cannot be removed.
Here he comes.   42

Enter PAROLLES.

2. Lord. [*Aside to Ber.*] O, for the love of
laughter, hinder not the honour of his design.   Let
him fetch off his drum in any hand.   45
Ber. How now, monsieur! this drum sticks sorely
in your disposition.
1. Lord. A pox on't, let it go; 'tis but a drum.   49
Par. "But a drum"! is't "but a drum"?   A
drum so lost!   There was excellent command, —
to charge in with our horse upon our own wings, and
to rend our own soldiers!   53
1. Lord. That was not to be blam'd in the command of the service; it was a disaster of war that

---

74. **brokes:** deals.   86. **places:** i.e., brothels.   92. **shrewdly:** keenly.   95. **ring-carrier:** go-between.   97. **host:** lodge.
enjoin'd penitents: pilgrims performing penance.   103. **of:** on.
    Sc. vi, 3. **hilding:** coward.   5. **bubble:** sham.   13. **entertainment:** employment.   16. **main:** very great.   20. **fetch off:**
retrieve.   26. **hoodwink:** blindfold.   27. **leaguer:** camp.   38. **[his]** (Rowe).   *this* F.   39. **[ore]** (Theobald).   *ours* F.
40. **John Drum's entertainment:** a beating.   See Introduction.   41. **inclining:** partiality.   45. **hand:** event.

Cæsar himself could not have prevented, if he had
been there to command.   57

Ber. Well, we cannot greatly condemn our success. Some dishonour we had in the loss of that
drum; but it is not to be recovered.

Par. It might have been recovered.   61

Ber. It might; but it is not now.

Par. It is to be recovered. But that the merit
of service is seldom attributed to the true and exact
performer, I would have that drum or another, or
"*hic jacet.*"   66

Ber. Why, if you have a stomach, to't, monsieur:
if you think your mystery in stratagem can bring
this instrument of honour again into his native
quarter, be magnanimous in the enterprise and   70
go on; I will grace the attempt for a worthy exploit.
If you speed well in it, the Duke shall both speak of
it, and extend to you what further becomes his
greatness, even to the utmost syllable of your
worthiness.   75

Par. By the hand of a soldier, I will undertake it.

Ber. But you must not now slumber in it.

Par. I'll about it this evening; and I will presently pen down my dilemmas, encourage myself   80
in my certainty, put myself into my mortal preparation; and by midnight look to hear further from me.

Ber. May I be bold to acquaint his Grace you are
gone about it?   85

Par. I know not what the success will be, my
lord; but the attempt I vow.

Ber. I know thou'rt valiant; and to the possibility
of thy soldiership will subscribe for thee. Farewell.   90

Par. I love not many words.   [*Exit.*

2. Lord. No more than a fish loves water. Is
not this a strange fellow, my lord, that so confidently seems to undertake this business, which he
knows is not to be done; damns himself to do, and
dares better be damned than to do't?   96

1. Lord. You do not know him, my lord, as we
do. Certain it is, that he will steal himself into a
man's favour and for a week escape a great deal of
discoveries; but when you find him out, you have
him ever after.   101

Ber. Why, do you think he will make no deed at
all of this that so seriously he does address himself
unto?   104

2. Lord. None in the world; but return with an
invention and clap upon you two or three probable
lies. But we have almost emboss'd him; you shall
see his fall to-night; for indeed he is not for your
lordship's respect.   109

1. Lord. We'll make you some sport with the fox
ere we case him. He was first smok'd by the old
lord Lafeu. When his disguise and he is parted,
tell me what a sprat you shall find him; which you
shall see this very night.   114

2. Lord. I must go look my twigs. He shall be
caught.

Ber. Your brother he shall go along with me.

2. Lord. As't please your lordship. I'll leave
you.   [*Exit.*]

Ber. Now will I lead you to the house, and show
you
The lass I spoke of.

1. Lord.   But you say she's honest.

Ber. That's all the fault. I spoke with her but
once   120
And found her wondrous cold; but I sent to her,
By this same coxcomb that we have i' the wind,
Tokens and letters which she did re-send;
And this is all I have done. She's a fair creature:
Will you go see her?

1. Lord.   With all my heart, my lord.   125
    [*Exeunt.*

[SCENE VII.   *Florence.   The Widow's house.*]

Enter HELENA *and* WIDOW.

Hel. If you misdoubt me that I am not she,
I know not how I shall assure you further
But I shall lose the grounds I work upon.

Wid. Though my estate be fallen, I was well born,
Nothing acquainted with these businesses,   5
And would not put my reputation now
In any staining act.

Hel.   Nor would I wish you.
First, give me trust, the Count he is my husband;
And what to your sworn counsel I have spoken
Is so from word to word; and then you cannot,   10
By the good aid that I of you shall borrow,
Err in bestowing it.

Wid.   I should believe you;
For you have show'd me that which well approves
You're great in fortune.

Hel.   Take this purse of gold,
And let me buy your friendly help thus far,   15
Which I will over-pay and pay again
When I have found it. The Count he wooes your
daughter,
Lays down his wanton siege before her beauty,
[Resolves] to carry her. Let her, in fine, consent
As we'll direct her how 'tis best to bear it.   20
Now his important blood will nought deny

---

66. "*hic jacet*": "here lies."   67. **stomach:** inclination, courage.   68. **mystery:** skill.   80. **dilemmas:** alternatives.
81–82. **put ... preparation:** prepare for my (possible) death.   88. **possibility:** capability.   107. **emboss'd:** cornered, trapped.
111. **case:** flay.   **smok'd:** detected.   113. **sprat:** a worthless fish.   115. **look my twigs:** i.e., get my snare ready (cf. III.v.25).
    Sc. vii, 3. **But ... upon:** i.e., without calling in Bertram, which would ruin her plan.   9. **counsel:** secrecy.   12. **it:** the aid.
19. [**Resolves**] F₂₋₄.   *Resolve* F₁.   **in fine:** in short.   21. **important:** importunate, urgent.

That she'll demand.   A ring the County wears,
That downward hath succeeded in his house
From son to son, some four or five descents
Since the first father wore it.   This ring he holds   25
In most rich choice; yet in his idle fire,
To buy his will, it would not seem too dear,
Howe'er repented after.
   Wid.   Now I see
The bottom of your purpose.
   Hel. You see it lawful, then.   It is no more   30
But that your daughter, ere she seems as won,
Desires this ring; appoints him an encounter;
In fine, delivers me to fill the time,
Herself most chastely absent.   After [this],
To marry her, I'll add three thousand crowns   35
To what is past already.
   Wid.   I have yielded.
Instruct my daughter how she shall persever,
That time and place with this deceit so lawful
May prove coherent.   Every night he comes
With musics of all sorts and songs compos'd   40
To her unworthiness.   It nothing steads us
To chide him from our eaves, for he persists
As if his life lay on't.
   Hel.   Why then to-night
Let us assay our plot; which, if it speed,
Is wicked meaning in a lawful deed   45
And lawful meaning in a lawful act,
Where both not sin, and yet a sinful fact.
But let's about it.   [*Exeunt.*]

ACT IV

[SCENE I.   *Without the Florentine camp.*]

Enter Second French LORD, *with five or six other*
SOLDIERS *in ambush.*

   2. Lord. He can come no other way but by this
hedge-corner.   When you sally upon him, speak
what terrible language you will.   Though you understand it not yourselves, no matter; for we must
not seem to understand him, unless some one among
us, whom we must produce for an interpreter.   7
   1. Sold. Good captain, let me be th' interpreter.
   2. Lord. Art not acquainted with him?   Knows
he not thy voice?   11
   1. Sold. No, sir, I warrant you.
   2. Lord. But what linsey-woolsey hast thou to
speak to us again?
   1. Sold. E'en such as you speak to me.   15
   2. Lord. He must think us some band of strangers
i' th' adversary's entertainment.   Now he hath a

smack of all neighbouring languages, therefore we
must every one be a man of his own fancy; not to
know what we speak one to another, so we seem   20
to know, is to know straight our purpose: choughs'
language, gabble enough, and good enough.   As
for you, interpreter, you must seem very politic.
But couch, ho! here he comes, to beguile two hours
in a sleep, and then to return and swear the lies
he forges.   26

Enter PAROLLES.

   Par. Ten o'clock: within these three hours 'twill
be time enough to go home.   What shall I say I
have done?   It must be a very plausive invention
that carries it.   They begin to smoke me, and   30
disgraces have of late knock'd too often at my door.
I find my tongue is too foolhardy; but my heart
hath the fear of Mars before it and of his creatures,
not daring the reports of my tongue.
   2. Lord. [*Aside, in ambush.*] This is the first
truth that e'er thine own tongue was guilty of.   36
   Par. What the devil should move me to undertake the recovery of this drum, being not ignorant
of the impossibility, and knowing I had no such
purpose?   I must give myself some hurts, and   40
say I got them in exploit.   Yet slight ones will not
carry it.   They will say, "Came you off with so
little?"   And great ones I dare not give.   Wherefore, what's the instance?   Tongue, I must put you
into a butter-woman's mouth and buy myself   45
another of Bajazet's mule, if you prattle me into
these perils.
   2. Lord. Is it possible he should know what he is,
and be that he is?   49
   Par. I would the cutting of my garments would
serve the turn, or the breaking of my Spanish
sword, —
   2. Lord. We cannot afford you so.
   Par. Or the baring of my beard; and to say it was
in stratagem.   55
   2. Lord. 'Twould not do.
   Par. Or to drown my clothes, and say I was
stripp'd.
   2. Lord. Hardly serve.
   Par. Though I swore I leap'd from the window
of the citadel —   61
   2. Lord. How deep?
   Par. Thirty fathom.
   2. Lord. Three great oaths would scarce make
that be believed.   65
   Par. I would I had any drum of the enemy's.   I
would swear I recover'd it.
   2. Lord. You shall hear one anon.

26. **choice:** esteem.   34. **[this]** F2.   Om. F1.   41. **To her unworthiness:** toward her undoing.
   Act IV, sc. i, 13. linsey-woolsey: jargon.   21. **know straight:** i.e., effect, realize.   **choughs':** jackdaws'.   29. **plausive:**
plausible.   44. **instance:** proof.   46. **Bajazet's mule.**   Perhaps, Balaam's ass.   52. **afford you so:** let you off that way.
54. **baring:** shaving.

Par. A drum now of the enemy's —
        [*Alarum within.*
2. Lord. *Throca movousus, cargo, cargo, cargo.* 71
All. *Cargo, cargo, cargo, villianda par corbo, cargo.*
Par. O, ransom, ransom! do not hide mine eyes.
        [*They seize and blindfold him.*]
1. Sold. *Bosko thromuldo boskos.* 75
Par. I know you are the Muskos' regiment,
And I shall lose my life for want of language.
If there be here German, or Dane, Low Dutch,
Italian, or French, let him speak to me; I'll 79
Discover that which shall undo the Florentine.
1. Sold. *Boskos vauvado:* I understand thee, and
can speak thy tongue. *Kerelybonto*, sir, betake
thee to thy faith, for seventeen poniards are at thy
bosom.
Par. O! 85
1. Sold. O, pray, pray, pray! *Manka revania
dulche.*
2. Lord. *Oscorbidulchos volivorco.*
1. Sold. The general is content to spare thee
yet; 89
And, hoodwink'd as thou art, will lead thee on
To gather from thee. Haply thou mayst inform
Something to save thy life.
Par. O, let me live!
And all the secrets of our camp I'll show,
Their force, their purposes; nay, I'll speak that
Which you will wonder at.
1. Sold. But wilt thou faithfully?
Par. If I do not, damn me. 96
1. Sold. *Acordo linta.*
Come on; thou art granted space.
    [*Exit [with Parolles guarded].* *A short
    alarum within.*
2. Lord. Go, tell the Count Rousillon, and my
brother,
We have caught the woodcock, and will keep him
muffled 100
Till we do hear from them.
2. Sold. Captain, I will.
2. Lord. 'A will betray us all unto ourselves:
Inform on that.
2. Sold. So I will, sir.
2. Lord. Till then I'll keep him dark and safely
lock'd. [*Exeunt.* 105

[SCENE II. *Florence. The Widow's house.*]

Enter BERTRAM *and the maid called* DIANA.

Ber. They told me that your name was Fontibell.
Dia. No, my good lord, Diana.
Ber. Titled goddess,
And worth it, with addition! But, fair soul,
In your fine frame hath love no quality?

If the quick fire of youth light not your mind 5
You are no maiden, but a monument.
When you are dead you should be such a one
As you are now, for you are cold and stern;
And now you should be as your mother was
When your sweet self was got. 10
Dia. She then was honest.
Ber. So should you be.
Dia. No;
My mother did but duty; such, my lord,
As you owe to your wife.
Ber. No more o' that.
I prithee, do not strive against my vows.
I was compell'd to her; but I love thee 15
By love's own sweet constraint, and will for ever
Do thee all rights of service.
Dia. Ay, so you serve us
Till we serve you; but when you have our roses,
You barely leave our thorns to prick ourselves,
And mock us with our bareness.
Ber. How have I sworn!
Dia. 'Tis not the many oaths that makes the
truth, 21
But the plain single vow that is vow'd true.
What is not holy, that we swear not by,
But take the High'st to witness. Then, pray you,
tell me,
If I should swear by Jove's great attributes 25
I lov'd you dearly, would you believe my oaths
When I did love you ill? This has no holding,
To swear by Him whom I protest to love,
That I will work against Him; therefore your oaths
Are words and poor conditions, but unseal'd, 30
At least in my opinion.
Ber. Change it, change it!
Be not so holy-cruel. Love is holy,
And my integrity ne'er knew the crafts
That you do charge men with. Stand no more off,
But give thyself unto my sick desires, 35
Who then recovers. Say thou art mine, and ever
My love, as it begins, shall so persever.
Dia. I see that men make rope's in such a scarre
That we'll forsake ourselves. Give me that ring.
Ber. I'll lend it thee, my dear; but have no
power 40
To give it from me.
Dia. Will you not, my lord?
Ber. It is an honour 'longing to our house,
Bequeathed down from many ancestors,
Which were the greatest obloquy i' th' world
In me to lose.
Dia. Mine honour's such a ring, 45
My chastity's the jewel of our house,
Bequeathed down from many ancestors,
Which were the greatest obloquy i' th' world

Sc. ii, 27. **holding:** consistency. 30. **unseal'd:** invalid (because lacking a seal). 38. **I...scarre.** This line is hopelessly corrupt.

In me to lose. Thus your own proper wisdom
Brings in the champion Honour on my part,   50
Against your vain assault.
      Ber.   Here, take my ring!
My house, mine honour, yea, my life, be thine,
And I'll be bid by thee.
      Dia. When midnight comes, knock at my cham-
ber-window.
I'll order take my mother shall not hear.   55
Now will I charge you in the band of truth,
When you have conquer'd my yet maiden bed,
Remain there but an hour, nor speak to me.
My reasons are most strong, and you shall know
      them
When back again this ring shall be deliver'd;   60
And on your finger in the night I'll put
Another ring, that what in time proceeds
May token to the future our past deeds.
Adieu, till then; then, fail not. You have won
A wife of me, though there my hope be done.   65
      Ber. A heaven on earth I have won by wooing
            thee.   [*Exit.*]
      Dia. For which live long to thank both Heaven
            and me!
You may so in the end.
My mother told me just how he would woo,
As if she sat in's heart. She says all men   70
Have the like oaths. He had sworn to marry me
When his wife's dead; therefore I'll lie with him
When I am buried. Since Frenchmen are so braid,
Marry that will, I live and die a maid.
Only in this disguise I think't no sin   75
To cozen him that would unjustly win.   [*Exit.*]

[SCENE III.   *The Florentine camp.*]

Enter the two French LORDS *and some two or three*
            Soldiers.

      2. Lord. You have not given him his mother's
letter?
      1. Lord. I have deliver'd it an hour since. There
is something in't that stings his nature; for on the
reading it he chang'd almost into another man.   6
      2. Lord. He has much worthy blame laid upon
him for shaking off so good a wife and so sweet a
lady.   9
      1. Lord. Especially he hath incurred the ever-
lasting displeasure of the King, who had even tun'd
his bounty to sing happiness to him. I will tell you
a thing, but you shall let it dwell darkly with you. 14
      2. Lord. When you have spoken it, 'tis dead, and
I am the grave of it.

      1. Lord. He hath perverted a young gentle-
woman here in Florence, of a most chaste renown;
and this night he fleshes his will in the spoil of her
honour. He hath given her his monumental   20
ring, and thinks himself made in the unchaste
composition.
      2. Lord. Now, God delay our rebellion! As we
are ourselves, what things are we!   24
      1. Lord. Merely our own traitors. And as in
the common course of all treasons, we still see them
reveal themselves, till they attain to their abhorr'd
ends, so he that in this action contrives against his
own nobility, in his proper stream o'erflows himself.   30
      2. Lord. Is it not meant damnable in us, to be
trumpeters of our unlawful intents? We shall not
then have his company to-night?
      1. Lord. Not till after midnight; for he is dieted
to his hour.   35
      2. Lord. That approaches apace. I would gladly
have him see his company anatomiz'd, that he
might take a measure of his own judgements,
wherein so curiously he had set this counterfeit.   40
      1. Lord. We will not meddle with him till he
come, for his presence must be the whip of the
other.
      2. Lord. In the mean time, what hear you of
these wars?   45
      1. Lord. I hear there is an overture of peace.
      2. Lord. Nay, I assure you, a peace concluded.
      1. Lord. What will Count Rousillon do then?
Will he travel higher, or return again into France? 51
      2. Lord. I perceive, by this demand, you are not
altogether of his counsel.
      1. Lord. Let it be forbid, sir; so should I be a
great deal of his act.   55
      2. Lord. Sir, his wife some two months since fled
from his house. Her pretence is a pilgrimage to
Saint Jaques le Grand; which holy undertaking with
most austere sanctimony she accomplish'd; and,
there residing, the tenderness of her nature be-   60
came as a prey to her grief; in fine, made a groan of
her last breath, and now she sings in heaven.
      1. Lord. How is this justified?   64
      2. Lord. The stronger part of it by her own
letters, which makes her story true, even to the
point of her death. Her death itself, which could
not be her office to say is come, was faithfully confirm'd by the rector of the place.   69
      1. Lord. Hath the Count all this intelligence?
      2. Lord. Ay, and the particular confirmations,
point from point, to the full arming of the verity.

---

49. **own proper:** very own.   71. **had:** would have.   73. **braid:** deceitful.   76. **cozen:** cheat.
      Sc. iii, 7. **worthy:** deserved.   19. **fleshes his will:** satiates his lust.   20. **monumental:** memorial.   22. **composition:**
bargain.   23. **delay our rebellion:** make us slow to rebel against his law.   24. **are ourselves:** i.e., without God's aid.   25.
our own traitors: traitors to ourselves.   31. **meant damnable:** a damnable intention.   34. **dieted:** prescribed, bound.   37.
company: companion, i.e., Parolles.   40. **curiously:** carefully.   **set.** The metaphor is from jewelry.   51. **higher:** farther into
Italy.   53. **of his counsel:** in his confidence.   57. **pretence:** intent.   64. **justified:** confirmed, proved.   65. **stronger:**
greater.   69. **rector:** ruler.

1. Lord. I am heartily sorry that he'll be glad of this. 75

2. Lord. How mightily sometimes we make us comforts of our losses!

1. Lord. And how mightily some other times we drown our gain in tears! The great dignity that his valour hath here acquir'd for him shall at home be encount'red with a shame as ample. 82

2. Lord. The web of our life is of a mingled yarn, good and ill together: our virtues would be proud, if our faults whipp'd them not; and our crimes would despair, if they were not cherish'd by our virtues. 87

Enter a MESSENGER.

How now! where's your master?

Mess. He met the Duke in the street, sir, of whom he hath taken a solemn leave. His lordship will next morning for France. The Duke 90 hath offered him letters of commendations to the King.

1. Lord. They shall be no more than needful there, if they were more than they can commend.

Enter BERTRAM.

2. Lord. They cannot be too sweet for the King's tartness. Here's his lordship now. How now, my lord! is't not after midnight? 97

Ber. I have to-night dispatch'd sixteen businesses, a month's length a-piece, by an abstract of success. I have congied with the Duke, done 100 my adieu with his nearest; buried a wife, mourn'd for her; writ to my lady mother I am returning; entertain'd my convoy; and between these main parcels of dispatch [effected] many nicer needs. The last was the greatest, but that I have not ended yet. 106

1. Lord. If the business be of any difficulty, and this morning your departure hence, it requires haste of your lordship. 109

Ber. I mean, the business is not ended, as fearing to hear of it hereafter. But shall we have this dialogue between the fool and the soldier? Come, bring forth this counterfeit module, has deceiv'd me, like a double-meaning prophesier. 115

1. Lord. Bring him forth. Has sat i' th' stocks all night, poor gallant knave.

Ber. No matter; his heels have deserv'd it, in usurping his spurs so long. How does he carry himself? 120

1. Lord. I have told your lordship already, the stocks carry him. But to answer you as you

would be understood, he weeps like a wench that had shed her milk. He hath confess'd himself to Morgan, whom he supposes to be a friar, from 125 the time of his remembrance to this very instant disaster of his setting i' th' stocks; and what think you he hath confess'd?

Ber. Nothing of me, has 'a? 129

1. Lord. His confession is taken, and it shall be read to his face. If your lordship be in't, as I believe you are, you must have the patience to hear it.

Enter PAROLLES *with* [FIRST SOLDIER *as*] *his Interpreter.*

Ber. A plague upon him! Muffled! He can say nothing of me. 135

2. Lord. Hush! hush! Hoodman comes! *Portotartarossa.*

1. Sold. He calls for the tortures. What will you say without 'em?

Par. I will confess what I know without constraint. If ye pinch me like a pasty, I can say no more. 141

1. Sold. Bosko chimurco.

2. Lord. Boblibindo chicurmurco.

1. Sold. You are a merciful general. Our general bids you answer to what I shall ask you out of a note. 146

Par. And truly, as I hope to live.

1. Sold. [*Reads.*] "First demand of him how many horse the Duke is strong." What say you to that? 150

Par. Five or six thousand; but very weak and unserviceable. The troops are all scattered, and the commanders very poor rogues, upon my reputation and credit and as I hope to live. 154

1. Sold. Shall I set down your answer so?

Par. Do: I'll take the sacrament on't, how and which way you will.

Ber. All's one to him. What a past-saving slave is this! 159

2. Lord. You're deceiv'd, my lord; this is Monsieur Parolles, the gallant militarist, — that was his own phrase, — that had the whole theoric of war in the knot of his scarf, and the practice in the chape of his dagger. 164

1. Lord. I will never trust a man again for keeping his sword clean, nor believe he can have everything in him by wearing his apparel neatly.

1. Sold. Well, that's set down. 169

Par. Five or six thousand horse, I said, — I will say true, — or thereabouts, set down, for I'll speak truth.

---

99. **abstract:** condensation. 100. **congied with:** taken leave of. 103. **entertain'd:** engaged. 104. [**effected**] F₂. *affected* F₁. 114. **module:** model. 126. **instant:** present. 136. **Hush! hush!** Cont. by F to Bertram. Rectified by Hanmer. **Hoodman comes.** A cry in blindman's buff. 156–57. **how . . . way:** i.e., either the Catholic or Protestant way. Parolles isn't sure about the religion of his captors. 158. **All's . . . him.** Cont. by F to Parolles. Rectified by Capell. 163. **chape:** metal part of sheath.

2. Lord. He's very near the truth in this.

Ber. But I con him no thanks for't, in the nature he delivers it.   175

Par. Poor rogues, I pray you, say.

1. Sold. Well, that's set down.

Par. I humbly thank you, sir. A truth's a truth; the rogues are marvellous poor.   179

1. Sold. [*Reads.*] "Demand of him, of what strength they are a-foot." What say you to that?

Par. By my troth, sir, if I were to live this present hour, I will tell true. Let me see: — Spurio, a hundred and fifty; Sebastian, so many; Corambus, so many; Jaques, so many; Guiltian, Cosmo,   185 Lodowick, and Gratii, two hundred fifty each; mine own company, Chitopher, Vaumond, Bentii, two hundred fifty each; so that the muster-file, rotten and sound, upon my life, amounts not to fifteen thousand poll; half of the which dare not shake   190 the snow from off their cassocks, lest they shake themselves to pieces.

Ber. What shall be done to him?   194

2. Lord. Nothing, but let him have thanks. Demand of him my condition, and what credit I have with the Duke.

1. Sold. Well, that's set down. [*Reads.*] "You shall demand of him, whether one Captain Dumain be i' th' camp, a Frenchman; what his reputation is with the Duke; what his   200 valour, honesty, and expertness in wars; or whether he thinks it were not possible, with well-weighing sums of gold, to corrupt him to a revolt." What say you to this? What do you know of it?   205

Par. I beseech you, let me answer to the particular of the inter'gatories. Demand them singly.   208

1. Sold. Do you know this Captain Dumain?

Par. I know him. 'A was a botcher's 'prentice in Paris, from whence he was whipp'd for getting the shrieve's fool with child, — a dumb innocent, that could not say him nay.   214

Ber. Nay, by your leave, hold your hands; though I know his brains are forfeit to the next tile that falls.

1. Sold. Well, is this captain in the Duke of Florence's camp?   219

Par. Upon my knowledge, he is, and lousy.

2. Lord. Nay, look not so upon me; we shall hear of your [lordship] anon.

1. Sold. What is his reputation with the Duke?   224

Par. The Duke knows him for no other but a poor officer of mine; and writ to me this other day

to turn him out o' th' band. I think I have his letter in my pocket.

1. Sold. Marry, we'll search.   229

Par. In good sadness, I do not know. Either it is there, or it is upon a file with the Duke's other letters in my tent.

1. Sold. Here 'tis; here's a paper. Shall I read it to you?

Par. I do not know if it be it or no.   235

Ber. Our interpreter does it well.

2. Lord. Excellently.

1. Sold. [*Reads.*] "Dian, the Count's a fool, and full of gold," —

Par. That is not the Duke's letter, sir; that is an advertisement to a proper maid in Florence,   240 one Diana, to take heed of the allurement of one Count Rousillon, a foolish idle boy, but for all that very ruttish. I pray you, sir, put it up again.

1. Sold. Nay, I'll read it first, by your favour.   245

Par. My meaning in't, I protest, was very honest in the behalf of the maid; for I knew the young Count to be a dangerous and lascivious boy, who is a whale to virginity and devours up all the fry it finds.   250

Ber. Damnable both-sides rogue!

1. Sold. [*Reads.*]

"When he swears oaths, bid him drop gold, and
    take it;
After he scores, he never pays the score.
Half won is match well made; match, and well
    make it;
He ne'er pays after-debts, take it before;   255
And say a soldier, Dian, told thee this,
Men are to mell with, boys are not to kiss;
For count of this, the Count's a fool, I know it,
Who pays before, but not when he does owe it.
    Thine, as he vow'd to thee in thine ear,   260
                                    PAROLLES."

Ber. He shall be whipp'd through the army with this rhyme in's forehead.

1. Lord. This is your devoted friend, sir, the manifold linguist and the armipotent soldier.   265

Ber. I could endure anything before but a cat; and now he's a cat to me.

1. Sold. I perceive, sir, by [our] general's looks, we shall be fain to hang you.   269

Par. My life, sir, in any case: not that I am afraid to die; but that, my offences being many, I would repent out the remainder of nature. Let me live, sir, in a dungeon, i' th' stocks, or anywhere, so I may live.   274

1. Sold. We'll see what may be done, so you

---

174. **con:** offer (lit. "know"). 182. **this:** i.e., only this. 191. **cassocks:** military cloaks. 196. **condition:** character. 210. **botcher:** mender of old clothes. 213. **shrieve's fool:** sheriff's idiot. In Shakespeare's time idiots were generally wards of the Crown or of some member of the Court, but the poor were sometimes placed under the guardianship of the sheriff. 222. **[lordship]** (Pope). *Lord* F. 230. **good sadness:** all seriousness. 243. **ruttish:** lustful. 254. **Half...it:** a bargain well-planned is half won, so plan yours well. 257. **mell:** embrace. 268. **[our]** (Capell). *your* F$_{1,2}$; *the* F$_{3,4}$. 272. **out...** **nature:** the rest of my life.

confess freely; therefore, once more to this Captain Dumain. You have answer'd to his reputation with the Duke, and to his valour; what is his honesty? 279

Par. He will steal, sir, an egg out of a cloister. For rapes and ravishments he parallels Nessus. He professes not keeping of oaths; in breaking 'em he is stronger than Hercules; he will lie, sir, with such volubility, that you would think Truth were a fool. Drunkenness is his best virtue, for he will be 285 swine drunk, and in his sleep he does little harm, save to his bed-clothes about him; but they know his conditions and lay him in straw. I have but little more to say, sir, of his honesty. He has everything that an honest man should not have; 290 what an honest man should have, he has nothing.

2. Lord. I begin to love him for this.

Ber. For this description of thine honesty? A pox upon him for me, he's more and more a cat. 295

1. Sold. What say you to his expertness in war?

Par. Faith, sir, has led the drum before the English tragedians. To belie him, I will not, and more of his soldiership I know not; except, in 300 that country he had the honour to be the officer at a place there called Mile-end, to instruct for the doubling of files. I would do the man what honour I can, but of this I am not certain. 304

2. Lord. He hath out-villain'd villainy so far, that the rarity redeems him.

Ber. A pox on him, he's a cat still.

1. Sold. His qualities being at this poor price, I need not to ask you if gold will corrupt him to revolt. 310

Par. Sir, for a *quart d'écu* he will sell the fee-simple of his salvation, the inheritance of it; and cut th' entail from all remainders, and a perpetual succession for it perpetually. 314

1. Sold. What's his brother, the other Captain Dumain?

1. Lord. Why does he ask him of me?

1. Sold. What's he? 318

Par. E'en a crow o' th' same nest; not altogether so great as the first in goodness, but greater a great deal in evil. He excels his brother for a coward, yet his brother is reputed one of the best that is. In a retreat he outruns any lackey; marry, in coming on he has the cramp. 324

1. Sold. If your life be saved, will you undertake to betray the Florentine?

Par. Ay, and the captain of his horse, Count Rousillon.

1. Sold. I'll whisper with the general, and know his pleasure. 330

Par. [*Aside.*] I'll no more drumming; a plague of all drums! Only to seem to deserve well, and to beguile the supposition of that lascivious young boy the Count, have I run into this danger. Yet who would have suspected an ambush where I was taken? 336

1. Sold. There is no remedy, sir, but you must die. The general says, you that have so traitorously discover'd the secrets of your army and made such pestiferous reports of men very nobly held, 340 can serve the world for no honest use; therefore you must die. Come, headsman, off with his head.

Par. O Lord, sir, let me live, or let me see my death! 345

1. Sold. That shall you, and take your leave of all your friends. [*Unblinding him.*] So, look about you. Know you any here?

Ber. Good morrow, noble captain. 349

1. Lord. God bless you, Captain Parolles.

2. Lord. God save you, noble captain.

1. Lord. Captain, what greeting will you to my Lord Lafeu? I am for France. 353

2. Lord. Good captain, will you give me a copy of the sonnet you writ to Diana in behalf of the Count Rousillon? An I were not a very coward, I'd compel it of you; but fare you well.

[*Exeunt* [*Bertram and Lords*].

1. Sold. You are undone, captain, all but your scarf; that has a knot on't yet.

Par. Who cannot be crush'd with a plot? 360

1. Sold. If you could find out a country where but women were that had received so much shame, you might begin an impudent nation. Fare ye well, sir; I am for France too. We shall speak of you there. [*Exit* [*with Soldiers*]. 365

Par. Yet am I thankful. If my heart were great, 'Twould burst at this. Captain I'll be no more; But I will eat and drink, and sleep as soft As captain shall. Simply the thing I am Shall make me live. Who knows himself a braggart, 370 Let him fear this; for it will come to pass That every braggart shall be found an ass. Rust, sword! cool, blushes! and, Parolles, live Safest in shame! Being fool'd, by fool'ry thrive! There's place and means for every man alive. I'll after them. [*Exit.* 376

[SCENE IV. *Florence. The Widow's house.*]

Enter HELENA, WIDOW, *and* DIANA.

Hel. That you may well perceive I have not
    wrong'd you,
One of the greatest in the Christian world

---

281. **Nessus:** the Centaur who tried to abduct Dejaneira, the wife of Hercules. 297. **led:** carried. 302. **Mile-end:** where the London militia drilled. 306. **rarity:** rare quality of his performance. 311. *quart d'écu:* a French coin worth eightpence. *Cardceue* F. **fee-simple:** absolute title. 333. **supposition:** imagination.

Shall be my surety; 'fore whose throne 'tis needful,
Ere I can perfect mine intents, to kneel.
Time was, I did him a desired office,   5
Dear almost as his life; which gratitude
Through flinty Tartar's bosom would peep forth
And answer thanks.   I duly am inform'd
His Grace is at Marseilles, to which place
We have convenient convoy.   You must know,   10
I am supposed dead.   The army breaking,
My husband hies him home; where, Heaven aiding,
And by the leave of my good lord the King,
We'll be before our welcome.
Wid.   Gentle madam,
You never had a servant to whose trust   15
Your business was more welcome.
Hel.   Nor you, mistress,
Ever a friend whose thoughts more truly labour
To recompense your love.   Doubt not but Heaven
Hath brought me up to be your daughter's dower,
As it hath fated her to be my motive   20
And helper to a husband.   But, O strange men!
That can such sweet use make of what they hate,
When saucy trusting of the cozen'd thoughts
Defiles the pitchy night; so lust doth play
With what it loathes for that which is away.   25
But more of this hereafter.   You, Diana,
Under my poor instructions yet must suffer
Something in my behalf.
Dia.   Let death and honesty
Go with your impositions, I am yours
Upon your will to suffer.
Hel.   Yet, I pray you.   30
But with the word the time will bring on summer,
When briers shall have leaves as well as thorns,
And be as sweet as sharp.   We must away.
Our waggon is prepar'd, and time revives us.
All's well that ends well!   Still the [fine's] the
          crown;   35
Whate'er the course, the end is the renown.
                                              [*Exeunt.*

[SCENE V.   *Rousillon.   The Count's palace.*]

Enter COUNTESS, LAFEU, *and* CLOWN.

Laf. No, no, no, your son was misled with a
snipt-taffeta fellow there, whose villanous saffron
would have made all the unbak'd and doughy youth
of a nation in his colour.   Your daughter-in-law had
been alive at this hour, and your son here at home,
more advanc'd by the King than by that red-tail'd
humble-bee I speak of.   7

Count. I would I had not known him.   It was
the death of the most virtuous gentlewoman that
ever Nature had praise for creating.   If she had
partaken of my flesh, and cost me the dearest groans
of a mother, I could not have owed her a more
rooted love.   13
Laf. 'Twas a good lady, 'twas a good lady.   We
may pick a thousand salads ere we light on such
another herb.   16
Clo. Indeed, sir, she was the sweet-marjoram of
the salad, or rather, the herb of grace.
Laf. They are not [salad] herbs, you knave; they
are nose-herbs.   20
Clo. I am no great Nebuchadnezzar, sir; I have
not much skill in [grass].
Laf. Whether dost thou profess thyself a knave
or a fool?
Clo. A fool, sir, at a woman's service, and a knave
at a man's.   26
Laf. Your distinction?
Clo. I would cozen the man of his wife and do his
service.
Laf. So you were a knave at his service, in-
deed.   31
Clo. And I would give his wife my bauble, sir, to
do her service.
Laf. I will subscribe for thee, thou art both
knave and fool.   35
Clo. At your service.
Laf. No, no, no.
Clo. Why, sir, if I cannot serve you, I can serve
as great a prince as you are.
Laf. Who's that?   A Frenchman?   40
Clo. Faith, sir, 'a has an English [name]; but his
fisnomy is more hotter in France than there.
Laf. What prince is that?
Clo. The Black Prince, sir; alias, the prince of
darkness; alias, the devil.   45
Laf. Hold thee, there's my purse.   I give thee
not this to suggest thee from thy master thou
talk'st of.   Serve him still.   48
Clo. I am a woodland fellow, sir, that always
loved a great fire; and the master I speak of ever
keeps a good fire.   But, sure, he is the prince of the
world; let his nobility remain in's court.   I am for
the house with the narrow gate, which I take to   53
be too little for pomp to enter.   Some that humble
themselves may; but the many will be too chill and
tender, and they'll be for the flow'ry way that leads
to the broad gate and the great fire.   58
Laf. Go thy ways, I begin to be aweary of thee;

Sc. iv, 11. **breaking**: disbanding.   14. **before our welcome**: i.e., before we are expected.   20. **motive**: agent.   23. **saucy**: wanton.   **cozen'd**: deceived.   30. **Yet**: i.e., yet a while.   31. **word**: i.e., promise.   Helena means to assure Diana that time will bring good out of all this scheming.   35. **the ... crown.**   Cf. *Finis coronat opus.*   [**fine's**] (Theobald).   *fine* F.
Sc. v, 2. **saffron**: yellow.   11. **dearest**: most grievous.   18. **herb of grace**: rue.   19. [**salad**] (Rowe).   Om. F.   20. **nose-herbs**: scented flowers.   22. [**grass**] (Rowe).   *grace* F.   Rowe's reading points the pun on "grace" (l.18).   41. [**name**] (Rowe).   *maine* F.   42. **fisnomy**: physiognomy.   47. **suggest**: lure.   55. **chill**: hesitating.

and I tell thee so before, because I would not fall out with thee. Go thy ways. Let my horses be well look'd to, without any tricks.   62

Clo. If I put any tricks upon 'em, sir, they shall be jades' tricks; which are their own right by the law of nature.   [*Exit.*

Laf. A shrewd knave and an unhappy.   66

Count. So 'a is. My lord that's gone made himself much sport out of him. By his authority he remains here, which he thinks is a patent for his sauciness; and, indeed, he has no pace, but runs where he will.   71

Laf. I like him well; 'tis not amiss. And I was about to tell you, since I heard of the good lady's death and that my lord your son was upon his return home, I moved the King my master to speak in the behalf of my daughter; which, in the mi-   76 nority of them both, his Majesty, out of a self-gracious remembrance, did first propose. His Highness hath promis'd me to do it; and, to stop up the displeasure he hath conceived against your son, there is no fitter matter. How does your ladyship like it?   82

Count. With very much content, my lord; and I wish it happily effected.

Laf. His Highness comes post from Marseilles, of as able body as when he number'd thirty. 'A will be here to-morrow, or I am deceiv'd by him that in such intelligence hath seldom fail'd.   88

Count. It rejoices me, that I hope I shall see him ere I die. I have letters that my son will be here to-night. I shall beseech your lordship to remain with me till they meet together.

Laf. Madam, I was thinking with what manners I might safely be admitted.   94

Count. You need but plead your honourable privilege.

Laf. Lady, of that I have made a bold charter; but I thank my God it holds yet.   98

Re-enter CLOWN.

Clo. O madam, yonder's my lord your son with a patch of velvet on's face. Whether there be a scar under't or no, the velvet knows; but 'tis a goodly patch of velvet. His left cheek is a cheek of two pile and a half, but his right cheek is worn bare.   104

Laf. A scar nobly got, or a noble scar, is a good livery of honour; so belike is that.

Clo. But it is your carbonado'd face.

Laf. Let us go see your son, I pray you. I long to talk with the young noble soldier.   109

Clo. 'Faith, there's a dozen of 'em, with delicate fine hats and most courteous feathers which bow the head and nod at every man.   [*Exeunt.*

ACT V

[SCENE I. *Marseilles. A street.*]

Enter HELENA, WIDOW, *and* DIANA, *with two Attendants.*

Hel. But this exceeding posting day and night
Must wear your spirits low; we cannot help it:
But since you have made the days and nights as one,
To wear your gentle limbs in my affairs,
Be bold you do so grow in my requital   5

Enter a [GENTLEMAN, A STRANGER].

As nothing can unroot you. In happy time!
This man may help me to his Majesty's ear,
If he would spend his power. God save you, sir.

Gent. And you.

Hel. Sir, I have seen you in the court of France.

Gent. I have been sometimes there.   11

Hel. I do presume, sir, that you are not fall'n
From the report that goes upon your goodness;
And therefore, goaded with most sharp occasions,
Which lay nice manners by, I put you to   15
The use of your own virtues, for the which
I shall continue thankful.

Gent.   What's your will?

Hel. That it will please you
To give this poor petition to the King,
And aid me with that store of power you have   20
To come into his presence.

Gent. The King's not here.

Hel.   Not here, sir!

Gent.   Not, indeed.
He hence remov'd last night, and with more haste
Than is his use.

Wid.   Lord, how we lose our pains!

Hel. All's well that ends well yet,   25
Though time seem so adverse and means unfit.
I do beseech you, whither is he gone?

Gent. Marry, as I take it, to Rousillon,
Whither I am going.

Hel.   I do beseech you, sir,
Since you are like to see the King before me,   30
Commend the paper to his gracious hand,
Which I presume shall render you no blame
But rather make you thank your pains for it.
I will come after you with what good speed

---

64. **jades' tricks:** sharp practices. Used punningly. 69. **patent:** license. 70. **pace:** training. 77. **self-gracious:** voluntary and gracious. 97. **charter:** claim of freedom. 103. **two...half.** A reference to the thickness of the nap of the velvet, "three pile" being the best quality. 107. **carbonado'd:** slashed.

Act V, sc. i, 5. **bold:** sure. 6. S.D. [GENTLEMAN, A STRANGER] F₃,₄. *gentle Astringer* F₁. *gentle Astranger* F₂. 14. **occasions:** necessities.

Our means will make us means.

Gent.   This I'll do for you.   35
Hel. And you shall find yourself to be well
thank'd,
Whate'er falls more.   We must to horse again.
Go, go, provide.   [*Exeunt.*]

[SCENE II. *Rousillon.   Inner court of the
Count's palace.*]

Enter CLOWN *and* PAROLLES.

Par. Good [*Monsieur*] Lavache, give my Lord
Lafeu this letter.   I have ere now, sir, been better
known to you, when I have held familiarity with
fresher clothes; but I am now, sir, muddied in
Fortune's mood, and smell somewhat strong of her
strong displeasure.   6
Clo. Truly, Fortune's displeasure is but sluttish,
if it smell so strongly as thou speak'st of.   I will
henceforth eat no fish of Fortune's butt'ring.
Prithee, allow the wind.   10
Par. Nay, you need not to stop your nose, sir;
I spake but by a metaphor.
Clo. Indeed, sir, if your metaphor stink, I will
stop my nose; or against any man's metaphor.
Prithee, get thee further.   15
Par. Pray you, sir, deliver me this paper.
Clo. Foh! prithee, stand away.   A paper from
Fortune's close-stool to give to a nobleman!   Look,
here he comes himself.   19

Enter LAFEU.

Here is a purr of Fortune's, sir, or of Fortune's
cat, — but not a musk-cat, — that has fall'n into
the unclean fishpond of her displeasure, and, as he
says, is muddied withal.   Pray you, sir, use the carp
as you may; for he looks like a poor, decayed,   24
ingenious, foolish, rascally knave.   I do pity his
distress in my [similes] of comfort and leave him
to your lordship.   [*Exit.*]
Par. My lord, I am a man whom Fortune hath
cruelly scratch'd.   29
Laf. And what would you have me to do?   'Tis
too late to pare her nails now.   Wherein have you
play'd the knave with Fortune that she should
scratch you, who of herself is a good lady and would
not have knaves thrive long under [her]?   There's
a *quart d'écu* for you.   Let the justices make   35
you and Fortune friends; I am for other business.
Par. I beseech your honour to hear me one
single word.

Laf. You beg a single penny more.   Come, you
shall ha' 't; save your word.   40
Par. My name, my good lord, is Parolles.
Laf. You beg more than word, then.   Cox my
passion! give me your hand.   How does your drum?
Par. O my good lord, you were the first that
found me!   46
Laf. Was I, in sooth?   And I was the first that
lost thee.
Par. It lies in you, my lord, to bring me in some
grace, for you did bring me out.   50
Laf. Out upon thee, knave!   Dost thou put
upon me at once both the office of God and the
devil? one brings thee in grace and the other brings
thee out.   [*Trumpets sound.*]   The King's coming;
I know by his trumpets.   Sirrah, inquire   55
further after me.   I had talk of you last night.
Though you are a fool and a knave, you shall eat;
go to, follow.
Par. I praise God for you.   [*Exeunt.*]

[SCENE III. *Rousillon.   The Count's palace.*]

Flourish.   Enter KING, COUNTESS, LAFEU, *the two
French* LORDS, *with Attendants.*

King. We lost a jewel of her, and our esteem
Was made much poorer by it; but your son,
As mad in folly, lack'd the sense to know
Her estimation home.
Count.   'Tis past, my liege;
And I beseech your Majesty to make it   5
Natural rebellion, done i' th' [blaze] of youth;
When oil and fire, too strong for reason's force,
O'erbears it and burns on.
King.   My honour'd lady,
I have forgiven and forgotten all;
Though my revenges were high bent upon him   10
And watch'd the time to shoot.
Laf.   This I must say
But first I beg my pardon, the young lord
Did to his Majesty, his mother, and his lady
Offence of mighty note; but to himself
The greatest wrong of all.   He lost a wife   15
Whose beauty did astonish the survey
Of richest eyes, whose words all ears took captive,
Whose dear perfection hearts that scorn'd to serve
Humbly call'd mistress.
King.   Praising what is lost
Makes the remembrance dear.   Well, call him
hither;   20
We are reconcil'd, and the first view shall kill

37. **falls:** befalls.
Sc. ii, 1. [*Monsieur*] Lavache.   *Mr Lavatch* F.   5. **mood:** anger.   Theobald emended to *moat.*   10. **allow the wind:** i.e.,
let me get to windward.   26. [similes] (Theobald).   *smiles* F.   34. [her] F₂.   Om. F₁.   35-36. **Let...friends:** i.e., by giving
you poor-relief.   **the justices:** who administered the poor laws.   42. **word.** Perhaps a pun on Parolles's name.   F₃,₄ read
one word.   **Cox my passion:** God's passion.
Sc. iii, 1. **esteem:** prestige.   4. **her estimation home:** her real value.   6. [blaze] (Theobald conj.).   *blade* F.   10. **high
bent:** bent taut (the metaphor is from archery).   17. **richest:** most experienced.

All repetition. Let him not ask our pardon.
The nature of his great offence is dead,
And deeper than oblivion we do bury
Th' incensing relics of it. Let him approach,   25
A stranger, no offender; and inform him
So 'tis our will he should.

   1. Lord.   I shall, my liege.
                                       [Exit.]
   King. What says he to your daughter? Have
   you spoke?
   Laf. All that he is hath reference to your High-
   ness.
   King. Then shall we have a match. I have let-
   ters sent me   30
That sets him high in fame.

                 Enter BERTRAM.

   Laf.   He looks well on't.
   King. I am not a day of season,
For thou mayst see a sunshine and a hail
In me at once. But to the brightest beams   34
Distracted clouds give way, so stand thou forth;
The time is fair again.

   Ber.   My high-repented blames,
Dear sovereign, pardon to me.

   King.   All is whole;
Not one word more of the consumed time.
Let's take the instant by the forward top;
For we are old, and on our quick'st decrees   40
Th' inaudible and noiseless foot of Time
Steals ere we can effect them. You remember
The daughter of this lord?

   Ber. Admiringly, my liege. At first
I stuck my choice upon her, ere my heart   45
Durst make too bold a herald of my tongue,
Where the impression of mine eye infixing,
Contempt his scornful perspective did lend me,
Which warp'd the line of every other favour,
Scorn'd a fair colour, or express'd it stol'n,   50
Extended or contracted all proportions
To a most hideous object. Thence it came
That she whom all men prais'd and whom myself,
Since I have lost, have lov'd, was in mine eye
The dust that did offend it.

   King.   Well excus'd.   55
That thou didst love her, strikes some scores away
From the great compt; but love that comes too late,
Like a remorseful pardon slowly carried,
To the great sender turns a sour offence,
Crying, "That's good that's gone." Our rash
   faults   60
Make trivial price of serious things we have,

Not knowing them until we know their grave.
Oft our displeasures, to ourselves unjust,
Destroy our friends and after weep their dust.
Our own love waking cries to see what's done,
While shameful hate sleeps out the afternoon.   66
Be this sweet Helen's knell, and now forget her.
Send forth your amorous token for fair Maudlin.
The main consents are had; and here we'll stay
To see our widower's second marriage-day,   70
Which better than the first, O dear Heaven, bless!
Or, ere they meet, in me, O nature, cease!

   Laf. Come on, my son, in whom my house's name
Must be digested; give a favour from you
To sparkle in the spirits of my daughter,   75
That she may quickly come. *[Bertram gives a ring.]*
               By my old beard,
And every hair that's on't, Helen, that's dead,
Was a sweet creature; such a ring as this,
The last that e'er I took her leave at court,
I saw upon her finger.

   Ber.   Hers it was not.   80
   King. Now, pray you, let me see it; for mine eye,
While I was speaking, oft was fasten'd to't.
This ring was mine; and, when I gave it Helen,
I bade her, if her fortunes ever stood
Necessitied to help, that by this token   85
I would relieve her. Had you that craft, to reave
   her
Of what should stand her most?

   Ber.   My gracious sovereign,
Howe'er it pleases you to take it so,
The ring was never hers.

   Count.   Son, on my life,
I have seen her wear it; and she reckon'd it   90
At her life's rate.

   Laf.   I am sure I saw her wear it.
   Ber. You are deceiv'd, my lord, she never saw it.
In Florence was it from a casement thrown me,
Wrapp'd in a paper, which contain'd the name
Of her that threw it. Noble she was, and thought
I stood engag'd; but when I had subscrib'd   96
To mine own fortune, and inform'd her fully
I could not answer in that course of honour
As she had made the overture, she ceas'd
In heavy satisfaction and would never   100
Receive the ring again.

   King.   Plutus himself,
That knows the tinct and multiplying med'cine,
Hath not in nature's mystery more science
Than I have in this ring. 'Twas mine, 'twas
   Helen's,
Whoever gave it you. Then, if you know   105

---

22. **repetition:** recollection. 29. **hath . . . to:** rests with. 32. **day of season:** seasonable day. 35. **Distracted:** parting.
39. **forward top:** forelock. 48. **perspective:** glass (producing optical illusions). 53. **she:** i.e., Helena. 57. **compt:** reckoning. 74. **digested:** absorbed. 79. **The . . . leave:** the last time she took leave of me. 96. **engag'd:** pledged. **subscrib'd To:** explained. 100. **heavy satisfaction:** sad conviction. 102. **tinct:** tincture. **multiplying med'cine:** the elixir by which alchemists hoped to change ("multiply") base metals into gold. 105. **if:** i.e., as sure as.

That you are well acquainted with yourself,
Confess't was hers, and by what rough enforcement
You got it from her. She call'd the saints to surety
That she would never put it from her finger,
Unless she gave it to yourself in bed,   110
Where you have never come, or sent it us
Upon her great disaster.

Ber.   She never saw it.

King. Thou speak'st it falsely, as I love mine
    honour;
And mak'st conjectural fears to come into me,
Which I would fain shut out. If it should prove   115
That thou art so inhuman, — 'twill not prove so; —
And yet I know not: thou didst hate her deadly,
And she is dead; which nothing but to close
Her eyes myself could win me to believe,
More than to see this ring. Take him away.   120
                [*Guards seize Bertram.*]
My fore-past proofs, howe'er the matter fall,
Shall [tax] my fears of little vanity,
Having vainly fear'd too little. Away with him!
We'll sift this matter further.

Ber.   If you shall prove
This ring was ever hers, you shall as easy   125
Prove that I husbanded her bed in Florence,
Where yet she never was.   [*Exit, guarded.*]

Enter a GENTLEMAN.

King. I am wrapp'd in dismal thinkings.

Gent.   Gracious sovereign,
Whether I have been to blame or no, I know not.
Here's a petition from a Florentine,   130
Who hath for four or five removes come short
To tender it herself. I undertook it,
Vanquish'd thereto by the fair grace and speech
Of the poor suppliant, who by this I know
Is here attending. Her business looks in her   135
With an importing visage; and she told me,
In a sweet verbal brief, it did concern
Your Highness with herself.

[*King. Reads*] *a letter.* "Upon his many protestations to marry me when his wife was dead, I blush
to say it, he won me. Now is the Count   140
Rousillon a widower; his vows are forfeited to me,
and my honour's paid to him. He stole from
Florence, taking no leave, and I follow him to his
country for justice. Grant it me, O king! In you
it best lies. Otherwise a seducer flourishes,   145
and a poor maid is undone. DIANA CAPILET."

Laf. I will buy me a son-in-law in a fair, and
toll for this. I'll none of him.

King. The heavens have thought well on thee,
    Lafeu,   150

To bring forth this discov'ry. Seek these suitors.
Go speedily and bring again the Count.
I am afeard the life of Helen, lady,
Was foully snatch'd.

Count.   Now, justice on the doers!

Re-enter BERTRAM [*guarded*].

King. I wonder, sir, [sith] wives are monsters to
    you,   155
And that you fly them as you swear them lordship,
Yet you desire to marry. What woman's that?

Enter WIDOW *and* DIANA.

Dia. I am, my lord, a wretched Florentine,
Derived from the ancient Capilet.
My suit, as I do understand, you know,   160
And therefore know how far I may be pitied.

Wid. I am her mother, sir, whose age and honour
Both suffer under this complaint we bring,
And both shall cease, without your remedy.

King. Come hither, Count; do you know these
    women?   165

Ber. My lord, I neither can nor will deny
But that I know them. Do they charge me further?

Dia. Why do you look so strange upon your wife?

Ber. She's none of mine, my lord.

Dia.   If you shall marry,
You give away this hand, and that is mine;   170
You give away heaven's vows, and those are mine;
You give away myself, which is known mine;
For I by vow am so embodied yours,
That she which marries you must marry me,
Either both or none.   175

Laf. Your reputation comes too short for my
daughter; you are no husband for her.

Ber. My lord, this is a fond and desp'rate
    creature,
Whom sometime I have laugh'd with. Let your
    Highness
Lay a more noble thought upon mine honour   180
Than for to think that I would sink it here.

King. Sir, for my thoughts, you have them ill to
    friend
Till your deeds gain them. Fairer prove your
    honour
Than in my thought it lies.

Dia.   Good my lord,
Ask him upon his oath, if he does think   185
He had not my virginity.

King. What say'st thou to her?

Ber.   She's impudent, my lord,
And was a common gamester to th' camp.

Dia. He does me wrong, my lord; if I were so,

---

122. **Shall ... vanity:** shall little accuse my fears of being vain.   [**tax**] F₂. *taze* F₁.   131. **removes:** stages of the journey.
135–36. **looks ... visage:** i.e., appears important.   148. **toll for this:** i.e., pay to sell this (Bertram). One was required to
register ("toll") horses officially at fairs to prevent fraudulent sales.   155. [**sith**] (Dyce): since.   *sir* F.   158. s.d. [*and*
DIANA] (Rowe). *Diana and Parolles* F.   164. **cease:** die.   188. **gamester:** harlot.

He might have bought me at a common price.
Do not believe him.   O, behold this ring,   191
Whose high respect and rich validity
Did lack a parallel; yet for all that
He gave it to a commoner o' th' camp,
If I be one.
    Count.   He blushes, and 'tis hit.   195
Of six preceding ancestors, that gem,
Conferr'd by testament to th' sequent issue,
Hath it been ow'd and worn.   This is his wife;
That ring's a thousand proofs.
    King.   Methought you said
You saw one here in court could witness it.   200
    Dia. I did, my lord, but loath am to produce
So bad an instrument.   His name's Parolles.
    Laf. I saw the man to-day, if man he be.
    King. Find him, and bring him hither.
                    [Exit an attendant.]
    Ber.   What of him?
He's quoted for a most perfidious slave,   205
With all the spots o' th' world tax'd and debauch'd,
Whose nature sickens but to speak a truth.
Am I or that or this for what he'll utter,
That will speak anything?
    King.   She hath that ring of yours.
    Ber. I think she has.   Certain it is I lik'd her, 210
And boarded her i' th' wanton way of youth.
She knew her distance and did angle for me,
Madding my eagerness with her restraint,
As all impediments in fancy's course
Are motives of more fancy; and, in fine,   215
Her [infinite cunning], with her modern grace,
Subdu'd me to her rate.   She got the ring;
And I had that which any inferior might
At market-price have bought.
    Dia.   I must be patient.
You, that have turn'd off a first so noble wife,
May justly diet me.   I pray you yet, —   221
Since you lack virtue, I will lose a husband, —
Send for your ring, I will return it home,
And give me mine again.
    Ber.   I have it not.
    King. What ring was yours, I pray you?
    Dia.   Sir, much like
The same upon your finger.   226
    King. Know you this ring?   This ring was his
of late.
    Dia. And this was it I gave him, being abed.
    King. The story then goes false, you threw it him
Out of a casement.
    Dia.   I have spoke the truth.   230

            Enter PAROLLES.

    Ber. My lord, I do confess the ring was hers.

    King. You boggle shrewdly, every feather starts
you.
Is this the man you speak of?
    Dia.   Ay, my lord.
    King. Tell me, sirrah, but tell me true, I charge
you,
Not fearing the displeasure of your master,   235
Which on your just proceeding I'll keep off,
By him and by this woman here what know you?
    Par. So please your Majesty, my master hath
been an honourable gentleman.   Tricks he hath
had in him, which gentlemen have.   240
    King. Come, come, to th' purpose.   Did he love
this woman?
    Par. Faith, sir, he did love her; but how?
    King. How, I pray you?
    Par. He did love her, sir, as a gentleman loves a
woman.   246
    King. How is that?
    Par. He lov'd her, sir, and lov'd her not.
    King. As thou art a knave, and no knave.
What an equivocal companion is this!   250
    Par. I am a poor man, and at your Majesty's
command.
    Laf. He's a good drum, my lord, but a naughty
orator.
    Dia. Do you know he promis'd me marriage? 255
    Par. Faith, I know more than I'll speak.
    King. But wilt thou not speak all thou know'st?
    Par. Yes, so please your Majesty.   I did go
between them, as I said; but more than that, he
lov'd her; for indeed he was mad for her, and
talk'd of Satan and of Limbo and of Furies and 260
I know not what.   Yet I was in that credit with
them at that time that I knew of their going to bed,
and of other motions, as promising her marriage,
and things which would derive me ill will to 265
speak of; therefore I will not speak what I know.
    King. Thou hast spoken all already, unless thou
canst say they are married.   But thou art too fine
in thy evidence; therefore stand aside.   This 270
ring, you say, was yours?
    Dia.   Ay, my good lord.
    King. Where did you buy it?   Or who gave it
you?
    Dia. It was not given me, nor I did not buy it.
    King. Who lent it you?
    Dia.   It was not lent me, neither.
    King. Where did you find it, then?
    Dia.   I found it not.
    King. If it were yours by none of all these
ways,   276
How could you give it him?
    Dia.   I never gave it him.

---

195. **'tis hit:** i.e., they've struck home.   199–200. **Methought,** etc.   Actually Diana has not said this.   208. **for:** because of.
211. **boarded:** accosted.   212. **distance:** space (a fencing term).   214. **fancy's:** love's.   216. **[infinite cunning]** (Singer).
insuite comming F.   **modern:** commonplace.   221. **diet:** discipline.   232. **boggle shrewdly:** switch about cursedly.   **starts:**
startles.   253. **drum:** drummer.   **naughty:** worthless.   269. **fine:** subtle.

Laf. This woman's an easy glove, my lord; she goes off and on at pleasure.

King. This ring was mine; I gave it his first wife.

Dia. It might be yours or hers, for aught I know.   281

King. Take her away; I do not like her now. To prison with her; and away with him. Unless thou tell'st me where thou hadst this ring, Thou diest within this hour.

Dia.   I'll never tell you.   285

King. Take her away.

Dia.   I'll put in bail, my liege.

King. I think thee now some common customer.

Dia. By Jove, if ever I knew man, 'twas you.

King. Wherefore hast thou accus'd him all this while?

Dia. Because he's guilty, and he is not guilty. He knows I am no maid, and he'll swear to't: 291 I'll swear I am a maid, and he knows not. Great king, I am no strumpet, by my life; I am either maid, or else this old man's wife.

King. She does abuse our ears. To prison with her!   295

Dia. Good mother, fetch my bail. Stay, royal sir.   *[Exit Widow.]* The jeweller that owes the ring is sent for, And he shall surety me. But for this lord, Who hath abus'd me, as he knows himself, Though yet he never harm'd me, here I quit him. He knows himself my bed he hath defil'd,   301 And at that time he got his wife with child. Dead though she be, she feels her young one kick. So there's my riddle: one that's dead is quick: And now behold the meaning.

Re-enter Widow, *with* HELENA.

King.   Is there no exorcist Beguiles the truer office of mine eyes?   306 Is't real that I see?

Hel.   No, my good lord; 'Tis but the shadow of a wife you see, The name and not the thing.

Ber.   Both, both. O, pardon!

Hel. O my good lord, when I was like this maid, I found you wondrous kind. There is your ring;   311 And, look you, here's your letter. This it says: "When from my finger you can get this ring And [are] by me with child," etc.   This is done. Will you be mine, now you are doubly won?   315

Ber. If she, my liege, can make me know this clearly, I'll love her dearly, ever, ever dearly.

Hel. If it appear not plain and prove untrue, Deadly divorce step between me and you! O my dear mother, do I see you living?   320

Laf. Mine eyes smell onions; I shall weep anon. *[To Parolles.]* Good Tom Drum, lend me a handkercher. So, I thank thee; wait on me home, I'll make sport with thee. Let thy courtesies alone, they are scurvy ones.

King. Let us from point to point this story know, To make the even truth in pleasure flow.   326 *[To Diana.]* If thou be'st yet a fresh uncropped flower, Choose thou thy husband, and I'll pay thy dower; For I can guess that by thy honest aid Thou kept'st a wife herself, thyself a maid.   330 Of that and all the progress, more and less, Resolvedly more leisure shall express. All yet seems well; and if it end so meet, The bitter past, more welcome is the sweet.   *[Flourish.*

[EPILOGUE]

[King.] The king's a beggar, now the play is done. All is well ended, if this suit be won,   336 That you express content; which we will pay, With strife to please you, day exceeding day. Ours be your patience then, and yours our parts; Your gentle hands lend us, and take our hearts.   340   *[Exeunt omnes.*

300. **quit:** acquit.   304. **quick:** alive.   305. **exorcist:** raiser of spirits.   314. **[are]** (Rowe). *is* F.   332. **resolvedly:** until all is explained.   338. **day exceeding day:** each day more than the day before.   340. **hands:** applause.

Measure for Measure

AN ENTRY in the Account Books of the Revels Office records a performance of *Measure for Measure* at Court on December 26, 1604, and it is reasonable to assign the composition of the play to that year. It was among the first of Shakespeare's plays to be given for James at Whitehall by Shakespeare's company, now the King's Men; and the lines in I.i.68–73 and II.iv.27–30, touching upon the annoyance which well-intentioned public throngs may cause their rulers, seem calculated to please James, whose aversion to crowds was well known. The central stratagem in the plot links the play directly with *All's Well*, and the splendid passages in II.iv.1–7 and III.i.4–41, 118–132 are unmistakably kin to famous speeches in *Hamlet*.

There is no trace of the play's having been printed before 1623, and a modern text is based perforce on the far from perfect version in the First Folio. The critical problems of the received text suggest that it was set up from a transcribed copy with confusions which in turn may point to revision at some time or other.

The most emphatic hints of revision lie in the speeches or silences of certain characters, yet the significance of some of these has been unduly magnified. It may be odd, for example, that the Duke informs Friar Thomas that Angelo believes him gone into Poland (I.iii.14–16) though he has said nothing about his intentions to Angelo when giving him his commission. This discrepancy, if it is one, is of no great moment; Shakespeare seems to be guilty of nothing more than giving his exposition gradually. Other matters, however, are genuinely strange. Mrs. Overdone, who has told Lucio and his companions about Claudio's arrest and its cause, appears curiously ignorant when shortly afterwards Pompey begins to talk about the same thing (I.ii.60–97); and presently Lucio, encountering Claudio in custody, seems to know nothing of what only a moment ago he has been told about. These inconsistencies are hard to explain. The letter-writing and operations of the Friar-Duke in IV.iii–v are not wholly clear. In IV.iv he has a rendezvous with one Varrius, who walks off with him as soon as they meet and who is on hand, according to the stage direction, in V.i; but his function is entirely obscure and he does not speak. There may be some muddling here owing to revision, though it would probably not be very apparent on the stage in the general excitement of the approaching dénouement. The text of *Measure*

for Measure may have undergone some changes during the years of performance, but it is very doubtful if the revision was ever extensive.

Stories containing the central situation of *Measure for Measure*, the perfidy of Angelo, are common in European literature. The direct source, however, of Shakespeare's play is clearly the double drama of *Promos and Cassandra* (1578) by George Whetstone, who later threw the plot into narrative form in his *Heptameron of Civil Discourses* (1582). Whetstone's source was the fifth novel of the tenth day in the *Hecatommithi* (1565) of Giraldi Cinthio, who dramatized the same story in his *Epitia* (1583). It is likely that Cinthio found the idea for the situation in an actual occurrence reported to have taken place in an Italian town near Milan in 1547. Other cases purporting to be historical are on record, and, indeed, no one can deny that the situation at the core of *Measure for Measure* is realistic enough to have been one or more times a matter of fact.

The scene of Whetstone's comedy is Julio in Hungary, governed by Promos (Angelo) as representative of Corvinus, King of Bohemia. The society of this city is described as seething with moral corruption, a picture transferred by Shakespeare to Vienna. But the typical characters chosen to represent this society are all re-created in *Measure for Measure*, Pompey alone bearing some resemblance to a prototype, the Rosko of Whetstone. The function of the King in the older play is practically confined to the redressing of wrongs in the last act, so that the Duke's disguise as a friar, all his activity in the intrigue, and his final offer of marriage to Isabella, are Shakespeare's. The Deputy in Whetstone is honest in his severity before he sees Cassandra (Isabella), but the subtle portrayal of his austerity, so carefully made in the earlier scenes of the present play, is altogether absent. Shakespeare has changed details of the plot in a way to mitigate the cruelty of Angelo. Whetstone's Promos gives a false pledge of marriage to seal his evil bargain, but with the invention of Mariana, Shakespeare could dispense with this element in his treachery. And whereas Promos ordered the head of the heroine's brother, Andrugio (Claudio), sent to her, Shakespeare avoids this sadism by having Angelo command only that the head be despatched to him. Actually the command is in both instances thwarted: in Whetstone a merciful gaoler defeats the intention by substituting the head of a newly executed felon; in Shakespeare the Duke persuades the Provost to send to Angelo the head of Ragozine, the pirate. The Provost is a development of Whetstone's gaoler, but Escalus, the sub-deputy, is the invention of Shakespeare to serve as a foil to Angelo.

The most profound change is in the creation of the rôle of Mariana. In the older forms of the story, the heroine yields to the Deputy, who is forced to marry her at the end. But for such an Isabella as Shakespeare conceived, this fate was clearly impossible. So the device of substitution, which Shakespeare had used in *All's Well*, was again employed, and a much loftier type of character made possible for the heroine. This elevation is apparent throughout the play, but since the characters of both Isabella and Mariana have been assailed because of their collaboration in this ruse, the whole matter must be examined more closely.

In the introduction to *All's Well* it was remarked that some of Shakespeare's plays contain elements which can be properly interpreted only when they are looked at against the background of popular stories, widely current in Shakespeare's day, in which these elements were accepted unquestioningly as common, traditional, and wholly respectable features. So regarded, the trick of the substituted bedfellow was felt to be in no way degrading to Helena. The same device, adopted by Isabella for different motives, is in no wise humiliating to her or to Mariana. Moreover, what Mariana does finds a sanction not alone in the conventions of popular narrative, but in current Elizabethan mores. For Mariana and Angelo had earlier been betrothed, and their betrothal had, according to Elizabethan custom, the validity of marriage. It was a "handfasting," a kind of pre-contract which bestowed marital rights, though individuals thus plighted would not necessarily avail themselves of them before the final marriage ceremony. (This custom is important also in considering the gravity of the offence of Claudio and Juliet.) These important matters are clearly in the mind of the Friar-Duke when he seeks to enlist the co-operation of Isabella and Mariana in the deception scheme (III.i.204–81 and IV.i.72–75) and rule out of court all charges against the purity or honor of Isabella and Mariana. Their action is lawful and the ruse signifies only in so far as it contributes to good and to a happy issue out of all their afflictions.

The Duke is another character who must not be misjudged. Trouble begins when one takes him too seriously, with moral scruples about his inconsistency and dishonesty. The Duke is created for the sake of the plot; without his shiftiness, his scheming, and his falsehoods there would be no

story running through five acts. He is responsible for the ultimate resolution of the complexities, and for the dispensation of happiness with which the play must end. His responsibility is dramatic, rather than moral, though in his own devious ways, like Providence, he brings good out of evil.

The character of Claudio is so admirably realized in the unforgettable first scene of the third act, that one must regret Shakespeare's failure to fill out his part. He appears but once before this (I.ii), when he passes across the scene under arrest and begs his friend Lucio to acquaint his sister with his situation. On that occasion he speaks well, but not with the vitality he exhibits when Isabella visits him in prison. Then his speech is moving and his conduct profoundly human. It is hard not to feel that Isabella, in the swift and crushing rebuke which she deals him, is somewhat insensible to her brother's misery. It is well to remember, however, that Isabella has a saintly horror of unchastity (even Lucio regards her as "a thing enskied and sainted," and she has already anticipated a vocation of celibacy), she has come to her brother with an agonizing message yet confident of his understanding, and now his plea that she comply with Angelo tortures her spirit. The anger in her reply comes not solely from outraged righteousness; it springs partly from her feeling that she has misjudged her brother and partly from the wretchedness of her own predicament. Sympathy must not be denied her because at the moment one feels intensely for Claudio. Claudio's repentant outcry after he has regained his poise, "Let me ask my sister pardon. I am so out of love with life that I will sue to be rid of it," would melt a stony heart, and one would feel better, perhaps, if Isabella made some reply to it. But she has moved aside, and there is no evidence that she hears. She and Claudio exchange no further words, not even at the end of the play when they are reunited and when speeches of reconciliation would seem appropriate. Nevertheless, feelings may be registered in gesture and expression.

Despite the tragic depths which it probes, *Measure for Measure* is a comedy and must, therefore, have a happy ending. The transition from darkness to light is abrupt for modern taste, but it would disturb Elizabethans not a jot. Yet we may believe that Shakespeare found a higher reason than the theatrical convention of a happy ending for the pardon of Angelo. Angelo had stood out for inflexible justice against all the pleas of mercy; Isabella proves her saintliness by begging mercy for the man who has injured her, and the Duke dispenses mercy all around. In spite of the title, the moral of the play is that justice should be tempered with mercy.

MEASURE FOR MEASURE

[DRAMATIS PERSONÆ]

VINCENTIO, *the Duke.*
ANGELO, *the Deputy.*
ESCALUS, *an ancient Lord.*
CLAUDIO, *a young gentleman.*
LUCIO, *a fantastic.*
Two other like gentlemen.
Provost.
THOMAS, }
PETER,   } *two friars.*
[A Justice.]
[VARRIUS.]

ELBOW, *a simple constable.*
FROTH, *a foolish gentleman.*
[POMPEY,] *clown* [*servant to Mistress Overdone*].
ABHORSON, *an executioner.*
BARNARDINE, *a dissolute prisoner.*

ISABELLA, *sister to Claudio.*
MARIANA, *betrothed to Angelo.*
JULIET, *beloved of Claudio.*
FRANCISCA, *a nun.*
MISTRESS OVERDONE, *a bawd.*

[Lords, Officers, Citizens, Boy, and Attendants.]

SCENE: *Vienna.*

ACT I

SCENE I. [*An apartment in the Duke's palace.*]

Enter DUKE, ESCALUS, Lords [*and Attendants*].

Duke. Escalus.
Escal. My lord.
Duke. Of government the properties to unfold
Would seem in me to affect speech and discourse,
Since I am put to know that your own science   5
Exceeds, in that, the lists of all advice
My strength can give you.   Then no more remains,
But that to your sufficiency . . . .
. . . . as your worth is able,
And let them work.   The nature of our people,   10
Our city's institutions, and the terms
For common justice, you're as pregnant in
As art and practice hath enriched any
That we remember.   There is our commission,
From which we would not have you warp.   Call
    hither,   15

I say, bid come before us Angelo.
                              [*Exit an attendant.*]
What figure of us think you he will bear?
For you must know, we have with special soul
Elected him our absence to supply,
Lent him our terror, dress'd him with our love,   20
And given his deputation all the organs
Of our own power.   What think you of it?
    Escal. If any in Vienna be of worth
To undergo such ample grace and honour,
It is Lord Angelo.

Enter ANGELO.

Duke.   Look where he comes.   **25**
    Ang. Always obedient to your Grace's will,
I come to know your pleasure.
    Duke.   Angelo,
There is a kind of character in thy life,
That to the observer doth thy history
Fully unfold.   Thyself and thy belongings   30

Act I, sc. i, 5. **put to know:** forced to acknowledge.   6. **lists:** bounds.   8–9. **But ... able.**   F prints as one line.   Something necessary to the sense apparently has been lost.   Since the line in F is a metrical monstrosity, perhaps the missing words stood originally between *sufficiency* and *as.*   12. **pregnant:** well versed.   15. **warp:** swerve.   17. **figure:** likeness.   18. **soul:** assurance.   28. **character:** stamp.   30. **belongings:** attributes.

Are not thine own so proper as to waste
Thyself upon thy virtues, they on thee.
Heaven doth with us as we with torches do,
Not light them for themselves; for if our virtues
Did not go forth of us, 'twere all alike   35
As if we had them not.   Spirits are not finely
    touch'd
But to fine issues, nor Nature never lends
The smallest scruple of her excellence
But, like a thrifty goddess, she determines
Herself the glory of a creditor,   40
Both thanks and use.   But I do bend my speech
To one that can my part in him advertise.
Hold therefore, Angelo:
In our remove be thou at full ourself.
Mortality and mercy in Vienna   45
Live in thy tongue and heart.   Old Escalus,
Though first in question, is thy secondary.
Take thy commission.
    Ang.   Now, good my lord,
Let there be some more test made of my metal
Before so noble and so great a figure   50
Be stamp'd upon it.
    Duke.   No more evasion.
We have with a leaven'd and prepared choice
Proceeded to you; therefore take your honours.
Our haste from hence is of so quick condition
That it prefers itself and leaves unquestion'd   55
Matters of needful value.   We shall write to you,
As time and our concernings shall importune,
How it goes with us, and do look to know
What doth befall you here.   So, fare you well.
To the hopeful execution do I leave you   60
Of your commissions.
    Ang.   Yet give leave, my lord,
That we may bring you something on the way.
    Duke. My haste may not admit it;
Nor need you, on mine honour, have to do
With any scruple.   Your scope is as mine own,   65
So to enforce or qualify the laws
As to your soul seems good.   Give me your hand;
I'll privily away.   I love the people,
But do not like to stage me to their eyes.
Though it do well, I do not relish well   70
Their loud applause and Aves vehement;
Nor do I think the man of safe discretion
That does affect it.   Once more, fare you well.
    Ang. The heavens give safety to your purposes!
    Escal. Lead forth and bring you back in happi-
        ness!   75
    Duke. I thank you.   Fare you well.   [*Exit.*

    Escal. I shall desire you, sir, to give me leave
To have free speech with you; and it concerns me
To look into the bottom of my place.
A power I have, but of what strength and nature   80
I am not yet instructed.
    Ang. 'Tis so with me.   Let us withdraw together,
And we may soon our satisfaction have
Touching that point.
    Escal. I'll wait upon your honour.   [*Exeunt.*

SCENE II. [*A street.*]

Enter LUCIO *and two other* GENTLEMEN.

    Lucio. If the Duke with the other dukes come
not to composition with the King of Hungary,
why then all the dukes fall upon the King.
    1. Gent. Heaven grant us its peace, but not the
King of Hungary's!   5
    2. Gent. Amen.
    Lucio. Thou conclud'st like the sanctimonious
pirate, that went to sea with the Ten Commandments, but scrap'd one out of the table.
    2. Gent. "Thou shalt not steal"?   10
    Lucio. Ay, that he raz'd.
    1. Gent. Why, 'twas a commandment to com-
mand the captain and all the rest from their functions; they put forth to steal.   There's not a
soldier of us all, that, in the thanksgiving before
meat, do relish the petition well that prays for
peace.   17
    2. Gent. I never heard any soldier dislike it.
    Lucio. I believe thee; for I think thou never wast
where grace was said.   20
    2. Gent. No?   A dozen times at least.
    1. Gent. What, in metre?
    Lucio. In any proportion or in any language.
    1. Gent. I think, or in any religion.   24
    Lucio. Ay, why not?   Grace is grace, despite
of all controversy; as, for example, thou thyself
art a wicked villain, despite of all grace.
    1. Gent. Well, there went but a pair of shears
between us.
    Lucio. I grant; as there may between the lists and
the velvet.   Thou art the list.   31
    1. Gent. And thou the velvet.   Thou art good
velvet; thou'rt a three-pil'd piece, I warrant thee.
I had as lief be a list of an English kersey as be pil'd,
as thou art pil'd, for a French velvet.   Do I speak
feelingly now?   36
    Lucio. I think thou dost; and, indeed, with most
painful feeling of thy speech.   I will, out of thine

---

31. **thine ... proper:** so entirely your own.   37. **But ... issues:** except to bring forth fine things.   38. **scruple:** i.e.,
particle ($\frac{1}{8}$ of a dram).   41. **use:** interest.   42. **can ... advertise:** can himself teach the rôle which is mine and which I am
assigning to him.   43. **Hold:** stand fast.   47. **question:** consideration (because the elder).   52. **leaven'd:** matured.   55. **un-**
question'd: undiscussed.   62. **bring:** escort.   66. **qualify:** modify.   71. **Aves:** Hails.

Sc. ii, 2. **composition:** terms.   28–29. **there ... us:** i.e., we were cut from the same cloth.   30. **lists:** the selvages (edges)
of cloth.   33. **three-pil'd:** superlative.   34. **kersey:** coarse woollen.   35. **pil'd:** peeled (i.e., *bald* from the "French disease").
36. **feelingly:** pointedly.   Lucio next implies that his companion speaks feelingly as a victim of the disease.

own confession, learn to begin thy health; but, whilst I live, forget to drink after thee.   40

1. Gent. I think I have done myself wrong, have I not?

2. Gent. Yes, that thou hast, whether thou art tainted or free.   44

Enter Bawd [MISTRESS OVERDONE].

Lucio. Behold, behold, where Madam Mitigation comes! I have purchas'd as many diseases under her roof as come to —

2. Gent. To what, I pray?

Lucio. Judge.   49

2. Gent. To three thousand dolours a year.

1. Gent. Ay, and more.

Lucio. A French crown more.

1. Gent. Thou art always figuring diseases in me; but thou art full of error; I am sound.   54

Lucio. Nay, not as one would say, healthy; but so sound as things that are hollow. Thy bones are hollow; impiety has made a feast of thee.

1. Gent. How now! which of your hips has the most profound sciatica?   59

Mrs. Ov. Well, well; there's one yonder arrested and carried to prison was worth five thousand of you all.

2. Gent. Who's that, I pray thee?

Mrs. Ov. Marry, sir, that's Claudio, Signior Claudio.   65

1. Gent. Claudio to prison? 'Tis not so.

Mrs. Ov. Nay, but I know 'tis so. I saw him arrested, saw him carried away; and, which is more, within these three days his head to be chopp'd off.   70

Lucio. But, after all this fooling, I would not have it so. Art thou sure of this?

Mrs. Ov. I am too sure of it; and it is for getting Madam Julietta with child.   74

Lucio. Believe me, this may be. He promis'd to meet me two hours since, and he was ever precise in promise-keeping.

2. Gent. Besides, you know, it draws something near to the speech we had to such a purpose.   79

1. Gent. But, most of all, agreeing with the proclamation.

Lucio. Away! let's go learn the truth of it.
          [*Exeunt* [*Lucio and Gentlemen*].

Mrs. Ov. Thus, what with the war, what with the sweat, what with the gallows, and what with poverty, I am custom-shrunk.   85

Enter Clown [POMPEY].

How now! what's the news with you?

Pom. Yonder man is carried to prison.

Mrs. Ov. Well; what has he done?

Pom. A woman.

Mrs. Ov. But what's his offence?   90

Pom. Groping for trouts in a peculiar river.

Mrs. Ov. What, is there a maid with child by him?

Pom. No, but there's a woman with maid by him. You have not heard of the proclamation, have you?   96

Mrs. Ov. What proclamation, man?

Pom. All houses in the suburbs of Vienna must be pluck'd down.

Mrs. Ov. And what shall become of those in the city?   101

Pom. They shall stand for seed. They had gone down too, but that a wise burgher put in for them.

Mrs. Ov. But shall all our houses of resort in the suburbs be pull'd down?   105

Pom. To the ground, mistress.

Mrs. Ov. Why, here's a change indeed in the commonwealth! What shall become of me?

Pom. Come, fear not you; good counsellors lack no clients. Though you change your place, you   110
need not change your trade. I'll be your tapster still. Courage! there will be pity taken on you. You that have worn your eyes almost out in the service, you will be considered.   115

Mrs. Ov. What's to do here, Thomas tapster? Let's withdraw.

Pom. Here comes Signior Claudio, led by the provost to prison; and there's Madam Juliet.
          [*Exeunt.*

Enter PROVOST, CLAUDIO, JULIET, *and* Officers.

Claud. Fellow, why dost thou show me thus to th' world?   120
Bear me to prison, where I am committed.

Prov I do it not in evil disposition,
But from Lord Angelo by special charge.

Claud. Thus can the demigod authority
Make us pay down for our offence by weight   125
The words of heaven: on whom it will, it will;
On whom it will not, so; yet still 'tis just.

          [*Re-enter* LUCIO *and two* Gentlemen.]

Lucio. Why, how now, Claudio! whence comes this restraint?

40. **after thee:** i.e., from the same (infected) cup. 50. **dolours:** (1) griefs, (2) dollars. 52. **French crown:** (1) gold coin, (2) bald head (cf. l. 35 n.). 53. **figuring:** imagining. 84. **sweat:** sweating sickness, a form of the plague. 98. **suburbs,** where the houses of ill-fame were. 103. **put in:** bid, applied. 119. **provost:** jailer. 120. S.D. F marks a new scene here, and gives Lucio and the two Gentlemen an entrance with the others at this point. Since Juliet says nothing in this scene, her appearance is strange; in fact much of what is said sounds odd if she herself is present (especially ll. 150 and 160). Perhaps she was meant to retire at l. 127, before which point she had had something to say which has somehow been lost. Furthermore, Lucio's questioning of Claudio about the cause of his arrest is queer, considering that only a few moments earlier Mrs. Overdone has informed him. The "two Gentlemen" are also mute in this scene. 126-27. **The . . . so.** Probably corrupt, though there seems to be an allusion to *Romans* ix.15.

Claud. From too much liberty, my Lucio, liberty.
As surfeit is the father of much fast, 130
So every scope by the immoderate use
Turns to restraint. Our natures do pursue,
Like rats that ravin down their proper bane,
A thirsty evil; and when we drink we die. 134
    Lucio. If I could speak so wisely under an
arrest, I would send for certain of my creditors;
and yet, to say the truth, I had as lief have the
foppery of freedom as the [morality] of imprison-
ment. What's thy offence, Claudio?
    Claud. What but to speak of would offend again.
    Lucio. What, is't murder? 141
    Claud. No.
    Lucio. Lechery?
    Claud. Call it so.
    Prov. Away, sir! you must go. 145
    Claud. One word, good friend. Lucio, a word
    with you.
    Lucio. A hundred, if they'll do you any good.
Is lechery so look'd after?
    Claud. Thus stands it with me: upon a true
    contract
I got possession of Julietta's bed. 150
You know the lady; she is fast my wife,
Save that we do the denunciation lack
Of outward order. This we came not to,
Only for propagation of a dower
Remaining in the coffer of her friends, 155
From whom we thought it meet to hide our love
Till time had made them for us. But it chances
The stealth of our most mutual entertainment
With character too gross is writ on Juliet.
    Lucio. With child, perhaps?
    Claud.   Unhappily, even so.
And the new deputy now for the Duke — 161
Whether it be the fault and glimpse of newness,
Or whether that the body public be
A horse whereon the governor doth ride,
Who, newly in the seat, that it may know 165
He can command, lets it straight feel the spur;
Whether the tyranny be in his place,
Or in his eminence that fills it up,
I stagger in: — but this new governor
Awakes me all the enrolled penalties 170
Which have, like unscour'd armour, hung by the
    wall
So long that nineteen zodiacs have gone round
And none of them been worn; and, for a name,
Now puts the drowsy and neglected act
Freshly on me. 'Tis surely for a name. 175

    Lucio. I warrant it is; and thy head stands so
tickle on thy shoulders that a milkmaid, if she be
in love, may sigh it off. Send after the Duke and
appeal to him.
    Claud. I have done so, but he's not to be found.
I prithee, Lucio, do me this kind service. 181
This day my sister should the cloister enter
And there receive her approbation.
Acquaint her with the danger of my state;
Implore her, in my voice, that she make friends 185
To the strict deputy; bid herself assay him.
I have great hope in that; for in her youth
There is a prone and speechless dialect,
Such as move men; beside, she hath prosperous art
When she will play with reason and discourse,
And well she can persuade. 191
    Lucio. I pray she may; as well for the encour-
agement of the like, which else would stand under
grievous imposition, as for the enjoying of thy life,
who I would be sorry should be thus foolishly lost
at a game of tick-tack. I'll to her. 196
    Claud. I thank you, good friend Lucio.
    Lucio. Within two hours.
    Claud.   Come, Officer, away!
                            [*Exeunt.*

Scene [III. *A monastery.*]

Enter Duke *and* Friar Thomas.

    Duke. No, holy father; throw away that thought.
Believe not that the dribbling dart of love
Can pierce a complete bosom. Why I desire thee
To give me secret harbour, hath a purpose
More grave and wrinkled than the aims and ends 5
Of burning youth.
    Fri. T.   May your Grace speak of it?
    Duke. My holy sir, none better knows than you
How I have ever lov'd the life removed,
And held in idle price to haunt assemblies
Where youth, and cost, [and] witless bravery keeps.
I have deliver'd to Lord Angelo, 11
A man of stricture and firm abstinence,
My absolute power and place here in Vienna,
And he supposes me travell'd to Poland;
For so I have strew'd it in the common ear, 15
And so it is receiv'd. Now, pious sir,
You will demand of me why I do this.
    Fri. T. Gladly, my lord.
    Duke. We have strict statutes and most biting
    laws,
The needful bits and curbs to headstrong [steeds],

---

131. **scope:** liberty. 133. **ravin:** gulp. **proper bane:** own poison. 138. **foppery:** folly. **[morality]** (Rowe). *mortality* F.
152. **denunciation:** proclamation. 154. **for:** i.e., for the sake of. **propagation:** increase. 157. **for:** favorable to. 162. **fault
and glimpse:** harmful glamour. 167. **place:** office. 169. **stagger in:** am not sure. 172. **nineteen zodiacs:** nineteen years.
In I.iii.21, the Duke says fourteen. 177. **tickle:** insecure. 183. **receive her approbation:** begin her novitiate. 194. **imposition:** punishment. 196. **tick-tack:** a kind of backgammon.
    Sc. iii, 2. **dribbling:** feeble. 10. **[and]** F2–4. Om. F1. **bravery:** finery. 12. **stricture:** strictness. 20. **[steeds]** (Theo-
bald). *weeds* F.

Which for this fourteen years we have let slip; 21
Even like an o'ergrown lion in a cave,
That goes not out to prey. Now, as fond fathers,
Having bound up the threatening twigs of birch,
Only to stick it in their children's sight 25
For terror, not to use, in time the rod
[Becomes] more mock'd than fear'd; so our decrees,
Dead to infliction, to themselves are dead,
And liberty plucks justice by the nose,
The baby beats the nurse, and quite athwart 30
Goes all decorum.
  Fri. T.   It rested in your Grace
To unloose this tied-up justice when you pleas'd:
And it in you more dreadful would have seem'd
Than in Lord Angelo.
  Duke.   I do fear, too dreadful.
Sith 'twas my fault to give the people scope, 35
'Twould be my tyranny to strike and gall them
For what I bid them do; for we bid this be done,
When evil deeds have their permissive pass
And not the punishment. Therefore indeed, my father,
I have on Angelo impos'd the office; 40
Who may, in th' ambush of my name, strike home,
And yet my nature never in the [sight]
To do [it] slander. And to behold his sway,
I will, as 'twere a brother of your order,
Visit both prince and people; therefore, I prithee,
Supply me with the habit and instruct me 46
How I may formally in person bear [me]
Like a true friar. Moe reasons for this action
At our more leisure shall I render you;
Only, this one: Lord Angelo is precise, 50
Stands at a guard with envy, scarce confesses
That his blood flows, or that his appetite
Is more to bread than stone; hence shall we see,
If power change purpose, what our seemers be.
                         [Exeunt.

Scene [IV. *A nunnery.*]

Enter ISABELLA *and* FRANCISCA, *a Nun.*

  Isab. And have you nuns no farther privileges?
  Fran. Are not these large enough?
  Isab. Yes, truly. I speak not as desiring more,
But rather wishing a more strict restraint
Upon the sisterhood, the votaries of Saint Clare. 5
  Lucio. (*Within.*) Ho! Peace be in this place!
  Isab.   Who's that which calls?
  Fran. It is a man's voice. Gentle Isabella,
Turn you the key, and know his business of him.

You may, I may not; you are yet unsworn.
When you have vow'd, you must not speak with men 10
But in the presence of the prioress;
Then, if you speak, you must not show your face,
Or, if you show your face, you must not speak.
He calls again; I pray you, answer him.   *[Exit.*
  Isab. Peace and prosperity! Who is't that calls? 15

[Enter LUCIO.]

  Lucio. Hail, virgin, if you be, as those cheek-roses
Proclaim you are no less! Can you so stead me
As bring me to the sight of Isabella,
A novice of this place and the fair sister
To her unhappy brother Claudio? 20
  Isab. Why her unhappy brother? let me ask,
The rather for I now must make you know
I am that Isabella and his sister.
  Lucio. Gentle and fair, your brother kindly greets you.
Not to be weary with you, he's in prison. 25
  Isab. Woe me! for what?
  Lucio. For that which, if myself might be his judge,
He should receive his punishment in thanks.
He hath got his friend with child.
  Isab. Sir, make me not your story.
  Lucio.   [It is] true.
I would not — though 'tis my familiar sin 31
With maids to seem the lapwing and to jest,
Tongue far from heart — play with all virgins so.
I hold you as a thing enskied and sainted,
By your renouncement an immortal spirit, 35
And to be talk'd with in sincerity,
As with a saint.
  Isab. You do blaspheme the good in mocking me.
  Lucio. Do not believe it. Fewness and truth, 'tis thus:
Your brother and his lover have embrac'd. 40
As those that feed grow full, as blossoming time
That from the seedness the bare fallow brings
To teeming foison, even so her plenteous womb
Expresseth his full tilth and husbandry.
  Isab. Some one with child by him? My cousin Juliet? 45
  Lucio. Is she your cousin?
  Isab. Adoptedly; as school-maids change their names
By vain though apt affection.

---

    23. **fond:** foolish. 27. **[Becomes]** (Pope). Om. F. 42–43. **[sight]** ... **[it]** (Hanmer). *fight ... in* F. Meaning obscure. Perhaps the idea is, Without injuring my character since I am out of sight. 47. **[me]** (Capell). Om. F. 48. **Moe:** more. 51. **with envy:** against malice.

    Sc. iv, 17. **stead:** aid. 25. **weary:** tedious. 30. **story:** i.e., jest. **[It is]** (Steevens). *'Tis* F. 32. **lapwing.** The lapwing tries to lead intruders from its nest by tricks. 39. **Fewness and truth:** briefly and honestly. 42. **seedness:** sowing. 43. **foison:** plenty. 48. **vain:** foolish. **apt:** spontaneous.

Lucio.   She it is.

Isab. O, let him marry her.

Lucio.   This is the point.
The Duke is very strangely gone from hence;   50
Bore many gentlemen, myself being one,
In hand, [in] hope of action; but we do learn
By those that know the very nerves of state,
His [givings-out] were of an infinite distance
From his true-meant design.   Upon his place,   55
And with full line of his authority,
Governs Lord Angelo, a man whose blood
Is very snow-broth, one who never feels
The wanton stings and motions of the sense,
But doth rebate and blunt his natural edge   60
With profits of the mind, study, and fast.
He — to give fear to use and liberty,
Which have for long run by the hideous law,
As mice by lions — hath pick'd out an act,
Under whose heavy sense your brother's life   65
Falls into forfeit; he arrests him on it;
And follows close the rigour of the statute,
To make him an example.   All hope is gone,
Unless you have the grace by your fair prayer
To soften Angelo.   And that's my pith   70
Of business 'twixt you and your poor brother.

Isab. Doth he so seek his life?

Lucio.   Has censur'd him
Already; and, as I hear, the Provost hath
A warrant for his execution.

Isab. Alas! what poor ability's in me   75
To do him good?

Lucio.   Assay the power you have.

Isab. My power?   Alas, I doubt —

Lucio.   Our doubts are traitors,
And makes us lose the good we oft might win
By fearing to attempt.   Go to Lord Angelo,
And let him learn to know, when maidens sue   80
Men give like gods; but when they weep and
   kneel,
All their petitions are as freely theirs
As they themselves would owe them.

Isab. I'll see what I can do.

Lucio.   But speedily.

Isab. I will about it straight,   85
No longer staying but to give the Mother
Notice of my affair.   I humbly thank you.
Commend me to my brother.   Soon at night
I'll send him certain word of my success.

Lucio. I take my leave of you.

Isab.   Good sir, adieu.   90
                                       [*Exeunt.*

ACT II

Scene I.   [*A hall in Angelo's house.*]

Enter Angelo, Escalus, *a* Justice, *and Servants.*

Ang. We must not make a scarecrow of the law,
Setting it up to fear the birds of prey,
And let it keep one shape, till custom make it
Their perch and not their terror.

Escal.   Ay, but yet
Let us be keen, and rather cut a little,   5
Than fall, and bruise to death.   Alas, this gentle-
   man
Whom I would save had a most noble father!
Let but your honour know,
Whom I believe to be most strait in virtue,
That, in the working of your own affections,   10
Had time coher'd with place or place with wishing,
Or that the resolute acting of [your] blood
Could have attain'd the effect of your own pur-
   pose,
Whether you had not sometime in your life
Err'd in this point which now you censure him,
And pull'd the law upon you.   16

Ang. 'Tis one thing to be tempted, Escalus,
Another thing to fall.   I not deny,
The jury, passing on the prisoner's life,
May in the sworn twelve have a thief or two   20
Guiltier than him they try.   What's open made to
   justice,
That justice seizes.   What knows the laws
That thieves do pass on thieves?   'Tis very preg-
   nant,
The jewel that we find, we stoop and take't
Because we see it; but what we do not see   25
We tread upon, and never think of it.
You may not so extenuate his offence
For I have had such faults; but rather tell me,
When I, that censure him, do so offend,   20
Let mine own judgement pattern out my death,
And nothing come in partial.   Sir, he must die.

Enter Provost.

Escal. Be it as your wisdom will.

Ang.   Where is the Provost?

Prov. Here, if it like your honour.

Ang.   See that Claudio
Be executed by nine to-morrow morning.
Bring him his confessor, let him be prepar'd;   35
For that's the utmost of his pilgrimage.
                                    [*Exit Provost.*]

51–52. **Bore ... In hand:** deluded.   52. **[in]** (Keightley).   *and* F.   **action:** i.e., war.   54. **[givings-out]** (Rowe).   *giving-out* F.   60. **rebate:** dull.   72. **censur'd:** sentenced.   83. **As:** as if.   **would owe:** possessed.   89. **my success:** the out-come.

Act II, sc. i, 6. **fall:** let fall (i.e., the sword of justice).   12. **[your]** (Rowe).   *our* F.   21. **open:** evident.   22–23. **What ... thieves:** i.e., the law ignores the hidden crimes of jurors.   23. **pregnant:** obvious.   28. **For:** because.   36. **pilgrimage:** i.e. of life.

Escal. [*Aside.*] Well, Heaven forgive him! and
forgive us all!
Some rise by sin, and some by virtue fall.
Some run from brakes of [vice] and answer
none;
And some condemned for a fault alone.   40

Enter ELBOW, FROTH, *Clown* [POMPEY, *and*]
Officers.

Elb. Come, bring them away. If these be good
people in a commonweal that do nothing but use
their abuses in common houses, I know no law.
Bring them away.   44
Ang. How now, sir! What's your name? and
what's the matter?
Elb. If it please your honour, I am the poor
Duke's constable, and my name is Elbow. I do
lean upon justice, sir, and do bring in here before
your honour two notorious benefactors.   50
Ang. Benefactors? Well, what benefactors are
they? Are they not malefactors?
Elb. If it please your honour, I know not well
what they are; but precise villains they are, that I
am sure of; and void of all profanation in the world
that good Christians ought to have.   56
Escal. This comes off well. Here's a wise officer.
Ang. Go to; what quality are they of? Elbow
is your name? Why dost thou not speak, Elbow?
Pom. He cannot, sir; he's out at elbow.   61
Ang. What are you, sir?
Elb. He, sir! A tapster, sir; parcel-bawd; one
that serves a bad woman, whose house, sir, was, as
they say, pluck'd down in the suburbs; and now she
professes a hot-house, which, I think, is a very ill
house too.   67
Escal. How know you that?
Elb. My wife, sir, whom I detest before Heaven
and your honour, —   70
Escal. How? Thy wife?
Elb. Ay, sir; whom, I thank Heaven, is an honest
woman, —
Escal. Dost thou detest her therefore?   74
Elb. I say, sir, I will detest myself also, as well
as she, that this house, if it be not a bawd's house,
it is pity of her life, for it is a naughty house.   78
Escal. How dost thou know that, constable?
Elb. Marry, sir, by my wife; who, if she had been
a woman cardinally given, might have been accus'd
in fornication, adultery, and all uncleanliness there.
Escal. By the woman's means?   84
Elb. Ay, sir, by Mistress Overdone's means; but
as she spit in his face, so she defi'd him.
Pom. Sir, if it please your honour, this is not so.

Elb. Prove it before these varlets here, thou
honourable man; prove it.
Escal. Do you hear how he misplaces?   90
Pom. Sir, she came in great with child, and longing, saving your honour's reverence, for stew'd
prunes. Sir, we had but two in the house, which
at that very distant time stood, as it were, in a
fruit-dish, a dish of some three-pence. Your
honours have seen such dishes; they are not china
dishes, but very good dishes, —   97
Escal. Go to, go to; no matter for the dish, sir.
Pom. No, indeed, sir, not of a pin; you are therein
in the right. But to the point. As I say, this Mistress Elbow, being, as I say, with child, and being
great-bellied, and longing, as I said, for prunes; 102
and having but two in the dish, as I said, Master
Froth here, this very man, having eaten the rest, as
I said, and, as I say, paying for them very honestly;
for, as you know, Master Froth, I could not give
you three-pence again.   107
Froth. No, indeed.
Pom. Very well; you being then, if you be rememb'red, cracking the stones of the foresaid
prunes, —   111
Froth. Ay, so I did indeed.
Pom. Why, very well. I telling you then, if you
be rememb'red, that such a one and such a one
were past cure of the thing you wot of, unless they
kept very good diet, as I told you, —   116
Froth. All this is true.
Pom. Why, very well, then, —
Escal. Come, you are a tedious fool. To the
purpose. What was done to Elbow's wife, that he
hath cause to complain of? Come me to what
was done to her.   122
Pom. Sir, your honour cannot come to that yet.
Escal. No, sir, nor I mean it not.
Pom. Sir, but you shall come to it, by your
honour's leave. And, I beseech you, look into
Master Froth here, sir; a man of fourscore pound
a year; whose father died at Hallowmas. Was't
not at Hallowmas, Master Froth?   129
Froth. All-hallond eve.
Pom. Why, very well; I hope here be truths.
He, sir, sitting, as I say, in a lower chair, sir; 'twas
in the Bunch of Grapes, where indeed you have
a delight to sit, have you not?   134
Froth. I have so; because it is an open room and
good for winter.
Pom. Why, very well, then; I hope here be truths.
Ang. This will last out a night in Russia,
When nights are longest there. I'll take my leave,
And leave you to the hearing of the cause,   141

---

39. **brakes:** thickets. **[vice]** (Rowe). *ice* F. **answer none:** are never called to account   40. **fault alone:** single
fault.   43. **abuses:** evil practices.   54. **precise:** puritanical.   63. **parcel-bawd:** partly bawd.   66. **hot-house:** bathing house.
69. **detest:** for *protest.*   81. **cardinally:** for *carnally.*   92. **saving . . . reverence:** begging your honour's pardon.   121. **Come:**
bring.   130. **All-hallond eve:** Hallowe'en.   132. **lower:** reclining.   133. **Bunch of Grapes:** name of a room at the inn.

Hoping you'll find good cause to whip them all.

Escal. I think no less. Good morrow to your
    lordship.

                          [Exit Angelo.
Now, sir, come on. What was done to Elbow's
wife, once more?   145

Pom. Once, sir? There was nothing done to her
once.

Elb. I beseech you, sir, ask him what this man
did to my wife.

Pom. I beseech your honour, ask me.   150

Escal. Well, sir; what did this gentleman to her?

Pom. I beseech you, sir, look in this gentleman's
face. Good Master Froth, look upon his honour;
'tis for a good purpose. Doth your honour mark
his face?   156

Escal. Ay, sir, very well.

Pom. Nay, I beseech you, mark it well.

Escal. Well, I do so.

Pom. Doth your honour see any harm in his
face?   161

Escal. Why, no.

Pom. I'll be suppos'd upon a book, his face is
the worst thing about him. Good, then; if his face
be the worst thing about him, how could Master
Froth do the constable's wife any harm? I would
know that of your honour.   167

Escal. He's in the right. Constable, what say
you to it?

Elb. First, an it like you, the house is a respected
house; next, this is a respected fellow; and his mistress is a respected woman.   172

Pom. By this hand, sir, his wife is a more respected person than any of us all.

Elb. Varlet, thou liest! Thou liest, wicked varlet! The time is yet to come that she was ever respected with man, woman, or child.   177

Pom. Sir, she was respected with him before he
married with her.

Escal. Which is the wiser here, Justice or Iniquity? Is this true?   181

Elb. O thou caitiff! O thou varlet! O thou
wicked Hannibal! I respected with her before I
was married to her! If ever I was respected with
her, or she with me, let not your worship think me
the poor Duke's officer. Prove this, thou wicked
Hannibal, or I'll have mine action of battery on
thee.   188

Escal. If he took you a box o' th' ear, you might
have your action of slander too.

Elb. Marry, I thank your good worship for it.
What is't your worship's pleasure I shall do with
this wicked caitiff?   193

Escal. Truly, officer, because he hath some offences in him that thou wouldst discover if thou
couldst, let him continue in his courses till thou
know'st what they are.   197

Elb. Marry, I thank your worship for it. Thou
seest, thou wicked varlet, now, what's come upon
thee. Thou art to continue now, thou varlet; thou
art to continue.   201

Escal. Where were you born, friend?

Froth. Here in Vienna, sir.

Escal. Are you of fourscore pounds a year?

Froth. Yes, an't please you, sir.   205

Escal. So. What trade are you of, sir?

Pom. A tapster; a poor widow's tapster.

Escal. Your mistress' name?

Pom. Mistress Overdone.

Escal. Hath she had any more than one husband?   211

Pom. Nine, sir; Overdone by the last.

Escal. Nine! Come hither to me, Master Froth.
Master Froth, I would not have you acquainted
with tapsters; they will draw you, Master Froth,
and you will hang them. Get you gone, and let
me hear no more of you.   217

Froth. I thank your worship. For mine own
part, I never come into any room in a tap-house, but
I am drawn in.   220

Escal. Well, no more of it, Master Froth. Farewell. *[Exit Froth.]* Come you hither to me,
Master tapster. What's your name, Master tapster?   224

Pom. Pompey.

Escal. What else?

Pom. Bum, sir.   227

Escal. Troth, and your bum is the greatest thing
about you, so that in the beastliest sense you are
Pompey the Great. Pompey, you are partly a
bawd, Pompey, howsoever you colour it in being a
tapster, are you not? Come, tell me true; it shall
be the better for you.   233

Pom. Truly, sir, I am a poor fellow that would
live.

Escal. How would you live, Pompey? By being
a bawd? What do you think of the trade, Pompey?
Is it a lawful trade?   238

Pom. If the law would allow it, sir.

Escal. But the law will not allow it, Pompey;
nor it shall not be allowed in Vienna.   241

Pom. Does your worship mean to geld and splay
all the youth of the city?

Escal. No, Pompey.   244

Pom. Truly, sir, in my poor opinion, they will
to't then. If your worship will take order for the
drabs and the knaves, you need not to fear the
bawds.

---

163. **suppos'd:** for *deposed*, i.e., sworn. 170. **respected:** for *suspected*, of ill fame. 180–81. **Justice or Iniquity:** i.e., Elbow
or Pompey, who are referred to as if they were characters in a morality play. 183. **Hannibal:** for *cannibal*. 215. **draw you:**
(1) draw liquor for you, (2) hang, draw, and quarter you. 242. **splay:** castrate.

Escal. There is pretty orders beginning, I can tell you. It is but heading and hanging. 250

Pom. If you head and hang all that offend that way but for ten year together, you'll be glad to give out a commission for more heads. If this law hold in Vienna ten year, I'll rent the fairest house in it after three-pence a bay. If you live to see this come to pass, say Pompey told you so. 257

Escal. Thank you, good Pompey; and, in re-quital of your prophecy, hark you: I advise you, let me not find you before me again upon any 260 complaint whatsoever; no, not for dwelling where you do. If I do, Pompey, I shall beat you to your tent, and prove a shrewd Cæsar to you; in plain dealing, Pompey, I shall have you whipt. So, for this time, Pompey, fare you well. 265

Pom. I thank your worship for your good coun-sel; [*aside*] but I shall follow it as the flesh and for-tune shall better determine.
Whip me? No, no; let carman whip his jade;
The valiant heart's not whipt out of his trade. 270
                [*Exit.*

Escal. Come hither to me, Master Elbow; come hither, Master constable. How long have you been in this place of constable?

Elb. Seven year and a half, sir. 274

Escal. I thought, by the readiness in the office, you had continued in it some time. You say, seven years together?

Elb. And a half, sir. 278

Escal. Alas, it hath been great pains to you. They do you wrong to put you so oft upon't. Are there not men in your ward sufficient to serve it?

Elb. Faith, sir, few of any wit in such matters. As they are chosen, they are glad to choose me for them. I do it for some piece of money, and go through with all. 285

Escal. Look you bring me in the names of some six or seven, the most sufficient of your parish.

Elb. To your worship's house, sir?

Escal. To my house. Fare you well.
              [*Exit Elbow.*]
What's o'clock, think you? 290

Just. Eleven, sir.

Escal. I pray you home to dinner with me.

Just. I humbly thank you.

Escal. It grieves me for the death of Claudio; But there's no remedy. 295

Just. Lord Angelo is severe.

Escal.   It is but needful.
Mercy is not itself, that oft looks so;
Pardon is still the nurse of second woe.
But yet, — poor Claudio! There is no remedy.
Come, sir.   [*Exeunt.* 300

SCENE II. [*Another room in the same.*]

Enter PROVOST *and a* SERVANT.

Serv. He's hearing of a cause; he will come straight.
I'll tell him of you.

Prov.   Pray you, do.
              [*Exit Servant.*]
                I'll know
His pleasure; may be he will relent. Alas,
He hath but as offended in a dream!
All sects, all ages smack of this vice; and he 5
To die for't!

Enter ANGELO.

Ang.   Now, what's the matter, Provost?

Prov. Is it your will Claudio shall die to-morrow?

Ang. Did not I tell thee yea? Hadst thou not order?
Why dost thou ask again?

Prov.   Lest I might be too rash.
Under your good correction, I have seen 10
When, after execution, judgement hath
Repented o'er his doom.

Ang.   Go to; let that be mine.
Do you your office, or give up your place,
And you shall well be spar'd.

Prov.   I crave your honour's pardon.
What shall be done, sir, with the groaning Juliet?
She's very near her hour.

Ang.   Dispose of her 16
To some more fitter place, and that with speed.

[*Re-enter* SERVANT.]

Serv. Here is the sister of the man condemn'd
Desires access to you.

Ang.   Hath he a sister?

Prov. Ay, my good lord; a very virtuous maid,
And to be shortly of a sisterhood, 21
If not already.

Ang.   Well, let her be admitted.
              [*Exit Servant.*]
See you the fornicatress be remov'd.
Let her have needful but not lavish **means**;
There shall be order for't.

Enter ISABELLA *and* LUCIO.

Prov.   [God] save your honour!

Ang. Stay a little while. [*To Isab.*] You're welcome; what's your will? 26

Isab. I am a woeful suitor to your honour,
Please but your honour hear me.

Ang.   Well; what's your suit?

Isab. There is a vice that most I do abhor,
And most desire should meet the blow of justice;

---

250. **heading**: beheading.   255. **after**: at. **bay**: a window with the space round it.   269. **jade**: nag. Sc. ii, 12. **doom**: sentence.   25. [God] **save** (Walker conj.). 'Save F.

For which I would not plead, but that I must; 31
For which I must not plead, but that I am
At war 'twixt will and will not.
    Ang.   Well; the matter?
    Isab. I have a brother is condemn'd to die.
I do beseech you, let it be his fault, 35
And not my brother.
    Prov. [*Aside.*] Heaven give thee moving graces!
    Ang. Condemn the fault, and not the actor of it?
Why, every fault's condemn'd ere it be done.
Mine were the very cipher of a function,
To fine the faults whose fine stands in record, 40
And let go by the actor.
    Isab.   O just but severe law!
I had a brother, then. Heaven keep your honour!
    Lucio. [*Aside to Isab.*] Give't not o'er so. To
    him again, entreat him,
Kneel down before him, hang upon his gown.
You are too cold. If you should need a pin, 45
You could not with more tame a tongue desire it.
To him, I say!
    Isab. Must he needs die?
    Ang.   Maiden, no remedy.
    Isab. Yes; I do think that you might pardon him,
And neither heaven nor man grieve at the mercy.
    Ang. I will not do't.
    Isab.   But can you, if you would? 51
    Ang. Look, what I will not, that I cannot do.
    Isab. But might you do't, and do the world no
    wrong,
If so your heart were touch'd with that remorse
As mine is to him?
    Ang.   He's sentenc'd; 'tis too late.
    Lucio. [*Aside to Isab.*] You are too cold. 56
    Isab. Too late? Why, no, I, that do speak a
    word,
May call it [back] again. Well, believe this,
No ceremony that to great ones longs, 59
Not the king's crown, nor the deputed sword,
The marshal's truncheon, nor the judge's robe,
Become them with one half so good a grace
As mercy does.
If he had been as you and you as he,
You would have slipt like him; but he, like you, 65
Would not have been so stern.
    Ang.   Pray you, be gone.
    Isab. I would to heaven I had your potency,
And you were Isabel! Should it then be thus?
No; I would tell what 'twere to be a judge,
And what a prisoner.
    Lucio. [*Aside to Isab.*] Ay, touch him; there's
    the vein. 70
    Ang. Your brother is a forfeit of the law,

And you but waste your words.
    Isab.   Alas, alas!
Why, all the souls that were were forfeit once;
And He that might the vantage best have took
Found out the remedy. How would you be 75
If He, which is the top of judgement, should
But judge you as you are? O, think on that;
And mercy then will breathe within your lips,
Like man new made.
    Ang.   Be you content, fair maid.
It is the law, not I condemn your brother. 80
Were he my kinsman, brother, or my son,
It should be thus with him. He must die to-
    morrow.
    Isab. To-morrow! O, that's sudden! Spare
    him, spare him!
He's not prepar'd for death. Even for our kitchens
We kill the fowl of season. Shall we serve Heaven
With less respect than we do minister 86
To our gross selves? Good, good my lord, bethink
    you:
Who is it that hath died for this offence?
There's many have committed it.
    Lucio.   [*Aside to Isab.*] Ay, well said.
    Ang. The law hath not been dead, though it
    hath slept. 90
Those many had not dar'd to do that evil,
If [but] the first that did th' edict infringe
Had answer'd for his deed. Now 'tis awake,
Takes note of what is done, and, like a prophet,
Looks in a glass that shows what future evils,
Either [new], or by remissness new-conceiv'd, 96
And so in progress to be hatch'd and born,
Are now to have no successive degrees,
But, [ere] they live, to end.
    Isab.   Yet show some pity.
    Ang. I show it most of all when I show justice,
For then I pity those I do not know, 101
Which a dismiss'd offence would after gall;
And do him right that, answering one foul wrong,
Lives not to act another. Be satisfied.
Your brother dies to-morrow. Be content. 105
    Isab. So you must be the first that gives this
    sentence,
And he, that suffers. O, it is excellent
To have a giant's strength; but it is tyrannous
To use it like a giant.
    Lucio. [*Aside to Isab.*] That's well said.
    Isab Could great men thunder 110
As Jove himself does, Jove would ne'er be quiet;
For every pelting, petty officer
Would use his heaven for thunder,
Nothing but thunder! Merciful Heaven, 114

---

35. **let ... fault:** i e., let his fault die. 40. **fine:** punish. **fine:** punishment. 54. **remorse:** pity. 58. **[back]** F₂₋₄. Om. F₁. 59. **longs:** belongs. 70. **vein:** style. 79. **Like ... made:** As God breathed life into Adam. See *Gen.* ii.7. 85. **of season:** i.e., fattened. 92. **[but]** (White). Om. F. 95. **glass:** i.e., magic crystal. 96. **[new]** (Dyce). *now* F. 98. **successive degrees:** development. 99. **[ere]** (Hanmer). *here* F. 112. **pelting:** paltry.

Thou rather with thy sharp and sulphurous bolt
Splits the unwedgeable and gnarled oak
Than the soft myrtle; but man, proud man,
Dress'd in a little brief authority,
Most ignorant of what he's most assur'd,
His glassy essence, like an angry ape,   120
Plays such fantastic tricks before high heaven
As makes the angels weep; who, with our spleens,
Would all themselves laugh mortal.

Lucio. [*Aside to Isab.*] O, to him, to him, wench!
    he will relent.
He's coming; I perceive't.

Prov. [*Aside.*] Pray Heaven she win him!   125

Isab. We cannot weigh our brother with ourself.
Great men may jest with saints; 'tis wit in them,
But in the less foul profanation.

Lucio. [*Aside.*] Thou'rt i' th' right, girl. More
    o' that.

Isab. That in the captain's but a choleric word,
Which in the soldier is flat blasphemy.   131

Lucio. [*Aside to Isab.*] Art avis'd o' that? More
    on't.

Ang. Why do you put these sayings upon me?

Isab. Because authority, though it err like others,
Hath yet a kind of medicine in itself,   135
That skins the vice o' th' top. Go to your bosom;
Knock there, and ask your heart what it doth know
That's like my brother's fault. If it confess
A natural guiltiness such as is his,
Let it not sound a thought upon your tongue   140
Against my brother's life.

Ang.   [*Aside.*] She speaks, and 'tis
Such sense, that my sense breeds with it. — Fare
    you well.

Isab. Gentle my lord, turn back.

Ang. I will bethink me. Come again to-morrow.

Isab. Hark how I'll bribe you. Good my lord,
    turn back.   145

Ang. How! bribe me?

Isab. Ay, with such gifts that Heaven shall
    share with you.

Lucio. [*Aside to Isab.*] You had marr'd all else.

Isab. Not with fond shekels of the tested gold,
Or stones whose [rates] are either rich or poor 150
As fancy values them; but with true prayers
That shall be up at heaven and enter there
Ere sun-rise, prayers from preserved souls,
From fasting maids whose minds are dedicate
To nothing temporal.

Ang.   Well, come to me to-morrow.

Lucio. [*Aside to Isab.*] Go to; 'tis well. Away!

Isab. Heaven keep your honour safe!

Ang.   [*Aside.*] Amen!   157

For I am that way going to temptation,
Where prayers cross.

Isab.   At what hour to-morrow
Shall I attend your lordship?

Ang.   At any time 'fore noon. 160

Isab. 'Save your honour!

        [*Exeunt Isabella, Lucio, and Provost.*]

Ang.   From thee, even from thy virtue.
What's this, what's this? Is this her fault or mine?
The tempter or the tempted, who sins most?
Ha!
Not she, nor doth she tempt; but it is I   165
That, lying by the violet in the sun,
Do as the carrion does, not as the flower,
Corrupt with virtuous season. Can it be
That modesty may more betray our sense
Than woman's lightness? Having waste ground
    enough,   170
Shall we desire to raze the sanctuary
And pitch our evils there? O, fie, fie, fie!
What dost thou, or what art thou, Angelo?
Dost thou desire her foully for those things
That make her good? O, let her brother live!
Thieves for their robbery have authority   176
When judges steal themselves. What, do I love
    her,
That I desire to hear her speak again
And feast upon her eyes? What is't I dream on?
O cunning enemy, that, to catch a saint,   180
With saints dost bait thy hook! Most dangerous
Is that temptation that doth goad us on
To sin in loving virtue. Never could the strumpet,
With all her double vigour, art and nature,
Once stir my temper; but this virtuous maid
Subdues me quite. Ever till now,   186
When men were fond, I smil'd and wond'red how.
                                        [*Exit.*

SCENE III. [*A room in a prison.*]

Enter [*severally*] DUKE [*disguised as a friar*]
    and PROVOST.

Duke. Hail to you, Provost! so I think you are.

Prov. I am the Provost. What's your will, good
    friar?

Duke. Bound by my charity and my blest order,
I come to visit the afflicted spirits
Here in the prison. Do me the common right   5
To let me see them and to make me know
The nature of their crimes, that I may minister
To them accordingly.

Prov. I would do more than that, if more were
    needful.

---

120. **glassy essence**: frail spirit. 122. **spleens.** The spleen was the supposed seat of laughter. 123. **mortal**: i.e., to death.
126. **weigh...ourself**: i.e., judge others by ourselves. 132. **avis'd**: aware. 142. **breeds**: is enlivened. 150. [**rates**]
(Johnson). *rate* F. 153. **preserved**: kept from evil. 159. **cross**: are at cross purposes. 168. **Corrupt...season**: i.e.,
decay with the (sun of) summer. 169. **betray our sense**: catch our sensual desire.

Enter JULIET.

Look, here comes one; a gentlewoman of mine,   10
Who, falling in the flaws of her own youth,
Hath blister'd her report.   She is with child;
And he that got it, sentenc'd; a young man
More fit to do another such offence
Than die for this.   15
   Duke. When must he die?
   Prov.   As I do think, to-morrow.
I have provided for you.   Stay awhile,
                                     [*To Juliet.*]
And you shall be conducted.
   Duke. Repent you, fair one, of the sin you carry?
   Jul. I do; and bear the shame most patiently. 20
   Duke. I'll teach you how you shall arraign your
      conscience,
And try your penitence, if it be sound
Or hollowly put on.
   Jul.   I'll gladly learn.
   Duke. Love you the man that wrong'd you? 24
   Jul. Yes, as I love the woman that wrong'd him.
   Duke. So then it seems your most offenceful act
Was mutually committed?
   Jul.   Mutually.
   Duke. Then was your sin of heavier kind than
      his.
   Jul. I do confess it, and repent it, father.
   Duke. 'Tis meet so, daughter; but lest you do
      repent   30
As that the sin hath brought you to this shame, —
Which sorrow is always towards ourselves, not
      heaven,
Showing we would not spare heaven as we love it,
But as we stand in fear, —
   Jul. I do repent me, as it is an evil,   35
And take the shame with joy.
   Duke.   There rest.
Your partner, as I hear, must die to-morrow,
And I am going with instruction to him.
Grace go with you, *Benedicite!*   [*Exit.*
   Jul. Must die to-morrow! O injurious [law], 40
That respites me a life whose very comfort
Is still a dying horror!
   Prov.   'Tis pity of him.   [*Exeunt.*

SCENE IV.   [*A room in Angelo's house.*]

Enter ANGELO.

   Ang. When I would pray and think, I think and
      pray

To several subjects.   Heaven hath my empty
      words,
Whilst my invention, hearing not my tongue,
Anchors on Isabel; Heaven in my mouth,
As if I did but only chew his name,   5
And in my heart the strong and swelling evil
Of my conception.   The state, whereon I studied,
Is like a good thing, being often read,
Grown [sear'd] and tedious; yea, my gravity,
Wherein — let no man hear me — I take pride, .o
Could I with boot change for an idle plume,
Which the air beats for vain.   O place, O form,
How often dost thou with thy case, thy habit,
Wrench awe from fools and tie the wiser souls
To thy false seeming!   Blood, thou art blood. 15
Let's write good angel on the devil's horn;
'Tis not the devil's crest.

Enter a SERVANT.

                        How now! who's there?
   Serv. One Isabel, a sister, desires access to you.
   Ang. Teach her the way.   [*Exit Serv.*] O
      heavens!
Why does my blood thus muster to my heart, 20
Making both it unable for itself,
And dispossessing all my other parts
Of necessary fitness?
So play the foolish throngs with one that swounds;
Come all to help him, and so stop the air   25
By which he should revive; and even so
The general, subject to a well-wish'd king,
Quit their own part, and in obsequious fondness
Crowd to his presence, where their untaught love
Must needs appear offence.

Enter ISABELLA.

                        How now, fair maid?
   Isab. I am come to know your pleasure.   31
   Ang. That you might know it, would much better
      please me
Than to demand what 'tis.   Your brother cannot
      live.
   Isab. Even so.   Heaven keep your honour!
   Ang. Yet may he live a while; and, it may be, 35
As long as you or I.   Yet he must die.
   Isab. Under your sentence?
   Ang. Yea.
   Isab. When, I beseech you? that in his reprieve,
Longer or shorter, he may be so fitted   40
That his soul sicken not.

Sc. iii, 11. **flaws:** flames.   12. **report:** reputation.   33. **spare heaven:** i.e., spare heaven the grievance of our sins.   38.
instruction: religious counsel.   40. **[law]** (Hanmer).   *love* F.
   Sc. iv, 2. **several subjects:** i.e., at cross purposes.   3. **invention:** imagination, conception.   5. **chew:** i.e., mouth, mumble.
9. **[sear'd]** (Hanmer): dry.   *fear'd* F.   12. **for vain:** vainly, idly.   13. **case:** outward garb.   16–17. **Let's ... crest.** Probably corrupt.   Angelo, talking about "false seeming," appears to say cynically, "Let hypocrisy thrive."   I.e., we may
(safely) write "good angel" on the devil's horn, because it ("good angel") is not the true crest (insignia) of the devil (and
thus will deceive).   20. **muster:** rush.   27. **general:** people.   32. **know.** Angelo takes *pleasure* (l. 31) in the sense of sexual
pleasure.

Ang. Ha! fie, these filthy vices! It were as good
To pardon him that hath from nature stol'n
A man already made, as to remit
Their saucy sweetness that do coin Heaven's image
In stamps that are forbid. 'Tis all as easy   46
Falsely to take away a life true made
As to put metal in restrained means
To make a false one.   49
    Isab. 'Tis set down so in heaven, but not in earth.
    Ang. Say you so? Then I shall pose you quickly.
Which had you rather, that the most just law
Now took your brother's life; [or], to redeem him,
Give up your body to such sweet uncleanness
As she that he hath stain'd?
    Isab.   Sir, believe this,
I had rather give my body than my soul.   56
    Ang. I talk not of your soul; our compell'd sins
Stand more for number than for accompt.
    Isab.   How say you?
    Ang. Nay, I'll not warrant that; for I can speak
Against the thing I say. Answer to this: 60
I, now the voice of the recorded law,
Pronounce a sentence on your brother's life.
Might there not be a charity in sin
To save this brother's life?
    Isab.   Please you to do't,
I'll take it as a peril to my soul,   65
It is no sin at all, but charity.
    Ang. Pleas'd you to do't at peril of your soul,
Were equal poise of sin and charity.
    Isab. That I do beg his life, if it be sin,
Heaven let me bear it! You granting of my suit,
If that be sin, I'll make it my morn prayer   71
To have it added to the faults of mine,
And nothing of your answer.
    Ang.   Nay, but hear me;
Your sense pursues not mine. Either you are ig-
          norant,
Or seem so [craftily]; and that's not good.   75
    Isab. Let [me] be ignorant, and in nothing
          good,
But graciously to know I am no better.
    Ang. Thus wisdom wishes to appear most bright
When it doth tax itself; as these black masks
Proclaim an enshield beauty ten times louder   80
Than beauty could, displayed. But mark me:
To be received plain, I'll speak more gross.
Your brother is to die.
    Isab. So.
    Ang. And his offence is so, as it appears,   85
Accountant to the law upon that pain.

Isab. True.
    Ang. Admit no other way to save his life, —
As I subscribe not that, nor any other,
But in the [loose] of question, — that you, his sister,
Finding yourself desir'd of such a person,   91
Whose credit with the judge, or own great place,
Could fetch your brother from the manacles
Of the [all-binding] law; and that there were
No earthly mean to save him, but that either   95
You must lay down the treasures of your body
To this supposed, or else to let him suffer;
What would you do?
    Isab. As much for my poor brother as myself:
That is, were I under the terms of death,   100
The impression of keen whips I'd wear as rubies,
And strip myself to death, as to a bed
That, longing, have been sick for, ere I'd yield
My body up to shame.
    Ang.   Then must your brother die.
    Isab. And 'twere the cheaper way.   105
Better it were a brother died at once,
Than that a sister, by redeeming him,
Should die for ever.
    Ang. Were not you then as cruel as the sentence
That you have slander'd so?   110
    Isab. Ignomy in ransom and free pardon
Are of two houses. Lawful mercy
Is nothing kin to foul redemption.
    Ang. You seem'd of late to make the law a tyrant;
And rather prov'd the sliding of your brother   115
A merriment than a vice.
    Isab. O, pardon me, my lord. It oft falls out,
To have what we would have, we speak not what
          we mean.
I something do excuse the thing I hate,
For his advantage that I dearly love.   120
    Ang. We are all frail.
    Isab.   Else let my brother die,
If not a fedary, but only he
Owe and succeed [this] weakness.
    Ang. Nay, women are frail too.
    Isab. Ay, as the glasses where they view them-
          selves;   125
Which are as easy broke as they make forms.
Women! Help, Heaven! men their creation mar
In profiting by them. Nay, call us ten times frail;
For we are soft as our complexions are,   129
And credulous to false prints.
    Ang.   I think it well;
And from this testimony of your own sex, —
Since I suppose we are made to be no stronger

44. **remit:** forgive. 46. **'Tis…easy:** i.e., it is morally the same. 48. **restrained:** prohibited. 51. **pose you:** put a puzzling question to you. 53. **[or]** (Rowe). *and* F. 58. **Stand…accompt:** are enumerated rather than scored against us. 68. **poise:** weight. 73. **nothing…answer:** you not accountable. 75. **[craftily]** (Rowe). *crafty* F. 76. **[me]** F₂. Om. F₁. 79. **tax:** accuse. 80. **enshield:** hidden. 86. **pain:** penalty. 90. **[loose]** (Singer conj.): freedom. *loss* F. **question:** talk. 94. **[all-binding]** (Theobald). *all-building* F. 103. **have:** I have. 115. **sliding:** backsliding. 122–23. **If… weakness:** if he has no fellow in this weakness but he alone inherits (succeed) and possesses (owe) it. **[this]** (Malone conj.) *thy* F. 127. **creation:** nature. 128. **profiting by:** taking advantage of. 130. **credulous:** susceptible. **prints:** impressions.

Than faults may shake our frames, — let me be
    bold.
I do arrest your words. Be that you are,
That is, a woman; if you be more, you're none; 135
If you be one, as you are well express'd
By all external warrants, show it now,
By putting on the destin'd livery.
    Isab. I have no tongue but one; gentle my lord,
Let me entreat you speak the former language. 140
    Ang. Plainly conceive, I love you.
    Isab. My brother did love Juliet,
And you tell me that he shall die for it.
    Ang. He shall not, Isabel, if you give me love.
    Isab. I know your virtue hath a license in't. 145
Which seems a little fouler than it is,
To pluck on others.
    Ang.   Believe me, on mine honour,
My words express my purpose.
    Isab. Ha! little honour to be much believ'd,
And most pernicious purpose! Seeming, seeming!
I will proclaim thee, Angelo. Look for 't! 151
Sign me a present pardon for my brother,
Or with an outstretch'd throat I'll tell the world
    aloud
What man thou art.
    Ang.   Who will believe thee, Isabel?
My unsoil'd name, th' austereness of my life, 155
My vouch against you, and my place i' th' state,
Will so your accusation overweigh,
That you shall stifle in your own report
And smell of calumny. I have begun,
And now I give my sensual race the rein. 160
Fit thy consent to my sharp appetite;
Lay by all nicety and prolixious blushes
That banish what they sue for; redeem thy brother
By yielding up thy body to my will;
Or else he must not only die the death, 165
But thy unkindness shall his death draw out
To ling'ring sufferance. Answer me to-morrow,
Or, by the affection that now guides me most,
I'll prove a tyrant to him. As for you, 169
Say what you can, my false o'erweighs your true.
                                [*Exit.*
    Isab. To whom should I complain? Did I tell
    this,
Who would believe me? O perilous mouths,
That bear in them one and the self-same tongue,
Either of condemnation or approof,
Bidding the law make curtsy to their will, 175
Hooking both right and wrong to th' appetite,
To follow as it draws! I'll to my brother.
Though he hath fall'n by prompture of the blood,

Yet hath he in him such a mind of honour
That, had he twenty heads to tender down 180
On twenty bloody blocks, he'd yield them up,
Before his sister should her body stoop
To such abhorr'd pollution.
Then, Isabel, live chaste, and, brother, die;
More than our brother is our chastity. 185
I'll tell him yet of Angelo's request,
And fit his mind to death, for his soul's rest.
                                [*Exit.*

ACT III

SCENE I. [*A room in the prison.*]

Enter DUKE [*disguised as before,*] CLAUDIO, *and*
    PROVOST.

    Duke. So then you hope of pardon from Lord
    Angelo?
    Claud. The miserable have no other medicine
But only hope.
I've hope to live, and am prepar'd to die.
    Duke. Be absolute for death; either death or
    life 5
Shall thereby be the sweeter. Reason thus with
    life:
If I do lose thee, I do lose a thing
That none but fools would keep. A breath thou
    art,
Servile to all the skyey influences,
That dost this habitation where thou keep'st 10
Hourly afflict. Merely, thou art Death's fool;
For him thou labour'st by thy flight to shun
And yet runn'st toward him still. Thou art not
    noble;
For all the accommodations that thou bear'st
Are nurs'd by baseness. Thou'rt by no means
    valiant; 15
For thou dost fear the soft and tender fork
Of a poor worm. Thy best of rest is sleep,
And that thou oft provok'st; yet grossly fear'st
Thy death, which is no more. Thou art not thy-
    self;
For thou exist'st on many a thousand grains 20
That issue out of dust. Happy thou art not;
For what thou hast not, still thou striv'st to get,
And what thou hast, forget'st. Thou art not cer
    tain,
For thy complexion shifts to strange effects 24
After the moon. If thou art rich, thou'rt poor;
For, like an ass whose back with ingots bows,
Thou bear'st thy heavy riches but a journey,

---

134. **arrest:** seize upon. 138. **livery:** i.e., frailty. 140. **the former language:** i.e., as you did before these lascivious advances.
150. **Seeming:** hypocrisy. 156. **vouch:** assertion. 162. **prolixious:** superfluous. 178. **prompture:** prompting, incitement.
    Act III, sc. i, 5. **absolute:** resolved. 9. **skyey:** i.e., astrological. 10. **keep'st:** livest. 11. **Merely:** absolutely. 14. **ac-
commodations:** qualities. 15. **nurs'd by baseness:** have rotten foundations. 16. **fork:** forked tongue. 17. **worm:** snake
18. **provok'st:** invitest. 24. **complexion:** disposition.

And Death unloads thee.   Friend hast thou none;
For thine own bowels, which do call thee sire,
The mere effusion of thy proper loins,   30
Do curse the gout, [serpigo], and the rheum,
For ending thee no sooner.   Thou hast nor youth
      nor age,
But, as it were, an after-dinner's sleep,
Dreaming on both; for all thy blessed youth
Becomes as aged, and doth beg the alms   35
Of palsied Eld; and when thou art old and rich,
Thou hast neither heat, affection, limb, nor beauty,
To make thy riches pleasant.   What's yet in this
That bears the name of life?   Yet in this life
Lie hid moe thousand deaths; yet death we fear 40
That makes these odds all even.
    Claud.   I humbly thank you.
To sue to live, I find I seek to die;
And, seeking death, find life.   Let it come on.
    Isab. [*Within.*] What, ho!   Peace here; grace
      and good company!
    Prov. Who's there?   Come in; the wish deserves
      a welcome.   45
    Duke. Dear sir, ere long I'll visit you again.
    Claud. Most holy sir, I thank you.

                   Enter ISABELLA.

    Isab. My business is a word or two with Claudio.
    Prov. And very welcome.   Look, signior, here's
      your sister.
    Duke. Provost, a word with you.   50
    Prov. As many as you please.
    Duke. Bring [me] to hear [them] speak, where I
may be conceal'd.   [*Exeunt Duke and Provost.*]
    Claud. Now, sister, what's the comfort?
    Isab.   Why,
As all comforts are; most good, most good indeed.
Lord Angelo, having affairs to heaven,   57
Intends you for his swift ambassador,
Where you shall be an everlasting leiger;
Therefore your best appointment make with speed,
To-morrow you set on.
    Claud.   Is there no remedy? 61
    Isab. None but such remedy as, to save a head,
To cleave a heart in twain.
    Claud.   But is there any?
    Isab. Yes, brother, you may live.
There is a devilish mercy in the judge,   65
If you'll implore it, that will free your life,
But fetter you till death.
    Claud.   Perpetual durance?

    Isab. Ay, just; perpetual durance, a restraint,
[Though] all the world's vastidity you had,
To a determin'd scope.
    Claud.   But in what nature? 70
    Isab. In such a one as, you consenting to't,
Would bark your honour from that trunk you bear,
And leave you naked.
    Claud.   Let me know the point.
    Isab. O, I do fear thee, Claudio; and I quake,
Lest thou a feverous life shouldst entertain,   75
And six or seven winters more respect
Than a perpetual honour.   Dar'st thou die?
The sense of death is most in apprehension;
And the poor beetle, that we tread upon,
In corporal sufferance finds a pang as great   80
As when a giant dies.
    Claud.   Why give you me this shame?
Think you I can a resolution fetch
From flow'ry tenderness?   If I must die,
I will encounter darkness as a bride,
And hug it in mine arms.   85
    Isab. There spake my brother; there my father's
      grave
Did utter forth a voice.   Yes, thou must die.
Thou art too noble to conserve a life
In base appliances.   This outward-sainted deputy,
Whose settled visage and deliberate word   90
Nips youth i' th' head and follies doth [enew]
As falcon doth the fowl, is yet a devil;
His filth within being cast, he would appear
A pond as deep as hell.
    Claud.   The prenzie Angelo!
    Isab. O, 'tis the cunning livery of hell,   95
The damned'st body to invest and cover
In prenzie guards!   Dost thou think, Claudio?
If I would yield him my virginity,
Thou mightst be freed.
    Claud.   O heavens! it cannot be.
    Isab. Yes, he would give't thee, from this rank
      offence,   100
So to offend him still.   This night's the time
That I should do what I abhor to name,
Or else thou diest to-morrow.
    Claud.   Thou shalt not do't.
    Isab. O, were it but my life,
I'd throw it down for your deliverance   105
As frankly as a pin.
    Claud.   Thanks, dear Isabel.
    Isab. Be ready, Claudio, for your death to-
      morrow.

29. **bowels:** i.e., offspring.   31. **[serpigo]** (Rowe): a skin disease.   *Sapego* F.   35–36. **Becomes...Eld:** grows old and
begs the charity that old age must beg.   The passage is very likely corrupt.   37. **limb:** i.e., strength.   40. **moe:** i.e.,
more than I have spoken of.   52. **[me]...[them]** (Steevens conj.).   *them...me* F.   59. **leiger:** ambassador.   60. **appointment:** preparation.   68. **just:** exactly.   69. **[Though]** (Rowe).   *Through* F.   69. **vastidity:** vastness.   70. **determin'd
scope:** fixed limit.   75. **entertain:** favor.   89. **in...appliances:** by base means.   90. **settled:** composed, grave.   91. **[enew]**
(New Camb. Edd.): pursue.   *emmew* F.   The literal meaning is to drive a fowl into the water.   93. **cast:** reckoned.   94, 97.
prenzie: (apparently) smooth, slick.   F$_{2-4}$ read *princely*.   97. **guards:** trimmings.   100–01. **give't...still:** grant you freedom, in exchange for my sin, to go on sinning.   106. **frankly:** freely.

Claud. Yes. Has he affections in him,
That thus can make him bite the law by the
          nose,
When he would force it? Sure, it is no sin;   110
Or of the deadly seven it is the least.
     Isab. Which is the least?
     Claud. If it were damnable, he being so wise,
Why would he for the momentary trick
Be perdurably fin'd? O Isabel!   115
     Isab. What says my brother?
     Claud.   Death is a fearful thing.
     Isab. And shamed life a hateful.
     Claud. Ay, but to die, and go we know not where;
To lie in cold obstruction and to rot;
This sensible warm motion to become   120
A kneaded clod, and the delighted spirit
To bathe in fiery floods, or to reside
In thrilling region of thick-ribbed ice;
To be imprison'd in the viewless winds,
And blown with restless violence round about   125
The pendent world; or to be — worse than worst —
Of those that lawless and incertain thought
Imagine howling, — 'tis too horrible!
The weariest and most loathed worldly life
That age, ache, [penury], and imprisonment   130
Can lay on nature is a paradise
To what we fear of death.
     Isab. Alas, alas!
     Claud.   Sweet sister, let me live.
What sin you do to save a brother's life,
Nature dispenses with the deed so far   135
That it becomes a virtue.
     Isab.   O you beast!
O faithless coward! O dishonest wretch!
Wilt thou be made a man out of my vice?
Is't not a kind of incest, to take life
From thine own sister's shame? What should I
          think?   140
Heaven shield my mother play'd my father fair!
For such a warped slip of wilderness
Ne'er issu'd from his blood. Take my defiance!
Die, perish! Might but my bending down
Reprieve thee from thy fate, it should proceed.
I'll pray a thousand prayers for thy death,   146
No word to save thee.
     Claud. Nay, hear me, Isabel.
     Isab.   O, fie, fie, fie!
Thy sin's not accidental, but a trade.
Mercy to thee would prove itself a bawd;   150
'Tis best that thou diest quickly.
     Claud.   O hear me, Isabella!

[Re-enter DUKE.]

     Duke. Vouchsafe a word, young sister, but one
          word.
     Isab. What is your will?   153
     Duke. Might you dispense with your leisure, I
would by and by have some speech with you. The
satisfaction I would require is likewise your own
benefit.
     Isab. I have no superfluous leisure; my stay must
be stolen out of other affairs; but I will attend you a
while.   *[Walks apart.]* 160
     Duke. Son, I have overheard what hath pass'd
between you and your sister. Angelo had never
the purpose to corrupt her; only he hath made an
assay of her virtue to practise his judgement with
the disposition of natures. She, having the   165
truth of honour in her, hath made him that gracious
denial which he is most glad to receive. I am confessor to Angelo, and I know this to be true; therefore prepare yourself to death. Do not satisfy your
resolution with hopes that are fallible; to-morrow
you must die. Go to your knees and make ready.
     Claud. Let me ask my sister pardon. I am   173
so out of love with life that I will sue to be rid of it.
     Duke. Hold you there! Farewell. *[Exit
Claudio.]* Provost, a word with you!

[Re-enter PROVOST.]

     Prov. What's your will, father?   178
     Duke. That now you are come, you will be gone.
Leave me a while with the maid. My mind promises with my habit no loss shall touch her by my
company.
     Prov. In good time.   183
          [Exit [Provost. Isabella comes forward].
     Duke. The hand that hath made you fair hath
made you good; the goodness that is cheap in
beauty makes beauty brief in goodness; but grace,
being the soul of your complexion, shall keep the
body of it ever fair. The assault that Angelo   188
hath made to you, fortune hath convey'd to my understanding; and, but that frailty hath examples
for his falling, I should wonder at Angelo. How
will you do to content this substitute, and to save
your brother?   193
     Isab. I am now going to resolve him. I had
rather my brother die by the law than my son
should be unlawfully born. But, O, how much is
the good Duke deceiv'd in Angelo! If ever he return and I can speak to him, I will open my lips in
vain, or discover his government.   199

---

110. **force**: enforce. 115. **perdurably fin'd**: eternally punished. 119. **obstruction**: stagnation (of the blood). 120. **sensible**: sensitive. **motion**: i.e., body. 121. **delighted**: capable of delight. 123. **thrilling**: piercing (with cold). 127. **Of**: among. 130. **[penury]** F₂. *periury* F₁. 135. **dispenses with**: condones. 141. **shield**: forbid. 142. **wilderness**: wild growth. 145. **it**: i.e., your fate. 155. **by and by**: directly. 164. **with**: respecting. 169. **satisfy**: feed, nourish. 175. **there**: to that. 183. **In good time**: very well. 187. **complexion**: disposition. 192. **substitute**: deputy. 199. **discover his government**: expose his conduct.

Duke. That shall not be much amiss; yet, as the matter now stands, he will avoid your accusation: he made trial of you only. Therefore fasten your ear on my advisings. To the love I have in doing good a remedy presents itself. I do make myself believe that you may most uprighteously do a   205 poor wronged lady a merited benefit, redeem your brother from the angry law, do no stain to your own gracious person, and much please the absent Duke, if peradventure he shall ever return to have hearing of this business.   211

Isab. Let me hear you speak farther. I have spirit to do anything that appears not foul in the truth of my spirit.   214

Duke. Virtue is bold, and goodness never fearful. Have you not heard speak of Mariana, the sister of Frederick, the great soldier who miscarried at sea?

Isab. I have heard of the lady, and good words went with her name.   220

Duke. She should this Angelo have married; was affianced to her [by] oath, and the nuptial appointed; between which time of the contract and limit of the solemnity, her brother Frederick was wreck'd at sea, having in that perished vessel   225 the dowry of his sister. But mark how heavily this befell to the poor gentlewoman. There she lost a noble and renowned brother, in his love toward her ever most kind and natural; with him, the portion and sinew of her fortune, her marriage-dowry; with both, her combinate husband, this well-seeming Angelo.   232

Isab. Can this be so? Did Angelo so leave her?

Duke. Left her in her tears, and dried not one of them with his comfort; swallowed his vows whole, pretending in her discoveries of dishonour; in few, bestow'd her on her own lamentation, which she yet wears for his sake; and he, a marble to her tears, is washed with them, but relents not.   239

Isab. What a merit were it in death to take this poor maid from the world! What corruption in this life, that it will let this man live! But how out of this can she avail?   243

Duke. It is a rupture that you may easily heal; and the cure of it not only saves your brother, but keeps you from dishonour in doing it.

Isab. Show me how, good father.   247

Duke. This forenamed maid hath yet in her the continuance of her first affection; his unjust unkindness, that in all reason should have quenched   250 her love, hath, like an impediment in the current, made it more violent and unruly. Go you to An-

gelo; answer his requiring with a plausible obedience; agree with his demands to the point; only refer yourself to this advantage, first, that   255 your stay with him may not be long; that the time may have all shadow and silence in it; and the place answer to convenience. This being granted in course, — and now follows all, — we shall advise this wronged maid to stead up your ap-   260 pointment, go in your place. If the encounter acknowledge itself hereafter, it may compel him to her recompense; and here, by this is your brother saved, your honour untainted, the poor Mariana advantaged, and the corrupt deputy scaled. The   264 maid will I frame and make fit for his attempt.   265 If you think well to carry this as you may, the doubleness of the benefit defends the deceit from reproof. What think you of it?   269

Isab. The image of it gives me content already; and I trust it will grow to a most prosperous perfection.   272

Duke. It lies much in your holding up. Haste you speedily to Angelo. If for this night he entreat you to his bed, give him promise of satisfaction. I will presently to Saint Luke's; there, at the moated grange, resides this dejected Mariana. At that place call upon me; and dispatch with Angelo, that it may be quickly.   279

Isab. I thank you for this comfort. Fare you well, good father.   *[Exeunt [Isabella and Duke].*

[Scene II.   *The street before the prison.*]

Enter [on one side, DUKE, *disguised as before; on the other,]* ELBOW, *and* Officers *with Clown [*POMPEY].

Elb. Nay, if there be no remedy for it but that you will needs buy and sell men and women like beasts, we shall have all the world drink brown and white bastard.

Duke. O heavens! what stuff is here?   5

Pom. 'Twas never merry world since, of two usuries, the merriest was put down, and the worser allow'd by order of law a furr'd gown to keep him warm; and furr'd with fox and lambskins too, to signify that craft, being richer than innocency, stands for the facing.   11

Elb. Come your way, sir. 'Bless you, good father friar.

Duke. And you, good brother father. What offence hath this man made you, sir?   15

Elb. Marry, sir, he hath offended the law; and, sir, we take him to be a thief too, sir, for we have

---

201-02. **avoid...he:** answer your charge by saying he (etc.).   218. **miscarried:** perished.   222. **[by]** F$_2$. Om. F$_1$. 224. **limit...solemnity:** date of the ceremony.   231. **combinate:** affianced.   255. **refer...to:** i.e., demand for yourself. 264. **scaled:** weighed.   265. **frame:** instruct.   276. **moated grange:** country house with a moat.

Sc. ii, 4. **bastard:** a sweet Spanish wine (used punningly).   6. **two usuries:** i.e., prostitution and money-lending.   11. **facing:** trimming.   Pompey means to say that the fox and lambskin facings of the usurer's gown signify that craft is **stronger** than innocence.

found upon him, sir, a strange picklock, which we
have sent to the deputy.

Duke. Fie, sirrah! a bawd, a wicked bawd!   20
The evil that thou causest to be done,
That is thy means to live. Do thou but think
What 'tis to cram a maw or clothe a back
From such a filthy vice; say to thyself,
From their abominable and beastly touches   25
I drink, I eat, [array] myself, and live.
Canst thou believe thy living is a life,
So stinkingly depending? Go mend, go mend.

Pom. Indeed, it does stink in some sort, sir; but
yet, sir, I would prove —   30

Duke. Nay, if the devil have given thee proofs
for sin,
Thou wilt prove his. Take him to prison, officer.
Correction and instruction must both work
Ere this rude beast will profit.   34

Elb. He must before the deputy, sir; he has given
him warning. The deputy cannot abide a whoremaster. If he be a whoremonger, and comes before
him, he were as good go a mile on his errand.

Duke. That we were all, as some would seem to
be,   40
[Free] from our faults, as [from faults] seeming free!

Enter LUCIO.

Elb. His neck will come to your waist, — a cord,
sir.

Pom. I spy comfort; I cry bail. Here's a gentleman and a friend of mine.   44

Lucio. How now, noble Pompey! What, at the
wheels of Cæsar? Art thou led in triumph? What,
is there none of Pygmalion's images, newly made
woman, to be had now, for putting the hand in the
pocket and extracting [it] clutch'd? What reply,
ha? What say'st thou to this tune, matter, and   50
method? Is't not drown'd i' the last rain, ha?
What say'st thou, Trot? Is the world as it was,
man? Which is the way? Is it sad, and few
words? or how? The trick of it?   54

Duke. Still thus, and thus; still worse!

Lucio. How doth my dear morsel, thy mistress?
Procures she still, ha?

Pom. Troth, sir, she hath eaten up all her beef,
and she is herself in the tub.   59

Lucio. Why, 'tis good; it is the right of it; it must
be so. Ever your fresh whore and your powder'd
bawd; an unshunn'd consequence; it must be so.
Art going to prison, Pompey?

Pom. Yes, faith, sir.   64

Lucio. Why, 'tis not amiss, Pompey. Farewell.

Go, say I sent thee thither. For debt, Pompey? or
how?

Elb. For being a bawd, for being a bawd.   68

Lucio. Well, then, imprison him. If imprisonment be the due of a bawd, why, 'tis his right.
Bawd is he doubtless, and of antiquity too; bawd-
born. Farewell, good Pompey. Commend me to
the prison, Pompey. You will turn good husband
now, Pompey; you will keep the house.   74

Pom. I hope, sir, your good worship will be my
bail.

Lucio. No, indeed, will I not, Pompey; it is not
the wear. I will pray, Pompey, to increase your
bondage. If you take it not patiently, why, your
mettle is the more. Adieu, trusty Pompey. 'Bless
you, friar.   81

Duke. And you.

Lucio. Does Bridget paint still, Pompey, ha?

Elb. Come your ways, sir; come.

Pom. You will not bail me, then, sir?   85

Lucio. Then, Pompey, nor now. What news
abroad, friar? what news?

Elb. Come your ways, sir; come.

Lucio. Go to kennel, Pompey; go. [*Exeunt Elbow, Pompey, and Officers.*] What news, friar, of
the Duke?   91

Duke. I know none. Can you tell me of any?

Lucio. Some say he is with the Emperor of
Russia; other some, he is in Rome; but where is he,
think you?   95

Duke. I know not where; but wheresoever, I wish
him well.

Lucio. It was a mad fantastical trick of him to
steal from the state, and usurp the beggary he was
never born to. Lord Angelo dukes it well in his
absence; he puts transgression to't.   101

Duke. He does well in't.

Lucio. A little more lenity to lechery would do
no harm in him. Something too crabbed that way,
friar.

Duke. It is too general a vice, and severity must
cure it.   107

Lucio. Yes, in good sooth, the vice is of a great
kindred, it is well allied; but it is impossible to extirp it quite, friar, till eating and drinking be put
down. They say this Angelo was not made by man
and woman after this downright way of creation.
Is it true, think you?   113

Duke. How should he be made, then?

Lucio. Some report a sea-maid spawn'd him;
some, that he was begot between two stock-fishes.
But it is certain that when he makes water his urine

---

26. [array] (Theobald). *away* F.   28. depending: supported.   38. he ... errand: he has no chance.   41. [Free]
F₂. Om. F₁. [from faults] (Hanmer). *faults from* F.   42. cord: friar's girdle. He will be hanged.   49. [it]
(Rowe). Om. F. clutch'd: clenched (holding money).   52. Trot: old woman (contemptuously).   59. tub: (1) for salting meat, (2) for sweating treatment in venereal disease.   61. powder'd: pickled.   62. unshunn'd: inevitable.   73. husband:
housekeeper.   78. wear: fashion.   80. mettle: i.e., shackles (with a pun).   110. extirp: eradicate.   116. stock-fishes:
codfish.

is congeal'd ice; that I know to be true: and he is a
motion generative; that's infallible.   119

Duke. You are pleasant, sir, and speak apace.

Lucio. Why, what a ruthless thing is this in him,
for the rebellion of a codpiece to take away the life
of a man! Would the Duke that is absent have
done this? Ere he would have hang'd a man for the
getting a hundred bastards, he would have paid   125
for the nursing a thousand. He had some feeling
of the sport; he knew the service, and that instructed him to mercy.

Duke. I never heard the absent Duke much
detected for women. He was not inclin'd that way.

Lucio. O, sir, you are deceived.   131

Duke. 'Tis not possible.

Lucio. Who? Not the Duke? Yes, your beggar of fifty; and his use was to put a ducat in her
clack-dish. The Duke had crotchets in him. He
would be drunk too; that let me inform you.   136

Duke. You do him wrong, surely.

Lucio. Sir, I was an inward of his. A shy fellow
was the Duke; and I believe I know the cause of
his withdrawing.   140

Duke. What, I prithee, might be the cause?

Lucio. No, pardon; 'tis a secret must be lock'd
within the teeth and the lips. But this I can let
you understand, the greater file of the subject held
the Duke to be wise.   145

Duke. Wise! Why, no question but he was.

Lucio. A very superficial, ignorant, unweighing
fellow.

Duke. Either this is envy in you, folly, or mistaking. The very stream of his life and the business he hath helmed must, upon a warranted   151
need, give him a better proclamation. Let him be
but testimonied in his own bringings-forth, and he
shall appear to the envious a scholar, a statesman,
and a soldier. Therefore you speak unskilfully; or
if your knowledge be more it is much dark'ned in
your malice.   157

Lucio. Sir, I know him, and I love him.

Duke. Love talks with better knowledge, and
knowledge with [dearer] love.

Lucio. Come, sir, I know what I know.   161

Duke. I can hardly believe that, since you know
not what you speak. But if ever the Duke return,
as our prayers are he may, let me desire you to
make your answer before him. If it be honest you
have spoke, you have courage to maintain it. I am
bound to call upon you; and, I pray you, your
name?   168

Lucio. Sir, my name is Lucio; well known to the
Duke.

Duke. He shall know you better, sir, if I may
live to report you.

Lucio. I fear you not.   173

Duke. O, you hope the Duke will return no more;
or you imagine me too unhurtful an opposite. But
indeed I can do you little harm; you'll forswear this
again.   177

Lucio. I'll be hang'd first; thou art deceiv'd in
me, friar. But no more of this. Canst thou tell if
Claudio die to-morrow or no?   180

Duke. Why should he die, sir?

Lucio. Why? For filling a bottle with a tun-dish.
I would the Duke we talk of were return'd again.
This ungenitur'd agent will unpeople the province
with continency. Sparrows must not build in   185
his house-eaves, because they are lecherous. The
Duke yet would have dark deeds darkly answered;
he would never bring them to light. Would he were
return'd! Marry, this Claudio is condemned for
untrussing. Farewell, good friar; I prithee,   190
pray for me. The Duke, I say to thee again, would
eat mutton on Fridays. He's now past it; yet (and
I say to thee) he would mouth with a beggar, though
she smelt brown bread and garlic. Say that I said
so. Farewell.   [*Exit.*   195

Duke. No might nor greatness in mortality
Can censure scape; back-wounding calumny
The whitest virtue strikes. What king so strong
Can tie the gall up in the slanderous tongue?
But who comes here?   200

Enter ESCALUS, PROVOST, *and* [Officers, *with*]
Bawd [MISTRESS OVERDONE].

Escal. Go; away with her to prison!

Mrs. Ov. Good my lord, be good to me; your
honour is accounted a merciful man. Good my
lord!   204

Escal. Double and treble admonition, and still
forfeit in the same kind! This would make mercy
swear and play the tyrant.

Prov. A bawd of eleven years' continuance, may
it please your honour.   209

Mrs. Ov. My lord, this is one Lucio's information
against me. Mistress Kate Keepdown was with
child by him in the Duke's time. He promis'd her
marriage. His child is a year and a quarter old,
come Philip and Jacob. I have kept it myself, and
see how he goes about to abuse me!   215

Escal. That fellow is a fellow of much license; let

---

119. **motion generative:** a male puppet. 130. **detected for:** accused of. 135. **clack-dish:** covered wooden dish, carried by
beggars for alms; they rattled the cover to get attention. **crotchets:** caprices. 138. **inward:** intimate. 144. **greater ...
subject:** majority of subjects. 147. **unweighing:** thoughtless. 149. **envy:** malice. 151. **helmed:** steered. **upon ...
need:** were assurance needed. 155. **unskilfully:** uncritically. 160. **[dearer]** *deare* F. 175. **opposite:** opponent.
182. **tun-dish:** funnel. 184. **ungenitur'd:** impotent. 190. **untrussing:** undressing. 192. **mutton.** Also meant *loose woman.*
196. **mortality:** human life. 206. **forfeit:** guilty. 214. **Philip and Jacob:** the day of St. Philip and St. James (May 1st).

him be call'd before us.   Away with her to prison!
Go to; no more words.   [*Exeunt Officers with Mis-*
tress Ov.]   Provost, my brother Angelo will not be
alter'd; Claudio must die to-morrow.   Let him   220
be furnish'd with divines, and have all charitable
preparation.   If my brother wrought by my pity, it
should not be so with him.

Prov.   So please you, this friar hath been with
him, and advis'd him for the entertainment of
death.   226

Escal.   Good even, good father.

Duke.   Bliss and goodness on you!

Escal.   Of whence are you?

Duke.   Not of this country, though my chance
    is now   230
To use it for my time.   I am a brother
Of gracious order, late come from the [See]
In special business from his Holiness.

Escal.   What news abroad i' th' world?   234

Duke.   None, but that there is so great a fever on
goodness, that the dissolution of it must cure it.
Novelty is only in request; and it is as dangerous to
be aged in any kind of course, as it is virtuous to be
constant in any undertaking.   There is scarce
truth enough alive to make societies secure;   240
but security enough to make fellowships accurst.
Much upon this riddle runs the wisdom of the
world.   This news is old enough, yet it is every
day's news.   I pray you, sir, of what disposition
was the Duke?   245

Escal.   One that, above all other strifes, con-
tended especially to know himself.

Duke.   What pleasure was he given to?   248

Escal.   Rather rejoicing to see another merry,
than merry at anything which profess'd to make him
rejoice; a gentleman of all temperance.   But leave
we him to his events, with a prayer they may prove
prosperous; and let me desire to know how you find
Claudio prepar'd.   I am made to understand that
you have lent him visitation.   255

Duke.   He professes to have received no sinister
measure from his judge, but most willingly humbles
himself to the determination of justice; yet had he
framed to himself, by the instruction of his frailty,
many deceiving promises of life, which I by my good
leisure have discredited to him, and now is he resolv'd to die.   262

Escal.   You have paid the heavens your function,
and the prisoner the very debt of your calling.   I
have labour'd for the poor gentleman to the extremest shore of my modesty; but my brother

justice have I found so severe, that he hath forc'd
me to tell him he is indeed Justice.   268

Duke.   If his own life answer the straitness of his
proceeding, it shall become him well; wherein if he
chance to fail, he hath sentenc'd himself.

Escal.   I am going to visit the prisoner.   Fare
you well.   273

Duke.   Peace be with you!

    [*Exeunt Escalus and Provost.*]
He who the sword of heaven will bear
Should be as holy as severe;
Pattern in himself to know,
Grace to stand, and virtue go;
More nor less to others paying
Than by self-offences weighing.   280
Shame to him whose cruel striking
Kills for faults of his own liking!
Twice treble shame on Angelo,
To weed my vice and let his grow!
O, what may man within him hide,   285
Though angel on the outward side!
How may likeness made in crimes,
Making practice on the times,
To draw with idle spiders' strings
Most ponderous and substantial things!   290
Craft against vice I must apply.
With Angelo to-night shall lie
His old betrothed but despised;
So disguise shall, by th' disguised,
Pay with falsehood false exacting,   295
And perform an old contracting.   [*Exit.*

ACT IV

SCENE I.   [*The moated grange at St. Luke's.*]

Enter MARIANA, *and* BOY *singing.*

SONG

Take, O, take those lips away,
    That so sweetly were forsworn;
And those eyes, the break of day,
    Lights that do mislead the morn;
But my kisses bring again, bring again;
Seals of love, but seal'd in vain, seal'd in vain.

Enter DUKE [*disguised as before*].

Mari.   Break off thy song, and haste thee quick
    away.
Here comes a man of comfort, whose advice
Hath often still'd my brawling discontent.

    [*Exit Boy.*]

232. [See] (Theobald): i.e., of Rome.   *Sea* F.   236. dissolution: death.   237. it is as F$_{3,4}$ *as it is as* F$_{1,2}$.
241. security: (demands for) surety.   fellowships: friendships.   252. events: affairs.   256. sinister: unfair.   259.
instruction: prompting.   266. shore: limit.   275-96. These octosyllabic lines have been widely proclaimed as un-Shakespearean.   They are as feeble as they are unnecessary.   278. go: to go ahead.   284. my: i.e., other people's.   287-90.
Probably corrupt and certainly unintelligible.   295. exacting: exaction.
    Act IV, sc. i, 9. brawling: clamorous.

I cry you mercy, sir; and well could wish   10
You had not found me here so musical.
Let me excuse me, and believe me so,
My mirth it much displeas'd, but pleas'd my woe.
    Duke. 'Tis good; though music oft hath such a
        charm
To make bad good, and good provoke to harm. 15
I pray you, tell me, hath anybody inquir'd for me
here to-day?   Much upon this time have I promis'd
here to meet.
    Mari. You have not been inquir'd after.   I have
sat here all day.   20

Enter ISABELLA.

    Duke. I do constantly believe you.   The time
is come even now.   I shall crave your forbearance a
little.   May be I will call upon you anon, for some
advantage to yourself.
    Mari. I am always bound to you.   [*Exit.* 25
    Duke. Very well met, and well come.
What is the news from this good deputy?
    Isab. He hath a garden circummur'd with brick,
Whose western side is with a vineyard back'd,
And to that vineyard is a planched gate   30
That makes his opening with this bigger key.
This other doth command a little door
Which from the vineyard to the garden leads;
There have I made my promise
Upon the heavy middle of the night   35
To call upon him.
    Duke. But shall you on your knowledge find this
        way?
    Isab. I have ta'en a due and wary note upon't.
With whispering and most guilty diligence,
In action all of precept, he did show me   40
The way twice o'er.
    Duke.   Are there no other tokens
Between you 'greed concerning her observance?
    Isab. No, none, but only a repair i' th' dark;
And that I have possess'd him my most stay
Can be but brief; for I have made him know   45
I have a servant comes with me along,
That stays upon me, whose persuasion is
I come about my brother.
    Duke.   'Tis well borne up.
I have not yet made known to Mariana
A word of this.   What ho, within! come forth! 50

Re-enter MARIANA.

I pray you, be acquainted with this maid;
She comes to do you good.

    Isab.   I do desire the like.
    Duke. Do you persuade yourself that I respect
        you?
    Mari. Good friar, I know you do, and have found
it.
    Duke. Take, then, this your companion by the
        hand,   55
Who hath a story ready for your ear.
I shall attend your leisure; but make haste;
The vaporous night approaches.
    Mari. Will't please you walk aside?
        [*Exeunt [Mariana and Isabella].*
    Duke. O place and greatness! millions of false
        eyes   60
Are stuck upon thee.   Volumes of report
Run with these false and most contrarious [quests]
Upon thy doings; thousand escapes of wit
Make thee the father of their idle dream
And rack thee in their fancies.

Re-enter MARIANA *and* ISABELLA.

                    Welcome, how agreed?
    Isab. She'll take the enterprise upon her,
        father,   66
If you advise it.
    Duke.   It is not my consent,
But my entreaty too.
    Isab.   Little have you to say
When you depart from him, but, soft and low,
"Remember now my brother."
    Mari.   Fear me not.   70
    Duke. Nor, gentle daughter, fear you not at all.
He is your husband on a pre-contract:
To bring you thus together, 'tis no sin,
Sith that the justice of your title to him
Doth flourish the deceit.   Come, let us go.   75
Our corn's to reap, for yet our [tilth]'s to sow.
        |*Exeunt.*

SCENE II. [*A room in the prison.*]

Enter PROVOST *and Clown* [POMPEY].

    Prov. Come hither, sirrah.   Can you cut off a
man's head?
    Pom. If the man be a bachelor, sir, I can; but if
he be a married man, he's his wife's head, and I can
never cut off a woman's head.   5
    Prov. Come, sir, leave me your snatches, and
yield me a direct answer.   To-morrow morning
are to die Claudio and Barnardine.   Here is in our
prison a common executioner, who in his office lacks

---

10. **cry you mercy:** beg your pardon.   21. **constantly:** certainly.   28. **circummur'd:** walled about.   30. **planched:** made
of planks.   35. **heavy:** sleepy.   40. **In . . . precept:** with demonstrative gestures.   42. **her:** i.e., Mariana's.   43. **repair:**
tryst.   44. **possess'd:** informed.   47. **persuasion:** understanding.   48. **borne up:** devised.   60. **false:** deceitful.   62.
[quests] F₂: the cries of the hounds upon the scent.   *quest* F₁.   63. **escapes:** sallies.   65. **rack:** distort.   75. **flourish:**
grace, justify.   76. **[tilth]'s** (Warburton): fallow land is.   *tithes* F.
    Sc. ii, 6. snatches: quips.   9. **common:** public.

a helper. If you will take it on you to assist him, 10
it shall redeem you from your gyves; if not, you
shall have your full time of imprisonment, and your
deliverance with an unpitied whipping, for you have
been a notorious bawd.   15

Pom. Sir, I have been an unlawful bawd time
out of mind; but yet I will be content to be a lawful
hangman. I would be glad to receive some instruction from my fellow partner.

Prov. What, ho! Abhorson! Where's Abhorson, there?   21

Enter ABHORSON.

Abhor. Do you call, sir?

Prov. Sirrah, here's a fellow will help you to-
morrow in your execution. If you think it meet,
compound with him by the year, and let him 25
abide here with you; if not, use him for the present
and dismiss him. He cannot plead his estimation
with you; he hath been a bawd.

Abhor. A bawd, sir? Fie upon him! he will discredit our mystery.   30

Prov. Go to, sir; you weigh equally. A feather
will turn the scale.   [*Exit.*

Pom. Pray, sir, by your good favour, — for
surely, sir, a good favour you have, but that you
have a hanging look, — do you call, sir, your occupation a mystery?   36

Abhor. Ay, sir; a mystery.

Pom. Painting, sir, I have heard say, is a mystery; and your whores, sir, being members of my
occupation, using painting, do prove my occupation
a mystery; but what mystery there should be in
hanging, if I should be hang'd, I cannot imagine. 43

Abhor. Sir, it is a mystery.

Pom. Proof?

Abhor. Every true man's apparel fits your thief.
If it be too little for your thief, your true man thinks
it big enough; if it be too big for your thief, your
thief thinks it little enough; so every true man's
apparel fits your thief.   50

Re-enter PROVOST.

Prov. Are you agreed?

Pom. Sir, I will serve him, for I do find your
hangman is a more penitent trade than your bawd;
he doth oftener ask forgiveness.   54

Prov. You, sirrah, provide your block and your
axe to-morrow four o'clock.

Abhor. Come on, bawd, I will instruct thee in
my trade. Follow.   58

Pom. I do desire to learn, sir; and I hope, if you
have occasion to use me for your own turn, you

shall find me yare; for truly, sir, for your kindness I
owe you a good turn.   [*Exit.*

Prov. Call hither Barnardine and Claudio.
                                  [*Exit Abhorson.*]
The one has my pity; not a jot the other,
Being a murderer, though he were my brother. 65

Enter CLAUDIO.

Look, here's the warrant, Claudio, for thy death.
'Tis now dead midnight, and by eight to-morrow
Thou must be made immortal. Where's Bar-
    nardine?

Claud. As fast lock'd up in sleep as guiltless
    labour
When it lies starkly in the traveller's bones. 70
He will not wake.

Prov.   Who can do good on him?
Well, go, prepare yourself. [*Knocking within.*]
    But, hark, what noise?
Heaven give your spirits comfort! [*Exit Clau-
    dio.*] By and by.
I hope it is some pardon or reprieve
For the most gentle Claudio.

Enter DUKE [*disguised as before*].
                                  Welcome, father.

Duke. The best and wholesom'st spirits of the
    night   76
Envelop you, good Provost! Who call'd here of
    late?

Prov. None, since the curfew rung.

Duke. Not Isabel?

Prov.   No.

Duke.   They will, then, ere't be long.

Prov. What comfort is for Claudio?   80

Duke. There's some in hope.

Prov.   It is a bitter deputy.

Duke. Not so, not so; his life is parallel'd
Even with the stroke and line of his great justice.
He doth with holy abstinence subdue
That in himself which he spurs on his power 85
To qualify in others. Were he meal'd with that
Which he corrects, then were he tyrannous;
But this being so, he's just. [*Knocking within.*]
                        Now are they come.
                                  [*Exit Provost.*]
This is a gentle Provost: seldom when
The steeled gaoler is the friend of men. 90
                                  [*Knocking within.*]
How now! what noise? That spirit's possess'd with
    haste
That wounds the unsisting postern with these
    strokes.

---

11. **gyves:** fetters. 14. **unpitied:** pitiless. 25. **compound:** make contract. 30. **mystery:** profession, trade. 33. **favour:** (1) grace, (2) face. 47-50. **If...thief.** F gives these lines to the Clown. The correction is Capell's. 61. **yare:** ready. 83. **stroke and line:** line marked out (possibly with allusion to the *stroke* of the executioner's axe and the hangman's *line*, i.e., rope). 86. **qualify:** moderate. **meal'd:** tainted. 92. **unsisting:** unresisting (?). Meaning doubtful.

[Re-enter PROVOST.]

Prov. There he must stay until the officer
Arise to let him in. He is call'd up.

Duke. Have you no countermand for Claudio
yet   95
But he must die to-morrow?

Prov.   None, sir, none.

Duke. As near the dawning, Provost, as it is,
You shall hear more ere morning.

Prov.   Happily
You something know, yet I believe there
comes
No countermand; no such example have we.   100
Besides, upon the very siege of justice
Lord Angelo hath to the public ear
Profess'd the contrary.

Enter a MESSENGER.

           This is his [lordship's] man.

[Duke.] And here comes Claudio's pardon.

Mes. [*Giving a paper.*] My lord hath sent   105
you this note; and by me this further charge, that
you swerve not from the smallest article of it,
neither in time, matter, or other circumstance.
Good morrow; for, as I take it, it is almost day.

Prov. I shall obey him. [*Exit Messenger.*]   110

Duke. [*Aside.*] This is his pardon, purchas'd by
such sin
For which the pardoner himself is in.
Hence hath offence his quick celerity,
When it is borne in high authority.
When vice makes mercy, mercy's so extended,   115
That for the fault's love is the offender friended.
Now, sir, what news?

Prov. I told you. Lord Angelo, belike thinking
me remiss in mine office, awakens me with this unwonted putting-on; methinks strangely, for he hath
not us'd it before.   121

Duke. Pray you, let's hear.

[*Prov. Reads*] *the letter.*

"Whatsoever you may hear to the contrary, let
Claudio be executed by four of the clock; and in the
afternoon Barnardine. For my better satisfac-   125
tion, let me have Claudio's head sent me by five.
Let this be duly performed, with a thought that
more depends on it than we must yet deliver. Thus
fail not to do your office, as you will answer it at
your peril."   130
What say you to this, sir?

Duke. What is that Barnardine who is to be
executed in the afternoon?

Prov. A Bohemian born, but here nurs'd up and

bred; one that is a prisoner nine years old.   135

Duke. How came it that the absent Duke had
not either deliver'd him to his liberty or executed
him? I have heard it was ever his manner to do
so.   139

Prov. His friends still wrought reprieves for him;
and, indeed, his fact, till now in the government of
Lord Angelo, came not to an undoubtful proof.

Duke. It is now apparent?   144

Prov. Most manifest, and not denied by himself.

Duke. Hath he borne himself penitently in
prison? How seems he to be touch'd?   148

Prov. A man that apprehends death no more
dreadfully but as a drunken sleep; careless, reckless, and fearless of what's past, present, or to come;
insensible of mortality, and desperately mortal.

Duke. He wants advice.   154

Prov. He will hear none. He hath evermore
had the liberty of the prison; give him leave to
escape hence, he would not; drunk many times a
day, if not many days entirely drunk. We have
very oft awak'd him, as if to carry him to execution,
and show'd him a seeming warrant for it; it hath
not moved him at all.   161

Duke. More of him anon. There is written in
your brow, Provost, honesty and constancy. If I
read it not truly, my ancient skill beguiles me; but,
in the boldness of my cunning, I will lay myself   165
in hazard. Claudio, whom here you have warrant
to execute, is no greater forfeit to the law than
Angelo who hath sentenc'd him. To make you
understand this in a manifested effect, I crave but
four days' respite; for the which you are to do me   170
both a present and a dangerous courtesy.   172

Prov. Pray, sir, in what?

Duke. In the delaying death.

Prov. Alack, how may I do it, having the hour
limited, and an express command, under penalty,
to deliver his head in the view of Angelo? I may
make my case as Claudio's, to cross this in the
smallest.   179

Duke. By the vow of mine order I warrant you,
if my instructions may be your guide. Let this
Barnardine be this morning executed, and his head
borne to Angelo.

Prov. Angelo hath seen them both, and will discover the favour.   185

Duke. O, death's a great disguiser, and you may
add to it. Shave the head, and tie the beard; and
say it was the desire of the penitent to be so bar'd
before his death. You know the course is common.
If anything fall to you upon this, more than thanks

---

98. **Happily:** haply, perhaps.   101. **siege:** seat.   103. **This...man.** So Tyrwhitt. F gives this to the Duke, and the next line to the Provost. **[lordship's]** (Pope). **lords** F.   120. **putting-on:** insistence.   141. **fact:** crime.   153. **mortality:** death. **desperately mortal:** in a desperate spiritual state, unlikely to be saved.   165. **cunning:** knowledge. **lay...hazard:** i.e., stake my very self.   169–70. **in...effect:** by direct evidence.   176. **limited:** prescribed.   180. **warrant you:** give you surety.   185. **discover the favour:** recognize the face.

and good fortune, by the saint whom I profess, I will plead against it with my life. 193

Prov. Pardon me, good father; it is against my oath.

Duke. Were you sworn to the Duke, or to the deputy? 197

Prov. To him, and to his substitutes.

Duke. You will think you have made no offence, if the Duke avouch the justice of your dealing?

Prov. But what likelihood is in that? 202

Duke. Not a resemblance, but a certainty. Yet since I see you fearful, that neither my coat, integrity, nor persuasion can with ease attempt 205 you, I will go further than I meant, to pluck all fears out of you. Look you, sir, here is the hand and seal of the Duke. You know the character, I doubt not; and the signet is not strange to you.

Prov. I know them both. 210

Duke. The contents of this is the return of the Duke. You shall anon over-read it at your pleasure; where you shall find, within these two days he will be here. This is a thing that Angelo knows not; for he this very day receives letters of strange tenour, perchance of the Duke's death, per- 215 chance entering into some monastery, but, by chance, nothing of what is here writ. Look, the unfolding star calls up the shepherd. Put not yourself into amazement how these things should be. 220 All difficulties are but easy when they are known. Call your executioner, and off with Barnardine's head. I will give him a present shrift and advise him for a better place. Yet you are amaz'd, but this shall absolutely resolve you. Come away; it is almost clear dawn. [*Exeunt.* 226

SCENE III. [*Another room in the same.*]

Enter Clown [POMPEY].

Pom. I am as well acquainted here as I was in our house of profession. One would think it were Mistress Overdone's own house, for here be many of her old customers. First, here's young Master Rash. He's in for a commodity of brown paper 5 and old ginger, nine-score and seventeen pounds; of which he made five marks, ready money. Marry, then ginger was not much in request, for the old women were all dead. Then is there here one Master Caper, at the suit of Master Three-pile the 10 mercer, for some four suits of peach-colour'd satin, which now peaches him a beggar. Then have we here young Dizzy, and young Master Deep-vow, and Master Copper-spur, and Master Starve-lackey the rapier and dagger man, and young 15 Drop-heir that killed lusty Pudding, and Master

Forthlight the tilter, and brave Master Shooty the great traveller, and wild Half-can that stabb'd Pots, and, I think, forty more; all great doers in our trade, and are now "for the Lord's sake." 21

Enter ABHORSON.

Abhor. Sirrah, bring Barnardine hither.

Pom. Master Barnardine! You must rise and be hang'd, Master Barnardine!

Abhor. What, ho, Barnardine! 25

Bar. (*Within.*) A pox o' your throats! Who makes that noise there? What are you?

Pom. Your friends, sir; the hangman. You must be so good, sir, to rise and be put to death.

Bar. [*Within.*] Away, you rogue, away! I am sleepy. 31

Abhor. Tell him he must awake, and that quickly too.

Pom. Pray, Master Barnardine, awake till you are executed, and sleep afterwards. 35

Abhor. Go in to him, and fetch him out.

Pom. He is coming, sir, he is coming. I hear his straw rustle.

Enter BARNARDINE.

Abhor. Is the axe upon the block, sirrah?

Pom. Very ready, sir.

Bar. How now, Abhorson? What's the news with you?

Abhor. Truly, sir, I would desire you to clap into your prayers; for, look you, the warrant's come. 45

Bar. You rogue, I have been drinking all night; I am not fitted for 't.

Pom. O, the better, sir; for he that drinks all night, and is hanged betimes in the morning, may sleep the sounder all the next day. 50

Enter DUKE [*disguised as before*].

Abhor. Look you, sir; here comes your ghostly father. Do we jest now, think you?

Duke. Sir, induced by my charity, and hearing how hastily you are to depart, I am come to advise you, comfort you, and pray with you. 55

Bar. Friar, not I. I have been drinking hard all night, and I will have more time to prepare me, or they shall beat out my brains with billets. I will not consent to die this day, that's certain.

Duke. O, sir, you must; and therefore I beseech you 60
Look forward on the journey you shall go.

Bar. I swear I will not die to-day for any man's persuasion.

Duke. But hear you. 64

Bar. Not a word. If you have anything to say

---

203. **resemblance:** probability. 218. **unfolding star:** morning star, at whose rising shepherds lead their flocks from the fold. Sc. iii, 5. **commodity:** quantity. 12. **peaches:** impeaches, denounces. 21. **for ... sake.** The cry of prisoners begging alms. 58. **billets:** logs of wood, cudgels.

to me, come to my ward; for thence will not I to-
day.   [*Exit.*

Re-enter PROVOST.

Duke. Unfit to live or die, O gravel heart!
After him, fellows; bring him to the block.
                    [*Exeunt Abhorson and Pompey.*]
Prov. Now sir, how do you find the prisoner?   70
Duke. A creature unprepar'd, unmeet for death;
And to transport him in the mind he is
Were damnable.
    Prov.   Here in the prison, father,
There died this morning of a cruel fever
One Ragozine, a most notorious pirate,   75
A man of Claudio's years; his beard and head
Just of his colour. What if we do omit
This reprobate till he were well inclin'd,
And satisfy the deputy with the visage
Of Ragozine, more like to Claudio?   80
Duke. O, 'tis an accident that Heaven provides!
Dispatch it presently. The hour draws on
Prefix'd by Angelo. See this be done,
And sent according to command, whiles I
Persuade this rude wretch willingly to die.   85
Prov. This shall be done, good father, presently.
But Barnardine must die this afternoon;
And how shall we continue Claudio,
To save me from the danger that might come
If he were known alive?
    Duke.   Let this be done.   90
Put them in secret holds, both Barnardine
And Claudio.
Ere twice the sun hath made his journal greeting
To [th' under] generation, you shall find
Your safety manifested.
    Prov. I am your free dependant.   95
Duke. Quick, dispatch, and send the head to
    Angelo.   [*Exit Provost.*
Now will I write letters to Angelo, —
The Provost, he shall bear them, — whose contents
Shall witness to him I am near at home,
And that, by great injunctions, I am bound   100
To enter publicly. Him I'll desire
To meet me at the consecrated fount
A league below the city; and from thence,
By cold gradation and [well-balanc'd] form,
We shall proceed with Angelo.   105

Re-enter PROVOST.

Prov. Here is the head; I'll carry it myself.
Duke. Convenient is it. Make a swift return;

For I would commune with you of such things
That want no ear but yours.
    Prov.   I'll make all speed.
                                              [*Exit.*
Isab. (*Within.*) Peace, ho, be here!   110
Duke. The tongue of Isabel. She's come to
    know
If yet her brother's pardon be come hither.
But I will keep her ignorant of her good,
To make her heavenly comforts of despair,
When it is least expected.

Enter ISABELLA.

Isab.   Ho, by your leave!
Duke. Good morning to you, fair and gracious
    daughter.   116
Isab. The better, given me by so holy a man.
Hath yet the deputy sent my brother's pardon?
Duke. He hath releas'd him, Isabel, from the
    world.
His head is off and sent to Angelo.   120
Isab. Nay, but it is not so.
Duke. It is no other. Show your wisdom,
    daughter,
In your close patience.
Isab. O, I will to him and pluck out his eyes!
Duke. You shall not be admitted to his sight. 125
Isab. Unhappy Claudio! Wretched Isabel!
Injurious world! Most damned Angelo!
Duke. This nor hurts him nor profits you a jot.
Forbear it therefore; give your cause to heaven.
Mark what I say, which you shall find   130
By every syllable a faithful verity.
The Duke comes home to-morrow; — nay, dry
    your eyes; —
One of our covent, and his confessor,
Gives me this instance. Already he hath carried
Notice to Escalus and Angelo,   135
Who do prepare to meet him at the gates,
There to give up their power. If you can, pace
    your wisdom
In that good path that I would wish it go,
And you shall have your bosom on this wretch,
Grace of the Duke, revenges to your heart,   140
And general honour.
    Isab.   I am directed by you.
Duke. This letter, then, to Friar Peter give;
'Tis that he sent me of the Duke's return.
Say, by this token, I desire his company
At Mariana's house to-night. Her cause and yours
I'll perfect him withal, and he shall bring you 146

77. **omit:** pass by. 88. **continue:** preserve. 93. **journal:** daily. 94. **[th' under]** generation: people underneath, i.e.,
antipodes; or, possibly, the people of this earth. **[th'under]** (Hanmer). 95. **your ... dependant:** entirely your
servant. 97. **to Angelo.** From ll. 134–36 below and IV.iv.6 it appears that Angelo had been instructed to meet the Duke
at the gates. At IV.v.11, however, it is Varrius who meets the Duke, obviously by appointment; perhaps, therefore, *Varrius* should be read for *Angelo* in this line. Nevertheless, note IV.iv.1. 104. **cold gradation:** deliberate steps. **[well-
balanc'd]** (Rowe). *weal-balanc'd* F. 123. **close:** silent. 133. **covent:** convent. 134. **instance:** news. 139. **bosom:**
heart's desire. 146. **perfect:** inform (fully).

Before the Duke, and to the head of Angelo
Accuse him home and home. For my poor self,
I am combined by a sacred vow
And shall be absent. Wend you with this letter.
Command these fretting waters from your eyes   151
With a light heart. Trust not my holy order
If I pervert your course. Who's here?

Enter LUCIO.

Lucio. Good even. Friar, where's the Provost?
Duke. Not within, sir.   156
Lucio. O pretty Isabella, I am pale at mine
heart to see thine eyes so red. Thou must be patient. I am fain to dine and sup with water and
bran; I dare not for my head fill my belly; one   160
fruitful meal would set me to't. But they say the
Duke will be here to-morrow. By my troth, Isabel,
I lov'd thy brother. If the old fantastical Duke
of dark corners had been at home, he had lived.   165
                            [Exit Isabella.]
Duke. Sir, the Duke is marvellous little beholding
to your reports; but the best is, he lives not in them.
Lucio. Friar, thou knowest not the Duke so well
as I do. He's a better woodman than thou tak'st
him for.   171
Duke. Well, you'll answer this one day. Fare ye
well.
Lucio. Nay, tarry; I'll go along with thee. I can
tell thee pretty tales of the Duke.   175
Duke. You have told me too many of him already, sir, if they be true; if not true, none were
enough.
Lucio. I was once before him for getting a wench
with child.   180
Duke. Did you such a thing?
Lucio. Yes, marry, did I; but I was fain to forswear it. They would else have married me to the
rotten medlar.   184
Duke. Sir, your company is fairer than honest.
Rest you well.
Lucio. By my troth, I'll go with thee to the
lane's end. If bawdy talk offend you, we'll have
very little of it. Nay, friar, I am a kind of burr; I
shall stick.   *[Exeunt.* 190

SCENE IV. *[A room in Angelo's house.]*

Enter ANGELO *and* ESCALUS.

Escal. Every letter he hath writ hath disvouch'd
other.
Ang. In most uneven and distracted manner.

His actions show much like to madness; pray
Heaven his wisdom be not tainted! And why meet
him at the gates, and [redeliver] our authorities
there?   7
Escal. I guess not.
Ang. And why should we proclaim it in an hour
before his entering, that if any crave redress of injustice, they should exhibit their petitions in the
street?   12
Escal. He shows his reason for that: to have a
dispatch of complaints, and to deliver us from de-
vices hereafter, which shall then have no power to
stand against us.   16
Ang. Well, I beseech you, let it be proclaim'd
betimes i' th' morn. I'll call you at your house.
Give notice to such men of sort and suit as are to
meet him.   20
Escal. I shall, sir. Fare you well.
                       [Exit Escalus
Ang. Good night.
This deed unshapes me quite, makes me unpreg-
    nant
And dull to all proceedings. A deflow'red maid!
And by an eminent body that enforc'd   25
The law against it! But that her tender shame
Will not proclaim against her maiden loss,
How might she tongue me! Yet reason dares her
    no;
For my authority bears a credent bulk,
That no particular scandal once can touch   30
But it confounds the breather. He should have
    liv'd,
Save that his riotous youth, with dangerous sense,
Might in the times to come have ta'en revenge,
By so receiving a dishonour'd life
With ransom of such shame. Would yet he had
    liv'd!   35
Alack, when once our grace we have forgot,
Nothing goes right; we would, and we would not.
                           [Exit.

SCENE V. *[Fields without the town.]*

Enter DUKE *[in his own habit,]* and FRIAR PETER.

Duke. These letters at fit time deliver me.
                       [Giving letters.]
The Provost knows our purpose and our plot.
The matter being afoot, keep your instruction,
And hold you ever to our special drift,   4
Though sometimes you do blench from this to that,
As cause doth minister. Go call at Flavius' house,

---

147. **head:** face. 149. **combined:** bound. 159. **fain:** obliged. 165. **dark corners:** i.e., for meeting women in. 167. **lives
... them:** is not like them. 170. **woodman:** hunter (of women). 184. **medlar:** a kind of apple, edible only at the point
of decay. 185. **fairer:** friendlier.
    Sc. iv, 1. **disvouch'd:** contradicted. 6. **[redeliver]** (Capell). *re-liver* F₁; *deliver* F₂₋₄. 15. **devices:** plots. 19. **sort:**
rank. **suit:** i.e., petitioners. 23. **unpregnant:** unready, inept. 28. **dares her no:** forbids her to dare. 29. **bears a**
(Theobald). *bears of a* F. **credent bulk:** weight of credit.
    Sc. v, 1. **me:** for me. 5. **blench:** swerve.

And tell him where I stay. Give the like notice
To [Valentinus], Rowland, and to Crassus,
And bid them bring the trumpets to the gate.
But send me Flavius first.
    Fri. P.   It shall be speeded well.
                                  [Exit.]

           Enter VARRIUS.

  Duke. I thank thee, Varrius; thou hast made
    good haste: 11
Come, we will walk. There's other of our friends
Will greet us here anon, my gentle Varrius.
                                [Exeunt.

    SCENE VI.   *[Street near the city gate.]*

      Enter ISABELLA *and* MARIANA.

  Isab. To speak so indirectly I am loath.
I would say the truth; but to accuse him so,
That is your part. Yet I am advis'd to do it;
He says, to veil full purpose.
  Mari.   Be rul'd by him.
  Isab. Besides, he tells me that, if peradventure   5
He speak against me on the adverse side,
I should not think it strange; for 'tis a physic
That's bitter to sweet end.

          Enter FRIAR PETER.

  Mari. I would Friar Peter —
  Isab.   O, peace! the friar is come.
  Fri. P. Come, I have found you out a stand most
    fit,   10
Where you may have such vantage on the Duke,
He shall not pass you. Twice have the trumpets
    sounded,
The generous and gravest citizens
Have hent the gates, and very near upon   14
The Duke is ent'ring; therefore, hence, away!
                                [Exeunt.

               ACT V

       SCENE I.   *[The city gate.]*

Enter DUKE, VARRIUS, *Lords,* ANGELO, ESCALUS,
    LUCIO, *[Provost, Officers, and]* Citizens, *at*
    several doors.

  Duke. My very worthy cousin, fairly met!
Our old and faithful friend, we are glad to see you.
  Ang. ⎫
  Escal. ⎬ Happy return be to your royal Grace!
  Duke. Many and hearty thankings to you both.

We have made inquiry of you, and we hear   5
Such goodness of your justice, that our soul
Cannot but yield you forth to public thanks,
Forerunning more requital.
  Ang.   You make my bonds still greater.
  Duke. O, your desert speaks loud; and I should
    wrong it
To lock it in the wards of covert bosom   10
When it deserves, with characters of brass,
A forted residence 'gainst the tooth of time
And razure of oblivion. Give [me] your hand,
And let the subject see, to make them know
That outward courtesies would fain proclaim   15
Favours that keep within. Come, Escalus,
You must walk by us on our other hand;
And good supporters are you.

      Enter FRIAR PETER *and* ISABELLA.

  Fri. P. Now is your time. Speak loud and kneel
    before him.   19
  Isab. Justice, O royal Duke! Vail your regard
Upon a wrong'd — I would fain have said a maid!
O worthy Prince, dishonour not your eye
By throwing it on any other object
Till you have heard me in my true complaint
And given me justice, justice, justice, justice!   25
  Duke. Relate your wrongs. In what? By
    whom? Be brief.
Here is Lord Angelo shall give you justice:
Reveal yourself to him.
  Isab.   O worthy Duke,
You bid me seek redemption of the devil.
Hear me yourself; for that which I must speak
Must either punish me, not being believ'd,   31
Or wring redress from you. Hear me, O hear me,
    [hear]!
  Ang. My lord, her wits, I fear me, are not firm.
She hath been a suitor to me for her brother,
Cut off by course of justice, —
  Isab.   By course of justice!
  Ang. And she will speak most bitterly and
    strange.   36
  Isab. Most strange, but yet most truly, will I
    speak.
That Angelo's forsworn, is it not strange?
That Angelo's a murderer, is't not strange?
That Angelo is an adulterous thief,   40
An hypocrite, a virgin-violator,
Is it not strange and strange?
  Duke.   Nay, it is ten times strange.
  Isab. It is not truer he is Angelo
Than this is all as true as it is strange.

---

  8. [Valentinus] (Capell). *Valencius* F. 9. trumpets: trumpeters.
Sc. vi, 10. stand: position. 13. generous: of noble birth. 14. hent: reached. near upon: soon.
Act V, sc. i, 1. cousin. A title used by men of high rank to one another. 8. bonds: indebtedness. 10. wards: prison
cells. covert: secret. 11. characters: letters. 13. razure: erasure. [me] F$_3$. *we* F$_1$. 20. Vail: lower. 32. [hear]
(Keightley). *heere* F.

Nay, it is ten times true; for truth is truth   45
To th' end of reckoning.
   Duke.   Away with her! Poor soul,
She speaks this in th' infirmity of sense.
   Isab. O Prince, I conjure thee, as thou believ'st
There is another comfort than this world,
That thou neglect me not, with that opinion   50
That I am touch'd with madness! Make not impossible
That which but seems unlike. 'Tis not impossible
But one, the wicked'st caitiff on the ground,
May seem as shy, as grave, as just, as absolute
As Angelo. Even so may Angelo,   55
In all his dressings, characts, titles, forms,
Be an arch-villain. Believe it, royal Prince!
If he be less, he's nothing; but he's more,
Had I more name for badness.
   Duke.   By mine honesty,
If she be mad, — as I believe no other, —   60
Her madness hath the oddest frame of sense,
Such a dependency of thing on thing,
As e'er I heard in madness.
   Isab.   O gracious Duke,
Harp not on that; nor do not banish reason
For inequality; but let your reason serve   65
To make the truth appear where it seems hid,
And hide the false seems true.
   Duke.   Many that are not mad
Have, sure, more lack of reason. What would you
   say?
   Isab. I am the sister of one Claudio,
Condemn'd upon the act of fornication   70
To lose his head; condemn'd by Angelo.
I, in probation of a sisterhood,
Was sent to by my brother; one Lucio
As then the messenger, —
   Lucio.   That's I, an't like your Grace.
I came to her from Claudio, and desir'd her   75
To try her gracious fortune with Lord Angelo
For her poor brother's pardon.
   Isab.   That's he indeed.
   Duke. You were not bid to speak.
   Lucio.   No, my good lord;
Nor wish'd to hold my peace.
   Duke.   I wish you now, then.
Pray you, take note of it; and when you have   80
A business for yourself, pray Heaven you then
Be perfect.
   Lucio. I warrant your honour.
   Duke. The warrant's for yourself; take heed to 't.
   Isab. This gentleman told somewhat of my
   tale, —
   Lucio. Right.   85

   Duke. It may be right, but you are i' the wrong
To speak before your time. Proceed.
   Isab.   I went
To this pernicious caitiff deputy, —
   Duke. That's somewhat madly spoken.
   Isab.   Pardon it;
The phrase is to the matter.   90
   Duke. Mended again. The matter; proceed.
   Isab. In brief, to set the needless process by,
How I persuaded, how I pray'd, and kneel'd,
How he refell'd me, and how I repli'd, —
For this was of much length, — the vile conclusion
I now begin with grief and shame to utter.   96
He would not, but by gift of my chaste body
To his concupiscible intemperate lust,
Release my brother; and, after much debatement,
My sisterly remorse confutes mine honour,   100
And I did yield to him; but the next morn betimes,
His purpose surfeiting, he sends a warrant
For my poor brother's head.
   Duke.   This is most likely!
   Isab. O, that it were as like as it is true!
   Duke. By heaven, fond wretch, thou know'st not
   what thou speak'st,   105
Or else thou art suborn'd against his honour
In hateful practice. First, his integrity
Stands without blemish. Next, it imports no
   reason
That with such vehemency he should pursue
Faults proper to himself. If he had so offended,
He would have weigh'd thy brother by himself,   111
And not have cut him off. Some one hath set you
   on.
Confess the truth, and say by whose advice
Thou cam'st here to complain.
   Isab.   And is this all?
Then, O you blessed ministers above,   115
Keep me in patience, and with rip'ned time
Unfold the evil which is here wrapt up
In countenance! Heaven shield your Grace from
   woe,
As I, thus wrong'd, hence unbelieved go!
   Duke. I know you'd fain be gone. An officer!
To prison with her! Shall we thus permit   121
A blasting and a scandalous breath to fall
On him so near us? This needs must be a practice.
Who knew of your intent and coming hither?
   Isab. One that I would were here, Friar Lodowick.   125
   Duke. A ghostly father, belike. Who knows
   that Lodowick?
   Lucio. My lord, I know him; 'tis a meddling
   friar.

---

52. **unlike**: unlikely. 54. **absolute**: perfect. 56. **characts**: characteristics, marks. 65. **inequality**: injustice. 67. **seems**: which seems. 90. **matter**: point, question. 94. **refell'd**: refuted. 98. **concupiscible**: sensual. 100. **remorse**: pity. 106. **suborn'd**: bribed as false witness. 107. **practice**: plotting. 108. **imports**: carries. 110. **proper to**: owned by. 118. **countenance**: support of authority.

I do not like the man. Had he been lay, my lord,
For certain words he spake against your Grace
In your retirement, I had swing'd him soundly.   130
   Duke. Words against me! That's a good friar,
    belike!
And to set on this wretched woman here
Against our substitute! Let this friar be found.
   Lucio. But yesternight, my lord, she and that
    friar,
I saw them at the prison. A saucy friar,   135
A very scurvy fellow.
   Fri. P. Blessed be your royal Grace!
I have stood by, my lord, and I have heard
Your royal ear abus'd. First, hath this woman
Most wrongfully accus'd your substitute,   140
Who is as free from touch or soil with her
As she from one ungot.
   Duke.   We did believe no less.
Know you that Friar Lodowick that she speaks of?
   Fri. P. I know him for a man divine and holy;
Not scurvy, nor a temporary meddler,   145
As he's reported by this gentleman;
And, on my trust, a man that never yet
Did, as he vouches, misreport your Grace.
   Lucio. My lord, most villanously; believe it.
   Fri. P. Well, he in time may come to clear him-
    self;   150
But at this instant he is sick, my lord,
Of a strange fever. Upon his mere request,
Being come to knowledge that there was complaint
Intended 'gainst Lord Angelo, came I hither,
To speak, as from his mouth, what he doth know
Is true and false; and what he with his oath   156
And all probation will make up full clear,
Whensoever he's convented. First, for this
    woman,
To justify this worthy nobleman,
So vulgarly and personally accus'd,   160
Her shall you hear disproved to her eyes,
Till she herself confess it.
   Duke.   Good friar, let's hear it.
    [Isabella is carried off guarded.]
Do you not smile at this, Lord Angelo?
O heaven, the vanity of wretched fools!
Give us some seats. Come, cousin Angelo;   165
In this I'll be impartial. Be you judge
Of your own cause. Is this the witness, friar?

     Enter MARIANA *[veiled].*

First, let her show [her] face, and after speak.
   Mari. Pardon, my lord; I will not show my face
Until my husband bid me.   170
   Duke. What, are you married?

   Mari. No, my lord.
   Duke. Are you a maid?
   Mari. No, my lord.
   Duke. A widow, then?   175
   Mari. Neither, my lord.
   Duke. Why, you are nothing then: neither maid,
widow, nor wife?
   Lucio. My lord, she may be a punk; for many of
them are neither maid, widow, nor wife.   180
   Duke. Silence that fellow. I would he had some
    cause
To prattle for himself.
   Lucio. Well, my lord.
   Mari. My lord, I do confess I ne'er was married;
And I confess besides I am no maid.   185
I have known my husband; yet my husband
Knows not that ever he knew me.
   Lucio. He was drunk then, my lord; it can be
    no better.
   Duke. For the benefit of silence, would thou
wert so too!   191
   Lucio. Well, my lord.
   Duke. This is no witness for Lord Angelo.
   Mari. Now I come to't, my lord.
She that accuses him of fornication,   195
In self-same manner doth accuse my husband,
And charges him, my lord, with such a time
When I'll depose I had him in mine arms
With all the effect of love.
   Ang. Charges she moe than me?
   Mari.   Not that I know.
   Duke. No? You say your husband.   201
   Mari. Why, just, my lord, and that is Angelo,
Who thinks he knows that he ne'er knew my body,
But knows he thinks that he knows Isabel's.
   Ang. This is a strange abuse. Let's see thy face.
   Mari. My husband bids me; now I will unmask.
     [Unveiling.]   206
This is that face, thou cruel Angelo,
Which once thou swor'st was worth the looking on;
This is the hand which, with a vow'd contract,
Was fast belock'd in thine; this is the body
That took away the match from Isabel,   211
And did supply thee at thy garden-house
In her imagin'd person.
   Duke.   Know you this woman?
   Lucio. Carnally, she says.
   Duke.   Sirrah, no more!
   Lucio. Enough, my lord.   215
   Ang. My lord, I must confess I know this woman;
And five years since there was some speech of mar-
    riage
Betwixt myself and her; which was broke off,

---

128. **lay:** a layman.   130. **swing'd:** beaten.   142. **ungot:** unbegotten, unborn.   145. **temporary:** in temporal affairs.
157. **probation:** proof.   158. **convented:** summoned.   160. **vulgarly:** publicly.   166. **be impartial:** take no part.   168. **[her]**
F₂.   *your* F₁.   179. **punk:** strumpet.   198. **depose:** swear.   200. **moe:** more.   205. **abuse:** deception.   211.
match: appointment.

Partly for that her promised proportions
Came short of composition, but in chief 220
For that her reputation was disvalued
In levity: since which time of five years
I never spake with her, saw her, nor heard from her,
Upon my faith and honour.
 Mari.   Noble Prince,
As there comes light from heaven and words from
  breath, 225
As there is sense in truth and truth in virtue,
I am affianc'd this man's wife as strongly
As words could make up vows; and, my good lord,
But Tuesday night last gone in's garden-house
He knew me as a wife. As this is true, 230
Let me in safety raise me from my knees,
Or else for ever be confixed here,
A marble monument!
 Ang.   I did but smile till now.
Now, good my lord, give me the scope of justice.
My patience here is touch'd. I do perceive 235
These poor informal women are no more
But instruments of some more mightier member
That sets them on. Let me have way, my lord,
To find this practice out.
 Duke.   Ay, with my heart;
And punish them unto your height of pleasure. 240
Thou foolish friar, and thou pernicious woman,
Compact with her that's gone, think'st thou thy
  oaths,
Though they would swear down each particular saint,
Were testimonies against his worth and credit
That's seal'd in approbation? You, Lord Escalus,
Sit with my cousin. Lend him your kind pains 246
To find out this abuse, whence 'tis deriv'd.
There is another friar that set them on;
Let him be sent for.
 Fri. P. Would he were here, my lord, for he in-
  deed 250
Hath set the women on to this complaint.
Your provost knows the place where he abides,
And he may fetch him.
 Duke. Go, do it instantly. [*Exit Provost.*]
And you, my noble and well-warranted cousin,
Whom it concerns to hear this matter forth, 255
Do with your injuries as seems you best,
In any chastisement. I for a while will leave you;
But stir not you till you have well determin'd
Upon these slanderers.
 Escal. My lord, we'll do it throughly. 260
            [*Exit Duke.*
Signior Lucio, did not you say you knew that
Friar Lodowick to be a dishonest person?
 Lucio. Cucullus non facit monachum: honest in

nothing but in his clothes; and one that hath spoke
most villanous speeches of the Duke. 265
 Escal. We shall entreat you to abide here till he
come and enforce them against him. We shall find
this friar a notable fellow.
 Lucio. As any in Vienna, on my word. 269
 Escal. Call that same Isabel here once again; I
would speak with her. [*Exit an attendant.*] Pray
you, my lord, give me leave to question; you shall
see how I'll handle her.
 Lucio. Not better than he, by her own report.
 Escal. Say you? 275
 Lucio. Marry, sir, I think, if you handled her
privately, she would sooner confess. Perchance,
publicly, she'll be asham'd.

Re-enter [Officers *with*] ISABELLA; *and* Provost *with
  the* DUKE [*in his friar's habit*].

 Escal. I will go darkly to work with her.
 Lucio. That's the way, for women are light at
midnight. 281
 Escal. Come on, mistress. Here's a gentlewoman
denies all that you have said.
 Lucio. My lord, here comes the rascal I spoke
of; here with the Provost. 285
 Escal. In very good time. Speak not you to
him till we call upon you.
 Lucio. Mum.
 Escal. Come, sir, did you set these women on to
slander Lord Angelo? They have confess'd you
did. 291
 Duke. 'Tis false.
 Escal. How! know you where you are?
 Duke. Respect to your great place! and let the
  devil
Be sometime honour'd for his burning throne! 295
Where is the Duke? 'Tis he should hear me speak.
 Escal. The Duke's in us; and we will hear you
  speak.
Look you speak justly.
 Duke. Boldly, at least. But, O, poor souls,
Come you to seek the lamb here of the fox? 300
Good night to your redress! Is the Duke gone?
Then is your cause gone too. The Duke's unjust
Thus to retort your manifest appeal,
And put your trial in the villain's mouth
Which here you come to accuse. 305
 Lucio. This is the rascal; this is he I spoke of.
 Escal. Why, thou unreverend and unhallowed
  friar,
Is't not enough thou hast suborn'd these women
To accuse this worthy man, but, in foul mouth
And in the witness of his proper ear, 310

---

219. **proportions:** dowry. 220. **composition:** agreement. 221–22. **disvalued in levity:** depreciated by lightness
of conduct. 236. **informal:** crazy, deranged. 242. **Compact:** confederate, leagued. 259. **determin'd:** judged. 263.
Cucullus . . . monachum: a cowl does not make a monk. 279. **darkly:** indirectly. 280. **light:** with pun on sense of *wan-
'on.* 303. **retort:** refer back (to Angelo). 310. **proper:** own.

To call him villain, and then to glance from him
To the Duke himself, to tax him with injustice?
Take him hence; to the rack with him! We'll touse
    you
Joint by joint, but we will know his purpose.
What, "unjust"!
    Duke.   Be not so hot. The Duke   315
Dare no more stretch this finger of mine than he
Dare rack his own. His subject am I not,
Nor here provincial. My business in this state
Made me a looker on here in Vienna,
Where I have seen corruption boil and bubble
Till it o'er-run the stew; laws for all faults,   321
But faults so countenanc'd, that the strong statutes
Stand like the forfeits in a barber's shop,
As much in mock as mark.
    Escal. Slander to the state! Away with him to
        prison!   325
    Ang. What can you vouch against him, Signior
        Lucio?
Is this the man that you did tell us of?
    Lucio. 'Tis he, my lord. Come hither, good-
man bald-pate. Do you know me?   329
    Duke. I remember you, sir, by the sound of your
voice. I met you at the prison, in the absence of
the Duke.
    Lucio. O, did you so? And do you remember
what you said of the Duke?
    Duke. Most notedly, sir.   335
    Lucio. Do you so, sir? And was the Duke a
fleshmonger, a fool, and a coward, as you then reported him to be?
    Duke. You must, sir, change persons with me,
ere you make that my report. You, indeed, spoke
so of him, and much more, much worse.   341
    Lucio. O thou damnable fellow! Did not I
pluck thee by the nose for thy speeches?
    Duke. I protest I love the Duke as I love myself.
    Ang. Hark, how the villain would close now, after
his treasonable abuses!   347
    Escal. Such a fellow is not to be talk'd withal.
Away with him to prison! Where is the Provost?
Away with him to prison! Lay bolts enough upon
him. Let him speak no more. Away with those
giglots too, and with the other confederate companion! [*The Provost lays hands on the Duke.*]   353
    Duke. Stay, sir; stay awhile.
    Ang. What, resists he? Help him, Lucio.
    Lucio. Come, sir; come, sir; come, sir; foh, sir!
Why, you bald-pated, lying rascal, you must be
hooded, must you? Show your knave's visage,
with a pox to you! Show your sheep-biting face,

and be hang'd an hour! Will't not off?   360
        [*Pulls off the friar's hood.*]
    Duke. Thou art the first knave that e'er mad'st
        a duke.
First Provost, let me bail these gentle three.
[*To Lucio.*] Sneak not away, sir; for the friar and
        you
Must have a word anon. Lay hold on him.
    Lucio. This may prove worse than hanging.
    Duke. [*To Escalus.*] What you have spoke I
        pardon. Sit you down;   366
We'll borrow place of him. Sir, [*taking Angelo's
        seat*] by your leave.
Hast thou or word, or wit, or impudence,
That yet can do thee office? If thou hast,
Rely upon it till my tale be heard,   370
And hold no longer out.
    Ang.   O my dread lord,
I should be guiltier than my guiltiness,
To think I can be undiscernible,
When I perceive your Grace, like power divine,
Hath look'd upon my passes. Then, good Prince,
No longer session hold upon my shame,   376
But let my trial be mine own confession.
Immediate sentence, then, and sequent death
Is all the grace I beg.
    Duke.   Come hither, Mariana.
Say, wast thou e'er contracted to this woman?
    Ang. I was, my lord.   381
    Duke. Go take her hence, and marry her in-
        stantly.
Do you the office, friar; which consummate,
Return him here again. Go with him, Provost.
        [*Exeunt [Angelo, Mariana, Friar Peter, and
            Provost*].
    Escal. My lord, I am more amaz'd at his dis-
        honour   385
Than at the strangeness of it.
    Duke.   Come hither, Isabel.
Your friar is now your prince. As I was then
Advertising and holy to your business,
Not changing heart with habit, I am still
Attorney'd at your service.
    Isab.   O, give me pardon,   390
That I, your vassal, have employ'd and pain'd
Your unknown sovereignty!
    Duke.   You are pardon'd, Isabel;
And now, dear maid, be you as free to us.
Your brother's death, I know, sits at your heart;
And you may marvel why I obscur'd myself,   395
Labouring to save his life, and would not rather
Make rash remonstrance of my hidden power

---

313. **touse:** tear. 318. **here provincial:** within this ecclesiastical province. 321. **stew:** (1) kettle, (2) brothel. 323.
forfeits. Apparently alluding to the teeth extracted by barbers, the dentists of the time, and hung up in their shops. 324.
As ... mark: as much spurned as heeded. 335. **notedly:** precisely. 346. **close:** make terms. 352. **giglots:** lewd women.
other: i.e., Friar Peter. 359. **sheep-biting:** thievish. 371. **hold ... out:** bluff no longer. 375. **passes:** acts. 388.
Advertising: attentive. **holy:** dedicated. 393. **free:** generous. 397. **rash remonstrance:** swift show.

Than let him so be lost.   O most kind maid,
It was the swift celerity of his death,
Which I did think with slower foot came on,   400
That brain'd my purpose.   But, peace be with him!
That life is better life, past fearing death,
Than that which lives to fear.   Make it your comfort
So happy is your brother.

Re-enter ANGELO, MARIANA, FRIAR PETER, *and*
PROVOST.

Isab.   I do, my lord.
Duke. For this new-married man approaching
   here,   405
Whose salt imagination yet hath wrong'd
Your well defended honour, you must pardon
For Mariana's sake; but as he adjudg'd your
   brother, —
Being criminal, in double violation
Of sacred chastity and of promise-breach   410
Thereon dependent, for your brother's life, —
The very mercy of the law cries out
Most audible, even from his proper tongue,
"An Angelo for Claudio, death for death!"   414
Haste still pays haste, and leisure answers leisure;
Like doth quit like, and *Measure* still *for Measure.*
Then, Angelo, thy fault's thus manifested;
Which, though thou wouldst deny, denies thee
   vantage.
We do condemn thee to the very block
Where Claudio stoop'd to death, and with like
   haste.   420
Away with him!
Mari.   O my most gracious lord,
I hope you will not mock me with a husband.
Duke. It is your husband mock'd you with a
   husband.
Consenting to the safeguard of your honour,
I thought your marriage fit; else imputation,   425
For that he knew you, might reproach your life
And choke your good to come.   For his possessions,
Although by [confiscation] they are ours,
We do instate and widow you withal,
To buy you a better husband.
Mari.   O my dear lord,
I crave no other, nor no better man.   431
Duke. Never crave him; we are definitive.
Mari. Gentle my liege, —   [*Kneeling.*]
Duke.   You do but lose your labour.
Away with him to death! [*To Lucio.*] Now, sir,
   to you.
Mari. O my good lord!   Sweet Isabel, take my
   part!   435
Lend me your knees, and all my life to come

I'll lend you all my life to do you service.
Duke. Against all sense you do importune her.
Should she kneel down in mercy of this fact,
Her brother's ghost his paved bed would break,
And take her hence in horror.
Mari.   Isabel,   441
Sweet Isabel, do yet but kneel by me.
Hold up your hands, say nothing; I'll speak all.
They say best men are moulded out of faults,
And, for the most, become much more the better
For being a little bad; so may my husband.   446
O Isabel, will you not lend a knee?
Duke. He dies for Claudio's death.
Isab.   [*Kneeling.*]   Most bounteous sir,
Look, if it please you, on this man condemn'd
As if my brother liv'd.   I partly think   450
A due sincerity govern'd his deeds,
Till he did look on me.   Since it is so,
Let him not die.   My brother had but justice,
In that he did the thing for which he died;
For Angelo,   455
His act did not o'ertake his bad intent,
And must be buried but as an intent
That perish'd by the way.   Thoughts are no sub-
   jects;
Intents, but merely thoughts.
Mari.   Merely, my lord.
Duke. Your suit's unprofitable; stand up, I say.
I have bethought me of another fault.   461
Provost, how came it Claudio was beheaded
At an unusual hour?
Prov.   It was commanded so.
Duke. Had you a special warrant for the deed?
Prov. No, my good lord; it was by private mes-
   sage.   465
Duke. For which I do discharge you of your office:
Give up your keys.
Prov.   Pardon me, noble lord.
I thought it was a fault, but knew it not;
Yet did repent me, after more advice.
For testimony whereof, one in the prison,   470
That should by private order else have died,
I have reserv'd alive.
Duke.   What's he?
Prov.   His name is Barnardine.
Duke. I would thou hadst done so by Claudio.
Go fetch him hither; let me look upon him.
                                     [*Exit Provost.*]
Escal. I am sorry, one so learned and so wise   475
As you, Lord Angelo, have still appear'd,
Should slip so grossly, both in the heat of blood,
And lack of temper'd judgement afterward.
Ang. I am sorry that such sorrow I procure;

---

401. **brain'd:** killed, defeated.   406. **salt:** lustful.   418. **vantage:** advantage, i.e., escape.   425. **imputation:** censure.
427. **For:** as for.   428. [confiscation] F₂.   *confutation* F₁.   429. **instate...withal:** confer upon you as a widow's estate.
432. **definitive:** resolved.   458. **subjects:** i.e., to the law.   468. **fault:** mistake.   469. **advice:** thought, consideration.
479. **procure:** cause.

And so deep sticks it in my penitent heart   480
That I crave death more willingly than mercy.
'Tis my deserving, and I do entreat it.

Re-enter PROVOST, *with* BARNARDINE, CLAUDIO
[*muffled*], *and* JULIET.
Duke. Which is that Barnardine?
Prov.   This, my lord.
Duke. There was a friar told me of this man.
Sirrah, thou art said to have a stubborn soul   485
That apprehends no further than this world,
And squar'st thy life according. Thou'rt con-
    demn'd;
But, for those earthly faults, I quit them all;
And pray thee take this mercy to provide
For better times to come. Friar, advise him;   490
I leave him to your hand. What muffl'd fellow's
    that?
Prov. This is another prisoner that I sav'd,
Who should have died when Claudio lost his head;
As like almost to Claudio as himself.
                    [*Unmuffles Claudio.*]
Duke. [*To Isabella.*] If he be like your brother, for
    his sake   495
Is he pardon'd; and, for your lovely sake —
Give me your hand and say you will be mine —
He is my brother too. But fitter time for that.
By this Lord Angelo perceives he's safe;
Methinks I see a quick'ning in his eye.   500
Well, Angelo, your evil quits you well.
Look that you love your wife; her worth worth
    yours.
I find an apt remission in myself;
And yet here's one in place I cannot pardon.
    [*To Lucio.*] You, sirrah, that knew me for a fool,
    a coward,   505
One all of luxury, an ass, a madman,
Wherein have I [deserved so] of you,
That you extol me thus?   508

Lucio. Faith, my lord, I spoke it but according
to the trick. If you will hang me for it, you may;
but I had rather it would please you I might be
whipp'd.   512
Duke. Whipp'd first, sir, and hang'd after.
Proclaim it, Provost, round about the city,
[Is] any woman wrong'd by this lewd fellow,   515
As I have heard him swear himself there's one
Whom he begot with child, let her appear,
And he shall marry her. The nuptial finish'd,
Let him be whipp'd and hang'd.   519
Lucio. I beseech your Highness do not marry me
to a whore. Your Highness said even now, I made
you a duke; good my lord, do not recompense me
in making me a cuckold.
Duke. Upon mine honour, thou shalt marry her.
Thy slanders I forgive; and therewithal   525
Remit thy other forfeits. Take him to prison;
And see our pleasure herein executed.
Lucio. Marrying a punk, my lord, is pressing to
death, whipping, and hanging.
Duke. Slandering a prince deserves it.   530
                    [*Exeunt Officers with Lucio.*]
She, Claudio, that you wrong'd, look you restore.
Joy to you, Mariana! Love her, Angelo!
I have confess'd her and I know her virtue.
Thanks, good friend Escalus, for thy much goodness;
There's more behind that is more gratulate.   535
Thanks, Provost, for thy care and secrecy;
We shall employ thee in a worthier place.
Forgive him, Angelo, that brought you home
The head of Ragozine for Claudio's;
The offence pardons itself. Dear Isabel,   540
I have a motion much imports your good;
Whereto if you'll a willing ear incline,
What's mine is yours and what is yours is mine.
So, bring us to our palace, where we'll show
What's yet behind, that['s] meet you all should
    know.   [*Exeunt.*]   545

488. quit: forgive. 501. quits: requites. 503. apt remission: readiness to pardon. 504. in place: present. 506. luxury: lust. 507. [deserved so] (Pope). *so deserv'd* F. 515. [Is] (Hart). *If* F. 526. forfeits: penalties. 535. behind: i.e., to come. gratulate: gratifying. 545. that['s] F₂. *that* F₁.

Pericles, Prince of Tyre

ON MAY 20, 1608, "the book of Pericles prynce of Tyre" was entered in the Stationers' Register to Edward Blount. Blount does not seem to have issued the play, nor was it included in the First Folio (1623), of which Blount was one of the publishers. It was likewise absent from the Second Folio (1632), but appeared (with six other additional plays, all of which were spurious) in the second impression of the Third Folio (1664), the text following that of the sixth Quarto. For in 1609 had been published an exceptionally corrupt and undoubtedly pirated Quarto, with Shakespeare's name upon the title page, purporting to give the play as it had been "diuers and sundry times acted by his Maiesties Seruants, at the Globe on the Banck-side." This Quarto was reissued in the same year, and reprinted in 1611, 1619, 1630, and 1635. The original Quarto is perforce the authority for any and all editions, but modern editors owe a special debt to Malone, who corrected many errors and worked out the generally accepted arrangements for many mislineated passages.

Clues for the date of *Pericles* are not very helpful. The registration entry argues the existence of the play in some condition prior to May 20, 1608, though a few scholars have maintained that the reference is not to Shakespeare's play but to another now lost. Some time between January 5, 1606 and November 23, 1608 the Venetian ambassador, Zorzi Giustinian, saw a play called *Pericles*; and in 1608 George Wilkins (who the previous year had written *The Miseries of Inforst Mariage* for Shakespeare's company) published a novel, *The Painfull Aduentures of Pericles Prince of Tyre. Being The true History of the Play of Pericles, as it was lately presented by the worthy and ancient Poet Iohn Gower.* The prefatory "Argument" recalls the theatrical performance "by the King's Maiesties Players excellently presented." On this meagre evidence one may venture late 1607 or early 1608 for the composition of the present play.

It is generally conceded today that *Pericles* is only in part Shakespeare's. The last three acts are usually held to be his, the first two being assigned to another hand. There is, however, no agreement as to the manner in which these elements came to be united. Shakespeare may have revised an earlier play, keeping the first two acts substantially unchanged; he may have left unfinished a play on Marina which a minor playwright completed; he may have co-operated with another writer from the outset. The occurrence even in the earlier acts of passages and phrases with a Shakespearean ring suggests the more usual method of collaboration, whereby joint authors discuss and retouch the whole play; on the other hand, it would seem that in the first two acts Shakespeare's interest was never more than superficially engaged. The collaborator cannot be identified. Whoever he was, he was once credited, in addition to the first two acts, with the brothel scenes in Act IV and all of the Gower Choruses. But the stews of Mytilene are no more repulsive than those of Vienna in *Measure for Measure*, and there is no sound reason for relieving Shakespeare of responsibility, especially since the experiences of Marina in the brothel are traditional elements in the story. The purity of Marina is enhanced, as that of Isabella had been, by her resistance to the toils and snares of corruption. With respect to the Gower Choruses, it is obvious that the archaic effects are deliberate, in deference to the "ancient poet." It is to be noted, nevertheless, that they are not all in the same class. The first three and the one in V.ii are in octosyllabic verse; those in Act IV and at the beginning and end of Act V are decasyllabic, and, with that in V.ii, are somewhat less crude in style. Yet to pronounce which ones were written by Shakespeare and which by the collaborator seems presumptuous. If the latter is held accountable for all the octosyllabic verse in the play, Cerimon's letter (III.ii.68–75) must be his also. It is conceivable that the Gower Choruses were all part of his assignment.

Pericles is a dramatization of the story of *Apollonius of Tyre*, one of the most widely diffused themes in fiction. The earliest known form is a Latin prose *Historia*, supposed to have been compiled from Greek sources about the fifth century, and extant in many MSS.; but the versions serving the playwrights were that of John Gower in his *Confessio Amantis* (VIII,271–2008), derived from the *Pantheon*, a twelfth-century verse chronicle by Godfrey of Viterbo, and that of Laurence Twine, *The Patterne of Painfull Aduentures* (registered 1576 and preserved in two editions, one of 1607, the other undated), based upon the rendering in the *Gesta Romanorum*. Certain features appear for the first time in the play: the substitution of a tournament for the ball game in which the hero distinguishes himself at Pentapolis, the playful trickery of Simonides in the scene where the marriage is arranged; the details of the scenes in the brothel; and the omission of the revenges of the hero upon the bawds and the treacherous foster-parents of Marina.

It is practically certain that George Wilkins wrote *The Painfull Aduentures* with access to the manuscript of *Pericles*, for the novel frequently reproduces the phrasing of the play more closely than memory alone could easily have achieved. Striking parallels also indicate a first-hand use of Twine. The relation of the novel to the play has led to the theory, now generally abandoned, that Wilkins had been in fact Shakespeare's collaborator. His having provided a play for the King's Men in 1607 is suggestive, but it seems more likely that through his association with the players he was able to get at Shakespeare's text.

Although the crudities of the text and the uncertainty about Shakespeare's part in the composition render dangerous any conclusions about the significance of *Pericles* in Shakespeare's development, certain affiliations of this play with others are not to be ignored. The theme of separation and reunion relates it to several, both early and late. Specifically, the restoration of Thaisa to Pericles recalls the discovery of Aemilia by Aegeon in *The Comedy of Errors* (where the frame story was suggested to Shakespeare by the sources of the present play), the revelation of Marina to Pericles is reminiscent of the reunion of Sebastian and Viola in *Twelfth Night*, and these recognition scenes in *Pericles* bear a family resemblance to those in *Cymbeline* and *The Winter's Tale*. One may remark also the element of shipwreck in *The Comedy of Errors*, *Twelfth Night*, *Pericles*, and *The Tempest*; in the first two the accident is a matter of report, but in the second pair it is rendered dramatically. However casual or incomplete may be the impress of Shakespeare's art upon the present play, one cannot escape the fact that *Pericles* bears an important relationship to Shakespeare's last work. There is reason for believing that in handling the material of *Pericles* Shakespeare glimpsed dramatic possibilities which were to be realized with growing sureness in *Cymbeline*, *The Winter's Tale*, and *The Tempest*, and that in bringing the experiences of Pericles and Marina to their happy outcome he gave expression to a spiritual attitude which was to make itself felt

with increasing emphasis and to have its perfect reflection in *The Tempest*. To say this is neither to find nor to seek particular implications in these last plays. But the importance given in their conclusions to triumphant human goodness and forgiveness and reconcilement is suggestive of a mood increasingly sustained. Not that Shakespeare had not stressed goodness and exploited happy endings before. From his earliest days as a writer of comedy he was careless of probability in order that joy might reign and wedding bells might ring. In a sense there is nothing really novel in the comedies of the last period. The elements of evil or mischance which load them with potential disaster are not new. *The Two Gentlemen of Verona* might easily have been conducted to a tragic end. In *Much Ado* action skirts the very borders of calamity. In *Measure for Measure* one listens for a space to the true accents of despair. Yet in all these plays, as in the final group, tragedy is averted. Since, then, neither the ultimate happiness, nor the element of potential disaster in Shakespeare's last comedies is an innovation, what differentiates them from their predecessors? The difference is mainly in the dominant temper, which is graver than that of the earlier comedies, with the exception of the "problem comedies," which form a special class, and possibly of *The Merchant of Venice*. Forces of evil threaten more ominously; the spirit of comedy has its way less readily (*Pericles* and *Cymbeline* are almost entirely without humor). The difference is felt, too, in the endings of these last plays. The happiness to which the main characters are finally brought has a peculiar quality. There is communicated, somehow, more than the mere fact of their happiness; subtle undercurrents of emotion in unforgettable passages convey a special glow (*Per.*, V.i.98–240; V.iii.40–48; *Cymb.*, V.v.261–64; *W. T.*, V.iii.109–28; *Temp.*, V.172–84). Moreover, in the final group of tragi-comedies, or dramatic romances, as they may appropriately be called, the sins and errors of the older generation are visited upon the children, but the faults of the old are expiated through repentance and pardon, and the young people escape from adversity to joy. Thus both parents and children share intimately in the consummation. And the power to move which these plays possess is owing not only to the variety of incident with which they are replete, and to the felicity which crowns their endings, but also to the intimation that the future opening up for the young is a kind of fulfillment. By itself *Pericles* would be a most untrustworthy witness with reference to Shakespeare's development, but regarded in conjunction with his last plays, it seems to foretell the new directions in which he was soon unmistakably to move.

PERICLES, PRINCE OF TYRE

[DRAMATIS PERSONÆ

ANTIOCHUS, *king of Antioch.*
PERICLES, *prince of Tyre.*
HELICANUS,
ESCANES, } *two lords of Tyre.*
SIMONIDES, *king of Pentapolis.*
CLEON, *governor of Tarsus.*
LYSIMACHUS, *governor of Mytilene.*
CERIMON, *a lord of Ephesus.*
THALIARD, *a lord of Antioch.*
PHILEMON, *servant to Cerimon.*
LEONINE, *servant to Dionyza.*
Marshal.

A Pandar.
BOULT, *his servant.*

The Daughter of Antiochus.
DIONYZA, *wife to Cleon.*
THAISA, *daughter to Simonides.*
MARINA, *daughter to Pericles and Thaisa.*
LYCHORIDA, *nurse to Marina.*
A Bawd.

DIANA.
GOWER, *as Chorus.*

Lords, Ladies, Knights, Gentlemen, Sailors, Pirates, Fishermen, and Messengers.

SCENE: *Dispersedly in various countries.*]

ACT I

Enter GOWER.

[*Before the palace of Antioch.   Heads and skulls of men over the gate.*]

Gow. To sing a song that old was sung,
From ashes ancient Gower is come,
Assuming man's infirmities,
To glad your ear and please your eyes.
It hath been sung at festivals,   5
On ember-eves and holidays;
And lords and ladies in their lives
Have read it for restoratives.
The purchase is to make men glorious;
Et bonum quo antiquius, eo melius.   10
If you, born in these latter times
When wit's more ripe, accept my rhymes,
And that to hear an old man sing
May to your wishes pleasure bring,
I life would wish, and that I might   15

Waste it for you like taper-light.
This Antioch, then, Antiochus the Great
Built up, this city, for his chiefest seat,
The fairest in all Syria;
I tell you what mine authors say.   20
This king unto him took a [fere],
Who died and left a female heir,
So buxom, blithe, and full of face
As heaven had lent her all his grace;
With whom the father liking took,   25
And her to incest did provoke, —
Bad child; worse father! to entice his own
To evil should be done by none.
[By] custom what they did begin
Was with long use account'd no sin.   30
The beauty of this sinful dame
Made many princes thither frame
To seek her as a bed-fellow,
In marriage-pleasures play-fellow;
Which to prevent he made a law   35

Act I, Prol., 6. **ember-eves:** evenings preceding ember-days, periods for fasting and prayer. **holidays.** Emended by Steevens and many editors to *holy-ales,* rural festivals. 9. **purchase:** gain. 10. *Et ... melius:* and the older a good thing, the better. 13. **that:** if. 21. **[fere]** (Malone): mate, partner. *Peere* Q. 23. **face:** i.e., beauty. 29. **[By]** (Malone). *But* Q. 32. **frame:** plan.

To keep her still and men in awe,
That whoso ask'd her for his wife,
His riddle told not, lost his life.
So for her many a wight did die,
As yon grim looks do testify.   40
What now ensues, to the judgement of your eye
I give, my cause who best can justify.   [*Exit.*

[SCENE I. *Antioch. A room in the palace.*]

Enter ANTIOCHUS, PRINCE PERICLES, *and followers.*

    Ant. Young Prince of Tyre, you have at large receiv'd
The danger of the task you undertake.
    Per. I have, Antiochus, and, with a soul
Embold'ned with the glory of her praise,
Think death no hazard in this enterprise.   5
    Ant. Bring in our daughter, clothed like a bride   [*Music.*
For embracements even of Jove himself;
At whose conception, till Lucina reign'd,
Nature this dowry gave to glad her presence,
The senate-house of planets all did sit,   10
To knit in her their best perfections.

Enter the DAUGHTER *of Antiochus.*

    Per. See where she comes, apparell'd like the spring,
Graces her subjects, and her thoughts the king
Of every virtue gives renown to men!
Her face the book of praises, where is read   15
Nothing but curious pleasures, as from thence
Sorrow were ever raz'd, and testy wrath
Could never be her mild companion.
You gods that made me man, and sway in love,
That have inflam'd desire in my breast   20
To taste the fruit of yon celestial tree
Or die in the adventure, be my helps,
As I am son and servant to your will,
To compass such a boundless happiness!
    Ant. Prince Pericles, —   25
    Per. That would be son to great Antiochus.
    Ant. Before thee stands this fair Hesperides,
With golden fruit, but dangerous to be touch'd,
For death-like dragons here affright thee hard.
Her face, like heaven, enticeth thee to view   30
Her countless glory, which desert must gain,
And which, without desert, because thine eye
Presumes to reach, all the whole heap must die.
Yon sometimes famous princes, like thyself,
Drawn by report, advent'rous by desire,   35
Tell thee, with speechless tongues and semblance pale,

That without covering, save yon field of stars,
Here they stand martyrs, slain in Cupid's wars;
And with dead cheeks advise thee to desist
For going on death's net, whom none resist.   40
    Per. Antiochus, I thank thee, who hath taught
My frail mortality to know itself,
And by those fearful objects to prepare
This body, like to them, to what I must;
For death remembered should be like a mirror,   45
Who tells us life's but breath, to trust it error.
I'll make my will then, and, as sick men do
Who know the world, see heaven, but, feeling woe,
Gripe not at earthly joys as erst they did;
So I bequeath a happy peace to you   50
And all good men, as every prince should do;
My riches to the earth from whence they came;
But my unspotted fire of love to you.
                        [*To the Princess.*]
Thus ready for the way of life or death,
I wait the sharpest blow, Antiochus.   55
    [*Ant.*] Scorning advice, read the conclusion then,
Which read and not expounded, 'tis decreed,
As these before thee, thou thyself shalt bleed.
    Daugh. Of all 'say'd yet, mayst thou prove prosperous!
Of all 'say'd yet I wish thee happiness!   60
    Per. Like a bold champion I assume the lists,
Nor ask advice of any other thought
But faithfulness and courage.

         THE RIDDLE.

I am no viper, yet I feed
On mother's flesh which did me breed.   65
I sought a husband, in which labour
I found that kindness in a father.
He's father, son, and husband mild;
I mother, wife, and yet his child.
How they may be, and yet in two,   70
As you will live, resolve it you.
[*Aside.*] Sharp physic is the last; but, O you powers
That give heaven countless eyes to view men's acts.
Why cloud they not their sights perpetually
If this be true which makes me pale to read it?   75
Fair glass of light, I lov'd you, and could still,
Were not this glorious casket stor'd with ill.
But I must tell you, now my thoughts revolt;
For he's no man on whom perfections wait
That, knowing sin within, will touch the gate.   80
You are a fair viol, and your sense the strings;
Who, finger'd to make man his lawful music,
Would draw heaven down and all the gods to hearken;
But being play'd upon before your time,

Sc. i, 1. **receiv'd:** heard.   8. **Lucina:** goddess of childbirth.   **till … reign'd:** i.e., before her birth.   9. **glad … presence:** make her beautiful.   14. **gives:** that gives.   18. **mild:** i.e., of her mildness.   33. **all … die:** you must perish wholly.   40. **For:** from.   56. **[*Ant.*]** (Malone). Q continues to Pericles.   **conclusion:** riddle.   59. **'say'd:** who have essayed, tried.   72. **last:** last line.

Hell only danceth at so harsh a chime.   85
Good sooth, I care not for you.
   Ant. Prince Pericles, touch not, upon thy life,
For that's an article within our law,
As dangerous as the rest.   Your time's expir'd.
Either expound now, or receive your sentence.   90
   Per. Great king,
Few love to hear the sins they love to act;
'Twould braid yourself too near for me to tell it.
Who has a book of all that monarchs do,
He's more secure to keep it shut than shown;   95
For vice repeated is like the wand'ring wind,
Blows dust in others' eyes, to spread itself;
And yet the end of all is bought thus dear,
The breath is gone, and the sore eyes see clear
To stop the air would hurt them.   The blind mole casts   100
Copp'd hills towards heaven, to tell the earth is throng'd
By man's oppression; and the poor worm doth die for't.
Kings are earth's gods; in vice their law's their will;
And if Jove stray, who dare say Jove doth ill?
It is enough you know; and it is fit,   105
What being more known grows worse, to smother it.
All love the womb that their first being bred,
Then give my tongue like leave to love my head.
   Ant. [*Aside.*] Heaven, that I had thy head!
   He has found the meaning.
But I will gloze with him. — Young Prince of Tyre,   110
Though by the tenour of [our] strict edict,
Your exposition misinterpreting,
We might proceed to [cancel off] your days;
Yet hope, succeeding from so fair a tree
As your fair self, doth tune us otherwise.   115
Forty days longer we do respite you;
If by which time our secret be undone,
This mercy shows we'll joy in such a son;
And until then your entertain shall be
As doth befit our honour and your worth.   120
                       [*Exeunt all but Pericles.*]
   Per. How courtesy would seem to cover sin,
When what is done is like an hypocrite,
The which is good in nothing but in sight!
If it be true that I interpret false,
Then were it certain you were not so bad   125
As with foul incest to abuse your soul;
Where now [you're] both a father and a son
By your untimely claspings with your child
(Which pleasures fits a husband, not a father),

And she an eater of her mother's flesh   130
By the defiling of her parent's bed;
And both like serpents are, who though they feed
On sweetest flowers, yet they poison breed.
Antioch, farewell! for wisdom sees, those men
Blush not in actions blacker than the night   135
Will [shun] no course to keep them from the light.
One sin, I know, another doth provoke;
Murder's as near to lust as flame to smoke;
Poison and treason are the hands of sin,
Ay, and the targets to put off the shame;   140
Then, lest my life be cropp'd to keep you clear,
By flight I'll shun the danger which I fear.   [*Exit.*]

             Re-enter ANTIOCHUS.

   Ant. He hath found the meaning,
For which we mean to have his head.
He must not live to trumpet forth my infamy,   145
Nor tell the world Antiochus doth sin
In such a loathed manner;
And therefore instantly this prince must die,
For by his fall my honour must keep high.
Who attends us there?

             Enter THALIARD.

   Thal.   Doth your Highness call?
   Ant. Thaliard,   151
You are of our chamber, and our mind partakes
Her private actions to your secrecy;
And for your faithfulness we will advance you.
Thaliard, behold, here's poison, and here's gold;   155
We hate the Prince of Tyre, and thou must kill him.
It fits thee not to ask the reason why,
Because we bid it.   Say, is it done?
   Thal.   My lord,
'Tis done.
   Ant.   Enough.   160

          Enter a MESSENGER.

Let your breath cool yourself, telling your haste.
   Mes. My lord, Prince Pericles is fled.   [*Exit.*]
   Ant.   As thou
Wilt live, fly after; and like an arrow shot
From a well-experienc'd archer hits the mark
His eye doth level at, so thou ne'er return   165
Unless thou say Prince Pericles is dead.
   Thal. My lord,
If I can get him within my pistol's length,
I'll make him sure enough; so farewell to your Highness.
   Ant. Thaliard, adieu! [*Exit Thal.*]   Till Pericles be dead,   170
My heart can lend no succour to my head. [*Exit.*]

---

93. **braid**: reproach.   96. **repeated**: reported.   101. **Copp'd**: peaked.   102. **worm**: i.e., the mole.   110. [**our**] F₃. *your* Q.   110. **gloze**: talk deceptively.   111. [**our**] F₃. *your* Q.   113. [**cancel off**] F₃. *counsell of* Q.   114. **succeeding**: issuing.   127. [**you're**] F₃. *you* Q.   135. **Blush**: who blush.   136. [**shun**] (Malone).   *shew* Q.   140. **targets**: shields.   152. **chamber.** Q inserts *Thaliard* after *chamber*.   **partakes**: imparts.   161. **telling**: showing.   165. **level**: aim.

[SCENE II. *Tyre. A room in the palace.*]

Enter PERICLES *with his* Lords.

Per. Let none disturb us. [*Exeunt Lords.*] — Why
 should this [charge] of thoughts,
The sad companion, dull-ey'd Melancholy,
[Be my] so us'd a guest as not an hour
In the day's glorious walk or peaceful night,
The tomb where grief should sleep, can breed me
 quiet?   5
Here pleasures court mine eyes, and mine eyes
 shun them;
And danger, which I feared, is at Antioch,
Whose arm seems far too short to hit me here.
Yet neither pleasure's art can joy my spirits,
Nor yet the other's distance comfort me.   10
Then it is thus: the passions of the mind,
That have their first conception by mis-dread,
Have after-nourishment and life by care;
And what was first but fear what might be done,
Grows elder now and cares it be not done.   15
And so with me. The great Antiochus,
'Gainst whom I am too little to contend,
Since he's so great can make his will his act,
Will think me speaking, though I swear to
 silence;
Nor boots it me to say I honour [him],   20
If he suspect I may dishonour him;
And what may make him blush in being known,
He'll stop the course by which it might be known.
With hostile forces he'll o'erspread the land,
And with [th' ostent] of war will look so huge   25
Amazement shall drive courage from the state,
Our men be vanquish'd ere they do resist,
And subjects punish'd that ne'er thought offence:
Which care of them, not pity of myself —
Who [am] no more but as the tops of trees,   30
Which fence the roots they grow by and defend
 them —
Makes both my body pine and soul to languish,
And punish that before that he would punish.

Enter [HELICANUS, *with other*] LORDS.

1. Lord. Joy and all comfort in your sacred
 breast!
2. Lord. And keep your mind, till you return
 to us,   35
Peaceful and comfortable!
Hel. Peace, peace, and give experience tongue.
They do abuse the King that flatter him,
For flattery is the bellows blows up sin,
The thing the which is flattered, but a spark   40

To which that [blast] gives heat and stronger
 glowing;
Whereas reproof, obedient and in order,
Fits kings as they are men, for they may err.
When Signior Sooth here does proclaim a peace,
He flatters you, makes war upon your life.   45
Prince, pardon me, or strike me, if you please;
I cannot be much lower than my knees. [*Kneels.*]
Per. All leave us else; but let your cares o'erlook
What shipping and what lading's in our haven,
And then return to us. [*Exeunt Lords.*] Heli-
 canus, thou   50
Hast mov'd us. What seest thou in our looks?
Hel. An angry brow, dread lord.
Per. If there be such a dart in princes' frowns,
How durst thy tongue move anger to our face?
Hel. How dares the plants look up to heaven,
 from whence   55
They have their nourishment?
Per.   Thou know'st I have power
To take thy life from thee.
Hel. I have ground the axe myself;
Do you but strike the blow.
Per.   Rise, prithee, rise.
Sit down. Thou art no flatterer.   60
I thank thee for't; and heaven forbid
That kings should let their ears hear their faults hid!
Fit counsellor and servant for a prince,
Who by thy wisdom makes a prince thy servant,
What wouldst thou have me do?
Hel.   To bear with patience
Such griefs as you yourself do lay upon yourself. 66
Per. Thou speak'st like a physician, Helicanus,
That ministers a potion unto me
That thou wouldst tremble to receive thyself.
Attend me, then. I went to Antioch,   70
Where, as thou know'st, against the face of death
I sought the purchase of a glorious beauty,
From whence an issue I might propagate
Are arms to princes and bring joys to subjects.
Her face was to mine eye beyond all wonder;   75
The rest — hark in thine ear — as black as incest;
Which by my knowledge found, the sinful father
Seem'd not to strike, but smooth. But thou know'st
 this,
'Tis time to fear when tyrants seem to kiss.
Which fear so grew in me, I hither fled   80
Under the covering of a careful night,
Who seem'd my good protector; and, being here,
Bethought me what was past, what might succeed.
I knew him tyrannous, and tyrants' fears
Decrease not, but grow faster than the years;   85

Sc. ii, 2. [charge] (Malone): burden. *chāge* Q. 3. [Be my] (Dyce). *By me* Q. us'd: accustomed. 12. mis-dread:
fear of evil. 20. boots: avails. [him] (Rowe). Om. Q. 25. [th' ostent] (Tyrwhitt conj.): display. *the stint* Q. 30. [am]
(Farmer conj.). *once* Q. 38. abuse: deceive. 41. [blast] (Mason conj.). *sparke* Q. 44. Sooth: Flattery. 49. lading:
cargo. 74. Are . . . subjects. It is conjectured that a line is missing before this one. If not, the meaning would seem to be
"who are" or "such as are." 78. smooth: flatter, cajole.

And should he [doubt it], as no doubt he doth,
That I should open to the list'ning air
How many worthy princes' bloods were shed
To keep his bed of blackness unlaid ope,
To lop that doubt, he'll fill this land with arms   90
And make pretence of wrong that I have done him;
When all for mine (if I may call) offence
Must feel war's blow, who spares not innocence:
Which love to all, of which thyself art one,
Who now reprov'dst me for it, —
   Hel.   Alas, sir!   95
   Per. Drew sleep out of mine eyes, blood from
    my cheeks,
Musings into my mind, with thousand doubts
How I might stop this tempest ere it came;
And finding little comfort to relieve them,
I thought it princely charity to grieve them.   100
   Hel. Well, my lord, since you have given me
    leave to speak,
Freely will I speak. Antiochus you fear;
And justly too, I think, you fear the tyrant,
Who either by public war or private treason
Will take away your life.   105
Therefore, my lord, go travel for a while,
Till that his rage and anger be forgot,
Or till the Destinies do cut his thread of life.
Your rule direct to any; if to me,
Day serves not light more faithful than I'll be.
   Per. I do not doubt thy faith;   111
But should he wrong my liberties in my absence?
   Hel. We'll mingle our bloods together in the
    earth,
From whence we had our being and our birth.
   Per. Tyre, I now look from thee then, and to
    Tarsus   115
Intend my travel, where I'll hear from thee,
And by whose letters I'll dispose myself.
The care I had and have of subjects' good
On thee I lay, whose wisdom's strength can bear it.
I'll take thy word for faith, not ask thine oath;   120
Who shuns not to break one will [sure] crack both;
But in our orbs we'll live so round and safe
That time of both this truth shall ne'er convince,
Thou show'dst a subject's shine, I a true prince.
                           [Exeunt.

[SCENE III. *Tyre. An ante-chamber in the palace.*]

Enter THALIARD.

   Thal. So this is Tyre, and this the court. Here
must I kill King Pericles; and if I do it not, I am
sure to be hang'd at home. 'Tis dangerous. Well,
I perceive he was a wise fellow and had good discretion that, being bid to ask what he would of   5

the King, desired he might know none of his secrets.
Now do I see he had some reason for't; for if a
king bid a man be a villain, he's bound by the indenture of his oath to be one. Hush! here comes
the lords of Tyre.   10

Enter HELICANUS *and* ESCANES, *with other* Lords.

   Hel. You shall not need, my fellow peers of Tyre,
Further to question me of your king's departure.
His seal'd commission, left in trust with me,
Doth speak sufficiently he's gone to travel.
   Thal. [*Aside.*] How? the King gone?   15
   Hel. If further yet you will be satisfied
Why, as it were unlicens'd of your loves,
He would depart, I'll give some light unto you.
Being at Antioch —
   Thal.   [*Aside.*] What from Antioch?
   Hel. Royal Antiochus — on what cause I know
    not —   20
Took some displeasure at him; at least he judg'd so;
And doubting lest [that] he had err'd or sinn'd,
To show his sorrow, he'd correct himself;
So puts himself unto the shipman's toil,
With whom each minute threatens life or death.
   Thal. [*Aside.*] Well, I perceive   26
I shall not be hang'd now, although I would;
But since he's gone, the King's [ears it] must please
He scap'd the land, to perish at the sea.
I'll present myself. — Peace to the lords of Tyre!
   Hel. Lord Thaliard from Antiochus is welcome.   31
   Thal. From him I come
With message unto princely Pericles;
But since my landing I have understood
Your lord has betook himself to unknown travels;   35
Now message must return from whence it came.
   Hel. We have no reason to desire it,
Commended to our master, not to us;
Yet, ere you shall depart, this we desire,
As friends to Antioch, we may feast in Tyre.   40
                            [Exeunt.

[SCENE IV. *Tarsus. A room in the Governor's
house.*]

Enter CLEON, *the Governor of Tarsus, with* [DIONYZA,]
his wife, and others.

   Cle. My Dionyza, shall we rest us here,
And by relating tales of others' griefs,
See if 'twill teach us to forget our own?
   Dio. That were to blow at fire in hope to quench
    it;
For who digs hills because they do aspire   5
Throws down one mountain to cast up a higher.
O my distressed lord, even such our griefs are.

86. **[doubt it]** (Malone): suspect it. *doo't* Q. 100. **them** Q₅. *for them* Q₁. 109. **direct:** depute. 112. **liberties:** rights,
prerogatives. 121. **[sure]** F₃. Om. Q. 123. **convince:** disprove. 124. **shine:** honor, glory.
Sc. iii, 22. **doubting:** fearing. **lest [that]** *lest* Q₁. *that* F₃. 28. **[ears it]** (Dyce). *seas* Q.

Here they're but felt and seen with mischief's
  eyes,
But like to groves, being topp'd, they higher rise.
  Cle. O Dionyza,   10
Who wanteth food and will not say he wants it,
Or can conceal his hunger till he famish?
Our tongues and sorrows [do] sound deep
Our woes into the air; our eyes [do] weep
Till tongues fetch breath that may proclaim them
  louder;   15
That, if heaven slumber while their creatures want,
They may awake their [helps] to comfort them.
I'll then discourse our woes, felt several years,
And, wanting breath to speak, help me with tears.
  Dio. I'll do my best, sir.   20
  Cle. This Tarsus, o'er which I have the govern-
  ment,
A city on whom Plenty held full hand,
For Riches strew'd herself even in the streets;
Whose towers bore heads so high they kiss'd the
  clouds,
And strangers ne'er beheld but wond'red at; 25
Whose men and dames so jetted and adorn'd,
Like one another's glass to trim them by.
Their tables were stor'd full, to glad the sight,
And not so much to feed on as delight.
All poverty was scorn'd, and pride so great, 30
The name of help grew odious to repeat.
  Dio. O, 'tis too true.
  Cle. But see what heaven can do! By this our
  change,
These mouths, who but of late, earth, sea, and air
Were all too little to content and please, 35
Although they gave their creatures in abundance,
As houses are defil'd for want of use,
They are now starv'd for want of exercise.
Those palates who, not yet [two summers] younger,
Must have inventions to delight the taste, 40
Would now be glad of bread and beg for it.
Those mothers who, to nuzzle up their babes,
Thought nought too curious, are ready now
To eat those little darlings whom they lov'd.
So sharp are hunger's teeth, that man and wife 45
Draw lots who first shall die to lengthen life.
Here stands a lord, and there a lady weeping.
Here many sink, yet those which see them fall
Have scarce strength left to give them burial.
Is not this true?   50
  Dio. Our cheeks and hollow eyes do witness it.
  Cle. O, let those cities that of Plenty's cup
And her prosperities so largely taste

With their superfluous riots, hear these tears!
The misery of Tarsus may be theirs. 55

      Enter a LORD.

  Lord. Where's the Lord Governor?
  Cle. Here.
Speak out thy sorrows which thou bring'st in haste,
For comfort is too far for us to expect.
  Lord. We have descried, upon our neighbouring
  shore,   60
A portly sail of ships make hitherward.
  Cle. I thought as much.
One sorrow never comes but brings an heir
That may succeed as his inheritor;
And so in ours. Some neighbouring nation, 65
Taking advantage of our misery,
[Hath] stuff'd these hollow vessels with their power
To beat us down, the which are down already;
And make a conquest of unhappy me,
Whereas no glory's got to overcome. 70
  Lord. That's the least fear; for, by the semblance
Of their white flags display'd, they bring us peace
And come to us as favourers, not as foes.
  Cle. Thou speak'st like [him's] untutor'd to
  repeat,   74
"Who makes the fairest show means most deceit."
But bring they what they will and what they can,
What need we [fear?
The] ground's the lowest, and we are half way there.
Go tell their general we attend him here,
To know for what he comes, and whence he comes,
And what he craves.   81
  Lord. I go, my lord.   [*Exit.*]
  Cle. Welcome is peace, if he on peace consist;
If wars, we are unable to resist.

    Enter PERICLES *with* Attendants.

  Per. Lord Governor, for so we hear you are, 85
Let not our ships and number of our men
Be like a beacon fir'd t' amaze your eyes.
We have heard your miseries as far as Tyre,
And seen the desolation of your streets;
Nor come we to add sorrow to your tears, 90
But to relieve them of their heavy load;
And these our ships, you happily may think
Are like the Troyan horse was stuff'd within
With bloody veins, expecting overthrow,
Are stor'd with corn to make your needy bread, 95
And give them life whom hunger starv'd half dead.
  All. The gods of Greece protect you!
And we'll pray for you.

Sc. iv, 8. **mischief's:** calamity's. 9. **topp'd:** lopped, pruned. 13. **[do]** Q₄. *to* Q₁. 14. **[do]** (Malone). *to* Q. 17. **[helps]** (Malone). *helpers* Q. 26. **jetted:** strutted. 27. **glass:** mirror. 39. **[two summers]** (Mason conj.). *too sauers* Q. 42. **nuzzle:** nurse, pamper. 43. **curious:** fine, nice. 54. **superfluous riots:** rioting in superfluity. 61. **portly:** stately. 67. **[Hath]** (Rowe). *That* Q. **power:** armed forces. 70. **Whereas:** in whose case. 74. **[him's]** (Malone): him who is. *himnes* Q. 77–78. **[fear? The]** (Malone). *leave our* Q₁; *feare, the* Q₄. 83. **on...consist:** means peace. 92. **happily:** perchance. 94. **expecting:** threatening.

Per.   Arise, I pray you, rise.
We do not look for reverence but for love,
And harbourage for ourself, our ships, and men. 100
    Cle. The which when any shall not gratify,
Or pay you with unthankfulness in thought,
Be it our wives, our children, or ourselves,
The curse of heaven and men succeed their evils!
Till when, — the which I hope shall ne'er be
    seen, —   105
Your Grace is welcome to our town and us.
    Per. Which welcome we'll accept; feast here a
    while,
Until our stars that frown lend us a smile.
                                    [*Exeunt.*

[ACT II]

Enter GOWER.

Gow. Here have you seen a mighty king
His child, i-wis, to incest bring;
A better prince and benign lord,
That will prove awful both in deed and word
Be quiet then as men should be,   5
Till he hath pass'd necessity.
I'll show you those in troubles reign,
Losing a mite, a mountain gain.
The good in conversation,
To whom I give my benison,   10
Is still at Tarsus, where each man
Thinks all is writ he spoken can;
And, to remember what he does,
Build his statue to make him glorious.
But tidings to the contrary   15
Are brought your eyes; what need speak I?

DUMB SHOW.

Enter at one door Pericles *talking with* Cleon; *all
the train with them. Enter at another door a
Gentleman, with a letter to* Pericles; Pericles
shows the letter to Cleon; *gives the* Messenger *a
reward, and knights him. Exit* Pericles *at one
door, and* Cleon *at another.*

Good Helicane, that stay'd at home,
Not to eat honey like a drone
From others' labours; for though he strive
To killen bad, keep good alive,   20
And to fulfil his prince' desire,
[Sends word] of all that haps in Tyre:
How Thaliard came full bent with sin
And had intent to murder him;
And that in Tarsus was not best   25
Longer for him to make his rest.

He, doing so, put forth to seas,
Where when men been, there's seldom ease.
For now the wind begins to blow;
Thunder above and deeps below   30
Makes such unquiet, that the ship
Should house him safe is wreck'd and split;
And he, good prince, having all lost,
By waves from coast to coast is tost.
All perishen of man, of pelf,   35
Ne aught escapen but himself;
Till Fortune, tir'd with doing bad,
Threw him ashore, to give him glad:
And here he comes. What shall be next,
Pardon old Gower, — this longs the text.   40
                                    [*Exit.*]

[SCENE I. *Pentapolis. An open place by the
sea-side.*]

Enter PERICLES, *wet.*

Per. Yet cease your ire, you angry stars of heaven!
Wind, rain, and thunder, remember earthly man
Is but a substance that must yield to you;
And I, as fits my nature, do obey you.
Alas, the seas hath cast me on the rocks,   5
Wash'd me from shore to shore, and left [me]
    breath
Nothing to think on but ensuing death.
Let it suffice the greatness of your powers
To have bereft a prince of all his fortunes;
And having thrown him from your watery grave, 10
Here to have death in peace is all he'll crave.

Enter three FISHERMEN.

    1. Fish. What [ho,] Pilch!
    2. Fish. Ha, come and bring away the nets!
    1. Fish. What, Patch-breech, I say!
    3. Fish. What say you, master?   15
    1. Fish. Look how thou stirr'st now! Come
away, or I'll fetch thee with a wanion.
    3. Fish. Faith, master, I am thinking of the poor
men that were cast away before us even now.   20
    1. Fish. Alas, poor souls; it grieved my heart
to hear what pitiful cries they made to us to help
them, when, well-a-day, we could scarce help
ourselves.   24
    3. Fish. Nay, master, said not I as much when
I saw the porpoise how he bounc'd and tumbled?
They say they're half fish, half flesh. A plague
on them, they ne'er come but I look to be wash'd.
Master, I marvel how the fishes live in the sea. 30
    1. Fish. Why, as men do a-land; the great ones
eat up the little ones. I can compare our rich

Act II, Prol., 2. **i-wis:** certainly. 6. **pass'd necessity:** experienced the utmost. 9. **conversation:** behavior. 12. **writ:**
holy scripture. 13. **remember:** commemorate. 19. **for ... strive.** Probably corrupt. 22. [Sends word] (Malone).
Sav'd one Q. 32. **Should:** which should. 40. **longs:** belongs to.
Sc. i, 6. [me] (Malone). *my* Q. 12. [ho] (Malone). *to* Q. 17. **wanion:** vengeance.

misers to nothing so fitly as to a whale; 'a plays
and tumbles, driving the poor fry before him, and
at last devour them all at a mouthful. Such
whales have I heard on o' th' land, who never leave
gaping till they swallow'd the whole parish, church,
steeple, bells, and all.   38

Per. [*Aside.*] A pretty moral.

3. *Fish.* But, master, if I had been the sexton,
I would have been that day in the belfry.

2. *Fish.* Why, man?   42

3. *Fish.* Because he should have swallowed me
too; and when I had been in his belly, I would
have kept such a jangling of the bells, that he
should never have left till he cast bells, steeple,
church, and parish, up again. But if the good King
Simonides were of my mind, —   48

Per. [*Aside.*] Simonides!

3. *Fish.* We would purge the land of these drones,
that rob the bee of her honey.   51

Per. [*Aside.*] How from the finny subject of the
                                         sea
These fishers tell the infirmities of men;
And from their wat'ry empire recollect
All that may men approve or men detect!   55
Peace be at your labour, honest fishermen.

2. *Fish.* Honest! good fellow, what's that? If
it be a day fits you, [scratch't] out of the calendar,
and nobody look after it.

Per. May see the sea hath cast upon your
                                         coast —   60

2. *Fish.* What a drunken knave was the sea to
cast thee in our way!

Per. A man whom both the waters and the wind,
In that vast tennis-court, hath made the ball
For them to play upon, entreats you pity him.   65
He asks of you that never us'd to beg.

1. *Fish.* No, friend, cannot you beg? Here's
them in our country of Greece gets more with
begging than we can do with working.

2. *Fish.* Canst thou catch any fishes, then?

Per. I never practis'd it.   71

2. *Fish.* Nay, then thou wilt starve, sure; for
here's nothing to be got now-a-days unless thou
canst fish for't.

Per. What I have been I have forgot to know,
But what I am want teaches me to think on, —   76
A man throng'd up with cold. My veins are chill,
And have no more of life than may suffice
To give my tongue that heat to ask your help;
Which if you shall refuse, when I am dead,
For that I am a man, pray see me buried.   81

1. *Fish.* Die, [quoth-a]? Now gods forbid't
an I have a gown here! Come, put it on; keep
thee warm. Now, afore me, a handsome fellow!

Come, thou shalt go home, and we'll have flesh
for [holidays], fish for fasting-days, and, [moreo'er],
puddings and flap-jacks, and thou shalt be wel-
come.   87

Per. I thank you, sir.

2. *Fish.* Hark you, my friend. You said you
could not beg?   90

Per. I did but crave.

2. *Fish.* But crave! Then I'll turn craver too,
and so I shall scape whipping.

Per. Why, are [all your] beggars whipp'd,
then?   94

2. *Fish.* O, not all, my friend, not all; for if all
your beggars were whipp'd, I would wish no better
office than to be beadle. But, master, I'll go draw
up the net.   [*Exit with Third Fisherman.*]

Per. [*Aside.*] How well this honest mirth becomes their labour!   99

1. *Fish.* Hark you, sir, do you know where ye
are?

Per. Not well.

1. *Fish.* Why, I'll tell you. This is called Pentapolis, and our king the good Simonides.   104

Per. The good Simonides, do you call him?

1. *Fish.* Ay, sir; and he deserves so to be call'd
for his peaceable reign and good government.

Per. He is a happy king, since he gains from his
subjects the name of good by his government.
How far is his court distant from this shore?   111

1. *Fish.* Marry, sir, half a day's journey. And
I'll tell you, he hath a fair daughter, and to-morrow
is her birthday; and there are princes and knights
come from all parts of the world to joust and
tourney for her love.   116

Per. Were my fortunes equal to my desires, I
could wish to make one there.

1. *Fish.* O, sir, things must be as they may;
and what a man cannot get, he may lawfully deal
for — his wife's soul.   121

Re-enter SECOND *and* THIRD FISHERMEN, *drawing
                              up a net.*

2. *Fish.* Help, master, help! here's a fish hangs
in the net, like a poor man's right in the law; 'twill
hardly come out. Ha! bots on't, 'tis come at last,
and 'tis turned to a rusty armour.   125

Per. An armour, friends! I pray you, let me
                                         see it.
Thanks, Fortune, yet, that, after all [thy] crosses,
Thou giv'st me somewhat to repair myself;
And though it was mine own, part of my heritage,
Which my dead father did bequeath to me,   130
With this strict charge, even as he left his life,
"Keep it, my Pericles; it hath been a shield

54. **recollect:** gather up. 55. **detect:** expose, condemn. 58. **[scratch't]** (Singer). *search* Q. 77. **throng'd:** shrunk.
81. **pray.** *pray you* Q. 82. **[quoth-a]** (Malone). *he-tha* Q. 85. **[holidays]** (Malone). *all day* Q. 86. **[moreo'er]** (Farmer
conj.). *more; or* Q. 94. **[all your]** Q₄. *you* Q₁₋₃. 124. **bots:** maggots, i.e., a plague. 127. **[thy]** (Delius). Om. Q.

'Twixt me and death,"—and pointed to this [brace]—
"For that it sav'd me, keep it.   In like necessity —
The which the gods protect thee [from! — may't]
  defend thee."   135
It kept where I kept, I so dearly lov'd it;
Till the rough seas, that spares not any man,
Took it in rage, though calm'd have given't again.
I thank thee for't.   My shipwreck now's no ill,
Since I have here my [father's gift] in his will.   140
  1. Fish. What mean you, sir?
  Per. To beg of you, kind friends, this coat of worth,
For it was sometime target to a king;
I know it by this mark.   He lov'd me dearly,
And for his sake I wish the having of it;   145
And that you'd guide me to your sovereign's court,
Where with't I may appear a gentleman;
And if that ever my low fortune's better,   148
I'll pay your bounties; till then rest your debtor.
  1. Fish. Why, wilt thou tourney for the lady?
  Per. I'll show the virtue I have borne in arms.
  1. Fish. Why, do 'e take it, and the gods give
thee good on't!   153
  2. Fish. Ay, but hark you, my friend; 'twas
we that made up this garment through the rough
seams of the waters.   There are certain condole-
ments, certain vails.   I hope, sir, if you thrive,
you'll remember from whence you had [it].
  Per. Believe't, I will.   159
By your furtherance I am cloth'd in steel;
And, spite of all the [rapture] of the sea,
This jewel holds his building on my arm.
Unto thy value I will mount myself
Upon a courser, whose [delightful] steps
Shall make the gazer joy to see him tread.   165
Only, my friend, I yet am unprovided
Of a pair of bases.
  2. Fish. We'll sure provide.   Thou shalt have
my best gown to make thee a pair; and I'll bring
thee to the court myself.   170
  Per. Then honour be but a goal to my will,
This day I'll rise, or else add ill to ill.   [*Exeunt.*]

[SCENE II.   *The same.   A public way or platform
leading to the lists.   A pavilion by the side of it
for the reception of the King, Princess, Lords, etc.*]

Enter SIMONIDES, THAISA, [LORDS] *and* Attendants.
  Sim. Are the knights ready to begin the triumph?
  1. Lord. They are, my liege;
And stay your coming to present themselves.

  Sim. Return them, we are ready; and our
  daughter,
In honour of whose birth these triumphs are,   5
Sits here like beauty's child, whom nature gat
For men to see and, seeing, wonder at.
                                            [*Exit a Lord.*]
  Thai. It pleaseth you, my royal father, to express
My commendations great, whose merit's less.
  Sim. It's fit it should be so, for princes are
A model which heaven makes like to itself.   11
As jewels lose their glory if neglected,
So princes their renowns if not respected.
'Tis now your honour, daughter, to entertain
The labour of each knight in his device.   15
  Thai. Which, to preserve mine honour, I'll
  perform.

The First Knight *passes by [and his* Squire *presents
his shield to the* Princess].

  Sim. Who is the first that doth prefer himself?
  Thai. A knight of Sparta, my renowned father;
And the device he bears upon his shield
Is a black Ethiope reaching at the sun;   20
The word, "*Lux tua vita mihi.*"
  Sim. He loves you well that holds his life of
  you.

The Second Knight [*passes by*].

Who is the second that presents himself?
  Thai. A prince of Macedon, my royal father;
And the device he bears upon his shield   25
Is an arm'd knight that's conquer'd by a lady;
The motto thus, in Spanish, "*Piu por dulzura
que por fuerza.*"

The Third Knight [*passes by*].

  Sim. And [what's] the third?
  Thai.   The third of Antioch;
And his device, a wreath of chivalry;
The word, "*Me pompæ provexit apex.*"   30

The Fourth Knight [*passes by*].

  Sim. What is the fourth?
  Thai. A burning torch that's turned upside
  down;
The word, "*Quod me alit, me extinguit.*"
  Sim. Which shows that beauty hath his power
  and will,
Which can as well inflame as it can kill.   35

---

133. [brace] (Malone).   *prayse* Q. 135. [from! — may't] (Staunton). *Fame may* Q. 140. [father's gift] (Malone). *Father
gave* Q. 157. condolements. Blunder for *dole.*   vails: tips. 158. [it] (Malone).   *them* Q. 161. [rapture] (Rowe): seizure.
rupture Q. 162. building: i.e., fixed place. 163. Unto: suiting. 164. [delightful] F₄.   *delight* Q. 167. pair of bases:
mantle, hanging from the waist to the knee, apparently in two parts, worn on horseback.
Sc. ii, 1. Sim. The speeches of Simonides are headed *King* in Q. 4. Return: answer. daughter. So Malone. Q
adds *heere.* 14. entertain: receive, review. 15. device: emblem. 17. prefer: present. 21. Lux...mihi: Thy light is my
life. 27. Piu...fuerza: More by gentleness than by force. 28. [what's] Q₄.   *with* Q₁. 29. of chivalry: with a chivalric
motto. 30. Me...apex: The crown of honor has led me on. 33. Quod...extinguit: That which nourishes me kil's me.

The Fifth Knight [*passes by*].

Thai. The fifth, an hand environed with clouds,
Holding out gold that's by the touchstone tried;
The motto thus, "*Sic spectanda fides.*"

The Sixth Knight [*Pericles, passes by*].

Sim. And what's
The sixth and last, the which the knight himself 40
With such a graceful courtesy deliver'd?
  Thai. He seems to be a stranger; but his present
        is
A withered branch, that's only green at top;
The motto, "*In hac spe vivo.*"
  Sim. A pretty moral.   45
From the dejected state wherein he is,
He hopes by you his fortunes yet may flourish.
  1. Lord. He had need mean better than his out-
        ward show
Can any way speak in his just commend;
For by his rusty outside he appears   50
To have practis'd more the whipstock than the
        lance.
  2. Lord. He well may be a stranger, for he comes
To an honour'd triumph strangely furnished.
  3. Lord. And on set purpose let his armour rust
Until this day, to scour it in the dust.   55
  Sim. Opinion's but a fool, that makes us scan
The outward habit by the inward man.
But stay, the knights are coming.   We will with-
        draw
Into the gallery.   [*Exeunt.*]
                [*Great shouts within, and all cry,*
                       "The mean knight!"]

[SCENE III. *The same.   A hall of state: a banquet
                      prepared.*]

Enter SIMONIDES, [THAISA, MARSHAL, Lords,
        Attendants] *and* KNIGHTS, *from tilting.*

  Sim. Knights,
To say you're welcome were superfluous.
[To] place upon the volume of your deeds,
As in a title-page, your worth in arms,
Were more than you expect, or more than's fit,
Since every worth in show commends itself.   6
Prepare for mirth, for mirth becomes a feast.
You are princes and my guests.
  Thai. But you, my knight and guest;
To whom this wreath of victory I give,   10
And crown you king of this day's happiness.
  Per. 'Tis more by fortune, lady, than my merit.
  Sim. Call it by what you will, the day is yours;

And here, I hope, is none that envies it.
In framing an artist, Art hath thus decreed   15
To make some good, but others to exceed;
And you are her labour'd scholar.   Come, queen
        o' th' feast, —
For, daughter, so you are, — here take your place.
Marshal the rest as they deserve their grace.
  Knights. We are honour'd much by good Simon-
        ides.   20
  Sim. Your presence glads our days.   Honour
        we love;
For who hates honour hates the gods above.
  Marshal. Sir, yonder is your place.
  Per.   Some other is more fit.
  1. Knight. Contend not, sir; for we are gentlemen
[That] neither in our hearts nor outward eyes   25
Envies the great nor shall the low despise.
  Per. You are right courteous knights.
  Sim.   Sit, sir, sit.
[*Aside.*] By Jove, I wonder, that is king of
        thoughts,
These cates resist me, he not thought upon.
  Thai. [*Aside.*] By Juno, that is queen of mar-
        riage,   30
All viands that I eat do seem unsavoury,
Wishing him my meat. — Sure, he's a gallant
        gentleman.
  Sim. [*Aside.*]   He's but a country gentleman,
Has done no more than other knights have done,
Has broken a staff or so; so let it pass.   35
  Thai. [*Aside.*] To me he seems like diamond to
        glass.
  Per. [*Aside.*] [Yon king's] to me like to my father's
        picture,
Which tells [me] in that glory once he was;
Had princes sit like stars about his throne,
And he the sun for them to reverence;   40
None that beheld him but, like lesser lights,
Did vail their crowns to his supremacy;
Where now his [son's] like a glow-worm in the
        night,
The which hath fire in darkness, none in light;
Whereby I see that Time's the king of men: 45
He's both their parent, and he is their grave,
And gives them what he will, not what they crave.
  Sim. What, are you merry, knights?
  Knights. Who can be other in this royal presence?
  Sim. Here, with a cup that's stor'd unto the
        brim, —   50
As [you do] love, fill to your mistress' lips, —
We drink this health to you.
  Knights.   We thank your Grace.

---

38. *Sic ... fides:* Thus is faith to be tested.   40. **himself:** i.e., without a Squire.   41. **courtesy:** bow.   42. **present:** device presented.   44. *In ... vivo:* In this hope I live.   56. **scan:** judge.   57. **The ... man.** A case of inversion.
  Sc. iii, 3. **[To]** F4.   1 Q.   25. **[That]** *Have* Q.   28. **wonder:** marvel.   29. **cates ... me:** delicacies are distasteful to me.   37. **[Yon king's]** Q2.   *You Kings* Q1.   38. **[me]** Q4.   Om. Q1.   42. **vail:** lower.   43. **[son's]** (Malone).   *sonne* Q.   51. **[you do]** Q4.   *do you* Q1.

Sim. Yet pause a while;
Yon knight doth sit too melancholy,
As if the entertainment in our court   55
Had not a show might countervail his worth.
Note it not you, Thaisa?
 Thai.   What is't
To me, my father?
 Sim.   O, attend, my daughter.
Princes in this should live like gods above,
Who freely give to every one that come   60
To honour them;
And princes not doing so are like to gnats,
Which make a sound, but, kill'd, are wond'red at.
Therefore to make his entrance more sweet,
Here, say we drink this standing-bowl of wine
 to him.   65
 Thai. Alas, my father, it befits not me
Unto a stranger knight to be so bold.
He may my proffer take for an offence,
Since men take women's gifts for impudence.
 Sim. How!   70
Do as I bid you, or you'll move me else.
 Thai. [*Aside.*] Now, by the gods, he could
 not please me better.
 Sim. And furthermore tell him we desire to
 know of him
Of whence he is, his name, and parentage.
 Thai. The King my father, sir, has drunk to
 you, —   75
 Per. I thank him.
 Thai. Wishing it so much blood unto your life.
 Per. I thank both him and you, and pledge him
 freely.
 Thai. And further he desires to know of you
Of whence you are, your name, and parentage.   80
 Per. A gentleman of Tyre; my name, Pericles;
My education been in arts and arms;
Who, looking for adventures in the world,
Was by the rough seas reft of ships and men,
And after shipwreck driven upon this shore.   85
 Thai. He thanks your Grace; names himself
 Pericles,
A gentleman of Tyre,
Who only by misfortune of the seas
Bereft of ships and men, cast on this shore.
 Sim. Now, by the gods, I pity his misfortune,
And will awake him from his melancholy.   91
Come, gentlemen, we sit too long on trifles,
And waste the time, which looks for other revels.
Even in your armours, as you are address'd,
Will [very] well become a soldier's dance.   95
I will not have excuse, with saying this
Loud music is too harsh for ladies' heads,

Since they love men in arms as well as beds.
         [*They dance.*
So, this was well ask'd, 'twas so well perform'd.
Come, sir,   100
Here is a lady that wants breathing too;
And I have heard you knights of Tyre
Are excellent in making ladies trip,
And that their measures are as excellent.
 Per. In those that practice them they are, my
 lord.   105
 Sim. O, that's as much as you would be denied
Of your fair courtesy.   [*They dance.*
    Unclasp, unclasp:
Thanks, gentlemen, to all; all have done well,
[*To Per.*] But you the best. — Pages and lights, to
 conduct
These knights unto their several lodgings! — [*To
 Per.*] Yours, sir,   110
We have given order to be next our own.
 Per. I am at your Grace's pleasure.
 [*Sim.*] Princes, it is too late to talk of love,
And that's the mark I know you level at.
Therefore each one betake him to his rest;   115
To-morrow all for speeding do their best. [*Exeunt.*

[SCENE IV. *Tyre. A room in the Governor's
house.*]

Enter HELICANUS *and* ESCANES.

 Hel. No, Escanes, know this of me,
Antiochus from incest lived not free;
For which, the most high gods not minding longer
To withhold the vengeance that they had in store,
Due to this heinous capital offence,   5
Even in the height and pride of all his glory,
When he was seated in a chariot
Of an inestimable value, and his daughter with him,
A fire from heaven came and shrivell'd up
[Their] bodies, even to loathing; for they so stunk,
That all those eyes ador'd them ere their fall   11
Scorn now their hand should give them burial.
 Esca. 'Twas very strange.
 Hel.   And yet but justice; for though
This king were great, his greatness was no guard
To bar heaven's shaft, but sin had his reward.   15
 Esca. 'Tis very true.

Enter two or three LORDS.

 1. Lord. See, not a man in private conference
Or council has respect with him but he.
 2. Lord. It shall no longer grieve without reproof.
 3. Lord. And curs'd be he that will not second
 it.

---

56. **countervail:** equal. 65. **standing-bowl:** bowl on a foot or stem. 94. **address'd:** equipped. 95. **[very]** F₃. Om. Q.
101. **breathing:** exercise. 106–107. **that's ... courtesy:** i.e., that's as much as to deny your own courtly skill. 116. **for speed-ing:** to be successful.
Sc. iv, 10. **[Their]** (Steevens). *those* Q. 19. **grieve:** i.e., offend us.

1. Lord. Follow me, then. Lord Helicane, a
   word.   21
Hel. With me? and welcome. Happy day, my
   lords.
1. Lord. Know that our griefs are risen to the top,
And now at length they overflow their banks.
   Hel. Your griefs! For what? Wrong not your
   prince you love.   25
   1. Lord. Wrong not yourself, then, noble Heli-
   cane;
But if the Prince do live, let us salute him,
Or know what ground's made happy by his breath.
If in the world he live, we'll seek him out;
If in his grave he rest, we'll find him there;   30
And be resolv'd he lives to govern us,
Or, dead, give's cause to mourn his funeral,
And leave us to our free election.
   2. Lord. Whose [death's] indeed the strongest in
   our censure;
And knowing this kingdom is without a head, — 35
Like goodly buildings left without a roof
Soon fall to ruin, — your noble self,
That best know how to rule and how to reign,
We thus submit unto, — our sovereign.
   All. Live, noble Helicane!   40
   Hel. [By] honour's cause, forbear your suffrages.
If that you love Prince Pericles, forbear.
Take I your wish, I leap into the seas,
Where's hourly trouble for a minute's ease.
A twelvemonth longer let me entreat you to   45
Forbear the absence of your king;
If in which time expir'd he not return,
I shall with aged patience bear your yoke.
But if I cannot win you to this love,
Go search like nobles, like noble subjects,   50
And in your search spend your adventurous worth;
Whom if you find, and win unto return,
You shall like diamonds sit about his crown.
   1. Lord. To wisdom he's a fool that will not yield;
And since Lord Helicane enjoineth us,   55
We with our travels will endeavour [thus].
   Hel. Then you love us, we you, and we'll clasp
   hands.
When peers thus knit, a kingdom ever stands.
                            [Exeunt.

[SCENE V. *Pentapolis. A room in the palace.*]

Enter SIMONIDES, *reading of a letter, at one
   door: the* KNIGHTS *meet him.*

   1. Knight. Good morrow to the good Simonides.
   Sim. Knights, from my daughter this I let you
   know,
That for this twelvemonth she'll not undertake
A married life.

Her reason to herself is only known,   5
Which from her by no means can I get.
   2. Knight. May we not get access to her, my
   lord?
   Sim. Faith, by no means; she hath so strictly
   tied
Her to her chamber that 'tis impossible.
One twelve moons more she'll wear Diana's livery;
This by the eye of Cynthia hath she vow'd,   11
And on her virgin honour will not break it.
   3. Knight. Loath to bid farewell, we take our
   leaves.   *[Exeunt Knights.]*
   Sim. So,
They are well dispatch'd; now to my daughter's
   letter.   15
She tells me here, she'll wed the stranger knight,
Or never more to view nor day nor light.
'Tis well, mistress; your choice agrees with mine;
I like that well. Nay, how absolute she's in't,
Not minding whether I dislike or no!   20
Well, I do commend her choice;
And will no longer have it be delay'd.
Soft! here he comes. I must dissemble it.

Enter PERICLES.

   Per. All fortune to the good Simonides!
   Sim. To you as much, sir! I am beholding to
   you   25
For your sweet music this last night. I do
Protest my ears were never better fed
With such delightful pleasing harmony.
   Per. It is your Grace's pleasure to commend;
Not my desert.
   Sim.   Sir, you are Music's master.   30
   Per. The worst of all her scholars, my good lord.
   Sim. Let me ask you one thing:
What do you think of my daughter, sir?
   Per. A most virtuous princess.
   Sim. And she is fair too, is she not?   35
   Per. As a fair day in summer; wondrous fair.
   Sim. Sir, my daughter thinks very well of you;
Ay, so well, that you must be her master,
And she will be your scholar; therefore look to it.
   Per. I am unworthy for her schoolmaster.   40
   Sim. She thinks not so; peruse this writing else.
   Per. [*Aside.*] What's here?
A letter, that she loves the knight of Tyre!
'Tis the King's subtilty to have my life.
O, seek not to entrap me, gracious lord,   45
A stranger and distressed gentleman,
That never aim'd so high to love your daughter,
But bent all offices to honour her.
   Sim. Thou hast bewitch'd my daughter, and
   thou art
A villain.   50

---

34. **[death's]** (Malone). *death* Q. **strongest:** likeliest. **censure:** opinion. 36. **Like:** as. 41. **[By]** (Dyce). *Try* Q.
46. **Forbear:** bear with. 56. **[thus]** Edd. Om. Q. *it* Malone.

Per.   By the gods, I have not.
Never did thought of mine levy offence;
Nor never did my actions yet commence
A deed might gain her love or your displeasure.
   Sim.   Traitor, thou liest.
   Per.   Traitor!
   Sim.   Ay, traitor.
   Per.   Even in his throat — unless it be the
     King —   56
That calls me traitor, I return the lie.
   Sim. [*Aside.*] Now, by the gods, I do applaud
his courage.
   Per.   My actions are as noble as my thoughts,
That never relish'd of a base descent.   60
I came unto your court for honour's cause,
And not to be a rebel to her state;
And he that otherwise accounts of me,
This sword shall prove he's honour's enemy.
   Sim.   No?   65
Here comes my daughter, she can witness it.

         Enter THAISA.

   Per.   Then, as you are as virtuous as fair,
Resolve your angry father if my tongue
Did e'er solicit, or my hand subscribe
To any syllable that made love to you.   70
   Thai.   Why, sir, say if you had,
Who takes offence at that would make me glad?
   Sim.   Yea, mistress, are you so peremptory?
[*Aside.*] I am glad on't with all my heart. —
I'll tame you; I'll bring you in subjection.   75
Will you, not having my consent,
Bestow your love and your affections
Upon a stranger? [*aside*] who, for aught I know,
May be, nor can I think the contrary,
As great in blood as I myself. —   80
Therefore hear you, mistress: either frame
Your will to mine, — and you, sir, hear you,
Either be rul'd by me, — or I will make you —
Man and wife.
Nay, come, your hands and lips must seal it too; 85
And being join'd, I'll thus your hopes destroy;
And for [a] further grief, — God give you joy!
What, are you both pleas'd?
   Thai.   Yes, if you love me, sir.
   Per.   Even as my life my blood that fosters it.
   Sim.   What, are you both agreed?   90
   Both.   Yes, if't please your Majesty.
   Sim.   It pleaseth me so well that I will see you
     wed;
Then with what haste you can, get you to bed.
                        [*Exeunt.*

[ACT III]

Enter GOWER.

   Gow.   Now sleep y-slaked hath the rout.
No din but snores [the house about],
Made louder by the o'er-fed breast
Of this most pompous marriage-feast.
The cat, with eyne of burning coal,   5
Now couches ['fore] the mouse's hole;
And crickets sing at the oven's mouth,
[E'er] the blither for their drouth.
Hymen hath brought the bride to bed,
Where, by the loss of maidenhead,   10
A babe is moulded.   Be attent,
And time that is so briefly spent
With your fine fancies quaintly [eche].
What's dumb in show I'll plain with speech.

[DUMB SHOW.]

Enter Pericles *and* Simonides, *at one door, with*
   Attendants.   *A* Messenger *meets them, kneels,*
   and gives Pericles *a letter.*   Pericles *shows it*
   Simonides; *the Lords kneel to him.   Then enter*
   Thaisa *with child, with* Lychorida *a nurse.   The*
   King *shows her the letter; she rejoices.   She and*
   Pericles *take leave of her father, and depart* [*with*
   Lychorida *and their Attendants.   Then exeunt*
   Simonides *and the rest*].

By many a dern and painful perch,   15
Of Pericles the careful search,
By the four opposing [coigns]
Which the world together joins,
Is made with all due diligence
That horse and sail and high expense   20
Can stead the quest.   At last from Tyre,
Fame answering the most strange inquire,
To the court of King Simonides
Are letters brought, the tenour these:
Antiochus and his daughter dead,   25
The men of Tyrus on the head
Of Helicanus would set on
The crown of Tyre, but he will none.
The mutiny he there hastes t' oppress;
Says to 'em, if King Pericles   30
Come not home in twice six moons,
He, obedient to their dooms,
Will take the crown.   The sum of this,
Brought hither to Pentapolis,
Y-ravished the regions round,   35
And every one with claps can sound,
"Our heir-apparent is a king!
Who dreamt, who thought of such a thing?"

   Sc. v, 60. **relish'd:** smacked.   68. **Resolve:** satisfy.   87. [a] (Malone).   Om. Q.   93. **Then** (Malone).   *And then* Q.
   Act III, Prol., 1. **rout:** company (of revellers).   2. [the house about] (Malone).   *about the house* Q.   6. ['fore] (Malone conj.).
from Q.   8. [E'er] (Dyce conj.)   *Are* Q.   13. [eche] (Malone); eke out.   *each* Q.   14. **plain:** explain.   15. **dern:** dark, drear.
perch: measure of land (5½ yards).   17. [coigns] (Rowe): corners.   *Crignes* Q.   21. **stead:** aid.   22. **Fame:** report.
strange: far-flung.   32. **dooms:** judgments.   36. **can:** began to.

Brief, he must hence depart to Tyre:
His queen with child makes her desire — 40
Which who shall cross? — along to go.
Omit we all their dole and woe.
Lychorida, her nurse, she takes,
And so to sea. Their vessel shakes
On Neptune's billow; half the flood 45
Hath their keel cut. But [fortune's mood]
Varies again. The grisled north
Disgorges such a tempest forth,
That, as a duck for life that dives,
So up and down the poor ship drives. 50
The lady shrieks, and well-a-near
Does fall in travail with her fear;
And what ensues in this fell storm
Shall for itself itself perform.
I nill relate, action may 55
Conveniently the rest convey,
Which might not what by me is told.
In your imagination hold
This stage the ship, upon whose deck
The sea-tost Pericles appears to speak. [*Exit.* 60

[SCENE I.]

Enter PERICLES, *on shipboard.*

Per. [Thou] god of this great vast, rebuke these surges,
Which wash both heaven and hell; and thou that hast
Upon the winds command, bind them in brass,
Having call'd them from the deep! O, still
Thy deaf'ning, dreadful thunders; gently quench 5
Thy nimble, sulphurous flashes! — O, how, Lychorida,
How does my queen? — [Thou stormest] venomously;
Wilt thou spit all thyself? The seaman's whistle
Is as a whisper in the ears of death,
Unheard. — Lychorida! — Lucina, O 10
Divinest patroness, and [midwife] gentle
To those that cry by night, convey thy deity
Aboard our dancing boat; make swift the pangs
Of my queen's travails!

Enter LYCHORIDA [*with an Infant*].
Now, Lychorida!
Lyc. Here is a thing too young for such a place,
Who, if it had conceit, would die, as I 16
Am like to do. Take in your arms this piece
Of your dead queen.

Per. How, how, Lychorida?
Lyc. Patience, good sir; do not assist the storm.
Here's all that is left living of your queen, 20
A little daughter. For the sake of it
Be manly, and take comfort.
Per. O you gods!
Why do you make us love your goodly gifts
And snatch them straight away? We here below
Recall not what we give, and therein may 25
Use honour with you.
Lyc. Patience, good sir,
Even for this charge.
Per. Now, mild may be thy life!
For a more blust'rous birth had never babe.
Quiet and gentle thy conditions! for
Thou art the rudeliest welcome to this world 30
That ever was prince's child. Happy what follows!
Thou hast as chiding a nativity
As fire, air, water, earth, and heaven can make
To herald thee from the womb. Even at the first
Thy loss is more than can thy portage quit 35
With all thou canst find here. Now, the good gods
Throw their best eyes upon't!

Enter two SAILORS.

1. Sail. What courage, sir? God save you!
Per. Courage enough. I do not fear the flaw;
It hath done to me the worst. Yet for the love
Of this poor infant, this fresh-new sea-farer, 41
I would it would be quiet.
1. Sail. Slack the bolins there! Thou wilt not, wilt thou? Blow, and split thyself.
2. Sail. But sea-room, an the brine and cloudy billow kiss the moon, I care not. 46
1. Sail. Sir, your queen must overboard. The sea works high, the wind is loud, and will not lie till the ship be clear'd of the dead.
Per. That's your superstition. 50
1. Sail. Pardon us, sir; with us at sea it hath been still observed, and we are strong in [custom]. Therefore briefly yield her; for she must overboard straight.
Per. As you think meet. Most wretched queen!
Lyc. Here she lies, sir. 56
Per. A terrible childbed hast thou had, my dear;
No light, no fire. Th' unfriendly elements
Forgot thee utterly; nor have I time
To give thee hallow'd to thy grave, but straight
Must cast thee, scarcely coffin'd, in [the ooze]; 61
Where, for a monument upon thy bones
[And aye-remaining] lamps, the belching whale

45–46. half ... cut: they have gone half way. 46. [fortune's mood] (Malone). *fortune mou'd* Q. 47. grisled: grisly. 51. well-a-near: alas. 55. nill: will not. 57. Which ... not: i.e., though action could not represent. Sc. i, 1. [Thou] (Rowe). *The* Q. vast: expanse. 7–8. [Thou stormest] (Dyce). *then storme* Q. 11. [midwife] (Malone). *my wife* Q. 16. conceit: understanding. 26. Use: contend in. 27. charge: care (i.e., the baby). 29. conditions: circumstances. 35. can ... quit: thy earnings can make up for. portage: seaman's wages. 39. flaw: squall. 43. bolins: bowlines. 52. [custom] (Boswell conj.). *easterne* Q. 53–54. for ... straight. Follows *meet* (l. 55) in Q. Corrected by Malone. 61. [the ooze] (Malone): bed of the sea. *oare* Q. 63. [And aye-remaining] (Steevens). *The ayre remaining* Q.

And humming water must o'erwhelm thy corpse
Lying with simple shells.   O Lychorida,   65
Bid Nestor bring me spices, ink and [paper],
My casket and my jewels; and bid Nicander
Bring me the satin coffin.   Lay the babe
Upon the pillow.   Hie thee, whiles I say
A priestly farewell to her.   Suddenly, woman.   70

[*Exit Lychorida.*]

2. Sail. Sir, we have a chest beneath the hatches,
caulk'd and bitumed ready.
   Per. I thank thee.   Mariner, say what coast is
this?
   2. Sail. We are near Tarsus.
   Per. Thither, gentle mariner,   75
Alter thy course for Tyre.   When canst thou reach
it?
   2. Sail. By break of day, if the wind cease.
   Per. O, make for Tarsus!
There will I visit Cleon, for the babe
Cannot hold out to Tyrus.   There I'll leave it   80
At careful nursing.   Go thy ways, good mariner.
I'll bring the body present.   [*Exeunt.*

[SCENE II. *Ephesus.   A room in Cerimon's
house.*]

Enter CERIMON, *with a* SERVANT [*and some
Persons who have been shipwrecked*].

   Cer. Philemon, ho!

Enter PHILEMON.

   Phil. Doth my lord call?
   Cer. Get fire and meat for these poor men.
'T has been a turbulent and stormy night.
   Serv. I have been in many; but such a night as
this   5
Till now I ne'er endured.
   Cer. Your master will be dead ere you return.
There's nothing can be minist'red to nature
That can recover him.   [*To Philemon.*]   Give this
to the 'pothecary,
And tell me how it works.

[*Exeunt all but Cerimon.*]

Enter two GENTLEMEN.

   1. Gent.   Good morrow.   10
   2. Gent. Good morrow to your lordship.
   Cer.   Gentlemen,
Why do you stir so early?
   1. Gent. Sir,
Our lodgings, standing bleak upon the sea,
Shook as the earth did quake;   15
The very principals did seem to rend,

And all to topple.   Pure surprise and fear
Made me to quit the house.
   2. Gent. That is the cause we trouble you so early;
'Tis not our husbandry.
   Cer.   O, you say well.   20
   1. Gent. But I much marvel that your lordship,
having
Rich tire about you, should at these early hours
Shake off the golden slumber of repose.
'Tis most strange
Nature should be so conversant with pain,   25
Being thereto not compelled.
   Cer.   I hold it ever
Virtue and cunning were endowments greater
Than nobleness and riches.   Careless heirs
May the two latter darken and expend,
But immortality attends the former,   30
Making a man a god.   'Tis known, I ever
Have studied physic, through which secret art,
By turning o'er authorities, I have,
Together with my practice, made familiar
To me and to my aid the blest infusions   35
That dwells in vegetives, in metals, stones;
And [I] can speak of the disturbances
That Nature works, and of her cures; which doth
give me
A more content in course of true delight
Than to be thirsty after tottering honour,   40
Or tie my pleasure up in silken bags,
To please the fool and Death.
   2. Gent. Your honour has through Ephesus
pour'd forth
Your charity, and hundreds call themselves
Your creatures, who by you have been restor'd;   45
And not your knowledge, your personal pain, but even
Your purse, still open, hath built Lord Cerimon
Such strong renown as time shall never [raze].

Enter two or three [SERVANTS] *with a chest.*

   [*1.*] *Serv.* So; lift there.
   Cer.   What is that?
   [*1.*] *Serv.*   Sir, even now
Did the sea toss up upon our shore this chest.   50
'Tis of some wreck.
   Cer.   Set 't down, let's look upon't.
   2. Gent. 'Tis like a coffin, sir.
   Cer.   Whate'er it be,
'Tis wondrous heavy.   Wrench it open straight.
If the sea's stomach be o'ercharg'd with gold,   54
'Tis a good constraint of fortune it belches upon us.
   2. Gent. 'Tis so, my lord.
   Cer.   How close 'tis caulk'd and [bitum'd]!
Did the sea cast it up?

---

66. [paper] Q₂. *Taper* Q₁.   68. coffin. Malone reads *coffer*.   70. Suddenly: swiftly.   72. bitumed: pitched.
   Sc. ii, 16. principals: chief supports.   20. husbandry: thrift.   21–22. having ... tire: living in luxury (?).   25. conversant with pain: willing to take trouble.   27. cunning: skill.   35. aid: assistants.   36. vegetives: herbs.   37. [I] (Malone).
Om. Q.   48. [raze] (Dyce).   Om. Q.   57. [bitum'd] (Malone).   Cf. III.i.72.   *bottomed* Q.

[*1.*] *Serv.* I never saw so huge a billow, sir,
As toss'd it upon shore.
    Cer.   Wrench it open.
Soft! it smells most sweetly in my sense.   60
  2. Gent. A delicate odour.
  Cer. As ever hit my nostril. So, up with it.
O you most potent gods! what's here? A corse!
  1. Gent. Most strange.
  Cer. Shrouded in cloth of state; balm'd and en-
    treasur'd   65
With full bags of spices! A passport too!
Apollo, perfect me in the characters!
                  [*Reads from a scroll.*]
  "Here I give to understand,
  If e'er this coffin drives a-land,
  I, King Pericles, have lost   70
  This queen, worth all our mundane cost.
  Who finds her, give her burying;
  She was the daughter of a king.
  Besides this treasure for a fee,
  The gods requite his charity!"   75
If thou liv'st, Pericles, thou hast a heart
That even cracks for woe! This chanc'd to-night.
  2. Gent. Most likely, sir.
  Cer.   Nay, certainly to-night;
For look how fresh she looks! They were too rough
That threw her in the sea. Make a fire within.
Fetch hither all my boxes in my closet.   81
                  [*Exit a Servant.*]
Death may usurp on nature many hours
And yet the fire of life kindle again
The o'erpress'd spirits. I heard of an Egyptian
That had nine hours lien dead,   85
Who was by good appliance recovered.

    Re-enter one [*with boxes,*] *napkins, and fire.*

Well said, well said. — The fire and cloths.
The rough and woeful music that we have,
Cause it to sound, beseech you.
The [vial] once more. How thou stirr'st, thou block!
The music there! I pray you, give her air.   91
Gentlemen,
This queen will live. Nature awakes; a warmth
[Breathes] out of her. She hath not been entranc'd
Above five hours. See how she gins to blow   95
Into life's flower again!
  1. Gent.   The heavens
Through you increase our wonder and set up
Your fame for ever.
  Cer.   She is alive; behold,
Her eyelids, cases to those heavenly jewels
Which Pericles hath lost, begin to part   100
Their fringes of bright gold. The diamonds
Of a most praised water doth appear

To make the world twice rich. Live, and make
Us weep to hear your fate, fair creature,
Rare as you seem to be.   [*She moves.*
  Thai.   O dear Diana,   105
Where am I? Where's my lord? What world is
  this?
  2. Gent. Is not this strange?
  1. Gent.   Most rare.
  Cer.   Hush, my gentle neighbours!
Lend me your hands. To the next chamber bear
  her.
Get linen. Now this matter must be look'd to,
For her relapse is mortal. Come, come;   110
And Æsculapius guide us!
           [*They carry her away. Exeunt omnes.*

[SCENE III. *Tarsus. A room in Cleon's house.*]

Enter PERICLES, CLEON, DIONYZA [*and* LYCHORIDA,
      with MARINA *in her arms*].

  Per. Most honour'd Cleon, I must needs be gone.
My twelve months are expir'd, and Tyrus stands
In a litigious peace. You and your lady
Take from my heart all thankfulness! The gods
Make up the rest upon you!   5
  Cle. Your [shafts] of fortune, though they [hurt]
  you mortally,
Yet glance full [wand'ringly] on us.
  Dion.   O your sweet queen!
That the strict fates had pleas'd you had brought
  her hither
To have bless'd mine eyes with her!
  Per.   We cannot but obey
The powers above us. Could I rage and roar   10
As doth the sea she lies in, yet the end
Must be as 'tis. My gentle babe Marina, whom,
For she was born at sea I have nam'd so, here
I charge your charity withal, leaving her
The infant of your care; beseeching you   15
To give her princely training, that she may be
Manner'd as she is born.
  Cle.   Fear not, my lord, but think
Your Grace, that fed my country with your corn,
For which the people's prayers still fall upon you,
Must in your child be thought on. If neglection   20
Should therein make me vile, the common body,
By you reliev'd, would force me to my duty;
But if to that my nature need a spur,
The gods revenge it upon me and mine
To the end of generation!   25
  Per.   I believe you.
Your honour and your goodness teach me to't
Without your vows. Till she be married, madam,
By bright Diana, whom we honour, all

---

  67. **characters:** writing. 87. **Well said:** well done. 90. **[vial]** Q₄. *Violl* Q₁. 93-94. **awakes ... [Breathes]** (Malone).
awakes a warmth breath Q. 102. **water:** lustre. 110. **is:** would be.
  Sc. iii, 6. **[shafts] ... [hurt]** (Steevens). *shakes ... hant* Q. 7. **[wand'ringly]** (Steevens). *wondringly* Q.

[Unscissor'd] shall this hair of mine remain,
Though I show [ill] in't.   So I take my leave.   30
Good madam, make me blessed in your care
In bringing up my child.
 Dion.   I have one myself,
Who shall not be more dear to my respect
Than yours, my lord.
 Per.   Madam, my thanks and prayers.
 Cle. We'll bring your Grace e'en to the edge o'
  th' shore,   35
Then give you up to the mask'd Neptune and
The gentlest winds of heaven.
 Per.   I will embrace
Your offer.   Come, dearest madam.   O, no tears,
Lychorida, no tears.
Look to your little mistress, on whose grace 40
You may depend hereafter. Come, my lord. [*Exeunt.*]

[SCENE IV. *Ephesus.   A room in Cerimon's house.*]

Enter CERIMON *and* THAISA.

 Cer. Madam, this letter and some certain jewels
Lay with you in your coffer, which are
At your command.   Know you the character?
 Thai. It is my lord's.
That I was shipp'd at sea I well remember, 5
Even on my [eaning] time; but whether there
Delivered, by the holy gods,
I cannot rightly say.   But since King Pericles,
My wedded lord, I ne'er shall see again,
A vestal livery will I take me to,   10
And never more have joy.
 Cer. Madam, if this you purpose as ye speak,
Diana's temple is not distant far,
Where you may abide till your date expire.
Moreover, if you please, a niece of mine 15
Shall there attend you.
 Thai. My recompense is thanks, that's all;
Yet my good will is great, though the gift small.
             [*Exeunt.*

[ACT IV]

Enter GOWER.

 Gow. Imagine Pericles arriv'd at Tyre,
Welcom'd and settled to his own desire.
His woeful queen we leave at Ephesus,
Unto Diana there 's a votaress.
Now to Marina bend your mind,   5
Whom our fast-growing scene must find
At Tarsus, and by Cleon train'd
In music, letters; who hath gain'd

Of education all the grace,
Which makes [her] both the [heart] and place 10
Of general wonder.   But, alack,
That monster Envy, oft the wrack
Of earned praise, Marina's life
Seeks to take off by treason's knife.
And in this kind [hath our Cleon   15
One daughter, and a wench full grown],
Even [ripe] for marriage-[rite].   This maid
Hight Philoten; and it is said
For certain in our story, she
Would ever with Marina be.   20
Be't when they weav'd the sleided silk
With fingers long, small, white as milk;
Or when she would with sharp needle wound
The cambric, which she made more sound
By hurting it; or when to th' lute   25
She sung, and made the [night-bird] mute
That still records with moan; or when
She would with rich and constant pen
Vail to her mistress Dian; still
This Philoten contends in skill   30
With absolute Marina: so
[With the dove of Paphos might the crow]
Vie feathers white.   Marina gets
All praises, which are paid as debts,
And not as given.   This so darks   35
In Philoten all graceful marks,
That Cleon's wife, with envy rare,
A present murderer does prepare
For good Marina, that her daughter
Might stand peerless by this slaughter. 40
The sooner her vile thoughts to stead,
Lychorida, our nurse, is dead;
And cursed Dionyza hath
The pregnant instrument of wrath
Prest for this blow.   The unborn event 45
I do commend to your content;
Only I [carry] winged time
Post on the lame feet of my rhyme;
Which never could I so convey.
Unless your thoughts went on my way. 50
Dionyza does appear,
With Leonine, a murderer.   [*Exit.*

[SCENE I. *Tarsus.   An open place near the seashore.*]

Enter DIONYZA *with* LEONINE.

 Dion. Thy oath remember; thou hast sworn to
  do't.
'Tis but a blow, which never shall be known.

---

29. [Unscissor'd] (Steevens).   *unsistred* Q.   30. [ill] (Malone conj.).   *will* Q.   36. **mask'd Neptune:** sea, wearing the mask of calm.
 Sc. iv, 6. [eaning] **time:** time of delivery.   [eaning] F₃.   *learning* Q.
 Act IV, Prol., 4. **'s:** as.   10. [her] ... [heart] (Malone).   *hie ... art* Q.   15–16. [hath ... grown] (Malone).   *our Cleon hath ... full growne wench* Q.   17. [ripe] Q₂.   *right* Q₁.   [rite] (Singer).   *sight* Q.   21. **sleided:** raw.   26. [night-bird] (Malone).   *night bed* Q.   29. **Vail:** do homage.   31. **absolute:** perfect.   32. [With ... crow] (Malone conj.).   *The Doue ... with the crow* Q.   35. **given:** i.e., unearned gifts.   44. **pregnant:** ready, apt.   45. **Prest:** ready.   47. [carry] (Steevens).   *carried* Q.

Thou canst not do a thing in the world so soon
To yield thee so much profit. Let not conscience,
Which is but cold, [inflaming love i' thy] bosom, 5
Inflame too nicely; nor let pity, which
Even women have cast off, melt thee, but be
A soldier to thy purpose.
  Leon. I will do't; but yet she is a goodly crea-
    ture.   9
  Dion. The fitter, then, the gods should have her.
Here she comes weeping for her only mistress'
death. Thou art resolv'd?
  Leon. I am resolv'd.

  Enter MARINA, *with a basket of flowers.*

  Mar. No, I will rob Tellus of her weed,
To strew thy green with flowers. The yellows,
    blues,   15
The purple violets, and marigolds
Shall as a carpet hang upon thy grave
While summer-days doth last. Ay me! poor maid,
Born in a tempest when my mother died,
This world to me is [like] a lasting storm,   20
Whirring me from my friends.
  Dion. How now, Marina! why do you keep alone?
How chance my daughter is not with you? Do not
Consume your blood with sorrowing; [you have]
A nurse of me. Lord, how your favour's chang'd
With this unprofitable woe!   26
Come, give me your flowers. [Near the sea margent]
Walk with Leonine; the air is quick there,
And it pierces and sharpens the stomach. Come,
Leonine, take her by the arm, walk with her.   30
  Mar. No, I pray you;
I'll not bereave you of your servant.
  Dion.   Come, come;
I love the King your father and yourself
With more than foreign heart. We every day
Expect him here. When he shall come and find   35
Our paragon to all reports thus blasted,
He will repent the breadth of his great voyage;
Blame both my lord and me that we have taken
No care to your best courses. Go, I pray you,
Walk, and be cheerful once again; reserve   40
That excellent complexion, which did steal
The eyes of young and old. Care not for me;
I can go home alone.
  Mar.   Well, I will go;
But yet I have no desire to it.
  Dion. Come, come, I know 'tis good for you.   45
Walk half an hour, Leonine, at the least.
Remember what I have said.
  Leon.   I warrant you, madam.

  Dion. I'll leave you, my sweet lady, for a while.
Pray, walk softly, do not heat your blood.   49
What! I must have a care of you.
  Mar.   My thanks, sweet madam.
                                    [*Exit Dionyza.*]
Is this wind westerly that blows?
  Leon.   South-west.
  Mar. When I was born, the wind was north.
  Leon.   Was't so?
  Mar. My father, as nurse says, did never fear,
But cried "Good seamen!" to the sailors, galling
His kingly hands haling ropes;   55
And, clasping to the mast, endured a sea
That almost burst the deck, —
  Leon. When was this?
  Mar. When I was born;
Never was waves nor wind more violent; —   60
And from the ladder-tackle washes off
A canvas-climber. "Ha!" says one, "wilt out?"
And with a dropping industry they skip
From [stem] to stern. The boatswain whistles, and
The master calls, and trebles their confusion.   65
  Leon. Come, say your prayers.
  Mar. What mean you?
  Leon. If you require a little space for prayer,
I grant it. Pray, but be not tedious;
For the gods are quick of ear, and I am sworn   70
To do my work with haste.
  Mar.   Why will you kill me?
  Leon. To satisfy my lady.
  Mar. Why would she have me kill'd?
Now, as I can remember, by my troth,
I never did her hurt in all my life.   75
I never spake bad word, nor did ill turn
To any living creature. Believe me, la,
I never kill'd a mouse, nor hurt a fly,
Aye, trod upon a worm against my will,
But I wept for it. How have I offended,   80
Wherein my death might yield her any profit,
Or my life imply her any danger?
  Leon. My commission
Is not to reason of the deed, but do't.
  Mar. You will not do't for all the world, I
    hope.
You are well favour'd, and your looks foreshow   86
You have a gentle heart. I saw you lately
When you caught hurt in parting two that fought;
Good sooth, it show'd well in you. Do so now.
Your lady seeks my life; come you between,   90
And save poor me, the weaker.
  Leon.   I am sworn,
And will dispatch.

Sc. i, 5. [inflaming ... thy] (Knight). *in flaming, thy love bosome* Q. 6. **nicely:** scrupulously. 14. **Tellus:** Earth. **weed:** garment. 15. **green:** grave. 20. [like] Q4. Om. Q1. 21. **Whirring:** sweeping. 24. **consume ... sorrowing.** Each sigh supposedly cost the heart a drop of blood. [you have] Q4. *Have you* Q1. 25. **favour's:** face is. 27. [Near ... margent]. *ere ... marre it* Q. *On ... margent* (Hudson). 28. **quick:** bracing. 29. **stomach:** spirits. 40. **reserve:** guard. 63. **dropping:** dripping. 64. [stem] (Malone). *sterne* Q.

Enter PIRATES.

1. Pirate. Hold, villain!   [*Leonine runs away.*]
2. Pirate. A prize! a prize!
3. Pirate. Half-part, mates, half-part.   95
Come, let's have her aboard suddenly.
                         [*Exeunt* [*Pirates with Marina.*]

Re-enter LEONINE.

Leon. These roguing thieves serve the great
     pirate Valdes,
And they have seiz'd Marina.   Let her go!
There's no hope she will return.   I'll swear she's
     dead
And thrown into the sea.   But I'll see further.   100
Perhaps they will but please themselves upon her,
Not carry her aboard.   If she remain,
Whom they have ravish'd must by me be slain.
                         [*Exit.*

[SCENE II.   *Mytilene.   A room in a brothel.*]

Enter PANDAR, BAWD, *and* BOULT.

Pand. Boult!
Boult. Sir?
Pand. Search the market narrowly; Mytilene is
full of gallants.   We lost too much money this mart
by being too wenchless.   5
Bawd. We were never so much out of creatures.
We have but poor three, and they can do no more
than they can do; and they with continual action
are even as good as rotten.   9
Pand. Therefore let's have fresh ones, whate'er
we pay for them.   If there be not a conscience to
be us'd in every trade, we shall never prosper.   13
Bawd. Thou say'st true.   'Tis not our bringing up
of poor bastards, — as I think, I have brought up
some eleven, —
Boult. Ay, to eleven; and brought them down
again.   But shall I search the market?   18
Bawd. What else, man?   The stuff we have, a
strong wind will blow it to pieces, they are so pitifully sodden.   21
Pand. Thou sayest true; [they're too] unwholesome, o' conscience.   The poor Transylvanian is
dead, that lay with the little baggage.
Boult Ay, she quickly poop'd him; she made him
roast-meat for worms.   But I'll go search the
market.   [*Exit.*   27
Pand. Three or four thousand chequins were as
pretty a proportion to live quietly and so give over.
Bawd. Why to give over, I pray you?   Is it a
shame to get when we are old?   32
Pand. O, our credit comes not in like the com-

modity, nor the commodity wages not with the
danger; therefore, if in our youths we could pick
up some pretty estate, 'twere not amiss to keep our
door hatch'd.   Besides, the sore terms we stand
upon with the gods will be strong with us for giving
o'er.   39
Bawd. Come, other sorts offend as well as we.
Pand. As well as we! Ay, and better too.   We
offend worse.   Neither is our profession any trade;
it's no calling.   But here comes Boult.

Re-enter BOULT, *with the* PIRATES *and* MARINA.

Boult. Come your ways, my masters.   You say
she's a virgin?   45
1. Pirate. O, sir, we doubt it not.
Boult. Master, I have gone through for this
piece you see.   If you like her, so; if not, I have lost
my earnest.
Bawd. Boult, has she any qualities?   50
Boult. She has a good face, speaks well, and has
excellent good clothes.   There's no further necessity
of qualities can make her be refus'd.
Bawd. What's her price, Boult?   54
Boult. I cannot be bated one doit of a thousand
pieces.
Pand. Well, follow me, my masters; you shall
have your money presently.   Wife, take her in.
Instruct her what she has to do, that she may not
be raw in her entertainment.   60
                         [*Exeunt Pandar and Pirates.*]
Bawd. Boult, take you the marks of her, the
colour of her hair, complexion, height, her age,
with warrant of her virginity; and cry, "He that
will give most shall have her first."   Such a maiden-
head were no cheap thing, if men were as they have
been.   Get this done as I command you.   66
Boult. Performance shall follow.   [*Exit.*
Mar. Alack that Leonine was so slack, so slow!
He should have struck, not spoke; or that these
     pirates,
Not enough barbarous, had not o'erboard thrown
     me   70
For to seek my mother!
Bawd. Why lament you, pretty one?
Mar. That I am pretty.
Bawd. Come, the gods have done their part in
you.   75
Mar. I accuse them not.
Bawd. You are light into my hands, where you
are like to live.
Mar. The more my fault
To scape his hands where I was [like] to die.   80
Bawd. Ay, and you shall live in pleasure.

Sc. ii, 22. [they're too] (Malone).   *ther's two* Q.   25. **poop'd:** foundered.   28. **chequins:** gold coins.   34. **commodity
wages not with:** profit is not equal to.   37. **hatch'd:** closed.   47. **gone through:** bid high.   49. **earnest:** advance payment.
52–53 **necessity . . . refus'd:** requirement she cannot meet.   55. **bated:** reduced.   60. **entertainment:** i.e., of customers.
79. **fault:** i.e., misfortune.   80. **[like]** Q$_4$.   Om. Q$_1$.

Mar. No.

Bawd. Yes, indeed shall you, and taste gentle-men of all fashions. You shall fare well; you shall have the difference of all complexions. What! do you stop your ears?   86

Mar. Are you a woman?

Bawd. What would you have me be, an I be not a woman?

Mar. An honest woman, or not a woman.   90

Bawd. Marry, whip thee, gosling. I think I shall have something to do with you. Come, you're a young foolish sapling, and must be bow'd as I would have you.

Mar. The gods defend me!   95

Bawd. If it please the gods to defend you by men, then men must comfort you, men must feed you, men stir you up. Boult's return'd.

[*Re-enter* BOULT.]

Now, sir, hast thou cried her through the mar-ket?   99

Boult. I have cried her almost to the number of her hairs; I have drawn her picture with my voice.

Bawd. And I prithee tell me, how dost thou find the inclination of the people, especially of the younger sort?   105

Boult. Faith, they listened to me as they would have hearkened to their father's testament. There was a Spaniard's mouth so wat'red! and he went to bed to her very description.   109

Bawd. We shall have him here to-morrow with his best ruff on.

Boult. To-night, to-night. But, mistress, do you know the French knight that cowers i' the hams?

Bawd. Who, Monsieur Verollus?   115

Boult. Ay, he; he offered to cut a caper at the proclamation; but he made a groan at it, and swore he would see her to-morrow.   118

Bawd. Well, well; as for him, he brought his disease hither; here he does but repair it. I know he will come in our shadow, to scatter his crowns in the sun.

Boult. Well, if we had of every nation a traveller, we should lodge them with this sign.   124

Bawd. [*To Mar.*] Pray you, come hither awhile. You have fortunes coming upon you. Mark me: you must seem to do that fearfully which you com-mit willingly, despise profit where you have most gain. To weep that you live as ye do makes pity in your lovers; seldom but that pity begets you a good opinion, and that opinion a mere profit.   132

Mar. I understand you not.

Boult. O, take her home, mistress, take her home.

These blushes of hers must be quench'd with some present practice.   136

[*Bawd.*] Thou say'st true, i' faith, so they must: for your bride goes to that with shame which is her way to go with warrant.

Boult. Faith, some do, and some do not. But, mistress, if I have bargain'd for the joint, —   141

Bawd. Thou mayst cut a morsel off the spit?

Boult. I may so.

Bawd. Who should deny it? Come, young one, I like the manner of your garments well.

Boult. Ay, by my faith, they shall not be chang'd yet.   147

Bawd. Boult, spend thou that in the town. Report what a sojourner we have; you'll lose nothing by custom. When Nature fram'd this piece, she meant thee a good turn; therefore say what a paragon she is, and thou hast the harvest out of thine own report.   153

Boult. I warrant you, mistress, thunder shall not so awake the beds of eels as my giving out her beauty stirs up the lewdly inclined. I'll bring home some to-night.

Bawd. Come your ways; follow me.   158

Mar. If fires be hot, knives sharp, or waters deep, Untied I still my virgin knot will keep. Diana, aid my purpose!

Bawd. What have we to do with Diana? Pray you, will you go with us?   [*Exeunt.* 163

[SCENE III. *Tarsus. A room in Cleon's house.*]

Enter CLEON *and* DIONYZA.

Dion. Why, are you foolish? Can it be undone?

Cle. O Dionyza, such a piece of slaughter The sun and moon ne'er look'd upon!

Dion.   I think You'll turn a child again.

Cle. Were I chief lord of all this spacious world, I'd give it to undo the deed. O lady,   6 Much less in blood than virtue, yet a princess To equal any single crown o' th' earth I' th' justice of compare! O villain Leonine! Whom thou hast pois'ned too.   10 If thou hadst drunk to him, 't had been a kindness Becoming well thy [fact]. What canst thou say When noble Pericles shall demand his child?

Dion. That she is dead. Nurses are not the fates, To foster it, nor ever to preserve.   15 She died at night; I'll say so. Who can cross it? Unless you play the [pious] innocent And for an honest attribute cry out She died by foul play.

Cle.   O, go to. Well, well,   19

92. **have...do:** have some trouble. 116. **offered:** tried. 132. **mere:** sure. 137. **[Bawd.]** F₃. *Mari.* Q.

Sc. iii, 9. **I'...compare:** by just comparison. 12. **[fact]** (Dyce): deed. *face* Q. 16. **cross:** deny. 17. **[pious]** (Mason conj.). *impious* Q.

Of all the faults beneath the heavens, the gods
Do like this worst.
   Dion.   Be one of those that thinks
The petty wrens of Tarsus will fly hence
And open this to Pericles. I do shame
To think of what a noble strain you are,   24
And of how coward a spirit.
   Cle.   To such proceeding
Who ever but his approbation added,
Though not his [prime] consent, he did not flow
From honourable [sources].
   Dion.   Be it so, then.
Yet none does know but you how she came dead,
Nor none can know, Leonine being gone.   30
She did [distain] my child, and stood between
Her and her fortunes. None would look on her,
But cast their gazes on Marina's face;
Whilst ours was blurted at and held a Malkin
Not worth the time of day. It pierc'd me thor-
    ough;   35
And though you call my course unnatural,
You not your child well loving, yet I find
It greets me as an enterprise of kindness
Perform'd to your sole daughter.
   Cle.   Heavens forgive it!
   Dion. And as for Pericles,   40
What should he say? We wept after her hearse,
And yet we mourn. Her monument
Is almost finish'd, and her epitaphs
In glittering golden characters express
A general praise to her, and care in us   45
At whose expense 'tis done.
   Cle.   Thou art like the harpy,
Which, to betray, dost, with thine angel's face,
Seize with thine eagle's talons.
   Dion. You are like one that superstitiously
Do swear to th' gods that winter kills the flies; 50
But yet I know you'll do as I advise.   [*Exeunt.*]

[SCENE IV.]

[*Enter* GOWER, *before the monument of Marina
at Tarsus.*]

   Gow. Thus time we waste, and [longest] leagues
    make short;
Sail seas in cockles, have [a] wish but for't;
Making, to take [your] imagination,
From bourn to bourn, region to region.
By you being pardoned, we commit no crime   5
To use one language in each several clime
Where our scenes seems to live. I do beseech you
To learn of me, who stand [i' th'] gaps to teach you,

The stages of our story. Pericles
Is now again thwarting the wayward seas,   10
Attended on by many a lord and knight,
To see his daughter, all his life's delight.
Old Helicanus goes along. Behind
Is left to govern it, you bear in mind,
Old Escanes, whom Helicanus late   15
Advanc'd in time to great and high estate,
Well-sailing ships and bounteous winds have
    brought
This king to Tarsus — think [his] pilot thought;
So with his steerage shall your thoughts [grow
    on] —
To fetch his daughter home, who first is gone.
Like motes and shadows see them move a while; 21
Your ears unto your eyes I'll reconcile.

[DUMB SHOW.]

Enter Pericles, *at one door, with all his train*: Cleon
    and Dionyza, *at the other. * Cleon *shows* Pericles
    the tomb; whereat Pericles *makes lamentation, puts
    on sackcloth, and in a mighty passion departs.
    *[*Then exeunt* Cleon *and* Dionyza.]

See how belief may suffer by foul show!
This borrowed passion stands for true old woe;
And Pericles, in sorrow all devour'd,   25
With sighs shot through and biggest tears o'er-
    shower'd,
Leaves Tarsus and again embarks. He swears
Never to wash his face, nor cut his hairs.
He puts on sackcloth, and to sea. He bears
A tempest, which his mortal vessel tears,   30
And yet he rides it out. Now please you wit
The epitaph is for Marina writ
By wicked Dionyza.
        [*Reads the inscription on Marina's monu-
        ment.*]
"The fairest, sweet'st, and best lies here,
Who withered in her spring of year.   35
She was of Tyrus the King's daughter,
On whom foul death hath made this slaughter.
Marina was she call'd; and at her birth,
Thetis, being proud, swallowed some part o' th'
    earth:
Therefore the earth, fearing to be o'erflowed,   40
Hath Thetis' birth-child on the heavens bestowed;
Wherefore she does, and swears she'll never stint,
Make raging battery upon shores of flint."
No visor does become black villainy
So well as soft and tender flattery.   45
Let Pericles believe his daughter's dead,

---

27. [prime] (Dyce): original. *prince* Q. 28. [sources] (Dyce). *courses* Q. 31. [distain] (Steevens conj.). *disdaine* Q.
34. **Malkin**: kitchen-maid.
    Sc. iv, 1. [longest] F₃: *long* Q. 2. [a] Edd. *and* Qq Ff. 3. [your] (Malone). *our* Qq Ff. 3. **Making:** i.e., proceeding. 8.
[i' th'] (Malone). *with* Q. 18. [his] (Malone). *this* Q. 19. [grow on] (Malone): keep pace. *grone* Q. 24. **borrowed
passion:** simulated grief. 30. **mortal vessel:** i.e., body. 41. **Thetis:** goddess of the sea.

And bear his courses to be ordered
By Lady Fortune; while our scene must play
His daughter's woe and heavy well-a-day
In her unholy service. Patience, then,   50
And think you now are all in Mytilene.   [*Exit.*

[SCENE V. *Mytilene. A street before the brothel.*]

Enter [*from the brothel*] *two* GENTLEMEN.

1. Gent. Did you ever hear the like?
2. Gent. No, nor never shall do in such a place as
this, she being once gone.
1. Gent. But to have divinity preach'd there!
Did you ever dream of such a thing?   5
2. Gent. No, no. Come, I am for no more
bawdy-houses. Shall 's go hear the vestals sing?
1. Gent. I'll do anything now that is virtuous;
but I am out of the road of rutting for ever.   10
[*Exeunt.*

[SCENE VI. *The same. A room in the brothel.*]

Enter PANDAR, BAWD, *and* BOULT.

Pand. Well, I had rather than twice the worth
of her she had ne'er come here.   2
Bawd. Fie, fie upon her! she's able to freeze the
god Priapus and undo a whole generation. We
must either get her ravished or be rid of her. When
she should do for clients her fitment, and do me the
kindness of our profession, she has me her quirks,
her reasons, her master reasons, her prayers, her
knees; that she would make a puritan of the devil
if he should cheapen a kiss of her.   10
Boult. Faith, I must ravish her, or she'll disfurnish us of all our [cavaliers], and make our swearers priests.
Pand. Now, the pox upon her green-sickness for
me!   15
Bawd. Faith, there's no way to be rid on't but
by the way to the pox. Here comes the Lord
Lysimachus disguised.
Boult. We should have both lord and lown, if
the peevish baggage would but give way to customers.   21

Enter LYSIMACHUS.

Lys. How now! How a dozen of virginities?
Bawd. Now, the gods to bless your honour!
Boult. I am glad to see your honour in good
health.   25
Lys. You may so; 'tis the better for you that
your resorters stand upon sound legs. How now,
wholesome iniquity! have you that a man may
deal withal and defy the surgeon?

Bawd. We have here one, sir, if she would —
but there never came her like in Mytilene.   31
Lys. If she'd do the deeds of darkness, thou
wouldst say.
Bawd. Your honour knows what 'tis to say well
enough.   35
Lys. Well, call forth, call forth.
Boult. For flesh and blood, sir, white and red,
you shall see a rose; and she were a rose indeed, if
she had but —
Lys. What, prithee?   40
Boult. O, sir, I can be modest.   [*Exit.*]
Lys. That dignifies the renown of a bawd, no
less than it gives a good report to a number to be
chaste.
Bawd. Here comes that which grows to the stalk;
never pluck'd yet, I can assure you.   46

[*Re-enter* BOULT *with* MARINA.]
Is she not a fair creature?
Lys. Faith, she would serve after a long voyage
at sea. Well, there's for you. Leave us.
Bawd. I beseech your honour, give me leave a
word, and I'll have done presently.   51
Lys. I beseech you, do.
Bawd. [*Aside to Marina.*] First, I would have
you note, this is an honourable man.
Mar. I desire to find him so, that I may worthily
note him.   56
Bawd. Next, he's the governor of this country,
and a man whom I am bound to.
Mar. If he govern the country, you are bound to
him indeed; but how honourable he is in that, I
know not.   61
Bawd. Pray you, without any more virginal
fencing, will you use him kindly? He will line your
apron with gold.
Mar. What he will do graciously, I will thank-
fully receive.   66
Lys. Ha' you done?
Bawd. My lord, she's not pac'd yet; you must
take some pains to work her to your manage.
Come, we will leave his honour and her together.   70
Go thy ways. [*Exeunt Bawd, Pandar, and Boult.*]
Lys. Now, pretty one, how long have you been
at this trade?
Mar. What trade, sir?   74
Lys. Why, I cannot name['t] but I shall offend.
Mar. I cannot be offended with my trade.
Please you to name it.
Lys. How long have you been of this profession?
Mar. E'er since I can remember.
Lys. Did you go to't so young? Were you a
gamester at five or at seven?   81

49. **well-a-day**: lamentation.
Sc. vi, 4. **Priapus**: god of generative power. 6. **fitment**: duty. 10. **cheapen**: bid for. 12. **[cavaliers]** F₂. *caualereea* Q.
14. **green-sickness**: anemia. 19. **lown**: low fellow. 43. **report**: reputation. **to be**: of being. 75. **['t]** F₃. Om. Q.

Mar. Earlier too, sir, if now I be one.

Lys. Why, the house you dwell in proclaims you
to be a creature of sale.   84

Mar. Do you know this house to be a place of
such resort and will come into't? I hear say you
are of honourable parts, and are the governor of
this place.   88

Lys. Why, hath your principal made known unto
you who I am?

Mar. Who is my principal?   91

Lys. Why, your herb-woman; she that sets seeds
and roots of shame and iniquity. O, you have
heard something of my power, and so stand [aloof]
for more serious wooing. But I protest to thee,
pretty one, my authority shall not see thee, or else
look friendly upon thee. Come, bring me to some
private place, come, come.   98

Mar. If you were born to honour, show it now;
If put upon you, make the judgement good
That thought you worthy of it.   101

Lys. How's this? how's this? Some more; be
    sage.

Mar.   For me,
That am a maid, though most ungentle fortune
Have plac'd me in this sty, where, since I came,
Diseases have been sold dearer than physic,   105
[O,] that the gods
Would set me free from this unhallowed place,
Though they did change me to the meanest bird
That flies i' th' purer air!

Lys.   I did not think
Thou couldst have spoke so well; ne'er dreamt thou
    couldst.   110
Had I brought hither a corrupted mind,
Thy speech had altered it. Hold, here's gold for thee.
Persever in that clear way thou goest,
And the gods strengthen thee!

Mar.   The good gods preserve you!

Lys. For me, be you thoughten   115
That I came with no ill intent; for to me
The very doors and windows savour vilely.
Fare thee well. Thou art a piece of virtue, and
I doubt not but thy training hath been noble.
Hold, here's more gold for thee.   120
A curse upon him, die he like a thief,
That robs thee of thy goodness! If thou dost
Hear from me, it shall be for thy good.

[Re-enter BOULT.]

Boult. I beseech your honour, one piece for me.

Lys. Avaunt, thou damned doorkeeper!   126
Your house, but for this virgin that doth prop it,
Would sink and overwhelm you. Away!   [*Exit.*]

Boult. How's this? We must take another

course with you. If your peevish chastity, which
is not worth a breakfast in the cheapest country
under the cope, shall undo a whole household, let
me be gelded like a spaniel. Come your ways. 134

Mar. Whither would you have me?

Boult. I must have your maidenhead taken off,
or the common hangman shall execute it. Come
your ways. We'll have no more gentlemen driven
away. Come your ways, I say.

Re-enter BAWD.

Bawd. How now! what's the matter?   140

Boult. Worse and worse, mistress; she has here
spoken holy words to the Lord Lysimachus.

Bawd. O abominable!

Boult. [She] makes our profession as it were to
stink afore the face of the gods.   145

Bawd. Marry, hang her up for ever!

Boult. The nobleman would have dealt with her
like a nobleman, and she sent him away as cold as
a snowball; saying his prayers too.   149

Bawd. Boult, take her away; use her at thy pleasure. Crack the glass of her virginity, and make the
rest malleable.

Boult. An if she were a thornier piece of ground
than she is, she shall be ploughed.

Mar. Hark, hark, you gods!   155

Bawd. She conjures; away with her! Would she
had never come within my doors! Marry, hang you!
She's born to undo us. Will you not go the way of
womenkind? Marry, come up, my dish of chastity
with rosemary and bays!   [*Exit.*] 160

Boult. Come, mistress; come your ways with me.

Mar. Whither wilt thou have me?

Boult. To take from you the jewel you hold so
dear.   165

Mar. Prithee, tell me one thing first.

Boult. Come now, your one thing.

Mar. What canst thou wish thine enemy to be?

Boult. Why, I could wish him to be my master,
or rather, my mistress.   170

Mar. Neither of these are so bad as thou art,
Since they do better thee in their command.
Thou hold'st a place for which the pained'st fiend
Of hell would not in reputation change.
Thou art the damned doorkeeper to every   175
Coistrel that comes inquiring for his Tib.
To the choleric fisting of every rogue
Thy ear is liable; thy food is such
As hath been belch'd on by infected lungs.   179

Boult. What would you have me do? Go to the
wars, would you, where a man may serve seven
years for the loss of a leg, and have not money
enough in the end to buy him a wooden one?

---

94. [aloof] (Rowe). *aloft* Q. 96. **my...thee:** I will not look upon you in my official capacity. 100. **If put:** i.e., if honor
were put. 106. [O] Q4. Om. Q1–3. 132. **cope:** heavens. 144. [She] (Rowe). *He* Q. 172. **better...command:** are better
than you, being in command. 176. **Coistrel:** knave.

Mar. Do anything but this thou doest.   Empty
Old receptacles, or common shores, of filth;   186
Serve by indenture to the common hangman.
Any of these ways are yet better than this;
For what thou professest, a baboon, could he speak,
Would own a name too dear.   O, that the gods
Would safely deliver me from this place!   191
Here, here's gold for thee.
If that thy master would gain by me,
Proclaim that I can sing, weave, sew, and dance,
With other virtues, which I'll keep from boast;
And [I] will undertake all these to teach.   196
I doubt not but this populous city will
Yield many scholars.
     Boult. But can you teach all this you speak of?
     Mar. Prove that I cannot, take me home again
And prostitute me to the basest groom   201
That doth frequent your house.
     Boult. Well, I will see what I can do for thee.   If
I can place thee, I will.
     Mar. But amongst honest women.   205
     Boult. Faith, my acquaintance lies little amongst
them.   But since my master and mistress hath
bought you, there's no going but by their consent.
Therefore I will make them acquainted with your
purpose, and I doubt not but I shall find them
tractable enough.   Come, I'll do for thee what I
can; come your ways.   [*Exeunt.* 212

ACT V

Enter GOWER.

Gow. Marina thus the brothel scapes, and
     chances
Into an honest house, our story says.
She sings like one immortal, and she dances
As goddess-like to her admired lays.
Deep clerks she dumbs; and with her neeld com-
     poses   5
Nature's own shape of bud, bird, branch, or berry,
That even her art sisters the natural roses.
Her inkle, silk, [twin] with the rubied cherry,
That pupils lacks she none of noble race,
Who pour their bounty on her; and her gain   10
She gives the cursed bawd.   Here we her place;
And to her father turn our thoughts again,
Where we left him, on the sea.   We there him [lost];
[Whence], driven before the winds, he is arriv'd
Here where his daughter dwells; and on this coast   15
Suppose him now at anchor.   The city striv'd
God Neptune's annual feast to keep; from whence

Lysimachus our Tyrian ship espies,
His banners sable, trimm'd with rich expense;
And to him in his barge with [fervour] hies.   20
In your supposing once more put your sight.
Of heavy Pericles think this his bark,
Where what is done in action, (more, if might)
Shall be discover'd.   Please you, sit and hark.
                              [*Exit.*

[SCENE I.   *On board* Pericles' *ship, off Mytilene.
A close pavilion on deck, with a curtain before it:*
Pericles *within it, reclined on a couch.   A barge
lying beside the Tyrian vessel.*]

Enter two SAILORS [*one belonging to the Tyrian
vessel, the other to the barge*]; *to them* HELICANUS.

     [*Tyr.*] *Sail.* [*To the Sailor of Mytilene.*]   Where
is Lord Helicanus?   He can resolve you.
O, here he is.
Sir, there's a barge put off from Mytilene,
And in it is Lysimachus the governor,
Who craves to come aboard.   What is your will?   5
     Hel. That he have his.   Call up some gentlemen.
     [*Tyr.*] *Sail.* Ho, gentlemen! my lord calls.

Enter two or three GENTLEMEN.

     1. Gent. Doth your lordship call?
     Hel. Gentlemen, there's some of worth would
          come aboard;
I pray, greet him fairly.   10
     [*The Gentlemen and the two Sailors descend,
          and go on board the barge.*]

Enter LYSIMACHUS [*and* LORDS; *with the* Gentlemen *and the two* Sailors].

     [*Tyr. Sail.*] Sir,
This is the man that can, in aught you would,
Resolve you.
     Lys. Hail, reverend sir!   The gods preserve you!
     Hel. And you, [sir], to outlive the age I am,   15
And die as I would do.
     Lys.   You wish me well.
Being on shore, honouring of Neptune's triumphs,
Seeing this goodly vessel ride before us,
I made to it to know of whence you are.
     Hel. First, what is your place?   20
     Lys. I am the governor of this place you lie be-
          fore.
     Hel. Sir,
Our vessel is of Tyre, in it the King;
A man who for this three months hath not spoken

186. **shores:** sewers.   190. **own...dear:** i.e., say his reputation could not stand such a name.   196. **[I]** (Rowe).
Om. Q.

Act V, Prol., 5. clerks: scholars.   **neeld:** needle.   8. **inkle:** thread.   **[twin]** (Malone).   *Twine* Q.   13. **[lost]** (Malone).
left Q.   14. **[Whence]** (Steevens).   *Where* Q.   20. **[fervour]** Q₂.   *former* Q₁.
Sc. i, 1, 7. **[Tyr.]** (Malone).   Q has 1, 2, respectively.   11. **[Tyr. Sail.]** (Malone).   *Hell* Q.   15. **[sir]** (Malone).   Om. Q.

To any one, nor taken sustenance.   25
But to prorogue his grief.
  Lys. Upon what ground is his distemperature?
  Hel. 'Twould be too tedious to repeat;
But the main grief springs from the loss
Of a beloved daughter and a wife.   30
  Lys. May we not see him?
  Hel. You may;
But bootless is your sight.   He will not speak
To any.
  [*Lys.*] Yet let me obtain my wish.   35
  [*Hel.*] Behold him.   [*Pericles discovered.*] This
    was a goodly person
Till the disaster that, one mortal [night],
Drove him to this.
  Lys. Sir king, all hail!   The gods preserve you!
Hail, royal sir!   40
  Hel. It is in vain; he will not speak to you.
  1. Lord. Sir,
We have a maid in Mytilene, I durst wager,
Would win some words of him.
  Lys.   'Tis well bethought.
She questionless with her sweet harmony   45
And other chosen attractions, would allure,
And make a batt'ry through his deafen'd parts,
Which now are midway stopp'd.
She is all happy as the fairest of all,
And, [with] her fellow maids, [is] now upon   50
The leafy shelter that abuts against
The island's side.
  [*Whispers a Lord, who goes off in the barge*
    of Lysimachus.]
  Hel. Sure, all effectless; yet nothing we'll omit
That bears recovery's name.   But since your kind-
    ness
We have stretch'd thus far, let us beseech you   55
That for our gold we may provision have,
Wherein we are not destitute for want,
But weary for the staleness.
  Lys.   O, sir, a courtesy
Which if we should deny, the most just God
For every graff would send a caterpillar,   60
And so inflict our province.   Yet once more
Let me entreat to know at large the cause
Of your king's sorrow.
  Hel.   Sit, sir; I will recount it to you.
But, see, I am prevented.

[*Re-enter, from the barge,* Lord, *with* MARINA, *and a*
    young Lady.]
  Lys.   O, here's
The lady that I sent for.   Welcome, fair one!   65

— Is't not a goodly [presence]?
  Hel.   She's a gallant lady.
  Lys. She's such a one, that, were I well assur'd
Came of a gentle kind and noble stock,
[I'd] wish no better choice, and think me rarely wed.
Fair one, all goodness that consists in [bounty]   70
Expect even here, where is a kingly patient.
If that thy prosperous and artificial [feat]
Can draw him but to answer thee in aught,
Thy sacred physic shall receive such pay
As thy desires can wish.
  Mar.   Sir, I will use   75
My utmost skill in his recovery,
Provided
That none but I and my companion maid
Be suffered to come near him.
  Lys.   Come, let us leave her;
And the gods make her prosperous!   [*Marina sings.*
  Lys. [Mark'd] he your music?   81
  Mar.   No, nor look'd on us.
  Lys. See, she will speak to him.
  Mar. Hail, sir! my lord, lend ear.
  Per. Hum, ha!   [*Pushing her back.*]
  Mar. I am a maid,   85
My lord, that ne'er before invited eyes,
But have been gaz'd on like a comet.   She speaks,
My lord, that, may be, hath endur'd a grief
Might equal yours, if both were justly weigh'd.
Though wayward fortune did malign my state,   90
My derivation was from ancestors
Who stood equivalent with mighty kings;
But time hath rooted out my parentage,
And to the world and awkward casualties
Bound me in servitude.   [*Aside.*] I will desist;   95
But there is something glows upon my cheek,
And whispers in mine ear, "Go not till he speak."
  Per. My fortunes — parentage — good parent-
    age —
To equal mine!   Was it not thus?   What say you?
  Mar. I said, my lord, if you did know my
    parentage,   100
You would not do me violence.
  Per. I do think so.   Pray you, turn your eyes
    upon me.
You are like something that — What country-
    woman?
Here of these [shores]?
  Mar.   No, nor of any [shores];
Yet I was mortally brought forth, and am   105
No other than I appear.
  Per. I am great with woe, and shall deliver
    weeping.

26. **prorogue:** prolong. 27. **distemperature:** disturbance of mind. 35. [*Lys.*] Q₄. Cont. to Helicanus in Q₁. 36. [*Hel.*] Q₄. Q₁ gives *Behold . . . person* to Lysimachus, and *Till . . . this* to Helicanus. 37. **[night]** (Malone). *wight* Q. 50. **[with]** (Malone).   Om. Q.   **[is]** (Malone).   Om. Q.   60. **graff:** graft (of trees).   61. **inflict:** afflict. 66. **[presence]** (Malone). *present* Q. 69. **[I'd]** F₃. *I do* Q. **wed:** to wed Q. 70. **[bounty]** (Malone). *beautie* Q. 72. **artificial:** cunning.   **[feat]** (Percy conj.). *fate* Q. 81. **[Mark'd]** Q₄. *Marke* Q₁. 94. **awkward:** adverse. 104. **[shores]** (Malone). *shewes* Q.

My dearest wife was like this maid, and such a one
My daughter might have been. My queen's
    square brows;
Her stature to an inch; as wand-like straight;   110
As silver-voic'd; her eyes as jewel-like
And cas'd as richly; in pace another Juno;
Who starves the ears she feeds, and makes them
    hungry,
The more she gives them speech. Where do you
    live?
Mar. Where I am but a stranger. From the
    deck   115
You may discern the place.
Per.   Where were you bred?
And how achiev'd you these endowments which
You make more rich to owe?
Mar. If I should tell my history, it would seem
Like lies disdain'd in the reporting.
Per.   Prithee, speak.
Falseness cannot come from thee; for thou look'st
Modest as Justice, and thou seem'st a [palace]   122
For the crown'd Truth to dwell in. I will believe
    thee,
And make [my] senses credit thy relation
To points that seem impossible; for thou look'st
Like one I lov'd indeed. What were thy
    friends?   126
Didst thou not [say], when I did push thee back —
Which was when I perceiv'd thee — that thou
    cam'st
From good descending?
Mar.   So indeed I did.
Per. Report thy parentage. I think thou
    said'st   130
Thou hadst been toss'd from wrong to injury,
And that thou thought'st thy griefs might equal
    mine,
If both were opened.
Mar.   Some such thing
I said, and said no more but what my thoughts
Did warrant me was likely.
Per.   Tell thy story;   135
If thine, considered, prove the thousand part
Of my endurance, thou art a man, and I
Have suffered like a girl. Yet thou dost look
Like Patience gazing on kings' graves, and smiling
Extremity out of act. What were thy friends?
How lost thou [them?] Thy name, my most kind
    virgin?   141
Recount, I do beseech thee. Come, sit by me.
Mar. My name is Marina.
Per.   O, I am mock'd,
And thou by some incensed god sent hither
To make the world to laugh at me.

Mar.   Patience, good sir,
Or here I'll cease.
Per.   Nay, I'll be patient.   146
Thou little know'st how thou dost startle me,
To call thyself Marina.
Mar. The name
Was given me by one that had some power,   150
My father, and a king.
Per.   How! a king's daughter?
And call'd Marina?
Mar.   You said you would believe me;
But, not to be a troubler of your peace,
I will end here.
Per.   But are you flesh and blood?
Have you a working pulse, and are no fairy?   155
Motion? Well, speak on. Where were you born?
And wherefore call'd Marina?
Mar.   Call'd Marina
For I was born at sea.
Per.   At sea! What mother?
Mar. My mother was the daughter of a king,
Who died the minute I was born,   160
As my good nurse Lychorida hath oft
Delivered weeping.
Per.   O, stop there a little!
[*Aside.*] This is the rarest dream that e'er dull
    sleep
Did mock sad fools withal. This cannot be;
My daughter['s] buried. — Well, where were you
    bred?   165
I'll hear you more, to th' bottom of your story,
And never interrupt you.
Mar. You scorn. Believe me, 'twere best I did
    give o'er.
Per. I will believe you by the syllable
Of what you shall deliver. Yet give me leave:
How came you in these parts? Where were you
    bred?   171
Mar. The King my father did in Tarsus leave
    me,
Till cruel Cleon, with his wicked wife,
Did seek to murder me; and having wooed
A villain to attempt it, who having drawn to do't,
A crew of pirates came and rescued me;   176
Brought me to Mytilene. But, good sir,
Whither will you have me? Why do you weep?
    It may be,
You think me an impostor. No, good faith;
I am the daughter to King Pericles,   180
If good King Pericles be.
[*Per.*] Ho, Helicanus!
Hel. Calls my lord?
Per. Thou art a grave and noble counsellor,
Most wise in general; tell me, if thou canst,   185

118. **to owe:** by possessing. 122. **[palace]** (Malone). *Pallas* Q. 124. **[my]** Q4. Om. Q1. **relation:** tale. 127. **[say]** (Malone).
stay Q. 137. **my endurance:** what I have endured. 140. **Extremity . . . act:** so that extreme danger cannot harm. 141.
[them?] (Malone). Om. Q. 165. **['s]** (Steevens). Om. Q. 169. **by the:** i.e., every. 182. **[Per.]** F3. *Hell* Q.

What this maid is, or what is like to be,
That thus hath made me weep?
Hel.   I know not; but
Here is the regent, sir, of Mytilene
Speaks nobly of her.
Lys.   She never would tell
Her parentage. Being demanded that,   190
She would sit still and weep.
Per. O Helicanus, strike me, honour'd sir;
Give me a gash, put me to present pain,
Lest this great sea of joys rushing upon me
O'erbear the shores of my mortality   195
And drown me with their sweetness. O, come
    hither,
Thou that beget'st him that did thee beget;
Thou that wast born at sea, buried at Tarsus,
And found at sea again! O Helicanus,
Down on thy knees, thank the holy gods as loud
As thunder threatens us. This is Marina.   201
What was thy mother's name? Tell me but that,
For truth can never be confirm'd enough,
Though doubts did ever sleep.
Mar.   First, sir, I pray,
What is your title?   205
Per. I am Pericles of Tyre; but tell me now
My drown'd queen's name, as in the rest you said
Thou hast been godlike perfect,
The heir of kingdoms and another like
To Pericles thy father.   210
Mar. Is it no more to be your daughter than
To say my mother's name was Thaisa?
Thaisa was my mother, who did end
The minute I began.
Per. Now blessing on thee! Rise; thou art my
    child.   215
Give me fresh garments. Mine own, Helicanus;
She is not dead at Tarsus, as she should have been,
By savage Cleon. She shall tell thee all;
When thou shalt kneel, and justify in knowledge
She is thy very princess. Who is this?   220
Hel. Sir, 'tis the governor of Mytilene
Who, hearing of your melancholy state,
Did come to see you.
Per.   I embrace you.
Give me my robes. I am wild in my beholding.
O heavens bless my girl! But, hark, what music?
Tell Helicanus, my Marina, tell him   226
O'er, point by point, for yet he seems to [doubt],
How sure you are my daughter. But, what music?
Hel. My lord, I hear none.
Per. None!   230
The music of the spheres! List, my Marina.
Lys. It is not good to cross him; give him way.
Per. Rarest sounds! Do ye not hear?
Lys. Music, my lord? I hear.

Per. Most heavenly music!
It nips me unto listening, and thick slumber   233
Hangs upon mine eyes. Let me rest.   [*Sleeps.*]
Lys. A pillow for his head.
So, leave him all. Well, my companion friends,
If this but answer to my just belief,
I'll well remember you.   240
    [*Exeunt all but Pericles.*]

DIANA [*appears to Pericles as in a vision*].
Dia. My temple stands in Ephesus; hie thee
    thither,
And do upon mine altar sacrifice.
There, when my maiden priests are met together
Before the people all,
Reveal how thou at sea didst lose thy wife.   245
To mourn thy crosses, with thy daughter's, call
And give them repetition to the [life].
Or perform my bidding, or thou liv'st in woe;
Do it, and happy, by my silver bow.
Awake, and tell thy dream.   [*Disappears.*]   250
Per. Celestial Dian, goddess argentine,
I will obey thee. Helicanus!

[*Re-enter* HELICANUS, LYSIMACHUS, *and* MARINA.]
Hel.   Sir?
Per. My purpose was for Tarsus, there to strike
The inhospitable Cleon; but I am
For other service first. Toward Ephesus   255
Turn our blown sails; eftsoons I'll tell thee why.
[*To Lysimachus.*] Shall we refresh us, sir, upon your
    shore,
And give you gold for such provision
As our intents will need?
Lys. Sir,   260
With all my heart; and, when you come ashore,
I have another suit.
Per.   You shall prevail,
Were it to woo my daughter; for it seems
You have been noble towards her.
Lys.   Sir, lend me your arm.
Per. Come, my Marina.   [*Exeunt.* 265

[SCENE II. *Enter* GOWER, *before the temple of
    Diana at Ephesus.*]

Gow. Now our sands are almost run;
More a little, and then dumb.
This, my last boon, give me,
For such kindness must relieve me,
That you aptly will suppose   5
What pageantry, what feats, what shows,
What minstrelsy, and pretty din,
The regent made in Mytilene
To greet the King. So he thrived

211. **Is it:** does it need.   217. **should:** was said to.   227. **[doubt]** (Malone). *doat* Q.   235. **nips:** forces.   247. **[life]** (Malone). *like* Q.   251. **argentine:** silvery.

That he is promis'd to be wived   10
To fair Marina, but in no wise
Till he had done his sacrifice,
As Dian bade; whereto being bound,
The interim, pray you, all confound.
In feather'd briefness sails are fill'd,   15
And wishes fall out as they're will'd.
At Ephesus the temple see,
Our king and all his company.
That he can hither come so soon
Is by your fancy's thankful doom.   [*Exit.*]   20

[SCENE III.   *The temple of Diana at Ephesus;*
THAISA *standing near the altar, as high priestess;*
a number of Virgins on each side; CERIMON *and*
other Inhabitants of Ephesus attending.

   Enter PERICLES, *with his train:* LYSIMACHUS,
      HELICANUS, MARINA, *and a Lady.*]

Per. Hail, Dian! to perform thy just com-
      mand,
I here confess myself the King of Tyre;
Who, frighted from my country, did wed
At Pentapolis the fair Thaisa.
At sea in childbed died she, but brought forth   5
A maid-child call'd Marina; who, O goddess,
Wears yet thy silver livery. She at Tarsus
Was nurs'd with Cleon; who at fourteen years
He sought to murder; but her better stars
Brought her to Mytilene, 'gainst whose shore   10
Riding, her fortunes brought the maid aboard us,
Where, by her own most clear remembrance, she
Made known herself my daughter.
   Thai.   Voice and favour!
You are, you are — O royal Pericles!   [*Faints.*]
   Per. What means the [nun]? She dies! Help,
      gentlemen!   15
   Cer. Noble sir,
If you have told Diana's altar true,
This is your wife.
   Per.   Reverend appearer, no.
I threw her overboard with these very arms.
   Cer. Upon this coast, I warrant you.
   Per.   'Tis most certain.
   Cer. Look to the lady; O, she's but overjoy'd.   21
Early in blustering morn this lady was
Thrown upon this shore. I op'd the coffin,
Found there rich jewels; recovered her, and plac'd
      her
Here in Diana's temple.
   Per.   May we see them?   25
   Cer. Great sir, they shall be brought you to my
      house,

Whither I invite you. Look, Thaisa is
Recovered.
   Thai.   O, let me look!
If he be none of mine, my sanctity
Will to my sense bend no licentious ear,   30
But curb it, spite of seeing. O, my lord,
Are you not Pericles? Like him you spake,
Like him you are! Did you not name a tempest,
A birth, and death?
   Per.   The voice of dead Thaisa!
   Thai. That Thaisa am I, supposed dead   35
And drown'd.
   Per. Immortal Dian!
   Thai.   Now I know you better.
When we with tears parted Pentapolis,
The King my father gave you such a ring.
                         [*Shows a ring.*]
   Per. This, this. No more, you gods! Your
      present kindness   40
Makes my past miseries sports. You shall do well
That on the touching of her lips I may
Melt and no more be seen. O, come, be buried
A second time within these arms.
   Mar.   My heart
Leaps to be gone into my mother's bosom.   45
                         [*Kneels to Thaisa.*]
   Per. Look who kneels here! Flesh of thy flesh,
      Thaisa;
Thy burden at the sea, and call'd Marina
For she was yielded there.
   Thai.   Blest, and mine own!
   Hel. Hail, madam, and my queen!
   Thai.   I know you not.
[*Per.*] You have heard me say, when I did fly
      from Tyre,   50
I left behind an ancient substitute.
Can you remember what I call'd the man?
I have nam'd him oft.
   Thai.   'Twas Helicanus then.
   Per. Still confirmation!
Embrace him, dear Thaisa; this is he.   55
Now do I long to hear how you were found,
How possibly preserv'd, and who to thank,
Besides the gods, for this great miracle.
   Thai. Lord Cerimon, my lord; this man,
Through whom the gods have shown their power;
      that can   60
From first to last resolve you.
   Per.   Reverend sir,
The gods can have no mortal officer
More like a god than you. Will you deliver
How this dead queen re-lives?
   Cer.   I will, my lord.

Sc. ii, 12. **he:** Pericles. 14. **confound:** destroy, omit.   15. **In... briefness:** with winged speed.   20. **thankful doom:**
gracious permission.
   Sc. iii, 11. **Riding.** Modifies "us."   15. [nun] (Collier). *num* Q.   24. **recovered:** revived.   42. **That:** if.   48. **yielded:**
born.   50. [*Per.*] F₃. *Hell* Q.

Beseech you, first go with me to my house,   65
Where shall be shown you all was found with her,
How she came plac'd here in the temple;
No needful thing omitted.
    Per. Pure Dian, bless thee for thy vision! [I]
Will offer night oblations to thee. Thaisa,   70
This prince, the fair-betrothed of your daughter,
Shall marry her at Pentapolis. And now,
This ornament
Makes me look dismal will I clip to form:
And what this fourteen years no razor touch'd,   75
To grace thy marriage-day, I'll beautify.
    Thai. Lord Cerimon hath letters of good credit,
    sir,
My father's dead.
    Per. Heavens make a star of him! Yet there, my
    queen,
We'll celebrate their nuptials, and ourselves   80
Will in that kingdom spend our following days.
Our son and daughter shall in Tyrus reign.
Lord Cerimon, we do our longing stay
To hear the rest untold. Sir, lead's the way.
                                                    [Exeunt.]

                                 [Enter GOWER.]
    Gow. In Antiochus and his daughter you have
    heard   85
Of monstrous lust the due and just reward.
In Pericles, his queen and daughter, seen,
Although assail'd with fortune fierce and keen,
Virtue [preserv'd] from fell destruction's blast,
Led on by heaven, and crown'd with joy at last.   90
In Helicanus may you well descry
A figure of truth, of faith, of loyalty.
In reverend Cerimon there well appears
The worth that learned charity aye wears.
For wicked Cleon and his wife, when fame   95
Had spread [their] cursed deed, [and] honour'd
    name
Of Pericles, to rage the city turn,
That him and his they in his palace burn;
The gods for murder seemed so content
To punish [them]; although not done, but meant. 100
So, on your patience evermore attending,
New joy wait on you! Here our play has ending.
                                                 [Exit.]

    69. [I] F₃. *and* Q. 73. **ornament:** hair and beard (which). 89. [**preserv'd**] (Malone). *preferd* Q. 96. [**their**] Q₄.
his Q. [**and**] F₃. *the* Q. 100. [**them**] (Malone). Om. Q.

Cymbeline

CYMBELINE FIRST APPEARED in print in the Folio of 1623, and there is no evidence of any previous attempt at publication. The text must therefore be based upon this original.

For the date of production the later limit is fixed by the death, on September 12, 1611, of Simon Forman, astrologer and quack physician, whose *Booke of Plaies* records a performance of *Cymbeline* which he had seen. The entry, undated, appears to have been made between notes on performances of *Macbeth* and *Richard II* (not Shakespeare's play) dated respectively Saturday, April 20, 1610, and Tuesday, April 30, 1611. But April 20th fell on a Saturday in 1611, not in 1610, and inasmuch as the entries of the other plays witnessed by Forman are headed 1611, it is likely that Forman made an error in the case of *Macbeth*, and that he saw both that play and *Cymbeline* in 1611. If this is true, it seems reasonable to suppose that, unless the play was very new, *Cymbeline* was composed some time in 1610, and features of style and metre support this date.

Cymbeline conforms in its general theatrical nature to the tragi-comic romances with which Beaumont and Fletcher were winning at about this time remarkable success, and to their *Philaster* (c. 1610) in particular, with which it exhibits some striking resemblances. The question of influence and indebtedness may never, perhaps, be unequivocally resolved, because the date of *Philaster* cannot be fixed with precision. In 1608 Beaumont and Fletcher had produced *The Faithful Shepherdess*, which, though a pastoral and written in couplets, may be regarded as anticipating the new kind of tragi-comedy to which both *Cymbeline* and *Philaster* belong. It may be conjectured that after writing *Cymbeline*, Shakespeare was encouraged to continue working the same vein in *The Winter's Tale* and *The Tempest*, not only because of his presumable satisfaction with *Cymbeline* but also because of the success of Beaumont and Fletcher. In such cases influence may be reciprocal. Furthermore, it may be recalled that *Pericles* (1608) has many of the features of the tragi-comic romance.

Doubt has been cast upon the authorship of the vision of Posthumus in V.iv. The device itself is paralleled by the spectacular elements in *The Winter's Tale* and *The Tempest*, but the vastly inferior quality of the verses has led most authorities to believe that many, at least, must be by another hand than Shakespeare's. Critics differ, however, in the amount they would assign to him. To consider V.iv.30–113 as un-Shakespearean is a conservative judgment, but that is all that one can relieve him of with any confidence, and lines 93–113 may be genuine. Moreover, one must see a collaborator here rather than an interpolator, for the extended reference to the vision in V.v.425–59 shows that Shakespeare was cognizant of what had gone before.

For the intricate plot of *Cymbeline* Shakespeare chose to place a familiar romantic tale in a semi-historical setting. Though the story of a man who makes a wager upon the chastity of his wife is widespread in Western Europe, the version in the ninth novel of the second day in Boccaccio's *Decameron* is assuredly the one which served Shakespeare. In the essential features of the story up to the point where the heroine sets out to seek her fortunes in disguise, Shakespeare closely follows his source, but the rest of her history bears no relation to Boccaccio's narrative. Moreover, Shakespeare has made two notable changes in the material he derived from Boccaccio. Whereas the prototype of Posthumus (Bernabo) is a merchant, Shakespeare makes Posthumus a noble; and Imogen, whose original (Ginevra) is, like her husband, bourgeois, Shakespeare makes the daughter of a king. In Boccaccio the wager is proposed by the husband himself; in the play the suggestion comes from the villain Iachimo. These alterations significantly affect characterization.

His romantic plot Shakespeare has skillfully woven into a background derived from Holinshed's *Chronicle*. This background is chiefly legendary; of authentic history there is little beyond the fact of the existence, about the beginning of the Christian era, of a British king, Cunobelinus. The *Chronicle* represents him as brought up at Rome and knighted by Augustus Caesar, who showed him great favor, and as the father of two sons, Guiderius and Arviragus. Conflicting stories are reported about the payment of tribute to Rome, but Holinshed stresses the friendship between Cymbeline and the Emperor, and makes the refusal of tribute come from Guiderius after his father's death. The references to previous conflicts between Rome and Britain are derived from the *Chronicle*. The account of the battle in the fifth act, and of the saving of the day by Belarius and the two princes, is based upon Holinshed's story of a fight between the Danes and the Scots, in which the fleeing Scots were rallied in a lane by a husbandman and his two sons. The names given to the Britons in the play, even the pseudonyms of the princes Shakespeare picked up in a variety of places in Holinshed.

In the matter of the stolen princes, their education according to nature by the banished Belarius, and their loving hospitality to their disguised sister, Shakespeare seems to have been largely original. Yet some hints he probably found in an old anonymous play, *The Rare Triumphs of Love and Fortune* (printed 1589), which presents one Hermione (whose name Shakespeare appropriated for the queen in *The Winter's Tale*) as a king's ward, who is banished for marrying the princess Fidelia against her father's wishes. Fidelia, seeking her lover, is succored at the cave of a hermit, a courtier who had been banished (like Belarius) on false charges. Fidelia, whose name seems to have inspired "Fidele" for the disguised Imogen, has a cowardly Brother (Armenio) who may have suggested to Shakespeare the character of Cloten. The relation of the Queen to her son and Imogen recalls the familiar stepmother motive of Germanic folk-lore. But whatever sources may have assisted Shakespeare in these various matters, the skillful interweaving and the atmosphere are all his own, and all the wealth of poetry and characterization which gives the drama its charm.

In the brand of tragi-comedy of which *Cymbeline* is typical the widest gamut of emotion, sensation, and surprise was enjoined, anything being permissible and welcome, provided only that ultimately tragic consequences should be avoided and the protagonists brought finally to complete happiness. The audience could surrender to the manifold adventure, sentiment, and pathos, safe in the assurance of a happy ending. To judge plays of this kind by realistic criteria is entirely wrong, yet this need not preclude observing where Shakespeare has evidently sought to make the extraordinary appear more natural.

Several of the characters in *Cymbeline* are more memorable than the dexterously contrived plot. The weak king and his wicked queen, indeed, are rather flat, but Cloten, a crass bully and coward is individualized. Vulgar, boastful, and stupid though he is, he is a patriot and speaks to the Roman Lucius in so honest and telling a fashion that one is almost persuaded he is more like his betters than he is known to be. One would be tempted to accuse Shakespeare of inconsistent characterization, if life did not amply confirm that vain and arrogant men often sincerely love their country.

The other villain, Iachimo, is of the subtle, crafty type. As a clever strategist and opportunist who takes an artist's satisfaction in the execution of his villainy, he may be called the Iago of Shakespearean comedy.

Posthumus plays a rôle so uncongenial to modern minds that he has been widely misjudged. He has been condemned for his compact with Iachimo, for his crediting Iachimo's story, and for his revenge upon Imogen. No Elizabethan, however, would have censured him. He is no simpleton and no criminal. Shakespeare takes pains to stress his fine traits through the conversation of the "first Gentleman" at court and the good report of Iachimo to his friends in Rome. Clearly his confidence in his wife's honor was construed as a virtue, and as a gentleman he was bound to go to any extreme in its defense. That the circumstantial detail supporting Iachimo's story is simply overwhelming, does not, of course, justify Posthumus in planning his wife's murder, but in the literature on which the Elizabethans fed, guilty women were not spared.

The lady whom he so trusts and wrongs is in truth a "heavenly angel," almost too bright and good for human nature's daily food. And yet she is completely human, a flesh and blood creature, at least most of the time. In her seem to be compacted the several excellences of Shakespeare's earlier romantic heroines: the dignity of Portia, the energy of Beatrice, the radiant high spirits of Rosalind, the sweetness of Viola. And she has courage beyond them all, as circumstances demand. It would be difficult to conceive words more compelling than those which spontaneously burst from her after she has read the false letter telling her to meet her lord at Milford Haven (III.ii.49–84), or those she utters when she is reunited with him at the last (V.v.261–263). The indignation with which she rejects the accusation of infidelity shows her fine mettle (III.iv.42–66); the mingled reserve and sharpness in her repulse of Cloten show her high breeding (II.iii.91–160). Only in the woodland scenes does Imogen's natural sweetness (cf. I.i.109–114 and I.iii.14–37) come perilously near to cloying, and her clear, strong voice sound thin — an impression accentuated by the artificiality of the situation and the sentimentality of the spotless youths, her brothers. In this respect the grafting of the Belarius branch upon the main plot proved unfortunate for the heroine. But while one may regret this, and her subordination in the finale where everything is made to serve the technical triumph of unravelling all the strands of the intricate web, one will hardly stint his devotion to Imogen, whom many have thought to stand supreme among the women of Shakespeare's comedies.

CYMBELINE

[DRAMATIS PERSONÆ

CYMBELINE, *king of Britain.*
CLOTEN, *son to the Queen by a former husband.*
POSTHUMUS LEONATUS, *a gentleman, husband to*
   Imogen.
BELARIUS, *a banished lord disguised under the*
   name of Morgan.
GUIDERIUS,   { *sons to Cymbeline, disguised under*
ARVIRAGUS,   { *the names of Polydore and Cad-*
          { *wal, supposed sons to Morgan.*
PHILARIO, *friend to Posthumus,* }
IACHIMO, *friend to Philario,*   } *Italians.*
CAIUS LUCIUS, *general of the Roman forces.*

PISANIO, *servant to Posthumus.*
CORNELIUS, *a physician.*
A Roman Captain.
Two British Captains.
A Frenchman, friend to Philario.
Two Lords of Cymbeline's court.
Two Gentlemen of the same.
Two Gaolers.

QUEEN, *wife to Cymbeline.*
IMOGEN, *daughter to Cymbeline by a former Queen.*
HELEN, *a lady attending on Imogen.*

Lords, Ladies, Roman Senators, Tribunes, a Soothsayer, a Dutchman, a Spaniard, Musicians,
    Officers, Captains, Soldiers, Messengers, and other Attendants.

Apparitions.

SCENE: *Britain; Rome.*]

ACT I

SCENE I. [*Britain. The garden of Cymbeline's*
    palace.]

Enter two GENTLEMEN.

1. Gent. You do not meet a man but frowns.
   Our bloods
No more obey the heavens than our courtiers
Still seem as does the [King].
  2. Gent.   But what's the matter?
  1. Gent. His daughter, and the heir of 's kingdom,
   whom
He purpos'd to his wife's sole son — a widow   5
That late he married — hath referr'd herself
Unto a poor but worthy gentleman. She's wedded,
Her husband banish'd, she imprison'd; all

Is outward sorrow, though I think the King
Be touch'd at very heart.
  2. Gent.   None but the King?
  1. Gent. He that hath lost her too; so is the
   Queen,   11
That most desir'd the match; but not a courtier,
Although they wear their faces to the bent
Of the King's looks, hath a heart that is not
Glad at the thing they scowl at.
  2. Gent.   And why so?
  1. Gent. He that hath miss'd the Princess is a
   thing   16
Too bad for bad report; and he that hath her —
I mean, that married her, alack, good man!
And therefore banish'd — is a creature such
As, to seek through the regions of the earth   20
For one his like, there would be something failing

Act I, sc. i, 1. bloods: moods.   3. **[King]** (Tyrwhitt conj.).   *kings* F.   4. *1. Gent.* From this point to l. 68 F designates
1. Gent. and *2. Gent.* as *1.* and *2.* This holds generally throughout the play.   6. **referr'd:** given.   13. **bent:** inclination-

In him that should compare. I do not think
So fair an outward and such stuff within
Endows a man but he.
   2. Gent.   You speak him far.
   1. Gent. I do extend him, sir, within himself, 25
Crush him together rather than unfold
His measure duly.
   2. Gent.   What's his name and birth?
   1. Gent. I cannot delve him to the root. His
     father
Was call'd Sicilius, who did gain his honour
Against the Romans with Cassibelan,   30
But had his titles by Tenantius whom
He serv'd with glory and admir'd success,
So gain'd the sur-addition Leonatus;
And had, besides this gentleman in question,
Two other sons, who in the wars o' th' time 35
Died with their swords in hand; for which their
     father,
Then old and fond of issue, took such sorrow
That he quit being, and his gentle lady,
Big of this gentleman our theme, deceas'd
As he was born. The King he takes the babe 40
To his protection, calls him Posthumus Leonatus,
Breeds him and makes him of his bed-chamber,
Puts to him all the learnings that his time
Could make him the receiver of; which he took,
As we do air, fast as 'twas minist'red,   45
And in 's spring became a harvest; liv'd in court —
Which rare it is to do — most prais'd, most lov'd,
A sample to the youngest, to the more mature
A glass that feated them, and to the graver
A child that guided dotards; to his mistress, 50
For whom he now is banish'd, — her own price
Proclaims how she esteem'd him and his virtue;
By her election may be truly read
What kind of man he is.
   2. Gent.   I honour him
Even out of your report. But, pray you, tell me, 55
Is she sole child to the King?
   1. Gent.   His only child.
He had two sons, — if this be worth your hearing,
Mark it — the eldest of them at three years old,
I' th' swathing-clothes the other, from their nursery
Were stol'n, and to this hour no guess in knowl-
     edge   60
Which way they went.
   2. Gent.   How long is this ago?
   1. Gent. Some twenty years.
   2. Gent. That a king's children should be so
     convey'd,
So slackly guarded, and the search so slow,
That could not trace them!
   1. Gent.   Howsoe'er 'tis strange, 65

Or that the negligence may well be laugh'd at,
Yet is it true, sir.
   2. Gent.   I do well believe you.
   1. Gent. We must forbear; here comes the gentle-
     man,
The Queen, and Princess.   *[Exeunt.*

   Enter the QUEEN, POSTHUMUS, *and* IMOGEN.

   Queen. No, be assur'd you shall not find me,
     daughter,   70
After the slander of most stepmothers,
Evil-ey'd unto you. You're my prisoner, but
Your gaoler shall deliver you the keys
That lock up your restraint. For you, Posthumus,
So soon as I can win th' offended King,   75
I will be known your advocate. Marry, yet
The fire of rage is in him, and 'twere good
You lean'd unto his sentence with what patience
Your wisdom may inform you.
   Post.   Please your Highness,
I will from hence to-day.
   Queen.   You know the peril.
I'll fetch a turn about the garden, pitying   81
The pangs of barr'd affections, though the King
Hath charg'd you should not speak together.
                               [Exit.
   Imo.   O
Dissembling courtesy! How fine this tyrant
Can tickle where she wounds! My dearest hus-
     band,   85
I something fear my father's wrath, but nothing —
Always reserv'd my holy duty — what
His rage can do on me. You must be gone;
And I shall here abide the hourly shot
Of angry eyes, not comforted to live,   90
But that there is this jewel in the world
That I may see again.
   Post.   My queen! my mistress!
O lady, weep no more, lest I give cause
To be suspected of more tenderness
Than doth become a man. I will remain   95
The loyal'st husband that did e'er plight troth.
My residence in Rome at one [Philario's],
Who to my father was a friend, to me
Known but by letter; thither write, my queen,
And with mine eyes I'll drink the words you
     send,   100
Though ink be made of gall.

   Re-enter QUEEN.

   Queen.   Be brief, I pray you.
If the King come, I shall incur I know not
How much of his displeasure. *[Aside.]* Yet I'll
     move him

---

24. **speak...far:** praise him very highly. F₂ reads *fair.* 33. **sur-addition:** added title. 37. **fond of issue:** desirous of offspring. 43. **time:** years. 49. **feated them:** gave them a flattering reflection. 51. **price:** valuation. 70. s.d. F begins Sc. ii here. 78. **lean'd:** submitted. 97. **[Philario's]** (Rowe). *Filorio's* F.

To walk this way. I never do him wrong
But he does buy my injuries, to be friends;　105
Pays dear for my offences.　　　　　[*Exit.*]
　　Post.　　　　　Should we be taking leave
As long a term as yet we have to live,
The loathness to depart would grow. Adieu!
　　Imo. Nay, stay a little;
Were you but riding forth to air yourself,　110
Such parting were too petty. Look here, love;
This diamond was my mother's. Take it, heart;
But keep it till you woo another wife,
When Imogen is dead.
　　Post.　　　　　How, how! another?
You gentle gods, give me but this I have,　115
And cere up my embracements from a next
With bonds of death!　　[*Putting on the ring.*]
　　　　Remain, remain thou here
While sense can keep it on. And, sweetest, fairest,
As I my poor self did exchange for you,
To your so infinite loss, so in our trifles　120
I still win of you; for my sake wear this.
It is a manacle of love; I'll place it
Upon this fairest prisoner.
　　　　　[*Putting a bracelet upon her arm.*]
　　Imo.　　　　　O the gods!
When shall we see again?

　　　　Enter CYMBELINE *and* Lords.
　　Post.　　　　　Alack, the King!
　　Cym. Thou basest thing, avoid! Hence, from
　　my sight!　125
If after this command thou fraught the court
With thy unworthiness, thou diest. Away!
Thou'rt poison to my blood.
　　Post.　　　　　The gods protect you!
And bless the good remainders of the court!
I am gone.　　　　　　　[*Exit.*
　　Imo.　　There cannot be a pinch in death　130
More sharp than this is.
　　Cym.　　　　　O disloyal thing,
That shouldst repair my youth, thou heap'st
A year's age on me.
　　Imo.　　　　　I beseech you, sir,
Harm not yourself with your vexation.
I am senseless of your wrath; a touch more rare　135
Subdues all pangs, all fears.
　　Cym.　　　　　Past grace? obedience?
　　Imo. Past hope, and in despair; that way, past
　　grace.
　　Cym. That mightst have had the sole son of my
　　queen!
　　Imo. O blest, that I might not! I chose an eagle,
And did avoid a puttock.　140

　　Cym. Thou took'st a beggar; wouldst have made
　　my throne
A seat for baseness.
　　Imo.　　　　　No; I rather added
A lustre to it.
　　Cym.　　　　　O thou vile one!
　　Imo.　　　　　Sir,
It is your fault that I have lov'd Posthumus.
You bred him as my playfellow, and he is　145
A man worth any woman; overbuys me
Almost the sum he pays.
　　Cym.　　　　　What, art thou mad?
　　Imo. Almost, sir; heaven restore me! Would
　　I were
A neat-herd's daughter, and my Leonatus
Our neighbour shepherd's son!

　　　　　Re-enter QUEEN.
　　Cym.　　　　　Thou foolish thing!
— They were again together; you have done　151
Not after our command. Away with her,
And pen her up.
　　Queen.　　　　Beseech your patience. Peace,
Dear lady daughter, peace! Sweet sovereign,
Leave us to ourselves; and make yourself some
　　comfort　155
Out of your best advice.
　　Cym.　　　　　Nay, let her languish
A drop of blood a day; and, being aged,
Die of this folly!　　[*Exeunt* [*Cymbeline and Lords*].

　　　　　Enter PISANIO.
　　Queen.　　　　Fie! you must give way.
Here is your servant. How now, sir! What
　　news?　159
　　Pis. My lord your son drew on my master.
　　Queen.　　　　Ha!
No harm, I trust, is done?
　　Pis.　　　　　There might have been,
But that my master rather play'd than fought
And had no help of anger. They were parted
By gentlemen at hand.
　　Queen.　　　　I am very glad on't.
　　Imo. Your son's my father's friend; he takes
　　his part　165
To draw upon an exile. O brave sir!
I would they were in Afric both together;
Myself by with a needle, that I might prick
The goer-back. Why came you from your master?
　　Pis. On his command. He would not suffer
　　me　170
To bring him to the haven; left these notes
Of what commands I should be subject to,

When't pleas'd you to employ me.

Queen.   This hath been
Your faithful servant. I dare lay mine honour
He will remain so.

Pis.   I humbly thank your Highness. 175

Queen. Pray, walk a while.

Imo. [*to Pis.*] About some half-hour hence,
[I] pray you, speak with me; you shall at least
Go see my lord aboard. For this time leave
me.   [*Exeunt.*

SCENE [II. *The same. A public place.*]

Enter CLOTEN *and two* LORDS.

1. Lord. Sir, I would advise you to shift a shirt;
the violence of action hath made you reek as a
sacrifice. Where air comes out, air comes in;
there's none abroad so wholesome as that you vent. 5

Clo. If my shirt were bloody, then to shift it.
Have I hurt him?

2. Lord. [*Aside.*] No, faith; not so much as his
patience.   9

1. Lord. Hurt him! His body's a passable
carcass, if he be not hurt; it is a throughfare for
steel, if it be not hurt.

2. Lord. [*Aside.*] His steel was in debt; it went
o' th' backside the town.

Clo. The villain would not stand me.   15

2. Lord. [*Aside.*] No; but he fled forward still,
toward your face.

1. Lord. Stand you! You have land enough of
your own, but he added to your having, gave you
some ground.   20

2. Lord. [*Aside.*] As many inches as you have
oceans. Puppies!

Clo. I would they had not come between us.

2. Lord. [*Aside.*] So would I, till you had measur'd how long a fool you were upon the ground. 26

Clo. And that she should love this fellow and
refuse me!

2. Lord. [*Aside.*] If it be a sin to make a true
election, she is damn'd.   30

1. Lord. Sir, as I told you always, her beauty
and her brain go not together. She's a good sign,
but I have seen small reflection of her wit.

2. Lord. [*Aside.*] She shines not upon fools,
lest the reflection should hurt her.   35

Clo. Come, I'll to my chamber. Would there
had been some hurt done!

2. Lord. [*Aside.*] I wish not so; unless it had been
the fall of an ass, which is no great hurt.

Clo. You'll go with us?   40

1. Lord. I'll attend your lordship.

Clo. Nay, come, let's go together.

2. Lord. Well, my lord.   [*Exeunt.*

SCENE [III. *A room in Cymbeline's palace.*]

Enter IMOGEN *and* PISANIO.

Imo. I would thou grew'st unto the shores o'
      th' haven,
And question'dst every sail. If he should write
And I not have it, 'twere a paper lost
As offer'd mercy is. What was the last   4
That he spake to thee?

Pis.   It was his queen, his queen!

Imo. Then wav'd his handkerchief?

Pis.   And kiss'd it, madam.

Imo. Senseless linen! happier therein than I!
And that was all?

Pis.   No, madam; for so long
As he could make me with [this] eye or ear
Distinguish him from others, he did keep   10
The deck, with glove or hat or handkerchief
Still waving, as the fits and stirs of 's mind
Could best express how slow his soul sail'd on,
How swift his ship.

Imo.   Thou shouldst have made him
As little as a crow, or less, ere left   15
To after-eye him.

Pis.   Madam, so I did.

Imo. I would have broke mine eye-strings,
      crack'd them, but
To look upon him, till the diminution
Of space had pointed him sharp as my needle;
Nay, follow'd him till he had melted from   20
The smallness of a gnat to air, and then
Have turn'd mine eye and wept. But, good
      Pisanio,
When shall we hear from him?

Pis.   Be assur'd, madam,
With his next vantage.   24

Imo. I did not take my leave of him, but had
Most pretty things to say. Ere I could tell him
How I would think on him at certain hours
Such thoughts and such, or I could make him swear
The shes of Italy should not betray
Mine interest and his honour, or have charg'd
      him,   30
At the sixth hour of morn, at noon, at midnight,
T' encounter me with orisons, for then
I am in heaven for him; or ere I could

176. **walk:** withdraw. 177. [I] (Capell). Om. F.
Sc. ii, 1. *1. Lord.* In this scene speeches of the Lords are designated in F merely *1.* and *2.* 5. **abroad:** outside you. 10.
passable: easy (for a rapier) to pass through. 13. **in debt:** i.e., paid no scores (blows). 13–14. **went...town:** was afraid
to go through the town; i.e., it missed. 32. **sign:** appearance.
Sc. iii, 4. **offer'd mercy:** pardon not received. 9. [this] (Theobald). *his* F. 24. **vantage:** opportunity. 32. **orisons:**
prayers.

Give him that parting kiss which I had set
Betwixt two charming words, comes in my father 35
And like the tyrannous breathing of the north
Shakes all our buds from growing.

Enter a LADY.

Lady.   The Queen, madam,
Desires your Highness' company.
Imo. Those things I bid you do, get them dis-
    patch'd.
I will attend the Queen.
Pis.   Madam, I shall.   40
                                              [*Exeunt.*

SCENE [IV. *Rome. Philario's house.*]

Enter PHILARIO, IACHIMO, *a* FRENCHMAN, *a* Dutch-
    man, *and a* Spaniard.

Iach. Believe it, sir, I have seen him in Britain.
He was then of a crescent note, expected to prove
so worthy as since he hath been allowed the name
of; but I could then have look'd on him without the
help of admiration, though the catalogue of his
endowments had been tabled by his side and I to
peruse him by items.   7
Phi. You speak of him when he was less furnish'd
than now he is with that which makes him both
without and within.
French. I have seen him in France. We had
very many there could behold the sun with as firm
eyes as he.   13
Iach. This matter of marrying his king's daughter, wherein he must be weighed rather by her
value than his own, words him, I doubt not, a great
deal from the matter.
French. And then his banishment.   18
Iach. Ay, and the approbation of those that
weep this lamentable divorce under her colours
are wonderfully to extend him, be it but to fortify
her judgement, which else an easy battery might
lay flat for taking a beggar without less quality.
But how comes it he is to sojourn with you? How
creeps acquaintance?   25
Phi. His father and I were soldiers together;
to whom I have been often bound for no less
than my life.

Enter POSTHUMUS.

Here comes the Briton. Let him be so entertained
amongst you as suits with gentlemen of your knowing to a stranger of his quality. — I beseech you 30
all, be better known to this gentleman, whom I
commend to you as a noble friend of mine. How
worthy he is I will leave to appear hereafter,
rather than story him in his own hearing.   35
French. Sir, we have known together in Orleans.
Post. Since when I have been debtor to you for
courtesies, which I will be ever to pay and yet
pay still.   40
French. Sir, you o'er-rate my poor kindness.
I was glad I did atone my countryman and you.
It had been pity you should have been put together with so mortal a purpose as then each bore,
upon importance of so slight and trivial a nature. 45
Post. By your pardon, sir, I was then a young
traveller; rather shunn'd to go even with what I
heard than in my every action to be guided by
others' experiences: but upon my mended judgement — if I offend [not] to say it is mended — my
quarrel was not altogether slight.   51
French. Faith, yes, to be put to the arbitrement
of swords, and by such two that would by all likelihood have confounded one the other, or have
fallen both.   55
Iach. Can we, with manners, ask what was the
difference?
French. Safely, I think; 'twas a contention in
public, which may, without contradiction, suffer
the report. It was much like an argument that   60
fell out last night, where each of us fell in praise of
our country-mistresses; this gentleman at that
time vouching — and upon warrant of bloody af-
firmation — his to be more fair, virtuous, wise,
chaste, constant, qualified, and less attemptable
than any the rarest of our ladies in France.   66
Iach. That lady is not now living, or this gentleman's opinion by this worn out.
Post. She holds her virtue still, and I my mind.
Iach. You must not so far prefer her 'fore ours
of Italy.   71
Post. Being so far provok'd as I was in France,
I would abate her nothing, though I profess myself
her adorer, not her friend.   74
Iach. As fair and as good — a kind of hand-in-
hand comparison — had been something too fair
and too good for any lady in Britain. If she went
before others I have seen, as that diamond of yours
outlustres many I have beheld, I could not [but]
believe she excelled many. But I have not seen
the most precious diamond that is, nor you the
lady.   82

35. **charming**: having a charm or spell.
  Sc. iv, 2. **crescent note**: growing distinction. 5. **admiration**: astonishment. 6. **tabled**: listed. 12–13. **many...he**:
many there as good as he. 16–17. **words...matter**: represents him as very different from what he really is. 20. **colours**:
banners; i.e., those on her side. 21. **extend**: magnify. 23. **without**. A mistake for *with*. 24. **quality**: rank. 36. **known**
together: been acquainted. 42. **atone**: reconcile. 43. **put together**: opposed (in a duel). 47. **go even**: agree. 50. [**not**]
(Rowe). Om. F. 54. **confounded**: destroyed. 65. **qualified**: endowed. **attemptable**: i.e., in virtue. 73. **abate**:
depreciate. 74. **friend**: lover. 75. **hand-in-hand comparison**: comparison of equals. 79. [**but**] (Malone). Om. F.

Post. I prais'd her as I rated her; so do I my stone.

Iach. What do you esteem it at?

Post. More than the world enjoys.

Iach. Either your unparagon'd mistress is dead, or she's outpriz'd by a trifle.   88

Post. You are mistaken. The one may be sold or given, or if there were wealth enough for the purchase, or merit for the gift; the other is not a thing for sale, and only the gift of the gods.

Iach. Which the gods have given you?

Post. Which, by their graces, I will keep.   95

Iach. You may wear her in title yours; but, you know, strange fowl light upon neighbouring ponds. Your ring may be stol'n too; so your brace of un- prizable estimations, the one is but frail and the other casual. A cunning thief, or a that-way- accomplish'd courtier, would hazard the winning both of first and last.   102

Post. Your Italy contains none so accomplish'd a courtier to convince the honour of my mistress, if, in the holding or loss of that, you term her frail. I do nothing doubt you have store of thieves; notwithstanding, I fear not my ring.   108

Phi. Let us leave here, gentlemen.

Post. Sir, with all my heart. This worthy signior, I thank him, makes no stranger of me; we are familiar at first.   112

Iach. With five times so much conversation, I should get ground of your fair mistress, make her go back, even to the yielding, had I admittance, and opportunity to friend.

Post. No, no.   117

Iach. I dare thereupon pawn the moiety of my estate to your ring; which, in my opinion, o'ervalues it something. But I make my wager rather against your confidence than her reputation; and, to bar your offence herein too, I durst attempt it against any lady in the world.   123

Post. You are a great deal abus'd in too bold a persuasion, and I doubt not you sustain what you're worthy of by your attempt.

Iach. What's that?

Post. A repulse; though your attempt, as you call it, deserve more, — a punishment too.   129

Phi. Gentlemen, enough of this; it came in too suddenly. Let it die as it was born, and, I pray you, be better acquainted.

Iach. Would I had put my estate and my neigh- bour's on th' approbation of what I have spoke!

Post. What lady would you choose to assail?   136

Iach. Yours, whom in constancy you think stands so safe. I will lay you ten thousand ducats to your ring that, commend me to the court where

your lady is, with no more advantage than the opportunity of a second conference, and I will bring from thence that honour of hers which you imagine so reserv'd.   143

Post. I will wage against your gold, gold to it. My ring I hold dear as my finger; 'tis part of it.

Iach. You are [afraid], and therein the wiser. If you buy ladies' flesh at a million a dram, you cannot preserve it from tainting. But I see you have some religion in you, that you fear.   149

Post. This is but a custom in your tongue; you bear a graver purpose, I hope.

Iach. I am the master of my speeches, and would undergo what's spoken, I swear.   153

Post. Will you? I shall but lend my diamond till your return. Let there be covenants drawn between 's. My mistress exceeds in goodness the hugeness of your unworthy thinking. I dare you to this match; here's my ring.

Phi. I will have it no lay.   159

Iach. By the gods, it is one. If I bring you no sufficient testimony that I have enjoy'd the dearest bodily part of your mistress, my ten thousand ducats are yours; so is your diamond too. If I come off and leave her in such honour as you have trust in, she your jewel, this your jewel, and my gold are yours; provided I have your commendation for my more free entertainment.   167

Post. I embrace these conditions; let us have articles betwixt us. Only, thus far you shall answer: if you make your voyage upon her and give me directly to understand you have prevail'd, I am no further your enemy; she is not worth our debate. If she remain unseduc'd, you not making it appear otherwise, for your ill opinion and the assault you have made to her chastity you shall answer me with your sword.   176

Iach. Your hand; a covenant. We will have these things set down by lawful counsel, and straight away for Britain, lest the bargain should catch cold and starve. I will fetch my gold and have our two wagers recorded.   181

Post. Agreed. [*Exeunt Posthumus and Iachimo.*]

French. Will this hold, think you?

Phi. Signior Iachimo will not from it. Pray, let us follow 'em.   [*Exeunt.*]

SCENE [V. *Britain. A room in Cymbeline's palace.*]

Enter QUEEN, LADIES, *and* CORNELIUS.

Queen. Whiles yet the dew's on ground, gather those flowers;

---

99. **unprizable estimations:** priceless values. 100. **casual:** subject to accident. 104. **convince:** overcome. 108. **fear:** fear for. 109. **leave:** desist. 116. **to friend:** as aid. 118. **moiety:** half. 124. **abus'd:** deceived. 125. **persuasion:** opinion. 134. **approbation:** proof. 146. **[afraid]** (Theobald). *a Friend* F. 149. **that:** because. 153. **undergo:** undertake. 159. **lay:** wager. 180. **starve:** die.

Make haste. Who has the note of them?
    [*1.*] *Lady.*   I, madam.
    Queen. Dispatch.   [*Exeunt Ladies.*
Now, master doctor, have you brought those drugs?
    Cor. Pleaseth your Highness, ay. Here they
    are, madam.   [*Presenting a small box.*]   5
But I beseech your Grace, without offence, —
My conscience bids me ask — wherefore you have
Commanded of me these most poisonous com-
    pounds,
Which are the movers of a languishing death,
But though slow, deadly.
    Queen.   I wonder, doctor,   10
Thou ask'st me such a question. Have I not been
Thy pupil long? Hast thou not learn'd me how
To make perfumes? distil? preserve? yea, so
That our great king himself doth woo me oft
For my confections? Having thus far pro-
    ceeded, —   15
Unless thou think'st me devilish — is't not meet
That I did amplify my judgement in
Other conclusions? I will try the forces
Of these thy compounds on such creatures as
We count not worth the hanging, — but none
    human —   20
To try the vigour of them and apply
Allayments to their act, and by them gather
Their several virtues and effects.
    Cor.   Your Highness
Shall from this practice but make hard your heart.
Besides, the seeing these effects will be   25
Both noisome and infectious.
    Queen.   O, content thee.

                 Enter PISANIO.

[*Aside.*] Here comes a flattering rascal; upon him
Will I first work. He's for his master,
And enemy to my son. How now, Pisanio!
Doctor, your service for this time is ended;   30
Take your own way.
    Cor.   [*Aside.*] I do suspect you, madam;
But you shall do no harm.
    Queen.   [*To Pisanio.*] Hark thee, a word.
    Cor. [*Aside.*] I do not like her. She doth think
    she has
Strange ling'ring poisons. I do know her spirit,
And will not trust one of her malice with   35
A drug of such damn'd nature. Those she has
Will stupefy and dull the sense a while,
Which first, perchance, she'll prove on cats and
    dogs,
Then afterward up higher; but there is
No danger in what show of death it makes,   40

More than the locking-up the spirits a time,
To be more fresh, reviving. She is fool'd
With a most false effect; and I the truer,
So to be false with her.
    Queen.   No further service, doctor,
Until I send for thee.
    Cor.   I humbly take my leave.   45
                          [*Exit.*
    Queen. Weeps she still, say'st thou? Dost
    thou think in time
She will not quench and let instructions enter
Where folly now possesses? Do thou work.
When thou shalt bring me word she loves my son,
I'll tell thee on the instant thou art then   50
As great as is thy master, — greater, for
His fortunes all lie speechless and his name
Is at last gasp. Return he cannot, nor
Continue where he is. To shift his being
Is to exchange one misery with another,   55
And every day that comes comes to decay
A day's work in him. What shalt thou expect
To be depender on a thing that leans,
Who cannot be new built, nor has no friends
So much as but to prop him? [*The Queen drops
    the box: Pisanio takes it up.*]
                 Thou tak'st up
Thou know'st not what; but take it for thy labour.
It is a thing I made, which hath the King   62
Five times redeem'd from death. I do not know
What is more cordial. Nay, I prithee, take it;
It is an earnest of a further good   65
That I mean to thee. Tell thy mistress how
The case stands with her; do't as from thyself.
Think what a chance thou changest on, but think
Thou hast thy mistress still; to boot, my son.
Who shall take notice of thee. I'll move the
    King   70
To any shape of thy preferment such
As thou'lt desire; and then myself, I chiefly,
That set thee on to this desert, am bound
To load thy merit richly. Call my women.
Think on my words.   [*Exit Pisanio.*
             A sly and constant knave,
Not to be shak'd; the agent for his master   76
And the remembrancer of her to hold
The hand-fast to her lord. I have given him that
Which, if he take, shall quite unpeople her
Of liegers for her sweet, and which she after,   80
Except she bend her humour, shall be assur'd
To taste of too.

         Re-enter PISANIO *and* Ladies.
    So, so; well done, well done.

Sc. v, 2. note: list. 18. conclusions: experiments. 22. Allayments: antidotes. 47. quench: cool off. instructions: counsel. 54. being: abode. 56. decay: destroy. 64. cordial: restorative. 65. earnest: token. 68. chance ... on: opportunity this change (of service) offers. 77. the ... her: her reminder. 78. hand-fast: marriage contract. 80. liegers ... sweet: ambassadors to her lover.

The violets, cowslips, and the primroses,
Bear to my closet. Fare thee well, Pisanio;
Think on my words.   [*Exeunt Queen and Ladies.*
  Pis.   And shall do;   85
But when to my good lord I prove untrue,
I'll choke myself. There's all I'll do for you.
                                [*Exit.*

SCENE [VI. *The same. Another room in the palace.*]

Enter IMOGEN *alone.*

  Imo. A father cruel, and a step-dame false;
A foolish suitor to a wedded lady
That hath her husband banish'd; — O, that husband!
My supreme crown of grief! and those repeated
Vexations of it! Had I been thief-stolen,   5
As my two brothers, happy! but most miserable
Is the desire that's glorious. Blessed be those,
How mean soe'er, that have their honest wills,
Which seasons comfort. Who may this be? Fie!

Enter PISANIO *and* IACHIMO.

  Pis. Madam, a noble gentleman of Rome,   10
Comes from my lord with letters.
  Iach.   Change you, madam?
The worthy Leonatus is in safety
And greets your Highness dearly.
                      [*Presents a letter.*]
  Imo.   Thanks, good sir;
You're kindly welcome.
  Iach. [*Aside.*] All of her that is out of door
    most rich!   15
If she be furnish'd with a mind so rare,
She is alone, th' Arabian bird, and I
Have lost the wager. Boldness be my friend!
Arm me, audacity, from head to foot!
Or, like the Parthian, I shall flying fight;   20
Rather, directly fly.
  Imo. (*Reads.*) " — He is one of the noblest note,
to whose kindnesses I am most infinitely tied.
Reflect upon him accordingly, as you value your
trust —   LEONATUS."   25
So far I read aloud —
But even the very middle of my heart
Is warm'd by th' rest — and take it thankfully.
You are as welcome, worthy sir, as I
Have words to bid you, and shall find it so   30
In all that I can do.
  Iach.   Thanks, fairest lady.
What, are men mad? Hath nature given them eyes

To see this vaulted arch and the rich crop
Of sea and land, which can distinguish 'twixt
The fiery orbs above and the twinn'd stones   35
Upon [th' unnumber'd] beach, and can we not
Partition make with spectacles so precious
'Twixt fair and foul?
  Imo.   What makes your admiration?
  Iach. It cannot be i' th' eye, for apes and
    monkeys
'Twixt two such shes would chatter this way
    and   40
Contemn with mows the other; nor i' th' judge-
    ment,
For idiots in this case of favour would
Be wisely definite; nor i' th' appetite;
Sluttery to such neat excellence oppos'd
Should make desire vomit emptiness,   45
Not so allur'd to feed.
  Imo. What is the matter, trow?
  Iach.   The cloyed will, —
That satiate yet unsatisfi'd desire, that tub
Both fill'd and running, — ravening first the lamb,
Longs after for the garbage.
  Imo.   What, dear sir,   50
Thus raps you? Are you well?
  Iach. Thanks, madam; well. [*To Pisanio.*]
    Beseech you, sir, desire
My man's abode where I did leave him. He
Is strange and peevish.
  Pis.   I was going, sir,
To give him welcome.   [*Exit.* 55
  Imo. Continues well my lord? His health,
    beseech you?
  Iach. Well, madam.
  Imo. Is he dispos'd to mirth? I hope he is.
  Iach. Exceeding pleasant; none a stranger there
So merry and so gamesome. He is call'd   60
The Briton reveller.
  Imo.   When he was here,
He did incline to sadness, and oft-times
Not knowing why.
  Iach.   I never saw him sad.
There is a Frenchman his companion, one
An eminent monsieur that, it seems, much loves   65
A Gallian girl at home. He furnaces
The thick sighs from him, whiles the jolly Briton —
Your lord, I mean — laughs from 's free lungs,
    cries "O,
Can my sides hold, to think that man, who knows
By history, report, or his own proof,   70
What woman is, yea, what she cannot choose
But must be, will his free hours languish for

Sc. vi, 4. **repeated:** which I have enumerated.   7. **that's glorious:** for glory.   8. **wills:** desires.   9. **seasons:** gives zest to. 11. **Change:** i.e., change color.   17. **alone:** unique.   **Arabian bird:** the phoenix, a fabulous bird, one only existing at a time. 24. **Reflect upon:** regard.   35. **twinn'd:** identical.   36. **[th' unnumber'd]** (Theobald). *the number'd* F.   37. **spectacles:** eyes.   38. **admiration:** wonder.   41. **mows:** grimaces.   42. **case of favour:** question of beauty.   49. **ravening:** devouring. 51. **raps:** transports.   52–53. **desire...abode:** ask my servant to remain.   54. **strange:** a stranger.   66. **Gallian:** Gallic.

Assured bondage?"
   Imo.   Will my lord say so?
   Iach. Ay, madam, with his eyes in flood with
      laughter.
It is a recreation to be by   75
And hear him mock the Frenchman. But, heavens
      know,
Some men are much to blame.
   Imo.   Not he, I hope.
   Iach. Not he; but yet heaven's bounty towards
      him might
Be us'd more thankfully. In himself, 'tis much;
In you — which I account his — beyond all
      talents.   80
Whilst I am bound to wonder, I am bound
To pity too.
   Imo.   What do you pity, sir?
   Iach. Two creatures heartily.
   Imo.   Am I one, sir?
You look on me; what wreck discern you in me
Deserves your pity?
   Iach.   Lamentable! What,   85
To hide me from the radiant sun, and solace
I' th' dungeon by a snuff!
   Imo.   I pray you, sir,
Deliver with more openness your answers
To my demands. Why do you pity me?
   Iach. That others do,   90
I was about to say, enjoy your — But
It is an office of the gods to venge it,
Not mine to speak on 't.
   Imo.   You do seem to know
Something of me, or what concerns me: pray you, —
Since doubting things go ill often hurts more   95
Than to be sure they do; for certainties
Either are past remedies, or, timely knowing,
The remedy then born — discover to me
What both you spur and stop.
   Iach.   Had I this cheek
To bathe my lips upon; this hand, whose touch,   100
Whose every touch, would force the feeler's soul
To the oath of loyalty; this object, which
Takes prisoner the wild motion of mine eye,
[Fixing] it only here; should I, damn'd then,
Slaver with lips as common as the stairs   105
That mount the Capitol; join gripes with hands
Made hard with hourly falsehood — falsehood, as
With labour; then [lie] peeping in an eye
Base and [illustrous] as the smoky light
That's fed with stinking tallow: it were fit   110
That all the plagues of hell should at one time

Encounter such revolt.
   Imo.   My lord, I fear,
Has forgot Britain.
   Iach.   And himself. Not I,
Inclin'd to this intelligence, pronounce
The beggary of his change; but 'tis your graces   115
That from my mutest conscience to my tongue
Charms this report out.
   Imo.   Let me hear no more.
   Iach. O dearest soul! your cause doth strike
      my heart
With pity that doth make me sick. A lady
So fair, and fasten'd to an empery   120
Would make the great'st king double, — to be
      partner'd
With tomboys hir'd with that self-exhibition
Which your own coffers yield! with diseas'd ven-
      tures
That play with all infirmities for gold
Which rottenness can lend nature! such boil'd
      stuff   125
As well might poison poison! Be reveng'd;
Or she that bore you was no queen, and you
Recoil from your great stock.
   Imo.   Reveng'd!
How should I be reveng'd? If this be true, —
As I have such a heart that both mine ears   130
Must not in haste abuse — if it be true,
How should I be reveng'd?
   Iach.   Should he make me
Live, like Diana's priest, betwixt cold sheets,
Whiles he is vaulting variable ramps,
In your despite, upon your purse? Revenge it.   135
I dedicate myself to your sweet pleasure,
More noble than that runagate to your bed,
And will continue fast to your affection,
Still close as sure.
   Imo.   What, ho, Pisanio!
   Iach. Let me my service tender on your lips.   140
   Imo. Away! I do condemn mine ears that have
So long attended thee. If thou wert honourable,
Thou wouldst have told this tale for virtue, not
For such an end thou seek'st, — as base as strange.
Thou wrong'st a gentleman, who is as far   145
From thy report as thou from honour, and
[Solicit'st] here a lady that disdains
Thee and the devil alike. What ho, Pisanio!
The King my father shall be made acquainted
Of thy assault. If he shall think it fit   150
A saucy stranger in his court to mart
As in a Romish stew, and to expound

---

80. **talents:** riches. 87. **snuff:** candle wick. 99. **spur and stop:** impel (to speak) and check. 104. [**Fixing**] F2. *Fiering* F1. 108. [**lie**] (Johnson conj.). *by* F. 109. [**illustrous**] (Collier); lack-lustre. *illustrious* F. 112. **Encounter:** befall. **revolt:** infidelity. 113-14. **Not . . . intelligence:** I, reluctant to give this news. 120. **empery:** empire. 122. **tomboys:** strumpets. 122-23. **with . . . yield:** with money from you. 123. **ventures:** adventuresses. 125. **Which:** referring to *infirmities*. **boil'd:** sweated, referring to the treatment for certain diseases. 128. **Recoil:** degenerate. 134. **ramps:** prostitutes. 137. **runagate:** renegade. 139. **close:** secret. 147. [**Solicit'st**]. *Solicites* F. 151. **mart:** bargain. 152. **stew:** brothel.

His beastly mind to us, he hath a court
He little cares for and a daughter who
He not respects at all. What, ho, Pisanio!   155
   Iach. O happy Leonatus! I may say.
The credit that thy lady hath of thee
Deserves thy trust, and thy most perfect goodness
Her assur'd credit. Blessed live you long
A lady to the worthiest sir that ever   160
Country call'd his! and you his mistress, only
For the most worthiest fit! Give me your pardon.
I have spoke this to know if your affiance
Were deeply rooted, and shall make your lord,
That which he is, new o'er; and he is one   165
The truest manner'd, such a holy witch
That he enchants societies into him;
Half all men's hearts are his.
   Imo.   You make amends.
   Iach. He sits 'mongst men like a [descended]
      god:
He hath a kind of honour sets him off,   170
More than a mortal seeming. Be not angry,
Most mighty princess, that I have adventur'd
To try your taking of a false report; which hath
Honour'd with confirmation your great judgement
In the election of a sir so rare,   175
Which you know cannot err. The love I bear him
Made me to fan you thus; but the gods made you,
Unlike all others, chaffless. Pray, your pardon.
   Imo. All's well, sir. Take my power i' th'
      court for yours.
   Iach. My humble thanks. I had almost forgot
To entreat your Grace but in a small request,   181
And yet of moment too, for it concerns
Your lord; myself, and other noble friends,
Are partners in the business.
   Imo.   Pray, what is't?
   Iach. Some dozen Romans of us and your
      lord —   185
The best feather of our wing — have mingled sums
To buy a present for the Emperor;
Which I, the factor for the rest, have done
In France. 'Tis plate of rare device, and jewels
Of rich and exquisite form, their values great;   190
And I am something curious, being strange,
To have them in safe stowage. May it please you
To take them in protection?
   Imo.   Willingly;
And pawn mine honour for their safety. Since
My lord hath interest in them, I will keep them   195
In my bedchamber.
   Iach.   They are in a trunk,
Attended by my men. I will make bold
To send them to you, only for this night;

I must aboard to-morrow.
   Imo.   O, no, no.   200
   Iach. Yes, I beseech; or I shall short my word
By length'ning my return. From Gallia
I cross'd the seas on purpose and on promise
To see your Grace.
   Imo.   I thank you for your pains:
But not away to-morrow!
   Iach.   O, I must, madam;
Therefore I shall beseech you, if you please   205
To greet your lord with writing, do't to-night.
I have outstood my time; which is material
To the tender of our present.
   Imo.   I will write.
Send your trunk to me; it shall safe be kept,
And truly yielded you. You're very welcome. 210
                    [*Exeunt.*

ACT II

Scene I. [*Britain. Before Cymbeline's palace.*]

Enter Cloten *and the two* Lords.

   Clo. Was there ever man had such luck! When
I kiss'd the jack, upon an up-cast to be hit away! I
had a hundred pound on't; and then a whoreson
jackanapes must take me up for swearing, as if I
borrowed mine oaths of him and might not spend
them at my pleasure.   6
   1. Lord. What got he by that? You have
broke his pate with your bowl.
   2. Lord. [*Aside.*] If his wit had been like him
that broke it, it would have run all out.   10
   Clo. When a gentleman is dispos'd to swear, it
is not for any standers-by to curtail his oaths, ha?
   2. Lord. No, my lord; [*aside*] nor crop the ears
of them.   15
   Clo. Whoreson dog! I gave him satisfaction!
Would he had been one of my rank!
   2. Lord. [*Aside.*] To have smelt like a fool.   18
   Clo. I am not vex'd more at anything in th'
earth; a pox on't! I had rather not be so noble as
I am. They dare not fight with me because of the
Queen my mother. Every Jack-slave hath his
bellyful of fighting, and I must go up and down like
a cock that nobody can match.   24
   2. Lord. [*Aside.*] You are cock and capon too;
and you crow, cock, with your comb on.
   Clo. Sayest thou?
   2. Lord. It is not fit your lordship should undertake every companion that you give offence to.   30
   Clo. No, I know that; but it is fit I should commit offence to my inferiors.

---

157. **credit:** trust.   166. **witch:** wizard, charmer.   169. [**descended**] F₂. *defended* F₁.   177. **fan:** winnow, i.e., test.   188.
factor: agent.   191. **curious . . . strange:** anxious, being a stranger.   200. **short:** fall short of.   208. **tender:** bestowing.
    Act II, sc. i, 2. **kiss'd the jack:** touched the target bowl.   **up-cast:** final shot.   4. **take me up:** rebuke me.   22. **Jack-**
slave: base fellow.   26. **comb:** coxcomb, fool's cap.   30. **companion:** fellow.

2. Lord. Ay, it is fit for your lordship only.
Clo. Why, so I say.
1. Lord. Did you hear of a stranger that's come
to court [to-night]?　　　　　　　　　　　　　36
Clo. A stranger, and I not know on't!
2. Lord. [*Aside.*] He's a strange fellow himself,
and knows it not.
1. Lord. There's an Italian come; and, 'tis
thought, one of Leonatus' friends.　　　　　　41
Clo. Leonatus! a banish'd rascal; and he's another, whatsoever he be. Who told you of this
stranger?
1. Lord. One of your lordship's pages.　　　45
Clo. Is it fit I went to look upon him? Is there
no derogation in't?
2. Lord. You cannot derogate, my lord.
Clo. Not easily, I think.　　　　　　　　49
2. Lord. [*Aside.*] You are a fool granted; therefore your issues, being foolish, do not derogate.
Clo. Come, I'll go see this Italian. What I have
lost to-day at bowls I'll win to-night of him.
Come, go.　　　　　　　　　　　　　　55
2. Lord. I'll attend your lordship.
　　　　　　[*Exeunt [Cloten and First Lord].*
That such a crafty devil as is his mother
Should yield the world this ass! A woman that
Bears all down with her brain; and this her son
Cannot take two from twenty, for his heart,　60
And leave eighteen. Alas, poor princess,
Thou divine Imogen, what thou endur'st,
Betwixt a father by thy step-dame govern'd,
A mother hourly coining plots, a wooer
More hateful than the foul expulsion is　　　65
Of thy dear husband, [than] that horrid act
Of the divorce he'd make! The heavens hold firm
The walls of thy dear honour, keep unshak'd
That temple, thy fair mind, that thou mayst stand,
T' enjoy thy banish'd lord and this great land!　70
　　　　　　　　　　　　　　　　[*Exit.*

SCENE II. [*Imogen's bedchamber in Cymbeline's
palace: a trunk in one corner of it.*]

IMOGEN *in her bed* [*reading*]; *and a* LADY [*attending*].

Imo. Who's there? My woman Helen?
Lady.　　　　　　　　　Please you, madam.
Imo. What hour is it?
Lady.　　　　　　Almost midnight, madam.
Imo. I have read three hours then. Mine eyes
　are weak.
Fold down the leaf where I have left. To bed.
Take not away the taper, leave it burning;　　5
And if thou canst awake by four o' th' clock,

I prithee, call me. Sleep hath seiz'd me wholly.
　　　　　　　　　　　　　　[*Exit Lady.*]
To your protection I commend me, gods.
From fairies and the tempters of the night
Guard me, beseech ye.　　　　　　　　10
　　[*Sleeps. Iachimo [comes] from the trunk.*
　Iach. The crickets sing, and man's o'er-labour'd
　　sense
Repairs itself by rest. Our Tarquin thus
Did softly press the rushes ere he waken'd
The chastity he wounded. Cytherea!
How bravely thou becom'st thy bed, fresh lily,　15
And whiter than the sheets! That I might touch!
But kiss one kiss! Rubies unparagon'd,
How dearly they do't! 'Tis her breathing that
Perfumes the chamber thus. The flame o' th' taper
Bows toward her, and would under-peep her lids　20
To see th' enclosed lights, now canopied
Under these windows white and azure, lac'd
With blue of heaven's own tinct. But my design,
To note the chamber. I will write all down:
Such and such pictures; there the window; such　25
Th' adornment of her bed; the arras, figures,
Why, such and such, and the contents o' th' story.
Ah, but some natural notes about her body,
Above ten thousand meaner moveables
Would testify, t' enrich mine inventory.　　30
O sleep, thou ape of death, lie dull upon her!
And be her sense but as a monument,
Thus in a chapel lying! Come off, come off!
　　　　　　　　　　[*Taking off her bracelet.*]
As slippery as the Gordian knot was hard!
'Tis mine; and this will witness outwardly,　35
As strongly as the conscience does within,
To th' madding of her lord. On her left breast
A mole cinque-spotted, like the crimson drops
I' th' bottom of a cowslip. Here's a voucher,
Stronger than ever law could make; this secret　40
Will force him think I have pick'd the lock and
　ta'en
The treasure of her honour. No more. To what
　end?
Why should I write this down, that's riveted,
Screw'd to my memory? She hath been reading
late
The tale of Tereus; here the leaf's turn'd down　45
Where Philomel gave up. I have enough.
To th' trunk again, and shut the spring of it.
Swift, swift, you dragons of the night, that dawning
May bare the raven's eye! I lodge in fear;
Though this a heavenly angel, hell is here.　　50
　　　　　　　　　　　　　　[*Clock strikes.*
One, two, three; time, time! [*Goes into the trunk.*]

36. [to-night] F₂. *night* F₁. 47. **derogation**: loss of dignity. 66. **husband, [than]** F₄. *husband. Then* F₁.
Sc. ii, 13. **rushes.** Floors of Elizabethan houses were covered with rushes (an anachronism). 14. **Cytherea:** Venus.
18. **they do't**: her lips kiss each other. 27. **story**: the picture on the arras. 29. **moveables**: pieces of furniture. 38. **cinque-spotted**: with five spots. 45. **Tereus**: a Thracian king who defiled his sister-in-law Philomela.

SCENE III. [*An ante-chamber adjoining Imogen's apartments.*]

Enter CLOTEN *and* LORDS.

1. Lord. Your lordship is the most patient man in loss, the most coldest that ever turn'd up ace.

Clo. It would make any man cold to lose. 4

1. Lord. But not every man patient after the noble temper of your lordship. You are most hot and furious when you win.

Clo. Winning will put any man into courage. If I could get this foolish Imogen, I should have gold enough. It's almost morning, is't not? 10

1. Lord. Day, my lord.

Clo. I would this music would come. I am advised to give her music o' mornings; they say it will penetrate. 14

Enter Musicians.

Come on; tune. If you can penetrate her with your fingering, so; we'll try with tongue too. If none will do, let her remain; but I'll never give o'er. First, a very excellent good-conceited thing; after, a wonderful sweet air, with admirable rich words to it; and then let her consider. 20

SONG.

Hark, hark! the lark at heaven's gate sings,
   And Phœbus gins arise
His steeds to water at those springs
   On chalic'd flowers that lies;
And winking Mary-buds begin   25
   To ope their golden eyes;
With every thing that pretty is,
   My lady sweet, arise,
      Arise, arise.   30

[*Clo.*] So, get you gone. If this penetrate, I will consider your music the better; if it do not, it is a [vice] in her ears, which horsehairs and calves' guts, nor the voice of unpaved eunuch to boot, can never amend.   [*Exeunt Musicians.*] 35

Enter CYMBELINE *and* QUEEN.

2. Lord. Here comes the King.

Clo. I am glad I was up so late, for that's the reason I was up so early. He cannot choose but take this service I have done fatherly. — Good morrow to your Majesty and to my gracious mother! 41

Cym. Attend you here the door of our stern daughter?
Will she not forth?

Clo. I have assail'd her with musics, but she vouchsafes no notice.   45

Cym. The exile of her minion is too new;
She hath not yet forgot him. Some more time
Must wear the print of his remembrance on't,
And then she's yours.

Queen.   You are most bound to th' King,
Who lets go by no vantages that may   50
Prefer you to his daughter. Frame yourself
To orderly [soliciting], and be friended
With aptness of the season; make denials
Increase your services; so seem as if
You were inspir'd to do those duties which   55
You tender to her, that you in all obey her,
Save when command to your dismission tends,
And therein you are senseless.

Clo.   Senseless! not so.

[*Enter a* MESSENGER.]

Mess. So like you, sir, ambassadors from Rome;
The one is Caius Lucius.

Cym.   A worthy fellow,   60
Albeit he comes on angry purpose now;
But that's no fault of his. We must receive him
According to the honour of his sender;
And towards himself, his goodness forespent on us,
We must extend our notice. Our dear son,   65
When you have given good morning to your mistress,
Attend the Queen and us; we shall have need
T' employ you towards this Roman. Come, our
     queen.   [*Exeunt [all but Cloten].*]

Clo. If she be up, I'll speak with her; if not,
Let her lie still and dream. [*Knocks.*] By your
     leave, ho!   70
I know her women are about her; what
If I do line one of their hands? 'Tis gold
Which buys admittance; oft it doth; yea, and makes
Diana's rangers false themselves, yield up   74
Their deer to th' stand o' th' stealer; and 'tis gold
Which makes the true man kill'd and saves the thief,
Nay, sometime hangs both thief and true man.
     What
Can it not do and undo? I will make
One of her women lawyer to me, for
I yet not understand the case myself.   80
By your leave.   [*Knocks.*

Enter a LADY.

Lady. Who's there that knocks?

Clo.   A gentleman.

Lady.   No more?

Clo. Yes, and a gentlewoman's son.

Lady.   That's more

Sc. iii, 2. **ace:** lowest throw of the dice. 18. **good-conceited:** fanciful. 25. **winking Mary-buds:** closed marigold buds. 32. **consider:** requite. 33. **[vice]** (Rowe). *voyce* F. **horsehairs:** bow strings. 33. **calves' guts:** violin strings. **unpaved:** castrated. 39. **fatherly.** Modifies *take.* 46. **minion:** darling. 48. **on't** F₁. *ou't* F₂. *out* Rowe. 51. **Prefer:** commend. 52. **[soliciting]** (Collier). *solicity* F. 58. **are senseless:** must fail to understand. 64. **forespent:** formerly bestowed. 74. **rangers:** gamekeepers; here, her nymphs. 75. **stand...stealer:** the stalking hunter.

Than some, whose tailors are as dear as yours,
Can justly boast of.   What's your lordship's pleas-
　　ure?   85
　Clo. Your lady's person.   Is she ready?
　Lady.   Ay,
To keep her chamber.
　Clo.   There is gold for you;
Sell me your good report.
　Lady. How! my good name?   Or to report of you
What I shall think is good? — The Princess!   90

　　　　　　Enter IMOGEN.

　Clo. Good morrow, fairest sister; your sweet
　　hand.   [*Exit Lady.*]
　Imo. Good morrow, sir.   You lay out too much
　　pains
For purchasing but trouble.   The thanks I give
Is telling you that I am poor of thanks
And scarce can spare them.
　Clo.   Still, I swear I love you.
　Imo. If you but said so, 'twere as deep with me.
If you swear still, your recompense is still   97
That I regard it not.
　Clo.   This is no answer.
　Imo. But that you shall not say I yield being
　　silent,
I would not speak.   I pray you, spare me.   Faith,
I shall unfold equal discourtesy   101
To your best kindness.   One of your great knowing
Should learn, being taught, forbearance.
　Clo. To leave you in your madness, 'twere my sin.
I will not.   105
　Imo. Fools are not mad folks.
　Clo.   Do you call me fool?
　Imo. As I am mad, I do.
If you'll be patient, I'll no more be mad;
That cures us both.   I am much sorry, sir,
You put me to forget a lady's manners,   110
By being so verbal; and learn now, for all,
That I, which know my heart, do here pronounce,
By th' very truth of it, I care not for you,
And am so near the lack of charity
To accuse myself I hate you; which I had rather 115
You felt than make 't my boast.
　Clo.   You sin against
Obedience, which you owe your father.   For
The contract you pretend with that base wretch,
One bred of alms and foster'd with cold dishes,
With scraps o' th' court — it is no contract, none;
And though it be allow'd in meaner parties —   121
Yet who than he more mean? — to knit their
　　souls —

On whom there is no more dependency
But brats and beggary, — in self-figur'd knot,
Yet you are curb'd from that enlargement by   125
The consequence o' th' crown, and must not foil
The precious note of it with a base slave,
A hilding for a livery, a squire's cloth,
A pantler, not so eminent.
　Imo.   Profane fellow!
Wert thou the son of Jupiter and no more   130
But what thou art besides, thou wert too base
To be his groom.   Thou wert dignified enough,
Even to the point of envy, if 'twere made
Comparative for your virtues, to be styl'd   134
The under-hangman of his kingdom, and hated
For being preferr'd so well.
　Clo.   The south-fog rot him!
　Imo. He never can meet more mischance than
　　come
To be but nam'd of thee.   His meanest garment
That ever hath but clipp'd his body, is dearer
In my respect than all the hairs above thee,   140
Were they all made such men.   How now? [*Miss-
ing the bracelet.*]   Pisanio!

　　　　　　Enter PISANIO.

　Clo. "His garment!"   Now the devil —
　Imo. To Dorothy my woman hie thee pre-
　　sently —
　Clo. "His garment!"
　Imo.   I am sprited with a fool,
Frighted, and ang'red worse.   Go bid my woman
Search for a jewel that too casually   146
Hath left mine arm.   It was thy master's.   Shrew me
If I would lose it for a revenue
Of any king's in Europe.   I do think
I saw 't this morning; confident I am   150
Last night 'twas on mine arm; I kiss'd it.
I hope it be not gone to tell my lord
That I kiss aught but he.
　Pis.   'Twill not be lost.
　Imo. I hope so; go and search.   [*Exit Pisanio.*]
　Clo.   You have abus'd me.
"His meanest garment!"
　Imo.   Ay, I said so, sir.   155
If you will make 't an action, call witness to 't.
　Clo. I will inform your father.
　Imo.   Your mother too.
She's my good lady, and will conceive, I hope,
But the worst of me.   So, I leave you, sir,
To the worst of discontent.   [*Exit.*
　Clo.   I'll be reveng'd.
"His meanest garment!"   Well.   [*Exit.* 161

---

86. **ready:** dressed.   111. **verbal:** profuse, plain-spoken.   123-24. **there . . . beggary:** no more people are dependent than brats and beggars.   124. **self-figur'd:** self-made.   125. **enlargement:** freedom.   126. **consequence:** succession.   **foil:** foul, mar.   127. **note:** distinction.   128. **hilding . . . livery:** worthless fellow fit for a livery.   129. **pantler:** pantry servant.   134. **Comparative for:** a comparison befitting.   139. **clipp'd:** embraced.   140. **respect:** regard.   144. **sprited:** haunted.   156. **action:** i.e., at law.

SCENE IV. [*Rome. Philario's house.*]

Enter POSTHUMUS *and* PHILARIO.

Post. Fear it not, sir. I would I were so sure
To win the King as I am bold her honour
Will remain hers.

Phi.   What means do you make to him?

Post. Not any, but abide the change of time,
Quake in the present winter's state, and wish
That warmer days would come. In these fear'd
    hopes   6
I barely gratify your love; they failing,
I must die much your debtor.

Phi. Your very goodness and your company
O'erpays all I can do. By this, your king   10
Hath heard of great Augustus. Caius Lucius
Will do 's commission throughly; and I think
He'll grant the tribute, send th' arrearages,
Or look upon our Romans, whose remembrance
Is yet fresh in their grief.

Post.   I do believe,   15
Statist though I am none, nor like to be,
That this will prove a war; and you shall hear
The legion now in Gallia sooner landed
In our not-fearing Britain than have tidings
Of any not penny tribute paid. Our countrymen   20
Are men more order'd than when Julius Cæsar
Smil'd at their lack of skill, but found their courage
Worthy his frowning at. Their discipline,
Now [mingled] with their courages, will make
    known
To their approvers they are people such   25
That mend upon the world.

Enter IACHIMO.

Phi.   See! Iachimo!

Post. The swiftest harts have posted you by land,
And winds of all the corners kiss'd your sails,
To make your vessel nimble.

Phi.   Welcome, sir.

Post. I hope the briefness of your answer made
The speediness of your return.

Iach.   Your lady   31
Is one of the fairest that I have look'd upon.

Post. And therewithal the best; or let her beauty
Look through a casement to allure false hearts
And be false with them.

Iach.   Here are letters for you.   35

Post. Their tenour good, I trust.

Iach.   'Tis very like.

[*Phi.*] Was Caius Lucius in the Britain court
When you were there?

Iach.   He was expected then,
But not approach'd.

Post.   All is well yet.

Sparkles this stone as it was wont, or is't not   40
Too dull for your good wearing?

Iach.   If I have lost it,
I should have lost the worth of it in gold.
I'll make a journey twice as far, to enjoy
A second night of such sweet shortness which
Was mine in Britain; for the ring is won.   45

Post. The stone's too hard to come by.

Iach.   Not a whit,
Your lady being so easy.

Post.   Make not, sir,
Your loss your sport. I hope you know that we
Must not continue friends.

Iach.   Good sir, we must,
If you keep covenant. Had I not brought   50
The knowledge of your mistress home, I grant
We were to question farther; but I now
Profess myself the winner of her honour,
Together with your ring; and not the wronger
Of her or you, having proceeded but   55
By both your wills.

Post.   If you can make't apparent
That you have tasted her in bed, my hand
And ring is yours; if not, the foul opinion
You had of her pure honour gains or loses
Your sword or mine, or masterless leaves both   60
To who shall find them.

Iach.   Sir, my circumstances,
Being so near the truth as I will make them,
Must first induce you to believe; whose strength
I will confirm with oath, which, I doubt not,
You'll give me leave to spare when you shall find   65
You need it not.

Post.   Proceed.

Iach.   First, her bedchamber, —
Where, I confess, I slept not, but profess
Had that was well worth watching — it was hang'd
With tapestry of silk and silver; the story
Proud Cleopatra, when she met her Roman,   70
And Cydnus swell'd above the banks, or for
The press of boats or pride; a piece of work
So bravely done, so rich, that it did strive
In workmanship and value; which I wonder'd
Could be so rarely and exactly wrought,   75
Since the true life on't was —

Post.   This is true;
And this you might have heard of here, by me,
Or by some other.

Iach.   More particulars
Must justify my knowledge.

Post.   So they must,
Or do your honour injury.

Iach.   The chimney   80
Is south the chamber, and the chimney-piece

Sc. iv, 6. fear'd: mistrustful. 7. gratify: requite. 14. Or: before. 16. Statist: statesman. 21. order'd: disciplined. 24. [mingled] F₂. *wing-led* F₁. 25. approvers: those who try them out. 37. [*Phi.*] (Capell). *Post.* F. 52. question· dispute (in a duel). 61. circumstances: particulars. 68. watching: keeping awake for. 73. bravely: splendidly.

Chaste Dian bathing.   Never saw I figures
So likely to report themselves.   The cutter
Was as another Nature, dumb; outwent her,
Motion and breath left out.
   Post.   This is a thing   85
Which you might from relation likewise reap,
Being, as it is, much spoke of.
   Iach.   The roof o' th' chamber
With golden cherubins is fretted.   Her andirons —
I had forgot them — were two winking Cupids
Of silver, each on one foot standing, nicely   90
Depending on their brands.
   Post.   This is her honour!
Let it be granted you have seen all this — and
   praise
Be given to your remembrance — the description
Of what is in her chamber nothing saves
The wager you have laid.
   Iach.   Then, if you can,   95
         [*Showing the bracelet.*]
Be pale.   I beg but leave to air this jewel; see!
And now 'tis up again.   It must be married
To that your diamond; I'll keep them.
   Post.   Jove!
Once more let me behold it.   Is it that
Which I left with her?
   Iach.   Sir — I thank her — that.
She stripp'd it from her arm.   I see her yet.   101
Her pretty action did outsell her gift,
And yet enrich'd it too.   She gave it me, and said
She priz'd it once.
   Post.   May be she pluck'd it off
To send it me.
   Iach.   She writes so to you, doth she? 105
   Post. O, no, no, no! 'tis true.   Here, take this too;
        [*Gives the ring.*]
It is a basilisk unto mine eye,
Kills me to look on't.   Let there be no honour
Where there is beauty; truth, where semblance;
   love,
Where there's another man.   The vows of women
Of no more bondage be to where they are made 111
Than they are to their virtues, which is nothing.
O, above measure false!
   Phi.   Have patience, sir,
And take your ring again; 'tis not yet won.
It may be probable she lost it; or   115
Who knows if one [of] her women, being corrupted,
Hath stol'n it from her?
   Post.   Very true;
And so, I hope, he came by't.   Back my ring!
Render to me some corporal sign about her,
More evident than this; for this was stol'n.   120

   Iach. By Jupiter, I had it from her arm.
   Post. Hark you, he swears; by Jupiter he swears.
'Tis true, — nay, keep the ring — 'tis true.   I am
   sure
She would not lose it.   Her attendants are
All sworn and honourable.   They induc'd to steal
   it?   125
And by a stranger?   No, he hath enjoy'd her.
The cognizance of her incontinency
Is this.   She hath bought the name of whore thus
   dearly.
There, take thy hire; and all the fiends of hell
Divide themselves between you!
   Phi.   Sir, be patient.
This is not strong enough to be believ'd   131
Of one persuaded well of —
   Post.   Never talk on't;
She hath been colted by him.
   Iach.   If you seek
For further satisfying, under her breast —
Worthy [the] pressing — lies a mole, right proud
Of that most delicate lodging.   By my life,   136
I kiss'd it; and it gave me present hunger
To feed again, though full.   You do remember
This stain upon her?
   Post.   Ay, and it doth confirm
Another stain, as big as hell can hold,   140
Were there no more but it.
   Iach.   Will you hear more?
   Post. Spare your arithmetic; never count the
   turns;
Once, and a million!
   Iach.   I'll be sworn —
   Post.   No swearing.
If you will swear you have not done't, you lie;
And I will kill thee if thou dost deny   145
Thou'st made me cuckold.
   Iach.   I'll deny nothing.
   Post. O, that I had her here, to tear her limb-
   meal!
I will go there and do't, i' th' court, before
Her father.   I'll do something —   [*Exit.*
   Phi.   Quite besides
The government of patience!   You have won.   150
Let's follow him and pervert the present wrath
He hath against himself.
   Iach.   With all my heart.
        [*Exeunt.*

[SCENE V.   *Another room in Philario's house.*]

Enter POSTHUMUS.

   Post. Is there no way for men to be, but women

---

  83. **So...themselves:** such speaking likenesses.   84. **dumb:** but could not give speech.   88. **fretted:** carved.   89. **wink**-ing: blind.   91. **Depending:** leaning.   **brands:** torches.   97. **up:** put away.   107. **basilisk:** a fabulous serpent, believed to kill by its glance.   111. **Of...made:** i.e., no more bind them to their men.   116. **[of]** F2. Om. F1.   127. **cognizance:** token.   135. **[the]** (Rowe).   *her* F.   147. **limbmeal:** limb from limb.   151. **pervert:** divert.

Must be half-workers? We are all bastards;
And that most venerable man which I
Did call my father, was I know not where
When I was stamp'd. Some coiner with his tools   5
Made me a counterfeit; yet my mother seem'd
The Dian of that time. So doth my wife
The nonpareil of this. O, vengeance, vengeance!
Me of my lawful pleasure she restrain'd
And pray'd me oft forbearance; did it with   10
A pudency so rosy the sweet view on't
Might well have warm'd old Saturn; that I thought
    her
As chaste as unsunn'd snow. O, all the devils!
This yellow Iachimo, in an hour, — was't not? —
Or less, — at first? — perchance he spoke not, but,
Like a full-acorn'd boar, a [German one],   16
Cried "O!" and mounted; found no opposition
But what he look'd for should oppose and she
Should from encounter guard. Could I find out
The woman's part in me! For there's no motion
That tends to vice in man, but I affirm   21
It is the woman's part: be it lying, note it,
The woman's flattering, hers; deceiving, hers;
Lust and rank thoughts, hers, hers; revenges, hers;
Ambitions, covetings, change of prides, disdain, 25
Nice longing, slanders, mutability,
All faults that [may be nam'd], nay, that hell knows,
Why, hers, in part or all; but rather, all.
For even to vice
They are not constant, but are changing still   30
One vice but of a minute old, for one
Not half so old as that. I'll write against them,
Detest them, curse them; yet 'tis greater skill
In a true hate, to pray they have their will;
The very devils cannot plague them better.   35
                                            [Exit.

ACT III

SCENE I. [Britain. A hall in Cymbeline's
                        palace.]

Enter in state, CYMBELINE, QUEEN, CLOTEN, and
Lords at one door, and at another, CAIUS LUCIUS
and Attendants.

Cym. Now say, what would Augustus Cæsar
    with us?
Luc. When Julius Cæsar, whose remembrance
    yet
Lives in men's eyes and will to ears and tongues
Be theme and hearing ever, was in this Britain
And conquer'd it, Cassibelan, thine uncle, —   5

Famous in Cæsar's praises, no whit less
Than in his feats deserving it — for him
And his succession granted Rome a tribute,
Yearly three thousand pounds, which by thee lately
Is left untender'd.
Queen.   And, to kill the marvel,   10
Shall be so ever.
Clo.   There be many Cæsars,
Ere such another Julius. Britain is
A world by itself, and we will nothing pay
For wearing our own noses.
Queen.   That opportunity
Which then they had to take from 's, to resume   15
We have again. Remember, sir, my liege,
The kings your ancestors, together with
The natural bravery of your isle, which stands
As Neptune's park, ribbed and paled in
With [rocks] unscaleable and roaring waters,   20
With sands that will not bear your enemies' boats
But suck them up to th' topmast. A kind of con-
    quest
Cæsar made here, but made not here his brag
Of "Came and saw and overcame." With shame —
The first that ever touch'd him — he was carried   25
From off our coast, twice beaten; and his shipping —
Poor ignorant baubles! — on our terrible seas,
Like egg-shells mov'd upon their surges, crack'd
As easily 'gainst our rocks; for joy whereof
The fam'd Cassibelan, who was once at point —   30
O giglot fortune! — to master Cæsar's sword,
Made Lud's town with rejoicing fires bright
And Britons strut with courage.
                                        33
Clo. Come, there's no more tribute to be paid.
Our kingdom is stronger than it was at that time;
and, as I said, there is no moe such Cæsars. Other
of them may have crook'd noses, but to owe such
straight arms, none.
Cym. Son, let your mother end.   39
Clo. We have yet many among us can gripe as
hard as Cassibelan. I do not say I am one, but I
have a hand. Why tribute? Why should we pay
tribute? If Cæsar can hide the sun from us with a
blanket, or put the moon in his pocket, we will pay
him tribute for light; else, sir, no more tribute, pray
you now.   46
Cym. You must know,
Till the injurious Romans did extort
This tribute from us, we were free. Cæsar's am-
    bition,
Which swell'd so much that it did almost stretch   50
The sides o' th' world, against all colour here
Did put the yoke upon 's; which to shake off

Sc. v, 2. **half-workers:** i.e., in procreation. 11. **pudency:** modesty. 16. **full-acorn'd:** full of acorns. [German one]
(Rowe). *Iarmen on* F. No convincing emendation has been proposed. 25. **prides:** vanities. 26. **Nice:** fastidious. 27.
[may be nam'd] F₂. *name* F₁.
    Act III, sc. i, 20. [rocks] (Seward conj.). *Oakes* F. 27. **ignorant:** silly. 31. **giglot:** wanton woman. 32. **Lud's town:**
London. Lud was a mythical king of Britain. 37. **owe:** own. 48. **injurious:** insulting. 51. **colour:** excuse.

Becomes a warlike people, whom we reckon
Ourselves to be. We do say then to Cæsar,
Our ancestor was that Mulmutius which   55
Ordain'd our laws, whose use the sword of Cæsar
Hath too much mangled, whose repair and franchise
Shall, by the power we hold, be our good deed,
Though Rome be therefore angry. Mulmutius
     made our laws,
Who was the first of Britain which did put   60
His brows within a golden crown and call'd
Himself a king.

     Luc.   I am sorry, Cymbeline,
That I am to pronounce Augustus Cæsar —
Cæsar, that hath moe kings his servants than
Thyself domestic officers — thine enemy.   65
Receive it from me, then: War and confusion
In Cæsar's name pronounce I 'gainst thee; look
For fury not to be resisted. Thus defi'd,
I thank thee for myself.

     Cym.   Thou art welcome, Caius.
Thy Cæsar knighted me; my youth I spent   70
Much under him; of him I gather'd honour,
Which he to seek of me again, perforce,
Behoves me keep at utterance. I am perfect
That the Pannonians and Dalmatians for
Their liberties are now in arms, a precedent
Which not to read would show the Britons cold.   76
So Cæsar shall not find them.

     Luc.   Let proof speak.

     Clo. His Majesty bids you welcome. Make
pastime with us a day or two, or longer. If you
seek us afterwards in other terms, you shall find us
in our salt-water girdle; if you beat us out of it, it is
yours; if you fall in the adventure, our crows shall
fare the better for you; and there's an end.   84

     Luc. So, sir.

     Cym. I know your master's pleasure and he mine:
All the remain is "Welcome!"   [*Exeunt.*

     SCENE II. [*Another room in the palace.*]

     Enter PISANIO, *reading a letter.*

     Pis. How? of adultery? Wherefore write you
     not
What [monster's her accuser]? Leonatus!
O master! what a strange infection
Is fall'n into thy ear! What false Italian,
As poisonous-tongu'd as handed, hath prevail'd   5
On thy too ready hearing? Disloyal? No!
She's punish'd for her truth, and undergoes,
More goddess-like than wife-like, such assaults
As would take in some virtue. O my master!

Thy mind to her is now as low as were   10
Thy fortunes. How? that I should murder her?
Upon the love and truth and vows which I
Have made to thy command? I, her? Her blood?
If it be so to do good service, never
Let me be counted serviceable. How look I   15
That I should seem to lack humanity
So much as this fact comes to? [*Reading.*] "Do't;
     the letter
That I have sent her, by her own command
Shall give thee opportunity." O damn'd paper,
Black as the ink that's on thee! Senseless bauble,
Art thou a fedary for this act, and look'st   21
So virgin-like without? Lo, here she comes.

     Enter IMOGEN.

I am ignorant in what I am commanded.

     Imo. How now, Pisanio!

     Pis. Madam, here is a letter from my lord.

     Imo. Who? Thy lord? That is my lord
     Leonatus!   26
O, learn'd indeed were that astronomer
That knew the stars as I his characters;
He'd lay the future open. You good gods,
Let what is here contain'd relish of love,   30
Of my lord's health, of his content, — yet not
That we two are asunder; let that grieve him:
Some griefs are med'cinable; that is one of them,
For it doth physic love — of his content,
All but in that! Good wax, thy leave. Blest be
You bees that make these locks of counsel! Lovers
And men in dangerous bonds pray not alike;   37
Though forfeiters you cast in prison, yet
You clasp young Cupid's tables. Good news,
     gods!   39
     [*Reads.*] "Justice, and your father's wrath should
he take me in his dominion, could not be so cruel to
me as you, O the dearest of creatures, would even
renew me with your eyes. Take notice that I am
in Cambria, at Milford-Haven; what your own love
will out of this advise you, follow. So he wishes
you all happiness, that remains loyal to his vow,
and your increasing in love
                 LEONATUS POSTHUMUS."   49
O, for a horse with wings! Hear'st thou, Pisanio?
He is at Milford-Haven. Read, and tell me
How far 'tis thither. If one of mean affairs
May plod it in a week, why may not I
Glide thither in a day? Then, true Pisanio, —
Who long'st like me to see thy lord; who long'st, —
O, let me bate, — but not like me — yet long'st,   56
But in a fainter kind; — O, not like me,

---

57. **franchise:** free use.   72. **he to seek:** his seeking.   73. **at utterance:** to the last extremity.   **perfect:** well informed.
Sc. ii 2. [**monster's her accuser**] (Capell). *Monsters her accuse* F.   9. **take in:** subdue.   10. **to:** compared to.   17. **fact:**
crime.   21. **fedary:** confederate.   23. **I . . . in:** I will act as if I knew not.   28. **characters:** handwriting.   30. **relish:** taste.
35. **Good . . . leave.** She breaks the seal.   36. **counsel:** secrets.   37. **pray not alike.** Lovers pray for blessings on the bees,
forfeiters for curses.   38. **forfeiters:** i.e., of bonds sealed with your wax.   39. **You . . . tables:** you seal love-letters.   42.
as: but that.   44. **Cambria:** Wales.   52. **mean affairs:** small business.   56. **bate:** abate, qualify.

For mine's beyond beyond — say, and speak
    thick, —
Love's counsellor should fill the bores of hearing, 59
To th' smothering of the sense — how far it is
To this same blessed Milford; and by th' way
Tell me how Wales was made so happy as
T' inherit such a haven; but first of all,
How we may steal from hence, and for the gap
That we shall make in time, from our hence-going
And our return, to excuse.   But first, how get
    hence?   66
Why should excuse be born or ere begot?
We'll talk of that hereafter.   Prithee, speak,
How many [score] of miles may we well ride
'Twixt hour and hour?
   Pis.   One score 'twixt sun and sun,
Madam, 's enough for you, and too much too.   71
   Imo.   Why, one that rode to's execution, man,
Could never go so slow.   I have heard of riding
    wagers,
Where horses have been nimbler than the sands
That run i' th' clock's behalf.   But this is foolery.
Go bid my woman feign a sickness, say   76
She'll home to her father; and provide me presently
A riding-suit, no costlier than would fit
A franklin's housewife.
   Pis.   Madam, you're best consider.
   Imo.   I see before me, man; nor here, [nor] here,
Nor what ensues, but have a fog in them   81
That I cannot look through.   Away, I prithee;
Do as I bid thee.   There's no more to say.
Accessible is none but Milford way.   [*Exeunt.*

    Scene III.   [*Wales: a mountainous country with
            a cave.*]

   Enter [from the cave] Belarius; Guiderius
        and Arviragus *[following].*

   Bel.   A goodly day not to keep house with such
Whose roof's as low as ours!   [Stoop], boys; this
    gate
Instructs you how t' adore the heavens and bows
    you
To a morning's holy office.   The gates of monarchs
Are arch'd so high that giants may jet through
And keep their impious turbans on without   6
Good morrow to the sun.   Hail, thou fair heaven!
We house i' th' rock, yet use thee not so hardly
As prouder livers do.
   Gui.   Hail, heaven!
   Arv.   Hail, heaven!

   Bel.   Now for our mountain sport.   Up to yond
    hill!   10
Your legs are young; I'll tread these flats.   Con-
    sider,
When you above perceive me like a crow,
That it is place which lessens and sets off;
And you may then revolve what tales I have told
    you
Of courts of princes, of the tricks in war;   15
This service is not service, so being done,
But being so allow'd.   To apprehend thus
Draws us a profit from all things we see;
And often, to our comfort, shall we find
The sharded beetle in a safer hold   20
Than is the full-wing'd eagle.   O, this life
Is nobler than attending for a check,
Richer than doing nothing for a [bribe],
Prouder than rustling in unpaid-for silk.
Such gains the cap of him that makes him fine, 25
Yet keeps his book uncross'd.   No life to ours.
   Gui.   Out of your proof you speak; we, poor un-
    fledg'd,
Have never wing'd from view o' th' nest, nor know
    not
What air's from home.   Haply this life is best,
If quiet life be best; sweeter to you   30
That have a sharper known; well corresponding
With your stiff age; but unto us it is
A cell of ignorance, travelling a-bed,
A prison [of] a debtor that not dares
To stride a limit.
   Arv.   What should we speak of 35
When we are old as you?   When we shall hear
The rain and wind beat dark December, how,
In this our pinching cave, shall we discourse
The freezing hours away?   We have seen nothing.
We are beastly; subtle as the fox for prey,   40
Like warlike as the wolf for what we eat.
Our valour is to chase what flies.   Our cage
We make a choir, as doth the prison'd bird,
And sing our bondage freely.
   Bel.   How you speak!
Did you but know the city's usuries,   45
And felt them knowingly; the art o' th' court,
As hard to leave as keep, whose top to climb
Is certain falling, or so slipp'ry that
The fear 's as bad as falling; the toil o' th' war,
A pain that only seems to seek out danger   50
I' th' name of fame and honour which dies i' th'
    search,
And hath as oft a slanderous epitaph

   58. **thick**: quickly.   63. **inherit**: possess.   67. **or ere begot**: before the thing has happened.   69. [score] F₂.   *store* F₁.
79. **franklin's**: small landowner's.   80. [nor] F₂.   *not* F₁.   80–82. I . . . through: i.e., I see only Milford; all else lies in a fog.
Sc. iii, 1. **keep house**: stay inside.   2. [Stoop] (Hanmer).   *Sleepe* F.   5. **jet**: strut.   13. **sets off**: enhances.   17. **allow'd**:
acknowledged.   20. **sharded**: with scaly wing covers.   22. **attending . . . check**: doing service only to get a rebuke.   23.
[bribe] (Hanmer).   *Babe* F.   25. **the cap . . . fine**: the salute of his tailor.   26. **book uncross'd**: account unpaid.   27. **proof**:
experience.   29. **Haply**: perhaps.   34. [of] (Vaughan).   *or* F.   35. **stride a limit**: over-step a boundary.   40. **beastly**:
like beasts.

As record of fair act; nay, many times,
Doth ill deserve by doing well; what's worse,
Must curtsy at the censure; — O boys, this story   55
The world may read in me.   My body's mark'd
With Roman swords, and my report was once
First with the best of note.   Cymbeline lov'd me,
And when a soldier was the theme, my name
Was not far off.   Then was I as a tree   60
Whose boughs did bend with fruit; but in one night,
A storm or robbery, call it what you will,
Shook down my mellow hangings, nay, my leaves,
And left me bare to weather.
      Gui.   Uncertain favour!
      Bel.   My fault being nothing — as I have told you
            oft —   65
But that two villains, whose false oaths prevail'd
Before my perfect honour, swore to Cymbeline
I was confederate with the Romans; so
Follow'd my banishment, and this twenty years
This rock and these demesnes have been my
            world,   70
Where I have liv'd at honest freedom, paid
More pious debts to heaven than in all
The fore-end of my time.   But up to th' moun-
            tains!
This is not hunters' language.   He that strikes
The venison first shall be the lord o' th' feast;
To him the other two shall minister;   76
And we will fear no poison, which attends
In place of greater state.   I'll meet you in the
            valleys.   [*Exeunt* [*Guiderius and Arviragus*].
How hard it is to hide the sparks of nature!
These boys know little they are sons to th' King,   80
Nor Cymbeline dreams that they are alive.
They think they're mine; and, though train'd up
            thus meanly
I' th' cave [wherein they bow], their thoughts do hit
The roofs of palaces, and nature prompts them
In simple and low things to prince it much   85
Beyond the trick of others.   This Polydore,
The heir of Cymbeline and Britain, who
The King his father call'd Guiderius, — Jove!
When on my three-foot stool I sit and tell
The warlike feats I have done, his spirits fly out   90
Into my story; say, "Thus mine enemy fell,
And thus I set my foot on's neck;" even then
The princely blood flows in his cheek, he sweats,
Strains his young nerves, and puts himself in posture
That acts my words.   The younger brother, Cad-
            wal,   95
Once Arviragus, in as like a figure,
Strikes life into my speech and shows much more
His own conceiving. — Hark, the game is rous'd! —
O Cymbeline! heaven and my conscience knows

Thou didst unjustly banish me; whereon,   100
At three and two years old, I stole these babes,
Thinking to bar thee of succession, as
Thou reft'st me of my lands.   Euriphile,
Thou wast their nurse; they took thee for their
            mother,
And every day do honour to her grave.   105
Myself, Belarius, that am Morgan call'd,
They take for natural father. — The game is up.
                                          [*Exit.*

SCENE IV.   [*Wales Country near Milford-Haven.*]

Enter PISANIO *and* IMOGEN.

      Imo.   Thou told'st me, when we came from horse,
            the place
Was near at hand.   Ne'er long'd my mother so
To see me first, as I have now.   Pisanio! man!
Where is Posthumus?   What is in thy mind
That makes thee stare thus?   Wherefore breaks
            that sigh   5
From th' inward of thee?   One but painted thus
Would be interpreted a thing perplex'd
Beyond self-explication.   Put thyself
Into a haviour of less fear, ere wildness
Vanquish my staider senses.   What's the matter?
Why tender'st thou that paper to me with   11
A look untender?   If 't be summer news,
Smile to 't before; if winterly, thou need'st
But keep that countenance still.   My husband's
            hand!
That drug-damn'd Italy hath out-crafted him,
And he's at some hard point.   Speak, man!   Thy
            tongue   16
May take off some extremity, which to read
Would be even mortal to me.
      Pis.   Please you, read;
And you shall find me, wretched man, a thing
The most disdain'd of fortune.   20
      Imo.   (*Reads.*)   "Thy mistress, Pisanio, hath
played the strumpet in my bed, the testimonies
whereof lie bleeding in me.   I speak not out of
weak surmises, but from proof as strong as my grief
and as certain as I expect my revenge.   That part
thou, Pisanio, must act for me, if thy faith be   25
not tainted with the breach of hers.   Let thine own
hands take away her life.   I shall give thee opportunity at Milford-Haven.   She hath my letter for
the purpose; where, if thou fear to strike and to
make me certain it is done, thou art the pander to
her dishonour and equally to me disloyal."   33
      Pis.   What shall I need to draw my sword?   The
            paper
Hath cut her throat already.   No, 'tis slander,

---

54. deserve: earn.   83. [wherein they bow] (Warburton).   *whereon the Bowe* F.   94. nerves: sinews.   98. conceiving:
imagination.
      Sc. iv, 9. of . . . fear: less fearsome.   wildness: madness.   16. hard point: crisis.   32. pander: go-between.

Whose edge is sharper than the sword, whose
    tongue   36
Outvenoms all the worms of Nile, whose breath
Rides on the posting winds and doth belie
All corners of the world. Kings, queens, and states,
Maids, matrons, nay, the secrets of the grave   40
This viperous slander enters. What cheer, madam?
  Imo. False to his bed! What is it to be false?
To lie in watch there and to think on him?
To weep 'twixt clock and clock? if sleep charge
    nature,
To break it with a fearful dream of him   45
And cry myself awake? That's false to 's bed, is it?
  Pis. Alas, good lady!
  Imo. I false! Thy conscience witness! —
    Iachimo,
Thou didst accuse him of incontinency;
Thou then look'dst like a villain; now methinks   50
Thy favour's good enough. Some jay of Italy,
Whose mother was her painting, hath betray'd him!
Poor I am stale, a garment out of fashion;
And, for I am richer than to hang by th' walls,
I must be ripp'd. — To pieces with me! — O,   55
Men's vows are women's traitors! All good seeming,
By thy revolt, O husband, shall be thought
Put on for villainy; not born where't grows,
But worn a bait for ladies.
  Pis.   Good madam, hear me.
  Imo. True honest men, being heard like false
    Æneas,   60
Were in his time thought false, and Sinon's weeping
Did scandal many a holy tear, took pity
From most true wretchedness; so thou, Posthumus,
Wilt lay the leaven on all proper men;
Goodly and gallant shall be false and perjur'd   65
From thy great fail. — Come, fellow, be thou hon-
    est!
Do thou thy master's bidding. When thou see'st
    him,
A little witness my obedience. Look!
I draw the sword myself. Take it, and hit
The innocent mansion of my love, my heart.   70
Fear not; 'tis empty of all things but grief.
Thy master is not there, who was indeed
The riches of it. Do his bidding; strike.
Thou mayst be valiant in a better cause,   74
But now thou seem'st a coward.
  Pis.   Hence, vile instrument!
Thou shalt not damn my hand.
  Imo.   Why, I must die;
And if I do not by thy hand, thou art

No servant of thy master's. Against self-slaughter
There is a prohibition so divine
That cravens my weak hand. Come, here's my
    heart,   80
(Something's [afore't], — soft, soft! we'll no de-
    fence,)
Obedient as the scabbard. What is here?
The scriptures of the loyal Leonatus,
All turn'd to heresy? Away, away,
Corrupters of my faith! you shall no more   85
Be stomachers to my heart. [*Drawing his letters
    from her bodice.*] Thus may poor fools
Believe false teachers. Though those that are
    betray'd
Do feel the treason sharply, yet the traitor
Stands in worse case of woe.
And thou, Posthumus, [thou] that didst set up
My disobedience 'gainst the King my father,   90
And make me put into contempt the suits
Of princely fellows, shalt hereafter find
It is no act of common passage, but
A strain of rareness; and I grieve myself   95
To think, when thou shalt be disedg'd by her
That now thou tirest on, how thy memory
Will then be pang'd by me. Prithee, dispatch!
The lamb entreats the butcher. Where's thy knife?
Thou art too slow to do thy master's bidding,   100
When I desire it too.
  Pis.   O gracious lady,
Since I receiv'd command to do this business
I have not slept one wink.
  Imo.   Do't, and to bed then.
  Pis. I'll wake mine eye-balls [out] first.
  Imo.   Wherefore then
Didst undertake it? Why hast thou abus'd   105
So many miles with a pretence? This place?
Mine action and thine own? Our horses' labour?
The time inviting thee? The perturb'd court
For my being absent? whereunto I never
Purpose return. Why hast thou gone so far,   110
To be unbent when thou hast ta'en thy stand,
Th' elected deer before thee?
  Pis.   But to win time
To lose so bad employment; in the which
I have consider'd of a course. Good lady,   114
Hear me with patience.
  Imo.   Talk thy tongue weary; speak.
I have heard I am a strumpet, and mine ear,
Therein false struck, can take no greater wound,
Nor tent to bottom that. But speak.
  Pis.   Then, madam,

37. **worms:** serpents. 38. **posting:** speeding. **belie:** calumniate. 39. **states:** statesmen. 51. **favour's:** countenance is.
jay: strumpet. 52. **Whose...painting:** i.e., born of the paint pot. 54. **richer than:** too rich. 60. **Æneas.** Æneas deserted Dido. 61. **Sinon's weeping.** By false pretenses Sinon caused the downfall of Troy. 62. **scandal:** make disreputable. 64. **lay...on:** discredit. 80. **cravens:** makes cowardly. 81. **[afore't]** (Rowe). **a-foot** F. 89. **[thou]** (Capell).
Om. F. **set up:** inspire, incite. 94. **It:** i.e., my choice. **passage:** occurrence. 96. **disedg'd:** satiated. 97. **tirest on:** de-
vourest. 104. **[out]** (Johnson conj.). Om. F. 111. **unbent:** i.e., with bow unbent. 118. **tent...that:** probe to reach the
bottom of that wound.

I thought you would not back again.

Imo.   Most like;
Bringing me here to kill me.

Pis.   Not so, neither;
But if I were as wise as honest, then   121
My purpose would prove well. It cannot be
But that my master is abus'd.
Some villain, ay, and singular in his art,
Hath done you both this cursed injury.   125

Imo. Some Roman courtezan.

Pis.   No, on my life.
I'll give but notice you are dead, and send him
Some bloody sign of it; for 'tis commanded
I should do so. You shall be miss'd at court,
And that will well confirm it.

Imo.   Why, good fellow,
What shall I do the while? Where bide? How
     live?   131
Or in my life what comfort, when I am
Dead to my husband?

Pis.   If you'll back to th' court —

Imo. No court, no father; nor no more ado   134
With that harsh, [nothing] noble, simple nothing,
That Cloten, whose love-suit hath been to me
As fearful as a siege.

Pis.   If not at court,
Then not in Britain must you bide.

Imo.   Where then?
Hath Britain all the sun that shines? Day, night,
Are they not but in Britain? I' th' world's volume
Our Britain seems as of it, but not in't;   141
In a great pool a swan's nest. Prithee, think
There's livers out of Britain.

Pis.   I am most glad
You think of other place. Th' ambassador,
Lucius the Roman, comes to Milford-Haven   145
To-morrow. Now, if you could wear a mind
Dark as your fortune is, and but disguise
That which, to appear itself, must not yet be
But by self-danger, you should tread a course
Pretty and full of view; yea, haply, near   150
The residence of Posthumus; so nigh at least
That though his actions were not visible, yet
Report should render him hourly to your ear
As truly as he moves.

Imo.   O, for such means,
Though peril to my modesty, not death on't,   155
I would adventure.

Pis.   Well, then, here's the point.
You must forget to be a woman; change
Command into obedience; fear and niceness —
The handmaids of all women, or, more truly,
Woman it pretty self — into a waggish courage;   160

Ready in gibes, quick-answer'd, saucy, and
As quarrelous as the weasel; nay, you must
Forget that rarest treasure of your cheek,
Exposing it — but, O, the harder heart!
Alack, no remedy! — to the greedy touch   165
Of common-kissing Titan, and forget
Your laboursome and dainty trims, wherein
You made great Juno angry.

Imo.   Nay, be brief.
I see into thy end and am almost
A man already.

Pis.   First, make yourself but like one.
Fore-thinking this, I have already fit —   171
'Tis in my cloak-bag — doublet, hat, hose, all
That answer to them. Would you in their serving,
And with what imitation you can borrow
From youth of such a season, 'fore noble Lucius   175
Present yourself, desire his service, tell him
Wherein you're happy, — which will make him
     know
If that his head have ear in music, — doubtless
With joy he will embrace you, for he's honourable,
And doubling that, most holy. Your means
     abroad —   180
You have me, rich; and I will never fail
Beginning nor supplyment.

Imo.   Thou art all the comfort
The gods will diet me with. Prithee, away.
There's more to be consider'd; but we'll even
All that good time will give us. This attempt   185
I am soldier to, and will abide it with
A prince's courage. Away, I prithee.

Pis. Well, madam, we must take a short farewell,
Lest, being miss'd, I be suspected of
Your carriage from the court. My noble mis-
     tress,   190
Here is a box — I had it from the Queen —
What's in't is precious. If you are sick at sea,
Or stomach-qualm'd at land, a dram of this
Will drive away distemper. To some shade,
And fit you to your manhood. May the gods   195
Direct you to the best!

Imo. Amen! I thank thee.

[Exeunt [severally]

SCENE V. [*Britain. A room in Cymbeline's
     palace.*]

Enter CYMBELINE, QUEEN, CLOTEN, LUCIUS,
     Lords [*and* ATTENDANTS].

Cym. Thus far; and so farewell.

Luc.   Thanks, royal sir.
My emperor hath wrote I must from hence,

---

123. **abus'd:** deceived.   124. **singular:** unique.   135. [nothing] (Dowden conj.).   Om. F.   147. **Dark:** lowly.   148. **That which:** i.e., her sex.   150. **view:** opportunity.   160. **it:** its.   164. **harder heart:** i.e., the too hard heart (that could demand this).   166. **Titan:** the sun.   167. **laboursome:** elaborate.   173. **in ... serving:** with their help.   175. **season:** age.   177. **happy:** accomplished.   184. **even:** avail ourselves fully of.

And am right sorry that I must report ye
My master's enemy.
      Cym.   Our subjects, sir,
Will not endure his yoke; and for ourself   5
To show less sovereignty than they, must needs
Appear unkinglike.
      Luc.   So, sir. I desire of you
A conduct over-land to Milford-Haven.
Madam, all joy befall your Grace, and you!
      Cym. My lords, you are appointed for that
      office;   10
The due of honour in no point omit.
So farewell, noble Lucius.
      Luc.   Your hand, my lord.
      Clo. Receive it friendly; but from this time forth
I wear it as your enemy.
      Luc.   Sir, the event
Is yet to name the winner. Fare you well.   15
      Cym. Leave not the worthy Lucius, good my
      lords,
Till he have cross'd the Severn. Happiness!
                    [*Exeunt Lucius and Lords.*
      Queen. He goes hence frowning; but it honours us
That we have given him cause.
      Clo.   'Tis all the better;
Your valiant Britons have their wishes in it.   20
      Cym. Lucius hath wrote already to the Emperor
How it goes here. It fits us therefore ripely
Our chariots and our horsemen be in readiness.
The powers that he already hath in Gallia
Will soon be drawn to head, from whence he moves
His war for Britain.   26
      Queen.   'Tis not sleepy business,
But must be look'd to speedily and strongly.
      Cym. Our expectation that it would be thus
Hath made us forward. But, my gentle queen,
Where is our daughter? She hath not appear'd   30
Before the Roman, nor to us hath tender'd
The duty of the day. She looks us like
A thing more made of malice than of duty;
We have noted it. Call her before us, for
We have been too slight in sufferance.
                          [*Exit an attendant.*
      Queen.   Royal sir,
Since the exile of Posthumus, most retir'd   36
Hath her life been; the cure whereof, my lord,
'Tis time must do. Beseech your Majesty,
Forbear sharp speeches to her; she's a lady
So tender of rebukes that words are strokes   40
And strokes death to her.

            Re-enter ATTENDANT.

      Cym.   Where is she, sir? How
Can her contempt be answer'd?
      Atten.   Please you, sir,

Her chambers are all lock'd; and there's no answer
That will be given to the [loudest] noises we make.
      Queen. My lord, when last I went to visit her,
She pray'd me to excuse her keeping close;   46
Whereto constrain'd by her infirmity,
She should that duty leave unpaid to you,
Which daily she was bound to proffer. This
She wish'd me to make known; but our great
      court   50
Made me to blame in memory.
      Cym.   Her doors lock'd?
Not seen of late? Grant, heavens, that which I fear
Prove false!   [*Exit.*
      Queen. Son, I say, follow the King.
      Clo. That man of hers, Pisanio, her old servant,
I have not seen these two days.   [*Exit.*
      Queen [*to attendant*].   Go, look after
Pisanio, thou, that stands so for Posthumus.   56
                          [*Exit attendant.*
He hath a drug of mine; I pray his absence
Proceed by swallowing that, for he believes
It is a thing most precious. But for her,
Where is she gone? Haply, despair hath seiz'd
      her,   60
Or, wing'd with fervour of her love, she's flown
To her desir'd Posthumus. Gone she is
To death or to dishonour; and my end
Can make good use of either. She being down,
I have the placing of the British crown.   65

            Re-enter CLOTEN.

How now, my son!
      Clo.   'Tis certain she is fled.
Go in and cheer the King. He rages; none
Dare come about him.
      Queen.   [*Aside.*] All the better. May
This night forestall him of the coming day!
                                      [*Exit.*
      Clo. I love and hate her; for she's fair and royal,
And that she hath all courtly parts more exqui-
      site   71
Than lady, ladies, woman; from every one
The best she hath, and she, of all compounded,
Outsells them all. I love her therefore; but
Disdaining me and throwing favours on   75
The low Posthumus slanders so her judgement
That what's else rare is chok'd; and in that point
I will conclude to hate her, nay, indeed,
To be reveng'd upon her. For when fools
Shall —

            Enter PISANIO.

Who is here? What, are you packing, sirrah?
Come hither. Ah, you precious pandar! Vil-
      lain,   81

Sc. v, 14. **event:** outcome.   22. **ripely:** urgently.   35. **slight in sufferance:** slack in allowing this.   44. **[loudest]** (Rowe).
'owd of F.   50. **great court:** i.e., the reception to Lucius.   69. **forestall:** deprive.   80. **packing:** plotting.

Where is thy lady?   In a word; or else
Thou art straightway with the fiends.
   Pis.   O, good my lord!
   Clo. Where is thy lady? or, by Jupiter,
I will not ask again.   Close villain,   85
I'll have this secret from thy heart, or rip
Thy heart to find it.   Is she with Posthumus,
From whose so many weights of baseness cannot
A dram of worth be drawn?
   Pis.   Alas, my lord,   89
How can she be with him?   When was she miss'd?
He is in Rome.
   Clo.   Where is she, sir?   Come nearer.
No further halting.   Satisfy me home
What is become of her.
   Pis. O, my all-worthy lord!
   Clo.   All-worthy villain!
Discover where thy mistress is at once,   95
At the next word.   No more of "worthy lord!"
Speak, or thy silence on the instant is
Thy condemnation and thy death.
   Pis.   Then, sir,
This paper is the history of my knowledge
Touching her flight.   [*Presenting a letter.*]
   Clo.   Let's see't.   I will pursue her 100
Even to Augustus' throne.
   Pis.   [*Aside.*] Or this, or perish.
She's far enough; and what he learns by this
May prove his travel, not her danger.
   Clo.   Hum!
   Pis. [*Aside.*] I'll write to my lord she's dead.   O
    Imogen,   104
Safe mayst thou wander, safe return again!
   Clo. Sirrah, is this letter true?
   Pis. Sir, as I think.   107
   Clo. It is Posthumus' hand; I know't.   Sirrah,
if thou wouldst not be a villain, but do me true service, undergo those employments wherein I should
have cause to use thee with a serious industry, that
is, what villainy soe'er I bid thee do, to perform it
directly and truly, I would think thee an honest
man.   Thou shouldst neither want my means for
thy relief nor my voice for thy preferment.   116
   Pis. Well, my good lord.
   Clo. Wilt thou serve me?   For since patiently
and constantly thou hast stuck to the bare fortune
of that beggar Posthumus, thou canst not, in the
course of gratitude, but be a diligent follower of
mine.   Wilt thou serve me?   122
   Pis. Sir, I will.
   Clo. Give me thy hand; here's my purse.   Hast
any of thy late master's garments in thy possession?   126
   Pis. I have, my lord, at my lodging, the same

suit he wore when he took leave of my lady and mistress.
   Clo. The first service thou dost me, fetch that
suit hither.   Let it be thy first service; go.   131
   Pis. I shall, my lord.   [*Exit.*
   Clo. Meet thee at Milford-Haven! — I forgot
to ask him one thing; I'll remember't anon; —
even there, thou villain Posthumus, will I kill   135
thee.   I would these garments were come.   She
said upon a time — the bitterness of it I now belch
from my heart — that she held the very garment
of Posthumus in more respect than my noble and
natural person, together with the adornment of 140
my qualities.   With that suit upon my back will I
ravish her, — first kill him, and in her eyes; there
shall she see my valour, which will then be a torment to her contempt, — he on the ground, my
speech of insultment ended on his dead body;   145
and when my lust hath dined, — which, as I say, to
vex her I will execute in the clothes that she so
prais'd, — to the court I'll knock her back, foot
her home again.   She hath despis'd me rejoicingly,
and I'll be merry in my revenge.   150

   Re-enter PISANIO [*with the clothes*].

Be those the garments?
   Pis. Ay, my noble lord.
   Clo. How long is't since she went to Milford-
Haven?
   Pis. She can scarce be there yet.   155
   Clo. Bring this apparel to my chamber; that is
the second thing that I have commanded thee; the
third is, that thou wilt be a voluntary mute to my
design.   Be but duteous, and true preferment shall
tender itself to thee.   My revenge is now at Milford;
would I had wings to follow it!   Come, and be
true.   [*Exit.* 162
   Pis. Thou bidd'st me to my loss; for true to thee
Were to prove false, which I will never be,
To him that is most true.   To Milford go,
And find not her whom thou pursuest.   Flow, flow,
You heavenly blessings, on her!   This fool's speed
Be cross'd with slowness; labour be his meed!   168
                         [*Exit.*

SCENE VI.   [*Wales.   Before the cave of Belarius.*]

   Enter IMOGEN, *alone* [*in boy's clothes*].

   Imo. I see a man's life is a tedious one.
I have tir'd myself, and for two nights together
Have made the ground my bed.   I should be sick,
But that my resolution helps me.   Milford,
When from the mountain-top Pisanio show'd thee,
Thou wast within a ken.   O Jove!   I think   6

---

85. **Close:** secretive. 91. **Come nearer:** answer more to the point. 92. **home:** completely. 148. **foot:** kick. 168.
cross'd: thwarted.
   Sc. vi, 6. **a ken:** view.

Foundations fly the wretched; such, I mean,
Where they should be reliev'd. Two beggars told
    me
I could not miss my way: will poor folks lie,
That have afflictions on them, knowing 'tis   10
A punishment or trial? Yes; no wonder,
When rich ones scarce tell true. To lapse in fulness
Is sorer than to lie for need; and falsehood
Is worse in kings than beggars. My dear lord!
Thou art one o' th' false ones. Now I think on
    thee,   15
My hunger's gone; but even before, I was
At point to sink for food. But what is this?
Here is a path to't. 'Tis some savage hold.
I were best not call; I dare not call; yet famine,
Ere clean it o'erthrow nature, makes it valiant. 20
Plenty and peace breeds cowards; hardness ever
Of hardiness is mother. Ho! who's here?
If anything that's civil, speak; if savage,
Take or lend. Ho! No answer? Then I'll enter.
Best draw my sword; and if mine enemy   25
But fear the sword like me, he'll scarcely look on't.
Such a foe, good heavens!   [*Exit [to the cave*].

Enter BELARIUS, GUIDERIUS, *and* ARVIRAGUS.

Bel. You, Polydore, have prov'd best woodman and
Are master of the feast. Cadwal and I
Will play the cook and servant; 'tis our match. 30
The sweat of industry would dry and die,
But for the end it works to. Come; our stomachs
Will make what's homely savoury; weariness
Can snore upon the flint, when resty sloth   34
Finds the down pillow hard. Now peace be here,
Poor house, that keep'st thyself!
Gui.   I am throughly weary.
Arv. I am weak with toil, yet strong in appetite.
Gui. There is cold meat i' th' cave; we'll browse
    on that,
Whilst what we have kill'd be cook'd.
Bel. [*Looking into the cave.*] Stay; come not in.
But that it eats our victuals, I should think   41
Here were a fairy.
Gui.   What's the matter, sir?
Bel. By Jupiter, an angel! or, if not,
An earthly paragon! Behold divineness
No elder than a boy!   45

Re-enter IMOGEN.

Imo. Good masters, harm me not.
Before I enter'd here I call'd, and thought
To have begg'd or bought what I have took. Good
    troth,

I have stol'n nought, nor would not, though I had
    found
Gold strew'd i' th' floor. Here's money for my
    meat.   50
I would have left it on the board so soon
As I had made my meal, and parted with
Prayers for the provider.
Gui.   Money, youth?
Arv. All gold and silver rather turn to dirt!
As 'tis no better reckon'd, but of those   55
Who worship dirty gods.
Imo.   I see you're angry.
Know, if you kill me for my fault, I should
Have died had I not made it.
Bel.   Whither bound?
Imo. To Milford-Haven.
Bel. What's your name?   60
Imo. Fidele, sir. I have a kinsman who
Is bound for Italy; he embark'd at Milford;
To whom being going, almost spent with hunger,
I am fall'n in this offence.
Bel.   Prithee, fair youth,
Think us no churls, nor measure our good minds
By this rude place we live in. Well encounter'd! 66
'Tis almost night: you shall have better cheer
Ere you depart; and thanks to stay and eat it.
Boys, bid him welcome.
Gui.   Were you a woman, youth,
I should woo hard but be your groom. In hon-
    esty,   70
I bid for you as [I'd] buy.
Arv.   I'll make't my comfort
He is a man; I'll love him as my brother;
And such a welcome as I'd give to him
After long absence, such is yours. Most welcome!
Be sprightly, for you fall 'mongst friends.
Imo.   'Mongst friends,
If brothers. [*Aside.*] Would it had been so, that
    they   76
Had been my father's sons! Then had my prize
Been less, and so more equal ballasting
To thee, Posthumus.
Bel.   He wrings at some distress.
Gui. Would I could free't!
Arv.   Or I, whate'er it be, 80
What pain it cost, what danger. Gods!
Bel.   Hark, boys.
                  [*Whispering.*]
Imo. [*Aside.*] Great men,
That had a court no bigger than this cave,
That did attend themselves and had the virtue
Which their own conscience seal'd them, laying by
That nothing-gift of differing multitudes,   86

---

7. **Foundations:** houses of charity. 11. **trial:** i.e., of their virtue. 21. **hardness:** hardship. 24. **Take or lend:** i.e., perhaps, blows. Obscure. 30. **match:** agreement. 34. **resty:** idle. 38. **browse:** nibble. 70. **but be:** but to be. 71. **[I'd]** (Tyrwhitt conj.). *I do* F. **buy:** pay. 77. **prize:** value. With her brothers alive, Imogen would not be heir. 79. **wrings:** writhes. 85. **seal'd:** assured. 86. **nothing...multitudes:** worthless gift of being attended by mobs of suitors.

Could not out-peer these twain.　Pardon me, gods!
I'd change my sex to be companion with them,
Since Leonatus false.
　　Bel.　　　　　　　It shall be so.
Boys, we'll go dress our hunt.　Fair youth, come
　　in.　　　　　　　　　　　　　　　　　90
Discourse is heavy, fasting; when we have supp'd,
We'll mannerly demand thee of thy story,
So far as thou wilt speak it.
　　Gui.　　　　　　　Pray, draw near.
　　Arv. The night to th' owl and morn to th' lark
　　less welcome.
　　Imo. Thanks, sir.　　　　　　　　　95
　　Arv. I pray, draw near.　　　　　*[Exeunt.*

SCENE VII.　[*Rome.　A public place.*]

Enter two Roman SENATORS *and* TRIBUNES.

　1. Sen. This is the tenour of the Emperor's writ:
That since the common men are now in action
'Gainst the Pannonians and Dalmatians,
And that the legions now in Gallia are
Full weak to undertake our wars against　　　5
The fall'n-off Britons, that we do incite
The gentry to this business.　He creates
Lucius proconsul; and to you the tribunes,
For this immediate levy, he commands
His absolute commission.　Long live Cæsar!　10
　1. Tri. Is Lucius general of the forces?
　2. Sen.　　　　　　　　　　　Ay.
　1. Tri. Remaining now in Gallia?
　1. Sen.　　　　　　With those legions
Which I have spoke of, whereunto your levy
Must be supplyant.　The words of your commis-
　sion
Will tie you to the numbers and the time　　15
Of their dispatch.
　1. Tri.　　　　We will discharge our duty.
　　　　　　　　　　　　　　　　　[Exeunt.

ACT IV

SCENE I.　[*Wales.　Near the cave of Belarius.*]

Enter CLOTEN *alone.*

　Clo. I am near to th' place where they should
meet, if Pisanio have mapp'd it truly.　How fit
his garments serve me!　Why should his mistress,
who was made by him that made the tailor, not be
fit too? the rather — saving reverence of the　5
word — for 'tis said a woman's fitness comes by
fits.　Therein I must play the workman.　I dare

speak it to myself — for it is not vain-glory for a
man and his glass to confer in his own chamber —
I mean, the lines of my body are as well drawn as
his; no less young, more strong, not beneath　10
him in fortunes, beyond him in the advantage of the
time, above him in birth, alike conversant in general services, and more remarkable in single oppositions; yet this imperceiverant thing loves him in　15
my despite.　What mortality is!　Posthumus, thy
head, which now is growing upon thy shoulders,
shall within this hour be off; thy mistress enforced;
thy garments cut to pieces before [her] face: and
all this done, spurn her home to her father; who　20
may haply be a little angry for my so rough usage;
but my mother, having power of his testiness, shall
turn all into my commendations.　My horse is
tied up safe.　Out, sword, and to a sore purpose!
Fortune, put them into my hand!　This is the　25
very description of their meeting-place; and the
fellow dares not deceive me.　　　　　*[Exit.*

SCENE II.　[*Before the cave of Belarius.*]

Enter BELARIUS, GUIDERIUS, ARVIRAGUS, *and*
　　　　IMOGEN, *from the cave.*

　Bel. [*To Imogen.*] You are not well.　Remain
　here in the cave;
We'll come to you after hunting.
　Arv.　　　　　　[*To Imogen.*] Brother, stay here.
Are we not brothers?
　Imo.　　　　So man and man should be;
But clay and clay differs in dignity,
Whose dust is both alike.　I am very sick.　　5
　Gui. Go you to hunting; I'll abide with him.
　Imo. So sick I am not, yet I am not well;
But not so citizen a wanton as
To seem to die ere sick.　So please you, leave me;
Stick to your journal course.　The breach of cus-
　tom　　　　　　　　　　　　　　　10
Is breach of all.　I am ill, but your being by me
Cannot amend me; society is no comfort
To one not sociable.　I am not very sick,
Since I can reason of it.　Pray you, trust me here.
I'll rob none but myself; and let me die,　　15
Stealing so poorly.
　Gui.　　　　　　I love thee; I have spoke it;
How much the quantity, the weight as much,
As I do love my father.
　Bel.　　　　　　What! how! how!
　Arv. If it be sin to say so, sir, I yoke me
In my good brother's fault.　I know not why　20
I love this youth; and I have heard you say,
Love's reason's without reason.　The bier at door,

87. out-peer: surpass.
Sc. vii, 6. fall'n-off: rebelling.　9. commands: commends.　14. supplyant: supplementary.　15. tie you to: inform you of.
Act IV, sc. i, 14. oppositions: combats.　imperceiverant: undiscerning.　19. [her] (Hanmer).　thy F.
Sc. ii, 8. citizen a wanton: delicate a spoiled child.　10. journal: daily.

And a demand who is't shall die, I'd say
My father, not this youth.
    Bel.   [*Aside.*] O noble strain!
O worthiness of nature! breed of greatness!   25
Cowards father cowards and base things sire base:
Nature hath meal and bran, contempt and grace.
I'm not their father; yet who this should be
Doth miracle itself, lov'd before me. —
'Tis the ninth hour o' th' morn.
    Arv.   Brother, farewell. 30
    Imo. I wish ye sport.
    Arv.   You health. — So please you, sir.
    Imo. [*Aside.*] These are kind creatures. Gods,
        what lies I have heard!
Our courtiers say all's savage but at court.
Experience, O, thou disprov'st report!
The imperious seas breed monsters; for the dish 35
Poor tributary rivers as sweet fish.
I am sick still, heart-sick. Pisanio,
I'll now taste of thy drug.   [*Swallows some.*]
    Gui.   I could not stir him.
He said he was gentle, but unfortunate;
Dishonestly afflicted, but yet honest.   40
    Arv. Thus did he answer me; yet said, hereafter
I might know more.
    Bel.   To th' field, to th' field!
We'll leave you for this time. Go in and rest.
    Arv. We'll not be long away.
    Bel.   Pray, be not sick,
For you must be our housewife.
    Imo.   Well or ill, 45
I am bound to you.   [*Exit [to the cave*].
    Bel.   And shalt be ever.
This youth, howe'er distress'd, appears he hath had
Good ancestors.
    Arv.   How angel-like he sings!
    Gui. But his neat cookery! He cut our roots
In characters,
And sauc'd our broths, as Juno had been sick 50
And he her dieter.
    Arv.   Nobly he yokes
A smiling with a sigh, as if the sigh
Was that it was for not being such a smile;
The smile mocking the sigh, that it would fly
From so divine a temple to commix 55
With winds that sailors rail at.
    Gui.   I do note
That grief and patience, rooted in [him] both,
Mingle their spurs together.
    Arv.   Grow, [patience]!
And let the stinking elder, grief, untwine
His perishing root with th' increasing vine! 60
    Bel. It is great morning. Come, away! —
    Who's there?

               Enter CLOTEN.
    Clo. I cannot find those runagates; that villain
Hath mock'd me. I am faint.
    Bel.   Those runagates!
Means he not us? I partly know him. 'Tis
Cloten, the son o' th' Queen. I fear some ambush.
I saw him not these many years, and yet   65
I know 'tis he. We are held as outlaws; hence!
    Gui. He is but one. You and my brother search
What companies are near. Pray you, away;
Let me alone with him.
          [*Exeunt Belarius and Arviragus.*]
    Clo.   Soft! What are you 70
That fly me thus? Some villain mountaineers?
I have heard of such. What slave art thou?
    Gui.   A thing
More slavish did I ne'er than answering
A "slave" without a knock.
    Clo.   Thou art a robber,
A law-breaker, a villain. Yield thee, thief. 75
    Gui. To who? To thee? What art thou?
    Have not I
An arm as big as thine? a heart as big?
Thy words, I grant, are bigger; for I wear not
My dagger in my mouth. Say what thou art,
Why I should yield to thee.
    Clo.   Thou villain base, 80
Know'st me not by my clothes?
    Gui.   No, nor thy tailor, rascal,
Who is thy grandfather. He made those clothes,
Which, as it seems, make thee.
    Clo.   Thou precious varlet,
My tailor made them not.
    Gui.   Hence, then, and thank
The man that gave them thee. Thou art some
    fool; 85
I am loath to beat thee.
    Clo.   Thou injurious thief,
Hear but my name, and tremble.
    Gui.   What's thy name?
    Clo. Cloten, thou villain.
    Gui. Cloten, thou double villain, be thy name,
I cannot tremble at it. Were it Toad, or Adder,
    Spider, 90
'Twould move me sooner.
    Clo.   To thy further fear,
Nay, to thy mere confusion, thou shalt know
I am son to th' Queen.
    Gui.   I am sorry for't; not seeming
So worthy as thy birth.
    Clo.   Art not afeard?
    Gui. Those that I reverence, those I fear, the
    wise. 95
At fools I laugh, not fear them.
    Clo.   Die the death!

---

29. **Doth miracle itself:** is miraculous. 39. **gentle:** nobly born. 49. **characters:** letters, emblems. 57. [him] (Pope)
them F. 58. **spurs:** roots. [patience] (Theobald). *patient* F. 92. **mere:** utter.

When I have slain thee with my proper hand,
I'll follow those that even now fled hence,
And on the gates of Lud's town set your heads.
Yield, rustic mountaineer. [*Fight and exeunt.* 100

Re-enter BELARIUS *and* ARVIRAGUS.

Bel. No company's abroad?
Arv. None in the world. You did mistake him,
    sure.
Bel. I cannot tell, — long is it since I saw him.
But time hath nothing blurr'd those lines of favour
Which then he wore. The snatches in his voice, 105
And burst of speaking, were as his. I am absolute
'Twas very Cloten.
    Arv. In this place we left them.
I wish my brother make good time with him,
You say he is so fell.
    Bel. Being scarce made up,
I mean, to man, he had not apprehension 110
Of roaring terrors; for the defect of judgement
Is oft the [cease] of fear.

Re-enter GUIDERIUS [*with Cloten's head*].
    But, see, thy brother.
Gui. This Cloten was a fool, an empty purse;
There was no money in't. Not Hercules
Could have knock'd out his brains, for he had none.
Yet I not doing this, the fool had borne 116
My head as I do his.
    Bel. What hast thou done?
Gui. I am perfect what: cut off one Cloten's head,
Son to the Queen, after his own report;
Who call'd me traitor, mountaineer, and swore
With his own single hand he'd take us in, 121
Displace our heads where — thank the gods! —
    they grow.
And set them on Lud's town.
    Bel. We are all undone.
Gui. Why, worthy father, what have we to lose,
But that he swore to take, our lives? The law 125
Protects not us; then why should we be tender
To let an arrogant piece of flesh threat us,
Play judge and executioner all himself,
For we do fear the law? What company
Discover you abroad?
    Bel. No single soul 130
Can we set eye on; but in all safe reason
He must have some attendants. Though his [hu-
    mour]
Was nothing but mutation, ay, and that
From one bad thing to worse, not frenzy, not
Absolute madness could so far have rav'd 135
To bring him here alone; although perhaps
It may be heard at court that such as we

Cave here, hunt here, are outlaws, and in time
May make some stronger head; the which he hear-
    ing —
As it is like him — might break out and swear 140
He'd fetch us in; yet is't not probable
To come alone, either he so undertaking,
Or they so suffering. Then on good ground we fear,
If we do fear this body hath a tail
More perilous than the head.
    Arv. Let ordinance 145
Come as the gods foresay it; howsoe'er,
My brother hath done well.
    Bel. I had no mind
To hunt this day; the boy Fidele's sickness
Did make my way long forth.
    Gui. With his own sword,
Which he did wave against my throat, I have ta'en
His head from him. I'll throw't into the creek 151
Behind our rock; and let it to the sea,
And tell the fishes he's the Queen's son, Cloten.
That's all I reck. [*Exit.*
    Bel. I fear 'twill be reveng'd.
Would, Polydore, thou hadst not done't! though
    valour 155
Becomes thee well enough.
    Arv. Would I had done't,
So the revenge alone pursu'd me! Polydore,
I love thee brotherly, but envy much
Thou hast robb'd me of this deed. I would re-
    venges,
That possible strength might meet, would seek us
    through 160
And put us to our answer.
    Bel. Well, 'tis done.
We'll hunt no more to-day, nor seek for danger
Where there's no profit. I prithee, to our rock;
You and Fidele play the cooks. I'll stay
Till hasty Polydore return, and bring him 165
To dinner presently.
    Arv. Poor sick Fidele!
I'll willingly to him. To gain his colour
I'd let a parish of such Clotens blood,
And praise myself for charity. [*Exit.*
    Bel. O thou goddess,
Thou divine Nature, [how] thyself thou blazon'st
In these two princely boys! They are as gentle
As zephyrs blowing below the violet, 172
Not wagging his sweet head; and yet as rough,
Their royal blood enchaf'd, as the rud'st wind
That by the top doth take the mountain pine 175
And make him stoop to th' vale. 'Tis wonder
That an invisible instinct should frame them
To royalty unlearn'd, honour untaught,
Civility not seen from other, valour

---

104. **favour**: appearance. 105. **snatches**: catches, breaks. 112. **[cease]** Herr. *cause* F. 129. **For**: because. 132. **[humour]** (Theobald). *honor* F. 139. **head**: armed force. 143. **suffering**: permitting. 145. **ordinance**: what is or-dained. 167. **gain his colour**: restore color to his cheeks. 170. **[how]** (Pope). *thou* F. 174. **enchaf'd**: heated.

That wildly grows in them but yields a crop   180
As if it had been sow'd.   Yet still it's strange
What Cloten's being here to us portends,
Or what his death will bring us.

Re-enter GUIDERIUS.

Gui.   Where's my brother?
I have sent Cloten's clotpoll down the stream
In embassy to his mother.   His body's hostage   185
For his return.   [*Solemn music.*
Bel.   My ingenious instrument!
Hark, Polydore, it sounds!   But what occasion
Hath Cadwal now to give it motion?   Hark!
Gui. Is he at home?
Bel.   He went hence even now.
Gui. What does he mean?   Since death of my
           dear'st mother   190
It did not speak before.   All solemn things
Should answer solemn accidents.   The matter?
Triumphs for nothing and lamenting toys
Is jollity for apes and grief for boys.
Is Cadwal mad?

Re-enter ARVIRAGUS, *with* IMOGEN [*as*] *dead,*
           bearing her in his arms.

Bel.   Look, here he comes,   195
And brings the dire occasion in his arms
Of what we blame him for.
Arv.   The bird is dead
That we have made so much on.   I had rather
Have skipp'd from sixteen years of age to sixty,
To have turn'd my leaping-time into a crutch,   200
Than have seen this.
Gui.   O sweetest, fairest lily!
My brother wears thee not the one half so well
As when thou grew'st thyself.
Bel.   O melancholy!
Who ever yet could sound thy bottom? find
The ooze, to show what coast thy sluggish [crare]
[Might] easiliest harbour in?   Thou blessed thing!
Jove knows what man thou mightst have made;
           but I,   207
Thou diedst, a most rare boy, of melancholy.
How found you him?
Arv.   Stark, as you see;
Thus smiling, as some fly had tickled slumber,   210
Not as death's dart, being laugh'd at; his right
           cheek
Reposing on a cushion.
Gui.   Where?
Arv.   O' th' floor,
His arms thus league'd.   I thought he slept, and put
My clouted brogues from off my feet, whose rude-
           ness

Answer'd my steps too loud.
Gui.   Why, he but sleeps!
If he be gone, he'll make his grave a bed.   216
With female fairies will his tomb be haunted,
And worms will not come to thee.
Arv.   With fairest flowers
Whilst summer lasts and I live here, Fidele,
I'll sweeten thy sad grave.   Thou shalt not lack   220
The flower that's like thy face, pale primrose, nor
The azur'd harebell, like thy veins, no, nor
The leaf of eglantine, whom not to slander,
Out-sweet'ned not thy breath.   The ruddock
           would,
With charitable bill, — O bill, sore shaming   225
Those rich-left heirs that let their fathers lie
Without a monument! — bring thee all this;
Yea, and furr'd moss besides, when flowers are none,
To winter-ground thy corse.
Gui.   Prithee, have done;
And do not play in wench-like words with that
Which is so serious.   Let us bury him,   231
And not protract with admiration what
Is now due debt.   To th' grave!
Arv.   Say, where shall's lay him?
Gui. By good Euriphile, our mother.
Arv.   Be't so;
And let us, Polydore, though now our voices   235
Have got the mannish crack, sing him to th' ground,
As once our mother; use like note and words,
Save that Euriphile must be Fidele.
Gui. Cadwal,
I cannot sing.   I'll weep, and word it with thee; 240
For notes of sorrow out of tune are worse
Than priests and fanes that lie.
Arv.   We'll speak it, then.
Bel. Great griefs, I see, med'cine the less; for
           Cloten
Is quite forgot.   He was a queen's son, boys;
And though he came our enemy, remember   245
He was paid for that.   Though mean and mighty,
           rotting
Together, have one dust, yet reverence,
That angel of the world, doth make distinction
Of place 'tween high and low.   Our foe was princely;
And though you took his life, as being our foe,   250
Yet bury him as a prince.
Gui.   Pray you, fetch him hither.
Thersites' body is as good as Ajax',
When neither are alive.
Arv.   If you'll go fetch him,
We'll say our song the whilst.   Brother, begin.
           [*Exit Belarius.*]
Gui. Nay, Cadwal, we must lay his head to the
           east;   255

184. **clotpoll**: blockhead.   192. **accidents**: events.   193. **toys**: trifles.   205. [crare] (Sympson conj.): small trading
vessel.   *care* F.   206. [**Might**] F₂.   *Might'st* F₁.   207. **but I**: but I know that.   But perhaps *I* should read *ay* or *ah*.   223.
eglantine: sweet briar.   224. **ruddock**: robin.   229. **winter-ground**: protect in winter.   237. **our** (Pope).   *to our* F.

My father hath a reason for't.
Arv.   'Tis true.
Gui. Come on then, and remove him.
Arv.   So. Begin.

SONG.

Gui. Fear no more the heat o' th' sun,
          Nor the furious winter's rages;
     Thou thy worldly task hast done,   260
          Home art gone, and ta'en thy wages.
     Golden lads and girls all must,
     As chimney-sweepers, come to dust.

Arv. Fear no more the frown o' th' great;
          Thou art past the tyrant's stroke.   265
     Care no more to clothe and eat;
          To thee the reed is as the oak.
     The sceptre, learning, physic, must
     All follow this, and come to dust.

Gui. Fear no more the lightning-flash,   270
Arv.   Nor the all-dreaded thunder-stone;
Gui. Fear not slander, censure rash;
Arv.   Thou hast finish'd joy and moan.
Both. All lovers young, all lovers must
     Consign to thee, and come to dust.   275

Gui. No exorciser harm thee!
Arv. Nor no witchcraft charm thee!
Gui. Ghost unlaid forbear thee!
Arv. Nothing ill come near thee!
Both. Quiet consummation have,   280
     And renowned be thy grave!

Re-enter BELARIUS, *with the body of Cloten.*

Gui. We have done our obsequies. Come, lay
     him down.
Bel. Here's a few flowers; but 'bout midnight,
     more.
The herbs that have on them cold dew o' th' night
Are strewings fitt'st for graves. Upon their faces.
You were as flowers, now wither'd; even so   286
These herblets shall, which we upon you strew.
Come on, away; apart upon our knees.
The ground that gave them first has them again.
Their pleasures here are past, so [is] their pain.   290
          [*Exeunt* [*Belarius, Guiderius, and Arvira-*
               gus].
Imo. [*Awaking.*] Yes, sir, to Milford-Haven;
     which is the way? —
I thank you. — By yond bush? — Pray, how far
     thither?
'Ods pittikins! can it be six mile yet?
I have gone all night. Faith, I'll lie down and sleep.

But, soft! no bedfellow! — O gods and god-
     desses!   [*Seeing the body of Cloten.*]   295
These flowers are like the pleasures of the world;
This bloody man, the care on't. I hope I dream;
For so I thought I was a cave-keeper
And cook to honest creatures. But 'tis not so.
'Twas but a bolt of nothing, shot at nothing,   300
Which the brain makes of fumes. Our very eyes
Are sometimes like our judgements, blind. Good
     faith,
I tremble still with fear; but if there be
Yet left in heaven as small a drop of pity
As a wren's eye, fear'd gods, a part of it!   305
The dream's here still, even when I wake. It is
Without me, as within me; not imagin'd, felt.
A headless man! The garments of Posthumus!
I know the shape of 's leg; this is his hand,
His foot Mercurial, his Martial thigh,   310
The brawns of Hercules; but his Jovial face —
Murder in heaven? — How! — 'Tis gone. Pisanio,
All curses madded Hecuba gave the Greeks,
And mine to boot, be darted on thee! Thou,
Conspir'd with that irregulous devil, Cloten,   315
Hath here cut off my lord. To write and read
Be henceforth treacherous! Damn'd Pisanio
Hath with his forged letters, — damn'd Pisanio —
From this most bravest vessel of the world
Struck the main-top! O Posthumus! alas,   320
Where is thy head? Where's that? Ay me!
     where's that?
Pisanio might have kill'd thee at the heart
And left this head on. How should this be? Pi-
     sanio?
'Tis he and Cloten. Malice and lucre in them
Have laid this woe here. O, 'tis pregnant, preg-
     nant!   325
The drug he gave me, which he said was precious
And cordial to me, have I not found it
Murd'rous to the senses? That confirms it home.
This is Pisanio's deed, and Cloten's. O!
Give colour to my pale cheek with thy blood,   330
That we the horrider may seem to those
Which chance to find us. O, my lord, my lord!
          [*Falls on the body.*]

Enter LUCIUS, CAPTAINS, *and a* SOOTHSAYER.

1. Cap. To him the legions garrison'd in Gallia,
After your will, have cross'd the sea, attending
You here at Milford-Haven with your ships.   335
They're here in readiness.
Luc.   But what from Rome?
1. Cap. The senate hath stirr'd up the confiners
And gentlemen of Italy, most willing spirits
That promise noble service; and they come

Under the conduct of bold Iachimo,   340
Sienna's brother.
   Luc.   When expect you them?
   1. Cap. With the next benefit o' th' wind.
   Luc.   This forwardness
Makes our hopes fair.   Command our present
    numbers
Be muster'd; bid the captains look to't.   Now, sir,
What have you dream'd of late of this war's pur-
    pose?   345
   Sooth. Last night the very gods show'd me a
    vision —
I fast and pray'd for their intelligence — thus:
I saw Jove's bird, the Roman eagle, wing'd
From the spongy south to this part of the west,
There vanish'd in the sunbeams; which portends —
Unless my sins abuse my divination —   351
Success to the Roman host.
   Luc.   Dream often so,
And never false.   Soft, ho! what trunk is here
Without his top?   The ruin speaks that sometime
It was a worthy building.   How! a page!   355
Or dead, or sleeping on him?   But dead rather;
For nature doth abhor to make his bed
With the defunct, or sleep upon the dead.
Let's see the boy's face.
   1. Cap.   He's alive, my lord.
   Luc. He'll then instruct us of this body.   Young
    one,   360
Inform us of thy fortunes, for it seems
They crave to be demanded.   Who is this
Thou mak'st thy bloody pillow?   Or who was he
That, otherwise than noble nature did,
Hath alter'd that good picture?   What's thy in-
    terest   365
In this sad wreck?   How came it?   Who is it?
What art thou?
   Imo.   I am nothing: or if not,
Nothing to be were better.   This was my master,
A very valiant Briton and a good,
That here by mountaineers lies slain.   Alas!   370
There is no more such masters.   I may wander
From east to occident, cry out for service,
Try many, all good, serve truly, never
Find such another master.
   Luc.   'Lack, good youth!
Thou mov'st no less with thy complaining than   375
Thy master in bleeding.   Say his name, good friend.
   Imo. Richard du Champ.   [*Aside.*] If I do lie
    and do
No harm by it, though the gods hear, I hope
They'll pardon it. — Say you, sir?
   Luc.   Thy name?
   Imo.   Fidele, sir.
   Luc. Thou dost approve thyself the very same;

Thy name well fits thy faith, thy faith thy name.
Wilt take thy chance with me?   I will not say   382
Thou shalt be so well master'd, but, be sure,
No less belov'd.   The Roman Emperor's letters,
Sent by a consul to me, should not sooner   385
Than thine own worth prefer thee.   Go with me.
   Imo. I'll follow, sir.   But first, an't please the
    gods,
I'll hide my master from the flies, as deep
As these poor pickaxes can dig; and when
With wild-wood leaves and weeds I ha' strew'd his
    grave,   390
And on it said a century of prayers,
Such as I can, twice o'er, I'll weep and sigh;
And leaving so his service, follow you,
So please you entertain me.
   Luc.   Ay, good youth;
And rather father thee than master thee.   395
My friends,
The boy hath taught us manly duties.   Let us
Find out the prettiest daisied plot we can,
And make him with our pikes and partisans
A grave.   Come, arm him.   Boy, he is preferr'd   400
By thee to us, and he shall be interr'd
As soldiers can.   Be cheerful; wipe thine eyes.
Some falls are means the happier to arise.
                          [*Exeunt.*

SCENE III.   [*Britain.   A room in Cymbeline's
palace.*]

Enter CYMBELINE, LORDS, PISANIO [*and Attendants*].

   Cym. Again; and bring me word how 'tis with
    her.   [*Exit an attendant.*]
A fever with the absence of her son,
A madness, of which her life's in danger.   Heavens,
How deeply you at once do touch me!   Imogen,
The great part of my comfort, gone; my queen   5
Upon a desperate bed, and in a time
When fearful wars point at me; her son gone,
So needful for this present: it strikes me, past
The hope of comfort.   But for thee, fellow,
Who needs must know of her departure and   10
Dost seem so ignorant, we'll enforce it from thee
By a sharp torture.
   Pis.   Sir, my life is yours;
I humbly set it at your will; but, for my mistress,
I nothing know where she remains, why gone,
Nor when she purposes return.   Beseech your High-
    ness,   15
Hold me your loyal servant.
   1. Lord.   Good my liege,
The day that she was missing he was here.
I dare be bound he's true and shall perform

---

341. **Sienna's:** i.e., the lord of Sienna's.   389. **pickaxes:** i.e., her fingers.   394. **entertain:** employ.   399. **partisans:**
long-handled weapons with a blade.   400. **arm him:** pick him up.   **preferr'd:** advanced.

All parts of his subjection loyally.   For Cloten,
There wants no diligence in seeking him,   20
And will, no doubt, be found.
    Cym.   The time is troublesome.
[*To Pisanio.*] We'll slip you for a season; but our
    jealousy
Does yet depend.
    1. Lord.   So please your Majesty,
The Roman legions, all from Gallia drawn,
Are landed on your coast, with a supply   25
Of Roman gentlemen, by the senate sent.
    Cym. Now for the counsel of my son and queen!
I am amaz'd with matter.
    1. Lord.   Good my liege,
Your preparation can affront no less
Than what you hear of.   Come more, for more
    you're ready;   30
The want is but to put those powers in motion
That long to move.
    Cym.   I thank you.   Let's withdraw,
And meet the time as it seeks us.   We fear not
What can from Italy annoy us; but
We grieve at chances here.   Away!   35
                [*Exeunt [all but Pisanio*].
    Pis. I heard no letter from my master since
I wrote him Imogen was slain.   'Tis strange.
Nor hear I from my mistress, who did promise
To yield me often tidings; neither know I
What is betid to Cloten; but remain   40
Perplex'd in all.   The heavens still must work.
Wherein I am false I am honest; not true, to be true.
These present wars shall find I love my country,
Even to the note o' th' King, or I'll fall in them.
All other doubts, by time let them be clear'd;   45
Fortune brings in some boats that are not steer'd.
                      [*Exit.*

SCENE IV. [*Wales.   Before the cave of Belarius.*]

    Enter BELARIUS, GUIDERIUS, *and* ARVIRAGUS.

    Gui. The noise is round about us.
    Bel.   Let us from it.
    Arv. What pleasure, sir, [find we] in life, to lock it
From action and adventure?
    Gui.   Nay, what hope
Have we in hiding us?   This way, the Romans
Must or for Britons slay us, or receive us   5
For barbarous and unnatural revolts
During their use, and slay us after.
    Bel.   Sons,
We'll higher to the mountains; there secure us.
To the King's party there's no going.   Newness

Of Cloten's death — we being not known, not mus-
    ter'd   10
Among the bands — may drive us to a render
Where we have liv'd, and so extort from 's that
Which we have done, whose answer would be death
Drawn on with torture.
    Gui.   This is, sir, a doubt
In such a time nothing becoming you,   15
Nor satisfying us.
    Arv.   It is not likely
That when they hear [the] Roman horses neigh,
Behold their quarter'd fires, have both their eyes
And ears so cloy'd importantly as now,
That they will waste their time upon our note,   20
To know from whence we are.
    Bel.   O, I am known
Of many in the army.   Many years,
Though Cloten then but young, you see, not wore
    him
From my remembrance.   And besides, the King
Hath not deserv'd my service nor your loves,   25
Who find in my exile the want of breeding,
The certainty of this hard life; aye hopeless
To have the courtesy your cradle promis'd,
But to be still hot Summer's tanlings and
The shrinking slaves of Winter.
    Gui.   Than be so   30
Better to cease to be.   Pray, sir, to th' army.
I and my brother are not known; yourself
So out of thought, and thereto so o'ergrown,
Cannot be question'd.
    Arv.   By this sun that shines,
I'll thither.   What thing is it that I never   35
Did see man die! scarce ever look'd on blood,
But that of coward hares, hot goats, and venison!
Never bestrid a horse, save one that had
A rider like myself, who ne'er wore rowel
Nor iron on his heel!   I am asham'd   40
To look upon the holy sun, to have
The benefit of his blest beams, remaining
So long a poor unknown.
    Gui.   By heavens, I'll go.
If you will bless me, sir, and give me leave,
I'll take the better care; but if you will not,   45
The hazard therefore due fall on me by
The hands of Romans!
    Arv.   So say I; amen.
    Bel. No reason I, since of your lives you set
So slight a valuation, should reserve
My crack'd one to more care.   Have with you,
    boys!   50
If in your country wars you chance to die,

    Sc. iii, 22. **slip**: release.   **jealousy**: suspicion.   23. **depend**: hang in suspense.   28. **amaz'd . . . matter**: confused with the
rush of affairs.   29. **affront**: encounter.   44. **note**: notice.
    Sc. iv, 2. **[find we]** F₂.   *we finde* F₁.   4. **This way**: i.e., if we hide.   6. **revolts**: rebels.   7. **During . . . use**: while they use
us.   11. **render**: confession.   17. **[the]** (Rowe).   *their* F.   18. **their . . . fires**: camp fires.   19. **cloy'd importantly**: filled
with urgent matters.   20. **upon our note**: noticing us.   29. **tanlings**: those tanned by.   33. **o'ergrown**: heavily bearded.

That is my bed too, lads, and there I'll lie.
Lead, lead! [*Aside*.] The time seems long; their
    blood thinks scorn
Till it fly out and show them princes born.
                              [*Exeunt*.

ACT V

Scene I. [*Britain. The Roman camp.*]

Enter POSTHUMUS [*with a bloody handkerchief*].

Post. Yea, bloody cloth, I'll keep thee, for I
    wish'd
Thou shouldst be colour'd thus. You married ones,
If each of you should take this course, how many
Must murder wives much better than themselves
For wrying but a little! O Pisanio!   5
Every good servant does not all commands;
No bond but to do just ones. Gods! if you
Should have ta'en vengeance on my faults, I never
Had liv'd to put on this; so had you sav'd
The noble Imogen to repent, and struck   10
Me, wretch, more worth your vengeance. But,
    alack,
You snatch some hence for little faults; that's love,
To have them fall no more: you some permit
To second ills with ills, each elder worse,
And make them dread it, to the doers' thrift.
But Imogen is your own; do your best wills,   16
And make me blest to obey! I am brought hither
Among th' Italian gentry, and to fight
Against my lady's kingdom. 'Tis enough
That, Britain, I have kill'd thy mistress; peace!   20
I'll give no wound to thee. Therefore, good
    heavens,
Hear patiently my purpose: I'll disrobe me
Of these Italian weeds and suit myself
As does a Briton peasant; so I'll fight
Against the part I come with; so I'll die   25
For thee, O Imogen, even for whom my life
Is every breath a death; and thus, unknown,
Pitied nor hated, to the face of peril
Myself I'll dedicate. Let me make men know
More valour in me than my habits show.   30
Gods, put the strength o' th' Leonati in me!
To shame the guise o' th' world, I will begin
The fashion: less without and more within. [*Exit*.

Scene II. [*Field between the British and Roman
camps.*]

Enter LUCIUS, IACHIMO, *and the* Roman Army *at
one door; and the* Briton Army *at another;* LEONA-
TUS POSTHUMUS *following, like a poor soldier.*

*They march over and go out. Then enter again, in
skirmish,* IACHIMO *and* POSTHUMUS: *he vanquisheth
and disarmeth* IACHIMO, *and then leaves him.*

Iach. The heaviness and guilt within my bosom
Takes off my manhood. I have belied a lady,
The Princess of this country, and the air on't
Revengingly enfeebles me; or could this carl,
A very drudge of Nature's, have subdu'd me   5
In my profession? Knighthoods and honours,
    borne
As I wear mine, are titles but of scorn.
If that thy gentry, Britain, go before
This lout as he exceeds our lords, the odds
Is that we scarce are men and you are gods.   10
                              [*Exit*.

The battle continues; the Britons *fly;* CYMBELINE
is taken: then enter, to his rescue, BELARIUS,
GUIDERIUS, *and* ARVIRAGUS.

Bel. Stand, stand! We have th' advantage of
    the ground;
The lane is guarded. Nothing routs us but
The villainy of our fears.
  Gui. }
  Arv. }   Stand, stand, and fight!

Re-enter POSTHUMUS, *and seconds the* Britons.
They rescue CYMBELINE, *and exeunt. Then re-
enter* LUCIUS, IACHIMO, *and* IMOGEN.

Luc. Away, boy, from the troops, and save thy-
    self;
For friends kill friends, and the disorder's such   15
As war were hoodwink'd.
  Iach.   'Tis their fresh supplies.
  Luc. It is a day turn'd strangely. Or betimes
Let's reinforce, or fly.   [*Exeunt*.

Scene III. [*Another part of the field.*]

Enter POSTHUMUS *and a* Briton LORD.

Lord. Cam'st thou from where they made the
    stand?
Post.   I did;
Though you, it seems, come from the fliers.
Lord.   I did.
Post. No blame be to you, sir, for all was lost
But that the heavens fought; the King himself
Of his wings destitute, the army broken,   5
And but the backs of Britons seen, all flying
Through a strait lane; the enemy full-hearted,
Lolling the tongue with slaught'ring, having work
More plentiful than tools to do 't, struck down
Some mortally, some slightly touch'd, some falling

Merely through fear; that the strait pass was
    damm'd   11
With dead men hurt behind, and cowards living
To die with length'ned shame.
   Lord.   Where was this lane?
   Post. Close by the battle, ditch'd, and wall'd with
    turf;
Which gave advantage to an ancient soldier,   15
(An honest one, I warrant) who deserv'd
So long a breeding as his white beard came to,
In doing this for 's country. Athwart the lane,
He, with two striplings — lads more like to run
The country base than to commit such slaughter, 20
With faces fit for masks, or rather fairer
Than those for preservation cas'd, or shame, —
Made good the passage; cried to those that fled,
"Our Britain's harts die flying, not our men.
To darkness fleet souls that fly backwards. Stand,
Or we are Romans and will give you that   26
Like beasts which you shun beastly, and may save
But to look back in frown. Stand, stand!" These
    three,
Three thousand confident, in act as many —
For three performers are the file when all   30
The rest do nothing — with this word "Stand,
    stand!"
Accommodated by the place, more charming
With their own nobleness, which could have turn'd
A distaff to a lance, gilded pale looks.
Part shame, part spirit renew'd; that some, turn'd
    coward   35
But by example — O, a sin in war,
Damn'd in the first beginners! — gan to look
The way that they did, and to grin like lions
Upon the pikes o' th' hunters. Then began
A stop i' th' chaser, a retire, anon   40
A rout, confusion thick. Forthwith they fly
Chickens, the way which they [stoop'd] eagles;
    slaves,
The strides [they] victors made: and now our cow-
    ards,
Like fragments in hard voyages, became
The life o' th' need. Having found the backdoor
    open   45
Of th' unguarded hearts, heavens, how they wound!
Some slain before; some dying; some their friends
O'er-borne i' th' former wave; then, chas'd by one,
Are now each one the slaughter-man of twenty.
Those that would die or ere resist are grown   50
The mortal bugs o' th' field.
   Lord.   This was strange chance.

A narrow lane, an old man, and two boys!
   Post. Nay, do not wonder at it; you are made
Rather to wonder at the things you hear
Than to work any. Will you rhyme upon 't,   55
And vent it for a mockery? Here is one:
"Two boys, an old man twice a boy, a lane,
Preserv'd the Britons, was the Romans' bane."
   Lord. Nay, be not angry, sir.
   Post.   'Lack, to what end?
Who dares not stand his foe, I'll be his friend;   60
For if he'll do as he is made to do,
I know he'll quickly fly my friendship too.
You have put me into rhyme.
   Lord.   Farewell; you're angry.
                                   [*Exit.*
   Post. Still going? This is a lord! O noble
    misery,
To be i' th' field, and ask "what news?" of me! 65
To-day how many would have given their honours
To have sav'd their carcases! took heel to do 't,
And yet died too! I, in mine own woe charm'd,
Could not find Death where I did hear him groan,
Nor feel him where he struck. Being an ugly mon-
    ster,   70
'Tis strange he hides him in fresh cups, soft beds,
Sweet words; or hath moe ministers than we
That draw his knives i' th' war. Well, I will find
    him;
For being now a favourer to the Briton,
No more a Briton, I have resum'd again   75
The part I came in. Fight I will no more,
But yield me to the veriest hind that shall
Once touch my shoulder. Great the slaughter is
Here made by th' Roman; great the answer be
Britons must take. For me, my ransom's death.
On either side I come to spend my breath;   81
Which neither here I'll keep nor bear again,
But end it by some means for Imogen.

    Enter two [British] CAPTAINS *and* Soldiers.

   1. [*Cap.*] Great Jupiter be prais'd! Lucius is
    taken.   84
'Tis thought the old man and his sons were angels.
   2. [*Cap.*] There was a fourth man, in a silly
    habit,
That gave the affront with them.
   1. [*Cap.*]   So 'tis reported;
But none of 'em can be found. Stand! who's there?
   Post. A Roman,
Who had not now been drooping here, if seconds   90
Had answer'd him.

Sc. iii, 19-20. **run...base:** play prisoner's base. 22. **cas'd:** masked. **shame:** modesty. 27-28. **save...frown:** avert
if you will only look back defiantly. Cf. ll. 36-38, below. 30. **file:** rank. 32. **charming:** bewitching. 35. **Part...part:**
some...others. 38. **they:** i.e., the three. 42. **[stoop'd]** (Rowe): swooped. *stopt* F. 43. **[they]** (Theobald). *the* F.
42-43. **slaves...made:** retrace like slaves the ground they strode like victors. 44. **fragments:** i.e., of food. 45. **life...
need:** i.e., food for life in (dire) need. 51. **mortal bugs:** deadly terrors. 64. **noble misery:** titled wretchedness. 68.
charm'd: made invulnerable. 86. **silly:** simple. 90. **seconds:** supporters.

2. [*Cap.*]   Lay hands on him; a dog!
A leg of Rome shall not return to tell
What crows have peck'd them here. He brags
    his service
As if he were of note. Bring him to th' King.

Enter Cymbeline, Belarius, Guiderius, Arviragus,
Pisanio [Soldiers, Attendants] *and* Roman
Captives. *The* Captains *present* Posthumus *to*
Cymbeline, *who delivers him over to a* Gaoler.
[*Then exeunt omnes.*]

SCENE IV. [*A British prison.*]

Enter POSTHUMUS *and* [*two*] GAOLER[S].

[*I.*] *Gaol.* You shall not now be stol'n, you have
    locks upon you;
So graze as you find pasture.
    2. *Gaol.*   Ay, or a stomach.
                                [*Exeunt Gaolers.*]
Post. Most welcome, bondage! for thou art a
    way,
I think, to liberty; yet am I better
Than one that's sick o' th' gout, since he had
    rather   5
Groan so in perpetuity than be cur'd
By th' sure physician, Death, who is the key
T' unbar these locks. My conscience, thou art
    fetter'd
More than my shanks and wrists. You good gods,
    give me
The penitent instrument to pick that bolt;   10
Then, free for ever! Is't enough I am sorry?
So children temporal fathers do appease;
Gods are more full of mercy. Must I repent
I cannot do it better than in gyves,
Desir'd more than constrain'd; to satisfy,   15
If of my freedom 'tis the main part, take
No stricter render of me than my all.
I know you are more clement than vile men,
Who of their broken debtors take a third,
A sixth, a tenth, letting them thrive again   20
On their abatement. That's not my desire.
For Imogen's dear life take mine; and though
'Tis not so dear, yet 'tis a life; you coin'd it.
'Tween man and man they weigh not every stamp;
Though light, take pieces for the figure's sake;   25
You rather mine, being yours; and so, great powers,
If you will take this audit, take this life,
And cancel these cold bonds. O Imogen!
I'll speak to thee in silence.   [*Sleeps.*]

Solemn music. Enter, as in an apparition, SICILIUS
LEONATUS, *father to Posthumus, an old man,*

*attired like a warrior; leading in his hand an
ancient matron, his wife and mother to Posthumus,
with music before them. Then, after other music,
follow the two young* LEONATI *brothers to Posthumus, with wounds as they died in the wars. They
circle Posthumus round, as he lies sleeping.*
Sici. No more, thou Thunder-master, show   30
        Thy spite on mortal flies:
    With Mars fall out, with Juno chide,
        That thy adulteries
            Rates and revenges.
    Hath my poor boy done aught but well,   35
        Whose face I never saw?
    I died whilst in the womb he stay'd
        Attending Nature's law;
    Whose father then, as men report
        Thou orphans' father art,   40
    Thou shouldst have been, and shielded him
        From this earth-vexing smart.

Moth. Lucina lent not me her aid,
        But took me in my throes;
    That from me was Posthumus ript,   45
        Came crying 'mongst his foes,
        A thing of pity!

Sici. Great Nature, like his ancestry,
        Moulded the stuff so fair,
    That he deserv'd the praise o' th' world,   50
        As great Sicilius' heir.

I. Bro. When once he was mature for man,
        In Britain where was he
    That could stand up his parallel,
        Or fruitful object be   55
    In eye of Imogen, that best
        Could deem his dignity?

Moth. With marriage wherefore was he mock'd,
        To be exil'd, and thrown
    From Leonati seat, and cast   60
        From her his dearest one,
            Sweet Imogen?

Sici. Why did you suffer Iachimo,
        Slight thing of Italy,
    To taint his nobler heart and brain   65
        With needless jealousy;
    And to become the geck and scorn
        O' th' other's villainy?

2. Bro. For this from stiller seats we came,
        Our parents and us twain,   70

Sc. iv, 14. **gyves:** fetters. 16–17. **If . . . me:** If it is essential for my freedom of conscience, take from me no greater
payment. 24. **stamp:** coin. 25. **figure's:** i.e., the image (or the amount) stamped on the coin. 26. **You . . . yours:** You
(gods) should sooner take the light coin of my life, since you made it. 34. **rates:** scolds. 38. **Attending:** awaiting. 43.
Lucina: goddess of childbirth. 67. **geck:** dupe.

That striking in our country's cause
    Fell bravely and were slain,
Our fealty and Tenantius' right
    With honour to maintain.

1. Bro. Like hardiment Posthumus hath   75
    To Cymbeline perform'd.
Then, Jupiter, thou king of gods,
    Why hast thou thus adjourn'd
The graces for his merits due,
    Being all to dolours turn'd?   80

Sici. Thy crystal window ope; look out;
    No longer exercise
Upon a valiant race thy harsh
    And potent injuries.

Moth. Since, Jupiter, our son is good,   85
    Take off his miseries.

Sici. Peep through thy marble mansion; help;
    Or we poor ghosts will cry
To th' shining synod of the rest
    Against thy deity.   90

Both Bro. Help, Jupiter; or we appeal,
    And from thy justice fly.

JUPITER *descends in thunder and lightning, sitting upon an eagle: he throws a thunderbolt. The Ghosts fall on their knees.*

Jup. No more, you petty spirits of region low,
    Offend our hearing; hush! How dare you ghosts
Accuse the Thunderer, whose bolt, you know, 95
    Sky-planted batters all rebelling coasts?
Poor shadows of Elysium, hence, and rest
    Upon your never-with'ring banks of flowers.
Be not with mortal accidents opprest;
    No care of yours it is; you know 'tis ours. 100
Whom best I love I cross; to make my gift,
    The more delay'd, delighted. Be content;
Your low-laid son our godhead will uplift.
    His comforts thrive, his trials well are spent.
Our jovial star reign'd at his birth, and in 105
    Our temple was he married. Rise, and fade.
He shall be lord of Lady Imogen,
    And happier much by his affliction made.
This tablet lay upon his breast, wherein
    Our pleasure his full fortune doth confine. 110
And so, away! No farther with your din
    Express impatience, lest you stir up mine.
Mount, eagle, to my palace crystalline.
                     [Ascends.
Sici. He came in thunder; his celestial breath
Was sulphurous to smell. The holy eagle 115

Stoop'd, as to foot us. His ascension is
More sweet than our blest fields. His royal bird
Prunes the immortal wing and cloys his beak,
As when his god is pleas'd.
All.   Thanks, Jupiter!
Sici. The marble pavement closes, he is enter'd
His radiant roof. Away! and, to be blest, 121
Let us with care perform his great behest.
                     [The Ghosts] vanish.
Post. [*Waking.*] Sleep, thou hast been a grandsire
    and begot
A father to me, and thou hast created
A mother and two brothers; but, O scorn! 125
Gone! they went hence so soon as they were born.
And so I am awake. Poor wretches that depend
On greatness' favour dream as I have done,
Wake and find nothing. But, alas, I swerve.
Many dream not to find, neither deserve, 130
And yet are steep'd in favours; so am I,
That have this golden chance and know not why.
What fairies haunt this ground? A book? O
    rare one!
Be not, as is our fangled world, a garment
Nobler than that it covers! Let thy effects 135
So follow, to be most unlike our courtiers,
As good as promise!
    (*Reads.*) "Whenas a lion's whelp shall, to himself unknown, without seeking find, and be embrac'd by a piece of tender air; and when from a stately cedar shall be lopp'd branches, which, 140 being dead many years, shall after revive, be jointed to the old stock and freshly grow; then shall Posthumus end his miseries, Britain be fortunate and flourish in peace and plenty." 145
'Tis still a dream, or else such stuff as madmen
Tongue and brain not; either both or nothing;
Or senseless speaking, or a speaking such
As sense cannot untie. Be what it is,
The action of my life is like it, which 150
I'll keep, if but for sympathy.

Re-enter GAOLER.

Gaol. Come, sir, are you ready for death?
Post. Over-roasted rather; ready long ago.
Gaol. Hanging is the word, sir. If you be ready
for that, you are well cook'd. 156
Post. So, if I prove a good repast to the spectators, the dish pays the shot.
Gaol. A heavy reckoning for you, sir. But the
comfort is, you shall be called to no more pay- 160
ments, fear no more tavern-bills, which are often
the sadness of parting, as the procuring of mirth.
You come in faint for want of meat, depart reeling
with too much drink; sorry that you have paid too

---

102. **delighted:** delightful. 116. **foot:** grasp with his talons. **ascension:** i.e., his breath when ascending. 118. **Prunes:** preens. **cloys:** claws. 125. **scorn:** mockery. 129. **swerve:** digress. 134. **fangled:** showy. 146. **brain:** understand. 151. **for sympathy:** because of the resemblance. 158. **shot:** reckoning.

much, and sorry that you are paid too much; 165
purse and brain both empty; the brain the heavier
for being too light, the purse too light, being drawn
of heaviness. O, of this contradiction you shall
now be quit. O, the charity of a penny cord! It
sums up thousands in a trice. You have no 170
true debitor and creditor but it; of what's past, is,
and to come, the discharge. Your neck, sir, is pen,
book, and counters; so the acquittance follows.

Post. I am merrier to die than thou art to live. 176
Gaol. Indeed, sir, he that sleeps feels not the
toothache; but a man that were to sleep your sleep,
and a hangman to help him to bed, I think he
would change places with his officer; for, look you,
sir, you know not which way you shall go.

Post. Yes indeed do I, fellow. 183
Gaol. Your Death has eyes in's head then; I have
not seen him so pictur'd. You must either be
directed by some that take upon them to know,
or to take upon yourself that which I am sure you
do not know, or jump the after-inquiry on your own
peril; and how you shall speed in your journey's
end, I think you'll never return to tell one. 191

Post. I tell thee, fellow, there are none want eyes
to direct them the way I am going, but such as
wink and will not use them. 194

Gaol. What an infinite mock is this, that a man
should have the best use of eyes to see the way of
blindness! I am sure hanging's the way of winking.

Enter a MESSENGER.

Mess. Knock off his manacles; bring your
prisoner to the King. 200

Post. Thou bring'st good news; I am call'd to
be made free.

Gaol. I'll be hang'd then.

Post. Thou shalt be then freer than a gaoler;
no bolts for the dead. 205

[*Exeunt all but the Gaoler.*]

Gaol. Unless a man would marry a gallows and
beget young gibbets, I never saw one so prone.
Yet, on my conscience, there are verier knaves
desire to live, for all he be a Roman; and there be
some of them too that die against their wills. 210
So should I, if I were one. I would we were all
of one mind, and one mind good. O, there were
desolation of gaolers and gallowses! I speak against
my present profit, but my wish hath a preferment
in't. [*Exit.* 215

SCENE V. [*Cymbeline's tent.*]

Enter CYMBELINE, BELARIUS, GUIDERIUS, ARVI-
RAGUS, PISANIO, Lords [Officers, *and* Attendants].

Cym. Stand by my side, you whom the gods have
made
Preservers of my throne. Woe is my heart
That the poor soldier that so richly fought,
Whose rags sham'd gilded arms, whose naked breast
Stepp'd before targes of proof, cannot be found. 5
He shall be happy that can find him, if
Our grace can make him so.

Bel.   I never saw
Such noble fury in so poor a thing;
Such precious deeds in one that promis'd nought
But beggary and poor looks.

Cym.   No tidings of him?

Pis. He hath been search'd among the dead and
living,
But no trace of him.   11

Cym.   To my grief, I am
The heir of his reward; [*to Belarius, Guiderius, and
Arviragus*] which I will add
To you, the liver, heart and brain of Britain,
By whom I grant she lives. 'Tis now the time
To ask of whence you are. Report it.

Bel.   Sir, 16
In Cambria are we born, and gentlemen.
Further to boast were neither true nor modest,
Unless I add we are honest.

Cym.   Bow your knees.
Arise my knights o' th' battle. I create you 20
Companions to our person and will fit you
With dignities becoming your estates.

Enter CORNELIUS *and* LADIES.

There's business in these faces. Why so sadly
Greet you our victory? You look like Romans,
And not o' th' court of Britain.

Cor.   Hail, great King!
To sour your happiness, I must report 26
The Queen is dead.

Cym.   Who worse than a physician
Would this report become? But I consider,
By med'cine life may be prolong'd, yet death
Will seize the doctor too. How ended she? 30

Cor. With horror, madly dying, like her life,
Which, being cruel to the world, concluded
Most cruel to herself. What she confess'd
I will report, so please you. These her women
Can trip me, if I err; who with wet cheeks 35
Were present when she finish'd.

Cym.   Prithee, say.

Cor. First, she confess'd she never lov'd you; only
Affected greatness got by you, not you;
Married your royalty, was wife to your place,
Abhorr'd your person.

Cym.   She alone knew this; 40

---

167. **drawn:** emptied.   171. **debitor and creditor:** accountant.   173. **counters:** metal discs used in counting.   188.
jump: risk.   194. **wink:** close.   207. **prone:** eager (to die).   214. **preferment:** promotion.
Sc. v, 5. **targes of proof:** shields proved impenetrable.   35. **trip:** refute.   38. **Affected:** loved.

And, but she spoke it dying, I would not
Believe her lips in opening it.   Proceed.
    Cor. Your daughter, whom she bore in hand to
      love
With such integrity, she did confess
Was as a scorpion to her sight; whose life,   45
But that her flight prevented it, she had
Ta'en off by poison.
    Cym.   O most delicate fiend!
Who is't can read a woman?   Is there more?
    Cor. More, sir, and worse.   She did confess she
      had
For you a mortal mineral, which, being took,   50
Should by the minute feed on life, and ling'ring,
By inches waste you; in which time she purpos'd,
By watching, weeping, tendance, kissing, to
O'ercome you with her show, and, in time,
When she had fitted you with her craft, to work   55
Her son into th' adoption of the crown;
But, failing of her end by his strange absence,
Grew shameless-desperate; open'd, in despite
Of heaven and men, her purposes; repented
The evils she hatch'd were not effected; so   60
Despairing died.
    Cym.   Heard you all this, her women?
    Lad. We did, so please your Highness.
    Cym.   Mine eyes
Were not in fault, for she was beautiful;
Mine ears, that [heard] her flattery; nor my heart,
That thought her like her seeming.   It had been
      vicious   65
To have mistrusted her; yet — O my daughter! —
That it was folly in me, thou mayst say,
And prove it in thy feeling.   Heaven mend all!

Enter LUCIUS, IACHIMO, [*the* SOOTHSAYER] *and other*
    Roman Prisoners [*guarded*]; POSTHUMUS *behind,*
    and IMOGEN.

Thou com'st not, Caius, now for tribute; that
The Britons have raz'd out, though with the loss   70
Of many a bold one, whose kinsmen have made suit
That their good souls may be appeas'd with
      slaughter
Of you their captives, which ourself have granted.
So think of your estate.
    Luc. Consider, sir, the chance of war.   The day
Was yours by accident.   Had it gone with us,   76
We should not, when the blood was cool, have
      threaten'd
Our prisoners with the sword.   But since the gods
Will have it thus, that nothing but our lives
May be call'd ransom, let it come.   Sufficeth   80
A Roman with a Roman's heart can suffer.
Augustus lives to think on't; and so much
For my peculiar care.   This one thing only

I will entreat: my boy, a Briton born,
Let him be ransom'd.   Never master had   85
A page so kind, so duteous, diligent,
So tender over his occasions, true,
So feat, so nurse-like.   Let his virtue join
With my request, which I'll make bold your High-
      ness
Cannot deny.   He hath done no Briton harm,   90
Though he have serv'd a Roman.   Save him, sir,
And spare no blood beside.
    Cym.   I have surely seen him;
His favour is familiar to me.   Boy,
Thou hast look'd thyself into my grace
And art mine own.   I know not why, wherefore,   95
To say "Live, boy."   Ne'er thank thy master; live,
And ask of Cymbeline what boon thou wilt,
Fitting my bounty and thy state, I'll give it,
Yea, though thou do demand a prisoner,   99
The noblest ta'en.
    Imo.   I humbly thank your Highness.
    Luc. I do not bid thee beg my life, good lad;
And yet I know thou wilt.
    Imo.   No, no, alack;
There's other work in hand.   I see a thing
Bitter to me as death; your life, good master,
Must shuffle for itself.
    Luc.   The boy disdains me;   105
He leaves me, scorns me.   Briefly die their joys
That place them on the truth of girls and boys.
Why stands he so perplex'd?
    Cym.   What wouldst thou, boy?
I love thee more and more; think more and more
What's best to ask.   Know'st him thou look'st on?
      Speak,   110
Wilt have him live?   Is he thy kin? thy friend?
    Imo. He is a Roman, no more kin to me
Than I to your Highness; who, being born your
      vassal,
Am something nearer.
    Cym.   Wherefore ey'st him so?
    Imo. I'll tell you, sir, in private, if you please   115
To give me hearing.
    Cym.   Ay, with all my heart,
And lend my best attention.   What's thy name?
    Imo. Fidele, sir.
    Cym.   Thou'rt my good youth, my page;
I'll be thy master.   Walk with me; speak freely.
           [*Cymbeline and Imogen talk apart.*]
    Bel. Is not this boy, reviv'd from death, —
    Arv.   One sand another
Not more resembles, — that sweet rosy lad   121
Who died, and was Fidele?   What think you?
    Gui. The same dead thing alive.
    Bel. Peace, peace! see further.   He eyes us not;
      forbear;

---

42. **opening:** revealing.   43. **bore in hand:** pretended.   47. **delicate:** artful.   55. **fitted:** prepared.   64. **[heard]** F3. *hearc*
F1.   83. **peculiar:** personal.   87. **occasions:** needs.   88. **feat:** adroit.

Creatures may be alike. Were 't he, I am sure 125
He would have spoke to us.
   Gui.   But we [saw] him dead.
   Bel. Be silent; let's see further.
   Pis.   [*Aside.*] It is my mistress.
Since she is living, let the time run on
To good or bad.
         [*Cymbeline and Imogen come forward.*]
   Cym.   Come, stand thou by our side;
Make thy demand aloud. [*To Iachimo.*]   Sir, step
    you forth;   130
Give answer to this boy, and do it freely;
Or, by our greatness and the grace of it,
Which is our honour, bitter torture shall
Winnow the truth from falsehood.   On, speak to
    him.
   Imo. My boon is, that this gentleman may
    render   135
Of whom he had this ring.
   Post.   [*Aside.*] What's that to him?
   Cym. That diamond upon your finger, say
How came it yours?
   Iach. Thou'lt torture me to leave unspoken that
Which, to be spoke, would torture thee.
   Cym.   How! me?
   Iach. I am glad to be constrain'd to utter that
Which torments me to conceal.   By villainy 142
I got this ring. 'Twas Leonatus' jewel,
Whom thou didst banish; and — which more may
    grieve thee,
As it doth me — a nobler sir ne'er liv'd   145
'Twixt sky and ground.   Wilt thou hear more,
    my lord?
   Cym. All that belongs to this.
   Iach.   That paragon, thy daughter, —
For whom my heart drops blood, and my false
    spirits
Quail to remember, — Give me leave; I faint.
   Cym. My daughter! what of her?   Renew thy
    strength.   150
I had rather thou shouldst live while Nature will
Than die ere I hear more.   Strive, man, and speak.
   Iach. Upon a time, — unhappy was the clock
That struck the hour! — it was in Rome, — ac-
    curs'd
The mansion where! — 'twas at a feast, — O,
    would   155
Our viands had been poison'd, or at least
Those which I heav'd to head! — the good Post-
    humus —
What should I say? He was too good to be
Where ill men were, and was the best of all
Amongst the rar'st of good ones, — sitting sadly,
Hearing us praise our loves of Italy   161

For beauty that made barren the swell'd boast
Of him that best could speak; for feature, lam-
    ing
The shrine of Venus or straight-pight Minerva,
Postures beyond brief nature; for condition,   165
A shop of all the qualities that man
Loves woman for, besides that hook of wiving,
Fairness which strikes the eye —
   Cym.   I stand on fire:
Come to the matter.
   Iach.   All too soon I shall,
Unless thou wouldst grieve quickly.   This Post-
    humus,   170
Most like a noble lord in love and one
That had a royal lover, took his hint;
And, not dispraising whom we prais'd, — therein
He was as calm as virtue, — he began
His mistress' picture; which by his tongue being
    made,   175
And then a mind put in't, either our brags
Were crack'd of kitchen-trulls, or his description
Prov'd us unspeaking sots.
   Cym.   Nay, nay, to th' purpose.
   Iach. Your daughter's chastity — there it begins.
He spake of her, as Dian had hot dreams,   180
And she alone were cold; whereat I, wretch,
Made scruple of his praise, and wager'd with him
Pieces of gold 'gainst this which then he wore
Upon his honour'd finger, to attain
In suit the place of 's bed and win this ring   185
By hers and mine adultery.   He, true knight,
No lesser of her honour confident
Than I did truly find her, stakes this ring;
And would so, had it been a carbuncle
Of Phœbus' wheel, and might so safely, had it 190
Been all the worth of 's car.   Away to Britain
Post I in this design.   Well may you, sir,
Remember me at court, where I was taught
Of your chaste daughter the wide difference
'Twixt amorous and villainous.   Being thus
    quench'd   195
Of hope, not longing, mine Italian brain
Gan in your duller Britain operate
Most vilely; for my vantage, excellent;
And, to be brief, my practice so prevail'd,
That I return'd with simular proof enough   200
To make the noble Leonatus mad,
By wounding his belief in her renown
With tokens thus, and thus; averring notes
Of chamber-hanging, pictures, this her bracelet, —
O cunning, how I got [it]! — nay, some marks
Of secret on her person, that he could not   206
But think her bond of chastity quite crack'd,
I having ta'en the forfeit.   Whereupon —

126. [saw] (Rowe). *see* F. 139. to leave: for leaving. 164. shrine: image. straight-pight: erect. 165. condition:
character. 167. hook of wiving: bait to marriage. 172. hint: occasion. 177. crack'd: boasted. 199. practice: plot.
200. simular: counterfeit. 205. got [it]. got F.

Methinks, I see him now —
  Post.   [*Advancing.*] Ay, so thou dost,
Italian fiend! Ay me, most credulous fool,   210
Egregious murderer, thief, anything
That's due to all the villains past, in being,
To come! O, give me cord, or knife, or poison,
Some upright justicer! Thou, King, send out
For torturers ingenious; it is I   215
That all th' abhorred things o' th' earth amend
By being worse than they. I am Posthumus,
That kill'd thy daughter: — villain-like, I lie —
That caused a lesser villain than myself,
A sacrilegious thief, to do't. The temple   220
Of Virtue was she; yea, and she herself.
Spit, and throw stones, cast mire upon me, set
The dogs o' th' street to bay me; every villain
Be call'd Posthumus Leonatus, and
Be villainy less than 'twas! O Imogen!   225
My queen, my life, my wife! O Imogen,
Imogen, Imogen!
  Imo.   Peace, my lord; hear, hear —
  Post. Shall 's have a play of this? Thou scornful page,
There lie thy part.   [*Striking her; she falls.*]
  Pis.   O, gentlemen, help
Mine and your mistress! O, my Lord Posthumus!
You ne'er kill'd Imogen till now. Help, help! 231
Mine honour'd lady!
  Cym.   Does the world go round?
  Post. How comes these staggers on me?
  Pis.   Wake, my mistress!
  Cym. If this be so, the gods do mean to strike me
To death with mortal joy.
  Pis.   How fares my mistress?
  Imo. O, get thee from my sight;   236
Thou gav'st me poison. Dangerous fellow, hence!
Breathe not where princes are.
  Cym.   The tune of Imogen!
  Pis. Lady,
The gods throw stones of sulphur on me, if   240
That box I gave you was not thought by me
A precious thing. I had it from the Queen.
  Cym. New matter still?
  Imo.   It poison'd me.
  Cor.   O gods!
I left out one thing which the Queen confess'd,
Which must approve thee honest. "If Pisanio
Have," said she, "given his mistress that confection
Which I gave him for cordial, she is serv'd   247
As I would serve a rat."
  Cym.   What's this, Cornelius?
  Cor. The Queen, sir, very oft importun'd me
To temper poisons for her, still pretending   250
The satisfaction of her knowledge only
In killing creatures vile, as cats and dogs,

Of no esteem. I, dreading that her purpose
Was of more danger, did compound for her
A certain stuff, which, being ta'en, would cease 255
The present power of life, but in short time
All offices of nature should again
Do their due functions. Have you ta'en of it?
  Imo. Most like I did, for I was dead.
  Bel.   My boys,
There was our error.
  Gui.   This is, sure, Fidele.   260
  Imo. Why did you throw your wedded lady from
      you?
Think that you are upon a [lock], and now
Throw me again.   [*Embracing him.*
  Post.   Hang there like fruit, my soul,
Till the tree die!
  Cym.   How now, my flesh, my child!
What, mak'st thou me a dullard in this act?
Wilt thou not speak to me?
  Imo.   [*Kneeling.*] Your blessing, sir. 266
  Bel. [*To Guiderius and Arviragus.*] Though you
      did love this youth, I blame ye not;
You had a motive for't.
  Cym.   My tears that fall
Prove holy water on thee! Imogen,
Thy mother's dead.
  Imo.   I am sorry for't, my lord.
  Cym. O, she was naught; and long of her it was
That we meet here so strangely; but her son   272
Is gone, we know not how nor where.
  Pis.   My lord,
Now fear is from me, I'll speak troth. Lord Cloten,
Upon my lady's missing, came to me   275
With his sword drawn; foam'd at the mouth and
      swore,
If I discover'd not which way she was gone,
It was my instant death. By accident
I had a feigned letter of my master's
Then in my pocket, which directed him   280
To seek her on the mountains near to Milford;
Where, in a frenzy, in my master's garments,
Which he enforc'd from me, away he posts
With unchaste purpose and with oath to violate
My lady's honour. What became of him   285
I further know not.
  Gui.   Let me end the story:
I slew him there.
  Cym.   Marry, the gods forfend!
I would not thy good deeds should from my lips
Pluck a hard sentence. Prithee, valiant youth,
Deny 't again.
  Gui.   I have spoke it, and I did it.   290
  Cym. He was a prince.
  Gui. A most incivil one. The wrongs he did me
Were nothing prince-like; for he did provoke me

---

221. **she herself:** Virtue herself.   238. **tune:** voice.   262. **[lock]** (Dowden): wrestling hold. *rock* F. 265. **dullard:** dummy. 271. **naught:** wicked.

With language that would make me spurn the sea
If it could so roar to me.　I cut off 's head;   295
And am right glad he is not standing here
To tell this tale of mine.
   Cym.   I am [sorry] for thee.
By thine own tongue thou art condemn'd, and must
Endure our law.　Thou'rt dead.
   Imo.   That headless man
I thought had been my lord.
   Cym.   Bind the offender   300
And take him from our presence.
   Bel.   Stay, sir King;
This man is better than the man he slew,
As well descended as thyself; and hath
More of thee merited than a band of Clotens
Had ever scar for.　[*To the Guard.*]　Let his arms
     alone;   305
They were not born for bondage.
   Cym.   Why, old soldier,
Wilt thou undo the worth thou art unpaid for,
By tasting of our wrath?　How of descent
As good as we?
   Arv.   In that he spake too far.
   Cym. And thou shalt die for't.
   Bel.   We will die all three
But I will prove that two on 's are as good   311
As I have given out him.　My sons, I must
For mine own part unfold a dangerous speech,
Though, haply, well for you.
   Arv.   Your danger's ours.
   Gui. And our good his.
   Bel.   Have at it then, by leave.
Thou hadst, great King, a subject who   316
Was call'd Belarius.
   Cym.   What of him?　He is
A banish'd traitor.
   Bel.   He it is that hath
Assum'd this age, indeed a banish'd man;
I know not how a traitor.
   Cym.   Take him hence.   320
The whole world shall not save him.
   Bel.   Not too hot.
First pay me for the nursing of thy sons;
And let it be confiscate all so soon
As I've receiv'd it.
   Cym.   Nursing of my sons!
   Bel. I am too blunt and saucy; here's my knee.
Ere I arise, I will prefer my sons;   326
Then spare not the old father.　Mighty sir,
These two young gentlemen, that call me father
And think they are my sons, are none of mine;
They are the issue of your loins, my liege,   330
And blood of your begetting.
   Cym.   How! my issue!
   Bel. So sure as you your father's.　I, old Morgan,

Am that Belarius whom you sometime banish'd.
Your pleasure was my mere offence, my punishment
Itself, and all my treason; that I suffer'd   335
Was all the harm I did.　These gentle princes —
For such and so they are — these twenty years
Have I train'd up.　Those arts they have as I
Could put into them; my breeding was, sir, as
Your Highness knows.　Their nurse, Euriphile,   340
Whom for the theft I wedded, stole these children.
Upon my banishment I mov'd her to't,
Having receiv'd the punishment before,
For that which I did then.　Beaten for loyalty
Excited me to treason.　Their dear loss,   345
The more of you 'twas felt, the more it shap'd
Unto my end of stealing them.　But, gracious sir,
Here are your sons again; and I must lose
Two of the sweet'st companions in the world.
The benediction of these covering heavens   350
Fall on their heads like dew! for they are worthy
To inlay heaven with stars.
   Cym.   Thou weep'st, and speak'st.
The service that you three have done is more
Unlike than this thou tell'st.　I lost my children;
If these be they, I know not how to wish   355
A pair of worthier sons.
   Bel.   Be pleas'd awhile.
This gentleman, whom I call Polydore,
Most worthy prince, as yours, is true Guiderius;
This gentleman, my Cadwal, Arviragus,
Your younger princely son.　He, sir, was lapp'd   360
In a most curious mantle, wrought by the hand
Of his queen mother, which for more probation
I can with ease produce.
   Cym.   Guiderius had
Upon his neck a mole, a sanguine star;
It was a mark of wonder.
   Bel.   This is he,   365
Who hath upon him still that natural stamp.
It was wise Nature's end in the donation,
To be his evidence now.
   Cym.   O, what, am I
A mother to the birth of three?　Ne'er mother
Rejoic'd deliverance more.　Blest pray you be,   370
That, after this strange starting from your orbs,
You may reign in them now!　O Imogen,
Thou hast lost by this a kingdom.
   Imo.   No, my lord;
I have got two worlds by't.　O my gentle brothers,
Have we thus met?　O, never say hereafter   375
But I am truest speaker.　You call'd me brother,
When I was but your sister; I you brothers,
When [ye] were so indeed.
   Cym.   Did you e'er meet?
   Arv. Ay, my good lord.
   Gui.   And at first meeting lov'd;

---

297. [sorry] F₂.　*sorrow* F₁.　319. **Assum'd:** reached.　334. **pleasure:** caprice.　**mere:** entire.　346. **shap'd:** suited.
354. **Unlike:** improbable.　362. **probation:** proof.　364. **sanguine:** red.　378. [ye] (Rowe).　*we* F.

Continu'd so, until we thought he died.   380
  Cor. By the Queen's dram she swallow'd.
  Cym.   O rare instinct!
When shall I hear all through? This fierce abridgement
Hath to it circumstantial branches, which
Distinction should be rich in. Where, how liv'd you?   384
And when came you to serve our Roman captive?
How parted with your brothers? How first met them?
Why fled you from the court? and whither? These
And your three motives to the battle, with
I know not how much more, should be demanded,
And all the other by-dependencies,   390
From chance to chance; but nor the time nor place
Will serve our long inter'gatories. See
Posthumus anchors upon Imogen,
And she, like harmless lightning, throws her eye
On him, her brothers, me, her master, hitting   395
Each object with a joy; the counterchange
Is severally in all. Let's quit this ground,
And smoke the temple with our sacrifices.
[*To Belarius.*] Thou art my brother; so we'll hold thee ever.
  Imo. You are my father too, and did relieve me
To see this gracious season.
  Cym.   All o'erjoy'd,   401
Save these in bonds. Let them be joyful too,
For they shall taste our comfort.
  Imo.   My good master,
I will yet do you service.
  Luc.   Happy be you!   404
  Cym. The forlorn soldier, that so nobly fought,
He would have well becom'd this place, and grac'd
The thankings of a king.
  Post.   I am, sir,
The soldier that did company these three
In poor beseeming; 'twas a fitment for
The purpose I then follow'd. That I was he,   410
Speak, Iachimo. I had you down and might
Have made you finish.
  Iach.   [*Kneeling.*] I am down again;
But now my heavy conscience sinks my knee,
As then your force did. Take that life, beseech you,
Which I so often owe; but your ring first,   415
And here the bracelet of the truest princess
That ever swore her faith.
  Post.   Kneel not to me.
The power that I have on you is to spare you,
The malice towards you to forgive you. Live,

And deal with others better.
  Cym.   Nobly doom'd!   420
We'll learn our freeness of a son-in-law;
Pardon's the word to all.
  Arv.   You holp us, sir,
As you did mean indeed to be our brother;
Joy'd are we that you are.
  Post. Your servant, Princes. Good my lord of Rome,   425
Call forth your soothsayer. As I slept, methought
Great Jupiter, upon his eagle back'd,
Appear'd to me, with other spritely shows
Of mine own kindred. When I wak'd, I found
This label on my bosom, whose containing   430
Is so from sense in hardness, that I can
Make no collection of it. Let him show
His skill in the construction.
  Luc.   Philarmonus!
  Sooth. Here, my good lord.
  Luc.   Read, and declare the meaning.   434
  [*Sooth.*] (*Reads.*) "Whenas a lion's whelp shall, to himself unknown, without seeking find, and be embrac'd by a piece of tender air; and when from a stately cedar shall be lopp'd branches, which, being dead many years, shall after revive, be jointed to the old stock, and freshly grow; then shall Posthumus end his miseries, Britain be fortunate and flourish in peace and plenty."   442
Thou, Leonatus, art the lion's whelp;
The fit and apt construction of thy name,
Being *leo-natus*, doth import so much.   445
[*To Cymbeline.*] The piece of tender air, thy virtuous daughter,
Which we call *mollis aer;* and *mollis aer*
We term it *mulier;* which *mulier* I divine
Is this most constant wife, who, even now,
Answering the letter of the oracle,   450
Unknown to you, unsought, were clipp'd about
With this most tender air.
  Cym.   This hath some seeming.
  Sooth. The lofty cedar, royal Cymbeline,
Personates thee; and thy lopp'd branches point
Thy two sons forth; who, by Belarius stol'n,   455
For many years thought dead, are now reviv'd,
To the majestic cedar join'd, whose issue
Promises Britain peace and plenty.
  Cym.   Well;
My peace we will begin. And, Caius Lucius,
Although the victor, we submit to Cæsar,   460
And to the Roman empire, promising
To pay our wonted tribute, from the which
We were dissuaded by our wicked queen;

382. **fierce abridgement:** extravagant entertainment. 383–84. **which...in:** which should be rich in interest. 388. **your three motives:** what incited you three. 391. **chance:** happening. 397. **severally in all:** in each according to his relationship. 400. **relieve:** rescue. 405. **forlorn:** lost. 409. **fitment:** outfit. 428. **spritely:** ghostly. 430. **label:** parchment. 432. **collection:** interpretation. 445. *leo-natus:* lion-born. 447. *mollis aer:* tender air, an imagined etymology of *mulier*, woman. 451. **clipp'd:** embraced. 452. **seeming:** likelihood.

Whom heavens, in justice, both on her and hers,
Have laid most heavy hand.   465
  Sooth. The fingers of the powers above do tune
The harmony of this peace.   The vision
Which I made known to Lucius, ere the stroke
Of [this yet] scarce-cold battle, at this instant
Is full accomplish'd; for the Roman eagle,   470
From south to west on wing soaring aloft,
Lessen'd herself, and in the beams o' th' sun
So vanish'd; which foreshow'd our princely eagle,
Th' imperial Cæsar, should again unite
His favour with the radiant Cymbeline,   475

Which shines here in the west.
  Cym.   Laud we the gods;
And let our crooked smokes climb to their nostrils
From our bless'd altars.   Publish we this peace
To all our subjects.   Set we forward.   Let
A Roman and a British ensign wave   480
Friendly together.   So through Lud's town march;
And in the temple of great Jupiter
Our peace we'll ratify; seal it with feasts.
Set on there!   Never was a war did cease,   484
Ere bloody hands were wash'd, with such a peace.
                                                        [*Exeunt.*

469. [this yet] F₃.   *yet this* F₁.

The Winter's Tale

NO QUARTO of *The Winter's Tale* was published, nor is the title found in the Stationers' Register before 1623. The earliest edition is that in the First Folio, in which it is the last of the Comedies. On this, which is unusually accurate, the present text is based. The bibliographical features which render the Folio text of *The Two Gentlemen of Verona* peculiar, prevail here, though to a less extent; and the same reasons for opposing the theory of an "assembled" text may be advanced in this instance also.

Simon Forman saw *The Winter's Tale* on May 15, 1611. It is highly probable that the dance of twelve satyrs (IV.iv.331–52), three of whom had "danced before the king," was suggested by the anti-masque in Jonson's *Masque of Oberon*, performed at court on January 1, 1611. There is, therefore, good reason for believing that the play was written within the early months of 1611, and all the metrical evidence, as well as the atmosphere and method of treatment, is in harmony with this late date.

The source of the plot is Robert Greene's euphuistic romance, *Pandosto. The Triumph of Time* (1588). Some of the changes wrought by Shakespeare in his material are interesting to note. For no discernible reason Bohemia and Sicily are interchanged, Greene's Pandosto (Leontes) being king of Bohemia, and Egistus (Polixenes), king of Sicily. Fawnia (Perdita) is put to sea in a rudderless boat, instead of being exposed on a desert shore. The proposal to consult the oracle comes from the queen (Bellaria) in the novel, from Leontes in the play; yet Pandosto accepts the answer of the oracle at once, while Leontes denies its truth until brought to his senses by the death of his son and the apparent death of Hermione. This latter change is significant because it touches upon the much-discussed problem of Leontes's jealousy, of which more must presently be said. In the novel the instant remorse of Pandosto upon hearing the oracle is succeeded by the announcement that his son Garinter (Mamillius) has suddenly died, at which news Bellaria (Hermione) falls dead. The old shepherd comes from Greene, but the Clown is substituted by Shake-

speare for the shepherd's wife. The wooing of Fawnia is related at great length in the novel, and the situation is complicated by Egistus's wish to marry his son to a princess of Denmark. In his flight from his father's court Dorastus (Florizel) has the assistance of a servant, Capnio, whom Shakespeare discards, but whose functions in the plot are divided between Camillo (Franion) and Autolycus. When the prince arrives at the court of Pandosto he conceals his identity, and is thrown into prison while the king makes love to Fawnia. This unpleasant incident of the courtship of the unrecognized daughter by her father Shakespeare omits, keeping Leontes faithful to the memory of Hermione. The omission makes possible the happy ending for all and does away with the depression and suicide of Pandosto with which Greene closes his narrative. The most important change made by Shakespeare is in saving the life of Hermione, thus opening the way for the situation which, though more defiant of likelihood than any of the improbabilities in the source, gives to the play its undeniably effective conclusion. The characters of Antigonus, Paulina, Emilia, Mopsa, Dorcas, the Clown, and Autolycus are all of Shakespeare's invention. And through the delightful rustic figures, particularly in the beautiful scene of the sheep-shearing feast, Shakespeare converts the artificial pastoralism of his source into something authentically of his own England.

Certain subsidiary indebtednesses may be mentioned. It seems clear that Shakespeare found the trick by which Autolycus picks the pocket of the shepherd's son (IV.iii.53–81) substantially described in Greene's *Second Part of Conny-Catching* (1592). The device of bringing an apparent statue to life could have been suggested by Lyly's *Woman in the Moon* (1597) or Marston's *Pygmalion's Image* (1598), but Shakespeare must have known the story of Pygmalion for years in Ovid's *Metamorphoses*. The names of Leontes, Antigonus, Cleomenes, Archidamus, and Mopsa are derived from Sidney's *Arcadia*; that of Florizel, probably, from *Amadis de Gaule*; and Autolycus from the *Odyssey* (XIX, 394) or from Ovid.

Ever since Ben Jonson remarked to Drummond

of Hawthornden that "Sheakspear in a play brought in a number of men saying they had suffered Shipwrack in Bohemia, wher ther is no Sea neer by some 100 Miles," critics have been amused or vexed by the fact. To worry about such a matter is to be a "snapper-up of unconsidered trifles" with a vengeance. Shakespeare's (and Greene's) error needs neither censure nor vindication in a play where Apollo's Delphic oracle, Whitsun pastorals, Puritans singing hymns to hornpipes, a queen who is the daughter of a Russian emperor, and "that rare Italian master, Julio Romano" are all charmingly contemporary.

Criticism has been concerned to better purpose with the jealousy of Leontes, a problem which merits consideration. As it is presented, the jealousy of Leontes is obviously a case of temporary insanity; when the requisite shock is administered, the termination of the seizure is as abrupt as the onslaught has been. The amazement of those intimate with Leontes indicates that nothing remotely like it has ever been seen in him before. In the novel, the jealousy of Pandosto appears, upon comparison, to be better motivated. Pandosto, having observed the familiarity of his wife and Egistus, becomes suspicious, but he ponders his fears before giving rein to them. His "doubtfull thoughtes a long time smoothering in his stomache, beganne at last to kindle in his minde a secret mistrust, which increased by suspition, grewe at last to be a flaming Iealousie, that so tormented him as he could take no rest." The necessity inherent in the source that the jealousy of Leontes must set the entire plot in motion presented a real problem in verisimilitude, which was made no easier by the fact that the delusions of Leontes are self-engendered. Leontes's sole enemy is his own imagination; the problem for the dramatist is simpler, and the attaining of plausibility easier, when the deceived character is, like Othello and Posthumus, the victim of another's machinations. Though Shakespeare must have been aware of the difficulties confronting him, it is doubtful if he let them trouble him. He must have felt confident that his audience, accustomed to accepting improbabilities in the very premises of romantic story and drama, would accept whatever was to be postulated in this one. And the jealousy of Leontes, demanded almost at the beginning of the play, is in the nature of a postulate. Psychiatrists might even argue today that the case of Leontes is credible. But to subject the matter to rigorous scrutiny is doubtless mistaken effort, for this kind of tragi-comedy asks by its very nature exemption from too close questioning. Indeed, it would seem that in the title of his play Shakespeare has sought to remind us of this fact. For a "winter's tale" is proverbially one "to drive away the time," a good story, that is, which is to be taken with just as much or as little seriousness as one will.

One must accept with a willing suspension of disbelief the incredible seclusion of Hermione for sixteen years. That is a thing which it is absurd to rationalize; it is there for the sake of the plot, for the sake of the striking climax which Shakespeare was reserving, the dramatic descent of Hermione from her pedestal, which, *coup de théâtre* though it is, is profoundly moving. For the sake of this scene, furthermore, Shakespeare sacrifices another which would have been almost as effective, namely, the revelation of Perdita's identity and her restoration to her father. He has been censured for describing these things through conversations (V.ii) instead of representing them dramatically, but surely, had he chosen the latter course, he would have rendered the scene with Hermione a conspicuous anti-climax. He paid the price of seeming ineptitude in order to keep the greater scene unrivalled.

The Winter's Tale is a play which takes a firmer hold upon one's affections with every reading. This is owing equally to certain of its characters and to the beauty of its poetry. With respect to characterization in general it may be said that, whatever the improbabilities in situation, the behavior of the characters is completely credible, once the situation is granted. Hermione is throughout nobly conceived. Her serene dignity, which almost raises her above pity, never deserts her, either in her hour of trial or in her exalted hour of reconcilement. In the final scene, Shakespeare exhibits a fine dramatic sense in according but one speech to Hermione. To her husband she says no word, expressing the fullness of her heart in her embrace; her words are reserved for the daughter whom she has never known. And the rich simplicity of her address to Perdita must stir the heart of the most stolid spectator or reader. Of Perdita it is hard to speak controlledly. She is exquisite, one with the beauty of the flowers she knows and loves so well, joining somehow an other-worldliness with the earthiness of the English countryside. Her gay rustic friends and, of course, Autolycus, one of the most engaging rogues in Shakespeare, contribute much to the realism of the pastoral scenes. Perdita is the queen of curds and cream, but there can be no doubt of the blood that runs in her veins. In her speech to Florizel after her dream has been shattered by the cruel words of Polixenes, are mingled courage and dignity inherited from her mother, and the simplicity derived from her environment (IV.iv.451–59). Nothing she says "but smacks of something greater than herself," and no strain is put upon the imagination picturing her moving with the same ease and charm in the new life to which the happy turn of fortune finally brings her.

THE WINTER'S TALE

ACT I

SCENE I. [*Sicilia. Ante-chamber in the palace of Leontes.*]

Enter CAMILLO *and* ARCHIDAMUS.

Arch. If you shall chance, Camillo, to visit Bohemia on the like occasion whereon my services are now on foot, you shall see, as I have said, great difference betwixt our Bohemia and your Sicilia. 5

Cam. I think, this coming summer, the King of Sicilia means to pay Bohemia the visitation which he justly owes him.

Arch. Wherein our entertainment shall shame us we will be justified in our loves; for indeed —

Cam. Beseech you, — 11

Arch. Verily, I speak it in the freedom of my knowledge. We cannot with such magnificence — in so rare — I know not what to say. We will give you sleepy drinks, that your senses, unintelligent of our insufficience, may, though they cannot praise us, as little accuse us. 17

Cam. You pay a great deal too dear for what's given freely.

Arch. Believe me, I speak as my understanding instructs me and as mine honesty puts it to utterance. 22

Cam. Sicilia cannot show himself over-kind to Bohemia. They were train'd together in their childhoods; and there rooted betwixt them then such an affection, which cannot choose but branch now. Since their more mature dignities and royal 28 necessities made separation of their society, their encounters, though not personal, hath been royally attorneyed with interchange of gifts, letters, loving embassies; that they have seem'd to be together, though absent; shook hands, as over a vast; and embrac'd, as it were, from the ends of opposed winds. The heavens continue their loves! 35

Arch. I think there is not in the world either malice or matter to alter it. You have an unspeakable comfort of your young prince Mamillius. It is a gentleman of the greatest promise that ever came into my note. 40

Act I, sc. i, 10. **be justified:** make amends. 30. **attorneyed:** performed by proxy. 32. **vast:** wide expanse. 40. **note:** observation (cf. Sc.ii.2).

Cam. I very well agree with you in the hopes of him. It is a gallant child; one that indeed physics the subject, makes old hearts fresh. They that went on crutches ere he was born desire yet their life to see him a man. 45

Arch. Would they else be content to die?

Cam. Yes; if there were no other excuse why they should desire to live.

Arch. If the King had no son, they would desire to live on crutches till he had one. 50

[*Exeunt.*

SCENE II. [*A room of state in the same.*]

Enter LEONTES, HERMIONE, MAMILLIUS, PO-LIXENES, CAMILLO [*and* Attendants].

Pol. Nine changes of the wat'ry star hath been
The shepherd's note since we have left our throne
Without a burden; time as long again
Would be fill'd up, my brother, with our thanks,
And yet we should, for perpetuity, 5
Go hence in debt; and therefore, like a cipher,
Yet standing in rich place, I multiply
With one "We thank you" many thousands moe
That go before it.

Leon.   Stay your thanks a while,
And pay them when you part.

Pol.   Sir, that's to-morrow.
I am question'd by my fears of what may chance
Or breed upon our absence; that may blow 12
No sneaping winds at home, to make us say,
"This is put forth too truly." Besides, I have stay'd
To tire your Royalty.

Leon.   We are tougher, brother,
Than you can put us to't.

Pol.   No longer stay. 16

Leon. One sev'n-night longer.

Pol.   Very sooth, to-morrow.

Leon. We'll part the time between's then; and in that
I'll no gainsaying.

Pol.   Press me not, beseech you, so.
There is no tongue that moves, none, none i' th' world, 20
So soon as yours could win me. So it should now,
Were there necessity in your request, although
'Twere needful I deni'd it. My affairs
Do even drag me homeward; which to hinder
Were, in your love, a whip to me; my stay 25
To you a charge and trouble. To save both,

Farewell, our brother.

Leon.   Tongue-tied our Queen? Speak you.

Her. I had thought, sir, to have held my peace until
You had drawn oaths from him not to stay. You, sir,
Charge him too coldly. Tell him you are sure 30
All in Bohemia's well; this satisfaction
The by-gone day proclaim'd. Say this to him,
He's beat from his best ward.

Leon.   Well said, Hermione.

Her. To tell he longs to see his son were strong;
But let him say so then, and let him go; 35
But let him swear so, and he shall not stay;
We'll thwack him hence with distaffs.
Yet of your royal presence I'll adventure
The borrow of a week. When at Bohemia
You take my lord, I'll give him my commission 40
To let him there a month behind the gest
Prefix'd for 's parting; yet, good deed, Leontes,
I love thee not a jar o' th' clock behind
What lady she her lord. You'll stay?

Pol.   No, madam.

Her. Nay, but you will?

Pol.   I may not, verily. 45

Her. Verily!
You put me off with limber vows; but I,
Though you would seek to unsphere the stars with oaths,
Should yet say, "Sir, no going." Verily,
You shall not go; a lady's "Verily" 's 50
As potent as a lord's. Will you go yet?
Force me to keep you as a prisoner,
Not like a guest? So you shall pay your fees
When you depart, and save your thanks. How say you?
My prisoner or my guest? By your dread "Verily,"
One of them you shall be.

Pol.   Your guest, then, madam. 56
To be your prisoner should import offending,
Which is for me less easy to commit
Than you to punish.

Her.   Not your gaoler, then,
But your kind hostess. Come, I'll question you 60
Of my lord's tricks and yours when you were boys.
You were pretty lordings then?

Pol.   We were, fair Queen,
Two lads that thought there was no more behind
But such a day to-morrow as to-day,
And to be boy eternal.

Her.   Was not my lord 65

42. **physics the subject:** does the people good.
Sc. ii, 1. wat'ry star: the moon (that governs the tides). 6. **like a cipher.** A cipher, though worthless itself, may, when added to a small number, increase it. 11. **question'd:** i.e., motivated. 12. **that may blow:** may there blow. 13. **sneaping:** nipping. 14. **"This ... truly":** our present fears are only too true. 16. **Than ... to't:** i.e., than anything you can lay upon us. 19. **I'll no gainsaying:** I'll take no denial. 25. **in your love:** i.e., though inspired by your love. **whip:** punishment. 32. **The ... day:** yesterday. 33. **ward:** position of defense. 40. **take:** charm (as in several passages in this play). 41. **let:** allow. **gest:** time. 53. **fees.** Prisoners leaving jail had to pay for their keep.

The verier wag o' th' two?
   Pol. We were as twinn'd lambs that did frisk i'
      th' sun,
And bleat the one at th' other. What we chang'd
Was innocence for innocence; we knew not
The doctrine of ill-doing, [no], nor dream'd   70
That any did. Had we pursu'd that life,
And our weak spirits ne'er been higher rear'd
With stronger blood, we should have answer'd
    Heaven
Boldly, "Not guilty"; the imposition clear'd
Hereditary ours.
   Her.   By this we gather   75
You have tripp'd since.
   Pol.   O my most sacred lady,
Temptations have since then been born to 's; for
In those unfledg'd days was my wife a girl;
Your precious self had then not cross'd the eyes
Of my young play-fellow.
   Her.   Grace to boot!   80
Of this make no conclusion, lest you say
Your Queen and I are devils. Yet go on;
Th' offences we have made you do we'll answer,
If you first sinn'd with us, and that with us
You did continue fault, and that you slipp'd not   85
With any but with us.
   Leon.   Is he won yet?
   Her. He'll stay, my lord.
   Leon.   At my request he would not.
Hermione, my dearest, thou never spok'st
To better purpose.
   Her.   Never?
   Leon.   Never, but once.
   Her. What! have I twice said well? When was 't
    before?   90
I prithee tell me; cram 's with praise, and make 's
As fat as tame things. One good deed dying
    tongueless
Slaughters a thousand waiting upon that.
Our praises are our wages; you may ride 's
With one soft kiss a thousand furlongs ere   95
With spur we heat an acre. But to th' goal:
My last good deed was to entreat his stay;
What was my first? It has an elder sister,
Or I mistake you. O, would her name were
    Grace!
But once before I spoke to th' purpose; when?   100
Nay, let me have 't; I long.
   Leon.   Why, that was when

Three crabbed months had sour'd themselves to
    death,
Ere I could make thee open thy white hand
And clap thyself my love; then didst thou utter,
"I am yours for ever."
   Her.   'Tis grace indeed.   105
Why, lo you now, I have spoke to th' purpose
    twice:
The one for ever earn'd a royal husband;
Th' other for some while a friend.
                [*Gives her hand to Polixenes.*]
   Leon.   [*Aside.*] Too hot, too hot!
To mingle friendship far is mingling bloods.
I have *tremor cordis* on me; my heart dances,   110
But not for joy; not joy. This entertainment
May a free face put on, derive a liberty
From heartiness, from bounty, fertile bosom,
And well become the agent; 't may, I grant;
But to be paddling palms and pinching fingers,   115
As now they are, and making practis'd smiles,
As in a looking-glass; and then to sigh, as 'twere
The mort o' th' deer; — O, that is entertainment
My bosom likes not, nor my brows! Mamillius,
Art thou my boy?
   Mam.   Ay, my good lord.
   Leon.   I' fecks!
Why, that's my bawcock. What, hast smutch'd
    thy nose?   121
They say it is a copy out of mine. Come, captain,
We must be neat; not neat, but cleanly, captain:
And yet the steer, the heifer, and the calf
Are all call'd neat. — Still virginalling   125
Upon his palm! — How now, you wanton calf!
Art thou my calf?
   Mam.   Yes, if you will, my lord.
   Leon. Thou want'st a rough pash and the shoots
    that I have,
To be full like me; yet they say we are
Almost as like as eggs; women say so,   130
That will say anything. But were they false
As o'er-dy'd blacks, as wind, as waters, false
As dice are to be wish'd by one that fixes
No bourn 'twixt his and mine, yet were it true
To say this boy were like me. Come, sir page,   135
Look on me with your welkin eye. Sweet villain!
Most dear'st! my collop! Can thy dam? — may 't
    be? —
Affection! thy intention stabs the centre.
Thou dost make possible things not so held,

---

70. [no] F$_2$. Om. F$_1$.   74–75. the ... ours: absolved even from our inherited guilt (i.e., original sin).   80. **Grace to boot:** heavenly grace help me.   96. **heat:** speed over.   104. **clap:** pledge (by handclasp).   110. *tremor cordis:* fluttering of the heart.   112. **free:** innocent.   113. **fertile:** generous.   118. **mort:** blast of a hunting horn, announcing the death of the deer.   119. **brows.** Referring to the horns of the cuckold (cf. ll. 146 and 186).   120. **I' fecks:** in faith.   121. **bawcock:** fine fellow.   123. **not neat.** *Neat*, cattle, suggests "horns" to Leontes.   125. **virginalling:** fingering (as upon the virginals, an early kind of piano).   128. **rough pash:** shaggy head.   **shoots:** horns.   132. **o'er-dy'd blacks:** black garments spoiled by too much dyeing.   136. **welkin:** sky-blue.   137. **my collop:** piece of my flesh.   138–43. **Affection ... something.** The general sense is: that since Desire can fix upon imagined objects so powerfully, it is all the more credible that it should pursue real ones.   138. **Affection:** sexual desire.   **centre:** soul.

Communicat'st with dreams; — how can this
  be? —   140
With what's unreal thou co-active art,
And fellow'st nothing.   Then 'tis very credent
Thou mayst co-join with something; and thou
  dost,
And that beyond commission, and I find it,
And that to the infection of my brains   145
And hardening of my brows.
    Pol.   What means Sicilia?
    Her. He something seems unsettled.
    Pol.   How, my lord!
What cheer?   How is 't with you, best brother?
    Her.   You look
As if you held a brow of much distraction.
Are you mov'd, my lord?
    Leon.   No, in good earnest.
How sometimes nature will betray its folly,   151
Its tenderness, and make itself a pastime
To harder bosoms!   Looking on the lines
Of my boy's face, methoughts I did [recoil]
Twenty-three years, and saw myself unbreech'd
In my green velvet coat, my dagger muzzl'd   156
Lest it should bite its master, and so prove,
As ornaments oft do, too dangerous.
How like, methought, I then was to this kernel,
This squash, this gentleman.   Mine honest friend,
Will you take eggs for money?   161
    Mam. No, my lord, I'll fight.
    Leon. You will!   Why, happy man be 's dole!
  My brother,
Are you so fond of your young prince as we
Do seem to be of ours?
    Pol.   If at home, sir,   165
He's all my exercise, my mirth, my matter,
Now my sworn friend and then mine enemy,
My parasite, my soldier, statesman, all.
He makes a July's day short as December,
And with his varying childness cures in me   170
Thoughts that would thick my blood.
    Leon.   So stands this squire
Offic'd with me.   We two will walk, my lord,
And leave you to your graver steps.   Hermione,
How thou lov'st us, show in our brother's welcome;
Let what is dear in Sicily be cheap.   175
Next to thyself and my young rover, he's
Apparent to my heart.
    Her.   If you would seek us,
We are yours i' th' garden.   Shall 's attend you
  there?
    Leon. To your own bents dispose you; you'll be
  found,

Be you beneath the sky.   [*Aside.*]   I am angling
  now,   180
Though you perceive me not how I give line.
Go to, go to!
How she holds up the neb, the bill to him!
And arms her with the boldness of a wife
To her allowing husband!
    [*Exeunt Polixenes, Hermione, and attend-
  ants.*]
                              Gone already!   185
Inch-thick, knee-deep, o'er head and ears a fork'd
  one!
Go, play, boy, play.   Thy mother plays, and I
Play too, but so disgrac'd a part, whose issue
Will hiss me to my grave; contempt and clamour
Will be my knell.   Go, play, boy, play.   There have
  been,   190
Or I am much deceiv'd, cuckolds ere now;
And many a man there is, even at this present,
Now while I speak this, holds his wife by th' arm,
That little thinks she has been sluic'd in 's absence
And his pond fish'd by his next neighbour, by   195
Sir Smile, his neighbour.   Nay, there's comfort in 't
Whiles other men have gates, and those gates
  open'd,
As mine, against their will.   Should all despair
That have revolted wives, the tenth of mankind
Would hang themselves.   Physic for 't there is
  none.   200
It is a bawdy planet, that will strike
Where 'tis predominant; and 'tis powerful, think it,
From east, west, north, and south.   Be it concluded,
No barricado for a belly; know 't;
It will let in and out the enemy   205
With bag and baggage.   Many thousand on 's
Have the disease, and feel 't not.   How now, boy!
    Mam. I am like you, [they] say.
    Leon.   Why, that's some comfort.
What, Camillo there?
    Cam. Ay, my good lord.   210
    Leon. Go play, Mamillius; thou 'rt an honest
  man.   [*Exeunt Mamillius.*]
Camillo, this great sir will yet stay longer.
    Cam. You had much ado to make his anchor
  hold.
When you cast out, it still came home.
    Leon.   Didst note it?
    Cam. He would not stay at your petitions; made
His business more material.
    Leon.   Didst perceive it? 216
[*Aside.*] They're here with me already, whispering,
  rounding,

142. **fellow'st nothing:** art companion to what does not exist.   144. **commission:** what is lawful.   148. **What ... brother**
(Rann).   F gives this line to Leontes.   153-55. **Looking ... years.**   These lines indicate that Leontes must be about
thirty.   154. [**recoil**] F₃.   *requoyle* F₁.   160. **squash:** unripe pea-pod.   161. **take ... money:** i.e., let yourself be cheated.
163. **happy ... dole:** may his lot be happy.   170. **childness:** childish ways.   171-72. **So ... me:** such is the part this boy
plays in my life.   177. **Apparent:** heir apparent.   185. **allowing:** approving.   186. **fork'd:** horned.   201. **strike:** spread
ruin.   202. **predominant:** in the ascendant.   208. [**they**] F₂.   Om. F₁.   214. **still ... home:** always failed to hold.   216.
material: urgent.   217. **here ... me:** i.e., mocking me.   **rounding:** whispering.

"Sicilia is a so-forth." 'Tis far gone,
When I shall gust it last. — How came 't, Camillo,
That he did stay?
   Cam.   At the good Queen's entreaty.
   Leon. At the Queen's be 't; "good" should be
     pertinent;   221
But, so it is, it is not. Was this taken
By any understanding pate but thine?
For thy conceit is soaking, — will draw in
More than the common blocks. Not noted, is 't,
But of the finer natures? By some severals 226
Of head-piece extraordinary? Lower messes
Perchance are to this business purblind? Say.
   Cam. Business, my lord! I think most under-
     stand
Bohemia stays here longer.
   Leon.   Ha!
   Cam.   Stays here longer.
   Leon. Ay, but why?   231
   Cam. To satisfy your Highness and the entreaties
Of our most gracious mistress.
   Leon.   Satisfy!
Th' entreaties of your mistress! Satisfy!
Let that suffice. I have trusted thee, Camillo, 235
With all the nearest things to my heart, as well
My chamber-counsels, wherein, priest-like, thou
Hast cleans'd my bosom, ay, from thee departed
Thy penitent reform'd; but we have been
Deceiv'd in thy integrity, deceiv'd   240
In that which seems so.
   Cam.   Be it forbid, my lord!
   Leon. To bide upon 't, thou art not honest, or,
If thou inclin'st that way, thou art a coward,
Which hoxes honesty behind, restraining
From course requir'd; or else thou must be counted
A servant grafted in my serious trust   246
And therein negligent; or else a fool
That seest a game play'd home, the rich stake
    drawn,
And tak'st it all for jest.
   Cam.   My gracious lord,
I may be negligent, foolish, and fearful;   250
In every one of these no man is free
But that his negligence, his folly, fear,
Among the infinite doings of the world,
Sometime puts forth. In your affairs, my lord,
If ever I were wilful-negligent,   255
It was my folly; if industriously
I play'd the fool, it was my negligence,
Not weighing well the end; if ever fearful
To do a thing, where I the issue doubted,
Whereof the execution did cry out   260

Against the non-performance, 'twas a fear
Which oft infects the wisest: these, my lord,
Are such allow'd infirmities that honesty
Is never free of. But, beseech your Grace,
Be plainer with me; let me know my trespass 265
By its own visage. If I then deny it,
'Tis none of mine.
   Leon.   Ha' not you seen, Camillo, —
But that's past doubt; you have, or your eye-glass
Is thicker than a cuckold's horn, — or heard, —
For to a vision so apparent rumour   270
Cannot be mute, — or thought, — for cogitation
Resides not in that man that does not think, —
My wife is slippery? If thou wilt confess,
Or else be impudently negative,
To have nor eyes nor ears nor thought, then say
My wife 's a hobby-horse, — deserves a name 276
As rank as any flax-wench that puts to
Before her troth-plight: say 't and justify 't.
   Cam. I would not be a stander-by to hear
My sovereign mistress clouded so, without 280
My present vengeance taken. Shrew my heart,
You never spoke what did become you less
Than this; which to reiterate were sin
As deep as that, though true.
   Leon.   Is whispering nothing?
Is leaning cheek to cheek? Is meeting noses?
Kissing with inside lip? stopping the career 286
Of laughter with a sigh? — a note infallible
Of breaking honesty; — horsing foot on foot?
Skulking in corners? wishing clocks more swift?
Hours, minutes? noon, midnight? and all eyes 290
Blind with the pin-and-web but theirs, theirs only,
That would unseen be wicked? Is this nothing?
Why, then the world and all that's in 't is nothing;
The covering sky is nothing; Bohemia nothing;
My wife is nothing; nor nothing have these no-
    things,   295
If this be nothing.
   Cam.   Good my lord, be cur'd
Of this diseas'd opinion, and betimes;
For 'tis most dangerous.
   Leon.   Say it be, 'tis true.
   Cam. No, no, my lord.
   Leon.   It is; you lie, you lie!
I say thou liest, Camillo, and I hate thee, 300
Pronounce thee a gross lout, a mindless slave,
Or else a hovering temporizer, that
Canst with thine eyes at once see good and evil,
Inclining to them both. Were my wife's liver
Infected as her life, she would not live 305
The running of one glass.

---

219. **gust:** taste, perceive. 222. **so it is:** as things are. 224. **conceit:** understanding. **soaking:** absorbent. 225. **blocks:** blockheads. 226. **severals:** individuals. 227. **Lower messes:** those occupying inferior seats at meals. 237. **chamber-counsels:** private concerns. 242. **bide:** insist. 244. **hoxes:** hamstrings. 254. **puts forth:** appears. 256. **industriously:** purposefully. 268. **eye-glass:** lens of the eye. 270. **vision so apparent:** sight so obvious. 277. **flax-wench:** a coarse woman. 284. **that...true:** that offense, if it were true. 286. **career:** swift course (equestrian figure). 288. **honesty:** chastity. **horsing:** setting. 291. **pin-and-web:** cataract. 302. **hovering:** wavering. 306. **glass:** hour-glass.

Cam.   Who does infect her?
Leon. Why, he that wears her like her medal
    hanging
About his neck, Bohemia; who, if I
Had servants true about me, that bare eyes
To see alike mine honour as their profits,   310
Their own particular thrifts, they would do that
Which should undo more doing; ay, and thou,
His cup-bearer, — whom I from meaner form
Have bench'd and rear'd to worship, who mayst see
Plainly as heaven sees earth and earth sees heaven,
How I am gall'd, — mightst bespice a cup,   316
To give mine enemy a lasting wink;
Which draught to me were cordial.
Cam.   Sir, my lord,
I could do this, and that with no rash potion,
But with a ling'ring dram that should not work   320
Maliciously like poison; but I cannot
Believe this crack to be in my dread mistress,
So sovereignly being honourable.
I have lov'd thee, —
Leon.   Make that thy question, and go rot!
Dost think I am so muddy, so unsettled,   325
To appoint myself in this vexation, sully
The purity and whiteness of my sheets,
Which to preserve is sleep, which being spotted
Is goads, thorns, nettles, tails of wasps,
Give scandal to the blood o' th' Prince my son,
Who I do think is mine and love as mine,   331
Without ripe moving to 't? Would I do this?
Could man so blench?
Cam.   I must believe you, sir;
I do; and will fetch off Bohemia for 't;
Provided that, when he's removed, your Highness
Will take again your queen as yours at first,   336
Even for your son's sake; and thereby forsealing
The injury of tongues in courts and kingdoms
Known and allied to yours.
Leon.   Thou dost advise me
Even so as I mine own course have set down.
I'll give no blemish to her honour, none.   341
Cam. My lord,
Go then; and with a countenance as clear
As friendship wears at feasts, keep with Bohemia
And with your queen. I am his cupbearer: 345
If from me he have wholesome beverage,
Account me not your servant.
Leon.   This is all.
Do 't and thou hast the one half of my heart;
Do 't not, thou split'st thine own.
Cam.   I'll do 't, my lord.

Leon. I will seem friendly, as thou hast advis'd
    me.   [*Exit.* 350
Cam. O miserable lady! But, for me,
What case stand I in? I must be the poisoner
Of good Polixenes; and my ground to do 't
Is the obedience to a master, one
Who, in rebellion with himself, will have   355
All that are his so too. To do this deed,
Promotion follows. If I could find example
Of thousands that had struck anointed kings
And flourish'd after, I'd not do 't; but since
Nor brass nor stone nor parchment bears not one,
Let villainy itself forswear 't. I must   361
Forsake the court. To do 't, or no, is certain
To me a break-neck. Happy star reign now!
Here comes Bohemia.

                    Re-enter POLIXENES.

Pol.   This is strange; methinks
My favour here begins to warp. Not speak!   365
Good day, Camillo.
Cam.   Hail, most royal sir!
Pol. What is the news i' th' court?
Cam.   None rare, my lord.
Pol. The King hath on him such a countenance
As he had lost some province and a region
Lov'd as he loves himself. Even now I met him
With customary compliment; when he,   371
Wafting his eyes to th' contrary and falling
A lip of much contempt, speeds from me, and
So leaves me to consider what is breeding
That changeth thus his manners.   375
Cam. I dare not know, my lord.
Pol. How! dare not? Do not! Do you know,
    and dare not?
Be intelligent to me: 'tis thereabouts;
For, to yourself, what you do know, you must,
And cannot say you dare not. Good Camillo,   380
Your chang'd complexions are to me a mirror
Which shows me mine chang'd too; for I must be
A party in this alteration, finding
Myself thus alter'd with 't.
Cam.   There is a sickness
Which puts some of us in distemper, but   385
I cannot name the disease; and it is caught
Of you that yet are well.
Pol.   How! caught of me!
Make me not sighted like the basilisk.
I have look'd on thousands, who have sped the
    better
By my regard, but kill'd none so. Camillo, —

311. **particular thrifts:** personal gains. 313. **meaner form:** lower seat. 314. **bench'd:** raised to an official seat. **worship:** dignity. 317. **wink:** sleep. 322. **dread:** revered. 324. **question:** topic. 326. **appoint...in:** bring myself into. 332. **ripe moving:** good reason. 333. **blench:** swerve (from sense). 334. **fetch off:** kill. 337. **forsealing:** sealing up tight. 372. **falling:** letting droop. 378. **Be intelligent:** make yourself clear. **thereabouts:** something like that. 379-80. **For ... not:** i.e., for, as to yourself, what you know must be clear to yourself, and you cannot say you dare not. 388. **basilisk:** fabulous snake, supposed to kill by its glance.

As you are certainly a gentleman, thereto   391
Clerk-like experienc'd, which no less adorns
Our gentry than our parents' noble names,
In whose success we are gentle, — I beseech you,
If you know aught which does behove my knowl-
    edge   395
Thereof to be inform'd, imprison 't not
In ignorant concealment.
    Cam.   I may not answer.
    Pol. A sickness caught of me, and yet I well!
I must be answer'd. Dost thou hear, Camillo?
I conjure thee, by all the parts of man   400
Which honour does acknowledge, whereof the least
Is not this suit of mine, that thou declare
What incidency thou dost guess of harm
Is creeping toward me; how far off, how near;
Which way to be prevented, if to be;   405
If not, how best to bear it.
    Cam.   Sir, I will tell you,
Since I am charg'd in honour and by him
That I think honourable; therefore mark my
    counsel,
Which must be even as swiftly follow'd as
I mean to utter it, or both yourself and me   410
Cry lost, and so good night!
    Pol.   On, good Camillo.
    Cam. I am appointed him to murder you.
    Pol. By whom, Camillo?
    Cam.   By the King.
    Pol.   For what?
    Cam. He thinks, nay, with all confidence he
    swears,
As he had seen 't or been an instrument   415
To vice you to 't, that you have touch'd his queen
Forbiddenly.
    Pol.   O, then my best blood turn
To an infected jelly, and my name
Be yok'd with his that did betray the Best!
Turn then my freshest reputation to   420
A savour that may strike the dullest nostril
Where I arrive, and my approach be shunn'd,
Nay, hated too, worse than the great'st infection
That e'er was heard or read!
    Cam.   Swear his thought over
By each particular star in heaven and   425
By all their influences, you may as well
Forbid the sea for to obey the moon
As or by oath remove or counsel shake
The fabric of his folly, whose foundation
Is pil'd upon his faith and will continue   430
The standing of his body.
    Pol.   How should this grow?

Cam. I know not; but I am sure 'tis safer to
Avoid what's grown than question how 'tis born.
If therefore you dare trust my honesty,
That lies enclosed in this trunk which you   435
Shall bear along impawn'd, away to-night!
Your followers I will whisper to the business,
And will by twos and threes at several posterns
Clear them o' th' city. For myself, I'll put
My fortunes to your service, which are here   440
By this discovery lost. Be not uncertain;
For, by the honour of my parents, I
Have utt'red truth, which if you seek to prove,
I dare not stand by; nor shall you be safer
Than one condemn'd by th' King's own mouth,
    thereon   445
His execution sworn.
    Pol.   I do believe thee;
I saw his heart in 's face. Give me thy hand.
Be pilot to me, and thy places shall
Still neighbour mine. My ships are ready and
My people did expect my hence departure   450
Two days ago. This jealousy
Is for a precious creature. As she 's rare,
Must it be great; and as his person 's mighty,
Must it be violent; and as he does conceive
He is dishonour'd by a man which ever   455
Profess'd to him, why, his revenges must
In that be made more bitter. Fear o'ershades me.
Good expedition be my friend, and comfort
The gracious queen, — part of his theme, but
    nothing
Of his ill-ta'en suspicion! Come, Camillo;   460
I will respect thee as a father if
Thou bear'st my life off hence. Let us avoid.
    Cam. It is in mine authority to command
The keys of all the posterns. Please your Highness
To take the urgent hour. Come, sir, away.   465
                                        [*Exeunt.*

ACT II

Scene I. [*Sicilia. A room in the palace.*]

Enter HERMIONE, MAMILLIUS, *and* LADIES.

Her. Take the boy to you; he so troubles me,
'Tis past enduring.
    [*1.*] *Lady.*   Come, my gracious lord,
Shall I be your playfellow?
    Mam.   No, I'll none of you.
    [*1.*] *Lady.* Why, my sweet lord?
    Mam. You'll kiss me hard and speak to me
    as if   5

392. Clerk-like: like a scholar. 394. In...gentle: from whom we inherit our noble rank. 400. parts: duties. 403. incidency: happening. 412. him: the one. 416. vice: force. 419. his...Best: i.e., the name of Judas. 424. Swear...over: though you seek to annul his thought by swearing. 431. The...body: whilst he lives. 435. trunk: body. 436. impawn'd: as a pledge of my honesty. 441. discovery: disclosure. 448-49. thy...mine: i.e., I shall keep you in offices ever close to me. 456. Profess'd: professed friendship.

I were a baby still. — I love you better.
  2. Lady. And why so, my lord?
  Mam.   Not for because
Your brows are blacker; yet black brows, they say,
Become some women best, so that there be not
Too much hair there, but in a semicircle,   10
Or a half-moon made with a pen.
  2. Lady.   Who **taught '** this?
  Mam. I learn'd it out of women's faces. Pray now
What colour are your eyebrows?
  [*1.*] *Lady.*   Blue, my lord.
  Mam. Nay, that's a mock. I have seen a lady's
    nose
That has been blue, but not her eyebrows.
  [*1.*] *Lady.*   Hark ye;
The Queen your mother rounds apace. We shall 16
Present our services to a fine new prince
One of these days; and then you'd wanton with us,
If we would have you.
  2. Lady.   She is spread of late
Into a goodly bulk. Good time encounter her! 20
  Her. What wisdom stirs amongst you? Come,
    sir, now
I am for you again. Pray you, sit by us,
And tell 's a tale.
  Mam.   Merry or sad shall't be?
  Her. As merry as you will.
  Mam. A sad tale's best for winter. I have one 25
Of sprites and goblins.
  Her.   Let's have that, good sir.
Come on, sit down; come on, and do your best
To fright me with your sprites; you're powerful at it.
  Mam. There was a man —
  Her.   Nay, come, sit down; then on.
  Mam. **D**welt by a churchyard. I will tell it
    softly;   30
Yond crickets shall not hear it.
  Her.   Come on, then,
And give 't me in mine ear.

    [*Enter* LEONTES, *with* ANTIGONUS, LORDS, *and
        others.*]

  Leon. Was he met there? his train? Camillo
    with him?
  [*1.*] *Lord.* Behind the tuft of pines I met them;
    never
Saw I men scour so on their way. I ey'd   35
Them even to their ships.
  Leon.   How blest am I
In my just censure, in my true opinion!
Alack, for lesser knowledge! How accurs'd
In being so blest! There may be in the cup
A spider steep'd, and one may drink, depart,   40

And yet partake no venom, for his knowledge
Is not infected; but if one present
Th' abhorr'd ingredient to his eye, make known
How he hath drunk, he cracks his gorge, his sides,
With violent hefts. I have drunk, and seen the
    spider.   45
Camillo was his help in this, his pander.
There is a plot against my life, my crown.
All's true that is mistrusted. That false villain
Whom I employ'd was pre-employ'd by him.
He has discover'd my design, and I   50
Remain a pinch'd thing; yea, a very trick
For them to play at will. How came the posterns
So easily open?
  [*1.*] *Lord.*   By his great authority;
Which often hath no less prevail'd than so
On your command.
  Leon.   I know 't too well.   55
Give me the boy. I am glad you did not nurse him.
Though he does bear some signs of me, yet you
Have too much blood in him.
  Her.   What is this? Sport?
  Leon. Bear the boy hence; he shall not come
    about her.
Away with him! and let her sport herself   60
With that she's big with; for 'tis Polixenes
Has made thee swell thus.
  Her.   But I'd say he had not,
And I'll be sworn you would believe my saying,
Howe'er you lean to th' nayward.
  Leon.   You, my lords,
Look on her, mark her well; be but about   65
To say she is a goodly lady, and
The justice of your hearts will thereto add
'Tis pity she's not honest, honourable.
Praise her but for this her without-door form,
Which on my faith deserves high speech, and
    straight   70
The shrug, the hum or ha, these petty brands
That calumny doth use — O, I am out —
That mercy does, for calumny will sear
Virtue itself; these shrugs, these hums and has,
When you have said she's goodly, come between 75
Ere you can say she's honest: but be't known,
From him that has most cause to grieve it should be,
She's an adultress.
  Her.   Should a villain say so,
The most replenish'd villain in the world,
He were as much more villain: you, my lord, 80
Do but mistake.
  Leon.   You have mistook, my lady,
Polixenes for Leontes. O thou thing!
Which I'll not call a creature of thy place,

Act II, sc. i, 18. **wanton:** play. 31. **crickets:** chattering women. 37. **censure:** judgment. 38. **for … knowledge:**
would that I knew less. 45. **hefts:** heavings, retchings. 48. **mistrusted:** suspected. 51. **pinch'd:** made ridiculous. 64. **to
th' nayward:** in the opposite direction. 68. **honest:** chaste. 69. **without-door:** outward. 72. **out:** wrong. 79. **replenish'd:** complete. 83. **Which … place:** a term I'll not apply to one of your rank.

Lest barbarism, making me the precedent,
Should a like language use to all degrees,   85
And mannerly distinguishment leave out
Betwixt the prince and beggar.   I have said
She's an adultress; I have said with whom;
More, she's a traitor, and Camillo is
A [fedary] with her, and one that knows   90
What she should shame to know herself
But with her most vile principal, that she's
A bed-swerver, even as bad as those
That vulgars give bold'st titles; ay, and privy
To this their late escape.
    Her.   No, by my life,   95
Privy to none of this.   How will this grieve you,
When you shall come to clearer knowledge, that
You thus have publish'd me!   Gentle, my lord,
You scarce can right me throughly then to say
You did mistake.
    Leon.   No; if I mistake   100
In those foundations which I build upon,
The centre is not big enough to bear
A school-boy's top.   Away with her, to prison!
He who shall speak for her is afar off guilty
But that he speaks.
    Her.   There's some ill planet reigns;
I must be patient till the heavens look   106
With an aspect more favourable.   Good my lords,
I am not prone to weeping, as our sex
Commonly are, the want of which vain dew
Perchance shall dry your pities; but I have   110
That honourable grief lodg'd here which burns
Worse than tears drown.   Beseech you all, my
    lords,
With thoughts so qualified as your charities
Shall best instruct you, measure me; and so
The King's will be perform'd!
    Leon.   Shall I be heard?
    Her.   Who is't that goes with me?   Beseech your
    Highness,   116
My women may be with me; for you see
My plight requires it.   Do not weep, good fools;
There is no cause.   When you shall know your
    mistress
Has deserv'd prison, then abound in tears   120
As I come out; this action I now go on
Is for my better grace.   Adieu, my lord.
I never wish'd to see you sorry; now
I trust I shall.   My women, come; you have leave.
    Leon.   Go, do our bidding; hence!   125
        [*Exit Queen guarded, with Ladies.*]
    [*1.*] *Lord.* Beseech your Highness, call the Queen
again.

    Ant. Be certain what you do, sir, lest your jus-
    tice
Prove violence; in the which three great ones suffer,
Yourself, your queen, your son.
    [*1.*] *Lord.*   For her, my lord,
I dare my life lay down, and will do't, sir,   130
Please you to accept it, that the Queen is spotless
I' th' eyes of Heaven and to you; I mean,
In this which you accuse her.
    Ant.   If it prove
She's otherwise, I'll keep my stables where
I lodge my wife; I'll go in couples with her;   135
Than when I feel and see her no farther trust her;
For every inch of woman in the world,
Ay, every dram of woman's flesh is false,
If she be.
    Leon.   Hold your peaces.
    [*1.*] *Lord.*   Good my lord, —
    Ant. It is for you we speak, not for ourselves.   140
You are abus'd, and by some putter-on
That will be damn'd for't; would I knew the villain,
I would land-damn him.   Be she honour-flaw'd,
I have three daughters; the eldest is eleven;
The second and the third, nine, and some five;
If this prove true, they'll pay for't.   By mine
    honour,   146
I'll geld 'em all; fourteen they shall not see
To bring false generations.   They are co-heirs;
And I had rather glib myself than they
Should not produce fair issue.
    Leon.   Cease; no more.
You smell this business with a sense as cold   151
As is a dead man's nose; but I do see't and feel't,
As you feel doing thus; and see withal
The instruments that feel.
    Ant.   If it be so,
We need no grave to bury honesty.   155
There's not a grain of it the face to sweeten
Of the whole dungy earth.
    Leon.   What! lack I credit?
    [*1.*] *Lord.* I had rather you did lack than I, my
    lord,
Upon this ground; and more it would content me
To have her honour true than your suspicion,   160
Be blam'd for't how you might.
    Leon.   Why, what need we
Commune with you of this, but rather follow
Our forceful instigation?   Our prerogative
Calls not your counsels, but our natural goodness
Imparts this; which if you, or stupefied   165
Or seeming so in skill, cannot or will not
Relish a truth like us, inform yourselves

---

    90. **[fedary]** (Dyce): confederate.   *Federarie* F.   102. **centre:** earth.   104–105. **afar . . . speaks:** indirectly guilty
merely through speaking.   113. **so qualified:** of such a nature.   115. **heard:** obeyed.   134–35. **I'll . . . wife:** i.e., I'll lock
up my wife like my mares.   141. **abus'd:** deceived.   **putter-on:** plotter.   143. **land-damn.** Probably corrupt.   149. **glib:**
geld.   153–54. **As . . . feel.** The usual stage business here is pulling Antigonus's nose.   159. **ground:** matter.   163. **instigation:** impulse.   164. **Calls not:** has no call for.   166. **skill:** craft.

We need no more of your advice.   The matter,
The loss, the gain, the ord'ring on't, is all
Properly ours.
    Ant.   And I wish, my liege,   170
You had only in your silent judgement tried it,
Without more overture.
    Leon.   How could that be?
Either thou art most ignorant by age,
Or thou wert born a fool.   Camillo's flight,
Added to their familiarity, —   175
Which was as gross as ever touch'd conjecture,
That lack'd sight only, nought for approbation
But only seeing, all other circumstances
Made up to th' deed, — doth push on this proceed-
    ing.
Yet, for a greater confirmation,   180
For in an act of this importance 'twere
Most piteous to be wild, I have dispatch'd in post
To sacred Delphos, to Apollo's temple,
Cleomenes and Dion, whom you know
Of stuff'd sufficiency.   Now from the oracle   185
They will bring all; whose spiritual counsel had,
I shall stop or spur me.   Have I done well?
    [*1.*] *Lord.* Well done, my lord.
    Leon. Though I am satisfi'd and need no more
Than what I know, yet shall the oracle   190
Give rest to th' minds of others, such as he
Whose ignorant credulity will not
Come up to th' truth.   So have we thought it
    good
From our free person she should be confin'd,
Lest that the treachery of the two fled hence   195
Be left her to perform.   Come, follow us;
We are to speak in public, for this business
Will raise us all.
    Ant. [*Aside.*] To laughter, as I take it,
If the good truth were known.   [*Exeunt.* 200

SCENE II.   [*Outer ward of a prison.*]

Enter PAULINA, *a Gentleman,* [*and* Attendants].

    Paul. The keeper of the prison, call to him;
Let him have knowledge who I am.   [*Exit Gent.*]
                          Good lady,
No court in Europe is too good for thee;
What dost thou then in prison?

    [*Re-enter* Gentleman, *with the* GAOLER.]

                          Now, good sir,
You know me, do you not?
    Gaol.   For a worthy lady,   5
And one who much I honour.
    Paul.   Pray you then,

Conduct me to the Queen.
    Gaol.   I may not, madam.
To the contrary I have express commandment.
    Paul. Here's ado,
To lock up honesty and honour from   10
Th' access of gentle visitors!   Is't lawful, pray
    you,
To see her women?   Any of them?   Emilia?
    Gaol. So please you, madam,
To put apart these your attendants, I
Shall bring Emilia forth.
    Paul.   I pray now, call her.
Withdraw yourselves.
                  [*Exeunt Gentleman and attendants.*]
    Gaol.   And, madam,   16
I must be present at your conference.
    Paul. Well, be't so, prithee.   [*Exit Gaoler.*]
Here's such ado to make no stain a stain
As passes colouring.

    [*Re-enter* GAOLER, *with* EMILIA.]
                  Dear gentlewoman,   20
How fares our gracious lady?
    Emil. As well as one so great and so forlorn
May hold together.   On her frights and griefs,
Which never tender lady hath borne greater,
She is something before her time deliver'd.   25
    Paul. A boy?
    Emil.   A daughter, and a goodly babe,
Lusty and like to live.   The Queen receives
Much comfort in't; says, "My poor prisoner,
I am innocent as you."
    Paul.   I dare be sworn.
These dangerous unsafe lunes i' th' King, beshrew
    them!   30
He must be told on't, and he shall.   The office
Becomes a woman best; I'll take't upon me.
If I prove honey-mouth'd, let my tongue blister
And never to my red-look'd anger be
The trumpet any more.   Pray you, Emilia,   35
Commend my best obedience to the Queen.
If she dares trust me with her little babe,
I'll show't the King and undertake to be
Her advocate to th' loud'st.   We do not know
How he may soften at the sight o' th' child.   40
The silence often of pure innocence
Persuades when speaking fails.
    Emil.   Most worthy madam,
Your honour and your goodness is so evident
That your free undertaking cannot miss
A thriving issue.   There is no lady living   45
So meet for this great errand.   Please your lady-
    ship
To visit the next room, I'll presently

172. **overture:** publicity.   176. **touch'd conjecture:** i.e., conjecture reached to.   177. **approbation:** proof.   182. **wild:** rash.
185. **stuff'd sufficiency:** complete competence.   194. **free:** accessible.   198. **raise:** rouse.
Sc. ii, 20. **colouring:** (1) dyeing, (2) excusing.   30. **lunes:** fits of lunacy.   47. **presently:** immediately.

Acquaint the Queen of your most noble offer;
Who but to-day hammer'd of this design,
But durst not tempt a minister of honour,   50
Lest she should be deni'd.
    Paul.   Tell her, Emilia,
I'll use that tongue I have.   If wit flow from 't
As boldness from my bosom, let 't not be doubted
I shall do good.
    Emil.   Now be you blest for it!
I'll to the Queen.   Please you, come something
    nearer.   55
    Gaol. Madam, if 't please the Queen to send the
    babe,
I know not what I shall incur to pass it,
Having no warrant.
    Paul.   You need not fear it, sir.
This child was prisoner to the womb and is
By law and process of great Nature thence   60
Freed and enfranchis'd, not a party to
The anger of the King nor guilty of,
If any be, the trespass of the Queen.
    Gaol. I do believe it.
    Paul. Do not you fear.   Upon mine honour, I
Will stand betwixt you and danger.   [*Exeunt.* 66

SCENE III.   [*A room in Leontes' palace.*]

Enter LEONTES, ANTIGONUS, LORDS, *and* SERVANTS.

    Leon. Nor night nor day no rest.   It is but weak-
    ness
To bear the matter thus; mere weakness.   If
The cause were not in being, — part o' th' cause,
She the adultress; for the harlot king
Is quite beyond mine arm, out of the blank   5
And level of my brain, plot-proof; but she
I can hook to me: say that she were gone,
Given to the fire, a moiety of my rest
Might come to me again.   Who's there?
    [*1.*] *Serv.*   My lord?
    Leon. How does the boy?
    [*1.*] *Serv.*   He took good rest to-night;
'Tis hop'd his sickness is discharg'd.   11
    Leon. To see his nobleness!
Conceiving the dishonour of his mother,
He straight declin'd, droop'd, took it deeply,
Fasten'd and fix'd the shame on 't in himself,
Threw off his spirit, his appetite, his sleep,   16
And downright languish'd.   Leave me solely; go,
See how he fares.   [*Exit Serv.*] Fie, fie! no thought
    of him;
The very thought of my revenges that way
Recoil upon me: in himself too mighty,   20
And in his parties, his alliance.   Let him be
Until a time may serve; for present vengeance,

Take it on her.   Camillo and Polixenes
Laugh at me, make their pastime at my sorrow.
They should not laugh if I could reach them,
    nor   25
Shall she within my power.

    Enter PAULINA [*with a babe*].

    [*1.*] *Lord.*   You must not enter.
    Paul. Nay, rather, good my lords, be second to
    me.
Fear you his tyrannous passion more, alas,
Than the Queen's life?   A gracious innocent soul,
More free than he is jealous.
    Ant.   That's enough.
    [*2.*] *Serv.* Madam, he hath not slept to-night,
    commanded   31
None should come at him.
    Paul.   Not so hot, good sir;
I come to bring him sleep.   'Tis such as you,
That creep like shadows by him and do sigh
At each his needless heavings, such as you   35
Nourish the case of his awaking.   I
Do come with words as med'cinal as true,
Honest as either, to purge him of that humour
That presses him from sleep.
    Leon.   [What] noise there, ho?
    Paul. No noise, my lord; but needful conference
About some gossips for your Highness.
    Leon.   How!   41
Away with that audacious lady!   Antigonus,
I charg'd thee that she should not come about me:
I knew she would.
    Ant.   I told her so, my lord,
On your displeasure's peril and on mine,   45
She should not visit you.
    Leon.   What, canst not rule her?
    Paul. From all dishonesty he can.   In this,
Unless he take the course that you have done,
Commit me for committing honour, trust it,
He shall not rule me.
    Ant.   La you now, you hear.
When she will take the rein I let her run;   51
But she'll not stumble.
    Paul.   Good my liege, I come;
And, I beseech you, hear me, who professes
Myself your loyal servant, your physician,
Your most obedient counsellor, yet that dares   55
Less appear so in comforting your evils,
Than such as most seem yours.   I say, I come
From your good queen.
    Leon.   Good queen!
    Paul.   Good queen, my lord,
Good queen; I say good queen;
And would by combat make her good, so were I   60

---

49. **hammer'd of:** deliberated.   52. **wit:** wisdom.
  Sc. iii, 5. **blank:** white spot in the centre of a target.   6. **level:** aim.   18. **him:** Polixenes.   39. **[What]** F$_2$.   *Who* F$_1$.
41. **gossips:** sponsors in baptism.   49. **Commit:** imprison.   57. **yours:** your loyal servants.

A man, the worst about you.
    Leon.   Force her hence.
    Paul. Let him that makes but trifles of his eyes
First hand me. On mine own accord I'll off,
But first I'll do my errand. The good queen,
For she is good, hath brought you forth a daughter;
Here 'tis; commends it to your blessing.
                        [*Laying down the child.*]
    Leon.   Out! 66
A mankind witch! Hence with her, out o' door!
A most intelligencing bawd!
    Paul.   Not so.
I am as ignorant in that as you
In so entitling me, and no less honest   70
Than you are mad; which is enough, I'll warrant,
As this world goes, to pass for honest.
    Leon.   Traitors!
Will you not push her out? Give her the bastard,
Thou dotard! thou art woman-tir'd, unroosted
By thy dame Partlet here. Take up the bastard;
Take 't up, I say; give 't to thy crone.
    Paul.   For ever
Unvenerable be thy hands, if thou   77
Tak'st up the Princess by that forced baseness
Which he has put upon't!
    Leon.   He dreads his wife.
    Paul. So I would you did; then 'twere past all
        doubt   80
You'd call your children yours.
    Leon.   A nest of traitors!
    Ant. I am none, by this good light.
    Paul.   Nor I, nor any
But one that's here, and that's himself; for he
The sacred honour of himself, his queen's,
His hopeful son's, his babe's, betrays to slander, 85
Whose sting is sharper than the sword's, and will
    not —
For, as the case now stands, it is a curse
He cannot be compell'd to't — once remove
The root of his opinion, which is rotten
As ever oak or stone was sound.
    Leon.   A callat   90
Of boundless tongue, who late hath beat her hus-
    band
And now baits me! This brat is none of mine;
It is the issue of Polixenes.
Hence with it, and together with the dam
Commit them to the fire!
    Paul.   It is yours;   95
And, might we lay th' old proverb to your charge,
So like you, 'tis the worse. Behold, my lords,
Although the print be little, the whole matter
And copy of the father, — eye, nose, lip,
The trick of 's frown, his forehead, nay, the valley,

The pretty dimples of his chin and cheek,   101
His smiles,
The very mould and frame of hand, nail, finger;
And thou, good goddess Nature, which hast made it
So like to him that got it, if thou hast   105
The ordering of the mind too, 'mongst all colours
No yellow in 't, lest she suspect, as he does,
Her children not her husband's!
    Leon.   A gross hag!
And, lozel, thou art worthy to be hang'd,   109
That wilt not stay her tongue.
    Ant.   Hang all the husbands
That cannot do that feat, you'll leave yourself
Hardly one subject.
    Leon.   Once more, take her hence.
    Paul. A most unworthy and unnatural lord
Can do no more.
    Leon.   I'll ha' thee burnt.
    Paul.   I care not;
It is an heretic that makes the fire,   115
Not she which burns in 't. I'll not call you tyrant;
But this most cruel usage of your queen,
Not able to produce more accusation
Than your own weak-hing'd fancy, something
    savours
Of tyranny, and will ignoble make you,   120
Yea, scandalous to the world.
    Leon.   On your allegiance,
Out of the chamber with her! Were I a tyrant,
Where were her life? She durst not call me so,
If she did know me one. Away with her!
    Paul. I pray you, do not push me; I'll be gone.
Look to your babe, my lord; 'tis yours. Jove send
    her   126
A better guiding spirit! What needs these hands?
You, that are thus so tender o'er his follies,
Will never do him good, not one of you.
So, so; farewell; we are gone.   [*Exit.* 130
    Leon. Thou, traitor, hast set on thy wife to this.
My child? Away with't! Even thou, that hast
A heart so tender o'er it, take it hence
And see it instantly consum'd with fire;
Even thou and none but thou. Take it up straight.
Within this hour bring me word 'tis done,   136
And by good testimony, or I'll seize thy life,
With what thou else call'st thine. If thou refuse
And wilt encounter with my wrath, say so;
The bastard brains with these my proper hands
Shall I dash out. Go, take it to the fire;   141
For thou set'st on thy wife.
    Ant.   I did not, sir.
These lords, my noble fellows, if they please,
Can clear me in't.
    Lords.   We can. My royal liege,

---

67. **mankind:** ferocious.   74. **woman-tir'd:** henpecked.   **unroosted:** driven off the perch.   75. **Partlet:** the hen in the fable of the cock and the fox.   78. **by...baseness:** i.e., under that false name of bastard.   90. **callat:** scold.   107. **yellow:** the color of jealousy.   109. **lozel:** scoundrel.   127. **What...hands:** i.e., you don't have to push me out.

He is not guilty of her coming hither.   145
  Leon. You're liars all.
  [*1.*] *Lord.* Beseech your Highness, give us better
    credit.
We have always truly serv'd you, and beseech
So to esteem of us; and on our knees we beg,
As recompense of our dear services   150
Past and to come, that you do change this pur-
    pose,
Which being so horrible, so bloody, must
Lead on to some foul issue. We all kneel.
  Leon. I am a feather for each wind that blows.
Shall I live on to see this bastard kneel   155
And call me father? Better burn it now
Than curse it then. But be it; let it live.
It shall not neither. You, sir, come you hither;
You that have been so tenderly officious
With Lady Margery, your midwife there,   160
To save this bastard's life, — for 'tis a bastard,
So sure as this beard's gray, — what will you ad-
    venture
To save this brat's life?
  Ant.   Anything, my lord,
That my ability may undergo
And nobleness impose; at least thus much: 165
I'll pawn the little blood which I have left
To save the innocent. Anything possible.
  Leon. It shall be possible. Swear by this sword
Thou wilt perform my bidding.
  Ant.   I will, my lord.
  Leon. Mark and perform it; see'st thou? for the
    fail   170
Of any point in 't shall not only be
Death to thyself but to thy lewd-tongu'd wife,
Whom for this time we pardon. We enjoin thee,
As thou art liege-man to us, that thou carry
This female bastard hence, and that thou bear it
To some remote and desert place quite out   176
Of our dominions, and that there thou leave it,
Without more mercy, to it own protection
And favour of the climate. As by strange fortune
It came to us, I do in justice charge thee,   180
On thy soul's peril and thy body's torture,
That thou commend it strangely to some place
Where chance may nurse or end it. Take it up.
  Ant. I swear to do this, though a present death
Had been more merciful. Come on, poor babe.   185
Some powerful spirit instruct the kites and ravens
To be thy nurses! Wolves and bears, they say,
Casting their savageness aside, have done
Like offices of pity. Sir, be prosperous
In more than this deed does require! And blessing
Against this cruelty fight on thy side,   191

Poor thing, condemn'd to loss!
                    [Exit [with the babe].
  Leon.   No, I'll not rear
Another's issue.

Enter a SERVANT.

  Serv.   Please your Highness, posts
From those you sent to th' oracle are come
An hour since. Cleomenes and Dion,   195
Being well arriv'd from Delphos, are both landed,
Hasting to the court.
  [*1.*] *Lord.*   So please you, sir, their speed
Hath been beyond accompt.
  Leon.   Twenty-three days
They have been absent; 'tis good speed; foretells
The great Apollo suddenly will have   200
The truth of this appear. Prepare you, lords;
Summon a session, that we may arraign
Our most disloyal lady, for, as she hath
Been publicly accus'd, so shall she have
A just and open trial. While she lives   205
My heart will be a burden to me. Leave me,
And think upon my bidding.   *[Exeunt.*

ACT III

SCENE I. [*A street in a Sicilian town.*]

Enter CLEOMENES *and* DION.

  Cleo. The climate's delicate, the air most sweet,
Fertile the isle, the temple much surpassing
The common praise it bears.
  Dion.   I shall report,
For most it caught me, the celestial habits
(Methinks I so should term them), and the rev-
    erence   5
Of the grave wearers. O, the sacrifice!
How ceremonious, solemn, and unearthly
It was i' th' off'ring!
  Cleo.   But of all, the burst
And the ear-deaf'ning voice o' th' oracle,
Kin to Jove's thunder, so surpris'd my sense,   10
That I was nothing.
  Dion.   If th' event o' th' journey
Prove as successful to the Queen, — O be 't so! —
As it hath been to us rare, pleasant, speedy,
The time is worth the use on't.
  Cleo.   Great Apollo
Turn all to th' best! These proclamations,   15
So forcing faults upon Hermione,
I little like.
  Dion.   The violent carriage of it
Will clear or end the business. When the oracle,

---

162. **So . . . gray.** Leontes perhaps plucks the beard of Antigonus. Cf. I.ii.153–55 and note.   182. **strangely:** as an alien.   190. **does require:** deserves.   192. **loss:** destruction.   198. **accompt:** precedent.   200. **suddenly:** at once.
    Act III, sc. i, 2. isle. Shakespeare repeats an error in his source, confusing Delos, the island sacred as Apollo's birthplace, with Delphi, the seat of his oracle.   4. **habits:** garments.   14. **worth . . . on't:** well spent.

Thus by Apollo's great divine seal'd up,
Shall the contents discover, something rare   20
Even then will rush to knowledge.   Go; fresh
     horses!
And gracious be the issue!   [*Exeunt.*

SCENE II.   [*Sicilia.   A place of justice.*]

Enter LEONTES, LORDS, *and* OFFICERS.

Leon.   This sessions (to our great grief we pro-
     nounce)
Even pushes 'gainst our heart, — the party tried
The daughter of a king, our wife, and one
Of us too much belov'd.   Let us be clear'd
Of being tyrannous, since we so openly   5
Proceed in justice, which shall have due course
Even to the guilt or the purgation.
Produce the prisoner.

Off.   It is his Highness' pleasure that the Queen
Appear in person here in court.   Silence!   10

[*Enter* HERMIONE (*as to her trial*); PAULINA *and*
     LADIES *attending.*]

Leon.   Read the indictment.

Off.   [*Reads.*]   "Hermione, Queen to the worthy
Leontes, King of Sicilia, thou art here accused and
arraigned of high treason, in committing adultery
with Polixenes, King of Bohemia, and conspiring   15
with Camillo to take away the life of our sovereign
lord the King, thy royal husband: the pretence
whereof being by circumstances partly laid open,
thou, Hermione, contrary to the faith and allegiance
of a true subject, didst counsel and aid them, for
their better safety, to fly away by night."   22

Her.   Since what I am to say must be but that
Which contradicts my accusation, and
The testimony on my part no other   25
But what comes from myself, it shall scarce boot me
To say "Not guilty."   Mine integrity
Being counted falsehood, shall, as I express it,
Be so receiv'd.   But thus: — If powers divine
Behold our human actions, as they do,   30
I doubt not then but innocence shall make
False accusation blush, and tyranny
Tremble at patience.   You, my lord, best know,
[Who] least will seem to do so, my past life
Hath been as continent, as chaste, as true,   35
As I am now unhappy; which is more
Than history can pattern, though devis'd
And play'd to take spectators.   For behold me,
A fellow of the royal bed, which owe
A moiety of the throne, a great king's daughter,

The mother to a hopeful prince, here standing   41
To prate and talk for life and honour 'fore
Who please to come and hear.   For life, I prize it
As I weigh grief, which I would spare; for honour,
'Tis a derivative from me to mine,   45
And only that I stand for.   I appeal
To your own conscience, sir, before Polixenes
Came to your court, how I was in your grace,
How merited to be so; since he came,
With what encounter so uncurrent I   50
Have strain'd t' appear thus; if one jot beyond
The bound of honour, or in act or will
That way inclining, hard'ned be the hearts
Of all that hear me, and my near'st of kin
Cry fie upon my grave!

Leon.   I ne'er heard yet   55
That any of these bolder vices wanted
Less impudence to gainsay what they did
Than to perform it first.

Her.   That's true enough;
Though 'tis a saying, sir, not due to me.

Leon.   You will not own it.

Her.   More than mistress of
Which comes to me in name of fault, I must not
At all acknowledge.   For Polixenes,   62
With whom I am accus'd, I do confess
I lov'd him as in honour he requir'd,
With such a kind of love as might become   65
A lady like me, with a love even such,
So and no other, as yourself commanded;
Which not t' have done I think had been in me
Both disobedience and ingratitude
To you and toward your friend, whose love had
     spoke,   70
Even since it could speak, from an infant, freely
That it was yours.   Now, for conspiracy,
I know not how it tastes, though it be dish'd
For me to try how.   All I know of it
Is that Camillo was an honest man;   75
And why he left your court, the gods themselves,
Wotting no more than I, are ignorant.

Leon.   You knew of his departure, as you know
What you have underta'en to do in 's absence.

Her.   Sir,   80
You speak a language that I understand not.
My life stands in the level of your dreams,
Which I'll lay down.

Leon.   Your actions are my dreams;
You had a bastard by Polixenes,
And I but dream'd it.   As you were past all
     shame, —   85
Those of your fact are so, — so past all truth,

19. **great divine:** high priest.
Sc. ii, 7. **purgation:** acquittal.   17. **pretence:** design.   34. [Who] (Rowe).   *Whom* F.   36. **which:** which unhappiness.
38. **take:** charm.   39. **owe:** own.   40. **moiety:** half.   43–44. **For . . . spare:** as for life, I esteem it as I do grief — a thing
I would do without.   50. **encounter:** behavior.   **uncurrent:** improper.   51. **strain'd . . . thus:** strained propriety, so that
I should so be brought to trial.   59. **due:** applicable.   60–61. **More . . . fault:** i.e., more than I am guilty of.   77. **Wotting:**
if they know.   82. **in . . . of:** within the range of, i.e., at the mercy of.   86. **fact:** crime.

Which to deny concerns more than avails; for as
Thy brat hath been cast out, like to itself,
No father owning it, — which is, indeed,
More criminal in thee than it, — so thou   90
Shalt feel our justice, in whose easiest passage
Look for no less than death.
    Her.   Sir, spare your threats.
The bug which you would fright me with I seek;
To me can life be no commodity.
The crown and comfort of my life, your favour,   95
I do give lost; for I do feel it gone,
But know not how it went. My second joy
And first-fruits of my body, from his presence
I am barr'd, like one infectious. My third comfort,
Starr'd most unluckily, is from my breast,   100
The innocent milk in it most innocent mouth,
Hal'd out to murder; myself on every post
Proclaim'd a strumpet; with immodest hatred
The child-bed privilege deni'd, which longs
To women of all fashion; lastly, hurried   105
Here to this place, i' th' open air, before
I have got strength of limit. Now, my liege,
Tell me what blessings I have here alive,
That I should fear to die? Therefore proceed.
But yet hear this: mistake me not; no life,   110
I prize it not a straw; but for mine honour,
Which I would free, — if I shall be condemn'd
Upon surmises, all proofs sleeping else
But what your jealousies awake, I tell you
'Tis rigour and not law. Your honours all,   115
I do refer me to the oracle:
Apollo be my judge!
    [*1.*] *Lord.*   This your request
Is altogether just; therefore bring forth,
And in Apollo's name, his oracle.
                  [*Exeunt certain Officers.*]
    Her. The Emperor of Russia was my father:
O that he were alive, and here beholding   121
His daughter's trial! that he did but see
The flatness of my misery, yet with eyes
Of pity, not revenge!

    [*Re-enter* OFFICERS, *with* CLEOMENES *and* DION.]
    Off. You here shall swear upon this sword of
        justice,   125
That you, Cleomenes and Dion, have
Been both at Delphos, and from thence have
        brought
This seal'd-up oracle, by the hand deliver'd
Of great Apollo's priest, and that since then
You have not dar'd to break the holy seal   130
Nor read the secrets in't.

    Cleo. Dion.   All this we swear.
    Leon. Break up the seals and read.
    Off. [*Reads.*]   "Hermione is chaste; Polixenes
blameless; Camillo a true subject; Leontes a jealous
tyrant; his innocent babe truly begotten; and the
King shall live without an heir, if that which is lost
be not found."   137
    Lords. Now blessed be the great Apollo!
    Her.   Praised!
    Leon. Hast thou read truth?
    Off.   Ay, my lord; even so
As it is here set down.   140
    Leon. There is no truth at all i' th' oracle.
The sessions shall proceed; this is mere falsehood.

                [*Enter a* SERVANT.]
    Serv. My lord the King, the King!
    Leon.   What is the business?
    Serv. O sir, I shall be hated to report it!
The Prince your son, with mere conceit and fear   145
Of the Queen's speed, is gone.
    Leon.   How! gone?
    Serv.   Is dead.
    Leon. Apollo's angry; and the heavens them-
        selves
Do strike at my injustice. [*Hermione swoons.*]
        How now there!
    Paul. This news is mortal to the Queen. Look
        down   149
And see what Death is doing.
    Leon.   Take her hence;
Her heart is but o'ercharg'd; she will recover.
I have too much believ'd mine own suspicion.
Beseech you, tenderly apply to her
Some remedies for life.
        [*Exeunt Paulina and Ladies, with Her-*
        mione.]
                    Apollo, pardon
My great profaneness 'gainst thine oracle!   155
I'll reconcile me to Polixenes,
New woo my queen, recall the good Camillo,
Whom I proclaim a man of truth, of mercy;
For, being transported by my jealousies
To bloody thoughts and to revenge, I chose   160
Camillo for the minister to poison
My friend Polixenes; which had been done,
But that the good mind of Camillo tardied
My swift command, though I with death and with
Reward did threaten and encourage him,   165
Not doing't and being done. He, most humane
And fill'd with honour, to my kingly guest
Unclasp'd my practice, quit his fortunes here,

---

87. **concerns...avails:** is more important to you than effective with me. 88. **like to itself:** i.e., as a bastard should be.
93. **bug:** bogey. 94. **commodity:** profit. 100. **Starr'd...unluckily:** born under a most unlucky star. 103. **immodest:**
immoderate. 104. **longs:** belongs. 105. **fashion:** sorts. 107. **of limit:** from the due time of rest after childbirth. 110.
no life: i.e., I do not ask for life. 115. **rigour:** tyranny. 123. **flatness:** completeness. 145. **conceit:** idea. 146. **speed:**
fortune. 168. **Unclasp'd my practice:** disclosed my plot.

Which you knew great, and to the [certain] hazard
Of all incertainties himself commended,   I70
No richer than his honour. How he glisters
Through my [dark] rust! And how his piety
Does my deeds make the blacker!

[*Re-enter* PAULINA.]

Paul.   Woe the while!
O, cut my lace, lest my heart, cracking it,
Break too!
  [*I.*] *Lord.* What fit is this, good lady?   I75
  Paul. What studied torments, tyrant, hast for
    me?
What wheels? racks? fires? What flaying? boiling
In leads or oils? What old or newer torture
Must I receive, whose every word deserves
To taste of thy most worst? Thy tyranny   I80
Together working with thy jealousies,
Fancies too weak for boys, too green and idle
For girls of nine, — O, think what they have done,
And then run mad indeed, stark mad! for all
Thy by-gone fooleries were but spices of it.   I85
That thou betray'dst Polixenes, 'twas nothing;
That did but show thee of a fool, inconstant
And damnable ingrateful; nor was 't much
Thou wouldst have poison'd good Camillo's honour,
To have him kill a king; poor trespasses,   I90
More monstrous standing by; whereof I reckon
The casting forth to crows thy baby-daughter
To be or none or little, though a devil
Would have shed water out of fire ere done't;
Nor is't directly laid to thee, the death   I95
Of the young Prince, whose honourable thoughts,
Thoughts high for one so tender, cleft the heart
That could conceive a gross and foolish sire
Blemish'd his gracious dam; this is not, no,
Laid to thy answer: but the last, — O lords,   200
When I have said, cry "Woe!" — the Queen, the
    Queen,
The sweet'st, dear'st creature's dead, and vengeance
    for't
Not dropp'd down yet.
  [*I.*] *Lord.*   The higher pow'rs forbid!
  Paul. I say she's dead; I'll swear't. If word nor
    oath
Prevail not, go and see. If you can bring   205
Tincture or lustre in her lip, her eye,
Heat outwardly or breath within, I'll serve you
As I would do the gods. But, O thou tyrant!
Do not repent these things, for they are heavier
Than all thy woes can stir; therefore betake thee   2I0
To nothing but despair. A thousand knees
Ten thousand years together, naked, fasting,

Upon a barren mountain, and still winter
In storm perpetual, could not move the gods
To look that way thou wert.
  Leon.   Go on, go on;   2I5
Thou canst not speak too much. I have deserv'd
All tongues to talk their bitt'rest.
  [*I.*] *Lord.*   Say no more.
Howe'er the business goes, you have made fault
I' th' boldness of your speech.
  Paul.   I am sorry for't.
All faults I make, when I shall come to know them,
I do repent. Alas! I have show'd too much
The rashness of a woman; he is touch'd   222
To th' noble heart. What's gone and what's past
    help
Should be past grief. Do not receive affliction
At my petition; I beseech you, rather   225
Let me be punish'd, that have minded you
Of what you should forget. Now, good my liege,
Sir, royal sir, forgive a foolish woman.
The love I bore your queen — lo, fool again! —
I'll speak of her no more, nor of your children;   230
I'll not remember you of my own lord,
Who is lost too. Take your patience to you,
And I'll say nothing.
  Leon.   Thou didst speak but well
When most the truth; which I receive much better
Than to be pitied of thee. Prithee, bring me   235
To the dead bodies of my queen and son.
One grave shall be for both; upon them shall
The causes of their death appear, unto
Our shame perpetual. Once a day I'll visit
The chapel where they lie, and tears shed there   240
Shall be my recreation. So long as nature
Will bear up with this exercise, so long
I daily vow to use it. Come and lead me
To these sorrows.   [*Exeunt.*

SCENE III. [*Bohemia. A desert country near
the sea.*]

Enter ANTIGONUS, *with the* Babe, *and a* MARINER.

  Ant. Thou art perfect then, our ship hath touch'd
    upon
The deserts of Bohemia?
  Mar.   Ay, my lord; and fear
We have landed in ill time: the skies look grimly
And threaten present blusters. In my conscience,
The heavens with that we have in hand are angry   5
And frown upon 's.
  Ant. Their sacred wills be done! Go, get aboard;
Look to thy bark. I'll not be long before
I call upon thee.

I69. [certain] F₂₋₄. Om. F₁.   I71. **No . . . honour:** with nothing but his honor.   I72. [dark] F₂₋₄. Om. F₁.   I85.
spices: samples.   I94. shed . . . fire: "dropped tears from burning eyes" (C. C. Clarke).   20I. said: spoken it.   2I0. stir:
remove, change.
Sc. iii, I. perfect: certain.

Mar. Make your best haste, and go not   10
Too far i' th' land; 'tis like to be loud weather.
Besides, this place is famous for the creatures
Of prey that keep upon 't.

Ant.   Go thou away;
I'll follow instantly.

Mar.   I am glad at heart
To be so rid o' th' business.   [*Exit.*

Ant.   Come, poor babe.
I have heard, but not believ'd, the spirits o' th'
    dead   16
May walk again. If such thing be, thy mother
Appear'd to me last night, for ne'er was dream
So like a waking. To me comes a creature,
Sometimes her head on one side, some another;
I never saw a vessel of like sorrow,   21
So fill'd and so becoming. In pure white robes,
Like very sanctity, she did approach
My cabin where I lay; thrice bow'd before me,
And, gasping to begin some speech, her eyes   25
Became two spouts; the fury spent, anon
Did this break from her: "Good Antigonus,
Since fate, against thy better disposition,
Hath made thy person for the thrower-out
Of my poor babe, according to thine oath,   30
Places remote enough are in Bohemia,
There weep and leave it crying; and, for the babe
Is counted lost for ever, Perdita,
I prithee, call 't. For this ungentle business,
Put on thee by my lord, thou ne'er shalt see   35
Thy wife Paulina more." And so, with shrieks,
She melted into air. Affrighted much,
I did in time collect myself and thought
This was so, and no slumber. Dreams are toys;
Yet for this once, yea, superstitiously,   40
I will be squar'd by this. I do believe
Hermione hath suffer'd death, and that
Apollo would, this being indeed the issue
Of King Polixenes, it should here be laid,
Either for life or death, upon the earth   45
Of its right father. Blossom, speed thee well!
There lie, and there thy character; there these,
Which may, if Fortune please, both breed thee,
    pretty,
    [*Laying down the babe, with a paper and a
    bundle.*]
And still rest thine. The storm begins. Poor wretch,
That for thy mother's fault art thus expos'd   50
To loss and what may follow! Weep I cannot,
But my heart bleeds; and most accurs'd am I
To be by oath enjoin'd to this. Farewell!
The day frowns more and more; thou 'rt like to have

A lullaby too rough. I never saw   55
The heavens so dim by day. — A savage clamour!
Well may I get aboard! This is the chase;
I am gone for ever.   [*Exit, pursued by a bear.*

[*Enter a* SHEPHERD.]

Shep. I would there were no age between ten and
three-and-twenty, or that youth would sleep   60
out the rest; for there is nothing in the between but
getting wenches with child, wronging the ancientry,
stealing, fighting — [*Horns.*] Hark you now!
Would any but these boil'd brains of nineteen and
two-and-twenty hunt this weather? They have   65
scar'd away two of my best sheep, which I fear the
wolf will sooner find than the master. If anywhere
I have them, 'tis by the seaside, browsing of ivy.
Good luck, an 't be thy will! what have we here?
Mercy on 's, a barne; a very pretty barne! A   70
boy or a child, I wonder? A pretty one; a very
pretty one: sure, some scape. Though I am not
bookish, yet I can read waiting-gentlewoman in the
scape. This has been some stair-work, some trunk-
work, some behind-door-work; they were warmer   75
that got this than the poor thing is here. I'll take
it up for pity: yet I'll tarry till my son come; he
halloo'd but even now. Whoa, ho, hoa!

Enter CLOWN.

Clo. Hilloa, loa!
Shep. What, art so near? If thou'lt see a thing   80
to talk on when thou art dead and rotten, come
hither. What ail'st thou, man?
Clo. I have seen two such sights, by sea and by   83
land! But I am not to say it is a sea, for it is now
the sky; betwixt the firmament and it you cannot
thrust a bodkin's point.
Shep. Why, boy, how is it?   88
Clo. I would you did but see how it chafes, how
it rages, how it takes up the shore! But that 's
not to the point. O, the most piteous cry of the
poor souls! Sometimes to see 'em, and not to see
'em; now the ship boring the moon with her main-
mast, and anon swallowed with yeast and froth, as
you'd thrust a cork into a hogshead. And then   95
for the land-service, to see how the bear tore out his
shoulder-bone; how he cried to me for help and said
his name was Antigonus, a nobleman. But to make
an end of the ship, to see how the sea flap-dragon'd
it; but, first, how the poor souls roared, and the   100
sea mock'd them; and how the poor gentleman
roared and the bear mock'd him, both roaring
louder than the sea or weather.   104

---

22. **So...becoming:** so complete (in sorrow) and yet so beautiful. 39. **toys:** trifles. 41. **squar'd:** ruled. 47. **character:** evidence of identity. **these:** the gold and jewels. 48–49. **both...thine:** both pay for thy upbringing and still leave
something for thine own. 57. **chase:** hunted animal. 58. s.d. It is quite likely that Shakespeare's company introduced
a tame bear upon the stage. 62. **ancientry:** old people. 64. **boil'd:** hot. 70. **barne:** child. 71. **child:** girl. 74. **scape:**
escapade. 99. **flap-dragon'd:** swallowed, as a flap-dragon (a raisin floating on burning brandy).

Shep. Name of mercy, when was this, boy?

Clo. Now, now; I have not wink'd since I saw these sights. The men are not yet cold under water, nor the bear half din'd on the gentleman. He's at it now.   109

Shep. Would I had been by, to have help'd the old man!

Clo. I would you had been by the ship side, to have help'd her; there your charity would have lack'd footing.   114

Shep. Heavy matters! heavy matters! But look thee here, boy. Now bless thyself; thou met'st with things dying, I with things new-born. Here's a sight for thee; look thee, a bearing-cloth for a squire's child! Look thee here; take up, take up, boy; open't. So, let's see. It was told me I should be rich by the fairies. This is some changeling; open't. What's within, boy?   123

Clo. You're a made old man; if the sins of your youth are forgiven you, you're well to live. Gold! all gold!   126

Shep. This is fairy gold, boy, and 'twill prove so. Up with't, keep it close. Home, home, the next way. We are lucky, boy; and to be so still requires nothing but secrecy. Let my sheep go. Come, good boy, the next way home.   131

Clo. Go you the next way with your findings. I'll go see if the bear be gone from the gentleman and how much he hath eaten. They are never curst but when they are hungry. If there be any of him left, I'll bury it.   136

Shep. That's a good deed. If thou mayest discern by that which is left of him what he is, fetch me to the sight of him.

Clo. Marry, will I; and you shall help to put him i' th' ground.   141

Shep. 'Tis a lucky day, boy, and we'll do good deeds on't.   [*Exeunt.*

ACT IV

SCENE I.

Enter TIME, *the* Chorus.

Time. I, that please some, try all, both joy and
    terror
Of good and bad, that makes and unfolds error,
Now take upon me, in the name of Time,
To use my wings. Impute it not a crime
To me or my swift passage, that I slide   5
O'er sixteen years and leave the growth untri'd
Of that wide gap, since it is in my power
To o'erthrow law and in one self-born hour

To plant and o'erwhelm custom. Let me pass
The same I am, ere ancient'st order was   10
Or what is now receiv'd. I witness to
The times that brought them in; so shall I do
To th' freshest things now reigning, and make stale
The glistering of this present, as my tale
Now seems to it. Your patience this allowing,   15
I turn my glass and give my scene such growing
As you had slept between. Leontes leaving,
Th' effects of his fond jealousies so grieving
That he shuts up himself, imagine me,
Gentle spectators, that I now may be   20
In fair Bohemia; and remember well,
I mention'd a son o' th' King's, which Florizel
I now name to you; and with speed so pace
To speak of Perdita, now grown in grace
Equal with wond'ring. What of her ensues   25
I list not prophesy; but let Time's news
Be known when 'tis brought forth. A shepherd's
    daughter,
And what to her adheres, which follows after,
Is th' argument of Time. Of this allow,
If ever you have spent time worse ere now;   30
If never, yet that Time himself doth say
He wishes earnestly you never may.   [*Exit.*

SCENE II. [*Bohemia. The palace of Polixenes.*]

Enter POLIXENES *and* CAMILLO.

Pol. I pray thee, good Camillo, be no more importunate. 'Tis a sickness denying thee anything; a death to grant this.   3

Cam. It is fifteen years since I saw my country; though I have for the most part been aired abroad, I desire to lay my bones there. Besides, the penitent king, my master, hath sent for me; to whose feeling sorrows I might be some allay, or I o'erween to think so, which is another spur to my departure.   10

Pol. As thou lov'st me, Camillo, wipe not out the rest of thy services by leaving me now. The need I have of thee thine own goodness hath made. Better not to have had thee than thus to want thee. Thou, having made me businesses which none   15
without thee can sufficiently manage, must either stay to execute them thyself or take away with thee the very services thou hast done; which if I have not enough considered (as too much I cannot), to be more thankful to thee shall be my study, and   20
my profit therein the heaping friendships. Of that fatal country, Sicilia, prithee speak no more; whose very naming punishes me with the remembrance of that penitent, as thou call'st him, and reconciled   25

---

118. **bearing-cloth:** christening-robe. 128. **close:** secret. **next:** nearest. 135. **curst:** fierce.
    Act IV, sc. i, 6. **untri'd:** unexamined. 8. **self-born:** self-same. 15. **seems:** seems stale. 25. **with wond'ring:** to the amazement it creates.
    Sc. ii, 4. **fifteen.** Cf. IV.i.6. 21. **heaping friendships:** piling up of favors.

king, my brother; whose loss of his most precious queen and children are even now to be afresh lamented. Say to me, when saw'st thou the Prince Florizel, my son? Kings are no less unhappy, their issue not being gracious, than they are in losing them when they have approved their virtues.   32

Cam. Sir, it is three days since I saw the Prince. What his happier affairs may be, are to me unknown: but I have missingly noted, he is of late much retired from court and is less frequent to his princely exercises than formerly he hath appeared.   38

Pol. I have considered so much, Camillo, and with some care; so far that I have eyes under my service which look upon his removedness; from whom I have this intelligence, that he is seldom from the house of a most homely shepherd, a man, they say, that from very nothing, and beyond the imagination of his neighbours, is grown into an unspeakable estate.   46

Cam. I have heard, sir, of such a man, who hath a daughter of most rare note. The report of her is extended more than can be thought to begin from such a cottage.   50

Pol. That's likewise part of my intelligence; but, I fear, the angle that plucks our son thither. Thou shalt accompany us to the place; where we will, not appearing what we are, have some question with the shepherd; from whose simplicity I think it not   55 uneasy to get the cause of my son's resort thither. Prithee, be my present partner in this business, and lay aside the thoughts of Sicilia.

Cam. I willingly obey your command.   60

Pol. My best Camillo! We must disguise ourselves.   [*Exeunt.*

SCENE III. [*A road near the Shepherd's cottage.*]

Enter AUTOLYCUS [*very ragged*], *singing.*

"When daffodils begin to peer,
    With heigh! the doxy over the dale,
Why, then comes in the sweet o' the year;
    For the red blood reigns in the winter's pale.

"The white sheet bleaching on the hedge,   5
    With heigh! the sweet birds, O, how they sing!
Doth set my pugging tooth on edge;
    For a quart of ale is a dish for a king.

"The lark, that tirra-lyra chants,
    With heigh! [with heigh!] the thrush and the
        jay,   10
Are summer songs for me and my aunts,
    While we lie tumbling in the hay."

I have serv'd Prince Florizel, and in my time wore three-pile; but now I am out of service.

"But shall I go mourn for that, my dear?   15
    The pale moon shines by night;
And when I wander here and there,
    I then do most go right.

"If tinkers may have leave to live,
    And bear the sow-skin budget,   20
Then my account I well may give,
    And in the stocks avouch it."

My traffic is sheets; when the kite builds, look to lesser linen. My father nam'd me Autolycus, who being, as I am, litter'd under Mercury, was like-   25 wise a snapper-up of unconsidered trifles. With die and drab I purchas'd this caparison, and my revenue is the silly cheat. Gallows and knock are too powerful on the highway; beating and hanging are terrors to me; for the life to come, I sleep out the thought of it. A prize! a prize!   32

Enter CLOWN.

Clo. Let me see: every 'leven wether tods; every tod yields pound and odd shilling; fifteen hundred shorn, what comes the wool to?

Aut. [*Aside.*] If the springe hold, the cock's mine.   37

Clo. I cannot do 't without compters. Let me see: what am I to buy for our sheep-shearing feast? Three pound of sugar, five pound of currants, rice, — what will this sister of mine do with rice?   40 But my father hath made her mistress of the feast, and she lays it on. She hath made me four-and-twenty nosegays for the shearers, three-man song-men all, and very good ones; but they are most of them means and bases; but one Puritan amongst   45 them, and he sings psalms to hornpipes. I must have saffron to colour the warden pies; mace; dates — none, that's out of my note; nutmegs, seven; a race or two of ginger, but that I may beg; four pounds of prunes, and as many of raisins o' th' sun.   52

32. **approved:** proved.   35. **missingly:** with a sense of loss.   40–41. **eyes ... removedness:** spies keeping watch upon his absences.   52. **angle:** baited hook.

Sc. iii, 2. **doxy:** beggar's wench.   4. **in ... pale:** in place of the winter's pale blood.   7. **pugging:** thievish.   10. **[with heigh]** F₂. Om. F₁.   11. **aunts:** wenches.   14. **three-pile:** costly velvet.   20. **budget:** wallet.   23–24. **My ... linen:** i.e., watch your sheets when I'm around, as you guard your smaller pieces from the kite, who likes to steal them.   25. **under Mercury.** The mythical Autolycus was the son of Mercury, god of thieves; Shakespeare's Autolycus was born when the planet Mercury was rising.   26–27. **With ... caparison:** through dice and women have I come into this outfit (i.e., rags).   28. **the ... cheat:** from petty thieving.   33. **every ... tods:** every eleven sheep yield a tod (28 lbs.) of wool.   36. **springe:** snare.   **cock:** woodcock (a proverbially silly bird).   37. **compters:** counters, metal discs used for counting.   43. **three ... men:** singers of catches.   45. **means:** tenors.   46. **hornpipes:** dance tunes.   47. **saffron:** orange-red coloring.   **warden:** made of winter pears.   49. **race:** root.   52. **o' th' sun:** sun-dried.

Aut. O that ever I was born!
                    [*Grovelling on the ground.*]
Clo. I' th' name of me —
Aut. O, help me, help me! Pluck but off these
rags, and then, death, death!   56
Clo. Alack, poor soul! thou hast need of more
rags to lay on thee, rather than have these off.
Aut. O sir, the loathsomeness of them offend me
more than the stripes I have received, which are
mighty ones and millions.   61
Clo. Alas, poor man! a million of beating may
come to a great matter.
Aut. I am robb'd, sir, and beaten; my money
and apparel ta'en from me, and these detestable
things put upon me.   66
Clo. What, by a horseman or a footman?
Aut. A footman, sweet sir, a footman.
Clo. Indeed, he should be a footman by the gar-
ments he has left with thee. If this be a horseman's
coat, it hath seen very hot service. Lend me thy
hand, I'll help thee. Come, lend me thy hand. 73
Aut. O, good sir, tenderly, O!
Clo. Alas, poor soul!
Aut. O, good sir, softly, good sir! I fear, sir, my
shoulder-blade is out.   77
Clo. How now! canst stand?
Aut. Softly, dear sir; [*picking his pocket*] good sir,
softly. You ha' done me a charitable office.
Clo. Dost lack any money? I have a little
money for thee.   83
Aut. No, good sweet sir; no, I beseech you, sir.
I have a kinsman not past three quarters of a mile
hence, unto whom I was going. I shall there have
money, or anything I want. Offer me no money, I
pray you; that kills my heart.
Clo. What manner of fellow was he that robb'd
you?   90
Aut. A fellow, sir, that I have known to go about
with troll-my-dames. I knew him once a servant
of the Prince. I cannot tell, good sir, for which of
his virtues it was, but he was certainly whipp'd out
of the court.   95
Clo. His vices, you would say; there's no virtue
whipp'd out of the court. They cherish it to make
it stay there; and yet it will no more but abide. 99
Aut. Vices, I would say, sir. I know this man
well. He hath been since an ape-bearer; then a
process-server, a bailiff; then he compass'd a motion of the Prodigal Son, and married a tinker's wife
within a mile where my land and living lies;
and, having flown over many knavish profes- 105

sions, he settled only in rogue. Some call him
Autolycus.
Clo. Out upon him! prig, for my life, prig. He
haunts wakes, fairs, and bear-baitings.
Aut. Very true, sir; he, sir, he. That's the rogue
that put me into this apparel.   111
Clo. Not a more cowardly rogue in all Bohemia.
If you had but look'd big and spit at him, he'd have
run.
Aut. I must confess to you, sir, I am no fighter.
I am false of heart that way; and that he knew, I
warrant him.   117
Clo. How do you now?
Aut. Sweet sir, much better than I was; I can
stand and walk. I will even take my leave of you,
and pace softly towards my kinsman's.   121
Clo. Shall I bring thee on the way?
Aut. No, good-fac'd sir; no, sweet sir.
Clo. Then fare thee well. I must go buy spices
for our sheep-shearing.   [*Exit.* 125
Aut. Prosper you, sweet sir! — Your purse is not
hot enough to purchase your spice. I'll be with
you at your sheep-shearing too. If I make not this
cheat bring out another and the shearers prove
sheep, let me be unroll'd and my name put in the
book of virtue!   131

(*Sings.*) "Jog on, jog on, the foot-path way,
          And merrily hent the stile-a;
        A merry heart goes all the day
          Your sad tires in a mile-a." [*Exit.* 135

SCENE IV. [*Bohemia. The Shepherd's cottage.*]

Enter FLORIZEL *and* PERDITA.

Flo. These your unusual weeds to each part of
          you
[Do] give a life; no shepherdess, but Flora,
Peering in April's front. This your sheep-shearing
Is as a meeting of the petty gods,
And you the queen on't.
Per.   Sir, my gracious lord,
To chide at your extremes it not becomes me. 6
O, pardon, that I name them! Your high self,
The gracious mark o' th' land, you have obscur'd
With a swain's wearing, and me, poor lowly maid,
Most goddess-like prank'd up. But that our feasts
In every mess have folly, and the feeders 11
Digest [it] with a custom, I should blush
To see you so attir'd; sworn, I think,
To show myself a glass.
Flo.   I bless the time

---

92. **troll-my-dames:** a game, something like bagatelle. 99. **abide:** stay briefly. 101. **ape-bearer:** man with a trained monkey. 102. **compass'd a motion:** obtained a puppet show. 108. **prig:** thief. 130. **unroll'd:** struck from the roll of thieves. 133. **hent:** take, leap over.
Sc. iv, 1. **weeds:** garments. 2. **[Do]** (Theobald). *Do's* F. 3. **Peering...front:** peeping in early April. 8. **mark:** pattern. 11. **mess:** group. 12. **Digest...custom:** accept from habit. **[it]** F₂. Om. F₁. 13–14. **sworn...glass:** bound to see myself as in a mirror. Many edd. follow Theobald in reading *swoon.*

When my good falcon made her flight across   15
Thy father's ground.
    Per.   Now Jove afford you cause!
To me the difference forges dread; your greatness
Hath not been us'd to fear.   Even now I tremble
To think your father, by some accident,
Should pass this way as you did.   O, the Fates!   20
How would he look to see his work, so noble,
Vilely bound up?   What would he say?   Or how
Should I, in these my borrowed flaunts, behold
The sternness of his presence?
    Flo.   Apprehend
Nothing but jollity.   The gods themselves,   25
Humbling their deities to love, have taken
The shapes of beasts upon them.   Jupiter
Became a bull and bellow'd; the green Neptune
A ram and bleated; and the fire-rob'd god,
Golden Apollo, a poor humble swain,   30
As I seem now.   Their transformations
Were never for a piece of beauty rarer,
Nor in a way so chaste, since my desires
Run not before mine honour, nor my lusts
Burn hotter than my faith.
    Per.   O, but, sir,   35
Your resolution cannot hold when 'tis
Oppos'd, as it must be, by th' power of the King.
One of these two must be necessities,
Which then will speak that you must change this
        purpose,
Or I my life.
    Flo.   Thou dearest Perdita,   40
With these forc'd thoughts, I prithee, darken not
The mirth o' th' feast.   Or I'll be thine, my fair,
Or not my father's; for I cannot be
Mine own, nor anything to any, if
I be not thine.   To this I am most constant,   45
Though destiny say no.   Be merry, gentle!
Strangle such thoughts as these with anything
That you behold the while.   Your guests are com-
        ing.
Lift up your countenance, as it were the day
Of celebration of that nuptial which   50
We two have sworn shall come.
    Per.   O lady Fortune,
Stand you auspicious!
    Flo.   See, your guests approach.
Address yourself to entertain them sprightly,
And let's be red with mirth.

[*Enter* SHEPHERD, CLOWN, MOPSA, DORCAS, *and*
    others, with POLIXENES *and* CAMILLO *disguised.*]
    Shep.   Fie, daughter! when my old wife liv'd,
        upon   55

This day she was both pantler, butler, cook,
Both dame and servant; welcom'd all, serv'd all;
Would sing her song and dance her turn; now here,
At upper end o' th' table, now i' th' middle;
On his shoulder, and his; her face o' fire   60
With labour; and the thing she took to quench it,
She would to each one sip.   You are retir'd,
As if you were a feasted one and not
The hostess of the meeting.   Pray you, bid   64
These unknown friends to 's welcome, for it is
A way to make us better friends, more known.
Come, quench your blushes, and present yourself
That which you are, mistress o' th' feast.   Come on,
And bid us welcome to your sheep-shearing,
As your good flock shall prosper.
    Per.   [*To Pol.*] Sir, welcome.
It is my father's will I should take on me   71
The hostess-ship o' th' day.   [*To Cam.*] You're
        welcome, sir.
Give me those flowers there, Dorcas.   Reverend sirs,
For you there's rosemary and rue; these keep
Seeming and savour all the winter long.   75
Grace and remembrance be to you both,
And welcome to our shearing!
    Pol.   Shepherdess, —
A fair one are you — well you fit our ages
With flowers of winter.
    Per.   Sir, the year growing ancient,
Not yet on summer's death, nor on the birth   80
Of trembling winter, the fairest flowers o' th' season
Are our carnations and streak'd [gillyflowers],
Which some call Nature's bastards.   Of that kind
Our rustic garden 's barren; and I care not   84
To get slips of them.
    Pol.   Wherefore, gentle maiden,
Do you neglect them?
    Per.   For I have heard it said
There is an art which in their piedness shares
With great creating Nature.
    Pol.   Say there be;
Yet Nature is made better by no mean
But Nature makes that mean; so, over that art   90
Which you say adds to Nature, is an art
That Nature makes.   You see, sweet maid, we
        marry
A gentler scion to the wildest stock,
And make conceive a bark of baser kind
By bud of nobler race.   This is an art   95
Which does mend Nature, change it rather, but
The art itself is Nature.
    Per.   So it is.
    Pol.   Then make [your] garden rich in gilly-
        flowers,

---

17. **difference:** i.e., between our ranks.   23. **flaunts:** finery.   33. **Nor ... chaste.** The reference is to "transformations,"
not to "piece."   41. **forc'd:** far-fetched.   56. **pantler:** pantry servant.   82. **[gillyflowers]** (Rowe); clove-scented pinks. The
name was also applied to wallflowers and stocks.   *Gilly-vors* F.   83. **Nature's bastards.**   Because grown artificially.
98. **[your]** F₂.   *you* F₁.

And do not call them bastards.

Per.   I'll not put
The dibble in earth to set one slip of them;   100
No more than were I painted I would wish
This youth should say 'twere well, and only there-
        fore
Desire to breed by me. Here's flowers for you;
Hot lavender, mints, savory, marjoram;
The marigold, that goes to bed wi' th' sun   105
And with him rises weeping. These are flowers
Of middle summer, and I think they are given
To men of middle age. You're very welcome.

Cam. I should leave grazing, were I of your flock,
And only live by gazing.

Per.   Out, alas!   110
You'd be so lean, that blasts of January
Would blow you through and through. Now, my
        fair'st friend,
I would I had some flowers o' th' spring that might
Become your time of day; and yours, and yours,
That wear upon your virgin branches yet   115
Your maidenheads growing. O Proserpina,
For the flowers now, that frighted thou let'st fall
From Dis's waggon! daffodils,
That come before the swallow dares, and take
The winds of March with beauty; violets dim,
But sweeter than the lids of Juno's eyes   121
Or Cytherea's breath; pale primroses,
That die unmarried, ere they can behold
Bright Phœbus in his strength — a malady
Most incident to maids; bold oxlips and   125
The crown imperial; lilies of all kinds,
The flower-de-luce being one! O, these I lack,
To make you garlands of, and my sweet friend,
To strew him o'er and o'er!

Flo.   What, like a corse?

Per. No, like a bank for love to lie and play on;
Not like a corse; or if, not to be buried,   131
But quick and in mine arms. Come, take your
        flowers.
Methinks I play as I have seen them do
In Whitsun pastorals. Sure this robe of mine
Does change my disposition.

Flo.   What you do   135
Still betters what is done. When you speak, sweet,
I'd have you do it ever; when you sing,
I'd have you buy and sell so, so give alms,
Pray so; and for the ord'ring your affairs,
To sing them too. When you do dance, I wish you
A wave o' th' sea, that you might ever do   141
Nothing but that; move still, still so,
And own no other function. Each your doing,
So singular in each particular,

Crowns what you are doing in the present deeds, 145
That all your acts are queens.

Per.   O Doricles,
Your praises are too large. But that your youth,
And the true blood which peeps [so] fairly through't,
Do plainly give you out an unstain'd shepherd,
With wisdom I might fear, my Doricles,   150
You woo'd me the false way.

Flo.   I think you have
As little skill to fear as I have purpose
To put you to 't. But come; our dance, I pray.
Your hand, my Perdita. So turtles pair,
That never mean to part.

Per.   I'll swear for 'em. 155

Pol. This is the prettiest low-born lass that ever
Ran on the green-sward. Nothing she does or
        seems
But smacks of something greater than herself,
Too noble for this place.

Cam.   He tells her something
That makes her blood look out. Good sooth, she is
The queen of curds and cream.

Clo.   Come on, strike up! 161

Dor. Mopsa must be your mistress; marry, garlic,
To mend her kissing with!

Mop.   Now, in good time!

Clo. Not a word, a word; we stand upon our
        manners.
Come, strike up!   165
        [*Music.*] *Here a dance of Shepherds and*
                Shepherdesses.

Pol. Pray, good shepherd, what fair swain is this
Which dances with your daughter?

Shep. They call him Doricles; and boasts himself
To have a worthy feeding; but I have it
Upon his own report, and I believe it.   170
He looks like sooth. He says he loves my daughter.
I think so too; for never gaz'd the moon
Upon the water as he'll stand and read,
As 'twere, my daughter's eyes; and, to be plain,
I think there is not half a kiss to choose   175
Who loves another best.

Pol.   She dances featly.

Shep. So she does anything, though I report it,
That should be silent. If young Doricles
Do light upon her, she shall bring him that
Which he not dreams of.   180

                Enter a SERVANT.

Serv. O master, if you did but hear the pedlar at
the door, you would never dance again after a tabor
and pipe; no, the bagpipe could not move you. He
sings several tunes faster than you'll tell money.

100. **dibble:** tool for making holes. 104. **Hot:** fragrant. 126. **crown imperial:** fritillary. 127. **flower-de-luce:** iris.
132. **quick:** alive. 134. **Whitsun pastorals:** morris dances at Whitsuntide. 144. **singular:** distinctly yours. 148. **[so]**
(Capell). Om. F. 152. **skill:** reason. 154. **turtles:** turtle-doves. 163. **in . .time.** An expression of indignation. 169.
feeding: pasture land. 171. **like sooth:** honest. 176. **featly:** gracefully. 182. **tabor:** small drum. 184. **tell:** count.

He utters them as he had eaten ballads and all men's ears grew to his tunes.   186

Clo. He could never come better; he shall come in. I love a ballad but even too well, if it be doleful matter merrily set down, or a very pleasant thing indeed and sung lamentably.   190

Serv. He hath songs for man or woman, of all sizes; no milliner can so fit his customers with gloves. He has the prettiest love-songs for maids; so without bawdry, which is strange; with such delicate burdens of dildos and fadings, "jump   195 her and thump her;" and where some stretch-mouth'd rascal would, as it were, mean mischief and break a foul gap into the matter, he makes the maid to answer, "Whoop, do me no harm, good man;" puts him off, slights him, with "Whoop, do me no harm, good man."   201

Pol. This is a brave fellow.

Clo. Believe me, thou talkest of an admirable conceited fellow. Has he any unbraided wares?   204

Serv. He hath ribbons of all the colours i' th' rainbow; points more than all the lawyers in Bohemia can learnedly handle, though they come to him by th' gross; inkles, caddises, cambrics, lawns. Why, he sings 'em over as they were gods or goddesses; you would think a smock were a she-angel, he so chants to the sleeve-hand and the work about the square on't.   212

Clo. Prithee bring him in; and let him approach singing.

Per. Forewarn him that he use no scurrilous words in 's tunes.   [*Exit Servant.*]   216

Clo. You have of these pedlars, that have more in them than you'd think, sister.

Per. Ay, good brother, or go about to think.

Enter AUTOLYCUS, *singing.*

"Lawn as white as driven snow;   220
Cypress black as e'er was crow;
Gloves as sweet as damask roses;
Masks for faces and for noses;
Bugle bracelet, necklace amber,
Perfume for a lady's chamber;   225
Golden quoifs and stomachers
For my lads to give their dears;
Pins and poking-sticks of steel;
What maids lack from head to heel.
Come buy of me, come; come buy, come buy;   230
Buy, lads, or else your lasses cry.
Come buy."

Clo. If I were not in love with Mopsa, thou shouldst take no money of me; but being enthrall'd as I am, it will also be the bondage of certain ribbons and gloves.   236

Mop. I was promis'd them against the feast; but they come not too late now.

Dor. He hath promis'd you more than that, or there be liars.   240

Mop. He hath paid you all he promis'd you. May be he has paid you more, which will shame you to give him again.   243

Clo. Is there no manners left among maids? Will they wear their plackets where they should bear their faces? Is there not milking-time, when you are going to bed, or kiln-hole, to whistle off these secrets, but you must be tittle-tattling before all our guests? 'Tis well they are whisp'ring. Clamour your tongues, and not a word more.   251

Mop. I have done. Come, you promis'd me a tawdry-lace and a pair of sweet gloves.

Clo. Have I not told thee how I was cozen'd by the way and lost all my money?   255

Aut. And indeed, sir, there are cozeners abroad; therefore it behoves men to be wary.

Clo. Fear not thou, man, thou shalt lose nothing here.   259

Aut. I hope so, sir; for I have about me many parcels of charge.

Clo. What hast here? Ballads?

Mop. Pray now, buy some. I love a ballad in print, o' life, for then we are sure they are true.   264

Aut. Here's one to a very doleful tune, how a usurer's wife was brought to bed of twenty money-bags at a burden, and how she long'd to eat adders' heads and toads carbonado'd.

Mop. Is it true, think you?

Aut. Very true, and but a month old.   270

Dor. Bless me from marrying a usurer!

Aut. Here's the midwife's name to't, one Mistress Tale-porter, and five or six honest wives that were present. Why should I carry lies abroad?   275

Mop. Pray you now, buy it.

Clo. Come on, lay it by, and let's first see moe ballads. We'll buy the other things anon.   278

Aut. Here's another ballad, of a fish that appeared upon the coast on Wednesday the fourscore of April, forty thousand fathom above water, and sung this ballad against the hard hearts of maids. It was thought she was a woman and was turned into a cold fish for she would not exchange

195. **dildos and fadings:** words familiar in ballad refrains.   196. **stretch-mouth'd:** foul-mouthed.   198. **break...matter:** thrust in a lewd phrase.   204. **conceited:** clever.   **unbraided:** fresh.   206. **points:** (1) metal-tagged laces, (2) arguments.   208. **inkles:** linen tapes.   **caddises:** worsted tapes for garters.   211. **sleeve-hand:** wrist-band.   212. **square:** yoke.   217. **You have:** there are some.   219. **go about:** intend.   221. **Cypress:** crepe.   224. **Bugle:** black-beaded.   226. **quoifs:** caps.   228. **poking-sticks:** metal rods for adjusting the plaits of ruffs.   237. **against:** for.   245. **plackets:** petticoats.   247. **kiln-hole:** furnace-room of a kiln.   251. **Clamour:** silence.   253. **tawdry-lace:** a silk neckerchief (named for St. Audrey).   261. **charge:** value.   268. **carbonado'd:** cut up for broiling.

flesh with one that lov'd her. The ballad is very pitiful and as true.   286

Dor. Is it true too, think you?

Aut. Five justices' hands at it, and witnesses more than my pack will hold.

Clo. Lay it by too. Another.

Aut. This is a merry ballad, but a very pretty one.   292

Mop. Let's have some merry ones.

Aut. Why, this is a passing merry one and goes to the tune of "Two maids wooing a man." There's scarce a maid westward but she sings it. 'Tis in request, I can tell you.   297

Mop. We can both sing it. If thou'lt bear a part, thou shalt hear. 'Tis in three parts.

Dor. We had the tune on't a month ago.   300

Aut. I can bear my part; you must know 'tis my occupation. Have at it with you.

SONG.

A. Get you hence, for I must go
    Where it fits not you to know.

D. Whither? *M.* O, whither? *D.* Whither?

    M. It becomes thy oath full well,   306
    Thou to me thy secrets tell.

D. Me too, let me go thither.

    M. Or thou goest to th' grange or mill.

D. If to either, thou dost ill.   310

A. Neither. *D.* What, neither? *A.* Neither.

D. Thou hast sworn my love to be.

M. Thou hast sworn it more to me.

Then whither goest? Say, whither?   314

Clo. We'll have this song out anon by ourselves. My father and the gentlemen are in sad talk, and we'll not trouble them. Come, bring away thy pack after me. Wenches, I'll buy for you both. Pedlar, let's have the first choice. Follow me, girls.   320
                    [*Exit with Dorcas and Mopsa.*]

Aut. And you shall pay well for 'em.

"Will you buy any tape,
    Or lace for your cape,
My dainty duck, my dear-a?
    Any silk, any thread,   325
    Any toys for your head,
Of the new'st and fin'st, fin'st wear-a?
    Come to the pedlar;
    Money's a meddler
That doth utter all men's ware-a." [*Exit.*   330

[*Re-enter* SERVANT.]

Serv. Master, there is three carters, three shepherds, three neat-herds, three swine-herds, that

have made themselves all men of hair. They call themselves Saltiers; and they have a dance which the wenches say is a gallimaufry of gambols,   335 because they are not in't; but they themselves are o' th' mind, if it be not too rough for some that know little but bowling, it will please plentifully. 339

Shep. Away! we'll none on't. Here has been too much homely foolery already. I know, sir, we weary you.

Pol. You weary those that refresh us. Pray, let's see these four threes of herdsmen.   344

Serv. One three of them, by their own report, sir, hath danc'd before the King; and not the worst of the three but jumps twelve foot and a half by the squire.

Shep. Leave your prating. Since these good men are pleas'd, let them come in; but quickly now.   351

Serv. Why, they stay at door, sir.   [*Exit.*]

Here a dance of twelve Satyrs.

Pol. O, father, you'll know more of that hereafter.

[*To Cam.*] Is it not too far gone? 'Tis time to part them.

He's simple and tells much. [*To Flor.*] How now, fair shepherd!   355

Your heart is full of something that does take Your mind from feasting. Sooth, when I was young And handed love as you do, I was wont To load my she with knacks. I would have ransack'd The pedlar's silken treasury and have pour'd it   360 To her acceptance; you have let him go And nothing marted with him. If your lass Interpretation should abuse and call this Your lack of love or bounty, you were straited For a reply; at least if you make a care   365 Of happy holding her.

Flo.   Old sir, I know She prizes not such trifles as these are. The gifts she looks from me are pack'd and lock'd Up in my heart; which I have given already, But not deliver'd. O, hear me breathe my life   370 Before this ancient sir, [who], it should seem, Hath sometime lov'd! I take thy hand, this hand, As soft as dove's down and as white as it, Or Ethiopian's tooth, or the fann'd snow that's bolted   374 By the northern blasts twice o'er.

Pol.   What follows this? How prettily the young swain seems to wash The hand was fair before! I have put you out. But to your protestation; let me hear What you profess.

316. **sad:** sober. 330. **utter:** put to sale. 333. **of hair:** clad in skins. 334. **Saltiers:** i.e., Satyrs. The servant calls them *saltiers* because they jumped (*sault:* leap). 335. **gallimaufry:** jumble. 348. **squire:** foot rule. 362. **marted:** trafficked. 364. **straited:** hard put. 371. **[who]** F₂. *whom* F₁. 374. **bolted:** sifted.

Flo.   Do, and be witness to 't.

Pol. And this my neighbour too?

Flo.   And he, and more
Than he, and men, the earth, the heavens, and
     all: 381
That, were I crown'd the most imperial monarch,
Thereof most worthy, were I the fairest youth
That ever made eye swerve, had force and knowl-
     edge
More than was ever man's, I would not prize them
Without her love; for her employ them all;   386
Commend them and condemn them to her service
Or to their own perdition.

Pol.   Fairly offer'd.

Cam. This shows a sound affection.

Shep.   But, my daughter,
Say you the like to him?

Per.   I cannot speak   390
So well, nothing so well; no, nor mean better.
By th' pattern of mine own thoughts I cut out
The purity of his.

Shep.   Take hands, a bargain!
And, friends unknown, you shall bear witness to 't:
I give my daughter to him, and will make   395
Her portion equal his.

Flo.   O, that must be
I' th' virtue of your daughter. One being dead,
I shall have more than you can dream of yet.
Enough then for your wonder. But, come on,
Contract us 'fore these witnesses.

Shep.   Come, your hand;   400
And, daughter, yours.

Pol.   Soft, swain, a while, beseech you.
Have you a father?

Flo.   I have; but what of him?

Pol. Knows he of this?

Flo.   He neither does nor shall.

Pol. Methinks a father
Is at the nuptial of his son a guest   405
That best becomes the table. Pray you once more,
Is not your father grown incapable
Of reasonable affairs? Is he not stupid
With age and alt'ring rheums? Can he speak?
     hear?
Know man from man? dispute his own estate?   410
Lies he not bed-rid? and again does nothing
But what he did being childish?

Flo.   No, good sir;
He has his health, and ampler strength indeed
Than most have of his age.

Pol.   By my white beard,
You offer him, if this be so, a wrong   415
Something unfilial. Reason my son

Should choose himself a wife, but as good reason
The father, all whose joy is nothing else
But fair posterity, should hold some counsel
In such a business.

Flo.   I yield all this;   420
But for some other reasons, my grave sir,
Which 'tis not fit you know, I not acquaint
My father of this business.

Pol.   Let him know 't.

Flo. He shall not.

Pol.   Prithee, let him.

Flo.   No, he must not.

Shep. Let him, my son. He shall not need to
     grieve   425
At knowing of thy choice.

Flo.   Come, come, he must not.
Mark our contract.

Pol.   Mark your divorce, young sir,
                              [*Discovering himself.*]
Whom son I dare not call. Thou art too base
To be acknowledg'd. Thou, a sceptre's heir,
That thus affects a sheep-hook! Thou old traitor,
I am sorry that by hanging thee I can   431
But shorten thy life one week. And thou, fresh
     piece
Of excellent witchcraft, [who] of force must know
The royal fool thou cop'st with, —

Shep.   O, my heart!

Pol. I'll have thy beauty scratch'd with briers
     and made   435
More homely than thy state. For thee, fond boy,
If I may ever know thou dost but sigh
That thou no more shalt see this knack, as never
I mean thou shalt, we'll bar thee from succession,
Not hold thee of our blood, no, not our kin,   440
Far than Deucalion off. Mark thou my words.
Follow us to the court. Thou, churl, for this time,
Though full of our displeasure, yet we free thee
From the dead blow of it. And you, enchant-
     ment, —
Worthy enough a herdsman, yea, him too,   445
That makes himself, but for our honour therein,
Unworthy thee, — if ever henceforth thou
These rural latches to his entrance open,
Or hoop his body more with thy embraces,
I will devise a death as cruel for thee   450
As thou art tender to 't.   [*Exit.*

Per.   Even here undone!
I was not much afeard; for once or twice
I was about to speak, and tell him plainly
The self-same sun that shines upon his court
Hides not his visage from our cottage, but   455
Looks on alike. Will 't please you, sir, be gone?

---

384. **made eye swerve:** attracted notice.   409. **alt'ring rheums:** weakening colds.   410. **dispute:** discuss.   416. **Reason:** it is reasonable.   433. **[who]** *whom* F₁.   434. **cop'st:** dealest.   436. **fond:** foolish.   438. **That:** because. **shalt** (Rowe). *shalt ne'er* F. **knack:** toy.   441. **Far:** farther (*Farre* F). **Deucalion:** the Noah of Greek mythology. 445-47. **him...thee:** i.e., worthy also of him, who (the question of our royalty aside) makes himself unworthy of thee.

I told you what would come of this.   Beseech you,
Of your own state take care.   This dream of mine,—
Being now awake, I'll queen it no inch farther,
But milk my ewes and weep.

Cam.   Why, how now, father!   460
Speak ere thou diest.

Shep.   I cannot speak, nor think,
Nor dare to know that which I know.   O sir!
You have undone a man of fourscore three,
That thought to fill his grave in quiet, yea,
To die upon the bed my father died,   465
To lie close by his honest bones; but now
Some hangman must put on my shroud and lay me
Where no priest shovels in dust. — O cursed
    wretch,
That knew'st this was the Prince, and wouldst
    adventure
To mingle faith with him!   Undone! undone!
If I might die within this hour, I have liv'd   471
To die when I desire.   [*Exit.*

Flo.   Why look you so upon me?
I am but sorry, not afeard; delay'd,
But nothing alt'red.   What I was, I am;
More straining on for plucking back, not following
My leash unwillingly.

Cam.   Gracious my lord,   476
You know your father's temper.   At this time
He will allow no speech, which I do guess
You do not purpose to him; and as hardly
Will he endure your sight as yet, I fear.   480
Then, till the fury of his Highness settle,
Come not before him.

Flo.   I not purpose it.
I think, Camillo?

Cam.   Even he, my lord.

Per. How often have I told you 'twould be thus!
How often said, my dignity would last   485
But till 'twere known!

Flo.   It cannot fail but by
The violation of my faith; and then
Let Nature crush the sides o' th' earth together
And mar the seeds within!   Lift up thy looks.
From my succession wipe me, father; I   490
Am heir to my affection.

Cam.   Be advis'd.

Flo. I am, and by my fancy.   If my reason
Will thereto be obedient, I have reason;
If not, my senses, better pleas'd with madness,
Do bid it welcome.

Cam.   This is desperate, sir.   495

Flo. So call it, but it does fulfil my vow;
I needs must think it honesty.   Camillo,
Not for Bohemia, nor the pomp that may
Be thereat gleaned, for all the sun sees or
The close earth wombs or the profound seas hides

In unknown fathoms, will I break my oath   501
To this my fair belov'd; therefore, I pray you,
As you have ever been my father's honour'd friend,
When he shall miss me, — as, in faith, I mean not
To see him any more, — cast your good counsels
Upon his passion; let myself and Fortune   506
Tug for the time to come.   This you may know
And so deliver: I am put to sea
With her who here I cannot hold on shore;
And most opportune to [our] need I have   510
A vessel rides fast by, but not prepar'd
For this design.   What course I mean to hold
Shall nothing benefit your knowledge, nor
Concern me the reporting.

Cam.   O my lord!
I would your spirit were easier for advice,   515
Or stronger for your need.

Flo.   Hark, Perdita!
                              [*Drawing her aside.*
I'll hear you [*to Cam.*] by and by.

Cam.   He's irremoveable,
Resolv'd for flight.   Now were I happy, if
His going I could frame to serve my turn,
Save him from danger, do him love and honour, 520
Purchase the sight again of dear Sicilia
And that unhappy king, my master, whom
I so much thirst to see.

Flo.   Now, good Camillo;
I am so fraught with curious business that
I leave out ceremony.

Cam.   Sir, I think   525
You have heard of my poor services i' th' love
That I have borne your father?

Flo.   Very nobly
Have you deserv'd.   It is my father's music
To speak your deeds, not little of his care
To have them recompens'd as thought on.

Cam.   Well, my lord,
If you may please to think I love the King   531
And through him what's nearest to him, which is
Your gracious self, embrace but my direction.
If your more ponderous and settled project
May suffer alteration, on mine honour,   535
I'll point you where you shall have such receiv-
    ing
As shall become your Highness; where you may
Enjoy your mistress, from the whom, I see,
There's no disjunction to be made, but by —
As heavens forefend! — your ruin; marry her, 540
And, with my best endeavours in your absence,
Your discontenting father strive to qualify
And bring him up to liking.

Flo.   How, Camillo,
May this, almost a miracle, be done?
That I may call thee something more than man 545

---

492. fancy: love.   507. Tug...come: combat for the future.   510. [our] (Theobald).   her F.   524. curious: anxious.
542. qualify: appease.   543. liking: i.e., approving your choice.

And after that trust to thee.
Cam.   Have you thought on
A place whereto you'll go?
Flo.   Not any yet:
But as th' unthought-on accident is guilty
To what we wildly do, so we profess
Ourselves to be the slaves of chance, and flies   550
Of every wind that blows.
Cam.   Then list to me.
This follows: if you will not change your purpose
But undergo this flight, make for Sicilia,
And there present yourself and your fair princess,
For so I see she must be, 'fore Leontes.   555
She shall be habited as it becomes
The partner of your bed. Methinks I see
Leontes opening his free arms and weeping
His welcomes forth; asks thee, the son, forgiveness,
As 'twere i' th' father's person; kisses the hands 560
Of your fresh princess; o'er and o'er divides him
'Twixt his unkindness and his kindness; the one
He chides to hell and bids the other grow
Faster than thought or time.
Flo.   Worthy Camillo,
What colour for my visitation shall I   565
Hold up before him?
Cam.   Sent by the King your father
To greet him and to give him comforts. Sir,
The manner of your bearing towards him, with
What you as from your father shall deliver,   569
Things known betwixt us three, I'll write you down;
The which shall point you forth at every sitting
What you must say; that he shall not perceive
But that you have your father's bosom there
And speak his very heart.
Flo.   I am bound to you.
There is some sap in this.
Cam.   A course more promising
Than a wild dedication of yourselves   576
To unpath'd waters, undream'd shores, most certain
To miseries enough; no hope to help you,
But as you shake off one to take another;
Nothing so certain as your anchors, who   580
Do their best office, if they can but stay you
Where you'll be loath to be. Besides, you know,
Prosperity's the very bond of love,
Whose fresh complexion and whose heart together
Affliction alters.
Per.   One of these is true.   585
I think affliction may subdue the cheek,
But not take in the mind.
Cam.   Yea, say you so?
There shall not at your father's house these seven
    years

Be born another such.
Flo.   My good Camillo,
She is as forward of her breeding as   590
She is i' th' rear o' our birth.
Cam.   I cannot say 'tis pity
She lacks instructions, for she seems a mistress
To most that teach.
Per.   Your pardon, sir; for this
I'll blush you thanks.
Flo.   My prettiest Perdita!
But O, the thorns we stand upon! Camillo,   595
Preserver of my father, now of me,
The medicine of our house, how shall we do?
We are not furnish'd like Bohemia's son,
Nor shall appear in Sicilia.
Cam.   My lord,
Fear none of this. I think you know my fortunes
Do all lie there. It shall be so my care   601
To have you royally appointed as if
The scene you play were mine. For instance, sir,
That you may know you shall not want, one
    word.   *[They talk aside.]* 604

Re-enter AUTOLYCUS.

Aut. Ha, ha! what a fool Honesty is! and Trust,
his sworn brother, a very simple gentleman! I
have sold all my trumpery; not a counterfeit stone,
not a ribbon, glass, pomander, brooch, table-book,
ballad, knife, tape, glove, shoe-tie, bracelet, horn-
ring, to keep my pack from fasting. They 610
throng who should buy first, as if my trinkets had
been hallowed and brought a benediction to the
buyer; by which means I saw whose purse was
best in picture, and what I saw, to my good use
I remem'bred. My clown, who wants but 615
something to be a reasonable man, grew so in
love with the wenches' song, that he would not
stir his pettitoes till he had both tune and words;
which so drew the rest of the herd to me that all
their other senses stuck in ears. You might 620
have pinched a placket, it was senseless; 'twas
nothing to geld a codpiece of a purse; I would
have fil'd keys off that hung in chains. No hearing, no feeling, but my sir's song, and admiring
the nothing of it. So that in this time of 625
lethargy I pick'd and cut most of their festival
purses; and had not the old man come in with a
whoo-bub against his daughter and the King's son
and scar'd my choughs from the chaff, I had not
left a purse alive in the whole army. 630
    [Camillo, Florizel, and Perdita come for-
    ward.]

---

558. **free:** gracious. 561. **him:** i.e., his speech. 565. **colour:** excuse. 571. **point you forth:** show you. **sitting:** conference. 586. **subdue:** i.e., with tears. 587. **take in:** overcome. 599. **appear:** i.e., appear as such. 608. **pomander:** scent-ball. **table-book:** notebook. 614. **picture:** looks. 618. **pettitoes:** pig's feet. 622. **geld ... codpiece:** rob a trouser pocket. 624. **my sir's:** i.e., the clown's. 629. **choughs:** jackdaws.

Cam. Nay, but my letters, by this means being
there
So soon as you arrive, shall clear that doubt.
Flo. And those that you'll procure from King
Leontes?
Cam. Shall satisfy your father.
Per.   Happy be you!
All that you speak shows fair.
Cam.   Who have we here?
                    [*Seeing Autolycus.*]
We'll make an instrument of this, omit   636
Nothing may give us aid.
Aut. [*Aside.*] If they have overheard me now,
why, hanging.   639
Cam. How now, good fellow! why shak'st thou
so?   Fear not, man; here's no harm intended to
thee.
Aut. I am a poor fellow, sir.   643
Cam. Why, be so still; here's nobody will steal
that from thee.   Yet for the outside of thy poverty
we must make an exchange; therefore discase thee
instantly, — thou must think there's a necessity
in't, — and change garments with this gentleman.
Though the pennyworth on his side be the worst,
yet hold thee, there's some boot.   650
Aut. I am a poor fellow, sir. [*Aside.*] I know ye
well enough.
Cam. Nay, prithee, dispatch.   The gentleman
is half [flay'd] already.
Aut. Are you in earnest, sir?   [*Aside.*] I smell
the trick on't.   656
Flo. Dispatch, I prithee.
Aut. Indeed, I have had earnest; but I cannot
with conscience take it.
Cam. Unbuckle, unbuckle.   660
[*Florizel and Autolycus exchange garments.*]
Fortunate mistress, — let my prophecy
Come home to ye! — you must retire yourself
Into some covert.   Take your sweetheart's hat
And pluck it o'er your brows, muffle your face,
Dismantle you, and, as you can, disliken   665
The truth of your own seeming; that you may —
For I do fear eyes over — to shipboard
Get undescri'd.
Per.   I see the play so lies
That I must bear a part.
Cam.   No remedy.   669
Have you done there?
Flo.   Should I now meet my father,
He would not call me son.
Cam.   Nay, you shall have no hat.
                    [*Giving it to Perdita.*]
Come, lady, come.   Farewell, my friend.
Aut.   Adieu, sir.

Flo. O Perdita, what have we twain forgot!
Pray you, a word.
Cam. [*Aside.*] What I do next shall be to tell
the King   675
Of this escape and whither they are bound;
Wherein my hope is I shall so prevail
To force him after; in whose company
I shall re-view Sicilia, for whose sight
I have a woman's longing.
Flo.   Fortune speed us!
Thus we set on, Camillo, to th' sea-side.   681
Cam. The swifter speed the better.
            [*Exeunt [Florizel, Perdita, and Camillo].*
Aut. I understand the business, I hear it.   To
have an open ear, a quick eye, and a nimble hand,
is necessary for a cut-purse; a good nose is   685
requisite also, to smell out work for th' other senses.
I see this is the time that the unjust man doth
thrive.   What an exchange had this been without
boot!   What a boot is here with this exchange!
Sure the gods do this year connive at us, and   690
we may do anything extempore.   The Prince himself is about a piece of iniquity, stealing away from
his father with his clog at his heels.   If I thought
it were a piece of honesty to acquaint the King
withal, I would not do 't.   I hold it the more   695
knavery to conceal it; and therein am I constant
to my profession.

Re-enter CLOWN *and* SHEPHERD.

Aside, aside; here is more matter for a hot brain.
Every lane's end, every shop, church, session,
hanging, yields a careful man work.   701
Clo. See, see; what a man you are now!   There
is no other way but to tell the King she's a changeling and none of your flesh and blood.   705
Shep. Nay, but hear me.
Clo. Nay, but hear me.
Shep. Go to, then.
Clo. She being none of your flesh and blood,
your flesh and blood has not offended the King;   710
and so your flesh and blood is not to be punish'd
by him.   Show those things you found about her,
those secret things, all but what she has with her.
This being done, let the law go whistle.   I warrant
you.   715
Shep. I will tell the King all, every word, yea,
and his son's pranks too; who, I may say, is no
honest man, neither to his father nor to me, to go
about to make me the King's brother-in-law.   720
Clo. Indeed, brother-in-law was the farthest off
you could have been to him, and then your blood
had been the dearer by I know how much an ounce.
Aut. [*Aside.*] Very wisely, puppies!   725

646. **discase:** undress.   649. **the pennyworth:** his side of the bargain.   650. **some boot:** something in addition.   654.
[flay'd] (Rowe): undressed.   *fled* F.   658. **earnest:** down-payment (to bind a bargain).   661. **prophecy:** i.e., as implied
in "Fortunate mistress."   665. **disliken:** disguise.   667. **eyes over:** spying eyes.   723. **know** F.   *know not* Hanmer.

Shep. Well, let us to the King. There is that in this fardel will make him scratch his beard.

Aut. [*Aside.*] I know not what impediment this complaint may be to the flight of my master.

Clo. Pray heartily he be at palace.   730

Aut. [*Aside.*] Though I am not naturally honest, I am so sometimes by chance. Let me pocket up my pedlar's excrement. [*Takes off his false beard.*] How now, rustics! whither are you bound?   735

Shep. To th' palace, an it like your worship.

Aut. Your affairs there? What, with whom, the condition of that fardel, the place of your dwelling, your names, your ages, of what having, breeding, and anything that is fitting to be known, discover?   741

Clo. We are but plain fellows, sir.

Aut. A lie; you are rough and hairy. Let me have no lying. It becomes none but tradesmen, and they often give us soldiers the lie; but we pay them for it with stamped coin, not stabbing steel; therefore they do not give us the lie.   748

Clo. Your worship had like to have given us one, if you had not taken yourself with the manner.

Shep. Are you a courtier, an't like you, sir?   752

Aut. Whether it like me or no, I am a courtier. Seest thou not the air of the court in these enfoldings? Hath not my gait in it the measure of the court? Receives not thy nose court-odour from me? Reflect I not on thy baseness court-contempt? Think'st thou, for that I insinuate, [or] touse from thee thy business, I am therefore no courtier? I am courtier cap-a-pie, and one that will either   760 push on or pluck back thy business there; whereupon I command thee to open thy affair.

Shep. My business, sir, is to the King.

Aut. What advocate hast thou to him?   765

Shep. I know not, an't like you.

Clo. Advocate's the court-word for a pheasant. Say you have none.

Shep. None, sir; I have no pheasant, cock nor hen.   770

Aut. How bless'd are we that are not simple men!
Yet Nature might have made me as these are,
Therefore I will not disdain.

Clo. This cannot be but a great courtier.

Shep. His garments are rich, but he wears them not handsomely.   776

Clo. He seems to be the more noble in being fantastical. A great man, I'll warrant; I know by the picking on 's teeth.

Aut. The fardel there? What's i' th' fardel?

Wherefore that box?   781

Shep. Sir, there lies such secrets in this fardel and box, which none must know but the King; and which he shall know within this hour, if I may come to th' speech of him.   785

Aut. Age, thou hast lost thy labour.

Shep. Why, sir?

Aut. The King is not at the palace. He is gone aboard a new ship to purge melancholy and air himself; for, if thou be'st capable of things serious, thou must know the King is full of grief.   791

Shep. So 'tis said, sir; about his son, that should have married a shepherd's daughter.

Aut. If that shepherd be not in hand-fast, let him fly. The curses he shall have, the tortures he shall feel, will break the back of man, the heart of monster.

Clo. Think you so, sir?   798

Aut. Not he alone shall suffer what wit can make heavy and vengeance bitter, but those that are germane to him, though remov'd fifty times, shall all come under the hangman; which though it be great pity, yet it is necessary. An old   803 sheep-whistling rogue, a ram-tender, to offer to have his daughter come into grace! Some say he shall be ston'd; but that death is too soft for him, say I. Draw our throne into a sheep-cote! All deaths are too few, the sharpest too easy.

Clo. Has the old man e'er a son, sir, do you hear, an't like you, sir?   810

Aut. He has a son, who shall be flay'd alive; then 'nointed over with honey, set on the head of a wasp's nest; then stand till he be three quarters and a dram dead; then recover'd again with aqua-vitæ or some other hot infusion; then, raw as   815 he is, and in the hottest day prognostication proclaims, shall he be set against a brick-wall, the sun looking with a southward eye upon him, where he is to behold him with flies blown to death. But what talk we of these traitorly rascals,   820 whose miseries are to be smil'd at, their offences being so capital? Tell me, for you seem to be honest plain men, what you have to the King. Being something gently consider'd, I'll bring you where he is aboard, tender your persons to his presence, whisper him in your behalfs; and if it be in man besides the King to effect your suits, here is man shall do it.   828

Clo. He seems to be of great authority. Close with him, give him gold; and though authority be a stubborn bear, yet he is oft led by the nose with gold. Show the inside of your purse to the

---

727. **fardel**: bundle.   733. **excrement**: beard.   739. **having**: property.   751. **with the manner**: in the act.   754. **enfoldings**: garments.   758. **insinuate**: wheedle.   [**or**] F₂.   *at* F₁.   **touse**: tear (*toaze* F₁).   760. **cap-a-pie**: from head to foot.   769. **pheasant**. Judges were sometimes bribed by gifts such as game.   779. **picking...teeth**: the way he picks his teeth.   794. **hand-fast**: custody.   814. **aqua-vitæ**: brandy.   816. **prognostication**: the almanac.   824. **Being...consider'd**: if nobly recompensed.

outside of his hand, and no more ado. Remember "ston'd," and "flay'd alive."   834

Shep. An't please you, sir, to undertake the business for us, here is that gold I have. I'll make it as much more, and leave this young man in pawn till I bring it you.

Aut. After I have done what I promised?

Shep. Ay, sir.   840

Aut. Well, give me the moiety. Are you a party in this business?

Clo. In some sort, sir; but though my case be a pitiful one, I hope I shall not be flay'd out of it.

Aut. O, that's the case of the shepherd's son. Hang him, he'll be made an example.   846

Clo. Comfort, good comfort! We must to the King and show our strange sights. He must know 'tis none of your daughter nor my sister; we are gone else. Sir, I will give you as much as this old man does when the business is performed, and remain, as he says, your pawn till it be brought you.   853

Aut. I will trust you. Walk before toward the sea-side; go on the right hand. I will but look upon the hedge and follow you.

Clo. We are blest in this man, as I may say, even blest.

Shep. Let's before as he bids us. He was provided to do us good.   860

[*Exeunt Shepherd and Clown.*]

Aut. If I had a mind to be honest, I see Fortune would not suffer me; she drops booties in my mouth. I am courted now with a double occasion, gold and a means to do the Prince my master good; which who knows how that may turn back to   865 my advancement? I will bring these two moles, these blind ones, aboard him. If he think it fit to shore them again, and that the complaint they have to the King concerns him nothing, let him call me rogue for being so far officious; for   870 I am proof against that title and what shame else belongs to't. To him will I present them. There may be matter in it.   [*Exit.*   873

ACT V

Scene I. [*Sicilia. A room in Leontes' palace.*]

Enter Leontes, Cleomenes, Dion, Paulina, *and Servants.*

Cleo. Sir, you have done enough, and have perform'd
A saint-like sorrow. No fault could you make
Which you have not redeem'd; indeed, paid down
More penitence than done trespass. At the last

Do as the heavens have done, forget your evil;   5
With them forgive yourself

Leon.   Whilst I remember
Her and her virtues, I cannot forget
My blemishes in them, and so still think of
The wrong I did myself; which was so much
That heirless it hath made my kingdom, and   10
Destroy'd the sweet'st companion that e'er man
Bred his hopes out of.

Paul.   True, too true, my lord.
If, one by one, you wedded all the world,
Or, from the all that are, took something good
To make a perfect woman, she you kill'd   15
Would be unparallel'd.

Leon.   I think so. Kill'd!
She I kill'd! I did so; but thou strik'st me
Sorely, to say I did. It is as bitter
Upon thy tongue as in my thought. Now, good
      now,
Say so but seldom.

Cleo.   Not at all, good lady.   20
You might have spoken a thousand things that
      would
Have done the time more benefit and grac'd
Your kindness better.

Paul.   You are one of those
Would have him wed again.

Dion.   If you would not so,
You pity not the state, nor the remembrance   25
Of his most sovereign name; consider little
What dangers, by his Highness' fail of issue,
May drop upon his kingdom and devour
Incertain lookers on. What were more holy
Than to rejoice the former queen is well?   30
What holier than, for royalty's repair,
For present comfort and for future good,
To bless the bed of majesty again
With a sweet fellow to't?

Paul.   There is none worthy,
Respecting her that's gone. Besides, the gods   35
Will have fulfill'd their secret purposes;
For has not the divine Apollo said,
Is't not the tenour of his oracle,
That King Leontes shall not have an heir
Till his lost child be found? which that it shall,   40
Is all as monstrous to our human reason
As my Antigonus to break his grave
And come again to me; who, on my life,
Did perish with the infant. 'Tis your counsel
My lord should to the heavens be contrary,   45
Oppose against their wills. [*To Leontes.*] Care
      not for issue;
The crown will find an heir. Great Alexander
Left his to th' worthiest; so his successor

---

843. **case:** (1) plight, (2) skin.

Act V, sc. i, 12. True, too true. Theobald. F continues the first *true* to Leontes. 29. **Incertain:** wavering. 35. **Respecting:** compared with.

Was like to be the best.

Leon.   Good Paulina,
Who hast the memory of Hermione,   50
I know, in honour, O, that ever I
Had squar'd me to thy counsel! then, even now,
I might have look'd upon my queen's full eyes,
Have taken treasure from her lips —

Paul.   And left them
More rich for what they yielded.

Leon.   Thou speak'st truth.
No more such wives; therefore, no wife. One
          worse,   56
And better us'd, would make her sainted spirit
Again possess her corpse, and on this stage,
(Where we offenders now appear) soul-vex'd,
Begin, "[And] why to me — ?"

Paul.   Had she such power, 60
She had just cause.

Leon.   She had; and would incense me
To murder her I married.

Paul.   I should so.
Were I the ghost that walk'd, I'd bid you mark
Her eye, and tell me for what dull part in't
You chose her; then I'd shriek, that even your
          ears   65
Should rift to hear me; and the words that follow'd
Should be "Remember mine."

Leon.   Stars, stars,
And all eyes else dead coals! Fear thou no wife;
I'll have no wife, Paulina.

Paul.   Will you swear
Never to marry but by my free leave?   70

Leon. Never, Paulina; so be blest my spirit!

Paul. Then, good my lords, bear witness to his
          oath.

Cleo. You tempt him over-much.

Paul.   Unless another,
As like Hermione as is her picture,   74
Affront his eye.

Cleo.   Good madam, —

Paul.   I have done.
Yet, if my lord will marry, — if you will, sir,
No remedy, but you will, — give me the office
To choose you a queen. She shall not be so
          young
As was your former; but she shall be such
As, walk'd your first queen's ghost, it should take
          joy   80
To see her in your arms.

Leon.   My true Paulina,
We shall not marry till thou bid'st us.

Paul.   That
Shall be when your first queen's again in breath;
Never till then.

Enter a SERVANT.

Serv. One that gives out himself Prince Florizel,
Son of Polixenes, with his princess, she   86
The fairest I have yet beheld, desires access
To your high presence.

Leon.   What with him? He comes not
Like to his father's greatness. His approach,
So out of circumstance and sudden, tells us   90
'Tis not a visitation fram'd, but forc'd
By need and accident. What train?

Serv.   But few,
And those but mean.

Leon.   His princess, say you, with him?

Serv. Ay, the most peerless piece of earth, I
          think,
That e'er the sun shone bright on.

Paul.   O Hermione,
As every present time doth boast itself   96
Above a better gone, so must thy grave
Give way to what's seen now! Sir, you yourself
Have said and writ so, but your writing now   99
Is colder than that theme, "She had not been,
Nor was not to be equall'd;" — thus your verse
Flow'd with her beauty once. 'Tis shrewdly ebb'd,
To say you have seen a better.

Serv.   Pardon, madam:
The one I have almost forgot, — your pardon, —
The other, when she has obtain'd your eye,   105
Will have your tongue too. This is a creature,
Would she begin a sect, might quench the zeal
Of all professors else, make proselytes
Of who she but bid follow.

Paul.   How? Not women!

Serv. Women will love her, that she is a woman
More worth than any man; men, that she is   111
The rarest of all women.

Leon.   Go, Cleomenes;
Yourself, assisted with your honour'd friends,
Bring them to our embracement. Still, 'tis strange
          [*Exeunt* [*Cleomenes and others*].
He thus should steal upon us.

Paul.   Had our prince, 115
Jewel of children, seen this hour, he had pair'd
Well with this lord. There was not full a month
Between their births.

Leon. Prithee, no more; cease. Thou know'st
He dies to me again when talk'd of. Sure,   120
When I shall see this gentleman, thy speeches
Will bring me to consider that which may
Unfurnish me of reason. They are come.

Re-enter CLEOMENES *and others, with* FLORIZEL
          and PERDITA.

Your mother was most true to wedlock, Prince,

---

52. **squar'd**: adjusted.   60. **Begin, [And]** (Capell).   *And begin* F.   **why to me**: i.e., why the insult you put upon me?
66. **rift**: split.   75. **Affront**: confront.   **I have done.** Capell.   F continues to Cleomenes.   91. **fram'd**: planned.   102.
shrewdly: grievously.   108. **professors else**: adherents of other sects.

For she did print your royal father off,   125
Conceiving you. Were I but twenty-one,
Your father's image is so hit in you,
His very air, that I should call you brother,   128
As I did him, and speak of something wildly
By us perform'd before. Most dearly welcome!
And your fair princess, — goddess! — O, alas!
I lost a couple, that 'twixt heaven and earth
Might thus have stood begetting wonder as
You, gracious couple, do; and then I lost —
All mine own folly — the society,   135
Amity too, of your brave father, whom,
Though bearing misery, I desire my life
Once more to look on him.
   Flo.   By his command
Have I here touch'd Sicilia, and from him
Give you all greetings that a king, at friend,
Can send his brother; and, but infirmity   141
Which waits upon worn times hath something seiz'd
His wish'd ability, he had himself
The lands and waters 'twixt your throne and his   144
Measur'd to look upon you; whom he loves —
He bade me say so — more than all the sceptres
And those that bear them living.
   Leon.   O my brother,
Good gentleman! the wrongs I have done thee stir
Afresh within me, and these thy offices,
So rarely kind, are as interpreters   150
Of my behind-hand slackness. Welcome hither,
As is the spring to th' earth. And hath he too
Expos'd this paragon to the fearful usage,
(At least ungentle,) of the dreadful Neptune,
To greet a man not worth her pains, much less   155
Th' adventure of her person?
   Flo.   Good my lord,
She came from Libya.
   Leon.   Where the warlike Smalus,
That noble honour'd lord, is fear'd and lov'd?
   Flo. Most royal sir, from thence; from him, whose
     daughter   159
His tears proclaim'd his, parting with her; thence,
A prosperous south-wind friendly, we have cross'd,
To execute the charge my father gave me
For visiting your Highness. My best train
I have from your Sicilian shores dismiss'd;
Who for Bohemia bend, to signify   165
Not only my success in Libya, sir,
But my arrival and my wife's in safety
Here where we are.
   Leon.   The blessed gods
Purge all infection from our air whilst you
Do climate here! You have a holy father,   170
A graceful gentleman, against whose person,
So sacred as it is, I have done sin;

For which the heavens, taking angry note,
Have left me issueless; and your father's blest,
As he from heaven merits it, with you   175
Worthy his goodness. What might I have been,
Might I a son and daughter now have look'd on,
Such goodly things as you?

       Enter a LORD.

   Lord.   Most noble sir,
That which I shall report will bear no credit,
Were not the proof so nigh. Please you, great sir,
Bohemia greets you from himself by me;   181
Desires you to attach his son, who has —
His dignity and duty both cast off —
Fled from his father, from his hopes, and with   184
A shepherd's daughter.
   Leon.   Where's Bohemia? Speak
   Lord. Here in your city; I now came from him.
I speak amazedly, and it becomes
My marvel and my message. To your court
Whiles he was hast'ning, in the chase, it seems,
Of this fair couple, meets he on the way   190
The father of this seeming lady and
Her brother, having both their country quitted
With this young prince.
   Flo.   Camillo has betray'd me;
Whose honour and whose honesty till now   194
Endur'd all weathers.
   Lord.   Lay 't so to his charge:
He's with the King your father.
   Leon.   Who? Camillo?
   Lord. Camillo, sir; I spake with him; who now
Has these poor men in question. Never saw I
Wretches so quake. They kneel, they kiss the
     earth,
Forswear themselves as often as they speak.   200
Bohemia stops his ears, and threatens them
With divers deaths in death.
   Per.   O my poor father!
The heaven sets spies upon us, will not have
Our contract celebrated.
   Leon.   You are married?
   Flo. We are not, sir, nor are we like to be.   205
The stars, I see, will kiss the valleys first;
The odds for high and low 's alike.
   Leon.   My lord,
Is this the daughter of a king?
   Flo.   She is,
When once she is my wife.
   Leon. That "once," I see by your good father's
     speed,   210
Will come on very slowly. I am sorry,
Most sorry, you have broken from his liking
Where you were tied in duty, and as sorry

---

129. **wildly:** boisterously. 140. **at friend:** in friendship. 142. **worn times:** old age. 149. **offices:** kindnesses. 170. **climate:** stay (in this climate). 182. **attach:** arrest. 187. **amazedly:** confusedly. 188. **marvel:** wonder. 202. **deaths in death:** i.e., tortures. 207. **The ... alike:** i.e., Fortune cheats high and low alike.

Your choice is not so rich in worth as beauty,
That you might well enjoy her.
 Flo.   **Dear, look up.**
Though Fortune, visible an enemy,   216
Should chase us with my father, pow'r no jot
Hath she to change our loves. Beseech you, sir,
Remember since you ow'd no more to time
Than I do now. With thought of such affections,
Step forth mine advocate. At your request 221
My father will grant precious things as trifles.
 Leon. Would he do so, I'd beg your precious mis-
    tress,
Which he counts but a trifle.
 Paul.   **Sir, my liege,**
Your eye hath too much youth in't. Not a month
'Fore your queen died, she was more worth such
   gazes   226
Than what you look on now.
 Leon.   **I thought of her,**
Even in these looks I made. [*To Florizel.*] But
  your petition
Is yet unanswer'd. I will to your father.
Your honour not o'erthrown by your desires, 230
I am friend to them and you; upon which errand
I now go toward him; therefore follow me
And mark what way I make. Come, good my lord.
             [*Exeunt.*

SCENE II. [*Before Leontes' palace.*]

Enter AUTOLYCUS *and a* GENTLEMAN.

 Aut. Beseech you, sir, were you present at this
relation?
 1. Gent. I was by at the opening of the fardel,
heard the old shepherd deliver the manner how he
found it; whereupon, after a little amazedness, we
were all commanded out of the chamber; only this
methought I heard the shepherd say, he found the
child.   8
 Aut. I would most gladly know the issue of it.
 1. Gent. I make a broken delivery of the business;
but the changes I perceived in the King and Camillo
were very notes of admiration. They seem'd almost, with staring on one another, to tear the cases
of their eyes. There was speech in their dumbness,
language in their very gesture; they look'd as 15
they had heard of a world ransom'd, or one destroyed. A notable passion of wonder appeared in
them; but the wisest beholder, that knew no more
but seeing, could not say if th' importance were joy
or sorrow; but in the extremity of the one, it must
needs be.   21

Enter another GENTLEMAN.

Here comes a gentleman that haply knows more.
The news, Rogero?
 2. Gent. Nothing but bonfires. The oracle is
fulfill'd; the King's daughter is found; such a deal
of wonder is broken out within this hour that ballad-
makers cannot be able to express it.   27

Enter a third GENTLEMAN.

Here comes the Lady Paulina's steward: he can 28
deliver you more. How goes it now, sir? This
news which is call'd true is so like an old tale, that
the verity of it is in strong suspicion. Has the
King found his heir?   32
 3. Gent. Most true, if ever truth were pregnant
by circumstance. That which you hear you'll
swear you see, there is such unity in the proofs.
The mantle of Queen Hermione's, her jewel about
the neck of it, the letters of Antigonus found with
it, which they know to be his character, the majesty
of the creature in resemblance of the mother, the
affection of nobleness which nature shows above 40
her breeding, and many other evidences proclaim
her with all certainty to be the King's daughter.
Did you see the meeting of the two kings?
 2. Gent. No.   45
 3. Gent. Then have you lost a sight which was to
be seen, cannot be spoken of. There might you
have beheld one joy crown another, so and in such
manner that it seem'd sorrow wept to take leave of
them, for their joy waded in tears. There was 50
casting up of eyes, holding up of hands, with countenance of such distraction that they were to be
known by garment, not by favour. Our king, being ready to leap out of himself for joy of his found
daughter, as if that joy were now become a loss, 55
cries, "O, thy mother, thy mother!" then asks
Bohemia forgiveness; then embraces his son-in-law;
then again worries he his daughter with clipping
her; now he thanks the old shepherd, which stands
by like a weather-bitten conduit of many kings' 60
reigns. I never heard of such another encounter,
which lames report to follow it and undoes description to do it.
 2. Gent. What, pray you, became of Antigonus,
that carried hence the child?   65
 3. Gent. Like an old tale still, which will have
matter to rehearse, though credit be asleep and not
an ear open. He was torn to pieces with a bear;
this avouches the shepherd's son, who has not only
his innocence, which seems much, to justify him,

---

214. **worth:** rank. 219-20. **since . . . now:** when you were as young as I am.
 Sc. ii, 10. broken delivery: incoherent story. 12. **notes of admiration:** exclamation points. 13. **cases:** sockets. 19.
importance: import. 33. **pregnant by circumstance:** clear from evidence. 38. **character:** handwriting. 40. **affection of:**
inclination to. 51. **countenance:** appearance. 53. **favour:** face. 58. **clipping:** embracing. 60. **weather-bitten conduit:**
weather-beaten fountain (in the form of a statue). 63. **do:** report. 70. **innocence:** simplicity.

but a handkerchief and rings of his that Paulina knows.   72

1. Gent. What became of his bark and his followers?

3. Gent. Wreck'd the same instant of their   75
master's death and in the view of the shepherd; so that all the instruments which aided to expose the child were even then lost when it was found. But O, the noble combat that 'twixt joy and sorrow was fought in Paulina!   She had one eye declin'd   80
for the loss of her husband, another elevated that the oracle was fulfill'd.   She lifted the Princess from the earth, and so locks her in embracing, as if she would pin her to her heart that she might no more be in danger of losing.   85

1. Gent. The dignity of this act was worth the audience of kings and princes; for by such was it acted.

3. Gent. One of the prettiest touches of all, and that which angl'd for mine eyes, caught the   90
water though not the fish, was when, at the relation of the Queen's death, with the manner how she came to't bravely confess'd and lamented by the King, how attentiveness wounded his daughter; till, from one sign of dolour to another, she did with an   95
"Alas," I would fain say, bleed tears, for I am sure my heart wept blood.   Who was most marble there changed colour; some swooned, all sorrowed.   If all the world could have seen 't, the woe had been universal.   100

1. Gent. Are they returned to the court?

3. Gent. No.   The Princess hearing of her mother's statue, which is in the keeping of Paulina, — a piece many years in doing and now newly perform'd by that rare Italian master, Julio Ro-   105
mano, who, had he himself eternity and could put breath into his work, would beguile Nature of her custom, so perfectly he is her ape.   He so near to Hermione hath done Hermione that they say one would speak to her and stand in hope of answer. Thither with all greediness of affection are they gone, and there they intend to sup.   112

2. Gent. I thought she had some great matter there in hand; for she hath privately twice or thrice a day, ever since the death of Hermione, visited that removed house.   Shall we thither and with our company piece the rejoicing?   117

1. Gent. Who would be thence that has the benefit of access?   Every wink of an eye some new grace will be born.   Our absence makes us unthrifty to our knowledge.   Let's along.   121

[Exeunt [Gentlemen].

Aut. Now, had I not the dash of my former life in me, would preferment drop on my head.   I

brought the old man and his son aboard the Prince, told him I heard them talk of a fardel and I   125
know not what; but he at that time, overfond of the shepherd's daughter, so he then took her to be, who began to be much sea-sick, and himself little better, extremity of weather continuing, this mystery remained undiscover'd.   But 'tis all one to me; for had I been the finder out of this secret, it would not have relish'd among my other discredits.   133

Enter SHEPHERD *and* CLOWN.

Here come those I have done good to against my will, and already appearing in the blossoms of their fortune.

Shep. Come, boy; I am past moe children, but thy sons and daughters will be all gentlemen born.   138

Clo. You are well met, sir.   You deni'd to fight with me this other day, because I was no gentleman born.   See you these clothes?   Say you see them not and think me still no gentleman born.   You were best say these robes are not gentlemen born. Give me the lie, do, and try whether I am not now a gentleman born.   145

Aut. I know you are now, sir, a gentleman born.

Clo. Ay, and have been so any time these four hours.   149

Shep. And so have I, boy.

Clo. So you have; but I was a gentleman born before my father.   For the King's son took me by the hand, and call'd me brother; and then the two kings call'd my father brother; and then the Prince my brother and the Princess my sister call'd my father father; and so we wept, and there was the first gentleman-like tears that ever we shed.   156

Shep. We may live, son, to shed many more.

Clo. Ay; or else 'twere hard luck, being in so preposterous estate as we are.   159

Aut. I humbly beseech you, sir, to pardon me all the faults I have committed to your worship, and to give me your good report to the Prince my master.

Shep. Prithee, son, do; for we must be gentle, now we are gentlemen.   165

Clo. Thou wilt amend thy life?

Aut. Ay, an it like your good worship.

Clo. Give me thy hand: I will swear to the Prince thou art as honest a true fellow as any is in Bohemia.   170

Shep. You may say it, but not swear it.

Clo. Not swear it, now I am a gentleman?   Let boors and franklins say it, I'll swear it.

Shep. How if it be false, son?   175

Clo. If it be ne'er so false, a true gentleman may swear it in the behalf of his friend; and I'll swear to

---

94. **attentiveness:** listening.   104. **perform'd:** completed.   105. **Julio Romano:** Italian artist (d. 1546).   107. **beguile:** rob.   108. **custom:** trade.   117. **piece:** increase.   133. **relish'd:** been acceptable.   174. **boors:** peasants.   **franklins:** small landowners.

the Prince thou art a tall fellow of thy hands and
that thou wilt not be drunk; but I know thou art no
tall fellow of thy hands and that thou wilt be drunk;
but I'll swear it, and I would thou wouldst be a tall
fellow of thy hands.   182
  Aut. I will prove so, sir, to my power.
  Clo. Ay, by any means prove a tall fellow. If I
do not wonder how thou dar'st venture to be drunk,
not being a tall fellow, trust me not. Hark! the
kings and the princes, our kindred, are going to see
the Queen's picture. Come, follow us; we'll be thy
good masters.   189
                                        [*Exeunt.*

SCENE III. [*A chapel in Paulina's house.*]

Enter LEONTES, POLIXENES, FLORIZEL, PER-
  DITA, CAMILLO, PAULINA, Lords, *etc.*

  Leon. O grave and good Paulina, the great com-
      fort
That I have had of thee!
  Paul.   What, sovereign sir,
I did not well I meant well. All my services
You have paid home; but that you have vouchsaf'd,
With your crown'd brother and these your con-
      tracted   5
Heirs of your kingdoms, my poor house to visit,
It is a surplus of your grace, which never
My life may last to answer.
  Leon.   O Paulina,
We honour you with trouble. But we came
To see the statue of our queen. Your gallery   10
Have we pass'd through, not without much content
In many singularities; but we saw not
That which my daughter came to look upon,
The statue of her mother.
  Paul.   As she liv'd peerless,
So her dead likeness, I do well believe,   15
Excels whatever yet you look'd upon
Or hand of man hath done; therefore I keep it
Lonely, apart. But here it is. Prepare
To see the life as lively mock'd as ever   19
Still sleep mock'd death. Behold, and say 'tis well.
      [*Paulina draws a curtain, and discovers
        Hermione standing like a statue.*]
I like your silence; it the more shows off
Your wonder; but yet speak. First, you, my liege;
Comes it not something near?
  Leon.   Her natural posture!
Chide me, dear stone, that I may say indeed
Thou art Hermione; or rather, thou art she   25
In thy not chiding, for she was as tender
As infancy and grace. But yet, Paulina,
Hermione was not so much wrinkled, nothing

So aged as this seems.
  Pol.   O, not by much.   29
  Paul. So much the more our carver's excellence,
Which lets go by some sixteen years and makes her
As she liv'd now.
  Leon.   As now she might have done,
So much to my good comfort as it is
Now piercing to my soul. O, thus she stood,
Even with such life of majesty, warm life,   35
As now it coldly stands, when first I woo'd her!
I am asham'd; does not the stone rebuke me
For being more stone than it? O royal piece
There's magic in thy majesty, which has
My evils conjur'd to remembrance, and   40
From thy admiring daughter took the spirits,
Standing like stone with thee.
  Per.   And give me leave,
And do not say 'tis superstition, that
I kneel and then implore her blessing. Lady,
Dear queen, that ended when I but began,   45
Give me that hand of yours to kiss.
  Paul.   O, patience!
The statue is but newly fix'd, the colour's
Not dry.
  Cam. My lord, your sorrow was too sore laid on,
Which sixteen winters cannot blow away,   50
So many summers dry. Scarce any joy
Did ever so long live; no sorrow
But kill'd itself much sooner.
  Pol.   Dear my brother,
Let him that was the cause of this have power
To take off so much grief from you as he   55
Will piece up in himself.
  Paul.   Indeed, my lord,
If I had thought the sight of my poor image
Would thus have wrought you, — for the stone is
      mine —
I'd not have show'd it.
  Leon.   Do not draw the curtain.
  Paul. No longer shall you gaze on't, lest your
      fancy   60
May think anon it moves.
  Leon.   Let be, let be.
Would I were dead but that, methinks, already —
What was he that did make it? See, my lord,
Would you not deem it breath'd, and that those
      veins
Did verily bear blood?
  Pol.   Masterly done!   65
The very life seems warm upon her lip.
  Leon. The fixure of her eye has motion in't,
As we are mock'd with art.
  Paul.   I'll draw the curtain
My lord 's almost so far transported that

---

178. **tall . . . hands:** brave fellow in action.
  Sc. iii, 4. **home:** fully. 12. **singularities:** rarities. 58. **wrought:** moved. 62. **Would . . . already:** i.e., may I die if it is
not beginning to move. 67. **fixure:** fixedness. 68. **As:** as if.

He'll think anon it lives.

Leon.   O sweet Paulina,   70
Make me to think so twenty years together!
No settled senses of the world can match
The pleasure of that madness. Let 't alone.

Paul. I am sorry, sir, I have thus far stirr'd you;
but
I could afflict you farther.

Leon.   Do, Paulina;   75
For this affliction has a taste as sweet
As any cordial comfort. Still, methinks,
There is an air comes from her. What fine chisel
Could ever yet cut breath? Let no man mock me,
For I will kiss her.

Paul.   Good my lord, forbear.   80
The ruddiness upon her lip is wet;
You'll mar it if you kiss it, stain your own
With oily painting. Shall I draw the curtain?

Leon. No, not these twenty years.

Per.   So long could I
Stand by, a looker on.

Paul.   Either forbear,   85
Quit presently the chapel, or resolve you
For more amazement. If you can behold it,
I'll make the statue move indeed, descend
And take you by the hand; but then you'll think —
Which I protest against — I am assisted   90
By wicked powers.

Leon.   What you can make her do,
I am content to look on; what to speak,
I am content to hear; for 'tis as easy
To make her speak as move.

Paul.   It is requir'd
You do awake your faith. Then all stand still;
[Or], those that think it is unlawful business   96
I am about, let them depart.

Leon.   Proceed;
No foot shall stir.

Paul.   Music, awake her; strike!
                                    [*Music.*]
'Tis time; descend; be stone no more; approach.   99
Strike all that look upon with marvel. Come,
I'll fill your grave up. Stir, nay, come away,
Bequeath to death your numbness; for from him
Dear life redeems you. You perceive she stirs.
                          [*Hermione comes down.*]
Start not; her actions shall be holy as
You hear my spell is lawful. Do not shun her
Until you see her die again, for then   106
You kill her double. Nay, present your hand.
When she was young you woo'd her; now in age
Is she become the suitor?

Leon.   O, she's warm!
If this be magic, let it be an art   110
Lawful as eating.

Pol.   She embraces him.

Cam. She hangs about his neck.
If she pertain to life let her speak too.

Pol. Ay, and make 't manifest where she has
    liv'd,
Or how stolen from the dead.

Paul.   That she is living,
Were it but told you, should be hooted at   116
Like an old tale; but it appears she lives,
Though yet she speak not. Mark a little while.
Please you to interpose, fair madam; kneel
And pray your mother's blessing. Turn, good
    lady;   120
Our Perdita is found.

Her.   You gods, look down
And from your sacred vials pour your graces
Upon my daughter's head! Tell me, mine own,
Where hast thou been preserv'd? where liv'd? how
    found
Thy father's court? for thou shalt hear that I,
Knowing by Paulina that th' oracle   126
Gave hope thou wast in being, have preserv'd
Myself to see the issue.

Paul.   There's time enough for that,
Lest they desire upon this push to trouble
Your joys with like relation. Go together,   130
You precious winners all; your exultation
Partake to every one. I, an old turtle,
Will wing me to some wither'd bough and there
My mate, that's never to be found again,
Lament till I am lost.

Leon.   O, peace, Paulina!   135
Thou shouldst a husband take by my consent,
As I by thine a wife; this is a match,
And made between 's by vows. Thou hast found
    mine;
But how, is to be question'd; for I saw her,   139
As I thought, dead, and have in vain said many
A prayer upon her grave. I'll not seek far —
For him, I partly know his mind — to find thee
An honourable husband. Come, Camillo,
And take her by the hand, whose worth and hon-
    esty
Is richly noted and here justified   145
By us, a pair of kings. Let's from this place.
What! look upon my brother. Both your pardons,
That e'er I put between your holy looks
My ill suspicion. This your son-in-law   149
And son unto the King, whom heavens directing,
Is troth-plight to your daughter. Good Paulina,
Lead us from hence, where we may leisurely
Each one demand and answer to his part
Perform'd in this wide gap of time since first
We were dissever'd. Hastily lead away.   155
                                    [*Exeunt.*

96. [Or] (Hanmer). *On* F. 129. upon ... push: under the pressure of these events. 130. relation: narrative. 132. Partake: impart. 145. justified: confirmed. 149. This: i.e., this is.

The Tempest

THE TEMPEST FIRST APPEARED in print as the opening play in the First Folio. It is generally held to be Shakespeare's last independent contribution to the stage, and the suggestion has been made that this distinction, coupled with the established success of the play, led to its eminence in the Folio. It was one of numerous plays performed at Court by Shakespeare's company during the winter of 1612–1613 as part of the wedding festivities of King James's daughter Elizabeth, who was betrothed to Frederick, the Elector Palatine, on December 27, and married on February 14. The play was written, however, somewhat earlier. An entry in the Revels Accounts, relieved by recent scholarship of a long-standing charge of forgery, records a performance of *The Tempest* before the King at Whitehall on Hallowmas Night (November 1) in 1611. Details in the play inspired by accounts of the wreck of Sir George Somers in the Bermudas (1609), about which more will be said, point to a date early in 1611, for no news of Somers's experiences reached England before September, 1610.

It is a reasonable assumption that the received text, a thoroughly good one, presents the drama as it was given on the occasion connected with the royal marriage, and the suggestion that its unusually full stage directions were prepared by Shakespeare himself with special care in anticipation of that performance has welcome plausibility.

For the main thread of the plot no source has been discovered. Resemblances to *Die Schöne Sidea* of Jacob Ayrer of Nuremberg, who died in 1605, are more interesting than significant. In both plays we have a dispossessed prince devoted to magic and driven into exile with a daughter who ultimately marries the son of his enemy; an attendant spirit; and, especially striking, the imposition of log-carrying upon the captive prince, and the fixing of his sword in its scabbard. But there is absolutely no similarity in character, and Ayrer's devil has nothing in common with Ariel, save his function as a supernatural servant. The fixing of the sword is a commonplace of magic, and even the carrying or splitting of logs is found as a task imposed by a magician on a captive prince in folktales having no connection with the present plays. Since English comedians were in Nuremberg in 1604, it is barely possible that Shakespeare learned the plot of Ayrer's play from some actor, but the more credible view is that both dramas may go back to a common origin, which, in all likelihood, was remote.

The origin of certain details can be pointed out with more assurance. Gonzalo's ideal commonwealth (II.i.147 ff.) was inspired by passages in Montaigne's essay "Of the Cannibales," which Shakespeare could have read in Florio's translation (1603). Prospero's abjuration speech (V.i.33–57) shows the influence of Ovid's *Metamorphoses* (VII.192 ff.), which Shakespeare could have known either through Golding's translation (1567), or in the original. The name of Setebos is taken from Richard Eden's *History of Travayle in the West and East Indies* (1577), where it occurs as that of the devil-god of the Patagonian giants, and in the same source are also to be found the names of Alonso, Sebastian, Antonio, Ferdinand, and Gonzalo. The names Prospero and Stephano were given to characters in the first edition of *Every Man in his Humour* (in which Shakespeare himself is reputed to have played a rôle) before Jonson substituted English for Italian ones; and Prospero is to be found also in William Thomas's *Historie of Italye* (1549). Ariel appears in *Isaiah*, and is the name of a prince of spirits in cabalistic literature. Caliban seems to be an anagram for "cannibal." Miranda is evidently a significant coinage, like Marina and Perdita. Finally, Shakespeare's interest in certain events which had but recently excited considerable public attention, is noteworthy.

On June 2, 1609, an expedition of nine ships set sail from Plymouth for the colony at Jamestown, Virginia, founded two years before. On July 25 a terrific storm dispersed the fleet. All the vessels reached Jamestown safely, however, with the exception of the *Sea Adventure*, which, with about one hundred and fifty aboard, including Sir George Somers (the Admiral), Sir Thomas Gates (the new Governor), and Sir Christopher Newport (one of the first founders), was believed lost. When, therefore, some months later (May 23, 1610), they all sailed into Jamestown, the others could hardly believe their eyes. The *Sea Adventure* had been driven south from her course until finally wrecked on the reefs of Bermuda. Not a life had been lost, and after considerable time, during which they made out a fair subsistence on the islands, the party built two small pinnaces in which they effected their own rescue. On June 10, 1610, Gates and Newport sailed back to England and, arriving in September, astonished London with the first news of their preservation.

The lively public interest in these events could be capitalized, and certain members of the *Sea Adventure's* party lent their aid. In October of 1610, Silvester Jourdan, one of the crew, published a pamphlet entitled *A Discovery of the Bermudas, otherwise called the Isle of Divels*. Soon afterwards there followed *A True Declaration of the Colonie in Virginia*, to which William Strachey, another member of the group, may have contributed data. Strachey was the writer of a letter, dated July 15, 1610, which was published only in 1625 in *Purchas his Pilgrimes* under the title, "A true reportory of the wracke, and redemption of Sir Thomas Gates, Knight." There can be no doubt, however, that it had circulated freely in manuscript and that somehow its contents reached Shakespeare. Numerous parallels and echoes in *The Tempest*, especially with reference to the storm, the climate, and the means of livelihood on Prospero's island, make it clear that Shakespeare had read the aforementioned narratives with keen attention, and may, indeed, have supplemented them with details gathered from some of the survivors. Nevertheless, it does not follow that Shakespeare intended to identify Prospero's island with Bermuda.

The Tempest is, with the exception of *The Comedy of Errors*, the shortest play Shakespeare wrote, and it is unique in the canon for its observance of the unity of time. The total action comprises little more than three hours. This compression suited Shakespeare's purpose, but he may still have taken a sly joy in proving to his classical friend, Ben Jonson, what he could do with a rule when he wished. He gave the freest possible rein to imagination, however, and Jonson, as if in retort, jovially slapped both *The Tempest* and *The Winter's Tale* in the Induction to his *Bartholomew Fair* (acted at Court, November 1, 1614): "If there bee never a *Seruant-monster* i' the Fayre; who can helpe it? he [Jonson] sayes; nor a nest of *Antiques*? Hee is loth to make Nature afraid in his *Playes*, like those that beget *Tales, Tempests*, and such like *Drolleries*."

The Tempest presents a comprehensive kind of entertainment: idyllic romance in the love of Ferdinand and Miranda, set against the background of Prospero's wrongs, of which, through his "rarer action" preferring virtue to vengeance, it is the benign outcome; realistic intrigue in the designs of Sebastian and Antonio upon Alonso, to which the conspiracy of Caliban and his confederates against Prospero is a kind of comic counterpart; excellent fooling in the trio of Caliban, Stephano, and Trinculo; overseeing wisdom and charity in Prospero, the master of the revels. For Prospero is master. It is clear from the beginning that the destinies of all, including his own, are in his hands, and we never doubt his providential guidance.

The harmony in which the heterogeneous elements of the play are blended, and the delicate poise maintained throughout between the illusions of fancy and reality, are miraculous. We surrender to the play as to a fairy tale of perennial charm, yet we do not entirely forget the world we live in.

Ariel, blithely serving out his time to win again his elemental freedom, enthralls the imagination, like the fairies of *A Midsummer Night's Dream*, to whom aesthetically he is kin. He has their vitality and their poetry, but while they make their own sport with foolish mortals, he performs the will of a human master.

If Ariel charms the imagination, Caliban, his gross opposite, teases it. The offspring of the Devil and a witch Sycorax, Caliban is a native of Prospero's island. His physique, kept by Shakespeare purposely indeterminate, it is impossible to visualize. Though he is "not honoured with a human shape," appears, in fact, to be "a strange fish," he is "legged like a man, and his fins [are] like arms" (II.ii.35); he has long nails and he can carry wood. That is about all that one can say. Prospero once calls him "tortoise" (I.ii.316), but this alludes to his sloth. Prospero has made him a slave, and he feels a peculiar hatred for this master, who has dispossessed him. There is a touch of pathos in Caliban's protesting claim to his island (I.ii.331–44). But his baser instincts have been his real enemy, for Prospero was fond of him at first and attempted to educate him (I.ii.353–65) with disappointing results. It would be interesting to know how much of Shakespeare's considered thought on the subject of the savage is reflected here. Indeed, when one recalls the fresh English interest in colonization and the reflections in *The Tempest* of the Virginia enterprise, it is tempting to see manifold problems adumbrated in the play: the relations of colonists with native populations, the question of government, the question of slavery, the missionary question, and so on. But all such speculation is perilous and can be indulged only with reserve and with a sense of humor to fall back upon. In a last word about Caliban it may be remarked that in his repudiation of his folly he is almost heroic (V.i.295–97).

Take it how one will, *The Tempest* remains an infinitely suggestive play, and not the least of its intimations concern the dramatist himself. Without resort to allegorical interpretation, of which there has been much, one may yet assert that Shakespeare's ripest thoughts upon life inform certain of the speeches of Prospero. The best known lines of the play (IV.i.148–58) constitute one of the most beautiful expressions in the language of the evanescence of earthly things. The words in which Prospero commends reason and virtue (V.i.25–30) express the goal of human wisdom. And when one reads Prospero's eloquent speech of abdication of his art (V.i.32–57), the notion that in penning it Shakespeare must have felt the analogy with the closing of his own career is too potent to be denied.

THE TEMPEST

[DRAMATIS PERSONÆ]

ALONSO, *king of Naples.*
SEBASTIAN, *his brother.*
PROSPERO, *the right duke of Milan.*
ANTONIO, *his brother, the usurping duke of Milan.*
FERDINAND, *son to the king of Naples.*
GONZALO, *an honest old Counsellor.*
ADRIAN, } *Lords.*
FRANCISCO, }
CALIBAN, *a savage and deformed Slave.*
TRINCULO, *a Jester.*

STEPHANO, *a drunken Butler.*
Master of a Ship.
Boatswain.
Mariners.
MIRANDA, *daughter to Prospero.*
ARIEL, *an airy Spirit.*
IRIS,
CERES,
JUNO, } *Spirits.*
Nymphs,
Reapers,

[Other Spirits attending on Prospero.]

SCENE: [*A ship at sea;*] *an uninhabited island.*

ACT I

SCENE I. [*On a ship at sea:*] *a tempestuous noise of thunder and lightning heard.*

Enter a SHIP-MASTER *and a* BOATSWAIN.

Mast. Boatswain!
Boats. Here, master; what cheer?
Mast. Good; speak to th' mariners. Fall to't, yarely, or we run ourselves aground. Bestir, bestir. [*Exit.* 5

Enter MARINERS.

Boats. Heigh, my hearts! cheerly, cheerly, my hearts! yare, yare! Take in the topsail. Tend to the master's whistle. — Blow till thou burst thy wind, if room enough!

Enter ALONSO, SEBASTIAN, ANTONIO, FERDINAND, GONZALO, *and others.*

Alon. Good boatswain, have care. Where's the master? Play the men. 11
Boats. I pray now, keep below.
Ant. Where is the master, bos'n?

Boats. Do you not hear him? You mar our labour. Keep your cabins; you do assist the storm.
Gon. Nay, good, be patient. 16
Boats. When the sea is. Hence! What cares these roarers for the name of king? To cabin! silence! trouble us not.
Gon. Good, yet remember whom thou hast aboard. 21
Boats. None that I more love than myself. You are a counsellor; if you can command these elements to silence, and work the peace of the present, we will not hand a rope more; use your authority. If you cannot, give thanks you have liv'd so long, and make yourself ready in your cabin for the mischance of the hour, if it so hap. — Cheerly, good hearts! — Out of our way, I say. [*Exit.* 29
Gon. I have great comfort from this fellow. Methinks he hath no drowning mark upon him; his complexion is perfect gallows. Stand fast, good Fate, to his hanging; make the rope of his destiny our cable, for our own doth little advantage. If he be not born to be hang'd, our case is miserable. [*Exeunt.* 36

Act I, sc. i, 4. **yarely:** nimbly. 16. **good:** i.e., good friend. 32. **his ... gallows:** his look shows he was born for hanging. **34. advantage:** help (us).

Re-enter BOATSWAIN.

Boats. Down with the topmast! yare! lower, lower! Bring her to try wi' th' main-course. A plague   (*A cry within.*)

Re-enter SEBASTIAN, ANTONIO, *and* GONZALO.

upon this howling! They are louder than the weather or our office. — Yet again! What do   40
you here? Shall we give o'er and drown? Have you a mind to sink?

Seb. A pox o' your throat, you bawling, blasphemous, incharitable dog!

Boats. Work you, then.   45

Ant. Hang, cur! hang, you whoreson, insolent noisemaker! We are less afraid to be drown'd than thou art.

Gon. I'll warrant him for drowning though the ship were no stronger than a nut-shell and as leaky as an unstanched wench.   51

Boats. Lay her a-hold, a-hold! Set her two courses off to sea again! Lay her off.

Enter MARINERS *wet.*

Mariners. All lost! To prayers, to prayers! All lost!   55

Boats. What, must our mouths be cold?

Gon. The King and Prince at prayers! Let's assist them,
For our case is as theirs.

Seb.   I'm out of patience.

Ant. We are merely cheated of our lives by drunkards.
This wide-chopp'd rascal — would thou mightst lie
    drowning   60
The washing of ten tides!

Gon.   He'll be hang'd yet,
Though every drop of water swear against it
And gape at wid'st to glut him.
                                    [*A confused noise within.*
                                    Mercy on us!
We split, we split! Farewell, my wife and chil-
    dren!   65
Farewell, brother! We split, we split, we split!

Ant. Let's all sink wi' th' King.

Seb. Let's take leave of him.
                                          [*Exit.*

Gon. Now would I give a thousand furlongs of sea for an acre of barren ground, long heath, brown [furze], anything. The wills above be done! but I would fain die a dry death.   72
                                          [*Exeunt.*

SCENE II. [*The island. Before Prospero's cell.*]

Enter PROSPERO *and* MIRANDA.

Mir. If by your art, my dearest father, you have
Put the wild waters in this roar, allay them.
The sky, it seems, would pour down stinking pitch,
But that the sea, mounting to th' welkin's cheek,
Dashes the fire out. O, I have suffer'd   5
With those that I saw suffer! A brave vessel,
Who had, no doubt, some noble creature in her,
Dash'd all to pieces! O, the cry did knock
Against my very heart. Poor souls, they perish'd.
Had I been any god of power, I would   10
Have sunk the sea within the earth or ere
It should the good ship so have swallow'd and
The fraughting souls within her.

Pros.   Be collected;
No more amazement. Tell your piteous heart
There's no harm done.

Mir.   O, woe the day!

Pros.   No harm.
I have done nothing but in care of thee,   16
Of thee, my dear one, thee, my daughter, who
Art ignorant of what thou art, nought knowing
Of whence I am, nor that I am more better
Than Prospero, master of a full poor cell,   20
And thy no greater father.

Mir.   More to know
Did never meddle with my thoughts.

Pros.   'Tis time
I should inform thee farther. Lend thy hand,
And pluck my magic garment from me. So,
                                    [*Lays down his mantle.*
Lie there, my art. Wipe thou thine eyes; have
    comfort.   25
The direful spectacle of the wreck, which touch'd
The very virtue of compassion in thee,
I have with such provision in mine art
So safely ordered that there is no soul —
No, not so much perdition as an hair   30
Betid to any creature in the vessel
Which thou heard'st cry, which thou saw'st sink.
    Sit down;
For thou must now know farther.

Mir.   You have often
Begun to tell me what I am, but stopp'd
And left me to a bootless inquisition,   35
Concluding, "Stay, not yet."

Pros.   The hour's now come;
The very minute bids thee ope thine ear.
Obey and be attentive. Canst thou remember
A time before we came unto this cell?

---

38. **Bring . . . try:** sail her near to the wind. **main-course:** mainsail. 49. **for:** against. 52. **a-hold:** close to the wind.
53. **courses:** points of the compass. **off:** i.e., away from shore. 59. **merely:** absolutely. 60. **wide-chopp'd:** wide-jawed.
63. **glut:** swallow. 71. **[furze]** (Hanmer). *firrs* F.
  Sc. ii, 4. **welkin's:** sky's. 6. **brave:** fine, gallant. 13. **fraughting:** making the cargo. 14. **amazement:** terror. **piteous:**
pitying. 22. **meddle:** mingle. 28. **provision:** foresight. 35. **bootless inquisition:** useless inquiry.

I do not think thou canst, for then thou wast not   40
Out three years old.
  Mir.   Certainly, sir, I can.
  Pros. By what? By any other house or person?
Of anything the image tell me, that
Hath kept with thy remembrance.
  Mir.   'Tis far off
And rather like a dream than an assurance   45
That my remembrance warrants. Had I not
Four or five women once that tended me?
  Pros. Thou hadst, and more, Miranda. But
   how is it
That this lives in thy mind? What seest thou else
In the dark backward and abysm of time?   50
If thou rememb'rest aught ere thou cam'st here,
How thou cam'st here thou may'st.
  Mir.   But that I do not.
  Pros. Twelve year since, Miranda, twelve year
   since,
Thy father was the Duke of Milan and   54
A prince of power.
  Mir.   Sir, are not you my father?
  Pros. Thy mother was a piece of virtue, and
She said thou wast my daughter; and thy father
Was Duke of Milan, and his only heir
And princess no worse issued.
  Mir.   O the heavens!
What foul play had we, that we came from thence?
Or blessed was 't we did?
  Pros.   Both, both, my girl.   61
By foul play, as thou say'st, were we heav'd thence,
But blessedly holp hither.
  Mir.   O, my heart bleeds
To think o' th' teen that I have turn'd you to,
Which is from my remembrance! Please you, far-
   ther.   65
  Pros. My brother and thy uncle, call'd Antonio —
I pray thee, mark me — that a brother should
Be so perfidious! — he whom next thyself
Of all the world I lov'd, and to him put
The manage of my state; as at that time   70
Through all the signories it was the first,
And Prospero the prime duke, being so reputed
In dignity, and for the liberal arts
Without a parallel; those being all my study,
The government I cast upon my brother   75
And to my state grew stranger, being transported
And rapt in secret studies. Thy false uncle —
Dost thou attend me?
  Mir.   Sir, most heedfully.
  Pros. Being once perfected how to grant suits,
How to deny them, who t' advance and who   80

To trash for overtopping, new created
The creatures that were mine, I say, or chang'd 'em,
Or else new form'd 'em; having both the key
Of officer and office, set all hearts i' th' state
To what tune pleas'd his ear; that now he was   85
The ivy which had hid my princely trunk,
And suck'd my verdure out on 't. Thou attend'st
  not.
  Mir. O, good sir, I do.
  Pros.   I pray thee, mark me.
I, thus neglecting worldly ends, all dedicated
To closeness and the bettering of my mind   90
With that which, but by being so retir'd,
O'er-priz'd all popular rate, in my false brother
Awak'd an evil nature; and my trust,
Like a good parent, did beget of him
A falsehood, in its contrary as great   95
As my trust was; which had indeed no limit,
A confidence sans bound. He being thus lorded,
Not only with what my revenue yielded,
But what my power might else exact, — like one
Who having into truth, by telling of it,   100
Made such a sinner of his memory
To credit his own lie, — he did believe
He was indeed the Duke. Out o' th' substitution,
And executing the outward face of royalty,   104
With all prerogative, hence his ambition growing —
Dost thou hear?
  Mir.   Your tale, sir, would cure deafness.
  Pros. To have no screen between this part he
   play'd
And him he play'd it for, he needs will be
Absolute Milan. Me, poor man! — my library
Was dukedom large enough — of temporal royal-
  ties   110
He thinks me now incapable; confederates —
So dry he was for sway — wi' th' King of Naples
To give him annual tribute, do him homage,
Subject his coronet to his crown, and bend
The dukedom yet unbow'd — alas, poor Milan! —
To most ignoble stooping.
  Mir.   O the heavens!   116
  Pros. Mark his condition and th' event, then tell
   me
If this might be a brother.
  Mir.   I should sin
To think but nobly of my grandmother.
Good wombs have borne bad sons.
  Pros.   Now the condition.
This King of Naples, being an enemy   121
To me inveterate, hearkens my brother's suit;
Which was, that he, in lieu o' th' premises,

---

41. **Out:** fully. 56. **piece:** masterpiece. 59. **issued:** born. 64. **teen:** trouble, grief. 79. **perfected:** expert.
81. **trash...overtopping:** check for going too far ahead (hunting term). 83. **key:** (1) key to office, (2) tuning key.
90. **closeness:** seclusion. 92. **rate:** estimation. 97. **sans:** without. 100–102. **Who...lie:** who, having told a lie so often,
came to believe it true. 107. **screen:** distinction. 108. **him...for:** i.e., himself. 109. **Absolute Milan:** the actual Duke.
112. **dry:** thirsty. 117. **condition:** compact. **event:** outcome. 123. **lieu...premises:** return for the stipulations.

Of homage, and I know not how much tribute,
Should presently extirpate me and mine   125
Out of the dukedom, and confer fair Milan
With all the honours on my brother; whereon,
A treacherous army levied, one midnight
Fated to th' purpose did Antonio open   129
The gates of Milan; and, i' th' dead of darkness,
The ministers for th' purpose hurried thence
Me and thy crying self.

Mir.   Alack, for pity!
I, not rememb'ring how I cried out then,
Will cry it o'er again.   It is a hint   134
That wrings mine eyes to't.

Pros.   Hear a little further,
And then I'll bring thee to the present business
Which now's upon 's, without the which this story
Were most impertinent.

Mir.   Wherefore did they not
That hour destroy us?

Pros.   Well demanded, wench;
My tale provokes that question.   Dear, they durst
    not   140
(So dear the love my people bore me) set
A mark so bloody on the business; but
With colours fairer painted their foul ends.
In few, they hurried us aboard a bark,
Bore us some leagues to sea; where they prepared
A rotten carcass of a butt, not rigg'd,   146
Nor tackle, sail, nor mast; the very rats
Instinctively have quit it.   There they hoist us,
To cry to th' sea that roar'd to us, to sigh
To th' winds whose pity, sighing back again,   150
Did us but loving wrong.

Mir.   Alack, what trouble
Was I then to you!

Pros.   O, a cherubin
Thou wast that did preserve me.   Thou didst smile,
Infused with a fortitude from heaven,   154
When I have deck'd the sea with drops full salt,
Under my burden groan'd; which rais'd in me
An undergoing stomach, to bear up
Against what should ensue.

Mir.   How came we ashore?

Pros.   By Providence divine.
Some food we had and some fresh water that   160
A noble Neapolitan, Gonzalo,
Out of his charity, who being then appointed
Master of this design, did give us, with
Rich garments, linens, stuffs, and necessaries,
Which since have steaded much; so, of his gentle-
    ness,   165
Knowing I lov'd my books, he furnish'd me
From mine own library with volumes that

I prize above my dukedom.

Mir.   Would I might
But ever see that man!

Pros.   Now I arise.
                                        [*Puts on his robe.*]
Sit still, and hear the last of our sea-sorrow.   170
Here in this island we arriv'd; and here
Have I, thy schoolmaster, made thee more profit
Than other princess can that have more time
For vainer hours and tutors not so careful.

Mir.   Heavens thank you for't!   And now, I
    pray you, sir,   175
For still 'tis beating in my mind, your reason
For raising this sea-storm?

Pros.   Know thus far forth.
By accident most strange, bountiful Fortune,
Now my dear lady, hath mine enemies
Brought to this shore; and by my prescience   180
I find my zenith doth depend upon
A most auspicious star, whose influence
If now I court not but omit, my fortunes
Will ever after droop.   Here cease more questions.
Thou art inclin'd to sleep; 'tis a good dulness,   185
And give it way.   I know thou canst not choose.
                                        [*Miranda sleeps.*]
Come away, servant, come; I am ready now.
Approach, my Ariel; come.

Enter ARIEL.

Ari.   All hail, great master! grave sir, hail! I come
To answer thy best pleasure, be't to fly,   190
To swim, to dive into the fire, to ride
On the curl'd clouds.   To thy strong bidding task
Ariel and all his quality.

Pros.   Hast thou, spirit,
Perform'd to point the tempest that I bade thee.

Ari.   To every article.   195
I boarded the king's ship; now on the beak,
Now in the waist, the deck, in every cabin,
I flam'd amazement.   Sometime I'd divide,
And burn in many places.   On the topmast,
The yards and bowsprit, would I flame distinctly,
Then meet and join.   Jove's lightnings, the pre-
    cursors   201
O' th' dreadful thunder-claps, more momentary
And sight-outrunning were not; the fire and cracks
Of sulphurous roaring the most mighty Neptune
Seem to besiege, and make his bold waves tremble,
Yea, his dread trident shake.

Pros.   My brave spirit!
Who was so firm, so constant, that this coil   207
Would not infect his reason?

Ari.   Not a soul

---

134. **hint:** occasion.   141. **set** (Wright conj.).   *nor set* F.   144. **few:** short.   146. **butt:** tub.   155. **deck'd:** sprinkled.   157. **undergoing stomach:** courage to undergo.   165. **steaded:** helped.   173. **princess:** i.e., princesses.   Rowe reads *princes.*   181. **zenith:** height of fortune.   183. **omit:** ignore.   193. **quality:** (1) skill, (2) profession (i.e., fellow spirits).   194. **to point:** in every detail.   207. **coil:** turmoil.

But felt a fever of the mad, and play'd
Some tricks of desperation.   All but mariners   210
Plung'd in the foaming brine and quit the vessel,
Then all afire with me.   The King's son, Fer-
    dinand,
With hair up-staring, — then like reeds, not hair, —
Was the first man that leap'd; cried, "Hell is
    empty,   214
And all the devils are here."
    Pros.   Why, that's my spirit!
But was not this nigh shore?
    Ari.   Close by, my master.
    Pros. But are they, Ariel, safe?
    Ari.   Not a hair perish'd;
On their sustaining garments not a blemish,
But fresher than before; and, as thou bad'st me,
In troops I have dispers'd them 'bout the isle.   220
The King's son have I landed by himself,
Whom I left cooling of the air with sighs
In an odd angle of the isle, and sitting,
His arms in this sad knot.
    Pros.   Of the King's ship
The mariners say how thou hast dispos'd,   225
And all the rest o' th' fleet.
    Ari.   Safely in harbour
Is the King's ship; in the deep nook, where once
Thou call'dst me up at midnight to fetch dew
From the still-vex'd Bermoothes, there she's hid;
The mariners all under hatches stow'd,   230
Who, with a charm join'd to their suff'red labour,
I have left asleep; and for the rest o' th' fleet,
Which I dispers'd, they all have met again
And are upon the Mediterranean float
Bound sadly home for Naples,   235
Supposing that they saw the King's ship wreck'd
And his great person perish.
    Pros.   Ariel, thy charge
Exactly is perform'd; but there's more work.
What is the time o' th' day?
    Ari.   Past the mid season.
    Pros. At least two glasses.   The time 'twixt six
    and now   240
Must by us both be spent most preciously.
    Ari. Is there more toil?   Since thou dost give me
    pains,
Let me remember thee what thou hast promis'd,
Which is not yet perform'd me.
    Pros.   How now? moody?
What is't thou canst demand?
    Ari.   My liberty.   245
    Pros. Before the time be out?   No more!
    Ari.   I prithee,
Remember I have done thee worthy service,
Told thee no lies, made thee no mistakings, serv'd

Without or grudge or grumblings.   Thou did
    promise
To bate me a full year.
    Pros.   Dost thou forget   250
From what a torment I did free thee?
    Ari.   No.
    Pros. Thou dost, and think'st it much to tread
    the ooze
Of the salt deep,
To run upon the sharp wind of the north,
To do me business in the veins o' th' earth   255
When it is bak'd with frost.
    Ari.   I do not, sir.
    Pros. Thou liest, malignant thing!   Hast thou
    forgot
The foul witch Sycorax, who with age and envy
Was grown into a hoop?   Hast thou forgot her?
    Ari. No, sir.
    Pros.   Thou hast.   Where was she born?
    Speak; tell me.   260
    Ari. Sir, in Argier.
    Pros.   O, was she so?   I must
Once in a month recount what thou hast been,
Which thou forget'st.   This damn'd witch Sycorax,
For mischiefs manifold and sorceries terrible
To enter human hearing, from Argier,   265
Thou know'st, was banish'd; for one thing she did
They would not take her life.   Is not this true?
    Ari. Ay, sir.
    Pros. This blue-ey'd hag was hither brought with
    child,
And here was left by th' sailors.   Thou, my slave,
As thou report'st thyself, was then her servant; 271
And, for thou wast a spirit too delicate
To act her earthly and abhorr'd commands,
Refusing her grand hests, she did confine thee,
By help of her more potent ministers   275
And in her most unmitigable rage,
Into a cloven pine; within which rift
Imprison'd thou didst painfully remain
A dozen years; within which space she died
And left thee there, where thou didst vent thy
    groans   280
As fast as mill-wheels strike.   Then was this
    island —
Save for the son that [she] did litter here,
A freckl'd whelp, hag-born, — not honour'd with
A human shape.
    Ari.   Yes, Caliban her son.
    Pros. Dull thing, I say so; he, that Caliban   285
Whom now I keep in service.   Thou best know'st
What torment I did find thee in; thy groans
Did make wolves howl, and penetrate the breasts
Of ever-angry bears.   It was a torment

---

218. **sustaining:** supporting.   229. **still-vex'd Bermoothes:** ever-stormy Bermudas.   234. **float:** sea.   240. **glasses:** hour-glasses.   242. **pains:** labor.   250. **bate:** remit.   258. **envy:** malice.   261. **Argier:** Algiers.   269. **blue-ey'd:** with dark circles round the eyes; frequently emended to *blear-eyed*.   274. **hests:** commands.   282. **[she]** (Dryden).   *he* F.

To lay upon the damn'd, which Sycorax   290
Could not again undo. It was mine art,
When I arriv'd and heard thee, that made gape
The pine, and let thee out.
   Ari.   I thank thee, master.
   Pros. If thou more murmur'st, I will rend an oak
And peg thee in his knotty entrails till   295
Thou hast howl'd away twelve winters.
   Ari.   Pardon, master;
I will be correspondent to command
And do my spriting gently.
   Pros.   Do so, and after two days
I will discharge thee.
   Ari.   That's my noble master!
What shall I do? say what. What shall I do?   300
   Pros. Go make thyself like a nymph o' th' sea;
      be subject
To no sight but thine and mine, invisible
To every eyeball else. Go take this shape
And hither come in't. Go, hence with diligence!
                         [*Exit Ariel.*
Awake, dear heart, awake! Thou hast slept well;
Awake!   306
   Mir. The strangeness of your story put
Heaviness in me.
   Pros.   Shake it off. Come on;
We'll visit Caliban my slave, who never
Yields us kind answer.
   Mir.   'Tis a villain, sir,
I do not love to look on.
   Pros.   But, as 'tis,   310
We cannot miss him. He does make our fire,
Fetch in our wood, and serves in offices
That profit us. What, ho! slave! Caliban!
Thou earth, thou! speak.
   Cal. (*Within.*) There's wood enough within.
   Pros. Come forth, I say! there's other business
      for thee.   315
Come, thou tortoise! when?

     Re-enter ARIEL *like a water-nymph.*

Fine apparition! My quaint Ariel,
Hark in thine ear.
   Ari.   My lord, it shall be done.
                           [*Exit.*
   Pros. Thou poisonous slave, got by the devil
      himself
Upon thy wicked dam, come forth!   320

        Enter CALIBAN.

   Cal. As wicked dew as e'er my mother brush'd
With raven's feather from unwholesome fen
Drop on you both! A south-west blow on ye
And blister you all o'er!

   Pros. For this, be sure, to-night thou shalt have
      cramps,   325
Side-stitches that shall pen thy breath up; urchins
Shall, for that vast of night that they may work,
All exercise on thee; thou shalt be pinch'd
As thick as honeycomb, each pinch more stinging
Than bees that made 'em.
   Cal.   I must eat my dinner.
This island's mine, by Sycorax my mother,   331
Which thou tak'st from me. When thou cam'st first,
Thou [strok'dst] me and made much of me, wouldst
      give me
Water with berries in't, and teach me how
To name the bigger light, and how the less,   335
That burn by day and night; and then I lov'd thee
And show'd thee all the qualities o' th' isle,
The fresh springs, brine-pits, barren place and
      fertile.
Curs'd be I that did so! All the charms
Of Sycorax, toads, beetles, bats, light on you!
For I am all the subjects that you have,   341
Which first was mine own king; and here you sty
      me
In this hard rock, whiles you do keep from me
The rest o' th' island.
   Pros.   Thou most lying slave,
Whom stripes may move, not kindness! I have
      us'd thee,   345
Filth as thou art, with human care, and lodg'd thee
In mine own cell, till thou didst seek to violate
The honour of my child.
   Cal. O ho, O ho! would 't had been done!
Thou didst prevent me; I had peopl'd else   350
This isle with Calibans.
   [*Pros.*]   Abhorred slave,
Which any print of goodness wilt not take,
Being capable of all ill! I pitied thee,
Took pains to make thee speak, taught thee each
      hour   354
One thing or other. When thou didst not, savage,
Know thine own meaning, but wouldst gabble like
A thing most brutish, I endow'd thy purposes
With words that made them known. But thy vile
      race,
Though thou didst learn, had that in't which good
      natures
Could not abide to be with; therefore wast thou
Deservedly confin'd into this rock,   361
Who hadst deserv'd more than a prison.
   Cal. You taught me language; and my profit
      on't
Is, I know how to curse. The red plague rid you
For learning me your language!
   Pros.   Hag-seed, hence!

---

297. **correspondent:** obedient. 311. **miss:** do without. 317. **quaint:** dainty. 326. **urchins:** goblins (lit., hedgehogs).
327. **vast:** dark void. 333. **[strok'dst]** (Rowe). *stroakst* F. 351. **[*Pros.*]** (Dryden). *Mira.* F. 358. **race:** inherited nature.
364. **rid:** destroy.

Fetch us in fuel; and be quick, thou 'rt best,   366
To answer other business.   Shrug'st thou, malice?
If thou neglect'st or dost unwillingly
What I command, I'll rack thee with old cramps,
Fill all thy bones with achës, make thee roar   370
That beasts shall tremble at thy din.
Cal.   No, pray thee.
[*Aside.*] I must obey.   His art is of such power
It would control my dam's god, Setebos,
And make a vassal of him.
Pros.   So, slave; hence!   375
                                     [*Exit Caliban.*

Re-enter ARIEL, *invisible, playing and singing;*
          FERDINAND [*following*].

ARIEL'S SONG.

Come unto these yellow sands,
     And then take hands.
Curtsied when you have, and kiss'd
     The wild waves whist,
Foot it featly here and there,   380
And, sweet sprites, the burden bear.
Burden (*dispersedly*). Hark, hark!
                              Bow-wow.
     The watch-dogs bark!
                              Bow-wow.
Ari. Hark, hark! I hear
     The strain of strutting chanticleer   385
     Cry, "Cock-a-diddle-dow."

Fer. Where should this music be?   I' th' air or
     th' earth?
It sounds no more; and, sure, it waits upon
Some god o' th' island.   Sitting on a bank,
Weeping again the King my father's wreck,   390
This music crept by me upon the waters,
Allaying both their fury and my passion
With its sweet air; thence I have follow'd it,
Or it hath drawn me rather.   But 'tis gone.
No, it begins again.   395

ARIEL'S SONG.

Full fathom five thy father lies;
     Of his bones are coral made;
Those are pearls that were his eyes:
     Nothing of him that doth fade
But doth suffer a sea-change   400
Into something rich and strange.
Sea-nymphs hourly ring his knell:
Burden.   Ding-dong.
Ari. Hark! now I hear them, — ding-dong, bell.
Fer. The ditty does remember my drown'd
     father.   405

This is no mortal business, nor no sound
That the earth owes.   I hear it now above me.
Pros. The fringed curtains of thine eye advance
And say what thou seest yond.
Mir.   What is 't?   A spirit?
Lord, how it looks about!   Believe me, sir,   410
It carries a brave form.   But 'tis a spirit.
Pros. No, wench; it eats and sleeps and hath such
     senses
As we have, such.   This gallant which thou seest
Was in the wreck; and, but he's something stain'd
With grief, that's beauty's canker, thou mightst
     call him   415
A goodly person.   He hath lost his fellows
And strays about to find 'em.
Mir.   I might call him
A thing divine; for nothing natural
I ever saw so noble.
Pros. [*Aside.*] It goes on, I see,
As my soul prompts it.   Spirit, fine spirit!   I'll free
     thee   420
Within two days for this.
Fer.   Most sure, the goddess
On whom these airs attend!   Vouchsafe my prayer
May know if you remain upon this island,
And that you will some good instruction give
How I may bear me here.   My prime request,   425
Which I do last pronounce, is, O you wonder!
If you be maid or no?
Mir.   No wonder, sir,
But certainly a maid.
Fer.   My language! heavens!
I am the best of them that speak this speech,   429
Were I but where 'tis spoken.
Pros.   How? the best?
What wert thou, if the King of Naples heard thee?
Fer. A single thing, as I am now, that wonders
To hear thee speak of Naples.   He does hear me;
And that he does I weep.   Myself am Naples,
Who with mine eyes, never since at ebb, beheld   435
The King my father wreck'd.
Mir.   Alack, for mercy!
Fer. Yes, faith, and all his lords; the Duke of
     Milan
And his brave son being twain.
Pros.   [*Aside.*] The Duke of Milan
And his more braver daughter could control thee,
If now 'twere fit to do 't.   At the first sight   440
They have chang'd eyes.   Delicate Ariel,
I'll set thee free for this.   [*To Fer.*] A word, good
     sir;
I fear you have done yourself some wrong; a word.
Mir. Why speaks my father so ungently?   This

---

370. **achës.** Pronounced "aitches."   379. **whist:** (being) silent.   380. **featly:** nimbly.   381. **the burden bear** Q 1674.
beare the burthen F.   382. s.d. **Burden:** refrain.   **dispersedly:** from several directions.   405. **remember:** commemorate.
407. **owes:** owns.   408. **advance:** raise.   415. **canker:** canker-worm.   432. **single:** solitary, helpless.   439. **control:** confute.
441. **chang'd eyes:** exchanged loving glances.

Is the third man that e'er I saw, the first   445
That e'er I sigh'd for.   Pity move my father
To be inclin'd my way!
    Fer.   O, if a virgin,
And your affection not gone forth, I'll make you
The Queen of Naples.
    Pros.   Soft, sir! one word more.
[*Aside.*] They are both in either's powers; but this
    swift business   450
I must uneasy make, lest too light winning
Make the prize light.   [*To Fer.*] One word more; I
    charge thee
That thou attend me.   Thou dost here usurp
The name thou ow'st not; and hast put thyself
Upon this island as a spy, to win it   455
From me, the lord on't.
    Fer.   No, as I am a man.
    Mir. There's nothing ill can dwell in such a
    temple.
If the ill spirit have so fair a house,
Good things will strive to dwell with 't.
    Pros.   Follow me.
Speak not you for him; he's a traitor.   Come,   460
I'll manacle thy neck and feet together.
Sea-water shalt thou drink; thy food shall be
The fresh-brook mussels, wither'd roots and husks
Wherein the acorn cradled.   Follow.
    Fer.   No;
I will resist such entertainment till   465
Mine enemy has more power.
        [*He draws, and is charmed from moving.*
    Mir.   O dear father,
Make not too rash a trial of him, for
He's gentle and not fearful.
    Pros.   What! I say;
My foot my tutor?   Put thy sword up, traitor,
Who mak'st a show but dar'st not strike, thy con-
    science   470
Is so possess'd with guilt.   Come from thy ward,
For I can here disarm thee with this stick
And make thy weapon drop.
    Mir.   Beseech you, father.
    Pros. Hence! hang not on my garments.
    Mir.   Sir, have pity;
I'll be his surety.
    Pros.   Silence! one word more   475
Shall make me chide thee if not hate thee.   What!
An advocate for an impostor! hush!
Thou think'st there is no more such shapes as he,
Having seen but him and Caliban.   Foolish wench!
To th' most of men this is a Caliban,   480
And they to him are angels.
    Mir.   My affections
Are then most humble; I have no ambition

To see a goodlier man.
    Pros.   Come on; obey
Thy nerves are in their infancy again
And have no vigour in them.
    Fer.   So they are.   485
My spirits, as in a dream, are all bound up.
My father's loss, the weakness which I feel,
The wreck of all my friends, nor this man's threats
To whom I am subdu'd, are but light to me,
Might I but through my prison once a day   490
Behold this maid.   All corners else o' th' earth
Let liberty make use of; space enough
Have I in such a prison.
    Pros. [*Aside.*] It works.   [*To Fer.*]   Come on.
— Thou hast done well, fine Ariel!   [*To Fer.*]   Fol-
    low me.
[*To Ari.*]   Hark what thou else shalt do me.
    Mir.   Be of comfort;
My father's of a better nature, sir,   496
Than he appears by speech.   This is unwonted
Which now came from him.
    Pros.   [*To Ari.*]   Thou shalt be as free
As mountain winds; but then exactly do
All points of my command.
    Ari.   To th' syllable.   500
    Pros. [*To Mir. and Fer.*]   Come, follow.   Speak
    not for him.   [*Exeunt.*

ACT II

Scene I.   [*Another part of the island.*]

Enter Alonso, Sebastian, Antonio, Gonzalo,
    Adrian, Francisco, *and others.*

    Gon. Beseech you, sir, be merry; you have cause,
So have we all, of joy; for our escape
Is much beyond our loss.   Our hint of woe
Is common; every day some sailor's wife,
The masters of some merchant, and the merchant   5
Have just our theme of woe; but for the miracle,
I mean our preservation, few in millions
Can speak like us.   Then wisely, good sir, weigh
Our sorrow with our comfort.
    Alon.   Prithee, peace.
    Seb. He receives comfort like cold porridge.   10
    Ant. The visitor will not give him o'er so.
    Seb. Look, he's winding up the watch of his wit;
by and by it will strike.
    Gon. Sir, —
    Seb. One.   Tell.   15
    Gon. When every grief is entertain'd that's
    offer'd,
Comes to th' entertainer —
    Seb. A dollar.

---

468. **fearful:** dangerous.   469. **foot:** subordinate, i.e., Miranda.   471. **Come ... ward:** drop your posture of defense.
484. **nerves:** sinews.   486. **spirits:** vital powers.
    Act II, sc. i, 5. **merchant:** merchant vessel.   11. **visitor:** spiritual guide.   15. **Tell:** count.

Gon. Dolour comes to him, indeed; you have spoken truer than you purpos'd.   20

Seb. You have taken it wiselier than I meant you should.

Gon. Therefore, my lord, —

Ant. Fie, what a spendthrift is he of his tongue!

Alon. I prithee, spare.   25

Gon. Well, I have done. But yet, —

Seb. He will be talking.

Ant. Which, of he or Adrian, for a good wager, first begins to crow?

Seb. The old cock.   30

Ant. The cock'rel.

Seb. Done. The wager?

Ant. A laughter.

Seb. A match!   34

Adr. Though this island seem to be desert, —

Seb. Ha, ha, ha! [Antonio]! So you're paid.

Adr. Uninhabitable and almost inaccessible, —

Seb. Yet, —

Adr. Yet, —

Ant. He could not miss't.   40

Adr. It must needs be of subtle, tender, and delicate temperance.

Ant. Temperance was a delicate wench.

Seb. Ay, and a subtle; as he most learnedly deliver'd.   45

Adr. The air breathes upon us here most sweetly.

Seb. As if it had lungs and rotten ones.

Ant. Or as 'twere perfum'd by a fen.

Gon. Here is everything advantageous to life.

Ant. True; save means to live.   50

Seb. Of that there's none, or little.

Gon. How lush and lusty the grass looks! How green!

Ant. The ground indeed is tawny.

Seb. With an eye of green in't.   55

Ant. He misses not much.

Seb. No; he doth but mistake the truth totally.

Gon. But the rarity of it is, — which is indeed almost beyond credit, —

Seb. As many vouch'd rarities are.   60

Gon. That our garments, being, as they were, drench'd in the sea, hold notwithstanding their freshness and glosses, being rather new-dy'd than stain'd with salt water.

Ant. If but one of his pockets could speak, would it not say he lies?   66

Seb. Ay, or very falsely pocket up his report.

Gon. Methinks our garments are now as fresh as when we put them on first in Afric, at the marriage of the King's fair daughter Claribel to the King of Tunis.   71

Seb. 'Twas a sweet marriage, and we prosper well in our return.

Adr. Tunis was never grac'd before with such a paragon to their queen.   75

Gon. Not since widow Dido's time.

Ant. Widow! a pox o' that! How came that widow in? Widow Dido!

Seb. What if he had said "widower Æneas" too? Good Lord, how you take it!   80

Adr. "Widow Dido" said you? You make me study of that. She was of Carthage, not of Tunis.

Gon. This Tunis, sir, was Carthage.

Adr. Carthage?

Gon. I assure you, Carthage.   85

Ant. His word is more than the miraculous harp.

Seb. He hath rais'd the wall and houses too.

Ant. What impossible matter will he make easy next?

Seb. I think he will carry this island home in his pocket and give it his son for an apple.   91

Ant. And, sowing the kernels of it in the sea, bring forth more islands.

Gon. Ay.

Ant. Why, in good time.   95

Gon. Sir, we were talking that our garments seem now as fresh as when we were at Tunis at the marriage of your daughter, who is now Queen.

Ant. And the rarest that e'er came there.

Seb. Bate, I beseech you, widow Dido.   100

Ant. O, widow Dido! ay, widow Dido.

Gon. Is not, sir, my doublet as fresh as the first day I wore it? I mean, in a sort.

Ant. That "sort" was well fish'd for.

Gon. When I wore it at your daughter's marriage?   105

Alon. You cram these words into mine ears against
The stomach of my sense. Would I had never
Married my daughter there! for, coming thence,
My son is lost and, in my rate, she too,
Who is so far from Italy removed   110
I ne'er again shall see her. O thou mine heir
Of Naples and of Milan, what strange fish
Hath made his meal on thee?

Fran.   Sir, he may live.
I saw him beat the surges under him
And ride upon their backs. He trod the water,   115
Whose enmity he flung aside, and breasted
The surge most swoln that met him. His bold head
'Bove the contentious waves he kept, and oar'd
Himself with his good arms in lusty stroke
To th' shore, that o'er his wave-worn basis bowed,
As stooping to relieve him. I not doubt   121

---

33. **laughter:** (1) a laugh, (2) sitting of eggs. 34. **match:** bargain. 36. **Ha ... paid.** Since Adrian speaks first, Sebastian loses the bet and pays Antonio his laugh. **[Antonio]** (Liddell). *Ant.* F (as speech-tag). 40. **miss't:** miss saying "yet," or, do without the island. 42. **temperance:** temperature. 55. **eye:** spot. 86. **harp:** the harp of Amphion, whose music raised the walls of Thebes. 100. **Bate:** except. 107. **stomach:** inclination. 100. **rate:** judgment.

He came alive to land.

Alon.   No, no, he's gone.

Seb. Sir, you may thank yourself for this great loss,
That would not bless our Europe with your daughter,
But rather loose her to an African;   125
Where she at least is banish'd from your eye,
Who hath cause to wet the grief on't.

Alon.   Prithee, peace.

Seb. You were kneel'd to and importun'd otherwise
By all of us, and the fair soul herself
Weigh'd between loathness and obedience, at
Which end o' th' beam should bow.   We have lost your son,   131
I fear, for ever.   Milan and Naples have
Moe widows in them of this business' making
Than we bring men to comfort them.
The fault's your own.

Alon.   So is the dear'st o' th' loss.

Gon. My lord Sebastian,   136
The truth you speak doth lack some gentleness
And time to speak it in.   You rub the sore,
When you should bring the plaster.

Seb.   Very well.

Ant. And most chirurgeonly.   140

Gon. It is foul weather in us all, good sir,
When you are cloudy.

Seb.   Foul weather?

Ant.   Very foul.

Gon. Had I plantation of this isle, my lord, —

Ant. He'd sow't with nettle-seed.

Seb.   Or docks, or mallows.

Gon. And were the king on't, what would I do?

Seb. Scape being drunk for want of wine.   146

Gon. I' th' commonwealth I would by contraries
Execute all things; for no kind of traffic
Would I admit; no name of magistrate;
Letters should not be known; riches, poverty,   150
And use of service, none; contract, succession,
Bourn, bound of land, tilth, vineyard, none;
No use of metal, corn, or wine, or oil;
No occupation; all men idle, all;
And women too, but innocent and pure;   155
No sovereignty; —

Seb.   Yet he would be king on't.

Ant. The latter end of his commonwealth forgets
the beginning.

Gon. All things in common nature should produce   159
Without sweat or endeavour: treason, felony,

Sword, pike, knife, gun, or need of any engine,
Would I not have; but nature should bring forth,
Of it own kind, all foison, all abundance,
To feed my innocent people.

Seb. No marrying 'mong his subjects?   165

Ant. None, man; all idle; whores and knaves.

Gon. I would with such perfection govern, sir,
T' excel the golden age.

Seb.   Save his Majesty!

Ant. Long live Gonzalo!

Gon.   And, — do you mark me, sir?

Alon. Prithee, no more; thou dost talk nothing to me.   171

Gon. I do well believe your Highness; and did it
to minister occasion to these gentlemen, who are of
such sensible and nimble lungs that they always use
to laugh at nothing.   175

Ant. 'Twas you we laugh'd at.

Gon. Who in this kind of merry fooling am nothing to you.   So you may continue and laugh at nothing still.

Ant. What a blow was there given!   180

Seb. An it had not fallen flatlong.

Gon. You are gentlemen of brave mettle; you
would lift the moon out of her sphere, if she would
continue in it five weeks without changing.

Enter ARIEL [*invisible*], *playing solemn music.*

Seb. We would so, and then go a bat-fowling.

Ant. Nay, good my lord, be not angry.   186

Gon. No, I warrant you; I will not adventure my
discretion so weakly.   Will you laugh me asleep,
for I am very heavy?

Ant. Go sleep, and hear us.   190

[*All sleep except Alon., Seb., and Ant.*]

Alon. What, all so soon asleep!   I wish mine eyes
Would, with themselves, shut up my thoughts.   I find
They are inclin'd to do so.

Seb.   Please you, sir,
Do not omit the heavy offer of it.
It seldom visits sorrow; when it doth,   195
It is a comforter.

Ant.   We two, my lord,
Will guard your person while you take your rest,
And watch your safety.

Alon.   Thank you.   Wondrous heavy.

[*Alonso sleeps.   Exit Ariel.*]

Seb. What a strange drowsiness possesses them!

Ant. It is the quality o' th' climate.

Seb.   Why   200

---

125. **loose her:** turn her loose. 127. **Who:** which (eye). 130. **Weigh'd:** poised. **loathness:** unwillingness. 135. **dear'st:** most keenly felt. 140. **chirurgeonly:** like a surgeon. 143. **plantation:** colonizing. 147. **by contraries:** contrary to custom. 150. **Letters:** learning. 151. **service:** servants. **succession:** inheritance. 152. **Bourn:** boundary. **tilth:** tilling of soil. 161. **engine:** instrument of war. 163. **it:** its. **foison:** plenty. 174. **sensible:** sensitive. 181. **flatlong:** with the flat of the sword. 185. **bat-fowling:** hunting birds by night.   *Bat* is a stick for knocking them down. 187. **adventure:** risk. 194. **omit:** neglect.

Doth it not then our eyelids sink? I find not
Myself dispos'd to sleep.
    Ant.   Nor I; my spirits are nimble.
They fell together all, as by consent;
They dropp'd, as by a thunder-stroke. What
    might,
Worthy Sebastian, O, what might —? No more:—
And yet methinks I see it in thy face,   206
What thou shouldst be. Th' occasion speaks thee,
    and
My strong imagination sees a crown
Dropping upon thy head.
    Seb.   What, art thou waking?
    Ant. Do you not hear me speak?
    Seb.   I do; and surely
It is a sleepy language, and thou speak'st   211
Out of thy sleep. What is it thou didst say?
This is a strange repose, to be asleep
With eyes wide open; standing, speaking, moving,
And yet so fast asleep.
    Ant.   Noble Sebastian,   215
Thou let'st thy fortune sleep — die, rather;
    wink'st
Whiles thou art waking.
    Seb.   Thou dost snore distinctly;
There's meaning in thy snores.
    Ant. I am more serious than my custom; you
Must be so too, if heed me; which to do   220
Trebles thee o'er.
    Seb.   Well, I am standing water.
    Ant. I'll teach you how to flow.
    Seb.   Do so. To ebb
Hereditary sloth instructs me.
    Ant.   O,
If you but knew how you the purpose cherish
Whiles thus you mock it! how, in stripping it,   225
You more invest it! Ebbing men, indeed,
Most often do so near the bottom run
By their own fear or sloth.
    Seb.   Prithee, say on.
The setting of thine eye and cheek proclaim
A matter from thee, and a birth indeed   230
Which throes thee much to yield.
    Ant.   Thus, sir:
Although this lord of weak remembrance, this
Who shall be of as little memory
When he is earth'd, hath here almost persuaded —
For he's a spirit of persuasion, only   235
Professes to persuade — the King his son's alive,
'Tis as impossible that he's undrown'd

As he that sleeps here swims.
    Seb.   I have no hope
That he's undrown'd.
    Ant.   O, out of that no hope
What great hope have you! No hope that way is
Another way so high a hope that even   241
Ambition cannot pierce a wink beyond,
But doubt discovery there. Will you grant with
    me
That Ferdinand is drown'd?
    Seb.   He's gone.
    Ant.   Then, tell me,
Who's the next heir of Naples?
    Seb.   Claribel.   245
    Ant. She that is Queen of Tunis; she that dwells
Ten leagues beyond man's life; she that from
    Naples
Can have no note, unless the sun were post —
The Man i' th' Moon's too slow — till newborn
    chins   249
Be rough and razorable; she that — from whom
We all were sea-swallow'd, though some cast again,
And by that destiny to perform an act
Whereof what's past is prologue, what to come
In yours and my discharge.
    Seb.   What stuff is this! How say you?
'Tis true, my brother's daughter 's Queen of
    Tunis;
So is she heir of Naples; 'twixt which regions   256
There is some space.
    Ant.   A space whose every cubit
Seems to cry out, "How shall that Claribel
Measure us back to Naples? Keep in Tunis,
And let Sebastian wake." Say this were death   260
That now hath seiz'd them; why, they were no
    worse
Than now they are. There be that can rule Naples
As well as he that sleeps; lords that can prate
As amply and unnecessarily
As this Gonzalo; I myself could make   265
A chough of as deep chat. O, that you bore
The mind that I do! what a sleep were this
For your advancement! Do you understand me?
    Seb. Methinks I do.
    Ant.   And how does your content
Tender your own good fortune?
    Seb.   I remember   270
You did supplant your brother Prospero.
    Ant.   True.
And look how well my garments sit upon me;

203. **consent:** agreement. 207. **speaks:** proclaims. 216. **wink'st:** closest thine eyes. 221. **Trebles...o'er:** triples thy greatness. **standing water:** between ebb and flow, i.e., undecided. 225-26. **in...it:** in making little of it, you give it more meaning. 231. **throes:** pains. 232. **this lord:** probably Francisco. See ll. 113 ff. 234. **earth'd:** buried. 242-43. **cannot...there:** cannot imagine anything higher beyond, but can only find it difficult to believe what it sees there. 247. **man's life:** a lifetime journey. 248. **note:** news. 250. **from:** coming from. 251. **cast:** (1) cast up, (2) cast as actors. 254. **discharge:** performance. 259. **Measure us:** travel over us (the cubits). **Keep:** i.e., let her stay. 260. **wake:** i.e., awake to fortune. 266. **chough...chat:** jackdaw chatter as wisely. 269. **content:** desire. 270. **Tender:** regard.

Much feater than before. My brother's servants
Were then my fellows; now they are my men.
   Seb. But, for your conscience? 275
   Ant. Ay, sir, where lies that? If 'twere a kibe,
'Twould put me to my slipper; but I feel not
This deity in my bosom. Twenty consciences,
That stand 'twixt me and Milan, candied be they
And melt ere they molest! Here lies your brother,
No better than the earth he lies upon 281
If he were that which now he's like, that's dead;
Whom I, with this obedient steel, three inches of it,
Can lay to bed for ever; whiles you, doing thus,
To the perpetual wink for aye might put 285
This ancient morsel, this Sir Prudence, who
Should not upbraid our course. For all the rest,
They'll take suggestion as a cat laps milk;
They'll tell the clock to any business that 289
We say befits the hour.
   Seb.   Thy case, dear friend,
Shall be my precedent; as thou got'st Milan,
I'll come by Naples. Draw thy sword. One stroke
Shall free thee from the tribute which thou payest,
And I the King shall love thee.
   Ant.   Draw together;
And when I rear my hand, do you the like, 295
To fall it on Gonzalo.
   Seb.   O, but one word.
                    [They talk apart.]

   Re-enter ARIEL *[invisible], with music and song.*
   Ari. My master through his art foresees the danger
That you, his friend, are in; and sends me forth —
For else his project dies — to keep them living.
                 [Sings in Gonzalo's ear.
   While you here do snoring lie, 300
   Open-ey'd Conspiracy
      His time doth take.
   If of life you keep a care,
   Shake off slumber, and beware;
      Awake, awake! 305
   Ant. Then let us both be sudden.
   Gon. [*Waking.*]   Now, good angels
Preserve the King!   [*Wakes Alon.*]
   Alon. Why, how now? — Ho, awake! — Why
   are you drawn? 308
Wherefore this ghastly looking?
   Gon.   What's the matter?
   Seb. Whiles we stood here securing your repose,
Even now, we heard a hollow burst of bellowing
Like bulls, or rather lions. Did 't not wake you?
It struck mine ear most terribly.
   Alon.   I heard nothing.
   Ant. O, 'twas a din to fright a monster's ear,
To make an earthquake! Sure, it was the roar 315

Of a whole herd of lions.
   Alon.   Heard you this, Gonzalo?
   Gon. Upon mine honour, sir, I heard a humming,
And that a strange one too, which did awake me.
I shak'd you, sir, and cried. As mine eyes open'd,
I saw their weapons drawn. There was a noise,
That's verily. 'Tis best we stand upon our guard,
Or that we quit this place. Let's draw our weap-
   ons. 322
   Alon. Lead off this ground; and let's make fur-
   ther search
For my poor son.
   Gon. Heavens keep him from these beasts!
For he is, sure, i' th' island.
   Alon.   Lead away. 325
   Ari. Prospero my lord shall know what I have
   done.
So, King, go safely on to seek thy son.   [*Exeunt.*

   SCENE II. [*Another part of the island.*]

   Enter CALIBAN *with a burden of wood. A noise
           of thunder heard.*

   Cal. All the infections that the sun sucks up
From bogs, fens, flats, on Prosper fall and make
   him
By inch-meal a disease! His spirits hear me
And yet I needs must curse. But they'll nor pinch,
Fright me with urchin-shows, pitch me i' th' mire,
Nor lead me, like a firebrand, in the dark 6
Out of my way, unless he bid 'em; but
For every trifle are they set upon me,
Sometime like apes that mow and chatter at me
And after bite me, then like hedgehogs which 10
Lie tumbling in my barefoot way and mount
Their pricks at my footfall; sometime am I
All wound with adders who with cloven tongues
Do hiss me into madness.

   Enter TRINCULO.
          Lo, now, lo!
Here comes a spirit of his, and to torment me 15
For bringing wood in slowly. I'll fall flat;
Perchance he will not mind me.
   Trin. Here's neither bush nor shrub to bear off
any weather at all, and another storm brewing; I
hear it sing i' th' wind. Yond same black cloud, 20
yond huge one, looks like a foul bombard that
would shed his liquor. If it should thunder as it
did before, I know not where to hide my head; yond
same cloud cannot choose but fall by pailfuls.
What have we here? A man or a fish? Dead 25
or alive? A fish; he smells like a fish; a very ancient and fish-like smell; a kind of not-of-the-newest
Poor-John. A strange fish! Were I in England

---

273. **feater:** more becomingly.   276. **kibe:** chilblain.   279. **candied:** frozen.   308. **Ho, awake!** To the other sleepers.
Sc. ii, 3. **By inch-meal:** inch by inch.   6. **like:** in the shape of.   21. **bombard:** leather bottle.   28. **Poor-John:** salted hake.

now, as once I was, and had but this fish painted, not a holiday fool there but would give a piece of 30 silver. There would this monster make a man; any strange beast there makes a man. When they will not give a doit to relieve a lame beggar, they will lay out ten to see a dead Indian. Legg'd like a man! and his fins like arms! Warm o' my troth! 35 I do now let loose my opinion, hold it no longer: this is no fish, but an islander, that hath lately suffered by a thunderbolt. [*Thunder.*] Alas, the storm is come again! My best way is to creep under his gaberdine; there is no other shelter hereabout. 40 Misery acquaints a man with strange bedfellows. I will here shroud till the dregs of the storm be past.

Enter STEPHANO, *singing* [: *a bottle in his hand*].

  Ste. "I shall no more to sea, to sea,
           Here shall I die ashore —"   45
This is a very scurvy tune to sing at a man's funeral. Well, here's my comfort.   [*Drinks.*

(*Sings.*) "The master, the swabber, the boatswain, and I,
       The gunner and his mate
Lov'd Moll, Meg, and Marian, and Margery,   50
       But none of us car'd for Kate;
       For she had a tongue with a tang,
       Would cry to a sailor, 'Go hang!'
She lov'd not the savour of tar nor of pitch,   54
Yet a tailor might scratch her where'er she did itch;
       Then to sea, boys, and let her go hang!"

This is a scurvy tune too; but here's my comfort.
                                [*Drinks.*
  Cal. Do not torment me! Oh!   58
  Ste. What's the matter? Have we devils here? Do you put tricks upon 's with savages and men of Ind, ha? I have not scap'd drowning to be afeard now of your four legs; for it hath been said, "As proper a man as ever went on four legs cannot make him give ground"; and it shall be said so again while Stephano breathes at nostrils.   65
  Cal. The spirit torments me! Oh!
  Ste. This is some monster of the isle with four legs, who hath got, as I take it, an ague. Where the devil should he learn our language? I will give him some relief, if it be but for that. If I can re- 70 cover him and keep him tame and get to Naples with him, he's a present for any emperor that ever trod on neat's-leather.
  Cal. Do not torment me, prithee; I'll bring my wood home faster.   75

  Ste. He's in his fit now and does not talk after the wisest. He shall taste of my bottle; if he have never drunk wine afore, it will go near to remove his fit. If I can recover him and keep him tame, I will not take too much for him; he shall pay for him that hath him, and that soundly.   81
  Cal. Thou dost me yet but little hurt; thou wilt anon, I know it by thy trembling. Now Prosper works upon thee.   84
  Ste. Come on your ways. Open your mouth; here is that which will give language to you, cat. Open your mouth; this will shake your shaking, I can tell you, and that soundly. You cannot tell who's your friend. Open your chaps again.   89
  Trin. I should know that voice; it should be — but he is drown'd; and these are devils. O defend me!   92
  Ste. Four legs and two voices; a most delicate monster! His forward voice now is to speak well of his friend; his backward voice is to utter foul speeches and to detract. If all the wine in my bottle will recover him, I will help his ague. Come. Amen! I will pour some in thy other mouth.   99
  Trin. Stephano!
  Ste. Doth thy other mouth call me? Mercy, mercy! This is a devil, and no monster. I will leave him; I have no long spoon.   103
  Trin. Stephano! If thou beest Stephano, touch me and speak to me; for I am Trinculo, — be not afeard — thy good friend Trinculo.   106
  Ste. If thou beest Trinculo, come forth. I'll pull thee by the lesser legs. If any be Trinculo's legs, these are they. Thou art very Trinculo indeed! How cam'st thou to be the siege of this moon-calf? Can he vent Trinculos?   111
  Trin. I took him to be kill'd with a thunder-stroke. But art thou not drown'd, Stephano? I hope now thou art not drown'd. Is the storm over-blown? I hid me under the dead mooncalf's gab-erdine for fear of the storm. And art thou living, Stephano? O Stephano, two Neapolitans scap'd!   117
  Ste. Prithee, do not turn me about; my stomach is not constant.
  Cal. [*Aside.*] These be fine things, an if they be not sprites.
That's a brave god and bears celestial liquor.
I will kneel to him.   122
  Ste. How didst thou scape? How cam'st thou hither? Swear by this bottle how thou cam'st hither, — I escap'd upon a butt of sack which the sailors heaved o'erboard — by this bottle, which I

---

31. **man:** i.e., man's fortune. 33. **doit:** Dutch coin worth less than a farthing. 40. **gaberdine:** cloak. 63. **proper:** hand-some. 71. **recover:** restore. 73. **neat's-leather:** cowhide. 83. **trembling.** Caliban takes this as a sign he is possessed of a devil. 86. **cat.** Allusion to the proverb, "Good liquor will make a cat speak." 93. **delicate:** charming. 103. **long spoon.** Allusion to the proverb, "It takes a long spoon to sup with the devil." 110. **siege:** stool, excrement. **moon-calf:** monstrosity (caused by the influence of the moon). 125. **sack:** sherry-like wine.

made of the bark of a tree with mine own hands
since I was cast ashore.   128

Cal. I'll swear upon that bottle to be thy true
subject, for the liquor is not earthly.

Ste. Here; swear then how thou escap'dst.

Trin. Swam ashore, man, like a duck. I can
swim like a duck, I'll be sworn.   133

Ste. Here, kiss the book. [*Passing the bottle.*]
Though thou canst swim like a duck, thou art made
like a goose.

Trin. O Stephano, hast any more of this?

Ste. The whole butt, man. My cellar is in a rock
by th' seaside where my wine is hid. How now,
moon-calf! how does thine ague?   139

Cal. Hast thou not dropp'd from heaven?

Ste. Out o' th' moon, I do assure thee. I was the
Man i' the Moon when time was.

Cal. I have seen thee in her and I do adore thee.
My mistress show'd me thee and thy dog and thy
bush.   144

Ste. Come, swear to that; kiss the book. I will
furnish it anon with new contents. Swear.

Trin. By this good light, this is a very shallow
monster! I afeard of him! A very weak monster!
The Man i' th' Moon! A most poor credulous
monster! Well drawn, monster, in good sooth! 150

Cal. I'll show thee every fertile inch o' th' island;
And I will kiss thy foot. I prithee, be my god.

Trin. By this light, a most perfidious and
drunken monster! When 's god 's asleep, he'll rob
his bottle.   155

Cal. I'll kiss thy foot. I'll swear myself thy subject.

Ste. Come on then; down, and swear.

Trin. I shall laugh myself to death at this puppy-
headed monster! A most scurvy monster! I could
find in my heart to beat him —   160

Ste. Come, kiss.

Trin. But that the poor monster's in drink. An
abominable monster!

Cal. I'll show thee the best springs; I'll pluck
thee berries;
I'll fish for thee and get thee wood enough.   165
A plague upon the tyrant that I serve!
I'll bear him no more sticks, but follow thee,
Thou wondrous man.

Trin. A most ridiculous monster, to make a wonder of a poor drunkard!   170

Cal. I prithee, let me bring thee where crabs
grow;
And I with my long nails will dig thee pig-nuts,
Show thee a jay's nest, and instruct thee how

To snare the nimble marmoset. I'll bring thee
To clust'ring filberts and sometimes I'll get thee
Young scamels from the rock. Wilt thou go with
me?   176

Ste. I prithee now, lead the way without any
more talking. Trinculo, the King and all our company else being drown'd, we will inherit here.
Here! bear my bottle. Fellow Trinculo, we'll fill
him by and by again.   181

Cal. (*Sings drunkenly.*)
Farewell, master; farewell, farewell!

Trin. A howling monster; a drunken monster!

Cal. No more dams I'll make for fish;
Nor fetch in firing   185
At requiring;
Nor scrape trenchering, nor wash dish.
'Ban, 'Ban, Ca-Caliban
Has a new master, get a new man.
Freedom, high-day! high-day, freedom! freedom,
high-day, freedom!   191

Ste. O brave monster! Lead the way.

[*Exeunt.*

ACT III

Scene I. [*Before Prospero's cell.*]

Enter Ferdinand, *bearing a log.*

Fer. There be some sports are painful, and their
labour
Delight in them [sets] off; some kinds of baseness
Are nobly undergone, and most poor matters
Point to rich ends. This my mean task
Would be as heavy to me as odious, but   5
The mistress which I serve quickens what's dead
And makes my labours pleasures. O, she is
Ten times more gentle than her father's crabbed,
And he's compos'd of harshness. I must remove
Some thousands of these logs and pile them up,
Upon a sore injunction. My sweet mistress   11
Weeps when she sees me work, and says such base-
ness
Had never like executor. I forget;
But these sweet thoughts do even refresh my la-
bours,   14
Most busy least when I do it.

Enter Miranda; *and* Prospero [*at a distance,
unseen*].

Mir.   Alas, now, pray you,
Work not so hard. I would the lightning had
Burnt up those logs that you are enjoin'd to pile!

---

142. **when...was:** once upon a time.   150. **drawn:** drunk.   171. **crabs:** crab-apples.   174. **marmoset:** monkey.   176.
scamels. Unexplained. *Seamells* (seagulls) is a common emendation.   187. **trenchering:** wooden plates.

Act III, sc. i, 2. [sets] **off:** cancels. [sets] (Theobald).   *set* F.   11. **sore injunction:** orders with a severe penalty for dis-
obeying.   15. **Most...it.** The passage may be corrupt, but the general sense seems to be: I feel the burden of my labors
least when occupied with these thoughts.   Holt reads *busiest* for F *busy lest.*

Pray, set it down and rest you. When this burns,
'Twill weep for having wearied you. My father
Is hard at study; pray now, rest yourself;   20
He's safe for these three hours.

Fer.   O most dear mistress,
The sun will set before I shall discharge
What I must strive to do.

Mir.   If you'll sit down,
I'll bear your logs the while. Pray, give me that;
I'll carry it to the pile.

Fer.   No, precious creature;   25
I had rather crack my sinews, break my back,
Than you should such dishonour undergo,
While I sit lazy by.

Mir.   It would become me
As well as it does you; and I should do it
With much more ease, for my good will is to it,   30
And yours it is against.

Pros.   Poor worm, thou art infected!
This visitation shows it.

Mir.   You look wearily.

Fer. No, noble mistress; 'tis fresh morning with
    me
When you are by at night. I do beseech you —
Chiefly that I might set it in my prayers —   35
What is your name?

Mir.   Miranda. — O my father,
I have broke your hest to say so!

Fer.   Admir'd Miranda!
Indeed the top of admiration! worth
What's dearest to the world! Full many a lady
I have ey'd with best regard, and many a time   40
Th' harmony of their tongues hath into bondage
Brought my too diligent ear; for several virtues
Have I lik'd several women, never any
With so full soul but some defect in her
Did quarrel with the noblest grace she ow'd   45
And put it to the foil; but you, O you,
So perfect and so peerless, are created
Of every creature's best!

Mir.   I do not know
One of my sex; no woman's face remember,
Save, from my glass, mine own; nor have I seen   50
More that I may call men than you, good friend,
And my dear father. How features are abroad,
I am skilless of; but, by my modesty,
The jewel in my dower, I would not wish
Any companion in the world but you,   55
Nor can imagination form a shape,
Besides yourself, to like of. But I prattle
Something too wildly, and my father's precepts
I therein do forget.

Fer.   I am in my condition
A prince, Miranda; I do think, a king;   60

I would, not so! — and would no more endure
This wooden slavery than to suffer
The flesh-fly blow my mouth. Hear my soul speak.
The very instant that I saw you, did
My heart fly to your service; there resides,   65
To make me slave to it; and for your sake
Am I this patient log-man.

Mir.   Do you love me?

Fer. O heaven, O earth, bear witness to this
    sound,
And crown what I profess with kind event
If I speak true! if hollowly, invert   70
What best is boded me to mischief! I,
Beyond all limit of what else i' th' world,
Do love, prize, honour you.

Mir.   I am a fool
To weep at what I am glad of.

Pros.   Fair encounter 74
Of two most rare affections! Heavens rain grace
On that which breeds between 'em!

Fer.   Wherefore weep you?

Mir. At mine unworthiness, that dare not offer
What I desire to give, and much less take
What I shall die to want. But this is trifling;
And all the more it seeks to hide itself,   80
The bigger bulk it shows. Hence, bashful cunning!
And prompt me, plain and holy innocence!
I am your wife, if you will marry me;
If not, I'll die your maid. To be your fellow
You may deny me; but I'll be your servant,   85
Whether you will or no.

Fer.   My mistress, dearest;
And I thus humble ever.

Mir.   My husband, then?

Fer. Ay, with a heart as willing
As bondage e'er of freedom. Here's my hand.

Mir. And mine, with my heart in't. And now
    farewell   90
Till half an hour hence.

Fer.   A thousand thousand!
          [*Exeunt* [*Fer. and Mir. severally*].

Pros. So glad of this as they I cannot be,
Who are surpris'd withal; but my rejoicing
At nothing can be more. I'll to my book,
For yet ere supper-time must I perform   95
Much business appertaining.   [*Exit.*

SCENE II. [*Another part of the island.*]

Enter CALIBAN, STEPHANO, *and* TRINCULO.

Ste. Tell not me. When the butt is out, we will
drink water; not a drop before; therefore bear up
and board 'em. Servant-monster, drink to me.   4

---

42. **several:** particular.   45. **ow'd:** owned.   46. **put...foil:** defeated it.   52. **abroad:** in the world.   53. **skilless:**
ignorant.   59. **condition:** status, rank.   69. **event:** outcome.   70. **invert:** convert.   71. **boded:** destined.   79. **to want:**
if I lack.   84. **maid:** handmaiden.   **fellow:** mate.

Trin. Servant-monster! the folly of this island! They say there's but five upon this isle: we are three of them; if the other two be brain'd like us, the state totters.

Ste. Drink, servant-monster, when I bid thee. Thy eyes are almost set in thy head.   10

Trin. Where should they be set else? He were a brave monster indeed, if they were set in his tail.   13

Ste. My man-monster hath drown'd his tongue in sack. For my part, the sea cannot drown me; I swam, ere I could recover the shore, five and thirty leagues off and on. By this light, thou shalt be my lieutenant, monster, or my standard.

Trin. Your lieutenant, if you list; he's no standard.   20

Ste. We'll not run, Monsieur Monster.

Trin. Nor go neither; but you'll lie like dogs and yet say nothing neither.

Ste. Moon-calf, speak once in thy life, if thou beest a good moon-calf.   25

Cal. How does thy honour? Let me lick thy shoe. I'll not serve him; he's not valiant.   27

Trin. Thou liest, most ignorant monster! I am in case to justle a constable. Why, thou debosh'd fish, thou, was there ever man a coward that hath drunk so much sack as I to-day? Wilt thou tell a monstrous lie, being but half a fish and half a monster?   33

Cal. Lo, how he mocks me! Wilt thou let him, my lord?

Trin. "Lord" quoth he! That a monster should be such a natural!   37

Cal. Lo, lo, again! Bite him to death, I prithee.

Ste. Trinculo, keep a good tongue in your head. If you prove a mutineer, — the next tree! The poor monster's my subject and he shall not suffer indignity.

Cal. I thank my noble lord. Wilt thou be pleas'd to hearken once again to the suit I made to thee?   45

Ste. Marry, will I; kneel and repeat it. I will stand, and so shall Trinculo.

Enter ARIEL, *invisible.*

Cal. As I told thee before, I am subject to a tyrant, a sorcerer, that by his cunning hath cheated me of the island.   50

Ari. Thou liest.

Cal. Thou liest, thou jesting monkey, thou. I would my valiant master would destroy thee! I do not lie.   54

Ste. Trinculo, if you trouble him any more in's tale, by this hand, I will supplant some of your teeth.

Trin. Why, I said nothing.

Ste. Mum, then, and no more. Proceed.

Cal. I say by sorcery he got this isle;   60
From me he got it. If thy greatness will
Revenge it on him, — for I know thou dar'st,
But this thing dare not, —

Ste. That's most certain.   64

Cal. Thou shalt be lord of it and I'll serve thee.

Ste. How now shall this be compass'd? Canst thou bring me to the party?

Cal. Yea, yea, my lord. I'll yield him thee asleep,
Where thou mayst knock a nail into his head.

Ari. Thou liest; thou canst not.   70

Cal. What a pied ninny's this! Thou scurvy patch!
I do beseech thy greatness, give him blows
And take his bottle from him. When that's gone
He shall drink nought but brine; for I'll not show him
Where the quick freshes are.   75

Ste. Trinculo, run into no further danger. Interrupt the monster one word further, and, by this hand, I'll turn my mercy out o' doors and make a stock-fish of thee.

Trin. Why, what did I? I did nothing. I'll go farther off.   81

Ste. Didst thou not say he lied?

Ari. Thou liest.

Ste. Do I so? Take thou that. [*Beats Trin.*]
As you like this, give me the lie another time.   85

Trin. I did not give the lie. Out o' your wits and hearing too? A pox o' your bottle! this can sack and drinking do. A murrain on your monster, and the devil take your fingers!

Cal. Ha, ha, ha!   90

Ste. Now, forward with your tale. Prithee, stand farther off.

Cal. Beat him enough. After a little time I'll beat him too.

Ste.   Stand farther. Come, proceed.   94

Cal. Why, as I told thee, 'tis a custom with him, I' th' afternoon to sleep. There thou mayst brain him,
Having first seiz'd his books, or with a log
Batter his skull, or paunch him with a stake,
Or cut his wezand with thy knife. Remember
First to possess his books; for without them   100
He's but a sot, as I am, nor hath not
One spirit to command. They all do hate him
As rootedly as I. Burn but his books.

Sc. ii, 10. **set:** fixed by drink.   18. **standard:** standard-bearer (with a pun in l. 20).   22. **go:** walk.   29. **case:** condition.   29. **debosh'd:** debauched.   37. **natural:** idiot.   71. **pied ninny:** jester in many-colored costume.   **patch:** fool.   75. **quick freshes:** springs of fresh water.   79. **stock-fish:** dried cod, which was beaten before cooking.   88. **murrain:** plague.   98 **paunch him:** stab him in the belly.   99. **wezand:** windpipe.

He has brave utensils, — for so he calls them, —
Which, when he has a house, he'll deck withal.   105
And that most deeply to consider is
The beauty of his daughter. He himself
Calls her a nonpareil. I never saw a woman
But only Sycorax my dam and she;
But she as far surpasseth Sycorax   110
As greatest does least.
     Ste.   Is it so brave a lass?
     Cal. Ay, lord; she will become thy bed, I warrant,
And bring thee forth brave brood.
     Ste. Monster, I will kill this man. His daughter
and I will be king and queen, — save our Graces! —
and Trinculo and thyself shall be viceroys. Dost
thou like the plot, Trinculo?   117
     Trin. Excellent.
     Ste. Give me thy hand. I am sorry I beat thee;
but, while thou liv'st, keep a good tongue in thy
head.   121
     Cal. Within this half hour will he be asleep.
Wilt thou destroy him then?
     Ste.   Ay, on mine honour.
     Ari. This will I tell my master.
     Cal. Thou mak'st me merry; I am full of pleasure.   125
Let us be jocund. Will you troll the catch
You taught me but while-ere?
     Ste. At thy request, monster, I will do reason,
any reason. Come on, Trinculo, let us sing.
                            [*Sings.*
       Flout 'em and [scout] 'em   130
       And scout 'em and flout 'em;
       Thought is free.
     Cal. That's not the tune.
       [*Ariel plays the tune on a tabor and pipe.*
     Ste. What is this same?
     Trin. This is the tune of our catch, played by the
picture of Nobody.   136
     Ste. If thou beest a man, show thyself in thy
likeness. If thou be'st a devil, take't as thou list.
     Trin. O, forgive me my sins!
     Ste. He that dies pays all debts. I defy thee.
Mercy upon us!   141
     Cal. Art thou afeard?
     Ste. No, monster, not I.
     Cal. Be not afeard. The isle is full of noises,
Sounds and sweet airs, that give delight and hurt
not.   145
Sometimes a thousand twangling instruments
Will hum about mine ears, and sometime voices
That, if I then had wak'd after long sleep,
Will make me sleep again; and then, in dreaming,
The clouds methought would open and show riches

Ready to drop upon me, that, when I wak'd,   151
I cried to dream again.
     Ste. This will prove a brave kingdom to me,
where I shall have my music for nothing.
     Cal. When Prospero is destroy'd.   155
     Ste. That shall be by and by. I remember the
story.
     Trin. The sound is going away. Let's follow it,
and after do our work.
     Ste. Lead, monster; we'll follow. I would I
could see this taborer; he lays it on.   161
     Trin. Wilt come? I'll follow Stephano.
                            [*Exeunt.*

SCENE III. [*Another part of the island.*]

Enter ALONSO, SEBASTIAN, ANTONIO, GONZALO,
     ADRIAN, FRANCISCO, *etc.*

     Gon. By'r lakin, I can go no further, sir;
My old bones ache. Here's a maze trod indeed
Through forth-rights and meanders! By your patience,
I needs must rest me.
     Alon.   Old lord, I cannot blame thee,
Who am myself attach'd with weariness   5
To th' dulling of my spirits. Sit down, and rest.
Even here I will put off my hope and keep it
No longer for my flatterer. He is drown'd
Whom thus we stray to find, and the sea mocks
Our frustrate search on land. Well, let him go.   10
     Ant. [*Aside to Seb.*] I am right glad that he's so
       out of hope.
Do not, for one repulse, forgo the purpose
That you resolv'd t' effect.
     Seb. [*Aside to Ant.*] The next advantage
Will we take throughly.
     Ant. [*Aside to Seb.*] Let it be to-night;
For, now they are oppress'd with travel, they   15
Will not, nor cannot, use such vigilance
As when they are fresh.

Solemn and strange music; and PROSPERO *on the top
     invisible. Enter several strange shapes, bringing in
     a banquet; and dance about it with gentle actions of
     salutation; and, inviting the King, etc., to eat, they
     depart.*

     Seb. [*Aside to Ant.*] I say, to-night. No more.
     Alon. What harmony is this? My good friends,
       hark!
     Gon. Marvellous sweet music!
     Alon. Give us kind keepers, heavens! What
       were these?   20
     Seb. A living drollery. Now I will believe
That there are unicorns, that in Arabia

---

126. **troll the catch**: sing the part-song.   130. **[scout]** (Rowe). *cout* F.   133. s.d. **tabor**: a small drum.
    Sc. iii, 1. **By'r lakin**: by our Lady (the Virgin Mary).   3. **forth-rights**: straight paths.   **meanders**: winding paths.   5.
attach'd: seized.   17. s.d. **top**: the upper stage.   21. **drollery**: puppet show.

There is one tree, the phœnix' throne, one phœnix
At this hour reigning there.
    Ant.   I'll believe both;
And what does else want credit, come to me,   25
And I'll be sworn 'tis true. Travellers ne'er did lie,
Though fools at home condemn 'em.
    Gon.   If in Naples
I should report this now, would they believe me?
If I should say, I saw such [islanders] —
For, certes, these are people of the island —   30
Who, though they are of monstrous shape, yet, note,
Their manners are more gentle, kind, than of
Our human generation you shall find
Many, nay, almost any.
    Pros.   [*Aside.*] Honest lord,   34
Thou hast said well; for some of you there present
Are worse than devils.
    Alon.   I cannot too much muse
Such shapes, such gesture, and such sound, express-
    ing,
Although they want the use of tongue, a kind
Of excellent dumb discourse.
    Pros.   [*Aside.*] Praise in departing.
    Fran. They vanish'd strangely.
    Seb.   No matter, since
They have left their viands behind, for we have
    stomachs.   41
Will't please you taste of what is here?
    Alon.   Not I.
    Gon. Faith, sir, you need not fear. When we
    were boys,
Who would believe that there were mountaineers
Dew-lapp'd like bulls, whose throats had hanging
    at 'em   45
Wallets of flesh? or that there were such men
Whose heads stood in their breasts? which now we
    find
Each putter-out of five for one will bring us
Good warrant of.
    Alon.   I will stand to and feed.
Although my last. No matter, since I feel   50
The best is past. Brother, my lord the Duke,
Stand to and do as we.

Thunder and lightning. Enter ARIEL, *like a harpy;*
    claps his wings upon the table; and, with a quaint
    device, the banquet vanishes.

    Ari. You are three men of sin, whom Destiny,
That hath to instrument this lower world
And what is in't, the never-surfeited sea   55
Hath caus'd to belch up you; and on this island

Where man doth not inhabit; you 'mongst men
Being most unfit to live. I have made you mad;
And even with such-like valour men hang and
    drown
Their proper selves.
          [*Alon., Seb., etc., draw their swords.*]
          You fools! I and my fellows
Are ministers of Fate. The elements,   61
Of whom your swords are temper'd, may as well
Wound the loud winds, or with bemock'd-at stabs
Kill the still-closing waters, as diminish
One dowle that's in my plume. My fellow-minis-
    ters   65
Are like invulnerable. If you could hurt,
Your swords are now too massy for your strengths
And will not be uplifted. But remember —
For that's my business to you — that you three
From Milan did supplant good Prospero;   70
Expos'd unto the sea, which hath requit it,
Him and his innocent child; for which foul deed
The powers, delaying, not forgetting, have
Incens'd the seas and shores, yea, all the creatures,
Against your peace. Thee of thy son, Alonso,   75
They have bereft; and do pronounce by me
Ling'ring perdition, worse than any death
Can be at once, shall step by step attend
You and your ways; whose wraths to guard you
    from —
Which here, in this most desolate isle, else falls   80
Upon your heads — is nothing but heart's sorrow
And a clear life ensuing.

He vanishes in thunder; then, to soft music, enter the
    shapes again, and dance, with mocks and mows,
    and carrying out the table.

    Pros. Bravely the figure of this harpy hast thou
Perform'd, my Ariel; a grace it had, devouring.
Of my instruction hast thou nothing bated   85
In what thou hadst to say; so, with good life
And observation strange, my meaner ministers
Their several kinds have done. My high charms
    work,
And these mine enemies are all knit up
In their distractions. They now are in my power;
And in these fits I leave them, while I visit   91
Young Ferdinand, whom they suppose is drown'd,
And his and mine lov'd darling.   [*Exit above.*]
    Gon. I' th' name of something holy, sir, why
    stand you   94
In this strange stare?
    Alon.   O, it is monstrous, monstrous!
Methought the billows spoke and told me of it;

---

29. [islanders] F₂. *Islands* F₁. 36. **muse:** marvel at. 39. **Praise in departing:** keep your praise until your entertainment is over (Proverbial). 45. **Dew-lapp'd:** with a fold of loose skin hanging from the throat (a reference to goitre). 48. **Each . . . one.** Travelers took out a kind of insurance, depositing money with an agent, who was bound to pay a specified number of times as much if they returned safely. 52. S.D. *harpy:* fabulous monster with woman's head and vulture's body. *quaint device:* ingenious mechanism. 54. **to:** for. 60. **proper:** own. 65. **dowle:** tiny feather. 67. **massy:** heavy. 71. **requit:** requited, avenged. 82. **clear:** blameless. 84. **devouring:** i.e., as you whisked it away. 86. **life:** likeness to life. 88. **kinds:** parts, rôles.

The winds did sing it to me, and the thunder,
That deep and dreadful organ-pipe, pronounc'd
The name of Prosper; it did bass my trespass.
Therefore my son i' th' ooze is bedded, and   100
I'll seek him deeper than e'er plummet sounded
And with him there lie mudded.   [*Exit.*]
    Seb.   But one fiend at a time,
I'll fight their legions o'er.
    Ant.   I'll be thy second.
                          [*Exeunt [Seb. and Ant.].*
    Gon. All three of them are desperate: their great
          guilt,
Like poison given to work a great time after,   105
Now gins to bite the spirits. I do beseech you
That are of suppler joints, follow them swiftly
And hinder them from what this ecstasy
May now provoke them to.
    Adr.   Follow, I pray you.
                                    [*Exeunt.*

ACT IV

SCENE I. [*Before Prospero's cell.*]

Enter PROSPERO, FERDINAND, *and* MIRANDA.

    Pros. If I have too austerely punish'd you,
Your compensation makes amends, for I
Have given you here a third of mine own life,
Or that for which I live; who once again
I tender to thy hand. All thy vexations   5
Were but my trials of thy love, and thou
Hast strangely stood the test. Here, afore Heaven,
I ratify this my rich gift. O Ferdinand,
Do not smile at me that I boast her off,
For thou shalt find she will outstrip all praise 10
And make it halt behind her.
    Fer.   I do believe it
Against an oracle.
    Pros. Then, as my [gift] and thine own acquisi-
          tion
Worthily purchas'd, take my daughter. But
If thou dost break her virgin-knot before   15
All sanctimonious ceremonies may
With full and holy rite be minist'red,
No sweet aspersion shall the heavens let fall
To make this contract grow; but barren Hate,
Sour-eyed Disdain, and Discord shall bestrew   20
The union of your bed with weeds so loathly
That you shall hate it both. Therefore take heed,
As Hymen's lamps shall light you.
    Fer.   As I hope

For quiet days, fair issue, and long life,
With such love as 'tis now, the murkiest den,   25
The most opportune place, the strong'st suggestion
Our worser genius can, shall never melt
Mine honour into lust, to take away
The edge of that day's celebration   29
When I shall think or Phœbus' steeds are founder'd
Or Night kept chain'd below.
    Pros.   Fairly spoke.
Sit then and talk with her; she is thine own.
What, Ariel! my industrious servant, Ariel!

Enter ARIEL.

    Ari. What would my potent master? Here I am.
    Pros. Thou and thy meaner fellows your last
          service   35
Did worthily perform; and I must use you
In such another trick. Go bring the rabble,
O'er whom I give thee power, here to this place.
Incite them to quick motion; for I must
Bestow upon the eyes of this young couple   40
Some vanity of mine art. It is my promise,
And they expect it from me.
    Ari.   Presently?
    Pros. Ay, with a twink.
    Ari. Before you can say "come" and "go,"
          And breathe twice and cry "so, so,"   45
          Each one, tripping on his toe,
          Will be here with mop and mow.
          Do you love me, master? No?
    Pros. Dearly, my delicate Ariel. Do not ap-
          proach
Till thou dost hear me call.
    Ari.   Well, I conceive.   50
                                    [*Exit.*
    Pros. Look thou be true; do not give dalliance
Too much the rein. The strongest oaths are straw
To th' fire i' th' blood. Be more abstemious,
Or else good night your vow!
    Fer.   I warrant you, sir;
The white cold virgin snow upon my heart   55
Abates the ardour of my liver.
    Pros.   Well.
Now come, my Ariel! bring a corollary,
Rather than want a spirit. Appear, and pertly!
No tongue! all eyes! Be silent.   [*Soft music.*

Enter IRIS.

    Iris. Ceres, most bounteous lady, thy rich leas
Of wheat, rye, barley, vetches, oats, and pease; 61
Thy turfy mountains, where live nibbling sheep,

---

    99. **bass:** proclaim in deep tones. 108. **ecstasy:** frenzy.
    Act IV, sc. i, 3. **third.** Variously explained. Perhaps the "thirds" are Prospero, his dukedom, and his daughter;
or, better, past, present, and future. 7. **strangely:** unusually well. 13. [**gift**] (Rowe). *guest* F. 18. **aspersion:** sprin-
kling (of dew). 26. **suggestion:** temptation. 27. **can:** i.e., can offer. 41. **vanity:** trifling illusion. 42. **Presently:** instantly.
47. **mop and mow.** Both words mean grimace. 50. **conceive:** understand. 56. **liver:** the supposed seat of love. 57.
corollary: surplus, extra. 58. **pertly:** briskly.

And flat meads thatch'd with stover, them to keep;
Thy banks with pioned and twilled brims,
Which spongy April at thy hest betrims   65
To make cold nymphs chaste crowns; and thy
          broom groves,
Whose shadow the dismissed bachelor loves,
Being lass-lorn; thy pole-clipp'd vineyard;
And thy sea-marge, sterile and rocky-hard,
Where thou thyself dost air; — the queen o' th' sky,
Whose wat'ry arch and messenger am I,   71
Bids thee leave these, and with her sovereign grace,
                    [*Juno descends.*
Here on this grass-plot, in this very place,
To come and sport; here peacocks fly amain.
Approach, rich Ceres, her to entertain.   75

          Enter CERES.

Cer. Hail, many-coloured messenger, that ne'er
Dost disobey the wife of Jupiter;
Who with thy saffron wings upon my flowers
Diffusest honey-drops, refreshing showers,
And with each end of thy blue bow dost crown   80
My bosky acres and my unshrubb'd down,
Rich scarf to my proud earth; why hath thy queen
Summon'd me hither, to this short-grass'd green?
Iris. A contract of true love to celebrate;
And some donation freely to estate   85
On the blest lovers.
Cer.   Tell me, heavenly bow,
If Venus or her son, as thou dost know,
Do now attend the Queen? Since they did plot
The means that dusky Dis my daughter got,
Her and her blind boy's scandal'd company   90
I have forsworn.
Iris.   Of her society
Be not afraid. I met her deity
Cutting the clouds towards Paphos, and her son
Dove-drawn with her. Here thought they to have
          done
Some wanton charm upon this man and maid,   95
Whose vows are, that no bed-right shall be paid
Till Hymen's torch be lighted; but in vain
Mars's hot minion is return'd again;
Her waspish-headed son has broke his arrows,
Swears he will shoot no more, but play with spar-
          rows   100
And be a boy right out.   [*Juno alights.*]
Cer.   Highest queen of state,
Great Juno, comes; I know her by her gait.
Juno. How does my bounteous sister? Go with
          me

To bless this twain, that they may prosperous be
And honour'd in their issue.   [*They sing.* 105
Juno. Honour, riches, marriage-blessing,
     Long continuance, and increasing,
     Hourly joys be still upon you!
     Juno sings her blessings on you.

[*Cer.*] Earth's increase, foison plenty,   110
     Barns and garners never empty,
     Vines with clust'ring bunches growing,
     Plants with goodly burden bowing.
     Spring come to you at the farthest
     In the very end of harvest!   115
     Scarcity and want shall shun you;
     Ceres' blessing so is on you.
Fer. This is a most majestic vision, and
Harmonious charmingly. May I be bold
To think these spirits?
Pros.   Spirits, which by mine art
I have from their confines call'd to enact   121
My present fancies.
Fer.   Let me live here ever;
So rare a wond'red father and a wise
Makes this place Paradise.
Pros.   Sweet, now, silence!
Juno and Ceres whisper seriously.   125
There's something else to do; hush and be mute,
Or else our spell is marr'd.
          [*Juno and Ceres whisper, and send Iris on*
               employment.
Iris. You nymphs, call'd Naiads, of the wind'ring
          brooks,
With your sedg'd crowns and ever-harmless looks,
Leave your crisp channels, and on this green land
Answer your summons; Juno does command.   131
Come, temperate nymphs, and help to celebrate
A contract of true love; be not too late.

          Enter certain Nymphs.

You sunburnt sicklemen, of August weary,
Come hither from the furrow and be merry.   135
Make holiday; your rye-straw hats put on
And these fresh nymphs encounter every one
In country footing.

Enter certain Reapers, *properly habited: they join*
     with the Nymphs in a graceful dance; towards the
     end whereof Prospero starts suddenly, and speaks;
     after which, to a strange, hollow, and confused noise,
     they heavily vanish.

---

63. **stover:** hay.   64. **pioned and twilled.** Meaning uncertain, the most satisfactory interpretation being "furrowed
and ridged." 66. **broom groves.** So F. *brown groves* Hanmer. 68. **pole-clipp'd:** surrounded by poles. 71. **wat'ry arch:**
rainbow. 72. S.D. As Juno does not seem to be present before l. 101, this F direction is the cue for operating the
machinery for her descent. 81. **bosky:** wooded. 85. **estate:** bestow. 89. **Dis:** Pluto, who abducted Proserpine to be
his queen in Hades. 90. **scandal'd:** scandalous. 98. **hot minion:** lustful darling (Venus). 99. **waspish-headed:** irritable.
110. [*Cer.*] (Theobald). Om. F. 123. **wond'red:** wonder-doing. **wise.** Some copies of F read *wife*. 128. **wind'ring:**
wandering or winding or both. *winding* (Rowe); *wand'ring* (Steevens). 138. S.D. **heavily:** reluctantly.

Pros. [*Aside.*] I had forgot that foul conspiracy
Of the beast Caliban and his confederates   140
Against my life. The minute of their plot
Is almost come. [*To the Spirits.*] Well done!
    avoid. No more!
Fer. This is strange. Your father's in some pas-
    sion
That works him strongly.
Mir.   Never till this day   144
Saw I him touch'd with anger, so distemper'd.
Pros. You do look, my son, in a mov'd sort,
As if you were dismay'd. Be cheerful, sir,
Our revels now are ended. These our actors,
As I foretold you, were all spirits, and
Are melted into air, into thin air;   150
And, like the baseless fabric of this vision,
The cloud-capp'd towers, the gorgeous palaces,
The solemn temples, the great globe itself,
Yea, all which it inherit, shall dissolve
And, like this insubstantial pageant faded,   155
Leave not a rack behind. We are such stuff
As dreams are made on, and our little life
Is rounded with a sleep. Sir, I am vex'd, —
Bear with my weakness — my old brain is troubled.
Be not disturb'd with my infirmity.   160
If you be pleas'd, retire into my cell
And there repose. A turn or two I'll walk,
To still my beating mind.
Fer. Mir.   We wish your peace.
                [*Exeunt.*
Pros. Come with a thought. I thank thee,
    Ariel; come.

Enter ARIEL.

Ari. Thy thoughts I cleave to. What's thy
    pleasure?
Pros.   Spirit,   165
We must prepare to meet with Caliban.
Ari. Ay, my commander. When I presented
    Ceres,
I thought to have told thee of it, but I fear'd
Lest I might anger thee.
Pros. Say again, where didst thou leave these
    varlets?   170
Ari. I told you, sir, they were red-hot with
    drinking;
So full of valour that they smote the air
For breathing in their faces; beat the ground
For kissing of their feet; yet always bending
Towards their project. Then I beat my tabor;
At which, like unback'd colts, they prick'd their
    ears,   176
Advanc'd their eyelids, lifted up their noses

As they smelt music. So I charm'd their ears
That calf-like they my lowing follow'd through
Tooth'd briers, sharp furzes, pricking [gorse] and
    thorns,   180
Which ent'red their frail shins. At last I left them
I' th' filthy-mantled pool beyond your cell,
There dancing up to the chins, that the foul lake
O'erstunk their feet.
Pros.   This was well done, my bird.
Thy shape invisible retain thou still.   185
The trumpery in my house, go bring it hither,
For stale to catch these thieves.
Ari.   I go, I go.
                [*Exit.*
Pros. A devil, a born devil, on whose nature
Nurture can never stick; on whom my pains,
Humanely taken, all, all lost, quite lost;   190
And as with age his body uglier grows,
So his mind cankers. I will plague them all,
Even to roaring.

Re-enter ARIEL, *loaden with glittering apparel,*
    etc.

        Come, hang [them on] this line.

[*Prospero and Ariel remain, invisible.*] Enter
CALIBAN, STEPHANO, *and* TRINCULO, *all wet.*

Cal. Pray you, tread softly, that the blind mole
    may not
Hear a foot fall; we now are near his cell.   195
Ste. Monster, your fairy, which you say is a
harmless fairy, has done little better than play'd
the Jack with us.
Trin. Monster, I do smell all horse-piss, at which
my nose is in great indignation.   200
Ste. So is mine. Do you hear, monster? If I
should take a displeasure against you, look you, —
Trin. Thou wert but a lost monster.
Cal. Good my lord, give me thy favour still.
Be patient, for the prize I'll bring thee to   205
Shall hoodwink this mischance; therefore speak
    softly.
All's hush'd as midnight yet.
Trin. Ay, but to lose our bottles in the pool, —
Ste. There is not only disgrace and dishonour in
that, monster, but an infinite loss.   210
Trin. That's more to me than my wetting; yet
this is your harmless fairy, monster!
Ste. I will fetch off my bottle, though I be o'er
ears for my labour,
Cal. Prithee, my king, be quiet. See'st thou
    here,   215
This is the mouth o' th' cell. No noise, and enter,

142. **avoid:** begone. 156. **rack:** cloud. 176. **unback'd:** unbroken. 180. **[gorse]** (Collier). *goss* F. 182. **filthy-mantled:**
slime covered. 186. **trumpery:** stuff, the "glittering apparel" of s.d. (l.193). 187. **stale:** decoy. 193. **[them on]** (Rowe).
on them F. **line:** lime-tree. 198. **Jack:** knave. 206. **hoodwink:** cover up, make you blind to.

Do that good mischief which may make this island
Thine own for ever, and I, thy Caliban,
For aye thy foot-licker.

Ste. Give me thy hand. I do begin to have
bloody thoughts.   221

Trin. O King Stephano! O peer! O worthy
Stephano! look what a wardrobe here is for thee!

Cal. Let it alone, thou fool; it is but trash.

Trin. O, ho, monster! we know what belongs to
a frippery. O King Stephano!   226

Ste. Put off that gown, Trinculo; by this hand,
I'll have that gown.

Trin. Thy Grace shall have it.

Cal. The dropsy drown this fool! what do you
    mean   230
To dote thus on such luggage? [Let 't] alone
And do the murder first. If he awake,
From toe to crown he'll fill our skins with pinches,
Make us strange stuff.   234

Ste. Be you quiet, monster. Mistress line, is not
this my jerkin? Now is the jerkin under the line.
Now, jerkin, you are like to lose your hair and
prove a bald jerkin.

Trin. Do, do; we steal by line and level, an't like
your Grace.   240

Ste. I thank thee for that jest; here's a garment
for't. Wit shall not go unrewarded while I am
king of this country. "Steal by line and level" is
an excellent pass of pate; there's another garment
for't.   245

Trin. Monster, come, put some lime upon your
fingers, and away with the rest.

Cal. I will have none on't. We shall lose our
    time,
And all be turn'd to barnacles, or to apes
With foreheads villainous low.   250

Ste. Monster, lay-to your fingers. Help to bear
this away where my hogshead of wine is, or I'll turn
you out of my kingdom. Go to, carry this.

Trin. And this.

Ste. Ay, and this.   255

*A noise of hunters heard. Enter divers Spirits, in
shape of dogs and hounds, hunting them about,
Prospero and Ariel setting them on.*

Pros. Hey, Mountain, hey!

Ari. Silver! there it goes, Silver!

Pros. Fury, Fury! there, Tyrant, there! hark!
    hark!

        [*Cal., Ste., and Trin. are driven out.*]
Go charge my goblins that they grind their joints

With dry convulsions, shorten up their sinews   260
With aged cramps, and more pinch-spotted make
    them
Than pard or cat o' mountain.

Ari.   Hark, they roar!

Pros. Let them be hunted soundly. At this hour
Lies at my mercy all mine enemies.
Shortly shall all my labours end, and thou   265
Shalt have the air at freedom. For a little
Follow, and do me service.   [*Exeunt.*

ACT V

SCENE I.   [*Before Prospero's cell.*]

Enter PROSPERO *in his magic robes, and* ARIEL.

Pros. Now does my project gather to a head.
My charms crack not; my spirits obey; and Time
Goes upright with his carriage. How's the day?

Ari. On the sixth hour; at which time, my lord,
You said our work should cease.

Pros.   I did say so,   5
When first I rais'd the tempest. Say, my spirit,
How fares the King and 's followers?

Ari.   Confin'd together
In the same fashion as you gave in charge,
Just as you left them; all prisoners, sir,
In the line-grove which weather-fends your cell;   10
They cannot budge till your release. The King,
His brother, and yours, abide all three distracted,
And the remainder mourning over them,
Brimful of sorrow and dismay; but chiefly
Him that you term'd, sir, "the good old lord, Gon-
    zalo,"   15
His tears run down his beard like winter's drops
From eaves of reeds. Your charm so strongly
    works 'em
That if you now beheld them, your affections
Would become tender.

Pros.   Dost thou think so, spirit?

Ari. Mine would, sir, were I human.

Pros.   And mine shall.
Hast thou, which art but air, a touch, a feeling   21
Of their afflictions, and shall not myself,
One of their kind, that relish all as sharply
Passion as they, be kindlier mov'd than thou art?
Though with their high wrongs I am struck to th'
    quick,   25
Yet with my nobler reason 'gainst my fury
Do I take part. The rarer action is
In virtue than in vengeance. They being penitent,

---

222. **King . . . peer.** Allusion to an old song beginning, "King Stephen was a worthy peer."   226. **frippery:** old clothes
shop.   231. **[Let 't]** (Rowe). *let's* F.   236. **line:** (1) lime-tree, (2) equator. Stephano has taken the jerkin down from
the lime-tree. The jerkin will "lose its hair" (fur trimming?), as men lose hair through tropical fevers.   239. **Do, do:** i.e.,
bravo! **by . . . level:** by plumb line and carpenter's level, i.e., systematically.   244. **pass of pate:** stroke of wit.   246. **lime:**
bird lime.   249. **barnacles:** wild geese, thought to be hatched from the shell fish.   262. **pard:** leopard.
  Act V, sc. i, 3. carriage: burden.   11. **your release:** you release them.   23. **relish:** am susceptible to.

The sole drift of my purpose doth extend
Not a frown further.   Go release them, Ariel.   30
My charms I'll break, their senses I'll restore,
And they shall be themselves.
   Ari.   I'll fetch them, sir.
             [*Exit.*
  Pros. Ye elves of hills, brooks, standing lakes,
   and groves,
And ye that on the sands with printless foot
Do chase the ebbing Neptune, and do fly him   35
When he comes back; you demi-puppets that
By moonshine do the green sour ringlets make,
Whereof the ewe not bites; and you whose pastime
Is to make midnight mushrooms, that rejoice
To hear the solemn curfew; by whose aid,   40
Weak masters though ye be, I have bedimm'd
The noontide sun, call'd forth the mutinous winds,
And 'twixt the green sea and the azur'd vault
Set roaring war; to the dread rattling thunder
Have I given fire, and rifted Jove's stout oak   45
With his own bolt; the strong-bas'd promontory
Have I made shake, and by the spurs pluck'd up
The pine and cedar; graves at my command
Have wak'd their sleepers, op'd, and let 'em forth
By my so potent art.   But this rough magic   50
I here abjure, and, when I have requir'd
Some heavenly music, which even now I do,
To work mine end upon their senses that
This airy charm is for, I'll break my staff,
Bury it certain fathoms in the earth,   55
And deeper than did ever plummet sound
I'll drown my book.   [*Solemn music.*

Here enters ARIEL *before: then* ALONSO, *with a frantic
gesture, attended by* GONZALO; SEBASTIAN *and
Antonio in like manner, attended by Adrian and
Francisco.   They all enter the circle which Pros-
pero had made, and there stand charmed; which
Prospero observing, speaks.*

A solemn air and the best comforter
To an unsettled fancy cure thy brains,
Now useless, boil'd within thy skull!   There stand,
For you are spell-stopp'd.   61
Holy Gonzalo, honourable man,
Mine eyes, ev'n sociable to the shew of thine,
Fall fellowly drops.   The charm dissolves apace,
And as the morning steals upon the night,   65
Melting the darkness, so their rising senses
Begin to chase the ignorant fumes that mantle
Their clearer reason.   O good Gonzalo,
My true preserver, and a loyal sir
To him thou follow'st! I will pay thy graces   70
Home both in word and deed.   Most cruelly

Did thou, Alonso, use me and my daughter.
Thy brother was a furtherer in the act.
Thou art pinch'd for't now, Sebastian.   Flesh and
  blood,
You, brother mine, that entertain'd ambition,   75
Expell'd remorse and nature, [who], with Sebastian,
Whose inward pinches therefore are most strong,
Would here have kill'd your king, I do forgive thee,
Unnatural though thou art. — Their understanding
Begins to swell, and the approaching tide   80
Will shortly fill the reasonable shore
That now [lies] foul and muddy.   Not one of them
That yet looks on me, or would know me!   Ariel,
Fetch me the hat and rapier in my cell;
I will discase me, and myself present   85
As I was sometime Milan.   Quickly, spirit;
Thou shalt ere long be free.   [*Exit Ariel.*]

  *Ariel [returning] sings and helps to attire
  him.*
  Ari. "Where the bee sucks, there suck I.
   In a cowslip's bell I lie;
    There I couch when owls do cry.   9(
   On the bat's back I do fly
   After summer merrily.
  Merrily, merrily shall I live now
  Under the blossom that hangs on the bough."

  Pros. Why, that's my dainty Ariel!   I shall miss
  thee;   95
But yet thou shalt have freedom.   So, so, so.
To the King's ship, invisible as thou art;
There shalt thou find the mariners asleep
Under the hatches.   The master and the boatswain
Being awake, enforce them to this place,   100
And presently, I prithee.
  Ari. I drink the air before me, and return
Or ere your pulse twice beat.   [*Exit.*
  Gon. All torment, trouble, wonder, and amaze-
  ment
Inhabits here.   Some heavenly power guide us   105
Out of this fearful country!
  Pros.   Behold, sir King,
The wronged Duke of Milan, Prospero.
For more assurance that a living prince
Does now speak to thee, I embrace thy body;
And to thee and thy company I bid   110
A hearty welcome.
  Alon.   Whe'er thou be'st he or no,
Or some enchanted trifle to abuse me,
As late I have been, I not know.   Thy pulse
Beats as of flesh and blood; and, since I saw thee,
Th' affliction of my mind amends, with which,   115

I fear, a madness held me. This must crave,
An if this be at all, a most strange story.
Thy dukedom I resign and do entreat
Thou pardon me my wrongs. But how should
    Prospero
Be living and be here?
   Pros.   First, noble friend,   120
Let me embrace thine age, whose honour cannot
Be measur'd or confin'd.
   Gon.   Whether this be
Or be not, I'll not swear.
   Pros.   You do yet taste
Some subtleties o' th' isle, that will not let you
Believe things certain. Welcome, my friends all!
[*Aside to Seb. and Ant.*] But you, my brace of lords,
    were I so minded,   126
I here could pluck his Highness' frown upon you
And justify you traitors. At this time
I will tell no tales.
   Seb.   [*Aside.*]   The devil speaks in him.
   Pros.   No.
For you, most wicked sir, whom to call brother 130
Would even infect my mouth, I do forgive
Thy rankest fault, — all of them; and require
My dukedom of thee, which perforce, I know,
Thou must restore.
   Alon.   If thou be'st Prospero,
Give us particulars of thy preservation,   135
How thou hast met us here, [who] three hours since
Were wreck'd upon this shore, where I have lost —
How sharp the point of this remembrance is! —
My dear son Ferdinand.
   Pros.   I am woe for't, sir.
   Alon. Irreparable is the loss, and Patience   140
Says it is past her cure.
   Pros.   I rather think
You have not sought her help, of whose soft grace
For the like loss I have her sovereign aid
And rest myself content.
   Alon.   You the like loss!   144
   Pros. As great to me as late; and, supportable
To make the dear loss, have I means much weaker
Than you may call to comfort you, for I
Have lost my daughter.
   Alon.   A daughter?
O heavens, that they were living both in Naples,
The King and Queen there! That they were, I
    wish   150
Myself were mudded in that oozy bed
Where my son lies. When did you lose your daugh-
    ter?
   Pros. In this last tempest. I perceive, these
    lords
At this encounter do so much admire
That they devour their reason and scarce think 155

Their eyes do offices of truth, their words
Are natural breath; but, howsoe'er you have
Been jostled from your senses, know for certain
That I am Prospero and that very duke
Which was thrust forth of Milan, who most
    strangely   160
Upon this shore, where you were wreck'd, was
    landed,
To be the lord on't. No more yet of this;
For 'tis a chronicle of day by day,
Not a relation for a breakfast nor
Befitting this first meeting. Welcome, sir;   165
This cell's my court. Here have I few attendants,
And subjects none abroad. Pray you, look in.
My dukedom since you have given me again,
I will requite you with as good a thing;
At least bring forth a wonder, to content ye   170
As much as me my dukedom.

   Here Prospero discovers FERDINAND *and* MIRANDA
               playing at chess.

   Mir. Sweet lord, you play me false.
   Fer.   No, my dearest love,
I would not for the world.
   Mir. Yes, for a score of kingdoms you should
    wrangle,
And I would call it fair play.
   Alon.   If this prove   175
A vision of the island, one dear son
Shall I twice lose.
   Seb.   A most high miracle!
   Fer. Though the seas threaten, they are merciful;
I have curs'd them without cause.
                          [*Kneels.*]
   Alon.   Now all the blessings
Of a glad father compass thee about!   180
Arise, and say how thou cam'st here.
   Mir.   O, wonder!
How many goodly creatures are there here!
How beauteous mankind is! O brave new world,
That has such people in't!
   Pros.   'Tis new to thee.
   Alon. What is this maid with whom thou wast at
    play?   185
Your eld'st acquaintance cannot be three hours.
Is she the goddess that hath sever'd us,
And brought us thus together?
   Fer.   Sir, she is mortal,
But by immortal Providence she's mine.
I chose her when I could not ask my father   190
For his advice, nor thought I had one. She
Is daughter to this famous Duke of Milan,
Of whom so often I have heard renown,
But never saw before; of whom I have
Receiv'd a second life; and second father   195

   124. **subtleties:** illusions.   128. **justify:** prove.   136. **[who]** F₂₋₄. *whom* F₁. 145. **late:** recent. 154. **admire:** wonder.
171. S.D. ***discovers:*** discloses. 186. **eld'st:** longest possible.

This lady makes him to me.
   Alon.   I am hers.
But, O, how oddly will it sound that I
Must ask my child forgiveness!
   Pros.   There, sir, stop.
Let us not burden our remembrances with
A heaviness that's gone.
   Gon.   I have inly wept,   200
Or should have spoke ere this. Look down, you gods,
And on this couple drop a blessed crown!
For it is you that have chalk'd forth the way
Which brought us hither.
   Alon.   I say, Amen, Gonzalo!
   Gon. Was Milan thrust from Milan, that his issue   205
Should become Kings of Naples? O, rejoice
Beyond a common joy, and set it down
With gold on lasting pillars: in one voyage
Did Claribel her husband find at Tunis,
And Ferdinand, her brother, found a wife   210
Where he himself was lost, Prospero his dukedom
In a poor isle, and all of us ourselves
When no man was his own.
   Alon. [*To Fer. and Mir.*] Give me your hands.
Let grief and sorrow still embrace his heart
That doth not wish you joy!
   Gon.   Be it so! Amen!

Re-enter ARIEL, *with the* Master *and* BOATSWAIN
amazedly following.

O, look, sir, look, sir! here is more of us.   216
I prophesi'd, if a gallows were on land,
This fellow could not drown. Now, blasphemy,
That swear'st grace o'erboard, not an oath on shore?
Hast thou no mouth by land? What is the news?
   Boats. The best news is, that we have safely found   221
Our king and company; the next, our ship —
Which, but three glasses since, we gave out split —
Is tight and yare and bravely rigg'd as when
We first put out to sea.
   Ari. [*Aside to Pros.*] Sir, all this service   225
Have I done since I went.
   Pros.   [*Aside to Ari.*] My tricksy spirit!
   Alon. These are not natural events; they strengthen
From strange to stranger. Say, how came you hither?
   Boats. If I did think, sir, I were well awake,
I'd strive to tell you. We were dead of sleep,
And — how we know not — all clapp'd under hatches;   231

Where but even now with strange and several noises
Of roaring, shrieking, howling, jingling chains,
And moe diversity of sounds, all horrible,
We were awak'd; straightway, at liberty;   235
Where we, in all [her] trim, freshly beheld
Our royal, good, and gallant ship, our master
Cap'ring to eye her. On a trice, so please you,
Even in a dream, were we divided from them
And were brought moping hither.
   Ari.   [*Aside to Pros.*] Was't well done?   240
   Pros. [*Aside to Ari.*]   Bravely, my diligence.
Thou shalt be free.
   Alon. This is as strange a maze as e'er men trod;
And there is in this business more than nature
Was ever conduct of. Some oracle
Must rectify our knowledge.
   Pros.   Sir, my liege,   245
Do not infest your mind with beating on
The strangeness of this business. At pick'd leisure,
Which shall be shortly, single I'll resolve you,
Which to you shall seem probable, of every
These happen'd accidents; till when, be cheerful
And think of each thing well. [*Aside to Ari.*] Come hither, spirit.   251
Set Caliban and his companions free;
Untie the spell. [*Exit Ariel.*] How fares my gracious sir?
There are yet missing of your company
Some few odd lads that you remember not.   255

Re-enter ARIEL, *driving in* CALIBAN, STEPHANO *and*
TRINCULO, *in their stolen apparel.*

   Ste. Every man shift for all the rest, and let no man take care for himself; for all is but fortune. Coragio, bully-monster, coragio!
   Trin. If these be true spies which I wear in my head, here's a goodly sight.   260
   Cal. O Setebos, these be brave spirits indeed!
How fine my master is! I am afraid
He will chastise me.
   Seb.   Ha, ha!
What things are these, my lord Antonio?
Will money buy 'em?
   Ant.   Very like; one of them   265
Is a plain fish, and, no doubt, marketable.
   Pros. Mark but the badges of these men, my lords,
Then say if they be true. This mis-shapen knave,
His mother was a witch, and one so strong
That could control the moon, make flows and ebbs,
And deal in her command without her power.   271
These three have robb'd me; and this demi-devil —
For he's a bastard one — had plotted with them
To take my life. Two of these fellows you

---

214. **still:** ever.   224. **yare:** ready.   236. [her] (Thirlby conj.). *our* F.   240. **moping:** dazed.   244. **conduct:** director.
245. **rectify:** verify, confirm.   246. **infest:** harass.   248. **single:** in private, or, one by one.   258. **Coragio:** courage.
267. **badges:** liveries; here, the stolen garments.   271. **deal...power:** act in the moon's domain independently.

Must know and own; this thing of darkness I 275
Acknowledge mine.
 Cal.   I shall be pinch'd to death.
 Alon. Is not this Stephano, my drunken butler?
 Seb. He is drunk now. Where had he wine?
 Alon. And Trinculo is reeling ripe. Where
  should they
Find this grand liquor that hath gilded 'em? 280
How cam'st thou in this pickle?
 Trin. I have been in such a pickle since I saw you
last that, I fear me, will never out of my bones. I
shall not fear fly-blowing.
 Seb. Why, how now, Stephano! 285
 Ste. O, touch me not; I am not Stephano, but a
  cramp.
 Pros. You'd be king o' the isle, sirrah?
 Ste. I should have been a sore one then,
 Alon. This is a strange thing as e'er I look'd on.
        [*Pointing to Caliban.*
 Pros. He is as disproportion'd in his manners
As in his shape. Go, sirrah, to my cell; 291
Take with you your companions. As you look
To have my pardon, trim it handsomely.
 Cal. Ay, that I will; and I'll be wise hereafter
And seek for grace. What a thrice-double ass 295
Was I, to take this drunkard for a god
And worship this dull fool!
 Pros.   Go to; away!
 Alon. Hence, and bestow your luggage where you
  found it.
 Seb. Or stole it, rather. 299
     [*Exeunt Cal., Ste., and Trin.*]
 Pros. Sir, I invite your Highness and your train
To my poor cell, where you shall take your rest
For this one night; which, part of it, I'll waste
With such discourse as, I not doubt, shall make it
Go quick away, — the story of my life
And the particular accidents gone by 305
Since I came to this isle. And in the morn
I'll bring you to your ship and so to Naples,

Where I have hope to see the nuptial
Of these our dear-belov'd solemnized;
And thence retire me to my Milan, where 310
Every third thought shall be my grave.
 Alon.   I long
To hear the story of your life, which must
Take the ear strangely.
 Pros.   I'll deliver all;
And promise you calm seas, auspicious gales,
And sail so expeditious that shall catch 315
Your royal fleet far off. [*Aside to Ari.*] My Ariel,
  chick,
That is thy charge. Then to the elements
Be free, and fare thou well! Please you, draw near.
          [*Exeunt omnes.*

EPILOGUE

SPOKEN BY PROSPERO.

Now my charms are all o'erthrown,
And what strength I have's mine own,
Which is most faint. Now, 'tis true,
I must be here confin'd by you,
Or sent to Naples. Let me not, 5
Since I have my dukedom got
And pardon'd the deceiver, dwell
In this bare island by your spell;
But release me from my bands
With the help of your good hands. 10
Gentle breath of yours my sails
Must fill, or else my project fails,
Which was to please. Now I want
Spirits to enforce, art to enchant,
And my ending is despair, 15
Unless I be reliev'd by prayer,
Which pierces so that it assaults
Mercy itself and frees all faults.
 As you from crimes would pardon'd be.
Let your indulgence set me free. [*Exit.* 20

280. **gilded:** intoxicated. 288. **sore:** (1) pained, (2) severe. 313. **deliver:** relate.
Epilogue, 10. hands: applause.

The Life and Death of King John

KING JOHN, like *The Taming of the Shrew*, is not entered in the Stationers' Register. The theory in the case of the comedy is that the copyright of its predecessor, *The Taming of a Shrew*, covered the revised play; and this suggests that a similar explanation of the failure to register the present play is to be found in the entry of the anonymous *Troublesome Raigne of John, King of England* in 1591. It does not appear that there was any edition of *King John* before it was printed in the First Folio, on which the present text is based.

The mention of the play by Francis Meres in his *Palladis Tamia* (1598) gives a later limit for the date, and an earlier limit is approximately fixed by the date of its source, which was published in 1591 but may have been written three or four years earlier. Within this range of ten years we have no good external evidence. Attempts to find allusions to current politics are negatived by the existence of the supposed allusions in the source also. "Basilisco-like" in I.i.244 is an allusion to *Soliman and Perseda* which was registered on Nov. 20, 1592. Most editors place the play between 1593 and 1596. The comparative absence of the so-called lyrical element has led some to place it after *Richard II*, but allowance must be made for the difference in theme and in the leading character. It is a fair guess to date it 1594.

In the time of Henry VIII, Bishop Bale had made the reign of John the subject of an historical morality with a virulently Protestant purpose; but it does not appear that this piece was used in any of the later dramatic treatments of the theme. *The Troublesome Raigne* is an anonymous play in two parts, written in blank verse of considerable power and showing ability to deal imaginatively with historical material. On this Shakespeare founded his *King John*, without seeking either to corroborate or to correct, by reference to the chronicles, the very legendary history of his source. The earlier author not only disregarded chronology, but invented, altered, or ignored the facts with the greatest freedom. Like Bale, though to a less degree, he gave

his work an anti-Papal bias. He invented the part played by the Bastard Faulconbridge; he combined in one person the Archduke of Austria, who had imprisoned Richard I and was dead at the time dealt with in the play, with the Viscount of Limoges, before whose castle Cœur-de-lion had received his mortal wound; he made Arthur younger than he was, and kept Constance a widow — both for purposes of dramatic effectiveness; and he omitted all mention of Magna Charta, and with it of the constitutional element in the quarrel between John and his barons. Such are a few of the departures from historical accuracy which mark almost every scene.

Shakespeare's method of treating the work of his predecessor was peculiar. He re-wrote practically every line, and he condensed the two parts (of thirteen and nine scenes respectively) into five acts. Yet the later play is only 300 lines shorter than the earlier. He selected some scenes and rejected others, but to the action he added almost nothing. On several occasions he economized by representing an action as just completed (e.g., the second coronation), instead of showing it on the stage. He cut out the long comic scene in which Faulconbridge exposes the immorality of the monasteries; and in general he gave up the attempt to picture John as a Protestant hero.

With much gain in compactness and rapidity of action, these changes also involved some loss. The play was left without a leading motive or a truly central character, and some details are not wholly intelligible. Thus the reasons for the Bastard's hatred of Austria, and for his ill-natured speech on the betrothal of Lewis and Blanch (II.i.504ff.) are not clear without the prominence given in *The Troublesome Raigne* to the legendary version of Cœur-de-lion's death at Austria's hands in the one case, and in the other to Eleanor's scheme for marrying Faulconbridge himself to Blanch. More serious is the weaker presentation of the motive for the poisoning of the King by the monk — a deed easily understood in the older play on account of the prominence given throughout to the hostility between John and the Church. Yet Shakespeare supplies the key to the careful reader in King John's instructions to Faulconbridge to "shake the bags of hoarding abbots" (III.iii.7–8), and in the Bastard's indication in IV.ii.141–142 that he has carried out his orders. See also I.i.48–49, and III.iv.171–173.

Shakespeare's additions consist chiefly in the elaboration of character, and in this field the creation of the Bastard Faulconbridge is outstanding. He is the one person in the play whose part one imagines Shakespeare writing with zest. Though at times what Doctor Johnson calls his "levity" approaches clowning, yet he embodies the sturdy sense and patriotism of the loyal Englishman. It is significant that it is to him and not to Prince Henry that the dramatist gives the last speech, which gives noble utterance to what comes as near being a central theme as the play possesses — the supreme importance of national unity.

The number and length of the speeches by Constance are also greatly increased, and at one time critics regarded them as the chief glory of the play and Constance herself as the supreme embodiment of mother-love. But the speeches at times come perilously near rant, and are heavily weighted with sentimentalism and hysteria. That Shakespeare was perfectly aware of this and that it was part of the characterization is made clear by the deadly remark of King Philip, "You are as fond of grief as of your child."

The character of the King presented the dramatist with a difficult problem. However able John may have been — and modern historians rank him high intellectually among English Kings — his vices and his tyranny, his cowardice and his shiftiness made him impossible as a hero, and it is manifest that Shakespeare found him hard to stand. In order to give core and stability to a play in which England stands in peril from foreign enemies, the wickedness of the king made the invention of a Faulconbridge imperative.

The omission of all mention of the Magna Charta is not surprising when we consider the prevailing political attitude of Elizabethan England. After the turmoil and suffering of the Wars of the Roses, the stability of the strong rule of the Tudors was very welcome, and in the sixteenth century Englishmen were content to give the sovereign a fairly free hand without raising the constitutional questions which in the next century again led to civil war.

DESCENDANTS OF HENRY II

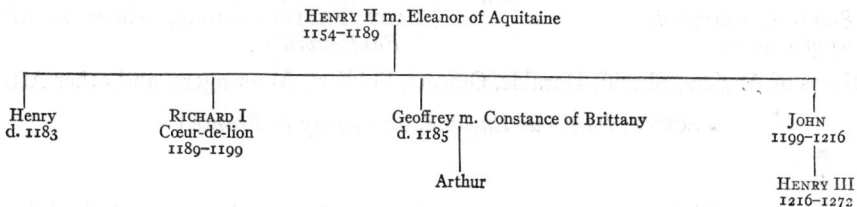

HENRY II m. Eleanor of Aquitaine
1154–1189

| Henry d. 1183 | RICHARD I Cœur-de-lion 1189–1199 | Geoffrey m. Constance of Brittany d. 1185 | JOHN 1199–1216 |

Arthur

HENRY III
1216–1272

THE LIFE AND DEATH OF
KING JOHN

[DRAMATIS PERSONÆ

KING JOHN.
PRINCE HENRY, *son to the king.*
ARTHUR, *duke of Bretagne, nephew to the king.*
The Earl of PEMBROKE.
The Earl of ESSEX.
The Earl of SALISBURY.
The Lord BIGOT.
HUBERT DE BURGH.
ROBERT FAULCONBRIDGE, *son of Sir Robert Faulconbridge.*
PHILIP the BASTARD, *his half-brother.*
JAMES GURNEY, *servant to Lady Faulconbridge.*
PETER of Pomfret, *a prophet.*
PHILIP, *king of France.*

LEWIS, *the Dauphin.*
LYMOGES, *duke of Austria.*
CARDINAL PANDULPH, *the Pope's legate.*
MELUN, *a French Lord.*
CHATILLON, *ambassador from France to King John.*

QUEEN ELEANOR, *widow of Henry II, mother to King John.*
CONSTANCE, *widow of Geoffrey, John's elder brother, mother to Arthur.*
BLANCH of Spain, *niece to King John.*
LADY FAULCONBRIDGE, *widow to Sir Robert Faulconbridge.*

Lords, Citizens of Angiers, Sheriff, Heralds, Officers, Soldiers, Messengers, and other Attendants.

SCENE: *Partly in England, and partly in France.*]

ACT I

SCENE I. [*King John's palace: a room of state.*]

Enter KING JOHN, QUEEN ELEANOR, PEMBROKE, ESSEX, SALISBURY [*and others*], *with* CHATILLON.

K. John. Now, say, Chatillon, what would France with us?

Chat. Thus, after greeting, speaks the King of France
In my behaviour to the majesty,
The borrowed majesty, of England here.

El. A strange beginning: "borrowed majesty!"

K. John. Silence, good mother; hear the embassy.   6

Chat. Philip of France, in right and true behalf
Of thy deceased brother Geoffrey's son,
Arthur Plantagenet, lays most lawful claim
To this fair island and the territories,   10
To Ireland, Poictiers, Anjou, Touraine, Maine,
Desiring thee to lay aside the sword
Which sways usurpingly these several titles,
And put the same into young Arthur's hand,
Thy nephew and right royal sovereign.   15

K. John. What follows if we disallow of this?

Chat. The proud control of fierce and bloody war,
To enforce these rights so forcibly withheld.

K. John. Here have we war for war and blood for blood,
Controlment for controlment: so answer France.

Chat. Then take my king's defiance from my mouth,   21
The farthest limit of my embassy.

K. John. Bear mine to him, and so depart in peace.
Be thou as lightning in the eyes of France;
For ere thou canst report I will be there,   25
The thunder of my cannon shall be heard.
So hence! Be thou the trumpet of our wrath
And sullen presage of your own decay.
An honourable conduct let him have.
Pembroke, look to't. Farewell, Chatillon.   30
[*Exeunt Chatillon and Pembroke.*

Act I, sc. i, 3. In my behaviour: through me.

El. What now, my son! have I not ever said
How that ambitious Constance would not cease
Till she had kindled France and all the world
Upon the right and party of her son?
This might have been prevented and made whole
With very easy arguments of love,   36
Which now the manage of two kingdoms must
With fearful bloody issue arbitrate.

K. John. Our strong possession and our right for
us.

El. Your strong possession much more than your
right,   40
Or else it must go wrong with you and me.
So much my conscience whispers in your ear,
Which none but heaven and you and I shall hear.

Enter a Sheriff [*and whispers to Essex*].

Essex. My liege, here is the strangest contro-
versy
Come from the country to be judg'd by you   45
That e'er I heard.   Shall I produce the men?

K. John. Let them approach.
— Our abbeys and our priories shall pay
This expedition's charge.

Enter ROBERT FAULCONBRIDGE *and* PHILIP
[THE BASTARD].
                        What men are you?

Bast. Your faithful subject I, a gentleman   50
Born in Northamptonshire, and eldest son,
As I suppose, to Robert Faulconbridge,
A soldier by the honour-giving hand
Of Cœur-de-lion knighted in the field.

K. John. What art thou?   55

Rob. The son and heir to that same Faulconbridge.

K. John. Is that the elder, and art thou the heir?
You came not of one mother then, it seems.

Bast. Most certain of one mother, mighty king;
That is well known; and, as I think, one father; 60
But for the certain knowledge of that truth
I put you o'er to heaven and to my mother.
Of that I doubt, as all men's children may.

El. Out on thee, rude man! thou dost shame thy
mother
And wound her honour with this diffidence.   65

Bast. I, madam?   No, I have no reason for it.
That is my brother's plea and none of mine;
The which if he can prove, 'a pops me out
At least from fair five hundred pounds a year.
Heaven guard my mother's honour and my land!

K. John. A good blunt fellow.   Why, being
younger born,   71

Doth he lay claim to thine inheritance?

Bast. I know not why, except to get the land;
But once he slander'd me with bastardy.
But whe'er I be as true begot or no,   75
That still I lay upon my mother's head;
But that I am as well begot, my liege, —
Fair fall the bones that took the pains for me! —
Compare our faces and be judge yourself.
If old Sir Robert did beget us both   80
And were our father, and this son like him,
O old Sir Robert, father, on my knee
I give heaven thanks I was not like to thee!

K. John. Why, what a madcap hath heaven lent
us here!

El. He hath a trick of Cœur-de-lion's face;   85
The accent of his tongue affecteth him.
Do you not read some tokens of my son
In the large composition of this man?

K. John. Mine eye hath well examined his parts
And finds them perfect Richard.   Sirrah, speak, 90
What doth move you to claim your brother's land?

Bast. Because he hath a half-face like my father,
With half that face would he have all my land, —
A half-fac'd groat five hundred pound a year!

Rob. My gracious liege, when that my father
liv'd,   95
Your brother did employ my father much, —

Bast. Well, sir, by this you cannot get my land.
Your tale must be how he employ'd my mother.

Rob. And once dispatch'd him in an embassy
To Germany, there with the Emperor   100
To treat of high affairs touching that time.
Th' advantage of his absence took the King
And in the meantime sojourn'd at my father's,
Where how he did prevail I shame to speak.
But truth is truth.   Large lengths of seas and shores
Between my father and my mother lay,   106
As I have heard my father speak himself,
When this same lusty gentleman was got.
Upon his death-bed he by will bequeath'd
His lands to me, and took it on his death   110
That this my mother's son was none of his;
And if he were, he came into the world
Full fourteen weeks before the course of time.
Then, good my liege, let me have what is mine,
My father's land, as was my father's will.   115

K. John. Sirrah, your brother is legitimate.
Your father's wife did after wedlock bear him,
And if she did play false, the fault was hers;
Which fault lies on the hazards of all husbands
That marry wives.   Tell me, how if my brother,
Who, as you say, took pains to get this son,   121
Had of your father claim'd this son for his?

37. **manage:** managers, governments. 50. *Bast.* Here and in 59, 66, 73, 92, 97, 132, F has *Philip* or *Phil.* Elsewhere
usually *Bast.* 62. **put you o'er:** refer you. 65. **diffidence:** mistrust. 81. **this son:** Robert. 86. **affecteth:** takes after.
92. **half-face:** (1) profile, (2) pinched face. 94. **half-fac'd groat:** groat (4*d.*) with the sovereign's head in profile. It was also
used as a term of contempt. 110. **took ... death:** swore solemnly. 113. **course:** due course. 119. **lies on:** is one of.

In sooth, good friend, your father might have kept
This calf bred from his cow from all the world;   124
In sooth he might; then, if he were my brother's,
My brother might not claim him, nor your father,
Being none of his, refuse him. This concludes:
My mother's son did get your father's heir;
Your father's heir must have your father's land.
    Rob. Shall then my father's will be of no force
To dispossess that child which is not his?   131
    Bast. Of no more force to dispossess me, sir,
Than was his will to get me, as I think.
    El. Whether hadst thou rather be a Faulcon-
      bridge
And like thy brother, to enjoy thy land,   135
Or the reputed son of Cœur-de-lion,
Lord of thy presence and no land beside?
    Bast. Madam, an if my brother had my shape
And I had his, Sir Robert's his, like him;
And if my legs were two such riding-rods,   140
My arms such eel-skins stuff'd, my face so thin
That in mine ear I durst not stick a rose
Lest men should say, Look, where three-farthings
    goes!
And, to his shape, were heir to all this land, —
Would I might never stir from off this place! —
I would give it every foot to have this face;   146
[I] would not be Sir Nob in any case.
    El. I like thee well. Wilt thou forsake thy for-
      tune,
Bequeath thy land to him and follow me?
I am a soldier, and now bound to France.   150
    Bast. Brother, take you my land, I'll take my
      chance.
Your face hath got five hundred pound a year,
Yet sell your face for five pence and 'tis dear.
Madam, I'll follow you unto the death.   154
    El. Nay, I would have you go before me thither.
    Bast. Our country manners give our betters way.
    K. John. What is thy name?
    Bast. Philip, my liege, so is my name begun;
Philip, good old Sir Robert's wife's eldest son.
    K. John. From henceforth bear his name whose
      form thou bearest.   160
Kneel thou down Philip, but rise [up] more great,
Arise Sir Richard and Plantagenet.
    Bast. Brother by th' mother's side, give me your
      hand;
My father gave me honour, yours gave land.
Now blessed be the hour by night or day   165
When I was got, Sir Robert was away!
    El. The very spirit of Plantagenet!

I am thy grandam, Richard; call me so.
    Bast. Madam, by chance but not by truth; what
      though?
Something about, a little from the right,   170
   In at the window, or else o'er the hatch.
Who dares not stir by day must walk by night,
   And have is have, however men do catch.
Near or far off, well won is still well shot,
And I am I, howe'er I was begot.   175
    K. John. Go, Faulconbridge, now hast thou thy
      desire;
A landless knight makes thee a landed squire.
Come, madam, and come, Richard, we must speed
For France, for France, for it is more than need.
    Bast. Brother, adieu; good fortune come to thee!
For thou wast got i' th' way of honesty.   181
                 [Exeunt all but Bastard.
A foot of honour better than I was;
But many a many foot of land the worse.
Well, now can I make any Joan a lady.   184
"Good den, Sir Richard!" "God-a-mercy, fellow!"
And if his name be George, I'll call him Peter;
For new-made honour doth forget men's names;
'Tis too respective and too sociable
For your conversion. Now your traveller,
He and his toothpick at my worship's mess,   190
— And when my knightly stomach is suffic'd,
Why then I suck my teeth and catechise
My picked man of countries. "My dear sir,"
Thus, leaning on mine elbow, I begin,
"I shall beseech you" — that is question now;   195
And then comes answer like an Absey book.
"O sir," says answer, "at your best command,
At your employment, at your service, sir."
"No, sir," says question, "I, sweet sir, at yours."
And so, ere answer knows what question would,
Saving in dialogue of compliment,   201
And talking of the Alps and Apennines,
The Pyrenean and the river Po,
It draws toward supper in conclusion so.
But this is worshipful society   205
And fits the mounting spirit like myself,
For he is but a bastard to the time
That doth not smack of observation.
And so am I, whether I smack or no;
And not alone in habit and device,   210
Exterior form, outward accoutrement,
But from the inward motion to deliver
Sweet, sweet, sweet poison for the age's tooth;
Which, though I will not practise to deceive,
Yet, to avoid deceit, I mean to learn;   215

    140. **riding-rods:** riding switch.   143. **three-farthings.** The coin of this value was stamped with a rose behind the Queen's head.   144. **to his shape:** with his appearance.   147. [I] F₂.   *It* F₁.   **Nob:** Bob.   161. **rise [up]** (Pope).   *rise* F.   *arise* Steevens.   171. **hatch:** the lower half of a door opening in two parts.   188–89. **'Tis . . . conversion:** It is showing too much respect and sociability for one just promoted.   193. **picked:** affectedly fastidious.   196. **Absey book:** A B C book, primer.   208. **smack of observation:** use flattery somewhat.   209. **am I:** i.e., not a true child of the time.   212. **from:** lacking.   215. **deceit:** being deceived.

For it shall strew the footsteps of my rising.
But who comes in such haste in riding-robes?
What woman-post is this? Hath she no husband
That will take pains to blow a horn before her?

Enter LADY FAULCONBRIDGE *and* JAMES
GURNEY.

O me! 'tis my mother. How now, good lady! 220
What brings you here to court so hastily?

  Lady F. Where is that slave, thy brother? Where
is he,
That holds in chase mine honour up and down?

  Bast. My brother Robert? Old Sir Robert's
son?
Colbrand the giant, that same mighty man? 225
Is it Sir Robert's son that you seek so?

  Lady F. Sir Robert's son! Ay, thou unreverend
boy,
Sir Robert's son. Why scorn'st thou at Sir Robert?
He is Sir Robert's son, and so art thou.

  Bast. James Gurney, wilt thou give us leave a
while? 230

  Gur. Good leave, good Philip.

  Bast.   Philip! sparrow! James,
There's toys abroad; anon I'll tell thee more.
                       [*Exit Gurney.*
Madam, I was not old Sir Robert's son.
Sir Robert might have eat his part in me
Upon Good-Friday and ne'er broke his fast. 235
Sir Robert could do well; marry, to confess,
Could he get me? Sir Robert could not do it;
We know his handiwork. Therefore, good mother,
To whom am I beholding for these limbs?
Sir Robert never holp to make this leg. 240

  Lady F. Hast thou conspired with thy brother
too,
That for thine own gain shouldst defend mine
honour?
What means this scorn, thou most untoward knave?

  Bast. "Knight, knight," good mother, Basilisco-
like. 244
What! I am dubb'd! I have it on my shoulder.
But, mother, I am not Sir Robert's son;
I have disclaim'd Sir Robert and my land;
Legitimation, name, and all is gone.
Then, good my mother, let me know my father;
Some proper man, I hope. Who was it, mother?

  Lady F. Hast thou denied thyself a Faulconbridge? 251

  Bast. As faithfully as I deny the devil.

  Lady F. King Richard Cœur-de-lion was thy
father.
By long and vehement suit I was seduc'd

To make room for him in my husband's bed. 255
Heaven lay not my transgression to my charge!
[Thou] art the issue of my dear offence,
Which was so strongly urg'd past my defence.

  Bast. Now, by this light, were I to get again,
Madam, I would not wish a better father. 260
Some sins do bear their privilege on earth,
And so doth yours; your fault was not your folly.
Needs must you lay your heart at his dispose,
Subjected tribute to commanding love,
Against whose fury and unmatched force 265
The aweless lion could not wage the fight
Nor keep his princely heart from Richard's hand.
He that perforce robs lions of their hearts
May easily win a woman's. Ay, my mother,
With all my heart I thank thee for my father! 270
Who lives and dares but say thou didst not well
When I was got, I'll send his soul to hell.
Come, lady, I will show thee to my kin;
  And they shall say, when Richard me begot,
If thou hadst said him nay, it had been sin. 275
  Who says it was, he lies; I say 'twas not.
                       [*Exeunt.*

[ACT II]

SCENE [I. *France.*] *Before Angiers.*

Enter AUSTRIA [*and forces, drums, etc., on one side:
on the other*] KING PHILIP *of France* [*and his
power*]; LEWIS, ARTHUR, CONSTANCE [*and attendants*].

  Lew. Before Angiers well met, brave Austria.
Arthur, that great forerunner of thy blood,
Richard, that robb'd the lion of his heart
And fought the holy wars in Palestine,
By this brave duke came early to his grave; 5
And for amends to his posterity,
At our importance hither is he come
To spread his colours, boy, in thy behalf,
And to rebuke the usurpation
Of thy unnatural uncle, English John. 10
Embrace him, love him, give him welcome hither.

  Arth. God shall forgive you Cœur-de-lion's death
The rather that you give his offspring life,
Shadowing their right under your wings of war.
I give you welcome with a powerless hand, 15
But with a heart full of unstained love.
Welcome before the gates of Angiers, Duke.

  Lew. A noble boy! Who would not do thee
right?

  Aust. Upon thy cheek lay I this zealous kiss
As seal to this indenture of my love 20
That to my home I will no more return

---

231. **Philip! sparrow!** Philip was a name commonly given to sparrows.   244. **Basilisco-like.** Theobald noted that Basi-
lisco, a character in Kyd's *Soliman and Perseda*, is quoted here.   257. **[Thou]** F4.   *That* F1-3.
  Act II, sc. i, 7. importance: importunity.

Till Angiers and the right thou hast in France,
Together with that pale, that white-fac'd shore,
Whose foot spurns back the ocean's roaring tides
And coops from other lands her islanders,   25
Even till that England, hedg'd in with the main,
That water-walled bulwark, still secure
And confident from foreign purposes,
Even till that utmost corner of the west
Salute thee for her king; till then, fair boy,   30
Will I not think of home, but follow arms.
 Const. O, take his mother's thanks, a widow's
  thanks,
Till your strong hand shall help to give him strength
To make a more requital to your love!
 Aust. The peace of heaven is theirs that lift their
  swords   35
In such a just and charitable war.
 K. Phi. Well then, to work! Our cannon shall
  be bent
Against the brows of this resisting town.
Call for our chiefest men of discipline
To cull the plots of best advantages.   40
We'll lay before this town our royal bones,
Wade to the market-place in Frenchmen's blood,
But we will make it subject to this boy.
 Const. Stay for an answer to your embassy,
Lest unadvis'd you stain your swords with blood.
My Lord Chatillon may from England bring   46
That right in peace which here we urge in war,
And then we shall repent each drop of blood
That hot rash haste so indirectly shed.

    Enter CHATILLON.

 K. Phi. A wonder, lady! Lo, upon thy wish,
Our messenger Chatillon is arriv'd!   51
What England says, say briefly, gentle lord;
We coldly pause for thee; Chatillon, speak.
 Chat. Then turn your forces from this paltry
  siege
And stir them up against a mightier task.   55
England, impatient of your just demands,
Hath put himself in arms. The adverse winds,
Whose leisure I have stay'd, have given him time
To land his legions all as soon as I;
His marches are expedient to this town,   60
His forces strong, his soldiers confident.
With him along is come the mother-queen,
An [Ate,] stirring him to blood and strife;
With her her niece, the Lady Blanch of Spain;
With them a bastard of the king's deceas'd;   65
And all th' unsettled humours of the land,
Rash, inconsiderate, fiery voluntaries
With ladies' faces and fierce dragons' spleens,

Have sold their fortunes at their native homes,
Bearing their birthrights proudly on their backs,
To make a hazard of new fortunes here.   71
In brief, a braver choice of dauntless spirits
Than now the English bottoms have waft o'er
Did never float upon the swelling tide
To do offence and scath in Christendom.   75
The interruption of their churlish drums
Cuts off more circumstance.   They are at hand
        [*Drum beats.*
To parley or to fight; therefore prepare.
 K. Phi. How much unlook'd for is this expedi-
  tion!
 Aust. By how much unexpected, by so much   80
We must awake endeavour for defence,
For courage mounteth with occasion.
Let them be welcome then; we are prepar'd.

  Enter KING JOHN, ELEANOR, BLANCH, *the*
   BASTARD, PEMBROKE, *and others.*

 K. John. Peace be to France, if France in
  peace permit
Our just and lineal entrance to our own;   85
If not, bleed France, and peace ascend to heaven,
Whiles we, God's wrathful agent, do correct
Their proud contempt that beats His peace to
  heaven.
 K. Phi. Peace be to England, if that war return
From France to England, there to live in peace.   90
England we love; and for that England's sake
With burden of our armour here we sweat.
This toil of ours should be a work of thine;
But thou from loving England art so far
That thou hast under-wrought his lawful king,   95
Cut off the sequence of posterity,
Out-faced infant state, and done a rape
Upon the maiden virtue of the crown.
Look here upon thy brother Geoffrey's face.
These eyes, these brows, were moulded out of his;
This little abstract doth contain that large   101
Which died in Geoffrey; and the hand of Time
Shall draw this brief into as huge a volume.
That Geoffrey was thy elder brother born,
And this his son; England was Geoffrey's right,   105
And this is Geoffrey's: in the name of God
How comes it then that thou art call'd a king,
When living blood doth in these temples beat,
Which owe the crown that thou o'ermasterest?
 K. John. From whom hast thou this great com-
  mission, France,   110
To draw my answer from thy articles?
 K. Phi. From that supernal judge that stirs good
  thoughts

---

 39. **discipline:** science of war. 40. **cull the plots:** select the plans. 60. **expedient to:** expeditiously approaching. 63.
[**Ate**] (Rowe): goddess of infatuation. *Ace* F. 77. **circumstance:** detail. 95. **under-wrought his:** undermined its. 97. **Out-
faced...state:** defied the authority of the child-king. 101. **abstract:** copy. 106. **this:** i.e., Arthur's. Rann emends to *his.*
109. **owe:** own. 111. **from thy articles.** John means that Philip speaks as if he were reading from a formal indictment.

In any breast of strong authority,
To look into the blots and stains of right.
That Judge hath made me guardian to this boy,
Under whose warrant I impeach thy wrong   116
And by whose help I mean to chastise it.
K. John. Alack, thou dost usurp authority.
K. Phi. Excuse it is to beat usurping down.
El. Who is it thou dost call usurper, France?   120
Const. Let me make answer; thy usurping son.
El. Out, insolent! thy bastard shall be king
That thou mayst be a queen, and check the world!
Const. My bed was ever to thy son as true
As thine was to thy husband; and this boy   125
Liker in feature to his father Geoffrey
Than thou and John in manners, being as like
As rain to water, or devil to his dam.
My boy a bastard! By my soul, I think
His father never was so true begot.   130
It cannot be, an if thou wert his mother.
El. There's a good mother, boy, that blots thy
    father.
Const. There's a good grandam, boy, that would
    blot thee.
Aust. Peace!
Bast.   Hear the crier.
Aust.   What the devil art thou?
Bast. One that will play the devil, sir, with you,
An 'a may catch your hide and you alone.   136
You are the hare of whom the proverb goes,
Whose valour plucks dead lions by the beard.
I'll smoke your skin-coat an I catch you right.
Sirrah, look to't; i' faith, I will, i' faith.   140
Blanch. O, well did he become that lion's robe,
That did disrobe the lion of that robe!
Bast. It lies as sightly on the back of him
As great [Alcides' shows] upon an ass.
But, ass, I'll take that burden from your back,   145
Or lay on that shall make your shoulders crack.
Aust. What cracker is this same that deafs our
    ears
With this abundance of superfluous breath?
King [Philip], determine what we shall do straight.
K. Phi. Women and fools, break off your con-
    ference.   150
King John, this is the very sum of all:
England and Ireland, Anjou, Touraine, Maine,
In right of Arthur do I claim of thee.
Wilt thou resign them and lay down thy arms?
K. John. My life as soon. I do defy thee,
    France.   155
Arthur of Bretagne, yield thee to my hand,
And out of my dear love I'll give thee more
Than e'er the coward hand of France can win.

Submit thee, boy.
El.   Come to thy grandam, child.
Const. Do, child, go to it grandam, child;   160
Give grandam kingdom, and it grandam will
Give it a plum, a cherry, and a fig.
There's a good grandam.
Arth.   Good my mother, peace.
I would that I were low laid in my grave;
I am not worth this coil that's made for me.   165
El. His mother shames him so, poor boy, he
    weeps.
Const. Now shame upon you, whe'er she does or
    no!
His grandam's wrongs, and not his mother's
    shames,
Draws those heaven-moving pearls from his poor
    eyes,
Which Heaven shall take in nature of a fee;   170
Ay, with these crystal beads Heaven shall be brib'd
To do him justice and revenge on you.
El. Thou monstrous slanderer of heaven and
    earth!
Const. Thou monstrous injurer of heaven and
    earth,
Call not me slanderer! Thou and thine usurp   175
The dominations, royalties, and rights
Of this oppressed boy. This is thy eldest son's son,
Infortunate in nothing but in thee.
Thy sins are visited in this poor child;
The canon of the law is laid on him,   180
Being but the second generation
Removed from thy sin-conceiving womb.
K. John. Bedlam, have done.
Const.   I have but this to say,
That he is not only plagued for her sin,
But God hath made her sin and her the plague
On this removed issue, plagu'd for her   186
And with her plague; her sin his injury,
Her injury the beadle to her sin,
All punish'd in the person of this child,
And all for her. A plague upon her!   190
El. Thou unadvised scold, I can produce
A will that bars the title of thy son.
Const. Ay, who doubts that? A will! a wicked
    will;
A woman's will; a cank'red grandam's will!
K. Phi. Peace, lady! pause, or be more temper-
    ate.   195
It ill beseems this presence to cry aim
To these ill-tuned repetitions.
Some trumpet summon hither to the walls
These men of Angiers. Let us hear them speak
Whose title they admit, Arthur's or John's.   200

136. **hide.** Austria was wearing Richard's lion-skin. 139. **smoke:** beat. 144. **[Alcides' shows]** (Theobald). The reference is to the skin of the Nemean lion worn by Hercules. *Alcides shooes* F. 147. **cracker:** boaster. 149. **[Philip]** (Theobald). *Lewis* F. 165. **coil:** turmoil. 183. **Bedlam:** lunatic. 187. **his injury:** the wrong done to him (Arthur). 188. **Her injury:** the wrong done by her (Eleanor). **beadle:** the parish whipper. 196. **cry aim:** encourage.

Trumpet sounds.   Enter a CITIZEN *upon the*
walls [*attended*].
Cit. Who is it that hath warn'd us to the walls?
K. Phi. 'Tis France, for England.
K. John.   England, for itself.
You men of Angiers, and my loving subjects, —
K. Phi. You loving men of Angiers, Arthur's
subjects,
Our trumpet call'd you to this gentle parle —   205
K. John. For our advantage; therefore hear us
first.
These flags of France, that are advanced here
Before the eye and prospect of your town,
Have hither march'd to your endamagement.
The cannons have their bowels full of wrath,   210
And ready mounted are they to spit forth
Their iron indignation 'gainst your walls.
All preparation for a bloody siege
And merciless proceeding by these French   214
[Confronts your] city's eyes, your winking gates;
And but for our approach those sleeping stones,
That as a waist doth girdle you about,
By the compulsion of their ordinance
By this time from their fixed beds of lime
Had been dishabited, and wide havoc made   220
For bloody power to rush upon your peace.
But on the sight of us, your lawful king,
Who painfully with much expedient march
Have brought a countercheck before your gates,
To save unscratch'd your city's threat'ned cheeks,
Behold, the French amaz'd vouchsafe a parle;   226
And now, instead of bullets wrapp'd in fire,
To make a shaking fever in your walls,
They shoot but calm words folded up in smoke,
To make a faithless error in your ears;   230
Which trust accordingly, kind citizens,
And let us in, your king, whose labour'd spirits,
Forwearied in this action of swift speed,
Crave harbourage within your city walls.
K. Phi. When I have said, make answer to us
both.   235
Lo, in this right hand, whose protection
Is most divinely vow'd upon the right
Of him it holds, stands young Plantagenet,
Son to the elder brother of this man,
And king o'er him and all that he enjoys.   240
For this down-trodden equity, we tread
In warlike march these greens before your town,
Being no further enemy to you
Than the constraint of hospitable zeal
In the relief of this oppressed child   245
Religiously provokes.   Be pleased then
To pay that duty which you truly owe
To him that owes it, namely this young prince;
And then our arms, like to a muzzled bear

Save in aspect, hath all offence seal'd up: 250
Our cannons' malice vainly shall be spent
Against the invulnerable clouds of heaven;
And with a blessed and unvex'd retire,
With unhack'd swords and helmets all unbruis'd,
We will bear home that lusty blood again   255
Which here we came to spout against your town,
And leave your children, wives, and you in peace.
But if you fondly pass our proffer'd offer,
'Tis not the roundure of your old-fac'd walls
Can hide you from our messengers of war,   260
Though all these English and their discipline
Were harbour'd in their rude circumference.
Then tell us, shall your city call us lord,
In that behalf which we have challeng'd it?
Or shall we give the signal to our rage   265
And stalk in blood to our possession?
Cit. In brief, we are the King of England's sub-
jects.
For him, and in his right, we hold this town.
K. John. Acknowledge then the King, and let
me in.
Cit. That can we not; but he that proves the
King,   270
To him will we prove loyal.   Till that time
Have we ramm'd up our gates against the world.
K. John. Doth not the crown of England prove
the King?
And if not that, I bring you witnesses,
Twice fifteen thousand hearts of England's breed, —
Bast. Bastards, and else.   276
K. John. To verify our title with their lives.
K. Phi. As many and as well-born bloods as
those —
Bast. Some bastards too.   279
K. Phi. Stand in his face to contradict his claim.
Cit. Till you compound whose right is worthiest,
We for the worthiest hold the right for both.
K. John. Then God forgive the sin of all those
souls
That to their everlasting residence,
Before the dew of evening fall, shall fleet   285
In dreadful trial of our kingdom's king!
K. Phi. Amen, amen!   Mount, chevaliers!   To
arms!
Bast. Saint George, that swing'd the dragon, and
e'er since
Sits on his horseback at mine hostess' door,
Teach us some fence! [*To Aust.*] Sirrah, were I at
home,   290
At your den, sirrah, with your lioness,
I would set an ox-head to your lion's hide,
And make a monster of you.
Aust.   Peace! no more.
Bast. O, tremble, for you hear the lion roar.

205. parle: parley.   215. [Confronts your] (Capell).   *Comfort yours* F.   winking: shut.   220. dishabited: dislodged.
253. retire: withdrawal.   259. roundure: circle.   276. else· others.   281. compound: settle.

K. John. Up higher to the plain, where we'll set
    forth   295
In best appointment all our regiments.
Bast. Speed then, to take advantage of the field.
K. Phi. It shall be so; and at the other hill
Command the rest to stand.   God and our right!
                            [*Exeunt.*

Here after excursions, enter the HERALD OF
FRANCE, *with trumpets, to the gates.*

F. Her. You men of Angiers, open wide your
    gates,   300
And let young Arthur, Duke of Bretagne, in,
Who by the hand of France this day hath made
Much work for tears in many an English mother,
Whose sons lie scattered on the bleeding ground.
Many a widow's husband grovelling lies,   305
Coldly embracing the discoloured earth;
And victory, with little loss, doth play
Upon the dancing banners of the French,
Who are at hand, triumphantly displayed,
To enter conquerors and to proclaim   310
Arthur of Bretagne England's king and yours.

Enter ENGLISH HERALD, *with trumpet.*

E. Her. Rejoice, you men of Angiers, ring your
    bells,
King John, your king and England's, doth ap-
    proach,
Commander of this hot malicious day.
Their armours, that march'd hence so silver-bright,
Hither return all gilt with Frenchmen's blood.   316
There stuck no plume in any English crest
That is removed by a staff of France.
Our colours do return in those same hands
That did display them when we first march'd forth;
And, like a jolly troop of huntsmen, come   321
Our lusty English, all with purpled hands,
Dy'd in the dying slaughter of their foes.
Open your gates and give the victors way.
  [*Cit.*] Heralds, from off our towers we might be-
    hold,   325
From first to last, the onset and retire
Of both your armies, whose equality
By our best eyes cannot be censured.
Blood hath bought blood and blows have answer'd
    blows;
Strength match'd with strength, and power con-
    fronted power.   330
Both are alike; and both alike we like.
One must prove greatest.   While they weigh so
    even,
We hold our town for neither, yet for both.

Re-enter the two KINGS, *with their powers, at
several doors.*

K. John. France, hast thou yet more blood to
    cast away?
Say, shall the current of our right [run] on?   335
Whose passage, vex'd with thy impediment,
Shall leave his native channel and o'erswell
With course disturb'd even thy confining shores,
Unless thou let his silver water keep
A peaceful progress to the ocean.   340
  K. Phi. England, thou hast not sav'd one drop
    of blood
In this hot trial more than we of France;
Rather, lost more.   And by this hand I swear,
That sways the earth this climate overlooks,
Before we will lay down our just-borne arms   345
We'll put thee down, 'gainst whom these arms we
    bear,
Or add a royal number to the dead,
Gracing the scroll that tells of this war's loss
With slaughter coupled to the name of kings.
  Bast. Ha, majesty! how high thy glory towers
When the rich blood of kings is set on fire!   351
O, now doth Death line his dead chaps with steel;
The swords of soldiers are his teeth, his fangs;
And now he feasts, mousing the flesh of men,
In undetermin'd differences of kings.   355
Why stand these royal fronts amazed thus?
Cry, havoc! kings.   Back to the stained field,
You equal potents, fiery-kindled spirits!
Then let confusion of one part confirm
The other's peace.   Till then, blows, blood, and
    death!   360
  K. John. Whose party do the townsmen yet
    admit?
  K. Phi. Speak, citizens, for England.   Who's
    your king?
  Cit. The King of England, when we know the
    King.
  K. Phi. Know him in us, that here hold up his
    right.
  K. John. In us, that are our own great deputy,
And bear possession of our person here,   366
Lord of our presence, Angiers, and of you.
  [*Cit.*] A greater power than we denies all this;
And till it be undoubted, we do lock
Our former scruple in our strong-barr'd gates,   370
Kings of our fear, until our fears, resolv'd,
Be by some certain king purg'd and depos'd.
  Bast. By heaven, these scroyles of Angiers flout
    you, kings,
And stand securely on their battlements
As in a theatre, whence they gape and point   375
At your industrious scenes and acts of death.
Your royal presences be rul'd by me:

Do like the mutines of Jerusalem,
Be friends a while, and both conjointly bend
Your sharpest deeds of malice on this town.　380
By east and west let France and England mount
Their battering cannon charged to the mouths,
Till their soul-fearing clamours have brawl'd down
The flinty ribs of this contemptuous city.
I'd play incessantly upon these jades,　385
Even till unfenced desolation
Leave them as naked as the vulgar air.
That done, dissever your united strengths,
And part your mingled colours once again;
Turn face to face and bloody point to point;　390
Then, in a moment, Fortune shall cull forth
Out of one side her happy minion,
To whom in favour she shall give the day,
And kiss him with a glorious victory.
How like you this wild counsel, mighty states?　395
Smacks it not something of the policy?
　　K. John. Now, by the sky that hangs above our
　　　heads,
I like it well.　France, shall we knit our powers
And lay this Angiers even with the ground;
Then after fight who shall be king of it?　400
　　Bast. An if thou hast the mettle of a king,
Being wrong'd as we are by this peevish town,
Turn thou the mouth of thy artillery,
As we will ours, against these saucy walls;
And when that we have dash'd them to the ground,
Why then defy each other, and pell-mell　406
Make work upon ourselves, for heaven or hell.
　　K. Phi. Let it be so.　Say, where will you as-
　　　sault?
　　K. John. We from the west will send destruction
Into this city's bosom.　410
　　Aust. I from the north.
　　K. Phi.　　　　Our thunder from the south
Shall rain their drift of bullets on this town.
　　Bast. O prudent discipline!　From north to
　　　south,
Austria and France shoot in each other's mouth.
I'll stir them to it.　Come, away, away!　415
　　[*Cit.*] Hear us, great kings!　Vouchsafe a while to
　　　stay,
And I shall show you peace and fair-fac'd league,
Win you this city without stroke or wound,
Rescue those breathing lives to die in beds,
That here come sacrifices for the field.　420
Persever not, but hear me, mighty kings.
　　K. John. Speak on with favour; we are bent to
　　　hear.
　　Cit. That daughter there of Spain, the Lady
　　　Blanch,
Is [niece] to England.　Look upon the years

Of Lewis the Dauphin and that lovely maid.　425
If lusty Love should go in quest of beauty,
Where should he find it fairer than in Blanch?
If zealous Love should go in search of virtue,
Where should he find it purer than in Blanch?
If Love ambitious sought a match of birth,　430
Whose veins bound richer blood than Lady Blanch?
Such as she is, in beauty, virtue, birth,
Is the young Dauphin every way complete;
If not complete, [I] say he is not she;
And she again wants nothing, to name want,　435
If want it be not that she is not he.
He is the half part of a blessed man,
Left to be finished by such as she;
And she a fair divided excellence,
Whose fulness of perfection lies in him.　440
O, two such silver currents, when they join,
Do glorify the banks that bound them in;
And two such shores to two such streams made one,
Two such controlling bounds shall you be, kings,
To these two princes, if you marry them.　445
This union shall do more than battery can
To our fast-closed gates; for at this match,
With swifter spleen than powder can enforce,
The mouth of passage shall we fling wide ope
And give you entrance; but without this match,
The sea enraged is not half so deaf,　451
Lions more confident, mountains and rocks
More free from motion, no, not Death himself
In mortal fury half so peremptory,
As we to keep this city.
　　Bast.　　　　Here's a stay　455
That shakes the rotten carcass of old Death
Out of his rags!　Here's a large mouth, indeed,
That spits forth death and mountains, rocks and
　　　seas,
Talks as familiarly of roaring lions
As maids of thirteen do of puppy-dogs!　460
What cannoneer begot this lusty blood?
He speaks plain cannon fire, and smoke, and
　　　bounce;
He gives the bastinado with his tongue:
Our ears are cudgell'd; not a word of his
But buffets better than a fist of France.　465
Zounds! I was never so bethump'd with words
Since I first call'd my brother's father dad.
　　El. Son, list to this conjunction, make this
　　　match;
Give with our niece a dowry large enough;
For by this knot thou shalt so surely tie　470
Thy now unsur'd assurance to the crown,
That yon green boy shall have no sun to ripe
The bloom that promiseth a mighty fruit.
I see a yielding in the looks of France;

---

378. **mutines:** mutineers — John of Giscala and Simon bar Gioras, who combined against the Romans.　392. **minion:** favorite.　396. **the policy:** i.e., the right policy.　424. **[niece]** (Singer).　*neere* F.　434. **[I]** (Kittredge).　*of* F.　447. **match.** A pun.　455. **stay:** stoppage.　462. **bounce:** sound of the cannon.

Mark, how they whisper. Urge them while their
    souls   475
Are capable of this ambition,
Lest zeal, now melted by the windy breath
Of soft petitions, pity, and remorse,
Cool and congeal again to what it was.
[*Cit.*] Why answer not the double majesties   480
This friendly treaty of our threat'ned town?
    K. Phi. Speak England first, that hath been for-
    ward first
To speak unto this city. What say you?
    K. John. If that the Dauphin there, thy princely
    son,
Can in this book of beauty read, "I love,"   485
Her dowry shall weigh equal with a queen;
For [Anjou] and fair Touraine, Maine, Poictiers,
And all that we upon this side the sea,
Except this city now by us besieg'd,
Find liable to our crown and dignity,   490
Shall gild her bridal bed, and make her rich
In titles, honours, and promotions,
As she in beauty, education, blood,
Holds hand with any princess of the world.
    K. Phi. What say'st thou, boy? Look in the
    lady's face.   495
    Lew. I do, my lord; and in her eye I find
A wonder, or a wondrous miracle,
The shadow of myself form'd in her eye;
Which, being but the shadow of your son,
Becomes a sun and makes your son a shadow.   500
I do protest I never lov'd myself
Till now infixed I beheld myself
Drawn in the flattering table of her eye.
                [*Whispers with Blanch.*
    Bast. "Drawn in the flattering table of her eye!"
    Hang'd in the frowning wrinkle of her brow!   505
And quarter'd in her heart! he doth espy
    Himself love's traitor. This is pity now,
That, hang'd and drawn and quarter'd, there
    should be
In such a love so vile a lout as he.
    Blanch. My uncle's will in this respect is mine.
If he see aught in you that makes him like,   511
That anything he sees, which moves his liking,
I can with ease translate it to my will;
Or if you will, to speak more properly,
I will enforce it easily to my love.   515
Further I will not flatter you, my lord,
That all I see in you is worthy love,
Than this, that nothing do I see in you,
Though churlish thoughts themselves should be
    your judge,
That I can find should merit any hate.   520
    K. John. What say these young ones? What
    say you, my niece?

    Blanch. That she is bound in honour still to do
What you in wisdom still vouchsafe to say.
    K. John. Speak then, Prince Dauphin. Can you
    love this lady?
    Lew. Nay, ask me if I can refrain from love;   525
For I do love her most unfeignedly.
    K. John. Then do I give Volquessen, Touraine,
    Maine,
Poictiers, and Anjou, these five provinces,
With her to thee; and this addition more,
Full thirty thousand marks of English coin.   530
Philip of France, if thou be pleas'd withal,
Command thy son and daughter to join hands.
    K. Phi. It likes us well. Young princes, close
    your hands.
    Aust. And your lips too; for I am well assur'd
That I did so when I was first assur'd.   535
    K. Phi. Now, citizens of Angiers, ope your gates,
Let in that amity which you have made;
For at Saint Mary's Chapel presently
The rites of marriage shall be solemniz'd.
Is not the Lady Constance in this troop?   540
I know she is not, for this match made up
Her presence would have interrupted much.
Where is she and her son? Tell me, who knows.
    Lew. She is sad and passionate at your Highness'
    tent.
    K. Phi. And, by my faith, this league that we
    have made   545
Will give her sadness very little cure.
Brother of England, how may we content
This widow lady? In her right we came,
Which we, God knows, have turn'd another way,
To our own vantage.
    K. John.   We will heal up all;   550
For we'll create young Arthur Duke of Bretagne
And Earl of Richmond; and this rich fair town
We make him lord of. Call the Lady Constance;
Some speedy messenger bid her repair
To our solemnity. I trust we shall,   555
If not fill up the measure of her will,
Yet in some measure satisfy her so
That we shall stop her exclamation.
Go we, as well as haste will suffer us,
To this unlook'd for, unprepared pomp.   560
          [*Exeunt [all but the Bastard].*
    Bast. Mad world! mad kings! mad composition!
John, to stop Arthur's title in the whole,
Hath willingly departed with a part;
And France, whose armour conscience buckled on,
Whom zeal and charity brought to the field   565
As God's own soldier, rounded in the ear
With that same purpose-changer, that sly devil,
That broker that still breaks the pate of faith,
That daily break-vow, he that wins of all,

---

487. [Anjou] (Pope). *Angiers* F.   494. **Holds...with:** equals.   519. **churlish:** grudging.   535. **assur'd:** betrothed.
538. **presently:** immediately.   555. **solemnity:** marriage ceremony.   561. **composition:** agreement.   563. **departed:** parted.
566. **rounded:** whispered.   568. **broker:** agent.

Of kings, of beggars, old men, young men, maids,
Who, having no external thing to lose   571
But the word "maid," cheats the poor maid of that,
That smooth-faced gentleman, tickling Commodity,
Commodity, the bias of the world, —
The world, who of itself is peised well,   575
Made to run even upon even ground,
Till this advantage, this vile-drawing bias,
This sway of motion, this Commodity,
Makes it take head from all indifferency,
From all direction, purpose, course, intent;   580
And this same bias, this Commodity,
This bawd, this broker, this all-changing word,
Clapp'd on the outward eye of fickle France,
Hath drawn him from his own determin'd aim,
From a resolv'd and honourable war   585
To a most base and vile-concluded peace.
And why rail I on this Commodity
But for because he hath not woo'd me yet?
Not that I have the power to clutch my hand
When his fair angels would salute my palm;   590
But for my hand, as unattempted yet,
Like a poor beggar, raileth on the rich.
Well, whiles I am a beggar, I will rail
And say there is no sin but to be rich;
And being rich, my virtue then shall be   595
To say there is no vice but beggary.
Since kings break faith upon Commodity,
Gain, be my lord, for I will worship thee.   [*Exit.*

ACT [III]

[SCENE I. *The French King's pavilion.*]

Enter CONSTANCE, ARTHUR, *and* SALISBURY

Const. Gone to be married! Gone to swear a peace!
False blood to false blood join'd! Gone to be friends!
Shall Lewis have Blanch, and Blanch those provinces?
It is not so; thou hast misspoke, misheard.
Be well advis'd, tell o'er thy tale again.   5
It cannot be; thou dost but say 'tis so.
I trust I may not trust thee, for thy word
Is but the vain breath of a common man.
Believe me, I do not believe thee, man;
I have a king's oath to the contrary.   10
Thou shalt be punish'd for thus frighting me,
For I am sick and capable of fears,

Oppress'd with wrongs, and therefore full of fears,
A widow, husbandless, subject to fears,
A woman, naturally born to fears;   15
And though thou now confess thou didst but jest,
With my vex'd spirits I cannot take a truce,
But they will quake and tremble all this day.
What dost thou mean by shaking of thy head?
Why dost thou look so sadly on my son?   20
What means that hand upon that breast of thine?
Why holds thine eye that lamentable rheum,
Like a proud river peering o'er his bounds?
Be these sad signs confirmers of thy words?
Then speak again; not all thy former tale,   25
But this one word, whether thy tale be true.
Sal. As true as I believe you think them false
That give you cause to prove my saying true.
Const. O, if thou teach me to believe this sorrow,
Teach thou this sorrow how to make me die,   30
And let belief and life encounter so
As doth the fury of two desperate men
Which in the very meeting fall and die.
Lewis marry Blanch! O boy, then where art thou?
France friend with England, what becomes of me?
Fellow, be gone! I cannot brook thy sight.   36
This news hath made thee a most ugly man.
Sal. What other harm have I, good lady, done,
But spoke the harm that is by others done?
Const. Which harm within itself so heinous is   40
As it makes harmful all that speak of it.
Arth. I do beseech you, madam, be content.
Const. If thou that bid'st me be content wert grim,
Ugly, and sland'rous to thy mother's womb,
Full of unpleasing blots and sightless stains,   45
Lame, foolish, crooked, swart, prodigious,
Patch'd with foul moles and eye-offending marks,
I would not care, I then would be content;
For then I should not love thee, no, nor thou
Become thy great birth nor deserve a crown.   50
But thou art fair, and at thy birth, dear boy,
Nature and Fortune join'd to make thee great.
Of Nature's gifts thou mayst with lilies boast
And with the half-blown rose. But Fortune, O,
She is corrupted, chang'd, and won from thee;   55
Sh' adulterates hourly with thine uncle John;
And with her golden hand hath pluck'd on France
To tread down fair respect of sovereignty,
And made his majesty the bawd to theirs.
France is a bawd to Fortune and King John,   60
That strumpet Fortune! that usurping John!
Tell me, thou fellow, is not France forsworn?
Envenom him with words, or get thee gone

573. **tickling**: flattering. **Commodity**: compromise, expediency. 574. **bias**: the piece of lead in the side of a bowl, making it take a curved course. 575. **peised**: balanced. 579. **take ... indifferency**: abandon a straight course. 590. **angels**: coins worth ten shillings. 591. **unattempted**: untempted.

Act III, sc. i. Act II in F, ending at l. 74, where Act III begins. 12. **capable of**: susceptible to. 14. **widow**. She was, in fact, married to her third husband. 45. **sightless**: unsightly. 46. **prodigious**: monstrous.

And leave those woes alone which I alone
Am bound to under-bear.
   Sal.   Pardon me, madam, 65
I may not go without you to the kings.
   Const. Thou mayst, thou shalt; I will not go
    with thee.
I will instruct my sorrows to be proud;
For Grief is proud and makes his owner stoop.
To me and to the state of my great grief 70
Let kings assemble; for my grief's so great
That no supporter but the huge firm earth
Can hold it up. Here I and sorrow sit;
Here is my throne, bid kings come bow to it.
              [Seats herself on the ground.]

Enter KING JOHN, KING PHILIP, LEWIS, BLANCH,
   ELEANOR, *the* BASTARD, AUSTRIA *[and Attend-
   ants].*

   K. Phi. 'Tis true, fair daughter; and this blessed
    day 75
Ever in France shall be kept festival.
To solemnize this day the glorious sun
Stays in his course and plays the alchemist,
Turning with splendour of his precious eye
The meagre cloddy earth to glittering gold. 80
The yearly course that brings this day about
Shall never see it but a holiday.
   Const. A wicked day, and not a holy day!
                         [Rising.]
What hath this day deserv'd? What hath it done,
That it in golden letters should be set 85
Among the high tides in the calendar?
Nay, rather turn this day out of the week,
This day of shame, oppression, perjury.
Or, if it must stand still, let wives with child
Pray that their burdens may not fall this day 90
Lest that their hopes prodigiously be cross'd;
But on this day let seamen fear no wrack;
No bargains break that are not this day made.
This day, all things begun come to ill end,
Yea, faith itself to hollow falsehood change! 95
   K. Phi. By heaven, lady, you shall have no cause
To curse the fair proceedings of this day.
Have I not pawn'd to you my majesty?
   Const. You have beguil'd me with a counterfeit
Resembling majesty, which, being touch'd and
    tried, 100
Proves valueless. You are forsworn, forsworn!
You came in arms to spill mine enemies' blood,
But now in arms you strengthen it with yours.
The grappling vigour and rough frown of war
Is cold in amity and painted peace, 105
And our oppression hath made up this league.

Arm, arm, you heavens, against these perjur'd
   kings!
A widow cries; be husband to me, heavens!
Let not the hours of this ungodly day
Wear out the day in peace; but, ere sunset, 110
Set armed discord 'twixt these perjur'd kings!
Hear me, O, hear me!
   Aust.   Lady Constance, peace!
   Const. War! war! no peace! Peace is to me a
    war.
O Lymoges! O Austria! thou dost shame
That bloody spoil. Thou slave, thou wretch, thou
    coward! 115
Thou little valiant, great in villainy!
Thou ever strong upon the stronger side!
Thou Fortune's champion that dost never fight
But when her humorous ladyship is by
To teach thee safety! thou art perjur'd too, 120
And sooth'st up greatness. What a fool art thou,
A ramping fool, to brag and stamp and swear
Upon my party! Thou cold-blooded slave,
Hast thou not spoke like thunder on my side,
Been sworn my soldier, bidding me depend 125
Upon thy stars, thy fortune, and thy strength,
And dost thou now fall over to my foes?
Thou wear a lion's hide! Doff it for shame,
And hang a calf's-skin on those recreant limbs.
   Aust. O, that a man should speak those words to
    me! 130
   Bast. And hang a calf's-skin on those recreant
    limbs.
   Aust. Thou dar'st not say so, villain, for thy life.
   Bast. And hang a calf's-skin on those recreant
    limbs.
   K. John. We like not this; thou dost forget thy-
    self. 134

               Enter PANDULPH.

   K. Phi. Here comes the holy legate of the Pope.
   Pand. Hail, you anointed deputies of heaven!
To thee, King John, my holy errand is.
I Pandulph, of fair Milan cardinal,
And from Pope Innocent the legate here,
Do in his name religiously demand 140
Why thou against the Church, our holy mother,
So wilfully dost spurn; and force perforce
Keep Stephen Langton, chosen Archbishop
Of Canterbury, from that holy see?
This, in our foresaid Holy Father's name, 145
Pope Innocent, I do demand of thee.
   K. John. What earthy name to interrogatories
Can [task] the free breath of a sacred king?
Thou canst not, Cardinal, devise a name

---

86. **high tides:** festival days.   92. **But:** except.   100. **touch'd:** tested by a touchstone.   106. **our oppression:** your
oppression of us.   114. **Lymoges ... Austria:** an unhistorical identification of two different men.   115. **bloody spoil:** the
lion's skin.   119. **humorous:** whimsical.   121. **sooth'st up:** flatterest.   129. **calf's-skin.** Domestic fools are said to have
been clothed in calfskin.   148. **[task]** (Theobald): force to answer. *tast* F.

So slight, unworthy, and ridiculous,   150
To charge me to an answer, as the Pope.
Tell him this tale; and from the mouth of England
Add thus much more, that no Italian priest
Shall tithe or toll in our dominions;
But as we, under Heaven, are supreme head,   155
So under Him that great supremacy,
Where we do reign, we will alone uphold,
Without the assistance of a mortal hand.
So tell the Pope, all reverence set apart
To him and his usurp'd authority.   160
   K. Phi. Brother of England, you blaspheme in
   this.
   K. John. Though you and all the kings of Chris-
   tendom
Are led so grossly by this meddling priest,
Dreading the curse that money may buy out;
And by the merit of vile gold, dross, dust,   165
Purchase corrupted pardon of a man
Who in that sale sells pardon from himself,
Though you and all the rest so grossly led
This juggling witchcraft with revenue cherish,
Yet I alone, alone do me oppose   170
Against the Pope and count his friends my foes.
   Pand. Then, by the lawful power that I have,
Thou shalt stand curs'd and excommunicate;
And blessed shall he be that doth revolt
From his allegiance to an heretic;   175
And meritorious shall that hand be call'd,
Canonized and worshipp'd as a saint,
That takes away by any secret course
Thy hateful life.
   Const.   O, lawful let it be
That I have room with Rome to curse a while!   180
Good father Cardinal, cry thou amen
To my keen curses; for without my wrong
There is no tongue hath power to curse him right.
   Pand. There's law and warrant, lady, for my
   curse.
   Const. And for mine too.   When law can do no
   right,   185
Let it be lawful that law bar no wrong.
Law cannot give my child his kingdom here,
For he that holds his kingdom holds the law;
Therefore, since law itself is perfect wrong,
How can the law forbid my tongue to curse?   190
   Pand. Philip of France, on peril of a curse,
Let go the hand of that arch-heretic
And raise the power of France upon his head,
Unless he do submit himself to Rome.
   El. Look'st thou pale, France?   Do not let go
   thy hand.   195
   Const. Look to that, devil, lest that France re-
   pent,
And, by disjoining hands, hell lose a soul.

   Aust. King Philip, listen to the Cardinal.
   Bast. And hang a calf's-skin on his recreant
   limbs.
   Aust. Well, ruffian, I must pocket up these
   wrongs,   200
Because —
   Bast.   Your breeches best may carry them.
   K. John. Philip, what say'st thou to the Cardi-
   nal?
   Const. What should he say, but as the Cardinal?
   Lew. Bethink you, father; for the difference
Is purchase of a heavy curse from Rome,   205
Or the light loss of England for a friend.
Forgo the easier.
   Blanch.   That's the curse of Rome.
   Const. O Lewis, stand fast!   The devil tempts
   thee here
In likeness of a new untrimmed bride.
   Blanch. The Lady Constance speaks not from
   her faith,   210
But from her need.
   Const.   O, if thou grant my need,
Which only lives but by the death of faith,
That need must needs infer this principle,
That faith would live again by death of need.
O then, tread down my need, and faith mounts up;
Keep my need up, and faith is trodden down!   216
   K. John. The King is mov'd, and answers not to
   this.
   Const. O, be remov'd from him, and answer well!
   Aust. Do so, King Philip; hang no more in doubt.
   Bast. Hang nothing but a calf's-skin, most sweet
   lout.   220
   K. Phi. I am perplex'd, and know not what to
   say.
   Pand. What canst thou say but will perplex thee
   more,
If thou stand excommunicate and curs'd?
   K. Phi. Good reverend father, make my person
   yours,
And tell me how you would bestow yourself.   225
This royal hand and mine are newly knit,
And the conjunction of our inward souls
Married in league, coupled and link'd together
With all religious strength of sacred vows.
The latest breath that gave the sound of words 230
Was deep-sworn faith, peace, amity, true love
Between our kingdoms and our royal selves;
And even before this truce, but new before,
No longer than we well could wash our hands
To clap this royal bargain up of peace,   235
Heaven knows, they were besmear'd and over-
   stain'd
With slaughter's pencil, where revenge did paint
The fearful difference of incensed kings:

180. **Rome.** Pronounced *room.*   209. **untrimmed:** virgin; or, with hair unbound.   213. **infer:** imply.   233. **new:** immediately.

And shall these hands, so lately purg'd of blood,
So newly join'd in love, so strong in both,   240
Unyoke this seizure and this kind regreet?
Play fast and loose with faith? So jest with heaven,
Make such unconstant children of ourselves,
As now again to snatch our palm from palm,
Unswear faith sworn, and on the marriage-bed   245
Of smiling Peace to march a bloody host,
And make a riot on the gentle brow
Of true Sincerity? O, holy sir,
My reverend father, let it not be so!
Out of your grace devise, ordain, impose   250
Some gentle order; and then we shall be blest
To do your pleasure and continue friends.
    Pand. All form is formless, order orderless,
Save what is opposite to England's love.   254
Therefore to arms! Be champion of our Church,
Or let the Church, our mother, breathe her curse,
A mother's curse, on her revolting son.
France, thou mayst hold a serpent by the tongue,
A [chafed] lion by the mortal paw,
A fasting tiger safer by the tooth,   260
Than keep in peace that hand which thou dost hold.
    K. Phi. I may disjoin my hand, but not my faith.
    Pand. So mak'st thou faith an enemy to faith,
And like a civil war set'st oath to oath,   264
Thy tongue against thy tongue. O, let thy vow
First made to heaven, first be to heaven perform'd,
That is, to be the champion of our Church!
What since thou swor'st is sworn against thyself
And may not be performed by thyself,
For that which thou hast sworn to do amiss   270
Is not amiss when it is truly done,
And being not done, where doing tends to ill
The truth is then most done not doing it.
The better act of purposes mistook
Is to mistake again; though indirect,   275
Yet indirection thereby grows direct,
And falsehood falsehood cures, as fire cools fire
Within the scorched veins of one new-burn'd.
It is religion that doth make vows kept;
But thou hast sworn against religion,   280
By what thou swear'st against the thing thou
    swear'st,
And makest an oath the surety for thy truth
Against an oath. The truth thou art unsure
To swear, swears only not to be forsworn;
Else what a mockery should it be to swear!   285
But thou dost swear only to be forsworn;
And most forsworn, to keep what thou dost swear.
Therefore thy later vows against thy first
Is in thyself rebellion to thyself;
And better conquest never canst thou make   290
Than arm thy constant and thy nobler parts

Against these giddy loose suggestions;
Upon which better part our prayers come in,
If thou vouchsafe them. But if not, then know
The peril of our curses light on thee   295
So heavy as thou shalt not shake them off,
But in despair die under their black weight.
    Aust. Rebellion, flat rebellion!
    Bast.   Will't not be?
Will not a calf's-skin stop that mouth of thine?
    Lew. Father, to arms!
    Blanch.   Upon thy wedding-day?   300
Against the blood that thou hast married?
What, shall our feast be kept with slaughtered men?
Shall braying trumpets and loud churlish drums,
Clamours of hell, be measures to our pomp?
O husband, hear me! Ay, alack, how new   305
Is husband in my mouth! Even for that name,
Which till this time my tongue did ne'er pronounce,
Upon my knee I beg, go not to arms
Against mine uncle.
    Const.   O, upon my knee,
Made hard with kneeling, I do pray to thee,   310
Thou virtuous Dauphin, alter not the doom
Forethought by Heaven!
    Blanch. Now shall I see thy love. What motive
        may
Be stronger with thee than the name of wife?
    Const. That which upholdeth him that thee up-
        holds,   315
His honour. O, thine honour, Lewis, thine honour!
    Lew. I muse your Majesty doth seem so cold,
When such profound respects do pull you on.
    Pand. I will denounce a curse upon his head.
    K. Phi. Thou shalt not need. England, I will
        fall from thee.   320
    Const. O fair return of banish'd majesty!
    El. O foul revolt of French inconstancy!
    K. John. France, thou shalt rue this hour within
        this hour.
    Bast. Old Time the clock-setter, that bald sexton
        Time,
Is it as he will? Well then, France shall rue.   325
    Blanch. The sun's o'ercast with blood; fair day,
        adieu!
Which is the side that I must go withal?
I am with both; each army hath a hand,
And in their rage, I having hold of both,
They whirl assunder and dismember me.   330
Husband, I cannot pray that thou mayst win;
Uncle, I needs must pray that thou mayst lose;
Father, I may not wish the fortune thine;
Grandam, I will not wish thy wishes thrive.
Whoever wins, on that side shall I lose;   335
Assured loss before the match be play'd.

---

240. **both:** i.e., battle and love. 241. **regreet:** greeting, friendship. 259. **[chafed]** (Theobald): enraged. *cased* F. 271.
not F. *most* Hanmer, followed by many edd. *Truly* is explained by *the truth,* etc. in 273. 304. **measures . . . pomp:** music
for our wedding. 317. **muse:** wonder. 318. **respects:** considerations. 319. **denounce:** call down.

Lew. Lady, with me, with me thy fortune lies.

Blanch. There where my fortune lives, there my
life dies.

K. John. Cousin, go draw our puissance together.
[*Exit Bastard.*]

France, I am burn'd up with inflaming wrath,   340
A rage whose heat hath this condition,
That nothing can allay, nothing but blood,
The blood and dearest-valued blood of France.

K. Phi. Thy rage shall burn thee up, and thou
shalt turn
To ashes, ere our blood shall quench that fire.   345
Look to thyself, thou art in jeopardy.

K. John. No more than he that threats. To
arms let's hie!   [*Exeunt.*

SCENE II. [*The same. Plains near Angiers.*]

Alarums, excursions. Enter the BASTARD, *with
Austria's head.*

Bast. Now, by my life, this day grows wondrous
hot.
Some airy devil hovers in the sky
And pours down mischief. Austria's head lie there,

Enter KING JOHN, ARTHUR, *and* HUBERT.

While Philip breathes.

K. John. Hubert, keep this boy. Philip, make
up.   5
My mother is assailed in our tent,
And ta'en, I fear.

Bast.   My lord, I rescued her;
Her Highness is in safety, fear you not.
But on, my liege; for very little pains
Will bring this labour to an happy end.   10
[*Exeunt.*

[SCENE III. *The same.*]

Alarums, excursions, retreat. Enter KING JOHN,
ELEANOR, ARTHUR, *the* BASTARD, HUBERT, *and*
Lords.

K. John. [*To Eleanor.*] So shall it be; your
Grace shall stay behind
So strongly guarded. [*To Arthur.*] Cousin, look
not sad.
Thy grandam loves thee; and thy uncle will
As dear be to thee as thy father was.

Arth. O, this will make my mother die with grief!

K. John. [*To the Bastard.*] Cousin, away for
England! haste before;   6
And, ere our coming, see thou shake the bags
Of hoarding abbots; imprisoned angels

Set at liberty. The fat ribs of peace
Must by the hungry now be fed upon.   10
Use our commission in his utmost force.

Bast. Bell, book, and candle shall not drive me
back,
When gold and silver becks me to come on.
I leave your Highness. Grandam, I will pray
(If ever I remember to be holy)   15
For your fair safety; so, I kiss your hand.

El. Farewell, gentle cousin.

K. John.   Coz, farewell.
[*Exit Bastard.*]

El. Come hither, little kinsman; hark, a word.

K. John. Come hither, Hubert. O my gentle
Hubert,
We owe thee much! Within this wall of flesh   20
There is a soul counts thee her creditor,
And with advantage means to pay thy love;
And, my good friend, thy voluntary oath
Lives in this bosom, dearly cherished.
Give me thy hand. I had a thing to say,   25
But I will fit it with some better [time].
By heaven, Hubert, I am almost asham'd
To say what good respect I have of thee.

Hub. I am much bounden to your Majesty.

K. John. Good friend, thou hast no cause to say
so yet,   30
But thou shalt have; and creep time ne'er so slow,
Yet it shall come for me to do thee good.
I had a thing to say, but let it go.
The sun is in the heaven, and the proud day,
Attended with the pleasures of the world,   35
Is all too wanton and too full of gawds
To give me audience. If the midnight bell
Did, with his iron tongue and brazen mouth,
Sound on into the drowsy [ear] of night;
If this same were a churchyard where we stand,   40
And thou possessed with a thousand wrongs;
Or if that surly spirit, melancholy,
Had bak'd thy blood and made it heavy, thick,
Which else runs tickling up and down the veins,
Making that idiot, laughter, keep men's eyes   45
And strain their cheeks to idle merriment —
A passion hateful to my purposes;
Or if that thou couldst see me without eyes,
Hear me without thine ears, and make reply
Without a tongue, using conceit alone,   50
Without eyes, ears, and harmful sound of words;
Then, in despite of brooded watchful day,
I would into thy bosom pour my thoughts.
But, ah, I will not! yet I love thee well;
And, by my troth, I think thou lov'st me well.   55

Hub. So well, that what you bid me undertake,

Sc. ii, 5. **make up:** hasten.
Sc. iii, 12. **Bell ... candle:** i.e., excommunication. **22. advantage:** interest. **26.** [time] (Pope). *tune* F. **36. gawds:** toys,
gay trifles. **39.** [ear] (Collier and Walker coni.). *race* F. **50. conceit:** thought. **52. brooded:** observing closely (like a
hen over her brood).

Though that my death were adjunct to my act
By heaven, I would do it.

K. John.   Do not I know thou wouldst?
Good Hubert, Hubert, Hubert, throw thine eye
On yon young boy. I'll tell thee what, my friend,
He is a very serpent in my way;   61
And wheresoe'er this foot of mine doth tread,
He lies before me. Dost thou understand me?
Thou art his keeper.

Hub.   And I'll keep him so,
That he shall not offend your Majesty.

K. John.   Death. 65
Hub. My lord?
K. John.   A grave.
Hub.   He shall not live.
K. John.   Enough.
I could be merry now. Hubert, I love thee.
Well, I'll not say what I intend for thee.
Remember. Madam, fare you well;
I'll send those powers o'er to your Majesty.   70

El. My blessing go with thee!

K. John.   For England, cousin, go.
Hubert shall be your man, attend on you
With all true duty. On toward Calais, ho!

                    [*Exeunt.*

SCENE [IV. *The same. The French king's tent.*]

Enter KING PHILIP, LEWIS, PANDULPH, *and*
Attendants.

K. Phi. So, by a roaring tempest on the flood,
A whole armado of convicted sail
Is scattered and disjoin'd from fellowship.

Pand. Courage and comfort! all shall yet go well.

K. Phi. What can go well, when we have run so
    ill?   5
Are we not beaten? Is not Angiers lost?
Arthur ta'en prisoner? Divers dear friends slain?
And bloody England into England gone,
O'erbearing interruption, spite of France?

Lew. What he hath won, that hath he fortified.
So hot a speed with such advice dispos'd,   11
Such temperate order in so fierce a cause,
Doth want example. Who hath read or heard
Of any kindred action like to this?

K. Phi. Well could I bear that England had this
    praise,   15
So we could find some pattern of our shame.

Enter CONSTANCE.

Look, who comes here! a grave unto a soul;
Holding th' eternal spirit, against her will,
In the vile prison of afflicted breath.
I prithee, lady, go away with me.   20

Const. Lo, now! now see the issue of your peace.

K. Phi. Patience, good lady! comfort, gentle
    Constance!

Const. No, I defy all counsel, all redress,
But that which ends all counsel, true redress,
Death, death. O amiable lovely death!   25
Thou odoriferous stench! sound rottenness!
Arise forth from the couch of lasting night,
Thou hate and terror to prosperity,
And I will kiss thy detestable bones,
And put my eyeballs in thy vaulty brows,   30
And ring these fingers with thy household worms,
And stop this gap of breath with fulsome dust,
And be a carrion monster like thyself.
Come, grin on me and I will think thou smil'st
And buss thee as thy wife. Misery's love,   35
O, come to me!

K. Phi.   O fair affliction, peace!

Const. No, no, I will not, having breath to cry.
O, that my tongue were in the thunder's mouth!
Then with a passion would I shake the world;
And rouse from sleep that fell anatomy   40
Which cannot hear a lady's feeble voice,
Which scorns a modern invocation.

Pand. Lady, you utter madness, and not sorrow.

Const. Thou art [not] holy to belie me so;
I am not mad. This hair I tear is mine;   45
My name is Constance; I was Geoffrey's wife;
Young Arthur is my son, and he is lost.
I am not mad; I would to heaven I were!
For then 'tis like I should forget myself.
O, if I could, what grief should I forget!   50
Preach some philosophy to make me mad,
And thou shalt be canoniz'd, Cardinal;
For being not mad, but sensible of grief,
My reasonable part produces reason
How I may be deliver'd of these woes,   55
And teaches me to kill or hang myself.
If I were mad, I should forget my son,
Or madly think a babe of clouts were he.
I am not mad; too well, too well I feel
The different plague of each calamity.   60

K. Phi. Bind up those tresses. O, what love I
    note
In the fair multitude of those her hairs!
Where but by chance a silver drop hath fallen,
Even to that drop ten thousand wiry [friends]
Do glue themselves in sociable grief,   65
Like true, inseparable, faithful loves,
Sticking together in calamity.

Const. To England, if you will.

K. Phi.   Bind up your hairs.

Const. Yes, that I will; and wherefore will I do it?
I tore them from their bonds and cried aloud,   70
"O that these hands could so redeem my son
As they have given these hairs their liberty!"

Sc. iv, 2. **convicted:** defeated.   11. **advice:** wisdom.   28. **prosperity:** the prosperous.   35. **buss:** kiss.   40. **anatomy:** skeleton.   42. **modern:** commonplace.   44. [not] F4. Om. F1–3.   64. [friends] (Rowe). *fiends* F.

But now I envy at their liberty
And will again commit them to their bonds
Because my poor child is a prisoner.   75
And, father Cardinal, I have heard you say
That we shall see and know our friends in heaven.
If that be true, I shall see my boy again;
For since the birth of Cain, the first male child,
To him that did but yesterday suspire,   80
There was not such a gracious creature born.
But now will canker sorrow eat my bud
And chase the native beauty from his cheek,
And he will look as hollow as a ghost,
As dim and meagre as an ague's fit,   85
And so he'll die; and, rising so again,
When I shall meet him in the court of heaven
I shall not know him: therefore never, never
Must I behold my pretty Arthur more.   89
    Pand. You hold too heinous a respect of grief.
    Const. He talks to me that never had a son.
    K. Phi. You are as fond of grief as of your child.
    Const. Grief fills the room up of my absent child,
Lies in his bed, walks up and down with me,
Puts on his pretty looks, repeats his words,   95
Remembers me of all his gracious parts,
Stuffs out his vacant garments with his form;
Then, have I reason to be fond of grief?
Fare you well! Had you such a loss as I,
I could give better comfort than you do.   100
I will not keep this form upon my head
                     [*tearing her hair*]
When there is such disorder in my wit.
O Lord! my boy, my Arthur, my fair son!
My life, my joy, my food, my all the world!
My widow-comfort, and my sorrows' cure!   105
                          [*Exit.*
    K. Phi. I fear some outrage, and I'll follow her.
                          [*Exit.*
    Lew. There's nothing in this world can make me
      joy.
Life is as tedious as a twice-told tale
Vexing the dull ear of a drowsy man;
And bitter shame hath spoil'd the sweet [world's]
    taste,   110
That it yields nought but shame and bitterness.
    Pand. Before the curing of a strong disease,
Even in the instant of repair and health,
The fit is strongest; evils that take leave,
On their departure most of all show evil.   115
What have you lost by losing of this day?
    Lew. All days of glory, joy, and happiness.
    Pand. If you had won it, certainly you had.
No, no; when Fortune means to men most good,
She looks upon them with a threat'ning eye.   120
'Tis strange to think how much King John hath lost
In this which he accounts so clearly won.

Are not you griev'd that Arthur is his prisoner?
    Lew. As heartily as he is glad he hath him.
    Pand. Your mind is all as youthful as your blood.
Now hear me speak with a prophetic spirit;   126
For even the breath of what I mean to speak
Shall blow each dust, each straw, each little rub,
Out of the path which shall directly lead
Thy foot to England's throne; and therefore mark.
John hath seiz'd Arthur; and it cannot be   131
That, whiles warm life plays in that infant's veins,
The misplac'd John should entertain an hour,
One minute, nay, one quiet breath of rest.
A sceptre snatch'd with an unruly hand   135
Must be as boisterously maintain'd as gain'd;
And he that stands upon a slipp'ry place
Makes nice of no vile hold to stay him up.
That John may stand, then Arthur needs must fall:
So be it; for it cannot be but so.   140
    Lew. But what shall I gain by young Arthur's
      fall?
    Pand. You, in the right of Lady Blanch your
      wife,
May then make all the claim that Arthur did.
    Lew. And lose it, life and all, as Arthur did.
    Pand. How green you are and fresh in this old
      world!   145
John lays you plots; the times conspire with you;
For he that steeps his safety in true blood
Shall find but bloody safety and untrue.
This act so evilly borne shall cool the hearts
Of all his people and freeze up their zeal,   150
That none so small advantage shall step forth
To check his reign, but they will cherish it;
No natural exhalation in the sky,
No scope of nature, no distemper'd day,
No common wind, no customed event,   155
But they will pluck away his natural cause
And call them meteors, prodigies, and signs,
Abortives, presages, and tongues of heaven,
Plainly denouncing vengeance upon John.
    Lew. May be he will not touch young Arthur's
      life,   160
But hold himself safe in his prisonment.
    Pand. O, sir, when he shall hear of your ap-
      proach,
If that young Arthur be not gone already,
Even at that news he dies; and then the hearts
Of all his people shall revolt from him,   165
And kiss the lips of unacquainted change,
And pick strong matter of revolt and wrath
Out of the bloody fingers' ends of John.
Methinks I see this hurly all on foot;
And, O, what better matter breeds for you   170
Than I have nam'd! The bastard Faulconbridge
Is now in England, ransacking the Church,

110. [world's] (Pope). *words* F. 128. rub: obstruction. 138. **Makes nice of:** is fastidious about. 146. **you:** by which you may benefit. 153. **exhalation:** meteor. 154. **scope of nature:** thing within natural limits. 158. **Abortives:** abnormalities.

Offending charity. If but a dozen French
Were there in arms, they would be as a call
To train ten thousand English to their side,   175
Or as a little snow, tumbled about,
Anon becomes a mountain. O noble Dauphin,
Go with me to the King. 'Tis wonderful
What may be wrought out of their discontent,
Now that their souls are topful of offence.   180
For England go; I will whet on the King.
   Lew. Strong reasons [make strong] actions; let us
     go.
If you say ay, the King will not say no.   [*Exeunt.*

ACT IV

Scene I. [*A room in a castle.*]

Enter Hubert *and* Executioners.

   Hub. Heat me these irons hot, and look thou
     stand
Within the arras. When I strike my foot
Upon the bosom of the ground, rush forth
And bind the boy which you shall find with me
Fast to the chair. Be heedful. Hence, and watch.
   1. Exec. I hope your warrant will bear out the
     deed.   6
   Hub. Uncleanly scruples! fear not you. Look
     to't.   [*Exeunt Executioners.*]
Young lad, come forth; I have to say with you.

Enter Arthur.

   Arth. Good morrow, Hubert.
   Hub.   Good morrow, little prince.
   Arth. As little prince, having so great a title   10
To be more prince, as may be. You are sad.
   Hub. Indeed, I have been merrier.
   Arth.   Mercy on me!
Methinks nobody should be sad but I.
Yet, I remember, when I was in France,
Young gentlemen would be as sad as night,   15
Only for wantonness. By my christendom,
So I were out of prison and kept sheep,
I should be merry as the day is long;
And so I would be here, but that I doubt
My uncle practises more harm to me.   20
He is afraid of me and I of him.
Is it my fault that I was Geoffrey's son?
No, indeed, is't not; and I would to heaven
I were your son, so you would love me, Hubert.
   Hub. [*Aside.*] If I talk to him, with his innocent
     prate   25
He will awake my mercy which lies dead;
Therefore I will be sudden and dispatch.

   Arth. Are you sick, Hubert? You look pale to-
     day.
In sooth, I would you were a little sick,
That I might sit all night and watch with you.   30
I warrant I love you more than you do me.
   Hub. [*Aside.*] His words do take possession of
     my bosom.
Read here, young Arthur.   [*Showing a paper.*]
           [*Aside.*] How now, foolish rheum!
Turning dispiteous torture out of door!
I must be brief, lest resolution drop   35
Out of mine eyes in tender womanish tears.
Can you not read it? Is it not fair writ?
   Arth. Too fairly, Hubert, for so foul effect.
Must you with hot irons burn out both mine eyes?
   Hub. Young boy, I must.
   Arth.   And will you?
   Hub.   And I will.   40
   Arth. Have you the heart? When your head did
     but ache,
I knit my handkercher about your brows,
The best I had, a princess wrought it me,
And I did never ask it you again;
And with my hand at midnight held your head,   45
And like the watchful minutes to the hour,
Still and anon cheer'd up the heavy time,
Saying, "What lack you?" and "Where lies your
     grief?"
Or "What good love may I perform for you?"
Many a poor man's son would have lien still   50
And ne'er have spoke a loving word to you;
But you at your sick service had a prince.
Nay, you may think my love was crafty love
And call it cunning. Do, an if you will;
If heaven be pleas'd that you must use me ill,   55
Why then you must. Will you put out mine eyes,
These eyes that never did nor never shall
So much as frown on you?
   Hub.   I have sworn to do it;
And with hot irons must I burn them out.
   Arth. Ah, none but in this iron age would do
     it!   60
The iron of itself, though heat red-hot,
Approaching near these eyes, would drink my tears,
And quench his fiery indignation
Even in the matter of mine innocence;
Nay, after that, consume away in rust   65
But for containing fire to harm mine eye.
Are you more stubborn-hard than hammer'd iron?
An if an angel should have come to me
And told me Hubert should put out mine eyes,
I would not have believ'd him,—no tongue but
     Hubert's.   70
   Hub. Come forth.   [*Stamps.*]

174. **call:** decoy.   175. **train:** draw.   182. **[make]** (Capell). *makes* F. **[strong]** F₂. *strange* F₁.
Act IV, sc. i, 16. wantonness: affectation.   20. **practises:** plots.   34. **dispiteous:** pitiless.   64. **matter...innocence:** my
tears.

[*Re-enter* EXECUTIONERS, *with a cord, irons, etc.*]
Do as I bid you do.
  Arth. O, save me, Hubert, save me! My eyes
    are out
Even with the fierce looks of these bloody men.
  Hub. Give me the iron, I say, and bind him here.
  Arth. Alas, what need you be so boisterous-
    rough?   76
I will not struggle, I will stand stone-still.
For heaven sake, Hubert, let me not be bound!
Nay, hear me, Hubert, drive these men away,
And I will sit as quiet as a lamb;   80
I will not stir, nor wince, nor speak a word,
Nor look upon the iron angerly.
Thrust but these men away, and I'll forgive you,
Whatever torment you do put me to.
  Hub. Go, stand within; let me alone with him.
  1. Exec. I am best pleas'd to be from such a
    deed.   [*Exeunt Executioners.*]   86
  Arth. Alas, I then have chid away my friend!
He hath a stern look, but a gentle heart.
Let him come back, that his compassion may
Give life to yours.
  Hub.   Come, boy, prepare yourself. 90
  Arth. Is there no remedy?
  Hub.   None, but to lose your eyes.
  Arth. O heaven, that there were but a mote in
    yours,
A grain, a dust, a gnat, a wandering hair,
Any annoyance in that precious sense!
Then feeling what small things are boisterous there,
Your vile intent must needs seem horrible.   96
  Hub. Is this your promise? Go to, hold your
    tongue.
  Arth. Hubert, the utterance of a brace of tongues
Must needs want pleading for a pair of eyes.
Let me not hold my tongue, let me not, Hubert;
Or, Hubert, if you will, cut out my tongue, 101
So I may keep mine eyes. O, spare mine eyes,
Though to no use but still to look on you!
Lo, by my troth, the instrument is cold
And would not harm me.
  Hub.   I can heat it, boy. 105
  Arth. No, in good sooth; the fire is dead with
    grief,
Being create for comfort, to be us'd
In undeserv'd extremes. See else yourself;
There is no malice in this burning coal;
The breath of heaven has blown his spirit out 110
And strew'd repentant ashes on his head.
  Hub. But with my breath I can revive it, boy.
  Arth. An if you do, you will but make it blush
And glow with shame of your proceedings, Hubert.
Nay, it perchance will sparkle in your eyes, 115
And, like a dog that is compell'd to fight,

Snatch at his master that doth tarre him on.
All things that you should use to do me wrong
Deny their office; only you do lack
That mercy which fierce fire and iron extends, 120
Creatures of note for mercy-lacking uses.
  Hub. Well, see to live; I will not touch thine eye
For all the treasure that thine uncle owes.
Yet am I sworn and I did purpose, boy,
With this same very iron to burn them out. 125
  Arth. O, now you look like Hubert! all this while
You were disguis'd.
  Hub.   Peace; no more. Adieu.
Your uncle must not know but you are dead.
I'll fill these dogged spies with false reports;
And, pretty child, sleep doubtless and secure 130
That Hubert, for the wealth of all the world,
Will not offend thee.
  Arth.   O heaven! I thank you, Hubert.
  Hub. Silence; no more. Go closely in with me.
Much danger do I undergo for thee.   [*Exeunt.*

SCENE II. [*King John's palace.*]

Enter KING JOHN, PEMBROKE, SALISBURY,
and other Lords.

  K. John. Here once again we sit, once again
    crown'd,
And look'd upon, I hope, with cheerful eyes.
  Pem. This "once again," but that your Highness
    pleas'd,
Was once superfluous. You were crown'd before,
And that high royalty was ne'er pluck'd off, 5
The faiths of men ne'er stained with revolt;
Fresh expectation troubled not the land
With any long'd-for change or better state.
  Sal. Therefore, to be possess'd with double pomp,
To guard a title that was rich before, 10
To gild refined gold, to paint the lily,
To throw a perfume on the violet,
To smooth the ice, or add another hue
Unto the rainbow, or with taper-light
To seek the beauteous eye of heaven to garnish,
Is wasteful and ridiculous excess. 16
  Pem. But that your royal pleasure must be done,
This act is as an ancient tale new told,
And in the last repeating troublesome,
Being urged at a time unseasonable. 20
  Sal. In this the antique and well noted face
Of plain old form is much disfigured;
And, like a shifted wind unto a sail,
It makes the course of thoughts to fetch about,
Startles and frights consideration, 25
Makes sound opinion sick, and truth suspected
For putting on so new a fashion'd robe.
  Pem. When workmen strive to do better than well,

117. tarre: urge. 129. dogged: surly. 130. doubtless...secure: free from fear and care. 133. closely: secretly.
Sc. ii, 10. guard: ornament.

They do confound their skill in covetousness;
And oftentimes excusing of a fault   30
Doth make the fault the worse by the excuse,
As patches set upon a little breach
Discredit more in hiding of the fault
Than did the fault before it was so patch'd.   34
    Sal. To this effect, before you were new crown'd,
We breath'd our counsel; but it pleas'd your Highness
To overbear it, and we are all well pleas'd,
Since all and every part of what we would
Doth make a stand at what your Highness will.   39
    K. John. Some reasons of this double coronation
I have possess'd you with, and think them strong;
And more, more strong, [when] lesser is my fear,
I shall indue you with. Meantime but ask
What you would have reform'd that is not well,
And well shall you perceive how willingly   45
I will both hear and grant you your requests.
    Pem. Then I — as one that am the tongue of
      these
To sound the purposes of all their hearts,
Both for myself and them, but, chief of all,
Your safety, for the which myself and them   50
Bend their best studies, — heartily request
Th' enfranchisement of Arthur; whose restraint
Doth move the murmuring lips of discontent
To break into this dangerous argument:
If what in rest you have in right you hold,   55
Why then your fears, which (as they say) attend
The steps of wrong, should move you to mew up
Your tender kinsman and to choke his days
With barbarous ignorance and deny his youth
The rich advantage of good exercise?   60
That the time's enemies may not have this
To grace occasions, let it be our suit
That you have bid us ask his liberty;
Which for our goods we do no further ask
Than whereupon our weal, on you depending,   65
Counts it your weal he have his liberty.

Enter HUBERT.

    K. John. Let it be so; I do commit his youth
To your direction. Hubert, what news with you?
                      [*Taking him apart.*]
    Pem. This is the man should do the bloody deed;
He show'd his warrant to a friend of mine.   70
The image of a wicked heinous fault
Lives in his eye; that close aspect of his
Does show the mood of a much troubled breast;
And I do fearfully believe 'tis done,
What we so fear'd he had a charge to do.   75
    Sal. The colour of the King doth come and go

Between his purpose and his conscience,
Like heralds 'twixt two dreadful battles set.
His passion is so ripe, it needs must break.
    Pem. And when it breaks, I fear will issue thence
The foul corruption of a sweet child's death.   81
    K. John. We cannot hold mortality's strong
      hand.
Good lords, although my will to give is living,
The suit which you demand is gone and dead.
He tells us Arthur is deceas'd to-night.   85
    Sal. Indeed we fear'd his sickness was past cure.
    Pem. Indeed we heard how near his death he was
Before the child himself felt he was sick.
This must be answer'd either here or hence.
    K. John. Why do you bend such solemn brows
      on me?   90
Think you I bear the shears of Destiny?
Have I commandment on the pulse of life?
    Sal. It is apparent foul play; and 'tis shame
That greatness should so grossly offer it.
So thrive it in your game! and so, farewell.   95
    Pem. Stay yet, Lord Salisbury; I'll go with thee,
And find th' inheritance of this poor child,
His little kingdom of a forced grave.
That blood which ow'd the breadth of all this isle,
Three foot of it doth hold; bad world the while!   100
This must not be thus borne. This will break out
To all our sorrows, and ere long I doubt.
                   [*Exeunt* [*Lords*].
    K. John. They burn in indignation. I repent.

Enter a MESSENGER.

There is no sure foundation set on blood,
No certain life achiev'd by others' death.   105
A fearful eye thou hast. Where is that blood
That I have seen inhabit in those cheeks?
So foul a sky clears not without a storm;
Pour down thy weather. How goes all in France?
    Mess. From France to England. Never such a
      power   110
For any foreign preparation
Was levied in the body of a land.
The copy of your speed is learn'd by them;
For when you should be told they do prepare,
The tidings comes that they are all arriv'd.   115
    K. John. O, where hath our intelligence been
      drunk?
Where hath it slept? Where is my mother's care,
That such an army could be drawn in France,
And she not hear of it?
    Mess.   My liege, her ear
Is stopp'd with dust; the first of April died   120
Your noble mother: and, as I hear, my lord,

---

39. **make a stand at:** be subservient to. 42. **[when]** (Steevens). *then* F. 56–57. **your fears ... should:** should your fears.
61. **the time's enemies:** enemies of the present state of affairs. 72. **close:** secretive. 100. **the while:** when such things
happen. 109. **weather:** storm. 116. **intelligence:** information service, spies. 117. **care.** The F reading is uncertain, and
may be *eare.*

The Lady Constance in a frenzy died
Three days before; but this from Rumour's tongue
I idly heard; if true or false I know not.   124
   K. John. Withhold thy speed, dreadful occasion!
O, make a league with me, till I have pleas'd
My discontented peers! What! mother dead!
How wildly then walks my estate in France!
Under whose conduct came those powers of France
That thou for truth giv'st out are landed here?   130
   Mess. Under the Dauphin.

      Enter the BASTARD *and* PETER *of Pomfret.*

   K. John.   Thou hast made me giddy
With these ill tidings. — Now, what says the world
To your proceedings? Do not seek to stuff
My head with more ill news, for it is full.
   Bast. But if you be afeard to hear the worst,   135
Then let the worst unheard fall on your head.
   K. John. Bear with me, cousin, for I was amaz'd
Under the tide; but now I breathe again
Aloft the flood, and can give audience
To any tongue, speak it of what it will.   140
   Bast. How I have sped among the clergymen
The sums I have collected shall express.
But as I travell'd hither through the land,
I find the people strangely fantasied;
Possess'd with rumours, full of idle dreams,   145
Not knowing what they fear, but full of fear.
And here's a prophet that I brought with me
From forth the streets of Pomfret, whom I found
With many hundreds treading on his heels;
To whom he sung, in rude harsh-sounding rhymes,
That, ere the next Ascension-day at noon,   151
Your Highness should deliver up your crown.
   K. John. Thou idle dreamer, wherefore didst
      thou so?
   Peter. Foreknowing that the truth will fall out so.
   K. John. Hubert, away with him; imprison him;
And on that day at noon, whereof he says   156
I shall yield up my crown, let him be hang'd.
Deliver him to safety, and return,
For I must use thee.   *[Exit Hubert with Peter.]*
               O my gentle cousin,
Hear'st thou the news abroad, who are arriv'd?   160
   Bast. The French, my lord; men's mouths are
      full of it.
Besides, I met Lord Bigot and Lord Salisbury,
With eyes as red as new-enkindled fire,
And others more, going to seek the grave
Of Arthur, whom they say is kill'd to-night   165
On your suggestion.
   K. John.   Gentle kinsman, go
And thrust thyself into their companies.
I have a way to win their loves again.
Bring them before me.
   Bast.   I will seek them out.

   K. John. Nay, but make haste; the better foot
      before.   170
O, let me have no subject enemies
When adverse foreigners affright my towns
With dreadful pomp of stout invasion!
Be Mercury, set feathers to thy heels,
And fly like thought from them to me again.   175
   Bast. The spirit of the time shall teach me speed.
                                      [Exit.
   K. John. Spoke like a sprightful noble gentleman.
Go after him; for he perhaps shall need
Some messenger betwixt me and the peers;
And be thou he.
   Mess.   With all my heart, my liege.   180
                                      [Exit.]
   K. John. My mother dead!

           Re-enter HUBERT.

   Hub. My lord, they say five moons were seen
      to-night;
Four fixed, and the fifth did whirl about
The other four in wondrous motion.
   K. John. Five moons!
   Hub.   Old men and beldams in the streets
Do prophesy upon it dangerously.   186
Young Arthur's death is common in their mouths;
And when they talk of him, they shake their heads
And whisper one another in the ear;
And he that speaks doth gripe the hearer's wrist,
Whilst he that hears makes fearful action   191
With wrinkled brows, with nods, with rolling eyes.
I saw a smith stand with his hammer, thus,
The whilst his iron did on the anvil cool,
With open mouth swallowing a tailor's news;   195
Who, with his shears and measure in his hand,
Standing on slippers, which his nimble haste
Had falsely thrust upon contrary feet,
Told of a many thousand warlike French
That were embattailed and rank'd in Kent.   200
Another lean unwash'd artificer
Cuts off his tale and talks of Arthur's death.
   K. John. Why seek'st thou to possess me with
      these fears?
Why urgest thou so oft young Arthur's death?
Thy hand hath murd'red him. I had a mighty
      cause   205
To wish him dead, but thou hadst none to kill him.
   Hub. No had, my lord! Why, did you not
      provoke me?
   K. John. It is the curse of kings to be attended
By slaves that take their humours for a warrant
To break within the bloody house of life,   210
And on the winking of authority
To understand a law, to know the meaning
Of dangerous majesty, when perchance it frowns
More upon humour than advis'd respect.

    137. **amaz'd:** dumbfounded.   177. **sprightful:** high-spirited.   201. **artificer:** artisan.   207. **provoke:** incite.

Hub. Here is your hand and seal for what I did.

K. John. O, when the last account 'twixt heaven and earth   216
Is to be made, then shall this hand and seal
Witness against us to damnation!
How oft the sight of means to do ill deeds
Make deeds ill done! Hadst not thou been by, 220
A fellow by the hand of nature mark'd,
Quoted, and sign'd to do a deed of shame,
This murder had not come into my mind;
But taking note of thy abhorr'd aspect,
Finding thee fit for bloody villainy,   225
Apt, liable to be employ'd in danger,
I faintly broke with thee of Arthur's death;
And thou, to be endeared to a king,
Made it no conscience to destroy a prince.

Hub. My lord, —   230

K. John. Hadst thou but shook thy head or made a pause
When I spake darkly what I purposed,
Or turn'd an eye of doubt upon my face,
As bid me tell my tale in express words,
Deep shame had struck me dumb, made me break off,   235
And those thy fears might have wrought fears in me.
But thou didst understand me by my signs
And didst in signs again parley with sin;
Yea, without stop, didst let thy heart consent,
And consequently thy rude hand to act   240
The deed, which both our tongues held vile to name.
Out of my sight, and never see me more!
My nobles leave me; and my state is brav'd,
Even at my gates, with ranks of foreign powers;
Nay, in the body of this fleshly land,   245
This kingdom, this confine of blood and breath,
Hostility and civil tumult reigns
Between my conscience and my cousin's death.

Hub. Arm you against your other enemies,
I'll make a peace between your soul and you. 250
Young Arthur is alive. This hand of mine
Is yet a maiden and an innocent hand,
Not painted with the crimson spots of blood.
Within this bosom never ent'red yet
The dreadful motion of a murderous thought; 255
And you have slander'd nature in my form,
Which, howsoever rude exteriorly,
Is yet the cover of a fairer mind
Than to be butcher of an innocent child.

K. John. Doth Arthur live? O, haste thee to the peers,   260
Throw this report on their incensed rage,
And make them tame to their obedience!
Forgive the comment that my passion made
Upon thy feature; for my rage was blind,
And foul imaginary eyes of blood   265
Presented thee more hideous than thou art.
O, answer not, but to my closet bring
The angry lords with all expedient haste.
I conjure thee but slowly; run more fast. *[Exeunt.*

SCENE III. *[Before the castle.]*

Enter ARTHUR, *on the walls.*

Arth. The wall is high, and yet will I leap down.
Good ground, be pitiful and hurt me not!
There's few or none do know me; if they did,
This ship-boy's semblance hath disguis'd me quite.
I am afraid, and yet I'll venture it.   5
If I get down, and do not break my limbs,
I'll find a thousand shifts to get away.
As good to die and go, as die and stay.
    [Leaps down.]
O me! my uncle's spirit is in these stones.
Heaven take my soul, and England keep my bones!   *[Dies.* 10

Enter PEMBROKE, SALISBURY, *and* BIGOT.

Sal. Lords, I will meet him at Saint Edmundsbury.
It is our safety, and we must embrace
This gentle offer of the perilous time.

Pem. Who brought that letter from the Cardinal?

Sal. The Count Melun, a noble lord of France;
Whose private with me of the Dauphin's love 16
Is much more general than these lines import.

Big. To-morrow morning let us meet him then.

Sal. Or rather then set forward; for 'twill be
Two long days' journey, lords, or ere we meet. 20

Enter the BASTARD.

Bast. Once more to-day well met, distemper'd lords!
The King by me requests your presence straight.

Sal. The King hath dispossess'd himself of us.
We will not line his thin bestained cloak
With our pure honours, nor attend the foot   25
That leaves the print of blood where'er it walks.
Return and tell him so. We know the worst.

Bast. Whate'er you think, good words, I think, were best.

Sal. Our griefs, and not our manners, reason now.

Bast. But there is little reason in your grief; 30
Therefore 'twere reason you had manners now.

Pem. Sir, sir, impatience hath his privilege.

Bast. 'Tis true, to hurt his master, no man else.

Sal. This is the prison. What is he lies here?
    [Seeing Arthur.]

---

222. **Quoted, and sign'd:** designated and marked. 226. **liable:** fit. 227. **broke:** broached the subject. 243. **state is brav'd:** authority is defied. 245-46. **body ... breath.** Referring to his own body. 265. **imaginary:** imaginative.
Sc. iii, 16. **private:** private communication. 21. **distemper'd:** disturbed, out of temper.

Pem. O death, made proud with pure and princely
    beauty!   35
The earth had not a hole to hide this deed.
    Sal. Murder, as hating what himself hath done,
Doth lay it open to urge on revenge.
    Big. Or, when he doom'd this beauty to a grave,
Found it too precious-princely for a grave.   40
    Sal. Sir Richard, what think you? [Have you]
    beheld,
Or have you read or heard, or could you think?
Or do you almost think, although you see,
That you do see? Could thought, without this
    object,
Form such another? This is the very top,   45
The height, the crest, or crest unto the crest,
Of murder's arms. This is the bloodiest shame,
The wildest savagery, the vilest stroke,
That ever wall-ey'd wrath or staring rage
Presented to the tears of soft remorse.   50
    Pem. All murders past do stand excus'd in this;
And this, so sole and so unmatchable,
Shall give a holiness, a purity,
To the yet unbegotten sin of times;
And prove a deadly bloodshed but a jest,   55
Exampled by this heinous spectacle.
    Bast. It is a damned and a bloody work;
The graceless action of a heavy hand,
If that it be the work of any hand.
    Sal. If that it be the work of any hand!   60
We had a kind of light what would ensue.
It is the shameful work of Hubert's hand,
The practice and the purpose of the King;
From whose obedience I forbid my soul,
Kneeling before this ruin of sweet life,   65
And breathing to his breathless excellence
The incense of a vow, a holy vow,
Never to taste the pleasures of the world,
Never to be infected with delight,
Nor conversant with ease and idleness,   70
Till I have set a glory to this hand,
By giving it the worship of revenge.
    Pem. Big. Our souls religiously confirm thy
    words.

    Enter HUBERT.

    Hub. Lords, I am hot with haste in seeking you.
Arthur doth live; the King hath sent for you.   75
    Sal. O, he is bold and blushes not at death.
Avaunt, thou hateful villain, get thee gone!
    Hub. I am no villain.
    Sal.   Must I rob the law?
    [*Drawing his sword.*]
    Bast. Your sword is bright, sir; put it up again.
    Sal. Not till I sheathe it in a murderer's skin.   80
    Hub. Stand back, Lord Salisbury, stand back,
    I say;

By heaven, I think my sword's as sharp as yours.
I would not have you, lord, forget yourself
Nor tempt the danger of my true defence,
Lest I, by marking of your rage, forget   85
Your worth, your greatness, and nobility.
    Big. Out, dunghill! dar'st thou brave a nobleman?
    Hub. Not for my life; but yet I dare defend
My innocent life against an emperor.   89
    Sal. Thou art a murderer.
    Hub.   Do not prove me so;
Yet I am none. Whose tongue soe'er speaks false,
Not truly speaks; who speaks not truly, lies.
    Pem. Cut him to pieces.
    Bast.   Keep the peace, I say.
    Sal. Stand by, or I shall gall you, Faulconbridge.
    Bast. Thou wert better gall the devil, Salisbury.
If thou but frown on me, or stir thy foot,   96
Or teach thy hasty spleen to do me shame,
I'll strike thee dead. Put up thy sword betime;
Or I'll so maul you and your toasting-iron,
That you shall think the devil is come from hell.   100
    Big. What wilt thou do, renowned Faulconbridge?
Second a villain and a murderer?
    Hub. Lord Bigot, I am none.
    Big.   Who kill'd this prince?
    Hub. 'Tis not an hour since I left him well.
I honour'd him, I lov'd him, and will weep   105
My date of life out for his sweet life's loss.
    Sal. Trust not those cunning waters of his eyes,
For villainy is not without such rheum;
And he, long traded in it, makes it seem
Like rivers of remorse and innocency.   110
Away with me, all you whose souls abhor
Th' uncleanly savours of a slaughter-house;
For I am stifled with this smell of sin.
    Big. Away toward Bury, to the Dauphin there!
    Pem. There, tell the King, he may inquire us
    out.   [*Exeunt Lords.* 115
    Bast. Here's a good world! Knew you of this
    fair work?
Beyond the infinite and boundless reach
Of mercy, if thou didst this deed of death,
Art thou damn'd, Hubert.
    Hub.   Do but hear me, sir.
    Bast. Ha! I'll tell thee what;   120
Thou'rt damn'd as black — nay, nothing is so black;
Thou art more deep damn'd than Prince Lucifer.
There is not yet so ugly a fiend of hell
As thou shalt be, if thou didst kill this child.
    Hub. Upon my soul —
    Bast.   If thou didst but consent
To this most cruel act, do but despair;   126
And if thou want'st a cord, the smallest thread
That ever spider twisted from her womb
Will serve to strangle thee; a rush will be a beam
To hang thee on; or wouldst thou drown thyself,   130

41. [Have you] F₃. *You have* F₁. 54. times: the future. 90. Do...so: i.e., by forcing me to kill you.

Put but a little water in a spoon,
And it shall be as all the ocean,
Enough to stifle such a villain up.
I do suspect thee very grievously.

 Hub. If I in act, consent, or sin of thought 135
Be guilty of the stealing that sweet breath
Which was embounded in this beauteous clay,
Let hell want pains enough to torture me.
I left him well.

 Bast.   Go, bear him in thine arms.
I am amaz'd, methinks, and lose my way 140
Among the thorns and dangers of this world.
How easy dost thou take all England up!
From forth this morsel of dead royalty,
The life, the right, and truth of all this realm
Is fled to heaven; and England now is left 145
To tug and scamble and to part by th' teeth
The unow'd interest of proud-swelling state.
Now for the bare-pick'd bone of majesty
Doth dogged war bristle his angry crest
And snarleth in the gentle eyes of peace. 150
Now powers from home and discontents at home
Meet in one line; and vast confusion waits,
As doth a raven on a sick-fallen beast,
The imminent decay of wrested pomp.
Now happy he whose cloak and [cincture] can 155
Hold out this tempest. Bear away that child,
And follow me with speed. I'll to the King.
A thousand businesses are brief in hand,
And heaven itself doth frown upon the land.
           [Exeunt.

ACT [V]

Scene I. [*King John's palace.*]

Enter King John, Pandulph, *and* Attendants.

 K. John. Thus have I yielded up into your hand
The circle of my glory. [*Giving the crown.*]

 Pand.   Take again
From this my hand, as holding of the Pope,
Your sovereign greatness and authority.

 K. John. Now keep your holy word. Go meet
  the French, 5
And from his Holiness use all your power
To stop their marches 'fore we are inflam'd.
Our discontented counties do revolt;
Our people quarrel with obedience,
Swearing allegiance and the love of soul 10
To stranger blood, to foreign royalty.
This inundation of mistemp'red humour
Rests by you only to be qualified.
Then pause not; for the present time's so sick,

That present medicine must be minist'red, 15
Or overthrow incurable ensues.

 Pand. It was my breath that blew this tempest
  up,
Upon your stubborn usage of the Pope;
But since you are a gentle convertite,
My tongue shall hush again this storm of war, 20
And make fair weather in your blust'ring land.
On this Ascension-day, remember well,
Upon your oath of service to the Pope,
Go I to make the French lay down their arms.
           [Exit.

 K. John. Is this Ascension-day? Did not the
  prophet 25
Say that before Ascension-day at noon
My crown I should give off? Even so I have.
I did suppose it should be on constraint;
But, heaven be thank'd, it is but voluntary.

Enter the Bastard.

 Bast. All Kent hath yielded; nothing there holds
  out 30
But Dover castle. London hath receiv'd,
Like a kind host, the Dauphin and his powers.
Your nobles will not hear you, but are gone
To offer service to your enemy,
And wild amazement hurries up and down 35
The little number of your doubtful friends.

 K. John. Would not my lords return to me again
After they heard young Arthur was alive?

 Bast. They found him dead and cast into the
  streets,
An empty casket, where the jewel of life 40
By some damn'd hand was robb'd and ta'en away.

 K. John. That villain Hubert told me he did live.

 Bast. So, on my soul, he did, for aught he knew.
But wherefore do you droop? Why look you sad?
Be great in act, as you have been in thought. 45
Let not the world see fear and sad distrust
Govern the motion of a kingly eye.
Be stirring as the time; be fire with fire;
Threaten the threat'ner and outface the brow
Of bragging Horror; so shall inferior eyes, 50
That borrow their behaviours from the great,
Grow great by your example and put on
The dauntless spirit of resolution.
Away, and glister like the god of war
When he intendeth to become the field. 55
Show boldness and aspiring confidence.
What, shall they seek the lion in his den
And fright him there, and make him tremble there?
O, let it not be said! Forage, and run
To meet displeasure farther from the doors, 60

---

 146. **scamble:** scramble. 147. **unow'd:** of uncertain ownership. 151. **powers from home:** foreign levies. 154. **wrested pomp:** usurped authority. 155. **[cincture]** (Pope). *center* F. 158. **brief in hand:** demanding prompt action.
 Act V, sc. i, 8. **counties:** perhaps nobles. 13. **qualified:** checked. 19. **convertite:** convert. 55. **become:** adorn. 59. **Forage:** raven.

And grapple with him ere he come so nigh.
   K. John. The legate of the Pope hath been with
     me,
And I have made a happy peace with him;
And he hath promis'd to dismiss the powers
Led by the Dauphin.
   Bast.   O inglorious league!   65
Shall we, upon the footing of our land,
Send fair-play orders and make compromise,
Insinuation, parley, and base truce
To arms invasive? Shall a beardless boy,
A cock'red silken wanton, brave our fields,   70
And flesh his spirit in a warlike soil,
Mocking the air with colours idly spread,
And find no check? Let us, my liege, to arms.
Perchance the Cardinal cannot make your peace;
Or if he do, let it at least be said   75
They saw we had a purpose of defence.
   K. John. Have thou the ordering of this present
     time.
   Bast. Away, then, with good courage! Yet, I
     know,
Our party may well meet a prouder foe. [*Exeunt.*

SCENE II. [*The Dauphin's camp at Saint
Edmundsbury.*]

Enter, in arms, LEWIS, SALISBURY, MELUN,
PEMBROKE, BIGOT, *and* Soldiers.

   Lew. My Lord Melun, let this be copied out,
And keep it safe for our remembrance.
Return the precedent to these lords again,
That, having our fair order written down,
Both they and we, perusing o'er these notes,   5
May know wherefore we took the sacrament
And keep our faiths firm and inviolable.
   Sal. Upon our sides it never shall be broken.
And, noble Dauphin, albeit we swear
A voluntary zeal and an unurg'd faith   10
To your proceedings, yet believe me, Prince,
I am not glad that such a sore of time
Should seek a plaster by contemn'd revolt,
And heal the inveterate canker of one wound
By making many O, it grieves my soul,   15
That I must draw this metal from my side
To be a widow-maker! O, and there
Where honourable rescue and defence
Cries out upon the name of Salisbury!
But such is the infection of the time,   20
That, for the health and physic of our right,
We cannot deal but with the very hand
Of stern injustice and confused wrong.

And is't not pity, O my grieved friends,
That we, the sons and children of this isle,   25
Were born to see so sad an hour as this;
Wherein we step after a stranger, march
Upon her gentle bosom, and fill up
Her enemies' ranks — I must withdraw and weep
Upon the spot of this enforced cause —   30
To grace the gentry of a land remote,
And follow unacquainted colours here?
What, here? O nation, that thou couldst remove!
That Neptune's arms, who clippeth thee about,
Would bear thee from the knowledge of thyself, 35
And [grapple] thee unto a pagan shore,
Where these two Christian armies might combine
The blood of malice in a vein of league,
And not to spend it so unneighbourly!
   Lew. A noble temper dost thou show in this; 40
And great affections wrestling in thy bosom
Doth make an earthquake of nobility.
O, what a noble combat hast [thou] fought
Between compulsion and a brave respect!
Let me wipe off this honourable dew,   45
That silverly doth progress on thy cheeks.
My heart hath melted at a lady's tears,
Being an ordinary inundation;
But this effusion of such manly drops,
This shower, blown up by tempest of the soul, 50
Startles mine eyes, and makes me more amaz'd
Than had I seen the vaulty top of heaven
Figur'd quite o'er with burning meteors.
Lift up thy brow, renowned Salisbury,
And with a great heart heave away the storm. 55
Commend these waters to those baby eyes
That never saw the giant world enrag'd,
Nor met with fortune other than at feasts,
Full [of warm] blood, of mirth, of gossiping.
Come, come; for thou shalt thrust thy hand as deep
Into the purse of rich prosperity   61
As Lewis himself; so, nobles, shall you all,
That knit your sinews to the strength of mine.

Enter PANDULPH.

And even there, methinks, an angel spake.
Look, where the holy legate comes apace,   65
To give us warrant from the hand of Heaven,
And on our actions set the name of right
With holy breath.
   Pand.   Hail, noble Prince of France!
The next is this, King John hath reconcil'd
Himself to Rome; his spirit is come in,   70
That so stood out against the Holy Church,
The great metropolis and see of Rome;

---

66. **upon ... land:** standing on our own soil. 71. **flesh:** initiate into slaughter.
   Sc. ii, 3. precedent: original document. 18–19. **Where ... Salisbury:** where those who are honorably defending their
country exclaim against Salisbury. 30. **spot:** stain. 36. **[grapple]** (Pope). *cripple* F. 43. **[thou]** F₄. Om. F₁₋₃. 44. **Between ... respect:** between what you are compelled to and gallant regard (for your country). 59. **[of warm]** Heath conj.
warm of F. 64. **an angel spake.** It has been suggested that a trumpet sounds here.

Therefore thy threat'ning colours now wind up,
And tame the savage spirit of wild war,
That, like a lion fostered up at hand,   75
It may lie gently at the foot of Peace,
And be no further harmful than in show.

Lew. Your Grace shall pardon me, I will not back.
I am too high-born to be propertied,
To be a secondary at control,   80
Or useful serving-man and instrument
To any sovereign state throughout the world.
Your breath first kindled the dead coal of wars
Between this chastis'd kingdom and myself,
And brought in matter that should feed this fire;   85
And now 'tis far too huge to be blown out
With that same weak wind which enkindled it.
You taught me how to know the face of right,
Acquainted me with interest to this land,
Yea, thrust this enterprise into my heart;   90
And come ye now to tell me John hath made
His peace with Rome?   What is that peace to me?
I, by the honour of my marriage-bed,
After young Arthur, claim this land for mine;
And, now it is half-conquer'd, must I back   95
Because that John hath made his peace with Rome?
Am I Rome's slave? What penny hath Rome borne,
What men provided, what munition sent,
To underprop this action?   Is't not I
That undergo this charge? Who else but I,   100
And such as to my claim are liable,
Sweat in this business and maintain this war?
Have I not heard these islanders shout out
"*Vive le roi!*" as I have bank'd their towns?
Have I not here the best cards for the game,   105
To win this easy match play'd for a crown?
And shall I now give o'er the yielded set?
No, on my soul, it never shall be said.

Pand. You look but on the outside of this work.

Lew. Outside or inside, I will not return   110
Till my attempt so much be glorified
As to my ample hope was promised
Before I drew this gallant head of war,
And cull'd these fiery spirits from the world,
To outlook conquest and to win renown   115
Even in the jaws of danger and of death.

                              [*Trumpet sounds.*]
What lusty trumpet thus doth summon us?

Enter the BASTARD, *attended.*

Bast. According to the fair play of the world,
Let me have audience. I am sent to speak,
My holy lord of Milan, from the King.   120
I come to learn how you have dealt for him;
And, as you answer, I do know the scope

And warrant limited unto my tongue.

Pand. The Dauphin is too wilful-opposite,
And will not temporize with my entreaties.   125
He flatly says he'll not lay down his arms.

Bast. By all the blood that ever fury breath'd,
The youth says well. Now hear our English King,
For thus his royalty doth speak in me.
He is prepar'd, and reason too he should.   130
This apish and unmannerly approach,
This harness'd masque and unadvised revel,
This [unhair'd] sauciness and boyish troops,
The King doth smile at, and is well prepar'd
To whip this dwarfish war, [these] pigmy arms,   135
From out the circle of his territories.
That hand which had the strength, even at your
        door,
To cudgel you and make you take the hatch,
To dive like buckets in concealed wells,
To crouch in litter of your stable planks,   140
To lie like pawns lock'd up in chests and trunks,
To hug with swine, to seek sweet safety out
In vaults and prisons, and to thrill and shake
Even at the crying of your nation's crow,
Thinking his voice an armed Englishman;   145
Shall that victorious hand be feebled here,
That in your chambers gave you chastisement?
No! Know the gallant monarch is in arms
And like an eagle o'er his aery towers,
To souse annoyance that comes near his nest.   150
And you degenerate, you ingrate revolts,
You bloody Neroes, ripping up the womb
Of your dear mother England, blush for shame;
For your own ladies and pale-visag'd maids
Like Amazons come tripping after drums,   155
Their thimbles into armed gauntlets change,
Their needles to lances, and their gentle hearts
To fierce and bloody inclination.

Lew. There end thy brave, and turn thy face in
        peace;
We grant thou canst outscold us.   Fare thee well!
We hold our time too precious to be spent   161
With such a brabbler.

Pand.   Give me leave to speak.

Bast. No, I will speak.

Lew.   We will attend to neither.
Strike up the drums; and let the tongue of war
Plead for our interest and our being here.   165

Bast. Indeed, your drums, being beaten, will
        cry out;
And so shall you, being beaten. Do but start
An echo with the clamour of thy drum,
And even at hand a drum is ready brac'd
That shall reverberate all as loud as thine.   170

<hr>

79. **propertied:** made a chattel of.   89. **interest:** my claim.   101. **liable:** subject.   104. **bank'd:** coasted along by.   107.
set: game.   113. **head of war:** army.   115. **outlook:** outstare, defy.   133. **[unhair'd]** (Theobald): unbearded. *un-heard*
F.   135. **[these]** (Rowe).   *this* F.   138. **take the hatch:** leap over the lower half of the door.   150. **souse:** swoop down
on.   159. **brave:** swaggering.   162. **brabbler:** loud talker.   169. **brac'd:** tightened.

Sound but another, and another shall
As loud as thine rattle the welkin's ear
And mock the deep-mouth'd thunder; for at hand,
Not trusting to this halting legate here,
Whom he hath us'd rather for sport than need,   175
Is warlike John; and in his forehead sits
A bare-ribb'd Death, whose office is this day
To feast upon whole thousands of the French.
   Lew. Strike up our drums, to find this danger out.
   Bast. And thou shalt find it, Dauphin, do not
    doubt.   [*Exeunt.* 180

SCENE III. [*The field of battle.*]

Alarums. Enter KING JOHN *and* HUBERT.

   K. John. How goes the day with us? O, tell
    me, Hubert.
   Hub. Badly, I fear. How fares your Majesty?
   K. John. This fever, that hath troubled me so
    long,
Lies heavy on me. O, my heart is sick!

Enter a MESSENGER.

   Mess. My lord, your valiant kinsman, Faul-
    conbridge,   5
Desires your Majesty to leave the field
And send him word by me which way you go.
   K. John. Tell him, toward Swinstead, to the
    abbey there.
   Mess. Be of good comfort; for the great supply
That was expected by the Dauphin here,   10
Are wreck'd three nights ago on Goodwin Sands.
This news was brought to Richard but even now.
The French fight coldly, and retire themselves.
   K. John. Ay me! this tyrant fever burns me up,
And will not let me welcome this good news.   15
Set on toward Swinstead. To my litter straight;
Weakness possesseth me, and I am faint. [*Exeunt.*

SCENE IV. [*Another part of the field.*]

Enter SALISBURY, PEMBROKE, *and* BIGOT.

   Sal. I did not think the King so stor'd with
    friends.
   Pem. Up once again! Put spirit in the French.
If they miscarry, we miscarry too.
   Sal. That misbegotten devil, Faulconbridge,
In spite of spite, alone upholds the day.   5
   Pem. They say King John sore sick hath left
    the field.

Enter MELUN, *wounded.*

   Mel. Lead me to the revolts of England here.

   Sal. When we were happy we had other names.
   Pem. It is the Count Melun.
   Sal.   Wounded to death.
   Mel. Fly, noble English, you are bought and
    sold!   10
Unthread the rude eye of rebellion
And welcome home again discarded faith.
Seek out King John and fall before his feet;
For if the French be lords of this loud day,
He means to recompense the pains you take   15
By cutting off your heads. Thus hath he sworn
And I with him, and many moe with me,
Upon the altar at Saint Edmundsbury;
Even on that altar where we swore to you
Dear amity and everlasting love.   20
   Sal. May this be possible? May this be true?
   Mel. Have I not hideous death within my view,
Retaining but a quantity of life,
Which bleeds away even as a form of wax
Resolveth from his figure 'gainst the fire?   25
What in the world should make me now deceive
Since I must lose the use of all deceit?
Why should I then be false, since it is true
That I must die here and live hence by truth?
I say again, if Lewis do win the day,   30
He is forsworn if e'er those eyes of yours
Behold another day break in the east;
But even this night, whose black contagious breath
Already smokes about the burning crest
Of the old, feeble, and day-wearied sun,   35
Even this ill night your breathing shall expire,
Paying the fine of rated treachery
Even with a treacherous fine of all your lives,
If Lewis by your assistance win the day.
Commend me to one Hubert with your king.   40
The love of him, and this respect besides,
For that my grandsire was an Englishman,
Awakes my conscience to confess all this;
In lieu whereof, I pray you, bear me hence
From forth the noise and rumour of the field,   45
Where I may think the remnant of my thoughts
In peace, and part this body and my soul
With contemplation and devout desires.
   Sal. We do believe thee; and beshrew my soul
But I do love the favour and the form   50
Of this most fair occasion, by the which
We will untread the steps of damned flight,
And like a bated and retired flood,
Leaving our rankness and irregular course,
Stoop low within those bounds we have o'erlook'd, 55
And calmly run on in obedience   56
Even to our ocean, to our great King John.

Sc. iii, 9. **supply:** reinforcement.

Sc. iv, 7. **revolts:** revolting nobles.   11. **Unthread...rebellion:** withdraw from rebellion, into which you have been drawn as a thread into the eye of a needle.   23. **quantity:** small portion.   25. **Resolveth:** melts.   27. **use:** benefit.   37–38. **fine...fine:** penalty...end.   **rated:** estimated at its true value.   41. **respect:** consideration.   50. **favour:** aspect.   54. **rankness:** flooding.   55. **o'erlook'd:** overflowed.

My arm shall give thee help to bear thee hence;
For I do see the cruel pangs of death
Right in thine eye. Away, my friends! New flight, 60
And happy newness, that intends old right.
      [*Exeunt [leading off Melun].*

SCENE V. [*The French camp.*]

Enter LEWIS *and his train.*

Lew. The sun of heaven methought was loath to set,
But stay'd and made the western welkin blush,
When English measure backward their own ground
In faint retire. O, bravely came we off,
When with a volley of our needless shot, 5
After such bloody toil, we bid good night;
And wound our tott'ring colours clearly up,
Last in the field, and almost lords of it!

Enter a MESSENGER.

Mess. Where is my prince, the Dauphin?
Lew.   Here: what news?
Mess. The Count Melun is slain; the English lords 10
By his persuasion are again fallen off,
And your supply, which you have wish'd so long,
Are cast away and sunk on Goodwin Sands.
 Lew. Ah, foul shrewd news! Beshrew thy very heart!
I did not think to be so sad to-night 15
As this hath made me. Who was he that said
King John did fly an hour or two before
The stumbling night did part our weary powers?
 Mess. Whoever spoke it, it is true, my lord.
 Lew. Well; keep good quarter and good care to-night. 20
The day shall not be up so soon as I,
To try the fair adventure of to-morrow. [*Exeunt.*

SCENE VI. [*An open place in the neighbourhood of Swinstead Abbey.*]

Enter the BASTARD *and* HUBERT, *severally.*

Hub. Who's there? Speak, ho! Speak quickly, or I shoot.
Bast. A friend. What art thou?
Hub.   Of the part of England.
Bast. Whither dost thou go?
Hub. What's that to thee? Why may not I demand
Of thine affairs, as well as thou of mine? 5
Bast. Hubert, I think?

Hub.   Thou hast a perfect thought.
I will upon all hazards well believe
Thou art my friend that know'st my tongue so well.
Who art thou?
Bast.   Who thou wilt; and if thou please,
Thou may'st befriend me so much as to think 10
I come one way of the Plantagenets.
 Hub. Unkind remembrance! thou and [eyeless] night
Have done me shame. Brave soldier, pardon me
That any accent breaking from thy tongue
Should scape the true acquaintance of mine ear. 15
 Bast. Come, come; sans compliment, what news abroad?
 Hub. Why, here walk I in the black brow of night,
To find you out.
 Bast.   Brief, then; and what's the news?
 Hub. O, my sweet sir, news fitting to the night,
Black, fearful, comfortless, and horrible. 20
 Bast. Show me the very wound of this ill news.
I am no woman, I'll not swoon at it.
 Hub. The King, I fear, is poison'd by a monk.
I left him almost speechless, and broke out
To acquaint you with this evil, that you might
The better arm you to the sudden time 26
Than if you had at leisure known of this.
 Bast. How did he take it? Who did taste to him?
 Hub. A monk, I tell you; a resolved villain,
Whose bowels suddenly burst out. The King 30
Yet speaks and peradventure may recover.
 Bast. Who didst thou leave to tend his Majesty?
 Hub. Why, know you not the lords are all come back,
And brought Prince Henry in their company?
At whose request the King hath pardon'd them, 35
And they are all about his Majesty.
 Bast. Withhold thine indignation, mighty heaven,
And tempt us not to bear above our power!
I'll tell thee, Hubert, half my power this night,
Passing these flats, are taken by the tide; 40
These Lincoln Washes have devoured them;
Myself, well mounted, hardly have escap'd.
Away before; conduct me to the King.
I doubt he will be dead or ere I come. [*Exeunt.*

SCENE VII. [*The orchard at Swinstead Abbey.*]

Enter PRINCE HENRY, SALISBURY, *and* BIGOT.

P. Hen. It is too late. The life of all his blood
Is touch'd corruptibly, and his pure brain,
Which some suppose the soul's frail dwelling-house,
Doth by the idle comments that it makes
Foretell the ending of mortality. 5

Sc. v, 7. **tott'ring:** flying in tatters. 14. **shrewd:** cursed. 20. **quarter:** watch.
Sc. vi, 11. **one way:** on one side. 12. **Unkind remembrance.** Reproaching himself for his bad memory. **[eyeless]** (Theobald). *endles* F. 28. **taste:** act as the taster (who ate of every dish offered the king to detect poison).
Sc. vii, 2. **pure.** Probably corrupt. White reads *poor.*

Enter PEMBROKE.

Pem. His Highness yet doth speak, and holds belief
That, being brought into the open air,
It would allay the burning quality
Of that fell poison which assaileth him.   9
P. Hen. Let him be brought into the orchard here.
Doth he still rage?   [*Exit Attendants.*]
Pem.   He is more patient
Than when you left him; even now he sung.
P. Hen. O vanity of sickness! fierce extremes
In their continuance will not feel themselves.
Death, having prey'd upon the outward parts,   15
Leaves them [insensible]; and his siege is now
Against the [mind], the which he pricks and wounds
With many legions of strange fantasies,
Which, in their throng and press to that last hold,
Confound themselves.   'Tis strange that death
          should sing.   20
I am the cygnet to this pale faint swan
Who chants a doleful hymn to his own death,
And from the organ-pipe of frailty sings
His soul and body to their lasting rest.
Sal. Be of good comfort, Prince; for you are born
To set a form upon that indigest   26
Which he hath left so shapeless and so rude.

KING JOHN *is brought in.*

K. John. Ay, marry, now my soul hath elbow-
          room;
It would not out at windows nor at doors.
There is so hot a summer in my bosom   30
That all my bowels crumble up to dust.
I am a scribbled form, drawn with a pen
Upon a parchment, and against this fire
Do I shrink up.
P. Hen.   How fares your Majesty?
K. John. Poison'd, — ill fare — dead, forsook,
          cast off;   35
And none of you will bid the Winter come
To thrust his icy fingers in my maw,
Nor let my kingdom's rivers take their course
Through my burn'd bosom, nor entreat the north
To make his bleak winds kiss my parched lips   40
And comfort me with cold. I do not ask you much,
I beg cold comfort; and you are so strait
And so ingrateful, you deny me that.
P. Hen. O that there were some virtue in my
          tears,
That might relieve you!
K. John.   The salt in them is hot.
Within me is a hell, and there the poison   46
Is as a fiend confin'd to tyrannize
On unreprievable condemned blood.

Enter the BASTARD.

Bast. O, I am scalded with my violent motion
And spleen of speed to see your Majesty!   50
K. John. O cousin, thou art come to set mine eye.
The tackle of my heart is crack'd and burn'd,
And all the shrouds wherewith my life should sail
Are turned to one thread, one little hair.
My heart hath one poor string to stay it by,   55
Which holds but till thy news be uttered;
And then all this thou seest is but a clod
And module of confounded royalty.
Bast. The Dauphin is preparing hitherward,
Where Heaven He knows how we shall answer him;
For in a night the best part of my power,   61
As I upon advantage did remove,
Were in the Washes all unwarily
Devoured by the unexpected flood. [*The king dies.*]
Sal. You breathe these dead news in as dead an
          ear.   65
My liege! my lord! But now a king, now thus.
P. Hen. Even so must I run on, and even so stop.
What surety of the world, what hope, what stay,
When this was now a king, and now is clay?
Bast. Art thou gone so? I do but stay behind
To do the office for thee of revenge,   71
And then my soul shall wait on thee to heaven,
As it on earth hath been thy servant still.
Now, now, you stars that move in your right spheres,
Where be your powers?   Show now your mended
          faiths,   75
And instantly return with me again
To push destruction and perpetual shame
Out of the weak door of our fainting land.
Straight let us seek, or straight we shall be sought;
The Dauphin rages at our very heels.   80
Sal. It seems you know not, then, so much as we.
The Cardinal Pandulph is within at rest,
Who half an hour since came from the Dauphin,
And brings from him such offers of our peace
As we with honour and respect may take,   85
With purpose presently to leave this war.
Bast. He will the rather do it when he sees
Ourselves well sinewed to our defence.
Sal. Nay, 'tis in a manner done already;
For many carriages he hath despatch'd   90
To the sea-side, and put his cause and quarrel
To the disposing of the Cardinal;
With whom yourself, myself, and other lords,
If you think meet, this afternoon will post
To consummate this business happily.   95
Bast. Let it be so; and you, my noble prince,
With other princes that may best be spar'd,
Shall wait upon your father's funeral.

16. [insensible] (Hanmer). *invisible* F. 17. [mind] (Rowe). *winde* F. 26. indigest: formless confusion. 42. strait:
niggardly. 50. spleen: passionate burst. 51. set: close. 58. module: model, image. confounded: shattered. 62.
upon advantage: taking advantage of a good opportunity. 74. you stars. Addressed to the repentant nobles.

P. Hen. At Worcester must his body be interr'd;
For so he will'd it.
    Bast.   Thither shall it then;   100
And happily may your sweet self put on
The lineal state and glory of the land!
To whom, with all submission, on my knee
I do bequeath my faithful services
And true subjection everlastingly.   105
    Sal. And the like tender of our love we make,
To rest without a spot for evermore.
    P. Hen. I have a kind soul that would [fain] give
       thanks

And knows not how to do it but with tears.
    Bast. O, let us pay the time but needful woe,   110
Since it hath been beforehand with our griefs.
This England never did, nor never shall,
Lie at the proud foot of a conqueror,
But when it first did help to wound itself.
Now these her princes are come home again,   115
Come the three corners of the world in arms,
And we shall shock them. Nought shall make us
     rue,
If England to itself do rest but true.
                             [*Exeunt.*

108. **[fain] give.** (Camb. edd. conj.).   *give* F.   *give you* Rowe.

The Tragedy of Richard the Second

RICHARD II WAS entered in the Stationers' Register on August 29, 1597, and the First Quarto was published anonymously the same year. Two other quartos appeared in 1598 (with Shakespeare's name on the title page), a fourth, containing the abdication scene for the first time (IV.i.154–318), in 1608, and a fifth in 1615. The present text is based upon that of the First Quarto, which was probably printed from the author's manuscript. For the abdication scene the First Folio has been used as a basis, since it seems to follow a corrected copy of the Fifth Quarto.

The date of composition of *Richard II* is tied up with the question of the relation of the play to Daniel's *Civil Wars between Lancaster and York*, which was registered on October 11, 1594, and published in 1595. There is, however, as yet no agreement among scholars as to whether there is any indebtedness between the poem and the play, and, if there is, on which side. A supposed allusion to *Richard II* has been found in an invitation sent to Sir Robert Cecil by Sir Edward Hoby to visit him at his house in Canon Row on December 9, 1595, where "a gate for your supper shal be open, and K. Richard present him selfe to your vewe." But it is by no means certain that the reference is to a play at all, or that, if it is, that it was to Shakespeare's, or that the Richard was Richard the second. On grounds of style and versification it is generally held that the date is close to that of *A Midsummer-Night's Dream* and of *King John*, and a reasonable conjecture is 1595.

The main source of the action is Holinshed's *Chronicles of England, Scotland, and Ireland*. Subsidiary sources are Froissart's *Chronicle*, which he knew in Lord Berners's translation; possibly one or two other French chronicles; and an earlier play on the Duke of Gloucester, known as *Thomas of Woodstock*. But the chief interest lies in those elements that are due to the dramatist's imagination. The parts played and the speeches uttered by the female characters are entirely Shakespeare's. Historically, the Queen was only eleven years old

at the date of her husband's deposition; and the Duchess of York was only the stepmother of Aumerle. The treatment of the character of John of Gaunt follows Froissart rather than Holinshed, but of the great speech on the glory of England there is no hint in the sources. This speech, with others such as the closing lines of *King John*, points to the inference that the dramatist deliberately used the opportunities given in the historical plays to appeal to the patriotic enthusiasm of the Elizabethan Englishman.

The greatest achievement in the play is in the creation, or interpretation, of the character of Richard himself, and in the poetry of his speeches. The chronicles supplied the outline of his action, but little characterization beyond charges of self-indulgence and subjection to unworthy favorites. Richard's love of the spectacular and his enjoyment of his own emotions even of misery and despair, along with his tendency to substitute fluent and poetical utterance for deeds, are all the conception of the dramatist. The resignation of the crown actually took place in the presence of a few lords in Richard's chamber in the Tower, so that the amazing exhibition of sentimental vanity in the abdication scene is purely Shakespearean. The hints of the character of Bolingbroke are also mainly invented, and prepare the ground for the more elaborate treatment in *1* and *2 Henry IV*. Holinshed speaks of his popularity, but gives nothing of such causes of it as are indicated in the description of his courtship of the common people in I.iv. 23–36. Throughout, even when the details of the episode are borrowed from the chronicle, as in the conspiracy in which Aumerle is involved, the speeches are purely imaginary, hardly a hint of the diction being derived from the sources.

The tragedy was highly successful when first produced, Queen Elizabeth herself being the authority for the statement that "this tragedy was played forty times in open streets and houses." It was in the same conversation with the keeper of the Tower records that she is reported as saying, "I am

Richard II, know ye not that?" The uncertainty of the succession to the throne, and the existence of factions favoring the various candidates, seem to have made the Queen sensitive about treatments of the deposition of kings. Grounds for her uneasiness may be found in the performance of the play at the Globe Theatre on February 7, 1601, the afternoon before the outbreak of Essex's rebellion. This was arranged for by partisans of Essex, who induced the Chamberlain's Men to give it (though they felt it was too old to draw an audience) by paying them a special honorarium of forty shillings. At the trial of Essex, this performance was adduced in evidence against him. The absence of the abdication scene in all the editions published during Elizabeth's lifetime is further evidence that the subject was felt to be a delicate one.

Shakespeare was, of course, fully aware that in the deposition and murder of Richard and the usurpation of Bolingbroke lay the seeds of the civil dissensions he had already presented in the three parts of *Henry VI* and *Richard III*. But it seems clear that his interest lay less in presenting a case for either side in the quarrels of York and Lancaster than in the human beings who were the agents or the victims in the long drawn out struggle. Richard's weaknesses and selfishness are not disguised, yet neither are they so emphasized as to lead us to deny him sympathy or to obscure his tragedy. Bolingbroke's grievances are palpable enough, yet we are shown clearly the steps by which he proceeds from seeking to vindicate his just claims to seizing the opportunities Fortune offers him till he becomes guilty of usurpation.

The spellings "Bullingbroke," "Herford," "Barkly," "Callice" (Calais), and "Cotshall" or "Coltshold" (Cotswold) in the old copies, indicate the Elizabethan pronunciation of these names.

SONS OF EDWARD III

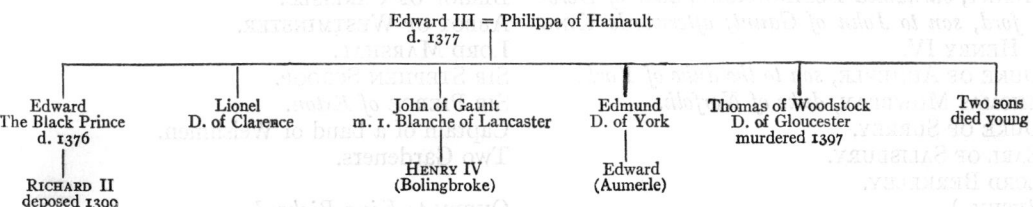

Edward III = Philippa of Hainault
d. 1377

Edward	Lionel	John of Gaunt	Edmund	Thomas of Woodstock	Two sons
The Black Prince	D. of Clarence	m. 1. Blanche of Lancaster	D. of York	D. of Gloucester	died young
d. 1376				murdered 1397	
RICHARD II		HENRY IV	Edward		
deposed 1399		(Bolingbroke)	(Aumerle)		

THE TRAGEDY OF
RICHARD THE SECOND

[DRAMATIS PERSONÆ

KING RICHARD II

JOHN OF GAUNT, *duke of Lancaster,* ⎱ *uncles*
EDMUND OF LANGLEY, *duke of York,* ⎰ *to the King.*

HENRY, *surnamed* BOLINGBROKE, *duke of Hereford, son to John of Gaunt; afterwards* KING HENRY IV.
DUKE OF AUMERLE, *son to the duke of York.*
THOMAS MOWBRAY, *duke of Norfolk.*
DUKE OF SURREY.
EARL OF SALISBURY.
LORD BERKELEY.
BUSHY, ⎫
BAGOT, ⎬ *servants to King Richard.*
GREEN, ⎭
EARL OF NORTHUMBERLAND.

HENRY PERCY, *surnamed* HOTSPUR, *his son.*
LORD ROSS.
LORD WILLOUGHBY.
LORD FITZWATER.
BISHOP OF CARLISLE.
ABBOT OF WESTMINSTER.
LORD MARSHAL.
SIR STEPHEN SCROOP.
SIR PIERCE *of Exton.*
Captain of a band of Welshmen.
Two Gardeners.

QUEEN *to King Richard.*
DUCHESS OF YORK.
DUCHESS OF GLOUCESTER.
Lady attending on the Queen.

Lords, Heralds, Officers, Soldiers, Keeper, Messenger, Groom, and other Attendants.

SCENE: *England and Wales.*]

ACT I

SCENE I. [*London. King Richard's palace.*]

Enter KING RICHARD, JOHN OF GAUNT, *with other* Nobles *and* Attendants.

K. Rich. Old John of Gaunt, time-honoured Lancaster,
Hast thou, according to thy oath and band,
Brought hither Henry Hereford thy bold son,
Here to make good the boist'rous late appeal,
Which then our leisure would not let us hear,   5
Against the Duke of Norfolk, Thomas Mowbray?
  Gaunt. I have, my liege.
  K. Rich. Tell me, moreover, hast thou sounded him
If he appeal the Duke on ancient malice,
Or worthily, as a good subject should,   10

On some known ground of treachery in him?
  Gaunt. As near as I could sift him on that argument,
On some apparent danger seen in him
Aim'd at your Highness, no inveterate malice.
  K. Rich. Then call them to our presence.
    [*Exeunt some Attendants.*] Face to face,   15
And frowning brow to brow, ourselves will hear
The accuser and the accused freely speak.
High-stomach'd are they both and full of ire,
In rage deaf as the sea, hasty as fire.

Enter BOLINGBROKE *and* MOWBRAY [*with Attendants*].

  Boling. Many years of happy days befall   20
My gracious sovereign, my most loving liege!
  Mow. Each day still better other's happiness

Act I, sc. i, 2. **band:** bond. 4. **appeal:** accusation.   18. **High-stomach'd:** haughty and wrathful.

Until the heavens, envying earth's good hap,
Add an immortal title to your crown!

K. Rich. We thank you both; yet one but flatters
   us,   25
As well appeareth by the cause you come,
Namely, to appeal each other of high treason.
Cousin of Hereford, what dost thou object
Against the Duke of Norfolk, Thomas Mowbray?

Boling. First, heaven be the record to my speech!
In the devotion of a subject's love,   31
Tend'ring the precious safety of my prince,
And free from other misbegotten hate,
Come I appellant to this princely presence.
Now, Thomas Mowbray, do I turn to thee,   35
And mark my greeting well; for what I speak
My body shall make good upon this earth,
Or my divine soul answer it in heaven.
Thou art a traitor and a miscreant,
Too good to be so, and too bad to live,   40
Since the more fair and crystal is the sky,
The uglier seem the clouds that in it fly.
Once more, the more to aggravate the note,
With a foul traitor's name stuff I thy throat
And wish, so please my sovereign, ere I move,   45
What my tongue speaks my right drawn sword may
   prove.

Mow. Let not my cold words here accuse my zeal.
'Tis not the trial of a woman's war,
The bitter clamour of two eager tongues,
Can arbitrate this cause betwixt us twain;   50
The blood is hot that must be cool'd for this.
Yet can I not of such tame patience boast
As to be hush'd and nought at all to say.
First, the fair reverence of your Highness curbs me
From giving reins and spurs to my free speech,   55
Which else would post until it had return'd
These terms of treason doubled down his throat.
Setting aside his high blood's royalty,
And let him be no kinsman to my liege,
I do defy him and I spit at him,   60
Call him a slanderous coward and a villain;
Which to maintain I would allow him odds
And meet him, were I tied to run afoot
Even to the frozen ridges of the Alps,
Or any other ground inhabitable   65
Where ever Englishman durst set his foot.
Meantime let this defend my loyalty:
By all my hopes, most falsely doth he lie.

Boling. Pale trembling coward, there I throw
   my gage,
Disclaiming here the kindred of the King,   70
And lay aside my high blood's royalty,

Which fear, not reverence, makes thee to except.
If guilty dread have left thee so much strength
As to take up mine honour's pawn, then stoop.
By that and all the rites of knighthood else,   75
Will I make good against thee, arm to arm,
What I have spoke or thou canst worse devise.

Mow. I take it up; and by that sword I swear
Which gently laid my knighthood on my shoulder,
I'll answer thee in any fair degree   80
Or chivalrous design of knightly trial;
And when I mount, alive may I not light
If I be traitor or unjustly fight!

K. Rich. What doth our cousin lay to Mowbray's
   charge?
It must be great that can inherit us   85
So much as of a thought of ill in him.

Boling. Look, what I speak, my life shall prove
   it true:
That Mowbray hath receiv'd eight thousand nobles
In name of lendings for your Highness' soldiers,
The which he hath detain'd for lewd employments,
Like a false traitor and injurious villain.   91
Besides I say, and will in battle prove,
Or here or elsewhere to the furthest verge
That ever was survey'd by English eye,
That all the treasons for these eighteen years   95
Complotted and contrived in this land
Fetch from false Mowbray their first head and
   spring.
Further I say, and further will maintain
Upon his bad life to make all this good,
That he did plot the Duke of Gloucester's death,
Suggest his soon-believing adversaries,   101
And consequently, like a traitor coward,
Sluic'd out his innocent soul through streams of
   blood;
Which blood, like sacrificing Abel's, cries,
Even from the tongueless caverns of the earth,   105
To me for justice and rough chastisement;
And, by the glorious worth of my descent,
This arm shall do it, or this life be spent.

K. Rich. How high a pitch his resolution soars!
Thomas of Norfolk, what say'st thou to this?   110

Mow. O, let my sovereign turn away his face
And bid his ears a little while be deaf,
Till I have told this slander of his blood
How God and good men hate so foul a liar.

K. Rich. Mowbray, impartial are our eyes and
   ears.   115
Were he my brother, nay, my kingdom's heir,
As he is but my father's brother's son,
Now, by [my] sceptre's awe, I make a vow,

---

32. **Tend'ring:** holding dear.   34. **appellant:** accuser.   43. **note:** stigma.   47. **accuse my zeal:** accuse me for lacking zeal.   49. **eager:** biting.   63. **tied:** obliged.   65. **inhabitable:** uninhabitable.   74. **pawn:** pledge (his glove).   85. **inherit us:** make us have.   88. **nobles:** coins worth 6s.8d.   90. **lewd:** base.   100. **Gloucester's.** Thomas of Woodstock, uncle of Richard and Bolingbroke, murdered at Calais, 1397.   101. **Suggest:** incite.   102. **consequently:** afterwards.   118. **[my]** F. Om. Q.

Such neighbour nearness to our sacred blood
Should nothing privilege him, nor partialize   120
The unstooping firmness of my upright soul.
He is our subject, Mowbray; so art thou.
Free speech and fearless I to thee allow.

   Mow. Then, Bolingbroke, as low as to thy heart,
Through the false passage of thy throat, thou liest.
Three parts of that receipt I had for Calais   126
Disburs'd I duly to his Highness' soldiers;
The other part reserv'd I by consent,
For that my sovereign liege was in my debt
Upon remainder of a dear account,   130
Since last I went to France to fetch his queen.
Now swallow down that lie. For Gloucester's
    death,
I slew him not; but to my own disgrace
Neglected my sworn duty in that case.
For you, my noble Lord of Lancaster,   135
The honourable father to my foe,
Once did I lay an ambush for your life,
A trespass that doth vex my grieved soul;
But ere I last receiv'd the sacrament
I did confess it, and exactly begg'd   140
Your Grace's pardon; and I hope I had it.
This is my fault. As for the rest appeal'd,
It issues from the rancour of a villain,
A recreant and most degenerate traitor;
Which in myself I boldly will defend;   145
And interchangeably hurl down my gage
Upon this overweening traitor's foot
To prove myself a loyal gentleman
Even in the best blood chamber'd in his bosom.
In haste whereof, most heartily I pray   150
Your Highness to assign our trial day.

   K. Rich. Wrath-kindled gentlemen, be rul'd by
    me;
Let's purge this choler without letting blood.
This we prescribe, though no physician;
Deep malice makes too deep incision;   155
Forget, forgive; conclude and be agreed;
Our doctors say this is no month to bleed.
Good uncle, let this end where it begun;
We'll calm the Duke of Norfolk, you your son.   159

   Gaunt. To be a make-peace shall become my age.
Throw down, my son, the Duke of Norfolk's gage.

   K. Rich. And, Norfolk, throw down his.

   Gaunt.   When, Harry, when!
Obedience bids I should not bid again.

   K. Rich. Norfolk, throw down, we bid; there is
    no boot.

   Mow. Myself I throw, dread sovereign, at thy
    foot;   165
My life thou shalt command, but not my shame.

The one my duty owes; but my fair name,
Despite of death that lives upon my grave,
To dark dishonour's use thou shalt not have.
I am disgrac'd, impeach'd, and baffl'd here,   170
Pierc'd to the soul with slander's venom'd spear,
The which no balm can cure but his heart-blood
Which breath'd this poison.

   K. Rich.   Rage must be withstood;
Give me his gage. Lions make leopards tame.

   Mow. Yea, but not change his spots. Take but
    my shame,   175
And I resign my gage. My dear dear lord,
The purest treasure mortal times afford
Is spotless reputation; that away,
Men are but gilded loam or painted clay.
A jewel in a ten-times-barr'd-up chest   180
Is a bold spirit in a loyal breast.
Mine honour is my life; both grow in one;
Take honour from me, and my life is done.
Then, dear my liege, mine honour let me try;
In that I live, and for that will I die.   185

   K. Rich. Cousin, throw up your gage. Do you
    begin.

   Boling. O, God defend my soul from such deep
    sin!
Shall I seem crest-fallen in my father's sight,
Or with pale beggar-fear impeach my height
Before this out-dar'd dastard? Ere my tongue   190
Shall wound my honour with such feeble wrong
Or sound so base a parle, my teeth shall tear
The slavish motive of recanting fear,
And spit it bleeding in his high disgrace,
Where shame doth harbour, even in Mowbray's
    face.   [*Exit Gaunt.*   195

   K. Rich. We were not born to sue, but to com-
    mand;
Which since we cannot do to make you friends,
Be ready, as your lives shall answer it,
At Coventry, upon Saint Lambert's day.
There shall your swords and lances arbitrate   200
The swelling difference of your settled hate.
Since we cannot atone you, we shall see
Justice design the victor's chivalry.
Lord Marshal, command our officers at arms
Be ready to direct these home alarms.   [*Exeunt.*   205

SCENE II. [*London. The Duke of Lancaster's
palace.*]

Enter JOHN OF GAUNT *with the* DUCHESS OF
GLOUCESTER.

   Gaunt. Alas, the part I had in Woodstock's blood
Doth more solicit me than your exclaims

126. **receipt:** money received. 130. **dear:** large. 150. **In haste whereof:** to hasten which. 156. **conclude:** come to terms. 164. **boot:** remedy, alternative. 170. **baffl'd:** put to shame. 174. **gage:** glove given as a challenge. 177. **mortal times: a** man's life. 189. **impeach my height:** disgrace my rank. 193. **motive:** i.e., his tongue. 199. **Saint Lambert's day:** Sept. 17. 202. **atone:** reconcile. 203. **design:** designate

To stir against the butchers of his life!
But since correction lieth in those hands
Which made the fault that we cannot correct,   5
Put we our quarrel to the will of Heaven;
Who, when they see the hours ripe on earth,
Will rain hot vengeance on offenders' heads.
 Duch. Finds brotherhood in thee no sharper spur?
Hath love in thy old blood no living fire?   10
Edward's seven sons, whereof thyself art one,
Were as seven vials of his sacred blood,
Or seven fair branches springing from one root.
Some of those seven are dried by nature's course,
Some of those branches by the Destinies cut;   15
But Thomas, my dear lord, my life, my Gloucester,
One vial full of Edward's sacred blood,
One flourishing branch of his most royal root,
Is crack'd, and all the precious liquor spilt,
Is hack'd down, and his summer leaves all faded,   20
By Envy's hand and Murder's bloody axe.
Ah, Gaunt, his blood was thine! That bed, that womb,
That mettle, that self-mould, that fashion'd thee
Made him a man; and though thou liv'st and breath'st,
Yet art thou slain in him. Thou dost consent   25
In some large measure to thy father's death,
In that thou seest thy wretched brother die,
Who was the model of thy father's life.
Call it not patience, Gaunt; it is despair.
In suff'ring thus thy brother to be slaught'red,
Thou show'st the naked pathway to thy life,   31
Teaching stern Murder how to butcher thee.
That which in mean men we entitle patience
Is pale cold cowardice in noble breasts.
What shall I say? To safeguard thine own life   35
The best way is to venge my Gloucester's death.
 Gaunt. God's is the quarrel; for God's substitute,
His deputy anointed in His sight,
Hath caus'd his death; the which if wrongfully,
Let Heaven revenge; for I may never lift   40
An angry arm against His minister.
 Duch. Where then, alas, may I complain myself?
 Gaunt. To God, the widow's champion and defence.
 Duch. Why, then, I will. Farewell, old Gaunt!
Thou go'st to Coventry, there to behold   45
Our cousin Hereford and fell Mowbray fight.
O, [sit] my husband's wrongs on Hereford's spear,
That it may enter butcher Mowbray's breast!
Or, if misfortune miss the first career,
Be Mowbray's sins so heavy in his bosom   50
That they may break his foaming courser's back,
And throw the rider headlong in the lists,
A caitiff recreant to my cousin Hereford!
Farewell, old Gaunt! Thy sometimes brother's wife

With her companion grief must end her life.   55
 Gaunt. Sister, farewell; I must to Coventry.
As much good stay with thee as go with me!
 Duch. Yet one word more! Grief boundeth where [it falls],
Not with the empty hollowness, but weight.
I take my leave before I have begun,   60
For sorrow ends not when it seemeth done.
Commend me to thy brother, Edmund York.
Lo, this is all: — nay, yet depart not so;
Though this be all, do not so quickly go;
I shall remember more. Bid him — ah, what? —
With all good speed at Plashy visit me.   66
Alack, and what shall good old York there see
But empty lodgings and unfurnish'd walls,
Unpeopled offices, untrodden stones?   69
And what hear there for welcome but my groans?
Therefore commend me; let him not come there
To seek out sorrow that dwells everywhere.
Desolate, desolate, will I hence and die.
The last leave of thee takes my weeping eye.
         [Exeunt.

SCENE III. *[The lists at Coventry.]*

Enter the LORD MARSHAL *and the* DUKE OF AUMERLE.

 Mar. My Lord Aumerle, is Harry Hereford arm'd?
 Aum. Yea, at all points; and longs to enter in.
 Mar. The Duke of Norfolk, sprightfully and bold,
Stays but the summons of the appellant's trumpet.
 Aum. Why, then, the champions are prepar'd, and stay   5
For nothing but his Majesty's approach.

The trumpets sound, and the KING *enters with his nobles,* GAUNT, BUSHY, BAGOT, GREEN, *and others. When they are set, enter* MOWBRAY *in arms, defendant, with a* HERALD.

 K. Rich. Marshal, demand of yonder champion
The cause of his arrival here in arms.
Ask him his name, and orderly proceed
To swear him in the justice of his cause.   10
 Mar. In God's name and the King's, say who thou art
And why thou com'st thus knightly clad in arms,
Against what man thou com'st, and what thy quarrel.
Speak truly, on thy knighthood and thy oath;
And so defend thee Heaven and thy valour!   15
 Mow. My name is Thomas Mowbray, Duke of Norfolk;
Who hither come engaged by my oath —

Sc. ii, 4. **those hands:** Richard's.   21. **Envy's:** Malice's.   28. **model:** copy.   46. **cousin:** kinsman; here, nephew.   47. [sit] F.   *set* Q.   49. **career:** charge.   58. [it falls] F.   *is fals* Q.   69. **offices:** service quarters.

Which God defend a knight should violate! —
Both to defend my loyalty and truth
To God, my King, and my succeeding issue,   20
Against the Duke of Hereford that appeals me;
And, by the grace of God and this mine arm,
To prove him, in defending of myself,
A traitor to my God, my King, and me:
And as I truly fight, defend me Heaven!   25

The trumpets sound. Enter BOLINGBROKE,
appellant, in armour, with a HERALD.

   K. Rich. Marshal, ask yonder knight in arms,
Both who he is and why he cometh hither
Thus plated in habiliments of war,
And formally, according to our law,
Depose him in the justice of his cause.   30
   Mar. What is thy name? and wherefore com'st
          thou hither
Before King Richard in his royal lists?
Against whom comest thou? and what's thy quarrel?
Speak like a true knight, so defend thee Heaven!
   Boling. Harry of Hereford, Lancaster, and Derby
Am I; who ready here do stand in arms   36
To prove, by God's grace and my body's valour
In lists on Thomas Mowbray, Duke of Norfolk,
That he's a traitor, foul and dangerous,
To God of heaven, King Richard, and to me;   40
And as I truly fight, defend me Heaven!
   Mar. On pain of death, no person be so bold
Or daring-hardy as to touch the lists,
Except the Marshal and such officers
Appointed to direct these fair designs.   45
   Boling. Lord Marshal, let me kiss my sovereign's
          hand
And bow my knee before his Majesty;
For Mowbray and myself are like two men
That vow a long and weary pilgrimage.
Then let us take a ceremonious leave   50
And loving farewell of our several friends.
   Mar. The appellant in all duty greets your
          Highness,
And craves to kiss your hand and take his leave.
   K. Rich. We will descend and fold him in our arms.
Cousin of Hereford, as thy cause is right   55
So be thy fortune in this royal fight!
Farewell, my blood; which if to-day thou shed,
Lament we may, but not revenge thee dead.
   Boling. O, let no noble eye profane a tear
For me, if I be gor'd with Mowbray's spear.   60
As confident as is the falcon's flight
Against a bird, do I with Mowbray fight.
My loving lord, I take my leave of you;
Of you, my noble cousin, Lord Aumerle;
Not sick, although I have to do with death,   65
But lusty, young, and cheerly drawing breath.

Lo, as at English feasts, so I regreet
The daintiest last, to make the end most sweet:
O thou, the earthly author of my blood,
Whose youthful spirit, in me regenerate,   70
Doth with a twofold vigour lift me up
To reach at victory above my head,
Add proof unto mine armour with thy prayers,
And with thy blessings steel my lance's point
That it may enter Mowbray's waxen coat,   75
And furbish new the name of John o' Gaunt,
Even in the lusty haviour of his son.
   Gaunt. God in thy good cause make thee pros-
          perous!
Be swift like lightning in the execution;
And let thy blows, doubly redoubled,   80
Fall like amazing thunder on the casque
Of thy adverse pernicious enemy.
Rouse up thy youthful blood, be valiant, and
          live.
   Boling. Mine innocency and Saint George to
          thrive!
   Mow. However God or Fortune cast my lot,   85
There lives or dies, true to King Richard's throne,
A loyal, just, and upright gentleman.
Never did captive with a freer heart
Cast off his chains of bondage and embrace
His golden uncontroll'd enfranchisement,   90
More than my dancing soul doth celebrate
This feast of battle with mine adversary.
Most mighty liege and my companion peers,
Take from my mouth the wish of happy years.
As gentle and as jocund as to jest   95
Go I to fight; truth hath a quiet breast.
   K. Rich. Farewell, my lord; securely I espy
Virtue with valour couched in thine eye.
Order the trial, Marshal, and begin.
   Mar. Harry of Hereford, Lancaster, and Derby,
Receive thy lance; and God defend the right!   101
   Boling. Strong as a tower in hope, I cry amen.
   Mar. [*To an officer.*] Go bear this lance to Thomas,
          Duke of Norfolk.
   1. Her. Harry of Hereford, Lancaster, and Derby,
Stands here for God, his sovereign, and himself,   105
On pain to be found false and recreant,
To prove the Duke of Norfolk, Thomas Mowbray,
A traitor to his God, his king, and him;
And dares him to set forward to the fight.
   2. Her. Here standeth Thomas Mowbray, Duke
          of Norfolk,   110
On pain to be found false and recreant,
Both to defend himself and to approve
Henry of Hereford, Lancaster, and Derby,
To God, his sovereign, and to him disloyal;
Courageously and with a free desire   115
Attending but the signal to begin.

Sc. iii, 18. **defend:** forbid. 30. **Depose:** swear. 67. **regreet:** salute. 73. **proof:** power of resistance. 81. **amazing:** be-
wildering. 112. **approve:** prove.

Mar. Sound, trumpets; and set forward, com-
   batants.   [*A charge sounded.*
Stay!   The King hath thrown his warder down.
   K. Rich. Let them lay by their helmets and their
      spears,
And both return back to their chairs again.   120
Withdraw with us; and let the trumpets sound
While we return these dukes what we decree.
   [*A long flourish.*
Draw near
And list what with our council we have done.
For that our kingdom's earth should not be soil'd
With that dear blood which it hath fostered;   126
And for our eyes do hate the dire aspect
Of civil wounds plough'd up with neighbours' sword;
And for we think the eagle-winged pride
Of sky-aspiring and ambitious thoughts,   130
With rival-hating envy, set on you
To wake our peace, which in our country's cradle
Draws the sweet infant breath of gentle sleep;
Which, so rous'd up with boist'rous untun'd drums,
With harsh-resounding trumpets' dreadful bray,
And grating shock of wrathful iron arms,   136
Might from our quiet confines fright fair Peace
And make us wade even in our kindred's blood;
Therefore, we banish you our territories.
You, cousin Hereford, upon pain of life,   140
Till twice five summers have enrich'd our fields
Shall not regreet our fair dominions,
But tread the stranger paths of banishment.
   Boling. Your will be done.   This must my com-
      fort be,
That sun that warms you here shall shine on me;   145
And those his golden beams to you here lent
Shall point on me and gild my banishment.
   K. Rich. Norfolk, for thee remains a heavier doom,
Which I with some unwillingness pronounce.
The sly, slow hours shall not determinate   150
The dateless limit of thy dear exile;
The hopeless word of "never to return"
Breathe I against thee, upon pain of life.
   Mow. A heavy sentence, my most sovereign liege,
And all unlook'd for from your Highness' mouth.
A dearer merit, not so deep a maim   156
As to be cast forth in the common air,
Have I deserved at your Highness' hands.
The language I have learn'd these forty years,
My native English, now I must forgo;   160
And now my tongue's use is to me no more
Than an unstringed viol or a harp,
Or like a cunning instrument cas'd up,
Or, being open, put into his hands
That knows no touch to tune the harmony.   165
Within my mouth you have engaol'd my tongue,
Doubly portcullis'd with my teeth and lips;

And dull unfeeling barren ignorance
Is made my gaoler to attend on me.
I am too old to fawn upon a nurse,   170
Too far in years to be a pupil now.
What is thy sentence [then] but speechless death,
Which robs my tongue from breathing native
      breath?
   K. Rich. It boots thee not to be compassionate.
After our sentence plaining comes too late   175
   Mow. Then thus I turn me from my country's
      light,
To dwell in solemn shades of endless night.
   K. Rich. Return again, and take an oath with thee.
Lay on our royal sword your banish'd hands;
Swear by the duty that you owe to God —   180
Our part therein we banish with yourselves —
To keep the oath that we administer:
You never shall, so help you truth and God!
Embrace each other's love in banishment;
Nor never look upon each other's face;   185
Nor never write, regreet, nor reconcile
This louring tempest of your home-bred hate;
Nor never by advised purpose meet
To plot, contrive, or complot any ill
'Gainst us, our state, our subjects, or our land.   190
   Boling. I swear.
   Mow. And I, to keep all this.
   Boling. Norfolk, so far as to mine enemy: —
By this time, had the King permitted us,
One of our souls had wand'red in the air,   195
Banish'd this frail sepulchre of our flesh
As now our flesh is banish'd from this land;
Confess thy treasons ere thou fly the realm;
Since thou hast far to go, bear not along
The clogging burden of a guilty soul.   200
   Mow. No, Bolingbroke; if ever I were traitor,
My name be blotted from the book of life,
And I from heaven banish'd as from hence!
But what thou art, God, thou, and I do know;
And all too soon, I fear, the King shall rue.   205
Farewell, my liege.   Now no way can I stray;
Save back to England, all the world's my way.
   [*Exit.*
   K. Rich. Uncle, even in the glasses of thine eyes
I see thy grieved heart.   Thy sad aspect
Hath from the number of his banish'd years   210
Pluck'd four away.   [*To Boling.*] Six frozen winters
      spent,
Return with welcome home from banishment.
   Boling. How long a time lies in one little word!
Four lagging winters and four wanton springs
End in a word: such is the breath of kings.   215
   Gaunt. I thank my liege that in regard of me
He shortens four years of my son's exile;
But little vantage shall I reap thereby,

118. **warder:** baton.   122. **return:** inform.   150. **determinate:** end.   151. **dear:** keenly felt.   156. **maim:** penalty.
172. **[then]** F.   Om. Q.   174. **compassionate:** self-pitying.   175. **plaining:** complaining.

For, ere the six years that he hath to spend
Can change their moons and bring their times about,
My oil-dri'd lamp and time-bewasted light 221
Shall be extinct with age and endless night;
My inch of taper will be burnt and done,
And blindfold Death not let me see my son.

 K. Rich. Why, uncle, thou hast many years to
  live. 225

 Gaunt. But not a minute, King, that thou canst
  give.
Shorten my days thou canst with sullen sorrow,
And pluck nights from me, but not lend a morrow.
Thou canst help Time to furrow me with age,
But stop no wrinkle in his pilgrimage. 230
Thy word is current with him for my death,
But dead, thy kingdom cannot buy my breath.

 K. Rich. Thy son is banish'd upon good advice,
Whereto thy tongue a party-verdict gave.
Why at our justice seem'st thou then to lour? 235

 Gaunt. Things sweet to taste prove in digestion
  sour.
You urg'd me as a judge; but I had rather
You would have bid me argue like a father.
O, had it been a stranger, not my child,
To smooth his fault I should have been more mild.
A partial slander sought I to avoid, 241
And in the sentence my own life destroy'd.
Alas, I look'd when some of you should say
I was too strict to make mine own away;
But you gave leave to my unwilling tongue 245
Against my will to do myself this wrong.

 K. Rich. Cousin, farewell; and, uncle, bid him so.
Six years we banish him, and he shall go.
   [*Flourish. Exeunt* [*King Richard and train*].

 Aum. Cousin, farewell! What presence must not
  know, 250
From where you do remain let paper show.

 Mar. My lord, no leave take I; for I will ride,
As far as land will let me, by your side.

 Gaunt. O, to what purpose dost thou hoard thy
  words,
That thou return'st no greeting to thy friends?

 Boling. I have too few to take my leave of you,
When the tongue's office should be prodigal 256
To breathe the abundant dolour of the heart.

 Gaunt. Thy grief is but thy absence for a time.

 Boling. Joy absent, grief is present for that time.

 Gaunt. What is six winters? They are quickly
  gone. 260

 Boling. To men in joy; but grief makes one hour
  ten.

 Gaunt. Call it a travel that thou tak'st for
  pleasure.

 Boling. My heart will sigh when I miscall it so,

Which finds it an enforced pilgrimage.

 Gaunt. The sullen passage of thy weary steps
Esteem as foil wherein thou art to set 266
The precious jewel of thy home return.

 Boling. Nay, rather, every tedious stride I make
Will but remember me what a deal of world
I wander from the jewels that I love. 270
Must I not serve a long apprenticehood
To foreign passages, and in the end,
Having my freedom, boast of nothing else
But that I was a journeyman to grief?

 Gaunt. All places that the eye of heaven visits
Are to a wise man ports and happy havens. 276
Teach thy necessity to reason thus:
There is no virtue like necessity.
Think not the King did banish thee,
But thou the King. Woe doth the heavier sit 280
Where it perceives it is but faintly borne.
Go, say I sent thee forth to purchase honour
And not the King exil'd thee; or suppose
Devouring pestilence hangs in our air
And thou art flying to a fresher clime. 285
Look, what thy soul holds dear, imagine it
To lie that way thou goest, not whence thou com'st.
Suppose the singing birds musicians,
The grass whereon thou tread'st the presence strew'd,
The flowers fair ladies, and thy steps no more 290
Than a delightful measure or a dance;
For gnarling sorrow hath less power to bite
The man that mocks at it and sets it light.

 Boling. O, who can hold a fire in his hand
By thinking on the frosty Caucasus? 295
Or cloy the hungry edge of appetite
By bare imagination of a feast?
Or wallow naked in December snow
By thinking on fantastic summer's heat?
O, no! the apprehension of the good 300
Gives but the greater feeling to the worse.
Fell Sorrow's tooth doth never rankle more
Than when he bites, but lanceth not the sore.

 Gaunt. Come, come, my son, I'll bring thee on
  thy way;
Had I thy youth and cause, I would not stay.

 Boling. Then, England's ground, farewell; sweet
  soil, adieu; 306
My mother, and my nurse, that bears me yet!
Where'er I wander, boast of this I can,
Though banish'd, yet a trueborn Englishman.
             [*Exeunt.*

SCENE IV. [*The Court.*]

Enter the KING, *with* BAGOT *and* GREEN *at one door;
and the* DUKE OF AUMERLE *at another.*

 K. Rich. We did observe. Cousin Aumerle,

---

234. **party-verdict:** vote with others. 241. **partial slander:** charge of partiality. 266. **foil:** metal-leaf placed under a precious stone. 289. **presence strew'd:** royal presence-chamber, strewed with rushes. 292. **gnarling:** snarling. 299. **fantastic:** imaginary. 305. **stay:** delay.

How far brought you high Hereford on his way?

Aum. I brought high Hereford, if you call him so,
But to the next highway, and there I left him.

K. Rich. And say, what store of parting tears
    were shed? 5

Aum. Faith, none for me; except the northeast
    wind,
Which then blew bitterly against our faces,
Awak'd the sleeping rheum, and so by chance
Did grace our hollow parting with a tear.

K. Rich. What said our cousin when you parted
    with him? 10

Aum. "Farewell!"
And, for my heart disdained that my tongue
Should so profane the word, that taught me craft
To counterfeit oppression of such grief
That words seem'd buried in my sorrow's grave. 15
Marry, would the word "farewell" have length'ned
    hours
And added years to his short banishment,
He should have had a volume of farewells;
But since it would not, he had none of me. 19

K. Rich. He is our [cousin, cousin]; but 'tis doubt,
When time shall call him home from banishment,
Whether our kinsman come to see his friends.
Ourself and Bushy, [Bagot here and Green]
Observ'd his courtship to the common people;
How he did seem to dive into their hearts 25
With humble and familiar courtesy,
What reverence he did throw away on slaves,
Wooing poor craftsmen with the craft of smiles
And patient underbearing of his fortune,
As 'twere to banish their affects with him. 30
Off goes his bonnet to an oyster-wench;
A brace of draymen bid God speed him well
And had the tribute of his supple knee,
With "Thanks, my countrymen, my loving friends,"
As were our England in reversion his, 35
And he our subjects' next degree in hope.

Green. Well, he is gone; and with him go these
    thoughts.
Now for the rebels which stand out in Ireland,
Expedient manage must be made, my liege,
Ere further leisure yield them further means 40
For their advantage and your Highness' loss.

K. Rich. We will ourself in person to this war;
And, for our coffers, with too great a court
And liberal largess, are grown somewhat light,
We are enforc'd to farm our royal realm; 45
The revenue whereof shall furnish us
For our affairs in hand. If that come short,
Our substitutes at home shall have blank charters;
Whereto, when they shall know what men are rich,

They shall subscribe them for large sums of gold 50
And send them after to supply our wants,
For we will make for Ireland presently.

Enter BUSHY.

[Bushy, what news?]

Bushy. Old John of Gaunt is grievous sick, my
    lord,
Suddenly taken; and hath sent post haste 55
To entreat your Majesty to visit him.

K. Rich. Where lies he?

Bushy. At Ely House.

K. Rich. Now put it, God, in the physician's
    mind
To help him to his grave immediately! 60
The lining of his coffers shall make coats
To deck our soldiers for these Irish wars.
Come, gentlemen, let's all go visit him.
Pray God we may make haste, and come too late!

[*All.*] Amen. [*Exeunt.* 65

ACT II

SCENE I. [*London. Ely House.*]

Enter JOHN OF GAUNT, *sick, with the* DUKE OF
YORK, *etc.*

Gaunt. Will the King come, that I may breathe
    my last
In wholesome counsel to his unstaid youth?

York. Vex not yourself, nor strive not with your
    breath;
For all in vain comes counsel to his ear.

Gaunt. O, but they say the tongues of dying men
Enforce attention like deep harmony. 6
Where words are scarce, they are seldom spent in vain,
For they breathe truth that breathe their words in
    pain.
He that no more must say is listened more
    Than they whom youth and ease have taught to
    glose. 10
More are men's ends mark'd than their lives before.
    The setting sun, and music at the close,
As the last taste of sweets, is sweetest last,
Writ in remembrance more than things long past.
Though Richard my life's counsel would not hear,
My death's sad tale may yet undeaf his ear. 16

York. No; it is stopp'd with other flattering
    sounds,
As praises, of whose taste the wise are found,
Lascivious metres, to whose venom sound
The open ear of youth doth always listen; 20
Report of fashions in proud Italy,

Sc. iv, 20. [cousin, cousin] F. *coosens coosin* Q. 23. [Bagot...Green] Q₆. Om. Q₁. 29. **underbearing:** endurance.
30. **affects:** affections. 39. **Expedient manage:** swift handling. 45. **farm:** lease the revenues. 48. **blank charters:** i.e., to
be filled in at the king's pleasure. 53. [Bushy, what news?] F. *with news* (as part of s.d.) Q. 65. [*All.*] (Staunton). Om. Q.
    Act II, sc. i, 10. **glose:** flatter. 18. **of...found** Q. *of his state: then there are found* Ff. Obviously corrupt. Many edd.
read *fond* for *found*.

Whose manners still our tardy, apish nation
Limps after in base imitation.
Where doth the world thrust forth a vanity —
So it be new, there's no respect how vile —   25
That is not quickly buzz'd into his ears?
Then all too late comes counsel to be heard
Where will doth mutiny with wit's regard.
Direct not him whose way himself will choose;
'Tis breath thou lack'st, and that breath wilt thou
          lose.   30
    Gaunt. Methinks I am a prophet new inspir'd
And thus expiring do foretell of him:
His rash fierce blaze of riot cannot last,
For violent fires soon burn out themselves;
Small showers last long, but sudden storms are
          short;   35
He tires betimes that spurs too fast betimes;
With eager feeding food doth choke the feeder;
Light vanity, insatiate cormorant,
Consuming means, soon preys upon itself.
This royal throne of kings, this sceptred isle,   40
This earth of majesty, this seat of Mars,
—This other Eden, demi-paradise,
This fortress built by Nature for herself
Against infection and the hand of war,
This happy breed of men, this little world,   45
This precious stone set in the silver sea,
Which serves it in the office of a wall
Or as a moat defensive to a house
Against the envy of less happier lands,
This blessed plot, this earth, this realm, this
          England,   50
This nurse, this teeming womb of royal kings,
Fear'd by their breed and famous by their birth,
Renowned for their deeds as far from home,
For Christian service and true chivalry,
As is the sepulchre in stubborn Jewry,   55
Of the world's ransom, blessed Mary's Son,
This land of such dear souls, this dear dear land,
Dear for her reputation through the world,
Is now leas'd out, I die pronouncing it,
Like to a tenement or pelting farm.   60
England, bound in with the triumphant sea,
Whose rocky shore beats back the envious siege
Of wat'ry Neptune, is now bound in with shame,
With inky blots and rotten parchment bonds.
That England, that was wont to conquer others,   65
Hath made a shameful conquest of itself.
Ah, would the scandal vanish with my life,
How happy then were my ensuing death!

    Enter KING RICHARD *and* QUEEN, AUMERLE,
BUSHY, GREEN, BAGOT, ROSS, *and* WILLOUGHBY.
    York. The King is come. Deal mildly with his
          youth;

For young hot colts being rag'd do rage the more.
    Queen. How fares our noble uncle Lancaster? 71
    K. Rich. What comfort, man? How is't with
          aged Gaunt?
    Gaunt. O, how that name befits my composition!
Old Gaunt indeed, and gaunt in being old.
Within me Grief hath kept a tedious fast;   75
And who abstains from meat that is not gaunt?
For sleeping England long time have I watch'd;
Watching breeds leanness, leanness is all gaunt.
The pleasure that some fathers feed upon,
Is my strict fast; I mean, my children's looks;   80
And therein fasting, hast thou made me gaunt.
Gaunt am I for the grave, gaunt as a grave,
Whose hollow womb inherits nought but bones.
    K. Rich. Can sick men play so nicely with their
          names?
    Gaunt. No, misery makes sport to mock itself. 85
Since thou dost seek to kill my name in me,
I mock my name, great King, to flatter thee.
    K. Rich. Should dying men flatter with those
          that live?
    Gaunt. No, no, men living flatter those that die.
    K. Rich. Thou, now a-dying, say'st thou flatterest
          me.   90
    Gaunt. O, no! thou diest, though I the sicker be.
    K. Rich. I am in health, I breathe, and see thee ill.
    Gaunt. Now He that made me knows I see thee ill;
Ill in myself to see, and in thee seeing ill.
Thy death-bed is no lesser than thy land   95
Wherein thou liest in reputation sick;
And thou, too careless patient as thou art,
Commit'st thy anointed body to the cure
Of those physicians that first wounded thee.
A thousand flatterers sit within thy crown,   100
Whose compass is no bigger than thy head;
And yet, [incaged] in so small a verge,
The waste is no whit lesser than thy land.
O, had thy grandsire with a prophet's eye
Seen how his son's son should destroy his sons,   105
From forth thy reach he would have laid thy shame,
Deposing thee before thou wert possess'd,
Which art possess'd now to depose thyself.
Why, cousin, wert thou regent of the world,
It were a shame to let this land by lease;   110
But for thy world enjoying but this land,
Is it not more than shame to shame it so?
Landlord of England art thou now, not king.
Thy state of law is bondslave to the law,
And thou —
    K. Rich. A lunatic lean-witted fool,   115
Presuming on an ague's privilege,
Dar'st with thy frozen admonition
Make pale our cheek, chasing the royal blood
With fury from his native residence.

25. no respect: no matter. 28. wit's regard: respect for reason. 52. by: for. 60. pelting: paltry. 73. composition: condition. 83. inherits: holds. 84. nicely: delicately, subtly. 102. [incaged] F. *inraged* Q. verge: circle.

Now, by my seat's right royal majesty, 120
Wert thou not brother to great Edward's son,
This tongue that runs so roundly in thy head
Should run thy head from thy unreverent shoulders.
    Gaunt. O, spare me not, my brother Edward's son,
For that I was his father Edward's son. 125
That blood already, like the pelican,
Hast thou tapp'd out and drunkenly carous'd.
My brother Gloucester, plain well-meaning soul,
Whom fair befall in heaven 'mongst happy souls!
May be a precedent and witness good 130
That thou respect'st not spilling Edward's blood.
Join with the present sickness that I have,
And thy unkindness be like crooked age,
To crop at once a too long withered flower.
Live in thy shame, but die not shame with thee!
These words hereafter thy tormentors be! 136
Convey me to my bed, then to my grave;
Love they to live that love and honour have.
    [*Exit [borne off by his Attendants].*
    K. Rich. And let them die that age and sullens have;
For both hast thou, and both become the grave.
    York. I do beseech your Majesty, impute his words 141
To wayward sickliness and age in him.
He loves you, on my life, and holds you dear
As Harry Duke of Hereford, were he here.
    K. Rich. Right, you say true. As Hereford's love, so his; 145
As theirs, so mine; and all be as it is.

    Enter NORTHUMBERLAND.

    North. My liege, old Gaunt commends him to your Majesty.
    K. Rich. What says he?
    North.   Nay, nothing; all is said.
His tongue is now a stringless instrument;
Words, life, and all, old Lancaster hath spent. 150
    York. Be York the next that must be bankrupt so!
Though death be poor, it ends a mortal woe.
    K. Rich. The ripest fruit first falls, and so doth he;
His time is spent, our pilgrimage must be.
So much for that. Now for our Irish wars. 155
We must supplant those rough rug-headed kerns,
Which live like venom where no venom else
But only they have privilege to live.
And for these great affairs do ask some charge,
Towards our assistance we do seize to us 160
The plate, coin, revenues, and moveables,
Whereof our uncle Gaunt did stand possess'd.

    York. How long shall I be patient? Ah, how long
Shall tender duty make me suffer wrong? 164
Not Gloucester's death, nor Hereford's banishment
Not Gaunt's rebukes, nor England's private wrongs,
Nor the prevention of poor Bolingbroke
About his marriage, nor my own disgrace,
Have ever made me sour my patient cheek,
Or bend one wrinkle on my sovereign's face. 170
I am the last of noble Edward's sons,
Of whom thy father, Prince of Wales, was first.
In war was never lion rag'd more fierce,
In peace was never gentle lamb more mild,
Than was that young and princely gentleman. 175
His face thou hast, for even so look'd he,
Accomplish'd with the number of thy hours;
But when he frown'd, it was against the French
And not against his friends. His noble hand
Did win what he did spend and spent not that 180
Which his triumphant father's hand had won.
His hands were guilty of no kindred blood,
But bloody with the enemies of his kin.
O Richard! York is too far gone with grief,
Or else he never would compare between. 185
    K. Rich. Why, uncle, what's the matter?
    York.   O my liege,
Pardon me, if you please; if not, I, pleas'd
Not to be pardon'd, am content withal.
Seek you to seize and gripe into your hands
The royalties and rights of banish'd Hereford? 190
Is not Gaunt dead, and doth not Hereford live?
Was not Gaunt just, and is not Harry true?
Did not the one deserve to have an heir?
Is not his heir a well-deserving son?
Take Hereford's rights away, and take from Time
His charters and his customary rights; 196
Let not to-morrow then ensue to-day;
Be not thyself; for how art thou a king
But by fair sequence and succession?
Now, afore God — God forbid I say true! — 200
If you do wrongfully seize Hereford's rights,
Call in the letters patents that he hath
By his attorneys general to sue
His livery, and deny his off'red homage,
You pluck a thousand dangers on your head, 205
You lose a thousand well-disposed hearts
And prick my tender patience to those thoughts
Which honour and allegiance cannot think.
    K. Rich. Think what you will, we seize into our hands
His plate, his goods, his money, and his lands. 210
    York. I'll not be by the while. My liege, farewell!

132–34. **Join . . . flower:** Let thy unkindness join with my sickness to end my life. 156. **rug-headed kerns:** shock-headed troops. 157. **venom:** venomous animals, the snakes St. Patrick banished. 159. **charge:** expense. 166. **Gaunt's rebukes:** insults to Gaunt. 167–68. **prevention . . . marriage.** Richard had intervened to prevent Bolingbroke's marriage to the cousin of the King of France. ⸙77 **Accomplish'd . . . hours:** at thy age. 203–04. **sue His livery:** claim his inheritance.

What will ensue hereof, there's none can tell;
But by bad courses may be understood
That their events can never fall out good.   [*Exit.*
  K. Rich. Go, Bushy, to the Earl of Wiltshire
       straight.   215
Bid him repair to us to Ely House
To see this business.   To-morrow next
We will for Ireland; and 'tis time, I trow:
And we create, in absence of ourself,
Our uncle York lord governor of England;   220
For he is just and always lov'd us well.
Come on, our queen; to-morrow must we part.
Be merry, for our time of stay is short.
       [*Flourish.   Exeunt King, Queen, Aumerle,*
                Bushy, Green, and Bagot.
  North. Well, lords, the Duke of Lancaster is dead.
  Ross. And living too; for now his son is duke. 225
  Willo. Barely in title, not in revenues.
  North. Richly in both, if Justice had her right.
  Ross. My heart is great; but it must break with
       silence,
Ere 't be disburden'd with a liberal tongue.
  North. Nay, speak thy mind; and let him ne'er
       speak more   230
That speaks thy words again to do thee harm!
  Willo. Tends that thou wouldst speak to the
       Duke of Hereford?
If it be so, out with it boldly, man;
Quick is mine ear to hear of good towards him.
  Ross. No good at all that I can do for him;   235
Unless you call it good to pity him,
Bereft and gelded of his patrimony.
  North. Now, afore God, 'tis shame such wrongs
       are borne
In him, a royal prince, and many moe
Of noble blood in this declining land.   240
The King is not himself, but basely led
By flatterers; and what they will inform,
Merely in hate, 'gainst any of us all,
That will the King severely prosecute
'Gainst us, our lives, our children, and our heirs. 245
  Ross. The commons hath he pill'd with grievous
       taxes,
And quite lost their hearts; the nobles hath he fin'd
For ancient quarrels, and quite lost their hearts.
  Willo. And daily new exactions are devis'd,
As blanks, benevolences, and I wot not what.   250
But what, o' God's name, doth become of this?
  North. Wars hath not wasted it, for warr'd he
       hath not,
But basely yielded upon compromise
That which his noble ancestors achiev'd with blows.
More hath he spent in peace than they in wars.   255
  Ross. The Earl of Wiltshire hath the realm in farm.

  Willo. The King's grown bankrupt, like a broken
       man.
  North. Reproach and dissolution hangeth over
       him.
  Ross. He hath not money for these Irish wars,
His burdenous taxations notwithstanding,   260
But by the robbing of the banish'd Duke.
  North. His noble kinsman: most degenerate king!
But, lords, we hear this fearful tempest sing,
Yet seek no shelter to avoid the storm;
We see the wind sit sore upon our sails,   265
And yet we strike not, but securely perish.
  Ross. We see the very wreck that we must suffer;
And unavoided is the danger now,
For suffering so the causes of our wreck.
  North. Not so; even through the hollow eyes of
       death   270
I spy life peering; but I dare not say
How near the tidings of our comfort is.
  Willo. Nay, let us share thy thoughts, as thou
       dost ours.
  Ross. Be confident to speak, Northumberland.
We three are but thyself; and, speaking so,   275
Thy words are but as thoughts; therefore, be
       bold.
  North. Then thus: I have from Le Port Blanc, a
       bay
In Brittany, receiv'd intelligence
That Harry Duke of Hereford, Rainold Lord
       Cobham,
[The son and heir of th' Earl of Arundel,]   280
That late broke from the Duke of Exeter,
His brother, Archbishop late of Canterbury,
Sir Thomas Erpingham, Sir John Ramston,
Sir John Norbery, Sir Robert Waterton, and
       Francis Coines,
All these, well furnish'd by the Duke of Bretagne 285
With eight tall ships, three thousand men of war,
Are making hither with all due expedience
And shortly mean to touch our northern shore.
Perhaps they had ere this, but that they stay
The first departing of the King for Ireland.   290
If then we shall shake off our slavish yoke,
Imp out our drooping country's broken wing,
Redeem from broking pawn the blemish'd crown,
Wipe off the dust that hides our sceptre's gilt,
And make high majesty look like itself,   295
Away with me in post to Ravenspurgh;
But if you faint, as fearing to do so,
Stay and be secret, and myself will go.
  Ross. To horse, to horse! urge doubts to them
       that fear.   299
  Willo. Hold out my horse, and I will first be there.
                                                   [*Exeunt.*

---

228. **great**: swollen, full.   229. **liberal**: free.   246. **pill'd**: robbed.   250. **blanks**. Cf. I.iv.48, note. **benevolences**:
forced loans.   265. **sit sore**: press hard.   266. **securely**: carelessly.   280. This line is substantially from Holinshed. Om. QF.
281. **broke from**: escaped the custody of.   292. **Imp out**: mend by grafting.   293. **broking pawn**: the pawnbroker.

SCENE II. [*Windsor Castle.*]

Enter QUEEN, BUSHY, *and* BAGOT.

Bushy. Madam, your Majesty is too much sad.
You promis'd, when you parted with the King,
To lay aside life-harming heaviness
And entertain a cheerful disposition.
  Queen. To please the King I did; to please myself
I cannot do it; yet I know no cause   6
Why I should welcome such a guest as Grief,
Save bidding farewell to so sweet a guest
As my sweet Richard.   Yet again, methinks,
Some unborn sorrow, ripe in fortune's womb,   10
Is coming towards me, and my inward soul
With nothing trembles.   At something it grieves,
More than with parting from my lord the King.
  Bushy. Each substance of a grief hath twenty
    shadows,
Which shows like grief itself, but is not so;   15
For sorrow's eye, glazed with blinding tears,
Divides one thing entire to many objects,
Like perspectives, which rightly gaz'd upon
Show nothing but confusion, ey'd awry
Distinguish form; so your sweet Majesty,   20
Looking awry upon your lord's departure,
Find shapes of grief, more than himself, to wail;
Which, look'd on as it is, is nought but shadows
Of what it is not.   Then, thrice-gracious Queen,
More than your lord's departure weep not.   More's
    not seen;   25
Or if it be, 'tis with false sorrow's eye,
Which for things true weeps things imaginary.
  Queen. It may be so; but yet my inward soul
Persuades me it is otherwise.   Howe'er it be,
I cannot but be sad; so heavy sad   30
As, though on thinking on no thought I think,
Makes me with heavy nothing faint and shrink.
  Bushy. 'Tis nothing but conceit, my gracious
    lady.
  Queen. 'Tis nothing less: conceit is still deriv'd
From some forefather grief; mine is not so,   35
For nothing hath begot my something grief,
Or something hath the nothing that I grieve,
'Tis in reversion that I do possess;
But what it is, that is not yet known; what,
I cannot name; 'tis nameless woe, I wot.   40

Enter GREEN.

  Green. God save your Majesty! and well met,
    gentlemen.
I hope the King is not yet shipp'd for Ireland.
  Queen. Why hop'st thou so? 'Tis better hope he is;
For his designs crave haste, his haste good hope.
Then wherefore dost thou hope he is not shipp'd? 45
  Green. That he, our hope, might have retir'd his
    power,

And driven into despair an enemy's hope,
Who strongly hath set footing in this land.
The banish'd Bolingbroke repeals himself,
And with uplifted arms is safe arriv'd   50
At Ravenspurgh.
  Queen.   Now God in heaven forbid!
  Green. Ah, madam, 'tis too true; and, that is
    worse,
The Lord Northumberland, his son young Henry
    Percy,
The Lords of Ross, Beaumond, and Willoughby,
With all their powerful friends, are fled to him. 55
  Bushy. Why have you not proclaim'd Northum-
    berland
And all the rest revolted faction traitors?
  Green. We have; whereupon the Earl of Worces-
    ter
Hath broken his staff, resign'd his stewardship,
And all the household servants fled with him   60
To Bolingbroke.
  Queen. So, Green, thou art the midwife to my
    woe,
And Bolingbroke my sorrow's dismal heir.
Now hath my soul brought forth her prodigy,
And I, a gasping new-deliver'd mother,   65
Have woe to woe, sorrow to sorrow join'd.
  Bushy. Despair not, madam.
  Queen.   Who shall hinder me?
I will despair, and be at enmity
With cozening hope.   He is a flatterer,
A parasite, a keeper back of death,   70
Who gently would dissolve the bands of life,
Which false hope lingers in extremity.

Enter YORK.

  Green. Here comes the Duke of York.
  Queen. With signs of war about his aged neck.
O, full of careful business are his looks!   75
Uncle, for God's sake, speak comfortable words.
  York. Should I do so, I should belie my thoughts.
Comfort's in heaven, and we are on the earth,
Where nothing lives but crosses, cares, and grief.
Your husband, he is gone to save far off,   80
Whilst others come to make him lose at home.
Here am I left to underprop his land,
Who, weak with age, cannot support myself.
Now comes the sick hour that his surfeit made;
Now shall he try his friends that flatter'd him.   85

Enter a SERVANT.

  Serv. My lord, your son was gone before I came.
  York. He was? Why, so! go all which way it will!
The nobles they are fled; the commons they are
    cold,
And will, I fear, revolt on Hereford's side.   89

Sc. ii, 18. **perspectives**: optical glasses. **rightly**: straight. 33. **conceit**: imagination. 34. **still**: always. 46. **retir'd**: brought back. 52. **that**: what. 69. **cozening**: cheating. 72. **lingers**: prolongs. 75. **careful**: anxious.

Sirrah, get thee to Plashy, to my sister Gloucester;
Bid her send me presently a thousand pound.
Hold, take my ring.
   Serv. My lord, I had forgot to tell your lordship,
To-day, as I came by, I called there, —
But I shall grieve you to report the rest.   95
   York. What is't, knave?
   Serv. An hour before I came, the Duchess died.
   York. God for his mercy! what a tide of woes
Comes rushing on this woeful land at once!
I know not what to do. I would to God,   100
So my untruth had not provok'd him to it,
The King had cut off my head with my brother's.
What, are there no posts dispatch'd for Ireland?
How shall we do for money for these wars?
Come, sister, — cousin, I would say, — pray,
   pardon me.   105
Go, fellow, get thee home, provide some carts
And bring away the armour that is there.
               [Exit Servant.]
Gentlemen, will you go muster men? If I
Know how or which way to order these affairs
Thus thrust disorderly into my hands,   110
Never believe me. Both are my kinsmen:
Th' one is my sovereign, whom both my oath
And duty bids defend; t'other again
Is my kinsman, whom the King hath wrong'd,
Whom conscience and my kindred bids to right.   115
Well, somewhat we must do. Come, cousin, I'll
Dispose of you.
Gentlemen, go, muster up your men,
And meet me presently at Berkeley.
I should to Plashy too,   120
But time will not permit. All is uneven,
And everything is left at six and seven.
           [Exeunt York and Queen.
   Bushy. The wind sits fair for news to go for
   Ireland,
But none returns. For us to levy power
Proportionable to the enemy   125
Is all unpossible.
   Green. Besides, our nearness to the King in love
Is near the hate of those love not the King.
   Bagot. And that's the wavering commons, for
   their love
Lies in their purses; and whoso empties them   130
By so much fills their hearts with deadly hate.
   Bushy. Wherein the King stands generally con-
   demn'd.
   Bagot. If judgement lie in them, then so do we,
Because we ever have been near the King.
   Green. Well, I will for refuge straight to Bristol
   castle: 135
The Earl of Wiltshire is already there.
   Bushy. Thither will I with you; for little office
The hateful commons [will] perform for us

Except like curs to tear us all to pieces.
Will you go along with us?   140
   Bagot. No; I will to Ireland to his Majesty.
Farewell! If heart's presages be not vain,
We three here part that ne'er shall meet again.
   Bushy. That's as York thrives to beat back
   Bolingbroke.
   Green. Alas, poor duke! the task he undertakes
Is numb'ring sands and drinking oceans dry.   146
Where one on his side fights, thousands will fly.
Farewell at once, for once, for all, and ever.
   Bushy. Well, we may meet again.
   Bagot.   I fear me, never.
           [Exeunt.

SCENE III. *[Wilds in Gloucestershire.]*

Enter BOLINGBROKE *and* NORTHUMBERLAND
        [with forces].

   Boling. How far is it, my lord, to Berkeley now?
   North. Believe me, noble lord,
I am a stranger here in Gloucestershire.
These high wild hills and rough uneven ways   4
Draws out our miles, and makes them wearisome;
And yet your fair discourse hath been as sugar,
Making the hard way sweet and delectable.
But I bethink me what a weary way
From Ravenspurgh to Cotswold will be found
In Ross and Willoughby, wanting your company,   10
Which, I protest, hath very much beguil'd
The tediousness and process of my travel.
But theirs is sweet'ned with the hope to have
The present benefit which I possess;
And hope to joy is little less in joy   15
Than hope enjoy'd. By this the weary lords
Shall make their way seem short, as mine hath done
By sight of what I have, your noble company.
   Boling. Of much less value is my company
Than your good words. But who comes here?   20

       Enter HENRY PERCY.

   North. It is my son, young Harry Percy,
Sent from my brother Worcester, whencesoever.
Harry, how fares your uncle?
   Percy. I had thought, my lord, to have learn'd
   his health of you.
   North. Why, is he not with the Queen?   25
   Percy. No, my good lord; he hath forsook the
   court,
Broken his staff of office, and dispers'd
The household of the King.
   North.   What was his reason?
He was not so resolv'd when last we spake together.
   Percy. Because your lordship was proclaimed
   traitor.   30
But he, my lord, is gone to Ravenspurgh

133. **do we:** i.e., stand condemned. 138. **hateful:** full of hate. **[will]** (Pope). Qq Ff place at beginning of line.

To offer service to the Duke of Hereford,
And sent me over by Berkeley, to discover
What power the Duke of York had levied there;
Then with directions to repair to Ravenspurgh. 35
  North. Have you forgot the Duke of Hereford,
    boy?
  Percy. No, my good lord, for that is not forgot
Which ne'er I did remember. To my knowledge,
I never in my life did look on him.
  North. Then learn to know him now; this is the
    Duke. 40
  Percy. My gracious lord, I tender you my
    service,
Such as it is, being tender, raw, and young;
Which elder days shall ripen and confirm
To more approved service and desert.
  Boling. I thank thee, gentle Percy; and be sure
I count myself in nothing else so happy 46
As in a soul rememb'ring my good friends;
And, as my fortune ripens with thy love,
It shall be still thy true love's recompense.
My heart this covenant makes, my hand thus
    seals it. 50
  North. How far is it to Berkeley? and what stir
Keeps good old York there with his men of war?
  Percy. There stands the castle, by yon tuft of
    trees,
Mann'd with three hundred men, as I have heard;
And in it are the Lords of York, Berkeley, and
    Seymour; 55
None else of name and noble estimate.

    Enter ROSS *and* WILLOUGHBY.

  North. Here come the Lords of Ross and Wil-
    loughby,
Bloody with spurring, fiery-red with haste.
  Boling. Welcome, my lords. I wot your love
    pursues
A banish'd traitor. All my treasury 60
Is yet but unfelt thanks, which more enrich'd
Shall be your love and labour's recompense.
  Ross. Your presence makes us rich, most noble
    lord.
  Willo. And far surmounts our labour to attain it.
  Boling. Evermore thanks, the exchequer of the
    poor, 65
Which, till my infant fortune comes to years,
Stands for my bounty. But who comes here?

    Enter BERKELEY.

  North. It is my Lord of Berkeley, as I guess.
  Berk. My Lord of Hereford, my message is to you.
  Boling. My lord, my answer is — to Lancaster;
And I am come to seek that name in England; 71

And I must find that title in your tongue,
Before I make reply to aught you say.
  Berk. Mistake me not, my lord; 'tis not my
    meaning
To raze one title of your honour out. 75
To you, my lord, I come, what lord you will,
From the most gracious regent of this land,
The Duke of York, to know what pricks you on
To take advantage of the absent time 79
And fright our native peace with [self-born] arms.

    Enter YORK [*attended*].

  Boling. I shall not need transport my words by
    you;
Here comes his Grace in person. My noble uncle!
               [*Kneels.*]
  York. Show me thy humble heart, and not thy
    knee,
Whose duty is deceiveable and false.
  Boling. My gracious uncle — 85
  York. Tut, tut!
Grace me no grace, nor uncle me no uncle.
I am no traitor's uncle; and that word "grace"
In an ungracious mouth is but profane.
Why have those banish'd and forbidden legs 90
Dar'd once to touch a dust of England's ground?
But then more "why?" Why have they dar'd to
    march
So many miles upon her peaceful bosom,
Frighting her pale-fac'd villages with war
And ostentation of despised arms? 95
Com'st thou because the anointed King is hence?
Why, foolish boy, the King is left behind,
And in my loyal bosom lies his power.
Were I but now the lord of such hot youth
As when brave Gaunt, thy father, and myself 100
Rescued the Black Prince, that young Mars of men,
From forth the ranks of many thousand French,
O, then how quickly should this arm of mine,
Now prisoner to the palsy, chastise thee
And minister correction to thy fault! 105
  Boling. My gracious uncle, let me know my fault.
On what condition stands it and wherein?
  York. Even in condition of the worst degree,
In gross rebellion and detested treason.
Thou art a banish'd man, and here art come 110
Before the expiration of thy time,
In braving arms against thy sovereign.
  Boling. As I was banish'd, I was banish'd Here-
    ford;
But as I come, I come for Lancaster.
And, noble uncle, I beseech your Grace 115
Look on my wrongs with an indifferent eye.
You are my father, for methinks in you

Sc. iii, 61. **unfelt:** which I cannot make you feel. 79. **absent time:** time of the King's absence. 80. **[self-born]** F₃: domestic. *selfeborne* Q. 84. **deceiveable:** deceptive. 95. **despised:** despicable. 107. **condition:** quality. 112. **braving:** defiant. 116. **indifferent:** impartial.

I see old Gaunt alive. O, then, my father,
Will you permit that I shall stand condemn'd
A wandering vagabond; my rights and royalties 120
Pluck'd from my arms perforce, and given away
To upstart unthrifts? Wherefore was I born?
If that my cousin king be King of England,
It must be granted I am Duke of Lancaster.
You have a son, Aumerle, my noble cousin; 125
Had you first died, and he been thus trod down,
He should have found his uncle Gaunt a father
To rouse his wrongs and chase them to the bay.
I am deni'd to sue my livery here,
And yet my letters patents give me leave. 130
My father's goods are all distrain'd and sold,
And these and all are all amiss employ'd.
What would you have me do? I am a subject
And I challenge law. Attorneys are denied me;
And therefore personally I lay my claim 135
To my inheritance of free descent.
    North. The noble Duke hath been too much
      abus'd.
    Ross. It stands your Grace upon to do him right.
    Willo. Base men by his endowments are made
      great.
    York. My lords of England, let me tell you this:
I have had feeling of my cousin's wrongs 141
And labour'd all I could to do him right;
But in this kind to come, in braving arms,
Be his own carver and cut out his way,
To find out right with wrong — it may not be; 145
And you that do abet him in this kind
Cherish rebellion and are rebels all.
    North. The noble Duke hath sworn his coming is
But for his own; and for the right of that
We all have strongly sworn to give him aid; 150
And let him ne'er see joy that breaks that oath!
    York. Well, well, I see the issue of these arms.
I cannot mend it, I must needs confess,
Because my power is weak and all ill left;
But if I could, by Him that gave me life, 155
I would attach you all and make you stoop
Unto the sovereign mercy of the King;
But since I cannot, be it known to you
I do remain as neuter. So, fare you well;
Unless you please to enter in the castle 160
And there repose you for this night.
    Boling. An offer, uncle, that we will accept.
But we must win your Grace to go with us
To Bristol castle, which they say is held
By Bushy, Bagot, and their complices, 165
The caterpillars of the commonwealth,
Which I have sworn to weed and pluck away.
    York. It may be I will go with you; but yet I'll
    pause,

For I am loath to break our country's laws.
Nor friends nor foes, to me welcome you are. 170
Things past redress are now with me past care.
                      [*Exeunt.*

SCENE IV. [*A camp in Wales.*]

Enter SALISBURY *and a* Welsh CAPTAIN.

    Cap. My Lord of Salisbury, we have stay'd ten
    days
And hardly kept our countrymen together,
And yet we hear no tidings from the King;
Therefore we will disperse ourselves. Farewell!
    Sal. Stay yet another day, thou trusty Welsh-
    man. 5
The King reposeth all his confidence in thee.
    Cap. 'Tis thought the King is dead; we will not
    stay.
The bay-trees in our country are all wither'd
And meteors fright the fixed stars of heaven;
The pale-fac'd moon looks bloody on the earth 10
And lean-look'd prophets whisper fearful change;
Rich men look sad and ruffians dance and leap,
The one in fear to lose what they enjoy,
The other to enjoy by rage and war.
These signs forerun the death or fall of kings. 15
Farewell! Our countrymen are gone and fled,
As well assur'd Richard their king is dead. [*Exit*
    Sal. Ah, Richard, with the eyes of heavy mind
I see thy glory like a shooting star
Fall to the base earth from the firmament. 20
Thy sun sets weeping in the lowly west,
Witnessing storms to come, woe, and unrest.
Thy friends are fled to wait upon thy foes,
And crossly to thy good all fortune goes. [*Exit.*

ACT III

SCENE I. [*Bristol. Before the castle.*]

Enter BOLINGBROKE, YORK, NORTHUMBERLAND,
    ROSS, PERCY, WILLOUGHBY, *with* BUSHY *and*
    GREEN, *prisoners.*

    Boling. Bring forth these men.
Bushy and Green, I will not vex your souls —
Since presently your souls must part your bodies
With too much urging your pernicious lives,
For 'twere no charity; yet, to wash your blood
From off my hands, here in the view of men
I will unfold some causes of your deaths.
You have misled a prince, a royal king,
A happy gentleman in blood and lineaments,
By you unhappied and disfigur'd clean. 10
You have in manner with your sinful hours

---

128. **to the bay:** to the extreme limit. 131. **distrain'd:** seized. 138. **stands ... upon:** is your Grace's duty. 156. **attach:** arrest.

Act III, sc. i, 3. **part:** leave.

Made a divorce betwixt his queen and him,
Broke the possession of a royal bed
And stain'd the beauty of a fair queen's cheeks
With tears drawn from her eyes by your foul wrongs.
Myself, a prince by fortune of my birth, 16
Near to the King in blood, and near in love
Till you did make him misinterpret me,
Have stoop'd my neck under your injuries,
And sigh'd my English breath in foreign clouds, 20
Eating the bitter bread of banishment;
Whilst you have fed upon my signories,
Dispark'd my parks and fell'd my forest woods,
From my own windows torn my household coat,
Raz'd out my imprese, leaving me no sign, 25
Save men's opinions and my living blood,
To show the world I am a gentleman.
This and much more, much more than twice all this,
Condemns you to the death. See them delivered
    over
To execution and the hand of death. 30
  Bushy. More welcome is the stroke of death to me
Than Bolingbroke to England. Lords, farewell!
  Green. My comfort is that heaven will take our
    souls
And plague injustice with the pains of hell.
  Boling. My Lord Northumberland, see them
    dispatch'd. 35
    [*Exeunt Northumberland and others, with
    the prisoners.*]
Uncle, you say the Queen is at your house.
For God's sake, fairly let her be entreated.
Tell her I send to her my kind commends;
Take special care my greetings be delivered.
  York. A gentleman of mine I have dispatch'd 40
With letters of your love to her at large.
  Boling. Thanks, gentle uncle. Come, lords,
    away,
To fight with Glendower and his complices.
A while to work, and after holiday.   [*Exeunt.*

SCENE II. [*The coast of Wales. A castle in view.*]

Drums: flourish and colours. Enter KING RICHARD,
the BISHOP OF CARLISLE, AUMERLE, *and Soldiers.*

  K. Rich. Barkloughly castle call they this at
    hand?
  Aum. Yea, my lord. How brooks your Grace the
    air,
After your late tossing on the breaking seas?
  K. Rich. Needs must I like it well; I weep for joy
To stand upon my kingdom once again. 5
Dear earth, I do salute thee with my hand,
Though rebels wound thee with their horses' hoofs.
As a long-parted mother with her child

Plays fondly with her tears and smiles in meeting,
So, weeping, smiling, greet I thee, my earth, 10
And do thee favours with my royal hands.
Feed not thy sovereign's foe, my gentle earth,
Nor with thy sweets comfort his ravenous sense;
But let thy spiders, that suck up thy venom,
And heavy-gaited toads lie in their way, 15
Doing annoyance to the treacherous feet
Which with usurping steps do trample thee.
Yield stinging nettles to mine enemies;
And when they from thy bosom pluck a flower,
Guard it, I pray thee, with a lurking adder 20
Whose double tongue may with a mortal touch
Throw death upon thy sovereign's enemies.
Mock not my senseless conjuration, lords.
This earth shall have a feeling, and these stones
Prove armed soldiers, ere her native king 25
Shall falter under foul rebellion's arms.
  Car. Fear not, my lord; that Power that made
    you king
Hath power to keep you king in spite of all.
The means that heavens yield must be embrac'd,
And not neglected; else, [if] heaven would 30
And we will not, heaven's offer we refuse,
The proffer'd means of succour and redress.
  Aum. He means, my lord, that we are too remiss,
Whilst Bolingbroke, through our security, 34
Grows strong and great in substance and in power.
  K. Rich. Discomfortable cousin! know'st thou not
That when the searching eye of heaven is hid
Behind the globe, that lights the lower world,
Then thieves and robbers range abroad unseen
In murders and in outrage boldly here; 40
But when from under this terrestrial ball
He fires the proud tops of the eastern pines
And darts his light through every guilty hole,
Then murders, treasons, and detested sins,
The cloak of night being pluck'd from off their
    backs, 45
Stand bare and naked, trembling at themselves?
So when this thief, this traitor, Bolingbroke,
Who all this while hath revell'd in the night
Whilst we were wand'ring with the antipodes,
Shall see us rising in our throne, the east, 50
His treasons will sit blushing in his face,
Not able to endure the sight of day,
But, self-affrighted, tremble at his sin.
Not all the water in the rough rude sea
Can wash the balm off from an anointed king; 55
The breath of worldly men cannot depose
The deputy elected by the Lord.
For every man that Bolingbroke hath press'd
To lift shrewd steel against our golden crown,
God for his Richard hath in heavenly pay 60

22. **signories:** estates. 23. **Dispark'd:** thrown open. 24. **coat:** coat of arms. 25. **imprese:** device with motto.
    Sc. ii, 2. brooks: enjoys. 21. **double:** forked. 23. **conjuration:** appeal. 25. **native:** by right of birth. 30. **[if]** (Pope).
Om. O. **34. security:** lack of care. 38. **that.** The antecedent is *eye.* 58. **press'd:** impressed, conscripted.

A glorious angel; then, if angels fight,
Weak men must fall, for Heaven still guards the
   right.

Enter SALISBURY.

Welcome, my lord.   How far off lies your power?
   Sal. Nor near nor farther off, my gracious lord,
Than this weak arm.   Discomfort guides my
   tongue   65
And bids me speak of nothing but despair.
One day too late, I fear me, noble lord,
Hath clouded all thy happy days on earth.
O, call back yesterday, bid time return,
And thou shalt have twelve thousand fighting men!
To-day, to-day, unhappy day, too late,   71
O'erthrows thy joys, friends, fortune, and thy state;
For all the Welshmen, hearing thou wert dead,
Are gone to Bolingbroke, dispers'd, and fled.
   Aum. Comfort, my liege; why looks your Grace
   so pale?   75
   K. Rich. But now the blood of twenty thousand
   men
Did triumph in my face, and they are fled;
And, till so much blood thither come again,
Have I not reason to look pale and dead?
All souls that will be safe fly from my side,   80
For time hath set a blot upon my pride.
   Aum. Comfort, my liege; remember who you are.
   K. Rich. I had forgot myself; am I not King?
Awake, thou coward majesty! thou sleepest.
Is not the King's name twenty thousand names? 85
Arm, arm, my name! a puny subject strikes
At thy great glory.   Look not to the ground,
Ye favourites of a king; are we not high?
High be our thoughts.   I know my uncle York
Hath power enough to serve our turn.   But who
   comes here?   90

Enter SCROOP.

   Scroop. More health and happiness betide my
   liege
Than can my care-tun'd tongue deliver him!
   K. Rich. Mine ear is open and my heart prepar'd.
The worst is worldly loss thou canst unfold.
Say, is my kingdom lost?   Why, 'twas my care; 95
And what loss is it to be rid of care?
Strives Bolingbroke to be as great as we?
Greater he shall not be; if he serve God,
We'll serve Him too and be his fellow so.
Revolt our subjects?   That we cannot mend;   100
They break their faith to God as well as us.
Cry woe, destruction, ruin, and decay:
The worst is death, and death will have his day.
   Scroop. Glad am I that your Highness is so arm'd
To bear the tidings of calamity.   105

Like an unseasonable stormy day
Which makes the silver rivers drown their shores
As if the world were all dissolv'd to tears,
So high above his limits swells the rage
Of Bolingbroke, covering your fearful land   110
With hard bright steel and hearts harder than steel.
White-beards have arm'd their thin and hairless
   scalps
Against thy majesty; boys, with women's voices,
Strive to speak big, and clap their female joints
In stiff unwieldy arms against thy crown;   115
Thy very beadsmen learn to bend their bows
Of double-fatal yew against thy state;
Yea, distaff-women manage rusty bills
Against thy seat: both young and old rebel,
And all goes worse than I have power to tell. 120
   K. Rich. Too well, too well thou tell'st a tale so ill.
Where is the Earl of Wiltshire?   Where is Bagot?
What is become of Bushy?   Where is Green?
That they have let the dangerous enemy
Measure our confines with such peaceful steps? 125
If we prevail, their heads shall pay for it.
I warrant they have made peace with Bolingbroke.
   Scroop. Peace have they made with him indeed,
   my lord.
   K. Rich. O villains, vipers, damn'd without re-
   demption!
Dogs, easily won to fawn on any man!   130
Snakes, in my heart-blood warm'd, that sting my
   heart!
Three Judases, each one thrice worse than Judas!
Would they make peace?   Terrible hell make war
Upon their spotted souls for this [offence]!
   Scroop. Sweet love, I see, changing his property,
Turns to the sourest and most deadly hate.   136
Again uncurse their souls; their peace is made
With heads, and not with hands.   Those whom you
   curse
Have felt the worst of death's destroying wound
And lie full low, grav'd in the hollow ground. 140
   Aum. Is Bushy, Green, and the Earl of Wiltshire
   dead?
   Scroop Ay, all of them at Bristol lost their heads.
   Aum. Where is the Duke my father with his
   power?
   K. Rich. No matter where; of comfort no man
   speak.
Let's talk of graves, of worms, and epitaphs; 145
Make dust our paper and with rainy eyes
Write sorrow on the bosom of the earth.
Let's choose executors and talk of wills;
And yet not so; for what can we bequeath
Save our deposed bodies to the ground?   150
Our lands, our lives, and all are Bolingbroke's,
And nothing can we call our own but death,

116. **beadsmen:** almsmen who prayed for the King.   117. **double-fatal:** causing death in two ways.   The wood was used
for bows, and the berries are poisonous.   118. **bills:** two-handed axes.   134. **[offence]** F.   Om. Q (ending line 133 with *hell*).

And that small model of the barren earth
Which serves as paste and cover to our bones.
For God's sake, let us sit upon the ground   155
And tell sad stories of the death of kings:
How some have been depos'd; some slain in war;
Some haunted by the ghosts they have depos'd;
Some poison'd by their wives; some sleeping kill'd;
All murdered: for within the hollow crown   160
That rounds the mortal temples of a king
Keeps Death his court, and there the antic sits,
Scoffing his state and grinning at his pomp,
Allowing him a breath, a little scene,
To monarchize, be fear'd, and kill with looks,   165
Infusing him with self and vain conceit,
As if this flesh which walls about our life
Were brass impregnable; and humour'd thus
Comes at the last and with a little pin
Bores through his castle wall, and — farewell
      king!   170
Cover your heads, and mock not flesh and blood
With solemn reverence.   Throw away respect,
Tradition, form, and ceremonious duty;
For you have but mistook me all this while.
I live with bread like you, feel want,   175
Taste grief, need friends: subjected thus,
How can you say to me I am a king?
      Car. My lord, wise men ne'er sit and wail their
            woes,
But presently prevent the ways to wail.
To fear the foe, since fear oppresseth strength,   180
Gives in your weakness strength unto your foe,
And so your follies fight against yourself.
Fear, and be slain; no worse can come to fight;
And fight and die is death destroying death,
Where fearing dying pays death servile breath.   185
      Aum. My father hath a power; inquire of him,
And learn to make a body of a limb.
      K. Rich. Thou chid'st me well.   Proud Boling-
            broke, I come
To change blows with thee for our day of doom.
This ague fit of fear is over-blown;   190
An easy task it is to win our own.
Say, Scroop, where lies our uncle with his power?
Speak sweetly, man, although thy looks be sour.
      Scroop. Men judge by the complexion of the sky
The state and inclination of the day;   195
So may you by my dull and heavy eye,
   My tongue hath but a heavier tale to say.
I play the torturer by small and small
To lengthen out the worst that must be spoken.
Your uncle York is join'd with Bolingbroke,   200
And all your northern castles yielded up,
And all your southern gentlemen in arms
Upon his party.
      K. Rich.   Thou hast said enough.

[*To Aumerle.*] Beshrew thee, cousin, which didst
      lead me forth
Of that sweet way I was in to despair!   205
What say you now?   What comfort have we now?
By heaven, I'll hate him everlastingly
That bids me be of comfort any more.
Go to Flint castle; there I'll pine away;
A king, woe's slave, shall kingly woe obey.   210
That power I have, discharge; and let them go
To ear the land that hath some hope to grow,
For I have none.   Let no man speak again
To alter this, for counsel is but vain.
      Aum. My liege, one word.
      K. Rich.   He does me double wrong   215
That wounds me with the flatteries of his tongue.
Discharge my followers; let them hence away,
From Richard's night to Bolingbroke's fair day.
                                             [*Exeunt.*]

SCENE III. [*Wales. Before Flint Castle.*]

Enter, with drum and colours, BOLINGBROKE, YORK,
   NORTHUMBERLAND, *Attendants* [*and forces*].

      Boling. So that by this intelligence we learn
The Welshmen are dispers'd, and Salisbury
Is gone to meet the King, who lately landed
With some few private friends upon this coast.
      North. The news is very fair and good, my lord.
Richard not far from hence hath hid his head.   6
      York. It would beseem the Lord Northumberland
To say King Richard.   Alack the heavy day
When such a sacred king should hide his head!
      North. Your Grace mistakes; only to be brief   10
Left I his title out.
      York.   The time hath been,
Would you have been so brief with him, he would
Have been so brief [with you], to shorten you,
For taking so the head, your whole head's length.
      Boling. Mistake not, uncle, further than you
            should.   15
      York. Take not, good cousin, further than you
            should,
Lest you mistake the heavens are o'er our heads.
      Boling. I know it, uncle, and oppose not myself
Against their will.   But who comes here?

Enter PERCY.

Welcome, Harry.   What, will not this castle yield?
      Percy. The castle royally is mann'd, my lord,   21
Against thy entrance.
      Boling. Royally!
Why, it contains no king?
      Percy.   Yes, my good lord,
It doth contain a king.   King Richard lies   25
Within the limits of yon lime and stone;

And with him are the Lord Aumerle, Lord Salisbury,
Sir Stephen Scroop, besides a clergyman
Of holy reverence; who, I cannot learn.
    North. O, belike it is the Bishop of Carlisle.   30
    Boling. Noble lords,
Go to the rude ribs of that ancient castle;
Through brazen trumpet send the breath of parley
Into his ruin'd ears, and thus deliver:
Henry Bolingbroke   35
On both his knees doth kiss King Richard's hand
And sends allegiance and true faith of heart
To his most royal person, hither come
Even at his feet to lay my arms and power,
Provided that my banishment repeal'd   40
And lands restor'd again be freely granted.
If not, I'll use the advantage of my power
And lay the summer's dust with showers of blood
Rain'd from the wounds of slaughtered Englishmen;
The which, how far off from the mind of Bolingbroke
It is, such crimson tempest should bedrench   46
The fresh green lap of fair King Richard's land,
My stooping duty tenderly shall show.
Go, signify as much, while here we march
Upon the grassy carpet of this plain.   50
Let's march without the noise of threat'ning drum,
That from this castle's tattered battlements
Our fair appointments may be well perus'd.
Methinks King Richard and myself should meet
With no less terror than the elements   55
Of fire and water, when their thund'ring shock
At meeting tears the cloudy cheeks of heaven.
Be he the fire, I'll be the yielding water;
The rage be his, whilst on the earth I rain
My waters — on the earth, and not on him.   60
March on, and mark King Richard how he looks.

Parle without, and answer within: then a flourish.
    Enter on the walls, KING RICHARD, *the* BISHOP OF
    CARLISLE, AUMERLE, SCROOP, *and* SALISBURY.

See, see, King Richard doth himself appear,
As doth the blushing discontented sun
From out the fiery portal of the east,
When he perceives the envious clouds are bent 65
To dim his glory and to stain the track
Of his bright passage to the occident.
    York. Yet looks he like a king! Behold, his eye,
As bright as is the eagle's, lightens forth
Controlling majesty. Alack, alack, for woe,   70
That any harm should stain so fair a show!
    K. Rich. We are amaz'd; and thus long have we
    stood   [*To North.*]
To watch the fearful bending of thy knee,
Because we thought ourself thy lawful king;
And if we be, how dare thy joints forget   75
To pay their awful duty to our presence?

If we be not, show us the hand of God
That hath dismiss'd us from our stewardship;
For well we know, no hand of blood and bone
Can gripe the sacred handle of our sceptre,   80
Unless he do profane, steal, or usurp.
And though you think that all, as you have done,
Have torn their souls by turning them from us,
And we are barren and bereft of friends,
Yet know, my master, God omnipotent,   85
Is mustering in his clouds on our behalf
Armies of pestilence; and they shall strike
Your children yet unborn and unbegot,
That lift your vassal hands against my head
And threat the glory of my precious crown.   90
Tell Bolingbroke — for yon methinks he stands —
That every stride he makes upon my land
Is dangerous treason. He is come to open
The purple testament of bleeding war;
But ere the crown he looks for live in peace,   95
Ten thousand bloody crowns of mothers' sons
Shall ill become the flower of England's face,
Change the complexion of her maid-pale peace
To scarlet indignation, and bedew
Her pastures' grass with faithful English blood.   100
    North. The King of heaven forbid our lord the
    King
Should so with civil and uncivil arms
Be rush'd upon! Thy thrice noble cousin
Harry Bolingbroke doth humbly kiss thy hand;
And by the honourable tomb he swears   105
That stands upon your royal grandsire's bones,
And by the royalties of both your bloods,
Currents that spring from one most gracious head,
And by the buried hand of warlike Gaunt,
And by the worth and honour of himself,   110
Comprising all that may be sworn or said,
His coming hither hath no further scope
Than for his lineal royalties, and to beg
Enfranchisement immediate on his knees;
Which on thy royal party granted once,   115
His glittering arms he will commend to rust,
His barbed steeds to stables, and his heart
To faithful service of your Majesty.
This swears he, as he is [a prince, is] just;
And, as I am a gentleman, I credit him.   120
    K. Rich. Northumberland, say thus the King
    returns:
His noble cousin is right welcome hither;
And all the number of his fair demands
Shall be accomplish'd without contradiction.
With all the gracious utterance thou hast   125
Speak to his gentle hearing kind commends.
    [*Northumberland withdraws to Bolingbroke.*]
    [*To Aumerle.*] We do debase ourselves, cousin, do
    we not,

73. **watch:** wait for. 102. **civil:** as in civil war. The other sense is played on in *uncivil.* 115. **party:** part. 119. **[a prince, is]** F₁. *princesse* Q. 121. **returns:** replies.

To look so poorly and to speak so fair?
Shall we call back Northumberland, and send
Defiance to the traitor, and so die?   130
  Aum. No, good my lord; let's fight with gentle
    words
Till time lend friends, and friends their helpful
    swords.
  K. Rich. O God, O God! that e'er this tongue of
    mine
That laid the sentence of dread banishment
On yon proud man, should take it off again   135
With words of sooth!   O that I were as great
As is my grief, or lesser than my name!
Or that I could forget what I have been,
Or not remember what I must be now!
Swell'st thou, proud heart?   I'll give thee scope to
    beat,   140
Since foes have scope to beat both thee and me.
  Aum. Northumberland comes back from Boling-
    broke.
  K. Rich. What must the King do now?   Must he
    submit?
The King shall do it.   Must he be depos'd?
The King shall be contented.   Must he lose   145
The name of king?   O' God's name, let it go.
I'll give my jewels for a set of beads,
My gorgeous palace for a hermitage,
My gay apparel for an almsman's gown,
My figur'd goblets for a dish of wood,   150
My sceptre for a palmer's walking-staff,
My subjects for a pair of carved saints,
And my large kingdom for a little grave,
A little little grave, an obscure grave;
Or I'll be buried in the King's highway,   155
Some way of common trade, where subjects' feet
May hourly trample on their sovereign's head;
For on my heart they tread now whilst I live,
And buried once, why not upon my head?
Aumerle, thou weep'st, my tender-hearted cousin!
We'll make foul weather with despised tears.   161
Our sighs and they shall lodge the summer corn,
And make a dearth in this revolting land.
Or shall we play the wantons with our woes
And make some pretty match with shedding tears?
As thus, to drop them still upon one place,   166
Till they have fretted us a pair of graves
Within the earth; and, therein laid, — there lies
Two kinsmen digg'd their graves with weeping eyes.
Would not this ill do well?   Well, well, I see   170
I talk but idly, and you laugh at me.
Most mighty prince, my Lord Northumberland,
What says King Bolingbroke?   Will his Majesty
Give Richard leave to live till Richard die?
You make a leg, and Bolingbroke says ay.   175
  North. My lord, in the base court he doth attend

To speak with you, may it please you to come down.
  K. Rich. Down, down I come; like glist'ring
    Phaethon,
Wanting the manage of unruly jades.
In the base court?   Base court, where kings grow
    base,   180
To come at traitors' calls and do them grace.
In the base court?   Come down?   Down, court!
    down, king!
For night-owls shriek where mounting larks should
    sing.   [*Exeunt from above.*]
  Boling. What says his Majesty?
  North.   Sorrow and grief of heart
Makes him speak fondly, like a frantic man;   185
Yet he is come.

[*Enter* KING RICHARD *and his* Attendants *below.*]

  Boling. Stand all apart,
And show fair duty to his Majesty.
                                        [*He kneels down.*
My gracious lord, —
  K. Rich. Fair cousin, you debase your princely
    knee   190
To make the base earth proud with kissing it.
Me rather had my heart might feel your love
Than my unpleas'd eye see your courtesy.
Up, cousin, up; your heart is up, I know,
Thus high at least [*touching his own head*], although
    your knee be low.   195
  Boling. My gracious lord, I come but for mine
    own.
  K. Rich. Your own is yours, and I am yours, and
    all.
  Boling. So far be mine, my most redoubted lord,
As my true service shall deserve your love.
  K. Rich. Well you deserve; they well deserve to
    have   200
That know the strong'st and surest way to get.
Uncle, give me your hands: nay, dry your eyes;
Tears show their love, but want their remedies.
Cousin, I am too young to be your father,
Though you are old enough to be my heir.   205
What you will have, I'll give, and willing too;
For do we must what force will have us do.
Set on towards London, cousin, is it so?
  Boling. Yea, my good lord.
  K. Rich.   Then I must not say no.
                                        [*Flourish. Exeunt.*

SCENE IV. [*Langley. The Duke of York's garden.*]

Enter the QUEEN *and two* LADIES.

  Queen. What sport shall we devise here in this
    garden
To drive away the heavy thought of care?

---

136. **words of sooth:** smooth words.   162. **lodge:** lay flat.   167. **fretted:** worn.   175. **leg:** obeisance.   176. **base court:**
lower (outer) courtyard.   179. **Wanting ... of:** lacking the ability to control.   185. **fondly:** foolishly.

Lady. Madam, we'll play at bowls.

Queen. 'Twill make me think the world is full of rubs,

And that my fortune runs against the bias.   5

Lady. Madam, we'll dance.

Queen. My legs can keep no measure in delight,

When my poor heart no measure keeps in grief;

Therefore, no dancing, girl; some other sport.

Lady. Madam, we'll tell tales.   10

Queen. Of sorrow or of [joy]?

Lady.   Of either, madam.

Queen. Of neither, girl;

For if of joy, being altogether wanting,

It doth remember me the more of sorrow;

Or if of grief, being altogether had,   15

It adds more sorrow to my want of joy;

For what I have I need not to repeat,

And what I want it boots not to complain.

Lady. Madam, I'll sing.

Queen.   'Tis well that thou hast cause;

But thou shouldst please me better wouldst thou weep.   20

Lady. I could weep, madam, would it do you good.

Queen. And I could sing, would weeping do me good,

And never borrow any tear of thee.

Enter a GARDENER *and two* SERVANTS.

But stay, here come the gardeners.

Let's step into the shadow of these trees.   25

My wretchedness unto a row of pins,

They'll talk of state; for every one doth so

Against a change; woe is forerun with woe.

                    [*Queen and Ladies retire.*]

Gard. Go, bind thou up yon dangling apricocks,

Which, like unruly children, make their sire   30

Stoop with oppression of their prodigal weight;

Give some supportance to the bending twigs.

Go thou, and like an executioner,

Cut off the heads of too fast growing sprays,

That look too lofty in our commonwealth;   35

All must be even in our government.

You thus employ'd, I will go root away

The noisome weeds, which without profit suck

The soil's fertility from wholesome flowers.

Serv. Why should we in the compass of a pale   40

Keep law and form and due proportion,

Showing, as in a model, our firm estate,

When our sea-walled garden, the whole land,

Is full of weeds, her fairest flowers chok'd up,

Her fruit-trees all unprun'd, her hedges ruin'd,   45

Her knots disorder'd and her wholesome herbs

Swarming with caterpillars?

Gard.   Hold thy peace.

He that hath suffer'd this disordered spring

Hath now himself met with the fall of leaf.

The weeds which his broad-spreading leaves did shelter,   50

That seem'd in eating him to hold him up,

Are pluck'd up root and all by Bolingbroke,

I mean the Earl of Wiltshire, Bushy, Green.

Serv. What, are they dead?

Gard.   They are; and Bolingbroke

Hath seiz'd the wasteful King. O, what pity is it

That he had not so trimm'd and dress'd his land   56

As we this garden! [We] at time of year

Do wound the bark, the skin of our fruit-trees,

Lest, being over-proud in sap and blood,

With too much riches it confound itself;   60

Had he done so to great and growing men,

They might have liv'd to bear and he to taste

Their fruits of duty. Superfluous branches

We lop away, that bearing boughs may live;

Had he done so, himself had borne the crown,   65

Which waste of idle hours hath quite thrown down.

Serv. What, think you the King shall be depos'd?

Gard. Depress'd he is already, and depos'd

'Tis doubt he will be. Letters came last night

To a dear friend of the good Duke of York's,   70

That tell black tidings.

Queen. O, I am press'd to death through want of speaking!   [*Coming forward.*]

Thou, old Adam's likeness, set to dress this garden,

How dares thy harsh rude tongue sound this unpleasing news?

What Eve, what serpent, hath suggested thee   75

To make a second fall of cursed man?

Why dost thou say King Richard is depos'd?

Dar'st thou, thou little better thing than earth,

Divine his downfall? Say, where, when, and how,

Cam'st thou by this ill tidings? Speak, thou wretch.

Gard. Pardon me, madam; little joy have I   81

To breathe this news; yet what I say is true.

King Richard, he is in the mighty hold

Of Bolingbroke. Their fortunes both are weigh'd.

In your lord's scale is nothing but himself,   85

And some few vanities that make him light;

But in the balance of great Bolingbroke,

Besides himself, are all the English peers,

And with that odds he weighs King Richard down.

Post you to London, and you'll find it so;   90

I speak no more than every one doth know.

Queen. Nimble Mischance, that art so light of foot,

Doth not thy embassage belong to me,

And am I last that knows it? O, thou think'st

To serve me last, that I may longest keep   95

Thy sorrow in my breast.   Come, ladies, go,
To meet at London London's king in woe.
What, was I born to this, that my sad look
Should grace the triumph of great Bolingbroke?
Gardener, for telling me these news of woe,   100
Pray God the plants thou graft'st may never grow.
                    [*Exeunt [Queen and Ladies*].
   Gard. Poor queen! so that thy state might be no
      worse,
I would my skill were subject to thy curse.
Here did she fall a tear; here in this place
I'll set a bank of rue, sour herb of grace.   105
Rue, even for ruth, here shortly shall be seen,
In the remembrance of a weeping queen. [*Exeunt.*

ACT IV

SCENE I. [*London. Westminster Hall.*]

Enter as to the Parliament BOLINGBROKE, AUMERLE,
   NORTHUMBERLAND, PERCY, FITZWATER, SURREY,
   the BISHOP OF CARLISLE, *the* ABBOT OF WEST-
   MINSTER [*and another* LORD], Herald, *and* Officers.

Boling. Call forth Bagot.

Enter BAGOT.

Now, Bagot, freely speak thy mind;
What thou dost know of noble Gloucester's death,
Who wrought it with the King, and who perform'd
The bloody office of his timeless end.   5
   Bagot. Then set before my face the Lord Aumerle.
   Boling. Cousin, stand forth, and look upon that
      man.
   Bagot. My Lord Aumerle, I know your daring
      tongue
Scorns to unsay what once it hath deliver'd.
In that dead time when Gloucester's death was
      plotted,   10
I heard you say, "Is not my arm of length,
That reacheth from the restful English court
As far as Calais, to mine uncle's head?"
Amongst much other talk, that very time,
I heard you say that you had rather refuse   15
The offer of an hundred thousand crowns
Than Bolingbroke's return to England;
Adding withal, how blest this land would be
In this your cousin's death.
   Aum.   Princes and noble lords,
What answer shall I make to this base man?   20
Shall I so much dishonour my fair stars
On equal terms to give [him] chastisement?
Either I must, or have mine honour soil'd
With the attainder of his slanderous lips.
There is my gage, the manual seal of death,   25
That marks thee out for hell.   I say, thou liest,

And will maintain what thou hast said is false
In thy heart-blood, though being all too base
To stain the temper of my knightly sword.   29
   Boling. Bagot, forbear; thou shalt not take it up.
   Aum. Excepting one, I would he were the best
In all this presence that hath mov'd me so.
   Fitz. If that thy valour stand on sympathy,
There is my gage, Aumerle, in gage to thine.
By that fair sun which shows me where thou stand'st,
I heard thee say, and vauntingly thou spak'st it,   36
That thou wert cause of noble Gloucester's death.
If thou deny'st it twenty times, thou liest;
And I will turn thy falsehood to thy heart,
Where it was forged, with my rapier's point.   40
   Aum. Thou dar'st not, coward, live to see that
      day.
   Fitz. Now, by my soul, I would it were this hour.
   Aum. Fitzwater, thou art damn'd to hell for this.
   Percy. Aumerle, thou liest; his honour is as true
In this appeal as thou art all unjust;   45
And that thou art so, there I throw my gage,
To prove it on thee to the extremest point
Of mortal breathing.   Seize it, if thou dar'st.
   Aum. An if I do not, may my hands rot off
And never brandish more revengeful steel   50
Over the glittering helmet of my foe!
   Another Lord. I task the earth to the like, for-
      sworn Aumerle;
And spur thee on with full as many lies
As may be holloa'd in thy treacherous ear
From sun to sun.   There is my honour's pawn;   55
Engage it to the trial, if thou dar'st.
   Aum. Who sets me else?   By heaven, I'll throw
      at all!
I have a thousand spirits in one breast,
To answer twenty thousand such as you.
   Surrey. My Lord Fitzwater, I do remember well
The very time Aumerle and you did talk.   61
   Fitz. 'Tis very true; you were in presence then,
And you can witness with me this is true.
   Surrey. As false, by heaven, as heaven itself is
      true.
   Fitz. Surrey, thou liest.
   Surrey.   Dishonourable boy!
That lie shall lie so heavy on my sword,   66
That it shall render vengeance and revenge
Till thou the lie-giver and that lie do lie
In earth as quiet as thy father's skull;
In proof whereof, there is my honour's pawn;
Engage it to the trial, if thou dar'st.   71
   Fitz. How fondly dost thou spur a forward horse!
If I dare eat, or drink, or breathe, or live,
I dare meet Surrey in a wilderness
And spit upon him, whilst I say he lies,   75
And lies, and lies.   There is [my] bond of faith,

Act IV, sc. i, 5. **timeless:** untimely.   10. **dead:** fatal.   21. **stars:** destiny.   22. **[him]** F.   *them* Q1, *my* Q2.   33. **sympathy:**
equality of rank.   57. **sets:** challenges.   76. **[my]** Q3.   Om. Q1.

To tie thee to my strong correction.
As I intend to thrive in this new world,
Aumerle is guilty of my true appeal;
Besides, I heard the banish'd Norfolk say   80
That thou, Aumerle, didst send two of thy men
To execute the noble Duke at Calais.
    Aum. Some honest Christian trust me with a
        gage
That Norfolk lies. Here do I throw down this,
If he may be repeal'd, to try his honour.   85
    Boling. These differences shall all rest under gage
Till Norfolk be repeal'd. Repeal'd he shall be,
And, though mine enemy, restor'd again
To all his lands and signories. When he's return'd,
Against Aumerle we will enforce his trial.   90
    Car. That honourable day shall ne'er be seen.
Many a time hath banish'd Norfolk fought
For Jesu Christ in glorious Christian field,
Streaming the ensign of the Christian cross
Against black pagans, Turks, and Saracens;   95
And, toil'd with works of war, retir'd himself
To Italy; and there at Venice gave
His body to that pleasant country's earth,
And his pure soul unto his captain Christ,
Under whose colours he had fought so long.   100
    Boling. Why, Bishop, is Norfolk dead?
    Car. As surely as I live, my lord.
    Boling. Sweet Peace conduct his sweet soul to
        the bosom
Of good old Abraham! Lords appellants,
Your differences shall all rest under gage   105
Till we assign you to your days of trial.

Enter YORK [*attended*].

    York. Great Duke of Lancaster, I come to thee
From plume-pluck'd Richard; who with willing soul
Adopts thee heir, and his high sceptre yields
To the possession of thy royal hand.   110
Ascend his throne, descending now from him;
And long live Henry, fourth of that name!
    Boling. In God's name, I'll ascend the regal
        throne.
    Car. Marry, God forbid!
Worst in this royal presence may I speak,   115
Yet best beseeming me to speak the truth.
Would God that any in this noble presence
Were enough noble to be upright judge
Of noble Richard! Then true noblesse would
Learn him forbearance from so foul a wrong.   120
What subject can give sentence on his king?
And who sits here that is not Richard's subject?
Thieves are not judg'd but they are by to hear,
Although apparent guilt be seen in them;
And shall the figure of God's majesty,   125
His captain, steward, deputy elect,

Anointed, crowned, planted many years,
Be judg'd by subject and inferior breath,
And he himself not present? O, forfend it, God,
That in a Christian climate souls refin'd   130
Should show so heinous, black, obscene a deed!
I speak to subjects, and a subject speaks,
Stirr'd up by God, thus boldly for his king.
My Lord of Hereford here, whom you call king,
Is a foul traitor to proud Hereford's king;   135
And if you crown him, let me prophesy,
The blood of English shall manure the ground,
And future ages groan for this foul act.
Peace shall go sleep with Turks and infidels,
And in this seat of peace tumultuous wars   140
Shall kin with kin and kind with kind confound.
Disorder, horror, fear, and mutiny
Shall here inhabit, and this land be call'd
The field of Golgotha and dead men's skulls.
O, if you raise this house against this house,   145
It will the woefullest division prove
That ever fell upon this cursed earth.
Prevent it, resist it, let it not be so,
Lest child, child's children, cry against you "woe!"
    North. Well have you argued, sir; and, for your
        pains   150
Of capital treason we arrest you here.
My Lord of Westminster, be it your charge
To keep him safely till his day of trial.
May it please you, lords, to grant the commons'
        suit?
    Boling. Fetch hither Richard, that in common
        view   155
He may surrender; so we shall proceed
Without suspicion.
    York.   I will be his conduct. [*Exit.*
    Boling. Lords, you that here are under our arrest,
Procure your sureties for your days of answer.
Little are we beholding to your love,   160
And little look'd for at your helping hands.

Re-enter YORK, *with* RICHARD [*and* Officers
        bearing the crown and sceptre].

    K. Rich. Alack, why am I sent for to a king
Before I have shook off the regal thoughts
Wherewith I reign'd? I hardly yet have learn'd
To insinuate, flatter, bow, and bend my knee.   165
Give sorrow leave a while to tutor me
To this submission. Yet I well remember
The favours of these men. Were they not mine?
Did they not sometime cry, "All hail!" to me?
So Judas did to Christ; but He, in twelve,   170
Found truth in all but one; I, in twelve thousand,
        none.
God save the King! — Will no man say amen?
Am I both priest and clerk? Well then, amen.

78. world: era. 96. toil'd: tired out. 115. Worst: humblest. 124. apparent: manifest. 130. climate: country. 131.
obscene: foul. 154–318. F₁. Om. Q₁Q₂. 168. favours: faces.

God save the King! although I be not he;
And yet, amen, if heaven do think him me. — 175
To do what service am I sent for hither?
  York. To do that office of thine own good will
Which tired majesty did make thee offer,
The resignation of thy state and crown
To Henry Bolingbroke.   180
  K. Rich. Give me the crown. Here, cousin,
    seize the crown;
Here, cousin,
On this side my hand, and on that side thine.
Now is this golden crown like a deep well
That owes two buckets, filling one another, 185
The emptier ever dancing in the air,
The other down, unseen, and full of water.
That bucket down and full of tears am I,
Drinking my griefs, whilst you mount up on high.
  Boling. I thought you had been willing to resign.
  K. Rich. My crown I am; but still my griefs are
    mine.   191
You may my glories and my state depose,
But not my griefs; still am I king of those.
  Boling. Part of your cares you give me with your
    crown.
  K. Rich. Your cares set up do not pluck my cares
    down.   195
My care is loss of care, by old care done;
Your care is gain of care, by new care won.
The cares I give I have, though given away;
They 'tend the crown, yet still with me they stay.
  Boling. Are you contented to resign the crown?
  K. Rich. Ay, no; no, ay; for I must nothing be;
Therefore no no, for I resign to thee.   202
Now mark me, how I will undo myself.
I give this heavy weight from off my head
And this unwieldy sceptre from my hand,   205
The pride of kingly sway from out my heart.
With mine own tears I wash away my balm,
With mine own hands I give away my crown,
With mine own tongue deny my sacred state,
With mine own breath release all duteous oaths. 210
All pomp and majesty I do forswear;
My manors, rents, revenues I forgo;
My acts, decrees, and statutes I deny.
God pardon all oaths that are broke to me!
God keep all vows unbroke are made to thee!   215
Make me, that nothing have, with nothing griev'd,
And thou with all pleas'd, that hast all achiev'd!
Long mayst thou live in Richard's seat to sit,
And soon lie Richard in an earthy pit!
God save King Henry, unking'd Richard says,   220
And send him many years of sunshine days!
— What more remains?
  North.   No more, but that you read
                              [*Presenting a paper.*]

These accusations and these grievous crimes
Committed by your person and your followers
Against the state and profit of this land;   225
That, by confessing them, the souls of men
May deem that you are worthily depos'd.
  K. Rich. Must I do so? and must I ravel out
My weav'd-up follies? Gentle Northumberland,
If thy offences were upon record,   230
Would it not shame thee in so fair a troop
To read a lecture of them? If thou wouldst,
There shouldst thou find one heinous article,
Containing the deposing of a king
And cracking the strong warrant of an oath,   235
Mark'd with a blot, damn'd in the book of heaven.
Nay, all of you that stand and look upon me
Whilst that my wretchedness doth bait myself,
Though some of you with Pilate wash your hands
Showing an outward pity; yet you Pilates   240
Have here deliver'd me to my sour cross,
And water cannot wash away your sin.
  North. My lord, dispatch; read o'er these articles.
  K. Rich. Mine eyes are full of tears, I cannot see;
And yet salt water blinds them not so much   245
But they can see a sort of traitors here.
Nay, if I turn mine eyes upon myself,
I find myself a traitor with the rest;
For I have given here my soul's consent
To undeck the pompous body of a king;   250
Made glory base, a sovereignty a slave,
Proud majesty a subject, state a peasant.
  North. My lord, —
  K. Rich. No lord of thine, thou haught insulting
    man,
Nor no man's lord. I have no name, no title;   255
No, not that name was given me at the font,
But 'tis usurp'd. Alack the heavy day,
That I have worn so many winters out
And know not now what name to call myself!
O that I were a mockery king of snow,   260
Standing before the sun of Bolingbroke,
To melt myself away in water-drops!
Good king, great king, and yet not greatly good,
An if my word be sterling yet in England,
Let it command a mirror hither straight,   265
That it may show me what a face I have
Since it is bankrupt of his majesty.
  Boling. Go some of you and fetch a looking-glass.
                              [*Exit an attendant.*]
  North. Read o'er this paper while the glass doth
    come.
  K. Rich. Fiend, thou torments me e'er I come to
    hell!   270
  Boling. Urge it no more, my Lord Northumber-
    land.
  North. The commons will not then be satisfi'd.

  246. **sort**: group.   250. **pompous**: glorious.   252. **state**: kingship.   254. **haught**: haughty, arrogant.   264. **sterling**:
current, valid.   269. **while**: till.

K. Rich. They shall be satisfi'd. I'll read enough,
When I do see the very book indeed
Where all my sins are writ, and that's myself.   275

Re-enter Attendant, *with a glass.*

Give me that glass, and therein will I read.
No deeper wrinkles yet? Hath sorrow struck
So many blows upon this face of mine,
And made no deeper wounds? O flatt'ring glass,
Like to my followers in prosperity,   280
Thou dost beguile me! Was this face the face
That every day under his household roof
Did keep ten thousand men? Was this the face
That, like the sun, did make beholders wink?
Is this the face which fac'd so many follies,   285
That was at last out-fac'd by Bolingbroke?
A brittle glory shineth in this face;
As brittle as the glory is the face,
      [*Dashes the glass against the ground.*]
For there it is, crack'd in an hundred shivers.
Mark, silent king, the moral of this sport,   290
How soon my sorrow hath destroy'd my face.
  Boling. The shadow of your sorrow hath destroy'd
The shadow of your face.
  K. Rich.   Say that again.
The shadow of my sorrow! Ha! let's see.
'Tis very true, my grief lies all within;
And these external manners of laments   295
Are merely shadows to the unseen grief
That swells with silence in the tortur'd soul.
There lies the substance; and I thank thee, King,
For thy great bounty, that not only giv'st   300
Me cause to wail but teachest me the way
How to lament the cause. I'll beg one boon,
And then be gone and trouble you no more.
Shall I obtain it?
  Boling.   Name it, fair cousin.
  K. Rich. "Fair cousin"? I am greater than a
    king;   305
For when I was a king my flatterers
Were then but subjects; being now a subject,
I have a king here to my flatterer.
Being so great, I have no need to beg.
  Boling. Yet ask.   310
  K. Rich. And shall I have?
  Boling. You shall.
  K. Rich. Then give me leave to go.
  Boling. Whither?
  K. Rich. Whither you will, so I were from your
    sights.   315
  Boling. Go, some of you convey him to the
    Tower.

  K. Rich. O, good! convey! Conveyers are you all,
That rise thus nimbly by a true king's fall.
    [*Exeunt King Richard, some Lords, and a
      Guard.*]
  Boling. On Wednesday next we solemnly proclaim
Our coronation. Lords, be ready all.   320
    [*Exeunt all but the Bishop of Carlisle, the
      Abbot of Westminster, and Aumerle.*
  Abbot. A woeful pageant have we here beheld.
  Car. The woe's to come; the children yet unborn
Shall feel this day as sharp to them as thorn.
  Aum. You holy clergymen, is there no plot
To rid the realm of this pernicious blot?   325
  Abbot. My lord,
Before I freely speak my mind herein,
You shall not only take the sacrament
To bury mine intents, but also to effect
Whatever I shall happen to devise.   330
I see your brows are full of discontent,
Your hearts of sorrow, and your eyes of tears.
Come home with me to supper; [and] I'll lay
A plot shall show us all a merry day.   [*Exeunt.*

ACT V

SCENE I. [*London. A street leading to the Tower.*]

Enter the QUEEN *with her* Attendants.

  Queen. This way the King will come; this is the
    way
To Julius Cæsar's ill-erected tower,
To whose flint bosom my condemned lord
Is doom'd a prisoner by proud Bolingbroke.
Here let us rest, if this rebellious earth   5
Have any resting for her true king's queen.

Enter RICHARD *and* Guard.

But soft, but see, or rather do not see,
My fair rose wither; yet look up, behold,
That you in pity may dissolve to dew
And wash him fresh again with true-love tears.   10
Ah, thou, the model where old Troy did stand,
Thou map of honour, thou King Richard's tomb,
And not King Richard; thou most beauteous inn,
Why should hard-favour'd Grief be lodg'd in thee,
When Triumph is become an alehouse guest?   15
  K. Rich. Join not with grief, fair woman, do
    not so,
To make my end too sudden. Learn, good soul,
To think our former state a happy dream,
From which awak'd, the truth of what we are
Shows us but this. I am sworn brother, sweet,   20

---

296. **to:** compared to.   308. **to:** as.   317. **Conveyers:** thieves.   319. **On** F₁. *Let it be so, and loe on* Q. **proclaim** Q.
set down F₁.   320. **be ready all** Q. *prepare yourselves* F₁.   333. **[and]** (Pope). Om. Qq Ff.
  Act V, sc. i, 2. **ill-erected:** erected for evil ends. The Tower was, in fact, built by William the Conqueror.   11. **model:**
ground plan. She compares Richard to a mere plan of a ruined city, then to a mere outline of majesty.

To grim Necessity; and he and I
Will keep a league till death.   Hie thee to France
And cloister thee in some religious house.
Our holy lives must win a new world's crown,
Which our profane hours here have thrown down.
    Queen. What, is my Richard both in shape and
        mind   26
Transform'd and weak'ned?   Hath Bolingbroke
        depos'd
Thine intellect?   Hath he been in thy heart?
The lion dying thrusteth forth his paw,
And wounds the earth, if nothing else, with rage 30
To be o'erpower'd; and wilt thou, pupil-like,
Take the correction, mildly kiss the rod,
And fawn on rage with base humility,
Which art a lion and the king of beasts?
    K. Rich. A king of beasts, indeed; if aught but
        beasts,   35
I had been still a happy king of men.
Good sometime queen, prepare thee hence for
        France.
Think I am dead, and that even here thou tak'st,
As from my death-bed, thy last living leave.
In winter's tedious nights sit by the fire   40
With good old folks and let them tell thee tales
Of woeful ages long ago betid;
And ere thou bid good night, to quite their griefs
Tell thou the lamentable tale of me
And send the hearers weeping to their beds.   45
For why, the senseless brands will sympathize
The heavy accent of thy moving tongue,
And in compassion weep the fire out;
And some will mourn in ashes, some coal-black,
For the deposing of a rightful king.   50

       Enter NORTHUMBERLAND [*and others*].

    North. My lord, the mind of Bolingbroke is
        chang'd;
You must to Pomfret, not unto the Tower.
And, madam, there is order ta'en for you;
With all swift speed you must away to France.
    K. Rich. Northumberland, thou ladder where-
        withal   55
The mounting Bolingbroke ascends my throne,
The time shall not be many hours of age
More than it is, ere foul sin gathering head
Shall break into corruption.   Thou shalt think,
Though he divide the realm and give thee half,   60
It is too little, helping him to all;
[And] he shall think that thou, which know'st the
        way
To plant unrightful kings, wilt know again,
Being ne'er so little urg'd, another way
To pluck him headlong from the usurped throne. 65

The love of wicked men converts to fear,
That fear to hate, and hate turns one or both
To worthy danger and deserved death.
    North. My guilt be on my head, and there an end.
Take leave and part; for you must part forthwith.
    K. Rich. Doubly divorc'd!   Bad men, you vio-
        late   71
A twofold marriage, 'twixt my crown and me,
And then betwixt me and my married wife.
Let me unkiss the oath 'twixt thee and me;
And yet not so, for with a kiss 'twas made.   75
Part us, Northumberland; I towards the north,
Where shivering cold and sickness pines the clime;
My wife to France; from whence, set forth in pomp,
She came adorned hither like sweet May,
Sent back like Hallowmas or short'st of day.   80
    Queen. And must we be divided?   Must we part?
    K. Rich. Ay, hand from hand, my love, and heart
        from heart.
    Queen. Banish us both, and send the King with
        me.
    [*North.*] That were some love but little policy.
    Queen. Then whither he goes, thither let me go.
    K. Rich. So two, together weeping, make one
        woe.   86
Weep thou for me in France, I for thee here;
Better far off than near, be ne'er the near.
Go, count thy way with sighs; I mine with groans.
    Queen. So longest way shall have the longest
        moans.   90
    K. Rich. Twice for one step I'll groan, the way
        being short,
And piece the way out with a heavy heart.
Come, come, in wooing sorrow let's be brief,
Since, wedding it, there is such length in grief.
One kiss shall stop our mouths, and dumbly part;
Thus give I mine, and thus take I thy heart.   96
    Queen. Give me mine own again; 'twere no good
        part
To take on me to keep and kill thy heart. —
So, now I have mine own again, be gone,
That I may strive to kill it with a groan.   100
    K. Rich. We make woe wanton with this fond
        delay.
Once more, adieu; the rest let sorrow say.
                                [*Exeunt.*

SCENE II.   [*London.   The Duke of York's palace.*]

       Enter YORK *and his* DUCHESS.

    Duch. My lord, you told me you would tell the
        rest,
When weeping made you break the story off,
Of our two cousins coming into London.

---

43. **quite ... griefs:** requite their sad tales.   62. **[And]** (Rowe).   Om. Qq Ff.   68. **worthy:** well-earned.   77. **pines:** makes
painful.   80. **Hallowmas ... day.** Nov. 1 or Dec. 21.   84. **[North.]** Ff.   *King* Q.   88. **be ... near:** if we can never meet.
Near is comparative.

York. Where did I leave?

Duch.   At that sad stop, my lord,
Where rude misgovern'd hands from windows' tops
Threw dust and rubbish on King Richard's head. 6

York. Then, as I said, the Duke, great Boling-
    broke,
Mounted upon a hot and fiery steed
Which his aspiring rider seem'd to know,
With slow but stately pace kept on his course, 10
Whilst all tongues cried, "God save thee, Boling-
    broke!"
You would have thought the very windows spake,
So many greedy looks of young and old
Through casements darted their desiring eyes
Upon his visage, and that all the walls 15
With painted imagery had said at once,
"Jesu preserve thee! Welcome, Bolingbroke!"
Whilst he, from the one side to the other turning,
Bareheaded, lower than his proud steed's neck,
Bespake them thus: "I thank you, countrymen."
And thus still doing, thus he pass'd along. 21

Duch. Alack, poor Richard! where rode he the
    whilst?

York. As in a theatre, the eyes of men,
After a well-grac'd actor leaves the stage,
Are idly bent on him that enters next, 25
Thinking his prattle to be tedious;
Even so, or with much more contempt, men's eyes
Did scowl on gentle Richard. No man cried,
"God save him!"
No joyful tongue gave him his welcome home;
But dust was thrown upon his sacred head, 30
Which with such gentle sorrow he shook off,
His face still combating with tears and smiles,
The badges of his grief and patience,
That had not God, for some strong purpose, steel'd
The hearts of men, they must perforce have melted,
And barbarism itself have pitied him. 36
But Heaven hath a hand in these events,
To whose high will we bow our calm contents.
To Bolingbroke are we sworn subjects now,
Whose state and honour I for aye allow. 40

Enter AUMERLE.

Duch. Here comes my son Aumerle.

York.   Aumerle that was;
But that is lost for being Richard's friend,
And, madam, you must call him Rutland now.
I am in parliament pledge for his truth
And lasting fealty to the new-made king. 45

Duch. Welcome, my son! Who are the violets now
That strew the green lap of the new come spring?

Aum. Madam, I know not, nor I greatly care not.
God knows I had as lief be none as one.

York. Well, bear you well in this new spring of
    time, 50

Lest you be cropp'd before you come to prime.
What news from Oxford? Do these jousts and
    triumphs hold?

Aum. For aught I know, my lord, they do.

York. You will be there, I know.

Aum. If God prevent not, I purpose so. 55

York. What seal is that, that hangs without thy
    bosom?
Yea, look'st thou pale? Let me see the writing.

Aum. My lord, 'tis nothing.

York.   No matter, then, who see it.
I will be satisfied; let me see the writing.

Aum. I do beseech your Grace to pardon me. 60
It is a matter of small consequence,
Which for some reasons I would not have seen.

York. Which for some reasons, sir, I mean to see.
I fear, I fear, ——

Duch.   What should you fear?
'Tis nothing but some band that he is ent'red into
For gay apparel 'gainst the triumph day. 66

York. Bound to himself! What doth he with a
    bond
That he is bound to? Wife, thou art a fool.
Boy, let me see the writing.

Aum. I do beseech you, pardon me. I may not
    show it. 70

York. I will be satisfied; let me see it, I say.
    [*He plucks it out of his bosom and reads it.*
Treason! foul treason! Villain! traitor! slave!

Duch. What is the matter, my lord?

York. Ho! who is within there?

           [*Enter a* Servant.]

                    Saddle my horse.
God for his mercy, what treachery is here! 75

Duch. Why, what is it, my lord?

York. Give me my boots, I say; saddle my horse.
                    [*Exit Servant.*
Now, by mine honour, by my life, by my troth,
I will appeach the villain.

Duch.   What is the matter?

York. Peace, foolish woman. 80

Duch. I will not peace. What is the matter,
    Aumerle?

Aum. Good mother, be content; it is no more
Than my poor life must answer.

Duch.   Thy life answer!

York. Bring me my boots; I will unto the King.

    Re-enter Servant *with boots.*

Duch. Strike him, Aumerle. Poor boy, thou art
    amaz'd. 85
— Hence, villain! never more come in my sight.

York. Give me my boots, I say.

Duch. Why, York, what wilt thou do?
Wilt thou not hide the trespass of thine own?

Have we more sons? or are we like to have?   90
Is not my teeming date drunk up with time,
And wilt thou pluck my fair son from mine age,
And rob me of a happy mother's name?
Is he not like thee?   Is he not thine own?
  York. Thou fond mad woman,   95
Wilt thou conceal this dark conspiracy?
A dozen of them here have ta'en the sacrament,
And interchangeably set down their hands,
To kill the King at Oxford.
  Duch.   He shall be none;
We'll keep him here; then what is that to him? 100
  York. Away, fond woman! were he twenty times
      my son,
I would appeach him.
  Duch.   Hadst thou groan'd for him
As I have done, thou wouldst be more pitiful.
But now I know thy mind; thou dost suspect
That I have been disloyal to thy bed,   105
And that he is a bastard, not thy son.
Sweet York, sweet husband, be not of that mind.
He is as like thee as a man may be,
Not like to me, or any of my kin,
And yet I love him.
  York.   Make way, unruly woman! 110
                                    [*Exit.*
  Duch. After, Aumerle! mount thou upon his
      horse;
Spur post, and get before him to the King,
And beg thy pardon ere he do accuse thee.
I'll not be long behind; though I be old,
I doubt not but to ride as fast as York.   115
And never will I rise up from the ground
Till Bolingbroke have pardon'd thee.   Away, be
      gone!   [*Exeunt.*

SCENE III.   [*Windsor Castle.*]

Enter BOLINGBROKE, PERCY, *and other* Lords.

  Boling. Can no man tell me of my unthrifty son?
'Tis full three months since I did see him last.
If any plague hang over us, 'tis he.
I would to God, my lords, he might be found.
Inquire at London, 'mongst the taverns there,   5
For there, they say, he daily doth frequent,
With unrestrained loose companions,
Even such, they say, as stand in narrow lanes
And beat our watch and rob our passengers;
Which he, young wanton and effeminate boy,   10
Takes on the point of honour to support
So dissolute a crew.
  Percy. My lord, some two days since I saw the
      Prince,
And told him of those triumphs held at Oxford.
  Boling. And what said the gallant?   15

  Percy. His answer was, he would unto the stews,
And from the common'st creature pluck a glove
And wear it as a favour; and with that
He would unhorse the lustiest challenger.
  Boling. As dissolute as desperate; yet through
      both   20
I see some sparks of better hope, which elder years
May happily bring forth.   But who comes here?

Enter AUMERLE, *amazed.*

  Aum. Where is the King?
  Boling. What means our cousin, that he stares
      and looks
So wildly?   25
  Aum. God save your Grace!   I do beseech your
      Majesty,
To have some conference with your Grace alone.
  Boling. Withdraw yourselves, and leave us here
      alone.   [*Exeunt Percy and Lords.*]
What is the matter with our cousin now?   29
  Aum. For ever may my knees grow to the earth,
                                [*Kneeling.*]
My tongue cleave to my roof within my mouth,
Unless a pardon ere I rise or speak.
  Boling. Intended or committed was this fault?
If on the first, how heinous e'er it be,
To win thy after-love I pardon thee.   35
  Aum. Then give me leave that [I] may turn the
      key,
That no man enter till my tale be done.
  Boling. Have thy desire.
        [*Aumerle locks the door.*]   *York knocks at
              the door and crieth.*
  York. (*Within.*)   My liege, beware!   Look to
      thyself;
Thou hast a traitor in thy presence there.   40
  Boling. Villain, I'll make thee safe.   [*Drawing.*]
  Aum. Stay thy revengeful hand; thou hast no
      cause to fear.
  York. [*Within.*]   Open the door, secure, fool-
      hardy King!
Shall I for love speak treason to thy face?
Open the door, or I will break it open.   45

Enter YORK.

  Boling. What is the matter, uncle?   Speak;
Recover breath; tell us how near is danger
That we may arm us to encounter it.
  York. Peruse this writing here, and thou shalt
      know
The treason that my haste forbids me show.   50
  Aum. Remember, as thou read'st, thy promise
      pass'd.
I do repent me; read not my name there.
My heart is not confederate with my hand.

91. **teeming:** child-bearing.
Sc. iii, 1. **unthrifty:** prodigal.   16. **stews:** houses of ill-fame.   36. **[I]** Om. Q.   43. **secure:** heedless.

York. It was, villain, ere thy hand did set it
    down.
I tore it from the traitor's bosom, King;   55
Fear, and not love, begets his penitence.
Forget to pity him, lest thy pity prove
A serpent that will sting thee to the heart.
    Boling. O heinous, strong, and bold conspiracy!
O loyal father of a treacherous son!   60
Thou sheer, immaculate, and silver fountain,
From whence this stream through muddy passages
Hath held his current and defil'd himself!
Thy overflow of good converts to bad,
And thy abundant goodness shall excuse   65
This deadly blot in thy digressing son.
    York. So shall my virtue be his vice's bawd;
And he shall spend mine honour with his shame,
As thriftless sons their scraping fathers' gold.
Mine honour lives when his dishonour dies,   70
Or my sham'd life in his dishonour lies.
Thou kill'st me in his life; giving him breath,
The traitor lives, the true man's put to death.
    Duch. (*Within.*) What ho, my liege! for God's
    sake, let me in.
    Boling. What shrill-voiced suppliant makes this
    eager cry?   75
    Duch. A woman, and thy aunt, great King; 'tis
    I.
Speak with me, pity me, open the door!
A beggar begs that never begg'd before.
    Boling. Our scene is alt'red from a serious thing,
And now chang'd to "The Beggar and the King."
My dangerous cousin, let your mother in: 81
I know she's come to pray for your foul sin.
    York. If thou do pardon, whosoever pray,
More sins for this forgiveness prosper may.
This fest'red joint cut off, the rest rest sound;   85
This let alone will all the rest confound.

    Enter DUCHESS.

    Duch. O King, believe not this hard-hearted
    man!
Love loving not itself none other can.
    York. Thou frantic woman, what dost thou make
    here?
Shall thy old dugs once more a traitor rear?   90
    Duch. Sweet York, be patient. Hear me, gentle
    liege.   [*Kneels.*]
    Boling. Rise up, good aunt.
    Duch.   Not yet, I thee beseech.
For ever will I walk upon my knees,
And never see day that the happy sees,
Till thou give joy; until thou bid me joy   95
By pardoning Rutland, my transgressing boy.
    Aum. Unto my mother's prayers I bend my
    knee.   [*Kneels.*]

    York. Against them both my true joints bended
    be.   [*Kneels.*]
Ill mayst thou thrive, if thou grant any grace!   99
    Duch. Pleads he in earnest? Look upon his face;
His eyes do drop no tears, his prayers are in jest;
His words come from his mouth, ours from our
    breast.
He prays but faintly and would be deni'd;
We pray with heart and soul and all beside.
His weary joints would gladly rise, I know;   105
Our knees [shall] kneel till to the ground they grow.
His prayers are full of false hypocrisy;
Ours of true zeal and deep integrity.
Our prayers do out-pray his; then let them have
That mercy which true prayer ought to have.   110
    Boling. Good aunt, stand up.
    Duch.   Nay, do not say, "Stand up";
Say "Pardon" first, and afterwards "Stand up."
An if I were thy nurse, thy tongue to teach,
"Pardon" should be the first word of thy speech.
I never long'd to hear a word till now.   115
Say "pardon," King; let pity teach thee how.
The word is short, but not so short as sweet;
No word like "pardon" for kings' mouths so meet.
    York. Speak it in French, King; say, "*Pardonne
    moi.*"
    Duch. Dost thou teach pardon pardon to de-
    stroy?   120
Ah, my sour husband, my hard-hearted lord,
That set'st the word itself against the word!
Speak "pardon" as 'tis current in our land;
The chopping French we do not understand.
Thine eye begins to speak; set thy tongue there;
Or in thy piteous heart plant thou thine ear;   126
That, hearing how our plaints and prayers do
    pierce,
Pity may move thee "pardon" to rehearse.
    Boling. Good aunt, stand up.
    Duch.   I do not sue to stand;
Pardon is all the suit I have in hand.   130
    Boling. I pardon him, as God shall pardon me.
    Duch. O happy vantage of a kneeling knee!
Yet am I sick for fear: speak it again.
Twice saying "pardon" doth not pardon twain,
But makes one pardon strong.
    Boling. I pardon him with all my heart.   135
    Duch. A god on earth thou art.
    Boling. But for our trusty brother-in-law and the
    abbot,
With all the rest of that consorted crew,
Destruction straight shall dog them at the heels.
Good uncle, help to order several powers   140
To Oxford, or where'er these traitors are.
They shall not live within this world, I swear,
But I will have them, if I once know where.

---

61. **sheer:** pure.   80. "The Beggar ... King": referring to the ballad of King Cophetua.   86. **confound:** destroy.   106. [shall] F₁. *still* Q.   119. "*Pardonne moi*": excuse me, i.e., No.   128. **rehearse:** say.   140. **powers:** bodies of troops.

Uncle, farewell; and, cousin, adieu!   144
Your mother well hath pray'd, and prove you true.
Duch. Come, my old son; I pray God make thee
new.   [*Exeunt.*

[SCENE IV.   *Another room in the same.*]

Enter EXTON *and* SERVANT.

Exton. Didst thou not mark the King, what
words he spake,
"Have I no friend will rid me of this living fear?"
Was it not so?
Serv.   These were his very words.
Exton. "Have I no friend?" quoth he.   He spake
it twice,
And urg'd it twice together, did he not?   5
Serv. He did.
Exton. And speaking it, he wishtly look'd on me
As who should say, "I would thou wert the man
That would divorce this terror from my heart;"
Meaning the King at Pomfret.   Come, let's go.
I am the King's friend, and will rid his foe.   11
[*Exeunt.*

SCENE [V.   *Pomfret Castle.   A ward room.*]

Enter KING RICHARD.

K. Rich. I have been studying how I may com-
pare
This prison where I live unto the world;
And for because the world is populous
And here is not a creature but myself,
I cannot do it; yet I'll hammer it out.   5
My brain I'll prove the female to my soul,
My soul the father; and these two beget
A generation of still-breeding thoughts,
And these same thoughts people this little world,
In humours like the people of this world.   10
For no thought is contented.   The better sort,
As thoughts of things divine, are intermix'd
With scruples and do set the word itself
Against the word:
As thus, "Come, little ones," and then again,
"It is as hard to come as for a camel   16
To thread the postern of a small needle's eye."
Thoughts tending to ambition, they do plot
Unlikely wonders: how these vain weak nails
May tear a passage through the flinty ribs   20
Of this hard world, my ragged prison walls,
And, for they cannot, die in their own pride.
Thoughts tending to content flatter themselves
That they are not the first of fortune's slaves,
Nor shall not be the last; like silly beggars   25

Who, sitting in the stocks, refuge their shame,
That many have and others must sit there;
And in this thought they find a kind of ease,
Bearing their own misfortunes on the back
Of such as have before endur'd the like.   30
Thus play I in one person many people,
And none contented.   Sometimes am I king;
Then treasons make me wish myself a beggar;
And so I am.   Then crushing penury
Persuades me I was better when a king;   35
Then am I king'd again: and by and by
Think that I am unking'd by Bolingbroke,
And straight am nothing.   But whate'er I be,
Nor I nor any man that but man is
With nothing shall be pleas'd, till he be eas'd   40
With being nothing.   Music do I hear?   [*Music.*
Ha, ha! keep time!   How sour sweet music is,
When time is broke and no proportion kept!
So is it in the music of men's lives.
And here have I the daintiness of ear   45
To check time broke in a disordered string;
But for the concord of my state and time
Had not an ear to hear my true time broke.
I wasted time, and now doth Time waste me;   49
For now hath Time made me his numb'ring clock.
My thoughts are minutes; and with sighs they jar
Their watches on unto mine eyes, the outward
watch,
Whereto my finger, like a dial's point,
Is pointing still, in cleansing them from tears.
Now sir, the sound that tells what hour it is   55
Are clamorous groans, which strike upon my heart,
Which is the bell.   So sighs and tears and groans
Show minutes, times, and hours; but my time
Runs posting on in Bolingbroke's proud joy,
While I stand fooling here, his Jack o' th' clock.   60
This music mads me; let it sound no more;
For though it have holp madmen to their wits,
In me it seems it will make wise men mad.
Yet blessing on his heart that gives it me!
For 'tis a sign of love; and love to Richard   65
Is a strange brooch in this all-hating world.

Enter a GROOM *of the Stable.*

Groom. Hail, royal prince!
K. Rich.   Thanks, noble peer!
The cheapest of us is ten groats too dear.
What art thou? and how com'st thou hither,
Where no man never comes but that sad dog   70
That brings me food to make misfortune live?
Groom. I was a poor groom of thy stable, King,
When thou wert king; who, travelling towards York,
With much ado at 'ength have gotten leave

Sc. iv, 7. **wishtly:** wistfully.   11. **rid:** destroy.
Sc. v, 8. **still-breeding:** ever-breeding.   10. **humours:** individual peculiarities.   21. **ragged:** rough.   46. **check:** object to.
51. **jar:** tick.   60. **Jack:** the figure that strikes the hours.   66. **brooch:** ornament.   67–68. **royal...noble...ten groats.**
Ten groats made 3*s.*4*d.*, the difference between a royal (10*s.*) and a noble (6*s.*8*d.*).

To look upon my sometimes royal master's face.   75
O, how it yearn'd my heart when I beheld
In London streets, that coronation-day,
When Bolingbroke rode on roan Barbary,
That horse that thou so often hast bestrid,
That horse that I so carefully have dress'd!   80
   K. Rich. Rode he on Barbary? Tell me, gentle
friend,
How went he under him?
   Groom. So proudly as if he disdain'd the ground.
   K. Rich. So proud that Bolingbroke was on his
back!
That jade hath eat bread from my royal hand;   85
This hand hath made him proud with clapping him.
Would he not stumble? Would he not fall down,
Since pride must have a fall, and break the neck
Of that proud man that did usurp his back?
Forgiveness, horse! why do I rail on thee,   90
Since thou, created to be aw'd by man,
Wast born to bear? I was not made a horse;
And yet I bear a burden like an ass,
Spurr'd, gall'd, and tir'd by jauncing Bolingbroke.

     Enter KEEPER, *with a dish.*

   Keep. Fellow, give place; here is no longer stay.
   K. Rich. If thou love me, 'tis time thou wert
away.   96
   Groom. What my tongue dares not, that my heart
shall say.   [*Exit.*
   Keep. My lord, will 't please you to fall to?
   K. Rich. Taste of it first, as thou art wont to do.
   Keep. My lord, I dare not. Sir Pierce of Exton,
who lately came from the King, commands the con-
trary.   102
   K. Rich. The devil take Henry of Lancaster and
thee!
Patience is stale, and I am weary of it.
   Keep. Help, help, help!   105

    Enter EXTON *and* Servants [*armed*].

   K. Rich. How now! what means death in this
rude assault?
Villain, thy own hand yields thy death's instru-
ment.
   [*Snatching an axe from a Servant and kill-
ing him.*]
Go thou, and fill another room in hell.
   [*He kills another.*] *Here Exton strikes him
down.*
That hand shall burn in never-quenching fire
That staggers thus my person. Exton, thy fierce
hand   110
Hath with the King's blood stain'd the King's own
land.
Mount, mount, my soul! thy seat is up on high;

Whilst my gross flesh sinks downward, here to die.
                     [*Dies.*]
   Exton. As full of valour as of royal blood!
Both have I spill'd; O would the deed were good!
For now the devil, that told me I did well,   116
Says that this deed is chronicled in hell.
This dead king to the living king I'll bear:
Take hence the rest, and give them burial here.
                    [*Exeunt.*

SCENE [VI. *Windsor Castle.*]

Flourish. Enter BOLINGBROKE, YORK, *with
other* Lords, *and* Attendants.

   Boling. Kind uncle York, the latest news we hear
Is that the rebels hath consum'd with fire
Our town of Cicester in Gloucestershire;
But whether they be ta'en or slain we hear not.

      Enter NORTHUMBERLAND.

Welcome, my lord, what is the news?   5
   North. First, to thy sacred state wish I all happi-
ness.
The next news is, I have to London sent
The heads of Oxford, Salisbury, Blunt, and Kent.
The manner of their taking may appear
At large discoursed in this paper here.   10
   Boling. We thank thee, gentle Percy, for thy
pains;
And to thy worth will add right worthy gains.

      Enter FITZWATER.

   Fitz. My lord, I have from Oxford sent to London
The heads of Brocas and Sir Bennet Seely,
Two of the dangerous consorted traitors   15
That sought at Oxford thy dire overthrow.
   Boling. Thy pains, Fitzwater, shall not be forgot;
Right noble is thy merit, well I wot.

   Enter PERCY, *and the* BISHOP OF CARLISLE.

   Percy. The grand conspirator, Abbot of West-
minster,
With clog of conscience and sour melancholy   20
Hath yielded up his body to the grave;
But here is Carlisle living, to abide
Thy kingly doom and sentence of his pride.
   Boling. Carlisle, this is your doom:
Choose out some secret place, some reverend room,
More than thou hast, and with it joy thy life.   26
So as thou liv'st in peace, die free from strife;
For though mine enemy thou hast ever been,
High sparks of honour in thee have I seen.

   Enter EXTON, *with* [Attendants *bearing*] *a coffin.*

   Exton. Great King, within this coffin I present

76. yearn'd: made ache.   94. jauncing: prancing.
Sc. vi, 26. joy: enjoy.

Thy buried fear.   Herein all breathless lies   31
The mightiest of thy greatest enemies,
Richard of Bordeaux, by me hither brought.
　Boling. Exton, I thank thee not; for thou hast
　　wrought
A deed of slander with thy fatal hand   35
Upon my head and all this famous land.
　Exton. From your own mouth, my lord, did I
　　this deed.
　Boling. They love not poison that do poison need,
Nor do I thee.   Though I did wish him dead,
I hate the murderer, love him murdered.   40

The guilt of conscience take thou for thy labour,
But neither my good word nor princely favour.
With Cain go wander through [the] shades of night,
And never show thy head by day nor light.
Lords, I protest, my soul is full of woe   45
That blood should sprinkle me to make me grow.
Come, mourn with me for what I do lament,
And put on sullen black incontinent.
I'll make a voyage to the Holy Land,
To wash this blood off from my guilty hand.   50
March sadly after; grace my mournings here
In weeping after this untimely bier.   [*Exeunt.*

he never does

43. [the] Q₂.   Om. Q₁.   48. incontinent: at once.

The First Part of Henry the Fourth

ON FEBRUARY 25, 1598, there was entered in the Stationers' Register *The historye of Henry the iiiith with his battaile of Shrewsburye against Henry Hottspurre of The Northe with the conceipted mirth of Sir John Ffalstoff.* The First Quarto appeared the same year, and others, each printed from the preceding one, followed in 1599, 1603, 1604, 1608, 1613, and 1622. The First Folio was printed from the Fifth Quarto. The basis for the present text is the First Quarto.

There is no evidence of the date of composition before the entry in the Stationers' Register, but the play was obviously written after *Richard II*, judging from the treatment of the character of Bolingbroke, which is clearly developed on the lines laid down in the earlier play. Meres lists *Henry IV* among the Tragedies, and may be presumed to refer to Part I. The date 1597 is generally accepted. The number of editions as well as the frequency of allusion to Falstaff show it to have been the most successful of the histories.

The political part of the plot is founded on Holinshed's *Chronicles* (2d edition, 1587), the speeches, as usually in the English historical plays, being elaborated from the merest hints. The outstanding creation in the serious plot, apart from the Prince, is the opposing figure of Hotspur, whom Shakespeare clearly conceived for the purpose of psychological contrast. In fact, Hotspur was slightly older than the King, and his age is reduced in order to match that of Hal, who is presented as older than his real age, which at the time of the battle of Shrewsbury was only sixteen. Prince Hal does not appear in *Richard II*, but the King speaks of him as "unthrifty," "young wanton and effeminate boy," "as dissolute as desperate," and the associate of ruffians and robbers, though with "sparks of better hope" (V.iii.1–22). This is a slightly darker picture than we get in the present play, for though some of its features are corroborated, Shakespeare is careful to keep the Prince's wildness within limits, however disreputable his associates. Elaborate preparation for his future greatness is made in the soliloquy in the end of I.ii, and this priggish and hypocritical speech has been defended or explained away as a kind of exposition by the author, the soliloquy serving the purpose of a chorus. Be this as it may, the fact that it is uttered by Hal himself leaves an unpleasant impression of insincerity on the reader.

For the comic scenes Shakespeare gathered some names and incidents from *The Famous Victories of Henry V*, a very crude history-comedy printed in 1598, but licensed in 1594, and acted certainly as early as 1588. The robbery at Gadshill, the Tavern in Eastcheap, Hal's relation to his boon companions and to the Lord Chief Justice, his reconciliation to his father, the episode of the crown, and the final abandonment of his tavern friends, are all presented in rude form in *The Famous Victories*. But the method of treatment is such as to offer barely more suggestion than the bald narrative of Holinshed. In the sixth scene a Sir John Oldcastle is introduced who speaks some half-dozen lines, including one referring to Henry IV: "He is a good old man, God take him to his mercy the sooner." This seems to be the germ of Falstaff, who was called Oldcastle when *I Henry IV* was first produced. The historical Sir John Oldcastle was a well-known nobleman of the time of Henry V, who was burned as a Lollard. His descendants were influential in the time of Elizabeth, and it is supposed that the change of name was made under pressure from them. The epilogue to the second part of *Henry IV* contains the explicit statement, "for Oldcastle died a martyr, and this is not the man." The name Falstaff seems to be derived from that of Sir John Fastolfe who appears (unhistorically) as a coward in *I Henry VI*.

The historical action presented occupied little more than a year (June, 1402–July, 1403), and in the play is compressed into a few months. Culminating as it does in the battle of Shrewsbury, the play has more unity and compactness than most of the histories. Its importance in the development of the chronicle history as a dramatic form lies in the great expansion of the comic element. In this, of course, the main element is Falstaff, the greatest of Shakespeare's comic creations, and in the opinion of many the greatest comic figure in literature. It is indeed difficult to find a parallel to the amazing vitality with which he is endowed, to his great gift of language, to his readiness of wit, to his imperturbable good humor, and to the charm which overcomes his grossness. Critical attention has been curiously attracted to the question as to whether he was a coward. The association of his name with that of Sir John Fastolfe, the Prince's upbraiding after the Gadshill affair, and his soliloquy on honor at the battle of Shrewsbury have led to this charge; while he has found valiant defenders who have explained all this away. There is evidence enough that he did not lack courage, but he practiced a discreet economy in its employment.

DESCENT OF THE MORTIMERS

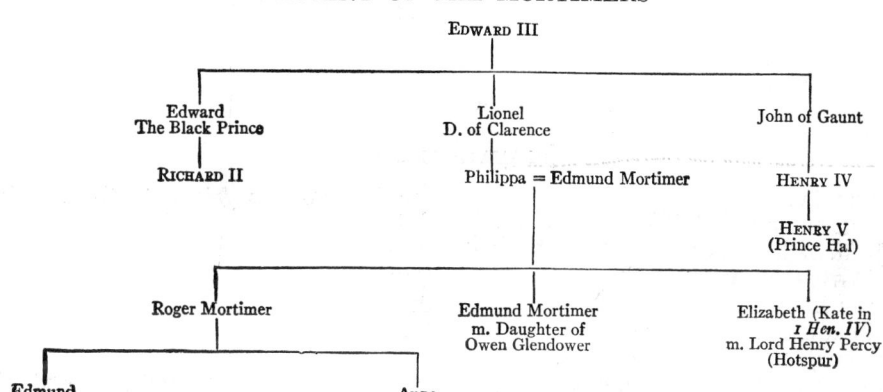

THE FIRST PART OF
HENRY THE FOURTH

[DRAMATIS PERSONÆ

KING HENRY IV.
HENRY, PRINCE OF WALES, } *sons to the King.*
PRINCE JOHN OF LANCASTER,
EARL OF WESTMORELAND.
SIR WALTER BLUNT.
THOMAS PERCY, *earl of Worcester.*
HENRY PERCY, *earl of Northumberland.*
HENRY PERCY, *surnamed* HOTSPUR, *his son.*
EDMUND MORTIMER, *earl of March.*
RICHARD SCROOP, *archbishop of York.*
ARCHIBALD, *earl of Douglas.*
OWEN GLENDOWER.
SIR RICHARD VERNON.
SIR JOHN FALSTAFF.

SIR MICHAEL, *a friend to the archbishop of York.*
POINS.
GADSHILL.
PETO.
BARDOLPH.

LADY PERCY, *wife to Hotspur, and sister to Mortimer.*
LADY MORTIMER, *daughter to Glendower, and wife to Mortimer.*
MISTRESS QUICKLY, *hostess of a tavern in Eastcheap.*

Lords, Officers, Sheriff, Vintner, Chamberlain, Drawers, two Carriers, Travellers, and Attendants.

SCENE: *England and Wales.*]

ACT I

SCENE I. [*London. The palace.*]

Enter KING HENRY, LORD JOHN OF LANCASTER, *the* EARL OF WESTMORELAND, [SIR WALTER BLUNT] *with others.*

King. So shaken as we are, so wan with care,
Find we a time for frighted Peace to pant
And breathe short-winded accents of new broils
To be commenc'd in strands afar remote.
No more the thirsty entrance of this soil   5
Shall daub her lips with her own children's blood;
No more shall trenching war channel her fields,
Nor bruise her flowerets with the armed hoofs
Of hostile paces.   Those opposed eyes,
Which, like the meteors of a troubled heaven,   10
All of one nature, of one substance bred,
Did lately meet in the intestine shock
And furious close of civil butchery,
Shall now, in mutual well-beseeming ranks,
March all one way and be no more oppos'd   15
Against acquaintance, kindred, and allies.
The edge of war, like an ill-sheathed knife,
No more shall cut his master.   Therefore, friends,
As far as to the sepulchre of Christ,
Whose soldier now, under whose blessed cross   20
We are impressed and engag'd to fight,
Forthwith a power of English shall we levy,
Whose arms were moulded in their mother's womb
To chase these pagans in those holy fields
Over whose acres walk'd those blessed feet   25
Which fourteen hundred years ago were nail'd
For our advantage on the bitter cross.
But this our purpose now is twelve month old,
And bootless 'tis to tell you we will go;

Act I, sc. i, 5. **thirsty entrance:** parched mouth.   12. **intestine:** internal.   14. **mutual:** united.   22. **power:** force.

Therefore we meet not now.   Then let me hear   30
Of you, my gentle cousin Westmoreland,
What yesternight our council did decree
In forwarding this dear expedience.

   West. My liege, this haste was hot in question
And many limits of the charge set down   35
But yesternight; when all athwart there came
A post from Wales loaden with heavy news;
Whose worst was, that the noble Mortimer,
Leading the men of Herefordshire to fight
Against the irregular and wild Glendower,   40
Was by the rude hands of that Welshman taken,
A thousand of his people butchered;
Upon whose dead corpse there was such misuse,
Such beastly shameless transformation,
By those Welshwomen done as may not be   45
Without much shame retold or spoken of.

   King. It seems then that the tidings of this broil
Brake off our business for the Holy Land.

   West. This match'd with other did, my gracious
    lord;
For more uneven and unwelcome news   50
Came from the north, and thus it did import:
On Holy-rood day, the gallant Hotspur there,
Young Harry Percy, and brave Archibald,
That ever-valiant and approved Scot,
At Holmedon met,   55
Where they did spend a sad and bloody hour,
As by discharge of their artillery
And shape of likelihood the news was told;
For he that brought them, in the very heat
And pride of their contention did take horse,   60
Uncertain of the issue any way.

   King. Here is a dear, a true industrious friend,
Sir Walter Blunt, new lighted from his horse,
Stain'd with the variation of each soil
Betwixt that Holmedon and this seat of ours;   65
And he hath brought us smooth and welcome news.
The Earl of Douglas is discomfited.
Ten thousand bold Scots, two and twenty knights,
Balk'd in their own blood did Sir Walter see
On Holmedon's plains.   Of prisoners, Hotspur took
Murdoch Earl of Fife and eldest son   71
To beaten Douglas; and the Earl of Athole,
Of Moray, Angus, and Menteith.
And is not this an honourable spoil?
A gallant prize, ha, cousin, is it not?   75

   West. In faith,
It is a conquest for a prince to boast of.

   King. Yea, there thou mak'st me sad, and mak'st
    me sin

In envy that my Lord Northumberland
Should be the father to so blest a son;   80
A son who is the theme of Honour's tongue,
Amongst a grove the very straightest plant,
Who is sweet Fortune's minion and her pride;
Whilst I, by looking on the praise of him,
See riot and dishonour stain the brow   85
Of my young Harry.   O that it could be prov'd
That some night-tripping fairy had exchang'd
In cradle-clothes our children where they lay,
And call'd mine Percy, his Plantagenet!
Then would I have his Harry and he mine.   90
But let him from my thoughts.   What think you,
   coz,
Of this young Percy's pride?   The prisoners
Which he in this adventure hath surpris'd
To his own use he keeps; and sends me word,
I shall have none but Murdoch Earl of Fife.   95

   West. This is his uncle's teaching; this is
   Worcester,
Malevolent to you in all aspects;
Which makes him prune himself and bristle up
The crest of youth against your dignity.

   King. But I have sent for him to answer this;
And for this cause awhile we must neglect   101
Our holy purpose to Jerusalem.
Cousin, on Wednesday next our council we
Will hold at Windsor.   So inform the lords;
But come yourself with speed to us again,   105
For more is to be said and to be done
Than out of anger can be uttered.

   West. I will, my liege.   [*Exeunt.*

SCENE II. [*London.   An apartment of the Prince's.*]

   Enter the PRINCE OF WALES *and* FALSTAFF.

   Fal. Now, Hal, what time of day is it, lad?

   Prince. Thou art so fat-witted, with drinking of
old sack and unbuttoning thee after supper and
sleeping upon benches after noon, that thou hast
forgotten to demand that truly which thou wouldest
truly know.   What a devil hast thou to do   6
with the time of the day?   Unless hours were cups
of sack, and minutes capons, and clocks the tongues
of bawds, and dials the signs of leaping-houses, and
the blessed sun himself a fair hot wench in flame-
coloured taffeta, I see no reason why thou shouldest
be so superfluous to demand the time of the day.   13

   Fal. Indeed, you come near me now, Hal; for
we that take purses go by the moon and the seven
stars, and not by Phœbus, he, "that wand'ring

---

30. **Therefore**: for this.   33. **dear expedience**: expedition close to my heart.   35. **charge**: expense.   36. **athwart**: across
(the plan).   43. **corpse**.   A plural.   Q spells *corpes*.   44. **transformation**: mutilation.   50. **uneven**.   Cf. *smooth*, l. 66.
52. **Holy-rood day**: Sept. 14 (1402).   Mortimer's defeat was on June 22.   69. **Balk'd**: piled up in ridges.   71–72. **eldest...
Douglas**.   In fact Murdoch was son to the Duke of Albany.   76–77. **In faith It is** (Malone).   Q gives these words to King.
83. **minion**: darling.   98. **prune**: preen.
Sc. ii, 3. **sack**: a sweet Spanish wine, sherry.   9. **leaping-houses**: brothels.   15. **seven stars**: Pleiades.

knight so fair." And, I prithee, sweet wag, when thou art a king, as, God save thy Grace, — Majesty I should say, for grace thou wilt have none, — 20

Prince. What, none?

Fal. No, by my troth, not so much as will serve to be prologue to an egg and butter.

Prince. Well, how then? Come, roundly, roundly. 25

Fal. Marry, then, sweet wag, when thou art king, let not us that are squires of the night's body be called thieves of the day's beauty. Let us be Diana's foresters, gentlemen of the shade, minions of the moon; and let men say we be men of good government, being govern'd, as the sea is, by our noble and chaste mistress the moon, under whose countenance we steal. 33

Prince. Thou say'st well, and it holds well too; for the fortune of us that are the moon's men doth ebb and flow like the sea, being governed, as the sea is, by the moon. As, for proof, now: a purse of gold most resolutely snatch'd on 38 Monday night and mostly dissolutely spent on Tuesday morning; got with swearing "Lay by" and spent with crying "Bring in;" now in as low an ebb as the foot of the ladder, and by and by in as high a flow as the ridge of the gallows. 43

Fal. By the Lord, thou say'st true, lad. And is not my hostess of the tavern a most sweet wench?

Prince. As the honey of Hybla, my old lad of the castle. And is not a buff jerkin a most sweet robe of durance? 49

Fal. How now, how now, mad wag! What, in thy quips and thy quiddities, what a plague have I to do with a buff jerkin?

Prince. Why, what a pox have I to do with my hostess of the tavern? 54

Fal. Well, thou hast call'd her to a reckoning many a time and oft.

Prince. Did I ever call for thee to pay thy part?

Fal. No; I'll give thee thy due, thou hast paid all there. 60

Prince. Yea, and elsewhere, so far as my coin would stretch; and where it would not, I have us'd my credit. 63

Fal. Yea, and so us'd it that, were it not here apparent that thou art heir apparent — But, I prithee, sweet wag, shall there be gallows standing in England when thou art king? and resolution thus fobb'd as it is with the rusty curb of old father antic the law? Do not thou, when thou art king, hang a thief. 70

Prince. No; thou shalt.

Fal. Shall I? O rare! By the Lord, I'll be a brave judge.

Prince. Thou judgest false already. I mean, thou shalt have the hanging of the thieves and so become a rare hangman. 76

Fal. Well, Hal, well; and in some sort it jumps with my humour as well as waiting in the court, I can tell you.

Prince. For obtaining of suits? 80

Fal. Yea, for obtaining of suits, whereof the hangman hath no lean wardrobe. 'Sblood, I am as melancholy as a gib cat or a lugg'd bear.

Prince. Or an old lion, or a lover's lute. 84

Fal. Yea, or the drone of a Lincolnshire bagpipe.

Prince. What sayest thou to a hare, or the melancholy of Moor-ditch? 88

Fal. Thou hast the most unsavoury similes and art indeed the most comparative, rascalliest, sweet young prince. But, Hal, I prithee, trouble me no more with vanity. I would to God thou and I knew where a commodity of good names were to be bought. An old lord of the council rated me 94 the other day in the street about you, sir, but I mark'd him not; and yet he talk'd very wisely, but I regarded him not; and yet he talk'd wisely, and in the street too.

Prince. Thou didst well; for wisdom cries out in the streets, and no man regards it. 100

Fal. O, thou hast damnable iteration and art indeed able to corrupt a saint. Thou hast done much harm upon me, Hal; God forgive thee for it! Before I knew thee, Hal, I knew nothing; and now am I, if a man should speak truly, little 105 better than one of the wicked. I must give over this life, and I will give it over. By the Lord, an I do not, I am a villain. I'll be damn'd for never a king's son in Christendom.

Prince. Where shall we take a purse tomorrow, Jack? 111

Fal. 'Zounds, where thou wilt, lad; I'll make one. An I do not, call me villain and baffle me.

Prince. I see a good amendment of life in thee; from praying to purse-taking.

Fal. Why, Hal, 'tis my vocation, Hal. 'Tis no sin for a man to labour in his vocation. 117

Enter POINS.

Poins! Now shall we know if Gadshill have set a match. O, if men were to be saved by merit, what hole in hell were hot enough for him? This

---

25. **roundly:** directly. 47. **Hybla:** a town in Sicily. 49. **durance:** (1) lasting stuff, (2) imprisonment (because worn by sheriff's officers). 51. **quiddities:** hairsplittings. 68. **fobb'd:** cheated. 69. **antic:** clown. 77. **jumps:** agrees. 82. **no... wardrobe.** The hangman inherited the clothes of his victims. 83. **gib cat:** tomcat. **lugg'd:** led. 88. **Moor-ditch:** a swamp just outside the walls. 90. **comparative:** comparison-making. 93. **commodity:** supply. 99–100. **wisdom...regards it.** *Proverbs* I.20–24. Om. Ff. 101. **damnable iteration:** quoting for an evil end. 113. **baffle:** disgrace. 118. **Gadshill.** This confusing name is taken from *The Famous Victories of Henry V.* **set a match:** arranged a meeting.

is the most omnipotent villain that ever cried "Stand!" to a true man.

Prince. Good morrow, Ned.   123

Poins. Good morrow, sweet Hal. What says Monsieur Remorse? What says Sir John Sack and Sugar? Jack! how agrees the devil and thee about thy soul, that thou soldest him on Good Friday last for a cup of Madeira and a cold capon's leg?   129

Prince. Sir John stands to his word, the devil shall have his bargain; for he was never yet a breaker of proverbs. He will give the devil his due.

Poins. Then art thou damn'd for keeping thy word with the devil.   135

Prince. Else he had been damn'd for cozening the devil.

Poins. But, my lads, my lads, to-morrow morning by four o'clock early, at Gadshill! There are pilgrims going to Canterbury with rich offerings, 140 and traders riding to London with fat purses. I have vizards for you all; you have horses for yourselves. Gadshill lies to-night in Rochester. I have bespoke supper to-morrow night in Eastcheap. We may do it as secure as sleep. If you will go, 145 I will stuff your purses full of crowns; if you will not, tarry at home and be hang'd.

Fal. Hear ye, Yedward; if I tarry at home and go not, I'll hang you for going.   150

Poins. You will, chops?

Fal. Hal, wilt thou make one?

Prince. Who, I rob? I a thief? Not I, by my faith.   154

Fal. There's neither honesty, manhood, nor good fellowship in thee, nor thou cam'st not of the blood royal, if thou dar'st not stand for ten shillings.

Prince. Well, then, once in my days I'll be a madcap.   160

Fal. Why, that's well said.

Prince. Well, come what will, I'll tarry at home.

Fal. By the lord, I'll be a traitor then, when thou art king.   165

Prince. I care not.

Poins. Sir John, I prithee, leave the Prince and me alone. I will lay him down such reasons for this adventure that he shall go.   169

Fal. Well, God give thee the spirit of persuasion and him the ears of profiting, that what thou speakest may move and what he hears may be believed, that the true prince may, for recreation sake, prove a false thief; for the poor abuses of the time want countenance. Farewell; you shall find me in Eastcheap.   176

Prince. Farewell, [thou] latter spring! Farewell, All-hallown summer!   [*Exit Falstaff*]

Poins. Now, my good sweet honey lord, ride with us to-morrow; I have a jest to execute that 180 I cannot manage alone. Falstaff [Bardolph, Peto,] and Gadshill shall rob those men that we have already waylaid; yourself and I will not be there; and when they have the booty, if you and I do not rob them, cut this head off from my shoulders.

Prince. How shall we part with them in setting forth?   188

Poins. Why, we will set forth before or after them and appoint them a place of meeting, wherein it is at our pleasure to fail, and then will they adventure upon the exploit themselves; which they shall have no sooner achieved, but we'll set upon them.   194

Prince. Yea, but 'tis like that they will know us by our horses, by our habits, and by every other appointment, to be ourselves.   197

Poins. Tut! our horses they shall not see — I'll tie them in the wood; our vizards we will change after we leave them; and, sirrah, I have cases of buckram for the nonce, to immask our noted outward garments.   202

Prince. Yea, but I doubt they will be too hard for us.

Poins. Well, for two of them, I know them to be as true-bred cowards as ever turn'd back; and for the third, if he fight longer than he sees 207 reason, I'll forswear arms. The virtue of this jest will be the incomprehensible lies that this same fat rogue will tell us when we meet at supper; how thirty, at least, he fought with; what wards, what blows, what extremities he endured; and in the reproof of this lies the jest.   213

Prince. Well, I'll go with thee. Provide us all things necessary and meet me to-morrow night in Eastcheap; there I'll sup. Farewell.

Poins. Farewell, my lord.   [*Exit.*

Prince. I know you all, and will a while uphold The unyok'd humour of your idleness.
Yet herein will I imitate the sun,   220
Who doth permit the base contagious clouds
To smother up his beauty from the world,
That when he please again to be himself
Being wanted, he may be more wond'red at
By breaking through the foul and ugly mists   225
Of vapours that did seem to strangle him.
If all the year were playing holidays,
To sport would be as tedious as to work;
But when they seldom come, they wish'd for come,
And nothing pleaseth but rare accidents.   230

So, when this loose behaviour I throw off
And pay the debt I never promised,
By how much better than my word I am,
By so much shall I falsify men's hopes;
And like bright metal on a sullen ground, 235
My reformation, glitt'ring o'er my fault,
Shall show more goodly and attract more eyes
Than that which hath no foil to set it off.
I'll so offend, to make offence a skill,
Redeeming time when men think least I will. 240
[Exit.

SCENE III. [London. The palace.]

Enter the KING, NORTHUMBERLAND, WORCESTER,
　HOTSPUR, SIR WALTER BLUNT, with others.

　King. My blood hath been too cold and tem-
　　perate,
Unapt to stir at these indignities,
And you have found me; for accordingly
You tread upon my patience. But be sure
I will from henceforth rather be myself, 5
Mighty and to be fear'd, than my condition;
Which hath been smooth as oil, soft as young down,
And therefore lost that title of respect
Which the proud soul ne'er pays but to the proud.
　Wor. Our house, my sovereign liege, little de-
　　serves 10
The scourge of greatness to be us'd on it;
And that same greatness too which our own hands
Have holp to make so portly.
　North. My lord, —
　King. Worcester, get thee gone; for I do see 15
Danger and disobedience in thine eye.
O, sir, your presence is too bold and peremptory,
And majesty might never yet endure
The moody frontier of a servant brow. 19
You have good leave to leave us. When we need
Your use and counsel, we shall send for you.
[Exit Worcester.
You were about to speak.
　North. 　　　　　Yea, my good lord.
Those prisoners in your Highness' name demanded,
Which Harry Percy here at Holmedon took,
Were, as he says, not with such strength denied 25
As is delivered to your Majesty.
Either envy, therefore, or misprision
Is guilty of this fault, and not my son.
　Hot. My liege, I did deny no prisoners.
But I remember, when the fight was done, 30
When I was dry with rage and extreme toil,

Breathless and faint, leaning upon my sword,
Came there a certain lord, neat, trimly dress'd,
Fresh as a bridegroom; and his chin new reap'd
Show'd like a stubble-land at harvest-home. 35
He was perfumed like a milliner;
And 'twixt his finger and his thumb he held
A pouncet-box, which ever and anon
He gave his nose and took't away again;
Who therewith angry, when it next came there, 40
Took it in snuff; and still he smil'd and talk'd,
And as the soldiers bore dead bodies by,
He call'd them untaught knaves, unmannerly,
To bring a slovenly unhandsome corse
Betwixt the wind and his nobility. 45
With many holiday and lady terms
He question'd me; amongst the rest, demanded
My prisoners in your Majesty's behalf.
I then, all smarting with my wounds being cold,
To be so pest'red with a popinjay, 50
Out of my grief and my impatience
Answer'd neglectingly — I know not what,
He should, or he should not; for he made me mad
To see him shine so brisk and smell so sweet
And talk so like a waiting-gentlewoman 55
Of guns and drums and wounds, — God save the
　mark! —
And telling me the sovereign'st thing on earth
Was parmaceti for an inward bruise;
And that it was great pity, so it was,
This villanous salt-petre should be digg'd 60
Out of the bowels of the harmless earth,
Which many a good tall fellow had destroy'd
So cowardly; and but for these vile guns,
He would himself have been a soldier.
This bald unjointed chat of his, my lord, 65
I answered indirectly, as I said;
And I beseech you, let not his report
Come current for an accusation
Betwixt my love and your high Majesty.
　Blunt. The circumstance considered, good my
　　lord, 70
Whate'er Lord Harry Percy then had said
To such a person and in such a place,
At such a time, with all the rest retold,
May reasonably die and never rise
To do him wrong or any way impeach 75
What then he said, so he unsay it now.
　King. Why, yet he doth deny his prisoners
But with proviso and exception
That we at our own charge shall ransom straight
His brother-in-law, the foolish Mortimer; 80

235. sullen: dark. 238. foil: leaf of metal under a gem.
Sc. iii, 6. condition: natural bent. 19. frontier: forehead. The word meant also outwork, fortification. 27. misprision: misunderstanding. 38. pouncet-box: perfume box. 40. Who: which (nose). 41. Took...snuff: was offended. 50. popinjay: parrot. 51. grief: pain. 58. parmaceti: spermaceti, sperm of the whale. 62. tall: brave. 66. indirectly: vaguely. 68. Come current: be accepted as valid. 75. impeach: call in question. 78. But...exception: unless on the condition.

Who, on my soul, hath wilfully betray'd
The lives of those that he did lead to fight
Against that great magician, damn'd Glendower,
Whose daughter, as we hear, the Earl of March
Hath lately married. Shall our coffers, then, 85
Be emptied to redeem a traitor home?
Shall we buy treason, and indent with fears,
When they have lost and forfeited themselves?
No, on the barren mountains let him starve;
For I shall never hold that man my friend 90
Whose tongue shall ask me for one penny cost
To ransom home revolted Mortimer.
  Hot. Revolted Mortimer!
He never did fall off, my sovereign liege,
But by the chance of war. To prove that true 95
Needs no more but one tongue for all those wounds,
Those mouthed wounds, which valiantly he took,
When on the gentle Severn's sedgy bank,
In single opposition, hand to hand,
He did confound the best part of an hour 100
In changing hardiment with great Glendower.
Three times they breath'd and three times did they
    drink,
Upon agreement, of swift Severn's flood;
Who then, affrighted with their bloody looks,
Ran fearfully among the trembling reeds, 105
And hid his crisp head in the hollow bank
Bloodstained with these valiant combatants.
Never did [base] and rotten policy
Colour her working with such deadly wounds,
Nor never could the noble Mortimer 110
Receive so many, and all willingly.
Then let not him be slandered with revolt.
  King. Thou dost belie him, Percy, thou dost
    belie him;
He never did encounter with Glendower.
I tell thee, 115
He durst as well have met the devil alone
As Owen Glendower for an enemy.
Art thou not asham'd? But, sirrah, henceforth
Let me not hear you speak of Mortimer.
Send me your prisoners with the speediest means,
Or you shall hear in such a kind from me 121
As will displease you. My Lord Northumberland,
We license your departure with your son.
Send us your prisoners, or you'll hear of it.
  [*Exeunt King Henry [Blunt, and train].*
  Hot. An if the devil come and roar for them, 125
I will not send them. I will after straight
And tell him so; for I will ease my heart,
Albeit I make a hazard of my head.
  North. What, drunk with choler? Stay and
    pause a while.
Here comes your uncle.

  Re-enter WORCESTER.

  Hot.   Speak of Mortimer! 130
'Zounds, I will speak of him; and let my soul
Want mercy if I do not join with him.
Yea, on his part I'll empty all these veins,
And shed my dear blood drop by drop in the dust,
But I will lift the down-trod Mortimer 135
As high in the air as this unthankful king,
As this ingrate and cank'red Bolingbroke.
  North. Brother, the King hath made your
    nephew mad.
  Wor. Who struck this heat up after I was gone?
  Hot. He will, forsooth, have all my prisoners; 140
And when I urg'd the ransom once again
Of my wife's brother, then his cheek look'd pale,
And on my face he turn'd an eye of death,
Trembling even at the name of Mortimer.
  Wor. I cannot blame him. Was not he pro-
    claim'd 145
By Richard, that dead is, the next of blood?
  North. He was; I heard the proclamation.
And then it was when the unhappy king, —
Whose wrongs in us God pardon! — did set forth
Upon his Irish expedition; 150
From whence he intercepted did return
To be depos'd and shortly murdered.
  Wor. And for whose death we in the world's wide
    mouth
Live scandaliz'd and foully spoken of.
  Hot. But, soft, I pray you; did King Richard then
Proclaim my brother Edmund Mortimer 156
Heir to the crown?
  North.   He did; myself did hear it.
  Hot. Nay, then I cannot blame his cousin king,
That wish'd him on the barren mountains starve.
But shall it be that you, that set the crown 160
Upon the head of this forgetful man
And for his sake wear the detested blot
Of murderous subornation, shall it be,
That you a world of curses undergo,
Being the agents or base second means, 165
The cords, the ladder, or the hangman rather?
O, pardon me that I descend so low
To show the line and the predicament
Wherein you range under this subtle king!
Shall it for shame be spoken in these days, 170
Or fill up chronicles in time to come,
That men of your nobility and power
Did gage them both in an unjust behalf,
As both of you — God pardon it! — have done,
To put down Richard, that sweet lovely rose, 175
And plant this thorn, this canker, Bolingbroke?
And shall it in more shame be further spoken,
That you are fool'd, discarded, and shook off

---

87. **indent:** make a contract. 100. **confound:** spend. 101. **hardiment:** valiant blows. 106. **crisp:** rippled. 108. **[base]** Ff. *bare* Qq. 137. **cank'red:** malignant. 163. **subornation:** persuading to commit a crime. 168. **predicament:** situation. 173. **gage:** engage.

By him for whom these shames ye underwent?
No; yet time serves wherein you may redeem   180
Your banish'd honours and restore yourselves
Into the good thoughts of the world again,
Revenge the jeering and disdain'd contempt
Of this proud king, who studies day and night
To answer all the debt he owes to you   185
Even with the bloody payment of your deaths.
Therefore, I say, —
   Wor.   Peace, cousin, say no more;
And now I will unclasp a secret book,
And to your quick-conceiving discontents
I'll read you matter deep and dangerous,   190
As full of peril and adventurous spirit
As to o'er-walk a current roaring loud
On the unsteadfast footing of a spear.
   Hot. If he fall in, good night! or sink or swim.
Send Danger from the east unto the west,   195
So Honour cross it from the north to south,
And let them grapple.   O, the blood more stirs
To rouse a lion than to start a hare!
   North. Imagination of some great exploit
Drives him beyond the bounds of patience.   200
   [*Hot.*] By heaven, methinks it were an easy leap,
To pluck bright Honour from the pale-fac'd moon,
Or dive into the bottom of the deep,
Where fathom-line could never touch the ground
And pluck up drowned Honour by the locks;   205
So he that doth redeem her thence might wear
Without corrival all her dignities.
But out upon this half-fac'd fellowship!
   Wor. He apprehends a world of figures here,
But not the form of what he should attend.   210
Good cousin, give me audience for a while.
   Hot. I cry you mercy.
   Wor.   Those same noble Scots
That are your prisoners, —
   Hot.   I'll keep them all!
By God, he shall not have a Scot of them;
No, if a Scot would save his soul, he shall not!   215
I'll keep them, by this hand.
   Wor.   You start away
And lend no ear unto my purposes.
Those prisoners you shall keep.
   Hot.   Nay, I will; that's flat.
He said he would not ransom Mortimer;
Forbade my tongue to speak of Mortimer;   220
But I will find him when he lies asleep
And in his ear I'll holla "Mortimer!"
Nay,
I'll have a starling shall be taught to speak
Nothing but "Mortimer," and give it him   225
To keep his anger still in motion.
   Wor. Hear you, cousin; a word.

   Hot. All studies here I solemnly defy,
Save how to gall and pinch this Bolingbroke;
And that same sword-and-buckler Prince of Wales,
But that I think his father loves him not   231
And would be glad he met with some mischance,
I would have him poison'd with a pot of ale.
   Wor. Farewell, kinsman!   I'll talk to you
When you are better temper'd to attend.   235
   North. Why, what a wasp-stung and impatient
      fool
Art thou to break into this woman's mood,
Tying thine ear to no tongue but thine own!
   Hot. Why, look you, I am whipp'd and scourg'd
      with rods,
Nettled and stung with pismires, when I hear   240
Of this vile politician, Bolingbroke.
In Richard's time, — what do you call the place? —
A plague upon it, it is in Gloucestershire;
'Twas where the madcap duke his uncle kept,
His uncle York; where I first bow'd my knee   245
Unto this king of smiles, this Bolingbroke, —
'Sblood! —
When you and he came back from Ravenspurgh —
   North. At Berkeley castle.
   Hot. You say true.   250
Why, what a candy deal of courtesy
This fawning greyhound then did proffer me!
Look, "when his infant fortune came to age,"
And "gentle Harry Percy," and "kind cousin;"
O, the devil take such cozeners! — God forgive me!
Good uncle, tell your tale; [for] I have done.   256
   Wor. Nay, if you have not, to't again;
We'll stay your leisure.
   Hot.   I have done, i' faith.
   Wor. Then once more to your Scottish prisoners.
Deliver them up without their ransom straight,   260
And make the Douglas' son your only mean
For powers in Scotland; which, for divers reasons
Which I shall send you written, be assur'd,
Will easily be granted.   You, my lord,
                 [*To Northumberland.*
Your son in Scotland being thus employ'd,   265
Shall secretly into the bosom creep
Of that same noble prelate, well belov'd,
The Archbishop.
   Hot. Of York, is it not?
   Wor. True; who bears hard   270
His brother's death at Bristol, the Lord Scroop.
I speak not this in estimation,
As what I think might be, but what I know
Is ruminated, plotted, and set down,
And only stays but to behold the face   275
Of that occasion that shall bring it on.
   Hot. I smell it.   Upon my life, it will do well.

183. disdain'd: full of disdain.   201. [Hot.] Q₅.   Om. Q₁₋₄.   208. half-fac'd: half-hearted.   228. defy: renounce.   240.
pismires: ants.   244. kept: lived.   251. candy: sugary.   256. [for] F. Om. Qq.   261. mean: agent.   272. estimation:
inference.

North. Before the game's afoot, thou still let'st
    slip.
Hot. Why, it cannot choose but be a noble plot.
And then the power of Scotland and of York,   280
To join with Mortimer, ha?
Wor.   And so they shall.
Hot. In faith, it is exceedingly well aim'd.
Wor. And 'tis no little reason bids us speed,
To save our heads by raising of a head;
For, bear ourselves as even as we can,   285
The King will always think him in our debt,
And think we think ourselves unsatisfied,
Till he hath found a time to pay us home.
And see already how he doth begin
To make us strangers to his looks of love.   290
Hot. He does, he does. We'll be reveng'd on him.
Wor. Cousin, farewell! No further go in this
Than I by letters shall direct your course.
When time is ripe, which will be suddenly,
I'll steal to Glendower and Lord Mortimer;   295
Where you and Douglas and our powers at once,
As I will fashion it, shall happily meet
To bear our fortunes in our own strong arms,
Which now we hold at much uncertainty.
North. Farewell, good brother! We shall thrive,
    I trust.   300
Hot. Uncle, adieu! O, let the hours be short
Till fields and blows and groans applaud our sport!
                      [*Exeunt.*

ACT II

Scene I. [*Rochester. An inn yard.*]

Enter a Carrier *with a lantern in his hand.*

1. Car. Heigh-ho! an it be not four by the day,
I'll be hang'd. Charles' wain is over the new
chimney, and yet our horse not pack'd. What,
ostler!   4
Ost. [*Within.*] Anon, anon.
1. Car. I prithee, Tom, beat Cut's saddle, put a
few flocks in the point. Poor jade, is wrung in
the withers out of all cess.   8

Enter another Carrier.

2. Car. Peas and beans are as dank here as a
dog, and that is the next way to give poor jades
the bots. This house is turned upside down since
Robin Ostler died.
1. Car. Poor fellow, never joy'd since the price
of oats rose; it was the death of him.   14
2. Car. I think this be the most villanous house
in all London road for fleas. I am stung like a
tench.

1. Car. Like a tench! by the mass, there is ne'er
a king christen could be better bit than I have
been since the first cock.   20
2. Car. Why, they will allow us ne'er a jordan,
and then we leak in your chimney; and your
chamber-lye breeds fleas like a loach.
1. Car. What, ostler! come away and be hang'd!
Come away.   25
2. Car. I have a gammon of bacon and two razes
of ginger, to be delivered as far as Charing-
cross.   28
1. Car. God's body! the turkeys in my pannier
are quite starved. What, ostler! A plague on
thee! hast thou never an eye in thy head? Canst
not hear? An't were not as good deed as drink,
to break the pate on thee, I am a very villain.
Come, and be hang'd! Hast no faith in thee?   35

Enter Gadshill.

Gads. Good morrow, carriers. What's o'clock?
[*1.*] *Car.* I think it be two o'clock.
Gads. I prithee, lend me thy lantern, to see my
gelding in the stable.
1. Car. Nay, by God, soft; I know a trick worth
two of that, i' faith.
Gads. I pray thee, lend me thine.
2. Car. Ay, when? canst tell? Lend me thy
lantern, quoth he? Marry, I'll see thee hang'd first.
Gads. Sirrah carrier, what time do you mean to
come to London?   46
2. Car. Time enough to go to bed with a candle,
I warrant thee. Come, neighbour Mugs, we'll
call up the gentlemen. They will along with
company, for they have great charge.   51
                  [*Exeunt Carriers*

Enter Chamberlain.

Gads. What, ho! chamberlain!
Cham. At hand, quoth pick-purse.
Gads. That's even as fair as — at hand, quoth
the chamberlain; for thou variest no more from
picking of purses than giving direction doth from
labouring; thou lay'st the plot how.   57
Cham. Good morrow, Master Gadshill. It holds
current that I told you yesternight: there's a
franklin in the Wild of Kent hath brought three
hundred marks with him in gold. I heard him
tell it to one of his company last night at supper;
a kind of auditor; one that hath abundance of
charge too, God knows what. They are up already, and call for eggs and butter. They will
away presently.   66
Gads. Sirrah, if they meet not with Saint
Nicholas' clerks, I'll give thee this neck.

Act II, sc. i, 2. **Charles' wain:** the Great Bear. 5. **Anon:** at once. 7. **flocks:** tufts of wool. 8. **cess:** measure. 11. **bots:** worms. 17. **tench:** a spotted fish. 23. **chamber-lye:** urine. **loach:** fish. 26. **razes:** bundles of roots. 40. **soft:** go slow. 51. **charge:** valuables. 60. **Wild:** Weald, forest. 61. **marks:** 13s.4d. 67-68. **Saint Nicholas' clerks:** highwaymen.

Cham. No, I'll none of it. I pray thee, keep that for the hangman; for I know thou worshipp'st Saint Nicholas as truly as a man of falsehood may.   72

Gads. What talkest thou to me of the hangman? If I hang, I'll make a fat pair of gallows; for if I hang, old Sir John hangs with me, and thou know'st he is no starveling. Tut! there are other Troians that thou dream'st not of, the which for sport sake are content to do the profession 78 some grace, that would, if matters should be look'd into, for their own credit sake, make all whole. I am joined with no foot land-rakers, no long-staff sixpenny strikers, none of these mad mustachio purple-hued malt-worms; but with nobility and tranquillity, burgomasters and great oneyers; such as can hold in, such as will strike sooner than 85 speak, and speak sooner than drink, and drink sooner than pray; and yet, 'zounds, I lie; for they pray continually to their saint, the commonwealth; or rather, not pray to her, but prey on her, for they ride up and down on her and make her their boots.   91

Cham. What, the commonwealth their boots? Will she hold out water in foul way?

Gads. She will, she will; justice hath liquor'd her. We steal as in a castle, cock-sure; we have the receipt of fern-seed, we walk invisible. 96

Cham. Nay, by my faith, I think you are more beholding to the night than to fern-seed for your walking invisible.

Gads. Give me thy hand. Thou shalt have a share in our purchase, as I am a true man.   101

Cham. Nay, rather let me have it as you are a false thief.

Gads. Go to; *homo* is a common name to all men. Bid the ostler bring my gelding out of the stable. Farewell, you muddy knave.   [*Exeunt.* 106

SCENE II. [*The highway, near Gadshill.*]

Enter PRINCE HENRY *and* POINS.

Poins. Come, shelter, shelter! I have remov'd Falstaff's horse, and he frets like a gumm'd velvet.
                                           [*They step back.*]

Prince. Stand close.

Enter FALSTAFF.

Fal. Poins! Poins, and be hang'd! Poins! 4

Prince. [*Coming forward.*] Peace, ye fat-kidney'd rascal! what a brawling dost thou keep!

Fal. Where's Poins, Hal?

Prince. He is walk'd up to the top of the hill; I'll go seek him.   [*Withdraws.*] 9

Fal. I am accurs'd to rob in that thief's company. The rascal hath removed my horse, and tied him I know not where. If I travel but four foot by the squire further afoot, I shall break my wind. Well, I doubt not but to die a fair death for all this, if I scape hanging for killing that 15 rogue. I have forsworn his company hourly any time this two and twenty years, and yet I am bewitch'd with the rogue's company. If the rascal have not given me medicines to make me love him, I'll be hang'd. It could not be else; I have 20 drunk medicines. Poins! Hal! a plague upon you both! Bardolph! Peto! I'll starve ere I'll rob a foot further. An 'twere not as good a deed as drink, to turn true man and to leave these rogues, I am the veriest varlet that ever chewed 25 with a tooth. Eight yards of uneven ground is threescore and ten miles afoot with me; and the stony-hearted villains know it well enough. A plague upon it when thieves cannot be true one to another! (*They whistle.*) Whew! A 30 plague upon you all! Give me my horse, you rogues; give me my horse, and be hang'd!

Prince. [*Coming forward.*] Peace, ye fat-guts! lie down. Lay thine ear close to the ground and list if thou canst hear the tread of travellers. 35

Fal. Have you any levers to lift me up again, being down? 'Sblood, I'll not bear mine own flesh so far afoot again for all the coin in thy father's exchequer. What a plague mean ye to colt me thus?   40

Prince. Thou liest; thou art not colted, thou art uncolted.

Fal. I prithee, good Prince Hal, help me to my horse, good king's son.

Prince. Out, ye rogue! shall I be your ostler? 45

Fal. Hang thyself in thine own heir-apparent garters! If I be ta'en, I'll peach for this. An I have not ballads made on you all and sung to filthy tunes, let a cup of sack be my poison. When a jest is so forward, and afoot too! I hate it. 50

Enter GADSHILL [BARDOLPH, *and* PETO *with him*].

Gads. Stand.

Fal. So I do, against my will.

Poins. [*Coming forward.*] O, 'tis our setter; I know his voice. Bardolph, what news?   54

Bard. Case ye, case ye; on with your vizards. There's money of the King's coming down the hill; 'tis going to the King's exchequer.

---

77. **Troians:** fellows.   81. **foot land-rakers:** footpads.   82. **long-staff … strikers:** petty thieves.   83. **mustachio … malt-worms:** topers with mustaches dyed with ale.   84. **oneyers:** ones.   91. **boots.** With a pun on *booty*.   93. **foul:** muddy.   94. **liquor'd:** waterproofed.   101. **purchase:** booty.

Sc. ii, 2. **gumm'd:** stiffened with gum.   13. **squire:** square, foot-rule.   15. **for:** in spite of.   39. **colt:** fool.   53. **setter:** arranger (Gadshill).

Fal. You lie, ye rogue; 'tis going to the King's tavern.

Gads. There's enough to make us all.   60

Fal. To be hang'd.

Prince. Sirs, you four shall front them in the narrow lane; Ned Poins and I will walk lower. If they scape from your encounter, then they light on us.   65

Peto. How many be there of them?

Gads. Some eight or ten.

Fal. 'Zounds, will they not rob us?

Prince. What, a coward, Sir John Paunch?

Fal. Indeed, I am not John of Gaunt, your grandfather; but yet no coward, Hal.   71

Prince. Well, we leave that to the proof.

Poins. Sirrah Jack, thy horse stands behind the hedge; when thou need'st him, there thou shalt find him. Farewell, and stand fast.   75

Fal. Now cannot I strike him, if I should be hang'd.

Prince. [*Aside.*] Ned, where are our disguises.

Poins. [*Aside.*] Here, hard by. Stand close.

[*Exeunt Prince and Poins.*]

Fal. Now, my masters, happy man be his dole, say I. Every man to his business.   81

Enter the TRAVELLERS.

[*1.*] *Trav.* Come, neighbour; the boy shall lead our horses down the hill. We'll walk afoot a while, and ease our legs.

Thieves. Stand!

Travellers. Jesus bless us!   86

Fal. Strike; down with them! Cut the villains' throats! Ah! whoreson caterpillars! bacon-fed knaves! they hate us youth. Down with them! Fleece them!

Travellers. O, we are undone, both we and ours for ever!   92

Fal. Hang ye, gorbellied knaves, are ye undone? No, ye fat chuffs; I would your store were here! On, bacons, on! What, ye knaves! young men must live. You are grandjurors, are ye? We'll jure ye, faith.   97

[*Here they rob them and bind them. Exeunt.*]

Re-enter PRINCE HENRY *and* POINS [*in buckram*].

Prince. The thieves have bound the true men. Now, could thou and I rob the thieves and go merrily to London, it would be argument for a week, laughter for a month, and a good jest for ever.

Poins. Stand close; I hear them coming.   103

Enter the Thieves again.

Fal. Come, my masters, let us share, and then

to horse before day. An the Prince and Poins be not two arrant cowards, there's no equity stirring. There's no more valour in that Poins than in a wild-duck.   108

Prince. Your money!

Poins. Villains!

[*As they are sharing, the Prince and Poins set upon them; they all run away; and Falstaff, after a blow or two, runs away too, leaving the booty behind them.*]

Prince. Got with much ease. Now merrily to horse.
The thieves are all scatt'red and possess'd with fear
So strongly that they dare not meet each other;
Each takes his fellow for an officer.
Away, good Ned. Falstaff sweats to death,   115
And lards the lean earth as he walks along.
Were't not for laughing, I should pity him.

Poins. How the [fat] rogue roar'd!   [*Exeunt.*

SCENE III. [*Warkworth Castle.*]

Enter HOTSPUR, *solus, reading a letter.*

Hot. "But, for mine own part, my lord, I could be well contented to be there, in respect of the love I bear your house." He could be contented: why is he not, then? In respect of the love he bears our house: he shows in this, he loves his   5
own barn better than he loves our house. Let me see some more. "The purpose you undertake is dangerous;" — why, that's certain. 'Tis dangerous to take a cold, to sleep, to drink; but I tell you, my lord fool, out of this nettle, danger, we   10
pluck this flower, safety. "The purpose you undertake is dangerous; the friends you have named uncertain; the time itself unsorted; and your whole plot too light for the counterpoise of so great an opposition." Say you so, say you so? I say   15
unto you again, you are a shallow, cowardly hind, and you lie. What a lack-brain is this! By the Lord, our plot is a good plot as ever was laid; our friends true and constant: a good plot, good friends, and full of expectation; an excellent plot, very good friends. What a frosty-   20
spirited rogue is this! Why, my Lord of York commends the plot and the general course of the action. 'Zounds, an I were now by this rascal, I could brain him with his lady's fan. Is there not my father, my uncle, and myself? Lord   25
Edmund Mortimer, my Lord of York, and Owen Glendower? Is there not besides the Douglas? Have I not all their letters to meet me in arms by the ninth of the next month? and are they

not some of them set forward already? What 30
a pagan rascal is this! an infidel! Ha! you shall
see now in very sincerity of fear and cold heart,
will he to the King and lay open all our proceedings. O, I could divide myself and go to buffets,
for moving such a dish of skim-milk with so 35
honourable an action! Hang him! let him tell
the King; we are prepared. I will set forward
to-night.

Enter LADY PERCY.

How now, Kate! I must leave you within these
two hours.
 Lady. O, my good lord, why are you thus alone?
For what offence have I this fortnight been 41
A banish'd woman from my Harry's bed?
Tell me, sweet lord, what is't that takes from thee
Thy stomach, pleasure, and thy golden sleep?
Why dost thou bend thine eyes upon the earth, 45
And start so often when thou sit'st alone?
Why hast thou lost the fresh blood in thy cheeks,
And given my treasures and my rights of thee
To thick-ey'd musing and curst melancholy?
In thy faint slumbers I by thee have watch'd, 50
And heard thee murmur tales of iron wars;
Speak terms of manage to thy bounding steed;
Cry "Courage! to the field!" And thou hast
 talk'd
Of sallies and retires, of trenches, tents,
Of palisadoes, frontiers, parapets, 55
Of basilisks, of cannon, culverin,
Of prisoners' ransom, and of soldiers slain,
And all the currents of a heady fight.
Thy spirit within thee hath been so at war
And thus hath so bestirr'd thee in thy sleep, 60
That beads of sweat have stood upon thy brow,
Like bubbles in a late-disturbed stream;
And in thy face strange motions have appear'd,
Such as we see when men restrain their breath
On some great sudden hest. O, what portents are
 these? 65
Some heavy business hath my lord in hand,
And I must know it, else he loves me not.
 Hot. What, ho!

[*Enter* SERVANT.]

    Is Gilliams with the packet gone?
 Serv. He is, my lord, an hour ago.
 Hot. Hath Butler brought those horses from the
 sheriff? 70
 Serv. One horse, my lord, he brought even
 now.
 Hot. What horse? Roan, a crop-ear, is it not?

 Serv. It is, my lord.
 Hot.   That roan shall be my throne.
Well, I will back him straight. O *Esperance!*
Bid Butler lead him forth into the park. 75
          [*Exit Servant.*]
 Lady. But hear you, my lord.
 Hot. What say'st thou, my lady?
 Lady. What is it carries you away?
 Hot. Why, my horse, my love, my horse.
 Lady. Out, you mad-headed ape! 80
A weasel hath not such a deal of spleen
As you are toss'd with. In faith,
I'll know your business, Harry, that I will.
I fear my brother Mortimer doth stir
About his title, and hath sent for you 85
To line his enterprise; but if you go, —
 Hot. So far afoot, I shall be weary, love.
 Lady. Come, come, you paraquito, answer me
Directly unto this question that I ask.
In faith, I'll break thy little finger, Harry, 90
An if thou wilt not tell me all things true.
 Hot. Away.
Away, you trifler! Love! I love thee not,
I care not for thee, Kate. This is no world
To play with mammets and to tilt with lips. 95
We must have bloody noses and crack'd crowns,
And pass them current too. God's me, my
 horse!
What say'st thou, Kate? What would'st thou
 have with me?
 Lady. Do you not love me? Do you not, indeed?
Well, do not then; for since you love me not, 100
I will not love myself. Do you not love me?
Nay, tell me if you speak in jest or no.
 Hot. Come, wilt thou see me ride?
And when I am o' horseback, I will swear
I love thee infinitely. But hark you, Kate; 105
I must not have you henceforth question me
Whither I go, nor reason whereabout.
Whither I must, I must; and, to conclude,
This evening must I leave you, gentle Kate.
I know you wise; but yet no farther wise 110
Than Harry Percy's wife. Constant you are,
But yet a woman; and for secrecy,
No lady closer; for I well believe
Thou wilt not utter what thou dost not know;
And so far will I trust thee, gentle Kate. 115
 Lady. How! so far?
 Hot. Not an inch further. But hark you, Kate:
Whither I go, thither shall you go too;
To-day will I set forth, to-morrow you.
Will this content you, Kate?
 Lady.   It must of force. 120
          [*Exeunt.*

44. **stomach:** appetite. 52. **manage:** horse-training. 55. **frontiers:** outworks. 56. **basilisks:** brass cannon. **culverin:** long cannon. 65. **hest:** demand. 74. *Esperance:* Hope; the Percy motto. 86. **line:** support. 95. **mammets:** dolls. 107. **whereabout:** about what.

SCENE IV. [*The Boar's-Head Tavern, Eastcheap.*]

Enter the PRINCE *and* POINS.

Prince. Ned, prithee, come out of that fat room, and lend me thy hand to laugh a little.

Poins. Where hast been, Hal?

Prince. With three or four loggerheads amongst three or four score hogsheads. I have sounded 5
the very base-string of humility. Sirrah, I am sworn brother to a leash of drawers; and can call them all by their christen names, as Tom, Dick, and Francis. They take it already upon their salvation, that though I be but Prince of Wales, 10
yet I am the king of courtesy; and tell me flatly I am no proud Jack, like Falstaff, but a Corinthian, a lad of mettle, a good boy, (by the Lord, so they call me,) and when I am King of England, I shall command all the good lads in Eastcheap. 15
They call drinking deep, dyeing scarlet; and when you breathe in your watering, they cry "hem!" and bid you play it off. To conclude, I am so good a proficient in one quarter of an hour, that I can drink with any tinker in his own language 20
during my life. I tell thee, Ned, thou hast lost much honour, that thou wert not with me in this action. But, sweet Ned,— to sweeten which name of Ned, I give thee this pennyworth of sugar, clapp'd even now into my hand by an under- 25
skinker, one that never spake other English in his life than "Eight shillings and sixpence," and "You are welcome," with this shrill addition, "Anon, anon, sir! Score a pint of bastard in the Half-moon," or so. But, Ned, to drive away the 30
time till Falstaff come, I prithee, do thou stand in some by-room, while I question my puny drawer to what end he gave me the sugar; and do thou never leave calling "Francis," that his tale to me may be nothing but "Anon." Step aside, 35
and I'll show thee a [precedent].

Poins. Francis!

Prince. Thou art perfect.

Poins. Francis!   [*Exit Poins.*] 40

Enter drawer [FRANCIS].

Fran. Anon, anon, sir. Look down into the Pomgarnet, Ralph.

Prince. Come hither, Francis.

Fran. My lord?

Prince. How long hast thou to serve, Francis? 45

Fran. Forsooth, five years, and as much as to —

Poins. [*Within.*] Francis!

Fran. Anon, anon, sir.   49

Prince. Five year! by 'r lady, a long lease for

the clinking of pewter. But, Francis, darest thou be so valiant as to play the coward with thy indenture and show it a fair pair of heels and run from it?   54

Fran. O Lord, sir, I'll be sworn upon all the books in England, I could find in my heart —

Poins. [*Within.*] Francis!

Fran. Anon, sir.

Prince. How old art thou, Francis?

Fran. Let me see — about Michaelmas next I shall be —   61

Poins. [*Within.*] Francis!

Fran. Anon, sir. Pray you, stay a little, my lord.

Prince. Nay, but hark you, Francis: for the sugar thou gavest me, 'twas a pennyworth, was 't not?   66

Fran. O Lord, I would it had been two!

Prince. I will give thee for it a thousand pound. Ask me when thou wilt, and thou shalt have it. 70

Poins. [*Within.*] Francis!

Fran. Anon, anon.

Prince. Anon, Francis? No, Francis; but tomorrow, Francis; or Francis, o' Thursday; or indeed, Francis, when thou wilt. But, Francis!

Fran. My lord?   76

Prince. Wilt thou rob this leathern jerkin, crystal-button, not-pated, agate-ring, puke-stocking, caddis-garter, smooth-tongue, Spanish-pouch, —   80

Fran. O Lord, sir, who do you mean?

Prince. Why, then, your brown bastard is your only drink; for look you, Francis, your white canvas doublet will sully. In Barbary, sir, it cannot come to so much.   85

Fran. What, sir?

Poins. [*Within.*] Francis!

Prince. Away, you rogue! dost thou not hear them call?   89

[*Here they both call him; the drawer stands amazed, not knowing which way to go.*

Enter VINTNER.

Vint. What, stand'st thou still, and hear'st such a calling? Look to the guests within. [*Exit Francis.*] My lord, old Sir John with half-a-dozen more are at the door; shall I let them in? 94

Prince. Let them alone a while, and then open the door. [*Exit Vintner.*] Poins!

Poins. [*Within.*] Anon, anon, sir.

Re-enter POINS.

Prince. Sirrah, Falstaff and the rest of the thieves are at the door; shall we be merry? 99

Sc. iv, 1. fat: vat. 12. Corinthian: a gay blade. 17. watering: drinking. 25. under-skinker: tapster's assistant. 29. bastard: a Spanish wine. Half-moon: name of a room in the inn, like *Pomgarnet* in l. 42. 36. [precedent] (Pope): example. *present* Q, *president* Ff. 42. Pomgarnet: Pomegranate. 53. indenture: apprentice's contract. 77–80. Describing the vintner (l. 90). 78. not-pated: close-cropped. puke: dark gray. 79. caddis: worsted. Spanish: of Spanish leather.

Poins. As merry as crickets, my lad. But hark ye; what cunning match have you made with this jest of the drawer? Come, what's the issue?   103

Prince. I am now of all humours that have showed themselves humours since the old days of goodman Adam to the pupil age of this present twelve o'clock at midnight.

[*Re-enter* FRANCIS.]

What's o'clock, Francis?

Fran. Anon, anon, sir.   [*Exit.*]   109

Prince. That ever this fellow should have fewer words than a parrot, and yet the son of a woman! His industry is upstairs and downstairs; his eloquence the parcel of a reckoning. I am not yet of Percy's mind, the Hotspur of the north; he that kills me some six or seven dozen of Scots at a   115 breakfast, washes his hands, and says to his wife, "Fie upon this quiet life! I want work." "O my sweet Harry," says she, "how many hast thou kill'd to-day?" "Give my roan horse a drench," says he; and answers, "Some fourteen," an   120 hour after; "a trifle, a trifle." I prithee, call in Falstaff. I'll play Percy, and that damn'd brawn shall play Dame Mortimer his wife. "Rivo!" says the drunkard. Call in ribs, call in tallow.   125

Enter FALSTAFF [GADSHILL, BARDOLPH, *and* PETO; FRANCIS *following with wine*].

Poins. Welcome, Jack! Where hast thou been?

Fal. A plague of all cowards, I say, and a vengeance too! marry, and amen! Give me a cup of sack, boy. Ere I lead this life long, I'll sew nether stocks, and mend them and foot them too. A plague of all cowards! Give me a cup of sack, rogue. Is there no virtue extant?   132

[*He drinketh.*

Prince. Didst thou never see Titan kiss a dish of butter, pitiful-hearted Titan, that melted at the sweet tale of the [sun]? If thou didst, then behold that compound.   136

Fal. You rogue, here's lime in this sack too. There is nothing but roguery to be found in villanous man; yet a coward is worse than a cup of sack with lime in it. A villanous coward! Go   140 thy ways, old Jack; die when thou wilt, if manhood, good manhood, be not forgot upon the face of the earth, then am I a shotten herring. There lives not three good men unhang'd in England; and one of them is fat and grows old. God help   145

the while! a bad world, I say. I would I were a weaver; I could sing psalms or anything. A plague of all cowards, I say still.

Prince. How now, wool-sack! what mutter you?   149

Fal. A king's son! If I do not beat thee out of thy kingdom with a dagger of lath, and drive all thy subjects afore thee like a flock of wild-geese, I'll never wear hair on my face more. You Prince of Wales!   154

Prince. Why, you whoreson round man, what's the matter?

Fal. Are not you a coward? Answer me to that; and Poins there?

Poins. 'Zounds, ye fat paunch, an ye call me coward, by the Lord, I'll stab thee.   160

Fal. I call thee coward! I'll see thee damn'd ere I call thee coward; but I would give a thousand pound I could run as fast as thou canst. You are straight enough in the shoulders; you care not who sees your back. Call you that backing of your friends? A plague upon such backing! give me them that will face me. Give me a cup of sack. I am a rogue, if I drunk to-day.   169

Prince. O villain! thy lips are scarce wip'd since thou drunk'st last.

Fal. All's one for that. (*He drinketh.*) A plague of all cowards, still say I.

Prince. What's the matter?   174

Fal. What's the matter! There be four of us here have ta'en a thousand pound this day morning.

Prince. Where is it, Jack? where is it?

Fal. Where is it! Taken from us it is; a hundred upon poor four of us.   180

Prince. What, a hundred, man?

Fal. I am a rogue, if I were not at half-sword with a dozen of them two hours together. I have scaped by miracle. I am eight times thrust through the doublet, four through the hose; my   185 buckler cut through and through; my sword hack'd like a hand-saw — *ecce signum!* I never dealt better since I was a man; all would not do. A plague of all cowards! Let them speak; if they speak more or less than truth, they are villains and the sons of darkness.   191

[*Prince.*] Speak, sirs; how was it?

[*Gads.*] We four set upon some dozen —

Fal. Sixteen at least, my lord.

[*Gads.*] And bound them.   195

Peto. No, no, they were not bound.

---

102. **match:** game. 106. **pupil age:** youth. 113. **parcel:** item. 119. **drench:** bran and water. 124. "**Rivo!**": a reveller's exclamation. 130. **nether stocks:** stockings. 133. **Titan:** Hyperion, the sun. 134. **that.** The antecedent is *butter.* 135. [sun] Q₃F₁. *sonnes* Q₁. 137. **lime:** used as a preservative. 143. **shotten:** having spawned. 146. **the while:** the times. 182. **at half-sword:** at close quarters. 187. *ecce signum:* behold the proof. 192. [*Prince*] Ff. *Gad.* Qq. 193, 195, 199. [*Gads.*] Ff. *Ross.* Qq. Cf. I.ii.181, note.

Fal. You rogue, they were bound, every man of them, or I am a Jew else, an Ebrew Jew.

[*Gads.*] As we were sharing, some six or seven fresh men set upon us — 200

Fal. And unbound the rest, and then come in the other.

Prince. What, fought you with them all? 203

Fal. All! I know not what you call all; but if I fought not with fifty of them, I am a bunch of radish. If there were not two or three and fifty upon poor old Jack, then am I no two-legg'd creature.

Prince. Pray God you have not murd'red some of them. 210

Fal. Nay, that's past praying for; I have pepper'd two of them. Two I am sure I have paid, two rogues in buckram suits. I tell thee what, Hal, if I tell thee a lie, spit in my face, call me horse. Thou knowest my old ward: here I lay, and thus I bore my point. Four rogues in buckram let drive at me — 217

Prince. What, four? Thou saidst but two even now.

Fal. Four, Hal; I told thee four.

Poins. Ay, ay, he said four. 221

Fal. These four came all a-front, and mainly thrust at me. I made me no more ado but took all their seven points in my target, thus.

Prince. Seven? why, there were but four even now. 226

Fal. In buckram?

Poins. Ay, four, in buckram suits.

Fal. Seven, by these hilts, or I am a villain else. 230

Prince. Prithee, let him alone; we shall have more anon.

Fal. Dost thou hear me, Hal?

Prince. Ay, and mark thee too, Jack. 234

Fal. Do so, for it is worth the listening to. These nine in buckram that I told thee of —

Prince. So, two more already.

Fal. Their points being broken, —

Poins. Down fell their hose. 239

Fal. Began to give me ground; but I followed me close, came in foot and hand, and with a thought seven of the eleven I paid.

Prince. O monstrous! eleven buckram men grown out of two! 244

Fal. But, as the devil would have it, three misbegotten knaves in Kendal green came at my back and let drive at me; for it was so dark, Hal, that thou couldst not see thy hand. 248

Prince. These lies are like their father that begets them; gross as a mountain, open, palpable.

Why thou clay-brain'd guts, thou knotty-pated fool, thou whoreson, obscene, greasy tallow-catch, — 253

Fal. What, art thou mad? art thou mad? Is not the truth the truth?

Prince. Why, how couldst thou know these men in Kendal green, when it was so dark thou couldst not see thy hand? Come, tell us your reason; what say'st thou to this? 259

Poins. Come, your reason, Jack, your reason.

Fal. What, upon compulsion? 'Zounds, an I were at the strappado, or all the racks in the world, I would not tell you on compulsion. Give you a reason on compulsion! If reasons were as plenty as blackberries, I would give no man a reason upon compulsion, I. 266

Prince. I'll be no longer guilty of this sin. This sanguine coward, this bed-presser, this horseback-breaker, this huge hill of flesh, — 269

Fal. 'Sblood, you starveling, you elf-skin, you dried neat's tongue, you bull's pizzle, you stock-fish! O for breath to utter what is like thee! you tailor's-yard, you sheath, you bowcase, you vile standing-tuck, — 274

Prince. Well, breathe a while, and then to it again; and when thou hast tired thyself in base comparisons, hear me speak but this: —

Poins. Mark, Jack. 278

Prince. We two saw you four set on four and bound them, and were masters of their wealth. Mark now, how a plain tale shall put you down. Then did we two set on you four; and, with a word out-fac'd you from your prize, and have it, yea, and can show it you here in the house; and, Falstaff, you carried your guts away as nimbly, with as 285 quick dexterity, and roar'd for mercy, and still run and roar'd, as ever I heard bull-calf. What a slave art thou, to hack thy sword as thou hast done, and then say it was in fight! What trick, what device, what starting-hole, canst thou now find out to hide thee from this open and apparent shame? 292

Poins. Come, let's hear, Jack; what trick hast thou now?

Fal. By the Lord, I knew ye as well as he that made ye. Why, hear you, my masters. Was it for me to kill the heir-apparent? Should I turn upon the true prince? Why, thou knowest I am as valiant as Hercules; but beware instinct; the lion will not touch the true prince. Instinct is a great matter; I was now a coward on in- 300 stinct. I shall think the better of myself and thee during my life; I for a valiant lion, and thou for a true prince. But, by the Lord, lads, I am

---

222. **mainly:** powerfully. 224. **target:** shield. 238. **points:** (1) of swords, (2) tagged laces, holding garments together 253. **catch:** tub. 262. **strappado:** a torture of Spanish origin. 271. **neat's:** ox's. 271. **stockfish:** dried cod. 274. **tuck:** rapier. 290. **starting-hole:** loophole.

glad you have the money. Hostess, clap to the doors! Watch to-night, pray to-morrow. 305 Gallants, lads, boys, hearts of gold, all the titles of good fellowship come to you! What, shall we be merry? Shall we have a play extempore?

Prince. Content; and the argument shall be thy running away. 311

Fal. Ah, no more of that, Hal, an thou lovest me!

Enter HOSTESS.

Host. O Jesu, my lord the Prince!

Prince. How now, my lady the hostess! what say'st thou to me? 316

Host. Marry, my lord, there is a nobleman of the court at door would speak with you. He says he comes from your father.

Prince. Give him as much as will make him a royal man, and send him back again to my mother.

Fal. What manner of man is he? 323

Host. An old man.

Fal. What doth Gravity out of his bed at midnight? Shall I give him his answer? 326

Prince. Prithee, do, Jack.

Fal. Faith, and I'll send him packing. [*Exit.*

Prince. Now, sirs, by 'r lady, you fought fair; so did you, Peto; so did you, Bardolph. You are lions too, you ran away upon instinct, you will not touch the true prince; no, fie! 332

Bard. Faith, I ran when I saw others run.

Prince. Faith, tell me now in earnest, how came Falstaff's sword so hack'd?

Peto. Why, he hack'd it with his dagger, and said he would swear truth out of England but he would make you believe it was done in fight, and persuaded us to do the like. 339

Bard. Yea, and to tickle our noses with speargrass to make them bleed, and then to beslubber our garments with it and swear it was the blood of true men. I did that I did not this seven year before, I blush'd, to hear his monstrous devices. 344

Prince. O villain, thou stolest a cup of sack eighteen years ago, and wert taken with the manner, and ever since thou hast blush'd extempore. Thou hadst fire and sword on thy side, and yet thou ran'st away; what instinct hadst thou for it? 350

Bard. My lord, do you see these meteors? Do you behold these exhalations?

[*Pointing to his own face.*]

Prince. I do.

Bard. What think you they portend?

Prince. Hot livers and cold purses. 355

Bard. Choler, my lord, if rightly taken.

Re-enter FALSTAFF.

Prince. No, if rightly taken, halter. Here comes lean Jack, here comes bare-bone. How now, my sweet creature of bombast! How long is 't ago, Jack, since thou sawest thine own knee? 361

Fal. My own knee? When I was about thy years, Hal, I was not an eagle's talon in the waist; I could have crept into any alderman's thumb-ring. A plague of sighing and grief! it blows a man up like a bladder. There's villanous news abroad. 366 Here was Sir John Bracy from your father; you must to the court in the morning. That same mad fellow of the north, Percy, and he of Wales that gave Amamon the bastinado and made Lucifer cuckold and swore the devil his true liegeman upon the cross of a Welsh hook — what a plague call you him? 373

Poins. O, Glendower.

Fal. Owen, Owen, the same; and his son-in-law Mortimer, and old Northumberland, and that sprightly Scot of Scots, Douglas, that runs o' horseback up a hill perpendicular, —

Prince. He that rides at high speed and with his pistol kills a sparrow flying. 380

Fal. You have hit it.

Prince. So did he never the sparrow.

Fal. Well, that rascal hath good mettle in him; he will not run. 384

Prince. Why, what a rascal art thou then, to praise him so for running!

Fal. O' horseback, ye cuckoo; but afoot he will not budge a foot.

Prince. Yes, Jack, upon instinct. 389

Fal. I grant ye, upon instinct. Well, he is there too, and one Murdoch, and a thousand blue-caps more. Worcester is stolen away tonight. Thy father's beard is turn'd white with the news. You may buy land now as cheap as stinking mackerel. 395

Prince. Why, then, it is like, if there come a hot June and this civil buffeting hold, we shall buy maidenheads as they buy hob-nails, by the hundreds. 399

Fal. By the mass, lad, thou say'st true; it is like we shall have good trading that way. But tell me, Hal, art not thou horrible afeard? Thou being heir-apparent, could the world pick thee out three such enemies again as that fiend Douglas, that spirit Percy, and that devil Glendower? Art thou not horribly afraid? Doth not thy blood thrill at it? 407

305. **Watch:** wake. 321. **royal:** A play on *noble* and *royal* as names of coins worth respectively 6s.8d. and 10s. 346. **with...manner:** in the act. 355. **Hot...purses:** drunkenness and poverty. 357. **halter:** with a pun on *choler, collar.* 360. **bombast:** cotton wadding. 370. **Amamon:** a devil. 372. **Welsh hook:** a bill with a curved blade. 391. **blue-caps:** blue bonnets, Scots.

Prince. Not a whit, i' faith; I lack some of thy instinct.

Fal. Well, thou wilt be horribly chid tomorrow when thou comest to thy father. If thou love me, practise an answer.   412

Prince. Do thou stand for my father, and examine me upon the particulars of my life.

Fal. Shall I? Content. This chair shall be my state, this dagger my sceptre, and this cushion my crown.   417

Prince. Thy state is taken for a join'd-stool, thy golden sceptre for a leaden dagger, and thy precious rich crown for a pitiful bald crown!   420

Fal. Well, an the fire of grace be not quite out of thee, now shalt thou be moved. Give me a cup of sack to make my eyes look red, that it may be thought I have wept; for I must speak in passion, and I will do it in King Cambyses' vein.   426

Prince. Well, here is my leg.

Fal. And here is my speech. Stand aside, nobility.

Host. O Jesu, this is excellent sport, i' faith!

Fal. Weep not, sweet queen; for trickling tears are vain.   431

Host. O, the father, how he holds his countenance!

Fal. For God's sake, lords, convey my [tristful] queen;

For tears do stop the flood-gates of her eyes.   435

Host. O Jesu, he doth it as like one of these harlotry players as ever I see!

Fal. Peace, good pint-pot; peace, good tickle-brain. Harry, I do not only marvel where thou spendest thy time, but also how thou art ac-   440 companied; for though the camomile, the more it is trodden on the faster it grows, [yet] youth, the more it is wasted the sooner it wears. That thou art my son, I have partly thy mother's word, partly my own opinion, but chiefly a villanous   445 trick of thine eye and a foolish hanging of thy nether lip, that doth warrant me. If then thou be son to me, here lies the point; why, being son to me, art thou so pointed at? Shall the blessed sun of heaven prove a micher and eat blackberries? a   450 question not to be ask'd. Shall the son of England prove a thief and take purses? a question to be ask'd. There is a thing, Harry, which thou hast often heard of and it is known to many in our land by the name of pitch. This pitch, as ancient   455 writers do report, doth defile; so doth the company thou keepest; for, Harry, now I do not speak to thee in drink but in tears; not in pleasure but in passion, not in words only, but in woes also; and yet there is a virtuous man whom I have often noted in thy company, but I know not his name.   461

Prince. What manner of man, an it like your Majesty?

Fal. A goodly portly man, i' faith, and a corpulent; of a cheerful look, a pleasing eye, and a   465 most noble carriage; and, as I think, his age some fifty, or, by 'r lady, inclining to threescore; and now I remember me, his name is Falstaff. If that man should be lewdly given, he deceiveth me; for, Harry, I see virtue in his looks. If then the tree   470 may be known by the fruit, as the fruit by the tree, then, peremptorily I speak it, there is virtue in that Falstaff; him keep with, the rest banish. And tell me now, thou naughty varlet, tell me, where hast thou been this month?   475

Prince. Dost thou speak like a king? Do thou stand for me, and I'll play my father.

Fal. Depose me? If thou dost it half so gravely, so majestically, both in word and matter, hang me up by the heels for a rabbit-sucker or a poulter's hare.   481

Prince. Well, here I am set.

Fal. And here I stand. Judge, my masters.

Prince. Now, Harry, whence come you?

Fal. My noble lord, from Eastcheap.   485

Prince. The complaints I hear of thee are grievous.

Fal. 'Sblood, my lord, they are false. — Nay, I'll tickle ye for a young prince, i' faith.   489

Prince. Swearest thou, ungracious boy? Henceforth ne'er look on me. Thou art violently carried away from grace. There is a devil haunts thee in the likeness of an old fat man; a tun of man is thy companion. Why dost thou converse with that trunk of humours, that bolting-hutch of beast-   495 liness, that swollen parcel of dropsies, that huge bombard of sack; that stuff'd cloak-bag of guts, that roasted Manningtree ox with the pudding in his belly, that reverend vice, that grey iniquity, that father ruffian, that vanity in years?   500 Wherein is he good, but to taste sack and drink it? wherein neat and cleanly, but to carve a capon and eat it? wherein cunning, but in craft? wherein crafty, but in villainy? wherein villanous, but in all things? wherein worthy, but in nothing?   505

Fal. I would your Grace would take me with you. Whom means your Grace?

Prince. That villanous abominable misleader of youth, Falstaff, that old white-bearded Satan.

Fal. My lord, the man I know.   510

---

416. **state:** throne.   418. **join'd-stool:** wooden stool.   426. **King Cambyses' vein:** Preston's *Cambyses* (1570) was the type of the bombastic tragedy. Falstaff imitates the style in ll. 431, 434-35.   427. **leg:** obeisance.   434. [tristful] (Rowe). *trustful* Q.   438. **tickle-brain:** strong drink.   441-475. In these speeches Falstaff parodies the style of Lyly's *Euphues.* 442. [yet] F. *so* Q.   450. **micher:** truant.   480. **rabbit-sucker:** young rabbit.   **poulter's:** poulterer's.   495. **bolting-hutch:** miller's chest.   497. **bombard:** a large leather vessel for liquor.   498. **Manningtree:** an agricultural town in Essex.

Prince. I know thou dost.

Fal. But to say I know more harm in him than in myself, were to say more than I know. That he is old, the more the pity, his white hairs do witness it; but that he is, saving your reverence, a 515 whoremaster, that I utterly deny. If sack and sugar be a fault, God help the wicked! If to be old and merry be a sin, then many an old host that I know is damn'd. If to be fat be to be hated, then Pharaoh's lean kine are to be loved. No, my 520 good lord; banish Peto, banish Bardolph, banish Poins; but for sweet Jack Falstaff, kind Jack Falstaff, true Jack Falstaff, valiant Jack Falstaff, and therefore more valiant, being, as he is, old Jack Falstaff, banish not him thy Harry's company, 525 banish not him thy Harry's company. Banish plump Jack, and banish all the world.

Prince. I do, I will.

    [*A knocking heard. Exeunt Hostess, Francis, and Bardolph.*]

Re-enter BARDOLPH, *running.*

Bard. O, my lord, my lord! the sheriff with a most monstrous watch is at the door.   530

Fal. Out, ye rogue! Play out the play; I have much to say in the behalf of that Falstaff.

Re-enter the HOSTESS.

Host. O Jesu, my lord, my lord!

Prince. Heigh, heigh! the devil rides upon a fiddlestick. What's the matter?   535

Host. The sheriff and all the watch are at the door; they are come to search the house. Shall I let them in?

Fal. Dost thou hear, Hal? Never call a true piece of gold a counterfeit. Thou art essentially mad, without seeming so.   541

Prince. And thou a natural coward, without instinct.

Fal. I deny your major. If you will deny the sheriff, so; if not, let him enter. If I become not a cart as well as another man, a plague on my bringing up! I hope I shall as soon be strangled with a halter as another.   548

Prince. Go, hide thee behind the arras; the rest walk up above. Now, my masters, for a true face and good conscience.

Fal. Both which I have had; but their date is out, and therefore I'll hide me.   [*Exit.* 553

Prince. Call in the sheriff.

    [*Exeunt all except the Prince and Peto.*]

Enter SHERIFF *and the* CARRIER.

Now, master sheriff, what is your will with me?

Sher. First, pardon me, my lord. A hue and cry
Hath followed certain men unto this house.

Prince. What men?

Sher. One of them is well known, my gracious lord,
A gross fat man.

Car.   As fat as butter.   560

Prince. The man, I do assure you, is not here,
For I myself at this time have employ'd him.
And, sheriff, I will engage my word to thee
That I will, by to-morrow dinner-time,
Send him to answer thee or any man   565
For anything he shall be charg'd withal.
And so let me entreat you leave the house.

Sher. I will, my lord. There are two gentlemen
Have in this robbery lost three hundred marks.

Prince. It may be so. If he have robb'd these men,   570
He shall be answerable; and so farewell.

Sher. Good night, my noble lord.

Prince. I think it is good morrow, is it not?

Sher. Indeed, my lord, I think it be two o'clock.
    [*Exeunt [Sheriff and Carrier].*

Prince. This oily rascal is known as well as Paul's. Go, call him forth.   576

Peto. Falstaff!— Fast asleep behind the arras, and snorting like a horse.

Prince. Hark, how hard he fetches breath. Search his pockets. (*He searcheth his pockets, and findeth certain papers.*) What hast thou found?   582

Peto. Nothing but papers, my lord.

Prince. Let's see what they be. Read them.

Peto. [*Reads.*]

Item, A capon	. . .	.	2s. 2d.
Item, Sauce	. . .	.	4d.
Item, Sack, two gallons	. .	.	5s. 8d.
Item, Anchovies and sack after supper			2s. 6d.
Item, Bread	. . . . .	.	ob.

Prince. O monstrous! but one half-penny- 591 worth of bread to this intolerable deal of sack! What there is else, keep close; we'll read it at more advantage. There let him sleep till day. I'll to the court in the morning. We must all to the 595 wars, and thy place shall be honourable. I'll procure this fat rogue a charge of foot; and I know his death will be a march of twelve-score. The money shall be paid back again with advantage. Be with [me] betimes in the morning; and so, good morrow, Peto.   601

Peto. Good morrow, good my lord.   [*Exeunt.*

---

544. **major:** major premise. 546. **cart:** the hangman's cart. 549. **arras:** tapestry hangings. 576. **Paul's:** St. Paul's Cathedral. 590. **ob.:** obolus; here, a halfpenny. 598. **death...twelve-score:** a march of 240 yards will kill him. 599. **advantage:** interest. 600. **[me]** F. *the* Q.

ACT III

SCENE I. [*Bangor. The Archdeacon's house.*]

Enter HOTSPUR, WORCESTER, MORTIMER, *and*
GLENDOWER.

Mort. These promises are fair, the parties sure,
And our induction full of prosperous hope.
  Hot. Lord Mortimer, and cousin Glendower,
Will you sit down?
And uncle Worcester, — a plague upon it!   5
I have forgot the map.
  Glend.   No, here it is.
Sit, cousin Percy; sit, good cousin Hotspur,
For by that name as oft as Lancaster
Doth speak of you, his cheek looks pale and with
A rising sigh he wisheth you in heaven.   10
  Hot. And you in hell, as oft as he hears Owen
Glendower spoke of.
  Glend. I cannot blame him. At my nativity
The front of heaven was full of fiery shapes,
Of burning cressets; and at my birth   15
The frame and huge foundation of the earth
Shak'd like a coward.
  Hot. Why, so it would have done at the same
season, if your mother's cat had but kitten'd,
though yourself had never been born.   20
  Glend. I say the earth did shake when I was born.
  Hot. And I say the earth was not of my mind,
If you suppose as fearing you it shook.
  Glend. The heavens were all on fire, the earth did
tremble.
  Hot. O, then the earth shook to see the heavens
on fire,   25
And not in fear of your nativity.
Diseased nature oftentimes breaks forth
In strange eruptions; oft the teeming earth
Is with a kind of colic pinch'd and vex'd
By the imprisoning of unruly wind   30
Within her womb; which, for enlargement striving,
Shakes the old beldam earth, and topples down
Steeples and moss-grown towers. At your birth
Our grandam earth, having this distemperature,
In passion shook.
  Glend.   Cousin, of many men   35
I do not bear these crossings. Give me leave
To tell you once again that at my birth
The front of heaven was full of fiery shapes,
The goats ran from the mountains, and the herds
Were strangely clamorous to the frighted fields.
These signs have mark'd me extraordinary;   41
And all the courses of my life do show
I am not in the roll of common men.
Where is he living, clipp'd in with the sea
That chides the banks of England, Scotland, Wales,

Which calls me pupil, or hath read to me?   46
And bring him out that is but woman's son
Can trace me in the tedious ways of art
And hold me pace in deep experiments.
  Hot. I think there's no man speaks better Welsh.
I'll to dinner.   51
  Mort. Peace, cousin Percy; you will make him
mad.
  Glend. I can call spirits from the vasty deep.
  Hot. Why, so can I, or so can any man;
But will they come when you do call for them?   55
  Glend. Why, I can teach you, cousin, to com-
mand
The devil.
  Hot. And I can teach thee, coz, to shame the
devil
By telling truth. "Tell truth and shame the devil."
If thou have power to raise him, bring him hither,
And I'll be sworn I have power to shame him
hence.   61
O, while you live, tell truth and shame the devil!
  Mort. Come, come, no more of this unprofitable
chat.
  Glend. Three times hath Henry Bolingbroke
made head
Against my power; thrice from the banks of Wye
And sandy-bottom'd Severn have I sent him   66
Bootless home and weather-beaten back.
  Hot. Home without boots, and in foul weather
too!
How scapes he agues, in the devil's name?
  Glend. Come, here's the map. Shall we divide
our right   70
According to our threefold order ta'en?
  Mort. The Archdeacon hath divided it
Into three limits very equally.
England, from Trent and Severn hitherto,
By south and east is to my part assign'd;   75
All westward, Wales beyond the Severn shore,
And all the fertile land within that bound,
To Owen Glendower; and, dear coz, to you
The remnant northward, lying off from Trent.
And our indentures tripartite are drawn;   80
Which being sealed interchangeably,
A business that this night may execute,
To-morrow, cousin Percy, you and I
And my good Lord of Worcester will set forth
To meet your father and the Scottish power,   85
As is appointed us, at Shrewsbury.
My father Glendower is not ready yet,
Nor shall we need his help these fourteen days.
Within that space you may have drawn together
Your tenants, friends, and neighbouring gentle-
men.   90
  Glend. A shorter time shall send me to you, lords;

Act III, sc. i, 2. **induction:** beginning.   15. **cressets:** fire baskets; here, meteors.   34. **distemperature:** disorder.   46.
read to: taught.   48. **trace:** follow.   **art:** magic.   67. **Bootless:** without advantage.   74. **hitherto:** to this point.

And in my conduct shall your ladies come,
From whom you now must steal and take no leave,
For there will be a world of water shed
Upon the parting of your wives and you.   95
   Hot. Methinks my moiety, north from Burton here,
In quantity equals not one of yours.
See how this river comes me cranking in,
And cuts me from the best of all my land
A huge half-moon, a monstrous cantle out.   100
I'll have the current in this place damm'd up;
And here the smug and silver Trent shall run
In a new channel, fair and evenly.
It shall not wind with such a deep indent,
To rob me of so rich a bottom here.   105
   Glend. Not wind? It shall, it must; you see it doth.
   Mort. Yea, but
Mark how he bears his course, and runs me up
With like advantage on the other side;
Gelding the opposed continent as much   110
As on the other side it takes from you.
   Wor. Yea, but a little charge will trench him here
And on this north side win this cape of land;
And then he runs straight and even.
   Hot. I'll have it so; a little charge will do it.   115
   Glend. I'll not have it alt'red.
   Hot.   Will not you?
   Glend. No, nor you shall not.
   Hot.   Who shall say me nay?
   Glend. Why, that will I.
   Hot. Let me not understand you, then; speak it in Welsh.   120
   Glend. I can speak English, lord, as well as you;
For I was train'd up in the English court;
Where, being but young, I framed to the harp
Many an English ditty lovely well
And gave the tongue a helpful ornament,   125
A virtue that was never seen in you.
   Hot. Marry,
And I am glad of it with all my heart.
I had rather be a kitten and cry mew
Than one of these same metre ballad-mongers.
I had rather hear a brazen canstick turn'd,   131
Or a dry wheel grate on the axle-tree,
And that would set my teeth nothing on edge,
Nothing so much as mincing poetry.
'Tis like the forc'd gait of a shuffling nag.   135
   Glend. Come, you shall have Trent turn'd.
   Hot. I do not care. I'll give thrice so much land
To any well-deserving friend;
But in the way of bargain, mark ye me,

I'll cavil on the ninth part of a hair.   140
Are the indentures drawn? Shall we be gone?
   Glend. The moon shines fair; you may away by night.
I'll haste the writer, and withal
Break with your wives of your departure hence.
I am afraid my daughter will run mad,   145
So much she doteth on her Mortimer.   [*Exit.*
   Mort. Fie, cousin Percy! how you cross my father!
   Hot. I cannot choose. Sometimes he angers me
With telling me of the moldwarp and the ant,
Of the dreamer Merlin and his prophecies,   150
And of a dragon and a finless fish,
A clip-wing'd griffin and a moulten raven,
A couching lion and a ramping cat,
And such a deal of skimble-skamble stuff
As puts me from my faith. I tell you what: 155
He held me last night at least nine hours
In reckoning up the several devils' names
That were his lackeys. I cried "hum," and "well, go to,"
But mark'd him not a word. O, he is as tedious
As a tired horse, a railing wife;   160
Worse than a smoky house. I had rather live
With cheese and garlic in a windmill, far,
Than feed on cates and have him talk to me
In any summer-house in Christendom.
   Mort. In faith, he is a worthy gentleman,   165
Exceedingly well read, and profited
In strange concealments, valiant as a lion
And wondrous affable, and as bountiful
As mines of India. Shall I tell you, cousin?
He holds your temper in a high respect   170
And curbs himself even of his natural scope
When you come 'cross his humour. Faith, he does.
I warrant you, that man is not alive
Might so have tempted him as you have done,
Without the taste of danger and reproof.   175
But do not use it oft, let me entreat you.
   Wor. In faith, my lord, you are too wilful-blame;
And since your coming hither have done enough
To put him quite besides his patience.
You must needs learn, lord, to amend this fault.   180
Though sometimes it show greatness, courage, blood, —
And that's the dearest grace it renders you, —
Yet oftentimes it doth present harsh rage,
Defect of manners, want of government,
Pride, haughtiness, opinion, and disdain;   185
The least of which haunting a nobleman
Loseth men's hearts and leaves behind a stain
Upon the beauty of all parts besides,

---

96. **moiety:** share. 100. **cantle:** piece, corner. 104. **indent:** indentation. 110. **Gelding:** cutting off from. **continent:** land. 112. **charge:** cost. 131. **canstick:** candlestick. 149. **moldwarp:** mole. This and the following lines refer to a prophecy mentioned by Holinshed. 163. **cates:** delicacies. 166. **profited:** proficient. 167. **concealments:** occult arts. 177. **wilful-blame:** wilfully to blame. 183. **present:** indicate. 184. **government:** self-control.

Beguiling them of commendation.

Hot. Well, I am school'd.   Good manners be
    your speed!   190

Here come our wives, and let us take our leave.

       Re-enter GLENDOWER *with the ladies.*

Mort. This is the deadly spite that angers me;

My wife can speak no English, I no Welsh.

Glend. My daughter weeps; she will not part
    with you.

She'll be a soldier too, she'll to the wars.   195

Mort. Good father, tell her that she and my aunt
    Percy

Shall follow in your conduct speedily.

      [*Glendower speaks to her in Welsh, and she
        answers him in the same.*

Glend. She is desperate here; a peevish self-
will'd harlotry, one that no persuasion can do good
upon.   [*The lady speaks in Welsh.*   200

Mort. I understand thy looks.   That pretty
    Welsh

Which thou pourest down from these swelling
    heavens

I am too perfect in; and, but for shame,

In such a parley should I answer thee.

      [*The lady speaks again in Welsh.*

I understand thy kisses and thou mine,   205

And that's a feeling disputation.

But I will never be a truant, love,

Till I have learn'd thy language; for thy tongue

Makes Welsh as sweet as ditties highly penn'd,

Sung by a fair queen in a summer's bower,   210

With ravishing division, to her lute.

Glend. Nay, if you melt, then will she run mad.

      [*The lady speaks again in Welsh.*

Mort. O, I am ignorance itself in this!

Glend. She bids you on the wanton rushes lay
    you down

And rest your gentle head upon her lap,   215

And she will sing the song that pleaseth you

And on your eyelids crown the god of sleep,

Charming your blood with pleasing heaviness,

Making such difference 'twixt wake and sleep

As is the difference 'twixt day and night   220

The hour before the heavenly-harness'd team

Begins his golden progress in the east.

Mort. With all my heart I'll sit and hear her
    sing.

By that time will our book, I think be drawn.

Glend. Do so;   225

And those musicians that shall play to you

Hang in the air a thousand leagues from hence,

And straight they shall be here.   Sit, and attend.

Hot. Come, Kate, thou art perfect in lying down.

Come, quick, quick, that I may lay my head in thy
lap.   231

Lady P. Go, ye giddy goose.   [*The music plays.*

Hot. Now I perceive the devil understands
    Welsh;

And 'tis no marvel he is so humorous.

By 'r lady, he is a good musician.   235

Lady P. Then should you be nothing but musical,
for you are altogether governed by humours.   Lie
still, ye thief, and hear the lady sing in Welsh.

Hot. I had rather hear Lady, my brach, howl in
Irish.   241

Lady P. Wouldst thou have thy head broken?

Hot. No.

Lady P. Then be still.

Hot. Neither; 'tis a woman's fault.   245

Lady P. Now God help thee!

Hot. To the Welsh lady's bed.

Lady P. What's that?

Hot. Peace! she sings.

      [*Here the lady sings a Welsh song.*

Hot. Come, Kate, I'll have your song too.   250

Lady P. Not mine, in good sooth.

Hot. Not yours, in good sooth!   Heart, you
swear like a comfit-maker's wife.   "Not you, in
good sooth," and "as true as I live," and "as God
shall mend me," and "as sure as day;"   255

And givest such sarcenet surety for thy oaths

As if thou never walk'st further than Finsbury.

Swear me, Kate, like a lady as thou art,

A good mouth-filling oath, and leave "in sooth,"

And such protest of pepper-gingerbread,   260

To velvet-guards and Sunday-citizens.

Come, sing.

Lady P. I will not sing.

Hot. 'Tis the next way to turn tailor, or be red-
breast teacher.   An the indentures be drawn,   265
I'll away within these two hours; and so, come in
when ye will.   [*Exit.*

Glend. Come, come, Lord Mortimer; you are as
    slow

As hot Lord Percy is on fire to go.

By this our book is drawn.   We'll but seal,   270

And then to horse immediately.

Mort.   With all my heart.

      [*Exeunt.*

SCENE II.   [*London.   The palace.*]

Enter the KING, PRINCE OF WALES, *and others.*

King. Lords, give us leave; the Prince of Wales
    and I

Must have some private conference; but be near
    at hand,

---

199. **harlotry:** hussy.   211. **division:** modulation.   224. **book:** the threefold agreement.   240. **brach:** bitch.   253. **comfit-
maker's:** confectioner's.   256. **sarcenet:** silky.   257. **Finsbury:** a recreation ground outside London.   261. **velvet-guards:**
velvet trimmings such as the citizens' wives wore.   265. **red-breast teacher:** teacher of song birds.

For we shall presently have need of you.
                            [*Exeunt Lords.*
I know not whether God will have it so,
For some displeasing service I have done,   5
That, in his secret doom, out of my blood
He'll breed revengement and a scourge for me;
But thou dost in thy passages of life
Make me believe that thou art only mark'd
For the hot vengeance and the rod of heaven   10
To punish my mistreadings. Tell me else,
Could such inordinate and low desires,
Such poor, such bare, such lewd, such mean
    attempts,
Such barren pleasures, rude society,
As thou art match'd withal and grafted to,   15
Accompany the greatness of thy blood
And hold their level with thy princely heart?
  Prince. So please your Majesty, I would I could
Quit all offences with as clear excuse
As well as I am doubtless I can purge   20
Myself of many I am charg'd withal.
Yet such extenuation let me beg,
As, in reproof of many tales devis'd,
Which oft the ear of greatness needs must hear,
By smiling pick-thanks and base newsmongers,   25
I may, for some things true, wherein my youth
Hath faulty wand'red and irregular,
Find pardon on my true submission.
  King. God pardon thee! yet let me wonder,
    Harry,
At thy affections, which do hold a wing   30
Quite from the flight of all thy ancestors.
Thy place in council thou hast rudely lost,
Which by thy younger brother is suppli'd,
And art almost an alien to the hearts
Of all the court and princes of my blood.   35
The hope and expectation of thy time
Is ruin'd, and the soul of every man
Prophetically do forethink thy fall.
Had I so lavish of my presence been,
So common-hackney'd in the eyes of men,   40
So stale and cheap to vulgar company,
Opinion, that did help me to the crown,
Had still kept loyal to possession
And left me in reputeless banishment,
A fellow of no mark nor likelihood.   45
By being seldom seen, I could not stir
But like a comet I was wond'red at;
That men would tell their children, "This is he;"
Others would say, "Where, which is Bolingbroke?"
And then I stole all courtesy from heaven,   50
And dress'd myself in such humility
That I did pluck allegiance from men's hearts,

Loud shouts and salutations from their mouths,
Even in the presence of the crowned King.
Thus did I keep my person fresh and new,   55
My presence, like a robe pontifical,
Ne'er seen but wond'red at; and so my state,
Seldom but sumptuous, show'd like a feast
And won by rareness such solemnity.
The skipping King, he ambled up and down   60
With shallow jesters and rash bavin wits,
Soon kindled and soon burnt; carded his state,
Mingled his royalty with cap'ring fools,
Had his great name profaned with their scorns,
And gave his countenance, against his name   65
To laugh at gibing boys and stand the push
Of every beardless vain comparative;
Grew a companion to the common streets,
Enfeoff'd himself to popularity;
That, being daily swallowed by men's eyes,   70
They surfeited with honey and began
To loathe the taste of sweetness, whereof a little
More than a little is by much too much.
So when he had occasion to be seen,
He was but as the cuckoo is in June,   75
Heard, not regarded; seen, but with such eyes
As, sick and blunted with community,
Afford no extraordinary gaze
Such as is bent on sun-like majesty
When it shines seldom in admiring eyes;   80
But rather drows'd and hung their eyelids down,
Slept in his face and rend'red such aspect
As cloudy men use to their adversaries,
Being with his presence glutted, gorg'd, and full.
And in that very line, Harry, standest thou;   85
For thou hast lost thy princely privilege
With vile participation. Not an eye
But is a-weary of thy common sight,
Save mine, which hath desir'd to see thee more;
Which now doth that I would not have it do,   90
Make blind itself with foolish tenderness.
  Prince. I shall hereafter, my thrice gracious lord,
Be more myself.
  King.   For all the world
As thou art to this hour was Richard then
When I from France set foot at Ravenspurgh,   95
And even as I was then is Percy now.
Now, by my sceptre and my soul to boot,
He hath more worthy interest to the state
Than thou, the shadow of succession.
For of no right, nor colour like to right,   100
He doth fill fields with harness in the realm,
Turns head against the lion's armed jaws,
And, being no more in debt to years than thou,
Leads ancient lords and reverend bishops on

Sc. ii, 6. **doom:** judgment. 19. **Quit:** clear myself of. 23. **reproof:** refutation. 25. **pick-thanks:** busybodies, flatterers. 36. **time:** reign. 43. **possession:** i.e., Richard II. 61. **bavin:** brushwood. 62. **carded:** diluted. 67. **comparative:** would-be wit. 69. **Enfeoff'd:** became a vassal. 77. **community:** familiarity. 87. **participation:** fellowship. 98. **interest:** claim. 101. **harness:** armor.

To bloody battles and to bruising arms.   105
What never-dying honour hath he got
Against renowned Douglas! whose high deeds,
Whose hot incursions and great name in arms
Holds from all soldiers chief majority
And military title capital   110
Through all the kingdoms that acknowledge Christ.
Thrice hath this Hotspur, Mars in swathling clothes,
This infant warrior, in his enterprises
Discomfited great Douglas, ta'en him once,
Enlarged him and made a friend of him,   115
To fill the mouth of deep defiance up
And shake the peace and safety of our throne.
And what say you to this? Percy, Northumberland,
The Archbishop's grace of York, Douglas, Morti-
    mer,
Capitulate against us and are up.   120
But wherefore do I tell these news to thee?
Why, Harry, do I tell thee of my foes,
Which art my near'st and dearest enemy?
Thou that art like enough, through vassal fear,
Base inclination, and the start of spleen,   125
To fight against me under Percy's pay,
To dog his heels and curtsy at his frowns,
To show how much thou art degenerate.
    Prince. Do not think so; you shall not find it so:
And God forgive them that so much have sway'd
Your Majesty's good thoughts away from me!   131
I will redeem all this on Percy's head,
And in the closing of some glorious day
Be bold to tell you that I am your son;
When I will wear a garment all of blood   135
And stain my favours in a bloody mask,
Which, wash'd away, shall scour my shame with it.
And that shall be the day, whene'er it lights,
That this same child of honour and renown,
This gallant Hotspur, this all-praised knight,   140
And your unthought-of Harry chance to meet.
For every honour sitting on his helm,
Would they were multitudes, and on my head
My shames redoubled! For the time will come
That I shall make this northern youth exchange   145
His glorious deeds for my indignities.
Percy is but my factor, good my lord,
To engross up glorious deeds on my behalf;
And I will call him to so strict account
That he shall render every glory up,   150
Yea, even the slightest worship of his time,
Or I will tear the reckoning from his heart.
This, in the name of God, I promise here;
The which if He be pleas'd I shall perform,
I do beseech your Majesty may salve   155

The long-grown wounds of my intemperance.
If not, the end of life cancels all bands;
And I will die a hundred thousand deaths
Ere break the smallest parcel of this vow.   159
    King. A hundred thousand rebels die in this.
Thou shalt have charge and sovereign trust herein.

Enter BLUNT.

How now, good Blunt? Thy looks are full of
    speed.
    Blunt. So hath the business that I come to
    speak of.
Lord Mortimer of Scotland hath sent word
That Douglas and the English rebels met   165
The eleventh of this month at Shrewsbury.
A mighty and a fearful head they are,
If promises be kept on every hand,
As ever off'red foul play in a state.
    King. The Earl of Westmoreland set forth to-
    day,   170
With him my son, Lord John of Lancaster,
For this advertisement is five days old.
On Wednesday next, Harry, you shall set forward;
On Thursday we ourselves will march. Our meet-
    ing
Is Bridgenorth: and, Harry, you shall march   175
Through Gloucestershire; by which account,
Our business valued, some twelve days hence
Our general forces at Bridgenorth shall meet.
Our hands are full of business; let's away.
Advantage feeds him fat, while men delay.   180
    [*Exeunt.*

SCENE III. [*Eastcheap. The Boar's-Head
Tavern.*]

Enter FALSTAFF *and* BARDOLPH.

    Fal. Bardolph, am I not fallen away vilely since
this last action? Do I not bate? Do I not dwindle?
Why, my skin hangs about me like an old lady's
loose gown; I am withered like an old apple-john.
Well, I'll repent, and that suddenly, while I am   5
in some liking. I shall be out of heart shortly, and
then I shall have no strength to repent. An I have
not forgotten what the inside of a church is made of,
I am a peppercorn, a brewer's horse. The inside of
a church! Company, villanous company, hath   10
been the spoil of me.
    Bard. Sir John, you are so fretful, you cannot
live long.   14
    Fal. Why, there is it. Come sing me a bawdy
song; make me merry. I was as virtuously given

---

109. **majority:** supremacy. 120. **Capitulate:** combine. **up:** in rebellion. 136. **favours:** features. 147. **factor:** agent. 148. **engross up:** gather. 164. **Lord ... Scotland:** Dunbar, the Scottish Earl of March, confused with the English Mortimer. 167. **head:** force. 172. **advertisement:** information. 177. **Our ... valued:** the time necessary for our business being considered.
    Sc. iii, 4. **apple-john:** an apple that keeps its flavor after it is shriveled. 6. **liking:** bodily condition.

as a gentleman need to be; virtuous enough, swore
little, dic'd not above seven times a week, went to a
bawdy-house not above once in a quarter — of an
hour, paid money that I borrowed — three or 20
four times, lived well and in good compass; and
now I live out of all order, out of all compass.

Bard. Why, you are so fat, Sir John, that you
must needs be out of all compass, out of all reasonable compass, Sir John.   26

Fal. Do thou amend thy face, and I'll amend my
life. Thou art our admiral; thou bearest the lantern in the poop, but 'tis in the nose of thee. Thou
art the Knight of the Burning Lamp.   30

Bard. Why, Sir John, my face does you no harm.

Fal. No, I'll be sworn; I make as good use of it
as many a man doth of a Death's-head or a *memento
mori;* I never see thy face but I think upon hell- 35
fire and Dives that lived in purple; for there he is
in his robes, burning, burning. If thou wert any
way given to virtue, I would swear by thy face; my
oath should be, "By this fire, that's God's angel;"
but thou art altogether given over, and wert 40
indeed, but for the light in thy face, the son of utter
darkness. When thou ran'st up Gadshill in the
night to catch my horse, if I did not think thou
hadst been an *ignis fatuus* or a ball of wildfire,
there's no purchase in money. O, thou art a 45
perpetual triumph, an everlasting bonfire-light!
Thou hast saved me a thousand marks in links and
torches, walking with thee in the night betwixt
tavern and tavern; but the sack that thou hast
drunk me would have bought me lights as good 50
cheap at the dearest chandler's in Europe. I have
maintain'd that salamander of yours with fire any
time this two and thirty years; God reward me
for it!   55

Bard. 'Sblood, I would my face were in your
belly!

Fal. God-a-mercy! so should I be sure to be
heart-burn'd.

Enter HOSTESS.

How now, Dame Partlet the hen! have you inquir'd yet who pick'd my pocket?   61

Host. Why, Sir John, what do you think, Sir
John? Do you think I keep thieves in my house?
I have search'd, I have inquired, so has my husband, man by man, boy by boy, servant by 65
servant. The [tithe] of a hair was never lost in my
house before.

Fal. Ye lie, hostess. Bardolph was shav'd and
lost many a hair; and I'll be sworn my pocket was
pick'd. Go to, you are a woman, go.   70

Host. Who? I? No; I defy thee. God's light,
I was never call'd so in mine own house before.

Fal. Go to, I know you well enough.

Host. No, Sir John; you do not know me, Sir
John. I know you, Sir John; you owe me 75
money, Sir John; and now you pick a quarrel to
beguile me of it. I bought you a dozen of shirts
to your back.

Fal. Dowlas, filthy dowlas. I have given them
away to bakers' wives; they have made bolters of
them.   81

Host. Now, as I am a true woman, holland of
eight shillings an ell. You owe money here besides, Sir John, for your diet and by-drinkings, and
money lent you, four and twenty pound.   86

Fal. He had his part of it; let him pay.

Host. He? Alas, he is poor; he hath nothing.

Fal. How! poor? Look upon his face; what call
you rich? Let them coin his nose, let them 90
coin his cheeks. I'll not pay a denier. What, will
you make a younker of me? Shall I not take mine
ease in mine inn but I shall have my pocket pick'd?
I have lost a seal-ring of my grandfather's worth
forty mark.   95

Host. O Jesu, I have heard the Prince tell him,
I know not how oft, that that ring was copper!

Fal. How! the Prince is a Jack, a sneak-cup.
'Sblood, an he were here, I would cudgel him like a
dog, if he would say so.   101

Enter the PRINCE [*and* PETO], *marching, and*
FALSTAFF *meets them playing on his truncheon
like a fife.*

How now, lad! is the wind in that door, i' faith?
Must we all march?

Bard. Yea, two and two, Newgate fashion.

Host. My lord, I pray you, hear me.   105

Prince. What say'st thou, Mistress Quickly?
How doth thy husband? I love him well; he is an
honest man.

Host. Good my lord, hear me.

Fal. Prithee, let her alone, and list to me.   110

Prince. What say'st thou, Jack?

Fal. The other night I fell asleep here behind the
arras and had my pocket pick'd. This house is
turn'd bawdy-house; they pick pockets.

Prince. What didst thou lose, Jack?   115

Fal. Wilt thou believe me, Hal? Three or four
bonds of forty pound a-piece, and a seal-ring of my
grandfather's.

Prince. A trifle, some eight-penny matter.

Host. So I told him, my lord, and I said I 120
heard your Grace say so; and, my lord, he speaks

---

28. **admiral**: flagship. 36. **Dives**: the rich man in *Luke* xvi.19–31. 44. *ignis fatuus:* will o' the wisp. 46. **triumph**: public celebration. 47. **links**: torches. 66. **[tithe]** (Theobald). *tight* Q. 79. **Dowlas**: coarse linen. 80. **bolters**: sieves for flour. 82. **holland**: fine linen. 84. **by-drinkings**: i.e., between meals. 91. **denier**: tenth of a penny. 92. **younker**: novice. 99. **Jack**: knave. **sneak-cup**: a shirker in drinking. 104. **Newgate**: a London prison.

most vilely of you, like a foul-mouth'd man as he is, and said he would cudgel you.

Prince. What! he did not?

Host. There's neither faith, truth, nor womanhood in me else. 126

Fal. There's no more faith in thee than in a stew'd prune; nor no more truth in thee than in a drawn fox; and for womanhood, Maid Marian may be the deputy's wife of the ward to thee. Go, you thing, go. 131

Host. Say, what thing? what thing?

Fal. What thing? Why, a thing to thank God on.

Host. I am no thing to thank God on, I 135 would thou shouldst know it. I am an honest man's wife; and, setting thy knighthood aside, thou art a knave to call me so.

Fal. Setting thy womanhood aside, thou art a beast to say otherwise. 140

Host. Say, what beast, thou knave, thou?

Fal. What beast? Why, an otter.

Prince. An otter, Sir John! Why an otter?

Fal. Why, she's neither fish nor flesh; a man knows not where to have her. 145

Host. Thou art an unjust man in saying so. Thou or any man knows where to have me, thou knave, thou!

Prince. Thou say'st true, hostess; and he slanders thee most grossly. 150

Host. So he doth you, my lord; and said this other day you ought him a thousand pound.

Prince. Sirrah, do I owe you a thousand pound?

Fal. A thousand pound, Hal! A million. 155 Thy love is worth a million; thou ow'st me thy love.

Host. Nay, my lord, he called you Jack, and said he would cudgel you.

Fal. Did I, Bardolph? 160

Bard. Indeed, Sir John, you said so.

Fal. Yea, if he said my ring was copper.

Prince. I say 'tis copper. Dar'st thou be as good as thy word now? 164

Fal. Why, Hal, thou know'st, as thou art but man, I dare; but as thou art Prince, I fear thee as I fear the roaring of the lion's whelp.

Prince. And why not as the lion?

Fal. The King himself is to be feared as the lion. Dost thou think I'll fear thee as I fear thy 170 father? Nay, an I do, I pray God my girdle break.

Prince. O, if it should, how would thy guts fall about thy knees! But, sirrah, there's no room for faith, truth, nor honesty in this bosom of thine;

it is all filled up with guts and midriff. Charge 175 an honest woman with picking thy pocket! Why, thou whoreson, impudent, emboss'd rascal, if there were anything in thy pocket but tavern-reckonings, memorandums of bawdy-houses, and one poor penny-worth of sugar-candy to make thee long- 180 winded, if thy pocket were enrich'd with any other injuries but these, I am a villain. And yet you will stand to it; you will not pocket up wrong. Art thou not asham'd? 184

Fal. Dost thou hear, Hal? Thou know'st in the state of innocency Adam fell; and what should poor Jack Falstaff do in the days of villany? Thou seest I have more flesh than another man, and therefore more frailty. You confess then, you pick'd my pocket? 190

Prince. It appears so by the story.

Fal. Hostess, I forgive thee. Go, make ready breakfast; love thy husband, look to thy servants, cherish thy guests. Thou shalt find me tractable to any honest reason; thou seest I am pacified 195 still. Nay, prithee, be gone. [*Exit Hostess.*

Now, Hal, to the news at court. For the robbery, lad, how is that answered?

Prince. O, my sweet beef, I must still be good angel to thee. The money is paid back again. 200

Fal. O, I do not like that paying back; 'tis a double labour.

Prince. I am good friends with my father and may do anything. 204

Fal. Rob me the exchequer the first thing thou doest, and do it with unwash'd hands too.

Bard. Do, my lord.

Prince. I have procured thee, Jack, a charge of foot. 209

Fal. I would it had been of horse. Where shall I find one that can steal well? O for a fine thief, of the age of two and twenty or thereabouts! I am heinously unprovided. Well, God be thanked for these rebels, they offend none but the virtues. I laud them, I praise them. 215

Prince. Bardolph!

Bard. My lord?

Prince. Go bear this letter to Lord John of Lancaster, to my brother John; this to my Lord of Westmoreland. [*Exit Bardolph.*] Go, Peto, 220 to horse, to horse; for thou and I have thirty miles to ride yet ere dinner time. [*Exit Peto.*] Jack, meet me to-morrow in the Temple hall at two o'clock in the afternoon.

There shalt thou know thy charge, and there 225
receive
Money and order for their furniture.

---

128. **stew'd prune:** harlot. 129. **drawn:** i.e., out of his hole, and seeking to trick his pursuers. **Maid Marian:** a character in Robin Hood ballads and May-games, not admired by Puritanical burgesses. 145. **have:** find, place. 152. **ought:** owed. 177. **emboss'd:** swollen. 182. **injuries:** incriminating articles. 206. **with unwash'd hands:** hastily. 226. **furniture:** equipment.

The land is burning; Percy stands on high;
And either we or they must lower lie.   [*Exit.*]
  Fal. Rare words! brave world! Hostess, my
    breakfast, come!
O, I could wish this tavern were my drum!   230
                            [*Exit.*

ACT IV

SCENE I. [*The rebel camp near Shrewsbury.*]

Enter HOTSPUR, WORCESTER, *and* DOUGLAS.

  Hot. Well said, my noble Scot! If speaking
    truth
In this fine age were not thought flattery,
Such attribution should the Douglas have
As not a soldier of this season's stamp
Should go so general current through the world.   5
By God, I cannot flatter; I do defy
The tongues of soothers; but a braver place
In my heart's love hath no man than yourself.
Nay, task me to my word; approve me, lord.
  Doug. Thou art the king of honour.   10
No man so potent breathes upon the ground
But I will beard him.

Enter a MESSENGER *with letters.*

  Hot.   Do so, and 'tis well. —
What letters hast thou there? — I can but thank
    you.
  Mess. These letters come from your father.
  Hot. Letters from him! Why comes he not
    himself?   15
  Mess. He cannot come, my lord; he is grievous
    sick.
  Hot. 'Zounds! how has he the leisure to be sick
In such a justling time? Who leads his power?
Under whose government come they along?
  Mess. His letters bears his mind, not I, my
    [lord].   20
  Wor. I prithee, tell me, doth he keep his bed?
  Mess. He did, my lord, four days ere I set forth;
And at the time of my departure thence
He was much fear'd by his physicians.
  Wor. I would the state of time had first been
    whole   25
Ere he by sickness had been visited.
His health was never better worth than now.
  Hot. Sick now! droop now! This sickness doth
    infect
The very life-blood of our enterprise;
'Tis catching hither, even to our camp.   30

He writes me here, that inward sickness —
And that his friends by deputation could not
So soon be drawn, nor did he think it meet
To lay so dangerous and dear a trust
On any soul remov'd but on his own.   35
Yet doth he give us bold advertisement
That with our small conjunction we should on
To see how fortune is dispos'd to us;
For, as he writes, there is no quailing now,
Because the King is certainly possess'd   40
Of all our purposes. What say you to it?
  Wor. Your father's sickness is a maim to us.
  Hot. A perilous gash, a very limb lopp'd off.
And yet, in faith, 'tis not; his present want
Seems more than we shall find it. Were it good   45
To set the exact wealth of all our states
All at one cast? to set so rich a main
On the nice hazard of one doubtful hour?
It were not good; for therein should we read
The very bottom and the soul of hope,   50
The very list, the very utmost bound
Of all our fortunes.
  Doug.   Faith, and so we should;
Where now remains a sweet reversion.
We may boldly spend upon the hope of what
[Is] to come in.   55
A comfort of retirement lives in this.
  Hot. A rendezvous, a home to fly unto,
If that the devil and mischance look big
Upon the maidenhead of our affairs.
  Wor. But yet I would your father had been
    here.   60
The quality and hair of our attempt
Brooks no division. It will be thought
By some that know not why he is away
That wisdom, loyalty, and mere dislike
Of our proceedings kept the earl from hence;   65
And think how such an apprehension
May turn the tide of fearful faction
And breed a kind of question in our cause.
For well you know we of the off'ring side
Must keep aloof from strict arbitrement,   70
And stop all sight-holes, every loop from whence
The eye of reason may pry in upon us.
This absence of your father's draws a curtain,
That shows the ignorant a kind of fear
Before not dreamt of.
  Hot.   You strain too far.   75
I rather of his absence make this use:
It lends a lustre and more great opinion,
A larger dare to our great enterprise,
Than if the earl were here; for men must think,

Act IV, sc. i, 7. **soothers:** flatterers. 9. **approve:** test. 20. [lord] (Capell). *mind* Q. 32. **deputation:** deputy, agent.
35. **remov'd:** other. 36. **advertisement:** advice. 37. **conjunction:** allied force. 44. **want:** absence. 46. **set:** stake.
47. **main:** stake. 48. **nice:** delicate. 51. **list:** limit. 53. **Where:** whereas. **reversion:** something to fall back on. 55.
[Is] F. *tis* Q. 58–59. **look . . . maidenhead:** frown upon the early stages. 61. **hair:** fiber, quality. 69. **off'ring:** attacking.
70. **arbitrement:** judicial decision.

If we without his help can make a head   80
To push against a kingdom, with his help
We shall o'erturn it topsy-turvy down.
Yet all goes well, yet all our joints are whole.
  Doug. As heart can think. There is not such a
    word
Spoke of in Scotland as this term of fear.   85

      Enter Sir Richard Vernon.

  Hot. My cousin Vernon! welcome, by my soul.
  Ver. Pray God my news be worth a welcome,
    lord.
The Earl of Westmoreland, seven thousand strong,
Is marching hitherwards; with him Prince John.
  Hot. No harm. What more?
  Ver.   And further, I have learn'd,
The King himself in person is set forth,   91
Or hitherwards intended speedily,
With strong and mighty preparation.
  Hot. He shall be welcome too. Where is his son,
The nimble-footed madcap Prince of Wales,   95
And his comrades, that daff'd the world aside
And bid it pass?
  Ver.   All furnish'd, all in arms;
All plum'd like estridges that with the wind
Bated, like eagles having lately bath'd;
Glittering in golden coats, like images;   100
As full of spirit as the month of May
And gorgeous as the sun at midsummer;
Wanton as youthful goats, wild as young bulls.
I saw young Harry with his beaver on,
His cuisses on his thighs, gallantly arm'd,   105
Rise from the ground like feathered Mercury,
And vaulted with such ease into his seat
As if an angel dropp'd down from the clouds
To turn and wind a fiery Pegasus
And witch the world with noble horsemanship. 110
  Hot. No more, no more! Worse than the sun
    in March,
This praise doth nourish agues. Let them come!
They come like sacrifices in their trim,
And to the fire-ey'd maid of smoky war
All hot and bleeding will we offer them.   115
The mailed Mars shall on his altar sit
Up to the ears in blood. I am on fire
To hear this rich reprisal is so nigh
And yet not ours. Come, let me taste my horse,
Who is to bear me like a thunderbolt   120
Against the bosom of the Prince of Wales.
Harry to Harry shall, hot horse to horse,
Meet and ne'er part till one drop down a corse.
O that Glendower were come!
  Ver.   There is more news.

I learn'd in Worcester, as I rode along,   125
He [cannot] draw his power this fourteen days.
  Doug. That's the worst tidings that I hear of
    [yet].
  Wor. Ay, by my faith, that bears a frosty
    sound.
  Hot. What may the King's whole battle reach
    unto?
  Ver. To thirty thousand.
  Hot.   Forty let it be!   130
My father and Glendower being both away,
The powers of us may serve so great a day.
Come, let us take a muster speedily.
Doomsday is near; die all, die merrily.
  Doug. Talk not of dying; I am out of fear   135
Of death or death's hand for this one half-year.
                            [Exeunt.

    Scene II. [*A public road near Coventry.*]

    Enter Falstaff *and* Bardolph.

  Fal. Bardolph, get thee before to Coventry; fill
me a bottle of sack. Our soldiers shall march
through; we'll to Sutton Cophill to-night.
  Bard. Will you give me money, captain?
  Fal. Lay out, lay out.   5
  Bard. This bottle makes an angel.
  Fal. An if it do, take it for thy labour; and if it
make twenty, take them all; I'll answer the coinage. Bid my lieutenant Peto meet me at town's
end.   10
  Bard. I will, captain; farewell.   [*Exit.*
  Fal. If I be not ashamed of my soldiers, I am a
sous'd gurnet. I have misus'd the King's press
damnably. I have got, in exchange of a hundred
and fifty soldiers, three hundred and odd pounds. 15
I press me none but good householders, yeoman's
sons; inquire me out contracted bachelors, such as
had been ask'd twice on the banns; such a commodity of warm slaves, as had as lieve hear the
devil as a drum; such as fear the report of a   20
caliver worse than a struck fowl or a hurt wild-
duck. I press'd me none but such toasts-and-
butter, with hearts in their bellies no bigger than
pins' heads; and they have bought out their
services; and now my whole charge consists of   25
ancients, corporals, lieutenants, gentlemen of
companies — slaves as ragged as Lazarus in the
painted cloth, where the glutton's dogs licked his
sores; and such as, indeed, were never soldiers, but
discarded unjust serving-men, younger sons   30
to younger brothers, revolted tapsters and ostlers
trade-fallen, the cankers of a calm world and a

---

  96. **daff'd:** thrust. 98. **estridges:** ostriches. 99. **Bated:** beat their wings. 104. **beaver:** (face part of the) helmet.
118. **reprisal:** prize. 126. **[cannot]** Q5. *can* Q1. 127. **[yet]** Q5. *it* Q1.
  Sc. ii, 6. angel: 10s. 13. **sous'd gurnet:** pickled fish. **press:** warrant for conscripting. 18. **commodity:** lot. 19.
warm: comfortable. 21. **caliver:** musket. 26. **ancients:** ensigns. 32. **trade-fallen:** out of work.

long peace, ten times more dishonourable ragged than an old feaz'd ancient: and such have I, to fill up the rooms of them as have bought out their 35 services, that you would think that I had a hundred and fifty tatter'd prodigals lately come from swine-keeping, from eating draff and husks. A mad fellow met me on the way and told me I had un-loaded all the gibbets and press'd the dead 40 bodies. No eye hath seen such scarecrows. I'll not march through Coventry with them, that's flat. Nay, and the villains march wide betwixt the legs, as if they had gyves on; for indeed I had the most of them out of prison. There's but a 45 shirt and a half in all my company; and the half shirt is two napkins tack'd together and thrown over the shoulders like an herald's coat without sleeves; and the shirt, to say the truth, stolen from my host at Saint Alban's, or the red-nose inn- 50 keeper of Daventry. But that's all one; they'll find linen enough on every hedge.

Enter the PRINCE *and* WESTMORELAND.

Prince. How now, blown Jack! how now, quilt! 54

Fal. What, Hal! how now, mad wag! What a devil dost thou in Warwickshire? My good Lord of Westmoreland, I cry you mercy! I thought your honour had already been at Shrewsbury. 59

West. Faith, Sir John, 'tis more than time that I were there, and you too; but my powers are there already. The King, I can tell you, looks for us all. We must away all night.

Fal. Tut, never fear me. I am as vigilant as a cat to steal cream. 65

Prince. I think, to steal cream indeed, for thy theft hath already made thee butter. But tell me, Jack, whose fellows are these that come after?

Fal. Mine, Hal, mine.

Prince. I did never see such pitiful rascals. 70

Fal. Tut, tut; good enough to toss; food for powder, food for powder; they'll fill a pit as well as better. Tush, man, mortal men, mortal men.

West. Ay, but, Sir John, methinks they are exceeding poor and bare, too beggarly. 75

Fal. Faith, for their poverty, I know not where they had that; and for their bareness, I am sure they never learn'd that of me.

Prince. No, I'll be sworn; unless you call three fingers on the ribs bare. But, sirrah, make haste. Percy is already in the field. 81

Fal. What, is the King encamp'd?

West. He is, Sir John. I fear we shall stay too long.

Fal. Well,

To the latter end of a fray and the beginning of a feast 85
Fits a dull fighter and a keen guest. [*Exeunt.*

SCENE III. [*The rebel camp near Shrewsbury.*]

Enter HOTSPUR, WORCESTER, DOUGLAS, *and* VERNON.

Hot. We'll fight with him to-night.
Wor. It may not be.
Doug. You give him then advantage.
Ver. Not a whit.
Hot. Why say you so? Looks he not for supply?
Ver. So do we.
Hot. His is certain, ours is doubtful.
Wor. Good cousin, be advis'd; stir not to-night. 5
Ver. Do not, my lord.
Doug. You do not counsel well.
You speak it out of fear and cold heart.
Ver. Do me no slander, Douglas. By my life,
And I dare well maintain it with my life,
If well-respected honour bid me on 10
I hold as little counsel with weak fear
As you, my lord, or any Scot that this day lives.
Let it be seen to-morrow in the battle
Which of us fears.
Doug. Yea, or to-night.
Ver. Content.
Hot. To-night, say I. 15
Ver. Come, come, it may not be. I wonder much,
Being men of such great leading as you are,
That you foresee not what impediments
Drag back our expedition. Certain horse
Of my cousin Vernon's are not yet come up. 20
Your uncle Worcester's horse came but to-day;
And now their pride and mettle is asleep,
Their courage with hard labour tame and dull,
That not a horse is half the half of himself.
Hot. So are the horses of the enemy 25
In general, journey-bated and brought low.
The better part of ours are full of rest.
Wor. The number of the King exceedeth ours.
For God's sake, cousin, stay till all come in.
[*The trumpet sounds a parley.*

Enter SIR WALTER BLUNT.

Blunt. I come with gracious offers from the King,
If you vouchsafe me hearing and respect. 31
Hot. Welcome, Sir Walter Blunt; and would to God
You were of our determination!
Some of us love you well; and even those some

---

34. **feaz'd ancient:** torn flag. 38. **draff:** swill. 44. **gyves:** fetters. 63. **all night:** marching all night. Ff read *all to night.* Sc. iii, 3. **supply:** reinforcements. 17. **leading:** leadership. 26. **journey-bated:** weary from travel. 33. **determination:** party.

Envy your great deservings and good name, 35
Because you are not of our quality,
But stand against us like an enemy.
   Blunt. And God defend but still I should stand so,
So long as out of limit and true rule
You stand against anointed majesty. 40
But to my charge. The King hath sent to know
The nature of your griefs, and whereupon
You conjure from the breast of civil peace
Such bold hostility, teaching his duteous land
Audacious cruelty. If that the King 45
Have any way your good deserts forgot,
Which he confesseth to be manifold,
He bids you name your griefs; and with all speed
You shall have your desires with interest
And pardon absolute for yourself and these 50
Herein misled by your suggestion.
   Hot. The King is kind; and well we know the King
Knows at what time to promise, when to pay.
My father and my uncle and myself
Did give him that same royalty he wears; 55
And when he was not six and twenty strong,
Sick in the world's regard, wretched and low,
A poor unminded outlaw sneaking home,
My father gave him welcome to the shore;
And when he heard him swear and vow to God 60
He came but to be Duke of Lancaster,
To sue his livery and beg his peace,
With tears of innocence and terms of zeal,
My father, in kind heart and pity mov'd,
Swore him assistance and perform'd it too. 65
Now when the lords and barons of the realm
Perceiv'd Northumberland did lean to him,
The more and less came in with cap and knee;
Met him in boroughs, cities, villages,
Attended him on bridges, stood in lanes, 70
Laid gifts before him, proffer'd him their oaths,
Gave him their heirs as pages, followed him
Even at the heels in golden multitudes.
He presently, as greatness knows itself,
Steps me a little higher than his vow 75
Made to my father, while his blood was poor,
Upon the naked shore at Ravenspurgh;
And now, forsooth, takes on him to reform
Some certain edicts and some strait decrees
That lie too heavy on the commonwealth, 80
Cries out upon abuses, seems to weep
Over his country's wrongs; and by this face,
This seeming brow of justice, did he win
The hearts of all that he did angle for;
Proceeded further; cut me off the heads 85
Of all the favourites that the absent king

In deputation left behind him here,
When he was personal in the Irish war.
   Blunt. Tut, I came not to hear this.
   Hot.   Then to the point.
In short time after, he depos'd the King; 90
Soon after that, depriv'd him of his life;
And in the neck of that, task'd the whole state.
To make that worse, suffer'd his kinsman March,
Who is, if every owner were well plac'd,
Indeed his king, to be engag'd in Wales, 95
There without ransom to lie forfeited;
Disgrac'd me in my happy victories,
Sought to entrap me by intelligence;
Rated mine uncle from the council-board;
In rage dismiss'd my father from the court; 100
Broke oath on oath, committed wrong on wrong,
And in conclusion drove us to seek out
This head of safety; and withal to pry
Into his title, the which we find
Too indirect for long continuance. 105
   Blunt. Shall I return this answer to the King?
   Hot. Not so, Sir Walter; we'll withdraw a while.
Go to the King; and let there be impawn'd
Some surety for a safe return again,
And in the morning early shall mine uncle 110
Bring him our purposes: and so farewell.
   Blunt. I would you would accept of grace and love.
   Hot. And may be so we shall.
   Blunt.   Pray God you do.
                          [Exeunt.

SCENE IV. [*York. The Archbishop's palace.*]

Enter the ARCHBISHOP OF YORK *and* SIR MICHAEL.

   Arch. Hie, good Sir Michael; bear this sealed brief
With winged haste to the Lord Marshal,
This to my cousin Scroop, and all the rest
To whom they are directed. If you knew
How much they do import, you would make haste.
   Sir M. My good lord, 6
I guess their tenour.
   Arch.   Like enough you do.
To-morrow, good Sir Michael, is a day
Wherein the fortune of ten thousand men
Must bide the touch; for, sir, at Shrewsbury, 10
As I am truly given to understand,
The King with mighty and quick-raised power
Meets with Lord Harry; and, I fear, Sir Michael,
What with the sickness of Northumberland,
Whose power was in the first proportion, 15
And what with Owen Glendower's absence thence,
Who with them was a rated sinew too

---

36. **quality:** party. 62. **sue his livery:** claim his inheritance. 79. **strait:** strict. 88. **personal:** in person. 92. **task'd:** taxed. 98. **intelligence:** spies. 99. **Rated:** scolded. 103. **head of safety:** safety by armed force.
   Sc. iv, 15. **proportion:** magnitude. 17. **rated sinew:** force counted on.

And comes not in, o'er-rul'd by prophecies,
I fear the power of Percy is too weak
To wage an instant trial with the King.   20
   Sir M. Why, my good lord, you need not fear;
There is Douglas and Lord Mortimer.
   Arch. No, Mortimer is not there.
   Sir M. But there is Murdoch, Vernon, Lord
     Harry Percy,
And there is my Lord of Worcester, and a head 25
Of gallant warriors, noble gentlemen.
   Arch. And so there is; but yet the King hath
     drawn
The special head of all the land together:
The Prince of Wales, Lord John of Lancaster,
The noble Westmoreland, and warlike Blunt;   30
And many moe corrivals and dear men
Of estimation and command in arms.
   Sir M. Doubt not, my lord, they shall be well
     oppos'd.
   Arch. I hope no less, yet needful 'tis to fear;
And, to prevent the worst, Sir Michael, speed; 35
For if Lord Percy thrive not, ere the King
Dismiss his power he means to visit us,
For he hath heard of our confederacy,
And 'tis but wisdom to make strong against him.
Therefore make haste. I must go write again   40
To other friends; and so farewell, Sir Michael.
                          [Exeunt.

ACT V

SCENE I. [*The King's camp near Shrewsbury.*]

Enter the KING, PRINCE OF WALES, LORD JOHN OF
   LANCASTER, SIR WALTER BLUNT, *and* FALSTAFF.

   King. How bloodily the sun begins to peer
Above yon [busky] hill! The day looks pale
At his distemperature.
   Prince.   The southern wind
Doth play the trumpet to his purposes,
And by his hollow whistling in the leaves   5
Foretells a tempest and a blust'ring day.
   King. Then with the losers let it sympathize,
For nothing can seem foul to those that win.
                     [The trumpet sounds.

Enter WORCESTER [*and* VERNON].

How now, my Lord of Worcester! 'tis not well
That you and I should meet upon such terms   10
As now we meet. You have deceiv'd our trust,
And made us doff our easy robes of peace,
To crush our old limbs in ungentle steel.
This is not well, my lord, this is not well.
What say you to it? Will you again unknit   15

This churlish knot of all-abhorred war?
And move in that obedient orb again
Where you did give a fair and natural light,
And be no more an exhal'd meteor,
A prodigy of fear and a portent   20
Of broached mischief to the unborn times?
   Wor. Hear me, my liege.
For mine own part, I could be well content
To entertain the lag-end of my life
With quiet hours; for I [do] protest,   25
I have not sought the day of this dislike.
   King. You have not sought it! How comes it,
     then?
   Fal. Rebellion lay in his way, and he found it.
   Prince. Peace, chewet, peace!
   Wor. It pleas'd your Majesty to turn your looks
Of favour from myself and all our house;   31
And yet I must remember you, my lord,
We were the first and dearest of your friends.
For you my staff of office did I break
In Richard's time; and posted day and night   35
To meet you on the way, and kiss your hand,
When yet you were in place and in account
Nothing so strong and fortunate as I.
It was myself, my brother, and his son,
That brought you home and boldly did outdare
The dangers of the time. You swore to us,   41
And you did swear that oath at Doncaster,
That you did nothing purpose 'gainst the state;
Nor claim no further than your new-fall'n right,
The seat of Gaunt, dukedom of Lancaster.   45
To this we swore our aid. But in short space
It rain'd down fortune show'ring on your head;
And such a flood of greatness fell on you,
What with our help, what with the absent King,
What with the injuries of a wanton time,   50
The seeming sufferances that you had borne,
And the contrarious winds that held the King
So long in his unlucky Irish wars
That all in England did repute him dead;
And from this swarm of fair advantages   55
You took occasion to be quickly woo'd
To gripe the general sway into your hand;
Forgot your oath to us at Doncaster;
And being fed by us you us'd us so
As that ungentle gull, the cuckoo's bird,   60
Useth the sparrow; did oppress our nest;
Grew by our feeding to so great a bulk
That even our love durst not come near your sight
For fear of swallowing; but with nimble wing
We were enforc'd, for safety sake, to fly   65
Out of your sight and raise this present head;
Whereby we stand opposed by such means
As you yourself have forg'd against yourself

31. moe: more. corrivals: associates.
  Act V, sc. i, S.D. SIR (Capell). *Earle of Westmorland, Sir* Qq Ff. 2. [busky] Ff: wooded. *bulky* Q. 3. distemperature:
abnormal appearance. 21. broached: set going. 25. [do] F. Om. Qq. 29. chewet: jackdaw. 60. gull, bird: nestling.

By unkind usage, dangerous countenance,
And violation of all faith and troth   70
Sworn to us in your younger enterprise.

King. These things indeed you have articulate,
Proclaim'd at market-crosses, read in churches,
To face the garment of rebellion
With some fine colour that may please the eye   75
Of fickle changelings and poor discontents,
Which gape and rub the elbow at the news
Of hurly-burly innovation.
And never yet did insurrection want
Such water-colours to impaint his cause;   80
Nor moody beggars, starving for a time
Of pell-mell havoc and confusion.

Prince. In both your armies there is many a
        soul
Shall pay full dearly for this encounter,
If once they join in trial. Tell your nephew,   85
The Prince of Wales doth join with all the world
In praise of Henry Percy. By my hopes,
This present enterprise set off his head,
I do not think a braver gentleman,
More active-valiant or more valiant-young,   90
More daring or more bold, is now alive
To grace this latter age with noble deeds.
For my part, I may speak it to my shame,
I have a truant been to chivalry;
And so I hear he doth account me too;   95
Yet this before my father's majesty:
I am content that he shall take the odds
Of his great name and estimation,
And will, to save the blood on either side,
Try fortune with him in a single fight.   100

King. And, Prince of Wales, so dare we venture
        thee,
Albeit considerations infinite
Do make against it. No, good Worcester, no,
We love our people well; even those we love
That are misled upon your cousin's part;   105
And, will they take the offer of our grace,
Both he and they and you, yea, every man
Shall be my friend again and I'll be his.
So tell your cousin, and bring me word
What he will do. But if he will not yield,   110
Rebuke and dread correction wait on us
And they shall do their office. So, be gone;
We will not now be troubled with reply.
We offer fair; take it advisedly.
                [*Exeunt Worcester* [*and Vernon*].

Prince. It will not be accepted, on my life.   115
The Douglas and the Hotspur both together
Are confident against the world in arms.

King. Hence, therefore, every leader to his
        charge,
For, on their answer, will we set on them;

And God befriend us, as our cause is just!   120
        [*Exeunt all but the Prince of Wales and
                Falstaff.*

Fal. Hal, if thou see me down in the battle and
bestride me, so; 'tis a point of friendship.

Prince. Nothing but a colossus can do thee that
friendship. Say thy prayers, and farewell.

Fal. I would 'twere bed-time, Hal, and all well.

Prince. Why, thou owest God a death.   127
                [*Exit.*]

Fal. 'Tis not due yet; I would be loath to pay
him before his day. What need I be so forward
with him that calls not on me? Well, 'tis no   130
matter; honour pricks me on. Yea, but how if
honour prick me off when I came on? How then?
Can honour set to a leg? No. Or an arm? No.
Or take away the grief of a wound? No. Honour
hath no skill in surgery, then? No. What is   135
honour? A word. What is in that word honour?
What is that honour? Air; a trim reckoning! Who
hath it? He that died o' Wednesday. Doth he
feel it? No. Doth he hear it? No. 'Tis insensible, then? Yea, to the dead. But will   140
[it] not live with the living? No. Why? Detraction will not suffer it. Therefore I'll none of it.
Honour is a mere scutcheon: and so ends my
catechism.   [*Exit.*

SCENE II. [*The rebel camp.*]

Enter WORCESTER *and* VERNON.

Wor. O, no, my nephew must not know, Sir
        Richard,
The liberal and kind offer of the King.

Ver. 'Twere best he did.

Wor.   Then are we all [undone].
It is not possible, it cannot be,
The King should keep his word in loving us.   5
He will suspect us still, and find a time
To punish this offence in other faults.
Supposition all our lives shall be stuck full of eyes;
For treason is but trusted like the fox,
Who, ne'er so tame, so cherish'd and lock'd up,   10
Will have a wild trick of his ancestors.
Look how we can, or sad or merrily,
Interpretation will misquote our looks,
And we shall feed like oxen at a stall,
The better cherish'd, still the nearer death.   15
My nephew's trespass may be well forgot;
It hath the excuse of youth and heat of blood,
And an adopted name of privilege,
A hare-brain'd Hotspur, govern'd by a spleen.
All his offences live upon my head   20
And on his father's. We did train him on,
And, his corruption being ta'en from us,

72. **articulate:** stated in articles. 78. **innovation:** rebellion. 88. **set . . . head:** apart. 141. **[it]** Q₂. Om. Q₁.
Sc. ii, 3. **[undone]** Q₅. *under one* Q₁. 8. **Supposition:** suspicion.

We, as the spring of all, shall pay for all.
Therefore, good cousin, let not Harry know,
In any case, the offer of the King.   25
  Ver. Deliver what you will; I'll say 'tis so.
Here comes your cousin.

Enter HOTSPUR [*and* DOUGLAS].

  Hot. My uncle is return'd;
Deliver up my Lord of Westmoreland.
Uncle, what news?   30
  Wor. The King will bid you battle presently.
  Doug. Defy him by the Lord of Westmoreland.
  Hot. Lord Douglas, go you and tell him so.
  Doug. Marry, and shall, and very willingly.
                                                 [*Exit.*
  Wor. There is no seeming mercy in the King. 35
  Hot. Did you beg any? God forbid!
  Wor. I told him gently of our grievances,
Of his oath-breaking; which he mended thus,
By now forswearing that he is forsworn.
He calls us rebels, traitors; and will scourge   40
With haughty arms this hateful name in us.

Re-enter DOUGLAS.

  Doug. Arm, gentlemen; to arms! for I have
    thrown
A brave defiance in King Henry's teeth,
And Westmoreland, that was engag'd, did bear it;
Which cannot choose but bring him quickly on.
  Wor. The Prince of Wales stepp'd forth before
    the King,   46
And, nephew, challeng'd you to single fight.
  Hot. O, would the quarrel lay upon our heads,
And that no man might draw short breath to-day
But I and Harry Monmouth! Tell me, tell me,   50
How show'd his tasking? Seem'd it in contempt?
  Ver. No, by my soul; I never in my life
Did hear a challenge urg'd more modestly,
Unless a brother should a brother dare
To gentle exercise and proof of arms.   55
He gave you all the duties of a man,
Trimm'd up your praises with a princely tongue,
Spoke your deservings like a chronicle,
Making you ever better than his praise
By still dispraising praise valued with you;   60
And, which became him like a prince indeed.
He made a blushing cital of himself,
And chid his truant youth with such a grace
As if he mast'red there a double spirit
Of teaching and of learning instantly.   65
There did he pause; but let me tell the world,
If he outlive the envy of this day,
England did never owe so sweet a hope,
So much misconstrued in his wantonness.
  Hot. Cousin, I think thou art enamoured   70

On his follies. Never did I hear
Of any prince so wild a liberty.
But be he as he will, yet once ere night
I will embrace him with a soldier's arm
That he shall shrink under my courtesy.   75
Arm, arm with speed! and, fellows, soldiers, friends,
Better consider what you have to do
Than I, that have not well the gift of tongue,
Can lift your blood up with persuasion.

Enter a MESSENGER.

  Mess. My lord, here are letters for you.   80
  Hot. I cannot read them now.
O gentlemen, the time of life is short!
To spend that shortness basely were too long,
If life did ride upon a dial's point,
Still ending at the arrival of an hour.   85
An if we live, we live to tread on kings;
If die, brave death, when princes die with us!
Now, for our consciences, the arms are fair
When the intent of bearing them is just.

Enter another MESSENGER.

  [*2.*] *Mess.* My lord, prepare; the King comes on
    apace.   90
  Hot. I thank him that he cuts me from my tale,
For I profess not talking; only this —
Let each man do his best; and here draw I
A sword, whose temper I intend to stain
With the best blood that I can meet withal   95
In the adventure of this perilous day.
Now *Esperance!* Percy! and set on.
Sound all the lofty instruments of war,
And by that music let us all embrace;
For, heaven to earth, some of us never shall   100
A second time do such a courtesy.
                             [*They embrace* [*and exeunt*].

[SCENE III. *Plain between the camps.*]

*The trumpets sound. The King enters with his power
  and passes over. Alarum to the battle. Then
  enter* DOUGLAS *and* SIR WALTER BLUNT.

  Blunt. What is thy name, that in the battle thus
Thou crossest me? What honour dost thou seek
Upon my head?
  Doug.   Know then, my name is Douglas;
And I do haunt thee in the battle thus
Because some tell me that thou art a king.   5
  Blunt. They tell thee true.
  Doug. The Lord of Stafford dear to-day hath
    bought
Thy likeness, for instead of thee, King Harry,
This sword hath ended him. So shall it thee,
Unless thou yield thee as my prisoner.   10

44. engag'd: held as hostage. 51. tasking: challenge. 56. duties: due merits. 60. valued: compared. 62. cital:
mention. 67. envy: malice. 68. owe: own.

Blunt. I was not born a yielder, thou proud Scot;
And thou shalt find a king that will revenge
Lord Stafford's death.
                    [*They fight. Douglas kills Blunt.*

                    Enter HOTSPUR.

Hot. O Douglas, hadst thou fought at Holmedon
    thus,
I never had triumph'd upon a Scot.   16
Doug. All's done, all's won; here breathless lies
    the King.
Hot. Where?
Doug. Here.
Hot. This, Douglas? No. I know this face
    full well.
A gallant knight he was, his name was Blunt;   20
Semblably furnish'd like the King himself.
Doug. Ah! "fool" go with thy soul, whither it
    goes!
A borrowed title hast thou bought too dear.
Why didst thou tell me that thou wert a king? 24
Hot. The King hath many marching in his coats.
Doug. Now, by my sword, I will kill all his coats;
I'll murder all his wardrobe, piece by piece,
Until I meet the King.
Hot.   Up, and away!
Our soldiers stand full fairly for the day.   29
                                        [*Exeunt.*

            Alarum. Enter FALSTAFF, *solus.*

Fal. Though I could scape shot-free at London,
I fear the shot here; here's no scoring but upon
the pate. Soft! who are you? Sir Walter Blunt.
There's honour for you! Here's no vanity! I
am as hot as molten lead, and as heavy too. God
keep lead out of me! I need no more weight 35
than mine own bowels. I have led my ragamuffins
where they are pepper'd. There's not three of
my hundred and fifty left alive; and they are for
the town's end, to beg during life. But who
comes here?   40

                Enter the PRINCE.

Prince. What, stands thou idle here? Lend me
    thy sword.
Many a nobleman lies stark and stiff
Under the hoofs of vaunting enemies,
Whose deaths are yet unreveng'd. I prithee, lend
    me thy sword.   44
Fal. O Hal, I prithee, give me leave to breathe
a while. Turk Gregory never did such deeds in
arms as I have done this day. I have paid Percy,
I have made him sure.

Prince. He is, indeed; and living to kill thee. I
prithee, lend me thy sword.   50
Fal. Nay, before God, Hal, if Percy be alive,
thou gets not my sword; but take my pistol, if thou
wilt.
Prince. Give it me. What, is it in the case?
Fal. Ay, Hal; 'tis hot, 'tis hot. There's that
will sack a city.   56
        [*The Prince draws it out, and finds it to
            be a bottle of sack.*
Prince. What, is it a time to jest and dally now?
                    [*He throws the bottle at him. Exit.*
Fal. Well, if Percy be alive, I'll pierce him. If
he do come in my way, so; if he do not, if I   60
come in his willingly, let him make a carbonado
of me. I like not such grinning honour as Sir
Walter hath. Give me life, which if I can save,
so; if not, honour comes unlook'd for, and there's
an end.   [*Exit.*   65

        SCENE [IV. *Another part of the field.*]

Alarum. Excursions. Enter the KING, *the* PRINCE
[*wounded*], LORD JOHN OF LANCASTER, *and* EARL
OF WESTMORELAND.

King. I prithee,
Harry, withdraw thyself; thou bleedest too much.
Lord John of Lancaster, go you with him.
Lan. Not I, my lord, unless I did bleed too.
Prince. I beseech your Majesty, make up,   5
Lest your retirement do amaze your friends.
King. I will do so.
My Lord of Westmoreland, lead him to his tent.
West. Come, my lord, I'll lead you to your tent.
Prince. Lead me, my lord? I do not need your
    help: 10
And God forbid a shallow scratch should drive
The Prince of Wales from such a field as this,
Where stain'd nobility lies trodden on,
And rebels' arms triumph in massacres!
Lan. We breathe too long. Come, cousin
    Westmoreland,   15
Our duty this way lies; for God's sake, come.
            [*Exeunt Prince John and Westmoreland.*]
Prince. By God, thou hast deceiv'd me, Lan-
    caster;
I did not think thee lord of such a spirit.
Before, I lov'd thee as a brother, John;
But now, I do respect thee as my soul.   20
King. I saw him hold Lord Percy at the point
With lustier maintenance than I did look for
Of such an ungrown warrior.
Prince.   O, this boy
Lends mettle to us all!   [*Exit.*

Sc. iii, 21. **Semblably:** similarly. 30. **shot-free:** without paying. 46. **Turk Gregory:** Pope Gregory VII (Hildebrand).
61. **carbonado:** meat slashed for broiling.
Sc. iv, 5. **make up:** advance. 6. **amaze:** confound. 22. **maintenance:** endurance.

Enter DOUGLAS.

Doug. Another king! they grow like Hydra's
   heads.   25
I am the Douglas, fatal to all those
That wear those colours on them.   What art thou,
That counterfeit'st the person of a king?
King. The King himself; who, Douglas, grieves
   at heart
So many of his shadows thou hast met   30
And not the very King.   I have two boys
Seek Percy and thyself about the field;
But, seeing thou fall'st on me so luckily,
I will assay thee; [so,] defend thyself.
Doug. I fear thou art another counterfeit;   35
And yet, in faith, thou bear'st thee like a king.
But mine I am sure thou art, whoe'er thou be,
And thus I win thee.

They fight; the King being in danger, re-enter
   PRINCE OF WALES.

Prince. Hold up thy head, vile Scot, or thou art
   like
Never to hold it up again!   The spirits   40
Of valiant Shirley, Stafford, Blunt, are in my arms.
It is the Prince of Wales that threatens thee,
Who never promiseth but he means to pay.
                 [They fight: Douglas flies.
Cheerly, my lord, how fares your Grace?
Sir Nicholas Gawsey hath for succour sent,   45
And so hath Clifton.   I'll to Clifton straight.
King. Stay, and breathe a while.
Thou hast redeem'd thy lost opinion,
And show'd thou mak'st some tender of my life
In this fair rescue thou hast brought to me.   50
Prince. O God! they did me too much injury
That ever said I heark'ned for your death.
If it were so, I might have let alone
The insulting hand of Douglas over you,
Which would have been as speedy in your end   55
As all the poisonous potions in the world,
And sav'd the treacherous labour of your son.
King. Make up to Clifton.   I'll to Sir Nicholas
   Gawsey.   *[Exit.*

Enter HOTSPUR.

Hot. If I mistake not, thou art Harry Monmouth.
Prince. Thou speak'st as if I would deny my
   name.   60
Hot. My name is Harry Percy.
Prince.   Why, then I see
A very valiant rebel of the name.
I am the Prince of Wales; and think not, Percy,
To share with me in glory any more.

Two stars keep not their motion in one sphere,   65
Nor can one England brook a double reign
Of Harry Percy and the Prince of Wales.
Hot. Nor shall it, Harry; for the hour is come
To end the one of us; and would to God
Thy name in arms were now as great as mine!   70
Prince. I'll make a greater ere I part from thee,
And all the budding honours on thy crest
I'll crop, to make a garland for my head.
Hot. I can no longer brook thy vanities.
                           [They fight.

Enter FALSTAFF.

Fal. Well said, Hal! to it, Hal!   Nay, you shall
find no boy's play here, I can tell you.   76

Re-enter Douglas; he fights with Falstaff, who falls
   down as if he were dead [and exit Douglas.   Hotspur
   is wounded, and falls].

Hot. O, Harry, thou hast robb'd me of my youth!
I better brook the loss of brittle life
Than those proud titles thou hast won of me.
They wound my thoughts worse than thy sword
   my flesh.   80
But thoughts, the slaves of life, and life, time's fool,
And time, that takes survey of all the world,
Must have a stop.   O, I could prophesy,
But that the earthy and cold hand of death
Lies on my tongue.   No, Percy, thou art dust,   85
And food for —   *[Dies.]*
Prince. For worms, brave Percy.   Fare thee
   well, great heart!
Ill-weav'd ambition, how much art thou shrunk!
When that this body did contain a spirit,
A kingdom for it was too small a bound;   90
But now two paces of the vilest earth
Is room enough.   This earth that bears thee dead
Bears not alive so stout a gentleman.
If thou wert sensible of courtesy,
I should not make so dear a show of zeal.   95
But let my favours hide thy mangled face;
And, even in thy behalf, I'll thank myself
For doing these fair rites of tenderness.
Adieu, and take thy praise with thee to heaven!
Thy ignominy sleep with thee in the grave,   100
But not remems'red in thy epitaph!
             [He spieth Falstaff on the ground.
What, old acquaintance! could not all this flesh
Keep in a little life?   Poor Jack, farewell!
I could have better spar'd a better man.
O, I should have a heavy miss of thee   105
If I were much in love with vanity!

---

34. **[so]** Ff. *and* Q.   48. **opinion:** reputation.   49. **mak'st ... of:** hast some regard for.   77. S.D. **[and ... falls]** (Steevens).
the Prince killeth Percie Qq Ff.   81. **thoughts, the slaves** Q.   F reads *thought's the slave.*   But probably *slaves* is in apposition
with *thoughts, fool* with *life,* and *thoughts, fool,* and *time* are all subjects of *Must.*   96. **favours.**   He covers Hotspur's face
with a scarf, or the like.   100. **ignominy:** pronounced *ignomy* which Ff read.

Death hath not struck so fat a deer to-day,
Though many dearer, in this bloody fray.
Embowell'd will I see thee by and by;   109
Till then in blood by noble Percy lie.   [*Exit.*

Fal. (*Rising up.*) Embowell'd! if thou embowel
me to-day, I'll give you leave to powder me and
eat me too to-morrow.   'Sblood, 'twas time to
counterfeit, or that hot termagant Scot had paid
me scot and lot too.   Counterfeit? I lie, I am   115
no counterfeit.   To die is to be a counterfeit, for
he is but the counterfeit of a man who hath not
the life of a man; but to counterfeit dying, when a
man thereby liveth, is to be no counterfeit, but the
true and perfect image of life indeed.   The   120
better part of valour is discretion; in the which
better part I have saved my life.   'Zounds, I am
afraid of this gunpowder Percy though he be dead.
How, if he should counterfeit too and rise? By
my faith, I am afraid he would prove the better   125
counterfeit.   Therefore I'll make him sure; yea,
and I'll swear I kill'd him.   Why may not he
rise as well as I? Nothing confutes me but eyes,
and nobody sees me.   Therefore, sirrah [*stabbing
him*], with a new wound in your thigh, come   130
you along with me.

[*Takes up Hotspur on his back.*

Re-enter the Prince of Wales *and* Lord John
of Lancaster.

Prince. Come, brother John; full bravely hast
      thou flesh'd
Thy maiden sword.
Lan.   But, soft! whom have we here?
Did you not tell me this fat man was dead?   135
Prince. I did; I saw him dead,
Breathless and bleeding on the ground.   Art thou
      alive?
Or is it fantasy that plays upon our eyesight?
I prithee, speak; we will not trust our eyes   139
Without our ears.   Thou art not what thou seem'st.
Fal. No, that's certain; I am not a double man;
but if I be not Jack Falstaff, then am I a Jack.
There is Percy [*throwing the body down*].   If your
father will do me any honour, so; if not, let him
kill the next Percy himself.   I look to be either earl
or duke, I can assure you.   146
Prince. Why, Percy I kill'd myself, and saw
      thee dead.
Fal. Didst thou? Lord, Lord, how this world
is given to lying! I grant you I was down and
out of breath, and so was he; but we rose both   150
at an instant and fought a long hour by Shrewsbury clock.   If I may be believed, so; if not, let
them that should reward valour bear the sin
upon their own heads.   I'll take it upon my death,
I gave him this wound in the thigh.   If the man   155

were alive and would deny it, 'zounds, I would
make him eat a piece of my sword.
Lan. This is the strangest tale that ever I
      heard.
Prince. This is the strangest fellow, brother John.
Come, bring your luggage nobly on your back. 160
For my part, if a lie may do thee grace,
I'll gild it with the happiest terms I have.

[*A retreat is sounded.*
The trumpet sounds retreat; the day is ours.
Come, brother, let us to the highest of the field,
To see what friends are living, who are dead. 165

[*Exeunt* [*Prince of Wales and Lancaster*].
Fal. I'll follow, as they say, for reward. He
that rewards me, God reward him! If I do grow
great, I'll grow less; for I'll purge, and leave
sack, and live cleanly as a nobleman should do.

[*Exit.*

Scene [V. *Another part of the field.*]

The trumpets sound.   Enter the King, Prince of
Wales, Lord John of Lancaster, Earl of
Westmoreland, *with* Worcester *and* Vernon
prisoners.

King. Thus ever did rebellion find rebuke.
Ill-spirited Worcester! did not we send grace,
Pardon, and terms of love to all of you?
And wouldst thou turn our offers contrary?
Misuse the tenour of thy kinsman's trust?   5
Three knights upon our party slain to-day,
A noble earl, and many a creature else
Had been alive this hour,
If like a Christian thou hadst truly borne
Betwixt our armies true intelligence.   10
Wor. What I have done my safety urg'd me to;
And I embrace this fortune patiently,
Since not to be avoided it falls on me.
King. Bear Worcester to the death and Vernon
      too.
Other offenders we will pause upon.   15

[*Exeunt Worcester and Vernon* [*guarded*].
How goes the field?
Prince. The noble Scot, Lord Douglas, when he
      saw
The fortune of the day quite turn'd from him,
The noble Percy slain, and all his men
Upon the foot of fear, fled with the rest;   20
And falling from a hill, he was so bruis'd
That the pursuers took him.   At my tent
The Douglas is; and I beseech your Grace
I may dispose of him.
King.   With all my heart.
Prince. Then, brother John of Lancaster, to
      you
This honourable bounty shall belong.   26

112. **powder:** salt. 115. **scot and lot:** completely. 141. **double:** referring to the body of Hotspur he is carrying.

Go to the Douglas, and deliver him
Up to his pleasure, ransomless and free.
His valours shown upon our crests to-day
Have taught us how to cherish such high deeds   30
Even in the bosom of our adversaries.
   Lan. I thank your Grace for this high courtesy,
Which I shall give away immediately.
   King. Then this remains, that we divide our
     power.
You, son John, and my cousin Westmoreland   35

Towards York shall bend you with your dearest
     speed,
To meet Northumberland and the prelate Scroop,
Who, as we hear, are busily in arms.
Myself and you, son Harry, will towards Wales,
To fight with Glendower and the Earl of March.
Rebellion in this land shall lose his sway,   41
Meeting the check of such another day;
And since this business so fair is done,
Let us not leave till all our own be won.   [*Exeunt.*

The Second Part of Henry the Fourth

ON THE TWENTY-THIRD OF AUGUST, 1600, the Second Part of *Henry IV* was entered in the Stationers' Register, and the first and only Quarto was published in the same year with the title: *The Second part of Henrie the fourth, continuing to his death, and coronation of Henri the fift. With the humours of Sir John Falstaffe, and Swaggering Pistoll.* Though the Quarto lacks about 170 lines which appear in the Folio, recent opinion tends to the conclusion that the earlier publication is nearer to Shakespeare's manuscript, and may have been printed from that manuscript. The Folio text lacks 40 lines given by the Quarto and bears marks of revision that suggest that it was printed from a transcript of a prompt-book. The present text is based upon the Quarto, except for the missing 170 lines for which the Folio is the only source. These are enclosed in brackets in the present text.

The reasons for the omissions in the Quarto have been the subject of much discussion. It is not likely, judging from the awkwardness with which the cuts are made, that they were intended merely to produce an acting version. Some may have been due to inadvertence and difficulty in reading the manuscript; others point to political reasons. Eleven references to Richard II appear in the Folio, all of which have been cut out of the Quarto, and it is impossible not to connect this with the Queen's attitude towards Richard's abdication discussed in the Introduction to *Richard II*. Other omissions, such as references to the right of rebellion, may have been due to the political tension during the trial of Essex.

It is evident that the writing of Part II followed closely on that of Part I, and there is general agreement on 1598 as the date of composition.

As in the case of Part I, the historical material is taken chiefly from Holinshed's *Chronicles*. The story of the attack on the Chief Justice follows the account given in Elyot's *Governour* (1531), which had been reproduced in Stow's *Annals*, in either of which Shakespeare may have read it. Suggestions for the scene of the recruiting in Gloucestershire and of the rejection of Falstaff are to be found in the old play, *The Famous Victories of Henry the Fifth*, from which he borrowed in Part I, but they are only suggestions.

Many critics have found Part II inferior to Part I, and it must be admitted that the serious part of the play provides no such dramatic contrast of character as that between Hotspur and the Prince in the earlier play. Nor does the victory over the rebels obtained by the treachery of Prince John compare in effectiveness with the climax provided by the battle of Shrewsbury. Shakespeare had the disadvantage also of having to make a plot out of the same kind of material as he had just used — the fomenting of conspiracy and the overthrow of rebellion. This difficulty is probably responsible for the increased amount of space given to comic scenes.

The theme of the relation of father and son is, however, developed much more fully and with much more emotional power. There is in the treatment of the King's despair over the Prince's wildness a characteristic strain of Shakespeare's favorite device of dramatic irony. The audience of Elizabeth's time all knew that Hal was to turn out all right, and Shakespeare made sure they would not forget it by making the Prince remind them of it as early as the end of I.ii of Part I. This does not detract from the pathos of Henry's anxiety and depression, but it makes possible a fuller enjoyment of the comedy element.

Whatever may be thought of the comparative merit of the historical scenes, there is no decline in the part of the play carried by Falstaff. The conversations between him and the Chief Justice, the Tavern riots in which Mrs. Quickly is developed from the sketch in Part I and Doll Tearsheet and Pistol are added to the group, and the scenes with Shallow and Silence in Gloucestershire are among the greatest triumphs of Shakespearean comedy. The part played by the Prince in these is a diminishing one, the dramatist clearly preparing him and us for his final withdrawal. When this occurs in the great scene following the coronation and the reconciliation with the Lord Chief Justice, the transformation of the wild prince into the hero-king is complete. This had obviously been contemplated by Shakespeare from the first and was, of course, inevitable. Yet few episodes in these plays have been more bitterly resented than the rejection of Falstaff. Much argument has been waged in attack and defense, all of which goes to show how completely and perhaps uniquely Shakespeare has succeeded in producing in his greatest comic creation the absolute illusion of reality.

THE SECOND PART OF
HENRY THE FOURTH

The Second Part of Henry the Fourth

[DRAMATIS PERSONÆ]

RUMOUR, *the Presenter.*
KING HENRY IV.
HENRY, PRINCE [OF WALES], *afterwards crowned*
   Henry V.
PRINCE JOHN OF LANCASTER, | *sons to Henry*
[PRINCE] HUMPHREY OF | *IV and breth-*
   GLOUCESTER, | *ren to Henry*
THOMAS [DUKE] OF CLARENCE, | *V.*
[EARL OF] NORTHUMBERLAND,
[SCROOP,] *archbishop of York,*
[LORD] MOWBRAY, | *opposites*
[LORD] HASTINGS, | *against King*
LORD BARDOLPH, | *Henry IV.*
TRAVERS, | *retainers of North-*
MORTON, | *umberland,*
[SIR JOHN] COLVILLE,
[EARL OF] WARWICK,
[EARL OF] WESTMORELAND,
[EARL OF] SURREY, | *of the King's*
GOWER, | *Party.*
HARCOURT,
LORD CHIEF JUSTICE,

[SIR JOHN] FALSTAFF,
HIS PAGE,
POINS,
BARDOLPH, | *irregular Humourists.*
PISTOL,
PETO,
SHALLOW, | *both country Justices.*
SILENCE,
DAVY, *servant to Shallow.*
FANG *and* SNARE, *two Sergeants.*
MOULDY,
SHADOW,
WART, | *country soldiers.*
FEEBLE,
BULLCALF,

NORTHUMBERLAND'S WIFE.
[LADY PERCY], *Percy's Widow.*
QUICKLY, *hostess* [*of a tavern in Eastcheap*].
DOLL TEARSHEET.

[Lords and attendants; Porter] Drawers, Beadles, Grooms [Servants, etc. A Dancer as] Epilogue.

[SCENE: *England.*]

INDUCTION

[*Warkworth. Before the castle.*]

Enter RUMOUR, *painted full of tongues.*

Rum. Open your ears; for which of you will stop
The vent of hearing when loud Rumour speaks?
I, from the orient to the drooping west,
Making the wind my post-horse, still unfold
The acts commenced on this ball of earth.   5
Upon my tongues continual slanders ride,
The which in every language I pronounce,
Stuffing the ears of men with false reports.
I speak of peace, while covert enmity
Under the smile of safety wounds the world;   10
And who but Rumour, who but only I,
Make fearful musters and prepar'd defence,
Whiles the big year, swoln with some other grief,
Is thought with child by the stern tyrant war,
And no such matter?   Rumour is a pipe   15
Blown by surmises, jealousies, conjectures,
And of so easy and so plain a stop

The list of Dramatis Personæ is substantially as given in F₁.

That the blunt monster with uncounted heads,
The still-discordant wav'ring multitude,
Can play upon it.   But what need I thus   20
My well-known body to anatomize
Among my household?   Why is Rumour here?
I run before King Harry's victory,
Who in a bloody field by Shrewsbury
Hath beaten down young Hotspur and his troops,
Quenching the flame of bold rebellion   26
Even with the rebel's blood.   But what mean I
To speak so true at first?   My office is
To noise abroad that Harry Monmouth fell
Under the wrath of noble Hotspur's sword,   30
And that the King before the Douglas' rage
Stoop'd his anointed head as low as death.
This have I rumour'd through the peasant towns
Between that royal field of Shrewsbury
And this worm-eaten [hold] of ragged stone,   35
[Where] Hotspur's father, old Northumberland,
Lies crafty-sick.   The posts come tiring on,
And not a man of them brings other news
Than they have learn'd of me.   From Rumour's
   tongues
They bring smooth comforts false, worse than true
   wrongs.   [*Exit.* 40

ACT I

SCENE [I. *The same.*]

Enter LORD BARDOLPH *at one door.*

L. Bard. Who keeps the gate here, ho?
   [*The* PORTER *opens the gate.*]
                    Where is the Earl?
Port. What shall I say you are?
L. Bard.   Tell thou the Earl
That the Lord Bardolph doth attend him here.
Port. His lordship is walk'd forth into the
   orchard.
Please it your honour, knock but at the gate,   5
And he himself will answer.

Enter NORTHUMBERLAND.

L. Bard.   Here comes the Earl.
                      [*Exit Porter.*]
North. What news, Lord Bardolph?   Every
   minute now
Should be the father of some stratagem.
The times are wild; contention, like a horse
Full of high feeding, madly hath broke loose   10
And bears down all before him.
L. Bard.   Noble Earl,
I bring you certain news from Shrewsbury.
North. Good, an God will!
L. Bard.   As good as heart can wish.
The King is almost wounded to the death;

And, in the fortune of my lord your son,   15
Prince Harry slain outright; and both the Blunts
Kill'd by the hand of Douglas; young Prince John
And Westmoreland and Stafford fled the field;
And Harry Monmouth's brawn, the hulk Sir John,
Is prisoner to your son.   O, such a day,   20
So fought, so followed, and so fairly won,
Came not till now to dignify the times,
Since Cæsar's fortunes!
North.   How is this deriv'd?
Saw you the field?   Came you from Shrewsbury?
L. Bard. I spake, with one, my lord, that came
   from thence,   25
A gentleman well bred and of good name,
That freely rend'red me these news for true.

Enter TRAVERS.

North. Here comes my servant Travers, who I
   sent
On Tuesday last to listen after news.
L. Bard. My lord, I over-rode him on the way;
And he is furnish'd with no certainties   31
More than he haply may retail from me.
North. Now, Travers, what good tidings comes
   with you?
Tra. My lord, Sir John Umfrevile turn'd me back
With joyful tidings; and, being better hors'd,   35
Out-rode me.   After him came spurring hard
A gentleman, almost forspent with speed,
That stopp'd by me to breathe his bloodied horse.
He ask'd the way to Chester; and of him
I did demand what news from Shrewsbury.   40
He told me that rebellion had bad luck,
And that young Harry Percy's spur was cold.
With that, he gave his able horse the head,
And bending forward struck his armed heels
Against the panting sides of his poor jade   45
Up to the rowel-head, and starting so
He seem'd in running to devour the way,
Staying no longer question.
North.   Ha! Again.
Said he young Harry Percy's spur was cold?
Of Hotspur Coldspur?   That rebellion   50
Had met ill luck?
L. Bard.   My lord, I'll tell you what:
If my young lord your son have not the day,
Upon mine honour, for a silken point
I'll give my barony.   Never talk of it.
North. Why should that gentleman that rode
   by Travers   55
Give then such instances of loss?
L. Bard.   Who, he?
He was some hilding fellow that had stolen
The horse he rode on, and, upon my life,
Spoke at a venture.   Look, here comes more news.

Ind., 18. **blunt**: stupid. 29. **Harry Monmouth**: Prince Henry. 35. **[hold]** (Theobald). *hole* QF. 36. **[Where]** F. *When* Q.
Act I, sc. i, 19. **brawn**: mass of flesh. 53. **point**: lace, tying doublet to breeches. 57. **hilding**: worthless.

Enter MORTON.

North. Yea, this man's brow, like to a title-leaf,
Foretells the nature of a tragic volume.   61
So looks the strand whereon the imperious flood
Hath left a witness'd usurpation.
Say, Morton, didst thou come from Shrewsbury?

Mor. I ran from Shrewsbury, my noble lord,   65
Where hateful Death put on his ugliest mask
To fright our party.

North.   How doth my son and brother?
Thou tremblest; and the whiteness in thy cheek
Is apter than thy tongue to tell thy errand.
Even such a man, so faint, so spiritless,   70
So dull, so dead in look, so woe-begone,
Drew Priam's curtain in the dead of night
And would have told him half his Troy was burnt;
But Priam found the fire ere he his tongue,
And I my Percy's death ere thou report'st it.   75
This thou wouldst say, "Your son did thus and
          thus;
Your brother thus; so fought the noble Douglas;"
Stopping my greedy ear with their bold deeds;
But in the end, to stop my ear indeed,
Thou hast a sigh to blow away this praise,   80
Ending with "Brother, son, and all are dead."

Mor. Douglas is living, and your brother yet;
But, for my lord your son, —

North.   Why, he is dead.
See what a ready tongue suspicion hath!
He that but fears the thing he would not know   85
Hath by instinct knowledge from others' eyes
That what he fear'd is chanc'd. Yet speak, Morton;
Tell thou an earl his divination lies,
And I will take it as a sweet disgrace
And make thee rich for doing me such wrong.   90

Mor. You are too great to be by me gainsaid;
Your spirit is too true, your fears too certain.

North. Yet, for all this, say not that Percy's dead.
I see a strange confession in thine eye.
Thou shak'st thy head and hold'st it fear or sin   95
To speak a truth. If he be slain, [say so;]
The tongue offends not that reports his death;
And he doth sin that doth belie the dead,
Not he which says the dead is not alive.
Yet the first bringer of unwelcome news   100
Hath but a losing office, and his tongue
Sounds ever after as a sullen bell,
Remem'red tolling a departing friend.

L. Bard. I cannot think, my lord, your son is
          dead.

Mor. I am sorry I should force you to believe   105
That which I would to God I had not seen;
But these mine eyes saw him in bloody state,
Rend'ring faint quittance, wearied and outbreath'd,

To Harry Monmouth; whose swift wrath beat down
The never-daunted Percy to the earth,   110
From whence with life he never more sprung up.
In few, his death, whose spirit lent a fire
Even to the dullest peasant in his camp,
Being bruited once, took fire and heat away
From the best-temper'd courage in his troops;   115
For from his metal was his party steel'd;
Which once in him abated, all the rest
Turn'd on themselves, like dull and heavy lead.
And as the thing that's heavy in itself
Upon enforcement flies with greatest speed,   120
So did our men, heavy in Hotspur's loss,
Lend to this weight such lightness with their fear
That arrows fled not swifter toward their aim
Than did our soldiers, aiming at their safety,
Fly from the field. Then was that noble Worcester
[Too] soon ta'en prisoner; and that furious Scot, 126
The bloody Douglas, whose well-labouring sword
Had three times slain th' appearance of the King,
Gan vail his stomach and did grace the shame
Of those that turn'd their backs, and in his flight,
Stumbling in fear, was took. The sum of all   131
Is that the King hath won, and hath sent out
A speedy power to encounter you, my lord,
Under the conduct of young Lancaster
And Westmoreland. This is the news at full.   135

North. For this I shall have time enough to
          mourn.
In poison there is physic; and these news,
Having been well, that would have made me sick,
Being sick, have in some measure made me well.
And as the wretch whose fever-weak'ned joints,
Like strengthless hinges, buckle under life,   141
Impatient of his fit, breaks like a fire
Out of his keeper's arms, even so my limbs,
Weak'ned with grief, being now enrag'd with grief,
Are thrice themselves. Hence, therefore, thou nice
          crutch!   145
A scaly gauntlet now with joints of steel
Must glove this hand; and hence, thou sickly quoif!
Thou art a guard too wanton for the head
Which princes, flesh'd with conquest, aim to hit.
Now bind my brows with iron; and approach   150
The ragged'st hour that time and spite dare bring
To frown upon th' enrag'd Northumberland!
Let heaven kiss earth! Now let not Nature's hand
Keep the wild flood confin'd! Let order die!
And let this world no longer be a stage   155
To feed contention in a ling'ring act;
But let one spirit of the first-born Cain
Reign in all bosoms, that, each heart being set
On bloody courses, the rude scene may end,
And darkness be the burier of the dead!   160

63. witness'd: witness of.   87. is chanc'd: has happened.   96. [say so] F. Om. Q.   112. In few: in short.   126. [Too]
F. *So* Q.   129. Gan ... stomach: began to lower his courage.   144. grief: pain. The second *grief* has its modern sense.
145. nice: effeminate.   147. quoif: cap.   148. wanton: luxurious.   149. flesh'd: made fierce.

[*Tra.*] This strained passion doth you wrong, my
lord.

L. Bard. Sweet Earl, divorce not wisdom from
your honour.

Mor. The lives of all your loving complices
[Lean] on your health; the which, if you give o'er
To stormy passion, must perforce decay.   165
[You cast th' event of war, my noble lord,
And summ'd the account of chance before you said,
"Let us make head." It was your presurmise
That in the dole of blows your son might drop.
You knew he walk'd o'er perils, on an edge,   170
More likely to fall in than to get o'er;
You were advis'd his flesh was capable
Of wounds and scars, and that his forward spirit
Would lift him where most trade of danger rang'd;
Yet did you say, "Go forth!" and none of this,   175
Though strongly apprehended, could restrain
The stiff-borne action. What hath then befall'n,
Or what hath this bold enterprise brought forth
More than that being which was like to be?]

L. Bard. We all that are engaged to this loss   180
Knew that we ventur'd on such dangerous seas
That if we wrought out life 'twas ten to one;
And yet we ventur'd, for the gain propos'd
Chok'd the respect of likely peril fear'd;
And since we are o'erset, venture again.   185
Come, we will all put forth, body and goods.

Mor. 'Tis more than time; and, my most noble
lord,
I hear for certain and [do] speak the truth,
[The gentle Archbishop of York is up
With well-appointed powers. He is a man   190
Who with a double surety binds his followers.
My lord your son had only but the corpse,
But shadows and the shows of men, to fight;
For that same word, rebellion, did divide
The action of their bodies from their souls;   195
And they did fight with queasiness, constrain'd
As men drink potions, that their weapons only
Seem'd on our side; but, for their spirits and souls,
This word, rebellion, it had froze them up,
As fish are in a pond. But now the Bishop   200
Turns insurrection to religion.
Suppos'd sincere and holy in his thoughts,
He's follow'd both with body and with mind;
And doth enlarge his rising with the blood
Of fair King Richard, scrap'd from Pomfret stones;   206
Derives from heaven his quarrel and his cause;
Tells them he doth bestride a bleeding land,
Gasping for life under great Bolingbroke;

And more and less do flock to follow him.]

North. I knew of this before; but, to speak truth,
This present grief had wip'd it from my mind.   211
Go in with me; and counsel every man
The aptest way for safety and revenge.
Get posts and letters, and make friends with
speed, —
Never so few, and never yet more need.   215

[*Exeunt.*

SCENE [II. *London. A street.*]

Enter FALSTAFF, *with his* PAGE *bearing his
sword and buckler.*

Fal. Sirrah, you giant, what says the doctor to
my water?

Page. He said, sir, the water itself was a good
healthy water; but, for the party that ow'd it,
he might have moe diseases than he knew for.   6

Fal. Men of all sorts take a pride to gird at me.
The brain of this foolish-compounded clay, man,
is not able to invent anything that intends to
laughter more than I invent or is invented on   10
me. I am not only witty in myself, but the cause
that wit is in other men. I do here walk before
thee like a sow that hath overwhelm'd all her
litter but one. If the Prince put thee into my
service for any other reason than to set me off,   15
why then I have no judgement. Thou whoreson
mandrake, thou art fitter to be worn in my cap
than to wait at my heels. I was never mann'd
with an agate till now; but I will inset you neither
in gold nor silver, but in vile apparel, and   20
send you back again to your master, for a jewel, —
the juvenal, the Prince your master, whose chin
is not yet fledg'd. I will sooner have a beard grow
in the palm of my hand than he shall get one off
his cheek; and yet he will not stick to say his   25
face is a face royal. God may finish it when he
will, 'tis not a hair amiss yet. He may keep it
still at a face royal, for a barber shall never earn
sixpence out of it; and yet he'll be crowing as if
he had writ man ever since his father was a   30
bachelor. He may keep his own grace, but he's
almost out of mine, I can assure him. What said
Master Dommelton about the satin for my short
cloak and my slops?   34

Page. He said, sir, you should procure him
better assurance than Bardolph. He would not
take his band and yours. He lik'd not the security.   38

161. [*Tra.*] (Capell). *Umfr.* Q. 164. [Lean] F. *Leave* Q. 166–79. F. Om. Q. 166. **cast th' event:** considered the
outcome. 168. **make head:** gather troops. 169. **dole:** dealing. 172. **advis'd:** aware. 172–73. **capable Of:** susceptible to.
180. **engaged to:** involved in. 182. **That … one:** that it was ten to one against our surviving. 184. **Chok'd the respect:**
checked consideration. 186. **put forth:** stake. 188. [do] F. *dare* Q. 189–209. F. Om. Q. 192. **corpse:** bodies. 196.
queasiness: nausea.

Sc. ii, 5. **ow'd:** owned. 17. **mandrake:** plant with a forked root. 19. **agate:** a stone often carved into little figures.
26, 28. **royal:** with a pun on *royal*, a coin bearing the king's head. 34. **slops:** wide breeches. 37. **band:** bond.

Fal. Let him be damn'd like the glutton! Pray God his tongue be hotter! A whoreson Achitophel! a rascally yea-for-sooth knave! to bear a gentleman in hand, and then stand upon security! The whoreson smooth-pates do now wear nothing but high shoes, and bunches of keys at their girdles; and if a man is through with them in honest 45 taking up, then they must stand upon security. I had as lief they would put ratsbane in my mouth as offer to stop it with security. I look'd 'a should have sent me two and twenty yards of satin, as I am a true knight, and he sends me security. 50 Well, he may sleep in security; for he hath the horn of abundance, and yet the lightness of his wife shines through it; and yet cannot he see, though he have his own lanthorn to light him. Where's Bardolph? 55

Page. He's gone [into] Smithfield to buy your worship a horse.

Fal. I bought him in Paul's, and he'll buy me a horse in Smithfield. An I could get me but a wife in the stews, I were mann'd, hors'd, and wiv'd. 61

Enter the LORD CHIEF JUSTICE *and* SERVANT.

Page. Sir, here comes the nobleman that committed the Prince for striking him about Bardolph.

Fal. Wait close; I will not see him. 65

Ch. Just. What's he that goes there?

Serv. Falstaff, an 't please your lordship.

Ch. Just. He that was in question for the robbery? 69

Serv. He, my lord; but he hath since done good service at Shrewsbury, and, as I hear, is now going with some charge to the Lord John of Lancaster.

Ch. Just. What, to York? Call him back again.

Serv. Sir John Falstaff! 76

Fal. Boy, tell him I am deaf.

Page. You must speak louder; my master is deaf. 79

Ch. Just. I am sure he is, to the hearing of anything good. Go, pluck him by the elbow; I must speak with him.

Serv. Sir John! 83

Fal. What! a young knave, and begging! Is there not wars? Is there not employment? Doth not the King lack subjects? Do not the rebels need soldiers? Though it be a shame to be on any side but one, it is worse shame to beg than to be on the worst side, were it worse than the name of rebellion can tell how to make it. 90

Serv. You mistake me, sir.

Fal. Why, sir, did I say you were an honest man? Setting my knighthood and my soldiership aside, I had lied in my throat, if I had said so. 94

Serv. I pray you, sir, then set your knighthood and your soldiership aside; and give me leave to tell you you lie in your throat if you say I am any other than an honest man. 98

Fal. I give thee leave to tell me so! I lay aside that which grows to me! If thou get'st any leave of me, hang me; if thou tak'st leave, thou wert better be hang'd. You hunt counter; hence! avaunt! 103

Serv. Sir, my lord would speak with you.

Ch. Just. Sir John Falstaff, a word with you.

Fal. My good lord! God give your lordship good time of day. I am glad to see your lordship abroad. I heard say your lordship was sick; I 108 hope your lordship goes abroad by advice. Your lordship, though not clean past your youth, [hath] yet some smack of [age] in you, some relish of the saltness of time in you; and I most humbly beseech your lordship to have a reverent care of your health. 114

Ch. Just. Sir John, I sent for you before your expedition to Shrewsbury.

Fal. An't please your lordship, I hear his Majesty is return'd with some discomfort from Wales. 119

Ch. Just. I talk not of his Majesty. You would not come when I sent for you.

Fal. And I hear, moreover, his Highness is fallen into this same whoreson apoplexy.

Ch. Just. Well, God mend him! I pray you, let me speak with you. 126

Fal. This apoplexy, as I take it, is a kind of lethargy, an't please your lordship, a kind of sleeping in the blood, a whoreson tingling.

Ch. Just. What tell you me of it? Be it as it is. 130

Fal. It hath it original from much grief, from study, and perturbation of the brain. I have read the cause of his effects in Galen. It is a kind of deafness. 134

Ch. Just. I think you are fallen into the disease; for you hear not what I say to you.

[*Fal.*] Very well, my lord, very well. Rather, an't please you, it is the disease of not listening, the malady of not marking, that I am troubled withal. 140

Ch. Just. To punish you by the heels would

39. **glutton:** Dives (*Luke* xvi.19). 40. **Achitophel:** Absalom's adviser (II *Samuel*, xv ff.). 41. **yea-for-sooth:** a mild oath. 42. **bear... in hand:** lead on. 45. **through:** straightforward. 46. **taking up:** ordering on credit. 52–54. **horn... lanthorn:** a play on *horn* (1) cornucopia, (2) the sign of the cuckold, and (3) the window of a lantern. 55. **Where's Bardolph?** Q inserts in l. 53, before *and yet.* 56. **[into]** F. *in* Q. 58. **Paul's.** Men seeking service paraded in St. Paul's. 60. **stews:** houses of ill fame. 72. **charge:** troops. 102. **counter:** in the wrong direction. 110. **[hath]** F. *have* Q. 111. **[age]** F. *an ague* Q. 137. **[Fal.]** F. *Old.* Q. A trace of Oldcastle, the earlier name for Falstaff. See Introduction to Part I.

amend the attention of your ears; and I care not if I do become your physician. 143

Fal. I am as poor as Job, my lord, but not so patient. Your lordship may minister the potion of imprisonment to me in respect of poverty; but how I should be your patient to follow your prescriptions, the wise may make some dram of a scruple, or indeed a scruple itself. 149

Ch. Just. I sent for you, when there were matters against you for your life, to come speak with me.

Fal. As I was then advis'd by my learned counsel in the laws of this land-service, I did not come. 155

Ch. Just. Well, the truth is, Sir John, you live in great infamy.

Fal. He that buckles himself in my belt cannot live in less.

Ch. Just. Your means are very slender, and your waste is great. 161

Fal. I would it were otherwise; I would my means were greater, and my waist [slenderer].

Ch. Just. You have misled the youthful prince.

Fal. The young prince hath misled me. I am the fellow with the great belly, and he my dog. 166

Ch. Just. Well, I am loath to gall a new-heal'd wound. Your day's service at Shrewsbury hath a little gilded over your night's exploit on Gadshill. You may thank th' unquiet time for your quiet o'er-posting that action. 171

Fal. My lord?

Ch. Just. But since all is well, keep it so. Wake not a sleeping wolf.

Fal. To wake a wolf is as bad as smell a fox. 176

Ch. Just. What! you are as a candle, the better part burnt out.

Fal. A wassail candle, my lord, all tallow. If I did say of wax, my growth would approve the truth. 181

Ch. Just. There is not a white hair in your face but should have his effect of gravity.

Fal. His effect of gravy, gravy, gravy.

Ch. Just. You follow the young prince up and down, like his ill angel. 186

Fal. Not so, my lord. Your ill angel is light; but I hope he that looks upon me will take me without weighing; and yet, in some respects, I grant, I cannot go. I cannot tell. Virtue is of 190 so little regard in these costermongers' times that true Valour is turned bear-herd; Pregnancy is made a tapster, and his quick wit wasted in giving reckonings; all the other gifts appertinent to man, as the malice of [this] age shapes them, are not 195 worth a gooseberry. You that are old consider not the capacities of us that are young; you do measure the heat of our livers with the bitterness of your galls; and we that are in the vaward of our youth, I must confess, are wags too. 200

Ch. Just. Do you set down your name in the scroll of youth, that are written down old with all the characters of age? Have you not a moist eye, a dry hand, a yellow cheek, a white beard, a decreasing leg, an increasing belly? Is not 205 your voice broken, your wind short, your chin double, your wit single, and every part about you blasted with antiquity? And will you yet call yourself young? Fie, fie, fie, Sir John! 209

Fal. My lord, I was born about three of the clock in the afternoon, with a white head and something a round belly. For my voice, I have lost it with hallooing and singing of anthems. To approve my youth further, I will not. The truth is, I am only old in judgement and understanding; 215 and he that will caper with me for a thousand marks, let him lend me the money, and have at him! For the box of the ear that the Prince gave you, he gave it like a rude prince, and you took it like a sensible lord. I have check'd him for it, and the young lion repents; marry, not in ashes and sackcloth, but in new silk and old sack. 222

Ch. Just. Well, God send the Prince a better companion!

Fal. God send the companion a better prince! I cannot rid my hands of him. 226

Ch. Just. Well, the King hath sever'd you [and Prince Harry]. I hear you are going with Lord John of Lancaster against the Archbishop and the Earl of Northumberland. 230

Fal. Yea, I thank your pretty sweet wit for it. But look you pray, all you that kiss my lady Peace at home, that our armies join not in a hot day; for, by the Lord, I take but two shirts out with me, and I mean not to sweat extraordinarily. 235 If it be a hot day, and I brandish anything but a bottle, I would I might never spit white again. There is not a dangerous action can peep out his head but I am thrust upon it. Well, I cannot last ever; but it was alway yet the trick of our 240 English nation, if they have a good thing, to make it too common. If ye will needs say I am an old man, you should give me rest. I would to God my name were not so terrible to the enemy as it is. I were better to be eaten to death with a rust than to be scoured to nothing with perpetual motion. 247

Ch. Just. Well, be honest, be honest; and God bless your expedition!

---

148. **dram of a scruple**: trifle of a doubt, punning on *scruple*, a small weight. 163. **[slenderer]** F. *slander* Q. 171. **o'er-posting**: getting over the results of. 179. **wassail**: festival. 187. **angel**: a pun on *angel*, the coin. **light**: underweight. 190. **go**: pass (as genuine). 191. **costermongers'**: i.e., commercial. 192. **Pregnancy**: readiness of wit. 195. **[this]** F. *his* Q. 199. **vaward**: vanguard. 222. **sack**: Spanish wine. 227. **[and Prince Harry]** F. Om. Q. 237. **spit white**. Not satisfactorily explained. "Be thirsty" is a possible meaning. 240–247. Q. Om. F.

Fal. Will your lordship lend me a thousand pound to furnish me forth?

Ch. Just. Not a penny, not a penny; you are too impatient to bear crosses. Fare you well! Commend me to my cousin Westmoreland.   254

[*Exeunt Chief Justice and Servant.*]

Fal. If I do, fillip me with a three-man beetle. A man can no more separate age and covetousness than 'a can part young limbs and lechery; but the gout galls the one, and the pox pinches the other, and so both the degrees prevent my curses.   Boy?

Page. Sir?   261

Fal. What money is in my purse?

Page. Seven groats and two pence.   263

Fal. I can get no remedy against this consumption of the purse. Borrowing only lingers and lingers it out, but the disease is incurable. Go bear this letter to my Lord of Lancaster; this to the Prince; this to the Earl of Westmoreland; and this to old Mistress Ursula, whom I have weekly sworn to marry since I perceiv'd the first white   270 hair of my chin. About it. You know where to find me. [*Exit Page.*] A pox of this gout! or, a gout of this pox! for the one or the other plays the rogue with my great toe. 'Tis no matter if I do halt; I have the wars for my colour, and my pension shall seem the more reasonable. A good wit will make use of anything. I will turn diseases to commodity.   [*Exit.* 278

Scene [III. *York. The Archbishop's palace.*]

Enter the Archbishop, *the* Lords Hastings, Mowbray (Earl Marshal), *and* Bardolph.

Arch. Thus have you heard our cause and known our means;
And, my most noble friends, I pray you all,
Speak plainly your opinions of our hopes.
And first, Lord Marshal, what say you to it?

Mowb. I well allow the occasion of our arms;   5
But gladly would be better satisfied
How in our means we should advance ourselves
To look with forehead bold and big enough
Upon the power and puissance of the King.

Hast. Our present musters grow upon the file   10
To five and twenty thousand men of choice;
And our supplies live largely in the hope
Of great Northumberland, whose bosom burns
With an incensed fire of injuries.

L. Bard. The question then, Lord Hastings, standeth thus: 15

Whether our present five and twenty thousand
May hold up head without Northumberland?

Hast. With him, we may.

L. Bard.   Yea, marry, there's the point!
But if without him we be thought too feeble,
My judgement is, we should not step too far   20
[Till we had his assistance by the hand;
For, in a theme so bloody-fac'd as this,
Conjecture, expectation, and surmise
Of aids incertain should not be admitted].

Arch. 'Tis very true, Lord Bardolph; for indeed
It was young Hotspur's case at Shrewsbury.   26

L. Bard. It was, my lord; who lin'd himself with hope,
Eating the air, and promise of supply,
Flatt'ring himself in project of a power
Much smaller than the smallest of his thoughts;   30
And so, with great imagination
Proper to madmen, led his powers to death,
And winking leap'd into destruction.

Hast. But, by your leave, it never yet did hurt
To lay down likelihoods and forms of hope.   35

L. Bard. [Yes, if this present quality of war
Needed the instant action. A cause on foot
Lives so in hope as in an early spring
We see th' appearing buds, which to prove fruit
Hope gives not so much warrant, as despair   40
That frosts will bite them. When we mean to build,
We first survey the plot, then draw the model;
And when we see the figure of the house,
Then must we rate the cost of the erection;
Which if we find outweighs ability,   45
What do we then but draw anew the model
In fewer offices, or at least desist
To build at all? Much more, in this great work,
Which is almost to pluck a kingdom down
And set another up, should we survey   50
The plot of situation and the model,
Consent upon a sure foundation,
Question surveyors, know our own estate,
How able such a work to undergo,
To weigh against his opposite; or else]   55
We fortify in paper and in figures,
Using the names of men instead of men;
Like one that draws the model of a house
Beyond his power to build it; who, half through,
Gives o'er and leaves his part-created cost   60
A naked subject to the weeping clouds
And waste for churlish winter's tyranny.

Hast. Grant that our hopes, yet likely of fair birth,

253. crosses: (1) afflictions, (2) coins.   255. fillip...beetle: toss me into the air from the end of a board, the other end being struck by a rammer worked by three men.   260. degrees: kinds (of disease).   prevent: anticipate.   275. colour: excuse.   278. commodity: advantage.
   Sc. iii, 10. file: list.   12. supplies: reinforcements.   21-24. F. Om. Q.   27. lin'd: supported.   29. project: idea.   33. winking: with eyes shut.   36-55. F. Om. Q.   37. Needed (Gould conj.).   Indeed F.   47. offices: rooms for service.   52. Consent: agree.   53. estate: resources.   55. weigh...opposite: balance the expenditure.   60. part-created cost: expensive half-built house.

Should be still-born, and that we now possess'd
The utmost man of expectation,   65
I think we are [a] body strong enough,
Even as we are, to equal with the King.

L. Bard. What, is the King but five and twenty
thousand?

Hast. To us no more; nay, not so much, Lord
Bardolph.
For his divisions, as the times do brawl,   70
[Are] in three heads: one power against the French,
And one against Glendower; perforce a third
Must take up us. So is the unfirm King
In three divided; and his coffers sound
With hollow poverty and emptiness.   75

Arch. That he should draw his several strengths
together
And come against us in full puissance,
Need not be dreaded.

Hast.   If he should do so,
[To] French and Welsh he leaves his back unarm'd,
They baying him at the heels. Never fear that.

L. Bard. Who is it like should lead his forces
hither?   81

Hast. The Duke of Lancaster and Westmoreland;
Against the Welsh, himself and Harry Monmouth;
But who is substituted 'gainst the French,
I have no certain notice.

[*Arch.*   Let us on,   85
And publish the occasion of our arms.
The commonwealth is sick of their own choice;
Their over-greedy love hath surfeited.
An habitation giddy and unsure
Hath he that buildeth on the vulgar heart.   90
O thou fond many, with what loud applause
Didst thou beat heaven with blessing Bolingbroke
Before he was what thou wouldst have him be!
And being now trimm'd in thine own desires,
Thou, beastly feeder, art so full of him,   95
That thou provok'st thyself to cast him up.
So, so, thou common dog, didst thou disgorge
Thy glutton bosom of the royal Richard;
And now thou wouldst eat thy dead vomit up,
And howl'st to find it. What trust is in these
times?   100
They that, when Richard liv'd, would have him die,
Are now become enamour'd on his grave.
Thou, that threw'st dust upon his goodly head
When through proud London he came sighing on
After th' admired heels of Bolingbroke,   105
Cri'st now, "O earth, yield us that king again,
And take thou this!" O thoughts of men accurs'd!
Past and to come seems best; things present
worst.]

Mowb. Shall we go draw our numbers and set on?
Hast. We are Time's subjects, and Time bids
be gone.   [*Exeunt.* 110

ACT II

Scene I. [*London.   A street.*]

Enter Hostess, Fang [*and his* Boy *with her,*]
and Snare *following.*

Host. Master Fang, have you ent'red the action?
Fang. It is ent'red.
Host. Where's your yeoman? Is't a lusty
yeoman? Will 'a stand to't?   5
Fang. Sirrah, where's Snare?
Host. O Lord, ay! good Master Snare.
Snare. Here, here.
Fang. Snare, we must arrest Sir John Falstaff.
Host. Yea, good Master Snare; I have ent'red
him and all.   11
Snare. It may chance cost some of us our lives,
for he will stab.
Host. Alas the day! take heed of him. He
stabb'd me in mine own house, [and that] most   15
beastly. In good faith, 'a cares not what mischief
he does, if his weapon be out. He will foin like
any devil; he will spare neither man, woman, nor
child.   19
Fang. If I can close with him, I care not for his
thrust.
Host. No, nor I neither. I'll be at your elbow.
Fang. An I but fist him once; an 'a come but
within my vice, —   24
Host. I am undone by his going; I warrant you,
he's an infinitive thing upon my score. Good
Master Fang, hold him sure. Good Master Snare,
let him not scape. 'A comes continually to Pie-
corner — saving your manhoods — to buy a saddle;
and he is indited to dinner to the Lubber's-head   30
in Lumbert street, to Master Smooth's the silk-
man. I pray you, since my exion is ent'red and
my case so openly known to the world, let him be
brought in to his answer. A hundred mark is a
long one for a poor lone woman to bear; and I   35
have borne, and borne, and borne, and have been
fubb'd off, and fubb'd off, and fubb'd off, from this
day to that day, that it is a shame to be thought on.
There is no honesty in such dealing; unless a woman
should be made an ass and a beast, to bear   40
every knave's wrong. Yonder he comes; and that
arrant malmsey-nose knave, Bardolph, with him.
Do your offices, do your offices, Master Fang and
Master Snare; do me, do me, do me your offices. 45

66. [a] F. *so* Q.   70. do brawl: are disturbed.   71. [Are] F.   *And* Q.   78. be F.   *to be* Q.   79. [To] (Capell). Om. Q.
85–108. F. Om. Q.   91. fond many: foolish multitude.
    Act II, sc. i, 10. ent'red: brought suit against.   15. [and that] F. Om. Q.   17. foin: thrust.   24. vice: grasp.   30. in-
dited: invited.   32. exion: action.   42. malmsey-nose: red nose from drinking wine.

Enter FALSTAFF, BARDOLPH, *and* PAGE.

Fal. How now! whose mare's dead? What's the matter?

Fang. [Sir John,] I arrest you at the suit of Mistress Quickly.

Fal. Away, varlets! Draw, Bardolph; cut me off the villain's head. Throw the quean in the channel.   52

Host. Throw me in the channel! I'll throw thee in the channel. Wilt thou? wilt thou? thou bastardly rogue! Murder, murder! Ah, thou honeysuckle villain! wilt thou kill God's officers and the King's? Ah, thou honey-seed rogue! thou art a honey-seed, a man-queller, and a woman-queller. 59

Fal. Keep them off, Bardolph.

Fang. A rescue! a rescue!

Host. Good people, bring a rescue or two. Thou wo't, wo't thou? thou wo't, wo't ta? Do, do, thou rogue! do, thou hempseed!   64

Page. Away, you scullion! you rampallian! you fustilarian! I'll tickle your catastrophe.

Enter the LORD CHIEF JUSTICE, *and his men.*

Ch. Just. What is the matter? Keep the peace here, ho!

Host. Good my lord, be good to me. I beseech you, stand to me.   70

Ch. Just. How now, Sir John! what, are you brawling here?
Doth this become your place, your time and business?
You should have been well on your way to York.
Stand from him, fellow; wherefore hang'st thou upon him?   74

Host. O my most worshipful lord, an't please your Grace, I am a poor widow of Eastcheap, and he is arrested at my suit.

Ch. Just. For what sum?   78

Host. It is more than for some, my lord; it is for all I have. He hath eaten me out of house and home; he hath put all my substance into that fat belly of his: but I will have some of it out again, or I will ride thee o' nights like the mare. 83

Fal. I think I am as like to ride the mare, if I have any vantage of ground to get up.

Ch. Just. How comes this, Sir John? [Fie!] what man of good temper would endure this tempest of exclamation? Are you not asham'd to enforce a poor widow to so rough a course to come by her own?   90

Fal. What is the gross sum that I owe thee?

Host. Marry, if thou wert an honest man, thyself and the money too. Thou didst swear to me upon a parcel-gilt goblet, sitting in my Dolphin chamber, at the round table, by a sea-coal fire, 95 upon Wednesday in Wheeson week, when the Prince broke thy head for liking his father to a singing-man of Windsor, thou didst swear to me then, as I was washing thy wound, to marry me and make me my lady thy wife. Canst thou 100 deny it? Did not goodwife Keech, the butcher's wife, come in then and call me gossip Quickly? coming in to borrow a mess of vinegar, telling us she had a good dish of prawns; whereby thou didst desire to eat some; whereby I told thee they 105 were ill for a green wound? And didst thou not, when she was gone downstairs, desire me to be no more so familiarity with such poor people, saying that ere long they should call me madam? And didst thou not kiss me and bid me fetch thee thirty shillings? I put thee now to thy book-oath. Deny it, if thou canst.   112

Fal. My lord, this is a poor mad soul; and she says up and down the town that her eldest son is like you. She hath been in good case, and the truth is, poverty hath distracted her. But for these foolish officers, I beseech you I may have redress against them.   118

Ch. Jus. Sir John, Sir John, I am well acquainted with your manner of wrenching the true cause the false way. It is not a confident brow, nor the throng of words that come with such more than impudent sauciness from you, can thrust me 123 from a level consideration. You have, as it appears to me, practis'd upon the easy-yielding spirit of this woman, and made her serve your uses both in purse and in person.

Host. Yea, in truth, my lord.   128

Ch. Just. Pray thee, peace. Pay her the debt you owe her, and unpay the villainy you have done with her. The one you may do with sterling money, and the other with current repentance. 132

Fal. My lord, I will not undergo this sneap without reply. You call honourable boldness impudent sauciness; if a man will make curtsy and say nothing, he is virtuous. No, my lord, my humble duty remem'red, I will not be your suitor. I say to you, I do desire deliverance from these officers, being upon hasty employment in the King's affairs.   140

Ch. Just. You speak as having power to do wrong; but answer in th' effect of your reputation, and satisfy the poor woman.

Fal. Come hither, hostess.   144

48. [Sir John] F. Om. Q. 51. **quean**: hussy. 52. **channel**: gutter. 55. **honey-suckle**: i.e., homicidal. 57. **honey-seed**: i.e., homicide. 66. **catastrophe**: end, backside. 83. **mare**: nightmare. 86. [**Fie**] F. Om. Q. 94. **parcel-gilt**: gilded on the inside. 96. **Wheeson**: Whitsun(day). 104. **prawns**: shrimps. 106. **green**: new. 115. **in good case**: prosperous. 124. **level**: just. 132. **current**: real. 133. **sneap**: rebuke. 142. **in th' effect of**: suitably to.

Enter GOWER.

Ch. Just. Now, Master Gower, what news?

Gow. The King, my lord, and Harry Prince of Wales
Are near at hand.   The rest the paper tells.

Fal. As I am a gentleman.

Host. Faith, you said so before.   149

Fal. As I am a gentleman.   Come, no more words of it.

Host. By this heavenly ground I tread on, I must be fain to pawn both my plate and the tapestry of my dining-chambers.   154

Fal. Glasses, glasses, is the only drinking; and for thy walls, a pretty slight drollery, or the story of the Prodigal, or the German hunting in water-work, is worth a thousand of these bed-hangers and these fly-bitten tapestries.   Let it be ten pound, if thou canst.   Come, an't were not   160 for thy humours, there's not a better wench in England.   Go, wash thy face, and draw the action. Come, thou must not be in this humour with me; dost not know me?   Come, come, I know thou wast set on to this.   165

Host. Pray thee, Sir John, let it be but twenty nobles.   I' faith, I am loath to pawn my plate, so God save me, la!

Fal. Let it alone; I'll make other shift.   You'll be a fool still.   170

Host. Well, you shall have it, though I pawn my gown.   I hope you'll come to supper.   You'll pay me altogether?

Fal. Will I live?   [*To Bardolph.*] Go, with her, with her; hook on, hook on.   175

Host. Will you have Doll Tearsheet meet you at supper?

Fal. No more words; let's have her.

[*Exeunt Hostess, Bardolph, Officers, and Boy.*]

Ch. Just. I have heard better news.

Fal. What's the news, my lord?   180

Ch. Just. Where lay the King to-night?

Gow. At [Basingstoke], my lord.

Fal. I hope, my lord, all's well.   What is the news, my lord?

Ch. Just. Come all his forces back?   185

Gow. No; fifteen hundred foot, five hundred horse,
Are march'd up to my Lord of Lancaster.
Against Northumberland and the Archbishop.

Fal. Comes the King back from Wales, my noble lord?

Ch. Just. You shall have letters of me presently. Come, go along with me, good Master Gower.   191

Fal. My lord!

Ch. Just. What's the matter?

Fal. Master Gower, shall I entreat you with me to dinner?   195

Gow. I must wait upon my good lord here; I thank you, good Sir John.

Ch. Just. Sir John, you loiter here too long, being you are to take soldiers up in counties as you go.   200

Fal. Will you sup with me, Master Gower?

Ch. Just. What foolish master taught you these manners, Sir John?

Fal. Master Gower, if they become me not, he was a fool that taught them me.   This is the right fencing grace, my lord; tap for tap, and so part fair.   207

Ch. Just. Now the Lord lighten thee! thou art a great fool.   [*Exeunt.*]

SCENE II.   [*London.   Another street.*]

Enter PRINCE HENRY *and* POINS.

Prince. Before God, I am exceeding weary.

Poins. Is't come to that?   I had thought weariness durst not have attach'd one of so high blood.   4

Prince. Faith, it does me, though it discolours the complexion of my greatness to acknowledge it.   Doth it not show vilely in me to desire small beer?

Poins. Why, a prince should not be so loosely studied as to remember so weak a composition.   10

Prince. Belike then my appetite was not princely got, for, by my troth, I do now remember the poor creature, small beer.   But, indeed, these humble considerations make me out of love with my greatness.   What a disgrace is it to me   15 to remember thy name! or to know thy face to-morrow! or to take note how many pair of silk stockings thou hast, [viz.], these, and those that were thy peach-colour'd [ones]! or to bear the inventory of thy shirts, as, one for superfluity,   and another for use!   But that the tennis-   20 court-keeper knows better than I; for it is a low ebb of linen with thee when thou keepest not racket there; as thou hast not done a great while, because the rest of the low countries have [made a shift to] eat up thy holland.   And God knows,   25 whether those that bawl out the ruins of thy linen shall inherit his kingdom: but the midwives say

---

155. **Glasses:** i.e., in place of silver goblets. 156. **drollery:** a comic scene. 157. **water-work:** water-color. 161. **humours:** whims, moods. 162. **draw:** withdraw. 182. **[Basingstoke]** F. *Billingsgate* Q. 199. **take ... up:** recruit.

Sc. ii, S.D. POINS. (Rowe). *Poins, sir Iohn Russel, with other* Q. 5–6. **discolours the complexion:** makes blush. 10. **studied:** disposed. 18. **[viz.]** F. *with* Q. 19. **[ones]** F. *once* Q. 25. **[made a shift to]** F. Om. Q. **holland:** linen, with ทนท or *Holland*. 26. **those ... linen:** his children, who wear his cast-off shirts. 26–30. Q. Om. F.

the children are not in the fault; whereupon the world increases, and kindreds are mightily strengthened.   30

Poins. How ill it follows, after you have laboured so hard, you should talk so idlely! Tell me, how many good young princes would do so, their fathers being so sick as yours at this time is?

Prince. Shall I tell thee one thing, Poins?   35

Poins. Yes, faith; and let it be an excellent good thing.

Prince. It shall serve among wits of no higher breeding than thine.

Poins. Go to; I stand the push of your one thing that you will tell.   41

Prince. Marry, I tell thee, it is not meet that I should be sad, now my father is sick; albeit I could tell to thee, as to one it pleases me, for fault of a better, to call my friend, I could be sad, and sad indeed too.

Poins. Very hardly upon such a subject.   47

Prince. By this hand, thou think'st me as far in the devil's book as thou and Falstaff for obduracy and persistency. Let the end try the man. But I tell thee, my heart bleeds inwardly that my father is so sick; and keeping such vile company as thou art hath in reason taken from me all ostentation of sorrow.   54

Poins. The reason?

Prince. What wouldst thou think of me, if I should weep?

Poins. I would think thee a most princely hypocrite.   59

Prince. It would be every man's thought; and thou art a blessed fellow to think as every man thinks. Never a man's thought in the world keeps the road-way better than thine. Every man would think me an hypocrite indeed. And what accites your most worshipful thought to think so?   65

Poins. Why, because you have been so lewd and so much engraffed to Falstaff.

Prince. And to thee.   68

Poins. By this light, I am well spoke on; I can hear it with mine own ears. The worst that they can say of me is that I am a second brother and that I am a proper fellow of my hands; and those two things, I confess, I cannot help. By the mass, here comes Bardolph.   74

Enter BARDOLPH *and* PAGE.

Prince. And the boy that I gave Falstaff. 'A had him from me Christian; and look, if the fat villain have not transform'd him ape.

Bard. God save your Grace!

Prince. And yours, most noble Bardolph!   79

Poins. Come, you virtuous ass, you bashful fool, must you be blushing? Wherefore blush you now? What a maidenly man-at-arms are you become! Is't such a matter to get a pottle-pot's maidenhead?   84

Page. 'A calls me e'en now, my lord, through a red lattice, and I could discern no part of his face from the window. At last I spied his eyes, and methought he had made two holes in the ale-wife's [new] petticoat and so peep'd through.

Prince. Has not the boy profited?   90

Bard. Away, you whoreson upright rabbit, away!

Page. Away, you rascally Althæa's dream, away!   94

Prince. Instruct us, boy; what dream, boy?

Page. Marry, my lord, Althæa dream'd she was delivered of a fire-brand; and therefore I call him her dream.

Prince. A crown's worth of good interpretation. There 'tis, boy.   100

Poins. O, that this [good] blossom could be kept from cankers! Well, there is sixpence to preserve thee.

Bard. An you do not make him hang'd among you, the gallows shall have wrong.   105

Prince. And how doth thy master, Bardolph?

Bard. Well, my lord. He heard of your Grace's coming to town. There's a letter for you.

Poins. Deliver'd with good respect. And how doth the martlemas, your master?   110

Bard. In bodily health, sir.

Poins. Marry, the immortal part needs a physician; but that moves not him. Though that be sick, it dies not.   114

Prince. I do allow this wen to be as familiar with me as my dog, and he holds his place, for look you how he writes.   117

Poins. [*Reads.*] "John Falstaff, knight,"— every man must know that, as oft as he has occasion to name himself; even like those that are kin to the King, for they never prick their finger but they say, "There's some of the King's blood spilt." "How comes that?" says he, that   124 takes upon him not to conceive. The answer is as ready as a [borrower's] cap, "I am the King's poor cousin, sir."

Prince. Nay, they will be kin to us, or they will fetch it from Japhet. But the letter: 128

"Sir John Falstaff, knight, to the son of the King nearest his father, Harry Prince of Wales, greeting."

Poins. Why, this is a certificate.

Prince. Peace!   133

---

64. **accites:** prompts.   83. **pottle-pot:** two-quart pot.   89. **[new]** F. Om. Q.   101. **[good]** F. Om. Q.   102. **cankers:** canker-worms.   110. **martlemas:** fatted ox, killed at Martinmas (Nov. 11).   115. **wen:** tumor.   126. **[borrower's]** (Theobald). *borrowed* QF.   128. **Japhet:** son of Noah.

"I will imitate the honourable Romans in brevity."

Poins. He sure means brevity in breath, short-winded.

[*Prince.*] "I commend me to thee, I commend thee, and I leave thee. Be not too familiar with Poins; for he misuses thy favours so much that he swears thou art to marry his sister Nell. Repent at idle times as thou mayest; and so, farewell. 141

"Thine, by yea and no, which is as much
    as to say, as thou usest him, JACK
    FALSTAFF with my [familiars,] JOHN
    with my brothers and sisters, and SIR
    JOHN with all Europe." 146

Poins. My lord, I'll steep this letter in sack and make him eat it.

Prince. That's to make him eat twenty of his words. But do you use me thus, Ned? Must I marry your sister? 151

Poins. God send the wench no worse fortune! But I never said so.

Prince. Well, thus we play the fools with the time, and the spirits of the wise sit in the clouds and mock us. Is your master here in London? 157

Bard. Yea, my lord.

Prince. Where sups he? Doth the old boar feed in the old frank? 161

Bard. At the old place, my lord, in Eastcheap.

Prince. What company?

Page. Ephesians, my lord, of the old church.

Prince. Sup any women with him?

Page. None, my lord, but old Mistress Quickly and Mistress Doll Tearsheet. 167

Prince. What pagan may that be?

Page. A proper gentlewoman, sir, and a kins-woman of my master's.

Prince. Even such kin as the parish heifers are to the town bull. Shall we steal upon them, Ned, at supper? 173

Poins. I am your shadow, my lord; I'll follow you.

Prince. Sirrah, you boy, and Bardolph, no word to your master that I am yet come to town. There's for your silence. 178

Bard. I have no tongue, sir.

Page. And for mine, sir, I will govern it.

Prince. Fare you well; go. [*Exeunt Bardolph and Page.*] This Doll Tearsheet should be some road. 183

Poins. I warrant you, as common as the way between Saint Alban's and London.

Prince. How might we see Falstaff bestow him-

self to-night in his true colours, and not ourselves be seen? 188

Poins. Put on two leathern jerkins and aprons, and wait upon him at his table as drawers. 191

Prince. From a God to a bull? a heavy descension! It was Jove's case. From a prince to a prentice? a low transformation! That shall be mine; for in everything the purpose must weigh with the folly. Follow me, Ned. [*Exeunt.* 196

SCENE III. [*Warkworth. Before the castle.*]

Enter NORTHUMBERLAND, LADY NORTHUM-
BERLAND, *and* LADY PERCY.

North. I pray thee, loving wife, and gentle
    daughter,
Give even way unto my rough affairs;
Put not you on the visage of the times
And be like them to Percy troublesome.

Lady N. I have given over, I will speak no
    more. 5
Do what you will; your wisdom be your guide.

North. Alas, sweet wife, my honour is at pawn;
And, but my going, nothing can redeem it.

Lady P. O yet, for God's sake, go not to these
    wars!
The time was, father, that you broke your word 10
When you were more endear'd to it than now;
When your own Percy, when my heart's dear
    Harry,
Threw many a northward look to see his father
Bring up his powers; but he did long in vain.
Who then persuaded you to stay at home? 15
There were two honours lost, yours and your son's.
For yours, the God of heaven brighten it!
For his, it stuck upon him as the sun
In the grey vault of heaven, and by his light
Did all the chivalry of England move 20
To do brave acts. He was indeed the glass
Wherein the noble youth did dress themselves.
[He had no legs, that practis'd not his gait;
And speaking thick, which nature made his blemish,
Became the accents of the valiant; 25
For those that could speak low and tardily
Would turn their own perfection to abuse
To seem like him; so that in speech, in gait,
In diet, in affections of delight,
In military rules, humours of blood, 30
He was the mark and glass, copy and book,
That fashion'd others. And him, O wondrous him!
O miracle of men! him did you leave,
Second to none, unseconded by you,

---

138. [*Prince*] (Theobald). Om. Q.   144. [familiars] F. *family* Q.   161. frank: sty.   164. Ephesians: boon companions. 168. pagan: harlot.   183. road: harlot.   186. bestow: behave.   192. God...bull: an allusion to the story of Jove and Europa.   196. weigh with: equal.
  Sc. iii, 11. endear'd: bound.   23-45. F. Om. Q.   24. thick: hurriedly.   29. affections of delight: favorite occupations. 30. humours of blood: temperament.

To look upon the hideous god of war   35
In disadvantage; to abide a field
Where nothing but the sound of Hotspur's name
Did seem defensible: so you left him.
Never, O never, do his ghost the wrong
To hold your honour more precise and nice   40
With others than with him! Let them alone.
The Marshal and the Archbishop are strong.
Had my sweet Harry had but half their numbers,
To-day might I, hanging on Hotspur's neck,
Have talk'd of Monmouth's grave.]

North.   Beshrew your heart,
Fair daughter, you do draw my spirits from me   46
With new lamenting ancient oversights.
But I must go and meet with danger there,
Or it will seek me in another place
And find me worse provided.

Lady N.   O, fly to Scotland
Till that the nobles and the armed commons   51
Have of their puissance made a little taste.

Lady P. If they get ground and vantage of the
        King,
Then join you with them, like a rib of steel,
To make strength stronger; but, for all our loves,   55
First let them try themselves. So did your son;
He was so suff'red; so came I a widow;
And never shall have length of life enough
To rain upon remembrance with mine eyes,
That it may grow and sprout as high as heaven,
For recordation to my noble husband.   61

North. Come, come, go in with me. 'Tis with
        my mind
As with the tide swell'd up unto his height,
That makes a still stand, running neither way.
Fain would I go to meet the Archbishop,   65
But many thousand reasons hold me back.
I will resolve for Scotland. There am I
Till time and vantage crave my company.

                                        [*Exeunt.*

SCENE IV. [*London. The Boar's-Head Tavern
        in Eastcheap.*]

Enter two DRAWERS.

[*1. Draw.*] What the devil hast thou brought
there? Apple-johns? Thou know'st Sir John
cannot endure an apple-john.   3

2. Draw. Mass, thou say'st true. The Prince
once set a dish of apple-johns before him, and told
him there were five more Sir Johns, and, putting
off his hat, said, "I will now take my leave of these
six dry, round, old, wither'd knights." It ang'red

him to the heart; but he hath forgot that.   10

[*1. Draw.*] Why, then, cover, and set them down;
and see if thou canst find out Sneak's noise. Mistress Tearsheet would fain hear some music. Dispatch! The room where they supped is too hot;
they'll come in straight.   15

[*2. Draw.*] Sirrah, here will be the Prince and
Master Poins anon; and they will put on two of
our jerkins and aprons; and Sir John must not
know of it. Bardolph hath brought word.   20

1. Draw. By the mass, here will be old utis; it
will be an excellent stratagem.

[*2. Draw.*] I'll see if I can find out Sneak. [*Exit.*

Enter HOSTESS *and* DOLL TEARSHEET.

Host. I' faith, sweetheart, methinks now you
are in an excellent good temperality. Your   25
pulsidge beats as extraordinarily as heart would
desire; and your colour, I warrant you, is as red
as any rose, in good truth, la! But, i' faith, you
have drunk too much canaries; and that's a marvellous searching wine, and it perfumes the blood ere
one can say, "What's this?" How do you now?   32

Dol. Better than I was. Hem!

Host. Why, that's well said; a good heart's
worth gold. Lo, here comes Sir John.   35

Enter FALSTAFF.

Fal. [*Singing.*] "When Arthur first in court" —
Empty the jordan. [*Exit 1. Drawer.*] — [*Singing.*]
"And was a worthy king." How now, Mistress
Doll!

Host. Sick of a calm; yea, good faith.   40

Fal. So is all her sect; an they be once in a calm,
they are sick.

Dol. A pox damn you, you muddy rascal, is that
all the comfort you give me?

Fal. You make fat rascals, Mistress Doll.   45

Dol. I make them? Gluttony and diseases make
[them]; I make them not.

Fal. If the cook help to make the gluttony, you
help to make the diseases, Doll. We catch of you,
Doll, we catch of you. Grant that, my poor virtue,
grant that.   51

Dol. Yea, joy, our chains and our jewels.

Fal. Your brooches, pearls, and ouches. For to
serve bravely is to come halting off, you know; to
come off the breach with his pike bent bravely, and
to surgery bravely; to venture upon the charg'd
chambers bravely, —   57

Dol. Hang yourself, you muddy conger, hang
yourself!

61. **recordation:** memorial.

Sc. iv, 1, 11. [*1. Draw.*] F. *Francis* Q. 2. **Apple-johns:** wrinkled winter apples. 12. **noise:** band of musicians. 14.
Dispatch (Pope). *Dra. Dispatch* Q. 16, 23. [*2. Draw.*] F. *Francis* Q. 20. **word** F. *word. Enter Will* Q. 21. **old utis:**
great sport. 36. "**When Arthur, etc.**" Fragment of the ballad *Sir Lancelot du Lake.* 37. **jordan:** chamber-pot.
40. **calm:** qualm. 47. [**them**] F. Om. Q. 53. **ouches:** jewels. 57. **chambers:** small cannon. 58. **conger:** eel.

Host. By my troth, this is the old fashion; you two never meet but you fall to some discord. You are both, i' good truth, as rheumatic as two dry   62
toasts; you cannot one bear with another's confirmities. What the good-year! one must bear, and that must be you; you are the weaker vessel, as they say, the emptier vessel.   66

Dol. Can a weak empty vessel bear such a huge full hogshead? There's a whole merchant's venture of Bourdeaux stuff in him; you have not seen a hulk better stuff'd in the hold. Come, I'll be friends with thee, Jack. Thou art going to the wars; and whether I shall ever see thee again or no, there is nobody cares.   73

Re-enter [First] Drawer.

[1.] *Draw.* Sir, Ancient Pistol's below, and would speak with you.

Dol. Hang him, swaggering rascal! let him not come hither. It is the foul-mouth'd'st rogue in England.   78

Host. If he swagger, let him not come here; no, by my faith. I must live among my neighbours; I'll no swaggerers. I am in good name and fame with the very best. Shut the door; there comes no swaggerers here. I have not liv'd all this while, to have swaggering now. Shut the door, I pray you.

Fal. Dost thou hear, hostess?   86

Host. Pray ye, pacify yourself, Sir John. There comes no swaggerers here.

Fal. Dost thou hear? It is mine ancient.   89

Host. Tilly-fally, Sir John, ne'er tell me; and your ancient swaggerer comes not in my doors. I was before Master Tisick, the deputy, t'other day; and, as he said to me, 'twas no longer ago than Wednesday last, "I' good faith, neighbour Quickly," says he; Master Dumbe, our minister,   95 was by then; "neighbour Quickly," says he, "receive those that are civil; for," said he, "you are in an ill name." Now 'a said so, I can tell whereupon; "for," says he, "you are an honest woman, and well thought on; therefore take heed what   100 guests you receive. Receive," says he, "no swaggering companions." There comes none here. You would bless you to hear what he said. No, I'll no swaggerers.   104

Fal. He's no swaggerer, hostess; a tame cheater, i' faith; you may stroke him as gently as a puppy greyhound. He'll not swagger with a Barbary hen, if her feathers turn back in any show of resistance. Call him up, drawer.   [*Exit* 1. *Drawer.*]   109

Host. Cheater, call you him? I will bar no honest man my house, nor no cheater; but I do not love swaggering, by my troth. I am the worse, when one says swagger. Feel, masters, how I shake; look you, I warrant you.   114

Dol. So you do, hostess.

Host. Do I? yea, in very truth, do I, an 'twere an aspen leaf. I cannot abide swaggerers.

Enter Pistol, Bardolph, *and* Page.

Pist. God save you, Sir John!   119

Fal. Welcome, Ancient Pistol. Here, Pistol, I charge you with a cup of sack; do you discharge upon mine hostess.

Pist. I will discharge upon her, Sir John, with two bullets.   124

Fal. She is pistol-proof, sir; you shall hardly offend her.

Host. Come, I'll drink no proofs nor no bullets I'll drink no more than will do me good, for no man's pleasure, I.   129

Pist. Then to you, Mistress Dorothy; I will charge you.

Dol. Charge me! I scorn you, scurvy companion. What! you poor, base, rascally, cheating, lack-linen mate! Away, you mouldy rogue, away! I am meat for your master.   135

Pist. I know you, Mistress Dorothy.

Dol. Away, you cut-purse rascal! you filthy bung, away! By this wine, I'll thrust my knife in your mouldy chaps, an you play the saucy cuttle with me. Away, you bottle-ale rascal! you basket-hilt stale juggler, you! Since when, I pray you, sir? God's light, with two points on your shoulder? Much!   143

Pist. God let me not live, but I will murder your ruff for this.

Fal. No more, Pistol; I would not have you go off here. Discharge yourself of our company, Pistol.

Host. No, good Captain Pistol; not here, sweet captain.   150

Dol. Captain! thou abominable damn'd cheater, art thou not ashamed to be call'd captain? An captains were of my mind, they would truncheon you out for taking their names upon you before you have earn'd them. You a captain! you   155 slave, for what? For tearing a poor whore's ruff in a bawdy-house? He a captain! Hang him, rogue! he lives upon mouldy stew'd prunes and dried cakes. A captain! God's light, these villains will make the word as odious as the word   160 "occupy"; which was an excellent good word before it was ill sorted; therefore captains had need look to't.

---

64. **What the good-year!** A common expletive.   74. **Ancient:** ensign.   102. **companions:** fellows.   105. **cheater:** swindler. Some have seen in l. 110, a confusion with *escheator*, a fiscal officer.   107. **Barbary hen:** Guinea hen.   138. **bung:** pickpocket.   139. **cuttle:** cut-purse.   142. **points:** laces.   161. **"occupy":** fornicate.   162. **ill sorted:** fallen into evil company.

Bard. Pray thee, go down, good ancient.

Fal. Hark thee hither, Mistress Doll.   165

Pist. Not I. I tell thee what, Corporal Bardolph, I could tear her. I'll be reveng'd of her.

Page. Pray thee, go down.

Pist. I'll see her damn'd first; to Pluto's damn'd lake, by this hand, to the infernal deep, with Erebus and tortures vile also. Hold hook and line, say I. Down, down, dogs! down, faitors! Have we not Hiren here?   173

Host. Good Captain Peesel, be quiet; 'tis very late, i' faith. I beseek you now, aggravate your choler.

Pist. These be good humours, indeed! Shall pack-horses
And hollow pamper'd jades of Asia,
Which cannot go but thirty mile a-day,   179
Compare with Cæsars and with Cannibals
And Troian Greeks? Nay, rather damn them with
King Cerberus, and let the welkin roar.
Shall we fall foul for toys?

Host. By my troth, captain, these are very bitter words.   185

Bard. Be gone, good ancient. This will grow to a brawl anon.

Pist. [Die] men like dogs! Give crowns like pins! Have we not Hiren here?   189

Host. O' my word, captain, there's none such here. What the good-year! do you think I would deny her? For God's sake, be quiet.

Pist. Then feed, and be fat, my fair Calipolis. Come, give 's some sack.   194
"*Si fortune me tormente, sperato me contento.*"
Fear we broadsides? No, let the fiend give fire.
Give me some sack; and, sweetheart, lie thou there.   [*Laying down his sword.*]
Come we to full points here; and are etceteras nothings?

Fal. Pistol, I would be quiet.   199

Pist. Sweet knight, I kiss thy neaf. What! we have seen the seven stars.

Dol. For God's sake, thrust him downstairs. I cannot endure such a fustian rascal.

Pist. Thrust him downstairs! Know we not Galloway nags?   205

Fal. Quoit him down, Bardolph, like a shove-groat shilling. Nay, an 'a do nothing but speak nothing, 'a shall be nothing here.

Bard. Come, get you downstairs.

Pist. What! shall we have incision? Shall we imbrue?   [*Snatching up his sword.*]   210
Then death rock me asleep, abridge my doleful days!

Why, then, let grievous, ghastly, gaping wounds
Untwine the Sisters Three! Come, Atropos, I say!

Host. Here's goodly stuff toward!   214

Fal. Give me my rapier, boy.

Dol. I pray thee, Jack, I pray thee, do not draw.

Fal. Get you downstairs.   218
    [*Drawing, and driving Pistol out.*]

Host. Here's a goodly tumult! I'll forswear keeping house, afore I'll be in these tirrits and frights. So; murder, I warrant now. Alas, alas! put up your naked weapons, put up your naked weapons.   [*Exeunt Pistol and Bardolph.*]   223

Dol. I pray thee, Jack, be quiet; the rascal's gone. Ah, you whoreson little valiant villain, you!

Host. Are you not hurt i' the groin? Methought 'a made a shrewd thrust at your belly.   228

[*Re-enter* BARDOLPH.]

Fal. Have you turn'd him out o' doors?

Bard. Yea, sir; the rascal's drunk. You have hurt him, sir, i' the shoulder.

Fal. A rascal! to brave me!   232

Dol. Ah, you sweet little rogue, you! Alas, poor ape, how thou sweat'st! Come, let me wipe thy face. Come on, you whoreson chops. Ah, rogue! i' faith, I love thee. Thou art as valorous as Hector of Troy, worth five of Agamemnon, and ten times better than the Nine Worthies. Ah, villain!   239

Fal. A rascally slave! I will toss the rogue in a blanket.

Dol. Do, an thou dar'st for thy heart. An thou dost, I'll canvass thee between a pair of sheets.   244

Enter Music.

Page. The music is come, sir.

Fal. Let them play. Play, sirs. Sit on my knee, Doll. A rascal bragging slave! The rogue fled from me like quicksilver.   248

Dol. I' faith, and thou follow'dst him like a church. Thou whoreson little tidy Bartholomew boar-pig, when wilt thou leave fighting o' days and foining o' nights, and begin to patch up thine old body for heaven?   253

Enter [*behind,*] PRINCE HENRY *and* POINS, *disguised.*

Fal. Peace, good Doll! do not speak like a death's-head. Do not bid me remember mine end.

Dol. Sirrah, what humour's the Prince of?

Fal. A good shallow young fellow. 'A would

---

172. **faitors:** swindlers. 173. **Hiren.** Not satisfactorily explained. 175. **aggravate.** As often, Quickly says the opposite of what she means. 188. [Die] F. Om. Q. 195. "If fortune torments me, hope contents me." 198. **points:** stops. 200. **neaf:** fist. 207. **shove-groat:** a game where coins were aimed at a mark. 213. **Atropos:** one of the three Fates. 214. **toward:** coming. 235. **chops:** fat face. 250. **Bartholomew boar-pig:** roast pig was the chief dish at the fair on St. Bartholomew's Day. 252. **foining:** thrusting.

have made a good pantler; 'a would ha' chipp'd
bread well.   259

Dol. They say Poins has a good wit.

Fal. He a good wit? Hang him, baboon! His
wit's as thick as Tewksbury mustard; there's no
more conceit in him than is in a mallet.   263

Dol. Why does the Prince love him so, then?

Fal. Because their legs are both of a bigness, and
he plays at quoits well, and eats conger and fennel,
and drinks off candles' ends for flap-dragons, and
rides the wild-mare with the boys, and jumps upon
join'd stools, and swears with a good grace, and
wears his boots very smooth, like unto the sign   270
of The Leg, and breeds no bate with telling of discreet stories; and such other gambol faculties 'a
has, that show a weak mind and an able body, for
the which the Prince admits him. For the Prince
himself is such another; the weight of a hair will
turn the scales between their avoirdupois.   277

Prince. Would not this nave of a wheel have his
ears cut off?

Poins. Let's beat him before his whore.

Prince. Look, whe'er the wither'd elder hath not
his poll claw'd like a parrot.   282

Poins. Is it not strange that desire should so
many years outlive performance?

Fal. Kiss me, Doll.

Prince. Saturn and Venus this year in conjunction! What says the almanac to that?   287

Poins. And, look, whether the fiery Trigon, his
man, be not lisping to his master's old tables, his
note-book, his counsel-keeper.

Fal. Thou dost give me flattering busses.

Dol. By my troth, I kiss thee with a most constant heart.   293

Fal. I am old, I am old.

Dol. I love thee better than I love e'er a scurvy
young boy of them all.   296

Fal. What stuff wilt have a kirtle of? I shall
receive money o' Thursday. Shalt have a cap to-
morrow. A merry song, come! It grows late;
we'll to bed. Thou't forget me when I am gone.   300

Dol. By my troth, thou't set me a-weeping, an
thou say'st so. Prove that ever I dress myself
handsome till thy return. Well, hearken a' th'
end.

Fal. Some sack, Francis.   305

Prince. ⎱
Poins. ⎰ Anon, anon, sir.

                              [*Coming forward.*]

Fal. Ha! a bastard son of the King's? And art
not thou Poins his brother?

Prince. Why, thou globe of sinful continents,
what a life dost thou lead!   310

Fal. A better than thou. I am a gentleman; thou
art a drawer.

Prince. Very true, sir; and I come to draw you
out by the ears.   314

Host. O, the Lord preserve thy Grace! By my
troth, welcome to London. Now, the Lord bless
that sweet face of thine! O Jesu, are you come
from Wales?

Fal. Thou whoreson mad compound of majesty,
by this light flesh and corrupt blood, thou art
welcome.   321

Dol. How, you fat fool! I scorn you.

Poins. My lord, he will drive you out of your
revenge and turn all to a merriment, if you take
not the heat.   325

Prince. You whoreson candle-mine, you, how
vilely did you speak of me even now before this
honest, virtuous, civil gentlewoman!

Host. God's blessing of your good heart! and
so she is, by my troth.   330

Fal. Didst thou hear me?

Prince. Yea, and you knew me, as you did when
you ran away by Gadshill. You knew I was at
your back, and spoke it on purpose to try my
patience.   335

Fal. No, no, no; not so; I did not think thou
wast within hearing.

Prince. I shall drive you then to confess the
wilful abuse, and then I know how to handle you.

Fal. No abuse, Hal, o' mine honour; no abuse.

Prince. Not to dispraise me, and call me pantler
and bread-chipper and I know not what?   342

Fal. No abuse, Hal.

Poins. No abuse?   344

Fal. No abuse, Ned, i' the world; honest Ned,
none. I disprais'd him before the wicked, that the
wicked might not fall in love with [him]; in which
doing, I have done the part of a careful friend and
a true subject, and thy father is to give me thanks
for it. No abuse, Hal; none, Ned, none; no, faith,
boys, none.   351

Prince. See now, whether pure fear and entire
cowardice doth not make thee wrong this virtuous
gentlewoman to close with us? Is she of the
wicked? Is thine hostess here of the wicked? Or
is thy boy of the wicked? Or honest Bardolph,
whose zeal burns in his nose, of the wicked?   357

Poins. Answer, thou dead elm, answer.

Fal. The fiend hath prick'd down Bardolph ir-
recoverable; and his face is Lucifer's privy-kitchen,

---

258. **pantler:** servant in the pantry. 263. **conceit:** wit. 267. **for flap-dragons:** floating on burning brandy. 268. **wild-mare:** see-saw. 271. **bate:** strife. 278. **nave:** hub, with pun on *knave.* 288. **fiery Trigon.** The Zodiac was divided into four "trigons" of three signs, characterized as fiery, airy, watery, and earthy. 289. **tables:** account book, i.e., Quickly. 291. **busses:** kisses. 320. **light ... blood:** i.e., Doll. 325. **take ... heat:** strike not when the iron is hot. 326. **candle-mine:** mass of tallow. 347. **[him]** F. *thee* Q. 353. **close with:** pacify. 359. **prick'd:** marked.

where he doth nothing but roast malt-worms. For the boy, there is a good angel about him; but the devil blinds him too.   363

Prince. For the women?

Fal. For one of them, she is in hell already, and burns poor souls. For the other, I owe her money; and whether she be damn'd for that, I know not.

Host. No, I warrant you.   369

Fal. No, I think thou art not; I think thou art quit for that. Marry, there is another indictment upon thee, for suffering flesh to be eaten in thy house, contrary to the law; for the which I think thou wilt howl.   374

Host. All victuallers do so. What's a joint of mutton or two in a whole Lent?

Prince. You, gentlewoman,—

Dol. What says your Grace?

Fal. His grace says that which his flesh rebels against.   [*Peto knocks at door.* 380

Host. Who knocks so loud at door? Look to th' door there, Francis.

Enter PETO.

Prince. Peto, how now! what news?

Peto. The King your father is at Westminster; And there are twenty weak and wearied posts 385 Come from the north; and, as I came along, I met and overtook a dozen captains, Bare-headed, sweating, knocking at the taverns, And asking every one for Sir John Falstaff.

Prince. By heaven, Poins, I feel me much to blame   390 So idly to profane the precious time, When tempest of commotion, like the south Borne with black vapour, doth begin to melt And drop upon our bare unarmed heads. 394 Give me my sword and cloak. Falstaff, good night.

[*Exeunt Prince Henry, Poins, [Peto, and Bardolph.]*

Fal. Now comes in the sweetest morsel of the night, and we must hence and leave it unpick'd. [*Knocking within.*] More knocking at the door!

[*Re-enter* BARDOLPH.]

How now! what's the matter?   400

Bard. You must away to court, sir, presently; A dozen captains stay at door for you.

Fal. [*To the Page.*] Pay the musicians, sirrah. Farewell, hostess; farewell, Doll. You see, my good wenches, how men of merit are sought after. The undeserver may sleep when the man of action is call'd on. Farewell, good wenches; if I be not sent away post, I will see you again ere I go. 408

Dol. I cannot speak. If my heart be not ready to burst, — well, sweet Jack, have a care of thyself.

Fal. Farewell, farewell.

[*Exeunt Falstaff [and Bardolph.]*

Host. Well, fare thee well. I have known thee these twenty-nine years, come peascod-time; but an honester and truer-hearted man, — well, fare thee well.   415

Bard. [*Within.*] Mistress Tearsheet!

Host. What's the matter?

Bard. [*Within.*] Bid Mistress Tearsheet come to my master.

Host. O, run, Doll, run; run, good Doll. Come. [*She comes blubbered.*] Yea, will you come, Doll?   [*Exeunt.* 421

ACT III

SCENE I. [*Westminster. The palace.*]

Enter the KING *in his nightgown, with a* Page.

King. Go call the Earls of Surrey and of Warwick; But, ere they come, bid them o'er-read these letters And well consider of them. Make good speed.

[*Exit Page.*

How many thousand of my poorest subjects Are at this hour asleep! O Sleep, O gentle Sleep, 5 Nature's soft nurse, how have I frighted thee That thou no more wilt weigh my eyelids down And steep my senses in forgetfulness? Why rather, Sleep, liest thou in smoky cribs, Upon uneasy pallets stretching thee,   10 And hush'd with buzzing night-flies to thy slumber, Than in the perfum'd chambers of the great Under the canopies of costly state, And lull'd with sound of sweetest melody? O thou dull god, why liest thou with the vile 15 In loathsome beds, and leav'st the kingly couch A watch-case or a common 'larum-bell? Wilt thou upon the high and giddy mast Seal up the ship-boy's eyes, and rock his brains In cradle of the rude imperious surge 20 And in the visitation of the winds, Who take the ruffian billows by the top, Curling their monstrous heads and hanging them With deaf'ning clamour in the slippery clouds, That, with the hurly, death itself awakes? 25 Canst thou, O partial Sleep, give thy repose To the wet [sea-boy] in an hour so rude, And in the calmest and most stillest night, With all appliances and means to boot, Deny it to a king? Then happy low, lie down! 30 Uneasy lies the head that wears a crown.

Enter WARWICK *and* SURREY.

War. Many good morrows to your Majesty!

King. Is it good morrow, lords?

War. 'Tis one o'clock, and past.

King. Why, then, good morrow to you all, my
    lords.   35
Have you read o'er the letters that I sent you?

War. We have, my liege.

King. Then you perceive the body of our king-
    dom
How foul it is; what rank diseases grow,
And with what danger, near the heart of it.   40

War. It is but as a body yet distemper'd;
Which to his former strength may be restor'd
With good advice and little medicine.
My Lord Northumberland will soon be cool'd.

King. O God! that one might read the book of
    fate,   45
And see the revolution of the times
Make mountains level, and the continent,
Weary of solid firmness, melt itself
Into the sea! and, other times, to see
The beachy girdle of the ocean   50
Too wide for Neptune's hips; how chances mock,
And changes fill the cup of alteration
With divers liquors! O, if this were seen,
The happiest youth, viewing his progress through,
What perils past, what crosses to ensue,   55
Would shut the book, and sit him down and die.
'Tis not ten years gone
Since Richard and Northumberland, great friends,
Did feast together, and in two years after
Were they at wars. It is but eight years since   60
This Percy was the man nearest my soul,
Who like a brother toil'd in my affairs
And laid his love and life under my foot;
Yea, for my sake, even to the eyes of Richard
Gave him defiance. But which of you was by —
You, cousin Nevil, as I may remember —   66
        [To Warwick.]
When Richard, with his eye brimful of tears,
Then check'd and rated by Northumberland,
Did speak these words, now prov'd a prophecy?
"Northumberland, thou ladder by the which   70
My cousin Bolingbroke ascends my throne, —"
Though then, God knows, I had no such intent,
But that necessity so bow'd the state
That I and greatness were compell'd to kiss; —
"The time shall come," thus did he follow it,   75
"The time will come, that foul sin, gathering head,
Shall break into corruption:" so went on,
Foretelling this same time's condition
And the division of our amity.

War. There is a history in all men's lives,   80
Figuring the nature of the times deceas'd;
The which observ'd, a man may prophesy,
With a near aim, of the main chance of things
As yet not come to life, [which] in their seeds
And weak beginnings lie intreasured.   85
Such things become the hatch and brood of time;
And by the necessary form of this
King Richard might create a perfect guess
That great Northumberland, then false to him,
Would of that seed grow to a greater falseness,   90
Which should not find a ground to root upon
Unless on you.

King.   Are these things then necessities?
Then let us meet them like necessities.
And that same word even now cries out on us.
They say the Bishop and Northumberland   95
Are fifty thousand strong.

War.   It cannot be, my lord.
Rumour doth double, like the voice and echo,
The numbers of the fear'd. Please it your Grace
To go to bed. Upon my soul, my lord,
The powers that you already have sent forth   100
Shall bring this prize in very easily.
To comfort you the more, I have receiv'd
A certain instance that Glendower is dead.
Your Majesty hath been this fortnight ill,
And these unseason'd hours perforce must add   105
Unto your sickness.

King.   I will take your counsel:
And were these inward wars once out of hand,
We would, dear lords, unto the Holy Land.
        [Exeunt.

SCENE II. [*Gloucestershire. Before Justice Shal-
    low's house.*]

Enter SHALLOW *and* SILENCE [*meeting*]; MOULDY,
SHADOW, WART, FEEBLE, BULLCALF [*a Servant
or two with them*].

Shal. Come on, come on, come on, sir; give me
your hand, sir, give me your hand, sir. An early
stirrer, by the rood! And how doth my good cousin Silence?

Sil. Good morrow, good cousin Shallow.   5

Shal. And how doth my cousin, your bedfellow?
and your fairest daughter and mine, my god-
daughter Ellen?

Sil. Alas, a black ousel, cousin Shallow!   9

Shal. By yea and no, sir, I dare say my cousin
William is become a good scholar. He is at Oxford
still, is he not?

Sil. Indeed, sir, to my cost.   13

Shal. 'A must, then, to the Inns o' Court shortly.

32. s.d. SURREY. F. *Surrey, and sir Iohn Blunt* Q. 70 ff. See *Rich. II*, V.i.55 ff. 84. [which] F. *who* Q. 103. instance
proof.
Sc. ii, 9. ousel: blackbird.

I was once of Clement's Inn, where I think they will talk of mad Shallow yet. 16

Sil. You were call'd lusty Shallow then, cousin.

Shal. By the mass, I was call'd anything; and I would have done anything indeed too, and roundly too. There was I, and little John Doit of Staffordshire, and black George Barnes, and Francis Pickbone, and Will Squele, a Cots'ol' man. You had not four such swingebucklers in all the Inns o' Court again; and I may say to you, we knew where 25 the bona robas were and had the best of them all at commandment. Then was Jack Falstaff, now Sir John, a boy, and page to Thomas Mowbray, Duke of Norfolk.

Sil. Cousin, this Sir John that comes hither anon about soldiers? 31

Shal. The same Sir John, the very same. I see him break Skogan's head at the court-gate, when 'a was a crack not thus high; and the very same day did I fight with one Sampson Stockfish, a fruiterer, behind Gray's Inn. Jesu, Jesu, the mad days that I have spent! And to see how many of my old acquaintance are dead! 38

Sil. We shall all follow, cousin.

Shal. Certain, 'tis certain; very sure, very sure. Death, as the Psalmist saith, is certain to all; all shall die. How a good yoke of bullocks at Stamford fair? 43

Sil. By my troth, I was not there.

Shal. Death is certain. Is old Double of your town living yet? 47

Sil. Dead, sir.

Shal. Jesu, Jesu, dead! 'A drew a good bow; and dead! 'A shot a fine shoot. John o' Gaunt loved him well, and betted much money on his head. Dead! 'a would have clapp'd i' th' clout at twelve score; and carried you a forehand shaft at fourteen and fourteen and a half, that it would have done a man's heart good to see. How a score of ewes now? 55

Sil. Thereafter as they be, a score of good ewes may be worth ten pounds.

Shal. And is old Double dead?

Sil. Here come two of Sir John Falstaff's men, as I think. 60

Enter BARDOLPH *and one with him.*

Good morrow, honest gentlemen.

Bard. I beseech you, which is Justice Shallow?

Shal. I am Robert Shallow, sir; a poor esquire of this county, and one of the King's justices of the peace. What is your good pleasure with me? 65

Bard. My captain, sir, commends him to you;

my captain, Sir John Falstaff, a tall gentleman, by heaven, and a most gallant leader.

Shal. He greets me well, sir. I knew him a good backsword man. How doth the good knight? May I ask how my lady his wife doth? 71

Bard. Sir, pardon; a soldier is better accommodated than with a wife.

Shal. It is well said, in faith, sir; and it is well said indeed too. Better accommodated! it is good; yea, indeed, is it. Good phrases are surely, and ever were, very commendable. Accommodated! it comes of *accommodo.* Very good; a good phrase.

Bard. Pardon, sir; I have heard the word. 80 Phrase call you it? By this day, I know not the phrase; but I will maintain the word with my sword to be a soldier-like word, and a word of exceeding good command, by heaven. Accommodated; 84 that is, when a man is, as they say, accommodated; or when a man is, being, whereby 'a may be thought to be accommodated; which is an excellent thing.

Enter FALSTAFF.

Shal. It is very just. Look, here comes good Sir John. Give me your good hand, give me your 90 worship's good hand. By my troth, you like well and bear your years very well. Welcome, good Sir John.

Fal. I am glad to see you well, good Master Robert Shallow. Master Surecard, as I think? 95

Shal. No, Sir John; it is my cousin Silence, in commission with me.

Fal. Good Master Silence, it well befits you should be of the peace.

Sil. Your good worship is welcome. 100

Fal. Fie! this is hot weather, gentlemen. Have you provided me here half a dozen sufficient men?

Shal. Marry, have we, sir. Will you sit?

Fal. Let me see them, I beseech you. 105

Shal. Where's the roll? where's the roll? where's the roll? Let me see, let me see, let me see. So, so, so, so, so, so, so; yea, marry, sir. Ralph Mouldy! Let them appear as I call; let them do so, let them do so. Let me see; where is Mouldy? 111

Moul. Here, an it please you.

Shal. What think you, Sir John? A good-limb'd fellow; young, strong, and of good friends.

Fal. Is thy name Mouldy? 115

Moul. Yea, an't please you.

Fal. 'Tis the more time thou wert us'd.

Shal. Ha, ha, ha! most excellent, i' faith! Things that are mouldy lack use. Very singular good! In faith, well said, Sir John, very well said.

Fal. Prick him. [*John pricks him.* 121

Moul. I was prick'd well enough before, an you

27. **bona robas:** harlots. 51–52. **clapp'd ... score:** hit the bull's-eye at 240 yards. 52. **forehand:** for straightforward shooting. 67. **tall:** brave. 70. **backsword man:** single-stick fencer. 72. **accommodated:** furnished. Shallow's remarks show that it was an innovation. 91. **like well:** are in good condition.

could have let me alone. My old dame will be undone now for one to do her husbandry and her
drudgery. You need not to have prick'd me; there
are other men fitter to go out than I.   126

Fal. Go to; peace, Mouldy; you shall go.
Mouldy, it is time you were spent.

Moul. Spent!

Shal. Peace, fellow, peace; stand aside; know
you where you are? For the other, Sir John, let
me see. Simon Shadow!   132

Fal. Yea, marry, let me have him to sit under;
he's like to be a cold soldier.

Shal. Where's Shadow?

Shad. Here, sir.

Fal. Shadow, whose son art thou?   137

Shad. My mother's son, sir.

Fal. Thy mother's son! like enough, and thy
father's shadow. So the son of the female is the
shadow of the male. It is often so, indeed; but
much of the father's substance!   142

Shal. Do you like him, Sir John?

Fal. Shadow will serve for summer. Prick
him, for we have a number of shadows to fill up
the muster-book.   146

Shal. Thomas Wart!

Fal. Where's he?

Wart. Here, sir.

Fal. Is thy name Wart?   150

Wart. Yea, sir.

Fal. Thou art a very ragged wart.

Shal. Shall I prick him, Sir John?

Fal. It were superfluous; for [his] apparel is
built upon his back and the whole frame stands
upon pins. Prick him no more.   156

Shal. Ha, ha, ha! you can do it, sir; you can do
it; I commend you well. Francis Feeble!

Fee. Here, sir.

[*Fal.*] What trade art thou, Feeble?   160

Fee. A woman's tailor, sir.

Shal. Shall I prick him, sir?

Fal. You may; but if he had been a man's
tailor, he'd ha' prick'd you. Wilt thou make as
many holes in an enemy's battle as thou hast done
in a woman's petticoat?   166

Fee. I will do my good will, sir; you can have no
more.

Fal. Well said, good woman's tailor! well said,
courageous Feeble! Thou wilt be as valiant as the
wrathful dove or most magnanimous mouse. Prick
the woman's tailor. Well, Master Shallow; deep,
Master Shallow.   173

Fee. I would Wart might have gone, sir.

Fal. I would thou wert a man's tailor, that thou
mightst mend him and make him fit to go. I cannot put him to a private soldier that is the leader

of so many thousands. Let that suffice, most
forcible Feeble.

Fee. It shall suffice, sir.   180

Fal. I am bound to thee, reverend Feeble. Who
is next?

Shal. Peter Bullcalf o' th' green!

Fal. Yea, marry, let's see Bullcalf.

Bull. Here, sir.   185

Fal. 'Fore God, a likely fellow! Come, prick
me Bullcalf till he roar again.

Bull. O Lord! good my lord captain, —

Fal. What, dost thou roar before thou art
prick'd?   190

Bull. O Lord, sir! I am a diseased man.

Fal. What disease hast thou?

Bull. A whoreson cold, sir, a cough, sir, which I
caught with ringing in the King's affairs upon his
coronation-day, sir.   195

Fal. Come, thou shalt go to the wars in a gown.
We will have away thy cold; and I will take such
order that thy friends shall ring for thee. Is here
all?   199

Shal. Here is two more call'd than your number;
you must have but four here, sir. And so, I pray
you, go in with me to dinner.

Fal. Come, I will go drink with you, but I cannot tarry dinner. I am glad to see you, by my
troth, Master Shallow.   205

Shal. O, Sir John, do you remember since we
lay all night in the windmill in Saint George's field?

Fal. No more of that, [good] Master Shallow
[no more of that].

Shal. Ha! 'twas a merry night. And is Jane
Nightwork alive?   211

Fal. She lives, Master Shallow.

Shal. She never could away with me.

Fal. Never, never; she would always say she
could not abide Master Shallow.   215

Shal. By the mass, I could anger her to the
heart. She was then a bona roba. Doth she hold
her own well?

Fal. Old, old, Master Shallow.   219

Shal. Nay, she must be old; she cannot choose
but be old; certain she's old; and had Robin Nightwork by old Nightwork before I came to Clement's
Inn.

Sil. That's fifty-five year ago.   224

Shal. Ha, cousin Silence, that thou hadst seen
that that this knight and I have seen! Ha, Sir
John, said I well?

Fal. We have heard the chimes at midnight,
Master Shallow.   229

Shal. That we have, that we have, that we have;
in faith, Sir John, we have. Our watchword was
"Hem, boys!" Come, let's to dinner; come, let's

to dinner. Jesu, the days that we have seen! Come, come.   234

[Exeunt [Falstaff and the Justices].

Bull. Good Master Corporate Bardolph, stand my friend; and here's four Harry ten shillings in French crowns for you. In very truth, sir, I had as lief be hang'd, sir, as go; and yet, for mine own part, sir, I do not care; but rather, because I   239
am unwilling, and, for mine own part, have a desire to stay with my friends; else, sir, I did not care, for mine own part, so much.

Bard. Go to; stand aside.   243

Moul. And, good master corporal captain, for my [old] dame's sake, stand my friend. She has nobody to do anything about her when I am gone; and she is old, and cannot help herself. You shall have forty, sir.

Bard. Go to; stand aside.   249

Fee. By my troth, I care not; a man can die but once; we owe God a death. I'll ne'er bear a base mind. An't be my destiny, so; an't be not, so. No man's too good to serve 's prince; and let it go which way it will, he that dies this year is quit for the next.   255

Bard. Well said; th' art a good fellow.

Fee. Faith, I'll bear no base mind.

Re-enter FALSTAFF *and the* JUSTICES.

Fal. Come, sir, which men shall I have?

Shal. Four of which you please.

Bard. [*Aside to Fal.*] Sir, a word with you. I have three pound to free Mouldy and Bullcalf.   261

Fal. Go to; well.

Shal. Come, Sir John, which four will you have?

Fal. Do you choose for me.

Shal. Marry, then, Mouldy, Bullcalf, Feeble, and Shadow.   267

Fal. Mouldy and Bullcalf! for you, Mouldy, stay at home till you are past service; and for your part, Bullcalf, grow till you come unto it. I will none of you.

Shal. Sir John, Sir John, do not yourself wrong. They are your likeliest men, and I would have you serv'd with the best.   274

Fal. Will you tell me, Master Shallow, how to choose a man? Care I for the limb, the thews, the stature, bulk, and big assemblance of a man! Give me the spirit, Master Shallow. Here's Wart; you see what a ragged appearance it is. 'A shall charge you and discharge you with the   280
motion of a pewterer's hammer, come off and on swifter than he that gibbets on the brewer's bucket. And this same half-fac'd fellow, Shadow; give me

this man. He presents no mark to the enemy; the foeman may with as great aim level at the   285
edge of a penknife. And for a retreat; how swiftly will this Feeble the woman's tailor run off! O, give me the spare men, and spare me the great ones. Put me a caliver into Wart's hand, Bardolph.   290

Bard. Hold, Wart, traverse; thus, thus, thus.

Fal. Come, manage me your caliver. So: very well; go to; very good, exceeding good. O, give me always a little, lean, old, chapt, bald shot. Well said, i' faith, Wart; thou'rt a good scab. Hold, there's a tester for thee.   296

Shal. He is not his craft's master; he doth not do it right. I remember at Mile-end Green, when I lay at Clement's Inn, — I was then Sir Dagonet in Arthur's show, — there was a little quiver fellow, and 'a would manage you his piece thus;   301
and 'a would about and about, and come you in and come you in. "Rah, tah, tah," would 'a say; "bounce" would 'a say; and away again would 'a go, and again would 'a come. I shall ne'er see such a fellow.   306

Fal. These fellows will do well, Master Shallow. God keep you, Master Silence; I will not use many words with you. Fare you well, gentlemen both; I thank you. I must a dozen mile to-night. Bardolph, give the soldiers coats.   311

Shal. Sir John, the Lord bless you! God prosper your affairs! God send us peace! At your return visit our house; let our old acquaintance be renewed. Peradventure I will with ye to the court.   316

Fal. 'Fore God, would you would [Master Shallow].

Shal. Go to; I have spoke at a word. God keep you!   320

Fal. Fare you well, gentle gentlemen. [*Exeunt Justices.*] On, Bardolph; lead the men away. [*Exeunt Bardolph, recruits, etc.*] As I return, I will fetch off these justices. I do see the bottom of Justice Shallow. Lord, Lord, how subject we old men are to this vice of lying! This same   326
starv'd justice hath done nothing but prate to me of the wildness of his youth, and the feats he hath done about Turnbull Street; and every third word a lie, duer paid to the hearer than the Turk's   330
tribute. I do remember him at Clement's Inn like a man made after supper of a cheese-paring. When 'a was naked, he was, for all the world, like a forked radish, with a head fantastically carv'd upon it with a knife. 'A was so forlorn,   335
that his dimensions to any thick sight were invincible. 'A was the very genius of famine, yet lecherous as a monkey, and the whores called him man-

245. [old] F. Om. Q.   277. assemblance: appearance.   282. gibbets: hangs on the yoke.   290. caliver: musket.   291. traverse: march.   296. tester: sixpence.   300. Arthur's show. A company of London archers gave an annual exhibition at Mile-End Green, each taking the name of one of King Arthur's knights. Sir Dagonet was the fool.   300. quiver: nimble. 317. [Master Shallow] F. Om. Q.   319. at a word: in one word.   324. fetch off: fleece.   330. duer: more duly.   337. invincible: not discernible.

drake. 'A came ever in the rearward of the fashion, and sung those tunes to the overscutch'd 340 huswives that he heard the carmen whistle, and sware they were his fancies or his good-nights. And now is this Vice's dagger become a squire, and talks as familiarly of John o' Gaunt as if he had been sworn brother to him; and I'll be sworn 345 'a ne'er saw him but once in the Tilt-yard; and then he burst his head for crowding among the marshal's men. I saw it, and told John o' Gaunt he beat his own name; for you might have thrust him and all his apparel into an eel-skin. The case of a 350 treble hautboy was a mansion for him, a court; and now has he land and beeves. Well, I'll be acquainted with him, if I return; and 't shall go hard but I will make him a philosopher's two stones to me. If the young dace be a bait for the old 355 pike, I see no reason in the law of nature but I may snap at him. Let time shape, and there an end.

[*Exit.*

ACT IV

Scene I. [*Yorkshire.*] *Within the Forest of Gaultree.*

Enter the Archbishop of York, Mowbray, Hastings [*and others*].

Arch. What is this forest call'd?

Hast. 'Tis Gaultree Forest, an't shall please your Grace.

Arch. Here stand, my lords; and send discoverers forth
To know the numbers of our enemies.

Hast. We have sent forth already.

Arch. 'Tis well done.
My friends and brethren in these great affairs, 6
I must acquaint you that I have receiv'd
New-dated letters from Northumberland;
Their cold intent, tenour, and substance, thus:
Here doth he wish his person, with such powers 10
As might hold sortance with his quality,
The which he could not levy; whereupon
He is retir'd, to ripe his growing fortunes,
To Scotland; and concludes in hearty prayers
That your attempts may overlive the hazard 15
And fearful meeting of their opposite.

Mowb. Thus do the hopes we have in him touch ground
And dash themselves to pieces.

Enter a Messenger.

Hast.   Now, what news?

Mess. West of this forest, scarcely off a mile,

In goodly form comes on the enemy; 20
And, by the ground they hide, I judge their number
Upon or near the rate of thirty thousand.

Mowb. The just proportion that we gave them out.
Let us sway on and face them in the field.

Arch. What well-appointed leader fronts us here? 25

Enter Westmoreland.

Mowb. I think it is my Lord of Westmoreland.

West. Health and fair greeting from our general,
The Prince, Lord John and Duke of Lancaster.

Arch. Say on, my Lord of Westmoreland, in peace,
What doth concern your coming.

West.   [Then, my lord,]
Unto your Grace do I in chief address 31
The substance of my speech. If that rebellion
Came like itself, in base and abject routs,
Led on by bloody youth, guarded with [rags,]
And countenanc'd by boys and beggary, — 35
I say, if damn'd commotion so appear'd
In his true, native, and most proper shape,
You, reverend father, and these noble lords
Had not been here to dress the ugly form
Of base and bloody insurrection 40
With your fair honours. You, Lord Archbishop,
Whose see is by a civil peace maintain'd,
Whose beard the silver hand of peace hath touch'd,
Whose learning and good letters peace hath tutor'd,
Whose white investments figure innocence, 45
The dove, and very blessed spirit of peace,
Wherefore do you so ill translate yourself
Out of the speech of peace that bears such grace,
Into the harsh and boist'rous tongue of war;
Turning your books to graves, your ink to blood,
Your pens to lances and your tongue divine 51
To a loud trumpet and a point of war?

Arch. Wherefore do I this? so the question stands.
Briefly to this end: we are all diseas'd,
[And with our surfeiting and wanton hours 55
Have brought ourselves into a burning fever,
And we must bleed for it; of which disease
Our late king, Richard, being infected, died.
But, my most noble Lord of Westmoreland,
I take not on me here as a physician, 60
Nor do I as an enemy to peace
Troop in the throngs of military men;
But rather show awhile like fearful war
To diet rank minds sick of happiness,
And purge the obstructions which begin to stop 65

---

339. **mandrake:** a plant with a forked root. 340. **overscutch'd huswives:** worn-out strumpets. 342. **fancies, good-nights:** types of songs. 343. **Vice:** a character in the morality plays who carried a dagger of lath. 351. **hautboy:** oboe. 354. **philosopher's two stones:** as valuable as two philosopher's stones, which were supposed to change base metals to gold.
  Act IV, sc. i, 11. **sortance:** accord. 23. **just...out:** exact number we estimated. 30. [**Then, my lord**] F. Om. Q. 34. **guarded:** dressed. [**rags**] (Singer). *rage* QF. 52. **point:** note of a trumpet. 55-79. F. Om. Q.

Our very veins of life.   Hear me more plainly.
I have in equal balance justly weigh'd
What wrongs our arms may do, what wrongs we
         suffer,
And find our griefs heavier than our offences.
We see which way the stream of time doth run,   70
And are enforc'd from our most quiet there
By the rough torrent of occasion;
And have the summary of all our griefs,
When time shall serve, to show in articles;
Which long ere this we offer'd to the King,   75
And might by no suit gain our audience.
When we are wrong'd and would unfold our griefs,
We are deni'd access unto his person
Even by those men that most have done us wrong.]
The dangers of the days but newly gone,   80
Whose memory is written on the earth
With yet appearing blood, and the examples
Of every minute's instance, present now,
Hath put us in these ill-beseeming arms,
Not to break peace or any branch of it,   85
But to establish here a peace indeed,
Concurring both in name and quality.
   West. When ever yet was your appeal denied?
Wherein have you been galled by the King?   89
What peer hath been suborn'd to grate on you
That you should seal this lawless bloody book
Of forg'd rebellion with a seal divine
And consecrate commotion's bitter edge?
   Arch. My brother general, the commonwealth,
To brother born an household cruelty.   95
I make my quarrel in particular.
   West. There is no need of any such redress;
Or if there were, it not belongs to you.
   Mowb. Why not to him in part, and to us all
That feel the bruises of the days before,   100
And suffer the condition of these times
To lay a heavy and unequal hand
Upon our honours?
   West.   [O, my good Lord Mowbray,
Construe the times to their necessities,
And you shall say indeed, it is the time,   105
And not the King, that doth you injuries.
Yet for your part, it not appears to me
Either from the King or in the present time
That you should have an inch of any ground
To build a grief on. Were you not restor'd   110
To all the Duke of Norfolk's signories,
Your noble and right well-rememb'red father's?
   Mowb. What thing, in honour, had my father
         lost,
That need to be reviv'd and breath'd in me?   114

The King that lov'd him, as the state stood then,
Was, force perforce, compell'd to banish him;
And then that Henry Bolingbroke and he,
Being mounted and both roused in their seats,
Their neighing coursers daring of the spur,   119
Their armed staves in charge, their beavers down,
Their eyes of fire sparkling through sights of steel,
And the loud trumpet blowing them together,
Then, then, when there was nothing could have stay'd
My father from the breast of Bolingbroke,   124
O, when the King did throw his warder down —
His own life hung upon the staff he threw, —
Then threw he down himself and all their lives
That by indictment and by dint of sword
Have since miscarried under Bolingbroke.
   West. You speak, Lord Mowbray, now you
         know not what.   130
The Earl of Hereford was reputed then
In England the most valiant gentleman.
Who knows on whom Fortune would then have
         smil'd?
But if your father had been victor there,
He ne'er had borne it out of Coventry;   135
For all the country in a general voice
Cried hate upon him; and all their prayers and love
Were set on Hereford, whom they doted on
And bless'd and grac'd and did, more than the
         King, —]
But this is mere digression from my purpose.   140
Here come I from our princely general
To know your griefs; to tell you from his Grace
That he will give you audience; and wherein
It shall appear that your demands are just,
You shall enjoy them, everything set off   145
That might so much as think you enemies.
   Mowb. But he hath forc'd us to compel this offer;
And it proceeds from policy, not love.
   West. Mowbray, you overween to take it so;
This offer comes from mercy, not from fear.   150
For, lo! within a ken our army lies,
Upon mine honour, all too confident
To give admittance to a thought of fear.
Our battle is more full of names than yours,
Our men more perfect in the use of arms,   155
Our armour all as strong, our cause the best;
Then reason will our hearts should be as good.
Say you not then our offer is compell'd.
   Mowb. Well, by my will we shall admit no parley.
   West. That argues but the shame of your offence.
A rotten case abides no handling.   161
   Hast. Hath the Prince John a full commission,
In very ample virtue of his father,

---

69. **griefs**: grievances.   94-96. These lines are obviously defective. F. omits 95. York's brother, Scroop, had been executed by Henry. 103-139. F. Om. Q.   104. **to**: according to.   114. **breath'd**: have life breathed into it.   115 ff. Cf.
Rich. II, I.iii.118 ff.   116. **force** (Theobald).   *forc'd* F.   120. **armed...charge**: lances in rest.   **beavers**: visors. 125.
warder: staff.   129. **miscarried**: perished.   131. **Hereford**: Bolingbroke.   145. **set off**: disregarded.   151. **a ken**: sight.
157. **will**: will show.   163. **virtue**: power.

To hear and absolutely to determine
Of what conditions we shall stand upon?   165
  West. That is intended in the general's name.
I muse you make so slight a question.
  Arch. Then take, my Lord of Westmoreland, this
    schedule,
For this contains our general grievances.
Each several article herein redress'd,   170
All members of our cause, both here and hence,
That are insinew'd to this action,
Acquitted by a true substantial form,
And present execution of our wills
To us and to our purposes confin'd,   175
We come within our awful banks again
And knit our powers to the arm of peace.
  West. This will I show the general. Please you,
    lords,
In sight of both our battles we may meet;
And either end in peace, which God so frame!   180
Or to the place of diff'rence call the swords
Which must decide it.   [*Exit West.*
  Arch.   My lord, we will do so.
  Mowb. There is a thing within my bosom tells
    me
That no conditions of our peace can stand.
  Hast. Fear you not that. If we can make our
    peace   185
Upon such large terms and so absolute
As our conditions shall consist upon,
Our peace shall stand as firm as rocky mountains.
  Mowb. Yea, but our valuation shall be such
That every slight and false-derived cause,   190
Yea, every idle, nice, and wanton reason
Shall to the King taste of this action;
That, were our royal faiths martyrs in love,
We shall be winnow'd with so rough a wind
That even our corn shall seem as light as chaff   195
And good from bad find no partition.
  Arch. No, no, my lord. Note this: the King is
    weary
Of dainty and such picking grievances;
For he hath found to end one doubt by death
Revives two greater in the heirs of life,   200
And therefore will he wipe his tables clean
And keep no tell-tale to his memory
That may repeat and history his loss
To new remembrance; for full well he knows
He cannot so precisely weed this land   205
As his misdoubts present occasion.
His foes are so enrooted with his friends
That, plucking to unfix an enemy,
He doth unfasten so and shake a friend;

So that this land, like an offensive wife   210
That hath enrag'd him on to offer strokes,
As he is striking, holds his infant up
And hangs resolv'd correction in the arm
That was uprear'd to execution.
  Hast. Besides, the King hath wasted all his rods
On late offenders, that he now doth lack   216
The very instruments of chastisement;
So that his power, like to a fangless lion,
May offer, but not hold.
  Arch.   'Tis very true;
And therefore be assur'd, my good Lord Marshal,
If we do now make our atonement well,   221
Our peace will, like a broken limb united,
Grow stronger for the breaking.
  Mowb.   Be it so.
Here is return'd my Lord of Westmoreland.

Re-enter WESTMORELAND.

  West. The Prince is here at hand. Pleaseth
    your lordship   225
To meet his Grace just distance 'tween our armies.
  Mowb. Your Grace of York, in God's name, then,
    set forward.
  Arch. Before, and greet his Grace. My lord,
    we come.   [*Exeunt*

[SCENE II. *Another part of the forest.*]

Enter [*from one side,* MOWBRAY, *attended; afterwards the* ARCHBISHOP, HASTINGS, *and others:
  from the other side,*] PRINCE JOHN OF LANCASTER
  [*and* WESTMORELAND; *Officers, and others with
  them*].

  Lan. You are well encount'red here, my cousin
    Mowbray.
Good day to you, gentle Lord Archbishop;
And so to you, Lord Hastings, and to all.
My Lord of York, it better show'd with you
When that your flock, assembled by the bell,   5
Encircled you to hear with reverence
Your exposition on the holy text
Than now to see you here an iron man,
Cheering a rout of rebels with your drum,
Turning the Word to sword and life to death.   10
That man that sits within a monarch's heart
And ripens in the sunshine of his favour,
Would he abuse the countenance of the King,
Alack, what mischiefs might he set abroach
In shadow of such greatness! With you, Lord
    Bishop,   15
It is even so. Who hath not heard it spoken

---

166. **intended:** implied.   172. **insinew'd to:** involved in.   174–75. The immediate carrying out of our wishes as regards ourselves and our plans.   176. **awful banks:** bounds of respect.   187. **upon:** of.   189. **valuation:** i.e., by the king.   193. **were...love:** though our fidelity to the king were as intense as the faith of martyrs.   198. **picking:** trifling.   203. **history:** record.   213. **hangs resolv'd correction:** checks intended punishment.   219. **offer:** threaten.   226. **just:** precise.
  Sc. ii, 8. man F.   *man talking* Q.   14. **set abroach:** start.

How deep you were within the books of God?
To us the speaker in His parliament;
To us the imagin'd voice of God himself;
The very opener and intelligencer   20
Between the grace, the sanctities, of Heaven
And our dull workings. O, who shall believe
But you misuse the reverence of your place,
[Employ] the countenance and grace of Heaven,
As a false favourite doth his prince's name,   25
In deeds dishonourable? You have ta'en up,
Under the counterfeited zeal of God,
The subjects of His substitute, my father,
And both against the peace of Heaven and him
Have here upswarm'd them.
     Arch.   Good my Lord of Lancaster,
I am not here against your father's peace;   31
But, as I told my Lord of Westmoreland,
The time misord'red doth, in common sense,
Crowd us and crush us to this monstrous form
To hold our safety up. I sent your Grace   35
The parcels and particulars of our grief,
The which hath been with scorn shov'd from the
     court,
Whereon this Hydra son of war is born;
Whose dangerous eyes may well be charm'd asleep
With grant of our most just and right desires;   40
And true obedience, of this madness cur'd,
Stoop tamely to the foot of majesty.
     Mowb. If not, we ready are to try our fortunes
To the last man.
     Hast.   And though we here fall down,
We have supplies to second our attempt.   45
If they miscarry, theirs shall second them;
And so success of mischief shall be born,
And heir from heir shall hold this quarrel up
Whiles England shall have generation.
     Lan. You are too shallow, Hastings, much too
     shallow,   50
To sound the bottom of the after-times.
     West. Pleaseth your Grace to answer them
     directly
How far forth you do like their articles.
     Lan. I like them all, and do allow them well,
And swear here, by the honour of my blood,   55
My father's purposes have been mistook,
And some about him have too lavishly
Wrested his meaning and authority.
My lord, these griefs shall be with speed redress'd;
Upon my soul, they shall. If this may please
     you,   60
Discharge your powers unto their several counties,
As we will ours; and here between the armies
Let's drink together friendly and embrace,
That all their eyes may bear those tokens home

Of our restored love and amity.   65
     Arch. I take your princely word for these re-
     dresses.
     Lan. I give it you, and will maintain my word;
And thereupon I drink unto your Grace.
     [*Hast.*] Go, captain, and deliver to the army
This news of peace. Let them have pay, and
     part.   70
I know it will well please them. Hie thee, captain.
                              [*Exit* [*Officer*].
     Arch. To you, my noble Lord of Westmoreland.
     West. I pledge your Grace; and, if you knew
     what pains
I have bestow'd to breed this present peace,
You would drink freely. But my love to ye   75
Shall show itself more openly hereafter.
     Arch. I do not doubt you.
     West.   I am glad of it.
Health to my lord and gentle cousin, Mowbray.
     Mowb. You wish me health in very happy
     season;
For I am, on the sudden, something ill.   80
     Arch. Against ill chances men are ever merry;
But heaviness foreruns the good event.
     West. Therefore be merry, coz; since sudden
     sorrow
Serves to say thus, some good thing comes to-
     morrow.
     Arch. Believe me, I am passing light in spirit. 85
     Mowb. So much the worse, if your own rule be
     true.   [*Shouts* [*within*].
     Lan. The word of peace is rend'red. Hark, how
     they shout!
     Mowb. This had been cheerful after victory.
     Arch. A peace is of the nature of a conquest;
For then both parties nobly are subdu'd,   90
And neither party loser.
     Lan.   Go, my lord,
And let our army be discharged too.
And, good my lord, so please you, let your trains
March by us, that we may peruse the men
                              [*Exit* [*Westmoreland*].
We should have cop'd withal.
     Arch.   Go, good Lord Hastings,
And, ere they be dismiss'd, let them march by. 96
                              [*Exit* [*Hastings*].

               Re-enter WESTMORELAND.

     Lan. I trust, lords, we shall lie to-night together.
Now cousin, wherefore stands our army still?
     West. The leaders, having charge from you to
     stand,
Will not go off until they hear you speak.   100
     Lan. They know their duties.

20. **opener:** interpreter. **intelligencer:** intermediary. 24. [**Employ**] F. *Imply* Q. 26. **ta'en up:** enlisted. 36. **parcels:**
details. 38. **Hydra:** many-headed. 47. **success:** succession. 69. [**Hast.**] F. *Prince* Q. 81. **Against:** before. 87. **ren-**
d'red: given out. 95. **cop'd:** fought.

Re-enter HASTINGS.

Hast. My lord, our army is dispers'd already.
Like youthful steers unyok'd, they take their
      courses
East, west, north, south; or, like a school broke up,
Each hurries toward his home and sporting-
      place.   105
West. Good tidings, my Lord Hastings; for the
      which
I do arrest thee, traitor, of high treason;
And you, Lord Archbishop, and you, Lord Mow-
      bray,
Of capital treason I attach you both.
Mowb. Is this proceeding just and honourable?
West. Is your assembly so?   111
Arch. Will you thus break your faith?
Lan.   I pawn'd thee none.
I promis'd you redress of these same grievances
Whereof you did complain; which, by mine honour,
I will perform with a most Christian care.   115
But for you, rebels, look to taste the due
Meet for rebellion [and such acts as yours].
Most shallowly did you these arms commence,
Fondly brought here and foolishly sent hence.
Strike up our drums, pursue the scatt'red stray.   120
God, and not we, hath safely fought to-day.
Some guard [these traitors] to the block of death,
Treason's true bed and yielder up of breath.
                                                  [*Exeunt.*

[SCENE III.   *Another part of the forest.*]

Alarums.   Excursion.   Enter FALSTAFF *and*
            COLVILLE [*meeting*].

Fal. What's your name, sir? Of what condition
are you, and of what place, [I pray]?
Col. I am a knight, sir; and my name is Colville
of the Dale.   4
Fal. Well, then, Colville is your name, a knight
is your degree, and your place the Dale. Colville
shall be still your name, a traitor your degree, and
the dungeon your place, a place deep enough; so
shall you be still Colville of the Dale.   10
Col. Are not you Sir John Falstaff?
Fal. As good a man as he, sir, whoe'er I am. Do
ye yield, sir? or shall I sweat for you? If I do
sweat, they are the drops of thy lovers, and they
weep for thy death; therefore rouse up fear and
trembling, and do observance to my mercy.   17
Col. I think you are Sir John Falstaff, and in
that thought yield me.
Fal. I have a whole school of tongues in this belly
of mine, and not a tongue of them all speaks any
other word but my name. An I had but a belly of
any indifferency, I were simply the most active   23
fellow in Europe. My womb, my womb, my
womb, undoes me. Here comes our general.

Enter PRINCE JOHN OF LANCASTER, WEST-
      MORELAND, [BLUNT] *and others.*

Lan. The heat is past; follow no further now.   27
Call in the powers, good cousin Westmoreland.
                                [*Exit Westmoreland.*]
Now, Falstaff, where have you been all this while?
When everything is ended, then you come.
These tardy tricks of yours will, on my life,
One time or other break some gallows' back.   32
Fal. I would be sorry, my lord, but it should be
thus. I never knew yet but rebuke and check was
the reward of valour. Do you think me a swallow,
an arrow, or a bullet? Have I, in my poor and old
motion, the expedition of thought? I have   37
speeded hither with the very extremest inch of
possibility; I have found'red ninescore and odd
posts; and here, travel-tainted as I am, have, in my
pure and immaculate valour, taken Sir John Colville of the Dale, a most furious knight and valor- 42
ous enemy. But what of that? He saw me, and
yielded; that I may justly say, with the hook-
nos'd fellow of Rome, "I came, saw, and overcame."
Lan. It was more of his courtesy than your deserving.   48
Fal. I know not. Here he is, and here I yield
him; and I beseech your Grace, let it be book'd
with the rest of this day's deeds; or, by the Lord, I
will have it in a particular ballad else, with mine
own picture on the top on't, Colville kissing my
foot; to the which course if I be enforc'd, if you do
not all show like gilt twopences to me, and I in   55
the clear sky of fame o'ershine you as much as the
full moon doth the cinders of the element, which
show like pins' heads to her, believe not the word
of the noble. Therefore let me have right, and let
desert mount.   61
Lan. Thine's too heavy to mount.
Fal. Let it shine, then.
Lan. Thine's too thick to shine.
Fal. Let it do something, my good lord, that
may do me good, and call it what you will.   66
Lan. Is thy name Colville?
Col. It is, my lord.
Lan. A famous rebel art thou, Colville.
Fal. And a famous true subject took him.   70
Col. I am, my lord, but as my betters are
That led me hither. Had they been rul'd by me,
You should have won them dearer than you have.
Fal. I know not how they sold themselves; but

117. [and ... yours] F. Om. Q.   120. stray: stragglers.   122. [these traitors] F. *this traitor* Q.
   Sc. iii, 1. condition: rank.   2. [I pray] F. Om. Q.   23. indifferency: moderate bulk.   37. expedition: speed.   40. posts:
horses.   45. Rome F. *Rome, there cosin* Q.   57. cinders of the element: stars.

thou, like a kind fellow, gav'st thyself away gratis;
and I thank thee for thee.   76

Re-enter WESTMORELAND.

Lan. Now, have you left pursuit?
West. Retreat is made and execution stay'd.
Lan. Send Colville with his confederates
To York, to present execution.   80
Blunt, lead him hence; and see you guard him sure.
            [*Exeunt [Blunt and others] with Colville.*
And now dispatch we toward the court, my lords;
I hear the King my father is sore sick.
Our news shall go before us to his Majesty,
Which, cousin, you shall bear to comfort him,
And we with sober speed will follow you.   86
Fal. My lord, I beseech you, give me leave to go
Through Gloucestershire; and, when you come to
            court,
Stand my good lord, [pray,] in your good report.
Lan. Fare you well, Falstaff. I, in my condi-
            tion,   90
Shall better speak of you than you deserve.
            [*Exeunt [all but Falstaff].*
Fal. I would you had [but] the wit; 'twere better
than your dukedom. Good faith, this same young
sober-blooded boy doth not love me, nor a man
cannot make him laugh; but that's no marvel,   95
he drinks no wine. There's never none of these
demure boys come to any proof; for thin drink doth
so over-cool their blood, and making many fish-
meals, that they fall into a kind of male green-
sickness; and then, when they marry, they get   100
wenches. They are generally fools and cowards;
which some of us should be too, but for inflammation. A good sherris-sack hath a two-fold operation in it. It ascends me into the brain; dries me
there all the foolish and dull and crudy vapours 105
which environ it; makes it apprehensive, quick,
forgetive, full of nimble, fiery, and delectable
shapes; which, delivered o'er to the voice, the
tongue, which is the birth, becomes excellent wit.
The second property of your excellent sherris 110
is, the warming of the blood; which, before cold and
settled, left the liver white and pale, which is the
badge of pusillanimity and cowardice; but the
sherris warms it and makes it course from the inwards to the parts extremes. It illumineth the 115
face, which as a beacon gives warning to all the
rest of this little kingdom, man, to arm; and then
the vital commoners and inland petty spirits
muster me all to their captain, the heart, who, 120
great and puff'd up with this retinue, doth any deed
of courage; and this valour comes of sherris. So

that skill in the weapon is nothing without sack,
for that sets it a-work; and learning a mere hoard
of gold kept by a devil, till sack commences it 125
and sets it in act and use. Hereof comes it that
Prince Harry is valiant; for the cold blood he did
naturally inherit of his father, he hath, like lean,
sterile, and bare land, manured, husbanded, and
till'd with excellent endeavour of drinking good 130
and good store of fertile sherris, that he is become
very hot and valiant. If I had a thousand sons,
the first humane principle I would teach them
should be, to forswear thin potations and to addict
themselves to sack.   135

Enter BARDOLPH
How now, Bardolph?
Bard. The army is discharged all and gone.
Fal. Let them go. I'll through Gloucestershire; and there will I visit Master Robert Shallow,
esquire. I have him already tempering between my
finger and my thumb, and shortly will I seal with
him. Come away.   [*Exeunt.* 142

SCENE [IV. *Westminster. The Jerusalem
            Chamber.*]

Enter the KING, *the* PRINCES THOMAS OF CLARENCE
and HUMPHREY OF GLOUCESTER, WARWICK [*and
others*].

King. Now, lords, if God doth give successful
            end
To this debate that bleedeth at our doors,
We will our youth lead on to higher fields,
And draw no swords but what are sanctifi'd.
Our navy is address'd, our power collected,   5
Our substitutes in absence well invested,
And everything lies level to our wish.
Only, we want a little personal strength;
And pause us, till these rebels, now afoot,
Come underneath the yoke of government.   10
War. Both which we doubt not but your Ma-
            jesty
Shall soon enjoy.
King.   Humphrey, my son of Gloucester,
Where is the Prince your brother?
Glou. I think he's gone to hunt, my lord, at
            Windsor.
King. And how accompanied?
Glou.   I do not know, my lord.
King. Is not his brother, Thomas of Clarence,
            with him?   16
Glou. No, my good lord; he is in presence here.
Clar. What would my lord and father?

89. [pray] F. Om. Q. 90. condition: official capacity. 92. [but] F. Om. Q. 97. come to any proof: develop
well. 99. green-sickness: anemia. 102. inflammation: i.e., by drink. 103. sherris-sack: sherry. 107. forgetive: inventive. 140. tempering: softening.
Sc. iv, 3. higher fields: Palestine. 5. address'd: ready.

King. Nothing but well to thee, Thomas of
   Clarence.
How chance thou art not with the Prince thy
   brother?   20
He loves thee, and thou dost neglect him, Thomas.
Thou hast a better place in his affection
Than all thy brothers.   Cherish it, my boy,
And noble offices thou mayst effect
Of mediation, after I am dead,   25
Between his greatness and thy other brethren.
Therefore omit him not; blunt not his love,
Nor lose the good advantage of his grace
By seeming cold or careless of his will.
For he is gracious, if he be observ'd;   30
He hath a tear for pity, and a hand
Open as day for [melting] charity;
Yet notwithstanding, being incens'd, he's flint,
As humorous as winter, and as sudden
As flaws congealed in the spring of day.   35
His temper, therefore, must be well observ'd.
Chide him for faults, and do it reverently
When you perceive his blood inclin'd to mirth;
But, being moody, give him time and scope,
Till that his passions, like a whale on ground,   40
Confound themselves with working.   Learn this,
   Thomas,
And thou shalt prove a shelter to thy friends,
A hoop of gold to bind thy brothers in,
That the united vessel of their blood,
Mingled with venom of suggestion,   45
(As, force perforce, the age will pour it in),
Shall never leak, though it do work as strong
As aconitum or rash gunpowder.
   Clar. I shall observe him with all care and love.
   King. Why art thou not at Windsor with him,
   Thomas?   50
   Clar. He is not there to-day; he dines in London.
   King. And how accompanied?   [Canst thou tell
   that?]
   Clar. With Poins, and other his continual fol-
   lowers.
   King. Most subject is the fattest soil to weeds,
And he, the noble image of my youth,   55
Is overspread with them; therefore my grief
Stretches itself beyond the hour of death.
The blood weeps from my heart when I do shape
In forms imaginary the unguided days
And rotten times that you shall look upon   60
When I am sleeping with my ancestors.
For when his headstrong riot hath no curb,
When rage and hot blood are his counsellors,
When means and lavish manners meet together,
O, with what wings shall his affections fly   65

Towards fronting peril and oppos'd decay!
   War. My gracious lord, you look beyond him
   quite.
The Prince but studies his companions
Like a strange tongue, wherein, to gain the lan-
   guage,
'Tis needful that the most immodest word   70
Be look'd upon and learn'd; which once attain'd,
Your Highness knows, comes to no further use
But to be known and hated.   So, like gross terms,
The Prince will in the perfectness of time
Cast off his followers; and their memory   75
Shall as a pattern or a measure live,
By which his Grace must mete the lives of others,
Turning past evils to advantages.
   King. 'Tis seldom when the bee doth leave her
   comb
In the dead carrion.

Enter WESTMORELAND.

                      Who's here?   Westmoreland?
   West. Health to my sovereign, and new happi-
   ness   81
Added to that that I am to deliver!
Prince John your son doth kiss your Grace's hand.
Mowbray, the Bishop Scroop, Hastings and all
Are brought to the correction of your law.   85
There is not now a rebel's sword unsheath'd,
But Peace puts forth her olive everywhere.
The manner how this action hath been borne
Here at more leisure may your Highness read,
With every course in his particular.   90
   King. O Westmoreland, thou art a summer bird,
Which ever in the haunch of winter sings
The lifting up of day.

Enter HARCOURT.

                      Look, here's more news.
   Har. From enemies heaven keep your Majesty;
And, when they stand against you, may they fall   95
As those that I am come to tell you of!
The Earl Northumberland and the Lord Bardolph,
With a great power of English and of Scots,
Are by the sheriff of Yorkshire overthrown.
The manner and true order of the fight   100
This packet, please it you, contains at large.
   King. And wherefore should these good news
   make me sick?
Will Fortune never come with both hands full,
But [write] her fair words still in foulest [letters]?
She either gives a stomach and no food;   105
Such are the poor, in health; or else a feast
And takes away the stomach; such are the rich,

---

27. omit: neglect.   30. observ'd: paid respect to.   32. [melting] F.   *meeting* Q.   34. humorous: capricious.   35. flaws:
blasts of wind.   45. suggestion: gossip.   48. aconitum: a poisonous plant.   52. [Canst . . . that] F. Om. Q.   66. oppos'd
decay: decay facing him.   67. look beyond: misinterpret.   92. haunch: latter end.   104. [write] . . . [letters] F.   *wet . . .
termes* Q.

That have abundance and enjoy it not.
I should rejoice now at this happy news;
And now my sight fails, and my brain is giddy.
O me! come near me; now I am much ill.   111
  Glou. Comfort, your Majesty!
  Clar.   O my royal father!
  West. My sovereign lord, cheer up yourself,
    look up.
  War. Be patient, Princes; you do know, these
    fits
Are with his Highness very ordinary.   115
Stand from him, give him air. He'll straight be
    well.
  Clar. No, no, he cannot long hold out these pangs.
The incessant care and labour of his mind
Hath wrought the mure that should confine it in
So thin that life looks through [and will break
    out].   120
  Glou. The people fear me; for they do observe
Unfather'd heirs and loathly births of nature.
The seasons change their manners, as the year
Had found some months asleep and leap'd them
    over.
  Clar. The river hath thrice flow'd, no ebb be-
    tween;   125
And the old folk, time's doting chronicles,
Say it did so a little time before
That our great-grandsire, Edward, sick'd and
    died.
  War. Speak lower, Princes, for the King re-
    covers.
  Glou. This apoplexy will certain be his end.   130
  King. I pray you, take me up, and bear me hence
Into some other chamber. [*Softly, pray.*]
        [*Exeunt. The King is borne out.*]

[SCENE V. *Another chamber.*

The KING *lying on a bed:* CLARENCE, GLOUCESTER,
WARWICK, *and others in attendance.*]

  King. Let there be no noise made, my gentle
    friends,
Unless some dull and favourable hand
Will whisper music to my weary spirit.
  Wor. Call for the music in the other room.
  King. Set me the crown upon my pillow here.   5
  Clar. His eye is hollow, and he changes much.
  War. Less noise, less noise!

Enter PRINCE HENRY.

  Prince.   Who saw the Duke of Clarence?
  Clar. I am here, brother, full of heaviness.
  Prince. How now! rain within doors, and none
    abroad!

How doth the King?   10
  Glou. Exceeding ill.
  Prince.   Heard he the good news yet?
Tell it him.
  Glou. He [alt'red] much upon the hearing it.
  Prince. If he be sick with joy, he'll recover with-
out physic.   15
  War. Not so much noise, my lords. Sweet
    Prince, speak low;
The King, your father, is dispos'd to sleep.
  Clar. Let us withdraw into the other room.
  War. Will't please your Grace to go along with
    us?
  Prince. No; I will sit and watch here by the
    King.   [*Exeunt all but the Prince.*]   20
Why doth the crown lie there upon his pillow,
Being so troublesome a bedfellow?
O polish'd perturbation! golden care!
That keep'st the ports of slumber open wide
To many a watchful night! Sleep with it now!   25
Yet not so sound and half so deeply sweet
As he whose brow with homely biggen bound
Snores out the watch of night. O majesty!
When thou dost pinch thy bearer, thou dost sit
Like a rich armour worn in heat of day,   30
That scald'st with safety. By his gates of breath
There lies a downy feather which stirs not.
Did he suspire, that light and weightless down
Perforce must move. My gracious lord! my father!
This sleep is sound indeed; this is a sleep   35
That from this golden rigol hath divorc'd
So many English kings. Thy due from me
Is tears and heavy sorrows of the blood,
Which nature, love, and filial tenderness
Shall, O dear father, pay thee plenteously.   40
My due from thee is this imperial crown,
Which, as immediate from thy place and blood,
Derives itself to me. [*Puts on the crown.*] Lo,
    where it sits,
Which God shall guard; and put the world's whole
    strength
Into one giant arm, it shall not force   45
This lineal honour from me. This from thee
Will I to mine leave, as 'tis left to me.   [*Exit.*
  King. Warwick! Gloucester! Clarence!

Re-enter WARWICK, GLOUCESTER, CLARENCE
[*and the rest*].

  Clar. Doth the King call?
  War. What would your Majesty? [How fares
    your Grace?]   50
  King. Why did you leave me here alone, my
    lords?

---

119. **wrought the mure:** worn away the wall.   120. [**and ... out**] F. Om. Q.   121. **fear:** frighten.   132. [**Softly, pray**] F. Om. Q.

Sc. v, 2. **dull:** soft.   27. **biggen:** nightcap.   31. **with:** giving.   36. **rigol:** circle.   50. [**How fares your Grace?**] F. Om. Q.

Clar. We left the Prince my brother here, my
    liege,
Who undertook to sit and watch by you.
  King. The Prince of Wales! Where is he? Let
    me see him.
He is not here.   55
  War. This door is open; he is gone this way.
  Glou. He came not through the chamber where
    we stay'd.
  King. Where is the crown? Who took it from
    my pillow?
  War. When we withdrew, my liege, we left it
    here.
  King. The Prince hath ta'en it hence. Go, seek
    him out.   60
Is he so hasty that he doth suppose
My sleep my death?
Find him, my Lord of Warwick; chide him hither.
                                [Exit Warwick.]
This part of his conjoins with my disease,
And helps to end me. See, sons, what things you
    are!   65
How quickly nature falls into revolt
When gold becomes her object!
For this the foolish over-careful fathers
Have broke their sleep with thoughts, their brains
    with care,
Their bones with industry;   70
For this they have engrossed and pil'd up
The cank'red heaps of strange-achieved gold;
For this they have been thoughtful to invest
Their sons with arts and martial exercises;
When, like the bee, tolling from every flower   75
[The virtuous sweets],
Our thighs pack'd with wax, our mouths with
    honey,
We bring it to the hive, and, like the bees,
Are murd'red for our pains. This bitter taste
Yields his engrossments to the ending father.   80

Re-enter WARWICK.

Now, where is he that will not stay so long
Till his friend sickness hath determin'd me?
  War. My lord, I found the Prince in the next
    room,
Washing with kindly tears his gentle cheeks,
With such a deep demeanour in great sorrow   85
That Tyranny, which never quaff'd but blood,
Would, by beholding him, have wash'd his knife
With gentle eye-drops. He is coming hither.
  King. But wherefore did he take away the crown?

Re-enter PRINCE HENRY.

Lo, where he comes. Come hither to me, Harry.   90

Depart the chamber, leave us here alone.
                  [Exeunt [Warwick and the rest].
  Prince. I never thought to hear you speak again.
  King. Thy wish was father, Harry, to that
    thought.
I stay too long by thee, I weary thee.
Dost thou so hunger for mine empty chair   95
That thou wilt needs invest thee with mine honours
Before thy hour be ripe? O foolish youth!
Thou seek'st the greatness that will overwhelm
    thee.
Stay but a little; for my cloud of dignity
Is held from falling with so weak a wind   100
That it will quickly drop. My day is dim.
Thou hast stol'n that which after some few hours
Were thine without offence; and at my death
Thou hast seal'd up my expectation.
Thy life did manifest thou lov'dst me not,   105
And thou wilt have me die assur'd of it.
Thou hid'st a thousand daggers in thy thoughts,
Which thou hast whetted on thy stony heart
To stab at half an hour of my life.
What! canst thou not forbear me half an hour?   110
Then get thee gone and dig my grave thyself,
And bid the merry bells ring to thine ear
That thou art crowned, not that I am dead.
Let all the tears that should bedew my hearse
Be drops of balm to sanctify thy head;   115
Only compound me with forgotten dust;
Give that which gave thee life unto the worms.
Pluck down my officers, break my decrees;
For now a time is come to mock at form.
Harry the Fifth is crown'd! Up, vanity!   120
Down, royal state! All you sage counsellors,
    hence!
And to the English court assemble now,
From every region, apes of idleness!
Now, neighbour confines, purge you of your scum!
Have you a ruffian that will swear, drink, dance,   125
Revel the night, rob, murder, and commit
The oldest sins the newest kind of ways?
Be happy, he will trouble you no more.
England shall double gild his treble guilt,
England shall give him office, honour, might;   130
For the fifth Harry from curb'd license plucks
The muzzle of restraint, and the wild dog
Shall flesh his tooth on every innocent.
O my poor kingdom, sick with civil blows!
When that my care could not withhold thy riots,
What wilt thou do when riot is thy care?   136
O, thou wilt be a wilderness again,
Peopled with wolves, thy old inhabitants!
  Prince. O, pardon me, my liege! but for my tears,
The moist impediments unto my speech,   140
I had forestall'd this dear and deep rebuke

64. **part:** deed.   69. **thoughts:** worries.   71. **engrossed:** accumulated.   72. **cank'red:** tarnished.   76. **[The ... sweets]**
F. Om. Q.   82. **determin'd:** ended.   84. **kindly:** natural.   104. **seal'd up:** confirmed.   141. **dear:** cutting to the heart.

indicates this will be joyfully received

Ere you with grief had spoke and I had heard
The course of it so far. There is your crown;
And He that wears the crown immortally
Long guard it yours! If I affect it more   145
Than as your honour and as your renown,
Let me no more from this obedience rise,   [*Kneels.*]
Which my most inward, true, and duteous spirit
Teacheth, this prostrate and exterior bending.
God witness with me, when I here came in,   150
And found no course of breath within your Majesty,
How cold it struck my heart! If I do feign,
O, let me in my present wildness die
And never live to show th' incredulous world
The noble change that I have purposed!   155
Coming to look on you, thinking you dead,
And dead almost, my liege, to think you were,
I spake unto this crown as having sense,
And thus upbraided it: "The care on thee depending
Hath fed upon the body of my father;   160
Therefore, thou best of gold art [worst of] gold.
Other, less fine in carat, [is] more precious,
Preserving life in medicine potable;
But thou, most fine, most honour'd, most renown'd,
Hast eat thy bearer up." Thus, my most royal
liege,   165
Accusing it, I put it on my head,
To try with it, as with an enemy
That had before my face murdered my father,
The quarrel of a true inheritor.
But if it did infect my blood with joy,   170
Or swell my thoughts to any strain of pride;
If any rebel or vain spirit of mine
Did with the least affection of a welcome
Give entertainment to the might of it,
Let God for ever keep it from my head   175
And make me as the poorest vassal is
That doth with awe and terror kneel to it!
    King. [O my son,]
God put it in thy mind to take it hence,
That thou mightst win the more thy father's love,
Pleading so wisely in excuse of it!   181
Come hither, Harry, sit thou by my bed;
And hear, I think, the very latest counsel
That ever I shall breathe. God knows, my son,
By what by-paths and indirect crook'd ways   185
I met this crown; and I myself know well
How troublesome it sat upon my head.
To thee it shall descend with better quiet,
Better opinion, better confirmation;
For all the soil of the achievement goes   190

With me into the earth. It seem'd in me
But as an honour snatch'd with boist'rous hand,
And I had many living to upbraid
My gain of it by their assistances;
Which daily grew to quarrel and to bloodshed,   195
Wounding supposed peace. All these bold fears
Thou see'st with peril I have answered;
For all my reign hath been but as a scene
Acting that argument; and now my death
Changes the mode; for what in me was purchas'd
Falls upon thee in a more fairer sort;   201
So thou the garland wear'st successively.
Yet, though thou stand'st more sure than I could do,
Thou art not firm enough, since griefs are green;
And all [my] friends, which thou must make thy
friends,   205
Have but their stings and teeth newly ta'en out,
By whose fell working I was first advanc'd
And by whose power I well might lodge a fear
To be again displac'd; which to avoid,
I cut them off; and had a purpose now   210
To lead out many to the Holy Land,
Lest rest and lying still might make them look
Too near unto my state. Therefore, my Harry,
Be it thy course to busy giddy minds
With foreign quarrels, that action, hence borne out, *abroad*
May waste the memory of the former days.   216
More would I, but my lungs are wasted so
That strength of speech is utterly deni'd me.
How I came by the crown, O God forgive;
And grant it may with thee in true peace live!   220
    Prince. [My gracious liege,]
You won it, wore it, kept it, gave it me;
Then plain and right must my possession be,
Which I with more than with a common pain *effort*
'Gainst all the world will rightfully maintain.   225

Enter LORD JOHN OF LANCASTER *and* WARWICK.

    King. Look, look, here comes my John of Lancaster.
    Lan. Health, peace, and happiness to my royal father!
    King. Thou bring'st me happiness and peace, son John;
But health, alack, with youthful wings is flown
From this bare wither'd trunk. Upon thy sight   230
My worldly business makes a period.
Where is my Lord of Warwick?
    Prince.   My Lord of Warwick!
    King. Doth any name particular belong
Unto the lodging where I first did swoon?
    War. 'Tis call'd Jerusalem, my noble lord.   235

145. **affect:** love. 161. [worst of] F. *worse than* Q. 162. [is] F. Om. Q. 163. **potable:** drinkable. Gold was valued as a medicine. 171. **strain:** tendency. 178. [O my son] F. Om. Q. 189. **opinion:** support of public opinion. 200. **purchas'd:** acquired (often wrongly). 202. **successively:** by inheritance. 205. [my] (Tyrwhitt conj.). *thy* QF. 207. **fell:** violent. 215. **hence:** abroad. 221. [My gracious liege] F. Om. Q. 224. **pain:** effort. 230. **Upon thy sight:** seeing thee. 235. **Jerusalem:** a chamber in Westminster Abbey.

King. Laud be to God! even there my life must end.
It hath been prophesi'd to me many years,
I should not die but in Jerusalem;
Which vainly I suppos'd the Holy Land.
But bear me to that chamber; there I'll lie;   240
In that Jerusalem shall Harry die.   *[Exeunt.*

ACT V

SCENE I. *[Gloucestershire. Shallow's house.]*

Enter SHALLOW, FALSTAFF, BARDOLPH, *and* Page.

Shal. By cock and pie, sir, you shall not away
to-night. What, Davy, I say!
Fal. You must excuse me, Master Robert
Shallow.   4
Shal. I will not excuse you; you shall not be
excus'd; excuses shall not be admitted; there is no
excuse shall serve; you shall not be excus'd. Why,
Davy!

[Enter DAVY.]

Davy. Here, sir.   9
Shal. Davy, Davy, Davy, Davy, let me see,
Davy; let me see, Davy; let me see. Yea, marry,
William cook, bid him come hither. Sir John, you
shall not be excus'd.
Davy. Marry, sir, thus; those precepts cannot
be serv'd; and, again, sir, shall we sow the headland
with wheat?   16
Shal. With red wheat, Davy. But for William
cook: are there no young pigeons?
Davy. Yes, sir. Here is now the smith's note for
shoeing and plough-irons.   20
Shal. Let it be cast and paid. Sir John, you
shall not be excus'd.
Davy. Now, sir, a new link to the bucket must
needs be had; and, sir, do you mean to stop any of
William's wages, about the sack he lost [the other
day] at Hinckley fair?   26
Shal. 'A shall answer it. Some pigeons, Davy,
a couple of short-legg'd hens, a joint of mutton, and
any pretty little tiny kickshaws, tell William cook.
Davy. Doth the man of war stay all night, sir? 31
Shal. Yea, Davy; I will use him well. A friend
i' th' court is better than a penny in purse. Use his
men well, Davy; for they are arrant knaves, and
will backbite.   36
Davy. No worse than they are backbitten, sir;
for they have marvellous foul linen.

Shal. Well conceited, Davy. About thy business, Davy.   40
Davy. I beseech you, sir, to countenance William
Visor of Woncot against Clement Perkes o' th' hill.
Shal. There is many complaints, Davy, against
that Visor. That Visor is an arrant knave, on my
knowledge.   46
Davy. I grant your worship that he is a knave,
sir; but yet, God forbid, sir, but a knave should
have some countenance at his friend's request. An
honest man, sir, is able to speak for himself, when a
knave is not. I have serv'd your worship truly, 51
sir, this eight years; and if I cannot once or twice in
a quarter bear out a knave against an honest man, I
have [but a very] little credit with your worship.
The knave is mine honest friend, sir; therefore, I
beseech you, let him be countenanc'd.   57
Shal. Go to; I say he shall have no wrong. Look
about, Davy. *[Exit Davy.]* Where are you, Sir
John? Come, come, come, off with your boots.
Give me your hand, Master Bardolph.   62
Bard. I am glad to see your worship.
Shal. I thank thee with [all] my heart, kind
Master Bardolph: and welcome, my tall fellow [*to
the Page*]. Come, Sir John.   66
Fal. I'll follow you, good Master Robert Shallow. *[Exit Shallow.]* Bardolph, look to our
horses. *[Exeunt Bardolph and Page.]* If I were
saw'd into quantities, I should make four dozen 70
of such bearded hermits' staves as Master Shallow.
It is a wonderful thing to see the semblable coherence of his men's spirits and his. They, by
observing him, do bear themselves like foolish
justices; he, by conversing with them, is turn'd 75
into a justice-like serving-man. Their spirits are
so married in conjunction with the participation of
society that they flock together in consent, like so
many wild-geese. If I had a suit to Master Shallow, I would humour his men with the imputa- 80
tion of being near their master; if to his men, I
would curry with Master Shallow that no man
could better command his servants. It is certain
that either wise bearing or ignorant carriage is
caught, as men take diseases, one of another; 85
therefore let men take heed of their company. I
will devise matter enough out of this Shallow to
keep Prince Harry in continual laughter the wearing out of six fashions, which is four terms, or two
actions, and 'a shall laugh without intervallums. 90
O, it is much that a lie with a slight oath and a jest
with a sad brow will do with a fellow that never had
the ache in his shoulders! O, you shall see him
laugh till his face be like a wet cloak ill laid up. 95

Act V, sc. i, 14. **precepts:** summonses. 21. **cast:** reckoned. 25-26. **[the other day]** F. Om. Q. 29. **kickshaws:** fancy
dishes. 39. **Well conceited:** wittily said. 41. **countenance:** favor. 54. **[but a very]** F. Om. Q. 64. **[all]** F. Om. Q.
72. **semblable coherence:** similarity. 78. **consent:** agreement. 89. **terms:** i.e., of court. 90. **actions:** lawsuits. 92. **sad:**
serious.

Shal. [*Within.*] Sir John!

Fal. I come, Master Shallow; I come, Master Shallow.   [*Exit.*

SCENE II. [*Westminster.   The palace.*]

Enter WARWICK *and the* LORD CHIEF JUSTICE [*meeting*].

War. How now, my Lord Chief Justice; whither away?

Ch. Just. How doth the King?

War. Exceeding well; his cares are now all ended.

Ch. Just. I hope, not dead.

War.   He's walk'd the way of nature;
And to our purposes he lives no more.   5

Ch. Just. I would his Majesty had call'd me with him.
The service that I truly did his life
Hath left me open to all injuries.

War. Indeed I think the young King loves you not.

Ch. Just. I know he doth not, and do arm myself   10
To welcome the condition of the time,
Which cannot look more hideously upon me
Than I have drawn it in my fantasy.

Enter LANCASTER, CLARENCE, GLOUCESTER [WESTMORELAND, *and others*].

War. Here come the heavy issue of dead Harry:
O that the living Harry had the temper   15
Of him, the worst of these three gentlemen!
How many nobles then should hold their places,
That must strike sail to spirits of vile sort!

Ch. Just. O God, I fear all will be overturn'd!

Lan. Good morrow, cousin Warwick, good morrow.   20

Glou. }
Clar. } Good morrow, cousin.

Lan. We meet like men that had forgot to speak.

War. We do remember; but our argument
Is all too heavy to admit much talk.

Lan. Well, peace be with him that hath made us heavy!   25

Ch. Just. Peace be with us, lest we be heavier!

Glou. O, good my lord, you have lost a friend indeed;
And I dare swear you borrow not that face
Of seeming sorrow; it is sure your own.

Lan. Though no man be assur'd what grace to find,   30
You stand in coldest expectation.
I am the sorrier; would 'twere otherwise!

Clar. Well, you must now speak Sir John Falstaff fair;
Which swims against your stream of quality.

Ch. Just. Sweet princes, what I did, I did in honour,   35
Led by th' impartial conduct of my soul;
And never shall you see that I will beg
A ragged and forestall'd remission.
If truth and upright innocency fail me,
I'll to the King my master that is dead,   40
And tell him who hath sent me after him.

War. Here comes the Prince.

Enter KING HENRY THE FIFTH [*attended*].

Ch. Just. Good morrow; and God save your Majesty!

King. This new and gorgeous garment, majesty,
Sits not so easy on me as you think.   45
Brothers, you mix your sadness with some fear.
This is the English, not the Turkish court;
Not Amurath an Amurath succeeds,
But Harry Harry.   Yet be sad, good brothers,
For, by my faith, it very well becomes you.   50
Sorrow so royally in you appears
That I will deeply put the fashion on
And wear it in my heart.   Why then, be sad;
But entertain no more of it, good brothers,
Than a joint burden laid upon us all.   55
For me, by heaven, I bid you be assur'd,
I'll be your father and your brother too.
Let me but bear your love, I'll bear your cares.
Yet weep that Harry's dead, and so will I;
But Harry lives, that shall convert those tears   60
By number into hours of happiness.

Princes. We hope no other from your Majesty.

King. You all look strangely on me, and you most.
You are, I think, assur'd I love you not.

Ch. Just. I am assur'd, if I be measur'd rightly,
Your Majesty hath no just cause to hate me.   66

King. No?
How might a prince of my great hopes forget
So great indignities you laid upon me?
What! rate, rebuke, and roughly send to prison   70
The immediate heir of England!   Was this easy?
May this be wash'd in Lethe, and forgotten?

Ch. Just. I then did use the person of your father;
The image of his power lay then in me;
And, in th' administration of his law,   75
Whiles I was busy for the commonwealth,
Your Highness pleased to forget my place,
The majesty and power of law and justice,
The image of the King whom I presented,
And struck me in my very seat of judgement;   80

Sc. ii, 23. **argument:** subject.   34. **stream of quality:** tendency of your character.   38. **ragged:** beggarly.   **forestall'd:** destined to be refused.   48. **Amurath:** a Turkish emperor who, on his accession, strangled his five brothers.   71. **easy:** a small thing.   73. **use the person of:** represent.

Whereon, as an offender to your father,
I gave bold way to my authority
And did commit you. If the deed were ill,
Be you contented, wearing now the garland,
To have a son set your decrees at nought?   85
To pluck down justice from your awful bench?
To trip the course of law and blunt the sword
That guards the peace and safety of your person?
Nay, more, to spurn at your most royal image
And mock your workings in a second body?   90
Question your royal thoughts, make the case yours:
Be now the father and propose a son,
Hear your own dignity so much profan'd,
See your most dreadful laws so loosely slighted,
Behold yourself so by a son disdained;   95
And then imagine me taking your part
And in your power soft silencing your son.
After this cold considerance, sentence me;
And, as you are a king, speak in your state
What I have done that misbecame my place,   100
My person, or my liege's sovereignty.
    King. You are right, Justice, and you weigh this
        well,
Therefore still bear the balance and the sword,
And I do wish your honours may increase,
Till you do live to see a son of mine   105
Offend you and obey you, as I did.
So shall I live to speak my father's words:
"Happy am I, that have a man so bold,
That dares do justice on my proper son;
And not less happy, having such a son   110
That would deliver up his greatness so
Into the hands of justice." You did commit me;
For which I do commit into your hand
Th' unstained sword that you have us'd to bear,
With this remembrance, that you use the same   115
With the like bold, just, and impartial spirit
As you have done 'gainst me. There is my hand.
You shall be as a father to my youth,
My voice shall sound as you do prompt mine ear,
And I will stoop and humble my intents   120
To your well-practis'd wise directions.
And, princes all, believe me, I beseech you,
My father is gone wild into his grave,
For in his tomb lie my affections;
And with his spirit sadly I survive,   125
To mock the expectation of the world,
To frustrate prophecies, and to raze out
Rotten opinion, who hath writ me down
After my seeming. The tide of blood in me
Hath proudly flow'd in vanity till now: 130
Now doth it turn and ebb back to the sea,
Where it shall mingle with the state of floods

And flow henceforth in formal majesty.
Now call we our high court of parliament;
And let us choose such limbs of noble counsel   135
That the great body of our state may go
In equal rank with the best govern'd nation;
That war, or peace, or both at once, may be
As things acquainted and familiar to us;
In which you, father, shall have foremost hand.   140
Our coronation done, we will accite,
As I before remem'bred, all our state;
And, God consigning to my good intents,
No prince nor peer shall have just cause to say,
God shorten Harry's happy life one day!   145
                                                [*Exeunt.*

SCENE III. [*Gloucestershire.   Shallow's orchard.*]

    Enter FALSTAFF, SHALLOW, SILENCE, DAVY,
            BARDOLPH, *and the* Page.

    Shal. Nay, you shall see my orchard, where,
in an arbour, we will eat a last year's pippin of
mine own graffing, with a dish of caraways, and
so forth, — come, cousin Silence, — and then to
bed.   5
    Fal. 'Fore God, you have here a goodly dwelling
and [a] rich.
    Shal. Barren, barren, barren; beggars all, beg-
gars all, Sir John: marry, good air. Spread,
Davy; spread, Davy. Well said, Davy.   10
    Fal. This Davy serves you for good uses; he is
your serving-man and your husband.
    Shal. A good varlet, a good varlet, a very good
varlet, Sir John. By the mass, I have drunk
too much sack at supper. A good varlet. Now
sit down, now sit down. Come, cousin.   16
    Sil. Ah, sirrah! quoth-a, we shall
[*Singing.*]
"Do nothing but eat, and make good cheer,
    And praise God for the merry year,
    When flesh is cheap and females dear,   20
    And lusty lads roam here and there
            So merrily,
    And ever among so merrily."
    Fal. There's a merry heart! Good Master
Silence, I'll give you a health for that anon.   25
    Shal. Give Master Bardolph some wine, Davy.
    Davy. Sweet sir, sit; I'll be with you anon;
most sweet sir, sit. Master page, good master
page, sit. Proface! What you want in meat, we'll
have in drink; but you must bear. The heart's
all.   [*Exit.*]   32
    Shal. Be merry, Master Bardolph; and, my little
soldier there, be merry.

90. **second body:** deputy. 92. **propose:** imagine. 98. **considerance:** consideration. 99. **state:** royal capacity. 109.
proper: own. 123. **wild:** carrying my wildness. 124. **affections:** previous inclinations. 125. **sadly:** soberly. 132. **state
of floods:** ocean's majesty. 141. **accite:** summon. 142. **remem'bred:** mentioned. 143. **consigning:** assenting.
    Sc. iii, 3. **graffing:** grafting. 10. **said:** done. 12. **husband:** manager. 29. **Proface:** your health!

Sil. [*Singing.*] "Be merry, be merry, my wife
      has all;
  For women are shrews, both short and
      tall.
'Tis merry in hall when beards wag all,
  And welcome merry Shrove-tide.
Be merry, be merry."   39

Fal. I did not think Master Silence had been a
man of this mettle.

Sil. Who? I? I have been merry twice and
once ere now.

Re-enter DAVY.

Davy. There's a dish of leather-coats for you.
                      [*To Bardolph.*]

Shal. Davy!   45

Davy. Your worship! I'll be with you straight.
A cup of wine, sir?

Sil. [*Singing.*] "A cup of wine that's brisk and
      fine,
  And drink unto the leman mine;
     And a merry heart lives long-a."   50

Fal. Well said, Master Silence.

Sil. An we shall be merry, now comes in the
sweet o' th' night.

Fal. Health and long life to you, Master
Silence.   55

Sil. [*Singing.*] "Fill the cup, and let it come;
  I'll pledge you a mile to the bottom."

Shal. Honest Bardolph, welcome. If thou
want'st anything, and wilt not call, beshrew thy
heart. Welcome, my little tiny thief [*to the Page*],
and welcome indeed too. I'll drink to Master Bardolph, and to all the cabileros about London.   63

Davy. I hope to see London once ere I die.

Bard. An I might see you there, Davy, —

Shal. By the mass, you'll crack a quart together,
ha! will you not, Master Bardolph?

Bard. Yea, sir, in a pottle-pot.   68

Shal. By God's liggens, I thank thee. The
knave will stick by thee, I can assure thee that.
'A will not out; [he is] true bred.

Bard. And I'll stick by him, sir.   72
                  [*One knocks at door.*]

Shal. Why, there spoke a king. Lack nothing;
be merry! Look who's at door there. Ho! who
knocks?   [*Exit Davy.*]

Fal. Why, now you have done me right.   76
    [*To Silence, seeing him take off a bumper.*]

Sil. [*Singing.*] "Do me right,
    And dub me knight:
      S'amingo."

Is't not so?   80

Fal. 'Tis so.

Sil. Is't so? Why then, say an old man can
do somewhat.

[*Re-enter* DAVY.]

Davy. An't please your worship, there's one
Pistol come from the court with news.   85

Fal. From the court! Let him come in.

Enter PISTOL.

How now, Pistol!

Pist. Sir John, God save you!

Fal. What wind blew you hither, Pistol?   89

Pist. Not the ill wind which blows no man to
good. Sweet knight, thou art now one of the
greatest men in this realm.

Sil. By 'r lady, I think 'a be, but goodman Puff
of Barson.

Pist. Puff!   95
Puff i' thy teeth, most recreant coward base!
Sir John, I am thy Pistol and thy friend,
And helter-skelter have I rode to thee,
And tidings do I bring, and lucky joys
And golden times and happy news of price.   100

Fal. I pray thee now, deliver them like a man
of this world.

Pist. A foutra for the world and worldlings base!
I speak of Africa and golden joys.

Fal. O base Assyrian knight, what is thy news?
Let King Cophetua know the truth thereof.   106

Sil. [*Singing.*] "And Robin Hood, Scarlet, and
    John."

Pist. Shall dunghill curs confront the Helicons?
And shall good news be baffled?
Then, Pistol, lay thy head in Furies' lap.   110

Sil. Honest gentleman, I know not your breeding.

Pist. Why then, lament therefore.

Shal. Give me pardon, sir. If, sir, you come
with news from the court, I take it there's but
two ways, either to utter them, or to conceal them.
I am, sir, under the King, in some authority.   118

Pist. Under which king, Besonian? Speak, or
    die.

Shal. Under King Harry.

Pist.   Harry the Fourth or Fifth?

Shal. Harry the Fourth.

Pist.   A foutra for thine office!
Sir John, thy tender lambkin now is king;   122
Harry the Fifth's the man. I speak the truth.
When Pistol lies, do this, and fig me like
The bragging Spaniard.

Fal. What, is the old king dead?   126

---

44. **leather-coats:** russet apples. 49. **leman:** sweetheart. 63. **cabileros:** gallants. 68. **pottle-pot:** two-quart tankard.
69. **liggens:** lifekins (?). 71. **[he is]** F. *a tis* Q. 76. **done me right:** matched me (in drinking). 79. **S'amingo:** San
Domingo. 93. **but:** except. 103. **foutra:** a coarse term of contempt. 119. **Besonian:** base fellow. 124. **fig:** insult by
thrusting the thumb between the fingers.

Pist. As nail in door. The things I speak are just.

Fal. Away, Bardolph! saddle my horse. Master Robert Shallow, choose what office thou wilt in the land, 'tis thine. Pistol, I will double-charge thee with dignities.   131

Bard. O joyful day!
I would not take a [knighthood] for my fortune.

Pist. What! I do bring good news.   134

Fal. Carry Master Silence to bed. Master Shallow, my Lord Shallow, — be what thou wilt; I am Fortune's steward — get on thy boots. We'll ride all night. O sweet Pistol! Away, Bardolph! [*Exit Bard.*] Come, Pistol, utter more to me; and withal devise something to do thyself good. Boot, boot, Master Shallow! 140 I know the young king is sick for me. Let us take any man's horses; the laws of England are at my commandment. Blessed are they that have been my friends; and woe to my Lord Chief Justice!   145

Pist. Let vultures vile seize on his lungs also! "Where is the life that late I led?" say they. Why here it is; welcome these pleasant days!
[*Exeunt.*

SCENE IV. [*London. A street.*]

Enter BEADLES, [*dragging in*] HOSTESS QUICKLY *and* DOLL TEARSHEET.

Host. No, thou arrant knave; I would to God that I might die, that I might have thee hang'd. Thou hast drawn my shoulder out of joint.

[*1. Bead.*] The constables have delivered her over to me; and she shall have whipping cheer enough, I warrant her. There hath been a man or two lately kill'd about her.   7

Dol. Nut-hook, nut-hook, you lie. Come on! I'll tell thee what, thou damn'd tripe-visag'd rascal, an the child I now go with do miscarry, thou wert better thou hadst struck thy mother, thou paper-fac'd villain!   12

Host. O the Lord, that Sir John were come! He would make this a bloody day to somebody. But I pray God the fruit of her womb miscarry.

[*1. Bead.*] If it do, you shall have a dozen of cushions again; you have but eleven now. Come, I charge you both go with me; for the man is dead that you and Pistol beat amongst you.   19

Dol. I'll tell you what, you thin man in a censer, I will have you as soundly swinged for this, — you blue-bottle rogue, you filthy famish'd correctioner, if you be not swinged, I'll forswear half-kirtles. 24

[*1. Bead.*] Come, come, you she knight-errant, come.

Host. O God, that right should thus overcome might! Well, of sufferance comes ease.

Dol. Come, you rogue, come; bring me to a justice.   30

Host. Ay, come, you starv'd blood-hound.

Dol. Goodman death, goodman bones!

Host. Thou atomy, thou!

Dol. Come, you thin thing; come, you rascal.

[*1. Bead.*] Very well.   [*Exeunt.* 35

SCENE V. [*A public place near Westminster Abbey.*]

Enter two GROOMS, *strewing rushes.*

1. Groom. More rushes, more rushes.

2. Groom. The trumpets have sounded twice.

1. Groom. 'Twill be two o'clock ere they come from the coronation. Dispatch, dispatch.   4
[*Exeunt.*

Trumpets sound, and the King and his train pass over the stage. After them enter FALSTAFF, SHALLOW, PISTOL, BARDOLPH, *and* PAGE.

Fal. Stand here by me, Master Robert Shallow; I will make the King do you grace. I will leer upon him as 'a comes by; and do but mark the countenance that he will give me.

Pist. God bless thy lungs, good knight.   9

Fal. Come here, Pistol; stand behind me. O, if I had time to have made new liveries, I would have bestowed the thousand pound I borrowed of you. But 'tis no matter; this poor show doth better; this doth infer the zeal I had to see him.

[*Shal.*] It doth so.   16

Fal. It shows my earnestness of affection, —

Shal. It doth so.

Fal. My devotion, —

Shal. It doth, it doth, it doth.   20

Fal. As it were, to ride day and night; and not to deliberate, not to remember, not to have patience to shift me, —

Shal. It is best, certain.   24

[*Fal.*] But to stand stained with travel and sweating with desire to see him; thinking of nothing else, putting all affairs else in oblivion, as if there were nothing else to be done but to see him. 29

---

133. **[knighthood]** F. *knight* Q.
Sc. iv, s.d. BEADLES F. Q reads *Sincklo*, the name of the actor. 4, 16, 25, 35. [*1. Bead.*] (Malone). *Sincklo* Q. *Off.* F.
8. **nut-hook:** catchpole. 8, 20, etc. **Dol.** F. *Whoore* Q. 17. **cushions:** i.e., to simulate pregnancy. 20. **thin...censer:** a figure in low relief embossed on the bottom of a censer. 22. **blue-bottle:** Beadles wore blue coats. 24. **half-kirtles:** short skirts. 28. **sufferance:** suffering. 33. **atomy:** confusion of *atom* and *anatomy*, skeleton.
Sc. v, 12. **bestowed:** used. 16. [**Shal.**] F. *Pist.* Q. 23. **shift me:** change my clothes. 25. **[Fal.]** F. Om. Q.

Pist. 'Tis "*semper idem*," for "*obsque hoc nihil est.*" 'Tis all in every part.

Shal. 'Tis so, indeed.

Pist. My knight, I will inflame thy noble liver,
And make thee rage.
Thy Doll, and Helen of thy noble thoughts,   35
Is in base durance and contagious prison;
Hal'd thither
By most mechanical and dirty hand.
Rouse up revenge from ebon den with fell Alecto's snake,
For Doll is in.   Pistol speaks nought but truth.   40

Fal. I will deliver her.

Pist. There roar'd the sea, and trumpet-clangor sounds.

The trumpets sound.   Enter the KING *and his train, the* LORD CHIEF JUSTICE [*among them*].

Fal. God save thy Grace, King Hal! my royal Hal!   44

Pist. The heavens thee guard and keep, most royal imp of fame!

Fal. God save thee, my sweet boy!

King. My Lord Chief Justice, speak to that vain man.

Ch. Just. Have you your wits? Know you what 'tis you speak?

Fal. My king! my Jove! I speak to thee, my heart!   50

King. I know thee not, old man; fall to thy prayers.
How ill white hairs become a fool and jester!
I have long dreamt of such a kind of man,
So surfeit-swell'd, so old, and so profane;
But, being awak'd, I do despise my dream.   55
Make less thy body hence, and more thy grace;
Leave gormandizing; know the grave doth gape
For thee thrice wider than for other men.
Reply not to me with a fool-born jest.
Presume not that I am the thing I was;   60
For God doth know, so shall the world perceive,
That I have turn'd away my former self;
So will I those that kept me company.
When thou dost hear I am as I have been,
Approach me, and thou shalt be as thou wast,   65
The tutor and the feeder of my riots.
Till then, I banish thee, on pain of death,
As I have done the rest of my misleaders,
Not to come near our person by ten mile.
For competence of life I will allow you,   70
That lack of means enforce you not to evils;
And, as we hear you do reform yourselves,
We will, according to your strengths and qualities,
Give you advancement. Be it your charge, my lord,

To see perform'd the tenour of my word.   75
Set on.   [*Exeunt King* [*etc.*].

Fal. Master Shallow, I owe you a thousand pound.

Shal. Yea, marry, Sir John; which I beseech you to let me have home with me.   80

Fal. That can hardly be, Master Shallow. Do not you grieve at this; I shall be sent for in private to him. Look you, he must seem thus to the world. Fear not your advancements; I will be the man yet that shall make you great.   85

Shal. I cannot well perceive how, unless you should give me your doublet and stuff me out with straw. I beseech you, good Sir John, let me have five hundred of my thousand.

Fal. Sir, I will be as good as my word. This that you heard was but a colour.   91

Shal. A colour that I fear you will die in, Sir John.

Fal. Fear no colours; go with me to dinner. Come, Lieutenant Pistol; come, Bardolph. I shall be sent for soon at night.   96

Re-enter PRINCE JOHN, *the* LORD CHIEF JUSTICE [*Officers with them*].

Ch. Just. Go, carry Sir John Falstaff to the Fleet.
Take all his company along with him.

Fal. My lord, my lord,—

Ch. Just. I cannot now speak; I will hear you soon.   100
Take them away.

Pist. Si fortuna me tormenta, spera contenta.
        [*Exeunt all but Prince John and the Chief Justice.*

Lan. I like this fair proceeding of the King's.
He hath intent his wonted followers
Shall all be very well provided for;   105
But all are banish'd till their conversations
Appear more wise and modest to the world.

Ch. Just. And so they are.

Lan. The King hath call'd his parliament, my lord.

Ch. Just. He hath.   110

Lan. I will lay odds that, ere this year expire,
We bear our civil swords and native fire
As far as France. I heard a bird so sing,
Whose music, to my thinking, pleas'd the King.
Come, will you hence?   [*Exeunt.*   115

EPILOGUE

[*Spoken by a* DANCER.]

First my fear; then my curtsy; last my speech.
My fear is, your displeasure; my curtsy, my duty;
and my speech, to beg your pardons. If you

30–31. **semper ... est:** "always the same" for "without this there is nothing." 38. **mechanical:** low-class. 39. **Alecto:** a Fury. 91–94. **colour ... colours:** pun on (1) pretext, (2) collar, (3) flags. 97. **Fleet:** a prison. 106. **conversations:** behavior.

look for a good speech now, you undo me; for
what I have to say is of mine own making; and 5
what indeed I should say will, I doubt, prove mine
own marring. But to the purpose, and so to the
venture. Be it known to you, as it is very well, I
was lately here in the end of a displeasing play,
to pray your patience for it and to promise you 10
a better. I meant indeed to pay you with this;
which, if like an ill venture it come unluckily home,
I break, and you, my gentle creditors, lose. Here
I promis'd you I would be, and here I commit my
body to your mercies. Bate me some and I 15
will pay you some and, as most debtors do, promise
you infinitely.

If my tongue cannot entreat you to acquit me,
will you command me to use my legs? And
yet that were but light payment, to dance out of

your debt. But a good conscience will make 20
any possible satisfaction, and so would I. All the
gentlewomen here have forgiven me; if the gentlemen will not, then the gentlemen do not agree
with the gentlewomen, which was never seen
[before] in such an assembly. 26

One word more, I beseech you. If you be not
too much cloy'd with fat meat, our humble author
will continue the story, with Sir John in it, and
make you merry with fair Katharine of France; 30
where, for anything I know, Falstaff shall die of
a sweat, unless already 'a be kill'd with your hard
opinions; for Oldcastle died a martyr, and this is
not the man. My tongue is weary; when my legs
are too, I will bid you good night; and so I kneel 35
down before you; but, indeed, to pray for the
Queen.

Epi., 9. **displeasing play.** Not identified. 13. **break:** go bankrupt. 15. **Bate:** abate, remit. 26. **[before]** F. Om. Q.
33. **Oldcastle.** See Introduction to Part I. 35–36. **and . . . Queen** F (omitting *I*). Q inserts at l. 17.

The Life of Henry the Fifth

OF FEW OF SHAKESPEARE'S PLAYS can the date of composition be fixed with such accuracy and precision as that of *Henry the Fifth*. The Prologue to Act V contains the following lines:

As, by a lower but loving likelihood,
Were now the general of our gracious Empress,
As in good time he may, from Ireland coming,
Bringing rebellion broached on his sword,

The allusion is clear to the expedition led by the Earl of Essex, who left for Ireland on March 27, 1599, and returned unannounced to London on September 28th of the same year. As Essex's failure had been foreseen for some time before his return, the passage must have been written by midsummer, 1599. The play is not listed by Meres.

Following the entry in the Stationers' Register of August 4, 1600, a Quarto edition appeared in that year and was reprinted in 1602 and 1619. It differs, however, in the source of the text from the First Folio, on which the present edition is based. The Quarto text is less than half the length of the version in the Folio, and is so badly mangled and corrupted that it is now generally agreed that it is a pirated edition printed from notes taken at a performance, and perhaps from other sources surreptitiously obtained. The theory that it represents an early draft of the play is not supported by a close comparison of the texts.

The source of the serious plot is, as usual in the Histories, the *Chronicles* of Holinshed. Shakespeare follows the main trend of actual events, altering the order only slightly, but condensing the action from six years. The long speeches throughout are, but for a few hints, altogether his, with the exception of the genealogical argument of the Archbishop of Canterbury, I.ii, which follows Holinshed with remarkable closeness. The following passage shows how little change was necessary to transform Holinshed's prose into blank verse:

"Hugh Capet also, (who usurped the crowne upon Charles duke of Loraine, the sole heire male of the line and stocke of Charles the great,) to make his title seeme true, and appeare good, (though in deed it was starke naught,) conveied himselfe as heire to the ladie Lingard, daughter to King Charlemaine, sonne to Lewes the emperour, that was son to Charles the great." (Holinshed, iii.545)

Hugh Capet also, who usurp'd the crown
Of Charles the Duke of Lorraine, sole heir male
Of the true line and stock of Charles the Great,
To find his title with some shows of truth,
Though, in pure truth, it was corrupt and naught,
Convey'd himself as th' heir to th' Lady Lingare,
Daughter to Charlemain, who was the son
To Lewis the Emperor, and Lewis the son
Of Charles the Great. (I.ii.69–77.)

On the other hand the spirited retort to the Dauphin on the tennis balls in I.ii.259–296, is elaborated from a single sentence. "Wherfore the K. wrote to him, that yer ought long, he would tosse him some London balles that perchance should shake the walles of the best court in France." (Holinshed, iii.545.) The scenes in which Pistol and his fellows appear have, of course, no original; and the group of subordinate officers, Fluellen, Macmorris, and Captain Jamy, with Bates and Williams and the glove episode, are all purely Shakespearean. The pardoning of the man who had railed against the king is a skillful invention to lead up to the unmasking and self-condemnation of the conspirators. The happy personal relations existing among the English are brought out in Henry's speeches to old Erpingham, in the description of the deaths of Suffolk and York, in the conversation between the king and the common soldiers, in the splendid eloquence of such speeches as those of Henry before Harfleur and on St Crispin's Day, all of which are absent from the chronicles; and, conversely, the vain boasting of the French lords before the battle is created out of a mere hint that they passed the night in merriment and were contemptuous of their opponents. Again, additional stress is laid by Shakespeare on Henry's piety, his soliloquy and prayer before Agincourt being without historical basis. Yet the main lines of his character are those laid down by Holinshed and earlier writers.

The French lesson of the Princess is original; but the wooing is foreshadowed in the crude play of *The Famous Victories of Henry the Fifth*, which had already supplied hints for *Henry IV*. This play also uses the Dauphin's gift of tennis balls, and contains dialect parts which may have suggested the Welsh, Scottish, and Irish parts here; and a scene in which a Frenchman tries to hold an Englishman for ransom bears a certain resemblance to Pistol's treatment of his French captive. The stealing of the pyx and the fate, though not the character, of Bardolph are historical. The Dauphin was not in fact present at the battle of Agincourt, nor were Bedford, Westmoreland, or Warwick. The simile of the bees in Canterbury's speech (I.ii.187–204) may have been suggested by a passage in Lyly's *Euphues and his England*, which in turn is based on Pliny.

As has been pointed out in previous introductions, Shakespeare had planned, while writing the immediately preceding histories, the ultimate development of Henry into the heroic figure of the ideal English king. The completion of his regeneration is explicitly announced by the Archbishop of Canterbury in the first scene of the present play. Henry is no longer exhibited as a master of spar-

kling repartee, but stress is laid on his judgment and his piety. He retains, however, his power over words, as is shown in the great heroic speeches, in the soliloquy on ceremony, and in the wooing of Katharine. His capacity for dealing with the common people is exhibited in the moving prose of the scene with Bates and Williams (IV.1), in which "mean and gentle all behold . . . a little touch of Harry in the night."

The Epilogue to the second part of *Henry the Fourth* had promised to continue "the story with Sir John in it," but it is obvious enough that the association of the king with Falstaff would have been impossible in a play with the temper of *Henry the Fifth*. In place of it we have the hostess's incomparable account of his death — a passage which owes much to the most celebrated of all textual emendations: the change by Theobald of "and a Table of greene fields" into "and 'a babbled of green fields."

With the exception of the collaborated *Henry VIII*, this play was the last to be written of Shakespeare's histories. The crises in English history before the Tudor period which gave good dramatic opportunity were well-nigh exhausted, and the limitations of the form of the chronicle play must have been increasingly irksome to Shakespeare's developed artistic sense. *Henry the Fifth* forms an appropriate close to the series, bringing, as it does, the patriotic fervor underlying them all to its highest expression.

THE CLAIM OF HENRY V TO THE FRENCH THRONE

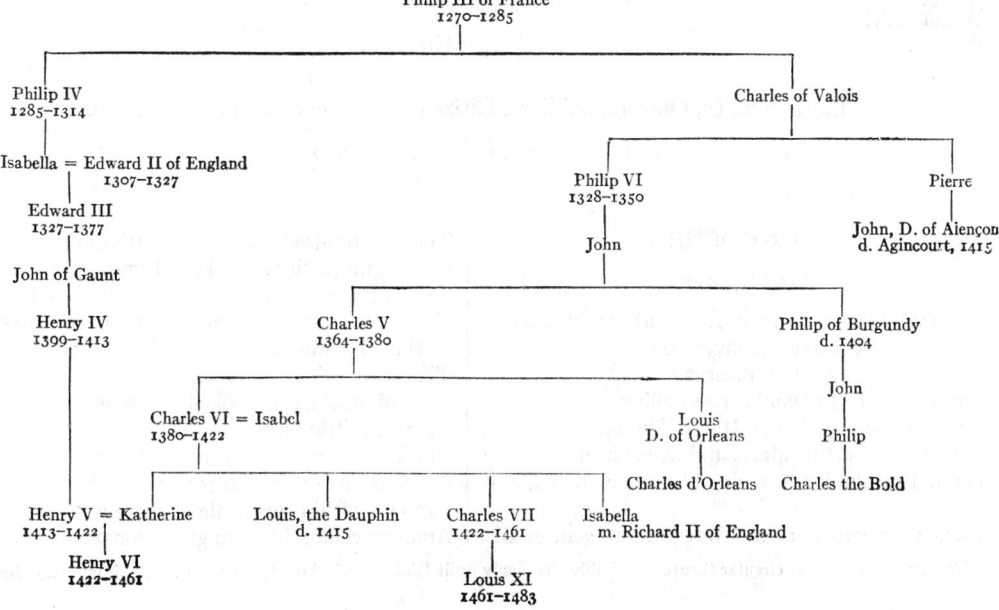

THE LIFE OF HENRY THE FIFTH

[DRAMATIS PERSONÆ

KING HENRY V.

DUKE OF GLOUCESTER,
DUKE OF BEDFORD, } *brothers to the King.*

DUKE OF EXETER, *uncle to the King.*

DUKE OF YORK, *cousin to the King.*

EARLS OF SALISBURY, WESTMORELAND, *and*
WARWICK.

ARCHBISHOP OF CANTERBURY.

BISHOP OF ELY.

EARL OF CAMBRIDGE.

LORD SCROOP.

SIR THOMAS GREY.

SIR THOMAS ERPINGHAM,
GOWER,
FLUELLEN, } *officers in King*
MACMORRIS, *Henry's army.*
JAMY,

BATES,
COURT, } *soldiers in the same.*
WILLIAMS,

PISTOL.

NYM.

BARDOLPH.

BOY.

A Herald.

CHARLES VI, *king of France.*

LEWIS, *the Dauphin.*

DUKES OF BURGUNDY, ORLEANS, *and* BOURBON.

The Constable of France.

RAMBURES,
GRANDPRÉ, } *French Lords.*

Governor of Harfleur.

MONTJOY, *a French Herald.*

Ambassadors to the King of England.

ISABEL, *queen of France.*

KATHARINE, *daughter to Charles and Isabel.*

ALICE, *a lady attending on her.*

HOSTESS *of a tavern in Eastcheap, formerly Mistress Quickly, and now married to Pistol.*

CHORUS.

Lords, Ladies, Officers, Soldiers, Citizens, Messengers, and Attendants.

SCENE: *England; afterwards France.*]

PROLOGUE

Enter [CHORUS].

[*Chor.*] O for a Muse of fire, that would ascend
The brightest heaven of invention,
A kingdom for a stage, princes to act,
And monarchs to behold the swelling scene!
Then should the warlike Harry, like himself,   5
Assume the port of Mars; and at his heels,
Leash'd in like hounds, should famine, sword, and
   fire
Crouch for employment. But pardon, gentles all,
The flat unraised spirits that hath dar'd
On this unworthy scaffold to bring forth   10
So great an object. Can this cockpit hold
The vasty fields of France? Or may we cram
Within this wooden O the very casques
That did affright the air at Agincourt?
O, pardon! since a crooked figure may   15
Attest in little place a million;
And let us, ciphers to this great accompt,
On your imaginary forces work.
Suppose within the girdle of these walls
Are now confin'd two mighty monarchies,   20

Prol., 13. **wooden O**: circular theater, probably the newly built Globe. 16. **Attest**: represent. 18. **imaginary**: imaginative.

Whose high upreared and abutting fronts
The perilous narrow ocean parts asunder;
Piece out our imperfections with your thoughts;
Into a thousand parts divide one man,
And make imaginary puissance;   25
Think, when we talk of horses, that you see them
Printing their proud hoofs i' th' receiving earth.
For 'tis your thoughts that now must deck our
    kings,
Carry them here and there, jumping o'er times,
Turning the accomplishment of many years   30
Into an hour-glass: for the which supply,
Admit me Chorus to this history;
Who, prologue-like, your humble patience pray
Gently to hear, kindly to judge, our play.   [*Exit*.

ACT I

SCENE I. [*London.   An ante-chamber in the
                King's palace.*]

Enter the ARCHBISHOP OF CANTERBURY *and the*
BISHOP OF ELY.

Cant. My lord, I'll tell you: that self bill is urg'd
Which in th' eleventh year of the last king's reign
Was like, and had indeed against us pass'd,
But that the scambling and unquiet time
Did push it out of farther question.   5
Ely. But how, my lord, shall we resist it now?
Cant. It must be thought on. If it pass against
    us,
We lose the better half of our possession;
For all the temporal lands which men devout
By testament have given to the Church   10
Would they strip from us; being valu'd thus:
As much as would maintain, to the King's honour,
Full fifteen earls and fifteen hundred knights,
Six thousand and two hundred good esquires;
And, to relief of lazars and weak age,   15
Of indigent faint souls past corporal toil,
A hundred almshouses right well suppli'd;
And to the coffers of the King beside,
A thousand pounds by th' year. Thus runs the
    bill.
Ely. This would drink deep.
Cant.   'Twould drink the cup and all.   20
Ely. But what prevention?
Cant. The King is full of grace and fair regard.
Ely. And a true lover of the holy Church.
Cant. The courses of his youth promis'd it not.
The breath no sooner left his father's body,   25
But that his wildness, mortifi'd in him,

Seem'd to die too; yea, at that very moment
Consideration like an angel came
And whipp'd th' offending Adam out of him,
Leaving his body as a paradise   30
T' envelop and contain celestial spirits.
Never was such a sudden scholar made;
Never came reformation in a flood
With such a heady currance, scouring faults;
Nor never Hydra-headed wilfulness   35
So soon did lose his seat, and all at once,
As in this king.
Ely.   We are blessed in the change.
Cant. Hear him but reason in divinity,
And, all-admiring, with an inward wish
You would desire the King were made a prelate;   40
Hear him debate of commonwealth affairs,
You would say it hath been all in all his study;
List his discourse of war, and you shall hear
A fearful battle rend'red you in music;
Turn him to any cause of policy,   45
The Gordian knot of it he will unloose,
Familiar as his garter; that, when he speaks,
The air, a charter'd libertine, is still,
And the mute wonder lurketh in men's ears
To steal his sweet and honey'd sentences;   50
So that the art and practic part of life
Must be the mistress to this theoric:
Which is a wonder how his Grace should glean it,
Since his addiction was to courses vain,
His companies unletter'd, rude, and shallow,   55
His hours fill'd up with riots, banquets, sports,
And never noted in him any study,
Any retirement, any sequestration
From open haunts and popularity.
Ely. The strawberry grows underneath the
        nettle,   60
And wholesome berries thrive and ripen best
Neighbour'd by fruit of baser quality;
And so the Prince obscur'd his contemplation
Under the veil of wildness; which, no doubt,
Grew like the summer grass, fastest by night,   65
Unseen, yet crescive in his faculty.
Cant. It must be so; for miracles are ceas'd,
And therefore we must needs admit the means
How things are perfected.
Ely.   But, my good lord,
How now for mitigation of this bill   70
Urg'd by the commons? Doth his Majesty
Incline to it, or no?
Cant.   He seems indifferent,
Or rather swaying more upon our part
Than cherishing th' exhibiters against us;
For I have made an offer to his Majesty,   75

31. **the which supply:** filling the gaps.
  Act I, sc. i, 1. **self:** same. 4. **scambling:** disorderly. 15. **lazars:** lepers. 28. **Consideration:** reflection. 34. **heady currance:** violent current. 45. **cause:** question. 48. **charter'd:** licensed. 59. **popularity:** association with common people. 66. **crescive ... faculty:** growing in its natural power. 74. **exhibiters:** promoters.

Upon our spiritual convocation
And in regard of causes now in hand,
Which I have open'd to his Grace at large,
As touching France, to give a greater sum
Than ever at one time the clergy yet   80
Did to his predecessors part withal.
   Ely. How did this offer seem receiv'd, my lord?
   Cant. With good acceptance of his Majesty;
Save that there was not time enough to hear,
As I perceiv'd his Grace would fain have done,   85
The severals and unhidden passages
Of his true titles to some certain dukedoms,
And generally to the crown and seat of France
Deriv'd from Edward, his great-grandfather.
   Ely. What was th' impediment that broke this
     off?   90
   Cant. The French ambassador upon that instant
Crav'd audience; and the hour, I think, is come
To give him hearing.   Is it four o'clock?
   Ely. It is.
   Cant. Then go we in, to know his embassy;   95
Which I could with a ready guess declare
Before the Frenchman speak a word of it.
   Ely. I'll wait upon you, and I long to hear it.
                        [Exeunt.

[SCENE II.   *The same.   The presence chamber.*]

Enter KING HENRY, GLOUCESTER, BEDFORD,
   EXETER, WARWICK, WESTMORELAND [*and*
   Attendants].

   K. Hen. Where is my gracious Lord of Canter-
     bury?
   Exe. Not here in presence.
   K. Hen.   Send for him, good uncle.
   West. Shall we call in th' ambassador, my liege?
   K. Hen. Not yet, my cousin.   We would be
     resolv'd,
Before we hear him, of some things of weight   5
That task our thoughts, concerning us and France.

Enter the ARCHBISHOP OF CANTERBURY *and the*
              BISHOP OF ELY

   Cant. God and his angels guard your sacred
     throne
And make you long become it!
   K. Hen.   Sure we thank you.
My learned lord, we pray you to proceed
And justly and religiously unfold   10
Why the law Salique that they have in France
Or should, or should not, bar us in our claim;

And God forbid, my dear and faithful lord,
That you should fashion, wrest, or bow your
     reading,
Or nicely charge your understanding soul   15
With opening titles miscreate, whose right
Suits not in native colours with the truth;
For God doth know how many now in health
Shall drop their blood in approbation
Of what your reverence shall incite us to.   20
Therefore take heed how you impawn our person,
How you awake our sleeping sword of war.
We charge you, in the name of God, take heed;
For never two such kingdoms did contend
Without much fall of blood, whose guiltless drops
Are every one a woe, a sore complaint   26
'Gainst him whose wrong gives edge unto the
     swords
That makes such waste in brief mortality.
Under this conjuration speak, my lord;
For we will hear, note, and believe in heart   30
That what you speak is in your conscience wash'd
As pure as sin with baptism.
   Cant. Then hear me, gracious sovereign, and you
     peers,
That owe yourselves, your lives, and services
To this imperial throne.   There is no bar   35
To make against your Highness' claim to France
But this, which they produce from Pharamond:
"In terram Salicam mulieres ne succedant,"
"No woman shall succeed in Salique land;"
Which Salique land the French unjustly gloze   40
To be the realm of France, and Pharamond
The founder of this law and female bar.
Yet their own authors faithfully affirm
That the land Salique is in Germany,
Between the floods of Sala and of Elbe;   45
Where Charles the Great, having subdu'd the
     Saxons,
There left behind and settled certain French;
Who, holding in disdain the German women
For some dishonest manners of their life,
Establish'd then this law, to wit, no female   50
Should be inheritrix in Salique land;
Which Salique, as I said, 'twixt Elbe and Sala,
Is at this day in Germany call'd Meisen.
Then doth it well appear the Salique law
Was not devised for the realm of France;   55
Nor did the French possess the Salique land
Until four hundred one and twenty years
After defunction of King Pharamond,
Idly suppos'd the founder of this law,
Who died within the year of our redemption   60

---

76. **Upon . . . convocation:** on behalf of the assembly of clergy.   86. **severals:** details.   **unhidden passages:** clear derivation.
   Sc. ii, 4. **resolv'd:** clear in our minds.   11. **law Salique.**   Henry's claim to the French throne was through Isabella, daughter of Philip IV of France and wife of Edward II, Henry's great-great-grandfather.   15. **nicely:** sophistically.   19-20. **approbation Of:** making good.   21. **impawn:** commit.   40. **gloze:** interpret.   49. **dishonest:** unchaste.   58. **defunction:** death.

Four hundred twenty-six; and Charles the Great
Subdu'd the Saxons, and did seat the French
Beyond the river Sala, in the year
Eight hundred five. Besides, their writers say,
King Pepin, which deposed Childeric,   65
Did, as heir general, being descended
Of Blithild, which was daughter to King Clothair,
Make claim and title to the crown of France.
Hugh Capet also, who usurp'd the crown
Of Charles the Duke of Lorraine, sole heir male   70
Of the true line and stock of Charles the Great,
To find his title with some shows of truth,
Though, in pure truth, it was corrupt and naught,
Convey'd himself as th' heir to th' Lady Lingare,
Daughter to Charlemain, who was the son   75
To Lewis the Emperor, and Lewis the son
Of Charles the Great.   Also, King Lewis the Tenth,
Who was sole heir to the usurper Capet,
Could not keep quiet in his conscience,
Wearing the crown of France, till satisfied   80
That fair Queen Isabel, his grandmother,
Was lineal of the Lady Ermengare,
Daughter to Charles, the foresaid Duke of Lor-
    raine;
By the which marriage the line of Charles the
    Great
Was re-united to the crown of France.   85
So that, as clear as is the summer's sun,
King Pepin's title and Hugh Capet's claim,
King Lewis his satisfaction, all appear
To hold in right and title of the female.
So do the kings of France unto this day,   90
Howbeit they would hold up this Salique law
To bar your Highness claiming from the female,
And rather choose to hide them in a net
Than amply to imbar their crooked titles
Usurp'd from you and your progenitors.   95
    K. Hen. May I with right and conscience make
        this claim?
    Cant. The sin upon my head, dread sovereign!
For in the book of Numbers is it writ,
When the man dies, let the inheritance
Descend unto the daughter.   Gracious lord,   100
Stand for your own!   Unwind your bloody flag!
Look back into your mighty ancestors!
Go, my dread lord, to your great-grandsire's tomb,
From whom you claim; invoke his warlike spirit,
And your great-uncle's, Edward the Black Prince,
Who on the French ground play'd a tragedy,   106
Making defeat on the full power of France,
Whiles his most mighty father on a hill
Stood smiling to behold his lion's whelp

Forage in blood of French nobility.   110
O noble English, that could entertain
With half their forces the full pride of France
And let another half stand laughing by,
All out of work and cold for action!
    Ely. Awake remembrance of these valiant dead,
And with your puissant arm renew their feats.   116
You are their heir; you sit upon their throne;
The blood and courage that renowned them
Runs in your veins; and my thrice-puissant liege
Is in the very May-morn of his youth,   120
Ripe for exploits and mighty enterprises.
    Exe. Your brother kings and monarchs of the
        earth
Do all expect that you should rouse yourself,
As did the former lions of your blood.
    West. They know your Grace hath cause and
        means and might;   125
So hath your Highness.   Never King of England
Had nobles richer and more loyal subjects,
Whose hearts have left their bodies here in England
And lie pavilion'd in the fields of France.   129
    Cant. O, let their bodies follow, my dear liege,
With blood and sword and fire to win your right;
In aid whereof we of the spiritualty
Will raise your Highness such a mighty sum
As never did the clergy at one time
Bring in to any of your ancestors.   135
    K. Hen. We must not only arm t' invade the
        French,
But lay down our proportions to defend
Against the Scot, who will make road upon us
With all advantages.
    Cant. They of those marches, gracious sovereign,
Shall be a wall sufficient to defend   141
Our inland from the pilfering borderers.
    K. Hen. We do not mean the coursing snatchers
        only,
But fear the main intendment of the Scot,
Who hath been still a giddy neighbour to us;   145
For you shall read that my great-grandfather
Never went with his forces into France
But that the Scot on his unfurnish'd kingdom
Came pouring, like the tide into a breach,
With ample and brim fullness of his force,   150
Galling the gleaned land with hot assays,
Girding with grievous siege castles and towns;
That England, being empty of defence,
Hath shook and trembled at th' ill neighbourhood.
    Cant. She hath been then more fear'd than
        harm'd, my liege;   155
For hear her but exampl'd by herself:

---

72. **find**: provide. 74. **Convey'd**: passed off. 75. **Charlemain**: really, Charles the Bald. 77. **Lewis the Tenth** should be
Louis IX. 82. **lineal of**: descended from. 94. **amply to imbar**: frankly to rule out. 106–114. Battle of Crecy, 1346.
114. **for**: for lack of. 137. **proportions**: division of forces. 138. **road**: inroad. 139. **With . . . advantages**: whenever he sees
a good chance. 143. **coursing snatchers**: raiders. 144. **intendment**: intention. 145. **still a giddy**: always a restless.
148. **unfurnish'd**: deprived of defenders. 151. **assays**: assaults. 155. **fear'd**: frightened.

When all her chivalry hath been in France,
And she a mourning widow of her nobles,
She hath herself not only well defended
But taken and impounded as a stray   160
The King of Scots; whom she did send to France
To fill King Edward's fame with prisoner kings,
And make her chronicle as rich with praise
As is the ooze and bottom of the sea
With sunken wrack and sumless treasuries.   165
   [*West.*] But there's a saying very old and true,
     "If that you will France win,
       Then with Scotland first begin."
For once the eagle England being in prey,
To her unguarded nest the weasel Scot   170
Comes sneaking and so sucks her princely eggs,
Playing the mouse in absence of the cat,
To [spoil] and havoc more than she can eat.
   Exe. It follows then the cat must stay at home;
Yet that is but a crush'd necessity,   175
Since we have locks to safeguard necessaries,
And pretty traps to catch the petty thieves.
While that the armed hand doth fight abroad,
Th' advised head defends itself at home;
For government, though high and low and lower,
Put into parts, doth keep in one consent,   181
Congreeing in a full and natural close,
Like music.
   Cant.   Therefore doth heaven divide
The state of man in divers functions,
Setting endeavour in continual motion,   185
To which is fixed, as an aim or butt,
Obedience; for so work the honey-bees,
Creatures that by a rule in nature teach
The act of order to a peopled kingdom.
They have a king and officers of sorts,   190
Where some, like magistrates, correct at home,
Others, like merchants, venture trade abroad,
Others, like soldiers, armed in their stings,
Make boot upon the summer's velvet buds,
Which pillage they with merry march bring
   home
To the tent-royal of their emperor;   196
Who, busied in his majesty, surveys
The singing masons building roofs of gold,
The civil citizens kneading up the honey,
The poor mechanic porters crowding in   200
Their heavy burdens at his narrow gate,
The sad-eyed justice, with his surly hum,
Delivering o'er to executors pale
The lazy yawning drone. I this infer,
That many things, having full reference   205
To one consent, may work contrariously.
As many arrows, loosed several ways,

Come to one mark; as many ways meet in one
   town;
As many fresh streams meet in one salt sea;
As many lines close in the dial's centre;   210
So may a thousand actions, once afoot,
End in one purpose, and be all well borne
Without defeat. Therefore to France, my liege!
Divide your happy England into four,
Whereof take you one quarter into France,   215
And you withal shall make all Gallia shake.
If we, with thrice such powers left at home,
Cannot defend our own doors from the dog,
Let us be worried and our nation lose
The name of hardiness and policy.   220
   K. Hen. Call in the messengers sent from the
   Dauphin.   [*Exeunt some Attendants.*]
Now are we well resolv'd; and by God's help
And yours, the noble sinews of our power,
France being ours, we'll bend it to our awe,
Or break it all to pieces. Or there we'll sit,   225
Ruling in large and ample empery
O'er France and all her almost kingly dukedoms,
Or lay these bones in an unworthy urn,
Tombless, with no remembrance over them.
Either our history shall with full mouth   230
Speak freely of our acts, or else our grave,
Like Turkish mute, shall have a tongueless mouth,
Not worshipp'd with a waxen epitaph.

       Enter AMBASSADORS *of France.*

Now are we well prepar'd to know the pleasure
Of our fair cousin Dauphin; for we hear   235
Your greeting is from him, not from the King.
   1. Amb. May 't please your Majesty to give us
   leave
Freely to render what we have in charge,
Or shall we sparingly show you far off
The Dauphin's meaning and our embassy?   240
   K. Hen. We are no tyrant, but a Christian king,
Unto whose grace our passion is as subject
As is our wretches fett'red in our prisons;
Therefore with frank and with uncurbed plainness
Tell us the Dauphin's mind.
   1. Amb.   Thus, then, in few.
Your Highness, lately sending into France,   246
Did claim some certain dukedoms, in the right
Of your great predecessor, King Edward the Third.
In answer of which claim, the prince our master
Says that you savour too much of your youth,   250
And bids you be advis'd there's nought in France
That can be with a nimble galliard won.
You cannot revel into dukedoms there.
He therefore sends you, meeter for your spirit,

161. **King of Scots:** David Bruce, 1346. 166. [*West.*] (Capell after Holinshed). *Bish. Ely* F. 169. **in prey:** in search
of prey. 173. [spoil] Q. *tame* F. *tear* Rowe. 175. **crush'd:** strained. 179. **advised:** judicious. 181. **consent:** harmony.
182. **Congreeing:** agreeing. **close:** cadence. 190. **sorts:** different kinds. 194. **boot:** booty. 226. **empery:** imperial
power. 233. **with . . . epitaph:** even with an epitaph written on wax. For *waxen* Q reads *paper.* 252. **galliard:** a dance.

This tun of treasure; and, in lieu of this,   255
Desires you let the dukedoms that you claim
Hear no more of you. This the Dauphin speaks.

    K. Hen. What treasure, uncle?

    Exe.   Tennis-balls, my liege.

    K. Hen. We are glad the Dauphin is so pleasant
     with us.
His present and your pains we thank you for.   260
When we have match'd our rackets to these balls,
We will, in France, by God's grace, play a set
Shall strike his father's crown into the hazard.
Tell him he hath made a match with such a wrangler
That all the courts of France will be disturb'd   265
With chaces. And we understand him well,
How he comes o'er us with our wilder days,
Not measuring what use we made of them.
We never valu'd this poor seat of England;
And therefore, living hence, did give ourself   270
To barbarous license; as 'tis ever common
That men are merriest when they are from home.
But tell the Dauphin I will keep my state,
Be like a king, and show my sail of greatness
When I do rouse me in my throne of France.   275
For that I have laid by my majesty
And plodded like a man for working-days,
But I will rise there with so full a glory
That I will dazzle all the eyes of France,
Yea, strike the Dauphin blind to look on us.   280
And tell the pleasant prince this mock of his
Hath turn'd his balls to gun-stones, and his soul
Shall stand sore charged for the wasteful vengeance
That shall fly with them; for many a thousand
     widows
Shall this his mock mock out of their dear hus-
     bands,   285
Mock mothers from their sons, mock castles down;
And some are yet ungotten and unborn
That shall have cause to curse the Dauphin's scorn.
But this lies all within the will of God,
To whom I do appeal; and in whose name   290
Tell you the Dauphin I am coming on
To venge me as I may, and to put forth
My rightful hand in a well-hallow'd cause.
So get you hence in peace; and tell the Dauphin
His jest will savour but of shallow wit,   295
When thousands weep more than did laugh at it. —
Convey them with safe conduct. — Fare you well.
                 [*Exeunt Ambassadors.*

    Exe. This was a merry message.

    K. Hen. We hope to make the sender blush at it.
Therefore, my lords, omit no happy hour   300
That may give furtherance to our expedition;
For we have now no thought in us but France,
Save those to God, that run before our business.
Therefore, let our proportions for these wars

Be soon collected, and all things thought upon   305
That may with reasonable swiftness add
More feathers to our wings; for, God before,
We'll chide this Dauphin at his father's door.
Therefore let every man now task his thought,
That this fair action may on foot be brought.   310
                       [*Exeunt.*

[ACT II]

[PROLOGUE.]

Flourish. Enter CHORUS.

[*Chor.*] Now all the youth of England are on fire,
And silken dalliance in the wardrobe lies.
Now thrive the armourers, and honour's thought
Reigns solely in the breast of every man.
They sell the pasture now to buy the horse,   5
Following the mirror of all Christian kings
With winged heels, as English Mercuries.
For now sits Expectation in the air,
And hides a sword from hilts unto the point
With crowns imperial, crowns, and coronets   10
Promis'd to Harry and his followers.
The French, advis'd by good intelligence
Of this most dreadful preparation,
Shake in their fear, and with pale policy
Seek to divert the English purposes.   15
O England! model to thy inward greatness,
Like little body with a mighty heart,
What mightst thou do, that honour would thee do,
Were all thy children kind and natural!
But see thy fault! France hath in thee found out
A nest of hollow bosoms, which he fills   21
With treacherous crowns; and three corrupted men,
One, Richard Earl of Cambridge, and the second,
Henry Lord Scroop of Masham, and the third,
Sir Thomas Grey, knight, of Northumberland,
Have, for the gilt of France, — O guilt indeed! — 26
Confirm'd conspiracy with fearful France;
And by their hands this grace of kings must die,
If hell and treason hold their promises,
Ere he take ship for France, and in Southampton.
Linger your patience on, and we'll digest   31
The abuse of distance, force a play.
The sum is paid; the traitors are agreed;
The King is set from London; and the scene
Is now transported, gentles, to Southampton.   35
There is the playhouse now, there must you sit;
And thence to France shall we convey you safe,
And bring you back, charming the narrow seas
To give you gentle pass; for, if we may,
We'll not offend one stomach with our play.   40
But, till the King come forth, and not till then,
Unto Southampton do we shift our scene.   [*Exit.*

263–266. **hazard, wrangler, courts, chaces:** terms of court tennis used punningly.   267. **comes o'er:** taunts.
Act II, Prol., 18. **would:** would have.   31–32. **digest ... distance:** take care of the violation of the unity of place.

[SCENE I. *London. A street.*]

Enter CORPORAL NYM *and* LIEUTENANT BARDOLPH.

Bard. Well met, Corporal Nym.

Nym. Good morrow, Lieutenant Bardolph.

Bard. What, are Ancient Pistol and you friends
yet?   4

Nym. For my part, I care not. I say little;
but when time shall serve, there shall be smiles;
but that shall be as it may. I dare not fight,
but I will wink and hold out mine iron. It is a
simple one, but what though? It will toast cheese,
and it will endure cold as another man's sword
will; and there's an end.   11

Bard. I will bestow a breakfast to make you
friends; and we'll be all three sworn brothers to
France. Let it be so, good Corporal Nym.   14

Nym. Faith, I will live so long as I may, that's
the certain of it; and when I cannot live any
longer, I will do as I may. That is my rest, that is
the rendezvous of it.

Bard. It is certain, corporal, that he is married
to Nell Quickly; and certainly she did you wrong,
for you were troth-plight to her.   21

Nym. I cannot tell. Things must be as they
may. Men may sleep, and they may have their
throats about them at that time; and some say
knives have edges. It must be as it may. Though
patience be a tired mare, yet she will plod. There
must be conclusions. Well, I cannot tell.   27

Enter PISTOL *and* HOSTESS.

Bard. Here come Ancient Pistol and his wife.
Good corporal, be patient here. How now, mine
host Pistol!   30

Pist. Base tike, call'st thou me host?
Now, by this hand, I swear, I scorn the term;
Nor shall my Nell keep lodgers.   33

Host. No, by my troth, not long; for we cannot
lodge and board a dozen or fourteen gentlewomen
that live honestly by the prick of their needles
but it will be thought we keep a bawdy house
straight. [*Nym and Pistol draw.*] O well a day,
Lady, if he be not [drawn] now! We shall see
wilful adultery and murder committed.   40

Bard. Good lieutenant! good corporal! offer
nothing here.

Nym. Pish!

Pist. Pish for thee, Iceland dog! thou prick-
ear'd cur of Iceland!

Host. Good Corporal Nym, show thy valour, and
put up your sword.   46

Nym. Will you shog off? I would have you
solus.

Pist. "Solus," egregious dog! O viper vile!
The "solus" in thy most mervailous face;   50
The "solus" in thy teeth, and in thy throat,
And in thy hateful lungs, yea, in thy maw, perdy,
And, which is worse, within thy nasty mouth!
I do retort the "solus" in thy bowels;
For I can take, and Pistol's cock is up,
And flashing fire will follow.   56

Nym. I am not Barbason; you cannot conjure
me. I have an humour to knock you indifferently
well. If you grow foul with me, Pistol, I will
scour you with my rapier, as I may, in fair terms.
If you would walk off, I would prick your guts a
little, in good terms, as I may; and that's the
humour of it.   63

Pist. O braggart vile and damned furious wight!
The grave doth gape, and doting death is near,
Therefore exhale.

Bard. Hear me, hear me what I say. He that
strikes the first stroke, I'll run him up to the hilts,
as I am a soldier.   [*Draws.*]

Pist. An oath of mickle might; and fury shall
    abate.   70
Give me thy fist, thy fore-foot to me give.
Thy spirits are most tall.

Nym. I will cut thy throat, one time or other,
in fair terms: that is the humour of it.

Pist. "*Couple a gorge!*"   75
That is the word. I thee defy again.
O hound of Crete, think'st thou my spouse to get?
No! to the spital go,
And from the powdering-tub of infamy
Fetch forth the lazar kite of Cressid's kind,   80
Doll Tearsheet she by name, and her espouse.
I have, and I will hold, the quondam Quickly
For the only she; and — *pauca*, there's enough.
Go to.   84

Enter the BOY.

Boy. Mine host Pistol, you must come to my
master, and you, hostess. He is very sick, and
would to bed. Good Bardolph, put thy face
between his sheets, and do the office of a warming-
pan. Faith, he's very ill.

Bard. Away, you rogue!   90

Host. By my troth, he'll yield the crow a pudding one of these days. The King has kill'd his
heart. Good husband, come home presently.
    [*Exeunt* [*Hostess and Boy*].

Bard. Come, shall I make you two friends? We

Sc. i, 3. **Ancient:** ensign. 8. **wink:** shut my eyes. 17. **rest:** what I put my stakes on. 18. **rendezvous.** It is useless to try
to explain all Nym's and Pistol's assaults on the language. 30. In Q it is Nym who calls Pistol "host." 31. **tike:** cur.
39. **[drawn]** (Hanmer). *hewne* F. 47. **shog:** jog. 52. **perdy:** *par Dieu.* 57. **Barbason:** a fiend. 66. **exhale:** draw out
(your sword). 75. *Couple a gorge: couper la gorge,* cut the throat. 78. **spital:** hospital. 79. **powdering-tub:** salting tub,
slang for the hot bath used in treating venereal disease. 80. **lazar ... kind.** A reference to Henryson's sequel to Chaucer's
Troilus, in which Cressida is smitten with leprosy. 83. *pauca:* few (words). 93. **presently:** at once.

must to France together; why the devil should we
keep knives to cut one another's throats?   96

Pist. Let floods o'erswell, and fiends for food
   howl on!

Nym. You'll pay me the eight shillings I won
of you at betting?

Pist. Base is the slave that pays.   100

Nym. That now I will have: that's the humour
of it.

Pist. As manhood shall compound. Push home.
                           [*They draw.*

Bard. By this sword, he that makes the first
thrust, I'll kill him; by this sword, I will.   105

Pist. Sword is an oath, and oaths must have their
   course.

Bard. Corporal Nym, an thou wilt be friends,
be friends; an thou wilt not, why, then, be enemies
with me too. Prithee, put up.

[*Nym.* I shall have my eight shillings I won from
you at betting?]   111

Pist. A noble shalt thou have, and present pay;
And liquor likewise will I give to thee,
And friendship shall combine, and brotherhood.
I'll live by Nym, and Nym shall live by me.   115
Is not this just? For I shall sutler be
Unto the camp, and profits will accrue.
Give me thy hand.

Nym. I shall have my noble?

Pist. In cash most justly paid.   120

Nym. Well, then, that's the humour of 't.

Re-enter HOSTESS.

Host. As ever you come of women, come in
quickly to Sir John. Ah, poor heart! he is so
shak'd of a burning quotidian tertian, that it is
most lamentable to behold. Sweet men, come to
him.   126

Nym. The King hath run bad humours on the
knight; that's the even of it.

Pist. Nym, thou hast spoke the right.
His heart is fracted and corroborate.   130

Nym. The king is a good King; but it must be
as it may; he passes some humours and careers.

Pist. Let us condole the knight; for, lambkins,
we will live.   [*Exeunt.*]

[SCENE II. *Southampton. A council-chamber.*]

Enter EXETER, BEDFORD, *and* WESTMORELAND.

Bed. 'Fore God, his Grace is bold, to trust these
traitors.

Exe. They shall be apprehended by and by.

West. How smooth and even they do bear them-
   selves!
As if allegiance in their bosoms sat
Crowned with faith and constant loyalty.   5

Bed. The King hath note of all that they intend,
By interception which they dream not of.

Exe. Nay, but the man that was his bedfellow,
Whom he hath dull'd and cloy'd with gracious
   favours,
That he should, for a foreign purse, so sell   10
His sovereign's life to death and treachery.

Trumpets sound. Enter KING HENRY, SCROOP,
         CAMBRIDGE, *and* GREY.

K. Hen. Now sits the wind fair, and we will
   aboard.
My Lord of Cambridge, and my kind Lord of
   Masham,
And you, my gentle knight, give me your thoughts.
Think you not that the powers we bear with us   15
Will cut their passage through the force of France,
Doing the execution and the act
For which we have in head assembled them?

Scroop. No doubt, my liege, if each man do his
   best.

K. Hen. I doubt not that, since we are well
   persuaded   20
We carry not a heart with us from hence
That grows not in a fair consent with ours,
Nor leave not one behind that doth not wish
Success and conquest to attend on us.

Cam. Never was monarch better fear'd and
   lov'd   25
Than is your Majesty. There's not, I think, a
   subject
That sits in heart-grief and uneasiness
Under the sweet shade of your government.

Grey. True; those that were your father's
   enemies
Have steep'd their galls in honey, and do serve you
With hearts create of duty and of zeal.   31

K. Hen. We therefore have great cause of
   thankfulness,
And shall forget the office of our hand
Sooner than quittance of desert and merit
According to the weight and worthiness.   35

Scroop. So service shall with steeled sinews toil,
And labour shall refresh itself with hope,
To do your Grace incessant services.

K. Hen. We judge no less. Uncle of Exeter,
Enlarge the man committed yesterday,   40
That rail'd against our person. We consider
It was excess of wine that set him on,

---

103. **compound:** decide. 110–111. [*Nym...betting*] Q. Om. F. 112. **noble:** 6s.8d. 116. **sutler:** seller of provisions.
124. **quotidian tertian:** confusion of medical terms for two kinds of fever. 130. **fracted:** broken. **corroborate:** lit., strengthened. 132. **passes:** lets pass. **careers:** a term of horsemanship.
    Sc. ii, 2. **by and by:** soon. 18. **head:** force. 34. **quittance:** reward. 40. **Enlarge:** set free.

And on his more advice we pardon him.
　Scroop. That's mercy, but too much security.
Let him be punish'd, sovereign, lest example　45
Breed, by his sufferance, more of such a kind.
　K. Hen. O, let us yet be merciful.
　Cam. So may your Highness, and yet punish too.
　Grey. Sir,
You show great mercy if you give him life　50
After the taste of much correction.
　K. Hen. Alas, your too much love and care of me
Are heavy orisons 'gainst this poor wretch!
If little faults, proceeding on distemper,
Shall not be wink'd at, how shall we stretch our eye
When capital crimes, chew'd, swallow'd and di-
　　gested,　56
Appear before us? We'll yet enlarge that man,
Though Cambridge, Scroop, and Grey, in their dear
　　care
And tender preservation of our person,
Would have him punish'd. And now to our French
　　causes.　60
Who are the late commissioners?
　Cam. I one, my lord.
Your Highness bade me ask for it to-day.
　Scroop. So did you me, my liege.
　Grey. And I, my royal sovereign.　65
　K. Hen. Then, Richard Earl of Cambridge, there
　　is yours;
There yours, Lord Scroop of Masham; and, sir
　　knight,
Grey of Northumberland, this same is yours.
Read them, and know I know your worthiness.
My Lord of Westmoreland, and uncle Exeter,　70
We will aboard to-night. — Why, how now, gentle-
　　men?
What see you in those papers that you lose
So much complexion? — Look ye, how they change!
Their cheeks are paper. — Why, what read you
　　there
That have so cowarded and chas'd your blood　75
Out of appearance?
　Cam.　　　　　I do confess my fault,
And do submit me to your Highness' mercy.
　Grey. ⎫
　Scroop. ⎬ To which we all appeal.
　K. Hen. The mercy that was quick in us but late,
By your own counsel is suppress'd and kill'd.　80
You must not dare, for shame, to talk of mercy,
For your own reasons turn into your bosoms,
As dogs upon their masters, worrying you.
See you, my princes and my noble peers,

These English monsters! My Lord of Cambridge
　　here,　85
You know how apt our love was to accord
To furnish him with all appertinents
Belonging to his honour; and this man
Hath, for a few light crowns, lightly conspir'd
And sworn unto the practices of France　90
To kill us here in Hampton; to the which
This knight, no less for bounty bound to us
Than Cambridge is, hath likewise sworn. But, O
What shall I say to thee, Lord Scroop? thou cruel,
Ingrateful, savage, and inhuman creature!　95
Thou that didst bear the key of all my counsels,
That knew'st the very bottom of my soul,
That almost mightst have coin'd me into gold,
Wouldst thou have practis'd on me for thy use, —
May it be possible that foreign hire　100
Could out of thee extract one spark of evil
That might annoy my finger? 'Tis so strange,
That, though the truth of it stands off as gross
As black and white, my eye will scarcely see it.
Treason and murder ever kept together,　105
As two yoke-devils sworn to either's purpose,
Working so grossly in a natural cause
That admiration did not whoop at them;
But thou, 'gainst all proportion, didst bring in
Wonder to wait on treason and on murder;　110
And whatsoever cunning fiend it was
That wrought upon thee so preposterously
Hath got the voice in hell for excellence;
And other devils that suggest by treasons
Do botch and bungle up damnation　115
With patches, colours, and with forms being fetch'd
From glist'ring semblances of piety.
But he that temper'd thee, bade thee stand up,
Gave thee no instance why thou shouldst do treason,
Unless to dub thee with the name of traitor.　120
If that same demon that hath gull'd thee thus
Should with his lion gait walk the whole world
He might return to vasty Tartar back,
And tell the legions, "I can never win
A soul so easy as that Englishman's."　125
O, how hast thou with jealousy infected
The sweetness of affiance! Show men dutiful?
Why, so didst thou. Seem they grave and learned?
Why, so didst thou. Come they of noble family?
Why, so didst thou. Seem they religious?　130
Why, so didst thou. Or are they spare in diet,
Free from gross passion or of mirth or anger,
Constant in spirit, not swerving with the blood,
Garnish'd and deck'd in modest complement,

---

43. **more advice:** thinking better of it. 44. **security:** lack of caution. 46. **his sufferance:** pardoning him. 53. **orisons:** prayers. 54. **on distemper:** from intoxication. 61. **late:** recently appointed. 63. **it:** my commission. 79. **quick:** alive. 86. **accord:** consent. 90. **practices:** plots. 103. **gross:** obvious. 108. **admiration...them:** they did not evoke wonder. 113. **voice:** vote. 114. **suggest:** seduce. 116. **colours:** pretexts. 118. **temper'd:** worked on your disposition. **bade... up.** The subject of *bade* is probably *that*. *Stand up* like *dub* (l. 120) is part of the formula used in knighting. 121. **gull'd:** fooled. 123. **Tartar:** Tartarus, Hell. 126. **jealousy:** suspicion. 127. **affiance:** trust. **show:** appear. 134. **complement:** demeanor.

Not working with the eye without the ear,   135
And but in purged judgement trusting neither?
Such and so finely bolted didst thou seem.
And thus thy fall hath left a kind of blot
To [mark the] full-fraught man and best indued
With some suspicion. I will weep for thee;   140
For this revolt of thine, methinks, is like
Another fall of man. Their faults are open.
Arrest them to the answer of the law;
And God acquit them of their practices!

Exe. I arrest thee of high treason, by the name
of Richard Earl of Cambridge.   146
I arrest thee of high treason, by the name of
[Henry] Lord Scroop of Masham.
I arrest thee of high treason, by the name of
Thomas Grey, knight, of Northumberland.   150

Scroop. Our purposes God justly hath discover'd,
And I repent my fault more than my death,
Which I beseech your Highness to forgive,
Although my body pay the price of it.

Cam. For me, the gold of France did not se-
     duce,   155
Although I did admit it as a motive
The sooner to effect what I intended.
But God be thanked for prevention,
Which I in sufferance heartily will rejoice,
Beseeching God and you to pardon me.   160

Grey. Never did faithful subject more rejoice
At the discovery of most dangerous treason
Than I do at this hour joy o'er myself,
Prevented from a damned enterprise.
My fault, but not my body, pardon, sovereign.   165

K. Hen. God quit you in his mercy! Hear your
     sentence.
You have conspir'd against our royal person,
Join'd with an enemy proclaim'd, and from his
     coffers
Receiv'd the golden earnest of our death;
Wherein you would have sold your king to slaugh-
     ter,   170
His princes and his peers to servitude,
His subjects to oppression and contempt,
And his whole kingdom into desolation.
Touching our person seek we no revenge;
But we our kingdom's safety must so tender,   175
Whose ruin you [have] sought, that to her laws
We do deliver you. Get you therefore hence,
Poor miserable wretches, to your death,
The taste whereof God of his mercy give
You patience to endure, and true repentance   180
Of all your dear offences! Bear them hence.

*[Exeunt [Cambridge, Scroop, and Grey
     guarded].*
Now, lords, for France; the enterprise whereof
Shall be to you, as us, like glorious.
We doubt not of a fair and lucky war,
Since God so graciously hath brought to light   185
This dangerous treason lurking in our way
To hinder our beginnings. We doubt not now
But every rub is smoothed on our way.
Then forth, dear countrymen! Let us deliver
Our puissance into the hand of God,   190
Putting it straight in expedition.
Cheerly to sea! The signs of war advance!
No king of England, if not king of France!
     [Flourish.

[SCENE III.   *London.   Before a tavern.*]

Enter PISTOL, NYM, BARDOLPH, BOY, *and*
     HOSTESS.

Host. Prithee honey, sweet husband, let me
bring thee to Staines.

Pist. No; for my manly heart doth ern.
Bardolph, be blithe; Nym, rouse thy vaunting
     veins;
Boy, bristle thy courage up; for Falstaff he is dead,
And we must ern therefore.   6

Bard. Would I were with him, wheresome'er he
is, either in heaven or in hell!

Host. Nay, sure, he's not in hell. He's in Arthur's bosom, if ever man went to Arthur's   10
bosom. 'A made a finer end and went away an it
had been any christom child. 'A parted even just
between twelve and one, even at the turning o' th'
tide: for after I saw him fumble with the sheets,
and play with flowers, and smile upon his fin-   15
gers' ends, I knew there was but one way; for his
nose was as sharp as a pen, and ['a babbled] of
green fields. "How now, Sir John!" quoth I;
"what, man! be o' good cheer." So 'a cried out,
"God, God, God!" three or four times. Now I,   20
to comfort him, bid him 'a should not think of
God; I hop'd there was no need to trouble himself
with any such thoughts yet. So 'a bade me lay
more clothes on his feet. I put my hand into the
bed and felt them, and they were as cold as   25
any stone; then I felt to his knees, [and they were
as cold as any stone;] and so upward and upward,
and all was as cold as any stone.

Nym. They say he cried out of sack.
Host. Ay, that 'a did.   30

---

135. Not judging a man by looks without talking with him.   137. **bolted**: sifted.   139. **[mark the]** (Theobald).   *make
thee* F.   **full-fraught**: loaded with good qualities.   148. **[Henry]** Q.   *Thomas* F.   151. **discover'd**: revealed.   159. **in sufferance**: though suffering punishment.   166. **quit**: absolve.   169. **earnest**: payment to bind a bargain.   175. **tender**: regard.
176. **[have]** Q. Om. F₁, *three* F₂.   181. **dear**: grievous.   188. **rub**: obstacle.   192. **signs of war**: banners.
   Sc. iii, 2. **Staines**: on the way to Southampton.   3. **ern**: grieve; the older form and meaning of *yearn*.   12. **christom**:
chrisom, newly christened.   17. **['a babbled]** (Theobald).   *a Table* F.   See Introduction.   26–27. **[and ... stone]** Q. Om. F
29. **sack**: a Spanish wine.

Bard. And of women.

Host. Nay, that 'a did not.

Boy. Yes, that 'a did; and said they were devils incarnate.

Host. 'A could never abide carnation; 'twas a colour he never lik'd.   36

Boy. 'A said once, the devil would have him about women.

Host. 'A did in some sort, indeed, handle women; but then he was rheumatic, and talk'd of the whore of Babylon.   41

Boy. Do you not remember, 'a saw a flea stick upon Bardolph's nose, and 'a said it was a black soul burning in [hell-fire]?   44

Bard. Well, the fuel is gone that maintain'd that fire. That's all the riches I got in his service.

Nym. Shall we shog? The King will be gone from Southampton.

Pist. Come, let's away. My love, give me thy lips.

Look to my chattels and my movables.   50
Let senses rule; the word is "Pitch and Pay."
Trust none;
For oaths are straws, men's faiths are wafer-
      cakes,
And hold-fast is the only dog, my duck;
Therefore, *Caveto* be thy counsellor.   55
Go, clear thy crystals. Yoke-fellows in arms,
Let us to France; like horse-leeches, my boys,
To suck, to suck, the very blood to suck!

Boy. And that's but unwholesome food, they say.   60

Pist. Touch her soft mouth, and march.

Bard. Farewell, hostess.   [*Kissing her.*]

Nym. I cannot kiss; that is the humour of it; but, adieu.

Pist. Let housewifery appear. Keep close, I
      thee command.   65

Host. Farewell; adieu.   [*Exeunt.*]

[SCENE IV. *France. The King's palace.*]

Flourish. Enter the FRENCH KING, *the* DAUPHIN, *the* DUKES OF BERRI *and* BRETAGNE [*the* CONSTABLE, *and others*].

Fr. King. Thus comes the English with full
      power upon us,
And more than carefully it us concerns
To answer royally in our defences.
Therefore the Dukes of Berri and of Bretagne,
Of Brabant and of Orleans, shall make forth,   5
And you, Prince Dauphin, with all swift dispatch,
To line and new repair our towns of war

With men of courage and with means defendant;
For England his approaches makes as fierce
As waters to the sucking of a gulf.   10
It fits us then to be as provident
As fears may teach us out of late examples
Left by the fatal and neglected English
Upon our fields.

Dau.   My most redoubted father,
It is most meet we arm us 'gainst the foe;   15
For peace itself should not so dull a kingdom
(Though war nor no known quarrel were in ques-
      tion)
But that defences, musters, preparations,
Should be maintain'd, assembled, and collected,
As were a war in expectation.   20
Therefore, I say, 'tis meet we all go forth
To view the sick and feeble parts of France.
And let us do it with no show of fear;
No, with no more than if we heard that England
Were busied with a Whitsun morris-dance;   25
For, my good liege, she is so idly king'd,
Her sceptre so fantastically borne
By a vain, giddy, shallow, humorous youth,
That fear attends her not.

Con.   O peace, Prince Dauphin!
You are too much mistaken in this king.   30
Question your Grace the late ambassadors
With what great state he heard their embassy,
How well supplied with noble counsellors,
How modest in exception, and withal
How terrible in constant resolution.   35
And you shall find his vanities forespent
Were but the outside of the Roman Brutus,
Covering discretion with a coat of folly,
As gardeners do with ordure hide those roots
That shall first spring and be most delicate.   40

Dau. Well, 'tis not so, my Lord High Constable;
But though we think it so, it is no matter.
In cases of defense 'tis best to weigh
The enemy more mighty than he seems,
So the proportions of defence are fill'd;   45
Which, of a weak and niggardly projection,
Doth, like a miser, spoil his coat with scanting
A little cloth.

Fr. King.   Think we King Harry strong;
And, Princes, look you strongly arm to meet him.
The kindred of him hath been flesh'd upon us;   50
And he is bred out of that bloody strain
That haunted us in our familiar paths.
Witness our too much memorable shame
When Cressy battle fatally was struck,
And all our princes captiv'd by the hand   55
Of that black name, Edward, Black Prince of Wales;

---

39. **handle:** talk of. 40. **rheumatic.** She probably means *lunatic.* 44. **[hell-fire]** Q. *Hell* F. 55. *Caveto:* be cautious. Sc. **iv,** 7. **line:** garrison. 10. **gulf:** whirlpool. 13. **fatal and:** fatally. 28. **humorous:** capricious. 34. **exception:** raising objections. 36. **forespent:** former. 37. Brutus pretended madness to conceal conspiracy against Tarquin. 46. **projection:** scale. 50. **flesh'd upon us:** fed on our flesh.

Whiles that his mountain sire, on mountain stand-
    ing,
Up in the air, crown'd with the golden sun,
Saw his heroical seed, and smil'd to see him,
Mangle the work of nature and deface   60
The patterns that by God and by French fathers
Had twenty years been made. This is a stem
Of that victorious stock; and let us fear
The native mightiness and fate of him.

Enter a MESSENGER.

Mess. Ambassadors from Harry King of England
Do crave admittance to your Majesty.   66
    Fr. King. We'll give them present audience.
    Go, and bring them.
        [Exeunt Messenger and certain Lords.]
You see this chase is hotly follow'd, friends.
    Dau. Turn head, and stop pursuit; for coward
    dogs
Most spend their mouths when what they seem to
    threaten   70
Runs far before them. Good my sovereign,
Take up the English short, and let them know
Of what a monarchy you are the head.
Self-love, my liege, is not so vile a sin
As self-neglecting.

Enter EXETER.

    Fr. King.   From our brother of England?
    Exe. From him; and thus he greets your Majesty:
He wills you, in the name of God Almighty,   77
That you divest yourself, and lay apart
The borrowed glories that by gift of heaven,
By law of nature and of nations, 'longs   80
To him and to his heirs; namely, the crown
And all wide-stretched honours that pertain
By custom and the ordinance of times
Unto the crown of France. That you may know
'Tis no sinister nor no awkward claim   85
Pick'd from the worm-holes of long-vanish'd days,
Nor from the dust of old oblivion rak'd,
He sends you this most memorable line,
In every branch truly demonstrative;
Willing you overlook this pedigree;   90
And when you find him evenly deriv'd
From his most fam'd of famous ancestors,
Edward the Third, he bids you then resign
Your crown and kingdom, indirectly held
From him, the native and true challenger.   95
    Fr. King. Or else what follows?
    Exe. Bloody constraint; for if you hide the crown
Even in your hearts, there will he rake for it.
Therefore in fierce tempest is he coming,

In thunder and in earthquake, like a Jove,   100
That, if requiring fail, he will compel;
And bids you, in the bowels of the Lord,
Deliver up the crown, and to take mercy
On the poor souls for whom this hungry war
Opens his vasty jaws; and on your head   105
Turning the widows' tears, the orphans' cries,
The dead men's blood, the [pining] maidens' groans,
For husbands, fathers, and betrothed lovers,
That shall be swallowed in this controversy.
This is his claim, his threat'ning, and my message;
Unless the Dauphin be in presence here,   111
To whom expressly I bring greeting too.
    Fr. King. For us, we will consider of this
    further.
To-morrow shall you bear our full intent   114
Back to our brother of England.
    Dau.   For the Dauphin,
I stand here for him. What to him from Eng-
    land?
    Exe. Scorn and defiance. Slight regard, con-
    tempt,
And anything that may not misbecome
The mighty sender, doth he prize you at.
Thus says my king: an if your father's Highness 120
Do not, in grant of all demands at large,
Sweeten the bitter mock you sent his Majesty,
He'll call you to so hot an answer of it
That caves and womby vaultages of France
Shall chide your trespass and return your mock 125
In second accent of his ordinance.
    Dau. Say, if my father render fair return,
It is against my will; for I desire
Nothing but odds with England. To that end,
As matching to his youth and vanity,   130
I did present him with the Paris balls.
    Exe. He'll make your Paris Louvre shake for it,
Were it the mistress-court of mighty Europe;
And, be assur'd, you'll find a difference,
As we his subjects have in wonder found,   135
Between the promise of his greener days
And these he masters now. Now he weighs time
Even to the utmost grain. That you shall read
In your own losses, if he stay in France.
    Fr. King. To-morrow shall you know our mind
    at full.   *[Flourish.* 140
    Exe. Dispatch us with all speed, lest that our
    king
Come here himself to question our delay;
For he is footed in this land already.
    Fr. King. You shall be soon dispatch'd with fair
    conditions.
A night is but small breath and little pause   145
To answer matters of this consequence.   *[Exeunt.*

57. **mountain:** imposing. 64. **fate of him:** what his destiny holds. 85. **sinister:** illegitimate. 88. **line:** genealogical
table. 94. **indirectly:** unjustly. 107. **[pining]** Q. *privy* F. 124. **womby vaultages:** hollow caverns. 126. **second...**
ordinance: echo of his ordnance, or artillery.

ACT [III]

[PROLOGUE]

Flourish. Enter CHORUS.

[*Chor.*] Thus with imagin'd wing our swift scene
    flies
In motion of no less celerity
Than that of thought. Suppose that you have seen
The well-appointed king at [Hampton] pier
Embark his royalty, and his brave fleet   5
With silken streamers the young Phœbus fanning.
Play with your fancies, and in them behold
Upon the hempen tackle ship-boys climbing;
Hear the shrill whistle which doth order give
To sounds confus'd; behold the threaden sails,   10
Borne with th' invisible and creeping wind,
Draw the huge bottoms through the furrowed sea,
Breasting the lofty surge. O, do but think
You stand upon the rivage and behold
A city on th' inconstant billows dancing;   15
For so appears this fleet majestical,
Holding due course to Harfleur. Follow, follow!
Grapple your minds to sternage of this navy,
And leave your England, as dead midnight still,
Guarded with grandsires, babies, and old women,
Either past or not arriv'd to pith and puissance. 21
For who is he, whose chin is but enrich'd
With one appearing hair, that will not follow
These cull'd and choice-drawn cavaliers to France?
Work, work your thoughts, and therein see a siege;
Behold the ordnance on their carriages,   26
With fatal mouths gaping on girded Harfleur.
Suppose th' ambassador from the French comes
    back,
Tells Harry that the King doth offer him
Katharine his daughter, and with her, to dowry, 30
Some petty and unprofitable dukedoms.
The offer likes not; and the nimble gunner
With linstock now the devilish cannon touches,
              [*Alarum, and chambers go off.*
And down goes all before them. Still be kind,
And eke out our performance with your mind. 35
                      [*Exit.*

[SCENE I. *France. Before*] Harfleur.

Alarum. Enter KING HENRY, EXETER, BEDFORD,
  GLOUCESTER, [*and* Soldiers, *with*] *scaling-ladders.*

K. Hen. Once more unto the breach, dear friends,
    once more,
Or close the wall up with our English dead.
In peace there's nothing so becomes a man
As modest stillness and humility;
But when the blast of war blows in our ears,   5
Then imitate the action of the tiger;
Stiffen the sinews, summon up the blood,
Disguise fair nature with hard-favour'd rage;
Then lend the eye a terrible aspect;
Let it pry through the portage of the head   10
Like the brass cannon; let the brow o'erwhelm it
As fearfully as doth a galled rock
O'erhang and jutty his confounded base,
Swill'd with the wild and wasteful ocean.
Now set the teeth and stretch the nostril wide,   15
Hold hard the breath, and bend up every spirit
To his full height. On, on, you [noblest] English,
Whose blood is fet from fathers of war-proof!
Fathers that, like so many Alexanders,
Have in these parts from morn till even fought, 20
And sheath'd their swords for lack of argument.
Dishonour not your mothers; now attest
That those whom you call'd fathers did beget you.
Be copy now to men of grosser blood,
And teach them how to war. And you, good yeo-
    men,   25
Whose limbs were made in England, show us here
The mettle of your pasture; let us swear
That you are worth your breeding, which I doubt
    not;
For there is none of you so mean and base
That hath not noble lustre in your eyes.   30
I see you stand like greyhounds in the slips,
[Straining] upon the start. The game's afoot!
Follow your spirit, and upon this charge
Cry, "God for Harry! England and Saint George!"
           [*Exeunt.*] *Alarum, and chambers go off.*

[SCENE II. *The same.*]

Enter NYM, BARDOLPH, PISTOL, *and* BOY.

Bard. On, on, on, on, on! To the breach, to
the breach!

Nym. Pray thee, corporal, stay. The knocks
are too hot; and, for mine own part, I have not a
case of lives. The humour of it is too hot; that is
the very plain-song of it.   6

Pist. The plain-song is most just, for humours
do abound.

"Knocks go and come; God's vassals drop and die;
      And sword and shield,
        In bloody field,   10
Doth win immortal fame."

Boy. Would I were in an alehouse in London!

Act III, Prol., 1. **imagin'd wing**: wing of imagination. 4. **[Hampton]** (Theobald). *Dover* F. 14. **rivage**: shore. 18.
sternage: the sterns. 32. **likes**: pleases. 33. **linstock**: stick holding the match. s.d. **chambers**: small cannon.
    Sc. i, 10. **portage**: port-holes. 11. **o'erwhelm**: overhang. 12. **galled**: worn away. 13. **jutty**: project over. **confounded**:
wasted away. 14. **Swill'd**: washed. 17. **[noblest]** F₂. *noblish* F₁. 18. **fet**: fetched. 21. **argument**: cause of quarrel.
31. **slips**: leash. 32. **[Straining]** (Rowe). *Straying* F.
    Sc. ii, 5. **case**: set. 6. **plain-song**: simple melody.

I would give all my fame for a pot of ale and safety.

Pist. And I.   15

"If wishes would prevail with me,
My purpose should not fail with me,
But thither would I hie."

Boy. "As duly, but not as truly,
     As bird doth sing on bough."   20

Enter FLUELLEN.

Flu. Up to the breach, you dogs! Avaunt, you
cullions!   [*Driving them forward.*]
Pist. Be merciful, great Duke, to men of mould.
Abate thy rage, abate thy manly rage,
Abate thy rage, great Duke!   25
Good bawcock, bate thy rage; use lenity, sweet
chuck!
Nym. These be good humours! Your honour
wins bad humours.   [*Exeunt [all but Boy].*]
Boy. As young as I am, I have observ'd these
three swashers. I am boy to them all three; but   30
all they three, though they would serve me, could
not be man to me; for indeed three such antics do
not amount to a man. For Bardolph, he is white-
liver'd and red-fac'd; by the means whereof 'a faces
it out, but fights not. For Pistol, he hath a   35
killing tongue and a quiet sword; by the means
whereof 'a breaks words, and keeps whole weapons.
For Nym, he hath heard that men of few words are
the best men; and therefore he scorns to say his
prayers, lest 'a should be thought a coward. But   40
his few bad words are match'd with as few good
deeds; for 'a never broke any man's head but his
own, and that was against a post when he was drunk.
They will steal anything, and call it purchase.
Bardolph stole a lute-case, bore it twelve   45
leagues, and sold it for three half-pence. Nym
and Bardolph are sworn brothers in filching, and
in Calais they stole a fire-shovel. I knew by that
piece of service the men would carry coals. They
would have me as familiar with men's pockets   50
as their gloves or their handkerchers; which makes
much against my manhood, if I should take from
another's pocket to put into mine; for it is plain
pocketing up of wrongs. I must leave them, and
seek some better service. Their villainy goes   55
against my weak stomach, and therefore I must
cast it up.   [*Exit.*

Enter GOWER [*and* FLUELLEN].

Gow. Captain Fluellen, you must come presently
to the mines. The Duke of Gloucester would
speak with you.   60

Flu. To the mines! Tell you the Duke, it is not
so good to come to the mines; for, look you, the
mines is not according to the disciplines of the war.
The concavities of it is not sufficient; for, look you,
the athversary, you may discuss unto the Duke,
look you, is digt himself four yard under [with]
countermines. By Cheshu, I think 'a will plow
up all, if there is not better directions.   68
Gow. The Duke of Gloucester, to whom the
order of the siege is given, is altogether directed
by an Irishman, a very valiant gentleman, i' faith.
Flu. It is Captain Macmorris, is it not?
Gow. I think it be.   73
Flu. By Cheshu, he is an ass, as in the world.
I will verify as much in his beard. He has no more
directions in the true disciplines of the wars, look
you, of the Roman disciplines, than is a puppy-dog.

Enter MACMORRIS *and* CAPTAIN JAMY.

Gow. Here 'a comes; and the Scots captain,
Captain Jamy with him.   80
Flu. Captain Jamy is a marvellous falorous
gentleman, that is certain; and of great expedition
and knowledge in th' aunchient wars, upon my
particular knowledge of his directions. By Cheshu,
he will maintain his argument as well as any military
man in the world, in the disciplines of the pristine
wars of the Romans.   87
Jamy. I say gud-day, Captain Fluellen.
Flu. God-den to your worship, good Captain
James.
Gow. How now, Captain Macmorris! have you
quit the mines? Have the pioners given o'er?   92
Mac. By Chrish, la! 'tish ill done. The work ish
give over, the trompet sound the retreat. By my
hand I swear, and my father's soul, the work ish ill
done; it ish give over. I would have blowed up the
town, so Chrish save me, la! in an hour. O, 'tish ill
done, 'tish ill done; by my hand, 'tish ill done!   99
Flu. Captain Macmorris, I beseech you now,
will you voutsafe me, look you, a few disputations
with you, as partly touching or concerning the disciplines of the war, the Roman wars, in the way of
argument, look you, and friendly communication;
partly to satisfy my opinion, and partly for the   105
satisfaction, look you, of my mind, as touching the
direction of the military discipline; that is the point.
Jamy. It sall be very gud, gud feith, gud captains bath: and I sall quit you with gud leve, as I
may pick occasion; that sall I, marry.   111
Mac. It is no time to discourse, so Chrish save
me. The day is hot, and the weather, and the wars,
and the King, and the Dukes. It is no time to discourse. The town is beseech'd, and the trumpet   115

---

22. **cullions:** scoundrels.   26. **bawcock:** Fr. *beau coq*, fine fellow.   32. **antics:** clowns.   49. **carry coals:** put up with an affront.   65. **discuss:** tell.   66. **[with]** (Vaughan). *the* F.   82. **expedition:** a blunder between *experience* and *erudition* (Evans).   92. **pioners:** trench and mine diggers.   110. **quit:** requite.

call us to the breach, and we talk, and, be Chrish, do
nothing. 'Tis shame for us all. So God sa' me, 'tis
shame to stand still; it is shame, by my hand; and
there is throats to be cut, and works to be done; and
there ish nothing done, so Chrish sa' me, la!   121

Jamy. By the mess, ere theise eyes of mine take
themselves to slomber, I'll de gud service, or I'll
lig i' the grund for it; ay, or go to death; and I'll
pay't as valourously as I may, that sall I suerly
do, that is the breff and the long. Marry, I wad
full fain heard some question 'tween you tway.   128

Flu. Captain Macmorris, I think, look you,
under your correction, there is not many of your
nation —   131

Mac. Of my nation! What ish my nation? Ish
a villain, and a bastard, and a knave, and a rascal?
What ish my nation? Who talks of my nation? 135

Flu. Look you, if you take the matter otherwise
than is meant, Captain Macmorris, peradventure
I shall think you do not use me with that affability
as in discretion you ought to use me, look you, being
as good a man as yourself, both in the disciplines of
war, and in the derivation of my birth, and in other
particularities.   142

Mac. I do not know you so good a man as myself. So Chrish save me, I will cut off your head.

Gow. Gentlemen both, you will mistake each
other.

Jamy. Ah! that's a foul fault.

[*A parley* [*sounded*].

Gow. The town sounds a parley.   149

Flu. Captain Macmorris, when there is more better opportunity to be required, look you, I will be
so bold as to tell you I know the disciplines of war;
and there is an end.   [*Exeunt.* 153

[SCENE III. *The same.*] *Before the gates.*

[*The* GOVERNOR *and some* Citizens *on the walls; the*
English forces below.] *Enter* KING HENRY *and his*
train.

K. Hen. How yet resolves the governor of the
town?
This is the latest parle we will admit;
Therefore to our best mercy give yourselves,
Or like to men proud of destruction
Defy us to our worst; for, as I am a soldier,   5
A name that in my thoughts becomes me best,
If I begin the batt'ry once again,
I will not leave the half-achieved Harfleur
Till in her ashes she lies buried.
The gates of mercy shall be all shut up,   10
And the flesh'd soldier, rough and hard of heart,
In liberty of bloody hand shall range

With conscience wide as hell, mowing like grass
Your fresh fair virgins and your flow'ring infants.
What is it then to me, if impious War,   15
Array'd in flames like to the prince of fiends,
Do with his smirch'd complexion all fell feats
Enlink'd to waste and desolation?
What is't to me, when you yourselves are cause,
If your pure maidens fall into the hand   20
Of hot and forcing violation?
What rein can hold licentious wickedness
When down the hill he holds his fierce career?
We may as bootless spend our vain command
Upon th' enraged soldiers in their spoil   25
As send precepts to the leviathan
To come ashore. Therefore, you men of Harfleur,
Take pity of your town and of your people,
Whiles yet my soldiers are in my command,
Whiles yet the cool and temperate wind of grace 30
O'erblows the filthy and contagious clouds
Of heady murder, spoil, and villainy.
If not, why, in a moment look to see
The blind and bloody soldier with foul hand
[Defile] the locks of your shrill-shrieking daughters;
Your fathers taken by the silver beards,   36
And their most reverend heads dash'd to the walls;
Your naked infants spitted upon pikes,
Whiles the mad mothers with their howls confus'd
Do break the clouds, as did the wives of Jewry 40
At Herod's bloody-hunting slaughtermen.
What say you? Will you yield and this avoid,
Or, guilty in defence, be thus destroy'd?

Gov. Our expectation hath this day an end.
The Dauphin, whom of succours we entreated, 45
Returns us that his powers are yet not ready
To raise so great a siege. Therefore, great King,
We yield our town and lives to thy soft mercy.
Enter our gates; dispose of us and ours;
For we no longer are defensible.   50

K. Hen. Open your gates. Come, uncle Exeter,
Go you and enter Harfleur; there remain,
And fortify it strongly 'gainst the French.
Use mercy to them all. For us, dear uncle,
The winter coming on, and sickness growing 55
Upon our soldiers, we will retire to Calais.
To-night in Harfleur will we be your guest;
To-morrow for the march are we addrest.

[*Flourish.* [*The King and his train*] *enter*
the town.

[SCENE IV. *The French King's palace.*]

Enter KATHARINE *and* [ALICE] *an old Gentlewoman.*

Kath. Alice, tu as été en Angleterre, et tu parles
bien le langage.

124. lig: lie.
Sc. iii, 32. **heady**: headstrong. 35. **[Defile]** (Rowe). *Desire* F. 41. **Herod's.** See *Matthew* II.16–18.
Sc. iv. The French of this scene has been corrected by successive editors. In F it is about as accurate as the Welsh, Irish,
and Scottish dialect in Sc. ii.

Alice. Un peu, madame.

Kath. Je te prie, m'enseignez; il faut que j'apprenne à parler.   Comment appelez-vous la main en Anglois?   6

Alice. La main?   Elle est appelée de hand.

Kath. De hand.   Et les doigts?

Alice. Les doigts?   Ma foi, j'oublie les doigts; mais je me souviendrai.   Les doigts?   Je pense qu'ils sont appelés de fingres; oui, de fingres.   11

Kath. La main, de hand; les doigts, de fingres. Je pense que je suis le bon écolier; j'ai gagné deux mots d'Anglois vîtement.   Comment appelez-vous les ongles?   15

Alice. Les ongles?   Nous les appelons de nails.

Kath. De nails.   Écoutez; dites-moi, si je parle bien: de hand, de fingres, et de nails.

Alice. C'est bien dit, madame; il est fort bon Anglois.   20

Kath. Dites-moi l'Anglois pour le bras.

Alice. De arm, madame.

Kath. Et le coude?

Alice. D'elbow.   24

Kath. D'elbow.   Je m'en fais la répétition de tous les mots que vous m'avez appris dès à présent.

Alice. Il est trop difficile, madame, comme je pense.

Kath. Excusez-moi, Alice; écoutez: D'hand, de fingres, de nails, d'arma, de bilbow.   31

Alice. D'elbow, madame.

Kath. O Seigneur Dieu, je m'en oublie!   D' elbow.   Comment appelez-vous le col?

Alice. De nick, madame.   35

Kath. De nick.   Et le menton?

Alice. De chin.

Kath. De sin.   Le col, de nick; le menton, de sin.

Alice. Oui.   Sauf votre honneur, en vérité,   40 vous prononcez les mots aussi droit que les natifs d'Angleterre.

Kath. Je ne doute point d'apprendre, par la grace de Dieu, et en peu de temps.   44

Alice. N'avez vous pas déjà oublié ce que je vous ai enseigné?

Kath. Non, je reciterai à vous promptement: d' hand, de fingres, de mails, —

Alice. De nails, madame.

Kath. De nails, de arm, de ilbow.   50

Alice. Sauf votre honneur, de elbow.

Kath. Ainsi dis-je; d'elbow, de nick, et de sin. Comment appelez-vous le pied et la robe?

Alice. De foot, madame; et de coun.   54

Kath. De foot et de coun!   O Seigneur Dieu! ce sont mots de son mauvais, corruptible, gros, et impudique, et non pour les dames d'honneur d'user. Je ne voudrais prononcer ces mots devant les seig-

neurs de France pour tout le monde.   Foh! le foot et le coun!   Néanmoins, je réciterai une autre   60 fois ma leçon ensemble: d'hand, de fingres, de nails, d'arm, d'elbow, de nick, de sin, de foot, de coun.

Alice. Excellent, madame!

Kath. C'est assez pour une fois: allons-nous à dîner.   *[Exeunt.* 66

[SCENE V. *The same.*]

Enter the KING OF FRANCE, *the* DAUPHIN, [*the* DUKE OF BOURBON,] *the* CONSTABLE OF FRANCE, *and others.*

Fr. King. 'Tis certain he hath pass'd the river Somme.

Con. An if he be not fought withal, my lord,
Let us not live in France; let us quit all
And give our vineyards to a barbarous people.

Dau. O Dieu vivant! shall a few sprays of us,   5
The emptying of our fathers' luxury,
Our scions put in wild and savage stock,
Spirt up so suddenly into the clouds
And overlook their grafters?

Bour. Normans, but bastard Normans, Norman
bastards!   10
Mort de ma vie! if they march along
Unfought withal, but I will sell my dukedom,
To buy a slobbery and a dirty farm
In that nook-shotten isle of Albion.

Con. Dieu de batailles! where have they this
mettle?   15
Is not their climate foggy, raw, and dull,
On whom, as in despite, the sun looks pale,
Killing their fruit with frowns?   Can sodden water,
A drench for sur-rein'd jades, their barley-broth,
Decoct their cold blood to such valiant heat?   20
And shall our quick blood, spirited with wine,
Seem frosty?   O, for honour of our land,
Let us not hang like roping icicles
Upon our houses' thatch, whiles a more frosty
people
Sweat drops of gallant youth in our rich fields!   25
Poor we [may] call them in their native lords.

Dau. By faith and honour,
Our madams mock at us, and plainly say
Our mettle is bred out, and they will give
Their bodies to the lust of English youth   30
To new-store France with bastard warriors.

Bour. They bid us to the English dancing-schools,
And teach lavoltas high and swift corantos,
Saying our grace is only in our heels,
And that we are most lofty runaways.   35

Fr. King. Where is Montjoy the herald?   Speed
him hence.

Sc. v, 6. **luxury:** lust.   7. **put in:** grafted upon.   14. **nook-shotten:** running out into corners.   18. **sodden:** boiled.   19. **drench...jades:** drink for over-worked horses.   20. **Decoct:** warm.   26. **[may]** F2.   Om. F1.   33. **lavoltas, corantos:** dances.

Let him greet England with our sharp defiance.
Up, princes! and, with spirit of honour edg'd
More sharper than your swords, hie to the field!
Charles Delabreth, High Constable of France;   40
You Dukes of Orleans, Bourbon, and of Berri,
Alençon, Brabant, Bar, and Burgundy;
Jacques Chatillon, Rambures, Vaudemont,
Beaumont, Grandpré, Roussi, and Fauconberg,
Foix, Lestrale, Bouciqualt, and Charolois;   45
High dukes, great princes, barons, lords, and
    [knights],
For your great seats now quit you of great shames.
Bar Harry England, that sweeps through our land
With pennons painted in the blood of Harfleur.
Rush on his host, as doth the melted snow   50
Upon the valleys, whose low vassal seat
The Alps doth spit and void his rheum upon.
Go down upon him, you have power enough,
And in a captive chariot into Rouen
Bring him our prisoner.
    Con.   This becomes the great.
Sorry am I his numbers are so few,   56
His soldiers sick and famish'd in their march;
For I am sure, when he shall see our army,
He'll drop his heart into the sink of fear
And for achievement offer us his ransom.   60
    Fr. King. Therefore, Lord Constable, haste on
        Montjoy,
And let him say to England that we send
To know what willing ransom he will give.
Prince Dauphin, you shall stay with us in Rouen.
    Dau. Not so, I do beseech your Majesty.   65
    Fr. King. Be patient, for you shall remain with
        us.
Now forth, Lord Constable and princes all,
And quickly bring us word of England's fall.
                    [*Exeunt.*

[SCENE VI. *The English camp in Picardy.*]

Enter GOWER *and* FLUELLEN [*meeting*].

    Gow. How now, Captain Fluellen! come you from
the bridge?
    Flu. I assure you, there is very excellent services
committed at the bridge.
    Gow. Is the Duke of Exeter safe?   5
    Flu. The Duke of Exeter is as magnanimous as
Agamemnon; and a man that I love and honour
with my soul, and my heart, and my duty, and my
live, and my living, and my uttermost power. He
is not — God be praised and blessed! — any   10
hurt in the world; but keeps the bridge most val-

iantly, with excellent discipline. There is an
aunchient lieutenant there at the pridge, I think
in my very conscience he is as valiant a man as
Mark Antony; and he is a man of no estimation   15
in the world, but I did see him do as gallant service.
    Gow. What do you call him?
    Flu. He is called Aunchient Pistol.
    Gow. I know him not.   20

Enter PISTOL.

    Flu. Here is the man.
    Pist. Captain, I thee beseech to do me favours.
The Duke of Exeter doth love thee well.
    Flu. Ay, I praise God; and I have merited some
love at his hands.   25
    Pist. Bardolph, a soldier, firm and sound of heart,
And of buxom valour, hath, by cruel fate,
And giddy Fortune's furious fickle wheel,
That goddess blind,
That stands upon the rolling restless stone —   30
    Flu. By your patience, Aunchient Pistol. For-
tune is painted blind, with a muffler afore his eyes,
to signify to you that Fortune is blind; and she is
painted also with a wheel, to signify to you, which
is the moral of it, that she is turning, and incon-   35
stant, and mutability, and variation; and her foot,
look you, is fixed upon a spherical stone, which
rolls, and rolls, and rolls. In good truth, the poet
makes a most excellent description of it. Fortune
is an excellent moral.   40
    Pist. Fortune is Bardolph's foe, and frowns on
    him;
For he hath stolen a pax, and hanged must 'a be, —
A damned death!
Let gallows gape for dog; let man go free,
And let not hemp his windpipe suffocate.   45
But Exeter hath given the doom of death
For pax of little price.
Therefore, go speak; the Duke will hear thy voice;
And let not Bardolph's vital thread be cut
With edge of penny cord and vile reproach.   50
Speak, captain, for his life, and I will thee requite.
    Flu. Aunchient Pistol, I do partly understand
your meaning.
    Pist. Why then, rejoice therefore.   54
    Flu. Certainly, aunchient, it is not a thing to
rejoice at; for if, look you, he were my brother, I
would desire the Duke to use his good pleasure, and
put him to execution; for discipline ought to be
used.
    Pist. Die and be damn'd! and *figo* for thy friend-
ship!   60

---

46. [knights] (Pope). *Kings* F.   47. quit: clear.   52. rheum: used of any watery discharge.   60. for achievement: in
place of victory.
    Sc. vi, 27. buxom: lively.   42. pax: a piece of metal with the figure of Christ stamped on it. It is probably a mistake for
Holinshed's *pyx*, the box containing the sacramental wafer.   60. *figo:* fig, a contemptuous gesture made by thrusting the
thumb between the next two fingers, or between the teeth.

Flu. It is well.

Pist. The fig of Spain.   [*Exit.*

Flu. Very good.

Gow. Why, this is an arrant counterfeit rascal.
I remember him now; a bawd, a cutpurse.   65

Flu. I'll assure you, 'a utt'red as prave words at
the pridge as you shall see in a summer's day. But
it is very well; what he has spoke to me, that is well,
I warrant you, when time is serve.   69

Gow. Why, 'tis a gull, a fool, a rogue, that now
and then goes to the wars, to grace himself at his
return into London under the form of a soldier.
And such fellows are perfect in the great commanders' names; and they will learn you by rote
where services were done; at such and such a   75
sconce, at such a breach, at such a convoy; who
came off bravely, who was shot, who disgrac'd, what
terms the enemy stood on; and this they con perfectly in the phrase of war, which they trick up with
new-tuned oaths: and what a beard of the   80
general's cut and a horrid suit of the camp will do
among foaming bottles and ale-wash'd wits, is
wonderful to be thought on. But you must learn
to know such slanders of the age, or else you may be
marvellously mistook.   85

Flu. I tell you what, Captain Gower; I do perceive he is not the man that he would gladly make
show to the world he is. If I find a hole in his coat,
I will tell him my mind. [*Drum heard.*] Hark you,
the King is coming, and I must speak with him from
the pridge.   91

Drum and colours. Enter KING HENRY,
[GLOUCESTER,] *and his poor* Soldiers.

God bless your Majesty!

K. Hen. How now, Fluellen! cam'st thou from
the bridge?

Flu. Ay, so please your Majesty. The Duke of
Exeter has very gallantly maintain'd the pridge. 95
The French is gone off, look you; and there is gallant
and most prave passages. Marry, th' athversary
was have possession of the pridge; but he is enforced to retire, and the Duke of Exeter is master of
the pridge. I can tell your Majesty, the Duke is a
prave man.   101

K. Hen. What men have you lost, Fluellen?

Flu. The perdition of th' athversary hath been
very great, reasonable great. Marry, for my part,
I think the Duke hath lost never a man, but one 105
that is like to be executed for robbing a church, one
Bardolph, if your Majesty know the man. His face
is all bubukles, and whelks, and knobs, and flames
o' fire; and his lips blows at his nose, and it is like a

coal of fire, sometimes plue and sometimes red; but
his nose is executed, and his fire's out.   112

K. Hen. We would have all such offenders so
cut off; and we give express charge, that in our
marches through the country, there be nothing   115
compell'd from the villages, nothing taken but paid
for, none of the French upbraided or abused in disdainful language; for when lenity and cruelty play
for a kingdom, the gentler gamester is the soonest
winner.   120

Tucket. Enter MONTJOY.

Mont. You know me by my habit.

K. Hen. Well then I know thee. What shall I
know of thee?

Mont. My master's mind.

K. Hen. Unfold it.   124

Mont. Thus says my King: Say thou to Harry of
England: Though we seem'd dead, we did but
sleep; advantage is a better soldier than rashness.
Tell him we could have rebuk'd him at Harfleur, but
that we thought not good to bruise an injury till it
were full ripe. Now we speak upon our cue,   130
and our voice is imperial. England shall repent
his folly, see his weakness, and admire our sufferance. Bid him therefore consider of his ransom;
which must proportion the losses we have borne, the
subjects we have lost, the disgrace we have   135
digested; which in weight to re-answer, his pettiness
would bow under. For our losses, his exchequer
is too poor; for th' effusion of our blood, the muster
of his kingdom too faint a number; and for our disgrace, his own person, kneeling at our feet, but   140
a weak and worthless satisfaction. To this add
defiance; and tell him, for conclusion, he hath betrayed his followers, whose condemnation is pronounc'd. So far my King and master; so much my
office.   145

K. Hen. What is thy name? I know thy quality.

Mont. Montjoy.

K. Hen. Thou dost thy office fairly. Turn thee
back
And tell thy King I do not seek him now,
But could be willing to march on to Calais   150
Without impeachment; for, to say the sooth,
Though 'tis no wisdom to confess so much
Unto an enemy of craft and vantage,
My people are with sickness much enfeebled,
My numbers lessen'd, and those few I have   155
Almost no better than so many French;
Who when they were in health, I tell thee, herald,
I thought upon one pair of English legs
Did march three Frenchmen. Yet, forgive me,
God,

70. gull: simpleton. 76. sconce: part of a fortification. 108. bubukles: carbuncles. whelks: pimples. 119. gamester: player. s.d. Tucket: trumpet call. MONTJOY: title of the chief herald of France. 121. habit: herald's costume. 129.
injury: boil. 136. digested: put up with. 146. quality: profession. 151. impeachment: hindrance.

That I do brag thus! This your air of France   160
Hath blown that vice in me. I must repent.
Go therefore, tell thy master here I am;
My ransom is this frail and worthless trunk,
My army but a weak and sickly guard;
Yet, God before, tell him we will come on,   165
Though France himself and such another neighbour
Stand in our way. There's for thy labour, Montjoy.
Go, bid thy master well advise himself.
If we may pass, we will; if we be hind'red,   169
We shall your tawny ground with your red blood
Discolour; and so, Montjoy, fare you well.
The sum of all our answer is but this:
We would not seek a battle, as we are;
Nor, as we are, we say we will not shun it.
So tell your master.   175
    Mont. I shall deliver so. Thanks to your High-
       ness.   [*Exit.*]
    Glou. I hope they will not come upon us now.
    K. Hen. We are in God's hands, brother, not in
       theirs.
March to the bridge; it now draws toward night.
Beyond the river we'll encamp ourselves,   180
And on to-morrow bid them march away.
                                [*Exeunt.*

[SCENE VII. *The French camp, near Agincourt.*]

Enter the CONSTABLE OF FRANCE, *the* LORD
RAMBURES, ORLEANS, DAUPHIN, *with others.*

    Con. Tut! I have the best armour of the world.
Would it were day!
    Orl. You have an excellent armour; but let my
horse have his due.
    Con. It is the best horse of Europe.   5
    Orl. Will it never be morning?
    Dau. My Lord of Orleans, and my Lord High
Constable, you talk of horse and armour?
    Orl. You are as well provided of both as any
prince in the world.   10
    Dau. What a long night is this! I will not change
my horse with any that treads but on four [pas-
terns]. *Ça, ha!* he bounds from the earth, as if his
entrails were hairs; *le cheval volant,* the Pegasus,
[*avec*] *les narines de feu!* When I bestride him, I   15
soar, I am a hawk; he trots the air; the earth sings
when he touches it; the basest horn of his hoof is
more musical than the pipe of Hermes.
    Orl. He's of the colour of the nutmeg.   20
    Dau. And of the heat of the ginger. It is a beast
for Perseus. He is pure air and fire; and the dull
elements of earth and water never appear in him,

but only in patient stillness while his rider mounts
him. He is indeed a horse, and all other jades you
may call beasts.   26
    Con. Indeed, my lord, it is a most absolute and
excellent horse.
    Dau. It is the prince of palfreys; his neigh is like
the bidding of a monarch, and his countenance
enforces homage.   31
    Orl. No more, cousin.
    Dau. Nay, the man hath no wit that cannot,
from the rising of the lark to the lodging of the
lamb, vary deserved praise on my palfrey. It is   35
a theme as fluent as the sea; turn the sands into eloquent tongues, and my horse is argument for them
all. 'Tis a subject for a sovereign to reason on, and
for a sovereign's sovereign to ride on; and for the
world, familiar to us and unknown, to lay apart   40
their particular functions and wonder at him. I
once writ a sonnet in his praise and began thus:
"Wonder of nature," —
    Orl. I have heard a sonnet begin so to one's
mistress.   45
    Dau. Then did they imitate that which I com-
pos'd to my courser, for my horse is my mistress.
    Orl. Your mistress bears well.
    Dau. Me well; which is the prescript praise and
perfection of a good and particular mistress.   50
    Con. Nay, for methought yesterday your mis-
tress shrewdly shook your back.
    Dau. So perhaps did yours.
    Con. Mine was not bridled.   54
    Dau. O then belike she was old and gentle; and
you rode, like a kern of Ireland, your French hose
off, and in your strait strossers.
    Con. You have good judgement in horsemanship.
    Dau. Be warn'd by me, then; they that ride   60
so and ride not warily, fall into foul bogs. I had
rather have my horse to my mistress.
    Con. I had as lief have my mistress a jade.
    Dau. I tell thee, Constable, my mistress wears
his own hair.   65
    Con. I could make as true a boast as that, if I had
a sow to my mistress.
    Dau. "*Le chien est retourné à son propre vomisse-
ment, et la truie lavée au bourbier.*" Thou mak'st
use of anything.   70
    Con. Yet do I not use my horse for my mistress,
or any such proverb so little kin to the purpose.
    Ram. My Lord Constable, the armour that I saw
in your tent to-night, are those stars or suns upon
it?   75
    Con. Stars, my lord.

---

161. **blown:** fanned.
Sc. vii, 13. [**pasterns**] F₂. *postures* F₁. 14. **hairs:** like the stuffing of a tennis ball. **Pegasus:** the winged horse ridden by
Perseus (l. 22). 15. [*avec*] (Nicholson conj.) *chez* F. 34. **lodging:** lying down. 49. **prescript:** prescribed, proper. 50.
particular: belonging to me alone. 56. **kern:** soldier. **French hose:** wide breeches. 57. **strait strossers:** tight trousers.
Theobald says the Irish kerns, like the Scotch Highlanders, wore no breeches. 68-69. "*Le chien,* etc." See II *Peter,* ii.22.

Dau. Some of them will fall to-morrow, I hope.

Con. And yet my sky shall not want.

Dau. That may be, for you bear a many superfluously, and 'twere more honour some were away.   81

Con. Even as your horse bears your praises; who would trot as well, were some of your brags dismounted.

Dau. Would I were able to load him with his desert! Will it never be day? I will trot to-morrow a mile, and my way shall be paved with English faces.   88

Con. I will not say so, for fear I should be fac'd out of my way. But I would it were morning; for I would fain be about the ears of the English. 92

Ram. Who will go to hazard with me for twenty prisoners?

Con. You must first go yourself to hazard, ere you have them.   96

Dau. 'Tis midnight; I'll go arm myself. [*Exit.*

Orl. The Dauphin longs for morning.

Ram. He longs to eat the English.

Con. I think he will eat all he kills.   100

Orl. By the white hand of my lady, he's a gallant prince.

Con. Swear by her foot that she may tread out the oath.

Orl. He is simply the most active gentleman of France.   106

Con. Doing is activity; and he will still be doing.

Orl. He never did harm, that I heard of.

Con. Nor will do none to-morrow. He will keep that good name still.   111

Orl. I know him to be valiant.

Con. I was told that by one that knows him better than you.

Orl. What's he?   115

Con. Marry, he told me so himself; and he said he car'd not who knew it.

Orl. He needs not; it is no hidden virtue in him.   119

Con. By my faith, sir, but it is; never anybody saw it but his lackey. 'Tis a hooded valour; and when it appears, it will bate.

Orl. "Ill will never said well."

Con. I will cap that proverb with "There is flattery in friendship."   125

Orl. And I will take up that with "Give the devil his due."

Con. Well plac'd. There stands your friend for the devil; have at the very eye of that proverb with "A pox of the devil."   130

Orl. You are the better at proverbs, by how

much "A fool's bolt is soon shot."

Con. You have shot over.

Orl. 'Tis not the first time you were overshot.

Enter a MESSENGER.

Mess. My Lord High Constable, the English lie within fifteen hundred paces of your tents.   136

Con. Who hath measur'd the ground?

Mess. The Lord Grandpré.

Con. A valiant and most expert gentleman Would it were day! Alas, poor Harry of England, he longs not for the dawning as we do.   141

Orl. What a wretched and peevish fellow is this King of England, to mope with his fat-brain'd followers so far out of his knowledge!

Con. If the English had any apprehension, they would run away.   146

Orl. That they lack; for if their heads had any intellectual armour, they could never wear such heavy head-pieces.

Ram. That island of England breeds very valiant creatures. Their mastiffs are of unmatchable courage.   152

Orl. Foolish curs, that run winking into the mouth of a Russian bear and have their heads crush'd like rotten apples! You may as well say, that's a valiant flea that dare eat his breakfast on the lip of a lion.   157

Con. Just, just; and the men do sympathize with the mastiffs in robustious and rough coming on, leaving their wits with their wives; and then, give them great meals of beef and iron and steel, they will eat like wolves and fight like devils.   162

Orl. Ay, but these English are shrewdly out of beef.

Con. Then shall we find to-morrow they have only stomachs to eat and none to fight. Now is the time to arm. Come, shall we about it?   167

Orl. It is now two o'clock; but, let me see, by ten We shall have each a hundred Englishmen.

[*Exeunt.*

ACT [IV]

[PROLOGUE]

[*Enter* CHORUS.]

Chor. Now entertain conjecture of a time When creeping murmur and the poring dark Fills the wide vessel of the universe. From camp to camp through the foul womb of night The hum of either army stilly sounds,   5 That the fix'd sentinels almost receive

121–122. **hooded ... bate.** A hawk was hooded till the game was in sight. **bate:** (1) to flap the wings, (2) to be downcast. 142. **peevish:** silly. 143. **mope:** wander in a daze. 158. **sympathize with:** resemble.

Act IV, Prol., 1. **conjecture:** supposition. 2. **poring dark:** the dark in which people strain to see.

The secret whispers of each other's watch;
Fire answers fire, and through their paly flames
Each battle sees the other's umber'd face;
Steed threatens steed, in high and boastful neighs 10
Piercing the night's dull ear; and from the tents
The armourers, accomplishing the knights,
With busy hammers closing rivets up,
Give dreadful note of preparation.
The country cocks do crow, the clocks do toll, 15
And the third hour of drowsy morning [name].
Proud of their numbers and secure in soul,
The confident and over-lusty French
Do the low-rated English play at dice;
And chide the cripple tardy-gaited Night 20
Who, like a foul and ugly witch, doth limp
So tediously away. The poor condemned English,
Like sacrifices, by their watchful fires
Sit patiently and inly ruminate
The morning's danger; and their gesture sad, 25
Investing lank-lean cheeks and war-worn coats,
Presented them unto the gazing moon
So many horrid ghosts. O now, who will behold
The royal captain of this ruin'd band
Walking from watch to watch, from tent to tent, 30
Let him cry, "Praise and glory on his head!"
For forth he goes and visits all his host,
Bids them good morrow with a modest smile,
And calls them brothers, friends, and countrymen.
Upon his royal face there is no note 35
How dread an army hath enrounded him;
Nor doth he dedicate one jot of colour
Unto the weary and all-watched night,
But freshly looks, and over-bears attaint
With cheerful semblance and sweet majesty; 40
That every wretch, pining and pale before,
Beholding him, plucks comfort from his looks.
A largess universal like the sun
His liberal eye doth give to every one,
Thawing cold fear, that mean and gentle all 45
Behold, as may unworthiness define,
A little touch of Harry in the night.
And so our scene must to the battle fly,
Where — O for pity! — we shall much disgrace
With four or five most vile and ragged foils, 50
Right ill-dispos'd in brawl ridiculous,
The name of Agincourt. Yet sit and see,
Minding true things by what their mockeries be.
                             [*Exit.*

[SCENE I. *The English camp at Agincourt.*]

Enter KING HENRY, BEDFORD, *and* GLOUCESTER.

  K. Hen. Gloucester, 'tis true that we are in great
    danger;

The greater therefore should our courage be.
Good morrow, brother Bedford. God Almighty!
There is some soul of goodness in things evil,
Would men observingly distil it out; 5
For our bad neighbour makes us early stirrers,
Which is both healthful and good husbandry.
Besides, they are our outward consciences
And preachers to us all, admonishing
That we should dress us fairly for our end. 10
Thus may we gather honey from the weed,
And make a moral of the devil himself.

          Enter ERPINGHAM.

Good morrow, old Sir Thomas Erpingham.
A good soft pillow for that good white head
Were better than a churlish turf of France. 15
  Erp. Not so, my liege; this lodging likes me
    better,
Since I may say, "Now lie I like a king."
  K. Hen. 'Tis good for men to love their present
    pains
Upon example; so the spirit is eas'd;
And when the mind is quick'ned, out of doubt, 20
The organs, though defunct and dead before,
Break up their drowsy grave and newly move,
With casted slough and fresh legerity.
Lend me thy cloak, Sir Thomas. Brothers both,
Commend me to the princes in our camp; 25
Do my good morrow to them, and anon
Desire them all to my pavilion.
  Glou. We shall, my liege.
  Erp. Shall I attend your Grace?
  K. Hen.   No, my good knight;
Go with my brothers to my lords of England. 30
I and my bosom must debate a while,
And then I would no other company.
  Erp. The Lord in heaven bless thee, noble Harry!
                   [*Exeunt all but King*].
  K. Hen. God-a-mercy, old heart! thou speak'st
    cheerfully.

          Enter PISTOL.

  Pist. Qui va là? 35
  K. Hen. A friend.
  Pist. Discuss unto me; art thou officer?
Or art thou base, common, and popular?
  K. Hen. I am a gentleman of a company.
  Pist. Trail'st thou the puissant pike? 40
  K. Hen. Even so. What are you?
  Pist. As good a gentleman as the Emperor.
  K. Hen. Then you are a better than the King.
  Pist. The King's a bawcock, and a heart of gold,
A lad of life, an imp of fame; 45
Of parents good, of fist most valiant.

9. umber'd: dusky. 12. accomplishing: equipping. 16. [name] (Tyrwhitt). nam'd F. 19. play: play for. 25. gesture: bearing. 39. over-bears attaint: resists stain. 46. as ... define: as well as their limitations permit. 53. Minding: conceiving. Sc. i, 19. Upon example: by comparison. 23. legerity: nimbleness. 37. Discuss: tell. 38. popular: of the people.

I kiss his dirty shoe, and from heart-string
I love the lovely bully.   What is thy name?
  K. Hen. Harry le Roy.
  Pist. Le Roy! a Cornish name.   Art thou of
    Cornish crew?   50
  K. Hen. No, I am a Welshman.
  Pist. Know'st thou Fluellen?
  K. Hen. Yes.
  Pist. Tell him, I'll knock his leek about his pate
Upon Saint Davy's day.   55
  K. Hen. Do not you wear your dagger in your
cap that day, lest he knock that about yours.
  Pist. Art thou his friend?
  K. Hen. And his kinsman too.
  Pist. The *figo* for thee, then!   60
  K. Hen. I thank you.   God be with you!
  Pist. My name is Pistol call'd.   [*Exit.*
  K. Hen. It sorts well with your fierceness.

          Enter FLUELLEN *and* GOWER.

  Gow. Captain Fluellen!   64
  Flu. So! in the name of Jesu Christ, speak fewer.
It is the greatest admiration in the universal world,
when the true and aunchient prerogatifes and laws
of the wars is not kept.   If you would take the
pains but to examine the wars of Pompey the Great,
you shall find, I warrant you, that there is no   70
tiddle taddle nor pibble babble in Pompey's camp.
I warrant you, you shall find the ceremonies of the
wars, and the cares of it, and the forms of it, and
the sobriety of it, and the modesty of it, to be
otherwise.   75
  Gow. Why, the enemy is loud; you hear him all
night.
  Flu. If the enemy is an ass and a fool and a prating coxcomb, is it meet, think you, that we should
also, look you, be an ass and a fool and a prating
coxcomb?   In your own conscience, now?   81
  Gow. I will speak lower.
  Flu. I pray you and beseech you that you will.
            [*Exeunt [Gower and Fluellen].*
  K. Hen. Though it appear a little out of fash-
    ion,   85
There is much care and valour in this Welshman.

  Enter three soldiers, JOHN BATES, ALEXANDER
  COURT, *and* MICHAEL WILLIAMS.

  Court. Brother John Bates, is not that the morning which breaks yonder?
  Bates. I think it be; but we have no great cause
to desire the approach of day.   90
  Will. We see yonder the beginning of the day,
but I think we shall never see the end of it.   Who
goes there?

  K. Hen. A friend.
  Will. Under what captain serve you?   95
  K. Hen. Under Sir [Thomas] Erpingham.
  Will. A good old commander and a most kind
gentleman.   I pray you, what thinks he of our
estate?
  K. Hen. Even as men wreck'd upon a sand,
that look to be wash'd off the next tide.   101
  Bates. He hath not told his thought to the King?
  K. Hen. No; nor it is not meet he should.   For,
though I speak it to you, I think the King is but a 105
man, as I am.   The violet smells to him as it does
to me; the element shows to him as it doth to me;
all his senses have but human conditions.   His
ceremonies laid by, in his nakedness he appears but
a man; and though his affections are higher   110
mounted than ours, yet, when they stoop, they
stoop with the like wing.   Therefore, when he sees
reason of fears as we do, his fears, out of doubt, be
of the same relish as ours are; yet, in reason, no
man should possess him with any appearance of
fear, lest he, by showing it, should dishearten his
army.   117
  Bates. He may show what outward courage he
will; but I believe, as cold a night as 'tis, he could
wish himself in Thames up to the neck; and so I
would he were, and I by him, at all adventures, so
we were quit here.   122
  K. Hen. By my troth, I will speak my conscience
of the King: I think he would not wish himself
anywhere but where he is.
  Bates. Then I would he were here alone; so
should he be sure to be ransomed, and a many poor
men's lives saved.   128
  K. Hen. I dare say you love him not so ill to
wish him here alone, howsoever you speak this to
feel other men's minds.   Methinks I could not die
anywhere so contented as in the King's company,
his cause being just and his quarrel honourable.   134
  Will. That's more than we know.
  Bates. Ay, or more than we should seek after;
for we know enough if we know we are the King's
subjects.   If his cause be wrong, our obedience to
the King wipes the crime of it out of us.   139
  Will. But if the cause be not good, the King himself hath a heavy reckoning to make, when all those
legs and arms and heads, chopp'd off in a battle,
shall join together at the latter day and cry all,
"We died at such a place"; some swearing, some
crying for a surgeon, some upon their wives   145
left poor behind them, some upon the debts they
owe, some upon their children rawly left.   I am
afeard there are few die well that die in a battle;
for how can they charitably dispose of anything,

54–55. **leek … day.** The Welsh wore leeks in their caps to commemorate a victory over the Saxons, as ordered by their patron saint, David.   96. **[Thomas]** (Pope).   *John* F.   107. **element:** sky.   109. **ceremonies:** ceremonial garments.   114. **relish:** kind, quality.   123. **conscience:** genuine opinion.   147. **rawly:** unprovided for.

when blood is their argument? Now, if these men do not die well, it will be a black matter for the King that led them to it; who to disobey were against all proportion of subjection.　153

K. Hen. So, if a son that is by his father sent about merchandise do sinfully miscarry upon the sea, the imputation of his wickedness, by your rule, should be imposed upon his father that sent him; or if a servant, under his master's command transporting a sum of money, be assailed by robbers and die in many irreconcil'd iniquities, you may 160 call the business of the master the author of the servant's damnation. But this is not so. The King is not bound to answer the particular endings of his soldiers, the father of his son, nor the master of his servant; for they purpose not their death 165 when they purpose their services. Besides, there is no king, be his cause never so spotless, if it come to the arbitrement of swords, can try it out with all unspotted soldiers. Some peradventure have on them the guilt of premeditated and contrived 170 murder; some, of beguiling virgins with the broken seals of perjury; some, making the wars their bulwark, that have before gored the gentle bosom of Peace with pillage and robbery. Now, if these men have defeated the law and outrun native pun- 175 ishment, though they can outstrip men, they have no wings to fly from God. War is his beadle, war is his vengeance; so that here men are punish'd for before-breach of the King's laws in now the King's quarrel. Where they feared the death, they 180 have borne life away; and where they would be safe, they perish. Then if they die unprovided, no more is the King guilty of their damnation than he was before guilty of those impieties for which they are now visited. Every subject's duty is 185 the King's; but every subject's soul is his own. Therefore should every soldier in the wars do as every sick man in his bed, wash every mote out of his conscience; and dying so, death is to him advantage; or not dying, the time was blessedly 190 lost wherein such preparation was gained; and in him that escapes, it were not sin to think that, making God so free an offer, He let him outlive that day to see His greatness and to teach others how they should prepare.　196

Will. 'Tis certain, every man that dies ill, the ill upon his own head, the King is not to answer it.

Bates. I do not desire he should answer for me; and yet I determine to fight lustily for him.　201

K. Hen. I myself heard the King say he would not be ransom'd.

Will. Ay, he said so, to make us fight cheerfully;

but when our throats are cut, he may be ransom'd, and we ne'er the wiser.

K. Hen. If I live to see it, I will never trust his word after.　208

Will. You pay him then. That's a perilous shot out of an elder-gun, that a poor and a private displeasure can do against a monarch! You may as well go about to turn the sun to ice with fanning in his face with a peacock's feather. You'll never trust his word after! Come, 'tis a foolish saying.　215

K. Hen. Your reproof is something too round. I should be angry with you, if the time were convenient.

Will. Let it be a quarrel between us, if you live.

K. Hen. I embrace it.　221

Will. How shall I know thee again?

K. Hen. Give me any gage of thine, and I will wear it in my bonnet; then, if ever thou dar'st acknowledge it, I will make it my quarrel.　225

Will. Here's my glove; give me another of thine.

K. Hen. There.

Wil. This will I also wear in my cap. If ever thou come to me and say, after to-morrow, "This is my glove," by this hand, I will take thee a box on the ear.　232

K. Hen. If ever I live to see it, I will challenge it.

Will. Thou dar'st as well be hang'd.

K. Hen. Well, I will do it, though I take thee in the King's company.　237

Will. Keep thy word; fare thee well.

Bates. Be friends, you English fools, be friends. We have French quarrels enow, if you could tell how to reckon.　241

K. Hen. Indeed, the French may lay twenty French crowns to one they will beat us, for they bear them on their shoulders; but it is no English treason to cut French crowns, and to-morrow the King himself will be a clipper. [*Exeunt soldiers.* 246
Upon the King! let us our lives, our souls,
Our debts, our careful wives,
Our children, and our sins lay on the King!
We must bear all. O hard condition,　250
Twin-born with greatness, subject to the breath
Of every fool whose sense no more can feel
But his own wringing! What infinite heart's-ease
Must kings neglect, that private men enjoy!
And what have kings, that privates have not too,
Save ceremony, save general ceremony?　256
And what art thou, thou idol Ceremony?
What kind of god art thou, that suffer'st more
Of mortal griefs than do thy worshippers?
What are thy rents? What are thy comings in?

---

153. **proportion of subjection:** proper relation of subject to sovereign. 155. **sinfully miscarry:** die in his sins. 175. **native:** at home. 197. **ill:** in sin. 210. **elder-gun:** pop-gun, made by removing the pith from a piece of elder. 216. **round:** harsh. 223. **gage:** pledge. 243, 245. **crowns:** (1) heads, (2) coins. 246. **clipper:** a pun on *clip* (1) to cut off, (2) to trim the edges of coins for the gold or silver. 248. **careful:** burdened by care. 253. **wringing:** writhing.

O Ceremony, show me but thy worth!   261
What is thy soul of adoration?
Art thou aught else but place, degree, and form,
Creating awe and fear in other men?
Wherein thou art less happy being fear'd   265
Than they in fearing.
What drink'st thou oft, instead of homage sweet,
But poison'd flattery? O, be sick, great greatness,
And bid thy Ceremony give thee cure!
Think'st thou the fiery fever will go out   270
With titles blown from adulation?
Will it give place to flexure and low bending?
Canst thou, when thou command'st the beggar's
       knee,
Command the health of it? No, thou proud dream,
That play'st so subtly with a king's repose;   275
I am a king that find thee, and I know
'Tis not the balm, the sceptre, and the ball,
The sword, the mace, the crown imperial,
The intertissued robe of gold and pearl,
The farced title running 'fore the King,   280
The throne he sits on, nor the tide of pomp
That beats upon the high shore of this world, —
No, not all these, thrice-gorgeous Ceremony,
Not all these, laid in bed majestical,
Can sleep so soundly as the wretched slave,   285
Who with a body fill'd and vacant mind
Gets him to rest, cramm'd with distressful bread,
Never sees horrid night, the child of hell,
But like a lackey from the rise to set
Sweats in the eye of Phœbus, and all night   290
Sleeps in Elysium; next day after dawn,
Doth rise and help Hyperion to his horse,
And follows so the ever-running year
With profitable labour to his grave:
And, but for ceremony, such a wretch,   295
Winding up days with toil and nights with sleep,
Had the fore-hand and vantage of a king.
The slave, a member of the country's peace,
Enjoys it, but in gross brain little wots
What watch the King keeps to maintain the peace,
Whose hours the peasant best advantages.   301

Enter ERPINGHAM.

  Erp. My lord, your nobles, jealous of your
       absence,
Seek through your camp to find you.
  K. Hen.   Good old knight,
Collect them all together at my tent.
I'll be before thee.
  Erp.   I shall do't, my lord.   305
                                            [*Exit.*

  K. Hen. O God of battles! steel my soldiers'
       hearts.
Possess them not with fear. Take from them now
The sense of reckoning, [if] th' opposed numbers
Pluck their hearts from them. Not to-day, O
       Lord,
O, not to-day, think not upon the fault   310
My father made in compassing the crown!
I Richard's body have interred new,
And on it have bestow'd more contrite tears,
Than from it issu'd forced drops of blood.
Five hundred poor I have in yearly pay,   315
Who twice a day their wither'd hands hold up
Toward heaven, to pardon blood; and I have built
Two chantries, where the sad and solemn priests
Sing still for Richard's soul. More will I do;
Though all that I can do is nothing worth,   320
Since that my penitence comes after all,
Imploring pardon.

Enter GLOUCESTER.

  Glou. My liege!
  K. Hen. My brother Gloucester's voice? Ay;
I know thy errand, I will go with thee.   325
The day, my friends, and all things stay for me.
                                          [*Exeunt.*

[SCENE II. *The French camp.*]

Enter the DAUPHIN, ORLEANS, RAMBURES,
       and others.

  Orl. The sun doth gild our armour; up, my lords!
  Dau. Montez à cheval! My horse, varlet!
       lackey! ha!
  Orl. O brave spirit!
  Dau. Via! les eaux et la terre.
  Orl. Rien puis? L'air et le feu.   5
  Dau. Ciel, cousin Orleans.

Enter CONSTABLE.

Now, my Lord Constable!
  Con. Hark, how our steeds for present service
       neigh!
  Dau. Mount them, and make incision in their
       hides,
That their hot blood may spin in English eyes, 10
And dout them with superfluous courage, ha!
  Ram. What, will you have them weep our horses'
       blood?
How shall we, then, behold their natural tears?

---

262. **thy ... adoration:** the secret of the adoration paid thee. 271. **from adulation:** by flatterers. 272. **flexure:** bowing.
277. **balm:** coronation oil. **ball:** symbol of sovereignty. 280. **farced:** stuffed, pompous. 287. **distressful:** hard earned.
298. **member:** sharer. 301. **best advantages:** employs most profitably, or profits (the peasant). 302. **jealous of:** nervous
about. 308. **[if]** (Tyrwhitt). *of* F. *lest* Theobald. 311. **compassing:** getting possession of.
  Sc. ii, 11. **dout:** put out.

Enter MESSENGER.

Mess. The English are embattl'd, you French
   peers.

Con. To horse, you gallant princes! straight to
   horse!   15
Do but behold yond poor and starved band,
And your fair show shall suck away their souls,
Leaving them but the shales and husks of men.
There is not work enough for all our hands;
Scarce blood enough in all their sickly veins   20
To give each naked curtle-axe a stain,
That our French gallants shall to-day draw out
And sheathe for lack of sport. Let us but blow on
   them,
The vapour of our valour will o'erturn them.
'Tis positive 'gainst all exceptions, lords,   25
That our superflucus lackeys and our peasants,
Who in unnecessary action swarm
About our squares of battle, were enow
To purge this field of such a hilding foe,
Though we upon this mountain's basis by   30
Took stand for idle speculation,
But that our honours must not. What's to say?
A very little little let us do,
And all is done. Then let the trumpets sound
The tucket sonance and the note to mount;   35
For our approach shall so much dare the field
That England shall crouch down in fear and yield.

Enter GRANDPRÉ.

Grand. Why do you stay so long, my lords of
   France?
Yond island carrions, desperate of their bones,
Ill-favouredly become the morning field.   40
Their ragged curtains poorly are let loose,
And our air shakes them passing scornfully.
Big Mars seems bankrupt in their beggar'd host
And faintly through a rusty beaver peeps;
The horsemen sit like fixed candlesticks   45
With torch-staves in their hand; and their poor
   jades
Lob down their heads, dropping the hides and hips,
The gum down-roping from their pale-dead eyes,
And in their pale dull mouths the gimmal'd bit
Lies foul with chew'd grass, still and motionless;   50
And their executors, the knavish crows,
Fly o'er them, all impatient for their hour.
Description cannot suit itself in words
To demonstrate the life of such a battle,
In life so lifeless as it shows itself.   55

Con. They have said their prayers, and they stay
   for death.

Dau. Shall we go send them dinners and fresh
   suits
And give their fasting horses provender,
And after fight with them?

Con. I stay but for my guard; on to the field!   60
I will the banner from a trumpet take,
And use it for my haste. Come, come, away!
The sun is high, and we outwear the day. [*Exeunt.*

[SCENE III. *The English camp.*]

Enter GLOUCESTER, BEDFORD, EXETER, ERPING-
HAM, *with all his host:* SALISBURY *and* WEST-
MORELAND.

Glou. Where is the King?

Bed. The King himself is rode to view their battle.

West. Of fighting men they have full threescore
   thousand.

Exe. There's five to one; besides, they all are
   fresh.

Sal. God's arm strike with us! 'tis a fearful odds.
God be wi' you, princes all; I'll to my charge.   6
If we no more meet till we meet in heaven,
Then, joyfully, my noble Lord of Bedford,
My dear Lord Gloucester, and my good Lord
   Exeter,
And my kind kinsman, warriors all, adieu!   10

Bed. Farewell, good Salisbury, and good luck go
   with thee!

Exe. Farewell, kind lord; fight valiantly to-day!
And yet I do thee wrong to mind thee of it,
For thou art fram'd of the firm truth of valour.
                    [*Exit Salisbury.*]

Bed. He is as full of valour as of kindness,   15
Princely in both.

Enter the KING.

West.   O that we now had here
But one ten thousand of those men in England
That do no work to-day!

K. Hen.   What's he that wishes so?
My cousin Westmoreland? No, my fair cousin.
If we are mark'd to die, we are enow   20
To do our country loss; and if to live,
The fewer men, the greater share of honour.
God's will! I pray thee, wish not one man more.
By Jove, I am not covetous for gold,
Nor care I who doth feed upon my cost;   25
It yearns me not if men my garments wear;
Such outward things dwell not in my desires;
But if it be a sin to covet honour
I am the most offending soul alive.   29
No, 'faith, my coz, wish not a man from England.

18. **shales:** shells. 21. **curtle-axe:** cutlass. 29. **hilding:** worthless. 31. **speculation:** on-looking. 35. **tucket sonance:** trumpet notes. 36. **dare the field:** daze the enemy (a figure from lark catching). 41. **curtains:** flags. 44. **beaver:** face part of a helmet. 47. **Lob:** hang. 49. **gimmal'd:** jointed.

   Sc. iii, 13, 14. **And . . . valour.** In F these lines follow l. 11. 26. **yearns:** grieves.

God's peace! I would not lose so great an honour
As one man more, methinks, would share from me
For the best hope I have. O, do not wish one more!
Rather proclaim it, Westmoreland, through my
    host,
That he which hath no stomach to this fight,   35
Let him depart. His passport shall be made,
And crowns for convoy put into his purse.
We would not die in that man's company
That fears his fellowship to die with us.
This day is call'd the feast of Crispian.   40
He that outlives this day and comes safe home
Will stand a tip-toe when this day is named,
And rouse him at the name of Crispian.
He that shall [live] this day, and [see] old age,
Will yearly on the vigil feast his neighbours,   45
And say, "To-morrow is Saint Crispian."
Then will he strip his sleeve and show his scars,
[And say, "These wounds I had on Crispin's day."]
Old men forget; yet all shall be forgot,
But he'll remember with advantages   50
What feats he did that day.   Then shall our names,
Familiar in his mouth as household words,
Harry the King, Bedford, and Exeter,
Warwick and Talbot, Salisbury and Gloucester,
Be in their flowing cups freshly rememb'red.   55
This story shall the good man teach his son;
And Crispin Crispian shall ne'er go by,
From this day to the ending of the world,
But we in it shall be remembered,
We few, we happy few, we band of brothers.   60
For he to-day that sheds his blood with me
Shall be my brother; be he ne'er so vile,
This day shall gentle his condition;
And gentlemen in England now a-bed   64
Shall think themselves accurs'd they were not here,
And hold their manhoods cheap whiles any speaks
That fought with us upon Saint Crispin's day.

Re-enter SALISBURY.

Sal. My sovereign lord, bestow yourself with
    speed.
The French are bravely in their battles set,
And will with all expedience charge on us.   70
K. Hen. All things are ready, if our minds be so.
West. Perish the man whose mind is backward
    now!
K. Hen. Thou dost not wish more help from
    England, coz?
West. God's will! my liege, would you and I alone,
Without more help, could fight this royal battle! 75
K. Hen. Why, now thou hast unwish'd five
    thousand men,

Which likes me better than to wish us one.
You know your places. God be with you all!

    Tucket. Enter MONTJOY.

Mont. Once more I come to know of thee, King
    Harry,
If for thy ransom thou wilt now compound,   80
Before thy most assured overthrow;
For certainly thou art so near the gulf,
Thou needs must be englutted. Besides, in mercy,
The Constable desires thee thou wilt mind
Thy followers of repentance; that their souls   85
May make a peaceful and a sweet retire
From off these fields, where, wretches, their poor
    bodies
Must lie and fester.
K. Hen.   Who hath sent thee now?
Mont. The Constable of France.
K. Hen. I pray thee, bear my former answer
    back: 90
Bid them achieve me and then sell my bones.
Good God! why should they mock poor fellows thus?
The man that once did sell the lion's skin
While the beast liv'd, was kill'd with hunting him.
A many of our bodies shall no doubt   95
Find native graves, upon the which, I trust,
Shall witness live in brass of this day's work;
And those that leave their valiant bones in France,
Dying like men, though buried in your dunghills,
They shall be fam'd; for there the sun shall greet
    them,   100
And draw their honours reeking up to heaven;
Leaving their earthly parts to choke your clime,
The smell whereof shall breed a plague in France.
Mark then abounding valour in our English,
That being dead, like to the bullet's grazing,   105
Break out into a second course of mischief,
Killing in relapse of mortality.
Let me speak proudly: tell the Constable
We are but warriors for the working-day.
Our gayness and our gilt are all besmirch'd   110
With rainy marching in the painful field;
There's not a piece of feather in our host —
Good argument, I hope, we will not fly —
And time hath worn us into slovenry;
But, by the mass, our hearts are in the trim;   115
And my poor soldiers tell me, yet ere night
They'll be in fresher robes, or they will pluck
The gay new coats o'er the French soldiers' heads
And turn them out of service. If they do this —
As, if God please, they shall, — my ransom then   120
Will soon be levied. Herald, save thou thy labour.
Come thou no more for ransom, gentle herald.

40, 48. Crispinus and Crispianus were the patron saints of shoemakers, celebrated Oct. 25.   44. [live] ... [see] (Pope).
see ... live F. 48. [And ... day] Q. Om. F. 62. vile: low born. 63. gentle his condition: make him a gentleman. 68. bestow yourself: take your position. 70. expedience: speed. 80. compound: make terms. 82. gulf: whirlpool. 83. englutted: swallowed. 91. achieve: capture, or kill. 105. grazing: glancing off. 107. relapse of mortality: mortal rebound.

They shall have none, I swear, but these my joints;
Which if they have as I will leave 'em them,
Shall yield them little, tell the Constable.   125
    Mont. I shall, King Harry. And so fare thee
     well;
Thou never shalt hear herald any more.   [*Exit.*
    K. Hen. I fear thou will once more come again
for ransom.

           Enter YORK.

    York. My lord, most humbly on my knee I beg
The leading of the vaward,   130
    K. Hen. Take it, brave York. Now, soldiers,
     march away;
And how thou pleasest, God, dispose the day!
                           [*Exeunt.*

      [SCENE IV. *The field of battle.*]

    Alarum. Excursions. Enter PISTOL, FRENCH
          SOLDIER, *and* BOY.

    Pist. Yield, cur!
    *Fr. Sol. Je pense que vous êtes le gentilhomme de
bonne qualité.*
    Pist. Qualtitie calmie custure me! Art thou a
gentleman? What is thy name? Discuss.   5
    Fr. Sol. O Seigneur Dieu!
    Pist. O, Signieur Dew should be a gentleman.
Perpend my words, O Signieur Dew, and mark:
O Signieur Dew, thou diest on point of fox,
Except, O signieur, thou do give to me   10
Egregious ransom.
    Fr. Sol. O, prenez miséricorde! ayez pitié de moi!
    Pist. Moy shall not serve; I will have forty moys,
Or I will fetch thy rim out at thy throat   15
In drops of crimson blood.
    *Fr. Sol. Est-il impossible d'échapper la force de
ton bras?*
    Pist. Brass, cur!
Thou damned and luxurious mountain goat,   20
Offer'st me brass?
    Fr. Sol. O pardonnez moi!
    Pist. Say'st thou me so? Is that a ton of moys?
Come hither, boy; ask me this slave in French
What is his name.   25
    Boy. Écoutez: comment êtes-vous appelé?
    Fr. Sol. Monsieur le Fer.
    Boy. He says his name is Master Fer.
    Pist. Master Fer! I'll fer him, and firk him, and
ferret him. Discuss the same in French unto him.
    Boy. I do not know the French for fer, and   32
ferret, and firk.
    Pist. Bid him prepare; for I will cut his throat.
    Fr. Sol. Que dit-il, monsieur?   35
    Boy. Il me commande à vous dire que vous faites

*vous prêt; car ce soldat ici est disposé tout à cette
heure de couper votre gorge.*
    Pist. Owy, cuppele gorge, permafoy,
Peasant, unless thou give me crowns, brave crowns;
Or mangled shalt thou be by this my sword.   41
    *Fr. Sol. O, je vous supplie, pour l'amour le Dieu,
me pardonner! Je suis le gentilhomme de bonne
maison; gardez ma vie, et je vous donnerai deux cents
écus.*   45
    Pist. What are his words?
    Boy. He prays you to save his life. He is a
gentleman of a good house; and for his ransom he
will give you two hundred crowns.
    Pist. Tell him my fury shall abate, and I   50
The crowns will take.
    Fr. Sol. Petit monsieur, que dit-il?
    *Boy. Encore qu'il est contre son jurement de par-
donner aucun prisonnier; néanmoins, pour les écus
que vous l'avez promis, il est content de vous donner la
liberté, le franchisement.*   56
    *Fr. Sol. Sur mes genoux je vous donne mille
remercîmens; et je m'estime heureux que je suis tombé
entre les mains d'un chevalier, je pense, le plus brave,
vaillant, et très distingué seigneur d'Angleterre.*   61
    Pist. Expound unto me, boy.
    Boy. He gives you upon his knees, a thousand
thanks; and he esteems himself happy that he hath
fallen into the hands of one (as he thinks) the most
brave, valorous, and thrice-worthy seigneur of
England.
    Pist. As I suck blood, I will some mercy show.
Follow me!   69
    Boy. Suivez-vous le grand capitaine. [*Exeunt
Pistol, and French Soldier.*] I did never know so
full a voice issue from so empty a heart; but the
saying is true, "The empty vessel makes the greatest sound." Bardolph and Nym had ten times
more valour than this roaring devil i' th' old   75
play, that every one may pare his nails with a
wooden dagger; and they are both hang'd; and so
would this be, if he durst steal anything adven-
turously. I must stay with the lackeys with the
luggage of our camp. The French might have a
good prey of us, if he knew of it; for there is none to
guard it but boys.   [*Exit.*   82

      [SCENE V. *Another part of the field.*]

    Enter CONSTABLE, ORLEANS, BOURBON,
        DAUPHIN, *and* RAMBURES.

    Con. O diable!
    Orl. O seigneur! le jour est perdu, tout est perdu!
    Dau. Mort de ma vie! all is confounded, all!
Reproach and everlasting shame

Sits mocking in our plumes. *O méchante for-*
    tune!   5
Do not run away.   [*A short alarum.*
  Con.   Why, all our ranks are broke.
  Dau. O perdurable shame! let's stab ourselves.
Be these the wretches that we play'd at dice for?
  Orl. Is this the king we sent to for his ransom?
  Bour. Shame and eternal shame, nothing but
    shame!   10
Let's die in [honour]! Once more back again!
And he that will not follow Bourbon now,
Let him go hence, and with his cap in hand
Like a base pandar hold the chamber door
Whilst [by a] slave, no gentler than my dog,   15
His fairest daughter is contaminated.
  Con. Disorder, that hath spoil'd us, friend us
    now!
Let us on heaps go offer up our lives.
  Orl. We are enow yet living in the field
To smother up the English in our throngs   20
If any order might be thought upon.
  Bour. The devil take order now! I'll to the
    throng.
Let life be short, else shame will be too long.
                            [*Exeunt.*

[SCENE VI. *Another part of the field.*]

Alarum. Enter KING HENRY *and his train,*
with prisoners.

  K. Hen. Well have we done, thrice valiant
    countrymen.
But all's not done; yet keep the French the field.
  Exe. The Duke of York commends him to your
    Majesty.
  K. Hen. Lives he, good uncle? Thrice within
    this hour
I saw him down; thrice up again, and fighting.   5
From helmet to the spur all blood he was.
  Exe. In which array, brave soldier, doth he lie,
Larding the plain; and by his bloody side,
Yoke-fellow to his honour-owing wounds,
The noble Earl of Suffolk also lies.   10
Suffolk first died; and York, all haggled over,
Comes to him where in gore he lay insteeped,
And takes him by the beard; kisses the gashes
That bloodily did yawn upon his face.
He cries aloud, "Tarry, my cousin Suffolk!   15
My soul shall thine keep company to heaven;
Tarry, sweet soul, for mine, then fly abreast,
As in this glorious and well-foughten field
We kept together in our chivalry!"
Upon these words I came and cheer'd him up.   20
He smil'd me in the face, raught me his hand,
And, with a feeble gripe, says, "Dear my lord,

Commend my service to my sovereign."
So did he turn and over Suffolk's neck
He threw his wounded arm and kiss'd his lips;   25
And so espous'd to death, with blood he seal'd
A testament of noble-ending love.
The pretty and sweet manner of it forc'd
Those waters from me which I would have stopp'd;
But I had not so much of man in me,   30
And all my mother came into mine eyes
And gave me up to tears.
  K. Hen.   I blame you not;
For, hearing this, I must perforce compound
With mistful eyes, or they will issue too.
                            [*Alarum.*
But, hark! what new alarum is this same?   35
The French have reinforc'd their scatter'd men.
Then every soldier kill his prisoners;
Give the word through.   [*Exeunt.*

[SCENE VII. *Another part of the field.*]

Enter FLUELLEN *and* GOWER.

  Flu. Kill the poys and the luggage! 'Tis expressly against the law of arms. 'Tis as arrant a
piece of knavery, mark you now, as can be offer't;
in your conscience, now, is it not?   4
  Gow. 'Tis certain there's not a boy left alive;
and the cowardly rascals that ran from the battle
ha' done this slaughter. Besides, they have
burned and carried away all that was in the King's
tent; wherefore the King, most worthily, hath
caus'd every soldier to cut his prisoner's throat.
O, 'tis a gallant king!   11
  Flu. Ay, he was porn at Monmouth, Captain
Gower. What call you the town's name where
Alexander the Pig was born!
  Gow. Alexander the Great.   15
  Flu. Why, I pray you, is not pig great? The
pig, or the great, or the mighty, or the huge, or the
magnanimous, are all one reckonings, save the
phrase is a little variations.   19
  Gow. I think Alexander the Great was born in
Macedon. His father was called Philip of Macedon, as I take it.
  Flu. I think it is in Macedon where Alexander
is porn. I tell you, captain, if you look in the
maps of the 'orld, I warrant you sall find, in the   25
comparisons between Macedon and Monmouth,
that the situations, look you, is both alike. There
is a river in Macedon; and there is also moreover a
river at Monmouth. It is call'd Wye at Monmouth; but it is out of my prains what is the name
of the other river; but 'tis all one, 'tis alike as   30
my fingers is to my fingers, and there is salmons in
both. If you mark Alexander's life well, Harry of

    Sc. **v**, 7. **perdurable**: lasting. 11. **[honour]** Q. Om. F. 15. **[by a]** Q. *a base* ʰ.
    Sc. **vi**, 8. **Larding**: fattening. 11. **haggled**: mangled. 21. **raught**: reached. 34. **issue**: weep.

Monmouth's life is come after it indifferent well; for there is figures in all things. Alexander, 35 God knows, and you know, in his rages, and his furies, and his wraths, and his cholers, and his moods, and his displeasures, and his indignations, and also being a little intoxicates in his prains, did, in his ales and his angers, look you, kill his best friend, Cleitus. 41

Gow. Our King is not like him in that. He never kill'd any of his friends.

Flu. It is not well done, mark you now, to take the tales out of my mouth, ere it is made and 45 finished. I speak but in the figures and comparisons of it. As Alexander kill'd his friend Cleitus, being in his ales and his cups; so also Harry Monmouth, being in his right wits and his good judgements, turn'd away the fat knight with the 50 great belly doublet. He was full of jests, and gipes, and knaveries, and mocks; I have forgot his name.

Gow. Sir John Falstaff.

Flu. That is he. I'll tell you there is good men porn at Monmouth. 56

Gow. Here comes his Majesty.

Alarum. Enter KING HENRY *and* [*forces;* WARWICK, GLOUCESTER, EXETER,] *with prisoners. Flourish.*

K. Hen. I was not angry since I came to France Until this instant. Take a trumpet, herald; Ride thou unto the horsemen on yond hill. 60 If they will fight with us, bid them come down, Or void the field; they do offend our sight. If they'll do neither, we will come to them And make them skirr away, as swift as stones Enforced from the old Assyrian slings. 65 Besides, we'll cut the throats of those we have, And not a man of them that we shall take Shall taste our mercy. Go and tell them so.

Enter MONTJOY.

Exe. Here comes the herald of the French, my liege.

Glou. His eyes are humbler than they us'd to be. 70

K. Hen. How now! what means this, herald? Know'st thou not That I have fin'd these bones of mine for ransom? Com'st thou again for ransom?

Mont.   No, great King; I come to thee for charitable license, That we may wander o'er this bloody field 75 To book our dead, and then to bury them; To sort our nobles from our common men. For many of our princes — woe the while! — Lie drown'd and soak'd in mercenary blood; So do our vulgar drench their peasant limbs 80

In blood of princes; and their wounded steeds Fret fetlock deep in gore, and with wild rage Yerk out their armed heels at their dead masters, Killing them twice. O, give us leave, great King, To view the field in safety, and dispose 85 Of their dead bodies!

K. Hen.   I tell thee truly, herald, I know not if the day be ours or no; For yet a many of your horsemen peer And gallop o'er the field.

Mont.   The day is yours.

K. Hen. Praised be God, and not our strength, for it! 90 What is this castle call'd that stands hard by?

Mont. They call it Agincourt.

K. Hen. Then call we this the field of Agincourt, Fought on the day of Crispin Crispianus. 94

Flu. Your grandfather of famous memory, an't please your Majesty, and your great-uncle Edward the Plack Prince of Wales, as I have read in the chronicles, fought a most prave pattle here in France.

K. Hen. They did, Fluellen. 100

Flu. Your Majesty says very true. If your Majesties is remember'd of it, the Welshmen did good service in a garden where leeks did grow, wearing leeks in their Monmouth caps; which, your Majesty know, to this hour is an honourable badge of the service; and I do believe your Majesty takes no scorn to wear the leek upon Saint Tavy's day. 108

K. Hen. I wear it for a memorable honour; For I am Welsh, you know, good countryman.

Flu. All the water in Wye cannot wash your Majesty's Welsh plood out of your pody, I can tell you that. God pless it and preserve it, as long as it pleases His grace, and His majesty too!

K. Hen. Thanks, good my countryman. 115

Flu. By Jeshu, I am your Majesty's countryman, I care not who know it. I will confess it to all the 'orld. I need not to be ashamed of your Majesty, praised be God, so long as your Majesty is an honest man. 120

K. Hen. God keep me so!

Enter WILLIAMS.

                    Our heralds go with him; Bring me just notice of the numbers dead On both our parts. Call yonder fellow hither. [*Exeunt Heralds with Montjoy.*]

Exe. Soldier, you must come to the King. 124

K. Hen. Soldier, why wear'st thou that glove in thy cap?

Will. An't please your Majesty, 'tis the gage of one that I should fight withal, if he be alive.

Sc. vii, 35. **figures:** similes. 64. **skirr:** scurry. 72. **fin'd:** pledged. 76. **hook:** list. 88. **peer:** appear. 122. **just notice:** exact record.

K. Hen. An Englishman?   129

Will. An't please your Majesty, a rascal that swagger'd with me last night; who, if alive and ever dare to challenge this glove, I have sworn to take him a box o' th' ear; or if I can see my glove in his cap, which he swore, as he was a soldier, he would wear if alive, I will strike it out soundly.   136

K. Hen. What think you, Captain Fluellen? Is it fit this soldier keep his oath?

Flu. He is a craven and a villain else, an't please your Majesty, in my conscience.   140

K. Hen. It may be his enemy is a gentleman of great sort, quite from the answer of his degree. 143

Flu. Though he be as good a gentleman as the devil is, as Lucifer and Belzebub himself, it is necessary, look your Grace, that he keep his vow and his oath. If he be perjur'd, see you now, his reputation is as arrant a villain and a Jack-sauce, as ever his black shoe trod upon God's ground and His earth, in my conscience, la!   150

K. Hen. Then keep thy vow, sirrah, when thou meet'st the fellow.

Will. So I will, my liege, as I live.

K. Hen. Who serv'st thou under?

Will. Under Captain Gower, my liege.   155

Flu. Gower is a good captain, and is good knowledge and literatured in the wars.

K. Hen. Call him hither to me, soldier.

Will. I will, my liege.   [*Exit.* 159

K. Hen. Here, Fluellen; wear thou this favour for me and stick it in thy cap. When Alençon and myself were down together, I pluck'd this glove from his helm. If any man challenge this, he is a friend to Alençon, and an enemy to our person. If thou encounter any such, apprehend him, an thou dost me love.   166

Flu. Your Grace doo's me as great honours as can be desir'd in the hearts of his subjects. I would fain see the man, that has but two legs, that shall find himself aggrief'd at this glove; that is all. But I would fain see it once, an please God of His grace that I might see.   172

K. Hen. Know'st thou Gower?

Flu. He is my dear friend, an please you.

K. Hen. Pray thee, go seek him, and bring him to my tent.   176

Flu. I will fetch him.   [*Exit.*

K. Hen. My Lord of Warwick, and my brother Gloucester,
Follow Fluellen closely at the heels.
The glove which I have given him for a favour
May haply purchase him a box o' th' ear.   181
It is the soldier's; I by bargain should
Wear it myself. Follow, good cousin Warwick.
If that the soldier strike him, as I judge

By his blunt bearing he will keep his word,   185
Some sudden mischief may arise of it;
For I do know Fluellen valiant
And, touch'd with choler, hot as gunpowder,
And quickly will return an injury.   189
Follow, and see there be no harm between them.
Go you with me, uncle of Exeter.   [*Exeunt.*

[SCENE VIII. *Before King Henry's pavilion.*]

Enter GOWER *and* WILLIAMS.

Will. I warrant it is to knight you, captain.

Enter FLUELLEN.

Flu. God's will and his pleasure, captain, I beseech you now, come apace to the King. There is more good toward you peradventure than is in your knowledge to dream of.   5

Will. Sir, know you this glove?

Flu. Know the glove! I know the glove is a glove.

Will. I know this; and thus I challenge it.
                                    [*Strikes him.*

Flu. 'Sblood! an arrant traitor as any is in the universal world, or in France, or in England!   11

Gow. How now, sir! you villain!

Will. Do you think I'll be forsworn?

Flu. Stand away, Captain Gower. I will give treason his payment into plows, I warrant you. 15

Will. I am no traitor.

Flu. That's a lie in thy throat. I charge you in his Majesty's name, apprehend him; he's a friend of the Duke Alençon's.   19

Enter WARWICK *and* GLOUCESTER.

War. How now, how now! what's the matter?

Flu. My Lord of Warwick, here is — praised be God for it! — a most contagious treason come to light, look you, as you shall desire in a summer's day. Here is his Majesty.

Enter KING HENRY *and* EXETER.

K. Hen. How now! what's the matter?   25

Flu. My liege, here is a villain and a traitor, that, look your Grace, has struck the glove which your Majesty is take out of the helmet of Alençon.   28

Will. My liege, this was my glove; here is the fellow of it; and he that I gave it to in change promis'd to wear it in his cap. I promis'd to strike him, if he did. I met this man with my glove in his cap, and I have been as good as my word.   34

Flu. Your Majesty hear now, saving your Majesty's manhood, what an arrant, rascally, beggarly, lousy knave it is. I hope your Majesty is pear me testimony and witness, and will

---

143. **sort:** rank. **quite ... degree:** far above answering the challenge of Williams's rank.   148. **Jack-sauce:** impudent fellow. Sc. viii, 38. **is pear:** will bear.

avouchment, that this is the glove of Alençon that your Majesty is give me; in your conscience, now?

K. Hen. Give me thy glove, soldier. Look, here is the fellow of it.   42
'Twas I, indeed, thou promisedst to strike;
And thou hast given me most bitter terms.

Flu. An it please your Majesty, let his neck answer for it, if there is any martial law in the world.   47

K. Hen. How canst thou make me satisfaction?

Will. All offences, my lord, come from the heart. Never came any from mine that might offend your Majesty.   51

K. Hen. It was ourself thou didst abuse.

Will. Your Majesty came not like yourself. You appear'd to me but as a common man; witness the night, your garments, your lowliness; and what   55
your Highness suffer'd under that shape, I beseech you take it for your own fault and not mine; for had you been as I took you for, I made no offence; therefore, I beseech your Highness, pardon me.   60

K. Hen. Here, uncle Exeter, fill this glove with
       crowns,
And give it to this fellow. Keep it, fellow;
And wear it for an honour in thy cap
Till I do challenge it. Give him his crowns;   65
And, captain, you must needs be friends with him.

Flu. By this day and this light, the fellow has mettle enough in his belly. Hold, there is twelve pence for you; and I pray you to serve God, and keep you out of prawls, and prabbles, and quarrels, and dissensions, and, I warrant you, it is the better for you.   71

Will. I will none of your money.

Flu. It is with a good will; I can tell you, it will serve you to mend your shoes. Come, wherefore should you be so pashful? Your shoes is not so good. 'Tis a good silling, I warrant you, or I will change it.   77

Enter [an English] HERALD.

K. Hen. Now, herald, are the dead numb'red?

Her. Here is the number of the slaught'red French.

K. Hen. What prisoners of good sort are taken,
       uncle?   80

Exe. Charles Duke of Orleans, nephew to the King;
John Duke of Bourbon, and Lord Bouciqualt:
Of other lords and barons, knights and squires,
Full fifteen hundred, besides common men.

K. Hen. This note doth tell me of ten thousand
       French   85
That in the field lie slain; of princes, in this number,
And nobles bearing banners, there lie dead
One hundred twenty-six; added to these,
Of knights, esquires, and gallant gentlemen,
Eight thousand and four hundred; of the which,   90

Five hundred were but yesterday dubb'd knights;
So that, in these ten thousand they have lost,
There are but sixteen hundred mercenaries;
The rest are princes, barons, lords, knights, squires,
And gentlemen of blood and quality.   95
The names of those their nobles that lie dead:
Charles Delabreth, High Constable of France;
Jacques of Chatillon, Admiral of France;
The master of the cross-bows, Lord Rambures;
Great Master of France, the brave Sir Guichard
       Dauphin,   100
John Duke of Alençon, Anthony Duke of Brabant,
The brother to the Duke of Burgundy,
And Edward Duke of Bar; of lusty earls,
Grandpré and Roussi, Fauconberg and Foix,
Beaumont and Marle, Vaudemont and Lestrale. 105
Here was a royal fellowship of death!
Where is the number of our English dead?

            [*Herald shows him another paper.*]
Edward the Duke of York, the Earl of Suffolk,
Sir Richard Ketly, Davy Gam, esquire;
None else of name; and of all other men   110
But five and twenty. — O God, thy arm was here;
And not to us, but to thy arm alone,
Ascribe we all! When, without stratagem,
But in plain shock and even play of battle,
Was ever known so great and little loss   115
On one part and on the other? Take it, God,
For it is none but thine!

Exe.   'Tis wonderful!

K. Hen. Come, go we in procession to the village;
And be it death proclaimed through our host
To boast of this or take that praise from God   120
Which is His only.

Flu. Is it not lawful, an please your Majesty, to tell how many is kill'd?

K. Hen. Yes, captain, but with this acknow-
       ledgement,
That God fought for us.   125

Flu. Yes, my conscience, He did us great good.

K. Hen. Do we all holy rites.
Let there be sung *Non nobis* and *Te Deum.*
The dead with charity enclos'd in clay,
And then to Calais; and to England then,   130
Where ne'er from France arriv'd more happy
       men.   [*Exeunt.*

ACT V

[PROLOGUE]

Enter CHORUS.

[*Chor.*] Vouchsafe to those that have not read
       the story,
That I may prompt them; and of such as have,
I humbly pray them to admit th' excuse

39. **avouchment:** testify.

Of time, of numbers, and due course of things,
Which cannot in their huge and proper life   5
Be here presented. Now we bear the King
Toward Calais; grant him there; there seen,
Heave him away upon your winged thoughts
Athwart the sea. Behold, the English beach
Pales in the flood with men, [with] wives and
    boys,   10
Whose shouts and claps out-voice the deep-mouth'd
    sea,
Which like a mighty whiffler 'fore the King
Seems to prepare his way. So let him land,
And solemnly see him set on to London.
So swift a pace hath thought that even now   15
You may imagine him upon Blackheath,
Where that his lords desire him to have borne
His bruised helmet and his bended sword
Before him through the city. He forbids it,
Being free from vainness and self-glorious pride; 20
Giving full trophy, signal, and ostent
Quite from himself to God. But now behold,
In the quick forge and working-house of thought,
How London doth pour out her citizens!
The mayor and all his brethren in best sort,   25
Like to the senators of th' antique Rome,
With the plebeians swarming at their heels,
Go forth and fetch their conqu'ring Cæsar in;
As, by a lower but loving likelihood,
Were now the general of our gracious empress, 30
As in good time he may, from Ireland coming,
Bringing rebellion broached on his sword,
How many would the peaceful city quit,
To welcome him! Much more, and much more cause,
Did they this Harry. Now in London place
    him;   35
As yet the lamentation of the French
Invites the King of England's stay at home, —
The Emperor 's coming in behalf of France,
To order peace between them; — and omit
All the occurrences, whatever chanc'd,   40
Till Harry's back-return again to France.
There must we bring him; and myself have play'd
The interim, by rememb'ring you 'tis past.
Then brook abridgement, and your eyes advance
After your thoughts, straight back again to France.
                        [*Exit.* 45

[SCENE I. *France. The English camp.*]

Enter FLUELLEN *and* GOWER.

Gow. Nay, that's right; but why wear you your
leek to-day? Saint Davy's day is past.

Flu. There is occasions and causes why and
wherefore in all things. I will tell you asse my
friend, Captain Gower. The rascally, scald, 5
beggarly, lousy, pragging knave, Pistol, which you
and yourself and all the world know to be no petter
than a fellow, look you now, of no merits, he is
come to me and prings me pread and salt yesterday,
look you, and bid me eat my leek. It was in 10
a place where I could not breed no contention with
him; but I will be so bold as to wear it in my cap
till I see him once again, and then I will tell him a
little piece of my desires.

Enter PISTOL.

Gow. Why, here he comes, swelling like a turkey-
cock.   16
Flu. 'Tis no matter for his swellings nor his
turkey-cocks. God pless you, Aunchient Pistol!
you scurfy, lousy knave, God pless you!
Pist. Ha! art thou bedlam? Dost thou thirst,
    base Troyan,   20
To have me fold up Parca's fatal web?
Hence! I am qualmish at the smell of leek.
Flu. I peseech you heartily, scurfy, lousy knave,
at my desires, and my requests, and my petitions,
to eat, look you, this leek. Because, look you, 25
you do not love it, nor your affections and your
appetites and your disgestions doo's not agree with
it, I would desire you to eat it.
Pist. Not for Cadwallader and all his goats.
Flu. There is one goat for you. (*Strikes him.*)
Will you be so good, scald knave, as eat it? 31
Pist. Base Troyan, thou shalt die.
Flu. You say very true, scald knave, when
God's will is. I will desire you to live in the mean
time, and eat your victuals. Come, there is 35
sauce for it. [*Strikes him.*] You call'd me yesterday mountain-squire; but I will make you to-day
a squire of low degree. I pray you, fall to; if you
can mock a leek, you can eat a leek.
Gow. Enough, captain; you have astonish'd
him.   41
Flu. I say, I will make him eat some part of my
leek, or I will peat his pate four days. Bite, I pray
you; it is good for your green wound and your
ploody coxcomb.   45
Pist. Must I bite?
Flu. Yes, certainly, and out of doubt and out
of question too, and ambiguities.
Pist. By this leek, I will most horribly revenge.
I eat and eat, I swear —   50
Flu. Eat, I pray you. Will you have some more

Act V, Prol., 10. **Pales:** fences. [with] F₂. Om. F₁. 12. **whiffler:** one who clears the way for a procession. 21. **signal, and ostent:** signs and shows of victory. 29. **loving** (Seymour). *by loving* F. 30. **general.** The Earl of Essex, who went to Ireland March 27, 1599, to put down Tyrone's rebellion, returning unsuccessful on Sept. 28 of same year. 32. **broached:** spitted. 38. **Emperor:** Sigismund.
Sc. i, 5. **scald:** scabby. 20. **bedlam:** crazy. 21. **Parca's:** Fate's. 29. **Cadwallader:** the last of the Welsh kings. 40 **astonish'd:** stunned.

sauce to your leek? There is not enough leek to swear by.

Pist. Quiet thy cudgel; thou dost see I eat. 54

Flu. Much good do you, scald knave, heartily. Nay, pray you, throw none away; the skin is good for your broken coxcomb. When you take occasions to see leeks hereafter, I pray you, mock at 'em; that is all.

Pist. Good. 60

Flu. Ay, leeks is good. Hold you, there is a groat to heal your pate.

Pist. Me a groat!

Flu. Yes, verily and in truth you shall take it; or I have another leek in my pocket, which you shall eat. 66

Pist. I take thy groat in earnest of revenge.

Flu. If I owe you anything, I will pay you in cudgels. You shall be a woodmonger, and buy nothing of me but cudgels. God be wi' you, and keep you, and heal your pate. [*Exit.* 71

Pist. All hell shall stir for this.

Gow. Go, go; you are a counterfeit cowardly knave. Will you mock at an ancient tradition, begun upon an honourable respect, and worn as a memorable trophy of predeceased valour, and 75 dare not avouch in your deeds any of your words? I have seen you gleeking and galling at this gentleman twice or thrice. You thought, because he could not speak English in the native garb, he 80 could not therefore handle an English cudgel. You find it otherwise; and henceforth let a Welsh correction teach you a good English condition. Fare ye well. [*Exit.*

Pist. Doth Fortune play the huswife with me now? 85

News have I, that my [Nell] is dead i' th' spital Of malady of France;

And there my rendezvous is quite cut off.

Old I do wax; and from my weary limbs

Honour is cudgell'd. Well, bawd I'll turn. 90

And something lean to cutpurse of quick hand.

To England will I steal, and there I'll steal;

And patches will I get unto these cudgell'd scars.

And swear I got them in the Gallia wars. [*Exit.*

[SCENE II. *France. A royal palace.*]

Enter, at one door, KING HENRY, EXETER, BEDFORD, [GLOUCESTER,] WARWICK, [WESTMORELAND,] *and other* Lords; *at another, the* FRENCH KING, QUEEN ISABEL, [*the* PRINCESS KATHARINE, ALICE, *and other* Ladies;] *the* DUKE OF BURGUNDY, *and other French.*

K. Hen. Peace to this meeting, wherefore we are met!

Unto our brother France, and to our sister,

Health and fair time of day; joy and good wishes

To our most fair and princely cousin Katharine;

And, as a branch and member of this royalty, 5

By whom this great assembly is contriv'd,

We do salute you, Duke of Burgundy;

And, princes French, and peers, health to you all!

Fr. King. Right joyous are we to behold your face,

Most worthy brother England; fairly met! 10

So are you, princes English, every one.

Q. Isa. So happy be the issue, brother [England],

Of this good day and of this gracious meeting,

As we are now glad to behold your eyes;

Your eyes, which hitherto have borne in them 15

Against the French that met them in their bent

The fatal balls of murdering basilisks.

The venom of such looks, we fairly hope,

Have lost their quality, and that this day

Shall change all griefs and quarrels into love. 20

K. Hen. To cry amen to that, thus we appear.

Q. Isa. You English princes all, I do salute you.

Bur. My duty to you both, on equal love,

Great Kings of France and England! That I have labour'd

With all my wits, my pains, and strong endeavours

To bring your most imperial Majesties 26

Unto this bar and royal interview,

Your mightiness on both parts best can witness.

Since then my office hath so far prevail'd

That, face to face and royal eye to eye, 30

You have congreeted, let it not disgrace me,

If I demand, before this royal view,

What rub or what impediment there is,

Why that the naked, poor, and mangled Peace,

Dear nurse of arts, plenties, and joyful births, 35

Should not in this best garden of the world,

Our fertile France, put up her lovely visage?

Alas, she hath from France too long been chas'd,

And all her husbandry doth lie on heaps,

Corrupting in it own fertility. 40

Her vine, the merry cheerer of the heart,

Unpruned dies; her hedges even-pleach'd,

Like prisoners wildly overgrown with hair,

Put forth disorder'd twigs; her fallow leas

The darnel, hemlock, and rank fumitory 45

Doth root upon, while that the coulter rusts

That should deracinate such savagery;

The even mead, that erst brought sweetly forth

The freckled cowslip, burnet, and green clover,

Wanting the scythe, [all] uncorrected, rank, 50

---

62. **groat**: fourpence.   77. **gleeking and galling**: sneering and scoffing.   85. **huswife**: hussy.   86. **[Nell]** (Johnson). *Doll* F. Sc. ii, 12. **[England]** F₂. *Ireland* F₁.   17. **basilisks**: (1) fabulous creatures which killed by a glance, (2) large cannon. 27. **bar**: court.   33. **rub**: obstacle.   40. **it**: its.   42. **even-pleach'd**: smoothly interwoven.   47. **deracinate**: uproot.   50. **[all]** (Rowe).   *withall* F.

Conceives by idleness, and nothing teems
But hateful docks, rough thistles, kexes, burs,
Losing both beauty and utility;
And all our vineyards, fallows, meads, and hedges,
Defective in their natures, grow to wildness.   55
Even so our houses and ourselves and children
Have lost, or do not learn for want of time,
The sciences that should become our country,
But grow like savages, — as soldiers will
That nothing do but meditate on blood, —   60
To swearing and stern looks, diffus'd attire,
And everything that seems unnatural.
Which to reduce into our former favour
You are assembled; and my speech entreats
That I may know the let why gentle Peace   65
Should not expel these inconveniences
And bless us with her former qualities.
   K. Hen. If, Duke of Burgundy, you would the
        peace,
Whose want gives growth to th' imperfections
Which you have cited, you must buy that peace   70
With full accord to all our just demands;
Whose tenours and particular effects
You have enschedul'd briefly in your hands.
   Bur. The King hath heard them; to the which as
        yet   74
There is no answer made.
   K. Hen.   Well, then, the peace,
Which you before so urg'd, lies in his answer.
   Fr. King. I have but with a cursory eye
O'erglanc'd the articles.   Pleaseth your Grace
To appoint some of your council presently
To sit with us once more, with better heed   80
To re-survey them, we will suddenly
Pass our accept and peremptory answer.
   K. Hen. Brother, we shall.   Go, uncle Exeter,
And brother Clarence, and you, brother Gloucester,
Warwick, and Huntingdon, go with the King;   85
And take with you free power to ratify,
Augment, or alter, as your wisdoms best
Shall see advantageable for our dignity,
Anything in or out of our demands,
And we'll consign thereto.   Will you, fair sister,   90
Go with the princes, or stay here with us?
   Q. Isa. Our gracious brother, I will go with them.
Haply a woman's voice may do some good,
When articles too nicely urg'd be stood on.
   K. Hen. Yet leave our cousin Katharine here
        with us: 95
She is our capital demand, compris'd
Within the fore-rank of our articles.
   Q. Isa. She hath good leave.
      [*Exeunt all except Henry, Katharine* [*and
         Alice*].

   K. Hen.   Fair Katharine, and most fair,
Will you vouchsafe to teach a soldier terms
Such as will enter at a lady's ear   100
And plead his love-suit to her gentle heart?
   Kath. Your Majesty shall mock at me; I cannot
speak your England.
   K. Hen. O fair Katharine, if you will love me
soundly with your French heart, I will be glad to
hear you confess it brokenly with your English
tongue.   Do you like me, Kate?   107
   Kath. Pardonnez-moi, I cannot tell wat is "like
me."
   K. Hen. An angel is like you, Kate, and you are
like an angel.   111
   *Kath. Que dit-il?   Que je suis semblable à les
anges?*
   Alice. Oui, vraiment, sauf votre grace, ainsi dit-il.
   K. Hen. I said so, dear Katharine; and I must
not blush to affirm it.   117
   *Kath. O bon Dieu! les langues des hommes sont
pleines de tromperies.*
   K. Hen. What says she, fair one?   That the
tongues of men are full of deceits?
   Alice. Oui, dat de tongues of de mans is be full
of deceits: dat is de Princess.   123
   K. Hen. The Princess is the better English-
woman.   I' faith, Kate, my wooing is fit for thy
understanding.   I am glad thou canst speak no
better English; for, if thou couldst, thou wouldst
find me such a plain king that thou wouldst think
I had sold my farm to buy my crown.   I know no
ways to mince it in love, but directly to say,   130
"I love you"; then if you urge me farther than to
say, "Do you in faith?"   I wear out my suit.
Give me your answer; i' faith, do; and so clap hands
and a bargain.   How say you, lady?
   Kath.   Sauf votre honneur, me understand
well.   136
   K. Hen. Marry, if you would put me to verses,
or to dance for your sake, Kate, why you undid me;
for the one, I have neither words nor measure, and
for the other I have no strength in measure,   140
yet a reasonable measure in strength.   If I could
win a lady at leap-frog, or by vaulting into my
saddle with my armour on my back, under the
correction of bragging be it spoken, I should quickly
leap into a wife.   Or if I might buffet for   145
my love, or bound my horse for her favours, I
could lay on like a butcher and sit like a jack-
an-apes, never off.   But, before God, Kate, I
cannot look greenly, nor gasp out my eloquence,
nor I have no cunning in protestation; only   150
downright oaths, which I never use till urg'd, nor
never break for urging.   If thou canst love a fellow

---

52. **kexes:** dry stalks.   61. **diffus'd:** ragged.   63. **favour:** looks.   65. **let:** hindrance.   77. **cursorary:** cursory.   F spells
curselarie.   81. **suddenly:** quickly.   82. **Pass...answer:** return our adopted and decisive reply.   90. **consign:** agree.   94.
nicely: punctiliously.   96. **capital:** chief.   139, 140, 141. **measure:** (1) meter, (2) dancing, (3) amount.

of this temper, Kate, whose face is not worth sun-
burning, that never looks in his glass for love of
anything he sees there, let thine eye be thy   155
cook.   I speak to thee plain soldier.   If thou
canst love me for this, take me; if not, to say to
thee that I shall die, is true; but for thy love, by
the Lord, no; yet I love thee too.   And while
thou liv'st, dear Kate, take a fellow of plain   160
and uncoined constancy; for he perforce must do
thee right, because he hath not the gift to woo
in other places; for these fellows of infinite tongue,
that can rhyme themselves into ladies' favours,
they do always reason themselves out again.   165
What! a speaker is but a prater; a rhyme is but a
ballad.   A good leg will fall; a straight back will
stoop; a black beard will turn white; a curl'd pate
will grow bald; a fair face will wither; a full eye
will wax hollow; but a good heart, Kate, is   170
the sun and the moon; or rather the sun and not
the moon; for it shines bright and never changes,
but keeps his course truly.   If thou would have
such a one, take me; and take me, take a soldier;
take a soldier, take a king.   And what say'st   175
thou then to my love?   Speak, my fair, and fairly,
I pray thee.

Kath.   Is it possible dat I should love de enemy
of France?   179

K. Hen.   No; it is not possible you should love
the enemy of France, Kate; but, in loving me, you
should love the friend of France; for I love France
so well that I will not part with a village of it,
I will have it all mine; and, Kate, when France is
mine and I am yours, then yours is France and
you are mine.   186

Kath.   I cannot tell wat is dat.

K. Hen.   No, Kate?   I will tell thee in French;
which I am sure will hang upon my tongue like a
new-married wife about her husband's neck,   190
hardly to be shook off.   *Je quand sur le possession
de France, et quand vous avez le possession de moi,* —
let me see, what then?   Saint Denis be my speed! —
donc votre est France et vous êtes mienne.   It is as
easy for me, Kate, to conquer the kingdom as   195
to speak so much more French.   I shall never
move thee in French, unless it be to laugh at
me.

Kath.   *Sauf votre honneur, le François que vous
parlez, il est meilleur que l'Anglois lequel je parle.*   201

K. Hen.   No, faith, is't not, Kate; but thy
speaking of my tongue, and I thine, most truly-
falsely, must needs be granted to be much at one.
But, Kate, dost thou understand thus much
English: canst thou love me?   206

Kath.   I cannot tell.

K. Hen.   Can any of your neighbours tell, Kate?

I'll ask them.   Come, I know thou lovest me;
and at night, when you come into your closet,   210
you'll question this gentlewoman about me; and
I know, Kate, you will to her disparise those parts
in me that you love with your heart.   But, good
Kate, mock me mercifully; the rather, gentle
princess, because I love thee cruelly.   If ever   215
thou beest mine, Kate, as I have a saving faith
within me tells me thou shalt, I get thee with
scambling, and thou must therefore needs prove
a good soldier-breeder.   Shalt not thou and I,
between Saint Denis and Saint George, com-   220
pound a boy, half French, half English, that shall
go to Constantinople and take the Turk by the
beard?   Shall we not?   What say'st thou, my fair
flower-de-luce?

Kath.   I do not know dat.   225

K. Hen.   No; 'tis hereafter to know, but now to
promise.   Do but now promise, Kate, you will
endeavour for your French part of such a boy;
and for my English moiety, take the word of a
king and a bachelor.   How answer you, *la plus
belle Katharine du monde, mon très cher et devin
déesse?*   232

Kath.   Your Majestee ave fausse French enough
to deceive de most sage demoiselle dat is en
France.   235

K. Hen.   Now, fie upon my false French!   By
mine honour, in true English, I love thee, Kate;
by which honour I dare not swear thou lovest me;
yet my blood begins to flatter me that thou dost,
notwithstanding the poor and untempering   240
effect of my visage.   Now, beshrew my father's
ambition! he was thinking of civil wars when he
got me; therefore was I created with a stubborn
outside, with an aspect of iron, that, when I come
to woo ladies, I fright them.   But, in faith,   245
Kate, the elder I wax, the better I shall appear.
My comfort is, that old age, that ill layer up of
beauty, can do no more spoil upon my face.   Thou
hast me, if thou hast me, at the worst; and thou
shalt wear me, if thou wear me, better and   250
better; and therefore tell me, most fair Katharine,
will you have me?   Put off your maiden blushes;
avouch the thoughts of your heart with the looks
of an empress; take me by the hand, and say,
Harry of England, I am thine; which word   255
thou shalt no sooner bless mine ear withal, but I
will tell thee aloud, England is thine, Ireland is
thine, France is thine, and Henry Plantagenet is
thine; who, though I speak it before his face, if
he be not fellow with the best king, thou shalt   260
find the best king of good fellows.   Come, your
answer in broken music; for thy voice is music
and thy English broken; therefore, queen of all,

---

155. **be thy cook**: add the garnishing.   161. **uncoined**: of metal not coined so that it can pass from one hand to another.
167. **fall**: lose shape.   210. **closet**: chamber.   218. **scambling**: fighting.   240. **untempering**: uningratiating.   262. **broken
music**: part-music.

Katharine, break thy mind to me in broken English.
Wilt thou have me?   266
  Kath. Dat is as it shall please de *roi mon père.*
  K. Hen. Nay, it will please him well, Kate;
it shall please him, Kate.
  Kath. Den it sall also content me.   270
  K. Hen. Upon that I kiss your hand, and call
you my queen.
  *Kath. Laissez, mon seigneur, laissez, laissez!
Ma foi, je ne veux point que vous abaissez votre
grandeur en baisant la main d'une [de votre seigneurie
indigne] serviteur. Excusez-moi, je vous supplie,
mon très-puissant seigneur.*   277
  K. Hen. Then I will kiss your lips, Kate.
  *Kath. Les dames et demoiselles pour être baisées
devant leur noces, il n'est pas la coutume de* 281
France.
  K. Hen. Madam my interpreter, what says she?
  Alice. Dat it is not be de fashion pour les ladies
of France, — I cannot tell wat is *baiser* en Anglish.
  K. Hen. To kiss.   287
  Alice. Your Majesty *entendre* bettre *que moi.*
  K. Hen. It is not the fashion for the maids in
France to kiss before they are married, would she
say?   291
  Alice. Oui, vraiment.
  K. Hen. O Kate, nice customs curtsy to great
kings. Dear Kate, you and I cannot be confined
within the weak list of a country's fashion. 295
We are the makers of manners, Kate; and the
liberty that follows our places stops the mouth
of all find-faults, as I will do yours, for upholding
the nice fashion of your country in denying me
a kiss; therefore, patiently and yielding. 300
[*Kissing her.*] You have witchcraft in your lips,
Kate; there is more eloquence in a sugar touch
of them than in the tongues of the French council;
and they should sooner persuade Harry of England
than a general petition of monarchs. Here comes
your father.   306

  Re-enter the FRENCH POWER *and the* ENGLISH
                LORDS.

  Bur. God save your Majesty! My royal cousin,
teach you our princess English?
  K. Hen. I would have her learn, my fair cousin,
how perfectly I love her; and that is good English.
  Bur. Is she not apt?   312
  K. Hen. Our tongue is rough, coz, and my
condition is not smooth; so that, having neither
the voice nor the heart of flattery about me, I
cannot so conjure up the spirit of love in her,
that he will appear in his true likeness. 317
  Bur. Pardon the frankness of my mirth, if I

answer you for that. If you would conjure in
her, you must make a circle; if conjure up Love
in her in his true likeness, he must appear naked
and blind. Can you blame her then, being a
maid yet ros'd over with the virgin crimson of
modesty, if she deny the appearance of a naked
blind boy in her naked seeing self? It were, my
lord, a hard condition for a maid to consign to. 326
  K. Hen. Yet they do wink and yield, as love is
blind and enforces.
  Bur. They are then excus'd, my lord, when they
see not what they do.
  K. Hen. Then, good my lord, teach your cousin
to consent winking.   332
  Bur. I will wink on her to consent, my lord, if
you will teach her to know my meaning; for maids,
well summer'd and warm kept, are like flies at
Bartholomew-tide, blind, though they have their
eyes; and then they will endure handling, which
before would not abide looking on.   338
  K. Hen. This moral ties me over to time and a
hot summer; and so I shall catch the fly, your
cousin, in the latter end, and she must be blind too.
  Bur. As love is, my lord, before it loves. 342
  K. Hen. It is so; and you may, some of you,
thank love for my blindness, who cannot see many
a fair French city for one fair French maid that
stands in my way.   346
  Fr. King. Yes, my lord, you see them perspectively, the cities turn'd into a maid; for they are
all girdled with maiden walls that war hath [never]
ent'red.   350
  K. Hen. Shall Kate be my wife?
  Fr. King. So please you.
  K. Hen. I am content, so the maiden cities you
talk of may wait on her; so the maid that stood in
the way for my wish shall show me the way to
my will.   356
  Fr. King. We have consented to all terms of
reason.
  K. Hen. Is't so, my lords of England?
  West. The King hath granted every article;
His daughter first, and then in sequel all,
According to their firm proposed natures. 362
  Exe. Only he hath not yet subscribed this:
where your Majesty demands, that the King of
France, having any occasion to write for matter
of grant, shall name your Highness in this form
and with this addition, in French, *Notre très-cher
fils Henri, Roi d'Angleterre, Héritier de France;* and
thus in Latin *Præcarissimus filius noster Henricus,
Rex Angliæ, et Hæres Franciæ.*   370
  Fr. King. Nor this I have not, brother, so denied
But your request shall make me let it pass.

---

265. **break:** open. 275. [*de ... indigne*] (Camb. edd.) *nostre Seigneur indignie* F. 295. **list:** boundary. 314. **condition:**
disposition. 327. **wink:** close the eyes. 336. **Bartholomew-tide:** Aug. 24. 347. **perspectively:** as through an optical glass
which produces illusions. 349. [**never**] (Rowe). Om. F. 367. **addition:** title. 360. *Præcarissimus. Præclarissimus* F.

K. Hen. I pray you then, in love and dear
   alliance,
Let that one article rank with the rest;
And thereupon give me your daughter.   375
   Fr. King. Take her, fair son, and from her blood
   raise up
Issue to me; that the contending kingdoms
Of France and England, whose very shores look pale
With envy of each other's happiness,
May cease their hatred, and this dear conjunction
Plant neighbourhood and Christian-like accord 381
In their sweet bosoms, that never war advance
His bleeding sword 'twixt England and fair France.
   Lords. Amen!
   K. Hen. Now, welcome, Kate; and bear me
   witness all,   385
That here I kiss her as my sovereign queen.
                         [Flourish.
   Q. Isa. God, the best maker of all marriages,
Combine your hearts in one, your realms in one!
As man and wife, being two, are one in love,
So be there 'twixt your kingdoms such a spousal,
That never may ill office, or fell jealousy, 391
Which troubles oft the bed of blessed marriage,
Thrust in between the paction of these kingdoms,
To make divorce of their incorporate league;
That English may as French, French Englishmen,
Receive each other. God speak this Amen! 396
   All. Amen!

K. Hen. Prepare we for our marriage; on which
   day,
My Lord of Burgundy, we'll take your oath,
And all the peers', for surety of our leagues.   400
Then shall I swear to Kate, and you to me;
And may our oaths well kept and prosperous be!
                     [Sennet. Exeunt.

[EPILOGUE]

Enter CHORUS.

[Chor.] Thus far, with rough and all-unable pen,
   Our bending author hath pursu'd the story,
In little room confining mighty men,
   Mangling by starts the full course of their glory.
Small time, but in that small most greatly liv'd 5
   This star of England. Fortune made his sword,
By which the world's best garden he achiev'd,
   And of it left his son imperial lord.
Henry the Sixth, in infant bands crown'd King
   Of France and England, did this king succeed; 10
Whose state so many had the managing,
   That they lost France and made his England
   bleed;
Which oft our stage hath shown; and, for their
   sake,
In your fair minds let this acceptance take.
                           [Exit.]

---

393. **paction:** agreement.
   Epi., 2. **bending:** i.e., under the weight of his theme. 4. **starts:** fragments. 7. **garden:** i.e., France. 14. **let . . . take:**
let this play find acceptance.

The First Part of Henry the Sixth

THE FIRST PART OF HENRY VI is not found in print till it appears in the First Folio, which is therefore the basis of all later texts. On November 8, 1623, Blount and Jaggard, who were among the publishers of the First Folio, entered in the Stationers' Register among other plays by Shakespeare "not formerly entered to other men," "the Thirde Part of Henry ye Sixt." For reasons connected with the entry and publication in quarto of the *Second* and *Third Parts*, this entry is generally regarded as referring to the present play.

Philip Henslowe, manager of the Rose Theatre, records in his *Diary* that on March 3, 1592, a "new enterlude," "harey the vj," was performed. The actors were Lord Strange's men, to which company Shakespeare then belonged. In Thomas Nashe's *Pierce Pennilesse*, published in 1592, appears the following passage:

"How would it have ioyed brave Talbot (the terror of the French), to think that after he had lyen two hundred yeare in his Toombe, hee should triumphe againe on the Stage and have his bones newe embalmed with teares of ten thousand spectators at least (at several times), who in the Tragedian that represents his person imagine that they behold him fresh bleeding."

It is more than probable that the allusion here is to the play mentioned by Henslowe, and that both are to be identified with some form of the play appearing in the Folio as *I Henry VI*. If this assumption is correct, the composition of the play may fairly be placed about 1591.

As to authorship, there is no external evidence but the fact of its inclusion by his fellow-actors, Heminge and Condell, in the First Folio. Nearly all scholars agree that considerable parts of the present play are by other hands than Shakespeare's, but there is little general agreement as to who the other dramatists were, and which parts ought to be assigned to each. Shakespeare is usually credited with the scene (II.iv) in the Temple Gardens, in which the red and white roses are chosen as emblems of the rival houses, and the summons of Talbot to the garrison of Bordeaux (IV.ii); others assign to him the scenes (IV.iii–vii) culminating in the death of Talbot and his son, the scene (II.v) between Mortimer and Plantagenet in the Tower, and the wooing of Margaret by Suffolk (V.iii). The final scene (V.v) may have been added later by Shakespeare to link the play with important elements in Parts II and III.

The non-Shakespearean scenes have been assigned to Marlowe and Greene, with less assurance to Peele, and with still less to Kyd, Lodge, and Chapman. The difficulty with such attributions is that the playwrights of the time imitated one another, and Shakespeare himself was then presumably more under the influence of his predecessors than later. Nor do we know whether the question is one of collaboration or revision.

The material for the plot was drawn chiefly from the *Chronicles* of Holinshed or from Halle, whose narrative for this period Holinshed paraphrases. A few details may have been derived from Fabian or Stowe. The facts thus obtained were treated with great freedom, and chronological sequence is often entirely disregarded. Thus the calamities to the English reported by the First Messenger in I.i as having occurred by the date of the funeral of Henry V in 1422 are either quite unhistorical, as in the case of the loss of Orleans and Poictiers, which were not held by the English at that time, or are antedated by from seven to twenty-nine years, as in the case of the loss of Rheims, Guysors, Paris, and Guienne. Again, Talbot's death in the drama precedes the capture of Jeanne d'Arc; but in fact he lived till 1453, while the Maid was burned in 1431. The reconciliation which she is represented as bringing about between Burgundy and Charles VII did not occur till four years after her death. Nor is there more care for internal consistency. Paris is represented as lost by the English in I.i, yet Henry VI is crowned there in IV.i, and in V.ii the Parisians are revolting to the French. Several picturesque incidents have no basis in the chronicle. Such are the interview of Talbot and the Countess of Auvergne in II.iii, and the plucking of the roses in II.iv.25 ff., with its sequel in IV.i.78–161. The device of disguising soldiers as countrymen bearing sacks for the capture of Rouen is unhistorical. Rouen was not lost by the English till 1449; but a trick similar to that in the play is described by Holinshed as having been used by the French for the capture of Cornill in 1441.

The operatic opening scene introduces the two main themes of the play: the loss of Henry V's conquests in France, and the disunity at home leading to the Wars of the Roses, which occupy Parts II and III. The former theme has two aspects, that repre- senting Talbot as an epic hero, and that vilifying Joan of Arc. In both, the play gives the view of these characters presented by the sources. The blaming of Somerset by York for the failure to rein- force Talbot connects the two themes. Though the drama lacks the unity Shakespeare obtained in his later histories by emphasis on a central figure, even the loose structure of this early chronicle play with its Senecan echoes — messengers, soliloquies, moral- izing — makes possible the presentation of great historical forces moving groups and masses of men, and prepares us for the tragic events which are to follow.

THE FIRST PART OF
HENRY THE SIXTH

[DRAMATIS PERSONÆ

KING HENRY VI.
DUKE OF GLOUCESTER, *uncle to the King, and Protector.*
DUKE OF BEDFORD, *uncle to the King, and Regent of France.*
THOMAS BEAUFORT, *duke of Exeter,* } *great-*
HENRY BEAUFORT, *bishop of Winchester, and afterwards cardinal.* } *uncles to the King.*
JOHN BEAUFORT, *earl, afterwards duke, of Somerset.*
RICHARD PLANTAGENET, *son of Richard, late earl of Cambridge, afterwards duke of York.*
EARL OF WARWICK.
EARL OF SALISBURY.
EARL OF SUFFOLK.
LORD TALBOT, *afterwards earl of Shrewsbury.*
JOHN TALBOT, *his son.*
EDMUND MORTIMER, *earl of March.*
SIR JOHN FASTOLFE.
SIR WILLIAM LUCY.
SIR WILLIAM GLANSDALE.
SIR THOMAS GARGRAVE.
Mayor of London.

WOODVILLE, *lieutenant of the Tower.*
VERNON, *of the White Rose or York faction.*
BASSET, *of the Red Rose or Lancaster faction.*
A Lawyer.   *Mortimer's Keepers.*

CHARLES, *Dauphin, and afterwards King, of France.*
REIGNIER, *duke of Anjou, and titular King of Naples.*
DUKE OF BURGUNDY.
DUKE OF ALENÇON.
BASTARD OF ORLEANS.
Governor of Paris.
Master-Gunner of Orleans and his Son.
General of the French forces in Bordeaux.
A French Sergeant.   *A Porter.*
An old Shepherd, *father to Joan la Pucelle.*

MARGARET, *daughter to Reignier, afterwards married to King Henry.*
COUNTESS OF AUVERGNE.
JOAN LA PUCELLE, *commonly called Joan of Arc.*

Lords, Wardens of the Tower, Heralds, Officers, Soldiers, Messengers, and Attendants, English and French.
Fiends appearing to La Pucelle.

SCENE: *Partly in England and partly in France.*]

ACT I

SCENE I. [*Westminster Abbey.*]

Dead March. Enter the Funeral of KING HENRY THE FIFTH, *attended on by the* DUKE OF BEDFORD, *Regent of France; the* DUKE OF GLOUCESTER, *Protector; the* DUKE OF EXETER, *the* EARL OF WARWICK, *the* BISHOP OF WINCHESTER, *Heralds,* etc.

Bed. Hung be the heavens with black, yield day to night!
Comets, importing change of times and states,
Brandish your crystal tresses in the sky,
And with them scourge the bad revolting stars
That have consented unto Henry's death!   5
King Henry the Fifth, too famous to live long!
England ne'er lost a king of so much worth.
   Glou. England ne'er had a king until his time.
Virtue he had, deserving to command.
His brandish'd sword did blind men with his beams;   10
His arms spread wider than a dragon's wings;
His sparkling eyes, replete with wrathful fire,

More dazzled and drove back his enemies
Than mid-day sun fierce bent against their faces.
What should I say? His deeds exceed all speech. 15
He ne'er lift up his hand but conquered.
　　Exe. We mourn in black; why mourn we not in
　　blood?
Henry is dead and never shall revive.
Upon a wooden coffin we attend,
And death's dishonourable victory　　　　　20
We with our stately presence glorify,
Like captives bound to a triumphant car.
What! shall we curse the planets of mishap
That plotted thus our glory's overthrow?
Or shall we think the subtle-witted French　25
Conjurers and sorcerers, that afraid of him
By magic verses have contriv'd his end?
　　Win. He was a king bless'd of the King of kings.
Unto the French the dreadful judgement-day
So dreadful will not be as was his sight.　30
The battles of the Lord of hosts he fought;
The Church's prayers made him so prosperous.
　　Glou. The Church! where is it? Had not
　　churchmen pray'd,
His thread of life had not so soon decay'd.
None do you like but an effeminate prince,　35
Whom, like a school-boy, you may over-awe.
　　Win. Gloucester, whate'er we like, thou art
　　Protector
And lookest to command the Prince and realm.
Thy wife is proud; she holdeth thee in awe,
More than God or religious churchmen may.　40
　　Glou. Name not religion, for thou lov'st the flesh,
And ne'er throughout the year to church thou go'st
Except it be to pray against thy foes.
　　Bed. Cease, cease these jars and rest your minds
　　in peace;
Let's to the altar. Heralds, wait on us.　45
Instead of gold we'll offer up our arms,
Since arms avail not now that Henry's dead.
Posterity, await for wretched years,
When at their mothers' [moist] eyes babes shall
　suck,
Our isle be made a [marish] of salt tears,　50
And none but women left to wail the dead.
Henry the Fifth, thy ghost I invocate:
Prosper this realm, keep it from civil broils,
Combat with adverse planets in the heavens!
A far more glorious star thy soul will make　55
Than Julius Cæsar or bright —

　　　　Enter a MESSENGER.

　　1. Mess. My honourable lords, health to you all!
Sad tidings bring I to you out of France
Of loss, of slaughter, and discomfiture.
Guienne, Champagne, Rheims, Orleans,　60

Paris, Guysors, Poictiers, are all quite lost.
　　Bed. What say'st thou, man, before dead Henry's
　　corse?
Speak softly, or the loss of those great towns
Will make him burst his lead and rise from death.
　　Glou. Is Paris lost? Is Rouen yielded up?　65
If Henry were recall'd to life again,
These news would cause him once more yield the
　ghost.
　　Exe. How were they lost? What treachery was
　　us'd?
　　1. Mess. No treachery, but want of men and
　　money.
Amongst the soldiers this is muttered,　70
That here you maintain several factions,
And whilst a field should be dispatch'd and fought
You are disputing of your generals.
One would have ling'ring wars with little cost;
Another would fly swift, but wanteth wings;　75
A third [man] thinks, without expense at all,
By guileful fair words peace may be obtain'd.
Awake, awake, English nobility!
Let not sloth dim your honours new-begot.
Cropp'd are the flower-de-luces in your arms;　80
Of England's coat one half is cut away.
　　Exe. Were our tears wanting to this funeral,
These tidings would call forth their flowing tides.
　　Bed. Me they concern; Regent I am of France.
Give me my steeled coat; I'll fight for France.　85
Away with these disgraceful wailing robes!
Wounds will I lend the French instead of eyes,
To weep their intermissive miseries.

　　　Enter to them a second MESSENGER.

　　2. Mess. Lords, view these letters full of bad
　　mischance.
France is revolted from the English quite,　90
Except some petty towns of no import.
The Dauphin Charles is crowned king in Rheims;
The Bastard of Orleans with him is join'd;
[Reignier], the Duke of Anjou, doth take his part;
The Duke of Alençon flieth to his side.　95
　　　　　　　　　　　　　　　　　　[*Exit.*
　　Exe. The Dauphin crowned king! All fly to him!
O, whither shall we fly from this reproach?
　　Glou. We will not fly but to our enemies' throats.
Bedford, if thou be slack, I'll fight it out.
　　Bed. Gloucester, why doubt'st thou of my for-
　　wardness?　100
An army have I muster'd in my thoughts,
Wherewith already France is overrun.

　　　　Enter a third MESSENGER.

　　3. Mess. My gracious lords, to add to your
　　laments

Act I, sc. i, 39. holdeth ... awe: overaweth thee. **49.** [moist] F₂. *moistned* F₁. **50.** [marish] (Pope). *nourish* F. **64. lead:** leaden coffin. **76.** [man] F₂. Om. F₁. **88. intermissive:** occurring at intervals. **92. *Dauphin*.** Dolphin F throughout.

Wherewith you now bedew King Henry's hearse,
I must inform you of a dismal fight   105
Betwixt the stout Lord Talbot and the French.
   Win. What! wherein Talbot overcame? Is't so?
   3. Mess. O, no; wherein Lord Talbot was o'er-
    thrown.
The circumstance I'll tell you more at large.
The tenth of August last this dreadful lord,   110
Retiring from the siege of Orleans,
Having full scarce six thousand in his troop,
By three and twenty thousand of the French
Was round encompassed and set upon.
No leisure had he to enrank his men.   115
He wanted pikes to set before his archers;
Instead whereof sharp stakes pluck'd out of hedges
They pitched in the ground confusedly,
To keep the horsemen off from breaking in.
More than three hours the fight continued,   120
Where valiant Talbot above human thought
Enacted wonders with his sword and lance.
Hundreds he sent to hell, and none durst stand him;
Here, there, and everywhere, enrag'd he slew.
The French exclaim'd the devil was in arms;   125
All the whole army stood agaz'd on him.
His soldiers, spying his undaunted spirit,
"A Talbot! a Talbot!" cri'd out amain
And rush'd into the bowels of the battle.
Here had the conquest fully been seal'd up,   130
If Sir John [Fastolfe] had not play'd the coward.
He, being in the vaward, plac'd behind
With purpose to relieve and follow them,
Cowardly fled, not having struck one stroke.
Hence grew the general wreck and massacre;   135
Enclosed were they with their enemies.
A base Walloon, to win the Dauphin's grace,
Thrust Talbot with a spear into the back,
Whom all France with their chief assembled
   strength
Durst not presume to look once in the face.   140
   Bed. Is Talbot slain? Then I will slay myself
For living idly here in pomp and ease
Whilst such a worthy leader, wanting aid,
Unto his dastard foeman is betray'd.   144
   3. Mess. O no, he lives, but is took prisoner,
And Lord Scales with him and Lord Hungerford.
Most of the rest slaughter'd or took likewise.
   Bed. His ransom there is none but I shall pay.
I'll hale the Dauphin headlong from his throne;
His crown shall be the ransom of my friend.   150
Four of their lords I'll change for one of ours.
Farewell, my masters! To my task will I.
Bonfires in France forthwith I am to make,
To keep our great Saint George's feast withal.
Ten thousand soldiers with me I will take,   155

Whose bloody deeds shall make all Europe quake.
   3. Mess. So you had need, for Orleans is be-
   sieg'd.
The English army is grown weak and faint.
The Earl of Salisbury craveth supply
And hardly keeps his men from mutiny,   160
Since they, so few, watch such a multitude.
   Exe. Remember, lords, your oaths to Henry
   sworn,
Either to quell the Dauphin utterly
Or bring him in obedience to your yoke.
   Bed. I do remember it; and here take my
   leave,   165
To go about my preparation.   [*Exit.*
   Glou. I'll to the Tower with all the haste I can,
To view th' artillery and munition;
And then I will proclaim young Henry king.
                      [*Exit.*
   Exe. To Eltham will I, where the young King
   is,   170
Being ordain'd his special governor,
And for his safety there I'll best devise.   [*Exit.*
   Win. Each hath his place and function to attend.
I am left out; for me nothing remains.
But long I will not be Jack out of office.   175
The King from Eltham I intend to [steal]
And sit at chiefest stern of public weal.   [*Exeunt.*

[SCENE II. *France.   Before Orleans.*]

A flourish.   Enter CHARLES, ALENÇON, *and*
   REIGNIER, *marching with drum and Soldiers.*

   Char. Mars his true moving, even as in the
   heavens
So in the earth, to this day is not known.
Late did he shine upon the English side;
Now we are victors, upon us he smiles.
What towns of any moment but we have?   5
At pleasure here we lie near Orleans;
Otherwhiles the famish'd English, like pale ghosts,
Faintly besiege us one hour in a month.
   Alen. They want their porridge and their fat
   bull-beeves.
Either they must be dieted like mules   10
And have their provender tied to their mouths,
Or piteous they will look, like drowned mice.
   Reig. Let's raise the siege; why live we idly here?
Talbot is taken, whom we wont to fear;
Remaineth none but mad-brain'd Salisbury,   15
And he may well in fretting spend his gall.
Nor men nor money hath he to make war.
   Char. Sound, sound alarum! We will rush on
   them.
Now for the honour of the forlorn French!

Him I forgive my death that killeth me   20
When he sees me go back one foot or fly.
                                    [*Exeunt.*

*Alarum; they are beaten back by the English with
great loss. Re-enter* CHARLES, ALENÇON, *and*
REIGNIER.

Char. Who ever saw the like?   What men have I!
Dogs! cowards! dastards! I would ne'er have fled,
But that they left me 'midst my enemies.
   Reig. Salisbury is a desperate homicide;   25
He fighteth as one weary of his life.
The other lords, like lions wanting food,
Do rush upon us as their hungry prey.
   Alen. Froissart, a countryman of ours, records
England all Olivers and Rolands bred   30
During the time Edward the Third did reign.
More truly now may this be verified,
For none but Samsons and Goliases
It sendeth forth to skirmish.   One to ten!
Lean raw-bon'd rascals! who would e'er suppose   35
They had such courage and audacity?
   Char. Let's leave this town; for they are hare-
      brain'd slaves,
And hunger will enforce them to be more eager.
Of old I know them; rather with their teeth
The walls they'll tear down than forsake the
      siege.   40
   Reig. I think, by some odd gimmers or device
Their arms are set like clocks, still to strike on;
Else ne'er could they hold out so as they do.
By my consent, we'll even let them alone.
   Alen. Be it so.   45

Enter the BASTARD *of Orleans.*

Bast. Where's the Prince Dauphin?   I have
      news for him.
   Char. Bastard of Orleans, thrice welcome to us.
   Bast. Methinks your looks are sad, your cheer
      appall'd.
Hath the late overthrow wrought this offence?
Be not dismay'd, for succour is at hand.   50
A holy maid hither with me I bring,
Which by a vision sent to her from heaven
Ordained is to raise this tedious siege
And drive the English forth the bounds of France.
The spirit of deep prophecy she hath,   55
Exceeding the nine sibyls of old Rome;
What's past and what's to come she can descry.
Speak, shall I call her in?   Believe my words,
For they are certain and unfallible.
   Char. Go, call her in. [*Exit Bastard.*] But first,
      to try her skill,   60

Reignier, stand thou as Dauphin in my place;
Question her proudly; let thy looks be stern.
By this means shall we sound what skill she hath.

Re-enter [the BASTARD *of Orleans, with]* JOAN
LA PUCELLE.

   Reig. Fair maid, is't thou wilt do these won-
      drous feats?
   Puc. Reignier, is't thou that thinkest to beguile
      me?   65
Where is the Dauphin?   Come, come from behind;
I know thee well, though never seen before.
Be not amaz'd, there's nothing hid from me.
In private will I talk with thee apart.
Stand back, you lords, and give us leave a while.   70
   Reig. She takes upon her bravely at first dash.
   Puc. Dauphin, I am by birth a shepherd's
      daughter,
My wit untrain'd in any kind of art.
Heaven and our Lady gracious hath it pleas'd
To shine on my contemptible estate.   75
Lo, whilst I waited on my tender lambs,
And to sun's parching heat display'd my cheeks,
God's mother deigned to appear to me,
And in a vision full of majesty
Will'd me to leave my base vocation   80
And free my country from calamity.
Her aid she promis'd and assur'd success;
In complete glory she reveal'd herself;
And, whereas I was black and swart before,
With those clear rays which she infus'd on me   85
That beauty am I bless'd with which you see.
Ask me what question thou canst possible,
And I will answer unpremeditated.
My courage try by combat, if thou dar'st,
And thou shalt find that I exceed my sex.   90
Resolve on this: thou shalt be fortunate
If thou receive me for thy warlike mate.
   Char. Thou hast astonish'd me with thy high
      terms.
Only this proof I'll of thy valour make,
In single combat thou shalt buckle with me,   95
And if thou vanquishest, thy words are true;
Otherwise I renounce all confidence.
   Puc. I am prepar'd: here is my keen-edg'd sword,
Deck'd with [five] flower-de-luces on each side;
The which at Touraine, in Saint Katharine's
      churchyard,   100
Out of a great deal of old iron I chose forth.
   Char. Then come, o' God's name; I fear no
      woman.
   Puc. And while I live, I'll ne'er fly from a man.
                  [*Here they fight, and Joan la Pucelle over-
                     comes.*

28. **hungry prey:** prey of their hunger.   30. **Olivers and Rolands:** the two most famous of Charlemagne's twelve peers.
35. **rascals:** lean worthless deer.   41. **gimmers:** mechanism.   85. **infus'd:** poured.   91. **Resolve on:** make up your mind
to.   99. **[five]**. So in Holinshed.   *fine* F.

Char. Stay, stay thy hands! Thou art an Amazon
And fightest with the sword of Deborah.   105
   Puc. Christ's mother helps me, else I were too weak.
   Char. Whoe'er helps thee, 'tis thou that must help me.
Impatiently I burn with thy desire;
My heart and hands thou hast at once subdu'd.
Excellent Pucelle, if thy name be so,   110
Let me thy servant and not sovereign be.
'Tis the French Dauphin sueth to thee thus.
   Puc. I must not yield to any rites of love,
For my profession's sacred from above.
When I have chased all thy foes from hence,   115
Then will I think upon a recompense.
   Char. Meantime look gracious on thy prostrate thrall.
   Reig. My lord, methinks, is very long in talk.
   Alen. Doubtless he shrives this woman to her smock;
Else ne'er could he so long protract his speech.
   Reig. Shall we disturb him, since he keeps no mean?   121
   Alen. He may mean more than we poor men do know.
These women are shrewd tempters with their tongues.
   Reig. My lord, where are you? What devise you on?
Shall we give over Orleans, or no?   125
   Puc. Why, no, I say, distrustful recreants!
Fight till the last gasp; I will be your guard.
   Char. What she says I'll confirm. We'll fight it out.
   Puc. Assign'd am I to be the English scourge.
This night the siege assuredly I'll raise.   130
Expect Saint Martin's summer, halcyon days,
Since I have entered into these wars.
Glory is like a circle in the water
Which never ceaseth to enlarge itself
Till by broad spreading it disperse to nought.   135
With Henry's death the English circle ends;
Dispersed are the glories it included.
Now am I like that proud insulting ship
Which Cæsar and his fortune bare at once.
   Char. Was Mahomet inspired with a dove?
Thou with an eagle art inspired then.   141
Helen, the mother of great Constantine,
Not yet Saint Philip's daughters, were like thee.
Bright star of Venus, fallen down on the earth,
How may I reverently worship thee enough?   145
   Alen. Leave off delays, and let us raise the siege.

   Reig. Woman, do what thou canst to save our honours.
Drive them from Orleans and be immortaliz'd.
   Char. Presently we'll try; come, let's away about it.
No prophet will I trust, if she prove false.   150
                                  [Exeunt.

[SCENE III. *London.   Before the Tower.*]

Enter the DUKE OF GLOUCESTER, *with his* SERVING-MEN [*in blue coats*].

   Glou. I am come to survey the Tower this day;
Since Henry's death, I fear, there is conveyance.
Where be these warders, that they wait not here?
Open the gates; 'tis Gloucester that calls.
   1. Warder. [*Within.*] Who's there that knocks so imperiously?   5
   1. Serv. It is the noble Duke of Gloucester.
   2. Warder. [*Within.*] Whoe'er he be, you may not be let in.
   1. Serv. Villains, answer you so the Lord Protector?
   1. Warder. [*Within.*] The Lord protect him! so we answer him.
We do no otherwise than we are will'd.   10
   Glou. Who willed you? or whose will stands but mine?
There's none Protector of the realm but I. —
Break up the gates, I'll be your warrantize.
Shall I be flouted thus by dunghill grooms?
      [*Gloucester's men rush at the Tower Gates, and Woodvile the Lieutenant speaks within.*
   Woodv. What noise is this? What traitors have we here?   15
   Glou. Lieutenant, is it you whose voice I hear?
Open the gates; here's Gloucester that would enter.
   Woodv. Have patience, noble Duke, I may not open;
The Cardinal of Winchester forbids.
From him I have express commandment   20
That thou nor none of thine shall be let in.
   Glou. Faint-hearted Woodvile, prizest him 'fore me?
Arrogant Winchester, that haughty prelate,
Whom Henry, our late sovereign, ne'er could brook?
Thou art no friend to God or to the King.   25
Open the gates, or I'll shut thee out shortly.
   Serving-men. Open the gates unto the Lord Protector,
Or we'll burst them open, if that you come not quickly.   *[They rush again at the gates.]*

---

121. **mean:** moderation.   124. **devise:** decide.   131. **Saint Martin's summer:** Indian summer.   139. **Cæsar.** The allusion is to Plutarch's story of Cæsar's attempt to cross the Adriatic.   143. **Saint Philip's daughters.** See *Acts* xxi.9.
Sc. iii, 2. **conveyance:** graft.   13. **warrantize:** guarantee.

Enter to the Lord Protector at the Tower Gates
WINCHESTER *and his men in tawny coats.*

Win. How now, ambitious Humphrey! what
    means this?

Glou. Peel'd priest, dost thou command me to
    be shut out?   30

Win. I do, thou most usurping proditor,
And not Protector, of the King or realm.

Glou. Stand back, thou manifest conspirator,
Thou that contriv'dst to murder our dead lord;
Thou that giv'st whores indulgences to sin.   35
I'll canvass thee in thy broad cardinal's hat,
If thou proceed in this thy insolence.

Win. Nay, stand thou back; I will not budge
    a foot.
This be Damascus, be thou cursed Cain
To slay thy brother Abel, if thou wilt.   40

Glou. I will not slay thee, but I'll drive thee
    back.
Thy scarlet robes as a child's bearing-cloth
I'll use to carry thee out of this place.

Win. Do what thou dar'st; I beard thee to thy
    face.

Glou. What! am I dar'd and bearded to my
    face?   45
Draw, men, for all this privileged place;
Blue coats to tawny coats! Priest, beware your
    beard;
I mean to tug it and to cuff you soundly.
Under my feet I stamp thy cardinal's hat.
In spite of Pope or dignities of church,   50
Here by the cheeks I'll drag thee up and down.

Win. Gloucester, thou wilt answer this before
    the Pope.

Glou. Winchester goose, I cry, "A rope! a rope!"
Now beat them hence; why do you let them stay?
Thee I'll chase hence, thou wolf in sheep's array.   55
Out, tawny coats! Out, scarlet hypocrite!

*Here Gloucester's men beat out the Cardinal's men,
and enter in the hurly-burly the* MAYOR *of London
and his* OFFICERS.

May. Fie, lords! that you, being supreme magis-
    trates,
Thus contumeliously should break the peace!

Glou. Peace, mayor, thou know'st little of my
    wrongs.
Here's Beaufort, that regards nor God nor king,   60
Hath here distrain'd the Tower to his use.

Win. Here's Gloucester, a foe to citizens,
One that still motions war and never peace,
O'ercharging your free purses with large fines,

That seeks to overthrow religion   65
Because he is Protector of the realm,
And would have armour here out of the Tower,
To crown himself king and suppress the Prince.

Glou. I will not answer thee with words, but
    blows.   [*Here they skirmish again.*

May. Nought rests for me in this tumultuous
    strife   70
But to make open proclamation.
Come, officer; as loud as e'er thou canst,
Cry.   73

[*1. Off.*] All manner of men assembled here in
arms this day against God's peace and the King's,
we charge and command you, in his Highness'
name, to repair to your several dwelling-places;
and not to wear, handle, or use any sword, weapon,
or dagger, henceforward, upon pain of death.   79

Glou. Cardinal, I'll be no breaker of the law;
But we shall meet, and break our minds at large.

Win. Gloucester, we'll meet to thy cost, be sure.
Thy heart-blood I will have for this day's work.

May. I'll call for clubs, if you will not away.
This cardinal's more haughty than the devil.   85

Glou. Mayor, farewell; thou dost but what thou
    mayst.

Win. Abominable Gloucester, guard thy head;
For I intend to have it ere long.

    [*Exeunt [severally, Gloucester and Win-
    chester with their Serving-men*].

May. See the coast clear'd, and then we will
    depart.
Good God, these nobles should such stomachs
    bear!   90
I myself fight not once in forty year.   [*Exeunt.*

[SCENE IV. *France.*   *Before Orleans.*]

Enter [on the walls,] a MASTER GUNNER *and
his* BOY.

M. Gun. Sirrah, thou know'st how Orleans is
    besieg'd,
And how the English have the suburbs won.

Boy. Father, I know; and oft have shot at them,
Howe'er unfortunate I miss'd my aim.

M. Gun. But now thou shalt not. Be thou rul'd
    by me.   5
Chief master-gunner am I of this town;
Something I must do to procure me grace.
The Prince's espials have informed me
How the English, in the suburbs close intrench'd,
Went through a secret grate of iron bars   10
In yonder tower to overpeer the city

---

30. **Peel'd:** shaven.   31. **proditor:** traitor.   35. **Thou . . . sin.** The brothels in Southwark were under the jurisdiction of
the Bishop of Winchester.   36. **canvass:** toss in a canvas sheet; belabor.   39. **Damascus:** believed to have been the scene
of the murder of Abel.   42. **bearing-cloth:** christening robe.   53. **Winchester goose:** slang name for a venereal disease.
"**A rope**": a halter to hang him.   61. **distrain'd:** seized.   63. **motions:** stirs up.   84. **clubs:** peace officers with staves.
90. **stomachs:** fighting dispositions.
    Sc. iv, 8. **espials:** spies.

And thence discover how with most advantage
They may vex us with shot or with assault.
To intercept this inconvenience,
A piece of ordnance 'gainst it I have plac'd;   15
And even these three days have I watch'd
If I could see them.
Now do thou watch, for I can stay no longer.
If thou spy'st any, run and bring me word;
And thou shalt find me at the governor's.   20
                                        [*Exit.*
  Boy. Father, I warrant you; take you no care.
I'll never trouble you, if I may spy them.   [*Exit.*

Enter, on the turret, the LORDS SALISBURY *and* TAL-
BOT, [SIR WILLIAM GLANSDALE, SIR THOMAS
GARGRAVE,] *and others.*

  Sal. Talbot, my life, my joy, again return'd!
How wert thou handled being prisoner?
Or by what means got'st thou to be releas'd?   25
Discourse, I prithee, on this turret's top.
  Tal. The Earl of Bedford had a prisoner
Call'd the brave Lord Ponton de Santrailles;
For him was I exchang'd and ransomed.
But with a baser man of arms by far   30
Once in contempt they would have barter'd me;
Which I disdaining scorn'd, and craved death
Rather than I would be so [vile] esteem'd.
In fine, redeem'd I was as I desir'd.
But, O! the treacherous Fastolfe wounds my
    heart,   35
Whom with my bare fists I would execute,
If I now had him brought into my power.
  Sal. Yet tell'st thou not how thou wert enter-
    tain'd.
  Tal. With scoffs and scorns and contumelious
    taunts.
In open market-place produc'd they me   40
To be a public spectacle to all.
Here, said they, is the terror of the French,
The scarecrow that affrights our children so.
Then broke I from the officers that led me,
And with my nails digg'd stones out of the
    ground
To hurl at the beholders of my shame.   46
My grisly countenance made others fly;
None durst come near for fear of sudden death.
In iron walls they deem'd me not secure;
So great fear of my name 'mongst them were
    spread   50
That they suppos'd I could rend bars of steel
And spurn in pieces posts of adamant;
Wherefore a guard of chosen shot I had
That walk'd about me every minute while;
And if I did but stir out of my bed,   55
Ready they were to shoot me to the heart.

Enter the Boy with a linstock.

  Sal. I grieve to hear what torments you endur'd,
But we will be reveng'd sufficiently.
Now it is supper-time in Orleans.
Here, through this secret grate, I count each one   60
And view the Frenchmen how they fortify.
Let us look in; the sight will much delight thee.
Sir Thomas Gargrave, and Sir William Glansdale,
Let me have your express opinions
Where is best place to make our batt'ry next.
  Gar. I think, at the north gate; for there stands
    lords.   66
  Glan. And I, here, at the bulwark of the
    bridge.
  Tal. For aught I see, this city must be famish'd,
Or with light skirmishes enfeebled.
    [*Shot [from the town], and Salisbury [and*
        Gargrave] fall.
  Sal. O Lord, have mercy on us, wretched sin-
    ners!   70
  Gar. O Lord, have mercy on me, woeful man!
  Tal. What chance is this that suddenly hath
    cross'd us?
Speak, Salisbury; at least, if thou canst, speak.
How far'st thou, mirror of all martial men?
One of thy eyes and thy cheek's side struck off!   75
Accursed tower! accursed fatal hand
That hath contriv'd this woeful tragedy!
In thirteen battles Salisbury o'ercame.
Henry the Fifth he first train'd to the wars.
Whilst any trump did sound, or drum struck up,   80
His sword did ne'er leave striking in the field.
Yet liv'st thou, Salisbury? Though thy speech
    doth fail,
One eye thou hast, to look to heaven for grace;
The sun with one eye vieweth all the world.
Heaven, be thou gracious to none alive   85
If Salisbury wants mercy at thy hands!
Bear hence his body; I will help to bury it.
Sir Thomas Gargrave, hast thou any life?
Speak unto Talbot; nay, look up to him.
Salisbury, cheer thy spirit with this comfort,   90
Thou shalt not die whiles —
He beckons with his hand and smiles on me,
As who should say, "When I am dead and gone,
Remember to avenge me on the French."
Plantagenet, I will; and like thee, [Nero,]   95
Play on the lute, beholding the towns burn.
Wretched shall France be only in my name.
    [*Here an alarum, and it thunders and lightens.*
What stir is this? What tumult's in the heavens?
Whence cometh this alarum and the noise?

Enter a MESSENGER.

  Mess. My lord, my lord, the French have
    gather'd head.   100

---

33. [vile] (Pope).   *pil'd* F.   56. s.d. **linstock:** stick to hold the gunner's match.   95. **[Nero]** (Malone).   Om. F.

The Dauphin, with one Joan la Pucelle join'd,
A holy prophetess new risen up,
Is come with a great power to raise the siege.
    [Here Salisbury lifteth himself up and groans.
Tal. Hear, hear how dying Salisbury doth
    groan!
It irks his heart he cannot be reveng'd.   105
Frenchmen, I'll be a Salisbury to you.
Pucelle or puzzel, dolphin or dogfish,
Your hearts I'll stamp out with my horse's heels,
And make a quagmire of your mingled brains.
Convey me Salisbury into his tent,   110
And then we'll try what these dastard Frenchmen
    dare.
    [Alarum. Exeunt [bearing out the bodies].

[SCENE V. *The same.*]

Here an alarum again; and TALBOT *pursueth the*
DAUPHIN, *and driveth him. Then enter* JOAN LA
PUCELLE, *driving Englishmen before her [and exit
after them]. Then re-enter* TALBOT.

Tal. Where is my strength, my valour, and my
    force?
Our English troops retire, I cannot stay them;
A woman clad in armour chaseth them.

Re-enter LA PUCELLE.

Here, here she comes. I'll have a bout with thee;
Devil or devil's dam, I'll conjure thee.   5
Blood will I draw on thee, thou art a witch,
And straightway give thy soul to him thou serv'st.
Puc. Come, come, 'tis only I that must dis-
    grace thee.   *[Here they fight.*
Tal. Heavens, can you suffer hell so to prevail?
My breast I'll burst with straining of my courage   10
And from my shoulders crack my arms asunder,
But I will chastise this high-minded strumpet.
    [They fight again.
Puc. Talbot, farewell; thy hour is not yet come.
I must go victual Orleans forthwith.
    *[A short alarum: then La Pucelle enters the
    town with soldiers.*
O'ertake me, if thou canst; I scorn thy strength.   15
Go, go, cheer up thy hungry, starved men;
Help Salisbury to make his testament.
This day is ours, as many more shall be.   *[Exit.*
Tal. My thoughts are whirled like a potter's
    wheel;
I know not where I am nor what I do.   20
A witch by fear, not force, like Hannibal,
Drives back our troops and conquers as she lists;
So bees with smoke and doves with noisome stench

Are from their hives and houses driven away.
They call'd us for our fierceness English dogs;   25
Now, like to whelps, we crying run away.
    [A short alarum.
Hark, countrymen! either renew the fight,
Or tear the lions out of England's coat,
Renounce your soil, give sheep in lions' stead.
Sheep run not half so treacherous from the wolf,   30
Or horse or oxen from the leopard,
As you fly from your oft-subdued slaves.
    [Alarum. Another skirmish.
It will not be. Retire into your trenches.
You all consented unto Salisbury's death,
For none would strike a stroke in his revenge.   35
Pucelle is ent'red into Orleans
In spite of us or aught that we could do.
O, would I were to die with Salisbury!
The shame hereof will make me hide my head.
    [Exit Talbot. Alarum; retreat; flourish.

[SCENE VI. *The same.*]

Enter, on the walls, LA PUCELLE, CHARLES,
REIGNIER, ALENÇON, *and Soldiers.*

Puc. Advance our waving colours on the walls;
Rescu'd is Orleans from the English!
Thus Joan la Pucelle hath perform'd her word.
Char. Divinest creature, Astræa's daughter,
How shall I honour thee for this success?   5
Thy promises are like Adonis' garden
That one day bloom'd and fruitful were the next.
France, triumph in thy glorious prophetess!
Recover'd is the town of Orleans.
More blessed hap did ne'er befall our state.   10
Reig. Why ring not out the bells aloud through-
    out the town?
Dauphin, command the citizens make bonfires
And feast and banquet in the open streets,
To celebrate the joy that God hath given us.
Alen. All France will be replete with mirth and
    joy   15
When they shall hear how we have play'd the men.
Char. 'Tis Joan, not we, by whom the day is
    won;
For which I will divide my crown with her,
And all the priests and friars in my realm
Shall in procession sing her endless praise.   20
A statelier pyramis to her I'll rear
Than Rhodope's [of] Memphis ever was.
In memory of her when she is dead,
Her ashes, in an urn more precious
Than the rich-jewell'd coffer of Darius,   25
Transported shall be at high festivals
Before the kings and queens of France.

Sc. v, 12. **high-minded:** haughty. 21. **Hannibal.** An allusion to his trick of fixing lighted twigs on the horns of oxen.
Sc. vi, 4. **Astræa:** goddess of justice. 22. **[of]** (Capell). *or* F. **Rhodope** was a famed Egyptian courtesan, who married the king of Memphis. 25. **coffer of Darius:** the casket in which Alexander the Great carried the poems of Homer.

No longer on Saint Denis will we cry,
But Joan la Pucelle shall be France's saint.
Come in, and let us banquet royally,   30
After this golden day of victory.
                        [*Flourish.   Exeunt.*

ACT II

Scene I. [*Before Orleans.*]

Enter a [French] Sergeant, *with two* Sentinels.

Serg. Sirs, take your places and be vigilant.
If any noise or soldier you perceive
Near to the walls, by some apparent sign
Let us have knowledge at the court of guard.
    1. Sent. Sergeant, you shall. [*Exit Sergeant.*]
            Thus are poor servitors,   5
When others sleep upon their quiet beds,
Constrain'd to watch in darkness, rain, and cold.

Enter Talbot, Bedford, Burgundy, [*and forces,*]
    *with scaling-ladders, their drums beating a dead
    march.*

Tal. Lord Regent, and redoubted Burgundy,
By whose approach the regions of Artois,
Wallon and Picardy are friends to us,   10
This happy night the Frenchmen are secure,
Having all day carous'd and banqueted.
Embrace we then this opportunity
As fitting best to quittance their deceit
Contriv'd by art and baleful sorcery.   15
    Bed. Coward of France! how much he wrongs
        his fame,
Despairing of his own arm's fortitude,
To join with witches and the help of hell!
    Bur. Traitors have never other company.   19
But what's that Pucelle whom they term so pure?
    Tal. A maid, they say.
    Bed.   A maid! and be so martial!
    Bur. Pray God she prove not masculine ere
        long,
If underneath the standard of the French
She carry armour as she hath begun.
    Tal. Well, let them practise and converse with
        spirits.   25
God is our fortress, in whose conquering name
Let us resolve to scale their flinty bulwarks.
    Bed. Ascend, brave Talbot; we will follow thee.
    Tal. Not all together. Better far, I guess,
That we do make our entrance several ways;   30
That, if it chance the one of us do fail,
The other yet may rise against their force.
    Bed. Agreed. I'll to yond corner.
    Bur.   And I to this.
    Tal. And here will Talbot mount, or make his
        grave.

Now, Salisbury, for thee, and for the right   35
Of English Henry, shall this night appear
How much in duty I am bound to both.
    Sent. Arm! arm! the enemy doth make assault!
        [*Cry:* "St. George," "A Talbot." [*The
        English scale the walls.*]

*The French leap over the walls in their shirts. Enter
    several ways, the* Bastard *of Orleans,* Alençon,
    and Reignier, *half ready, and half unready.*

Alen. How now, my lords! what, all unready so?
    Bast. Unready! Ay, and glad we scap'd so well.
    Reig. 'Twas time, I trow, to wake and leave our
        beds,   41
Hearing alarums at our chamber-doors.
    Alen. Of all exploits since first I follow'd arms,
Ne'er heard I of a warlike enterprise
More venturous or desperate than this.   45
    Bast. I think this Talbot be a fiend of hell.
    Reig. If not of hell, the heavens, sure, favour him.
    Alen. Here cometh Charles; I marvel how he
        sped.

Enter Charles *and* La Pucelle.

Bast. Tut, holy Joan was his defensive guard.
    Char. Is this thy cunning, thou deceitful dame?
Didst thou at first, to flatter us withal,   51
Make us partakers of a little gain,
That now our loss might be ten times so much?
    Puc. Wherefore is Charles impatient with his
        friend?
At all times will you have my power alike?   55
Sleeping or waking must I still prevail,
Or will you blame and lay the fault on me?
Improvident soldiers! had your watch been good,
This sudden mischief never could have fall'n.
    Char. Duke of Alençon, this was your default, 60
That, being captain of the watch to-night,
Did look no better to that weighty charge.
    Alen. Had all your quarters been as safely kept
As that whereof I had the government,
We had not been thus shamefully surpris'd.   65
    Bast. Mine was secure.
    Reig.   And so was mine, my lord.
    Char. And, for myself, most part of all this
        night,
Within her quarter and mine own precinct
I was employ'd in passing to and fro,
About relieving of the sentinels.   70
Then how or which way should they first break in?
    Puc. Question, my lords, no further of the case,
How or which way. 'Tis sure they found some
        place
But weakly guarded, where the breach was made.
And now there rests no other shift but this,   75

Act II, sc. i, 11. **secure:** careless. 14. **quittance:** repay. 15. **art:** the black art, magic. 38. s.d. **ready:** dressed.

To gather our soldiers, scatter'd and dispers'd,
And lay new platforms to endamage them.

Alarum.   Enter an [English] Soldier, crying, "A Talbot! a Talbot!" They fly, leaving their clothes behind.

Sold. I'll be so bold to take what they have left.
The cry of Talbot serves me for a sword;
For I have loaden me with many spoils,   80
Using no other weapon but his name.   [*Exit.*

[SCENE II.   *Orleans.   Within the town.*]

Enter Talbot, Bedford, Burgundy [*a* Captain, *and others*].

Bed. The day begins to break, and night is fled,
Whose pitchy mantle over-veil'd the earth.
Here sound retreat, and cease our hot pursuit.
                           [*Retreat sounded.*
Tal. Bring forth the body of old Salisbury,
And here advance it in the market-place,   5
The middle centre of this cursed town.
Now have I paid my vow unto his soul;
For every drop of blood was drawn from him
There hath at least five Frenchmen died tonight.
And that hereafter ages may behold   10
What ruin happened in revenge of him,
Within their chiefest temple I'll erect
A tomb, wherein his corpse shall be interr'd;
Upon the which, that every one may read,
Shall be engrav'd the sack of Orleans,   15
The treacherous manner of his mournful death,
And what a terror he had been to France.
But, lords, in all our bloody massacre,
I muse we met not with the Dauphin's grace,
His new-come champion, virtuous Joan of Arc,   20
Nor any of his false confederates.
Bed. 'Tis thought, Lord Talbot, when the fight began,
Rous'd on the sudden from their drowsy beds,
They did amongst the troops of armed men
Leap o'er the walls for refuge in the field.   25
Bur. Myself, as far as I could well discern
For smoke and dusky vapours of the night,
Am sure I scar'd the Dauphin and his trull,
When arm in arm they both came swiftly running,
Like to a pair of loving turtle-doves   30
That could not live asunder day or night.
After that things are set in order here,
We'll follow then with all the power we have.

Enter a Messenger.

Mess. All hail, my lords! Which of this princely train

Call ye the warlike Talbot, for his acts   35
So much applauded through the realm of France?
Tal. Here is the Talbot; who would speak with him?
Mess. The virtuous lady, Countess of Auvergne,
With modesty admiring thy renown,
By me entreats, great lord, thou wouldst vouch-
safe   40
To visit her poor castle where she lies,
That she may boast she hath beheld the man
Whose glory fills the world with loud report.
Bur. Is it even so? Nay, then, I see our wars
Will turn unto a peaceful comic sport,   45
When ladies crave to be encount'red with.
You may not, my lord, despise her gentle suit.
Tal. Ne'er trust me then; for when a world of men
Could not prevail with all their oratory,
Yet hath a woman's kindness over-rul'd;   50
And therefore tell her I return great thanks,
And in submission will attend on her.
Will not your honours bear me company?
Bed. No, truly, 'tis more than manners will;
And I have heard it said, unbidden guests   55
Are often welcomest when they are gone.
Tal. Well then, alone, since there's no remedy,
I mean to prove this lady's courtesy.
Come hither, captain. (*Whispers.*) You perceive my mind?
Capt. I do, my lord, and mean accordingly.   60
                                      [*Exeunt.*

[SCENE III.   *Auvergne.   The Countess's castle.*]

Enter the Countess [*and her* Porter].

Count. Porter, remember what I gave in charge.
And when you have done so, bring the keys to me;
Port. Madam, I will.   [*Exit.*
Count. The plot is laid. If all things fall out right
I shall as famous be by this exploit   5
As Scythian Tomyris by Cyrus' death.
Great is the rumour of this dreadful knight,
And his achievements of no less account;
Fain would mine eyes be witness with mine ears
To give their censure of these rare reports.   10

Enter Messenger *and* Talbot.

Mess. Madam.
According as your ladyship desir'd,
By message crav'd, so is Lord Talbot come.
Count. And he is welcome. What! is this the man?
Mess. Madam, it is.

---

77. **platforms:** plans.
Sc. ii, 5. **advance:** raise. 28. **trull:** harlot.
Sc. iii, 6. **Tomyris:** Queen of the Massagetæ, who killed Cyrus. 10. **censure:** judgment.

Count.   Is this the scourge of France?
Is this the Talbot, so much fear'd abroad   16
That with his name the mothers still their babes?
I see report is fabulous and false.
I thought I should have seen some Hercules,
A second Hector, for his grim aspect   20
And large proportion of his strong-knit limbs.
Alas, this is a child, a silly dwarf!
It cannot be this weak and writhled shrimp
Should strike such terror to his enemies.
  Tal. Madam, I have been bold to trouble you; 25
But since your ladyship is not at leisure
I'll sort some other time to visit you.   [*Going.*]
  Count. What means he now? Go ask him
    whither he goes.
  Mess. Stay, my Lord Talbot; for my lady craves
To know the cause of your abrupt departure. 30
  Tal. Marry, for that she's in a wrong belief,
I go to certify her Talbot's here.

      Re-enter Porter *with keys.*

  Count. If thou be he, then art thou prisoner.
  Tal. Prisoner! To whom?
  Count.   To me, blood-thirsty lord;
And for that cause I train'd thee to my house. 35
Long time thy shadow hath been thrall to me,
For in my gallery thy picture hangs;
But now the substance shall endure the like,
And I will chain these legs and arms of thine
That hast by tyranny these many years   40
Wasted our country, slain our citizens,
And sent our sons and husbands captivate.
  Tal. Ha, ha, ha!
  Count. Laughest thou, wretch? Thy mirth
    shall turn to moan.
  Tal. I laugh to see your ladyship so fond 45
To think that you have aught but Talbot's shadow
Whereon to practise your severity.
  Count. Why, art not thou the man?
  Tal.   I am indeed.
  Count. Then have I substance too.
  Tal. No, no, I am but shadow of myself. 50
You are deceiv'd, my substance is not here;
For what you see is but the smallest part
And least proportion of humanity.
I tell you, madam, were the whole frame here,
It is of such a spacious lofty pitch, 55
Your roof were not sufficient to contain 't.
  Count. This is a riddling merchant for the nonce;
He will be here, and yet he is not here.
How can these contrarieties agree?
  Tal. That will I show you presently. 60
    [*Winds his horn. Drums strike up: a
      peal of ordnance.* [*The gates are forced.*]

              Enter Soldiers.

How say you, madam? Are you now persuaded
That Talbot is but shadow of himself?
These are his substance, sinews, arms, and strength,
With which he yoketh your rebellious necks,
Razeth your cities and subverts your towns 65
And in a moment makes them desolate.
  Count. Victorious Talbot! pardon my abuse.
I find thou art no less than fame hath bruited
And more than may be gathered by thy shape.
Let my presumption not provoke thy wrath; 70
For I am sorry that with reverence
I did not entertain thee as thou art.
  Tal. Be not dismay'd, fair lady; nor misconster
The mind of Talbot, as you did mistake
The outward composition of his body. 75
What you have done hath not offended me;
Nor other satisfaction do I crave,
But only, with your patience, that we may
Taste of your wine and see what cates you have;
For soldiers' stomachs always serve them well. 80
  Count. With all my heart, and think me honoured
To feast so great a warrior in my house. [*Exeunt.*

   [SCENE IV. *London. The Temple-garden.*]

Enter the EARLS OF SOMERSET, SUFFOLK, *and*
  WARWICK; RICHARD PLANTAGENET [VERNON,
  and another Lawyer].

  [*Plan.*] Great lords and gentlemen, what means
    this silence?
Dare no man answer in a case of truth?
  Suf. Within the Temple-hall we were too loud;
The garden here is more convenient.
  Plan. Then say at once if I maintain'd the
    truth;   5
Or else was wrangling Somerset in th' error?
  Suf. Faith, I have been a truant in the law,
And never yet could frame my will to it;
And therefore frame the law unto my will.
  Som. Judge you, my Lord of Warwick, then,
    between us.   10
  War. Between two hawks, which flies the higher
    pitch;
Between two dogs, which hath the deeper mouth;
Between two blades, which bears the better temper;
Between two horses, which doth bear him best;
Between two girls, which hath the merriest eye; 15
I have perhaps some shallow spirit of judgement;
But in these nice sharp quillets of the law,
Good faith, I am no wiser than a daw.
  Plan. Tut, tut, here is a mannerly forbearance.
The truth appears so naked on my side 20

---

23. **writhled:** wrinkled. 27. **sort:** choose. 45. **fond:** foolish. 57. **merchant:** fellow. 65. **subverts:** overthrows. 68.
bruited: reported. 73. **misconster:** misconstrue. 79. **cates:** dainties.
  Sc. iv, 1 and throughout this scene. [*Plan.*] (Rowe). *Yorke* F. 17. **quillets:** subtleties.

That any purblind eye may find it out.

Som. And on my side it is so well apparell'd,
So clear, so shining, and so evident
That it will glimmer through a blind man's eye.

Plan. Since you are tongue-tied and so loath to
    speak,   25
In dumb significants proclaim your thoughts.
Let him that is a true-born gentleman
And stands upon the honour of his birth,
If he suppose that I have pleaded truth,
From off this brier pluck a white rose with me.   30

Som. Let him that is no coward nor no flatterer,
But dare maintain the party of the truth,
Pluck a red rose from off this thorn with me.

War. I love no colours, and without all colour
Of base insinuating flattery   35
I pluck this white rose with Plantagenet.

Suf. I pluck this red rose with young Somerset,
And say withal I think he held the right.

Ver. Stay, lords and gentlemen, and pluck no
    more
Till you conclude that he upon whose side   40
The fewest roses are cropp'd from the tree
Shall yield the other in the right opinion.

Som. Good Master Vernon, it is well objected.
If I have fewest, I subscribe in silence.

Plan. And I.   45

Ver. Then for the truth and plainness of the case,
I pluck this pale and maiden blossom here,
Giving my verdict on the white rose side.

Som. Prick not your finger as you pluck it off,
Lest bleeding you do paint the white rose red   50
And fall on my side so, against your will.

Ver. If I, my lord, for my opinion bleed,
Opinion shall be surgeon to my hurt
And keep me on the side where still I am.

Som. Well, well, come on; who else?   55

Law. Unless my study and my books be false,
The argument you held was wrong in you;
                       [*To Somerset.*]
In sign whereof I pluck a white rose too.

Plan. Now, Somerset, where is your argument?

Som. Here in my scabbard, meditating that
Shall dye your white rose in a bloody red.   61

Plan. Meantime your cheeks do counterfeit our
    roses;
For pale they look with fear, as witnessing
The truth on our side.

Som.   No, Plantagenet,
'Tis not for fear, but anger, that thy cheeks   65
Blush for pure shame to counterfeit our roses,
And yet thy tongue will not confess thy error.

Plan. Hath not thy rose a canker, Somerset?

Som. Hath not thy rose a thorn, Plantagenet?

Plan. Ay, sharp and piercing, to maintain his
    truth;   70
Whiles thy consuming canker eats his falsehood.

Som. Well, I'll find friends to wear my bleeding
    roses,
That shall maintain what I have said is true,
Where false Plantagenet dare not be seen.

Plan. Now, by this maiden blossom in my hand,
I scorn thee and thy [faction], peevish boy.   76

Suf. Turn not thy scorns this way, Plantagenet.

Plan. Proud Pole, I will, and scorn both him
    and thee.

Suf. I'll turn my part thereof into thy throat.

Som. Away, away, good William de la Pole!   80
We grace the yeoman by conversing with him.

War. Now, by God's will, thou wrong'st him,
    Somerset;
His grandfather was Lionel Duke of Clarence,
Third son to the third Edward King of England.
Spring crestless yeomen from so deep a root? 85

Plan. He bears him on the place's privilege,
Or durst not, for his craven heart, say thus.

Som. By Him that made me, I'll maintain my
    words
On any plot of ground in Christendom.
Was not thy father, Richard Earl of Cambridge, 90
For treason executed in our late king's days?
And, by his treason, stand'st not thou attainted,
Corrupted, and exempt from ancient gentry?
His trespass yet lives guilty in thy blood;
And, till thou be restor'd, thou art a yeoman. 95

Plan. My father was attached, not attainted,
Condemn'd to die for treason, but no traitor;
And that I'll prove on better men than Somerset,
Were growing time once ripened to my will.
For your partaker Pole and you yourself,   100
I'll note you in my book of memory
To scourge you for this apprehension.
Look to it well and say you are well warn'd.

Som. Ah, thou shalt find us ready for thee still;
And know us by these colours for thy foes,   105
For these my friends in spite of thee shall wear.

Plan. And, by my soul, this pale and angry rose,
As cognizance of my blood-drinking hate,
Will I for ever and my faction wear,
Until it wither with me to my grave   110
Or flourish to the height of my degree.

Suf. Go forward and be chok'd with thy ambi-
    tion!
And so farewell until I meet thee next.   [*Exit.*

Som. Have with thee, Pole. Farewell, ambi-
    tious Richard.   [*Exit.*

21. **purblind:** dim-sighted. 26. **significants:** signs. 34. **colours:** pretences. 43. **it...objected:** the point is well raised. 68. **canker:** canker-worm. 76. **[faction]** (Theobald). *fashion* F. 83. **Lionel.** A mistake for Edmund, D. of York. 86. **the place's privilege.** It seems to be assumed that the Temple-garden afforded sanctuary (which, in fact, it did not). 92. **attainted:** disgraced. 96. **attached:** arrested. 102. **apprehension:** opinion. 108. **cognizance:** badge.

Plan. How I am brav'd and must perforce en-
    dure it!   115
War. This blot that they object against your
    house
Shall be wip'd out in the next parliament
Call'd for the truce of Winchester and Gloucester;
And if thou be not then created York
I will not live to be accounted Warwick.   120
Meantime, in signal of my love to thee,
Against proud Somerset and William Pole,
Will I upon thy party wear this rose;
And here I prophesy: this brawl to-day,
Grown to this faction in the Temple-garden,   125
Shall send between the red rose and the white
A thousand souls to death and deadly night.
    Plan. Good Master Vernon, I am bound to you
That you on my behalf would pluck a flower.
    Ver. In your behalf still will I wear the same. 130
    Law. And so will I.
    Plan. Thanks, gentle sir.
Come, let us four to dinner. I dare say
This quarrel will drink blood another day.
                           [Exeunt.

[SCENE V. *The Tower of London.*]

Enter MORTIMER, *brought in a chair, and* GAOLERS.

    Mor. Kind keepers of my weak decaying age,
Let dying Mortimer here rest himself.
Even like a man new haled from the rack,
So fare my limbs with long imprisonment;
And these grey locks, the pursuivants of death,   5
Nestor-like aged in an age of care,
Argue the end of Edmund Mortimer.
These eyes, like lamps whose wasting oil is spent,
Wax dim, as drawing to their exigent;
Weak shoulders, overborne with burdening grief,   10
And pithless arms, like to a withered vine
That droops his sapless branches to the ground.
Yet are these feet, whose strengthless stay is numb,
(Unable to support this lump of clay)
Swift-winged with desire to get a grave,   15
As witting I no other comfort have.
But tell me, keeper, will my nephew come?
    1. Gaol. Richard Plantagenet, my lord, will come.
We sent unto the Temple, unto his chamber;
And answer was return'd that he will come.   20
    Mor. Enough; my soul shall then be satisfied.
Poor gentleman! his wrong doth equal mine.
Since Henry Monmouth first began to reign,
Before whose glory I was great in arms,
This loathsome sequestration have I had;   25
And even since then hath Richard been obscur'd,
Deprived of honour and inheritance.

But now the arbitrator of despairs,
Just Death, kind umpire of men's miseries,
With sweet enlargement doth dismiss me hence.   30
I would his troubles likewise were expir'd,
That so he might recover what was lost.

    Enter RICHARD PLANTAGENET.

    1. Gaol. My lord, your loving nephew now is
    come.
    Mor. Richard Plantagenet, my friend, is he come?
    [*Plan.*] Ay, noble uncle, thus ignobly us'd,   35
Your nephew, late despised Richard, comes.
    Mor. Direct mine arms I may embrace his neck,
And in his bosom spend my latter gasp.
O, tell me when my lips do touch his cheeks,
That I may kindly give one fainting kiss.   40
And now declare, sweet stem from York's great
    stock,
Why didst thou say, of late thou wert despis'd?
    Plan. First, lean thine aged back against mine
    arm;
And in that ease I'll tell thee my dis-ease.
This day, in argument upon a case,   45
Some words there grew 'twixt Somerset and me;
Among which terms he us'd his lavish tongue
And did upbraid me with my father's death;
Which obloquy set bars before my tongue,
Else with the like I had requited him.   50
Therefore, good uncle, for my father's sake,
In honour of a true Plantagenet
And for alliance sake, declare the cause
My father, Earl of Cambridge, lost his head.
    Mor. That cause, fair nephew, that imprison'd
    me   55
And hath detain'd me all my flow'ring youth
Within a loathsome dungeon, there to pine,
Was cursed instrument of his decease.
    Plan. Discover more at large what cause that
    was,
For I am ignorant and cannot guess.   60
    Mor. I will, if that my fading breath permit
And death approach not ere my tale be done.
Henry the Fourth, grandfather to this king,
Deposed his nephew Richard, Edward's son,
The first-begotten and the lawful heir   65
Of Edward king, the third of that descent;
During whose reign the Percies of the north,
Finding his usurpation most unjust,
Endeavour'd my advancement to the throne.
The reason mov'd these warlike lords to this   70
Was, for that — young King Richard thus remov'd,
Leaving no heir begotten of his body —
I was the next by birth and parentage;
For by my mother I derived am

115. brav'd: defied.   118. for the truce of: to make peace between.
Sc. v, 5. pursuivants: heralds.   9. exigent: end.   25. sequestration: imprisonment.   30. enlargement: release.   35.
[*Plan.*] In this scene and III. 1, F reads *Rich.*   64. nephew: cousin.   74. mother: historically, grandmother (Philippa).

From Lionel Duke of Clarence, the third son   75
To King Edward the Third; whereas he
From John of Gaunt doth bring his pedigree,
Being but fourth of that heroic line.
But mark: as in this haughty great attempt
They laboured to plant the rightful heir,   80
I lost my liberty and they their lives.
Long after this, when Henry the Fifth,
Succeeding his father Bolingbroke, did reign,
Thy father, Earl of Cambridge, then deriv'd
From famous Edmund Langley, Duke of York,   85
Marrying my sister that thy mother was,
Again in pity of my hard distress
Levied an army, weening to redeem
And have install'd me in the diadem.
But, as the rest, so fell that noble earl   90
And was beheaded. Thus the Mortimers,
In whom the title rested, were suppress'd.
    Plan. Of which, my lord, your honour is the last.
    Mor. True; and thou seest that I no issue have
And that my fainting words do warrant death.   95
Thou art my heir; the rest I wish thee gather,
But yet be wary in thy studious care.
    Plan. Thy grave admonishments prevail with me.
But yet, methinks, my father's execution
Was nothing less than bloody tyranny.   100
    Mor. With silence, nephew, be thou politic.
Strong-fixed is the house of Lancaster
And like a mountain, not to be remov'd.
But now thy uncle is removing hence,
As princes do their courts, when they are cloy'd 105
With long continuance in a settled place.
    Plan. O, uncle, would some part of my young
        years
Might but redeem the passage of your age!
    Mor. Thou dost then wrong me, as that slaugh-
        terer doth
Which giveth many wounds when one will kill. 110
Mourn not, except thou sorrow for my good:
Only give order for my funeral.
And so farewell, and fair be all thy hopes
And prosperous be thy life in peace and war!
                                    [*Dies.*
    Plan. And peace, no war, befall thy parting
        soul!   115
In prison hast thou spent a pilgrimage
And like a hermit overpass'd thy days.
Well, I will lock his counsel in my breast;
And what I do imagine, let that rest.
Keepers, convey him hence, and I myself   120
Will see his burial better than his life.
        [*Exeunt [Gaolers, bearing out the body of
            Mortimer].*
Here dies the dusky torch of Mortimer,
Chok'd with ambition of the meaner sort;
And for those wrongs, those bitter injuries

Which Somerset hath offer'd to my house,   125
I doubt not but with honour to redress.
And therefore haste I to the parliament,
Either to be restored to my blood,
Or make my ill th' advantage of my good.   [*Exit.*

ACT III

SCENE I. [*London.   The Parliament-house.*]

Flourish.   Enter KING, EXETER, GLOUCESTER,
    WARWICK, SOMERSET, *and* SUFFOLK; *the* BISHOP
    OF WINCHESTER, RICHARD PLANTAGENET [*and
    others*].   *Gloucester offers to put up a bill; Win-
    chester snatches it, and tears it.*

    Win. Com'st thou with deep premeditated lines,
With written pamphlets studiously devis'd,
Humphrey of Gloucester? If thou canst accuse,
Or aught intend'st to lay unto my charge,
Do it without invention, suddenly;   5
As I with sudden and extemporal speech
Purpose to answer what thou canst object.
    Glou. Presumptuous priest! this place com-
        mands my patience
Or thou shouldst find thou hast dishonour'd me.
Think not, although in writing I preferr'd   10
The manner of thy vile outrageous crimes,
That therefore I have forg'd, or am not able
Verbatim to rehearse the method of my pen.
No, prelate; such is thy audacious wickedness,
Thy lewd, pestiferous, and dissentious pranks, 15
As very infants prattle of thy pride.
Thou art a most pernicious usurer,
Froward by nature, enemy to peace;
Lascivious, wanton, more than well beseems
A man of thy profession and degree;   20
And for thy treachery, what's more manifest?
In that thou laid'st a trap to take my life,
As well at London Bridge as at the Tower.
Beside, I fear me, if thy thoughts were sifted,
The King, thy sovereign, is not quite exempt   25
From envious malice of thy swelling heart.
    Win. Gloucester, I do defy thee.   Lords,
        vouchsafe
To give me hearing what I shall reply.
If I were covetous, ambitious, or perverse,
As he will have me, how am I so poor?   30
Or how haps it I seek not to advance
Or raise myself, but keep my wonted calling?
And for dissension, who preferreth peace
More than I do? — except I be provok'd.
No, my good lords, it is not that offends;   35
It is not that that hath incens'd the Duke.
It is because no one should sway but he,
No one but he should be about the King;
And that engenders thunder in his breast

Act III, sc. i, S.D. *bill:* written statement.   13. **Verbatim:** orally.   16. **As:** that.

And makes him roar these accusations forth.   40
But he shall know I am as good —
   Glou.   As good!
Thou bastard of my grandfather!
   Win. Ay, lordly sir; for what are you, I pray,
But one imperious in another's throne?
   Glou. Am I not Protector, saucy priest?   45
   Win. And am not I a prelate of the Church?
   Glou. Yes, as an outlaw in a castle keeps
And useth it to patronage his theft.
   Win. Unreverent Gloucester!
   Glou.   Thou art reverend
Touching thy spiritual function, not thy life.   50
   Win. Rome shall remedy this.
   War.   Roam thither, then.
   [*Som.*] My lord, it were your duty to forbear.
   [*War.*] Ay, see the Bishop be not overborne.
   Som. Methinks my lord should be religious
And know the office that belongs to such.   55
   War. Methinks his lordship should be humbler;
It fitteth not a prelate so to plead.
   Som. Yes, when his holy state is touch'd so near.
   War. State holy or unhallow'd, what of that?
Is not his Grace Protector to the King?   60
   Plan. [*Aside.*] Plantagenet, I see, must hold his
      tongue,
Lest it be said, "Speak, sirrah, when you should;
Must your bold verdict enter talk with lords?"
Else would I have a fling at Winchester.
   King. Uncles of Gloucester and of Winchester,   65
The special watchmen of our English weal,
I would prevail, if prayers might prevail,
To join your hearts in love and amity.
O, what a scandal is it to our crown
That two such noble peers as ye should jar!   70
Believe me, lords, my tender years can tell
Civil dissension is a viperous worm
That gnaws the bowels of the commonwealth.
   [*A noise within,* "Down with the tawny-
      coats!"
What tumult's this?
   War.   An uproar, I dare warrant,   75
Begun through malice of the Bishop's men.
           [*A noise again,* "Stones! stones!"

   Enter the MAYOR [*of London, attended*].

   May. O, my good lords, and virtuous Henry,
Pity the city of London, pity us!
The Bishop and the Duke of Gloucester's men,
Forbidden late to carry any weapon,
Have fill'd their pockets full of pebble stones   80
And banding themselves in contrary parts
Do pelt so fast at one another's pate
That many have their giddy brains knock'd out.

Our windows are broke down in every street
And we for fear compell'd to shut our shops.   85

   Enter [SERVING-MEN *of both parties,*] *in skirmish,
      with bloody pates.*

   King. We charge you, on allegiance to ourself,
To hold your slaught'ring hands and keep the peace.
Pray uncle Gloucester, mitigate this strife.
   1. Serv. Nay, if we be forbidden stones, we'll
fall to it with our teeth.   90
   2. Serv. Do what ye dare, we are as resolute.
           [*Skirmish again.*
   Glou. You of my household, leave this peevish
      broil
And set this unaccustom'd fight aside.
   3. Serv. My lord, we know your Grace to be a
      man
Just and upright; and, for your royal birth,   95
Inferior to none but to his Majesty:
And ere that we will suffer such a prince,
So kind a father of the commonweal,
To be disgraced by an inkhorn mate,
We and our wives and children all will fight   100
And have our bodies slaught'red by thy foes.
   1. Serv. Ay, and the very parings of our nails
Shall pitch a field when we are dead. [*Begin again.*
   Glou.   Stay, stay, I say!
And if you love me, as you say you do,
Let me persuade you to forbear a while.   105
   King. O, how this discord doth afflict my soul!
Can you, my Lord of Winchester, behold
My sighs and tears and will not once relent?
Who should be pitiful, if you be not?
Or who should study to prefer a peace,   110
If holy churchmen take delight in broils?
   War. Yield, my Lord Protector; yield, Win-
      chester;
Except you mean with obstinate repulse
To slay your sovereign and destroy the realm.
You see what mischief and what murder too   115
Hath been enacted through your enmity.
Then be at peace, except ye thirst for blood.
   Win. He shall submit, or I will never yield.
   Glou. Compassion on the King commands me
      stoop;
Or I would see his heart out ere the priest   120
Should ever get that privilege of me.
   War. Behold, my Lord of Winchester, the Duke
Hath banish'd moody discontented fury,
As by his smoothed brows it doth appear.
Why look you still so stern and tragical?   125
   Glou. Here, Winchester, I offer thee my hand.
   King. Fie, uncle Beaufort! I have heard you
      preach
That malice was a great and grievous sin;

---

48. **patronage:** defend.   52. [*Som.*] (Theobald).   Om. F.   53. [*War.*] (Theobald).   *Som.* F.   92. **peevish:** childish.
99. **inkhorn mate:** writing fellow.

And will not you maintain the thing you teach,
But prove a chief offender in the same?   130
 War. Sweet king! the Bishop hath a kindly gird.
For shame, my Lord of Winchester, relent!
What, shall a child instruct you what to do?
 Win. Well, Duke of Gloucester, I will yield to
  thee;
Love for thy love and hand for hand I give.   135
 Glou. [*Aside.*] Ay, but, I fear me, with a hollow
  heart.—
See here, my friends and loving countrymen,
This token serveth for a flag of truce
Betwixt ourselves and all our followers.
So help me God, as I dissemble not!   140
 Win. [*Aside.*] So help me God, as I intend it not!
 King. O loving uncle, kind Duke of Gloucester,
How joyful am I made by this contract!
Away, my masters! trouble us no more;
But join in friendship, as your lords have done.   145
 1. Serv. Content; I'll to the surgeon's.
 2. Serv.   And so will I.
 3. Serv. And I will see what physic the tavern
affords.   [*Exeunt* [*Serving-men, Mayor, etc.*].
 War. Accept this scroll, most gracious sovereign,
Which in the right of Richard Plantagenet   150
We do exhibit to your Majesty.
 Glou. Well urg'd, my Lord of Warwick; for,
  sweet prince,
An if your Grace mark every circumstance,
You have great reason to do Richard right;
Especially for those occasions   155
At Eltham Place I told your Majesty.
 King. And those occasions, uncle, were of force.
Therefore, my loving lords, our pleasure is
That Richard be restored to his blood.
 War. Let Richard be restored to his blood;   160
So shall his father's wrongs be recompens'd.
 Win. As will the rest, so willeth Winchester.
 King. If Richard will be true, not that alone
But all the whole inheritance I give
That doth belong unto the house of York,   165
From whence you spring by lineal descent.
 Plan. Thy humble servant vows obedience
And humble service till the point of death.
 King. Stoop then and set your knee against my
  foot;
And, in reguerdon of that duty done,   170
I gird thee with the valiant sword of York.
Rise, Richard, like a true Plantagenet,
And rise created princely Duke of York.
 Plan. And so thrive Richard as thy foes may fall!
And as my duty springs, so perish they   175
That grudge one thought against your Majesty!
 All. Welcome, high prince, the mighty Duke of
  York!

 Som. [*Aside.*] Perish, base prince, ignoble Duke
  of York!
 Glou. Now will it best avail your Majesty
To cross the seas and to be crown'd in France.   180
The presence of a king engenders love
Amongst his subjects and his loyal friends,
As it disanimates his enemies.
 King. When Gloucester says the word, King
  Henry goes;
For friendly counsel cuts off many foes.   185
 Glou. Your ships already are in readiness.
   [*Sennet. Flourish. Exeunt* [*all but Exeter*].
 Exe. Ay, we may march in England or in France,
Not seeing what is likely to ensue.
This late dissension grown betwixt the peers
Burns under feigned ashes of forg'd love,   190
And will at last break out into a flame:
As fest'red members rot but by degree
Till bones and flesh and sinews fall away,
So will this base and envious discord breed.
And now I fear that fatal prophecy   195
Which in the time of Henry nam'd the Fifth
Was in the mouth of every sucking babe,
That Henry born at Monmouth should win all,
And Henry born at Windsor [should] lose all.
Which is so plain that Exeter doth wish   200
His days may finish ere that hapless time. [*Exit.*

SCENE II. [*France. Before Rouen.*]

Enter LA PUCELLE *disguised, with four* SOLDIERS
with sacks upon their backs.

 Puc. These are the city gates, the gates of Rouen,
Through which our policy must make a breach.
Take heed, be wary how you place your words;
Talk like the vulgar sort of market men
That come to gather money for their corn.   5
If we have entrance, as I hope we shall,
And that we find the slothful watch but weak,
I'll by a sign give notice to our friends,
That Charles the Dauphin may encounter them.
 1. Sol. Our sacks shall be a mean to sack the city,
And we be lords and rulers over Rouen;   11
Therefore we'll knock.   [*Knock.*
 Watch. [*Within.*] Qui est là?
 Puc. Paysans, pauvres gens de France;
Poor market folks that come to sell their corn.   15
 Watch. Enter, go in; the market bell is rung.
 Puc. Now, Rouen, I'll shake thy bulwarks to the
  ground.   [*Exeunt* [*to the town*].

Enter CHARLES, *the* BASTARD *of Orleans,*
ALENÇON [REIGNIER, *and forces*].

 Char. Saint Denis bless this happy stratagem!
And once again we'll sleep secure in Rouen.

---

131. **gird:** rebuke. 170. **reguerdon:** reward. 176. **grudge one thought:** think one grudge. 199. **[should]** F₂. Om. P₁.
Sc. ii, 2. policy: stratagem.

Bast. Here ent'red Pucelle and her practisants.
Now she is there, how will she specify   21
Where is the best and safest passage in?
    Reig. By thrusting out a torch from yonder
tower;
Which, once discern'd, shows that her meaning is,
No way to that, for weakness, which she ent'red.   25

Enter LA PUCELLE *on the top, thrusting out a torch
burning.*

    Puc. Behold, this is the happy wedding torch
That joineth Rouen unto her countrymen,
But burning fatal to the Talbotites!   [*Exit.*]
    Bast. See, noble Charles, the beacon of our
friend;
The burning torch in yonder turret stands.   30
    Char. Now shine it like a comet of revenge,
A prophet to the fall of all our foes!
    Reig. Defer no time, delays have dangerous ends.
Enter, and cry "The Dauphin!" presently,
And then do execution on the watch.   35
                          [*Alarum.* [*Exeunt.*]

An alarm.   Enter TALBOT *in an excursion.*

    Tal. France, thou shalt rue this treason with thy
tears,
If Talbot but survive thy treachery.
Pucelle, that witch, that damned sorceress,
Hath wrought this hellish mischief unawares,
That hardly we escap'd the pride of France.   40
                          [*Exit.*

An alarum: excursions. BEDFORD, *brought in sick in
a chair.   Enter* TALBOT *and* BURGUNDY *without:
within* LA PUCELLE, CHARLES, BASTARD, [ALEN-
ÇON,] *and* REIGNIER, *on the walls.*

    Puc. Good morrow, gallants! want ye corn for
bread?
I think the Duke of Burgundy will fast
Before he'll buy again at such a rate.
'Twas full of darnel; do you like the taste?
    Bur. Scoff on, vile fiend and shameless cour-
tezan!   45
I trust ere long to choke thee with thine own
And make thee curse the harvest of that corn.
    Char. Your Grace may starve perhaps before
that time.
    Bed. O, let no words, but deeds, revenge this
treason!
    Puc. What will you do, good grey-beard?
Break a lance,   50
And run a tilt at Death within a chair?
    Tal. Foul fiend of France, and hag of all despite,

Encompass'd with thy lustful paramours!
Becomes it thee to taunt his valiant age
And twit with cowardice a man half dead?   55
Damsel, I'll have a bout with you again,
Or else let Talbot perish with this shame.
    Puc. Are ye so hot, sir?   Yet, Pucelle, hold thy
peace;
If Talbot do but thunder, rain will follow.
          [*The English whisper together in council*
God speed the parliament!   Who shall be the
speaker?   60
    Tal. Dare ye come forth and meet us in the field?
    Puc. Belike your lordship takes us then for fools,
To try if that our own be ours or no.
    Tal. I speak not to that railing Hecate,
But unto thee, Alençon, and the rest.   65
Will ye, like soldiers, come and fight it out?
    Alen. Signior, no.
    Tal. Signior, hang!   Base muleteers of France!
Like peasant foot-boys do they keep the walls
And dare not take up arms like gentlemen.   70
    Puc. Away, captains! let's get us from the walls
For Talbot means no goodness by his looks.
God b'uy, my lord! we came but to tell you
That we are here.
          [*Exeunt* [*La Pucelle, etc.,*] *from the walls.*
    Tal. And there will we be too, ere it be long,
Or else reproach be Talbot's greatest fame!   76
Vow, Burgundy, by honour of thy house,
Prick'd on by public wrongs sustain'd in France,
Either to get the town again or die:
And I, as sure as English Henry lives   80
And as his father here was conqueror,
As sure as in this late-betrayed town
Great Cœur-de-lion's heart was buried,
So sure I swear to get the town or die.
    Bur. My vows are equal partners with thy
vows.   85
    Tal. But, ere we go, regard this dying prince,
The valiant Duke of Bedford.   Come, my lord,
We will bestow you in some better place,
Fitter for sickness and for crazy age.
    Bed. Lord Talbot, do not so dishonour me.   90
Here will I sit before the walls of Rouen
And will be partner of your weal or woe.
    Bur. Courageous Bedford, let us now persuade
you —
    Bed. Not to be gone from hence; for once I read
That stout Pendragon in his litter sick   95
Came to the field and vanquished his foes.
Methinks I should revive the soldiers' hearts,
Because I ever found them as myself.
    Tal. Undaunted spirit in a dying breast!
Then be it so.   Heavens keep old Bedford safe!
And now no more ado, brave Burgundy,   101

20. **practisants:** fellow-conspirators.   25. **to that:** compared to that.   40. **pride:** princes.   44. **darnel:** a weed.   52.
hag ... despite: malicious witch.   89. **crazy:** infirm.   95. **Pendragon:** Uther Pendragon, King Arthur's father.

But gather we our forces out of hand
And set upon our boasting enemy.
        [*Exeunt* [*into the town all but Bedford and
                Attendants*].

        An alarum: excursions.   Enter SIR JOHN
                FASTOLFE *and a* CAPTAIN.

Cap. Whither away, Sir John Fastolfe, in such
        haste?
Fast. Whither away! to save myself by flight. 105
We are like to have the overthrow again.
Cap. What! will you fly, and leave Lord Talbot?
Fast.   Ay,
All the Talbots in the world, to save my life.
                                        [*Exit.*
Cap. Cowardly knight! ill fortune follow thee!
                        [*Exit* [*into the town*].

        Retreat: excursions. LA PUCELLE, ALENÇON, *and*
                CHARLES [*enter from the town and*] *fly.*

Bed. Now, quiet soul, depart when heaven please,
For I have seen our enemies' overthrow.   111
What is the trust or strength of foolish man?
They that of late were daring with their scoffs
Are glad and fain by flight to save themselves.
        [*Bedford dies, and is carried in by two in his
                chair.*

        An alarum.   Re-enter TALBOT, BURGUNDY,
                and the rest.

Tal. Lost, and recovered in a day again!   115
This is a double honour, Burgundy;
Yet heavens have glory for this victory!
Bur. Warlike and martial Talbot, Burgundy
Enshrines thee in his heart and there erects
Thy noble deeds as valour's monuments.   120
Tal. Thanks, gentle duke.   But where is Pucelle
        now?
I think her old familiar is asleep.
Now where's the Bastard's braves, and Charles his
        gleeks?
What, all amort?   Rouen hangs her head for grief
That such a valiant company are fled.   125
Now will we take some order in the town,
Placing therein some expert officers,
And then depart to Paris to the King,
For there young Henry with his nobles lie.
Bur. What wills Lord Talbot pleaseth Bur-
        gundy.   130
Tal. But yet, before we go, let's not forget
The noble Duke of Bedford late deceas'd,
But see his exequies fulfill'd in Rouen.
A braver soldier never couched lance,
A gentler heart did never sway in court.   135

But kings and mightiest potentates must die,
For that's the end of human misery.   [*Exeunt.*

        SCENE III. [*The plains near Rouen.*]

        Enter CHARLES, *the* BASTARD *of* Orleans,
                ALENÇON, LA PUCELLE [*and forces*].

Puc. Dismay not, princes, at this accident,
Nor grieve that Rouen is so recovered.
Care is no cure, but rather corrosive,
For things that are not to be remedi'd.
Let frantic Talbot triumph for a while   5
And like a peacock sweep along his tail;
We'll pull his plumes and take away his train,
If Dauphin and the rest will be but rul'd.
Char. We have been guided by thee hitherto
And of thy cunning had no diffidence.   10
One sudden foil shall never breed distrust.
Bast. Search out thy wit for secret policies,
And we will make thee famous through the world.
Alen. We'll set thy statue in some holy place,
And have thee reverenc'd like a blessed saint. 15
Employ thee then, sweet virgin, for our good.
Puc. Then thus it must be; this doth Joan devise:
By fair persuasions mix'd with sug'red words
We will entice the Duke of Burgundy
To leave the Talbot and to follow us.   20
Char. Ay, marry, sweeting, if we could do that,
France were no place for Henry's warriors;
Nor should that nation boast it so with us,
But be extirped from our provinces.
Alen. For ever should they be expuls'd from
        France   25
And not have title of an earldom here.
Puc. Your honours shall perceive how I will work
To bring this matter to the wished end.
                        [*Drum sounds afar off.*
Hark! by the sound of drum you may perceive
Their powers are marching unto Paris-ward. 30

        Here sound an English march. [*Enter, and pass
                over at a distance,* TALBOT *and his forces.*]
There goes the Talbot, with his colours spread,
And all the troops of English after him.

        French march. [*Enter the* DUKE OF BURGUNDY
                and forces.]
Now in the rearward comes the Duke and his.
Fortune in favour makes him lag behind.
Summon a parley; we will talk with him.   35
                        [*Trumpets sound a parley.*
Char. A parley with the Duke of Burgundy!
Bur. Who craves a parley with the Burgundy?

---

122. **familiar:** attendant spirit.   123. **braves:** boasts.   **gleeks:** scoffs.   124. **amort:** downcast.   133. **exequies:** funeral
rites.
Sc. iii, 10. **diffidence:** distrust.   11. **foil:** defeat.   24. **extirped:** extirpated.   34. **favour:** i.e., to us.

Puc. The princely Charles of France, thy coun-
    tryman.
Bur. What say'st thou, Charles? for I am march-
    ing hence.
Char. Speak, Pucelle, and enchant him with thy
    words.   40
Puc. Brave Burgundy, undoubted hope of
    France!
Stay, let thy humble handmaid speak to thee.
Bur. Speak on; but be not over-tedious.
Puc. Look on thy country, look on fertile France,
And see the cities and the towns defac'd   45
By wasting ruin of the cruel foe.
As looks the mother on her lowly babe
When death doth close his tender dying eyes,
See, see the pining malady of France!
Behold the wounds, the most unnatural wounds,   50
Which thou thyself hast given her woeful breast.
O, turn thy edged sword another way;
Strike those that hurt, and hurt not those that help.
One drop of blood drawn from thy country's bosom
Should grieve thee more than streams of foreign
    gore.   55
Return thee therefore with a flood of tears,
And wash away thy country's stained spots.
Bur. Either she hath bewitch'd me with her
    words,
Or nature makes me suddenly relent.
Puc. Besides, all French and France exclaims on
    thee,   60
Doubting thy birth and lawful progeny.
Who join'st thou with but with a lordly nation
That will not trust thee but for profit's sake?
When Talbot hath set footing once in France
And fashion'd thee that instrument of ill,   65
Who then but English Henry will be lord
And thou be thrust out like a fugitive?
Call we to mind, and mark but this for proof,
Was not the Duke of Orleans thy foe?
And was he not in England prisoner?   70
But when they heard he was thine enemy,
They set him free without his ransom paid,
In spite of Burgundy and all his friends.
See, then, thou fight'st against thy countrymen
And join'st with them will be thy slaughtermen.   75
Come, come, return; return, thou wandering lord!
Charles and the rest will take thee in their arms.
Bur. [*Aside.*] I am vanquished. These haughty
    words of hers
Have batt'red me like roaring cannon-shot,
And made me almost yield upon my knees. —   80
Forgive me, country, and sweet countrymen,
And, lords, accept this hearty kind embrace;
My forces and my power of men are yours.
So farewell, Talbot; I'll no longer trust thee.

Puc. [*Aside.*] Done like a Frenchman; turn, and
    turn again!   85
Char. Welcome, brave duke! thy friendship
    makes us fresh.
Bast. And doth beget new courage in our breasts.
Alen. Pucelle hath bravely play'd her part in
    this,
And doth deserve a coronet of gold.
Char. Now let us on, my lords, and join our
    powers,   90
And seek how we may prejudice the foe. [*Exeunt.*

SCENE IV. [*Paris. The palace.*]

Enter KING HENRY, GLOUCESTER, BISHOP OF WIN-
CHESTER, YORK, SUFFOLK, SOMERSET, WARWICK,
EXETER [VERNON, BASSET, *and others*]. *To them
with his* Soldiers, TALBOT.

Tal. My gracious prince, and honourable peers,
Hearing of your arrival in this realm,
I have a while given truce unto my wars
To do my duty to my sovereign;
In sign whereof, this arm, that hath reclaim'd   5
To your obedience fifty fortresses,
Twelve cities, and seven walled towns of strength,
Beside five hundred prisoners of esteem,
Lets fall his sword before your Highness' feet,
And with submissive loyalty of heart   10
Ascribes the glory of his conquest got
First to my God and next unto your Grace.
    [*Kneels.*]
King. Is this the Lord Talbot, uncle Gloucester,
That hath so long been resident in France?
Glou. Yes, if it please your Majesty, my liege.   15
King. Welcome, brave captain and victorious
    lord!
When I was young, as yet I am not old,
I do remember how my father said
A stouter champion never handled sword.
Long since we were resolved of your truth,   20
Your faithful service, and your toil in war;
Yet never have you tasted our reward,
Or been reguerdon'd with so much as thanks,
Because till now we never saw your face.
Therefore, stand up; and, for these good deserts,   25
We here create you Earl of Shrewsbury;
And in our coronation take your place.
    [*Sennet. Flourish. Exeunt all but Vernon
    and Basset.*

Ver. Now, sir, to you, that were so hot at sea,
Disgracing of these colours that I wear
In honour of my noble Lord of York: 30
Dar'st thou maintain the former words thou
    spak'st?
Bas. Yes, sir; as well as you dare patronage

---

61. **progeny:** descent.   67. **fugitive:** renegade.
Sc. iv, 27. s.d. **Sennet:** set of notes on a trumpet.

The envious barking of your saucy tongue
Against my lord the Duke of Somerset.

   Ver. Sirrah, thy lord I honour as he is.   35

   Bas. Why, what is he? As good a man as York.

   Ver. Hark ye, not so; in witness, take ye that
                       [Strikes him.

   Bas. Villain, thou know'st the law of arms is such
That whoso draws a sword, 'tis present death,
Or else this blow should broach thy dearest blood.
But I'll unto his Majesty, and crave   41
I may have liberty to venge this wrong;
When thou shalt see I'll meet thee to thy cost.

   Ver. Well, miscreant, I'll be there as soon as you;
And, after, meet you sooner than you would.   45
                       [Exeunt.

ACT IV

Scene I. [*Paris. A hall of state.*]

Enter King Henry, Gloucester, Bishop of Winchester, York, Suffolk, Somerset, Warwick,
Talbot, Exeter, *the* Governor of Paris [*and
others*].

   Glou. Lord Bishop, set the crown upon his head.

   Win. God save King Henry, of that name the
      sixth!

   Glou. Now, governor of Paris, take your oath,
That you elect no other king but him;
                  [Governor kneels.]
Esteem none friends but such as are his friends,   5
And none your foes but such as shall pretend
Malicious practices against his state.
This shall ye do, so help you righteous God!
               [Exeunt Governor, etc.]

Enter Sir John Fastolfe.

   Fast. My gracious sovereign, as I rode from
      Calais,
To haste unto your coronation,   10
A letter was deliver'd to my hands,
Writ to your Grace from th' Duke of Burgundy.

   Tal. Shame to the Duke of Burgundy and thee!
I vow'd, base knight, when I did meet thee next,
To tear the Garter from thy craven's leg,   15
                  [Plucking it off.]
Which I have done, because unworthily
Thou wast installed in that high degree.
Pardon me, princely Henry, and the rest.
This dastard, at the battle of [Patay],
When but in all I was six thousand strong   20
And that the French were almost ten to one,
Before we met or that a stroke was given,
Like to a trusty squire did run away;
In which assault we lost twelve hundred men;

Myself and divers gentlemen beside   25
Were there surpris'd and taken prisoners.
Then judge, great lords, if I have done amiss;
Or whether that such cowards ought to wear
This ornament of knighthood, yea or no.

   Glou. To say the truth, this fact was infamous   30
And ill beseeming any common man,
Much more a knight, a captain, and a leader.

   Tal. When first this order was ordain'd, my lords,
Knights of the Garter were of noble birth,
Valiant and virtuous, full of haughty courage,   35
Such as were grown to credit by the wars;
Not fearing death, nor shrinking for distress,
But always resolute in most extremes.
He then that is not furnish'd in this sort
Doth but usurp the sacred name of knight,   40
Profaning this most honourable order,
And should, if I were worthy to be judge,
Be quite degraded, like a hedge-born swain
That doth presume to boast of gentle blood.

   King. Stain to thy countrymen, thou hear'st thy
      doom!   45
Be packing, therefore, thou that wast a knight;
Henceforth we banish thee, on pain of death.
                  [Exit Fastolfe.]
And now, [my] Lord Protector, view the letter
Sent from our uncle Duke of Burgundy.

   Glou. What means his Grace, that he hath
      chang'd his style?   50
No more but, plain and bluntly, "To the King!"
Hath he forgot he is his sovereign?
Or doth this churlish superscription
Pretend some alteration in good will?
What's here?
   [*Reads.*]   "I have, upon especial cause,   55
Mov'd with compassion of my country's wrack,
Together with the pitiful complaints
Of such as your oppression feeds upon,
Forsaken your pernicious faction
And join'd with Charles, the rightful King of
      France."   60
O monstrous treachery! can this be so,
That in alliance, amity, and oaths,
There should be found such false dissembling guile?

   King. What! doth my uncle Burgundy revolt?

   Glou. He doth, my lord, and is become your
      foe.   65

   King. Is that the worst this letter doth contain?

   Glou. It is the worst, and all, my lord, he writes.

   King. Why, then, Lord Talbot there shall talk
      with him
And give him chastisement for this abuse.
How say you, my lord? Are you not content?   70

   Tal. Content, my liege? Yes. But that I am
      prevented,

   Act IV, sc. i, 6. **pretend:** intend.   19. **[Patay]** (Capell).   *Poictiers* F.   Poictiers was fought in 1357, Patay in 1428.   38.
most: greatest.   48. **[my]** Om. F.   54. **Pretend:** indicate.   71. **prevented:** anticipated.

I should have begg'd I might have been employ'd.
   King. Then gather strength and march unto him
     straight.
Let him perceive how ill we brook his treason,
And what offence it is to flout his friends.   75
   Tal. I go, my lord, in heart desiring still
You may behold confusion of your foes.   [*Exit.*

     Enter VERNON *and* BASSET.

   Ver. Grant me the combat, gracious sovereign.
   Bas. And me, my lord, grant me the combat too.
   York. This is my servant; hear him, noble
     prince.   80
   Som. And this is mine; sweet Henry, favour him.
   K. Hen. Be patient, lords; and give them leave to
     speak.
Say, gentlemen, what makes you thus exclaim?
And wherefore crave you combat? or with whom?
   Ver. With him, my lord; for he hath done me
     wrong.   85
   Bas. And I with him; for he hath done me wrong.
   K. Hen. What is that wrong whereof you both
     complain?
First let me know, and then I'll answer you.
   Bas. Crossing the sea from England into France,
This fellow here, with envious carping tongue,   90
Upbraided me about the rose I wear,
Saying the sanguine colour of the leaves
Did represent my master's blushing cheeks
When stubbornly he did repugn the truth
About a certain question in the law   95
Argued betwixt the Duke of York and him;
With other vile and ignominious terms;
In confutation of which rude reproach
And in defence of my lord's worthiness,
I crave the benefit of law of arms.   100
   Ver. And that is my petition, noble lord.
For though he seem with forged quaint conceit
To set a gloss upon his bold intent,
Yet know, my lord, I was provok'd by him;
And he first took exceptions at this badge,   105
Pronouncing that the paleness of this flower
Bewray'd the faintness of my master's heart.
   York. Will not this malice, Somerset, be left?
   Som. Your private grudge, my Lord of York,
     will out,
Though ne'er so cunningly you smother it.   110
   K. Hen. Good Lord, what madness rules in
     brainsick men
When for so slight and frivolous a cause
Such factious emulations shall arise!
Good cousins both, of York and Somerset,
Quiet yourselves, I pray, and be at peace.   115
   York. Let this dissension first be tried by fight,

And then your Highness shall command a peace.
   Som. The quarrel toucheth none but us alone;
Betwixt ourselves let us decide it then.
   York. There is my pledge; accept it, Somerset.
   Ver. Nay, let it rest where it began at first.   121
   Bas. Confirm it so, mine honourable lord.
   Glou. Confirm it so! Confounded be your strife!
And perish ye, with your audacious prate!
Presumptuous vassals, are you not asham'd   125
With this immodest clamorous outrage
To trouble and disturb the King and us?
And you, my lords, methinks you do not well
To bear with their perverse objections;
Much less to take occasion from their mouths   130
To raise a mutiny betwixt yourselves.
Let me persuade you take a better course.
   Exe. It grieves his Highness. Good my lords, be
     friends.
   K. Hen. Come hither, you that would be com-
     batants.
Henceforth I charge you, as you love our favour,
Quite to forget this quarrel and the cause.   136
And you, my lords, remember where we are;
In France, amongst a fickle, wavering nation.
If they perceive dissension in our looks
And that within ourselves we disagree,   140
How will their grudging stomachs be provok'd
To wilful disobedience, and rebel!
Beside, what infamy will there arise,
When foreign princes shall be certified
That for a toy, a thing of no regard,   145
King Henry's peers and chief nobility
Destroy'd themselves, and lost the realm of France!
O, think upon the conquest of my father,
My tender years, and let us not forgo
That for a trifle that was bought with blood!   150
Let me be umpire in this doubtful strife.
I see no reason, if I wear this rose,
               [*Putting on a red rose.*]
That any one should therefore be suspicious
I more incline to Somerset than York.
Both are my kinsmen, and I love them both.   155
As well they may upbraid me with my crown,
Because, forsooth, the King of Scots is crown'd.
But your discretions better can persuade
Than I am able to instruct or teach;
And therefore, as we hither came in peace,   160
So let us still continue peace and love.
Cousin of York, we institute your Grace
To be our regent in these parts of France;
And, good my Lord of Somerset, unite
Your troops of horsemen with his bands of foot;   165
And, like true subjects, sons of your progenitors,
Go cheerfully together and digest

---

   94. **repugn:** reject.   98. **confutation:** refutation.   102. **forged quaint conceit:** cleverly contrived invention.   103. **gloss:**
fair appearance.   107. **Bewray'd:** showed.   129. **objections:** proposals.   141. **grudging stomachs:** discontented tempers.
167. **digest:** dissipate.

Your angry choler on your enemies.
Ourself, my Lord Protector, and the rest
After some respite will return to Calais;   170
From thence to England; where I hope ere long
To be presented, by your victories,
With Charles, Alençon, and that traitorous rout.
            [Exeunt all but York, Warwick, Exeter and
                    Vernon.
   War. My Lord of York, I promise you, the King
Prettily, methought, did play the orator.   175
   York. And so he did; but yet I like it not,
In that he wears the badge of Somerset.
   War. Tush, that was but his fancy, blame him
        not.
I dare presume, sweet prince, he thought no harm.
   York. An if I [wist] he did, — but let it rest;
Other affairs must now be managed.   181
                [Flourish. Exeunt all but Exeter.
   Exe. Well didst thou, Richard, to suppress thy
        voice;
For, had the passions of thy heart burst out,
I fear we should have seen decipher'd there
More rancorous spite, more furious raging broils,
Than yet can be imagin'd or suppos'd.   186
But howsoe'er, no simple man that sees
This jarring discord of nobility,
This shouldering of each other in the court,
This factious bandying of their favourites,   190
But that it doth presage some ill event.
'Tis much when sceptres are in children's hands;
But more when envy breeds unkind division.
There comes the ruin, there begins confusion. [Exit.

[SCENE II.]   Before Bordeaux.

Enter TALBOT, *with trump and drum.*

   Tal. Go to the gates of Bordeaux, trumpeter;
Summon their general unto the wall.

Trumpet sounds.   Enter GENERAL [*and others,*] *aloft.*

English John Talbot, captains, calls you forth,
Servant in arms to Harry King of England,
And thus he would: Open your city gates;   5
Be humble to us; call my sovereign yours,
And do him homage as obedient subjects;
And I'll withdraw me and my bloody power.
But, if you frown upon this proffer'd peace,
You tempt the fury of my three attendants,   10
Lean famine, quartering steel, and climbing fire;
Who in a moment even with the earth
Shall lay your stately and air-braving towers,
If you forsake the offer of their love.
   Gen. Thou ominous and fearful owl of death,   15
Our nation's terror and their bloody scourge!

The period of thy tyranny approacheth.
On us thou canst not enter but by death;
For, I protest, we are well fortified
And strong enough to issue out and fight.   20
If thou retire, the Dauphin, well appointed,
Stands with the snares of war to tangle thee.
On either hand thee there are squadrons pitch'd,
To wall thee from the liberty of flight;
And no way canst thou turn thee for redress   25
But death doth front thee with apparent spoil,
And pale destruction meets thee in the face.
Ten thousand French have ta'en the sacrament
To rive their dangerous artillery
Upon no Christain soul but English Talbot.   30
Lo, there thou stand'st, a breathing valiant man,
Of an invincible unconquer'd spirit!
This is the latest glory of thy praise
That I, thy enemy, due thee withal;
For ere the glass, that now begins to run,   35
Finish the process of his sandy hour,
These eyes, that see thee now well coloured,
Shall see thee withered, bloody, pale, and dead.
                            [Drum afar off.
Hark! hark! the Dauphin's drum, a warning bell,
Sings heavy music to thy timorous soul;   40
And mine shall ring thy dire departure out.
                    [Exeunt [General, etc.].
   Tal. He fables not; I hear the enemy.
Out, some light horsemen, and peruse their wings.
O, negligent and heedless discipline!
How are we park'd and bounded in a pale,   45
A little herd of England's timorous deer,
Maz'd with a yelping kennel of French curs!
If we be English deer, be then in blood;
Not rascal-like, to fall down with a pinch,
But rather, moody, mad, and desperate stags,   50
Turn on the bloody hounds with heads of steel
And make the cowards stand aloof at bay.
Sell every man his life as dear as mine,
And they shall find dear deer of us, my friends.
God and Saint George, Talbot and England's right,
Prosper our colours in this dangerous fight!   56
                            [Exeunt.]

[SCENE III.   Plains in Gascony.]

Enter YORK, *with trumpet and many* Soldiers: *to
            him a* MESSENGER.

   York. Are not the speedy scouts return'd again
That dogg'd the mighty army of the Dauphin?
   Mess. They are return'd, my lord, and give it out
That he is march'd to Bordeaux with his power
To fight with Talbot. As he march'd along,   5

---

170. **respite:** rest.   180. **[wist]** (Capell).   *wish* F.   184. **decipher'd:** displayed.   193. **unkind:** unnatural.
   Sc. ii, 11. **quartering:** slaughtering.   29. **rive:** burst.   34. **due:** endue.   45. **pale:** enclosure.   47. **Maz'd:** dazed.   48.
in blood: in good condition.   49. **rascal-like:** like a worthless deer.   50. **moody:** in dangerous mood.

By your espials were discovered
Two mightier troops than that the Dauphin led,
Which join'd with him and made their march for
    Bordeaux.
    York. A plague upon that villain Somerset
That thus delays my promised supply   10
Of horsemen that were levied for this siege!
Renowned Talbot doth expect my aid,
And I am louted by a traitor villain
And cannot help the noble chevalier.
God comfort him in this necessity!   15
If he miscarry, farewell wars in France!

    Enter another Messenger [SIR WILLIAM LUCY.

    [*Lucy.*] Thou princely leader of our English
    strength,
Never so needful on the earth of France,
Spur to the rescue of the noble Talbot,
Who now is girdled with a waist of iron   20
And hemm'd about with grim destruction.
To Bordeaux, warlike duke! to Bordeaux, York!
Else, farewell Talbot, France, and England's
    honour!
    York. O God, that Somerset, who in proud heart
Doth stop my cornets, were in Talbot's place! 25
So should we save a valiant gentleman
By forfeiting a traitor and a coward.
Mad ire and wrathful fury makes me weep,
That thus we die, while remiss traitors sleep.
    [*Lucy.*] O, send some succour to the distress'd
    lord!   30
    York. He dies, we lose; I break my warlike word;
We mourn, France smiles; we lose, they daily get;
All long of this vile traitor Somerset.
    [*Lucy.*] Then God take mercy on brave Talbot's
    soul,
And on his son young John, who two hours since 35
I met in travel toward his warlike father!
This seven years did not Talbot see his son,
And now they meet where both their lives are done.
    York. Alas, what joy shall noble Talbot have
To bid his young son welcome to his grave?   40
Away! vexation almost stops my breath,
That sund'red friends greet in the hour of death.
Lucy, farewell; no more my fortune can,
But curse the cause I cannot aid the man.
Maine, Blois, Poictiers, and Tours, are won away,
Long all of Somerset and his delay.   46
            [*Exit* [*with his soldiers*].
    [*Lucy.*] Thus, while the vulture of sedition
Feeds in the bosom of such great commanders,
Sleeping neglection doth betray to loss
The conquest of our scarce cold conqueror,   50
That ever living man of memory,

Henry the Fifth. Whiles they each other cross,
Lives, honours, lands, and all hurry to loss.
                            [*Exit.*]

    [SCENE IV. *Other plains in Gascony.*]

    Enter SOMERSET, *with his army* [*a* CAPTAIN *of*
    Talbot's *with him*].

    Som. It is too late; I cannot send them now.
This expedition was by York and Talbot
Too rashly plotted. All our general force
Might with a sally of the very town
Be buckled with. The over-daring Talbot   5
Hath sullied all his gloss of former honour
By this unheedful, desperate, wild adventure.
York set him on to fight and die in shame,
That, Talbot dead, great York might bear the name.
    Cap. Here is Sir William Lucy, who with me 10
Set from our o'ermatch'd forces forth for aid.

    Enter SIR WILLIAM LUCY.

    Som. How now, Sir William! whither were you
    sent?
    Lucy. Whither, my lord? From bought and sold
    Lord Talbot;
Who, ring'd about with bold adversity,
Cries out for noble York and Somerset   15
To beat assailing death from his weak [legions];
And whiles the honourable captain there
Drops bloody sweat from his war-wearied limbs,
And, in advantage ling'ring, looks for rescue,
You, his false hopes, the trust of England's honour,
Keep off aloof with worthless emulation.   21
Let not your private discord keep away
The levied succours that should lend him aid,
While he, renowned noble gentleman,
Yield up his life unto a world of odds.   25
Orleans the Bastard, Charles, Burgundy,
Alençon, Reignier, compass him about,
And Talbot perisheth by your default.
    Som. York set him on; York should have sent
    him aid.
    Lucy. And York as fast upon your Grace ex-
    claims,   30
Swearing that you withhold his levied host,
Collected for this expedition.
    Som. York lies; he might have sent and had the
    horse.
I owe him little duty, and less love,
And take foul scorn to fawn on him by sending. 35
    Lucy. The fraud of England, not the force of
    France,
Hath now entrapp'd the noble-minded Talbot.
Never to England shall he bear his life,
But dies, betray'd to fortune by your strife.

Sc. iii, 13. **louted**: mocked. 17. [*Lucy*]. **2. Mes.** F. 25. **cornets**: squadrons of cavalry. 33. **long**: because.
Sc. iv, 4. **of ... town**: merely of the town. 5. **buckled with**: engaged in combat. 16. [**legions**] (Rowe). *Regions* F.

Som. Come, go; I will dispatch the horsemen
    straight.   40
Within six hours they will be at his aid.
  Lucy. Too late comes rescue. He is ta'en or slain;
For fly he could not, if he would have fled;
And fly would Talbot never, though he might.
  Som. If he be dead, brave Talbot, then adieu! 45
  Lucy. His fame lives in the world, his shame
    in you.   [*Exeunt.*

[SCENE V. *The English camp near Bordeaux.*]

Enter TALBOT *and* [JOHN] *his son.*

  Tal. O young John Talbot! I did send for thee
To tutor thee in stratagems of war,
That Talbot's name might be in thee reviv'd
When sapless age and weak unable limbs
Should bring thy father to his drooping chair. 5
But, O malignant and ill-boding stars!
Now thou art come unto a feast of death,
A terrible and unavoided danger.
Therefore, dear boy, mount on my swiftest horse;
And I'll direct thee how thou shalt escape 10
By sudden flight. Come, dally not, be gone.
  John. Is my name Talbot? and am I your son?
And shall I fly? O, if you love my mother,
Dishonour not her honourable name
To make a bastard and a slave of me! 15
The world will say, he is not Talbot's blood,
That basely fled when noble Talbot stood.
  Tal. Fly, to revenge my death, if I be slain.
  John. He that flies so will ne'er return again.
  Tal. If we both stay, we both are sure to die. 20
  John. Then let me stay; and, father, do you fly.
Your loss is great, so your regard should be;
My worth unknown, no loss is known in me.
Upon my death the French can little boast;
In yours they will, in you all hopes are lost. 25
Flight cannot stain the honour you have won,
But mine it will, that no exploit have done.
You fled for vantage, every one will swear;
But, if I bow, they'll say it was for fear.
There is no hope that ever I will stay 30
If the first hour I shrink and run away.
Here on my knee I beg mortality,
Rather than life preserv'd with infamy.
  Tal. Shall all thy mother's hopes lie in one
    tomb?
  John. Ay, rather than I'll shame my mother's
    womb. 35
  Tal. Upon my blessing, I command thee go.
  John. To fight I will, but not to fly the foe.
  Tal. Part of thy father may be sav'd in thee.
  John. No part of him but will be shame in me.

  Tal. Thou never hadst renown, nor canst not
    lose it. 40
  John. Yes, your renowned name. Shall flight
    abuse it?
  Tal. Thy father's charge shall clear thee from
    that stain.
  John. You cannot witness for me, being slain.
If death be so apparent, then both fly.
  Tal. And leave my followers here to fight and
    die? 45
My age was never tainted with such shame.
  John. And shall my youth be guilty of such
    blame?
No more can I be severed from your side
Than can yourself yourself in twain divide.
Stay, go, do what you will, the like do I; 50
For live I will not if my father die.
  Tal. Then here I take my leave of thee, fair son,
Born to eclipse thy life this afternoon.
Come, side by side together live and die;
And soul with soul from France to heaven fly. 55
    [*Exeunt.*

[SCENE VI. *A field of battle.*]

Alarum: excursions, wherein JOHN TALBOT *is
hemmed about, and* TALBOT *rescues him.*

  Tal. Saint George and victory! fight, soldiers,
    fight!
The Regent hath with Talbot broke his word
And left us to the rage of France his sword.
Where is John Talbot? Pause, and take thy breath;
I gave thee life and rescu'd thee from death. 5
  John. O, twice my father, twice am I thy son!
The life thou gav'st me first was lost and done
Till with thy warlike sword, despite of fate,
To my determin'd time thou gav'st new date.
  Tal. When from the Dauphin's crest thy sword
    struck fire, 10
It warm'd thy father's heart with proud desire
Of bold-fac'd victory. Then leaden age,
Quicken'd with youthful spleen and warlike rage,
Beat down Alençon, Orleans, Burgundy,
And from the pride of Gallia rescued thee. 15
The ireful bastard Orleans, that drew blood
From thee, my boy, and had the maidenhood
Of thy first fight, I soon encountered,
And interchanging blows I quickly shed
Some of his bastard blood; and in disgrace 20
Bespoke him thus: "Contaminated, base,
And misbegotten blood I spill of thine,
Mean and right poor, for that pure blood of mine
Which thou didst force from Talbot, my brave boy."
Here, purposing the Bastard to destroy, 25
Came in strong rescue. Speak, thy father's care,

Art thou not weary, John?   How dost thou fare?
Wilt thou yet leave the battle, boy, and fly,
Now thou art seal'd the son of chivalry?
Fly, to revenge my death when I am dead;   30
The help of one stands me in little stead.
O, too much folly is it, well I wot,
To hazard all our lives in one small boat!
If I to-day die not with Frenchmen's rage,
To-morrow I shall die with mickle age.   35
By me they nothing gain an if I stay;
'Tis but the short'ning of my life one day.
In thee thy mother dies, our household's name,
My death's revenge, thy youth, and England's
    fame.
All these and more we hazard by thy stay;   40
All these are sav'd if thou wilt fly away.
    John. The sword of Orleans hath not made me
        smart;
These words of yours draw life-blood from my heart.
On that advantage, bought with such a shame,
To save a paltry life and slay bright fame,   45
Before young Talbot from old Talbot fly
The coward horse that bears me fall and die!
And like me to the peasant boys of France,
To be shame's scorn and subject of mischance!
Surely, by all the glory you have won,   50
An if I fly, I am not Talbot's son.
Then talk no more of flight, it is no boot;
If son to Talbot, die at Talbot's foot.
    Tal. Then follow thou thy desperate sire of Crete,
Thou Icarus. Thy life to me is sweet.   55
If thou wilt fight, fight by thy father's side;
And, commendable prov'd, let's die in pride.
                                    [*Exeunt.*

[SCENE VII. *Another part of the field.*]

Alarum: excursions.   Enter old TALBOT *led [by a*
    SERVANT].

    Tal. Where is my other life? mine own is gone.
O, where's young Talbot? where is valiant John?
Triumphant Death, smear'd with captivity,
Young Talbot's valour makes me smile at thee.
When he perceiv'd me shrink and on my knee,   5
His bloody sword he brandish'd over me,
And, like a hungry lion, did commence
Rough deeds of rage and stern impatience;
But when my angry guardant stood alone,
Tend'ring my ruin and assail'd of none,   10
Dizzy-ey'd fury and great rage of heart
Suddenly made him from my side to start
Into the clust'ring battle of the French;
And in that sea of blood my boy did drench

His over-mounting spirit, and there died,   15
My Icarus, my blossom, in his pride.

Enter [Soldiers,] *with the body of* JOHN TALBOT.

    Serv. O my dear lord, lo, where your son is borne!
    Tal. Thou antic Death, which laugh'st us here
        to scorn,
Anon, from thy insulting tyranny,
Coupled in bonds of perpetuity,   20
Two Talbots, winged through the lither sky,
In thy despite shall scape mortality.
O thou, whose wounds become hard-favoured Death,
Speak to thy father ere thou yield thy breath!
Brave Death by speaking, whether he will or no;   25
Imagine him a Frenchman and thy foe.
Poor boy! he smiles, methinks, as who should say,
Had Death been French, then Death had died to-
        day.
Come, come, and lay him in his father's arms.
My spirit can no longer bear these harms.   30
Soldiers, adieu! I have what I would have,
Now my old arms are young John Talbot's grave.
                                    [*Dies.*

Enter CHARLES, ALENÇON, BURGUNDY, BASTARD,·
    LA PUCELLE [*and forces*].

    Char. Had York and Somerset brought rescue in,
We should have found a bloody day of this.
    Bast. How the young whelp of Talbot's, raging
        wood,   35
Did flesh his puny sword in Frenchmen's blood!
    Puc. Once I encount'red him, and thus I said:
"Thou maiden youth, be vanquish'd by a maid!"
But, with a proud majestical high scorn,
He answer'd thus: "Young Talbot was not born   40
To be the pillage of a giglot wench."
So, rushing in the bowels of the French,
He left me proudly, as unworthy fight.
    Bur. Doubtless he would have made a noble
        knight.
See, where he lies inhearsed in the arms   45
Of the most bloody nurser of his harms!
    Bast. Hew them to pieces, hack their bones
        asunder,
Whose life was England's glory, Gallia's wonder.
    Char. O, no, forbear! for that which we have fled
During the life, let us not wrong it dead.   50

Enter SIR WILLIAM LUCY [*attended; Herald of the*
    French *preceding*].

    Lucy. Herald, conduct me to the Dauphin's tent
To know who hath obtain'd the glory of the day.

---

44. **On that advantage:** taking such an opportunity. 48. **like:** liken. 54. **sire of Crete:** Dædalus, who made wings
of wax for his son, Icarus. He, flying too near the sun, fell into the sea.
  Sc. vii, 3. **smear'd with captivity:** which would be a stain if accompanied by captivity. 9. **guardant:** protector. 10.
Tend'ring my ruin: anxiously protecting me in my fall. 18. **antic:** buffoon. 21. **lither:** yielding. 25. **Brave:** defy. 35.
wood: mad. 41. **giglot:** wanton.

Char. On what submissive message art thou
    sent?
Lucy. Submission, Dauphin! 'tis a mere French
    word;
We English warriors wot not what it means.   55
I come to know what prisoners thou hast ta'en
And to survey the bodies of the dead.
Char. For prisoners ask'st thou? Hell our prison
    is.
But tell me whom thou seek'st.
Lucy. But where's the great Alcides of the
    field,   60
Valiant Lord Talbot, Earl of Shrewsbury,
Created, for his rare success in arms,
Great Earl of Washford, Waterford, and Valence;
Lord Talbot of Goodrig and Urchinfield,
Lord Strange of Blackmere, Lord Verdun of
    Alton,   65
Lord Cromwell of Wingfield, Lord Furnival of
    Sheffield,
The thrice-victorious Lord of Falconbridge;
Knight of the noble Order of Saint George,
Worthy Saint Michael, and the Golden Fleece;
Great marshal to Henry the Sixth   70
Of all his wars within the realm of France?
Puc. Here is a silly stately style indeed!
The Turk, that two and fifty kingdoms hath,
Writes not so tedious a style as this.
Him that thou magnifi'st with all these titles   75
Stinking and fly-blown lies here at our feet.
Lucy. Is Talbot slain, the Frenchmen's only
    scourge,
Your kingdom's terror and black Nemesis?
O, were mine eye-balls into bullets turn'd,
That I in rage might shoot them at your faces! 80
O, that I could but call these dead to life!
It were enough to fright the realm of France.
Were but his picture left amongst you here,
It would amaze the proudest of you all.
Give me their bodies, that I may bear them hence
And give them burial as beseems their worth.   86
Puc. I think this upstart is old Talbot's ghost,
He speaks with such a proud commanding spirit.
For God's sake, let him have him. To keep them
    here,
They would but stink, and putrefy the air.   90
Char. Go, take their bodies hence.
Lucy. I'll bear them hence; but from their ashes
    shall be rear'd
A phœnix that shall make all France afeard.
Char. So we be rid of them, do with them what
    thou wilt.
And now to Paris, in this conquering vein;   95
All will be ours, now bloody Talbot's slain.
                     [*Exeunt.*

[ACT V]

SCENE [I. *London. The palace.*]

Sennet. Enter KING, GLOUCESTER, *and* EXETER.

King. Have you perus'd the letters from the
    Pope,
The Emperor, and the Earl of Armagnac?
Glou. I have, my lord; and their intent is this:
They humbly sue unto your excellence
To have a godly peace concluded of   5
Between the realms of England and of France.
King. How doth your Grace affect their motion?
Glou. Well, my good lord; and as the only means
To stop effusion of our Christian blood
And stablish quietness on every side.   10
King. Ay. marry, uncle; for I always thought
It was both impious and unnatural
That such immanity and bloody strife
Should reign among professors of one faith.
Glou. Beside, my lord, the sooner to effect   15
And surer bind this knot of amity,
The Earl of Armagnac, near knit to Charles,
A man of great authority in France,
Proffers his only daughter to your Grace
In marriage, with a large and sumptuous dowry.
King. Marriage, uncle! Alas, my years are
    young!   21
And fitter is my study and my books
Than wanton dalliance with a paramour.
Yet call th' ambassadors; and, as you please,
So let them have their answers every one.   25
I shall be well content with any choice
Tends to God's glory and my country's weal.

Enter WINCHESTER [*in Cardinal's habit, a* LEGATE,
and two] Ambassadors.

Exe. What! is my Lord of Winchester install'd,
And call'd unto a cardinal's degree?
Then I perceive that will be verified   30
Henry the Fifth did sometime prophesy,
"If once he come to be a cardinal,
He'll make his cap co-equal with the crown."
King. My lords ambassadors, your several suits
Have been consider'd and debated on.   35
Your purpose is both good and reasonable;
And therefore are we certainly resolv'd
To draw conditions of a friendly peace;
Which by my Lord of Winchester we mean
Shall be transported presently to France.   40
Glou. And for the proffer of my lord your master,
I have inform'd his Highness so at large;
As liking of the lady's virtuous gifts,
Her beauty, and the value of her dower,
He doth intend she shall be England's queen. 45

60. **Alcides:** Hercules. 72. **style:** title.
Act V, sc. i, 7. **affect their motion:** like their proposal. 13. **immanity:** ferocity.

King. [*To the Amb.*]   In argument and proof of
  which contract,
Bear her this jewel, pledge of my affection.
And so, my Lord Protector, see them guarded
And safely brought to Dover; where inshipp'd
Commit them to the fortune of the sea.   50
          [*Exeunt [all but Winchester and Legate*].
Win. Stay, my lord legate; you shall first receive
The sum of money which I promised
Should be delivered to his Holiness
For clothing me in these grave ornaments.
Leg. I will attend upon your lordship's leisure.
Win. [*Aside.*] Now Winchester will not submit,
  I trow,   56
Or be inferior to the proudest peer.
Humphrey of Gloucester, thou shalt well perceive
That, neither in birth or for authority,
The Bishop will be overborne by thee.   60
I'll either make thee stoop and bend thy knee,
Or sack this country with a mutiny.   [*Exeunt.*

SCENE [II.   *France.   Plains in Anjou.*]

Enter CHARLES, BURGUNDY, ALENÇON, BASTARD,
  REIGNIER, LA PUCELLE [*and forces*].

Char. These news, my lords, may cheer our
  drooping spirits.
'Tis said the stout Parisians do revolt
And turn again unto the warlike French.
Alen. Then march to Paris, royal Charles of
  France,
And keep not back your powers in dalliance.   5
Puc. Peace be amongst them, if they turn to us;
Else, ruin combat with their palaces!

Enter SCOUT.

Scout. Success unto our valiant general,
And happiness to his accomplices!
Char. What tidings send our scouts?   I prithee,
  speak.   10
Scout. The English army, that divided was
Into two parties, is now conjoin'd in one,
And means to give you battle presently.
Char. Somewhat too sudden, sirs, the warning
  is;
But we will presently provide for them.   15
Bur. I trust the ghost of Talbot is not there.
Now he is gone, my lord, you need not fear.
Puc. Of all base passions, fear is most accurs'd.
Command the conquest, Charles, it shall be thine,
Let Henry fret and all the world repine.   20
Char. Then on, my lords; and France be for-
  tunate!   [*Exeunt.*

[SCENE III.   *Before Angiers.*]

Alarum.   Excursions.   Enter LA PUCELLE.

Puc. The Regent conquers, and the Frenchmen
  fly.
Now help, ye charming spells and periapts;
And ye choice spirits that admonish me
And give me signs of future accidents.   [*Thunder.*
You speedy helpers, that are substitutes   5
Under the lordly monarch of the north,
Appear and aid me in this enterprise.

Enter Fiends.

This speedy and quick appearance argues proof
Of your accustom'd diligence to me.
Now, ye familiar spirits, that are cull'd   10
Out of the powerful regions under earth,
Help me this once that France may get the field.
              [*They walk, and speak not.*
O, hold me not with silence over-long!
Where I was wont to feed you with my blood,
I'll lop a member off and give it you   15
In earnest of a further benefit,
So you do condescend to help me now.
                    [*They hang their heads.*
No hope to have redress?   My body shall
Pay recompense, if you will grant my suit.
                    [*They shake their heads.*
Cannot my body nor blood-sacrifice   20
Entreat you to your wonted furtherance?
Then take my soul, my body, soul, and all,
Before that England give the French the foil.
                          [*They depart.*
See, they forsake me!   Now the time is come
That France must vail her lofty-plumed crest   25
And let her head fall into England's lap.
My ancient incantations are too weak,
And hell too strong for me to buckle with.
Now, France, thy glory droopeth to the dust.
                              [*Exit.*

Excursions.   Enter BURGUNDY *and* YORK *fighting
  hand to hand.   The French fly.* [LA PUCELLE
  is brought in captive.]

York. Damsel of France, I think I have you
  fast.   30
Unchain your spirits now with spelling charms
And try if they can gain your liberty.
A goodly prize, fit for the devil's grace!
See, how the ugly wench doth bend her brows,
As if with Circe she would change my shape!   35
Puc. Chang'd to a worser shape thou canst not be.
York. O, Charles the Dauphin is a proper man;
No shape but his can please your dainty eye.

Sc. iii, 2. periapts: inscribed amulets.   3. admonish: warn.   4. accidents: happenings.   6. north: home of evil spirits.
16. earnest: advance payment.   21. furtherance: help.   23. foil: defeat.   25. vail: lower.

Puc. A plaguing mischief light on Charles and
thee!
And may ye both be suddenly surpris'd   40
By bloody hands, in sleeping on your beds!
   York. Fell banning hag, enchantress, hold thy
tongue!
   Puc. I prithee, give me leave to curse a while.
   York. Curse, miscreant, when thou comest to
the stake.   [*Exeunt.*

Alarum. Enter SUFFOLK, *with* MARGARET *in his
hand.*

   Suf. Be what thou wilt, thou art my prisoner.
                                 [*Gazes on her.*
O fairest beauty, do not fear nor fly,   46
For I will touch thee but with reverent hands.
I kiss these fingers for eternal peace,
And lay them gently on thy tender side.
Who art thou? say, that I may honour thee.   50
   Mar. Margaret my name, and daughter to a
king,
The King of Naples, whosoe'er thou art.
   Suf. An earl I am, and Suffolk am I call'd.
Be not offended, nature's miracle,
Thou art allotted to be ta'en by me;   55
So doth the swan her downy cygnets save,
Keeping them prisoner underneath her wings.
Yet, if this servile usage once offend,
Go and be free again as Suffolk's friend.
                          [*She is going.*
O, stay! [*Aside.*] I have no power to let her pass; 60
My hand would free her, but my heart says no.
As plays the sun upon the glassy streams,
Twinkling another counterfeited beam,
So seems this gorgeous beauty to mine eyes.
Fain would I woo her, yet I dare not speak.   65
I'll call for pen and ink, and write my mind.
Fie, De la Pole! disable not thyself.
Hast not a tongue? Is she not here?
Wilt thou be daunted at a woman's sight?
Ay, beauty's princely majesty is such,   70
Confounds the tongue and makes the senses rough.
   Mar. Say, Earl of Suffolk — if thy name be so —
What ransom must I pay before I pass?
For I perceive I am thy prisoner.
   Suf. [*Aside.*] How canst thou tell she will deny
thy suit,   75
Before thou make a trial of her love?
   Mar. Why speak'st thou not? What ransom
must I pay?
   Suf. [*Aside.*] She's beautiful and therefore to be
woo'd;
She is a woman, therefore to be won.
   Mar. Wilt thou accept of ransom? yea, or no. 80

   Suf. [*Aside.*] Fond man, remember that thou
hast a wife;
Then how can Margaret be thy paramour?
   Mar. I were best to leave him, for he will not
hear.
   Suf. [*Aside.*] There all is marr'd; there lies a
cooling card.
   Mar. He talks at random; sure, the man is
mad.   85
   Suf. [*Aside.*] And yet a dispensation may be had.
   Mar. And yet I would that you would answer me.
   Suf. [*Aside.*] I'll win this Lady Margaret. For
whom?
Why, for my king. Tush, that's a wooden thing!
   Mar. He talks of wood; it is some carpenter. 90
   Suf. [*Aside.*] Yet so my fancy may be satisfied,
And peace established between these realms.
But there remains a scruple in that too;
For though her father be the King of Naples,
Duke of Anjou and Maine, yet is he poor,   95
And our nobility will scorn the match.
   Mar. Hear ye, captain? Are you not at leisure?
   Suf. [*Aside.*] It shall be so, disdain they ne'er so
much.
Henry is youthful and will quickly yield.
Madam, I have a secret to reveal.   100
   Mar. [*Aside.*] What though I be enthrall'd? He
seems a knight,
And will not any way dishonour me.
   Suf. Lady, vouchsafe to listen what I say.
   Mar. [*Aside.*] Perhaps I shall be rescu'd by the
French;
And then I need not crave his courtesy.   105
   Suf. Sweet madam, give me hearing in a cause —
   Mar. [*Aside.*] Tush, women have been captivate
ere now.
   Suf. Lady, wherefore talk you so?
   Mar. I cry you mercy, 'tis but *quid* for *quo.*
   Suf. Say, gentle princess, would you not sup-
pose   110
Your bondage happy, to be made a queen?
   Mar. To be a queen in bondage is more vile
Than is a slave in base servility;
For princes should be free.
   Suf.   And so shall you,
If happy England's royal king be free.   115
   Mar. Why, what concerns his freedom unto me?
   Suf. I'll undertake to make thee Henry's queen,
To put a golden sceptre in thy hand
And set a precious crown upon thy head,
If thou wilt condescend to be my —
   Mar.   What?   120
   Suf. His love.
   Mar. I am unworthy to be Henry's wife.
   Suf. No, gentle madam; I unworthy am

---

42. **banning:** cursing. 67. **disable:** disparage. 71. **rough:** dull. 84. **cooling card:** one that checks the courage. 91.
fancy: love. 107. **captivate:** taken prisoner. 109. **cry you mercy:** beg your pardon.

To woo so fair a dame to be his wife
And have no portion in the choice myself.   125
How say you, madam, are ye so content?
  Mar. An if my father please, I am content.
  Suf. Then call our captains and our colours forth.
And, madam, at your father's castle walls
We'll crave a parley, to confer with him.   130

A parley sounded. Enter REIGNIER *on the walls.*

See, Reignier, see, thy daughter prisoner!
  Reig. To whom?
  Suf.   To me.
  Reig.   Suffolk, what remedy?
I am a soldier and unapt to weep
Or to exclaim on Fortune's fickleness.
  Suf. Yes, there is remedy enough, my lord.   135
Consent, and for thy honour give consent,
Thy daughter shall be wedded to my king,
Whom I with pain have woo'd and won thereto;
And this her easy-held imprisonment
Hath gain'd thy daughter princely liberty.   140
  Reig. Speaks Suffolk as he thinks?
  Suf.   Fair Margaret knows
That Suffolk doth not flatter, face, or feign.
  Reig. Upon thy princely warrant, I descend
To give thee answer of thy just demand.
                     [*Exit from the walls.*]
  Suf. And here I will expect thy coming.   145

Trumpets sound. Enter REIGNIER [*below*].

  Reig. Welcome, brave earl, into our territories!
Command in Anjou what your honour pleases.
  Suf. Thanks, Reignier, happy for so sweet a child,
Fit to be made companion with a king.
What answer makes your Grace unto my suit?   150
  Reig. Since thou dost deign to woo her little
     worth
To be the princely bride of such a lord,
Upon condition I may quietly
Enjoy mine own, the country Maine and Anjou,
Free from oppression or the stroke of war,   155
My daughter shall be Henry's, if he please.
  Suf. That is her ransom; I deliver her;
And those two counties I will undertake
Your Grace shall well and quietly enjoy.
  Reig. And I again, in Henry's royal name,   160
As deputy unto that gracious king,
Give thee her hand, for sign of plighted faith.
  Suf. Reignier of France, I give thee kingly
thanks,
Because this is in traffic of a king.   164
[*Aside.*] And yet, methinks, I could be well content
To be mine own attorney in this case.
I'll over then to England with this news,
And make this marriage to be solemniz'd.

So farewell, Reignier! Set this diamond safe
In golden palaces, as it becomes.   170
  Reig. I do embrace thee, as I would embrace
The Christian prince, King Henry, were he here.
  Mar. Farewell, my lord! Good wishes, praise,
    and prayers
Shall Suffolk ever have of Margaret.   [*Going.*
  Suf. Farewell, sweet madam! But hark you,
    Margaret;   175
No princely commendations to my king?
  Mar. Such commendations as becomes a maid,
A virgin, and his servant, say to him.
  Suf. Words sweetly plac'd and modestly directed.
But, madam, I must trouble you again;   180
No loving token to his Majesty?
  Mar. Yes, my good lord, a pure unspotted heart,
Never yet taint with love, I send the King.
  Suf. And this withal.   [*Kisses her.*
  Mar. That for thyself; I will not so presume   185
To send such peevish tokens to a king.
               [*Exeunt Reignier and Margaret.*]
  Suf. O, wert thou for myself! But, Suffolk, stay,
Thou mayst not wander in that labyrinth;
There Minotaurs and ugly treasons lurk.
Solicit Henry with her wondrous praise;   190
Bethink thee on her virtues that surmount,
And natural graces that extinguish art;
Repeat their semblance often on the seas,   193
That, when thou com'st to kneel at Henry's feet,
Thou mayst bereave him of his wits with wonder.
                      [*Exit.*

[SCENE IV. *Camp of the Duke of York in Anjou.*]

Enter YORK, WARWICK [*and others*].

  York. Bring forth that sorceress condemn'd to
    burn.

[*Enter* LA PUCELLE, *guarded, and a* SHEPHERD.]

  Shep. Ah, Joan, this kills thy father's heart out-
    right!
Have I sought every country far and near,
And, now it is my chance to find thee out,
Must I behold thy timeless cruel death?   5
Ah, Joan, sweet daughter Joan, I'll die with thee!
  Puc. Decrepit miser! base ignoble wretch!
I am descended of a gentler blood.
Thou art no father nor no friend of mine.
  Shep. Out, out! My lords, an please you, 'tis
    not so.   10
I did beget her, all the parish knows.
Her mother liveth yet, can testify
She was the first fruit of my bach'lorship.
  War. Graceless! wilt thou deny thy parentage?

133. **unapt:** not given. 142. **face:** deceive. 186. **peevish:** foolish.
Sc. iv, 5. **timeless:** untimely. 7. **miser:** wretch. 9. **friend:** relative.

York. This argues what her kind of life hath
    been,   15
Wicked and vile; and so her death concludes.
  Shep. Fie, Joan, that thou wilt be so obstacle!
God knows thou art a collop of my flesh,
And for thy sake have I shed many a tear.
Deny me not, I prithee, gentle Joan.   20
  Puc. Peasant, avaunt! — You have suborn'd
    this man
Of purpose to obscure my noble birth.
  Shep. 'Tis true, I gave a noble to the priest
The morn that I was wedded to her mother.
Kneel down and take my blessing, good my girl. 25
Wilt thou not stoop? Now cursed be the time
Of thy nativity! I would the milk
Thy mother gave thee when thou suck'dst her
    breast,
Had been a little ratsbane for thy sake!
Or else, when thou didst keep my lambs a-field, 30
I wish some ravenous wolf had eaten thee!
Dost thou deny thy father, cursed drab?
O, burn her, burn her! hanging is too good. [*Exit.*
  York. Take her away; for she hath liv'd too long
To fill the world with vicious qualities.   35
  Puc. First, let me tell you whom you have con-
    demn'd:
Not me begotten of a shepherd swain,
But issued from the progeny of kings;
Virtuous and holy; chosen from above,
By inspiration of celestial grace,   40
To work exceeding miracles on earth.
I never had to do with wicked spirits;
But you, that are polluted with your lusts,
Stain'd with the guiltless blood of innocents,
Corrupt and tainted with a thousand vices, 45
Because you want the grace that others have,
You judge it straight a thing impossible
To compass wonders but by help of devils.
No; misconceived! Joan of Arc hath been
A virgin from her tender infancy,   50
Chaste and immaculate in very thought;
Whose maiden blood, thus rigorously effus'd,
Will cry for vengeance at the gates of heaven.
  York. Ay, ay; away with her to execution!
  War. And hark ye, sirs; because she is a maid 55
Spare for no faggots, let there be enow.
Place barrels of pitch upon the fatal stake,
That so her torture may be shortened.
  Puc. Will nothing turn your unrelenting hearts?
Then, Joan, discover thine infirmity,   60
That warranteth by law to be thy privilege.
I am with child, ye bloody homicides!
Murder not then the fruit within my womb,
Although ye hale me to a violent death.
  York. Now heaven forfend! the holy maid with
    child!   65

  War. The greatest miracle that e'er ye wrought!
Is all your strict preciseness come to this?
  York. She and the Dauphin have been juggling.
I did imagine what would be her refuge.
  War. Well, go to; we'll have no bastards live, 70
Especially since Charles must father it.
  Puc. You are deceiv'd; my child is none of his.
It was Alençon that enjoy'd my love.
  York. Alençon! that notorious Machiavel!
It dies, an if it had a thousand lives.   75
  Puc. O, give me leave, I have deluded you.
'Twas neither Charles nor yet the duke I nam'd,
But Reignier, King of Naples, that prevail'd.
  War. A married man! that's most intolerable.
  York. Why, here's a girl! I think she knows
    not well,   80
There were so many, whom she may accuse.
  War. It's sign she hath been liberal and free.
  York. And yet, forsooth, she is a virgin pure.
Strumpet, thy words condemn thy brat and thee.
Use no entreaty, for it is in vain.   85
  Puc. Then lead me hence, with whom I leave
    my curse:
May never glorious sun reflex his beams
Upon the country where you make abode,
But darkness and the gloomy shade of death
Environ you, till mischief and despair   90
Drive you to break your necks or hang yourselves!
                       [*Exit* [*guarded*].
  York. Break thou in pieces and consume to ashes,
Thou foul accursed minister of hell!

Enter CARDINAL [BEAUFORT, Bishop of Winchester,
    attended].

  Car. Lord Regent, I do greet your excellence
With letters of commission from the King. 95
For know, my lords, the states of Christendom,
Mov'd with remorse of these outrageous broils,
Have earnestly implor'd a general peace
Betwixt our nation and the aspiring French;
And here at hand the Dauphin and his train 100
Approacheth, to confer about some matter.
  York. Is all our travail turn'd to this effect?
After the slaughter of so many peers,
So many captains, gentlemen, and soldiers,
That in this quarrel have been overthrown 105
And sold their bodies for their country's benefit,
Shall we at last conclude effeminate peace?
Have we not lost most part of all the towns,
By treason, falsehood, and by treachery,
Our great progenitors had conquered?   110
O, Warwick, Warwick! I foresee with grief
The utter loss of all the realm of France.
  War. Be patient, York. If we conclude a peace,
It shall be with such strict and severe covenants
As little shall the Frenchmen gain thereby. 115

---

    17. **obstacle:** obstinate.   18. **collop:** slice.   52. **rigorously effus'd:** cruelly shed.   82. **liberal:** loose.

Enter CHARLES, ALENÇON, BASTARD, REIGNIER
    [*and others*].

Char. Since, lords of England, it is thus agreed
That peaceful truce shall be proclaim'd in France,
We come to be informed by yourselves
What the conditions of that league must be.

York. Speak, Winchester; for boiling choler
    chokes   120
The hollow passage of my poison'd voice,
By sight of these our baleful enemies.

Car. Charles, and the rest, it is enacted thus:
That, in regard King Henry gives consent,
Of mere compassion and of lenity,   125
To ease your country of distressful war
And suffer you to breathe in fruitful peace,
You shall become true liegemen to his crown;
And, Charles, upon condition thou wilt swear
To pay him tribute and submit thyself,   130
Thou shalt be plac'd as viceroy under him,
And still enjoy thy regal dignity.

Alen. Must he be then as shadow of himself?
Adorn his temples with a coronet,
And yet, in substance and authority,   135
Retain but privilege of a private man?
This proffer is absurd and reasonless.

Char. 'Tis known already that I am possess'd
With more than half the Gallian territories,
And therein reverenc'd for their lawful king.   140
Shall I, for lucre of the rest unvanquish'd,
Detract so much from that prerogative
As to be call'd but viceroy of the whole?
No, lord ambassador, I'll rather keep
That which I have than, coveting for more,   145
Be cast from possibility of all.

York. Insulting Charles! hast thou by secret
    means
Us'd intercession to obtain a league,
And, now the matter grows to compromise,
Stand'st thou aloof upon comparison?   150
Either accept the title thou usurp'st,
Of benefit proceeding from our king
And not of any challenge of desert,
Or we will plague thee with incessant wars.

Reig. My lord, you do not well in obstinacy   155
To cavil in the course of this contract.
If once it be neglected, ten to one
We shall not find like opportunity.

Alen. To say the truth, it is your policy
To save your subjects from such massacre   160
And ruthless slaughters as are daily seen
By our proceeding in hostility;
And therefore take this compact of a truce,
Although you break it when your pleasure serves.

War. How say'st thou, Charles?   Shall our
    condition stand?   165

Char. It shall;

Only reserv'd, you claim no interest
In any of our towns of garrison.

York. Then swear allegiance to his Majesty,
As thou art knight, never to disobey   170
Nor be rebellious to the crown of England,
Thou, nor thy nobles, to the crown of England.
    [*Charles and his party give signs of fealty.*]
So, now dismiss your army when ye please;
Hang up your ensigns, let your drums be still,
For here we entertain a solemn peace.   175
    [*Exeunt.*

[SCENE] V. [*London.   The palace.*]

Enter SUFFOLK *in conference with the* KING;
    GLOUCESTER *and* EXETER [*following*].

King. Your wondrous rare description, noble earl,
Of beauteous Margaret hath astonish'd me.
Her virtues graced with external gifts
Do breed love's settled passions in my heart;
And like as rigour of tempestuous gusts   5
Provokes the mightiest hulk against the tide,
So am I driven by breath of her renown
Either to suffer shipwreck or arrive
Where I may have fruition of her love.

Suf. Tush, my good lord, this superficial tale   10
Is but a preface of her worthy praise.
The chief perfections of that lovely dame,
Had I sufficient skill to utter them,
Would make a volume of enticing lines,
Able to ravish any dull conceit;   15
And, which is more, she is not so divine,
So full-replete with choice of all delights,
But with as humble lowliness of mind
She is content to be at your command;
Command, I mean, of virtuous chaste intents,   20
To love and honour Henry as her lord.

King. And otherwise will Henry ne'er presume.
Therefore, my Lord Protector, give consent
That Margaret may be England's royal queen.

Glou. So should I give consent to flatter sin.   25
You know, my lord, your Highness is betroth'd
Unto another lady of esteem.
How shall we then dispense with that contract,
And not deface your honour with reproach?

Suf. As doth a ruler with unlawful oaths;   30
Or one that, at a triumph having vow'd
To try his strength, forsaketh yet the lists
By reason of his adversary's odds.
A poor earl's daughter is unequal odds,
And therefore may be broke without offence.   35

Glou. Why, what, I pray, is Margaret more than
    that?
Her father is no better than an earl,
Although in glorious titles he excel.

Suf. Yes, my lord, her father is a king,

121. **poison'd.** Theobald's emendation to *prison'd* is probably right.   125. **Of:** out of.   152. **Of benefit:** as a favor.

The King of Naples and Jerusalem;   40
And of such great authority in France
As his alliance will confirm our peace
And keep the Frenchmen in allegiance.
   Glou. And so the Earl of Armagnac may do,
Because he is near kinsman unto Charles.   45
   Exe. Beside, his wealth doth warrant a liberal
     dower,
Where Reignier sooner will receive than give.
   Suf. A dower, my lords! disgrace not so your
     king,
That he should be so abject, base, and poor,
To choose for wealth and not for perfect love.   50
Henry is able to enrich his queen
And not to seek a queen to make him rich.
So worthless peasants bargain for their wives,
As market-men for oxen, sheep, or horse.
Marriage is a matter of more worth   55
Than to be dealt in by attorneyship.
Not whom we will, but whom his Grace affects,
Must be companion of his nuptial bed.
And therefore, lords, since he affects her most,
[It] most of all these reasons bindeth us   60
In our opinions she should be preferr'd.
For what is wedlock forced but a hell,
An age of discord and continual strife?
Whereas the contrary bringeth bliss,
And is a pattern of celestial peace.   65
Whom should we match with Henry, being a king,
But Margaret, that is daughter to a king?
Her peerless feature, joined with her birth,
Approves her fit for none but for a king.
Her valiant courage and undaunted spirit,   70
More than in women commonly is seen,
Will answer our hope in issue of a king;
For Henry, son unto a conqueror,
Is likely to beget more conquerors

If with a lady of so high resolve   75
As is fair Margaret he be link'd in love.
Then yield, my lords; and here conclude with me
That Margaret shall be Queen, and none but she.
   King. Whether it be through force of your report,
My noble Lord of Suffolk, or for that   80
My tender youth was never yet attaint
With any passion of inflaming love,
I cannot tell; but this I am assur'd,
I feel such sharp dissension in my breast,
Such fierce alarums both of hope and fear,   85
As I am sick with working of my thoughts.
Take, therefore, shipping; post, my lord, to France;
Agree to any covenants, and procure
That Lady Margaret do vouchsafe to come
To cross the seas to England and be crown'd   90
King Henry's faithful and anointed queen.
For your expenses and sufficient charge,
Among the people gather up a tenth.
Be gone, I say; for, till you do return,
I rest perplexed with a thousand cares.   95
And you, good uncle, banish all offence.
If you do censure me by what you were,
Not what you are, I know it will excuse
This sudden execution of my will.
And so, conduct me where, from company,   100
I may revolve and ruminate my grief.   [*Exit.*
   Glou. Ay, grief, I fear me, both at first and last.
           [*Exeunt Gloucester [and Exeter].*
   Suf. Thus Suffolk hath prevail'd; and thus he
     goes,
As did the youthful Paris once to Greece,
With hope to find the like event in love   105
But prosper better than the Troyan did.
Margaret shall now be Queen, and rule the King;
But I will rule both her, the King, and realm.
                  [*Exit.*

Sc. v, 60. [It] (Rowe). Om. F.   64. contrary. Pronounced *conterary*.   97. censure ... were: judge me by your own youth.

The Second Part of Henry the Sixth

THE QUESTION of the authorship of the *Second* and *Third Parts* of *Henry VI* has been greatly complicated by the existence of two plays published in Quarto before *2* and *3 Henry VI* appeared in the First Folio, and containing a large amount of matter in common with them. *The First Part of the Contention betwixt the two famous Houses of Yorke and Lancaster, with the death of the good Duke Humphrey: And the banishment and death of the Duke of Suffolke, and the Tragicall end of the proud Cardinall of Winchester with the notable Rebellion of Iacke Cade: And the Duke of Yorkes first claime vnto the Crowne* was entered in the Stationers' Register on March 12, 1594, printed in the same year, and reissued in 1600. *The true Tragedie of Richard Duke of Yorke, and the death of good King Henrie the Sixt* appeared in 1595 and again in 1600. In 1619 the two plays were issued as *The Whole Contention betweene the two Famous Houses, Lancaster and Yorke — Written by William Shakespeare, Gent.* Since the end of the eighteenth century until comparatively recently the majority of scholars regarded these Quartos as the work of Marlowe, Greene, and perhaps others, and as the basis on which Shakespeare constructed *2* and *3 Henry VI.* In the third decade of the twentieth century, however, opinion changed, and now there is fairly general agreement that these early Quartos represent a pirated report of a heavily cut acting version of the plays printed in the Folio. There is little evidence as to the agency through which these surreptitious editions were obtained, the chief conjectures being the actor who had played Suffolk and Cade for the *Second Part* and he who had played Warwick and Clifford for the *Third*, or a prompter.

The *First Part of the Contention* is much shorter than *2 Henry VI* and its text is corrupted in every possible way. The reporter, whoever he was, had a very capricious memory and mangled the grammar, the sense, and the meter unmercifully. Modern editors must rely for the text almost entirely on the First Folio.

The evidence which formerly was supposed to point to the authorship of Marlowe and others in the Quarto tends now to be regarded as showing rather the influence of the style of his predecessors upon the young Shakespeare.

There is no clear proof of the date of composition of *2 Henry VI*, but 1591 is probably not more than a year wrong either way. Some scholars conjecture a revival of the plays on Henry VI about 1594, at which time they may have undergone some revision, which would give an additional explanation of differences between the Quarto and Folio versions.

As compared with *Part I*, the *Second Part of Henry VI* shows some development in the treatment of the chronicle play. As before, the material is mainly from Holinshed and Halle. The episode of the pretended miracle at St. Alban's (II.i) is found in Grafton's *Chronicle*, which derives it from a story told to Sir Thomas More by his father and recorded in More's *Dialogue of the Worship of Images*. On the whole there is less violation of historical accuracy than in Part I, but events are still varied and rearranged for dramatic effect. Two of the more extreme instances of such distortion are the scenes between Queen Margaret and Eleanor, though the date of Margaret's arrival in England makes them impossible; and the feats of the future Richard III at the battle of St. Alban's, though he was then only two years old.

The characterization in *Part II* is clearer and firmer than in *Part I*, and in the opening scene there is a not unsuccessful attempt to bring together the main strands of the action: the relation of Suffolk and Margaret; the conflict between Gloucester and Winchester; and the putting forth by York of his claims to the crown. But some of these are allowed to disappear for acts at a time; and the most successful piece of theater in the play, the rebellion of Jack Cade, is almost a detached episode.

THE HOUSE OF LANCASTER

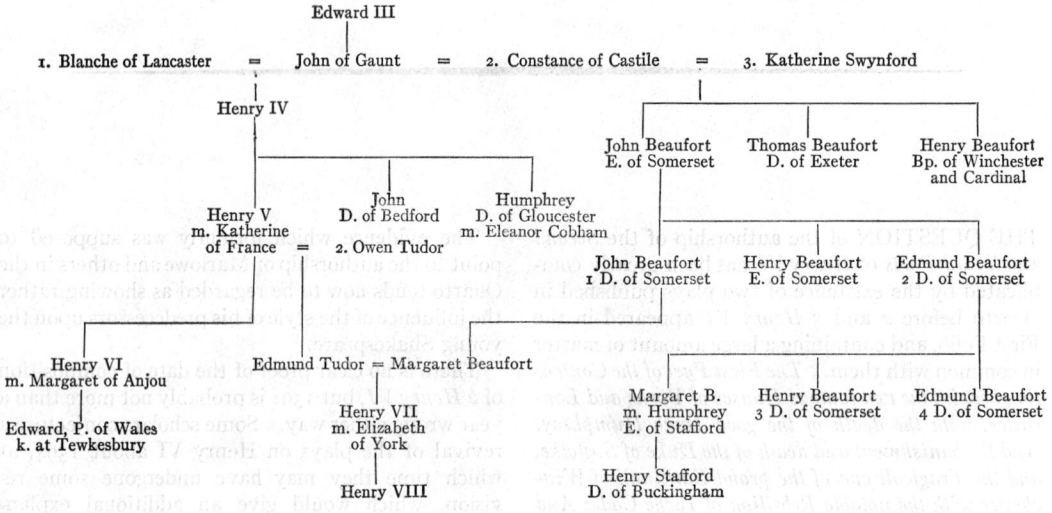

FAMILY OF WARWICK, THE KING–MAKER

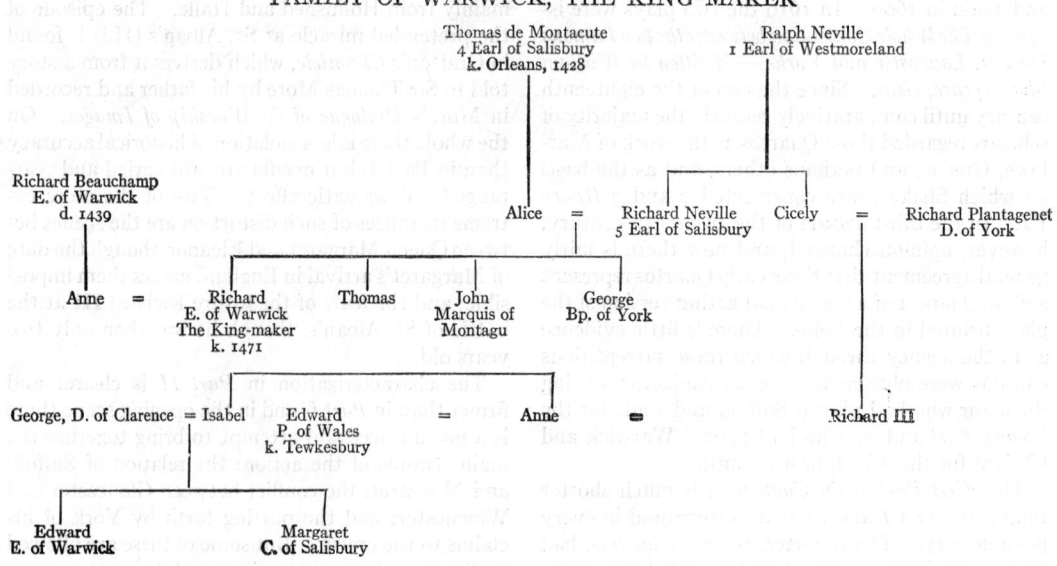

THE SECOND PART OF
HENRY THE SIXTH

[DRAMATIS PERSONÆ

KING HENRY VI.
HUMPHREY, *duke of Gloucester, his uncle.*
CARDINAL BEAUFORT, *bishop of Winchester,*
  great-uncle to the King.
RICHARD PLANTAGENET, *duke of York.*
EDWARD *and* RICHARD, *his sons.*
DUKE OF SOMERSET.
DUKE OF SUFFOLK.
DUKE OF BUCKINGHAM.
LORD CLIFFORD.
Young CLIFFORD, *his son.*
EARL OF SALISBURY.
EARL OF WARWICK.
LORD SCALES.
LORD SAY.
SIR HUMPHREY STAFFORD, *and* WILLIAM STAF-
  FORD, *his brother.*
SIR JOHN STANLEY.
VAUX.
MATTHEW GOFFE.
ALEXANDER IDEN, *a Kentish gentleman.*

A Lieutenant, Master, and Master's Mate, and
  WALTER WHITMORE.
Two Gentlemen, *prisoners with Suffolk.*
JOHN HUME *and* JOHN SOUTHWELL, *priests.*
ROGER BOLINGBROKE, *a conjurer.*
THOMAS HORNER, *an armourer.*
PETER, *his man.*
Clerk of Chatham.   Mayor of Saint Alban's.
SIMPCOX, *an impostor.*
JACK CADE, *a rebel.*
GEORGE BEVIS, JOHN HOLLAND, DICK *the*
  butcher, SMITH *the weaver,* MICHAEL, *etc., fol-*
  lowers of Cade.
Two Murderers.

MARGARET, *Queen to King Henry.*
ELEANOR, *duchess of Gloucester.*
MARGERY JORDAN, *a witch.*
Wife to Simpcox.

A Spirit.

Lords, Ladies, and Attendants, Petitioners, Aldermen, a Herald, a Beadle, Sheriff, and
  Officers, Citizens, Apprentices, Falconers, Guards, Soldiers, Messengers, etc.

SCENE: *England.*]

ACT I

SCENE I. [*London.   The palace.*]

Flourish of trumpets: then hautboys.   Enter the
KING, HUMPHREY DUKE OF GLOUCESTER,
SALISBURY, WARWICK, *and* CARDINAL BEAU-
FORT, *on the one side; the* QUEEN, SUFFOLK, YORK,
SOMERSET, *and* BUCKINGHAM, *on the other.*

Suf. As by your high imperial Majesty
I had in charge at my depart for France,

As procurator to your Excellence,
To marry Princess Margaret for your Grace,
So, in the famous ancient city Tours,   5
In presence of the Kings of France and Sicil,
The Dukes of Orleans, Calaber, Bretagne, and
    Alençon,
Seven earls, twelve barons, and twenty reverend
    bishops,
I have perform'd my task and was espous'd;
And humbly now upon my bended knee,   10
In sight of England and her lordly peers,

Act I, sc. i, 3. procurator: deputy.

Deliver up my title in the Queen
To your most gracious hands, that are the substance
Of that great shadow I did represent;
The happiest gift that ever marquess gave,   15
The fairest queen that ever king receiv'd.
   King. Suffolk, arise. Welcome, Queen Margaret.
I can express no kinder sign of love
Than this kind kiss. O Lord, that lends me life,
Lend me a heart replete with thankfulness!   20
For thou hast given me in this beauteous face
A world of earthly blessings to my soul,
If sympathy of love unite our thoughts.
   Queen. Great King of England and my gracious
      lord,
The mutual conference that my mind hath had,   25
By day, by night, waking and in my dreams,
In courtly company or at my beads,
With you, mine alder-liefest sovereign,
Makes me the bolder to salute my king
With ruder terms, such as my wit affords   30
And over-joy of heart doth minister.
   King. Her sight did ravish; but her grace in
      speech,
Her words y-clad with wisdom's majesty,
Makes me from wond'ring fall to weeping joys,
Such is the fulness of my heart's content.   35
Lords, with one cheerful voice welcome my love.
   All (*kneeling*). Long live Queen Margaret, Eng-
      land's happiness!
   Queen. We thank you all.   [*Flourish.*
   Suf. My Lord Protector, so it please your Grace,
Here are the articles of contracted peace   40
Between our sovereign and the French king Charles,
For eighteen months concluded by consent.
   Glou. (*Reads.*) "*Imprimis,* It is agreed between
the French king Charles, and William de la Pole,
Marquess of Suffolk, ambassador for Henry King
of England, that the said Henry shall espouse   45
the Lady Margaret, daughter unto Reignier King
of Naples, Sicilia, and Jerusalem, and crown her
Queen of England ere the thirtieth of May next
ensuing. *Item,* that the duchy of Anjou and the
county of Maine shall be released and delivered to
the King her father" —   [*Lets the paper fall.* 52
   King. Uncle, how now?
   Glou.   Pardon me, gracious lord;
Some sudden qualm hath struck me at the heart
And dimm'd mine eyes, that I can read no further.
   King. Uncle of Winchester, I pray, read on. 56
   Car. [*Reads.*] "*Item,* It is further agreed between
them, that the duchies of Anjou and Maine shall
be released and delivered over to the King her
father, and she sent over of the King of England's
own proper cost and charges, without having any
dowry."   62

   King. They please us well. Lord Marquess,
      kneel down.
We here create thee the first Duke of Suffolk,
And gird thee with the sword. Cousin of York,
We here discharge your Grace from being regent
I' th' parts of France, till term of eighteen months
Be full expir'd. Thanks, uncle Winchester,
Gloucester, York, Buckingham, Somerset,
Salisbury, and Warwick;   70
We thank you all for this great favour done
In entertainment to my princely queen.
Come, let us in, and with all speed provide
To see her coronation be perform'd.
      [*Exeunt King, Queen, and Suffolk.*
   Glou. Brave peers of England, pillars of the state,
To you Duke Humphrey must unload his grief,   76
Your grief, the common grief of all the land.
What! did my brother Henry spend his youth,
His valour, coin, and people, in the wars?
Did he so often lodge in open field,   80
In winter's cold and summer's parching heat,
To conquer France, his true inheritance?
And did my brother Bedford toil his wits,
To keep by policy what Henry got?
Have you yourselves, Somerset, Buckingham,   85
Brave York, Salisbury, and victorious Warwick,
Receiv'd deep scars in France and Normandy?
Or hath mine uncle Beaufort and myself,
With all the learned council of the realm,
Studied so long, sat in the council-house   90
Early and late, debating to and fro
How France and Frenchmen might be kept in awe,
And hath his Highness in his infancy
Crowned in Paris in despite of foes?
And shall these labours and these honours die? 95
Shall Henry's conquest, Bedford's vigilance,
Your deeds of war, and all our counsel die?
O peers of England, shameful is this league,
Fatal this marriage, cancelling your fame,
Blotting your names from books of memory,   100
Razing the characters of your renown,
Defacing monuments of conquer'd France,
Undoing all, as all had never been!
   Car. Nephew, what means this passionate dis-
      course,
This peroration with such circumstance?   105
For France, 'tis ours; and we will keep it still.
   Glou. Ay, uncle, we will keep it, if we can;
But now it is impossible we should.
Suffolk, the new-made duke that rules the roast,
Hath given the duchy of Anjou and Maine   110
Unto the poor King Reignier, whose large style
Agrees not with the leanness of his purse.
   Sal. Now, by the death of Him that died for
      all,

---

28. **alder-liefest:** dearest of all. 33. **y-clad:** clad. 43. *Imprimis:* Lat. in the first place. 49. *Item:* (Lat.) also. 60. **of:** at.
80. **lodge:** lie. 111. **large style:** grand title.

These counties were the keys of Normandy.
But wherefore weeps Warwick, my valiant son?
   War. For grief that they are past recovery; 116
For, were there hope to conquer them again,
My sword should shed hot blood, mine eyes no
   tears.
Anjou and Maine! myself did win them both.
Those provinces these arms of mine did conquer;
And are the cities that I got with wounds 121
Deliver'd up again with peaceful words?
Mort Dieu!
   York. For Suffolk's duke, may he be suffocate,
That dims the honour of this warlike isle! 125
France should have torn and rent my very heart
Before I would have yielded to this league.
I never read but England's kings have had
Large sums of gold and dowries with their wives;
And our King Henry gives away his own 130
To match with her that brings no vantages.
   Glou. A proper jest, and never heard before,
That Suffolk should demand a whole fifteenth
For costs and charges in transporting her!
She should have stay'd in France and starv'd in
   France 135
Before —
   Car. My Lord of Gloucester, now ye grow too
   hot.
It was the pleasure of my lord the King.
   Glou. My Lord of Winchester, I know your
   mind.
'Tis not my speeches that you do mislike, 140
But 'tis my presence that doth trouble ye.
Rancour will out. Proud prelate, in thy face
I see thy fury. If I longer stay,
We shall begin our ancient bickerings.
Lordings, farewell; and say, when I am gone,
I prophesied France will be lost ere long. 146
                         [*Exit.*
   Car. So, there goes our Protector in a rage.
'Tis known to you he is mine enemy,
Nay, more, an enemy unto you all,
And no great friend, I fear me, to the King. 150
Consider, lords, he is the next of blood,
And heir apparent to the English crown.
Had Henry got an empire by his marriage,
And all the wealthy kingdoms of the west,
There's reason he should be displeas'd at it. 155
Look to it, lords! Let not his smoothing words
Bewitch your hearts. Be wise and circumspect.
What though the common people favour him,
Calling him "Humphrey, the good Duke of
   Gloucester,"
Clapping their hands, and crying with loud voice,
"Jesu maintain your royal Excellence!" 161
With "God preserve the good Duke Humphrey!"

I fear me, lords, for all this flattering gloss,
He will be found a dangerous protector.
   Buck. Why should he, then, protect our sov-
   ereign, 165
He being of age to govern of himself?
Cousin of Somerset, join you with me,
And all together, with the Duke of Suffolk,
We'll quickly hoise Duke Humphrey from his seat.
   Car. This weighty business will not brook
   delay. 170
I'll to the Duke of Suffolk presently. [*Exit.*
   Som. Cousin of Buckingham, though Hum-
   phrey's pride
And greatness of his place be grief to us,
Yet let us watch the haughty Cardinal.
His insolence is more intolerable 175
Than all the princes in the land beside.
If Gloucester be displac'd, he'll be Protector.
   Buck. Or thou or I, Somerset, will be Protectors,
Despite Duke Humphrey or the Cardinal.
        [*Exeunt Buckingham and Somerset.*
   Sal. Pride went before, ambition follows him. 180
While these do labour for their own preferment,
Behoves it us to labour for the realm.
I never saw but Humphrey Duke of Gloucester
Did bear him like a noble gentleman.
Oft have I seen the haughty Cardinal, 185
More like a soldier than a man o' th' church,
As stout and proud as he were lord of all,
Swear like a ruffian, and demean himself
Unlike the ruler of a commonweal.
Warwick, my son, the comfort of my age, 190
Thy deeds, thy plainness, and thy housekeeping,
Hath won the greatest favour of the commons,
Excepting none but good Duke Humphrey;
And, brother York, thy acts in Ireland,
In bringing them to civil discipline, 195
Thy late exploits done in the heart of France
When thou wert regent for our sovereign,
Have made thee fear'd and honour'd of the people.
Join we together, for the public good,
In what we can to bridle and suppress 200
The pride of Suffolk and the Cardinal,
With Somerset's and Buckingham's ambition;
And, as we may, cherish Duke Humphrey's deeds
While they do tend the profit of the land.
   War. So God help Warwick, as he loves the land
And common profit of his country! 206
   York. [*Aside.*] And so says York, for he hath
   greatest cause.
   Sal. Then let's make haste away, and look unto
   the main.
   War. Unto the main! O father, Maine is lost!
That Maine which by main force Warwick did
   win, 210

---

123. **Mort Dieu:** Fr. (by the) death of God (Christ). 145. **Lordings:** gentlemen (without contemptuous implication).
169. **hoise:** hoist. 171. **presently:** at once. 188. **demean:** behave. 191. **housekeeping:** hospitality.

And would have kept so long as breath did last!
Main chance, father, you meant; but I meant
    Maine,
Which I will win from France, or else be slain.
          [Exeunt Warwick and Salisbury.
York. Anjou and Maine are given to the French;
Paris is lost; the state of Normandy   215
Stands on a tickle point now they are gone.
Suffolk concluded on the articles,
The peers agreed, and Henry was well pleas'd
To change two dukedoms for a duke's fair daughter.
I cannot blame them all; what is't to them?   220
'Tis thine they give away, and not their own;
Pirates may make cheap pennyworths of their
    pillage
And purchase friends and give to courtezans,
Still revelling like lords till all be gone;
While as the silly owner of the goods   225
Weeps over them and wrings his hapless hands
And shakes his head and trembling stands aloof,
While all is shar'd and all is borne away,
Ready to starve and dare not touch his own;
So York must sit and fret and bite his tongue   230
While his own lands are bargain'd for and sold.
Methinks the realms of England, France, and Ire-
    land
Bear that proportion to my flesh and blood
As did the fatal brand Althæa burn'd
Unto the Prince's heart of Calydon.   235
Anjou and Maine both given unto the French!
Cold news for me, for I had hope of France,
Even as I have of fertile England's soil.
A day will come when York shall claim his own;
And therefore I will take the Nevils' parts   240
And make a show of love to proud Duke Hum-
    phrey;
And when I spy advantage claim the crown,
For that's the golden mark I seek to hit.
Nor shall proud Lancaster usurp my right,
Nor hold the sceptre in his childish fist,   245
Nor wear the diadem upon his head,
Whose church-like humours fits not for a crown.
Then, York, be still a while, till time do serve.
Watch thou and wake when others be asleep,
To pry into the secrets of the state;   250
Till Henry, surfeiting in joys of love
With his new bride and England's dear-bought
    queen,
And Humphrey with the peers be fallen at jars.
Then will I raise aloft the milk-white rose,
With whose sweet smell the air shall be perfum'd,
And in my standard bear the arms of York   256
To grapple with the house of Lancaster;
And, force perforce, I'll make him yield the crown,

Whose bookish rule hath pull'd fair England down.
                    [Exit.

[SCENE II. *The Duke of Gloucester's house.*]

Enter DUKE HUMPHREY *and his wife* ELEANOR.

Duch. Why droops my lord, like over-ripen'd corn
Hanging the head at Ceres' plenteous load?
Why doth the great Duke Humphrey knit his
    brows,
As frowning at the favours of the world?
Why are thine eyes fix'd to the sullen earth,   5
Gazing on that which seems to dim thy sight?
What seest thou there? King Henry's diadem,
Enchas'd with all the honours of the world?
If so, gaze on, and grovel on thy face,
Until thy head be circled with the same.   10
Put forth thy hand, reach at the glorious gold.
What, is't too short? I'll lengthen it with mine;
And, having both together heav'd it up,
We'll both together lift our heads to heaven
And never more abase our sight so low   15
As to vouchsafe one glance unto the ground.
    Glou. O Nell, sweet Nell, if thou dost love thy
    lord,
Banish the canker of ambitious thoughts!
And may that thought, when I imagine ill
Against my king and nephew, virtuous Henry,   20
Be my last breathing in this mortal world!
My troublous dreams this night doth make me sad.
    Duch. What dream'd my lord? Tell me, and
    I'll requite it
With sweet rehearsal of my morning's dream.
    Glou. Methought this staff, mine office-badge in
    court,   25
Was broke in twain; by whom I have forgot,
But, as I think, it was by th' Cardinal;
And on the pieces of the broken wand
Were plac'd the heads of Edmund Duke of Somer-
    set,
And William de la Pole, first Duke of Suffolk.   30
This was my dream; what it doth bode, God knows.
    Duch. Tut, this was nothing but an argument
That he that breaks a stick of Gloucester's grove
Shall lose his head for his presumption.
But list to me, my Humphrey, my sweet Duke.
Methought I sat in seat of majesty   36
In the cathedral church of Westminster,
And in that chair where kings and queens are
    crown'd,
Where Henry and Dame Margaret kneel'd to me
And on my head did set the diadem.   40
    Glou. Nay, Eleanor, then must I chide outright.
Presumptuous dame, ill-nurtur'd Eleanor,

216. **tickle:** ticklish, precarious. 221. **thine:** i.e., York's. 233. **proportion:** relation. 234. **Althæa:** mother of Meleager, whose life was fated to end with that of the brand. 247. **church-like humours:** pious disposition.
    Sc. ii, 8. Enchas'd: decorated. 18. **canker:** ulcer.

Art thou not second woman in the realm,
And the Protector's wife, belov'd of him?
Hast thou not worldly pleasure at command   45
Above the reach or compass of thy thought?
And wilt thou still be hammering treachery
To tumble down thy husband and thyself
From top of honour to disgrace's feet?
Away from me, and let me hear no more!   50
  Duch. What, what, my lord! are you so choleric
With Eleanor, for telling but her dream?
Next time I'll keep my dreams unto myself,
And not be check'd.
  Glou. Nay, be not angry; I am pleas'd again.

Enter a MESSENGER.

  Mess. My Lord Protector, 'tis his Highness'
    pleasure   56
You do prepare to ride unto Saint Alban's,
Where as the King and Queen do mean to hawk.
  Glou. I go. Come, Nell, thou wilt ride with us?
  Duch. Yes, my good lord, I'll follow presently. 60
    [Exeunt Gloucester [and Messenger].
Follow I must; I cannot go before
While Gloucester bears this base and humble mind.
Were I a man, a duke, and next of blood,
I would remove these tedious stumbling-blocks
And smooth my way upon their headless necks;
And, being a woman, I will not be slack   66
To play my part in Fortune's pageant.
Where are you there? Sir John! Nay, fear not,
    man,
We are alone; here's none but thee and I.

Enter HUME.

  Hume. Jesus preserve your royal Majesty!   70
  Duch. What say'st thou? Majesty? I am but
    Grace.
  Hume. But, by the grace of God and Hume's ad-
    vice,
Your Grace's title shall be multiplied.
  Duch. What say'st thou, man? Hast thou as yet
    conferr'd
With Margery Jordan, the cunning witch,   75
With Roger Bolingbroke, the conjurer?
And will they undertake to do me good?
  Hume. This they have promised, to show your
    Highness
A spirit rais'd from depth of under-ground,
That shall make answer to such questions   80
As by your Grace shall be propounded him.
  Duch. It is enough; I'll think upon the questions.
When from Saint Alban's we do make return,
We'll see these things effected to the full.
Here, Hume, take this reward. Make merry, man,

With thy confederates in this weighty cause.   86
    [Exit.
  Hume. Hume must make merry with the Duch-
    ess' gold;
Marry, and shall. But, how now, Sir John Hume!
Seal up your lips, and give no words but mum;
The business asketh silent secrecy.   90
Dame Eleanor gives gold to bring the witch;
Gold cannot come amiss, were she a devil.
Yet have I gold flies from another coast,
I dare not say from the rich Cardinal
And from the great and new-made Duke of Suffolk,
Yet I do find it so; for, to be plain,   96
They, knowing Dame Eleanor's aspiring humour,
Have hired me to undermine the Duchess
And buzz these conjurations in her brain.
They say, "A crafty knave does need no broker;"
Yet am I Suffolk and the Cardinal's broker.   101
Hume, if you take not heed, you shall go near
To call them both a pair of crafty knaves.
Well, so it stands; and thus, I fear, at last
Hume's knavery will be the Duchess' wreck,   105
And her attainture will be Humphrey's fall.
Sort how it will, I shall have gold for all.   *[Exit.*

[SCENE III. *The palace.*]

Enter three or four PETITIONERS, [PETER] *the
Armourer's man being one.*

  1. Petit. My masters, let's stand close. My
Lord Protector will come this way by and by, and
then we may deliver our supplications in the quill.
  2. Petit. Marry, the Lord protect him, for he's a
good man! Jesu bless him!   6

Enter SUFFOLK *and* QUEEN.

  Peter. Here 'a comes, methinks, and the Queen
with him. I'll be the first, sure.
  2. Petit. Come back, fool. This is the Duke of
Suffolk and not my Lord Protector.
  Suf. How now, fellow! wouldst anything with
me?   12
  1. Petit. I pray, my lord, pardon me. I took ye
for my Lord Protector.
  Queen. [*Reading.*] "To my Lord Protector!"
Are your supplications to his lordship? Let me see
them. What is thine?   17
  1. Petit. Mine is, an't please your Grace, against
John Goodman, my Lord Cardinal's man, for keeping my house, and lands, and wife, and all from
me.   21
  Suf. Thy wife too! that's some wrong, indeed.
What's yours? What's here! [*Reads.*] "Against
the Duke of Suffolk, for enclosing the commons of
Melford." How now, sir knave?   25

---

71. **Grace:** i.e., a Duchess. 106. **attainture:** conviction.
Sc. iii, 3. **in the quill:** all together.

2. Petit. Alas, sir, I am but a poor petitioner of our whole township.

Peter. [*Giving his petition.*] Against my master, Thomas Horner, for saying that the Duke of York was rightful heir to the crown. 30

Queen. What say'st thou? Did the Duke of York say he was rightful heir to the crown?

Peter. That my [master] was? No, forsooth. My master said that he was, and that the King was an usurper. 35

Suf. Who is there? (*Enter Servant.*) Take this fellow in, and send for his master with a pursuivant presently. We'll hear more of your matter before the King. [*Exit [Servant with Peter].*

Queen. And as for you, that love to be protected Under the wings of our Protector's grace, 41 Begin your suits anew, and sue to him.

                   [*Tears the supplications.*
Away, base cullions! Suffolk, let them go.

All. Come, let's be gone. [*Exeunt.*

Queen. My Lord of Suffolk, say, is this the guise, Is this the fashion in the court of England? 46 Is this the government of Britain's isle, And this the royalty of Albion's king? What, shall King Henry be a pupil still Under the surly Gloucester's governance? 50 Am I a queen in title and in style And must be made a subject to a duke? I tell thee, Pole, when in the city Tours Thou ran'st a tilt in honour of my love And stol'st away the ladies' hearts of France, 55 I thought King Henry had resembled thee In courage, courtship, and proportion. But all his mind is bent to holiness, To number Ave-Maries on his beads. His champions are the prophets and apostles, 60 His weapons holy saws of sacred writ, His study is his tilt-yard, and his loves Are brazen images of canoniz'd saints. I would the college of the cardinals Would choose him Pope and carry him to Rome, 65 And set the triple crown upon his head. That were a state fit for his holiness.

Suf. Madam, be patient. As I was cause Your Highness came to England, so will I In England work your Grace's full content. 70

Queen. Beside the haughty Protector, have we Beaufort The imperious churchman, Somerset, Buckingham, And grumbling York; and not the least of these But can do more in England than the King.

Suf. And he of these that can do most of all 75 Cannot do more in England than the Nevils. Salisbury and Warwick are no simple peers.

Queen. Not all these lords do vex me half so much

As that proud dame, the Lord Protector's wife. She sweeps it through the court with troops of ladies, 80 More like an empress than Duke Humphrey's wife. Strangers in court do take her for the Queen. She bears a duke's revenues on her back, And in her heart she scorns our poverty. Shall I not live to be aveng'd on her? 85 Contemptuous base-born callet as she is, She vaunted 'mongst her minions t'other day, The very train of her worst wearing gown Was better worth than all my father's lands, Till Suffolk gave two dukedoms for his daughter. 90

Suf. Madam, myself have lim'd a bush for her, And placed a choir of such enticing birds That she will light to listen to the lays, And never mount to trouble you again. So, let her rest; and, madam, list to me, 95 For I am bold to counsel you in this. Although we fancy not the Cardinal, Yet must we join with him and with the lords, Till we have brought Duke Humphrey in disgrace. As for the Duke of York, this late complaint 100 Will make but little for his benefit. So, one by one, we'll weed them all at last, And you yourself shall steer the happy helm.

Sound a sennet. Enter the KING, DUKE HUMPHREY, CARDINAL BEAUFORT, BUCKINGHAM, YORK, [SOMERSET,] SALISBURY, WARWICK, *and the* DUCHESS OF GLOUCESTER.

King. For my part, noble lords, I care not which; Or Somerset or York, all's one to me. 105

York. If York have ill demean'd himself in France, Then let him be denay'd the regentship.

Som. If Somerset be unworthy of the place, Let York be Regent; I will yield to him.

War. Whether your Grace be worthy, yea or no, Dispute not that York is the worthier. 111

Car. Ambitious Warwick, let thy betters speak.

War. The Cardinal's not my better in the field.

Buck. All in this presence are thy betters, Warwick.

War. Warwick may live to be the best of all. 115

Sal. Peace, son! and show some reason, Buckingham, Why Somerset should be preferr'd in this.

Queen. Because the King, forsooth, will have it so.

Glou. Madam, the King is old enough himself To give his censure. These are no women's matters. 120

Queen. If he be old enough, what needs your Grace To be Protector of his Excellence?

33. [master] (Warburton). *Mistresse* F. 43. cullions: wretches. 86. callet: strumpet. 91. lim'd: smeared with birdlime. 107. denay'd: refused. 120. censure: opinion.

Glou. Madam, I am Protector of the realm;
And, at his pleasure, will resign my place.
  Suf. Resign it then and leave thine insolence. 125
Since thou wert king — as who is king but thou? —
The commonwealth hath daily run to wrack,
The Dauphin hath prevail'd beyond the seas,
And all the peers and nobles of the realm
Have been as bondmen to thy sovereignty. 130
  Car. The commons hast thou rack'd; the clergy's
    bags
Are lank and lean with thy extortions.
  Som. Thy sumptuous buildings and thy wife's
    attire
Have cost a mass of public treasury.
  Buck. Thy cruelty in execution 135
Upon offenders hath exceeded law
And left thee to the mercy of the law.
  Queen. Thy sale of offices and towns in France,
If they were known, as the suspect is great,
Would make thee quickly hop without thy head. 140
    [*Exit Gloucester.* [*The Queen drops her fan.*]
Give me my fan. What, minion! can ye not?
    [*She gives the Duchess a box on the ear.*
I cry you mercy, madam; was it you?
  Duch. Was't I! Yea, I it was, proud French-
    woman.
Could I come near your beauty with my nails,
I'd set my ten commandments in your face. 145
  King. Sweet aunt, be quiet; 'twas against her
    will.
  Duch. Against her will! Good king, look to't
    in time;
She'll hamper thee, and dandle thee like a baby.
Though in this place most master wear no breeches,
She shall not strike Dame Eleanor unreveng'd. 150
    [*Exit.*
  Buck. Lord Cardinal, I will follow Eleanor,
And listen after Humphrey, how he proceeds.
She's tickled now; her fume needs no spurs,
She'll gallop far enough to her destruction. [*Exit.*

Re-enter GLOUCESTER.

  Glou. Now, lords, my choler being overblown 155
With walking once about the quadrangle,
I come to talk of commonwealth affairs.
As for your spiteful false objections,
Prove them, and I lie open to the law;
But God in mercy so deal with my soul 160
As I in duty love my king and country!
But to the matter that we have in hand.
I say, my sovereign, York is meetest man
To be your regent in the realm of France.
  Suf. Before we make election, give me leave 165

To show some reason, of no little force,
That York is most unmeet of any man.
  York. I'll tell thee, Suffolk, why I am unmeet.
First, for I cannot flatter thee in pride;
Next, if I be appointed for the place, 170
My Lord of Somerset will keep me here
Without discharge, money, or furniture,
Till France be won into the Dauphin's hands.
Last time, I danc'd attendance on his will
Till Paris was besieg'd, famish'd, and lost. 175
  War. That can I witness; and a fouler fact
Did never traitor in the land commit.
  Suf. Peace, headstrong Warwick!
  War. Image of pride, why should I hold my
    peace?

Enter [HORNER, *the*] *Armourer, and his man*
    [PETER, *guarded*].

  Suf. Because here is a man accus'd of treason. 180
Pray God the Duke of York excuse himself!
  York. Doth any one accuse York for a traitor?
  King. What mean'st thou, Suffolk? Tell me,
    what are these?
  Suf. Please if your Majesty, this is the man
That doth accuse his master of high treason. 185
His words were these: that Richard Duke of York
Was rightful heir unto the English crown
And that your Majesty was an usurper.
  King. Say, man, were these thy words? 189
  Hor. An't shall please your Majesty, I never said
nor thought any such matter. God is my witness,
I am falsely accus'd by the villain.
  Pet. By these ten bones, my lords [*holding up his
hands*] he did speak them to me in the garret one
night, as we were scouring my Lord of York's
armour. 195
  York. Base dunghill villain and mechanical, I'll
have thy head for this thy traitor's speech. I do beseech your royal Majesty,
Let him have all the rigour of the law. 199
  Hor. Alas, my lord, hang me, if ever I spake the
words. My accuser is my 'prentice; and when I did
correct him for his fault the other day, he did vow
upon his knees he would be even with me. I have
good witness of this; therefore I beseech your Majesty, do not cast away an honest man for a villain's
accusation. 206
  King. Uncle, what shall we say to this in law?
  Glou. This doom, my lord, if I may judge:
Let Somerset be regent o'er the French,
Because in York this breeds suspicion; 210
And let these have a day appointed them
For single combat in convenient place,

131. **rack'd:** impoverished by extortion. 142. **cry you mercy:** beg your pardon. 145. **ten commandments:** ten fingers.
149. **most master:** i.e., the Queen. 172. **furniture:** military equipment. 176. **fact:** deed. 196. **mechanical:** artisan (used
in contempt). 205. **cast away:** destroy.

For he hath witness of his servant's malice.
This is the law, and this Duke Humphrey's doom.
Som. I humbly thank your royal Majesty.   215
Hor. And I accept the combat willingly.
Pet. Alas, my lord, I cannot fight; for God's sake,
pity my case.   The spite of man prevaileth against
me.   O Lord, have mercy upon me!   I shall never
be able to fight a blow.   O Lord, my heart!   221
Glou. Sirrah, or you must fight, or else be hang'd.
King. Away with them to prison; and the day of
combat shall be the last of the next month.   Come,
Somerset, we'll see thee sent away.   226
[Flourish.   Exeunt.

[SCENE IV. *Gloucester's garden.*]

Enter the witch [MARGERY JORDAN], *the two priests,*
[HUME *and* SOUTHWELL], *and* BOLINGBROKE.

Hume. Come, my masters; the Duchess, I tell
you, expects performance of your promises.
Boling. Master Hume, we are therefor provided.
Will her ladyship behold and hear our exorcisms?
Hume. Ay, what else?   Fear you not her
courage.   7
Boling. I have heard her reported to be a woman
of an invincible spirit; but it shall be convenient,
Master Hume, that you be by her aloft, while we be
busy below; and so, I pray you, go, in God's name,
and leave us. [*Exit Hume.*]   Mother Jordan, be
you prostrate and grovel on the earth; John Southwell, read you; and let us to our work.   15

Enter DUCHESS *aloft* [HUME *following*].

Duch. Well said, my masters, and welcome all.
To this gear, the sooner the better.
Boling. Patience, good lady; wizards know their
times.
Deep night, dark night, the silent of the night,
The time of night when Troy was set on fire,   20
The time when screech-owls cry and ban-dogs
howl
And spirits walk and ghosts break up their graves,
That time best fits the work we have in hand.
Madam, sit you and fear not.   Whom we raise,
We will make fast within a hallow'd verge.   25
[Here they do the ceremonies belonging, and
make the circle; Bolingbroke or Southwell
reads, "Conjuro te," etc.   It thunders and
lightens terribly; then the Spirit riseth.
Spir. Adsum.
M. Jord. Asmath,
By the eternal God, whose name and power
Thou tremblest at, answer that I shall ask;
For, till thou speak, thou shalt not pass from hence.

Spir. Ask what thou wilt.   That I had said and
done!   31
Boling. "First of the King: what shall of him
become?"   [*Reading out of a paper.*]
Spir. The duke yet lives that Henry shall depose;
But him outlive, and die a violent death.
[As the Spirit speaks, Bolingbroke writes
the answer.]
Boling. "What fates await the Duke of Suffolk?"
Spir. By water shall he die, and take his end.   36
Boling. "What shall befall the Duke of Somer-
set?"
Spir. Let him shun castles.
Safer shall he be upon the sandy plains
Than where castles mounted stand.   40
Have done, for more I hardly can endure.
Boling. Descend to darkness and the burning
lake!
False fiend, avoid!
[Thunder and lightning.   Exit Spirit.

Enter the DUKE OF YORK *and the* DUKE OF
BUCKINGHAM *with their* Guard, *and break in.*

York. Lay hands upon these traitors and their
trash.
Beldam, I think we watch'd you at an inch.   45
What, madam, are you there?   The King and com-
monweal
Are deeply indebted for this piece of pains.
My Lord Protector will, I doubt it not,
See you well guerdon'd for these good deserts.
Duch. Not half so bad as thine to England's
king,   50
Injurious duke, that threatest where's no cause.
Buck. True, madam, none at all.   What call you
this?   [*Showing the papers.*]
Away with them! let them be clapp'd up close,
And kept asunder.   You, madam, shall with us.
Stafford, take her to thee.   55
[Exeunt above Duchess and Hume, guarded.]
We'll see your trinkets here all forthcoming.
All, away!
[Exeunt [guard with Jordan, Southwell, etc.].]
York. Lord Buckingham, methinks you watch'd
her well.
A pretty plot, well chosen to build upon!
Now, pray, my lord, let's see the devil's writ.   60
What have we here?   [*Reads.*
"The duke yet lives that Henry shall depose;
But him outlive, and die a violent death."
Why, this is just
"*Aio* [te,] *Æacida, Romanos vincere posse.*"   65
Well, to the rest:
"Tell me what fate awaits the Duke of Suffolk?"

Sc. iv, 4. **exorcisms:** conjurations.   16. **Well said:** well done.   17. **gear:** business.   21. **ban-dogs:** chained dogs.   45. **Beldam:** hag.   **at an inch:** closely.   65. "*Aio ... posse*": the ambiguous answer given by the Pythian Apollo to Pyrrhus, "I say that you, descendant of Æacus, the Romans can conquer,"

By water shall he die, and take his end.
What shall betide the Duke of Somerset?
Let him shun castles;   70
Safer shall he be upon the sandy plains
Than where castles mounted stand."
Come, come, my lords;
These oracles are hardly attain'd,
And hardly understood.   75
The King is now in progress towards Saint Alban's,
With him the husband of this lovely lady.
Thither goes these news, as fast as horse can carry
   them,
A sorry breakfast for my Lord Protector.
   Buck. Your Grace shall give me leave, my Lord of
   York,   80
To be the post, in hope of his reward.
   York. At your pleasure, my good lord. Who's
   within there, ho!

Enter a Servingman.

Invite my Lords of Salisbury and Warwick
To sup with me to-morrow night. Away!
                             [*Exeunt.*

ACT II

[SCENE I. *Saint Alban's.*]

Enter the KING, QUEEN, GLOUCESTER, CARDINAL,
   and SUFFOLK, *with* Falconers, *halloing.*

   Queen. Believe me, lords, for flying at the
   brook
I saw not better sport these seven years' day;
Yet, by your leave, the wind was very high,
And, ten to one, old Joan had not gone out.
   King. But what a point, my lord, your falcon
   made,   5
And what a pitch she flew above the rest!
To see how God in all His creatures works!
Yea, man and birds are fain of climbing high.
   Suf. No marvel, an it like your Majesty,
My Lord Protector's hawks do tower so well.   10
They know their master loves to be aloft
And bears his thoughts above his falcon's pitch.
   Glou. My lord, 'tis but a base ignoble mind
That mounts no higher than a bird can soar.
   Car. I thought as much. He would be above the
   clouds.   15
   Glou. Ay, my Lord Cardinal? How think you by
   that?
Were it not good your Grace could fly to heaven?

   King. The treasury of everlasting joy.
   Car. Thy heaven is on earth; thine eyes and
   thoughts
Beat on a crown, the treasure of thy heart,   20
Pernicious Protector, dangerous peer,
That smooth'st it so with king and commonweal!
   Glou. What, Cardinal, is your priesthood grown
   peremptory?
Tantæne animis cælestibus iræ?
Churchmen so hot? Good uncle, hide such malice.
With such holiness can you do it?   26
   Suf. No malice, sir; no more than well becomes
So good a quarrel and so bad a peer.
   Glou. As who, my lord?
   Suf.   Why, as you, my lord,
An't like your lordly Lord-protectorship.   30
   Glou. Why, Suffolk, England knows thine inso-
   lence.
   Queen. And thy ambition, Gloucester.
   King. I prithee, peace, good queen,
And whet not on these furious peers;
For blessed are the peacemakers on earth.   35
   Car. Let me be blessed for the peace I make
Against this proud Protector with my sword!
   Glou. [*Aside to Car.*] Faith, holy uncle, would
   'twere come to that!
   Car. [*Aside to Glou.*] Marry, when thou dar'st.
   Glou. [*Aside to Car.*] Make up no factious num-
   bers for the matter;   40
In thine own person answer thy abuse.
   Car. [*Aside to Glou.*] Ay, where thou dar'st not
   peep. An if thou dar'st,
This evening, on the east side of the grove.
   King. How now, my lords!
   Car.   Believe me, cousin Gloucester,
Had not your man put up the fowl so suddenly,   45
We had had more sport. [*Aside to Glou.*] Come
   with thy two-hand sword.
   Glou. True, uncle.
   [*Car. Aside to Glou.*] Are ye advis'd? The east
   side of the grove.
   Glou. [*Aside to Car.*] Cardinal, I am with you.
   King.   Why, how now, uncle Gloucester!
   Glou. Talking of hawking; nothing else, my lord.
[*Aside to Car.*] Now, by God's mother, priest, I'll
   shave your crown for this,   51
Or all my fence shall fail.
   Car. [*Aside to Glou.*] *Medice, teipsum —*
Protector, see to't well, protect yourself.
   King. The winds grow high; so do your stomachs,
   lords.
How irksome is this music to my heart!   55

74, 75. **hardly:** with difficulty.

   Act II, sc. i, 4. **old ... out:** the old hawk Joan would not have taken her flight.   5. **point:** the action of rising vertically above the prey.   22. **smooth'st:** flatterest.   24. *Tantæne ... iræ:* Is there such anger in heavenly minds (*Æneid* I.11). 47–48. **Are ... you** (Theobald). Continued to Glou. F.   47. **Are ye advis'd:** Do you understand?   52. **fence:** skill in fencing. *Medice, teipsum:* Physician, [heal] thyself. *Luke* iv.23.   54. **stomachs:** tempers.

When such strings jar, what hope of harmony?
I pray, my lords, let me compound this strife.

Enter [a TOWNSMAN *of Saint Alban's,] crying,*
"A miracle!"

Glou. What means this noise?
Fellow, what miracle dost thou proclaim?   60
Towns. A miracle! a miracle!
Suf. Come to the King and tell him what miracle.
Towns. Forsooth, a blind man at Saint Alban's
shrine,
Within this half-hour, hath receiv'd his sight;
A man that ne'er saw in his life before.   65
King. Now, God be prais'd, that to believing
souls
Gives light in darkness, comfort in despair!

Enter the MAYOR *of Saint Alban's and his brethren,
bearing the man [*SIMPCOX] *between two in a chair
[*SIMPCOX'S *WIFE *and others following*].

Car. Here comes the townsmen on procession,
To present your Highness with the man.
King. Great is his comfort in this earthly vale,   70
Although by his sight his sin be multiplied.
Glou. Stand by, my masters. Bring him near the
King;
His Highness' pleasure is to talk with him.
King. Good fellow, tell us here the circumstance,
That we for thee may glorify the Lord.   75
What, hast thou been long blind and now restor'd?
Simp. Born blind, an't please your Grace.
Wife. Ay, indeed, was he.
Suf. What woman is this?
Wife. His wife, an't like your worship.   80
Glou. Hadst thou been his mother, thou couldst
have better told.
King. Where wert thou born?
Simp. At Berwick in the north, an't like your
Grace.
King. Poor soul, God's goodness hath been great
to thee.
Let never day nor night unhallowed pass,   85
But still remember what the Lord hath done.
Queen. Tell me, good fellow, cam'st thou here by
chance
Or of devotion, to this holy shrine?
Simp. God knows, of pure devotion; being call'd
A hundred times and oftener, in my sleep,   90
By good Saint Alban, who said, "[Simpcox], come;
Come, offer at my shrine, and I will help thee."
Wife. Most true, forsooth; and many time and
oft
Myself have heard a voice to call him so.   94
Car. What, art thou lame?
Simp.   Ay, God Almighty help me!

Suf. How cam'st thou so?
Simp.   A fall off of a tree.
Wife. A plum-tree, master.
Glou.   How long hast thou been blind?
Simp. O, born so, master.
Glou.   What, and wouldst climb a tree?
Simp. But that in all my life, when I was a youth.
Wife. Too true; and bought his climbing very
dear.   100
Glou. Mass, thou lov'dst plums well, that wouldst
venture so.
Simp. Alas, good master, my wife desir'd some
damsons,
And made me climb, with danger of my life.
Glou. A subtle knave! but yet it shall not serve.
Let me see thine eyes. Wink now; now open them.
In my opinion yet thou see'st not well.   106
Simp. Yes, master, clear as day, I thank God
and Saint Alban.
Glou. Say'st thou me so? What colour is this
cloak of?
Simp. Red, master; red as blood.   110
Glou. Why, that's well said. What colour is my
gown of?
Simp. Black, forsooth; coal-black as jet.
King. Why, then, thou know'st what colour jet
is of?
Suf. And yet, I think, jet did he never see.
Glou. But cloaks and gowns, before this day, a
many.   115
Wife. Never, before this day, in all his life.
Glou. Tell me, sirrah, what's my name?
Simp. Alas, master, I know not.
Glou. What's his name?
Simp. I know not.   120
Glou. Nor his?
Simp. No, indeed, master.
Glou. What's thine own name?
Simp. Saunder Simpcox, an if it please you,
master.   124
Glou. Then, Saunder, sit there, the lying'st knave
in Christendom. If thou hadst been born blind,
thou mightst as well have known all our names as
thus to name the several colours we do wear. Sight
may distinguish of colours, but suddenly to nomi-
nate them all, it is impossible. My lords, Saint
Alban here hath done a miracle; and would ye not
think [his] cunning to be great, that could restore
this cripple to his legs again?   133
Simp. O master, that you could!
Glou. My masters of Saint Alban's, have you not
beadles in your town, and things call'd whips?
May. Yes, my lord, if it please your Grace.
Glou. Then send for one presently.   139
May. Sirrah, go fetch the beadle hither straight.
[*Exit [an Attendant*].

91. [Simpcox] (Pope). *Svmon* F. 132. [his] Q. *it* F.

Glou. Now fetch me a stool hither by and by. [*A stool brought.*] Now, sirrah, if you mean to save yourself from whipping, leap me over this stool and run away.

Simp. Alas, master, I am not able to stand alone.   145
You go about to torture me in vain.

Enter a BEADLE *with whips.*

Glou. Well, sir, we must have you find your legs. Sirrah beadle, whip him till he leap over that same stool.

Bead. I will, my lord. Come on, sirrah; off with your doublet quickly.   151

Simp. Alas, master, what shall I do? I am not able to stand.

    [*After the Beadle hath hit him once, he leaps over the stool and runs away; and they follow and cry, "A miracle!"*

King. O God, seest Thou this, and bearest so long?

Queen. It made me laugh to see the villain run.   155

Glou. Follow the knave; and take this drab away.

Wife. Alas, sir, we did it for pure need.

Glou. Let them be whipp'd through every market-town, till they come to Berwick, from whence they came.   160
    [*Exeunt* [*Wife, Beadle, Mayor, etc.*].

Car. Duke Humphrey has done a miracle today.

Suf. True; made the lame to leap and fly away.

Glou. But you have done more miracles than I;
You made in a day, my lord, whole towns to fly.

Enter BUCKINGHAM.

King. What tidings with our cousin Buckingham?   165

Buck. Such as my heart doth tremble to unfold.
A sort of naughty persons, lewdly bent,
Under the countenance and confederacy
Of Lady Eleanor, the Protector's wife,
The ringleader and head of all this rout,   170
Have practis'd dangerously against your state,
Dealing with witches and with conjurers;
Whom we have apprehended in the fact,
Raising up wicked spirits from under ground,
Demanding of King Henry's life and death,   175
And other of your Highness' privy-council,
As more at large your Grace shall understand.

Car. [*Aside to Glou.*] And so, my Lord Protector, by this means
Your lady is forthcoming yet at London.

This news, I think, hath turn'd your weapon's edge;   180
'Tis like, my lord, you will not keep your hour.

Glou. Ambitious churchman, leave to afflict my heart.
Sorrow and grief have vanquish'd all my powers;
And, vanquish'd as I am, I yield to thee,
Or to the meanest groom.   185

King. O God, what mischiefs work the wicked ones,
Heaping confusion on their own heads thereby!

Queen. Gloucester, see here the tainture of thy nest,
And look thyself be faultless, thou wert best.

Glou. Madam, for myself, to heaven I do appeal,
How I have lov'd my king and commonweal;   191
And, for my wife, I know not how it stands.
Sorry I am to hear what I have heard.
Noble she is, but if she have forgot
Honour and virtue, and convers'd with such   195
As, like to pitch, defile nobility,
I banish her my bed and company
And give her as a prey to law and shame,
That hath dishonoured Gloucester's honest name.

King. Well, for this night we will repose us here;
To-morrow toward London back again,   201
To look into this business thoroughly
And call these foul offenders to their answers,
And poise the cause in justice' equal scales,
Whose beam stands sure, whose rightful cause prevails.   [*Flourish. Exeunt.* 205

[SCENE II. *London. The Duke of York's garden.*]

Enter YORK, SALISBURY, *and* WARWICK.

York. Now, my good Lords of Salisbury and Warwick,
Our simple supper ended, give me leave
In this close walk to satisfy myself
In craving your opinion of my title,
Which is infallible, to England's crown.   5

Sal. My lord, I long to hear it at full.

War. Sweet York, begin; and if thy claim be good,
The Nevils are thy subjects to command.

York. Then thus:
Edward the Third, my lords, had seven sons: 10
The first, Edward the Black Prince, Prince of Wales;
The second, William of Hatfield; and the third,
Lionel Duke of Clarence; next to whom
Was John of Gaunt, the Duke of Lancaster;
The fifth was Edmund Langley, Duke of York;   15
The sixth was Thomas of Woodstock, Duke of Gloucester;

---

141. by and by: at once.   167. sort: gang. **lewdly bent:** wickedly disposed.   181. hour: appointment.   188. **tainture:** defilement.   204. poise: weigh.

William of Windsor was the seventh and last.
Edward the Black Prince died before his father
And left behind him Richard, his only son,
Who after Edward the Third's death reign'd as
    king   20
Till Henry Bolingbroke, Duke of Lancaster,
The eldest son and heir of John of Gaunt,
Crown'd by the name of Henry the Fourth,
Seiz'd on the realm, depos'd the rightful king,
Sent his poor queen to France, from whence she
    came,   25
And him to Pomfret; where, as all you know,
Harmless Richard was murdcrcd traitorously.
   War. Father, the Duke hath told the truth;
Thus got the house of Lancaster the crown.
   York. Which now they hold by force and not
    by right;   30
For Richard, the first son's heir, being dead,
The issue of the next son should have reign'd.
   Sal. But William of Hatfield died without an
    heir.
   York. The third son, Duke of Clarence, from
    whose line
I claim the crown, had issue, Philippe, a daugh-
    ter,   35
Who married Edmund Mortimer, Earl of March;
Edmund had issue, Roger Earl of March;
Roger had issue, Edmund, Anne, and Eleanor.
   Sal. This Edmund, in the reign of Bolingbroke,
As I have read, laid claim unto the crown;   40
And, but for Owen Glendower, had been king,
Who kept him in captivity till he died.
But to the rest.
   York.   His eldest sister, Anne,
My mother, being heir unto the crown,
Married Richard Earl of Cambridge, who was
    [son]   45
To Edmund Langley, Edward the Third's fifth [son]
By her I claim the kingdom. She was heir
To Roger Earl of March, who was the son
Of Edmund Mortimer, who married Philippe,
Sole daughter unto Lionel Duke of Clarence;   50
So, if the issue of the elder son
Succeed before the younger, I am king.
   War. What plain proceeding is more plain than
    this?
Henry doth claim the crown from John of Gaunt,
The fourth son; York claims it from the third. 55
Till Lionel's issue fails, his should not reign.
It fails not yet, but flourishes in thee
And in thy sons, fair slips of such a stock.
Then, father Salisbury, kneel we together;
And in this private plot be we the first   60
That shall salute our rightful sovereign
With honour of his birthright to the crown.

   Both. Long live our sovereign Richard, Eng-
    land's king!
   York. We thank you, lords. But I am not your
    king
Till I be crown'd, and that my sword be stain'd 65
With heart-blood of the house of Lancaster;
And that's not suddenly to be perform'd,
But with advice and silent secrecy.
Do you as I do in these dangerous days;
Wink at the Duke of Suffolk's insolence,   70
At Beaufort's pride, at Somerset's ambition,
At Buckingham and all the crew of them,
Till they have snar'd the shepherd of the flock,
That virtuous prince, the good Duke Humphrey.
'Tis that they seek, and they in seeking that   75
Shall find their deaths, if York can prophesy.
   Sal. My lord, break we off; we know your mind
    at full.
   War. My heart assures me that the Earl of War-
    wick
Shall one day make the Duke of York a king.
   York. And, Nevil, this I do assure myself,   80
Richard shall live to make the Earl of Warwick
The greatest man in England but the King.
                        [Exeunt.

        [SCENE III.   *A hall of justice.*]

Sound trumpets.   Enter the KING [*the* QUEEN,
  GLOUCESTER, YORK, SUFFOLK, *and* SALISBURY;
  the DUCHESS OF GLOUCESTER, MARGERY JORDAN,
  SOUTHWELL, HUME, *and* BOLINGBROKE, *under
  guard*].

   King. Stand forth, Dame Eleanor Cobham,
    Gloucester's wife.
In sight of God and us, your guilt is great.
Receive the sentence of the law for sins
Such as by God's book are adjudg'd to death.
You four, from hence to prison back again;   5
From thence unto the place of execution.
The witch in Smithfield shall be burn'd to ashes,
And you three shall be strangled on the gallows.
You, madam, for you are more nobly born,
Despoiled of your honour in your life,   10
Shall, after three days' open penance done,
Live in your country here in banishment,
With Sir John Stanley, in the Isle of Man.
   Duch. Welcome is banishment; welcome were
    my death.
   Glou. Eleanor, the law, thou see'st, hath judged
    thee.   15
I cannot justify whom the law condemns.
      [Exeunt Duchess and other prisoners, guarded.]
Mine eyes are full of tears, my heart of grief.
Ah, Humphrey, this dishonour in thine age

Will bring thy head with sorrow to the ground!
I beseech your Majesty, give me leave to go;   20
Sorrow would solace, and mine age would ease.
   King. Stay, Humphrey Duke of Gloucester! Ere thou go,
Give up thy staff.   Henry will to himself
Protector be; and God shall be my hope,
My stay, my guide, and lantern to my feet;   25
And go in peace, Humphrey, no less belov'd
Than when thou wert Protector to thy king.
   Queen. I see no reason why a king of years
Should be to be protected like a child.
God and King Henry govern England's realm.   30
Give up your staff, sir, and the King his realm.
   Glou. My staff?   Here, noble Henry, is my staff.
As willingly do I the same resign
As e'er thy father Henry made it mine;
And even as willingly at thy feet I leave it   35
As others would ambitiously receive it.
Farewell, good king!   When I am dead and gone,
May honourable peace attend thy throne!   [*Exit.*
   Queen. Why, now is Henry king and Margaret
    queen;
And Humphrey Duke of Gloucester scarce him-
    self,   40
That bears so shrewd a maim: two pulls at once —
His lady banish'd, and a limb lopp'd off.
This staff of honour raught, there let it stand
Where it best fits to be, in Henry's hand.
   Suf. Thus droops this lofty pine and hangs his
    sprays;   45
Thus Eleanor's pride dies in her youngest days.
   York. Lords, let him go.   Please it your Majesty,
This is the day appointed for the combat;
And ready are the appellant and defendant,
The armourer and his man, to enter the lists,   50
So please your Highness to behold the fight.
   Queen. Ay, good my lord; for purposely therefore
Left I the court, to see this quarrel tried.
   King. O' God's name, see the lists and all things
fit.
Here let them end it; and God defend the right!   55
   York. I never saw a fellow worse bested
Or more afraid to fight, than is the appellant,
The servant of this armourer, my lords.

Enter at one door [HORNER,] *the Armourer, and his*
NEIGHBOURS, *drinking to him so much that he is*
drunk: and he enters with a drum before him and his
staff with a sand-bag fastened to it; and at the other
door [PETER,] *his man, with a drum and sand-bag,*
and 'PRENTICES *drinking to him.*

   1. Neigh. Here, neighbour Horner, I drink to

you in a cup of sack; and fear not, neighbour, you
shall do well enough.   61
   2. Neigh. And here, neighbour, here's a cup of
charneco.
   3. Neigh. And here's a pot of good double beer,
neighbour.   Drink, and fear not your man.
   Hor. Let it come, i' faith, and I'll pledge you all;
and a fig for Peter!   66
   1. 'Pren. Here, Peter, I drink to thee; and be
not afraid.
   2. 'Pren. Be merry, Peter, and fear not thy
master.   Fight for credit of the 'prentices.   71
   Peter. I thank you all.   Drink, and pray for me,
I pray you; for I think I have taken my last draught
in this world.   Here, Robin, an if I die, I give thee
my apron; and, Will, thou shalt have my hammer;
and here, Tom, take all the money that I have.   O
Lord bless me!   I pray God! for I am never able to
deal with my master, he hath learnt so much fence
already.   79
   Sal. Come, leave your drinking, and fall to blows.
Sirrah, what's thy name?
   Peter. Peter, forsooth.
   Sal. Peter!   What more?
   Peter. Thump.
   Sal. Thump!   Then see thou thump thy master
well.   86
   Hor. Masters, I am come hither, as it were, upon
my man's instigation, to prove him a knave and
myself an honest man; and touching the Duke of
York, I will take my death, I never meant him any
ill, nor the King, nor the Queen; and therefore,
Peter, have at thee with a downright blow!   93
   York. Dispatch.   This knave's tongue begins to
    double.
Sound, trumpets, alarum to the combatants!
    [*Alarum.*]   *They fight, and Peter strikes him*
    down.
   Hor. Hold, Peter, hold!   I confess, I confess
treason.   [*Dies.*]
   York. Take away his weapon.   Fellow, thank
God, and the good wine in thy master's way.   99
   Peter. O God, have I overcome mine enemy in
this presence?   O Peter, thou hast prevail'd in
right!
   King. Go, take hence that traitor from our
    sight,
For by his death we do perceive his guilt;
And God in justice hath reveal'd to us   105
The truth and innocence of this poor fellow,
Which he had thought to have murder'd wrong-
    fully.
Come, fellow, follow us for thy reward.
    [*Sound a flourish.   Exeunt.*

Sc. iii, 41. **so shrewd a maim:** so severe a mutilation.   43. **raught:** torn from him (past tense of *reach*).   49. **appellant:**
challenger.   63. **charneco:** a sweet wine.   90. **take my death:** pledge my life.   94. **double:** speak thick, stammer.

[SCENE IV. *A street.*]

Enter GLOUCESTER *and his* SERVING-MEN, *in mourning cloaks.*

Glou. Thus sometimes hath the brightest day a
    cloud;
And after summer evermore succeeds
Barren winter, with his wrathful nipping cold;
So cares and joys abound, as seasons fleet.
Sirs, what's o'clock?
    Serv.   Ten, my lord.   5
    Glou. Ten is the hour that was appointed me
To watch the coming of my punish'd duchess.
Uneath may she endure the flinty streets,
To tread them with her tender-feeling feet.
Sweet Nell, ill can thy noble mind abrook   10
The abject people gazing on thy face,
With envious looks laughing at thy shame,
That erst did follow thy proud chariot-wheels
When thou didst ride in triumph through the
    streets.
But, soft! I think she comes; and I'll prepare 15
My tear-stain'd eyes to see her miseries.

Enter the DUCHESS OF GLOUCESTER [bare-foot], *in a
white sheet [with verses pinned upon her back], and
a taper burning in her hand; with* [SIR JOHN
STANLEY,] *the* SHERIFF, *and* Officers.

    Serv. So please your Grace, we'll take her from
    the sheriff.
    Glou. No, stir not, for your lives; let her pass by.
    Duch. Come you, my lord, to see my open
    shame?
Now thou dost penance too. Look how they
    gaze!   20
See how the giddy multitude do point
And nod their heads and throw their eyes on thee!
Ah, Gloucester, hide thee from their hateful looks,
And, in thy closet pent up, rue my shame
And ban thine enemies, both mine and thine! 25
    Glou. Be patient, gentle Nell; forget this grief.
    Duch. Ah, Gloucester, teach me to forget myself!
For whilst I think I am thy married wife
And thou a prince, Protector of this land,
Methinks I should not thus be led along, 30
Mail'd up in shame, with papers on my back,
And follow'd with a rabble that rejoice
To see my tears and hear my deep-fet groans.
The ruthless flint doth cut my tender feet,
And when I start, the envious people laugh 35
And bid me be advised how I tread.
Ah, Humphrey, can I bear this shameful yoke?
Trow'st thou that e'er I'll look upon the world,
Or count them happy that enjoys the sun?

No; dark shall be my light and night my day; 40
To think upon my pomp shall be my hell.
Sometime I'll say, I am Duke Humphrey's wife,
And he a prince and ruler of the land;
Yet so he rul'd and such a prince he was
As he stood by whilst I, his forlorn duchess, 45
Was made a wonder and a pointing-stock
To every idle rascal follower.
But be thou mild and blush not at my shame,
Nor stir at nothing till the axe of death
Hang over thee, as, sure, it shortly will; 50
For Suffolk, he that can do all in all
With her that hateth thee and hates us all,
And York and impious Beaufort, that false priest,
Have all lim'd bushes to betray thy wings,
And, fly thou how thou canst, they'll tangle thee. 55
But fear not thou, until thy foot be snar'd,
Nor never seek prevention of thy foes.
    Glou. Ah, Nell, forbear! thou aimest all awry.
I must offend before I be attainted;
And had I twenty times so many foes, 60
And each of them had twenty times their power,
All these could not procure me any scath
So long as I am loyal, true, and crimeless.
Wouldst have me rescue thee from this reproach?
Why, yet thy scandal were not wip'd away, 65
But I in danger for the breach of law.
Thy greatest help is quiet, gentle Nell.
I pray thee, sort thy heart to patience;
These few days' wonder will be quickly worn.

Enter a HERALD.

    Her. I summon your Grace to his Majesty's
    parliament,   70
Holden at Bury the first of this next month.
    Glou. And my consent ne'er ask'd herein before!
This is close dealing. Well, I will be there.
                        [Exit Herald.]
My Nell, I take my leave; and, master sheriff,
Let not her penance exceed the King's commis-
    sion.   75
    Sher. An't please your Grace, here my commis-
    sion stays,
And Sir John Stanley is appointed now
To take her with him to the Isle of Man.
    Glou. Must you, Sir John, protect my lady here?
    Stan. So am I given in charge, may't please your
    Grace.   80
    Glou. Entreat her not the worse in that I pray
You use her well. The world may laugh again,
And I may live to do you kindness if
You do it her. And so, Sir John, farewell!
    Duch. What, gone, my lord, and bid me not fare-
    well!   85

Sc. iv. 8. Uneath: scarcely. **10. abrook:** endure. **12. envious:** spiteful. **31. Mail'd up:** wrapped up. **33. deep-fet:**
deep-fetched. **36. advised:** careful. **46. pointing-stock:** butt. **58. thou...awry:** thy view is all wrong. **62. scath:**
harm. **68. sort:** fit, adapt. **73. close:** underhand. **81. in that:** because.

Glou. Witness my tears, I cannot stay to speak.
    [*Exeunt Gloucester [and Serving-men].*
Duch. Art thou gone too?   All comfort go with
    thee,
For none abides with me.   My joy is death;
Death, at whose name I oft have been afear'd,
Because I wish'd this world's eternity.   90
Stanley, I prithee, go, and take me hence,
I care not whither, for I beg no favour,
Only convey me where thou art commanded.
    Stan. Why, madam, that is to the Isle of Man;
There to be us'd according to your state.   95
    Duch. That's bad enough, for I am but reproach;
And shall I then be us'd reproachfully?
    Stan. Like to a duchess, and Duke Humphrey's
    lady.
According to that state you shall be us'd.
    Duch. Sheriff, farewell; and better than I fare,
Although thou hast been conduct of my shame.   101
    Sher. It is my office; and, madam, pardon me.
    Duch. Ay, ay, farewell; thy office is discharg'd.
Come, Stanley, shall we go?
    Stan. Madam, your penance done, throw off this
    sheet,   105
And go we to attire you for our journey.
    Duch. My shame will not be shifted with my
    sheet.
No, it will hang upon my richest robes
And show itself, attire me how I can.
Go, lead the way; I long to see my prison.   110
    [*Exeunt.*

[ACT III]

[SCENE I.   *The Abbey at Bury St. Edmund's.*]

A sennet.   Enter the KING, *the* QUEEN, CARDINAL,
SUFFOLK, YORK, BUCKINGHAM, SALISBURY, *and*
WARWICK *to the Parliament.*

    King. I muse my Lord of Gloucester is not come;
'Tis not his wont to be the hindmost man,
Whate'er occasion keeps him from us now.
    Queen. Can you not see, or will ye not observe
The strangeness of his alter'd countenance?   5
With what a majesty he bears himself,
How insolent of late he is become,
How proud, how peremptory, and unlike himself?
We know the time since he was mild and affable,
And if we did but glance a far-off look,   10
Immediately he was upon his knee,
That all the court admir'd him for submission;
But meet him now, and, be it in the morn,
When every one will give the time of day,
He knits his brow and shows an angry eye   15

And passeth by with stiff unbowed knee,
Disdaining duty that to us belongs.
Small curs are not regarded when they grin,
But great men tremble when the lion roars;
And Humphrey is no little man in England.   20
First note that he is near you in descent,
And should you fall, he is the next will mount.
Me seemeth then it is no policy,
Respecting what a rancorous mind he bears
And his advantage following your decease,   25
That he should come about your royal person
Or be admitted to your Highness' council.
By flattery hath he won the commons' hearts,
And when he please to make commotion,
'Tis to be fear'd they all will follow him.   30
Now 'tis the spring, and weeds are shallow-rooted;
Suffer them now, and they'll o'ergrow the garden
And choke the herbs for want of husbandry.
The reverent care I bear unto my lord
Made me collect these dangers in the Duke.   35
If it be fond, call it a woman's fear;
Which fear if better reasons can supplant,
I will subscribe and say I wrong'd the Duke.
My Lord of Suffolk, Buckingham, and York,
Reprove my allegation if you can,   40
Or else conclude my words effectual.
    Suf. Well hath your Highness seen into this
    duke;
And, had I first been put to speak my mind,
I think I should have told your Grace's tale.
The Duchess by his subornation,   45
Upon my life, began her devilish practices;
Or, if he were not privy to those faults,
Yet, by reputing of his high descent,
As next the King he was successive heir,
And such high vaunts of his nobility,   50
Did instigate the bedlam brain-sick Duchess
By wicked means to frame our sovereign's fall.
Smooth runs the water where the brook is deep;
And in his simple show he harbours treason.
The fox barks not when he would steal the lamb.
No, no, my sovereign; Gloucester is a man   56
Unsounded yet and full of deep deceit.
    Car. Did he not, contrary to form of law,
Devise strange deaths for small offences done?
    York. And did he not, in his protectorship,   60
Levy great sums of money through the realm
For soldiers' pay in France, and never sent it,
By means whereof the towns each day revolted?
    Buck. Tut, these are petty faults to faults un-
    known
Which time will bring to light in smooth Duke
    Humphrey.   65
    King. My lords, at once; the care you have of us

95. **state**: rank.   101. **conduct**: guide.
    Act III, sc. i, 1. muse: wonder.   18. **grin**: show the teeth, snarl.   36. **fond**: foolish.   38. **subscribe**: yield.   40. **Reprove**:
disprove.   45. **subornation**: instigation.   48. **reputing**: boasting.   51. **bedlam**: crazy.   64. **to**: compared to.

To mow down thorns that would annoy our foot
Is worthy praise; but, shall I speak my conscience,
Our kinsman Gloucester is as innocent
From meaning treason to our royal person   70
As is the sucking lamb or harmless dove.
The Duke is virtuous, mild, and too well given
To dream on evil or to work my downfall.

    Queen. Ah, what's more dangerous than this fond
        affiance!
Seems he a dove? His feathers are but bor-
      row'd,   75
For he's disposed as the hateful raven.
Is he a lamb? His skin is surely lent him,
For he's inclin'd as is the ravenous [wolf].
Who cannot steal a shape that means deceit?
Take heed, my lord; the welfare of us all   80
Hangs on the cutting short that fraudful man.

      Enter SOMERSET.

    Som. All health unto my gracious sovereign!
    King. Welcome, Lord Somerset. What news
      from France?
    Som. That all your interest in those territories
Is utterly bereft you. All is lost.   85
    King. Cold news, Lord Somerset; but God's
      will be done!
    York. [*Aside.*] Cold news for me; for I had
      hope of France
As firmly as I hope for fertile England.
Thus are my blossoms blasted in the bud
And caterpillars eat my leaves away.   90
But I will remedy this gear ere long,
Or sell my title for a glorious grave.

      Enter GLOUCESTER.

    Glou. All happiness unto my lord the King!
Pardon, my liege, that I have stay'd so long.
    Suf. Nay, Gloucester, know that thou art come
      too soon,   95
Unless thou wert more loyal than thou art.
I do arrest thee of high treason here.
    Glou. Well, Suffolk, thou shalt not see me blush
Nor change my countenance for this arrest;
A heart unspotted is not easily daunted.   100
The purest spring is not so free from mud
As I am clear from treason to my sovereign.
Who can accuse me? Wherein am I guilty?
    York. 'Tis thought, my lord, that you took
      bribes of France,   104
And, being Protector, stay'd the soldiers' pay,
By means whereof his Highness hath lost France.
    Glou. Is it but thought so? What are they that
      think it?
I never robb'd the soldiers of their pay,
Nor ever had one penny bribe from France.

So help me God, as I have watch'd the night,   110
Ay, night by night, in studying good for England.
That doit that e'er I wrested from the King,
Or any groat I hoarded to my use,
Be brought against me at my trial-day!
No; many a pound of mine own proper store,   115
Because I would not tax the needy commons,
Have I dispursed to the garrisons,
And never ask'd for restitution.
    Car. It serves you well, my lord, to say so much.
    Glou. I say no more than truth, so help me
      God!   120
    York. In your protectorship you did devise
Strange tortures for offenders never heard of,
That England was defam'd by tyranny.
    Glou. Why, 'tis well known that, whiles I was
      Protector,
Pity was all the fault that was in me;   125
For I should melt at an offender's tears,
And lowly words were ransom for their fault.
Unless it were a bloody murderer;
Or foul felonious thief that fleec'd poor passengers,
I never gave them condign punishment.   130
Murder indeed, that bloody sin, I tortur'd
Above the felon or what trespass else.
    Suf. My lord, these faults are easy, quickly
      answer'd;
But mightier crimes are laid unto your charge,
Whereof you cannot easily purge yourself.   135
I do arrest you in his Highness' name;
And here commit you to my Lord Cardinal
To keep, until your further time of trial.
    King. My Lord of Gloucester, 'tis my special
      hope
That you will clear yourself from all [suspect].   140
My conscience tells me you are innocent.
    Glou. Ah, gracious lord, these days are dangerous.
Virtue is chok'd with foul ambition,
And charity chas'd hence by rancour's hand.
Foul subornation is predominant,   145
And equity exil'd your Highness' land.
I know their complot is to have my life,
And if my death might make this island happy
And prove the period of their tyranny,
I would expend it with all willingness;   150
But mine is made the prologue to their play;
For thousands more, that yet suspect no peril,
Will not conclude their plotted tragedy.
Beaufort's red sparkling eyes blab his heart's malice,
And Suffolk's cloudy brow his stormy hate;   155
Sharp Buckingham unburdens with his tongue
The envious load that lies upon his heart;
And dogged York, that reaches at the moon,
Whose overweening arm I have pluck'd back,
By false accuse doth level at my life;   160

---

67. **annoy**: hurt. 72. **given**: disposed. 74. **affiance**: confidence. 78. [wolf] (Rowe). *wolves* F. 112. **doit**: coin worth one eighth of a penny. 140. [suspect] (Capell). *suspense* F. 160. **level**: aim.

And you, my sovereign lady, with the rest,
Causeless have laid disgraces on my head
And with your best endeavour have stirr'd up
My liefest liege to be mine enemy.
Ay, all of you have laid your heads together —
Myself had notice of your conventicles —   166
And all to make away my guiltless life.
I shall not want false witness to condemn me,
Nor store of treasons to augment my guilt.
The ancient proverb will be well effected,   170
"A staff is quickly found to beat a dog."
  Car. My liege, his railing is intolerable.
If those that care to keep your royal person
From treason's secret knife and traitors' rage
Be thus upbraided, chid, and rated at,   175
And the offender granted scope of speech,
'Twill make them cool in zeal unto your Grace.
  Suf. Hath he not twit our sovereign lady here
With ignominious words, though clerkly couch'd,
As if she had suborned some to swear   180
False allegations to o'erthrow his state?
  Queen. But I can give the loser leave to chide.
  Glou. Far truer spoke than meant. I lose, indeed.
Beshrew the winners, for they play'd me false!
And well such losers may have leave to speak.
  Buck. He'll wrest the sense and hold us here
    all day.   186
Lord Cardinal, he is your prisoner.
  Car. Sirs, take away the Duke, and guard him
    sure.
  Glou. Ah! thus King Henry throws away his
    crutch
Before his legs be firm to bear his body.   190
Thus is the shepherd beaten from thy side
And wolves are gnarling who shall gnaw thee first.
Ah, that my fear were false! Ah, that it were!
For, good King Henry, thy decay I fear.
        [*Exit* [*guarded*].
  King. My lords, what to your wisdoms seemeth
    best,   195
Do or undo, as if ourself were here.
  Queen. What, will your Highness leave the
    parliament?
  King. Ay, Margaret; my heart is drown'd with
    grief,
Whose flood begins to flow within mine eyes,
My body round engirt with misery,   200
For what's more miserable than discontent?
Ah, uncle Humphrey! in thy face I see
The map of honour, truth, and loyalty;
And yet, good Humphrey, is the hour to come
That e'er I prov'd thee false or fear'd thy faith.   205
What louring star now envies thy estate,
That these great lords and Margaret our queen

Do seek subversion of thy harmless life?
Thou never didst them wrong nor no man wrong;
And as the butcher takes away the calf   210
And binds the wretch and beats it when it strays,
Bearing it to the bloody slaughter-house,
Even so remorseless have they borne him hence;
And as the dam runs lowing up and down,   214
Looking the way her harmless young one went,
And can do nought but wail her darling's loss,
Even so myself bewails good Gloucester's case
With sad unhelpful tears, and with dimm'd eyes
Look after him and cannot do him good,
So mighty are his vowed enemies.   220
His fortunes I will weep, and 'twixt each groan
Say, "Who's a traitor? Gloucester he is none."
        [*Exeunt* [*all but Queen, Cardinal, Suffolk,
            and York; Somerset remains apart*].
  Queen. Free lords, cold snow melts with the
    sun's hot beams.
Henry my lord is cold in great affairs,
Too full of foolish pity, and Gloucester's show
Beguiles him as the mournful crocodile   226
With sorrow snares relenting passengers,
Or as the snake roll'd in a flow'ring bank,
With shining checker'd slough, doth sting a child
That for the beauty thinks it excellent.   230
Believe me, lords, were none more wise than I —
And yet herein I judge mine own wit good —
This Gloucester should be quickly rid the world,
To rid us from the fear we have of him.
  Car. That he should die is worthy policy,   235
But yet we want a colour for his death.
'Tis meet he be condemn'd by course of law.
  Suf. But, in my mind, that were no policy.
The King will labour still to save his life,
The commons haply rise, to save his life;   240
And yet we have but trivial argument,
More than mistrust, that shows him worthy death.
  York. So that, by this you would not have him
    die.
  Suf. Ah, York, no man alive so fain as I!
  York. 'Tis York that hath more reason for his
    death.   245
But, my Lord Cardinal, and you, my Lord of Suffolk,
Say as you think, and speak it from your souls,
Were't not all one, an empty eagle were set
To guard the chicken from a hungry kite,
As place Duke Humphrey for the King's Protector?   250
  Queen. So the poor chicken should be sure of
    death.
  Suf. Madam, 'tis true; and, were't not madness,
    then,
To make the fox surveyor of the fold?

164. **liefest:** dearest.   166. **conventicles:** secret meetings.   179. **clerkly:** cleverly.   192. **gnarling:** snarling.   229. **slough:** skin.   236. **colour:** pretext.

Who being accus'd a crafty murderer,
His guilt should be but idly posted over   255
Because his purpose is not executed.
No; let him die, in that he is a fox,
By nature prov'd an enemy to the flock,
Before his chaps be stain'd with crimson blood,
As Humphrey, prov'd by reasons, to my liege.   260
And do not stand on quillets how to slay him;
Be it by gins, by snares, by subtlety,
Sleeping or waking, 'tis no matter how,
So he be dead; for that is good deceit
Which mates him first that first intends de-
ceit.   265
          Queen. Thrice-noble Suffolk, 'tis resolutely
spoke.
          Suf. Not resolute, except so much were done,
For things are often spoke and seldom meant;
But that my heart accordeth with my tongue,
Seeing the deed is meritorious,   270
And to preserve my sovereign from his foe,
Say but the word, and I will be his priest.
          Car. But I would have him dead, my Lord of
Suffolk,
Ere you can take due orders for a priest.
Say you consent and censure well the deed,   275
And I'll provide his executioner,
I tender so the safety of my liege.
          Suf. Here is my hand, the deed is worthy doing.
          Queen. And so say I.
          York. And I; and now we three have spoke
it,   280
It skills not greatly who impugns our doom.

                    Enter a Post.

          Post. Great lords, from Ireland am I come
amain,
To signify that rebels there are up
And put the Englishmen unto the sword.
Send succours, lords, and stop the rage be-
time,   285
Before the wound do grow uncurable;
For, being green, there is great hope of help.
          Car. A breach that craves a quick expedient
stop!
What counsel give you in this weighty cause?
          York. That Somerset be sent as Regent thither.
'Tis meet that lucky ruler be employ'd;   291
Witness the fortune he hath had in France.
          Som. If York, with all his far-fet policy,
Had been the Regent there instead of me,
He never would have stay'd in France so long.   295
          York. No, not to lose it all, as thou hast done.
I rather would have lost my life betimes
Than bring a burden of dishonour home

By staying there so long till all were lost.
Show me one scar character'd on thy skin.   300
Men's flesh preserv'd so whole do seldom win.
          Queen. Nay, then, this spark will prove a raging
fire,
If wind and fuel be brought to feed it with.
No more, good York; sweet Somerset, be still.
Thy fortune, York, hadst thou been Regent
there,   305
Might happily have prov'd far worse than his.
          York. What, worse than nought? Nay, then, a
shame take all!
          Som. And, in the number, thee that wishest
shame!
          Car. My Lord of York, try what your fortune is.
Th' uncivil kerns of Ireland are in arms   310
And temper clay with blood of Englishmen.
To Ireland will you lead a band of men,
Collected choicely, from each county some,
And try your hap against the Irishmen?
          York. I will, my lord, so please his Majesty.   315
          Suf. Why, our authority is his consent,
And what we do establish he confirms.
Then, noble York, take thou this task in hand.
          York. I am content. Provide me soldiers, lords,
Whiles I take order for mine own affairs.   320
          Suf. A charge, Lord York, that I will see per-
form'd.
But now return we to the false Duke Humphrey.
          Car. No more of him; for I will deal with him
That henceforth he shall trouble us no more.
And so break off; the day is almost spent.   325
Lord Suffolk, you and I must talk of that event.
          York. My Lord of Suffolk, within fourteen days
At Bristol I expect my soldiers;
For there I'll ship them all for Ireland.
          Suf. I'll see it truly done, my Lord of York.   330
                    [*Exeunt all but York.*
          York. Now, York, or never, steel thy fearful
thoughts,
And change misdoubt to resolution.
Be that thou hop'st to be, or what thou art
Resign to death; it is not worth th' enjoying.
Let pale-fac'd fear keep with the mean-born
man,   335
And find no harbour in a royal heart.
Faster than spring-time showers comes thought on
thought,
And not a thought but thinks on dignity.
My brain more busy than the labouring spider
Weaves tedious snares to trap mine enemies.   340
Well, nobles, well, 'tis politicly done,
To send me packing with an host of men.
I fear me you but warm the starved snake,

---

255. **posted over:** hurriedly considered.   261. **quillets:** subtle disputes.   265. **mates:** subdues.   281. **skills:** matters.
impugns our doom: assails our decision.   282. **amain:** quickly.   287. **green:** fresh.   293. **far-fet:** far-fetched.   310. **uncivil
kerns:** uncivilized foot soldiers.   311. **temper:** mix.

Who, cherish'd in your breasts, will sting your
   hearts.
'Twas men I lack'd and you will give them me. 345
I take it kindly; yet be well assur'd
You put sharp weapons in a madman's hands.
Whiles I in Ireland nourish a mighty band,
I will stir up in England some black storm
Shall blow ten thousand souls to heaven or hell; 350
And this fell tempest shall not cease to rage
Until the golden circuit on my head,
Like to the glorious sun's transparent beams,
Do calm the fury of this mad-bred flaw.
And, for a minister of my intent, 355
I have seduc'd a headstrong Kentishman,
John Cade of Ashford,
To make commotion, as full well he can,
Under the title of John Mortimer.
In Ireland have I seen this stubborn Cade 360
Oppose himself against a troop of kerns,
And fought so long, till that his thighs with darts
Were almost like a sharp-quill'd porpentine;
And, in the end being rescued, I have seen
Him caper upright like a wild Morisco, 365
Shaking the bloody darts as he his bells.
Full often, like a shag-hair'd crafty kern,
Hath he conversed with the enemy,
And undiscover'd come to me again
And given me notice of their villainies. 370
This devil here shall be my substitute,
For that John Mortimer, which now is dead,
In face, in gait, in speech, he doth resemble.
By this I shall perceive the commons' mind,
How they affect the house and claim of York. 375
Say he be taken, rack'd, and tortured,
I know no pain they can inflict upon him
Will make him say I mov'd him to those arms.
Say that he thrive, as 'tis great like he will,
Why, then from Ireland come I with my strength
And reap the harvest which that rascal sow'd; 381
For Humphrey being dead, as he shall be,
And Henry put apart, the next for me. [*Exit.*

[SCENE II. *Bury St. Edmund's. A room of state.*]

Enter two or three [MURDERERS] *running over the
  stage, from the murder of Duke Humphrey.*

  1. Mur. Run to my Lord of Suffolk; let him
   know
We have dispatch'd the Duke, as he commanded.
  2. Mur. O that it were to do! What have we
   done?
Didst ever hear a man so penitent?

Enter SUFFOLK.

  1. Mur. Here comes my lord. 5

  Suf. Now, sirs, have you dispatch'd this thing?
  1. Mur. Ay, my good lord, he's dead.
  Suf. Why, that's well said. Go, get you to my
   house;
I will reward you for this venturous deed.
The King and all the peers are here at hand. 10
Have you laid fair the bed? Is all things well,
According as I gave directions?
  1. Mur. 'Tis, my good lord.
  Suf. Away! be gone. [*Exeunt [Murderers].*

Sound trumpets. Enter the KING, *the* QUEEN,
  CARDINAL, SOMERSET, *with Attendants.*

  King. Go, call our uncle to our presence straight.
Say we intend to try his Grace to-day, 16
If he be guilty, as 'tis published.
  Suf. I'll call him presently, my noble lord.
                        [*Exit.*
  King. Lords, take your places; and, I pray you
   all,
Proceed no straiter 'gainst our uncle Gloucester 20
Than from true evidence of good esteem
He be approv'd in practice culpable.
  Queen. God forbid any malice should prevail,
That faultless may condemn a nobleman!
Pray God he may acquit him of suspicion! 25
  King. I thank thee, [Meg;] these words content
   me much.

Re-enter SUFFOLK.

How now! why look'st thou pale? Why tremblest
   thou?
Where is our uncle? What's the matter, Suffolk?
  Suf. Dead in his bed, my lord; Gloucester is
   dead.
  Queen. Marry, God forfend! 30
  Car. God's secret judgement. I did dream to-
   night
The Duke was dumb and could not speak a word.
                   [*The King swoons.*
  Queen. How fares my lord? Help, lords! the
   King is dead.
  Som. Rear up his body; wring him by the nose.
  Queen. Run, go, help, help! O Henry, ope thine
   eyes! 35
  Suf. He doth revive again. Madam, be patient.
  King. O heavenly God!
  Queen.   How fares my gracious lord?
  Suf. Comfort, my sovereign! gracious Henry,
   comfort!
  King. What, doth my Lord of Suffolk comfort
   me?
Came he right now to sing a raven's note, 40
Whose dismal tune bereft my vital powers;
And thinks he that the chirping of a wren,

---

354. flaw: squall. 363. porpentine: porcupine. 365. **Morisco:** morris-dancer.
Sc. ii, 20. straiter: more rigorously. 26. [Meg] (Capell). *Nell* F.

By crying comfort from a hollow breast,
Can chase away the first-conceived sound?
Hide not thy poison with such sug'red words.   45
Lay not thy hands on me; forbear, I say!
Their touch affrights me as a serpent's sting.
Thou baleful messenger, out of my sight!
Upon thy eye-balls murderous tyranny
Sits in grim majesty, to fright the world.   50
Look not upon me, for thine eyes are wounding.
Yet do not go away.   Come, basilisk,
And kill the innocent gazer with thy sight;
For in the shade of death I shall find joy;
In life but double death, now Gloucester's dead.   55
  Queen.   Why do you rate my Lord of Suffolk thus?
Although the Duke was enemy to him,
Yet he most Christian-like laments his death;
And for myself, foe as he was to me,
Might liquid tears or heart-offending groans   60
Or blood-consuming sighs recall his life,
I would be blind with weeping, sick with groans,
Look pale as primrose with blood-drinking sighs,
And all to have the noble Duke alive.
What know I how the world may deem of me,   65
For it is known we were but hollow friends?
It may be judg'd I made the Duke away;
So shall my name with slander's tongue be wounded,
And princes' courts be fill'd with my reproach.
This get I by his death.   Ay me, unhappy!   70
To be a queen, and crown'd with infamy!
  King.   Ah, woe is me for Gloucester, wretched
      man!
  Queen.   Be woe for me, more wretched than he is.
What, dost thou turn away and hide thy face?
I am no loathsome leper; look on me.   75
What! art thou, like the adder, waxen deaf?
Be poisonous too and kill thy forlorn queen.
Is all thy comfort shut in Gloucester's tomb?
Why, then, Dame [Margaret] was ne'er thy joy.
Erect his statuë and worship it,   80
And make my image but an alehouse sign.
Was I for this nigh wreck'd upon the sea
And twice by awkward wind from England's bank
Drove back again unto my native clime?
What boded this but well forewarning wind   85
Did seem to say, "Seek not a scorpion's nest,
Nor set no footing on this unkind shore"?
What did I then, but curs'd the gentle gusts
And he that loos'd them forth their brazen caves;
And bid them blow towards England's blessed
      shore,   90
Or turn our stern upon a dreadful rock?
Yet Æolus would not be a murderer,
But left that hateful office unto thee.
The pretty-vaulting sea refus'd to drown me,

Knowing that thou wouldst have me drown'd on
      shore   95
With tears as salt as sea, through thy unkindness.
The splitting rocks cower'd in the sinking sands
And would not dash me with their ragged sides,
Because thy flinty heart, more hard than they,
Might in thy palace perish [Margaret].   100
As far as I could ken thy chalky cliffs,
When from thy shore the tempest beat us back,
I stood upon the hatches in the storm;
And when the dusky sky began to rob
My earnest-gaping sight of thy land's view,   105
I took a costly jewel from my neck,
A heart it was, bound in with diamonds,
And threw it towards thy land.   The sea receiv'd it,
And so I wish'd thy body might my heart.
And even with this I lost fair England's view,   110
And bid mine eyes be packing with my heart
And call'd them blind and dusky spectacles,
For losing ken of Albion's wished coast.
How often have I tempted Suffolk's tongue,
The agent of thy foul inconstancy,   115
To sit and [witch] me, as Ascanius did
When he to madding Dido would unfold
His father's acts commenc'd in burning Troy!
Am I not witch'd like her? or thou not false like him?
Ay me, I can no more! Die, [Margaret!]   120
For Henry weeps that thou dost live so long.

  Noise within.   Enter WARWICK, [SALISBURY,]
      and many COMMONS.

  War.   It is reported, mighty sovereign,
That good Duke Humphrey traitorously is murd'red
By Suffolk and the Cardinal Beaufort's means.
The commons, like an angry hive of bees   125
That want their leader, scatter up and down
And care not who they sting in his revenge.
Myself have calm'd their spleenful mutiny,
Until they hear the order of his death.
  King.   That he is dead, good Warwick, 'tis too
      true;   130
But how he died God knows, not Henry.
Enter his chamber, view his breathless corpse,
And comment then upon his sudden death.
  War.   That shall I do, my liege.   Stay, Salisbury,
With the rude multitude till I return.   135
      [*Exit Warwick and Salisbury, severally.*]
  King.   O Thou that judgest all things, stay my
      thoughts,
My thoughts that labour to persuade my soul
Some violent hands were laid on Humphrey's life,
If my suspect be false, forgive me, God,
For judgement only doth belong to thee.   140
Fain would I go to chafe his paly lips

---

52. **basilisk:** a fabulous serpent.   61, 63. **blood-consuming, blood-drinking sighs:** each sigh was believed to draw a drop
of blood from the heart.   79, 100, 120. **[Margaret]** (Rowe).   *Elianor* F.   83. **awkward:** contrary.   92. **Æolus:** god of the
winds.   116. **[witch]** (Theobald).   *watch* F.   **Ascanius:** son of Æneas.   129. **order:** manner.

With twenty thousand kisses, and to drain
Upon his face an ocean of salt tears,
To tell my love unto his dumb deaf trunk
And with my fingers feel his hand unfeeling.   145
But all in vain are these mean obsequies;

[*Re-enter* WARWICK *and others, bearing Gloucester's
body on a bed.*]

And to survey his dead and earthy image,
What were it but to make my sorrow greater?
   War. Come hither, gracious sovereign, view this
    body.
   King. That is to see how deep my grave is
   made;   150
For with his soul fled all my worldly solace,
And seeing him I see my life in death.
   War. As surely as my soul intends to live
With that dread King that took our state upon him
To free us from His Father's wrathful curse,   155
I do believe that violent hands were laid
Upon the life of this thrice-famed duke.
   Suf. A dreadful oath, sworn with a solemn
   tongue!
What instance gives Lord Warwick for his vow?
   War. See how the blood is settled in his face.
Oft have I seen a timely-parted ghost,   161
Of ashy semblance, meagre, pale, and bloodless,
Being all descended to the labouring heart;
Who, in the conflict that it holds with death,
Attracts the same for aidance 'gainst the enemy;
Which with the heart there cools and ne'er re-
   turneth   166
To blush and beautify the cheek again.
But see, his face is black and full of blood,
His eye-balls further out than when he liv'd,
Staring full ghastly like a strangled man;   170
His hair uprear'd, his nostrils stretch'd with strug-
   gling;
His hands abroad display'd, as one that grasp'd
And tugg'd for life and was by strength subdu'd.
Look, on the sheets his hair, you see, is sticking;
His well-proportion'd beard made rough and
   rugged,   175
Like to the summer's corn by tempest lodg'd.
It cannot be but he was murd'red here;
The least of all these signs were probable.
   Suf. Why, Warwick, who should do the Duke to
   death?
Myself and Beaufort had him in protection,   180
And we, I hope, sir, are no murderers.
   War. But both of you were vow'd Duke Hum-
   phrey's foes,
And you, forsooth, had the good Duke to keep.

'Tis like you would not feast him like a friend;
And 'tis well seen he found an enemy.   185
   Queen. Then you, belike, suspect these noblemen
As guilty of Duke Humphrey's timeless death.
   War. Who finds the heifer dead and bleeding
   fresh
And sees fast by a butcher with an axe,
But will suspect 'twas he that made the slaughter?
Who finds the partridge in the puttock's nest,   191
But may imagine how the bird was dead,
Although the kite soar with unbloodied beak?
Even so suspicious is this tragedy.
   Queen. Are you the butcher, Suffolk? Where's
   your knife?   195
Is Beaufort term'd a kite? Where are his talons?
   Suf. I wear no knife to slaughter sleeping men;
But here's a vengeful sword, rusted with ease,
That shall be scoured in his rancorous heart
That slanders me with murder's crimson badge.
Say, if thou dar'st, proud Lord of Warwickshire,   201
That I am faulty in Duke Humphrey's death.
     [*Exeunt Cardinal, Somerset, and others.*]
   War. What dares not Warwick, if false Suffolk
   dare him?
   Queen. He dares not calm his contumelious spirit
Nor cease to be an arrogant controller,   205
Though Suffolk dare him twenty thousand times.
   War. Madam, be still, with reverence may I say;
For every word you speak in his behalf
Is slander to your royal dignity.
   Suf. Blunt-witted lord, ignoble in demeanour!
If ever lady wrong'd her lord so much,   211
Thy mother took into her blameful bed
Some stern, untutor'd churl, and noble stock
Was graft with crab-tree slip; whose fruit thou art
And never of the Nevils' noble race.   215
   War. But that the guilt of murder bucklers thee
And I should rob the deathsman of his fee,
Quitting thee thereby of ten thousand shames,
And that my sovereign's presence makes me mild,
I would, false murd'rous coward, on thy knee   220
Make thee beg pardon for thy passed speech
And say it was thy mother that thou meant'st,
That thou thyself wast born in bastardy;
And after all this fearful homage done,
Give thee thy hire and send thy soul to hell,   225
Pernicious blood-sucker of sleeping men!
   Suf. Thou shalt be waking while I shed thy blood,
If from this presence thou dar'st go with me.
   War. Away even now, or I will drag thee hence.
Unworthy though thou art, I'll cope with thee   230
And do some service to Duke Humphrey's ghost.
     [*Exeunt* [*Suffolk and Warwick*].

146. s.d. **[Re-enter . . . bed]** Camb. edd. (after 148). *Bed put forth* F. *Werwicke draws the curtaines and showes Duke Humphrey in his bed* Q. 159. **instance**: evidence. 161. **timely-parted ghost**: a person who has died a natural death. 165. **aidance**: aid. 176. **lodg'd**: laid, beaten down. 187. **timeless**: untimely. 191. **puttock**: kite. 213. **stern**: rough. 221. **passed**: uttered.

King. What stronger breastplate than a heart untainted!
Thrice is he arm'd that hath his quarrel just,
And he but naked, though lock'd up in steel,
Whose conscience with injustice is corrupted.

[*A noise within.*

Queen. What noise is this?   236

Re-enter SUFFOLK *and* WARWICK, *with their weapons drawn.*

King. Why, how now, lords! your wrathful weapons drawn
Here in our presence!   Dare you be so bold?
Why, what tumultuous clamour have we here?

Suf. The traitorous Warwick with the men of Bury   240
Set all upon me, mighty sovereign.

Enter SALISBURY.

Sal. [*To the Commons.*] Sirs, stand apart; the King shall know your mind.
Dread lord, the commons send you word by me,
Unless Lord Suffolk straight be done to death,
Or banished fair England's territories,   245
They will by violence tear him from your palace
And torture him with grievous ling'ring death.
They say, by him the good Duke Humphrey died;
They say, in him they fear your Highness' death;
And mere instinct of love and loyalty,   250
Free from a stubborn opposite intent,
As being thought to contradict your liking,
Makes them thus forward in his banishment.
They say, in care of your most royal person,
That if your Highness should intend to sleep,   255
And charge that no man should disturb your rest
In pain of your dislike or pain of death,
Yet, notwithstanding such a strait edict,
Were there a serpent seen, with forked tongue,
That slily glided towards your Majesty,   260
It were but necessary you were wak'd,
Lest, being suffer'd in that harmful slumber,
The mortal worm might make the sleep eternal;
And therefore do they cry, though you forbid,
That they will guard you, whe'er you will or no,
From such fell serpents as false Suffolk is,   266
With whose envenomed and fatal sting,
Your loving uncle, twenty times his worth,
They say, is shamefully bereft of life.

Commons. (*Within.*) An answer from the King, my Lord of Salisbury!   270

Suf. 'Tis like the commons, rude unpolish'd hinds,
Could send such message to their sovereign.
But you, my lord, were glad to be employ'd,
To show how quaint an orator you are;

But all the honour Salisbury hath won   275
Is, that he was the lord ambassador
Sent from a sort of tinkers to the King.

Commons. (*Within.*) An answer from the King, or we will all break in!

King. Go, Salisbury, and tell them all from me,
I thank them for their tender loving care;   280
And had I not been cited so by them,
Yet did I purpose as they do entreat,
For, sure, my thoughts do hourly prophesy
Mischance unto my state by Suffolk's means;
And therefore, by His majesty I swear,   285
Whose far unworthy deputy I am,
He shall not breathe infection in this air
But three days longer, on the pain of death.

[*Exit Salisbury.*]

Queen. O Henry, let me plead for gentle Suffolk!

King. Ungentle queen, to call him gentle Suffolk!   290
No more, I say!   If thou dost plead for him,
Thou wilt but add increase unto my wrath.
Had I but said, I would have kept my word;
But when I swear, it is irrevocable.
If, after three days' space, thou here be'st found
On any ground that I am ruler of,   296
The world shall not be ransom for thy life.
Come, Warwick, come, good Warwick, go with me;
I have great matters to impart to thee.

[*Exeunt [all but Queen and Suffolk*].

Queen. Mischance and Sorrow go along with you!   300
Heart's Discontent and sour Affliction
Be playfellows to keep you company!
There's two of you; the devil make a third!
And threefold vengeance tend upon your steps!

Suf. Cease, gentle queen, these execrations,   305
And let thy Suffolk take his heavy leave.

Queen. Fie, coward woman and soft-hearted wretch!
Hast thou not spirit to curse thine enemy?

Suf. A plague upon them! wherefore should I curse them?
Would curses kill, as doth the mandrake's groan,
I would invent as bitter searching terms,   311
As curst, as harsh and horrible to hear,
Deliver'd strongly through my fixed teeth,
With full as many signs of deadly hate,
As lean-faced Envy in her loathsome cave.   315
My tongue should stumble in mine earnest words;
Mine eyes should sparkle like the beaten flint;
Mine hair be fix'd on end, as one distract;
Ay, every joint should seem to curse and ban;
And even now my burden'd heart would break,   320
Should I not curse them.   Poison be their drink!
Gall, worse than gall, the daintiest that they taste!

274. **quaint:** skillful.   281. **cited:** incited.   287. **in:** into.   310. **mandrake's groan.** The mandrake was supposed to shriek when torn up, and the sound to kill or drive the hearer mad.   313. **fixed:** clenched.

Their sweetest shade a grove of cypress trees!
Their chiefest prospect murd'ring basilisks!
Their softest touch as smart as lizards' stings! 325
Their music frightful as the serpent's hiss,
And boding screech-owls make the consort full!
All the foul terrors in dark-seated hell —
    Queen. Enough, sweet Suffolk! Thou torment'st
      thyself;
And these dread curses, like the sun 'gainst glass,
Or like an overcharged gun, recoil, 331
And turn the force of them upon thyself.
    Suf. You bade me ban, and will you bid me
      leave?
Now, by the ground that I am banish'd from,
Well could I curse away a winter's night, 335
Though standing naked on a mountain top
Where biting cold would never let grass grow,
And think it but a minute spent in sport.
    Queen. O, let me entreat thee cease. Give me
      thy hand,
That I may dew it with my mournful tears; 340
Nor let the rain of heaven wet this place
To wash away my woeful monuments.
O, could this kiss be printed in thy hand,
That thou mightst think upon these by the seal
Through whom a thousand sighs are breath'd for
    thee! 345
So, get thee gone, that I may know my grief.
'Tis but surmis'd whiles thou art standing by,
As one that surfeits thinking on a want.
I will repeal thee, or, be well assur'd,
Adventure to be banished myself; 350
And banished I am, if but from thee.
Go; speak not to me; even now be gone.
O, go not yet! Even thus two friends condemn'd
Embrace and kiss and take ten thousand leaves,
Loather a hundred times to part than die. 355
Yet now farewell; and farewell life with thee!
    Suf. Thus is poor Suffolk ten times banished;
Once by the King, and three times thrice by thee.
'Tis not the land I care for, wert thou thence.
A wilderness is populous enough, 360
So Suffolk had thy heavenly company;
For where thou art, there is the world itself,
With every several pleasure in the world,
And where thou art not, desolation.
I can no more. Live thou to joy thy life; 365
Myself no joy in nought but that thou liv'st.

        Enter VAUX.

    Queen. Whither goes Vaux so fast? What news,
      I prithee?
    Vaux. To signify unto his Majesty
That Cardinal Beaufort is at point of death;
For suddenly a grievous sickness took him, 370
That makes him gasp and stare and catch the air,

Blaspheming God and cursing men on earth.
Sometime he talks as if Duke Humphrey's ghost
Were by his side; sometime he calls the King
And whispers to his pillow as to him 375
The secrets of his overcharged soul;
And I am sent to tell his Majesty
That even now he cries aloud for him.
    Queen. Go tell this heavy message to the King.
                      [*Exit Vaux.*
Ay me! what is this world! What news are
    these! 380
But wherefore grieve I at an hour's poor loss,
Omitting Suffolk's exile, my soul's treasure?
Why only, Suffolk, mourn I not for thee,
And with the southern clouds contend in tears,
Theirs for the earth's increase, mine for my sor-
    row's? 385
Now get thee hence; the King, thou know'st, is
    coming.
If thou be found by me, thou art but dead.
    Suf. If I depart from thee, I cannot live;
And in thy sight to die, what were it else
But like a pleasant slumber in thy lap? 390
Here could I breathe my soul into the air,
As mild and gentle as the cradle-babe
Dying with mother's dug between its lips;
Where, from thy sight, I should be raging mad
And cry out for thee to close up mine eyes, 395
To have thee with thy lips to stop my mouth.
So shouldst thou either turn my flying soul,
Or I should breathe it so into thy body,
And then it liv'd in sweet Elysium.
To die by thee were but to die in jest; 400
From thee to die were torture more than death.
O, let me stay, befall what may befall!
    Queen. Away! though parting be a fretful cor-
      rosive,
It is applied to a deathful wound.
To France, sweet Suffolk! Let me hear from thee;
For wheresoe'er thou art in this world's globe, 406
I'll have an Iris that shall find thee out.
    Suf. I go.
    Queen.   And take my heart with thee.
    Suf. A jewel, lock'd into the woefull'st cask
That ever did contain a thing of worth. 410
Even as a splitted bark, so sunder we;
This way fall I to death.
    Queen.   This way for me.
                    [*Exeunt [severally]*

[SCENE III. *London. Beaufort's bedchamber.*]

    Enter the KING, SALISBURY, WARWICK, *to the*
             CARDINAL *in bed.*

    King. How fares my lord? Speak, Beaufort,
      to thy sovereign.

327. **consort:** concert. 342. **monuments:** memorials. 344. **seal:** i.e., her kiss. 350. **Adventure:** risk. 403. **fretful:** gnawing. 407. **Iris:** messenger of the gods. 409. **cask:** casket.

Car. If thou be'st death, I'll give thee England's
    treasure,
Enough to purchase such another island,
So thou wilt let me live, and feel no pain.
    King. Ah, what a sign it is of evil life,   5
Where death's approach is seen so terrible!
    War. Beaufort, it is thy sovereign speaks to thee.
    Car. Bring me unto my trial when you will.
Died he not in his bed? Where should he die?
Can I make men live, whe'er they will or no?   10
O, torture me no more! I will confess.
Alive again? Then show me where he is;
I'll give a thousand pound to look upon him.
He hath no eyes, the dust hath blinded them.
Comb down his hair; look, look! it stands up-
    right,   15
Like lime-twigs set to catch my winged soul.
Give me some drink; and bid the apothecary
Bring the strong poison that I bought of him.
    King. O thou eternal Mover of the heavens,
Look with a gentle eye upon this wretch!   20
O, beat away the busy meddling fiend
That lays strong siege unto this wretch's soul,
And from his bosom purge this black despair!
    War. See, how the pangs of death do make him
    grin!
    Sal. Disturb him not; let him pass peaceably.   25
    King. Peace to his soul, if God's good pleasure
    be!
Lord Cardinal, if thou think'st on heaven's bliss,
Hold up thy hand, make signal of thy hope. —
He dies, and makes no sign. O God, forgive him!
    War. So bad a death argues a monstrous life.   30
    King. Forbear to judge, for we are sinners all.
Close up his eyes and draw the curtain close;
And let us all to meditation.   [*Exeunt.*

ACT IV

[Scene I. *The coast of Kent.*]

Alarum. Fight at sea. Ordnance goes off. Enter a
Lieutenant, [*a* Master, *a* Master's Mate,
Walter Whitmore, *and others; with them*]
Suffolk [*disguised, and other gentlemen, pris-*
oners].

    Lieu. The gaudy, blabbing, and remorseful day
Is crept into the bosom of the sea;
And now loud-howling wolves arouse the jades
That drag the tragic melancholy night;   4
Who, with their drowsy, slow, and flagging wings,
Clip dead men's graves, and from their misty jaws
Breathe foul contagious darkness in the air.
Therefore bring forth the soldiers of our prize;

For, whilst our pinnace anchors in the Downs
Here shall they make their ransom on the sand,   10
Or with their blood stain this discoloured shore.
Master, this prisoner freely give I thee;
And thou that art his mate, make boot of this;
The other, Walter Whitmore, is thy share.
    1. Gent. What is my ransom, master? Let me
    know.   15
    Mast. A thousand crowns, or else lay down your
    head.
    Mate. And so much shall you give, or off goes
    yours.
    Lieu. What, think you much to pay two thousand
    crowns,
And bear the name and port of gentlemen?
Cut both the villains' throats; for die you shall.   20
The lives of those which we have lost in fight
Be counterpois'd with such a petty sum!
    1. Gent. I'll give it, sir; and therefore spare my
    life.
    2. Gent. And so will I, and write home for it
    straight.
    Whit. I lost mine eye in laying the prize aboard,
And therefore to revenge it shalt thou die;   26
                [*To Suffolk.*
And so should these, if I might have my will.
    Lieu. Be not so rash; take ransom, let him
    live.
    Suf. Look on my George; I am a gentleman.
Rate me at what thou wilt, thou shalt be paid.   30
    Whit. And so am I; my name is Walter Whit-
    more.
How now! why start'st thou? What, doth death
    affright?
    Suf. Thy name affrights me, in whose sound is
    death.
A cunning man did calculate my birth
And told me that by water I should die: 35
Yet let not this make thee be bloody-minded;
Thy name is Gualtier, being rightly sounded.
    Whit. Gualtier, or Walter, which it is, I care
    not.
Never yet did base dishonour blur our name
But with our sword we wip'd away the blot;   40
Therefore, when merchant-like I sell revenge
Broke be my sword, my arms torn and defac'd,
And I proclaim'd a coward through the world!
             [*Lays hold of Suffolk.*
    Suf. Stay, Whitmore; for thy prisoner is a prince,
The Duke of Suffolk, William de la Pole.   45
    Whit. The Duke of Suffolk muffled up in rags!
    Suf. Ay, but these rags are no part of the duke:
[Jove sometime went disguised, and why not I?]
    Lieu. But Jove was never slain, as thou shalt be.

Sc. iii, 24. **grin:** grimace.
Act IV, sc. i, 1. **blabbing:** revealing secrets of the dark.   6. **Clip:** embrace.   13. **boot:** booty.   25. **laying...aboard:**
tackling.   34. **birth:** horoscope.   35. **water.** Walter was pronounced "water."   48. Pope inserted this line from Q.

[*Suf.*] Obscure and lousy swain, King Henry's
  blood,   50
The honourable blood of Lancaster,
Must not be shed by such a jaded groom.
Hast thou not kiss'd thy hand and held my stirrup?
Bare-headed plodded by my foot-cloth mule
And thought thee happy when I shook my head? 55
How often hast thou waited at my cup,
Fed from my trencher, kneel'd down at the board,
When I have feasted with Queen Margaret?
Remember it and let it make thee crest-fall'n,
Ay, and allay this thy abortive pride,   60
How in our voiding lobby hast thou stood
And duly waited for my coming forth.
This hand of mine hath writ in thy behalf
And therefore shall it charm thy riotous tongue.
  Whit. Speak, captain, shall I stab the forlorn
    swain?   65
  Lieu. First let my words stab him, as he hath
    me.
  Suf. Base slave, thy words are blunt and so art
    thou.
  Lieu. Convey him hence and on our longboat's
    side
Strike off his head.
  Suf.   Thou dar'st not, for thy own.
[*Lieu.* Yes, Pole,
  Suf.   Pole!]
  Lieu.   Pool! Sir Pool! lord! 70
Ay, kennel, puddle, sink; whose filth and dirt
Troubles the silver spring where England drinks.
Now will I dam up this thy yawning mouth
For swallowing the treasure of the realm.
Thy lips that kiss'd the Queen shall sweep the
  ground;   75
And thou that smil'd'st at good Duke Humphrey's
  death
Against the senseless winds shalt grin in vain,
Who in contempt shall hiss at thee again;
And wedded be thou to the hags of hell,
For daring to affy a mighty lord   80
Unto the daughter of a worthless king,
Having neither subject, wealth, nor diadem.
By devilish policy art thou grown great
And, like ambitious Sylla, overgorg'd
With gobbets of thy mother's bleeding heart. 85
By thee Anjou and Maine were sold to France,
The false revolting Normans thorough thee
Disdain to call us lord, and Picardy
Hath slain their governors, surpris'd our forts,
And sent the ragged soldiers wounded home. 90

The princely Warwick, and the Nevils all,
Whose dreadful swords were never drawn in vain,
As hating thee, are rising up in arms;
And now the house of York, thrust from the crown
By shameful murder of a guiltless king   95
And lofty, proud, encroaching tyranny,
Burns with revenging fire; whose hopeful colours
Advance our half-fac'd sun, striving to shine,
Under the which is writ, "*Invitis nubibus.*"
The commons here in Kent are up in arms; 100
And, to conclude, reproach and beggary
Is crept into the palace of our king,
And all by thee. Away! convey him hence.
  Suf. O that I were a god, to shoot forth thunder
Upon these paltry, servile, abject drudges! 105
Small things make base men proud. This villain
  here,
Being captain of a pinnace, threatens more
Than Bargulus the strong Illyrian pirate.
Drones suck not eagles' blood, but rob beehives.
It is impossible that I should die   110
By such a lowly vassal as thyself.
Thy words move rage and not remorse in me.
I go of message from the Queen to France;
I charge thee waft me safely cross the Channel.
  Lieu. Walter, —   115
  Whit. Come, Suffolk, I must waft thee to thy
    death.
  Suf. Gelidus timor occupat artus: it is thee I fear.
  Whit. Thou shalt have cause to fear before I
leave thee.
What, are ye daunted now? Now will ye stoop?
  1. Gent. My gracious lord, entreat him, speak
    him fair.   120
  Suf. Suffolk's imperial tongue is stern and rough,
Us'd to command, untaught to plead for favour.
Far be it we should honour such as these
With humble suit. No, rather let my head
Stoop to the block than these knees bow to any
Save to the God of heaven and to my king, 126
And sooner dance upon a bloody pole
Than stand uncover'd to the vulgar groom.
True nobility is exempt from fear;
More can I bear than you dare execute.   130
  Lieu. Hale him away, and let him talk no
    more.
  [*Suf.*] Come, soldiers, show what cruelty ye can,
That this my death may never be forgot!
Great men oft die by vile besonians.
A Roman sworder and banditto slave   135
Murder'd sweet Tully; Brutus' bastard hand

---

50. [*Suf.*] (Pope). F continues this line to *Lieu.* 52. **jaded:** contemptible. Perhaps, having to do with horses. 54. **foot-
cloth:** wearing housings. 60. **abortive:** monstrous. 61. **voiding lobby:** anteroom. 65. **forlorn:** lost. 70. [*Lieu. ... Pole*]
Supplied by Capell from Q. 71. **kennel:** gutter. 74. **For:** to prevent. 79. **hags of hell:** Furies. 80. **affy:** betroth. 85.
gobbets: chunks. 98. **our.** Apparently corrupt, since the half-risen sun was Suffolk's device. 99. *Invitis nubibus:* in spite of
clouds. 108. **Bargulus.** Referred to by Cicero. 117. *Gelidus ... artus:* Cold fear seizes my limbs. F reads *Pine gelidus*, an
apparent misprint. 132. [*Suf.*] (Hanmer). F continues to *Lieu.* 134. **besonians:** scoundrels.

Stabb'd Julius Cæsar; savage islanders
Pompey the Great; and Suffolk dies by pirates.

[Exeunt Whitmore with Suffolk.

Lieu. And as for these whose ransom we have
   set,
It is our pleasure one of them depart;   140
Therefore come you with us and let him go.

[Exeunt all but the First Gentleman.

Re-enter WHITMORE *with Suffolk's body.*

Whit. There let his head and lifeless body lie,
Until the Queen his mistress bury it.   *[Exit.*

1. Gent. O barbarous and bloody spectacle!
His body will I bear unto the King.   145
If he revenge it not, yet will his friends;
So will the Queen, that living held him dear.

[Exit with the body.]

[SCENE II. *Blackheath.*]

Enter GEORGE BEVIS *and* JOHN HOLLAND.

Bevis. Come, and get thee a sword, though
made of a lath. They have been up these two days.

Holl. They have the more need to sleep now,
then.   4

Bevis. I tell thee, Jack Cade the clothier means
to dress the commonwealth, and turn it, and set a
new nap upon it.

Holl. So he had need, for 'tis threadbare. Well,
I say it was never merry world in England since
gentlemen came up.   10

Bevis. O miserable age! virtue is not regarded
in handicrafts-men.

Holl. The nobility think scorn to go in leather
aprons.

Bevis. Nay, more, the King's council are no good
workmen.   16

Holl. True; and yet it is said, labour in thy
vocation; which is as much to say as, let the magistrates be labouring men; and therefore should we
be magistrates.   20

Bevis. Thou hast hit it; for there's no better sign
of a brave mind than a hard hand.

Holl. I see them! I see them! There's Best's
son, the tanner of Wingham, —

Bevis. He shall have the skins of our enemies,
to make dog's-leather of.   26

Holl. And Dick the Butcher, —

Bevis. Then is sin struck down like an ox, and
iniquity's throat cut like a calf.

Holl. And Smith the weaver, —   30

Bevis. Argo, their thread of life is spun.

Holl. Come, come, let's fall in with them.

Drum. Enter CADE, DICK *the Butcher,* SMITH *the
Weaver, and a Sawyer, with infinite numbers.*

Cade. We John Cade, so term'd of our supposed
father, —

Dick. [*Aside.*] Or rather, of stealing a cade of
herrings.   36

Cade. For our enemies shall [fall] before us, inspired with the spirit of putting down kings and
princes, —— Command silence.

Dick. Silence!   40

Cade. My father was a Mortimer, —

Dick. [*Aside.*] He was an honest man, and a
good bricklayer.

Cade. My mother a Plantagenet, —   44

Dick. [*Aside.*] I knew her well; she was a midwife.

Cade. My wife descended of the Lacies, —

Dick. [*Aside.*] She was, indeed, a pedler's daughter, and sold many laces.   49

Smith. [*Aside.*] But now of late, not able to
travel with her furr'd pack, she washes bucks here
at home.

Cade. Therefore am I of an honourable house.

Dick. [*Aside.*] Ay, by my faith, the field is
honourable; and there was he born, under a hedge,
for his father had never a house but the cage.   56

Cade. Valiant I am.

Smith. [*Aside.*] 'A must needs; for beggary is
valiant.

Cade. I am able to endure much.   60

Dick. [*Aside.*] No question of that; for I have
seen him whipp'd three market-days together.

Cade. I fear neither sword nor fire.

Smith. [*Aside.*] He need not fear the sword; for
his coat is of proof.   65

Dick. [*Aside.*] But methinks he should stand in
fear of fire, being burnt i' th' hand for stealing of
sheep.   68

Cade. Be brave, then; for your captain is brave,
and vows reformation. There shall be in England
seven halfpenny loaves sold for a penny; the three-
hoop'd pot shall have ten hoops, and I will make it
felony to drink small beer. All the realm shall be
in common, and in Cheapside shall my palfrey go
to grass; and when I am king, as king I will be, —

All. God save your Majesty!   77

Cade. I thank you, good people, — there shall
be no money. All shall eat and drink on my score;
and I will apparel them all in one livery, that they
may agree like brothers and worship me their lord.

Dick. The first thing we do, let's kill all the
lawyers.   84

Cade. Nay, that I mean to do. Is not this a
lamentable thing, that of the skin of an innocent
lamb should be made parchment? that parch-

Sc. ii, 31. **Argo:** *ergo,* therefore. 35. **cade:** cask. 37. **[fall]** F₄. *faile* F₁. A pun on Cade's name, as if from Lat. *cadere,*
to fall. 51. **bucks:** soiled linen. 56. **cage:** jail. 65. **of proof:** a pun on the two senses (1) not to be pierced, (2) badly worn.
67. **burnt:** branded with T as a thief. 72. **three-hoop'd pot:** the wooden drinking cup, holding a quart.

ment, being scribbl'd o'er, should undo a man?
Some say the bee stings; but I say, 'tis the bee's
wax; for I did but seal once to a thing, and I was
never mine own man since.   How now! who's
there?   91

*Enter [some, bringing forward the] Clerk [of
Chatham].*

Smith. The clerk of Chatham.   He can write
and read and cast account.
Cade. O monstrous!
Smith. We took him setting of boys' copies.
Cade. Here's a villain!   96
Smith. Has a book in his pocket with red letters
in't.
Cade. Nay, then, he is a conjurer.
Dick. Nay, he can make obligations, and write
court-hand.   101
Cade. I am sorry for't.   The man is a proper
man, of mine honour; unless I find him guilty, he
shall not die.   Come hither, sirrah, I must examine
thee.   What is thy name?
Clerk. Emmanuel.   106
Dick. They use to write it on the top of letters;
'twill go hard with you.
Cade. Let me alone.   Dost thou use to write thy
name, or hast thou a mark to thyself, like an honest
plain-dealing man?   111
Clerk. Sir, I thank God, I have been so well
brought up that I can write my name.
All. He hath confess'd!   Away with him!
He's a villain and a traitor.   115
Cade. Away with him, I say!   Hang him with
his pen and ink-horn about his neck.
                        [*Exit one with the Clerk.*

Enter Michael.

Mich. Where's our general?
Cade. Here I am, thou particular fellow.   119
Mich. Fly, fly, fly!   Sir Humphrey Stafford and
his brother are hard by, with the King's forces.
Cade. Stand, villain, stand, or I'll fell thee down.
He shall be encount'red with a man as good as him-
self.   He is but a knight, is 'a?   125
Mich. No.
Cade. To equal him, I will make myself a knight
presently.   [*Kneels.*]   Rise up Sir John Mortimer.
[*Rises.*]   Now have at him!

*Enter Sir Humphrey Stafford and his Brother,
with drum and soldiers.*

Staf. Rebellious hinds, the filth and scum of
Kent,   130

Mark'd for the gallows, lay your weapons down!
Home to your cottages, forsake this groom!
The King is merciful, if you revolt.
Bro. But angry, wrathful, and inclin'd to blood,
If you go forward; therefore yield, or die.   135
Cade. As for these silken-coated slaves, I pass not.
It is to you, good people, that I speak,
Over whom, in time to come, I hope to reign,
For I am rightful heir unto the crown.
Staf. Villain, thy father was a plasterer,   140
And thou thyself a shearman, art thou not?
Cade. And Adam was a gardener.
Bro. And what of that?
Cade. Marry, this: Edmund Mortimer, Earl of
March,
Married the Duke of Clarence' daughter, did he
not?   145
Staf. Ay, sir.
Cade. By her he had two children at one birth.
Bro. That's false.
Cade. Ay, there's the question; but I say, 'tis
true.
The elder of them, being put to nurse,   150
Was by a beggar-woman stol'n away;
And, ignorant of his birth and parentage,
Became a bricklayer when he came to age.
His son am I; deny it, if you can.
Dick. Nay, 'tis too true; therefore he shall be
king.   155
Smith. Sir, he made a chimney in my father's
house, and the bricks are alive at this day to testify
it; therefore deny it not.
Staf. And will you credit this base drudge's
words,
That speaks he knows not what?   160
All. Ay, marry, will we; therefore get ye gone.
Bro. Jack Cade, the Duke of York hath taught
you this.
Cade. [*Aside.*] He lies; for I invented it myself. —
Go to, sirrah, tell the King from me, that, for   164
his father's sake, Henry the Fifth, in whose time
boys went to span-counter for French crowns, I
am content he shall reign; but I'll be Protector over
him.
Dick. And furthermore, we'll have the Lord
Say's head for selling the dukedom of Maine.   170
Cade. And good reason; for thereby is England
main'd, and fain to go with a staff, but that my
puissance holds it up.   Fellow kings, I tell you that
that Lord Say hath gelded the commonwealth, and
made it an eunuch; and more than that, he can
speak French, and therefore he is a traitor.   177
Staf. O gross and miserable ignorance!

90. **seal...thing:** put my name to a bond.   106. **Emmanuel:** "God with us," formerly prefixed to documents and letters.
133. **revolt:** desert (Cade).   136. **pass:** care.   141. **shearman:** a man who sheared woollen cloth.   166. **span-counter:** a
game in which the player tosses a coin, trying to land it within a span of another coin.   172. **main'd:** an old spelling of
maim'd. for the sake of the pun.

Cade. Nay, answer, if you can. The Frenchmen are our enemies. Go to, then, I ask but this: can he that speaks with the tongue of an enemy be a good counsellor, or no?

All. No, no; and therefore we'll have his head.

Bro. Well, seeing gentle words will not prevail, Assail them with the army of the King.   185

Staf. Herald, away; and throughout every town Proclaim them traitors that are up with Cade; That those which fly before the battle ends May, even in their wives' and children's sight, Be hang'd up for example at their doors.   190 And you that be the King's friends, follow me.

    [Exeunt [the two Staffords, and soldiers].

Cade. And you that love the commons, follow me. Now show yourselves men; 'tis for liberty. We will not leave one lord, one gentleman; Spare none but such as go in clouted shoon;   195 For they are thrifty honest men and such As would, but that they dare not, take our parts.

Dick. They are all in order and march toward us.

Cade. But then are we in order when we are most out of order. Come, march forward.   200

    [Exeunt.]

[SCENE III. *Another part of Blackheath.*]

Alarums to the fight, wherein both the STAFFORDS *are slain. Enter* CADE *and the rest.*

Cade. Where's Dick, the butcher of Ashford?

Dick. Here, sir.

Cade. They fell before thee like sheep and oxen, and thou behavedst thyself as if thou hadst been in thine own slaughter-house; therefore thus will I reward thee: the Lent shall be as long again as it is; and thou shalt have a license to kill for a hundred lacking one.   9

Dick. I desire no more.

Cade. And, to speak truth, thou deservest no less. This monument of the victory will I bear [*putting on Stafford's armour*]; and the bodies shall be dragg'd at my horse heels till I do come to London, where we will have the mayor's sword borne before us.   16

Dick. If we mean to thrive and do good, break open the gaols and let out the prisoners.

Cade. Fear not that, I warrant thee. Come, let's march towards London.   *[Exeunt.* 20

[SCENE IV. *London. The palace.*]

Enter the KING *with a supplication, and the* QUEEN *with Suffolk's head; the* DUKE OF BUCKINGHAM *and the* LORD SAY.

Queen. Oft have I heard that grief softens the mind

And makes it fearful and degenerate; Think therefore on revenge and cease to weep. But who can cease to weep and look on this? Here may his head lie on my throbbing breast;   5 But where's the body that I should embrace?

Buck. What answer makes your Grace to the rebels' supplication?

King. I'll send some holy bishop to entreat, For God forbid so many simple souls   10 Should perish by the sword! And I myself, Rather than bloody war shall cut them short, Will parley with Jack Cade their general. But stay, I'll read it over once again.

Queen. Ah, barbarous villains! hath this lovely face   15 Rul'd, like a wandering planet, over me. And could it not enforce them to relent, That were unworthy to behold the same?

King. Lord Say, Jack Cade hath sworn to have thy head.

Say. Ay, but I hope your Highness shall have his.   20

King. How now, madam! Still lamenting and mourning for Suffolk's death? I fear me, love, if that I had been dead, Thou wouldest not have mourn'd so much for me.

Queen. No, my love, I should not mourn, but die for thee.   25

Enter a MESSENGER.

King. How now! what news? Why com'st thou in such haste?

Mess. The rebels are in Southwark; fly, my lord! Jack Cade proclaims himself Lord Mortimer, Descended from the Duke of Clarence' house, And calls your Grace usurper openly,   30 And vows to crown himself in Westminster. His army is a ragged multitude Of hinds and peasants, rude and merciless. Sir Humphrey Stafford and his brother's death Hath given them heart and courage to proceed.   35 All scholars, lawyers, courtiers, gentlemen, They call false caterpillars and intend their death.

King. O graceless men! they know not what they do.

Buck. My gracious lord, retire to Killingworth Until a power be rais'd to put them down.   40

Queen. Ah, were the Duke of Suffolk now alive, These Kentish rebels would be soon appeas'd!

King. Lord Say, the traitors hate thee; Therefore away with us to Killingworth.

Say. So might your Grace's person be in danger.   45 The sight of me is odious in their eyes, And therefore in this city will I stay And live alone as secret as I may.

Sc. iii, 7. **license.** During Lent a special license was required for slaughtering, and the number of animals was restricted.

Enter another MESSENGER.

Mess. Jack Cade hath gotten London Bridge.
The citizens fly and forsake their houses.   50
The rascal people, thirsting after prey,
Join with the traitor, and they jointly swear
To spoil the city and your royal court.

Buck. Then linger not, my lord; away, take
    horse.

King. Come, Margaret. God, our hope, will
    succour us.   55

Queen. My hope is gone, now Suffolk is deceas'd.

King. Farewell, my lord; trust not the Kentish
    rebels.

Buck. Trust nobody, for fear you be betray'd.

Say. The trust I have is in mine innocence,
And therefore am I bold and resolute. [*Exeunt.* 60

[SCENE V. *London. The Tower.*]

Enter LORD SCALES *upon the Tower, walking.
Then enter two or three* CITIZENS *below.*

Scales. How now! is Jack Cade slain?

1. Cit. No, my lord, nor likely to be slain; for
they have won the Bridge, killing all those that
withstand them. The Lord Mayor craves aid of
your honour from the Tower to defend the city
from the rebels.   6

Scales. Such aid as I can spare you shall com-
mand,
But I am troubled here with them myself.
The rebels have assay'd to win the Tower.
But get you to Smithfield and gather head,   10
And thither I will send you Matthew Goffe.
Fight for your king, your country, and your lives;
And so, farewell, for I must hence again. [*Exeunt.*

[SCENE VI. *London. Cannon Street.*]

Enter JACK CADE *and the rest, and strikes his staff
on London-stone.*

Cade. Now is Mortimer lord of this city. And
here, sitting upon London-stone, I charge and command that, of the city's cost, the pissing-conduit
run nothing but claret wine this first year of our
reign. And now henceforward it shall be treason
for any that calls me other than Lord Mortimer. 7

Enter a SOLDIER, *running.*

Sold. Jack Cade! Jack Cade!

Cade. Knock him down there.   [*They kill him.*

Smith. If this fellow be wise, he'll never call ye
Jack Cade more. I think he hath a very fair
warning.   12

Dick. My lord, there's an army gathered together
in Smithfield.

Cade. Come, then, let's go fight with them.
But first go and set London Bridge on fire; and, if
you can, burn down the Tower too. Come, let's
away.   [*Exeunt.* 18

[SCENE VII. *London. Smithfield.*]

*Alarums. Matthew Goffe is slain, and all the rest.
Then enter* JACK CADE *with his company.*

Cade. So, sirs. Now go some and pull down the
Savoy; others to the inns of court; down with them
all.

Dick. I have a suit unto your lordship.

Cade. Be it a lordship, thou shalt have it for that
word.   6

Dick. Only that the laws of England may come
out of your mouth.

Holl. [*Aside.*] Mass, 'twill be sore law, then; for
he was thrust in the mouth with a spear, and 'tis
not whole yet.   11

Smith. [*Aside.*] Nay, John, it will be stinking
law; for his breath stinks with eating toasted cheese.

Cade. I have thought upon it; it shall be so.
Away, burn all the records of the realm. My
mouth shall be the parliament of England.   17

Holl. [*Aside.*] Then we are like to have biting
statutes, unless his teeth be pull'd out.

Cade. And henceforward all things shall be in
common.   21

Enter a MESSENGER.

Mess. My lord, a prize, a prize! Here's the Lord
Say, which sold the towns in France; he that made
us pay one and twenty fifteens, and one shilling to
the pound, the last subsidy.   25

Enter GEORGE BEVIS, *with the* LORD SAY.

Cade. Well, he shall be beheaded for it ten times.
Ah, thou say, thou serge, nay, thou buckram lord!
now art thou within point-blank of our jurisdiction
regal. What canst thou answer to my Majesty for
giving up of Normandy unto Mounsieur Basi- 30
mecu, the Dauphin of France? Be it known unto
thee by these presence, even the presence of Lord
Mortimer, that I am the besom that must sweep
the court clean of such filth as thou art. Thou
hast most traitorously corrupted the youth 35
of the realm in erecting a grammar school; and
whereas, before, our forefathers had no other books
but the score and the tally, thou hast caused printing to be us'd, and, contrary to the King, his crown

and dignity, thou hast built a paper-mill. It 40
will be proved to thy face that thou hast men about
thee that usually talk of a noun and a verb, and
such abominable words as no Christian ear can endure to hear.   Thou hast appointed justices of
peace, to call poor men before them about mat- 45
ters they were not able to answer.   Moreover, thou
hast put them in prison; and because they could not
read, thou hast hang'd them; when, indeed, only
for that cause they have been most worthy to live.
Thou dost ride in a foot-cloth, dost thou not? 52
    Say. What of that?
    Cade. Marry, thou oughtest not to let thy
horse wear a cloak, when honester men than thou
go in their hose and doublets.
    Dick. And work in their shirt too; as myself, for
example, that am a butcher.
    Say. You men of Kent, —
    Dick. What say you of Kent? 60
    Say. Nothing but this; 'tis "*bona terra, mala
        gens.*"
    Cade. Away with him, away with him! he speaks
Latin.
    Say. Hear me but speak, and bear me where
        you will.
Kent, in the Commentaries Cæsar writ, 65
Is term'd the civil'st place of all this isle.
Sweet is the country, because full of riches;
The people liberal, valiant, active, wealthy;
Which makes me hope you are not void of pity.
I sold not Maine, I lost not Normandy, 70
Yet, to recover them, would lose my life.
Justice with favour have I always done;
Prayers and tears have mov'd me, gifts could
    never.
When have I aught exacted at your hands
[But] to maintain the King, the realm, and you? 75
Large gifts have I bestow'd on learned clerks,
Because my book preferr'd me to the King;
And seeing ignorance is the curse of God,
Knowledge the wing wherewith we fly to heaven,
Unless you be possess'd with devilish spirits 80
You cannot but forbear to murder me.
This tongue hath parley'd unto foreign kings
For your behoof, —
    Cade. Tut, when struck'st thou one blow in the
field? 85
    Say. Great men have reaching hands.   Oft have
        I struck
Those that I never saw and struck them dead.
    Geo. O monstrous coward!   What, to come be-
hind folks?
    Say. These cheeks are pale for watching for
        your good. 90

    Cade. Give him a box o' th' ear and that will
make 'em red again.
    Say. Long sitting to determine poor men's
        causes
Hath made me full of sickness and diseases.
    Cade. Ye shall have a hempen [caudle] then and
the help of hatchet. 96
    Dick. Why dost thou quiver, man?
    Say. The palsy, and not fear, provokes me.
    Cade. Nay, he nods at us, as who should say, I'll
be even with you.   I'll see if his head will stand
steadier on a pole, or no.   Take him away, and be-
head him. 102
    Say. Tell me wherein have I offended most?
Have I affected wealth or honour?   Speak.
Are my chests fill'd up with extorted gold?
Is my apparel sumptuous to behold? 106
Whom have I injur'd that ye seek my death?
These hands are free from guiltless blood-shedding,
This breast from harbouring foul deceitful thoughts.
O, let me live! 110
    Cade. [*Aside.*] I feel remorse in myself with his
words; but I'll bridle it.   He shall die, an it be but
for pleading so well for his life.   Away with him!
he has a familiar under his tongue; he speaks not o'
God's name.   Go, take him away, I say, and strike
off his head presently; and then break into his son-
in-law's house, Sir James Cromer, and strike off
his head, and bring them both upon two poles
hither. 119
    All. It shall be done.
    Say. Ah, countrymen! if when you make your
        prayers,
God should be so obdurate as yourselves,
How would it fare with your departed souls?
And therefore yet relent, and save my life. 124
    Cade. Away with him! and do as I command ye.
[*Exeunt some with Lord Say.*] The proudest peer in
the realm shall not wear a head on his shoulders,
unless he pay me tribute.   There shall not a maid
be married, but she shall pay to me her maidenhead
ere they have it.   Men shall hold of me *in capite;*
and we charge and command that their wives be as
free as heart can wish or tongue can tell. 133
    Dick. My lord, when shall we go to Cheapside
and take up commodities upon our bills?
    Cade. Marry, presently.
    All. O, brave! 137

Re-enter one with the heads [of Say and Cromer].

    Cade. But is not this braver?   Let them kiss one
another, for they lov'd well when they were alive.
Now part them again, lest they consult about the
giving up of some more towns in France.   Soldiers,

---

61. **bona … gens:** good land, bad people.   72. **favour:** mercy.   75. **[But]** (Rann).   *Kent* F.   95. **[caudle]** F₄: a warm
drink.   *candle* F₁.   **hempen caudle** is a jocular expression for hangman's rope.   104. **affected:** loved.   131. *in capite:* in
chief, by direct grant from the Crown.   135. **commodities:** goods.   **bills:** a pun on *bill*, a weapon.

defer the spoil of the city until night; for with
these borne before us, instead of maces, will we ride
through the streets; and at every corner have them
kiss. Away!   [*Exeunt.* 145

[SCENE VIII. *Southwark.*]

Alarum and retreat. Enter again CADE *and all
his rabblement.*

Cade. Up Fish Street! down Saint Magnus'
Corner! Kill and knock down! Throw them into
Thames! (*Sound a parley.*) What noise is this I
hear? Dare any be so bold to sound retreat or parley, when I command them kill?   5

Enter BUCKINGHAM *and old* CLIFFORD [*attended*].

Buck. Ay, here they be that dare and will disturb
thee.
Know, Cade, we come ambassadors from the King
Unto the commons whom thou hast misled;
And here pronounce free pardon to them all
That will forsake thee and go home in peace. 10
Clif. What say ye, countrymen? Will ye relent
And yield to mercy whilst 'tis offered you,
Or let a [rebel] lead you to your deaths?
Who loves the King and will embrace his pardon,
Fling up his cap, and say, "God save his Maj-
esty!"   15
Who hateth him and honours not his father,
Henry the Fifth, that made all France to quake,
Shake he his weapon at us and pass by.
All. God save the King! God save the King! 19
Cade. What, Buckingham and Clifford, are ye
so brave? And you, base peasants, do ye believe
him? Will you needs be hang'd with your pardons
about your necks? Hath my sword therefore
broke through London gates, that you should leave
me at the White Hart in Southwark? I thought 25
ye would never have given out these arms till you
had recovered your ancient freedom. But you are
all recreants and dastards, and delight to live in
slavery to the nobility. Let them break your
backs with burdens, take your houses over your
heads, ravish your wives and daughters before your
faces. For me, I will make shift for one; and so,
God's curse light upon you all!   34
All. We'll follow Cade, we'll follow Cade!
Clif. Is Cade the son of Henry the Fifth,
That thus you do exclaim you'll go with him?
Will he conduct you through the heart of France
And make the meanest of you earls and dukes?
Alas, he hath no home, no place to fly to;   40
Nor knows he how to live but by the spoil,
Unless by robbing of your friends and us.
Were 't not a shame that, whilst you live at jar,

The fearful French, whom you late vanquished,
Should make a start o'er seas and vanquish you? 45
Methinks already in this civil broil
I see them lording it in London streets,
Crying "*Villiago!*" unto all they meet.
Better ten thousand base-born Cades miscarry
Than you should stoop unto a Frenchman's mercy.
To France, to France, and get what you have
lost!   51
Spare England, for it is your native coast.
Henry hath money, you are strong and manly;
God on our side, doubt not of victory.
All. A Clifford! a Clifford! We'll follow the
King and Clifford.   56
Cade. [*Aside.*] Was ever feather so lightly blown
to and fro as this multitude? The name of Henry
the Fifth hales them to an hundred mischiefs and
makes them leave me desolate. I see them lay 60
their heads together to surprise me. My sword
make way for me, for here is no staying. In despite of the devils and hell, have through the very
middest of you! And heavens and honour be witness that no want of resolution in me, but only my
followers' base and ignominious treasons, makes me
betake me to my heels.   [*Exit.* 67
Buck. What, is he fled? Go some, and follow
him;
And he that brings his head unto the King
Shall have a thousand crowns for his reward.
                         [*Exeunt some of them.*
Follow me, soldiers; we'll devise a mean   71
To reconcile you all unto the King.   [*Exeunt.*

[SCENE IX. *Kenilworth Castle.*]

Trumpets. Enter KING, QUEEN, *and* SOMERSET,
on the terrace.

King. Was ever king that joy'd an earthly
throne
And could command no more content than I?
No sooner was I crept out of my cradle
But I was made a king, at nine months old.
Was never subject long'd to be a king   5
As I do long and wish to be a subject.

Enter BUCKINGHAM *and old* CLIFFORD.

Buck. Health and glad tidings to your Majesty!
King. Why, Buckingham, is the traitor Cade
surpris'd?
Or is he but retir'd to make him strong?

Enter [*below,*] *multitudes with halters about their necks.*

Clif. He is fled, my lord, and all his powers do
yield,   10
And humbly thus, with halters on their necks,

Sc. viii, 13. [rebel] (Singer). *rabble* F. 21. **brave:** arrogant. 26. **out:** up. 48. *Villiago:* (Ital.) rascal. 61. **surprise:**
capture.

Expect your Highness' doom, of life or death.
King. Then, heaven, set ope thy everlasting gates
To entertain my vows of thanks and praise!
Soldiers, this day have you redeem'd your lives 15
And show'd how well you love your prince and country.
Continue still in this so good a mind,
And Henry, though he be infortunate,
Assure yourselves, will never be unkind.
And so, with thanks and pardon to you all, 20
I do dismiss you to your several countries.
All. God save the King! God save the King!

Enter a MESSENGER.

Mess. Please it your Grace to be advertised
The Duke of York is newly come from Ireland,
And with a puissant and a mighty power 25
Of gallowglasses and stout kerns
Is marching hitherward in proud array,
And still proclaimeth, as he comes along,
His arms are only to remove from thee
The Duke of Somerset, whom he terms a traitor. 30
King. Thus stands my state, 'twixt Cade and York distress'd;
Like to a ship that, having scap'd a tempest,
Is straightway calm'd and boarded with a pirate.
But now is Cade driven back, his men dispers'd,
And now is York in arms to second him. 35
I pray thee, Buckingham, go and meet him,
And ask him what's the reason of these arms.
Tell him I'll send Duke Edmund to the Tower;
And, Somerset, we will commit thee hither,
Until his army be dismiss'd from him. 40
Som. My lord,
I'll yield myself to prison willingly,
Or unto death, to do my country good.
King. In any case, be not too rough in terms;
For he is fierce and cannot brook hard language. 45
Buck. I will, my lord; and doubt not so to deal
As all things shall redound unto your good.
King. Come, wife, let's in, and learn to govern better;
For yet may England curse my wretched reign.
                 [*Flourish. Exeunt.*

[SCENE X. *Kent. Iden's garden.*]

Enter CADE.

Cade. Fie on ambition! Fie on myself, that have a sword, and yet am ready to famish! These five days have I hid me in these woods and durst not peep out, for all the country is laid for me; but now

am I so hungry that if I might have a lease of my 5
life for a thousand years I could stay no longer.
Wherefore, on a brick wall have I climb'd into this
garden, to see if I can eat grass, or pick a sallet another while, which is not amiss to cool a man's
stomach this hot weather. And I think this 10
word "sallet" was born to do me good; for many
a time, but for a sallet, my brain-pan had been
cleft with a brown bill; and many a time, when I
have been dry and bravely marching, it hath
serv'd me instead of a quart pot to drink in; and
now the word "sallet" must serve me to feed on. 17

Enter IDEN.

Iden. Lord, who would live turmoiled in the court
And may enjoy such quiet walks as these?
This small inheritance my father left me 20
Contenteth me, and worth a monarchy.
I seek not to wax great by others' [waning],
Or gather wealth, I care not, with what envy.
Sufficeth that I have maintains my state
And sends the poor well pleased from my gate. 25
Cade. [*Aside.*] Here's the lord of the soil come to
seize me for a stray, for entering his fee-simple with-
out leave. — Ah, villain, thou wilt betray me, and
get a thousand crowns of the King by carrying my
head to him; but I'll make thee eat iron like an
ostrich, and swallow my sword like a great pin, ere
thou and I part. 32
Iden. Why, rude companion, whatsoe'er thou be,
I know thee not; why, then, should I betray thee?
Is't not enough to break into my garden, 35
And, like a thief, to come to rob my grounds,
Climbing my walls in spite of me the owner,
But thou wilt brave me with these saucy terms? 38
Cade. Brave thee? Ay, by the best blood that
ever was broach'd, and beard thee too. Look on
me well. I have eat no meat these five days; yet,
come thou and thy five men, and if I do not leave
you all as dead as a doornail, I pray God I may
never eat grass more. 44
Iden. Nay, it shall ne'er be said, while England stands,
That Alexander Iden, an esquire of Kent,
Took odds to combat a poor famish'd man.
Oppose thy steadfast-gazing eyes to mine,
See if thou canst outface me with thy looks.
Set limb to limb, and thou art far the lesser; 50
Thy hand is but a finger to my fist,
Thy leg a stick compared with this truncheon;
My foot shall fight with all the strength thou hast;
And if mine arm be heaved in the air,

Sc. ix, 23. **advertised:** informed. 26. **gallowglasses:** heavy-armed Irish foot-soldiers. 44. **terms:** language.
Sc. x, 4. **laid:** set with snares. 11. **sallet:** (1) salad, (2) helmet. 13. **brown bill:** halberd. 22. [waning] (Rowe). *warning* F. 27. **stray:** vagabond. **fee-simple:** property. 33. **companion:** fellow. 40. **broach'd:** shed. 47. **odds:** advantage.

Thy grave is digg'd already in the earth.   55
As for words, whose greatness answers words,
Let this my sword report what speech forbears.
  Cade. By my valour, the most complete champion that ever I heard!   Steel, if thou turn the
edge, or cut not out the burly-bon'd clown in chines
of beef ere thou sleep in thy sheath, I beseech Jove
on my knees thou mayst be turn'd to hobnails. 63
        [*Here they fight.* [*Cade falls.*]
O, I am slain! Famine and no other hath slain
me. Let ten thousand devils come against me, and
give me but the ten meals I have lost, and I'd defy
them all.   Wither, garden, and be henceforth a
burying-place to all that do dwell in this house, because the unconquered soul of Cade is fled.   70
  Iden. Is't Cade that I have slain, that monstrous
      traitor?
Sword, I will hallow thee for this thy deed,
And hang thee o'er my tomb when I am dead.
Ne'er shall this blood be wiped from thy point,
But thou shalt wear it as a herald's coat,   75
To emblaze the honour that thy master got.
  Cade. Iden, farewell, and be proud of thy victory.
Tell Kent from me, she hath lost her best man, and
exhort all the world to be cowards; for I, that never
feared any, am vanquished by famine, not by
valour.   [*Dies.* 81
  Iden. How much thou wrong'st me, heaven be
      my judge.
Die, damned wretch, the curse of her that bare thee;
And as I thrust thy body in with my sword,
So wish I, I might thrust thy soul to hell.   85
Hence will I drag thee headlong by the heels
Unto a dunghill which shall be thy grave,
And there cut off thy most ungracious head;
Which I will bear in triumph to the King,
Leaving thy trunk for crows to feed upon.   90
                        [*Exit.*

[ACT V]

[SCENE I. *Fields between Dartford and Blackheath.*]

Enter YORK, *and his army of Irish, with drum and
colours.*

  York. From Ireland thus comes York to claim
      his right
And pluck the crown from feeble Henry's head.
Ring, bells, aloud! burn, bonfires, clear and bright
To entertain great England's lawful king!
Ah! *sancta majestas,* who would not buy thee dear?
Let them obey that knows not how to rule;   6
This hand was made to handle nought but gold.
I cannot give due action to my words

Except a sword or sceptre balance it.
A sceptre shall it have, have I a soul,   10
On which I'll toss the flower-de-luce of France.

            Enter BUCKINGHAM.
Whom have we here? Buckingham, to disturb me?
The King hath sent him, sure. I must dissemble.
  Buck. York, if thou meanest well, I greet thee
      well.
  York. Humphrey of Buckingham, I accept thy
      greeting.   15
Art thou a messenger, or come of pleasure?
  Buck. A messenger from Henry, our dread liege,
To know the reason of these arms in peace;
Or why thou, being a subject as I am,
Against thy oath and true allegiance sworn,   20
Should raise so great a power without his leave,
Or dare to bring thy force so near the court.
  York. [*Aside.*] Scarce can I speak, my choler is
      so great.
O, I could hew up rocks and fight with flint,
I am so angry at these abject terms;   25
And now, like Ajax Telamonius,
On sheep or oxen could I spend my fury.
I am far better born than is the King,
More like a king, more kingly in my thoughts;
But I must make fair weather yet a while,   30
Till Henry be more weak and I more strong. —
Buckingham, I prithee, pardon me,
That I have given no answer all this while;
My mind was troubled with deep melancholy.
The cause why I have brought this army hither 35
Is to remove proud Somerset from the King,
Seditious to his Grace and to the state.
  Buck. That is too much presumption on thy
      part;
But if thy arms be to no other end,
The King hath yielded unto thy demand.   40
The Duke of Somerset is in the Tower.
  York. Upon thine honour, is he prisoner?
  Buck. Upon mine honour, he is prisoner.
  York. Then, Buckingham, I do dismiss my
      powers.
Soldiers, I thank you all; disperse yourselves.   45
Meet me to-morrow in Saint George's field,
You shall have pay and everything you wish.
And let my sovereign, virtuous Henry,
Command my eldest son, nay, all my sons,
As pledges of my fealty and love;   50
I'll send them all as willing as I live.
Lands, goods, horse, armour, anything I have,
Is his to use, so Somerset may die.
  Buck. York, I commend this kind submission.
We twain will go into his Highness' tent.   55

56. **answers words:** equals your words. 61. **chines:** saddles.
  Act V, sc. i, 26. **Ajax Telamonius,** who went mad and slew sheep and oxen, supposing them his enemies. 30. **make fair
weather:** put on friendliness.

Enter KING *and* Attendants.

King. Buckingham, doth York intend no harm
    to us
That thus he marcheth with thee arm in arm?
York. In all submission and humility
York doth present himself unto your Highness.
    King. Then what intends these forces thou dost
    bring?   60
York. To heave the traitor Somerset from hence,
And fight against that monstrous rebel Cade,
Who since I heard to be discomfited.

Enter IDEN, *with Cade's head.*

Iden. If one so rude and of so mean condition
May pass into the presence of a king,   65
Lo, I present your Grace a traitor's head,
The head of Cade, whom I in combat slew.
    King. The head of Cade! Great God, how just
    art Thou!
O, let me view his visage, being dead,
That living wrought me such exceeding trouble. 70
Tell me, my friend, art thou the man that slew him?
    Iden. I was, an't like your Majesty.
    King. How art thou call'd, and what is thy
    degree?
    Iden. Alexander Iden, that's my name;
A poor esquire of Kent, that loves his king.   75
    Buck. So please it you, my lord, 'twere not amiss
He were created knight for his good service.
    King. Iden, kneel down. [*He kneels.*] Rise up
    a knight.
We give thee for reward a thousand marks,
And will that thou henceforth attend on us.   80
    Iden. May Iden live to merit such a bounty,
And never live but true unto his liege! [*Rises.*]

Enter QUEEN *and* SOMERSET.

King. See, Buckingham, Somerset comes with
    the Queen.
Go, bid her hide him quickly from the Duke.
    Queen. For thousand Yorks he shall not hide his
    head,   85
But boldly stand and front him to his face.
    York. How now! is Somerset at liberty?
Then, York, unloose thy long-imprisoned thoughts,
And let thy tongue be equal with thy heart.
Shall I endure the sight of Somerset?   90
False king! why hast thou broken faith with me,
Knowing how hardly I can brook abuse?
King did I call thee? No, thou art not King,
Not fit to govern and rule multitudes,
Which dar'st not, no, nor canst not rule a traitor. 95
That head of thine doth not become a crown,
Thy hand is made to grasp a palmer's staff
And not to grace an awful princely sceptre.
That gold must round engirt these brows of mine,

Whose smile and frown, like to Achilles' spear, 100
Is able with the change to kill and cure.
Here is a hand to hold a sceptre up
And with the same to act controlling laws.
Give place! By heaven, thou shalt rule no more
O'er him whom heaven created for thy ruler.   105
    Som. O monstrous traitor! I arrest thee, York,
Of capital treason 'gainst the King and crown.
Obey, audacious traitor; kneel for grace.
    York. Wouldst have me kneel? First let me ask
    of [these]
If they can brook I bow a knee to man.   110
Sirrah, call in my sons to be my bail.
                      [*Exit Attendant.*]
I know, ere they will have me go to ward,
They'll pawn their swords for my enfranchisement.
    Queen. Call hither Clifford; bid him come amain,
To say if that the bastard boys of York   115
Shall be the surety for their traitor father.
                    [*Exit Buckingham.*]
    York. O blood-besotted Neapolitan,
Outcast of Naples, England's bloody scourge!
The sons of York, thy betters in their birth,
Shall be their father's bail; and bane to those 120
That for my surety will refuse the boys!

Enter EDWARD *and* RICHARD, *with forces.*

See where they come; I'll warrant they'll make it
    good.

Enter CLIFFORD [*and his Son,* YOUNG CLIFFORD,
    with forces].

Queen. And here comes Clifford to deny their
    bail.
    Clif. Health and all happiness to my lord the
    King!   [*Kneels.*]
    York. I thank thee, Clifford. Say, what news
    with thee?   125
Nay, do not fright us with an angry look.
We are thy sovereign, Clifford, kneel again;
For thy mistaking so, we pardon thee.
    Clif. This is my king, York, I do not mistake;
But thou mistakes me much to think I do.   130
To Bedlam with him! Is the man grown mad?
    King. Ay, Clifford; a bedlam and ambitious
    humour
Makes him oppose himself against his king.
    Clif. He is a traitor; let him to the Tower,
And chop away that factious pate of his.   135
    Queen. He is arrested, but will not obey.
His sons, he says, shall give their words for him.
    York. Will you not, sons?
    Edw. Ay, noble father, if our words will serve.
    Rich. And if words will not, then our weapons
    shall.   140
    Clif. Why, what a brood of traitors have we here!

79. **marks.** A mark was 13*s.*4*d.* 109. **[these]** (Theobald). *thee* F.

York. Look in a glass, and call thy image so.
I am thy king, and thou a false-heart traitor.
Call hither to the stake my two brave bears,
That with the very shaking of their chains   145
They may astonish these fell-lurking curs.
Bid Salisbury and Warwick come to me.

Enter the EARLS OF WARWICK *and* SALISBURY
[*with forces*].

Clif. Are these thy bears? We'll bait thy bears
to death
And manacle the bear-ward in their chains
If thou dar'st bring them to the baiting place.   150
Rich. Oft have I seen a hot o'erweening cur
Run back and bite, because he was withheld;
Who being suffer'd, with the bear's fell paw
Hath clapp'd his tail between his legs and cried;
And such a piece of service will you do,   155
If you oppose yourselves to match Lord Warwick.
Clif. Hence, heap of wrath, foul indigested lump,
As crooked in thy manners as thy shape!
York. Nay, we shall heat you thoroughly anon.
Clif. Take heed, lest by your heat you burn your-
selves.   160
King. Why, Warwick, hath thy knee forgot to
bow?
Old Salisbury, shame to thy silver hair,
Thou mad misleader of thy brain-sick son!
What, wilt thou on thy death-bed play the ruffian,
And seek for sorrow with thy spectacles?   165
O, where is faith? O, where is loyalty?
If it be banish'd from the frosty head,
Where shall it find a harbour in the earth?
Wilt thou go dig a grave to find out war,
And shame thine honourable age with blood?   170
Why art thou old and want'st experience?
Or wherefore dost abuse it if thou hast it?
For shame! In duty bend thy knee to me
That bows unto the grave with mickle age.
Sal. My lord, I have considered with myself   175
The title of this most renowned duke,
And in my conscience do repute his Grace
The rightful heir to England's royal seat.
King. Hast thou not sworn allegiance unto me?
Sal. I have.   180
King. Canst thou dispense with heaven for such
an oath?
Sal. It is great sin to swear unto a sin,
But greater sin to keep a sinful oath.
Who can be bound by any solemn vow
To do a murd'rous deed, to rob a man,   185
To force a spotless virgin's chastity,
To reave the orphan of his patrimony,

To wring the widow from her custom'd right,
And have no other reason for this wrong
But that he was bound by a solemn oath?   190
Queen. A subtle traitor needs no sophister.
King. Call Buckingham, and bid him arm him-
self.
York. Call Buckingham, and all the friends thou
hast,
I am resolv'd for death [or] dignity.
Clif. The first I warrant thee, if dreams prove
true.   195
War. You were best to go to bed and dream
again,
To keep thee from the tempest of the field.
Clif. I am resolv'd to bear a greater storm
Than any thou canst conjure up to-day;
And that I'll write upon thy burgonet,   200
Might I but know thee by thy [house's] badge.
War. Now, by my father's badge, old Nevil's
crest,
The rampant bear chain'd to the ragged staff,
This day I'll wear aloft my burgonet,
As on a mountain top the cedar shows   205
That keeps his leaves in spite of any storm,
Even to affright thee with the view thereof.
Clif. And from thy burgonet I'll rend thy bear
And tread it under foot with all contempt,
Despite the bear-ward that protects the bear.   210
Y. Clif. And so to arms, victorious father,
To quell the rebels and their complices.
Rich. Fie! charity, for shame! speak not in spite,
For you shall sup with Jesu Christ to-night.
Y. Clif. Foul stigmatic, that's more than thou
canst tell.   215
Rich. If not in heaven, you'll surely sup in hell.
[*Exeunt* [*severally*].

[SCENE II. *Saint Alban's, near the Castle inn.*]

[*Alarums to the battle.*]   Enter WARWICK.

War. Clifford of Cumberland, 'tis Warwick calls!
An if thou dost not hide thee from the bear,
Now, when the angry trumpet sounds alarum
And dead men's cries do fill the empty air,
Clifford, I say, come forth and fight with me.   5
Proud northern lord, Clifford of Cumberland,
Warwick is hoarse with calling thee to arms.

Enter YORK.

How now, my noble lord! what, all afoot?
York. The deadly-handed Clifford slew my
steed,
But match to match I have encount'red him   10

---

146. **fell-lurking:** lying in wait to be cruel.   153. **suffer'd:** permitted to attack. **with:** smitten by.   157, 158. The first
of the endless references to Richard's deformity.   181. **dispense with:** obtain dispensation from.   187. **reave:** bereave.
194. **[or]** (Rowe).   *and* F.   200. **burgonet:** helmet.   201. **[house's]** F₂.   *housed* F₁; *household* Qq.   215. **stigmatic:** marked
with deformity.

And made a prey for carrion kites and crows
Even of the bonny beast he lov'd so well.

Enter old CLIFFORD.

War. Of one or both of us the time is come.
York. Hold, Warwick, seek thee out some other chase,
For I myself must hunt this deer to death.   15
War. Then, nobly, York; 'tis for a crown thou fight'st.
As I intend, Clifford, to thrive to-day,
It grieves my soul to leave thee unassail'd. [*Exit.*
Clif. What seest thou in me, York? Why dost thou pause?
York. With thy brave bearing should I be in love,   20
But that thou art so fast mine enemy.
Clif. Nor should thy prowess want praise and esteem,
But that 'tis shown ignobly and in treason.
York. So let it help me now against thy sword
As I in justice and true right express it.   25
Clif. My soul and body on the action both!
York. A dreadful lay! Address thee instantly.
[*They fight, and Clifford falls.*]
Clif. La fin couronne les œuvres.   [*Dies.*]
York. Thus war hath given thee peace, for thou art still.
Peace with his soul, Heaven, if it be thy will!   30
[*Exit.*]

Enter YOUNG CLIFFORD.

Y. Clif. Shame and confusion! all is on the rout;
Fear frames disorder, and disorder wounds
Where it should guard. O war, thou son of hell,
Whom angry heavens do make their minister,
Throw in the frozen bosoms of our part   35
Hot coals of vengeance! Let no soldier fly.
He that is truly dedicate to war
Hath no self-love, nor he that loves himself
Hath not essentially but by circumstance
The name of valour.   [*Seeing his dead father.*]
O, let the vile world end,   40
And the premised flames of the last day
Knit earth and heaven together!
Now let the general trumpet blow his blast,
Particularities and petty sounds
To cease! Wast thou ordain'd, dear father,   45
To lose thy youth in peace, and to achieve
The silver livery of advised age,
And, in thy reverence and thy chair-days, thus
To die in ruffian battle? Even at this sight
My heart is turn'd to stone; and while 'tis mine,   50

It shall be stony. York not our old men spares;
No more will I their babes. Tears virginal
Shall be to me even as the dew to fire,
And beauty, that the tyrant oft reclaims,
Shall to my flaming wrath be oil and flax.   55
Henceforth I will not have to do with pity.
Meet I an infant of the house of York,
Into as many gobbets will I cut it
As wild Medea young Absyrtus did.
In cruelty will I seek out my fame.   60
Come, thou new ruin of old Clifford's house.
As did Æneas old Anchises bear,
So bear I thee upon my manly shoulders;
But then Æneas bare a living load,
Nothing so heavy as these woes of mine.   65
[*Exit, bearing off his father.*]

Enter RICHARD *and* SOMERSET *to fight.* [SOMERSET *is killed.*]

Rich. So, lie thou there;
For underneath an alehouse' paltry sign,
The Castle in Saint Alban's, Somerset
Hath made the wizard famous in his death.
Sword, hold thy temper; heart, be wrathful still.   70
Priests pray for enemies, but princes kill.   [*Exit.*]

Fight: excursions. Enter KING, QUEEN, *and others.*
Queen. Away, my lord! you are slow; for shame, away!
King. Can we outrun the heavens? Good Margaret, stay.
Queen. What are you made of? You'll nor fight nor fly.
Now is it manhood, wisdom, and defence   75
To give the enemy way, and to secure us
By what we can, which can no more but fly.
[*Alarum afar off.*
If you be ta'en, we then should see the bottom
Of all our fortunes; but if we haply scape,
As well we may, if not through your neglect,   80
We shall to London get, where you are lov'd,
And where this breach now in our fortunes made
May readily be stopp'd.

Re-enter YOUNG CLIFFORD.

Y. Clif. But that my heart's on future mischief set,
I would speak blasphemy ere bid you fly.   85
But fly you must. Uncurable discomfit
Reigns in the hearts of all our present parts.
Away, for your relief! and we will live
To see their day and them our fortune give.
Away, my lord, away!   [*Exeunt.*   90

Sc. ii, 14. **chase**: game. 27. **lay**: wager. 28. *La fin*, etc.: The end crowns the work. 35. **part**: side. 41. **premised**: pre-ordained. 47. **advised**: wise. 53. **dew to fire.** Dew was supposed to make fire burn more fiercely. 54. **reclaims**: restrains. 59. **Absyrtus**: brother of Medea. 68. **Castle.** See I.iv.67. 89. **our ... give**: Fortune give to us.

[SCENE III. *Fields near Saint Alban's.*]

Alarum.   Retreat.   Enter YORK, RICHARD, WAR-
WICK, *and* Soldiers, *with drum and colours.*

York. Of Salisbury, who can report of him,
That winter lion, who in rage forgets
Aged contusions and all brush of time,
And, like a gallant in the brow of youth,
Repairs him with occasion?   This happy day   5
Is not itself, nor have we won one foot,
If Salisbury be lost.
     Rich.   My noble father,
Three times to-day I holp him to his horse,
Three times bestrid him; thrice I led him off,
Persuaded him from any further act: 10
But still, where danger was, still there I met
     him;
And like rich hangings in a homely house,
So was his will in his old feeble body.
But, noble as he is, look where he comes.

Enter SALISBURY.

     Sal. Now, by my sword, well hast thou fought
     to-day;   15
By the mass, so did we all.   I thank you, Richard.
God knows how long it is I have to live,
And it hath pleas'd Him that three times to-day
You have defended me from imminent death.
Well, lords, we have not got that which we have.   20
'Tis not enough our foes are this time fled,
Being opposites of such repairing nature.
     York. I know our safety is to follow them;
For, as I hear, the King is fled to London
To call a present court of parliament.   25
Let us pursue him ere the writs go forth.
What says Lord Warwick?   Shall we after them?
     War. After them?   Nay, before them, if we can.
Now, by my hand, lords, 'twas a glorious day.
Saint Alban's battle won by famous York   30
Shall be eterniz'd in all age to come.
Sound drum and trumpets, and to London all;
And more such days as these to us befall!   [*Exeunt.*

Sc. iii, 4. in: with.   **22. of such repairing nature:** having such power of recovery.

The Third Part of Henry the Sixth

IN THE INTRODUCTION to the previous play the relation of the *Third Part of Henry VI* to the Quarto dealing with the same theme has already been discussed. The Quarto was published in 1595 with the title of *The true Tragedie of Richard Duke of Yorke, and the death of good King Henrie the Sixt, with the whole contention between the two Houses Lancaster and Yorke, as it was sundrie times acted by the Right Honourable the Earle of Pembrooke his servants.* A second Quarto appeared in 1600, and it was reissued, along with the *First part of the Contention*, in 1619 with the title of *The Whole Contention between the two Famous Houses, Lancaster and Yorke.*

As was stated in the Introduction to the *Second Part*, the theory that *The True Tragedy* was the foundation of the *Third Part of Henry VI* as printed in the First Folio has been generally abandoned in favor of the view of *The True Tragedy* as a pirated version of the Folio play, reported, mainly from memory, by some actor or prompter who took part in the performance. This reporting was very badly done, much of the play being missing and the rest often ungrammatical, unmetrical, and incoherent. The source of all modern texts is the First Folio.

A later limit for the date of *3 Henry VI* is found in the well-known passage from *Greenes Groats-worth of Wit* (1592) quoted in the Biographical Sketch. The "upstart crow, beautified with our feathers, that with his *Tygers hart wrapt in a Players hyde*, supposes he is as well able to bombast out a blanke verse as the best of you" is unquestionably Shakespeare, and the line quoted occurs in *3 Henry VI*, I.iv.137, and also in *The True Tragedy*. Greene died on September 3, 1592. The probable date of composition is 1591 or early in 1592.

As in most of the other English histories, the main source is the Chronicles of Holinshed and Halle, and the same freedom is used in the manipulation of historical events for dramatic purposes. Thus Henry's acknowledgment of York's succession to the throne, which was made five years after the battle of St. Alban's (1455), is represented as following it immediately, and a similar telescoping occurs when the league of Margaret and Warwick is made to follow at once on Edward's marriage to Lady Grey (III.iii).

In *3 Henry VI* one can perceive a growing mastery over his material on the part of the dramatist. The leading characters, King Henry, Margaret, Warwick, and Richard of Gloucester stand out more clearly, and a greater degree of unity is achieved through the gradual growth in power of the House of York. In the third act, Richard, who has hitherto been a vigorous partisan and warrior, begins to take on the character of the Machiavellian villain into which he develops completely in the next play. The influence of Marlowe in the somewhat violent treatment of the main figures and in the swelling rhetoric of the blank verse is still evident, but more and more the distinctively Shakespearean accent begins to be perceptible.

THE HOUSE OF YORK

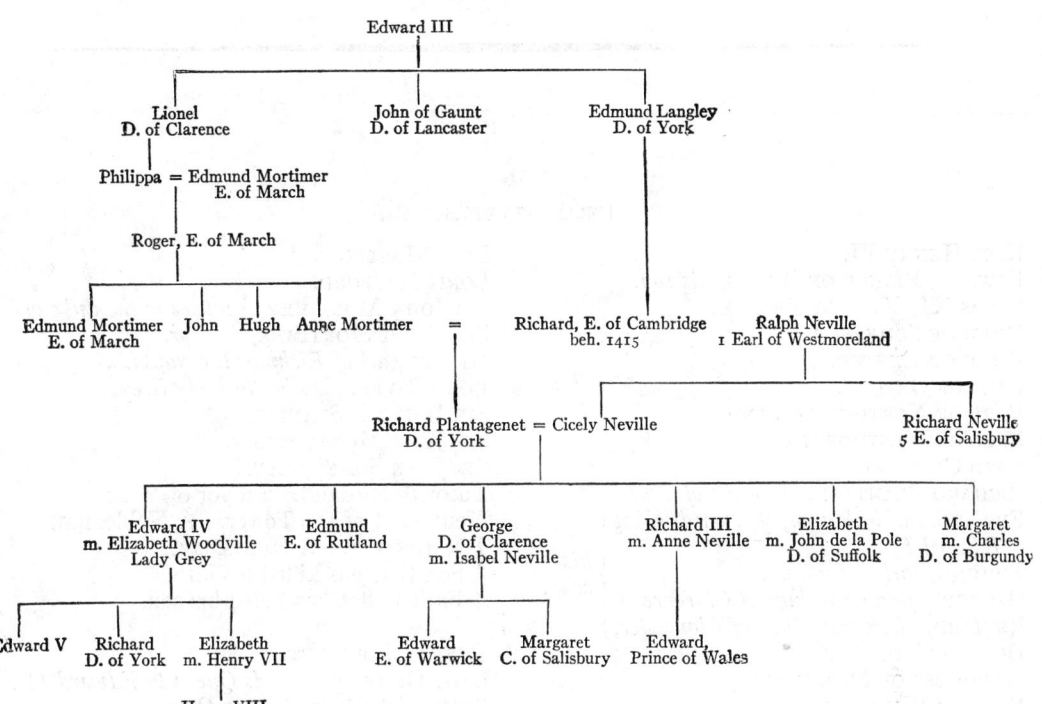

Edward III

Lionel
D. of Clarence

John of Gaunt
D. of Lancaster

Edmund Langley
D. of York

Philippa = Edmund Mortimer
E. of March

Roger, E. of March

Edmund Mortimer   John   Hugh   Anne Mortimer   =   Richard, E. of Cambridge   Ralph Neville
E. of March   beh. 1415   1 Earl of Westmoreland

Richard Plantagenet = Cicely Neville
D. of York

Richard Neville
5 E. of Salisbury

Edward IV
m. Elizabeth Woodville
Lady Grey

Edmund
E. of Rutland

George
D. of Clarence
m. Isabel Neville

Richard III
m. Anne Neville

Elizabeth
m. John de la Pole
D. of Suffolk

Margaret
m. Charles
D. of Burgundy

Edward V   Richard   Elizabeth
D. of York   m. Henry VII

Edward
E. of Warwick

Margaret
C. of Salisbury

Edward,
Prince of Wales

Henry VIII

THE THIRD PART OF
HENRY THE SIXTH

ACT I

SCENE I. [*London.   The Parliament-house.*]

Alarum. Enter the DUKE OF YORK, EDWARD, RICHARD, NORFOLK, MONTAGUE, WARWICK, *and Soldiers.*

War. I wonder how the King escap'd our hands.
York. While we pursu'd the horsemen of the
    north,
He slily stole away and left his men;
Whereat the great Lord of Northumberland,
Whose warlike ears could never brook retreat,   5
Cheer'd up the drooping army; and himself,
Lord Clifford and Lord Stafford, all abreast,
Charg'd our main battle's front, and breaking in
Were by the swords of common soldiers slain.
   Edw. Lord Stafford's father, Duke of Bucking-
    ham,   10
Is either slain or wounded dangerous;
I cleft his beaver with a downright blow.
That this is true, father, behold his blood.
   Mont. And, brother, here's the Earl of Wiltshire's
    blood,
Whom I encount'red as the battles join'd.   15
   Rich. Speak thou for me and tell them what I
    did. [*Showing the Duke of Somerset's head.*]
   York. Richard hath best deserv'd of all my sons.

Act I, sc. i, 5. **retreat:** the trumpet call for retreat.   8. **main battle's:** of the main body of the army.   12. **beaver:** here, helmet.

But is your Grace dead, my Lord of Somerset?
  Norf. Such hope have all the line of John of
    Gaunt!
  Rich. Thus do I hope to shake King Henry's
    head.   20
  War. And so do I. Victorious prince of York,
Before I see thee seated in that throne
Which now the house of Lancaster usurps,
I vow by heaven these eyes shall never close.
This is the palace of the fearful king,   25
And this the regal seat. Possess it, York;
For this is thine and not King Henry's heirs'.
  York. Assist me, then, sweet Warwick, and I
    will;
For hither we have broken in by force.   29
  Norf. We'll all assist you; he that flies shall die.
  York. Thanks, gentle Norfolk. Stay by me, my
    lords;
And, soldiers, stay and lodge by me this night.
                           [They go up.
  War. And when the King comes, offer him no
    violence
Unless he seek to thrust you out perforce.
  York. The Queen this day here holds her parlia-
    ment,   35
But little thinks we shall be of her council.
By words or blows here let us win our right.
  Rich. Arm'd as we are, let's stay within this
    house.
  War. The bloody parliament shall this be call'd,
Unless Plantagenet, Duke of York, be king, 40
And bashful Henry depos'd, whose cowardice
Hath made us by-words to our enemies.
  York. Then leave me not, my lords; be resolute;
I mean to take possession of my right.
  War. Neither the King, nor he that loves him
    best,   45
The proudest he that holds up Lancaster,
Dares stir a wing if Warwick shake his bells.
I'll plant Plantagenet, root him up who dares.
Resolve thee, Richard; claim the English crown.
                  [York takes the throne.

Flourish. Enter KING HENRY, CLIFFORD, NORTH-
UMBERLAND, WESTMORELAND, EXETER, *and the
rest [wearing red roses].*

  K. Hen. My lords, look where the sturdy rebel
    sits,   50
Even in the chair of state. Belike he means,
Back'd by the power of Warwick, that false peer,
To aspire unto the crown and reign as king.
Earl of Northumberland, he slew thy father,
And thine, Lord Clifford; and you both have vow'd
    revenge   55
On him, his sons, his favourites, and his friends.
  North. If I be not, heavens be reveng'd on me!

  Clif. The hope thereof makes Clifford mourn in
    steel.
  West. What, shall we suffer this? Let's pluck
    him down.
My heart for anger burns; I cannot brook it. 60
  K. Hen. Be patient, gentle Earl of Westmore-
    land.
  Clif. Patience is for poltroons, such as he.
He durst not sit there, had your father liv'd.
My gracious lord, here in the parliament
Let us assail the family of York.   65
  North. Well hast thou spoken, cousin; be it so.
  K. Hen. Ah, know you not the city favours them,
And they have troops of soldiers at their beck?
  [Exe.] But when the Duke is slain, they'll
    quickly fly.
  K. Hen. Far be the thought of this from Henry's
    heart,   70
To make a shambles of the parliament-house!
Cousin of Exeter, frowns, words, and threats
Shall be the war that Henry means to use.
Thou factious Duke of York, descend my throne,
And kneel for grace and mercy at my feet. 75
I am thy sovereign.
  York.   I am thine.
  Exe. For shame, come down. He made thee
    Duke of York.
  York. ['Twas] my inheritance, as the earldom
    was.
  Exe. Thy father was a traitor to the crown.
  War. Exeter, thou art a traitor to the crown 80
In following this usurping Henry.
  Clif. Whom should he follow but his natural
    king?
  War. True, Clifford; and that's Richard Duke of
    York.
  K. Hen. And shall I stand, and thou sit in my
    throne?   84
  York. It must and shall be so. Content thyself.
  War. Be Duke of Lancaster; let him be King.
  West. He is both King and Duke of Lancaster,
And that the Lord of Westmoreland shall maintain.
  War. And Warwick shall disprove it. You for-
    get   89
That we are those which chas'd you from the field
And slew your fathers, and with colours spread
March'd through the city to the palace gates.
  North. No, Warwick, I remember it to my grief;
And, by his soul, thou and thy house shall rue it.
  West. Plantagenet, of thee and these thy
    sons,   95
Thy kinsmen and thy friends, I'll have more lives
Than drops of blood were in my father's veins.
  Clif. Urge it no more; lest that, instead of words,
I send thee, Warwick, such a messenger
As shall revenge his death before I stir.   100

---

47. **shake his bells:** i.e., like a falcon.   69. **[Exe.]** (Theobald).   *Westm.* F.   78. **['Twas]** Q.   *It was* F.

War. Poor Clifford! how I scorn his worthless
     threats!
York. Will you we show our title to the crown?
If not, our swords shall plead it in the field.
     K. Hen. What title hast thou, traitor, to the
     crown?
[Thy] father was, as thou art, Duke of York;   105
Thy grandfather, Roger Mortimer, Earl of March:
I am the son of Henry the Fifth,
Who made the Dauphin and the French to stoop
And seiz'd upon their towns and provinces.
     War. Talk not of France, sith thou hast lost it
     all.   110
     K. Hen. The Lord Protector lost it, and not I.
When I was crown'd I was but nine months old.
     Rich. You are old enough now, and yet, me-
     thinks, you lose.
Father, tear the crown from the usurper's head.
     Edw. Sweet father, do so; set it on your head.   115
     Mont. Good brother, as thou lov'st and honour-
     est arms,
Let's fight it out and not stand cavilling thus.
     Rich. Sound drums and trumpets, and the King
     will fly.
     York. Sons, peace!
     K. Hen. Peace, thou! and give King Henry leave
     to speak.   120
     War. Plantagenet shall speak first. Hear him,
     lords;
And be you silent and attentive too,
For he that interrupts him shall not live.
     K. Hen. Think'st thou that I will leave my kingly
     throne,
Wherein my grandsire and my father sat?   125
No! First shall war unpeople this my realm;
Ay, and their colours, often borne in France,
And now in England to our heart's great sorrow,
Shall be my winding-sheet. Why faint you, lords?
My title's good, and better far than his.   130
     War. Prove it, Henry, and thou shalt be King.
     K. Hen. Henry the Fourth by conquest got the
     crown.
     York. 'Twas by rebellion against his king.
     K. Hen. [*Aside.*] I know not what to say; my
     title's weak. —
Tell me, may not a king adopt an heir?   135
     York. What then?
     K. Hen. An if he may, then am I lawful king;
For Richard, in the view of many lords,
Resign'd the crown to Henry the Fourth,
Whose heir my father was, and I am his.   140
     York. He rose against him, being his sovereign,
And made him to resign his crown perforce.
     War. Suppose, my lords, he did it unconstrain'd,
Think you 'twere prejudicial to his crown?
     Exe. No; for he could not so resign his crown   145

But that the next heir should succeed and reign.
     K. Hen. Art thou against us, Duke of Exeter?
     Exe. His is the right, and therefore pardon me.
     York. Why whisper you, my lords, and answer
     not?   149
     Exe. My conscience tells me he is lawful king.
     K. Hen. [*Aside.*] All will revolt from me and
     turn to him.
     North. Plantagenet, for all the claim thou lay'st,
Think not that Henry shall be so depos'd.
     War. Depos'd he shall be, in despite of all.
     North. Thou art deceiv'd. 'Tis not thy southern
     power   155
Of Essex, Norfolk, Suffolk, nor of Kent,
Which makes thee thus presumptuous and proud,
Can set the Duke up in despite of me.
     Clif. King Henry, be thy title right or wrong,
Lord Clifford vows to fight in thy defence.   160
May that ground gape and swallow me alive,
Where I shall kneel to him that slew my father!
     K. Hen. O Clifford, how thy words revive my
     heart!
     York. Henry of Lancaster, resign thy crown.
What mutter you, or what conspire you, lords?   165
     War. Do right unto this princely Duke of York,
Or I will fill the house with armed men,
And over the chair of state, where now he sits,
Write up his title with usurping blood.
       [*He stamps with his foot, and the Soldiers
       show themselves.*
     K. Hen. My Lord of Warwick, hear but one
     word.   170
Let me for this my life-time reign as king.
     York. Confirm the crown to me and to mine
     heirs,
And thou shalt reign in quiet while thou liv'st.
     King. I am content. Richard Plantagenet,
Enjoy the kingdom after my decease.   175
     Clif. What wrong is this unto the Prince your
     son!
     War. What good is this to England and him-
     self!
     West. Base, fearful, and despairing Henry!
     Clif. How hast thou injur'd both thyself and us!
     West. I cannot stay to hear these articles.   180
     North. Nor I.
     Clif. Come, cousin, let us tell the Queen these
     news.
     West. Farewell, faint-hearted and degenerate
     king,
In whose cold blood no spark of honour bides.
     North. Be thou a prey unto the house of York,
And die in bands for this unmanly deed!   186
     Clif. In dreadful war mayst thou be overcome,
Or live in peace abandon'd and despis'd!
       [*Exeunt North., Cliff., and West.*]

105. [Thy] Q. *My* F.   186. **bands:** bonds.

War. Turn this way, Henry, and regard them
    not.
Exe. They seek revenge and therefore will not
    yield.   190
K. Hen. Ah, Exeter!
War.   Why should you sigh, my lord?
K. Hen. Not for myself, Lord Warwick, but my
    son,
Whom I unnaturally shall disinherit.
But be it as it may. [*To York.*] I here entail
The crown to thee and to thine heirs for ever, 195
Conditionally that here thou take an oath
To cease this civil war, and whilst I live
To honour me as thy king and sovereign,
And neither by treason nor hostility
To seek to put me down and reign thyself.   200
York. This oath I willingly take and will per-
    form.
War. Long live King Henry! Plantagenet, em-
    brace him.
K. Hen. And long live thou, and these thy for-
    ward sons!
York. Now York and Lancaster are reconcil'd.
Exe. Accurs'd be he that seeks to make them
    foes! [*Sennet. Here they come down.* 205
York. Farewell, my gracious lord; I'll to my
    castle.
War. And I'll keep London with my soldiers.
Norf. And I to Norfolk with my followers.
Mont. And I unto the sea from whence I came.
K. Hen. And I with grief and sorrow to the court.
    [*Exeunt York and his sons, Warwick, Nor-
    folk, Montague, their Soldiers, and At-
    tendants.*]

Enter QUEEN MARGARET [*and the* PRINCE OF
    WALES].

Exe. Here comes the Queen, whose looks bewray
    her anger.   211
I'll steal away.
K. Hen.   Exeter, so will I.
Q. Mar. Nay, go not from me; I will follow thee.
K. Hen. Be patient, gentle queen, and I will stay.
Q. Mar. Who can be patient in such extremes?
Ah, wretched man! would I had died a maid   216
And never seen thee, never borne thee son,
Seeing thou hast prov'd so unnatural a father!
Hath he deserv'd to lose his birthright thus?
Hadst thou but lov'd him half so well as I,   220
Or felt that pain which I did for him once,
Or nourish'd him as I did with my blood,
Thou wouldst have left thy dearest heart-blood
    there
Rather than have made that savage duke thine heir
And disinherited thine only son.   225

Prince. Father, you cannot disinherit me.
If you be King, why should not I succeed?
K. Hen. Pardon me, Margaret; pardon me, sweet
    son.
The Earl of Warwick and the Duke enforc'd me.
Q. Mar. Enforc'd thee! Art thou King, and wilt
    be forc'd?   230
I shame to hear thee speak. Ah, timorous wretch!
Thou hast undone thyself, thy son, and me;
And giv'n unto the house of York such head
As thou shalt reign but by their sufferance.
To entail him and his heirs unto the crown,   235
What is it, but to make thy sepulchre
And creep into it far before thy time?
Warwick is chancellor and the lord of Calais;
Stern Falconbridge commands the narrow seas;
The Duke is made Protector of the realm;   240
And yet shalt thou be safe? Such safety finds
The trembling lamb environed with wolves.
Had I been there, which am a silly woman,
The soldiers should have toss'd me on their pikes
Before I would have granted to that act.   245
But thou preferr'st thy life before thine honour;
And seeing thou dost, I here divorce myself
Both from thy table, Henry, and thy bed,
Until that act of parliament be repeal'd
Whereby my son is disinherited.   250
The northern lords that have forsworn thy colours
Will follow mine, if once they see them spread;
And spread they shall be, to thy foul disgrace
And utter ruin of the house of York.
Thus do I leave thee. Come, son, let's away.   255
Our army is ready; come, we'll after them.
K. Hen. Stay, gentle Margaret, and hear me
    speak.
Q. Mar. Thou hast spoke too much already; get
    thee gone.
K. Hen. Gentle son Edward, thou wilt stay with
    me?
Q. Mar. Ay, to be murder'd by his enemies. 260
Prince. When I return with victory [from] the
    field
I'll see your Grace; till then I'll follow her.
Q. Mar. Come, son, away; we may not linger
    thus.
    [*Exeunt Queen Margaret and the Prince.*]
K. Hen. Poor queen! how love to me and to her
    son
Hath made her break out into terms of rage!   265
Reveng'd may she be on that hateful duke,
Whose haughty spirit, winged with desire,
Will cost my crown, and like an empty eagle
Tire on the flesh of me and of my son!
The loss of those three lords torments my heart. 270
I'll write unto them and entreat them fair.

205. S.D. *Sennet:* a set of notes on a trumpet. 211. bewray: show. 233. head: freedom of action (term from horseman-ship). 243. silly: feeble. 261. [from] Q. *to* F. 269. Tire: feed ravenously.

Come, cousin, you shall be the messenger.
  Exe. And I, I hope, shall reconcile them all.
                                      [*Exeunt.*

[SCENE II. *Sandal Castle.*]

Enter RICHARD, EDWARD, *and* MONTAGUE.

  Rich. Brother, though I be youngest, give me
leave.
  Edw. No, I can better play the orator.
  Mont. But I have reasons strong and forcible.

Enter the DUKE OF YORK

  York. Why, how now, sons and brother! at a
strife?
What is your quarrel! How began it first?   5
  Edw. No quarrel, but a slight contention.
  York. About what?
  Rich. About that which concerns your Grace and
us;
The crown of England, father, which is yours. 9
  York. Mine, boy? Not till King Henry be dead.
  Rich. Your right depends not on his life or death.
  Edw. Now you are heir, therefore enjoy it now.
By giving the house of Lancaster leave to breathe,
It will outrun you, father, in the end.   14
  York. I took an oath that he should quietly reign.
  Edw. But for a kingdom any oath may be broken.
I would break a thousand oaths to reign one year.
  Rich. No; God forbid your Grace should be fore-
sworn.
  York. I shall be, if I claim by open war.
  Rich. I'll prove the contrary, if you'll hear me
speak.   20
  York. Thou canst not, son; it is impossible.
  Rich. An oath is of no moment, being not took
Before a true and lawful magistrate
That hath authority over him that swears.
Henry had none, but did usurp the place.   25
Then, seeing 'twas he that made you to depose,
Your oath, my lord, is vain and frivolous.
Therefore, to arms! And, father, do but think
How sweet a thing it is to wear a crown,
Within whose circuit is Elysium   30
And all that poets feign of bliss and joy.
Why do we linger thus? I cannot rest
Until the white rose that I wear be dy'd
Even in the lukewarm blood of Henry's heart.
  York. Richard, enough; I will be King, or die. 35
Brother, thou shalt to London presently,
And whet on Warwick to this enterprise.
Thou, Richard, shalt to the Duke of Norfolk
And tell him privily of our intent.
You, Edward, shall unto my Lord Cobham, 40
With whom the Kentishmen will willingly rise.

In them I trust; for they are soldiers,
Witty, courteous, liberal, full of spirit.
While you are thus employ'd, what resteth more
But that I seek occasion how to rise,   45
And yet the King not privy to my drift,
Nor any of the house of Lancaster?

Enter [*a* MESSENGER].

But, stay, — What news? Why com'st thou in
such post?
  [*Mess.*] The Queen with all the northern earls and
lords
Intend here to besiege you in your castle.   50
She is hard by with twenty thousand men;
And therefore fortify your hold, my lord.
  York. Ay, with my sword. What! think'st thou
that we fear them?
Edward and Richard, you shall stay with me;
My brother Montague shall post to London. 55
Let noble Warwick, Cobham, and the rest,
Whom we have left protectors of the King,
With powerful policy strengthen themselves,
And trust not simple Henry nor his oaths.
  Mont. Brother, I go; I'll win them, fear it not. 60
And thus most humbly I do take my leave. [*Exit.*

Enter SIR JOHN MORTIMER *and* SIR HUGH
MORTIMER.

  York. Sir John and Sir Hugh Mortimer, mine
uncles,
You are come to Sandal in a happy hour;
The army of the Queen mean to besiege us.
  Sir John. She shall not need; we'll meet her in
the field.   65
  York. What, with five thousand men?
  Rich. Ay, with five hundred, father, for a need.
A woman 's general; what should we fear?
                              [*A march afar off.*
  Edw. I hear their drums. Let's set our men in
order,
And issue forth and bid them battle straight. 70
  York. Five men to twenty! Though the odds be
great,
I doubt not, uncle, of our victory.
Many a battle have I won in France
Whenas the enemy hath been ten to one;
Why should I not now have the like success? 75
                          [*Alarum. Exeunt.*

[SCENE III. *Field of battle betwixt Sandal Castle
and Wakefield.*]

[*Alarums.*] *Enter* RUTLAND *and his* TUTOR.

  Rut. Ah, whither shall I fly to scape their hands?
Ah, tutor, look where bloody Clifford comes!

Sc. ii, 37. **whet on:** incite. 44. **resteth:** remaineth. 47. S.D. [*a* MESSENGER] Q. *Gabriel* F. Perhaps the name of the
actor Gabriel Spencer.

Enter CLIFFORD [*and* Soldiers].

Clif. Chaplain, away! thy priesthood saves thy
        life.
As for the brat of this accursed duke,
Whose father slew my father, he shall die.   5
Tut. And I, my lord, will bear him company.
Clif. Soldiers, away with him!
Tut. Ah, Clifford, murder not this innocent child,
Lest thou be hated both of God and man!
        [*Exit* [*dragged off by soldiers*].
Clif. How now, is he dead already? Or is it fear
That makes him close his eyes? I'll open them.   11
Rut. So looks the pent-up lion o'er the wretch
That trembles under his devouring paws;
And so he walks, insulting o'er his prey,
And so he comes, to rend his limbs asunder.   15
Ah, gentle Clifford, kill me with thy sword
And not with such a cruel threat'ning look.
Sweet Clifford, hear me speak before I die.
I am too mean a subject for thy wrath.
Be thou reveng'd on men, and let me live.   20
    Clif. In vain thou speak'st, poor boy; my father's
        blood
Hath stopp'd the passage where thy words should
        enter.
Rut. Then let my father's blood open it again.
He is a man, and, Clifford, cope with him.
Clif. Had I thy brethren here, their lives and
        thine   25
Were not revenge sufficient for me;
No, if I digg'd up thy forefathers' graves
And hung their rotten coffins up in chains,
It could not slake mine ire nor ease my heart.
The sight of any of the house of York   30
Is as a fury to torment my soul;
And till I root out their accursed line
And leave not one alive, I live in hell.
Therefore —   [*Lifting his hand.*]
Rut. O, let me pray before I take my death!   35
To thee I pray; sweet Clifford, pity me!
Clif. Such pity as my rapier's point affords.
Rut. I never did thee harm; why wilt thou slay
        me?
Clif. Thy father hath.
Rut.   But 'twas ere I was born.
Thou hast one son; for his sake pity me,   40
Lest in revenge thereof, sith God is just,
He be as miserably slain as I.
Ah, let me live in prison all my days;
And when I give occasion of offence,
Then let me die, for now thou hast no cause.   45
    Clif. No cause!
Thy father slew my father; therefore, die.
                                    [*Stabs him.*]

Rut. Di faciant laudis summa sit ista tuæ! [*Dies.*]
Clif. Plantagenet! I come, Plantagenet!
And this thy son's blood cleaving to my blade   50
Shall rust upon my weapon, till thy blood,
Congeal'd with this, do make me wipe off both.
                                        [*Exit.*

[SCENE IV. *Another part of the field.*]

Alarum. Enter the DUKE OF YORK.

York. The army of the Queen hath got the field.
My uncles both are slain in rescuing me,
And all my followers to the eager foe
Turn back and fly, like ships before the wind
Or lambs pursu'd by hunger-starved wolves.   5
My sons, God knows what hath bechanced them;
But this I know, they have demean'd themselves
Like men born to renown by life or death.
Three times did Richard make a lane to me,
And thrice cried, "Courage, father! fight it out!" 10
And full as oft came Edward to my side
With purple falchion, painted to the hilt
In blood of those that had encount'red him.
And when the hardiest warriors did retire,
Richard cried, "Charge! and give no foot of
        ground!"   15
And cried, "A crown, or else a glorious tomb!
A sceptre, or an earthly sepulchre!"
With this we charg'd again; but, out, alas!
We budg'd again; as I have seen a swan
With bootless labour swim against the tide   20
And spend her strength with over-matching waves.
                            [*A short alarum within.*
Ah, hark! the fatal followers do pursue,
And I am faint and cannot fly their fury;
And were I strong, I would not shun their fury.
The sands are numb'red that makes up my life;   25
Here must I stay, and here my life must end.

Enter QUEEN MARGARET, CLIFFORD, NORTHUM-
    BERLAND, *the young* PRINCE, *and* Soldiers.

Come bloody Clifford, rough Northumberland,
I dare your quenchless fury to more rage.
I am your butt, and I abide your shot.
North. Yield to our mercy, proud Plantagenet.   30
Clif. Ay, to such mercy as his ruthless arm
With downright payment show'd unto my father.
Now Phaëthon hath tumbled from his car,
And made an evening at the noontide prick.
York. My ashes, as the phœnix, may bring forth
A bird that will revenge upon you all;   36
And in that hope I throw mine eyes to heaven,
Scorning whate'er you can afflict me with.
Why come you not? What! multitudes, and fear?

Sc. iii, 48. *Di ... tuæ:* "The gods grant that this be the summit of thy glory." (Ovid.)
Sc. iv, 2. **uncles:** Sir John and Sir Hugh Mortimer. 19. **budg'd:** gave way. 29. **butt:** target. 34. **prick:** point. 36.
bird: young one.

Clif. So cowards fight when they can fly no
    further;   40
So doves do peck the falcon's piercing talons;
So desperate thieves, all hopeless of their lives,
Breathe out invectives 'gainst the officers.
    York. O Clifford, but bethink thee once again,
And in thy thought o'er-run my former time;   45
And, if thou canst for blushing, view this face,
And bite thy tongue, that slanders him with cow-
    ardice,
Whose frown hath made thee faint and fly ere this!
    Clif. I will not bandy with thee word for word,
But buckle with thee blows, twice two for one. 50
    Q. Mar. Hold, valiant Clifford! for a thousand
    causes
I would prolong a while the traitor's life.
Wrath makes him deaf; speak thou, Northumber-
    land.
    North. Hold, Clifford! do not honour him so
    much
To prick thy finger, though to wound his heart. 55
What valour were it, when a cur doth grin,
For one to thrust his hand between his teeth
When he might spurn him with his foot away?
It is war's prize to take all vantages;
And ten to one is no impeach of valour.   60
    [They lay hands on York, who struggles.]
    Clif. Ay, ay, so strives the woodcock with the gin.
    North. So doth the cony struggle in the net.
    York. So triumph thieves upon their conquer'd
    booty;
So true men yield, with robbers so o'ermatch'd.
    North. What would your Grace have done unto
    him now?   65
    Q. Mar. Brave warriors, Clifford and Northum-
    berland,
Come, make him stand upon this molehill here
That raught at mountains with outstretched arms,
Yet parted but the shadow with his hand.
What! was it you that would be England's king? 70
Was't you that revell'd in our parliament,
And made a preachment of your high descent?
Where are your mess of sons to back you now,
The wanton Edward, and the lusty George?
And where's that valiant crook-back prodigy, 75
Dicky your boy, that with his grumbling voice
Was wont to cheer his dad in mutinies?
Or, with the rest, where is your darling Rutland?
Look, York! I stain'd this napkin with the blood
That valiant Clifford with his rapier's point 80
Made issue from the bosom of the boy;
And if thine eyes can water for his death,
I give thee this to dry thy cheeks withal.
Alas, poor York! but that I hate thee deadly,

I should lament thy miserable state.   85
I prithee, grieve, to make me merry, York.
What, hath thy fiery heart so parch'd thine entrails
That not a tear can fall for Rutland's death?
Why art thou patient, man? Thou shouldst be
    mad;
And I to make thee mad do mock thee thus. 90
Stamp, rave, and fret, that I may sing and dance.
Thou wouldst be fee'd, I see, to make me sport.
York cannot speak unless he wear a crown.
A crown for York! and, lords, bow low to him;
Hold you his hands whilst I do set it on. 95
    [Putting a paper crown on his head.]
Ay, marry, sir, now looks he like a king!
Ay, this is he that took King Henry's chair,
And this is he was his adopted heir.
But how is it that great Plantagenet
Is crown'd so soon, and broke his solemn oath? 100
As I bethink me, you should not be King
Till our King Henry had shook hands with death.
And will you pale your head in Henry's glory,
And rob his temples of the diadem
Now in his life, against your holy oath? 105
O, 'tis a fault too too unpardonable!
Off with the crown; and, with the crown, his head;
And, whilst we breathe, take time to do him dead.
    Clif. That is my office, for my father's sake.
    Q. Mar. Nay, stay; let's hear the orisons he
    makes.   110
    York. She-wolf of France, but worse than wolves
    of France,
Whose tongue more poisons than the adder's tooth!
How ill-beseeming is it in thy sex
To triumph like an Amazonian trull
Upon their woes whom fortune captivates! 115
But that thy face is visard-like, unchanging,
Made impudent with use of evil deeds,
I would assay, proud queen, to make thee blush.
To tell thee whence thou cam'st, of whom deriv'd,
Were shame enough to shame thee, wert thou not
    shameless.   120
Thy father bears the type of King of Naples,
Of both the Sicils and Jerusalem,
Yet not so wealthy as an English yeoman.
Hath that poor monarch taught thee to insult?
It needs not, nor it boots thee not, proud queen, 125
Unless the adage must be verifi'd,
That beggars mounted run their horse to death.
'Tis beauty that doth oft make women proud,
But God he knows thy share thereof is small.
'Tis virtue that doth make them most admir'd;
The contrary doth make thee wond'red at. 131
'Tis government that makes them seem divine;
The want thereof makes thee abominable.

---

45. **o'er-run:** survey. 50. **buckle:** engage. 60. **impeach:** accusation (of lack of). 68. **raught:** reached. 71. **revell'd:**
rioted. 73. **mess:** set of four. 103. **pale:** enclose. 114. **trull:** virago. 115. **captivates:** subdues. 121. **type:** title. 132.
government: self-control.

Thou art as opposite to every good
As the Antipodes are unto us,   135
Or as the south to the septentrion.
O tiger's heart wrapt in a woman's hide!
How couldst thou drain the life-blood of the child,
To bid the father wipe his eyes withal,
And yet be seen to wear a woman's face?   140
Women are soft, mild, pitiful, and flexible.
Thou stern, obdurate, flinty, rough, remorseless.
Bid'st thou me rage? Why, now thou hast thy
   wish.
Wouldst have me weep? Why, now thou hast thy
   will;
For raging wind blows up incessant showers,   145
And when the rage allays the rain begins.
These tears are my sweet Rutland's obsequies;
And every drop cries vengeance for his death
'Gainst thee, fell Clifford, and thee, false French-
   woman.
   North. Beshrew me, but his passion moves me so
That hardly can I check my eyes from tears.   151
   York. That face of his the hungry cannibals
Would not have touch'd, would not have stain'd
   with blood;
But you are more inhuman, more inexorable,
O, ten times more, than tigers of Hyrcania.   155
See, ruthless queen, a hapless father's tears!
This cloth thou dipp'dst in blood of my sweet boy,
And I with tears do wash the blood away.
Keep thou the napkin and go boast of this;
And if thou tell'st the heavy story right,   160
Upon my soul, the hearers will shed tears,
Yea, even my foes will shed fast-falling tears,
And say, "Alas, it was a piteous deed!"
There, take the crown, and, with the crown, my
   curse;
And in thy need such comfort come to thee   165
As now I reap at thy too cruel hand!
Hard-hearted Clifford, take me from the world.
My soul to heaven, my blood upon your heads!
   North. Had he been slaughter-man to all my kin,
I should not for my life but weep with him,   170
To see how inly sorrow gripes his soul.
   Q. Mar. What, weeping-ripe, my Lord North-
   umberland?
Think but upon the wrong he did us all,
And that will quickly dry thy melting tears.
   Clif. Here's for my oath, here's for my father's
   death.   [*Stabbing him.*] 175
   Q. Mar. And here's to right our gentle-hearted
   king.   [*Stabbing him.*]
   York. Open Thy gate of mercy, gracious God!
My soul flies through these wounds to seek out Thee.
                                                      [*Dies.*]

   Q. Mar. Off with his head, and set it on York
   gates;
So York may overlook the town of York.   180
                                   [*Flourish. Exeunt.*]

[ACT II]

[SCENE I. *A plain near Mortimer's Cross in
   Herefordshire.*]

A march.   Enter EDWARD, RICHARD, *and their
   power.*

   Edw. I wonder how our princely father scap'd,
Or whether he be scap'd away or no
From Clifford's and Northumberland's pursuit:
Had he been ta'en, we should have heard the news;
Had he been slain, we should have heard the news:
Or had he scap'd, methinks we should have heard   6
The happy tidings of his good escape.
How fares my brother? Why is he so sad?
   Rich. I cannot joy, until I be resolv'd
Where our right valiant father is become.   10
I saw him in the battle range about,
And watch'd him how he singled Clifford forth.
Methought he bore him in the thickest troop
As doth a lion in a herd of neat;
Or as a bear, encompass'd round with dogs,   15
Who having pinch'd a few and made them cry,
The rest stand all aloof and bark at him.
So far'd our father with his enemies;
So fled his enemies my warlike father.
Methinks, 'tis prize enough to be his son.   20
See how the morning opes her golden gates,
And takes her farewell of the glorious sun!
How well resembles it the prime of youth,
Trimm'd like a younker prancing to his love!
   Edw. Dazzle mine eyes, or do I see three suns? 25
   Rich. Three glorious suns, each one a perfect sun,
Not separated with the racking clouds,
But sever'd in a pale clear-shining sky.
See, see! they join, embrace, and seem to kiss,
As if they vow'd some league inviolable.   30
Now are they but one lamp, one light, one sun.
In this the heaven figures some event.
   Edw. 'Tis wondrous strange, the like yet never
   heard of.
I think it cites us, brother, to the field,
That we, the sons of brave Plantagenet,   35
Each one already blazing by our meeds,
Should notwithstanding join our lights together
And over-shine the earth as this the world.
Whate'er it bodes, henceforward will I bear
Upon my target three fair-shining suns.   40

136. **septentrion:** north.   155. **Hyrcania.** South of the Caspian Sea.   171. **inly:** inward.
   Act II, sc. i, 14. **neat:** oxen.   24. **younker:** stripling.   27. **racking:** driving.   32. **figures:** prefigures, portends.   34. **cites:**
urges.   36. **meeds:** deserts.

Rich. Nay, bear three daughters; by your leave I
    speak it,
You love the breeder better than the male.

Enter [a MESSENGER] *blowing.*

But what art thou, whose heavy looks foretell
Some dreadful story hanging on thy tongue?
   Mess. Ah, one that was a woeful looker-on   45
When as the noble Duke of York was slain,
Your princely father and my loving lord!
   Edw. O, speak no more, for I have heard too
    much.
   Rich. Say how he died, for I will hear it all.
   Mess. Environed he was with many foes,   50
And stood against them, as the hope of Troy
Against the Greeks that would have ent'red Troy.
But Hercules himself must yield to odds;
And many strokes, though with a little axe,
Hews down and fells the hardest-timber'd oak.   55
By many hands your father was subdu'd;
But only slaught'red by the ireful arm
Of unrelenting Clifford and the Queen,
Who crown'd the gracious duke in high despite,
Laugh'd in his face; and when with grief he wept,   60
The ruthless queen gave him to dry his cheeks
A napkin steeped in the harmless blood
Of sweet young Rutland, by rough Clifford slain.
And after many scorns, many foul taunts,
They took his head, and on the gates of York   65
They set the same; and there it doth remain,
The saddest spectacle that e'er I view'd.
   Edw. Sweet Duke of York, our prop to lean upon,
Now thou art gone we have no staff, no stay.
O Clifford, boist'rous Clifford! thou hast slain   70
The flower of Europe for his chivalry;
And treacherously hast thou vanquish'd him,
For hand to hand he would have vanquish'd thee.
Now my soul's palace is become a prison;
Ah, would she break from hence, that this my body
Might in the ground be closed up in rest!   76
For never henceforth shall I joy again,
Never, O never, shall I see more joy!
   Rich. I cannot weep, for all my body's moisture
Scarce serves to quench my furnace-burning heart;
Nor can my tongue unload my heart's great burden,
For self-same wind that I should speak withal   82
Is kindling coals that fires all my breast
And burns me up with flames that tears would
    quench.
To weep is to make less the depth of grief.   85
Tears then for babes; blows and revenge for me.
Richard, I bear thy name; I'll venge thy death,
Or die renowned by attempting it.
   Edw. His name that valiant duke hath left with
    thee;

His dukedom and his chair with me is left.   90
   Rich. Nay, if thou be that princely eagle's bird,
Show thy descent by gazing 'gainst the sun;
For chair and dukedom, throne and kingdom say,
Either that is thine, or else thou wert not his.

March. Enter WARWICK, MARQUESS OF MON-
    TAGUE, *and their army.*

   War. How now, fair lords! What fare? What
    news abroad?   95
   Rich. Great Lord of Warwick, if we should re-
    count
Our baleful news, and at each word's deliverance
Stab poniards in our flesh till all were told,
The words would add more anguish than the
    wounds.
O valiant lord, the Duke of York is slain!   100
   Edw. O Warwick, Warwick! that Plantagenet,
Which held thee dearly as his soul's redemption,
Is by the stern Lord Clifford done to death.
   War. Ten days ago I drown'd these news in
    tears;
And now, to add more measure to your woes,   105
I come to tell you things sith then befall'n.
After the bloody fray at Wakefield fought,
Where your brave father breath'd his latest gasp,
Tidings, as swiftly as the posts could run,
Were brought me of your loss and his depart.   110
I, then in London, keeper of the King,
Muster'd my soldiers, gathered flocks of friends,
[And very well appointed, as I thought,]
March'd toward Saint Alban's to intercept the
    Queen,
Bearing the King in my behalf along;   115
For by my scouts I was advertised
That she was coming with a full intent
To dash our late decree in parliament
Touching King Henry's oath and your succession.
Short tale to make, we at Saint Alban's met,   120
Our battles join'd, and both sides fiercely fought.
But whether 'twas the coldness of the King,
Who look'd full gently on his warlike queen,
That robb'd my soldiers of their heated spleen;
Or whether 'twas report of her success;   125
Or more than common fear of Clifford's rigour,
Who thunders to his captives blood and death,
I cannot judge; but, to conclude with truth,
Their weapons like to lightning came and went;
Our soldiers', like the night-owl's lazy flight,   130
Or like [an idle] thresher with a flail,
Fell gently down, as if they struck their friends.
I cheer'd them up with justice of our cause,
With promise of high pay and great rewards;
But all in vain; they had no heart to fight,   135
And we in them no hope to win the day,

---

42. S.D. [a MESSENGER] (Rowe). *one* F.   51. **hope of Troy:** Hector.   70. **boist'rous:** savage.   113. [And ... thought] Q.
Om. F.   131. [an idle] Q.   *a lazy* F.

So that we fled; the King unto the Queen;
Lord George your brother, Norfolk, and myself,
In haste, post-haste, are come to join with you;
For in the marches here we heard you were,   140
Making another head to fight again.
    Edw. Where is the Duke of Norfolk, gentle War-
    wick?
And when came George from Burgundy to England?
    War. Some six miles off the Duke is with the
    soldiers;
And for your brother, he was lately sent   145
From your kind aunt, Duchess of Burgundy,
With aid of soldiers to this needful war.
    Rich. 'Twas odds, belike, when valiant Warwick
    fled.
Oft have I heard his praises in pursuit,
But ne'er till now his scandal of retire.   150
    War. Nor now my scandal, Richard, dost thou
    hear;
For thou shalt know this strong right hand of
    mine
Can pluck the diadem from faint Henry's head,
And wring the awful sceptre from his fist,
Were he as famous and as bold in war   155
As he is famed for mildness, peace, and prayer.
    Rich. I know it well, Lord Warwick; blame me
    not.
'Tis love I bear thy glories make me speak.
But in this troublous time what's to be done?
Shall we go throw away our coats of steel   160
And wrap our bodies in black mourning gowns,
Numb'ring our Ave-Maries with our beads?
Or shall we on the helmets of our foes
Tell our devotion with revengeful arms?
If for the last, say ay, and to it, lords.   165
    War. Why, therefore Warwick came to seek you
    out;
And therefore comes my brother Montague.
Attend me, lords. The proud insulting queen,
With Clifford and the haught Northumberland,
And of their feather many moe proud birds,   170
Have wrought the easy-melting king like wax.
He swore consent to your succession,
His oath enrolled in the parliament;
And now to London all the crew are gone
To frustrate both his oath and what beside   175
May make against the house of Lancaster.
Their power, I think, is thirty thousand strong.
Now, if the help of Norfolk and myself,
With all the friends that thou, brave Earl of March,
Amongst the loving Welshmen canst procure,   180
Will but amount to five and twenty thousand,
Why, Via! to London will we march,
And once again bestride our foaming steeds,
And once again cry "Charge!" upon our foes
But never once again turn back and fly.   185

    Rich. Ay, now methinks I hear great Warwick
    speak.
Ne'er may he live to see a sunshine day
That cries "Retire!" if Warwick bid him stay.
    Edw. Lord Warwick, on thy shoulder will I lean;
And when thou fail'st — as God forbid the hour! —
Must Edward fall, which peril Heaven forfend!   191
    War. No longer Earl of March, but Duke of
    York;
The next degree is England's royal throne,
For King of England shalt thou be proclaim'd
In every borough as we pass along;   195
And he that throws not up his cap for joy
Shall for the fault make forfeit of his head.
King Edward, valiant Richard, Montague,
Stay we no longer, dreaming of renown,
But sound the trumpets, and about our task.   200
    Rich. Then, Clifford, were thy heart as hard as
    steel,
As thou hast shown it flinty by thy deeds,
I come to pierce it or to give thee mine.
    Edw. Then strike up drums. God and Saint
    George for us!

         Enter a MESSENGER

    War. How now! what news?   205
    Mess. The Duke of Norfolk sends you word by
    me
The Queen is coming with a puissant host;
And craves your company for speedy counsel.
    War. Why then it sorts. Brave warriors, let's
    away.   [*Exeunt.*

         [SCENE II. *Before York.*]

Flourish. Enter KING HENRY, QUEEN MARGARET,
    the PRINCE OF WALES, CLIFFORD, *and* NORTHUM-
    BERLAND, *with drum and trumpets.*

    Q. Mar. Welcome, my lord, to this brave town of
    York.
Yonder's the head of that arch-enemy
That sought to be encompass'd with your crown.
Doth not the object cheer your heart, my lord?
    K. Hen. Ay, as the rocks cheer them that fear
    their wreck.   5
To see this sight, it irks my very soul.
Withhold revenge, dear God! 'tis not my fault,
Nor wittingly have I infring'd my vow.
    Clif. My gracious liege, this too much lenity
And harmful pity must be laid aside.   10
To whom do lions cast their gentle looks?
Not to the beast that would usurp their den.
Whose hand is that the forest bear doth lick?
Not his that spoils her young before her face.
Who scapes the lurking serpent's mortal sting?   15
Not he that sets his foot upon her back.

---

140. **marches:** border-country.   170. **moe:** more.   182. **Via!:** On!   191. **forfend:** forbid.   209. **sorts:** fits.

The smallest worm will turn being trodden on,
And doves will peck in safeguard of their brood.
Ambitious York did level at thy crown,
Thou smiling while he knit his angry brows;　20
He, but a duke, would have his son a king,
And raise his issue like a loving sire;
Thou, being a king, blest with a goodly son,
Didst yield consent to disinherit him,
Which argued thee a most unloving father.　25
Unreasonable creatures feed their young;
And though man's face be fearful to their eyes,
Yet, in protection of their tender ones,
Who hath not seen them, even with those wings
Which sometime they have us'd with fearful flight,
Make war with him that climb'd unto their nest,　31
Offering their own lives in their young's defence?
For shame, my liege, make them your precedent!
Were it not pity that this goodly boy
Should lose his birthright by his father's fault,　35
And long hereafter say unto his child,
"What my great-grandfather and grandsire got
My careless father fondly gave away"?
Ah, what a shame were this!　Look on the boy;
And let his manly face, which promiseth　40
Successful fortune, steel thy melting heart
To hold thine own and leave thine own with him.
　K. Hen. Full well hath Clifford play'd the orator,
Inferring arguments of mighty force.
But, Clifford, tell me, didst thou never hear　45
That things ill-got had ever bad success?
And happy always was it for that son
Whose father for his hoarding went to hell?
I'll leave my son my virtuous deeds behind,
And would my father had left me no more!　50
For all the rest is held at such a rate
As brings a thousand-fold more care to keep
Than in possession any jot of pleasure.
Ah, cousin York! would thy best friends did know
How it doth grieve me that thy head is here!　55
　Q. Mar. My lord, cheer up your spirits! Our foes
　　are nigh,
And this soft courage makes your followers faint.
You promis'd knighthood to our forward son.
Unsheathe your sword, and dub him presently.
Edward, kneel down.　60
　K. Hen. Edward Plantagenet, arise a knight;
And learn this lesson, draw thy sword in right.
　Prince. My gracious father, by your kingly leave,
I'll draw it as apparent to the crown,
And in that quarrel use it to the death.　65
　Clif. Why, that is spoken like a toward prince.

Enter a MESSENGER.

　Mess. Royal commanders, be in readiness;
For with a band of thirty thousand men

Comes Warwick, backing of the Duke of York;
And in the towns, as they do march along,　70
Proclaims him king, and many fly to him.
Darraign your battle, for they are at hand.
　Clif. I would your Highness would depart the
　　field;
The Queen hath best success when you are absent.
　Q. Mar. Ay, good my lord, and leave us to our
　　fortune.　75
　K. Hen. Why, that's my fortune too; therefore
　　I'll stay.
　North. Be it with resolution then to fight.
　Prince. My royal father, cheer these noble lords
And hearten those that fight in your defence.
Unsheathe your sword, good father; cry "Saint
　　George!"　80

March. Enter EDWARD, GEORGE, RICHARD, WAR-
WICK, NORFOLK, MONTAGUE, *and* Soldiers.

　Edw. Now, perjur'd Henry! wilt thou kneel for
　　grace
And set thy diadem upon my head,
Or bide the mortal fortune of the field?
　Q. Mar. Go, rate thy minions, proud insulting
　　boy!
Becomes it thee to be thus bold in terms　85
Before thy sovereign and thy lawful king?
　Edw. I am his king, and he should bow his knee.
I was adopted heir by his consent;
Since when, his oath is broke; for, as I hear,
You, that are king though he do wear the crown,　90
Have caus'd him, by new act of parliament,
To blot out me, and put his own son in.
　Clif. And reason too.
Who should succeed the father but the son?
　Rich. Are you there, butcher?　O, I cannot
　　speak!　95
　Clif. Ay, crook-back, here I stand to answer thee,
Or any he the proudest of thy sort.
　Rich. 'Twas you that kill'd young Rutland, was
　　it not?
　Clif. Ay, and old York, and yet not satisfied.
　Rich. For God's sake, lords, give signal to the
　　fight.　100
　War. What say'st thou, Henry, wilt thou yield
　　the crown?
　Q. Mar. Why, how now, long-tongu'd Warwick!
　　dare you speak?
When you and I met at Saint Alban's last,
Your legs did better service than your hands.
　War. Then 'twas my turn to fly, and now 'tis
　　thine.　105
　Clif. You said so much before, and yet you fled.
　War. 'Twas not your valour, Clifford, drove me
　　thence.

Sc. ii, 19. level: aim.　44. Inferring: adducing.　59. presently: at once.　66. toward: bold.　72. Darraign: order.　89.
Since F2　Cla. Since F1.　97. sort: gang.

North. No, nor your manhood that durst make
    you stay.
Rich. Northumberland, I hold thee reverently.
Break off the parley; for scarce I can refrain   110
The execution of my big-swoln heart
Upon that Clifford, that cruel child-killer.
    Clif. I slew thy father, call'st thou him a child?
    Rich. Ay, like a dastard and a treacherous
    coward,
As thou didst kill our tender brother Rutland;   115
But ere sun set I'll make thee curse the deed.
    K. Hen. Have done with words, my lords, and
    hear me speak.
    Q. Mar. Defy them then, or else hold close thy
    lips.
    K. Hen. I prithee, give no limits to my tongue.
I am a king, and privileg'd to speak.   120
    Clif. My liege, the wound that bred this meeting
    here
Cannot be cur'd by words; therefore be still.
    Rich. Then, executioner, unsheathe thy sword.
By Him that made us all, I am resolv'd
That Clifford's manhood lies upon his tongue.   125
    Edw. Say, Henry, shall I have my right, or no?
A thousand men have broke their fasts to-day
That ne'er shall dine unless thou yield the crown.
    War. If thou deny, their blood upon thy head;
For York in justice puts his armour on.   130
    Prince. If that be right which Warwick says is
    right,
There is no wrong, but everything is right.
    [*Rich.*] Whoever got thee, there thy mother
    stands;
For, well I wot, thou hast thy mother's tongue.
    Q. Mar. But thou art neither like thy sire nor
    dam,   135
But like a foul mis-shapen stigmatic,
Mark'd by the destinies to be avoided
As venom toads, or lizards' dreadful stings.
    Rich. Iron of Naples hid with English gilt,
Whose father bears the title of a king, —   140
As if a channel should be call'd the sea —
Sham'st thou not, knowing whence thou art ex-
    traught,
To let thy tongue detect thy base-born heart?
    Edw. A wisp of straw were worth a thousand
    crowns
To make this shameless callet know herself.   145
Helen of Greece was fairer far than thou,
Although thy husband may be Menelaus;
And ne'er was Agamemnon's brother wrong'd
By that false woman as this king by thee.
His father revell'd in the heart of France   150

And tam'd the King and made the Dauphin stoop;
And had he match'd according to his state,
He might have kept that glory to this day;
But when he took a beggar to his bed,
And grac'd thy poor sire with his bridal-day,   155
Even then that sunshine brew'd a shower for him,
That wash'd his father's fortunes forth of France
And heap'd sedition on his crown at home.
For what hath broach'd this tumult but thy pride?
Hadst thou been meek, our title still had slept;   160
And we, in pity of the gentle king,
Had slipp'd our claim until another age.
    Geo. But when we saw our sunshine made thy
    spring,
And that thy summer bred us no increase,
We set the axe to thy usurping root;   165
And though the edge hath something hit ourselves,
Yet, know thou, since we have begun to strike,
We'll never leave till we have hewn thee down,
Or bath'd thy growing with our heated bloods.
    Edw. And, in this resolution, I defy thee,   170
Not willing any longer conference,
Since thou denied'st the gentle king to speak.
Sound trumpets! Let our bloody colours wave!
And either victory, or else a grave.
    Q. Mar. Stay, Edward.   175
    Edw. No, wrangling woman, we'll no longer stay.
These words will cost ten thousand lives this day.
                          [*Exeunt.*

[SCENE III.   *A field of battle between Towton and*
                    Saxton, in Yorkshire.]

    Alarum. Excursions. Enter WARWICK.

    War. Forspent with toil, as runners with a race,
I lay me down a little while to breathe;
For strokes receiv'd and many blows repaid
Have robb'd my strong-knit sinews of their strength,
And spite of spite needs must I rest a while.   5

    Enter EDWARD, *running.*

    Edw. Smile, gentle heaven! or strike, ungentle
    death!
For this world frowns, and Edward's sun is clouded.
    War. How now, my lord! what hap? What hope
    of good?

    Enter GEORGE

    Geo. Our hap is loss, our hope but sad despair;
Our ranks are broke and ruin follows us.   10
What counsel give you? Whither shall we fly?

---

133. [*Rich.*] Q. *War.* F. 136. **stigmatic:** one marked with deformity. 141. **channel:** gutter. 142. **extraught:** extracted,
derived. 143. **detect:** expose. 144. **wisp of straw:** mark of disgrace for a scold. 145. **callet:** strumpet. 150. **broach'd:**
set going; lit., tapped and left running. 162. **slipp'd:** let slide.
    Sc. iii, 1. **Forspent:** exhausted.

Edw. Bootless is flight, they follow us with wings;
And weak we are and cannot shun pursuit.

Enter RICHARD.

Rich. Ah, Warwick, why hast thou withdrawn
     thyself?
Thy brother's blood the thirsty earth hath
     drunk,   15
Broach'd with the steely point of Clifford's lance;
And in the very pangs of death he cried,
Like to a dismal clangor heard from far,
"Warwick, revenge! brother, revenge my death!"
So, underneath the belly of their steeds,   20
That stain'd their fetlocks in his smoking blood,
The noble gentleman gave up the ghost.
War. Then let the earth be drunken with our
     blood!
I'll kill my horse, because I will not fly.
Why stand we like soft-hearted women here,   25
Wailing our losses, whiles the foe doth rage;
And look upon, as if the tragedy
Were play'd in jest by counterfeiting actors?
Here on my knee I vow to God above
I'll never pause again, never stand still,   30
Till either death hath clos'd these eyes of mine
Or fortune given me measure of revenge.
Edw. O Warwick, I do bend my knee with thine;
And in this vow do chain my soul to thine!
— And, ere my knee rise from the earth's cold
     face,   35
I throw my hands, mine eyes, my heart to Thee,
Thou setter up and plucker down of kings,
Beseeching Thee, if with Thy will it stands
That to my foes this body must be prey,
Yet that Thy brazen gates of heaven may ope   40
And give sweet passage to my sinful soul!
Now, lords, take leave until we meet again,
Where'er it be, in heaven or in earth.
Rich. Brother, give me thy hand; and, gentle
     Warwick,
Let me embrace thee in my weary arms.   45
I, that did never weep, now melt with woe
That winter should cut off our spring-time so.
War. Away, away! Once more, sweet lords,
     farewell.
Geo. Yet let us all together to our troops,
And give them leave to fly that will not stay, 50
And call them pillars that will stand to us;
And, if we thrive, promise them such rewards
As victors wear at the Olympian games.
This may plant courage in their quailing breast;
For yet is hope of life and victory.   55
Forslow no longer, make we hence amain.
                                        [*Exeunt.*

[SCENE IV.   *Another part of the field.*]

Excursions. Enter RICHARD *and* CLIFFORD.

Rich. Now, Clifford, I have singled thee alone.
Suppose this arm is for the Duke of York,
And this for Rutland; both bound to revenge,
Wert thou environ'd with a brazen wall.
Clif. Now, Richard, I am with thee here alone. 5
This is the hand that stabb'd thy father York;
And this the hand that slew thy brother Rutland;
And here's the heart that triumphs in their death
And cheers these hands that slew thy sire and
     brother
To execute the like upon thyself.   10
And so, have at thee!
          [*They fight. Warwick comes; Clifford flies.*
Rich. Nay, Warwick, single out some other chase;
For I myself will hunt this wolf to death. [*Exeunt.*

[SCENE V.   *Another part of the field.*]

Alarum. Enter KING HENRY *alone.*

K. Hen. This battle fares like to the morning's
     war,
When dying clouds contend with growing light,
What time the shepherd, blowing of his nails,
Can neither call it perfect day nor night.
Now sways it this way, like a mighty sea   5
Forc'd by the tide to combat with the wind;
Now sways it that way, like the self-same sea
Forc'd to retire by fury of the wind.
Sometime the flood prevails, and then the wind;
Now one the better, then another best;   10
Both tugging to be victors, breast to breast,
Yet neither conqueror nor conquered;
So is the equal poise of this fell war.
Here on this molehill will I sit me down.
To whom God will, there be the victory!   15
For Margaret my queen, and Clifford too,
Have chid me from the battle; swearing both
They prosper best of all when I am thence.
Would I were dead! if God's good will were so;
For what is in this world but grief and woe?   20
O God! methinks it were a happy life
To be no better than a homely swain;
To sit upon a hill, as I do now,
To carve out dials quaintly, point by point,
Thereby to see the minutes how they run,   25
How many makes the hour full complete,
How many hours brings about the day,
How many days will finish up the year,
How many years a mortal man may live.
When this is known, then to divide the times: 30
So many hours must I tend my flock,
So many hours must I take my rest.

16. **Broach'd.** See II.ii.159, note. 56. **Forslow:** delay.
Sc. iv, 1. singled: chosen. 12. **chase:** game.

So many hours must I contemplate,
So many hours must I sport myself;
So many days my ewes have been with young, 35
So many weeks ere the poor fools will ean,
So many years ere I shall shear the fleece.
So minutes, hours, days, months, and years,
Pass'd over to the end they were created,
Would bring white hairs unto a quiet grave. 40
Ah, what a life were this! how sweet! how lovely!
Gives not the hawthorn-bush a sweeter shade
To shepherds looking on their silly sheep
Than doth a rich embroider'd canopy
To kings that fear their subjects' treachery? 45
O, yes, it doth, a thousand-fold it doth.
And to conclude, the shepherd's homely curds,
His cold thin drink out of his leather bottle,
His wonted sleep under a fresh tree's shade,
All which secure and sweetly he enjoys, 50
Is far beyond a prince's delicates, —
His viands sparkling in a golden cup,
His body couched in a curious bed,
When Care, Mistrust, and Treason waits on him.

Alarum. Enter a SON *that hath killed his father*
[dragging in the dead body].

  Son. Ill blows the wind that profits nobody. 55
This man whom hand to hand I slew in fight
May be possessed with some store of crowns;
And I, that haply take them from him now,
May yet ere night yield both my life and them
To some man else, as this dead man doth me. 60
Who's this? O God! it is my father's face,
Whom in this conflict I unwares have kill'd.
O heavy times, begetting such events!
From London by the King was I press'd forth;
My father, being the Earl of Warwick's man, 65
Came on the part of York, press'd by his master;
And I, who at his hands receiv'd my life,
Have by my hands of life bereaved him.
Pardon me, God, I knew not what I did!
And pardon, father, for I knew not thee! 70
My tears shall wipe away these bloody marks;
And no more words till they have flow'd their fill.
  K. Hen. O piteous spectacle! O bloody times!
Whiles lions war and battle for their dens,
Poor harmless lambs abide their enmity. 75
Weep, wretched man, I'll aid thee tear for tear;
And let our hearts and eyes, like civil war,
Be blind with tears, and break o'ercharg'd with
  grief.

Enter a FATHER, *bearing of his son.*

  Fath. Thou that so stoutly hast resisted me,
Give me thy gold, if thou hast any gold, 80
For I have bought it with an hundred blows.

But let me see: is this our foeman's face?
Ah, no, no, no, it is mine only son!
Ah, boy, if any life be left in thee,
Throw up thine eye! See, see what showers arise,
Blown with the windy tempest of my heart 86
Upon thy wounds, that kills mine eye and heart!
O, pity, God, this miserable age!
What stratagems, how fell, how butcherly,
Erroneous, mutinous, and unnatural, 90
This deadly quarrel daily doth beget!
O boy, thy father gave thee life too soon,
And hath bereft thee of thy life too late!
  K. Hen. Woe above woe! grief more than com-
  mon grief!
O that my death would stay these ruthful deeds! 95
O, pity, pity, gentle heaven, pity!
The red rose and the white are on his face,
The fatal colours of our striving houses;
The one his purple blood right well resembles,
The other his pale cheeks, methinks, presenteth. 100
Wither one rose, and let the other flourish;
If you contend, a thousand lives must wither.
  Son. How will my mother for a father's death
Take on with me and ne'er be satisfi'd!
  Fath. How will my wife for slaughter of my son
Shed seas of tears and ne'er be satisfi'd! 106
  K. Hen. How will the country for these woeful
  chances
Misthink the King and not be satisfi'd!
  Son. Was ever son so ru'd a father's death?
  Fath. Was ever father so bemoan'd his son? 110
  K. Hen. Was ever king so griev'd for subjects'
  woe?
Much is your sorrow; mine ten times so much.
  Son. I'll bear thee hence, where I may weep my
  fill.   *[Exit with the body.*
  Fath. These arms of mine shall be thy winding-
  sheet;
My heart, sweet boy, shall be thy sepulchre, 115
For from my heart thine image ne'er shall go;
My sighing breast shall be thy funeral bell;
And so obsequious will thy father be,
[E'en] for the loss of thee, having no more,
As Priam was for all his valiant sons. 120
I'll bear thee hence; and let them fight that will,
For I have murdered where I should not kill.
                 [Exit [with the body].
  K. Hen. Sad-hearted men, much overgone with
  care,
Here sits a king more woeful than you are.

Alarums. Excursions. Enter QUEEN MARGARET,
the PRINCE, *and* EXETER.

  Prince. Fly, father, fly! for all your friends are
  fled, 125

Sc. v, 36. **ean:** yean, bring forth. 43. **silly:** feeble, helpless. 51. **delicates:** delicacies. 53. **curious:** elaborate. 54, 66.
press'd: impressed, conscripted. 90. **Erroneous:** criminal. 108. **Misthink:** think ill of. 119. **[E'en]** (Collier MS.). *Men* F.

And Warwick rages like a chafed bull.
Away! for death doth hold us in pursuit.
    Q. Mar. Mount you, my lord; towards Berwick
      post amain.
Edward and Richard, like a brace of greyhounds
Having the fearful flying hare in sight,   130
With fiery eyes sparkling for very wrath,
And bloody steel grasp'd in their ireful hands,
Are at our backs; and therefore hence amain.
    Exe. Away! for vengeance comes along with
      them.
Nay, stay not to expostulate, make speed;   135
Or else come after. I'll away before.
    K. Hen. Nay, take me with thee, good sweet
      Exeter;
Not that I fear to stay, but love to go
Whither the Queen intends.   Forward; away!
                             [Exeunt.

       [SCENE VI. *Another part of the field.*]

    A loud alarum. Enter CLIFFORD, *wounded.*

    Clif. Here burns my candle out; ay, here it
      dies,
Which, whiles it lasted, gave King Henry light.
O Lancaster, I fear thy overthrow
More than my body's parting with my soul!
My love and fear glu'd many friends to thee,   5
And, now I fall, thy tough commixtures melts,
Impairing Henry, strength'ning misproud York.
[The common people swarm like summer flies;]
And whither fly the gnats but to the sun?
And who shines now but Henry's enemies?   10
O Phœbus, hadst thou never given consent
That Phaëthon should check thy fiery steeds,
Thy burning car never had scorch'd the earth!
And, Henry, hadst thou sway'd as kings should do,
Or as thy father and his father did,   15
Giving no ground unto the house of York,
They never then had sprung like summer flies;
I and ten thousand in this luckless realm
Had left no mourning widows for our death;
And thou this day hadst kept thy chair in peace.   20
For what doth cherish weeds but gentle air?
And what makes robbers bold but too much lenity?
Bootless are plaints, and cureless are my wounds.
No way to fly, nor strength to hold out flight.
The foe is merciless, and will not pity,   25
For at their hands I have deserv'd no pity.
The air hath got into my deadly wounds,
And much effuse of blood doth make me faint.
Come, York and Richard, Warwick and the rest;
I stabb'd your fathers' bosoms, split my breast.
                         [He faints.]

    Alarum and retreat. Enter EDWARD, GEORGE,
      RICHARD, MONTAGUE, WARWICK, *and* Soldiers.
    Edw. Now breathe we, lords; good fortune bids
      us pause   31
And smooth the frowns of war with peaceful looks.
Some troops pursue the bloody-minded queen
That led calm Henry, though he were a king,
As doth a sail, fill'd with a fretting gust,   35
Command an argosy to stem the waves.
But think you, lords, that Clifford fled with them?
    War. No, 'tis impossible he should escape;
For, though before his face I speak the words,
Your brother Richard mark'd him for the grave;   40
And wheresoe'er he is, he's surely dead.
              [Clifford groans [and dies].
    Rich. Whose soul is that which takes her heavy
      leave?
A deadly groan, like life and death's departing.
See who it is.
    Edw.   And, now the battle's ended,
If friend or foe, let him be gently used.   45
    Rich. Revoke that doom of mercy, for 'tis Clifford
Who, not contented that he lopp'd the branch
In hewing Rutland when his leaves put forth,
But set his murd'ring knife unto the root
From whence that tender spray did sweetly spring,
I mean our princely father, Duke of York.   51
    War. From off the gates of York fetch down the
      head,
Your father's head, which Clifford placed there;
Instead whereof let this supply the room.
Measure for measure must be answered.   55
    Edw. Bring forth that fatal screech-owl to our
      house
That nothing sung but death to us and ours.
Now death shall stop his dismal threat'ning sound,
And his ill-boding tongue no more shall speak.
    War. I think his understanding is bereft.   60
Speak, Clifford, dost thou know who speaks to
    thee?
Dark cloudy death o'ershades his beams of life,
And he nor sees nor hears us what we say.
    Rich. O, would he did! and so perhaps he doth.
'Tis but his policy to counterfeit   65
Because he would avoid such bitter taunts
Which in the time of death he gave our father.
    Geo. If so thou think'st, vex him with eager
      words.
    Rich. Clifford, ask mercy and obtain no grace.
    Edw. Clifford, repent in bootless penitence.   70
    War. Clifford, devise excuses for thy faults.
    Geo. While we devise fell tortures for thy faults.
    Rich. Thou didst love York, and I am son to
      York.
    Edw. Thou pitied'st Rutland; I will pity thee.

   Sc. vi, **7. misproud:** arrogant. **8. [The ... flies]** Q. Om. F. **28. effuse:** pouring out. **36. argosy:** large merchant ship.
60. bereft: destroyed. **68. eager:** biting.

Geo. Where's Captain Margaret, to fence you
   now?   75
War. They mock thee, Clifford; swear as thou
   wast wont.
Rich. What, not an oath? Nay, then the world
   goes hard
When Clifford cannot spare his friends an oath.
I know by that he's dead; and, by my soul,
If this right hand would buy two hours' life   80
That I in all despite might rail at him,
This hand should chop it off, and with the issuing
   blood
Stifle the villain whose unstanched thirst
York and young Rutland could not satisfy.
   War. Ay, but he's dead. Off with the traitor's
   head,   85
And rear it in the place your father's stands.
And now to London with triumphant march,
There to be crowned England's royal king;
From whence shall Warwick cut the sea to France,
And ask the Lady Bona for thy queen.   90
So shalt thou sinew both these lands together;
And, having France thy friend, thou shalt not dread
The scatt'red foe that hopes to rise again;
For though they cannot greatly sting to hurt,
Yet look to have them buzz to offend thine ears.   95
First will I see the coronation;
And then to Brittany I'll cross the sea
To effect this marriage, so it please my lord.
   Edw. Even as thou wilt, sweet Warwick, let it be;
For in thy shoulder do I build my seat,   100
And never will I undertake the thing
Wherein thy counsel and consent is wanting.
Richard, I will create thee Duke of Gloucester,
And George, of Clarence. Warwick, as ourself,
Shall do and undo as him pleaseth best.   105
   Rich. Let me be Duke of Clarence, George of
   Gloucester;
For Gloucester's dukedom is too ominous.
   War. Tut, that's a foolish observation.
Richard, be Duke of Gloucester. Now to London
To see these honours in possession. [*Exeunt.* 110

[ACT III]

[Scene I. *A forest in the north of England.*]

Enter [*two* Keepers,] *with cross-bows in their
hands.*

[*1. Keep.*] Under this thick-grown brake we'll
   shroud ourselves,
For through this laund anon the deer will come;
And in this covert will we make our stand,
Culling the principal of all the deer.

[*2. Keep.*] I'll stay above the hill, so both may
   shoot.   5
   1. Keep. That cannot be; the noise of thy cross-
   bow
Will scare the herd, and so my shoot is lost.
Here stand we both and aim we at the best;
And, for the time shall not seem tedious,
I'll tell thee what befell me on a day   10
In this self place where now we mean to stand.
   2. Keep. Here comes a man; let's stay till he be
   past.

Enter King Henry *disguised, with a prayer-book.*

   K. Hen. From Scotland am I stol'n, even of pure
   love,
To greet mine own land with my wishful sight.
No, Harry, Harry, 'tis no land of thine;   15
Thy place is fill'd, thy sceptre wrung from thee,
Thy balm wash'd off wherewith thou was anointed.
No bending knee will call thee Cæsar now,
No humble suitors press to speak for right,
No, not a man comes for redress of thee;   20
For how can I help them and not myself?
   1. Keep. Ay, here's a deer whose skin's a keeper's
   fee.
This is the quondam king; let's seize upon him.
   K. Hen. Let me embrace [thee, sour Adversity],
For wise men say it is the wisest course.   25
   2. Keep. Why linger we? Let us lay hands upon
   him.
   1. Keep. Forbear a while; we'll hear a little more.
   K. Hen. My queen and son are gone to France
   for aid;
And, as I hear, the great commanding Warwick
Is thither gone to crave the French king's sister   30
To wife for Edward. If this news be true,
Poor queen and son, your labour is but lost;
For Warwick is a subtle orator,
And Lewis a prince soon won with moving words.
By this account, then, Margaret may win him,   35
For she's a woman to be pitied much.
Her sighs will make a batt'ry in his breast;
Her tears will pierce into a marble heart;
The tiger will be mild whiles she doth mourn;
And Nero will be tainted with remorse   40
To hear and see her plaints, her brinish tears.
Ay, but she's come to beg, Warwick, to give;
She, on his left side, craving aid for Henry,
He, on his right, asking a wife for Edward.
She weeps and says her Henry is depos'd;   45
He smiles, and says his Edward is install'd;
That she, poor wretch, for grief can speak no more;
Whiles Warwick tells his title, smooths the wrong,
Inferreth arguments of mighty strength,

Act III, sc. i, s.d. [*two* Keepers] Q. *Sinklo, and Humphrey* F. The names of these two actors appear in F as speech-tags throughout the scene for *1. Keep.* and *2. Keep.* respectively. 2. **laund:** glade. 24. [**thee, sour Adversity**] (Singer). *the sower Adversaries* F. 40. **tainted:** touched.

And in conclusion wins the King from her   50
With promise of his sister and what else,
To strengthen and support King Edward's place.
O Margaret, thus 'twill be; and thou, poor soul,
Art then forsaken, as thou went'st forlorn!

2. Keep. Say, what art thou [that] talk'st of
kings and queens?   55

K. Hen. More than I seem, and less than I was
born to.
A man at least, for less I should not be;
And men may talk of kings, and why not I?

2. Keep. Ay, but thou talk'st as if thou wert a
king.

K. Hen. Why, so I am, in mind; and that's
enough.   60

2. Keep. But, if thou be a king, where is thy
crown?

K. Hen. My crown is in my heart, not on my
head;
Not deck'd with diamonds and Indian stones,
Nor to be seen.   My crown is called content;
A crown it is that seldom kings enjoy.   65

2. Keep. Well, if you be a king crown'd with con-
tent,
Your crown content and you must be contented
To go along with us; for, as we think,
You are the king King Edward hath depos'd;
And we his subjects sworn in all allegiance   70
Will apprehend you as his enemy.

K. Hen. But did you never swear and break an
oath?

2. Keep. No, never such an oath; nor will not now.

K. Hen. Where did you dwell when I was King of
England?

2. Keep. Here in this country where we now remain.   75

K. Hen. I was anointed king at nine months old;
My father and my grandfather were kings,
And you were sworn true subjects unto me;
And tell me, then, have you not broke your oaths?

1. Keep. No;   80
For we were subjects but while you were king.

K. Hen. Why, am I dead?   Do I not breathe a
man?
Ah, simple men, you know not what you swear!
Look, as I blow this feather from my face,
And as the air blows it to me again,   85
Obeying with my wind when I do blow
And yielding to another when it blows,
Commanded always by the greater gust,
Such is the lightness of you common men.
But do not break your oaths; for of that sin   90
My mild entreaty shall not make you guilty.
Go where you will, the King shall be commanded;
And be you kings, command, and I'll obey.

1. Keep. We are true subjects to the King, King
Edward.

K. Hen. So would you be again to Henry   95
If he were seated as King Edward is.

1. Keep. We charge you, in God's name and the
King's
To go with us unto the officers.

K. Hen. In God's name, lead; your king's name
be obey'd.
And what God will, that let your king perform;   100
And what He will, I humbly yield unto.   [*Exeunt.*

[SCENE II.   *London.   The palace.*]

Enter KING EDWARD, GLOUCESTER, CLARENCE,
and LADY GREY.

K. Edw. Brother of Gloucester, at Saint Alban's
field
This lady's husband, Sir Richard Grey, was slain,
His land then seiz'd on by the conqueror.
Her suit is now to repossess those lands,
Which we in justice cannot well deny,   5
Because in quarrel of the house of York
The worthy gentleman did lose his life.

Glou. Your Highness shall do well to grant her suit.
It were dishonour to deny it her.

K. Edw. It were no less; but yet I'll make a
pause.   10

Glou. [*Aside to Clar.*]   Yea, is it so?
I see the lady hath a thing to grant
Before the King will grant her humble suit.

Clar. [*Aside to Glou.*]   He knows the game; how
true he keeps the wind!

Glou. [*Aside to Clar.*]   Silence!   15

K. Edw. Widow, we will consider of your suit;
And come some other time to know our mind.

[*L. Grey.*]   Right gracious lord, I cannot brook
delay.
May it please your Highness to resolve me now,
And what your pleasure is shall satisfy me.   20

Glou. [*Aside to Clar.*]   Ay, widow?   Then I'll
warrant you all your lands
An if what pleases him shall pleasure you.
Fight closer or, good faith, you'll catch a blow.

Clar. [*Aside to Glou.*]   I fear her not, unless she
chance to fall.

Glou. [*Aside to Clar.*]   God forbid that! for he'll
take vantages.   25

K. Edw. How many children hast thou, widow?
Tell me.

Clar. [*Aside to Glou.*]   I think he means to beg a
child of her.

Glou. [*Aside to Clar.*]   Nay, then whip me; he'll
rather give her two.

L. Grey. Three, my most gracious lord.

55. [that] Q.   Om. F.
Sc. ii, 18. *[L. Grey]*.   *Wid.* F. throughout the scene.   23. catch a blow: incur disgrace.

Glou. [*Aside to Clar.*] You shall have four if
  you'll be rul'd by him.   30
K. Edw. 'Twere pity they should lose their
  father's lands.
L. Grey. Be pitiful, dread lord, and grant it then.
K. Edw. Lords, give us leave. I'll try this
  widow's wit.
Glou. [*Aside to Clar.*] Ay, good leave have you;
  for you will have leave
Till youth take leave and leave you to the crutch. 35
              [*Glou. and Clar. retire.*]
K. Edw. Now tell me, madam, do you love your
  children?
L. Grey. Ay, full as dearly as I love myself.
K. Edw. And would you not do much to do them
  good?
L. Grey. To do them good I would sustain some
  harm.
K. Edw. Then get your husband's lands, to do
  them good.   40
L. Grey. Therefore I came unto your Majesty.
K. Edw. I'll tell you how these lands are to be
  got.
L. Grey. So shall you bind me to your Highness'
  service.
K. Edw. What service wilt thou do me if I give
  them?
L. Grey. What you command that rests in me to
  do.   45
K. Edw. But you will take exceptions to my boon.
L. Grey. No, gracious lord, except I cannot do it.
K. Edw. Ay, but thou canst do what I mean to
  ask.
L. Grey. Why, then I will do what your Grace
  commands.
Glou. [*Aside to Clar.*] He plies her hard; and
  much rain wears the marble.   50
Clar. [*Aside to Glou.*] As red as fire! Nay, then
  her wax must melt.
L. Grey. Why stops my lord? Shall I not hear
  my task?
K. Edw. An easy task; 'tis but to love a king.
L. Grey. That's soon perform'd, because I am a
  subject.
K. Edw. Why, then, thy husband's lands I freely
  give thee.   55
L. Grey. I take my leave with many thousand
  thanks.
Glou. [*Aside to Clar.*] The match is made; she
  seals it with a curtsy.
K. Edw. But stay thee, 'tis the fruits of love I
  mean.
L. Grey. The fruits of love I mean, my loving
  liege.
K. Edw. Ay, but, I fear me, in another sense. 60
What love, think'st thou, I sue so much to get?

L. Grey. My love till death, my humble thanks,
  my prayers;
That love which virtue begs and virtue grants.
K. Edw. No, by my troth, I did not mean such
  love.
L. Grey. Why, then you mean not as I thought
  you did.   65
K. Edw. But now you partly may perceive my
  mind.
L. Grey. My mind will never grant what I per-
  ceive
Your Highness aims at, if I aim aright.
K. Edw. To tell thee plain, I aim to lie with thee.
L. Grey. To tell you plain, I had rather lie in
  prison.   70
K. Edw. Why, then thou shalt not have thy
  husband's lands.
L. Grey. Why, then mine honesty shall be my
  dower;
For by that loss I will not purchase them.
K. Edw. Therein thou wrong'st thy children
  mightily.
L. Grey. Herein your Highness wrongs both them
  and me.   75
But, mighty lord, this merry inclination
Accords not with the sadness of my suit.
Please you dismiss me, either with ay or no.
K. Edw. Ay, if thou wilt say ay to my request;
No, if thou dost say no to my demand.   80
L. Grey. Then, no, my lord. My suit is at an end.
Glou. [*Aside to Clar.*] The widow likes him not,
  she knits her brows.
Clar. [*Aside to Glou.*] He is the bluntest wooer in
  Christendom.
K. Edw. [*Aside.*] Her looks doth argue her re-
  plete with modesty;
Her words doth show her wit incomparable; 85
All her perfections challenge sovereignty.
One way or other, she is for a king;
And she shall be my love or else my queen. —
Say that King Edward take thee for his queen?
L. Grey. 'Tis better said than done, my gracious
  lord.   90
I am a subject fit to jest withal,
But far unfit to be a sovereign.
K. Edw. Sweet widow, by my state I swear to
  thee
I speak no more than what my soul intends;
And that is, to enjoy thee for my love.   95
L. Grey. And that is more than I will yield unto.
I know I am too mean to be your queen,
And yet too good to be your concubine.
K. Edw. You cavil, widow. I did mean, my
  queen.
L. Grey. 'Twill grieve your Grace my sons should
  call you father.   100

---

72. honesty: chastity.

K. Edw. No more than when my daughters call
    thee mother.
Thou art a widow, and thou hast some children;
And, by God's mother, I, being but a bachelor,
Have other some. Why, 'tis a happy thing
To be the father unto many sons. 105
Answer no more, for thou shalt be my queen.
    Glou. [*Aside to Clar.*] The ghostly father now
    hath done his shrift.
    Clar. [*Aside to Glou.*] When he was made a
    shriver, 'twas for shift.
K. Edw. Brothers, you muse what chat we two
    have had.
Glou. The widow likes it not, for she looks very
    sad. 110
K. Edw. You'd think it strange if I should marry
    her.
Clar. To who, my lord?
K. Edw.   Why, Clarence, to myself.
Glou. That would be ten days' wonder at the
    least.
Clar. That's a day longer than a wonder lasts.
Glou. By so much is the wonder in extremes. 115
K. Edw. Well, jest on, brothers. I can tell you
    both
Her suit is granted for her husband's lands.

        Enter a NOBLEMAN.

    Nob. My gracious lord, Henry your foe is taken
And brought your prisoner to your palace gate.
K. Edw. See that he be convey'd unto the Tower;
And go we, brothers, to the man that took him 121
To question of his apprehension.
Widow, go you along. Lords, use her honourably.
        [*Exeunt all but Gloucester.*
    Glou. Ay, Edward will use women honourably.
Would he were wasted, marrow, bones, and all, 125
That from his loins no hopeful branch may spring,
To cross me from the golden time I look for!
And yet, between my soul's desire and me —
The lustful Edward's title buried —
Is Clarence, Henry, and his son young Edward, 130
And all the unlook'd for issue of their bodies
To take their rooms, ere I can place myself:
A cold premeditation for my purpose!
Why, then, I do but dream on sovereignty,
Like one that stands upon a promontory 135
And spies a far-off shore where he would tread,
Wishing his foot were equal with his eye,
And chides the sea that sunders him from thence,
Saying, he'll lade it dry to have his way.
So do I wish the crown, being so far off; 140
And so I chide the means that keeps me from it;

And so I say, I'll cut the causes off,
Flattering me with impossibilities.
My eye's too quick, my heart o'erweens too
    much,
Unless my hand and strength could equal them. 145
Well, say there is no kingdom then for Richard;
What other pleasure can the world afford?
I'll make my heaven in a lady's lap,
And deck my body in gay ornaments,
And witch sweet ladies with my words and looks.
O miserable thought! and more unlikely 151
Than to accomplish twenty golden crowns!
Why, love forswore me in my mother's womb;
And, for I should not deal in her soft laws,
She did corrupt frail nature with some bribe, 155
To shrink mine arm up like a wither'd shrub;
To make an envious mountain on my back,
Where sits deformity to mock my body;
To shape my legs of an unequal size;
To disproportion me in every part, 160
Like to a chaos, or an unlick'd bear-whelp
That carries no impression like the dam.
And am I then a man to be belov'd?
O monstrous fault, to harbour such a thought!
Then, since this earth affords no joy to me 165
But to command, to check, to o'erbear such
As are of better person than myself,
I'll make my heaven to dream upon the crown
And, whiles I live, t' account this world but hell
Until my mis-shap'd trunk that bears this head 170
Be round impaled with a glorious crown.
And yet I know not how to get the crown,
For many lives stand between me and home;
And I, — like one lost in a thorny wood,
That rends the thorns and is rent with the thorns,
Seeking a way and straying from the way, 176
Not knowing how to find the open air
But toiling desperately to find it out, —
Torment myself to catch the English crown;
And from that torment I will free myself 180
Or hew my way out with a bloody axe.
Why, I can smile, and murder whiles I smile,
And cry "Content" to that which grieves my
    heart,
And wet my cheeks with artificial tears,
And frame my face to all occasions. 185
I'll drown more sailors than the mermaid shall;
I'll slay more gazers than the basilisk;
I'll play the orator as well as Nestor,
Deceive more slily than Ulysses could,
And, like a Sinon, take another Troy. 190
I can add colours to the chameleon,
Change shapes with Proteus for advantages,

---

107. **ghostly:** spiritual.   108. **shift:** trick.   129. **buried:** out of the way.   131. **unlook'd for:** that cannot be foreseen.
161. **unlick'd bear-whelp.** It was popularly believed that a bear-cub was born a shapeless lump of flesh and licked into shape
by the mother.   187. **basilisk:** a fabulous serpent that killed with a glance.   190. **Sinon,** who introduced the wooden
horse into Troy.

And set the murderous Machiavel to school.
Can I do this, and cannot get a crown?
Tut, were it farther off, I'll pluck it down.   195
                                        [*Exit.*

[SCENE III. *France.   The King's palace.*]

Flourish.   Enter LEWIS *the French King, his sister*
BONA, *his Admiral, call'd* BOURBON: PRINCE
EDWARD, QUEEN MARGARET, *and the* EARL OF
OXFORD.   LEWIS *sits, and riseth up again.*

K. Lew. Fair Queen of England, worthy Mar-
    garet,
Sit down with us.   It ill befits thy state
And birth that thou shouldst stand while Lewis doth
    sit.
Q. Mar. No, mighty King of France; now Mar-
    garet
Must strike her sail and learn a while to serve   5
Where kings command.   I was, I must confess,
Great Albion's queen in former golden days;
But now mischance hath trod my title down
And with dishonour laid me on the ground,
Where I must take like seat unto my fortune   10
And to my humble seat conform myself.
K. Lew. Why, say, fair queen, whence springs
    this deep despair?
Q. Mar. From such a cause as fills mine eyes with
    tears
And stops my tongue, while heart is drown'd in
    cares.
K. Lew. Whate'er it be, be thou still like thy-
    self   15
And sit thee by our side. (*Seats her by him.*)   Yield
    not thy neck
To fortune's yoke, but let thy dauntless mind
Still ride in triumph over all mischance.
Be plain, Queen Margaret, and tell thy grief;
It shall be eas'd if France can yield relief.   20
Q. Mar. Those gracious words revive my drooping
    thoughts
And give my tongue-tied sorrows leave to speak.
Now, therefore, be it known to noble Lewis,
That Henry, sole possessor of my love,
Is of a king become a banish'd man,   25
And forc'd to live in Scotland a forlorn;
While proud ambitious Edward, Duke of York,
Usurps the regal title and the seat
Of England's true-anointed lawful king.
This is the cause that I, poor Margaret,   30
With this my son, Prince Edward, Henry's heir,
Am come to crave thy just and lawful aid;
And if thou fail us, all our hope is done.
Scotland hath will to help, but cannot help.
Our people and our peers are both misled,   35
Our treasure seiz'd, our soldiers put to flight,

And, as thou see'st, ourselves in heavy plight.
K. Lew. Renowned queen, with patience calm
    the storm
While we bethink a means to break it off.
Q. Mar. The more we stay, the stronger grows
    our foe.   40
K. Lew. The more I stay, the more I'll succour
    thee.
Q. Mar. O, but impatience waiteth on true sor-
    row.
And see where comes the breeder of my sorrow!

Enter WARWICK.

K. Lew. What's he approacheth boldly to our
    presence?
Q. Mar. Our Earl of Warwick, Edward's greatest
    friend.   45
K. Lew. Welcome, brave Warwick!   What
    brings thee to France?
                        [*He descends.   She ariseth.*
Q. Mar. Ay, now begins a second storm to rise,
For this is he that moves both wind and tide.
War. From worthy Edward, King of Albion,
My lord and sovereign and thy vowed friend,   50
I come, in kindness and unfeigned love,
First, to do greetings to thy royal person,
And then to crave a league of amity;
And lastly, to confirm that amity
With nuptial knot, if thou vouchsafe to grant   55
That virtuous Lady Bona, thy fair sister,
To England's king in lawful marriage.
Q. Mar. [*Aside.*]   If that go forward, Henry's
    hope is done.
War. [*To Bona.*]   And, gracious madam, in our
    king's behalf
I am commanded, with your leave and favour,   60
Humbly to kiss your hand and with my tongue
To tell the passion of my sovereign's heart,
Where fame, late entering at his heedful ears
Hath plac'd thy beauty's image and thy virtue.
Q. Mar. King Lewis and Lady Bona, hear me
    speak   65
Before you answer Warwick.   His demand
Springs not from Edward's well-meant honest love,
But from deceit bred by necessity;
For how can tyrants safely govern home
Unless abroad they purchase great alliance?   70
To prove him tyrant this reason may suffice,
That Henry liveth still; but were he dead,
Yet here Prince Edward stands, King Henry's
    son.
Look, therefore, Lewis, that by this league and mar-
    riage
Thou draw not on thy danger and dishonour;   75
For though usurpers sway the rule a while,
Yet heavens are just and time suppresseth wrongs.

Sc. iii, 5. **strike her sail:** humble herself.   25. **of a king:** from being a king.   26. **forlorn:** lost creature.   40. **stay:** delay.

War. Injurious Margaret!
Prince.   And why not Queen?
War. Because thy father Henry did usurp,
And thou no more art prince than she is queen.   80
Oxf. Then Warwick disannuls great John of
    Gaunt,
Which did subdue the greatest part of Spain;
And after John of Gaunt, Henry the Fourth,
Whose wisdom was a mirror to the wisest;
And after that wise prince, Henry the Fifth,   85
Who by his prowess conquered all France.
From these our Henry lineally descends.
War. Oxford, how haps it in this smooth discourse
You told not how Henry the Sixth hath lost
All that which Henry the Fifth had gotten?   90
Methinks these peers of France should smile at that.
But for the rest, you tell a pedigree
Of threescore and two years; a silly time
To make prescription for a kingdom's worth.
Oxf. Why, Warwick, canst thou speak against
    thy liege,   95
Whom thou obeyed'st thirty and six years,
And not bewray thy treason with a blush?
War. Can Oxford, that did ever fence the right,
Now buckler falsehood with a pedigree?   99
For shame! Leave Henry, and call Edward king.
Oxf. Call him my king by whose injurious doom
My elder brother, the Lord Aubrey Vere,
Was done to death? and more than so, my father,
Even in the downfall of his mellow'd years,
When nature brought him to the door of death?   105
No, Warwick, no; while life unholds this arm,
This arm upholds the house of Lancaster.
War. And I the house of York.
K. Lew. Queen Margaret, Prince Edward, and
    Oxford,
Vouchsafe, at our request, to stand aside,   110
While I use further conference with Warwick.
                        [*They stand aloof.*
Q. Mar. Heavens grant that Warwick's words
    bewitch him not!
K. Lew. Now, Warwick, tell me, even upon thy
    conscience,
Is Edward your true king? for I were loath
To link with him that were not lawful chosen.   115
War. Thereon I pawn my credit and mine honour.
K. Lew. But is he gracious in the people's eye?
War. The more that Henry was unfortunate.
K. Lew. Then further, all dissembling set aside,
Tell me for truth the measure of his love   120
Unto our sister Bona.
War.   Such it seems
As may beseem a monarch like himself.
Myself have often heard him say and swear
That this his love was an [eternal] plant,
Whereof the root was fix'd in virtue's ground,   125

The leaves and fruit maintain'd with beauty's sun,
Exempt from envy, but not from disdain
Unless the Lady Bona quit his pain.
K. Lew. Now, sister, let us hear your firm resolve.
Bona. Your grant, or your denial, shall be
    mine;
Yet I confess that often ere this day,   [*To War.* 131
When I have heard your king's desert recounted,
Mine ear hath tempted judgement to desire.
K. Lew. Then, Warwick, thus: our sister shall
    be Edward's;
And now forthwith shall articles be drawn   135
Touching the jointure that your king must make,
Which with her dowry shall be counterpois'd.
Draw near, Queen Margaret, and be a witness
That Bona shall be wife to the English king.   139
Prince. To Edward, but not to the English king.
Q. Mar. Deceitful Warwick! it was thy device
By this alliance to make void my suit.
Before thy coming Lewis was Henry's friend.
K. Lew. And still is friend to him and Margaret.
But if your title to the crown be weak,   145
As may appear by Edward's good success,
Then 'tis but reason that I be releas'd
From giving aid which late I promised.
Yet shall you have all kindness at my hand
That your estate requires and mine can yield.   150
War. Henry now lives in Scotland at his ease,
Where having nothing, nothing can he lose.
And as for you, yourself, our quondam queen,
You have a father able to maintain you;
And better 'twere you troubled him than France.
Q. Mar. Peace, impudent and shameless War-
    wick, peace,   156
Proud setter up and puller down of kings!
I will not hence till with my talk and tears,
Both full of truth, I make King Lewis behold
Thy sly conveyance and thy lord's false love;   160
                        [*Post blows a horn within.*
For both of you are birds of self-same feather.
K. Lew. Warwick, this is some post to us or thee.

                    Enter a POST.

Post. My lord ambassador, these letters are for
    you.   [*To War.*
Sent from your brother, Marquess Montague:
These from our king unto your Majesty: 165
                                [*To Lewis.*
And, madam, these for you; from whom I know not.
                                [*To Margaret.*
                        [*They all read their letters.*
Oxf. I like it well that our fair queen and mistress
Smiles at her news, while Warwick frowns at his.
Prince. Nay, mark how Lewis stamps as he were
    nettled.
I hope all's for the best.   170

78. **Injurious:** insulting.   93. **silly:** absurdly short.   124. **[eternal]** Q.   *externall* F.   160. **conveyance:** deceit.

K. Lew. Warwick, what are thy news? and yours
 fair queen?
Q. Mar. Mine such as fill my heart with unhop'd
 joys.
War. Mine full of sorrow and heart's discontent.
K. Lew. What! has your king married the Lady
 Grey?
And now, to soothe your forgery and his, 175
Sends me a paper to persuade me patience?
Is this th' alliance that he seeks with France?
Dare he presume to scorn us in this manner?
 Q. Mar. I told your Majesty as much before.
This proveth Edward's love and Warwick's honesty.
 War. King Lewis, I here protest in sight of
 heaven, 181
And by the hope I have of heavenly bliss,
That I am clear from this misdeed of Edward's,
No more my king, for he dishonours me,
But most himself if he could see his shame. 185
Did I forget that by the house of York
My father came untimely to his death?
Did I let pass th' abuse done to my niece?
Did I impale him with the regal crown?
Did I put Henry from his native right? 190
And an I guerdon'd at the last with shame?
Shame on himself! for my desert is honour;
And to repair my honour lost for him,
I here renounce him and return to Henry.
My noble queen, let former grudges pass, 195
And henceforth I am thy true servitor.
I will revenge his wrong to Lady Bona
And replant Henry in his former state.
 Q. Mar. Warwick, these words have turn'd my
 hate to love;
And I forgive and quite forget old faults, 200
And joy that thou becom'st King Henry's friend.
 War. So much his friend, ay, his unfeigned
 friend,
That, if King Lewis vouchsafe to furnish us
With some few bands of chosen soldiers,
I'll undertake to land them on our coast 205
And force the tyrant from his seat by war.
'Tis not his new-made bride shall succour him;
And as for Clarence, as my letters tell me,
He's very likely now to fall from him
For matching more for wanton lust than honour, 210
Or than for strength and safety of our country.
 Bona. Dear brother, how shall Bona be reveng'd
But by thy help to this distressed queen?
 Q. Mar. Renowned prince, how shall poor Henry
 live
Unless thou rescue him from foul despair? 215
 Bona. My quarrel and this English queen's are
 one.
 War. And mine, fair Lady Bona, joins with yours.

K. Lew. And mine with hers, and thine, and
 Margaret's.
Therefore at last I firmly am resolv'd
You shall have aid. 220
 Q. Mar. Let me give humble thanks for all at once.
 K. Lew. Then, England's messenger, return in
 post,
And tell false Edward, thy supposed king,
That Lewis of France is sending over masquers
To revel it with him and his new bride. 225
Thou seest what's past, go fear thy king withal.
 Bona. Tell him, in hope he'll prove a widower
 shortly,
I wear the willow garland for his sake.
 Q. Mar. Tell him, my mourning weeds are laid
 aside,
And I am ready to put armour on. 230
 War. Tell him from me that he hath done me
 wrong,
And therefore I'll uncrown him ere 't be long.
There's thy reward; be gone. [*Exit Post.*
 K. Lew.   But, Warwick,
Thou and Oxford with five thousand men
Shall cross the seas and bid false Edward battle; 235
And, as occasion serves, this noble queen
And prince shall follow with a fresh supply.
Yet, ere thou go, but answer me one doubt:
What pledge have we of thy firm loyalty?
 War. This shall assure my constant loyalty, 240
That if our queen and this young prince agree,
I'll join mine eldest daughter and my joy
To him forthwith in holy wedlock bands.
 Q. Mar. Yes, I agree, and thank you for your
 motion.
Son Edward, she is fair and virtuous, 245
Therefore delay not, give thy hand to Warwick;
And, with thy hand, thy faith irrevocable
That only Warwick's daughter shall be thine.
 Prince. Yes, I accept her, for she well deserves it;
And here, to pledge my vow, I give my hand. 250
    [*He gives his hand to Warwick.*
 K. Lew. Why stay we now? These soldiers shall
 be levied,
And thou, Lord Bourbon, our high admiral,
Shall waft them over with our royal fleet.
I long till Edward fall by war's mischance
For mocking marriage with a dame of France. 255
    [*Exeunt all but Warwick.*
 War. I came from Edward as ambassador
But I return his sworn and mortal foe.
Matter of marriage was the charge he gave me,
But dreadful war shall answer his demand.
Had he none else to make a stale but me? 260
Then none but I shall turn his jest to sorrow.
I was the chief that rais'd him to the crown,

---

175. **soothe your forgery:** palliate your deceit. 189. **impale him:** encircle his head. 226. **fear:** frighten. 228. **willow garland:** token of being forsaken. 260. **stale:** laughing-stock.

And I'll be the chief to bring him down again;
Not that I pity Henry's misery,
But seek revenge on Edward's mockery. [*Exit.*] 265

[ACT IV]

[SCENE I. *London.   The palace.*]

Enter GLOUCESTER, CLARENCE, SOMERSET, *and*
MONTAGUE.

Glou. Now tell me, brother Clarence, what think
    you
Of this new marriage with the Lady Grey?
Hath not our brother made a worthy choice?
    Clar. Alas, you know, 'tis far from hence to
    France;
How could he stay till Warwick made return?   5
    Som. My lords, forbear this talk; here comes the
    King.

Flourish.   Enter KING EDWARD [*attended*], LADY
GREY [*as Queen*], PEMBROKE, STAFFORD, HAS-
TINGS [*and others*].   *Four stand on one side, and
four on the other.*

    Glou. And his well-chosen bride.
    Clar. I mind to tell him plainly what I think.
    K. Edw. Now, brother of Clarence, how like you
    our choice,
That you stand pensive as half malcontent?   10
    Clar. As well as Lewis of France or the Earl of
    Warwick,
Which are so weak of courage and in judgement
That they'll take no offence at our abuse.
    K. Edw. Suppose they take offence without a
    cause,   14
They are but Lewis and Warwick.   I am Edward,
Your king and Warwick's, and must have my will.
    Glou. And [you] shall have your will, because our
    king.
Yet hasty marriage seldom proveth well.
    K. Edw. Yea, brother Richard, are you offended
    too?
    Glou. Not I.   20
No, God forbid that I should wish them sever'd
Whom God hath join'd together; ay, and 'twere pity
To sunder them that yoke so well together.
    K. Edw. Setting your scorns and your mislike
    aside,
Tell me some reason why the Lady Grey   25
Should not become my wife and England's queen.
And you too, Somerset and Montague,
Speak freely what you think.
    Clar. Then this is mine opinion: that King Lewis
Becomes your enemy, for mocking him   30
About the marriage of the Lady Bona.

    Glou. And Warwick, doing what you gave in
    charge,
Is now dishonoured by this new marriage.
    K. Edw. What if both Lewis and Warwick be
    appeas'd
By such invention as I can devise?   35
    Mont. Yet, to have join'd with France in such
    alliance
Would more have strength'ned this our common-
    wealth
'Gainst foreign storms than any home-bred marriage.
    Hast. Why, knows not Montague that of itself
England is safe, if true within itself?   40
    Mont. [Yes] but the safer when 'tis back'd with
    France.
    Hast. 'Tis better using France than trusting
    France.
Let us be back'd with God and with the seas
Which He hath given for fence impregnable,
And with their helps only defend ourselves.   45
In them and in ourselves our safety lies.
    Clar. For this one speech Lord Hastings well
    deserves
To have the heir of the Lord Hungerford.
    K. Edw. Ay, what of that?   It was my will and
    grant,
And for this once my will shall stand for law.   50
    Glou. And yet methinks your Grace hath not
    done well
To give the heir and daughter of Lord Scales
Unto the brother of your loving bride.
She better would have fitted me or Clarence;
But in your bride you bury brotherhood.   55
    Clar. Or else you would not have bestow'd the
    heir
Of the Lord Bonville on your new wife's son,
And leave your brothers to go speed elsewhere.
    K. Edw. Alas, poor Clarence! is it for a wife
That thou art malcontent?   I will provide thee.   60
    Clar. In choosing for yourself, you show'd your
    judgement,
Which being shallow, you shall give me leave
To play the broker in mine own behalf;
And to that end I shortly mind to leave you.
    K. Edw. Leave me or tarry, Edward will be king
And not be tied unto his brother's will.   66
    Q. Eliz. My lords, before it pleas'd his Majesty
To raise my state to title of a queen,
Do me but right, and you must all confess
That I was not ignoble of descent,   70
And meaner than myself have had like fortune.
But as this title honours me and mine,
So your dislikes, to whom I would be pleasing,
Doth cloud my joys with danger and with sorrow.
    K. Edw. My love, forbear to fawn upon their
    frowns.   75

Act IV, sc. i, 17. [you] (Rowe).   Om. F.   41. [Yes] F₂.   Om. F₁.

What danger or what sorrow can befall thee
So long as Edward is thy constant friend
And their true sovereign whom they must obey?
Nay, whom they shall obey, and love thee too,
Unless they seek for hatred at my hands;   80
Which if they do, yet will I keep thee safe,
And they shall feel the vengeance of my wrath.
    Glou. I hear, yet say not much, but think the
      more.   [*Aside.*]

Enter a POST.

    K. Edw. Now, messenger, what letters or what
      news
From France?   85
    Post. My sovereign liege, no letters; and few
      words
But such as I, without your special pardon,
Dare not relate.
    K. Edw. Go to, we pardon thee; therefore in brief
Tell me their words as near as thou canst guess them.
What answer makes King Lewis unto our letters?   91
    Post. At my depart, these were his very words:
"Go tell false Edward, the supposed king,
That Lewis of France is sending over masquers
To revel it with him and his new bride."   95
    K. Edw. Is Lewis so brave? Belike he thinks me
      Henry.
But what said Lady Bona to my marriage?
    Post. These were her words, utt'red with mild
      disdain:
"Tell him, in hope he'll prove a widower shortly,
I'll wear the willow garland for his sake."   100
    K. Edw. I blame not her, she could say little less;
She had the wrong. But what said Henry's queen?
For I have heard that she was there in place.
    Post. "Tell him," quoth she, "my mourning
      weeds are done,
And I am ready to put armour on."   105
    K. Edw. Belike she minds to play the Amazon.
But what said Warwick to these injuries?
    Post. He, more incens'd against your Majesty
Than all the rest, discharg'd me with these words:
"Tell him from me that he hath done me wrong,   110
And therefore I'll uncrown him ere 't be long."
    K. Edw. Ha! durst the traitor breathe out so
      proud words?
Well, I will arm me, being thus forewarn'd.
They shall have wars and pay for their presumption.
But say, is Warwick friends with Margaret?   115
    Post. Ay, gracious sovereign; they are so link'd in
      friendship
That young Prince Edward marries Warwick's
    daughter.
    Clar. Belike the elder; Clarence will have the
      younger.
Now, brother king, farewell, and sit you fast,

For I will hence to Warwick's other daughter;   120
That, though I want a kingdom, yet in marriage
I may not prove inferior to yourself.
You that love me and Warwick, follow me.
        [*Exit Clarence, and Somerset follows.*
    Glou. [*Aside.*] Not I;
My thoughts aim at a further matter. I   125
Stay not for the love of Edward, but the crown.
    K. Edw. Clarence and Somerset both gone to
      Warwick!
Yet am I arm'd against the worst can happen;
And haste is needful in this desperate case.
Pembroke and Stafford, you in our behalf   130
Go levy men, and make prepare for war;
They are already or quickly will be landed.
Myself in person will straight follow you.
        [*Exeunt Pembroke and Stafford.*
But, ere I go, Hastings and Montague,
Resolve my doubt. You twain, of all the rest,   135
Are near to Warwick by blood and by alliance.
Tell me if you love Warwick more than me?
If it be so, then both depart to him;
I rather wish you foes than hollow friends.
But if you mind to hold your true obedience,   140
Give me assurance with some friendly vow,
That I may never have you in suspect.
    Mont. So God help Montague as he proves true!
    Hast. And Hastings as he favours Edward's
      cause!
    K. Edw. Now, brother Richard, will you stand
      by us?   145
    Glou. Ay, in despite of all that shall withstand
      you.
    K. Edw. Why, so! then am I sure of victory.
Now therefore let us hence, and lose no hour,
Till we meet Warwick with his foreign power.
               [*Exeunt.*

[SCENE II. *A plain in Warwickshire.*]

Enter WARWICK *and* OXFORD, *with* French soldiers.
    War. Trust me, my lord, all hitherto goes well;
The common people by numbers swarm to us.

Enter CLARENCE *and* SOMERSET.

But see where Somerset and Clarence comes!
Speak suddenly my lords, are we all friends?
    Clar. Fear not that, my lord.   5
    War. Then, gentle Clarence, welcome unto War-
      wick,
And welcome, Somerset! I hold it cowardice
To rest mistrustful where a noble heart
Hath pawn'd an open hand in sign of love;
Else might I think that Clarence, Edward's brother,
Were but a feigned friend to our proceedings.   11

      Sc. ii, 9. pawn'd: pledged.

But welcome, sweet Clarence; my daughter shall be
    thine.
And now what rests but, in night's coverture,
Thy brother being carelessly encamp'd,
His soldiers lurking in the town about,   15
And but attended by a simple guard,
We may surprise and take him at our pleasure?
Our scouts have found the adventure very easy,
That as Ulysses and stout Diomede
With sleight and manhood stole to Rhesus' tents   20
And brought from thence the Thracian fatal
    steeds,
So we, well cover'd with the night's black mantle,
At unawares may beat down Edward's guard
And seize himself; I say not, slaughter him,
For I intend but only to surprise him.   25
You that will follow me to this attempt,
Applaud the name of Henry with your leader.
             [*They all cry*, "Henry!"
Why, then, let's on our way in silent sort.
For Warwick and his friends, God and Saint George!
                   [*Exeunt.*

[SCENE III. *Edward's camp, near Warwick.*]

Enter three WATCHMEN, *to guard the King's tent.*

  1. Watch. Come on, my masters, each man take
    his stand.
The King by this is set him down to sleep.
  2. Watch. What, will he not to bed?
  1. Watch. Why, no; for he hath made a solemn
    vow
Never to lie and take his natural rest   5
Till Warwick or himself be quite suppress'd.
  2. Watch. To-morrow then belike shall be the day,
If Warwick be so near as men report.
  3. Watch. But say, I pray, what nobleman is that
That with the King here resteth in his tent?   10
  1. Watch. 'Tis the Lord Hastings, the King's
    chiefest friend.
  3. Watch. O, is it so? But why commands the
    King
That his chief followers lodge in towns about him,
While he himself keeps in the cold field?
  2. Watch. 'Tis the more honour, because more
    dangerous.   15
  3. Watch. Ay, but give me worship and quietness;
I like it better than a dangerous honour.
If Warwick knew in what estate he stands,
'Tis to be doubted he would waken him.
  1. Watch. Unless our halberds did shut up his
    passage.   20
  2. Watch. Ay, wherefore else guard we his royal
    tent
But to defend his person from night-foes?

Enter WARWICK, CLARENCE, OXFORD, SOMERSET,
    and French soldiers, *silent all.*

  War. This is his tent; and see where stand his
    guard.
Courage, my masters! honour now or never!
But follow me, and Edward shall be ours.   25
  1. Watch. Who goes there?
  2. Watch. Stay, or thou diest!
      [*Warwick and the rest cry all*, "Warwick!
      Warwick!" *and set upon the Guard, who
      fly, crying*, "Arm! arm!" *Warwick and
      the rest following them.*

The drum playing and trumpet sounding, re-enter
  WARWICK, SOMERSET, *and the rest, bringing the*
  KING *out in his gown, sitting in a chair.* Richard
  and Hastings *fly over the stage.*

  Som. What are they that fly there?
  War. Richard and Hastings. Let them go; here
    is
The Duke.
  K. Edw. The Duke! Why, Warwick, when we
    parted,   30
Thou call'dst me king.
  War.   Ay, but the case is alter'd.
When you disgrac'd me in my embassade
Then I degraded you from being king,
And come now to create you Duke of York.
Alas! how should you govern any kingdom,   35
That know not how to use ambassadors,
Nor how to be contented with one wife,
Nor how to use your brothers brotherly,
Nor how to study for the people's welfare,
Nor how to shroud yourself from enemies?   40
  K. Edw. Yea, brother of Clarence, art thou here
    too?
Nay, then I see that Edward needs must down.
Yet, Warwick, in despite of all mischance,
Of thee thyself and all thy complices,
Edward will always bear himself as king.   45
Though Fortune's malice overthrow my state,
My mind exceeds the compass of her wheel.
  War. Then, for his mind, be Edward England's
    king: [*Takes off his crown.*
But Henry now shall wear the English crown
And be true king indeed, thou but the shadow. 50
My Lord of Somerset, at my request,
See that forthwith Duke Edward be convey'd
Unto my brother, Archbishop of York.
When I have fought with Pembroke and his
    fellows
I'll follow you, and tell what answer   55
Lewis and the Lady Bona send to him.
Now, for a while farewell, good Duke of York.
             [*They lead him out forcibly.*

---

13. rests: remains. coverture: shadow. 15. lurking: lodging. 28. sort: fashion.
Sc. iii, 16. worship: ease and dignity. 32. embassade: embassy.

K. Edw. What fates impose, that men must needs abide;
It boots not to resist both wind and tide.
[Exit [guarded].
Oxf. What now remains, my lords, for us to do 60
But march to London with our soldiers?
War. Ay, that's the first thing that we have to do,
To free King Henry from imprisonment
And see him seated in the regal throne. *[Exeunt.*

[SCENE IV. *London. The palace.*]

Enter QUEEN ELIZABETH *and* RIVERS.

Riv. Madam, what makes you in this sudden change?
Q. Eliz. Why, brother Rivers, are you yet to learn
What late misfortune is befall'n King Edward?
Riv. What! loss of some pitch'd battle against Warwick?
Q. Eliz. No, but the loss of his own royal person.
Riv. Then is my sovereign slain? 6
Q. Eliz. Ay, almost slain, for he is taken prisoner,
Either betray'd by falsehood of his guard
Or by his foe surpris'd at unawares;
And, as I further have to understand, 10
Is new committed to the Bishop of York,
Fell Warwick's brother and by that our foe.
Riv. These news I must confess are full of grief;
Yet gracious madam, bear it as you may.
Warwick may lose, that now hath won the day. 15
Q. Eliz. Till then fair hope must hinder life's decay;
And I the rather wean me from despair
For love of Edward's offspring in my womb.
This is it that makes me bridle passion
And bear with mildness my misfortune's cross; 20
Ay, ay, for this I draw in many a tear
And stop the rising of blood-sucking sighs,
Lest with my sighs or tears I blast or drown
King Edward's fruit, true heir to th' English crown.
Riv. But, madam, where is Warwick then become? 25
Q. Eliz. I am inform'd that he comes towards London
To set the crown once more on Henry's head.
Guess thou the rest; King Edward's friends must down,
But, to prevent the tyrant's violence, —
For trust not him that hath once broken faith, — 30
I'll hence forthwith unto the sanctuary,
To save at least the heir of Edward's right;
There shall I rest secure from force and fraud.
Come, therefore, let us fly while we may fly;
If Warwick take us we are sure to die. *[Exeunt.* 35

[SCENE V. *A park near Middleham Castle in Yorkshire.*]

Enter GLOUCESTER, LORD HASTINGS, *and* SIR WILLIAM STANLEY.

Glou. Now, my Lord Hastings and Sir William Stanley,
Leave off to wonder why I drew you hither
Into this chiefest thicket of the park.
Thus stands the case: you know our king, my brother,
Is prisoner to the Bishop here, at whose hands 5
He hath good usage and great liberty;
And, often but attended with weak guard,
Comes hunting this way to disport himself.
I have advertis'd him by secret means
That if about this hour he make this way 10
Under the colour of his usual game,
He shall here find his friends with horse and men
To set him free from his captivity.

Enter KING EDWARD *and a* HUNTSMAN *with him.*

Hunt. This way, my lord; for this way lies the game.
K. Edw. Nay, this way, man; see where the huntsmen stand. 15
Now, brother of Gloucester, Lord Hastings, and the rest,
Stand you thus close to steal the Bishop's deer?
Glou. Brother, the time and case requireth haste.
Your horse stands ready at the park-corner.
K. Edw. But whither shall we then?
Hast.   To Lynn, my lord, 20
And, shipp'd from thence, to Flanders.
Glou. Well guess'd, believe me; for that was my meaning.
K. Edw. Stanley, I will requite thy forwardness.
Glou. But wherefore stay we? 'Tis no time to talk.
K. Edw. Huntsman, what say'st thou? Wilt thou go along? 25
Hunt. Better do so than tarry and be hang'd.
Glou. Come then, away; let's ha' no more ado.
K. Edw. Bishop, farewell! Shield thee from Warwick's frown,
And pray that I may repossess the crown. *[Exeunt.*

[SCENE VI. *London. The Tower.*]

Flourish. Enter KING HENRY, CLARENCE, WARWICK, SOMERSET, *young* RICHMOND, OXFORD, MONTAGUE, *and* LIEUTENANT of the Tower.

K. Hen. Master lieutenant, now that God and friends
Have shaken Edward from the regal seat,

Sc. iv, 22. **blood-sucking. It was believed that each sigh cost the heart a drop of blood.**
Sc. v, 17. **close: hidden.**

And turn'd my captive state to liberty,
My fear to hope, my sorrows unto joys,
At our enlargement what are thy due fees?   5
    Lieu. Subjects may challenge nothing of their
      sovereigns;
But if an humble prayer may prevail,
I then crave pardon of your Majesty.
    K. Hen. For what, lieutenant? For well using
    me?
Nay, be thou sure, I'll well requite thy kindness,   10
For that it made my imprisonment a pleasure;
Ay, such a pleasure as incaged birds
Conceive when, after many moody thoughts,
At last by notes of household harmony
They quite forget their loss of liberty.   15
But, Warwick, after God, thou set'st me free,
And chiefly therefore I thank God and thee.
He was the author, thou the instrument.
Therefore, that I may conquer Fortune's spite
By living low, where Fortune cannot hurt me,   20
And that the people of this blessed land
May not be punish'd with my thwarting stars,
Warwick, although my head still wear the crown,
I here resign my government to thee,
For thou art fortunate in all thy deeds.   25
    War. Your Grace hath still been fam'd for vir-
    tuous;
And now may seem as wise as virtuous
By spying and avoiding Fortune's malice,
For few men rightly temper with the stars.
Yet in this one thing let me blame your Grace,   30
For choosing me when Clarence is in place.
    Clar. No, Warwick, thou art worthy of the sway,
To whom the heavens in thy nativity
Adjudg'd an olive branch and laurel crown,
As likely to be blest in peace and war;   35
And therefore I yield thee my free consent.
    War. And I choose Clarence only for Protector.
    K. Hen. Warwick and Clarence, give me both
    your hands.
Now join your hands, and with your hands your
    hearts,
That no dissension hinder government.   40
I make you both Protectors of this land,
While I myself will lead a private life
And in devotion spend my latter days
To sin's rebuke and my Creator's praise.
    War. What answers Clarence to his sovereign's
    will?   45
    Clar. That he consents, if Warwick yield consent,
For on thy fortune I repose myself.
    War. Why, then, though loath, yet must I be
    content.
We'll yoke together like a double shadow
To Henry's body, and supply his place;   50
I mean, in bearing weight of government,

While he enjoys the honour and his ease.
And, Clarence, now then it is more than needful
Forthwith that Edward be pronounc'd a traitor,
And all his lands and goods be confiscate.   55
    Clar. What else? and that succession be deter-
    mined.
    War. Ay, therein Clarence shall not want his
    part.
    K. Hen. But, with the first of all your chief
    affairs,
Let me entreat, for I command no more,
That Margaret your queen and my son Edward   60
Be sent for, to return from France with speed;
For, till I see them here, by doubtful fear
My joy of liberty is half eclips'd.
    Clar. It shall be done, my sovereign, with all
    speed.
    K. Hen. My Lord of Somerset, what youth is
    that   65
Of whom you seem to have so tender care?
    Som. My liege, it is young Henry, Earl of Rich-
    mond.
    K. Hen. Come hither, England's hope. (*Lays
    his hand on his head.*) If secret powers
Suggest but truth to my divining thoughts,
This pretty lad will prove our country's bliss.   70
His looks are full of peaceful majesty,
His head by nature fram'd to wear a crown,
His hand to wield a sceptre, and himself
Likely in time to bless a regal throne.
Make much of him, my lords, for this is he   75
Must help you more than you are hurt by me.

                  Enter a POST.

    War. What news, my friend?
    Post. That Edward is escaped from your brother,
And fled, as he hears since, to Burgundy.
    War. Unsavoury news! but how made he escape?
    Post. He was convey'd by Richard Duke of
    Gloucester   81
And the Lord Hastings, who attended him
In secret ambush on the forest side
And from the Bishop's huntsmen rescu'd him;
For hunting was his daily exercise.   85
    War. My brother was too careless of his charge.
But let us hence, my sovereign, to provide
A salve for any sore that may betide.
    [*Exeunt all but Somerset, Richmond, and
    Oxford.*
    Som. My lord, I like not of this flight of Edward's;
For doubtless Burgundy will yield him help,   90
And we shall have more wars before 't be long.
As Henry's late presaging prophecy
Did glad my heart with hope of this young Rich-
    mond,
So doth my heart misgive me, in these conflicts

Sc. vi, 29. **temper . . . stars**: adjust themselves to their destiny.   67. **Henry**: later Henry VII.   82. **attended**: waited for.

What may befall him to his harm and ours.   95
Therefore, Lord Oxford, to prevent the worst,
Forthwith we'll send him hence to Brittany,
Till storms be past of civil enmity.

Oxf. Ay, for if Edward repossess the crown,
'Tis like that Richmond with the rest shall down.

Som. It shall be so; he shall to Brittany.   101
Come, therefore, let's about it speedily.   [*Exeunt.*

[SCENE VII.   *Before York.*]

Flourish.   Enter KING EDWARD, GLOUCESTER,
HASTINGS, *and* Soldiers.

K. Edw. Now, brother Richard, Lord Hastings,
and the rest,
Yet thus far Fortune maketh us amends,
And says that once more I shall interchange
My waned state for Henry's regal crown.
Well have we pass'd and now repass'd the seas   5
And brought desired help from Burgundy.
What then remains, we being thus arriv'd
From Ravenspurgh haven before the gates of York,
But that we enter as into our dukedom?

Glou. The gates made fast!   Brother, I like not
this;   10
For many men that stumble at the threshold
Are well foretold that danger lurks within.

K. Edw. Tush, man, abodements must not now
affright us.
By fair or foul means we must enter in,
For hither will our friends repair to us.   15

Hast. My liege, I'll knock once more to summon
them.

Enter, on the walls, the MAYOR *of York, and his*
Brethren.

May. My lords, we were forewarned of your
coming,
And shut the gates for safety of ourselves,
For now we owe allegiance unto Henry.

K. Edw. But, master mayor, if Henry be your
king,   20
Yet Edward at the least is Duke of York.

May. True, my good lord; I know you for no less.

K. Edw. Why, and I challenge nothing but my
dukedom,
As being well content with that alone.

Glou. [*Aside.*] But when the fox hath once got in
his nose,   25
He'll soon find means to make the body follow.

Hast. Why, master mayor, why stand you in a
doubt?
Open the gates; we are King Henry's friends.

May. Ay, say you so?   The gates shall then be
opened.   [*They descend.*

Glou. A wise stout captain, and soon persuaded!

Hast. The good old man would fain that all were
well,   31
So 'twere not long of him; but being ent'red,
I doubt not, I, but we shall soon persuade
Both him and all his brothers unto reason.

Enter the MAYOR *and two* Aldermen, *below.*

K. Edw. So, master mayor; these gates must not
be shut   35
But in the night or in the time of war.
What! fear not, man, but yield me up the keys;
[*Takes his keys.*
For Edward will defend the town and thee,
And all those friends that deign to follow me.

March.   Enter MONTGOMERY, *with drum and*
SOLDIERS.

Glou. Brother, this is Sir John Montgomery,   40
Our trusty friend, unless I be deceiv'd.

K. Edw. Welcome, Sir John!   But why come you
in arms?

Mont. To help King Edward in his time of storm,
As every loyal subject ought to do.

K. Edw. Thanks, good Montgomery; but we
now forget   45
Our title to the crown and only claim
Our dukedom till God please to send the rest.

Mont. Then fare you well, for I will hence again;
I came to serve a king and not a duke.
Drummer, strike up, and let us march away.   50
[*The drum begins to march.*

K. Edw. Nay, stay, Sir John, a while, and we'll
debate
By what safe means the crown may be recover'd.

Mont. What talk you of debating?   In few
words,
If you'll not here proclaim yourself our king,
I'll leave you to your fortune and be gone   55
To keep them back that come to succour you.
Why shall we fight if you pretend no title?

Glou. Why, brother, wherefore stand you on
nice points?

K. Edw. When we grow stronger, then we'll make
our claim.
Till then, 'tis wisdom to conceal our meaning.   60

Hast. Away with scrupulous wit!   Now arms
must rule.

Glou. And fearless minds climb soonest unto
crowns.
Brother, we will proclaim you out of hand;
The bruit thereof will bring you many friends.

K. Edw. Then be it as you will; for 'tis my right,
And Henry but usurps the diadem.   66

Mont. Ay, now my sovereign speaketh like himself;
And now will I be Edward's champion.

Sc. vii, 13. **abodements:** evil omens.   64. **bruit:** report.

Hast. Sound trumpet; Edward shall be here pro-
claim'd.   69
Come, fellow-soldier, make thou proclamation.
                              [*Giving him a paper.*] *Flourish.*
  Sold. [Reads.] "Edward the Fourth, by the grace
of God, King of England and France, and Lord of
Ireland," etc.
  Mont. And whosoe'er gainsays King Edward's
    right,
By this I challenge him to single fight.   75
                              [*Throws down his gauntlet.*
  All. Long live Edward the Fourth!
  K. Edw. Thanks, brave Montgomery, and thanks
    unto you all.
If fortune serve me, I'll requite this kindness.
Now, for this night, let's harbour here in York;
And when the morning sun shall raise his car   80
Above the border of this horizon,
We'll forward towards Warwick and his mates;
For well I wot that Henry is no soldier.
Ah, froward Clarence! how evil it beseems thee
To flatter Henry and forsake thy brother!   85
Yet, as we may, we'll meet both thee and War-
    wick.
Come on, brave soldiers! doubt not of the day,
And, that once gotten, doubt not of large pay.
                              [*Exeunt.*

[SCENE VIII. *London. The palace.*]

Flourish. Enter KING HENRY, WARWICK, MON-
TAGUE, CLARENCE, [EXETER,] *and* OXFORD.

  War. What counsel, lords?   Edward from
    Belgia,
With hasty Germans and blunt Hollanders,
Hath pass'd in safety through the narrow seas
And with his troops doth march amain to London;
And many giddy people flock to him.   5
  K. Hen. Let's levy men, and beat him back
    again.
  Clar. A little fire is quickly trodden out,
Which, being suffer'd, rivers cannot quench.
  War. In Warwickshire I have true-hearted friends
Not mutinous in peace yet bold in war;   10
Those will I muster up; and thou, son Clarence,
Shalt stir up in Suffolk, Norfolk, and in Kent,
The knights and gentlemen to come with thee.
Thou, brother Montague, in Buckingham,
Northampton, and in Leicestershire, shalt find   15
Men well inclin'd to hear what thou command'st;
And thou, brave Oxford, wondrous well belov'd,
In Oxfordshire shalt muster up thy friends.
My sovereign, with the loving citizens,
Like to his island girt in with the ocean,   20
Or, modest Dian, circled with her nymphs,
Shall rest in London till we come to him.

Fair lords, take leave and stand not to reply.
Farewell, my sovereign.
  K. Hen. Farewell, my Hector, and my Troy's true
    hope.   25
  Clar. In sign of truth, I kiss your Highness' hand.
  K. Hen. Well-minded Clarence, be thou fortunate!
  Mont. Comfort, my lord! and so I take my
    leave.
  Oxf. And thus [*kissing Henry's hand*] I seal my
    truth, and bid adieu.
  K. Hen. Sweet Oxford, and my loving Montague,
And all at once, once more a happy farewell.   31
  War. Farewell, sweet lords! Let's meet at
    Coventry.
                  [*Exeunt [all but King Henry and Exeter*].
  K. Hen. Here at the palace will I rest a while.
Cousin of Exeter, what thinks your lordship?
Methinks the power that Edward hath in field   35
Should not be able to encounter mine.
  Exe. The doubt is that he will seduce the rest.
  K. Hen. That's not my fear; my meed hath got
    me fame.
I have not stopp'd mine ears to their demands,
Nor posted off their suits with slow delays.   40
My pity hath been balm to heal their wounds,
My mildness hath allay'd their swelling griefs,
My mercy dri'd their water-flowing tears.
I have not been desirous of their wealth,
Nor much oppress'd them with great subsidies,   45
Nor forward of revenge, though they much err'd.
Then why should they love Edward more than
    me?
No, Exeter, these graces challenge grace;
And when the lion fawns upon the lamb,
The lamb will never cease to follow him.   50
            [*Shout within, "A Lancaster! A Lan-
              caster!"*
  Exe. Hark, hark, my lord! what shouts are these?

Enter KING EDWARD, [GLOUCESTER,] *and soldiers.*

  K. Edw. Seize on the shame-fac'd Henry, bear
    him hence;
And once again proclaim us King of England.
You are the fount that makes small brooks to flow;
Now stops thy spring, my sea shall suck them dry
And swell so much the higher by their ebb.   56
Hence with him to the Tower, let him not speak.
                              [*Exeunt some with King Henry.*
And, lords, towards Coventry bend we our course,
Where peremptory Warwick now remains.
The sun shines hot; and, if we use delay,   60
Cold biting winter mars our hop'd-for hay.
  Glou. Away betimes, before his forces join,
And take the great-grown traitor unawares.
Brave warriors, march amain towards Coventry.
                              [*Exeunt.*

[ACT V]

[SCENE I. Coventry.]

Enter WARWICK, *the* MAYOR of Coventry, *two*
MESSENGERS, *and others upon the walls.*

War. Where is the post that came from valiant
Oxford?
How far hence is thy lord, mine honest fellow?
  [*1.*] *Mess.* By this at Dunsmore, marching
hitherward.
War. How far off is our brother Montague?
Where is the post that came from Montague?   5
  [*2.*] *Mess.* By this at Daintry with a puissant
troop.

Enter SIR JOHN SOMERVILLE.

War. Say, Somerville, what says my loving son?
And, by thy guess, how nigh is Clarence now?
Som. At Southam I did leave him with his forces,
And do expect him here some two hours hence.   10
                              [*Drum heard.*]
War. Then Clarence is at hand; I hear his drum.
Som. It is not his, my lord; here Southam lies.
The drum your honour hears marcheth from War-
wick.
War. Who should that be? Belike unlook'd-for
friends.
Som. They are at hand, and you shall quickly
know.   15

March. Flourish. Enter KING EDWARD,
GLOUCESTER, *and soldiers.*

K. Edw. Go, trumpet, to the walls, and sound a
parle.
Glou. See how the surly Warwick mans the wall!
War. O unbid spite! is sportful Edward come?
Where slept our scouts, or how are they seduc'd
That we could hear no news of his repair?   20
K. Edw. Now, Warwick, wilt thou ope the city
gates,
Speak gentle words and humbly bend thy knee,
Call Edward king and at his hands beg mercy,
And he shall pardon thee these outrages.
War. Nay, rather, wilt thou draw thy forces
hence,   25
Confess who set thee up and pluck'd thee down,
Call Warwick patron, and be penitent,
And thou shalt still remain the Duke of York.
Glou. I thought, at least, he would have said the
King;
Or did he make the jest against his will?   30
War. Is not a dukedom, sir, a goodly gift?
Glou. Ay, by my faith, for a poor earl to give.
I'll do thee service for so good a gift.

War. 'Twas I that gave the kingdom to thy
brother.
K. Edw. Why then 'tis mine, if but by Warwick's
gift.   35
War. Thou art no Atlas for so great a weight;
And, weakling, Warwick takes his gift again,
And Henry is my king, Warwick his subject.
K. Edw. But Warwick's king is Edward's pris-
oner.
And, gallant Warwick, do but answer this: 40
What is the body when the head is off?
Glou. Alas, that Warwick had no more forecast,
But, whiles he thought to steal the single ten,
The king was slily finger'd from the deck!
You left poor Henry at the Bishop's palace,   45
And, ten to one, you'll meet him in the Tower.
K. Edw. 'Tis even so; yet you are Warwick still.
Glou. Come Warwick, take the time; kneel down,
kneel down.
Nay, when? strike now, or else the iron cools.
War. I had rather chop this hand off at a blow   50
And with the other fling it at thy face
Than bear so low a sail to strike to thee.
K. Edw. Sail how thou canst, have wind and tide
thy friend,
This hand, fast wound about thy coal-black hair,
Shall, whiles thy head is warm and new cut off,   55
Write in the dust this sentence with thy blood:
"Wind-changing Warwick now can change no more."

Enter OXFORD, *with drum and colours.*

War. O cheerful colours! see where Oxford comes!
Oxf. Oxford, Oxford, for Lancaster!
                    [*He and his forces enter the city.*]
Glou. The gates are open, let us enter too.   60
K. Edw. So other foes may set upon our backs.
Stand we in good array; for they no doubt
Will issue out again and bid us battle.
If not, the city being but of small defence,
We'll quickly rouse the traitors in the same.   65
War. O, welcome, Oxford! for we want thy help.

Enter MONTAGUE, *with drum and colours.*

Mont. Montague, Montague, for Lancaster!
                    [*He and his forces enter the city.*]
Glou. Thou and thy brother both shall buy this
treason
Even with the dearest blood your bodies bear.
K. Edw. The harder match'd, the greater victory.
My mind presageth happy gain and conquest.   71

Enter SOMERSET, *with drum and colours.*

Som. Somerset, Somerset, for Lancaster!
                    [*He and his forces enter the city.*]
Glou. Two of thy name, both Dukes of Somerset,

Act V, sc. i, 6. **Daintry:** Daventry. 13. **Warwick:** the town. 20. **repair:** approach. 43. **single:** simple. 48. **time:**
opportunity. 52. **bear ... sail:** be so humble. **strike:** lower (sail) in salute.

Have sold their lives unto the house of York;
And thou shalt be the third, if this sword hold. 75

Enter CLARENCE, *with drum and colours.*

War. And lo, where George of Clarence sweeps
     along,
Of force enough to bid his brother battle;
With whom an upright zeal to right prevails
More than the nature of a brother's love!
Come, Clarence, come; thou wilt, if Warwick
     call.   80
Clar. Father of Warwick, know you what this
     means?
               [*Taking his red rose out of his hat.*
Look here, I throw my infamy at thee.
I will not ruinate my father's house,
Who gave his blood to lime the stones together,
And set up Lancaster. Why, trow'st thou, War-
     wick,   85
That Clarence is so harsh, so blunt, unnatural,
To bend the fatal instruments of war
Against his brother and his lawful king?
Perhaps thou wilt object my holy oath.
To keep that oath were more impiety   90
Than Jephthah's when he sacrific'd his daughter.
I am so sorry for my trespass made
That, to deserve well at my brother's hands,
I here proclaim myself thy mortal foe,
With resolution, wheresoe'er I meet thee —   95
As I will meet thee, if thou stir abroad —
To plague thee for thy foul misleading me.
And so, proud-hearted Warwick, I defy thee,
And to my brother turn my blushing cheeks.
Pardon me, Edward, I will make amends;   100
And, Richard, do not frown upon my faults,
For I will henceforth be no more unconstant.
K. Edw. Now welcome more, and ten times more
     belov'd.
Than if thou never hadst deserv'd our hate.
Glou. Welcome, good Clarence; this is brother-
     like.   105
War. O passing traitor, perjur'd and unjust!
K. Edw. What, Warwick, wilt thou leave the
     town and fight?
Or shall we beat the stones about thine ears?
War. Alas, I am not coop'd here for defence!
I will away towards Barnet presently,   110
And bid thee battle, Edward, if thou dar'st.
K. Edw. Yes, Warwick, Edward dares, and leads
     the way.
Lords, to the field! Saint George and victory!
          [*Exeunt [King Edward and his company].*
          March.   Warwick and his company
          follow.

Alarum and excursions.   Enter KING EDWARD,
     bringing forth WARWICK *wounded.*

K. Edw. So, lie thou there. Die thou, and die
     our fear;
For Warwick was a bug that fear'd us all.
Now, Montague, sit fast; I seek for thee
That Warwick's bones may keep thine company.
                                          [*Exit.*
War. Ah, who is nigh? Come to me, friend or
     foe,   5
And tell me who is victor, York or Warwick?
Why ask I that? My mangled body shows,
My blood, my want of strength, my sick heart shows
That I must yield my body to the earth
And, by my fall, the conquest to my foe.   10
Thus yields the cedar to the axe's edge
Whose arms gave shelter to the princely eagle
Under whose shade the ramping lion slept,
Whose top-branch overpeer'd Jove's spreading tree
And kept low shrubs from winter's powerful wind.
These eyes, that now are dimm'd with death's black
     veil,   16
Have been as piercing as the mid-day sun
To search the secret treasons of the world.
The wrinkles in my brows, now fill'd with blood,
Were lik'ned oft to kingly sepulchres;   20
For who liv'd king, but I could dig his grave?
And who durst smile when Warwick bent his brow?
Lo, now my glory smear'd in dust and blood!
My parks, my walks, my manors that I had,
Even now forsake me, and of all my lands   25
Is nothing left me but my body's length.
Why, what is pomp, rule, reign, but earth and dust?
And, live we how we can, yet die we must.

Enter OXFORD *and* SOMERSET.

Som. Ah, Warwick, Warwick! wert thou as we are,
We might recover all our loss again.   30
The Queen from France hath brought a puissant
     power;
Even now we heard the news. Ah, couldst thou fly!
War. Why, then I would not fly. Ah, Montague,
If thou be there, sweet brother, take my hand,
And with thy lips keep in my soul a while!   35
Thou lov'st me not; for, brother, if thou didst,
Thy tears would wash this cold congealed blood
That glues my lips and will not let me speak.
Come quickly, Montague, or I am dead.
Som. Ah, Warwick! Montague hath breath'd
     his last: 40
And to the latest gasp cried out for Warwick,
And said, "Commend me to my valiant brother."
And more he would have said, and more he spoke,

84. lime: cement. 85. set up: i.e., I will not set up. 91. Jephthah's. See *Judges* xi.30.
Sc. ii, 2. bug: bugbear. fear'd: frightened.

Which sounded like a [clamour] in a vault,
That might not be distinguish'd; but at last   45
I well might hear, delivered with a groan,
"O, farewell, Warwick!"
 War. Sweet rest his soul! Fly, lords, and save
  yourselves;
For Warwick bids you all farewell, to meet in
  heaven.   [*Dies.*]
 Oxf. Away, away, to meet the Queen's great
  power!   50
  [*Here they bear away his body. Exeunt.*

[SCENE III. *Another part of the field.*]

Flourish. Enter KING EDWARD *in triumph; with*
GLOUCESTER, CLARENCE, *and the rest.*

 K. Edw. Thus far our fortune keeps an upward
  course
And we are grac'd with wreaths of victory.
But, in the midst of this bright-shining day
I spy a black, suspicious, threat'ning cloud,
That will encounter with our glorious sun 5
Ere he attain his easeful western bed.
I mean, my lords, those powers that the Queen
Hath rais'd in Gallia have arriv'd our coast
And, as we hear, march on to fight with us.
 Clar. A little gale will soon disperse that cloud   10
And blow it to the source from whence it came.
Thy very beams will dry those vapours up,
For every cloud engenders not a storm.
 Glou. The Queen is valued thirty thousand
  strong,
And Somerset, with Oxford, fled to her. 15
If she have time to breathe, be well assur'd
Her faction will be full as strong as ours.
 K. Edw. We are advertis'd by our loving friends
That they do hold their course toward Tewksbury.
We, having now the best at Barnet field, 20
Will thither straight, for willingness rids way;
And, as we march, our strength will be augmented
In every county as we go along.
Strike up the drum! Cry, "Courage!" and away.
           [*Exeunt.*

[SCENE IV. *Plains near Tewksbury.*]

March. Enter QUEEN MARGARET, PRINCE EDWARD,
SOMERSET, OXFORD, *and soldiers.*

 Q. Mar. Great lords, wise men ne'er sit and wail
  their loss,
But cheerly seek how to redress their harms.
What though the mast be now blown overboard,
The cable broke, the holding-anchor lost,
And half our sailors swallow'd in the flood? 5
Yet lives our pilot still. Is't meet that he

Should leave the helm and like a fearful lad
With tearful eyes add water to the sea
And give more strength to that which hath too
  much,
Whiles, in his moan, the ship splits on the rock,   10
Which industry and courage might have sav'd?
Ah, what a shame! ah, what a fault were this!
Say Warwick was our anchor; what of that?
And Montague our topmast; what of him?
Our slaught'red friends the tackles; what of these?
Why, is not Oxford here another anchor? 16
And Somerset another goodly mast?
The friends of France our shrouds and tacklings?
And, though unskillful, why not Ned and I
For once allow'd the skillful pilot's charge? 20
We will not from the helm to sit and weep,
But keep our course, though the rough wind say no,
From shelves and rocks that threaten us with
  wreck.
As good to chide the waves as speak them fair.
And what is Edward but a ruthless sea? 25
What Clarence but a quicksand of deceit?
And Richard but a [ragged] fatal rock?
All these the enemies to our poor bark.
Say you can swim; alas, 'tis but a while!
Tread on the sand; why, there you quickly sink.   30
Bestride the rock; the tide will wash you off,
Or else you famish; that's a threefold death.
This speak I, lords, to let you understand,
If case some one of you would fly from us,
That there's no hop'd-for mercy with the brothers
More than with ruthless waves, with sands and
  rocks.   36
Why, courage then! What cannot be avoided
'Twere childish weakness to lament or fear.
 Prince. Methinks a woman of this valiant spirit
Should, if a coward heard her speak these words,   40
Infuse his breast with magnanimity
And make him, naked, foil a man at arms.
I speak not this as doubting any here;
For did I but suspect a fearful man,
He should have leave to go away betimes 45
Lest in our need he might infect another
And make him of like spirit to himself.
If any such be here — as God forbid! —
Let him depart before we need his help.
 Oxf. Women and children of so high a courage,   50
And warriors faint! Why, 'twere perpetual shame.
O brave young prince! thy famous grandfather
Doth live again in thee. Long may'st thou live
To bear his image and renew his glories!
 Som. And he that will not fight for such a hope
Go home to bed, and like the owl by day, 56
If he arise, be mock'd and wond'red at.

---

44. [clamour] Q. *cannon* F.
Sc. iii, 21. **rids way**: shortens the road.
Sc. iv, 27. [ragged] (Rowe). *raged* F.

Q. Mar. Thanks, gentle Somerset; sweet Oxford, thanks.

Prince. And take his thanks that yet hath nothing else.

Enter a MESSENGER

Mess. Prepare you, lords, for Edward is at hand
Ready to fight; therefore be resolute.   61

Oxf. I thought no less. It is his policy
To haste thus fast, to find us unprovided.

Som. But he's deceiv'd, we are in readiness.

Q. Mar. This cheers my heart, to see your forwardness.   65

Oxf. Here pitch our battle; hence we will not budge.

Flourish and march. Enter KING EDWARD,
GLOUCESTER, CLARENCE, *and soldiers.*

K. Edw. Brave followers, yonder stands the thorny wood
Which, by the heavens' assistance and your strength,
Must by the roots be hewn up yet ere night.
I need not add more fuel to your fire,   70
For well I wot ye blaze to burn them out.
Give signal to the fight, and to it, lords!

Q. Mar. Lords, knights, and gentlemen, what I should say
My tears gainsay; for, every word I speak,
Ye see, I drink the water of my eye.   75
Therefore, no more but this: Henry, your sovereign
Is prisoner to the foe; his state usurp'd,
His realm a slaughter-house, his subjects slain,
His statutes cancell'd, and his treasure spent;
And yonder is the wolf that makes this spoil.   80
You fight in justice; then, in God's name, lords,
Be valiant and give signal to the fight.

[*Alarum. Retreat. Excursions. Exeunt.*

[SCENE V. *Another part of the field.*]

Flourish. Enter KING EDWARD, GLOUCESTER,
CLARENCE, [*and soldiers; with*] QUEEN MARGARET,
OXFORD, *and* SOMERSET [*prisoners*].

K. Edw. Now here a period of tumultuous broils.
Away with Oxford to Hames Castle straight;
For Somerset, off with his guilty head.
Go, bear them hence; I will not hear them speak.

Oxf. For my part, I'll not trouble thee with words.

Som. Nor I, but stoop with patience to my fortune.   6

[*Exeunt [Oxford and Somerset, guarded*].

Q. Mar. So part we sadly in this troublous world,
To meet with joy in sweet Jerusalem.

K. Edw. Is proclamation made, that who finds Edward
Shall have a high reward, and he his life?   10

Glou. It is; and lo, where youthful Edward comes!

Enter [*soldiers, with*] PRINCE EDWARD.

K. Edw. Bring forth the gallant, let us hear him speak.
What! can so young a thorn begin to prick?
Edward, what satisfaction canst thou make
For bearing arms, for stirring up my subjects,   15
And all the trouble thou hast turn'd me to?

Prince. Speak like a subject, proud ambitious York!
Suppose that I am now my father's mouth;
Resign thy chair, and where I stand kneel thou,
Whilst I propose the self-same words to thee,   20
Which, traitor, thou wouldst have me answer to.

Q. Mar. Ah, that thy father had been so resolv'd!

Glou. That you might still have worn the petticoat,
And ne'er have stolen the breech from Lancaster.

Prince. Let Æsop fable in a winter's night;   25
His currish riddles sorts not with this place.

Glou. By heaven, brat, I'll plague ye for that word.

Q. Mar. Ay, thou wast born to be a plague to men.

Glou. For God's sake, take away this captive scold.

Prince. Nay, take away this scolding crook-back rather.   30

K. Edw. Peace, wilful boy, or I will charm your tongue.

Clar. Untutor'd lad, thou art too malapert.

Prince. I know my duty; you are all undutiful.
Lascivious Edward, and thou perjur'd George,
And thou mis-shapen Dick, I tell ye all   35
I am your better, traitors as ye are;
And thou usurp'st my father's right and mine.

K. Edw. Take that, the likeness of this railer here.
[*Stabs him.*

Glou. Sprawl'st thou? Take that, to end thy agony.   [*Stabs him.*

Clar. And there's for twitting me with perjury.
[*Stabs him.*

Q. Mar. O, kill me too!   41

Glou. Marry, and shall.   [*Offers to kill her.*

K. Edw. Hold, Richard, hold; for we have done too much.

Glou. Why should she live, to fill the world with words?

K. Edw. What, doth she swoon? Use means for her recovery.   45

Glou. Clarence, excuse me to the King my brother;
I'll hence to London on a serious matter.
Ere ye come there, be sure to hear some news.

Clar. What? what?

Glou. [The] Tower, the Tower.   [*Exit.* 50

Q. Mar. O Ned, sweet Ned! speak to thy mother, boy!

Sc. v, 1. **period:** end.   25. Æsop was said to have been deformed.   31. **charm:** silence.   38. **this railer:** Margaret.   50.
[The] (Capell). Om. F.

Canst thou not speak? O traitors! murderers!
They that stabb'd Cæsar shed no blood at all,
Did not offend, nor were not worthy blame,
If this foul deed were by to equal it.   55
He was a man; this, in respect, a child,
And men ne'er spend their fury on a child.
What's worse than murderer, that I may name it?
No, no, my heart will burst an if I speak,
And I will speak that so my heart may burst.   60
Butchers and villains! bloody cannibals!
How sweet a plant have you untimely cropp'd!
You have no children, butchers! if you had,
The thought of them would have stirr'd up remorse;
But if you ever chance to have a child,   65
Look in his youth to have him so cut off
As, deathsmen, you have rid this sweet young prince!
   K. Edw. Away with her! Go, bear her hence
    perforce.
   Q. Mar. Nay, never bear me hence, dispatch me
    here;   69
Here sheathe thy sword, I'll pardon thee my death.
What, wilt thou not? Then, Clarence, do it thou.
   Clar. By heaven I will not do thee so much ease.
   Q. Mar. Good Clarence, do; sweet Clarence, do
    thou do it.
   Clar. Didst thou not hear me swear I would not
    do it?
   Q. Mar. Ay, but thou usest to forswear thyself;
'Twas sin before, but now 'tis charity.   76
What, wilt thou not? Where is that devil's
    butcher, Richard,
Hard-favour'd Richard? Richard, where art thou?
Thou art not here. Murder is thy alms-deed;
Petitioners for blood thou ne'er put'st back.   80
   K. Edw. Away, I say; I charge ye, bear her hence.
   Q. Mar. So come to you and yours, as to this
    prince!   [*Exit* [*led out forcibly*].
   K. Edw. Where's Richard gone?
   Clar. To London, all in post; and, as I guess,
To make a bloody supper in the Tower.   85
   K. Edw. He's sudden, if a thing comes in his head.
Now march we hence. Discharge the common sort
With pay and thanks, and let's away to London
And see our gentle queen how well she fares.
By this, I hope, she hath a son for me. [*Exeunt.* 90

[SCENE VI. *London. The Tower.*]

Enter KING HENRY *and* GLOUCESTER *with the*
Lieutenant, *on the walls.*

   Glou. Good day, my lord. What, at your book so
    hard?
   K. Hen. Ay, my good lord: — my lord, I should
    say rather.

'Tis sin to flatter; "good" was little better.
"Good Gloucester" and "good devil" were alike,
And both preposterous; therefore, not "good lord."
   Glou. Sirrah, leave us to ourselves. We must con-
    fer.   [*Exit Lieutenant.* 6
   K. Hen. So flies the reckless shepherd from the
    wolf;
So first the harmless sheep doth yield his fleece
And next his throat unto the butcher's knife.
What scene of death hath Roscius now to act?   10
   Glou. Suspicion always haunts the guilty mind.
The thief doth fear each bush an officer.
   K. Hen. The bird that hath been limed in a bush
With trembling wings misdoubteth every bush;
And I, the hapless male to one sweet bird,   15
Have now the fatal object in my eye
Where my poor young was lim'd, was caught, and
    kill'd.
   Glou. Why, what a peevish fool was that of Crete
That taught his son the office of a fowl!
And yet, for all his wings, the fool was drown'd.   20
   K. Hen. I, Dædalus; my poor boy, Icarus;
Thy father, Minos, that deni'd our course;
The sun that sear'd the wings of my sweet boy,
Thy brother Edward; and thyself, the sea
Whose envious gulf did swallow up his life.   25
Ah, kill me with thy weapon, not with words!
My breast can better brook thy dagger's point
Than can my ears that tragic history.
But wherefore dost thou come? Is't for my life?
   Glou. Think'st thou I am an executioner?   30
   K. Hen. A persecutor, I am sure, thou art.
If murdering innocents be executing,
Why, then thou art an executioner.
   Glou. Thy son I kill'd for his presumption.
   K. Hen. Hadst thou been kill'd when first thou
    didst presume,   35
Thou hadst not liv'd to kill a son of mine.
And thus I prophesy, that many a thousand
Which now mistrust no parcel of my fear,
And many an old man's sigh and many a widow's,
And many an orphan's water-standing eye —   40
Men for their sons, wives for their husbands,
And orphans for their parents' timeless death —
Shall rue the hour that ever thou wast born.
The owl shriek'd at thy birth, an evil sign;
The night-crow cried, aboding luckless time;   45
Dogs howl'd, and hideous tempest shook down trees;
The raven rook'd her on the chimney's top,
And chattering pies in dismal discords sung.
Thy mother felt more than a mother's pain,
And yet brought forth less than a mother's hope,   50
To wit, an indigested and deformed lump,
Not like the fruit of such a goodly tree.

---

67. **deathsmen:** executioners. 78. **Hard-favour'd:** ugly. 84. **all in post:** post-haste.
  Sc. vi, 10. **Roscius:** a great Roman actor. 18. **peevish:** foolish. **that of Crete:** Dædalus, who made wings for his son.
40. **water-standing:** tear-flooded. 42. **timeless:** untimely. 45. **aboding:** foreboding. 47. **rook'd her:** croaked.

Teeth hadst thou in thy head when thou wast born,
To signify thou cam'st to bite the world;
And, if the rest be true which I have heard,   55
Thou cam'st —
   Glou. I'll hear no more; die, prophet, in thy
      speech.   [*Stabs him.*
For this, amongst the rest, was I ordain'd.
   K. Hen. Ay, and for much more slaughter after
      this.
O, God forgive my sins, and pardon thee! [*Dies.* 60
   Glou. What, will the aspiring blood of Lancaster
Sink in the ground?   I thought it would have
     mounted.
See how my sword weeps for the poor king's death!
O, may such purple tears be alway shed
From those that wish the downfall of our house!   65
If any spark of life be yet remaining,
Down, down to hell; and say I sent thee thither,
                    [*Stabs him again.*
I, that have neither pity, love, nor fear.
Indeed, 'tis true that Henry told me of;
For I have often heard my mother say   70
I came into the world with my legs forward.
Had I not reason, think ye, to make haste,
And seek their ruin that usurp'd our right?
The midwife wonder'd and the women cri'd,
"O, Jesus bless us, he is born with teeth!"   75
And so I was; which plainly signified
That I should snarl and bite and play the dog.
Then, since the heavens have shap'd my body so,
Let hell make crook'd my mind to answer it.
I have no brother, I am like no brother;   80
And this word "love," which greybeards call divine,
Be resident in men like one another
And not in me. I am myself alone.
Clarence, beware! Thou keep'st me from the light,
But I will sort a pitchy day for thee;   85
For I will buzd abroad such prophecies
That Edward shall be fearful of his life,
And then, to purge his fear, I'll be thy death.
King Henry and the Prince his son are gone.
Clarence, thy turn is next, and then the rest,   90
Counting myself but bad till I be best.
I'll throw thy body in another room
And triumph, Henry, in thy day of doom.
                    [*Exit* [*with the body*].

    [SCENE VII. *London. The palace.*]

Flourish. KING EDWARD, [*upon the throne;*] QUEEN
   ELIZABETH, CLARENCE, GLOUCESTER, HASTINGS,
   a Nurse [*with the young Prince,*] and Attendants.
   K. Edw. Once more we sit in England's royal
      throne.

Re-purchas'd with the blood of enemies.
What valiant foemen, like to autumn's corn,
Have we mow'd down in tops of all their pride!
Three Dukes of Somerset, threefold renown'd   5
For hardy and undoubted champions;
Two Cliffords, as the father and the son,
And two Northumberlands; two braver men
Ne'er spurr'd their coursers at the trumpet's sound;
With them, the two brave bears, Warwick and
     Montague,   10
That in their chains fetter'd the kingly lion
And made the forest tremble when they roar'd.
Thus have we swept suspicion from our seat
And made our footstool of security.
Come hither, Bess, and let me kiss my boy.   15
Young Ned, for thee, thine uncles and myself
Have in our armours watch'd the winter's night.
Went all afoot in summer's scalding heat,
That thou mightst repossess the crown in peace;
And of our labours thou shalt reap the gain.   20
   Glou. [*Aside.*] I'll blast his harvest, if your head
     were laid,
For yet I am not look'd on in the world.
This shoulder was ordain'd so thick to heave;
And heave it shall some weight, or break my
     back.
Work thou the way, — and thou shalt execute.   25
   K. Edw. Clarence and Gloucester, love my lovely
     queen;
And kiss your princely nephew, brothers both.
   Clar. The duty that I owe unto your Majesty
I seal upon the lips of this sweet babe.
   [*Q. Eliz.*] Thanks, noble Clarence; worthy
     brother, thanks.   30
   Glou. And, that I love the tree from whence thou
     sprang'st,
Witness the loving kiss I give the fruit.
[*Aside.*] To say the truth, so Judas kiss'd his
     master
And cried, "All hail!" whenas he meant all harm.
   K. Edw. Now am I seated as my soul delights,   35
Having my country's peace and brothers' loves.
   Clar. What will your Grace have done with
     Margaret?
Reignier, her father, to the King of France
Hath pawn'd the Sicils and Jerusalem,
And hither have they sent it for her ransom.   40
   K. Edw. Away with her, and waft her hence to
     France.
And now what rests but that we spend the time
With stately triumphs, mirthful comic shows,
Such as befits the pleasure of the court?
Sound drums and trumpets! Farewell sour annoy!
For here, I hope, begins our lasting joy. [*Exeunt.* 46

85. sort: pick.
   Sc. vii, 4. in tops: at the height.   21. your ... laid: you were dead.   22. look'd on: i.e., as important.   25. thou ... thou:
my head ... my hand (indicated by gesture).   40. it: the money.

The Tragedy of Richard the Third

THE ONLY EXTERNAL evidence for the date of *Richard III* is the publication of the First Quarto in 1597. The marks of Shakespeare's early style, and especially of the influence of Marlowe, are, however, so pronounced as to have led to a general agreement that the play was composed some years before that date, probably about 1593.

The Quarto of 1597 was reprinted in 1598, with the name of Shakespeare on the title page, but without further change. Other Quartos appeared in 1602, 1605, 1612, 1622, 1629, and 1634, but all derive ultimately from the text of 1597. The version in the First Folio is independent, and differs widely in detail from the text of the Quartos. The question of the comparative authority of these texts is exceedingly complicated. Each contains passages essential to the context but lacking in the other. The Folio has besides many additions quite apposite and in the manner of Shakespeare, though the corresponding place in the Quarto shows no lacuna. The difficulty is thus to determine which goes back to the earlier original, and whether Shakespeare himself is responsible for the variations. Opinions still differ widely on these points, but are for the most part agreed that the Folio is to be regarded as the more authentic version; and it is, accordingly, made the basis of the present text. A striking peculiarity of the case is that the variations are too numerous to be plausibly accounted for as mistakes of copyist or printer, and are often so slight in their effect on meaning or rhythm that it is hard to believe them the result of conscious revision. They are very frequently such differences as might be explained by lapse of memory; and it is probable that in the First Quarto we have an exceptionally correct short-hand writer's report of the play, the variations being largely due to the slips of the actors; though some hold that the Quarto is from a transcript of the acting copy, perhaps made by a prompter who often followed his recollection of what he had heard the actors say rather than the manuscript before him.

The chief basis of the action is, as usual, Holin-shed, who, in dealing with the events of Acts I, II, III, and part of IV, follows the history of the reigns of Edward V and Richard III ascribed to Sir Thomas More, and the *Historia Anglica* of Polydore Vergil, as transmitted in the Chronicle of Halle; and who in the story corresponding to the rest of Act IV and to Act V, follows Halle. But before Shakespeare's there had been two, if not more, dramatic treatments of the theme. The *Richardus Tertius* of Dr. Legge is a Latin chronicle play written, perhaps as early as 1573, for performance at the University of Cambridge. *The True Tragedie of Richard III* is anonymous and of uncertain date, but was apparently a sequel to *3 Henry VI*. Both of these contributed to the dramatic tradition of Richard, but that they affected Shakespeare directly or at all remains to be proved. Some details seem to have been gathered from such narratives as those in *The Mirror for Magistrates*.

But it was the Chronicles of Holinshed or Halle which supplied almost all the episodes and the outlines of most of the characters, especially the men. These outlines, however, are in every case filled in by Shakespeare, whose imagination caught up and vitalized the merest hints of character. Most of the famous speeches are purely the invention of the dramatist. The opening soliloquy, the wooing of Anne, the two great cursing scenes in which Margaret of Anjou plays the chief part, the dream and the murder scene of Clarence, and the exchange of repartee between Gloucester and the little Duke of York, are all without foundation in Holinshed. Gloucester's hypocritical pre-occupation with holy exercises on the occasion of the visit of the Mayor and Buckingham with the offer of the crown, is based on the parenthetical phrase, "with a bishop on every hand of him." The substance and tone of the addresses of the rival leaders to their armies in V.iii. are suggested by the Chronicle.

The historical accuracy, in its main lines, of the portrait of Richard is still a matter of dispute among historians. But the falsification, if such there be, is only in a small degree due to Shakespeare; it had already occurred in the authorities from whom he drew the facts for which he supplied a plausible psychological explanation. It is important to remember that Henry Richmond, Richard's final rival, was the grandfather of Queen Elizabeth, and that the stamp of the Machiavellian villain had already been placed on Richard by Tudor historians like More and Polydore Vergil.

It is mainly through the tremendous emphasis on the central figure that Shakespeare passes from the loose structure that had characterized the earlier chronicle plays to the unity that was recognized in calling this drama *The Tragedy of Richard III*. The merely episodic scenes which made up the epic structure of a *Tamburlaine* give place to a series ascending to a climax. For a time it was common to ascribe to Marlowe at least a part in the authorship of *Richard III*, and the fact of his influence is still generally recognized. But Shakespeare had learned from Seneca and Kyd as well as from Marlowe, and in the present play he achieved a theatrical success beyond that of any predecessor.

The play was very popular in his time, as is shown by the large number of quartos, and it has held the stage down to the present day. The tremendous energy embodied in the main character, the biting quality of his speeches, and the opportunity for full-throated elocution have made the rôle a favorite one with actors; while the lack of subtlety and shading have made Richard vivid to every level of audience. In the histories which followed from *Richard II* to *Henry V*, Shakespeare maintained the structural advances shown in the present play, but abated the melodramatic intensity in the interest of a greater realism.

THE WOODVILLE FAMILY

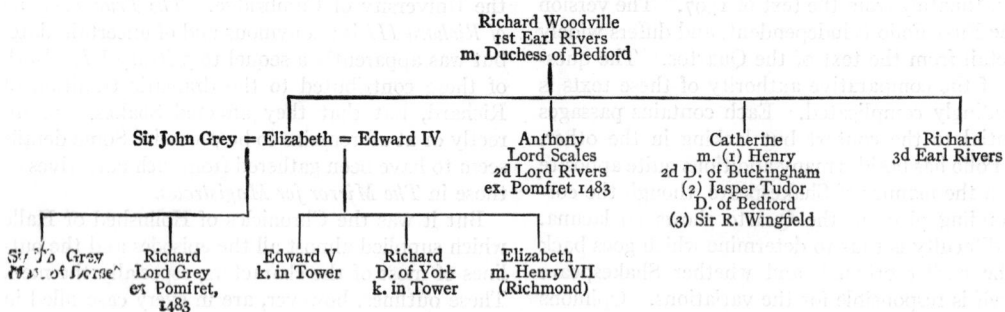

THE TRAGEDY OF
RICHARD THE THIRD

Margaret & Richard direct action [handwritten]
punishment they providential plan [handwritten]

p. 866 → [handwritten]
890 [handwritten]
902 l.27 [handwritten]

[DRAMATIS PERSONÆ

KING EDWARD IV.
EDWARD, PRINCE OF WALES, afterwards KING EDWARD V, } *sons to the King.*
RICHARD, *duke of York*,
GEORGE, *duke of Clarence*, } *brothers to the King.*
RICHARD, *duke of Gloucester*, afterwards KING RICHARD III,
A young son of Clarence (Edward, E. of Warwick).
HENRY, *earl of Richmond, afterwards* KING HENRY VII.
CARDINAL BOURCHIER, *archbishop of Canterbury*
THOMAS ROTHERHAM, *archbishop of York*.
JOHN MORTON, *bishop of Ely*.
DUKE OF BUCKINGHAM.
DUKE OF NORFOLK.
EARL OF SURREY, *his son*.
EARL RIVERS, *brother to Elizabeth*.
MARQUIS OF DORSET, } *sons to Elizabeth.*
LORD GREY,
EARL OF OXFORD,
LORD HASTINGS, *Lord Chamberlain*.
LORD STANLEY, *called also* EARL OF DERBY.
LORD LOVEL.

SIR THOMAS VAUGHAN.
SIR RICHARD RATCLIFF.
SIR WILLIAM CATESBY.
SIR JAMES TYRREL.
SIR JAMES BLUNT.
SIR WALTER HERBERT.
SIR ROBERT BRAKENBURY, *lieutenant of the Tower*.
SIR WILLIAM BRANDON, *Keeper in the Tower*.
CHRISTOPHER URSWICK, *a priest*.
Another Priest.
TRESSEL and BERKELEY, *gentlemen attending on the Lady Anne*.
Lord Mayor of London.
Sheriff of Wiltshire.

ELIZABETH, *queen to King Edward IV*.
MARGARET, *widow of King Henry VI*.
DUCHESS OF YORK, *mother to King Edward IV and King Richard III*.
LADY ANNE, *widow of Edward Prince of Wales, son to King Henry VI; afterwards married to Richard*.
A young Daughter of Clarence (MARGARET PLANTAGENET, *Countess of Salisbury*).

Ghosts of those murdered by Richard III; Lords and other Attendants, a Pursuivant, a Page, Scrivener, Citizens, Bishops, Aldermen, Murderers, Messengers, Soldiers, etc.

SCENE: *England.*]

ACT I

SCENE I. [*London. A street.*]

Enter RICHARD, DUKE OF GLOUCESTER, *solus.*

Glou. Now is the winter of our discontent
Made glorious summer by this sun of York;
And all the clouds that lour'd upon our house
In the deep bosom of the ocean buried.

Now are our brows bound with victorious wreaths;   6
Our bruised arms hung up for monuments;
Our stern alarums chang'd to merry meetings,
Our dreadful marches to delightful measures.
Grim-visag'd War hath smooth'd his wrinkled front;
And now, instead of mounting barbed steeds   10
To fright the souls of fearful adversaries,
He capers nimbly in a lady's chamber
To the lascivious pleasing of a lute.

Act I, sc. i, 2. **sun:** a pun on *son* and *sun.* King Edward's badge was a sun. Cf. *3 Henry VI*, II.i.25-40, V.iii.5. 8.
measures: dances. 10. **barbed:** armoured.

But I, that am not shap'd for sportive tricks,
Nor made to court an amorous looking-glass;   15
I, that am rudely stamp'd, and want love's majesty
To strut before a wanton ambling nymph;
I, that am curtail'd of this fair proportion,
Cheated of feature by dissembling nature,
Deform'd, unfinish'd, sent before my time   20
Into this breathing world, scarce half made up,
And that so lamely and unfashionable
That dogs bark at me as I halt by them;
Why, I, in this weak piping time of peace,
Have no delight to pass away the time,   25
Unless to see my shadow in the sun
And descant on mine own deformity.
And therefore, since I cannot prove a lover
To entertain these fair well-spoken days,
I am determined to prove a villain   30
And hate the idle pleasures of these days.
Plots have I laid, inductions dangerous,
By drunken prophecies, libels, and dreams,
To set my brother Clarence and the King
In deadly hate the one against the other;   35
And if King Edward be as true and just
As I am subtle, false, and treacherous,
This day should Clarence closely be mew'd up
About a prophecy, which says that G
Of Edward's heirs the murderer shall be.   40
Dive, thoughts, down to my soul! Here Clarence
    comes.

Enter CLARENCE, *guarded, and* BRAKENBURY.

Brother, good day. What means this armed guard
That waits upon your Grace?
   Clar.   His Majesty,
Tend'ring my person's safety, hath appointed
This conduct to convey me to the Tower.   45
   Glou. Upon what cause?
   Clar.   Because my name is George.
   Glou. Alack, my lord, that fault is none of yours;
He should, for that, commit your godfathers.
O, belike his Majesty hath some intent
That you should be new christ'ned in the Tower.   50
But what's the matter, Clarence? May I know?
   Clar. Yea, Richard, when I know, [for] I protest
As yet I do not; but, as I can learn,
He hearkens after prophecies and dreams,
And from the cross-row plucks the letter G,   55
And says a wizard told him that by G
His issue disinherited should be;
And, for my name of George begins with G,
It follows in his thought that I am he.
These, as I learn, and such like toys as these   60

Have mov'd his Highness to commit me now.
   Glou. Why, this it is, when men are rul'd by
    women.
'Tis not the King that sends you to the Tower;
My Lady Grey his wife, Clarence, 'tis she
That tempts him to this harsh extremity.   65
Was it not she and that good man of worship,
Anthony Woodville, her brother there,
That made him send Lord Hastings to the Tower,
From whence this present day he is delivered?
We are not safe, Clarence; we are not safe.   70
   Clar. By heaven, I think there is no man secure
But the Queen's kindred, and night-walking heralds
That trudge betwixt the King and Mistress Shore.
Heard you not what an humble suppliant
Lord Hastings was [to her for his] delivery?   75
   Glou. Humbly complaining to her deity
Got my Lord Chamberlain his liberty.
I'll tell you what; I think it is our way,
If we will keep in favour with the King,
To be her men and wear her livery.   80
The jealous o'erworn widow and herself,
Since that our brother dubb'd them gentlewomen,
Are mighty gossips in our monarchy.
   Brak. I beseech your Graces both to pardon me;
His Majesty hath straitly given in charge   85
That no man shall have private conference,
Of what degree soever, with your brother.
   Glou. Even so? An't please your worship,
    Brakenbury,
You may partake of anything we say.
We speak no treason, man. We say the King   90
Is wise and virtuous, and his noble queen
Well struck in years, fair, and not jealous;
We say that Shore's wife hath a pretty foot,
A cherry lip, a bonny eye, a passing pleasing tongue;
And that the Queen's kindred are made gentlefolks.
How say you, sir? Can you deny all this?   96
   Brak. With this, my lord, myself have nought
    to do.
   Glou. Naught to do with Mistress Shore! I tell
    thee, fellow,
He that doth naught with her, excepting one,
Were best to do it secretly, alone.   100
   Brak. What one, my lord?
   Glou. Her husband, knave. Wouldst thou
    betray me?
   Brak. I do beseech your Grace to pardon me,
    and withal
Forbear your conference with the noble Duke.
   Clar. We know thy charge, Brakenbury, and
    will obey.   105

19. **feature**: general appearance. **dissembling**: cheating.   22. **unfashionable**: badly made.   25. **to pass**: in passing. 27. **descant**: comment variously.   32. **inductions**: preparations.   38. **mew'd up**: caged (like a hawk).   44. **Tend'ring**: caring for.   52. **[for]** Q. *but* F.   55. **cross-row**: alphabet.   60. **toys**: trifles.   73. **Mistress Shore**: Jane Shore, wife of a London goldsmith and mistress of Edward.   75. **[to her for his]** Q. *for her* F.   78. **way**: best policy.   81. **widow**: Queen Elizabeth.   83. **mighty gossips**: powerful busybodies.   92. **Well struck**: advanced.

Glou. We are the Queen's abjects and must obey.
Brother, farewell! I will unto the King;
And whatsoe'er you will employ me in,
Were it to call King Edward's widow sister,
I will perform it to enfranchise you. 110
Meantime, this deep disgrace in brotherhood
Touches me deeper than you can imagine.
   Clar. I know it pleaseth neither of us well.
   Glou. Well, your imprisonment shall not be long;
I will deliver you, or else lie for you. 115
Meantime, have patience.
   Clar.   I must perforce. Farewell.
   [Exeunt Clarence [Brackenbury, and Guard].
   Glou. Go, tread the path that thou shalt ne'er return,
Simple, plain Clarence! I do love thee so
That I will shortly send thy soul to heaven,
If heaven will take the present at our hands. 120
But who comes here? The new-delivered Hastings?

Enter LORD HASTINGS.

   Hast. Good time of day unto my gracious lord!
   Glou. As much unto my good Lord Chamberlain!
Well are you welcome to the open air.
How hath your lordship brook'd imprisonment?
   Hast. With patience, noble lord, as prisoners must; 126
But I shall live, my lord, to give them thanks
That were the cause of my imprisonment.
   Glou. No doubt, no doubt; and so shall Clarence too;
For they that were your enemies are his 130
And have prevail'd as much on him as you.
   Hast. More pity that the eagles should be mew'd
Whiles kites and buzzards play at liberty.
   Glou. What news abroad?
   Hast. No news so bad abroad as this at home: 135
The King is sickly, weak, and melancholy,
And his physicians fear him mightily.
   Glou. Now, by Saint John, that news is bad indeed.
O, he hath kept an evil diet long,
And overmuch consum'd his royal person. 140
'Tis very grievous to be thought upon.
Where is he? In his bed?
   Hast. He is.
   Glou. Go you before, and I will follow you.
              [Exit Hastings.
He cannot live, I hope; and must not die 145
Till George be pack'd with post-horse up to heaven.
I'll in, to urge his hatred more to Clarence
With lies well steel'd with weighty arguments;
And, if I fail not in my deep intent,

Clarence hath not another day to live; 150
Which done, God take King Edward to his mercy,
And leave the world for me to bustle in!
For then I'll marry Warwick's youngest daughter.
What though I kill'd her husband and her father?
The readiest way to make the wench amends 155
Is to become her husband and her father,
The which will I; not all so much for love
As for another secret close intent
By marrying her which I must reach unto.
But yet I run before my horse to market: 160
Clarence still breathes; Edward still lives and reigns;
When they are gone, then must I count my gains.
                     [Exit.

SCENE II. *[The same. Another street.]*

Enter the corpse of KING HENRY VI, *[*GENTLEMEN*]
with halberds to guard it, [among them* TRESSEL
and BERKELEY;*]* LADY ANNE *being the mourner.*

   Anne. Set down, set down your honourable load,
If honour may be shrouded in a hearse,
Whilst I a while obsequiously lament
Th' untimely fall of virtuous Lancaster.
             [The coffin is set down.]
Poor key-cold figure of a holy king! 5
Pale ashes of the house of Lancaster!
Thou bloodless remnant of that royal blood!
Be it lawful that I invocate thy ghost
To hear the lamentations of poor Anne,
Wife to thy Edward, to thy slaught'red son, 10
Stabb'd by the self-same hand that made these wounds!
Lo, in these windows that let forth thy life
I pour the helpless balm of my poor eyes.
O cursed be the hand that made these holes!
Cursed the heart that had the heart to do it! 15
Cursed the blood that let this blood from hence!
More direful hap betide that hated wretch
That makes us wretched by the death of thee
Than I can wish to wolves, to spiders, toads,
Or any creeping venom'd thing that lives! 20
If ever he have child, abortive be it,
Prodigious, and untimely brought to light,
Whose ugly and unnatural aspect
May fright the hopeful mother at the view;
And that be heir to his unhappiness! 25
If ever he have wife, let her be made
More miserable by the death of him
Than I am made by my young lord and thee!
Come, now towards Chertsey with your holy load,
Taken from Paul's to be interred there; 30

---

106. **abjects:** servile subjects. 115. **lie:** i.e., in prison, with a play on the sense of prevaricate. 137. **fear:** fear for.
148. **steel'd:** hardened.
    Sc. ii, 3. obsequiously: mournfully.

And still, as you are weary of this weight,
Rest you, whiles I lament King Henry's corse.

                [The bearers take up the coffin.]

         Enter GLOUCESTER

Glou. Stay, you that bear the corse, and set it
    down.
Anne. What black magician conjures up this
    fiend
To stop devoted charitable deeds?   35
    Glou. Villains, set down the corse; or, by Saint
    Paul,
I'll make a corse of him that disobeys.
    Gent. My lord, stand back, and let the coffin
    pass.
    Glou. Unmanner'd dog! stand thou, when I
    command.
Advance thy halberd higher than my breast   40
Or, by Saint Paul, I'll strike thee to my foot
And spurn upon thee, beggar, for thy boldness.
             [The coffin is set down again.]
    Anne. What, do you tremble?   Are you all
    afraid?
Alas, I blame you not, for you are mortal
And mortal eyes cannot endure the devil.   45
Avaunt, thou dreadful minister of hell!
Thou hadst but power over his mortal body,
His soul thou canst not have; therefore, be gone.
    Glou. Sweet saint, for charity, be not so curst.
    Anne. Foul devil, for God's sake, hence, and
    trouble us not;   50
For thou hast made the happy earth thy hell,
Fill'd it with cursing cries and deep exclaims.
If thou delight to view thy heinous deeds,
Behold this pattern of thy butcheries.
O, gentlemen, see, see! dead Henry's wounds   55
Open their congeal'd mouths and bleed afresh!
Blush, blush, thou lump of foul deformity;
For 'tis thy presence that exhales this blood
From cold and empty veins, where no blood dwells.
Thy deed, inhuman and unnatural,   60
Provokes this deluge most unnatural.
O God, which this blood mad'st, revenge his death!
O earth, which this blood drink'st, revenge his
    death!
Either heaven with lightning strike the murd'rer
    dead,
Or earth gape open wide and eat him quick,   65
As thou dost swallow up this good king's blood
Which his hell-govern'd arm hath butchered!
    Glou. Lady, you know no rules of charity,
Which renders good for bad, blessings for curses.
    Anne. Villain, thou know'st nor law of God nor
    man.   70
No beast so fierce but knows some touch of pity.

    Glou. But I know none, and therefore am no beast.
    Anne. O wonderful, when devils tell the truth!
    Glou. More wonderful, when angels are so angry.
Vouchsafe, divine perfection of a woman,   75
Of these supposed crimes to give me leave
By circumstance but to acquit myself.
    Anne. Vouchsafe, defus'd infection of [a] man,
[For] these known evils but to give me leave
By circumstance to curse thy cursed self.   80
    Glou. Fairer than tongue can name thee, let me
    have
Some patient leisure to excuse myself.
    Anne. Fouler than heart can think thee, thou
    canst make
No excuse current but to hang thyself.
    Glou. By such despair I should accuse myself. 85
    Anne. And by despairing shalt thou stand excus'd
For doing worthy vengeance on thyself,
That didst unworthy slaughter upon others.
    Glou. Say that I slew them not?
    Anne.   Then say they were not slain.
But dead they are, and, devilish slave, by thee. 90
    Glou. I did not kill your husband.
    Anne.   Why, then he is alive.
    Glou. Nay, he is dead; and slain by Edward's
    hands.
    Anne. In thy foul throat thou liest! Queen
    Margaret saw
Thy murd'rous falchion smoking in his blood;
The which thou once didst bend against her breast,
But that thy brothers beat aside the point.   96
    Glou. I was provoked by her sland'rous tongue
That laid their guilt upon my guiltless shoulders.
    Anne. Thou wast provoked by thy bloody mind
That never dreamst on aught but butcheries.   100
Didst thou not kill this king?
    Glou.   I grant ye.
    Anne. Dost grant me, hedgehog?   Then, God
    grant me too
Thou mayst be damned for that wicked deed!
O, he was gentle, mild, and virtuous!
    Glou. The better for the King of heaven, that
    hath him.   105
    Anne. He is in heaven, where thou shalt never
    come.
    Glou. Let him thank me, that holp to send him
    ⁺hither,
For he was fitter for that place than earth.
    Anne. And thou unfit for any place but hell.
    Glou. Yes, one place else, if you will hear me
    name it.   110
    Anne. Some dungeon.
    Glou.   Your bed-chamber.
    Anne. Ill rest betide the chamber where thou
    liest!

54. **pattern**: example.   56. **bleed afresh** — as the bodies of murdered persons were believed to do in the presence of the murderer. 58. **exhales**: draws out. 78. **defus'd**: misshapen. [a] Q. Om. F. 79. [For] Q. *Of* F. 84. **current**: that will pass.

Glou. So will it, madam, till I lie with you.
Anne. I hope so.
Glou.   I know so. But, gentle Lady Anne,
To leave this keen encounter of our wits   115
And fall something into a slower method,
Is not the causer of the timeless deaths
Of these Plantagenets, Henry and Edward,
As blameful as the executioner?
     Anne. Thou wast the cause, and most accurs'd
          effect.   120
     Glou. Your beauty was the cause of that effect;
Your beauty, that did haunt me in my sleep
To undertake the death of all the world
So I might live one hour in your sweet bosom.
     Anne. If I thought that, I tell thee, homicide,   125
These nails should rend that beauty from my
          cheeks.
     Glou. These eyes could not endure that beauty's
          wreck;
You should not blemish it if I stood by.
As all the world is cheered by the sun,
So I by that; it is my day, my life.   130
     Anne. Black night o'ershade thy day, and death
          thy life!
     Glou. Curse not thyself, fair creature; thou art
          both.
     Anne. I would I were, to be reveng'd on thee.
     Glou. It is a quarrel most unnatural,
To be reveng'd on him that loveth thee.   135
     Anne. It is a quarrel just and reasonable,
To be reveng'd on him that kill'd my husband.
     Glou. He that bereft thee, lady, of thy husband
Did it to help thee to a better husband.
     Anne. His better doth not breathe upon the
          earth.   140
     Glou. He lives that loves thee better than he
          could.
     Anne. Name him.
     Glou.   Plantagenet.
     Anne.   Why, that was he.
     Glou. The self-same name, but one of better
          nature.
     Anne. Where is he?
     Glou.   Here. (*She spits at him.*) Why
          dost thou spit at me?   145
     Anne. Would it were mortal poison for thy sake!
     Glou. Never came poison from so sweet a place.
     Anne. Never hung poison on a fouler toad.
Out of my sight! Thou dost infect mine eyes.
     Glou. Thine eyes, sweet lady, have infected mine.
     Anne. Would they were basilisks, to strike thee
          dead!   151
     Glou. I would they were, that I might die at once,
For now they kill me with a living death.
Those eyes of thine from mine have drawn salt tears,
Sham'd their aspects with store of childish drops.

These eyes, which never shed remorseful tear,   156
No, when my father York and Edward wept
To hear the piteous moan that Rutland made
When black-fac'd Clifford shook his sword at
          him;
Nor when thy warlike father, like a child,   160
Told the sad story of my father's death,
And twenty times made pause to sob and weep
That all the standers-by had wet their cheeks
Like trees bedash'd with rain, — in that sad time
My manly eyes did scorn an humble tear;   165
And what these sorrows could not thence exhale
Thy beauty hath, and made them blind with
          weeping.
I never sued to friend nor enemy;
My tongue could never learn sweet smoothing
          words;
But, now thy beauty is propos'd my fee,   170
My proud heart sues and prompts my tongue to
          speak.   [*She looks scornfully at him.*
Teach not thy lip such scorn, for it was made
For kissing, lady, not for such contempt.
If thy revengeful heart cannot forgive,
Lo, here I lend thee this sharp-pointed sword,   175
Which if thou please to hide in this true breast
And let the soul forth that adoreth thee,
I lay it naked to the deadly stroke
And humbly beg the death upon my knee.
     [*He lays his breast open: she offers at it with
          his sword.*
Nay, do not pause; for I did kill King Henry,   180
But 'twas thy beauty that provoked me.
Nay, now dispatch; 'twas I that stabb'd young
          Edward,
But 'twas thy heavenly face that set me on.
                              [*She falls the sword.*
Take up the sword again, or take up me.
     Anne. Arise, dissembler! Though I wish thy
          death   185
I will not be thy executioner.
     Glou. Then bid me kill myself and I will do it.
     Anne. I have already.
     Glou.   That was in thy rage.
Speak it again, and even with the word
This hand, which for thy love did kill thy love,
Shall for thy love kill a far truer love;   191
To both their deaths shalt thou be accessary.
     Anne. I would I knew thy heart.
     Glou. 'Tis figur'd in my tongue.
     Anne. I fear me both are false.   195
     Glou. Then never man was true.
     Anne. Well, well, put up your sword.
     Glou. Say, then, my peace is made.
     Anne. That shalt thou know hereafter.
     Glou. But shall I live in hope?   200
     Anne. All men, I hope, live so.

117. **timeless:** untimely.   151. **basilisks:** fabulous serpents which killed by a glance.   194. **figur'd:** expressed.

[*Glou.*] Vouchsafe to wear this ring.
[*Anne.* To take is not to give.]

[*Puts on the ring.*]

Glou. Look, how my ring encompasseth thy finger,
Even so thy breast encloseth my poor heart.   205
Wear both of them, for both of them are thine.
And if thy poor devoted servant may
But beg one favour at thy gracious hand,
Thou dost confirm his happiness for ever.
   Anne. What is it?   210
   Glou. That it may please you leave these sad designs
To him that hath most cause to be a mourner,
And presently repair to Crosby House;
Where, after I have solemnly interr'd
At Chertsey monastery this noble king,   215
And wet his grave with my repentant tears,
I will with all expedient duty see you.
For divers unknown reasons, I beseech you,
Grant me this boon.
   Anne. With all my heart; and much it joys me too,   220
To see you are become so penitent.
Tressel and Berkeley, go along with me.
   Glou. Bid me farewell.
   Anne.   'Tis more than you deserve;
But since you teach me how to flatter you,
Imagine I have said farewell already.   225
         [*Exeunt Lady Anne, Tressel, and Berkeley.*
[*Glou.* Sirs, take up the corse.]
Gent.   Towards Chertsey, noble lord?
Glou. No, to White-Friars; there attend my coming.   [*Exeunt all but Gloucester.*
Was ever woman in this humour woo'd?
Was ever woman in this humour won?
I'll have her, but I will not keep her long.   230
What! I, that kill'd her husband and his father,
To take her in her heart's extremest hate,
With curses in her mouth, tears in her eyes,
The bleeding witness of my hatred by;
Having God, her conscience, and these bars against me,   235
And I no friends to back my suit withal
But the plain devil and dissembling looks,
And yet to win her, all the world to nothing!
Ha!
Hath she forgot already that brave prince,   240
Edward, her lord, whom I some three months since
Stabb'd in my angry mood at Tewksbury?
A sweeter and a lovelier gentleman,
Fram'd in the prodigality of nature,

Young, valiant, wise, and, no doubt, right royal,
The spacious world cannot again afford.   246
And will she yet abase her eyes on me,
That cropp'd the golden prime of this sweet prince
And made her widow to a woeful bed?
On me, whose all not equals Edward's moiety?   250
On me, that halts and am misshapen thus?
My dukedom to a beggarly denier,
I do mistake my person all this while.
Upon my life, she finds, although I cannot,
Myself to be a marvellous proper man.   255
I'll be at charges for a looking-glass,
And entertain a score or two of tailors
To study fashions to adorn my body.
Since I am crept in favour with myself,
I will maintain it with some little cost.   260
But first I'll turn yon fellow in his grave;
And then return lamenting to my love.
Shine out, fair sun, till I have bought a glass,
That I may see my shadow as I pass.   [*Exit.*

SCENE III. [*The palace.*]

Enter QUEEN ELIZABETH, LORD RIVERS, *and* LORD GREY.

Riv. Have patience, madam; there's no doubt his Majesty
Will soon recover his accustom'd health.
   Grey. In that you brook it ill, it makes him worse;
Therefore, for God's sake, entertain good comfort,
And cheer his Grace with quick and merry eyes. 5
   Q. Eliz. If he were dead, what would betide on me?
   Grey. No other harm but loss of such a lord.
   Q. Eliz. The loss of such a lord includes all harms.
   Grey. The heavens have bless'd you with a goodly son
To be your comforter when he is gone.   10
   Q. Eliz. Ah, he is young, and his minority
Is put unto the trust of Richard Gloucester,
A man that loves not me, nor none of you.
   Riv. Is it concluded he shall be Protector?
   Q. Eliz. It is determin'd, not concluded yet;   15
But so it must be, if the King miscarry.

Enter BUCKINGHAM *and* DERBY.

   Grey. Here comes the lords of Buckingham and Derby.
   Buck. Good time of day unto your royal Grace!
   Der. God make your Majesty joyful as you have been!
   Q. Eliz. The Countess Richmond, good my Lord of Derby,   20

202. [*Glou.*] Q. Om. F. 203. [*Anne...ring*] Q. Om. F. 213. **presently:** at once. 217. **expedient:** speedy. 226. [*Glou....* **corse**] Q. Om. F. 250. **Edward's moiety:** half of Edward. 252. **denier:** a small copper coin.
Sc. iii, 5. **quick:** lively. 15. **concluded:** put in operation. 20. **Countess Richmond:** Margaret Beaufort, great-grand-daughter of John of Gaunt, widow of Edmund Tudor, Earl of Richmond, and mother of the future Henry VII, had married the Earl of Derby.

To your good prayer will scarcely say amen.
Yet, Derby, notwithstanding she's your wife
And loves not me, be you, good lord, assur'd
I hate not you for her proud arrogance.

Der. I do beseech you, either not believe   25
The envious slanders of her false accusers;
Or, if she be accus'd on true report,
Bear with her weakness, which, I think, proceeds
From wayward sickness and no grounded malice.

Q. Eliz. Saw you the King to-day, my Lord of
Derby?   30

Der. But now the Duke of Buckingham and I
Are come from visiting his Majesty.

Q. Eliz. What likelihood of his amendment, lords?

Buck. Madam, good hope; his Grace speaks
cheerfully.

Q. Eliz. God grant him health! Did you confer
with him?   35

Buck. Ay, madam. He desires to make atonement
Between the Duke of Gloucester and your brothers,
And between them and my Lord Chamberlain;
And sent to warn them to his royal presence.

Q. Eliz. Would all were well! but that will never
be.   40
I fear our happiness is at the height.

Enter GLOUCESTER [HASTINGS, *and* DORSET].

Glou. They do me wrong and I will not endure it.
Who is it that complains unto the King
That I, forsooth, am stern and love them not?
By holy Paul, they love his Grace but lightly   45
That fill his ears with such dissentious rumours.
Because I cannot flatter and look fair,
Smile in men's faces, smooth, deceive, and cog,
Duck with French nods and apish courtesy,
I must be held a rancorous enemy.   50
Cannot a plain man live and think no harm
But thus his simple truth must be abus'd
With silken, sly, insinuating Jacks?

Grey. To who in all this presence speaks your
Grace?   54

Glou. To thee, that hast nor honesty nor grace.
When have I injur'd thee? When done thee wrong?
Or thee? or thee? or any of your faction?
A plague upon you all! His royal Grace —
Whom God preserve better than you would wish! —
Cannot be quiet scarce a breathing-while   60
But you must trouble him with lewd complaints.

Q. Eliz. Brother of Gloucester, you mistake the
matter.
The King on his own royal disposition,
And not provok'd by any suitor else,
Aiming, belike, at your interior hatred,   65
That in your outward action shows itself

Against my children, brothers, and myself,
Makes him to send that he may learn the ground.

Glou. I cannot tell. The world is grown so bad   70
That wrens make prey where eagles dare not perch.
Since every Jack became a gentleman,
There's many a gentle person made a Jack.

Q. Eliz. Come, come, we know your meaning,
brother Gloucester;
You envy my advancement and my friends'.   75
God grant we never may have need of you!

Glou. Meantime, God grants that I have need
of you.
Our brother is imprison'd by your means,
Myself disgrac'd, and the nobility
Held in contempt; while great promotions   80
Are daily given to ennoble those
That scarce, some two days since, were worth a
noble.

Q. Eliz. By Him that rais'd me to this careful
height
From that contented hap which I enjoy'd,
I never did incense his Majesty   85
Against the Duke of Clarence, but have been
An earnest advocate to plead for him.
My lord, you do me shameful injury
Falsely to draw me in these vile suspects.

Glou. You may deny that you were not the mean
Of my Lord Hastings' late imprisonment.   91

Riv. She may, my lord, for —

Glou. She may, Lord Rivers! Why, who knows
not so?
She may do more, sir, than denying that.
She may help you to many fair preferments   95
And then deny her aiding hand therein,
And lay those honours on your high desert.
What may she not? She may, ay, marry, may
she, —

Riv. What, marry, may she?

Glou. What, marry may she! Marry with a king,
A bachelor, and a handsome stripling too.   101
I wis your grandam had a worser match.

Q. Eliz. My Lord of Gloucester, I have too long
borne
Your blunt upbraidings and your bitter scoffs.
By heaven, I will acquaint his Majesty   105
Of those gross taunts that oft I have endur'd.
I had rather be a country servant-maid
Than a great queen with this condition,
To be thus baited, scorn'd, and stormed at.
Small joy have I in being England's Queen.   110

Enter old QUEEN MARGARET.

Q. Mar. And less'ned be that small, God I
beseech Him!

---

29. **wayward:** whimsical. 36. **atonement:** reconciliation. 39. **warn:** summon. 48. **cog:** cheat. 53. **Jacks:** fellows. 61. **lewd:** base. 77. **of you:** because of you. 82. **noble:** 6s.8d. 83. **careful:** full of care. 89. **suspects:** suspicions. 102. **wis:** assuredly.

Thy honour, state, and seat is due to me.
   Glou. What! threat you me with telling of the
     King?
[Tell him, and spare not. Look, what I have said]
I will avouch't in presence of the King.   115
I dare adventure to be sent to th' Tower.
'Tis time to speak; my pains are quite forgot.
   Q. Mar. Out, devil! I do remember them too
     well:
Thou kill'dst my husband Henry in the Tower,
And Edward, my poor son, at Tewksbury.   120
   Glou. Ere you were queen, ay, or your husband
     king,
I was a pack-horse in his great affairs,
A weeder-out of his proud adversaries,
A liberal rewarder of his friends.
To royalize his blood I spent mine own.   125
   Q. Mar. Ay, and much better blood than his or
     thine.
   Glou. In all which time you and your husband
     Grey
Were factious for the house of Lancaster;
And, Rivers, so were you. Was not your husband
In Margaret's battle at Saint Alban's slain?   130
Let me put in your minds, if you forget,
What you have been ere this and what you are;
Withal, what I have been and what I am.
   Q. Mar. A murd'rous villain, and so still thou art.
   Glou. Poor Clarence did forsake his father,
     Warwick,   135
Ay, and forswore himself — which Jesu pardon! —
   Q. Mar. Which God revenge!
   Glou. To fight on Edward's party for the crown;
And for his meed, poor lord, he is mew'd up.
I would to God my heart were flint, like Edward's;
Or Edward's soft and pitiful, like mine.   141
I am too childish-foolish for this world.
   Q. Mar. Hie thee to hell for shame, and leave
     this world,
Thou cacodemon! there thy kingdom is.
   Riv. My Lord of Gloucester, in those busy days
Which here you urge to prove us enemies,   146
We follow'd then our lord, our sovereign king.
So should we you if you should be our king.
   Glou. If I should be! I had rather be a pedlar.
Far be it from my heart, the thought thereof!   150
   Q. Eliz. As little joy, my lord, as you suppose
You should enjoy, were you this country's king,
As little joy you may suppose in me
That I enjoy, being the queen thereof.
   Q. Mar. A little joy enjoys the queen thereof;
For I am she, and altogether joyless.   156
I can no longer hold me patient.   [*Advancing.*]
Hear me, you wrangling pirates, that fall out
In sharing that which you have pill'd from me!
Which of you trembles not that looks on me?   160

If not that I am queen, you bow like subjects,
Yet that by you depos'd, you quake like rebels?
Ah, gentle villain, do not turn away!
   Glou. Foul wrinkled witch, what mak'st thou in
     my sight?
   Q. Mar. But repetition of what thou hast marr'd;
That will I make before I let thee go.   166
   Glou. Wert thou not banished on pain of death?
   Q. Mar. I was; but I do find more pain in ban-
     ishment
Than death can yield me here by my abode.
A husband and a son thou ow'st to me;   170
And thou a kingdom; all of you allegiance.
This sorrow that I have by right is yours,
And all the pleasures you usurp are mine.
   Glou. The curse my noble father laid on thee
When thou didst crown his warlike brows with
     paper   175
And with thy scorns drew'st rivers from his eyes
And then, to dry them, gav'st the Duke a clout
Steep'd in the faultless blood of pretty Rutland, —
His curses, then from bitterness of soul
Denounc'd against thee, are all fall'n upon thee;   180
And God, not we, hath plagu'd thy bloody deed.
   Q. Eliz. So just is God, to right the innocent.
   Hast. O, 'twas the foulest deed to slay that babe,
And the most merciless that e'er was heard of!
   Riv. Tyrants themselves wept when it was re-
     ported.   185
   Dor. No man but prophesied revenge for it.
   Buck. Northumberland, then present, wept to
     see it.
   Q. Mar. What! were you snarling all before I
     came,
Ready to catch each other by the throat,
And turn you all your hatred now on me?   190
Did York's dread curse prevail so much with heaven
That Henry's death, my lovely Edward's death,
Their kingdom's loss, my woeful banishment,
Should all but answer for that peevish brat?
Can curses pierce the clouds and enter heaven?   195
Why, then, give way, dull clouds, to my quick
     curses!
Though not by war, by surfeit die your king,
As ours by murder to make him a king!
Edward thy son, that now is Prince of Wales,
For Edward our son, that was Prince of Wales,   200
Die in his youth by like untimely violence!
Thyself a queen, for me that was a queen,
Outlive thy glory like my wretched self!
Long mayst thou live to wail thy children's death
And see another, as I see thee now,   205
Deck'd in thy rights as thou art stall'd in mine!
Long die thy happy days before thy death
And, after many length'ned hours of grief,
Die neither mother, wife, nor England's Queen!

114. Q. Om. F.   135. **father:** father-in-law.   144. **cacodemon:** evil spirit.   159. **pill'd:** pillaged.   206. **stall'd:** installed.

Rivers and Dorset, you were standers by   210
And so wast thou, Lord Hastings, when my son
Was stabb'd with bloody daggers: God I pray him,
That none of you may live his natural age,
But by some unlook'd accident cut off!
    Glou. Have done thy charm, thou hateful wither'd
      hag!   215
    Q. Mar. And leave out thee? Stay, dog, for
      thou shalt hear me.
If heaven have any grievous plague in store
Exceeding those that I can wish upon thee,
O, let them keep it till thy sins be ripe,
And then hurl down their indignation   220
On thee, the troubler of the poor world's peace!
The worm of conscience still begnaw thy soul!
Thy friends suspect for traitors while thou liv'st
And take deep traitors for thy dearest friends!
No sleep close up that deadly eye of thine   225
Unless it be while some tormenting dream
Affrights thee with a hell of ugly devils!
Thou elvish-mark'd, abortive, rooting hog!
Thou that wast seal'd in thy nativity
The slave of nature and the son of hell!   230
Thou slander of thy heavy mother's womb!
Thou loathed issue of thy father's loins!
Thou rag of honour! thou detested —
    Glou. Margaret.
    Q. Mar.   Richard!
    Glou.   Ha!
    Q. Mar.   I call thee not.
    Glou. I cry thee mercy then, for I did think   235
That thou hadst call'd me all these bitter names.
    Q. Mar. Why, so I did; but look'd for no reply.
O, let me make the period to my curse!
    Glou. 'Tis done by me, and ends in "Margaret."
    Q. Eliz. Thus have you breath'd your curse
      against yourself.   240
    Q. Mar. Poor painted queen, vain flourish of my
      fortune!
Why strew'st thou sugar on that bottl'd spider
Whose deadly web ensnareth thee about?
Fool, fool! thou whet'st a knife to kill thyself.
The day will come that thou shalt wish for me   245
To help thee curse this poisonous bunch-back'd
    toad.
    Hast. False-boding woman, end thy frantic curse,
Lest to thy harm thou move our patience.
    Q. Mar. Foul shame upon you! you have all
      mov'd mine.
    Riv. Were you well serv'd you would be taught
      your duty.   250
    Q. Mar. To serve me well you all should do me
      duty,
Teach me to be your queen and you my subjects.

O, serve me well and teach yourselves that duty!
    Dor. Dispute not with her; she is lunatic.
    Q. Mar. Peace, master marquess, you are mala-
      pert;   255
Your fire-new stamp of honour is scarce current.
O, that your young nobility could judge
What 'twere to lose it and be miserable!
They that stand high have many blasts to shake
    them;
And if they fall, they dash themselves to pieces.   260
    Glou. Good counsel, marry; learn it, learn it,
      marquess.
    Dor. It touches you, my lord, as much as me.
    Glou. Ay, and much more; but I was born so high,
Our aery buildeth in the cedar's top
And dallies with the wind and scorns the sun.   265
    Q. Mar. And turns the sun to shade; alas! alas!
Witness my son, now in the shade of death,
Whose bright out-shining beams thy cloudy wrath
Hath in eternal darkness folded up.
Your aery buildeth in our aery's nest.   270
O God that seest it, do not suffer it!
As it is won with blood, lost be it so!
    Buck. Peace, peace! for shame, if not for charity.
    Q. Mar. Urge neither charity nor shame to me.
Uncharitably with me have you dealt,   275
And shamefully my hopes by you are butcher'd.
My charity is outrage, life my shame;
And in that shame still live my sorrow's rage!
    Buck. Have done, have done.
    Q. Mar. O princely Buckingham, I'll kiss thy
      hand   280
In sign of league and amity with thee.
Now fair befall thee and thy noble house!
Thy garments are not spotted with our blood
Nor thou within the compass of my curse.
    Buck. Nor no one here; for curses never pass   285
The lips of those that breathe them in the air.
    Q. Mar. I will not think but they ascend the sky
And there awake God's gentle-sleeping peace.
[*Aside to Buck.*] O Buckingham, take heed of
      yonder dog!
Look, when he fawns he bites, and when he bites
His venom tooth will rankle to the death.   291
Have not to do with him, beware of him;
Sin, death, and hell have set their marks on him,
And all their ministers attend on him.
    Glou. What doth she say, my Lord of Bucking-
      ham?   295
    Buck. Nothing that I respect, my gracious lord.
    Q. Mar. What, dost thou scorn me for my gentle
      counsel
And soothe the devil that I warn thee from?
O, but remember this another day,

---

214. **unlook'd:** unexpected.   228. **elvish-mark'd:** deformed by elves.   230. **slave of nature:** born wretch.   241. **vain...
fortune:** empty ornament of the position which belongs to me.   242. **bottl'd:** big-bellied.   256. **fire-new:** brand new.
264. **aery:** eagle's brood.

When he shall split thy very heart with sorrow, 300
And say poor Margaret was a prophetess!
Live each of you the subjects to his hate,
And he to yours, and all of you to God's!   [Exit.
    Buck. My hair doth stand on end to hear her
        curses.
    Riv. And so doth mine.   I muse why she's at
        liberty.   305
    Glou. I cannot blame her.   By God's holy
        mother,
She hath had too much wrong, and I repent
My part thereof that I have done to her.
    Q. Eliz. I never did her any to my knowledge.
    Glou. Yet you have all the vantage of her wrong.
I was too hot to do somebody good   311
That is too cold in thinking of it now.
Marry, as for Clarence, he is well repaid;
He is frank'd up to fatting for his pains.
God pardon them that are the cause thereof!   315
    Riv. A virtuous and a Christian-like conclusion,
To pray for them that have done scathe to us.
    Glou. So do I ever, being well advis'd.
                            [Speaks to himself.
For had I curs'd now, I had curs'd myself.

            Enter CATESBY.

    Cates. Madam, his Majesty doth call for you;
And for your Grace; and yours, my noble lord. 321
    Q. Eliz. Catesby, I come.   Lords, will you go
        with me?
    Riv. We wait upon your Grace.
                        [Exeunt all but Gloucester.
    Glou. I do the wrong, and first begin to brawl.
The secret mischiefs that I set abroach   325
I lay unto the grievous charge of others.
Clarence, who I, indeed, have cast in darkness,
I do beweep to many simple gulls,
Namely, to Derby, Hastings, Buckingham;
And tell them 'tis the Queen and her allies   330
That stir the King against the Duke my brother.
Now, they believe it; and withal whet me
To be reveng'd on Rivers, Dorset, Grey.
But then I sigh, and, with a piece of scripture,
Tell them that God bids us do good for evil;   335
And thus I clothe my naked villainy
With odd old ends stol'n forth of holy writ,
And seem a saint when most I play the devil.

            Enter two MURDERERS.

But, soft! here come my executioners.
How now, my hardy, stout, resolved mates!   340
Are you now going to dispatch this thing?
    [I. Murd.] We are, my lord; and come to have
        the warrant

That we may be admitted where he is.
    Glou. Well thought upon; I have it here about me.
                        [Gives the warrant.]
When you have done, repair to Crosby Place.   345
But, sirs, be sudden in the execution;
Withal obdurate, do not hear him plead;
For Clarence is well-spoken and perhaps
May move your hearts to pity if you mark him.
    [I. Murd.] Tut, tut, my lord, we will not stand to
        prate.   351
Talkers are no good doers; be assur'd
We go to use our hands and not our tongues.
    Glou. Your eyes drop millstones, when fools' eyes
        fall tears.
I like you, lads; about your business straight. 355
Go, go, dispatch.
    [I. Murd.]   We will, my noble lord. [Exeunt.]

        SCENE IV.   [London.   The Tower.]

            Enter CLARENCE and KEEPER.

    Keep. Why looks your Grace so heavily today?
    Clar. O, I have pass'd a miserable night,
So full of fearful dreams, of ugly sights,
That, as I am a Christian faithful man,
I would not spend another such a night   5
Though 'twere to buy a world of happy days,
So full of dismal terror was the time.
    Keep. What was your dream, my lord?   I pray
        you, tell me.
    Clar. Methoughts that I had broken from the
        Tower
And was embark'd to cross to Burgundy;   10
And in my company my brother Gloucester,
Who from my cabin tempted me to walk
Upon the hatches.   There we look'd toward Eng-
        land,
And cited up a thousand heavy times
During the wars of York and Lancaster   15
That had befall'n us.   As we pac'd along
Upon the giddy footing of the hatches,
Methought that Gloucester stumbled, and in falling
Struck me, that thought to stay him, overboard
Into the tumbling billows of the main.   20
O Lord! methought what pain it was to drown!
What dreadful noise of water in mine ears!
What sights of ugly death within mine eyes!
Methoughts I saw a thousand fearful wrecks,
A thousand men that fishes gnaw'd upon,   25
Wedges of gold, great anchors, heaps of pearl,
Inestimable stones, unvalued jewels,
All scatt'red in the bottom of the sea.
Some lay in dead men's skulls; and, in the holes
Where eyes did once inhabit, there were crept,   30

---

305. muse: wonder.   314. frank'd up: shut up as in a sty.   317. scathe: harm.   325. abroach: a-going.   328. gulls: dupes.
342, 351, 356. [I. Murd.] (Capell).   Vil. F.
  Sc. iv, 27. unvalued: invaluable.

("and seem a saint" — handwritten margin note)

As 'twere in scorn of eyes, reflecting gems,
That woo'd the slimy bottom of the deep
And mock'd the dead bones that lay scatt'red by.
  Keep. Had you such leisure in the time of death
To gaze upon these secrets of the deep?   35
  Clar. Methought I had. And often did I strive
To yield the ghost; but still the envious flood
Stopp'd in my soul and would not let it forth
To find the empty, vast, and wand'ring air,
But smother'd it within my panting bulk,   40
Who almost burst to belch it in the sea.
  Keep. Awak'd you not in this sore agony?
  Clar. No, no, my dream was lengthen'd after
    life.
O, then began the tempest to my soul.
I pass'd, methought, the melancholy flood   45
With that sour ferryman which poets write of,
Unto the kingdom of perpetual night.
The first that there did greet my stranger soul
Was my great father-in-law, renowned Warwick,
Who spake aloud, "What scourge for perjury   50
Can this dark monarchy afford false Clarence?"
And so he vanish'd. Then came wand'ring by
A shadow like an angel, with bright hair
Dabbl'd in blood; and he shriek'd out aloud,
"Clarence is come; false, fleeting, perjur'd Clarence,
That stabb'd me in the field by Tewksbury.   56
Seize on him, Furies, take him unto torment!"
With that, methought, a legion of foul fiends
Environ'd me, and howled in mine ears
Such hideous cries that with the very noise   60
I trembling wak'd, and for a season after
Could not believe but that I was in hell,
Such terrible impression made my dream.
  Keep. No marvel, lord, though it affrighted you;
I am afraid, methinks, to hear you tell it.   65
  Clar. Ah! Keeper, Keeper, I have done these
    things
That now give evidence against my soul
For Edward's sake; and see how he requites me!
O God! if my deep prayers cannot appease thee,
But thou wilt be aveng'd on my misdeeds,   70
Yet execute thy wrath in me alone!
O, spare my guiltless wife and my poor children!
Keeper, I prithee, sit by me a while.
My soul is heavy, and I fain would sleep.
  Keep. I will, my lord. God give your Grace
    good rest!   [*Clarence sleeps.*] 75

     Enter BRAKENBURY, *the Lieutenant.*

  Brak. Sorrow breaks seasons and reposing hours,
Makes the night morning and the noon-tide night.
Princes have but their titles for their glories,
An outward honour for an inward toil;
And for unfelt imaginations   80

They often feel a world of restless cares,
So that between their titles and low name
There's nothing differs but the outward fame.

     Enter the two MURDERERS.

  1. Murd. Ho! who's here?
  Brak. What wouldst thou, fellow, and how cam'st
    thou hither?   85
  2. Murd. I would speak with Clarence, and I
came hither on my legs.
  Brak. What, so brief?
  1. Murd. 'Tis better, sir, than to be tedious.
Let him see our commission, and talk no more.   91
                     [*Brakenbury reads it.*
  Brak. I am in this commanded to deliver
The noble Duke of Clarence to your hands.
I will not reason what is meant hereby,
Because I will be guiltless from the meaning.   95
There lies the Duke asleep, and there the keys.
I'll to the King and signify to him
That thus I have resign'd to you my charge.
                   [*Exit* [*with Keeper*].
  1. Murd. You may, sir; 'tis a point of wisdom.
Fare you well.   100
  2. Murd. What, shall we stab him as he sleeps?
  1. Murd. No; he'll say 'twas done cowardly when
he wakes.
  2. Murd. Why, he shall never wake until the
great judgement-day.   106
  1. Murd. Why, then he'll say we stabb'd him
sleeping.
  2. Murd. The urging of that word "judgement"
hath bred a kind of remorse in me.   110
  1. Murd. What, art thou afraid?
  2. Murd. Not to kill him, having a warrant; but
to be damn'd for killing him, from the which no
warrant can defend me.
  1. Murd. I thought thou hadst been resolute.   116
  2. Murd. So I am, to let him live.
  1. Murd. I'll back to the Duke of Gloucester and
tell him so.
  2. Murd. Nay, I prithee, stay a little. I hope
this passionate humour of mine will change. It
was wont to hold me but while one tells twenty. 122
  1. Murd. How dost thou feel thyself now?
  2. Murd. Some certain dregs of conscience are
yet within me.
  1. Murd. Remember our reward when the deed's
done.
  2. Murd. ['Zounds], he dies! I had forgot the
reward.
  1. Murd. Where's thy conscience now?   130
  2. Murd. O, in the Duke of Gloucester's purse.
  1. Murd. When he opens his purse to give us
our reward, thy conscience flies out.

---

37. **envious:** malicious. 45. **flood:** the river Styx. 46. **ferryman:** Charon. 55. **fleeting:** inconstant. 80. **for unfelt imaginations:** in place of glories imagined but not experienced. 121. **passionate:** compassionate. 128. **['Zounds]** Q. *Come* F.

2. Murd. 'Tis no matter; let it go.   There's few
or none will entertain it.   135
1. Murd. What if it come to thee again?
2. Murd. I'll not meddle with it; [it is a dangerous thing;] it makes a man a coward.   A man
cannot steal but it accuseth him; a man cannot
swear but it checks him; a man cannot lie with
his neighbour's wife but it detects him.   'Tis a   140
blushing shamefac'd spirit that mutinies in a man's
bosom.   It fills a man full of obstacles.   It made
me once restore a purse of gold that by chance I
found.   It beggars any man that keeps it.   It is
turn'd out of towns and cities for a dangerous   145
thing; and every man that means to live well endeavours to trust to himself and live without it.
['Zounds,] 'tis even now at my elbow, persuading
me not to kill the Duke.   150
[*1.*] *Murd.* Take the devil in thy mind, and
believe him not; he would insinuate with thee but
to make thee sigh.
[*2.*] *Murd.* I am strong-fram'd, he cannot prevail
with me.   155
[*1.*] *Murd.* Spoke like a tall man that respects
thy reputation.   Come, shall we fall to work?
[*2.*] *Murd.* Take him on the costard with the
hilts of thy sword, and then throw him into the
malmsey-butt in the next room.   161
[*1.*] *Murd.* O excellent device! and make a sop
of him.
[*2.*] *Murd.* Soft!   He wakes.
[*1.*] *Murd.* Strike!
[*2.*] *Murd.* No, we'll reason with him.   165
Clar. Where art thou, Keeper?   Give me a cup
of wine.
[*1.*] *Murd.* You shall have wine enough, my lord,
anon.
Clar. In God's name, what art thou?
[*2.*] *Murd.* A man, as you are.   170
Clar. But not, as I am, royal.
[*2.*] *Murd.* Nor you, as we are, loyal.
Clar. Thy voice is thunder but thy looks are
humble.
[*2.*] *Murd.* My voice is now the King's, my looks
mine own.
Clar. How darkly and how deadly dost thou
speak!   175
Your eyes do menace me.   Why look you pale?
Who sent you hither?   Wherefore do you come?
2. Murd. To, to, to —
Clar. To murder me?
Both. Ay, ay.

Clar. You scarcely have the hearts to tell me so,
And therefore cannot have the hearts to do it.   181
Wherein, my friends, have I offended you?
1. Murd. Offended us you have not, but the
King.
Clar. I shall be reconcil'd to him again.
2. Murd. Never, my lord; therefore prepare to
die.   185
Clar. Are you drawn forth among a world of men
To slay the innocent?   What is my offence?
Where is the evidence that doth accuse me?
What lawful quest have given their verdict up
Unto the frowning judge? or who pronounc'd   190
The bitter sentence of poor Clarence' death?
Before I be convict by course of law,
To threaten me with death is most unlawful.
I charge you, as you hope [to have redemption
By Christ's dear blood shed for our grievous sins,]
That you depart and lay no hands on me.   196
The deed you undertake is damnable.
1. Murd. What we will do, we do upon command.
2. Murd. And he that hath commanded is our
King.
Clar. Erroneous vassals! the great King of kings
Hath in the table of his law commanded   201
That thou shalt do no murder.   Will you, then,
Spurn at His edict and fulfil a man's?
Take heed; for He holds vengeance in His hand,
To hurl upon their heads that break His law.   205
2. Murd. And that same vengeance doth He
hurl on thee
For false forswearing and for murder too,
Thou didst receive the sacrament to fight
In quarrel of the house of Lancaster.
1. Murd. And like a traitor to the name of God
Didst break that vow; and with thy treacherous
blade   211
Unripp'd'st the bowels of thy sovereign's son.
2. Murd. Whom thou wast sworn to cherish and
defend.
1. Murd. How canst thou urge God's dreadful
law to us,
When thou hast broke it in such dear degree?   215
Clar. Alas! for whose sake did I that ill deed?
For Edward, for my brother, for his sake.
He sends you not to murder me for this,
For in that sin he is as deep as I.   220
If God will be avenged for the deed,
O, know you yet, He doth it publicly.
Take not the quarrel from His powerful arm;
He needs no indirect or lawless course

---

137. [it ... thing] Q. Om. F. 148. ['Zounds] Q. Om. F. QF give this sentence to *1. Murd.* 151. the devil: i.e., your conscience. Or, if devil means Satan, taking him into your mind will enable you not to believe your conscience. 151, 156, 162, 167. [*1.*] *2.* QF. 152. insinuate: ingratiate himself. 154, 158. [*2.*] *1.* QF. 158. costard: head. 161. malmsey-butt: wine cask. 162. sop: cake soaked in wine. 163. [*2.*] *1.* F. 165, 170, 172, 174. [*2.*] *1.* F. In these speeches the ascriptions of F have been departed from to maintain the consistency of the characters. 189. quest: inquest. 192. convict: convicted. 194–95. [to ... sins] Q. *for any goodnesse* F. 215. dear: grievous.

To cut off those that have offended Him. 225
  1. Murd. Who made thee then a bloody minister,
When gallant-springing brave Plantagenet,
That princely novice, was struck dead by thee?
  Clar. My brother's love, the devil, and my rage.
  1. Murd. Thy brother's love, our duty, and thy
    faults 230
Provoke us hither now to slaughter thee.
  Clar. If you do love my brother, hate not me!
I am his brother and I love him well.
If you are hir'd for meed, go back again,
And I will send you to my brother Gloucester, 235
Who shall reward you better for my life
Than Edward will for tidings of my death.
  2. Murd. You are deceiv'd. Your brother
    Gloucester hates you.
  Clar. O, no, he loves me and he holds me dear.
Go you to him from me.
  1. Murd.   Ay, so we will. 240
  Clar. Tell him, when that our princely father
    York
Bless'd his three sons with his victorious arm
[And charg'd us from his soul to love each other]
He little thought of this divided friendship.
Bid Gloucester think on this, and he will weep. 245
  1. Murd. Ay, millstones; as he lesson'd us to weep.
  Clar. O, do not slander him, for he is kind.
  1. Murd. Right; as snow in harvest.
Come, you deceive yourself;
'Tis he that sends us to destroy you here. 250
  Clar. It cannot be; for he bewept my fortune
And hugg'd me in his arms and swore with sobs
That he would labour my delivery.
  1. Murd. Why, so he doth, when he delivers you
From this earth's thraldom to the joys of heaven.
  2. Murd. Make peace with God, for you must
    die, my lord. 256
  Clar. Have you that holy feeling in your souls
To counsel me to make my peace with God
And are you yet to your own souls so blind
That you will war with God by murd'ring me? 260
O, sirs, consider, they that set you on
To do this deed will hate you for the deed.
  2. Murd. What shall we do?
  Clar.   Relent, and save your souls.
  1. Murd. Relent! No! 'tis cowardly and womanish.
  Clar. Not to relent is beastly, savage, devilish.
Which of you, if you were a prince's son, 266
Being pent from liberty as I am now,
If two such murderers as yourselves came to you,
Would not entreat for life?
My friend, I spy some pity in thy looks. 270
O, if thine eye be not a flatterer,
Come thou on my side and entreat for me,

As you would beg, were you in my distress.
A begging prince what beggar pities not?
  2. Murd. Look behind you, my lord. 275
  1. Murd. Take that, and that. If all this will
    not do.   *[Stabs him.*
I'll drown you in the malmsey-butt within.
        [Exit [with the body].
  2. Murd. A bloody deed, and desperately dis-
    patch'd!
How fain, like Pilate, would I wash my hands
Of this most grievous murder! 280

Re-enter First Murderer.

  1. Murd. How now! what mean'st thou, that
    thou help'st me not?
By heaven, the Duke shall know how slack you
    have been!
  2. Murd. I would he knew that I had sav'd his
    brother!
Take thou the fee and tell him what I say,
For I repent me that the Duke is slain. 285
        [Exit.
  1. Murd. So do not I. Go, coward as thou art.
Well, I'll go hide the body in some hole
Till that the Duke give order for his burial;
And when I have my meed I will away;
For this will out, and then I must not stay. 290
        [Exit.

ACT II

Scene I. [London. The palace.]

Flourish. Enter King Edward *sick,* Queen Elizabeth, Dorset, Rivers, Hastings, Buckingham
[Grey, *and others*].

  K. Edw. Why, so: now have I done a good day's
    work.
You peers, continue this united league.
I every day expect an embassage
From my Redeemer to redeem me hence; 4
And more [in] peace my soul shall part to heaven
Since I have made my friends at peace on earth.
[Hastings] and Rivers, take each other's hand;
Dissemble not your hatred, swear your love.
  Riv. By heaven, my soul is purg'd from grudging
    hate;
And with my hand I seal my true heart's love. 10
  Hast. So thrive I as I truly swear the like!
  K. Edw. Take heed you dally not before your
    king
Lest He that is the supreme King of kings
Confound your hidden falsehood and award
Either of you to be the other's end. 15
  Hast. So prosper I as I swear perfect love!

---

243. [And ... other] Q. Om. F. 253. labour: work for. 264-65. *1. Murd.* ... devilish. So Q. After 273 in F. 267. pent: shut up. 270-72. Before 274 in F.
Act II, sc. i, 5. [in] Q. *to* F. 7. [Hastings] Q. *Dorset* F.

Riv. And I, as I love Hastings with my heart!
K. Edw. Madam, your self is not exempt from
     this,
Nor you, son Dorset, Buckingham, nor you;
You have been factious one against the other.   20
Wife, love Lord Hastings, let him kiss your hand;
And what you do, do it unfeignedly.
    Q. Eliz. There, Hastings; I will never more re-
     member
Our former hatred, so thrive I and mine!
    K. Edw. Dorset, embrace him; Hastings, love
     lord marquess.   25
    Dor. This interchange of love, I here protest,
Upon my part shall be inviolable.
    Hast. And so swear I.   [*They embrace.*]
    K. Edw. Now, princely Buckingham, seal thou
     this league
With thy embracements to my wife's allies,   30
And make me happy in your unity.
    Buck. Whenever Buckingham doth turn his hate
Upon your Grace [*to the Queen*], but with all duteous
     love
Doth cherish you and yours, God punish me
With hate in those where I expect most love!   35
When I have most need to employ a friend,
And most assured that he is a friend,
Deep, hollow, treacherous, and full of guile
Be he unto me! This do I beg of Heaven,
When I am cold in love to you or yours.   40
                             [*They embrace.*
    K. Edw. A pleasing cordial, princely Bucking-
     ham,
Is this thy vow unto my sickly heart.
There wanteth now our brother Gloucester here
To make the blessed period of this peace.
    Buck. And, in good time,   45
Here comes Sir Richard Ratcliff and the Duke.

        Enter GLOUCESTER *and* RATCLIFF.

    Glou. Good morrow to my sovereign king and
     queen;   46
And, princely peers, a happy time of day!
    K. Edw. Happy, indeed, as we have spent the day.
Gloucester, we have done deeds of charity,
Made peace of enmity, fair love of hate,   50
Between these swelling wrong-incensed peers.
    Glou. A blessed labour, my most sovereign lord.
Among this princely heap, if any here
By false intelligence or wrong surmise
Hold me a foe;   55
If I [unwittingly], or in my rage,
Have aught committed that is hardly borne
By any in this presence, I desire
To reconcile me to his friendly peace.

'Tis death to me to be at enmity;   60
I hate it, and desire all good men's love.
First, madam, I entreat true peace of you,
Which I will purchase with my duteous service;
Of you, my noble cousin Buckingham,
If ever any grudge were lodg'd between us;   65
Of you and you, Lord Rivers and of Dorset;
That all without desert have frown'd on me;
Dukes, earls, lords, gentlemen — indeed, of all.
I do not know that Englishman alive
With whom my soul is any jot at odds   70
More than the infant that is born to-night.
I thank my God for <u>my humility.</u>
    Q. Eliz. A holy day shall this be kept hereafter.
I would to God all strifes were well compounded.
My sovereign lord, I do beseech your Highness   75
To take our brother Clarence to your grace.
    Glou. Why, madam, have I off'red love for this,
To be so flouted in this royal presence?
Who knows not that the gentle Duke is dead?
                          [*They all start.*
You do him injury to scorn his corse.   80
    K. Edw. Who knows not he is dead! Who knows
     he is?
    Q. Eliz. All-seeing Heaven, what a world is this!
    Buck. Look I so pale, Lord Dorset, as the rest?
    Dor. Ay, my good lord; and no man in the pres-
     ence
But his red colour hath forsook his cheeks.   85
    K. Edw. Is Clarence dead? The order was
     revers'd.
    Glou. But he, poor man, by your first order died,
And that a winged Mercury did bear;
Some tardy cripple bare the countermand,
That came too lag to see him buried.   90
God grant that some, less noble and less loyal,
Nearer in bloody thoughts, but not in blood,
Deserve not worse than wretched Clarence did,
And yet go current from suspicion!   94

                Enter DERBY.

    Der. A boon, my sovereign, for my service done!
                                 [*Kneels.*]
    K. Edw. I prithee, peace; my soul is full of sorrow.
    Der. I will not rise, unless your Highness hear me.
    K. Edw. Then say at once what is it thou re-
     quests.
    Der. The forfeit, sovereign, of my servant's life,
Who slew to-day a riotous gentleman   100
Lately attendant on the Duke of Norfolk.
    K. Edw. Have I a tongue to doom my brother's
     death
And shall that tongue give pardon to a slave?
My brother kill'd no man; his fault was thought,

---

53. **heap:** band.   56. **[unwittingly]** Q.   *unwillingly* F.   57. **hardly borne:** resented.   67. **all without desert:** entirely
without my having deserved it. After this line F inserts, "Of you, Lord Woodville, and, Lord Scales, of you."   90. **lag:**
late.   99. **forfeit:** i.e., remission of the forfeit.

And yet his punishment was bitter death. 105
Who sued to me for him? Who, in my wrath,
Kneel'd at my feet and bid me be advis'd?
Who spoke of brotherhood? Who spoke of love?
Who told me how the poor soul did forsake
The mighty Warwick and did fight for me? 110
Who told me, in the field at Tewksbury,
When Oxford had me down, he rescued me
And said, "Dear brother, live, and be a king"?
Who told me, when we both lay in the field
Frozen almost to death, how he did lap me 115
Even in his garments, and did give himself,
All thin and naked, to the numb cold night?
All this from my remembrance brutish wrath
Sinfully pluck'd, and not a man of you
Had so much grace to put it in my mind. 120
But when your carters or your waiting-vassals
Have done a drunken slaughter, and defac'd
The precious image of our dear Redeemer,
You straight are on your knees for pardon, pardon;
And I, unjustly too, must grant it you. 125
                              [*Derby rises.*]
But for my brother not a man would speak,
Nor I, ungracious, speak unto myself
For him, poor soul. The proudest of you all
Have been beholding to him in his life;
Yet none of you would once beg for his life. 130
O God, I fear thy justice will take hold
On me and you, and mine and yours for this!
Come, Hastings, help me to my closet. Ah, poor
    Clarence! [*Exeunt some with King and Queen.*
Glou. This is the fruit of rashness! Mark'd you
    not
How that the guilty kindred of the Queen 135
Look'd pale when they did hear of Clarence' death?
O, they did urge it still unto the King!
God will revenge it. Come, lords, will you go
To comfort Edward with our company.
    Buck. We wait upon your Grace. [*Exeunt.* 140

SCENE II. [The palace.]

Enter the old DUCHESS OF YORK, *with the two*
    CHILDREN *of Clarence.*

    Boy. Good grandam, tell us, is our father dead?
    Duch. No, boy.
    Girl. Why do you weep so oft, and beat your
    breast,
And cry, "O Clarence, my unhappy son!"
    Boy. Why do you look on us, and shake your
    head, 5
And call us orphans, wretches, castaways,
If that our noble father were alive?

    Duch. My pretty cousins, you mistake me both.
I do lament the sickness of the King,
As loath to lose him, not your father's death; 10
It were lost sorrow to wail one that's lost.
    Boy. Then you conclude, my grandam, he is dead.
The King mine uncle is to blame for it.
God will revenge it, whom I will importune
With earnest prayers all to that effect. 15
    Girl. And so will I.
    Duch. Peace, children, peace! the King doth love
    you well.
Incapable and shallow innocents,
You cannot guess who caus'd your father's death.
    Boy. Grandam, we can; for my good uncle
    Gloucester 20
Told me the King, provok'd to it by the Queen,
Devis'd impeachments to imprison him.
And when my uncle told me so he wept,
And pitied me and kindly kiss'd my cheek;
Bade me rely on him as on my father, 25
And he would love me dearly as a child.
    Duch. Ah, that deceit should steal such gentle
    shape
And with a virtuous vizor hide deep vice!
He is my son, ay, and therein my shame;
Yet from my dugs he drew not this deceit. 30
    Boy. Think you my uncle did dissemble, gran-
    dam?
    Duch. Ay, boy.
    Boy. I cannot think it. Hark! what noise is this?

Enter QUEEN ELIZABETH, *with her hair about her*
    ears; RIVERS *and* DORSET *after her.*

    Q. Eliz. Ah, who shall hinder me to wail and weep,
To chide my fortune, and torment myself? 35
I'll join with black despair against my soul
And to myself become an enemy.
    Duch. What means this scene of rude impatience?
    Q. Eliz. To make an act of tragic violence.
Edward, my lord, thy son, our king, is dead. 40
Why grow the branches when the root is gone?
Why wither not the leaves that want their sap?
If you will live, lament; if die, be brief,
That our swift-winged souls may catch the King's,
Or, like obedient subjects, follow him 45
To his new kingdom of ne'er-changing night.
    Duch. Ah, so much interest have I in thy sorrow
As I had title in thy noble husband!
I have bewept a worthy husband's death,
And liv'd with looking on his images; 50
But now two mirrors of his princely semblance
Are crack'd in pieces by malignant death,
And I for comfort have but one false glass,
That grieves me when I see my shame in him.

---

107. **advis'd:** cautious. 137. **still:** continually.
Sc. ii, 8. **cousins.** Used of any relatives outside the immediate family. 18. **Incapable:** not able to understand. 50. **images:**
sons.

Thou art a widow; yet thou art a mother,   55
And hast the comfort of thy children left:
But death hath snatch'd my husband from mine
    arms
And pluck'd two crutches from my feeble hands,
Clarence and Edward. O, what cause have I,
Thine being but a moiety of my moan,   60
To overgo thy woes and drown thy cries!
　　Boy. Ah! aunt, you wept not for our father's
    death;
How can we aid you with our kindred tears?
　　Girl. Our fatherless distress was left unmoan'd;
Your widow-dolour likewise be unwept!   65
　　Q. Eliz. Give me no help in lamentation,
I am not barren to bring forth complaints.
All springs reduce their currents to mine eyes,
That I, being govern'd by the watery moon,
May send forth plenteous tears to drown the world!
Ah for my husband, for my dear lord Edward!   71
　　Chil. Ah for our father, for our dear lord Clarence!
　　Duch. Alas for both, both mine, Edward and
    Clarence!
　　Q. Eliz. What stay had I but Edward? and he's
    gone.
　　Chil. What stay had we but Clarence? and he's
    gone.   75
　　Duch. What stays had I but they? and they are
    gone.
　　Q. Eliz. Was never widow had so dear a loss!
　　Chil. Were never orphans had so dear a loss!
　　Duch. Was never mother had so dear a loss!
Alas, I am the mother of these griefs!   80
Their woes are parcell'd, mine is general.
She for an Edward weeps, and so do I;
I for a Clarence weep, so doth not she;
These babes for Clarence weep, [and so do I;
I for an Edward weep,] so do not they.   85
Alas, you three, on me, threefold distress'd,
Pour all your tears! I am your sorrow's nurse,
And I will pamper it with lamentation.
　　Dor. Comfort, dear mother. God is much dis-
    pleas'd
That you take with unthankfulness His doing.   90
In common worldly things 'tis call'd ungrateful
With dull unwillingness to repay a debt
Which with a bounteous hand was kindly lent;
Much more to be thus opposite with heaven,
For it requires the royal debt it lent you.   95
　　Riv. Madam, bethink you, like a careful mother,
Of the young prince your son. Send straight for
    him;
Let him be crown'd; in him your comfort lives.
Drown desperate sorrow in dead Edward's grave,
And plant your joys in living Edward's throne.   100

Enter GLOUCESTER, BUCKINGHAM, DERBY,
　　HASTINGS, *and* RATCLIFF.

　　Glou. Sister, have comfort. All of us have cause
To wail the dimming of our shining star,
But none can help our harms by wailing them.
Madam, my mother, I do cry you mercy;
I did not see your Grace. Humbly on my knee   105
I crave your blessing.
　　Duch. God bless thee, and put meekness in thy
    breast,
Love, charity, obedience, and true duty!
　　Glou. [*Aside.*] Amen; and make me die a good
    old man!
That is the butt-end of a mother's blessing.   110
I marvel that her Grace did leave it out.
　　Buck. You cloudy princes and heart-sorrowing
    peers
That bear this heavy mutual load of moan,
Now cheer each other in each other's love.
Though we have spent our harvest of this king,   115
We are to reap the harvest of his son.
The broken rancour of your high-swoln hates,
But lately splinter'd, knit, and join'd together,
Must gently be preserv'd, cherish'd, and kept.
Me seemeth good, that, with some little train,   120
Forthwith from Ludlow the young prince be fet
Hither to London, to be crown'd our king.
　　Riv. Why with some little train, my Lord of
    Buckingham?
　　Buck. Marry, my lord, lest, by a multitude,
The new-heal'd wound of malice should break out,
Which would be so much the more dangerous,   126
By how much the estate is green and yet ungovern'd.
Where every horse bears his commanding rein
And may direct his course as please himself,
As well the fear of harm, as harm apparent,   130
In my opinion, ought to be prevented.
　　Glou. I hope the King made peace with all of us;
And the compact is firm and true in me.
　　Riv. And so in me; and so, I think, in all.
Yet, since it is but green, it should be put   135
To no apparent likelihood of breach,
Which haply by much company might be urg'd;
Therefore I say with noble Buckingham,
That it is meet so few should fetch the Prince.
　　Hast. And so say I.   140
　　Glou. Then be it so; and go we to determine
Who they shall be that straight shall post to [Lud-
    low].
Madam, and you, my sister, will you go
To give your censures in this business?
[*Q. Eliz.*⎫
[*Duch.*⎬ With all our hearts.]   145
　　　　⎭
[*Exeunt all but Buckingham and Gloucester.*

---

68. **All springs reduce:** let all springs lead.   84–85. **[and ... weep]** Q. Om. F.   104. **do ... mercy:** beg your pardon.
112. **cloudy:** gloomy.   118. **splinter'd:** bound in splints.   121. **fet:** fetched.   127. **estate is green:** government is newly
established.   128. **bears:** controls.   142, 154. **[Ludlow]** Q. *London* F.   144. **censures:** judgments.   145. Q. Om. F.

Buck. My lord, whoever journeys to the Prince,
For God's sake, let not us two stay at home;
For, by the way, I'll sort occasion,
As index to the story we late talk'd of,
To part the Queen's proud kindred from the Prince.
    Glou. My other self, my counsel's consistory, 151
My oracle, my prophet, my dear cousin,
I, as a child, will go by thy direction.
Toward [Ludlow] then, for we'll not stay behind.
                            [Exeunt.

SCENE III. [*London. A street.*]

Enter one CITIZEN *at one door, and* another *at the other*.

    1. Cit. Good morrow, neighbour; whither away
so fast?
    2. Cit. I promise you, I scarcely know myself.
Hear you the news abroad?
    1. Cit.   Yes, that the King is dead.
    2. Cit. Ill news, by 'r lady; seldom comes the
better.
I fear, I fear 'twill prove a giddy world.   5

Enter another CITIZEN.

    3. Cit. Neighbours, God speed!
    1. Cit.   Give you good morrow, sir.
    3. Cit. Doth the news hold of good King Edward's
death?
    2. Cit. Ay, sir, it is too true; God help the while!
    3. Cit. Then, masters, look to see a troublous
world.
    1. Cit. No, no; by God's good grace his son shall
reign.   10
    3. Cit. Woe to that land that's govern'd by a
child!
    2. Cit. In him there is a hope of government,
That in his nonage, council under him,
And in his full and ripened years himself,
No doubt, shall then and till then govern well. 15
    1. Cit. So stood the state when Henry the Sixth
Was crown'd in Paris but at nine months old.
    3. Cit. Stood the state so? No, no, good friends,
God wot;
For then this land was famously enrich'd
With politic grave counsel; then the King   20
Had virtuous uncles to protect his Grace.
    1. Cit. Why, so hath this, both by his father and
mother.
    2. Cit. Better it were they all came by his father,
Or by his father there were none at all;
For emulation who shall now be nearest   25
Will touch us all too near, if God prevent not.
O, full of danger is the Duke of Gloucester,

And the Queen's sons and brothers haught and
proud!
And were they to be rul'd, and not to rule,
This sickly land might solace as before.   30
    1. Cit. Come, come, we fear the worst; all will be
well.
    3. Cit. When clouds are seen, wise men put on
their cloaks;
When great leaves fall, then winter is at hand;
When the sun sets, who doth not look for night?
Untimely storms makes men expect a dearth. 35
All may be well; but, if God sort it so,
'Tis more than we deserve or I expect.
    2. Cit. Truly, the hearts of men are full of fear.
You cannot reason almost with a man
That looks not heavily and full of dread.   40
    3. Cit. Before the days of change still is it so.
By a divine instinct men's minds mistrust
Ensuing danger; as by proof we see
The water swell before a boist'rous storm.
But leave it all to God. Whither away?   45
    2. Cit. Marry, we were sent for to the justices.
    3. Cit. And so was I. I'll bear you company.
                            [Exeunt.

SCENE IV. [*London. The palace.*]

Enter the ARCHBISHOP OF YORK, *the young* DUKE
OF YORK, QUEEN ELIZABETH, *and the* DUCHESS
OF YORK.

    Arch. Last night, I heard, they lay at [North-
ampton;
At Stony-Stratford] they do rest to-night.
To-morrow, or next day, they will be here.
    Duch. I long with all my heart to see the Prince.
I hope he is much grown since last I saw him. 5
    Q. Eliz. But I hear, no; they say my son of York
Has almost overta'en him in his growth.
    York. Ay, mother; but I would not have it so.
    Duch. Why, my good cousin, it is good to grow.
    York. Grandam, one night, as we did sit at sup-
per,   10
My uncle Rivers talk'd how I did grow
More than my brother. "Ay," quoth my uncle
Gloucester,
"Small herbs have grace, great weeds do grow
apace;"
And since, methinks I would not grow so fast,
Because sweet flowers are slow and weeds make
haste.   15
    Duch. Good faith, good faith, the saying did not
hold
In him that did object the same to thee.

---

148. **sort occasion:** make opportunity. 149. **index:** introduction. 151. **consistory:** high court.
Sc. iii, 8. **the while:** the times. 13. **nonage:** minority. 30. **solace:** be happy. 36. **sort:** arrange. 39. **reason:** talk.
42. **mistrust:** suspect. 43. **Ensuing.** So in Q and in catchword at foot of page in F. *Pursuing* in text.
Sc. iv, 1, 2. [**Northampton . . . Stony-Stratford**] Q. *Stony Stratford, and at Northampton* F.

He was the wretched'st thing when he was young,
So long a-growing and so leisurely
That, if his rule were true, he should be gracious. 20
   [*Arch.*] And so, no doubt, he is, my gracious
     madam.
   Duch. I hope he is; but yet let mothers doubt.
   York. Now, by my troth, if I had been remem-
     b'red
I could have given my uncle's Grace a flout,
To touch his growth nearer than he touch'd mine. 25
   Duch. How, my young York? I prithee, let me
     hear it.
   York. Marry, they say my uncle grew so fast
That he could gnaw a crust at two hours old;
'Twas full two years ere I could get a tooth.
Grandam, this would have been a biting jest. 30
   Duch. I prithee, pretty York, who told thee this?
   York. Grandam, his nurse.
   Duch. His nurse! why, she was dead ere thou
     wast born.
   York. If 'twere not she, I cannot tell who told me.
   Q. Eliz. A parlous boy! Go to, you are too
     shrewd. 35
   Duch. Good madam, be not angry with the child.
   Q. Eliz. Pitchers have ears.

Enter a MESSENGER.

   Arch. Here comes a messenger. What news?
   Mess. Such news, my lord, as grieves me to re-
     port.
   Q. Eliz. How doth the Prince?
   Mess.   Well, madam, and in health.
   Duch. What is thy news? 41
   Mess. Lord Rivers and Lord Grey are sent to
     Pomfret,
With them Sir Thomas Vaughan, prisoners.
   Duch. Who hath committed them?
   Mess.   The mighty dukes
Gloucester and Buckingham.
   Arch.   For what offence? 45
   Mess. The sum of all I can I have disclos'd.
Why or for what the nobles were committed
Is all unknown to me, my gracious lord.
   Q. Eliz. Ay me, I see the ruin of my house!
The tiger now hath seiz'd the gentle hind; 50
Insulting tyranny begins to jut
Upon the innocent and aweless throne.
Welcome, destruction, blood, and massacre!
I see, as in a map, the end of all.
   Duch. Accursed and unquiet wrangling days, 55
How many of you have mine eyes beheld!
My husband lost his life to get the crown,
And often up and down my sons were toss'd

For me to joy and weep their gain and loss;
And being seated and domestic broils 60
Clean over-blown, themselves, the conquerors,
Make war upon themselves, brother to brother,
Blood to blood, self against self. O, preposterous
And frantic outrage, end thy damned spleen;
Or let me die, to look on earth no more! 65
   Q. Eliz. Come, come, my boy; we will to sanc-
     tuary.
Madam, farewell.
   Duch.   Stay, I will go with you.
   Q. Eliz. You have no cause.
   Arch. [*To the Queen.*] My gracious lady, go;
And thither bear your treasure and your goods.
For my part, I'll resign unto your Grace 70
The seal I keep; and so betide to me
As well I tender you and all of yours!
Go, I'll conduct you to the sanctuary.   [*Exeunt.*

ACT III

SCENE I. [*London. A street.*]

The trumpets sound. Enter the young PRINCE, *the*
DUKES OF GLOUCESTER *and* BUCKINGHAM,
CARDINAL [BOURCHIER, CATESBY,] *and others.*

   Buck. Welcome, sweet prince, to London, to your
     chamber.
   Glou. Welcome, dear cousin, my thoughts'
     sovereign.
The weary way hath made you melancholy.
   Prince. No, uncle; but our crosses on the way
Have made it tedious, wearisome, and heavy. 5
I want more uncles here to welcome me.
   Glou. Sweet prince, the untainted virtue of your
     years
Hath not yet div'd into the world's deceit.
No more can you distinguish of a man
Than of his outward show, which, God he knows, 10
Seldom or never jumpeth with the heart.
Those uncles which you want were dangerous;
Your Grace attended to their sug'red words
But look'd not on the poison of their hearts.
God keep you from them, and from such false
     friends! 15
   Prince. God keep me from false friends! but they
     were none.
   Glou. My lord, the Mayor of London comes to
     greet you.

Enter the LORD MAYOR [*and his train*].

   May. God bless your Grace with health and
     happy days!

---

   21. [*Arch.*] (Capell). *Car.* Q. *Yor.* F. 25. **touch:** twit on. 35. **parlous:** mischievous. **shrewd:** keen. 46. **can:** know. 51.
Insulting: arrogant. 51–52. **jut Upon:** threaten. 52. **aweless:** not feared. 64. **spleen:** malevolence. 72. **tender:** cherish.
   Act III, sc. i, 1. **chamber.** London was called "The King's Chamber." 4. **crosses:** unfortunate happenings, i.e., the
arrests. 11. **jumpeth:** agreeth.

Prince. I thank you, good my lord, and thank
    you all.   [*Mayor and train retire.*]
I thought my mother and my brother York   20
Would long ere this have met us on the way.
Fie, what a slug is Hastings, that he comes not
To tell us whether they will come or no!

        Enter LORD HASTINGS.

Buck. And, in good time, here comes the sweating
    lord.
Prince. Welcome, my lord.   What, will our
    mother come?   25
Hast. On what occasion, God he knows, not I,
The Queen your mother and your brother York
Have taken sanctuary.   The tender prince
Would fain have come with me to meet your Grace,
But by his mother was perforce withheld.   30
Buck. Fie, what an indirect and peevish course
Is this of hers!   Lord Cardinal, will your Grace
Persuade the Queen to send the Duke of York
Unto his princely brother presently?
If she deny, Lord Hastings, go with him   35
And from her jealous arms pluck him perforce.
Card. My Lord of Buckingham, if my weak
    oratory
Can from his mother win the Duke of York,
Anon expect him here; but if she be obdurate
To mild entreaties, God [in heaven] forbid   40
We should infringe the holy privilege
Of blessed sanctuary!   Not for all this land
Would I be guilty of so great a sin.
Buck. You are too senseless-obstinate, my lord,
Too ceremonious and traditional.   45
Weigh it but with the grossness of this age,
You break not sanctuary in seizing him.
The benefit thereof is always granted
To those whose dealings have deserv'd the place
And those who have the wit to claim the place.   50
This prince hath neither claim'd it nor deserv'd it,
And therefore, in mine opinion, cannot have it.
Then, taking him from thence that is not there,
You break no privilege nor charter there.
Oft have I heard of sanctuary men,   55
But sanctuary children ne'er till now.
Card. My lord, you shall o'er-rule my mind for
    once.
Come on, Lord Hastings, will you go with me?
Hast. I go, my lord.
Prince. Good lords, make all the speedy haste
    you may.   [*Exeunt Cardinal and Hastings.*
Say, uncle Gloucester, if our brother come,   61
Where shall we sojourn till our coronation?
Glou. Where it think'st best unto your royal self.

If I may counsel you, some day or two
Your Highness shall repose you at the Tower;   65
Then where you please, and shall be thought most
    fit
For your best health and recreation.
Prince. I do not like the Tower, of any place.
Did Julius Cæsar build that place, my lord?
Buck. He did, my gracious lord, begin that place;
Which, since, succeeding ages have re-edifi'd.   71
Prince. Is it upon record, or else reported
Successively from age to age, he built it?
Buck. Upon record, my gracious lord.   74
Prince. But say, my lord, it were not regist'red,
Methinks the truth should live from age to age,
As 'twere retail'd to all posterity
Even to the general all-ending day.
Glou. [*Aside.*] So wise so young, they say, do
    never live long.
Prince. What say you, uncle?   80
Glou. I say, without characters, fame lives long.
[*Aside.*] Thus, like the formal Vice, Iniquity,
I moralize two meanings in one word.
Prince. That Julius Cæsar was a famous man;
With what his valour did enrich his wit   85
His wit set down to make his valour live.
Death makes no conquest of [this] conqueror,
For now he lives in fame, though not in life.
I'll tell you what, my cousin Buckingham, —
Buck. What, my gracious lord?   90
Prince. An if I live until I be a man,
I'll win our ancient right in France again
Or die a soldier as I liv'd a king.
Glou. [*Aside.*] Short summers lightly have a for-
    ward spring.

    Enter young YORK, HASTINGS, *and the* CARDINAL.

Buck. Now, in good time, here comes the Duke of
    York.   95
Prince. Richard of York! how fares our noble
    brother?
York. Well, my [dread] lord; so must I call you
    now.
Prince. Ay, brother, to our grief, as it is yours.
Too late he died that might have kept that title,
Which by his death hath lost much majesty.   100
Glou. How fares our cousin, noble Lord of York?
York. I thank you gentle uncle.   O, my lord,
You said that idle weeds are fast in growth:
The Prince my brother hath outgrown me far.
Glou. He hath, my lord.
York.   And therefore is he idle?   105
Glou. O, my fair cousin, I must not say so.
York. Then is he more beholding to you than I.

---

22. **slug:** snail.   31. **indirect and peevish:** irregular and silly.   40. **[in heaven]** Q. Om. F.   46. **grossness:** laxness,
unscrupulousness.   63. **think'st:** seems.   75. **regist'red:** written down.   81. **characters:** (1) writing, (2) moral qualities.
82. **formal Vice:** regular Vice (of the Moralities).   87. **[this]** Q. *his* F.   94. **lightly:** easily, i.e., are likely to.   97. **[dread]** Q.
deare F.   99. **late:** recently.

Glou. He may command me as my sovereign;
But you have power in me as in a kinsman.
    York. I pray you, uncle, give me this dagger.
    Glou. My dagger, little cousin? With all my
      heart.   III
    Prince. A beggar, brother?
    York. Of my kind uncle, that I know will give,
And being but a toy which is no grief to give.   114
    Glou. A greater gift than that I'll give my cousin.
    York. A greater gift! O, that's the sword to it.
    Glou. Ay, gentle cousin, were it light enough.
    York. O, then, I see, you will part but with light
      gifts;
In weightier things you'll say a beggar nay.
    Glou. It is too weighty for your Grace to wear.
    York. I weigh it lightly, were it heavier.   121
    Glou. What, would you have my weapon, little
      lord?
    York. I would, that I might thank you as you call
      me.
    Glou. How?
    York. Little.   125
    Prince. My Lord of York will still be cross in talk.
Uncle, your Grace knows how to bear with him.
    York. You mean, to bear me, not to bear with me.
Uncle, my brother mocks both you and me.
Because that I am little, like an ape,   130
He thinks that you should bear me on your shoulders.
    Buck. [*Aside to Hastings.*] With what a sharp-
      provided wit he reasons!
To migitate the scorn he gives his uncle,
He prettily and aptly taunts himself.
So cunning and so young is wonderful.   135
    Glou. My lord, will't please you pass along?
Myself and my good cousin Buckingham
Will to your mother, to entreat of her
To meet you at the Tower and welcome you.
    York. What, will you go unto the Tower, my
      lord?   140
    Prince. My Lord Protector [needs] will have it so.
    York. I shall not sleep in quiet at the Tower.
    Glou. Why, what should you fear?
    York. Marry, my uncle Clarence' angry ghost.
My grandam told me he was murder'd there.   145
    Prince. I fear no uncles dead.
    Glou. Nor none that live, I hope.
    Prince. An if they live, I hope I need not fear.
But come, my lord; and with a heavy heart,
Thinking on them, go I unto the Tower.   150
    [*A Sennet. Exeunt all but Gloucester,
      Buckingham, and Catesby.*
    Buck. Think you, my lord, this little prating
      York

Was not incensed by his subtle mother
To taunt and scorn you thus opprobriously?
    Glou. No doubt, no doubt. O, 'tis a perilous boy,
Bold, quick, ingenious, forward, capable.   155
He is all the mother's, from the top to toe.
    Buck. Well, let them rest. Come hither,
      Catesby.
Thou art sworn as deeply to effect what we intend
As closely to conceal what we impart.
Thou know'st our reasons urg'd upon the way;   160
What think'st thou? Is it not an easy matter
To make William Lord Hastings of our mind
For the instalment of this noble duke
In the seat royal of this famous isle?
    Cate. He for his father's sake so loves the Prince
That he will not be won to aught against him.   166
    Buck. What think'st thou, then, of Stanley?
      Will not he?
    Cate. He will do all in all as Hastings doth.
    Buck. Well, then, no more but this: go, gentle
      Catesby,
And, as it were far off, sound thou Lord Hastings
How he doth stand affected to our purpose;   171
And summon him to-morrow to the Tower
To sit about the coronation.
If thou dost find him tractable to us,
Encourage him and tell him all our reasons.   175
If he be leaden, icy, cold, unwilling,
Be thou so too; and so break off the talk,
And give us notice of his inclination;
For we to-morrow hold divided councils,
Wherein thyself shalt highly be employ'd.   180
    Glou. Commend me to Lord William. Tell him,
      Catesby,
His ancient knot of dangerous adversaries
To-morrow are let blood at Pomfret Castle;
And bid my lord, for joy of this good news,
Give Mistress Shore one gentle kiss the more.   185
    Buck. Good Catesby, go, effect this business
      soundly.
    Cate. My good lords both, with all the heed I
      can.
    Glou. Shall we hear from you, Catesby, ere we
      sleep?
    Cate. You shall, my lord.
    Glou. At Crosby House, there shall you find us
      both.   [*Exit Catesby.* 190
    Buck. Now, my lord, what shall we do if we per-
      ceive
Lord Hastings will not yield to our complots?
    Glou. Chop off his head; something we will de-
      termine.
And, look, when I am king, claim thou of me

114. toy: trifle. 121. lightly: as a trifle. 131. bear. It was common to have a bear carry an ape on his back. A slur on Richard's shape. 141. [needs] Q. Om. F. 150. s.d. Sennet: a set of notes on a trumpet. 152. incensed: incited. 173. sit about: discuss. 179. divided councils. Richard and Buckingham consulted separately. 182. knot: group. 185. Mistress Shore, who became Hastings' mistress after Edward IV's death. 192. complots: conspiracies.

The earldom of Hereford, and all the movables
Whereof the King my brother was possess'd.   196
  Buck. I'll claim that promise at your Grace's
    hand.
  Glou. And look to have it yielded with all kind-
    ness.
Come, let us sup betimes, that afterwards
We may digest our complots in some form.   200
                            [Exeunt.

SCENE II. *Before Lord Hastings' house.*

Enter a MESSENGER.

  Mess. My lord! my lord!
  Hast. [*Within.*] Who knocks?
  Mess. One from the Lord Stanley.
  Hast. [*Within.*] What is 't o'clock?
  Mess. Upon the stroke of four.   5

Enter LORD HASTINGS.

  Hast. Can't my lord Stanley sleep these tedious
    nights?
  Mess. So it appears by that I have to say.
First, he commends him to your noble self.
  Hast. What then?
  Mess. Then certifies your lordship that this
    night   10
He dreamt the boar had razed off his helm.
Besides, he says there are two councils kept;
And that may be determin'd at the one
Which may make you and him to rue at th' other.
Therefore he sends to know your lordship's pleas-
    ure,   15
If you will presently take horse with him,
And with all speed post with him toward the north
To shun the danger that his soul divines.
  Hast. Go, fellow, go, return unto thy lord;
Bid him not fear the separated councils.   20
His honour and myself are at the one,
And at the other is my good friend Catesby,
Where nothing can proceed that toucheth us
Whereof I shall not have intelligence.
Tell him his fears are shallow, without instance;   25
And for his dreams, I wonder he's so simple
To trust the mock'ry of unquiet slumbers.
To fly the boar before the boar pursues
Were to incense the boar to follow us
And make pursuit where he did mean no chase.
Go, bid thy master rise and come to me;   31
And we will both together to the Tower,
Where, he shall see, the boar will use us kindly.
  Mess. I'll go, my lord, and tell him what you say.
                            [Exit.

Enter CATESBY.

  Cate. Many good morrows to my noble lord!   35
  Hast. Good morrow, Catesby; you are early stir-
    ring.
What news, what news, in this our tott'ring state?
  Cate. It is a reeling world, indeed, my lord,
And, I believe, will never stand upright
Till Richard wear the garland of the realm.   40
  Hast. How! wear the garland! Dost thou mean
    the crown?
  Cate. Ay, my good lord.
  Hast. I'll have this crown of mine cut from my
    shoulders
Before I'll see the crown so foul misplac'd.
But canst thou guess that he doth aim at it?   45
  Cate. Ay, on my life; and hopes to find you for-
    ward
Upon his party for the gain thereof;
And thereupon he sends you this good news,
That this same very day your enemies,
The kindred of the Queen, must die at Pomfret.   50
  Hast. Indeed, I am no mourner for that news
Because they have been still my adversaries;
But, that I'll give my voice on Richard's side,
To bar my master's heirs in true descent,
God knows I will not do it, to the death.   55
  Cate. God keep your lordship in that gracious
    mind!
  Hast. But I shall laugh at this a twelve-month
    hence,
That they which brought me in my master's hate,
I live to look upon their tragedy.
Well, Catesby, ere a fortnight make me older,   60
I'll send some packing that yet think not on 't.
  Cate. 'Tis a vile thing to die, my gracious lord,
When men are unprepar'd and look not for it.   65
  Hast. O monstrous, monstrous! and so falls it out
With Rivers, Vaughan, Grey; and so 'twill do
With some men else, that think themselves as safe
As thou and I; who, as thou know'st, are dear
To princely Richard and to Buckingham.   70
  Cate. The Princes both make high account of you,
[*Aside.*] For they account his head upon the bridge.
  Hast. I know they do, and I have well deserv'd it.

Enter LORD STANLEY.

— Come on, come on [*to Stanley*]; where is your
    boar-spear, man?
Fear you the boar, and go so unprovided?   75
  Stan. My lord, good morrow; good morrow,
    Catesby.
You may jest on, but, by the holy rood,
I do not like these several councils, I.

---

200. **digest:** work out.
Sc. ii, 11. **boar:** Richard. 25. **instance:** grounds. 72. **bridge:** London Bridge, where the heads of traitors were exhibited.

Hast. My lord, I hold my life as dear as yours;
And never in my days, I do protest,   81
Was it so precious to me as 'tis now.
Think you, but that I know our state secure,
I would be so triumphant as I am?
    Stan. The lords at Pomfret, when they rode from
        London,   85
Were jocund, and suppos'd their states were sure,
And they indeed had no cause to mistrust;
But yet, you see, how soon the day o'ercast.
This sudden stab of rancour I misdoubt.
Pray God, I say, I prove a needless coward!   90
What, shall we toward the Tower?   The day is
    spent.
    Hast. Come, come, have with you.   Wot you
        what, my lord?
To-day the lords you talk of are beheaded.
    Stan. They, for their truth, might better wear
        their heads
Than some that have accus'd them wear their hats.
But come, my lord, let us away.   96

Enter a PURSUIVANT.

    Hast. Go on before; I'll talk with this good fel-
        low.   [*Exeunt Stanley and Catesby.*
How now, sirrah! how goes the world with thee?
    Purs. The better that your lordship please to
        ask.   99
    Hast. I tell thee, man, 'tis better with me now
Than when thou met'st me last where now we meet.
Then was I going prisoner to the Tower
By the suggestion of the Queen's allies;
But now, I tell thee — keep it to thyself —
This day those enemies are put to death,   105
And I in better state than e'er I was.
    Purs. God hold it, to your honour's good con-
        tent!
    Hast. Gramercy, fellow.   There, drink that for
        me.   [*Throws him his purse.*
    Purs. I thank your honour.   [*Exit.*

Enter a PRIEST.

    Priest. Well met, my lord; I am glad to see your
        honour.   110
    Hast. I thank thee, good Sir John, with all my
        heart.
I am in your debt for your last exercise;
Come the next Sabbath, and I will content you.
    Priest. I'll wait upon your lordship.

Enter BUCKINGHAM.

    Buck. What, talking with a priest, Lord Cham-
        berlain?
Your friends at Pomfret, they do need the priest;

Your honour hath no shriving work in hand.   116
    Hast. Good faith, and when I met this holy man
The men you talk of came into my mind.
What, go you toward the Tower?
    Buck. I do, my lord; but long I cannot stay there.
I shall return before your lordship thence.   121
    Hast. Nay, like enough, for I stay dinner there.
    Buck. [*Aside.*]   And supper too, although thou
        know'st it not.
Come, will you go?
    Hast. I'll wait upon your lordship.   125
                                   [*Exeunt.*

SCENE III.   *Pomfret [Castle].*

Enter SIR RICHARD RATCLIFF, *with halberds, carry-*
    ing RIVERS, GREY, *and* VAUGHAN *to death.*

    [*Rat.* Come, bring forth the prisoners.]
    Riv. Sir Richard Ratcliff, let me tell thee this:
To-day shalt thou behold a subject die
For truth, for duty, and for loyalty.
    Grey. God bless the Prince from all the pack of
        you!   5
A knot you are of damned blood-suckers.
    Vaug. You live that shall cry woe for this here-
        after.
    Rat. Dispatch; the limit of your lives is out.
    Riv. O Pomfret, Pomfret!   O thou bloody prison,
Fatal and ominous to noble peers!   10
Within the guilty closure of thy walls
Richard the Second here was hack'd to death;
And, for more slander to thy dismal seat,
We give to thee our guiltless blood to drink.
    Grey. Now Margaret's curse is fall'n upon our
        heads,   15
When she exclaim'd on Hastings, you, and I
For standing by when Richard stabb'd her son.
    Riv. Then curs'd she Richard, then curs'd she
        Buckingham,
Then curs'd she Hastings.   O, remember, God,
To hear her prayer for them, as now for us!
And for my sister and her princely sons,   20
Be satisfi'd, dear God, with our true blood,
Which, as thou know'st, unjustly must be spilt.
    Rat. Make haste; the hour of death is expiate.
    Riv. Come, Grey, come, Vaughan, let us here
        embrace.
Farewell, until we meet again in heaven.   25
                                   [*Exeunt.*

SCENE IV.   [*The Tower of London.*]

Enter BUCKINGHAM, DERBY, HASTINGS, *the* BISHOP
    OF ELY, RATCLIFF, LOVEL, *with others,* [*and take*
    their seats] *at a table.*

---

80. **as yours.** Q reading *as you do yours* is more explicit. 92. **have with you:** come along. 96. S.D. PURSUIVANT: attendant on a herald. 111. **Sir John.** Priests were habitually called Sir. 112. **exercise:** sermon. 116. **shriving work:** confession and absolution.
    Sc. iii, 1. [*Rat. . . . prisoners*] Q.   Om. F.   13. **slander:** evil reputation.   23. **expiate:** fully come.

Hast. Now, noble peers, the cause why we are met
Is to determine of the coronation.
In God's name speak, when is the royal day?
   Buck. Is all things ready for the royal time?
   Der. It is, and wants but nomination.   5
   Ely. To-morrow, then, I judge a happy day.
   Buck. Who knows the Lord Protector's mind herein?
Who is most inward with the royal Duke?
   Ely. Your Grace, we think, should soonest know his mind.
   Buck. [Who, I, my lord?]   10
We know each other's faces; for our hearts,
He knows no more of mine than I of yours,
Or I of his, my lord, than you of mine.
Lord Hastings, you and he are near in love.
   Hast. I thank his Grace, I know he loves me well;
But for his purpose in the coronation   16
I have not sounded him, nor he deliver'd
His gracious pleasure any way therein:
But you, my honourable lords, may name the time;
And in the Duke's behalf I'll give my voice,   20
Which, I presume, he'll take in gentle part.

     Enter GLOUCESTER.

   Ely. In happy time, here comes the Duke himself.
   Glou. My noble lords and cousins all, good morrow.
I have been long a sleeper; but, I trust,
My absence doth neglect no great design   25
Which by my presence might have been concluded.
   Buck. Had not you come upon your cue, my lord,
William Lord Hastings had pronounc'd your part,—
I mean, your voice, — for crowning of the King.
   Glou. Than my Lord Hastings no man might be bolder;   30
His lordship knows me well and loves me well.
   [*Hast.* I thank your Grace.]
   Glou.   My lord of Ely!
   [*Ely.*   My lord?]
   Glou. When I was last in Holborn,
I saw good strawberries in your garden there.
I do beseech you send for some of them.   35
   Ely. Marry, and will, my lord, with all my heart.
                        [*Exit.*
   Glou. Cousin of Buckingham, a word with you.
                [*Drawing him aside.*]
Catesby hath sounded Hastings in our business
And finds the testy gentleman so hot
That he will lose his head ere give consent   40
His master's child, as worshipfully he terms it,

Shall lose the royalty of England's throne.
   Buck. Withdraw yourself a while; I'll go with you.   [*Exeunt [Gloucester and Buckingham].*
   Der. We have not yet set down this day of triumph.
To-morrow, in my judgement, is too sudden;   45
For I myself am not so well provided
As else I would be were the day prolong'd.

     Re-enter BISHOP OF ELY.

   Ely. Where is my Lord, the Duke of Gloucester?
I have sent for these strawberries.
   Hast. His Grace looks cheerfully and smooth this morning.   50
There's some conceit or other likes him well
When that he bids good morrow with such spirit.
I think there's never a man in Christendom
Can lesser hide his love or hate than he;   54
For by his face straight shall you know his heart.
   Der. What of his heart perceive you in his face
By any [likelihood] he show'd to-day?
   Hast. Marry, that with no man here he is offended;
For, were he, he had shown it in his looks.
   [*Der.* I pray God he be not, I say.]   60

     Re-enter GLOUCESTER *and* BUCKINGHAM.

   Glou. I pray you all, tell me what they deserve
That do conspire my death with devilish plots
Of damned witchcraft, and that have prevail'd
Upon my body with their hellish charms?
   Hast. The tender love I bear your Grace, my lord,   65
Makes me most forward in this princely presence
To doom th' offenders, whosoe'er they be.
I say, my lord, they have deserved death.
   Glou. Then be your eyes the witness of their evil.
Look how I am bewitch'd; behold mine arm   70
Is, like a blasted sapling, wither'd up.
And this is Edward's wife, that monstrous witch,
Consorted with that harlot strumpet Shore,
That by their witchcraft thus have marked me.
   Hast. If they have done this deed, my noble lord, —   75
   Glou. If! Thou protector of this damned strumpet,
Talk'st thou to me of "ifs"? Thou art a traitor!
Off with his head! Now, by Saint Paul I swear,
I will not dine until I see the same.
Lovel and Ratcliff, look that it be done.   80
The rest, that love me, rise and follow me.
       [*Exeunt all but Hastings, Ratcliff, and Lovel.*

Sc. iv, 5. **nomination:** fixing. 8. **inward:** intimate. 10. [**Who ... lord?**] Q. Om. F. 20. **voice:** vote. 32. [*Hast. ...* Grace] [*Ely ... lord?*] Q. Om. F. 47. **prolong'd:** postponed. 51. **conceit:** fancy. **likes:** pleases. 57. [**likelihood**] Q. *livelihood* F. 60. [*Der. ... say*] Q. Om. F.

Hast. Woe, woe for England! not a whit for me;
For I, too fond, might have prevented this.
Stanley did dream the boar did raze our helms,
And I did scorn it and disdain to fly.   85
Three times to-day my foot-cloth horse did stumble,
And started when he look'd upon the Tower,
As loath to bear me to the slaughter-house.
O, now I need the priest that spake to me!
I now repent I told the pursuivant,   90
As too triumphing, how mine enemies
To-day at Pomfret bloodily were butcher'd,
And I myself secure in grace and favour.
O Margaret, Margaret, now thy heavy curse
Is lighted on poor Hastings' wretched head!   95
Rat. Come, come, dispatch; the Duke would be at dinner.
Make a short shrift; he longs to see your head.
Hast. O momentary grace of mortal men,
Which we more hunt for than the grace of God!
Who builds his hope in air of your good looks
Lives like a drunken sailor on a mast,   101
Ready, with every nod, to tumble down
Into the fatal bowels of the deep.
Lov. Come, come, dispatch; 'tis bootless to exclaim.
Hast. O bloody Richard! miserable England!
I prophesy the fearfull'st time to thee   106
That ever wretched age hath look'd upon.
Come, lead me to the block; bear him my head.
They smile at me who shortly shall be dead.
[*Exeunt.*

[SCENE V. *The Tower-walls.*]

Enter GLOUCESTER *and* BUCKINGHAM, *in rotten armour, marvellous ill-favoured.*

Glou. Come, cousin, canst thou quake and change thy colour,
Murder thy breath in middle of a word,
And then again begin, and stop again,
As if thou were distraught and mad with terror?
Buck. Tut, I can counterfeit the deep tragedian,
Speak and look back, and pry on every side,   6
Tremble and start at wagging of a straw,
Intending deep suspicion. Ghastly looks
Are at my service, like enforced smiles;
And both are ready in their offices   10
At any time to grace my stratagems.
But what, is Catesby gone?
Glou. He is; and, see, he brings the Mayor along.

Enter the MAYOR *and* CATESBY.

Buck. Lord Mayor, —

Glou. Look to the drawbridge there!   15
Buck. Hark! a drum.
Glou. Catesby, o'erlook the walls.
Buck. Lord Mayor, the reason we have sent —
Glou. Look back, defend thee, here are enemies.
Buck. God and our innocency defend and guard us!   20

Enter LOVEL *and* RATCLIFF, *with Hastings' head.*

Glou. Be patient, they are friends, Ratcliff and Lovel.
Lov. Here is the head of that ignoble traitor,
The dangerous and unsuspected Hastings.
Glou. So dear I lov'd the man that I must weep.
I took him for the plainest harmless creature   25
That breath'd upon the earth a Christian,
Made him my book wherein my soul recorded
The history of all her secret thoughts.
So smooth he daub'd his vice with show of virtue
That, his apparent open guilt omitted,   30
I mean his conversation with Shore's wife,
He liv'd from all attainder of suspects.
Buck. Well, well, he was the covert'st shelt'red traitor
That ever liv'd.
Would you imagine, or almost believe,   35
Were 't not that by great preservation
We live to tell it, that the subtle traitor
This day had plotted, in the council-house
To murder me and my good lord of Gloucester?
May. Had he done so?   40
Glou. What, think you we are Turks or infidels?
Or that we would, against the form of law,
Proceed thus rashly in the villain's death,
But that the extreme peril of the case,
The peace of England, and our persons' safety   45
Enforc'd us to this execution?
May. Now, fair befall you! he deserv'd his death;
And your good Graces both have well proceeded
To warn false traitors from the like attempts.
I never look'd for better at his hands   50
After he once fell in with Mistress Shore.
Buck. Yet had we not determin'd he should die
Until your lordship came to see his end;
Which now the loving haste of these our friends,
Something against our meanings, have prevented;
Because, my lord, I would have had you heard   56
The traitor speak, and timorously confess
The manner and the purpose of his treasons;
That you might well have signifi'd the same
Unto the citizens, who haply may   60
Misconstrue us in him and wail his death.
May. But, my good lord, your Grace's words shall serve

As well as I had seen and heard him speak;
And do not doubt, right noble princes both,
That I'll acquaint our duteous citizens   65
With all your just proceedings in this case.
   Glou. And to that end we wish'd your lordship here,
T' avoid the censures of the carping world.
   Buck. [But] since you come too late of our intent,
Yet witness what you hear we did intend.   70
And so, my good Lord Mayor, we bid farewell.
                    [Exit Mayor.
   Glou. Go, after, after, cousin Buckingham.
The mayor towards Guildhall hies him in all post.
There, at your meetest vantage of the time,
Infer the bastardy of Edward's children.   75
Tell them how Edward put to death a citizen
Only for saying he would make his son
Heir to the Crown; meaning indeed his house,
Which, by the sign thereof, was termed so.
Moreover, urge his hateful luxury   80
And bestial appetite in change of lust,
Which stretch'd unto their servants, daughters, wives,
Even where his raging eye or savage heart,
Without control, lusted to make a prey.
Nay, for a need, thus far come near my person: 85
Tell them, when that my mother went with child
Of that insatiate Edward, noble York
My princely father then had wars in France;
And, by true computation of the time,
Found that the issue was not his begot;   90
Which well appeared in his lineaments,
Being nothing like the noble Duke my father.
Yet touch this sparingly, as 'twere far off;
Because, my lord, you know my mother lives.
   Buck. Doubt not, my lord, I'll play the orator 95
As if the golden fee for which I plead
Were for myself; and so, my lord, adieu.
   Glou. If you thrive well, bring them to Baynard's Castle,
Where you shall find me well accompanied
With reverend fathers and well-learned bishops.
   Buck. I go; and towards three or four o'clock 101
Look for the news that the Guildhall affords. *[Exit.*
   Glou. Go, Lovel, with all speed to Doctor Shaw;
[*To Cate.*] Go thou to Friar Penker; bid them both
Meet me within this hour at Baynard's Castle.
             [Exeunt [all but Gloucester].
Now will I go to take some privy order   106
To draw the brats of Clarence out of sight;
And to give [notice] that no manner person
Have any time recourse unto the princes.   *[Exit.*

[SCENE VI.   *The same. A street.*]

Enter a SCRIVENER *with a paper in his hand.*
   Scriv. Here is the indictment of the good Lord Hastings,
Which in a set hand fairly is engross'd
That it may be to-day read o'er in Paul's.
And mark how well the sequel hangs together:
Eleven hours I've spent to write it over,   5
For yesternight by Catesby was it sent me;
The precedent was full as long a-doing;
And yet within these five hours Hastings liv'd,
Untainted, unexamin'd, free, at liberty.
Here's a good world the while! Who is so gross 10
That cannot see this palpable device?
Yet who so bold but says he sees it not?
Bad is the world; and all will come to nought
When such ill dealing must be seen in thought.
                     [Exit.

[SCENE VII.   *Baynard's Castle.*]

Enter GLOUCESTER *and* BUCKINGHAM, *at several doors.*
   Glou. How now, how now, what say the citizens?
   Buck. Now, by the holy mother of our Lord,
The citizens are mum, say not a word.
   Glou. Touch'd you the bastardy of Edward's children?
   Buck. I did; with his contract with Lady Lucy,
And his contract by deputy in France;   6
Th' unsatiate greediness of his desire,
And his enforcement of the city wives;
His tyranny for trifles; his own bastardy,
As being got, your father then in France,   10
And his resemblance, being not like the Duke.
Withal I did infer your lineaments,
Being the right idea of your father,
Both in your form and nobleness of mind;
Laid open all your victories in Scotland,   15
Your discipline in war, wisdom in peace,
Your bounty, virtue, fair humility;
Indeed, left nothing fitting for your purpose
Untouch'd or slightly handled in discourse.
And when my oratory drew toward end,   20
I bid them that did love their country's good
Cry, "God save Richard, England's royal king!"
   Glou. And did they so?
   Buck. No, so God help me, they spake not a word;
But, like dumb statues or breathing stones,   25
Star'd each on other and look'd deadly pale;
Which when I saw, I reprehended them,
And ask'd the Mayor what meant this wilful silence.

---

   69. [But] Q. *Which* F.   74. **meetest...time:** fittest opportunity.   75. **Infer:** assert.   80. **luxury:** sensuality.   85. **for a need:** if necessary.   108. [notice] Q.   *order* F.
   Sc. vi, 7. **precedent:** first draft.   10. **gross:** stupid.
   Sc. vii, 12. **infer:** adduce.

His answer was, the people were not used
To be spoke to but by the Recorder.   30
Then he was urg'd to tell my tale again,
"Thus saith the Duke, thus hath the Duke inferr'd;"
But nothing spoke in warrant from himself.
When he had done, some followers of mine own,
At lower end of th' hall, hurl'd up their caps,   35
And some ten voices cried, "God save King Rich-
    ard!"
And thus I took the vantage of those few,
"Thanks, gentle citizens and friends," quoth I;
"This general applause and cheerful shout
Argues your wisdom and your love to Richard:"   40
And even here brake off, and came away.
    Glou. What tongueless blocks were they! Would
      they not speak?
    [*Buck.* No, by my troth, my lord.]
    Glou. Will not the Mayor then and his brethren
      come?
    Buck. The Mayor is here at hand. Intend some
      fear;   45
Be not you spoke with but by mighty suit;
And look you get a prayer-book in your hand
And stand between two churchmen, good my lord,—
For on that ground I'll make a holy descant —
And be not easily won to our requests.   50
Play the maid's part, still answer nay and take it.
    Glou. I go; and if you plead as well for them
As I can say nay to thee for myself,
No doubt we'll bring it to a happy issue.
    Buck. Go, go up to the leads; the Lord Mayor
      knocks.   [*Exit* [*Gloucester*].   55

Enter the MAYOR *and* Citizens.

Welcome, my lord! I dance attendance here;
I think the Duke will not be spoke withal.

Enter CATESBY [*from the castle*].

[Here comes his servant.]
Now, Catesby, what says your lord to my request?
    Cate. He doth entreat your Grace, my noble lord,
To visit him to-morrow or next day.   60
He is within, with two right reverend **fathers,**
Divinely bent to meditation;
And in no worldly suits would he be **mov'd**
To draw him from his holy exercise.
    Buck. Return, good Catesby, to **the** gracious
      Duke;   65
Tell him, myself, the Mayor and Aldermen,
In deep designs, in matter of great moment,
No less importing than our general good,
Are come to have some conference with his Grace.
    Cate. I'll signify so much unto him straight.   70
                                           [*Exit.*

    Buck. Ah, ha, my lord, this prince is not an
      Edward!
He is not lolling on a lewd love-bed,
But on his knees at meditation;
Not dallying with a brace of courtezans,
But meditating with two deep divines;   75
Not sleeping, to engross his idle body,
But praying, to enrich his watchful soul.
Happy were England would this virtuous prince
Take on his Grace the sovereignty thereof;
But, sure, I fear, we shall not win him to it.   80
    May. Marry, God defend his Grace should say us
      nay!
    Buck. I fear he will. Here Catesby comes again.

Re-enter CATESBY.

Now, Catesby, what says his Grace?
    Cate.   [My lord,]
He wonders to what end you have assembled
Such troops of citizens to come to him,   85
His Grace not being warn'd thereof before.
He fears, my lord, you mean no good to him.
    Buck. Sorry I am my noble cousin should
Suspect me that I mean no good to him.
By heaven, we come to him in perfect love;   90
And so once more return and tell his Grace.
                                 [*Exit Catesby.*
When holy and devout religious men
Are at their beads, 'tis much to draw them thence,
So sweet is zealous contemplation.

Enter GLOUCESTER *aloft, between two* Bishops.
       [CATESBY *returns.*]

    May. See, where his Grace stands 'tween two
      clergymen!   95
    Buck. Two props of virtue for a Christian prince,
To stay him from the fall of vanity;
And, see, a book of prayer in his hand,
True ornaments to know a holy man.
Famous Plantagenet, most gracious prince,   100
Lend favourable ear to our requests,
And pardon us the interruption
Of thy devotion and right Christian zeal.
    Glou. My lord, there needs no such apology.
I do beseech your Grace to pardon me,   105
Who, earnest in the service of my God,
Deferr'd the visitation of my friends.
But, leaving this, what is your Grace's pleasure?
    Buck. Even that, I hope, which pleaseth God above
And all good men of this ungovern'd isle.   110
    Glou. I do suspect I have done some offence
That seems disgracious in the city's eye,
And that you come to reprehend my ignorance.
    Buck. You have, my lord. Would it might
      please your Grace,

---

43. [*Buck....* lord] Q. Om. F.   49. **make...descant:** play a tune with variations.   55. **leads:** roof.   57. [**Here...**
servant] Q. Om. F.   76. **engross:** fatten.   81. **defend:** forbid.   83. [**My lord,**] Q. Om. F.   97. **fall of:** falling into.

On our entreaties, to amend your fault!   115
   Glou. Else wherefore breathe I in a Christian
    land?
   Buck. Know then, it is your fault that you resign
The supreme seat, the throne majestical,
The scep'tred office of your ancestors,
Your state of fortune, and your due of birth,   120
The lineal glory of your royal house,
To the corruption of a blemish'd stock;
Whiles, in the mildness of your sleepy thoughts,
Which here we waken to our country's good,
The noble isle doth want his proper limbs;   125
His face defac'd with scars of infamy,
His royal stock graft with ignoble plants,
And almost should'red in the swallowing gulf
Of dark forgetfulness and deep oblivion.
Which to recure, we heartily solicit   130
Your gracious self to take on you the charge
And kingly government of this your land,
Not as protector, steward, substitute,
Or lowly factor for another's gain;
But as successively, from blood to blood,   135
Your right of birth, your empery, your own.
For this, consorted with the citizens,
Your very worshipful and loving friends,
And by their vehement instigation,
In this just cause come I to move your Grace.   140
   Glou. I cannot tell if to depart in silence
Or bitterly to speak in your reproof
Best fitteth my degree or your condition.
If not to answer, you might haply think
Tongue-ti'd ambition, not replying, yielded   145
To bear the golden yoke of sovereignty
Which fondly you would here impose on me.
If to reprove you for this suit of yours,
So season'd with your faithful love to me,
Then, on the other side, I check'd my friends.   150
Therefore, to speak, and to avoid the first,
And then, in speaking, not to incur the last,
Definitively thus I answer you:
Your love deserves my thanks; but my desert
Unmeritable shuns your high request.   155
First, if all obstacles were cut away,
And that my path were even to the crown
As [my right] revenue and due of birth,
Yet so much is my poverty of spirit,
So mighty and so many my defects,   160
That I would rather hide me from my greatness,
Being a bark to brook no mighty sea,
Than in my greatness covet to be hid
And in the vapour of my glory smother'd.
But, God be thank'd, there is no need of me,   165
And much I need to help you, were there need.
The royal tree hath left us royal fruit

Which, mellow'd by the stealing hours of time,
Will well become the seat of majesty,
And make, no doubt, us happy by his reign.   170
On him I lay that you would lay on me,
The right and fortune of his happy stars,
Which God defend that I should wring from him!
   Buck. My lord, this argues conscience in your
    Grace;
But the respects thereof are nice and trivial,   175
All circumstances well considered.
You say that Edward is your brother's son:
So say we too, but not by Edward's wife;
For first was he contract to Lady Lucy —
Your mother lives a witness to his vow —   180
And afterward by substitute betroth'd
To Bona, sister to the King of France.
These both put off, a poor petitioner,
A care-craz'd mother to a many sons,
A beauty-waning and distressed widow,   185
Even in the afternoon of her best days,
Made prize and purchase of his wanton eye,
Seduc'd the pitch and height of his degree
To base declension and loath'd bigamy.
By her, in his unlawful bed, he got   190
This Edward, whom our manners call the Prince.
More bitterly could I expostulate
Save that, for reverence to some alive,
I give a sparing limit to my tongue.
Then, good my lord, take to your royal self   195
This proffer'd benefit of dignity;
If not to bless us and the land withal,
Yet to draw forth your noble ancestry
From the corruption of abusing times
Unto a lineal true-derived course.   200
   May. Do, good my lord, your citizens entreat
    you.
   Buck. Refuse not, mighty lord, this proffer'd love.
   Cate. O, make them joyful, grant their lawful
    suit!
   Glou. Alas, why would you heap this care on me?
I am unfit for state and majesty.   205
I do beseech you, take it not amiss;
I cannot nor I will not yield to you.
   Buck. If you refuse it, — as, in love and zeal,
Loath to depose the child, your brother's son;
As well we know your tenderness of heart   210
And gentle, kind, effeminate remorse,
Which we have noted in you to your kindred
And equally indeed to all estates, —
Yet know, whe'er you accept our suit or no,
Your brother's son shall never reign our king;   215
But we will plant some other in the throne
To the disgrace and downfall of your house;
And in this resolution here we leave you. —

---

128. **should'red in:** plunged into.   130. **recure:** remedy.   158. **[my right]** Q2.   *the ripe* F.   *my ripe* Q1.   166. **much I**
need: I am greatly lacking in ability.   175. **nice:** over-scrupulous.   187. **purchase:** booty.   189. **declension:** decline.
192. **expostulate:** discuss.   199. **of abusing times:** caused by the abuses of the times.   211. **remorse:** pity.   213. **estates:** ranks.

Come, citizens! ['Zounds!] we'll entreat no more.
  [*Glou.* O, do not swear, my Lord of Buckingham.]
                    [*Exit Buckingham* [*with the Citizens*].
Cate. Call them again, sweet prince, accept their
    suit.   221
If you deny them all the land will rue it.
  Glou. Will you enforce me to a world of cares?
Call them again. [*Catesby goes to the Mayor, and
    exit.*] I am not made of stones,
But penetrable to your kind entreaties,   225
Albeit against my conscience and my soul.

Re-enter BUCKINGHAM, [CATESBY] *and the rest.*

Cousin of Buckingham, and sage, grave men,
Since you will buckle Fortune on my back
To bear her burden whe'er I will or no,
I must have patience to endure the load.   230
But if black scandal or foul-fac'd reproach
Attend the sequel of your imposition,
Your mere enforcement shall acquittance me
From all the impure blots and stains thereof;
For God doth know, and you may partly see,   235
How far I am from the desire of this.
  May. God bless your Grace! we see it and will say
    it.
  Glou. In saying so you shall but say the truth.
  Buck. Then I salute you with this royal title:
Long live King Richard, England's worthy king!
  All. Amen.   241
  Buck. To-morrow may it please you to be
    crown'd?
  Glou. Even when you please, for you will have it
    so.
  Buck. To-morrow, then, we will attend your
    Grace;
And so most joyfully we take our leave.   245
  Glou. [*To the Bishops.*] Come, let us to our holy
    work again.
Farewell, my cousins; farewell, gentle friends.
                                                  [*Exeunt.*

ACT IV

SCENE I. [*Before the Tower.*]

Enter QUEEN ELIZABETH, *the* DUCHESS OF YORK,
    and MARQUESS OF DORSET *at one door;* ANNE,
    DUCHESS OF GLOUCESTER, [*leading* LADY MAR-
    GARET PLANTAGENET, *Clarence's young Daughter*]
    at another door.

  Duch. Who meets us here? My niece Plantage-
    net
Led in the hand of her kind aunt of Gloucester?
Now, for my life, she's wandering to the Tower
On pure heart's love to greet the tender prince.

Daughter, well met.
  Anne.   God give your Graces both   5
A happy and a joyful time of day!
  Q. Eliz. As much to you, good sister! Whither
    away?
  Anne. No farther than the Tower; and, as I
    guess,
Upon the like devotion as yourselves,
To gratulate the gentle princes there.   10
  Q. Eliz. Kind sister, thanks; we'll enter all to-
    gether.

Enter the lieutenant [BRAKENBURY].

And, in good time, here the lieutenant comes.
Master lieutenant, pray you, by your leave,
How doth the Prince and my young son of York?
  Brak. Right well, dear madam. By your pa-
    tience,   15
I may not suffer you to visit them;
The King hath strictly charg'd the contrary.
  Q. Eliz. The King! Who's that?
  Brak. [I cry you mercy!] I mean the Lord Pro-
    tector.
  Q. Eliz. The Lord protect him from that kingly
    title!   20
Hath he set bounds between their love and me?
I am their mother; who shall bar me from them?
  Duch. I am their father's mother; I will see them.
  Anne. Their aunt I am in law, in love their
    mother;
Then bring me to their sights. I'll bear thy blame
And take thy office from thee, on my peril.   26
  Brak. No, madam, no; I may not leave it so.
I am bound by oath, and therefore pardon me.
                                                  [*Exit.*

Enter LORD STANLEY

  Stan. Let me but meet you, ladies, one hour
    hence,
And I'll salute your Grace of York as mother   30
And reverend looker on of two fair queens.
  [*To Anne.*] Come, madam, you must straight to
    Westminster.
There to be crowned Richard's royal queen.
  Q. Eliz. O, cut my lace asunder that my pent
    heart
May have some scope to beat, or else I swoon   35
With this dead-killing news!
  Anne. Despiteful tidings! O unpleasing news!
  Dor. Be of good cheer. Mother, how fares your
    Grace?
  Q. Eliz. O Dorset, speak not to me, get thee gone!
Death and destruction dogs thee at thy heels;   40
Thy mother's name is ominous to children.
If thou wilt outstrip death, go cross the seas,

219, 220. ['Zounds] [*Glou. . . . Buckingham*] Q. Om. F.   233. acquittance: acquit.
Act IV, sc. i, 1. niece: granddaughter.   19. [I . . . mercy] Q. Om. F.

And live with Richmond, from the reach of hell.
Go, hie thee, hie thee from this slaughter-house,
Lest thou increase the number of the dead,   45
And make me die the thrall of Margaret's curse,
Nor mother, wife, nor England's counted queen.
   Stan. Full of wise care is this your counsel,
madam.
Take all the swift advantage of the hours;
You shall have letters from me to my son   50
In your behalf, to meet you on the way.
Be not ta'en tardy by unwise delay.
   Duch. O ill-dispersing wind of misery!
O my accursed womb, the bed of death!
A cockatrice hast thou hatch'd to the world,   55
Whose unavoided eye is murderous.
   Stan. Come, madam, come; I in all haste was
sent.
   Anne. And I with all unwillingness will go.
O, would to God that the inclusive verge
Of golden metal that must round my brow   60
Were red-hot steel, to sear me to the brains!
Anointed let me be with deadly venom,
And die ere men can say, "God save the Queen!"
   Q. Eliz. Go, go, poor soul, I envy not thy glory;
To feed my humour wish thyself no harm.   65
   Anne. No! why? When he that is my husband
now
Came to me as I follow'd Henry's corse,
When scarce the blood was well wash'd from his
hands
Which issued from my other angel husband
And that dear saint which then I weeping follow'd;
O, when, I say, I look'd on Richard's face,   71
This was my wish: "Be thou," quoth I, "accurs'd
For making me, so young, so old a widow!
And, when thou wed'st, let sorrow haunt thy bed;
And be thy wife — if any be so mad —   75
More miserable by the life of thee
Than thou hast made me by my dear lord's death!"
Lo, ere I can repeat this curse again,
Within so small a time, my woman's heart
Grossly grew captive to his honey words   80
And prov'd the subject of mine own soul's curse,
Which hitherto hath held mine eyes from rest;
For never yet one hour in his bed
Did I enjoy the golden dew of sleep,
But with his timorous dreams was still awak'd.   85
Besides, he hates me for my father Warwick,
And will, no doubt, shortly be rid of me.
   Q. Eliz. Poor heart, adieu! I pity thy complain-
ing.
   Anne. No more than with my soul I mourn for
yours.

   Dor. Farewell, thou woeful welcomer of glory! 90
   Anne. Adieu, poor soul, that tak'st thy leave of it!
   Duch. [*To Dorset.*] Go thou to Richmond, and
good fortune guide thee!
   [*To Anne.*] Go thou to Richard, and good angels
tend thee!
   [*To Queen Eliz.*] Go thou to sanctuary, and good
thoughts possess thee!
I to my grave, where peace and rest lie with me!   95
Eighty odd years of sorrow have I seen.
And each hour's joy wreck'd with a week of teen.
   Q. Eliz. Stay, yet look back with me unto the
Tower.
Pity, you ancient stones, those tender babes
Whom envy hath immur'd within your walls,   100
Rough cradle for such little pretty ones!
Rude ragged nurse, old sullen playfellow
For tender princes, use my babies well!
So foolish sorrow bids your stones farewell. [*Exeunt.*

SCENE II. [*London.   The palace.*]

Sennet.   Enter RICHARD, *in pomp, crowned;* BUCK-
INGHAM, CATESBY [*a* PAGE, *and others*].

   K. Rich. Stand all apart. Cousin of Bucking-
ham!
   Buck. My gracious sovereign?
   K. Rich. Give me thy hand. (*Here he ascendeth
the throne.   Sound.*) Thus high, by thy
advice
And thy assistance, is King Richard seated;
But shall we wear these glories for a day;   5
Or shall they last, and we rejoice in them?
   Buck. Still live they, and for ever let them last!
   K. Rich. Ah, Buckingham, now do I play the
touch
To try if thou be current gold indeed.
Young Edward lives: think now what I would speak.
   Buck. Say on, my loving lord.   11
   K. Rich. Why, Buckingham, I say, I would be
king.
   Buck. Why, so you are, my thrice renowned lord.
   K. Rich. Ha! am I king? 'Tis so: but Edward
lives.
   Buck. True, noble prince.
   K. Rich.   O bitter consequence,
That Edward still should live! "True, noble
prince!"   16
Cousin, thou wast not wont to be so dull.
Shall I be plain? I wish the bastards dead;
And I would have it suddenly perform'd.
What say'st thou now? Speak suddenly; be brief.
   Buck. Your Grace may do your pleasure.   21

---

43. **Richmond:** Henry Tudor, son of Margaret Beaufort, later Henry VII. 50. **son:** step-son. Stanley married Henry
Tudor's mother. 55. **cockatrice:** a fabulous monster. 59. **verge:** rim. 80. **Grossly:** stupidly. 97. **teen:** sorrow.
Sc. ii, 8. **touch:** touchstone. 15. **consequence:** (1) answer, (2) fact.

K. Rich. Tut, tut, thou art all ice, thy kindness
    freezes.
Say, have I thy consent that they shall die?
    Buck. Give me some little breath, some pause,
        dear lord,
Before I positively speak in this.   25
I will resolve you herein presently.   [*Exit.*
    Cate. [*Aside to a stander by.*] The King is angry;
        see, he gnaws his lip.
    K. Rich. I will converse with iron-witted fools
And unrespective boys; none are for me
That look into me with considerate eyes.   30
High-reaching Buckingham grows circumspect.
Boy!
    Page. My lord?
    K. Rich. Know'st thou not any whom corrupting
        gold
Will tempt unto a close exploit of death?   35
    Page. I know a discontented gentleman
Whose humble means match not his haughty spirit.
Gold were as good as twenty orators,
And will, no doubt, tempt him to anything.   39
    K. Rich. What is his name?
    Page.   His name, my lord, is Tyrrel.
    K. Rich. I partly know the man; go, call him
        hither.   [*Exit Page.*
The deep-revolving witty Buckingham
No more shall be the neighbour to my counsels.
Hath he so long held out with me untir'd
And stops he now for breath? Well, be it so.   45

Enter STANLEY.

How now, Lord Stanley, what's the news?
    Stan. Know, my loving lord,
The Marquis Dorset, as I hear, is fled
To Richmond, in the parts where he abides.
                        [*Stands apart.*
    K. Rich. Come hither, Catesby. Rumour it
        abroad   51
That Anne, my wife, is very grievous sick;
I will take order for her keeping close.
Inquire me out some mean poor gentleman
Whom I will marry straight to Clarence' daughter;
The boy is foolish and I fear not him.   56
Look, how thou dream'st! I say again, give out
That Anne my queen is sick and like to die.
About it; for it stands me much upon
To stop all hopes whose growth may damage me.
                        [*Exit Catesby.*
I must be married to my brother's daughter,   61
Or else my kingdom stands on brittle glass.
Murder her brothers and then marry her!
Uncertain way of gain! But I am in

So far in blood that sin will pluck on sin!   65
Tear-falling pity dwells not in this eye.

Re-enter [*Page, with* SIR JAMES] TYRREL.

Is thy name Tyrrel?
    Tyr. James Tyrrel, and your most obedient
        subject.
    K. Rich. Art thou, indeed?
    Tyr.   Prove me, my gracious lord.
    K. Rich. Dar'st thou resolve to kill a friend of
        mine?   70
    Tyr. Please you;
But I had rather kill two enemies.
    K. Rich. Why, there thou hast it; two deep
        enemies,
Foes to my rest and my sweet sleep's disturbers
Are they that I would have thee deal upon.   75
Tyrrel, I mean those bastards in the Tower.
    Tyr. Let me have open means to come to them,
And soon I'll rid you from the fear of them.
    K. Rich. Thou sing'st sweet music. Hark, come
        hither, Tyrrel.
Go, by this token. Rise and lend thine ear. 80
                        [*Whispers.*
There is no more but so; say it is done,
And I will love thee and prefer thee for it.
    Tyr. I will despatch it straight.
    [*K. Rich.* Shall we hear from thee, Tyrrel, ere we
        sleep?
    Tyr. Ye shall, my lord.]   [*Exit.* 85

Re-enter BUCKINGHAM.

    Buck. My lord, I have consider'd in my mind
The late request that you did sound me in.
    K. Rich. Well, let that rest. Dorset is fled to
        Richmond.
    Buck. I hear the news, my lord.
    K. Rich. Stanley, he is your wife's son: well, look
        unto it.   90
    Buck. My lord, I claim the gift, my due by
        promise.
For which your honour and your faith is pawn'd;
The earldom of Hereford and the movables
Which you have promised I shall possess.
    K. Rich. Stanley, look to your wife. If she con-
        vey   95
Letters to Richmond, you shall answer it.
    Buck. What says your Highness to my just re-
        quest?
    K. Rich. I do remember me, Henry the Sixth
Did prophesy that Richmond should be king,
When Richmond was a little peevish boy.   100
A king, perhaps, [perhaps, —

26. resolve: inform. 29. unrespective: thoughtless. 30. considerate: thoughtful. 35. close exploit: secret undertaking.
42. witty: cunning. 53. close: confined. 59. stands ... upon: is of great concern to me. 61. my brother's daughter:
Edward IV's daughter Elizabeth. 84–85. [K. Rich. ... lord.] Q. Om. F. 101–121. [perhaps, — ... tut] Q. Buck. May
it please you to resolve me in my suit. Rich. F.

Buck. My lord!

K. Rich. How chance the prophet could not at
  that time
Have told me, I being by, that I should kill him?

Buck. My lord, your promise for the earldom, —

K. Rich. Richmond! When last I was at Exeter,
The mayor in courtesy show'd me the castle   107
And call'd it Rougemont; at which name I started,
Because a bard of Ireland told me once
I should not live long after I saw Richmond.   110

Buck. My lord!

K. Rich. Ay, what's o'clock?

Buck. I am thus bold to put your Grace in mind
Of what you promis'd me.

K. Rich.   Well, but what 's o'clock?

Buck. Upon the stroke of ten.

K. Rich.   Well, let it strike.

Buck. Why let it strike?   116

K. Rich. Because that, like a Jack, thou keep'st
  the stroke
Betwixt thy begging and my meditation.
I am not in the giving vein to-day.

Buck. Why, then resolve me whether you will or
  no.   120

K. Rich. Tut, tut,]
Thou troublest me; I am not in the vein.
          [*Exeunt all but Buckingham.*

Buck. And is it thus? Repays he my deep service
With such contempt? Made I him king for this?
O, let me think on Hastings, and be gone   125
To Brecknock while my fearful head is on! [*Exit.*

[SCENE III. *The same.*]

Enter TYRREL.

Tyr. The tyrannous and bloody act is done,
The most arch deed of piteous massacre
That ever yet this land was guilty of.
Dighton and Forrest, who I did suborn
To do this piece of ruthless butchery,   5
Albeit they were flesh'd villains, bloody dogs,
Melted with tenderness and mild compassion,
Wept like two children in their death's sad story.
"O, thus," quoth Dighton, "lay the gentle babes;"
"Thus, thus," quoth Forrest, "girdling one another
Within their alabaster innocent arms.   11
Their lips were four red roses on a stalk,
Which in their summer beauty kiss'd each other.
A book of prayers on their pillow lay,
Which once," quoth Forrest, "almost chang'd my
  mind;   15
But O! the devil" — there the villain stopp'd;
When Dighton thus told on: "We smothered

The most replenished sweet work of Nature
That from the prime creation e'er she fram'd."
Hence both are gone with conscience and remorse 20
They could not speak; and so I left them both,
To bear this tidings to the bloody King.

Enter KING RICHARD.

And here he comes. All health, my sovereign lord!

K. Rich. Kind Tyrrel, am I happy in thy news?

Tyr. If to have done the thing you gave in charge
Beget your happiness, be happy then,   26
For it is done.

K. Rich.   But didst thou see them dead?

Tyr. I did, my lord.

K. Rich.   And buried, gentle Tyrrel?

Tyr. The chaplain of the Tower hath buried
  them;
But where, to say the truth, I do not know.   30

K. Rich. Come to me, Tyrrel, soon, [at] after-
  supper,
When thou shalt tell the process of their death.
Meantime, but think how I may do thee good
And be inheritor of thy desire.
Farewell till then.   35

Tyr. I humbly take my leave.   [*Exit.*

K. Rich. The son of Clarence have I pent up close;
His daughter meanly have I match'd in marriage;
The sons of Edward sleep in Abraham's bosom,
And Anne my wife hath bid this world good-night.
Now, for I know the Breton Richmond aims   40
At young Elizabeth, my brother's daughter,
And by that knot looks proudly on the crown,
To her go I, a jolly thriving wooer.

Enter RATCLIFF.

Rat. My lord!

K. Rich. Good or bad news, that thou com'st in
  so bluntly?   45

Rat. Bad news, my lord. Morton is fled to Rich-
  mond;
And Buckingham, back'd with the hardy Welshmen,
Is in the field, and still his power increaseth.

K. Rich. Ely with Richmond troubles me more
  near
Than Buckingham and his rash-levied strength. 50
Come, I have learn'd that fearful commenting
Is leaden servitor to dull delay;
Delay leads impotent and snail-pac'd beggary.
Then fiery expedition be my wing,
Jove's Mercury, and herald for a king!   55
Go, muster men! My counsel is my shield;
We must be brief when traitors brave the field.
          [*Exeunt.*

117. **Jack:** a figure in old clocks that strikes the bell. The general sense is, make an end of begging and leave me to my
meditation.
Sc. iii, 2. **arch:** extreme. 6. **flesh'd:** accustomed to slaughter. 18. **replenished:** complete. 31. [at] Q. *and* F. **after-
supper:** dessert. 34. **inheritor:** possessor. 42. **knot:** alliance. 50. **rash-levied:** hastily raised. 53. **leads:** leads to.

Scene [IV. *Before the palace.*]

Enter old Queen Margaret.

Q. Mar. So, now prosperity begins to mellow
And drop into the rotten mouth of death.
Here in these confines slily have I lurk'd
To watch the waning of mine enemies.
A dire induction am I witness to,   5
And will to France, hoping the consequence
Will prove as bitter, black, and tragical.
Withdraw thee, wretched Margaret; who comes
        here?   [*Retires.*]

Enter Queen Elizabeth *and the* Duchess of York.

Q. Eliz. Ah, my poor princes! ah, my tender
        babes!
My [unblown] flowers, new-appearing sweets!   10
If yet your gentle souls fly in the air
And be not fix'd in doom perpetual,
Hover about me with your airy wings
And hear your mother's lamentation!
Q. Mar. Hover about her; say that right for
        right   15
Hath dimm'd your infant morn to aged night.
Duch. So many miseries have craz'd my voice
That my woe-wearied tongue is still and mute.
Edward Plantagenet, why art thou dead?
Q. Mar. Plantagenet doth quit Plantagenet.   20
Edward for Edward pays a dying debt.
Q. Eliz. Wilt thou, O God, fly from such gentle
        lambs
And throw them in the entrails of the wolf?
When didst thou sleep when such a deed was done?
Q. Mar. When holy Harry died, and my sweet
        son.   25
Duch. Dead life, blind sight, poor mortal living
        ghost,
Woe's scene, world's shame, grave's due by life
        usurp'd,
Brief abstract and record of tedious days,
Rest thy unrest on England's lawful earth,
                              [*Sitting down.*]
Unlawfully made drunk with innocent blood!   30
Q. Eliz. Ah, that thou wouldst as soon afford a
        grave
As thou canst yield a melancholy seat!
Then would I hide my bones, not rest them here.
Ah, who hath any cause to mourn but we?
                          [*Sitting down by her.*]
Q. Mar. [*Coming forward.*] If ancient sorrow be
        most reverend,   35
Give mine the benefit of seniory,
And let my griefs frown on the upper hand.

If sorrow can admit society,
                        [*Sitting down with them.*]
[Tell o'er your woes again by viewing mine.]
I had an Edward, till a Richard kill'd him;   40
I had a [Harry], till a Richard kill'd him:
Thou hadst an Edward, till a Richard kill'd him;
Thou hadst a Richard, till a Richard kill'd him.
Duch. I had a Richard too, and thou didst kill
        him;
I had a Rutland too, thou holp'st to kill him.   45
Q. Mar. Thou hadst a Clarence too, and Richard
        kill'd him.
From forth the kennel of thy womb hath crept
A hell-hound that doth hunt us all to death.
That dog, that had his teeth before his eyes
To worry lambs and lap their gentle blood,   50
That foul defacer of God's handiwork,
That excellent grand tyrant of the earth
That reigns in galled eyes of weeping souls,
Thy womb let loose, to chase us to our graves.
O upright, just, and true-disposing God,   55
How do I thank thee that this carnal cur
Preys on the issue of his mother's body
And makes her pew-fellow with others' moan!
Duch. O Harry's wife, triumph not in my woes!
God witness with me, I have wept for thine.   60
Q. Mar. Bear with me; I am hungry for revenge,
And now I cloy me with beholding it.
Thy Edward he is dead, that kill'd my Edward;
The other Edward dead, to quit my Edward;
Young York he is but boot, because both they   65
Match not the high perfection of my loss.
Thy Clarence he is dead that stabb'd my Edward;
And the beholders of this frantic play,
The adulterate Hastings, Rivers, Vaughan, Grey,
Untimely smother'd in their dusky graves.   70
Richard yet lives, hell's black intelligencer,
Only reserv'd their factor to buy souls
And send them thither; but at hand, at hand,
Ensues his piteous and unpitied end.
Earth gapes, hell burns, fiends roar, saints pray, 75
To have him suddenly convey'd from hence.
Cancel his bond of life, dear God, I pray,
That I may live to say, "The dog is dead!"
Q. Eliz. O, thou didst prophesy the time would
        come
That I should wish for thee to help me curse   80
That bottl'd spider, that foul bunch-back'd toad!
Q. Mar. I call'd thee then vain flourish of my
        fortune;
I call'd thee then poor shadow, painted queen;
The presentation of but what I was;
The flattering index of a direful pageant;   85

Sc. iv, 5. **induction:** beginning. 6. **consequence:** sequel. 10. **[unblown]** Q. *unblowed* F. 15. **right for right:** avenging justice. 17. **craz'd:** cracked. 39. **[Tell ... mine]** Q. Om. F. 41. **[Harry]** (Camb. edd.). *Husband* F. *Richard* Q. 52, 53. **That ... souls.** So Capell. Transposed in F. 56. **carnal:** carnivorous. 58. **pew-fellow:** companion. 65. **boot:** something added to equalize a bargain. 69. **adulterate:** adulterous, with perhaps the added idea of base metal. 71. **intelligencer:** agent. 85. **index:** beginning.

One heav'd a-high, to be hurl'd down below;
A mother only mock'd with two fair babes;
A dream of what thou wast; a garish flag
To be the aim of every dangerous shot;
A sign of dignity, a breath, a bubble;   90
A queen in jest, only to fill the scene.
Where is thy husband now? Where be thy brothers?
Where be thy two sons? Wherein dost thou joy?
Who sues, and kneels, and says, "God save the
     Queen"?
Where be the bending peers that flattered thee? 95
Where be the thronging troops that followed thee?
Decline all this, and see what now thou art:
For happy wife, a most distressed widow;
For joyful mother, one that wails the name;
For queen, a very caitiff crown'd with care;   100
For one being sued to, one that humbly sues;
For she that scorn'd at me, now scorn'd of me;
For she being fear'd of all, now fearing one;
For she commanding all, obey'd of none.
Thus hath the course of justice whirl'd about   105
And left thee but a very prey to time,
Having no more but thought of what thou wast
To torture thee the more, being what thou art.
Thou didst usurp my place, and dost thou not
Usurp the just proportion of my sorrow?   110
Now thy proud neck bears half my burden'd yoke
From which even here I slip my wearied head
And leave the burden of it all on thee.
Farewell, York's wife, and queen of sad mischance;
These English woes shall make me smile in France.
  Q. Eliz. O thou well skill'd in curses, stay a while
And teach me how to curse mine enemies!   117
  Q. Mar. Forbear to sleep the night, and fast the
     day;
Compare dead happiness with living woe;
Think that thy babes were sweeter than they were
And he that slew them fouler than he is.   121
Bett'ring thy loss makes the bad causer worse;
Revolving this will teach thee how to curse.
  Q. Eliz. My words are dull; O, quicken them with
     thine!
  Q. Mar. Thy woes will make them sharp and
     pierce like mine.   [*Exit.* 125
  Duch. Why should calamity be full of words?
  Q. Eliz. Windy attorneys to their [client] woes,
Airy succeeders of [intestate] joys,
Poor breathing orators of miseries,
Let them have scope! though what they will impart
Help nothing else, yet do they ease the heart. 131
  Duch. If so, then be not tongue-ti'd; go with me
And in the breath of bitter words let's smother

My damned son that thy two sweet sons smother'd.
The trumpet sounds; be copious in exclaims.   135

Enter KING RICHARD *and his train, marching,
with drums and trumpets.*

  K. Rich. Who intercepts me in my expedition?
  Duch. O, she that might have intercepted thee,
By strangling thee in her accursed womb,
From all the slaughters, wretch, that thou hast done!
  Q. Eliz. Hid'st thou that forehead with a golden
     crown   140
Where should be branded, if that right were right,
The slaughter of the prince that ow'd that crown,
And the dire death of my poor sons and brothers?
Tell me, thou villain slave, where are my children?
  Duch. Thou toad, thou toad, where is thy brother
     Clarence?   145
And little Ned Plantagenet, his son?
  Q. Eliz. Where is the gentle Rivers, Vaughan,
     Grey?
  Duch. Where is kind Hastings?
  K. Rich. A flourish, trumpets! strike alarum,
     drums!
Let not the heavens hear these tell-tale women
Rail on the Lord's anointed. Strike, I say!   150
     [*Flourish. Alarums.*
Either be patient and entreat me fair,
Or with the clamorous report of war
Thus will I drown your exclamations.
  Duch. Art thou my son?
  K. Rich. Ay, I thank God, my father, and your-
     self.   155
  Duch. Then patiently hear my impatience.
  K. Rich. Madam, I have a touch of your condi-
     tion,
That cannot brook the accent of reproof.
  Duch. O, let me speak!
  K. Rich.   Do then; but I'll not hear.
  Duch. I will be mild and gentle in my words.
  K. Rich. And brief, good mother, for I am in
     haste.   161
  Duch. Art thou so hasty? I have stay'd for thee,
God knows, in torment and in agony.
  K. Rich. And came I not at last to comfort you?
  Duch. No, by the holy rood, thou know'st it well,
Thou cam'st on earth to make the earth my hell. 166
A grievous burden was thy birth to me;
Tetchy and wayward was thy infancy;
Thy school-days frightful, desp'rate, wild, and
     furious,   169
Thy prime of manhood daring, bold, and venturous,
Thy age confirm'd proud, subtle, sly, and bloody,

---

90. **sign:** symbol, not the thing itself. 97. **Decline:** recite in order. 100, 101. **For . . . me.** So Q. Transposed in F.
111. **burden'd:** burdensome. 127. **[client]** (Hanmer). *clients* F. 128. **[intestate]** Q: dead without bequeathing anything.
intestine F. 136. **expedition:** haste. 142. **ow'd:** owned. 146. **Ned Plantagenet:** Edward, Earl of Warwick, referred to in
IV.ii.56, but not as a victim of Richard's. 157. **condition:** disposition. 168. **Tetchy:** fretful. 171. **age confirm'd:** settled
middle age.

More mild, but yet more harmful, kind in hatred.
What comfortable hour canst thou name
That ever grac'd me with thy company?
    K. Rich. Faith, none, but Humphrey Hour, that
        call'd your Grace   175
To breakfast once forth of my company.
If I be so disgracious in your eye
Let me march on and not offend you, madam.
Strike up the drum.
    Duch.   I prithee, hear me speak.
    K. Rich. You speak too bitterly.
    Duch.   Hear me a word,
For I shall never speak to thee again.   181
    K. Rich. So.
    Duch. Either thou wilt die by God's just ordinance
Ere from this war thou turn a conqueror,
Or I with grief and extreme age shall perish   185
And never more behold thy face again.
Therefore take with thee my most grievous curse,
Which in the day of battle tire thee more
Than all the complete armour that thou wear'st!
My prayers on the adverse party fight;   190
And there the little souls of Edward's children
Whisper the spirits of thine enemies
And promise them success and victory.
Bloody thou art, bloody will be thy end;
Shame serves thy life and doth thy death attend.
                          [*Exit.*
    Q. Eliz. Though far more cause, yet much less
        spirit to curse   196
Abides in me; I say amen to her.
    K. Rich. Stay, madam; I must talk a word with
        you.
    Q. Eliz. I have no more sons of the royal blood
For thee to slaughter; for my daughters, Richard,
They shall be praying nuns, not weeping queens; 201
And therefore level not to hit their lives.
    K. Rich. You have a daughter call'd Elizabeth,
Virtuous and fair, royal and gracious.
    Q. Eliz. And must she die for this? O, let her
        live   205
And I'll corrupt her manners, stain her beauty,
Slander myself as false to Edward's bed,
Throw over her the veil of infamy.
So she may live unscarr'd of bleeding slaughter,
I will confess she was not Edward's daughter. 210
    K. Rich. Wrong not her birth, she is a royal
        princess.
    Q. Eliz. To save her life, I'll say she is not so.
    K. Rich. Her life is safest only in her birth.
    Q. Eliz. And only in that safety died her brothers.
    K. Rich. Lo, at their birth good stars were op-
        posite.   215

    Q. Eliz. No, to their lives ill friends were con-
        trary.
    K. Rich. All unavoided is the doom of destiny.
    Q. Eliz. True, when avoided grace makes destiny.
My babes were destin'd to a fairer death
If grace had bless'd thee with a fairer life.   220
    K. Rich. You speak as if that I had slain my
        cousins.
    Q. Eliz. Cousins, indeed; and by their uncle
        cozen'd
Of comfort, kingdom, kindred, freedom, life.
Whose hand soever lanc'd their tender hearts,
Thy head, all indirectly, gave direction.   225
No doubt the murd'rous knife was dull and blunt
Till it was whetted on thy stone-hard heart
To revel in the entrails of my lambs.
But that still use of grief makes wild grief tame,
My tongue should to thy ears not name my boys
Till that my nails were anchor'd in thine eyes; 230
And I, in such a desp'rate bay of death,
Like a poor bark of sails and tackling reft,
Rush all to pieces on thy rocky bosom.
    K. Rich. Madam, so thrive I in my enterprise 235
And dangerous success of bloody wars,
As I intend more good to you and yours
Than ever you or yours by me were harm'd!
    Q. Eliz. What good is cover'd with the face of
        heaven.
To be discover'd, that can do me good?   240
    K. Rich. Th' advancement of your children,
        gentle lady.
    Q. Eliz. Up to some scaffold, there to lose their
        heads?
    K. Rich. Unto the dignity and height of fortune,
The high imperial type of this earth's glory.
    Q. Eliz. Flatter my sorrow with report of it; 245
Tell me what state, what dignity, what honour,
Canst thou demise to any child of mine?
    K. Rich. Even all I have; ay, and myself and all
Will I withal endow a child of thine;
So in the Lethe of thy angry soul   250
Thou drown the sad remembrance of those wrongs
Which thou supposest I have done to thee.
    Q. Eliz. Be brief, lest that the process of thy
        kindness
Last longer telling than thy kindness' date.
    K. Rich. Then know, that from my soul I love
        thy daughter.   255
    Q. Eliz. My daughter's mother thinks it with her
        soul.
    K. Rich. What do you think?
    Q. Eliz. That thou dost love my daughter from
        thy soul.

175. **Humphrey Hour.** Not explained. To dine with Duke Humphrey was to go hungry. 195. **serves:** attends. 202. **level:** aim. 217. **unavoided:** unavoidable. 218. **avoided grace:** lack of grace. 222. **cozen'd:** cheated. 229. **still:** continual. 244. **type:** symbol. 247. **demise:** transfer. 250. **Lethe:** the river of forgetfulness. 253. **process:** story. 258, 259, 260. **from:** apart from.

So from thy soul's love didst thou love her brothers,
And from my heart's love I do thank thee for it. 260
    K. Rich. Be not so hasty to confound my meaning.
I mean, that with my soul I love thy daughter,
And do intend to make her Queen of England.
    Q. Eliz. Well then, who dost thou mean shall be
      her king?
    K. Rich. Even he that makes her queen. Who
      else should be? 265
    Q. Eliz. What, thou?
    K. Rich. Even so. How think you of it?
    Q. Eliz. How canst thou woo her?
    K. Rich.   That I would learn of you,
As one being best acquainted with her humour.
    Q. Eliz. And wilt thou learn of me?
    K. Rich.   Madam, with all my heart.
    Q. Eliz. Send to her by the man that slew her
      brothers 271
A pair of bleeding hearts; thereon engrave
Edward and York; then haply will she weep.
Therefore present to her, — as sometime Margaret
Did to thy father, steep'd in Rutland's blood, — 275
A handkerchief; which, say to her, did drain
The purple sap from her sweet brother's body;
And bid her wipe her weeping eyes withal.
If this inducement move her not to love,
Send her a letter of thy noble deeds. 280
Tell her thou mad'st away her uncle Clarence,
Her uncle Rivers; ay, and, for her sake,
Mad'st quick conveyance with her good aunt Anne.
    K. Rich. You mock me, madam; this is not the
      way 284
To win your daughter.
    Q. Eliz.   There is no other way,
Unless thou couldst put on some other shape
And not be Richard that hath done all this.
    K. Rich. Say that I did all this for love of her.
    Q. Eliz. Nay, then indeed she cannot choose but
      hate thee,
Having bought love with such a bloody spoil. 290
    K. Rich. Look, what is done cannot be now
      amended.
Men shall deal unadvisedly sometimes,
Which after hours gives leisure to repent.
If I did take the kingdom from your sons,
To make amends I'll give it to your daughter. 295
If I have kill'd the issue of your womb,
To quicken your increase, I will beget
Mine issue of your blood upon your daughter.
A grandam's name is little less in love
Than is the doting title of a mother; 300
They are as children but one step below,
Even of your mettle, of your very blood;
Of all one pain, save for a night of groans
Endur'd of her, for whom you bid like sorrow.

Your children were vexation to your youth, 305
But mine shall be a comfort to your age.
The loss you have is but a son being king,
And by that loss your daughter is made queen.
I cannot make you what amends I would,
Therefore accept such kindness as I can. 310
Dorset your son, that with a fearful soul
Leads discontented steps in foreign soil,
This fair alliance quickly shall call home
To high promotions and great dignity.
The King, that calls your beauteous daughter wife,
Familiarly shall call thy Dorset brother; 316
Again shall you be mother to a king,
And all the ruins of distressful times
Repair'd with double riches of content.
What! we have many goodly days to see. 320
The liquid drops of tears that you have shed
Shall come again, transform'd to orient pearl,
Advantaging their [loan] with interest
Of ten times double gain of happiness.
Go, then, my mother, to thy daughter go; 325
Make bold her bashful years with your experience;
Prepare her ears to hear a wooer's tale;
Put in her tender heart th' aspiring flame
Of golden sovereignty; acquaint the princess
With the sweet silent hours of marriage joys; 330
And when this arm of mine hath chastised
The petty rebel, dull-brain'd Buckingham,
Bound with triumphant garlands will I come
And lead thy daughter to a conqueror's bed;
To whom I will retail my conquest won. 335
And she shall be sole victress, Cæsar's Cæsar.
    Q. Eliz. What were I best to say? Her father's
      brother
Would be her lord? Or shall I say, her uncle?
Or, he that slew her brothers and her uncles?
Under what title shall I woo for thee, 340
That God, the law, my honour, and her love
Can make seem pleasing to her tender years?
    K. Rich. Infer fair England's peace by this alliance.
    Q. Eliz. Which she shall purchase with still lasting
      war.
    K. Rich. Tell her the King, that may command,
      entreats. 345
    Q. Eliz. That at her hands which the King's king
      forbids.
    K. Rich. Say she shall be a high and mighty
      queen.
    Q. Eliz. To wail the title, as her mother doth.
    K. Rich. Say, I will love her everlastingly.
    Q. Eliz. But how long shall that title "ever"
      last? 350
    K. Rich. Sweetly in force unto her fair life's end.
    Q. Eliz. But how long fairly shall her sweet life
      last?

---

283. **conveyance:** riddance.   290. **spoil:** booty.   304. **bid:** did bide, suffered.   323. **[loan]** (Theobald). *loue* F.   335.
retail: relate.   343. **Infer:** allege.

K. Rich. As long as heaven and nature lengthens it.

Q. Eliz. As long as hell and Richard likes of it.

K. Rich. Say, I, her sovereign, am her subject low.

Q. Eliz. But she, your subject, loathes such sovereignty.   356

K. Rich. Be eloquent in my behalf to her.

Q. Eliz. An honest tale speeds best being plainly told.

K. Rich. Then plainly to her tell my loving tale.

Q. Eliz. Plain and not honest is too harsh a style.

K. Rich. Your reasons are too shallow and too quick.   361

Q. Eliz. O no, my reasons are too deep and dead;
Too deep and dead, poor infants, in their graves.

K. Rich. Harp not on that string, madam; that is past.

Q. Eliz. Harp on it still shall I till heartstrings break.   365

K. Rich. Now, by my George, my Garter, and my crown, —

Q. Eliz. Profan'd, dishonour'd, and the third usurp'd.

K. Rich. I swear —

Q. Eliz.   By nothing; for this is no oath.
Thy George, profan'd, hath lost his lordly honour;
Thy Garter, blemish'd, pawn'd his knightly virtue;
Thy crown, usurp'd, disgrac'd his kingly glory.   371
If something thou wouldst swear to be believ'd,
Swear then by something that thou hast not wrong'd.

K. Rich. Now, by the world —

Q. Eliz.   'Tis full of thy foul wrongs.

K. Rich. My father's death —

Q. Eliz.   Thy life hath it dishonour'd.   375

K. Rich. Then, by myself —

Q. Eliz.   Thyself [thyself misusest].

K. Rich. Why then, by [God] —

Q. Eliz.   [God's] wrong is most of all.
If thou did'st fear to break an oath with Him,
The unity the King my husband made
Thou hadst not broken, nor my brothers died.   380
If thou hadst fear'd to break an oath by Him,
Th' imperial metal, circling now thy head,
Had grac'd the tender temples of my child,
And both the Princes had been breathing here,
Which now, two tender bedfellows for dust,   385
Thy broken faith hath made the prey for worms.
What canst thou swear by now?

K. Rich.   The time to come.

Q. Eliz. That thou hast wronged in the time o'erpast;
For I myself have many tears to wash

Hereafter time, for time past wrong'd by thee.   390
The children live whose fathers thou hast slaughter'd,
Ungovern'd youth, to wail it with their age;
The parents live whose children thou hast butcher'd,
Old barren plants, to wail it with their age.
Swear not by time to come; for that thou hast
Misus'd ere us'd, by times ill-us'd [o'erpast].   396

K. Rich. As I intend to prosper and repent,
So thrive I in my dangerous affairs
Of hostile arms! Myself myself confound!
Heaven and fortune bar me happy hours!   400
Day, yield me not thy light, nor, night, thy rest!
Be opposite all planets of good luck
To my proceeding, if, with dear heart's love,
Immaculate devotion, holy thoughts,
I tender not thy beauteous princely daughter!   405
In her consists my happiness and thine;
Without her, follows to myself and thee,
Herself, the land, and many a Christian soul,
Death, desolation, ruin, and decay.
It cannot be avoided but by this;   410
It will not be avoided but by this.
Therefore, dear mother, — I must call you so —
Be the attorney of my love to her.
Plead what I will be, not what I have been;
Not my deserts, but what I will deserve.   415
Urge the necessity and state of times,
And be not [peevish-fond] in great designs.

Q. Eliz. Shall I be tempted of the devil thus?

K. Rich. Ay, if the devil tempt you to do good.

Q. Eliz. Shall I forget myself to be myself?   420

K. Rich. Ay, if yourself's remembrance wrong yourself.

Q. Eliz. Yet thou didst kill my children.

K. Rich. But in your daughter's womb I bury them;
Where in that nest of spicery they will breed
Selves of themselves to your recomforture.   425

Q. Eliz. Shall I go win my daughter to thy will?

K. Rich. And be a happy mother by the deed.

Q. Eliz. I go. Write to me very shortly,
And you shall understand from me her mind.

K. Rich. Bear me her true love's kiss; and so, farewell.   [*Exit Queen Elizabeth.* 430
Relenting fool, and shallow changing woman!

Enter RATCLIFF [CATESBY *following*].

How now! what news?

Rat. Most mighty sovereign, on the western coast
Rideth a puissant navy; to our shores
Throng many doubtful hollow-hearted friends,   435
Unarm'd, and unresolv'd to beat them back.

---

361. **quick:** hasty, but in l. 362 it is taken as *living.* 366. **George:** the pendant of St. George and the Dragon which hung from the collar of the Order of the Garter. 376. **K. Rich. . . . misusest**]. So Q. After 373 in F. [**thyself misusest**] Q. *is self misus'd* F. 377. [**God**] — [**God's**], Q. *Heaven. Heavens* F. 396. [**o'erpast**] Q. *repast* F. 405. **tender:** cherish. 417. [**peevish-fond**] (Staunton). *pievish, fond* Q. *peevish found* F. 424. **nest of spicery:** a reference to the nest of the Phœnix.

'Tis thought that Richmond is their admiral;
And there they hull, expecting but the aid
Of Buckingham to welcome them ashore.
    K. Rich. Some light-foot friend post to the Duke
      of Norfolk;   440
Ratcliff, thyself, or Catesby; where is he?
    Cate. Here, my good lord.
    K. Rich.   Catesby, fly to the Duke.   442a
    Cate. I will, my lord, with all convenient
      haste.   442b
    K. Rich. [Ratcliff], come hither. Post to Salis-
      bury.
When thou com'st thither, — [*To Catesby.*] Dull
    unmindful villain,
Why stay'st thou here, and go'st not to the Duke?
    Cate. First, mighty liege, tell me your Highness'
      pleasure,   446
What from your Grace I shall deliver to him.
    K. Rich. O, true, good Catesby. Bid him levy
      straight
The greatest strength and power that he can make,
And meet me suddenly at Salisbury.   450
    Cate. I go.   [*Exit.*
    Rat. What, may it please you, shall I do at
      Salisbury?
    K. Rich. Why, what wouldst thou do there before
      I go?
    Rat. Your Highness told me I should post before.
    K. Rich. My mind is chang'd.   456

             Enter LORD STANLEY.

             Stanley, what news with you?
    Stan. None good, my liege, to please you with
      the hearing;
Nor none so bad but may well be reported.
    K. Rich. Hoyday, a riddle! neither good nor bad!
What need'st thou run so many miles about   461
When thou mayst tell thy tale the nearest way?
Once more, what news?
    Stan.   Richmond is on the seas.
    K. Rich. There let him sink, and be the seas on
      him!
White-liver'd runagate, what doth he there?   465
    Stan. I know not, mighty sovereign, but by guess.
    K. Rich. Well, as you guess?
    Stan. Stirr'd up by Dorset, Buckingham, and
      Morton,
He makes for England, here to claim the crown.
    K. Rich. Is the chair empty? Is the sword un-
      sway'd?   470
Is the King dead? the empire unpossess'd?
What heir of York is there alive but we?
And who is England's king but great York's heir?
Then, tell me, what makes he upon the seas?   474
    Stan. Unless for that, my liege, I cannot guess.

    K. Rich. Unless for that he comes to be your liege
You cannot guess wherefore the Welshman comes?
Thou wilt revolt, and fly to him, I fear.
    Stan. No, my good lord, therefore mistrust me
      not.
    K. Rich. Where is thy power, then, to beat him
      back?   480
Where be thy tenants and thy followers?
Are they not now upon the western shore,
Safe-conducting the rebels from their ships?
    Stan. No, my good lord, my friends are in the
      north.
    K. Rich. Cold friends to me! What do they in
      the north   485
When they should serve their sovereign in the west?
    Stan. They have not been commanded, mighty
      King.
Pleaseth your Majesty to give me leave,
I'll muster up my friends and meet your Grace
Where and what time your Majesty shall please.
    K. Rich. Ay, ay, thou wouldst be gone to join
      with Richmond;   491
But I'll not trust thee.
    Stan.   Most mighty sovereign,
You have no cause to hold my friendship doubtful.
I never was nor never will be false.
    K. Rich. Go, then, and muster men; but leave
      behind   496
Your son, George Stanley. Look your heart be
    firm,
Or else his head's assurance is but frail.
    Stan. So deal with him as I prove true to you.
                                 [*Exit.*

            Enter a Messenger.

    1. Mess. My gracious sovereign, now in Devon-
      shire,   500
As I by friends am well advertised,
Sir Edward Courtney, and the haughty **prelate,**
Bishop of Exeter, his elder brother,
With many moe confederates, are in arms.

            Enter another MESSENGER.

    2. Mess. In Kent, my liege, the Guildfords are in
      arms;   505
And every hour more competitors
Flock to the rebels, and their power grows strong.

            Enter another MESSENGER.

    3. Mess. My lord, the army of great Bucking-
      ham —
    K. Rich. Out on ye, owls! nothing but songs of
      death?   [*He striketh him.* 509
There, take thou that till thou bring better news.
    3. Mess. The news I have to tell your Majesty

---

    438. **hull:** drift.   443. [Ratcliff] (Rowe). *Catesby* F.   465. **runagate:** renegade.   477. **Welshman:** the Tudors were Welsh.
501. **advertised:** informed.   506. **competitors:** associates.

Is that by sudden floods and fall of waters
Buckingham's army is dispers'd and scatter'd:
And he himself wand'red away alone,
No man knows whither.
 K. Rich.   I cry thee mercy; 515
There is my purse to cure that blow of thine.
Hath any well-advised friend proclaim'd
Reward to him that brings the traitor in?
 3. Mess. Such proclamation hath been made, my
  lord.

    Enter another MESSENGER.

 4. Mess. Sir Thomas Lovel and Lord Marquis
  Dorset, 520
'Tis said, my liege, in Yorkshire are in arms.
But this good comfort bring I to your Highness,
The Breton navy is dispers'd by tempest.
Richmond in Dorsetshire sent out a boat
Unto the shore, to ask those on the banks 525
If they were his assistants, yea or no;
Who answer'd him, they came from Buckingham
Upon his party. He, mistrusting them,
Hois'd sail and made his course again for Brittany.
 K. Rich. March on, march on, since we are up in
  arms; 530
If not to fight with foreign enemies,
Yet to beat down these rebels here at home.

    Re-enter CATESBY.

 Cate. My liege, the Duke of Buckingham is
  taken;
That is the best news. That the Earl of Richmond
Is with a mighty power landed at Milford, 535
Is colder news, but yet they must be told.
 K. Rich. Away towards Salisbury! While we
  reason here
A royal battle might be won and lost.
Some one take order Buckingham be brought
To Salisbury; the rest march on with me. 540
      [*Flourish. Exeunt.*

   SCENE [V. *Lord Derby's house.*]

Enter DERBY *and* SIR CHRISTOPHER [URSWICK].

 Der. Sir Christopher, tell Richmond this from
  me,
That in the sty of the most deadly boar
My son George Stanley is frank'd up in hold;
If I revolt, off goes young George's head.
The fear of that holds off my present aid. 5
So get thee gone; commend me to thy lord.
Withal say that the Queen hath heartily consented
He should espouse Elizabeth her daughter.
But, tell me, where is princely Richmond now?

 Chris. At Pembroke or at Ha'rford-west in
  Wales. 10
 Der. What men of name resort to him?
 Chris. Sir Walter Herbert, a renowned soldier;
Sir Gilbert Talbot, Sir William Stanley,
Oxford, redoubted Pembroke, Sir James Blunt,
And Rice ap Thomas, with a valiant crew, 15
And many other of great name and worth;
And towards London do they bend their power
If by the way they be not fought withal.
 Der. Well, hie thee to thy lord; I kiss his hand.
My letter will resolve him of my mind. 20
Farewell.   [*Gives letter, and*] *exeunt.*

      ACT V

  SCENE I. [*Salisbury. An open place.*]

Enter [*the* SHERIFF, *and*] BUCKINGHAM, *with halberds,*
    led to execution.

 Buck. Will not King Richard let me speak with
  him?
 Sher. No, my good lord; therefore be patient.
 Buck. Hastings, and Edward's children, Grey
  and Rivers,
Holy King Henry and thy fair son Edward,
Vaughan, and all that have miscarried 5
By underhand corrupted foul injustice,
If that your moody discontented souls
Do through the clouds behold this present hour,
Even for revenge mock my destruction!
This is All-Souls' day, fellow, is it not? 10
 Sher. It is [my lord].
 Buck. Why, then All-Souls' day is my body's
  doomsday.
This is the day which, in King Edward's time,
I wish'd might fall on me when I was found
False to his children and his wife's allies; 15
This is the day wherein I wish'd to fall
By the false faith of him whom most I trusted;
This, this All-Souls' day to my fearful soul
Is the determin'd respite of my wrongs.
That high All-Seer, which I dallied with, 20
Hath turn'd my feigned prayer on my head
And given in earnest what I begg'd in jest;
Thus doth He force the swords of wicked men
To turn their own points in their masters' bosoms.
Now Margaret's curse falls heavy on my neck: 25
"When he," quoth she, "shall split thy heart with
  sorrow,
Remember Margaret was a prophetess."
Come, lead me, officers, to the block of shame;
Wrong hath but wrong, and blame the due of
  blame.
        [*Exeunt.*

Sc. v, 3. **frank'd:** penned. **hold:** prison.
Act V, sc. i, 7. **moody:** angry. 11. **[my lord]** Q. Om. F. 19. **determin'd ... wrongs:** date fixed to end my wrong-doing.

SCENE II. [*The camp near Tamworth.*]

Enter RICHMOND, OXFORD, BLUNT, HERBERT, *and others, with drum and colours.*

Richm. Fellows in arms, and my most loving
    friends,
Bruis'd underneath the yoke of tyranny,
Thus far into the bowels of the land
Have we march'd on without impediment;
And here receive we from our father Stanley   5
Lines of fair comfort and encouragement.
The wretched, bloody, and usurping boar,
That spoil'd your summer fields and fruitful vines,
Swills your warm blood like wash and makes his
    trough
In your embowell'd bosoms, this foul swine   10
Is now even in the centre of this isle,
Near to the town of Leicester as we learn.
From Tamworth thither is but one day's march.
In God's name, cheerly on, courageous friends,
To reap the harvest of perpetual peace   15
By this one bloody trial of sharp war.
    Oxf. Every man's conscience is a thousand men
To fight against this guilty homicide.
    Herb. I doubt not but his friends will turn to us.
    Blunt. He hath no friends but what are friends for
    fear,   20
Which in his dearest need will fly from him.
    Richm. All for our vantage. Then, in God's name,
    march!
True hope is swift and flies with swallow's wings,
Kings it makes gods and meaner creatures kings.
                                  [*Exeunt.*

[SCENE III. *Bosworth Field.*]

Enter KING RICHARD, *in arms, with* NORFOLK, *the* EARL OF SURREY, RATCLIFF [*and others*].

    K. Rich. Here pitch our tent, even here in Bos-
    worth field.
My Lord of Surrey, why look you so sad?
    Sur. My heart is ten times lighter than my looks.
    K. Rich. My Lord of Norfolk, —
    Nor.   Here, most gracious liege.
    K. Rich. Norfolk, we must have knocks; ha!
    must we not?   5
    Nor. We must both give and take, my loving
    lord.
    K. Rich. Up with my tent! Here will I lie to-
    night —
But where to-morrow? Well, all's one for that.
Who hath descried the number of the traitors?
    Nor. Six or seven thousand is their utmost
    power.   10

    K. Rich. Why, our battalia treble that account;
Besides, the King's name is a tower of strength
Which they upon the adverse faction want.
Up with the tent! Come, noble gentlemen,
Let us survey the vantage of the ground.   15
Call for some men of sound direction;
Let's lack no discipline, make no delay;
For, lords, to-morrow is a busy day.   [*Exeunt.*

Enter [*on the other side of the field*] RICHMOND, SIR
    WILLIAM BRANDON, OXFORD, DORSET [BLUNT,
    and others]. *Some of the* Soldiers *pitch Richmond's*
    tent].

    Richm. The weary sun hath made a golden set
And by the bright [track] of his fiery car   20
Gives token of a goodly day to-morrow.
Sir William Brandon, you shall bear my standard.
Give me some ink and paper in my tent;
I'll draw the form and model of our battle,
Limit each leader to his several charge,   25
And part in just proportion our small power.
My Lord of Oxford, you, Sir William Brandon,
And you, Sir Walter Herbert, stay with me.
The Earl of Pembroke keeps his regiment;
Good Captain Blunt, bear my good-night to him 30
And by the second hour in the morning
Desire the Earl to see me in my tent.
Yet one thing more, good captain, do for me:
Where is Lord Stanley quarter'd, do you know?
    Blunt. Unless I have mista'en his colours much,
Which well I am assur'd I have not done,   36
His regiment lies half a mile at least
South from the mighty power of the King.
    Richm. If without peril it be possible,
Sweet Blunt, make some good means to speak with
    him.   40
And give him from me this most needful note.
    Blunt. Upon my life, my lord, I'll undertake it,
And so, God give you quiet rest to-night!
    Richm. Good-night, good Captain Blunt. Come,
    gentlemen,   [*Exit Blunt.*]
Let us consult upon to-morrow's business.   45
Into my tent; the dew is raw and cold.
                       [*They withdraw into the tent.*

Enter [*to his tent*] KING RICHARD, NORFOLK, RAT-
    CLIFF, CATESBY [*and others*].

    K. Rich. What is't o'clock?
    Cate.   It's supper-time, my lord;
It's nine o'clock.
    K. Rich.   I will not sup to-night.
Give me some ink and paper.
What, is my beaver easier than it was,   50
And all my armour laid into my tent?

Sc. ii, 5. **father**: stepfather. 9. **wash**: swill. 10. **embowell'd**: disembowelled.
Sc. iii, 11. **battalia**: army. 16. **direction**: military judgment. 20. [**track**] Q. *tract* F. 25. **Limit**: appoint. 29. **keeps**: stays with. 50. **beaver**: face part of the helmet.

Cate. It is, my liege; and all things are in readiness.

K. Rich. Good Norfolk, hie thee to thy charge;
Use careful watch, choose trusty sentinels.

Nor. I go, my lord.   55

K. Rich. Stir with the lark to-morrow, gentle
Norfolk.

Nor. I warrant you, my lord.   [*Exit.*

K. Rich. [Catesby!

Cate.] My lord?

K. Rich.   Send out a pursuivant at arms
To Stanley's regiment; bid him bring his power
Before sunrising, lest his son George fall   61
Into the blind cave of eternal night.

[*Exit Catesby.*]

Fill me a bowl of wine. Give me a watch.
Saddle white Surrey for the field to-morrow.
Look that my staves be sound, and not too heavy.
Ratcliff!   66

Rat. My lord?

K. Rich. Saw'st the melancholy Lord Northumberland?

Rat. Thomas the Earl of Surrey, and himself,
Much about cock-shut time, from troop to troop   70
Went through the army, cheering up the soldiers.

K. Rich. So, I am satisfied. Give me a bowl of
wine.
I have not that alacrity of spirit
Nor cheer of mind that I was wont to have.
Set it down. Is ink and paper ready?   75

Rat. It is, my lord.

K. Rich.   Bid my guard watch; leave me.
Ratcliff, about the mid of night come to my tent
And help to arm me. Leave me, I say.

[*Exeunt Ratcliff [and the other Attendants.
Richard sleeps*].

Enter DERBY *to* RICHMOND *in his tent.* [*Lords and
others attending.*]

Der. Fortune and victory sit on thy helm!

Richm. All comfort that the dark night can afford
Be to thy person, noble father-in-law!   81
Tell me, how fares our [loving] mother?

Der. I, by attorney, bless thee from thy mother,
Who prays continually for Richmond's good.
So much for that. The silent hours steal on   85
And flaky darkness breaks within the east.
In brief, — for so, the season bids us be, —
Prepare thy battle early in the morning,
And put thy fortune to th' arbitrement
Of bloody strokes and mortal-staring war.   90
I, as I may — that which I would I cannot, —
With best advantage will deceive the time

And aid thee in this doubtful shock of arms;
But on thy side I may not be too forward
Lest, being seen, thy brother, tender George,   95
Be executed in his father's sight.
Farewell! The leisure and the fearful time
Cuts off the ceremonious vows of love
And ample interchange of sweet discourse
Which so long sund'red friends should dwell upon.
God give us leisure for these rites of love!   101
Once more, adieu! Be valiant, and speed well!

Richm. Good lords, conduct him to his regiment.
I'll strive with troubled noise to take a nap
Lest leaden slumber peise me down to-morrow   105
When I should mount with wings of victory.
Once more, good-night, kind lords and gentlemen.

[*Exeunt all but Richmond.*

O Thou whose captain I account myself,
Look on my forces with a gracious eye!
Put in their hands thy bruising irons of wrath   110
That they may crush down with a heavy fall
The usurping helmets of our adversaries!
Make us thy ministers of chastisement
That we may praise Thee in the victory!
To Thee I do commend my watchful soul   115
Ere I let fall the windows of mine eyes.
Sleeping and waking, O, defend me still!   [*Sleeps.*

Enter the Ghost of PRINCE EDWARD, *son to
Henry the Sixth.*

Ghost. (*To Richard.*) Let me sit heavy on thy
soul to-morrow!
Think, how thou stabb'dst me in my prime of youth
At Tewksbury. Despair, therefore, and die!   120
(*To Richmond.*) Be cheerful, Richmond; for the
wronged souls
Of butcher'd princes fight in thy behalf.
King Henry's issue, Richmond, comforts thee.

Enter the Ghost of HENRY THE SIXTH.

Ghost. (*To Richard.*) When I was mortal, my
anointed body
By thee was punched full of [deadly] holes.   125
Think on the Tower and me. Despair, and die!
Harry the Sixth bids thee despair and die.
(*To Richmond.*) Virtuous and holy, be thou con-
queror!
Harry, that prophesied thou shouldst be king,
Doth comfort thee in sleep. Live, and flourish!

Enter the Ghost of CLARENCE.

Ghost. [*To Richard.*] Let me sit heavy in thy soul
to-morrow!   131
I, that was wash'd to death with fulsome wine,

58. [Catesby! *Cate.*] Q. *Ratcliffe. Rat.* F. 63. **watch:** watch-light, candle. 65. **staves:** shafts of my lances. 70.
cock-shut: sunset. 81. **father-in-law:** stepfather. 82. [loving] Q. *noble* F. 89. **arbitrement:** decision. 92. **With . . .
time:** cheat Richard at the best opportunity. 97. **leisure:** lack of leisure. 105. **peise:** weigh. 125. [deadly] Q. Om. F.
132. **fulsome:** cloying.

Poor Clarence, by thy guile betray'd to death!
To-morrow in the battle think on me
And fall thy edgeless sword. Despair, and die!
(*To Richmond.*) Thou offspring of the house of
    Lancaster,   136
The wronged heirs of York do pray for thee.
Good angels guard thy battle! Live, and flourish!

Enter the Ghosts of RIVERS, GREY, *and* VAUGHAN.

Ghost of R. [*To Richard.*] Let me sit heavy in thy
    soul to-morrow,
Rivers, that died at Pomfret! Despair, and die! 140
  Ghost of G. [*To Richard.*] Think upon Grey, and
    let thy soul despair!
Ghost of V. [*To Richard.*] Think upon Vaughan,
    and with guilty fear
Let fall thy lance. Despair, and die!
  All. (*To Richmond.*) Awake, and think our
    wrongs in Richard's bosom
Will conquer him! Awake, and win the day!   145

Enter the Ghost of HASTINGS.

Ghost. [*To Richard.*] Bloody and guilty, guiltily
    awake,
And in a bloody battle end thy days!
Think on Lord Hastings. Despair, and die!
(*To Richmond.*) Quiet untroubled soul, awake,
    awake!
Arm, fight, and conquer, for fair England's sake! 150

Enter the Ghosts of the two young Princes.

Ghosts. (*To Richard.*) Dream on thy cousins
    smothered in the Tower.
Let us be lead within thy bosom, Richard,
And weigh thee down to ruin, shame, and death!
Thy nephews' souls bid thee despair and die!
(*To Richmond.*) Sleep, Richmond, sleep in peace
    and wake in joy.   155
Good angels guard thee from the boar's annoy!
Live, and beget a happy race of kings!
Edward's unhappy sons do bid thee flourish.

Enter the Ghost of LADY ANNE.

Ghost. (*To Richard.*) Richard, thy wife, that
    wretched Anne thy wife,
That never slept a quiet hour with thee,   160
Now fills thy sleep with perturbations.
To-morrow in the battle think on me
And fall thy edgeless sword. Despair, and die!
(*To Richmond.*) Thou quiet soul, sleep thou a quiet
    sleep;
Dream of success and happy victory!   165
Thy adversary's wife doth pray for thee.

Enter the Ghost of BUCKINGHAM.

Ghost. (*To Richard.*) The first was I that help'd
    thee to the crown;
The last was I that felt thy tyranny.
O, in the battle think on Buckingham,
And die in terror of thy guiltiness!   170
Dream on, dream on, of bloody deeds and death;
Fainting, despair; despairing, yield thy breath!
(*To Richmond.*) I died for hope ere I could lend thee
    aid;
But cheer thy heart, and be thou not dismay'd.
God and good angels fight on Richmond's side,
And Richard fall in height of all his pride!   176
    [*The Ghosts vanish. King*] *Richard starts
    out of his dream.*
  K. Rich. Give me another horse! Bind up my
    wounds!
Have mercy, Jesu! — Soft! I did but dream.
O coward conscience, how dost thou afflict me!
The lights burn blue. It is now dead midnight. 180
Cold fearful drops stand on my trembling flesh.
What! do I fear myself? There's none else by.
Richard loves Richard; that is, I am I.
Is there a murderer here? No. Yes, I am.
Then fly. What, from myself? Great reason
    why,   185
Lest I revenge. What, myself upon myself?
Alack, I love myself. Wherefore? For any good
That I myself have done unto myself?
O, no! alas, I rather hate myself
For hateful deeds committed by myself!   190
I am a villain: yet I lie, I am not.
Fool, of thyself speak well; fool, do not flatter.
My conscience hath a thousand several tongues,
And every tongue brings in a several tale,
And every tale condemns me for a villain.   195
Perjury, [perjury,] in the high'st degree;
Murder, stern murder, in the dir'st degree;
All several sins, all us'd in each degree,
Throng to the bar, crying all, Guilty! guilty!
I shall despair. There is no creature loves me;
And if I die no soul shall pity me.   201
Nay, wherefore should they, since that I myself
Find in myself no pity to myself?
Methought the souls of all that I had murder'd
Came to my tent; and every one did threat   205
To-morrow's vengeance on the head of Richard.

Enter RATCLIFF.

  Rat. My lord!
  K. Rich. ['Zounds!] who's there?
  Rat. Ratcliff, my lord; 'tis I. The early village-
    cock
Hath twice done salutation to the morn;   210
Your friends are up and buckle on their armour.

156. **boar's annoy:** harm from Richard.   173. **for hope:** hoping to give aid.   180. **burn blue:** sign of a ghost's presence.
196. **[perjury]** Q. Om. F.   198. **us'd:** committed.   208. **['Zounds]** Q. Om. F.

K. Rich. [O Ratcliff, I have dream'd a fearful
    dream!
What thinkest thou, will our friends prove all true?
    Rat. No doubt, my lord.]
    K. Rich.   O Ratcliff, I fear, I fear, —
    Rat. Nay, good my lord, be not afraid of shadows.
    K. Rich. By the apostle Paul, shadows to-
    night   216
Have struck more terror to the soul of Richard
Than can the substance of ten thousand soldiers
Armed in proof and led by shallow Richmond.
It is not yet near day. Come, go with me;   220
Under our tents I'll play the eaves-dropper,
To hear if any mean to shrink from me. [*Exeunt.*

Enter the LORDS *to* RICHMOND, *sitting in his tent.*

    Lords. Good morrow, Richmond!
    Richm. Cry mercy, lords and watchful gentlemen,
That you have ta'en a tardy sluggard here.   225
    Lords. How have you slept, my lord?
    Richm. The sweetest sleep and fairest-boding
    dreams
That ever ent'red in a drowsy head
Have I since your departure had, my lords.
Methought their souls whose bodies Richard
    murder'd   230
Came to my tent and cried on victory.
I promise you, my heart is very jocund
In the remembrance of so fair a dream.
How far into the morning is it, lords?
    Lords. Upon the stroke of four.   235
    Richm. Why, then 'tis time to arm and give
    direction.

His oration to his soldiers.

More than I have said, loving countrymen,
The leisure and enforcement of the time
Forbids to dwell upon; yet remember this,
God and our good cause fight upon our side;   240
The prayers of holy saints and wronged souls,
Like high-rear'd bulwarks, stand before our faces.
Richard except, those whom we fight against
Had rather have us win than him they follow.
For what is he they follow? Truly, gentlemen,
A bloody tyrant and a homicide;   246
One rais'd in blood, and one in blood establish'd;
One that made means to come by what he hath
And slaughter'd those that were the means to help
    him;
A base foul stone, made precious by the foil   250
Of England's chair, where he is falsely set;
One that hath ever been God's enemy.
Then, if you fight against God's enemy,
God will in justice ward you as his soldiers;

If you do [sweat] to put a tyrant down,   255
You sleep in peace, the tyrant being slain;
If you do fight against your country's foes,
Your country's fat shall pay your pains the hire;
If you do fight in safeguard of your wives,
Your wives shall welcome home the conquerors;   260
If you do free your children from the sword,
Your children's children quits it in your age.
Then, in the name of God and all these rights,
Advance your standards, draw your willing swords.
For me, the ransom of my bold attempt   265
Shall be this cold corpse on the earth's cold face;
But if I thrive, the gain of my attempt
The least of you shall share his part thereof.
Sound drums and trumpets boldly and cheer-
    fully;   269
God and Saint George! Richmond and victory!
    [*Exeunt.*

Re-enter KING RICHARD, RATCLIFF, CATESBY
    [*Attendants and Forces*].

    K. Rich. What said Northumberland as touch-
    ing Richmond?
    Rat. That he was never trained up in arms.
    K. Rich. He said the truth; and what said
    Surrey then?
    Rat. He smil'd and said, "The better for our
    purpose."
    K. Rich. He was in the right; and so indeed it
    is.   [*Clock strikes.* 275
Tell the clock there. Give me a calendar.
Who saw the sun to-day?
    Rat.   Not I, my lord.
    K. Rich. Then he disdains to shine, for by the
    book
He should have brav'd the east an hour ago.
A black day will it be to somebody.   280
Ratcliff!
    Rat. My lord?
    K. Rich. The sun will not be seen to-day;
The sky doth frown and lour upon our army.
I would these dewy tears were from the ground.
Not shine to-day! Why, what is that to me   285
More than to Richmond? for the self-same heaven
That frowns on me looks sadly upon him.

Enter NORFOLK.

    Nor. Arm, arm, my lord; the foe vaunts in the field.
    K. Rich. Come, bustle, bustle; caparison my
    horse.
Call up Lord Stanley, bid him bring his power.   290
I will lead forth my soldiers to the plain,
And thus my battle shall be ordered:
My foreward shall be drawn [out all] in length,

212–214. [O . . . lord] Q. Om. F.   219. **proof**: tested armor.   250. **foil**: leaf of metal placed under a precious stone to
increase its brilliance.   255. [sweat] Q and Holinshed.   *sweare* F.   265. **ransom**: price.   276. **Tell**: count (the strokes).
279. brav'd: made splendid.   288. **vaunts**: swaggers.   293. **foreward**: vanguard.   [out all] Q. Om. F.

Consisting equally of horse and foot;
Our archers shall be placed in the midst;   295
John Duke of Norfolk, Thomas Earl of Surrey,
Shall have the leading of the foot and horse.
They thus directed, we will follow
In the main battle, whose puissance on either side
Shall be well winged with our chiefest horse.   300
This, and Saint George to boot! What think'st
  thou, Norfolk?
  Nor. A good direction, warlike sovereign.
This found I on my tent this morning.
                    [*He sheweth him a paper.*
  [*K. Rich. Reads.*] "Jockey of Norfolk, be not so
  bold,
For Dickon thy master is bought and sold."   305
A thing devised by the enemy.
Go, gentlemen, every man to his charge.
Let not our babbling dreams affright our souls,
For conscience is a word that cowards use,
Devis'd at first to keep the strong in awe.   310
Our strong arms be our conscience, swords our law!
March on, join bravely, let us to't pell-mell;
If not to heaven, then hand in hand to hell.

            His oration to his Army.

What shall I say more than I have inferr'd?
Remember whom you are to cope withal;   315
A sort of vagabonds, rascals, and runaways,
A scum of Bretons and base lackey peasants,
Whom their o'er-cloyed country vomits forth
To desperate [ventures] and assur'd destruction.
You sleeping safe, they bring you to unrest;   320
You having lands, and blest with beauteous wives,
They would restrain the one, distain the other.
And who doth lead them but a paltry fellow,
Long kept in Bretagne at our mother's cost?
A milk-sop, one that never in his life   325
Felt so much cold as over shoes in snow?
Let's whip these stragglers o'er the seas again;
Lash hence these overweening rags of France,
These famish'd beggars, weary of their lives,
Who, but for dreaming on this fond exploit,   330
For want of means, poor rats, had hang'd them-
  selves.
If we be conquered, let men conquer us
And not these bastard Bretons whom our fathers
Have in their own land beaten, bobb'd, and
  thump'd,
And on record, left them the heirs of shame.   335
Shall these enjoy our lands? lie with our wives?
Ravish our daughters? (*Drum afar off.*) Hark!
  I hear their drum.
[Fight], gentlemen of England! fight, [bold] yeomen!

Draw, archers, draw your arrows to the head!
Spur your proud horses hard and ride in blood;   340
Amaze the welkin with your broken staves!

            Enter a MESSENGER.

What says Lord Stanley? Will he bring his power?
  Mess. My lord, he doth deny to come.
  K. Rich. Off with his son George's head!
  Nor. My lord, the enemy is past the marsh;   345
After the battle let George Stanley die.
  K. Rich. A thousand hearts are great within my
  bosom.
Advance our standards, set upon our foes;
Our ancient word of courage, fair Saint George,
Inspire us with the spleen of fiery dragons!   350
Upon them! Victory sits on our [helms].
                              [*Exeunt.*]

            [SCENE IV. *Another part of the field.*]

Alarum. Excursions. Enter [NORFOLK *and forces
            fighting; to him*] CATESBY.

  Cate. Rescue, my Lord of Norfolk, rescue, rescue!
The King enacts more wonders than a man,
Daring an opposite to every danger.
His horse is slain, and all on foot he fights,
Seeking for Richmond in the throat of death.   5
Rescue, fair lord, or else the day is lost!

            Alarums. Enter KING RICHARD.

  K. Rich. A horse! a horse! my kingdom for a
  horse!
  Cate. Withdraw, my lord; I'll help you to a horse.
  K. Rich. Slave, I have set my life upon a cast
And I will stand the hazard of the die.   10
I think there be six Richmonds in the field;
Five have I slain to-day instead of him.
A horse! a horse! my kingdom for a horse!
                              [*Exeunt.*]

            [SCENE V. *Another part of the field.*]

*Alarum. Enter Richard and Richmond; they fight;
Richard is slain. Retreat and flourish. Re-enter*
RICHMOND, DERBY, *bearing the crown, with divers
            other Lords.*

  Richm. God and your arms be prais'd, victorious
  friends;
The day is ours, the bloody dog is dead.
  Der. Courageous Richmond, well hast thou
  acquit thee.
Lo, here, these long-usurped royalties
From the dead temples of this bloody wretch   5

302. **direction:** plan of battle. 304. [**K. Rich. Reads**] (Capell). Om. F. 314. **inferr'd:** stated. 316. **sort:** gang.
319. [**ventures**] (Capell). *adventures* Q F. 322. **restrain:** deprive you of. **distain:** outrage. 334. **bobb'd:** thrashed. 338.
[**Fight**] Q. *Right* F. [**bold**] Q. *boldly* F. 350. **spleen:** anger. 351. [**helms**] Q. *helpes* F.
  Sc. iv, 3. **opposite:** enemy. 9. **cast:** throw of the dice.

Have I pluck'd off to grace thy brows withal.
Wear it, [enjoy it,] and make much of it.

   Richm. Great God of heaven, say amen to all!
But, tell me, is young George Stanley living?

   Der. He is, my lord, and safe in Leicester town;
Whither, if [it please you], we may [now] with-
    draws us.   11

   Richm. What men of name are slain on either
    side?

   Der. John Duke of Norfolk, Walter Lord
    Ferrers,
Sir Robert Brakenbury, and Sir William Bran-
    don.

   Richm. Inter their bodies as become their births.
Proclaim a pardon to the soldiers fled   16
That in submission will return to us;
And then, as we have ta'en the sacrament,
We will unite the white rose and the red.
Smile heaven upon this fair conjunction,   20
That long have frown'd upon their enmity!
What traitor hears me, and says not amen?

England hath long been mad and scarr'd herself;
The brother blindly shed the brother's blood,
The father rashly slaughtered his own son,   25
The son, compell'd, been butcher to the sire.
All this divided York and Lancaster,
Divided in their dire division,
O, now, let Richmond and Elizabeth,
The true succeeders of each royal house,   30
By God's fair ordinance conjoin together!
And let [their] heirs, God, if thy will be so,
Enrich the time to come with smooth-fac'd Peace,
With smiling Plenty and fair prosperous days!
Abate the edge of traitors, gracious Lord,   35
That would reduce these bloody days again
And make poor England weep in streams of blood!
Let them not live to taste this land's increase
That would with treason wound this fair land's
    peace!
Now civil wounds are stopp'd, Peace lives again;
That she may long live here, God say amen!   41
                         [*Exeunt.*

   Sc. v, 7. [enjoy it] Q. Om. F. **11.** [it please you] Q₂. *you please* F. [now] Q. Om. F. **32.** [their] Q. *thy* F. **35. Abate:** blunt. **36. reduce:** bring back.

The Life of Henry the Eighth

A PLAY CALLED *Henry VIII or All is True* was being played in the Globe Theatre on June 29, 1613, when the theatre caught fire and was burned down. Contemporary descriptions of this piece fit the present history so exactly that there remains no doubt that the Shakespearean drama is meant. Sir Henry Wotton, writing to his nephew Sir Edmund Bacon on July 2 of the same year, gives the following account of the disaster:

Now to let matters of state sleep, I will entertain you at the present with what hath happened this week at the Bank's side. The King's Players had a new play, called *All is True*, representing some principal pieces of the reign of Henry 8, which was set forth with many extraordinary circumstances of pomp and majesty, even to the matting of the stage, the Knights of the Order, with their Georges and Garters, the Guards with their embroidered coats, and the like: sufficient in truth within a while to make greatness very familiar, if not ridiculous. Now, King Henry making a Masque at the Cardinal Wolsey's house, and certain chambers being shot off at his entry, some of the paper, or other stuff wherewith one of them was stopped, did light on the thatch, where being thought at first but an idle smoke, and their eyes more attentive to the show, it kindled inwardly, and ran round like a train, consuming within less than an hour the whole house to the very grounds.

This was the fatal period of that virtuous fabric, wherein yet nothing did perish but wood and straw, and a few forsaken cloaks; only one man had his breeches set on fire, that would perhaps have broiled him, if he had not by the benefit of a provident wit put it out with bottle ale.

Thomas Larkin, in a letter written the day after the fire, calls the play *Henry The Eighth*.

It is to be noted that Wotton calls *All is True* "a new play," so that we may conclude that the date of composition was 1613. The chief reason urged against this date lies in the reference to Elizabeth in III.ii. 50-52, and in the eulogy in V.v.18-39, 57-63, to which the praise of James may have been added

later. But eulogies of the great queen did not cease with her death; and there is much in the treatment of her parents that could hardly have been pleasing to her. In the style and metre of the undoubted Shakespearean part of the drama we find nothing pointing to a date before 1603, but much to the latest years of his activity; and it is a fairly safe conclusion that in the parts of the present play written by him we have the last of his extant work.

No edition of *Henry VIII* appeared till it was published in the First Folio, and on that version the present text is based.

The chief historical basis for the play is Holinshed's Chronicles. Some details seem to have come direct from Halle; and the scenes presenting the attempt to crush Cranmer (V.i,ii,iii) are taken from Foxe's *Actes and Monuments*, better known as *The Book of Martyrs*. These sources are followed at times almost slavishly, much of the actual diction being derived from the prose narratives. An instance may be cited from the beginning of Queen Katherine's speech in II.iv.13 ff. The account in Holinshed runs thus:

"Sir," quoth she, "I desire you to doo me iustice and right, and take some pitie upon me, for I am a poore woman, and a stranger, borne out of your dominion; having heere no indifferent counsell, and lesse assurance of friendship. Alas, sir, in what have I offended you, or what occasion of displeasure have I shewed you?"

Compare Shakespeare:

"Sir, I desire you do me right and justice
And to bestow your pity on me; for
I am a most poor woman, and a stranger,
Born out of your dominions, having here
No judge indifferent, nor no more assurance
Of equal friendship and proceeding. Alas, sir,
In what have I offended you? What cause
Hath my behaviour given to your displeasure?"

Yet with all this borrowing of detail, much freedom is used in the selection and arrangement of incident, historical time is disregarded, and even the identity of personages is confused.

The characterization of Queen Katherine alone shows any great creative imagination. Though all her acts and much of her language are taken from the Chronicles, the dramatist has bestowed on her a pathetic dignity which elevates her to such a pitch that in spite of her passive rôle she stands out as the real heroine of the play. Wolsey's farewell speech (except III.ii.455–457) is also invented; but his other important utterances and almost all of his actions are based directly on Holinshed, who here drew from a variety of sources varying much in their estimate of the Cardinal. Some details seem to have been suggested by Samuel Rowley's *When You See Me You Know Me* (printed 1605). The low comedy scenes in the palace yard and Cranmer's closing prophecies are, of course, without historical basis.

This drama is singularly lacking in unity. The material is simply translated into dialogue or pageant; and there results a succession of brilliant stage pictures, sketches of character, and fine speeches, entirely without dramatic coherence. Buckingham, Katherine, the King, Wolsey, and Cranmer hold in succession the centre of the stage, but no causal connection is apparent in the sequence; nor is there consistency in the demand for sympathy with men or factions. This fragmentary quality alone is sufficient to suggest a doubt as to unity of authorship; and examination of the technical qualities of style and metre has confirmed this suspicion. It is now fairly generally, though not universally, conceded that the greater number of scenes is to be credited to John Fletcher, and to Shakespeare only I.i,ii; II.iii, iv; III.ii.1–203; and, with less assurance of purity, V.i.

Attempts have been made to deny to Shakespeare any share in the authorship, and to assign it to other authors, especially to Massinger. But various internal reasons, besides the unchallenged appearance of the play in the First Folio, prevent the acceptance of this extreme view.

No speculation on the method of collaboration has resulted in anything more than mere conjecture. The fact that Shakespeare introduces most of the main characters, leaving the second author to carry them on, seems to exclude Shakespeare as a reviser, and suggests either an unfinished play completed by Fletcher, or, more probably, actual discussion and assignment of tasks.

THE LIFE OF
HENRY THE EIGHTH

[DRAMATIS PERSONÆ

KING HENRY VIII.
CARDINAL WOLSEY.
CARDINAL CAMPEIUS.
CAPUCIUS, *ambassador from the Emperor Charles V.*
CRANMER, *archbishop of Canterbury.*
DUKE OF NORFOLK.
DUKE OF BUCKINGFORD.
DUKE OF SUFFOLK.
EARL OF SURREY.
Lord Chamberlain.
Lord Chancellor.
GARDINER, *bishop of Winchester.*
Bishop of Lincoln.
LORD ABERGAVENNY.
LORD SANDYS (called also SIR WILLIAM SANDYS).
SIR HENRY GUILDFORD.
SIR THOMAS LOVELL.
SIR ANTHONY DENNY.
SIR NICHOLAS VAUX.

CROMWELL, *servant to Wolsey.*
Secretaries to Wolsey.
GRIFFITH, *gentleman usher to Queen Katherine.*
Three Gentlemen.
DOCTOR BUTTS, *physician to the King.*
Garter King-at-Arms.
Surveyor to the Duke of Buckingham.
BRANDON, *and a Sergeant-at-Arms.*
Door-keeper of the Council-chamber. *Porter, and his Man.*
Page to Gardiner. *A Crier.*

QUEEN KATHERINE, *wife to King Henry, afterwards divorced.*
ANNE BULLEN, *her Maid of Honour, afterwards Queen.*
An old Lady, *friend to Anne Bullen.*
PATIENCE, *woman to Queen Katherine.*

Spirits.

Several Bishops, Lords and Ladies in the Dumb Shows; Women attending upon the Queen; Scribes, Officers, Guards, and other Attendants.

SCENE: *London; Westminster; Kimbolton.*]

THE PROLOGUE

I COME no more to make you laugh: things now
That bear a weighty and a serious brow,
Sad, high, and working, full of state and woe,
Such noble scenes as draw the eye to flow,
We now present. Those that can pity, here   5
May (if they think it well) let fall a tear;
The subject will deserve it. Such as give
Their money out of hope they may believe
May here find truth too. Those that come to see
Only a show or two, and so agree   10
The play may pass, if they be still and willing,
I'll undertake may see away their shilling
Richly in two short hours. Only they
That come to hear a merry bawdy play,
A noise of targets, or to see a fellow   15
In a long motley coat guarded with yellow,
Will be deceiv'd. For, gentle hearers, know,
To rank our chosen truth with such a show
As fool and fight is, beside forfeiting
Our own brains and the opinion that we bring   20
To make that only true we now intend,
Will leave us never an understanding friend.

Prol., 3. working: moving. **15. noise of targets:** clashing of shields. **16. motley coat:** i.e., of a fool. **guarded:** trimmed **20–21. opinion . . . intend:** reputation we have of planning to give a true picture.

Therefore, for goodness' sake, and as you are known
The first and happiest hearers of the town,
Be sad, as we would make ye.   Think ye see   25
The very persons of our noble story
As they were living.   Think you see them great
And follow'd with the general throng and sweat
Of thousand friends; then, in a moment, see
How soon this mightiness meets misery;   30
And, if you can be merry then, I'll say
A man may weep upon his wedding-day.

ACT I

SCENE I. [*London.   An ante-chamber in the
palace.*]

Enter the DUKE OF NORFOLK *at one door; at the
other, the* DUKE OF BUCKINGHAM *and the* LORD
ABERGAVENNY.

Buck . Good morrow and well met.   How have ye
done
Since last we saw in France?
Nor.   I thank your Grace,
Healthful; and ever since a fresh admirer
Of what I saw there.
Buck.   An untimely ague
Stay'd me a prisoner in my chamber when   5
Those suns of glory, those two lights of men,
Met in the vale of Andren.
Nor.   'Twixt Guynes and Arde.
I was then present, saw them salute on horseback;
Beheld them when they lighted, how they clung
In their embracement, as they grew together;   10
Which had they, what four thron'd ones could have
weigh'd
Such a compounded one?
Buck.   All the whole time
I was my chamber's prisoner.
Nor.   Then you lost
The view of earthly glory.   Men might say
Till this time pomp was single, but now married   15
To one above itself.   Each following day
Became the next day's master, till the last
Made former wonders its.   To-day the French,
All clinquant, all in gold, like heathen gods,
Shone down the English; and, to-morrow, they   20
Made Britain India: every man that stood
Show'd like a mine.   Their dwarfish pages were
As cherubins, all gilt; the madams too,
Not us'd to toil, did almost sweat to bear
The pride upon them, that their very labour   25

Was to them as a painting.   Now this masque
Was cried incomparable; and th' ensuing night
Made it a fool and beggar.   The two kings,
Equal in lustre, were now best, now worst,
As presence did present them; him in eye   30
Still him in praise; and being present both,
'Twas said they saw but one; and no discerner
Durst wag his tongue in censure.   When these
suns —
For so they phrase 'em — by their heralds chal-
leng'd
The noble spirits to arms, they did perform   35
Beyond thought's compass, that former fabulous
story,
Being now seen possible enough, got credit,
That Bevis was believ'd.
Buck.   O, you go far.
Nor. As I belong to worship and affect
In honour honesty, the tract of everything   40
Would by a good discourser lose some life,
Which action's self was tongue to.   All was royal;
To the disposing of it nought rebell'd,
Order gave each thing view; the office did
Distinctly his full function.
Buck.   Who did guide,   45
I mean, who set the body and the limbs
Of this great sport together, as you guess?
Nor. One, certes, that promises no element
In such a business.
Buck.   I pray you, who, my lord?
Nor. All this was ord'red by the good discretion
Of the right reverend Cardinal of York.   50
Buck. The devil speed him! no man's pie is freed
From his ambitious finger.   What had he
To do in these fierce vanities?   I wonder
That such a keech can with his very bulk   55
Take up the rays o' th' beneficial sun
And keep it from the earth.
Nor.   Surely, sir,
There's in him stuff that puts him to these ends;
For, being not propp'd by ancestry, whose grace
Chalks successors their way, nor call'd upon   60
For high feats done to th' crown; neither allied
To eminent assistants; but spider-like
Out of his self-drawing web, [he] gives us note
The force of his own merit makes his way —
A gift that heaven gives for him, which buys   65
A place next to the King.
Aber.   I cannot tell
What heaven hath given him, — let some graver eye
Pierce into that; but I can see his pride

Act I, sc. i, 2. **saw:** i.e., each other.   6. **suns of glory:** Henry VIII and Francis I.   7. **Guynes and Arde:** towns in Picardy
belonging to England and France respectively.   19. **clinquant:** glittering.   26. **as a painting:** flushed, as if rouged.   33.
censure: judgment that one was better than the other.   38. **Bevis,** of Hampton, hero of a popular romance.   39. **worship:**
the nobility.   **affect:** love.   40. **tract:** course.   42–47. **All ... guess.** (Theobald).   In F, Buckingham's speech begins with
All and ends with *together.*   43. **rebell'd:** was inconsistent, inharmonious.   44. **office:** officials.   48. **promises no element:**
would not be expected to have part.   55. **keech:** lump of suet, alluding to the fact that Wolsey was a butcher's son.   56.
sun: the king.   63. **[he]** (Capell).   *O* F.

Peep through each part of him.   Whence has he
    that?
If not from hell, the devil is a niggard   70
Or has given all before, and he begins
A new hell in himself.
    Buck.   Why the devil,
Upon this French going out, took he upon him,
(Without the privity o' th' King) t' appoint
Who should attend on him?   He makes up the file
Of all the gentry, for the most part such   76
To whom as great a charge as little honour
He meant to lay upon; and his own letter,
The honourable board of council out,
Must fetch him in he papers.
    Aber.   I do know   80
Kinsmen of mine, three at the least, that have
By this so sicken'd their estates, that never
They shall abound as formerly.
    Buck.   O, many
Have broke their backs with laying manors on 'em
For this great journey.   What did this vanity   85
But minister communication of
A most poor issue?
    Nor.   Grievingly I think
The peace between the French and us not values
The cost that did conclude it.
    Buck.   Every man,
After the hideous storm that follow'd, was   90
A thing inspir'd; and, not consulting, broke
Into a general prophecy, that this tempest,
Dashing the garment of this peace, aboded
The sudden breach on't.
    Nor.   Which is budded out;
For France hath flaw'd the league, and hath
    attach'd   95
Our merchants' goods at Bourdeaux.
    Aber.   Is it therefore
The ambassador is silenc'd?
    Nor.   Marry, is't.
    Aber. A proper title of a peace, and purchas'd
At a superfluous rate!
    Buck.   Why, all this business
Our reverend Cardinal carried.
    Nor.   Like it your Grace, 100
The state takes notice of the private difference
Betwixt you and the Cardinal.   I advise you —
And take it from a heart that wishes towards you
Honour and plenteous safety — that you read
The Cardinal's malice and his potency   105
Together, to consider further that
What his high hatred would effect wants not

A minister in his power.   You know his nature,
That he's revengeful, and I know his sword
Hath a sharp edge; it's long, and 't may be said   110
It reaches far, and where 'twill not extend,
Thither he darts it.   Bosom up my counsel;
You'll find it wholesome.   Lo, where comes that
    rock
That I advise your shunning.

Enter CARDINAL WOLSEY, *the purse borne before him,
certain of the* Guard, *and two* SECRETARIES, *with
papers.   The Cardinal in his passage fixeth his eye
on Buckingham, and Buckingham on him, both full
of disdain.*

    Wol. The Duke of Buckingham's surveyor, ha?
Where's his examination?
    1. Secr.   Here, so please you. 116
    Wol. Is he in person ready?
    1. Secr.   Ay, please your Grace.
    Wol. Well, we shall then know more; and Buck-
    ingham
Shall lessen this big look.   119
               [Exeunt Wolsey and his train.
    Buck. This butcher's cur is venom-mouth'd, and I
Have not the power to muzzle him; therefore best
Not wake him in his slumber.   A beggar's book
Outworths a noble's blood.
    Nor.   What, are you chaf'd?
Ask God for temperance; that's th' appliance only
Which your disease requires.
    Buck.   I read in 's looks 125
Matter against me, and his eye revil'd
Me as his abject object.   At this instant
He bores me with some trick.   He's gone to th'
    King;
I'll follow and outstare him.
    Nor.   Stay, my lord,
And let your reason with your choler question   130
What 'tis you go about.   To climb steep hills
Requires slow pace at first.   Anger is like
A full hot horse, who being allow'd his way,
Self-mettle tires him.   Not a man in England
Can advise me like you; be to yourself   135
As you would to your friend.
    Buck.   I'll to the King;
And from a mouth of honour quite cry down
This Ipswich fellow's insolence, or proclaim
There's difference in no persons.
    Nor.   Be advis'd;
Heat not a furnace for your foe so hot   140
That it do singe yourself.   We may outrun

---

74. **privity**: knowledge (of something private).   75. **file**: list.   79. **out**: not consulted.   80. **he papers**: whom he puts on the list.   84. **broke . . . manors**: ruined themselves by spending their estates on costly clothes.   86–87. **minister . . . issue**: serve a useless conference.   91. **not consulting**: independently.   93. **aboded**: foreboded.   95. **flaw'd**: broken.   **attach'd**: seized.   97. **ambassador is silenc'd.**   The French ambassador was commanded to "keep his house."   100. **carried**: managed.   **Like it**: may it please.   104. **read**: consider.   107. **wants**: lacks.   112. **Bosom up**: hide in your bosom.   114. S.D. *purse*, containing the great seal.   115. **surveyor**: overseer.   He was Buckingham's cousin.   122. **beggar's book**: a poor scholar.   123. **Outworths**: is more powerful than.   **chaf'd**: angry.   128. **bores**: gets the better of.   134. **Self-mettle**: his own high spirit.

By violent swiftness that which we run at,
And lose by over-running. Know you not
The fire that mounts the liquor till 't run o'er
In seeming to augment it wastes it? Be advis'd.
I say again, there is no English soul   146
More stronger to direct you than yourself
If with the sap of reason you would quench,
Or but allay, the fire of passion.
    Buck.   Sir,
I am thankful to you; and I'll go along   150
By your prescription; but this top-proud fellow,
Whom from the flow of gall I name not, but
From sincere motions, by intelligence,
And proofs as clear as founts in July when
We see each grain of gravel, I do know   155
To be corrupt and treasonous.
    Nor.   Say not "treasonous."
    Buck. To th' King I'll say't, and make my vouch
        as strong
As shore of rock. Attend. This holy fox,
Or wolf, or both, — for he is equal rav'nous
As he is subtle, and as prone to mischief   160
As able to perform 't; his mind and place
Infecting one another, yea, reciprocally —
Only to show his pomp as well in France
As here at home, suggests the King our master
To this last costly treaty, th' interview   165
That swallowed so much treasure, and like a glass
Did break i' th' [rinsing].
    Nor.   Faith, and so it did.
    Buck. Pray, give me favour, sir. This cunning
        Cardinal
The articles o' th' combination drew
As himself pleas'd; and they were ratified   170
As he cried, "Thus let be!" to as much end
As give a crutch to th' dead. But our count-
        cardinal
Has done this, and 'tis well; for worthy Wolsey,
Who cannot err, he did it. Now this follows, —
Which, as I take it, is a kind of puppy   175
To th' old dam, treason, — Charles the Emperor,
Under pretence to see the Queen his aunt, —
For 'twas indeed his colour, but he came
To whisper Wolsey, — here makes visitation.
His fears were that the interview betwixt   180
England and France might through their amity
Breed him some prejudice; for from this league
Peep'd harms that menac'd him. [He] privily
Deals with our Cardinal; and, as I trow, —
Which I do well, for I am sure the Emperor   185
Paid ere he promis'd, whereby his suit was granted
Ere it was ask'd — but when the way was made

And pav'd with gold, the Emperor thus desir'd
That he would please to alter the King's course,
And break the foresaid peace. Let the King know,
As soon he shall by me, that thus the Cardinal   191
Does buy and sell his honour as he pleases
And for his own advantage.
    Nor.   I am sorry
To hear this of him; and could wish he were
Something mistaken in't.
    Buck.   No, not a syllable: 195
I do pronounce him in that very shape
He shall appear in proof.

        Enter BRANDON, *a* SERGEANT-AT-ARMS *before
        him, and two or three of the* Guard.

    Bran. Your office, sergeant; execute it.
    Serg.   Sir,
My lord the Duke of Buckingham and Earl
Of Hereford, Stafford, and Northampton, I   200
Arrest thee of high treason, in the name
Of our most sovereign king.
    Buck.   Lo you, my lord,
The net has fall'n upon me! I shall perish
Under device and practice.
    Bran.   I am sorry
To see you ta'en from liberty, to look on   205
The business present. 'Tis his Highness' pleasure
You shall to the Tower.
    Buck.   It will help me nothing
To plead mine innocence; for that dye is on me
Which makes my whit'st part black. The will of
        Heaven
Be done in this and all things! I obey.   210
O my Lord Abergavenny, fare you well!
    Bran. Nay, he must bear you company. The
        King   [*To Abergavenny.*]
Is pleas'd you shall to th' Tower, till you know
How he determines further.
    Aber.   As the Duke said,
The will of Heaven be done, and the King's pleasure
By me obey'd!
    Bran.   Here is a warrant from   216
The King t' attach Lord Montacute, and the bodies
Of the Duke's confessor, John de la Car,
One Gilbert Peck, his [chancellor], —
    Buck.   So, so;
These are the limbs o' th' plot. No more, I hope?
    Bran. A monk o' th' Chartreux.
    Buck.   O, [Nicholas] Hopkins?
    Bran.   He. 221
    Buck. My surveyor is false; the o'er-great
        Cardinal

152–153. **Whom ... motions:** whom I mention not from spite but from pure motives.   157. **vouch:** testimony.   164.
suggests: prompts.   167. [rinsing] (Pope).   *wrenching* F.   178. **colour:** pretext.   183. [He] (Capell).   Om. F.   195. **mistaken:** misinterpreted.   204. **device and practice:** schemes and plots.   211. **Abergavenny.** The F spelling *Aburgany* shows
the pronunciation.   217. **attach:** arrest.   219. [chancellor] (Pope).   *Councellour* F.   221. **o' th' Chartreux:** Carthusian.
[**Nicholas**] (Pope).   *Michaell* F.

Hath show'd him gold; my life is spann'd already.
I am the shadow of poor Buckingham,
Whose figure even this instant cloud puts on
By dark'ning my clear sun. My lord, farewell.   226
                                        [*Exeunt.*

SCENE II. [*The same. The council-chamber.*]

Cornets. Enter the KING, *leaning on the* CARDINAL'S
shoulder, the Nobles, *and* SIR THOMAS LOVELL;
*the Cardinal places himself under the King's feet on
his right side.*

King. My life itself, and the best heart of it,
Thanks you for this great care. I stood i' th' level
Of a full-charg'd confederacy, and give thanks
To you that chok'd it. Let be call'd before us
That gentleman of Buckingham's; in person   5
I'll hear him his confessions justify,
And point by point the treasons of his master
He shall again relate.

A noise within, crying, "Room for the Queen!"
Enter QUEEN KATHERINE, *usher'd by the* DUKE
OF NORFOLK *and the* DUKE OF SUFFOLK: *she
kneels. The King riseth from his state, takes her up,
kisses and placeth her by him.*

Q. Kath. Nay, we must longer kneel; I am a
    suitor.
King. Arise and take place by us. Half your suit
Never name to us, you have half our power;   11
The other moiety ere you ask is given.
Repeat your will and take it.
  Q. Kath.   Thank your Majesty.
That you would love yourself, and in that love
Not unconsidered leave your honour nor   15
The dignity of your office, is the point
Of my petition.
  King.   Lady mine, proceed.
  Q. Kath. I am solicited, not by a few,
And those of true condition, that your subjects
Are in great grievance. There have been commis-
    sions   20
Sent down among 'em, which hath flaw'd the heart
Of all their loyalties; wherein, although,
My good Lord Cardinal, they vent reproaches
Most bitterly on you as putter on
Of these exactions, yet the King our master —   25
Whose honour Heaven shield from soil! — even he
    escapes not
Language unmannerly, yea, such which breaks
The sides of loyalty and almost appears

In loud rebellion.
  Nor.   Not "almost appears:"
It doth appear; for, upon these taxations,   30
The clothiers all, not able to maintain
The many to them 'longing, have put off
The spinsters, carders, fullers, weavers, who,
Unfit for other life, compell'd by hunger
And lack of other means, in desperate manner   35
Daring the event to th' teeth, are all in uproar,
And danger serves among them.
  King.   Taxation!
Wherein? and what taxation? My Lord Cardinal
You that are blam'd for it alike with us,
Know you of this taxation?
  Wol.   Please you, sir,   40
I know but of a single part in aught
Pertains to th' state; and front but in that file
Where others tell steps with me.
  Q. Kath.   No, my lord?
You know no more than others? But you frame
Things that are known alike, which are not whole-
    some   45
To those which would not know them, and yet must
Perforce be their acquaintance. These exactions,
(Whereof my sovereign would have note) they are
Most pestilent to th' hearing; and, to bear 'em,
The back is sacrifice to th' load. They say   50
They are devis'd by you; or else you suffer
Too hard an exclamation.
  King.   Still exaction!
The nature of it? In what kind, let's know,
Is this exaction?
  Q. Kath.   I am much too venturous
In tempting of your patience; but am bold'ned   55
Under your promis'd pardon. The subjects' grief
Comes through commissions, which compels from
    each
The sixth part of his substance, to be levied
Without delay; and the pretence for this
Is nam'd, your wars in France. This makes bold
    mouths;   60
Tongues spit their duties out, and cold hearts freeze
Allegiance in them; their curses now
Live where their prayers did; and it's come to pass
This tractable obedience is a slave
To each incensed will. I would your Highness   65
Would give it quick consideration, for
There is no primer [business].
  King.   By my life,
This is against our pleasure.
  Wol.   And for me,

---

223. **spann'd:** ended.   225–226. **Whose ... sun:** whose shape is determined by the threatening cloud that comes between me and the sun. *Sun* may refer to the king as in l. 56.   Johnson conjectured *puts out* (obscures) for *puts on.*
  Sc. ii, 2. **level:** aim.   3. **full-charg'd confederacy:** heavily loaded conspiracy.   12. **moiety:** half.   18. **solicited:** informed by petitioners.   32. **put off:** discharged.   33. **spinsters:** spinners.   **fullers:** men who full (shrink) cloth.   42. **front:** have a place in the front rank.   43. **tell:** keep.   45. **alike:** to all.   45–46. **wholesome To:** approved by.   48. **note:** knowledge. 52. **exclamation:** reproach.   64. **a slave:** subordinated.   67. **primer:** more urgent. **[business]** (Warburton). *baseness* F.

I have no further gone in this than by
A single voice; and that not pass'd me but 70
By learned approbation of the judges. If I am
Traduc'd by ignorant tongues, which neither know
My faculties nor person yet will be
The chronicles of my doing, let me say
'Tis but the fate of place, and the rough brake 75
That virtue must go through. We must not stint
Our necessary actions in the fear
To cope malicious censurers; which ever,
As rav'nous fishes, do a vessel follow
That is new-trimm'd, but benefit no further 80
Than vainly longing. What we oft do best,
By sick interpreters, once weak ones, is
Not ours, or not allow'd; what worst, as oft,
Hitting a grosser quality, is cried up
For our best act. If we shall stand still, 85
In fear our motion will be mock'd or carp'd at,
We should take root here where we sit, or sit
State-statues only.
    King.   Things done well
And with a care exempt themselves from fear;
Things done without example, in their issue 90
Are to be fear'd. Have you a precedent
Of this commission? I believe, not any.
We must not rend our subjects from our laws
And stick them in our will. Sixth part of each?
A trembling contribution! Why, we take 95
From every tree lop, bark, and part o' th' timber;
And, though we leave it with a root, thus hack'd,
The air will drink the sap. To every county
Where this is question'd send our letters, with
Free pardon to each man that has deni'd 100
The force of this commission. Pray, look to't;
I put it to your care.
    Wol.   A word with you.
               [*To the Secretary, aside.*]
Let there be letters writ to every shire,
Of the King's grace and pardon. The grieved
    commons
Hardly conceive of me; let it be nois'd 105
That through our intercession this revokement
And pardon comes. I shall anon advise you
Further in the proceeding.   [*Exit Secretary.*

          Enter SURVEYOR.

    Q. Kath. I am sorry that the Duke of Bucking-
ham
Is run in your displeasure.
    King.   It grieves many. 110
The gentleman is learn'd, and a most rare speaker;
To nature none more bound; his training such

That he may furnish and instruct great teachers
And never seek for aid out of himself. Yet see,
When these so noble benefits shall prove 115
Not well dispos'd, the mind growing once corrupt,
They turn to vicious forms, ten times more ugly
Than ever they were fair. This man so complete,
Who was enroll'd 'mongst wonders, and when we,
Almost with ravish'd list'ning, could not find 120
His hour of speech a minute — he, my lady,
Hath into monstrous habits put the graces
That once were his, and is become as black
As if besmear'd in hell. Sit by us; you shall hear —
This was his gentleman in trust — of him 125
Things to strike honour sad. Bid him recount
The fore-recited practices, whereof
We cannot feel too little, hear too much.
    Wol. Stand forth, and with bold spirit relate
    what you,
Most like a careful subject, have collected 130
Out of the Duke of Buckingham.
    King.   Speak freely.
    Surv. First, it was usual with him, every day
It would infect his speech, that if the King
Should without issue die, he'll carry it so
To make the sceptre his. These very words 135
I've heard him utter to his son-in-law,
Lord Abergavenny, to whom by oath he menac'd
Revenge upon the Cardinal.
    Wol.   Please your Highness, note
This dangerous conception in this point.
Not friended by his wish, to your high person 140
His will is most malignant, and it stretches
Beyond you to your friends.
    Q. Kath.   My learn'd Lord Cardinal,
Deliver all with charity.
    King.   Speak on.
How grounded he his title to the crown?
Upon our fail? To this point hast thou heard him
At any time speak aught?
    Surv.   He was brought to this 146
By a vain prophecy of Nicholas [Hopkins].
    King. What was that [Hopkins]?
    Surv.   Sir, a Chartreux friar,
His confessor, who fed him every minute
With words of sovereignty.
    King.   How know'st thou this?
    Surv. Not long before your Highness sped to
    France, 151
The Duke being at the Rose, within the parish
Saint Lawrence Poultney, did of me demand
What was the speech among the Londoners
Concerning the French journey. I repli'd, 155

70. **voice:** vote. 78. **cope:** encounter. 80. **new-trimm'd:** in repair, seaworthy. 82. **sick:** incapable. **once:** indeed. 83. **Not...allow'd:** not credited to us or not approved. 84. **Hitting...quality:** appealing to coarser natures. 94. **stick...will:** subject them to our caprice. 95. **trembling:** causing apprehension. 96. **lop:** smaller branches. 101. **force:** validity. 105. **Hardly conceive:** think harshly. 140. **Not...wish:** not favored by having his wish granted (that the king die without issue). 145. **fail:** failure of issue. 147, 148. **[Hopkins]** (Pope). *Henton* F.

Men fear the French would prove perfidious,
To the King's danger. Presently the Duke
Said, 'twas the fear, indeed; and that he doubted
'Twould prove the verity of certain words
Spoke by a holy monk "that oft," says he,   160
"Hath sent to me, wishing me to permit
John de la Car, my chaplain, a choice hour
To hear from him a matter of some moment;
Whom after under the [confession's] seal
He solemnly had sworn that what he spoke   165
My chaplain to no creature living but
To me should utter, with demure confidence
This pausingly ensu'd: 'Neither the King nor 's
      heirs,
Tell you the Duke, shall prosper. Bid him strive
To [gain] the love o' th' commonalty. The Duke
Shall govern England.'"
      Q. Kath.   If I know you well,   171
You were the Duke's surveyor, and lost your office
On the complaint o' th' tenants. Take good heed
You charge not in your spleen a noble person
And spoil your nobler soul; I say, take heed;   175
Yes, heartily beseech you.
      King.   Let him on.
Go forward.
      Surv.   On my soul, I'll speak but truth.
I told my lord the Duke, by th' devil's illusions
The monk might be deceiv'd; and that 'twas danger-
      ous for [him]
To ruminate on this so far, until   180
It forg'd him some design; which, being believ'd,
It was much like to do. He answer'd, "Tush,
It can do me no damage;" adding further
That, had the King in his last sickness fail'd,
The Cardinal's and Sir Thomas Lovell's heads   185
Should have gone off.
      King.   Ha! what, so rank? Ah ha!
There's mischief in this man. Canst thou say
      further?
      Surv. I can, my liege.
      King.   Proceed.
      Surv.   Being at Greenwich,
After your Highness had reprov'd the Duke
About Sir William Bulmer, —
      King.   I remember   190
Of such a time; being my sworn servant,
The Duke retain'd him his. But on; what hence?
      Surv. "If," quoth he, "I for this had been com-
      mitted,"
— As, to the Tower, I thought, — "I would have
      play'd
The part my father meant to act upon   195

Th' usurper Richard; who, being at Salisbury,
Made suit to come in 's presence; which if granted
As he made semblance of his duty, would
Have put his knife into him."
      King.   A giant traitor!
      Wol. Now, madam, may his Highness live in
      freedom,   200
And this man out of prison?
      Q. Kath.   God mend all!
      King. There's something more would out of thee;
      what say'st?
      Surv. After "the Duke his father," with "the
      knife,"
He stretch'd him, and, with one hand on his dagger,
Another spread on 's breast, mounting his eyes,   205
He did discharge a horrible oath, whose tenour
Was, were he evil us'd, he would outgo
His father by as much as a performance
Does an irresolute purpose.
      King.   There's his period,
To sheathe his knife in us. He is attach'd.   210
Call him to present trial. If he may
Find mercy in the law, 'tis his; if none,
Let him not seek 't of us. By day and night,
He's traitor to the height.   [*Exeunt.*

SCENE III. [*An ante-chamber in the palace.*]

Enter the LORD CHAMBERLAIN *and* LORD SANDYS.

      Cham. Is't possible the spells of France should
      juggle
Men into such strange mysteries?
      San.   New customs,
Though they be never so ridiculous,
Nay, let 'em be unmanly, yet are follow'd.
      Cham. As far as I see, all the good our English   5
Have got by the late voyage is but merely
A fit or two o' th' face; but they are shrewd ones;
For when they hold 'em, you would swear directly
Their very noses had been counsellors
To Pepin or Clotharius, they keep state so.   10
      San. They have all new legs, and lame ones. One
      would take it,
That never saw 'em pace before, the spavin
[Or] springhalt reign'd among 'em.
      Cham.   Death! my lord,
Their clothes are after such a pagan cut too,
That, sure, they've worn out Christendom.

Enter SIR THOMAS LOVELL.

                                  How now!   15
What news, Sir Thomas Lovell?
      Lov.   Faith, my lord

I hear of none, but the new proclamation
That's clapp'd upon the court-gate.
    Cham.   What is't for?
    Lov. The reformation of our travell'd gallants,
That fill the court with quarrels, talk, and tailors.
    Cham. I'm glad 'tis there. Now I would pray
       our monsieurs   21
To think an English courtier may be wise
And never see the Louvre.
    Lov.   They must either,
For so run the conditions, leave those remnants
Of fool and feather that they got in France,   25
With all their honourable points of ignorance
Pertaining thereunto, as fights and fireworks,
Abusing better men than they can be,
Out of a foreign wisdom, renouncing clean
The faith they have in tennis and tall stockings, 30
Short blist'red breeches, and those types of travel,
And understand again like honest men,
Or pack to their old playfellows. There, I take it,
They may, *"cum privilegio,"* [wear] away
The lag end of their lewdness and be laugh'd at. 35
    San. 'Tis time to give 'em physic, their diseases
Are grown so catching.
    Cham.   What a loss our ladies
Will have of these trim vanities!
    Lov.   Ay, marry,
There will be woe indeed, lords; the sly whoresons
Have got a speeding trick to lay down ladies.   40
A French song and a fiddle has no fellow.
    San. The devil fiddle 'em! I am glad they are
       going,
For, sure, there's no converting of 'em. Now
An honest country lord, as I am, beaten
A long time out of play, may bring his plain-song 45
And have an hour of hearing; and, by 'r Lady,
Held current music too.
    Cham.   Well said, Lord Sandys;
Your colt's tooth is not cast yet.
    San.   No, my lord;
Nor shall not, while I have a stump.
    Cham.   Sir Thomas,
Whither were you a-going?
    Lov.   To the Cardinal's.   50
Your lordship is a guest too.
    Cham.   O, 'tis true:
This night he makes a supper, and a great one,
To many lords and ladies; there will be
The beauty of this kingdom, I'll assure you.
    Lov. That churchman bears a bounteous mind
indeed.   55
A hand as fruitful as the land that feeds us;
His dews fall everywhere.

    Cham.   No doubt he's noble;
He had a black mouth that said other of him.
    San. He may, my lord; has wherewithal; in him
Sparing would show a worse sin than ill doctrine. 60
Men of his way should be most liberal;
They are set here for examples.
    Cham.   True, they are so;
But few now give so great ones. My barge stays;
Your lordship shall along. Come, good Sir Thomas,
We shall be late else; which I would not be,   65
For I was spoke to, with Sir Henry Guildford
This night to be comptrollers.
    San.   I am your lordship's.
                                   [*Exeunt.*

SCENE IV. [*A Hall in York Place.*]

Hautboys. A small table under a state for the Cardi-
nal, a longer table for the guests. Then enter
ANNE BULLEN *and divers other* Ladies *and* Gentlemen *as guests, at one door; at another door, enter*
SIR HENRY GUILDFORD.

    Guild. Ladies, a general welcome from his Grace
Salutes ye all; this night he dedicates
To fair content and you. None here, he hopes,
In all this noble bevy, has brought with her
One care abroad. He would have all as merry   5
As, first, good company, good wine, good welcome,
Can make good people.

Enter LORD CHAMBERLAIN, LORD SANDYS, *and*
SIR THOMAS LOVELL.

                O, my lord, you're tardy;
The very thought of this fair company
Clapp'd wings to me.
    Cham.   You are young, Sir Harry Guildford.
    San. Sir Thomas Lovell, had the Cardinal   10
But half my lay thoughts in him, some of these
Should find a running banquet ere they rested
I think would better please 'em. By my life,
They are a sweet society of fair ones.
    Lov. O, that your lordship were but now confessor
To one or two of these!
    San.   I would I were;   16
They should find easy penance.
    Lov.   Faith, how easy?
    San. As easy as a down-bed would afford it.
    Cham. Sweet ladies, will it please you sit? Sir
       Harry,
Place you that side; I'll take the charge of this. 20
His Grace is ent'ring. Nay, you must not freeze;
Two women plac'd together makes cold weather.
My Lord Sandys, you are one will keep 'em waking;

---

31. **blist'red:** puffed. **types:** signs. 34. **[wear]** F₂. *wee* F₁. 38. **trim vanities:** finely dressed fools. 40. **speeding:** successful.   44–45. **beaten...play:** long out of the game.   45. **plain-song:** simple melody.   48. **colt's tooth:** youthful impulses.
67. **comptrollers:** masters of ceremonies.
    Sc. iv, 12. running banquet: hasty refreshment (fig.).

Pray, sit between these ladies.

San.   By my faith,
And thank your lordship.   By your leave, sweet
    ladies.   25
If I chance to talk a little wild, forgive me;
I had it from my father.

Anne.   Was he mad, sir?

San. O, very mad, exceeding mad; in love too;
But he would bite none.   Just as I do now,
He would kiss you twenty with a breath.
                                    [*Kisses her.*]

Cham.   Well said, my lord.
So, now you're fairly seated.   Gentlemen,   31
The penance lies on you if these fair ladies
Pass away frowning.

San.   For my little cure,
Let me alone.

Hautboys.   Enter CARDINAL WOLSEY, *and takes
    his state.*

Wol. You're welcome, my fair guests.   That
    noble lady   35
Or gentleman that is not freely merry
Is not my friend.   This, to confirm my welcome;
And to you all, good health.   [*Drinks.*]

San.   Your Grace is noble.
Let me have such a bowl may hold my thanks,
And save me so much talking.

Wol.   My Lord Sandys,   40
I am beholding to you; cheer your neighbours.
Ladies, you are not merry.   Gentlemen,
Whose fault is this?

San.   The red wine first must rise
In their fair cheeks, my lord; then we shall have 'em
Talk us to silence.

Anne.   You are a merry gamester,   45
My Lord Sandys.

San.   Yes, if I make my play.
Here's to your ladyship; and pledge it, madam,
For 'tis to such a thing, —

Anne.   You cannot show me.

San. I told your Grace they would talk anon.
        [*Drum and trumpet, chambers discharged.*

Wol.   What's that?

Cham. Look out there, some of ye.
                                    [*Exit Servant.*]

Wol.   What warlike voice
And to what end is this?   Nay, ladies, fear not;   51
By all the laws of war you're privileg'd.

Re-enter SERVANT.

Cham. How now! what is't?

Serv.   A noble troop of strangers,

For so they seem.   They've left their barge and
    landed,
And hither make as great ambassadors   55
From foreign princes.

Wol.   Good Lord Chamberlain,
Go, give 'em welcome; you can speak the French
    tongue;
And, pray, receive 'em nobly and conduct 'em
Into our presence, where this heaven of beauty   59
Shall shine at full upon them.   Some attend him.
        [*Exit Chamberlain, attended.*]   *All rise, and
            tables remov'd.*
You have now a broken banquet; but we'll mend it.
A good digestion to you all; and once more
I shower a welcome on ye.   Welcome all!

Hautboys.   Enter the KING *and others, as masquers,
    habited like shepherds, usher'd by the* LORD CHAM-
    BERLAIN.   *They pass directly before the Cardinal,
    and gracefully salute him.*

A noble company!   What are their pleasures?

Cham. Because they speak no English, thus they
    pray'd   65
To tell your Grace, that, having heard by fame
Of this so noble and so fair assembly
This night to meet here, they could do no less,
Out of the great respect they bear to beauty,
But leave their flocks, and under your fair conduct
Crave leave to view these ladies and entreat   71
An hour of revels with 'em.

Wol.   Say, Lord Chamberlain,
They have done my poor house grace; for which I
    pay 'em
A thousand thanks, and pray 'em take their
    pleasures.
        [*They choose Ladies [for the dance*].   *The
            King chooses Anne Bullen.*

King. The fairest hand I ever touch'd!   O
    beauty,   75
Till now I never knew thee!   [*Music.   Dance.*

Wol. My lord!

Cham.   Your Grace?

Wol. Pray, tell 'em thus much from me:
There should be one amongst 'em, by his person
More worthy this place than myself; to whom,
If I but knew him, with my love and duty   80
I would surrender it.

Cham.   I will, my lord.
                    [*Whispers [the Masquers*].

Wol. What say they?

Cham.   Such a one, they all confess,
There is indeed; which they would have your Grace
Find out, and he will take it.

Wol.   Let me see, then.

By all your good leaves, gentlemen; here I'll make
My royal choice.
　　King.　　　　Ye have found him, Cardinal. 86
　　　　　　　　　　　　[*Unmasking.*]
You hold a fair assembly; you do well, lord.
You are a churchman, or, I'll tell you, Cardinal,
I should judge now unhappily.
　　Wol.　　　　I am glad 89
Your Grace is grown so pleasant.
　　King.　　　　My Lord Chamberlain,
Prithee, come hither.　What fair lady's that?
　　Cham. An't please your Grace, Sir Thomas
　　　Bullen's daughter, —
The Viscount Rochford, — one of her Highness'
　　　women.
　　King. By heaven, she is a dainty one.　Sweet-
　　　heart,
I were unmannerly to take you out 95
And not to kiss you.　A health, gentlemen!
Let it go round.
　　Wol. Sir Thomas Lovell, is the banquet ready
I' th' privy chamber?
　　Lov.　　　　Yes, my lord.
　　Wol.　　　　Your Grace,
I fear, with dancing is a little heated. 100
　　King. I fear, too much.
　　Wol.　　　　There's fresher air, my lord,
In the next chamber.
　　King. Lead in your ladies, every one.　Sweet
　　　partner,
I must not yet forsake you; let's be merry.
Good my Lord Cardinal, I have half a dozen
　　　healths 105
To drink to these fair ladies, and a measure
To lead 'em once again; and then let's dream
Who's best in favour.　Let the music knock it.
　　　　　　　　　　　[*Exeunt with trumpets.*

ACT II

SCENE I. [*Westminster. A street.*]

Enter two GENTLEMEN *at several doors.*

　　1. Gent. Whither away so fast?
　　2. Gent.　　　　O, God save ye!
Ev'n to the hall, to hear what shall become
Of the great Duke of Buckingham.
　　1. Gent.　　　　I'll save you
That labour, sir.　All's now done but the ceremony
Of bringing back the prisoners.
　　2. Gent.　　　　Were you there? 5
　　1. Gent. Yes, indeed, was I.
　　2. Gent.　　　Pray, speak what has happen'd.
　　1. Gent. You may guess quickly what.

　　2. Gent.　　　　Is he found guilty?
　　1. Gent. Yes, truly is he, and condemn'd upon 't.
　　2. Gent. I am sorry for 't.
　　1. Gent.　　　　So are a number more.
　　2. Gent. But, pray, how pass'd it? 10
　　1. Gent. I'll tell you in a little.　The great Duke
Came to the bar; where to his accusations
He pleaded still not guilty and alleged
Many sharp reasons to defeat the law.
The King's attorney on the contrary 15
Urg'd on the examinations, proofs, confessions
Of divers witnesses; which the Duke desir'd
To have brought *vivâ voce* to his face;
At which appear'd against him his surveyor;
Sir Gilbert Peck his chancellor; and John Car, 20
Confessor to him; with that devil-monk,
Hopkins, that made this mischief.
　　2. Gent.　　　　That was he
That fed him with his prophecies?
　　1. Gent.　　　　The same.
All these accus'd him strongly; which he fain
Would have flung from him, but, indeed, he could
　　　not. 25
And so his peers upon this evidence
Have found him guilty of high treason.　Much
He spoke, and learnedly, for life; but all
Was either pitied in him or forgotten.
　　2. Gent. After all this, how did he bear himself? 30
　　1. Gent. When he was brought again to the bar,
　　　to hear
His knell rung out, his judgement, he was stirr'd
With such an agony he sweat extremely,
And something spoke in choler, ill, and hasty.
But he fell to himself again, and sweetly 35
In all the rest show'd a most noble patience.
　　2. Gent. I do not think he fears death.
　　1. Gent.　　　　Sure, he does not;
He never was so womanish.　The cause
He may a little grieve at.
　　2. Gent.　　　　Certainly
The Cardinal is the end of this.
　　1. Gent.　　　　'Tis likely 40
By all conjectures: first, Kildare's attainder,
Then deputy of Ireland; who remov'd,
Earl Surrey was sent thither, and in haste too,
Lest he should help his father.
　　2. Gent.　　　　That trick of state
Was a deep envious one.
　　1. Gent.　　　　At his return 45
No doubt he will requite it.　This is noted,
And generally, whoever the King favours,
The Cardinal instantly will find employment,
And far enough from court too.
　　2. Gent.　　　　All the commons

---

89. **unhappily:** unfavorably.　90. **pleasant:** jocular.　108. **knock it:** strike up.
　Act II, sc. i, 34. **choler:** anger.　40. **end:** ultimate cause　41. **Kildare's attainder.** Wolsey had the Earl of Kildare, Deputy of Ireland, arrested for maladministration.　44. **father.** Buckingham was Surrey's father-in-law.　45. **envious:** malicious.

Hate him perniciously, and, o' my conscience,   50
Wish him ten fathom deep. This duke as much
They love and dote on; call him bounteous Bucking-
    ham,
The mirror of all courtesy, —

Enter BUCKINGHAM *from his arraignment; tipstaves
before him; the axe with the edge towards him;
halberds on each side: accompanied with* SIR
THOMAS LOVELL, SIR NICHOLAS VAUX, Sir
[William] Sandys, *and common people.*

    1. Gent.   Stay there, sir,
And see the noble ruin'd man you speak of.
    2. Gent. Let's stand close, and behold him.
    Buck.   All good people,   55
You that thus far have come to pity me,
Hear what I say, and then go home and lose me.
I have this day receiv'd a traitor's judgement,
And by that name must die; yet, Heaven bear
    witness,
And if I have a conscience, let it sink me,   60
Even as the axe falls, if I be not faithful!
The law I bear no malice for my death;
'T has done, upon the premises, but justice;
But those that sought it I could wish more Chris-
    tians.
Be what they will, I heartily forgive 'em;   65
Yet let 'em look they glory not in mischief
Nor build their evils on the graves of great men,
For then my guiltless blood must cry against 'em.
For further life in this world I ne'er hope,
Nor will I sue, although the King have mercies 70
More than I dare make faults. You few that lov'd
    me
And dare be bold to weep for Buckingham,
His noble friends and fellows, whom to leave
Is only bitter to him, only dying,
Go with me, like good angels, to my end;   75
And, as the long divorce of steel falls on me,
Make of your prayers one sweet sacrifice,
And lift my soul to heaven. Lead on, o' God's
    name.
    Lov. I do beseech your Grace, for charity,
If ever any malice in your heart   80
Were hid against me, now to forgive me frankly.
    Buck. Sir Thomas Lovell, I as free forgive you
As I would be forgiven. I forgive all.
There cannot be those numberless offences
'Gainst me, that I cannot take peace with; no
    black envy   85
Shall [mark] my grave. Commend me to his
    Grace;
And, if he speak of Buckingham, pray, tell him

You met him half in heaven. My vows and prayers
Yet are the King's; and, till my soul forsake,
Shall cry for blessings on him. May he live   90
Longer than I have time to tell his years!
Ever belov'd and loving may his rule be!
And when old Time shall lead him to his end,
Goodness and he fill up one monument!
    Lov. To th' water side I must conduct your
    Grace;   95
Then give my charge up to Sir Nicholas Vaux,
Who undertakes you to your end.
    Vaux.   Prepare there,
The Duke is coming. See the barge be ready;
And fit it with such furniture as suits   99
The greatness of his person.
    Buck.   Nay, Sir Nicholas,
Let it alone; my state now will but mock me.
When I came hither, I was Lord High Constable
And Duke of Buckingham; now, poor Edward
    Bohun.
Yet I am richer than my base accusers,
That never knew what truth meant. I now seal
    it;   105
And with that blood will make 'em one day groan
    for 't.
My noble father, Henry of Buckingham,
Who first rais'd head against usurping Richard,
Flying for succour to his servant Banister,
Being distress'd, was by that wretch betray'd, 110
And without trial fell; God's peace be with him!
Henry the Seventh succeeding, truly pitying
My father's loss, like a most royal prince
Restor'd me to my honours, and, out of ruins,
Made my name once more noble. Now his son, 115
Henry the Eighth, life, honour, name, and all
That made me happy, at one stroke has taken
For ever from the world. I had my trial,
And, must needs say, a noble one; which makes me
A little happier than my wretched father.   120
Yet thus far we are one in fortunes: both
Fell by our servants, by those men we lov'd most;
A most unnatural and faithless service.
Heaven has an end in all; yet, you that hear me,
This from a dying man receive as certain: 125
Where you are liberal of your loves and counsels
Be sure you be not loose; for those you make friends
And give your hearts to, when they once perceive
Th' least rub in your fortunes, fall away
Like water from ye; never found again   130
But where they mean to sink ye. All good people,
Pray for me! I must now forsake ye. The last
    hour
Of my long weary life is come upon me.

53. s.d. *tipstaves:* bailiffs. **[William]** (Theobald). *Walter* F. 57. **lose:** forget. 60. **sink:** ruin. 67. **evils:** hovels or
privies. 74. **only...dying:** the bitterness of death lies only in separation from friends. 85. **envy:** malignity. 86. **[mark]**
(Warburton). *make* F. 91. **tell:** count. 103. **Bohun.** So Holinshed, but his family name was Stafford. 105. **it:** truth.
108. **head:** armed force. 124. **end:** purpose. 127. **loose:** careless. 129. **rub:** check.

Farewell!
And when you would say something that is sad, 135
Speak how I fell. I have done; and God forgive me!
                    [Exeunt Duke and train.
   1. Gent. O, this is full of pity! Sir, it calls,
I fear, too many curses on their heads
That were the authors.
   2. Gent.   If the Duke be guiltless,
'Tis full of woe; yet I can give you inkling 140
Of an ensuing evil, if it fall,
Greater than this.
   1. Gent.   Good angels keep it from us!
What may it be? You do not doubt my faith, sir?
   2. Gent. This secret is so weighty, 'twill require
A strong faith to conceal it.
   1. Gent.   Let me have it. 145
I do not talk much.
   2. Gent.   I am confident;
You shall, sir. Did you not of late days hear
A buzzing of a separation
Between the King and Katherine?
   1. Gent.   Yes, but it held not:
For when the King once heard it, out of anger 150
He sent command to the Lord Mayor straight
To stop the rumour, and allay those tongues
That durst disperse it.
   2. Gent.   But that slander, sir,
Is found a truth now; for it grows again
Fresher than e'er it was, and held for certain 155
The King will venture at it. Either the Cardinal,
Or some about him near, have out of malice
To the good Queen possess'd him with a scruple
That will undo her. To confirm this too,
Cardinal Campeius is arriv'd, and lately; 160
As all think, for this business.
   1. Gent.   'Tis the Cardinal;
And merely to revenge him on the Emperor
For not bestowing on him at his asking
The archbishopric of Toledo, this is purpos'd.
   2. Gent. I think you have hit the mark; but is't
      not cruel 165
That she should feel the smart of this? The
      Cardinal
Will have his will, and she must fall.
   1. Gent.   'Tis woful.
We are too open here to argue this;
Let's think in private more.   *[Exeunt.*

   SCENE II. [*An ante-chamber in the palace.*]

Enter the LORD CHAMBERLAIN, *reading this letter:*

   [*Cham.*] "My lord, the horses your lordship sent
for, with all the care I had, I saw well chosen,
ridden, and furnish'd. They were young and
handsome, and of the best breed in the north.

When they were ready to set out for London, a 5
man of my Lord Cardinal's, by commission and
main power, took 'em from me, with this reason:
His master would be serv'd before a subject, if not
before the King; which stopp'd our mouths,
sir." 10
I fear he will indeed. Well, let him have them;
He will have all, I think.

   Enter, to the Lord Chamberlain, the DUKES OF
         NORFOLK *and* SUFFOLK.

   Nor. Well met, my Lord Chamberlain.
   Cham. Good day to both your Graces. 14
   Suf. How is the King employ'd?
   Cham.   I left him private,
Full of sad thoughts and troubles.
   Nor.   What's the cause?
   Cham. It seems the marriage with his brother's
      wife
Has crept too near his conscience.
   Suf. [*Aside.*]   No, his conscience
Has crept too near another lady.
   Nor.   'Tis so.
This is the Cardinal's doing, the king-cardinal. 20
That blind priest, like the eldest son of Fortune,
Turns what he list. The King will know him one
      day.
   Suf. Pray God he do! he'll never know himself
      else.
   Nor. How holily he works in all his business!
And with what zeal! for, now he has crack'd the
      league 25
Between us and the Emperor, the Queen's great
      nephew,
He dives into the King's soul, and there scatters
Dangers, doubts, wringing of the conscience,
Fears, and despairs; and all these for his marriage.
And out of all these to restore the King, 30
He counsels a divorce; a loss of her
That, like a jewel, has hung twenty years
About his neck, yet never lost her lustre;
Of her that loves him with that excellence
That angels love good men with; even of her 35
That, when the greatest stroke of fortune falls,
Will bless the King. And is not this course pious?
   Cham. Heaven keep me from such counsel! 'Tis
      most true
These news are everywhere; every tongue speaks
      'em,
And every true heart weeps for 't. All that dare 40
Look into these affairs see this main end,
The French king's sister. Heaven will one day open
The King's eyes, that so long have slept upon
This bold bad man.
   Suf.   And free us from his slavery.

---

148. **buzzing:** rumor. 152. **allay:** silence. 158. **possess'd him with:** put into his mind.
Sc. ii, 21–22. **blind ... Turns:** allusions to Fortune's blindness and her wheel.

Nor. We had need pray,   45
And heartily, for our deliverance,
Or this imperious man will work us all
From princes into pages.   All men's honours
Lie like one lump before him, to be fashion'd
Into what pitch he please.
    Suf.   For me, my lords,   50
I love him not, nor fear him; there's my creed.
As I am made without him, so I'll stand,
If the King please; his curses and his blessings
Touch me alike, they're breath I not believe in.
I knew him, and I know him; so I leave him   55
To him that made him proud, the Pope.
    Nor.   Let's in;
And with some other business put the King
From these sad thoughts that work too much upon
    him.
My lord, you'll bear us company?
    Cham.   Excuse me;
The King has sent me otherwhere.   Besides,   60
You'll find a most unfit time to disturb him.
Health to your lordships.
    Nor.   Thanks, my good Lord Chamberlain.
    [*Exit Lord Chamberlain; [Norfolk] draws
    the curtain, and [discovers] the King read-
    ing pensively.*
    Suf. How sad he looks!   Sure, he is much
afflicted.
    King. Who's there, ha?
    Nor.   Pray God he be not angry.
    King. Who's there, I say?   How dare you thrust
    yourselves   65
Into my private meditations?
Who am I? ha?
    Nor. A gracious king that pardons all offences
Malice ne'er meant.   Our breach of duty this way
Is business of estate; in which we come   70
To know your royal pleasure.
    King.   Ye are too bold.
Go to; I'll make ye know your times of business.
Is this an hour for temporal affairs, ha?

Enter WOLSEY *and* CAMPEIUS, *with a commission.*

Who's there?   My good Lord Cardinal?   O my
    Wolsey,
The quiet of my wounded conscience,   75
Thou art a cure fit for a king.   [*To Camp.*] You're
    welcome,
Most learned reverend sir, into our kingdom;
Use us and it.   [*To Wol.*] My good lord, have
    great care
I be not found a talker.
    Wol.   Sir, you cannot.
I would your Grace would give us but an hour   80

Of private conference.
    King. [*To Nor. and Suf.*] We are busy; go.
    Nor. [*Aside to Suf.*] This priest has no pride in
    him?
    Suf. [*Aside to Nor.*] Not to speak of.
I would not be so sick, though, for his place.
But this cannot continue.
    Nor. [*Aside to Suf.*]   If it do,
I'll venture one have-at-him.
    Suf. [*Aside to Nor.*]   I another.   85
                                   [*Exeunt Nor. and Suf.*
    Wol. Your Grace has given a precedent of wisdom
Above all princes, in committing freely
Your scruple to the voice of Christendom.
Who can be angry now?   What envy reach you?
The Spaniard, tied by blood and favour to her,   91
Must now confess, if they have any goodness,
The trial just and noble.   All the clerks,
I mean the learned ones, in Christian kingdoms
Have their free voices.   Rome, the nurse of judge-
    ment,
Invited by your noble self, hath sent   95
One general tongue unto us, this good man,
This just and learned priest, Cardinal Campeius,
Whom once more I present unto your Highness.
    King. And once more in mine arms I bid him
    welcome,
And thank the holy conclave for their loves.   100
They have sent me such a man I would have wish'd
    for.
    Cam. Your Grace must needs deserve all
    strangers' loves,
You are so noble.   To your Highness' hand
I tender my commission; by whose virtue,
The court of Rome commanding, you, my Lord   105
Cardinal of York, are join'd with me their servant
In the unpartial judging of this business.
    King. Two equal men.   The Queen shall be
    acquainted
Forthwith for what you come.   Where's Gardiner?
    Wol. I know your Majesty has always lov'd her
So dear in heart not to deny her that   111
A woman of less place might ask by law,
Scholars allow'd freely to argue for her.
    King. Ay, and the best she shall have, and my
    favour
To him that does best; God forbid else.   Car-
    dinal,   115
Prithee, call Gardiner to me, my new secretary.
I find him a fit fellow.   [*Exit Wolsey.*

    Re-enter [WOLSEY, *with*] GARDINER.

    Wol. [*Aside to Gard.*] Give me your hand.   Much
    joy and favour to you;

50. **pitch:** degree of dignity. 70. **estate:** state. 83. **I … place.** I would not have his place at the cost of being so sick
with pride. 85. **have-at-him:** thrust. 94. **voices:** votes. 96. **general:** universal. 100. **conclave:** College of Cardinals.
108. **equal:** impartial.

You are the King's now.

Gard. [*Aside to Wol.*] But to be commanded
For ever by your Grace, whose hand has rais'd me.

King. Come hither, Gardiner.   121
                                                        [*Walks and whispers.*

Cam. My Lord of York, was not one Doctor Pace
In this man's place before him?

Wol.   Yes, he was.

Cam. Was he not held a learned man?

Wol.   Yes, surely.

Cam. Believe me, there's an ill opinion spread
then   125
Even of yourself, Lord Cardinal.

Wol.   How! of me?

Cam. They will not stick to say you envi'd him,
And fearing he would rise, he was so virtuous,
Kept him a foreign man still; which so griev'd him,
That he ran mad and died.

Wol.   Heaven's peace be with him!
That's Christian care enough. For living mur-
murers   131
There's places of rebuke. He was a fool,
For he would needs be virtuous. That good fel-
low,
If I command him, follows my appointment;
I will have none so near else. Learn this, brother,
We live not to be grip'd by meaner persons.   136

King. Deliver this with modesty to the Queen.
                                                        [*Exit Gardiner.*
The most convenient place that I can think of
For such receipt of learning is Black-Friars;
There ye shall meet about this weighty business. 140
My Wolsey, see it furnish'd. O, my lord,
Would it not grieve an able man to leave
So sweet a bedfellow? But, conscience, conscience!
O, 'tis a tender place; and I must leave her.
                                                        [*Exeunt.*

SCENE III. [*An ante-chamber of the Queen's
apartments.*]

Enter ANNE BULLEN *and an* OLD LADY.

Anne. Not for that neither. Here's the pang
that pinches:
His Highness having liv'd so long with her, and she
So good a lady that no tongue could ever
Pronounce dishonour of her, — by my life,
She never knew harm-doing — O, now, after   5
So many courses of the sun enthroned,
Still growing in a majesty and pomp, the which
To leave a thousand-fold more bitter than
'Tis sweet at first t' acquire, — after this process,

To give her the avaunt, it is a pity   10
Would move a monster.

Old L.   Hearts of most hard temper
Melt and lament for her.

Anne.   O, God's will, much better
She ne'er had known pomp! Though 't be tem-
poral,
Yet, if that quarrel, Fortune, do divorce
It from the bearer, 'tis a sufferance panging   15
As soul and body's severing.

Old L.   Alas, poor lady!
She's a stranger now again.

Anne.   So much the more
Must pity drop upon her. Verily,
I swear, 'tis better to be lowly born
And range with humble livers in content   20
Than to be perk'd up in a glist'ring grief
And wear a golden sorrow.

Old L.   Our content
Is our best having.

Anne.   By my troth and maidenhead,
I would not be a queen.

Old L.   Beshrew me, I would,
And venture maidenhead for 't; and so would you
For all this spice of your hypocrisy.   26
You, that have so fair parts of woman on you,
Have too a woman's heart, which ever yet
Affected eminence, wealth, sovereignty;
Which, to say sooth, are blessings; and which gifts,
Saving your mincing, the capacity   31
Of your soft cheveril conscience would receive
If you might please to stretch it.

Anne.   Nay, good troth.

Old L. Yes, troth, and troth. You would not be
a queen?

Anne. No, not for all the riches under heaven.   35

Old L. 'Tis strange. A three-pence bow'd would
hire me,
Old as I am, to queen it. But, I pray you,
What think you of a duchess? Have you limbs
To bear that load of title?

Anne.   No, in truth.

Old L. Then you are weakly made; pluck off a
little.   40
I would not be a young count in your way
For more than blushing comes to. If your back
Cannot vouchsafe this burden, 'tis too weak
Ever to get a boy.

Anne.   How you do talk!
I swear again, I would not be a queen   45
For all the world.

Old L.   In faith, for little England

You'd venture an emballing. I myself
Would for Carnarvonshire, although there long'd
No more to th' crown but that. Lo, who comes
here?

Enter the LORD CHAMBERLAIN.

Cham. Good morrow, ladies. What were't worth
to know   50
The secret of your conference?
Anne.   My good lord,
Not your demand; it values not your asking.
Our mistress' sorrows we were pitying.
Cham. It was a gentle business, and becoming
The action of good women. There is hope   55
All will be well.
Anne.   Now, I pray God, amen!
Cham. You bear a gentle mind, and heavenly
blessings
Follow such creatures. That you may, fair lady,
Perceive I speak sincerely, and high note 's
Ta'en of your many virtues, the King's Majesty 60
Commends his good opinion of you, and
Does purpose honour to you no less flowing
Than Marchioness of Pembroke; to which title
A thousand pound a year, annual support,
Out of his grace he adds.
Anne.   I do not know   65
What kind of my obedience I should tender.
More than my all is nothing; nor my prayers
Are not words duly hallowed, nor my wishes
More worth than empty vanities; yet prayers and
wishes
Are all I can return. Beseech your lordship,   70
Vouchsafe to speak my thanks and my obedience,
As from a blushing handmaid, to his Highness;
Whose health and royalty I pray for.
Cham.   Lady,
I shall not fail t' approve the fair conceit
The King hath of you. [*Aside.*] I have perus'd her
well.   75
Beauty and honour in her are so mingled
That they have caught the King; and who knows
yet
But from this lady may proceed a gem
To lighten all this isle? I'll to the King,
And say I spoke with you.
                    [*Exit Lord Chamberlain.*
Anne.   My honour'd lord.   80
Old L. Why, this it is; see, see!
I have been begging sixteen years in court,
Am yet a courtier beggarly, nor could
Come pat betwixt too early and too late
For any suit of pounds; and you, O fate!   85

A very fresh fish here — fie, fie, fie upon
This compell'd fortune! — have your mouth fill'd
up
Before you open it.
Anne.   This is strange to me.
Old L. How tastes it? Is it bitter? Forty pence, no.
There was a lady once ('tis an old story)   90
That would not be a queen, that would she not,
For all the mud in Egypt. Have you heard it?
Anne. Come, you are pleasant.
Old L.   With your theme, I could
O'ermount the lark. The Marchioness of Pem-
broke!
A thousand pounds a year for pure respect!   95
No other obligation! By my life,
That promises moe thousands; Honour's train
Is longer than his foreskirt. By this time
I know your back will bear a duchess. Say,
Are you not stronger than you were?
Anne.   Good lady,
Make yourself mirth with your particular fancy 101
And leave me out on't. Would I had no being,
If this salute my blood a jot. It faints me,
To think what follows.
The Queen is comfortless, and we forgetful   105
In our long absence. Pray, do not deliver
What here you've heard to her.
Old L.   What do you think me?
                                        [*Exeunt.*

SCENE IV. [*A hall in Black-Friars.*]

Trumpets, sennet, and cornets. Enter two Vergers,
with short silver wands; next them, two SCRIBES,
in the habit of doctors; after them, the [ARCH]BISHOP
OF CANTERBURY *alone; after him, the* BISHOPS OF
LINCOLN, ELY, ROCHESTER, *and* SAINT ASAPH;
next them, with some small distance, follows a
Gentleman *bearing the purse, with the great seal,
and a cardinal's hat; then two* Priests, *bearing each
a silver cross; then a* GENTLEMAN USHER *bare-
headed, accompanied with a* Sergeant-at-arms
bearing a silver mace; then two Gentlemen *bearing
two great silver pillars; after them, side by side, the
two* CARDINALS; *two* Noblemen *with the sword and
mace. The* KING *takes place under the cloth of
state; the two Cardinals sit under him as judges.
The* QUEEN *takes place some distance from the
King. The Bishops place themselves on each side
the court, in manner of a consistory; below them,
the Scribes. The Lords sit next the Bishops. The
rest of the Attendants stand in convenient order
about the stage.*

---

47. **emballing:** investment with the ball, symbol of sovereignty.   61. **of you** (Capell).   *of you to you* F.   74. **approve:**
confirm.   78. **gem.**   This compliment to Elizabeth has been used as evidence of an early date for the play.   85. **suit of**
pounds: petition for money.   87. **compell'd:** forced upon you.   89. **Forty pence:** a wager.   103. **salute:** stir.
Sc. iv, S.D.   *sennet:* a set of notes on a trumpet.

Wol. Whilst our commission from Rome is read,
Let silence be commanded.
    King.   What's the need?
It hath already publicly been read,
And on all sides th' authority allow'd;   4
You may, then, spare that time.
    Wol.   Be't so. Proceed.
    Scribe. Say, Henry King of England, come into
the court.
    Crier. Henry King of England, etc.
    King. Here.
    Scribe. Say, Katherine Queen of England, come
into the court.   11
    Crier. Katherine Queen of England, etc.
    [*The Queen makes no answer, rises out of
      her chair, goes about the court, comes to
      the King, and kneels at his feet; then
      speaks.*
    [*Q. Kath.*] Sir, I desire you do me right and justice
And to bestow your pity on me; for
I am a most poor woman, and a stranger,   15
Born out of your dominions, having here
No judge indifferent, nor no more assurance
Of equal friendship and proceeding. Alas, sir,
In what have I offended you? What cause
Hath my behaviour given to your displeasure 20
That thus you should proceed to put me off
And take your good grace from me? Heaven wit-
    ness
I have been to you a true and humble wife,
At all times to your will conformable;
Ever in fear to kindle your dislike,   25
Yea, subject to your countenance, glad or sorry
As I saw it inclin'd. When was the hour
I ever contradicted your desire,
Or made it not mine too? Or which of your friends
Have I not strove to love although I knew   30
He were mine enemy? What friend of mine
That had to him deriv'd your anger did I
Continue in my liking? nay, gave notice
He was from thence discharg'd? Sir, call to mind
That I have been your wife in this obedience 35
Upward of twenty years, and have been blest
With many children by you. If, in the course
And process of this time, you can report,
And prove it too, against mine honour aught,
My bond to wedlock or my love and duty, 40
Against your sacred person, in God's name,
Turn me away; and let the foul'st contempt
Shut door upon me, and so give me up
To the sharp'st kind of justice. Please you, sir,
The King, your father, was reputed for   45
A prince most prudent, of an excellent
And unmatch'd wit and judgement; Ferdinand,
My father, King of Spain, was reckon'd one

The wisest prince that there had reign'd by many
A year before; it is not to be question'd   50
That they had gather'd a wise council to them
Of every realm, that did debate this business,
Who deem'd our marriage lawful; wherefore I
    humbly
Beseech you, sir, to spare me, till I may
Be by my friends in Spain advis'd, whose counsel 55
I will implore. If not, i' th' name of God,
Your pleasure be fulfill'd!
    Wol.   You have here, lady,
And of your choice, these reverend fathers; men
Of singular integrity and learning,
Yea, the elect o' th' land, who are assembled 60
To plead your cause. It shall be therefore bootless
That longer you desire the court; as well
For your own quiet, as to rectify
What is unsettled in the King.
    Cam.   His Grace
Hath spoken well and justly; therefore, madam, 65
It's fit this royal session do proceed,
And that without delay their arguments
Be now produc'd and heard.
    Q. Kath.   Lord Cardinal,
To you I speak.
    Wol.   Your pleasure, madam?
    Q. Kath.   Sir,
I am about to weep; but, thinking that   70
We are a queen, or long have dream'd so, certain
The daughter of a king, my drops of tears
I'll turn to sparks of fire.
    Wol.   Be patient yet.
    Q. Kath. I will, when you are humble; nay, be-
      fore,
Or God will punish me. I do believe,   75
Induc'd by potent circumstances, that
You are mine enemy, and make my challenge
You shall not be my judge; for it is you
Have blown this coal betwixt my lord and me,
Which God's dew quench! Therefore I say again,
I utterly abhor, yea, from my soul   81
Refuse you for my judge; whom, yet once more,
I hold my most malicious foe, and think not
At all a friend to truth.
    Wol.   I do profess
You speak not like yourself, who ever yet 85
Have stood to charity, and display'd th' effects
Of disposition gentle, and of wisdom
O'ertopping woman's power. Madam, you do me
    wrong.
I have no spleen against you, nor injustice
For you or any. How far I have proceeded, 90
Or how far further shall, is warranted
By a commission from the consistory,
Yea, the whole consistory of Rome. You charge me

---

    17. **indifferent:** impartial. 32. **deriv'd:** drawn. 33. **gave.** A negative is understood. 62. **desire:** i.e., to delay. 81.
abhor: a legal term for protest against.

That I have blown this coal. I do deny it.
The King is present: if it be known to him   95
That I gainsay my deed, how may he wound,
And worthily, my falsehood! yea, as much
As you have done my truth. If he know
That I am free of your report, he knows
I am not of your wrong. Therefore in him   100
It lies to cure me; and the cure is to
Remove these thoughts from you; the which before
His Highness shall speak in, I do beseech
You, gracious madam, to unthink your speaking
And to say so no more.
     Q. Kath.   My lord, my lord,   105
I am a simple woman, much too weak
T' oppose your cunning. You're meek and
          humble-mouth'd;
You sign your place and calling, in full seeming,
With meekness and humility; but your heart
Is cramm'd with arrogancy, spleen, and pride.   110
You have, by fortune and his Highness' favours,
Gone slightly o'er low steps and now are mounted
Where powers are your retainers, and your words
(Domestics to you) serve your will as 't please
Yourself pronounce their office. I must tell you,
You tender more your person's honour than   116
Your high profession spiritual; that again
I do refuse you for my judge; and here,
Before you all, appeal unto the Pope,
To bring my whole cause 'fore his Holiness,   120
And to be judg'd by him.
     [*She curtsies to the King, and offers to de-
          part.*
     Cam.   The Queen is obstinate,
Stubborn to justice, apt to accuse it, and
Disdainful to be tried by't: 'tis not well.
She's going away.
     King. Call her again.   125
     Crier. Katherine, Queen of England, come into
          the court.
     Gent. Ush. Madam, you are call'd back.
     Q. Kath. What need you note it? Pray you,
          keep your way;
When you are call'd, return. Now, the Lord help!
They vex me past my patience. Pray you, pass on.
I will not tarry; no, nor ever more   131
Upon this business my appearance make
In any of their courts.
     [*Exeunt Queen, and her Attendants.*
     King.   Go thy ways, Kate.
That man i' th' world who shall report he has
A better wife, let him in nought be trusted   135
For speaking false in that. Thou art alone

(If thy rare qualities, sweet gentleness,
Thy meekness saint-like, wife-like government,
Obeying in commanding, and thy parts
Sovereign and pious else, could speak thee out)
The queen of earthly queens. She's noble born;   141
And like her true nobility she has
Carried herself towards me.
     Wol.   Most gracious sir,
In humblest manner I require your Highness
That it shall please you to declare, in hearing   145
Of all these ears, — for, where I am robb'd and
          bound,
There must I be unloos'd, although not there
At once and fully satisfi'd, — whether ever I
Did broach this business to your Highness, or
Laid any scruple in your way which might   150
Induce you to the question on't? or ever
Have to you, but with thanks to God for such
A royal lady, spake one the least word that might
Be to the prejudice of her present state,
Or touch of her good person?
     King.   My Lord Cardinal,
I do excuse you; yea, upon mine honour,   156
I free you from 't. You are not to be taught
That you have many enemies, that know not
Why they are so, but, like to village-curs,
Bark when their fellows do: by some of these   160
The Queen is put in anger. You're excus'd;
But will you be more justifi'd? You ever
Have wish'd the sleeping of this business; never
          desir'd
It to be stirr'd; but oft have hind'red, oft,
The passages made toward it. On my honour, 165
I speak my good Lord Cardinal to this point,
And thus far clear him. Now, what mov'd me to't,
I will be bold with time and your attention:
Then mark the inducement. Thus it came; give
          heed to't:
My conscience first receiv'd a tenderness,   170
Scruple, and prick, on certain speeches utter'd
By th' Bishop of Bayonne, then French ambas-
          sador;
Who had been hither sent on the debating
[A] marriage 'twixt the Duke of Orleans and
Our daughter Mary. I' th' progress of this busi-
          ness,   175
Ere a determinate resolution, he,
I mean the Bishop, did require a respite;
Wherein he might the King his lord advertise
Whether our daughter were legitimate,
Respecting this our marriage with the dowager,   180
Sometimes our brother's wife. This respite shook

---

99. **free ... report:** innocent of what you accuse me of. 108. **sign:** have the appearance of. 112. **slightly:** easily.
113. **powers:** influential persons. **words.** Tyrwhitt conjectured *wards.* 116. **tender:** care for. 140. **speak thee out:** describe you fully. 155. **touch ... person:** taint of her good reputation. 166. **I ... point:** I speak about the Cardinal's attitude in this matter. 174. **[A]** (Rowe). *And* F. 176. **determinate resolution:** final decision. 178. **advertise:** inform.
181. Sometimes: formerly.

The bosom of my conscience, enter'd me,
Yea, with a [splitting] power, and made to tremble
The region of my breast; which forc'd such way,
That many maz'd considerings did throng　185
And press'd in with this caution. First, methought
I stood not in the smile of Heaven; who had
Commanded nature, that my lady's womb,
If it conceiv'd a male child by me, should
Do no more offices of life to't than　190
The grave does to the dead; for her male issue
Or died where they were made, or shortly after
This world had air'd them. Hence I took a thought
This was a judgement on me; that my kingdom,
Well worthy the best heir o' th' world, should not
Be gladded in't by me. Then follows, that　196
I weigh'd the danger which my realms stood in
By this my issue's fail; and that gave to me
Many a groaning throe. Thus hulling in
The wild sea of my conscience, I did steer　200
Toward this remedy, whereupon we are
Now present here together; that's to say,
I meant to rectify my conscience, — which
I then did feel full sick, and yet not well, —
By all the reverend fathers of the land　205
And doctors learn'd. First I began in private
With you, my Lord of Lincoln. You remember
How under my oppression I did reek,
When I first mov'd you.
　　Lin.　　　　　　　　Very well, my liege.
　　King. I have spoke long; be pleas'd yourself to
　　　say　210
How far you satisfi'd me.
　　Lin.　　　　　　So please your Highness,
The question did at first so stagger me,
Bearing a state of mighty moment in't
And consequence of dread, that I committed
The daring'st counsel which I had to doubt;　215
And did entreat your Highness to this course
Which you are running here.
　　King.　　　　　　I then mov'd you,
My Lord of Canterbury; and got your leave
To make this present summons. Unsolicited
I left no reverend person in this court;　220
But by particular consent proceeded
Under your hands and seals. Therefore, go on;
For no dislike i' th' world against the person
Of the good queen, but the sharp thorny points
Of my alleged reasons, drives this forward.　225
Prove but our marriage lawful, by my life
And kingly dignity, we are contented
To wear our mortal state to come with her,
Katherine our queen, before the primest creature
That's paragon'd o' th' world.
　　Cam.　　　　　　So please your Highness,　230

The Queen being absent, 'tis a needful fitness
That we adjourn this court till further day.
Meanwhile must be an earnest motion
Made to the Queen to call back her appeal
She intends unto his Holiness.
　　King.　　　　　　[*Aside.*] I may perceive
These Cardinals trifle with me; I abhor　236
This dilatory sloth and tricks of Rome.
My learn'd and well-beloved servant, Cranmer,
Prithee, return. With thy approach, I know,　239
My comfort comes along. — Break up the court!
I say, set on.　[*Exeunt in manner as they enter'd.*]

ACT III

SCENE I. [*London. The Queen's apartments.*]

The QUEEN *and her women, as at work.*

Q. Kath. Take thy lute, wench; my soul grows
　sad with troubles.
Sing, and disperse 'em, if thou canst. Leave work-
　ing.

SONG.

Orpheus with his lute made trees
And the mountain tops that freeze
　Bow themselves when he did sing.　5
To his music plants and flowers
Ever sprung as sun and showers
　There had made a lasting spring.

Everything that heard him play,
Even the billows of the sea,　10
　Hung their heads, and then lay by.
In sweet music is such art,
Killing care and grief of heart
　Fall asleep, or hearing, die.

Enter a GENTLEMAN.

Q. Kath. How now!　15
Gent. An't please your Grace, the two great
　Cardinals
Wait in the presence.
Q. Kath.　　　　Would they speak with me?
Gent. They will'd me say so, madam.
Q. Kath.　　　　　　Pray their Graces
To come near. [*Exit Gent.*] What can be their
　business
With me, a poor weak woman, fallen from favour?
I do not like their coming. Now I think on't,　21
They should be good men, their affairs as righteous.
But all hoods make not monks.

Enter the two Cardinals, WOLSEY *and* CAMPEIUS.

Wol.　　　　　　Peace to your Highness!

183. [splitting]. *spitting* F.　199. hulling: drifting to and fro.　208. reek: sweat.　209. mov'd: approached.　230.
paragon'd: regarded as paragon.
Act III, sc. i, 16. An't: if it.　17. presence: presence-chamber.

Q. Kath. Your Graces find me here part of a
    housewife;
I would be all, against the worst may happen.   25
What are your pleasures with me, reverend lords?
    Wol. May it please you, noble madam, to with-
    draw
Into your private chamber, we shall give you
The full cause of our coming.
    Q. Kath.   Speak it here;
There's nothing I have done yet, o' my conscience,
Deserves a corner. Would all other women   31
Could speak this with as free a soul as I do!
My lords, I care not, so much I am happy
Above a number, if my actions
Were tried by ev'ry tongue, ev'ry eye saw 'em,   35
Envy and base opinion set against 'em,
I know my life so even. If your business
Seek me out, and that way I am wife in,
Out with it boldly. Truth loves open dealing.
    Wol. Tanta est erga te mentis integritas, regina
    serenissima, —   41
    Q. Kath. O, good my lord, no Latin;
I am not such a truant since my coming,
As not to know the language I have liv'd in.
A strange tongue makes my cause more strange,
    suspicious;   45
Pray, speak in English. Here are some will thank
    you,
If you speak truth, for their poor mistress' sake.
Believe me, she has had much wrong. Lord Car-
    dinal
The willing'st sin I ever yet committed
May be absolv'd in English.
    Wol.   Noble lady,   50
I am sorry my integrity should breed
(And service to his Majesty and you)
So deep suspicion, where all faith was meant.
We come not by the way of accusation
To taint that honour every good tongue blesses,   55
Nor to betray you any way to sorrow;
You have too much, good lady; but to know
How you stand minded in the weighty difference
Between the King and you; and to deliver,
Like free and honest men, our just opinions   60
And comforts to your cause.
    Cam.   Most honour'd madam,
My Lord of York, out of his noble nature,
Zeal and obedience he still bore your Grace,
Forgetting like a good man your late censure
Both of his truth and him (which was too far),   65
Offers, as I do, in a sign of peace,
His service and his counsel.
    Q. Kath.   [*Aside.*] To betray me. —

My lords, I thank you both for your good wills.
Ye speak like honest men; pray God, ye prove so!
But how to make ye suddenly an answer   70
In such a point of weight, so near mine honour, —
More near my life, I fear, — with my weak wit,
And to such men of gravity and learning,
In truth I know not. I was set at work
Among my maids; full little, God knows, looking   75
Either for such men or such business.
For her sake that I have been, — for I feel
The last fit of my greatness — good your Graces,
Let me have time and counsel for my cause.
Alas, I am a woman, friendless, hopeless!   80
    Wol. Madam, you wrong the King's love with
    these fears.
Your hopes and friends are infinite.
    Q. Kath.   In England
But little for my profit. Can you think, lords,
That any Englishman dare give me counsel?
Or be a known friend, 'gainst his Highness' pleas-
    ure,   85
Though he be grown so desperate to be honest,
And live a subject? Nay, forsooth; my friends,
They that must weigh out my afflictions,
They that my trust must grow to, live not here.
They are, as all my other comforts, far hence   90
In mine own country, lords.
    Cam.   I would your Grace
Would leave your griefs, and take my counsel.
    Q. Kath.   How, sir?
    Cam. Put your main cause into the King's pro-
    tection;
He's loving and most gracious. 'Twill be much
Both for your honour better and your cause;   95
For if the trial of the law o'ertake ye,
You'll part away disgrac'd.
    Wol.   He tells you rightly.
    Q. Kath. Ye tell me what ye wish for both, — my
    ruin.
Is this your Christian counsel? Out upon ye!
Heaven is above all yet; there sits a judge   100
That no king can corrupt.
    Cam.   Your rage mistakes us.
    Q. Kath. The more shame for ye! Holy men I
    thought ye,
Upon my soul, two reverend cardinal virtues;
But cardinal sins and hollow hearts I fear ye.
Mend 'em, for shame, my lords! Is this your com-
    fort,   105
The cordial that ye bring a wretched lady,
A woman lost among ye, laugh'd at, scorn'd?
I will not wish ye half my miseries;
I have more charity; but say, I warn'd ye.

---

25. **all**: entirely given up to housekeeping. 31. **a corner**: i.e., to hide in. 37. **even**: consistent. 38. **that...in**: the
matter of the divorce. 41. So great is (my) integrity of mind toward you, most serene queen. 52, 53. Perhaps these two
lines should be transposed. (Edwards.) 78. **fit**: canto, chapter. 86. **so desperate to be**: so reckless as to be. 88. **weigh
out**: outweigh. 101. **mistakes**: misjudges.

Take heed, for heaven's sake, take heed, lest at
    once   110
The burden of my sorrows fall upon ye.
    Wol. Madam, this is a mere distraction;
You turn the good we offer into envy.
    Q. Kath. Ye turn me into nothing! Woe upon ye
And all such false professors! Would you have
    me —   115
If you have any justice, any pity,
If ye be anything but churchmen's habits —
Put my sick cause into his hands that hates me?
Alas, he's banish'd me his bed already,
His love, too, long ago! I am old, my lords,   120
And all the fellowship I hold now with him
Is only my obedience. What can happen
To me above this wretchedness? All your studies
Make me a curse like this!
    Cam.   Your fears are worse.
    Q. Kath. Have I liv'd thus long — let me speak
    myself,   125
Since virtue finds no friends — a wife, a true one?
A woman, I dare say without vain-glory,
Never yet branded with suspicion?
Have I with all my full affections
Still met the King? loved him next Heaven? obey'd
    him?   130
Been, out of fondness, superstitious to him?
Almost forgot my prayers to content him?
And am I thus rewarded! 'Tis not well, lords.
Bring me a constant woman to her husband,
One that ne'er dream'd a joy beyond his pleasure;
And to that woman, when she has done most,   136
Yet will I add an honour, — a great patience.
    Wol. Madam, you wander from the good we aim
    at.
    Q. Kath. My lord, I dare not make myself so
    guilty
To give up willingly that noble title   140
Your master wed me to. Nothing but **death**
Shall e'er divorce my dignities.
    Wol.   Pray, hear me.
    Q. Kath. Would I had never trod this English earth
Or felt the flatteries that grow upon it!
Ye have angels' faces, but Heaven knows your
    hearts.   145
What will become of me now, wretched lady!
I am the most unhappy woman living.
Alas, poor wenches, where are now your fortunes!
Shipwreck'd upon a kingdom, where no pity,
No friends, no hope; no kindred weep for me;   150
Almost no grave allow'd me. Like the lily,
That once was mistress of the field and flourish'd,
I'll hang my head and perish.
    Wol.   If your Grace

Could but be brought to know our ends are honest,
You'd feel more comfort. Why should we, good
    lady,   155
Upon what cause, wrong you? Alas, our places,
The way of our profession is against it;
We are to cure such sorrows, not to sow 'em.
For goodness' sake, consider what you do;
How you may hurt yourself, ay, utterly   160
Grow from the King's acquaintance, by this car-
    riage.
The hearts of princes kiss obedience,
So much they love it; but to stubborn spirits
They swell, and grow as terrible as storms.
I know you have a gentle, noble temper,   165
A soul as even as a calm; pray, think us
Those we profess, peacemakers, friends, and
    servants.
    Cam. Madam, you'll find it so. You wrong your
    virtues
With these weak women's fears. A noble spirit
As yours was, put into you, ever casts   170
Such doubts, as false coin, from it. The King
    loves you;
Beware you lose it not. For us, if you please
To trust us in your business, we are ready
To use our utmost studies in your service.
    Q. Kath. Do what ye will, my lords; and, pray,
    forgive me   175
If I have us'd myself unmannerly.
You know I am a woman, lacking wit
To make a seemly answer to such persons.
Pray, do my service to his Majesty;
He has my heart yet and shall have my prayers   180
While I shall have my life. Come, reverend fathers,
Bestow your counsels on me. She now begs,
That little thought, when she set footing here,
She should have bought her dignities so dear.
                [*Exeunt.*

SCENE II. [*Ante-chamber to the King's apartment.*]

Enter the DUKE OF NORFOLK, *the* DUKE OF SUFFOLK,
    the EARL OF SURREY, *and the* LORD CHAMBERLAIN.

    Nor. If you will now unite in your complaints
And force them with a constancy, the Cardinal
Cannot stand under them. If you omit
The offer of this time, I cannot promise
But that you shall sustain moe new disgraces   5
With these you bear already.
    Sur.   I am joyful
To meet the least occasion that may give me
Remembrance of my father-in-law, the Duke,
To be reveng'd on him.
    Suf.   Which of the peers

---

    113. **envy:** malice.   123–124. **All ... this:** I defy all your studies to make, etc.   131. **superstitious:** idolatrous.   161.
carriage: behavior.   176. **us'd myself:** behaved.
    Sc. ii, 2. **force:** urge.   3. **omit:** neglect.   8. **the Duke:** Buckingham.

Have uncontemn'd gone by him, or at least   10
Strangely neglected?   When did he regard
The stamp of nobleness in any person
Out of himself?
  Cham.   My lords, you speak your pleasures.
What he deserves of you and me I know;
What we can do to him, though now the time   15
Gives way to us, I much fear.   If you cannot
Bar his access to th' King, never attempt
Anything on him; for he hath a witchcraft
Over the King in 's tongue.
  Nor.   O, fear him not;
His spell in that is out.   The King hath found   20
Matter against him that for ever mars
The honey of his language.   No, he's settled,
Not to come off, in his displeasure.
  Sur.   Sir,
I should be glad to hear such news as this
Once every hour.
  Nor.   Believe it, this is true.   25
In the divorce his contrary proceedings
Are all unfolded; wherein he appears
As I would wish mine enemy.
  Sur.   How came
His practices to light?
  Suf.   Most strangely.
  Sur.   O, how, how?
  Suf. The Cardinal's letters to the Pope mis-
    carried   30
And came to th' eye o' th' King; wherein was read,
How that the Cardinal did entreat his Holiness
To stay the judgement o' th' divorce; for if
It did take place, "I do," quoth he, "perceive
My king is tangled in affection to   35
A creature of the Queen's, Lady Anne Bullen."
  Sur. Has the King this?
  Suf.   Believe it.
  Sur.   Will this work?
  Cham. The King in this perceives him, how he
    coasts
And hedges his own way.   But in this point
All his tricks founder, and he brings his physic   40
After his patient's death.   The King already
Hath married the fair lady.
  Sur.   Would he had!
  Suf. May you be happy in your wish, my lord!
For, I profess, you have it.
  Sur.   Now, all my joy   44
Trace the conjunction!
  Suf.   My amen to't!
  Nor.   All men's!
  Suf. There's order given for her coronation.
Marry, this is yet but young, and may be left

To some ears unrecounted.   But, my lords,
She is a gallant creature, and complete
In mind and feature.   I persuade me, from her   50
Will fall some blessing to this land, which shall
In it be memoriz'd.
  Sur.   But, will the King
Digest this letter of the Cardinal's?
The Lord forbid!
  Nor.   Marry, amen!
  Suf.   No, no;
There be moe wasps that buzz about his nose   55
Will make this sting the sooner.   Cardinal Cam-
    peius
Is stolen away to Rome, hath ta'en no leave;
He's left the cause o' th' King unhandled, and
Is posted, as the agent of our Cardinal,
To second all his plot.   I do assure you   60
The King cried "Ha!" at this.
  Cham.   Now, God incense him,
And let him cry "Ha!" louder!
  Nor.   But, my lord,
When returns Cranmer?
  Suf. He is return'd in his opinions; which
Have satisfied the King for his divorce,   65
Together with all famous colleges'
Almost in Christendom.   Shortly, I believe,
His second marriage shall be publish'd, and
Her coronation.   Katherine no more
Shall be call'd Queen, but Princess Dowager   70
And widow to Prince Arthur.
  Nor.   This same Cranmer's
A worthy fellow, and hath ta'en much pain
In the King's business.
  Suf.   He has; and we shall see him
For it an archbishop.
  Nor.   So I hear.
  Suf.   'Tis so.

    Enter WOLSEY *and* CROMWELL.

The Cardinal!
  Nor.   Observe, observe, he's moody.   75
  Wol. The packet, Cromwell,
Gave't you the King?
  Crom.   To his own hand, in 's bedchamber.
  Wol. Look'd he o' th' inside of the paper?
  Crom.   Presently
He did unseal them; and the first he view'd,
He did it with a serious mind; a heed   80
Was in his countenance.   You he bade
Attend him here this morning.
  Wol.   Is he ready
To come abroad?
  Crom.   I think by this he is.

11. **neglected.** The negative in *uncontemn'd* carries over to *neglected*. 13. **Out of:** besides. 16. **Gives way to:** favors. 23.
Not ... off: not to change, if *he* refers to the king; not to escape, if to the Cardinal. 29. **practices:** plots. 38–39. **coasts And hedges:** follows indirect courses, as by coasts and hedgerows. 45. **Trace:** follow. 52. **memoriz'd:** made memorable. 53.
Digest: put up with. 64. **He ... opinions:** he has sent his opinions in advance.

Wol. Leave me a while.   [*Exit Cromwell.*
[*Aside.*] It shall be to the Duchess of Alençon, 85
The French king's sister; he shall marry her.
Anne Bullen! No; I'll no Anne Bullens for him;
There's more in 't than fair visage. Bullen!
No, we'll no Bullens. Speedily I wish
To hear from Rome. The Marchioness of Pem-
    broke!   90
  Nor. He's discontented.
  Suf.   May be, he hears the King
Does whet his anger to him.
  Sur.   Sharp enough,
Lord, for thy justice!
  Wol. [*Aside.*] The late queen's gentlewoman,
    a knight's daughter,
To be her mistress' mistress! the Queen's queen! 95
This candle burns not clear: 'tis I must snuff it;
Then out it goes. What though I know her vir-
    tuous
And well deserving? yet I know her for
A spleeny Lutheran; and not wholesome to
Our cause, that she should lie i' th' bosom of   100
Our hard-rul'd king. Again, there is sprung up
An heretic, an arch one, Cranmer; one
Hath crawl'd into the favour of the King,
And is his oracle.
  Nor.   He's vex'd at something.

Enter the KING, *reading a schedule* [*and* LOVELL].

  Sur. I would 'twere something that would fret
    the string,   105
The master-cord on 's heart!
  Suf.   The King, the King!
  King. What piles of wealth hath he accumu-
    lated
To his own portion! and what expense by th' hour
Seems to flow from him! How, i' th' name of thrift,
Does he rake this together! Now, my lords,   110
Saw you the Cardinal?
  Nor.   My lord, we have
Stood here observing him. Some strange com-
    motion
Is in his brain; he bites his lip, and starts;
Stops on a sudden, looks upon the ground,
Then lays his finger on his temple; straight   115
Springs out into fast gait; then stops again,
Strikes his breast hard, and anon he casts
His eye against the moon. In most strange pos-
    tures
We have seen him set himself.
  King.   It may well be;
There is a mutiny in 's mind. This morning   120
Papers of state he sent me to peruse,
As I requir'd; and wot you what I found
There, — on my conscience, put unwittingly?

Forsooth, an inventory, thus importing
The several parcels of his plate, his treasure,   125
Rich stuffs, and ornaments of household; which
I find at such proud rate, that it out-speaks
Possession of a subject.
  Nor.   It's Heaven's will!
Some spirit put this paper in the packet,
To bless your eye withal.
  King.   If we did think   130
His contemplation were above the earth,
And fix'd on spiritual object, he should still
Dwell in his musings; but I am afraid
His thinkings are below the moon, not worth
His serious considering.
    [*King takes his seat; whispers Lovell, who*
    goes to the Cardinal.
  Wol.   Heaven forgive me!   135
Ever God bless your Highness!
  King.   Good my lord,
You are full of heavenly stuff, and bear the inven-
    tory
Of your best graces in your mind; the which
You were now running o'er. You have scarce time
To steal from spiritual leisure a brief span   140
To keep your earthly audit. Sure, in that
I deem you an ill husband, and am glad
To have you therein my companion.
  Wol.   Sir,
For holy offices I have a time; a time
To think upon the part of business which   145
I bear i' th' state; and Nature does require
Her times of preservation, which perforce
I, her frail son, amongst my brethren mortal,
Must give my tendance to.
  King.   You have said well.
  Wol. And ever may your Highness yoke to-
    gether,   150
As I will lend you cause, my doing well
With my well saying!
  King.   'Tis well said again;
And 'tis a kind of good deed to say well;
And yet words are no deeds. My father lov'd you;
He said he did; and with his deed did crown   155
His word upon you. Since I had my office,
I have kept you next my heart; have not alone
Employ'd you where high profits might come home,
But par'd my present havings, to bestow   159
My bounties upon you.
  Wol.   [*Aside.*] What should this mean?
  Sur. [*Aside.*] The Lord increase this business!
  King.   Have I not made you
The prime man of the state? I pray you, tell me,
If what I now pronounce you have found true;
And, if you may confess it, say withal,
If you are bound to us or no. What say you? 165

99. **spleeny:** ardent. 101. **hard-rul'd:** difficult to guide. 105. **fret:** gnaw through. 124. **thus importing:** giving this information. 127. **out-speaks:** exceeds. 132. **should still:** should continue to. 142. **husband:** manager.

Wol. My sovereign, I confess your royal graces
Shower'd on me daily have been more than could
My studied purposes requite, which went
Beyond all man's endeavours. My endeavours
Have ever come too short of my desires, 170
Yet [fil'd] with my abilities. Mine own ends
Have been mine so that evermore they pointed
To the good of your most sacred person and
The profit of the state. For your great graces
Heap'd upon me, poor undeserver, I 175
Can nothing render but allegiant thanks,
My prayers to heaven for you, my loyalty,
Which ever has and ever shall be growing,
Till death, that winter, kill it.
     King.   Fairly answer'd.
A loyal and obedient subject is 180
Therein illustrated. The honour of it
Does pay the act of it, as i' th' contrary,
The foulness is the punishment. I presume
That, as my hand has open'd bounty to you,
My heart dropp'd love, my power rain'd honour,
     more 185
On you than any, so your hand and heart,
Your brain, and every function of your power,
Should, notwithstanding that your bond of duty,
As 'twere in love's particular, be more
To me, your friend, than any.
     Wol.   I do profess 190
That for your Highness' good I ever labour'd
More than mine own, that am, have, and will be —
Though all the world should crack their duty to you
And throw it from their soul; though perils did
Abound, as thick as thought could make 'em, and
Appear in forms more horrid, — yet my duty, 196
As doth a rock against the chiding flood,
Should the approach of this wild river break,
And stand unshaken yours.
     King.   'Tis nobly spoken.
Take notice, lords, he has a loyal breast, 200
For you have seen him open 't. Read o'er this;
     [*Giving him papers.*]
And, after, this; and then to breakfast with
What appetite you have.
     [*Exit King, frowning upon Cardinal
     Wolsey: the Nobles throng after him,
     smiling and whispering.*
     Wol.   What should this mean?
What sudden anger 's this? How have I reap'd it?
He parted frowning from me, as if ruin 205
Leap'd from his eyes. So looks the chafed lion
Upon the daring huntsman that has gall'd him;
Then makes him nothing. I must read this paper;
I fear, the story of his anger. 'Tis so!
This paper has undone me. 'Tis the account 210

Of all that world of wealth I have drawn together
For mine own ends; indeed, to gain the popedom
And fee my friends in Rome. O negligence,
Fit for a fool to fall by! What cross devil
Made me put this main secret in the packet 215
I sent the King? Is there no way to cure this?
No new device to beat this from his brains?
I know 'twill stir him strongly; yet I know
A way, if it take right, in spite of fortune
Will bring me off again. What's this? "To th'
     Pope!" 220
The letter, as I live, with all the business
I writ to 's Holiness. Nay then, farewell!
I have touch'd the highest point of all my great-
     ness;
And, from that full meridian of my glory,
I haste now to my setting. I shall fall 225
Like a bright exhalation in the evening,
And no man see me more.

Re-enter to Wolsey, the DUKES OF NORFOLK *and*
     SUFFOLK, *the* EARL OF SURREY, *and the* LORD
     CHAMBERLAIN.

     Nor. Hear the King's pleasure, Cardinal! who
          commands you
To render up the great seal presently
Into our hands; and to confine yourself 230
To Asher House, my Lord of Winchester's,
Till you hear further from his Highness.
     Wol.   Stay!
Where's your commission, lords? Words cannot carry
Authority so weighty.
     Suf.   Who dare cross 'em, 234
Bearing the King's will from his mouth expressly?
     Wol. Till I find more than will or words to do it,
I mean your malice, know, officious lords,
I dare and must deny it. Now I feel
Of what coarse metal ye are moulded, envy.
How eagerly ye follow my disgraces 240
As if it fed ye! and how sleek and wanton
Ye appear in everything may bring my ruin!
Follow your envious courses, men of malice!
You have Christian warrant for 'em, and, no doubt,
In time will find their fit rewards. That seal 245
You ask with such a violence, the King,
Mine and your master, with his own hand gave me;
Bade me enjoy it, with the place and honours,
During my life; and, to confirm his goodness,
Tied it by letters-patents. Now, who'll take it? 250
     Sur. The King, that gave it.
     Wol.   It must be himself, then.
     Sur. Thou art a proud traitor, priest.
     Wol.   Proud lord, thou liest!
Within these forty hours Surrey durst better

---

171. [fil'd] (Hanmer). *fill'd* F. fil'd with: ranked with, been proportionate to. 176. allegiant: loyal. 189. in love's partic-ular: in the special case of a person you loved. 192–199. More . . . yours. The grammatical incoherence shows Wolsey's emotion. 207. gall'd: wounded. 214. cross: perverse. 226. exhalation: meteor.

Have burnt that tongue than said so.

Sur.   Thy ambition,
Thou scarlet sin, robb'd this bewailing land   255
Of noble Buckingham, my father-in-law.
The heads of all thy brother cardinals,
With thee and all thy best parts bound together,
Weigh'd not a hair of his.   Plague of your policy!
You sent me deputy for Ireland,   260
Far from his succour, from the King, from all
That might have mercy on the fault thou gav'st
    him;
Whilst your great goodness, out of holy pity,
Absolv'd him with an axe.

Wol.   This, and all else
This talking lord can lay upon my credit,   265
I answer is most false.   The Duke by law
Found his deserts.   How innocent I was
From any private malice in his end,
His noble jury and foul cause can witness.
If I lov'd many words, lord, I should tell you   270
You have as little honesty as honour,
That in the way of loyalty and truth
Toward the King, my ever royal master,
Dare mate a sounder man than Surrey can be,
And all that love his follies.

Sur.   By my soul,   275
Your long coat, priest, protects you; thou shouldst
    feel
My sword i' th' life-blood of thee else.   My lords,
Can ye endure to hear this arrogance?
And from this fellow?   If we live thus tamely,
To be thus jaded by a piece of scarlet,   280
Farewell nobility!   Let his Grace go forward,
And dare us with his cap like larks.

Wol.   All goodness
Is poison to thy stomach.

Sur.   Yes, that goodness
Of gleaning all the land's wealth into one,
Into your own hands, Cardinal, by extortion;   285
The goodness of your intercepted packets
You writ to th' Pope against the King.   Your good-
    ness,
Since you provoke me, shall be most notorious.
My Lord of Norfolk, as you are truly noble,
As you respect the common good, the state   290
Of our despis'd nobility, our issues,
Who, if he live, will scarce be gentlemen,
Produce the grand sum of his sins, the articles
Collected from his life.   I'll startle you
Worse than the sacring bell, when the brown wench
Lay kissing in your arms, Lord Cardinal.   296

Wol. How much, methinks, I could despise this
    man,

But that I am bound in charity against it!

Nor. Those articles, my lord, are in the King's
    hand:
But, thus much, they are foul ones.

Wol.   So much fairer
And spotless shall mine innocence arise   301
When the King knows my truth.

Sur.   This cannot save you.
I thank my memory, I yet remember
Some of these articles; and out they shall.
Now, if you can blush and cry "guilty," Cardinal,
You'll show a little honesty.

Wol.   Speak on, sir;   306
I dare your worst objections.   If I blush,
It is to see a nobleman want manners.

Sur. I had rather want those than my head.
    Have at you!
First, that, without the King's assent or knowledge,
You wrought to be a legate; by which power   311
You maim'd the jurisdiction of all bishops.

Nor. Then, that in all you writ to Rome, or else
To foreign princes, "*Ego et Rex meus*"
Was still inscrib'd; in which you brought the King
To be your servant.

Suf.   Then, that, without the knowledge
Either of king or council, when you went   317
Ambassador to the Emperor, you made bold
To carry into Flanders the great seal.

Sur. Item, you sent a large commission   320
To Gregory de Cassado, to conclude,
Without the King's will or the state's allowance,
A league between his Highness and Ferrara.

Suf. That, out of mere ambition, you have caus'd
Your holy hat to be stamp'd on the King's coin.

Sur. Then, that you have sent innumerable sub-
    stance —   326
By what means got, I leave to your own con-
    science —
To furnish Rome, and to prepare the ways
You have for dignities; to the mere undoing
Of all the kingdom.   Many more there are;   330
Which, since they are of you and odious,
I will not taint my mouth with.

Cham.   O my lord,
Press not a falling man too far! 'tis virtue.
His faults lie open to the laws; let them,   334
Not you, correct him.   My heart weeps to see him
So little of his great self.

Sur.   I forgive him.

Suf. Lord Cardinal, the King's further pleasure is,
Because all those things you have done of late
By your power legatine within this kingdom
Fall into th' compass of a *præmunire*.   340

---

262. **gav'st him**: charged him with.   272. **That.** The antecedent is *I*, l. 270, and the predicate *Dare*, l. 274.   274. **mate:** match.   280. **jaded:** ridden.   282. **dare:** daze.   A piece of red cloth and a mirror were used to catch larks.   295. **sacring:** consecrating.   329. **mere:** complete.   340. *præmunire:* a statute making it illegal to carry to a foreign court matters belonging to the king's court.

That therefore such a writ be sued against you;
To forfeit all your goods, lands, tenements,
[Chattels], and whatsoever, and to be
Out of the King's protection. This is my charge.
   Nor. And so we'll leave you to your meditations
How to live better. For your stubborn answer 346
About the giving back the great seal to us,
The King shall know it, and, no doubt, shall thank you.
So fare you well, my little good Lord Cardinal.
                            [Exeunt all but Wolsey.
   Wol. So farewell to the little good you bear me.
Farewell! a long farewell, to all my greatness! 351
This is the state of man: to-day he puts forth
The tender leaves of hopes; to-morrow blossoms,
And bears his blushing honours thick upon him;
The third day comes a frost, a killing frost,   355
And, when he thinks, good easy man, full surely
His greatness is a-ripening, nips his root,
And then he falls, as I do. I have ventur'd,
Like little wanton boys that swim on bladders,
This many summers in a sea of glory,   360
But far beyond my depth. My high-blown pride
At length broke under me, and now has left me,
Weary and old with service, to the mercy
Of a rude stream that must for ever hide me.
Vain pomp and glory of this world, I hate ye! 365
I feel my heart new open'd. O, how wretched
Is that poor man that hangs on princes' favours!
There is, betwixt that smile we would aspire to,
That sweet aspect of princes, and their ruin,
More pangs and fears than wars or women have; 370
And when he falls, he falls like Lucifer,
Never to hope again.

      Enter CROMWELL, *standing amazed.*
              Why, how now, Cromwell!
   Crom. I have no power to speak, sir.
   Wol.   What, amaz'd
At my misfortunes? Can thy spirit wonder   374
A great man should decline? Nay, an you weep
I am fall'n indeed.
   Crom.   How does your Grace?
   Wol.   Why, well,
Never so truly happy, my good Cromwell.
I know myself now; and I feel within me
A peace above all earthly dignities,
A still and quiet conscience. The King has cur'd
   me,   380
I humbly thank his Grace; and from these shoulders,
These ruin'd pillars, out of pity taken
A load would sink a navy, too much honour.
O, 'tis a burden, Cromwell, 'tis a burden
Too heavy for a man that hopes for heaven!   385
   Crom. I am glad your Grace has made that right
     use of it.

   Wol. I hope I have. I am able now, methinks,
Out of a fortitude of soul I feel,
To endure more miseries and greater far
Than my weak-hearted enemies dare offer.   390
What news abroad?
   Crom.   The heaviest and the worst
Is your displeasure with the King.
   Wol.   God bless him!
   Crom. The next is, that Sir Thomas More is
    chosen
Lord Chancellor in your place.
   Wol.   That's somewhat sudden;
But he's a learned man. May he continue   395
Long in his Highness' favour, and do justice
For truth's sake and his conscience, that his bones,
When he has run his course and sleeps in blessings,
May have a tomb of orphans' tears wept on 'em!
What more?
   Crom.   That Cranmer is return'd with wel-
    come,   400
Install'd Lord Archbishop of Canterbury.
   Wol. That's news indeed.
   Crom.   Last, that the Lady Anne,
Whom the King hath in secrecy long married,
This day was view'd in open as his queen,
Going to chapel; and the voice is now   405
Only about her coronation.
   Wol. There was the weight that pull'd me down.
     O, Cromwell,
The King has gone beyond me! All my glories
In that one woman I have lost for ever.
No sun shall ever usher forth mine honours   410
Or gild again the noble troops that waited
Upon my smiles. Go, get thee from me, Cromwell!
I am a poor fallen man, unworthy now
To be thy lord and master. Seek the King!
That sun, I pray, may never set! I have told
   him   415
What and how true thou art. He will advance
   thee;
Some little memory of me will stir him —
I know his noble nature — not to let
Thy hopeful service perish too. Good Cromwell,
Neglect him not; make use now, and provide 420
For thine own future safety.
   Crom.   O my lord,
Must I, then, leave you? Must I needs forgo
So good, so noble, and so true a master?
Bear witness, all that have not hearts of iron,
With what a sorrow Cromwell leaves his lord. 425
The King shall have my service; but my prayers
For ever and for ever shall be yours.
   Wol. Cromwell, I did not think to shed a tear
In all my miseries; but thou hast forc'd me,
Out of thy honest truth, to play the woman. 430

---

343. [Chattels] (Theobald). *castles* F. 369. their ruin the ruin they cause. 405. voice: talk. 408. gone beyond: overreached. 420. make use: take the opportunity.

Let's dry our eyes; and thus far hear me, Cromwell,
And, when I am forgotten, as I shall be,
And sleep in dull cold marble where no mention
Of me more must be heard of, say, I taught thee;
Say, Wolsey, that once trod the ways of glory, 435
And sounded all the depths and shoals of honour,
Found thee a way, out of his wreck, to rise in;
A sure and safe one, though thy master miss'd it.
Mark but my fall, and that that ruin'd me.
Cromwell, I charge thee, fling away ambition! 440
By that sin fell the angels; how can man, then,
The image of his Maker, hope to win by it?
Love thyself last. Cherish those hearts that hate
  thee;
Corruption wins not more than honesty.
Still in thy right hand carry gentle peace 445
To silence envious tongues. Be just, and fear not.
Let all the ends thou aim'st at be thy country's,
Thy God's, and truth's; then if thou fall'st, O Crom-
  well,
Thou fall'st a blessed martyr! Serve the King!
And, prithee, lead me in. 450
There take an inventory of all I have,
To the last penny; 'tis the King's. My robe,
And my integrity to Heaven, is all
I dare now call mine own. O Cromwell, Cromwell!
Had I but serv'd my God with half the zeal 455
I serv'd my king, He would not in mine age
Have left me naked to mine enemies.
  Crom. Good sir, have patience.
  Wol.   So I have. Farewell
The hopes of court! My hopes in heaven do dwell.
          [*Exeunt.*

ACT IV

SCENE I. [*A street in Westminster.*]

Enter two GENTLEMEN *meeting one another.*

  1. Gent. You're well met once again.
  2. Gent.   So are you.
  1. Gent. You come to take your stand here, and
  behold
The Lady Anne pass from her coronation?
  2. Gent. 'Tis all my business. At our last encounter,
The Duke of Buckingham came from his trial. 5
  1. Gent. 'Tis very true; but that time offer'd
  sorrow;
This, general joy.
  2. Gent.   'Tis well. The citizens,
I am sure, have shown at full their royal minds —
As, let 'em have their rights, they are ever forward —
In celebration of this day with shows, 10
Pageants, and sights of honour.

  1. Gent.   Never greater,
Nor, I'll assure you, better taken, sir.
  2. Gent. May I be bold to ask what that contains,
That paper in your hand?
  1. Gent.   Yes; 'tis the list 15
Of those that claim their offices this day
By custom of the coronation.
The Duke of Suffolk is the first, and claims
To be High Steward; next, the Duke of Norfolk,
He to be Earl Marshal. You may read the rest.
  2. Gent. I thank you, sir; had I not known those
  customs 20
I should have been beholding to your paper.
But, I beseech you, what's become of Katherine,
The Princess Dowager? How goes her business?
  1. Gent. That I can tell you too. The Archbishop
Of Canterbury, accompanied with other 25
Learned and reverend fathers of his order,
Held a late court at Dunstable, six miles off
From Ampthill where the Princess lay; to which
She was often cited by them, but appear'd not;
And, to be short, for not appearance and 30
The King's late scruple, by the main assent
Of all these learned men she was divorc'd,
And the late marriage made of none effect:
Since which she was remov'd to Kimbolton,
Where she remains now sick.
  2. Gent.   Alas, good lady! 35
          [*Trumpets.*]
The trumpets sound; stand close, the Queen is
  coming.   [*Hautboys.*

THE ORDER OF THE CORONATION.

1. *A lively flourish of Trumpets.*
2. Then, *two Judges.*
3. Lord Chancellor, *with the purse and mace before
  him.*
4. Choristers, *singing.*   Music.
5. Mayor of London, *bearing the mace. Then
  Garter, in his coat of arms, and on his head
  he wore a gilt copper crown.*
6. Marquess Dorset, *bearing a sceptre of gold, on
  his head a demi-coronal of gold. With him,
  the* Earl of Surrey, *bearing the rod of silver
  with the dove, crowned with an earl's coronet.
  Collars of SS.*
7. Duke of Suffolk, *in his robe of estate, his coronet
  on his head, bearing a long white wand, as
  high steward. With him, the* Duke of Norfolk,
  *with the rod of marshalship, a coronet on his
  head. Collars of SS.*
8. *A canopy borne by four of the* Cinque-ports;
  under it, the QUEEN *in her robe, in her hair
  richly adorned with pearl, crowned. On each
  side her, the* Bishops of London *and* Winchester.

Act IV, sc. i, 9. **let . . . rights:** to do them justice. 31. **main:** firm. 36. S.D. *Collars of SS:* i.e., with S-shaped links. **Cinque-ports:** the wardens of Dover, Hastings, Romney, Hythe, and Sandwich. *in her hair:* with her hair hanging.

9. *The old* Duchess of Norfolk, *in a coronal of gold, wrought with flowers, bearing the Queen's train.*

10. *Certain* Ladies *or* Countesses, *with plain circlets of gold without flowers.*

Exeunt, first passing over the stage in order and state, and then a great flourish of trumpets.

2. Gent. A royal train, believe me. These I know.
Who's that that bears the sceptre?

1. Gent.   Marquess Dorset;
And that the Earl of Surrey, with the rod.

2. Gent. A bold brave gentleman. That should be   40
The Duke of Suffolk?

1. Gent.   'Tis the same: High Steward.

2. Gent. And that my Lord of Norfolk?

1. Gent.   Yes.

2. Gent.   Heaven bless thee!
[*Looking on the Queen.*]
Thou hast the sweetest face I ever look'd on.
Sir, as I have a soul, she is an angel;
Our king has all the Indies in his arms,   45
And more and richer, when he strains that lady.
I cannot blame his conscience.

1. Gent.   They that bear
The cloth of honour over her, are four barons
Of the Cinque-ports.

2. Gent. Those men are happy; and so are all are near her.   50
I take it, she that carries up the train
Is that old noble lady, Duchess of Norfolk.

1. Gent. It is; and all the rest are countesses.

2. Gent. Their coronets say so. These are stars indeed;
And sometimes falling ones.

1. Gent.   No more of that. 55
[*Exit the last of the procession.*]

Enter a third GENTLEMAN.

1. Gent. God save you, sir! Where have you been broiling?

3. Gent. Among the crowd i' th' Abbey, where a finger
Could not be wedg'd in more. I am stifled
With the mere rankness of their joy.

2. Gent.   You saw
The ceremony?

3. Gent.   That I did.

1. Gent.   How was it? 60

3. Gent. Well worth the seeing.

2. Gent.   Good sir, speak it to us.

3. Gent. As well as I am able. The rich stream
Of lords and ladies, having brought the Queen
To a prepar'd place in the choir, fell off

A distance from her; while her Grace sat down 65
To rest a while, some half an hour or so,
In a rich chair of state, opposing freely
The beauty of her person to the people, —
Believe me, sir, she is the goodliest woman
That ever lay by man; — which when the people
Had the full view of, such a noise arose   71
As the shrouds make at sea in a stiff tempest,
As loud and to as many tunes. Hats, cloaks, —
Doublets, I think, — flew up; and had their faces
Been loose, this day they had been lost. Such joy
I never saw before. Great-belli'd women 76
That had not half a week to go, like rams
In the old time of war, would shake the press
And make 'em reel before 'em. No man living
Could say "This is my wife" there; all were woven
So strangely in one piece.

2. Gent.   But what follow'd? 81

3. Gent. At length her Grace rose and with modest paces
Came to the altar, where she kneel'd and saint-like
Cast her fair eyes to heaven and pray'd devoutly;
Then rose again and bow'd her to the people, 85
When by the Archbishop of Canterbury
She had all the royal makings of a queen,
As holy oil, Edward Confessor's crown,
The rod and bird of peace and all such emblems
Laid nobly on her; which perform'd, the choir, 90
With all the choicest music of the kingdom,
Together sung "Te Deum." So she parted,
And with the same full state pac'd back again
To York Place, where the feast is held.

1. Gent.   Sir,
You must no more call it York Place, that's past; 95
For since the Cardinal fell that title's lost.
'Tis now the King's, and call'd Whitehall.

3. Gent.   I know it,
But 'tis so lately alter'd that the old name
Is fresh about me.

2. Gent.   What two reverend bishops
Were those that went on each side of the Queen? 100

3. Gent. Stokesly and Gardiner; the one of Winchester,
Newly preferr'd from the King's secretary,
The other, London.

2. Gent.   He of Winchester
Is held no great good lover of the Archbishop's,
The virtuous Cranmer.

3. Gent.   All the land knows that.
However, yet there is no great breach; when it comes, 106
Cranmer will find a friend will not shrink from him.

2. Gent. Who may that be, I pray you?

3. Gent.   Thomas Cromwell;
A man in much esteem with th' King, and truly

47. **conscience.** Cf. II.ii.17-19. 67. **opposing:** exhibiting. 72. **shrouds:** ropes. 77. **rams:** battering rams. 92. **parted:** departed.

A worthy friend. The King has made him Master
O' th' Jewel House,   111
And one, already, of the Privy Council.
    2. Gent. He will deserve more.
    3. Gent.   Yes, without all doubt.
Come, gentlemen, ye shall go my way, which
Is to th' court, and there ye shall be my guests; 115
Something I can command. As I walk thither,
I'll tell ye more.
    Both.   You may command us, sir.
                                        [*Exeunt.*

SCENE II. [*Kimbolton.*]

Enter KATHERINE, *Dowager, sick; led between*
    GRIFFITH, *her gentleman usher, and* PATIENCE, *her*
    woman.

    Grif. How does your Grace?
    Kath.   O Griffith, sick to death!
My legs, like loaden branches, bow to th' earth,
Willing to leave their burden. Reach a chair.
So; now, methinks, I feel a little ease.
Didst thou not tell me, Griffith, as thou led'st me, 5
That the great child of honour, Cardinal Wolsey,
Was dead?
    Grif. Yes, madam; but I think your Grace,
Out of the pain you suffer'd, gave no ear to't.
    Kath. Prithee, good Griffith, tell me how he died.
If well, he stepp'd before me, happily   10
For my example.
    Grif.   Well, the voice goes, madam:
For after the stout Earl Northumberland
Arrested him at York, and brought him forward,
As a man sorely tainted, to his answer,
He fell sick suddenly and grew so ill   15
He could not sit his mule.
    Kath.   Alas, poor man!
    Grif. At last, with easy roads, he came to Leices-
        ter,
Lodg'd in the abbey; where the reverend abbot
With all his covent honourably receiv'd him;
To whom he gave these words: "O, father abbot, 20
An old man, broken with the storms of state,
Is come to lay his weary bones among ye;
Give him a little earth for charity!"
So went to bed, where eagerly his sickness
Pursu'd him still; and, three nights after this, 25
About the hour of eight, which he himself
Foretold should be his last, full of repentance,
Continual meditations, tears, and sorrows,
He gave his honours to the world again,
His blessed part to heaven, and slept in peace. 30
    Kath. So may he rest; his faults lie gently on
        him!

Yet thus far, Griffith, give me leave to speak him,
And yet with charity. He was a man
Of an unbounded stomach, ever ranking
Himself with princes; one that, by suggestion 35
Tied all the kingdom. Simony was fair-play;
His own opinion was his law; i' th' presence
He would say untruths; and be ever double
Both in his words and meaning. He was never,
But where he meant to ruin, pitiful.   40
His promises were, as he then was, mighty;
But his performance, as he is now, nothing.
Of his own body he was ill, and gave
The clergy ill example.
    Grif.   Noble madam,
Men's evil manners live in brass; their virtues 45
We write in water. May it please your Highness
To hear me speak his good now?
    Kath.   Yes, good Griffith;
I were malicious else.
    Grif.   This Cardinal,
Though from an humble stock, undoubtedly
Was fashion'd to much honour from his cradle. 50
He was a scholar, and a ripe and good one;
Exceeding wise, fair-spoken, and persuading;
Lofty and sour to them that lov'd him not,
But to those men that sought him, sweet as summer.
And though he were unsatisfied in getting,   55
Which was a sin, yet in bestowing, madam,
He was most princely: ever witness for him
Those twins of learning that he rais'd in you,
Ipswich and Oxford! one of which fell with him,
Unwilling to outlive the good that did it;   60
The other, though unfinish'd, yet so famous,
So excellent in art, and still so rising,
That Christendom shall ever speak his virtue.
His overthrow heap'd happiness upon him;
For then, and not till then, he felt himself   65
And found the blessedness of being little;
And, to add greater honours to his age
Than man could give him, he died fearing God.
    Kath. After my death I wish no other herald,
No other speaker of my living actions   70
To keep mine honour from corruption,
But such an honest chronicler as Griffith.
Whom I most hated living, thou hast made me,
With thy religious truth and modesty,
Now in his ashes honour. Peace be with him! 75
Patience, be near me still, and set me lower;
I have not long to trouble thee. Good Griffith,
Cause the musicians play me that sad note
I nam'd my knell, whilst I sit meditating
On that celestial harmony I go to.   80
                        [*Sad and solemn music.*

Sc. ii, 10. **happily:** haply. 14. **tainted:** discredited. 17. **roads:** stages. 19. **covent:** convent, monastery. 34. **stomach:**
pride. 35. **suggestion:** underhand methods. 36. **Tied:** bound, got into his clutches. 37. **presence:** i.e., of the king. 43.
ill: ill-behaved. 60. **the good ... it:** the good man that founded it. 61. **The other:** Christ Church, originally Cardinal College. 74. **modesty:** moderation.

Grif. She is asleep. Good wench, let's sit down quiet
For fear we wake her; softly, gentle Patience.

The vision. Enter, solemnly tripping one after another, six personages, clad in white robes, wearing on their heads garlands of bays, and golden vizards on their faces; branches of bays or palm in their hands. They first congee unto her, then dance; and, at certain changes, the first two hold a spare garland over her head; at which the other four make reverent curtsies. Then the two that held the garland deliver the same to the other next two, who observe the same order in their changes, and holding the garland over her head; which done, they deliver the same garland to the last two, who likewise observe the same order; at which, as it were by inspiration, she makes in her sleep signs of rejoicing, and holdeth up her hands to heaven: and so in their dancing vanish, carrying the garland with them. The music continues.

Kath. Spirits of peace, where are ye? Are ye all gone
And leave me here in wretchedness behind ye?

Grif. Madam, we are here.

Kath. 　　　　　　　It is not you I call for.
Saw ye none enter since I slept?

Grif. 　　　　　　　None, madam. 86

Kath. No? Saw you not, even now, a blessed troop
Invite me to a banquet, whose bright faces
Cast thousand beams upon me, like the sun?
They promis'd me eternal happiness, 　　90
And brought me garlands, Griffith, which I feel
I am not worthy yet to wear. I shall, assuredly.

Grif. I am most joyful, madam, such good dreams
Possess your fancy.

Kath. 　　　　Bid the music leave, 　94
They are harsh and heavy to me. [*Music ceases.*

Pat. 　　　　　　　Do you note
How much her Grace is alter'd on the sudden?
How long her face is drawn! How pale she looks,
And of an earthy cold! Mark her eyes!

Grif. She is going, wench. Pray, pray.

Pat. 　　　　　　　Heaven comfort her!

Enter a MESSENGER.

Mess. An't like your Grace, —

Kath. 　　　　　You are a saucy fellow. 100
Deserve we no more reverence?

Grif. 　　　　　　You are to blame,
Knowing she will not lose her wonted greatness,
To use so rude behaviour. Go to, kneel.

Mess. I humbly do entreat your Highness' pardon;

My haste made me unmannerly. There is staying 　　105
A gentleman, sent from the King, to see you.

Kath. Admit him entrance, Griffith; but this fellow
Let me ne'er see again. 　　　[*Exit Messenger.*

Enter CAPUCIUS.

　　　　　　　If my sight fail not,
You should be lord ambassador from the Emperor,
My royal nephew, and your name Capucius. 110

Cap. Madam, the same; your servant.

Kath. 　　　　　　　O, my lord,
The times and titles now are alter'd strangely
With me since first you knew me. But, I pray you,
What is your pleasure with me?

Cap. 　　　　　　Noble lady,
First, mine own service to your Grace; the next,
The King's request that I would visit you; 　116
Who grieves much for your weakness and by me
Sends you his princely commendations
And heartily entreats you take good comfort.

Kath. O my good lord, that comfort comes too late; 　　120
'Tis like a pardon after execution.
That gentle physic given in time had cur'd me;
But now I am past all comforts here but prayers.
How does his Highness?

Cap. 　　　Madam, in good health.

Kath. So may he ever do! and ever flourish, 125
When I shall dwell with worms, and my poor name
Banish'd the kingdom! Patience, is that letter
I caused you write yet sent away?

Pat. 　　　　　　　No, madam.
　　　　　　　[*Giving it to Katherine.*]

Kath. Sir, I most humbly pray you to deliver
This to my lord the King.

Cap. 　　　Most willing, madam.

Kath. In which I have commended to his goodness 　131
The model of our chaste loves, his young daughter;
The dews of heaven fall thick in blessings on her!
Beseeching him to give her virtuous breeding, —
She is young, and of a noble modest nature, 135
I hope she will deserve well, — and a little
To love her for her mother's sake that lov'd him
Heaven knows how dearly. My next poor petition
Is, that his noble Grace would have some pity
Upon my wretched women, that so long 　140
Have follow'd both my fortunes faithfully;
Of which there is not one, I dare avow
And now I should not lie, but will deserve,
For virtue and true beauty of the soul,
For honesty and decent carriage, 　　145
A right good husband; let him be a noble;
And, sure, those men are happy that shall have 'em.

---

82. s.d. *congee:* curtsey. *changes:* figures. 94. **music leave:** musicians cease. 102. **lose:** give up. 132. **model:** image.

The last is, for my men, — they are the poorest,
But poverty could never draw 'em from me —
That they may have their wages duly paid 'em,
And something over to remember me by.   151
If Heaven had pleas'd to have given me longer life
And able means, we had not parted thus.
These are the whole contents; and, good my lord,
By that you love the dearest in this world,   155
As you wish Christian peace to souls departed,
Stand these poor people's friend, and urge the King
To do me this last right.
    Cap.   By heaven, I will,
Or let me lose the fashion of a man!
    Kath. I thank you, honest lord. Remember
        me   160
In all humility unto his Highness.
Say his long trouble now is passing
Out of this world; tell him, in death I bless'd him,
For so I will. Mine eyes grow dim. Farewell,
My lord. Griffith, farewell. Nay, Patience,   165
You must not leave me yet. I must to bed;
Call in more women. When I am dead, good
        wench,
Let me be us'd with honour. Strew me over
With maiden flowers that all the world may know
I was a chaste wife to my grave. Embalm me,
Then lay me forth. Although unqueen'd, yet
        like   171
A queen and daughter to a king inter me.
I can no more.   [*Exeunt, leading Katherine.*

ACT V

Scene I. [*London. A gallery in the palace.*]

Enter GARDINER, Bishop of Winchester, *a* PAGE
    with a torch before him, met by SIR THOMAS
    LOVELL.

    Gar. It's one o'clock, boy, is't not?
    Page.   It hath struck.
    Gar. These should be hours for necessities,
Not for delights; times to repair our nature
With comforting repose, and not for us
To waste these times. Good hour of night, Sir
        Thomas!   5
Whither so late?
    Lov.   Came you from the King, my lord?
    Gar. I did, Sir Thomas; and left him at primero
With the Duke of Suffolk.
    Lov.   I must to him too,
Before he go to bed. I'll take my leave.
    Gar. Not yet, Sir Thomas Lovell. What's the
        matter?   10
It seems you are in haste. An if there be
No great offence belongs to't, give your friend

Some touch of your late business. Affairs, that walk,
As they say spirits do, at midnight, have
In them a wilder nature than the business   15
That seeks dispatch by day.
    Lov.   My lord, I love you;
And durst commend a secret to your ear
Much weightier than this work. The Queen's
    in labour,
They say in great extremity; and fear'd
She'll with the labour end.
    Gar.   The fruit she goes with
I pray for heartily, that it may find   21
Good time, and live; but for the stock, Sir Thomas,
I wish it grubb'd up now.
    Lov.   Methinks I could
Cry the amen; and yet my conscience says
She's a good creature, and, sweet lady, does   25
Deserve our better wishes.
    Gar.   But, sir, sir,
Hear me, Sir Thomas. You're a gentleman
Of mine own way; I know you wise, religious;
And, let me tell you, it will ne'er be well,
'Twill not, Sir Thomas Lovell, take 't of me,   30
Till Cranmer, Cromwell, her two hands, and she
Sleep in their graves.
    Lov.   Now, sir, you speak of two
The most remark'd i' th' kingdom. As for Crom-
        well,
Beside that of the Jewel House, is made Master
O' th' Rolls, and the King's secretary; further, sir, 35
Stands in the gap and trade of moe preferments,
With which the time will load him. Th' Archbishop
Is the King's hand and tongue; and who dare speak
One syllable against him?
    Gar.   Yes, yes, Sir Thomas,
There are that dare; and I myself have ventur'd 40
To speak my mind of him: and indeed this day,
Sir, I may tell it you, I think I have
Incens'd the lords o' th' council that he is
(For so I know he is, they know he is)
A most arch heretic, a pestilence   45
That does infect the land; with which they mov'd
Have broken with the King, who hath so far
Given ear to our complaint, of his great grace
And princely care forseeing those fell mischiefs
Our reasons laid before him, hath commanded
To-morrow morning to the council-board   51
He be convented. He's a rank weed, Sir Thomas,
And we must root him out. From your affairs
I hinder you too long. Good-night, Sir Thomas.
    Lov. Many good-nights, my lord! I rest your
        servant.   [*Exeunt Gardiner and Page.* 55

Enter the KING *and* SUFFOLK.

    King. Charles, I will play no more to-night.

Act V, sc. i, 7. **primero:** a card game.   13. **touch:** inkling.   22. **time:** fortune.   28. **way:** religious belief.   36. **gap and trade:** open road.   43. **Incens'd:** led to believe.   47. **broken:** communicated.   52. **convented:** summoned.

My mind 's not on't; you are too hard for me.
Suf. Sir, I did never win of you before.
King. But little, Charles;
Nor shall not, when my fancy's on my play.   60
Now, Lovell, from the Queen what is the news?
Lov. I could not personally deliver to her
What you commanded me, but by her woman
I sent your message; who return'd her thanks
In the great'st humbleness, and desir'd your Highness   65
Most heartily to pray for her.
King.   What say'st thou, ha?
To pray for her? What, is she crying out?
Lov. So said her woman; and that her sufferance made
Almost each pang a death.
King.   Alas, good lady!
Suf. God safely quit her of her burden, and
With gentle travail, to the gladding of   71
Your Highness with an heir!
King.   'Tis midnight, Charles;
Prithee, to bed; and in thy prayers remember
Th' estate of my poor queen. Leave me alone;
For I must think of that which company   75
Would not be friendly to.
Suf.   I wish your Highness
A quiet night; and my good mistress will
Remember in my prayers.
King.   Charles, good-night.
                    [*Exit Suffolk.*

Enter SIR ANTHONY DENNY.
Well, sir, what follows?
Den. Sir, I have brought my lord the Archbishop,
As you commanded me.
King.   Ha! Canterbury?   81
Den. Ay, my good lord.
King.   'Tis true; where is he, Denny?
Den. He attends your Highness' pleasure.
King.   Bring him to us.
                    [*Exit Denny.*]
Lov. [*Aside.*] This is about that which the bishop spake.
I am happily come hither.   85

Re-enter DENNY, *with* CRANMER.
King. Avoid the gallery. (*Lovell seems to stay.*)
     Ha! I have said. Be gone.
What!   [*Exeunt Lovell and Denny.*
Cran. [*Aside.*] I am fearful; wherefore frowns
     he thus?
'Tis his aspect of terror. All's not well.

King. How now, my lord! you do desire to
     know   89
Wherefore I sent for you.
Cran.   [*Kneeling.*] It is my duty
To attend your Highness' pleasure.
King.   Pray you, arise,
My good and gracious Lord of Canterbury.
Come, you and I must walk a turn together;
I have news to tell you. Come, come, give me your
     hand.
Ah, my good lord, I grieve at what I speak   95
And am right sorry to repeat what follows.
I have, and most unwillingly, of late
Heard many grievous, I do say, my lord,
Grievous complaints of you; which, being considered,
Have mov'd us and our council, that you shall   100
This morning come before us; where, I know,
You cannot with such freedom purge yourself
But that, till further trial in those charges
Which will require your answer, you must take
Your patience to you, and be well contented   105
To make your house our Tower. You a brother of us,
It fits we thus proceed, or else no witness
Would come against you.
Cran. [*Kneeling.*] I humbly thank your Highness;
And am right glad to catch this good occasion
Most throughly to be winnowed, where my chaff   110
And corn shall fly asunder; for I know
There's none stands under more calumnious tongues
Than I myself, poor man.
King.   Stand up, good Canterbury!
Thy truth and thy integrity is rooted
In us, thy friend. Give me thy hand, stand up;   115
Prithee, let's walk. Now, by my holidame,
What manner of man are you? My lord, I look'd
You would have given me your petition, that
I should have ta'en some pains to bring together
Yourself and your accusers, and to have heard
     you   120
Without indurance further.
Cran.   Most dread liege,
The good I stand on is my truth and honesty.
If they shall fail, I, with mine enemies,
Will triumph o'er my person; which I weigh not,
Being of those virtues vacant. I fear nothing   125
What can be said against me.
King.   Know you not
How your state stands i' th' world, with the whole
     world?
Your enemies are many, and not small; their practices

---

68. **sufferance:** suffering. 74. **estate:** condition. 86. **Avoid:** leave. 106. **brother of us:** member of the Council. 116. **holidame:** halidom, holiness. 121. **indurance:** durance, imprisonment; or, perhaps, suffering. 124-125. **which...vacant:** which does not interest me if it is void of truth and honesty.

Must bear the same proportion; and not ever
The justice and the truth o' th' question carries 130
The due o' th' verdict with it.   At what ease
Might corrupt minds procure knaves as corrupt
To swear against you?   Such things have been done.
You are potently oppos'd, and with a malice
Of as great size.   Ween you of better luck,   135
I mean, in perjur'd witness, than your Master,
Whose minister you are, whiles here He liv'd
Upon this naughty earth?   Go to, go to!
You take a precipice for no leap of danger,
And woo your own destruction.
 Cran.   God and your Majesty
Protect mine innocence, or I fall into   141
The trap is laid for me!
 King.   Be of good cheer;
They shall no more prevail than we give way to.
Keep comfort to you; and this morning see
You do appear before them.   If they shall chance,
In charging you with matters, to commit you,   146
The best persuasions to the contrary
Fail not to use, and with what vehemency
Th' occasion shall instruct you.   If entreaties
Will render you no remedy, this ring   150
Deliver them, and your appeal to us
There make before them.   Look, the good man
  weeps!
He's honest, on mine honour.   God's blest mother!
I swear he is true-hearted; and a soul
None better in my kingdom.   Get you gone,   155
And do as I have bid you.   (*Exit Cranmer.*)   He
  has strangled
His language in his tears.

  Enter OLD LADY [LOVELL *following*].
 Gent. (*Within.*)   Come back!   What mean you?
 Old L.   I'll not come back; the tidings that I bring
Will make my boldness manners.   Now, good
  angels
Fly o'er thy royal head, and shade thy person   160
Under their blessed wings!
 King.   Now, by thy looks
I guess thy message.   Is the Queen deliver'd?
Say, ay; and of a boy.
 Old L.   Ay, ay, my liege;
And of a lovely boy.   The God of heaven
Both now and ever bless her! 'tis a girl,   165
Promises boys hereafter.   Sir, your queen
Desires your visitation, and to be
Acquainted with this stranger.   'Tis as like you
As cherry is to cherry.
 King.   Lovell!
 Lov.   Sir?
 King.   Give her an hundred marks.   I'll to the
  Queen.   [*Exit.*   170

 Old L.   An hundred marks!   By this light, I'll ha'
  more.
An ordinary groom is for such payment.
I will have more or scold it out of him.
Said I for this, the girl was like to him?
I will have more, or else unsay 't; and now,   175
While it is hot, I'll put it to the issue.   [*Exeunt.*

SCENE II.   [*Lobby before the council-chamber.*]

 [*Pursuivants, Pages, etc., attending.*]   *Enter*
  CRANMER, Archbishop of Canterbury.
 Cran.   I hope I am not too late; and yet the
  gentleman
That was sent to me from the council pray'd me
To make great haste.   All fast?   what means this?
  Ho!
Who waits there?   Sure, you know me?

    Enter KEEPER.
 Keep.   Yes, my lord;
But yet I cannot help you.   5
 Cran.   Why?
 Keep.   Your Grace must wait till you be call'd for.

    Enter DOCTOR BUTTS.
 Cran.   So.
 Butts. [*Aside.*]   This is a piece of malice.   I am
  glad
I came this way so happily; the King
Shall understand it presently.   [*Exit.*
 Cran.   [*Aside.*]   'Tis Butts,   10
The King's physician.   As he pass'd along,
How earnestly he cast his eyes upon me!
Pray Heaven, he sound not my disgrace!   For
  certain,
This is of purpose laid by some that hate me —
God turn their hearts!   I never sought their
  malice —   15
To quench mine honour; they would shame to make
  me
Wait else at door, a fellow-counsellor,
'Mong boys, grooms, and lackeys.   But their pleas-
  ures
Must be fulfill'd, and I attend with patience.

  Enter the KING *and* BUTTS, *at a window above.*
 Butts.   I'll show your Grace the strangest sight —
 King.   What's that, Butts?   20
 Butts.   I think your Highness saw this many a
  day.
 King.   Body o' me, where is it?
 Butts.   There, my lord:
The high promotion of his Grace of Canterbury,
Who holds his state at door, 'mongst pursuivants,

---

129. **ever**: always.   131. **due o' th' verdict**: the just verdict.   170. **mark**: 13s.4d.   172. **is for**: is entitled to.
 Sc. ii, 13. sound: proclaim.   24. **pursuivants**: heralds' assistants, messengers.

Pages, and footboys.
  King.   Ha! 'tis he, indeed.   25
Is this the honour they do one another?
'Tis well there's one above 'em yet. I had thought
They had parted so much honesty among 'em,
At least, good manners, as not thus to suffer
A man of his place and so near our favour   30
To dance attendance on their lordships' pleasures,
And at the door too, like a post with packets.
By holy Mary, Butts, there's knavery.
Let 'em alone, and draw the curtain close;
We shall hear more anon.   [*Exeunt.*] 35

[SCENE III. *The Council-chamber.*]

A council-table brought in with chairs and stools,
and placed under the state. Enter LORD CHAN-
CELLOR; *places himself at the upper end of the*
table on the left hand; a seat being left void above him,
*as for Canterbury's seat. *DUKE OF SUFFOLK,
DUKE OF NORFOLK, SURREY, LORD CHAMBER-
LAIN, GARDINER, *seat themselves in order on each*
*side. *CROMWELL *at lower end, as secretary.*
[KEEPER *at the door.*]
  Chan. Speak to the business, master secretary.
Why are we met in council?
  Crom.   Please your honours,
The chief cause concerns his Grace of Canter-
    bury.
  Gar. Has he had knowledge of it?
  Crom.   Yes.
  Nor.   Who waits there?
  Keep. Without, my noble lords?
  Gar.   Yes.
  Keep.   My Lord Archbishop;
And has done half an hour, to know your pleasures. 6
  Chan. Let him come in.
  Keep.   Your Grace may enter now.

CRANMER [*enters and*] *approaches the council-*
table.

  Chan. My good Lord Archbishop, I'm very sorry
To sit here at this present, and behold
That chair stand empty; but we all are men,   10
In our own natures frail, and capable
Of our flesh; few are angels: out of which frailty
And want of wisdom, you, that best should teach
    us,
Have misdemean'd yourself, and not a little,
Toward the King first, then his laws, in filling   15
The whole realm by your teaching and your chap-
    lains'
(For so we are inform'd) with new opinions

Divers and dangerous, which are heresies
And, not reform'd, may prove pernicious.   19
  Gar. Which reformation must be sudden too,
My noble lords; for those that tame wild horses
Pace 'em not in their hands to make 'em gentle,
But stop their mouths with stubborn bits and spur
    'em
Till they obey the manage. If we suffer,
Out of our easiness and childish pity   25
To one man's honour, this contagious sickness,
Farewell all physic! And what follows then?
Commotions, uproars, with a general taint
Of the whole state; as, of late days, our neighbours,
The upper Germany, can dearly witness,   30
Yet freshly pitied in our memories.
  Cran. My good lords, hitherto, in all the progress
Both of my life and office, I have labour'd
And with no little study, that my teaching
And the strong course of my authority   35
Might go one way, and safely; and the end
Was ever to do well; nor is there living,
I speak it with a single heart, my lords,
A man that more detests, more stirs against,
Both in his private conscience and his place,   40
Defacers of a public peace than I do.
Pray Heaven, the King may never find a heart
With less allegiance in it! Men that make
Envy and crooked malice nourishment
Dare bite the best. I do beseech your lordships,   45
That, in this case of justice, my accusers,
Be what they will, may stand forth face to face,
And freely urge against me.
  Suf.   Nay, my lord,
That cannot be. You are a councillor,
And, by that virtue, no man dare accuse you.   50
  Gar. My lord, because we have business of more
    moment,
We will be short with you. 'Tis his Highness'
    pleasure
And our consent, for better trial of you,
From hence you be committed to the Tower;
Where, being but a private man again,   55
You shall know many dare accuse you boldly,
More than, I fear, you are provided for.
  Cran. Ah, my good Lord of Winchester, I thank
    you.
You are always my good friend; if your will pass,
I shall both find your lordship judge and juror,
You are so merciful. I see your end;   61
'Tis my undoing. Love and meekness, lord,
Become a churchman better than ambition;
Win straying souls with modesty again,
Cast none away. That I shall clear myself,   65

---

28. **parted:** shared.
    Sc. iii, 9. **present:** present time.   11. **capable:** susceptible to the weaknesses.   22. **Pace ... hands:** do not train them by
leading them.   24. **manage:** training.   39. **more stirs:** is more active.   48. **urge against:** accuse.   50. **by that virtue:** because of your being a Privy Councillor.

Lay all the weight ye can upon my patience,
I make as little doubt as you do conscience
In doing daily wrongs. I could say more,
But reverence to your calling makes me modest.

    Gar. My lord, my lord, you are a sectary,   70
That's the plain truth. Your painted gloss discovers,
To men that understand you, words and weakness.

    Crom. My Lord of Winchester, you are a little,
By your good favour, too sharp; men so noble,
However faulty, yet should find respect   75
For what they have been. 'Tis a cruelty
To load a falling man.

    Gar.   Good master secretary,
I cry your honour mercy. You may, worst
Of all this table, say so.

    Crom.   Why, my lord?

    Gar. Do not I know you for a favourer   80
Of this new sect? Ye are not sound.

    Crom.   Not sound?

    Gar. Not sound, I say.

    Crom.   Would you were half so honest!
Men's prayers then would seek you, not their fears.

    Gar. I shall remember this bold language.

    Crom.   Do.
Remember your bold life too.

    [*Chan.*]   This is too much.   85
Forbear for shame, my lords.

    Gar.   I have done.

    Crom.   And I.

    [*Chan.*] Then thus for you, my lord: it stands
    agreed,
I take it, by all voices, that forthwith
You be convey'd to th' Tower a prisoner;
There to remain till the King's further pleasure   90
Be known unto us. Are you all agreed, lords?

    All. We are.

    Cran.   Is there no other way of mercy
But I must needs to th' Tower, my lords?

    Gar.   What other
Would you expect? You are strangely troublesome.
Let some o' th' guard be ready there.

              Enter Guard.

    Cran.   For me?   95
Must I go like a traitor thither?

    Gar.   Receive him,
And see him safe i' th' Tower.

    Cran.   Stay, good my lords,
I have a little yet to say. Look there, my lords;
By virtue of that ring, I take my cause
Out of the gripes of cruel men, and give it   100
To a most noble judge, the King my master.

    Cham. This is the King's ring.

    Sur.   'Tis no counterfeit.

    Suf. 'Tis the right ring, by heaven! I told ye all,
When we first put this dangerous stone a-rolling,
'Twould fall upon ourselves.

    Nor.   Do you think, my lords,
The King will suffer but the little finger   106
Of this man to be vex'd?

    Cham.   'Tis now too certain.
How much more is his life in value with him?
Would I were fairly out on't!

    Crom.   My mind gave me,
In seeking tales and informations   110
Against this man, whose honesty the devil
And his disciples only envy at,
Ye blew the fire that burns ye. Now have at ye!

    Enter KING, *frowning on them; takes his seat.*

    Gar. Dread sovereign, how much are we bound
    to Heaven
In daily thanks, that gave us such a prince;   115
Not only good and wise but most religious;
One that, in all obedience, makes the Church
The chief aim of his honour; and, to strengthen
That holy duty, out of dear respect,
His royal self in judgement comes to hear   120
The cause betwixt her and this great offender.

    King. You were ever good at sudden commendations,
Bishop of Winchester. But know, I come not
To hear such flattery now, and in my presence;
They are too thin and [bare] to hide offences.   125
To me you cannot reach you play the spaniel,
And think with wagging of your tongue to win
    me;
But, whatsoe'er thou tak'st me for, I'm sure
Thou hast a cruel nature and a bloody.
[*To Cranmer.*] Good man, sit down. Now let me
    see the proudest   130
He, that dares most, but wag his finger at thee:
By all that's holy, he had better starve
Than but once think [this] place becomes thee not.

    Sur. May it please your Grace, —

    King.   No, sir, it does not please me.
I had thought I had had men of some understanding   135
And wisdom of my council; but I find none.
Was it discretion, lords, to let this man,
This good man, — few of you deserve that title, —
This honest man, wait like a lousy footboy
At chamber-door? and one as great as you are?   140
Why, what a shame was this? Did my commission
Bid ye so far forget yourselves? I gave ye
Power as he was a counsellor to try him, —
Not as a groom. There's some of ye, I see,
More out of malice than integrity,   145

70. **sectary:** schismatic. 71. **painted gloss:** fine disingenuous speech. **discovers:** reveals. 78. **worst:** with least right. 85, 87. [*Chan.*] (Capell). *Cham.* F. 109. gave: told. 125. [bare] (Malone). base F. 132. **starve:** die. 133. [this] (Rowe). *his* F.

Would try him to the utmost had ye mean;
Which ye shall never have while I live.
 Chan.   Thus far,
My most dread sovereign, may it like your Grace
To let my tongue excuse all. What was purpos'd
Concerning his imprisonment was rather, 150
If there be faith in men, meant for his trial
And fair purgation to the world, than malice,
I'm sure, in me.
 King. Well, well, my lords, respect him;
Take him, and use him well, he's worthy of it. 155
I will say thus much for him, if a prince
May be beholding to a subject, I
Am for his love and service so to him.
Make me no more ado, but all embrace him.
Be friends, for shame, my lords! My Lord of
  Canterbury,   160
I have a suit which you must not deny me;
That is, a fair young maid that yet wants baptism,
You must be godfather, and answer for her.
 Cran. The greatest monarch now alive may
  glory
In such an honour; how may I deserve it, 165
That am a poor and humble subject to you?
 King. Come, come, my lord, you'd spare your
spoons. You shall have two noble partners with
you, the old Duchess of Norfolk and Lady Marquess
Dorset. Will these please you?   170
Once more, my Lord of Winchester, I charge you,
Embrace and love this man.
 Gar.   With a true heart
And brother-love I do it.
 Cran.   And let Heaven
Witness how dear I hold this confirmation.
 King. Good man, those joyful tears show thy
  true heart.   175
The common voice, I see, is verified
Of thee, which says thus, "Do my Lord of Can-
  terbury
A shrewd turn, and he is your friend for ever."
Come, lords, we trifle time away; I long
To have this young one made a Christian. 180
As I have made ye one, lords, one remain;
So I grow stronger, you more honour gain.
               [Exeunt.

  Scene [IV. *The palace yard.*]

Noise and tumult within. Enter PORTER *and*
his MAN.

 Port. You'll leave your noise anon, ye rascals;
do you take the court for Paris-garden? Ye rude
slaves, leave your gaping.

 (*Within.*) Good master porter, I belong to th'
larder.   5
 Port. Belong to th' gallows, and be hang'd, ye
rogue! Is this a place to roar in? Fetch me a dozen
crab-tree staves, and strong ones; these are but
switches to 'em. I'll scratch your heads. You
must be seeing christenings? Do you look for ale
and cakes here, you rude rascals?   11
 Man. Pray, sir, be patient. 'Tis as much im-
  possible —
Unless we sweep 'em from the door with cannons —
To scatter 'em, as 'tis to make 'em sleep
On May-day morning, which will never be. 15
We may as well push against Powle's as stir 'em.
 Port. How got they in, and be hang'd?
 Man. Alas, I know not; how gets the tide in?
As much as one sound cudgel of four foot —
You see the poor remainder — could distribute, 20
I made no spare, sir.
 Port.   You did nothing, sir.
 Man. I am not Samson, nor Sir Guy, nor Col-
  brand,
To mow 'em down before me; but if I spar'd any
That had a head to hit, either young or old,
He or she, cuckold or cuckold-maker,   25
Let me ne'er hope to see a chine again;
And that I would not for a cow, God save her!
 (*Within.*) Do you hear, master porter?
 Port. I shall be with you presently, good master
puppy. — Keep the door close, sirrah.
 Man. What would you have me do?   31
 Port. What should you do, but knock 'em down
by th' dozens? Is this Moorfields to muster in?
Or have we some strange Indian with the great
tool come to court, the women so besiege us? Bless
me, what a fry of fornication is at door! On my
Christian conscience, this one christening will beget
a thousand; here will be father, godfather, and all
together.   39
 Man. The spoons will be the bigger, sir. There
is a fellow somewhat near the door, he should be a
brazier by his face, for, o' my conscience, twenty of
the dog-days now reign in 's nose; all that stand
about him are under the line, they need no other
penance: that firedrake did I hit three times on 45
the head, and three times was his nose discharged
against me; he stands there, like a mortar-piece, to
blow us. There was a haberdasher's wife of small
wit near him, that rail'd upon me till her pink'd
porringer fell off her head, for kindling such a 50
combustion in the state. I miss'd the meteor
once, and hit that woman; who cried out "Clubs!"

---

146. **mean:** means. 168. **spoons:** the customary gift from a godfather. 178. **shrewd:** ill.
 Sc. iv, 2. **Paris-garden:** a bear-garden near the Globe Theatre. 3. **gaping:** bawling. 16. **Powle's:** St. Paul's Cathedral.
22. **Guy.** In the romance of Guy of Warwick, Sir Guy kills the Danish giant, Colbrand. 26. **chine:** strictly, backbone;
used for a joint of beef. 27. **for a cow.** A proverbial phrase. 33. **Moorfields:** a recreation field on the outskirts. 42.
brazier: (1) a worker in brass, (2) a charcoal stove. 44. **line:** equator. 45. **firedrake:** meteor. 50. **pink'd porringer:** a
round cap ornamented with small holes. 52. **"Clubs!":** the rallying cry of the apprentices.

when I might see from far some forty truncheoners
draw to her succour, which were the hope o' the
Strand, where she was quartered. They fell on; 55
I made good my place; at length they came to th'
broomstaff to me; I defi'd 'em still; when suddenly
a file of boys behind 'em, loose shot, deliver'd such a
shower of pebbles, that I was fain to draw mine
honour in, and let 'em win the work. The devil
was amongst 'em, I think, surely.   62

Port. These are the youths that thunder at a
playhouse and fight for bitten apples, that no
audience but the tribulation of Tower-hill or the
limbs of Limehouse, their dear brothers, are able to
endure. I have some of 'em in *Limbo Patrum*, and
there they are like to dance these three days; besides the running banquet of two beadles that is to
come.   70

Enter LORD CHAMBERLAIN.

Cham. Mercy o' me, what a multitude are here!
They grow still too; from all parts they are coming
As if we kept a fair here! Where are these porters,
These lazy knaves? Y' have made a fine hand,
        fellows;
There's a trim rabble let in. Are all these   75
Your faithful friends o' th' suburbs? We shall
        have
Great store of room, no doubt, left for the ladies,
When they pass back from the christening.
Port.   An't please your honour,
We are but men; and what so many may do,
Not being torn a-pieces, we have done.   80
An army cannot rule 'em.
Cham.   As I live,
If the King blame me for't, I'll lay ye all
By th' heels, and suddenly; and on your heads
Clap round fines for neglect. Ye're lazy knaves;
And here ye lie baiting of bombards, when   85
Ye should do service. Hark! the trumpets sound;
They're come already from the christening.
Go, break among the press, and find a way out
To let the troop pass fairly; or I'll find   89
A Marshalsea shall hold ye play these two months.
Port. Make way there for the princess.
Man.   You great fellow,
Stand close up, or I'll make your head ache.
Port. You i' th' camlet, get up o' th' rail;
I'll peck you o'er the pales else.   [*Exeunt.*

SCENE [V. *The palace.*]

Enter trumpets, sounding; then two Aldermen,
    Lord Mayor, GARTER, CRANMER, Duke of
    Norfolk *with his marshal's staff,* Duke of Suf-
    folk, *two* Noblemen *bearing great standing-
    bowls for the christening-gifts; then four* Noblemen
    bearing a canopy, under which the Duchess of
    Norfolk, *godmother, bearing the child richly habited
    in a mantle, etc., train borne by a* Lady; *then fol-
    lows the* Marchioness Dorset, *the other godmother,
    and* Ladies. *The troop pass once about the stage,
    and Garter speaks.*

Gart. Heaven, from thy endless goodness send
prosperous life, long, and ever happy, to the high
and mighty Princess of England, Elizabeth!

Flourish. Enter KING *and* Guard.

Cran. [*Kneeling.*] And to your royal Grace and
        the good queen,   5
My noble partners and myself thus pray:
All comfort, joy in this most gracious lady
Heaven ever laid up to make parents happy
May hourly fall upon ye!
King.   Thank you, good Lord Archbishop.
What is her name?
Cran.   Elizabeth.
King.   Stand up, lord. 10
                  [*The King kisses the child.*
With this kiss take my blessing: God protect thee!
Into whose hand I give thy life.
Cran.   Amen.
King. My noble gossips, ye have been too prodi-
        gal.
I thank ye heartily; so shall this lady,   14
When she has so much English.
Cran.   Let me speak, sir,
For Heaven now bids me; and the words I utter
Let none think flattery for they'll find 'em truth.
This royal infant — Heaven still move about
        her! —
Though in her cradle, yet now promises
Upon this land a thousand thousand blessings 20
Which time shall bring to ripeness. She shall
        be —
But few now living can behold that goodness —
A pattern to all princes living with her,
And all that shall succeed. Saba was never
More covetous of wisdom and fair virtue   25

57. **to th' broomstaff:** to close quarters. 58. **loose shot:** throwers at random. 61. **work:** fortification. 65. **tribulation . . . Limehouse.** Not explained. *limbs* probably means limbs of the devil. 68. *Limbo Patrum:* the place bordering
on Hell where the souls of the saints abode who had died before Christ came. 69. **running banquet:** public whipping. 74.
hand: success (ironical). 76. **suburbs,** where disreputable people lived. 85. **baiting of bombards:** drinking from leathern
bottles. *Baiting* may be the word meaning *feed,* or that meaning *set the dogs on,* in which case the picture is that of them
crowding round like dogs at a bear-baiting. 90. **Marshalsea:** a prison in Southwark. 93. **camlet:** a rough cloth. 94.
peck . . . pales: pitch you over the palings.
    Sc. v, 13. **gossips:** god-parents. 24. **Saba:** the queen of Sheba.

Than this pure soul shall be.   All princely graces
That mould up such a mighty piece as this is,
With all the virtues that attend the good,
Shall still be doubled on her.   Truth shall nurse
    her,
Holy and heavenly thoughts still counsel her.   30
She shall be lov'd and fear'd: her own shall bless
    her;
Her foes shake like a field of beaten corn
And hang their heads with sorrow.   Good grows
    with her.
In her days every man shall eat in safety
Under his own vine what he plants, and sing   35
The merry songs of peace to all his neighbours.
God shall be truly known; and those about her
From her shall read the perfect ways of honour
And by those claim their greatness, not by blood.
Nor shall this peace sleep with her; but as when
The bird of wonder dies, the maiden phœnix,   41
Her ashes new create another heir
As great in admiration as herself;
So shall she leave her blessedness to one,
When heaven shall call her from this cloud of dark-
    ness,   45
Who from the sacred ashes of her honour
Shall star-like rise as great in fame as she was,
And so stand fix'd.   Peace, plenty, love, truth,
    terror,
That were the servants to this chosen infant,
Shall then be his, and like a vine grow to him.   50
Wherever the bright sun of heaven shall shine
His honour and the greatness of his name
Shall be, and make new nations.   He shall flourish,
And like a mountain cedar reach his branches
To all the plains about him.   Our children's chil-
    dren   55
Shall see this, and bless Heaven.
    King.   Thou speakest wonders.

Cran. She shall be, to the happiness of England,
An aged princess; many days shall see her,
And yet no day without a deed to crown it.
Would I had known no more! but she must die, 60
She must, the saints must have her; yet a virgin,
A most unspotted lily shall she pass
To the ground, and all the world shall mourn her.
    King. O Lord Archbishop,
Thou hast made me now a man! Never, before
This happy child, did I get anything.   66
This oracle of comfort has so pleas'd me
That when I am in heaven I shall desire
To see what this child does, and praise my Maker.
I thank ye all.   To you, my good Lord Mayor,
And you, good brethren, I am much beholding;   71
I have receiv'd much honour by your presence,
And ye shall find me thankful.   Lead the way, lords.
Ye must all see the Queen and she must thank ye,
She will be sick else.   This day, no man think   75
'Has business at his house; for all shall stay.
This little one shall make it holiday.   [*Exeunt.*

EPILOGUE

'Tis ten to one this play can never please
All that are here.   Some come to take their ease
And sleep an act or two; but those, we fear,
We've frighted with our trumpets; so, 'tis clear,
They'll say 'tis naught; others, to hear the city 5
Abus'd extremely, and to cry, "That's witty!"
Which we have not done neither: that, I fear,
All the expected good we're like to hear
For this play at this time, is only in
The merciful construction of good women;   10
For such a one we show'd 'em.   If they smile
And say 'twill do, I know, within a while
All the best men are ours; for 'tis ill hap
If they hold when their ladies bid 'em clap.

27. **piece:** personage.   44. **one:** James I.

The Tragedy of Titus Andronicus

UNDER THE DATE January 24, 1594, Henslowe's *Diary* marks "ne" (i.e., new, or newly revised) a play, *Titus & Ondronicous*, performed by the Earl of Sussex's Men, who played it again twice within the following fortnight. This is now generally recognized as the present play and identical with "A Noble Roman Historye of Tytus Andronicus," which, on February 6, 1594, was entered in the Stationers' Register to John Danter, though it has been suggested that the latter is an early edition of an eighteenth-century chapbook on the same subject, now in the Folger Library. Later in 1594 Danter printed a Quarto with a title page reading, *The most Lamentable Romaine Tragedie of Titus Andronicus: As it was Plaide by the Right Honourable the Earle of Darbie, Earle of Pembrooke, and Earle of Sussex their Seruants*. A Second Quarto with some changes was published in 1600, and a third, printed from the second, appeared in 1611. The text of the First Folio, derived from the Third Quarto, includes for the first time Act III, scene ii. The present text is based upon the First Quarto. A number of speech prefixes in the First Quarto are printed in the center of the page above the speeches they introduce. Whatever this may imply, the generous stage directions, many of which are descriptive and imperative, suggest a theatrical manuscript (perhaps the author's) as the origin of the text.

Despite Henslowe's designation of *Titus Andronicus* as new, the play was certainly written well before 1594. An anonymous play, *A Knacke to Know a Knave*, printed in 1594 but performed by Lord Strange's Men on June 10, 1592 (according to Henslowe, who marks it "ne"), contains positive allusions to Titus's "conquest on the Goths" and the offer made to him of the imperial crown. On April 11, 1592 (and six times thereafter up to June 6th), Lord Strange's Men performed for Henslowe a "new" play called *Tittus & Vespacia* [Vespasian]. Some scholars think that that play, which has not survived under that name, dealt with the conquest of Jerusalem by the emperor Vespasian and his son Titus; others, however, are inclined to identify it with *Titus Andronicus*, since in the same season of 1592 Lord Strange's Men twice performed a play called *Jerusallei.*, and it seems improbable that they would be presenting currently two plays on the same material. Furthermore, in *Eine sehr klägliche Tragaedia von Tito Andronico* (1620), a derivative of *Titus Andronicus* performed some time by English actors traveling in Germany, Lucius is named Vespasian. This fact suggests that the English play once had a Vespasian in it and may even have been called *Titus and Vespasian*. Henslowe's record that in January, 1592, Lord Strange's Men also performed a play called simply *Titus*, tends to confirm this possibility. In the Induction to *Bartholomew Fair* (1614) Ben Jonson took his now famous fling at *Titus Andronicus*: "He that will swear *Jeronimo* or *Andronicus* are the best plays yet, shall pass unexcepted at here, as a man whose judgment shews it is constant, and hath stood still these five-and-twenty or thirty years. Though it be an ignorance, it is a virtuous and staid ignorance...." A literal interpretation of Jonson's words would push the date of *Titus Andronicus* back to some time between 1585 and 1589, but it is hardly to be supposed that in his jesting mood Jonson was careful to be precise. The play could perhaps have been written as early as 1589, but 1591 or the early months of 1592 would seem a better conjecture.

Titus Andronicus has been commonly held to be Shakespeare's revision of an earlier play, but there has been no general agreement concerning the original author, or authors. There is, however, no necessity for looking beyond Shakespeare. The play, we know, was a hit, and one may reasonably suppose that the First Quarto, apparently printed from a theatrical manuscript, represents it as it was performed in 1594 and substantially as it was written. Scruples about the authenticity of the play have been fostered by the ambiguities in Henslowe's *Diary*, by revulsion at the enormities of the plot, and by a strange confidence in the veracity of the dramatist, Edward Ravenscroft, who produced an adaptation, *Titus Andronicus, or the Rape of Lavinia* (acted 1678, printed 1687). In his prefatory Address Ravenscroft asserted, "I have been told by some anciently conversant with the Stage, that it was not Originally his [Shakespeare's], but brought by a private Author to be Acted, and he only gave some Master-touches to one or two of the Principal Parts or Characters...." It is interesting, however, that Ravenscroft's doubt was not mirrored in his title page, which calls his play "A Tragedy, Alter'd from Mr. Shakespear's Works." To offset the evidence of Ravenscroft there is the authority of Meres, who in 1598 included the play in his list of Shakespeare's tragedies, and that of Heminge and Condell, who admitted it into the First Folio. And for what it is worth, there is the witness of Gerard Langbaine, who in his *English Dramatick Poets* (1691) rebukes Ravenscroft for plagiarism and indicates his belief in Shakespeare's authorship.

Material from several classical stories is woven into the bloodshot design of *Titus Andronicus*. The most conspicuous contribution is from Ovid's tale of Philomela (*Metamorphoses*, VI) whose rape and mutilation are avenged in a cannibalistic feast which the victim herself, like Lavinia, helps to prepare. Remembered, too, is the similar banquet crowning the revenge of Atreus in Seneca's *Thyestes*. The sacrifice of Alarbus, the root of all succeeding evils, was suggested by Seneca's *Troades*. When Titus kills Lavinia, he cites the deed of Virginius as his "pattern, precedent, and lively warrant."

Like Kyd's *Spanish Tragedy*, with which Jonson advisedly coupled it, *Titus Andronicus* is a tragedy of blood designed to impress by the accumulation of horrors. This amassing of cruelties, from which generations of critics have recoiled, certain that the gentle Shakespeare could not have been responsible, is in fact not inconsistent with his authorship. For a young playwright, eager to make his mark, might be expected to serve the public the kind of fare it had shown itself pleased to feed upon. That he should run into excess in the business is not surprising, allowing, as doubtless one should, for a beginner's zeal and excitement in the play of his own powers. In his *Comedy of Errors* Shakespeare increases the range of confusions by adding a second pair of twins to the one provided by his source; in *Love's Labour's Lost*, satirizing linguistic fads and fashions, he overloads with verbal extravagance; similarly here, writing his first revenge play, he assembles horrors with a lavish hand. And it is fair to say that what the aforenamed plays are to Shakespeare's mature comedies, *Titus Andronicus* is to his mature tragedies. Furthermore, violence and cruelty are not alien to Shakespeare's later plays. To note but a few examples, one may recall the savagery of Hamlet in his motive for sparing Claudius at prayer, the blinding of Gloucester in *King Lear*, and the brutal slaying of Macduff's wife and children upon the order of Macbeth. These resemblances, however, are only incidental, by no means implying that *Titus Andronicus* provides any close foreshadowing of Shakespeare's great tragedies. The major characters in this play bear only superficial likeness to memorable figures in later ones, beside whom they are flat and obvious. One may perhaps feel in Tamora something of the fierce energy with which Shakespeare endows his wicked women, but she is remote from Lady Macbeth; Titus is not really like Lear, despite his pride and his madness, which, being feigned, is akin, rather, to Hamlet's; Aaron may remind us of Iago by his villainy, but he has nothing of Iago's brain and cunning. The person genuinely prophetic of figures to come is the Clown (IV.iii), who, in his miscomprehensions and his very accent, anticipates a long line of witless and genial bumpkins.

The gory details of *Titus Andronicus* presumably contributed to its original success. Today, however, the play makes no appeal, not so much because it is aesthetically or morally offensive as because it is dull. One cannot believe in it. Its progress is too artificial; its horrors are too mechanical; and to modern taste the play is absurdly melodramatic. The hero elicits slight interest or sympathy. Though he has motive enough for vengeance, he shows himself, before his miseries begin, to be self-righteous and impetuous (I.i.276 ff.), and suffering brings forth no redeeming traits. Though capable of sentiment (I.i.104–20; II.iii.9–29), Tamora is a harsh figure, drawn with little shading. Aaron comes close to the motiveless malignity of which Coleridge blindly accused Iago, for he is cast in the Machiavellian mould of absolute villainy. He is a brash, cool devil who lives for evil (III.i.203–06; V.i.121–50; V.iii.184–90), yet his idiom is somehow more natural than one would expect in this unnatural drama, and he betrays human instinct and emotion when he is confronted with his own black infant (IV.ii. 52 ff.).

The signal weakness of *Titus Andronicus*, as a play of Shakespeare's apprenticeship, is that it is too contrived; its interest is purely external. Nevertheless, it contains some memorable passages which are more than rhetoric. Most notable, perhaps, are the words of Tamora pleading for Alarbus (I.i.116–19), which hold the quintessence of Portia's famous speech on mercy; the elegiac lines of Titus spoken over his dead sons (I.i.150–56); and the speech of Titus which ends the gruesome colloquies of Act III on a note of mournful beauty (III.ii.81–85).

THE TRAGEDY OF
TITUS ANDRONICUS

[DRAMATIS PERSONÆ

SATURNINUS, *son to the late Emperor of Rome, and afterwards declared Emperor.*

BASSIANUS, *brother to Saturninus; in love with Lavinia.*

TITUS ANDRONICUS, *a noble Roman, general against the Goths.*

MARCUS ANDRONICUS, *tribune of the people, and brother to Titus.*

LUCIUS,
QUINTUS,
MARTIUS, } *sons to Titus Andronicus.*
MUTIUS,

YOUNG LUCIUS, *a boy, son to Lucius.*

ÆMILIUS, *a noble Roman.*

PUBLIUS, *son to Marcus the Tribune.*

SEMPRONIUS,
CAIUS, } *kinsmen to Titus.*
VALENTINE,

ALARBUS
DEMETRIUS, } *sons to Tamora.*
CHIRON,

AARON, *a Moor, beloved by Tamora.*

A Clown.

A Captain and a Messenger.

Goths and Romans.

TAMORA, *Queen of the Goths.*

LAVINIA, *daughter to Titus Andronicus.*

A Nurse, *and a black child.*

Senators, Tribunes, Officers, Soldiers, and Attendants.

SCENE: *Rome, and the country near it.*]

ACT I

SCENE I. [*Rome.   Before the Senate-house.   The Tomb of the Andronici appearing.*]

Enter the TRIBUNES *and Senators aloft, and then enter* SATURNINUS *and his* Followers *at one door, and* BASSIANUS *and his* Followers *at the other; with drums and trumpets.*

  Sat. Noble patricians, patrons of my right,
Defend the justice of my cause with arms,
And, countrymen, my loving followers,
Plead my successive title with your swords.
I am his first-born son, that was the last   5
That wore the imperial diadem of Rome;
Then let my father's honours live in me,
Nor wrong mine age with this indignity.
  Bas. Romans, friends, followers, favourers of my right,

If ever Bassianus, Cæsar's son,   10
Were gracious in the eyes of royal Rome,
Keep then this passage to the Capitol,
And suffer not dishonour to approach
The imperial seat, to virtue consecrate,
To justice, continence, and nobility;   15
But let desert in pure election shine,
And, Romans, fight for freedom in your choice.

Enter MARCUS ANDRONICUS, *aloft, with the crown.*

  Marc. Princes, that strive by factions and by friends
Ambitiously for rule and empery,
Know that the people of Rome, for whom we stand   20
A special party, have, by common voice,
In election for the Roman empery,
Chosen Andronicus, surnamed Pius
For many good and great deserts to Rome.

Act I, sc. i, 4. **successive title:** title to the succession. 8. **age:** seniority. 16. **pure:** free. 21. **special party:** representatives of a particular group. 22-23. **In election ... Chosen.** Nomination rather than election is implied.

A nobler man, a braver warrior, 25
Lives not this day within the city walls.
He by the senate is accited home
From weary wars against the barbarous Goths;
That, with his sons, a terror to our foes,
Hath yok'd a nation strong, train'd up in arms. 30
Ten years are spent since first he undertook
This cause of Rome and chastised with arms
Our enemies' pride; five times he hath return'd
Bleeding to Rome, bearing his valiant sons
In coffins from the field; 35
And now at last, laden with honour's spoils,
Returns the good Andronicus to Rome,
Renowned Titus, flourishing in arms.
Let us entreat, by honour of his name
Whom worthily you would have now succeed, 40
And in the Capitol and senate's right,
Whom you pretend to honour and adore,
That you withdraw you and abate your strength,
Dismiss your followers, and, as suitors should,
Plead your deserts in peace and humbleness. 45
  Sat. How fair the tribune speaks to calm my
    thoughts!
  Bas. Marcus Andronicus, so I do affy
In thy uprightness and integrity,
And so I love and honour thee and thine,
Thy noble brother Titus and his sons, 50
And her to whom my thoughts are humbled all,
Gracious Lavinia, Rome's rich ornament,
That I will here dismiss my loving friends,
And to my fortunes and the people's favour
Commit my cause in balance to be weigh'd. 55
              [*Exeunt soldiers [of Bassianus].*
  Sat. Friends, that have been thus forward in
    my right,
I thank you all and here dismiss you all,
And to the love and favour of my country
Commit myself, my person, and the cause.
              [*Exeunt soldiers of Saturninus.*
Rome, be as just and gracious unto me 60
As I am confident and kind to thee.
Open the gates and let me in.
  Bas. Tribunes, and me, a poor competitor.
    [*Flourish. They go up into the Senate-
    house.*

              Enter a CAPTAIN.

  Cap. Romans, make way! The good Andronicus,
Patron of virtue, Rome's best champion, 65
Successful in the battles that he fights,
With honour and with fortune is return'd

From where he circumscribed with his sword
And brought to yoke the enemies of Rome.

*Sound drums and trumpets, and then enter two of
  Titus's sons [*MARTIUS and MUTIUS*]; and then
  two Men bearing a coffin covered with black; then
  two other sons [*LUCIUS and QUINTUS*]. Then
  TITUS ANDRONICUS; and then TAMORA, the Queen
  of Goths and her [three] sons [*Alarbus,*] DEMETRIUS,
  and CHIRON; and with AARON the Moor, and others
  as many as can be. Then set down the coffin, and
  Titus speaks.*

  Tit. Hail, Rome, victorious in thy mourning
    weeds! 70
Lo, as the bark that hath discharg'd her fraught
Returns with precious lading to the bay
From whence at first she weigh'd her anchorage,
Cometh Andronicus, bound with laurel boughs,
To re-salute his country with his tears, 75
Tears of true joy for his return to Rome.
Thou great defender of this Capitol,
Stand gracious to the rites that we intend!
Romans, of five and twenty valiant sons,
Half of the number that King Priam had, 80
Behold the poor remains, alive and dead!
These that survive let Rome reward with love,
These that I bring unto their latest home,
With burial amongst their ancestors.
Here Goths have given me leave to sheathe my
    sword. 85
Titus, unkind and careless of thine own,
Why suffer'st thou thy sons, unburied yet,
To hover on the dreadful shore of Styx?
Make way to lay them by their brethren.
              [*They open the tomb.*
There greet in silence, as the dead are wont, 90
And sleep in peace, slain in your country's wars!
O sacred receptacle of my joys,
Sweet cell of virtue and nobility,
How many sons hast thou of mine in store,
That thou wilt never render to me more! 95
  Luc. Give us the proudest prisoner of the Goths,
That we may hew his limbs and on a pile
Ad manes fratrum sacrifice his flesh
Before this earthy prison of their bones;
That so the shadows be not unappeas'd, 100
Nor we disturb'd with prodigies on earth.
  Tit. I give him you, the noblest that survives,
The eldest son of this distressed queen.
  Tam. Stay, Roman brethren! Gracious con-
    queror,
Victorious Titus, rue the tears I shed, 105

---

27. **accited:** summoned. 30. **yok'd:** put under yoke. 35. **In ... field.** Following these words Q₁ has 3½ lines, which
the later texts omit; *and at this day/ To the Monument of that Androniçi/ Done sacrifice of expiation/ And slaine the Noblest
prisoner of the Gothes.* 39. **his:** the late emperor's. 42. **pretend:** profess. 47. **affy:** trust. 61. **confident:** confiding. 68.
circumscribed: restrained. 69. s.d. **[three].** *two* Q₁. 71. **fraught:** freight. 77. **defender:** i.e., Jupiter Capitolinus. 98.
Ad ... fratrum: to the shades of (our) brothers. 100. **shadows:** ghosts.

parallel to Portia's speech

A mother's tears in passion for her son;
And if thy sons were ever dear to thee,
O, think my son to be as dear to me!
Sufficeth not that we are brought to Rome,
To beautify thy triumphs and return,   110
Captive to thee and to thy Roman yoke,
But must my sons be slaughtered in the streets
For valiant doings in their country's cause?
O, if to fight for king and commonweal
Were piety in thine, it is in these.   115
Andronicus, stain not thy tomb with blood!
Wilt thou draw near the nature of the gods?
Draw near them, then, in being merciful;
Sweet mercy is nobility's true badge.
Thrice noble Titus, spare my first-born son!   120
   Tit. Patient yourself, madam, and pardon me.
These are their brethren, whom your Goths beheld
Alive and dead; and for their brethren slain
Religiously they ask a sacrifice.
To this your son is mark'd, and die he must   125
T' appease their groaning shadows that are gone.
   Luc. Away with him! and make a fire straight;
And with our swords, upon a pile of wood,
Let's hew his limbs till they be clean consum'd.

     [*Exeunt* [*Lucius, Quintus, Martius, and*
       Mutius], *with Alarbus.*

   Tam. O cruel, irreligious piety!   130
   Chi. Was never Scythia half so barbarous.
   Dem. Oppose not Scythia to ambitious Rome
Alarbus goes to rest; and we survive
To tremble under Titus' threat'ning look.
Then, madam, stand resolv'd, but hope withal   135
The self-same gods that arm'd the Queen of Troy
With opportunity of sharp revenge
Upon the Thracian tyrant in his tent,
May favour Tamora, the Queen of Goths —
When Goths were Goths and Tamora was queen —
To quit the bloody wrongs upon her foes.   140

Re-enter LUCIUS, QUINTUS, MARTIUS, *and* MUTIUS
     [*with their swords bloody*].

   Luc. See, lord and father, how we have perform'd
Our Roman rites. Alarbus' limbs are lopp'd,
And entrails feed the sacrificing fire,
Whose smoke, like incense, doth perfume the sky.
Remaineth nought but to inter our brethren   146
And with loud 'larums welcome them to Rome.
   Tit. Let it be so; and let Andronicus
Make this his latest farewell to their souls.

     [*Sound trumpets, and lay the coffin in the
       tomb.*

In peace and honour rest you here, my sons;   150
Rome's readiest champions, repose you here in rest,
Secure from worldly chances and mishaps!

Here lurks no treason, here no envy swells.
Here grow no damned drugs; here are no storms,
No noise, but silence and eternal sleep.   155
In peace and honour rest you here, my sons!

       Enter LAVINIA.

   Lav. In peace and honour live Lord Titus long!
My noble lord and father, live in fame!
Lo, at this tomb my tributary tears
I render for my brethren's obsequies;   160
And at thy feet I kneel, with tears of joy
Shed on this earth for thy return to Rome.
O, bless me here with thy victorious hand
Whose fortunes Rome's best citizens applaud!
   Tit. Kind Rome, that hast thus lovingly re-
     serv'd   165
The cordial of mine age to glad my heart!
Lavinia, live; outlive thy father's days
And fame's eternal date, for virtue's praise!

[*Re-enter, below,* MARCUS ANDRONICUS *and* TRI-
BUNES; *also* SATURNINUS *and* BASSIANUS, *at-*
tended.]

   Marc. Long live Lord Titus, my beloved brother,
Gracious triumpher in the eyes of Rome!   170
   Tit. Thanks, gentle tribune, noble brother
     Marcus.
   Marc. And welcome, nephews, from successful
     wars,
You that survive, and you that sleep in fame!
Fair lords, your fortunes are alike in all,
That in your country's service drew your swords;
But safer triumph is this funeral pomp,   176
That hath aspir'd to Solon's happiness
And triumphs over chance in honour's bed.
Titus Andronicus, the people of Rome,
Whose friend in justice thou hast ever been,   180
Send thee by me, their tribune and their trust,
This palliament of white and spotless hue;
And name thee in election for the empire,
With these our late-deceased emperor's sons.
Be *candidatus* then, and put it on,   185
And help to set a head on headless Rome.
   Tit. A better head her glorious body fits
Than his that shakes for age and feebleness.
What should I don this robe and trouble you,
Be chosen with proclamations to-day,   190
To-morrow yield up rule, resign my life,
And set abroad new business for you all?
Rome, I have been thy soldier forty years,
And led my country's strength successfully,
And buried one and twenty valiant sons,   195
Knighted in field, slain manfully in arms
In right and service of their noble country.

---

106. **passion**: grief.   132. **Oppose**: compare.   136. **Queen of Troy**: Hecuba, who avenged the death of her son Poly-
dorus, slain by Polymnestor, "the Thracian tyrant" (l. 138).   166. **cordial**: comfort.   177. **Solon's happiness.** The
philosopher Solon is reputed to have said that no man is happy until he is dead.   182. **palliament**: cloak.   189. **What**: why.

Give me a staff of honour for mine age,
But not a sceptre to control the world;
Upright he held it, lords, that held it last.   200
    Marc. Titus, thou shalt obtain and ask the
        empery.
    Sat. Proud and ambitious tribune, canst thou tell?
    Tit. Patience, Prince Saturninus.
    Sat.   Romans, do me right.
Patricians, draw your swords, and sheathe them not
Till Saturninus be Rome's emperor.   205
Andronicus, would thou were shipp'd to hell
Rather than rob me of the people's hearts!
    Luc. Proud Saturnine, interrupter of the good
That noble-minded Titus means to thee!
    Tit. Content thee, Prince; I will restore to thee
The people's hearts, and wean them from them-
        selves.   211
    Bas. Andronicus, I do not flatter thee,
But honour thee, and will do till I die.
My faction if thou strengthen with thy friends,
I will most thankful be; and thanks to men   215
Of noble minds is honourable meed.
    Tit. People of Rome, and people's tribunes here,
I ask your voices and your suffrages.
Will ye bestow them friendly on Andronicus?
    Tribunes. To gratify the good Andronicus,   220
And gratulate his safe return to Rome,
The people will accept whom he admits.
    Tit. Tribunes, I thank you; and this suit I make,
That you create our emperor's eldest son,
Lord Saturnine; whose virtues will, I hope,   225
Reflect on Rome as [Titan's] rays on earth,
And ripen justice in this commonweal.
Then, if you will elect by my advice,
Crown him and say, "Long live our emperor!"
    Marc. With voices and applause of every sort, 230
Patricians and plebeians, we create
Lord Saturninus Rome's great emperor,
And say, "Long live our Emperor Saturnine!"
        [*A long flourish till they come down.*
    Sat. Titus Andronicus, for thy favours done
To us in our election this day,   235
I give thee thanks in part of thy deserts,
And will with deeds requite thy gentleness;
And, for an onset, Titus, to advance
Thy name and honourable family,
Lavinia will I make my emperess,   240
Rome's royal mistress, mistress of my heart,
And in the sacred Pantheon her espouse.
Tell me, Andronicus, doth this motion please thee?
    Tit. It doth, my worthy lord; and in this match
I hold me highly honoured of your Grace: 245
And here in sight of Rome to Saturnine,

King and commander of our commonweal,
The wide world's emperor, do I consecrate
My sword, my chariot, and my prisoners;
Presents well worthy Rome's imperious lord,   250
Receive them then, the tribute that I owe,
Mine honour's ensigns humbled at thy feet.
    Sat. Thanks, noble Titus, father of my life!
How proud I am of thee and of thy gifts
Rome shall record, and when I do forget   255
The least of these unspeakable deserts,
Romans, forget your fealty to me.
    Tit. [*To Tamora.*] Now, madam, are you
        prisoner to an emperor;
To him that, for your honour and your state,
Will use you nobly and your followers.   260
    Sat. [*Aside.*] A goodly lady, trust me, of the hue
That I would choose, were I to choose anew. —
Clear up, fair queen, that cloudy countenance;
Though [chance] of war hath wrought this change
        of cheer,
Thou com'st not to be made a scorn in Rome; 265
Princely shall be thy usage every way.
Rest on my word, and let not discontent
Daunt all your hopes. Madam, he comforts you
Can make you greater than the Queen of Goths.
Lavinia, you are not displeas'd with this?   270
    Lav. Not I, my lord, sith true nobility
Warrants these words in princely courtesy.
    Sat. Thanks, sweet Lavinia. Romans, let us go;
Ransomless here we set our prisoners free.
Proclaim our honours, lords, with trump and
        drum.   275
        [*Flourish. Saturninus courts Tamora in
            dumb show.*]
    Bas. Lord Titus, by your leave, this maid is
        mine.   [*Seizing Lavinia.*]
    Tit. How, sir! Are you in earnest then, my lord?
    Bas. Ay, noble Titus; and resolv'd withal
To do myself this reason and this right.
    Marc. "*Suum cuique*" is our Roman justice; 280
This prince in justice seizeth but his own.
    Luc. And that he will, and shall, if Lucius live.
    Tit. Traitors, avaunt! Where is the Emperor's
        guard?
Treason, my lord! Lavinia is surpris'd!
    Sat. Surpris'd! By whom?
    Bas.   By him that justly may
Bear his betroth'd from all the world away.   286
        [*Exeunt Bassianus and Marcus with
            Lavinia.*]
    Mut. Brothers, help to convey her hence away,
And with my sword I'll keep this door safe.
        [*Exeunt Lucius, Quintus, and Martius.*]

201. **obtain and ask:** obtain by merely asking.   221. **gratulate:** celebrate.   224. **create:** i.e., elect.   226. [Titan's] Q₂:
the sun's. *Tytus* Q₁. 237. **gentleness:** noble action. 238. **onset:** beginning. 250. **imperious:** imperial. 264. [chance] Q₂.
change Q₁. **cheer:** (1) mood, (2) entertainment. 268. **he:** he who. 271. **sith:** since. 280. "*Suum cuique* ": to every one
his own.

Tit. Follow, my lord, and I'll soon bring her back.
Mut. My lord, you pass not here.
Tit.   What, villain boy! 290
Barr'st me my way in Rome?
Mut.   Help, Lucius, help!
                              [*Titus kills him.*
[*During the fray, exeunt Saturninus, Ta-
mora, Demetrius, Chiron, and Aaron.*]

[*Re-enter* LUCIUS.]

Luc. My lord, you are unjust, and, more than so,
In wrongful quarrel you have slain your son.
Tit. Nor thou, nor he, are any sons of mine;
My sons would never so dishonour me.   295
Traitor, restore Lavinia to the Emperor.
Luc. Dead, if you will; but not to be his wife
That is another's lawful promis'd love.   [*Exit.*]

Re-enter aloft SATURNINUS *with* TAMORA *and her
two sons, and* AARON.

Sat. No, Titus, no; the Emperor needs her not.
Nor her, nor thee, nor any of thy stock.   300
I'll trust, by leisure, him that mocks me once;
Thee never, nor thy traitorous haughty sons,
Confederates all thus to dishonour me.
Was [there] none [else] in Rome to make a stale,
But Saturnine? Full well, Andronicus,   305
Agree these deeds with that proud brag of thine,
That said'st I begg'd the empire at thy hands.
Tit. O monstrous! what reproachful words are
   these?
Sat. But go thy ways; go, give that changing
   piece
To him that flourish'd for her with his sword.   310
A valiant son-in-law thou shalt enjoy,
One fit to bandy with thy lawless sons,
To ruffle in the commonwealth of Rome.
Tit. These words are razors to my wounded
   heart.
Sat. And therefore, lovely Tamora, Queen of
   Goths,   315
That like the stately [Phœbe] 'mongst her nymphs
Dost overshine the gallant'st dames of Rome,
If thou be pleas'd with this my sudden choice,
Behold, I choose thee, Tamora, for my bride,
And will create thee Empress of Rome.   320
Speak, Queen of Goths, dost thou applaud my
   choice?
And here I swear by all the Roman gods,
Sith priest and holy water are so near
And tapers burn so bright and everything
In readiness for Hymenæus stand.   325

I will not re-salute the streets of Rome,
Or climb my palace, till from forth this place
I lead espous'd my bride along with me.
   Tam. And here, in sight of heaven, to Rome
   I swear,
If Saturnine advance the Queen of Goths,   330
She will a handmaid be to his desires,
A loving nurse, a mother to his youth.
   Sat. Ascend, fair queen, Pantheon; lords, ac-
   company
Your noble emperor and his lovely bride,
Sent by the heavens for Prince Saturnine,   335
Whose wisdom hath her fortune conquered;
There shall we consummate our spousal rites.
                    [*Exeunt all* [*but Titus*].
   Tit. I am not bid to wait upon this bride.
Titus, when wert thou wont to walk alone,
Dishonoured thus, and challenged of wrongs? 340

Re-enter MARCUS, LUCIUS, QUINTUS, *and* MARTIUS.
   Marc. O Titus, see, O, see what thou hast done!
In a bad quarrel slain a virtuous son.
   Tit. No, foolish tribune, no; no son of mine,
Nor thou, nor these, confederates in the deed
That hath dishonoured all our family;   345
Unworthy brother, and unworthy sons!
   Luc. But let us give him burial, as becomes;
Give Mutius burial with our brethren.
   Tit. Traitors, away! he rests not in this tomb.
This monument five hundred years hath stood, 350
Which I have sumptuously re-edified.
Here none but soldiers and Rome's servitors
Repose in fame; none basely slain in brawls.
Bury him where you can; he comes not here.
   Marc. My lord, this is impiety in you.   355
My nephew Mutius' deeds do plead for him;
He must be buried with his brethren.
   [*Quin.*] } And shall, or him we will accompany.
   [*Mart.*] }
   Tit. "And shall!" What villain was it spake
   that word?
   [*Quin.*] He that would vouch it in any place
   but here.   360
   Tit. What, would you bury him in my despite?
   Marc. No, noble Titus, but entreat of thee
To pardon Mutius and to bury him.
   Tit. Marcus, even thou hast struck upon my
   crest,
And, with these boys, mine honour thou hast
   wounded.   365
My foes I do repute you every one;
So, trouble me no more, but get you gone.

---

301. **by leisure:** i.e., not at all.   304. **[there] none [else]** F₂.   *none* Qq F₁.   **stale:** laughing stock.   309. **piece:** wench.
312. **bandy:** contend.   313. **ruffle:** swagger, brawl.   316. **[Phœbe]** F₂: Diana.   *Thebe* Qq F₁.   325. **Hymenæus:** god of
marriage.   338. **bid:** invited.   340. **challenged:** accused.   358. **[Quin.] [Mart.]** (Capell).   *Titus two sonnes speakes* Q₁.
360. **[Quin.]** (Rowe).   *Titus sonne speakes* Q₁.

[*Luc.*] He is not with himself; let us withdraw.

[*Mart.*] Not I, till Mutius' bones be buried.

      [*Marcus and the sons of Titus kneel.*

Marc. Brother, for in that name doth nature
  plead, —   370

[*Mart.*] Father, and in that name doth nature
  speak, —

Tit. Speak thou no more; if all the rest will
  speed —

Marc. Renowned Titus, more than half my soul, —

Luc. Dear father, soul and substance of us all, —

Marc. Suffer thy brother Marcus to inter   375
His noble nephew here in virtue's nest,
That died in honour and Lavinia's cause.
Thou art a Roman, be not barbarous.
The Greeks upon advice did bury Ajax
That slew himself; and wise Laertes' son   380
Did graciously plead for his funerals.
Let not young Mutius, then, that was thy joy,
Be barr'd his entrance here.

Tit.   Rise, Marcus, rise.
The dismall'st day is this that e'er I saw,
To be dishonoured by my sons in Rome!   385
Well, bury him, and bury me the next.

      [*Mutius is put into the tomb.*

Luc. There lie thy bones, sweet Mutius, with
  thy friends,
Till we with trophies do adorn thy tomb.

All. (*Kneeling.*) No man shed tears for noble
  Mutius;
He lives in fame that died in virtue's cause.   390

      [*Exeunt all but Marcus and Titus.*

Marc. My lord, to step out of these dreary dumps,
How comes it that the subtle Queen of Goths
Is of a sudden thus advanc'd in Rome?

Tit. I know not, Marcus, but I know it is;
Whether by device or no, the heavens can tell.   395
Is she not then beholding to the man
That brought her for this high good turn so far?
[Yes, and will nobly him remunerate.]

Flourish. Re-enter SATURNINUS, TAMORA, DEME-
TRIUS, CHIRON, *and* AARON *at one door; enter,*
at the other door, BASSIANUS, LAVINIA, *with others.*

Sat. So, Bassianus, you have play'd your prize.
God give you joy, sir, of your gallant bride!   400

Bas. And you of yours, my lord! I say no more,
Nor wish no less; and so I take my leave.

Sat. Traitor, if Rome have law or we have power,
Thou and thy faction shall repent this rape.

Bas. Rape call you it, my lord, to seize my
  own,   405

My true betrothed love and now my wife?
But let the laws of Rome determine all;
Meanwhile I am possess'd of that is mine.

Sat. 'Tis good, sir; you are very short with us;
But, if we live, we'll be as sharp with you.   410

Bas. My lord, what I have done, as best I may
Answer I must, and shall do with my life.
Only thus much I give your Grace to know:
By all the duties that I owe to Rome,
This noble gentleman, Lord Titus here,   415
Is in opinion and in honour wrong'd;
That in the rescue of Lavinia
With his own hand did slay his youngest son,
In zeal to you and highly mov'd to wrath
To be controll'd in that he frankly gave.   420
Receive him, then, to favour, Saturnine,
That hath express'd himself in all his deeds
A father and a friend to thee and Rome.

Tit. Prince Bassianus, leave to plead my deeds;
'Tis thou and those that have dishonoured me.   425
Rome and the righteous heavens be my judge,
How I have lov'd and honoured Saturnine!

Tam. My worthy lord, if ever Tamora
Were gracious in those princely eyes of thine,
Then hear me speak indifferently for all;   430
And at my suit, sweet, pardon what is past.

Sat. What, madam! be dishonoured openly
And basely put it up without revenge?

Tam. Not so, my lord; the gods of Rome forfend
I should be author to dishonour you!   435
But on mine honour dare I undertake
For good Lord Titus' innocence in all,
Whose fury not dissembled speaks his griefs.
Then, at my suit, look graciously on him;
Lose not so noble a friend on vain suppose,   440
Nor with sour looks afflict his gentle heart.
[*Aside to Sat.*] My lord, be rul'd by me, be won at
  last;
Dissemble all your griefs and discontents.
You are but newly planted in your throne;
Lest, then, the people, and patricians too,   445
Upon a just survey take Titus' part,
And so supplant you for ingratitude,
Which Rome reputes to be a heinous sin,
Yield at entreats; and then let me alone:
I'll find a day to massacre them all   450
And raze their faction and their family,
The cruel father and his traitorous sons,
To whom I sued for my dear son's life,
And make them know what 'tis to let a queen
Kneel in the streets and beg for grace in vain.   455

      [*Again speaking openly to Sat.*

368. [*Luc.*] (Rowe). 3. *Sonne* Q₁. **not . . . himself**: beside himself. 369. [*Mart.*] (Capell). 2. *Sonne* Q₁. Many edd. assign to Quintus. 371. [*Mart.*] (Capell). 2. *Sonne* Q₁. 379. **advice**: deliberation. 380. **Laertes' son**: Ulysses. 395. **device**: scheming. 396. **beholding**: indebted. 398. [**Yes . . . remunerate**] Ff. Om. Qq. 399. **play'd**: won. 416. **opinion**: reputation. 420. **To be controll'd**: at being restrained. 430. **indifferently**: impartially. 433. **put it up**: endure it. 436. **undertake**: vouch.

Come, come, sweet emperor; — come, Andro-
　　nicus; —
Take up this good old man, and cheer the heart
That dies in tempest of thy angry frown.
　　Sat. Rise, Titus, rise; my empress hath prevail'd.
　　Tit. I thank your Majesty, and her, my lord.　460
These words, these looks, infuse new life in me.
　　Tam. Titus, I am incorporate in Rome,
A Roman now adopted happily,
And must advise the Emperor for his good.
This day all quarrels die, Andronicus;　　465
And let it be mine honour, good my lord,
That I have reconcil'd your friends and you.
For you, Prince Bassianus, I have pass'd
My word and promise to the Emperor
That you will be more mild and tractable.　470
And fear not, lords, and you, Lavinia;
By my advice, all humbled on your knees,
You shall ask pardon of his Majesty.
　　　　[*Marcus, Lavinia, and the others kneel.*]
　　[*Luc.*] We do, and vow to heaven and to his
　　　　Highness
That what we did was mildly as we might,　475
Tend'ring our sister's honour and our own.
　　Marc. That, on mine honour, here do I protest.
　　Sat. Away, and talk not; trouble us no more.
　　Tam. Nay, nay, sweet emperor, we must all be
　　　　friends;
The tribune and his nephews kneel for grace.　480
I will not be denied; sweetheart, look back.
　　Sat. Marcus, for thy sake and thy brother's here,
And at my lovely Tamora's entreats,
I do remit these young men's heinous faults.
Stand up!　　[*Marcus and the others rise.*]　485
Lavinia, though you left me like a churl,
I found a friend, and sure as death I swore
I would not part a bachelor from the priest.
Come, if the Emperor's court can feast two brides,
You are my guest, Lavinia, and your friends.　490
This day shall be a love-day, Tamora.
　　Tit. To-morrow, an it please your Majesty
To hunt the panther and the hart with me,
With horn and hound we'll give your Grace *bonjour.*
　　Sat. Be it so, Titus, and gramercy too.　495
　　　　[*Flourish. Exeunt.*]

ACT II

[SCENE I. *Rome. Before the palace.*]

Enter AARON.

　　Aar. Now climbeth Tamora Olympus' top,
Safe out of Fortune's shot; and sits aloft,

Secure of thunder's crack or lightning flash,
Advanc'd above pale envy's threat'ning reach.
As when the golden sun salutes the morn　　5
And, having gilt the ocean with his beams,
Gallops the zodiac in his glistering coach
And overlooks the highest-peering hills;
So Tamora:
Upon her wit doth earthly honour wait,　　10
And virtue stoops and trembles at her frown.
Then, Aaron, arm thy heart and fit thy thoughts
To mount aloft with thy imperial mistress,
And mount her pitch, whom thou in triumph long
Hast prisoner held, fett'red in amorous chains　15
And faster bound to Aaron's charming eyes
Than is Prometheus tied to Caucasus.
Away with slavish weeds and servile thoughts!
I will be bright and shine in pearl and gold
To wait upon this new-made emperess.　　20
To wait, said I? To wanton with this queen,
This goddess, this Semiramis, this nymph,
This siren, that will charm Rome's Saturnine
And see his shipwreck and his commonweal's.
Holloa! what storm is this?　　25

　　　Enter DEMETRIUS *and* CHIRON, *braving.*

　　Dem. Chiron, thy years wants wit, thy [wit]
　　　　wants edge
And manners, to intrude where I am grac'd;
And may, for aught thou know'st, affected be.
　　Chi. Demetrius, thou dost over-ween in all;
And so in this, to bear me down with braves.　30
'Tis not the difference of a year or two
Makes me less gracious or thee more fortunate.
I am as able and as fit as thou
To serve, and to deserve my mistress' grace;
And that my sword upon thee shall approve,　35
And plead my passions for Lavinia's love.
　　Aar. [*Aside.*] Clubs, clubs! these lovers will not
　　　　keep the peace.
　　Dem. Why, boy, although our mother, un-
　　　　advis'd,
Gave you a dancing-rapier by your side,
Are you so desperate grown, to threat your friends?
Go to; have your lath glued within your sheath　41
Till you know better how to handle it.
　　Chi. Meanwhile, sir, with the little skill I have,
Full well shalt thou perceive how much I dare.
　　Dem. Ay, boy, grow ye so brave?　[*They draw.*
　　Aar. [*Coming forward.*] Why, how now, lords!　45
So near the Emperor's palace dare ye draw,
And maintain such a quarrel openly?
Full well I wot the ground of all this grudge.

474. [*Luc.*] (Rowe). Om. Q₁, All Q₃, *Son* F.　476. **Tend'ring:** having regard to.　486. **churl:** worthless person.　491.
love-day: day for the friendly settlement of disputes.　495. **gramercy:** many thanks.
　　Act II, sc. i. Q₁ marks no act or scene divisions.　14. **pitch:** height of a falcon's flight.　22. **Semiramis:** a cruel and voluptuous queen of Assyria.　25. s.d. **braving:** defying each other.　26. [**wit**] Q₂.　**wits** Q₁.　27. **grac'd:** favored.　28. **affected:**
loved.　35. **approve:** prove.　37. **Clubs, clubs:** rallying cry of the London apprentices.　39. **dancing-rapier:** a sword carried
for ornament.

I would not for a million of gold
The cause were known to them it most concerns;   50
Nor would your noble mother for much more
Be so dishonoured in the court of Rome.
For shame, put up.
    Dem.   Not I, till I have sheath'd
My rapier in his bosom, and withal
Thrust those reproachful speeches down his throat
That he hath breath'd in my dishonour here.   56
    Chi. For that I am prepar'd and full resolv'd,
Foul-spoken coward, that thund'rest with thy
        tongue
And with thy weapon nothing dar'st perform!
    Aar. Away, I say!   60
Now, by the gods that warlike Goths adore,
This petty brabble will undo us all.
Why, lords, and think you not how dangerous
It is to jet upon a prince's right?
What, is Lavinia then become so loose,   65
Or Bassianus so degenerate,
That for her love such quarrels may be broach'd
Without controlment, justice, or revenge?
Young lords, beware! an should the Empress
        know
This discord's ground, the music would not please.
    Chi. I care not, I, knew she and all the world;   71
I love Lavinia more than all the world.
    Dem. Youngling, learn thou to make some
        meaner choice;
Lavinia is thine elder brother's hope.
    Aar. Why, are ye mad? or know ye not, in
        Rome   75
How furious and impatient they be,
And cannot brook competitors in love?
I tell you, lords, you do but plot your deaths
By this device.
    Chi.   Aaron, a thousand deaths
Would I propose to achieve her whom I love.   80
    Aar. To achieve her! how?
    Dem.   Why makes thou it so strange?
She is a woman, therefore may be woo'd;
She is a woman, therefore may be won;
She is Lavinia, therefore must be lov'd.
What, man! more water glideth by the mill   85
Than wots the miller of; and easy it is
Of a cut loaf to steal a shive, we know.
Though Bassianus be the Emperor's brother,
Better than he have worn Vulcan's badge.
    Aar. [*Aside.*] Ay, and as good as Saturninus
        may.   90
    Dem. Then why should he despair that knows
        to court it

With words, fair looks, and liberality?
What, hast not thou full often struck a doe,
And borne her cleanly by the keeper's nose?
    Aar. Why, then, it seems, some certain snatch
        or so   95
Would serve your turns.
    Chi.   Ay, so the turn were serv'd.
    Dem. Aaron, thou hast hit it.
    Aar.   Would you had hit it too!
Then should not we be tir'd with this ado.
Why, hark ye, hark ye! and are you such fools
To square for this? Would it offend you, then,   100
That both should speed?
    Chi. Faith, not me.
    Dem.   Nor me, so I were one.
    Aar. For shame, be friends, and join for that you
        jar.
'Tis policy and stratagem must do
That you affect; and so must you resolve   105
That what you cannot as you would achieve
You must perforce accomplish as you may.
Take this of me: Lucrece was not more chaste
Than this Lavinia, Bassianus' love.
A speedier course [than] ling'ring languishment   110
Must we pursue, and I have found the path.
My lords, a solemn hunting is in hand:
There will the lovely Roman ladies troop;
The forest walks are wide and spacious;
And many unfrequented plots there are,   115
Fitted by kind for rape and villainy.
Single you thither then this dainty doe,
And strike her home by force, if not by words.
This way, or not at all, stand you in hope.
Come, come, our empress, with her sacred wit   120
To villainy and vengeance consecrate,
Will we acquaint [with all that] we intend,
And she shall file our engines with advice,
That will not suffer you to square yourselves,
But to your wishes' height advance you both.   125
The Emperor's court is like the house of Fame,
The palace full of tongues, of eyes, and ears;
The woods are ruthless, dreadful, deaf, and
        dull;
There speak, and strike, brave boys, and take your
        turns;
There serve your lust, shadowed from heaven's
        eye,   130
And revel in Lavinia's treasury.
    Chi. Thy counsel, lad, smells of no cowardice.
    Dem. *Sit fas aut nefas,* till I find the stream
To cool this heat, a charm to calm these fits,
Per Styga, per manes vehor.   [*Exeunt.* 135

---

62. **brabble:** squabble.   64. **jet:** encroach.   80. **propose:** face.   87. **shive:** slice.   89. **Vulcan's badge:** the horns of the cuckold.   100. **square:** quarrel.   103. **join ... jar:** cooperate for the thing you quarrel about.   110. **[than]** (Rowe).   *this* Q₁.   112. **solemn:** grand.   116. **kind:** nature.   117. **Single:** single out.   120. **sacred:** devoted.   122. **[with all that]** Q₂. *withal what* Q₁.   123. **file:** perfect.   **engines:** schemes.   126. **Fame:** Rumor.   133. *Sit ... nefas:* be it right or wrong.   135. *Per ... vehor:* I am borne across the Styx, among the shades.   These quotations are from Seneca's *Hippolytus.*

[SCENE II. *A forest near Rome.*]

Enter TITUS ANDRONICUS, *and his three sons*
[LUCIUS, QUINTUS, *and* MARTIUS], *making a
noise with hounds and horns, and* MARCUS.

Tit. The hunt is up, the morn is bright and grey,
The fields are fragrant and the woods are green.
Uncouple here and let us make a bay,
And wake the Emperor and his lovely bride,
And rouse the Prince, and ring a hunter's peal   5
That all the court may echo with the noise.
Sons, let it be your charge, as it is ours,
To attend the Emperor's person carefully.
I have been troubled in my sleep this night,
But dawning day new comfort hath inspir'd.   10

Here a cry of hounds, and wind horns in a peal.
Enter SATURNINUS, TAMORA, BASSIANUS, LAVINIA,
CHIRON, DEMETRIUS, *and their* Attendants.

Many good morrows to your Majesty;
Madam, to you as many and as good.
I promised your Grace a hunter's peal.
Sat. And you have rung it lustily, my lords;
Somewhat too early for new-married ladies.   15
Bas. Lavinia, how say you?
Lav.   I say, no;
I have been broad awake two hours and more.
Sat. Come on, then; horse and chariots let us
have,
And to our sport. [*To Tamora.*] Madam, now
shall ye see
Our Roman hunting.
Marc.   I have dogs, my lord,   20
Will rouse the proudest panther in the chase
And climb the highest promontory top.
Tit. And I have horse will follow where the game
Makes way, and run like swallows o'er the plain.
Dem. Chiron, we hunt not, we, with horse nor
hound,   25
But hope to pluck a dainty doe to ground.
                                        [*Exeunt.*

[SCENE III. *A lonely part of the forest.*]

Enter AARON [*with a bag of gold*].

Aar. He that had wit would think that I had
none
To bury so much gold under a tree
And never after to inherit it.
Let him that thinks of me so abjectly
Know that this gold must coin a stratagem,   5
Which, cunningly effected, will beget

A very excellent piece of villainy.
And so repose, sweet gold, for their unrest
                              [*Hides the gold.*]
That have their alms out of the Empress' chest.

Enter TAMORA.

Tam. My lovely Aaron, wherefore look'st thou
sad   10
When everything doth make a gleeful boast?
The birds chant melody on every bush,
The snake lies rolled in the cheerful sun,
The green leaves quiver with the cooling wind
And make a chequer'd shadow on the ground.   15
Under their sweet shade, Aaron, let us sit,
And, whilst the babbling echo mocks the hounds,
Replying shrilly to the well-tun'd horns
As if a double hunt were heard at once,
Let us sit down and mark their [yelping] noise;   20
And, after conflict such as was suppos'd
The wand'ring prince and Dido once enjoy'd,
When with a happy storm they were surpris'd
And curtain'd with a counsel-keeping cave,
We may, each wreathed in the other's arms,   25
Our pastimes done, possess a golden slumber;
Whiles hounds and horns and sweet melodious birds
Be unto us as is a nurse's song
Of lullaby to bring her babe asleep.
Aar. Madam, though Venus govern your de-
sires,   30
Saturn is dominator over mine.
What signifies my deadly-standing eye,
My silence and my cloudy melancholy,
My fleece of woolly hair that now uncurls
Even as an adder when she doth unroll   35
To do some fatal execution?
No, madam, these are no venereal signs.
Vengeance is in my heart, death in my hand,
Blood and revenge are hammering in my head.
Hark, Tamora, the empress of my soul,   40
Which never hopes more heaven than rests in thee,
This is the day of doom for Bassianus.
His Philomel must lose her tongue to-day,
Thy sons make pillage of her chastity
And wash their hands in Bassianus' blood.   45
Seest thou this letter? Take it up, I pray thee,
And give the King this fatal-plotted scroll.
Now question me no more; we are espied.
Here comes a parcel of our hopeful booty,
Which dreads not yet their lives' destruction.   50

Enter BASSIANUS *and* LAVINIA.

Tam. Ah, my sweet Moor, sweeter to me than
life!

Sc. ii, 3. **Uncouple:** unleash the hounds.
Sc. iii, 3. **inherit:** possess. 9. **alms . . . chest.** Obscure; possibly meaning that Aaron had received the gold from Tamora.
20. **[yelping]** F₁. *yellowing* Qq. 22. **prince:** Æneas. 23. **happy:** lucky. 32. **deadly-standing:** fixedly staring. 37. **ve-**
nereal: erotic. 43. **Philomel.** Philomel was ravished by Tereus, husband of her sister Progne, who cut out her tongue to
prevent detection (cf. II.iv.38).

Aar. No more, great Empress; Bassianus comes.
Be cross with him; and I'll go fetch thy sons
To back thy quarrels, whatsoe'er they be.   [*Exit.*]
   Bas. Who have we here?   Rome's royal Em-
     press,   55
Unfurnish'd of her well-beseeming troop?
Or is it Dian, habited like her,
Who hath abandoned her holy groves
To see the general hunting in this forest?
   Tam. Saucy controller of my private steps!   60
Had I the power that some say Dian had,
Thy temples should be planted presently
With horns, as was Actæon's; and the hounds
Should drive upon thy new-transformed limbs,
Unmannerly intruder as thou art!   65
   Lav. Under your patience, gentle Empress,
'Tis thought you have a goodly gift in horning;
And to be doubted that your Moor and you
Are singled forth to try experiments.
Jove shield your husband from his hounds to-day!   70
'Tis pity they should take him for a stag.
   Bas. Believe me, Queen, your [swarth] Cim-
     merian
Doth make your honour of his body's hue,
Spotted, detested, and abominable.
Why are you sequest'red from all your train,   75
Dismounted from your snow-white goodly steed,
And wand'red hither to an obscure plot,
Accompanied but with a barbarous Moor,
If foul desire had not conducted you?
   Lav. And, being intercepted in your sport,   80
Great reason that my noble lord be rated
For sauciness.   I pray you, let us hence,
And let her joy her raven-coloured love;
This valley fits the purpose passing well.
   Bas. The King, my brother, shall have note of
     this.   85
   Lav. Ay, for these slips have made him noted
     long,
Good king, to be so mightily abused.
   Tam. Why [have I] patience to endure all this?

Enter CHIRON *and* DEMETRIUS.

   Dem. How now, dear sovereign and our gracious
     mother!
Why doth your Highness look so pale and wan?   90
   Tam. Have I not reason, think you, to look pale?
These two have 'tic'd me hither to this place;
A barren detested vale you see it is;
The trees, though summer, yet forlorn and lean,
O'ercome with moss and baleful mistletoe.   95

Here never shines the sun; here nothing breeds,
Unless the nightly owl or fatal raven;
And when they show'd me this abhorred pit,
They told me, here, at dead time of the night,
A thousand fiends, a thousand hissing snakes,   100
Ten thousand swelling toads, as many urchins,
Would make such fearful and confused cries
As any mortal body hearing it
Should straight fall mad, or else die suddenly.
No sooner had they told this hellish tale   105
But straight they told me they would bind me here
Unto the body of a dismal yew,
And leave me to this miserable death.
And then they call'd me foul adulteress,
Lascivious Goth, and all the bitterest terms   110
That ever ear did hear to such effect;
And, had you not by wondrous fortune come,
This vengeance on me had they executed.
Revenge it, as you love your mother's life,
Or be ye not henceforth call'd my children.   115
   Dem. This is a witness that I am thy son.
               [*Stabs Bassianus.*
   Chi. And this for me, struck home to show my
     strength.
       [*Also stabs Bassianus, who dies.*]
   Lav. Ay, come, Semiramis, nay, barbarous
     Tamora,
For no name fits thy nature but thy own!
   Tam. Give me thy poniard; you shall know,
     my boys,   120
Your mother's hand shall right your mother's wrong.
   Dem. Stay, madam; here is more belongs to her.
First thrash the corn, then after burn the straw.
This minion stood upon her chastity,
Upon her nuptial vow, her loyalty,   125
And with that painted hope braves your mightiness;
And shall she carry this unto her grave?
   Chi. An if she do, I would I were an eunuch.
Drag hence her husband to some secret hole,
And make his dead trunk pillow to our lust.   130
   Tam. But when ye have the honey ye desire,
Let not this wasp outlive us both to sting.
   Chi. I warrant you, madam, we will make that
     sure.
Come, mistress, now perforce we will enjoy
That nice-preserved honesty of yours.   135
   Lav. O Tamora! thou bear'st a woman's face, —
   Tam. I will not hear her speak; away with her!
   Lav. Sweet lords, entreat her hear me but a word.
   Dem. Listen, fair madam: let it be your glory
To see her tears; but be your heart to them   140
As unrelenting flint to drops of rain.

---

56. **well-beseeming troop:** appropriate guard.   57. **habited:** dressed.   63. **Actæon's.** Actæon, while hunting, inad-vertently came upon Diana bathing, and was transformed by her into a stag.   He was then set upon by his own dogs and killed.   64. **drive:** rush.   69. **try** Q₂.   *try thy* Q₁.   72. **[swarth]** F₁.   *swartie* Qq.   **Cimmerian.** According to Homer, the Cimmerians lived in a land of darkness.   86. **slips:** offenses.   88. **[have I]** F₂.   *I have* Qq F₁.   95. **O'ercome with:** covered by.   101. **urchins:** hedgehogs.   124. **minion:** saucy wench.   **stood:** prided herself.   126. **painted:** unreal. The faulty meter suggests that the passage is corrupt.   135. **nice-preserved honesty:** fastidiously kept chastity.

Lav. When did the tiger's young ones teach the
    dam?
O, do not learn her wrath; she taught it thee;
The milk thou suck'dst from her did turn to marble;
Even at thy teat thou hadst thy tyranny.   145
Yet every mother breeds not sons alike.
[*To Chiron.*] Do thou entreat her show a woman's
    pity.
Chi. What, wouldst thou have me prove myself
    a bastard?
Lav. 'Tis true; the raven doth not hatch a lark.
Yet have I heard — O, could I find it now! —   150
The lion, mov'd with pity, did endure
To have his princely paws par'd all away;
Some say that ravens foster forlorn children
The whilst their own birds famish in their nests;
O, be to me, though thy hard heart say no,   155
Nothing so kind, but something pitiful!
Tam. I know not what it means; away with her!
Lav. O, let me teach thee! For my father's
    sake,
That gave thee life when well he might have slain
    thee,
Be not obdurate, open thy deaf ears.   160
Tam. Hadst thou in person ne'er offended me,
Even for his sake am I pitiless.
Remember, boys, I pour'd forth tears in vain
To save your brother from the sacrifice;
But fierce Andronicus would not relent.   165
Therefore, away with her, and use her as you will;
The worse to her, the better lov'd of me.
Lav. O Tamora, be call'd a gentle queen,
And with thine own hands kill me in this place!
For 'tis not life that I have begg'd so long;   170
Poor I was slain when Bassianus died.
Tam. What begg'st thou, then? Fond woman,
    let me go.
Lav. 'Tis present death I beg, and one thing
    more
That womanhood denies my tongue to tell.
O, keep me from their worse than killing lust,   175
And tumble me into some loathsome pit
Where never man's eye may behold my body.
Do this, and be a charitable murderer.
Tam. So should I rob my sweet sons of their fee.
No, let them satisfy their lust on thee.   180
Dem. Away! for thou hast stay'd us here too long.
Lav. No grace? no womanhood? Ah, beastly
    creature!
The blot and enemy to our general name!
Confusion fall —
Chi. Nay, then I'll stop your mouth. Bring
    thou her husband;   185
This is the hole where Aaron bid us hide him.

[*Demetrius throws the body of Bassianus
    into the pit; then exeunt Demetrius and
    Chiron, dragging off Lavinia.*]
Tam. Farewell, my sons; see that you make
    her sure.
Ne'er let my heart know merry cheer indeed
Till all the Andronici be made away.
Now will I hence to seek my lovely Moor,   190
And let my spleenful sons this trull deflow'r.
    [*Exit.*

Re-enter AARON, *with* [QUINTUS *and* MARTIUS].
Aar. Come on, my lords, the better foot before.
Straight will I bring you to the loathsome pit
Where I espied the panther fast asleep.
Quin. My sight is very dull, whate'er it bodes.
Mart. And mine, I promise you; were't not for
    shame,   196
Well could I leave our sport to sleep a while.
    [*Falls into the pit.*]
Quin. What, art thou fallen? What subtle hole
    is this,
Whose mouth is covered with rude-growing briers,
Upon whose leaves are drops of new-shed blood   200
As fresh as morning dew distill'd on flowers?
A very fatal place it seems to me.
Speak, brother, hast thou hurt thee with the fall?
Mart. O brother, with the dismall'st object hurt
That ever eye with sight made heart lament!   205
Aar. [*Aside.*] Now will I fetch the King to find
    them here,
That he thereby may have a likely guess
How these were they that made away his brother.
    [*Exit.*
Mart. Why dost not comfort me and help me
    out
From this unhallow'd and blood-stained hole?   210
Quin. I am surprised with an uncouth fear;
A chilling sweat o'er-runs my trembling joints;
My heart suspects more than mine eye can see.
Mart. To prove thou hast a true-divining heart,
Aaron and thou look down into this den   215
And see a fearful sight of blood and death.
Quin. Aaron is gone; and my compassionate
    heart
Will not permit mine eyes once to behold
The thing whereat it trembles by surmise.
O, tell me who it is; for ne'er till now   220
Was I a child to fear I know not what.
Mart. Lord Bassianus lies [embrued] in blood,
All on a heap, like to a slaughtered lamb,
In this detested, dark, blood-drinking pit.
Quin. If it be dark, how dost thou know 'tis
    he?   225

---

143. **learn her wrath:** teach wrath to her. 152. **paws:** claws. 172. **Fond:** foolish. 173. **present:** instant. 191. **spleenful:** passionate. 211. **uncouth:** strange. 222. [embrued] **in blood:** blood-stained. *bereaud in blood* Q1. *embrued here* Q2. The unique Q1 has the marginal emendation *heere reav'd of lyfe.*

Mart. Upon his bloody finger he doth wear
A precious ring that lightens all this hole,
Which, like a taper in some monument,
Doth shine upon the dead man's earthy cheeks
And shows the ragged entrails of this pit.   230
So pale did shine the moon on [Pyramus]
When he by night lay bath'd in maiden blood.
O brother, help me with thy fainting hand —
If fear hath made thee faint, as me it hath —
Out of this fell devouring receptacle,   235
As hateful as Cocytus' misty mouth.

    Quin. Reach me thy hand, that I may help
      thee out;
Or, wanting strength to do thee so much good,
I may be pluck'd into the swallowing womb
Of this deep pit, poor Bassianus' grave.   240
I have no strength to pluck thee to the brink.

    Mart. Nor I no strength to climb without thy
      help.

    Quin. Thy hand once more; I will not loose again
Till thou art here aloft or I below.
Thou canst not come to me; I come to thee.   245
                              [Falls in.

Enter SATURNINUS *with* AARON.

    Sat. Along with me; I'll see what hole is here,
And what he is that now is leap'd into it.
Say, who art thou that lately didst descend
Into this gaping hollow of the earth?

    Mart. The unhappy sons of old Andronicus,   250
Brought hither in a most unlucky hour
To find thy brother Bassianus dead.

    Sat. My brother dead! I know thou dost but jest.
He and his lady both are at the lodge
Upon the north side of this pleasant chase;   255
'Tis not an hour since I left them there.

    Mart. We know not where you left them all
      alive;
But, out, alas! here have we found him dead.

Re-enter TAMORA [*with* Attendants; TITUS]
    ANDRONICUS, *and* LUCIUS

    Tam. Where is my lord the King?

    Sat. Here, Tamora, though griev'd with killing
      grief.   260

    Tam. Where is thy brother Bassianus?

    Sat. Now to the bottom dost thou search my
      wound;
Poor Bassianus here lies murdered.

    Tam. Then all too late I bring this fatal writ,
The complot of this timeless tragedy;   265
And wonder greatly that man's face can fold
In pleasing smiles such murderous tyranny.
            [She giveth Saturnine a letter.

    Sat. (*Reads.*) "An if we miss to meet him hand-
      somely —
Sweet huntsman, Bassianus 'tis we mean —
Do thou so much as dig the grave for him.   270
Thou know'st our meaning. Look for thy reward
Among the nettles at the elder-tree
Which overshades the mouth of that same pit
Where we decreed to bury Bassianus.
Do this, and purchase us thy lasting friends."   275
O Tamora! was ever heard the like?
This is the pit, and this the elder-tree.
Look, sirs, if you can find the huntsman out
That should have murdered Bassianus here.

    Aar. My gracious lord here is the bag of gold.   280

    Sat. [*To Titus.*] Two of thy whelps, fell curs of
      bloody kind,
Have here bereft my brother of his life. —
Sirs, drag them from the pit unto the prison.
There let them bide until we have devis'd
Some never-heard-of torturing pain for them.   285

    Tam. What, are they in this pit? O wondrous
      thing!
How easily murder is discovered!

    Tit. High Emperor, upon my feeble knee
I beg this boon, with tears not lightly shed,
That this fell fault of my accursed sons, —   290
Accursed, if the fault be prov'd in them, —

    Sat. If it be prov'd! You see it is apparent.
Who found this letter? Tamora, was it you?

    Tam. Andronicus himself did take it up.

    Tit. I did, my lord; yet let me be their bail,   295
For, by my father's reverend tomb, I vow
They shall be ready at your Highness' will
To answer their suspicion with their lives.

    Sat. Thou shalt not bail them; see thou follow
      me.
Some bring the murdered body, some the mur-
      derers.   300
Let them not speak a word; the guilt is plain;
For, by my soul, were there worse end than death,
That end upon them should be executed.

    Tam. Andronicus, I will entreat the King.
Fear not thy sons; they shall do well enough.   305

    Tit. Come, Lucius, come; stay not to talk with
      them.   *[Exeunt.*

[SCENE IV. *Another part of the forest.*]

Enter [DEMETRIUS *and* CHIRON], *with* LAVINIA,
ravished; her hands cut off, and her tongue cut out.

    Dem. So, now go tell, an if thy tongue can speak,
Who 'twas that cut thy tongue and ravish'd thee.

    Chi. Write down thy mind, bewray thy meaning
      so,

227. **ring.** Probably a carbuncle, formerly believed to shine in the dark.   231. [Pyramus] Q₂. *Priamus* Q₁. See *Mid-summer Night's Dream,* III.i.50 ff.   236. **Cocytus:** a river in Hades.   255. **chase:** hunting ground.   265. **timeless:** untimely.   305. **Fear not:** fear not for.

An if thy stumps will let thee play the scribe.
　Dem. See how with signs and tokens she can
　　scrowl.　　　　　　　　　　　　　　　5
　Chi. Go home, call for sweet water, wash thy
　　hands.
　Dem. She hath no tongue to call, nor hands to
　　wash;
And so let's leave her to her silent walks.
　Chi. An't were my case, I should go hang myself.
　Dem. If thou hadst hands to help thee knit the
　　cord.　　*[Exeunt Demetrius and Chiron.* 10

Horns winded. Enter MARCUS *from hunting.*

　Mar. Who is this — my niece? — that flies
　　away so fast?
Cousin, a word; where is your husband?
If I do dream, would all my wealth would wake me!
If I do wake, some planet strike me down,
That I may slumber an eternal sleep!　　15
Speak, gentle niece; what stern ungentle hands
Hath lopp'd and hew'd and made thy body bare
Of her two branches, those sweet ornaments
Whose circling shadows kings have sought to sleep
　in,
And might not gain so great a happiness　　20
As [have] thy love?　Why dost not speak to me?
Alas, a crimson river of warm blood,
Like to a bubbling fountain stirr'd with wind,
Doth rise and fall between thy rosed lips,
Coming and going with thy honey breath.　　25
But, sure, some Tereus hath deflow'red thee
And, lest thou shouldst detect him, cut thy tongue.
Ah, now thou turn'st away thy face for shame!
And, notwithstanding all this loss of blood,
As from a conduit with three issuing spouts,　　30
Yet do thy cheeks look red as Titan's face
Blushing to be encount'red with a cloud.
Shall I speak for thee?　Shall I say 'tis so?
O, that I knew thy heart; and knew the beast,
That I might rail at him to ease my mind!　　35
Sorrow concealed, like an oven stopp'd,
Doth burn the heart to cinders where it is.
Fair Philomel, why, she but lost her tongue,
And in a tedious sampler sew'd her mind;
But, lovely niece, that mean is cut from thee;　　40
A craftier Tereus, cousin, hast thou met,
And he hath cut those pretty fingers off
That could have better sew'd than Philomel.
O, had the monster seen those lily hands
Tremble, like aspen-leaves, upon a lute　　45
And make the silken strings delight to kiss them,
He would not then have touch'd them for his life!
Or, had he heard the heavenly harmony

Which that sweet tongue hath made,
He would have dropp'd his knife, and fell asleep　50
As Cerberus at the Thracian poet's feet.
Come, let us go, and make thy father blind,
For such a sight will blind a father's eye.
One hour's storm will drown the fragrant meads;
What will whole months of tears thy father's eyes?
Do not draw back, for we will mourn with thee.　56
O, could our mourning ease thy misery!　　*[Exeunt.*

ACT III

[SCENE I. *Rome. A street.*]

Enter Judges, Senators [*and* Tribunes], *with Martius
　and Quintus, bound, passing on the stage to the
　place of execution;* TITUS *going before, pleading.*

　Tit. Hear me, grave fathers! noble tribunes, stay!
For pity of mine age, whose youth was spent
In dangerous wars whilst you securely slept,
For all my blood in Rome's great quarrel shed,
For all the frosty nights that I have watch'd,　　5
And for these bitter tears which now you see
Filling the aged wrinkles in my cheeks,
Be pitiful to my condemned sons,
Whose souls are not corrupted as 'tis thought.
For two and twenty sons I never wept,　　10
Because they died in honour's lofty bed.
　　　　*[Lieth down; the Judges, etc., pass by him
　　　　　[and exeunt].*
For these, tribunes, in the dust I write
My heart's deep languor and my soul's sad tears.
Let my tears stanch the earth's dry appetite;
My sons' sweet blood will make it shame and
　blush.　　　　　　　　　　　　　　　15
O earth, I will befriend thee more with rain,
That shall distil from these two ancient urns,
Than youthful April shall with all his show'rs.
In summer's drought I'll drop upon thee still;
In winter with warm tears I'll melt the snow　　20
And keep eternal spring-time [on thy] face,
So thou refuse to drink my dear sons' blood.

Enter LUCIUS, *with his weapon drawn.*

O reverend tribunes!　O gentle, aged men!
Unbind my sons, reverse the doom of death;
And let me say, that never wept before,　　25
My tears are now prevailing orators.
　Luc. O noble father, you lament in vain.
The tribunes hear you not; no man is by;
And you recount your sorrows to a stone.
　Tit. Ah, Lucius, for thy brothers let me plead.　30
Grave tribunes, once more I entreat of you, —

Sc. iv, 5. **scrowl:** scrawl.　6. **sweet:** perfumed.　12. **Cousin.**　Used of any near relation, outside of the immediate family.
21. **[have]** Q₂.　*halfe* Q₁.　40. **mean:** means.　51. **As...feet.**　When Orpheus descended into Hades to retrieve Eurydice,
he quieted the dog Cerberus, three-headed guardian of the gates, with his music.
　Act III, sc. i, 21. **[on thy]** Q₂.　*out by* Q₁.

Luc. My gracious lord, no tribune hears you
     speak.

Tit. Why, 'tis no matter, man; if they did hear,
They would not mark me; [or] if they did mark,
They would not pity me; yet plead I must,   35
And bootless unto them.
Therefore I tell my sorrows to the stones,
Who, though they cannot answer my distress,
Yet in some sort they are better than the tribunes,
For that they will not intercept my tale.   40
When I do weep, they humbly at my feet
Receive my tears and seem to weep with me;
And, were they but attired in grave weeds,
Rome could afford no tribunes like to these.
A stone is soft as wax, tribunes more hard than
     stones;   45
A stone is silent, and offendeth not,
And tribunes with their tongues doom men to
     death.   [*Rises.*]
But wherefore stand'st thou with thy weapon
     drawn?

Luc. To rescue my two brothers from their death;
For which attempt the judges have pronounc'd   50
My everlasting doom of banishment.

Tit. O happy man! they have befriended thee.
Why, foolish Lucius, dost thou not perceive
That Rome is but a wilderness of tigers?
Tigers must prey, and Rome affords no prey   55
But me and mine. How happy art thou, then,
From these devourers to be banished!
But who comes with our brother Marcus here?

Enter MARCUS *and* LAVINIA.

Marc. Titus, prepare thy aged eyes to weep;
Or, if not so, thy noble heart to break.   60
I bring consuming sorrow to thine age.

Tit. Will it consume me? Let me see it, then.

Marc. This was thy daughter.

Tit.   Why, Marcus, so she is.

Luc. Ay me, this object kills me!

Tit. Faint-hearted boy, arise, and look upon
     her.   65
Speak, [my] Lavinia, what accursed hand
Hath made thee handless in thy father's sight?
What fool hath added water to the sea,
Or brought a faggot to bright-burning Troy?
My grief was at the height before thou cam'st,   70
And now, like Nilus, it disdaineth bounds.
Give me a sword, I'll chop off my hands too;
For they have fought for Rome, and all in vain;
And they have nurs'd this woe, in feeding life;
In bootless prayer have they been held up,   75
And they have serv'd me to effectless use.
Now all the service I require of them
Is that the one will help to cut the other.

'Tis well, Lavinia, that thou hast no hands;
For hands to do Rome service is but vain.   80

Luc. Speak, gentle sister; who hath martyr'd
     thee?

Marc. O, that delightful engine of her thoughts,
That blabb'd them with such pleasing eloquence,
Is torn from forth that pretty hollow cage,
Where, like a sweet melodious bird, it sung   85
Sweet varied notes, enchanting every ear!

Luc. O, say thou for her, who hath done this
     deed?

Marc. O, thus I found her, straying in the park,
Seeking to hide herself, as doth the deer
That hath receiv'd some unrecuring wound.   90

Tit. It was my deer, and he that wounded her
Hath hurt me more than had he kill'd me dead.
For now I stand as one upon a rock
Environ'd with a wilderness of sea,
Who marks the waxing tide grow wave by wave,   95
Expecting ever when some envious surge
Will in his brinish bowels swallow him.
This way to death my wretched sons are gone,
Here stands my other son, a banish'd man,
And here my brother, weeping at my woes;   100
But that which gives my soul the greatest spurn
Is dear Lavinia, dearer than my soul.
Had I but seen thy picture in this plight,
It would have madded me; what shall I do
Now I behold thy lively body so?   105
Thou hast no hands to wipe away thy tears;
Nor tongue to tell me who hath martyr'd thee.
Thy husband he is dead; and for his death
Thy brothers are condemn'd, and dead by this.
Look, Marcus! ah, son Lucius, look on her!   110
When I did name her brothers, then fresh tears
Stood on her cheeks, as doth the honey-dew
Upon a gath'red lily almost withered.

Marc. Perchance she weeps because they kill'd
     her husband;
Perchance because she knows them innocent.   115

Tit. If they did kill thy husband, then be joyful,
Because the law hath ta'en revenge on them.
No, no, they would not do so foul a deed;
Witness the sorrow that their sister makes.
Gentle Lavinia, let me kiss thy lips,   120
Or make some sign how I may do thee ease.
Shall thy good uncle and thy brother Lucius
And thou and I sit round about some fountain,
Looking all downwards, to behold our cheeks
How they are stain'd, like meadows yet not dry   125
With miry slime left on them by a flood?
And in the fountain shall we gaze so long
Till the fresh taste be taken from that clearness,
And made a brine-pit with our bitter tears?
Or shall we cut away our hands, like thine?   130

34. [or] Q₂. Om. Q₁.   66. [my] F₂. Om. Qq F₁.   71. **Nilus:** the river Nile.   90. **unrecuring:** incurable.   96. **envious:**
malicious.   101. **spurn:** blow.   105. **lively:** living.

Or shall we bite our tongues, and in dumb shows
Pass the remainder of our hateful days?
What shall we do?   Let us that have our tongues
Plot some device of further misery,
To make us wond'red at in time to come.   135
    Luc. Sweet father, cease your tears; for, at your grief
See how my wretched sister sobs and weeps.
    Marc. Patience, dear niece.   Good Titus, dry thine eyes.
    Tit. Ah, Marcus, Marcus! brother, well I wot
Thy napkin cannot drink a tear of mine,   140
For thou, poor man, hast drown'd it with thine own.
    Luc. Ah, my Lavinia, I will wipe thy cheeks.
    Tit. Mark, Marcus, mark!   I understand her signs.
Had she a tongue to speak, now would she say
That to her brother which I said to thee: 145
His napkin, with [his] true tears all bewet,
Can do no service on her sorrowful cheeks.
O, what a sympathy of woe is this,
As far from help as Limbo is from bliss!

        Enter AARON *the Moor.*

    Aar. Titus Andronicus, my lord the Emperor   150
Sends thee this word, — that, if thou love thy sons,
Let Marcus, Lucius, or thyself, old Titus,
Or any one of you, chop off your hand
And send it to the King; he for the same
Will send thee hither both thy sons alive;   155
And that shall be the ransom for their fault.
    Tit. O gracious emperor!   O gentle Aaron!
Did ever raven sing so like a lark
That gives sweet tidings of the sun's uprise?
With all my heart I'll send the Emperor   160
My hand.
Good Aaron, wilt thou help to chop it off?
    Luc. Stay, father! for that noble hand of thine
That hath thrown down so many enemies
Shall not be sent.   My hand will serve the turn.   165
My youth can better spare my blood than you,
And therefore mine shall save my brothers' lives.
    Marc. Which of your hands hath not defended Rome
And rear'd aloft the bloody battle-axe,
Writing destruction on the enemy's castle?   170
O, none of both but are of high desert.
My hand hath been but idle; let it serve
To ransom my two nephews from their death;
Then have I kept it to a worthy end.
    Aar. Nay, come, agree whose hand shall go along,   175
For fear they die before their pardon come.
    Marc. My hand shall go.
    Luc.   By heaven, it shall not go!

    Tit. Sirs, strive no more: such with'red herbs as these
Are meet for plucking up, and therefore mine.
    Luc. Sweet father, if I shall be thought thy son,   180
Let me redeem my brothers both from death.
    Marc. And, for our father's sake and mother's care,
Now let me show a brother's love to thee.
    Tit. Agree between you; I will spare my hand.
    Luc. Then I'll go fetch an axe.   185
    Marc. But I will use the axe.
                   [Exeunt [Lucius and Marcus]
    Tit. Come hither, Aaron; I'll deceive them both.
Lend me thy hand, and I will give thee mine.
    Aar. [Aside.] If that be call'd deceit, I will be honest
And never, whilst I live, deceive men so;   190
But I'll deceive you in another sort,
And that you'll say, ere half an hour pass.
                [Cuts off Titus's hand.

       Re-enter LUCIUS *and* MARCUS.
    Tit. Now stay your strife; what shall be is dispatch'd.
Good Aaron, give his Majesty my hand.
Tell him it was a hand that warded him   195
From thousand dangers; bid him bury it:
More hath it merited; that let it have.
As for my sons, say I account of them
As jewels purchas'd at an easy price;
And yet dear too, because I bought mine own.   200
    Aar. I go, Andronicus; and for thy hand
Look by and by to have thy sons with thee.
[Aside.] Their heads, I mean.   O, how this villainy
Doth fat me with the very thoughts of it!
Let fools do good, and fair men call for grace,   205
Aaron will have his soul black like his face. *[Exit.*
    Tit. O, here I lift this one hand up to heaven
And bow this feeble ruin to the earth;
If any power pities wretched tears,
To that I call! *[To Lav.]* What, wouldst thou kneel with me?   210
Do, then, dear heart; for Heaven shall hear our prayers;
Or with our sighs we'll breathe the welkin dim
And stain the sun with fog, as sometime clouds
When they do hug him in their melting bosoms.
    Marc. O brother, speak with possibility,   215
And do not break into these deep extremes.
    Tit. Is not my sorrow deep, having no bottom?
Then be my passions bottomless with them!
    Marc. But yet let reason govern thy lament.
    Tit. If there were reason for these miseries,   220
Then into limits could I bind my woes.

---

140. **napkin:** handkerchief.   146. **[his]** F₄. *her* Q₁.   149. **Limbo:** purgatory.

When heaven doth weep, doth not the earth o'er-
    flow?
If the winds rage, doth not the sea wax mad,
Threat'ning the welkin with his big-swoln face?
And wilt thou have a reason for this coil?   225
I am the sea; hark, how her sighs [do blow]!
She is the weeping welkin, I the earth;
Then must my sea be moved with her sighs;
Then must my earth with her continual tears
Become a deluge, overflow'd and drown'd;   230
For why my bowels cannot hide her woes,
But like a drunkard must I vomit them.
Then give me leave, for losers will have leave
To ease their stomachs with their bitter tongues.

Enter a MESSENGER, *with two heads and a hand.*

  Mess. Worthy Andronicus, ill art thou repaid   235
For that good hand thou sent'st the Emperor.
Here are the heads of thy two noble sons;
And here's thy hand, in scorn to thee sent back, —
Thy grief their sports, thy resolution mock'd,
That woe is me to think upon thy woes   240
More than remembrance of my father's death.
                           [*Exit.*
  Marc. Now let hot Ætna cool in Sicily,
And be my heart an ever-burning hell!
These miseries are more than may be borne.
To weep with them that weep doth ease some
    deal,   245
But sorrow flouted at is double death.
  Luc. Ah, that this sight should make so deep a
    wound
And yet detested life not shrink thereat!
That ever death should let life bear his name
Where life hath no more interest but to breathe!   250
                  [*Lavinia kisses Titus.*]
  Marc. Alas, poor heart, that kiss is comfortless
As frozen water to a starved snake.
  Tit. When 'will this fearful slumber have an
    end?
  Marc. Now, farewell, flatt'ry; die, Andronicus.
Thou dost not slumber; see, thy two sons' heads,   255
Thy warlike hand, thy mangled daughter here,
Thy other banish'd son with this dear sight
Struck pale and bloodless; and thy brother, I,
Even like a stony image, cold and numb.
Ah, now no more will I control thy griefs.   260
Rend off thy silver hair, thy other hand
Gnawing with thy teeth; and be this dismal sight
The closing up of our most wretched eyes.
Now is a time to storm; why art thou still?
  Tit. Ha, ha, ha!   265

  Marc. Why dost thou laugh? It fits not with
    this hour.
  Tit. Why, I have not another tear to shed.
Besides, this sorrow is an enemy,
And would usurp upon my wat'ry eyes
And make them blind with tributary tears;   270
Then which way shall I find Revenge's cave?
For these two heads do seem to speak to me
And threat me I shall never come to bliss
Till all these mischiefs be return'd again
Even in their throats that [have] committed them.
Come, let me see what task I have to do.   276
You heavy people, circle me about,
That I may turn me to each one of you
And swear unto my soul to right your wrongs.
The vow is made. Come, brother, take a head;   280
And in this hand the other will I bear.
Lavinia, thou shalt be employ'd in these [things]!
Bear thou my hand, sweet wench, between thy
    teeth.
As for thee, boy, go, get thee from my sight;
Thou art an exile, and thou must not stay.   285
Hie to the Goths, and raise an army there;
And, if [you] love me, as I think you do,
Let's kiss and part, for we have much to do.
        [*Exeunt [Titus, Marcus, and Lavinia].*
  Luc. Farewell, Andronicus, my noble father,
The woefull'st man that ever liv'd in Rome.   290
Farewell, proud Rome; till Lucius come again,
He [leaves] his pledges dearer than his life.
Farewell, Lavinia, my noble sister;
O, would thou wert as thou tofore hast been!
But now nor Lucius nor Lavinia lives   295
But in oblivion and hateful griefs.
If Lucius live, he will requite your wrongs
And make proud Saturnine and his emperess
Beg at the gates, like Tarquin and his queen.
Now will I to the Goths, and raise a pow'r,   300
To be reveng'd on Rome and Saturnine.   [*Exit.*

[SCENE II. *A room in Titus's house. A banquet
set out.*

Enter TITUS, MARCUS, LAVINIA, *and young* LUCIUS.

  Tit. So, so; now sit; and look you eat no more
Than will preserve just so much strength in us
As will revenge these bitter woes of ours.
Marcus, unknit that sorrow-wreathen knot;
Thy niece and I, poor creatures, want our hands   5
And cannot passionate our tenfold grief
With folded arms. This poor right hand of mine
Is left to tyrannize upon my breast;

---

225. **coil:** confusion.   226. **[do blow]** F₂.   *doth flow* Q₁.   231. **For why:** because.   245. **some deal:** somewhat.   252.
starved: numb with cold.   257. **dear:** grievous.   275. **[have]** Q₂.   *hath* Q₁.   282. **[things]** F₁.   *Armes* Qq.   287. **[you]**
Q₂.   *yee* Q₁.   292. **[leaves]** (Rowe).   *loves* Q₁.   300. **pow'r:** army.
  Sc. ii. This scene, omitted in Qq, is supplied from F₁.   4. **sorrow-wreathen knot:** i.e.. arms crossed in a pose of deep grief
6. **passionate:** passionately express

Who, when my heart, all mad with misery,
Beats in this hollow prison of my flesh,   10
Then thus I thump it down.
[*To Lavinia.*] Thou map of woe, that thus dost
    talk in signs!
When thy poor heart beats with outrageous beating,
Thou canst not strike it thus to make it still.
Wound it with sighing, girl, kill it with groans;   15
Or get some little knife between thy teeth,
And just against thy heart make thou a hole,
That all the tears that thy poor eyes let fall
May run into that sink, and soaking in
Drown the lamenting fool in sea-salt tears.   20
   Marc. Fie, brother, fie! teach her not thus to lay
Such violent hands upon her tender life.
    Tit. How now! has sorrow made thee dote al-
    ready?
Why, Marcus, no man should be mad but I.
What violent hands can she lay on her life?   25
Ah, wherefore dost thou urge the name of hands,
To bid Æneas tell the tale twice o'er
How Troy was burnt and he made miserable?
O, handle not the theme, to talk of hands
Lest we remember still that we have none.   30
Fie, fie, how franticly I square my talk,
As if we should forget we had no hands
If Marcus did not name the word of hands!
Come, let's fall to; and, gentle girl, eat this.
Here is no drink! Hark, Marcus, what she says;   35
I can interpret all her martyr'd signs:
She says she drinks no other drink but tears,
Brew'd with her sorrow, mash'd upon her cheeks.
Speechless complainer, I will learn thy thought;
In thy dumb action will I be as perfect   40
As begging hermits in their holy prayers.
Thou shalt not sigh, nor hold thy stumps to heaven,
Nor wink, nor nod, nor kneel, nor make a sign,
But I of these will wrest an alphabet
And by still practice learn to know thy meaning.   45
   Young Luc. Good grandsire, leave these bitter
    deep laments.
Make my aunt merry with some pleasing tale.
   Marc. Alas, the tender boy, in passion mov'd,
Doth weep to see his grandsire's heaviness.
   Tit. Peace, tender sapling; thou art made of
    tears,   50
And tears will quickly melt thy life away.
         [*Marcus strikes the dish with a knife.*
What dost thou strike at, Marcus, with thy knife?
   Marc. At that that I have kill'd, my lord; a fly.
   Tit. Out on thee, murderer! thou kill'st my heart;
Mine eyes are cloy'd with view of tyranny.   55
A deed of death done on the innocent
Becomes not Titus' brother. Get thee gone;

I see thou art not for my company.
   Marc. Alas, my lord, I have but kill'd a fly.
   Tit. "But!" How, if that fly had a father and
    mother?   60
How would he hang his slender gilded wings
And buzz lamenting doings in the air!
Poor harmless fly,
That, with his pretty buzzing melody,
Came here to make us merry! and thou hast kill'd
    him.   65
   Marc. Pardon me, sir, it was a black ill-favour'd
    fly,
Like to the Empress' Moor; therefore I kill'd him.
   Tit. O, O, O,
Then pardon me for reprehending thee,
For thou hast done a charitable deed.   70
Give me thy knife, I will insult on him,
Flattering myself, as if it were the Moor
Come hither purposely to poison me. —
There's for thyself, and that's for Tamora.
Ah, sirrah!   75
Yet, I think, we are not brought so low
But that between us we can kill a fly
That comes in likeness of a coal-black Moor.
   Marc. Alas, poor man! grief has so wrought on
    him
He takes false shadows for true substances.   80
   Tit. Come, take away. Lavinia, go with me.
I'll to thy closet, and go read with thee
Sad stories chanced in the times of old.
Come, boy, and go with me; thy sight is young,
And thou shalt read when mine begin to dazzle.]   85
                    [*Exeunt.*

ACT IV

[SCENE I. *Rome. Titus's garden.*]

Enter young LUCIUS, *and* LAVINIA *running after
him, and the boy flies from her, with his books
under his arm. Then enter* TITUS *and* MARCUS.

   Young Luc. Help, grandsire, help! my aunt
    Lavinia
Follows me everywhere, I know not why.
Good uncle Marcus, see how swift she comes.
Alas, sweet aunt, I know not what you mean.
   Marc. Stand by me, Lucius; do not fear thine
    aunt.   5
   Tit. She loves thee, boy, too well to do thee harm.
   Young Luc. Ay, when my father was in Rome
    she did.
   Marc. What means my niece Lavinia by these
    signs?
   Tit. Fear her not, Lucius; somewhat doth she
    mean.

---

12. **map:** picture. 15. **Wound . . . sighing.** It was believed that every sigh cost a drop of blood. 31. **square:** fashion.
38. **Brew'd . . . mash'd.** Metaphors of the brewery. 44. **of:** from. 45. **still:** constant. 62. **lamenting doings:** lamentable tales. 71. **insult on:** exult over. 81. **take away:** clear the table. 85. **mine:** my eyes. **dazzle:** be dazzled.

See, Lucius, see how much she makes of thee;   10
Somewhither would she have thee go with her.
Ah, boy, Cornelia never with more care
Read to her sons than she hath read to thee
Sweet poetry and Tully's Orator.
Canst thou not guess wherefore she plies thee
    thus?   15
    Young Luc. My lord, I know not, I, nor can I
    guess,
Unless some fit or frenzy do possess her;
For I have heard my grandsire say full oft
Extremity of griefs would make men mad,
And I have read that Hecuba of Troy   20
Ran mad for sorrow. That made me to fear;
Although, my lord, I know my noble aunt
Loves me as dear as e'er my mother did,
And would not, but in fury, fright my youth;
Which made me down to throw my books, and
    fly, —   25
Causeless, perhaps. But pardon me, sweet aunt;
And, madam, if my uncle Marcus go,
I will most willingly attend your ladyship.
    Marc. Lucius, I will.
    [*Lavinia turns over with her stumps the
    books which Lucius has let fall.*]
    Tit. How now, Lavinia! Marcus, what means
    this?   30
Some book there is that she desires to see.
Which is it, girl, of these? — Open them, boy. —
But thou art deeper read, and better skill'd;
Come, and take choice of all my library,
And so beguile thy sorrow, till the heavens   35
Reveal the damn'd contriver of this deed.
Why lifts she up her arms in sequence thus?
    Marc. I think she means that there were more
    than one
Confederate in the fact. Ay, more there was;
Or else to heaven she heaves them for revenge. 40
    Tit. Lucius, what book is that she tosseth so?
    Young Luc. Grandsire, 'tis Ovid's Metamor-
    phoses;
My mother gave it me.
    Marc.   For love of her that's gone,
Perhaps she cull'd it from among the rest.
    Tit. Soft! so busily she turns the leaves! Help
    her.   45
What would she find? Lavinia, shall I read?
This is the tragic tale of Philomel,
And treats of Tereus' treason and his rape;
And rape, I fear, was root of thy annoy.
    Marc. See, brother, see; note how she quotes
    the leaves.   50
    Tit. Lavinia, wert thou thus surpris'd, sweet girl,

Ravish'd and wrong'd, as Philomela was,
Forc'd in the ruthless, vast, and gloomy woods?
See, see!
Ay, such a place there is where we did hunt — 55
O, had we never, never hunted there! —
Pattern'd by that the poet here describes,
By nature made for murders and for rapes.
    Marc. O, why should nature build so foul a den,
Unless the gods delight in tragedies?   60
    Tit. Give signs, sweet girl, for here are none but
    friends,
What Roman lord it was durst do the deed;
Or slunk not Saturnine, as Tarquin erst,
That left the camp to sin in Lucrece' bed?
    Marc. Sit down, sweet niece; brother, sit down
    by me.   65
Apollo, Pallas, Jove, or Mercury,
Inspire me, that I may this treason find!
My lord, look here; look here, Lavinia.
    [*He writes his name with his staff, and
    guides it with feet and mouth.*
This sandy plot is plain; guide, if thou canst,
This after me. I have writ my name   70
Without the help of any hand at all.
Curs'd be that heart that forc'd us to this shift!
Write thou, good niece; and here display at last
What God will have discovered for revenge.
Heaven guide thy pen to print thy sorrows plain, 75
That we may know the traitors and the truth!
    [*She takes the staff in her mouth, and
    guides it with her stumps, and writes.*
    Tit. O, do ye read, my lord, what she hath writ?
"*Stuprum* — Chiron — Demetrius."
    Marc. What, what! the lustful sons of Tamora
Performers of this heinous, bloody deed?   80
    Tit. Magni Dominator poli,
Tam lentus audis scelera? tam lentus vides?
    Marc. O, calm thee, gentle lord; although I know
There is enough written upon this earth
To stir a mutiny in the mildest thoughts,   85
And arm the minds of infants to exclaims.
My lord, kneel down with me; Lavinia, kneel;
And kneel, sweet boy, the Roman Hector's hope;
And swear with me, — as, with the woeful fere
And father of that chaste dishonoured dame, 90
Lord Junius Brutus sware for Lucrece' rape, —
That we will prosecute by good advice
Mortal revenge upon these traitorous Goths,
And see their blood, or die with this reproach.
    Tit. 'Tis sure enough, an you knew how. 95
But if you hunt these bear-whelps, then beware!
The dam will wake; and, if she wind you once,
She's with the lion deeply still in league,

Act IV, sc. i, 12. **Cornelia:** mother of the Gracchi. 14. **Tully's Orator:** Cicero's *De Oratore.* 15. **plies:** importunes. 24.
fury: madness. 39. **fact:** deed. 49. **annoy:** suffering. 50. **quotes:** examines. 57. **Pattern'd by:** on the pattern of. 78.
Stuprum: rape. 81–82. *Magni ... vides:* Ruler of the great heaven, dost thou so calmly hear of crimes, so calmly witness
them? 89. **fere:** companion, husband. 97. **wind:** scent.

And lulls him whilst she playeth on her back,
And when he sleeps will she do what she list.   100
You are a young huntsman, Marcus; let alone;
And, come, I will go get a leaf of brass,
And with a gad of steel will write these words,
And lay it by. The angry northern wind
Will blow these sands, like Sibyl's leaves, abroad,
And where's our lesson, then? Boy, what say
     you?   106
     Young Luc. I say, my lord, that if I were a man,
Their mother's bed-chamber should not be safe
For these base bondmen to the yoke of Rome.
     Marc. Ay, that's my boy! Thy father hath
     full oft   110
For his ungrateful country done the like.
     Young Luc. And, uncle, so will I, an if I live.
     Tit. Come, go with me into mine armoury;
Lucius, I'll fit thee; and withal, my boy
Shall carry from me to the Empress' sons   115
Presents that I intend to send them both.
Come, come; thou'lt do my message, wilt thou not?
     Young Luc. Ay, with my dagger in their bosoms,
     grandsire.
     Tit. No, boy, not so; I'll teach thee another
     course.
Lavinia, come. Marcus, look to my house;   120
Lucius and I'll go brave it at the court.
Ay, marry, will we, sir; and we'll be waited on.
          [*Exeunt* [*Titus, Lavinia, and young Lucius*].
     Marc. O heavens, can you hear a good man
     groan
And not relent or not compassion him?
Marcus, attend him in his ecstasy,   125
That hath more scars of sorrow in his heart
Than foemen's marks upon his batt'red shield;
But yet so just that he will not revenge.
Revenge the heavens for old Andronicus!   [*Exit.*

[SCENE II. *The same. A room in the palace.*]

Enter AARON, DEMETRIUS, *and* CHIRON, *at one
door; and at another door, young* LUCIUS, *and
another, with a bundle of weapons, and verses writ
upon them.*

     Chi. Demetrius, here's the son of Lucius;
He hath some message to deliver us.
     Aar. Ay, some mad message from his mad grand-
father.
     Young Luc. My lords, with all the humbleness
     I may,
I greet your honours from Andronicus.   5
[*Aside.*] And pray the Roman gods confound you
     both!

     Dem. Gramercy, lovely Lucius. What's the
     news?
     Young Luc. [*Aside.*] That you are both de-
     cipher'd, that's the news,
For villains mark'd with rape. — May it please you,
My grandsire, well advis'd, hath sent by me   10
The goodliest weapons of his armoury
To gratify your honourable youth,
The hope of Rome; for so he bid me say;
And so I do, and with his gifts present
Your lordships, that, whenever you have need,   15
You may be armed and appointed well:
And so I leave you both — [*Aside*] like bloody
     villains.
          [*Exeunt* [*young Lucius and Attendant*].
     Dem. What's here? A scroll; and written round
     about.
Let's see:
[*Reads.*] "*Integer vitæ, scelerisque purus,*   20
          Non eget Mauri jaculis, nec arcu."
     Chi. O, 'tis a verse in Horace; I know it well.
I read it in the grammar long ago.
     Aar. Ay, just; a verse in Horace; right, you have
     it.
[*Aside.*] Now, what a thing it is to be an ass!   25
Here's no sound jest! The old man hath found
     their guilt;
And sends them weapons wrapp'd about with lines
That wound, beyond their feeling, to the quick.
But were our witty empress well afoot,
She would applaud Andronicus' conceit;   30
But let her rest in her unrest a while. —
And now, young lords, was't not a happy star
Led us to Rome, strangers, and more than so,
Captives, to be advanced to this height?
It did me good, before the palace gate   35
To brave the tribune in his brother's hearing.
     Dem. But me more good to see so great a lord
Basely insinuate and send us gifts.
     Aar. Had he not reason, Lord Demetrius?
Did you not use his daughter very friendly?   40
     Dem. I would we had a thousand Roman dames
At such a bay, by turn to serve our lust.
     Chi. A charitable wish and full of love.
     Aar. Here lacks but your mother for to say amen.
     Chi. And that would she for twenty thousand
     more.   45
     Dem. Come, let us go and pray to all the gods
For our beloved mother in her pains.
     Aar. [*Aside.*] Pray to the devils; the gods have
     given us over.   [*Trumpets sound within.*
     Dem. Why do the Emperor's trumpets flourish
     thus?

---

     103. **gad:** point. 105. **Sibyl's leaves:** i.e., of the prophetic books of the Cumæan Sibyl. 125. **ecstasy:** frenzy.
     Sc. ii, 16. **appointed:** equipped. 20–21. *Integer ... arcu:* He who is pure in life and free from crime needs not the arrows
of the Moor, nor the bow. (Horace, *Odes,* Book I, XXII). 26. **sound:** wholesome. 38. **insinuate:** flatter. 42. **At ... bay:**
brought so to bay.

Chi. Belike, for joy the Emperor hath a son. 50
Dem. Soft! who comes here?

Enter a NURSE, *with a blackamoor* Child.

Nur.   Good morrow, lords.
O, tell me, did you see Aaron the Moor?
Aar. Well, more or less, or ne'er a whit at all,
Here Aaron is; and what with Aaron now?
Nur. O gentle Aaron, we are all undone! 55
Now help, or woe betide thee evermore!
Aar. Why, what a caterwauling dost thou keep!
What dost thou wrap and fumble in thy arms?
Nur. O, that which I would hide from heaven's
eye,
Our empress' shame, and stately Rome's disgrace!
She is delivered, lords; she is delivered. 61
Aar. To whom?
Nur.   I mean, she is brought a-bed.
Aar. Well, God give her good rest! What hath
he sent her?
Nur. A devil.
Aar. Why, then she is the devil's dam; a joyful
issue. 65
Nur. A joyless, dismal, black, and sorrowful issue!
Here is the babe, as loathsome as a toad
Amongst the fairest breeders of our clime.
The Empress sends it thee, thy stamp, thy seal,
And bids thee christen it with thy dagger's point. 70
Aar. 'Zounds, ye whore! is black so base a hue?
Sweet blowse, you are a beauteous blossom, sure.
Dem. Villain, what hast thou done?
Aar. That which thou canst not undo.
Chi. Thou hast undone our mother. 75
Aar. Villain, I have done thy mother.
Dem. And therein, hellish dog, thou hast undone
her.
Woe to her chance, and damn'd her loathed choice!
Accurs'd the offspring of so foul a fiend!
Chi. It shall not live. 80
Aar. It shall not die.
Nur. Aaron, it must; the mother wills it so.
Aar. What, must it, nurse? then let no man but I
Do execution on my flesh and blood.
Dem. I'll broach the tadpole on my rapier's
point. 85
Nurse, give it me; my sword shall soon dispatch it.
Aar. Sooner this sword shall plough thy bowels up.
[*Takes the Child from the Nurse, and draws.*]
Stay, murderous villains! will you kill your brother?
Now, by the burning tapers of the sky,
That shone so brightly when this boy was got, 90
He dies upon my scimitar's sharp point
That touches this my first-born son and heir!

I tell you, younglings, not Enceladus
With all his threat'ning band of Typhon's brood,
Nor great Alcides, nor the god of war, 95
Shall seize this prey out of his father's hands.
What, what, ye sanguine, shallow-hearted boys!
Ye white-lim'd walls! ye alehouse painted signs!
Coal-black is better than another hue,
In that it scorns to bear another hue; 100
For all the water in the ocean
Can never turn the swan's black legs to white
Although she lave them hourly in the flood.
Tell the Empress from me, I am of age
To keep mine own, excuse it how she can. 105
Dem. Wilt thou betray thy noble mistress thus?
Aar. My mistress is my mistress; this myself,
The vigour and the picture of my youth.
This before all the world do I prefer;
This maugre all the world will I keep safe, 110
Or some of you shall smoke for it in Rome.
Dem. By this our mother is for ever sham'd.
Chi. Rome will despise her for this foul escape.
Nur. The Emperor, in his rage, will doom her
death.
Chi. I blush to think upon this ignomy. 115
Aar. Why, there's the privilege your beauty bears.
Fie, treacherous hue, that will betray with blushing
The close enacts and counsels of thy heart!
Here's a young lad fram'd of another leer;
Look, how the black slave smiles upon the father,
As who should say, "Old lad, I am thine own." 121
He is your brother, lords, sensibly fed
Of that self blood that first gave life to you,
And from that womb where you imprisoned were
He is enfranchised and come to light. 125
Nay, he is your brother by the surer side,
Although my seal be stamped in his face.
Nur. Aaron, what shall I say unto the Empress?
Dem. Advise thee, Aaron, what is to be done,
And we will all subscribe to thy advice. 130
Save thou the child, so we may all be safe.
Aar. Then sit we down, and let us all consult.
My son and I will have the wind of you;
Keep there. Now talk at pleasure of your safety.
[*They sit.*]
Dem. How many women saw this child of his? 135
Aar. Why, so, brave lords! when we join in league,
I am a lamb; but if you brave the Moor,
The chafed boar, the mountain lioness,
The ocean swells not so as Aaron storms.
But say, again, how many saw the child? 140
Nur. Cornelia the midwife and myself;
And no one else but the delivered Empress.
Aar. The Emperess, the midwife, and yourself.

---

71. **'Zounds:** God's wounds. 73. **blowse.** Elsewhere used of a ruddy, plump-faced wench. 93. **Enceladus:** one of the Titans. 94. **Typhon's brood:** the Titans. 95. **Alcides:** Hercules. 97. **sanguine:** ruddy. 98. **white-lim'd:** whitewashed. 110. **maugre:** in spite of. 113. **escape:** escapade. 118. **enacts:** workings. 119. **leer:** complexion. 122. **sensibly:** manifestly. 129. **Advise thee:** consider. 133. **wind of you:** advantage of position.

Two may keep counsel when the third's away.
Go to the Empress, tell her this I said.   145
                                   [*He kills her.*
Weke, weke! so cries a pig prepared to the spit.
Dem. What mean'st thou, Aaron? Wherefore
    didst thou this?
Aar. O Lord, sir, 'tis a deed of policy.
Shall she live to betray this guilt of ours,
A long-tongu'd babbling gossip? No, lords, no;   150
And now be it known to you my full intent.
Not far, one [Muli lives], my countryman;
His wife but yesternight was brought to bed;
His child is like to her, fair as you are.
Go pack with him, and give the mother gold,   155
And tell them both the circumstance of all;
And how by this their child shall be advanc'd,
And be received for the Emperor's heir,
And substituted in the place of mine
To calm this tempest whirling in the court;   160
And let the Emperor dandle him for his own.
Hark ye, lords; you see I have given her physic,
                              [*Pointing to the Nurse.*]
And you must needs bestow her funeral;
The fields are near, and you are gallant grooms.
This done, see that you take no longer days,   165
But send the midwife presently to me.
The midwife and the nurse well made away,
Then let the ladies tattle what they please.
Chi. Aaron, I see thou wilt not trust the air
With secrets.
Dem.   For this care of Tamora,   170
Herself and hers are highly bound to thee.
        [*Exeunt [Dem. and Chi., bearing off the
          Nurse's body*].
Aar. Now to the Goths, as swift as swallow flies;
There to dispose this treasure in mine arms,
And secretly to greet the Empress' friends.
Come on, you thick-lipp'd slave, I'll bear you
    hence;   175
For it is you that puts us to our shifts.
I'll make you feed on berries and on roots,
And feed on curds and whey, and suck the goat,
And cabin in a cave, and bring you up
To be a warrior, and command a camp. [*Exit.*   180

[SCENE III.   *The same.   A public place.*]

Enter TITUS, *bearing arrows with letters at the ends
    of them: with him,* MARCUS, *young* LUCIUS,
    [PUBLIUS, SEMPRONIUS, CAIUS] *and other* Gentle-
    men, *with bows.*

Tit. Come, Marcus, come; kinsmen, this is the
way.

Sir boy, let me see your archery.
Look ye draw home enough, and 'tis there straight.
Terras Astræa reliquit;   4
Be you rememb'red, Marcus, she's gone, she's fled.
Sirs, take you to your tools. You, cousins, shall
Go sound the ocean, and cast your nets;
Happily you may catch her in the sea;
Yet there's as little justice as at land.
No; Publius and Sempronius, you must do it;   10
'Tis you must dig with mattock and with spade,
And pierce the inmost centre of the earth;
Then, when you come to Pluto's region,
I pray you, deliver him this petition.
Tell him, it is for Justice and for aid,   15
And that it comes from old Andronicus,
Shaken with sorrows in ungrateful Rome.
Ah, Rome! Well, well; I made thee miserable
What time I threw the people's suffrages
On him that thus doth tyrannize o'er me.   20
Go, get you gone; and pray be careful all,
And leave you not a man-of-war unsearch'd.
This wicked emperor may have shipp'd her hence;
And, kinsmen, then we may go pipe for Justice.
Marc. O Publius, is not this a heavy case,   25
To see thy noble uncle thus distract?
Pub. Therefore, my lords, it highly us concerns
By day and night to attend him carefully,
And feed his humour kindly as we may,
Till time beget some careful remedy.   30
Marc. Kinsmen, his sorrows are past remedy.
Join with the Goths; and with revengeful war
Take wreak on Rome for this ingratitude,
And vengeance on the traitor Saturnine.
Tit. Publius, how now! how now, my masters!   35
What, have you met with her?
Pub. No, my good lord; but Pluto sends you
    word,
If you will have Revenge from hell, you shall.
Marry, for Justice, she is so employ'd,
He thinks, with Jove in heaven, or somewhere
    else,
So that perforce you must needs stay a time.   41
Tit. He doth me wrong to feed me with delays.
I'll dive into the burning lake below
And pull her out of Acheron by the heels.
Marcus, we are but shrubs, no cedars we,   45
No big-bon'd men fram'd of the Cyclops' size;
But metal, Marcus, steel to the very back,
Yet wrung with wrongs more than our backs can
    bear.
And, sith there's no justice in earth nor hell,
We will solicit heaven and move the gods   50
To send down Justice for to wreak our wrongs.

Come, to this gear. You are a good archer, Marcus;
[He gives them the arrows.
"*Ad Jovem*," that's for you; here, "*Ad Apollinem;*"
"*Ad Martem*," that's for myself;
Here, boy, to Pallas; here, to Mercury; 55
To Saturn, Caius, not to Saturnine, —
You were as good to shoot against the wind.
To it, boy! Marcus, loose when I bid.
Of my word, I have written to effect;
There's not a god left unsolicited. 60
Marc. Kinsmen, shoot all your shafts into the court;
We will afflict the Emperor in his pride.
Tit. Now, masters, draw. [*They shoot.*] O, well said, Lucius!
Good boy, in Virgo's lap; give it Pallas.
Marc. My lord, I aim a mile beyond the moon; 65
Your letter is with Jupiter by this.
Tit. Ha, ha!
Publius, Publius, what hast thou done?
See, see, thou hast shot off one of Taurus' horns.
Marc. This was the sport, my lord. When Publius shot, 70
The Bull, being gall'd, gave Aries such a knock
That down fell both the Ram's horns in the court;
And who should find them but the Empress' villain?
She laugh'd, and told the Moor he should not choose
But give them to his master for a present. 75
Tit. Why, there it goes; God give his lordship joy!

Enter a CLOWN, *with a basket, and two pigeons in it.*

News, news from heaven! Marcus, the post is come.
Sirrah, what tidings? Have you any letters?
Shall I have justice? What says Jupiter? 79
Clo. O, the gibbet-maker! he says that he hath taken them down again, for the man must not be hang'd till the next week.
Tit. But what says Jupiter, I ask thee? 83
Clo. Alas, sir, I know not Jupiter; I never drank with him in all my life.
Tit. Why, villain, art not thou the carrier?
Clo. Ay, of my pigeons, sir; nothing else. 87
Tit. Why, didst thou not come from heaven?
Clo. From heaven! alas, sir, I never came there. God forbid I should be so bold to press to heaven in my young days. Why, I am going with my pigeons to the tribunal plebs, to take up a matter of brawl betwixt my uncle and one of the emperal's men. 94

Marc. Why, sir, that is as fit as can be to serve for your oration; and let him deliver the pigeons to the Emperor from you.
Tit. Tell me, can you deliver an oration to the Emperor with a grace? 99
Clo. Nay, truly, sir, I could never say grace in all my life.
Tit. Sirrah, come hither; make no more ado, But give your pigeons to the Emperor.
By me thou shalt have justice at his hands.
Hold, hold; meanwhile here's money for thy charges. 105
Give me pen and ink. Sirrah, can you with a grace deliver up a supplication?
Clo. Ay, sir. 108
Tit. Then here is a supplication for you. And when you come to him, at the first approach you must kneel, then kiss his foot, then deliver up your pigeons, and then look for your reward. I'll be at hand, sir; see you do it bravely.
Clo. I warrant you, sir, let me alone.
Tit. Sirrah, hast thou a knife? Come, let me see it. 115
Here, Marcus, fold it in the oration;
For thou hast made it like an humble suppliant.
And when thou hast given it the Emperor,
Knock at my door and tell me what he says.
Clo. God be with you, sir; I will. [*Exit.* 120
Tit. Come, Marcus, let us go. Publius, follow me. [*Exeunt.*

[SCENE IV. *The same. Before the palace.*]

Enter SATURNINUS, TAMORA, DEMETRIUS, CHIRON [*Lords, and others*]; SATURNINUS *brings the arrows in his hand that Titus shot at him.*

Sat. Why, lords, what wrongs are these! Was ever seen
An emperor in Rome thus overborne,
Troubled, confronted thus; and, for the extent
Of egal justice, us'd in such contempt?
My lords, you know, [as know] the mightful gods, 5
However these disturbers of our peace
Buzz in the people's ears, there nought hath pass'd,
But even with law, against the wilful sons
Of old Andronicus. And what an if
His sorrows have so overwhelm'd his wits, 10
Shall we be thus afflicted in his wreaks,
His fits, his frenzy, and his bitterness?
And now he writes to heaven for his redress.
See, here's to Jove, and this to Mercury;
This to Apollo; this to the god of war; 15
Sweet scrolls to fly about the streets of Rome!

What's this but libelling against the senate,
And blazoning our unjustice everywhere?
A goodly humour, is it not, my lords?
As who would say, in Rome no justice were.   20
But if I live, his feigned ecstasies
Shall be no shelter to these outrages;
But he and his shall know that justice lives
In Saturninus' health, whom, if he sleep,
He'll so awake as he in fury shall   25
Cut off the proud'st conspirator that lives.
   Tam. My gracious lord, my lovely Saturnine,
Lord of my life, commander of my thoughts,
Calm thee, and bear the faults of Titus' age,
Th' effects of sorrow for his valiant sons,   30
Whose loss hath pierc'd him deep and scarr'd his
    heart;
And rather comfort his distressed plight
Than prosecute the meanest or the best
For these contempts. (*Aside.*) Why, thus it shall
    become
High-witted Tamora to gloze with all;   35
But, Titus, I have touch'd thee to the quick.
Thy life-blood out, if Aaron now be wise,
Then is all safe, the anchor in the port.

        Enter CLOWN.

How now, good fellow! wouldst thou speak with us?
   Clo. Yea, forsooth, an your mistriship be em-
perial.   40
   Tam. Empress I am, but yonder sits the Emperor.
   Clo. 'Tis he. God and Saint Stephen give you
god-den. I have brought you a letter and a couple
of pigeons here.   [*Saturninus reads the letter.*
   Sat. Go, take him away, and hang him presently.
   Clo. How much money must I have?   46
   Tam. Come, sirrah, you must be hang'd.
   Clo. Hang'd! by 'r lady, then I have brought up
a neck to a fair end.   [*Exit [guarded].*
   Sat. Despiteful and intolerable wrongs!   50
Shall I endure this monstrous villainy?
I know from whence this same device proceeds.
May this be borne? As if his traitorous sons,
That died by law for murder of our brother,
Have by my means been butcher'd wrongfully!   55
Go, drag the villain hither by the hair;
Nor age nor honour shall shape privilege;
For this proud mock I'll be thy slaughter-man;
Sly frantic wretch, that holp'st to make me great
In hope thyself should govern Rome and me.   60

     Enter Nuntius ÆMILIUS.

What news with thee, Æmilius?
   Æmil. Arm, my lords! Rome never had more
    cause.

The Goths have gather'd head; and with a power
Of high-resolved men, bent to the spoil,
They hither march amain, under conduct   65
Of Lucius, son to old Andronicus;
Who threats, in course of this revenge, to do
As much as ever Coriolanus did.
   Sat. Is warlike Lucius general of the Goths?
These tidings nip me, and I hang the head   70
As flowers with frost or grass beat down with
    storms.
Ay, now begins our sorrows to approach.
'Tis he the common people love so much;
Myself hath often heard them say,
When I have walked like a private man,   75
That Lucius' banishment was wrongfully,
And they have wish'd that Lucius were their em-
    peror.
   Tam. Why should you fear? Is not your city
    strong?
   Sat. Ay, but the citizens favour Lucius
And will revolt from me to succour him.   80
   Tam. King, be thy thoughts imperious, like thy
    name.
Is the sun dimm'd, that gnats do fly in it?
The eagle suffers little birds to sing
And is not careful what they mean thereby,
Knowing that with the shadow of his wings   85
He can at pleasure stint their melody;
Even so mayst thou the giddy men of Rome.
Then cheer thy spirit; for know, thou emperor,
I will enchant the old Andronicus
With words more sweet, and yet more dangerous,
Than baits to fish, or honey-stalks to sheep,   91
Whenas the one is wounded with the bait,
The other rotted with delicious [feed].
   Sat. But he will not entreat his son for us.
   Tam. If Tamora entreat him, then he will;   95
For I can smooth and fill his aged ears
With golden promises; that, were his heart
Almost impregnable, his old ears deaf,
Yet should both ear and heart obey my tongue.
[*To Æmilius.*] Go thou before, be our ambassador.
Say that the Emperor requests a parley   101
Of warlike Lucius, and appoint the meeting
Even at his father's house, the old Andronicus.
   Sat. Æmilius, do this message honourably;
And if he stand on hostage for his safety,   105
Bid him demand what pledge will please him best.
   Æmil. Your bidding shall I do effectually.
                     [*Exit.*
   Tam. Now will I to that old Andronicus,
And temper him with all the art I have
To pluck proud Lucius from the warlike Goths.
And now, sweet emperor, be blithe again,   111

---

   21. **ecstasies**: madness. 35. **High-witted**: cunning. **gloze**: talk smoothly. 43. **god-den**: good evening. 57. **shape privilege**: cause exemption. 86. **stint**: stop. 91. **honey-stalks**: clover flowers. 93. [**feed**] Q₃. *seede* Q₁. 96. **smooth**: flatter. 105. **stand on**: demand. 109. **temper**: work on.

And bury all thy fear in my devices.
Sat. Then go successantly, and plead to him.
[*Exeunt.*

ACT V

[SCENE I. *Plains near Rome.*]

Enter LUCIUS *with an army of* GOTHS, *with drums and*
[*colours*].

Luc. Approved warriors, and my faithful friends,
I have received letters from great Rome
Which signifies what hate they bear their emperor
And how desirous of our sight they are.
Therefore, great lords, be, as your titles witness, 5
Imperious and impatient of your wrongs,
And wherein Rome hath done you any scath,
Let him make treble satisfaction.
[*I.*] *Goth.* Brave slip, sprung from the great
Andronicus,
Whose name was once our terror, now our com-
fort,   10
Whose high exploits and honourable deeds
Ingrateful Rome requites with foul contempt,
Be bold in us; we'll follow where thou lead'st,
Like stinging bees in hottest summer's day
Led by their master to the flow'red fields,   15
And be aveng'd on cursed Tamora.
[*All the Goths.*] And as he saith, so say we all with
him.
Luc. I humbly thank him, and I thank you all.
But who comes here, led by a lusty Goth?

Enter a GOTH, *leading of* AARON *with his* Child
in his arms.

[*2.*] *Goth.* Renowned Lucius, from our troops I
stray'd   20
To gaze upon a ruinous monastery;
And, as I earnestly did fix mine eye
Upon the wasted building, suddenly
I heard a child cry underneath a wall.
I made unto the noise; when soon I heard   25
The crying babe controll'd with this discourse:
"Peace, tawny slave, half me and half thy [dam]!
Did not thy hue bewray whose brat thou art,
Had nature lent thee but thy mother's look,
Villain, thou mightst have been an emperor.   30
But where the bull and cow are both milk-white,
They never do beget a coal-black calf.
Peace, villain, peace!" — even thus he rates the
babe, —
"For I must bear thee to a trusty Goth;
Who, when he knows thou art the Empress' babe,

Will hold thee dearly for thy mother's sake."   36
With this, my weapon drawn, I rush'd upon him,
Surpris'd him suddenly, and brought him hither
To use as you think needful of the man.
Luc. O worthy Goth, this is the incarnate devil
That robb'd Andronicus of his good hand;   41
This is the pearl that pleas'd your empress' eye,
And here's the base fruit of her burning lust.
Say, wall-eyed slave, whither wouldst thou convey
This growing image of thy fiend-like face?   45
Why dost not speak? What, deaf? Not a word?
A halter, soldiers! Hang him on this tree,
And by his side his fruit of bastardy.
Aar. Touch not the boy; he is of royal blood.
Luc. Too like the sire for ever being good.   50
First hang the child, that he may see it sprawl;
A sight to vex the father's soul withal.
Get me a ladder.
[*A ladder brought, which Aaron is made to
ascend.*]
Aar.   Lucius, save the child
And bear it from me to the Emperess.
If thou do this, I'll show thee wondrous things 55
That highly may advantage thee to hear.
If thou wilt not, befall what may befall,
I'll speak no more but "Vengeance rot you all!"
Luc. Say on; an if it please me which thou
speak'st,
Thy child shall live, and I will see it nourish'd. 60
Aar. An if it please thee! Why, assure thee,
Lucius,
'Twill vex thy soul to hear what I shall speak;
For I must talk of murders, rapes, and massacres,
Acts of black night, abominable deeds,
Complots of mischief, treason, villainies,   65
Ruthful to hear, yet piteously perform'd.
And this shall all be buried in my death
Unless thou swear to me my child shall live.
Luc. Tell on thy mind; I say thy child shall live.
Aar. Swear that he shall, and then I will begin.
Luc. Who should I swear by? Thou believ'st no
god: 71
That granted, how canst thou believe an oath?
Aar. What if I do not? as, indeed, I do not;
Yet, for I know thou art religious
And hast a thing within thee called conscience, 75
With twenty popish tricks and ceremonies
Which I have seen thee careful to observe,
Therefore I urge thy oath; for that I know
An idiot holds his bauble for a god
And keeps the oath which by that god he swears, 80
To that I'll urge him. Therefore thou shalt vow
By that same god, what god soe'er it be,

113. **successantly:** successfully.
Act V, sc. i, S.D. [*colours*] (Capell). *Souldiers* Qq Ff. 1. **Approved:** tried. 7. **scath:** harm. 9, 121, 162. [*I.*] (Capell).
Om. Q₁. 9. **slip:** scion. 20. [*2.*] (Capell). Om. Q₁. 26. **controll'd:** soothed. 27. [**dam**] Q₂. *Dame* Q₁. 33. **rates:** scolds.
50. **for ... being:** ever to be. 53. **Get ... ladder.** To Aaron in Q₁. 78. **urge:** insist upon.

That thou ador'st and hast in reverence,
To save my boy, to nourish and bring him up;
Or else I will discover nought to thee.   85
 Luc. Even by my God I swear to thee I will.
 Aar. First know thou, I begot him on the Empress.
 Luc. O most insatiate and luxurious woman!
 Aar. Tut, Lucius, this was but a deed of charity
To that which thou shalt hear of me anon.   90
'Twas her two sons that murdered Bassianus;
They cut thy sister's tongue, and ravish'd her,
And cut her hands, and trimm'd her as thou saw'st.
 Luc. O detestable villain! call'st thou that
  trimming?
 Aar. Why, she was wash'd and cut and trimm'd,
  and 'twas   95
Trim sport for them which had the doing of it.
 Luc. O barbarous, beastly villains like thyself!
 Aar. Indeed, I was their tutor to instruct them.
That codding spirit had they from their mother,
As sure a card as ever won the set;   100
That bloody mind, I think, they learn'd of me,
As true a dog as ever fought at head.
Well, let my deeds be witness of my worth.
I train'd thy brethren to that guileful hole
Where the dead corpse of Bassianus lay;   105
I wrote the letter that thy father found,
And hid the gold within that letter mention'd,
Confederate with the Queen and her two sons;
And what not done, that thou hast cause to rue,
Wherein I had no stroke of mischief in it?   110
I play'd the cheater for thy father's hand,
And, when I had it, drew myself apart
And almost broke my heart with extreme laughter.
I pried me through the crevice of a wall
When, for his hand, he had his two sons' heads;   115
Beheld his tears, and laugh'd so heartily
That both mine eyes were rainy like to his;
And when I told the Empress of this sport,
She swounded almost at my pleasing tale
And for my tidings gave me twenty kisses.   120
 [*1.*] *Goth.* What, canst thou say all this and never
  blush?
 Aar. Ay, like a black dog, as the saying is.
 Luc. Art thou not sorry for these heinous deeds?
 Aar. Ay, that I had not done a thousand more.
Even now I curse the day — and yet, I think,   125
Few come within the compass of my curse —
Wherein I did not some notorious ill,
As kill a man, or else devise his death,
Ravish a maid, or plot the way to do it,
Accuse some innocent and forswear myself,   130
Set deadly enmity between two friends,
Make poor men's cattle break their necks,

Set fire on barns and hay-stacks in the night,
And bid the owners quench them with their tears.
Oft have I digg'd up dead men from their graves   135
And set them upright at their dear friends' door,
Even when their sorrow almost was forgot;
And on their skins, as on the bark of trees,
Have with my knife carved in Roman letters,
"Let not your sorrow die, though I am dead."   140
[Tut], I have done a thousand dreadful things
As willingly as one would kill a fly,
And nothing grieves me heartily indeed
But that I cannot do ten thousand more.
 Luc. Bring down the devil, for he must not die
So sweet a death as hanging presently.   146
 Aar. If there be devils, would I were a devil,
To live and burn in everlasting fire,
So I might have your company in hell
But to torment you with my bitter tongue!   150
 Luc. Sirs, stop his mouth, and let him speak no
  more.

[*Enter a* GOTH.]

 [*3.*] *Goth.* My lord, there is a messenger from
  Rome
Desires to be admitted to your presence.
 Luc. Let him come near.

Enter ÆMILIUS.

Welcome, Æmilius! What's the news from Rome?
 Æmil. Lord Lucius, and you princes of the
  Goths,   156
The Roman Emperor greets you all by me;
And, for he understands you are in arms,
He craves a parley at your father's house,
Willing you to demand your hostages,   160
And they shall be immediately delivered.
 [*1.*] *Goth.* What says our general?
 Luc. Æmilius, let the Emperor give his pledges
Unto my father and my uncle Marcus,
And we will come. March away.   165
       [*Flourish. Exeunt.*

[SCENE II. *Rome. Before Titus's house.*]

Enter TAMORA, DEMETRIUS, *and* CHIRON, *disguised*

 Tam. Thus, in this strange and sad habiliment,
I will encounter with Andronicus
And say I am Revenge, sent from below
To join with him and right his heinous wrongs.
Knock at his study, where, they say, he keeps   5
To ruminate strange plots of dire revenge;
Tell him Revenge is come to join with him,
And work confusion on his enemies.
         [*They knock.*

---

88. **luxurious:** lustful. 99. **codding:** lecherous. 100. **set:** trick. 104. **train'd:** lured. ' 141. [Tut] Q2. *But* Q1. 152.
[*3.*] (Capell). Om. Q1.
Sc. ii, 5. keeps: lives.

Titus [*above*] *opens his study door.*

Tit. Who doth molest my contemplation?
Is it your trick to make me ope the door   10
That so my sad decrees may fly away
And all my study be to no effect?
You are deceiv'd, for what I mean to do
See here in bloody lines I have set down,
And what is written shall be executed.   15
Tam. Titus, I am come to talk with thee.
Tit. No, not a word; how can I grace my talk,
Wanting a hand to give it action?
Thou hast the odds of me; therefore no more.
Tam. If thou didst know me, thou would'st talk
with me.   20
Tit. I am not mad; I know thee well enough.
Witness this wretched stump, witness these crimson
lines;
Witness these trenches made by grief and care;
Witness the tiring day and heavy night;
Witness all sorrow, that I know thee well   25
For our proud empress, mighty Tamora.
Is not thy coming for my other hand?
Tam. Know, thou sad man, I am not Tamora;
She is thy enemy, and I thy friend.
I am Revenge, sent from th' infernal kingdom   30
To ease the gnawing vulture of thy mind
By working wreakful vengeance on thy foes.
Come down, and welcome me to this world's light;
Confer with me of murder and of death.
There's not a hollow cave or lurking-place,   35
No vast obscurity or misty vale,
Where bloody murder or detested rape
Can couch for fear, but I will find them out,
And in their ears tell them my dreadful name,
Revenge, which makes the foul offender quake.   40
Tit. Art thou Revenge? and art thou sent to me,
To be a torment to mine enemies?
Tam. I am; therefore come down and welcome
me.
Tit. Do me some service ere I come to thee.
Lo, by thy side where Rape and Murder stands: 45
Now give some surance that thou art Revenge;
Stab them, or tear them on thy chariot-wheels,
And then I'll come and be thy waggoner,
And whirl along with thee about the globes.
Provide two proper palfreys, black as jet,   50
To hale thy vengeful waggon swift away
And find out murderers in their guilty caves;
And when thy car is loaden with their heads,
I will dismount, and by thy waggon-wheel
Trot, like a servile footman, all day long,   55
Even from Hyperion's rising in the east
Until his very downfall in the sea;
And day by day I'll do this heavy task,

So thou destroy Rapine and Murder there.
Tam. These are my ministers, and come with
me.   60
Tit. Are [these] thy ministers? What are they
call'd?
Tam. Rape and Murder; therefore called so,
'Cause they take vengeance of such kind of men.
Tit. Good Lord, how like the Empress' sons they
are!
And you, the Empress! but we worldly men   65
Have miserable, mad, mistaking eyes.
O sweet Revenge, now do I come to thee;
And, if one arm's embracement will content thee,
I will embrace thee in it by and by.   [*Exit above.*]
Tam. This closing with him fits his lunacy.   70
Whate'er I forge to feed his brain-sick humours,
Do you uphold and maintain in your speeches,
For now he firmly takes me for Revenge;
And, being credulous in this mad thought,
I'll make him send for Lucius his son;   75
And, whilst I at a banquet hold him sure,
I'll find some cunning practice out of hand
To scatter and disperse the giddy Goths,
Or, at the least, make them his enemies.
See, here he comes, and I must ply my theme.   80

[*Enter* Titus *below.*]

Tit. Long have I been forlorn, and all for thee.
Welcome, dread Fury, to my woeful house;
Rapine and Murder, you are welcome too.
How like the Empress and her sons you are!
Well are you fitted, had you but a Moor,   85
Could not all hell afford you such a devil?
For well I wot the Empress never wags
But in her company there is a Moor;
And, would you represent our queen aright,
It were convenient you had such a devil.   90
But welcome, as you are. What shall we do?
Tam. What wouldst thou have us do, Androni-
cus?
Dem. Show me a murderer, I'll deal with him.
Chi. Show me a villain that hath done a rape,
And I am sent to be reveng'd on him.   95
Tam. Show me a thousand that [have] done thee
wrong,
And I will be revenged on them all.
Tit. Look round about the wicked streets of
Rome;
And when thou find'st a man that's like thyself,
Good Murder, stab him; he's a murderer.   100
Go thou with him; and when it is thy hap
To find another that is like to thee,
Good Rapine, stab him; he's a ravisher.
Go thou with them; and in the Emperor's court

11. **sad decrees:** sober resolutions.   50. **Provide.** *Provide thee* Qq Ff.   56. **Hyperion:** the sun god.   61. **[these]** (Dyce). *them* Q₁.   65. **worldly:** mortal.   70. **closing:** agreeing.   ᵗ. **humours:** whims.   77. **practice:** stratagem.   96. [have] Q₂.   *hath* Q₁.

There is a queen, attended by a Moor;   105
Well shalt thou know her by thine own proportion,
For up and down she doth resemble thee.
I pray thee, do on them some violent death;
They have been violent to me and mine.
 Tam. Well hast thou lesson'd us; this shall we
  do.   110
But would it please thee, good Andronicus,
To send for Lucius, thy thrice-valiant son,
Who leads towards Rome a band of warlike Goths,
And bid him come and banquet at thy house;
When he is here, even at thy solemn feast,   115
I will bring in the Empress and her sons,
The Emperor himself and all thy foes;
And at thy mercy shall they stoop and kneel,
And on them shalt thou ease thy angry heart.
What says Andronicus to this device?   120
 Tit. Marcus, my brother! 'tis sad Titus calls.

Enter MARCUS.

Go, gentle Marcus, to thy nephew Lucius;
Thou shalt inquire him out among the Goths:
Bid him repair to me, and bring with him
Some of the chiefest princes of the Goths.   125
Bid him encamp his soldiers where they are.
Tell him the Emperor and the Empress too
Feast at my house, and he shall feast with them.
This do thou for my love; and so let him,
As he regards his aged father's life.   130
 Marc. This will I do, and soon return again.
              [*Exit.*
 Tam. Now will I hence about thy business,
And take my ministers along with me.
 Tit. Nay, nay, let Rape and Murder stay with
  me;
Or else I'll call my brother back again   135
And cleave to no revenge but Lucius.
 Tam. [*Aside to her sons.*] What say you, boys?
  Will you abide with him
Whiles I go tell my lord the Emperor
How I have govern'd our determin'd jest?
Yield to his humour, smooth and speak him fair,
And tarry with him till I turn again.   141
 Tit. [*Aside.*] I knew them all though they sup-
  pos'd me mad,
And will o'erreach them in their own devices.
A pair of cursed hell-hounds and their dam!   144
 Dem. Madam, depart at pleasure; leave us here.
 Tam. Farewell, Andronicus! Revenge now goes
To lay a complot to betray thy foes.
 Tit. I know thou dost; and, sweet Revenge, fare-
  well.   [*Exit Tamora.*]
 Chi. Tell us, old man, how shall we be employ'd?
 Tit. Tut, I have work enough for you to do. 150
Publius, come hither! Caius and Valentine!

[*Enter* PUBLIUS *and others.*]

 Pub. What is your will?
 Tit. Know you these two?
 Pub. The Empress' sons I take them, Chiron,
  Demetrius.   155
 Tit. Fie, Publius, fie! thou art too much deceiv'd.
The one is Murder, Rape is the other's name;
And therefore bind them, gentle Publius.
Caius and Valentine, lay hands on them.   159
Oft have you heard me wish for such an hour,
And now I find it; therefore bind them sure,
And stop their mouths if they begin to cry.
  [*Exit Titus. Publius, etc., lay hold on
   Chiron and Demetrius.*]
 Chi. Villains, forbear! we are the Empress' sons.
 Pub. And therefore do we what we are com-
  manded.   164
Stop close their mouths, let them not speak a word.
Is he sure bound? Look that you bind them fast.

Re-enter TITUS *with a knife, and* Lavinia *with a
basin.*

 Tit. Come, come, Lavinia; look, thy foes are
  bound.
Sirs, stop their mouths, let them not speak to me,
But let them hear what fearful words I utter.
O villains, Chiron and Demetrius!   170
Here stands the spring whom you have stain'd with
  mud,
This goodly summer with your winter mix'd.
You kill'd her husband, and for that vile fault
Two of her brothers were condemn'd to death,
My hand cut off and made a merry jest;   175
Both her sweet hands, her tongue, and that more
  dear
Than hands or tongue, her spotless chastity,
Inhuman traitors, you constrain'd and forc'd.
What would you say if I should let you speak?
Villains, for shame you could not beg for grace. 180
Hark, wretches! how I mean to martyr you.
This one hand yet is left to cut your throats,
Whiles that Lavinia 'tween her stumps doth hold
The basin that receives your guilty blood.
You know your mother means to feast with me,   185
And calls herself Revenge, and thinks me mad.
Hark, villains! I will grind your bones to dust,
And with your blood and it I'll make a paste;
And of the paste a coffin I will rear   189
And make two pasties of your shameful heads,
And bid that strumpet, your unhallowed dam,
Like to the earth swallow her own increase.
This is the feast that I have bid her to,
And this the banquet she shall surfeit on;
For worse than Philomel you us'd my daughter,
And worse than Progne I will be reveng'd.   196

---

139. **govern'd:** managed. **determin'd:** planned. 141. **turn:** return. 157. **Rape** Q₂. *and Rape* Q₁. 189. **coffin:** pie-crust. 192. **increase:** offspring. 196. **Progne:** sister of Philomela. See II.iii.43 note.

And now prepare your throats. Lavinia, come,
Receive the blood; and when that they are dead,
Let me go grind their bones to powder small
And with this hateful liquor temper it;   200
And in that paste let their vile heads be bak'd.
Come, come, be every one officious
To make this banquet, which I wish may prove
More stern and bloody than the Centaurs' feast.
                          [*He cuts their throats.*
So! Now bring them in, for I'll play the cook,   205
And see them ready against their mother comes.
                          [*Exeunt [bearing the dead bodies].*

[SCENE III. *Court of Titus's house.*]

Enter LUCIUS, MARCUS, *and* GOTHS [*with* AARON
prisoner and his child].

Luc. Uncle Marcus, since 'tis my father's mind
That I repair to Rome, I am content.
[*1.*] *Goth.* And ours with thine, befall what for-
    tune will.
Luc. Good uncle, take you in this barbarous
    Moor,
This ravenous tiger, this accursed devil;   5
Let him receive no sust'nance; fetter him,
Till he be brought unto the Empress' face
For testimony of her foul proceedings.
And see the ambush of our friends be strong;
I fear the Emperor means no good to us.   10
Aar. Some devil whisper curses in mine ear
And prompt me, that my tongue may utter forth
The venomous malice of my swelling heart!
Luc. Away, inhuman dog! unhallowed slave!
Sirs, help our uncle to convey him in.   15
    [*Exeunt Goths, with Aaron.*] *Flourish*
    [*within*].
The trumpets show the Emperor is at hand.

Sound trumpets. Enter SATURNINUS *and* TAMORA,
with [ÆMILIUS,] *Tribunes,* [*Senators*] *and others.*

Sat. What, hath the firmament moe suns than one?
Luc. What boots it thee to call thyself a sun?
Marc. Rome's emperor, and nephew, break the
    parle;
These quarrels must be quietly debated.   20
The feast is ready which the careful Titus
Hath ordain'd to an honourable end,
For peace, for love, for league, and good to Rome.
Please you, therefore, draw nigh, and take your
    places.
Sat. Marcus, we will.   25
    [*Hautboys. A table brought in. [The
    company sit down.*]

Sound trumpets. Enter TITUS *like a cook, placing
the meat on the table;* LAVINIA *with a veil over her
face;* [*young* LUCIUS *and others*].

Tit. Welcome, my [gracious] lord; welcome,
    dread queen;
Welcome, ye warlike Goths; welcome, Lucius;
And welcome, all! Although the cheer be poor,
'Twill fill your stomachs; please you eat of it.
Sat. Why art thou thus attir'd, Andronicus? 30
Tit. Because I would be sure to have all well,
To entertain your Highness and your empress.
Tam. We are beholding to you, good Andronicus.
Tit. An if your Highness knew my heart, you
    were.
My lord the Emperor, resolve me this: 35
Was it well done of rash Virginius
To slay his daughter with his own right hand,
Because she was enforc'd, stain'd, and deflower'd?
Sat. It was, Andronicus.
Tit. Your reason, mighty lord?   40
Sat. Because the girl should not survive her
    shame
And by her presence still renew his sorrows.
Tit. A reason mighty, strong, and effectual;
A pattern, precedent, and lively warrant
For me, most wretched, to perform the like.   45
Die, die, Lavinia, and thy shame with thee;
And, with thy shame, thy father's sorrow die!
                          [*Kills Lavinia.*
Sat. What hast thou done, unnatural and un-
    kind?
Tit. Kill'd her for whom my tears have made me
    blind.
I am as woeful as Virginius was,   50
And have a thousand times more cause than he
To do this outrage; and it now is done.
Sat. What, was she ravish'd? Tell who did the
    deed.
Tit. Will't please you eat? Will't please your
    Highness feed?
Tam. Why hast thou slain thine only daughter
    thus?   55
Tit. Not I; 'twas Chiron and Demetrius.
They ravish'd her, and cut away her tongue;
And they, 'twas they, that did her all this wrong.
Sat. Go fetch them hither to us presently.
Tit. Why, there they are both, baked in that pie;
Whereof their mother daintily hath fed,   61
Eating the flesh that she herself hath bred.
'Tis true, 'tis true; witness my knife's sharp point.
                          [*Stabs Tamora.*
Sat. Die, frantic wretch, for this accursed deed!
                          [*Kills Titus.*

---

200. **temper:** mix. 202. **officious:** zealous. 204. **Centaurs' feast.** The wedding feast of Hippodamia and Pirithous, at which occurred the battle between the Centaurs and Lapithæ. 206. **against:** just before.

Sc. iii, 3. **ours with thine:** i.e., we are also satisfied. 17. **moe:** more. 19. **break the parle:** stop the dispute. 26. [gra-cious] Q₂. Om. Q₁.

Luc. Can the son's eye behold his father bleed?
There's meed for meed, death for a deadly deed!
    [*Kills Saturninus. A great tumult. Lucius,*
       Marcus, and others go up into the bal-
       cony.]

  Marc. You sad-fac'd men, people and sons of
    Rome,   67
By uproars sever'd, as a flight of fowl
Scatter'd by winds and high tempestuous gusts,
O, let me teach you how to knit again   70
This scatt'red corn into one mutual sheaf,
These broken limbs again into one body;
[Lest] Rome herself be bane unto herself,
And she whom mighty kingdoms curtsy to,
Like a forlorn and desperate castaway,   75
Do shameful execution on herself.
But if my frosty signs and chaps of age,
Grave witnesses of true experience,
Cannot induce you to attend my words,
[*To Lucius.*] Speak, Rome's dear friend, as erst our
    ancestor,   80
When with his solemn tongue he did discourse
To love-sick Dido's sad attending ear
The story of that baleful burning night
When subtle Greeks surpris'd King Priam's Troy.
Tell us what Sinon hath bewitch'd our ears,   85
Or who hath brought the fatal engine in
That gives our Troy, our Rome, the civil wound.
My heart is not compact of flint nor steel;
Nor can I utter all our bitter grief,
But floods of tears will drown my oratory   90
And break my utt'rance, even in the time
When it should move ye to attend me most,
And force you to commiseration.
Here's Rome's young captain, let him tell the tale;
While I stand by and weep to hear him speak. 95
  Luc. Then, gracious auditory, be it known to
    you
That Chiron and the damn'd Demetrius
Were they that murd'red our emperor's brother,
And they it were that ravished our sister.
For their fell faults our brothers were beheaded; 100
Our father's tears despis'd, and basely cozen'd
Of that true hand that fought Rome's quarrel out
And sent her enemies unto the grave.
Lastly, myself unkindly banished,
The gates shut on me, and turn'd weeping out 105
To beg relief among Rome's enemies,
Who drown'd their enmity in my true tears
And op'd their arms to embrace me as a friend.
I am the turned forth, be it known to you,
That have preserv'd her welfare in my blood 110

And from her bosom took the enemy's point,
Sheathing the steel in my advent'rous body.
Alas, you know I am no vaunter, I;
My scars can witness, dumb although they are,
That my report is just and full of truth.   115
But, soft! methinks I do digress too much,
Citing my worthless praise. O, pardon me;
For when no friends are by, men praise themselves.
  Marc. Now is my turn to speak. Behold the
    child:
      [*Pointing to Aaron's Child in the arms of*
       an Attendant.]
Of this was Tamora delivered,   120
The issue of an irreligious Moor,
Chief architect and plotter of these woes.
The villain is alive in Titus' house,
[Damn'd] as he is, to witness this is true.
Now judge what [cause] had Titus to revenge 125
These wrongs unspeakable, past patience,
Or more than any living man could bear.
Now have you heard the truth, what say you,
    Romans?
Have we done aught amiss? Show us wherein,
And, from the place where you behold us pleading.
The poor remainder of Andronici   131
Will, hand in hand, all headlong hurl ourselves,
And on the ragged stones beat forth our souls,
And make a mutual closure of our house.
Speak, Romans, speak; and if you say we shall, 135
Lo, hand in hand, Lucius and I will fall.
  Æmil. Come, come, thou reverend man of Rome,
And bring our Emperor gently in thy hand,
Lucius our Emperor; for well I know
The common voice do cry it shall be so. 140
  [*All.*] Lucius, all hail, Rome's royal Emperor!
  Marc. Go, go into old Titus' sorrowful house,
                          [*To Attendants.*]
And hither hale that misbelieving Moor
To be ad·udg'd some direful slaught'ring death,
As punishment for his most wicked life. 145
                      [*Exeunt Attendants.*]

  [Lucius, Marcus, *and the others descend.*]
  [*All.*] Lucius, all hail, Rome's gracious governor!
  Luc. Thanks, gentle Romans; may I govern so,
To heal Rome's harms and wipe away her woe!
But, gentle people, give me aim a while,
For nature puts me to a heavy task. 150
Stand all aloof, but, uncle, draw you near
To shed obsequious tears upon this trunk.
O, take this warm kiss on thy pale cold lips,
                        [*Kissing Titus.*]

---

    66. **meed:** measure. 73. [**Lest**] (Capell). *Romane Lord.* Let Qq. *Goth.* Let Ff. 77. **chaps:** wrinkles. 80. **ancestor:** Æneas. 85. **Sinon:** the Greek who persuaded the Trojans to take the wooden horse into their city. 88. **compact:** composed. 93. **And...to** Q₁. *Lending your kind* Q₂. 94. **Here's...young** Q₁. *Here is a* Q₂. 95. **While...by** Q₁. *Your hearts will throb* Q₂. 100. **fell:** cruel. 101. **cozen'd:** cheated. 124. [**Damn'd**] (Theobald). *And* Qq Ff. 125. [**cause**] F₄. *course* Qq. 133. **souls** Q₁. *brains* Q₂. 134. **closure:** end. 141, 146. [**All.**] (Capell). *Marcus* Q₁. 149. **aim.** Obscure: "room and scope for my thoughts" (Schmidt). 152. **obsequious:** such as befit obsequies.

These sorrowful drops upon thy blood-stain'd face,
The last true duties of thy noble son!   155
  Marc. Tear for tear, and loving kiss for kiss,
Thy brother Marcus tenders on thy lips.
O, were the sum of these that I should pay
Countless and infinite, yet would I pay them!
  Luc. Come hither, boy; come, come, and learn
     of us   160
To melt in showers; thy grandsire lov'd thee well.
Many a time he danc'd thee on his knee,
Sung thee asleep, his loving breast thy pillow;
Many a story hath he told to thee,
And bid thee bear his pretty tales in mind   165
And talk of them when he was dead and gone.
  Marc. How many thousand times hath these
     poor lips
When they were living warm'd themselves on thine!
O, now, sweet boy, give them their latest kiss!
Bid him farewell; commit him to the grave;   170
Do [him] that kindness, and take leave of [him].
  Young Luc. O grandsire, grandsire! ev'n with all
     my heart
Would I were dead, so you did live again!
O Lord, I cannot speak to him for weeping;
My tears will choke me if I ope my mouth.   175

     [*Re-enter* Attendants *with* AARON.]

  A Roman. You sad Andronici, have done with
     woes.
Give sentence on this execrable wretch
That hath been breeder of these dire events.
  Luc. Set him breast-deep in earth and famish
     him;
There let him stand and rave and cry for food.   180
If any one relieves or pities him,
For the offence he dies. This is our doom.
Some stay to see him fast'ned in the earth.
  Aar. Ah, why should wrath be mute and fury
     dumb?
I am no baby, I, that with base prayers   185
I should repent the evils I have done.
Ten thousand worse than ever yet I did
Would I perform if I might have my will.
If one good deed in all my life I did,
I do repent it from my very soul.   190
  Luc. Some loving friends convey the Emperor
     hence,
And give him burial in his father's grave.
My father and Lavinia shall forthwith
Be closed in our household's monument.
As for that ravenous tiger, Tamora,   195
No funeral rite, nor man in mourning weed;
No mournful bell shall ring her burial;
But throw her forth to beasts and birds to prey.
Her life was beastly and devoid of pity,
And, being dead, let birds on her take pity.   200
[See justice done on Aaron, that damn'd Moor,
By whom our heavy haps had their beginning.
Then, afterwards, to order well the state,
That like events may ne'er it ruinate.]   [*Exeunt.*

165–69. **And bid ... kiss** Q₁. *Meet and agreeing with thine infancy: /In that respect, then, like a loving child,/Shed yet some small drops from thy tender spring,/Because kind nature doth require it so:/Friends should associate friends in grief and wo.* Q₂. 171. **[him] ... [him]** Ff. *them ... them* Qq. 200. **dead ... take** Q₁. *so, shall have like want of* Q₂. 201–204. **[See ... ruinate]** Q₂. Om. Q₁.

The Tragedy of Romeo and Juliet

THE FIRST QUARTO of *Romeo and Juliet* was printed in 1597 with a title page stating that "it hath been often (with great applause) plaid publiquely, by the right Honourable the L. of Hunsdon his Seruants." This notice proves it to have been on the stage between July 22, 1596 and March 17, 1597, for only during that interval did Shakespeare's company go by the name of "Lord Hunsdon's servants." Further evidence for date is purely internal. Undue attention has been paid to the Nurse's remark (I.iii.23,35), "'tis since the earthquake now eleven years," which has been held to point to 1591 as the date of composition, because there was an earthquake in London in 1580. But Shakespeare is giving the Nurse a realistic basis for computing Juliet's age, and although he may have been reminded of the actual earthquake, the figure eleven is probably fortuitous. More compelling with reference to date, is the pervasive lyrical impulse. For despite the abundance of quibbling and of "conceited" verse, the play has much lyric beauty of a high order. The affinity of *Romeo and Juliet* with Shakespeare's Sonnets has often been remarked, and, though a tragedy, the play is a kind of hymn to the omnipotence of love. A proper date, therefore, would seem to be 1595, which would associate it with *Love's Labour's Lost, A Midsummer Night's Dream* and *Richard II*, in all of which plays lyricism is a marked feature.

The First Quarto prints a mangled text, copy for which was apparently provided by a reporter whose memory was perhaps eked out by some notes. Very likely he was a minor player, though he does not reveal himself by such superior rendering of particular parts as betrays the piratical actors behind the "bad" Quartos of *Hamlet* and *The Merry Wives*. The text is disfigured by mislineation and corrupt metre, by transposition of lines and phrases, and by paraphrase. In 1599 appeared the Second Quarto, "Newly corrected, augmented, and amended," but it was carelessly set up, with the result that it contains some errors which, paradoxically, can be rectified by readings from the First. The Second Quarto

contains 775 more lines than the First. From this discrepancy it has been argued that the First Quarto represents an earlier version of the play. It is more likely, however, that the texts of both Quartos derive ultimately from the same acting version, and that the brevity of the First Quarto is owing to the reporter's sins of omission and, perhaps, to a few cuts made for performances in 1597. Certain typographical likenesses suggest that the Second Quarto may have been set up in part from a corrected copy of the First. A Third Quarto was printed (1609) from the Second, and a Fourth (undated) from the Third, and a Fifth (1637) from the Fourth. The Folio reprints the Third Quarto. The Second Quarto is consequently the authority, and forms the basis of the present edition.

The story of Romeo and Juliet, who stand among the great lovers in the world's literature, has a long and fascinating lineage. The device of escaping from an unwelcome marriage by means of a sleeping potion is found in the *Ephesiaca* of Xenophon of Ephesus about the fourth century. At some time or other this element became merged with a tragic tale of ill-fated lovers, who were the forbears of Romeo and Juliet. Such a tale is the thirty-third in a collection by Masuccio of Salerno (1476), but the earliest version which is a direct ancestor of Shakespeare's plot is the *Historia di due nobili Amanti* by Luigi da Porto (c. 1530). The progress of the story toward its Shakespearean form continues through a version in the *Novelle* of Matteo Bandello (1554), a translation of the same by Boisteau in his *Histoires Tragiques* (1559), an English poem by Arthur Brooke, *The Tragicall Historye of Romeus and Juliet* (1562), and a prose tale in Painter's *Palace of Pleasure* (1567).

The main lines of the action and of the chief characters were thus already laid down before Shakespeare worked on the story. The dramatic essentials are present, indeed, in the version of da Porto, who sets the scene in Verona, introduces the feud of the Montecchi and Cappelletti, and gives the names Romeo and Giulietta, Tebaldo (Tybalt), and

Lorenzo (the Friar). But in this version Romeo goes to the Capulets' feast in pursuit of a cruel mistress (though he falls in love with Juliet there); Romeo is already in possession of poison; Juliet revives in the tomb before Romeo expires, and kills herself, not with her lover's dagger, but by holding her breath until she dies. In Bandello a new stress is given to Romeo's antecedent love affair; Romeo goes to the Capulets', not in pursuit of his cruel lady but in order to see new beauties; the undesired bridegroom is named Paris; and Juliet's Nurse is introduced as the lovers' go-between. The major contribution of Boisteau is the scene with the Apothecary (from a hint in Bandello) and an alteration in the ending whereby Juliet is made to awake after the death of Romeo and to kill herself with his dagger. The poem of Brooke is tedious and pedestrian, but in it the Nurse is developed as a comic character, and the episode of Romeo's distraction at the Friar's cell and a picture of his misery in exile are added. In an address "To the Reader" Brooke states that he "saw the same argument lately set forth on stage," but the play he mentions has not survived. The notion that Shakespeare was indebted to this lost play is superfluous, for Shakespeare's drama is derived directly and, to all appearances, exclusively from the poem of Brooke.

Shakespeare works a notable transformation in his material. He compresses the action, which in Brooke had covered nine months, to five days, and reduces Juliet's age from sixteen to thirteen. The important changes, however, lie in the enrichment of characterization. Tybalt's hatred is underscored by his early introduction at the Capulets' ball, where he recognizes Romeo. Romeo fights Tybalt to avenge the death of Mercutio, whom he had striven to pacify (III.i.87–136), not, as in Brooke, because Tybalt challenges him in one of the common brawls of Montagues and Capulets. Mercutio is Shakespeare's brilliant creation from a mere supernumerary in Brooke. The Nurse is perfected as a comic figure. Shakespeare expands the rôle of Paris, ennobling his character and adding his death at Juliet's tomb, and he develops the characters of Benvolio, Lady Capulet, Montague, and Lady Montague from hints in Brooke. The crowning achievement is the poetry. This tragedy of star-crossed lovers is one of the great love poems in an age rich in amorous poetry. Shakespeare has "loaded every rift with ore." It is not, on the other hand, of uniform quality. There is considerable verbal extravagance and mere rhetoric (e.g., I.i.170–201; III.iii.17–51); there are bravura pieces (e.g., I.iv.53–94; III.ii.1–31; IV.iii.14–58); but the finest passages, though they may lack the deep tonal qualities of Shakespeare's mature verse, are very beautiful indeed.

The lyric vitality of this play is in accord with the youthful passion it celebrates. For there can be no doubt about Shakespeare's attitude toward the lovers. He has written *con amore*, sympathetic with them at every turn. To seek the cause of their "piteous overthrow" in some inherent guilt or tragic flaw, in filial disobedience or sensuality or rashness, is entirely mistaken. To know Shakespeare's feelings one need only consult one's own, which, unless one is an incorrigible moralist or has never been in love, will not be expressed in an ethical judgment. Shakespeare has written it clear in his text that his drama is a tragedy of fate. The Prologue announces the fact unambiguously, and many other passages express the hostility of Fortune and the stars, or are fraught with foreboding (I.iv. 106–11; I.v.119–22; II.ii.116–20; II.vi.6–8; III.i. 124–25, 141; III.v.54–59; V.i.24; V.iii.108–12). Romeo's exultant image of a pilot adventuring for rich merchandise (II.ii.82–84) has its fateful transmutation in the "desperate pilot" shattering upon the rocks his "sea-sick weary bark" (V.iii.117–18). The imminence of Fate is enhanced by the feud; indeed, in the perspective of the victims the feud is Fate, for without it there would have been no obstacle to their happiness. The "ancient grudge" breaks out ominously in the first (and theatrically admirable) scene of the play; Mercutio, dying because of it, cries "a plague o' both your houses"; and Tybalt's death and Romeo's banishment are owing to it. The death of the lovers is in reality, however indirectly, a consequence; for the accident preventing the delivery of the Friar's letter is subservient to a Fate already too well implemented. And after this chastening fulfillment the grieving families are reconciled. In the wickedness of this mortal enmity lies the moral of the play, if Shakespeare intended any at all.

Romeo and Juliet is a genuinely moving rather than a great play. It has emotional intensity rather than spiritual depth. The lives of the protagonists are not wrecked through dangerous propensities within themselves. Shakespeare is not here picturing the moral havoc which is unleashed through base desires or guilty passions, through ruinous self-deception, or through malice poisoning the very springs of virtue in men. Neither experience nor inclination, presumably, yet summoned him to such endeavor. But when, nearly a decade later, Shakespeare came to treat of these things, the time very likely had passed when he could portray so affectingly the simple passion and heartbreak of youth.

THE TRAGEDY OF
ROMEO AND JULIET

see Act I. Mid. Dream
"jaws of darkness"

[DRAMATIS PERSONÆ

ESCALUS, *Prince of Verona.*
PARIS, *a young nobleman, kinsman to the prince.*
MONTAGUE,⎫ *heads of two houses at variance*
CAPULET, ⎭ *with each other.*
An old man, *of the Capulet family.*
ROMEO, *son to Montague.*
MERCUTIO, *kinsman to the prince, and friend to Romeo.*
BENVOLIO, *nephew to Montague, and cousin to Romeo.*
TYBALT, *nephew to Lady Capulet.*
FRIAR LAURENCE,⎫ *Franciscans.*
FRIAR JOHN, ⎭
BALTHASAR, *servant to Romeo.*
ABRAHAM, *servant to Montague.*

SAMPSON,⎫ *servants to Capulet.*
GREGORY,⎭
PETER, *servant to Juliet's nurse.*
An Apothecary.
Three Musicians.
Page to Paris; *another Page.*
An Officer.

LADY MONTAGUE, *wife to Montague.*
LADY CAPULET, *wife to Capulet.*
JULIET, *daughter to Capulet.*
Nurse to Juliet.

Chorus.

Citizens of Verona; several Men and Women, kinsfolk to both houses; Maskers, Guards,
Watchmen, and Attendants.

SCENE: *Verona; Mantua.*]

PROLOGUE

Two households, both alike in dignity,
  In fair Verona, where we lay our scene,
From ancient grudge break to new mutiny,
  Where civil blood makes civil hands unclean.
From forth the fatal loins of these two foes   5
  A pair of star-cross'd lovers take their life;
Whose misadventur'd piteous overthrows
  Doth with their death bury their parents' strife.
The fearful passage of their death-mark'd love,
  And the continuance of their parents' rage,   10
Which, but their children's end, nought could re-
move,
  Is now the two hours' traffic of our stage;
The which if you with patient ears attend,
What here shall miss, our toil shall strive to
mend.

ACT I

SCENE I. [*Verona. A public place.*]

Enter SAMPSON *and* GREGORY, *of the house of Capulet, with swords and bucklers.*

Sam. Gregory, on my word, we'll not carry coals.
Gre. No, for then we should be colliers.
Sam. I mean, an we be in choler, we'll draw.   5
Gre. Ay, while you live, draw your neck out of collar.
Sam. I strike quickly, being mov'd.
Gre. But thou art not quickly mov'd to strike.
Sam. A dog of the house of Montague moves me.   10
Gre. To move is to stir, and to be valiant is to stand; therefore, if thou art mov'd, thou run'st away.

Prol., 3. **mutiny:** discord. 6. **star-cross'd:** doomed by the stars.
Act I, sc. i, 1. **carry coals:** submit to insult. 7. **mov'd:** angered.

Sam. A dog of that house shall move me to stand. I will take the wall of any man or maid of Montague's.   16

Gre. That shows thee a weak slave; for the weakest goes to the wall.

Sam. 'Tis true; and therefore women, being the weaker vessels, are ever thrust to the wall; therefore I will push Montague's men from the wall, and thrust his maids to the wall.   22

Gre. The quarrel is between our masters and us their men.

Sam. 'Tis all one, I will show myself a tyrant. When I have fought with the men, I will be [cruel] with the maids; I will cut off their heads.   28

Gre. The heads of the maids?

Sam. Ay, the heads of the maids, or their maidenheads; take it in what sense thou wilt.

Gre. They must take it in sense that feel it.

Sam. Me they shall feel while I am able to stand; and 'tis known I am a pretty piece of flesh.   35

Gre. 'Tis well thou art not fish; if thou hadst, thou hadst been poor John. Draw thy tool; here comes [two] of the house of Montagues.

Enter two other serving-men [ABRAHAM *and* BALTHASAR].

Sam. My naked weapon is out. Quarrel! I will back thee.   40

Gre. How! turn thy back and run?

Sam. Fear me not.

Gre. No, marry; I fear thee!

Sam. Let us take the law of our sides; let them begin.   45

Gre. I will frown as I pass by, and let them take it as they list.

Sam. Nay, as they dare. I will bite my thumb at them; which is disgrace to them, if they bear it.   50

Abr. Do you bite your thumb at us, sir?

Sam. I do bite my thumb, sir.

Abr. Do you bite your thumb at us, sir?

Sam. [*Aside to Gre.*] Is the law of our side, if I say ay?   55

Gre. No.

Sam. No, sir, I do not bite my thumb at you, sir; but I bite my thumb, sir.

Gre. Do you quarrel, sir?

Abr. Quarrel, sir? No, sir.   60

Sam. But if you do, sir, I am for you. I serve as good a man as you.

Abr. No better.

Sam. Well, sir.

Enter BENVOLIO.

Gre. Say "better"; here comes one of my master's kinsmen.   66

Sam. Yes, better, sir.

Abr. You lie.

Sam. Draw, if you be men. Gregory, remember thy [swashing] blow.   [*They fight.* 70

Ben. Part, fools!

Put up your swords; you know not what you do.

[*Beats down their swords.*]

Enter TYBALT.

Tyb. What, art thou drawn among these heartless hinds?

Turn thee, Benvolio, look upon thy death.

Ben. I do but keep the peace. Put up thy sword,   75

Or manage it to part these men with me.

Tyb. What, drawn, and talk of peace! I hate the word

As I hate hell, all Montagues, and thee.

Have at thee, coward!   [*They fight.*

Enter three or four Citizens [*and* OFFICERS], *with clubs or partisans.*

Off. Clubs, bills, and partisans! Strike! Beat them down!   80

Down with the Capulets! down with the Montagues!

Enter CAPULET *in his gown, and* LADY CAPULET.

Cap. What noise is this? Give me my long sword, ho!

La. Cap. A crutch, a crutch! why call you for a sword?

Cap. My sword, I say! Old Montague is come,

And flourishes his blade in spite of me.   85

Enter MONTAGUE *and* LADY MONTAGUE.

Mon. Thou villain Capulet, — Hold me not, let me go.

La. Mon. Thou shalt not stir one foot to seek a foe.

Enter PRINCE ESCALUS, *with his train.*

Prin. Rebellious subjects, enemies to peace,

Profaners of this neighbour-stained steel, —

Will they not hear? — What, ho! you men, you beasts,   90

---

15. take the wall. Keeping to the side of the walk next to the wall was the pedestrian's best protection in the dirty streets of Shakespeare's day. To "take the wall" could be insulting, just as to yield it was courteous.   **27.** [cruel] Q₄. *civil* Q₂.   **37. poor John:** salt hake.   **38.** [two] Q₁. Om. Q₂.   **66. here...kinsmen.** Tybalt is sighted.   **70.** [swashing] Q₄: crushing.   *washing* Q₂.   **73. heartless hinds:** cowardly servants.   **80. Clubs:** a cry of the London apprentices, who wielded clubs.   **bills:** battle-axes.   **partisans:** pikes or spears with two-edged knives affixed.   **85. spite:** defiance.   **89 neighbour-stained:** stained with neighbor's blood.

That quench the fire of your pernicious rage
With purple fountains issuing from your veins,
On pain of torture, from those bloody hands
Throw your mistemper'd weapons to the ground,
And hear the sentence of your moved prince.   95
Three civil brawls, bred of an airy word,
By thee, old Capulet, and Montague,
Have thrice disturb'd the quiet of our streets,
And made Verona's ancient citizens
Cast by their grave beseeming ornaments   100
To wield old partisans, in hands as old,
Cank'red with peace, to part your cank'red hate;
If ever you disturb our streets again
Your lives shall pay the forfeit of the peace.
For this time, all the rest depart away.   105
You, Capulet, shall go along with me;
And, Montague, come you this afternoon,
To know our farther pleasure in this case,
To old Free-town, our common judgement-place.
Once more, on pain of death, all men depart.   110
    [*Exeunt [all but Montague, Lady Montague,
      and Benvolio*].
  Mon. Who set this ancient quarrel new abroach?
Speak, nephew, were you by when it began?
  Ben. Here were the servants of your adversary,
And yours, close fighting ere I did approach.
I drew to part them. In the instant came   115
The fiery Tybalt, with his sword prepar'd,
Which, as he breath'd defiance to my ears,
He swung about his head and cut the winds,
Who, nothing hurt withal, hiss'd him in scorn.
While we were interchanging thrusts and blows,   120
Came more and more and fought on part and part,
Till the Prince came, who parted either part.
  La. Mon. O, where is Romeo? Saw you him
to-day?
Right glad I am he was not at this fray.
  Ben. Madam, an hour before the worshipp'd
sun   125
Peer'd forth the golden window of the east,
A troubled mind [drave] me to walk abroad;
Where, underneath the grove of sycamore
That westward rooteth from [the city's] side,
So early walking did I see your son.   130
Towards him I made, but he was ware of me
And stole into the covert of the wood.
I, measuring his affections by my own,
Which then most sought where most might not be
    found,
Being one too many by my weary self,
Pursued my humour not pursuing his,   135
And gladly shunn'd who gladly fled from me.
  Mon. Many a morning hath he there been seen,
With tears augmenting the fresh morning's dew,

Adding to clouds more clouds with his deep sighs;
But all so soon as the all-cheering sun   140
Should in the farthest east begin to draw
The shady curtains from Aurora's bed,
Away from light steals home my heavy son,
And private in his chamber pens himself,
Shuts up his windows, locks fair daylight out,   145
And makes himself an artificial night.
Black and portentous must this humour prove
Unless good counsel may the cause remove.
  Ben. My noble uncle, do you know the cause?
  Mon. I neither know it nor can learn of him.   150
  Ben. Have you importun'd him by any means?
  Mon. Both by myself and many other friends;
But he, his own affections' counsellor,
Is to himself — I will not say how true —
But to himself so secret and so close,   155
So far from sounding and discovery,
As is the bud bit with an envious worm
Ere he can spread his sweet leaves to the air
Or dedicate his beauty to the [sun].
Could we but learn from whence his sorrows grow,
We would as willingly give cure as know.   161

         Enter ROMEO.

  Ben. See, where he comes! So please you, step
aside;
I'll know his grievance, or be much deni'd.
  Mon. I would thou wert so happy by thy stay
To hear true shrift. Come, madam, let's away.   165
         [*Exeunt [Montague and Lady*].
  Ben. Good morrow, cousin.
  Rom.   Is the day so young?
  Ben. But new struck nine.
  Rom.   Ay me! sad hours seem long.
Was that my father that went hence so fast?
  Ben. It was. What sadness lengthens Romeo's
hours?
  Rom. Not having that which, having, makes
them short.   170
  Ben. In love?
  Rom. Out —
  Ben. Of love?
  Rom. Out of her favour, where I am in love.
  Ben. Alas, that love, so gentle in his view,   175
Should be so tyrannous and rough in proof!
  Rom. Alas, that love, whose view is muffled still,
Should, without eyes, see pathways to his will!
Where shall we dine? O me! What fray was here?
Yet tell me not, for I have heard it all.   180
Here's much to do with hate, but more with love.
Why, then, O brawling love! O loving hate!
O anything, of nothing first [create]!
O heavy lightness! serious vanity!

---

94. **mistemper'd**: angry. 102. **Cank'red**: (1) rusted, (2) malignant. 111. **set...abroach**: tap and leave running. 127. [**drave**] F. *drive* Q₂. 129. [**the city's**] Q₁. *this city* Q₂. 133. **affections**: inclinations. 134. **where...found**: the most unfrequented place. 157. **envious**: malicious. 159. [**sun**] (Theobald). *same* Q₂. 165. **shrift**: confession. 175. **view**: looks. 176. **proof**: experience. 183. [**create**] Q₁. *created* Q₂.

Mis-shapen chaos of [well-seeming] forms!   185
Feather of lead, bright smoke, cold fire, sick health!
Still-waking sleep, that is not what it is!
This love feel I, that feel no love in this.
Dost thou not laugh?
   Ben.   No, coz, I rather weep.
   Rom. Good heart, at what?
   Ben.   At thy good heart's oppression.   190
   Rom. Why, such is love's transgression.
Griefs of mine own lie heavy in my breast,
Which thou wilt propagate to have it prest
With more of thine.   This love that thou hast shown
Doth add more grief to too much of mine own.   195
Love is a smoke made with the fume of sighs;
Being purg'd, a fire sparkling in lovers' eyes;
Being vex'd, a sea nourish'd with [lovers'] tears.
What is it else?   A madness most discreet,
A choking gall, and a preserving sweet.   200
Farewell, my coz.
   Ben.   Soft! I will go along.
An if you leave me so, you do me wrong.
   Rom. Tut, I have [left] myself; I am not here.
This is not Romeo; he's some otherwhere.
   Ben. Tell me in sadness, who is that you love?   205
   Rom. What, shall I groan and tell thee?
   Ben.   Groan! why, no;
But sadly tell me who.
   Rom. [Bid a] sick man in sadness [make] his
     will, —
Ah, word ill urg'd to one that is so ill!
In sadness, cousin, I do love a woman.   210
   Ben. I aim'd so near when I suppos'd you lov'd.
   Rom. A right good mark-man! And she's fair I
    love.
   Ben. A right fair mark, fair coz, is soonest hit.
   Rom. Well, in that hit you miss.   She'll not be
    hit
With Cupid's arrow; she hath Dian's wit;   215
And, in strong proof of chastity well arm'd,
From Love's weak childish bow she lives [un-
    harm'd].
She will not stay the siege of loving terms,
Nor bide th' encounter of assailing eyes,
Nor ope her lap to saint-seducing gold.   220
O, she is rich in beauty, only poor
That, when she dies, with beauty dies her store.
   Ben. Then she hath sworn that she will still live
    chaste?
   Rom. She hath, and in that sparing make huge
    waste;
For beauty starv'd with her severity   225
Cuts beauty off from all posterity.

She is too fair, too wise, wisely too fair,
To merit bliss by making me despair.
She hath forsworn to love, and in that vow
Do I live dead that live to tell it now.   230
   Ben. Be rul'd by me, forget to think of her.
   Rom. O, teach me how I should forget to think.
   Ben. By giving liberty unto thine eyes;
Examine other beauties.
   Rom.   'Tis the way
To call hers, exquisite, in question more.   235
These happy masks that kiss fair ladies' brows,
Being black, puts us in mind they hide the fair;
He that is strucken blind cannot forget
The precious treasure of his eyesight lost.
Show me a mistress that is passing fair,   240
What doth her beauty serve, but as a note
Where I may read who pass'd that passing fair?
Farewell! Thou canst not teach me to forget.
   Ben. I'll pay that doctrine, or else die in debt.
                        [Exeunt.

[SCENE II.   *A street.*]

Enter CAPULET, PARIS, *and the Clown* [*a* SERVANT].

   Cap. But Montague is bound as well as I,
In penalty alike; and 'tis not hard, I think,
For men so old as we to keep the peace.
   Par. Of honourable reckoning are you both;
And pity 'tis you liv'd at odds so long.   5
But now, my lord, what say you to my suit?
   Cap. But saying o'er what I have said before.
My child is yet a stranger in the world;
She hath not seen the change of fourteen years.
Let two more summers wither in their pride,   10
Ere we may think her ripe to be a bride.
   Par. Younger than she are happy mothers made.
   Cap. And too soon marr'd are those so early made.
[The] earth hath swallow'd all my hopes but she;
She is the hopeful lady of my earth;   15
But woo her, gentle Paris, get her heart,
My will to her consent is but a part;
An she [agree], within her scope of choice
Lies my consent and fair according voice.
This night I hold an old accustom'd feast,   20
Whereto I have invited many a guest,
Such as I love; and you, among the store
One more, most welcome, makes my number more.
At my poor house look to behold this night
Earth-treading stars that make dark heaven light. 25
Such comfort as do lusty young men feel
When well-apparell'd April on the heel
Of limping winter treads, even such delight

185. **[well-seeming]** Q₄. *well-seeing* Q₂. 193. **to have:** by having. 198. **[lovers']** (Pope). *a lovers* Q₁. *loving* Q₂.
203. **[left]** (Allen conj.). *lost* Q₂. 205. **sadness:** seriousness. 208. **[Bid a]**... **[make]** Q₁. *A ... makes* Q₂. 215. **wit:**
mind, purpose. 216. **proof:** armor. 217. **[unharm'd]** Q₁. *uncharm'd* Q₂. 218. **stay:** bide. 222. **store:** riches. 235.
in ... more: into greater consideration. 244. **pay ... doctrine:** teach that lesson.
  Sc. ii. 4. **reckoning:** repute. 14. **[The]** Q₄. Om. Q₂. 15. **earth:** body, or world. 18. **[agree]** F. *agreed* Q₂.

Among fresh [female] buds shall you this night
Inherit at my house. Hear all, all see,   30
And like her most whose merit most shall be;
Which [on] more view of, many, mine being one,
May stand in number, though in reckoning none.
Come, go with me. [*To Servant.*] Go, sirrah, trudge
     about
Through fair Verona; find those persons out   35
Whose names are written there, and to them say
My house and welcome on their pleasure stay.
                         [*Exeunt [Capulet and Paris]*].
     Serv. Find them out whose names are written
here! It is written that the shoemaker should
meddle with his yard and the tailor with his last, the
fisher with his pencil and the painter with his nets;
but I am sent to find those persons whose names are
here writ, and can never find what names the writing
person hath here writ. I must to the learned. — In
good time.   45

               Enter BENVOLIO *and* ROMEO.

     Ben. Tut, man, one fire burns out another's burn-
          ing,
One pain is less'ned by another's anguish;
Turn giddy, and be holp by backward turning;
One desperate grief cures with another's languish.
Take thou some new infection to thy eye,   50
And the rank poison of the old will die.
     Rom. Your plaintain-leaf is excellent for that.
     Ben. For what, I pray thee?
     Rom.   For your broken shin.
     Ben. Why, Romeo, art thou mad?
     Rom. Not mad, but bound more than a madman
          is;   55
Shut up in prison, kept without my food,
Whipp'd and tormented and — God-den, good fellow.
     Serv. God gi' god-den. I pray, sir, can you read?
     Rom. Ay, mine own fortune in my misery.   60
     Serv. Perhaps you have learn'd it without book.
But, I pray, can you read anything you see?
     Rom. Ay, if I know the letters and the language.
     Serv. Ye say honestly. Rest you merry!
     Rom. Stay, fellow; I can read.   66
     (*Reads.*) "Signior Martino and his wife and
daughters; County Anselme and his beauteous sisters;
the lady widow of Vitruvio; Signior Placentio and
his lovely nieces; Mercutio and his brother Valentine; mine uncle Capulet, his wife, and daughters;
my fair niece Rosaline; Livia; Signior Valentio and
his cousin Tybalt; Lucio and the lively Helena." 74
A fair assembly: whither should they come?
     Serv. Up.

     Rom. Whither? To supper?
     Serv. To our house.
     Rom. Whose house?
     Serv. My master's.   80
     Rom. Indeed, I should have ask'd you that before.
     Serv. Now I'll tell you without asking. My master
is the great rich Capulet; and if you be not of the
house of Montagues, I pray, come and crush a cup of
wine. Rest you merry!   [*Exit.*   86
     Ben. At this same ancient feast of Capulet's
Sups the fair Rosaline whom thou so loves,
With all the admired beauties of Verona.
Go thither; and with unattainted eye   90
Compare her face with some that I shall show,
And I will make thee think thy swan a crow.
     Rom. When the devout religion of mine eye
Maintains such falsehood, then turn tears to [fires];
And these, who, often drown'd, could never die, 95
     Transparent heretics, be burnt for liars!
One fairer than my love! The all-seeing sun
Ne'er saw her match since first the world begun.
     Ben. Tut, you saw her fair, none else being by,
Herself pois'd with herself in either eye;   100
But in that crystal scales let there be weigh'd
Your lady's love against some other maid
That I will show you shining at this feast,
And she shall scant show well that now seems best.
     Rom. I'll go along no such sight to be shown, 105
But to rejoice in splendour of mine own. [*Exeunt.*]

          [SCENE III. *A room in Capulet's house.*]

          Enter LADY CAPULET *and* NURSE.

     La. Cap. Nurse, where's my daughter? Call
          her forth to me.
     Nurse. Now, by my maidenhead at twelve year
          old.
I bade her come. What, lamb! What, ladybird!
God forbid! — Where's this girl? What, Juliet!

                    Enter JULIET.

     Jul. How now! Who calls?
     Nurse.   Your mother.
     Jul.   Madam, I am here.
What is your will?   6
     La. Cap. This is the matter. — Nurse, give leave a
          while,
We must talk in secret. — Nurse, come back again;
I have remem'bred me, thou 's hear our counsel.
Thou know'st my daughter 's of a pretty age.   10
     Nurse. Faith, I can tell her age unto an hour.
     La. Cap. She's not fourteen.

     29. **[female]** Q₁. *fennell* Q₂. 30. **Inherit:** possess. 32. **[on]** Q₄. *one* Q₂. 48. **backward:** in the reverse direction. 57.
God-den: good evening. 84. **crush:** drink. 87. **ancient:** customary. 90. **unattainted:** unprejudiced. 94. **[fires]** (Pope).
fire Q₂. 95. **these:** i.e., my eyes. 100. **pois'd:** balanced.
     Sc. iii, 4. **God forbid:** i.e., that anything is wrong. 2–78. Q₂ prints the Nurse's speeches in prose and in italics. 9. **thou's:**
thou shalt.

Nurse.   I'll lay fourteen of my teeth, —
And yet, to my teen be it spoken, I have but four, —
She 's not fourteen.   How long is it now
To Lammas-tide?
La. Cap.   A fortnight and odd days.   15
Nurse. Even or odd, of all days in the year,
Come Lammas-eve at night shall she be fourteen.
Susan and she — God rest all Christian souls! —
Were of an age.   Well, Susan is with God;
She was too good for me.   But, as I said,   20
On Lammas-eve at night shall she be fourteen;
That shall she, marry; I remember it well.
'Tis since the earthquake now eleven years,
And she was wean'd, — I never shall forget it —
Of all the days of the year, upon that day;   25
For I had then laid wormwood to my dug,
Sitting in the sun under the dove-house wall;
My lord and you were then at Mantua; —
Nay, I do bear a brain; — but, as I said,
When it did taste the wormwood on the nipple   30
Of my dug and felt it bitter, pretty fool,
To see it tetchy and fall out wi' the dug!
Shake, quoth the dove-house; 'twas no need, I trow,
To bid me trudge.
And since that time it is eleven years;   35
For then she could stand high-lone; nay, by the rood,
She could have run and waddled all about;
For even the day before, she broke her brow;
And then my husband — God be with his soul!
'A was a merry man — took up the child.   40
"Yea," quoth he, "dost thou fall upon thy face?
Thou wilt fall backward when thou hast more wit;
Wilt thou not, Jule?" and, by my holidame,
The pretty wretch left crying and said, "Ay."
To see, now, how a jest shall come about!   45
I warrant, an I should live a thousand years,
I never should forget it.   "Wilt thou not, Jule?"
     quoth he;
And, pretty fool, it stinted and said, "Ay."
La. Cap. Enough of this; I pray thee, hold thy
     peace.
Nurse. Yes, madam; yet I cannot choose but
     laugh   50
To think it should leave crying and say, "Ay."
And yet, I warrant, it had upon it brow
A bump as big as a young cock'rel's stone;
A perilous knock; and it cried bitterly.
"Yea," quoth my husband, "fall'st upon thy face?
Thou wilt fall backward when thou comest to age;   56
Wilt thou not, Jule?" It stinted and said, "Ay."
Jul. And stint thou too, I pray thee, nurse, say I.
Nurse. Peace, I have done.   God mark thee to his
     grace!

Thou wast the prettiest babe that e'er I nurs'd.   60
An I might live to see thee married once,
I have my wish.
La. Cap. Marry, that "marry" is the very theme
I came to talk of.   Tell me, daughter Juliet,
How stands your dispositions to be married?   65
Jul. It is an [honour] that I dream not of.
Nurse. An [honour]! were not I thine only nurse,
I would say thou hadst suck'd wisdom from thy teat
La. Cap. Well, think of marriage now; younger
     than you,
Here in Verona, ladies of esteem,   70 .
Are made already mothers.   By my count,
I was your mother much upon these years
That you are now a maid.   Thus then in brief:
The valiant Paris seeks you for his love.
Nurse. A man, young lady! Lady, such a man   75
As all the world — why, he's a man of wax.
La. Cap. Verona's summer hath not such a flower.
Nurse. Nay, he's a flower; in faith, a very flower.
La. Cap. What say you?   Can you love the gentle-
     man?
This night you shall behold him at our feast;   80
Read o'er the volume of young Paris' face
And find delight writ there with beauty's pen;
Examine every married lineament
And see how one another lends content,
And what obscur'd in this fair volume lies   85
Find written in the margent of his eyes.
This precious book of love, this unbound lover,
To beautify him, only lacks a cover.
The fish lives in the sea, and 'tis much pride
For fair without the fair within to hide.   90
That book in many's eyes doth share the glory,
That in gold clasps locks in the golden story;
So shall you share all that he doth possess,
By having him, making yourself no less.   94
Nurse. No less! nay, bigger; women grow by men.
La. Cap. Speak briefly, can you like of Paris' love?
Jul. I'll look to like, if looking liking move;
But no more deep will I endart mine eye
Than your consent gives strength to make [it] fly.   99

Enter SERVANT.

Serv. Madam, the guests are come, supper serv'd
up, you call'd, my young lady ask'd for, the nurse
curs'd in the pantry, and everything in extremity.   I
must hence to wait; I beseech you, follow straight.
                        [*Exit.*
La. Cap. We follow thee.   Juliet, the County
     stays.   105
Nurse. Go, girl, seek happy nights to happy days.
                       [*Exeunt.*

---

12. **lay:** wager.   13. **teen:** sorrow.   15. **Lammas-tide:** August 1st.   29. **bear a brain:** i.e., have a great memory.   32. **tetchy:** fretful.   36. **high-lone:** quite alone.   **rood:** cross.   43. **holidame:** i.e., halidom, holiness.   48. **stinted:** ceased.   53. **cock'rel's:** a young cock's.   66, 67. [**honour**] Q₁.   *houre* Q₂.   76. **man of wax:** as handsome as a wax figure.   83. **married:** harmonious.   86. **margent:** margin.   89. **The ... sea:** i.e., the lover is yet uncaught.   99. [**it**] Q₁.   Om. Q₂.   105. **stays:** waits.

[SCENE IV. *A street.*]

Enter ROMEO, MERCUTIO, BENVOLIO, *with five
or six other* Maskers, Torch-bearers.

Rom. What, shall this speech be spoke for our
excuse?
Or shall we on without apology?
Ben. The date is out of such prolixity.
We'll have no Cupid hoodwink'd with a scarf,
Bearing a Tartar's painted bow of lath,   5
Scaring the ladies like a crow-keeper;
[Nor no without-book prologue, faintly spoke
After the prompter, for our entrance;]
But let them measure us by what they will,
We'll measure them a measure and be gone.   10
Rom. Give me a torch. I am not for this ambling;
Being but heavy, I will bear the light.
Mer. Nay, gentle Romeo, we must have you dance.
Rom. Not I, believe me. You have dancing shoes
With nimble soles; I have a soul of lead   15
So stakes me to the ground I cannot move.
Mer. You are a lover; borrow Cupid's wings,
And soar with them above a common bound.
Rom. I am too sore enpierced with his shaft
To soar with his light feathers, and so bound   20
I cannot bound a pitch above dull woe.
Under love's heavy burden do I sink.
[*Mer.*] And, to sink in it, should you burden love;
Too great oppression for a tender thing.
Rom. Is love a tender thing? It is too rough, 25
Too rude, too boist'rous, and it pricks like thorn.
Mer. If love be rough with you, be rough with
love;
Prick love for pricking, and you beat love down. —
Give me a case to put my visage in, [*Puts on a mask.*]
A visor for a visor! what care I   30
What curious eye doth quote deformities?
Here are the beetle brows shall blush for me.
Ben. Come, knock and enter; and no sooner in,
But every man betake him to his legs.
Rom. A torch for me; let wantons light of heart 35
Tickle the senseless rushes with their heels,
For I am proverb'd with a grandsire phrase:
I'll be a candle-holder, and look on.
The game was ne'er so fair, and I am [done].
Mer. Tut, dun's the mouse, the constable's own
word.   40
If thou art Dun, we'll draw thee from the mire

Or, save your reverence, love, wherein thou stickest
Up to the ears. Come, we burn daylight, ho!
Rom. Nay, that's not so.
Mer.   I mean, sir, in delay
We waste our lights in vain, [like] lights by day.   45
Take our good meaning, for our judgement sits
Five times in that ere once in our [five] wits.
Rom. And we mean well in going to this mask;
But 'tis no wit to go.
Mer.   Why, may one ask?   49
Rom. I dream'd a dream to-night.
Mer.   And so did I.
Rom. Well, what was yours?
Mer.   That dreamers often lie.
Rom. In bed asleep, while they do dream things
true.
Mer. O, then, I see Queen Mab hath been with
you.
She is the fairies' midwife, and she comes
In shape no bigger than an agate-stone   55
On the fore-finger of an alderman,
Drawn with a team of little atomies
Over men's noses as they lie asleep;
Her waggon-spokes made of long spinners' legs,
The cover of the wings of grasshoppers,   60
Her traces of the smallest spider web,
Her collars of the moonshine's wat'ry beams,
Her whip of cricket's bone, the lash of film,
Her waggoner a small grey-coated gnat,
Not half so big as a round little worm   65
Prick'd from the lazy finger of a [maid];
Her chariot is an empty hazel-nut
Made by the joiner squirrel, or old grub,
Time out o' mind the fairies' coachmakers.
And in this state she gallops night by night   70
Through lovers' brains, and then they dream of love;
On courtiers' knees, that dream on curtsies straight;
O'er lawyers' fingers, who straight dream on fees;
O'er ladies' lips, who straight on kisses dream,
Which oft the angry Mab with blisters plagues, 75
Because their breath with sweetmeats tainted are.
Sometime she gallops o'er a courtier's nose,
And then dreams he of smelling out a suit;
And sometime comes she with a tithe-pig's tail
Tickling a parson's nose as 'a lies asleep,   80
Then he dreams of another benefice.
Sometime she driveth o'er a soldier's neck,
And then dreams he of cutting foreign throats,

Sc. iv, 1. speech. Maskers used to be preceded by one who made a speech. 4. **hoodwink'd**: blindfolded. 6. **crow-keeper**: scarecrow. 7–8. [**Nor ... entrance**] Q₁. Om. Q₂. 10. **measure**: dance. 23. [*Mer.*] Q₄. *Horatio* Q₂. 29. **case**: mask. 30. **visor ... visor**: mask for a mask-like (i.e., ugly) face. 31. **quote**: notice. 36. **rushes**. Rushes were used as floor covering. 37. **grandsire phrase**: old proverb, viz., "A good candle-holder (i.e., onlooker) proves a good gamester" (l. 38). Another seems to be echoed in l. 39: "He is wise who gives over (is done) when the game is fairest." 39. [**done**] Q₁. *dum* Q₂. *dun* Q₃. 40. **dun's the mouse.** A stock phrase apparently meaning "keep still." 41. **Dun.** Alluding to an old Christmas game, "Dun is in the mire." A heavy log representing a horse stuck in the mud is hauled out by the players. 42. **Or ... love.** Many edd. read *Of this sir-reverence love*, from Q₁. 45. [**like**] (Johnson). *lights* Q₂. 47. [**five**] (Wilbraham conj.). *fine* Q₂. 53–91. **O ... bodes.** So Q₁. Prose Q₂. 66. [**maid**] Q₁. *man* Q₂. 79. **tithe-pig's**: pig paid as part of parish dues.

Of breaches, ambuscadoes, Spanish blades,
Of healths five fathom deep; and then anon   85
Drums in his ear, at which he starts and wakes,
And being thus frighted swears a prayer or two
And sleeps again. This is that very Mab
That plats the manes of horses in the night,
And bakes the elf-locks in foul sluttish hairs,   90
Which, once untangled, much misfortune bodes.
This is the hag, when maids lie on their backs,
That presses them and learns them first to bear,
Making them women of good carriage.
This is she —
   Rom.   Peace, peace, Mercutio, peace!   95
Thou talk'st of nothing.
   Mer.   True, I talk of dreams,
Which are the children of an idle brain,
Begot of nothing but vain fantasy,
Which is as thin of substance as the air
And more inconstant than the wind, who wooes   100
Even now the frozen bosom of the north,
And, being anger'd, puffs away from thence,
Turning his [face] to the dew-dropping south.
   Ben. This wind you talk of blows us from our-
selves.
Supper is done, and we shall come too late.   105
   Rom. I fear, too early; for my mind misgives
Some consequence yet hanging in the stars
Shall bitterly begin his fearful date
With this night's revels, and expire the term
Of a despised life clos'd in my breast   110
By some vile forfeit of untimely death.
But He that hath the steerage of my course
Direct my [sail]! On, lusty gentlemen!
   Ben. Strike, drum.   [*They march about the stage.*
                    [*Exeunt.*]

[SCENE V. *A hall in Capulet's house.*]

[Musicians *waiting.*] *Enter* SERVING-MEN, *with*
napkins.

   [*1.*] *Serv.* Where's Potpan, that he helps not to
take away? He shift a trencher! He scrape a
trencher!
   [*2.*] *Serv.* When good manners shall lie all in one
or two men's hands, and they unwash'd too, 'tis a
foul thing.   6
   [*1.*] *Serv.* Away with the joint-stools, remove the
court-cupboard, look to the plate. Good thou, save
me a piece of marchpane; and, as thou loves me, let
the porter let in Susan Grindstone and Nell. Antony
and Potpan!   11
   2. Serv. Ay, boy, ready.
   [*1.*] *Serv.* You are look'd for and call'd for, ask'd
for and sought for, in the great chamber.

   3. Serv. We cannot be here and there too. Cheerly,
boys; be brisk a while, and the longer liver take
all.   [*They retire.*]   17

Enter [CAPULET, *with* JULIET, TYBALT, *and others of*
his house, meeting] *the* Guests, ROMEO, *and other*
Maskers.

   Cap. Welcome, gentlemen! Ladies that have
their toes
Unplagu'd with corns will walk [a bout] with you.
Ah, my mistresses, which of you all   20
Will now deny to dance? She that makes dainty,
She, I'll swear, hath corns. Am I come near ye
now?
Welcome, gentlemen! I have seen the day
That I have worn a visor and could tell
A whispering tale in a fair lady's ear,   25
Such as would please; 'tis gone, 'tis gone, 'tis gone.
You are welcome, gentlemen! Come, musicians,
play.   [*Music plays, and they dance.*
A hall, a hall! give room! and foot it, girls.
More light, you knaves; and turn the tables up,
And quench the fire, the room is grown too hot.   30
Ah, sirrah, this unlook'd-for sport comes well.
Nay, sit, nay, sit, good cousin Capulet,
For you and I are past our dancing days.
How long is't now since last yourself and I
Were in a mask?
   2. Cap.   By 'r lady, thirty years.   35
   Cap. What, man! 'tis not so much, 'tis not so much.
'Tis since the nuptial of Lucentio,
Come Pentecost as quickly as it will,
Some five and twenty years; and then we mask'd.
   2. Cap. 'Tis more, 'tis more. His son is elder, sir;
His son is thirty.
   Cap.   Will you tell me that?   41
His son was but a ward two years ago.
   Rom. [*To a Serving-man.*] What lady's that which
doth enrich the hand
Of yonder knight?
   Serv. I know not, sir.   45
   Rom. O, she doth teach the torches to burn bright!
It seems she hangs upon the cheek of night
As a rich jewel in an Ethiop's ear;
Beauty too rich for use, for earth too dear!
So shows a snowy dove trooping with crows,   50
As yonder lady o'er her fellows shows.
The measure done, I'll watch her place of stand,
And, touching hers, make blessed my rude hand.
Did my heart love till now? Forswear it, sight!
For I ne'er saw true beauty till this night.   55
   Tyb. This, by his voice, should be a Montague.
Fetch me my rapier, boy. What dares the slave
Come hither, cover'd with an antic face,

---

90. **elf-locks**: hair tangled by elves. 103. [face] Q$_1$. *side* Q$_2$. **dew-dropping**: rainy. 113. [sail] Q$_1$. *sute* Q$_2$.
Sc. v, 7. **joint-stools**: folding stools. 8. **court-cupboard**: sideboard. 9. **marchpane**: marzipan, cake made of almond
paste. 19. [a bout] (Daniel). *about* Q$_2$. To "walk a bout" is to tread a measure. 28. **A hall**: make room.

To fleer and scorn at our solemnity?
Now, by the stock and honour of my kin,   60
To strike him dead I hold it not a sin.
    Cap. Why, how now, kinsman! wherefore storm
      you so?
    Tyb. Uncle, this is a Montague, our foe,
A villain that is hither come in spite
To scorn at our solemnity this night.   65
    Cap. Young Romeo is it?
    Tyb.   'Tis he, that villain Romeo.
    Cap. Content thee, gentle coz, let him alone,
'A bears him like a portly gentleman;
And, to say truth, Verona brags of him
To be a virtuous and well-govern'd youth.   70
I would not for the wealth of all this town
Here in my house do him disparagement;
Therefore be patient, take no note of him;
It is my will, the which if thou respect,
Show a fair presence and put off these frowns,   75
An ill-beseeming semblance for a feast.
    Tyb. It fits, when such a villain is a guest.
I'll not endure him.
    Cap.   He shall be endur'd.
What, goodman boy! I say he shall; go to!
Am I the master here, or you? Go to!   80
You'll not endure him! God shall mend my soul!
You'll make a mutiny among my guests!
You will set cock-a-hoop! You'll be the man!
    Tyb. Why, uncle, 'tis a shame.
    Cap.   Go to, go to;
You are a saucy boy. Is't so, indeed?   85
This trick may chance to scathe you; I know what.
You must contrary me! Marry, 'tis time. —
Well said, my hearts! — You are a princox; go;
Be quiet, or — More light, more light! — for shame!
I'll make you quiet. — What, cheerly, my hearts! 90
    Tyb. Patience perforce with wilful choler meeting
Makes my flesh tremble in their different greeting.
I will withdraw; but this intrusion shall
Now seeming sweet convert to bitt'rest gall. [*Exit.*
    Rom. [*To Juliet.*] If I profane with my unworthiest
      hand   95
This holy shrine, the gentle [fine] is this:
My lips, two blushing pilgrims, ready stand
To smooth that rough touch with a tender kiss.
    Jul. Good pilgrim, you do wrong your hand too
      much,
Which mannerly devotion shows in this;   100
For saints have hands that pilgrims' hands do touch,
And palm to palm is holy palmers' kiss.
    Rom. Have not saints lips, and holy palmers too?
    Jul. Ay, pilgrim, lips that they must use in
      prayer.

    Rom. O, then, dear saint, let lips do what hands
      do;   105
They pray, grant thou, lest faith turn to despair.
    Jul. Saints do not move, though grant for prayers'
      sake.
    Rom. Then move not while my prayer's effect I
      take.
Thus from my lips, by thine, my sin is purg'd.
                      [*Kissing her.*]
    Jul. Then have my lips the sin that they have
      took.   110
    Rom. Sin from my lips? O trespass sweetly urg'd!
Give me my sin again.   [*Kissing her again.*
    Jul.   You kiss by the book.
    Nurse. Madam, your mother craves a word with
      you.
    Rom. What is her mother?
    Nurse.   Marry, bachelor,
Her mother is the lady of the house,   115
And a good lady, and a wise and virtuous.
I nurs'd her daughter, that you talk'd withal;
I tell you, he that can lay hold of her
Shall have the chinks.
    Rom.   Is she a Capulet?
O dear account! my life is my foe's debt.   120
    Ben. Away, be gone; the sport is at the best.
    Rom. Ay, so I fear; the more is my unrest.
    Cap. Nay, gentlemen, prepare not to be gone;
We have a trifling foolish banquet towards.
Is it e'en so? Why, then, I thank you all;   125
I thank you, honest gentlemen; good-night.
More torches here! Come on then, let's to bed.
Ah, sirrah, by my fay, it waxes late;
I'll to my rest.
    [*All but Juliet and Nurse begin to go out.*]
    Jul. Come hither, nurse. What is yond gentle-
      man?   130
    Nurse. The son and heir of old Tiberio.
    Jul. What's he that now is going out of door?
    Nurse. Marry, that, I think, be young Petruchio.
    Jul. What's he that follows here, that would not
      dance?
    Nurse. I know not.   135
    Jul. Go, ask his name. — If he be married,
My grave is like to be my wedding-bed.
    Nurse. His name is Romeo, and a Montague;
The only son of your great enemy.
    Jul. My only love sprung from my only hate! 140
Too early seen unknown, and known too late!
Prodigious birth of love it is to me
That I must love a loathed enemy.
    Nurse. What's this? what's this?
    Jul.   A rhyme I learn'd even now

---

    59. **fleer**: mock. **solemnity**: feast.   68. **portly**: dignified.   83. **set cock-a-hoop**: throw things into disorder.   88. **princox**: saucy boy.   91. **perforce**: enforced.   95–108. These lines make a sonnet in the Shakespearean form.   96. **[fine]** (Theobald). **sin** Q₂.   97. **ready** Q₁. *did readie* Q₂.   112. **by the book**: methodically.   119. **chinks**: money.   120. **my foe's debt**: i.e., in the power of my foe.   124. **towards**: coming.   142. **Prodigious**: ominous.

Of one I danc'd withal.

[One calls within, "Juliet."]

Nurse.   Anon, anon!   145
Come, let's away; the strangers all are gone.

[Exeunt.

[ACT II]

[PROLOGUE]

[Enter] CHORUS.

[Chor.] Now old Desire doth in his death-bed lie,
    And young Affection gapes to be his heir;
That fair for which love groan'd for and would die,
    With tender Juliet [match'd] is now not fair.
Now Romeo is belov'd and loves again,   5
    Alike bewitched by the charm of looks,
But to his foe suppos'd he must complain,
    And she steal love's sweet bait from fearful hooks.
Being held a foe, he may not have access
    To breathe such vows as lovers use to swear;   10
And she as much in love, her means much less
    To meet her new-beloved anywhere.
But passion lends them power, time means, to meet,
Temp'ring extremities with extreme sweet. *[Exit.]*

[SCENE I. *A lane by the wall of Capulet's orchard.*]

Enter ROMEO, *alone.*

Rom. Can I go forward when my heart is here?
Turn back, dull earth, and find thy centre out.

[He climbs the wall, and leaps down within it.]

Enter BENVOLIO *with* MERCUTIO.

Ben. Romeo! my cousin Romeo!
Mer.   He is wise;
And, on my life, hath stol'n him home to bed.
Ben. He ran this way, and leap'd this orchard
    wall.   5
Call, good Mercutio.
    [Mer.]   Nay, I'll conjure too.
Romeo! humours! madman! passion! lover!
Appear thou in the likeness of a sigh!
Speak but one rhyme, and I am satisfied;
Cry but "Ay me!" [pronounce] but "love" and
    ["dove"];   10
Speak to my gossip Venus one fair word,
One nick-name for her purblind son and [heir],
Young [Adam] Cupid, he that shot so [trim],
When King Cophetua lov'd the beggar-maid!
He heareth not, he stirreth not, he moveth not;   15

The ape is dead, and I must conjure him.
I conjure thee by Rosaline's bright eyes,
By her high forehead and her scarlet lip,
By her fine foot, straight leg, and quivering thigh,
And the demesnes that there adjacent lie,   20
That in thy likeness thou appear to us!
    Ben. An if he hear thee, thou wilt anger him.
    Mer. This cannot anger him; 'twould anger him
To raise a spirit in his mistress' circle,
Of some strange nature, letting it there stand   25
Till she had laid it and conjur'd it down.
That were some spite; my invocation
Is fair and honest; in his mistress' name
I conjure only but to raise up him.
    Ben. Come, he hath hid himself among these
        trees   30
To be consorted with the humorous night.
Blind is his love and best befits the dark.
    Mer. If Love be blind, Love cannot hit the mark.
Now will he sit under a medlar tree
And wish his mistress were that kind of fruit   35
As maids call medlars, when they laugh alone.
O, Romeo, that she were, O, that she were
An open [*et cetera*], thou a poperin pear!
Romeo, good-night; I'll to my truckle-bed;
This field-bed is too cold for me to sleep.   40
Come, shall we go?
    Ben.   Go, then; for 'tis in vain
To seek him here that means not to be found.

[Exeunt [Ben. and Mer.].

[SCENE II. *Capulet's orchard.*

ROMEO *advances from the wall.*]

Rom. He jests at scars that never felt a wound.

[Juliet appears above at her window.]

But, soft! what light through yonder window
    breaks?
It is the east, and Juliet is the sun.
Arise, fair sun, and kill the envious moon,
Who is already sick and pale with grief   5
That thou, her maid, art far more fair than she.
Be not her maid, since she is envious;
Her vestal livery is but sick and green,
And none but fools do wear it; cast it off.
It is my lady, O, it is my love!   10
O, that she knew she were!
She speaks, yet she says nothing; what of that?
Her eye discourses; I will answer it. —
I am too bold, 'tis not to me she speaks.
Two of the fairest stars in all the heaven,   15

Act II, Prol., 4. [match'd] F. *match* Q₂.
   Sc., i, 2. dull earth. Romeo means himself. 6. [Mer.] Q₁. Continued to Benvolio Q₂. 10. [pronounce] Q₁. *provaunt* Q₂.
["dove"] Q₁. *day* Q₂. 11. gossip: friend. 12. purblind: totally blind. [heir] Q₁. *her* Q₂. 13. [Adam] (Upton conj.). *Abraham* Q₂. Adam is Adam Bell, famous archer of the old ballads. [trim] Q₁. *true* Q₂. *Trim* is the word used in the ballad of King Cophetua. 27. spite: vexation. 31. humorous: damp. 34. medlar: a fruit like an apple. 38. [et cetera] Q₁. *or* Q₂. poperin: a Flemish variety of pear. 39. truckle-bed: small bed (made to slip under a larger).

Having some business, [do] entreat her eyes
To twinkle in their spheres till they return.
What if her eyes were there, they in her head?
The brightness of her cheek would shame those
    stars,
As daylight doth a lamp; her eyes in heaven   20
Would through the airy region stream so bright
That birds would sing and think it were not night.
See, how she leans her cheek upon her hand!
O, that I were a glove upon that hand,
That I might touch that cheek!
    Jul.   Ay me!
    Rom.   She speaks!
O, speak again, bright angel! for thou art   26
As glorious to this night, being o'er my head,
As is a winged messenger of heaven
Unto the white-upturned wond'ring eyes
Of mortals that fall back to gaze on him   30
When he bestrides the lazy-[pacing] clouds
And sails upon the bosom of the air.
    Jul. O Romeo, Romeo! wherefore art thou
    Romeo?
Deny thy father and refuse thy name;
Or, if thou wilt not, be but sworn my love,   35
And I'll no longer be a Capulet.
    Rom. [*Aside.*] Shall I hear more, or shall I speak
    at this?
    Jul. 'Tis but thy name that is my enemy;
Thou art thyself, though not a Montague.
What's Montague? It is nor hand, nor foot,   40
Nor arm, nor face, [nor any other part]
Belonging to a man. O, be some other name!
What's in a name? That which we call a rose
By any other word would smell as sweet;
So Romeo would, were he not Romeo call'd,   45
Retain that dear perfection which he owes
Without that title. Romeo, doff thy name,
And for thy name, which is no part of thee,
Take all myself.
    Rom.   I take thee at thy word.
Call me but love, and I'll be new baptiz'd;   50
Henceforth I never will be Romeo.
    Jul. What man art thou that thus bescreen'd in
    night
So stumblest on my counsel?
    Rom.   By a name
I know not how to tell thee who I am.
My name, dear saint, is hateful to myself,   55
Because it is an enemy to thee;
Had I it written, I would tear the word.
    Jul. My ears have yet not drunk a hundred words
Of thy tongue's uttering, yet I know the sound.
Art thou not Romeo, and a Montague?   60

    Rom. Neither, fair maid, if either thee dislike.
    Jul. How cam'st thou hither, tell me, and where-
    fore?
The orchard walls are high and hard to climb,
And the place death, considering who thou art,
If any of my kinsmen find thee here.   65
    Rom. With love's light wings did I o'erperch
    these walls;
For stony limits cannot hold love out,
And what love can do, that dares love attempt;
Therefore thy kinsmen are no stop to me.
    Jul. If they do see thee, they will murder thee.   70
    Rom. Alack, there lies more peril in thine eye
Than twenty of their swords! Look thou but sweet,
And I am proof against their enmity.
    Jul. I would not for the world they saw thee here.
    Rom. I have night's cloak to hide me from their
    eyes;   75
And but thou love me, let them find me here.
My life were better ended by their hate,
Than death prorogued, wanting of thy love.
    Jul. By whose direction found'st thou out this
    place?
    Rom. By Love, that first did prompt me to in-
    quire;   80
He lent me counsel and I lent him eyes.
I am no pilot; yet, wert thou as far
As that vast shore [wash'd] with the farthest sea,
I should adventure for such merchandise.
    Jul. Thou know'st the mask of night is on my
    face,   85
Else would a maiden blush bepaint my cheek
For that which thou hast heard me speak to-night.
Fain would I dwell on form, fain, fain deny
What I have spoke; but farewell compliment!
Dost thou love me? I know thou wilt say "Ay,"
And I will take thy word; yet, if thou swear'st,   91
Thou mayst prove false. At lovers' perjuries,
They say, Jove laughs. O gentle Romeo,
If thou dost love, pronounce it faithfully;
Or if thou think'st I am too quickly won,   95
I'll frown and be perverse and say thee nay, —
So thou wilt woo; but else, not for the world.
In truth, fair Montague, I am too fond,
And therefore thou mayst think my ['haviour] light;
But trust me, gentleman, I'll prove more true   100
Than those that have [more cunning] to be strange.
I should have been more strange, I must confess,
But that thou overheard'st, ere I was ware,
My true love's passion; therefore pardon me,
And not impute this yielding to light love,   105
Which the dark night hath so discovered.
    Rom. Lady, by yonder blessed moon I vow

Sc. ii, 16. **[do]** F. *to* Q₂. 31. **[pacing]** Q₁. *puffing* Q₂. 41. **[nor ... part]** Q₁. Om. Q₂. 42. **O ... name.** After *face* in l. 41 Q₂. Q₁ omits 42. 44. **word** Q₂. *name* Q₁. 46. **owes:** possesses. 61. **dislike:** displease. 78. **prorogued:** postponed. 83. **[wash'd]** Q₄. *washeth* Q₂. 89. **compliment:** convention. 99. **['haviour]** *haviour* Q₁. *behaviour* Q₂. 101. **[more cunning]** Q₁. *coying* Q₂. **strange:** reserved, distant. 107. **vow** Q₂. *swear* Q₁.

That tips with silver all these fruit-tree tops —
  Jul. O, swear not by the moon, the inconstant moon,
That monthly changes in her circled orb,   110
Lest that thy love prove likewise variable.
  Rom. What shall I swear by?
  Jul.   Do not swear at all;
Or, if thou wilt, swear by thy gracious self,
Which is the god of my idolatry,   114
And I'll believe thee.
  Rom.   If my heart's dear love —
  Jul. Well, do not swear. Although I joy in thee,
I have no joy of this contract to-night;
It is too rash, too unadvis'd, too sudden,
Too like the lightning, which doth cease to be
Ere one can say it lightens. Sweet, good-night!
This bud of love, by summer's ripening breath,   121
May prove a beauteous flower when next we meet.
Good-night, good-night! as sweet repose and rest
Come to thy heart as that within my breast!
  Rom. O, wilt thou leave me so unsatisfied?   125
  Jul. What satisfaction canst thou have to-night?
  Rom. Th' exchange of thy love's faithful vow for mine.
  Jul. I gave thee mine before thou didst request it;
And yet I would it were to give again.
  Rom. Wouldst thou withdraw it? For what purpose, love?   130
  Jul. But to be frank, and give it thee again.
And yet I wish but for the thing I have.
My bounty is as boundless as the sea,
My love as deep; the more I give to thee,
The more I have, for both are infinite.   135
                     [Nurse] calls within.
I hear some noise within; dear love, adieu!
Anon, good nurse! Sweet Montague, be true.
Stay but a little, I will come again.   *[Exit, above.]*
  Rom. O blessed, blessed night! I am afeard,
Being in night, all this is but a dream,   140
Too flattering-sweet to be substantial.

          [Re-enter JULIET, *above.]*

  Jul. Three words, dear Romeo, and good-night indeed.
If that thy bent of love be honourable,
Thy purpose marriage, send me word to-morrow,
By one that I'll procure to come to thee,   145
Where and what time thou wilt perform the rite;
And all my fortunes at thy foot I'll lay
And follow thee my lord throughout the world.
  [Nurse]. (*Within.*) Madam!
  Jul. I come, anon. — But if thou mean'st not well,   150
I do beseech thee —

  [Nurse]. (*Within.*) Madam!
  Jul.   By and by, I come: —
To cease thy suit, and leave me to my grief.
To-morrow will I send.
  Rom.   So thrive my soul —
  Jul. A thousand times good-night! *[Exit [above].*
  Rom. A thousand times the worse, to want thy light.   155
Love goes toward love, as schoolboys from their books,
But love from love, toward school with heavy looks.
                     [Retiring.]

        Re-enter JULIET, *above.*

  Jul. Hist! Romeo, hist! O, for a falconer's voice,
To lure this tassel-gentle back again!   160
Bondage is hoarse, and may not speak aloud;
Else would I tear the cave where Echo lies,
And make her airy tongue more hoarse than [mine],
With repetition of my [Romeo's name.]
Romeo!
  Rom. It is my soul, that calls upon my name.
How silver-sweet sound lovers' tongues by night, 166
Like softest music to attending ears!
  Jul. Romeo!
  Rom.   My [dear]?
  Jul.   What o'clock to-morrow
Shall I send to thee?
  Rom.   By the hour of nine.
  Jul. I will not fail; 'tis twenty year till then.   170
I have forgot why I did call thee back.
  Rom. Let me stand here till thou remember it.
  Jul. I shall forget, to have thee still stand there,
Rememb'ring how I love thy company.
  Rom. And I'll still stay, to have thee still forget,
Forgetting any other home but this.   176
  Jul. 'Tis almost morning, I would have thee gone; —
And yet no farther than a wanton's bird,
That lets it hop a little from [her] hand,
Like a poor prisoner in his twisted gyves,   180
And with a [silk] thread plucks it back again,
So loving-jealous of his liberty.
  Rom. I would I were thy bird.
  Jul.   Sweet, so would I;
Yet I should kill thee with much cherishing.
Good-night, good-night! Parting is such sweet sorrow,   185
That I shall say good-night till it be morrow.
                    [Exit, above.]
  Rom. Sleep dwell upon thine eyes, peace in thy breast!
Would I were sleep and peace, so sweet to rest!

---

131. **frank:** generous.   143. **bent:** inclination.   149, 151. [*Nurse*] (Capell). Om. Q₂.   151. **By and by:** immediately. 160. **tassel-gentle:** male hawk.   163. [mine] Q₄. Om. Q₂.   164. [**Romeo's name**] Q₁. Om. Q₂.   168. [**dear**] Q₄. *Neece* Q₂.   179. [**her**] Q₁. *his* Q₂.   180. **gyves:** fetters.   181. [**silk**] Q₁. *silken* Q₂.   188. After *rest* Q₂ inserts iii.1–4.

Hence will I to my ghostly [father's] cell,
His help to crave, and my dear hap to tell.   190
                                        [*Exit.*

[SCENE III.   *Friar Laurence's cell.*]

Enter FRIAR [LAURENCE], *with a basket.*

Fri. L. The grey-ey'd morn smiles on the frown-
        ing night,
Chequ'ring the eastern clouds with streaks of light,
And flecked darkness like a drunkard reels
From forth day's path and Titan's [fiery] wheels.
Now, ere the sun advance his burning eye,   5
The day to cheer and night's dank dew to dry,
I must up-fill this osier cage of ours
With baleful weeds and precious-juiced flowers.
The earth, that's nature's mother, is her tomb;
What is her burying grave, that is her womb;   10
And from her womb children of divers kind
We sucking on her natural bosom find:
Many for many virtues excellent,
None but for some, and yet all different.
O, mickle is the powerful grace that lies   15
In plants, herbs, stones, and their true qualities;
For nought so vile that on the earth doth live
But to the earth some special good doth give,
Nor aught so good but, strain'd from that fair use,
Revolts from true birth, stumbling on abuse.   20
Virtue itself turns vice, being misapplied;
And vice [sometime's] by action dignified.

Enter ROMEO.

Within the infant rind of this weak flower
Poison hath residence and medicine power;
For this, being smelt, with that part cheers each
        part;   25
Being tasted, [slays] all senses with the heart.
Two such opposed kings encamp them still
In man as well as herbs, grace and rude will;
And where the worser is predominant,
Full soon the canker death eats up that plant.   30
Rom. Good morrow, father.
Fri. L.   *Benedicite!*
What early tongue so sweet saluteth me?
Young son, it argues a distempered head
So soon to bid good morrow to thy bed.
Care keeps his watch in every old man's eye,   35
And where care lodges, sleep will never lie;
But where unbruised youth with unstuff'd brain
Doth couch his limbs, there golden sleep doth reign;
Therefore thy earliness doth me assure
Thou art up-rous'd with some distemp'rature;   40
Or if not so, then here I hit it right,

Our Romeo hath not been in bed to-night.
Rom. That last is true; the sweeter rest was mine.
Fri. L. God pardon sin! Wast thou with Rosa-
        line?
Rom. With Rosaline, my ghostly father? No!
I have forgot that name, and that name's woe.   46
Fri. L. That's my good son; but where hast thou
        been, then?
Rom. I'll tell thee ere thou ask it me again.
I have been feasting with mine enemy,
Where on a sudden one hath wounded me   50
That's by me wounded; both our remedies
Within thy help and holy physic lies.
I bear no hatred, blessed man, for, lo,
My intercession likewise steads my foe.
Fri. L. Be plain, good son, and homely in thy
        drift;   55
Riddling confession finds but riddling shrift.
Rom. Then plainly know my heart's dear love is
        set
On the fair daughter of rich Capulet.
As mine on hers, so hers is set on mine;
And all combin'd, save what thou must combine   60
By holy marriage. When and where and how
We met, we woo'd, and made exchange of vow,
I'll tell thee as we pass; but this I pray,
That thou consent to marry us to-day.
Fri. L. Holy Saint Francis, what a change is
        here!   65
Is Rosaline, that thou didst love so dear,
So soon forsaken? Young men's love then lies
Not truly in their hearts, but in their eyes.
Jesu Maria, what a deal of brine
Hath wash'd thy sallow cheeks for Rosaline!   70
How much salt water thrown away in waste,
To season love, that of it doth not taste!
The sun not yet thy sighs from heaven clears,
Thy old groans yet [ring] in mine ancient ears;
Lo, here upon thy cheek the stain doth sit   75
Of an old tear that is not wash'd off yet.
If e'er thou wast thyself and these woes thine,
Thou and these woes were all for Rosaline.
And art thou chang'd? Pronounce this sentence
        then:
Women may fall, when there's no strength in men.
Rom. Thou chid'st me oft for loving Rosaline.   81
Fri. L. For doting, not for loving, pupil mine.
Rom. And bad'st me bury love.
Fri. L.   Not in a grave,
To lay one in, another out to have.
Rom. I pray thee, chide me not. Her I love
        now   85
Doth grace for grace and love for love allow;

---

189. **ghostly:** spiritual. **[father's]** Q₁. *Friers close* Q₂. 190. **dear hap:** good fortune.
Sc. iii, 4. **[fiery]** Q₁. *burning* Q₂. 7. **osier cage:** willow basket. 22. **[sometime's]** (Capell). *sometimes* Q₁. *sometime* Q₂.
25. **that part:** i.e., the odor. 26. **[slays]** F. *stays* Q₂. 30. **canker:** canker-worm. 33. **distempered:** sick. 56. **shrift:**
absolution. 74. **[ring]** Q₄. *ringing* Q₂.

The other did not so.

Fri. L.   O, she knew well
Thy love did read by rote that could not spell.
But come, young waverer, come, go with me,
In one respect I'll thy assistant be;   90
For this alliance may so happy prove
To turn your households' rancour to pure love.

Rom. O, let us hence; I stand on sudden haste.

Fri. L. Wisely and slow; they stumble that run
    fast.   [*Exeunt.*

[SCENE IV. *A street.*]

Enter BENVOLIO *and* MERCUTIO.

Mer. Where the devil should this Romeo be?
Came he not home to-night?

Ben. Not to his father's; I spoke with his man.

Mer. Why, that same pale hard-hearted wench,
    that Rosaline,
Torments him so, that he will sure run mad.   5

Ben. Tybalt, the kinsman of old Capulet,
Hath sent a letter to his father's house.

Mer. A challenge, on my life.

Ben. Romeo will answer it.

Mer. Any man that can write may answer a letter.   10

Ben. Nay, he will answer the letter's master,
how he dares, being dared.

Mer. Alas, poor Romeo! he is already dead;
stabb'd with a white wench's black eye; run through
the ear with a love song; the very pin of his heart
cleft with the blind bow-boy's butt-shaft: and is he
a man to encounter Tybalt?   17

Ben. Why, what is Tybalt?

Mer. More than prince of cats. O, he's the
courageous captain of compliments. He fights
as you sing prick-song; keeps time, distance, and
proportion; he rests his minim rests, one, two,   22
and the third in your bosom: the very butcher of a
silk button; a duellist, a duellist; a gentleman of the
very first house, of the first and second cause. Ah,
the immortal *passado!* the *punto reverso!* the *hai!*

Ben. The what?   28

Mer. The pox of such antic, lisping, affecting
[fantasticoes]; these new tuners of accent! "By
Jesu, a very good blade! a very tall man! a very
good whore!" Why, is not this a lamentable thing,
grandsire, that we should be thus afflicted with these
strange flies, these fashion-mongers, these [*perdona-
mi's*], who stand so much on the new form, that
they cannot sit at ease on the old bench? O, their
bones, their bones!   37

Enter ROMEO.

Ben. Here comes Romeo, here comes Romeo.

Mer. Without his roe, like a dried herring: O
flesh, flesh, how art thou fishified! Now is he for the
numbers that Petrarch flowed in. Laura to his lady
was a kitchen-wench (marry, she had a better
love to be-rhyme her); Dido a dowdy; Cleopatra   43
a gipsy; Helen and Hero hildings and harlots;
Thisbe, a grey eye or so, but not to the purpose.
Signior Romeo, *bonjour!* There's a French salutation to your French slop. You gave us the counterfeit fairly last night.

Rom. Good morrow to you both. What counterfeit did I give you?   50

Mer. The slip, sir, the slip; can you not conceive?

Rom. Pardon, good Mercutio, my business was
great; and in such a case as mine a man may strain
courtesy.   55

Mer. That's as much as to say, such a case as
yours constrains a man to bow in the hams.

Rom. Meaning, to curtsy.

Mer. Thou hast most kindly hit it.

Rom. A most courteous exposition.   60

Mer. Nay, I am the very pink of courtesy.

Rom. Pink for flower.

Mer. Right.

Rom. Why, then is my pump well flower'd.   64

Mer. Sure wit! Follow me this jest now till thou
hast worn out thy pump, that, when the single sole
of it is worn, the jest may remain, after the wearing,
solely singular.

Rom. O single-sol'd jest, solely singular for the
singleness!   70

Mer. Come between us, good Benvolio; my wits
faint.

Rom. Switch and spurs, switch and spurs; or I'll
cry a match.   74

Mer. Nay, if our wits run the wild-goose chase,
I am done, for thou hast more of the wild-goose in
one of thy wits than, I am sure, I have in my whole
five. Was I with you there for the goose?   80

Rom. Thou wast never with me for anything
when thou wast not there for the goose.

---

88. **rote:** memory. 93. **stand on:** insist on.

  Sc. iv, 15. **pin:** peg in center of a target. 16. **butt-shaft:** blunt arrow. 19. **prince of cats.** The king of the cats in *Reynard the Fox* was called Tibalt. 21. **prick-song:** music sung from written notes. 25. **first house:** best school (of fencing). 26. **of ... cause:** i.e., very ready to quarrel. A satirical reference to the manuals which codified the reasons for quarreling. 27. *passado:* forward thrust; *punto reverso:* back-handed thrust; *hai:* home thrust. 30. [fantasticoes] Q₁; coxcombs. *phantacies* Q₂. 31. **tall:** brave. 34. [*perdona-mi's*] Q₄: pardon me's (Ital.). *pardons mees* Q₂. 36. **form:** (1) fashion, (2) bench. 37. **bones.** Pun on *bons* (Fr.). 41. **numbers:** verses. 44. **hildings:** good-for-nothings. 47. **slop:** loose breeches (French fashion). 50–51. **counterfeit ... slip.** Counterfeit coins were called *slips*. 59. **kindly:** naturally. 70. **singleness:** silliness. 75. **wild-goose chase:** a cross-country riding game, in which the leader could pick whatever course he chose and the others had to follow. The object was to capture the lead.

Mer. I will bite thee by the ear for that jest.

Rom. Nay, good goose, bite not.

Mer. Thy wit is a very bitter sweeting; it is a most sharp sauce.

Rom. And is it not, then, well serv'd in to a sweet goose?　　86

Mer. O, here's a wit of cheveril, that stretches from an inch narrow to an ell broad!

Rom. I stretch it out for that word "broad"; which added to the goose, proves thee far and wide a broad goose.　　91

Mer. Why, is not this better now than groaning for love? Now art thou sociable, now art thou Romeo, now art thou what thou art, by art as well as by nature; for this drivelling love is like a great natural, that runs lolling up and down to hide his bauble in a hole.　　97

Ben. Stop there, stop there.

Mer. Thou desir'st me to stop in my tale against the hair.

Ben. Thou wouldst else have made thy tale large.　　102

Mer. O, thou art deceiv'd; I would have made it short; for I was come to the whole depth of my tale, and meant, indeed, to occupy the argument no longer.　　106

Rom. Here's goodly gear!

Enter NURSE *and her man* [PETER].

A sail, a sail!

Mer. Two, two; a shirt and a smock.

Nurse. Peter!　　110

Peter. Anon!

Nurse. My fan, Peter.

Mer. Good Peter, to hide her face; for her fan's the fairer face.

Nurse. God ye good morrow, gentlemen.　　115

Mer. God ye good den, fair gentlewoman.

Nurse. Is it good den?

Mer. 'Tis no less, I tell ye; for the bawdy hand of the dial is now upon the prick of noon.

Nurse. Out upon you! what a man are you!　　120

Rom. One, gentlewoman, that God hath made [for] himself to mar.

Nurse. By my troth, it is well said; "for himself to mar," quoth 'a! Gentlemen, can any of you tell me where I may find the young Romeo?　　125

Rom. I can tell you; but young Romeo will be older when you have found him than he was when you sought him. I am the youngest of that name, for fault of a worse.

Nurse. You say well.　　130

Mer. Yea, is the worst well? Very well took, i' faith; wisely, wisely.

Nurse. If you be he, sir, I desire some confidence with you.

Ben. She will indite him to some supper.　　135

Mer. A bawd, a bawd, a bawd! So ho!

Rom. What hast thou found?

Mer. No hare, sir; unless a hare, sir, in a lenten pie, that is something stale and hoar ere it be spent.　　[*Sings.*]　140

"An old hare hoar,
　And an old hare hoar,
Is very good meat in lent;
　But a hare that is hoar
Is too much for a score,　　145
When it hoars ere it be spent."

Romeo, will you come to your father's? We'll to dinner thither.

Rom. I will follow you.

Mer. Farewell, ancient lady; farewell, [*singing*] "lady, lady, lady."　　151

[*Exeunt Mercutio and Benvolio.*

Nurse. I pray you, sir, what saucy merchant was this, that was so full of his ropery?

Rom. A gentleman, nurse, that loves to hear himself talk, and will speak more in a minute than he will stand to in a month.　　157

Nurse. An 'a speak anything against me, I'll take him down, an 'a were lustier than he is, and twenty such Jacks; and if I cannot, I'll find those that shall. Scurvy knave! I am none of his flirt-gills; I am none of his skains-mates. — And thou must stand by too, and suffer every knave to use me at his pleasure!　　164

Peter. I saw no man use you at his pleasure; if I had, my weapon should quickly have been out. I warrant you, I dare draw as soon as another man, if I see occasion in a good quarrel, and the law on my side.　　169

Nurse. Now, afore God, I am so vex'd that every part about me quivers. Scurvy knave! Pray you, sir, a word: and as I told you, my young lady bid me inquire you out; what she bid me say, I will keep to myself. But first let me tell ye, if ye should lead her [into] a fool's paradise, as they say, it [175 were a very gross kind of behaviour, as they say; for the gentlewoman is young, and, therefore, if you should deal double with her, truly it were an ill thing to be off'red to any gentlewoman, and very weak dealing.　　181

Rom. Nurse, commend me to thy lady and mistress. I protest unto thee —

---

85. **sweeting:** a variety of apple.　87. **cheveril:** kid leather.　88. **ell:** 45 inches.　96. **natural:** idiot.　100. **hair:** i.e., grain.　102. **large:** i.e., with a pun on sense of *gross, lewd.*　107. **gear:** matter.　122. **[for]** Q₁. Om. Q₂.　134. **confidence:** blunder for *conference.*　135. **indite:** Benvolio's intentional malapropism for *invite.*　136. **So ho:** hunter's cry when sighting a hare.　153. **ropery:** roguery.　160. **Jacks:** saucy fellows.　162. **flirt-gills:** flirting women.　**skains-mates.** A derogatory term not occurring elsewhere.　175. **[into]** Q₁.　*in* Q₂.

Nurse. Good heart, and, i' faith, I will tell her as much. Lord, Lord, she will be a joyful woman.   186
Rom. What wilt thou tell her, nurse? Thou dost not mark me.
Nurse. I will tell her, sir, that you do protest; which, as I take it, is a gentlemanlike offer.
Rom. Bid her devise   191
Some means to come to shrift this afternoon;
And there she shall at Friar Laurence' cell
Be shriv'd and married. Here is for thy pains.
Nurse. No, truly, sir; not a penny.   195
Rom. Go to; I say you shall.
Nurse. This afternoon, sir? Well, she shall be there.
Rom. And stay, good nurse; — behind the abbey wall
Within this hour my man shall be with thee,   200
And bring thee cords made like a tackled stair;
Which to the high top-gallant of my joy
Must be my convoy in the secret night.
Farewell; be trusty, and I'll quit thy pains.
Farewell; commend me to thy mistress.   205
Nurse. Now God in heaven bless thee! Hark you, sir.
Rom. What say'st thou, my dear nurse?
Nurse. Is your man secret? Did you ne'er hear say,
"Two may keep counsel, putting one away"?
Rom. [I] warrant thee, my man's as true as steel.   210
Nurse. Well, sir; my mistress is the sweetest lady — Lord, Lord! when 'twas a little prating thing, — O, there is a nobleman in town, one Paris, that would fain lay knife aboard; but she, good soul, had as lief see a toad, a very toad, as see   215
him. I anger her sometimes and tell her that Paris is the properer man; but, I'll warrant you, when I say so, she looks as pale as any clout in the versal world. Doth not rosemary and Romeo begin both with a letter?   220
Rom. Ay, nurse; what of that? Both with an R.
Nurse. Ah, mocker! that's the dog's name. R is for the — No; I know it begins with some other letter — and she hath the prettiest sententious of it, of you and rosemary, that it would do you good to hear it.   227
Rom. Commend me to thy lady.
Nurse. Ay, a thousand times. [*Exit Romeo.*]
Peter!
Pet. Anon!
Nurse. Before, and apace.   [*Exeunt.* 232

[SCENE V. *Capulet's orchard.*]

Enter JULIET.

Jul. The clock struck nine when I did send the nurse;
In half an hour she promis'd to return.
Perchance she cannot meet him: that's not so.
O, she is lame! Love's heralds should be thoughts,
Which ten times faster [glide] than the sun's beams   5
Driving back shadows over louring hills;
Therefore do nimble-pinion'd doves draw Love,
And therefore hath the wind-swift Cupid wings.
Now is the sun upon the highmost hill
Of this day's journey, and from nine till twelve 10
Is three long hours, yet she is not come.
Had she affections and warm youthful blood,
She would be as swift in motion as a ball;
My words would bandy her to my sweet love,
And his to me;   15
But old folks, [marry,] feign as they were dead,
Unwieldy, slow, heavy and pale as lead.

Enter NURSE [*and* PETER].

O God, she comes! O honey nurse, what news?
Hast thou met with him? Send thy man away.
Nurse. Peter, stay at the gate. [*Exit Peter.* 20
Jul. Now, good sweet nurse, — O Lord, why look'st thou sad?
Though news be sad, yet tell them merrily;
If good, thou sham'st the music of sweet news
By playing it to me with so sour a face.
Nurse. I am a-weary, give me leave a while. 25
Fie, how my bones ache! What a jaunce have I [had]!
Jul. I would thou hadst my bones, and I thy news.
Nay, come, I pray thee, speak; good, good nurse, speak.
Nurse. Jesu, what haste! Can you not stay a while?
Do you not see that I am out of breath?   30
Jul. How art thou out of breath, when thou hast breath
To say to me that thou art out of breath?
Th' excuse that thou dost make in this delay
Is longer than the tale thou dost excuse.
Is thy news good, or bad? Answer to that;   35
Say either, and I'll stay the circumstance.
Let me be satisfied, is't good or bad?
Nurse. Well, you have made a simple choice; you know not how to choose a man. Romeo! no, not he. Though his face be better than any man's, 40

yet his leg excels all men's; and for a hand, and a foot, and a body, though they be not to be talk'd on, yet they are past compare. He is not the flower of courtesy, but, I'll warrant him, as gentle as a lamb. Go thy ways, wench; serve God. What, have you din'd at home?   46

Jul. No, no! But all this did I know before. What says he of our marriage? What of that?

Nurse. Lord, how my head aches! What a head have I!

It beats as it would fall in twenty pieces.   50
My back o' t' other side, — O, my back, my back! Beshrew your heart for sending me about To catch my death with jauncing up and down!

Jul. I' faith, I am sorry that thou art not well. Sweet, sweet, sweet nurse, tell me, what says my love?   55

Nurse. Your love says, like an honest gentleman, and a courteous, and a kind, and a handsome, and, I warrant, a virtuous, — Where is your mother?

Jul. Where is my mother! why, she is within;   60
Where should she be? How oddly thou repliest! "Your love says, like an honest gentleman, 'Where is your mother?'"

Nurse.   O God's lady dear!
Are you so hot? Marry, come up, I trow; Is this the poultice for my aching bones?   65
Henceforward do your messages yourself.

Jul. Here's such a coil! — Come, what says Romeo?

Nurse. Have you got leave to go to shrift today?

Jul. I have.

Nurse. Then hie you hence to Friar Laurence' cell;   70
There stays a husband to make you a wife. Now comes the wanton blood up in your cheeks; They'll be in scarlet straight at any news. Hie you to church; I must another way, To fetch a ladder, by the which your love   75
Must climb a bird's nest soon when it is dark. I am the drudge and toil in your delight, But you shall bear the burden soon at night. Go; I'll to dinner; hie you to the cell.

Jul. Hie to high fortune! Honest nurse, farewell.   [*Exeunt.* 80

[SCENE VI. *Friar Laurence's cell.*]

Enter FRIAR LAURENCE *and* ROMEO.

Fri. L. So smile the heavens upon this holy act, That after-hours with sorrow chide us not!

Rom. Amen, amen! but come what sorrow can, It cannot countervail th' exchange of joy

That one short minute gives me in her sight.   5
Do thou but close our hands with holy words, Then love-devouring Death do what he dare; It is enough I may but call her mine.

Fri. L. These violent delights have violent ends, And in their triumph die, like fire and powder,   10
Which as they kiss consume. The sweetest honey Is loathsome in his own deliciousness And in the taste confounds the appetite: Therefore love moderately; long love doth so; Too swift arrives as tardy as too slow.   15

Enter JULIET.

Here comes the lady. O, so light a foot Will ne'er wear out the everlasting flint. A lover may bestride the gossamer That idles in the wanton summer air, And yet not fall; so light is vanity.   20

Jul. Good even to my ghostly confessor.

Fri. L. Romeo shall thank thee, daughter, for us both.

Jul. As much to him, else is his thanks too much.

Rom. Ah, Juliet, if the measure of thy joy Be heap'd like mine, and that thy skill be more   25
To blazon it, then sweeten with thy breath This neighbour air, and let rich music's tongue Unfold the imagin'd happiness that both Receive in either by this dear encounter.

Jul. Conceit, more rich in matter than in words, Brags of his substance, not of ornament.   31
They are but beggars that can count their worth; But my true love is grown to such excess I cannot sum up sum of half my wealth.

Fri. L. Come, come with me, and we will make short work;   35
For, by your leaves, you shall not stay alone Till Holy Church incorporate two in one. [*Exeunt.*

[ACT III]

[SCENE I. *A public place.*]

Enter MERCUTIO, BENVOLIO, *and men.*

Ben. I pray thee, good Mercutio, let's retire. The day is hot, the Capulets abroad, And, if we meet, we shall not scape a brawl, For now, these hot days, is the mad blood stirring. 4

Mer. Thou art like one of these fellows that, when he enters the confines of a tavern, claps me his sword upon the table and says, "God send me no need of thee!" and by the operation of the second cup draws him on the drawer, when indeed there is no need.   10

Ben. Am I like such a fellow?

Mer. Come, come, thou art as hot a Jack in thy

---

67. coil: fuss.

Sc. vi, 4. **countervail**: equal.   13. **confounds**: destroys.   26. **blazon**: proclaim.   30. **Conceit**: imagination.

Act III, sc. i, 9. **drawer**: tapster.

mood as any in Italy, and as soon moved to be moody, and as soon moody to be moved.

Ben. And what to?   15

Mer. Nay, an there were two such, we should have none shortly, for one would kill the other. Thou! why, thou wilt quarrel with a man that hath a hair more or a hair less in his beard than thou hast. Thou wilt quarrel with a man for cracking nuts,   20 having no other reason but because thou hast hazel eyes. What eye but such an eye would spy out such a quarrel? Thy head is as full of quarrels as an egg is full of meat, and yet thy head hath been beaten as addle as an egg for quarrelling. Thou hast quarrell'd with a man for coughing in the   26 street, because he hath wakened thy dog that hath lain asleep in the sun. Didst thou not fall out with a tailor for wearing his new doublet before East-   30 er? with another for tying his new shoes with old riband? And yet thou wilt tutor me for quarrelling!

Ben. An I were so apt to quarrel as thou art, any man should buy the fee-simple of my life for an hour and a quarter.   36

Mer. The fee-simple! O simple!

Enter TYBALT, Petruchio, *and others.*

Ben. By my head, here comes the Capulets.

Mer. By my heel, I care not.

Tyb. Follow me close, for I will speak to them. Gentlemen, good den; a word with one of you.   41

Mer. And but one word with one of us? Couple it with something; make it a word and a blow.

Tyb. You shall find me apt enough to that, sir, an you will give occasion.

Mer. Could you not take some occasion without giving?   47

Tyb.] Mercutio, thou consortest with Romeo, —

Mer. Consort! what, dost thou make us min- strels? An thou make minstrels of us, look to hear nothing but discords. Here's my fiddlestick; here's that shall make you dance. 'Zounds, con- sort!   52

Ben. We talk here in the public haunt of men. Either withdraw unto some private place, Or reason coldly of your grievances,   55 Or else depart; here all eyes gaze on us.

Mer. Men's eyes were made to look, and let them gaze; I will not budge for no man's pleasure, I.

Enter ROMEO.

Tyb. Well, peace be with you, sir; here comes my man.

Mer. But I'll be hang'd, sir, if he wear your liv- ery.   60 Marry, go before to field, he'll be your follower; Your worship in that sense may call him "man."

Tyb. Romeo, the love I bear thee can afford No better term than this: thou art a villain.

Rom. Tybalt, the reason that I have to love thee   65 Doth much excuse the appertaining rage To such a greeting. Villain am I none; Therefore farewell; I see thou know'st me not.

Tyb. Boy, this shall not excuse the injuries That thou hast done me; therefore turn and draw.

Rom. I do protest I never injur'd thee,   71 But love thee better than thou canst devise Till thou shalt know the reason of my love; And so, good Capulet, — which name I tender As dearly as mine own, — be satisfied.   75

Mer. O calm, dishonourable, vile submission! *Alla stoccata* carries it away.   [*Draws.*] Tybalt, you rat-catcher, will you walk?

Tyb. What wouldst thou have with me?   79

Mer. Good king of cats, nothing but one of your nine lives; that I mean to make bold withal, and, as you shall use me hereafter, dry-beat the rest of the eight. Will you pluck your sword out of his pilcher by the ears? Make haste, lest mine be about your ears ere it be out.   85

Tyb. I am for you.   [*Drawing.*]

Rom. Gentle Mercutio, put thy rapier up.

Mer. Come, sir, your *passado.*   [*They fight.*]

Rom. Draw, Benvolio; beat down their weapons. Gentlemen, for shame, forbear this outrage!   90 Tybalt, Mercutio, the Prince expressly hath Forbid this bandying in Verona streets. Hold, Tybalt! Good Mercutio!
       [*Tybalt under Romeo's arm thrusts Mercu-
              tio, and flies.*]

Mer.   I am hurt. A plague o' both [your] houses! I am sped. Is he gone, and hath nothing?

Ben.   What, art thou hurt?

Mer. Ay, ay, a scratch, a scratch; marry, 'tis enough.   96 Where is my page? Go, villain, fetch a surgeon.
                                        [*Exit Page.*]

Rom. Courage, man; the hurt cannot be much.

Mer. No, 'tis not so deep as a well, nor so wide as a church-door; but 'tis enough, 'twill serve. Ask for me to-morrow, and you shall find me a grave [101 man. I am pepper'd, I warrant, for this world. A plague o' both your houses! 'Zounds, a dog, a rat, a mouse, a cat, to scratch a man to death! a brag- gart, a rogue, a villain, that fights by the book of

14. moody: angry.   35. fee-simple: absolute possession.   52. 'Zounds: by God's wounds.   61. field: i.e., for duelling.
77. *Alla stoccata:* "with the thrust" — meaning Tybalt. Cf. II.iv.19-27.   carries it away: wins.   82. dry-beat: thrash
without drawing blood.   84. pilcher: scabbard.   94. [your] (Dyce). Om. Q₂; the F.   sped: done for.

arithmetic! Why the devil came you between us?
I was hurt under your arm. 108
    Rom. I thought all for the best.
    Mer. Help me into some house, Benvolio,
Or I shall faint. A plague o' both your houses!
They have made worms' meat of me. I have it,
And soundly too. Your houses! 113
        [*Exeunt* [*Mercutio and Benvolio*].
    Rom. This gentleman, the Prince's near ally,
My very friend, hath got this mortal hurt
In my behalf; my reputation stain'd
With Tybalt's slander, — Tybalt, that an hour
Hath been my cousin! O sweet Juliet,
Thy beauty hath made me effeminate
And in my temper soft'ned valour's steel! 120

Re-enter BENVOLIO.

    Ben. O Romeo, Romeo, brave Mercutio's dead!
That gallant spirit hath aspir'd the clouds,
Which too untimely here did scorn the earth.
    Rom. This day's black fate on moe days doth
        depend;
This but begins the woe others must end. 125
    Ben. Here comes the furious Tybalt back again.

Re-enter TYBALT.

    Rom. [Alive], in triumph! and Mercutio slain!
Away to heaven, respective lenity,
And [fire-eyed] fury be my conduct now!
Now, Tybalt, take the "villain" back again 130
That late thou gav'st me; for Mercutio's soul
Is but a little way above our heads,
Staying for thine to keep him company.
Either thou, or I, or both, must go with him.
    Tyb. Thou, wretched boy, that didst consort him
        here, 135
Shalt with him hence.
    Rom.   This shall determine that.
            [*They fight; Tybalt falls.*
    Ben. Romeo, away, be gone!
The citizens are up, and Tybalt slain.
Stand not amaz'd; the Prince will doom thee death
 f thou art taken. Hence, be gone, away! 140
    Rom. O, I am fortune's fool!
    Ben.   Why dost thou stay?
            [*Exit Romeo.*

Enter CITIZENS.

    [*A*] *Cit.* Which way ran he that kill'd Mercutio?
Tybalt, that murderer, which way ran he?
    Ben. There lies that Tybalt.
    [*A*] *Cit.*   Up, sir, go with me;
I charge thee in the Prince's name, obey. 145

Enter PRINCE, MONTAGUE, CAPULET, *their*
            WIVES, *and all.*

    Prin. Where are the vile beginners of this fray?
    Ben. O noble Prince, I can discover all
The unlucky manage of this fatal brawl.
There lies the man, slain by young Romeo,
That slew thy kinsman, brave Mercutio. 150
    La. Cap. Tybalt, my cousin! O my brother's
        child!
O Prince! O cousin! husband! O, the blood is
        spilt
Of my dear kinsman! Prince, as thou art true,
For blood of ours, shed blood of Montague.
O cousin, cousin! 155
    Prin. Benvolio, who began this bloody fray?
    Ben. Tybalt, here slain, whom Romeo's hand did
        slay!
Romeo that spoke him fair, bid him bethink
How nice the quarrel was, and urg'd withal
Your high displeasure; all this, uttered 160
With gentle breath, calm look, knees humbly bow'd,
Could not take truce with the unruly spleen
Of Tybalt deaf to peace, but that he tilts
With piercing steel at bold Mercutio's breast,
Who, all as hot, turns deadly point to point, 165
And, with a martial scorn, with one hand beats
Cold death aside, and with the other sends
It back to Tybalt, whose dexterity
Retorts it. Romeo he cries aloud,
"Hold, friends! friends, part!" and, swifter than
        his tongue, 170
His [agile] arm beats down their fatal points,
And 'twixt them rushes; underneath whose arm
An envious thrust from Tybalt hit the life
Of stout Mercutio, and then Tybalt fled;
But by and by comes back to Romeo, 175
Who had but newly entertain'd revenge,
And to't they go like lightning, for, ere I
Could draw to part them, was stout Tybalt slain,
And, as he fell, did Romeo turn and fly.
This is the truth, or let Benvolio die. 180
    La. Cap. He is a kinsman to the Montague;
Affection makes him false; he speaks not true.
Some twenty of them fought in this black strife,
And all those twenty could but kill one life.
I beg for justice, which thou, Prince, must give;
Romeo slew Tybalt, Romeo must not live. 186
    Prin. Romeo slew him, he slew Mercutio;
Who now the price of his dear blood doth owe?
    [*Mon.*] Not Romeo, Prince, he was Mercutio's
        friend;
His fault concludes but what the law should end,
The life of Tybalt.

---

114. **ally:** kinsman. 122. **aspir'd:** mounted to. 124. **moe:** more. 127. [**Alive**] Q₁. *He gan* Q₂. 128. **respective:** considerate. 129. [**fire-eyed**] Q₁. *fier end* Q₂; *fire and* F. **conduct:** guide. 139. **amaz'd:** stupefied. 147. **discover:** reveal. 148. **manage:** conduct. 159. **nice:** foolish. 171. [**agile**] Q₁. *aged* Q₂. 189. [**Mon.**] Q₄. *Capu* Q₂.

Prin.   And for that offence   191
Immediately we do exile him hence.
I have an interest in your [hate's] proceeding,
My blood for your rude brawls doth lie a-bleeding;
But I'll amerce you with so strong a fine   195
That you shall all repent the loss of mine.
[I] will be deaf to pleading and excuses;
Nor tears nor prayers shall purchase out abuses;
Therefore use none.   Let Romeo hence in haste,
Else, when he's found, that hour is his last.   200
Bear hence this body and attend our will.
Mercy but murders, pardoning those that kill.
                                                  [*Exeunt.*

[SCENE II. *Capulet's orchard.*]

Enter JULIET, *alone.*

Jul. Gallop apace, you fiery-footed steeds,
Towards Phœbus' lodging; such a waggoner
As Phaethon would whip you to the west,
And bring in cloudy night immediately.
Spread thy close curtain, love-performing night,   5
That runaway's eyes may wink, and Romeo
Leap to these arms untalk'd of and unseen!
Lovers can see to do their amorous rites
By their own beauties; or, if love be blind,
It best agrees with night.   Come, civil night,   10
Thou sober-suited matron, all in black,
And learn me how to lose a winning match,
Play'd for a pair of stainless maidenhoods.
Hood my unmann'd blood, bating in my cheeks,
With thy black mantle, till strange love grow bold,
Think true love acted simple modesty.   16
Come, night; come, Romeo; come, thou day in
    night;
For thou wilt lie upon the wings of night,
Whiter than new snow [on] a raven's back.
Come, gentle night, come, loving, black-brow'd
    night,   20
Give me my Romeo; and, when [he] shall die,
Take him and cut him out in little stars,
And he will make the face of heaven so fine
That all the world will be in love with night
And pay no worship to the garish sun.   25
O, I have bought the mansion of a love,
But not possess'd it, and, though I am sold,
Not yet enjoy'd.   So tedious is this day
As is the night before some festival
To an impatient child that hath new robes   30
And may not wear them.   O, here comes my nurse,

Enter NURSE, *with cords.*

And she brings news; and every tongue that speaks
But Romeo's name speaks heavenly eloquence.
Now, nurse, what news?   What hast thou there?
    The cords
That Romeo bid thee fetch?
    Nurse.   Ay, ay, the cords. 35
                                  [*Throws them down.*]
Jul. Ay me! what news?   Why dost thou wring
    thy hands?
    Nurse. Ah, well-a-day! he's dead, he's dead, he's
    dead!
We are undone, lady, we are undone!
Alack the day! he's gone, he's kill'd, he's dead!
    Jul. Can heaven be so envious?
    Nurse.   Romeo can, 40
Though heaven cannot.   O Romeo, Romeo!
Who ever would have thought it?   Romeo!
    Jul. What devil art thou, that dost torment me
    thus?
This torture should be roar'd in dismal hell.
Hath Romeo slain himself?   Say thou but ay,   45
And that bare vowel *I* shall poison more
Than the death-darting eye of cockatrice.
I am not I, if there be such an ay;
Or those eyes shut, that makes thee answer ay.
If he be slain, say ay; or if not, no.   50
Brief sounds determine [of] my weal or woe.
    Nurse. I saw the wound, I saw it with mine
    eyes, —
God save the mark! — here on his manly breast.
A piteous corse, a bloody piteous corse!
Pale, pale as ashes, all bedaub'd in blood,   55
All in gore-blood; I swounded at the sight.
    Jul. O, break, my heart! poor bankrupt, break
    at once!
To prison, eyes, ne'er look on liberty!
Vile earth, to earth resign; end motion here;
And thou and Romeo press [one] heavy bier!   60
    Nurse. O Tybalt, Tybalt, the best friend I
    had!
O courteous Tybalt! honest gentleman!
That ever I should live to see thee dead!
    Jul. What storm is this that blows so contrary?
Is Romeo slaught'red, and is Tybalt dead?   65
My dearest cousin, and my dearer lord?
Then, dreadful trumpet, sound the general doom!
For who is living, if those two are gone?
    Nurse. Tybalt is gone, and Romeo banished;
Romeo that kill'd him, he is banished.   70

193. [hate's] Q₁. *hearts* Q₂. 195. amerce: punish by fine. 197. [I] Q₁. *It* Q₂.
Sc. ii, 6. runaway's. Unexplained and probably corrupt. There is no apostrophe in the early texts. The stars, sun,
moon, Phaeton, Cupid, and many others have been suggested as the runaway. wink: close. 9. By Q₄. *And by* Q₂. 10.
civil: grave. 14. Hood: cover; unmann'd: untamed; bating: fluttering. Terms from falconry. The hawk was blindfolded to
keep it quiet. 19. [on] F₂. *upon* Q₂. 21. [he] Q₄. *I* Q₂. 47. cockatrice: fabulous animal which killed by its glance.
49. those eyes: i.e., Romeo's. 51. [of] F. *Om.* Q₂. 60. [one] Q₄. *on* Q₂.

Jul. O God! did Romeo's hand shed Tybalt's
    blood?

Nurse. It did, it did; alas the day, it did!

Jul. O serpent heart, hid with a flow'ring face!
Did ever dragon keep so fair a cave?
Beautiful tyrant! fiend angelical!   75
[Dove-feather'd] raven! wolvish ravening lamb!
Despised substance of divinest show!
Just opposite to what thou justly seem'st,
A [damned] saint, an honourable villain!
O nature, what hadst thou to do in hell,   80
When thou didst bower the spirit of a fiend
In mortal paradise of such sweet flesh?
Was ever book containing such vile matter
So fairly bound? O, that deceit should dwell
In such a gorgeous palace!

Nurse.   There's no trust,   85
No faith, no honesty in men; all perjur'd,
All forsworn, all naught, all dissemblers.
Ah, where's my man? Give me some *aqua vitæ;*
These griefs, these woes, these sorrows make me old.
Shame come to Romeo!

Jul.   Blister'd be thy tongue
For such a wish! he was not born to shame.   91
Upon his brow shame is asham'd to sit;
For 'tis a throne where honour may be crown'd
Sole monarch of the universal earth.
O, what a beast was I to chide at him!   95

Nurse. Will you speak well of him that kill'd
    your cousin?

Jul. Shall I speak ill of him that is my husband?
Ah, poor my lord, what tongue shall smooth thy
    name,
When I, thy three-hours wife, have mangled it?
But, wherefore, villain, didst thou kill my cousin?
That villain cousin would have kill'd my hus-
    band.   101
Back, foolish tears, back to your native spring;
Your tributary drops belong to woe,
Which you, mistaking, offer up to joy.
My husband lives that Tybalt would have slain;
And Tybalt's dead that would have slain my hus-
    band.   106
All this is comfort; wherefore weep I then?
Some word there was, worser than Tybalt's death,
That murd'red me; I would forget it fain;
But, O, it presses to my memory   110
Like damned guilty deeds to sinners' minds:
"Tybalt is dead, and Romeo — banished."
That "banished," that one word "banished,"
Hath slain ten thousand Tybalts. Tybalt's death
Was woe enough, if it had ended there;   115
Or, if sour woe delights in fellowship
And needly will be rank'd with other griefs,

Why follow'd not, when she said, "Tybalt's dead,"
Thy father, or thy mother, nay, or both,   119
Which modern lamentation might have mov'd?
But with a rear-ward following Tybalt's death,
"Romeo is banished," to speak that word,
Is father, mother, Tybalt, Romeo, Juliet,
All slain, all dead. "Romeo is banished!"
There is no end, no limit, measure, bound,   125
In that word's death; no words can that woe sound.
Where is my father and my mother, nurse?

Nurse. Weeping and wailing over Tybalt's corse.
Will you go to them? I will bring you thither.

Jul. Wash they his wounds with tears? Mine
    shall be spent,   130
When theirs are dry, for Romeo's banishment.
Take up those cords. Poor ropes, you are beguil'd,
Both you and I, for Romeo is exil'd.
He made you for a highway to my bed,
But I, a maid, die maiden-widowed.   135
Come, cords, come, nurse; I'll to my wedding-bed;
And death, not Romeo, take my maidenhead!

Nurse. Hie to your chamber. I'll find Romeo
To comfort you; I wot well where he is.
Hark ye, your Romeo will be here at night.   140
I'll to him; he is hid at Laurence' cell.

Jul. O, find him! Give this ring to my true
    knight,
And bid him come to take his last farewell.

                                [*Exeunt.*

[Scene III. *Friar Laurence's cell.*]

Enter FRIAR LAURENCE, ROMEO [*following*].

Fri. L. Romeo, come forth; come forth, thou
    fearful man:
Affliction is enamour'd of thy parts,
And thou art wedded to calamity.

Rom. Father, what news? What is the Prince's
    doom?
What sorrow craves acquaintance at my hand,   5
That I yet know not?

Fri. L.   Too familiar
Is my dear son with such sour company.
I bring thee tidings of the Prince's doom.

Rom. What less than dooms-day is the Prince's
    doom?

Fri. L. A gentler judgement vanish'd from his
    lips,   10
Not body's death, but body's banishment.

Rom. Ha, banishment! Be merciful, say
    "death";
For exile hath more terror in his look,
Much more than death. Do not say "banish-
    ment"!

---

76. **[Dove-feather'd]** (Theobald). *Ravenous dovefeatherd* Q₂.   78. **Just:** exact.   79. **[damned]** Q₄. *dimme* Q₂.   81.
bower: lodge.   117. **needly:** necessarily.   120. **modern:** ordinary.   126. **sound:** (1) express, (2) fathom.
Sc. iii, 1. **fearful:** full of fear.   10. **vanish'd:** issued.

Fri. L. Here from Verona art thou banished. 15
Be patient, for the world is broad and wide.
Rom. There is no world without Verona walls,
But purgatory, torture, hell itself.
Hence "banished" is banish'd from the world,
And world's exile is death; then "banished" 20
Is death mis-term'd. Calling death "banishment,"
Thou cut'st my head off with a golden axe,
And smil'st upon the stroke that murders me.
Fri. L. O deadly sin! O rude unthankfulness!
Thy fault our law calls death; but the kind prince,
Taking thy part, hath rush'd aside the law, 26
And turn'd that black word "death" to "banish-
    ment."
This is dear mercy, and thou seest it not.
Rom. 'Tis torture, and not mercy. Heaven is
    here,
Where Juliet lives; and every cat and dog 30
And little mouse, every unworthy thing,
Live here in heaven and may look on her;
But Romeo may not. More validity,
More honourable state, more courtship lives
In carrion-flies than Romeo; they may seize 35
On the white wonder of dear Juliet's hand
And steal immortal blessing from her lips,
Who, even in pure and vestal modesty,
Still blush, as thinking their own kisses sin;
But Romeo may not; he is banished. 40
This may flies do, when I from this must fly;
They are free men, but I am banished:
And say'st thou yet that exile is not death?
Hadst thou no poison mix'd, no sharp-ground knife,
No sudden mean of death, though ne'er so mean,
But "banished" to kill me? — "Banished"? 46
O friar, the damned use that word in hell;
Howling attends it. How hast thou the heart,
Being a divine, a ghostly confessor,
A sin-absolver, and my friend profess'd, 50
To mangle me with that word "banished"?
Fri. L. [Thou] fond mad man, hear me a little
    speak.
Rom. O, thou wilt speak again of banishment.
Fri. L. I'll give thee armour to keep off that
    word;
Adversity's sweet milk, philosophy, 55
To comfort thee, though thou art banished.
Rom. Yet "banished"? Hang up philosophy!
Unless philosophy can make a Juliet,
Displant a town, reverse a prince's doom,
It helps not, it prevails not. Talk no more. 60
Fri. L. O, then I see that madmen have no ears.
Rom. How should they, when that wise men
    have no eyes?
Fri. L. Let me dispute with thee of thy estate.

Rom. Thou canst not speak of that thou dost
    not feel.
Wert thou as young as I, Juliet thy love, 65
An hour but married, Tybalt murdered,
Doting like me and like me banished,
Then mightst thou speak, then mightst thou tear
    thy hair,
And fall upon the ground, as I do now,
Taking the measure of an unmade grave. 70
        [*Knocking within.*
Fri. L. Arise; one knocks. Good Romeo, hide
    thyself.
Rom. Not I; unless the breath of heart-sick
    groans,
Mist-like, infold me from the search of eyes.
        [*Knocking.*
Fri. L. Hark, how they knock! Who's there?
    Romeo, arise;
Thou wilt be taken. — Stay a while! — Stand
    up;   [*Knocking.* 75
Run to my study. — By and by! — God's will,
What simpleness is this! — I come, I come!
        [*Knocking.*
Who knocks so hard? Whence come you? What's
    your will?

        Enter NURSE.

Nurse. Let me come in, and you shall know my
    errand.
I come from Lady Juliet.
Fri. L.   Welcome, then. 80
Nurse. O holy friar, O, tell me, holy friar,
Where is my lady's lord, where's Romeo?
Fri. L. There on the ground, with his own tears
    made drunk.
Nurse. O, he is even in my mistress' case,
Just in her case! O woeful sympathy! 85
Piteous predicament! Even so lies she,
Blubb'ring and weeping, weeping and blubb'ring.
Stand up, stand up; stand, an you be a man.
For Juliet's sake, for her sake, rise and stand;
Why should you fall into so deep an O? 90
Rom. Nurse!
Nurse. Ah sir! ah sir! Death's the end of all.
Rom. Spak'st thou of Juliet? How is it with
    her?
Doth not she think me an old murderer,
Now I have stain'd the childhood of our joy 95
With blood remov'd but little from her own?
Where is she? and how doth she? and what says
My conceal'd lady to our cancell'd love?
Nurse. O, she says nothing, sir, but weeps and
    weeps;
And now falls on her bed; and then starts up, 100

---

17. **without:** outside.   33. **validity:** worth.   40–43. **But...death.** In Q$_2$ the order of the lines is 41, **43,** 40, **(41), 42.**
(41) reads *Flies may do this,* etc.   45. **mean...mean:** means...base.   52. **[Thou]** Q$_1$.   *Then* Q$_2$.   **fond:** foolish.   63. **dis-**
pute: discuss.   **estate:** situation.   90. **O:** i.e., groan.   98. **conceal'd:** secretly married.

And Tybalt calls; and then on Romeo cries,
And then down falls again.
   Rom.   As if that name,
Shot from the deadly level of a gun,
Did murder her, as that name's cursed hand
Murder'd her kinsman. O, tell me, friar, tell me,
In what vile part of this anatomy   106
Doth my name lodge? Tell me, that I may sack
The hateful mansion.
    [*He offers to stab himself, and the Nurse
      snatches the dagger away.*
   Fri. L.   Hold thy desperate hand!
Art thou a man? Thy form cries out thou art;
Thy tears are womanish; thy wild acts denote 110
The unreasonable fury of a beast.
Unseemly woman in a seeming man,
And ill-beseeming beast in seeming both,
Thou hast amaz'd me! By my holy order,
I thought thy disposition better temper'd.   115
Hast thou slain Tybalt? Wilt thou slay thyself,
And slay thy lady that in thy life [lives],
By doing damned hate upon thyself?
Why rail'st thou on thy birth, the heaven, and
    earth?
Since birth, and heaven, and earth, all three do
    meet   120
In thee at once, which thou at once wouldst lose.
Fie, fie, thou sham'st thy shape, thy love, thy wit;
Which, like a usurer, abound'st in all,
And usest none in that true use indeed
Which should bedeck thy shape, thy love, thy wit.
Thy noble shape is but a form of wax,   126
Digressing from the valour of a man;
Thy dear love sworn but hollow perjury,
Killing that love which thou hast vow'd to cherish;
Thy wit, that ornament to shape and love,   130
Mis-shapen in the conduct of them both,
Like powder in a skilless soldier's flask,
Is set a-fire by thine own ignorance,
And thou dismemb'red with thine own defence.
What, rouse thee, man! thy Juliet is alive, 135
For whose dear sake thou wast but lately dead:
There art thou happy. Tybalt would kill thee,
But thou slewest Tybalt: there art thou happy.
The law that threat'ned death becomes thy friend
And turns it to exile: there art thou happy. 140
A pack of blessings light upon thy back;
Happiness courts thee in her best array;
But, like a misbehav'd and sullen wench,
Thou [pout'st upon] thy fortune and thy love.
Take heed, take heed, for such die miserable. 145
Go, get thee to thy love, as was decreed;
Ascend her chamber; hence, and comfort her.
But look thou stay not till the watch be set,

For then thou canst not pass to Mantua,
Where thou shalt live till we can find a time 150
To blaze your marriage, reconcile your friends,
Beg pardon of the Prince, and call thee back
With twenty hundred thousand times more joy
Than thou went'st forth in lamentation.
Go before, nurse; commend me to thy lady; 155
And bid her hasten all the house to bed,
Which heavy sorrow makes them apt unto.
Romeo is coming.
   Nurse. O Lord, I could have stay'd here all the
    night
To hear good counsel. O, what learning is! 160
My lord, I'll tell my lady you will come.
   Rom. Do so, and bid my sweet prepare to chide.
      [*Nurse offers to go in, and turns again.*
   Nurse. Here, sir, a ring she bid me give you, sir.
Hie you, make haste, for it grows very late.
   Rom. How well my comfort is reviv'd by this!
      [*Exit Nurse.*
   Fri. L. Go hence; good-night; and here stands all
    your state: 166
Either be gone before the watch be set,
Or by the break of day disguis'd from hence.
Sojourn in Mantua; I'll find out your man,
And he shall signify from time to time 170
Every good hap to you that chances here.
Give me thy hand; 'tis late. Farewell; good-night.
   Rom. But that a joy past joy calls out on me,
It were a grief, so brief to part with thee.
Farewell.   [*Exeunt.* 175

[SCENE IV. *A room in Capulet's house.*]

Enter CAPULET, LADY CAPULET, *and* PARIS.

   Cap. Things have fallen out, sir, so unluckily
That we have had no time to move our daughter.
Look you, she lov'd her kinsman Tybalt dearly,
And so did I. Well, we were born to die.
'Tis very late, she'll not come down to-night; 5
I promise you, but for your company,
I would have been a-bed an hour ago.
   Par. These times of woe afford no times to woo.
Madam, good-night; commend me to your daughter.
   La. Cap. I will, and know her mind early to-
    morrow;   10
To-night she's mewed up to her heaviness.
   Cap. Sir Paris, I will make a desperate tender
Of my child's love. I think she will be rul'd
In all respects by me; nay, more, I doubt it not.
Wife, go you to her ere you go to bed; 15
Acquaint her here of my son Paris' love;
And bid her — mark you me? — on Wednesday
    next —

117. **[lives]** F4. *lies* Q2. 123. **Which:** who. 134. **defence:** weapon. 144. **[pout'st upon]** Q5. *puts up* Q2. 151. **blaze:** announce. 166. **here ... state:** i.e., this is the situation. 174. **brief:** hastily.
   Sc. iv, 11. mewed: shut. 12. **desperate tender:** bold offer.

But, soft! what day is this?

Par.   Monday, my lord.

Cap. Monday! ha, ha!   Well, Wednesday is too
    soon,

O' Thursday let it be, — o' Thursday, tell her,   20

She shall be married to this noble earl.

Will you be ready?   Do you like this haste?

We'll keep no great ado, — a friend or two;

For, hark you, Tybalt being slain so late,

It may be thought we held him carelessly,   25

Being our kinsman, if we revel much;

Therefore we'll have some half a dozen friends,

And there an end.   But what say you to Thursday?

Par. My lord, I would that Thursday were to-
    morrow.

Cap. Well, get you gone; o' Thursday be it,
    then.   30

Go you to Juliet ere you go to bed;

Prepare her, wife, against this wedding-day.

Farewell, my lord.   Light to my chamber, ho!

Afore me! it is so very late that we

May call it early by and by.   Good-night.   35

                                [Exeunt.

[SCENE V.   *Capulet's orchard.*]

Enter ROMEO *and* JULIET, *aloft.*

Jul. Wilt thou be gone? it is not yet near day.

It was the nightingale, and not the lark,

That pierc'd the fearful hollow of thine ear;

Nightly she sings on yond pomegranate-tree.

Believe me, love, it was the nightingale.   5

Rom. It was the lark, the herald of the morn,

No nightingale.   Look, love, what envious streaks

Do lace the severing clouds in yonder east.

Night's candles are burnt out, and jocund day

Stands tiptoe on the misty mountain tops.   10

I must be gone and live, or stay and die.

Jul. Yond light is not day-light, I know it, I;

It is some meteor that the sun exhales

To be to thee this night a torch-bearer

And light thee on thy way to Mantua;   15

Therefore stay yet; thou need'st not to be gone.

Rom. Let me be ta'en, let me be put to death;

I am content, so thou wilt have it so.

I'll say yon grey is not the morning's eye,

'Tis but the pale reflex of Cynthia's brow;   20

Nor that is not the lark, whose notes do beat

The vaulty heaven so high above our heads.

I have more care to stay than will to go.

Come, death, and welcome!   Juliet wills it so.

How is't, my soul?   Let's talk; it is not day.   25

Jul. It is, it is!   Hie hence, be gone, away!

It is the lark that sings so out of tune,

Straining harsh discords and unpleasing sharps.

Some say the lark makes sweet division;

This doth not so, for she divideth us.   30

Some say the lark and loathed toad change eyes;

O, now I would they had chang'd voices too,

Since arm from arm that voice doth us affray,

Hunting thee hence with hunt's-up to the day.

O, now be gone; more light and light it grows.   35

Rom. More light and light; more dark and dark
    our woes!

Enter NURSE [*from the chamber*].

Nurse. Madam!

Jul. Nurse?

Nurse. Your lady mother is coming to your
    chamber.

The day is broke; be wary, look about.   [*Exit.*   40

Jul. Then, window, let day in, and let life out.

Rom. Farewell, farewell!   One kiss, and I'll
    descend.   [*He goeth down.*

Jul. Art thou gone so?   Love, lord, ay, husband,
    friend!

I must hear from thee every day in the hour,

For in a minute there are many days.   45

O, by this count I shall be much in years

Ere I again behold my Romeo!

Rom. [*From below.*]   Farewell!

I will omit no opportunity

That may convey my greetings, love, to thee.   50

Jul. O, think'st thou we shall ever meet again?

Rom. I doubt it not; and all these woes shall
    serve

For sweet discourses in our times to come.

Jul. O God, I have an ill-divining soul!

Methinks I see thee, now thou art [below],   55

As one dead in the bottom of a tomb.

Either my eyesight fails, or thou look'st pale.

Rom. And trust me, love, in my eye so do you;

Dry sorrow drinks our blood.   Adieu, adieu!

Jul. O Fortune, Fortune! all men call thee
    fickle;   60

If thou art fickle, what dost thou with him

That is renown'd for faith?   Be fickle, Fortune;

For then, I hope, thou wilt not keep him long,

But send him back.

Enter LADY CAPULET.

La. Cap. Ho, daughter! are you up?   65

Jul. Who is't that calls?   It is my lady mother.

Is she not down so late, or up so early?

What unaccustom'd cause procures her hither?

La. Cap. Why, how now, Juliet?

Jul.   Madam, I am not well.

Sc. v, 20. Cynthia's: the moon's.   **23. care:** desire.   **28. sharps:** high notes.   **29. division:** melody.   **34. hunt's-up:** a song to waken hunters.   **54. ill-divining:** foreboding evil.   **55. [below]** Q₁.   *so low* Q₂.   **59. Dry sorrow.**   Sorrow was believed to dry up the blood.

La. Cap. Evermore weeping for your cousin's
    death?   70
What, wilt thou wash him from his grave with
    tears?
An if thou couldst, thou couldst not make him live;
Therefore, have done. Some grief shows much of
    love,
But much of grief shows still some want of wit.
Jul. Yet let me weep for such a feeling loss. 75
La. Cap. So shall you feel the loss, but not the
    friend
Which you weep for.
Jul.   Feeling so the loss,
I cannot choose but ever weep the friend.
La. Cap. Well, girl, thou weep'st not so much
    for his death, 79
As that the villain lives which slaughter'd him.
Jul. What villain, madam?
La. Cap.   That same villain, Romeo.
Jul. [*Aside.*] Villain and he be many miles
    asunder. —
God pardon [him]! I do, with all my heart;
And yet no man like he doth grieve my heart.
La. Cap. That is, because the traitor murderer
    lives. 85
Jul. Ay, madam, from the reach of these my
    hands.
Would none but I might venge my cousin's death!
La. Cap. We will have vengeance for it, fear thou
    not;
Then weep no more. I'll send to one in Mantua,
Where that same banish'd runagate doth live, 90
Shall give him such an unaccustom'd dram
That he shall soon keep Tybalt company;
And then, I hope, thou wilt be satisfied.
Jul. Indeed, I never shall be satisfied
With Romeo, till I behold him — dead — 95
Is my poor heart, so for a kinsman vex'd.
Madam, if you could find out but a man
To bear a poison, I would temper it
That Romeo should, upon receipt thereof, 99
Soon sleep in quiet. O, how my heart abhors
To hear him nam'd, and cannot come to him
To wreak the love I bore my cousin [Tybalt]
Upon his body that hath slaughter'd him!
La. Cap. Find thou the means, and I'll find such
    a man.
But now I'll tell thee joyful tidings, girl. 105
Jul. And joy comes well in such a needy time.
What are they, [I] beseech your ladyship?
La. Cap. Well, well, thou hast a careful father,
    child;
One who, to put thee from thy heaviness,

Hath sorted out a sudden day of joy 110
That thou expects not nor I look'd not for.
Jul. Madam, in happy time, what day is that?
La. Cap. Marry, my child, early next Thursday
    morn
The gallant, young, and noble gentleman,
The County Paris, at Saint Peter's Church, 115
Shall happily make thee there a joyful bride.
Jul. Now, by Saint Peter's Church and Peter
    too,
He shall not make me there a joyful bride.
I wonder at this haste that I must wed
Ere he that should be husband comes to woo. 120
I pray you, tell my lord and father, madam,
I will not marry yet; and, when I do, I swear,
It shall be Romeo, whom you know I hate,
Rather than Paris. These are news indeed!
La. Cap. Here comes your father; tell him so
    yourself, 125
And see how he will take it at your hands.

Enter CAPULET *and* NURSE

Cap. When the sun sets, the [air] doth drizzle
    dew;
But for the sunset of my brother's son
It rains downright.
How now! a conduit, girl? What, still in tears?
Evermore show'ring? In one little body 131
Thou counterfeits a bark, a sea, a wind:
For still thy eyes, which I may call the sea,
Do ebb and flow with tears; the bark thy body is,
Sailing in this salt flood; the winds, thy sighs, 135
Who, raging with thy tears, and they with them,
Without a sudden calm, will overset
Thy tempest-tossed body. How now, wife!
Have you delivered to her our decree?
La. Cap. Ay, sir; but she will none, she gives you
    thanks. 140
I would the fool were married to her grave!
Cap. Soft! take me with you, take me with you,
    wife.
How! will she none? Doth she not give us thanks?
Is she not proud? Doth she not count her blest,
Unworthy as she is, that we have wrought 145
So worthy a gentleman to be her bride?
Jul. Not proud you have; but thankful that you
    have.
Proud can I never be of what I hate;
But thankful even for hate that is meant love.
Cap. How how, how how, chop-logic! What is
    this? 150
"Proud," and "I thank you," and "I thank you
    not;"

75. **feeling:** affecting. 83. [him] Q₄. Om. Q₂. 84. **like:** as much as. 95. **dead.** Juliet intends this word to make sense both with what precedes and what follows it. 102. [Tybalt] F₂. Om. Q₂. 107. [I] Q₄. Om. Q₂. 127. [air] Q₄. *earth* Q₂. 130. **conduit:** water-pipe. 145. **wrought:** secured. 146. **bride.** Used of either man or woman in Shakespeare's day. 150. **chop-logic:** sophist.

And yet "not proud." Mistress minion, you,
Thank me no thankings, nor proud me no prouds,
But fettle your fine joints 'gainst Thursday next,
To go with Paris to Saint Peter's Church,   155
Or I will drag thee on a hurdle thither.
Out, you green-sickness carrion! Out, you baggage!
You tallow-face!
   La. Cap.   Fie, fie! what, are you mad?
   Jul. Good father, I beseech you on my knees,
Hear me with patience but to speak a word.   160
   Cap. Hang thee, young baggage! disobedient
     wretch!
I tell thee what: get thee to church o' Thursday,
Or never after look me in the face.
Speak not, reply not, do not answer me!
My fingers itch. Wife, we scarce thought us blest
That God had lent us but this only child;   166
But now I see this one is one too much,
And that we have a curse in having her.
Out on her, hilding!
   Nurse.   God in heaven bless her!
You are to blame, my lord, to rate her so.   170
   Cap. And why, my lady Wisdom? Hold your
     tongue,
Good prudence; smatter with your gossips, go.
   Nurse. I speak no treason.
   [*Cap.*]   O, God ye god-den.
   [*Nurse.*] May not one speak?
   Cap.   Peace, you mumbling fool!
Utter your gravity o'er a gossip's bowl;   175
For here we need it not.
   La. Cap.   You are too hot.
   Cap. God's bread! it makes me mad.
Day, night, hour, tide, time, work, play,
Alone, in company, still my care hath been
To have her match'd; and having now provided 180
A gentleman of noble parentage,
Of fair demesnes, youthful and nobly [train'd],
Stuff'd, as they say, with honourable parts,
Proportion'd as one's thought would wish a man;
And then to have a wretched puling fool,   185
A whining mammet, in her fortune's tender
To answer, "I'll not wed; I cannot love,
I am too young; I pray you, pardon me."
But, an you will not wed, I'll pardon you.
Graze where you will, you shall not house with me.
Look to't, think on't, I do not use to jest.   191
Thursday is near; lay hand on heart, advise.
An you be mine, I'll give you to my friend;
An you be not, hang, beg, starve, die in the streets,
For, by my soul, I'll ne'er acknowledge thee,   195
Nor what is mine shall never do thee good.

Trust to't, bethink you; I'll not be forsworn.
                        [*Exit.*
   Jul. Is there no pity sitting in the clouds,
That sees into the bottom of my grief?
O, sweet my mother, cast me not away!   200
Delay this marriage for a month, a week;
Or, if you do not, make the bridal bed
In that dim monument where Tybalt lies.
   La. Cap. Talk not to me, for I'll not speak a word.
Do as thou wilt, for I have done with thee.   205
                        [*Exit.*
   Jul. O God! — O nurse, how shall this be prevented?
My husband is on earth, my faith in heaven;
How shall that faith return again to earth,
Unless that husband send it me from heaven
By leaving earth? Comfort me, counsel me!   210
Alack, alack, that heaven should practise stratagems
Upon so soft a subject as myself!
What say'st thou? Hast thou not a word of joy?
Some comfort, nurse.
   Nurse.   Faith, here it is.
Romeo is banish'd; and all the world to nothing 215
That he dares ne'er come back to challenge you;
Or, if he do, it needs must be by stealth.
Then, since the case so stands as now it doth,
I think it best you married with the County.
O, he's a lovely gentleman!   220
Romeo's a dishclout to him. An eagle, madam,
Hath not so green, so quick, so fair an eye
As Paris hath. Beshrew my very heart,
I think you are happy in this second match,
For it excels your first; or if it did not,   225
Your first is dead; or 'twere as good he were
As living here and you no use of him.
   Jul. Speak'st thou from thy heart?
   Nurse. And from my soul too; else beshrew them
     both.
   Jul. Amen!
   Nurse. What?
   Jul. Well, thou hast comforted me marvellous
     much.   230
Go in; and tell my lady I am gone,
Having displeas'd my father, to Laurence' cell,
To make confession and to be absolv'd.
   Nurse. Marry, I will; and this is wisely done.
                        [*Exit.*]
   Jul. Ancient damnation! O most wicked fiend!
Is it more sin to wish me thus forsworn,   236
Or to dispraise my lord with that same tongue
Which she hath prais'd him with above compare
So many thousand times? Go, counsellor;

152. **minion:** spoiled child. 154. **fettle:** prepare. 156. **hurdle:** conveyance for criminals. 157. **green-sickness:** anemia (suggesting Juliet's paleness). 172. **smatter:** chatter. 173. [*Cap.*] Q4. Given to Nurse in Q2. 182. **demesnes:** estates. [**train'd**] Q1. *liand* Q2. *allied* F. 186. **mammet:** doll. **in... tender:** when good fortune is offered her. 192. **advise:** consider. 227. **here:** i.e., in this world.

Thou and my bosom henceforth shall be twain.
I'll to the friar, to know his remedy;   241
If all else fail, myself have power to die.   [*Exit.*

[ACT IV]

[SCENE I. *Friar Laurence's cell.*]

Enter FRIAR LAURENCE *and* PARIS.

Fri. L. On Thursday, sir? The time is very
   short.
Par. My father Capulet will have it so,
And I am nothing slow to slack his haste.
Fri. L. You say you do not know the lady's
   mind.
Uneven is the course, I like it not.   5
Par. Immoderately she weeps for Tybalt's
   death,
And therefore have I little [talk'd] of love,
For Venus smiles not in a house of tears.
Now, sir, her father counts it dangerous
That she do give her sorrow so much sway,   10
And in his wisdom hastes our marriage
To stop the inundation of her tears;
Which, too much minded by herself alone,
May be put from her by society.
Now do you know the reason of this haste.   15
Fri. L. [*Aside.*] I would I knew not why it should
   be slow'd.
Look, sir, here comes the lady toward my cell.

Enter JULIET.

Par. Happily met, my lady and my wife!
Jul. That may be, sir, when I may be a wife.
Par. That may be must be, love, on Thursday
   next.   20
Jul. What must be shall be.
Fri. L.   That's a certain text.
Par. Come you to make confession to this
   father?
Jul. To answer that, I should confess to you.
Par. Do not deny to him that you love me.
Jul. I will confess to you that I love him.   25
Par. So will ye, I am sure, that you love me.
Jul. If I do so, it will be of more price,
Being spoke behind your back, than to your face.
Par. Poor soul, thy face is much abus'd with tears.
Jul. The tears have got small victory by that,   30
For it was bad enough before their spite.
Par. Thou wrong'st it, more than tears, with
   that report.
Jul. That is no slander, sir, which is a truth;
And what I spake, I spake it to my face.

Par. Thy face is mine, and thou hast sland'red
   it.   35
Jul. It may be so, for it is not mine own.
Are you at leisure, holy father, now;
Or shall I come to you at evening mass?
Fri. L. My leisure serves me, pensive daughter,
   now.
My lord, we must entreat the time alone.   40
Par. God shield I should disturb devotion!
Juliet, on Thursday early will I rouse ye;
Till then, adieu; and keep this holy kiss.   [*Exit.*
Jul. O, shut the door! and when thou hast done
   so,
Come weep with me, past hope, past care, past
   help!   45
Fri. L. O Juliet, I already know thy grief;
It strains me past the compass of my wits.
I hear thou must, and nothing may prorogue it,
On Thursday next be married to this County.
Jul. Tell me not, friar, that thou hear'st of this, 50
Unless thou tell me how I may prevent it.
If, in thy wisdom, thou canst give no help,
Do thou but call my resolution wise,
And with this knife I'll help it presently.
God join'd my heart and Romeo's, thou our hands;
And ere this hand, by thee to Romeo's seal'd,   56
Shall be the label to another deed,
Or my true heart with treacherous revolt
Turn to another, this shall slay them both.
Therefore, out of thy long-experienc'd time,   60
Give me some present counsel, or, behold,
'Twixt my extremes and me this bloody knife
Shall play the umpire, arbitrating that
Which the commission of thy years and art
Could to no issue of true honour bring.   65
Be not so long to speak; I long to die
If what thou speak'st speak not of remedy.
Fri. L. Hold, daughter! I do spy a kind of hope,
Which craves as desperate an execution
As that is desperate which we would prevent.   70
If, rather than to marry County Paris,
Thou hast the strength of will to [slay] thyself,
Then is it likely thou wilt undertake
A thing like death to chide away this shame,
That cop'st with Death himself to scape from it;   75
And, if thou dar'st, I'll give thee remedy.
Jul. O, bid me leap, rather than marry Paris,
From off the battlements of any tower,
Or walk in thievish ways, or bid me lurk
Where serpents are; chain me with roaring bears, 80
Or hide me nightly in a charnel-house,
O'er-cover'd quite with dead men's rattling bones,
With reeky shanks and yellow chapless skulls;
Or bid me go into a new-made grave

Act IV, sc. i, 5. **Uneven**: irregular. 7. **[talk'd]** Q₅. *talke* Q₂. 41. **shield**: forbid. 45. **care** Q₂. *cure* Q₁. 57. **label**: seal.
62. **extremes**: extremities. 64. **commission**: authority. 72. **[slay]** Q₁. *stay* Q₂. 75. **cop'st with**: wouldest encounter.
79. **thievish**: full of thieves. 81. **hide** Q₂. *shut* Q₁. 83. **reeky**: foul smelling. **chapless**: jawless.

And hide me with a dead man in his [shroud], —
Things that, to hear them told, have made me trem-
ble;   86
And I will do it without fear or doubt,
To live an unstain'd wife to my sweet love.
   Fri. L. Hold, then. Go home, be merry, give
consent
To marry Paris. Wednesday is to-morrow.   90
To-morrow night look that thou lie alone;
Let not the nurse lie with thee in thy chamber.
Take thou this vial, being then in bed,
And this [distilled] liquor drink thou off;
When presently through all thy veins shall run   95
A cold and drowsy humour; for no pulse
Shall keep his native progress, but surcease;
No warmth, no [breath] shall testify thou livest;
The roses in thy lips and cheeks shall fade
To [paly] ashes, thy eyes' windows fall,   100
Like death when he shuts up the day of life;
Each part, depriv'd of supple government,
Shall, stiff and stark and cold, appear like death:
And in this borrowed likeness of shrunk death
Thou shalt continue two and forty hours,   105
And then awake as from a pleasant sleep.
Now, when the bridegroom in the morning comes
To rouse thee from thy bed, there art thou dead.
Then, as the manner of our country is,
[In] thy best robes uncovered on the bier   110
Thou shall be borne to that same ancient vault
Where all the kindred of the Capulets lie.
In the mean time, against thou shalt awake,
Shall Romeo by my letters know our drift,
And hither shall he come; and he and I   115
Will watch thy waking, and that very night
Shall Romeo bear thee hence to Mantua.
And this shall free thee from this present shame;
If no inconstant toy, nor womanish fear,
Abate thy valour in the acting it.   120
   Jul. Give me, give me! O, tell not me of fear!
   Fri. L. Hold; get you gone, be strong and pros-
perous
In this resolve. I'll send a friar with speed
To Mantua, with my letters to thy lord.
   Jul. Love give me strength! and strength shall
help afford.   125
Farewell, dear father!   [*Exeunt.*

[SCENE II. *Hall in Capulet's house.*]

Enter CAPULET, LADY CAPULET, NURSE, *and*
SERVING-MEN, *two or three.*

   Cap. So many guests invite as here are writ.
                                       [*Exit 1. Servant.*]

Sirrah, go hire me twenty cunning cooks.
   [*2.*] *Serv.* You shall have none ill, sir; for I'll try
if they can lick their fingers.
   Cap. How canst thou try them so?   5
   [*2.*] *Serv.* Marry, sir, 'tis an ill cook that cannot
lick his own fingers; therefore he that cannot lick his
fingers goes not with me.
   Cap. Go, be gone.   [*Exit 2. Servant.*]
We shall be much unfurnish'd for this time.   10
What, is my daughter gone to Friar Laurence?
   Nurse. Ay, forsooth.
   Cap. Well, he may chance to do some good on
her.
A peevish self-will'd harlotry it is.

               Enter JULIET.

   Nurse. See where she comes from shrift with
merry look.   15
   Cap. How now, my headstrong! where have you
been gadding?
   Jul. Where I have learn'd me to repent the sin
Of disobedient opposition
To you and your behests, and am enjoin'd
By holy Laurence to fall prostrate here   20
And beg your pardon. Pardon, I beseech you!
Henceforward I am ever rul'd by you.
   Cap. Send for the County; go tell him of this.
I'll have this knot knit up to-morrow morning.
   Jul. I met the youthful lord at Laurence' cell 25
And gave him what becomed love I might,
Not stepping o'er the bounds of modesty.
   Cap. Why, I am glad on't; this is well; stand
up.
This is as 't should be. Let me see the County;
Ay, marry, go, I say, and fetch him hither.   30
Now, afore God! this reverend holy friar,
All our whole city is much bound to him.
   Jul. Nurse, will you go with me into my closet
To help me sort such needful ornaments
As you think fit to furnish me to-morrow?   35
   La. Cap. No, not till Thursday; there is time
enough.
   Cap. Go, nurse, go with her; we'll to church to-
morrow.   [*Exeunt Juliet and Nurse.*
   La. Cap. We shall be short in our provision;
'Tis now near night.
   Cap.   Tush, I will stir about,
And all things shall be well, I warrant thee, wife;
Go thou to Juliet, help to deck up her.   41
I'll not to bed to-night; let me alone;
I'll play the housewife for this once. What, ho!
They are all forth. Well, I will walk myself
To County Paris, to prepare up him   45

85. [shroud] Q4. Om. Q2. 94. [distilled] Q1. *distilling* Q2. 98. [breath] Q1. *breast* Q2. 100. [paly] Q5. *many* Q2.
110. [In] *Is* Q2. bier. After l. 110 Qq Ff print a line "Be borne to burial in thy kindreds grave," probably an unerased
alternative for l. 111. 113. against: in preparation for the time when. 119. toy: whim.
Sc. ii, 14. peevish: refractory. harlotry: wench. 26. becomed: fitting.

Against to-morrow. My heart is wondrous light,
Since this same wayward girl is so reclaim'd.

                    [*Exeunt.*

[SCENE III. *Juliet's chamber.*]

Enter JULIET *and* NURSE.

Jul. Ay, those attires are best; but, gentle nurse,
I pray thee, leave me to myself to-night;
For I have need of many orisons
To move the heavens to smile upon my state,
Which, well thou know'st, is cross and full of sin. 5

Enter LADY CAPULET.

La. Cap. What, are you busy, ho? Need you my
   help?
Jul. No, madam; we have cull'd such necessaries
As are behoveful for our state to-morrow.
So please you, let me now be left alone,
And let the nurse this night sit up with you;   10
For, I am sure, you have your hands full all,
In this so sudden business.
   La. Cap.   Good-night.
Get thee to bed, and rest; for thou hast need.

        [*Exeunt* [*Lady Capulet and Nurse*].
Jul. Farewell! God knows when we shall meet
   again.
I have a faint cold fear thrills through my veins, 15
That almost freezes up the heat of life.
I'll call them back again to comfort me.
Nurse! — What should she do here?
My dismal scene I needs must act alone.
Come, vial.   20
What if this mixture do not work at all?
Shall I be married then to-morrow morning?
No, no; this shall forbid it. Lie thou there.

        [*Laying down her dagger.*]
What if it be a poison, which the friar
Subtly hath minist'red to have me dead,   25
Lest in this marriage he should be dishonour'd
Because he married me before to Romeo?
I fear it is; and yet, methinks, it should not,
For he hath still been tried a holy man.
How if, when I am laid into the tomb,   30
I wake before the time that Romeo
Come to redeem me? There's a fearful point!
Shall I not then be stifled in the vault,
To whose foul mouth no healthsome air breathes in,
And there die strangled ere my Romeo comes? 35
Or, if I live, is it not very like
The horrible conceit of death and night,
Together with the terror of the place, —

As in a vault, an ancient receptacle,
Where, for this many hundred years, the bones   40
Of all my buried ancestors are pack'd;
Where bloody Tybalt, yet but green in earth,
Lies fest'ring in his shroud; where, as they say,
At some hours in the night spirits resort; —
Alack, alack, is it not like that I,   45
So early waking, — what with loathsome smells,
And shrieks like mandrakes' torn out of the earth,
That living mortals, hearing them, run mad; —
O, if I wake, shall I not be distraught,
Environed with all these hideous fears,   50
And madly play with my forefathers' joints,
And pluck the mangled Tybalt from his shroud,
And, in this rage, with some great kinsman's bone
As with a club, dash out my desperate brains?
O, look! methinks I see my cousin's ghost   55
Seeking out Romeo, that did spit his body
Upon a rapier's point. Stay, Tybalt, stay!
Romeo, [I come! This do I] drink to thee.

   [*She falls upon her bed, within the curtains.*

[SCENE IV. *Hall in Capulet's house.*]

Enter LADY CAPULET *and* NURSE.

La. Cap. Hold, take these keys and fetch more
   spices, nurse.
Nurse. They call for dates and quinces in the
   pastry.

Enter CAPULET.

Cap. Come, stir, stir, stir! the second cock hath
   crow'd,
The curfew-bell hath rung, 'tis three o'clock.
Look to the bak'd meats, good Angelica;   5
Spare not for cost.
   Nurse.   Go, you cot-quean, go,
Get you to bed. Faith, you'll be sick to-morrow
For this night's watching.
   Cap. No, not a whit! What! I have watch'd ere
   now
All night for lesser cause, and ne'er been sick.   10
   La. Cap. Ay, you have been a mouse-hunt in
   your time;
But I will watch you from such watching now.

        [*Exeunt Lady Capulet and Nurse.*
   Cap. A jealous-hood, a jealous-hood!

Enter three or four [SERVING-MEN,] *with spits, logs, and baskets.*

                      Now, fellow,
What's there?

     Sc. iii, 5. **cross:** perverse.   8. **behoveful:** needful.   29. **still:** ever.   **tried:** proved.'   37. **conceit:** idea.   47. **mandrakes'.**
The root of the mandrake plant was believed to utter a shriek when pulled up.   58. **[I come! This do I]** Q₁. *Romeo, Romeo,*
heeres drinke, I Q₂.
     Sc. iv, 2. **pastry:** pastry-room, pantry.   5. **bak'd meats:** meat pies.   6. **cot-quean:** man who plays housewife.   11.
mouse-hunt: woman-chaser.   13. **jealous-hood:** jealous person.

[*1. Serv.*] Things for the cook, sir; but I know not
   what.
Cap. Make haste, make haste. [*Exit 1. Serv.*]
   Sirrah, fetch drier logs: 15
Call Peter, he will show thee where they are.
   [*2. Serv.*] I have a head, sir, that will find out logs,
And never trouble Peter for the matter.
Cap. Mass, and well said; a merry whoreson, ha!
Thou shalt be logger-head. [*Exit 2. Serv.*] Good
   [faith], 'tis day.   20
The County will be here with music straight,
For so he said he would.   I hear him near.
                          [*Music within.*
Nurse! Wife! What, ho! What, nurse, I say!

Re-enter NURSE.

Go waken Juliet, go and trim her up;
I'll go and chat with Paris. Hie, make haste,   25
Make haste; the bridegroom he is come already.
Make haste, I say.   [*Exeunt.*]

[SCENE V. *Juliet's chamber.*]

[*Enter* NURSE.]

Nurse. Mistress! what, mistress!   Juliet! —
   Fast, I warrant her, she. —
Why, lamb! why, lady! fie, you slug-a-bed!
Why, love! I say, madam! sweetheart! why, bride!
What, not a word?   You take your penny-worths
   now;
Sleep for a week; for the next night, I warrant,   5
The County Paris hath set up his rest
That you shall rest but little.   God forgive me!
Marry, and amen, how sound is she asleep!
I needs must wake her.   Madam, madam, madam!
Ay, let the County take you in your bed;   10
He'll fright you up, i' faith.   Will it not be?
               [*Draws back the curtains.*]
What, dress'd, and in your clothes! and down again!
I must needs wake you.   Lady! lady! lady!
Alas, alas! Help, help! my lady's dead!
O, well-a-day, that ever I was born!   15
Some *aqua vitæ*, ho!   My lord! my lady!

Enter LADY CAPULET.

La. Cap. What noise is here?
Nurse.   O lamentable day!
La. Cap. What is the matter?
Nurse.   Look, look! O heavy day!
La. Cap. O me, O me! My child, my only life,
Revive, look up, or I will die with thee!   20
Help, help! Call help.

Enter CAPULET.

Cap. For shame, bring Juliet forth; her lord is
   come.
Nurse. She's dead, deceas'd, she's dead; alack
   the day!
La. Cap. Alack the day, she's dead, she's dead,
   she's dead!
Cap. Ha! let me see her. Out, alas! she's cold;
Her blood is settled, and her joints are stiff;   26
Life and these lips have long been separated.
Death lies on her like an untimely frost
Upon the sweetest flower of all the field.
Nurse. O lamentable day!
La. Cap.   O woeful time!   30
Cap. Death, that hath ta'en her hence to make
   me wail,
Ties up my tongue, and will not let me speak.

Enter FRIAR LAURENCE *and* PARIS, *with*
MUSICIANS.

Fri. L. Come, is the bride ready to go to church?
Cap. Ready to go, but never to return. —
O son! the night before thy wedding-day   35
Hath Death lain with thy wife.   There she lies,
Flower as she was, deflowered by him.
Death is my son-in-law, Death is my heir;
My daughter he hath wedded.   I will die
And leave him all; life, living, all is Death's.   40
Par. Have I thought [long] to see this morning's
   face,
And doth it give me such a sight as this?
La. Cap. Accurs'd, unhappy, wretched, hateful
   day!
Most miserable hour that e'er Time saw
In lasting labour of his pilgrimage!   45
But one, poor one, one poor and loving child,
But one thing to rejoice and solace in,
And cruel Death hath catch'd it from my sight!
Nurse. O woe! O woeful, woeful, woeful day!
Most lamentable day, most woeful day,   50
That ever, ever, I did yet behold!
O day! O day! O day! O hateful day!
Never was seen so black a day as this.
O woeful day, O woeful day!
Par. Beguil'd, divorced, wronged, spited, slain!
Most detestable Death, by thee beguil'd,   56
By cruel cruel thee quite overthrown!
O love! O life! not life, but love in death!
Cap. Despis'd, distressed, hated, martyr'd,
   kill'd!
Uncomfortable time, why cam'st thou now   60
To murder, murder our solemnity?
O child! O child! my soul, and not my child!

---

14. [*1. Serv.*] (Capell). *Fel.* (i.e., Fellow) Q₂.   17. [*2. Serv.*] (Capell). *Fel.* Q₂.   20. **logger-head**: blockhead.   [**faith**]
Q₄.   *father* Q₂.
Sc. v, 2. Fast: i.e., fast asleep.   6. **set . . . rest**: resolved.   41. **thought [long]** Q₃: longed.   *thought love* Q₂.

Dead art thou! Alack! my child is dead;
And with my child my joys are buried.

　　Fri. L. Peace, ho, for shame! Confusion's
[cure] lives not　　　　　　　　　　　　　65
In these confusions.　Heaven and yourself
Had part in this fair maid; now heaven hath all,
And all the better is it for the maid.
Your part in her you could not keep from death,
But heaven keeps his part in eternal life.　　70
The most you sought was her promotion,
For 'twas your heaven she should be advanc'd;
And weep ye now, seeing she is advanc'd
Above the clouds, as high as heaven itself?
O, in this love, you love your child so ill　　75
That you run mad, seeing that she is well.
She's not well married that lives married long;
But she's best married that dies married young.
Dry up your tears, and stick your rosemary
On this fair corse; and, as the custom is,　　80
[In all] her best array bear her to church;
For though [fond] nature bids us all lament,
Yet nature's tears are reason's merriment.

　　Cap. All things that we ordained festival,
Turn from their office to black funeral;　　85
Our instruments to melancholy bells,
Our wedding cheer to a sad burial feast,
Our solemn hymns to sullen dirges change,
Our bridal flowers serve for a buried corse,
And all things change them to the contrary.　　90

　　Fri. L. Sir, go you in; and, madam, go with him;
And go, Sir Paris; every one prepare
To follow this fair corse unto her grave.
The heavens do lour upon you for some ill;
Move them no more by crossing their high will.　95
　　　*[Exeunt [Capulet, Lady Capulet, Paris, and
　　　　Friar].*

　　[*1.*] *Mus.* Faith, we may put up our pipes and be
gone.

　　Nurse. Honest good fellows, ah, put up, put up;
For, well you know, this is a pitiful case.　　*[Exit.*

　　[*1.*] *Mus.* Ay, by my troth, the case may be
amended.　　　　　　　　　　　　　　101

Enter [PETER].

　　Pet. Musicians, O, musicians, "Heart's ease,
Heart's ease!"　O, an you will have me live, play
"Heart's ease."

　　[*1.*] *Mus.* Why "Heart's ease"?　　　　105

　　Pet. O, musicians, because my heart itself plays
"My heart is full [of woe]."　O, play me some merry
dump to comfort me.

　　[*1.*] *Mus.* Not a dump we; 'tis no time to play
now.　　　　　　　　　　　　　　　　　110

　　Pet. You will not, then?

　　[*1.*] *Mus.* No.

　　Pet. I will then give it you soundly.

　　[*1.*] *Mus.* What will you give us?

　　Pet. No money, on my faith, but the gleek; I will
give you the minstrel.　　　　　　　　116

　　[*1.*] *Mus.* Then will I give you the serving-creature.

　　Pet. Then will I lay the serving-creature's dagger
on your pate.　I will carry no crotchets; I'll *re* you,
I'll *fa* you.　Do you note me?　　　　121

　　[*1.*] *Mus.* An you *re* us and *fa* us, you note us.

　　[*2.*] *Mus.* Pray you, put up your dagger, and put
out your wit.

　　Pet. Then have at you with my wit! I will dry-
beat you with an iron wit, and put up my iron dagger.　Answer me like men:　　　　　　127
　　"When griping griefs the heart doth wound,
　　　[And doleful dumps the mind oppress,]
　　Then music with her silver sound" —　　130
why "silver sound"?　Why "music with her silver
sound"?　What say you, Simon Catling?

　　[*1.*] *Mus.* Marry, sir, because silver hath a sweet
sound.　　　　　　　　　　　　　　　134

　　Pet. [Pretty!] What say you, Hugh Rebeck?

　　2. Mus. I say, "silver sound," because musicians sound for silver.

　　Pet. [Pretty] too! What say you, James Sound-
post?

　　3. Mus. Faith, I know not what to say.　　140

　　Pet. O, I cry you mercy; you are the singer; I will
say for you.　It is "music with her silver sound,"
because musicians have no gold for sounding:
　　"Then music with her silver sound　　145
　　　With speedy help doth lend redress."　　*[Exit.*

　　1. Mus. What a pestilent knave is this same!

　　2. Mus. Hang him, Jack! Come, we'll in here,
tarry for the mourners, and stay dinner.　　150
　　　　　　　　　　　　　　　　[Exeunt.

[ACT V]

[SCENE I. *Mantua. A street.*]

Enter ROMEO.

　　Rom. If I may trust the flattering truth of sleep,
My dreams presage some joyful news at hand.
My bosom's lord sits lightly in his throne,
And all this day an unaccustom'd spirit

---

65. **[cure]** (Theobald).　*care* Q₂.　79. **rosemary:** an herb (symbolic of remembrance).　81. **[In all]** Q₁.　*And in* Q₂.
82. **[fond]** F₂.　*some* Q₂.　102. s.d. **[PETER]** Q₄.　*Will Kemp* Q₂.　Kemp, the low comedian in Shakespeare's company,
apparently acted Peter.　107. **[of woe]** Q₄.　Om. Q₂.　108. **dump:** mournful tune.　115. **gleek:** gibe.　120. **carry:** endure.　**crotchets:** (1) whims, (2) quarter notes.　124. **put out:** exert.　125. **Then... wit.** So Q₄.　Cont. to *2. Mus.* in Q₂.
129. **[And...oppress]** Q₁.　Om. Q₂.　135, 138. **[Pretty]** (Pope).　*Prates* Q₂.　141. **singer.** Peter's joke is that as a singer
the musician can only *sing*, not *say*.
Act V, sc. i, 3. bosom's lord: heart.

Lifts me above the ground with cheerful thoughts.
I dreamt my lady came and found me dead —   6
Strange dream, that gives a dead man leave to
    think! —
And breath'd such life with kisses in my lips
That I reviv'd and was an emperor.
Ah me! how sweet is love itself possess'd,   10
When but love's shadows are so rich in joy!

Enter BALTHASAR, *his man, booted.*

News from Verona! — How now, Balthasar!
Dost thou not bring me letters from the friar?
How doth my lady?   Is my father well?
How [fares my] Juliet? that I ask again;   15
For nothing can be ill, if she be well.
  Bal. Then she is well, and nothing can be ill.
Her body sleeps in Capel's monument,
And her immortal part with angels lives.
I saw her laid low in her kindred's vault,   20
And presently took post to tell it you.
O, pardon me for bringing these ill news,
Since you did leave it for my office, sir.
  Rom. Is it [even] so?   Then I [defy] you,
    stars!
Thou know'st my lodging; get me ink and paper 25
And hire post-horses; I will hence to-night.
  Bal. I do beseech you, sir, have patience.
Your looks are pale and wild, and do import
Some misadventure.
  Rom.   Tush, thou art deceiv'd:
Leave me, and do the thing I bid thee do.   30
Hast thou no letters to me from the friar?
  Bal. No, my good lord.
  Rom.   No matter; get thee gone
And hire those horses; I'll be with thee straight.
                      [Exit Balthasar.
Well, Juliet, I will lie with thee to-night.
Let's see for means.   O mischief, thou art swift 35
To enter in the thoughts of desperate men!
I do remember an apothecary, —
And hereabouts 'a dwells, — which late I noted
In tatt'red weeds, with overwhelming brows,
Culling of simples; meagre were his looks,   40
Sharp misery had worn him to the bones;
And in his needy shop a tortoise hung,
An alligator stuff'd, and other skins
Of ill-shap'd fishes; and about his shelves
A beggarly account of empty boxes,   45
Green earthen pots, bladders and musty seeds,
Remnants of packthread and old cakes of roses
Were thinly scattered, to make up a show.
Noting this penury, to myself I said,
"An if a man did need a poison now,   50
Whose sale is present death in Mantua,
Here lives a caitiff wretch would sell it him."

O, this same thought did but forerun my need;
And this same needy man must sell it me.
As I remember, this should be the house.   55
Being holiday, the beggar's shop is shut.
What, ho! apothecary!

Enter APOTHECARY.

  Ap.   Who calls so loud?
  Rom. Come hither, man.   I see that thou art
    poor.
Hold, there is forty ducats.   Let me have
A dram of poison, such soon-speeding gear   60
As will disperse itself through all the veins
That the life-weary taker may fall dead,
And that the trunk may be discharg'd of breath
As violently as hasty powder fir'd
Doth hurry from the fatal cannon's womb.   65
  Ap. Such mortal drugs I have; but Mantua's law
Is death to any he that utters them.
  Rom. Art thou so bare and full of wretchedness,
And fear'st to die?   Famine is in thy cheeks,
Need and oppression starveth in thy eyes,   70
Contempt and beggary hangs upon thy back;
The world is not thy friend nor the world's law;
The world affords no law to make thee rich;
Then be not poor, but break it, and take this.
  Ap. My poverty, but not my will, consents. 75
  Rom. I [pay] thy poverty, and not thy will.
  Ap. Put this in any liquid thing you will,
And drink it off; and, if you had the strength
Of twenty men, it would dispatch you straight.
  Rom. There is thy gold, worse poison to men's
    souls,
                          80
Doing more murder in this loathsome world,
Than these poor compounds that thou mayst not
    sell.
I sell thee poison; thou hast sold me none.
Farewell!   Buy food, and get thyself in flesh.
Come, cordial and not poison, go with me   85
To Juliet's grave; for there must I use thee.
                         [Exeunt.

[SCENE II.   *Verona.   Friar Laurence's cell.*]

Enter FRIAR JOHN.

  Fri. J. Holy Franciscan friar! brother, ho!

Enter FRIAR LAURENCE.

  Fri. L. This same should be the voice of Friar
    John.
Welcome from Mantua!   What says Romeo?
Or, if his mind be writ, give me his letter.
  Fri. J. Going to find a bare-foot brother out,   5
One of our order, to associate me,
Here in this city visiting the sick,

---

15. [fares my] Q₁.   *doth my Lady* Q₂.   24. [even] F.   *in* Q₂.   [defy] Q₁.   *denie* Q₂.   40. simples: medicinal herbs.   63. trunk: body.   67. utters: sells.   76. [pay] Q₁.   *pray* Q₂.   85. cordial: restorative.

And finding him, the searchers of the town,
Suspecting that we both were in a house
Where the infectious pestilence did reign,   10
Seal'd up the doors and would not let us forth,
So that my speed to Mantua there was stay'd.
   Fri. L. Who bare my letter, then, to Romeo?
   Fri. J. I could not send it, — here it is again, —
Nor get a messenger to bring it thee,   15
So fearful were they of infection.
   Fri. L. Unhappy fortune! By my brotherhood,
The letter was not nice but full of charge
Of dear import, and the neglecting it
May do much danger. Friar John, go hence;   20
Get me an iron crow, and bring it straight
Unto my cell.
   Fri. J. Brother, I'll go and bring it thee. [*Exit.*
   Fri. L. Now must I to the monument alone;
Within this three hours will fair Juliet wake.   25
She will beshrew me much that Romeo
Hath had no notice of these accidents;
But I will write again to Mantua,
And keep her at my cell till Romeo come;
Poor living corse, clos'd in a dead man's tomb!   30
                     [*Exit.*

[SCENE III. *A churchyard; in it a tomb belonging to the Capulets.*]

Enter PARIS, *and his* PAGE *with flowers and sweet water* [*and a torch*].

   Par. Give me thy torch, boy. Hence, and stand
    aloof.
Yet put it out, for I would not be seen.
Under yond [yew-tree] lay thee all along,
Holding [thine] ear close to the hollow ground;
So shall no foot upon the churchyard tread,   5
Being loose, unfirm, with digging up of graves,
But thou shalt hear it. Whistle then to me,
As signal that thou hear'st something approach.
Give me those flowers. Do as I bid thee, go.
   Page. [*Aside.*] I am almost afraid to stand alone
Here in the churchyard; yet I will adventure.   11
                    [*Retires.*]
   Par. Sweet flower, with flowers thy bridal bed I
    strew, —
O woe! thy canopy is dust and stones —
Which with sweet water nightly I will dew,
   Or, wanting that, with tears distill'd by moans.
The obsequies that I for thee will keep   16
Nightly shall be to strew thy grave and weep.
                [*The Page whistles.*
The boy gives warning something doth approach.
What cursed foot wanders this way to-night,
To cross my obsequies and true love's rite?   20

What, with a torch! Muffle me, night, a while.
                    [*Retires.*]

Enter ROMEO *and* [BALTHASAR], *with a torch, a mattock, and a crow of iron.*

   Rom. Give me that mattock and the wrenching
    iron.
Hold, take this letter; early in the morning
See thou deliver it to my lord and father.
Give me the light. Upon thy life I charge thee,   25
Whate'er thou hear'st or seest, stand all aloof,
And do not interrupt me in my course.
Why I descend into this bed of death
Is partly to behold my lady's face,
But chiefly to take thence from her dead finger   30
A precious ring, a ring that I must use
In dear employment; therefore hence, be gone.
But if thou, jealous, dost return to pry
In what I farther shall intend to do,
By heaven, I will tear thee joint by joint   35
And strew this hungry churchyard with thy limbs.
The time and my intents are savage-wild,
More fierce and more inexorable far
Than empty tigers or the roaring sea.
   [*Bal.*] I will be gone, sir, and not trouble ye. 40
   Rom. So shalt thou show me friendship. Take
    thou that;
Live, and be prosperous; and farewell, good fellow.
   [*Bal.*] [*Aside.*] For all this same, I'll hide me
    hereabout.
His looks I fear, and his intents I doubt. [*Retires.*]
   Rom. Thou detestable maw, thou womb of
    death,   45
Gorg'd with the dearest morsel of the earth,
Thus I enforce thy rotten jaws to open,
And, in despite, I'll cram thee with more food!
                [*Opens the tomb.*]
   Par. This is that banish'd haughty Montague,
That murd'red my love's cousin, with which grief,
It is supposed, the fair creature died;   51
And here is come to do some villanous shame
To the dead bodies. I will apprehend him.
                [*Comes forward.*]
Stop thy unhallowed toil, vile Montague!
Can vengeance be pursued further than death?   55
Condemned villain, I do apprehend thee.
Obey, and go with me; for thou must die.
   Rom. I must indeed; and therefore came I
    hither.
Good gentle youth, tempt not a desperate man.
Fly hence, and leave me; think upon these gone,   60
Let them affright thee. I beseech thee, youth,
Put not another sin upon my head,
By urging me to fury: O, be gone!

   Sc. ii, 8. **searchers:** i.e., health officers. 18. **nice:** trivial. **charge:** importance. 21. **crow:** crowbar. 26. **beshrew:** censure.
   Sc. iii, 3. **[yew-tree]** Q₁. *young trees* Q₂. **all along:** prone. 4. **[thine]** Q₁. *thy* Q₂. 14. **sweet:** perfumed. 22. S.D.
[BALTHASAR] Q₁. *Peter* Q₂. 33. **jealous:** suspicious. 40, 43. [*Bal.*] Q₄. *Pet.* Q₂.

By heaven, I love thee better than myself;
For I come hither arm'd against myself.   65
Stay not, be gone; live, and hereafter say
A madman's mercy bid thee run away.
  Par. I do defy thy [conjurations]
And apprehend thee for a felon here.
  Rom. Wilt thou provoke me? Then have at
    thee, boy!   [*They fight.* 70
  [*Page.*] O Lord, they fight! I will go call the
    watch.   [*Exit.*]
  Par. O, I am slain! [*Falls.*] If thou be merciful,
Open the tomb, lay me with Juliet.   [*Dies.*]
  Rom. In faith, I will. Let me peruse this
    face.
Mercutio's kinsman, noble County Paris!   75
What said my man, when my betossed soul
Did not attend him as we rode? I think
He told me Paris should have married Juliet.
Said he not so? Or did I dream it so?
Or am I mad, hearing him talk of Juliet,   80
To think it was so? O, give me thy hand,
One writ with me in sour misfortune's book!
I'll bury thee in a triumphant grave.
A grave? O, no! a lantern, slaught'red youth,
For here lies Juliet, and her beauty makes   85
This vault a feasting presence full of light.
Death, lie thou there, by a dead man interr'd.
            [*Laying Paris in the tomb.*]
How oft when men are at the point of death
Have they been merry! which their keepers call
A lightning before death. O, how may I   90
Call this a lightning? O my love! my wife!
Death, that hath suck'd the honey of thy breath,
Hath had no power yet upon thy beauty.
Thou art not conquer'd; beauty's ensign yet
Is crimson in thy lips and in thy cheeks,   95
And death's pale flag is not advanced there.
Tybalt, li'st thou there in thy bloody sheet?
O, what more favour can I do to thee,
Than with that hand that cut thy youth in twain
To sunder his that was thine enemy?   100
Forgive me, cousin! Ah, dear Juliet,
Why art thou yet so fair? Shall I believe
That unsubstantial Death is amorous,
And that the lean abhorred monster keeps
Thee here in dark to be his paramour?   105
For fear of that, I still will stay with thee,
And never from this [palace] of dim night
Depart again. Here, here will I remain
With worms that are thy chamber-maids; O, here
Will I set up my everlasting rest,   110
And shake the yoke of inauspicious stars

From this world-wearied flesh. Eyes, look your
    last!
Arms, take your last embrace! and, lips, O you
The doors of breath, seal with a righteous kiss
A dateless bargain to engrossing death!   115
Come, bitter conduct, come, unsavoury guide!
Thou desperate pilot, now at once run on
The dashing rocks thy sea-sick weary bark!
Here's to my love! [*Drinks.*] O true apothe-
    cary!
Thy drugs are quick. Thus with a kiss I die. 120
                                    [*Dies.*]

    Enter FRIAR LAURENCE, *with lantern, crow,*
                and spade.

  Fri. L. Saint Francis be my speed! how oft to-
    night
Have my old feet stumbled at graves! Who's
    there?
  Bal. Here's one, a friend, and one that knows
    you well.
  Fri. L. Bliss be upon you! Tell me, good my
    friend,
What torch is yond, that vainly lends his light
To grubs and eyeless skulls? As I discern,   126
It burneth in the Capels' monument.
  Bal. It doth so, holy sir; and there's my master,
One that you love.
  Fri. L.   Who is it?
  Bal.   Romeo.   129
  Fri. L. How long hath he been there?
  Bal.   Full half an hour.
  Fri. L. Go with me to the vault.
  Bal.   I dare not, sir.
My master knows not but I am gone hence;
And fearfully did menace me with death
If I did stay to look on his intents.
  Fri. L. Stay, then; I'll go alone. Fear comes
    upon me: 135
O, much I fear some ill unthrifty thing.
  Bal. As I did sleep under this [yew]-tree here,
I dreamt my master and another fought,
And that my master slew him.
  Fri. L.   Romeo!
                                [*Advances.*]
Alack, alack, what blood is this, which stains   140
The stony entrance of this sepulchre?
What mean these masterless and gory swords
To lie discolour'd by this place of peace?
                            [*Enters the tomb.*]
Romeo! O, pale! Who else? What, Paris too?
And steep'd in blood? Ah, what an unkind hour

---

68. [conjurations] Q₁. *commiration* Q₂. 71. [*Page.*] Q₄. Om. Q₂. *Pet.* F. 86. **presence:** presence-chamber. 89. **keepers:** nurses. 107. [palace] Q₁. *pallat* Q₂. After this line, and before l. 108, Q₂ and F insert: "Depart againe, come lye thou in my arme,/Heer's to thy health, where ere thou tumblest in./O true Appothecarie!/Thy drugs are quicke. Thus with a kisse I die." 115. **dateless:** eternal. **engrossing:** monopolizing. 136. **unthrifty:** unlucky (which F reads). 137. [yew] (Pope). *yong* Q₂.

Is guilty of this lamentable chance!   146
The lady stirs.   *[Juliet rises.*

  Jul. O comfortable friar! where is my lord?
I do remember well where I should be,
And there I am. Where is my Romeo?   150
                   [Noise within.]

  Fri. L. I hear some noise. Lady, come from
    that nest
Of death, contagion, and unnatural sleep.
A greater power than we can contradict
Hath thwarted our intents. Come, come away.
Thy husband in thy bosom there lies dead;   155
And Paris too. Come, I'll dispose of thee
Among a sisterhood of holy nuns.
Stay not to question, for the watch is coming;
Come, go, good Juliet *[Noise again]*, I dare no longer
    stay.   *[Exit Fri. Lau.*

  Jul. Go, get thee hence, for I will not away. 160
What's here? A cup, clos'd in my true love's hand?
Poison, I see, hath been his timeless end.
O churl! drunk all, and left no friendly drop
To help me after? I will kiss thy lips;
Haply some poison yet doth hang on them,   165
To make me die with a restorative.
Thy lips are warm.

    Enter WATCH, *with the* PAGE *of Paris.*

  [*1.*] *Watch.* Lead, boy; which way?

  Jul. Yea, noise? Then I'll be brief. O happy
    dagger!   *[Snatching Romeo's dagger.]*
This is thy sheath (*Stabs herself*); there rust, and
    let me die.   170
         [Falls on Romeo's body, and dies].

  [*Page.*] This is the place; there, where the torch
    doth burn.

  [*1.*] *Watch.* The ground is bloody; search about
    the churchyard.
Go, some of you, whoe'er you find attach.
                  [Exeunt some.]
Pitiful sight! here lies the County slain;
And Juliet bleeding, warm, and newly dead,   175
Who here hath lain this two days buried.
Go, tell the Prince; run to the Capulets;
Raise up the Montagues; some others search.
                 [Exeunt others.]
We see the ground whereon these woes do lie;
But the true ground of all these piteous woes   180
We cannot without circumstance descry.

  Re-enter [*some of the* WATCH, *with*] BALTHASAR.

  [*2.*] *Watch.* Here's Romeo's man; we found him
    in the churchyard.

  [*1.*] *Watch.* Hold him in safety till the Prince
    come hither.

  Re-enter another WATCHMAN, *with* FRIAR LAURENCE.

  [*3.*] *Watch.* Here is a friar, that trembles, sighs,
    and weeps.
We took this mattock and this spade from him,   185
As he was coming from this churchyard's side.

  [*1.*] *Watch.* A great suspicion. Stay the friar too.

    Enter the PRINCE [*and* Attendants].

  Prince. What misadventure is so early up,
That calls our person from our morning rest?

  Enter CAPULET, LADY CAPULET, *and others.*

  Cap. What should it be, that [they] so shriek
    abroad?   190

  La. Cap. Oh! the people in the street cry Romeo,
Some Juliet, and some Paris; and all run,
With open outcry, toward our monument.

  Prince. What fear is this which startles in [our]
    ears?

  [*1.*] *Watch.* Sovereign, here lies the County Paris
    slain;   195
And Romeo dead; and Juliet, dead before,
Warm and new kill'd.

  Prince. Search, seek, and know how this foul
    murder comes.

  [*1.*] *Watch.* Here is a friar, and slaughter'd
    Romeo's man,
With instruments upon them, fit to open   200
These dead men's tombs.

  Cap. O heavens! O wife, look how our daughter
    bleeds!
This dagger hath mista'en, — for, lo, his house
Is empty on the back of Montague, —
And it mis-sheathed in my daughter's bosom! 205

  La. Cap. O me! this sight of death is as a bell,
That warns my old age to a sepulchre.

    Enter MONTAGUE [*and others*].

  Prince. Come, Montague; for thou art early up
To see thy son and heir [more early] down.

  Mon. Alas, my liege, my wife is dead to-night; 210
Grief of my son's exile hath stopp'd her breath.
What further woe conspires against mine age?

  Prince. Look, and thou shalt see.

  Mon. O thou untaught! what manners is in this,
To press before thy father to a grave?   215

  Prince. Seal up the mouth of outrage for a while,
Till we can clear these ambiguities,
And know their spring, their head, their true de-
    scent;
And then will I be general of your woes
And lead you even to death. Meantime forbear,
And let mischance be slave to patience.   221

Bring forth the parties of suspicion.

Fri. L. I am the greatest, able to do least,
Yet most suspected, as the time and place
Doth make against me, of this direful murder; 225
And here I stand, both to impeach and purge
Myself condemned and myself excus'd.

Prince. Then say at once what thou dost know
    in this.

Fri. L. I will be brief, for my short date of breath
Is not so long as is a tedious tale. 230
Romeo, there dead, was husband to that Juliet;
And she, there dead, [that] Romeo's faithful wife.
I married them; and their stol'n marriage-day
Was Tybalt's dooms-day, whose untimely death
Banish'd the new-made bridegroom from this city,
For whom, and not for Tybalt, Juliet pin'd. 236
You, to remove that siege of grief from her,
Betroth'd and would have married her perforce
To County Paris. Then comes she to me,
And, with wild looks, bid me devise some mean
To rid her from this second marriage, 241
Or in my cell there would she kill herself.
Then gave I her, so tutor'd by my art,
A sleeping potion; which so took effect
As I intended, for it wrought on her 245
The form of death. Meantime I writ to Romeo,
That he should hither come as this dire night
To help to take her from her borrowed grave,
Being the time the potion's force should cease.
But he which bore my letter, Friar John, 250
Was stay'd by accident, and yesternight
Return'd my letter back. Then all alone
At the prefixed hour of her waking,
Came I to take her from her kindred's vault;
Meaning to keep her closely at my cell, 255
Till I conveniently could send to Romeo;
But when I came, some minutes ere the time
Of her awak'ning, here untimely lay
The noble Paris and true Romeo dead.
She wakes; and I entreated her come forth 260
And bear this work of heaven with patience.
But then a noise did scare me from the tomb;
And she, too desperate, would not go with me,
But, as it seems, did violence on herself.
All this I know; and to the marriage 265
Her nurse is privy; and, if aught in this
Miscarried by my fault, let my old life
Be sacrific'd, some hour before his time,

Unto the rigour of severest law. 269

Prince. We still have known thee for a holy man.
Where's Romeo's man? What can he say to
    this?

Bal. I brought my master news of Juliet's death;
And then in post he came from Mantua
To this same place, to this same monument.
This letter he early bid me give his father, 275
And threat'ned me with death, going in the vault,
If I departed not and left him there.

Prince. Give me the letter; I will look on it.
Where is the County's page, that rais'd the watch?
Sirrah, what made your master in this place? 280

Page. He came with flowers to strew his lady's
    grave;
And bid me stand aloof, and so I did.
Anon comes one with light to ope the tomb,
And by and by my master drew on him;
And then I ran away to call the watch. 285

Prince. This letter doth make good the friar's
    words,
Their course of love, the tidings of her death.
And here he writes that he did buy a poison
Of a poor 'pothecary, and therewithal
Came to this vault to die, and lie with Juliet. 290
Where be these enemies? Capulet! Montague!
See, what a scourge is laid upon your hate,
That Heaven finds means to kill your joys with
    love.
And I for winking at your discords too 294
Have lost a brace of kinsmen. All are punish'd.

Cap. O brother Montague, give me thy hand.
This is my daughter's jointure, for no more
Can I demand.

Mon. But I can give thee more;
For I will raise her statue in pure gold;
That whiles Verona by that name is known, 300
There shall no figure at such rate be set
As that of true and faithful Juliet.

Cap. As rich shall Romeo's by his lady's lie,
Poor sacrifices of our enmity!

Prince. A glooming peace this morning with it
    brings; 305
The sun, for sorrow, will not show his head.
Go hence, to have more talk of these sad things;
    Some shall be pardon'd, and some punished:
For never was a story of more woe
Than this of Juliet and her Romeo. [*Exeunt.* 310

232. [that] Q4. *thats* Q2. 247. **as this:** this very. 255. **closely:** secretly. 297. **jointure:** marriage portion. 301. **rate:** value.

The Tragedy of Julius Cæsar

IN THE ABSENCE of any Quarto, the text of *Julius Cæsar* must be based upon the First Folio (1623), which prints the play with gratifying accuracy, probably from the theatre manuscript. Several pieces of evidence point convincingly to 1599 as the date of composition. The first of these is negative, the omission of the tragedy in Meres's list of Shakespeare's plays in his *Palladis Tamia* (1598), where we should confidently expect its inclusion if it had been on the stage before the fall of that year. On September 21, 1599, Thomas Platter, a German Swiss traveling in England, saw a "Tragedy vom ersten Keyser Julio Caesare," which is generally presumed to have been Shakespeare's. There is an unequivocal allusion to the speeches of Brutus and Antony to the citizens (III.ii.) in *The Mirror of Martyrs* by John Weever which, though published in 1601, was "made fit for the print," the author declares, some two years earlier. In Jonson's *Every Man Out of his Humour* (acted 1599), Clove, a talker of fustian, is made to say (III.iv.33), "reason long since is fled to animals, you know," perhaps echoing Antony's words, "O judgement! thou art fled to brutish beasts" (III.ii.109).

The relative brevity of the present play, and the number of short lines, have led some critics to surmise that the received text is an abridgment, although the soundness and cohesion of its parts point as plausibly to intentional economy. There is, however, a suggestion of incidental revision. Brutus, who himself tells Cassius about the death of Portia, behaves as if he knew nothing of it when, only a few minutes later, Messala brings news (IV.iii.147–57, 181–95). In all probability the first of these passages was entered in the manuscript as substitute for the second, and a mark cancelling the latter was overlooked by the printer.

The history of Julius Cæsar had been treated on the Elizabethan stage before Shakespeare wrote his tragedy, but there is no indication that he used anything by way of source beyond Plutarch's *Lives* — of Cæsar, Brutus, and Antonius — which he read in the translation by Sir Thomas North (1579, 1595).

Shakespeare follows his source so faithfully that in many passages he is merely turning North's prose into blank verse, with a characteristic heightening of imagination and language. With the exception of Lucius, every character comes from Plutarch, who supplies also several of their individualizing traits, such as the leanness of Cassius, the studiousness of Brutus, and Cæsar's "falling sickness." So, too, with the main events and a multitude of particulars. Yet within these confines of indebtedness Shakespeare is still admirably free, selecting, suppressing, and rearranging details for dramatic effect. Thus he juggles chronology, compressing into the compass of five days (though they are not consecutive) action which in fact covered three years, from the triumph of Cæsar in October, 45 B.C. to the battle at Philippi in October, 42 B.C. The murder of Cæsar, actually committed in the Senate House, Shakespeare transfers to the Capitol. Antony's compact with the conspirators and his demagogic speech, which in the play follow directly upon the murder, came two days later, according to Plutarch, in whose account (*The Life of Brutus*) the reading of the will precedes the speech. Finally, there were in actuality two battles at Philippi, about three weeks apart; the death of Cassius following the first, and the suicide of Brutus, the second. These two engagements Shakespeare unites. Shakespeare also added to what his source provided. The characters of Casca and Lepidus are only hinted at in Plutarch; Cassius's description of the swimming match and of Cæsar's fever, the soliloquy of Brutus rationalizing the need for killing Cæsar, the parley of the conspirators in his orchard, the incident of the assassins' bathing their arms in Cæsar's blood, and the speech of Antony over Cæsar's dead body are wholly Shakespeare's; while the orations of Brutus and Antony at Cæsar's funeral, and the quarrel of Brutus and Cassius, are elaborated from slight suggestions.

It has frequently been asserted that the play is misnamed and is weak in structure because the titular hero is taken off in the middle of the action.

This notion has even inspired the thesis that Shakespeare amalgamated two lost plays dealing respectively with the death and the avenging of Cæsar. That Shakespeare's title is a misnomer may be, theoretically, true, for the central figure in the action, the individual in whose mind there is conflict and upon whom our interest is mainly fixed, is Marcus Brutus. But the name of republican Brutus neither has today, nor had in Shakespeare's day, the éclat of imperial Cæsar's; and Shakespeare not unnaturally gave to this play the sovereign title, just as he had named his Histories after the Kings in whose reigns the chief events took place, regardless of the dramatic prominence of their rôles. The charge of disunity, however, is insubstantial, for if Brutus is the tragic protagonist, Cæsar and what he stands for constitute his problem. It is Cæsar's ambition that he fears. He tells the conspirators that they "all stand up against the spirit of Cæsar," and wishes that they could "come by Cæsar's spirit" without killing him (II.i.167–70). That being impossible, they do kill him, but "Cæsar's spirit ranging for revenge," as Antony prophesies (III.i.270), pursues Brutus as his Nemesis. Appearing to him at Sardis, the ghost of Cæsar proclaims itself his evil spirit (IV.iii.282). And Brutus acknowledges its victory before he dies (V.iii.94–96; V.v.50–51). Thus the spirit of Cæsar, dominant and avenged at the close, gives dramatic warrant for the title of Shakespeare's tragedy.

The character of Cæsar is deliberately foreshortened in the play for dramatic purposes. Since Cæsar is to be assassinated, Shakespeare must stress those qualities in him which can justify the deed in the eyes of those who commit it and who must, temporarily, have the sympathy of the audience. Consequently, Cæsar is presented without reference to the genuine springs of his greatness, emphasis being placed upon his arrogance and megalomania. This autocrat is a potential tyrant; he would be the Great Dictator. So, at least, it seems to Brutus and his friends. Such pride must have its fall, and Cæsar's murder accords with the ancient belief that those who affect godhead will be destroyed.

The danger embodied in Cæsar is most emphatically and resentfully expressed by Cassius, who is the dynamic personality among the rebels. His patriotism cannot be impugned, but it is not disinterested. He is mindful that Cæsar bears him hard, and his dislike of Cæsar is tainted with envy. His speech has occasionally a mordant, derisive tone, remotely suggestive of Iago's or Edmund's. Cæsar estimates him shrewdly, noting his supercilious mien, his humorless solemnity, his sharp intelligence.

For Cassius is a realist, tutored by reading and keen observation, "and he looks quite through the deeds of men" (I.ii.190 ff.). He perceives the need for winning Brutus to the cause, and the means by which he may be won. Yet he is mildly scornful of Brutus for being won. The situation, however, is to have its irony, for at crucial moments later on, Cassius yields his sounder judgment to the ill-calculated wishes of his friend. He sees the peril in allowing Antony to give the funeral oration, and he protests the error of marching to Philippi instead of waiting for the enemy at Sardis. The deference of Cassius to the nobility he feels in Brutus bespeaks a strain of gentleness in him, but it insures the final catastrophe.

The figure of Brutus, the tragically conscientious patriot, Shakespeare draws with sympathy. His integrity and gentility, to which Antony himself bears witness in an elegiac tribute at the close (V.v.68–75), are recognized by everybody and are expressed in all he says and does. To emphasize his goodness more fully, Shakespeare lets us see him in his private as well as his public relationships, giving us the touching pictures of his wife's solicitude and his expression of affection for her (II.i.233–303), and creating young Lucius to reveal his kindliness toward those who serve him. Studious by nature, and an adherent of the Stoic philosophy (IV.iii. 144–47), Brutus is not passion's slave, nor is he lightly to be moved in serious matters. He is above petty considerations and self-interest, but he is not without a dangerous kind of pride. Cassius plays upon this weakness deftly when he praises Brutus and reminds him of his illustrious ancestry (I.ii. 54–161). And when Brutus has cast the die and joined the conspiracy, this pride makes him perversely self-confident. As has been noted, some of his judgments are fatal, yet he never admits to himself the error of his ways. He dies in the high Roman fashion, "the noblest Roman of them all," but a little too aware of superior virtue.

Julius Cæsar is distinguished by a simplicity of outline and of language befitting its classical theme. There are no secondary elements in its rather austere design. The abundant eloquence is disciplined. The great speeches, memorable passages of poised and skillful rhetoric, invite declamation almost too readily. The art which here disguises art likewise restricts effects; the play rather thrills us mechanically than moves us deeply. Nevertheless, it looks forward directly to *Hamlet*, and Brutus the Roman, reflective, scrupulous, idealistic, is related to the Dane. But he never touches us so nearly.

THE TRAGEDY OF
JULIUS CÆSAR

[DRAMATIS PERSONÆ

JULIUS CÆSAR.
OCTAVIUS CÆSAR, ⎫
MARCUS ANTONIUS, ⎬ *triumvirs after the*
M. ÆMILIUS LEPIDUS, ⎭ *death of Julius Cæsar.*
CICERO, ⎫
PUBLIUS, ⎬ *senators.*
POPILIUS LENA, ⎭
MARCUS BRUTUS, ⎫
CASSIUS, ⎪
CASCA, ⎪
TREBONIUS, ⎬ *conspirators against Jul-*
CAIUS LIGARIUS, ⎪ *ius Cæsar.*
DECIUS BRUTUS, ⎪
METELLUS CIMBER, ⎪
CINNA, ⎭
FLAVIUS and MARULLUS, *tribunes.*
ARTEMIDORUS of Cnidos, *a teacher of Rhetoric.*
A Soothsayer.

CINNA, *a poet.*
Another Poet.
LUCILIUS, ⎫
TITINIUS, ⎪
MESSALA, ⎬ *friends to Brutus and Cassius.*
Young CATO, ⎪
VOLUMNIUS, ⎭
VARRO, ⎫
CLITUS, ⎪
CLAUDIUS, ⎬ *servants to Brutus.*
STRATO, ⎪
LUCIUS, ⎪
DARDANIUS, ⎭
PINDARUS, *servant to Cassius.*

CALPURNIA, *wife to Cæsar.*
PORTIA, *wife to Brutus.*

Senators, Citizens, Guards, Attendants, etc.

SCENE: *Rome; the neighbourhood of Sardis; the neighbourhood of Philippi.*]

ACT I

SCENE I. [*Rome. A street.*]

Enter FLAVIUS, MARULLUS, *and certain* COMMON-
ERS *over the stage.*

Flav. Hence! home, you idle creatures, get you
    home!
Is this a holiday? What! know you not,
Being mechanical, you ought not walk
Upon a labouring day without the sign
Of your profession? Speak, what trade art thou? 5
Car. Why, sir, a carpenter.
Mar. Where is thy leather apron and thy rule?
What dost thou with thy best apparel on?
You, sir, what trade are you?

Cob. Truly, sir, in respect of a fine workman, I am
but, as you would say, a cobbler. 11
Mar. But what trade art thou? Answer me
    directly.
Cob. A trade, sir, that I hope I may use with a
safe conscience; which is, indeed, sir, a mender of
bad soles. 15
[*Mar.*] What trade, thou knave? thou naughty
    knave, what trade?
Cob. Nay, I beseech you, sir, be not out with me;
yet, if you be out, sir, I can mend you.
Mar. What mean'st thou by that? Mend me,
thou saucy fellow! 21
Cob. Why, sir, cobble you.
Flav. Thou art a cobbler, art thou?
Cob. Truly, sir, all that I live by is with the awl.

Act I, sc. i, 3. **mechanical:** laborers. 10. **in respect of:** compared with. 11. **cobbler:** (1) mender of shoes, (2) botcher. 16. [*Mar.*] (Capell). *Flav.* F. **naughty:** worthless. 18. **out:** angry. 19. **you be out:** i.e., your shoes have holes.

I meddle with no tradesman's matters, nor 25
women's matters, but with all. I am, indeed, sir,
a surgeon to old shoes; when they are in great
danger, I re-cover them. As proper men as ever
trod upon neat's leather have gone upon my handiwork. 30
Flav. But wherefore art not in thy shop to-day?
Why dost thou lead these men about the streets?
Cob. Truly, sir, to wear out their shoes, to
get myself into more work. But, indeed, sir, we
make holiday, to see Cæsar and to rejoice in his
triumph. 36
Mar. Wherefore rejoice? What conquest brings
he home?
What tributaries follow him to Rome
To grace in captive bonds his chariot-wheels?
You blocks, you stones, you worse than senseless
things! 40
O you hard hearts, you cruel men of Rome,
Knew you not Pompey? Many a time and oft
Have you climb'd up to walls and battlements,
To tow'rs and windows, yea, to chimney-tops,
Your infants in your arms, and there have sat 45
The live-long day, with patient expectation,
To see great Pompey pass the streets of Rome;
And when you saw his chariot but appear
Have you not made an universal shout,
That Tiber trembled underneath her banks 50
To hear the replication of your sounds
Made in her concave shores?
And do you now put on your best attire?
And do you now cull out a holiday?
And do you now strew flowers in his way 55
That comes in triumph over Pompey's blood?
Be gone!
Run to your houses, fall upon your knees,
Pray to the gods to intermit the plague
That needs must light on this ingratitude. 60
Flav. Go, go, good countrymen, and, for this
fault,
Assemble all the poor men of your sort;
Draw them to Tiber banks, and weep your tears
Into the channel, till the lowest stream
Do kiss the most exalted shores of all. 65
          [*Exeunt all the Commoners.*
See, whe'er their basest metal be not mov'd;
They vanish tongue-tied in their guiltiness.
Go, you down that way towards the Capitol;
This way will I. Disrobe the images
If you do find them deck'd with ceremonies. 70
Mar. May we do so?
You know it is the feast of Lupercal.

Flav. It is no matter; let no images
Be hung with Cæsar's trophies. I'll about
And drive away the vulgar from the streets; 75
So do you too, where you perceive them thick.
These growing feathers pluck'd from Cæsar's wing
Will make him fly an ordinary pitch,
Who else would soar above the view of men
And keep us all in servile fearfulness. [*Exeunt.* 80

[SCENE II. *A public place.*]

Enter CÆSAR; ANTONY, *for the course;* CALPURNIA,
Portia, Decius, Cicero, BRUTUS, CASSIUS, *and*
CASCA; [*a great crowd following, among them*] *a*
SOOTHSAYER: *after them* Marullus *and* Flavius.

Cæs. Calpurnia!
Casca.   Peace, ho! Cæsar speaks.
Cæs.   Calpurnia!
Cal. Here, my lord.
Cæs. Stand you directly in Antonius' way
When he doth run his course. Antonius!
Ant. Cæsar, my lord? 5
Cæs. Forget not, in your speed, Antonius,
To touch Calpurnia; for our elders say,
The barren, touched in this holy chase,
Shake off their sterile curse.
Ant.   I shall remember:
When Cæsar says, "Do this," it is perform'd. 10
Cæs. Set on; and leave no ceremony out.
          [*Flourish.*
Sooth. Cæsar!
Cæs. Ha! who calls?
Casca. Bid every noise be still; peace yet again!
Cæs. Who is it in the press that calls on me? 15
I hear a tongue, shriller than all the music,
Cry "Cæsar!" Speak; Cæsar is turn'd to hear.
Sooth. Beware the ides of March.
Cæs.   What man is that?
Bru. A soothsayer bids you beware the ides of
March.
Cæs. Set him before me; let me see his face. 20
Cas. Fellow, come from the throng; look upon
Cæsar.
Cæs. What say'st thou to me now? Speak once
again.
Sooth. Beware the ides of March.
Cæs. He is a dreamer; let us leave him. Pass.
          [*Sennet. Exeunt all but Brutus and Cassius.*
Cas. Will you go see the order of the course? 25
Bru. Not I.
Cas. I pray you, do.
Bru. I am not gamesome; I do lack some part

28. **proper:** handsome. 29. **neat's leather:** cowhide. 36. **triumph:** triumphal procession. 56. **blood:** offspring. Cæsar had just defeated Pompey's sons. 59. **intermit:** withhold. 65. **most...all:** highest flood level. 66. **whe'er:** whether. *where* F. 70. **ceremonies:** festal ornaments. 72. **feast of Lupercal:** the Lupercalia, a festival honoring Lupercus, god of farmers. 75. **vulgar:** populace.
Sc. ii, S.D. *for the course:* ready for the race. See ll. 7-9. 18. **ides of March:** March 15th.

Of that quick spirit that is in Antony.
Let me not hinder, Cassius, your desires;   30
I'll leave you.
    Cas. Brutus, I do observe you now of late;
I have not from your eyes that gentleness
And show of love as I was wont to have.
You bear too stubborn and too strange a hand   35
Over your friend that loves you.
    Bru.   Cassius,
Be not deceiv'd. If I have veil'd my look,
I turn the trouble of my countenance
Merely upon myself. Vexed I am
Of late with passions of some difference,   40
Conceptions only proper to myself,
Which give some soil perhaps to my behaviours;
But let not therefore my good friends be griev'd —
Among which number, Cassius, be you one —
Nor construe any further my neglect,   45
Than that poor Brutus, with himself at war,
Forgets the shows of love to other men.
    Cas. Then, Brutus, I have much mistook your
     passion;
By means whereof this breast of mine hath buried
Thoughts of great value, worthy cogitations.   50
Tell me, good Brutus, can you see your face?
    Bru. No, Cassius; for the eye sees not itself
But by reflection, by some other things.
    Cas. 'Tis just;
And it is very much lamented, Brutus,   55
That you have no such mirrors as will turn
Your hidden worthiness into your eye
That you might see your shadow. I have heard
Where many of the best respect in Rome,
Except immortal Cæsar, speaking of Brutus   60
And groaning underneath this age's yoke,
Have wish'd that noble Brutus had his eyes.
    Bru. Into what dangers would you lead me,
     Cassius,
That you would have me seek into myself
For that which is not in me?   65
    Cas. Therefore, good Brutus, be prepar'd to
     hear;
And since you know you cannot see yourself
So well as by reflection, I, your glass,
Will modestly discover to yourself
That of yourself which you yet know not of.   70
And be not jealous on me, gentle Brutus.
Were I a common laugher, or did use
To stale with ordinary oaths my love
To every new protester; if you know
That I do fawn on men and hug them hard   75
And after scandal them, or if you know

That I profess myself in banqueting
To all the rout, then hold me dangerous.
                   [*Flourish and shout.*
    Bru. What means this shouting? I do fear, the
     people
Choose Cæsar for their king.
    Cas.   Ay, do you fear it?   80
Then must I think you would not have it so.
    Bru. I would not, Cassius; yet I love him well.
But wherefore do you hold me here so long?
What is it that you would impart to me?
If it be aught toward the general good,   85
Set honour in one eye and death i' th' other,
And I will look on both indifferently;
For let the gods so speed me as I love
The name of honour more than I fear death.
    Cas. I know that virtue to be in you, Brutus,   90
As well as I do know your outward favour.
Well, honour is the subject of my story.
I cannot tell what you and other men
Think of this life; but, for my single self,
I had as lief not be as live to be   95
In awe of such a thing as I myself.
I was born free as Cæsar, so were you;
We both have fed as well, and we can both
Endure the winter's cold as well as he;
For once, upon a raw and gusty day,   100
The troubled Tiber chafing with her shores,
Cæsar said to me, "Dar'st thou, Cassius, now
Leap in with me into this angry flood,
And swim to yonder point?" Upon the word,
Accoutred as I was, I plunged in   105
And bade him follow; so indeed he did.
The torrent roar'd, and we did buffet it
With lusty sinews, throwing it aside
And stemming it with hearts of controversy;
But ere we could arrive the point propos'd,   110
Cæsar cried, "Help me, Cassius, or I sink!"
I, as Æneas, our great ancestor,
Did from the flames of Troy upon his shoulder
The old Anchises bear, so from the waves of Tiber
Did I the tired Cæsar. And this man   115
Is now become a god, and Cassius is
A wretched creature, and must bend his body
If Cæsar carelessly but nod on him.
He had a fever when he was in Spain,
And when the fit was on him, I did mark   120
How he did shake — 'tis true, this god did shake.
His coward lips did from their colour fly,
And that same eye whose bend doth awe the world
Did lose his lustre; I did hear him groan.
Ay, and that tongue of his that bade the Romans

---

35. **stubborn:** rough.   38–39. **turn...myself:** keep the cause of my sad expression entirely to myself.   40. **of...difference:** conflicting.   42. **soil:** stain.   54. **just:** true.   58. **shadow:** image.   59. **respect:** repute.   69. **modestly:** without exaggeration.   74. **protester:** person professing friendship.   77. **profess myself:** profess friendship.   78. **rout:** crowd.   87. **indifferently:** impartially.   91. **favour:** appearance.   109. **of controversy:** excited by rivalry.   122. **His...fly.** The inversion makes clearer the pun on *colour* as (1) hue, (2) flag.   123. **bend:** glance.

Mark him and write his speeches in their books, 126
Alas, it cried, "Give me some drink, Titinius,"
As a sick girl. Ye gods, it doth amaze me
A man of such a feeble temper should
So get the start of the majestic world   130
And bear the palm alone.   [*Shout. Flourish.*

Bru. Another general shout!
I do believe that these applauses are
For some new honours that are heap'd on Cæsar.

Cas. Why, man, he doth bestride the narrow world
Like a Colossus, and we petty men   136
Walk under his huge legs, and peep about
To find ourselves dishonourable graves.
Men at some time are masters of their fates;
The fault, dear Brutus, is not in our stars, 140
But in ourselves, that we are underlings.
Brutus and Cæsar: what should be in that "Cæsar"?
Why should that name be sounded more than yours?
Write them together, yours is as fair a name;
Sound them, it doth become the mouth as well; 145
Weigh them, it is as heavy; conjure with 'em,
"Brutus" will start a spirit as soon as "Cæsar."
Now, in the names of all the gods at once,
Upon what meat doth this our Cæsar feed
That he is grown so great? Age, thou art sham'd!
Rome, thou hast lost the breed of noble bloods! 151
When went there by an age since the great flood
But it was fam'd with more than with one man?
When could they say, till now, that talk'd of Rome,
That her wide [walls] encompass'd but one man? 155
Now is it Rome indeed and room enough,
When there is in it but one only man.
O, you and I have heard our fathers say
There was a Brutus once that would have brook'd
Th' eternal devil to keep his state in Rome   160
As easily as a king.

Bru. That you do love me, I am nothing jealous;
What you would work me to, I have some aim.
How I have thought of this and of these times,
I shall recount hereafter; for this present,   165
I would not, so with love I might entreat you,
Be any further mov'd. What you have said
I will consider; what you have to say
I will with patience hear, and find a time
Both meet to hear and answer such high things. 170
Till then, my noble friend, chew upon this:
Brutus had rather be a villager
Than to repute himself a son of Rome
Under these hard conditions as this time
Is like to lay upon us.   175

Cas. I am glad that my weak words
Have struck but thus much show of fire from
    Brutus.

Re-enter CÆSAR *and his train.*

Bru. The games are done and Cæsar is returning.

Cas. As they pass by, pluck Casca by the sleeve;
And he will, after his sour fashion, tell you   180
What hath proceeded worthy note to-day.

Bru. I will do so. But, look you, Cassius,
The angry spot doth glow on Cæsar's brow,
And all the rest look like a chidden train.
Calpurnia's cheek is pale; and Cicero   185
Looks with such ferret and such fiery eyes
As we have seen him in the Capitol,
Being cross'd in conference by some senators.

Cas. Casca will tell us what the matter is.

Cæs. Antonius!   190

Ant. Cæsar?

Cæs. Let me have men about me that are fat,
Sleek-headed men and such as sleep o' nights.
Yond Cassius has a lean and hungry look,
He thinks too much; such men are dangerous. 195

Ant. Fear him not, Cæsar; he's not dangerous;
He is a noble Roman and well given.

Cæs. Would he were fatter! but I fear him not.
Yet if my name were liable to fear,
I do not know the man I should avoid   200
So soon as that spare Cassius. He reads much,
He is a great observer, and he looks
Quite through the deeds of men. He loves no plays
As thou dost, Antony; he hears no music;
Seldom he smiles, and smiles in such a sort   205
As if he mock'd himself and scorn'd his spirit
That could be mov'd to smile at anything.
Such men as he be never at heart's ease
Whiles they behold a greater than themselves,
And therefore are they very dangerous.   210
I rather tell thee what is to be fear'd
Than what I fear; for always I am Cæsar.
Come on my right hand, for this ear is deaf,
And tell me truly what thou think'st of him.
        [*Sennet. Exeunt Cæsar and all his train*
            [*but Casca*].

Casca. You pull'd me by the cloak; would you
speak with me?   215

Bru. Ay, Casca; tell us what hath chanc'd to-day
That Cæsar looks so sad.

Casca. Why, you were with him, were you not?

Bru. I should not then ask Casca what had
    chanc'd.   219

Casca. Why, there was a crown offer'd him; and
being offer'd him, he put it by with the back of his
hand, thus; and then the people fell a-shouting.

Bru. What was the second noise for?

Casca. Why, for that too.   225

147. **start**: raise. 152. **flood**: the classical flood, of which Deucalion was the Noah. 155. **[walls]** (Rowe). *walkes* F.
156. **Rome...room.** The words were pronounced alike. (Cf. III.i.288–89). 159. **a Brutus once.** Lucius Junius Brutus,
who drove out the Tarquins. **brook'd**: tolerated. 162. **nothing jealous**: by no means doubtful. 163. **aim**: guess.
186. **ferret**: red, angry (like a ferret's). 197. **given**: disposed. 199. **my name**: i.e., I myself. 217. **sad**: serious.

Cas. They shouted thrice; what was the last cry for?

Casca. Why, for that too.

Bru. Was the crown offer'd him thrice?

Casca. Ay, marry, was't, and he put it by thrice, every time gentler than other; and at every putting-by mine honest neighbours shouted. 231

Cas. Who offer'd him the crown?

Casca. Why, Antony.

Bru. Tell us the manner of it, gentle Casca. 234

Casca. I can as well be hang'd as tell the manner of it. It was mere foolery; I did not mark it. I saw Mark Antony offer him a crown — yet 'twas not a crown neither, 'twas one of these coronets — and, as I told you, he put it by once; but, for all that, to my thinking, he would fain have had it. 240 Then he offered it to him again; then he put it by again, but, to my thinking, he was very loath to lay his fingers off it. And then he offered it the third time; he put it the third time by; and still as he refus'd it, the rabblement hooted and 245 clapp'd their chapp'd hands and threw up their sweaty night-caps and uttered such a deal of stinking breath because Cæsar refus'd the crown, that it had almost choked Cæsar, for he swounded and fell down at it; and for mine own part, I durst not laugh, for fear of opening my lips and receiving the bad air. 252

Cas. But, soft, I pray you; what, did Cæsar swound?

Casca. He fell down in the market-place, and foam'd at mouth, and was speechless.

Bru. 'Tis very like; he hath the falling sickness.

Cas. No, Cæsar hath it not; but you and I And honest Casca, we have the falling sickness. 258

Casca. I know not what you mean by that, but I am sure Cæsar fell down. If the tag-rag people did not clap him and hiss him, according as he pleas'd and displeas'd them, as they use to do the players in the theatre, I am no true man.

Bru. What said he when he came unto himself? 264

Casca. Marry, before he fell down, when he perceiv'd the common herd was glad he refus'd the crown, he pluck'd me ope his doublet and offer'd them his throat to cut. An I had been a man of any occupation, if I would not have taken him at a word, I would I might go to hell among 270 the rogues. And so he fell. When he came to himself again, he said, if he had done or said any-thing amiss, he desir'd their worships to think it was his infirmity. Three or four wenches, where I stood, cried, "Alas, good soul!" and forgave him with all their hearts. But there's no heed to be 276

taken of them; if Cæsar had stabb'd their mothers, they would have done no less.

Bru. And after that, he came, thus sad, away?

Casca. Ay. 280

Cas. Did Cicero say anything?

Casca. Ay, he spoke Greek.

Cas. To what effect? 283

Casca. Nay, an I tell you that, I'll ne'er look you i' th' face again; but those that understood him smil'd at one another and shook their heads; but, for mine own part, it was Greek to me. I could tell you more news too. Marullus and Flavius, for pulling scarfs off Cæsar's images, are put to silence. Fare you well. There was more foolery yet, if I could remember it. 291

Cas. Will you sup with me to-night, Casca?

Casca. No, I am promis'd forth.

Cas. Will you dine with me to-morrow?

Casca. Ay, if I be alive and your mind hold and your dinner worth the eating. 296

Cas. Good; I will expect you.

Casca. Do so. Farewell, both.

[*Exit.*

Bru. What a blunt fellow is this grown to be! He was quick mettle when he went to school. 300

Cas. So is he now in execution Of any bold or noble enterprise, However he puts on this tardy form. This rudeness is a sauce to his good wit, Which gives men stomach to digest his words 305 With better appetite.

Bru. And so it is. For this time I will leave you; To-morrow, if you please to speak with me, I will come home to you; or, if you will, Come home to me, and I will wait for you. 310

Cas. I will do so; till then, think of the world.

[*Exit Brutus.*

Well, Brutus, thou art noble; yet, I see, Thy honourable metal may be wrought From that it is dispos'd; therefore it is meet That noble minds keep ever with their likes; 315 For who so firm that cannot be seduc'd? Cæsar doth bear me hard, but he loves Brutus. If I were Brutus now and he were Cassius, He should not humour me. I will this night, In several hands, in at his windows throw, 320 As if they came from several citizens, Writings all tending to the great opinion That Rome holds of his name; wherein obscurely Cæsar's ambition shall be glanced at; And after this let Cæsar seat him sure, 325 For we will shake him, or worse days endure.

[*Exit.*

256. **falling sickness**: epilepsy. 269. **man...occupation**: working man. 270. **at a word**: at his word. 289. **scarfs**: streamers, wreaths. 300. **quick mettle**: lively and gifted. 303. **tardy form**: sluggish manner. 314. **that...dispos'd**: its natural temper. 317. **hard**: i.e., ill-will. 320. **hands**: handwritings.

[SCENE III. *The same. A street.*]

Thunder and lightning. Enter [from opposite sides]
CASCA [*with his sword drawn*] *and* CICERO.

Cic. Good even, Casca; brought you Cæsar home?
Why are you breathless, and why stare you so?

Casca. Are not you mov'd, when all the sway of
    earth
Shakes like a thing unfirm? O Cicero,
I have seen tempests when the scolding winds   5
Have riv'd the knotty oaks, and I have seen
Th' ambitious ocean swell and rage and foam
To be exalted with the threat'ning clouds;
But never till to-night, never till now,
Did I go through a tempest dropping fire.   10
Either there is a civil strife in heaven,
Or else the world, too saucy with the gods,
Incenses them to send destruction.

Cic. Why, saw you anything more wonderful?

Casca. A common slave — you know him well
    by sight —   15
Held up his left hand, which did flame and burn
Like twenty torches join'd, and yet his hand,
Not sensible of fire, remain'd unscorch'd.
Besides — I ha' not since put up my sword —
Against the Capitol I met a lion,   20
Who glaz'd upon me, and went surly by
Without annoying me; and there were drawn
Upon a heap a hundred ghastly women,
Transformed with their fear, who swore they saw
Men all in fire walk up and down the streets.   25
And yesterday the bird of night did sit
Even at noon-day upon the market-place,
Hooting and shrieking.   When these prodigies
Do so conjointly meet, let not men say,
"These are their reasons; they are natural";   30
For, I believe, they are portentous things
Unto the climate that they point upon.

Cic. Indeed, it is a strange-disposed time;
But men may construe things after their fashion
Clean from the purpose of the things themselves. 35
Comes Cæsar to the Capitol to-morrow?

Casca. He doth; for he did bid Antonius
Send word to you he would be there to-morrow.

Cic. Good-night then, Casca; this disturbed sky
Is not to walk in.

Casca.   Farewell, Cicero.   40

[*Exit Cicero.*

Enter CASSIUS.

Cas. Who's there?

Casca.   A Roman.

Cas.   Casca, by your voice.

Casca. Your ear is good. Cassius, what night is
    this!

Cas. A very pleasing night to honest men.

Casca. Who ever knew the heavens menace so?

Cas. Those that have known the earth so full of
    faults.   45
For my part, I have walk'd about the streets,
Submitting me unto the perilous night,
And, thus unbraced, Casca, as you see,
Have bar'd my bosom to the thunder-stone;
And when the cross blue lightning seem'd to open
The breast of heaven, I did present myself   51
Even in the aim and very flash of it.

Casca. But wherefore did you so much tempt the
    heavens?
It is the part of men to fear and tremble
When the most mighty gods by tokens send   55
Such dreadful heralds to astonish us.

Cas. You are dull, Casca, and those sparks of life
That should be in a Roman you do want,
Or else you use not.   You look pale and gaze
And put on fear and cast yourself in wonder   60
To see the strange impatience of the heavens;
But if you would consider the true cause
Why all these fires, why all these gliding ghosts,
Why birds and beasts from quality and kind,
Why old men, fools, and children calculate,   65
Why all these things change from their ordinance
Their natures and preformed faculties
To monstrous quality, why, you shall find
That Heaven hath infus'd them with these spirits,
To make them instruments of fear and warning   70
Unto some monstrous state.
Now could I, Casca, name to thee a man
Most like this dreadful night,
That thunders, lightens, opens graves, and roars
As doth the lion in the Capitol, —   75
A man no mightier than thyself or me
In personal action, yet prodigious grown
And fearful, as these strange eruptions are.

Casca. 'Tis Cæsar that you mean; is it not, Cas-
    sius?

Cas. Let it be who it is; for Romans now   80
Have thews and limbs like to their ancestors,
But, woe the while! our fathers' minds are dead,
And we are govern'd with our mothers' spirits;
Our yoke and sufferance show us womanish.

Casca. Indeed, they say the senators to-morrow
Mean to establish Cæsar as a king;   86
And he shall wear his crown by sea and land,
In every place, save here in Italy.

Cas. I know where I will wear this dagger then:
Cassius from bondage will deliver Cassius.   90

Sc. iii, 21. **glaz'd:** stared. 22. **annoying:** harming. 26. **bird of night:** owl. 32. **climate:** region. 48. **unbraced:** with
doublet unfastened. 50. **cross:** zigzag. 64. **from . . . kind:** act contrary to their true nature. 65. **calculate:** forecast,
prophesy. 66. **ordinance:** established order. 67. **preformed:** original. 81. **thews:** sinews. 82. **woe the while:** woe to the
age. 84. **sufferance:** submission

Therein, ye gods, you make the weak most strong;
Therein, ye gods, you tyrants do defeat;
Nor stony tower, nor walls of beaten brass,
Nor airless dungeon, nor strong links of iron,
Can be retentive to the strength of spirit;   95
But life, being weary of these worldly bars,
Never lacks power to dismiss itself.
If I know this, know all the world besides,
That part of tyranny that I do bear
I can shake off at pleasure.   [*Thunder still.*
    Casca.   So can I;   100
So every bondman in his own hand bears
The power to cancel his captivity.
    Cas. And why should Cæsar be a tyrant then?
Poor man! I know he would not be a wolf,
But that he sees the Romans are but sheep;   105
He were no lion, were not Romans hinds.
Those that with haste will make a mighty fire
Begin it with weak straws: what trash is Rome,
What rubbish and what offal, when it serves
For the base matter to illuminate   110
So vile a thing as Cæsar! But, O grief,
Where hast thou led me? I perhaps speak this
Before a willing bondman; then I know
My answer must be made. But I am arm'd,
And dangers are to me indifferent.   115
    Casca. You speak to Casca, and to such a
       man
That is no fleering tell-tale. Hold, — my hand.
Be factious for redress of all these griefs,
And I will set this foot of mine as far
As who goes farthest.
    Cas.   There's a bargain made. 120
Now know you, Casca, I have mov'd already
Some certain of the noblest-minded Romans
To undergo with me an enterprise
Of honourable-dangerous consequence;
And I do know, by this they stay for me   125
In Pompey's Porch; for now, this fearful night,
There is no stir or walking in the streets;
And the complexion of the element
In favour's like the work we have in hand,
Most bloody, fiery, and most terrible.   130

Enter CINNA.

    Casca. Stand close a while, for here comes one in
       haste.
    Cas. 'Tis Cinna, I do know him by his gait;
He is a friend. Cinna, where haste you so?
    Cin. To find out you. Who's that? Metellus
       Cimber?
    Cas. No, it is Casca; one incorporate   135
To our attempts. Am I not stay'd for, Cinna?

    Cin. I am glad on't. What a fearful night is this!
There's two or three of us have seen strange sights.
    Cas. Am I not stay'd for? tell me.
    Cin.   Yes, you are.
O Cassius, if you could   140
But win the noble Brutus to our party —
    Cas. Be you content. Good Cinna, take this
       paper,
And look you lay it in the prætor's chair,
Where Brutus may but find it; and throw this
In at his window; set this up with wax   145
Upon old Brutus' statue. All this done,
Repair to Pompey's Porch, where you shall find us
Is Decius Brutus and Trebonius there?
    Cin. All but Metellus Cimber; and he's gone
To seek you at your house. Well, I will hie   150
And so bestow these papers as you bade me.
    Cas. That done, repair to Pompey's Theatre.
                              [*Exit Cinna.*
Come, Casca, you and I will yet ere day
See Brutus at his house. Three parts of him
Is ours already, and the man entire   155
Upon the next encounter yields him ours.
    Casca. O, he sits high in all the people's hearts;
And that which would appear offence in us,
His countenance, like richest alchemy,
Will change to virtue and to worthiness.   160
    Cas. Him and his worth and our great need of
       him
You have right well conceited. Let us go,
For it is after midnight; and ere day
We will awake him and be sure of him.   [*Exeunt.*

ACT II

[SCENE I. *Rome.*]

Enter BRUTUS *in his orchard.*

    Bru. What, Lucius, ho!
I cannot by the progress of the stars
Give guess how near to-day. Lucius, I say!
I would it were my fault to sleep so soundly.
When, Lucius, when! Awake, I say! What,
       Lucius!   5

Enter LUCIUS.

    Luc. Call'd you, my lord?
    Bru. Get me a taper in my study, Lucius.
When it is lighted, come and call me here.
    Luc. I will, my lord.   [*Exit*
    Bru. It must be by his death; and for my part, 10
I know no personal cause to spurn at him
But for the general. He would be crown'd:

---

106. **hinds:** female deer. 117. **fleering:** flattering. 118. **Be factious:** form a party. 126. **Pompey's Porch:** the portico
of Pompey's Theatre. 128. **element:** i.e., sky. 131. **close:** concealed. 143. **prætor's:** magistrate's. 162. **conceited:**
understood.
    Act II, sc. i, 12. **for the general:** for the sake of the public.

How that might change his nature, there's the
    question.
It is the bright day that brings forth the adder,
And that craves wary walking. Crown him?
    That —   15
And then, I grant, we put a sting in him
That at his will he may do danger with.
Th' abuse of greatness is when it disjoins
Remorse from power; and, to speak truth of Cæsar,
I have not known when his affections sway'd   20
More than his reason. But 'tis a common proof
That lowliness is young Ambition's ladder,
Whereto the climber-upward turns his face;
But when he once attains the upmost round,
He then unto the ladder turns his back,   25
Looks in the clouds, scorning the base degrees
By which he did ascend. So Cæsar may;
Then, lest he may, prevent. And, since the quarrel
Will bear no colour for the thing he is,
Fashion it thus: that what he is, augmented,   30
Would run to these and these extremities;
And therefore think him as a serpent's egg
Which, hatch'd, would, as his kind, grow mischievous,
And kill him in the shell.

Re-enter LUCIUS.

Luc. The taper burneth in your closet, sir.   35
Searching the window for a flint, I found
This paper, thus seal'd up; and I am sure
It did not lie there when I went to bed.
                   [Gives him the letter.
Bru. Get you to bed again; it is not day.
Is not to-morrow, boy, the [ides] of March?   40
Luc. I know not, sir.
Bru. Look in the calendar, and bring me word.
Luc. I will, sir.   *[Exit.*
Bru. The exhalations whizzing in the air
Gives so much light that I may read by them.   45
                [Opens the letter and reads.
"Brutus, thou sleep'st; awake, and see thyself!
Shall Rome, etc. Speak, strike, redress!"
"Brutus, thou sleep'st; awake!"
Such instigations have been often dropp'd
Where I have took them up.   50
"Shall Rome, etc." Thus must I piece it out:
Shall Rome stand under one man's awe? What,
    Rome?
My ancestors did from the streets of Rome
The Tarquin drive when he was call'd a king.
"Speak, strike, redress!" Am I entreated   55
To speak and strike? O Rome, I make thee promise,
If the redress will follow, thou receivest
Thy full petition at the hand of Brutus!

Re-enter LUCIUS.

Luc. Sir, March is wasted fifteen days.
                [Knocking within.
Bru. 'Tis good. Go to the gate; somebody
    knocks.   *[Exit Lucius.]* 60
Since Cassius first did whet me against Cæsar,
I have not slept.
Between the acting of a dreadful thing
And the first motion, all the interim is
Like a phantasma or a hideous dream.   65
The Genius and the mortal instruments
Are then in council; and the state of a man,
Like to a little kingdom, suffers then
The nature of an insurrection.

Re-enter LUCIUS.

Luc. Sir, 'tis your brother Cassius at the door,   70
Who doth desire to see you.
Bru.   Is he alone?
Luc. No, sir, there are more with him.
Bru.   Do you know them?
Luc. No, sir; their hats are pluck'd about their
    ears
And half their faces buried in their cloaks,
That by no means I may discover them   75
By any mark of favour.
Bru.   Let 'em enter.
                  [Exit Lucius.]
They are the faction. O Conspiracy,
Sham'st thou to show thy dangerous brow by night,
When evils are most free? O, then by day
Where wilt thou find a cavern dark enough   80
To mask thy monstrous visage? Seek none, Con-
    spiracy!
Hide it in smiles and affability;
For if thou path, thy native semblance on,
Not Erebus itself were dim enough
To hide thee from prevention.   85

Enter the conspirators, CASSIUS, CASCA, DECIUS,
    CINNA, METELLUS CIMBER, *and* TREBONIUS.

Cas. I think we are too bold upon your rest.
Good morrow, Brutus; do we trouble you?
Bru. I have been up this hour, awake all night.
Know I these men that come along with you?
Cas. Yes, every man of them; and no man here
But honours you; and every one doth wish   91
You had but that opinion of yourself
Which every noble Roman bears of you.
This is Trebonius.
Bru.   He is welcome hither.
Cas. This, Decius Brutus.
Bru.   He is welcome too.

---

19. **Remorse:** compassion, conscience. 20. **affections:** passions. 21. **proof:** experience. 29. **Will…is:** i.e., is not warranted by his conduct so far. 40. **[ides]** (Theobald). *first* F. 44. **exhalations:** meteors. 64. **motion:** proposal. 65. **phantasma:** hectic vision. 66–67. **The…council:** i.e., a man's mind deliberates over the deadly means at his disposal. 70. **brother.** Cassius had married a sister of Brutus. 83. **path:** goest about. 84. **Erebus:** Hades. 85. **prevention:** being forestalled.

Cas. This, Casca; this, Cinna; and this, Metel-
    lus Cimber.   96
Bru. They are all welcome.
What watchful cares do interpose themselves
Betwixt your eyes and night?
    Cas. Shall I entreat a word?   [*They whisper.* 100
Dec. Here lies the east; doth not the day break
    here?
Casca. No.
Cin. O, pardon, sir, it doth; and yon grey lines
That fret the clouds are messengers of day.
    Casca. You shall confess that you are both
    deceiv'd.   105
Here, as I point my sword, the sun arises,
Which is a great way growing on the south,
Weighing the youthful season of the year.
Some two months hence up higher toward the north
He first presents his fire; and the high east   110
Stands, as the Capitol, directly here.
    Bru. Give me your hands all over, one by one.
    Cas. And let us swear our resolution.
    Bru. No, not an oath! If not the face of men,
The sufferance of our souls, the time's abuse, —
If these be motives weak, break off betimes,   116
And every man hence to his idle bed;
So let high-sighted tyranny range on,
Till each man drop by lottery. But if these,
As I am sure they do, bear fire enough   120
To kindle cowards and to steel with valour
The melting spirits of women, then, countrymen,
What need we any spur but our own cause
To prick us to redress? what other bond
Than secret Romans, that have spoke the word   125
And will not palter? and what other oath
Than honesty to honesty engag'd
That this shall be, or we will fall for it?
Swear priests and cowards and men cautelous,
Old feeble carrions and such suffering souls   130
That welcome wrongs; unto bad causes swear
Such creatures as men doubt; but do not stain
The even virtue of our enterprise,
Nor th' insuppressive mettle of our spirits,
To think that or our cause or our performance   135
Did need an oath; when every drop of blood
That every Roman bears, and nobly bears,
Is guilty of a several bastardy,
If he do break the smallest particle
Of any promise that hath pass'd from him.   140
    Cas. But what of Cicero? Shall we sound him?
I think he will stand very strong with us.
    Casca. Let us not leave him out.
    Cin.   No, by no means.
    Met. O, let us have him, for his silver hairs

Will purchase us a good opinion   145
And buy men's voices to commend our deeds.
It shall be said his judgement rul'd our hands;
Our youths and wildness shall no whit appear,
But all be buried in his gravity.
    Bru. O, name him not; let us not break with him,
For he will never follow anything   151
That other men begin.
    Cas.   Then leave him out.
    Casca. Indeed he is not fit.
    Dec. Shall no man else be touch'd but only Cæsar?
    Cas. Decius, well urg'd. I think it is not meet,
Mark Antony, so well belov'd of Cæsar,   156
Should outlive Cæsar. We shall find of him
A shrewd contriver; and, you know, his means,
If he improve them, may well stretch so far
As to annoy us all; which to prevent,   160
Let Antony and Cæsar fall together.
    Bru. Our course will seem too bloody, Caius
    Cassius,
To cut the head off and then hack the limbs,
Like wrath in death and envy afterwards;
For Antony is but a limb of Cæsar.   165
Let's be sacrificers, but not butchers, Caius.
We all stand up against the spirit of Cæsar,
And in the spirit of men there is no blood;
O, that we then could come by Cæsar's spirit,
And not dismember Cæsar! But, alas,   170
Cæsar must bleed for it! And, gentle friends,
Let's kill him boldly, but not wrathfully;
Let's carve him as a dish fit for the gods,
Not hew him as a carcass fit for hounds;
And let our hearts, as subtle masters do,   175
Stir up their servants to an act of rage,
And after seem to chide 'em. This shall make
Our purpose necessary and not envious;
Which so appearing to the common eyes,
We shall be call'd purgers, not murderers.   180
And for Mark Antony, think not of him;
For he can do no more than Cæsar's arm
When Cæsar's head is off.
    Cas.   Yet I fear him;
For in the ingrafted love he bears to Cæsar —
    Bru. Alas, good Cassius, do not think of him. 185
If he love Cæsar, all that he can do
Is to himself — take thought and die for Cæsar;
And that were much he should, for he is given
To sports, to wildness, and much company.
    Treb. There is no fear in him; let him not die; 190
For he will live, and laugh at this hereafter.
                       [*Clock strikes.*
    Bru. Peace! count the clock.
    Cas.   The clock hath stricken three.

107. **growing on:** toward.   118. **high-sighted:** arrogant.   127. **honesty:** personal honor.   129. **cautelous:** deceitful. 130. **suffering:** submissive.   134. **insuppressive:** irrepressible.   150. **break with:** broach the matter to him.   157. **of:** in. 160. **annoy:** injure.   164. **envy:** malice (cf. *envious,* l. 178).   176. **their servants:** i.e., our hands.   187. **take thought:** become melancholy.   188. **were ... should:** is a great deal to expect.   190. **no fear:** nothing to fear.

Treb. 'Tis time to part.

Cas.   But it is doubtful yet
Whether Cæsar will come forth to-day or no;
For he is superstitious grown of late,   195
Quite from the main opinion he held once
Of fantasy, of dreams, and ceremonies.
It may be these apparent prodigies,
The unaccustom'd terror of this night,
And the persuasion of his augurers   200
May hold him from the Capitol to-day.

Dec. Never fear that. If he be so resolv'd,
I can o'ersway him; for he loves to hear
That unicorns may be betray'd with trees,
And bears with glasses, elephants with holes,   205
Lions with toils, and men with flatterers;
But when I tell him he hates flatterers
He says he does, being then most flattered.
Let me work;
For I can give his humour the true bent,   210
And I will bring him to the Capitol.

Cas. Nay, we will all of us be there to fetch him.

Bru. By the eighth hour; is that the uttermost?

Cin. Be that the uttermost, and fail not then.

Met. Caius Ligarius doth bear Cæsar hard,   215
Who rated him for speaking well of Pompey.
I wonder none of you have thought of him.

Bru. Now, good Metellus, go along by him.
He loves me well, and I have given him reasons;
Send him but hither, and I'll fashion him.   220

Cas. The morning comes upon 's. We'll leave you, Brutus,
And, friends, disperse yourselves; but all remember
What you have said, and show yourselves true
    Romans.

Bru. Good gentlemen, look fresh and merrily.
Let not our looks put on our purposes,   225
But bear it as our Roman actors do,
With untir'd spirits and formal constancy.
And so good morrow to you every one.

                    [*Exeunt all but Brutus.*
Boy! Lucius! Fast asleep? It is no matter;
Enjoy the honey-heavy dew of slumber.   230
Thou hast no figures nor no fantasies
Which busy care draws in the brains of men;
Therefore thou sleep'st so sound.

                    Enter PORTIA.

Por.   Brutus, my lord!

Bru. Portia, what mean you? Wherefore rise
    you now?
It is not for your health thus to commit   235
Your weak condition to the raw cold morning.

Por. Nor for yours neither. You've ungently,
    Brutus,
Stole from my bed; and yesternight at supper
You suddenly arose and walk'd about,
Musing and sighing, with your arms across;   240
And when I ask'd you what the matter was,
You star'd upon me with ungentle looks.
I urg'd you further; then you scratch'd your head
And too impatiently stamp'd with your foot.
Yet I insisted; yet you answer'd not,   245
But with an angry [wafture] of your hand
Gave sign for me to leave you. So I did,
Fearing to strengthen that impatience
Which seem'd too much enkindled, and withal
Hoping it was but an effect of humour,   250
Which sometime hath his hour with every man.
It will not let you eat, nor talk, nor sleep,
And could it work so much upon your shape
As it hath much prevail'd on your condition,
I should not know you, Brutus. Dear my lord,   255
Make me acquainted with your cause of grief.

Bru. I am not well in health, and that is all.

Por. Brutus is wise, and, were he not in health,
He would embrace the means to come by it.

Bru. Why, so I do. Good Portia, go to bed.   260

Por. Is Brutus sick? and is it physical
To walk unbraced and suck up the humours
Of the dank morning? What, is Brutus sick,
And will he steal out of his wholesome bed
To dare the vile contagion of the night,   265
And tempt the rheumy and unpurged air
To add unto his sickness? No, my Brutus;
You have some sick offence within your mind,
Which, by the right and virtue of my place,
I ought to know of; and upon my knees   270
I charm you, by my once commended beauty,
By all your vows of love, and that great vow
Which did incorporate and make us one,
That you unfold to me, yourself, your half,
Why you are heavy, and what men to-night   275
Have had resort to you; for here have been
Some six or seven, who did hide their faces
Even from darkness.

Bru.   Kneel not, gentle Portia.

Por. I should not need, if you were gentle Brutus.
Within the bond of marriage, tell me, Brutus,   280
Is it excepted I should know no secrets
That appertain to you? Am I yourself
But, as it were, in sort or limitation,
To keep with you at meals, comfort your bed,
And talk to you sometimes? Dwell I but in the
    suburbs   285

196. **main:** strong. 197. **ceremonies,** such as those performed by augurs. 198. **apparent:** manifest. 204. **unicorns . . . trees.** It was believed that a unicorn could be caught if, when it charged, the hunter jumped behind a tree, making it bury its horn in the trunk. 205. **glasses:** mirrors. **holes:** pitfalls. 206. **toils:** nets. 218. **by him:** by his house. 225. **put on:** reveal. 231. **figures:** imaginings. 236. **condition:** constitution. 237. **ungently:** unkindly. 246. **[wafture]** (Rowe): waving. *wafter* F. 261. **physical:** good for the health. 266. **rheumy:** dank. **unpurged:** not yet purified by the sun. 271. **charm:** conjure. 275. **heavy:** depressed. 283. **in . . . limitation:** in a limited manner only.

Of your good pleasure? If it be no more,
Portia is Brutus' harlot, not his wife.
  Bru. You are my true and honourable wife,
As dear to me as are the ruddy drops
That visit my sad heart.   290
  Por. If this were true, then should I know this
    secret.
I grant I am a woman; but withal
A woman that Lord Brutus took to wife.
I grant I am a woman; but withal
A woman well-reputed, Cato's daughter.   295
Think you I am no stronger than my sex,
Being so father'd and so husbanded?
Tell me your counsels, I will not disclose 'em.
I have made strong proof of my constancy,
Giving myself a voluntary wound   300
Here, in the thigh; can I bear that with patience,
And not my husband's secrets?
  Bru.   O ye gods!
Render me worthy of this noble wife!
                 [*Knocking within.*
Hark, hark! one knocks. Portia, go in a while,
And by and by thy bosom shall partake   305
The secrets of my heart.
All my engagements I will construe to thee,
All the charactery of my sad brows.
Leave me with haste.
                  [*Exit Portia.*
        Lucius, who's that knocks?

      Re-enter LUCIUS *with* LIGARIUS.

  Luc. Here is a sick man that would speak with
    you.   310
  Bru. Caius Ligarius, that Metellus spake of.
Boy, stand aside. Caius Ligarius! how?
  Lig. Vouchsafe good morrow from a feeble
    tongue.
  Bru. O, what a time have you chose out, brave
    Caius,
To wear a kerchief! Would you were not sick!   315
  Lig. I am not sick, if Brutus have in hand
Any exploit worthy the name of honour.
  Bru. Such an exploit have I in hand, Ligarius,
Had you a healthful ear to hear of it.
  Lig. By all the gods that Romans bow before,
I here discard my sickness! Soul of Rome!   322
Brave son, deriv'd from honourable loins!
Thou, like an exorcist, hast conjur'd up
My mortified spirit. Now bid me run,
And I will strive with things impossible;   325
Yea, get the better of them. What's to do?
  Bru. A piece of work that will make sick men
    whole.

  Lig. But are not some whole that we must make
    sick?
  Bru. That must we also. What it is, my Caius,
I shall unfold to thee as we are going   330
To whom it must be done.
  Lig.   Set on your foot,
And with a heart new-fir'd I follow you,
To do I know not what; but it sufficeth
That Brutus leads me on.   [*Thunder.*
  Bru.   Follow me, then.
                  [*Exeunt.*

     [SCENE II. *Cæsar's house.*]

 Thunder and lightning. Enter CÆSAR, *in his
          night-gown.*

  Cæs. Nor heaven nor earth have been at peace
    to-night.
Thrice hath Calpurnia in her sleep cried out,
"Help! ho! they murder Cæsar!" Who's within?

         Enter a SERVANT.

  Serv. My lord?
  Cæs. Go bid the priests do present sacrifice   5
And bring me their opinions of success.
  Serv. I will, my lord.   [*Exit.*

        Enter CALPURNIA.

  Cal. What mean you, Cæsar? Think you to
    walk forth?
You shall not stir out of your house to-day.
  Cæs. Cæsar shall forth. The things that
    threaten'd me   10
Ne'er look'd but on my back; when they shall see
The face of Cæsar, they are vanished.
  Cal. Cæsar, I never stood on ceremonies,
Yet now they fright me. There is one within,
Besides the things that we have heard and seen, 15
Recounts most horrid sights seen by the watch.
A lioness hath whelped in the streets,
And graves have yawn'd and yielded up their dead;
Fierce fiery warriors [fought] upon the clouds
In ranks and squadrons and right form of war,   20
Which drizzl'd blood upon the Capitol;
The noise of battle hurtled in the air,
Horses [did] neigh, and dying men did groan,
And ghosts did shriek and squeal about the streets.
O Cæsar! these things are beyond all use,   25
And I do fear them.
  Cæs.   What can be avoided
Whose end is purpos'd by the mighty gods?
Yet Cæsar shall go forth; for these predictions
Are to the world in general as to Cæsar.

---

  298. counsels: secrets. **308. charactery:** meaning (lit., handwriting). **313. Vouchsafe:** deign to accept. **324. mortified:** deadened.
  Sc. ii, S.D. **night-gown:** dressing gown. **5. present:** immediate. **6. success:** the outcome. **13. stood on ceremonies:** heeded omens. **19. [fought]** (Grant White). *fight* F. **23. [did]** F₂. *do* F₁. **25. use:** custom.

Cal. When beggars die there are no comets seen.
The heavens themselves blaze forth the death of
   princes,   31
Cæs. Cowards die many times before their
   deaths;
The valiant never taste of death but once.
Of all the wonders that I yet have heard,
It seems to me most strange that men should fear, 35
Seeing that death, a necessary end,
Will come when it will come.

Re-enter SERVANT.

               What say the augurers?
Serv. They would not have you to stir forth to-
   day.
Plucking the entrails of an offering forth,
They could not find a heart within the beast.   40
Cæs. The gods do this in shame of cowardice;
Cæsar should be a beast without a heart,
If he should stay at home to-day for fear.
No, Cæsar shall not; Danger knows full well
That Cæsar is more dangerous than he.   45
We [are] two lions litter'd in one day,
And I the elder and more terrible;
And Cæsar shall go forth.
Cal.   Alas, my lord,
Your wisdom is consum'd in confidence.
Do not go forth to-day; call it my fear   50
That keeps you in the house, and not your own.
We'll send Mark Antony to the Senate House,
And he shall say you are not well to-day.
Let me, upon my knee, prevail in this.
Cæs. Mark Antony shall say I am not well;   55
And, for thy humour, I will stay at home.

Enter DECIUS.

Here's Decius Brutus, he shall tell them so.
Dec. Cæsar, all hail! good morrow, worthy
   Cæsar;
I come to fetch you to the Senate House.
Cæs. And you are come in very happy time   60
To bear my greetings to the Senators
And tell them that I will not come to-day.
Cannot, is false, and that I dare not, falser;
I will not come to-day.   Tell them so, Decius.
Cal. Say he is sick.
Cæs.   Shall Cæsar send a lie?   65
Have I in conquest stretch'd mine arm so far,
To be afeard to tell greybeards the truth?
Decius, go tell them Cæsar will not come.
Dec. Most mighty Cæsar, let me know some
   cause,
Lest I be laugh'd at when I tell them so.   70
Cæs. The cause is in my will; I will not come;
That is enough to satisfy the Senate.

But for your private satisfaction,
Because I love you, I will let you know:
Calpurnia here, my wife, stays me at home.   75
She dreamt to-night she saw my statuë,
Which, like a fountain with an hundred spouts,
Did run pure blood; and many lusty Romans
Came smiling and did bathe their hands in it;
And these does she apply for warnings and portents
And evils imminent, and on her knee   81
Hath begg'd that I will stay at home to-day.
   Dec. This dream is all amiss interpreted;
It was a vision fair and fortunate.
Your statue spouting blood in many pipes,   85
In which so many smiling Romans bath'd,
Signifies that from you great Rome shall suck
Reviving blood, and that great men shall press
For tinctures, stains, relics, and cognizance.
This by Calpurnia's dream is signified.   90
   Cæs. And this way have you well expounded it.
   Dec. I have, when you have heard what I can say;
And know it now.   The Senate have concluded
To give this day a crown to mighty Cæsar.
If you shall send them word you will not come, 95
Their minds may change.   Besides, it were a mock
Apt to be render'd, for some one to say,
"Break up the Senate till another time,
When Cæsar's wife shall meet with better dreams."
If Cæsar hide himself, shall they not whisper, 100
"Lo, Cæsar is afraid"?
Pardon me, Cæsar; for my dear dear love
To your proceeding bids me tell you this;
And reason to my love is liable.
   Cæs. How foolish do your fears seem now, Cal-
   purnia!   105
I am ashamed I did yield to them.
Give me my robe, for I will go.

Enter PUBLIUS, BRUTUS, LIGARIUS, METELLUS,
CASCA, TREBONIUS, *and* CINNA.

And look where Publius is come to fetch me.
   Pub. Good morrow, Cæsar.
   Cæs.   Welcome, Publius.
What, Brutus, are you stirr'd so early too?   110
Good morrow, Casca.   Caius Ligarius,
Cæsar was ne'er so much your enemy
As that same ague which hath made you lean.
What is't o'clock?
   Bru.   Cæsar, 'tis strucken eight.
   Cæs. I thank you for your pains and courtesy.

Enter ANTONY.

See! Antony, that revels long o' nights,   116
Is notwithstanding up.   Good morrow, Antony.
   Ant. So to most noble Cæsar.
   Cæs.   Bid them prepare within;

---

46. **[are]** (Capell).   *heare* F.   49. **wisdom... confidence:** over-confidence gets the better of wisdom.   56. **humour:** whim.
75. **stays:** detains.   76. **to-night:** last night.   89. **cognizance:** tokens.   103. **proceeding:** career.   104. **liable:** subservient.

I am to blame to be thus waited for.
Now, Cinna; now, Metellus.   What, Trebonius!
I have an hour's talk in store for you;   121
Remember that you call on me to-day;
Be near me, that I may remember you.
  Treb. Cæsar, I will; [*aside*] and so near will I be,
That your best friends shall wish I had been further.
  Cæs. Good friends, go in, and taste some wine
with me;   126
And we, like friends, will straightway go together.
  Bru. [*Aside.*] That every like is not the same, O
Cæsar,
The heart of Brutus earns to think upon! [*Exeunt.*

[SCENE III. *A street near the Capitol.*]

Enter ARTEMIDORUS [*reading a paper*].

  Art. "Cæsar, beware of Brutus; take heed of
Cassius; come not near Casca; have an eye to Cin-
na; trust not Trebonius; mark well Metellus Cim-
ber: Decius Brutus loves thee not: thou hast wrong'd
Caius Ligarius. There is but one mind in all these   5
men, and it is bent against Cæsar. If thou beest
not immortal, look about you; security gives way to
conspiracy. The mighty gods defend thee! Thy
lover,
ARTEMIDORUS." 10
Here will I stand till Cæsar pass along,
And as a suitor will I give him this.
My heart laments that virtue cannot live
Out of the teeth of emulation.
If thou read this, O Cæsar, thou mayst live;   15
If not, the Fates with traitors do contrive. [*Exit.*

[SCENE IV. *Another part of the same street,
before the house of Brutus.*]

Enter PORTIA *and* LUCIUS.

  Por. I prithee, boy, run to the Senate House;
Stay not to answer me, but get thee gone.
Why dost thou stay?
  Luc.   To know my errand, madam.
  Por. I would have had thee there and here again
Ere I can tell thee what thou shouldst do there.   5
O constancy, be strong upon my side,
Set a huge mountain 'tween my heart and tongue!
I have a man's mind, but a woman's might.
How hard it is for women to keep counsel!
Art thou here yet?
  Luc.   Madam, what should I do?   10
Run to the Capitol, and nothing else?
And so return to you, and nothing else?
  Por. Yes, bring me word, boy, if thy lord look
well,

For he went sickly forth; and take good note
What Cæsar doth, what suitors press to him.   15
Hark, boy! what noise is that?
  Luc. I hear none, madam.
  Por.   Prithee, listen well;
I heard a bustling rumour, like a fray,
And the wind brings it from the Capitol.
  Luc. Sooth, madam, I hear nothing.   20

Enter the SOOTHSAYER.

  Por. Come hither, fellow; which way hast thou
been?
  Sooth. At mine own house, good lady.
  Por. What is't o'clock?
  Sooth.   About the ninth hour, lady.
  Por. Is Cæsar yet gone to the Capitol?
  Sooth. Madam, not yet; I go to take my stand, 25
To see him pass on to the Capitol.
  Por. Thou hast some suit to Cæsar, hast thou
not?
  Sooth. That I have, lady; if it will please Cæsar
To be so good to Cæsar as to hear me,
I shall beseech him to befriend himself.   30
  Por. Why, know'st thou any harm 's intended
towards him?
  Sooth. None that I know will be, much that I
fear may chance.
Good morrow to you.   Here the street is narrow;
The throng that follows Cæsar at the heels,
Of senators, of prætors, common suitors,   35
Will crowd a feeble man almost to death.
I'll get me to a place more void, and there
Speak to great Cæsar as he comes along.   [*Exit.*
  Por. I must go in.   Ay me, how weak a thing
The heart of woman is!   O Brutus,   40
The heavens speed thee in thine enterprise!
[*To herself.*] Sure, the boy heard me. [*To Lucius.*]
Brutus hath a suit
That Cæsar will not grant.   O, I grow faint.
Run, Lucius, and commend me to my lord;
Say I am merry.   Come to me again   45
And bring me word what he doth say to thee.
[*Exeunt* [*severally*].

ACT III

[SCENE I. *Rome.   Before the Capitol.*]

[*A crowd of people; among them*] ARTEMIDORUS
and the SOOTHSAYER. *Flourish. Enter* CÆSAR,
BRUTUS, CASSIUS, CASCA, DECIUS, METELLUS,
TREBONIUS, CINNA, ANTONY, LEPIDUS, PUB-
LIUS [*and* POPILIUS].

  Cæs. [*To the Soothsayer.*] The ides of **March** are
come.

128. **every ... same:** every apparent friend is not one in fact.   129. **earns:** grieves.
Sc. iii, 7. **security:** over-confidence.   14. **emulation:** envy.
Sc. iv, 6. **constancy:** firmness.   45. **merry:** in good spirits.

Sooth. Ay, Cæsar; but not gone.
Art. Hail, Cæsar! read this schedule.
Dec. Trebonius doth desire you to o'er-read,
At your best leisure, this his humble suit.   5
Art. O Cæsar, read mine first; for mine's a suit
That touches Cæsar nearer.   Read it, great Cæsar.
Cæs. What touches us ourself shall be last serv'd.
Art. Delay not, Cæsar; read it instantly.
Cæs. What, is the fellow mad?
Pub.   Sirrah, give place.
Cas. What, urge you your petitions in the
    street?   11
Come to the Capitol.
    [*Cæsar goes up to the Senate-House, the
        rest following.*]
Pop. I wish your enterprise to-day may thrive.
Cas. What enterprise, Popilius?
Pop.   Fare you well.
    [*Advances to Cæsar.*]
Bru. What said Popilius Lena?   15
Cas. He wish'd to-day our enterprise might
    thrive.
I fear our purpose is discovered.
Bru. Look, how he makes to Cæsar; mark him.
Cas. Casca, be sudden, for we fear prevention.
Brutus, what shall be done?   If this be known,   20
Cassius or Cæsar never shall turn back,
For I will slay myself.
Bru.   Cassius, be constant;
Popilius Lena speaks not of our purposes,
For, look, he smiles, and Cæsar doth not change.
Cas. Trebonius knows his time; for, look you,
    Brutus,   25
He draws Mark Antony out of the way.
    [*Exeunt Antony and Trebonius.*]
Dec. Where is Metellus Cimber?   Let him go
And presently prefer his suit to Cæsar.
Bru. He is address'd; press near and second him.
Cin. Casca, you are the first that rears your
    hand.   30
Cæs. Are we all ready?   What is now amiss
That Cæsar and his senate must redress?
Met. Most high, most mighty, and most puissant
    Cæsar,
Metellus Cimber throws before thy seat
An humble heart, —   [*Kneeling.*]
Cæs.   I must prevent thee, Cimber.
These couchings and these lowly courtesies   36
Might fire the blood of ordinary men,
And turn pre-ordinance and first decree
Into the [law] of children.   Be not fond
To think that Cæsar bears such rebel blood   40
That will be thaw'd from the true quality

With that which melteth fools; I mean, sweet
    words,
Low-crooked curtsies and base spaniel-fawning.
Thy brother by decree is banished;
If thou dost bend and pray and fawn for him,   45
I spurn thee like a cur out of my way.
Know, Cæsar doth not wrong, nor without cause
Will he be satisfied.
Met. Is there no voice more worthy than my
    own,
To sound more sweetly in great Cæsar's ear   50
For the repealing of my banish'd brother?
Bru. I kiss thy hand, but not in flattery, Cæsar;
Desiring thee that Publius Cimber may
Have an immediate freedom of repeal.
Cæs. What, Brutus!
Cas.   Pardon, Cæsar; Cæsar, pardon!   55
As low as to thy foot doth Cassius fall,
To beg enfranchisement for Publius Cimber.
Cæs. I could well be mov'd, if I were as you;
If I could pray to move, prayers would move
    me;
But I am constant as the northern star,   60
Of whose true-fix'd and resting quality
There is no fellow in the firmament.
The skies are painted with unnumb'red sparks,
They are all fire and every one doth shine;
But there's but one in all doth hold his place.   65
So in the world; 'tis furnish'd well with men,
And men are flesh and blood, and apprehensive;
Yet in the number I do know but one
That unassailable holds on his rank,
Unshak'd of motion; and that I am he,   70
Let me a little show it, even in this:
That I was constant Cimber should be banish'd,
And constant do remain to keep him so.
Cin. O Cæsar, —
Cæs.   Hence! wilt thou lift up Olympus?
Dec. Great Cæsar, —
Cæs.   Doth not Brutus bootless kneel?
Casca. Speak, hands, for me!   76
    [*They stab Cæsar.*
Cæs. Et tu Brute!   Then fall, Cæsar!   [*Dies.*
Cin. Liberty!   Freedom!   Tyranny is dead!
Run hence, proclaim, cry it about the streets.
Cas. Some to the common pulpits, and cry out,   80
"Liberty, freedom, and enfranchisement!"
Bru. People and senators, be not affrighted;
Fly not; stand still; ambition's debt is paid.
Casca. Go to the pulpit, Brutus.
Dec.   And Cassius too.
Bru. Where's Publius?   85
Cin. Here, quite confounded with this mutiny.

Act III, sc. i, 3. **schedule:** document.   28. **presently prefer:** at once present.   29. **address'd:** ready.   36. **couchings:** prostrations.   38. **first:** previous.   39. **[law]** (Johnson conj.).   *lane* F.   40. **rebel:** i.e., ready to violate law.   51. **repealing:** recall.   54. **freedom of:** permission for.   61. **resting quality:** stability.   67. **apprehensive:** intelligent.   80. **common pulpits:** public platforms.   86. **mutiny:** uproar.

Met. Stand fast together, lest some friend of Cæsar's
Should chance —

Bru. Talk not of standing. Publius, good cheer;
There is no harm intended to your person,   90
Nor to no Roman else. So tell them, Publius.

Cas. And leave us, Publius; lest that the people,
Rushing on us, should do your age some mischief.

Bru. Do so: and let no man abide this deed,
But we the doers.

Re-enter TREBONIUS.

Cas.   Where is Antony?   95
Treb. Fled to his house amaz'd.
Men, wives, and children stare, cry out, and run,
As it were doomsday.

Bru.   Fates, we will know your pleasures.
That we shall die, we know; 'tis but the time
And drawing days out, that men stand upon.   100

Cas. Why, he that cuts off twenty years of life
Cuts off so many years of fearing death.

Bru. Grant that, and then is death a benefit;
So are we Cæsar's friends, that have abridg'd
His time of fearing death. Stoop, Romans, stoop,
And let us bathe our hands in Cæsar's blood   106
Up to the elbows, and besmear our swords;
Then walk we forth, even to the market-place,
And, waving our red weapons o'er our heads,
Let's all cry, "Peace, freedom, and liberty!"   110

Cas. Stoop, then, and wash. How many ages hence
Shall this our lofty scene be acted over
In states unborn and accents yet unknown!

Bru. How many times shall Cæsar bleed in sport,
That now on Pompey's basis lies along   115
No worthier than the dust!

Cas.   So oft as that shall be,
So often shall the knot of us be call'd
The men that gave their country liberty.

Dec. What, shall we forth?

Cas.   Ay, every man away.
Brutus shall lead; and we will grace his heels   120
With the most boldest and best hearts of Rome.

Enter a SERVANT.

Bru. Soft! who comes here? A friend of Antony's.

Serv. Thus, Brutus, did my master bid me kneel,
Thus did Mark Antony bid me fall down;
And, being prostrate, thus he bade me say: 125
Brutus is noble, wise, valiant, and honest;
Cæsar was mighty, bold, royal, and loving;
Say I love Brutus, and I honour him;

Say I fear'd Cæsar, honour'd him, and lov'd him.
If Brutus will vouchsafe that Antony   130
May safely come to him, and be resolv'd
How Cæsar hath deserv'd to lie in death,
Mark Antony shall not love Cæsar dead
So well as Brutus living; but will follow
The fortunes and affairs of noble Brutus   135
Thorough the hazards of this untrod state
With all true faith. So says my master Antony.

Bru. Thy master is a wise and valiant Roman;
I never thought him worse.
Tell him, so please him come unto this place,   140
He shall be satisfied; and, by my honour,
Depart untouch'd.

Serv.   I'll fetch him presently. [*Exit.*

Bru. I know that we shall have him well to friend.

Cas. I wish we may; but yet have I a mind
That fears him much, and my misgiving still   145
Falls shrewdly to the purpose.

Re-enter ANTONY.

Bru. But here comes Antony. Welcome, Mark Antony!

Ant. O mighty Cæsar! dost thou lie so low?
Are all thy conquests, glories, triumphs, spoils,
Shrunk to this little measure? Fare thee well!   150
I know not, gentlemen, what you intend,
Who else must be let blood, who else is rank;
If I myself, there is no hour so fit
As Cæsar's death's hour, nor no instrument
Of half that worth as those your swords, made rich   155
With the most noble blood of all this world.
I do beseech ye, if you bear me hard,
Now, whilst your purpled hands do reek and smoke,
Fulfil your pleasure. Live a thousand years,
I shall not find myself so apt to die;   160
No place will please me so, no mean of death,
As here by Cæsar, and by you cut off,
The choice and master spirits of this age.

Bru. O Antony, beg not your death of us.
Though now we must appear bloody and cruel,   165
As by our hands and this our present act
You see we do, yet see you but our hands
And this the bleeding business they have done.
Our hearts you see not; they are pitiful;
And pity to the general wrong of Rome —   170
As fire drives out fire, so pity pity —
Hath done this deed on Cæsar. For your part,
To you our swords have leaden points, Mark Antony;
Our arms, in strength of malice, and our hearts

Of brothers' temper, do receive you in   175
With all kind love, good thoughts, and reverence.
   Cas. Your voice shall be as strong as any man's
In the disposing of new dignities.
   Bru. Only be patient till we have appeas'd
The multitude, beside themselves with fear,   180
And then we will deliver you the cause
Why I, that did love Cæsar when I struck him,
Have thus proceeded.
   Ant.   I doubt not of your wisdom.
Let each man render me his bloody hand.
First, Marcus Brutus, will I shake with you;   185
Next, Caius Cassius, do I take your hand;
Now, Decius Brutus, yours; now yours, Metellus;
Yours, Cinna; and, my valiant Casca, yours;
Though last, not least in love, yours, good Tre-
     bonius.
Gentlemen all, — alas, what shall I say?   190
My credit now stands on such slippery ground
That one of two bad ways you must conceit me,
Either a coward or a flatterer.
That I did love thee, Cæsar, O, 'tis true;
If then thy spirit look upon us now,   195
Shall it not grieve thee dearer than thy death,
To see thy Antony making his peace,
Shaking the bloody fingers of thy foes,
Most noble! in the presence of thy corse?
Had I as many eyes as thou hast wounds,   200
Weeping as fast as they stream forth thy blood,
It would become me better than to close
In terms of friendship with thine enemies.
Pardon me, Julius! Here wast thou bay'd, brave
     hart;
Here didst thou fall; and here thy hunters stand, 205
Sign'd in thy spoil, and crimson'd in thy lethe.
O world, thou wast the forest to this hart;
And this, indeed, O world, the heart of thee.
How like a deer, strucken by many princes,
Dost thou here lie!   210
   Cas. Mark Antony, —
   Ant.   Pardon me, Caius Cassius!
The enemies of Cæsar shall say this;
Then, in a friend, it is cold modesty.
   Cas. I blame you not for praising Cæsar so;
But what compact mean you to have with us?   215
Will you be prick'd in number of our friends;
Or shall we on, and not depend on you?
   Ant. Therefore I took your hands, but was, in-
     deed,
Sway'd from the point, by looking down on Cæsar.
Friends am I with you all and love you all,   220
Upon this hope, that you shall give me reasons
Why and wherein Cæsar was dangerous.
   Bru. Or else were this a savage spectacle.

Our reasons are so full of good regard
That were you, Antony, the son of Cæsar,   225
You should be satisfied.
   Ant.   That's all I seek;
And am, moreover, suitor that I may
Produce his body to the market-place
And in the pulpit, as becomes a friend,
Speak in the order of his funeral.   230
   Bru. You shall, Mark Antony.
   Cas.   Brutus, a word with you.
[*Aside to Bru.*] You know not what you do. Do
     not consent
That Antony speak in his funeral.
Know you how much the people may be mov'd
By that which he will utter?
   Bru.   By your pardon. 235
I will myself into the pulpit first
And show the reason of our Cæsar's death.
What Antony shall speak, I will protest
He speaks by leave and by permission,
And that we are contented Cæsar shall   240
Have all true rites and lawful ceremonies.
It shall advantage more than do us wrong.
   Cas. I know not what may fall; I like it not.
   Bru. Mark Antony, here, take you Cæsar's body.
You shall not in your funeral speech blame us, 245
But speak all good you can devise of Cæsar,
And say you do't by our permission;
Else shall you not have any hand at all
About his funeral. And you shall speak
In the same pulpit whereto I am going,   250
After my speech is ended.
   Ant.   Be it so;
I do desire no more.
   Bru. Prepare the body then, and follow us.
             [*Exeunt all but Antony.*
   Ant. O, pardon me, thou bleeding piece of earth.
That I am meek and gentle with these butchers! 255
Thou art the ruins of the noblest man
That ever lived in the tide of times.
Woe to the hand that shed this costly blood!
Over thy wounds now do I prophesy,
Which, like dumb mouths, do ope their ruby lips 260
To beg the voice and utterance of my tongue:
A curse shall light upon the limbs of men;
Domestic fury and fierce civil strife
Shall cumber all the parts of Italy;
Blood and destruction shall be so in use   265
And dreadful objects so familiar
That mothers shall but smile when they behold
Their infants quartered with the hands of war;
All pity chok'd with custom of fell deeds;
And Cæsar's spirit, ranging for revenge,   270
With Ate by his side come hot from hell,

---

192. **conceit**: regard. 196. **dearer**: more keenly. 204. **bay'd**: brought to bay. 206. **Sign'd ... spoil**: marked with the signs of death. **lethe**: death. 213. **modesty**: moderation. 216. **prick'd**: marked on the list. 224. **full ... regard**: worthy of approval. 230. **order**: ceremony. 241. **true**: due. 243. **fall**: happen. 269. **fell**: cruel. 271. **Ate**: goddess of discord

Shall in these confines with a monarch's voice
Cry "Havoc," and let slip the dogs of war,
That this foul deed shall smell above the earth
With carrion men, groaning for burial.   275

Enter Octavius' SERVANT.

You serve Octavius Cæsar, do you not?
   Serv. I do, Mark Antony.
   Ant. Cæsar did write for him to come to Rome.
   Serv. He did receive his letters, and is coming;
And bid me say to you by word of mouth —   280
O Cæsar! —   *[Seeing the body.]*
   Ant. Thy heart is big; get thee apart and weep.
Passion, I see, is catching; [for] mine eyes,
Seeing those beads of sorrow stand in thine,
Began to water. Is thy master coming?   285
   Serv. He lies to-night within seven leagues of
     Rome.
   Ant. Post back with speed and tell him what hath
     chanc'd.
Here is a mourning Rome, a dangerous Rome,
No Rome of safety for Octavius yet;
Hie hence, and tell him so. Yet, stay a while;   290
Thou shalt not back till I have borne this corse
Into the market-place. There shall I try,
In my oration, how the people take
The cruel issue of these bloody men;
According to the which thou shalt discourse   295
To young Octavius of the state of things.
Lend me your hand.   *[Exeunt [with Cæsar's body].*

[SCENE II. *The Forum.*]

Enter BRUTUS and CASSIUS, with the PLEBEIANS.

   Pleb. We will be satisfied! Let us be satisfied!
   Bru. Then follow me, and give me audience,
     friends.
Cassius, go you into the other street,
And part the numbers.
Those that will hear me speak, let 'em stay here;   5
Those that will follow Cassius, go with him;
And public reasons shall be rendered
Of Cæsar's death.
   1. Pleb.   I will hear Brutus speak.
   2. Pleb. I will hear Cassius; and compare their
     reasons
When severally we hear them rendered.   10
     [Exit Cassius, with some of the Plebeians.]
     Brutus goes into the pulpit.
   3. Pleb. The noble Brutus is ascended; silence!
   Bru. Be patient till the last.
     Romans, countrymen and lovers! hear me for
my cause, and be silent, that you may hear; believe

me for mine honour, and have respect to mine   15
honour, that you may believe; censure me in your
wisdom, and awake your senses, that you may the
better judge. If there be any in this assembly, any
dear friend of Cæsar's, to him I say, that Brutus'
love to Cæsar was no less than his. If then   20
that friend demand why Brutus rose against Cæsar,
this is my answer: Not that I lov'd Cæsar less, but
that I lov'd Rome more. Had you rather Cæsar
were living and die all slaves, than that Cæsar were
dead, to live all free men? As Cæsar lov'd   25
me, I weep for him; as he was fortunate, I rejoice at
it; as he was valiant, I honour him; but, as he was
ambitious, I slew him. There is tears for his love;
joy for his fortune; honour for his valour; and
death for his ambition. Who is here so base   30
that would be a bondman? If any, speak; for
him have I offended. Who is here so rude that
would not be a Roman? If any, speak; for him
have I offended. Who is here so vile that will not
love his country? If any, speak; for him have I
offended. I pause for a reply.   37
   All. None, Brutus, none.
   Bru. Then none have I offended. I have done
no more to Cæsar than you shall do to Brutus.
The question of his death is enroll'd in the Capitol;
his glory not extenuated, wherein he was worthy,
nor his offences enforc'd, for which he suffered
death.   44

Enter ANTONY [and others], with Cæsar's body.

Here comes his body, mourn'd by Mark Antony;
who, though he had no hand in his death, shall
receive the benefit of his dying, a place in the commonwealth; as which of you shall not? With this
I depart, that, as I slew my best lover for the good
of Rome, I have the same dagger for myself, when
it shall please my country to need my death.   52
   All. Live, Brutus! live, live!
   1. Pleb. Bring him with triumph home unto his
     house.
   2. Pleb. Give him a statue with his ancestors.   55
   3. Pleb. Let him be Cæsar. *can't get rid of tyrant*
   4. Pleb.   Cæsar's better parts
Shall be crown'd in Brutus.
   1. Pleb.   We'll bring him to his house
With shouts and clamours.
   Bru.   My countrymen, —
   2. Pleb. Peace, silence! Brutus speaks.
   1. Pleb.   Peace, ho!
   Bru. Good countrymen, let me depart alone,   60
And, for my sake, stay here with Antony.
Do grace to Cæsar's corpse, and grace his speech
Tending to Cæsar's glories, which Mark Antony,

   272. **confines**: regions.   273. **"Havoc"**: No quarter!   283. **Passion**: grief.   **[for]** F₂. *from* F₁.   294. **issue**: deed.
   Sc. ii, 13. lovers: dear friends.   16. **censure**: judge.   32. **rude**: barbarous.   41. **question ... enroll'd**: justification for his
death is on record.   43. **enforc'd**: exaggerated.   56. **parts**: qualities.

By our permission, is allow'd to make.
I do entreat you, not a man depart   65
Save I alone, till Antony have spoke.   [*Exit.*
    1. Pleb. Stay, ho! and let us hear Mark Antony,
    3. Pleb. Let him go up into the public chair;
We'll hear him.   Noble Antony, go up.   69
    Ant. For Brutus' sake, I am beholding to you.
                              [*Goes into the pulpit.*]
    4. Pleb. What does he say of Brutus?
    3. Pleb.   He says, for Brutus' sake
He finds himself beholding to us all.
    4. Pleb. 'Twere best he speak no harm of Brutus
        here.
    1. Pleb. This Cæsar was a tyrant.
    3. Pleb.   Nay, that's certain:
We are blest that Rome is rid of him.   75
    2. Pleb. Peace! let us hear what Antony can say.
    Ant. You gentle Romans, —
    All.   Peace, ho! let us hear him.
    Ant. Friends, Romans, countrymen, lend me
        your ears!
I come to bury Cæsar, not to praise him.
The evil that men do lives after them,   80
The good is oft interred with their bones;
So let it be with Cæsar.   The noble Brutus
Hath told you Cæsar was ambitious;
If it were so, it was a grievous fault,
And grievously hath Cæsar answer'd it. —   85
Here, under leave of Brutus and the rest —
For Brutus is an honourable man;
So are they all, all honourable men —
Come I to speak in Cæsar's funeral.
He was my friend, faithful and just to me;   90
But Brutus says he was ambitious,
And Brutus is an honourable man.
He hath brought many captives home to Rome,
Whose ransoms did the general coffers fill;
Did this in Cæsar seem ambitious?   95
When that the poor have cried, Cæsar hath wept;
Ambition should be made of sterner stuff:
Yet Brutus says he was ambitious,
And Brutus is an honourable man.
You all did see that on the Lupercal   100
I thrice presented him a kingly crown,
Which he did thrice refuse.   Was this ambition?
Yet Brutus says he was ambitious,
And, sure, he is an honourable man.
I speak not to disprove what Brutus spoke,   105
But here I am to speak what I do know.
You all did love him once, not without cause;
What cause withholds you then to mourn for
        him?
O judgement! thou art fled to brutish beasts,
And men have lost their reason.   Bear with me;
My heart is in the coffin there with Cæsar,   111
And I must pause till it come back to me.

    1. Pleb. Methinks there is much reason in his
        sayings.
    2. Pleb. If thou consider rightly of the matter,
Cæsar has had great wrong.
    3. Pleb.   Has he, masters?   115
I fear there will a worse come in his place.
    4. Pleb. Mark'd ye his words?   He would not
        take the crown;
Therefore 'tis certain he was not ambitious.
    1. Pleb. If it be found so, some will dear abide it.
    2. Pleb. Poor soul! his eyes are red as fire with
        weeping.   120
    3. Pleb. There's not a nobler man in Rome than
        Antony.
    4. Pleb. Now mark him, he begins again to speak.
    Ant. But yesterday the word of Cæsar might
Have stood against the world; now lies he there,
And none so poor to do him reverence.   125
O masters, if I were dispos'd to stir
Your hearts and minds to mutiny and rage,
I should do Brutus wrong, and Cassius wrong,
Who, you all know, are honourable men.
I will not do them wrong; I rather choose   130
To wrong the dead, to wrong myself and you,
Than I will wrong such honourable men.
But here's a parchment with the seal of Cæsar;
I found it in his closet; 'tis his will.
Let but the commons hear this testament —   135
Which, pardon me, I do not mean to read —
And they would go and kiss dead Cæsar's wounds
And dip their napkins in his sacred blood,
Yea, beg a hair of him for memory,
And, dying, mention it within their wills,   140
Bequeathing it as a rich legacy
Unto their issue.
    4. Pleb. We'll hear the will.   Read it, Mark
        Antony.
    All. The will, the will! we will hear Cæsar's will.
    Ant. Have patience, gentle friends, I must not
        read it;   145
It is not meet you know how Cæsar lov'd you.
You are not wood, you are not stones, but men;
And, being men, hearing the will of Cæsar,
It will inflame you, it will make you mad.
'Tis good you know not that you are his heirs;   150
For, if you should, O, what would come of it!
    4. Pleb. Read the will; we'll hear it, Antony.
You shall read us the will, Cæsar's will.
    Ant. Will you be patient?   Will you stay a while?
I have o'ershot myself to tell you of it.   155
I fear I wrong the honourable men
Whose daggers have stabb'd Cæsar; I do fear it.
    4. Pleb. They were traitors; honourable men!
    All. The will! the testament!
    2. Pleb. They were villains, murderers.   The
will!   Read the will!   160

70. **beholding:** indebted.   134. **closet:** chamber.   135. **commons:** common people.   138. **napkins:** handkerchiefs.

Ant. You will compel me, then, to read the will?
Then make a ring about the corpse of Cæsar,
And let me show you him that made the will.
Shall I descend? and will you give me leave?
All. Come down.   165
2. Pleb. Descend.
3. Pleb. You shall have leave.
                    [*Antony comes down from the pulpit.*]
4. Pleb. A ring; stand round.
1. Pleb. Stand from the hearse, stand from the
    body.
2. Pleb. Room for Antony, most noble Antony.
Ant. Nay, press not so upon me; stand far off. 171
All. Stand back; room; bear back!
Ant. If you have tears, prepare to shed them now.
You all do know this mantle; I remember
The first time ever Cæsar put it on.   175
'Twas on a summer's evening, in his tent,
That day he overcame the Nervii.
Look, in this place ran Cassius' dagger through;
See what a rent the envious Casca made;
Through this the well-beloved Brutus stabb'd,   180
And as he pluck'd his cursed steel away,
Mark how the blood of Cæsar followed it,
As rushing out of doors to be resolv'd
If Brutus so unkindly knock'd or no;
For Brutus, as you know, was Cæsar's angel.   185
Judge, O you gods, how dearly Cæsar lov'd him!
This was the most unkindest cut of all;
For when the noble Cæsar saw him stab,
Ingratitude, more strong than traitors' arms,
Quite vanquish'd him.   Then burst his mighty
    heart;   190
And, in his mantle muffling up his face,
Even at the base of Pompey's statuë,
Which all the while ran blood, great Cæsar fell.
O, what a fall was there, my countrymen!
Then I, and you, and all of us fell down,   195
Whilst bloody treason flourish'd over us.
O, now you weep, and I perceive you feel
The dint of pity.   These are gracious drops.
Kind souls, what, weep you when you but behold
Our Cæsar's vesture wounded? Look you here: 200
                    [*Lifting Cæsar's mantle.*]
Here is himself, marr'd, as you see, with traitors.
1. Pleb. O piteous spectacle!
2. Pleb. O noble Cæsar!
3. Pleb. O woeful day!
4. Pleb. O traitors, villains!   205
1. Pleb. O most bloody sight!
2. Pleb. We will be reveng'd!
[*All.*]   Revenge!   About!
Seek! Burn! Fire! Kill! Slay!
Let not a traitor live!
Ant.   Stay, countrymen. 210

1. Pleb. Peace there! hear the noble Antony.
2. Pleb. We'll hear him, we'll follow him, we'll
die with him.
Ant. Good friends, sweet friends, let me not stir
    you up
To such a sudden flood of mutiny.   215
They that have done this deed are honourable.
What private griefs they have, alas, I know not,
That made them do it; they are wise and honourable
And will, no doubt, with reasons answer you.
I come not, friends, to steal away your hearts. 220
I am no orator, as Brutus is;
But, as you know me all, a plain blunt man
That love my friend; and that they know full well
That gave me public leave to speak of him;
For I have neither [wit], nor words, nor worth, 225
Action, nor utterance, nor the power of speech
To stir men's blood; I only speak right on.
I tell you that which you yourselves do know;
Show you sweet Cæsar's wounds, poor, poor, dumb
    mouths,
And bid them speak for me. But were I Brutus, 230
And Brutus Antony, there were an Antony
Would ruffle up your spirits, and put a tongue
In every wound of Cæsar, that should move
The stones of Rome to rise and mutiny.
All. We'll mutiny.   235
1. Pleb. We'll burn the house of Brutus.
3. Pleb. Away, then! come, seek the conspirators.
Ant. Yet hear me, countrymen; yet hear me
    speak.
All. Peace, ho! hear Antony, most noble An-
    tony!
Ant. Why, friends, you go to do you know not
    what.   240
Wherein hath Cæsar thus deserv'd your loves?
Alas, you know not; I must tell you, then.
You have forgot the will I told you of.
All. Most true.   The will!   Let's stay and hear
    the will.
Ant. Here is the will, and under Cæsar's seal. 245
To every Roman citizen he gives,
To every several man, seventy-five drachmas.
2. Pleb. Most noble Cæsar! We'll revenge his
    death.
3. Pleb. O Royal Cæsar!
Ant. Hear me with patience.   250
All. Peace, ho!
Ant. Moreover, he hath left you all his walks,
His private arbours and new-planted orchards,
On this side Tiber; he hath left them you
And to your heirs forever, common pleasures,   255
To walk abroad and recreate yourselves.
Here was a Cæsar! When comes such another?
1. Pleb. Never, never! Come, away, away!

169. **hearse:** bier. 177. **Nervii:** a Belgian tribe. 208. **[All.]** (Grant White). 2 F. 225. **[wit]** F₂: intellectual capacity.
writ F₁. 226. **utterance:** eloquence. 232. **ruffle:** rouse. 255. **pleasures:** pleasure grounds.

We'll burn his body in the holy place,
And with the brands fire the traitors' houses.　260
Take up the body.

　2. Pleb. Go fetch fire.

　3. Pleb. Pluck down benches.

　4. Pleb. Pluck down forms, windows, anything.
　　　　　　　[Exeunt Plebeians [with the body].

　Ant. Now let it work. Mischief, thou art afoot,
Take thou what course thou wilt!　266

　　　　　Enter a SERVANT.

　　　　　　　　　How now, fellow?

　Serv. Sir, Octavius is already come to Rome.

　Ant. Where is he?

　Serv. He and Lepidus are at Cæsar's house.

　Ant. And thither will I straight to visit him;　270
He comes upon a wish. Fortune is merry,
And in this mood will give us anything.

　Serv. I heard him say, Brutus and Cassius
Are rid like madmen through the gates of Rome.

　Ant. Belike they had some notice of the people,　275
How I had mov'd them. Bring me to Octavius.
　　　　　　　　　　　　　[Exeunt.

　　　　[SCENE III. *A street.*]

Enter CINNA *the poet, and after him the* PLEBEIANS.

　Cin. I dreamt to-night that I did feast with
　　　Cæsar,
And things unluckily charge my fantasy.
I have no will to wander forth of doors,
Yet something leads me forth.

　1. Pleb. What is your name?　5

　2. Pleb. Whither are you going?

　3. Pleb. Where do you dwell?

　4. Pleb. Are you a married man or a bachelor?

　2. Pleb. Answer every man directly.　10

　1. Pleb. Ay, and briefly.

　4. Pleb. Ay, and wisely.

　3. Pleb. Ay, and truly, you were best.

　Cin. What is my name? Whither am I going?
Where do I dwell? Am I a married man or a　15
bachelor? Then, to answer every man directly and
briefly, wisely and truly: wisely I say, I am a bachelor.

　2. Pleb. That's as much as to say, they are fools
that marry. You'll bear me a bang for that, I fear.
Proceed; directly.　21

　Cin. Directly, I am going to Cæsar's funeral.

　1. Pleb. As a friend or an enemy?

　Cin. As a friend.

　2. Pleb. That matter is answered directly.　25

　4. Pleb. For your dwelling, — briefly.

　Cin. Briefly, I dwell by the Capitol.

　3. Pleb. Your name, sir, truly.

　Cin. Truly, my name is Cinna.　30

　1. Pleb. Tear him to pieces; he's a conspirator.

　Cin. I am Cinna the poet, I am Cinna the poet.

　4. Pleb. Tear him for his bad verses, tear him for
　　his bad verses.　35

　Cin. I am not Cinna the conspirator.

　4. Pleb. It is no matter, his name's Cinna. Pluck
but his name out of his heart, and turn him going.　39

　3. Pleb. Tear him, tear him! Come, brands,
ho! fire-brands! To Brutus', to Cassius'; burn
all! Some to Decius' house, and some to Casca's;
some to Ligarius'. Away, go!　　　　*[Exeunt.*

　　　　　　　ACT IV

　　　[SCENE I. *A house in Rome.*]

ANTONY, OCTAVIUS, *and* LEPIDUS [*seated at a table*].

　Ant. These many, then, shall die; their names
　　are prick'd.

　Oct. Your brother too must die; consent you,
　　Lepidus?

　Lep. I do consent, —

　Oct.　　　　　　Prick him down, Antony.

　Lep. Upon condition Publius shall not live,
Who is your sister's son, Mark Antony.　5

　Ant. He shall not live; look, with a spot I damn
　　him.
But, Lepidus, go you to Cæsar's house;
Fetch the will hither, and we shall determine
How to cut off some charge in legacies.

　Lep. What, shall I find you here?　10

　Oct. Or here, or at the Capitol.　*[Exit Lepidus.*

　Ant. This is a slight unmeritable man,
Meet to be sent on errands; is it fit,
The threefold world divided, he should stand
One of the three to share it?

　Oct.　　　　　　So you thought him;
And took his voice who should be prick'd to die,　16
In our black sentence and proscription.

　Ant. Octavius, I have seen more days than you;
And though we lay these honours on this man
To ease ourselves of divers sland'rous loads,　20
He shall but bear them as the ass bears gold,
To groan and sweat under the business,
Either led or driven, as we point the way;
And having brought our treasure where we will,
Then take we down his load, and turn him off,　25
Like to the empty ass, to shake his ears
And graze in commons.

　Oct.　　　　　　You may do your will;
But he's a tried and valiant soldier.

　Ant. So is my horse, Octavius; and for that
I do appoint him store of provender.　30
It is a creature that I teach to fight,

　　Sc. iii, 2. **unluckily:** ominously.　20. **bear ... bang:** get a blow from me.
　　Act IV, sc. i, 9. **charge:** cost.　20. **sland'rous loads:** burdens of slander.　26. **empty:** unburdened

To wind, to stop, to run directly on,
His corporal motion govern'd by my spirit.
And, in some taste, is Lepidus but so;
He must be taught and train'd and bid go forth;   35
A barren-spirited fellow; one that feeds
On abjects, orts, and imitations,
Which, out of use and stal'd by other men,
Begin his fashion. Do not talk of him
But as a property. And now, Octavius,   40
Listen great things. Brutus and Cassius
Are levying powers; we must straight make head;
Therefore let our alliance be combin'd,
Our best friends made, our means stretch'd;
And let us presently go sit in council   45
How covert matters may be best disclos'd
And open perils surest answered.

Oct. Let us do so; for we are at the stake
And bay'd about with many enemies;
And some that smile have in their hearts, I fear,   50
Millions of mischiefs.   [*Exeunt.*

[SCENE II.   *Camp near Sardis. Before Brutus's tent.*]

Drum.   Enter BRUTUS, LUCILIUS, [LUCIUS,] *and the army.* Titinius *and* PINDARUS *meet them.*

Bru. Stand, ho!
Lucil. Give the word, ho! and stand.
Bru. What now, Lucilius! is Cassius near?
Lucil. He is at hand; and Pindarus is come
To do you salutation from his master.   5
Bru. He greets me well. Your master, Pindarus,
In his own change, or by ill officers,
Hath given me some worthy cause to wish
Things done undone; but, if he be at hand,
I shall be satisfied.
Pin.   I do not doubt   10
But that my noble master will appear
Such as he is, full of regard and honour.
Bru. He is not doubted. A word, Lucilius:
How he receiv'd you let me be resolv'd.
Lucil. With courtesy and with respect enough;
But not with such familiar instances,   16
Nor with such free and friendly conference,
As he hath us'd of old.
Bru.   Thou hast describ'd
A hot friend cooling. Ever note, Lucilius,
When love begins to sicken and decay   20
It useth an enforced ceremony.
There are no tricks in plain and simple faith;
But hollow men, like horses hot at hand,

Make gallant show and promise of their mettle;
      [*Low march within.*
But when they should endure the bloody spur   25
They fall their crests, and, like deceitful jades,
Sink in the trial. Comes his army on?
Lucil. They mean this night in Sardis to be quarter'd.
The greater part, the horse in general,
Are come with Cassius.

Enter CASSIUS *and his Powers.*

Bru.   Hark! he is arriv'd   30
March gently on to meet him.
Cas. Stand, ho!
Bru. Stand, ho! Speak the word along.
[*1. Sol.*] Stand!
[*2. Sol.*] Stand!   35
[*3. Sol.*] Stand!
Cas. Most noble brother, you have done me wrong.
Bru. Judge me, you gods! wrong I mine enemies?
And, if not so, how should I wrong a brother?
Cas. Brutus, this sober form of yours hides wrongs;   40
And when you do them —
Bru.   Cassius, be content;
Speak your griefs softly; I do know you well.
Before the eyes of both our armies here,
Which should perceive nothing but love from us,
Let us not wrangle. Bid them move away;   45
Then in my tent, Cassius, enlarge your griefs,
And I will give you audience.
Cas.   Pindarus,
Bid our commanders lead their charges off
A little from this ground.   49
Bru. [Lucius], do you the like; and let no man
Come to our tent till we have done our conference.
[Lucilius] and Titinius, guard our door.   [*Exeunt.*

[SCENE III.   *Brutus's tent.*]

[*Enter*] BRUTUS *and* CASSIUS.

Cas. That you have wrong'd me doth appear in this:
You have condemn'd and noted Lucius Pella
For taking bribes here of the Sardians;
Wherein my letters, praying on his side,
Because I knew the man was slighted off, —   5
Bru. You wrong'd yourself to write in such a case.
Cas. In such a time as this it is not meet
That every nice offence should bear his comment.
Bru. Let me tell you, Cassius, you yourself
Are much condemn'd to have an itching palm,   10

32. **wind:** turn.   34. **taste:** degree.   40. **property:** tool.   42. **make head:** raise an army.   44. **our...stretch'd.** F₂ reads *and our best means stretch'd out.*   47. **answered:** met.

     Sc. ii, 16. familiar instances: tokens of intimacy.   23. **hollow:** insincere.   **hot at hand:** fiery when held back.   26. **fall:** droop.   31. **gently:** slowly.   46. **enlarge:** express fully.   50. **[Lucius]** (Craik). *Lucilius* F.   52. **[Lucilius]** (Craik). *Let Lucius* F.

     Sc. iii, 2. noted: branded with disgrace.   8. **nice:** trivial.   **bear his comment:** receive attention.   10. **to have:** for having

To sell and mart your offices for gold
To undeservers.
 Cas.   I an itching palm!
You know that you are Brutus that speaks this,
Or, by the gods, this speech were else your last.
 Bru. The name of Cassius honours this corrup- 15
  tion,
And Chastisement doth therefore hide his head.
 Cas. Chastisement!
 Bru. Remember March, the ides of March re-
  member:
Did not great Julius bleed for justice' sake?
What villain touch'd his body, that did stab 20
And not for justice? What, shall one of us,
That struck the foremost man of all this world
But for supporting robbers, shall we now
Contaminate our fingers with base bribes,
And sell the mighty space of our large honours 25
For so much trash as may be grasped thus?
I had rather be a dog, and bay the moon,
Than such a Roman.
 Cas.   Brutus, bait not me;
I'll not endure it. You forget yourself
To hedge me in. I am a soldier, I, 30
Older in practice, abler than yourself
To make conditions.
 Bru. Go to; you are not, Cassius.
 Cas. I am.
 Bru. I say you are not.
 Cas. Urge me no more, I shall forget myself; 35
Have mind upon your health, tempt me no farther.
 Bru. Away, slight man!
 Cas. Is't possible?
 Bru.   Hear me, for I will speak.
Must I give way and room to your rash choler?
Shall I be frighted when a madman stares? 40
 Cas. O ye gods, ye gods! must I endure all this?
 Bru. All this! ay, more. Fret till your proud
  heart break;
Go show your slaves how choleric you are,
And make your bondmen tremble. Must I budge?
Must I observe you? Must I stand and crouch 45
Under your testy humour? By the gods,
You shall digest the venom of your spleen,
Though it do split you; for, from this day forth,
I'll use you for my mirth, yea, for my laughter,
When you are waspish.
 Cas.   Is it come to this? 50
 Bru. You say you are a better soldier:
Let it appear so; make your vaunting true,
And it shall please me well. For mine own part,
I shall be glad to learn of noble men.
 Cas. You wrong me every way; you wrong me,
  Brutus; 55

I said an elder soldier, not a better.
Did I say "better"?
 Bru.   If you did, I care not.
 Cas. When Cæsar liv'd, he durst not thus have
  mov'd me.
 Bru. Peace, peace! you durst not so have
  tempted him.
 Cas. I durst not! 60
 Bru. No.
 Cas. What, durst not tempt him!
 Bru.   For your life you durst not.
 Cas. Do not presume too much upon my love;
I may do that I shall be sorry for.
 Bru. You have done that you should be sorry for.
There is no terror, Cassius, in your threats, 66
For I am arm'd so strong in honesty
That they pass by me as the idle wind,
Which I respect not. I did send to you
For certain sums of gold, which you deni'd me; 70
For I can raise no money by vile means. —
By heaven, I had rather coin my heart
And drop my blood for drachmas than to wring
From the hard hands of peasants their vile trash
By any indirection. — I did send 75
To you for gold to pay my legions,
Which you deni'd me. Was that done like Cassius?
Should I have answer'd Caius Cassius so?
When Marcus Brutus grows so covetous
To lock such rascal counters from his friends, 80
Be ready, gods, with all your thunderbolts;
Dash him to pieces!
 Cas.   I deni'd you not.
 Bru. You did.
 Cas. I did not. He was but a fool that brought
My answer back. Brutus hath riv'd my heart. 85
A friend should bear his friend's infirmities,
But Brutus makes mine greater than they are.
 Bru. I do not, till you practise them on me.
 Cas. You love me not.
 Bru.   I do not like your faults.
 Cas. A friendly eye could never see such faults. 90
 Bru. A flatterer's would not, though they do
  appear
As huge as high Olympus.
 Cas. Come, Antony, and young Octavius, come,
Revenge yourselves alone on Cassius,
For Cassius is aweary of the world; 95
Hated by one he loves; brav'd by his brother;
Check'd like a bondman; all his faults observ'd,
Set in a note-book, learn'd and conn'd by rote
To cast into my teeth. O, I could weep
My spirit from mine eyes! There is my dagger, 10c
And here my naked breast; within, a heart
Dearer than [Plutus'] mine, richer than gold.

11. **mart:** market. 30. **hedge me in:** curb me. 32. **make conditions:** manage affairs. 35. **Urge:** press. 36. **tempt:** try
45. **observe:** be obsequious to. 75. **indirection:** crooked means. 80. **rascal counters:** worthless coins. 85. **riv'd:** split.
broken. 97. **Check'd:** rebuked. 102. [**Plutus'**] (Pope): the god of wealth. *Pluto's* F.

If that thou be'st a Roman, take it forth;
I, that deni'd thee gold, will give my heart.
Strike, as thou didst at Cæsar; for, I know,   105
When thou didst hate him worst, thou lov'dst him
    better
Than ever thou lov'dst Cassius.
    Bru.   Sheathe your dagger.
Be angry when you will, it shall have scope.
Do what you will, dishonour shall be humour.
O Cassius, you are yoked with a lamb   110
That carries anger as the flint bears fire;
Who, much enforced, shows a hasty spark,
And straight is cold again.
    Cas.   Hath Cassius liv'd
To be but mirth and laughter to his Brutus,
When grief and blood ill-temper'd vexeth him?   115
    Bru. When I spoke that, I was ill-temper'd too.
    Cas. Do you confess so much? Give me your
    hand.
    Bru. And my heart too.
    Cas.   O Brutus!
    Bru.   What's the matter?
    Cas. Have not you love enough to bear with me,
When that rash humour which my mother gave me
Makes me forgetful?
    Bru.   Yes, Cassius; and, from henceforth,
When you are over earnest with your Brutus,   122
He'll think your mother chides, and leave you so.
    Poet. [*Within.*] Let me go in to see the generals.
There is some grudge between 'em; 'tis not meet
They be alone.   126
    Lucil. [*Within.*] You shall not come to them.
    Poet. [*Within.*] Nothing but death shall stay me.

Enter POET [*followed by* LUCILIUS, TITINIUS,
    and LUCIUS].

    Cas. How now! what's the matter?
    Poet. For shame, you generals! what do you
    mean?   130
Love, and be friends, as two such men should be;
For I have seen more years, I'm sure, than ye.
    Cas. Ha, ha! how vilely doth this cynic rhyme!
    Bru. Get you hence, sirrah; saucy fellow, hence!
    Cas. Bear with him, Brutus; 'tis his fashion. 135
    Bru. I'll know his humour, when he knows his
    time.
What should the wars do with these jigging fools?
Companion, hence!
    Cas.   Away, away, be gone!
                            [*Exit Poet.*
    Bru. Lucilius and Titinius, bid the commanders
Prepare to lodge their companies to-night.   140

    Cas. And come yourselves, and bring Messala
    with you
Immediately to us.
                        [*Exeunt Lucilius and Titinius.*]
    Bru.   Lucius, a bowl of wine!
                                    [*Exit Lucius.*]
    Cas. I did not think you could have been so
    angry.
    Bru. O Cassius, I am sick of many griefs.
    Cas. Of your philosophy you make no use   145
If you give place to accidental evils.
    Bru. No man bears sorrow better. Portia is
    dead.
    Cas. Ha! Portia!
    Bru. She is dead.
    Cas. How scap'd I killing when I cross'd you
    so?   150
O insupportable and touching loss!
Upon what sickness?
    Bru.   Impatient of my absence,
And grief that young Octavius with Mark Antony
Have made themselves so strong, — for with her
    death
That tidings came, — with this she fell distract, 155
And, her attendants absent, swallow'd fire.
    Cas. And died so?
    Bru.   Even so.
    Cas.   O ye immortal gods!

    Re-enter Boy [Lucius], *with wine and tapers.*

    Bru. Speak no more of her. Give me a bowl of
    wine.
In this I bury all unkindness, Cassius. [*Drinks.*
    Cas. My heart is thirsty for that noble pledge.
Fill, Lucius, till the wine o'erswell the cup;   161
I cannot drink too much of Brutus' love. [*Drinks.*]

    Re-enter TITINIUS, *with* MESSALA.

    Bru. Come in, Titinius!   [*Exit Lucius.*]
                            Welcome, good Messala.
Now sit we close about this taper here,
And call in question our necessities.   165
    Cas. Portia, art thou gone?
    Bru.   No more, I pray you.
Messala, I have here received letters
That young Octavius and Mark Antony
Come down upon us with a mighty power,
Bending their expedition toward Philippi.   170
    Mes. Myself have letters of the self-same [tenour].
    Bru. With what addition?
    Mes. That by proscription and bills of outlawry,

---

109. **dishonour...humour:** I shall count your insults merely as caprice.   110. **yoked with:** like.   115. **blood ill-temper'd:** a bad disposition.   123. **leave you so:** stop at that.   133. **cynic:** rude fellow.   136. **I'll...time:** I'll countenance his eccentricity when he chooses the proper time for it.   138. **Companion:** fellow.   146. **give...evils:** yield to accidents.
154. **her death:** news of her death.   156. **fire.** Plutarch says "hot, burning coals."   165. **call in question:** discuss.
171. **[tenour]** (Theobald). *Tenure* F.

Octavius, Antony, and Lepidus
Have put to death an hundred senators.   175
   Bru. Therein our letters do not well agree;
Mine speak of seventy senators that died
By their proscriptions, Cicero being one.
   Cas. Cicero one!
   Mes.   Cicero is dead,
And by that order of proscription.   180
Had you your letters from your wife, my lord?
   Bru. No, Messala.
   Mes. Nor nothing in your letters writ of her?
   Bru. Nothing, Messala.
   Mes.   That, methinks, is strange.
   Bru. Why ask you?   Hear you aught of her in
   yours?   185
   Mes. No, my lord.
   Bru. Now, as you are a Roman, tell me true.
   Mes. Then like a Roman bear the truth I tell:
For certain she is dead, and by strange manner.
   Bru. Why, farewell, Portia.   We must die,
   Messala.   190
With meditating that she must die once,
I have the patience to endure it now.
   Mes. Even so great men great losses should
   endure.
   Cas. I have as much of this in art as you,
But yet my nature could not bear it so.   195
   Bru. Well, to our work alive.   What do you
   think
Of marching to Philippi presently?
   Cas. I do not think it good.
   Bru.   Your reason?
   Cas.   This it is:
'Tis better that the enemy seek us.
So shall he waste his means, weary his soldiers, 200
Doing himself offence; whilst we, lying still,
Are full of rest, defence, and nimbleness.
   Bru. Good reasons must, of force, give place to
   better.
The people 'twixt Philippi and this ground
Do stand but in a forc'd affection,   205
For they have grudg'd us contribution.
The enemy, marching along by them,
By them shall make a fuller number up,
Come on refresh'd, new-added, and encourag'd;
From which advantage shall we cut him off   210
If at Philippi we do face him there,
These people at our back.
   Cas.   Hear me, good brother.
   Bru. Under your pardon.   You must note
   beside
That we have tried the utmost of our friends;
Our legions are brim-full, our cause is ripe.   215

The enemy increaseth every day;
We, at the height, are ready to decline.
There is a tide in the affairs of men
Which, taken at the flood, leads on to fortune;
Omitted, all the voyage of their life   220
Is bound in shallows and in miseries.
On such a full sea are we now afloat,
And we must take the current when it serves
Or lose our ventures.
   Cas.   Then, with your will, go on.
We'll along ourselves, and meet them at Philippi.
   Bru. The deep of night is crept upon our talk   226
And nature must obey necessity,
Which we will niggard with a little rest.
There is no more to say?
   Cas.   No more.   Good-night.
Early to-morrow will we rise, and hence.   230
   Bru. Lucius! (*Re-enter Lucius.*) My gown.
          [*Exit Lucius.*] Farewell, good Messala;
Good-night, Titinius.   Noble, noble Cassius,
Good-night, and good repose.
   Cas.   O my dear brother!
This was an ill beginning of the night.
Never come such division 'tween our souls!   235
Let it not, Brutus.

       Re-enter Lucius, *with the gown.*
   Bru.   Everything is well.
   Cas. Good-night, my lord.
   Bru.   Good-night, good brother.
   Tit. Mes. Good-night, Lord Brutus.
   Bru.   Farewell, every one.
          [*Exeunt [all but Brutus and Lucius].*
Give me the gown.   Where is thy instrument?
   Luc. Here in the tent.
   Bru.   What, thou speak'st drowsily? 240
Poor knave, I blame thee not; thou art o'erwatch'd.
Call [Claudius] and some other of my men;
I'll have them sleep on cushions in my tent.
   Luc. [Varro] and [Claudius]!

       Enter Varro *and* Claudius.
   Var. Calls my lord?   245
   Bru. I pray you, sirs, lie in my tent and sleep;
It may be I shall raise you by and by
On business to my brother Cassius.
   Var. So please you, we will stand and watch your
   pleasure.
   Bru. I will not have it so: lie down, good sirs;   250
It may be I shall otherwise bethink me.
          [*Varro and Claudius lie down.*
Look, Lucius, here's the book I sought for so;
I put it in the pocket of my gown.

---

184. **Nothing, Messala.**   To explain away this lie by Brutus, it has been suggested that ll. 147 ff. are a later addition.
192. **patience:** fortitude.   194. **art:** philosophic theory.   209. **new-added:** reinforced.   224. **with your will:** as you wish.
228. **niggard:** submit to sparingly.   241. **knave:** boy.   **o'er-watch'd:** worn out by keeping awake.   242. **[Claudius]** (Rowe).
Claudio F.   So in subsequent lines.   244. **[Varro]** (Rowe).   *Varrus* F.

Luc. I was sure your lordship did not give it me.

Bru. Bear with me, good boy, I am much forgetful. 255
Canst thou hold up thy heavy eyes a while,
And touch thy instrument a strain or two?

Luc. Ay, my lord, an't please you.

Bru. It does, my boy.
I trouble thee too much, but thou art willing.

Luc. It is my duty, sir. 260

Bru. I should not urge thy duty past thy might;
I know young bloods look for a time of rest.

Luc. I have slept, my lord, already.

Bru. It was well done; and thou shalt sleep again;
I will not hold thee long. If I do live, 265
I will be good to thee. [Music, and a song.
This is a sleepy tune. O murd'rous slumber,
Lay'st thou thy leaden mace upon my boy,
That plays thee music? Gentle knave, good-night;
I will not do thee so much wrong to wake thee. 270
If thou dost nod, thou break'st thy instrument.
I'll take it from thee; and, good boy, good-night.
Let me see, let me see; is not the leaf turn'd down
Where I left reading? Here it is, I think.

Enter the GHOST *of Cæsar.*

How ill this taper burns! Ha! who comes here?
I think it is the weakness of mine eyes 276
That shapes this monstrous apparition.
It comes upon me. Art thou anything?
Art thou some god, some angel, or some devil,
That mak'st my blood cold and my hair to stare? 280
Speak to me what thou art.

Ghost. Thy evil spirit, Brutus.

Bru. Why com'st thou?

Ghost. To tell thee thou shalt see me at Philippi.

Bru. Well; then I shall see thee again? 285

Ghost. Ay, at Philippi.

Bru. Why, I will see thee at Philippi, then.
[Exit Ghost.
Now I have taken heart thou vanishest.
Ill spirit, I would hold more talk with thee.
Boy, Lucius! Varro! Claudius! Sirs, awake! 290
Claudius!

Luc. The strings, my lord, are false.

Bru. He thinks he still is at his instrument.
Lucius, awake!

Luc. My lord? 295

Bru. Didst thou dream, Lucius, that thou so criedst out?

Luc. My lord, I do not know that I did cry.

Bru. Yes, that thou didst. Didst thou see anything?

Luc. Nothing, my lord.

Bru. Sleep again, Lucius. Sirrah Claudius! 300
Fellow thou, awake!

Var. My lord?

Clau. My lord?

Bru. Why did you so cry out, sirs, in your sleep?

Var. Clau. Did we, my lord?

Bru. Ay. Saw you anything? 305

Var. No, my lord, I saw nothing.

Clau. Nor I, my lord.

Bru. Go and commend me to my brother Cassius;
Bid him set on his powers betimes before,
And we will follow.

Var. Clau. It shall be done, my lord.
[Exeunt.

ACT V

[SCENE I. *The plains of Philippi.*]

Enter OCTAVIUS, ANTONY, *and their army.*

Oct. Now, Antony, our hopes are answered.
You said the enemy would not come down,
But keep the hills and upper regions.
It proves not so: their battles are at hand;
They mean to warn us at Philippi here, 5
Answering before we do demand of them.

Ant. Tut, I am in their bosoms, and I know
Wherefore they do it. They could be content
To visit other places, and come down
With fearful bravery, thinking by this face 10
To fasten in our thoughts that they have courage;
But 'tis not so.

Enter a MESSENGER.

Mess. Prepare you, Generals.
The enemy comes on in gallant show;
Their bloody sign of battle is hung out,
And something to be done immediately. 15

Ant. Octavius, lead your battle softly on,
Upon the left hand of the even field.

Oct. Upon the right hand I; keep thou the left.

Ant. Why do you cross me in this exigent?

Oct. I do not cross you; but I will do so. 20
[March.

Drum. Enter BRUTUS, CASSIUS, *and their army*
[LUCILIUS, TITINIUS, MESSALA, *and others*].

Bru. They stand, and would have parley.

Cas. Stand fast, Titinius; we must out and talk.

Oct. Mark Antony, shall we give sign of battle?

Ant. No, Cæsar, we will answer on their charge.
Make forth; the generals would have some words. 25

Oct. Stir not until the signal.

280. stare: stand on end.
Act V, sc. i, 4. battles: battalions. 5. warn: challenge. 7. am...bosoms: know their secrets. 10. With...bravery:
with a show of bravery, though afraid. face: exhibition. 19. exigent: emergency.

Bru. Words before blows; is it so, countrymen?

Oct. Not that we love words better, as you do.

Bru. Good words are better than bad strokes, Octavius.

Ant. In your bad strokes, Brutus, you give good words;   30
Witness the hole you made in Cæsar's heart,
Crying, "Long live! hail, Cæsar!"

Cas.   Antony,
The posture of your blows are yet unknown;
But for your words, they rob the Hybla bees,
And leave them honeyless.

Ant.   Not stingless too?   35

Bru. O, yes, and soundless too;
For you have stolen their buzzing, Antony,
And very wisely threat before you sting.

Ant. Villains, you did not so, when your vile daggers
Hack'd one another in the sides of Cæsar.   40
You show'd your teeth like apes, and fawn'd like hounds,
And bow'd like bondmen, kissing Cæsar's feet;
Whilst damned Casca, like a cur, behind
Struck Cæsar on the neck. O you flatterers!

Cas. Flatterers! Now, Brutus, thank yourself;   45
This tongue had not offended so to-day
If Cassius might have rul'd.

Oct. Come, come, the cause! If arguing make us sweat,
The proof of it will turn to redder drops.
Look!   50
I draw a sword against conspirators;
When think you that the sword goes up again?
Never, till Cæsar's three and thirty wounds
Be well aveng'd; or till another Cæsar
Have added slaughter to the sword of traitors.   55

Bru. Cæsar, thou canst not die by traitors' hands
Unless thou bring'st them with thee.

Oct.   So I hope;
I was not born to die on Brutus' sword.

Bru. O, if thou wert the noblest of thy strain,
Young man, thou couldst not die more honourable.

Cas. A peevish schoolboy, worthless of such honour,   61
Join'd with a masker and a reveller!

Ant. Old Cassius still!

Oct.   Come, Antony, away!
Defiance, traitors, hurl we in your teeth.
If you dare fight to-day, come to the field;   65
If not, when you have stomachs.

[*Exeunt Octavius, Antony, and army.*]

Cas. Why, now, blow wind, swell billow, and swim bark!
The storm is up, and all is on the hazard.

Bru. Ho, Lucilius! hark, a word with you.

Lucil.   (*Standing forth.*) My lord?
[*Brutus and Lucilius converse apart.*]

Cas. Messala!

Mes. (*Standing forth.*) What says my general?   70

Cas. Messala,
This is my birthday; as this very day
Was Cassius born. Give me thy hand, Messala.
Be thou my witness that against my will,
As Pompey was, am I compell'd to set   75
Upon one battle all our liberties.
You know that I held Epicurus strong
And his opinion; now I change my mind,
And partly credit things that do presage.
Coming from Sardis, on our former ensign   80
Two mighty eagles fell, and there they perch'd,
Gorging and feeding from our soldiers' hands,
Who to Philippi here consorted us.
This morning are they fled away and gone;
And in their steads do ravens, crows, and kites   85
Fly o'er our heads and downward look on us,
As we were sickly prey. Their shadows seem
A canopy most fatal, under which
Our army lies, ready to give up the ghost.

Mes. Believe not so.

Cas.   I but believe it partly;   90
For I am fresh of spirit, and resolv'd
To meet all perils very constantly.

Bru. Even so, Lucilius.

Cas.   Now, most noble Brutus,
The gods to-day stand friendly, that we may,
Lovers in peace, lead on our days to age!   95
But since the affairs of men rest still uncertain,
Let's reason with the worst that may befall.
If we do lose this battle, then is this
The very last time we shall speak together.
What are you then determined to do?   100

Bru. Even by the rule of that philosophy
By which I did blame Cato for the death
Which he did give himself, — I know not how,
But I do find it cowardly and vile,
For fear of what might fall, so to prevent   105
The time of life: — arming myself with patience
To stay the providence of some high powers
That govern us below.

Cas.   Then, if we lose this battle,
You are contented to be led in triumph
Thorough the streets of Rome?   110

Bru. No, Cassius, no. Think not, thou noble Roman,
That ever Brutus will go bound to Rome;

34. **Hybla:** a town in Sicily.   41. **show'd ... teeth:** grinned.   48. **cause:** i.e., to our real business.   52. **goes up:** will be sheathed.   55. **added ... to:** been slain by.   66. **stomachs:** courage.   80. **former:** foremost.   83. **consorted:** accompanied.   97. **reason with:** consider.   105–106. **prevent ... life:** anticipate death.

He bears too great a mind. But this same day
Must end that work the ides of March begun;
And whether we shall meet again I know not, 115
Therefore our everlasting farewell take.
For ever, and for ever, farewell, Cassius!
If we do meet again, why, we shall smile;
If not, why then, this parting was well made.
  Cas. For ever, and for ever, farewell, Brutus! 120
If we do meet again, we'll smile indeed;
If not, 'tis true this parting was well made.
  Bru. Why, then, lead on. O, that a man might
     know
The end of this day's business ere it come!
But it sufficeth that the day will end, 125
And then the end is known. Come, ho! away!
        [*Exeunt.*

[SCENE II. *The same. The field of battle.*]

  Alarum. Enter BRUTUS *and* MESSALA.

  Bru. Ride, ride, Messala, ride, and give these
     bills
Unto the legions on the other side. [*Loud alarum.*
Let them set on at once; for I perceive
But cold demeanour in Octavius' wing,
And sudden push gives them the overthrow. 5
Ride, ride, Messala: let them all come down.
        [*Exeunt.*

[SCENE III. *Another part of the field.*]

  Alarums. Enter CASSIUS *and* TITINIUS.

  Cas. O, look, Titinius, look, the villains fly!
Myself have to mine own turn'd enemy.
This ensign here of mine was turning back;
I slew the coward, and did take it from him.
  Tit. O Cassius, Brutus gave the word too early;
Who, having some advantage on Octavius, 6
Took it too eagerly. His soldiers fell to spoil,
Whilst we by Antony are all enclos'd.

        Enter PINDARUS.

  Pin. Fly further off, my lord, fly further off;
Mark Antony is in your tents, my lord; 10
Fly, therefore, noble Cassius, fly far off.
  Cas. This hill is far enough. Look, look, Titi-
     nius;
Are those my tents where I perceive the fire?
  Tit. They are, my lord.
  Cas.   Titinius, if thou lovest me
Mount thou my horse, and hide thy spurs in him 15
Till he have brought thee up to yonder troops
And here again; that I may rest assur'd
Whether yond troops are friend or enemy.

  Tit. I will be here again, even with a thought.
        [*Exit.*
  Cas. Go, Pindarus, get higher on that hill; 20
My sight was ever thick; regard Titinius,
And tell me what thou not'st about the field.
        [*Pindarus ascends the hill.*]
This day I breathed first; time is come round,
And where I did begin, there shall I end;
My life is run his compass. Sirrah, what news? 25
  Pin. (*Above.*) O my lord!
  Cas. What news?
  Pin. Titinius is enclosed round about
With horsemen, that make to him on the spur;
Yet he spurs on. Now they are almost on him. 30
Now, Titinius! Now some light. O, he lights too.
He's ta'en. (*Shout.*) And, hark! they shout for
     joy.
  Cas. Come down, behold no more.
O, coward that I am, to live so long
To see my best friend ta'en before my face! 35
        [*Pindarus [descends].*
Come hither, sirrah.
In Parthia did I take thee prisoner;
And then I swore thee, saving of thy life,
That whatsoever I did bid thee do,
Thou shouldst attempt it. Come now, keep thine
     oath; 40
Now be a freeman; and with this good sword,
That ran through Cæsar's bowels, search this
     bosom.
Stand not to answer; here, take thou the hilts,
And, when my face is cover'd, as 'tis now,
Guide thou the sword. [*Pindarus stabs him.*] Cæsar,
     thou art reveng'd, 45
Even with the sword that kill'd thee. [*Dies.*]
  Pin. So, I am free; yet would not so have been,
Durst I have done my will. O Cassius,
Far from this country Pindarus shall run,
Where never Roman shall take note of him. 50
        [*Exit.*]

        Re-enter TITINIUS *with* MESSALA.

  Mes. It is but change, Titinius; for Octavius
Is overthrown by noble Brutus' power,
As Cassius' legions are by Antony.
  Tit. These tidings will well comfort Cassius.
  Mes. Where did you leave him?
  Tit.   All disconsolate,
With Pindarus his bondman, on this hill. 56
  Mes. Is not that he that lies upon the ground?
  Tit. He lies not like the living. O my heart!
  Mes. Is not that he?
  Tit.   No, this was he, Messala,
But Cassius is no more. O setting sun, 60

Sc. ii, 1. **bills:** orders.
Sc. iii, 3. **ensign:** standard-bearer. 31. **light:** dismount. 38. **swore thee:** made thee swear. 51. **change:** exchange (of gains).

As in thy red rays thou dost sink to-night,
So in his red blood Cassius' day is set;
The sun of Rome is set! Our day is gone;
Clouds, dews, and dangers come; our deeds are
   done!
Mistrust of my success hath done this deed.   65
   Mes. Mistrust of good success hath done this
   deed.
O hateful error, melancholy's child,
Why dost thou show to the apt thoughts of men
The things that are not? O error, soon conceiv'd,
Thou never com'st unto a happy birth,   70
But kill'st the mother that engend'red thee!
   Tit. What, Pindarus! Where art thou, Pin-
   darus?
   Mes. Seek him, Titinius, whilst I go to meet
The noble Brutus, thrusting this report
Into his ears; I may say, "thrusting" it;   75
For piercing steel and darts envenomed
Shall be as welcome to the ears of Brutus
As tidings of this sight.
   Tit.   Hie you, Messala,
And I will seek for Pindarus the while.
                  [*Exit Messala.*]
Why didst thou send me forth, brave Cassius?   80
Did I not meet thy friends? and did not they
Put on my brows this wreath of victory
And bid me give it thee? Didst thou not hear their
   shouts?
Alas, thou hast misconstrued everything!
But, hold thee, take this garland on thy brow;   85
Thy Brutus bid me give it thee, and I
Will do his bidding. Brutus, come apace,
And see how I regarded Caius Cassius.
By your leave, gods! — this is a Roman's part.
Come, Cassius' sword, and find Titinius' heart.   90
                   [*Kills himself.*

Alarum. Re-enter MESSALA, *with* BRUTUS, *young*
  CATO, STRATO, VOLUMNIUS, LUCILIUS [*and*
  others].
   Bru. Where, where, Messala, doth his body lie?
   Mes. Lo, yonder, and Titinius mourning it.
   Bru. Titinius' face is upward.
   Cato.   He is slain.
   Bru. O Julius Cæsar, thou art mighty yet!
Thy spirit walks abroad, and turns our swords   95
In our own proper entrails.   [*Low alarums.*
   Cato.   Brave Titinius!
Look, whe'er he have not crown'd dead Cassius!
   Bru. Are yet two Romans living such as these?
The last of all the Romans, fare thee well!
It is impossible that ever Rome   100
Should breed thy fellow. Friends, I owe moe tears

To this dead man than you shall see me pay.
I shall find time, Cassius, I shall find time.
Come, therefore, and to [Thassos] send his body;
His funerals shall not be in our camp,   105
Lest it discomfort us. Lucilius, come;
And come, young Cato; let us to the field.
Labeo and [Flavius], set our battles on.
'Tis three o'clock; and, Romans, yet ere night
We shall try fortune in a second fight.   110
                   [*Exeunt.*

[SCENE IV. *Another part of the field.*]

Alarum. Enter BRUTUS, Messala, *young* CATO,
     LUCILIUS, *and* Flavius.
   Bru. Yet, countrymen, O, yet hold up your
   heads!
   Cato. What bastard doth not? Who will go with
   me?
I will proclaim my name about the field.
I am the son of Marcus Cato, ho!
A foe to tyrants, and my country's friend;   5
I am the son of Marcus Cato, ho!

Enter SOLDIERS, *and fight.*

   [*Bru.*] And I am Brutus, Marcus Brutus, I;
Brutus, my country's friend; know me for Brutus!
                     [*Exit.*]
   Lucil. O young and noble Cato, art thou down?
Why, now thou diest as bravely as Titinius,   10
And mayst be honour'd, being Cato's son.
   [*1.*] *Sol.* Yield, or thou diest.
   Lucil.   Only I yield to die:
There is so much that thou wilt kill me straight;
                 [*Offering money.*]
Kill Brutus, and be honour'd in his death.
   [*1.*] *Sol.* We must not. A noble prisoner!   15

Enter ANTONY.

   2. Sol. Room, ho! Tell Antony, Brutus is ta'en.
   1. Sol. I'll tell the news. Here comes the gen-
   eral.
Brutus is ta'en, Brutus is ta'en, my lord!
   Ant. Where is he?
   Lucil. Safe, Antony; Brutus is safe enough.   20
I dare assure thee that no enemy
Shall ever take alive the noble Brutus;
The gods defend him from so great a shame!
When you do find him, or alive or dead,
He will be found like Brutus, like himself.   25
   Ant. This is not Brutus, friend; but, I assure you,
A prize no less in worth. Keep this man safe,
Give him all kindness; I had rather have
Such men my friends than enemies. Go on,

---

65. **Mistrust:** i.e., on Cassius' part. 71. **mother:** person. 104. **[Thassos]** (Theobald). *Tharsus* F. 106. **discomfort:** dis-
courage. 108. **[Flavius]** F₂. *Flavio* F₁.
Sc. iv, 12. **Only I yield:** I yield only.

And see whe'er Brutus be alive or dead;   30
And bring us word unto Octavius' tent
How everything is chanc'd.   [*Exeunt.*

SCENE V. [*Another part of the field.*]

Enter BRUTUS, DARDANIUS, CLITUS, STRATO,
and VOLUMNIUS.

Bru. Come, poor remains of friends, rest on this
    rock.
Cli. Statilius show'd the torchlight, but, my
    lord,
He came not back.   He is or ta'en or slain.
Bru. Sit thee down, Clitus; slaying is the word,
It is a deed in fashion.   Hark thee, Clitus.   5
                              [*Whispering.*]
Cli. What, I, my lord?   No, not for all the world.
Bru. Peace then! no words.
Cli.   I'll rather kill myself.
Bru. Hark thee, Dardanius.   [*Whispering.*]
Dar.   Shall I do such a deed?
Cli. O Dardanius!
Dar. O Clitus!   10
Cli. What ill request did Brutus make to thee?
Dar. To kill him, Clitus.   Look, he meditates.
Cli. Now is that noble vessel full of grief,
That it runs over even at his eyes.
Bru. Come hither, good Volumnius; list a word.
Vol. What says my lord?
Bru.   Why, this, Volumnius: 16
The ghost of Cæsar hath appear'd to me
Two several times by night; at Sardis once,
And, this last night, here in Philippi fields.
I know my hour is come.
Vol.   Not so, my lord.   20
Bru. Nay, I am sure it is, Volumnius.
Thou seest the world, Volumnius, how it goes;
Our enemies have beat us to the pit.   [*Low alarums.*
It is more worthy to leap in ourselves
Than tarry till they push us.   Good Volumnius, 25
Thou know'st that we two went to school together;
Even for that our love of old, I prithee,
Hold thou my sword-hilts, whilst I run on it.
Vol. That's not an office for a friend, my lord.
                              [*Alarum still.*
Cli. Fly, fly, my lord; there is no tarrying here. 30
Bru. Farewell to you, and you, and you, Volum-
    nius.
Strato, thou hast been all this while asleep;
Farewell to thee too, Strato.   Countrymen,
My heart doth joy that yet in all my life
I found no man but he was true to me.   35
I shall have glory by this losing day
More than Octavius and Mark Antony
By this vile conquest shall attain unto.

So fare you well at once; for Brutus' tongue
Hath almost ended his life's history.   40
Night hangs upon mine eyes; my bones would rest,
That have but labour'd to attain this hour.
            [*Alarum.   Cry within,* "Fly, fly, fly!"
Cli. Fly, my lord, fly.
Bru.   Hence! I will follow.
        [*Exeunt Clitus, Dardanius, and Volum-
            nius.*]
I prithee, Strato, stay thou by thy lord.
Thou art a fellow of a good respect;   45
Thy life hath had some smatch of honour in it.
Hold then my sword, and turn away thy face,
While I do run upon it.   Wilt thou, Strato?
Stra. Give me your hand first.   Fare you well,
    my lord.
Bru. Farewell, good Strato.   [*Runs on his
    sword.*]   Cæsar, now be still;   50
I kill'd not thee with half so good a will.   [*Dies.*

Alarum.   Retreat.   Enter OCTAVIUS, ANTONY,
    MESSALA, LUCILIUS, *and the army.*

Oct. What man is that?
Mes. My master's man.   Strato, where is thy
    master?
Stra. Free from the bondage you are in, Mes-
    sala;
The conquerors can but make a fire of him,   55
For Brutus only overcame himself,
And no man else hath honour by his death.
Lucil. So Brutus should be found.   I thank thee,
    Brutus,
That thou hast prov'd Lucilius' saying true.
Oct. All that serv'd Brutus, I will entertain them.
Fellow, wilt thou bestow thy time with me?   6r
Stra. Ay, if Messala will prefer me to you.
Oct. Do so, good Messala.
Mes. How died my master, Strato?
Stra. I held the sword, and he did run on it.   65
Mes. Octavius, then take him to follow thee,
That did the latest service to my master.
Ant. This was the noblest Roman of them all.
All the conspirators, save only he,
Did that they did in envy of great Cæsar;   70
He only, in a general honest thought
And common good to all, made one of them.
His life was gentle, and the elements
So mix'd in him that Nature might stand up
And say to all the world, "This was a man!"   75
Oct. According to his virtue let us use him,
With all respect and rites of burial.
Within my tent his bones to-night shall lie,
Most like a soldier, ordered honourably.
So call the field to rest; and let's away   80
To part the glories of this happy day. [*Exeunt omnes.*

Sc. v, 23. **pit:** i.e., of destruction.   46. **smatch:** smack.   60. **entertain:** take into service.   62. **prefer:** recommend.   73
gentle: noble.   80. **field:** army.   81. **part:** share.

The Tragedy of Hamlet, Prince of Denmark

THE FIRST SURVIVING NOTICE of a Shakespearean *Hamlet* is an entry in the Stationers' Register for July 26, 1602: "The Revenge of Hamlett Prince Denmarke as yt was latelie Acted by the Lord Chamberleyne his servantes." In 1603 appeared the First Quarto, a pirated and badly mutilated text only a little more than half the length of that in the Second Quarto (1604). The Second Quarto, printed "according to the true and perfect Coppie," gives the authorized text of the play as currently performed by Shakespeare's company. This text differs significantly from that in the First Folio; it contains about 218 lines absent in the Folio, but lacks some 85 lines which the Folio has. Since the passages in question are all assuredly genuine, the natural conclusion is that both sets of omissions represent cuts made at different periods for acting purposes. It is likely that the Second Quarto was printed from Shakespeare's manuscript, in which the earlier set of cuts had been marked off. The Folio text, which has more numerous and more explicit stage directions, may have been set up from a transcript which had served as a prompt copy. Both the Second Quarto and the Folio have substantial authority, but the Folio appears to present the later, and therefore perhaps the more approved, acting version utilized by Shakespeare's fellows. The present text is consequently based upon the Folio.

The relationship of the First Quarto to the authoritative texts is a controversial problem. It was once generally held that the First Quarto preserves a corrupt reporting of an earlier handling by Shakespeare of the Hamlet story. The best of recent opinion, however, regards it as a debased rendering of an abridgment of the true text, made for a company on tour. Since the First Quarto reproduces the speeches of Marcellus with striking accuracy, in contrast to the bungling of other parts, it seems almost certain that the pirate was an actor who had played Marcellus. Bad though it is, the First Quarto is not negligible, for at a few points it provides a sound reading where the good texts are unsatisfactory.

The date of composition is conjectural. The entry in the Stationers' Register gives one terminus. A note by Gabriel Harvey in his edition of Speght's Chaucer is suggestive. Harvey remarks the pleasure afforded "the wiser sort" by Shakespeare's *Hamlet*, and since he also mentions commendation of *Albion's England* by the Earl of Essex, it is argued that his note was penned prior to the Earl's death (February 25, 1601). Late 1600 or 1601 is a likely date for the play.

The origin of the Hamlet story lies in the obscure regions of Scandinavian legend. It appears that Hamlet (Amlothi) was the hero of a tale as old as the Old English *Beowulf*, but what his story was like in its ancient form can only be vaguely guessed. The earliest literary account of Hamlet occurs in the *Historia Danica* (c. 1200) by Saxo Grammaticus, who drew upon tradition and the lost Scandinavian sagas. Saxo's narrative was adapted by Belleforest as one of his *Histoires Tragiques* (1576). In Belleforest the story lay ready to the hand of a dramatist. The essential features familiar in Shakespeare's play are present: adultery, fratricide, revenge, the hero's feigned madness, prototypes of Ophelia, Horatio, Polonius, Rosencrantz, and Guildenstern (though Shakespeare's characterization utterly transforms these figures), the journey to England, and the exchange of letters. There are, however, signal differences. In Belleforest the murder of the elder Hamlet is public knowledge. His brother successfully defended it, asserting that he had caught the dead king on the point of murdering his queen and that he had killed him in order to save the queen's life. Hamlet is but a youth, entirely at the mercy of his unscrupulous uncle. He pretends madness as his only means of self-protection until he can avenge his father. His uncle suspects him, however, and is resolved to have him killed if he can prove him sane. The devices employed foreshadow episodes in the play. An effort is made to trap the boy through the agency of a girl whom he loves; later a spy is set in the queen's chamber when Hamlet is to come for an interview with his mother. The first attempt is frustrated because Hamlet has been warned by a friend. On the second occasion Hamlet, still feigning madness, enters the chamber crowing like a cock and waving his arms about; in this fashion he beats the hangings, detects the intruder behind them, and kills him. To his repentant mother Hamlet confides his plan for revenge. On his way to England Hamlet not only procures the death of his companions by the exchange of letters, but requests the king of England to give him his daughter in marriage. After about a year in England Hamlet returns to Denmark and, resuming his feigned madness, enters his uncle's palace during a feast celebrating his own supposed death. He gets the courtiers drunk, sets fire to the hall, and kills the king. Then going before the people with a speech explaining everything, he is proclaimed king. The rest of the story is irrelevant to the play.

The indebtedness of Shakespeare, and his originality, would be easy to determine if this were all one had to consider, but between Belleforest's story and Shakespeare's drama stands a lost play. To its existence there are several witnesses. Henslowe records a performance on June 11, 1594; Lodge alludes in his *Wits Miserie* (1596) to "ye ghost which cried so miserally at ye Theator, like an oister wife, *Hamlet, revenge.*" But the play dates from the previous decade, for Nashe, in the Preface to Greene's *Menaphon* (1589), proclaims that "English *Seneca* read by Candle light yeelds many good sentences... and if you intreate him faire in a frostie morning, hee will affoord you whole *Hamlets*, I should say handfuls of Tragicall speeches." The author of this lost play is unknown, but evidence points to Kyd. It was clearly a play of the Senecan mode, like *The Spanish Tragedy*, though it may have been by an imitator of Kyd. In any event, it is certain that this lost play had already added to the existent source material the Ghost, probably the play within the play, and the fencing match involving Hamlet's death. Shakespeare must have been indebted to the old play, whatever its content; he may have worked from it directly, though that would presuppose that his company owned the "book," for there is no evidence that the old play was ever printed.

In *Hamlet* the character of the protagonist commands interest above everything else. It is significant that when the Prince is first introduced to us his tragedy has already begun. His impassioned soliloquy (I.ii.129–59) reveals the depth of misery and despair into which the death of a loved father and the hasty and "incestuous" marriage of his mother have plunged him. Because of these things life has lost its savor for him, the world seems contaminated, and he wishes he were dead. Hamlet's condition argues a nature of abnormal sensitivity; he has been, evidently, an idealist, and all that one

can learn of what he was like before disillusion transformed him assumes manifest interest and importance. Through the remarks of others and through speeches of Hamlet himself in relaxed or unguarded moments Shakespeare takes pains to inform us. The famous speech of Ophelia (III.i.158 ff.), wrung from her very heart, describes the noble attributes of the real Hamlet. From this testimony we learn that Hamlet was the embodiment of all courtly virtues, the incarnation of gentility as conceived by the Renaissance. The normal Hamlet can be seen also in the rare moments of gaiety or spontaneity when sudden pleasure makes him forget his melancholy; for example, in his joyous reception of Horatio (I.ii.160 ff.), his hearty welcome to Rosencrantz and Guildenstern (II.ii.226 ff.), and his delight at the arrival of the players (II.ii.440 ff.). In his true nature Hamlet is healthy, frank, and generous, and Claudius, laying his treacherous plot with Laertes, honors his integrity (IV.vii.135–37). Through this very integrity, however, Hamlet is vulnerable at the beginning of the play, as at its close; for it is because he is in morals and in honor finely tuned that his mother's new marriage so offends him. He who had worshiped his father (I.ii.139–53, 187–88; III.iv.55–62) sees his mother's act as treason to an ideal. It is to a mind already depressed and brooding that the Ghost's dread message is imparted.

For Hamlet the Ghost's revelation is a double shock, since he learns not only that his father had been foully murdered, but that his mother, who in his estimation has already fallen so low, had been adulterous while his father was still alive. That Hamlet had never suspected the murder is clear from his exclamation (I.v.26). That he was ignorant of the adultery is equally certain, though he says nothing. Horrified and overcome with pity for his wronged father, Hamlet is speechless, and this silence of grief is one of Shakespeare's finest effects. For fifty lines (I.v.41–91) the Ghost speaks without interruption, while Hamlet stands tense with emotion, and not until the Ghost has vanished does Hamlet find words again.

Hamlet accepts the commission of vengeance with an alacrity which the Ghost commends. To "sweep" to his revenge is his filial duty and his express desire, but he does not do so, and his delay has been the subject of voluminous critical discussion. One must recognize that the postponement of vengeance is a dramatic necessity; without Hamlet's delay there would be no play. Shakespeare's problem was to motivate the delay, and though the motivation he has provided may seem to modern critics unsatisfactory or incomplete, it must be accepted with whatever implications it may carry. When Hamlet swears vengeance, his faith in the authenticity of the Ghost is absolute. Nevertheless, there is the possibility, a commonplace in Elizabethan ghost lore, that the apparition may not be the spirit of his father at all, but rather a demon in the likeness of his father seeking to draw him into evil. This possibility, explicit in the warning of Horatio (I.iv.69 ff.), has already occurred to Hamlet (I.ii.244–46; I.iv.40), though in the moving colloquy with the Ghost suspicion is swept away. Doubt returns subsequently, however, finding memorable expression in the soliloquy of Hamlet inspired by the stirring recitation of his player-friend (II.ii.627–33). To hold, as some critics have, that Hamlet suddenly invents this scruple about the honesty of the Ghost as a pretext for deferring a deed that is repugnant to him is unjust to Hamlet and to Shakespeare. We have heard nothing about this scruple, it is true, since Hamlet swore vengeance, yet it is arbitrary to assume that it recurs for the first time on this occasion. Though Shakespeare does not indicate how soon after the conversation with the Ghost Hamlet's doubt began again to assail him, about two months have passed since that event (cf. I.ii.138 and III.ii.133–36), and one may reasonably suppose that alternate moods of conviction and of uncertainty have possessed Hamlet for some time. Moved by the emotion of the player, Hamlet reviews his own cue for passion, scourges himself for his inaction, and hits upon the play within the play as a means for resolving, once for all, the now insistent question of the Ghost's authenticity.

After the success of Hamlet's "mouse trap" his first opportunity to kill the King comes when he discovers him at prayer, but Hamlet refuses this chance, wishing to take Claudius "in some act that has no relish of salvation in it" and so to damn his soul. Some critics, finding this savage reasoning incompatible with the qualities they admire in Hamlet, construe it as another excuse for procrastination. Nevertheless, one must take Hamlet at his word. To us, this cruel wish is inconsistent with Hamlet's native refinement, but it is no more so than Hamlet's accepting the obligation of vengeance in the first place, and the line of reasoning was familiar to Shakespeare's audience. Individuals in the Renaissance may have outgrown the primitive code of vengeance, but everybody in that period was familiar with it, and the popularity of the contemporary revenge plays, in which vindictiveness touched extremes, gave it fresh notoriety. *Hamlet* is a revenge play, and the fact is that although Shakespeare marvelously transcended the genre, and gave to his hero superior dignity and nobility, he did not eradicate all the earlier crudity of the type. Moreover, Hamlet's particular motive for sparing Claudius was entirely comprehensible to Elizabethans.

With fine skill Shakespeare makes the fact of delay itself dramatic. The play within the play is intensely exciting; the audience is identified with Hamlet in seeking corroboration of the Ghost. Hamlet spares Claudius at prayer, but Claudius has been unable to pray, and thus, ironically, Hamlet loses an opportunity on his own expressed terms. Presently, in his mother's chamber, Hamlet kills Polonius, striking swiftly in the belief that it is the King (III.iv.25, 32). With this mistake his cause is lost, and would have remained forever so had not accident favored him on the voyage to England. Accident, however, merely presents the occasion for action; the energy and the sureness with which Hamlet acts show his mettle. After his return to Denmark, Hamlet kills Claudius at his first real opportunity; for of course he would not attack him at Ophelia's grave. It is easy to convert the simple dramatic necessity of Hamlet's delay into an intricate problem of character, especially in view of Hamlet's melancholy and his habit of self-analysis, but one must be careful not to work these factors too hard. On two notable occasions Hamlet denounces himself for inaction (II.ii.576 ff.; IV.iv.32 ff.) and, unpacking his heart with words, renews his resolve. Like any sensitive man, he can castigate himself unduly; at every crucial point, however, there is a plain reason why his task has not been fulfilled. And letting Hamlet renew his resolve at significant moments is good drama, for it increases suspense as to when and how he will carry it out.

There is no question whatsoever about Hamlet's sanity; his madness is only feigned. His decision to put an antic disposition on when and as he shall see fit, is taken suddenly (I.v.168 ff.), and he never gives any reason for it. This is not the case in Belleforest, where the feigned madness is clearly motivated. There Hamlet, a mere youth, pretends madness as a protection against an uncle who would slay him without hesitation if he could be sure of his sanity. How the madness was motivated in the lost play we do not know. But in Shakespeare, where the deed of Claudius is not known, and where Claudius is eager to be on good terms with Hamlet, this device is not necessary. The fact would seem to be that Shakespeare accepted the feigned madness as an integral factor in his inherited material, either without realizing that with his re-creation of the hero it needed a different motivation, or without caring to invent one. Very likely Shakespeare believed that audiences in the playhouse would be content to assume that Hamlet had reasons of his own. Certainly he knew that the feigned madness would afford moments of comic relief, for he uses it most skillfully to that end. Though Hamlet utters "wild and whirling words" on a few occasions when it is clear that his speech is not a display of the antic disposition (e.g., I.v.117 ff.; III.ii. 282 ff.; V.i.297 ff.), his conduct at such times is no more than the recoil from emotional strain, such as any normal person might exhibit. To particularize briefly, if the nonsensical jingle which Hamlet spouts after the success of the "mouse trap" betrays a neurotic state, we should certainly expect Hamlet to be highly excited when instructing the player in the delivery of the lines he has composed for him and in talking with Horatio before the play begins; but then he is conspicuously calm. For his unseemly conduct at Ophelia's grave he manfully repents; the showy grief of Laertes revolted him and made him forget himself.

Dramatically the rôle of Claudius is the equal of Hamlet's. Urbane, diplomatic, intelligent, courageous, and masterful in the face of danger, Claudius is a worthy antagonist for Hamlet. His self-control is consummate. After the dumb show has revealed to him Hamlet's knowledge of his secret and his consequent imminent peril, Claudius elects to sit out the play, and nearly succeeds. It is not so much the argument of the play as the relentless focus of Hamlet's eyes and his menacing irony that breaks

him down. His intrepidity when Laertes storms the palace with the mob at his back is crowned by the skill with which he subdues that rash and misguided young man to his designs. Claudius is the villain of the play, but he is no ordinary villain. For all his apparent callousness, his conscience is alive, and it is the irony of his fate that he cannot relish the fruits of his crime, or expiate it by living at peace with the nephew he has injured, as it had been his honest hope to do.

The Ghost of Hamlet's father is a remarkable creation. He is no horrific apparition, but "the beauteous majesty of buried Denmark." He is seen in his natural and wonted dignity, dressed as he had been dressed in life. "So excellent a king"; all that Hamlet has said of him (I.ii.139-44) is confirmed for us by his courteous action, his graceful speaking, and his noble solicitude for his queen. Shakespeare makes us feel pity, admiration, and affection for the Ghost. Indeed, the personality of the dead king, along with the character of the protagonist, contributes notably to the distinctive refinement of this tragedy of revenge, which stands today as Shakespeare's most popular and most frequently acted play.

THE TRAGEDY OF HAMLET,
PRINCE OF DENMARK

[DRAMATIS PERSONÆ

CLAUDIUS, *King of Denmark.*
HAMLET, *son to the late, and nephew to the present, King.*
POLONIUS, *Lord Chamberlain.*
HORATIO, *friend to Hamlet.*
LAERTES, *son to Polonius.*
VOLTIMAND,
CORNELIUS,
ROSENCRANTZ,
GUILDENSTERN, *courtiers.*
OSRIC,
A Gentleman,
MARCELLUS,
BERNARDO, *officers.*

FRANCISCO, *a soldier.*
REYNALDO, *servant to Polonius.*
A Priest.
Players.
Two Clowns, *grave-diggers.*
FORTINBRAS, *Prince of Norway.*
A Norwegian Captain.
English Ambassadors.

GERTRUDE, *Queen of Denmark, and mother to Hamlet.*
OPHELIA, *daughter to Polonius.*

Ghost of Hamlet's Father.

Lords, Ladies, Officers, Soldiers, Sailors, Messengers, and other Attendants.

SCENE: *Elsinore, Denmark.*]

ACT I

SCENE I. [*Elsinore. A platform before the castle.*]

FRANCISCO [*at his post. Enter to him*] BERNARDO.

Ber. Who's there?
Fran. Nay, answer me. Stand, and unfold yourself.
Ber. Long live the king!
Fran. Bernardo?
Ber. He. 5
Fran. You come most carefully upon your hour.
Ber. 'Tis now struck twelve. Get thee to bed, Francisco.
Fran. For this relief much thanks. 'Tis bitter cold,
And I am sick at heart.
Ber. Have you had quiet guard?
Fran. Not a mouse stirring. 10
Ber. Well, good-night.

If you do meet Horatio and Marcellus,
The rivals of my watch, bid them make haste.

Enter HORATIO *and* MARCELLUS.

Fran. I think I hear them. Stand! Who's there?
Hor. Friends to this ground.
Mar. And liegemen to the Dane. 15
Fran. Give you good-night.
Mar. O, farewell, honest soldier.
Who hath reliev'd you?
Fran. Bernardo has my place.
Give you good-night. [*Exit.*
Mar. Holla! Bernardo!
Ber. Say,
What, is Horatio there?
Hor. A piece of him.
Ber. Welcome, Horatio; welcome, good Marcellus. 20
Mar. What, has this thing appear'd again tonight?

Act I, sc. i, 3. **Long ... king.** A password. 13. **rivals:** partners. 21. **Mar.** F Q₁. *Hora* Q₂.

Ber. I have seen nothing.

Mar. Horatio says 'tis but our fantasy,
And will not let belief take hold of him
Touching this dreaded sight, twice seen of us;   25
Therefore I have entreated him along
With us to watch the minutes of this night,
That, if again this apparition come,
He may approve our eyes and speak to it.

Hor. Tush, tush, 'twill not appear.

Ber.   Sit down a while,   30
And let us once again assail your ears,
That are so fortified against our story,
What we two nights have seen.

Hor.   Well, sit we down,
And let us hear Bernardo speak of this.

Ber. Last night of all,   35
When yond same star that's westward from the pole
Had made his course t' illume that part of heaven
Where now it burns, Marcellus and myself,
The bell then beating one, —

Enter the Ghost.

Mar. Peace, break thee off!   Look, where it
comes again!   40

Ber. In the same figure, like the King that's
dead.

Mar. Thou art a scholar; speak to it, Horatio.

Ber. Looks it not like the King?   Mark it,
Horatio.

Hor. Most like; it harrows me with fear and
wonder.

Ber. It would be spoke to.

Mar.   Question it, Horatio.   45

Hor. What art thou that usurp'st this time of
night,
Together with that fair and warlike form
In which the majesty of buried Denmark
Did sometimes march?   By heaven I charge thee,
speak!

Mar. It is offended.

Ber.   See, it stalks away!   50

Hor. Stay!   Speak, speak!   I charge thee,
speak!   [*Exit Ghost.*

Mar. 'Tis gone, and will not answer.

Ber. How now, Horatio! You tremble and look
pale.
Is not this something more than fantasy?
What think you on't?   55

Hor. Before my God, I might not this believe
Without the sensible and true avouch
Of mine own eyes.

Mar.   Is it not like the King?

Hor. As thou art to thyself.
Such was the very armour he had on   60
When [he] th' ambitious Norway combated.
So frown'd he once, when, in an angry parle,
He smote the sledded [Polacks] on the ice.
'Tis strange.

Mar. Thus twice before, and [jump] at this
dead hour,   65
With martial stalk hath he gone by our watch.

Hor. In what particular thought to work I
know not;
But, in the gross and scope of my opinion,
This bodes some strange eruption to our state.

Mar. Good now, sit down, and tell me, he that
knows,   70
Why this same strict and most observant watch
So nightly toils the subject of the land,
And why such daily cast of brazen cannon,
And foreign mart for implements of war;
Why such impress of shipwrights, whose sore task
Does not divide the Sunday from the week.   76
What might be toward, that this sweaty haste
Doth make the night joint-labourer with the day,
Who is't that can inform me?

Hor.   That can I;
At least, the whisper goes so.   Our last king,   80
Whose image even but now appear'd to us,
Was, as you know, by Fortinbras of Norway,
Thereto prick'd on by a most emulate pride,
Dar'd to the combat; in which our valiant Ham-
let —   84
For so this side of our known world esteem'd him —
Did slay this Fortinbras; who, by a seal'd compact
Well ratified by law and heraldry,
Did forfeit, with his life, all those his lands
Which he stood seiz'd on, to the conqueror;
Against the which, a moiety competent   90
Was gaged by our king; which had return'd
To the inheritance of Fortinbras,
Had he been vanquisher; as, by the same covenant
And carriage of the [articled] design
His fell to Hamlet.   Now, sir, young Fortinbras,   95
Of unimproved mettle hot and full,
Hath in the skirts of Norway here and there
Shark'd up a list of landless resolutes,
For food and diet, to some enterprise
That hath a stomach in't; which is no other —   100
[As] it doth well appear unto our state —
But to recover of us, by strong hand
And terms compulsative, those foresaid lands
So by his father lost; and this, I take it,
Is the main motive of our preparations,   105

29. **approve:** confirm.   42. **scholar.** One had to address spirits in Latin.   57. **sensible:** of the senses.   61. **[he]** Q₂. Om. F.   63. **sledded:** using sleds or sledges.   **[Polacks]** (Malone): Poles.   *Pollax* F.   *pollax* Q₂.   65. **[jump]** Q₂: precisely. *just* F.   68. **gross and scope:** main drift.   72. **toils:** causes to work.   **subject:** people.   75. **impress:** forced service.   83. **emulate:** envious.   89. **seiz'd on:** possessed of.   90. **moiety competent:** equal share.   91. **gaged:** pledged.   94. **[articled] design** (Edd.).   *article designe* F₁.   *article design'd* F₂.   The line means: the plan conveyed by the articles of the treaty.   96. **unimproved:** untried.   98. **Shark'd up:** collected swiftly.   **landless** F₁.   *lawless* Q₂.   100. **hath . . . in't:** takes courage.   101. **[As]** Q₂.   *And* F.

The source of this our watch, and the chief head
Of this post-haste and romage in the land.
  [*Ber.* I think it be no other but e'en so.
Well may it sort that this portentous figure
Comes armed through our watch, so like the King
That was and is the question of these wars.   111
  Hor. A mote it is to trouble the mind's eye.
In the most high and palmy state of Rome,
A little ere the mightiest Julius fell,
The graves stood tenantless and the sheeted dead 115
Did squeak and gibber in the Roman streets.

. . . .

As stars with trains of fire and dews of blood,
Disasters in the sun; and the moist star
Upon whose influence Neptune's empire stands
Was sick almost to doomsday with eclipse.   120
And even the like precurse of fierce events,
As harbingers preceding still the fates
And prologue to the omen coming on,
Have heaven and earth together demonstrated
Unto our climatures and countrymen.]   125

Re-enter Ghost.

But soft, behold! Lo, where it comes again!
I'll cross it, though it blast me. Stay, illusion!
If thou hast any sound, or use of voice,
Speak to me;
If there be any good thing to be done   130
That may to thee do ease and grace to me,
Speak to me;
If thou art privy to thy country's fate,
Which, happily, foreknowing may avoid,
O speak!   135
Or if thou hast uphoarded in thy life
Extorted treasure in the womb of earth,
For which, they say, you spirits oft walk in death,
Speak of it; stay, and speak! (*Cock crows.*) Stop
  it, Marcellus.
  Mar. Shall I strike at it with my partisan?   140
  Hor. Do, if it will not stand.
  Ber.   'Tis here!
  Hor.   'Tis here!
  Mar. 'Tis gone!   [*Exit Ghost.*
We do it wrong, being so majestical,
To offer it the show of violence;
For it is, as the air, invulnerable,   145
And our vain blows malicious mockery.
  Ber. It was about to speak, when the cock crew.
  Hor. And then it started like a guilty thing
Upon a fearful summons. I have heard
The cock, that is the trumpet to the [morn],   150

Doth with his lofty and shrill-sounding throat
Awake the god of day; and, at his warning,
Whether in sea or fire, in earth or air,
The extravagant and erring spirit hies
To his confine; and of the truth herein   155
This present object made probation.
  Mar. It faded on the crowing of the cock.
Some [say] that ever 'gainst that season comes
Wherein our Saviour's birth is celebrated,
The bird of dawning singeth all night long;   160
And then, they say, no spirit can walk abroad;
The nights are wholesome; then no planets strike,
No fairy [takes], nor witch hath power to charm,
So hallow'd and so gracious is the time.
  Hor. So have I heard and do in part believe it.
But, look, the morn, in russet mantle clad,   166
Walks o'er the dew of yon high eastern hill.
Break we our watch up; and, by my advice,
Let us impart what we have seen to-night
Unto young Hamlet; for, upon my life,   170
This spirit, dumb to us, will speak to him.
Do you consent we shall acquaint him with it,
As needful in our loves, fitting our duty?
  Mar. Let's do't, I pray; and I this morning
    know
Where we shall find him most conveniently.   175
                                 [*Exeunt.*

SCENE II. [*A room of state in the castle.*]

Flourish.   *Enter the* KING, QUEEN, HAMLET,
POLONIUS, LAERTES, OPHELIA, *Lords, and At-*
tendants.

  King. Though yet of Hamlet our dear brother's
    death
The memory be green, and that it us befitted
To bear our hearts in grief, and our whole kingdom
To be contracted in one brow of woe,
Yet so far hath discretion fought with nature   5
That we with wisest sorrow think on him
Together with remembrance of ourselves.
Therefore our sometime sister, now our queen,
Th' imperial jointress of this warlike state,
Have we, as 'twere with a defeated joy, —   10
With one auspicious and one dropping eye,
With mirth in funeral and with dirge in marriage,
In equal scale weighing delight and dole, —
Taken to wife; nor have we herein barr'd
Your better wisdoms, which have freely gone   15
With this affair along. For all, our thanks.
Now follows that you know: young Fortinbras,

---

106. **head:** source. 107. **romage:** bustle. 108–25. [*Ber.* ... **countrymen**] Q₂. Om. F. 109. **sort:** fit. 115. **tenant-less** Q₄. *tennatlesse* Q₂. 116. **Did ... streets.** Probably a line has dropped out after l. 116. 118. **Disasters:** unfavorable aspects. **moist star:** moon. 121. **precurse:** precursor. 125. **climatures:** regions. 127. Q₂ adds S.D. *It spreads his arms.* 140. **partisan:** long-handled spear. 150. **trumpet:** trumpeter. [morn] Q₂. *day* F. 154. **extravagant:** vagrant. **erring:** wandering. 156. **probation:** proof. 158. [say] Q₂. *sayes* F. 161. **can walk** F. *dare sturre* Q₂. 163. [takes] Q₂: **charms.** *talks* F.

Sc. ii, 9. jointress: joint sovereign. 10. **defeated:** impaired.

Holding a weak supposal of our worth,
Or thinking by our late dear brother's death
Our state to be disjoint and out of frame, 20
Colleagued with the dream of his advantage,
He hath not fail'd to pester us with message
Importing the surrender of those lands
Lost by his father, with all bonds of law,
To our most valiant brother. So much for him. 25

   Enter VOLTIMAND *and* CORNELIUS.
Now for ourself and for this time of meeting,
Thus much the business is: we have here writ
To Norway, uncle of young Fortinbras, —
Who, impotent and bed-rid, scarcely hears
Of this his nephew's purpose, — to suppress 30
His further gait herein, in that the levies,
The lists, and full proportions are all made
Out of his subject; and we here dispatch
You, good Cornelius, and you, Voltimand,
For bearing of this greeting to old Norway; 35
Giving to you no further personal power
To business with the king, more than the scope
Of these delated articles allow. [*Giving a paper.*]
Farewell, and let your haste commend your duty.
 [*Cor.*] ⎱ In that and all things will we show our
 Vol. ⎰ duty. 40
 King. We doubt it nothing; heartily farewell.
      [*Exeunt Voltimand and Cornelius.*
And now, Laertes, what's the news with you?
You told us of some suit; what is't, Laertes?
You cannot speak of reason to the Dane
And lose your voice. What wouldst thou beg,
  Laertes, 45
That shall not be my offer, not thy asking?
The head is not more native to the heart,
The hand more instrumental to the mouth,
Than is the throne of Denmark to thy father.
What wouldst thou have, Laertes?
 Laer.   Dread my lord, 50
Your leave and favour to return to France;
From whence though willingly I came to Denmark
To show my duty in your coronation,
Yet now, I must confess, that duty done,
My thoughts and wishes bend again towards
  France 55
And bow them to your gracious leave and pardon.
 King. Have you your father's leave? What
  says Polonius?
 Pol. He hath, my lord, [wrung from me my slow
  leave
By laboursome petition, and at last
Upon his will I seal'd my hard consent.] 60
I do beseech you, give him leave to go.

 King. Take thy fair hour, Laertes. Time be
  thine,
And thy best graces spend it at thy will!
But now, my cousin Hamlet, and my son, —
 Ham. [*Aside.*] A little more than kin, and less
  than kind. 65
 King. How is it that the clouds still hang on you?
 Ham. Not so, my lord; I am too much i' th' sun.
 Queen. Good Hamlet, cast thy [nighted] colour
  off,
And let thine eye look like a friend on Denmark.
Do not for ever with thy vailed lids 70
Seek for thy noble father in the dust.
Thou know'st 'tis common; all that lives must die,
Passing through nature to eternity.
 Ham. Ay, madam, it is common.
 Queen.   If it be,
Why seems it so particular with thee? 75
 Ham. Seems, madam! Nay, it is; I know not
  "seems."
'Tis not alone my inky cloak, good mother,
Nor customary suits of solemn black,
Nor windy suspiration of forc'd breath,
No, nor the fruitful river in the eye, 80
Nor the dejected haviour of the visage,
Together with all forms, moods, shows of grief,
That can denote me truly. These indeed seem,
For they are actions that a man might play;
But I have that within which passeth show, 85
These but the trappings and the suits of woe.
 King. 'Tis sweet and commendable in your
  nature, Hamlet,
To give these mourning duties to your father.
But, you must know, your father lost a father;
That father lost, lost his; and the survivor bound 90
In filial obligation for some term
To do obsequious sorrow. But to persever
In obstinate condolement is a course
Of impious stubbornness; 'tis unmanly grief;
It shows a will most incorrect to heaven, 95
A heart unfortified, a mind impatient,
An understanding simple and unschool'd;
For what we know must be, and is as common
As any the most vulgar thing to sense,
Why should we in our peevish opposition 100
Take it to heart? Fie! 'tis a fault to heaven,
A fault against the dead, a fault to nature,
To reason most absurd, whose common theme
Is death of fathers, and who still hath cried,
From the first corse till he that died to-day, 105
"This must be so." We pray you, throw to earth
This unprevailing woe, and think of us
As of a father; for, let the world take note,

You are the most immediate to our throne,
And with no less nobility of love   110
Than that which dearest father bears his son
Do I impart towards you. For your intent
In going back to school in Wittenberg,
It is most retrograde to our desire;
And we beseech you, bend you to remain   115
Here in the cheer and comfort of our eye,
Our chiefest courtier, cousin, and our son.
    Queen. Let not thy mother lose her prayers, Hamlet.
I prithee, stay with us; go not to Wittenberg.
    Ham. I shall in all my best obey you, madam. 120
    King. Why, 'tis a loving and a fair reply.
Be as ourself in Denmark. Madam, come;
This gentle and unforc'd accord of Hamlet
Sits smiling to my heart; in grace whereof,
No jocund health that Denmark drinks to-day, 125
But the great cannon to the clouds shall tell,
And the King's rouse the heavens shall bruit again,
Re-speaking earthly thunder. Come away.
             [*Flourish. Exeunt all but Hamlet.*
    Ham. O, that this too too solid flesh would melt,
Thaw, and resolve itself into a dew!   130
Or that the Everlasting had not fix'd
His canon 'gainst self-slaughter! O God! God!
How weary, stale, flat, and unprofitable,
Seems to me all the uses of this world!
Fie on't! oh fie, fie! 'Tis an unweeded garden, 135
That grows to seed; things rank and gross in nature
Possess it merely. That it should come to this!
But two months dead! Nay, not so much, not two.
So excellent a king; that was, to this,
Hyperion to a satyr; so loving to my mother 140
That he might not beteem the winds of heaven
Visit her face too roughly. Heaven and earth!
Must I remember? Why, she would hang on him
As if increase of appetite had grown
By what it fed on; and yet, within a month, — 145
Let me not think on't! — Frailty, thy name is woman! —
A little month, or e'er those shoes were old
With which she followed my poor father's body,
Like Niobe, all tears, — why she, even she —
O [God]! a beast, that wants discourse of reason, 150
Would have mourn'd longer — married with mine uncle,
My father's brother, but no more like my father
Than I to Hercules; within a month,
Ere yet the salt of most unrighteous tears
Had left the flushing of her galled eyes, 155
She married. O, most wicked speed, to post

With such dexterity to incestuous sheets!
It is not, nor it cannot come to good. —
But break my heart, for I must hold my tongue.

    Enter HORATIO, MARCELLUS, *and* BERNARDO.

    Hor. Hail to your lordship!
    Ham.   I am glad to see you well. 160
Horatio! — or I do forget myself.
    Hor. The same, my lord, and your poor servant ever.
    Ham. Sir, my good friend; I'll change that name with you.
And what make you from Wittenberg, Horatio?
Marcellus?   165
    Mar. My good lord!
    Ham. I am very glad to see you. [*To Ber.*]
    Good even, sir. —
But what, in faith, make you from Wittenberg?
    Hor. A truant disposition, good my lord.
    Ham. I would not have your enemy say so, 170
Nor shall you do mine ear that violence,
To make it truster of your own report
Against yourself. I know you are no truant.
But what is your affair in Elsinore?
We'll teach you to drink deep ere you depart. 175
    Hor. My lord, I came to see your father's funeral.
    Ham. I pray thee, do not mock me, fellow-student
I think it was to see my mother's wedding.
    Hor. Indeed, my lord, it followed hard upon.
    Ham. Thrift, thrift, Horatio! The funeral bak'd-meats   180
Did coldly furnish forth the marriage tables.
Would I had met my dearest foe in heaven
Ere I had ever seen that day, Horatio!
My father! — methinks I see my father.   184
    Hor. Oh, where, my lord?
    Ham.   In my mind's eye, Horatio.
    Hor. I saw him once; he was a goodly king.
    Ham. He was a man, take him for all in all, I
shall not look upon his like again.
    Hor. My lord, I think I saw him yesternight.
    Ham. Saw? Who?   190
    Hor. My lord, the King your father.
    Ham.   The King my father!
    Hor. Season your admiration for a while
With an attent ear, till I may deliver,
Upon the witness of these gentlemen,
This marvel to you.
    Ham.   For [God's] love, let me hear. 195
    Hor. Two nights together had these gentlemen,
Marcellus and Bernardo, on their watch,
In the dead [waste] and middle of the night,

---

112. **impart.** The object understood is perhaps the succession. 127. **rouse:** bumper. **bruit:** loudly declare. 129. **solid** F. *sallied* Q₂. 132. **canon:** law. 134. **uses:** customs. 137. **merely:** utterly. 140. **Hyperion:** Apollo. 141. **beteem:** allow. 149. **even she** F. Om. Q₂. 150. **[God]** Q₂. *Heaven* F. The same change by F occurs in many other passages, owing to the statute against profanity. **discourse:** power. 155. **flushing:** redness. 170. **have** F. *hear* Q₂. 192. **Season:** temper. **admiration:** astonishment. 198. **[waste]** F₂. *mast* Q₂ F.

Been thus encount'red. A figure like your father,
Arm'd at all points exactly, cap-a-pie,   200
Appears before them, and with solemn march
Goes slow and stately by them.   Thrice he walk'd
By their oppress'd and fear-surprised eyes,
Within his truncheon's length; whilst they, [dis-
    till'd]
Almost to jelly with the act of fear,   205
Stand dumb and speak not to him.   This to me
In dreadful secrecy impart they did,
And I with them the third night kept the watch;
Where, as they had deliver'd, both in time,
Form of the thing, each   word made true and
    good,
The apparition comes. I knew your father;   211
These hands are not more like.
    Ham.   But where was this?
    Mar. My lord, upon the platform where we
    watch'd.
    Ham. Did you not speak to it?
    Hor.   My lord, I did;
But answer made it none. Yet once methought 215
It lifted up it head and did address
Itself to motion, like as it would speak;
But even then the morning cock crew loud,
And at the sound it shrunk in haste away,
And vanish'd from our sight.
    Ham.   'Tis very strange. 220
    Hor. As I do live, my honour'd lord, 'tis true,
And we did think it writ down in our duty
To let you know of it.
    Ham. Indeed, indeed, sirs. But this troubles me.
Hold you the watch to-night?
    Mar. }
    Ber. }   We do, my lord. 225
    Ham. Arm'd, say you?
    Mar. }
    Ber. } Arm'd, my lord.
    Ham. From top to toe?
    Mar. }
    Ber. }   My lord, from head to foot.
    Ham. Then saw you not his face?
    Hor. O, yes, my lord; he wore his beaver up. 229
    Ham. What, look'd he frowningly?
    Hor.   A countenance more
In sorrow than in anger.
    Ham.   Pale, or red?
    Hor. Nay, very pale.
    Ham.   And fix'd his eyes upon you?
    Hor. Most constantly.
    Ham.   I would I had been there. 235
    Hor. It would have much amaz'd you.
    Ham. Very like, very like. Stay'd it long?

    Hor. While one with moderate haste might tell
    a hundred.
    Mar. } Longer, longer.
    Ber. }
    Hor. Not when I saw 't.
    Ham.   His beard was grizzly? No? 240
    Hor. It was, as I have seen it in his life,
A sable silver'd.
    Ham.   I will watch to-night;
Perchance 'twill [walk] again.
    Hor.   I warrant you it will.
    Ham. If it assume my noble father's person,
I'll speak to it, though hell itself should gape 245
And bid me hold my peace. I pray you all,
If you have hitherto conceal'd this sight,
Let it be [tenable] in your silence still;
And whatsoever else shall hap to-night,
Give it an understanding, but no tongue.   250
I will requite your loves.   So, fare ye well.
Upon the platform 'twixt eleven and twelve,
I'll visit you.
    All.   Our duty to your honour.
    Ham. Your love, as mine to you; farewell.
                    [*Exeunt* [*all but Hamlet*].
My father's spirit in arms! All is not well; 255
I doubt some foul play.   Would the night were
    come!
Till then sit still, my soul.   Foul deeds will rise,
Though all the earth o'erwhelm them, to men's
    eyes.   [*Exit.*

SCENE III.   [*A room in Polonius's house.*]

        Enter LAERTES *and* OPHELIA.

    Laer. My necessaries are embark'd, farewell;
And, sister, as the winds give benefit
And convoy is assistant, do not sleep,
But let me hear from you.
    Oph.   Do you doubt that?
    Laer. For Hamlet and the trifling of his fa-
    vours,   5
Hold it a fashion and a toy in blood,
A violet in the youth of primy nature,
Forward, not permanent, sweet, not lasting,
The [perfume and] suppliance of a minute;
No more.
    Oph. No more but so?
    Laer.   Think it no more: 10
For nature crescent does not grow alone
In thews and bulk, but, as [this] temple waxes,
The inward service of the mind and soul
Grows wide withal.   Perhaps he loves you now,
And now no soil nor cautel doth besmirch   15

200. **cap-a-pie:** from head to foot. 204. **[distill'd]** Q₂. *bestil'd* F. 211. **knew:** recognized. 229. **beaver:** visor.
238. **tell:** count. 243. **[walk]** Q₂. *wake* F. 248. **[tenable]** Q₂: held close. *treble* F. 256. **doubt:** suspect.
  Sc. iii, 6. toy in blood: trifle of passion. 7. **primy:** springlike. 9. **[perfume and]** Q₂. Om. F. **suppliance:** pastime.
11. **crescent:** growing. 12. **[this]** Q₂. *his* F 15. **cautel:** deceit.

The virtue of his [will]; but you must fear,
His greatness weigh'd, his will is not his own;
For he himself is subject to his birth.
He may not, as unvalued persons do,
Carve for himself, for on his choice depends   20
The [sanity] and health of the whole state;
And therefore must his choice be circumscrib'd
Unto the voice and yielding of that body
Whereof he is the head.   Then, if he says he loves you,
It fits your wisdom so far to believe it   25
As he in his [particular act and place]
May give his saying deed; which is no further
Than the main voice of Denmark goes withal.
Then weigh what loss your honour may sustain
If with too credent ear you list his songs,   30
Or lose your heart, or your chaste treasure open
To his unmast'red importunity.
Fear it, Ophelia, fear it, my dear sister,
And keep within the rear of your affection,
Out of the shot and danger of desire.   35
The chariest maid is prodigal enough,
If she unmask her beauty to the moon.
Virtue itself scapes not calumnious strokes.
The canker galls the infants of the spring
Too oft before the buttons be disclos'd,   40
And in the morn and liquid dew of youth
Contagious blastments are most imminent.
Be wary then; best safety lies in fear;
Youth to itself rebels, though none else near.
    Oph. I shall th' effect of this good lesson keep,   45
As watchman to my heart.   But, good my brother,
Do not, as some ungracious pastors do,
Show me the steep and thorny way to heaven,
Whilst, like a puff'd and reckless libertine,
Himself the primrose path of dalliance treads,   50
And recks not his own rede.
    Laer.   O, fear me not.

          Enter POLONIUS.

I stay too long: but here my father comes.
A double blessing is a double grace;
Occasion smiles upon a second leave.
    Pol. Yet here, Laertes? Aboard, aboard, for
    shame!   55
The wind sits in the shoulder of your sail,
And you are stay'd for.   There; my blessing with you!
And these few precepts in thy memory
See thou character.   Give thy thoughts no tongue,
Nor any unproportion'd thought his act.   60
Be thou familiar, but by no means vulgar.

The friends thou hast, and their adoption tried,
Grapple them to thy soul with hoops of steel;
But do not dull thy palm with entertainment
Of each [new]-hatch'd, unfledg'd comrade.   Beware   65
Of entrance to a quarrel; but being in,
Bear 't that the opposed may beware of thee.
Give every man thine ear, but few thy voice;
Take each man's censure, but reserve thy judgement.
Costly thy habit as thy purse can buy,   70
But not express'd in fancy; rich, not gaudy;
For the apparel oft proclaims the man,
And they in France of the best rank and station
Are most select and generous in that.
Neither a borrower nor a lender be;   75
For loan oft loses both itself and friend,
And borrowing dulls the edge of husbandry.
This above all: to thine own self be true,
And it must follow, as the night the day,
Thou canst not then be false to any man.   80
Farewell; my blessing season this in thee!
    Laer. Most humbly do I take my leave, my lord.
    Pol. The time invites you; go, your servants tend.
    Laer. Farewell, Ophelia, and remember well
What I have said to you.
    Oph.   'Tis in my memory lock'd,   85
And you yourself shall keep the key of it.
    Laer. Farewell.   [*Exit.*
    Pol. What is't, Ophelia, he hath said to you?
    Oph. So please you, something touching the
    Lord Hamlet.
    Pol. Marry, well bethought.   90
'Tis told me, he hath very oft of late
Given private time to you, and you yourself
Have of your audience been most free and bounteous.
If it be so — as so 'tis put on me,
And that in way of caution — I must tell you   95
You do not understand yourself so clearly
As it behoves my daughter and your honour.
What is between you?   Give me up the truth.
    Oph. He hath, my lord, of late made many tenders
Of his affection to me.   100
    Pol. Affection! pooh! You speak like a green girl,
Unsifted in such perilous circumstance.
Do you believe his tenders, as you call them?
    Oph. I do not know, my lord, what I should think.

---

16. [will] Q₂. *feare* F.   19. **unvalued:** of low rank.   21. [sanity] (Theobald). *sanctity* F; *safety* Q₂.   26. [particular act and place] Q₂. *peculiar Sect and force* F.   34. **within** F. *you in* Q₂.   39. **canker:** canker-worm.   40. **buttons:** buds.   47. **ungracious:** graceless.   51. **rede:** counsel.   59. **character:** inscribe.   65. [new]-hatch'd Q₂. *unhatch't* F.   69. **censure:** opinion.   74. **Are...in that** (Grant White). *Are of a...cheff in that* F.   The passage is corrupt.   77. **husbandry:** thrift. 99. **tenders:** offers.   102. **Unsifted:** untried.

Pol. Marry, I'll teach you: think yourself a
baby   105
That you have ta'en his tenders for true pay,
Which are not sterling. Tender yourself more
dearly,
Or — not to crack the wind of the poor phrase,
[Running] it thus — you'll tender me a fool.
   Oph. My lord, he hath importun'd me with
love   110
In honourable fashion.
   Pol. Ay, fashion you may call it. Go to, go to.
   Oph. And hath given countenance to his speech,
my lord,
With [almost] all the [holy] vows of heaven.
   Pol. Ay, springes to catch woodcocks. I do
know,   115
When the blood burns, how prodigal the soul
Gives the tongue vows. These blazes, daughter,
Giving more light than heat, extinct in both
Even in their promise, as it is a-making,
You must not take for fire. [From] this time,
daughter,   120
Be somewhat scanter of your maiden presence.
Set your entreatments at a higher rate
Than a command to parley. For Lord Hamlet,
Believe so much in him, that he is young,
And with a larger tether may he walk   125
Than may be given you. In few, Ophelia,
Do not believe his vows; for they are brokers,
Not of [that dye] which their investments show,
But mere imploratos of unholy suits,
Breathing like sanctified and pious [bawds],   130
The better to beguile. This is for all:
I would not, in plain terms, from this time forth,
Have you so slander any moment leisure
As to give words or talk with the Lord Hamlet.
Look to't, I charge you. Come your ways.   135
   Oph. I shall obey, my lord.   [*Exeunt.*

[SCENE IV. *The platform.*]

Enter HAMLET, HORATIO, *and* MARCELLUS.

Ham. The air bites shrewdly; [it is] very cold.
Hor. It is a nipping and an eager air.
Ham. What hour now?
Hor.   I think it lacks of twelve.
Mar. No, it is struck.
Hor. Indeed? I heard it not. Then it draws
near the season   5

Wherein the spirit held his wont to walk.
    [*A flourish of trumpets, and two pieces go
off* [*within*].
What does this mean, my lord?
   Ham. The King doth wake to-night and takes
his rouse,
Keeps wassails, and the swagg'ring up-spring reels;
And, as he drains his draughts of Rhenish down,   10
The kettle-drum and trumpet thus bray out
The triumph of his pledge.
   Hor.   Is it a custom?
   Ham. Ay, marry, is't,
[But] to my mind, though I am native here
And to the manner born, it is a custom   15
More honour'd in the breach than the observance.
[This heavy-headed revel east and west
Makes us traduc'd and tax'd of other nations.
They clepe us drunkards, and with swinish phrase
Soil our addition; and indeed it takes   20
From our achievements, though perform'd at
height,
The pith and marrow of our attribute.
So, oft it chances in particular men,
That for some vicious mole of nature in them,
As, in their birth — wherein they are not guilty,   25
Since nature cannot choose his origin —
By their o'ergrowth of some complexion
Oft breaking down the pales and forts of reason,
Or by some habit that too much o'er-leavens
The form of plausive manners, that these men,   30
Carrying, I say, the stamp of one defect,
Being nature's livery, or fortune's star, —
His virtues else — be they as pure as grace,
As infinite as man may undergo —
Shall in the general censure take corruption   35
From that particular fault. The dram of evil
Doth all the noble substance often dout
To his own scandal.]

Enter Ghost.

   Hor.   Look, my lord, it comes!
   Ham. Angels and ministers of grace defend us!
Be thou a spirit of health or goblin damn'd,   40
Bring with thee airs from heaven or blasts from hell,
Be thy [intents] wicked or charitable,
Thou com'st in such a questionable shape
That I will speak to thee. I'll call thee Hamlet,
King, father; royal Dane, O, answer me!   45
Let me not burst in ignorance, but tell

107. **Tender:** hold. 109. **[Running]** (Collier conj.). *Roaming* F; *Wrong* Q₂. 114. **[almost]** Q₂. Om. F. **[holy]** Q₂. Om. F. 115. **springes:** snares. **woodcocks:** proverbially stupid birds. 117. **Gives** F. *Lends* Q₂. 120. **[From]** Q₂. *For* F. 122. **entreatments:** interviews. 127. **brokers:** procurers. 128. **[that dye]** Q₂. *the eye* F. **investments:** garments. 130. **[bawds]** (Theobald). *bonds* Q₂ F.
   Sc. iv, 1. **[it is]** Q₂. *is it* F. 2. **eager:** sharp. 8. **wake:** hold revels. 9. **up-spring:** a boisterous dance. 14. **[But]** Q₂. *And* F. 17–38. **[This ... scandal]** Q₂. Om. F. 18. **tax'd:** blamed. 19. **clepe:** call. 20. **addition:** title, distinction. 22. **attribute:** reputation. 24. **mole:** defect. 27. **their** Q₂. *the* Pope. **complexion:** disposition. 28. **pales:** fences. 30. **plausive:** pleasing. 35. **general:** popular. 36. **evil** (Keightley conj.). *eale* Q₂. 37. **often dout** (Steevens). *of a doubt* Q₂ **dout:** drive out, cancel. 42. **[intents]** Q₂. *events* F. 43. **questionable:** inviting talk. 45. **O** Q₂. *Oh, oh* F.

Why thy canoniz'd bones, hearsed in death,
Have burst their cerements; why the sepulchre,
Wherein we saw thee quietly inurn'd,
Hath op'd his ponderous and marble jaws   50
To cast thee up again. What may this mean,
That thou, dead corse, again in complete steel
Revisits thus the glimpses of the moon,
Making night hideous, and we fools of nature
So horridly to shake our disposition   55
With thoughts beyond the reaches of our souls?
Say, why is this? Wherefore? What should we
do?   [Ghost beckons Hamlet.
     Hor. It beckons you to go away with it,
As if it some impartment did desire
To you alone.
     Mar.   Look, with what courteous action   60
It wafts you to a more removed ground.
But do not go with it.
     Hor.   No, by no means.
     Ham. It will not speak; then will I follow it.
     Hor. Do not, my lord.
     Ham.   Why, what should be the fear?
I do not set my life at a pin's fee,   65
And for my soul, what can it do to that,
Being a thing immortal as itself?
It waves me forth again. I'll follow it.
     Hor. What if it tempt you toward the flood,
my lord,
Or to the dreadful summit of the cliff   70
That beetles o'er his base into the sea,
And there assume some other, horrible form,
Which might deprive your sovereignty of reason
And draw you into madness? Think of it.
[The very place puts toys of desperation,   75
Without more motive, into every brain
That looks so many fathoms to the sea
And hears it roar beneath.]
     Ham.   It wafts me still.
Go on, I'll follow thee.
     Mar. You shall not go, my lord.
     Ham.   Hold off your hand.   80
     Hor. Be rul'd; you shall not go.
     Ham.   My fate cries out,
And makes each petty artery in this body
As hardy as the Nemean lion's nerve.
Still am I call'd. Unhand me, gentlemen.
By heaven, I'll make a ghost of him that lets me!   85
I say, away! — Go on, I'll follow thee.
       [Exeunt Ghost and Hamlet.
     Hor. He waxes desperate with imagination.
     Mar. Let's follow. 'Tis not fit thus to obey
him.
     Hor. Have after. To what issue will this come?

     Mar. Something is rotten in the state of Den-
mark.   90
     Hor. Heaven will direct it.
     Mar.   Nay, let's follow him.
       [Exeunt.

[SCENE V. Another part of the platform.]

Enter GHOST and HAMLET.

     Ham. Where wilt thou lead me? Speak, I'll
go no further.
     Ghost. Mark me.
     Ham.   I will.
     Ghost.   My hour is almost come,
When I to sulphurous and tormenting flames
Must render up myself.
     Ham.   Alas, poor ghost!
     Ghost. Pity me not, but lend thy serious hearing   5
To what I shall unfold.
     Ham.   Speak; I am bound to hear.
     Ghost. So art thou to revenge, when thou shalt
hear.
     Ham. What?
     Ghost. I am thy father's spirit,
Doom'd for a certain term to walk the night,   10
And for the day confin'd to fast in fires,
Till the foul crimes done in my days of nature
Are burnt and purg'd away. But that I am forbid
To tell the secrets of my prison-house,
I could a tale unfold whose lightest word   15
Would harrow up thy soul, freeze thy young blood,
Make thy two eyes, like stars, start from their
spheres,
Thy knotty and combined locks to part
And each particular hair to stand on end,
Like quills upon the fretful porpentine.   20
But this eternal blazon must not be
To ears of flesh and blood. List, Hamlet, O, list!
If thou didst ever thy dear father love —
     Ham. O [God]!
     Ghost. Revenge his foul and most unnatural
murder.   25
     Ham. Murder!
     Ghost. Murder most foul, as in the best it is,
But this most foul, strange, and unnatural.
     Ham. [Haste] me to know't, that [I], with wings
as swift
As meditation or the thoughts of love,   30
May sweep to my revenge.
     Ghost.   I find thee apt;
And duller shouldst thou be than the fat weed
That rots itself in ease on Lethe wharf,
Wouldst thou not stir in this. Now, Hamlet, hear.

47. canoniz'd: sainted.   75–78. [The ... beneath] Q2. Om. F.   75. toys: impulses.   83. Nemean lion: lion slain
by Hercules.   nerve: sinew.   85. lets: hinders.
     Sc. v, 20. porpentine: porcupine.   21. eternal blazon: revelation of eternal things.   29. [Haste] Q2.   Hast, hast F.   [I]
Q2. Om. F.

It's given out that, sleeping in mine orchard,　35
A serpent stung me; so the whole ear of Denmark
Is by a forged process of my death
Rankly abus'd; but know, thou noble youth,
The serpent that did sting thy father's life
Now wears his crown.
　　Ham.　　　　　　O my prophetic soul!　40
Mine uncle?
　　Ghost. Ay, that incestuous, that adulterate beast,
With witchcraft of his wit, [with] traitorous gifts, —
O wicked wit and gifts, that have the power
So to seduce! — won [to his] shameful lust　45
The will of my most seeming-virtuous queen.
O Hamlet, what a falling-off was there!
From me, whose love was of that dignity
That it went hand in hand even with the vow
I made to her in marriage, and to decline　50
Upon a wretch whose natural gifts were poor
To those of mine!
But virtue, as it never will be mov'd,
Though lewdness court it in a shape of heaven,
So lust, though to a radiant angel link'd,　55
Will sate itself in a celestial bed
And prey on garbage.
But, soft! methinks I scent the morning's air.
Brief let me be. Sleeping within mine orchard,
My custom always in the afternoon,　60
Upon my secure hour thy uncle stole,
With juice of cursed hebenon in a vial,
And in the porches of mine ears did pour
The leperous distilment; whose effect
Holds such an enmity with blood of man　65
That swift as quicksilver it courses through
The natural gates and alleys of the body,
And with a sudden vigour it doth posset
And curd, like eager droppings into milk,
The thin and wholesome blood. So did it mine,　70
And a most instant tetter [bark'd] about,
Most lazar-like, with vile and loathsome crust,
All my smooth body.
Thus was I, sleeping, by a brother's hand
Of life, of crown, and queen, at once dispatch'd;　75
Cut off even in the blossoms of my sin,
Unhousel'd, disappointed, unanel'd,
No reck'ning made, but sent to my account
With all my imperfections on my head.
O, horrible! O, horrible! most horrible!　80
If thou hast nature in thee, bear it not;
Let not the royal bed of Denmark be
A couch for luxury and damned incest.
But, howsoever thou pursuest this act,
Taint not thy mind, nor let thy soul contrive　85

Against thy mother aught. Leave her to heaven,
And to those thorns that in her bosom lodge
To prick and sting her. Fare thee well at once!
The glow-worm shows the matin to be near,
And 'gins to pale his uneffectual fire.　90
Adieu, adieu! Hamlet, remember me.　[*Exit.*
　　Ham. O all you host of heaven! O earth!
What else?
And shall I couple hell? O, fie! Hold, my heart,
And you, my sinews, grow not instant old,
But bear me stiffly up. Remember thee!　95
Ay, thou poor ghost, while memory holds a seat
In this distracted globe. Remember thee!
Yea, from the table of my memory
I'll wipe away all trivial fond records,
All saws of books, all forms, all pressures past,　100
That youth and observation copied there,
And thy commandment all alone shall live
Within the book and volume of my brain,
Unmix'd with baser matter. Yes, yes, by heaven!
O most pernicious woman!　105
O villain, villain, smiling, damned villain!
My tables, my tables, — meet it is I set it down
That one may smile, and smile, and be a villain!
At least I'm sure it may be so in Denmark.
So, uncle, there you are. Now to my word;　110
It is "Adieu, adieu! remember me."
I have sworn 't.
　　Mar. ⎫ [*Within.*] My lord, my lord!
　　Hor. ⎭
　　Mar.　　　[*Within.*] Lord Hamlet!
　　Hor.　　　　　[*Within.*] Heaven secure him!
[*Ham.*] So be it!
　　Hor. [*Within.*] Illo, ho, ho, my lord!　115
　　Ham. Hillo, ho, ho, boy! Come, bird, come.

　　　　Enter HORATIO *and* MARCELLUS.

　　Mar. How is't, my noble lord?
　　Hor.　　　　　　What news, my lord?
　　Ham. O, wonderful!
　　Hor. Good my lord, tell it.
　　Ham.　　　　　　No, you'll reveal it.
　　Hor. Not I, my lord, by heaven.
　　Mar.　　　　　　Nor I, my lord.　120
　　Ham. How say you, then, would heart of man
　　　once think it? —
But you'll be secret?
　　Hor. ⎫
　　Mar. ⎭　　　Ay, by heaven, my lord.
　　Ham. There's ne'er a villain dwelling in all
　　　Denmark —
But he's an arrant knave.

37. **process:** account. 38. **abus'd:** deceived. 43. [with] Q2. *hath* F. 45. [to his] Q2. *to to this* F. 61. **secure:** care-free. 62. **hebenon:** yew, considered poisonous. 68. **posset:** curdle. 69. **eager:** sour. 71. **tetter:** scab. [bark'd] Q2. *bak'd* F. 72. **lazar-like:** leper-like. 77. **Unhousel'd:** without the Sacrament. **disappointed:** unabsolved. **un-anel'd:** lacking extreme unction. 83. **luxury:** lust. 97. **globe:** head. 98. **table:** tablet. 99. **fond:** foolish. 100. **pressures:** impressions. 110. **word:** motto. 114. [*Ham.*] Q2. *Mar.* F. 115. **Illo, ho, ho:** a falconer's call.

Hor. There needs no ghost, my lord, come from
    the grave   125
To tell us this.
    Ham.   Why, right, you are i' the right.
And so, without more circumstance at all,
I hold it fit that we shake hands and part;
You, as your business and desires shall point you,
For every man has business and desire,   130
Such as it *is*; and for mine own poor part,
Look you, I'll go pray.
    Hor. These are but wild and [whirling] words,
    my lord.
    Ham. I'm sorry they offend you, heartily;
Yes, faith, heartily.
    Hor.   There's no offence, my lord.   135
    Ham. Yes, by Saint Patrick, but there is,
[Horatio],
And much offence too. Touching this vision here,
It is an honest ghost, that let me tell you.
For your desire to know what is between us,
O'ermaster 't as you may. And now, good friends,
As you are friends, scholars, and soldiers,   141
Give me one poor request.
    Hor. What is 't, my lord? We will.
    Ham. Never make known what you have seen
    to-night.
    Hor. ⎫
    Mar. ⎬ My lord, we will not.
    Ham.   Nay, but swear 't.
    Hor.   In faith,   145
My lord, not I.
    Mar.   Nor I, my lord, in faith.
    Ham. Upon my sword.
    Mar.   We have sworn, my lord, already.
    Ham. Indeed, upon my sword, indeed.
    Ghost. Swear!   [*Ghost cries under the stage.*
    Ham. Ah, ha, boy! say'st thou so? Art thou
    there, truepenny?   150
Come on; you hear this fellow in the cellarage.
Consent to swear.
    Hor.   Propose the oath, my lord.
    Ham. Never to speak of this that you have seen.
Swear by my sword.
    Ghost. [*Beneath.*] Swear.   155
    Ham. Hic et ubique? Then we'll shift [our] ground.
Come hither, gentlemen,
And lay your hands again upon my sword.
Never to speak of this that you have heard,
Swear by my sword.   160
    Ghost. [*Beneath.*] Swear.
    Ham. Well said, old mole! Canst work i' th'
    ground so fast?
A worthy pioner! Once more remove, good friends.

Hor. O day and night, but this is wondrous
    strange!
    Ham. And therefore as a stranger give it wel-
    come.   165
There are more things in heaven and earth, Horatio,
Than are dreamt of in our philosophy.
But come;
Here, as before, never, so help you mercy,
How strange or odd soe'er I bear myself, —   170
As I perchance hereafter shall think meet
To put an antic disposition on —
That you, at such time seeing me, never shall,
With arms encumb'red thus, or [this] headshake,
Or by pronouncing of some doubtful phrase,   175
As "Well, we know," or "We could, an if we
    would,"
Or "If we list to speak," or "There be, an if they
    might."
Or such ambiguous giving out, to note
That you know aught of me, — this not to do,
So grace and mercy at your most need help you,   180
Swear.
    Ghost. [*Beneath.*] Swear.
    Ham. Rest, rest, perturbed spirit! [*They swear.*]
    So, gentlemen,
With all my love I do commend me to you;
And what so poor a man as Hamlet is   185
May do, t' express his love and friending to you,
God willing, shall not lack. Let us go in together;
And still your fingers on your lips, I pray.
The time is out of joint; — O cursed spite,
That ever I was born to set it right!   190
Nay, come, let's go together.   [*Exeunt.*

ACT II

[SCENE I. *A room in Polonius's house.*]

Enter POLONIUS *and* REYNALDO.

Pol. Give him his money and these notes, Rey-
    naldo.
    Rey. I will, my lord.
    Pol. You shall do marvellous wisely, good Rey-
    naldo,
Before you visit him, [to] make inquiry
Of his behaviour.
    Rey.   My lord, I did intend it.   5
    Pol. Marry, well said, very well said. Look
    you, sir,
Inquire me first what Danskers are in Paris,
And how, and who, what means, and where they
    keep,
What company, at what expense; and finding

133. **[whirling]** Q₂ (whurling). *hurling* F.   136. **[Horatio]** Q₂.   *my Lord* F.   156. *Hic et ubique:* here and everywhere.
[our] Q₂.   *for* F.   159-60. **Never . . . sword** F.   Q₂ prints the lines in reverse order.   162. **ground** F.   *earth* Q₂.   167.
our F.   *your* Q₂.   172. **antic:** fantastic.   174. **[this]** Q₂.   *thus* F.
    Act II, sc. i, 4. **[to]** Q₂.   *you* F.   7. **Danskers:** Danes.   8. **keep:** lodge.

By this encompassment and drift of question   10
That they do know my son, come you more nearer
Than your particular demands will touch it.
Take you, as 'twere, some distant knowledge of
     him,
[As] thus, "I know his father and his friends,
And in part him." Do you mark this, Reynaldo?
  Rey. Ay, very well, my lord.   16
  Pol. "And in part him; but," you may say,
     "not well.
But, if 't be he I mean, he's very wild,
Addicted so and so;" and there put on him
What forgeries you please; marry, none so rank   20
As may dishonour him, — take heed of that;
But, sir, such wanton, wild, and usual slips
As are companions noted and most known
To youth and liberty.
  Rey.   As gaming, my lord?
  Pol. Ay, or drinking, fencing, swearing, quarrel-
     ling,   25
Drabbing; you may go so far.
  Rey. My lord, that would dishonour him.
  Pol. Faith, no, as you may season it in the
     charge.
You must not put another scandal on him,
That he is open to incontinency.   30
That's not my meaning. But breathe his faults
     so quaintly
That they may seem the taints of liberty,
The flash and outbreak of a fiery mind,
A savageness in unreclaimed blood,
Of general assault.
  Rey.   But, my good lord, —   35
  Pol. Wherefore should you do this?
  Rey.   Ay, my lord,
I would know that.
  Pol.   Marry, sir, here's my drift,
And, I believe, it is a fetch of warrant:
You laying these slight sullies on my son,
As 'twere a thing a little soil'd i' th' working,   40
Mark you,
Your party in converse, him you would sound,
Having ever seen in the prenominate crimes
The youth you breathe of guilty, be assur'd
He closes with you in this consequence: 45
"Good sir," or so, or "friend," or "gentleman,"
According to the phrase and the addition
Of man and country —
  Rey.   Very good, my lord.
  Pol. And then, sir, does he this — he does —   50
What was I about to say? [By the mass,] I was
about to say something. Where did I leave?

  Rey. At "closes in the consequence," at "friend
or so," and "gentleman."
  Pol. At "closes in the consequence," ay, marry.
He closes with you thus: "I know the gentleman.   55
I saw him yesterday, or t' other day,
Or then, or then, with such and such; and, as you
     say,
There was he gaming; there o'ertook in 's rouse;
There falling out at tennis;" or, perchance,
"I saw him enter such a house of sale,"   60
Videlicet, a brothel, or so forth.
See you now,
Your bait of falsehood takes this [carp] of truth;
And thus do we of wisdom and of reach,
With windlasses and with assays of bias,   65
By indirections find directions out.
So by my former lecture and advice,
Shall you my son. You have me, have you not?
  Rey. My lord, I have.
  Pol.   God buy you; fare you well.
  Rey. Good my lord.   70
  Pol. Observe his inclination in yourself.
  Rey. I shall, my lord.
  Pol. And let him ply his music.
  Rey.   Well, my lord.
  Pol. Farewell!   [*Exit Reynaldo.*

Enter OPHELIA.

               How now, Ophelia! what's the matter?
  Oph. Alas, my lord, I have been so affrighted!   75
  Pol. With what, in the name of [God]?
  Oph. My lord, as I was sewing in my chamber,
Lord Hamlet, with his doublet all unbrac'd,
No hat upon his head, his stockings foul'd,
Ungart'red, and down-gyved to his ankle,   80
Pale as his shirt, his knees knocking each other,
And with a look so piteous in purport
As if he had been loosed out of hell
To speak of horrors, — he comes before me.
  Pol. Mad for thy love?
  Oph.   My lord, I do not know,
But truly, I do fear it.
  Pol.   What said he?   86
  Oph. He took me by the wrist and held me hard;
Then goes he to the length of all his arm,
And, with his other hand thus o'er his brow,
He falls to such perusal of my face   90
As he would draw it. Long stay'd he so.
At last, a little shaking of mine arm,
And thrice his head thus waving up and down,
He rais'd a sigh so piteous and profound
That it did seem to shatter all his bulk   95

14. [As] Q₂. *And* F.   30. **incontinency:** notorious lewdness.   31. **quaintly:** ingeniously.   35. **Of ... assault:** universal (with youth).   38. **fetch of warrant:** guaranteed device.   43. **prenominate:** aforenamed.   45. **closes:** falls in. **consequence:** conclusion.   51. [By the mass] Q₂. Om. F.   61. *Videlicet:* namely.   63. [carp] Q₂ (carpe). *cape* F.   64. **reach:** ability.   65. **windlasses:** roundabout ways. **assays of bias:** indirect attempts.   71. **in:** by.   80. **down-gyved:** hanging down like fetters.

And end his being. That done, he lets me go;
And, with his head over his shoulder turn'd,
He seem'd to find his way without his eyes,
For out o' doors he went without their help,
And to the last bended their light on me.   100
Pol. [Come,] go with me, I will go seek the King.
This is the very ecstasy of love,
Whose violent property fordoes itself
And leads the will to desperate undertakings
As oft as any passion under heaven   105
That does afflict our natures. I am sorry, —
What, have you given him any hard words of late?
Oph. No, my good lord, but, as you did command,
I did repel his letters and deni'd
His access to me.
    Pol.   That hath made him mad.   110
I am sorry that with better [heed] and judgement
I had not quoted him. I fear'd he did but trifle
And meant to wreck thee; but beshrew my jealousy!
It seems it is as proper to our age
To cast beyond ourselves in our opinions   115
As it is common for the younger sort
To lack discretion. Come, go we to the King.
This must be known, which, being kept close, might
    move
More grief to hide than hate to utter love.   119
[Come.]   [*Exeunt.*

SCENE II. [*A room in the castle.*]

Flourish. Enter KING, QUEEN, ROSENCRANTZ,
    GUILDENSTERN, *with others.*

King. Welcome, dear Rosencrantz and Guilden-
    stern!
Moreover that we much did long to see you,
The need we have to use you did provoke
Our hasty sending. Something have you heard
Of Hamlet's transformation; so I call it,   5
Since not th' exterior nor the inward man
Resembles that it was. What it should be,
More than his father's death, that thus hath put
    him
So much from th' understanding of himself,
I cannot [dream] of. I entreat you both   10
That, being of so young days brought up with him
And since so neighbour'd to his youth and humour,
That you vouchsafe your rest here in our court
Some little time; so by your companies
To draw him on to pleasures, and to gather   15
So much as from occasions you may glean,
[Whether aught, to us unknown, afflicts him thus,]
That, open'd, lies within our remedy.

Queen. Good gentlemen, he hath much talk'd
    of you;
And sure I am two men there are not living   20
To whom he more adheres. If it will please you
To show us so much gentry and good will
As to expend your time with us a while
For the supply and profit of our hope,
Your visitation shall receive such thanks   25
As fits a king's remembrance.
    Ros.   Both your Majesties
Might, by the sovereign power you have of us,
Put your dread pleasures more into command
Than to entreaty.
    Guil.   We both obey,
And here give up ourselves, in the full bent   30
To lay our services freely at your feet,
To be commanded.
    King. Thanks, Rosencrantz and gentle Guild-
    enstern.
    Queen. Thanks, Guildenstern and gentle Rosen-
    crantz;
And I beseech you instantly to visit   35
My too much changed son. Go, some of ye,
And bring the gentlemen where Hamlet is.
    Guil. Heavens make our presence and our
    practices
Pleasant and helpful to him!
    Queen.   Amen!
        [*Exeunt* [*Rosencrantz, Guildenstern, and*
           some Attendants].

Enter POLONIUS.

Pol. Th' ambassadors from Norway, my good
    lord,   40
Are joyfully return'd.
    King. Thou still hast been the father of good
    news.
    Pol. Have I, my lord? Assure you, my good
    liege,
I hold my duty as I hold my soul,
Both to my God [and] to my gracious king.   45
And I do think, or else this brain of mine
Hunts not the trail of policy so sure
As [it hath] us'd to do, that I have found
The very cause of Hamlet's lunacy.
    King. O, speak of that; that I do long to hear.   50
    Pol. Give first admittance to th' ambassadors.
My news shall be the [fruit] to that great feast.
    King. Thyself do grace to them, and bring
    them in.   [*Exit Polonius.*]
He tells me, my sweet queen, that he hath found
The head and source of all your son's distemper.   55

101. [Come] Q₂. Om. F. 102. ecstasy: madness. 103. property: quality. fordoes: destroys. 111. [heed] Q₂. *speed*
F. 112. quoted: observed. 115. cast... ourselves: over-calculate. 120. [Come] Q₂. Om. F.
    Sc. ii, 10. [dream] Q₂. *deeme* F. 11. of: from. 17. [Whether...thus] Q₂. Om. F. 22. gentry: courtesy. 30. in...
bent: to our utmost. 42. still: ever. 45. [and] Q₂. *one* F. 48. [it hath] Q₂. *I have* F. 52. [fruit] Q₂; dessert. *Newes* F.

Queen. I doubt it is no other but the main,
His father's death and our o'erhasty marriage.

Re-enter POLONIUS, *with* VOLTIMAND *and* CORNELIUS.

King. Well, we shall sift him. — Welcome, good friends!
Say, Voltimand, what from our brother Norway?
Volt. Most fair return of greetings and desires. 60
Upon our first, he sent out to suppress
His nephew's levies, which to him appear'd
To be a preparation 'gainst the Polack,
But, better look'd into, he truly found
It was against your Highness. Whereat griev'd,
That so his sickness, age, and impotence 66
Was falsely borne in hand, sends out arrests
On Fortinbras; which he, in brief, obeys,
Receives rebuke from Norway, and in fine
Makes vow before his uncle never more 70
To give th' assay of arms against your Majesty.
Whereon old Norway, overcome with joy,
Gives him three thousand crowns in annual fee,
And his commission to employ those soldiers,
So levied as before, against the Polack; 75
With an entreaty, herein further shown,
[Giving a paper.]
That it might please you to give quiet pass
Through your dominions for his enterprise,
On such regards of safety and allowance
As therein are set down.
King. It likes us well; 80
And at our more consider'd time we'll read,
Answer, and think upon this business.
Meantime we thank you for your well-took labour.
Go to your rest; at night we'll feast together.
Most welcome home!
[Exeunt Voltimand and Cornelius.
Pol. This business is well ended. 85
My liege, and madam, to expostulate
What majesty should be, what duty is,
Why day is day, night night, and time is time,
Were nothing but to waste night, day, and time;
Therefore, since brevity is the soul of wit, 90
And tediousness the limbs and outward flourishes,
I will be brief. Your noble son is mad.
Mad call I it; for, to define true madness,
What is't but to be nothing else but mad?
But let that go.
Queen. More matter, with less art. 95
Pol. Madam, I swear I use no art at all.
That he is mad, 'tis true; 'tis true 'tis pity,
And pity ['tis 'tis] true. A foolish figure!
But farewell it, for I will use no art.

Mad let us grant him then; and now remains 100
That we find out the cause of this effect,
Or rather say, the cause of this defect,
For this effect defective comes by cause.
Thus it remains, and the remainder thus.
Perpend. 105
I have a daughter — have whilst she is mine —
Who, in her duty and obedience, mark,
Hath given me this. Now gather, and surmise.
[Reads] the letter.
"To the celestial and my soul's idol, the most beautified Ophelia," — 110
That's an ill phrase, a vile phrase; "beautified" is a vile phrase. But you shall hear. [Thus]:
"In her excellent white bosom, these."
Queen. Came this from Hamlet to her?
Pol. Good madam, stay a while. I will be faithful. *[Reads.]* 115
"Doubt thou the stars are fire,
Doubt that the sun doth move,
Doubt truth to be a liar,
But never doubt I love. 119
"O dear Ophelia, I am ill at these numbers. I have not art to reckon my groans; but that I love thee best, O most best, believe it. Adieu.
Thine evermore, most dear lady,
Whilst this machine is to him,
HAMLET."
This in obedience hath my daughter show'd me, 125
And more above, hath his solicitings,
As they fell out by time, by means, and place,
All given to mine ear.
King. But how hath she
Receiv'd his love?
Pol. What do you think of me?
King. As of a man faithful and honourable. 130
Pol. I would fain prove so. But what might you think,
When I had seen this hot love on the wing, —
As I perceiv'd it, I must tell you that,
Before my daughter told me, — what might you,
Or my dear Majesty your queen here, think, 135
If I had play'd the desk or table-book,
Or given my heart a winking, mute and dumb,
Or look'd upon this love with idle sight,
What might you think? No, I went round to work,
And my young mistress thus I did bespeak: 140
"Lord Hamlet is a prince, out of thy star.
This must not be;" and then I precepts gave her,
That she should lock herself from his resort,
Admit no messengers, receive no tokens.
Which done, she took the fruits of my advice; 145
And he, repulsed — a short tale to make —

56. **main:** main cause. 67. **borne in hand:** taken advantage of. 80. **likes:** pleases. 81. **more...time:** greater leisure for thought. 85. **well** Q2. *very well* F. 86. **expostulate:** expound. 98. **['tis 'tis]** Q2. *it is* F. 112. **[Thus]** Q2. *these* F. 124. **machine:** body. 136. **play'd...table-book:** i.e., noted the matter secretly. 139. **round:** openly. 141. **star:** i.e., sphere.

Fell into a sadness, then into a fast,
Thence to a watch, thence into a weakness,
Thence to a lightness, and, by this declension,
Into the madness whereon now he raves,   150
And all we wail for.

King.   Do you think 'tis this?

Queen. It may be, very likely.

Pol. Hath there been such a time — I'd fain
    know that —
That I have positively said, "'Tis so,"
When it prov'd otherwise?

King.   Not that I know.   155

Pol. Take this from this, if this be otherwise.
If circumstances lead me, I will find
Where truth is hid, though it were hid indeed
Within the centre.

King.   How may we try it further?

Pol. You know sometimes he walks four hours
    together   160
Here in the lobby.

Queen.   So he has, indeed.

Pol. At such a time I'll loose my daughter to him.
Be you and I behind an arras then;
Mark the encounter. If he love her not,
And be not from his reason fall'n thereon,   165
Let me be no assistant for a state,
[But] keep a farm and carters.

King.   We will try it.

Enter HAMLET, *reading on a book.*

Queen. But look where sadly the poor wretch
    comes reading.

Pol. Away, I do beseech you, both away.
I'll board him presently.
        [*Exeunt King, Queen* [*and Attendants*].
               O, give me leave,   170
How does my good Lord Hamlet?

Ham. Well, God-a-mercy.

Pol. Do you know me, my lord?

Ham. Excellent well; you are a fishmonger.

Pol. Not I, my lord.   175

Ham. Then I would you were so honest a man.

Pol. Honest, my lord!

Ham. Ay, sir. To be honest, as this world goes,
is to be one man pick'd out of two thousand.

Pol. That's very true, my lord.   180

Ham. For if the sun breed maggots in a dead
dog, being a good kissing carrion, — Have you a
daughter?

Pol. I have, my lord.   184

Ham. Let her not walk i' th' sun. Conception
is a blessing, but not as your daughter may conceive. Friend, look to't.   187

Pol. [*Aside.*] How say you by that? Still harping
on my daugher. Yet he knew me not at first; he
said I was a fishmonger. He is far gone, far
gone. And truly in my youth I suff'red much extremity for love; very near this. I'll speak to him
again. — What do you read, my lord?   193

Ham. Words, words, words.

Pol. What is the matter, my lord?

Ham. Between who?

Pol. I mean, the matter you [read] my lord.   197

Ham. Slanders, sir; for the satirical slave says
here that old men have grey beards, that their faces
are wrinkled, their eyes purging thick amber or
plum-tree gum, and that they have a plentiful lack
of wit, together with weak hams; all which, sir,
though I most powerfully and potently believe, yet
I hold it not honesty to have it thus set down; for
you yourself, sir, should be old as I am, if like a
crab you could go backward.   206

Pol. [*Aside.*] Though this be madness, yet there
is method in't. — Will you walk out of the air,
my lord?

Ham. Into my grave?   210

Pol. Indeed, that is out o' th' air. [*Aside.*]
How pregnant sometimes his replies are! a happiness
that often madness hits on, which reason and sanity
could not so prosperously be deliver'd of. I will
leave him, and suddenly contrive the means of
meeting between him and my daughter. — My
honourable lord, I will most humbly take my leave
of you.   218

Ham. You cannot, sir, take from me anything
that I will more willingly part withal, — [*Aside*]
except my life, my life.   221

Pol. Fare you well, my lord.

Ham. These tedious old fools!

Enter ROSENCRANTZ *and* GUILDENSTERN.

Pol. You go to seek my Lord Hamlet? There
    he is.

Ros. [*To Polonius.*] God save you, sir!   225
                    [*Exit Polonius.*]

Guil. Mine honour'd lord!

Ros. My most dear lord!

Ham. My excellent good friends! How dost
thou, Guildenstern? Oh, Rosencrantz! Good
lads, how do ye both?   230

Ros. As the indifferent children of the earth.

Guil. Happy, in that we are not over-happy.
On Fortune's cap we are not the very button.

Ham. Nor the soles of her shoe?

Ros. Neither, my lord.   235

Ham. Then you live about her waist, or in the middle of her favour?

Guil. Faith, her privates we.

Ham. In the secret parts of Fortune? Oh, most true; she is a strumpet. What's the news?   240

Ros. None, my lord, but that the world's grown honest.

Ham. Then is doomsday near. But your news is not true. Let me question more in particular. What have you, my good friends, deserved at the hands of Fortune, that she sends you to prison hither?   247

Guil. Prison, my lord?

Ham. Denmark's a prison.

Ros. Then is the world one.   250

Ham. A goodly one, in which there are many confines, wards, and dungeons, Denmark being one o' th' worst.

Ros. We think not so, my lord.   254

Ham. Why, then, 'tis none to you; for there is nothing either good or bad, but thinking makes it so. To me it is a prison.

Ros. Why, then, your ambition makes it one. 'Tis too narrow for your mind.   259

Ham. O God, I could be bounded in a nutshell and count myself a king of infinite space, were it not that I have bad dreams.

Guil. Which dreams indeed are ambition, for the very substance of the ambitious is merely the shadow of a dream.   265

Ham. A dream itself is but a shadow.

Ros. Truly, and I hold ambition of so airy and light a quality that it is but a shadow's shadow.

Ham. Then are our beggars bodies, and our monarchs and outstretch'd heroes the beggars' shadows. Shall we to the court? for, by my fay, I cannot reason.   272

Ros. ⎫
Guil. ⎭ We'll wait upon you.

Ham. No such matter. I will not sort you with the rest of my servants, for, to speak to you like an honest man, I am most dreadfully attended. But in the beaten way of friendship, what make you at Elsinore?   278

Ros. To visit you, my lord; no other occasion.

Ham. Beggar that I am, I am even poor in thanks, but I thank you; and sure, dear friends, my thanks are too dear a halfpenny. Were you not sent for? Is it your own inclining? Is it a free visitation? Come, deal justly with me. Come, come. Nay, speak.   285

Guil. What should we say, my lord?

Ham. Why, anything, but to the purpose. You were sent for; and there is a kind [of] confession in your looks which your modesties have not craft enough to colour. I know the good king and queen have sent for you.

Ros. To what end, my lord?   292

Ham. That you must teach me. But let me conjure you by the rights of our fellowship, by the consonancy of our youth, by the obligation of our ever-preserved love, and by what more dear a better proposer could charge you withal, whether you were sent for or no!   299

Ros. [*Aside to Guil.*] What say you?

Ham. [*Aside.*] Nay, then, I have an eye of you. — If you love me, hold not off.

Guil. My lord, we were sent for.   303

Ham. I will tell you why; so shall my anticipation prevent your discovery, [and] your secrecy to the King and Queen moult no feather. I have of late — but wherefore I know not — lost all my mirth, forgone all custom of exercise; and indeed it goes so [heavily] with my disposition that this goodly frame, the earth, seems to me a sterile   310 promontory, this most excellent canopy, the air, look you, this brave o'erhanging [firmament] this majestical roof fretted with golden fire, why, it appears no other thing to me than a foul and pestilent congregation of vapours. What a piece of   315 work is a man! How noble in reason! How infinite in faculty, in form and moving! How express and admirable in action! How like an angel in apprehension! How like a god! The beauty of the world! The paragon of animals! And yet, to me, what is this quintessence of dust?   320 Man delights not me, — no, nor woman neither, though by your smiling you seem to say so.

Ros. My lord, there was no such stuff in my thoughts.   325

Ham. Why did you laugh [then], when I said, "Man delights not me"?

Ros. To think, my lord, if you delight not in man, what lenten entertainment the players shall receive from you. We coted them on the way, and hither are they coming to offer you service.   331

Ham. He that plays the king shall be welcome; his majesty shall have tribute of me; the adventurous knight shall use his foil and target; the lover shall not sigh gratis; the humorous man shall end his part in peace; the clown shall make those laugh whose lungs are tickle o' the sere; and the lady shall

---

244–76. Let...attended F. Om. Q₂.   288. [of] Q₂. Om. F.   289. modesties: sense of shame.   305. discovery: disclosure. [and] Q₂. of F.   309. [heavily] Q₂. heavenly F.   312. [firmament] Q₂. Om. F.   313. fretted: ornamented.   316–19. Our punctuation here substantially follows Q₂. F has question marks after reason, faculty, admirable, action, angel, god.   317. express: exact.   326. [then] Q₂. Om. F.   329. lenten: meager.   330. coted: outstripped.   337. tickle...sere: hair-triggered.

say her mind freely, or the blank verse shall halt
for't. What players are they?   340
 Ros. Even those you were wont to take delight
in, the tragedians of the city.
 Ham. How chances it they travel? Their residence, both in reputation and profit, was better
both ways.   345
 Ros. I think their inhibition comes by the means
of the late innovation.
 Ham. Do they hold the same estimation they
did when I was in the city? Are they so fol-
low'd?   350
 Ros. No, indeed, they are not.
 Ham. How comes it? Do they grow rusty?
 Ros. Nay, their endeavour keeps in the wonted
pace; but there is, sir, an aery of children, little
eyases, that cry out on the top of question,   355
and are most tyrannically clapp'd for't. These
are now the fashion, and so berattle the common
stages — so they call them — that many wearing
rapiers are afraid of goose-quills and dare scarce
come thither.   360
 Ham. What, are they children? Who maintains
'em? How are they escoted? Will they pursue
the quality no longer than they can sing? Will
they not say afterwards, if they should grow themselves to common players, — as it is [most like],
if their means are no better — their writers do them
wrong, to make them exclaim against their own
succession?   368
 Ros. Faith, there has been much to do on both
sides, and the nation holds it no sin to tarre them
to controversy. There was for a while no money
bid for argument unless the poet and the player
went to cuffs in the question.   373
 Ham. Is't possible?
 Guil. O, there has been much throwing about of
brains.
 Ham. Do the boys carry it away?
 Ros. Ay, that they do, my lord; Hercules and
his load too.   379
 Ham. It is not strange; for mine uncle is King of
Denmark, and those that would make mows at
him while my father lived, give twenty, forty, an
hundred ducats apiece for his picture in little.
['Sblood,] there is something in this more than
natural, if philosophy could find it out.   385

                [Flourish for the Players.

 Guil. There are the players.
 Ham. Gentlemen, you are welcome to Elsinore.
Your hands, come. The appurtenance of welcome
is fashion and ceremony. Let me comply with
you in the garb, lest my extent to the players,   390
which, I tell you, must show fairly outward, should
more appear like entertainment than yours. You
are welcome; but my uncle-father and aunt-mother
are deceiv'd.
 Guil. In what, my dear lord?   395
 Ham. I am but mad north-north-west. When
the wind is southerly I know a hawk from a hand-
saw.

                Enter POLONIUS.

 Pol. Well be with you, gentlemen!
 Ham. [*Aside to them.*] Hark you, Guildenstern, and you too, at each ear a hearer: that great
baby you see there is not yet out of his swathing-
clouts.   401
 Ros. Happily he is the second time come to them,
for they say an old man is twice a child.
 Ham. I will prophesy he comes to tell me of the
players; mark it. [*Aloud.*] You say right, sir; for
o' Monday morning 'twas so indeed.   407
 Pol. My lord, I have news to tell you.
 Ham. My lord, I have news to tell you. When
Roscius [was] an actor in Rome, —
 Pol. The actors are come hither, my lord.
 Ham. Buzz, buzz!
 Pol. Upon mine honour, —   413
 Ham. "Then [came] each actor on his ass," —
 Pol. The best actors in the world, either for
tragedy, comedy, history, pastoral, pastoral-comi-
cal, historical-pastoral, tragical-historical, tragical-
comical-historical-pastoral, scene individable, or
poem unlimited; Seneca cannot be too heavy, nor
Plautus too light. For the law of writ and the
liberty, these are the only men.   421
 Ham. O Jephthah, judge of Israel, what a
treasure hadst thou!
 Pol. What a treasure had he, my lord?
 Ham. Why,   425
    "One fair daughter, and no more,
       The which he loved passing well."
 Pol. [*Aside.*] Still on my daughter.
 Ham. Am I not i' the right, old Jephthah?
 Pol. If you call me Jephthah, my lord, I have a
daughter that I love passing well.   431

339. **halt**: i.e., if she is forced to omit vulgarities. 346. **inhibition**: hindrance. 347. **innovation**: the rise of the companies of child actors which proved serious rivals to the adult companies in the opening years of the century. 352–79.
How...load too F. Om. Q₂. 354. **aery**: nest. 355. **eyases**: young hawks. 355. **cry...question**: cry shrilly above
others in controversy. 357. **berattle**: satirize. 358. **common stages**: public theaters, which it became unfashionable to
visit. 359. **goose-quills**: i.e., the pens of satirical playwrights. 362. **escoted**: supported. 363. **quality**: profession.
366. **[most like]** (Pope). *like most* F. 368. **succession**: future. 370. **tarre**: provoke. 372. **argument**: plot of a play.
378–79. **Hercules...too.** Referring to the Globe Theatre, which had a sign showing Hercules with a globe. 381. **mows**:
grimaces. 384. **['Sblood]** Q₂: God's blood. Om. F. 390. **extent**: reception. 398. **handsaw.** With a quibble on "hern-
shaw" (heron). 410. **[was]** Q₂. Om. F. 414. **[came]** Q₂. *can* F. 418. **scene individable.** Probably a reference to
the dramatic unities. 420–21. **law...liberty**: strict regulation versus literary freedom, or, standing by the text versus im-
provising. 422. **O...Israel**: title of a ballad.

Ham. Nay, that follows not.

Pol. What follows, then, my lord?

Ham. Why,

      "As by lot, God wot,"   435

and then, you know,

   "It came to pass, as most like it was," —

The first row of the [pious] chanson will show you

more, for look where my abridgements come.   439

Enter four or five PLAYERS.

You're welcome, masters, welcome all.   I am glad
to see thee well.   Welcome, good friends.   O, my
old friend!   Thy face is [valanc'd] since I saw thee
last; com'st thou to beard me in Denmark?   What,
my young lady and mistress!   By 'r lady, your
ladyship is nearer heaven than when I saw you   445
last, by the altitude of a chopine.   Pray God, your
voice, like a piece of uncurrent gold, be not crack'd
within the ring.   Masters, you are all welcome.
We'll e'en to't like French falconers — fly at anything we see; we'll have a speech straight.   450
Come, give us a taste of your quality; come, a passionate speech.

1. Play. What speech, my lord?

Ham. I heard thee speak me a speech once,
but it was never acted; or, if it was, not above   455
once.   For the play, I remember, pleas'd not the
million; 'twas caviare to the general; but it was —
as I receiv'd it, and others, whose judgement in
such matters cried in the top of mine — an excellent
play, well digested in the scenes, set down with   460
as much modesty as cunning.   I remember, one
said there [were] no sallets in the lines to make the
matter savoury, nor no matter in the phrase that
might indict the author of affectation; but call'd it
an honest method, [as wholesome as sweet, and   465
by very much more handsome than fine.]   One
speech in it I chiefly lov'd; 'twas Æneas' tale to
Dido, and thereabout of it especially where he
speaks of Priam's slaughter.   If it live in your memory, begin at this line: let me see, let me see —   471
"The rugged Pyrrhus, like th' Hyrcanian beast," —
— It is not so. It begins with Pyrrhus: —
"The rugged Pyrrhus, he whose sable arms,
Black as his purpose, did the night resemble   475
When he lay couched in the ominous horse,
Hath now this dread and black complexion smear'd
With heraldry more dismal.   Head to foot
Now is he [total] gules, horribly trick'd

With blood of fathers, mothers, daughters, sons,   480
Bak'd and impasted with the parching streets,
That lend a tyrannous and damned light
To their vile murders.   Roasted in wrath and fire,
And thus o'er-sized with coagulate gore,
With eyes like carbuncles, the hellish Pyrrhus   485
Old grandsire Priam seeks."

[So, proceed you.]

Pol. 'Fore God, my lord, well spoken, with good
accent and good discretion.

1. Play.   "Anon he finds him
Striking too short at Greeks.   His antique sword,
Rebellious to his arm, lies where it falls,   492
Repugnant to command.   Unequal match,
Pyrrhus at Priam drives, in rage strikes wide,
But with the whiff and wind of his fell sword   495
Th' unnerved father falls.   Then senseless Ilium,
Seeming to feel his blow, with flaming top
Stoops to his base, and with a hideous crash
Takes prisoner Pyrrhus' ear; for, lo! his sword,
Which was declining on the milky head   500
Of reverend Priam, seem'd i' th' air to stick.
So, as a painted tyrant, Pyrrhus stood
And, like a neutral to his will and matter,
Did nothing.
But, as we often see, against some storm,   505
A silence in the heavens, the rack stand still,
The bold winds speechless, and the orb below
As hush as death, anon the dreadful thunder
Doth rend the region; so, after Pyrrhus' pause,
Aroused vengeance sets him new a-work;   510
And never did the Cyclops' hammers fall
On Mars his armour forg'd for proof eterne
With less remorse than Pyrrhus' bleeding sword
Now falls on Priam.
Out, out, thou strumpet Fortune!   All you gods,
In general synod take away her power!   516
Break all the spokes and fellies from her wheel,
And bowl the round nave down the hill of heaven
As low as to the fiends!"

Pol. This is too long.   520

Ham. It shall to the barber's, with your beard.
Prithee, say on; he's for a jig or a tale of bawdry, or
he sleeps.   Say on; come to Hecuba.

1. Play. "But who, O, who had seen the [mobled]
       queen" —   525

Ham. "The [mobled] queen"?

Pol. That's good; "[mobled] queen" is good.

1. Play. "Run barefoot up and down, threat-
       'ning the flame

---

438. **row:** stanza.   **[pious]** Q₂.   *Pons* F.   439. **abridgements:** (1) entertainments, (2) interrupters.   442. **[valanc'd]** Q₂: fringed, i.e., bearded.   *valiant* F.   446. **chopine:** thick-soled shoe.   457. **caviare . . . general:** i.e., too choice for the multitude.   459. **cried . . . of:** had more authority than.   462. **[were]** Q₂.   *was* F.   **sallets:** salads, i.e., spicy jokes. 465–66. **[as wholesome . . . fine]** Q₂.   Om. F.   467. **speech** Q₂.   *cheefe speech* F.   472. **Hyrcanian beast:** tiger of Hyrcania in the Caucasus.   479. **[total]** Q₂.   *to take* F.   **gules:** red.   **trick'd:** adorned.   481. **impasted:** crusted.   484. **o'er-sized:** varnished.   487. **[So . . . you]** Q₂.   Om. F.   503. **matter:** task.   506. **rack:** cloud.   509. **region:** i.e., air.   512. **proof:** endurance.   517. **fellies:** rims.   525–26. **[mobled]** Q₂ F₂: muffled.   *inobled* F₁.   527. **[mobled] . . . good** F₂.   *inobled . . . good* F₁. Om. Q₂.

With bisson rheum, a clout about that head
Where late the diadem stood, and for a robe, 530
About her lank and all o'er-teemed loins,
A blanket, in the alarm of fear caught up; —
Who this had seen, with tongue in venom steep'd
'Gainst Fortune's state would treason have pro-
    nounc'd.
But if the gods themselves did see her then, 535
When she saw Pyrrhus make malicious sport
In mincing with his sword her husband's limbs,
The instant burst of clamour that she made,
Unless things mortal move them not at all,
Would have made milch the burning eyes of heaven,
And passion in the gods." 541

Pol. Look, whe'er he has not turn'd his colour and
has tears in 's eyes. Pray you, no more.

Ham. 'Tis well; I'll have thee speak out the 545
rest soon. Good my lord, will you see the players
well bestow'd? Do ye hear? Let them be well us'd,
for they are the abstracts and brief chronicles of the
time; after your death you were better have a bad
epitaph than their ill report while you lived. 551

Pol. My lord, I will use them according to their
desert.

Ham. God's bodykins, man, better. Use every
man after his desert, and who should scape whipping? Use them after your own honour and dignity.
The less they deserve, the more merit is in your
bounty. Take them in.

Pol. Come, sirs. [*Exit.* 559

Ham. Follow him, friends; we'll hear a play to-
morrow. [*Exeunt all the Players but the First.*]
Dost thou hear me, old friend? Can you play "The
Murder of Gonzago"?

I. Play. Ay, my lord. 564

Ham. We'll ha' 't to-morrow night. You could,
for a need, study a speech of some dozen or sixteen
lines, which I would set down and insert in't, could
ye not?

I. Play. Ay, my lord. 569

Ham. Very well. Follow that lord, — and look
you mock him not. [*Exit I. Player.*] My good
friends, I'll leave you till night. You are welcome to
Elsinore.

Ros. Good my lord!
        [*Exeunt [Rosencrantz and Guildenstern.*]

Ham. Ay, so, God buy ye. — Now I am alone.
O, what a rogue and peasant slave am I! 576
Is it not monstrous that this player here,
But in a fiction, in a dream of passion,
Could force his soul so to his [own] conceit
That from her working all his visage [wann'd], 580

Tears in his eyes, distraction in 's aspect,
A broken voice, and his whole function suiting
With forms to his conceit? And all for nothing!
For Hecuba!
What's Hecuba to him, or he to Hecuba, 585
That he should weep for her? What would he do,
Had he the motive and the cue for passion
That I have? He would drown the stage with tears
And cleave the general ear with horrid speech,
Make mad the guilty and appall the free, 590
Confound the ignorant, and amaze indeed
The very faculty of eyes and ears.
Yet I,
A dull and muddy-mettled rascal, peak
Like John-a-dreams, unpregnant of my cause, 595
And can say nothing; no, not for a king,
Upon whose property and most dear life
A damn'd defeat was made. Am I a coward?
Who calls me villain, breaks my pate across,
Plucks off my beard and blows it in my face, 600
Tweaks me by th' nose, gives me the lie i' th' throat
As deep as to the lungs? Who does me this?
Ha!
['Swounds,] I should take it; for it cannot be
But I am pigeon-liver'd and lack gall 605
To make oppression bitter, or ere this
I should ha' fatted all the region kites
With this slave's offal. Bloody, bawdy villain!
Remorseless, treacherous, lecherous, kindless villain!
O, vengeance! 610
[Why,] what an ass am I! This is most brave,
That I, the son of [a] dear [father] murder'd,
Prompted to my revenge by heaven and hell,
Must, like a whore, unpack my heart with words,
And fall a-cursing, like a very drab, 615
A scullion!
Fie upon't! Foh! About, my brain! I have
    heard
That guilty creatures sitting at a play
Have by the very cunning of the scene
Been struck so to the soul that presently 620
They have proclaim'd their malefactions;
For murder, though it have no tongue, will speak
With most miraculous organ. I'll have these play-
    ers
Play something like the murder of my father
Before mine uncle. I'll observe his looks; 625
I'll tent him to the quick. If he but blench,
I know my course. The spirit that I have seen
May be the devil; and the devil hath power
T' assume a pleasing shape; yea, and perhaps
Out of my weakness and my melancholy, 630

---

529. **bisson rheum:** blinding tears. 531. **o'er-teemed:** worn out by child-bearing. 540. **milch:** moist. 579. **[own]** Q₂.
whole F. **conceit:** imagination. 580. **[wann'd]** Q₂ (*wand*). *warm'd* F. 590. **free:** innocent. 591. **amaze:** confound. 594.
muddy-mettled: irresolute. **peak:** mope. 595. **John-a-dreams:** a sleepy fellow. **unpregnant of:** unstirred by. 604.
['Swounds] Q₂. *Why* F. 609. **kindless:** unnatural. 611. **[Why]** Q₂. *Who* F. **This** Q₂. *I sure this* F. 612. **[a] dear
[father]** Q₄. *the Deere* F, *a deere* Q₂. 617. **About:** to work. 626. **tent:** probe.

As he is very potent with such spirits,
Abuses me to damn me. I'll have grounds
More relative than this. The play's the thing
Wherein I'll catch the conscience of the King.
                                           [Exit.

[ACT III]

[Scene I. *A room in the castle.*]

Enter King, Queen, Polonius, Ophelia,
Rosencrantz, *and* Guildenstern.

King. And can you, by no drift of circumstance,
Get from him why he puts on this confusion,
Grating so harshly all his days of quiet
With turbulent and dangerous lunacy?
  Ros. He does confess he feels himself distracted;
But from what cause he will by no means speak. 6
  Guil. Nor do we find him forward to be sounded,
But with a crafty madness keeps aloof
When we would bring him on to some confession
Of his true state.
  Queen.   Did he receive you well?   10
  Ros. Most like a gentleman.
  Guil. But with much forcing of his disposition.
  Ros. Niggard of question; but of our demands
Most free in his reply.
  Queen.   Did you assay him
To any pastime?   15
  Ros. Madam, it so fell out, that certain players
We o'er-raught on the way; of these we told him,
And there did seem in him a kind of joy
To hear of it. They are about the court,
And, as I think, they have already order   20
This night to play before him.
  Pol.   'Tis most true.
And he beseech'd me to entreat your Majesties
To hear and see the matter.
  King. With all my heart; and it doth much con-
    tent me
To hear him so inclin'd.   25
Good gentlemen, give him a further edge,
And drive his purpose on to these delights.
  Ros. We shall, my lord.
        [Exeunt [Rosencrantz and Guildenstern.]
  King.   Sweet Gertrude, leave us too,
For we have closely sent for Hamlet hither,
That he, as 'twere by accident, may [here]   30
Affront Ophelia.
Her father and myself, lawful espials,
Will so bestow ourselves that, seeing unseen,
We may of their encounter frankly judge,
And gather by him, as he is behav'd,   35

If 't be th' affliction of his love or no
That thus he suffers for.
  Queen.   I shall obey you.
And for your part, Ophelia, I do wish
That your good beauties be the happy cause
Of Hamlet's wildness. So shall I hope your virtues
Will bring him to his wonted way again,   41
To both your honours.
  Oph.   Madam, I wish it may.
                  [Exit Queen.]
  Pol. Ophelia, walk you here. Gracious, so please
    ye,
We will bestow ourselves. *[To Ophelia.]* Read on
    this book,
That show of such an exercise may colour   45
Your loneliness. We are oft to blame in this, —
'Tis too much prov'd — that with devotion's visage
And pious action we do [sugar] o'er
The devil himself.
  King.   O, 'tis true!
[Aside.] How smart a lash that speech doth give my
    conscience!   50
The harlot's cheek, beautied with plast'ring art,
Is not more ugly to the thing that helps it
Than is my deed to my most painted word.
O heavy burden!
  Pol. I hear him coming. Let's withdraw, my
    lord.   *[Exeunt [King and Polonius].* 55

Enter Hamlet.

  Ham. To be, or not to be: that is the question.
Whether 'tis nobler in the mind to suffer
The slings and arrows of outrageous fortune,
Or to take arms against a sea of troubles,
And by opposing end them. To die; to sleep; 60
No more; and by a sleep to say we end
The heart-ache and the thousand natural shocks
That flesh is heir to. 'Tis a consummation
Devoutly to be wish'd. To die; to sleep; —
To sleep? Perchance to dream! Ay, there's the
    rub;   65
For in that sleep of death what dreams may
    come,
When we have shuffl'd off this mortal coil,
Must give us pause. There's the respect
That makes calamity of so long life.
For who would bear the whips and scorns of time,
The oppressor's wrong, the [proud] man's con-
    tumely,   71
The pangs of dispriz'd love, the law's delay,
The insolence of office, and the spurns
That patient merit of the unworthy takes,
When he himself might his quietus make   75

---

631. **spirits:** moods. 633. **relative:** definite.
    Act III, sc. i, 13. **question:** conversation. 26. **edge:** incitement. 29. **closely:** secretly. 30. **[here]** Q₂. *there* F. 31.
Affront: meet. 48. **[sugar]** Q₂. *surge* F. 52. **to:** in comparison with. 67. **coil:** turmoil. 68. **respect:** consideration.
69. **of . . . life:** so long-lived. 71. **[proud]** Q₂. *poore* F. 72. **dispriz'd** F. *despiz'd* Q₂. 75. **quietus:** discharge (legal term).

With a bare bodkin? Who would fardels bear,
To grunt and sweat under a weary life,
But that the dread of something after death,
The undiscover'd country from whose bourn
No traveller returns, puzzles the will   80
And makes us rather bear those ills we have
Than fly to others that we know not of?
Thus conscience does make cowards of us all;
And thus the native hue of resolution
Is sicklied o'er with the pale cast of thought,   85
And enterprises of great pith and moment
With this regard their currents turn [awry],
And lose the name of action. — Soft you now!
The fair Ophelia! Nymph, in thy orisons
Be all my sins remem'bred.

Oph.   Good my lord,   90
How does your honour for this many a day?

Ham. I humbly thank you, well, well, well.

Oph. My lord, I have remembrances of yours
That I have longed long to re-deliver.
I pray you, now receive them.

Ham.   No, no;   95
I never gave you aught.

Oph. My honour'd lord, I know right well you
          did,
And, with them, words of so sweet breath compos'd
As made the things more rich. [Their] perfume
          [lost],
Take these again; for to the noble mind   100
Rich gifts wax poor when givers prove unkind.
There, my lord.

Ham. Ha, ha! are you honest?

Oph. My lord!

Ham. Are you fair?   105

Oph. What means your lordship?

Ham. That if you be honest and fair, your
honesty should admit no discourse to your beauty.

Oph. Could beauty, my lord, have better commerce than [with] honesty?   110

Ham. Ay, truly; for the power of beauty will
sooner transform honesty from what it is to a
bawd than the force of honesty can translate
beauty into his likeness. This was sometime a
paradox, but now the time gives it proof. I did
love you once.   116

Oph. Indeed, my lord, you made me believe so.

Ham. You should not have believ'd me, for
virtue cannot so inoculate our old stock but we
shall relish of it. I loved you not.   120

Oph. I was the more deceived.

Ham. Get thee to a nunnery; why wouldst thou

be a breeder of sinners? I am myself indifferent
honest, but yet I could accuse me of such things
that it were better my mother had not borne me.   125
I am very proud, revengeful, ambitious, with more
offences at my beck than I have thoughts to put
them in, imagination to give them shape, or time to
act them in. What should such fellows as I do
crawling between heaven and earth? We are   130
arrant knaves all; believe none of us. Go thy ways
to a nunnery. Where's your father?

Oph. At home, my lord.

Ham. Let the doors be shut upon him, that he
may play the fool [nowhere] but in 's own house.
Farewell!   137

Oph. O, help him, you sweet heavens!

Ham. If thou dost marry, I'll give thee this
plague for thy dowry: be thou as chaste as ice,   140
as pure as snow, thou shalt not escape calumny.
Get thee to a nunnery, go. Farewell! Or, if thou
wilt needs marry, marry a fool; for wise men know
well enough what monsters you make of them. To
a nunnery, go, and quickly too. Farewell!   146

Oph. O heavenly powers, restore him!

Ham. I have heard of your [paintings] too, well
enough. God has given you one [face], and you
make yourself another. You [jig], you amble,   150
and you lisp and nick-name God's creatures and
make your wantonness your ignorance. Go to, I'll
no more on't; it hath made me mad. I say, we will
have no more marriages. Those that are married
already (all but one) shall live; the rest shall keep as
they are. To a nunnery, go.   [*Exit.*   157

Oph. O, what a noble mind is here o'erthrown!
The courtier's, soldier's, scholar's, eye, tongue,
          sword;
The expectancy and rose of the fair state,   160
The glass of fashion and the mould of form,
The observ'd of all observers, quite, quite down!
[And] I, of ladies most deject and wretched,
That suck'd the honey of his music vows,
Now see that noble and most sovereign reason,   165
Like sweet bells jangled, out of tune and harsh;
That unmatch'd form and feature of blown youth
Blasted with ecstasy. O, woe is me,
T' have seen what I have seen, see what I see!   169

Re-enter KING *and* POLONIUS.

King. Love! his affections do not that way tend;
Nor what he spake, though it lack'd form a little,
Was not like madness. There's something in his soul
O'er which his melancholy sits on brood,

76. **bodkin:** dagger. **fardels** Q2: burdens. *these Fardles* F. 83. **conscience:** reflection. 85. **thought:** i.e., melancholy thought, brooding. 86. **pith** F. *pitch* Q2. 87. [awry] Q2. *away* F. 97. **I know** F. *you know* Q2. 99. [Their] Q2. *then* F. [lost] Q2. *left* F. 103. **honest:** chaste. 110. [with] Q2. *your* F. 119. **inoculate:** engraft. 120. **relish:** have a trace. **it:** i.e., the old stock. 136. [nowhere] Q2. *no way* F. 148. [paintings] Q2. *pratlings* F. 149. [face] Q2. *pace* F. 150. [jig] Q2 (*gig*). *gidge* F. 152. **make...ignorance:** excuse your wantonness as ignorance. 163. [And] Q2. *Have* F. 167. **blown:** blooming. 170. **affections:** emotions.

And I do doubt the hatch and the disclose
Will be some danger; which [for] to prevent, 175
I have in quick determination
Thus set it down: he shall with speed to England
For the demand of our neglected tribute.
Haply the seas and countries different
With variable objects shall expel 180
This something-settled matter in his heart,
Whereon his brains still beating puts him thus
From fashion of himself. What think you on't?
Pol. It shall do well; but yet do I believe
The origin and commencement of this grief 185
Sprung from neglected love. How now, Ophelia!
You need not tell us what Lord Hamlet said;
We heard it all. My lord, do as you please,
But, if you hold it fit, after the play
Let his queen mother all alone entreat him 190
To show his griefs. Let her be round with him,
And I'll be plac'd, so please you, in the ear
Of all their conference. If she find him not,
To England send him, or confine him where
Your wisdom best shall think.
King. It shall be so. 195
Madness in great ones must not unwatch'd go.
[*Exeunt.*

[SCENE II. *A hall in the castle.*]

Enter HAMLET *and* PLAYERS.

Ham. Speak the speech, I pray you, as I pronounc'd it to you, trippingly on the tongue; but if
you mouth it, as many of your players do, I had
as lief the town-crier had spoke my lines. Nor do
not saw the air too much [with] your hand, thus, 5
but use all gently; for in the very torrent, tempest,
and, as I may say, the whirlwind of passion, you
must acquire and beget a temperance that may
give it smoothness. O, it offends me to the soul to
see a robustious periwig-pated fellow tear a pas- 10
sion to tatters, to very rags, to split the ears of the
groundlings, who for the most part are capable of
nothing but inexplicable dumb-shows and noise. I
could have such a fellow whipp'd for o'erdoing Termagant. It out-herods Herod. Pray you, avoid
it. 16
[*1.*] *Play.* I warrant your honour.
Ham. Be not too tame neither, but let your own
discretion be your tutor. Suit the action to the
word, the word to the action; with this special 20
observance, that you [o'erstep] not the modesty of
nature. For anything so overdone is from the purpose of playing, whose end, both at the first and

now, was and is, to hold, as 'twere, the mirror up to
nature; to show virtue her own feature, scorn her 25
own image, and the very age and body of the time
his form and pressure. Now this overdone, or come
tardy off, though it make the unskillful laugh, cannot
but make the judicious grieve; the censure of the
which one must, in your allowance, o'erweigh a 30
whole theatre of others. O, there be players that I
have seen play, and heard others praise, and that
highly, not to speak it profanely, that, neither
having the accent of Christians nor the gait of
Christian, pagan, [nor man,] have so strutted and 35
bellowed that I have thought some of Nature's
journeymen had made men and not made them well,
they imitated humanity so abominably.
1. Play. I hope we have reform'd that indifferently with us, sir. 41
Ham. O, reform it altogether. And let those that
play your clowns speak no more than is set down
for them; for there be of them that will themselves
laugh to set on some quantity of barren specta- 45
tors to laugh too, though in the mean time some
necessary question of the play be then to be considered. That's villanous, and shows a most pitiful
ambition in the Fool that uses it. Go, make you
ready. [*Exeunt Players.* 50

Enter POLONIUS, ROSENCRANTZ, *and* GUILDEN-
STERN.

How now, my lord! Will the King hear this piece
of work?
Pol. And the Queen too, and that presently.
Ham. Bid the players make haste.
[*Exit Polonius.*
Will you two help to hasten them? 55
Ros. }
Guil. } We will, my lord.

[*Exeunt Rosencrantz and Guildenstern.*
Ham. What ho! Horatio.

Enter HORATIO.

Hor. Here, sweet lord, at your service.
Ham. Horatio, thou art e'en as just a man
As e'er my conversation cop'd withal. 60
Hor. O, my dear lord, —
Ham. Nay, do not think I flatter,
For what advancement may I hope from thee
That no revenue hast but thy good spirits
To feed and clothe thee? Why should the poor be
flatter'd?
No, let the candied tongue [lick] absurd pomp, 65
And crook the pregnant hinges of the knee

175. [for] Q₂. Om. F. 193. find him: learn the truth about him.
Sc. ii, 5. [with] Q₂. Om. F. 12. groundlings: those who stood in the "pit" of the theatre, the cheapest place. 15.
Termagant: a violent character in the Mystery plays, a god of the Saracens. Herod, represented in the Mystery plays as
bombastic. 21. [o'erstep] Q₂. ore-stop F. 28. tardy: i.e., ineffectually. 35. [nor man] Q₂. or Norman F. 40. indifferently: tolerably. 60. conversation: intercourse. cop'd: met. 65. candied: i.e., flattering. [lick] Q₂. like F. 66. pregnant: ready, pliant.

Where thrift may follow [fawning]. Dost thou
  hear?
Since my dear soul was mistress of my choice
And could of men distinguish, her election
Hath seal'd thee for herself; for thou hast been   70
As one, in suffering all, that suffers nothing,
A man that Fortune's buffets and rewards
Hath ta'en with equal thanks; and blest are those
Whose blood and judgement are so well commingled,
That they are not a pipe for Fortune's finger   75
To sound what stop she please. Give me that man
That is not passion's slave, and I will wear him
In my heart's core, ay, in my heart of heart,
As I do thee. — Something too much of this. —
There is a play to-night before the King.   80
One scene of it comes near the circumstance
Which I have told thee of my father's death.
I prithee, when thou seest that act a-foot,
Even with the very comment of [thy] soul
Observe mine uncle. If his occulted guilt   85
Do not itself unkennel in one speech,
It is a damned ghost that we have seen,
And my imaginations are as foul
As Vulcan's stithy. Give him [heedful] note;
For I mine eyes will rivet to his face,   90
And after we will both our judgements join
To censure of his seeming.
Hor.   Well, my lord.
If he steal aught the whilst this play is playing,
And scape detecting, I will pay the theft.

Danish march. A flourish. Enter KING, QUEEN,
POLONIUS, OPHELIA, ROSENCRANTZ, GUILDEN-
STERN, *and other Lords attendant, with the guard
carrying torches.*

Ham. They are coming to the play; I must be
  idle.   95
Get you a place.
King. How fares our cousin Hamlet?
Ham. Excellent, i' faith, — of the chameleon's
dish. I eat the air, promise-cramm'd. You cannot
feed capons so.   100
King. I have nothing with this answer, Hamlet;
these words are not mine.
Ham. No, nor mine now. [*To Polonius.*] My
lord, you play'd once i' th' university, you say?
Pol. That I did, my lord, and was accounted a
good actor.   106
Ham. And what did you enact?
Pol. I did enact Julius Cæsar. I was kill'd i' th'
Capitol; Brutus kill'd me.
Ham. It was a brute part of him to kill so capital
a calf there. Be the players ready?   111

Ros. Ay, my lord, they stay upon your patience.
Queen. Come hither, my good Hamlet, sit   115
by me.
Ham. No, good mother, here's metal more at-
tractive.   [*Lying down at Ophelia's feet.*]
Pol. [*To the King.*] O, ho! do you mark that?
Ham. Lady, shall I lie in your lap?
Oph. No, my lord.   120
Ham. I mean, my head upon your lap?
Oph. Ay, my lord.
Ham. Do you think I meant country matters?
Oph. I think nothing, my lord.
Ham. That's a fair thought to lie between maids'
legs.   126
Oph. What is, my lord?
Ham. Nothing.
Oph. You are merry, my lord.
Ham. Who, I?   130
Oph. Ay, my lord.
Ham. O God, your only jig-maker. What
should a man do but be merry? For, look you, how
cheerfully my mother looks, and my father died
within 's two hours.   135
Oph. Nay, 'tis twice two months, my lord.
Ham. So long? Nay then, let the devil wear
black, for I'll have a suit of sables. O heavens! die
two months ago, and not forgotten yet? Then
there's hope a great man's memory may outlive   140
his life half a year; but, by 'r lady; he must build
churches then, or else shall he suffer not thinking on,
with the hobby-horse, whose epitaph is, "For, O,
for, O, the hobby-horse is forgot."   145

Hautboys play. The dumb-show enters.

*Enter a King and Queen very lovingly, the Queen
  embracing him. She kneels and makes show of
  protestation unto him. He takes her up and declines his head upon her neck; lays him down upon
  a bank of flowers. She, seeing him asleep, leaves
  him. Anon comes in a fellow, takes off his crown,
  kisses it, and pours poison in the King's ears, and
  exit. The Queen returns, finds the King dead, and
  makes passionate action. The poisoner, with some
  two or three Mutes, comes in again, seeming to
  lament with her. The dead body is carried away.
  The poisoner woos the Queen with gifts; she seems
  loath and unwilling a while, but in the end accepts
  his love.   [Exeunt.*

Oph. What means this, my lord?
Ham. Marry, this is miching mallecho; that
means mischief.
Oph. Belike this show imports the argument of
the play?   150

67. **thrift:** profit. [**fawning**] Q₂. *faining* F. 74. **blood:** passions. 84. [**thy**] Q₂. *my* F. 85. **occulted:** hidden. 86.
unkennel: bring into the open. 89. [**heedful**] Q₂. *needfull* F. 92. **censure:** judgment. 101. **have ... with:** do not
understand. 138. **sables:** fine fur — with a quibble on *sable* as mourning black. 144-45. "**For ... forgot.**" A line
from an old ballad. 147. **miching mallecho:** sneaking mischief.

Enter PROLOGUE.

Ham. We shall know by [this fellow]. The players cannot keep counsel; they'll tell all.

Oph. Will they tell us what this show meant?

Ham. Ay, or any show that you'll show him. Be not you asham'd to show, he'll not shame to tell you what it means. 156

Oph. You are naught, you are naught. I'll mark the play.

Pro. For us, and for our tragedy,
Here stooping to your clemency, 160
We beg your hearing patiently.   [*Exit.*]

Ham. Is this a prologue, or the posy of a ring?

Oph. 'Tis brief, my lord.

Ham. As woman's love.

Enter [*two Players,*] KING *and his* QUEEN.

P. King. Full thirty times hath Phœbus' cart gone round 165
Neptune's salt wash and Tellus' orbed ground,
And thirty dozen moons with borrowed sheen
About the world have times twelve thirties been,
Since love our hearts and Hymen did our hands
Unite commutual in most sacred bands. 170
[*P. Queen.*] So many journeys may the sun and moon
Make us again count o'er ere love be done!
But, woe is me, you are so sick of late,
So far from cheer and from your former state,
That I distrust you. Yet, though I distrust, 175
Discomfort you, my lord, it nothing must;
For women's fear and love holds quantity,
In neither aught, or in extremity.
Now, what my love is, proof hath made you know;
And as my love is siz'd, my fear is so. 180
[Where love is great, the littlest doubts are fear;
Where little fears grow great, great love grows there.]

P. King. Faith, I must leave thee, love, and shortly too.
My operant powers [their] functions leave to do;
And thou shalt live in this fair world behind, 185
Honour'd, belov'd; and haply one as kind
For husband shalt thou —

P. Queen.   O, confound the rest!
Such love must needs be treason in my breast!
In second husband let me be accurst!
None wed the second but who kill'd the first.

Ham. [*Aside.*] Wormwood, wormwood! 191

P. Queen. The instances that second marriage move
Are base respects of thrift, but none of love.

A second time I kill my husband dead,
When second husband kisses me in bed. 195

P. King. I do believe you think what now you speak,
But what we do determine oft we break.
Purpose is but the slave to memory,
Of violent birth, but poor validity;
Which now, like fruit unripe, sticks on the tree, 200
But fall unshaken when they mellow be.
Most necessary 'tis that we forget
To pay ourselves what to ourselves is debt.
What to ourselves in passion we propose,
The passion ending, doth the purpose lose. 205
The violence of [either] grief or joy
Their own enactures with themselves destroy.
Where joy most revels, grief doth most lament;
Grief joys, joy grieves, on slender accident.
This world is not for aye, nor 'tis not strange 210
That even our loves should with our fortunes change,
For 'tis a question left us yet to prove,
Whether love lead fortune, or else fortune love.
The great man down, you mark his favourite flies;
The poor advanc'd makes friends of enemies. 215
And hitherto doth love on fortune tend,
For who not needs shall never lack a friend;
And who in want a hollow friend doth try,
Directly seasons him his enemy.
But, orderly to end where I begun, 220
Our wills and fates do so contrary run
That our devices still are overthrown;
Our thoughts are ours, their ends none of our own.
So think thou wilt no second husband wed;
But die thy thoughts when thy first lord is dead. 225

P. Queen. Nor earth to [me give] food, nor heaven light!
Sport and repose lock from me day and night!
[To desperation turn my trust and hope!
An anchor's cheer in prison be my scope!]
Each opposite that blanks the face of joy 230
Meet what I would have well and it destroy!
Both here and hence pursue me lasting strife,
If, once a widow, ever I be wife!

Ham. If she should break it now!

P. King. 'Tis deeply sworn. Sweet, leave me here a while. 235
My spirits grow dull, and fain I would beguile
The tedious day with sleep.   [*Sleeps.*

P. Queen.   Sleep rock thy brain,
And never come mischance between us twain! [*Exit.*

Ham. Madam, how like you this play?

Queen. The lady protests too much, methinks.

151. [this fellow] Q₂. *these fellowes* F. 157. **naught:** naughty. 162. **posy:** motto. 171. [**P. Queen**] (Steevens). *Bap.* F. *Quee.* Q₂. 175. **distrust:** fear for. 177. **quantity:** proportion. Q₂ inserts before *women's*, "For women feare too much, even as they love, and." 181–82. [Where … there] Q₂. Om. F. 184. **operant:** active. [**their**] Q₂. *my* F. 192. **move:** induce. 199. **validity:** strength. 206. [**either**] Q₂. *other* F. 207. **enactures:** acts. 219. **seasons:** changes into. 226. [**me give**] Q₂. *give me* F. 228–29. [**To … scope**] Q₂. Om. F. 229. **anchor's cheer:** hermit's fare. 230. **blanks:** makes pale.

Ham. O, but she'll keep her word.   241
    King. Have you heard the argument? Is there no offence in't?
    Ham. No, no, they do but jest, poison in jest. No offence i' th' world.   245
    King. What do you call the play?
    Ham. "The Mouse-trap." Marry, how? Tropically. This play is the image of a murder done in Vienna. Gonzago is the duke's name; his wife, Baptista. You shall see anon. 'Tis a knavish 250 piece of work, but what o' that? Your Majesty and we that have free souls, it touches us not. Let the gall'd jade wince, our withers are unwrung.

Enter LUCIANUS.

This is one Lucianus, nephew to the king.
    Oph. You are a good chorus, my lord.   255
    Ham. I could interpret between you and your love, if I could see the puppets dallying.
    Oph. You are keen, my lord, you are keen.
    Ham. It would cost you a groaning to take off my edge.   260
    Oph. Still better, and worse.
    Ham. So you mistake husbands. Begin, murderer; pox, leave thy damnable faces and begin. Come, "the croaking raven doth bellow for revenge."   265
    Luc. Thoughts black, hands apt, drugs fit, and time agreeing;
Confederate season, else no creature seeing.
Thou mixture rank, of midnight weeds collected,
With Hecate's ban thrice blasted, thrice infected,
Thy natural magic and dire property   270
On wholesome life usurp immediately.

     [*Pours the poison in* [*to the sleeper's*] *ears.*
    Ham. He poisons him i' th' garden for 's estate. His name's Gonzago; the story is extant, and writ in choice Italian. You shall see anon how the murderer gets the love of Gonzago's wife.   275
    Oph. The King rises.
    Ham. What, frighted with false fire?
    Queen. How fares my lord?
    Pol. Give o'er the play.
    King. Give me some light. Away!   280
    All. Lights, lights, lights!

     [*Exeunt all but Hamlet and Horatio.*
    Ham. Why, let the strucken deer go weep,
       The hart ungalled play;
    For some must watch, while some must sleep, —
       So runs the world away.   285
Would not this, sir, and a forest of feathers — if the

rest of my fortunes turn Turk with me — with two Provincial roses on my raz'd shoes, get me a fellowship in a cry of players, sir?
    Hor. Half a share.   290
    Ham. A whole one, I.
      For thou dost know, O Damon dear,
        This realm dismantled was
      Of Jove himself; and now reigns here
        A very, very — pajock.   295
    Hor. You might have rhym'd.
    Ham. O good Horatio, I'll take the ghost's word for a thousand pound. Didst perceive?
    Hor. Very well, my lord.
    Ham. Upon the talk of the poisoning?   300
    Hor. I did very well note him.

Re-enter ROSENCRANTZ *and* GUILDENSTERN.

    Ham. Ah, ha! Come, some music! Come, the recorders!
      For if the king like not the comedy,
      Why then, belike, he likes it not, perdy.   305
Come, some music!
    Guil. Good my lord, vouchsafe me a word with you.
    Ham. Sir, a whole history.
    Guil. The King, sir, —   310
    Ham. Ay, sir, what of him?
    Guil. Is in his retirement marvellous distemper'd.
    Ham. With drink, sir?
    Guil. No, my lord, rather with choler.   315
    Ham. Your wisdom should show itself more richer to signify this to his doctor; for, for me to put him to his purgation would perhaps plunge him into far more choler.   319
    Guil. Good my lord, put your discourse into some frame, and start not so wildly from my affair.
    Ham. I am tame, sir; pronounce.
    Guil. The Queen, your mother, in most great affliction of spirit, hath sent me to you.
    Ham. You are welcome.   325
    Guil. Nay, good my lord, this courtesy is not of the right breed. If it shall please you to make me a wholesome answer I will do your mother's commandment; if not, your pardon and my return shall be the end of my business.   330
    Ham. Sir, I cannot.
    Guil. What, my lord?
    Ham. Make you a wholesome answer. My wit's diseas'd. But, sir, such answers as I can make, you shall command, or, rather, [as] you say, my mother. Therefore no more, but to the matter. My mother, you say, —   337

---

247. **Tropically:** figuratively. 253. **gall'd jade:** chafed horse. 261. **better, and worse:** i.e., more pointed and less chaste. 262. **mistake** F. *mistake your* Q₂. *must take your* (*husband*) Q₁. 286. **feathers.** Tragic actors wore plumes. 287. **turn Turk:** go bad. 288. **Provincial roses:** rosettes like the rose of Provence. **raz'd:** slashed. 289. **cry:** company. 295. **pajock:** peacock. 315. **choler:** anger; but Hamlet (l. 319) plays upon the other meaning, biliousness. 335. **[as]** Q₂. Om. F.

Ros. Then thus she says: your behaviour hath struck her into amazement and admiration.

Ham. O wonderful son, that can so astonish a mother! But is there no sequel at the heels of this mother-admiration? [*Impart.*]   342

Ros. She desires to speak with you in her closet ere you go to bed.

Ham. We shall obey, were she ten times our mother. Have you any further trade with us?

Ros. My lord, you once did love me.   348

Ham. So I do still, by these pickers and stealers.

Ros. Good my lord, what is your cause of distemper? You do [surely] bar the door of your own liberty if you deny your griefs to your friend.

Ham. Sir, I lack advancement.   354

Ros. How can that be, when you have the voice of the King himself for your succession in Denmark?

Ham. Ay, but "While the grass grows," — the proverb is something musty.   359

Re-enter one with a recorder.

O, the recorder! Let me see. — To withdraw with you: — why do you go about to recover the wind of me, as if you would drive me into a toil?

Guil. O, my lord, if my duty be too bold, my love is too unmannerly.   364

Ham. I do not well understand that. Will you play upon this pipe?

Guil. My lord, I cannot.

Ham. I pray you.

Guil. Believe me, I cannot.

Ham. I do beseech you.   370

Guil. I know no touch of it, my lord.

Ham. 'Tis as easy as lying. Govern these ventages with your finger and thumb, give it breath with your mouth, and it will discourse most excellent music. Look you, these are the stops.   376

Guil. But these cannot I command to any utterance of harmony. I have not the skill.

Ham. Why, look you now, how unworthy a thing you make of me! You would play upon me,   380 you would seem to know my stops, you would pluck out the heart of my mystery, you would sound me from my lowest note to the top of my compass; and there is much music, excellent voice, in this little organ, yet cannot you make it [speak. 'Sblood,]   385 do you think that I am easier to be play'd on than a pipe? Call me what instrument you will, though you can fret me, you cannot play upon me.

Enter POLONIUS.

God bless you, sir.   390

Pol. My lord, the Queen would speak with you, and presently.

Ham. Do you see that cloud that's almost in shape like a camel?

Pol. By the mass, and it's like a camel, indeed.

Ham. Methinks it is like a weasel.   396

Pol. It is back'd like a weasel.

Ham. Or like a whale?

Pol. Very like a whale.   399

Ham. Then will I come to my mother by and by. [*Aside.*] They fool me to the top of my bent. — I will come by and by.

Pol. I will say so.   [*Exit.*

Ham. "By and by" is easily said. Leave me,   friends.   [*Exeunt all but Hamlet.*]   405

'Tis now the very witching time of night
When churchyards yawn and hell itself breathes out
Contagion to this world. Now could I drink hot
     blood,
And do such bitter business as the day
Would quake to look on. Soft! now to my mother.
O heart, lose not thy nature! Let not ever   411
The soul of Nero enter this firm bosom;
Let me be cruel, not unnatural.
I will speak daggers to her, but use none.
My tongue and soul in this be hypocrites;   415
How in my words soever she be shent
To give them seals never, my soul, consent! [*Exit.*

[SCENE III. *A room in the castle.*]

Enter KING, ROSENCRANTZ, *and* GUILDENSTERN.

King. I like him not, nor stands it safe with us
To let his madness range. Therefore prepare you.
I your commission will forthwith dispatch,
And he to England shall along with you.
The terms of our estate may not endure   5
Hazard so dangerous as doth hourly grow
Out of his lunacies.

Guil.   We will ourselves provide.
Most holy and religious fear it is
To keep those many many bodies safe
That live and feed upon your Majesty.   10

Ros. The single and peculiar life is bound
With all the strength and armour of the mind
To keep itself from noyance, but much more
That spirit upon whose [weal] depends and rests
The lives of many. The cease of majesty   15
Dies not alone, but, like a gulf, doth draw

339. **admiration:** wonder. 342. **mother-admiration** F₄. *Mother admiration* F₁. *mother's admiration* Q₂. [*Impart*] Q₂. Om. F. 343. **closet:** chamber. 349. **pickers and stealers:** i.e., hands. 351. [**surely**] Q₂. *freely* F. 359. **proverb:** "While the grass grows, the steed starves." 360. **withdraw:** speak privately. 361–62. **recover the wind:** get to windward. 362. **toil:** snare. 373. **ventages:** stops. 385. [**speak. 'Sblood**] Q₂. *Why* F. 388. **fret:** (1) finger, (2) vex. 401. **They . . . bent:** they let me play the fool to the limit. 411. **nature:** natural affection. 412. **Nero.** He murdered his mother. 416. **shent:** rebuked. 417. **give . . . seals:** confirm them by deeds.
     Sc. iii, 5. terms: condition. 11. **peculiar:** private. 14. [**weal**] Q₂. *spirit* F. 15. **cease:** death. 16. **gulf:** whirlpool.

What's near it with it.   It is a massy wheel,
Fixed on the summit of the highest mount,
To whose huge spokes ten thousand lesser things
Are mortis'd and adjoin'd; which, when it falls,   20
Each small annexment, petty consequence,
Attends the boisterous ruin.   Never alone
Did the King sigh, but with a general groan.
    King. Arm you, I pray you, to this speedy voy-
        age,
For we will fetters put upon this fear,   25
Which now goes too free-footed.
    Ros. ⎫
    Guil. ⎭   We will haste us.
        [Exeunt Rosencrantz and Guildenstern.

        Enter POLONIUS.

    Pol. My lord, he's going to his mother's closet.
Behind the arras I'll convey myself
To hear the process.   I'll warrant she'll tax him
    home;
And, as you said, and wisely was it said,   30
'Tis meet that some more audience than a mother,
Since nature makes them partial, should o'erhear
The speech, of vantage.   Fare you well, my liege.
I'll call upon you ere you go to bed
And tell you what I know.
    King.   Thanks, dear my lord.
                      [Exit Polonius.]
O, my offence is rank, it smells to heaven;   36
It hath the primal eldest curse upon't,
A brother's murder.   Pray can I not,
Though inclination be as sharp as will.
My stronger guilt defeats my strong intent,   40
And, like a man to double business bound,
I stand in pause where I shall first begin,
And both neglect.   What if this cursed hand
Were thicker than itself with brother's blood,
Is there not rain enough in the sweet heavens   45
To wash it white as snow?   Whereto serves mercy
But to confront the visage of offence?
And what's in prayer but this twofold force,
To be forestalled ere we come to fall,
Or pardon'd being down?   Then I'll look up;   50
My fault is past.   But, O, what form of prayer
Can serve my turn?   "Forgive me my foul mur-
    der"?
That cannot be; since I am still possess'd
Of those effects for which I did the murder,
My crown, mine own ambition, and my queen.   55
May one be pardon'd and retain th' offence?
In the corrupted currents of this world
Offence's gilded hand may shove by justice,
And oft 'tis seen the wicked prize itself

Buys out the law.   But 'tis not so above: 60
There is no shuffling, there the action lies
In his true nature; and we ourselves compell'd,
Even to the teeth and forehead of our faults,
To give in evidence.   What then?   What rests?
Try what repentance can.   What can it not?   65
Yet what can it when one cannot repent?
O wretched state!   O bosom black as death!
O limed soul, that, struggling to be free,
Art more engag'd!   Help, angels!   Make assay!
Bow, stubborn knees, and, heart with strings of
    steel,   70
Be soft as sinews of the new-born babe!
All may be well.   *[Retires and] kneels.*

        Enter HAMLET.

    Ham. Now might I do it pat, now he is pray-
        ing;
And now I'll do't — And so he goes to heaven;
And so am I reveng'd.   That would be scann'd.
A villain kills my father, and for that   76
I, his [sole] son, do this same villain send
To heaven.
Oh, this is hire and salary, not revenge.
He took my father grossly, full of bread,   80
With all his crimes broad blown, as [flush] as May;
And how his audit stands who knows save Heaven?
But in our circumstance and course of thought
'Tis heavy with him.   And am I then reveng'd,
To take him in the purging of his soul,   85
When he is fit and season'd for his passage?
No!
Up, sword, and know thou a more horrid hent.
When he is drunk asleep, or in his rage,
Or in th' incestuous pleasure of his bed,   90
At gaming, swearing, or about some act
That has no relish of salvation in't, —
Then trip him, that his heels may kick at heaven,
And that his soul may be as damn'd and black
As hell, whereto it goes.   My mother stays.   95
This physic but prolongs thy sickly days.   *[Exit.*
    King. *[Rising.]* My words fly up, my thoughts
        remain below.
Words without thoughts never to heaven go.
                            [Exit.

    [SCENE IV.   *The Queen's closet.*]

      Enter QUEEN *and* POLONIUS.

    Pol. He will come straight.   Look you lay home
    to him.
Tell him his pranks have been too broad to bear
    with,

---

24. **Arm:** prepare.   29. **tax:** censure.   33. **of vantage:** from a favorable position.   58. **gilded:** ready to bribe.   64. **rests:** remains.   68. **limed:** caught (as in bird lime).   75. **would be scann'd:** demands scrutiny.   77. [**sole**] Q₂. *foule* F.   81. [**flush**] Q₂: lusty.   *fresh* F.   88. **hent:** grip.   96. **physic:** i.e., prayer.
    Sc. iv, 2. broad: unrestrained.

And that your Grace hath screen'd and stood be-
        tween
Much heat and him. I'll silence me e'en here.
Pray you, be round with him.   5
    Ham. [*Within.*] Mother, mother, mother!
    Queen. I'll warrant you, fear me not. With-
draw, I hear him coming.

                 [*Polonius hides behind the arras.*]

                   Enter HAMLET.

    Ham. Now, mother, what's the matter?
    Queen. Hamlet, thou hast thy father much of-
fended.
    Ham. Mother, you have my father much of-
fended.   10
    Queen. Come, come, you answer with an idle
        tongue.
    Ham. Go, go, you question with [a wicked]
        tongue.
    Queen. Why, how now, Hamlet!
    Ham.   What's the matter now?
    Queen. Have you forgot me?
    Ham.   No, by the rood, not so.
You are the Queen, your husband's brother's wife;
But — would you were not so! — you are my
        mother.   16
    Queen. Nay, then, I'll set those to you that can
        speak.
    Ham. Come, come, and sit you down. You
        shall not budge.
You go not till I set you up a glass
Where you may see the inmost part of you.   20
    Queen. What wilt thou do? Thou wilt not mur-
        der me?
Help, help, ho!
    Pol. [*Behind.*] What, ho! help, help, help!
    Ham. [*Drawing.*] How now! A rat? Dead,
        for a ducat, dead!

                 [*Kills Polonius [through the arras].*]
    Pol. [*Behind.*] O, I am slain!
    Queen. O me, what hast thou done?
    Ham.   Nay, I know not.
Is it the King?   26
    Queen. O, what a rash and bloody deed is this!
    Ham. A bloody deed! Almost as bad, good
        mother,
As kill a king, and marry with his brother.   29
    Queen. As kill a king!
    Ham.   Ay, lady, 'twas my word.

         [*Lifts up the arras and discovers Polonius.*]
Thou wretched, rash, intruding fool, farewell!
I took thee for thy better. Take thy fortune.
Thou find'st to be too busy is some danger.

— Leave wringing of your hands. Peace! Sit you
        down,
And let me wring your heart; for so I shall,   35
If it be made of penetrable stuff,
If damned custom have not braz'd it so
That it is proof and bulwark against sense.
    Queen. What have I done, that thou dar'st wag
        thy tongue
In noise so rude against me?
    Ham.   Such an act   40
That blurs the grace and blush of modesty,
Calls virtue hypocrite, takes off the rose
From the fair forehead of an innocent love
And [sets] a blister there, makes marriage-vows
As false as dicers' oaths; O, such a deed   45
As from the body of contraction plucks
The very soul, and sweet religion makes
A rhapsody of words. Heaven's face doth glow,
Yea, this solidity and compound mass,
With tristful visage, as against the doom,   50
Is thought-sick at the act.
    Queen.   Ay me, what act,
That roars so loud and thunders in the index?
    Ham. Look here, upon this picture, and on this,
The counterfeit presentment of two brothers.
See, what a grace was seated on his brow: 55
Hyperion's curls, the front of Jove himself,
An eye like Mars, to threaten or command,
A station like the herald Mercury
New-lighted on a heaven-kissing hill,
A combination and a form indeed,   60
Where every god did seem to set his seal
To give the world assurance of a man.
This was your husband. Look you now what fol-
        lows:
Here is your husband, like a mildew'd ear,
Blasting his wholesome [brother]. Have you
        eyes?
Could you on this fair mountain leave to feed,   66
And batten on this moor? Ha! have you eyes?
You cannot call it love, for at your age
The hey-day in the blood is tame, it's humble,
And waits upon the judgement; and what judge-
        ment   70
Would step from this to this? [Sense sure you
        have,
Else could you not have motion; but sure, that
        sense
Is apoplex'd; for madness would not err,
Nor sense to ecstasy was ne'er so thrall'd
But it reserv'd some quantity of choice,   75
To serve in such a difference.] What devil was't
That thus hath cozen'd you at hoodman-blind?

---

12. [a wicked] Q₂. *an idle* F.   14. rood: cross.   37. braz'd: hardened (like brass).   38. sense: feeling.   44. [sets]
Q₂. *makes* F.   46. contraction: betrothal.   49. this ... mass: the earth.   50. tristful: sorrowful.   doom: Judgement Day.
52. index: prologue.   58. station: bearing.   65. [brother] Q₂. *breath* F.   67. batten: gorge.   71–76. [Sense ... difference]
Q₂. Om. F.   73. apoplex'd: paralyzed.   77. cozen'd: cheated.   hoodman-blind: blind-man's buff.

[Eyes without feeling, feeling without sight,
Ears without hands or eyes, smelling sans all,
Or but a sickly part of one true sense   80
Could not so mope.]
O shame! where is thy blush? Rebellious hell,
If thou canst mutine in a matron's bones,
To flaming youth let virtue be as wax
And melt in her own fire. Proclaim no shame   85
When the compulsive ardour gives the charge,
Since frost itself as actively doth burn,
[And] reason panders will.
     Queen.   O Hamlet, speak no more!
Thou turn'st mine eyes into my very soul,
And there I see such black and grained spots   90
As will not leave their tint.
     Ham.   Nay, but to live
In the rank sweat of an enseamed bed,
Stew'd in corruption, honeying and making love
Over the nasty sty, —
     Queen.   O, speak to me no more!
These words like daggers enter in mine ears.   95
No more, sweet Hamlet!
     Ham.   A murderer and a villain!
A slave that is not twentieth part the tithe
Of your precedent lord! A vice of kings!
A cutpurse of the empire and the rule,
That from a shelf the precious diadem stole,   100
And put it in his pocket!
     Queen.   No more!

          Enter GHOST.

     Ham. A king of shreds and patches! —
Save me, and hover o'er me with your wings,
You heavenly guards! What would you, gracious
     figure?
     Queen. Alas, he's mad!   105
     Ham. Do you not come your tardy son to chide,
That, laps'd in time and passion, lets go by
Th' important acting of your dread command?
O, say!
     Ghost. Do not forget! This visitation   110
Is but to whet thy almost blunted purpose.
But, look, amazement on thy mother sits.
O, step between her and her fighting soul.
Conceit in weakest bodies strongest works.
Speak to her, Hamlet.
     Ham.   How is it with you, lady?
     Queen. Alas, how is't with you,   116
That you [do] bend your eye on vacancy
And with [th' incorporal] air do hold discourse?
Forth at your eyes your spirits wildly peep,

And, as the sleeping soldiers in th' alarm,   120
Your bedded hair, like life in excrements,
Start up and stand on end. O gentle son,
Upon the heat and flame of thy distemper
Sprinkle cool patience. Whereon do you look?
     Ham. On him, on him! Look you, how pale he
     glares!   125
His form and cause conjoin'd, preaching to stones,
Would make them capable. — Do not look upon
     me,
Lest with this piteous action you convert
My stern effects; then what I have to do
Will want true colour, tears perchance for blood. 130
     Queen. To [whom] do you speak this?
     Ham.   Do you see nothing there?
     Queen. Nothing at all, yet all that is I see.
     Ham. Nor did you nothing hear?
     Queen.   No, nothing but ourselves.
     Ham. Why, look you there! Look, how it steals
     away!
My father, in his habit as he lived!   135
Look, where he goes, even now, out at the portal!
                                   [*Exit Ghost.*
     Queen. This is the very coinage of your brain.
This bodiless creation ecstasy
Is very cunning in.
     Ham.   Ecstasy!
My pulse, as yours, doth temperately keep time. 140
And makes as healthful music. It is not madness
That I have utt'red. Bring me to the test,
And I the matter will re-word, which madness
Would gambol from. Mother, for love of grace,
Lay not [that] flattering unction to your soul,   145
That not your trespass, but my madness speaks.
It will but skin and film the ulcerous place,
Whilst rank corruption, mining all within,
Infects unseen. Confess yourself to Heaven;
Repent what's past, avoid what is to come,   150
And do not spread the compost on the weeds
To make them rank. Forgive me this my virtue,
For in the fatness of [these] pursy times
Virtue itself of vice must pardon beg,
Yea, curb and woo for leave to do him good,   155
     Queen. O Hamlet, thou hast cleft my heart in
     twain.
     Ham. O, throw away the worser part of it,
And live the purer with the other half.
Good-night; but go not to mine uncle's bed.
Assume a virtue, if you have it not.   160
[That monster, custom, who all sense doth eat
Of habits evil, is angel yet in this,

78–81. [**Eyes . . . mope**] Q₂. Om. F. 81. **mope:** be dazed. 88. [**And**] Q₂. *As* F. **will:** lust. 90. **grained:** ingrained. 92. **enseamed:** greasy. 98. **vice:** the Vice, the mischievous buffoon of the Morality plays. 107. **laps'd . . . passion:** having let slip time and the desire for revenge. 117. [**do**] Q₂. Om. F. 118. [**th' incorporal**] Q₂. *their corporal* F. 121. **bedded:** lying flat. **excrements:** growths, i.e., hair. 129. **effects:** i.e., accomplishment of purpose. 131. [**whom**] Q₂. *who* F. 135. **habit:** garb. 138. **ecstasy:** madness. 145. [**that**] Q₂. *a* F. **unction:** salve. 151. **compost:** manure. 153. [**these**] Q₂. *this* F. **pursy:** short-winded, out of condition. 155. **curb:** bow. 161–65. [**That . . . on**] Q₂. Om. F. 162. **evil** (Thirlby conj.). *devill* Q₂.

That to the use of actions fair and good
He likewise gives a frock or livery,
That aptly is put on.] Refrain to-night,　　165
And that shall lend a kind of easiness
To the next abstinence; [the next more easy;
For use almost can change the stamp of nature,
And either master the devil or throw him out,
With wondrous potency.] Once more, good-night;
And when you are desirous to be blest,　　171
I'll blessing beg of you. For this same lord,
　　　　　　　　　　　[Pointing to Polonius.]
I do repent; but Heaven hath pleas'd it so,
To punish me with this and this with me,
That I must be their scourge and minister.　　175
I will bestow him, and will answer well
The death I gave him. So, again, good-night.
I must be cruel, only to be kind.
Thus bad begins and worse remains behind.
[One word more, good lady.]
　　Queen.　　　　　　What shall I do?　　180
　　Ham. Not this, by no means, that I bid you
　　do:
Let the [bloat] king tempt you again to bed,
Pinch wanton on your cheek, call you his mouse,
And let him, for a pair of reechy kisses,
Or paddling in your neck with his damn'd fingers,
Make you to ravel all this matter out,　　186
That I essentially am not in madness,
But mad in craft. 'Twere good you let him know;
For who, that's but a queen, fair, sober, wise,
Would from a paddock, from a bat, a gib,　　190
Such dear concernings hide? Who would do so?
No, in despite of sense and secrecy,
Unpeg the basket on the house's top,
Let the birds fly, and like the famous ape,
To try conclusions, in the basket creep,　　195
And break your own neck down.
　　Queen. Be thou assur'd, if words be made of
　　breath,
And breath of life, I have no life to breathe
What thou hast said to me.
　　Ham. I must to England; you know that?
　　Queen.　　　　　　　　　　Alack,
I had forgot. 'Tis so concluded on.　　201
　　Ham. [There's letters sealed, and my two school-
　　fellows,
Whom I will trust as I will adders fang'd,
They bear the mandate. They must sweep my way,
And marshal me to knavery. Let it work;　　205
For 'tis the sport to have the enginer
Hoist with his own petar; and 't shall go hard
But I will delve one yard below their mines,

And blow them at the moon. O, 'tis most sweet,
When in one line two crafts directly meet.]　　210
This man shall set me packing.
I'll lug the guts into the neighbour room.
Mother, good-night. Indeed this counsellor
Is now most still, most secret, and most grave,
Who was in life a foolish prating knave. —　　215
Come, sir, to draw toward an end with you. —
Good-night, mother.
　　　　　　[Exeunt [severally,] Hamlet tugging in
　　　　　　Polonius.

[ACT IV]

[SCENE I.　A room in the castle.]

Enter KING [QUEEN, Rosencrantz, and Guild-
enstern].

　　King. There's matter in these sighs; these pro-
　　found heaves
You must translate; 'tis fit we understand them.
Where is your son?
　　Queen. [Bestow this place on us a little while.]
　　　　　　[Exeunt Rosencrantz and Guildenstern.]
Ah, my good lord, what have I seen to-night!　　5
　　King. What, Gertrude? How does Hamlet?
　　Queen. Mad as the seas and wind, when both
　　contend
Which is the mightier. In his lawless fit,
Behind the arras hearing something stir,
He whips his rapier out, and cries, "A rat, a rat!"　10
And, in his brainish apprehension, kills
The unseen good old man.
　　King.　　　　　　　　O heavy deed!
It had been so with us, had we been there.
His liberty is full of threats to all,
To you yourself, to us, to every one.　　15
Alas, how shall this bloody deed be answer'd?
It will be laid to us, whose providence
Should have kept short, restrain'd, and out of
　　haunt
This mad young man. But so much was our love,
We would not understand what was most fit,　　20
But, like the owner of a foul disease,
To keep it from divulging, let it feed
Even on the pith of life. Where is he gone?
　　Queen. To draw apart the body he hath kill'd,
O'er whom his very madness, like some ore　　25
Among a mineral of metals base,
Shows itself pure; he weeps for what is done.
　　King. O Gertrude, come away!
The sun no sooner shall the mountains touch,

But we will ship him hence, and this vile deed   30
We must, with all our majesty and skill,
Both countenance and excuse.   Ho, Guildenstern!

[*Re-*]*enter* Rosencrantz *and* Guildenstern.

Friends both, go join you with some further aid.
Hamlet in madness hath Polonius slain,
And from his mother's closet hath he dragg'd him.
Go seek him out; speak fair, and bring the body   36
Into the chapel.   I pray you, haste in this.

        [*Exeunt Rosencrantz and Guildenstern.*
Come, Gertrude, we'll call up our wisest friends
To let them know both what we mean to do
And what's untimely done; [so, haply, slander].   40
[Whose whisper o'er the world's diameter,
As level as the cannon to his blank,
Transports his poisoned shot, may miss our name,
And hit the woundless air.]   O, come away!
My soul is full of discord and dismay.   45

                   [*Exeunt.*

[SCENE II.   *Another room in the castle.*]

Enter HAMLET.

Ham. Safely stow'd.
Ros. }
Guil. } (*Within.*)   Hamlet!   Lord Hamlet!
Ham. What noise?   Who calls on Hamlet?   O,
here they come.

Enter ROSENCRANTZ *and* GUILDENSTERN.

Ros. What have you done, my lord, with the dead
    body?   5
Ham. Compounded it with dust, whereto 'tis kin.
Ros. Tell us where 'tis, that we may take it
    thence
And bear it to the chapel.
Ham. Do not believe it.
Ros. Believe what?   10
Ham. That I can keep your counsel and not mine
own.   Besides, to be demanded of a sponge!
What replication should be made by the son of a
king?
Ros. Take you me for a sponge, my lord?   15
Ham. Ay, sir, that soaks up the King's coun-
tenance, his rewards, his authorities.   But such
officers do the King best service in the end.   He
keeps them, [as an ape doth nuts], in the corner of
his jaw; first mouth'd, to be last swallowed.   When
he needs what you have glean'd, it is but squeezing
you, and, sponge, you shall be dry again.   23

Ros. I understand you not, my lord.
Ham. I am glad of it.   A knavish speech sleeps
in a foolish ear.
Ros. My lord, you must tell us where the body
is, and go with us to the King.   28
Ham. The body is with the King, but the King
is not with the body.   The King is a thing —
Guil. A thing, my lord!
Ham. Of nothing.   Bring me to him.   Hide fox,
and all after.   [*Exeunt.* 33

[SCENE III.   *Another room in the castle.*]

Enter KING [*and two or three*].

King. I have sent to seek him, and to find the
    body.
How dangerous is it that this man goes loose!
Yet must not we put the strong law on him.
He's lov'd of the distracted multitude,
Who like not in their judgement, but their eyes;   5
And where 'tis so, th' offender's scourge is weigh'd,
But never the offence.   To bear all smooth and
    even,
This sudden sending him away must seem
Deliberate pause.   Diseases desperate grown
By desperate appliance are reliev'd,   10
Or not at all.

Enter ROSENCRANTZ.

          How now!   What hath befall'n?
Ros. Where the dead body is bestow'd, my lord,
We cannot get from him.
King.   But where is he?
Ros. Without, my lord, guarded, to know your
    pleasure.
King. Bring him before us.   15
Ros. Ho, Guildenstern! bring in my lord.

Enter HAMLET *and* Guildenstern.

King. Now, Hamlet, where's Polonius?
Ham. At supper.
King. At supper!   Where?   19
Ham. Not where he eats, but where he is eaten.
A certain convocation of [politic] worms are e'en at
him.   Your worm is your only emperor for diet.
We fat all creatures else to fat us, and we fat our-
selves for maggots.   Your fat king and your lean
beggar is but variable service, two dishes, but to one
table; that's the end.   26
   [*King.* Alas, alas!
Ham. A man may fish with the worm that hath

---

40. [so ... slander] (Capell).   Om. Q2 F.   41–44. [Whose ... air] Q2.   Om. F.   42. blank: target.   44. woundless: invulnerable.

Sc. ii, 12. demanded of: questioned by.   19. [as ... nuts] Q1.   *like an ape* F.   *like an apple* Q2.   32. Hide fox: a game like hide-and-seek.

Sc. iii, 9. pause: i.e., planning.   21. [politic] Q2: statesmanlike.   Om. F.   25. variable service: i.e., different ways of serving the same food.   27–30. [King ... worm] Q2.   Om. F.

eat of a king, and eat of the fish that hath fed of
that worm.]   30

King. What dost thou mean by this?

Ham. Nothing but to show you how a king may
go a progress through the guts of a beggar.

King. Where is Polonius?   34

Ham. In heaven; send thither to see. If your
messenger find him not there, seek him i' th' other
place yourself. But indeed, if you find him not
[within] this month, you shall nose him as you go
up the stairs into the lobby.

King. Go seek him there.   40

                                  [To some Attendants.]

Ham. He will stay till ye come.

                                [Exeunt Attendants.]

King. Hamlet, this deed, for thine especial
    safety, —

Which we do tender, as we dearly grieve

For that which thou hast done, — must send **thee**
    hence

With fiery quickness; therefore prepare thyself. 45

The bark is ready, and the wind at help.

Th' associates tend, and everything is bent

For England.

Ham. For England?

King.   Ay, Hamlet.

Ham.   Good.

King. So is it, if thou knew'st our purposes.

Ham. I see a cherub that sees [them]. But,
come, for England! Farewell, dear mother. 51

King. Thy loving father, Hamlet.

Ham. My mother. Father and mother is man
and wife, man and wife is one flesh, and so, my
mother. Come, for England!   *[Exit.* 55

King. Follow him at foot, tempt him with speed
    aboard.

Delay it not; I'll have him hence to-night.

Away! for everything is seal'd and done

That else leans on th' affair. Pray you, make
haste. *[Exeunt Rosencrantz and Guildenstern.]*

And, England, if my love thou hold'st at aught, — 60

As my great power thereof may give thee sense,

Since yet thy cicatrice looks raw and red

After the Danish sword, and thy free awe

Pays homage to us — thou mayst not coldly set

Our sovereign process, which imports at full,   65

By letters conjuring to that effect,

The present death of Hamlet. Do it, England;

For like the hectic in my blood he rages,

And thou must cure me. Till I know 'tis done,

Howe'er my haps, my joys were ne'er begun.   70

                                       [Exit.

[SCENE IV. *A plain in Denmark.*]

Enter FORTINBRAS, [*a* CAPTAIN,] *and army,*
               [*marching*].

For. Go, captain, from me greet the Danish king.

Tell him that, by his license, Fortinbras

Claims the conveyance of a promis'd march

Over his kingdom. You know the rendezvous.

If that his Majesty would aught with us,   5

We shall express our duty in his eye;

And let him know so.

Cap.   I will do't, my lord.

For. Go [softly] on.

                 [Exeunt Fortinbras [and Soldiers]

[Enter HAMLET, ROSENCRANTZ, *and others.*

Ham. Good sir, whose powers are these?

Cap. They are of Norway, sir.   10

Ham. How purpos'd, sir, I pray you?

Cap. Against some part of Poland.

Ham. Who commands them, sir?

Cap. The nephew to old Norway, Fortinbras.

Ham. Goes it against the main of Poland, sir,   15
Or for some frontier?

Cap. Truly to speak, and with no addition,

We go to gain a little patch of ground

That hath in it no profit but the name.

To pay five ducats, five, I would not farm it;   20

Nor will it yield to Norway or the Pole

A ranker rate, should it be sold in fee.

Ham. Why, then the Polack never will defend it.

Cap. Yes, it is already garrison'd.

Ham. Two thousand souls and twenty thousand
    ducats   25

Will not debate the question of this straw.

This is th' imposthume of much wealth and peace,

That inward breaks, and shows no cause without

Why the man dies. I humbly thank you, sir.

Cap. God buy you, sir.   *[Exit.]*

Ros.   Will 't please you go, my lord? 30

Ham. I'll be with you straight. Go a little
    before.   *[Exeunt all except Hamlet.]*

How all occasions do inform against me,

And spur my dull revenge! What is a man,

If his chief good and market of his time

Be but to sleep and feed? A beast, no more.   35

Sure, He that made us with such large discourse,

Looking before and after, gave us not

That capability and god-like reason

To fust in us unus'd. Now, whether it be

Bestial oblivion, or some craven scruple   40

Of thinking too precisely on th' event, —

---

    33. **progress:** royal journey.   38. **[within]** Q₂. Om. F.   42. **deed** Q₂. *deed of thine* F.   46. **at help:** favorable.
50. **[them]** Q₂. *him* F.   56. **at foot:** close.   62. **cicatrice:** scar.   63-64. **thy ... Pays:** thy fear makes thee pay voluntarily.
64. **set:** regard.   65. **process:** command.   68. **hectic:** fever.

    Sc. iv, 3. **conveyance of:** escort for.   6. **eye:** presence.   8. **[softly]** Q₂: slowly.   *safely* F.   9-66. **[Enter ... worth]** Q₂.
Om. F.   22. **ranker:** higher.   **in fee:** outright.   27. **imposthume:** abscess.   36. **discourse:** reasoning power.   40. *oblivion:*
forgetfulness.   41. **event:** outcome.

A thought which, quarter'd, hath but one part wis-
dom
And ever three parts coward, — I do not know
Why yet I live to say, "This thing's to do,"
Sith I have cause and will and strength and means 45
To do't. Examples gross as earth exhort me;
Witness this army of such mass and charge
Led by a delicate and tender prince,
Whose spirit with divine ambition puff'd
Makes mouths at the invisible event,   50
Exposing what is mortal and unsure
To all that fortune, death, and danger dare,
Even for an egg-shell.   Rightly to be great
Is not to stir without great argument,
But greatly to find quarrel in a straw   55
When honour's at the stake.   How stand I then,
That have a father kill'd, a mother stain'd,
Excitements of my reason and my blood,
And let all sleep, while to my shame I see
The imminent death of twenty thousand men,   60
That for a fantasy and trick of fame
Go to their graves like beds, fight for a plot
Whereon the numbers cannot try the cause,
Which is not tomb enough and continent
To hide the slain?   O, from this time forth,   65
My thoughts be bloody, or be nothing worth!]
                         [*Exit.*

[SCENE V.   *Elsinore.*   *A room in the castle.*]

Enter QUEEN, HORATIO [*and a* GENTLEMAN].

Queen. I will not speak with her.
[*Gent.*] She is importunate, indeed distract.
Her mood will needs be pitied.
     Queen.   What would she have?
[*Gent.*] She speaks much of her father; says she
hears
There's tricks i' th' world, and hems, and beats her
heart,
Spurns enviously at straws, speaks things in doubt 5
That carry but half sense.   Her speech is nothing,
Yet the unshaped use of it doth move
The hearers to collection.   They aim at it
And botch the words up fit to their own thoughts; 10
Which, as her winks and nods and gestures yield
them,
Indeed would make one think there would be
thought,
Though nothing sure, yet much unhappily.
[*Hor.*] 'Twere good she were spoken with, for she
may strew
Dangerous conjectures in ill-breeding minds.   15

Let her come in.   [*Exit Gentleman.*]
   Queen. [*Aside.*] To my sick soul, as sin's true
nature is,
Each toy seems prologue to some great amiss;
So full of artless jealousy is guilt,
It spills itself in fearing to be spilt.   20

Enter OPHELIA, *distracted.*

Oph. Where is the beauteous majesty of Den-
mark?
Queen. How now, Ophelia!
Oph. [*Sings.*]
   "How should I your true love know
       From another one?
   By his cockle hat and staff,   25
       And his sandal shoon."
Queen. Alas, sweet lady, what imports this song?
Oph. Say you?   Nay, pray you, mark.
[*Sings.*]   "He is dead and gone, lady,
       He is dead and gone;   30
   At his head a grass-green turf
       At his heels a stone."

Enter KING.

[O, ho!]
   Queen. Nay, but, Ophelia, —
   Oph. Pray you, mark.
[*Sings.*]   "White his shroud as the mountain
                 snow," —   35
   Queen. Alas, look here, my lord.
   Oph. [*Sings.*]
   "Larded with sweet flowers;
   Which bewept to the grave did not go
       With true-love showers."
   King. How do you, pretty lady?
   Oph. Well, God 'ild you!   They say the owl 40
was a baker's daughter.   Lord, we know what we
are, but know not what we may be.   God be at
your table!
   King. Conceit upon her father.
   Oph. Pray you, let's have no words of this, but 45
when they ask you what it means, say you this:
[*Sings.*]   "To-morrow is Saint Valentine's day,
       All in the morning betime,
   And I a maid at your window,   50
       To be your Valentine.

   "Then up he rose and donn'd his clothes,
       And dupp'd the chamber door;
   Let in the maid, that out a maid
       Never departed more."   55
   King. Pretty Ophelia!

---

54. **argument:** cause.   64. **continent:** receptacle.
   Sc. v, 2, 4. [*Gent.*] Q₂. *Hor.* F (which has no *Gent.* in this scene).   6. **Spurns enviously:** takes offense spitefully. **in doubt:**
ambiguously.   9. **collection:** conjecture. **aim:** guess.   14. [*Hor.*] Q. *Qu.* F (which gives ll. 14–20 to the Queen).   19. **jealousy:** suspicion.   20. **spills:** destroys.   25. **cockle ... staff:** marks of a pilgrim.   33. [O, ho] Q₂. Om. F.   37. **Larded:**
decked.   41. **owl.** Legend tells of a baker's daughter whom Jesus turned into an owl when she complied stingily with his
request for bread.   45. **Conceit:** brooding.   54. **dupp'd:** opened.

Oph. Indeed, la, without an oath I'll make an
end on't.

  "By Gis, and by Saint Charity,
    Alack! and, Fie for shame!   60
  Young men will do't, if they come to't;
    By Cock, they are to blame.

  "Quoth she, 'Before you tumbled me,
    You promis'd me to wed.'
  'So would I ha' done, by yonder sun,   65
    An thou hadst not come to my bed.'"
King. How long hath she been thus?
Oph. I hope all will be well. We must be patient;
but I cannot choose but weep, to think they should
lay him i' th' cold ground. My brother shall   70
know of it; and so I thank you for your good counsel.
Come, my coach! Good-night, ladies; good-night,
sweet ladies; good-night, good-night.   [*Exit.*
  King. Follow her close; give her good watch, I
    pray you.   [*Exeunt some.*] 75
O, this is the poison of deep grief; it springs
All from her father's death. O Gertrude, Gertrude,
When sorrows come, they come not single spies,
But in battalions. First, her father slain;   79
Next, your son gone; and he most violent author
Of his own just remove; the people muddied,
Thick and unwholesome in their thoughts and whis-
    pers,
For good Polonius' death; and we have done but
    greenly
In hugger-mugger to inter him; poor Ophelia
Divided from herself and her fair judgement,   85
Without the which we are pictures, or mere beasts;
Last, and as much containing as all these,
Her brother is in secret come from France,
[Feeds] on his wonder, keeps himself in clouds,
And wants not buzzers to infect his ear   90
With pestilent speeches of his father's death,
Wherein necessity, of matter beggar'd,
Will nothing stick our persons to arraign
In ear and ear. O my dear Gertrude, this,
Like to a murd'ring-piece, in many places   95
Gives me superfluous death.   [*A noise within.*

        Enter a MESSENGER.

  Queen.   Alack, what noise is this?
King. Where are my Switzers? Let them guard
    the door.
What is the matter?
  Mess.   Save yourself, my lord!
The ocean, overpeering of his list,
Eats not the flats with more impetuous haste 100

Than young Laertes, in a riotous head,
O'erbears your officers. The rabble call him lord;
And, as the world were now but to begin,
Antiquity forgot, custom not known,
(The ratifiers and props of every word,)   105
They cry, "Choose we! Laertes shall be king!"
Caps, hands, and tongues applaud it to the clouds,
"Laertes shall be king, Laertes king!"
  Queen. How cheerfully on the false trail they
    cry!
O, this is counter, you false Danish dogs!   110

    Enter LAERTES [*armed;* DANES *following*].

King. The doors are broke.   [*Noise within.*
Laer. Where is [this] king? Sirs, stand you all
    without.
[*Danes.*] No, let's come in.
Laer.   I pray you, give me leave.
[*Danes.*] We will, we will.
         [*They retire without the door.*]
Laer. I thank you; keep the door. O thou vile
    king,   115
Give me my father!
  Queen.   Calmly, good Laertes.
Laer. That drop of blood [that's calm] proclaims
    me bastard,
Cries cuckold to my father, brands the harlot
Even here, between the chaste unsmirched brows
Of my true mother.
  King.   What is the cause, Laertes, 120
That thy rebellion looks so giant-like?
Let him go, Gertrude; do not fear our person.
There's such divinity doth hedge a king
That treason can but peep to what it would,
Acts little of his will. Tell me, Laertes,   125
Why thou art thus incens'd. Let him go, Gertrude.
Speak, man.
  Laer. Where's my father?
  King.   Dead.
  Queen.   But not by him.
  King. Let him demand his fill.
  Laer. How came he dead? I'll not be juggl'd
    with.   130
To hell, allegiance! Vows, to the blackest devil!
Conscience and grace, to the profoundest pit!
I dare damnation. To this point I stand,
That both the worlds I give to negligence,
Let come what comes; only I'll be reveng'd   135
Most throughly for my father.
  King.   Who shall stay you?
  Laer. My will, not all the world.
And for my means, I'll husband them so well,

---

59. **Gis:** contraction of Jesus. 62. **Cock:** corruption of God. 81. **muddied:** confused. 83. **greenly:** foolishly. 84.
In hugger-mugger: secretly and hastily. 89. **[Feeds]** Q₂. *Keepes* F. 90. **buzzers:** whisperers. 95. **murd'ring-piece:**
cannon which shoots a kind of shrapnel. 97. **Switzers:** Swiss Guards. 99. **list:** boundary, shore. 101. **in...head:** with
a rebellious force. 110. **counter:** off the scent. 112. **[this]** Q₂. *the* F. 113, 114. **[Danes]** (Capell). *All* F. 117. **[that's
calm]** Q₂. *that calmes* F.

They shall go far with little.

King.   Good Laertes,
If you desire to know the certainty   140
Of your dear father's death, [is't] writ in your
          revenge
That, swoopstake, you will draw both friend and
          foe,
Winner and loser?

Laer. None but his enemies.

King.   Will you know them then?

Laer. To his good friends thus wide I'll ope my
          arms.   145
And like the kind life-rend'ring [pelican],
Repast them with my blood.

King.   Why, now you speak
Like a good child and a true gentleman.
That I am guiltless of your father's death,
And am most [sensibly] in grief for it,   150
It shall as level to your judgement pierce
As day does to your eye.

          [*A noise within:* "Let her come in!"

          Re-enter OPHELIA.

Laer. How now! what noise is that?
O heat, dry up my brains! Tears seven times salt
Burn out the sense and virtue of mine eye!   155
By heaven, thy madness shall be paid by weight
Till our scale turns the beam. O rose of May!
Dear maid, kind sister, sweet Ophelia!
O heavens! is't possible a young maid's wits
Should be as mortal as an old man's life?   160
Nature is fine in love, and where 'tis fine,
It sends some precious instance of itself
After the thing it loves.

Oph. [*Sings.*]
    "They bore him barefac'd on the bier;
      Hey non nonny, nonny, hey nonny;   165
    And on his grave rains many a tear," —
Fare you well, my dove!

Laer. Hadst thou thy wits and didst persuade
          revenge,
It could not move thus.

Oph. You must sing, "Down a-down, and   170
you call him a-down-a." O, how the wheel becomes it! It is the false steward, that stole his
master's daughter.

Laer. This nothing's more than matter.   174

Oph. There's rosemary, that's for remembrance;
pray, love, remember; and there is pansies, that's
for thoughts.

Laer. A document in madness, thoughts and
remembrance fitted.   179

Oph. There's fennel for you, and columbines;
there's rue for you, and here's some for me; we may
call it herb [of] grace o' Sundays. O, you must
wear your rue with a difference. There's a daisy.
I would give you some violets, but they wither'd
all when my father died. They say he made a
good end, —   186
[*Sings.*] "For bonny sweet Robin is all my joy."

Laer. Thought and affliction, passion, hell itself,
She turns to favour and to prettiness.

Oph. [*Sings.*]
    "And will he not come again?   190
      And will he not come again?
        No, no, he is dead;
        Go to thy death-bed;
      He never will come again.

    "His beard as white as snow,   195
      All flaxen was his poll.
        He is gone, he is gone,
        And we cast away moan.
      [God 'a' mercy] on his soul!"
And of all Christian souls, I pray God. God buy
          ye.   [*Exit.* 200

Laer. Do you see this, you gods?

King. Laertes, I must commune with your grief,
Or you deny me right. Go but apart,
Make choice of whom your wisest friends you will,
And they shall hear and judge 'twixt you and me. 205
If by direct or by collateral hand
They find us touch'd, we will our kingdom give,
Our crown, our life, and all that we call ours,
To you in satisfaction; but if not,
Be you content to lend your patience to us,   210
And we shall jointly labour with your soul
To give it due content.

Laer.   Let this be so.
His means of death, his obscure burial —
No trophy, sword, nor hatchment o'er his bones,
No noble rite nor formal ostentation —   215
Cry to be heard, as 'twere from heaven to earth,
That I must call ['t] in question.

King.   So you shall;
And where the offence is let the great axe fall.
I pray you, go with me.   [*Exeunt.*

          [SCENE VI.   *Another room in the castle.*]

          Enter HORATIO *with an* ATTENDANT.

Hor. What are they that would speak with me?

Att. Sailors, sir. They say they have letters for
          you.

141. [is't] Q₂. *if* F. 146. [pelican] Q₂. *politician* F. The female pelican was believed to feed its own blood to its young. 150. [sensibly] Q₂. *sensible* F. 161. fine: delicate. 171. wheel: (1) refrain, (2) the spinning wheel, at which women sang ballads. 178. document: lesson. 182. [of] Q₂. Om. F. 183. difference: heraldic term for a variation in a coat of arms as borne by different members of a family. 188. Thought: melancholy. passion: suffering. 189. favour: beauty. 199. [God 'a' mercy] Q₂. *Gramercy* F. 207. touch'd: guilty. 214. hatchment: heraldic tablet. 217. ['t] Q₂. Om. F.

Hor. Let them come in.   [*Exit Attendant.*]
I do not know from what part of the world
I should be greeted, if not from Lord Hamlet.   5

Enter SAILOR.

Sail. God bless you, sir.
Hor. Let Him bless thee too.
Sail. He shall, sir, an't please Him.   There's
a letter for you, sir — it comes from the ambassador that was bound for England — if your name
be Horatio, as I am let to know it is.   11
[*Hor.*] (*Reads.*) "Horatio, when thou shalt have
overlook'd this, give these fellows some means to
the King; they have letters for him.   Ere we were
two days old at sea, a pirate of very warlike ap-   15
pointment gave us chase.   Finding ourselves too
slow of sail, we put on a compelled valour.   In
the grapple I boarded them.   On the instant they
got clear of our ship, so I alone became their prisoner.   They have dealt with me like thieves of   20
mercy, but they knew what they did: I am to do a
good turn for them.   Let the King have the letters I
have sent, and repair thou to me with as much haste
as thou wouldest fly death.   I have words to speak
in your ear will make thee dumb, yet are they   25
much too light for the bore of the matter.   These
good fellows will bring thee where I am.   Rosencrantz and Guildenstern hold their course for England; of them I have much to tell thee.   Farewell. 30
    "He that thou knowest thine,
                    HAMLET."
Come, I will give you way for these your letters;
And do't the speedier, that you may direct me
To him from whom you brought them.   [*Exeunt.*

[SCENE VII.   *Another room in the castle.*]

Enter KING *and* LAERTES.

King. Now must your conscience my acquit-
        tance seal;
And you must put me in your heart for friend,
Sith you have heard, and with a knowing ear,
That he which hath your noble father slain
Pursued my life.
    Laer.   It well appears.   But tell me   5
Why you proceeded not against these feats,
So crimeful and so capital in nature,
As by your safety, wisdom, all things else
You mainly were stirr'd up.
    King.   O, for two special reasons,
Which may to you, perhaps, seem much un-
        sinew'd,   10

And yet to me they are strong.   The Queen his
        mother
Lives almost by his looks; and for myself —
My virtue or my plague, be it either which —
She's so conjunctive to my life and soul,
That, as the star moves not but in his sphere,   15
I could not but by her.   The other motive
Why to a public count I might not go
Is the great love the general gender bear him;
Who, dipping all his faults in their affection,
Would, like the spring that turneth wood to stone, 20
Convert his gyves to graces; so that my arrows,
Too slightly timb'red for so loud a wind,
Would have reverted to my bow again,
And not where I had aim'd them.
    Laer.   And so have I a noble father lost,   25
A sister driven into desperate terms,
[Whose worth], if praises may go back again,
Stood challenger on mount of all the age
For her perfections.   But my revenge will come.
    King.   Break not your sleeps for that.   You
        must not think   30
That we are made of stuff so flat and dull
That we can let our beard be shook with danger
And think it pastime.   You shortly shall hear more.
I lov'd your father, and we love ourself,
And that, I hope, will teach you to imagine —   35

Enter a MESSENGER *with letters*

How now!   What news?
    Mess.   Letters, my lord, from Hamlet.
This to your Majesty; this to the Queen.
    King.   From Hamlet!   Who brought them?
    Mess.   Sailors, my lord, they say; I saw them not.
They were given me by Claudio.   He receiv'd
        them   40
[Of him that brought them].
    King.   Laertes, you shall hear them.
Leave us.   [*Exit Messenger.*
    [*Reads.*] "High and mighty, You shall know I
am set naked on your kingdom.   To-morrow shall
I beg leave to see your kingly eyes, when I shall,
first asking your pardon thereunto, recount the
occasions of my sudden and more strange re-
turn.   48
                    HAMLET."
What should this mean?   Are all the rest come
        back?
Or is it some abuse, or no such thing?
    Laer.   Know you the hand?
    King.   'Tis Hamlet's character.   "Naked!"
And in a postscript here, he says, "alone."
Can you advise me?

Sc. vi, 20–21. **thieves of mercy:** merciful thieves.   26. **bore:** size, importance.
Sc. vii, 17. **count:** reckoning.   18. **general gender:** common people.   21. **gyves:** fetters.   27. **[Whose worth]** Q2.   *Who was* F.   41. **[Of ... them]** Q2.   Om. F.   43. **naked:** destitute.   50. **abuse:** deceit.   52. **character:** handwriting.

Laer. I'm lost in it, my lord. But let him come.
It warms the very sickness in my heart   56
That I shall live and tell him to his teeth,
"Thus didest thou."
   King.   If it be so, Laertes, —
As how should it be so? How otherwise? —
Will you be rul'd by me?
   Laer.   [Ay, my lord,]   60
If so you'll not o'errule me to a peace.
   King. To thine own peace. If he be now re-
    turn'd,
As checking at his voyage, and that he means
No more to undertake it, I will work him
To an exploit, now ripe in my device,   65
Under the which he shall not choose but fall;
And for his death no wind of blame shall breathe,
But even his mother shall uncharge the practice
And call it accident.
   [*Laer.*   My lord, I will be rul'd;
The rather, if you could devise it so   70
That I might be the organ.
   King.   It falls right.
You have been talk'd of since your travel much,
And that in Hamlet's hearing, for a quality
Wherein, they say, you shine. Your sum of parts
Did not together pluck such envy from him   75
As did that one, and that, in my regard,
Of the unworthiest siege.
   Laer.   What part is that, my lord?
   King. A very riband in the cap of youth,
Yet needful too; for youth no less becomes
The light and careless livery that it wears   80
Than settled age his sables and his weeds,
Importing health and graveness.] Two months
    [since]
Here was a gentleman of Normandy; —
I've seen myself, and serv'd against, the French,
And they [can] well on horseback; but this gallant
Had witchcraft in't. He grew into his seat,   86
And to such wondrous doing brought his horse,
As had he been incorps'd and demi-natur'd
With the brave beast. So far he pass'd my thought,
That I, in forgery of shapes and tricks,   90
Come short of what he did.
   Laer.   A Norman, was't?
   King. A Norman.
   Laer. Upon my life, Lamound.
   King.   The very same.
   Laer. I know him well. He is the brooch indeed
And gem of all [the] nation.   95
   King. He made confession of you,
And gave you such a masterly report

For art and exercise in your defence,
And for your rapier most especially
That he cried out 'twould be a sight indeed   100
If one could match you. [The scrimers of their
    nation,
He swore, had neither motion, guard, nor eye
If you oppos'd them.] Sir, this report of his
Did Hamlet so envenom with his envy
That he could nothing do but wish and beg   105
Your sudden coming o'er to play with him.
Now, out of this —
   Laer.   [What] out of this, my lord?
   King. Laertes, was your father dear to you?
Or are you like the painting of a sorrow,
A face without a heart?
   Laer.   Why ask you this?   110
   King. Not that I think you did not love your
    father,
But that I know love is begun by time,
And that I see, in passages of proof,
Time qualifies the spark and fire of it.
[There lives within the very flame of love   115
A kind of wick or snuff that will abate it,
And nothing is at a like goodness still;
For goodness, growing to a plurisy,
Dies in his own too much. That we would do,
We should do when we would; for this "would"
    changes,   120
And hath abatements and delays as many
As there are tongues, are hands, are accidents;
And then this "should" is like a spendthrift
    sigh,
That hurts by easing. But, to the quick o' th'
    ulcer: —]
Hamlet comes back. What would you undertake,
To show yourself your father's son in deed   126
More than in words?
   Laer.   To cut his throat i' th' church.
   King. No place, indeed, should murder sanc-
    tuarize;
Revenge should have no bounds. But, good
    Laertes,
Will you do this, keep close within your chamber?
Hamlet return'd shall know you are come home.   131
We'll put on those shall praise your excellence
And set a double varnish on the fame
The Frenchman gave you, bring you in fine to-
    gether
And wager on your heads. He, being remiss,   135
Most generous and free from all contriving,
Will not peruse the foils, so that, with ease,
Or with a little shuffling, you may choose

---

60. **[Ay, my lord]** Q₂. *Om.* F.   63. **checking at:** turning from (as a falcon forsakes its prey). 68. **uncharge the practice:** i.e., fail to see a plot. 69–82. [*Laer. . . . graveness*] Q₂. *Om.* F.   77. **siege:** rank. 82. **Two** Q₂. *Some two* F. **[since]** Q₂. *hence* F. 85. **[can]** Q₂. *ran* F. 88. **incorps'd:** of one body. 90. **forgery:** imagining. 94. **brooch:** ornament. 95. **[the]** Q₂. *our* F. 96. **confession:** acknowledgment. 101–103. [**The . . . them**] Q₂. *Om.* F. 101. **scrimers:** fencers. 107. **[What]** Q₂. *Why* F. 115–24. [**There . . . ulcer**] Q₂. *Om.* F. 118. **plurisy:** excess. 123. **sigh.** A sigh was supposed to draw blood from the heart. 128. **sanctuarize:** offer asylum to. 134. **in fine:** finally.

A sword unbated, and in a pass of practice
Requite him for your father.
    Laer.   I will do't;   140
And, for that purpose, I'll anoint my sword.
I bought an unction of a mountebank,
So mortal [that, but dip] a knife in it,
Where it draws blood no cataplasm so rare,
Collected from all simples that have virtue   145
Under the moon, can save the thing from death
That is but scratch'd withal.   I'll touch my point
With this contagion, that, if I gall him slightly,
It may be death.
    King.   Let's further think of this,
Weigh what convenience both of time and means
May fit us to our shape.   If this should fail,   151
And that our drift look through our bad perform-
         ance,
'Twere better not assay'd; therefore this project
Should have a back or second, that might hold
If this should blast in proof.   Soft! let me see.
We'll make a solemn wager on your cunnings —   156
I ha 't!
When in your motion you are hot and dry —
As make your bouts more violent to that end —
And [that] he calls for drink, I'll have prepar'd him
A chalice for the nonce, whereon but sipping,   161
If he by chance escape your venom'd stuck,
Our purpose may hold there.

               Enter QUEEN.

               How, sweet queen!
    Queen. One woe doth tread upon another's heel,
So fast they follow.   Your sister's drown'd, Laertes.
    Laer. Drown'd! O, where?   166
    Queen. There is a willow grows aslant a brook,
That shows his hoar leaves in the glassy stream.
There with fantastic garlands did she come
Of crow-flowers, nettles, daisies, and long purples
That liberal shepherds give a grosser name,   171
But our cold maids do dead men's fingers call them;
There, on the pendent boughs her coronet weeds
Clamb'ring to hang, an envious sliver broke,
When down the weedy trophies and herself   175
Fell in the weeping brook.   Her clothes spread
         wide,
And, mermaid-like, a while they bore her up;
Which time she chanted snatches of old tunes,
As one incapable of her own distress,
Or like a creature native and indued   180
Unto that element.   But long it could not be

Till that her garments, heavy with [their] drink,
Pull'd the poor wretch from her melodious [lay]
To muddy death.
    Laer.   Alas, then, is she drown'd?
    Queen. Drown'd, drown'd.   185
    Laer. Too much of water hast thou, poor
         Ophelia,
And therefore I forbid my tears.   But yet
It is our trick.   Nature her custom holds,
Let shame say what it will; when these are gone,
The woman will be out.   Adieu, my lord;   190
I have a speech of fire that fain would blaze,
But that this folly douts it.   [*Exit.*
    King.   Let's follow, Gertrude.
How much I had to do to calm his rage!
Now fear I this will give it start again,
Therefore let's follow.   [*Exeunt.* 195

               [ACT V]

        [SCENE I.   *A churchyard.*]

    Enter two CLOWNS [*with spades and pickaxes*].

    1. Clo. Is she to be buried in Christian burial that
wilfully seeks her own salvation?
    2. Clo. I tell thee she is, and therefore make her
grave straight.   The crowner hath sat on her, and
finds it Christian burial.   5
    1. Clo. How can that be, unless she drown'd her-
self in her own defence?
    2. Clo. Why, 'tis found so.
    1. Clo. It must be "*se offendendo*," it cannot be
else.   For here lies the point: if I drown myself   10
wittingly, it argues an act, and an act hath three
branches; it is [to] act, to do, and to perform; argal,
she drown'd herself wittingly.
    2. Clo. Nay, but hear you, goodman delver, —   15
    1. Clo. Give me leave.   Here lies the water;
good.   Here stands the man; good.   If the man
go to this water and drown himself, it is, will he,
nill he, he goes, — mark you that?   But if the
water come to him and drown him, he drowns not
himself; argal, he that is not guilty of his own death
shortens not his own life.   22
    2. Clo. But is this law?
    1. Clo. Ay, marry, is't; crowner's quest law.
    2. Clo. Will you ha' the truth on't?   If this had
not been a gentlewoman, she should have been
buried out of Christian burial.   28

---

   139. **unbated:** not blunted.   **pass of practice:** treacherous thrust.   142. **mountebank:** quack.   143. [that ... dip] Q₂. *I but dipt* F.   144. **cataplasm:** poultice.   145. **simples:** medicinal herbs.   155. **blast in proof:** burst in testing.   160. [that] Q₂. *the* F.   161. **nonce:** purpose.   162. **stuck:** thrust.   168. **hoar:** grey-white.   170. **long purples:** orchids.   171. **liberal:** free-spoken.   182. [their] Q₂. *her* F.   183. [lay] Q₂. *buy* F.   188. **trick:** trait, way.   190. **woman:** feminine quality.   192. **douts:** puts out.

   Act V, sc. i, 1. **1. Clo.** F consistently designates *1. Clo.* as *Clown* and *2. Clo.* as *Other.*   4. **crowner:** coroner.   9. **se offendendo:** blunder for *se defendendo*, self-defence.   12. [to] act Q₂. *an Acte* F.   **argal:** blunder for *ergo* (therefore).   24. **quest:** inquest.

1. Clo. Why, there thou say'st; and the more pity that great folk should have countenance in this world to drown or hang themselves, more than their even Christian. Come, my spade. There is no ancient gentlemen but gardeners, ditchers, and gravemakers; they hold up Adam's profession. 35

2. Clo. Was he a gentleman?

1. Clo. He was the first that ever bore arms.

2. Clo. Why, he had none. 39

1. Clo. What, art a heathen? How dost thou understand the Scripture? The Scripture says Adam digg'd; could he dig without arms? I'll put another question to thee. If thou answerest me not to the purpose, confess thyself —

2. Clo. Go to. 45

1. Clo. What is he that builds stronger than either the mason, the shipwright, or the carpenter?

2. Clo. The gallows-maker; for that frame outlives a thousand tenants. 50

1. Clo. I like thy wit well, in good faith. The gallows does well; but how does it well? It does well to those that do ill. Now, thou dost ill to say the gallows is built stronger than the church; argal, the gallows may do well to thee. To't again, come. 56

2. Clo. "Who builds stronger than a mason, a shipwright, or a carpenter?"

1. Clo. Ay, tell me that, and unyoke.

2. Clo. Marry, now I can tell. 60

1. Clo. To't.

2. Clo. Mass, I cannot tell.

Enter HAMLET *and* HORATIO, *afar off.*

1. Clo. Cudgel thy brains no more about it, for your dull ass will not mend his pace with beating; and, when you are ask'd this question next, say "a grave-maker"; the houses that he makes lasts till doomsday. Go, get thee to Yaughan; fetch me a stoup of liquor. 68

[*Exit 2. Clown.*]

[*He digs, and*] *sings.*

"In youth, when I did love, did love,
　Methought it was very sweet,
To contract, O, the time for, ah, my behove,
　O, methought, there was nothing meet." 72

Ham. Has this fellow no feeling of his business, that he sings at grave-making?

Hor. Custom hath made it in him a property of easiness.

Ham. 'Tis e'en so. The hand of little employment hath the daintier sense. 78

1. Clo. (*Sings.*)
"But age with his stealing steps
　Hath caught me in his clutch,
And hath shipped me intil the land,
　As if I had never been such." 82

[*Throws up a skull.*]

Ham. That skull had a tongue in it, and could sing once. How the knave jowls it to the ground, as if it were Cain's jaw-bone, that did the first murder! It might be the pate of a politician, which this ass [now o'erreaches]; one that [would] circumvent God, might it not?

Hor. It might, my lord. 89

Ham. Or of a courtier, which could say, "Good morrow, sweet lord! How dost thou, good lord?" This might be my Lord Such-a-one, that prais'd my Lord Such-a-one's horse, when he meant to beg it; might it not?

Hor. Ay, my lord. 95

Ham. Why, e'en so; and now my Lady Worm's; chapless, and knock'd about the mazzard with a sexton's spade. Here's fine revolution, if we had the trick to see 't. Did these bones cost no more the breeding, but to play at loggats with 'em? Mine ache to think on't. 101

1. Clo. (*Sings.*)
"A pick-axe and a spade, a spade,
　For and a shrouding sheet;
O, a pit of clay for to be made
　For such a guest is meet." 105

[*Throws up another skull.*]

Ham. There's another. Why might not that be the skull of a lawyer? Where be his quiddits now, his quillets, his cases, his tenures, and his tricks? Why does he suffer this rude knave now to knock him about the sconce with a dirty shovel, and will not tell him of his action of battery? Hum! This fellow might be in's time a great buyer of land, with his statutes, his recognizances, his fines, his double vouchers, his recoveries. Is this the fine of his fines, and the recovery of his recoveries, to have his fine pate full of fine dirt? Will his vouchers vouch him no more of his purchases, and double ones too, than the length and breadth of a pair of indentures? The very conveyances of his lands will hardly lie in this box, and must the inheritor himself have no more, ha? 121

Hor. Not a jot more, my lord.

Ham. Is not parchment made of sheep-skins?

Hor. Ay, my lord, and of calf-skins too.

Ham. They are sheep and calves that seek out assurance in that. I will speak to this fellow.

---

33. **even:** fellow.　59. **unyoke:** i.e., have done.　67. **Yaughan:** an ale-house keeper.　71. **behove:** advantage.　87. [**now o'erreaches**] Q₂.　*O're offices* F.　[**would**] Q₂.　*could* F.　97. **chapless:** without the lower jaw.　**mazzard:** head. 100. **loggats:** a game in which blocks were thrown at a stake.　107. **quiddits:** quibbles.　108. **quillets:** subtleties.　110. **sconce:** head.　113–14. *Statutes* and *recognizances* were bonds securing debts by attaching land and property; *fines* and *recoveries* were legal modes for putting an estate into fee simple.　114. **fine:** end.

Whose grave's this, sir? 127

1. Clo. Mine, sir.

[*Sings.*] "O, a pit of clay for to be made

For such a guest is meet."

Ham. I think it be thine indeed, for thou liest
in't. 132

1. Clo. You lie out on't, sir, and therefore it is
not yours. For my part, I do not lie in't, and yet
it is mine.

Ham. Thou dost lie in't, to be in't and say 'tis
thine. 'Tis for the dead, not for the quick, therefore thou liest. 138

1. Clo. 'Tis a quick lie, sir; 'twill away again,
from me to you.

Ham. What man dost thou dig it for?

1. Clo. For no man, sir.

Ham. What woman, then?

1. Clo. For none, neither.

Ham. Who is to be buried in't? 145

1. Clo. One that was a woman, sir; but, rest her
soul, she's dead.

Ham. How absolute the knave is! We must
speak by the card, or equivocation will undo us.
By the Lord, Horatio, these three years I have 150
taken note of it; the age is grown so picked that the
toe of the peasant comes so near the heels of our
courtier, he galls his kibe. How long hast thou
been a grave-maker? 154

1. Clo. Of all the days i' the year, I came to't
that day that our last king Hamlet o'ercame
Fortinbras.

Ham. How long is that since? 158

1. Clo. Cannot you tell that? Every fool can
tell that. It was the very day that young Hamlet
was born; he that was mad, and sent into England? 164

Ham. Ay, marry, why was he sent into England?

1. Clo. Why, because 'a was mad. He shall recover his wits there; or, if he do not, it's no great
matter there.

Ham. Why?

1. Clo. 'Twill not be seen in him [there]; there the
men are as mad as he. 170

Ham. How came he mad?

1. Clo. Very strangely, they say.

Ham. How "strangely"?

1. Clo. Faith, e'en with losing his wits.

Ham. Upon what ground? 175

1. Clo. Why, here in Denmark. I have been
[sexton] here, man and boy, thirty years.

Ham. How long will a man lie i' th' earth ere he
rot? 179

1. Clo. I' faith, if he be not rotten before he die
— as we have many pocky corses now-a-days, that

will scarce hold the laying in — he will last you
some eight year or nine year. A tanner will last
you nine year.

Ham. Why he more than another? 185

1. Clo. Why, sir, his hide is so tann'd with his
trade that he will keep out water a great while, and
your water is a sore decayer of your whoreson dead
body. Here's a skull now; this skull has lain in
the earth three and twenty years. 191

Ham. Whose was it?

1. Clo. A whoreson mad fellow's it was. Whose
do you think it was? 195

Ham. Nay, I know not.

1. Clo. A pestilence on him for a mad rogue!
'A pour'd a flagon of Rhenish on my head once.
This same skull, sir, was Yorick's skull, the King's
jester.

Ham. This? 200

1. Clo. E'en that.

Ham. Let me see. [*Takes the skull.*] Alas, poor
Yorick! I knew him, Horatio; a fellow of infinite
jest, of most excellent fancy. He hath borne me on
his back a thousand times. And [now] how 205
abhorred [in] my imagination [it] is! My gorge
rises at it. Here hung those lips that I have kiss'd
I know not how oft. Where be your gibes now,
your gambols, your songs, your flashes of merriment, that were wont to set the table on a roar? 210
No one now, to mock your own jeering? Quite
chop-fall'n? Now get you to my lady's chamber,
and tell her, let her paint an inch thick, to this
favour she must come. Make her laugh at that.
Prithee, Horatio, tell me one thing. 216

Hor. What's that, my lord?

Ham. Dost thou think Alexander look'd o' this
fashion i' th' earth?

Hor. E'en so. 220

Ham. And smelt so? Puh!

[*Puts down the skull.*]

Hor. E'en so, my lord.

Ham. To what base uses we may return, Horatio! Why may not imagination trace the noble
dust of Alexander, till he find it stopping a bung-
hole? 226

Hor. 'Twere to consider too curiously, to consider so.

Ham. No, faith, not a jot; but to follow him
thither with modesty enough and likelihood to 230
lead it; as thus: Alexander died, Alexander was
buried, Alexander returneth into dust, the dust is
earth, of earth we make loam, and why of that loam
whereto he was converted might they not stop a
beer-barrel? 235
Imperial Cæsar, dead and turn'd to clay,

---

149. **card:** compass, i.e., punctiliously. 151. **picked:** refined. 153. **kibe:** chilblain. 169. **[there]** Q2. Om. F. 177.
[sexton] Q4. *sixeteene* F. 198. **This ... sir.** F repeats these words. 205. **[now]** Q2. Om. F. 206. **[in]** Q2. Om. F. **[it]** Q2.
Om. F. 211. **jeering** F. *grinning* Q2. 215. **favour:** appearance. 227. **curiously:** minutely. 230. **modesty:** moderation.

Might stop a hole to keep the wind away.
O, that that earth which kept the world in awe
Should patch a wall t' expel the winter's flaw!
But soft! but soft! Aside! Here comes the King,

Enter [PRIESTS, *etc., in procession;*] KING, QUEEN,
LAERTES, *and a Coffin, with Lords attendant.*

The Queen, the courtiers. Who is that they fol-
low?   241
And with such maimed rites? This doth betoken
The corse they follow did with desperate hand
Fordo it own life. 'Twas [of] some estate.
Couch we a while, and mark.   245
                               [*Retiring with Horatio.*]
  Laer. What ceremony else?
  Ham. That is Laertes, a very noble youth.
Mark.
  Laer. What ceremony else?
  Priest. Her obsequies have been as far enlarg'd
As we have warrantise. Her death was doubtful;
And, but that great command o'ersways the order,
She should in ground unsanctified have lodg'd 252
Till the last trumpet; for charitable prayer,
Shards, flints, and pebbles should be thrown on her.
Yet here she is allowed her virgin rites,   255
Her maiden strewments, and the bringing home
Of bell and burial.
  Laer. Must there no more be done?
  Priest.   No more be done.
We should profane the service of the dead
To sing sage requiem and such rest to her   260
As to peace-parted souls.
  Laer.   Lay her i' th' earth,
And from her fair and unpolluted flesh
May violets spring! I tell thee, churlish priest,
A minist'ring angel shall my sister be,
When thou liest howling.
  Ham.   What, the fair Ophelia!
  Queen. Sweets to the sweet; farewell!   266
                               [*Scattering flowers.*]
I hop'd thou shouldst have been my Hamlet's wife.
I thought thy bride-bed to have deck'd, sweet maid,
And not t' have strew'd thy grave.
  Laer.   O, [treble woe]
Fall ten times treble on that cursed head   270
Whose wicked deed thy most ingenious sense
Depriv'd thee of! Hold off the earth a while,
Till I have caught her once more in mine arms.
                           [*Leaps in the grave.*
Now pile your dust upon the quick and dead,
Till of this flat a mountain you have made   275
To o'ertop old Pelion, or the skyish head
Of blue Olympus.

  Ham. [*Advancing.*] What is he whose grief
Bears such an emphasis, whose phrase of sorrow
Conjures the wand'ring stars and makes them stand
Like wonder-wounded hearers? This is I,   280
Hamlet, the Dane!   [*Leaps into the grave.*]
  Laer. The devil take thy soul!
                              [*Grappling with him.*]
  Ham.   Thou pray'st not well.
I prithee, take thy fingers from my throat.
Sir, though I am not splenitive and rash,
Yet have I something in me dangerous,   285
Which let thy wiseness fear. Away thy hand!
  King. Pluck them asunder.
  Queen.   Hamlet, Hamlet!
  [*All.*]   Gentlemen] —
  [*Hor.*] Good my lord, be quiet.
        [*The Attendants part them, and they come
        out of the grave.*]
  Ham. Why, I will fight with him upon this theme
Until my eyelids will no longer wag.   290
  Queen. O my son, what theme?
  Ham. I lov'd Ophelia. Forty thousand brothers
Could not, with all their quantity of love,
Make up my sum. What wilt thou do for her?
  King. O, he is mad, Laertes.   295
  Queen. For love of God, forbear him.
  Ham. ['Swounds,] show me what thou'lt do.
Woo 't weep? Woo 't fight? [Woo 't fast?]
      Woo 't tear thyself?
Woo 't drink up eisel? Eat a crocodile?
I'll do 't. Dost thou come here to whine?   300
To outface me with leaping in her grave?
Be buried quick with her, and so will I;
And, if thou prate of mountains, let them throw
Millions of acres on us, till our ground,
Singeing his pate against the burning zone,   305
Make Ossa like a wart! Nay, an thou'lt mouth,
I'll rant as well as thou.
  [*Queen.*]   This is mere madness,
And thus a while the fit will work on him.
Anon, as patient as the female dove,
When that her golden couplets are disclos'd,   310
His silence will sit drooping.
  Ham.   Hear you, sir,
What is the reason that you use me thus?
I lov'd you ever. But it is no matter.
Let Hercules himself do what he may,
The cat will mew and dog will have his day.   315
                                [*Exit.*
  King. I pray you, good Horatio, wait upon him.
                               [*Exit Horatio.*]
  [*To Laertes.*] Strengthen your patience in our last
    night's speech;

---

239. **flaw:** gust. 244. [of] Q2. Om. F. estate: rank. 250. **doubtful:** suspicious. 253. **for:** instead of. 260. **sage:** solemn. 269. [treble woe] Q2. *terrible woer* F. 284. **splenitive:** hot-tempered. 288. [*All.* Gentlemen] Q2. Om. F. 289. [*Hor.*] Q2. *Gen.* F. 297. ['Swounds] Q2. *Come* F. 298. [Woo 't fast] Q2. Om. F. 299. **eisel:** vinegar. 305. **burning zone:** sun's sphere. 307. [*Queen*] Q2. *Kin.* F. 310. **couplets:** twins.

We'll put the matter to the present push.
Good Gertrude, set some watch over your son.
This grave shall have a living monument.   320
An hour of quiet shortly shall we see;
Till then, in patience our proceeding be.   [*Exeunt.*

[SCENE II. *A hall in the castle.*]

Enter HAMLET *and* HORATIO.

Ham. So much for this, sir; now let me see the
    other.
You do remember all the circumstance?
    Hor. Remember it, my lord!
    Ham. Sir, in my heart there was a kind of fight-
    ing
That would not let me sleep. Methought I lay   5
Worse than the mutines in the bilboes. Rashly, —
And prais'd be rashness for it; let us know
Our indiscretion sometimes serves us well
When our dear plots do pall; and that should teach
    us
There's a divinity that shapes our ends,   10
Rough-hew them how we will, —
    Hor.   That is most certain.
    Ham. Up from my cabin,
My sea-gown scarf'd about me, in the dark
Grop'd I to find out them; had my desire;
Finger'd their packet; and in fine withdrew   15
To mine own room again, making so bold,
My fears forgetting manners, to unseal
Their grand commission; where I found, Horatio, —
O royal knavery! — an exact command,
Larded with many several sorts of reason   20
Importing Denmark's health and England's too,
With, ho! such bugs and goblins in my life,
That, on the supervise, no leisure bated,
No, not to stay the grinding of the axe,
My head should be struck off.
    Hor.   Is't possible?   25
    Ham. Here's the commission; read it at more
    leisure.
But wilt thou hear me how I did proceed?
    Hor. I beseech you.
    Ham. Being thus be-netted round with vil-
    lanies, —
Ere I could make a prologue to my brains,   30
They had begun the play, — I sat me down,
Devis'd a new commission, wrote it fair.
I once did hold it, as our statists do,
A baseness to write fair, and labour'd much
How to forget that learning; but, sir, now   35

It did me yeoman's service.   Wilt thou know
Th' effects of what I wrote?
    Hor.   Ay, good my lord.
    Ham. An earnest conjuration from the King,
As England was his faithful tributary,
As love between them as the palm should flourish,
As Peace should still her wheaten garland wear   41
And stand a comma 'tween their amities,
And many such-like *as*-es of great charge,
That, on the view and know of these contents,
Without debatement further, more or less,   45
He should the bearers put to sudden death,
Not shriving time allow'd.
    Hor.   How was this seal'd?
    Ham. Why, even in that was Heaven [ordinant].
I had my father's signet in my purse,
Which was the model of that Danish seal;   50
Folded the writ up in [the] form of th' other,
Subscrib'd it, gave't th' impression, plac'd it safely,
The changeling never known.   Now, the next
    day
Was our sea-fight; and what to this was [sequent]
Thou know'st already.   55
    Hor. So Guildenstern and Rosencrantz go to't.
    Ham. Why, man, they did make love to this em-
    ployment;
They are not near my conscience.   Their [defeat]
Doth by their own insinuation grow.
'Tis dangerous when the baser nature comes   60
Between the pass and fell incensed points
Of mighty opposites.
    Hor.   Why, what a king is this!
    Ham. Does it not, thinks 't thee, stand me now
    upon —
He that hath kill'd my king and whor'd my mother,
Popp'd in between th' election and my hopes,   65
Thrown out his angle for my proper life,
And with such cozenage — is't not perfect con-
    science,
To quit him with this arm?   And is't not to be
    damn'd,
To let this canker of our nature come
In further evil?   70
    Hor. It must be shortly known to him from
    England
What is the issue of the business there.
    Ham. It will be short; the interim is mine,
And a man's life's no more than to say "One."
But I am very sorry, good Horatio,   75
That to Laertes I forgot myself,
For by the image of my cause I see
The portraiture of his.   I'll [court] his favours.

---

318. **present push:** immediate act.
  Sc. ii, 6. **mutines:** mutineers. **bilboes:** fetters. 23. **supervise:** reading. **bated:** allowed (lit., subtracted). 33. **statists:**
statesmen. 42. **comma:** link. 43. **charge:** burden. 47. **shriving:** absolution. 48. [**ordinant**] Q₂. *ordinate* F. 51. [**the**]
Q₂. Om. F. 54. [**sequent**] Q₂. *sement* F. 58. [**defeat**] Q₂. *debate* F. 59. **insinuation:** meddling. 61. **pass:** thrust.
fell: cruel. 63. **thinks 't:** seems it to. 78. [**court**] (Theobald). *count* F.

But, sure, the bravery of his grief did put me
Into a tow'ring passion.
   Hor.   Peace! who comes here?   80

       Enter young OSRIC.

   Osr. Your lordship is right welcome back to
Denmark.
   Ham. I humbly thank you, sir. — Dost know
this water-fly?
   Hor. No, my good lord.
   Ham. Thy state is the more gracious, for 'tis 85
a vice to know him. He hath much land, and fer-
tile; let a beast be lord of beasts, and his crib shall
stand at the King's mess. 'Tis a chough, but, as I
[say], spacious in the possession of dirt. 90
   Osr. Sweet lord, if your [lordship] were at leisure,
I should impart a thing to you from his Majesty.
   Ham. I will receive it with all diligence of spirit.
Put your bonnet to his right use; 'tis for the head.
   Osr. I thank your lordship, 'tis very hot. 97
   Ham. No, believe me, 'tis very cold; the wind is
northerly.
   Osr. It is indifferent cold, my lord, indeed. 100
   Ham. Methinks it is very sultry and hot for my
complexion.
   Osr. Exceedingly, my lord; it is very sultry, —
as 'twere, — I cannot tell how. But, my lord, his
Majesty bade me signify to you that he has laid a
great wager on your head. Sir, this is the matter, —
   Ham. I beseech you, remember — 108
      [*Hamlet moves him to put on his hat.*]
   Osr. Nay, in good faith; for mine ease, in good
faith. [Sir, here is newly come to court Laertes; 110
believe me, an absolute gentleman, full of most excellent differences, of very soft society and great
showing; indeed, to speak feelingly of him, he is the
card or calendar of gentry, for you shall find in him
the continent of what part a gentleman would
see. 116
   Ham. Sir, his definement suffers no perdition in
you; though, I know, to divide him inventorially
would dizzy the arithmetic of memory, and yet but
yaw neither, in respect of his quick sail. But, 120
in ᵗhe verity of extolment, I take him to be a soul
of great article; and his infusion of such dearth and
rareness as, to make true diction of him, his semblable is his mirror; and who else would trace him,
his umbrage, nothing more. 125
   Osr. Your lordship speaks most infallibly of him.
   Ham. The concernancy, sir? Why do we wrap

the gentleman in our more rawer breath?
   Osr. Sir? 130
   Hor. Is't not possible to understand in another
tongue? You will do't, sir, really.
   Ham. What imports the nomination of this
gentleman?
   Osr. Of Laertes? 135
   Hor. His purse is empty already. All's golden
words are spent.
   Ham. Of him, sir.
   Osr. I know you are not ignorant — 139
   Ham. I would you did, sir; yet, in faith, if you
did, it would not much approve me. Well, sir?]
   Osr. You are not ignorant of what excellence
Laertes is — 144
[*Ham.* I dare not confess that, lest I should com-
pare with him in excellence; but to know a man well
were to know himself.
   Osr. I mean, sir, for his weapon; but in the imputation laid on him by them, in his meed he's
unfellowed.] 150
   Ham. What's his weapon?
   Osr. Rapier and dagger.
   Ham. That's two of his weapons; but well.
   Osr. The King, sir, has wag'd with him six Bar-
bary horses, against the which he impon'd, as I 155
take it, six French rapiers and poniards, with their
assigns, as girdle, hangers, or so. Three of the
carriages, in faith, are very dear to fancy, very responsive to the hilts, most delicate carriages, and
of very liberal conceit. 160
   Ham. What call you the carriages?
[*Hor.* I knew you must be edified by the margent ere you had done.]
   Osr. The carriages, sir, are the hangers. 164
   Ham. The phrase would be more germane to the
matter, if we could carry cannon by our sides; I
would it might be hangers till then. But, on: six
Barbary horses against six French swords, their
assigns, and three liberal-conceited carriages; that's
the French [bet] against the Danish. Why is this
"impon'd," as you call it? 171
   Osr. The King, sir, hath laid that in a dozen
passes between you and him, he shall not exceed
you three hits; he hath [laid on twelve for nine];
and that would come to immediate trial, if your
lordship would vouchsafe the answer.
   Ham. How if I answer no? 177
   Osr. I mean, my lord, the opposition of your person in trial.
   Ham. Sir, I will walk here in the hall; if it

89. **chough:** jackdaw. 90. **[say]** Q₂. *saw* F. 91. **[lordship]** Q₂. *friendship* F. 110–50. **[Sir ... unfellowed]** Q₂. Om.
F., which substitutes only ll. 143–44. 115. **continent:** summary. 119. **dizzy** Q₄. *dosie* Q₂. 120. **yaw:** falter, stagger.
122. **article:** importance. **infusion:** essence. **dearth:** rarity. 123. **semblable:** likeness. 125. **umbrage:** shadow. 131–32.
another tongue: i.e., when someone else speaks your lingo. **do't** Q₃. *too't* Q₂. 148. **his** Q₆. *this* Q₂. 149. **meed:**
merit. 155. **impon'd:** staked. 157. **assigns:** appurtenances. **hangers:** straps. 158. **responsive:** harmonious (in design).
160. **liberal conceit:** elegant design. 162–63. **[Hor. ... done]** Q₂. Om. F. 163. **margent:** marginal note. 170. **[bet]**
Q₂. *but* F. 174. **[laid ... nine]** Q₂. *one twelve for mine* F. 176. **answer:** encounter.

please his Majesty, 'tis the breathing time of day
with me.   Let the foils be brought, the gentleman
willing, and the King hold his purpose, I will win
for him if I can; if not, I'll gain nothing but my
shame and the odd hits.   185
   Osr. Shall I re-deliver you e'en so?
   Ham. To this effect, sir; after what flourish your
nature will.   188
   Osr. I commend my duty to your lordship.
   Ham. Yours, yours.   [*Exit Osric.*]   He does well
to commend it himself; there are no tongues else
for 's [turn].
   Hor. This lapwing runs away with the shell on
his head.   194
   Ham. He did comply with his dug before he
suck'd it.   Thus had he, and [many] more of the
same bevy that I know the drossy age dotes on,
only got the tune of the time and outward habit of
encounter; a kind of yeasty collection, which carries them through and through the most fond   200
and winnowed opinions; and do but blow them to
their trials, the bubbles are out.

[*Enter a* LORD.]

   Lord. My lord, his Majesty commended him
to you by young Osric, who brings back to him,
that you attend him in the hall.   He sends to know
if your pleasure hold to play with Laertes, or that
you will take longer time.   207
   Ham. I am constant to my purposes; they follow
the King's pleasure.   If his fitness speaks, mine is
ready, now or whensoever, provided I be so able as
now.   211
   Lord. The King and Queen and all are coming
down.
   Ham. In happy time.   214
   Lord. The Queen desires you to use some gentle
entertainment to Laertes before you fall to play.
   Ham. She well instructs me.]   [*Exit Lord.*]
   Hor. You will lose this wager, my lord.   219
   Ham. I do not think so; since he went into
France I have been in continual practice.   I shall
win at the odds.   But thou wouldst not think how
[ill all's] here about my heart.   But it is no matter.
   Hor. Nay, good my lord, —   224
   Ham. It is but foolery; but it is such a kind of
gain-giving, as would perhaps trouble a woman.
   Hor. If your mind dislike anything, obey [it].
I will forestall their repair hither, and say you are
not fit.   229
   Ham. Not a whit; we defy augury.   There's a
special providence in the fall of a sparrow.   If it

be now, 'tis not to come; if it be not to come, it will
be now; if it be not now, yet it will come; the readiness is all.   Since no man has aught of what he
leaves, what is't to leave betimes?   [Let be.]   235

Enter KING, QUEEN, LAERTES, [OSRIC,] *Lords,
and other Attendants with foils and gauntlets;
a table and flagons of wine on it.*

   King. Come, Hamlet, come, and take this hand
      from me.
            [*The King puts Laertes's hand into Ham-
               let's.*]
   Ham. Give me your pardon, sir.   I've done you
      wrong,
But pardon 't, as you are a gentleman.
This presence knows,
And you must needs have heard, how I am pun-
      ish'd   240
With sore distraction.   What I have done
That might your nature, honour, and exception
Roughly awake, I here proclaim was madness.
Was't Hamlet wrong'd Laertes?   Never Hamlet!
If Hamlet from himself be ta'en away,   245
And when he's not himself does wrong Laertes,
Then Hamlet does it not, Hamlet denies it.
Who does it, then?   His madness.   If 't be so,
Hamlet is of the faction that is wrong'd;
His madness is poor Hamlet's enemy.   250
Sir, in this audience,
Let my disclaiming from a purpos'd evil
Free me so far in your most generous thoughts,
That I have shot mine arrow o'er the house
And hurt my [brother].
   Laer.   I am satisfied in nature,
Whose motive, in this case, should stir me most 256
To my revenge; but in my terms of honour
I stand aloof, and will no reconcilement
Till by some elder masters of known honour
I have a voice and precedent of peace   260
To keep my name [ungor'd].   But till that time
I do receive your offer'd love like love,
And will not wrong it.
   Ham.   I do embrace it freely,
And will this brother's wager frankly play.
Give us the foils.   Come on.
   Laer.   Come, one for me.
   Ham. I'll be your foil, Laertes; in mine igno-
      rance   266
Your skill shall, like a star i' th' darkest night,
Stick fiery off indeed.
   Laer.   You mock me, sir.
   Ham. No, by this hand.

181. **breathing time:** time for exercise.   192. **[turn]** Q₂. *tongue* F.   196. **[many]** Q₂. *mine* F.   199. **yeasty:** frothy.   202-
18. **[*Enter . . . me*]** Q₂.   Om. F.   223. **[ill all's]** Q₂.   *all* F.   226. **gain-giving:** misgiving.   227. **[it]** Q₂.   Om. F.   231. **it:**
death.   235. **[Let be]** Q₂.   Om. F.   239. **presence:** assembled court.   242. **exception:** resentment, disapproval.   255.
[brother] Q₂.   *Mother* F.   260. **voice and precedent:** opinion backed by precedent.   261. **[ungor'd]** Q₂. *ungorg'd* F.
266. **foil:** (1) rapier, (2) something which, by contrast, enhances a jewel.

King. Give them the foils, young Osric. Cousin
Hamlet, 270
You know the wager?
Ham. Very well, my lord.
Your Grace hath laid the odds o' th' weaker side.
King. I do not fear it, I have seen you both;
But since he is better'd, we have therefore odds.
Laer. This is too heavy, let me see another.
Ham. This likes me well. These foils have all a
length? [*They prepare to play.* 276
Osr. Ay, my good lord.
King. Set me the stoups of wine upon that table.
If Hamlet give the first or second hit,
Or quit in answer of the third exchange, 280
Let all the battlements their ordnance fire.
The King shall drink to Hamlet's better breath,
And in the cup an union shall he throw,
Richer than that which four successive kings
In Denmark's crown have worn. Give me the
cups, 285
And let the kettle to the trumpets speak,
The trumpet to the cannoneer without,
The cannons to the heavens, the heaven to earth,
"Now the King drinks to Hamlet." Come,
begin;
And you, the judges, bear a wary eye. 290
Ham. Come on, sir.
Laer. Come, [my lord]. [*They play.*
Ham. One.
Laer. No.
Ham. Judgement.
Osr. A hit, a very palpable hit.
Laer. Well; again.
King. Stay, give me drink. Hamlet, this pearl
is thine;
Here's to thy health! Give him the cup. 294
[*Trumpets sound, and shot goes off* [with-
in].
Ham. I'll play this bout first; set [it] by a while.
Come. [*They play.*] Another hit; what say you?
Laer. A touch, a touch, I do confess.
King. Our son shall win.
Queen. He's fat, and scant of breath.
[Here, Hamlet, take my] napkin, rub thy brows.
The Queen carouses to thy fortune, Hamlet. 300
Ham. Good madam!
King. Gertrude, do not drink.
Queen. I will, my lord; I pray you, pardon me.
King. [*Aside.*] It is the poison'd cup; it is too
late.
Ham. I dare not drink yet, madam; by and
by.
Queen. Come, let me wipe thy face. 305
Laer. My lord, I'll hit him now.
King. I do not think 't.

Laer. [*Aside.*] And yet 'tis almost 'gainst my
conscience.
Ham. Come, for the third, Laertes; you but dally.
I pray you, pass with your best violence.
I am afeard you make a wanton of me. 310
Laer. Say you so? Come on. [*They play.*
Osr. Nothing, neither way.
Laer. Have at you now!
[*Laertes wounds Hamlet; then,*] in scuffling,
they change rapiers.
King. Part them; they are incens'd.
Ham. Nay, come, again.
[*Hamlet wounds Laertes. The Queen
falls.*]
Osr. Look to the Queen there! Ho!
Hor. They bleed on both sides. How is 't, my
lord! 315
Osr. How is 't, Laertes?
Laer. Why, as a woodcock to mine [own] springe,
Osric;
I am justly kill'd with mine own treachery.
Ham. How does the Queen?
King. She swounds to see them bleed.
Queen. No, no, the drink, the drink, — O my
dear Hamlet, — 320
The drink, the drink! I am poison'd. [*Dies.*]
Ham. O villainy! Ho! let the door be lock'd:
Treachery! Seek it out.
Laer. It is here, Hamlet. Hamlet, thou art slain.
No medicine in the world can do thee good; 325
In thee there is not half an hour of life.
The treacherous instrument is in thy hand,
Unbated and envenom'd. The foul practice
Hath turn'd itself on me. Lo, here I lie,
Never to rise again. Thy mother's poison'd. 330
I can no more: — the King, the King's to blame.
Ham. The point envenom'd too!
Then, venom, to thy work. [*Hurts the King.*
All. Treason! treason!
King. O, yet defend me, friends; I am but hurt.
Ham. Here, thou incestuous, murderous, damned
Dane, 336
Drink off this potion! Is thy union here?
Follow my mother! [*King dies.*
Laer. He is justly serv'd;
It is a poison temp'red by himself.
Exchange forgiveness with me, noble Hamlet. 340
Mine and my father's death come not upon thee,
Nor thine on me! [*Dies.*
Ham. Heaven make thee free of it! I follow
thee.
I am dead, Horatio. Wretched queen, adieu!
You that look pale and tremble at this chance, 345
That are but mutes or audience to this act,
Had I but time — as this fell sergeant, Death,

283. union: pearl. 286. kettle: kettle-drum. 291. [my lord] Q₂. *on sir* F. 295. [it] Q₂. Om. F. 298. fat: out of
training. 299. [Here ... my] Q₂. *Heere's a* F. 310. wanton: spoiled child. 317. [own] Q₂. Om. F.

Is strict in his arrest — O, I could tell you —
But let it be. Horatio, I am dead;
Thou liv'st. Report me and my [cause aright]   350
To the unsatisfied.
    Hor.   Never believe it.
I am more an antique Roman than a Dane;
Here's yet some liquor left.
    Ham.   As thou'rt a man,
Give me the cup. Let go! By heaven, I'll have't!
O good Horatio, what a wounded name,   355
Things standing thus unknown, shall live behind
    me!
If thou didst ever hold me in thy heart,
Absent thee from felicity a while
And in this harsh world draw thy breath in pain
To tell my story. [*March afar off, and shot within.*
             What warlike noise is this?   360
    Osr. Young Fortinbras, with conquest come
    from Poland,
To the ambassadors of England gives
This warlike volley.
    Ham.   O, I die, Horatio;
The potent poison quite o'er-crows my spirit.
I cannot live to hear the news from England   365
But I do prophesy th' election lights
On Fortinbras; he has my dying voice.
So tell him, with the occurrents, more and less,
Which have solicited — The rest is silence. [*Dies.*
    Hor. Now cracks a noble heart. Good-night,
    sweet prince,   370
And flights of angels sing thee to thy rest!
Why does the drum come hither? [*March within.*]

    Enter FORTINBRAS *and the* English AMBASSA-
    DOR, *with drum, colours, and Attendants.*

    Fort. Where is this sight?
    Hor.   What is it ye would see?
If aught of woe or wonder, cease your search.
    Fort. [This] quarry cries on havoc. O proud
    Death,   375
What feast is toward in thine eternal cell,
That thou so many princes at a shot
So bloodily hast struck?

    Amb.   The sight is dismal,
And our affairs from England come too late.
The ears are senseless that should give us hearing,
To tell him his commandment is fulfill'd,   381
That Rosencrantz and Guildenstern are dead.
Where should we have our thanks?
    Hor.   Not from his mouth,
Had it th' ability of life to thank you.
He never gave commandment for their death.   385
But since, so jump upon this bloody question,
You from the Polack wars, and you from England,
Are here arriv'd, give order that these bodies
High on a stage be placed to the view;
And let me speak to th' yet unknowing world   390
How these things came about. So shall you hear
Of carnal, bloody, and unnatural acts,
Of accidental judgements, casual slaughters,
Of deaths put on by cunning and forc'd cause,
And, in this upshot, purposes mistook   395
Fall'n on the inventors' heads: all this can I
Truly deliver.
    Fort.   Let us haste to hear it,
And call the noblest to the audience.
For me, with sorrow I embrace my fortune.
I have some rights of memory in this kingdom,   400
Which [now] to claim, my vantage doth invite me.
    Hor. Of that I shall have [also] cause to speak,
And from his mouth whose voice will draw on more.
But let this same be presently perform'd
Even while men's minds are wild, lest more mis-
    chance,   405
On plots and errors, happen.
    Fort.   Let four captains
Bear Hamlet, like a soldier, to the stage,
For he was likely, had he been put on,
To have prov'd most royally; and, for his passage,
The soldiers' music and the rites of war   410
Speak loudly for him.
Take up the body. Such a sight as this
Becomes the field, but here shows much amiss.
Go, bid the soldiers shoot.
        [*Exeunt marching; after which a peal of
        ordnance are shot off.*

---

  350. **[cause aright]** Q₂. *causes right* F. 352. **Roman.** Alluding to the Roman custom of suicide. 367. **voice:** approval, vote. 369. **solicited:** caused them. **silence.** F adds *O, o, o, o.* 375. **[This]** Q₂. *His* F. **quarry . . . havoc:** heap of dead proclaims a massacre. 383. **his:** the King's. 389. **stage:** platform. 400. **of memory:** unforgotten. 401. **[now]** Q₂. *are* F. 402. **[also]** Q₂. *alwayes* F. 408. **put on:** tested. 409. **passage:** i.e., death. 413. **field:** battlefield.

Othello, the Moor of Venice

OTHELLO IS NOTABLE among Shakespeare's plays as being the only one published between his death and the appearance of the First Folio. No First Quarto had been issued after 1609 till that of *Othello* was printed in 1622. The title page carried Shakespeare's name and stated that the tragedy had been "diuerse times acted at the Globe, and at the Black Friers, by his Maiesties Seruants." The text in the First Quarto is a good one, though it is shorter by some 160 lines than that in the First Folio. On the other hand, there are minor omissions and numerous variants in the Folio. Both texts appear to have been printed from manuscripts used in the theatre. The omissions in the Quarto presumably represent cuts, though a few may have been accidental; the preponderance in the Quarto of oaths that have been removed or modified in the Folio suggests that the manuscript from which that edition was printed may have antedated the law of 1606 against profanity on the stage. The text of the present edition is based upon the Folio, with deference to the Quarto where a better reading can be supplied.

There was a performance of *Othello* at Court on November 1, 1604, and authorities are in accord that the composition belongs to an earlier part of that year. There is a possible reference to the death of Desdemona in I.i.37 of Part I of *The Honest Whore* by Dekker and Middleton (1604), and metrical tests indicate a position between *Hamlet* and *Lear*.

The plot of the tragedy is drawn from a tale (the seventh of the third decade) in the *Hecatommithi* (1565) of Giraldi Cinthio, but, as usual, Shakespeare's work is a marvelous transmutation of crude ore. In the Italian story, Desdemona alone is given a name (Disdemona), and the outlines of her character, with those of Othello ("the Moor"), Iago ("the Ensign"), and Cassio ("the Captain") are there faintly indicated. Hardly so much can be said of Emilia and Bianca; for the character of Brabantio there is only the hint that Disdemona's parents opposed her marriage; and Roderigo and the official persons in Venice and Cyprus are Shakespeare's creations. The threat of a Turkish attack upon Cyprus, the separate voyages of Othello and Desdemona, the episode of Cassio's drunkenness, Emilia's part in the stealing of the handkerchief and Bianca's connection with it, are all lacking in the novel. There too, certain of the elements crucial in the drama are quite differently handled. Thus the villain is a disappointed lover of Disdemona's, whose failure turns his passion to hate. Only a trace of this is left in Iago, and the character of Roderigo is built up on the suggestion it affords. In the novel, the handkerchief is stolen by the Ensign himself, who removes it from Disdemona's sash when she is fondling his little girl. The Ensign's wife is aware of his criminal scheming. The Captain (Cassio) is married, and the ocular proof of Disdemona's guilt is given by the Ensign's bringing the Moor to see the Captain's wife sitting at a window making a copy of the lost handkerchief. The Captain is on his way to visit a courtezan when he is attacked by the Ensign, and it is apparently from this hint that Shakespeare creates Bianca, omitting the Captain's wife; although there may be a trace of the latter remaining, perhaps through an oversight, in the cryptic reference to Cassio (I.i.21) as "A fellow almost damn'd in a fair wife."

In the Italian, the arrangement of the catastrophe is also very different. There the Ensign, carrying out a plan approved by the Moor, beats Disdemona to death with a stocking filled with sand, and the two men disguise their crime by pulling down the ceiling and making it appear that she was killed by a falling beam. After a time, however, the Moor, brooding on the memory of Disdemona, comes to hate the Ensign and discharges him; then, in revenge, the Ensign tells the Captain that it was the Moor who wounded him and who caused Disdemona's death. The Moor is accused before the Signiory, is tried and tortured, but refuses to confess. He is banished and is subsequently killed by his wife's relatives. The Ensign goes free, but ultimately dies from the effects of torture inflicted in connection with another charge. The contrast between this sordid and dragged-out conclusion and the swiftness and dignity of Shakespeare's terrible close need not be detailed. The tone of the novel may be gathered from a remark made by the heroine: "I fear I shall prove an example to young girls not to marry against the wishes of their parents, and that the Italian ladies may learn from me not to marry a man whom nature, heaven, and manner of life have separated from us."

Out of this sordid and melodramatic tale, Shakespeare has created a tragic drama of terrifying plausibility. The conviction of reality is extraordinary, considering that the action, regarded in the light of reason, is full of improbability. But Shakespeare knew how easily the light of reason is extinguished in men, especially in certain types of men, and he was, in 1604, so sure a master of characterization and of theatrical illusion, that he could make acceptable in his medium what would not be so in another. He further strengthens credibility by building the action upon relentlessly simple lines. There is no more powerful a destroyer of human happiness than sexual jealousy, which has wrecked the lives of all sorts and conditions of men. Because it is precisely this which ruins Othello, whose happiness with Desdemona seemed ideally perfect, and because Othello, recovering his senses when it is too late, pathetically acknowledges the fact, his tragedy, however peculiar the circumstances, becomes a catastrophe by no means unfamiliar. His tragedy, however, is fraught with uncommon pity and terror, both elements being augmented by an extreme concentration of emotional force. No secondary interest or comic relief is permitted to take our attention from the main course of affairs.

The pathos of Othello's situation is especially acute because he is not constitutionally prone to jealousy. In the early scenes Shakespeare is careful to show us that Othello is a man of high integrity, of commanding presence and simple eloquence, and, most important, of complete self-mastery. When Iago recommends that he avoid Desdemona's irate father, he chooses, rather, to confront him honestly, confident that his perfect record and untarnished conscience will "manifest him rightly." When soon embroilment threatens, he suppresses it with a word. His speech before the Senators, recounting with a winning frankness the history of his courtship, reflects the essential nobility of his character. Furthermore, Othello's story reveals the important fact that Brabantio had respected him and had entertained him often at his house (I.iii.127-31). To be sure, Brabantio had never dreamed that his daughter would fall in love with Othello, but in the impression of Othello's nature which Shakespeare is seeking to convey, his relations with others, including Brabantio, and their opinions of him, are most significant.

How comes it, then, that a man of Othello's confirmed steadiness can be so rankly abused and can so completely lose his true self? Under normal circumstances, doubtless, the calamity would be impossible, but the circumstances are not normal. Othello becomes the victim of an incomparably ingenious and unscrupulous villain, whose hatred of him is increased by contempt for the very qualities which distinguish him. Thus Othello's natural goodness, the native honor which makes duplicity as alien to him as cowardice, becomes a weakness for Iago to play upon (I.iii.405-408). Furthermore, the essential simplicity of Othello's nature is complemented by a lack of certain kinds of experience. His career has been military, and his accomplishments belong to the field rather than to the drawing room (I.iii.81 ff.; III.iii.263-66). He is unacquainted with the ways of Venetian society, as Iago once powerfully reminds him (III.iii.199-204). Because the hero's credulity seems monstrous, one must not underestimate the skill of the intriguer. Nor must one suppose that the hero's noble nature is overcome without a struggle; Othello's mind fights the horrid coil that is being thrown around it (III.iii.176-92; 359-73). Once, however, conviction of Desdemona's guilt is planted in Othello's mind, its consequences are swift and deadly. To gnawing jealousy is added the force of shattered idealism. Desdemona, who has seemed to Othello the embodiment of purity, now seems to him corrupted and defiled. Since hers is now an infectious, not a healthful beauty, she must die, "else she'll betray more men." In this belief, even anger is finally consumed, leaving only unfathomable sorrow; so that when Othello enters Desdemona's chamber to kill her, he conceives of himself as the agent not of vengeance but of divine justice (V.ii.16-22).

The credulity of Othello, his confidence in the "honesty" of Iago, and his failure to place at least an equal trust in his newly wedded wife, when one frank talk would have cleared up everything, are, of course, contrary to reason and common sense. Othello's behavior completely belies his "free and noble nature." It must be remembered, however, that psychological inconsistency of this kind is not felt in the theatre. It may even be possible in real life, for idealists are often easily imposed upon by hypocrites. Men may become for a time "insane with jealousy," and it is conceivable that a man of Othello's make-up might be prevented by a sense of shame from speaking of his jealousy to the person who could logically allay it. In any event, Othello's judgment upon himself is utterly plain and simple. "Oh fool! fool! fool!" he cries, when his eyes are opened to the grossness of his deception. That is all that need be said, except, in fairness, that he was "one not easily jealous, but, being wrought, Perplex'd in the extreme." It is fitting that Othello should pass sentence and execute justice upon himself. In his final moments he recovers his essential nobility and that felicity of language which he commands so well, and his suicide is a kind of atonement.

Iago has become a by-word for consummate villainy. The motives for his evil-doing are explicit. The primary one is professional resentment. Othello has promoted Cassio to the lieutenantcy which he craved and for which he thinks he was better fitted (I.i.8 ff.). The sense of injustice rankles, and if what Iago says about Cassio's military experience in comparison with his own is true, he has something on his side. To supplement this grievance, there is some sexual jealousy (I.iii.392–96; II.i.300–11). At the outset, Iago's aim is only to humiliate Othello, to get Cassio's place, and thus to repair his wounded self-esteem. He has no preconceived plan, but shapes his intrigue gradually from what time and chance afford, becoming more and more deeply involved, until a retreat is finally impossible. In working upon Othello, Iago employs a skillful technique of insinuation and evasion, distilling the poison of jealousy drop by drop, hinting obliquely at evil, recoiling from the suggestion in apparent alarm, but returning to the theme again, each time a little more emphatically. Luck befriends him too. Thus, for example, it is propitious for his scheming that Othello proclaims an evening of revelry in Cyprus (II.ii.), for it becomes easy to get Cassio drunk and ripe for indiscretion. Cassio's leaving Desdemona so self-consciously when Othello and Iago approach (III.iii.29–40) gives the latter a perfect cue for beginning his evil suggestions. The supreme accident is, of course, the dropping of the handkerchief, for with it Iago comes into possession of "ocular proof" of Desdemona's guilt. Finally, however, Iago's luck deserts him, for Roderigo fails to kill Cassio, and his own wife turns out to be his Nemesis. Part of Iago's early good fortune is his reputation. How so wicked a man could acquire and maintain a name for honesty it is futile to wonder, but everybody believes in "honest Iago," and his reputation is at once a primary asset and a hideous irony. The word "honest" becomes a kind of motif, introduced repeatedly in its two meanings, "honorable" and "chaste." The play is charged

with irony too pervasive to be detailed. At points it becomes almost intolerable (e.g., III.iii.106–108; 213–20; III.iv.26–31; IV.ii.148–71), and the spell is not broken until Othello tells Iago's horrified wife that her husband knew all about Desdemona's infidelity. "I say thy husband," he cries. "My friend, thy husband, honest, honest Iago" (V.ii. 154).

Desdemona is essentially a passive heroine, created to love and to suffer. That she is not without spirit is proved by her defiance of convention in marrying Othello, but later when her lover is estranged and her happiness is imperiled, she is impractical and unresisting. For the change in Othello she assumes she must be to blame, though she cannot imagine how. Othello, she is certain, cannot be jealous, and women who would deceive their husbands are beyond her comprehension. Her only refuge is bewilderment and grief. Desdemona is sublimely pure and sublimely innocent, and inexperience is her undoing.

Something should be said about Emilia, and it should be in appreciation. Her relation to the heroine is such that, had the play been a comedy, she might have had a merry rôle. As things are, her capacity for banter is exhibited in two notable passages (II.i.96 ff.; IV.iii.60 ff.). But she is cast in a tragedy and plays an unhappy part. Romance has long since been over for her, though she gets along well enough with her husband. Her "stealing" Desdemona's handkerchief is a grave mistake, but she has only innocent intentions. Iago has expressed a desire for it, and she thinks she may gratify his whim. She purposes to keep it only long enough to make a copy of it, and when Iago snatches the original from her, she protests (III.iii.290 ff.). When Desdemona misses her handkerchief, Emilia (as Desdemona herself is presently to do) tells a venial lie. The only thing that it is difficult to forgive is her later negligence, not to say stupidity, in failing to connect Othello's distemper with the handkerchief and to clear matters up before there is serious trouble. It is only after Desdemona is dead and Othello refers to the handkerchief as proof of her guilt that Emilia comprehends. "O God!" she cries then, "O Heavenly God!" (V.ii.217). The horror in her exclamation proves her innocence, if any proof were needed. Her courageous defiance of Iago in solving the mystery, once her own ignorance has been dispelled, makes us take her to our hearts, and her death by his hand redeems her completely.

OTHELLO, THE MOOR OF VENICE

[DRAMATIS PERSONÆ]

DUKE OF VENICE.
BRABANTIO, [a senator,] father to Desdemona.
[Other] Senators.
GRATIANO, [brother to Brabantio,] } two noble
LODOVICO, [kinsman to Brabantio,] } Venetians.
OTHELLO, the Moor [in the military service of Venice].
CASSIO, an honourable lieutenant.
IAGO, [an ensign,] a villain.

RODERIGO, a gulled gentleman.
MONTANO, governor of Cyprus [before Othello].
CLOWN [servant to Othello].

DESDEMONA, [daughter to Brabantio and] wife to Othello.
EMILIA, wife to Iago.
BIANCA, a courtezan.

Gentlemen of Cyprus, Sailors [Officers, Messenger, Herald, Musicians, and Attendants].

[SCENE: Venice; a sea-port in Cyprus.]

ACT I

SCENE I. [Venice. A street.]

Enter RODERIGO *and* IAGO.

Rod. [Tush]! never tell me! I take it much un-
  kindly
That thou, Iago, who hast had my purse
As if the strings were thine, shouldst know of this.
  Iago. ['Sblood], but you'll not hear me.
If ever I did dream of such a matter,   5
Abhor me.
  Rod. Thou told'st me thou didst hold him in thy
  hate.
  Iago. Despise me if I do not. Three great ones
  of the city,
In personal suit to make me his lieutenant,
Off-capp'd to him; and, by the faith of man,   10
I know my price; I am worth no worse a place.
But he, as loving his own pride and purposes,
Evades them with a bombast circumstance
Horribly stuff'd with epithets of war,
[And, in conclusion,]   15

Nonsuits my mediators; for, "Certes," says he,
"I have already chose my officer."
And what was he?
Forsooth, a great arithmetician,
One Michael Cassio, a Florentine,   20
(A fellow almost damn'd in a fair wife)
That never set a squadron in the field,
Nor the division of a battle knows
More than a spinster, unless the bookish theoric,
Wherein the [toged] consuls can propose   25
As masterly as he. Mere prattle without practice
Is all his soldiership. But he, sir, had th' elec-
  tion;
And I, of whom his eyes had seen the proof
At Rhodes, at Cyprus, and on other grounds
Christen'd and heathen, must be be-lee'd and
  calm'd   30
By debitor and creditor; this counter-caster,
He, in good time, must his lieutenant be,
And I — [God] bless the mark! — his Moorship's
  ancient.
  Rod. By heaven, I rather would have been his
  hangman.

Act I, sc. i, 1. **[Tush]** Q. Om. F.   3. **this:** Desdemona's elopement.   4. **['Sblood]** Q. Om. F. Profane exclamations in brackets, such as this and that in I.i.33, were omitted in F on account of the Act of 1605 against swearing. Frequently *Heaven* was substituted for *God.*   13. **circumstance:** discourse.   15. **[And ... conclusion]** Q. Om. F.   21. **wife.** See Introduction.   23. **division:** array.   25. **[toged]** Q: wearing a toga. *tongued* F.   31. **counter-caster:** accountant.   33. **[God]** Q. Om. F.

Iago. Why, there's no remedy. 'Tis the curse of
service, 35
Preferment goes by letter and affection,
And not by old gradation, where each second
Stood heir to th' first. Now, sir, be judge yourself
Whether I in any just term am affin'd
To love the Moor.
Rod. I would not follow him then. 40
Iago. O, sir, content you;
I follow him to serve my turn upon him.
We cannot all be masters, nor all masters
Cannot be truly follow'd. You shall mark
Many a duteous and knee-crooking knave 45
That, doting on his own obsequious bondage,
Wears out his time, much like his master's ass,
For nought but provender, and when he's old,
cashier'd.
Whip me such honest knaves. Others there are
Who, trimm'd in forms and visages of duty, 50
Keep yet their hearts attending on themselves,
And, throwing but shows of service on their lords,
Do well thrive by them and, when they have lin'd
their coats,
Do themselves homage. These fellows have some
soul;
And such a one do I profess myself. For, sir, 55
It is as sure as you are Roderigo,
Were I the Moor, I would not be Iago.
In following him, I follow but myself;
Heaven is my judge, not I for love and duty,
But seeming so, for my peculiar end; 60
For when my outward action doth demonstrate
The native act and figure of my heart
In compliment extern, 'tis not long after
But I will wear my heart upon my sleeve
For daws to peck at. I am not what I am. 65
Rod. What a full fortune does the thick-lips owe,
If he can carry 't thus!
Iago. Call up her father,
Rouse him. Make after him, poison his delight,
Proclaim him in the streets. Incense her kins-
men,
And, though he in a fertile climate dwell, 70
Plague him with flies. Though that his joy be joy,
Yet throw such [changes] of vexation on 't,
As it may lose some colour.
Rod. Here is her father's house; I'll call aloud.
Iago. Do, with like timorous accent and dire yell
As when, by night and negligence, the fire 76
Is spied in populous cities.
Rod. What, ho, Brabantio! Signior Brabantio,
ho!

Iago. Awake! what, ho, Brabantio! thieves!
thieves!
Look to your house, your daughter, and your bags!
Thieves! thieves! 81

BRABANTIO [*appears*] *above, at a window.*

Bra. What is the reason of this terrible summons?
What is the matter there?
Rod. Signior, is all your family within?
Iago. Are your doors lock'd?
Bra. Why, wherefore ask you this?
Iago. ['Zounds], sir, you're robb'd! For shame,
put on your gown. 86
Your heart is burst, you have lost half your soul;
Even now, now, very now, an old black ram
Is tupping your white ewe. Arise, arise!
Awake the snorting citizens with the bell, 90
Or else the devil will make a grandsire of you.
Arise, I say!
Bra. What, have you lost your wits?
Rod. Most reverend signior, do you know my
voice?
Bra. Not I. What are you?
Rod. My name is Roderigo.
Bra. The worser welcome;
I have charg'd thee not to haunt about my doors. 96
In honest plainness thou hast heard me say
My daughter is not for thee; and now, in madness,
Being full of supper and distemp'ring draughts,
Upon malicious [bravery] dost thou come 100
To start my quiet.
Rod. Sir, sir, sir, —
Bra. But thou must needs be sure
My spirits and my place have in their power
To make this bitter to thee.
Rod. Patience, good sir.
Bra. What tell'st thou me of robbing? This is
Venice; 105
My house is not a grange.
Rod. Most grave Brabantio,
In simple and pure soul I come to you.
Iago. ['Zounds], sir, you are one of those that will
not serve God, if the devil bid you. Because we
come to do you service and you think we are 110
ruffians, you'll have your daughter cover'd with a
Barbary horse; you'll have your nephews neigh to
you; you'll have coursers for cousins, and gennets
for germans.
Bra. What profane wretch art thou? 115
Iago. I am one, sir, that comes to tell you your
daughter and the Moor are [now] making the beast
with two backs.

36. **letter:** i.e., of recommendation. 37. **old gradation:** seniority. 39. **affin'd:** bound. 48. **cashier'd:** dismissed. 50.
visages: semblances. 60. **peculiar:** private. 63. **compliment extern:** external show. 66. **thick-lips:** i.e., the Moor. **owe:**
own. 72. **[changes]** Q. *chances* F. 75. **timorous:** terrifying. 90. **snorting:** snoring. 99. **distemp'ring:** intoxicating.
100. **[bravery]** Q: swaggering. *knavery* F. 101. **start:** startle. 106. **grange:** isolated farm. 112. **nephews:** grandsons.
113. **gennets:** Spanish horses. 114. **germans:** relatives. 117. **[now]** Q. Om. F.

Bra. Thou art a villain.

Iago.   You are — a senator.

Bra. This thou shalt answer; I know thee, Roderigo.   120

Rod. Sir, I will answer anything. But, I beseech
you,
If 't be your pleasure and most wise consent,
As partly I find it is, that your fair daughter,
At this odd-even and dull watch o' th' night,
Transported, with no worse nor better guard   125
But with a knave of common hire, a gondolier,
To the gross clasps of a lascivious Moor, —
If this be known to you and your allowance,
We then have done you bold and saucy wrongs;
But if you know not this, my manners tell me   130
We have your wrong rebuke. Do not believe
That, from the sense of all civility,
I thus would play and trifle with your reverence.
Your daughter, if you have not given her leave,
I say again, hath made a gross revolt,   135
Tying her duty, beauty, wit, and fortunes
In an extravagant and wheeling stranger
Of here and everywhere. Straight satisfy your-
self.
If she be in her chamber or your house,
Let loose on me the justice of the state   140
For thus deluding you.

Bra.   Strike on the tinder, ho!
Give me a taper! Call up all my people!
This accident is not unlike my dream;
Belief of it oppresses me already.   144
Light, I say! light!   *[Exit [above].*

Iago.   Farewell; for I must leave you.
It seems not meet, nor wholesome to my place,
To be produc'd — as, if I stay, I shall —
Against the Moor; for, I do know, the state,
However this may gall him with some check,
Cannot with safety cast him, for he's embark'd 150
With such loud reason to the Cyprus wars,
Which even now [stand] in act, that, for their
souls,
Another of his fathom they have none
To lead their business; in which regard,
Though I do hate him as I do hell-pains,   155
Yet, for necessity of present life,
I must show out a flag and sign of love,
Which is indeed but sign. That you shall surely
find him,
Lead to the Sagittary the raised search;
And there will I be with him. So, farewell.   160
                                 [Exit.

Enter [below,] BRABANTIO *in his night-gown, and
Servants with torches.*

Bra. It is too true an evil; gone she is;
And what's to come of my despised time
Is nought but bitterness. Now, Roderigo,
Where didst thou see her? O unhappy girl!
With the Moor, say'st thou? Who would be a
father!   165
How didst thou know 'twas she? O, she deceives
me
Past thought! What said she to you? Get moe
tapers;
Raise all my kindred. Are they married, think you?

Rod. Truly, I think they are.

Bra. O heaven! How got she out? O treason of
the blood!   170
Fathers, from hence trust not your daughters' minds
By what you see them act. Is there not charms
By which the property of youth and maidhood
May be abus'd? Have you not read, Roderigo,
Of some such thing?

Rod.   Yes, sir, I have indeed.   175

Bra. Call up my brother. — O, would you had
had her! —
Some one way, some another. — Do you know
Where we may apprehend her and the Moor?

Rod. I think I can discover him, if you please
To get good guard and go along with me.   180

Bra. Pray you, lead on. At every house I'll call;
I may command at most. Get weapons, ho!
And raise some special officers of [night].
On, good Roderigo; I'll deserve your pains. *[Exeunt.*

SCENE II. *[Another street.]*

Enter OTHELLO, IAGO, *and Attendants with
torches.*

Iago. Though in the trade of war I have slain
men,
Yet do I hold it very stuff o' th' conscience
To do no contriv'd murder. I lack iniquity
Sometimes to do me service. Nine or ten times
I'd thought to have yerk'd him here under the ribs.

Oth. 'Tis better as it is.

Iago.   Nay, but he prated,   6
And spoke such scurvy and provoking terms
Against your honour
That, with the little godliness I have,
I did full hard forbear him. But, I pray you, sir, 10
Are you fast married? Be assur'd of this,

---

124. **odd-even:** midnight. **dull:** dead. 128. **your allowance:** has your approval. 132. **from:** contrary to. 137. **extrava-**
gant: vagabond. **wheeling:** roving. 149. **check:** rebuke. 150. **cast:** dismiss. 152. **[stand]** (Pope). *stands* QF. 153.
fathom: capacity. 159. **Sagittary:** an inn (with a Centaur on its sign). It has also been proposed that the word is a
translation of *Frezzaria*, the Street of the Arrow-makers in Venice. 161. s.d. **night-gown:** dressing gown. 173. **property:**
nature. 174. **abus'd:** deceived. 183. **[night]** Q. *might* F. 184. **deserve:** reward.
    Sc. ii, 5. **yerk'd:** stabbed.

That the magnifico is much belov'd,
And hath in his effect a voice potential
As double as the Duke's.   He will divorce you,
Or put upon you what restraint or grievance   15
The law, with all his might to enforce it on,
Will give him cable.
   Oth.   Let him do his spite;
My services which I have done the signiory
Shall out-tongue his complaints.   'Tis yet to know, —
Which, when I know that boasting is an honour,   20
I shall promulgate — I fetch my life and being
From men of royal siege, and my demerits
May speak unbonneted to as proud a fortune
As this that I have reach'd; for know, Iago,
But that I love the gentle Desdemona,   25
I would not my unhoused free condition
Put into circumscription and confine
For the sea's worth.   But, look! what lights come
    yond?

   Enter CASSIO, *with lights*, Officers, *and torches.*

   Iago. Those are the raised father and his friends.
You were best go in.
   Oth.   Not I; I must be found.   30
My parts, my title, and my perfect soul
Shall manifest me rightly.   Is it they?
   Iago. By Janus, I think no.
   Oth. The servants of the Duke, and my lieutenant.
The goodness of the night upon you, friends!   35
What is the news?
   Cas.   The Duke does greet you, general,
And he requires your haste-post-haste appearance,
Even on the instant.
   Oth.   What is the matter, think you?
   Cas. Something from Cyprus, as I may divine;
It is a business of some heat.   The galleys   40
Have sent a dozen sequent messengers
This very night at one another's heels,
And many of the consuls, rais'd and met,
Are at the Duke's already.   You have been hotly
    call'd for;
When, being not at your lodging to be found,   45
The Senate hath sent about three several quests
To search you out.
   Oth.   'Tis well I am found by you.
I will but spend a word here in the house.
And go with you.   [*Exit.*
   Cas.   Ancient, what makes he here?
   Iago. Faith, he to-night hath boarded a land
    carack.   50
If it prove lawful prize, he's made for ever.

   Cas. I do not understand.
   Iago.   He's married.
   Cas.   To who?

          [*Re-enter* OTHELLO.]

   Iago. Marry, to — Come, captain, will you go?
   Oth.   Have with you.
   Cas. Here comes another troop to seek for you.

   Enter BRABANTIO, RODERIGO, *and* OFFICERS
       with torches and weapons.

   Iago. It is Brabantio.   General, be advis'd;   55
He comes to bad intent.
   Oth.   Holla! stand there!
   Rod. Signior, it is the Moor.
   Bra.   Down with him, thief!
             [*They draw on both sides.*]
   Iago. You, Roderigo! come, sir, I am for you.
   Oth. Keep up your bright swords, for the dew will
    rust them.
Good signior, you shall more command with years
Than with your weapons.   61
   Bra. O thou foul thief, where hast thou stow'd
    my daughter?
Damn'd as thou art, thou hast enchanted her;
For I'll refer me to all things of sense,
If she in chains of magic were not bound,   65
Whether a maid so tender, fair, and happy,
So opposite to marriage that she shunn'd
The wealthy curled darlings of our nation,
Would ever have, t' incur a general mock,
Run from her guardage to the sooty bosom   70
Of such a thing as thou — to fear, not to delight.
Judge me the world, if 'tis not gross in sense
That thou hast practis'd on her with foul charms,
Abus'd her delicate youth with drugs or minerals
That weakens motion.   I'll have 't disputed on;   75
'Tis probable, and palpable to thinking.
I therefore apprehend and do attach thee
For an abuser of the world, a practiser
Of arts inhibited and out of warrant.
Lay hold upon him; if he do resist,   80
Subdue him at his peril.
   Oth.   Hold your hands,
Both you of my inclining, and the rest.
Were it my cue to fight, I should have known it
Without a prompter.   [Where] will you that I go
To answer this your charge?
   Bra.   To prison, till fit time
Of law and course of direct session   86
Call thee to answer.
   Oth.   What if [I] do obey?

---

14. **double:** strong.   22. **siege:** rank. **demerits:** deserts.   23. **unbonneted:** without taking my hat off, on equal terms.
26. **unhoused:** unconfined.   31. **perfect soul:** clear conscience.   40. **galleys:** i.e., officers of the galleys.   50. **carack:** large
trading ship.   72. **gross in sense:** perfectly clear.   75. **motion:** will power. **disputed on:** argued legally.   77. **attach:** arrest.
79. **inhibited:** prohibited. **out of warrant:** unjustifiable.   82. **inclining:** party.   84. **[Where]** Q. *Whether* F. *Whither* F₂.
86. **course . . . session:** due course of law.   87. **[I]** Q. Om. F.

How may the Duke be therewith satisfi'd,
Whose messengers are here about my side
Upon some present business of the state   90
To bring me to him?
    Off.   'Tis true, most worthy signior.
The Duke 's in council; and your noble self,
I am sure, is sent for.
    Bra.   How! the Duke in council!
In this time of the night! Bring him away;
Mine's not an idle cause. The Duke himself,   95
Or any of my brothers of the state,
Cannot but feel this wrong as 'twere their own;
For if such actions may have passage free,
Bond-slaves and pagans shall our statesmen be.
                              [*Exeunt.*

SCENE III. [*A council-chamber.*]

The DUKE *and* SENATORS *set at a table, with
lights;* OFFICERS *attending.*

    Duke. There is no composition in [these] news
That gives them credit.
    1. Sen.   Indeed, they are disproportion'd;
My letters say a hundred and seven galleys.
    Duke. And mine, a hundred forty.
    2. Sen.   And mine, two hundred!
But though they jump not on a just account, —   5
As in these cases, where the aim reports,
'Tis oft with difference — yet do they all confirm
A Turkish fleet, and bearing up to Cyprus.
    Duke. Nay, it is possible enough to judgement.
I do not so secure me in the error   10
But the main article I do approve
In fearful sense.
    Sailor. (*Within.*) What, ho! what, ho! what, ho!

Enter a SAILOR.

    Off. A messenger from the galleys.
    Duke.   Now, what's the business?
    Sail. The Turkish preparation makes for Rhodes;
So was I bid report here to the state   15
By Signior Angelo.
    Duke. How say you by this change?
    1. Sen.   This cannot be,
By no assay of reason; 'tis a pageant,
To keep us in false gaze. When we consider
Th' importancy of Cyprus to the Turk,   20
And let ourselves again but understand
That, as it more concerns the Turk than Rhodes,
So may he with more facile question bear it,
For that it stands not in such warlike brace,
But altogether lacks th' abilities   25
That Rhodes is dress'd in; if we make thought of
    this,

We must not think the Turk is so unskilful
To leave that latest which concerns him first,
Neglecting an attempt of ease and gain
To wake and wage a danger profitless.   30
    Duke. Nay, in all confidence, he's not for Rhodes.
    Off. Here is more news.

Enter a MESSENGER.

    Mess. The Ottomites, reverend and gracious,
Steering with due course towards the isle of Rhodes,
Have there injointed them with an after fleet.   35
    1. Sen. Ay, so I thought. How many, as you
    guess?
    Mess. Of thirty sail; and now they do restem
Their backward course, bearing with frank appear-
    ance
Their purposes toward Cyprus. Signior Montano,
Your trusty and most valiant servitor,   40
With his free duty recommends you thus,
And prays you to believe him.
    Duke. 'Tis certain, then, for Cyprus.
Marcus Luccicos, is not he in town?
    1. Sen. He's now in Florence.   45
    Duke. Write from us to him; post-post-haste dis-
    patch.
    1. Sen. Here comes Brabantio and the valiant
    Moor.

Enter BRABANTIO, OTHELLO, CASSIO, IAGO, RODERIGO, *and* Officers.

    Duke. Valiant Othello, we must straight employ
    you
Against the general enemy Ottoman.
[*To Brabantio.*] I did not see you; welcome, gentle
    signior;   50
We lack'd your counsel and your help to-night.
    Bra. So did I yours. Good your Grace, pardon
    me;
Neither my place nor aught I heard of business
Hath rais'd me from my bed, nor doth the general
    care
Take hold on me; for my particular grief   55
Is of so flood-gate and o'erbearing nature
That it engluts and swallows other sorrows
And it is still itself.
    Duke.   Why, what's the matter?
    Bra. My daughter! O, my daughter!
    Sen.   Dead?
    Bra.   Ay, to me;
She is abus'd, stol'n from me, and corrupted   60
By spells and medicines bought of mountebanks;
For nature so prepost'rously to err,
Being not deficient, blind, or lame of sense,
Sans witchcraft could not.

Sc. iii, 1. **composition:** consistency. **[these]** Q. *this* F. 5. **jump:** agree. **just:** exact. 6. **the...reports:** the reports are conjectural. 10. **so...error:** take such assurance from the disagreement. 11. **approve:** assent to. 18. **pageant:** pretence. 23. **with...it:** capture it more easily. 24. **brace:** defense. 35. **after:** i.e., sent after. 55. **particular:** personal.

Duke. Whoe'er he be that in this foul proceeding
Hath thus beguil'd your daughter of herself   66
And you of her, the bloody book of law
You shall yourself read in the bitter letter
After your own sense, yea, though our proper son
Stood in your action.
    Bra.   Humbly I thank your Grace.
Here is the man, — this Moor, whom now, it seems,
Your special mandate for the state affairs   72
Hath hither brought.
    All.   We are very sorry for 't.
    Duke. [*To Othello.*] What, in your own part, can
        you say to this?
    Bra. Nothing, but this is so.   75
    Oth. Most potent, grave, and reverend signiors,
My very noble and approv'd good masters,
That I have ta'en away this old man's daughter,
It is most true; true, I have married her:
The very head and front of my offending   80
Hath this extent, no more.   Rude am I in my
        speech,
And little bless'd with the soft phrase of peace;
For since these arms of mine had seven years' pith
Till now, some nine moons wasted, they have us'd
Their dearest action in the tented field,   85
And little of this great world can I speak
More than pertains to feats of broils and battle,
And therefore little shall I grace my cause
In speaking for myself.   Yet, by your gracious
        patience,
I will a round unvarnish'd tale deliver   90
Of my whole course of love — what drugs, what
        charms,
What conjuration, and what mighty magic,
(For such proceeding I am charg'd withal,)
I won his daughter.
    Bra.   A maiden never bold;
Of spirit so still and quiet that her motion   95
Blush'd at herself; and she, in spite of nature,
Of years, of country, credit, everything,
To fall in love with what she fear'd to look on!
It is a judgement maim'd and most imperfect
That will confess perfection so could err   100
Against all rules of nature, and must be driven
To find out practices of cunning hell,
Why this should be.   I therefore vouch again
That with some mixtures powerful o'er the blood,
Or with some dram conjur'd to this effect,   105
He wrought upon her.
    [*Duke.*]   To vouch this is no proof,
Without more wider and more overt test
Than these thin habits and poor likelihoods
Of modern seeming do prefer against him.

    [*1.*] *Sen.* But, Othello, speak.   110
Did you by indirect and forced courses
Subdue and poison this young maid's affections?
Or came it by request and such fair question
As soul to soul affordeth?
    Oth.   I do beseech you,
Send for the lady to the Sagittary,   115
And let her speak of me before her father.
If you do find me foul in her report,
The trust, the office I do hold of you,
Not only take away, but let your sentence
Even fall upon my life.
    Duke.   Fetch Desdemona hither.
                                    [*Exeunt two or three.*
    Oth. Ancient, conduct them; you best know the
        place.   [*Exit Iago.*]   121
And, till she come, as truly as to heaven
I do confess the vices of my blood,
So justly to your grave ears I'll present
How I did thrive in this fair lady's love,   125
And she in mine.
    Duke. Say it, Othello.
    Oth. Her father lov'd me; oft invited me;
Still question'd me the story of my life
From year to year, the battles, sieges, fortunes,   130
That I have pass'd.
I ran it through, even from my boyish days
To the very moment that he bade me tell it;
Wherein I spoke of most disastrous chances,
Of moving accidents by flood and field,   135
Of hair-breadth scapes i' th' imminent deadly
        breach,
Of being taken by the insolent foe
And sold to slavery, of my redemption thence
And portance in my travel's history;
Wherein of antres vast and deserts idle,   140
Rough quarries, rocks, [and] hills whose heads touch
        heaven,
It was my hint to speak, — such was my process, —
And of the Cannibals that each other eat,
The Anthropophagi, and men whose heads
[Do grow] beneath their shoulders.   These to hear
Would Desdemona seriously incline;   146
But still the house-affairs would draw her thence,
Which ever as she could with haste dispatch,
She'd come again, and with a greedy ear
Devour up my discourse: which I observing,   150
Took once a pliant hour, and found good means
To draw from her a prayer of earnest heart
That I would all my pilgrimage dilate,
Whereof by parcels she had something heard,
But not [intentively].   I did consent,   155
And often did beguile her of her tears

---

90. **round**: plain.   95. **motion**: impulses.   106. [*Duke*] Q.   Om. F.   108. **thin habits**: slight semblances.   109. **modern**: ordinary, trivial.   139. **portance**: behavior.   140. **antres**: caves.   **idle**: barren.   141. [**and**] Q.   Om. F.   142. **hint**: occasion.   145. [**Do grow**] Q.   *Grew* F.   **These** Q₂.   *These things* F.   151. **pliant**: convenient.   155. [**intentively**] Q: attentively.   *instinctively* F.

When I did speak of some distressful stroke
That my youth suffer'd. My story being done,
She gave me for my pains a world of [sighs].
She swore, in faith, 'twas strange, 'twas passing
    strange,   160
'Twas pitiful, 'twas wondrous pitiful.
She wish'd she had not heard it; yet she wish'd
That Heaven had made her such a man. She
    thank'd me,
And bade me, if I had a friend that lov'd her,
I should but teach him how to tell my story,   165
And that would woo her. Upon this hint I spake:
She lov'd me for the dangers I had pass'd,
And I lov'd her that she did pity them.
This only is the witchcraft I have us'd.
Here comes the lady; let her witness it.   170

     Enter DESDEMONA, IAGO, *and Attendants.*

  Duke. I think this tale would win my daughter too.
Good Brabantio,
Take up this mangled matter at the best;
Men do their broken weapons rather use
Than their bare hands.
  Bra.   I pray you, hear her speak.
If she confess that she was half the wooer,   176
Destruction on my head if my bad blame
Light on the man! Come hither, gentle mistress.
Do you perceive in all this noble company
Where most you owe obedience?
  Des.   My noble father,
I do perceive here a divided duty.   181
To you I am bound for life and education;
My life and education both do learn me
How to respect you; you are the lord of duty;
I am hitherto your daughter. But here's my hus-
    band;   185
And so much duty as my mother show'd
To you, preferring you before her father,
So much I challenge that I may profess
Due to the Moor, my lord.
  Bra.   God be with you! I have done.
Please it your Grace, on to the state-affairs.   190
I had rather to adopt a child than get it.
Come hither, Moor.
I here do give thee that with all my heart
Which, but thou hast already, with all my heart
I would keep from thee. For your sake, jewel, 195
I am glad at soul I have no other child;
For thy escape would teach me tyranny,
To hang clogs on them. I have done, my lord.
  Duke. Let me speak like yourself, and lay a sen-
    tence,

Which, as a grise or step, may help these lovers 200
[Into your favour.]
When remedies are past, the griefs are ended
By seeing the worst, which late on hopes depended.
To mourn a mischief that is past and gone
Is the next way to draw new mischief on.   205
What cannot be preserv'd when fortune takes,
Patience her injury a mock'ry makes.
The robb'd that smiles steals something from the
    thief;
He robs himself that spends a bootless grief.
  Bra. So let the Turk of Cyprus us beguile;   210
We lose it not, so long as we can smile.
He bears the sentence well that nothing bears
But the free comfort which from thence he hears,
But he bears both the sentence and the sorrow
That, to pay grief, must of poor patience borrow.
These sentences, to sugar or to gall   216
Being strong on both sides, are equivocal.
But words are words; I never yet did hear
That the bruis'd heart was pierced through the
    ear.
I humbly beseech you, proceed to the affairs of
    state.   220
  Duke. The Turk with a most mighty preparation
makes for Cyprus. Othello, the fortitude of the
place is best known to you; and though we have
there a substitute of most allowed sufficiency, yet
opinion, a sovereign mistress of effects, throws a
more safer voice on you. You must therefore be
content to slubber the gloss of your new fortunes
with this more stubborn and boist'rous expedi-
tion.   229
  Oth. The tyrant custom, most grave senators,
Hath made the flinty and steel couch of war
My thrice-driven bed of down. I do agnize
A natural and prompt alacrity
I find in hardness, and do undertake
These present wars against the Ottomites.   235
Most humbly therefore bending to your state,
I crave fit disposition for my wife,
Due reference of place and exhibition,
With such accommodation and besort
As levels with her breeding.
  Duke.   [If you please, 240
Be 't at her father's.]
  Bra.   I'll not have it so.
  Oth. Nor I.
  Des.   Nor I; [I would not] there reside,
To put my father in impatient thoughts
By being in his eye. Most gracious Duke,
To my unfolding lend your prosperous ear;   245

---

159. [sighs] Q. *kisses* F.   166. hint: opportunity (not consciously given). Cf. l. 142.   199. like yourself: as you should.
200. grise: degree.   201. [Into ... favour] Q. Om. F.   216. sentences: maxims.   217. equivocal: equal.   222. fortitude:
strength, fortification.   224. allowed: admitted.   225. sovereign Q. *more sovereign* F.   227. slubber: sully.   232. thrice
driven: thoroughly sifted.   agnize: acknowledge.   238. reference: assignment.   exhibition: provision.   239. besort: company.   240. levels with: befits.   240-41. [If ... father's] Q. *Why at her Fathers?* F.   242. [I ... not] Q. *would I* F.
245. prosperous: propitious.

And let me find a charter in your voice
T' assist my simpleness.

Duke. What would you, Desdemona?

Des. That I [did] love the Moor to live with him,
My downright violence and storm of fortunes 250
May trumpet to the world. My heart's subdu'd
Even to the very quality of my lord.
I saw Othello's visage in his mind,
And to his honours and his valiant parts
Did I my soul and fortunes consecrate. 255
So that, dear lords, if I were left behind,
A moth of peace, and he go to the war,
The rites for [which] I love him are bereft me,
And I a heavy interim shall support
By his dear absence. Let me go with him. 260

Oth. Let her have your voice.
Vouch with me, Heaven, I therefore beg it not
To please the palate of my appetite,
Nor to comply with heat, the young affects
In my defunct and proper satisfaction, 265
But to be free and bounteous to her mind;
And Heaven defend your good souls, that you think
I will your serious and great business scant
When she is with me. No, when light-wing'd toys
Of feather'd Cupid seel with wanton dullness 270
My speculative and offic'd instruments
That my disports corrupt and taint my business,
Let housewives make a skillet of my helm,
And all indign and base adversities
Make head against my estimation! 275

Duke. Be it as you shall privately determine,
Either for her stay or going. Th' affair cries haste,
And speed must answer it.

1. Sen.   You must away to-night.

[Des. To-night, my lord?

Duke.   This night.]

Oth.   With all my heart.

Duke. At nine i' th' morning here we'll meet
again. 280
Othello, leave some officer behind,
And he shall our commission bring to you,
And such things else of quality and respect
As doth import you.

Oth.   So please your Grace, my ancient;
A man he is of honesty and trust. 285
To his conveyance I assign my wife,
With what else needful your good Grace shall think
To be sent after me.

Duke.   Let it be so.
Good-night to every one. *[To Bra.]* And, noble
signior,

If virtue no delighted beauty lack, 290
Your son-in-law is far more fair than black.

1. Sen. Adieu, brave Moor; use Desdemona well.

Bra. Look to her, Moor, if thou hast eyes to see;
She has deceiv'd her father, and may thee.
[Exeunt [Duke, Senators, Officers, etc.].

Oth. My life upon her faith! Honest Iago, 295
My Desdemona must I leave to thee.
I prithee, let thy wife attend on her;
And bring them after in the best advantage.
Come, Desdemona; I have but an hour
Of love, of worldly matters and direction, 300
To spend with thee. We must obey the time.
[Exeunt Othello and Desdemona.

Rod. Iago,—

Iago. What say'st thou, noble heart?

Rod. What will I do, think'st thou?

Iago. Why, go to bed and sleep. 305

Rod. I will incontinently drown myself.

Iago. If thou dost, I shall never love thee after.
Why, thou silly gentleman!

Rod. It is silliness to live when to live is torment;
and then have we a prescription to die when Death is
our physician. 311

Iago. O villanous! I have look'd upon the world
for four times seven years; and since I could distinguish betwixt a benefit and an injury, I never
found man that knew how to love himself. Ere I
would say I would drown myself for the love of a
guinea-hen, I would change my humanity with a
baboon. 318

Rod. What should I do? I confess it is my
shame to be so fond, but it is not in my virtue to
amend it. 321

Iago. Virtue! a fig! 'tis in ourselves that we are
thus or thus. Our bodies are our gardens, to the
which our wills are gardeners; so that if we will plant
nettles or sow lettuce, set hyssop and weed up 325
thyme, supply it with one gender of herbs or distract
it with many, either to have it sterile with idleness
or manured with industry, why, the power and corrigible authority of this lies in our wills. If the
[balance] of our lives had not one scale of reason 330
to poise another of sensuality, the blood and baseness of our natures would conduct us to most preposterous conclusions; but we have reason to cool
our raging motions, our carnal stings, our unbitted
lusts, whereof I take this that you call love to be a
sect or scion. 337

Rod. It cannot be.

Iago. It is merely a lust of the blood and a per-

---

246. **charter:** privilege. 249. **[did]** Q. Om. F. 250. **My...fortunes:** my precipitate assault upon my fortunes. 258.
[which] Q. *why* F. 265. **defunct.** The modern meaning is here excluded, and no convincing explanation has been found.
267. **defend:** forbid. 270. **seel:** blind (from falconry). 271. **My...instruments:** my faculties whose office is to perceive.
274. **indign:** unworthy. 275. **estimation:** reputation. 279. *[Des.* **To-night...night]** Q. Om. F. 284. **import:** concern.
290. **delighted:** delightful. 298. **advantage:** opportunity. 306. **incontinently:** straightway. 325. **hyssop:** fragrant herb.
326. **gender:** kind. 329. **corrigible authority:** corrective power. 330. **[balance]** Q. *braine* F. 335. **motions:** appetites.
337. **sect or scion:** cutting or off-shoot.

mission of the will. Come, be a man! Drown thyself? drown cats and blind puppies! I have profess'd me thy friend, and I confess me knit to thy
deserving with cables of perdurable toughness; I
could never better stead thee than now. Put
money in thy purse; follow thou the wars; defeat 345
thy favour with an usurp'd beard. I say, put
money in thy purse. It cannot be long that Desdemona should continue her love to the Moor, — put
money in thy purse, — nor he his to her. It was a
violent commencement in her, and thou shalt 350
see an answerable sequestration. Put but money
in thy purse. These Moors are changeable in their
wills — fill thy purse with money; — the food that
to him now is as luscious as locusts, shall be to him
shortly as bitter as coloquintida. She must 355
change for youth; when she is sated with his body,
she will find the error of her choice; [she must have
change, she must:] therefore put money in thy
purse. If thou wilt needs damn thyself, do it a
more delicate way than drowning. Make all 360
the money thou canst. If sanctimony and a frail
vow betwixt an erring barbarian and a super-subtle
Venetian be not too hard for my wits and all the
tribe of hell, thou shalt enjoy her; therefore make
money. A pox of drowning thyself! it is clean 365
out of the way. Seek thou rather to be hang'd in
compassing thy joy than to be drown'd and go
without her.

Rod. Wilt thou be fast to my hopes, if I depend
on the issue?   370

Iago. Thou art sure of me. Go, make money.
I had told thee often, and I re-tell thee again and
again, I hate the Moor. My cause is hearted; thine
hath no less reason. Let us be conjunctive in our
revenge against him. If thou canst cuckold 375
him, thou dost thyself a pleasure, me a sport. There
are many events in the womb of time which will be
delivered. Traverse! go, provide thy money. We
will have more of this to-morrow. Adieu.   380

Rod. Where shall we meet i' th' morning?

Iago. At my lodging.

Rod. I'll be with thee betimes.

Iago. Go to; farewell. Do you hear, Roderigo?
[*Rod.* What say you?   386

Iago. No more of drowning, do you hear?

Rod. I am chang'd;] I'll sell all my land. [*Exit.*

Iago. Thus do I ever make my fool my purse;
For I mine own gain'd knowledge should profane
If I would time expend with such a snipe   391
But for my sport and profit. I hate the Moor;

And it is thought abroad that 'twixt my sheets
He has done my office. I know not if 't be true;
But I, for mere suspicion in that kind,   395
Will do as if for surety. He holds me well;
The better shall my purpose work on him.
Cassio's a proper man: let me see now:
To get his place and to plume up my will
In double knavery — How, how? — Let's see: —
After some time, to abuse Othello's ear   401
That he is too familiar with his wife.
He hath a person and a smooth dispose
To be suspected, fram'd to make women false.
The Moor is of a free and open nature,   405
That thinks men honest that but seem to be so,
And will as tenderly be led by th' nose
As asses are.
I have't. It is engend'red. Hell and night
Must bring this monstrous birth to the world's
    light.   [*Exit.* 410

ACT II

Scene I. [*A sea-port in Cyprus. An open
place near the quay.*]

Enter Montano *and two* Gentlemen.

Mon. What from the cape can you discern at sea?

1. Gent. Nothing at all; it is a high-wrought flood.
I cannot, 'twixt the heaven and the main,
Descry a sail.

Mon. Methinks the wind hath spoke aloud at
    land;   5
A fuller blast ne'er shook our battlements.
If it hath ruffian'd so upon the sea,
What ribs of oak, when mountains melt on them,
Can hold the mortise? What shall we hear of this?

2. Gent. A segregation of the Turkish fleet.   10
For do but stand upon the foaming shore,
The chidden billow seems to pelt the clouds;
The wind-shak'd surge, with high and monstrous
    mane,
Seems to cast water on the burning Bear
And quench the guards of th' ever-fixed Pole.   15
I never did like molestation view
On the enchafed flood.

Mon.   If that the Turkish fleet
Be not enshelter'd and embay'd, they are drown'd;
It is impossible to bear it out.

Enter a third Gentleman.

3. Gent. News, lads! our wars are done.   20

---

343. **perdurable**: eternal. 345-46. **defeat thy favour**: disguise thy face. 351. **sequestration**: separation. 354. **locusts**:
the fruit of the carob tree. 355. **coloquintida**: a bitter fruit. 357-58. [she ... she must] Q. Om. F. 369-70. **depend ...
issue**: rely on the outcome. 373. **hearted**: heart-felt. 374. **conjunctive**: united. 379. **Traverse**: forward. 386-88. [*Rod.*
What ... chang'd] Q. Om. F. 391. **snipe**: woodcock, a silly bird. 398. **proper**: handsome. 399-400. **plume ... In**: brace
myself to. 403. **dispose**: disposition.
    Act II, sc. i, 9. **hold the mortise**: hold their joints together. 10. **segregation**: dispersion. 15. **guards**: stars in the Little
Bear in line with the pole star.

The desperate tempest hath so bang'd the Turks,
That their designment halts.   A noble ship of
    Venice
Hath seen a grievous wreck and sufferance
On most part of their fleet.
    Mon. How! is this true?
    3. Gent.   The ship is here put in.
A Veronese, Michael Cassio,   26
Lieutenant to the warlike Moor Othello,
Is come on shore; the Moor himself at sea,
And is in full commission here for Cyprus.
    Mon. I am glad on't; 'tis a worthy governor.   30
    3. Gent. But this same Cassio, though he speak of
    comfort
Touching the Turkish loss, yet he looks sadly
And prays the Moor be safe, for they were parted
With foul and violent tempest.
    Mon.   Pray heavens he be;
For I have serv'd him, and the man commands   35
Like a full soldier.   Let's to the seaside, ho!
As well to see the vessel that's come in
As to throw out our eyes for brave Othello,
Even till we make the main and th' aerial blue
An indistinct regard.
    3. Gent.   Come, let's do so;   40
For every minute is expectancy
Of more arrivance.

            Enter CASSIO.

    Cas. Thanks, you the valiant of this warlike isle,
That so approve the Moor!   O, let the heavens
Give him defence against the elements,   45
For I have lost him on a dangerous sea.
    Mon. Is he well shipp'd?
    Cas. His bark is stoutly timber'd, and his pilot
Of very expert and approv'd allowance;
Therefore my hopes, not surfeited to death,   50
Stand in bold cure.   [*Within,* "A sail, a sail, a sail!"

        Enter a [*fourth* GENTLEMAN].

    Cas. What noise?
    [*4.*] *Gent.* The town is empty; on the brow o' th'
    sea
Stand ranks of people, and they cry, "A sail!"   54
    Cas. My hopes do shape him for the governor.
                                    [*A shot.*
    2. Gent. They do discharge their shot of courtesy.
Our friends at least.
    Cas.   I pray you, sir, go forth,
And give us truth who 'tis that is arriv'd.
    2. Gent. I shall.   [*Exit.*

    Mon. But, good Lieutenant, is your General
    wiv'd?   60
    Cas. Most fortunately.   He hath achiev'd a maid
That paragons description and wild fame;
One that excels the quirks of blazoning pens,
And in th' essential vesture of creation
Does tire the [ingener].

        Re-enter second GENTLEMAN.

                        How now! who has put in?
    2. Gent. 'Tis one Iago, ancient to the general. 66
    Cas. He has had most favourable and happy
    speed.
Tempests themselves, high seas, and howling winds,
The gutter'd rocks and congregated sands,
Traitors ensteep'd to enclog the guiltless keel,   70
As having sense of beauty, do omit
Their mortal natures, letting go safely by
The divine Desdemona.
    Mon.   What is she?
    Cas. She that I spake of, our great captain's cap-
    tain,
Left in the conduct of the bold Iago,   75
Whose footing here anticipates our thoughts
A se'nnight's speed.   Great Jove, Othello guard,
And swell his sail with thine own powerful breath,
That he may bless this bay with his tall ship,
Make love's quick pants in Desdemona's arms,   80
Give renew'd fire to our extinced spirits,
[And bring all Cyprus comfort!]

    Enter DESDEMONA, EMILIA, IAGO, RODERIGO
            [*and Attendants*].

                            O, behold,
The riches of the ship is come on shore!
You men of Cyprus, let her have your knees.
Hail to thee, lady! and the grace of heaven,   85
Before, behind thee, and on every hand,
Enwheel thee round!
    Des.   I thank you, valiant Cassio.
What tidings can you tell [me] of my lord?
    Cas. He is not yet arriv'd; nor know I aught
But that he's well and will be shortly here.   90
    Des. O, but I fear — How lost you company?
    Cas. The great contention of sea and skies
Parted our fellowship. — But, hark! a sail.
            [*Within,* "A sail, a sail!"] [*Guns heard.*]
    2. Gent. They give [their] greeting to the citadel.
This likewise is a friend.
    Cas.   See for the news.   96
                            [*Exit Gentleman.*]

---

23. **sufferance**: disaster.   26. **A Veronese.** In I.i.20 Cassio is called a Florentine.   49. **approv'd allowance**: tested repute.
50–51. **my hopes . . . cure.**   The sense seems to be: "My hopes, though far from being nourished to excess, yet stand a good
chance of being fulfilled."   62. **paragons**: excels.   63. **quirks**: flourishes.   **blazoning**: praising.   64. **essential . . . creation**:
i.e., just as she is, in her essential quality.   65. [**ingener**] (Steevens conj.): inventor (of praise).   *Ingeniver* F.   For *tire the*
[*ingener*] Q reads *beare an excellency.*   69. **gutter'd**: furrowed, jagged.   70. **ensteep'd**: submerged.   72. **mortal**: deadly.
82. [**And . . . comfort**] Q. Om. F.   88. [**me**] Q. Om. F.   95. [**their**] Q. *this* F.

Good ancient, you are welcome. *[To Emilia.]*
    Welcome, mistress.
Let it not gall your patience, good Iago,
That I extend my manners; 'tis my breeding
That gives me this bold show of courtesy.   100
                                    [Kissing her.]
    Iago. Sir, would she give you so much of her lips
As of her tongue she oft bestows on me,
You'd have enough.
    Des.   Alas, she has no speech.
    Iago. In faith, too much;
I find it still, when I have [list] to sleep.   105
Marry, before your ladyship, I grant,
She puts her tongue a little in her heart,
And chides with thinking.
    Emil. You have little cause to say so.
    Iago. Come on, come on; you are pictures out of
    door,   110
Bells in your parlours, wild-cats in your kitchens,
Saints in your injuries, devils being offended,
Players in your housewifery, and housewives in your
    beds.
    Des. O, fie upon thee, slanderer!
    Iago. Nay, it is true, or else I am a Turk.   115
You rise to play and go to bed to work.
    Emil. You shall not write my praise.
    Iago.   No, let me not.
    Des. What wouldst thou write of me, if thou
    shouldst praise me?
    Iago. O gentle lady, do not put me to't;
For I am nothing if not critical.   120
    Des. Come on, assay. — There's one gone to the
    harbour?
    Iago. Ay, madam.
    Des. I am not merry; but I do beguile
The thing I am by seeming otherwise. —
Come, how wouldst thou praise me?   125
    Iago. I am about it; but indeed my invention
Comes from my pate as birdlime does from frieze;
It plucks out brains and all. But my Muse labours,
And thus she is deliver'd:
If she be fair and wise, fairness and wit,   130
The one 's for use, the other useth it.
    Des. Well prais'd! How if she be black and
    witty?
    Iago. If she be black, and thereto have a wit,
She'll find a white that shall her blackness fit.
    Des. Worse and worse.   135
    Emil. How if fair and foolish?
    Iago. She never yet was foolish that was fair;
For even her folly help'd her to an heir.

    Des. These are old fond paradoxes to make fools
laugh i' th' alehouse. What miserable praise hast
thou for her that's foul and foolish?   141
    Iago. There's none so foul and foolish thereunto,
But does foul pranks which fair and wise ones do.
    Des. O heavy ignorance! thou praisest the worst
best. But what praise couldst thou bestow on a
deserving woman indeed, one that, in the authority
of her merit, did justly put on the vouch of very
malice itself?   148
    Iago. She that was ever fair and never proud,
Had tongue at will and yet was never loud,
Never lack'd gold and yet went never gay,
Fled from her wish and yet said, "Now I may;"
She that being ang'red, her revenge being nigh,
Bade her wrong stay and her displeasure fly;
She that in wisdom never was so frail   155
To change the cod's head for the salmon's tail;
She that could think and ne'er disclose her mind,
See suitors following and not look behind,
She was a wight, if ever such wights were, —
    Des. To do what?   160
    Iago. To suckle fools and chronicle small beer.
    Des. O most lame and impotent conclusion! Do
not learn of him, Emilia, though he be thy husband.
How say you, Cassio? Is he not a most profane and
liberal counsellor?   165
    Cas. He speaks home, madam. You may relish
him more in the soldier than in the scholar.
    Iago. *[Aside.]* He takes her by the palm; ay,
well said, whisper. With as little a web as this will
I ensnare as great a fly as Cassio. Ay, smile   170
upon her, do; I will gyve thee in thine own courtship.
— You say true; 'tis so, indeed. — If such tricks as
these strip you out of your lieutenantry, it had been
better you had not kiss'd your three fingers so oft,
which now again you are most apt to play the sir   175
in. Very good; well kiss'd! an excellent curtsy! 'Tis
so, indeed. Yet again your fingers to your lips?
Would they were clyster-pipes for your sake!
(Trumpet within.) — The Moor! I know his
trumpet.   180
    Cas. 'Tis truly so.
    Des. Let's meet him and receive him.
    Cas. Lo, where he comes!

            Enter OTHELLO *and Attendants.*

    Oth. O my fair warrior!
    Des.   My dear Othello!
    Oth. It gives me wonder great as my content   185
To see you here before me. O my soul's joy!

---

105. **[list]** Q: inclination. *leave* F. 108. **with thinking**: i.e., without words. 110-13. **Come ... beds.** So Q. Prose in F.
111. **Bells**: i.e., clanging tongues. 112. **Saints ... injuries**: i.e., you offend sanctimoniously. 113. **Players**: triflers.
housewives: hussies. 126-29. **I am ... deliver'd.** So Q. Prose in F. 132. **black**: brunette. 134. **white**: with a pun on
wight (person). 147-48. **put ... vouch**: compel the testimony. 156. **To ... tail**: to take the worthless in exchange for the
worthy. 161. **chronicle small beer**: i.e., to keep petty accounts. 165. **liberal**: free-spoken. 169. **well said**: well done.
171. **gyve**: fetter, entangle. **courtship**: courtesy. 175. **sir**: gentleman. 178. **clyster-pipes**: syringes.

If after every tempest come such calms,
May the winds blow till they have waken'd
  death!
And let the labouring bark climb hills of seas
Olympus-high, and duck again as low   190
As hell's from heaven! If it were now to die,
'Twere now to be most happy; for, I fear,
My soul hath her content so absolute
That not another comfort like to this
Succeeds in unknown fate.
  Des.   The heavens forbid 195
But that our loves and comforts should increase,
Even as our days do grow!
  Oth.   Amen to that, sweet powers!
I cannot speak enough of this content;
It stops me here; it is too much of joy.
And this, and this, the greatest discords be   200
                                  [*Kissing her.*
That e'er our hearts shall make!
  Iago. [*Aside.*] O, you are well tun'd now!
But I'll set down the pegs that make this music,
As honest as I am.
  Oth.   Come, let us to the castle.
News, friends: our wars are done, the Turks are
  drown'd.
How does my old acquaintance of this isle?   205
Honey, you shall be well desir'd in Cyprus;
I have found great love amongst them. O my sweet,
I prattle out of fashion, and I dote
In mine own comforts. I prithee, good Iago,
Go to the bay and disembark my coffers.   210
Bring thou the master to the citadel;
He is a good one, and his worthiness
Does challenge much respect. Come, Desdemona,
Once more, well met at Cyprus.   214
        [*Exeunt Othello, Desdemona [and Attendants].*
  Iago. Do thou meet me presently at the harbour.
— Come [hither]. If thou be'st valiant, — as, they
say, base men being in love have then a nobility in
their natures more than is native to them, — list me.
The lieutenant to-night watches on the court of
guard; — first, I must tell thee this: Desdemona is
directly in love with him.   221
  Rod. With him! why, 'tis not possible.
  Iago. Lay thy finger thus, and let thy soul be instructed. Mark me with what violence she first
lov'd the Moor, but for bragging and telling her 225
fantastical lies. To love him still for prating, —
let not thy discreet heart think it. Her eye must be
fed; and what delight shall she have to look on the
devil? When the blood is made dull with the act of
sport, there should be, [again] to inflame it and 230
to give satiety a fresh appetite, loveliness in favour,
sympathy in years, manners, and beauties; all

which the Moor is defective in. Now, for want of
these requir'd conveniences, her delicate tenderness
will find itself abus'd, begin to heave the gorge, 235
disrelish and abhor the Moor. Very nature will instruct her in it and compel her to some second
choice. Now, sir, this granted, — as it is a most
pregnant and unforc'd position — who stands so
eminent in the degree of this fortune as Cassio 240
does? a knave very voluble; no further conscionable than in putting on the mere form of civil and
humane seeming, for the better compassing of his
salt and most hidden loose affection? Why, none;
why, none; a slipper and subtle knave, a finder 245
of occasion, that has an eye can stamp and counterfeit advantages, though true advantage never present itself; a devilish knave. Besides, the knave is
handsome, young, and hath all those requisites 250
in him that folly and green minds look after; a pestilent complete knave, and the woman hath found him
already.
  Rod. I cannot believe that in her; she's full of
most bless'd condition.   255
  Iago. Bless'd fig's-end! The wine she drinks is
made of grapes. If she had been bless'd, she would
never have lov'd the Moor. Bless'd pudding!
Didst thou not see her paddle with the palm of his
hand? Didst not mark that?   260
  Rod. Yes, that I did; but that was but courtesy.
  Iago. Lechery, by this hand; an index and
obscure prologue to the history of lust and foul
thoughts. They met so near with their lips
that their breaths embrac'd together. Villan-   265
ous thoughts, Roderigo! When these [mutualities]
so marshal the way, hard at hand comes the master
and main exercise, th' incorporate conclusion.
Pish! But, sir, be you rul'd by me; I have   270
brought you from Venice. Watch you to-night; for
the command, I'll lay 't upon you. Cassio knows
you not. I'll not be far from you. Do you find
some occasion to anger Cassio, either by speaking
too loud, or tainting his discipline; or from what 275
other course you please, which the time shall more
favourably minister.
  Rod. Well?
  Iago. Sir, he's rash and very sudden in choler,
and haply may strike at you. Provoke him,
that he may; for even out of that will I cause   280
these of Cyprus to mutiny, whose qualification shall
come into no true taste again but by the displanting
of Cassio. So shall you have a shorter journey to
your desires by the means I shall then have to 285
prefer them; and the impediment most profitably
removed, without the which there were no expectation of our prosperity.

206. **desir'd**: beloved. 211. **master**: ship's master. 216. **[hither]** Q. *thither* F. 230. **[again]** Q. *a game* F. 235.
heave the gorge: be nauseated. 239. **pregnant**: evident. 241. **conscionable**: conscientious. 244. **salt**: lewd. 245. **slipper**:
slippery. 255. **condition**: character. 266. **[mutualities]** Q: exchanges. *mutabilities* F. 281. **qualification**: appeasement.

Rod. I will do this, if you can bring it to any
opportunity. 290

Iago. I warrant thee. Meet me by and by at the
citadel; I must fetch his necessaries ashore. Farewell.

Rod. Adieu. [*Exit.*

Iago. That Cassio loves her, I do well believe 't;
That she loves him, 'tis apt and of great credit; 296
The Moor, howbeit that I endure him not,
Is of a constant, loving, noble nature,
And I dare think he'll prove to Desdemona
A most dear husband. Now, I do love her too; 300
Not out of absolute lust, though peradventure
I stand accountant for as great a sin,
But partly led to diet my revenge,
For that I do suspect the lusty Moor
Hath leap'd into my seat; the thought whereof 305
Doth, like a poisonous mineral, gnaw my inwards;
And nothing can or shall content my soul
Till I am even'd with him, wife for [wife];
Or failing so, yet that I put the Moor
At least into a jealousy so strong 310
That judgement cannot cure. Which thing to do,
If this poor trash of Venice, whom I [trash]
For his quick hunting, stand the putting on,
I'll have our Michael Cassio on the hip,
Abuse him to the Moor in the [rank] garb — 315
For I fear Cassio with my night-cap too —
Make the Moor thank me, love me, and reward me
For making him egregiously an ass
And practising upon his peace and quiet
Even to madness. 'Tis here, but yet confus'd; 320
Knavery's plain face is never seen till us'd. [*Exit.*

SCENE II. [*A street.*]

Enter Othello's HERALD, *with a proclamation*
[*People following*].

Her. It is Othello's pleasure, our noble and
valiant general, that, upon certain tidings now
arriv'd importing the mere perdition of the Turkish
fleet, every man put himself into triumph; some
to dance, some to make bonfires, each man to 5
what sport and revels his [addiction] leads him; for,
beside these beneficial news, it is the celebration of
his nuptial. So much was his pleasure should be
proclaimed. All offices are open, and there is full
liberty of feasting from this present hour of five 10
till the bell have told eleven. [Heaven] bless the isle
of Cyprus and our noble general Othello! [*Exeunt.*

[SCENE III. *A hall in the castle.*]

Enter OTHELLO, DESDEMONA, CASSIO, *and*
Attendants.

Oth. Good Michael, look you to the guard to-
night.
Let's teach ourselves that honourable stop,
Not to outsport discretion.

Cas. Iago hath direction what to do;
But, notwithstanding, with my personal eye 5
Will I look to't.

Oth. Iago is most honest.
Michael, good-night; to-morrow with your earliest
Let me have speech with you. [*To Desdemona.*]
Come, my dear love,
The purchase made, the fruits are to ensue;
That profit's yet to come 'tween me and you. 10
Good-night.
[*Exeunt [Othello, Desdemona, and Attend-*
ants].

Enter IAGO.

Cas. Welcome, Iago; we must to the watch.

Iago. Not this hour, Lieutenant; 'tis not yet ten
o' th' clock. Our general cast us thus early for the
love of his Desdemona; who let us not therefore
blame. He hath not yet made wanton the night
with her; and she is sport for Jove. 17

Cas. She's a most exquisite lady.

Iago. And, I'll warrant her, full of game.

Cas. Indeed, she's a most fresh and delicate
creature. 21

Iago. What an eye she has! Methinks it sounds
a parley to provocation.

Cas. An inviting eye; and yet methinks right
modest.

Iago. And when she speaks, is it not an alarum to
love? 27

Cas. She is indeed perfection.

Iago. Well, happiness to their sheets! Come,
lieutenant, I have a stoup of wine; and here without
are a brace of Cyprus gallants that would fain have
a measure to the health of black Othello. 33

Cas. Not to-night, good Iago. I have very poor
and unhappy brains for drinking; I could well wish
courtesy would invent some other custom of entertainment.

Iago. O, they are our friends. But one cup; I'll
drink for you. 39

Cas. I have drunk but one cup to-night, and that

296. **apt:** natural. **of ... credit:** most credible. 308. **[wife]** Q. *wist* F. 312. **trash:** worthless fellow. **[trash]** (Steevens):
check. *trace* F. *crush* Q. 313. **putting on:** inciting. 315. **[rank]** Q: gross. *right* F. **garb:** manner. 319. **practising**
upon: plotting against.
Sc. ii, 3. **mere:** utter. 6. **[addiction]** Q₂: inclination. *addition* F. *minde* Q. 9. **offices:** kitchens, etc. 11. **[Heaven]** Q
Om. F.
Sc. iii, 14. **cast:** dismissed.

was craftily qualified too, and, behold, what innova-
tion it makes here. I am unfortunate in the infirm-
ity, and dare not task my weakness with any
more.   44
  Iago. What, man! 'tis a night of revels. The
gallants desire it.
  Cas. Where are they?
  Iago. Here at the door; I pray you, call them in.
  Cas. I'll do't; but it dislikes me.   [*Exit.*
  Iago. If I can fasten but one cup upon him,   50
With that which he hath drunk to-night already,
He'll be as full of quarrel and offence
As my young mistress' dog. Now, my sick fool
    Roderigo,
Whom love hath turn'd almost the wrong side out,
To Desdemona hath to-night carous'd   55
Potations pottle-deep; and he's to watch.
Three [lads] of Cyprus, noble swelling spirits
That hold their honours in a wary distance,
The very elements of this warlike isle,
Have I to-night fluster'd with flowing cups,   60
And they watch too. Now, 'mongst this flock of
    drunkards
Am I to put our Cassio in some action
That may offend the isle. But here they come.

  Re-enter CASSIO; *with him* MONTANO *and*
  GENTLEMEN [*Servants follow with wine*].

If consequence do but approve my dream,
My boat sails freely, both with wind and stream. 65
  Cas. 'Fore [God], they have given me a rouse
already.
  Mon. Good faith, a little one; not past a pint, as I
am a soldier.
  Iago. Some wine, ho!   70
[*Sings.*] "And let me the canakin clink, clink;
    And let me the canakin clink.
      A soldier's a man;
      O, man's life's but a span;
    Why, then, let a soldier drink."   75
Some wine, boys!
  Cas. 'Fore [God], an excellent song.
  Iago. I learn'd it in England, where, indeed, they
are most potent in potting; your Dane, your Ger-
man, and your swag-belli'd Hollander — Drink, ho!
— are nothing to your English.   81
  Cas. Is your Englishman so exquisite in his
drinking?
  Iago. Why, he drinks you, with facility, your
Dane dead drunk; he sweats not to overthrow your
Almain; he gives your Hollander a vomit ere the
next pottle can be fill'd.   87
  Cas. To the health of our general!

  Mon. I am for it, Lieutenant; and I'll do you
justice.   90
  Iago. O sweet England!
  "King Stephen was and-a worthy peer,
    His breeches cost him but a crown;
  He held them sixpence all too dear,
    With that he call'd the tailor lown.   95

  "He was a wight of high renown,
    And thou art but of low degree.
  'Tis pride that pulls the country down;
    And take thy auld cloak about thee."
Some wine, ho!   100
  Cas. Why, this is a more exquisite song than the
other.
  Iago. Will you hear 't again?
  Cas. No; for I hold him to be unworthy of his
place that does those things. Well, [God's] above
all; and there be souls must be saved, and there be
souls must not be saved.   107
  Iago. It's true, good Lieutenant.
  Cas. For mine own part — no offence to the
general, nor any man of quality — I hope to be
saved.   111
  Iago. And so do I too, Lieutenant.
  Cas. Ay, but, by your leave, not before me; the
lieutenant is to be saved before the ancient. Let's
have no more of this; let's to our affairs. —   115
[God] forgive us our sins! — Gentlemen, let's look to
our business. Do not think, gentlemen, I am drunk.
This is my ancient; this is my right hand, and this
is my left. I am not drunk now; I can stand well
enough, and I speak well enough.   120
  Gent. Excellent well.
  Cas. Why, very well then; you must not think
then that I am drunk.   [*Exit.*
  Mon. To the platform, masters; come, let's set
the watch.   125
  Iago. You see this fellow that is gone before:
He is a soldier fit to stand by Cæsar
And give direction; and do but see his vice.
'Tis to his virtue a just equinox,
The one as long as th' other; 'tis pity of him.   130
I fear the trust Othello puts him in,
On some odd time of his infirmity,
Will shake this island.
  Mon.   But is he often thus?
  Iago. 'Tis evermore his prologue to his sleep.
He'll watch the horologe a double set   135
If drink rock not his cradle.
  Mon.   It were well
The general were put in mind of it.
Perhaps he sees it not; or his good nature

---

  41. **craftily qualified:** slyly diluted. 49. **it dislikes me:** I don't want to. 56. **pottle-deep:** to the bottom of the tankard.
57. **[lads]** Q. *else* F. 58. **hold...distance:** i.e., are quick to quarrel. 59. **very elements:** true representatives. 66.
rouse: bumper. 86. **Almain:** German. 95. **lown:** fellow, rascal. 129. **equinox:** counterpart, equivalent. 135. **horologe...set:** clock twice around.

Prizes the virtue that appears in Cassio,
And looks not on his evils. Is not this true?   140

Enter RODERIGO.

Iago. [*Aside to him.*] How now, Roderigo!
I pray you, after the lieutenant; go.
                                            [*Exit Roderigo.*
Mon. And 'tis great pity that the noble Moor
Should hazard such a place as his own second
With one of an ingraft infirmity.   145
It were an honest action to say
So to the Moor.
Iago.   Not I, for this fair island.
I do love Cassio well; and would do much
To cure him of this evil. — But, hark! what noise?
            [*Cry within: "Help! help!"*]

Re-enter CASSIO, *pursuing* RODERIGO.

Cas. 'Zounds, you rogue! you rascal!
Mon.   What's the matter, Lieutenant?   150
Cas. A knave teach me my duty!
I'll beat the knave into a twiggen bottle.
Rod. Beat me!
Cas.   Dost thou prate, rogue?
                                            [*Striking Roderigo.*]
Mon.   Nay, good Lieutenant;
                                            [*Staying him.*]
I pray you, sir, hold your hand.
Cas.   Let me go, sir,
Or I'll knock you o'er the mazzard.
Mon.   Come, come, you're drunk.   155
Cas. Drunk!   [*They fight.*
Iago. [*Aside to Roderigo.*] Away, I say; go out,
    and cry a mutiny.   [*Exit Roderigo.*
Nay, good Lieutenant, — [God's will], gentle-
    men; —
Help, ho! — Lieutenant, — sir, — Montano, —
    [sir]; —
Help, masters! — Here's a goodly watch indeed!
                                            [*Bell rings.*
Who's that which rings the bell? — Diablo, ho!   160
The town will rise. Fie, fie, Lieutenant, [hold]!
You will be sham'd for ever.

Re-enter OTHELLO *and Attendants.*

Oth.   What is the matter here?
Mon. ['Zounds], I bleed still; I am hurt to the
    death. He dies!   165
Oth. Hold, for your lives!
Iago. Hold, ho! Lieutenant, — sir, — Mon-
    tano, — gentlemen, —
Have you forgot all [sense of place] and duty?
Hold! the general speaks to you; hold, for shame!

Oth. Why, how now, ho! from whence ariseth
    this?
Are we turn'd Turks, and to ourselves do that   170
Which Heaven hath forbid the Ottomites?
For Christian shame, put by this barbarous brawl.
He that stirs next to carve for his own rage
Holds his soul light; he dies upon his motion.
Silence that dreadful bell; it frights the isle   175
From her propriety. What is the matter, masters?
Honest Iago, that looks dead with grieving,
Speak, who began this? On thy love, I charge thee.
Iago. I do not know. Friends all but now, even
    now,
In quarter, and in terms like bride and groom   180
Devesting them for bed; and then, but now —
As if some planet had unwitted men —
Swords out, and tilting one at other's breast,
In opposition bloody. I cannot speak
Any beginning to this peevish odds;   185
And would in action glorious I had lost
Those legs that brought me to a part of it!
Oth. How comes it, Michael, you are thus forgot?
Cas. I pray you, pardon me; I cannot speak.
Oth. Worthy Montano, you were wont to be
    civil;   190
The gravity and stillness of your youth
The world hath noted, and your name is great
In mouths of wisest censure. What's the matter
That you unlace your reputation thus,
And spend your rich opinion for the name   195
Of a night-brawler? Give me answer to it.
Mon. Worthy Othello, I am hurt to danger.
Your officer, Iago, can inform you —
While I spare speech, which something now offends
    me —
Of all that I do know; nor know I aught   200
By me that's said or done amiss this night,
Unless self-charity be sometimes a vice,
And to defend ourselves it be a sin
When violence assails us.
Oth.   Now, by heaven,
My blood begins my safer guides to rule;   205
And passion, having my best judgement collied,
Assays to lead the way. If I once stir
Or do but lift this arm, the best of you
Shall sink in my rebuke. Give me to know
How this foul rout began, who set it on;   210
And he that is approv'd in this offence,
Though he had twinn'd with me, both at a birth,
Shall lose me. What! in a town of war,
Yet wild, the people's hearts brimful of fear,
To manage private and domestic quarrel,   215
In night, and on the court and guard of safety!

152. **twiggen:** wicker-covered. 155. **mazzard:** head. 157. [God's will] Q. *Alas* F. 158. [sir] Q. Om. F. 161. [hold]
Q. Om. F. 167. [sense of place] (Hanmer). *place of sense* QF. 173. **carve . . . rage:** act on his own impulse. 180.
quarter: peace. 185. **peevish odds:** stupid quarrel. 193. **censure:** judgment. 195. **opinion:** reputation. 199. **offends:**
pains. 206. **collied:** darkened. 211. **approv'd:** found guilty. 215. **manage:** carry on.

'Tis monstrous. Iago, who began 't?
   Mon. If partially affin'd, or leagu'd in office,
Thou dost deliver more or less than truth,
Thou art no soldier.
   Iago.   Touch me not so near.   220
I had rather have this tongue cut from my mouth
Than it should do offence to Michael Cassio;
Yet, I persuade myself, to speak the truth
Shall nothing wrong him. [Thus] it is, General:
Montano and myself being in speech,   225
There comes a fellow crying out for help;
And Cassio following him with determin'd sword
To execute upon him. Sir, this gentleman
Steps in to Cassio and entreats his pause;
Myself the crying fellow did pursue,   230
Lest by his clamour — as it so fell out —
The town might fall in fright. He, swift of foot,
Outran my purpose; and I return'd the rather
For that I heard the clink and fall of swords,
And Cassio high in oath; which till to-night   235
I ne'er might say before. When I came back —
For this was brief — I found them close together,
At blow and thrust; even as again they were
When you yourself did part them.
More of this matter cannot I report.   240
But men are men; the best sometimes forget.
Though Cassio did some little wrong to him,
As men in rage strike those that wish them best,
Yet surely Cassio, I believe, receiv'd
From him that fled some strange indignity   245
Which patience could not pass.
   Oth.   I know, Iago,
Thy honesty and love doth mince this matter,
Making it light to Cassio. Cassio, I love thee;
But never more be officer of mine.

     Re-enter DESDEMONA, *attended.*

Look, if my gentle love be not rais'd up!   250
I'll make thee an example.
   Des.   What's the matter, dear?
   Oth. All's well [now], sweeting; come away to bed.
Sir, for your hurts, myself will be your surgeon. —
Lead him off.   [*To Montano, who is led off.*]
Iago, look with care about the town,   255
And silence those whom this vile brawl distracted.
Come, Desdemona; 'tis the soldiers' life
To have their balmy slumbers wak'd with strife.
         [*Exeunt all but Iago and Cassio.*
   Iago. What, are you hurt, Lieutenant?
   Cas. Ay, past all surgery.   260
   Iago. Marry, God forbid!
   Cas. Reputation, reputation, reputation! O,
I have lost my reputation! I have lost the im-
mortal part of myself, and what remains is bestial.
My reputation, Iago, my reputation!   265

   Iago. As I am an honest man, I thought you had
received some bodily wound; there is more sense in
that than in reputation. Reputation is an idle
and most false imposition; oft got without merit,
and lost without deserving. You have lost no   270
reputation at all, unless you repute yourself such a
loser. What, man! there are more ways to recover
the general again. You are but now cast in his
mood, a punishment more in policy than in malice;
even so as one would beat his offenceless dog to affright an imperious lion. Sue to him again, and he's
yours.   277
   Cas. I will rather sue to be despis'd than to deceive so good a commander with so slight, so
drunken, and so indiscreet an officer. Drunk?
and speak parrot? and squabble? swagger? swear?
and discourse fustian with one's own shadow? O
thou invisible spirit of wine, if thou hast no name
to be known by, let us call thee devil!   284
   Iago. What was he that you follow'd with your
sword? What had he done to you?
   Cas. I know not.
   Iago. Is't possible?   288
   Cas. I remember a mass of things, but nothing
distinctly; a quarrel, but nothing wherefore. O
[God], that men should put an enemy in their
mouths to steal away their brains! That we should,
with joy, pleasance, revel, and applause, transform
ourselves into beasts!   294
   Iago. Why, but you are now well enough. How
came you thus recovered?
   Cas. It hath pleas'd the devil drunkenness to give
place to the devil wrath. One unperfectness shows
me another, to make me frankly despise myself.   300
   Iago. Come, you are too severe a moraler. As
the time, the place, and the condition of this country stands, I could heartily wish this had not befallen; but since it is as it is, mend it for your own
good.   305
   Cas. I will ask him for my place again; he shall
tell me I am a drunkard! Had I as many mouths
as Hydra, such an answer would stop them all.
To be now a sensible man, by and by a fool, and
presently a beast! O strange! Every inordinate
cup is unbless'd and the ingredient is a devil.   312
   Iago. Come, come, good wine is a good familiar
creature, if it be well us'd; exclaim no more against
it. And, good Lieutenant, I think you think I love
you.   316
   Cas. I have well approved it, sir. I drunk!
   Iago. You or any man living may be drunk at a
time, man. [I'll] tell you what you shall do. Our
general's wife is now the general; — I may say   320
so in this respect, for that he hath devoted and
given up himself to the contemplation, mark, and

[denotement] of her parts and graces; — confess yourself freely to her; importune her help to put you in your place again. She is of so free, so kind, so apt, so blessed a disposition, she holds 325 it a vice in her goodness not to do more than she is requested. This broken joint between you and her husband entreat her to splinter; and, my fortunes against any lay worth naming, this crack of your love shall grow stronger than it was before. 331

Cas. You advise me well.

Iago. I protest, in the sincerity of love and honest kindness. 334

Cas. I think it freely; and betimes in the morning I will beseech the virtuous Desdemona to undertake for me. I am desperate of my fortunes if they check me [here].

Iago. You are in the right. Good-night, lieutenant; I must to the watch. 340

Cas. Good-night, honest Iago. [*Exit.*

Iago. And what's he then that says I play the villain?
When this advice is free I give and honest,
Probal to thinking and indeed the course
To win the Moor again? For 'tis most easy 345
Th' inclining Desdemona to subdue
In any honest suit; she's fram'd as fruitful
As the free elements. And then for her
To win the Moor, [were't] to renounce his baptism,
All seals and symbols of redeemed sin, 350
His soul is so enfetter'd to her love,
That she may make, unmake, do what she list,
Even as her appetite shall play the god
With his weak function. How am I then a villain
To counsel Cassio to this parallel course, 355
Directly to his good? Divinity of hell!
When devils will the blackest sins put on,
They do suggest at first with heavenly shows,
As I do now; for whiles this honest fool
Plies Desdemona to repair his fortune 360
And she for him pleads strongly to the Moor,
I'll pour this pestilence into his ear,
That she repeals him for her body's lust;
And by how much she strives to do him good,
She shall undo her credit with the Moor. 365
So will I turn her virtue into pitch,
And out of her own goodness make the net
That shall enmesh them all.

Re-enter RODERIGO.

How now, Roderigo!

Rod. I do follow here in the chase, not like a hound that hunts, but one that fills up the cry. 370
My money is almost spent; I have been to-night

exceedingly well cudgell'd; and I think the issue will be, I shall have so much experience for my pains; and so, with no money at all and a little more wit, return again to Venice. 375

Iago. How poor are they that have not patience!
What wound did ever heal but by degrees?
Thou know'st we work by wit, and not by witchcraft;
And wit depends on dilatory time.
Does't not go well? Cassio hath beaten thee, 380
And thou, by that small hurt, hast cashier'd Cassio.
Though other things grow fair against the sun,
Yet fruits that blossom first will first be ripe.
Content thyself a while. In troth, 'tis morning;
Pleasure and action make the hours seem short.
Retire thee; go where thou art billeted. 386
Away, I say; thou shalt know more hereafter.
Nay, get thee gone. [*Exit Roderigo.*] Two things are to be done:
My wife must move for Cassio to her mistress;
I'll set her on; 390
Myself a while to draw the Moor apart,
And bring him jump when he may Cassio find
Soliciting his wife. Ay, that's the way;
Dull not device by coldness and delay. [*Exit.*

ACT III

SCENE I. [*Cyprus before the castle.*]

Enter CASSIO, *with* MUSICIANS.

Cas. Masters, play here; I will content your pains;
Something that's brief; and bid "Good morrow, general." [*They play.*

Enter CLOWN.

Clo. Why, masters, have your instruments been in Naples, that they speak i' th' nose thus?

1. Mus. How, sir, how? 5

Clo. Are these, I pray you, wind-instruments?

1. Mus. Ay, marry, are they, sir.

Clo. O, thereby hangs a tail.

1. Mus. Whereby hangs a tale, sir? 9

Clo. Marry, sir, by many a wind-instrument that I know. But, masters, here's money for you; and the General so likes your music, that he desires you, for love's sake, to make no more noise with it.

1. Mus. Well, sir, we will not. 15

Clo. If you have any music that may not be heard, to't again; but, as they say, to hear music the General does not greatly care.

---

322. [denotement] Q₂. *devotement* QF. 328. **splinter:** bind with splints. 330. **lay:** wager. 338. **[here]** Q. Om. F. 344. **Probal:** probable. 347. **fruitful:** generous. 349. **[were't]** Q. *were* F. 354. **function:** mental faculties. 357. **put on:** incite. 370. **cry:** pack. 392. **jump:** at the precise moment.
Act III, sc. i, 1. **content:** requite.

1. Mus. We have none such, sir.

Clo. Then put up your pipes in your bag, for
I'll away. Go, vanish into air, away!   21
                          [Exeunt Musicians.

Cas. Dost thou hear mine honest friend?

Clo. No, I hear not your honest friend; I hear
you.   24

Cas. Prithee, keep up thy quillets. There's a
poor piece of gold for thee. If the gentlewoman
that attends the [General's wife] be stirring, tell her
there's one Cassio entreats her a little favour of
speech. Wilt thou do this?

Clo. She is stirring, sir. If she will stir hither, I
shall seem to notify unto her.   31

Cas. [Do, good my friend.]   *[Exit Clown.*

Enter IAGO.

                In happy time, Iago.

Iago. You have not been a-bed, then?

Cas. Why, no; the day had broke
Before we parted. I have made bold, Iago,   35
To send in to your wife. My suit to her
Is that she will to virtuous Desdemona
Procure me some access.

Iago.   I'll send her to you presently;
And I'll devise a mean to draw the Moor
Out of the way, that your converse and business   40
May be more free.

Cas. I humbly thank you for't.   *[Exit Iago.]*
    I never knew
A Florentine more kind and honest.

Enter EMILIA.

Emil. Good morrow, good Lieutenant. I am
    sorry
For your displeasure; but all will sure be well.   45
The General and his wife are talking of it,
And she speaks for you stoutly. The Moor replies
That he you hurt is of great fame in Cyprus
And great affinity, and that in wholesome wisdom
He might not but refuse you; but he protests he
    loves you,   50
And needs no other suitor but his likings
[To take the safest occasion by the front]
To bring you in again.

Cas.   Yet, I beseech you,
If you think fit, or that it may be done,
Give me advantage of some brief discourse   55
With Desdemon alone.

Emil.   Pray you, come in.
I will bestow you where you shall have time

To speak your bosom freely.

Cas.   I am much bound to you.
                          [Exeunt.

SCENE II. *[A room in the castle.]*

Enter OTHELLO, IAGO, *and* GENTLEMEN.

Oth. These letters give, Iago, to the pilot;
And by him do my duties to the Senate.
That done, I will be walking on the works;
Repair there to me.

Iago.   Well, my good lord, I'll do't.

Oth. This fortification, gentlemen, shall we
    see't?   5

Gent. We'll wait upon your lordship.   *[Exeunt.*

SCENE III. *[The garden of the castle.]*

Enter DESDEMONA, CASSIO, *and* EMILIA.

Des. Be thou assur'd, good Cassio, I will do
All my abilities in thy behalf.

Emil. Good madam, do. I warrant it grieves my
    husband
As if the cause were his.

Des. O, that's an honest fellow. Do not doubt,
    Cassio,   5
But I will have my lord and you again
As friendly as you were.

Cas.   Bounteous madam,
Whatever shall become of Michael Cassio,
He's never anything but your true servant.

Des. I know 't; I thank you. You do love my
    lord;   10
You have known him long; and be you well assur'd
He shall in strangeness stand no farther off
Than in a politic distance.

Cas.   Ay, but, lady,
That policy may either last so long,
Or feed upon such nice and waterish diet,   15
Or breed itself so out of circumstances,
That, I being absent and my place supplied,
My general will forget my love and service.

Des. Do not doubt that; before Emilia here
I give thee warrant of thy place. Assure thee,   20
If I do vow a friendship, I'll perform it
To the last article. My lord shall never rest;
I'll watch him tame, and talk him out of patience;
His bed shall seem a school, his board a shrift;
I'll intermingle everything he does   25
With Cassio's suit. Therefore be merry, Cassio;
For thy solicitor shall rather die
Than give thy cause away.

22. **hear** Q. *hear me* F. 25. **quillets:** quibbles. 27. **[General's wife]** Q. *general* F. 32. **[Do … friend]** Q. Om. F. 45.
displeasure: disgrace. 49. **affinity:** connections. 52. **[To … front]** Q. Om. F. **front:** forelock.
    Sc. ii, 3. **works:** fortifications.
    Sc. iii, 12. **strangeness:** aloofness. 19. **doubt:** fear. 23. **watch him tame:** keep him awake till he gives in. 24. **shrift:**
confessional.

Enter OTHELLO *and* IAGO.

Emil. Madam, here comes my lord.

Cas. Madam, I'll take my leave.   30

Des. Why, stay, and hear me speak.

Cas. Madam, not now; I am very ill at ease,
Unfit for mine own purposes.

Des. Well, do your discretion.   [*Exit Cassio.*

Iago. Ha! I like not that.

Oth.   What dost thou say?

Iago. Nothing, my lord; or if — I know not
what.   36

Oth. Was not that Cassio parted from my wife?

Iago. Cassio, my lord! No, sure, I cannot
think it,
That he would steal away so guilty-like,
Seeing your coming.

Oth.   I do believe 'twas he.   40

Des. How now, my lord!
I have been talking with a suitor here,
A man that languishes in your displeasure.

Oth. Who is't you mean?

Des. Why, your lieutenant, Cassio. Good my
lord,   45
If I have any grace or power to move you,
His present reconciliation take;
For if he be not one that truly loves you,
That errs in ignorance and not in cunning,
I have no judgement in an honest face.   50
I prithee, call him back.

Oth.   Went he hence now?

Des. Yes, faith; so humbled
That he hath left part of his grief with me
To suffer with him. Good love, call him back.

Oth. Not now, sweet Desdemon; some other
time.   55

Des. But shall't be shortly?

Oth.   The sooner, sweet, for you.

Des. Shall't be to-night at supper?

Oth.   No, not to-night.

Des. To-morrow dinner, then?

Oth.   I shall not dine at home;
I meet the captains at the citadel.

Des. Why, then, to-morrow night; on Tuesday
morn;   60
On Tuesday noon, or night; on Wednesday
morn.
I prithee, name the time, but let it not
Exceed three days. In faith, he's penitent;
And yet his trespass, in our common reason —
Save that, they say, the wars must make example 65
Out of [their] best — is not almost a fault
T' incur a private check. When shall he come?
Tell me, Othello. I wonder in my soul
What you would ask me that I should deny,

Or stand so mamm'ring on. What! Michael
Cassio,   70
That came a-wooing with you, and so many a time,
When I have spoke of you dispraisingly,
Hath ta'en your part, — to have so much to do
To bring him in! Trust me, I could do much, —

Oth. Prithee, no more; let him come when he
will,   75
I will deny thee nothing.

Des.   Why, this is not a boon.
'Tis as I should entreat you wear your gloves,
Or feed on nourishing dishes, or keep you warm,
Or sue to you to do a peculiar profit
To your own person. Nay, when I have a suit   80
Wherein I mean to touch your love indeed,
It shall be full of poise and difficult weight
And fearful to be granted.

Oth.   I will deny thee nothing;
Whereon, I do beseech thee, grant me this,
To leave me but a little to myself.   85

Des. Shall I deny you? No. Farewell, my
lord.

Oth. Farewell, my Desdemona; I'll come to thee
straight.

Des. Emilia, come. — Be as your fancies teach
you;
Whate'er you be, I am obedient.

                    [*Exeunt Desdemona and Emilia.*

Oth. Excellent wretch! Perdition catch my
soul,   90
But I do love thee! and when I love thee not,
Chaos is come again.

Iago. My noble lord, —

Oth.   What dost thou say, Iago?

Iago. Did Michael Cassio, when [you] woo'd my
lady,
Know of your love?   95

Oth. He did, from first to last. Why dost thou
ask?

Iago. But for a satisfaction of my thought;
No further harm.

Oth.   Why of thy thought, Iago?

Iago. I did not think he had been acquainted
with her.

Oth. O, yes; and went between us very oft.   100

Iago. Indeed!

Oth. Indeed! ay, indeed. Discern'st thou
aught in that?
Is he not honest?

Iago.   Honest, my lord?

Oth.   Honest! ay, honest.

Iago. My lord, for aught I know.

Oth. What dost thou think?

Iago.   Think, my lord?

Oth.   Think, my lord!

66. [their] (Rowe). *her* QF. not almost: hardly. 70. **mamm'ring**: hesitating. 74. **bring...in**: i.e., into your favor.
82. poise: weight. 94. [you] Q. *he* F.

[By heaven, he echoes] me,   106
As if there were some monster in [his] thought
Too hideous to be shown. — Thou dost mean something.
I heard thee say even now, thou lik'st not that,
When Cassio left my wife. What didst not like? 110
And when I told thee he was of my counsel
[In] my whole course of wooing, thou criedst, "Indeed!"
And didst contract and purse thy brow together,
As if thou then hadst shut up in thy brain
Some horrible conceit. If thou dost love me, 115
Show me thy thought.
  Iago. My lord, you know I love you.
  Oth.   I think thou dost;
And, for I know thou'rt full of love and honesty,
And weigh'st thy words before thou giv'st them breath,
Therefore these stops of thine fright me the more;
For such things in a false disloyal knave   121
Are tricks of custom; but in a man that's just
They're close dilations, working from the heart
That passion cannot rule.
  Iago.   For Michael Cassio,
I dare be sworn I think that he is honest.   125
  Oth. I think so too.
  Iago.   Men should be what they seem;
Or those that be not, would they might seem none!
  Oth. Certain, men should be what they seem.
  Iago. Why, then, I think Cassio's an honest man.
  Oth. Nay, yet there's more in this.   130
I prithee, speak to me as to thy thinkings,
As thou dost ruminate, and give thy worst of thoughts
The worst of words.
  Iago.   Good my lord, pardon me.
Though I am bound to every act of duty,
I am not bound to that all slaves are free to. 135
Utter my thoughts? Why, say they are vile and false;
As where's that palace whereinto foul things
Sometimes intrude not? Who has that breast so pure
[But some] uncleanly apprehensions
Keep leets and law-days and in sessions sit   140
With meditations lawful?
  Oth. Thou dost conspire against thy friend, Iago,
If thou but think'st him wrong'd and mak'st his ear
A stranger to thy thoughts.
  Iago.   I do beseech you —
Though I perchance am vicious in my guess,   145
As, I confess, it is my nature's plague
To spy into abuses, and [oft] my jealousy

Shapes faults that are not — that your wisdom yet,
From one that so imperfectly conceits,
Would take no notice, nor build yourself a trouble
Out of his scattering and unsure observance.   151
It were not for your quiet nor your good,
Nor for my manhood, honesty, and wisdom,
To let you know my thoughts.
  Oth.   What dost thou mean?
  Iago. Good name in man and woman, dear my lord,   155
Is the immediate jewel of their souls.
Who steals my purse steals trash; 'tis something, nothing;
'Twas mine, 'tis his, and has been slave to thousands;
But he that filches from me my good name
Robs me of that which not enriches him,   160
And makes me poor indeed.
  Oth. [By heaven,] I'll know thy thoughts.
  Iago. You cannot, if my heart were in your hand;
Nor shall not, whilst 'tis in my custody.
  Oth. Ha!
  Iago.   O, beware, my lord, of jealousy!   165
It is the green-ey'd monster which doth mock
The meat it feeds on. That cuckold lives in bliss
Who, certain of his fate, loves not his wronger;
But, O, what damned minutes tells he o'er
Who dotes, yet doubts, suspects, yet soundly loves!
  Oth. O misery!   171
  Iago. Poor and content is rich, and rich enough;
But riches fineless is as poor as winter
To him that ever fears he shall be poor.
Good heaven, the souls of all my tribe defend 175
From jealousy!
  Oth.   Why, why is this?
Think'st thou I'd make a life of jealousy,
To follow still the changes of the moon
With fresh suspicions? No! to be once in doubt
Is [once] to be resolv'd. Exchange me for a goat
When I shall turn the business of my soul   181
To such exsufflicate and [blown] surmises,
Matching thy inference. 'Tis not to make me jealous
To say my wife is fair, feeds well, loves company,
Is free of speech, sings, plays, and dances [well]; 185
Where virtue is, these are more virtuous.
Nor from mine own weak merits will I draw
The smallest fear or doubt of her revolt;
For she had eyes, and chose me. No, Iago;
I'll see before I doubt; when I doubt, prove; 190
And on the proof, there is no more but this, —
Away at once with love or jealousy!
  Iago. I am glad of this, for now I shall have reason

---

106. [By ... echoes] Q. *Alas, thou eccho'st* F.   107. [his] Q.   *thy* F.   112. [In] Q.   *of* F.   123. **close dilations:** secret (i.e., unconscious) expressions.   139. [But some] Q.   *Wherein* F.   140. **leets:** court-days.   147. [oft] Q.   *of* F.   **jealousy:** suspicion. 151. **scattering:** random.   173. **fineless:** unlimited.   180. [once] Q.   Om. F.   182. **exsufflicate:** inflated.   [blown] Q. *blowed* F.   185. [well] Q.   Om. F.

To show the love and duty that I bear you
With franker spirit; therefore, as I am bound,   195
Receive it from me.   I speak not yet of proof.
Look to your wife; observe her well with Cassio;
Wear your eyes thus, not jealous nor secure.
I would not have your free and noble nature,
Out of self-bounty, be abus'd; look to't.   200
I know our country disposition well;
In Venice they do let Heaven see the pranks
They dare not show their husbands.   Their best
     conscience
Is not to leave 't undone, but keep 't unknown.
   Oth.   Dost thou say so?   205
   Iago.   She did deceive her father, marrying you;
And when she seem'd to shake and fear your looks,
She lov'd them most.
   Oth.   And so she did.
   Iago.   Why, go to then.
She that, so young, could give out such a seeming,
To seel her father's eyes up close as oak —   210
He thought 'twas witchcraft — but I am much to
     blame.
I humbly do beseech you of your pardon
For too much loving you.
   Oth.   I am bound to thee for ever.
   Iago.   I see this hath a little dash'd your spirits.
   Oth.   Not a jot, not a jot.
   Iago.   Trust me!   I fear it has.
I hope you will consider what is spoke   216
Comes from [my] love.   But I do see you're mov'd.
I am to pray you not to strain my speech
To grosser issues nor to larger reach
Than to suspicion.   220
   Oth.   I will not.
   Iago.   Should you do so, my lord,
My speech should fall into such vile success
Which my thoughts aim'd not at.   Cassio's my
     worthy friend, —
My lord, I see you're mov'd.
   Oth.   No, not much mov'd.
I do not think but Desdemona's honest.   225
   Iago.   Long live she so! and long live you to think
     so!
   Oth.   And yet, how nature erring from itself, —
   Iago.   Ay, there's the point; as — to be bold with
     you —
Not to affect many proposed matches
Of her own clime, complexion, and degree,   230
Whereto we see in all things nature tends —
Foh! one may smell in such, a will most rank,
Foul disproportions, thoughts unnatural.
But pardon me; I do not in position

Distinctly speak of her; though I may fear   235
Her will, recoiling to her better judgement,
May fall to match you with her country forms,
And happily repent.
   Oth.   Farewell, farewell!
If more thou dost perceive, let me know more;
Set on thy wife to observe.   Leave me, Iago.   240
   Iago.   [*Going.*] My lord, I take my leave.
   Oth.   Why did I marry?   This honest creature
     doubtless
Sees and knows more, much more, than he unfolds.
   Iago.   [*Returning.*]   My lord, I would I might
     entreat your honour
To scan this thing no farther; leave it to time.   245
Although 'tis fit that Cassio have his place,
For, sure, he fills it up with great ability,
Yet, if you please to [hold] him off a while,
You shall by that perceive him and his means.
Note if your lady strain his entertainment   250
With any strong or vehement importunity;
Much will be seen in that.   In the mean time,
Let me be thought too busy in my fears —
As worthy cause I have to fear I am —
And hold her free, I do beseech your honour.   255
   Oth.   Fear not my government.
   Iago.   I once more take my leave.   [*Exit.*
   Oth.   This fellow 's of exceeding honesty,
And knows all [qualities], with a learn'd spirit,
Of human dealings.   If I do prove her haggard,   260
Though that her jesses were my dear heartstrings,
I'd whistle her off and let her down the wind
To prey at fortune.   Haply, for I am black
And have not those soft parts of conversation
That chamberers have, or for I am declin'd   265
Into the vale of years, — yet that's not much —
She's gone.   I am abus'd; and my relief
Must be to loathe her.   O curse of marriage,
That we can call these delicate creatures ours,
And not their appetites!   I had rather be a toad 270
And live upon the vapour of a dungeon
Than keep a corner in the thing I love
For others' uses.   Yet, 'tis the plague [of] great
     ones;
Prerogativ'd are they less than the base.
'Tis destiny unshunnable, like death.   275
Even then this forked plague is fated to us
When we do quicken.   Look where she comes,

       Re-enter DESDEMONA *and* EMILIA.

If she be false, [O, then heaven mocks] itself!
I'll not believe 't.
   Des.   How now, my dear Othello!

---

     198. **secure:** careless.   200. **self-bounty:** inherent generosity.   217. [my] Q.   *your* F.   222. **success:** consequence.   225. **honest:** chaste.   232, 236. **will:** desire, appetite.   232. **rank:** foul.   234. **position:** i.e., conviction.   248. [hold] Q. Om. F.   250. **strain his entertainment:** press his reappointment.   255. **free:** guiltless.   256. **government:** management.   259. [qualities] Q.   *quantities* F.   260. **haggard:** wild.   261. **jesses:** strings by which hawks were held.   264. **parts of conversation:** social graces.   265. **chamberers:** gallants.   273. [of] Q.   *to* F.   276. **forked plague:** curse of cuckold's horns.   277 **quicken:** begin to live.   278. [O ... mocks] Q.   *Heaven mock'd* F.

Your dinner, and the generous islanders   280
By you invited, do attend your presence.
  Oth. I am to blame.
  Des.   Why do you speak so faintly?
Are you not well?
  Oth. I have a pain upon my forehead here.
  Des. Why, that's with watching; 'twill away
    again.   285
Let me but bind it hard, within this hour
It will be well.
  Oth.   Your napkin is too little;
    *[He puts the handkerchief from him; and it
    drops.]*
Let it alone. Come, I'll go in with you.
  Des. I am very sorry that you are not well.
        [Exeunt [Othello and Desdemona].
  Emil. I am glad I have found this napkin;   290
This was her first remembrance from the Moor.
My wayward husband hath a hundred times
Woo'd me to steal it; but she so loves the token,
For he conjur'd her she should ever keep it,
That she reserves it evermore about her   295
To kiss and talk to. I'll have the work ta'en out
And give 't Iago. What he will do with it
Heaven knows, not I;
I nothing but to please his fantasy.

      Re-enter IAGO.

  Iago. How now! what do you here alone?   300
  Emil. Do not you chide; I have a thing for you.
  Iago. A thing for me? It is a common thing —
  Emil. Ha!
  Iago. To have a foolish wife.
  Emil. O, is that all? What will you give me
    now   305
For that same handkerchief?
  Iago.   What handkerchief?
  Emil. What handkerchief!
Why, that the Moor first gave to Desdemona;
That which so often you did bid me steal.
  Iago. Hast stol'n it from her?   310
  Emil. No, [faith;] she let it drop by negligence,
And, to th' advantage, I, being here, took 't up.
Look, here it is.
  Iago.   A good wench; give it me.
  Emil. What will you do with 't, that you have
    been so earnest
To have me filch it?
  Iago. [Snatching it.] Why, what is that to you?
  Emil. If it be not for some purpose of import, 316
Give 't me again. Poor lady, she'll run mad
When she shall lack it.
  Iago. Be not acknown on't; I have use for it.
Go, leave me.   *[Exit Emilia.* 320

I will in Cassio's lodging lose this napkin,
And let him find it. Trifles light as air
Are to the jealous confirmations strong
As proofs of holy writ; this may do something.
The Moor already changes with my poison.   325
Dangerous conceits are, in their natures poisons,
Which at the first are scarce found to distaste,
But with a little act upon the blood
Burn like the mines of sulphur. I did say so.

      Re-enter OTHELLO.

Look, where he comes! Not poppy, nor mandra-
    gora,   330
Nor all the drowsy syrups of the world
Shall ever medicine thee to that sweet sleep
Which thou ow'dst yesterday.
  Oth.   Ha! ha! false to me?
  Iago. Why, how now, General! no more of that.
  Oth. Avaunt! be gone! thou hast set me on the
    rack.   335
I swear 'tis better to be much abus'd
Than but to know 't a little.
  Iago.   How now, my lord!
  Oth. What sense had I [of] her stol'n hours of
    lust?
I saw 't not, thought it not, it harm'd not me.
I slept the next night well, fed well, was free and
    merry;   340
I found not Cassio's kisses on her lips.
He that is robb'd, not wanting what is stolen,
Let him not know 't, and he's not robb'd at all.
  Iago. I am sorry to hear this.
  Oth. I had been happy, if the general camp,   345
Pioners and all, had tasted her sweet body,
So I had nothing known. O, now, for ever
Farewell the tranquil mind! farewell content!
Farewell the plumed troops and the big wars
That make ambition virtue! O, farewell!   350
Farewell the neighing steed and the shrill trump,
The spirit-stirring drum, th' ear-piercing fife,
The royal banner, and all quality,
Pride, pomp, and circumstance of glorious war!
And, O you mortal engines, whose rude throats 355
Th' immortal Jove's dread clamours counterfeit,
Farewell! Othello's occupation 's gone!
  Iago. Is 't possible, my lord?
  Oth. Villain, be sure thou prove my love a whore;
Be sure of it. Give me the ocular proof;   360
Or, by the worth of mine eternal soul,
Thou hadst been better have been born a dog
Than answer my wak'd wrath!
  Iago.   Is 't come to this?
  Oth. Make me to see 't; or, at the least, so prove
    it

turning point

280. **generous**: noble. 287. **napkin**: handkerchief. 288. **it**: i.e., his forehead. 296. **work … out**: pattern copied. 311. [**faith**] Q. *but* F. 312. **to th' advantage**: opportunely. 319. **acknown**: aware. 328. **act**: action. 330. **mandragora**: a soporific. 333. **ow'dst**: hadst. 338. [**of**] Q. *in* F. 346. **Pioners**: the lowest rank of soldiers.

That the probation bear no hinge nor loop　　365
To hang a doubt on; or woe upon thy life!
　Iago. My noble lord, —
　Oth. If thou dost slander her and torture me,
Never pray more; abandon all remorse;
On horror's head horrors accumulate;　　370
Do deeds to make heaven weep, all earth amaz'd;
For nothing canst thou to damnation add
Greater than that.
　Iago.　　　　O grace! O Heaven forgive me!
Are you a man? Have you a soul or sense?
God buy you; take mine office. O wretched fool, 375
That lov'st to make thine honesty a vice!
O monstrous world! Take note, take note, O world,
To be direct and honest is not safe.
I thank you for this profit; and from hence
I'll love no friend, sith love breeds such offence. 380
　Oth. Nay, stay. Thou shouldst be honest.
　Iago. I should be wise, for honesty 's a fool
And loses that it works for.
　Oth.　　　　　　By the world,
I think my wife be honest and think she is not;
I think that thou art just and think thou art not.　　385
I'll have some proof. [Her] name, that was as fresh
As Dian's visage, is now begrim'd and black
As mine own face. If there be cords, or knives,
Poison, or fire, or suffocating streams,
I'll not endure it. Would I were satisfied!　　390
　Iago. I see, [sir], you are eaten up with passion;
I do repent me that I put it to you.
You would be satisfied?
　Oth.　　　　Would! nay, I will.
　Iago. And may; but, how? How satisfied, my lord?
Would you, the [supervisor], grossly gape on —　　395
Behold her topp'd?
　Oth.　　　　Death and damnation! O!
　Iago. It were a tedious difficulty, I think,
To bring them to that prospect; [damn] them then,
If ever mortal eyes do see them bolster
More than their own! What then? How then?　400
What shall I say? Where's satisfaction?
It is impossible you should see this,
Were they as prime as goats, as hot as monkeys,
As salt as wolves in pride, and fools as gross
As ignorance made drunk. But yet, I say,　　405
If imputation and strong circumstances
Which lead directly to the door of truth
Will give you satisfaction, you might have't.
　Oth. Give me a living reason she's disloyal.

　Iago. I do not like the office;　　410
But, sith I am ent'red in this cause so far,
Prick'd to't by foolish honesty and love,
I will go on. I lay with Cassio lately;
And, being troubled with a raging tooth,
I could not sleep.　　415
There are a kind of men so loose of soul,
That in their sleeps will mutter their affairs;
One of this kind is Cassio.
In sleep I heard him say, "Sweet Desdemona,
Let us be wary, let us hide our loves;"　　420
And then, sir, would he gripe and wring my hand,
Cry, "O sweet creature!" then kiss me hard,
As if he pluck'd up kisses by the roots
That grew upon my lips; then lay his leg
Over my thigh, and sigh, and kiss; and then　425
Cry, "Cursed fate that gave thee to the Moor!"
　Oth. O monstrous! monstrous!
　Iago.　　　　Nay, this was but his dream.
　Oth. But this denoted a foregone conclusion.
'Tis a shrewd doubt, though it be but a dream.　429
　Iago. And this may help to thicken other proofs
That do demonstrate thinly.
　Oth.　　　　I'll tear her all to pieces.
　Iago. Nay, [but] be wise; yet we see nothing done.
She may be honest yet. Tell me but this,
Have you not sometimes seen a handkerchief
Spotted with strawberries in your wife's hand?　435
　Oth. I gave her such a one; 'twas my first gift.
　Iago. I know not that; but such a handkerchief —
I am sure it was your wife's — did I to-day
See Cassio wipe his beard with.
　Oth.　　　　If it be that, —
　Iago. If it be that, or any [that] was hers,　440
It speaks against her with the other proofs.
　Oth. O, that the slave had forty thousand lives!
One is too poor, too weak for my revenge.
Now do I see 'tis true. Look here, Iago;
All my fond love thus do I blow to heaven.　445
'Tis gone.
Arise, black vengeance, from the hollow hell!
Yield up, O love, thy crown and hearted throne
To tyrannous hate! Swell, bosom, with thy fraught,
For 'tis of aspics' tongues!
　Iago.　　　　Yet be content.　450
　Oth. O, blood, blood, blood!
　Iago. Patience, I say; your mind [perhaps] may change.
　Oth. Never, Iago. Like to the Pontic Sea,
Whose icy current and compulsive course
Ne'er [feels] retiring ebb, but keeps due on　455

---

375. **buy:** be with. 376. **lov'st** F. *livest* Q. 386. **[Her]** Q. *My* F. 391. **[sir]** Q. Om. F. 393. **nay** Q. *Nay, and* F. 395. **[supervisor]** Q. *supervision* F. 398. **[damn]** Q. Om. F. 399. **bolster:** lie on a bolster (together). 403. **prime:** lecherous. 404. **pride:** heat. 428. **foregone conclusion:** earlier act. 429. **shrewd doubt:** strong reason for suspicion. 432. **[but]** Q. *yet* F. 440. **[that]** (Malone). *it* QF. 449. **fraught:** burden. 450. **aspics':** asps'. 452. **[perhaps]** Q. Om. F. 453. **Pontic Sea:** Black Sea. 455. **[feels]** Q₂. *keeps* F.

To the Propontic and the Hellespont,
Even so my bloody thoughts, with violent pace,
Shall ne'er look back, ne'er ebb to humble love,
Till that a capable and wide revenge   459
Swallow them up.   Now, by yond marble heaven,
In the due reverence of a sacred vow   [*Kneels.*]
I here engage my words.
   Iago.   Do not rise yet.
Witness, you ever-burning lights above,
You elements that clip us round about,   [*Kneels.*]
Witness that here Iago doth give up   465
The execution of his wit, hands, heart,
To wrong'd Othello's service!   Let him command,
And to obey shall be in me remorse,
What bloody business ever.   [*They rise.*]
   Oth.   I greet thy love,
Not with vain thanks, but with acceptance bounteous,   470
And will upon the instant put thee to't:
Within these three days let me hear thee say
That Cassio's not alive.
   Iago. My friend is dead; 'tis done at your request.
But let her live.
   Oth. Damn her, lewd minx!   O, damn her!
   damn her!   475
Come, go with me apart; I will withdraw
To furnish me with some swift means of death
For the fair devil.   Now art thou my lieutenant.
   Iago. I am your own for ever.   [*Exeunt.*

SCENE IV.   [*Before the castle.*]

Enter DESDEMONA, EMILIA, *and* CLOWN.

   Des. Do you know, sirrah, where Lieutenant
Cassio lies?
   Clo. I dare not say he lies anywhere.
   Des. Why, man?
   Clo. He's a soldier, and for me to say a soldier
lies, 'tis stabbing.   6
   Des. Go to!   Where lodges he?
   Clo. To tell you where he lodges, is to tell you
where I lie.
   Des. Can anything be made of this?   10
   Clo. I know not where he lodges, and for me to
devise a lodging and say he lies here or he lies there,
were to lie in mine own throat.
   Des. Can you inquire him out, and be edified by
report?   15
   Clo. I will catechize the world for him; that is,
make questions, and by them answer.
   Des. Seek him, bid him come hither.   Tell him
I have mov'd my lord on his behalf, and hope all
will be well.   20

   Clo. To do this is within the compass of man's
wit; and therefore I will attempt the doing it. [*Exit.*
   Des. Where should I lose the handkerchief,
   Emilia?
   Emil. I know not, madam.
   Des. Believe me, I had rather have lost my
   purse   25
Full of crusadoes; and, but my noble Moor
Is true of mind and made of no such baseness
As jealous creatures are, it were enough
To put him to ill thinking.
   Emil.   Is he not jealous?
   Des. Who, he?   I think the sun where he was
   born   30
Drew all such humours from him.
   Emil.   Look, where he comes.

Enter OTHELLO.

   Des. I will not leave him now till Cassio
Be call'd to him. — How is't with you, my lord?
   Oth. Well, my good lady. [*Aside.*] O, hardness
   to dissemble! —
How do you, Desdemona?
   Des.   Well, my good lord.   35
   Oth. Give me your hand.   This hand is moist, my
   lady.
   Des. It [yet] hath felt no age nor known no sorrow.
   Oth. This argues fruitfulness and liberal heart;
Hot, hot, and moist.   This hand of yours requires
A sequester from liberty, fasting and prayer,   40
Much castigation, exercise devout;
For here's a young and sweating devil here
That commonly rebels.   'Tis a good hand,
A frank one.
   Des.   You may, indeed, say so;
For 'twas that hand that gave away my heart.   45
   Oth. A liberal hand.   The hearts of old gave
   hands;
But our new heraldry is hands, not hearts.
   Des. I cannot speak of this.   Come now, your
   promise.
   Oth. What promise, chuck?
   Des. I have sent to bid Cassio come speak with
   you.   50
   Oth. I have a salt and sorry rheum offends me;
Lend me thy handkerchief.
   Des.   Here, my lord.
   Oth. That which I gave you.
   Des.   I have it not about me.
   Oth. Not?
   Des.   No, indeed, my lord.
   Oth. That's a fault.   That handkerchief   55
Did an Egyptian to my mother give;
She was a charmer, and could almost read

---

459. **capable:** comprehensive.   464. **clip:** embrace.   466. **execution:** action.   468. **remorse:** obligation.
Sc. iv, 2. **lies:** lodges.   26. **crusadoes:** Portuguese coins stamped with a cross.   37. **[yet]** Q. Om. F.   40. **sequester:** separation.
47. **our new heraldry.** Probably a topical allusion.   51. **sorry:** distressing.   56. **Egyptian:** gypsy.   57. **charmer:** sorcerer.

The thoughts of people.   She told her, while she
    kept it
'Twould make her amiable and subdue my father
Entirely to her love, but if she lost it,   60
Or made a gift of it, my father's eye
Should hold her loathed and his spirits should hunt
After new fancies.   She, dying, gave it me
And bid me, when my fate would have me wiv'd,
To give it her.   I did so; and take heed on't;   65
Make it a darling like your precious eye.
To lose't or give't away were such perdition
As nothing else could match.
    Des.   Is't possible?
    Oth. 'Tis true; there's magic in the web of it.
A sibyl, that had numb'red in the world   70
The sun to course two hundred compasses,
In her prophetic fury sew'd the work;
The worms were hallowed that did breed the
    silk;
And it was dy'd in mummy which the skilful
Conserv'd of maidens' hearts.
    Des.   Indeed! is't true?
    Oth. Most veritable; therefore look to't well.   76
    Des. Then would to [God] that I had never seen
    't!
    Oth. Ha! wherefore?
    Des. Why do you speak so startingly and rash?
    Oth. Is't lost? Is't gone? Speak, is't out o' th'
    way?   80
    Des. [Heaven] bless us!
    Oth. Say you?
    Des. It is not lost; but what an if it were?
    Oth. How?
    Des. I say, it is not lost.
    Oth.   Fetch 't, let me see 't.   85
    Des. Why, so I can, [sir,] but I will not now.
This is a trick to put me from my suit.
Pray you, let Cassio be receiv'd again.
    Oth. Fetch me the handkerchief; my mind mis-
    gives.
    Des. Come, come;   90
You'll never meet a more sufficient man.
    Oth. The handkerchief!
    [*Des.*   I pray, talk me of Cassio.
    Oth. The handkerchief!]
    Des.   A man that all his time
Hath founded his good fortunes on your love,
Shar'd dangers with you, —   95
    Oth. The handkerchief!
    Des. In sooth, you are to blame.
    Oth. ['Zounds!]   [*Exit.*
    Emil. Is not this man jealous?
    Des. I ne'er saw this before.   100
Sure, there's some wonder in this handkerchief;

I am most unhappy in the loss of it.
    Emil. 'Tis not a year or two shows us a man.
They are all but stomachs, and we all but food;
They eat us hungerly, and when they are full   105
They belch us.

        Enter CASSIO *and* IAGO.

        Look you, Cassio and my husband!
    Iago. There is no other way, 'tis she must do't;
And, lo, the happiness!   Go, and importune her.
    Des. How now, good Cassio!   What's the news
    with you?
    Cas. Madam, my former suit.   I do beseech
    you   110
That by your virtuous means I may again
Exist, and be a member of his love
Whom I with all the office of my heart
Entirely honour.   I would not be delay'd.
If my offence be of such mortal kind   115
That nor my service past, nor present sorrows,
Nor purpos'd merit in futurity
Can ransom me into his love again,
But to know so must be my benefit;
So shall I clothe me in a forc'd content,   120
And shut myself up in some other course,
To fortune's alms.
    Des.   Alas, thrice-gentle Cassio!
My advocation is not now in tune.
My lord is not my lord; nor should I know him
Were he in favour as in humour alter'd.   125
So help me every spirit sanctified
As I have spoken for you all my best
And stood within the blank of his displeasure
For my free speech!   You must a while be pa-
    tient.
What I can do I will; and more I will   130
Than for myself I dare.   Let that suffice you.
    Iago. Is my lord angry?
    Emil.   He went hence but now,
And certainly in strange unquietness.
    Iago. Can he be angry?   I have seen the cannon
When it hath blown his ranks into the air,   135
And, like the devil, from his very arm
Puff'd his own brother: — and is he angry?
Something of moment then.   I will go meet him.
There's matter in't indeed, if he be angry.
                     [*Exit Iago.*
    Des. I prithee, do so.   Something, sure, of state,
Either from Venice, or some unhatch'd practice   141
Made demonstrable here in Cyprus to him,
Hath puddled his clear spirit; and in such cases
Men's natures wrangle with inferior things,
Though great ones are their object.   'Tis even so;
For let our finger ache, and it indues   146

59. **amiable:** lovable.   74. **mummy:** embalming fluid.   75. **Conserv'd:** prepared.   86. [sir] Q.   Om. F.   92–93. [*Des.* I...handkerchief] Q.   Om. F.   98. ['Zounds] Q. *Away* F.   108. **happiness:** luck.   111. **virtuous:** effective.   125. **favour:** appearance.   128. **blank:** target; strictly, the white spot in the center.   141. **practice:** plot.

Our other, healthful members even to a sense
Of pain. Nay, we must think men are not gods,
Nor of them look for such observancy
As fits the bridal. Beshrew me much, Emilia, 150
I was, unhandsome warrior as I am,
Arraigning his unkindness with my soul;
But now I find I had suborn'd the witness,
And he's indicted falsely.

  Emil. Pray Heaven it be state-matters, as you
    think,   155
And no conception nor no jealous toy
Concerning you.

  Des. Alas the day! I never gave him cause.

  Emil. But jealous souls will not be answer'd so;
They are not ever jealous for the cause,   160
But jealous for they're jealous. It is a monster
Begot upon itself, born on itself.

  Des. Heaven keep the monster from Othello's
    mind!

  Emil. Lady, amen.

  Des. I will go seek him. Cassio, walk here-
    about;   165
If I do find him fit, I'll move your suit
And seek to effect it to my uttermost.

  Cas. I humbly thank your ladyship.
              [*Exeunt* [*Desdemona and Emilia*].

Enter BIANCA.

  Bian. Save you, friend Cassio!

  Cas.   What make you from home?
How is it with you, my most fair Bianca?   170
Indeed, sweet love, I was coming to your house.

  Bian. And I was going to your lodging, Cassio.
What, keep a week away? seven days and nights?
Eightscore eight hours? and lovers' absent hours,
More tedious than the dial eightscore times?   175
O weary reck'ning!

  Cas.   Pardon me, Bianca.
I have this while with leaden thoughts been press'd;
But I shall, in a more continuate time,
Strike off this score of absence. Sweet Bianca,
        [*Giving her Desdemona's handkerchief.*]
Take me this work out.

  Bian.   O Cassio, whence came this?
This is some token from a newer friend;   181
To the felt absence now I feel a cause.
Is't come to this? Well, well.

  Cas.   Go to, woman!
Throw your vile guesses in the devils' teeth,
From whence you have them. You are jealous
    now   185
That this is from some mistress, some remembrance.
No, in good troth, Bianca.

  Bian.   Why, whose is it?

  Cas. I know not, [sweet]; I found it in my
    chamber.

I like the work well; ere it be demanded —
As like enough it will — I'd have it copied.   190
Take it, and do't; and leave me for this time.

  Bian. Leave you! Wherefore?

  Cas. I do attend here on the General;
And think it no addition, nor my wish,   194
To have him see me woman'd.

  Bian.   Why, I pray you?

  Cas. Not that I love you not.

  Bian.   But that you do not love me.
I pray you, bring me on the way a little,
And say if I shall see you soon at night.

  Cas. 'Tis but a little way that I can bring you,
For I attend here; but I'll see you soon.   200

  Bian. 'Tis very good; I must be circumstanc'd.
                                    [*Exeunt.*

ACT IV

SCENE I. [*Cyprus. Before the castle.*]

Enter OTHELLO *and* IAGO.

  Iago. Will you think so?

  Oth.   Think so, Iago!

  Iago.   What,
To kiss in private?

  Oth.   An unauthoriz'd kiss.

  Iago. Or to be naked with her friend in bed
An hour or more, not meaning any harm?

  Oth. Naked in bed, Iago, and not mean harm! 5
It is hypocrisy against the devil.
They that mean virtuously, and yet do so,
The devil their virtue tempts, and they tempt
    heaven.

  Iago. If they do nothing, 'tis a venial slip;
But if I give my wife a handkerchief, —   10

  Oth. What then?

  Iago. Why, then, 'tis hers, my lord; and, being
    hers,
She may, I think, bestow 't on any man.

  Oth. She is protectress of her honour too;
May she give that?   15

  Iago. Her honour is an essence that's not seen;
They have it very oft that have it not:
But, for the handkerchief, —

  Oth. By heaven, I would most gladly have forgot
    it.
Thou said'st — O, it comes o'er my memory,   20
As doth the raven o'er the infectious house,
Boding to all — he had my handkerchief.

  Iago. Ay, what of that?

  Oth.   That's not so good now.

  Iago.   What
If I had said I had seen him do you wrong?
Or heard him say, — as knaves be such abroad,   25
Who having, by their own importunate suit,

Or voluntary dotage of some mistress,
Convinced or suppli'd them, cannot choose
But they must blab ——
  Oth.   Hath he said anything? 29
  Iago. He hath, my lord; but be you well assur'd,
No more than he'll unswear.
  Oth.   What hath he said?
  Iago. Why, that he did — I know not what he
    did.
  Oth. What? what?
  Iago. Lie ——
  Oth.   With her?
  Iago.   With her, on her; what you will.
  Oth. Lie with her! lie on her! We say lie on 35
her, when they belie her. Lie with her! ['Zounds,]
that's fulsome! — Handkerchief — confessions —
handkerchief! — To confess, and be hang'd for his
labour; — first to be hang'd, and then to confess. —
I tremble at it. Nature would not invest herself 40
in such shadowing passion without some in-
struction. It is not words that shakes me thus.
Pish! Noses, ears, and lips. — Is't possible? —
Confess — handkerchief! — O devil!
                    [*Falls in a trance.*
  Iago. Work on, 45
My medicine, work! Thus credulous fools are
    caught;
And many worthy and chaste dames even thus,
All guiltless, meet reproach. — What, ho! my lord!
My lord, I say! Othello!

                    Enter CASSIO.

                    How now, Cassio!
  Cas. What's the matter? 50
  Iago. My lord is fall'n into an epilepsy.
This is his second fit; he had one yesterday.
  Cas. Rub him about the temples.
  Iago.   [No, forbear;]
The lethargy must have his quiet course;
If not, he foams at mouth and by and by 55
Breaks out to savage madness. Look, he stirs.
Do you withdraw yourself a little while;
He will recover straight. When he is gone,
I would on great occasion speak with you. 59
                    [*Exit Cassio.*
How is it, General? Have you not hurt your
    head?
  Oth. Dost thou mock me?
  Iago.   I mock you not, by heaven.
Would you would bear your fortune like a man!
  Oth. A horned man's a monster and a beast.
  Iago. There's many a beast then in a populous
    city,

And many a civil monster. 65
  Oth. Did he confess it?
  Iago.   Good sir, be a man;
Think every bearded fellow that's but yok'd
May draw with you. There's millions now alive
That nightly lie in those unproper beds
Which they dare swear peculiar; your case is
    better. 70
O, 'tis the spite of hell, the fiend's arch-mock,
To lip a wanton in a secure couch,
And to suppose her chaste! No, let me know;
And knowing what I am, I know what she shall
    be.
  Oth. O, thou art wise; 'tis certain.
  Iago.   Stand you a while apart; 75
Confine yourself but in a patient list.
Whilst you were here o'erwhelmed with your
    grief —
A passion most [unsuiting] such a man —
Cassio came hither. I shifted him away,
And laid good 'scuse upon your ecstasy; 80
Bade him anon return and here speak with me,
The which he promis'd. Do but encave yourself,
And mark the fleers, the gibes, and notable scorns
That dwell in every region of his face;
For I will make him tell the tale anew, 85
Where, how, how oft, how long ago, and when
He hath, and is again to cope your wife.
I say, but mark his gesture. Marry, patience;
Or I shall say you're all in all in spleen,
And nothing of a man.
  Oth.   Dost thou hear, Iago? 90
I will be found most cunning in my patience;
But — dost thou hear? — most bloody.
  Iago.   That's not amiss;
But yet keep time in all. Will you withdraw?
                    [*Othello retires.*]
Now will I question Cassio of Bianca,
A housewife that by selling her desires 95
Buys herself bread and clothes. It is a creature
That dotes on Cassio, as 'tis the strumpet's plague
To beguile many and be beguil'd by one.
He, when he hears of her, cannot [refrain]
From the excess of laughter. Here he comes. 100
                    Re-enter CASSIO.
As he shall smile, Othello shall go mad;
And his unbookish jealousy must [conster]
Poor Cassio's smiles, gestures, and light behaviours
Quite in the wrong. How do you, Lieutenant?
  Cas. The worser that you give me the addition
Whose want even kills me. 106
  Iago. Ply Desdemona well, and you are sure on't.

Act IV, sc. i, 40–41. **invest . . . instruction:** i.e., create such imaginings unless to teach me. 53. **[No, forbear]** Q. Om. F. 55. **by and by:** straightway. 65. **civil:** civilized. 69. **unproper:** not exclusively their own. 70. **peculiar:** their own. 72. **secure:** supposed safe from others. 76. **a patient list:** the bounds of patience. 78. **[unsuiting]** Q. *resulting* F. 80. **e'stasy:** trance. 89. **spleen:** anger, passion. 99. **[refrain]** Q. *restraine* F. 102. **[conster]** Q: construe. *conserve* F.

[*Speaking lower.*] Now, if this suit lay in Bianca's [power].
How quickly should you speed!

Cas.   Alas, poor caitiff!

Oth. Look how he laughs already!   110

Iago. I never knew woman love man so.

Cas. Alas, poor rogue! I think, indeed, she loves me.

Oth. Now he denies it faintly, and laughs it out.

Iago. Do you hear, Cassio?   115

Oth. Now he importunes him
To tell it o'er. Go to; well said, well said.

Iago. She gives it out that you shall marry her. Do you intend it?

Cas. Ha, ha, ha!   120

Oth. Do ye triumph, Roman? Do you triumph?

Cas. I marry [her]!! What? a customer! Prithee, bear some charity to my wit; do not think it so unwholesome. Ha, ha, ha!   125

Oth. So, so so, so; they laugh that win.

Iago. Why, the cry goes that you [shall] marry her.

Cas. Prithee, say true.

Iago. I am a very villain else.

Oth. Have you scor'd me? Well.   130

Cas. This is the monkey's own giving out. She is persuaded I will marry her, out of her own love and flattery, not out of my promise.

Oth. Iago [beckons] me; now he begins the story.   135

Cas. She was here even now; she haunts me in every place. I was the other day talking on the sea-bank with certain Venetians; and thither comes the bauble, and, falls me thus about my neck — 140

Oth. Crying, "O dear Cassio!" as it were; his gesture imports it.

Cas. So hangs, and lolls, and weeps upon me; so shakes and pulls me. Ha, ha, ha!   144

Oth. Now he tells how she pluck'd him to my chamber. Oh, I see that nose of yours, but not that dog I shall throw it to.

Cas. Well, I must leave her company.

Iago. Before me! look, where she comes.   149

Enter BIANCA.

Cas. 'Tis such another fitchew! Marry, a perfum'd one. — What do you mean by this haunting of me?

Bian. Let the devil and his dam haunt you! What did you mean by that same handkerchief you gave me even now? I was a fine fool to take it. 155
I must take out the work? — A likely piece of work, that you should find it in your chamber, and know not who left it there! This is some minx's token, and I must take out the work? There; give it

your hobby-horse. Wheresoever you had it, I'll take out no work on't.   161

Cas. How now, my sweet Bianca! how now! how now!

Oth. By heaven, that should be my handkerchief!   165

Bian. If you'll come to supper to-night, you may; if you will not, come when you are next prepar'd for.   [*Exit.*

Iago. After her, after her.

Cas. [Faith,] I must; she'll rail in the streets else.

Iago. Will you sup there?   172

Cas. Yes, I intend so.

Iago. Well, I may chance to see you; for I would very fain speak with you.   175

Cas. Prithee, come; will you?

Iago. Go to; say no more.   [*Exit Cassio.*

Oth. [*Advancing.*] How shall I murder him, Iago?

Iago. Did you perceive how he laugh'd at his vice?   181

Oth. O Iago!

Iago. And did you see the handkerchief?

Oth. Was that mine?

Iago. Yours, by this hand. And to see how he prizes the foolish woman your wife! She gave it him, and he hath given it his whore.   187

Oth. I would have him nine years a-killing. A fine woman! a fair woman! a sweet woman!

Iago. Nay, you must forget that.   190

Oth. Ay, let her rot, and perish, and be damn'd to-night; for she shall not live. No, my heart is turn'd to stone; I strike it, and it hurts my hand. O, the world hath not a sweeter creature! She might lie by an emperor's side and command him tasks.   196

Iago. Nay, that's not your way.

Oth. Hang her! I do but say what she is. So delicate with her needle! an admirable musician! O! she will sing the savageness out of a bear. Of so high and plenteous wit and invention!   201

Iago. She's the worse for all this.

Oth. O, a thousand thousand times. And then, of so gentle a condition!

Iago. Ay, too gentle.   205

Oth. Nay, that's certain. But yet the pity of it, Iago! O Iago, the pity of it, Iago!

Iago. If you are so fond over her iniquity, give her patent to offend; for if it touch not you, it comes near nobody.   210

Oth. I will chop her into messes. Cuckold me!

Iago. O, 'tis foul in her.

Oth. With mine officer!

Iago. That's fouler.   215

Oth. Get me some poison, Iago; this night. I'll not expostulate with her, lest her body and beauty

---

108. [power] Q. *dowre* F. 122. [her] Q. Om. F. **customer:** harlot. 127. [shall] Q. Om. F. 130. **scor'd:** branded.
134. [beckons] Q. *becomes* F. 150. **fitchew:** polecat. 211. **messes:** portions of food.

unprovide my mind again. This night, Iago. 219

Iago. Do it not with poison; strangle her in her bed, even the bed she hath contaminated.

Oth. Good, good; the justice of it pleases; very good.

Iago. And for Cassio, let me be his undertaker. You shall hear more by midnight. 225

[*A trumpet.*]

Enter LODOVICO, DESDEMONA, *and Attendants.*

Oth. Excellent good. What trumpet is that same?

Iago. I warrant, something from Venice. 'Tis Lodovico, this, comes from the Duke. See, your wife's with him.

Lod. Save you, worthy General!

Oth. With all my heart, sir.

Lod. The Duke and Senators of Venice greet you. [*Gives him a letter.*] 230

Oth. I kiss the instrument of their pleasures.

[*Opens the letter, and reads.*]

Des. And what's the news, good cousin Lodovico?

Iago. I am very glad to see you, signior; Welcome to Cyprus.

Lod. I thank you. How does Lieutenant Cassio? 235

Iago. Lives, sir.

Des. Cousin, there 's fall'n between him and my lord

An unkind breach; but you shall make all well.

Oth. Are you sure of that?

Des. My lord?

Oth. [*Reads.*] "This fail you not to do, as you will." — 240

Lod. He did not call; he's busy in the paper. Is there division 'twixt my lord and Cassio?

Des. A most unhappy one. I would do much T' atone them, for the love I bear to Cassio.

Oth. Fire and brimstone!

Des. My lord?

Oth. Are you wise? 245

Des. What, is he angry?

Lod. May be the letter mov'd him; For, as I think, they do command him home, Deputing Cassio in his government.

Des. Trust me, I am glad on 't.

Oth. Indeed!

Des. My lord?

Oth. I am glad to see you mad.

Des. Why, sweet Othello, —

Oth. [*Striking her.*] Devil! 251

Des. I have not deserv'd this.

Lod. My lord, this would not be believ'd in Venice

Though I should swear I saw 't. 'Tis very much. Make her amends: she weeps.

Oth. O devil, devil! 255

If that the earth could teem with woman's tears, Each drop she falls would prove a crocodile. Out of my sight!

Des. I will not stay to offend you.

[*Going.*]

Lod. Truly, [an] obedient lady: I do beseech your lordship, call her back. 260

Oth. Mistress!

Des. My lord?

Oth. What would you with her, sir?

Lod. Who, I, my lord?

Oth. Ay; you did wish that I would make her turn.

Sir, she can turn, and turn, and yet go on, And turn again; and she can weep, sir, weep; 265

And she's obedient, as you say, obedient,

Very obedient. Proceed you in your tears.

Concerning this, sir, — O well-painted passion! —

I am commanded home. — Get you away;

I'll send for you anon. — Sir, I obey the mandate, 270

And will return to Venice. — Hence, avaunt! —

[*Exit Desdemona.*]

Cassio shall have my place. And, sir, to-night I do entreat that we may sup together.

You are welcome, sir, to Cyprus. — Goats and monkeys! [*Exit.*

Lod. Is this the noble Moor whom our full Senate 275

Call all in all sufficient? Is this the nature Whom passion could not shake? whose solid virtue The shot of accident nor dart of chance Could neither graze nor pierce?

Iago. He is much chang'd.

Lod. Are his wits safe? Is he not light of brain?

Iago. He's that he is; I may not breathe my censure 281

What he might be. If what he might he is not, I would to heaven he were!

Lod. What, strike his wife!

Iago. Faith, that was not so well; yet would I knew

That stroke would prove the worst!

Lod. Is it his use? 285

Or did the letters work upon his blood And new-create [this] fault?

Iago. Alas, alas!

It is not honesty in me to speak

What I have seen and known. You shall observe him,

And his own courses will denote him so 290

That I may save my speech. Do but go after, And mark how he continues.

Lod. I am sorry that I am deceiv'd in him.

[*Exeunt.*

224. **undertaker:** dispatcher. 244. **atone:** reconcile. 256. **teem:** breed. 259. **[an]** Q. Om. F. 287. **[this]** Q. *his* F.

SCENE II. [*A room in the castle.*]

Enter OTHELLO *and* EMILIA.

Oth. You have seen nothing then?
Emil. Nor ever heard, nor ever did suspect.
Oth. Yes, you have seen Cassio and she together.
Emil. But then I saw no harm, and then I heard
Each syllable that breath made up between them.
Oth. What, did they never whisper?
Emil.   Never, my lord.   6
Oth. Nor send you out o' th' way?
Emil. Never.
Oth. To fetch her fan, her gloves, her mask, nor
  nothing?
Emil. Never, my lord.   10
Oth. That's strange.
Emil. I durst, my lord, to wager she is honest,
Lay down my soul at stake. If you think other,
Remove your thought; it doth abuse your bosom.
If any wretch have put this in your head,   15
Let Heaven requite it with the serpent's curse!
For, if she be not honest, chaste, and true,
There's no man happy; the purest of their wives
Is foul as slander.
Oth.   Bid her come hither; go.
                              [*Exit Emilia.*
She says enough; yet she's a simple bawd   20
That cannot say as much. This is a subtle whore,
A closet lock and key of villanous secrets;
And yet she'll kneel and pray; I have seen her do't.

Enter DESDEMONA *with* EMILIA.

Des. My lord, what is your will?
Oth.   Pray, chuck, come hither.
Des. What is your pleasure?
Oth.   Let me see your eyes;   25
Look in my face.
Des.   What horrible fancy's this?
Oth. [*To Emilia.*] Some of your function, mistress;
Leave procreants alone and shut the door;
Cough, or cry "hem," if anybody come.
Your mystery, your mystery; nay, dispatch.   30
                              [*Exit Emilia.*
Des. Upon my knee, what doth your speech
  import?
I understand a fury in your words,
[But not the words.]
Oth. Why, what art thou?
Des.   Your wife, my lord; your true
And loyal wife.
Oth.   Come, swear it, damn thyself,   35
Lest, being like one of heaven, the devils themselves

Should fear to seize thee; therefore be double
  damn'd,
Swear thou art honest.
Des.   Heaven doth truly know it.
Oth. Heaven truly knows that thou art false as
  hell.
Des. To whom, my lord? With whom? How
  am I false?   40
Oth. Ah, Desdemon! Away! away! away!
Des. Alas the heavy day! Why do you weep?
Am I the motive of these tears, my lord?
If haply you my father do suspect
An instrument of this your calling back,   45
Lay not your blame on me. If you have lost him,
[Why,] I have lost him too.
Oth.   Had it pleas'd Heaven
To try me with affliction; had they rain'd
All kind of sores and shames on my bare head,
Steep'd me in poverty to the very lips,   50
Given to captivity me and my utmost hopes,
I should have found in some place of my soul
A drop of patience; but, alas, to make me
The fixed figure for the time of scorn
To point his slow and moving finger at!   55
Yet could I bear that too, well, very well;
But there, where I have garner'd up my heart,
Where either I must live or bear no life;
The fountain from the which my current runs
Or else dries up; to be discarded thence!   60
Or keep it as a cistern for foul toads
To knot and gender in! Turn thy complexion
  there,
Patience, thou young and rose-lipp'd cherubin,
[Ay, there] look grim as hell!
Des. I hope my noble lord esteems me honest.   65
Oth. O, ay; as summer flies are in the shambles,
That quicken even with blowing. O thou weed,
Who art so lovely fair and smell'st so sweet
That the sense aches at thee, would thou hadst
  ne'er been born!   69
Des. Alas, what ignorant sin have I committed?
Oth. Was this fair paper, this most goodly book,
Made to write "whore" upon? What committed!
Committed! O thou public commoner!
I should make very forges of my cheeks,
That would to cinders burn up modesty,   75
Did I but speak thy deeds. What committed!
Heaven stops the nose at it, and the moon winks;
The bawdy wind, that kisses all it meets,
Is hush'd within the hollow mine of earth
And will not hear it. What committed!   80
[Impudent strumpet!]
Des.   By heaven, you do me wrong.

Oth. Are not you a strumpet?
Des.   No, as I am a Christian.
If to preserve this vessel for my lord
From any other foul unlawful touch
Be not to be a strumpet, I am none.   85
Oth. What, not a whore?
Des.   No, as I shall be sav'd.
Oth. Is't possible?
Des. O, Heaven forgive us!
Oth.   I cry you mercy, then.
I took you for that cunning whore of Venice
That married with Othello. [*Raising his voice.*] —
    You, mistress,   90

Re-enter EMILIA.

That have the office opposite to Saint Peter,
And keeps the gate of hell! You, you, ay, you!
We have done our course; there's money for your
    pains.
I pray you, turn the key and keep our counsel.
                                        [*Exit.*
Emil. Alas, what does this gentleman conceive?
How do you, madam? How do you, my good
    lady?   96
Des. Faith, half asleep.
Emil. Good madam, what's the matter with my
    lord?
Des. With who?
Emil. Why, with my lord, madam.   100
Des. Who is thy lord?
Emil.   He that is yours, sweet lady.
Des. I have none. Do not talk to me, Emilia;
I cannot weep, nor answers have I none
But what should go by water. Prithee, tonight
Lay on my bed my wedding sheets, remember;   105
And call thy husband hither.
Emil.   Here's a change indeed!
                                        [*Exit.*
Des. 'Tis meet I should be us'd so, very meet.
How have I been behav'd, that he might stick
The small'st opinion on my least misuse?

Re-enter EMILIA *with* IAGO

Iago. What is your pleasure, madam? How
    is't with you?   110
Des. I cannot tell. Those that do teach young
    babes
Do it with gentle means and easy tasks.
He might have chid me so; for, in good faith,
I am a child to chiding.
Iago.   What's the matter, lady?
Emil. Alas, Iago, my lord hath so bewhor'd her,
Thrown such despite and heavy terms upon her, 116
That true hearts cannot bear it.
Des. Am I that name, Iago?

Iago.   What name, fair lady?
Des. Such as she said my lord did say I was.
Emil. He call'd her whore. A beggar in his
    drink   120
Could not have laid such terms upon his callet.
Iago. Why did he so?
Des. I do not know; I am sure I am none such.
Iago. Do not weep, do not weep. Alas the day!
Emil. Hath she forsook so many noble matches, 126
Her father and her country and her friends,
To be call'd whore? Would it not make one weep?
Des. It is my wretched fortune.
Iago.   Beshrew him for't!
How comes this trick upon him?
Des.   Nay, Heaven doth know.
Emil. I will be hang'd if some eternal villain,
Some busy and insinuating rogue,   131
Some cogging, cozening slave, to get some office,
Have not devis'd this slander. I'll be hang'd else.
Iago. Fie, there is no such man; it is impossible.
Des. If any such there be, Heaven pardon him!
Emil. A halter pardon him! and hell gnaw his
    bones!   136
Why should he call her whore? Who keeps her
    company?
What place? what time? what form? what likeli-
    hood?
The Moor's abus'd by some most villanous knave,
Some base notorious knave, some scurvy fellow. 140
O heavens, that such companions thou'dst unfold,
And put in every honest hand a whip
To lash the rascals naked through the world
Even from the east to th' west!
Iago.   Speak within door.
Emil. O, fie upon them! Some such squire he
    was   145
That turn'd your wit the seamy side without,
And made you to suspect me with the Moor.
Iago. You are a fool; go to.
Des.   Alas, Iago,
What shall I do to win my lord again?
Good friend, go to him; for, by this light of heaven,
I know not how I lost him. Here I kneel: 151
If e'er my will did trespass 'gainst his love,
Either in discourse of thought or actual deed,
Or that mine eyes, mine ears, or any sense
Delighted them [in] any other form;   155
Or that I do not yet, and ever did,
And ever will — though he do shake me off
To beggarly divorcement — love him dearly,
Comfort forswear me! Unkindness may do much;
And his unkindness may defeat my life,   160
But never taint my love. I cannot say "whore."
It does abhor me now I speak the word;
To do the act that might the addition earn

104. **go by water:** be rendered by tears.   109. **opinion:** censure.   **misuse:** misconduct.   121. **callet:** whore.   132. **cog-ging:** lying.   **cozening:** cheating.   141. **unfold:** expose.   153. **discourse:** course.   155. **[in]** Q₂. *or* F.   160. **defeat:** destroy.

Not the world's mass of vanity could make me.

Iago. I pray you, be content; 'tis but his humour.
The business of the state does him offence, 166
[And he does chide with you.]

Des. If 'twere no other, —

Iago.   It is but so, I warrant.
                 [*Trumpets within.*]
Hark, how these instruments summon to supper!
The messengers of Venice stay the meat. 170
Go in, and weep not; all things shall be well.
         [*Exeunt Desdemona and Emilia.*

Enter RODERIGO.

How now, Roderigo!

Rod. I do not find that thou deal'st justly with
me.

Iago. What in the contrary? 175

Rod. Every day thou daff'st me with some device,
Iago; and rather, as it seems to me now, keep'st
from me all conveniency than suppliest me with
the least advantage of hope. I will indeed no
longer endure it, nor am I yet persuaded to put up
in peace what already I have foolishly suff'red. 182

Iago. Will you hear me, Roderigo?

Rod. I have heard too much, and your words and
performances are no kin together.

Iago. You charge me most unjustly. 186

Rod. With nought but truth. I have wasted
myself out of my means. The jewels you have had
from me to deliver Desdemona would half have
corrupted a votarist. You have told me she hath
receiv'd them and return'd me expectations and
comforts of sudden respect and acquaintance, but
I find none. 193

Iago. Well; go to; very well.

Rod. Very well! go to! I cannot go to, man;
nor 'tis not very well. Nay, I think it is scurvy,
and begin to find myself fopp'd in it.

Iago. Very well. 198

Rod. I tell you 'tis not very well. I will make
myself known to Desdemona. If she will return
me my jewels, I will give over my suit and repent
my unlawful solicitation; if not, assure yourself I
will seek satisfaction of you.

Iago. You have said now.

Rod. Ay, and said nothing but what I protest
intendment of doing. 206

Iago. Why, now I see there's mettle in thee, and
even from this instant do build on thee a better
opinion than ever before. Give me thy hand,
Roderigo. Thou hast taken against me a most
just exception; but yet, I protest, I have dealt most
directly in thy affair.

Rod. It hath not appear'd.

Iago. I grant indeed it hath not appear'd, and

your suspicion is not without wit and judgement.
But, Roderigo, if thou hast that in thee indeed, 216
which I have greater reason to believe now than
ever, I mean purpose, courage, and valour, this
night show it. If thou the next night following
enjoy not Desdemona, take me from this world
with treachery and devise engines for my life. 222

Rod. Well, what is it? Is it within reason and
compass?

Iago. Sir, there is especial commission come
from Venice to depute Cassio in Othello's place.

Rod. Is that true? Why, then Othello and
Desdemona return again to Venice. 228

Iago. O, no; he goes into Mauritania and taketh
away with him the fair Desdemona, unless his
abode be ling'red here by some accident; wherein
none can be so determinate as the removing of
Cassio. 233

Rod. How do you mean, removing him?

Iago. Why, by making him uncapable of Othello's
place; knocking out his brains.

Rod. And that you would have me to do? 237

Iago. Ay, if you dare do yourself a profit and a
right. He sups to-night with a harlotry, and
thither will I go to him; he knows not yet of his 240
honourable fortune. If you will watch his going
thence, which I will fashion to fall out between
twelve and one, you may take him at your pleasure.
I will be near to second your attempt, and he shall
fall between us. Come, stand not amaz'd at it, 245
but go along with me; I will show you such a necessity in his death that you shall think yourself
bound to put it on him. It is now high supper-
time, and the night grows to waste. About it. 250

Rod. I will hear further reason for this.

Iago. And you shall be satisfi'd.   [*Exeunt.*

SCENE III. [*Another room in the castle.*]

Enter OTHELLO, LODOVICO, DESDEMONA,
EMILIA, *and Attendants.*

Lod. I do beseech you, sir, trouble yourself no
further.

Oth. O, pardon me; 'twill do me good to walk.

Lod. Madam, good-night; I humbly thank your
ladyship.

Des. Your honour is most welcome.

Oth.   Will you walk, sir?
O, — Desdemona, —

Des. My lord?

Oth. Get you to bed on th' instant; I will
return'd forthwith. Dismiss your attendant there.
Look 't be done.

Des. I will, my lord. 10
       [*Exeunt* [*Othello, Lodovico, and Attendants*].

---

167. [And ... you] Q. Om. F.   170. **stay the meat:** wait to dine.   176. **daff'st me:** puttest me off.   190. **votarist:**
nun.   192. **sudden respect:** speedy notice.   197. **fopp'd:** duped.   222. **engines:** plots.

Emil. How goes it now? He looks gentler than
  he did.

Des. He says he will return incontinent;
And hath commanded me to go to bed,
And bid me to dismiss you.

Emil.   Dismiss me!

Des. It was his bidding; therefore, good Emilia,
Give me my nightly wearing, and adieu.   16
We must not now displease him.

Emil. I would you had never seen him!

Des. So would not I. My love doth so approve
  him,
That even his stubbornness, his checks, his
  frowns, —   20
Prithee, unpin me, — have grace and favour [in
  them].

Emil. I have laid those sheets you bade me on
  the bed.

Des. All's one. Good [faith], how foolish are
  our minds!
If I do die before, prithee, shroud me   24
In one of these same sheets.

Emil.   Come, come, you talk.

Des. My mother had a maid call'd Barbary;
She was in love, and he she lov'd prov'd mad
And did forsake her. She had a song of "Willow";
An old thing 'twas, but it express'd her fortune,
And she died singing it. That song to-night   30
Will not go from my mind; I have much to do
But to go hang my head all at one side
And sing it like poor Barbary. Prithee, dispatch.

Emil. Shall I go fetch your night-gown?

Des.   No, unpin me here.
This Lodovico is a proper man.   35

Emil. A very handsome man.

Des. He speaks well.

Emil. I know a lady in Venice would have
walk'd barefoot to Palestine for a touch of his
nether lip.   40

Des. [*Singing.*]
"The poor soul sat [sighing] by a sycamore tree,
  Sing all a green willow;
Her hand on her bosom, her head on her knee,
  Sing willow, willow, willow.
The fresh streams ran by her, and murmur'd her
    moans;   45
  Sing willow, willow, willow;
Her salt tears fell from her, and soft'ned the stones;
  Sing willow, willow, willow;"
Lay by these; —
[*Singing.*] "Willow, willow;" —
Prithee, hie thee; he'll come anon; —   50
[*Singing.*]
"Sing all a green willow must be my garland.

Let nobody blame him, his scorn I approve," —
Nay, that's not next. — Hark! who is't that
  knocks?

Emil. It's the wind.

Des. [*Singing.*]
"I call'd my love false love; but what said he
  then?   55
  Sing willow, willow, willow.
If I court moe women, you'll couch with moe
  men."
So, get thee gone; good-night. Mine eyes do itch;
Doth that bode weeping?

Emil.   'Tis neither here nor there.

Des. I have heard it said so. O, these men,
  these men!   60
Dost thou in conscience think, — tell me, Emilia, —
That there be women do abuse their husbands
In such gross kind?

Emil.   There be some such, no question.

Des. Wouldst thou do such a deed for all the
  world?   64

Emil. Why, would not you?

Des.   No, by this heavenly light!

Emil. Nor I neither by this heavenly light;
I might do't as well i' th' dark.

Des. Wouldst thou do such a deed for all the
  world?

Emil. The world's a huge thing; it is a great
  price   69
For a small vice.

Des.   In troth, I think thou wouldst not.

Emil. In troth, I think I should; and undo't
when I had done. Marry, I would not do such a
thing for a joint-ring, nor for measures of lawn, nor
for gowns, petticoats, nor caps, nor any petty exhibition; but, for all the whole world, — ['ud's
pity], who would not make her husband a   75
cuckold to make him a monarch? I should venture
purgatory for't.

Des. Beshrew me, if I would do such a wrong
For the whole world.   79

Emil. Why, the wrong is but a wrong i' th'
world; and having the world for your labour, 'tis a
wrong in your own world, and you might quickly
make it right.

Des. I do not think there is any such woman.   84

Emil. Yes, a dozen; and as many to th' vantage
as would store the world they play'd for.
But I do think it is their husbands' faults
If wives do fall. Say that they slack their duties
And pour our treasures into foreign laps,
Or else break out in peevish jealousies,   90
Throwing restraint upon us; or say they strike us,
Or scant our former having in despite;

Sc. iii, 20. stubbornness: roughness. 21. **[in them]** Q. Om. F. 23. **[faith]** Q. *Father* F. 41. **[sighing]** Q₂. *singing* F.
73. **joint-ring:** ring made in separable halves. 74. **exhibition:** allowance. 75. **['ud's pity]** Q: God's pity. *Why* F. 85.
to th' vantage: more, to boot. 90. **peevish:** silly. 92. **having:** allowance.

Why, we have galls, and though we have some
    grace,
Yet have we some revenge. Let husbands know
Their wives have sense like them; they see and
    smell   95
And have their palates both for sweet and sour
As husbands have. What is it that they do
When they change us for others? Is it sport?
I think it is. And doth affection breed it?
I think it doth. Is't frailty that thus errs?   100
It is so too. And have not we affections,
Desires for sport, and frailty, as men have?
Then let them use us well; else let them know,
The ills we do, their ills instruct us so.
Des. Good-night, good-night. Heaven me such
    uses send,   105
Not to pick bad from bad, but by bad mend.
                             [*Exeunt.*

ACT V

Scene I. [*Cyprus. A street.*]

Enter Iago *and* Roderigo.

Iago. Here, stand behind this [bulk]; straight
    will he come.
Wear thy good rapier bare, and put it home.
Quick, quick; fear nothing; I'll be at thy elbow.
It makes us, or it mars us; think on that,
And fix most firm thy resolution.   5
Rod. Be near at hand; I may miscarry in't.
Iago. Here, at thy hand; be bold, and take thy
    stand.   [*Retires.*]
Rod. I have no great devotion to the deed,
And yet he hath given me satisfying reasons.
'Tis but a man gone. Forth, my sword: he dies.   10
Iago. I have rubb'd this young quat almost to
    the sense,
And he grows angry. Now, whether he kill Cassio,
Or Cassio him, or each do kill the other,
Every way makes my gain. Live Roderigo,
He calls me to a restitution large   15
Of gold and jewels that I bobb'd from him
As gifts to Desdemona;
It must not be. If Cassio do remain,
He hath a daily beauty in his life
That makes me ugly; and, besides, the Moor   20
May unfold me to him; there stand I in much peril.
No, he must die. But so; I heard him coming.

Enter Cassio.

Rod. I know his gait, 'tis he. — Villain, thou
    diest!   [*Makes a pass at Cassio.*]

Cas. That thrust had been mine enemy indeed,
But that my coat is better than thou know'st.   25
I will make proof of thine.
             [*Draws, and wounds Roderigo.*]
Rod.   O, I am slain.
    [*Iago from behind wounds Cassio in the leg,
        and exit.*]
Cas. I am maim'd for ever. Help, ho! murder!
    murder!   [*Falls.*]

Enter Othello.

Oth. The voice of Cassio! Iago keeps his word.
Rod. O, villain that I am!
Oth.   It is even so.
Cas. O, help, ho! light! a surgeon!   30
Oth. 'Tis he! — O brave Iago, honest and just,
That hast such noble sense of thy friend's wrong!
Thou teachest me. Minion, your dear lies dead,
And your unblest fate hies; strumpet, I come.
[Forth] of my heart those charms, thine eyes, are
    blotted;   35
Thy bed, lust-stain'd, shall with lust's blood be
    spotted.   [*Exit.*

Enter Lodovico *and* Gratiano.

Cas. What, ho! no watch? no passage? Murder!
    murder!
Gra. 'Tis some mischance; the voice is very dire-
    ful.
Cas. O, help!
Lod. Hark!   40
Rod. O wretched villain!
Lod. Two or three groan. 'Tis heavy night,
These may be counterfeits; let's think 't unsafe
To come in to the cry without more help.
Rod. Nobody come? Then shall I bleed to
    death.   45

Re-enter Iago, *with a light.*

Lod. Hark!
Gra. Here's one comes in his shirt, with light and
    weapons.
Iago. Who's there? Whose noise is this that
    cries on murder?
Lod. We do not know.
Iago.   Do not you hear a cry?
Cas. Here, here! for Heaven's sake, help me!
Iago.   What's the matter?   50
Gra. This is Othello's ancient, as I take it.
Lod. The same indeed; a very valiant fellow.
Iago. What are you here that cry so grievously?
Cas. Iago? O, I am spoil'd, undone by villains!
Give me some help.   55

---

93. **galls:** spirits to resent injury.
  Act V, sc. i, 1. [**bulk**] Q: jutting part of a building. *barke* F. 11. **quat:** pimple. **the sense:** the quick. 16. **bobb'd:**
cheated, swindled. 25. **coat:** i.e., of mail (worn under outer clothing). 33. **Minion:** hussy. 35. [**Forth**] Q. *For* F. 37.
passage: passers-by. 42. **heavy:** dark.

Iago. O me, Lieutenant! what villains have done
this?

Cas. I think that one of them is hereabout
And cannot make away.

Iago.   O treacherous villains!
What are you there? — Come in, and give some
help.   [*To Lodovico and Gratiano.*]

Rod. O, help me there!   60

Cas. That's one of them.

Iago.   O murd'rous slave! O villain!
                [*Thrusts [Roderigo] in.*]

Rod. O damn'd Iago! O inhuman dog!

Iago. Kill men i' th' dark! — Where be these
bloody thieves? —
How silent is this town! — Ho! murder! murder! —
What may you be? Are you of good or evil? 65

Lod. As you shall prove us, praise us.

Iago. Signior Lodovico?

Lod. He, sir.

Iago. I cry you mercy. Here's Cassio hurt by
villains.

Gra. Cassio!   70

Iago. How is't, brother!

Cas. My leg is cut in two.

Iago.   Marry, heaven forbid!
Light, gentlemen! I'll bind it with my shirt.

Enter BIANCA.

Bian. What is the matter, ho? Who is't that
cried?

Iago. Who is't that cried!   75

Bian. O my dear Cassio! my sweet Cassio!
O Cassio, Cassio, Cassio!

Iago. O notable strumpet! Cassio, may you
suspect
Who they should be that have thus mangled you?

Cas. No.   80

Gra. I am sorry to find you thus; I have been
to seek you.

Iago. Lend me a garter. So. O, for a chair,
To bear him easily hence!

Bian. Alas, he faints! O Cassio, Cassio, Cassio!

Iago. Gentlemen all, I do suspect this trash 85
To be a party in this injury.
Patience a while, good Cassio. Come, come;
Lend me a light. Know we this face or no?
Alas, my friend and my dear countryman
Roderigo! No: — yes, sure: — yes, 'tis Roderigo.

Gra. What, of Venice?   91

Iago. Even he, sir; did you know him?

Gra.   Know him! ay.

Iago. Signior Gratiano? I cry your gentle
pardon;
These bloody accidents must excuse my manners
That so neglected you.

Gra.   I am glad to see you. 95

Iago. How do you, Cassio? O, a chair, a chair!

Gra. Roderigo!

Iago. He, he, 'tis he. [*A chair brought in.*] O,
that's well said; the chair.
Some good man bear him carefully from hence;
I'll fetch the General's surgeon.   [*To Bianca.*]
For you, mistress,   100
Save you your labour. He that lies slain here,
Cassio,
Was my dear friend. What malice was between
you?

Cas. None in the world; nor do I know the man.

Iago. [*To Bian.*] What, look you pale? O, bear
him out o' th' air.
         [*Cassio and Roderigo are borne off.*]
Stay you, good gentlemen. Look you pale, mis-
tress?   105
Do you perceive the gastness of her eye?
Nay, if you stare, we shall hear more anon.
Behold her well; I pray you, look upon her.
Do you see, gentlemen? Nay, guiltiness will speak,
Though tongues were out of use.   110

Enter EMILIA.

Emil. Alas, what's the matter? What's the
matter, husband?

Iago. Cassio hath here been set on in the dark
By Roderigo and fellows that are scap'd.
He's almost slain, and Roderigo quite dead.

Emil. Alas, good gentleman! alas, good Cassio!

Iago. This is the fruits of whoring. Prithee,
Emilia,   116
Go know of Cassio where he supp'd to-night.
[*To Bianca.*] What, do you shake at that?

Bian. He supp'd at my house; but I therefore
shake not.

Iago. O, did he so? I charge you, go with me. 120

Emil. Oh, fie upon thee, strumpet!

Bian. I am no strumpet, but of life as honest
As you that thus abuse me.

Emil.   As I? Fie upon thee!

Iago. Kind gentlemen, let's go see poor Cassio
dress'd.
Come, mistress, you must tell's another tale. 125
Emilia, run you to the citadel,
And tell my lord and lady what hath happ'd.
Will you go on afore? [*Aside.*] This is the night
That either makes me or fordoes me quite.
                   [*Exeunt.*

SCENE II.   [*A bedchamber in the castle:*] DESDEMONA
in bed [*asleep*].

Enter OTHELLO *with a light.*

Oth. It is the cause, it is the cause, my soul, —
Let me not name it to you, you chaste stars! —

---

82. **chair:** sedan chair.   106. **gastness:** ghastliness.   129. **fordoes:** destroys.

It is the cause. Yet I'll not shed her blood,
Nor scar that whiter skin of hers than snow,
And smooth as monumental alabaster.   5
Yet she must die, else she'll betray more men.
Put out the light, and then put out the light.
If I quench thee, thou flaming minister,
I can again thy former light restore,
Should I repent me; but once put out thy light,   10
Thou cunning'st pattern of excelling nature,
I know not where is that Promethean heat
That can thy light relume. When I have pluck'd
    the rose
I cannot give it vital growth again,
It needs must wither. I'll smell [it] on the tree.   15
                 [*Kisses her.*
Oh, balmy breath, that dost almost persuade
Justice to break her sword! One more, one more.
Be thus when thou art dead, and I will kill thee
And love thee after. One more, and that's the last;
So sweet was ne'er so fatal. I must weep,   20
But they are cruel tears. This sorrow's heavenly;
It strikes where it doth love. She wakes.
   Des. Who's there? Othello?
   Oth.   Ay, Desdemona.
   Des. Will you come to bed, my lord?
   Oth. Have you pray'd to-night, Desdemon?
   Des.   Ay, my lord.
   Oth. If you bethink yourself of any crime   26
Unreconcil'd as yet to Heaven and grace,
Solicit for it straight.
   Des. Alack, my lord, what may you mean by
    that?
   Oth. Well, do it, and be brief; I will walk by.   30
I would not kill thy unprepared spirit;
No; heavens forfend! I would not kill thy soul.
   Des. Talk you of killing?
   Oth.   Ay, I do.
   Des.   Then Heaven
Have mercy on me!
   Oth.   Amen, with all my heart!
   Des. If you say [so], I hope you will not kill
    me.   35
   Oth. Hum!
   Des. And yet I fear you; for you're fatal then
When your eyes roll so. Why I should fear I know
    not,
Since guiltiness I know not; but yet I feel I fear.
   Oth. Think on thy sins.
   Des.   They are loves I bear to you.   40
   Oth. Ay, and for that thou diest.
   Des. That death's unnatural that kills for loving.
Alas, why gnaw you so your nether lip?
Some bloody passion shakes your very frame.
These are portents; but yet I hope, I hope,   45
They do not point on me.

   Oth.   Peace, and be still!
   Des. I will so. What's the matter?
   Oth. That handkerchief which I so lov'd and
    gave thee
Thou gav'st to Cassio.
   Des.   No, by my life and soul!
Send for the man, and ask him.
   Oth.   Sweet soul, take heed,   50
Take heed of perjury; thou art on thy deathbed.
   Des. Ay, but not yet to die.
   Oth.   [Yes], presently:
Therefore confess thee freely of thy sin;
For to deny each article with oath
Cannot remove nor choke the strong conception   55
That I do groan withal. Thou art to die.
   Des. O, Heaven, have mercy on me!
   Oth.   I say, amen.
   Des. And have you mercy too! I never did
Offend you in my life; never lov'd Cassio
But with such general warranty of heaven   60
As I might love; I never gave him token.
   Oth. By heaven, I saw my handkerchief in 's hand.
O perjur'd woman! thou dost stone my heart,
And makes me call what I intend to do
A murder, which I thought a sacrifice.   65
I saw the handkerchief.
   Des.   He found it then;
I never gave it him. Send for him hither;
Let him confess a truth.
   Oth.   He hath confess'd.
   Des. What, my lord?   69
   Oth. That he hath us'd thee.
   Des.   How? unlawfully?
   Oth.   Ay.
   Des. He will not say so.
   Oth.   No, his mouth is stopp'd;
Honest Iago hath ta'en order for't.
   Des. O! my fear interprets. What, is he dead?
   Oth. Had all his hairs been lives, my great
    revenge
Had stomach for them all.   75
   Des. Alas! he is betray'd and I undone.
   Oth. Out, strumpet! weep'st thou for him to
    my face?
   Des. O, banish me, my lord, but kill me not!
   Oth. Down, strumpet!
   Des. Kill me to-morrow; let me live to-night!   80
   Oth. Nay, if you strive, —
   Des. But half an hour!
   Oth.   Being done, there is no pause.
   Des. But while I say one prayer!
   Oth.   It is too late.
                      [*He smothers her.*
   Emil. (*At the door.*) My lord, my lord!
     What, ho! my lord, my lord!

Sc. ii, 12. **Promethean heat:** divine fire.   15. [it] Q.   *thee* F.   35. [so] Q.   Om. F.   52. [Yes] Q.   Om. F.   55. **concep**
tion: purpose.

Oth. What noise is this?   Not dead? not yet
    quite dead?   85
I that am cruel am yet merciful;
I would not have thee linger in thy pain.
So, so.
   Emil. (*Within.*) What, ho! my lord, my lord!
   Oth.   Who's there?
   Emil. [*Within.*] O, good my lord, I would speak
    a word with you!   90
   Oth. Yes: — 'tis Emilia. — By and by. — She's
    dead.
'Tis like she comes to speak of Cassio's death.
The noise was high.   Ha! no more moving?
Still as the grave.   Shall she come in?   Were't
    good? —
I think she stirs again: — no.   What's best to
    do?   95
If she come in, she'll sure speak to my wife.
My wife! my wife! what wife?   I have no wife.
O, insupportable!   O heavy hour!
Methinks it should be now a huge eclipse
Of sun and moon, and that th' affrighted globe   100
Did yawn at alteration.
   Emil.   [*Within.*] I do beseech you
That I may speak with you, O, good my lord!
   Oth. I had forgot thee.   O, come in, Emilia.
Soft; by and by. — Let me the curtains draw. —
Where art thou?   [*Unlocks the door.*]

Enter EMILIA.

          What's the matter with thee now?   105
   Emil. O, my good lord, yonder's foul murders
    done!
   Oth. What, now?
   Emil. But now, my lord.
   Oth. It is the very error of the moon;
She comes more nearer earth than she was wont,   110
And makes men mad.
   Emil. Cassio, my lord, hath kill'd a young
    Venetian
Call'd Roderigo.
   Oth.   Roderigo kill'd!
And Cassio kill'd!
   Emil.   No, Cassio is not kill'd.
   Oth. Not Cassio kill'd!   Then murder's out
    of tune,   115
And sweet revenge grows harsh.
   Des. O, falsely, falsely murder'd!
   Emil.   O Lord, what cry is that?
   Oth. That! what?
   Emil. Out, and alas! that was my lady's voice.
Help! help, ho! help!   O lady, speak again!   120
Sweet Desdemona!   O sweet mistress, speak!
   Des. A guiltless death I die.
   Emil. O, who hath done this deed?
   Des. Nobody; I myself.   Farewell!

Commend me to my kind lord.   O, farewell!   125
                            [*Dies.*
   Oth. Why, how should she be murd'red?
   Emil.   Alas, who knows?
   Oth. You hear her say herself, it was not I.
   Emil. She said so; I must needs report the truth.
   Oth. She's, like a liar, gone to burning hell.
'Twas I that kill'd her.
   Emil.   O, the more angel she,   130
And you the blacker devil!
   Oth. She turn'd to folly, and she was a whore.
   Emil. Thou dost belie her, and thou art a devil.
   Oth. She was false as water.
   Emil.   Thou art rash as fire to say
That she was false: O, she was heavenly true!   135
   Oth. Cassio did top her; ask thy husband else.
O, I were damn'd beneath all depth in hell
But that I did proceed upon just grounds
To this extremity.   Thy husband knew it all.
   Emil. My husband!   140
   Oth. Thy husband.
   Emil. That she was false to wedlock?
   Oth. Ay, with Cassio.   Had she been true,
If Heaven would make me such another world
Of one entire and perfect chrysolite,   145
I'd not have sold her for it.
   Emil.   My husband!
   Oth. Ay, 'twas he that told me on her first.
An honest man he is, and hates the slime
That sticks on filthy deeds.
   Emil.   My husband!
   Oth. What needs this iterance, woman?   I say
    thy husband.   150
   Emil. O mistress, villainy hath made mocks
    with love!
My husband say [that] she was false!
   Oth.   He, woman;
I say thy husband; dost understand the word?
My friend, thy husband, honest, honest Iago.
   Emil. If he say so, may his pernicious soul   155
Rot half a grain a day!   He lies to the heart.
She was too fond of her most filthy bargain.
   Oth. Ha!
   Emil. Do thy worst!
This deed of thine is no more worthy heaven   160
Than thou wast worthy her.
   Oth.   Peace, you were best.
   Emil. Thou hast not half that power to do me
    harm
As I have to be hurt.   O gull! O dolt!
As ignorant as dirt!   Thou hast done a deed —
I care not for thy sword; I'll make thee known   165
Though I lost twenty lives. — Help! help, ho!
    help!
The Moor hath kill'd my mistress!   Murder!
    murder!

---

109. **error:** aberration.   145. **chrysolite:** a precious stone.   150. **iterance:** repetition.   152. **[that]** Q₂. Om. F.

Enter MONTANO, GRATIANO, IAGO, *and others.*

Mon. What is the matter? How now, general!

Emil. O, are you come, Iago? You have done well,

That men must lay their murders on your neck. 170

Gra. What is the matter?

Emil. Disprove this villain, if thou be'st a man.

He says thou told'st him that his wife was false.

I know thou didst not, thou'rt not such a villain.

Speak, for my heart is full. 175

Iago. I told him what I thought, and told no more

Than what he found himself was apt and true.

Emil. But did you ever tell him she was false?

Iago. I did.

Emil. You told a lie, an odious, damned lie; 180

Upon my soul, a lie, a wicked lie.

She false with Cassio! — did you say with Cassio?

Iago. With Cassio, mistress. Go to, charm your tongue.

Emil. I will not charm my tongue; I am bound to speak.

My mistress here lies murdered in her bed, — 185

All. O heavens forfend!

Emil. And your reports have set the murderer on.

Oth. Nay, stare not, masters; it is true, indeed.

Gra. 'Tis a strange truth.

Mon. O monstrous act!

Emil.   Villany, villany, villany! 190

I think upon't, — I think I smell 't, — O villany!

I thought so then, — I'll kill myself for grief —

O villany, villany!

Iago. What, are you mad? I charge you, get you home.

Emil. Good gentlemen, let me have leave to speak; 195

'Tis proper I obey him, but not now.

Perchance, Iago, I will ne'er go home.

Oth. O! O! O!   [*He falls on the bed.*

Emil.   Nay, lay thee down and roar;

For thou hast kill'd the sweetest innocent

That e'er did lift up eye.

Oth.   [*Rising.*] O, she was foul! 200

I scarce did know you, uncle; there lies your niece,

Whose breath, indeed, these hands have newly stopp'd.

I know this act shows horrible and grim.

Gra. Poor Desdemon! I am glad thy father's dead.

Thy match was mortal to him, and pure grief 205

Shore his old thread in twain. Did he live now,

This sight would make him do a desperate turn,

Yea, curse his better angel from his side,

And fall to reprobance.

Oth. 'Tis pitiful; but yet Iago knows 210

That she with Cassio hath the act of shame

A thousand times committed. Cassio confess'd it;

And she did gratify his amorous works

With that recognizance and pledge of love

Which I first gave her. I saw it in his hand; 215

It was a handkerchief, an antique token

My father gave my mother.

Emil. O [God]! O heavenly [God]!

Iago. ['Zounds,] hold your peace.

Emil.   'Twill out, 'twill out! I peace!

No, I will speak as liberal as the north. 220

Let Heaven and men and devils, let them all,

All, all, cry shame against me, yet I'll speak.

Iago. Be wise, and get you home.

Emil.   I will not.

[*Iago offers to stab Emilia.*]

Gra.   Fie!

Your sword upon a woman?

Emil. O thou dull Moor! that handkerchief thou speak'st of 225

I found by fortune and did give my husband;

For often, with a solemn earnestness,

More than indeed belong'd to such a trifle,

He begg'd of me to steal 't.

Iago.   Villanous whore! 229

Emil. She give it Cassio! No, alas! I found it,

And I did give't my husband.

Iago.   Filth, thou liest!

Emil. By heaven, I do not, I do not, gentlemen.

O murd'rous coxcomb! what should such a fool

Do with so good a wife?

Oth.   Are there no stones in heaven

But what serves for the thunder? — Precious villain! 235

[*He runs at Iago: Iago kills Emilia.*

Gra. The woman falls; sure, he hath kill'd his wife.

Emil. Ay, ay! O, lay me by my mistress' side.

[*Exit Iago.*

Gra. He's gone, but his wife's kill'd.

Mon. 'Tis a notorious villain. Take you this weapon

Which I have [here] recover'd from the Moor. 240

Come, guard the door without; let him not pass,

But kill him rather. I'll after that same villain,

For 'tis a damned slave.

[*Exeunt Montano and Gratiano.*

Oth.   I am not valiant neither,

But every puny whipster gets my sword.

But why should honour outlive honesty? 245

Let it go all.

Emil.   What did thy song bode, lady?

Hark, canst thou hear me? I will play the swan,

192. **I...then.** See IV.ii.130–33.   209. **reprobance:** damnation.   218. **[God] ... [God]** Q. *Heaven ... Powers* F.
219. **['Zounds]** Q. *Come* F.   220. **liberal:** freely.   234. **stones:** bolts.   240. **[here]** Q. Om. F.   244. **whipster:** term of contempt.

And die in music. [*Singing.*] "Willow, willow,
     willow!" —
Moor, she was chaste; she lov'd thee, cruel Moor;
So come my soul to bliss, as I speak true;   250
So speaking as I think, alas, I die.   [*Dies.*
   Oth. I have another weapon in this chamber;
It was a sword of Spain, the ice-brook's temper, —
O, here it is. Uncle, I must come forth.
   Gra. (*Within.*) If thou attempt it, it will cost
     thee dear: 255
Thou hast no weapon, and perforce must suffer.
   Oth. Look in upon me then and speak with me,
Or, naked as I am, I will assault thee.

[*Re-enter* GRATIANO.]

   Gra. What is the matter?
   Oth.   Behold, I have a weapon;
A better never did itself sustain   260
Upon a soldier's thigh. I have seen the day
That, with this little arm and this good sword,
I have made my way through more impediments
Than twenty times your stop. But, O vain boast!
Who can control his fate? 'tis not so now.   265
Be not afraid though you do see me weapon'd;
Here is my journey's end, here is my butt
And very sea-mark of my utmost sail.
Do you go back dismay'd? 'Tis a lost fear;
Man but a rush against Othello's breast   270
And he retires. Where should Othello go?
Now, how dost thou look now? O ill-starr'd wench!
Pale as thy smock! when we shall meet at compt,
This look of thine will hurl my soul from heaven,
And fiends will snatch at it. Cold, cold, my girl!   275
Even like thy chastity. O cursed, cursed slave!
Whip me, ye devils,
From the possession of this heavenly sight!
Blow me about in winds! roast me in sulphur!
Wash me in steep-down gulfs of liquid fire!   280
O Desdemon! dead, Desdemon! dead!
Oh! Oh!

Enter LODOVICO, MONTANO, CASSIO *carried in a
chair, and* Officers, *with* IAGO [*prisoner*].

   Lod. Where is this rash and most unfortunate
     man?
   Oth. That's he that was Othello; here I am.
   Lod. Where is that viper? Bring the villain
     forth.   285
   Oth. I look down towards his feet; but that's a
     fable.
If that thou be'st a devil, I cannot kill thee.
                    [*Wounds Iago.*]
   Lod. Wrench his sword from him.
   Iago.   I bleed, sir; but not kill'd.

   Oth. I am not sorry neither. I'd have thee live;
For, in my sense, 'tis happiness to die.   290
   Lod. O thou Othello, that [wast] once so good,
Fall'n in the practice of a cursed slave,
What shall be said to thee?
   Oth.   Why, anything.
An honourable murderer, if you will;
For nought I did in hate, but all in honour.   295
   Lod. This wretch hath part confess'd his villainy.
Did you and he consent in Cassio's death?
   Oth. Ay.
   Cas. Dear General, I never gave you cause.
   Oth. I do believe it, and I ask your pardon.   300
Will you, I pray, demand that demi-devil
Why he hath thus ensnar'd my soul and body?
   Iago. Demand me nothing; what you know, you
     know.
From this time forth I never will speak word.
   Lod. What, not to pray?
   Gra.   Torments will ope your lips.   305
   Oth. Well, thou dost best.
   Lod. Sir, you shall understand what hath befall'n,
Which, as I think, you know not. Here is a letter
Found in the pocket of the slain Roderigo,
And here another. The one of them imports   310
The death of Cassio to be undertook
By Roderigo.
   Oth. O villain!
   Cas.   Most heathenish and most gross!
   Lod. Now here's another discontented paper,
Found in his pocket too; and this, it seems,   315
Roderigo meant t' have sent this damned villain;
But that, belike, Iago in the interim
Came in and satisfi'd him.
   Oth.   O thou pernicious caitiff! —
How came you, Cassio, by that handkerchief
That was my wife's?
   Cas.   I found it in my chamber,   320
And he himself confess'd but even now
That there he dropp'd it for a special purpose
Which wrought to his desire.
   Oth.   O fool! fool! fool!
   Cas. There is besides in Roderigo's letter,
How he upbraids Iago, that he made him   325
Brave me upon the watch, whereon it came
That I was cast; and even but now he spake,
After long seeming dead, Iago hurt him,
Iago set him on.
   Lod. You must forsake this room and go with
     us.   330
Your power and your command is taken off,
And Cassio rules in Cyprus. For this slave,
If there be any cunning cruelty
That can torment him much and hold him long,

---

253. **ice-brook's temper:** its steel tempered in icy water. 258. **naked:** unarmed. 264. **stop:** power to stop. 267. **butt:**
goal. 273. **compt:** accounting, i.e., Judgment Day. 286. **I...feet:** i.e., to see if they are cloven. 291. **[wast]** *was* F. *wert*
Q. 292. **practice:** plot. 321. **but** Q. *it but* F.

It shall be his. You shall close prisoner rest, 335
Till that the nature of your fault be known
To the Venetian state. Come, bring away.

    Oth. Soft you; a word or two before you go.
I have done the state some service, and they know 't.
No more of that. I pray you, in your letters, 340
When you shall these unlucky deeds relate,
Speak of me as I am; nothing extenuate,
Nor set down aught in malice. Then must you
    speak
Of one that lov'd not wisely but too well;
Of one not easily jealous, but, being wrought, 345
Perplex'd in the extreme; of one whose hand,
Like the base [Indian], threw a pearl away
Richer than all his tribe; of one whose subdu'd
    eyes,
Albeit unused to the melting mood,
Drops tears as fast as the Arabian trees 350
Their medicinal gum. Set you down this;
And say besides, that in Aleppo once,
Where a malignant and a turban'd Turk
Beat a Venetian and traduc'd the state,

I took by th' throat the circumcised dog, 355
And smote him — thus.   *[Stabs himself.*
    Lod. O bloody period!
    Gra.   All that's spoke is marr'd.
    Oth. I kiss'd thee ere I kill'd thee: no way but
    this,
Killing myself, to die upon a kiss.
         [Falls on the bed, and] dies.
    Cas. This did I fear, but thought he had no
    weapon; 360
For he was great of heart.
    Lod.   *[To Iago.]* O Spartan dog,
More fell than anguish, hunger, or the sea!
Look on the tragic loading of this bed;
This is thy work. The object poisons sight;
Let it be hid. Gratiano, keep the house, 365
And seize upon the fortunes of the Moor,
For they succeed on you. To you, Lord Governor,
Remains the censure of this hellish villain;
The time, the place, the torture. O, enforce it!
Myself will straight aboard; and to the state 370
This heavy act with heavy heart relate. *[Exeunt.*

346. **Perplex'd:** distraught.   347. **[Indian]** Q. *Iudean* F. The allusion has not been identified. 356. **period:** end. 361. **Spartan dog:** bloodhound. 366. **seize upon:** take legal possession of. 368. **censure:** sentencing.

The Tragedy of King Lear

ON NOVEMBER 26, 1607, "Master William Shakespeare his historye of Kinge Lear" was entered in the Stationers' Register "as yt was played before the Kinges maiestie at Whitehall vppon Sainct Stephens night at Christmas Last." The First Quarto, appearing in 1608, repeats upon its title page Shakespeare's name and the notice of the command performance. This Quarto, known as the "Pied Bull" Quarto because it was printed for Nathaniel Butter and "sold at his shop in Pauls Church-yard at the signe of the Pide Bull," exists in a variety of states, owing to the fact that corrections were made while the work was being printed, corrected and uncorrected sheets being bound up together in several different combinations. A Second Quarto, reprinting the First, has been shown to belong to the year 1619, though the date upon its title page is 1608. The text in the First Quarto is very poorly printed, but it contains some 300 lines absent from the Folio. The Folio text, much more accurate, has, in turn, over one hundred lines lacking in the Quarto. Except for the Fool's prophecy (III.ii.79–95), which the Folio supplies and which is commonly regarded as spurious, all of the passages are held to be authentic, and it is reasonable to suppose that both texts derive from a single original, and that their respective omissions are, at least for the most part, cuts made for acting purposes. Certain features of the Quarto, especially the confounding of prose as verse and verse as prose, may point to a short-hand report as the source of the copy. The present text is based upon the Folio as the more accurately printed version, although the Quarto supplies not only its unique passages but numerous good readings.

For the date of King Lear the later limit is fixed by the record of the performance on Saint Stephen's night (December 26) in 1606. An earlier limit is provided by Harsnett's *Declaration of Egregious Popish Impostures* (Stationers' Register, March 16, 1603), from which Shakespeare took the names of the devils in the pretended ravings of Edgar. If, as seems most likely, "these late eclipses" (I.ii.112)

were inspired by the eclipses of the sun and moon on October 2 and September 27, 1605 respectively, then the close of 1605 or early 1606 would seem to be a sound conjecture for the date of composition. The chronological relation of *King Lear* to *Macbeth* (1606) cannot be ascertained, but in the light of the available evidence the priority of the former seems more probable.

In its remote origins the story of Lear appears to be a variant of the Cinderella tale, widespread in folklore. Attached to the name of Lear, the legend appears in a fully developed form in the pseudo-historical chronicle, *Historia Regum Britanniae*, by Geoffrey of Monmouth (c. 1135). Thereafter it became an oft-told tale, especially in Tudor days, the most conspicuous versions being those in Holinshed's *Chronicle*, in *The First parte of the Mirrour for Magistrates* by John Higgins, and in Spenser's *Faerie Queene* (II.x.27–32). The story had already been dramatized in an anonymous play, *The True Chronicle History of King Leir* (1605). This play, however, was an old one, having been registered on May 14, 1594 and having been acted, according to Henslowe's records, during the month preceding. It was registered again on May 8, 1605, before its publication in that year as "diuers and sundry times lately acted." It has been urged that the old play was belatedly published to take advantage of the success of Shakespeare's play, but it is easier to believe that the printing, or the revival, of the former moved Shakespeare to handle the time-honored story.

Shakespeare owes little to earlier accounts beyond the broad outlines of the traditional story. From Spenser he may have taken the present form of Cordelia's name, which earlier had been Cordeilla or Cordella. From the old play come minor verbal echoes and perhaps the suggestion for the characters of Kent and Oswald. Comparison of Shakespeare's version with its predecessors, however, reveals mainly his distinctive originality.

Shakespeare transforms the story by substituting a tragic catastrophe for the traditional happy ending, according to which the French forces are victorious and Lear is restored to his kingdom, where he dies in peace after reigning two more years. The old play closes with the restoration of the king. The earlier versions, however, carry the "history" beyond the death of Lear to a calamitous ending involving Cordelia. According to their story, Cordelia and her husband succeed to the throne, but after about five years the sons of Goneril and Regan make war upon Cordelia and cast her into prison, where she kills herself in grief and despair. This appendage to the main story presumably gave Shakespeare the idea for a tragic conclusion to the fortunes of Lear. Having resolved upon this fundamental change, Shakespeare directs all his resources to making the catastrophe terrible. He doubles the pity of it by making not only Lear's death but Cordelia's follow the failure of their cause; he adds immeasurable tragic force through the invention of Lear's madness; he augments pathos and irony through the banishment of the loyal Kent and the creation of the faithful Fool. Finally, he enlarges the dimensions of the tragedy and deepens its intensity by introducing the story of Gloucester and his sons.

This skillfully interwoven underplot is developed from the incident of the King of Paphlagonia in Sidney's *Arcadia* (II.x). The romance tells of a king turned against his legitimate son by the slanders of his bastard, the usurpation of his kingdom and his blinding by the bastard, his rescue by the good son whom he has sought to murder, and the foiling of his attempt at suicide by leaping from a rock. But the pretended madness of Edgar is entirely owing to Shakespeare, as is, of course, the deftness by which this minor plot is engrafted on the story of Lear through the activities of Edgar as Poor Tom and the love of Lear's wicked daughters for Edmund.

By this minor plot Shakespeare not only increases the tragic impact of his drama and deepens the conflict of love and hate in its world, but he both complicates and clarifies the structure through the symmetry of dominant elements. Both Lear and Gloucester suffer from the ingratitude of the children whom they have trusted and are succored by the ones they have cast off. Both meet their injured offspring without recognizing them. Both learn wisdom through adversity — too late. Then there is the remarkable instrumentation upon the theme of madness in the delirium of Lear, in the feigned insanity of Edgar, and in the cracked intelligence of the Fool. *King Lear* is a splendid achievement in dramatic counterpoint.

The much discussed opening affords a perfect illustration of Shakespeare's power to throw the illusion of reality over the improbable and to develop a world of human significance from a core of fable.

The initial situation in the traditional story, the division of Lear's kingdom among his daughters according to their expressions of love for him, involves a double improbability; first that a man of intelligence would do what Lear does, secondly that Cordelia, who loves her father so much, would so risk offending him. This implausibility Shakespeare was bound by as a postulate in his inherited material. As such we too must accept it; but at the same time we should appreciate his skill in disguising it, so that in the clean speed and poise of the opening action it is but faintly perceived. Certain details modify the situation and our impressions of it. For one thing, it is apparent that Lear has fixed his intentions in the division of the Kingdom before the occasion set for the announcement of them (I.i.1–7, 37–39, 84–88, 196–204, 245–47). He has envisaged the proclamation as an official act, duly witnessed, and as an opportunity for a public display of gratitude pleasing to his pride. It is apparent, too, that the portion reserved for Cordelia, his favorite daughter, is richer ("more opulent"), not more extensive, than the territories allotted to her sisters (ll. 81–88), and that Lear's preference for Cordelia, injudiciously stressed, has dictated this "largest bounty" and his expectations of a surpassing avowal of affection from her. When, therefore, Cordelia fails him, he is taken completely by surprise. His pride, both regal and paternal, is sharply wounded, he feels defied and publicly humiliated, and he breaks into a paroxysm of anger. His behavior is unpardonably extreme; on the other hand, he is a king accustomed to obedience, and Cordelia seems blunt in excess of what is needful. She might have indulged him. Our feelings toward her, however, are tempered by her "asides" which express to us the feelings she will not utter (ll. 63, 78–80); we suspect already and are soon to know the hypocrisy in her sisters which sickens her (ll. 271–84); and her defense by Kent and France (ll. 153–56, 185–88, 238–40) makes us understand her. The upshot of all this is that at the end of this first scene of swift and sturdy dialogue we are conscious not of inherent improbability but of grievous misunderstanding, and we sense the threat of worse things to come.

The self-will of Lear which blinds him to the true values about him and drives him to such acts of rashness as the disinheriting of Cordelia and the banishment of Kent, is deeply ingrained and has been fostered by years of autocratic rule. Its grip upon him is shown by his aggressive behavior at the home of Goneril before Goneril herself has begun to show her hand, and by his imprecations upon her after she has done so; and the folly into which it has now betrayed him is irreparable because it has delivered him, in the autumn of his life, into the power of ruthless people. From the wrongs unloosed by his monstrous daughters there is no rescue, but there is redemption for Lear's nature. Through his purgatory of suffering he attains to humble self-knowledge, and when he dies he is transfigured.

The change in Lear is gradual, but there are several points at which its progress is registered. Even at the house of Goneril, though he is still his domineering self and his pride is as yet unyielding, there is an intimation that his mind has begun to glimpse its folly (I.iv.288–94). At Gloucester's castle, where the antipathy of his daughters is becoming clearer every minute, Lear tries to master his rising passion (II.iv.56–58, 122), and this effort at patience and self-control, doubtless unaccustomed, is symptomatic of the transformation that adversity is preparing. Here, though he can still curse Goneril, he kneels to Regan, and when she too shows a heart of stone, Lear knows that he is forsaken. Out in the storm Lear defies the elements with all the vehemence of the passion surging in his heart, resolved to endure what to him is easier to bear than the malice of his daughters. Here his suffering is the beginning of wisdom. An outcast now himself, exposed and wretched, Lear feels bound to all the poor and afflicted for whom he has never before taken thought (III.iv.28–36); and presently, delirium having set in, he would make a philosopher of Poor Tom, who seems to him one of those stricken many whom he has just apostrophized and from whom, therefore, he can tardily learn. This is the new Lear, in whom pride and arrogance are extinguished, a Lear who feels his kinship with common mortals. It is in his reunion with Cordelia, however, that the seal is set upon his transformation. Shakespeare has written nothing more moving than the scene of recognition in which Lear acknowledges his fault and begs his daughter's forgiveness (IV.vii. 45 ff.). The lines, remarkable for their absolute simplicity, are carried "alive into the heart." All Lear cares for now is a refuge in Cordelia's love (V.iii.8–19). After this, the cruelty which parts them is almost too much to bear.

It has been truly noted that Lear's madness is an acute case of delirium brought on by physical exposure and nervous strain. This is clearly understood by the doctor who successfully prescribes for him. There is no hint of earlier mental weakness; Lear's despotic ways are royal prerogatives, not insanity. It is interesting, however, that Shakespeare artistically foreshadows what is to happen, in Lear's repeated dread lest his suffering unhinge his mind (I.V.50–51; II.iv.221, 286–89; III.ii.67; III.iv.21–22).

Shakespeare acknowledges no principle demanding poetic justice at the end of a play in which the powers of injustice have cruelly prevailed. Even Cordelia, whose taking off has seemed to many gratuitously wanton, must be sacrificed, for the wickedness upon which Shakespeare meditates is a perverse and a heartless scourge. Nevertheless, Shakespeare did not conceive this tragedy in a spirit of total negation. The picture of disaster upon which we are made to look is not a denial of good. The wickedness of Goneril and Regan and Edmund is matched by the virtue of Cordelia and Kent and Edgar, and there is a world of difference between the sordid ends of the evil characters and the passing of Lear and Cordelia, purged and reunited. The miserable words of Gloucester (IV.i.38–39),

As flies to wanton boys, are we to th' gods,
They kill us for their sport,

have often been quoted as if they abstracted the spirit of the play, in forgetfulness that Gloucester himself learned to think otherwise and, reconciled to affliction, later cried (IV.vi.221–23),

You ever-gentle gods, take my breath from me;
Let not my worser spirit tempt me again
To die before you please!

The meaning of this play is not to be plucked from isolated passages. Indeed, it is difficult to say specifically what the meaning of the play is, unless it be that when reason is abandoned, when natural ties and duties are violated, havoc and suffering are certain to follow. And perhaps one may also discern the implication that suffering may be a way to salvation. For the Lear who expires with Cordelia dead in his arms is a man whom sorrow has ennobled.

THE TRAGEDY OF KING LEAR

[DRAMATIS PERSONÆ

LEAR, *King of Britain.*
KING OF FRANCE.
DUKE OF BURGUNDY.
DUKE OF CORNWALL.
DUKE OF ALBANY.
EARL OF KENT.
EARL OF GLOUCESTER
EDGAR, *son to Gloucester.*
EDMUND, *bastard son to Gloucester.*
CURAN, *a courtier.*
Old Man, *tenant to Gloucester.*

Doctor.
Fool.
OSWALD, *steward to Goneril.*
A Captain employed by Edmund.
Gentleman attendant on Cordelia.
A Herald.
Servants to Cornwall.

GONERIL,
REGAN, } *daughters to Lear.*
CORDELIA,

Knights of Lear's train, Captains, Messengers, Soldiers, and Attendants.

SCENE: *Britain.*]

ACT I

SCENE I. [*King Lear's palace.*]

Enter KENT, GLOUCESTER, *and* EDMUND.

Kent. I thought the King had more affected the
Duke of Albany than Cornwall.

Glou. It did always seem so to us; but now, in
the division of the kingdom, it appears not which
of the Dukes he values most; for qualities are so
weigh'd, that curiosity in neither can make choice
of either's moiety.   7

Kent. Is not this your son, my lord?

Glou. His breeding, sir, hath been at my charge.
I have so often blush'd to acknowledge him, that
now I am braz'd to't.   11

Kent. I cannot conceive you.

Glou. Sir, this young fellow's mother could;
whereupon she grew round-womb'd, and had, indeed, sir, a son for her cradle ere she had a husband
for her bed.   Do you smell a fault?

Kent. I cannot wish the fault undone, the issue
of it being so proper.   18

Glou. But I have a son, sir, by order of law, some
year elder than this, who yet is no dearer in my
account.   Though this knave came something
saucily to the world before he was sent for, yet
was his mother fair; there was good sport at his
making, and the whoreson must be acknowledged.
Do you know this noble gentleman, Edmund?   25

Edm. No, my lord.

Glou. My Lord of Kent.   Remember him hereafter as my honourable friend.

Edm. My services to your lordship.

Kent. I must love you, and sue to know you
better.   31

Edm. Sir, I shall study deserving.

Glou. He hath been out nine years, and away he
shall again.   The King is coming.

Sennet.   Enter one bearing a coronet, then KING
LEAR, *then the* DUKES OF ALBANY *and* CORNWALL,
next GONERIL, REGAN, CORDELIA, *with followers.*

Lear. Attend the lords of France and Burgundy,
Gloucester.   35

Glou. I shall, my lord.
                    [*Exeunt* [*Gloucester and Edmund*].
Lear. Meantime we shall express our darker
    purpose.
Give me the map there.   Know that we have di-
    vided
In three our kingdom; and 'tis our fast intent
To shake all cares and business from our age,   40
Conferring them on younger strengths, while we
Unburden'd crawl toward death.   Our son of Corn-
    wall,
And you, our no less loving son of Albany,
We have this hour a constant will to publish
Our daughters' several dowers, that future strife   45
May be prevented now.   The Princes, France and
    Burgundy,
Great rivals in our youngest daughter's love,
Long in our court have made their amorous so-
    journ,
And here are to be answer'd.   Tell me, my daugh-
    ters, —
Since now we will divest us both of rule,   50
Interest of territory, cares of state, —
Which of you shall we say doth love us most,
That we our largest bounty may extend
Where nature doth with merit challenge? Goneril,
Our eldest-born, speak first.   55
    Gon. Sir, I love you more than word can wield
    the matter;
Dearer than eye-sight, space, and liberty;
Beyond what can be valued, rich or rare;
No less than life, with grace, health, beauty,
    honour;
As much as child e'er lov'd, or father found;   60
A love that makes breath poor, and speech unable:
Beyond all manner of so much I love you.
    Cor. [*Aside.*] What shall Cordelia speak?   Love
    and be silent.
    Lear. Of all these bounds, even from this line to
    this,
With shadowy forests and with champains rich'd,   65
With plenteous rivers and wide-skirted meads,
We make thee lady.   To thine and Albany's issues
Be this perpetual.   What says our second daughter,
Our dearest Regan, wife of Cornwall?   [Speak.]
    Reg. I am made of that self metal as my sister,   71
And prize me at her worth.   In my true heart
I find she names my very deed of love;
Only she comes too short, that I profess
Myself an enemy to all other joys   75
Which the most precious square of sense [possesses],

And find I am alone felicitate
In your dear Highness' love.
    Cor.   [*Aside.*] Then poor Cordelia!
And yet not so; since, I am sure, my love's
More ponderous than my tongue.   80
    Lear. To thee and thine hereditary ever
Remain this ample third of our fair kingdom;
No less in space, validity, and pleasure,
Than that conferr'd on Goneril.   Now, our joy,
Although our last and least, to whose young love   85
The vines of France and milk of Burgundy
Strive to be interess'd, what can you say to draw
A third more opulent than your sisters?   Speak.
    Cor. Nothing, my lord.
    Lear. Nothing!   90
    Cor. Nothing.
    Lear. Nothing will come of nothing.   Speak
    again.
    Cor. Unhappy that I am, I cannot heave
My heart into my mouth.   I love your Majesty
According to my bond; no more nor less.   95
    Lear. How, how, Cordelia!   Mend your speech
    a little,
Lest you may mar your fortunes.
    Cor.   Good my lord,
You have begot me, bred me, lov'd me: I
Return those duties back as are right fit;
Obey you, love you, and most honour you.   100
Why have my sisters husbands, if they say
They love you all?   Haply, when I shall wed,
That lord whose hand must take my plight shall
    carry
Half my love with him, half my care and duty.
Sure, I shall never marry like my sisters   105
[To love my father all].
    Lear. But goes thy heart with this?
    Cor.   Ay, my good lord.
    Lear. So young, and so untender?
    Cor. So young, my lord, and true.
    Lear. Let it be so; thy truth, then, be thy dower!
For, by the sacred radiance of the sun,   111
The [mysteries] of Hecate and the night;
By all the operation of the orbs
From whom we do exist and cease to be;
Here I disclaim all my paternal care,   115
Propinquity and property of blood,
And as a stranger to my heart and me
Hold thee from this for ever.   The barbarous
    Scythian,
Or he that makes his generation messes
To gorge his appetite, shall to my bosom   120

---

51. **Interest:** possession.   54. **Where ... challenge:** to the one whose nature and deserts make the best claim.
65. **champains:** plains.   70. [**Speak**] Q.   Om. F.   72. **prize ... worth:** estimate myself as her equal (in affection).
76. **most ... sense:** most exquisite region of my senses.   [**possesses**] Q.   *professes* F.   77. **felicitate:** made happy.
83. **validity:** value.   85. **our ... least** F.   *the last not least* Q.   87. **be interess'd:** establish a claim.   95. **bond:** duty.   103.
plight: troth-plight.   106. [**To ... all**] Q.   Om. F.   112. [**mysteries**] F₂.   *miseries* F₁ *mistresse* Q.   **Hecate:** goddess of the
infernal regions.   113. **operation:** influence.   119. **generation:** children.   But Herodotus says the Scythians ate the aged.

Be as well neighbour'd, piti'd, and reliev'd,
As thou my sometime daughter.
   Kent.   Good my liege, —
   Lear. Peace, Kent!
Come not between the dragon and his wrath.
I lov'd her most, and thought to set my rest   125
On her kind nursery. [*To Cor.*] Hence, and avoid
   my sight! —
So be my grave my peace, as here I give
Her father's heart from her! Call France. — Who
   stirs?
Call Burgundy. Cornwall and Albany,
With my two daughters' dowers digest the third;
Let pride, which she calls plainness, marry her.   131
I do invest you jointly with my power,
Pre-eminence, and all the large effects
That troop with majesty. Ourself, by monthly
   course,
With reservation of an hundred knights   135
By you to be sustain'd, shall our abode
Make with you by due turn. Only we shall
   retain
The name, and all th' addition to a king;
The sway, revenue, execution of the rest,
Beloved sons, be yours; which to confirm,   140
This coronet part between you.
   Kent.   Royal Lear,
Whom I have ever honour'd as my king,
Lov'd as my father, as my master follow'd,
As my great patron thought on in my prayers, —
   Lear. The bow is bent and drawn; make from
   the shaft.   145
   Kent. Let it fall rather, though the fork invade
The region of my heart. be Kent unmannerly
When Lear is mad. What wouldst thou do, old
   man?
Thinkest thou that duty shall have dread to speak
When power to flattery bows? To plainness hon-
   our's bound   150
When majesty falls to folly. Reserve thy state;
And in thy best consideration check
This hideous rashness. Answer my life my judge-
   ment,
Thy youngest daughter does not love thee least;
Nor are those empty-hearted whose low sounds
Reverb no hollowness.
   Lear.   Kent, on thy life, no more.   156
   Kent. My life I never held but as a pawn
To wage against thine enemies, [nor] fear to lose it,
Thy safety being motive.
   Lear.   Out of my sight!
   Kent. See better, Lear; and let me still remain
The true blank of thine eye.   160
   Lear. Now, by Apollo, —

   Kent.   Now, by Apollo, king,
Thou swear'st thy gods in vain.
   Lear.   O, vassal! miscreant!
                [*Laying his hand on his sword.*]
   Alb. ⎫
          ⎬ Dear sir, forbear.   164
   Corn.⎭
   Kent. Kill thy physician, and thy fee bestow
Upon the foul disease. Revoke thy gift,
Or, whilst I can vent clamour from my throat,
I'll tell thee thou dost evil.
   Lear.   Hear me, recreant!
On thine allegiance, hear me!   170
That thou hast sought to make us break our vows,
Which we durst never yet, and with strain'd pride
To come betwixt our sentence and our power,
Which nor our nature nor our place can bear,
Our potency made good, take thy reward.   175
Five days we do allot thee, for provision
To shield thee from disasters of the world;
And on the sixth to turn thy hated back
Upon our kingdom. If, on the tenth day follow-
   ing,   179
Thy banish'd trunk be found in our dominions,
The moment is thy death. Away! By Jupiter,
This shall not be revok'd.
   Kent. Fare thee well, king! Sith thus thou wilt
   appear,
Freedom lives hence, and banishment is here.
[*To Cordelia.*] The gods to their dear shelter take
   thee, maid,   185
That justly think'st and hast most rightly said!
[*To Regan and Goneril.*] And your large speeches
   may your deeds approve,
That good effects may spring from words of love.
Thus Kent, O princes, bids you all adieu;
He'll shape his old course in a country new.   190
                        [*Exit.*

   Flourish. Re-enter GLOUCESTER, *with* FRANCE,
       BURGUNDY, *and Attendants.*

   Glou. Here's France and Burgundy, my noble
   lord.
   Lear. My Lord of Burgundy,
We first address toward you, who with this king
Hath rivall'd for our daughter. What, in the least,
Will you require in present dower with her,   195
Or cease your quest of love?
   Bur.   Most royal Majesty,
I crave no more than what your Highness offer'd,
Nor will you tender less.
   Lear.   Right noble Burgundy,
When she was dear to us, we did hold her so;
But now her price is fall'n. Sir, there she stands:
If aught within that little-seeming substance,   201

---

125. **set my rest**: stake my all. 126. **nursery**: cherishing. 130. **digest**: absorb. 138. **addition**: title. 146. **fork**: barb.
158. **[nor]** Q. *nere* F. 161. **blank**: center of the target. 172. **strain'd**: exaggerated. 175. **Our...good**: to prove my
power. 183. **Sith**: since. 187. **approve**: justify. 198. **tender**: offer.

Or all of it, with our displeasure piec'd,
And nothing more, may fitly like your Grace,
She's there, and she is yours.
    Bur.   I know no answer.
  Lear. Will you, with those infirmities she owes,
Unfriended, new-adopted to our hate,   206
Dower'd with our curse, and stranger'd with our
    oath,
Take her, or leave her?
    Bur.   Pardon me, royal sir;
Election makes not up in such conditions.
  Lear. Then leave her, sir; for, by the power that
    made me,   210
I tell you all her wealth. [*To France.*] For you,
    great king,
I would not from your love make such a stray
To match you where I hate; therefore beseech you
T' avert your liking a more worthier way
Than on a wretch whom Nature is asham'd   215
Almost t' acknowledge hers.
  France.   This is most strange,
That she, whom even but now was your [best]
    object,
The argument of your praise, balm of your age,
The best, the dearest, should in this trice of time
Commit a thing so monstrous, to dismantle   220
So many folds of favour. Sure her offence
Must be of such unnatural degree
That monsters it, or your fore-vouch'd affection
Fallen into taint; which to believe of her,
Must be a faith that reason without miracle] 225
Should never plant in me.
  Cor.   I yet beseech your Majesty, —
If for I want that glib and oily art
To speak and purpose not, since what I [well] in-
    tend,
I'll do't before I speak, — that you make known
It is no vicious blot, murder, or foulness,   230
No unchaste action, or dishonoured step,
That hath depriv'd me of your grace and favour;
But even for want of that for which I am richer,
A still-soliciting eye, and such a tongue
That I am glad I have not, though not to have it 235
Hath lost me in your liking.
  Lear.   Better thou
Hadst not been born than not t' have pleas'd me
    better.
  France. Is it but this, — a tardiness in nature
Which often leaves the history unspoke   239
That it intends to do? My Lord of Burgundy,
What say you to the lady? Love 's not love

When it is mingled with regards that stands
Aloof from th' entire point. Will you have her?
She is herself a dowry.
  Bur.   Royal king,
Give but that portion which yourself propos'd,
And here I take Cordelia by the hand,   246
Duchess of Burgundy.
  Lear. Nothing. I have sworn; I am firm.
  Bur. I am sorry, then, you have so lost a father
That you must lose a husband.
  Cor.   Peace be with Burgundy!
Since that respect and fortunes are his love,   251
I shall not be his wife.
  France. Fairest Cordelia, that art most rich
    being poor,
Most choice forsaken, and most lov'd despis'd!
Thee and thy virtues here I seize upon,   255
Be it lawful I take up what 's cast away.
Gods, gods! 'tis strange that from their cold'st
    neglect
My love should kindle to inflam'd respect.
Thy dowerless daughter, king, thrown to my chance,
Is queen of us, of ours, and our fair France.   260
Not all the dukes of waterish Burgundy
Can buy this unpriz'd precious maid of me.
Bid them farewell, Cordelia, though unkind;
Thou losest here, a better where to find.
  Lear. Thou hast her, France. Let her be thine;
    for we   265
Have no such daughter, nor shall ever see
That face of hers again. — [*To Cor.*] Therefore be
    gone
Without our grace, our love, our benison. —
Come, noble Burgundy.
       [*Flourish. Exeunt [all but France, Goneril,*
              Regan, and Cordelia].
  France. Bid farewell to your sisters.   270
  Cor. The jewels of our father, with wash'd eyes
Cordelia leaves you. I know you what you are;
And like a sister am most loath to call
Your faults as they are nam'd. Love well our
    father.
To your professed bosoms I commit him;   275
But yet, alas, stood I within his grace,
I would prefer him to a better place.
So, farewell to you both.
  Reg. Prescribe not us our duty.
  Gon.   Let your study 279
Be to content your lord, who hath receiv'd you
At fortune's alms. You have obedience scanted,
And well are worth the want that you have wanted.

203. **like**: please. 205. **owes**: owns. 209. **Election...conditions**: one cannot make a choice on these terms. 212. **stray**: departure. 217. [**best**] Q. Om. F. 218. **argument**: theme. 223. **monsters**: makes monstrous. 224. **Fallen into taint**: must have decayed. 228. [**well**] Q. *will* F. 242. **regards**: considerations. 251. **respect and**: consideration of. 259. **thrown...chance**: fallen to my lot. 261. **waterish**: (1) well-watered, (2) poor. 264. **where**: place. 271. **wash'd**: tear-washed. 275. **professed**: making professions (of love). 281. **scanted**: come short in. 282. And have well deserved the loss of that affection in which you were lacking.

Cor. Time shall unfold what plighted cunning
    hides;
Who covers faults, at last shame [them] derides.
Well may you prosper!
    France.   Come, my fair Cordelia. 285
        [*Exeunt* [*France and Cordelia*].
Gon. Sister, it is not little I have to say of what
most nearly appertains to us both. I think our
father will hence to-night.
    Reg. That's most certain, and with you; next
month with us. 290
    Gon. You see how full of changes his age is; the
observation we have made of it hath [not] been
little. He always lov'd our sister most; and with
what poor judgement he hath now cast her off appears too grossly.
    Reg. 'Tis the infirmity of his age; yet he hath ever
but slenderly known himself. 297
    Gon. The best and soundest of his time hath been
but rash; then must we look from his age to receive
not alone the imperfections of long-engraffed condition, but therewithal the unruly waywardness that
infirm and choleric years bring with them. 303
    Reg. Such unconstant starts are we like to have
from him as this of Kent's banishment.
    Gon. There is further compliment of leave-taking
between France and him. Pray you, let['s hit] together; if our father carry authority with such disposition as he bears, this last surrender of his will
but offend us. 310
    Reg. We shall further think of it.
    Gon. We must do something, and i' th' heat.
        [*Exeunt.*

SCENE II. [*The Earl of Gloucester's castle.*]

Enter Bastard [EDMUND *with a letter*].

Edm. Thou, Nature, art my goddess; to thy law
My services are bound. Wherefore should I
Stand in the plague of custom, and permit
The curiosity of nations to deprive me,
For that I am some twelve or fourteen moonshines 5
Lag of a brother? Why bastard? Wherefore base?
When my dimensions are as well compact,
My mind as generous, and my shape as true,
As honest madam's issue? Why brand they us
With base? with baseness? bastardy? base, base? 10
Who, in the lusty stealth of nature, take
More composition and fierce quality
Than doth, within a dull, stale, tired bed,
Go to the creating a whole tribe of fops,

Got 'tween asleep and wake? Well, then, 15
Legitimate Edgar, I must have your land.
Our father's love is to the bastard Edmund
As to th' legitimate. Fine word, "legitimate!"
Well, my legitimate, if this letter speed
And my invention thrive, Edmund the base 20
Shall [top] th' legitimate. I grow; I prosper.
Now, gods, stand up for bastards!

Enter GLOUCESTER.

Glou. Kent banish'd thus! and France in choler
    parted!
And the King gone tonight! [subscrib'd] his power!
Confin'd to exhibition! All this done 25
Upon the gad! Edmund, how now! what news?
    Edm. So please your lordship, none.
        [*Putting up the letter.*]
    Glou. Why so earnestly seek you to put up that
    letter?
    Edm. I know no news, my lord.
    Glou. What paper were you reading? 30
    Edm. Nothing, my lord.
    Glou. No? What needed, then, that terrible
dispatch of it into your pocket? The quality of
nothing hath not such need to hide itself. Let's
see. Come, if it be nothing, I shall not need spectacles. 36
    Edm. I beseech you, sir, pardon me. It is a
letter from my brother that I have not all o'er-
read; and for so much as I have perus'd, I find it
not fit for your o'er-looking. 40
    Glou. Give me the letter, sir.
    Edm. I shall offend either to detain or give it.
The contents, as in part I understand them, are to
blame.
    Glou. Let's see, let's see. 45
    Edm. I hope, for my brother's justification, he
wrote this but as an essay or taste of my virtue.
    Glou. (*Reads.*) "This policy and reverence of
age makes the world bitter to the best of our times;
keeps our fortunes from us till our oldness can- 50
not relish them. I begin to find an idle and fond
bondage in the oppression of aged tyranny; who
sways, not as it hath power, but as it is suffer'd.
Come to me, that of this I may speak more. If
our father would sleep till I wak'd him, you 55
should enjoy half his revenue for ever, and live the
beloved of your brother,   EDGAR."
Hum — conspiracy! — "Sleep till I wake him, you
should enjoy half his revenue!" — My son Edgar!
Had he a hand to write this? a heart and brain to

---

283. **plighted**: folded, complicated.   284. **shame** [them] Q. *with shame* F.   292. [not] Q. Om. F.   295. **grossly:** obviously.   304. **starts**: impulsive actions.   308. **let['s hit]** Q: let us agree. *let us sit* F.   312. **i' th' heat:** while the iron is hot.

    Sc. ii, 3. **plague:** vexation.   4. **curiosity of nations:** i.e., the absurd law favoring the first-born.   6. **Lag of:** younger than. 19. **speed:** succeed.   21. **[top]** (Edwards conj.). *to'* F.   24. **[subscrib'd]** Q: surrendered. *prescrib'd* F.   25. **exhibition:** an allowance.   26. **gad:** spur of the moment.   47. **essay or taste:** trial or test.   48. **policy and reverence:** policy of revering. 49. **times:** lives.   51. **fond:** foolish.

breed it in? — When came this to you? Who brought it?   62

Edm. It was not brought me, my lord; there's the cunning of it. I found it thrown in at the casement of my closet.

Glou. You know the character to be your brother's?   67

Edm. If the matter were good, my lord, I durst swear it were his; but, in respect of that, I would fain think it were not.

Glou. It is his.

Edm. It is his hand, my lord; but I hope his heart is not in the contents.   73

Glou. Has he never before sounded you in this business?

Edm. Never, my lord; but I have heard him oft maintain it to be fit that, sons at perfect age and fathers declin'd, the father should be as ward to the son, and the son manage his revenue.   79

Glou. O villain, villain! His very opinion in the letter! Abhorred villain! Unnatural, detested, brutish villain! worse than brutish! Go, sirrah, seek him; I'll apprehend him. Abominable villain! Where is he?   84

Edm. I do not well know, my lord. If it shall please you to suspend your indignation against my brother till you can derive from him better testimony of his intent, you should run a certain course; where, if you violently proceed against him, mistaking his purpose, it would make a great gap   90 in your own honour and shake in pieces the heart of his obedience. I dare pawn down my life for him that he hath writ this to feel my affection to your honour, and to no other pretence of danger.   95

Glou. Think you so?

Edm. If your honour judge it meet, I will place you where you shall hear us confer of this, and by an auricular assurance have your satisfaction; and that without any further delay than this very evening.   101

Glou. He cannot be such a monster —

[*Edm.* Nor is not, sure.

Glou. To his father, that so tenderly and entirely loves him. Heaven and earth!] Ed-   105 mund, seek him out; wind me into him, I pray you. Frame the business after your own wisdom. I would unstate myself to be in a due resolution.

Edm. I will seek him, sir, presently; convey the business as I shall find means, and acquaint you withal.   111

Glou. These late eclipses in the sun and moon portend no good to us. Though the wisdom of nature can reason it thus and thus, yet nature finds itself scourg'd by the sequent effects.   115 Love cools, friendship falls off, brothers divide: in cities, mutinies; in countries, discord; in palaces, treason; and the bond crack'd 'twixt son and father. This villain of mine comes under the prediction; there's son against father: the King falls from   120 bias of nature; there's father against child. We have seen the best of our time; machinations, hollowness, treachery, and all ruinous disorders, follow us disquietly to our graves. Find out this villain, Edmund; it shall lose thee nothing; do it care-   125 fully. And the noble and true-hearted Kent banish'd! his offence, honesty! 'Tis strange.

[*Exit.*

Edm. This is the excellent foppery of the world, that, when we are sick in fortune, — often the surfeits of our own behaviour, — we make guilty   130 of our disasters the sun, the moon, and stars, as if we were villains on necessity, fools by heavenly compulsion, knaves, thieves, and treachers by spherical predominance, drunkards, liars, and adulterers by an enforc'd obedience of planetary   135 influence, and all that we are evil in, by a divine thrusting on. An admirable evasion of whoremaster man, to lay his goatish disposition on the charge of a star! My father compounded with my mother under the dragon's tail, and my nativity   140 was under *Ursa major;* so that it follows, I am rough and lecherous. Fut, I should have been that I am, had the maidenliest star in the firmament twinkled on my bastardizing. [Edgar —]   145

Enter EDGAR.

pat he comes like the catastrophe of the old comedy. My cue is villanous melancholy, with a sigh like Tom o' Bedlam. — O, these eclipses do portend these divisions! *fa, sol, la, mi.*

Edg. How now, brother Edmund! what serious contemplation are you in?   151

Edm. I am thinking, brother, of a prediction I read this other day, what should follow these eclipses.

Edg. Do you busy yourself with that?   155

Edm. I promise you, the effects he writes of succeed unhappily; [as of unnaturalness between the child and the parent; death, dearth, dissolutions of ancient amities; divisions in state, menaces and maledictions against king and nobles; needless diffidences, banishment of friends, dissipation of cohorts, nuptial breaches, and I know not what.   163

---

66. **character:** handwriting.   78. **declin'd:** failed.   89. **where:** whereas.   94. **feel:** sound.   95. **pretence of danger:** dangerous intent.   103-105. Q. Om. F.   106. **wind ... him:** gain his confidence.   108. **unstate ... resolution:** forfeit my position to be properly assured.   109. **presently:** at once.   **convey:** carry on.   120-21. **falls ... nature:** acts against his natural disposition.   128. **foppery:** foolishness.   133. **treachers:** traitors.   134. **spherical predominance:** influence of the planets.   145. **[Edgar —]** Q. Om. F.   148. **Tom o' Bedlam:** a lunatic beggar.   157-166. Q. Om. F.   161. **diffidences:** suspicions.

Edg. How long have you been a sectary astronomical?

Edm. Come, come;] when saw you my father last?

Edg. The night gone by.   168

Edm. Spake you with him?

Edg. Ay, two hours together.

Edm. Parted you in good terms? Found you no displeasure in him by word nor countenance?

Edg. None at all.   173

Edm. Bethink yourself wherein you may have offended him; and at my entreaty forbear his presence until some little time hath qualified the heat of his displeasure, which at this instant so rageth in him, that with the mischief of your person it would scarcely allay.

Edg. Some villain hath done me wrong.   180

Edm. That's my fear. I pray you, have a continent forbearance till the speed of his rage goes slower; and, as I say, retire with me to my lodging, from whence I will fitly bring you to hear my lord speak. Pray ye, go; there's my key. If you do stir abroad, go arm'd.   186

Edg. Arm'd, brother!

Edm. Brother, I advise you to the best; I am no honest man if there be any good meaning toward you. I have told you what I have seen and heard; but faintly, nothing like the image and horror of it. Pray you, away.   192

Edg. Shall I hear from you anon?

Edm. I do serve you in this business.

                          [Exit Edgar.

A credulous father and a brother noble,   195
Whose nature is so far from doing harms
That he suspects none; on whose foolish honesty
My practices ride easy. I see the business.
Let me, if not by birth, have lands by wit:
All with me 's meet that I can fashion fit.   200
                          [Exit.

SCENE III. [*The Duke of Albany's palace.*]

Enter GONERIL, *and* [OSWALD, *her*] *Steward.*

Gon. Did my father strike my gentleman for chiding of his Fool?

Osw. Ay, madam.

Gon. By day and night he wrongs me; every hour
He flashes into one gross crime or other
That sets us all at odds. I'll not endure it.   5
His knights grow riotous, and himself upbraids us
On every trifle. When he returns from hunting
I will not speak with him; say I am sick.
If you come slack of former services,

You shall do well; the fault of it I'll answer.   10

Osw. He's coming, madam; I hear him.

                        [Horns within.]

Gon. Put on what weary negligence you please,
You and your fellows; I'd have it come to question.
If he distaste it, let him to my sister,
Whose mind and mine, I know, in that are one,   15
[Not to be over-rul'd. Idle old man,
That still would manage those authorities
That he hath given away! Now, by my life,
Old fools are babes again, and must be us'd
With checks as flatteries, when they are seen abus'd.]
Remember what I have said.

Osw.   Well, madam.   21

Gon. And let his knights have colder looks among you;
What grows of it, no matter. Advise your fellows so.
[I would breed from hence occasions, and I shall,
That I may speak.] I'll write straight to my sister
To hold my [very] course. Prepare for dinner.   26
                          [Exeunt.

SCENE IV. [*A hall in the same.*]

Enter KENT [*disguised*].

Kent. If but as well I other accents borrow,
That can my speech defuse, my good intent
May carry through itself to that full issue
For which I raz'd my likeness. Now, banish'd Kent,
If thou canst serve where thou dost stand condemn'd,   5
So may it come, thy master, whom thou lov'st,
Shall find thee full of labours.

    Horns within. Enter LEAR, [KNIGHTS] *and Attendants.*

Lear. Let me not stay a jot for dinner; go get it ready. [*Exit an attendant.*] How now! what art thou?   10

Kent. A man, sir.

Lear. What dost thou profess? What wouldst thou with us?   13

Kent. I do profess to be no less than I seem; to serve him truly that will put me in trust; to love him that is honest; to converse with him that is wise and says little; to fear judgement; to fight when I cannot choose; and to eat no fish.   18

Lear. What art thou?

Kent. A very honest-hearted fellow, and as poor as the King.

Lear. If thou be'st as poor for a subject as he's

---

164. **sectary astronomical:** student of astrology. 176. **qualified:** moderated. 178. **mischief:** injury. 198. **practices:** plots.

Sc. iii, 13. **question:** discussion. 16-20. [**Not ... abus'd**] Q. Om. F. 20. **as:** as well as. **abus'd:** misled. 24-25. [I ... speak] Q. Om. F. 26. [**very**] Q: identical. Om. F.

Sc. iv, 2. **defuse:** disguise. 4. **raz'd my likeness:** changed my appearance. 18. **eat no fish:** be a Protestant.

for a king, thou art poor enough. What wouldst
thou? 24

Kent. Service.

Lear. Who wouldst thou serve?

Kent. You.

Lear. Dost thou know me, fellow?

Kent. No, sir; but you have that in your countenance which I would fain call master. 30

Lear. What's that?

Kent. Authority.

Lear. What services canst thou do? 33

Kent. I can keep honest counsel, ride, run, mar a
curious tale in telling it, and deliver a plain message
bluntly. That which ordinary men are fit for, I
am qualified in; and the best of me is diligence. 38

Lear. How old art thou?

Kent. Not so young, sir, to love a woman for
singing, nor so old to dote on her for anything. I
have years on my back forty-eight. 42

Lear. Follow me; thou shalt serve me. If I like
thee no worse after dinner, I will not part from thee
yet. Dinner, ho, dinner! Where's my knave? my
Fool? Go you, and call my Fool hither. 47

[*Exit an attendant.*

Enter Steward [OSWALD].

You, you, sirrah, where's my daughter?

Osw. So please you, — [*Exit.*

Lear. What says the fellow there? Call the
clotpoll back. [*Exit a knight.*] Where's my Fool,
ho? I think the world's asleep. 52

[*Re-enter* KNIGHT.]

How now! where's that mongrel?

Knight. He says, my lord, your daughter is not
well. 55

Lear. Why came not the slave back to me when
I call'd him?

Knight. Sir, he answered me in the roundest
manner, he would not.

Lear. He would not! 60

Knight. My lord, I know not what the matter is;
but, to my judgement, your Highness is not entertain'd with that ceremonious affection as you
were wont. There's a great abatement of kindness
appears as well in the general dependants as in the
Duke himself also and your daughter. 67

Lear. Ha! say'st thou so?

Knight. I beseech you, pardon me, my lord, if I
be mistaken; for my duty cannot be silent when I
think your Highness wrong'd. 71

Lear. Thou but rememb'rest me of mine own
conception. I have perceived a most faint neglect
of late, which I have rather blamed as mine own
jealous curiosity than as a very pretence and pur-

pose of unkindness. I will look further into't.
But where's my Fool? I have not seen him this
two days. 78

Knight. Since my young lady's going into France,
sir, the Fool hath much pined away.

Lear. No more of that; I have noted it well.
Go you, and tell my daughter I would speak with
her. [*Exit an attendant.*] Go you, call hither my
Fool. [*Exit an attendant.*] 84

Re-enter Steward [OSWALD].

O, you sir, you, come you hither, sir. Who am I,
sir?

Osw. My lady's father.

Lear. "My lady's father"! My lord's knave!
You whoreson dog! you slave! you cur! 89

Osw. I am none of these, my lord; I beseech your
pardon.

Lear. Do you bandy looks with me, you rascal?
[*Striking him.*]

Osw. I'll not be strucken, my lord. 94

Kent. Nor tripp'd neither, you base foot-ball
player. [*Tripping up his heels.*]

Lear. I thank thee, fellow. Thou serv'st me,
and I'll love thee. 98

Kent. Come, sir, arise, away! I'll teach you
differences. Away, away! If you will measure
your lubber's length again, tarry; but away! go to.
Have you wisdom? So. [*Pushes Oswald out.*]

Lear. Now, my friendly knave, I thank thee.
There's earnest of thy service. 104

[*Giving Kent money.*]

Enter FOOL.

Fool. Let me hire him too; here's my coxcomb.
[*Offering Kent his cap.*]

Lear. How now, my pretty knave! how dost
thou?

Fool. Sirrah, you were best take my coxcomb.
[*Kent.* Why, Fool?] 110

Fool. Why? For taking one's part that's out
of favour. Nay, an thou canst not smile as the
wind sits, thou'lt catch cold shortly. There, take
my coxcomb. Why, this fellow has banish'd two
on 's daughters, and did the third a blessing against
his will; if thou follow him, thou must needs wear
my coxcomb. — How now, nuncle! Would I had
two coxcombs and two daughters! 118

Lear. Why, my boy?

Fool. If I gave them all my living, I'd keep my
coxcombs myself. There's mine; beg another of
thy daughters.

Lear. Take heed, sirrah; the whip. 123

Fool. Truth's a dog must to kennel; he must be

---

51. **clotpoll:** blockhead. 75. **jealous curiosity:** suspicious fussiness. **very pretence:** real intention. 104. **earnest:** advance payment. 110. [**Kent . . . Fool**] Q. *Lear. Why my Boy?* F.

whipp'd out, when [Lady the] brach may stand by
the fire and stink.

Lear. A pestilent gall to me!

Fool. Sirrah, I'll teach thee a speech.

Lear. Do.

Fool. Mark it, nuncle: 130

"Have more than thou showest,
   Speak less than thou knowest,
   Lend less than thou owest,
   Ride more than thou goest,
   Learn more than thou trowest,   135
   Set less than thou throwest;
   Leave thy drink and thy whore,
   And keep in-a-door,
   And thou shalt have more
   Than two tens to a score."   140

Kent. This is nothing, Fool.

Fool. Then 'tis like the breath of an unfee'd
lawyer; you gave me nothing for't. Can you make
no use of nothing, nuncle?

Lear. Why, no, boy; nothing can be made out
of nothing.   146

Fool. [*To Kent.*] Prithee, tell him so much the
rent of his land comes to. He will not believe a
Fool.

Lear. A bitter fool!   150

Fool. Dost thou know the difference, my boy,
between a bitter fool and a sweet one?

Lear. No, lad; teach me.

[*Fool.* "That lord that counsell'd thee
     To give away thy land,   155
   Come place him here by me,
   Do thou for him stand:
   The sweet and bitter fool
     Will presently appear;
   The one in motley here,   160
     The other found out there."

Lear. Dost thou call me fool, boy?

Fool. All thy other titles thou hast given away;
that thou wast born with.

Kent. This is not altogether fool, my lord.   165

Fool. No, faith, lords and great men will not let
me; if I had a monopoly out, they would have part
on't. And ladies, too, they will not let me have all
the fool to myself; they'll be snatching.] Nuncle,
give me an egg, and I'll give thee two crowns.

Lear. What two crowns shall they be?   172

Fool. Why, after I have cut the egg i' th' middle
and eat up the meat, the two crowns of the egg.
When thou clovest thy crown i' th' middle and
gav'st away both parts, thou bor'st thine ass on thy
back o'er the dirt. Thou hadst little wit in thy
bald crown when thou gav'st thy golden one away.

If I speak like myself in this, let him be whipp'd
that first finds it so.   180

"Fools had ne'er less grace in a year;
   For wise men are grown foppish,
   And know not how their wits to wear,
     Their manners are so apish."

Lear. When were you wont to be so full of songs,
sirrah?   186

Fool. I have used it, nuncle, e'er since thou
mad'st thy daughters thy mothers; for when thou
gav'st them the rod, and puttest down thine own
breeches,   190

"Then they for sudden joy did weep,
     And I for sorrow sung,
   That such a king should play bo-peep,
     And go the fools among."   194

Prithee, nuncle, keep a schoolmaster that can teach
thy Fool to lie. I would fain learn to lie.

Lear. And you lie, sirrah, we'll have you
whipp'd.   198

Fool. I marvel what kin thou and thy daughters
are. They'll have me whipp'd for speaking true,
thou'lt have me whipp'd for lying; and sometimes
I am whipp'd for holding my peace. I had rather
be any kind o' thing than a Fool; and yet I would
not be thee, nuncle; thou hast pared thy wit o' both
sides, and left nothing i' th' middle. Here comes
one o' the parings.   206

Enter GONERIL.

Lear. How now, daughter! what makes that
frontlet on? [Methinks] you are too much of late
i' th' frown.   209

Fool. Thou wast a pretty fellow when thou hadst
no need to care for her frowning; now thou art an O
without a figure. I am better than thou art now;
I am a Fool, thou art nothing. [*To Gon.*] Yes, forsooth, I will hold my tongue; so your face bids me,
though you say nothing. Mum, mum,   216

"He that keeps nor crust nor crumb,
   Weary of all, shall want some."

[*Pointing to Lear.*] That's a sheal'd peascod.

Gon. Not only, sir, this your all-licens'd Fool,
But other of your insolent retinue   221
Do hourly carp and quarrel, breaking forth
In rank and not-to-be-endured riots. Sir,
I had thought, by making this well known unto
   you,
To have found a safe redress; but now grow fearful,
By what yourself, too, late have spoke and done, 226
That you protect this course and put it on
By your allowance; which if you should, the fault
Would not scape censure, nor the redresses sleep,

---

125. [**Lady the**] (Malone). *The Lady* F. **brach:** bitch.   133. **owest:** ownest.   134. **goest:** walkest.   136. **Set:** stake.
throwest: win at a throw of the dice.   154–170. [*Fool . . . snatching*] Q. Om. F.   208. **frontlet:** frown.   219. **sheal'd:** empty.   227. **put it on:** encourage it.   228. **allowance:** approval.
band). [**Methinks**] Q. Om. F.   219. **sheal'd:** empty.   227. **put it on:** encourage it.   228. **allowance:** approval.

Which, in the tender of a wholesome weal,   230
Might in their working do you that offence,
Which else were shame, that then necessity
Will call discreet proceeding.
   Fool. For, you know, nuncle,
   "The hedge-sparrow fed the cuckoo so long, 235
    That it had it head bit off by it young."
So, out went the candle, and we were left dark-
   ling.
   Lear. Are you our daughter?
   Gon. [Come, sir,]
I would you would make use of your good wis-
   dom,   240
Whereof I know you are fraught, and put away
These dispositions which of late transport you
From what you rightly are.
   Fool. May not an ass know when the cart draws
the horse? "Whoop, Jug! I love thee."
   Lear. Doth any here know me? This is not
   Lear.   246
Doth Lear walk thus? speak thus? Where are his
   eyes?
Either his notion weakens, his discernings
Are lethargied — Ha! waking? 'Tis not so.
Who is it that can tell me who I am?   250
   Fool. Lear's shadow.
   [*Lear.* I would learn that; for, by the marks of
sovereignty, knowledge, and reason, I should be
false persuaded I had daughters.
   Fool. Which they will make an obedient father.]
   Lear. Your name, fair gentlewoman?   257
   Gon. This admiration, sir, is much o' the savour
Of other your new pranks. I do beseech you
To understand my purposes aright.   260
As you are old and reverend, should be wise.
Here do you keep a hundred knights and squires,
Men so disorder'd, so debosh'd and bold,
That this our court, infected with their manners,
Shows like a riotous inn. Epicurism and lust 265
Makes it more like a tavern or a brothel
Than a grac'd palace. The shame itself doth speak
For instant remedy. Be then desir'd
By her, that else will take the thing she begs,
A little to disquantity your train;   270
And the remainders that shall still depend
To be such men as may besort your age,
Which know themselves and you.
   Lear.   Darkness and devils!
Saddle my horses; call my train together!
Degenerate bastard! I'll not trouble thee;   275
Yet have I left a daughter.

   Gon. You strike my people; and your disorder'd
   rabble
Make servants of their betters.

          Enter ALBANY.

   Lear. Woe, that too late repents! — [O, sir, are
   you come?]
Is it your will? Speak, sir. — Prepare my horses. —
Ingratitude, thou marble-hearted fiend,   281
More hideous when thou show'st thee in a child
Than the sea-monster!
   Alb.   Pray, sir, be patient.
   Lear. [*To Gon.*] Detested kite! thou liest.
My train are men of choice and rarest parts,   285
That all particulars of duty know,
And in the most exact regard support
The worships of their name. O most small fault,
How ugly didst thou in Cordelia show!   289
Which, like an engine, wrench'd my frame of nature
From the fix'd place; drew from my heart all love
And added to the gall. O Lear, Lear, Lear!
Beat at this gate, that let thy folly in
                [*Striking his head.*]
And thy dear judgement out! Go, go, my people.
   Alb. My lord, I am guiltless as I am ignorant 295
Of what hath moved you.
   Lear.   It may be so, my lord.
Hear, Nature! hear, dear goddess, hear!
Suspend thy purpose, if thou didst intend
To make this creature fruitful!
Into her womb convey sterility!   300
Dry up in her the organs of increase,
And from her derogate body never spring
A babe to honour her! If she must teem,
Create her child of spleen, that it may live
And be a thwart disnatur'd torment to her!   305
Let it stamp wrinkles in her brow of youth,
With cadent tears fret channels in her cheeks,
Turn all her mother's pains and benefits
To laughter and contempt, that she may feel
How sharper than a serpent's tooth it is   310
To have a thankless child! — Away, away!   [*Exit.*
   Alb. Now, gods that we adore, whereof comes
   this?
   Gon. Never afflict yourself to know more of it,
But let his disposition have that scope
As dotage gives it.   315

          Re-enter LEAR.

   Lear. What, fifty of my followers at a clap!
Within a fortnight!

---

230. **tender of:** care for. **weal:** commonweal. 236. **it:** its. 237. **darkling:** in the dark. 239. **[Come, sir]** Q. Om. F. 241. **fraught:** furnished with. 248. **notion:** mental power. 252-256. [*Lear*...*father*] Q. Om. F. 252. **by...of:** tested by. 258. **admiration:** (pretended) surprise. 263. **debosh'd:** debauched. 265. **Epicurism:** gluttony. 270. **disquantity:** reduce. 271. **depend:** be your dependants. 272. **besort:** suit. 279. [O...come] Q. Om. F. 288. **worships...name:** their honorable reputation. 290. **engine:** rack. 302. **derogate:** debased. 305. **thwart:** distorted, perverse. **disnatur'd:** unnatural. 307. **cadent:** falling. 313. **more of it:** F. *the cause* Q.

Alb.   What's the matter, sir?

Lear. I'll tell thee.   [*To Gon.*] Life and death!
I am asham'd
That thou hast power to shake my manhood thus;
That these hot tears, which break from me per-
    force,   320
Should make thee worth them.   Blasts and fogs
    upon thee!
Th' untented woundings of a father's curse
Pierce every sense about thee!   Old fond eyes,
Beweep this cause again, I'll pluck ye out,
And cast you, with the waters that you loose,   325
To temper clay.   Ha! [is it come to this?]
Let it be so: I have another daughter,
Who, I am sure, is kind and comfortable.
When she shall hear this of thee, with her nails
She'll flay thy wolvish visage.   Thou shalt find   330
That I'll resume the shape which thou dost think
I have cast off for ever.   [Thou shalt, I warrant
    thee.]   [*Exeunt [Lear, Kent, and attendants*].

Gon. Do you mark that?

Alb. I cannot be so partial, Goneril,
To the great love I bear you, —   335

Gon. Pray you, content. — What, Oswald, ho!
[*To the Fool.*] You, sir, more knave than fool, after
    your master.

Fool. Nuncle Lear, nuncle Lear, tarry! Take
the Fool with thee.

     A fox, when one has caught her,   340
     And such a daughter,
     Should sure to the slaughter,
     If my cap would buy a halter.
     So the Fool follows after.   [*Exit.*

Gon. This man hath had good counsel, — a
    hundred knights!   345
'Tis politic and safe to let him keep
At point a hundred knights; yes, that, on every
    dream,
Each buzz, each fancy, each complaint, dislike,
He may enguard his dotage with their powers,
And hold our lives in mercy.   Oswald, I say!   350

Alb. Well, you may fear too far.

Gon.   Safer than trust too far.
Let me still take away the harms I fear,
Not fear still to be taken.   I know his heart.
What he hath utter'd I have writ my sister.
If she sustain him and his hundred knights,   355
When I have show'd th' unfitness, —

        Re-enter Steward [OSWALD].

                   How now, Oswald!
What, have you writ that letter to my sister?

Osw. Ay, madam.

Gon. Take you some company, and away to horse.
Inform her full of my particular fear;   360
And thereto add such reasons of your own
As may compact it more.   Get you gone;
And hasten your return.   [*Exit Oswald.*] No, no,
    my lord,
This milky gentleness and course of yours
Though I condemn not, yet, under pardon,   365
You are much more at task for want of wisdom
Than prais'd for harmful mildness.

Alb. How far your eyes may pierce I cannot tell.
Striving to better, oft we mar what's well.

Gon. Nay, then —   370

Alb. Well, well; th' event.   [*Exeunt.*

SCENE V. [*Court before the same.*]

Enter LEAR, KENT, *and* FOOL.

Lear. Go you before to Gloucester with these
letters.   Acquaint my daughter no further with
anything you know than comes from her demand
out of the letter.   If your diligence be not speedy,
I shall be there afore you.   5

Kent. I will not sleep, my lord, till I have delivered your letter.   [*Exit.*

Fool. If a man's brains were in 's heels, were't
not in danger of kibes?

Lear. Ay, boy.   10

Fool. Then, I prithee, be merry; thy wit shall not
go slip-shod.

Lear. Ha, ha, ha!

Fool. Shalt see thy other daughter will use thee
kindly; for though she's as like this as a crab's like
an apple, yet I can tell what I can tell.   16

Lear. What canst tell, boy?

Fool. She will taste as like this as a crab does to a
crab.   Thou canst tell why one's nose stands i' th'
middle on 's face?   20

Lear. No.

Fool. Why, to keep one's eyes of either side 's
nose, that what a man cannot smell out, he may
spy into.

Lear. I did her wrong —   25

Fool. Canst tell how an oyster makes his shell?

Lear. No.

Fool. Nor I neither; but I can tell why a snail
has a house.   30

Lear. Why?

Fool. Why, to put 's head in; not to give it away
to his daughters and leave his horns without a
case.   34

---

322. **untented:** not to be probed.   326. [**is it come to this?**] Q.   Om. F.   328. **comfortable:** comforting.   332. [**Thou . . .
thee**] Q.   Om. F.   347. **At point:** armed.   350. **in mercy:** at his mercy.   362. **compact:** confirm.   366. **at task:** to be
blamed.   371. **th' event:** (we'll see) the outcome.

Sc. **v,** 1. **Gloucester:** the city.   9. **kibes:** chilblains.   11. **thy . . . slip-shod:** i.e., because there is no sense in your proposed
journey.   15. **kindly:** (1) in friendly fashion, (2) according to her nature.

Lear. I will forget my nature. So kind a father!
Be my horses ready?

Fool. Thy asses are gone about 'em. The reason
why the seven stars are no moe than seven is a
pretty reason.

Lear. Because they are not eight?   40

Fool. Yes, indeed. Thou wouldst make a good
Fool.

Lear. To take 't again perforce! Monster ingratitude!

Fool. If thou wert my Fool, nuncle, I'd have
thee beaten for being old before thy time.   46

Lear. How's that?

Fool. Thou shouldst not have been old till thou
hadst been wise.

Lear. O, let me not be mad, not mad, sweet
     heaven!   50
Keep me in temper; I would not be mad!

[*Enter* GENTLEMAN.]

How now! are the horses ready?

Gent. Ready, my lord.

Lear. Come, boy.

Fool. She that's a maid now, and laughs at my
     departure,   55
Shall not be a maid long, unless things be cut
     shorter.   [*Exeunt.*

ACT II

SCENE I. [*The Earl of Gloucester's castle.*]

Enter Bastard [EDMUND] *and* CURAN, *severally.*

Edm. Save thee, Curan.

Cur. And you, sir. I have been with your father,
and given him notice that the Duke of Cornwall and
Regan his duchess will be here with him this night.

Edm. How comes that?   6

Cur. Nay, I know not. You have heard of the
news abroad; I mean the whisper'd ones, for they
are yet but ear-kissing arguments?

Edm. Not I. Pray you, what are they?   10

Cur. Have you heard of no likely wars toward,
'twixt the Dukes of Cornwall and Albany?

Edm. Not a word.

Cur. You may do, then, in time. Fare you well,
sir.   [*Exit.* 15

Edm. The Duke be here to-night? The better!
best!
This weaves itself perforce into my business.
My father hath set guard to take my brother;
And I have one thing, of a queasy question,
Which I must act. Briefness and fortune, work! 20

Enter EDGAR.

Brother, a word; descend. Brother, I say!
My father watches; O sir, fly this place;
Intelligence is given where you are hid;
You have now the good advantage of the night.
Have you not spoken 'gainst the Duke of Corn-
     wall?   25
He's coming hither, now, i' th' night, i' th' haste,
And Regan with him. Have you nothing said
Upon his party 'gainst the Duke of Albany?
Advise yourself.

Edg.   I am sure on't, not a word.

Edm. I hear my father coming. Pardon me, 30
In cunning I must draw my sword upon you.
Draw; seem to defend yourself; now quit you well.
Yield! Come before my father. Light, ho, here! —
Fly, brother. — Torches, torches! — So, farewell.
     [*Exit Edgar.*
Some blood drawn on me would beget opinion 35
     [*Wounds his arm.*
Of my more fierce endeavour. I have seen drunk-
     ards
Do more than this in sport. — Father, father! —
Stop, stop! — No help?

Enter GLOUCESTER, *and* Servants *with torches.*

Glou. Now, Edmund, where's the villain?

Edm. Here stood he in the dark, his sharp sword
     out,   40
Mumbling of wicked charms, conjuring the moon
To stand ['s] auspicious mistress, —

Glou.   But where is he?

Edm. Look, sir, I bleed.

Glou.   Where is the villain, Edmund?

Edm. Fled this way, sir. When by no means he
     could —

Glou. Pursue him, ho! Go after. [*Exeunt some
     Servants.*] By no means what?   45

Edm. Persuade me to the murder of your lord-
     ship;
But that I told him, the revenging gods
'Gainst parricides did all the thunder bend;
Spoke, with how manifold and strong a bond
The child was bound to th' father; sir, in fine, 50
Seeing how loathly opposite I stood
To his unnatural purpose, in fell motion,
With his prepared sword he charges home
My unprovided body, latch'd mine arm;
And when he saw my best alarum'd spirits,   55
Bold in the quarrel's right, rous'd to th' encounter,
Or whether gasted by the noise I made,
Full suddenly he fled.

Glou.   Let him fly far.

Act II, sc. i, 9. **ear-kissing arguments:** whispered topics. 11. **toward:** imminent. 19. **of ... question:** requiring delicate
handling. 29. **Advise yourself:** consider. 42. ['s] Q: his. Om. F. **stand ... mistress:** to shed favorable influence on him.
52. **in fell motion:** with a fierce stab. 54. **latch'd:** caught. 57. **gasted:** scared.

Not in this land shall he remain uncaught;
And found, — dispatch.   The noble Duke my
   master,   60
My worthy arch and patron, comes to-night.
By his authority I will proclaim it,
That he which finds him shall deserve our thanks,
Bringing the murderous coward to the stake;
He that conceals him, death.   65
  Edm.   When I dissuaded him from his intent,
And found him pight to do it, with curst speech
I threaten'd to discover him; he replied,
"Thou unpossessing bastard! dost thou think,
If I would stand against thee, would the reposal   70
Of any trust, virtue, or worth in thee
Make thy words faith'd?   No! what [I should]
   deny, —
As this I would; [ay,] though thou didst produce
My very character, — I'd turn it all
To thy suggestion, plot, and damned practice;   75
And thou must make a dullard of the world
If they not thought the profits of my death
Were very pregnant and potential [spurs]
To make thee seek it."
  Glou.   O strange and fast'ned villain!
Would he deny his letter?   [I never got him.]   80
                          [*Tucket within.*
Hark, the Duke's trumpets!   I know not [why] he
   comes.
All ports I'll bar, the villain shall not scape;
The Duke must grant me that.   Besides, his
   picture
I will send far and near, that all the kingdom
May have due note of him; and of my land,   85
Loyal and natural boy, I'll work the means
To make thee capable.

    Enter CORNWALL, REGAN, *and Attendants.*

  Corn.   How now, my noble friend! since I came
   hither,
Which I can call but now, I have heard [strange
   news].
  Reg.   If it be true, all vengeance comes too
   short   90
Which can pursue th' offender.   How dost, my lord?
  Glou.   O, madam, my old heart is crack'd, it's
   crack'd!
  Reg.   What, did my father's godson seek your
   life?
He whom my father nam'd? your Edgar?
  Glou.   O, lady, lady, shame would have it hid!   95
  Reg.   Was he not companion with the riotous
   knights

That tended upon my father?
  Glou.   I know not, madam.   'Tis too bad, too bad.
  Edm.   Yes, madam, he was of that consort.
  Reg.   No marvel, then, though he were ill af-
   fected: 100
'Tis they have put him on the old man's death,
To have th' expense and waste of his revenues.
I have this present evening from my sister
Been well inform'd of them; and with such cautions,
That if they come to sojourn at my house,   105
I'll not be there.
  Corn.   Nor I, assure thee, Regan.
Edmund, I hear that you have shown your father
A child-like office.
  Edm.   'Twas my duty, sir.
  Glou.   He did bewray his practice; and receiv'd
This hurt you see, striving to apprehend him.   110
  Corn.   Is he pursued?
  Glou.   Ay, my good lord.
  Corn.   If he be taken he shall never more
Be fear'd of doing harm.   Make your own purpose,
How in my strength you please.   For you, Edmund,
Whose virtue and obedience doth this instant   115
So much commend itself, you shall be ours.
Natures of such deep trust we shall much need;
You we first seize on.
  Edm.   I shall serve you, sir,
Truly, however else.
  Glou.   For him I thank your Grace.
  Corn.   You know not why we came to visit you, —
  Reg.   Thus out of season, threading dark-ey'd
   night?   121
Occasions, noble Gloucester, of some [poise],
Wherein we must have use of your advice.
Our father he hath writ, so hath our sister,
Of differences, which I best thought it fit   125
To answer from our home; the several messengers
From hence attend dispatch.   Our good old friend,
Lay comforts to your bosom; and bestow
Your needful counsel to our businesses,
Which craves the instant use.
  Glou.   I serve you, madam.
Your Graces are right welcome.   131
                  [*Exeunt.   Flourish.*

    SCENE II.   [*Before Gloucester's castle.*]

    Enter KENT *and Steward* [OSWALD], *severally.*

  Osw.   Good dawning to thee, friend.   Art of this
   house?
  Kent.   Ay.
  Osw.   Where may we set our horses?

---

61. **arch:** chief.   66. **dissuaded:** tried to dissuade.   67. **pight:** pitched, determined.   68. **discover:** reveal.   72. **faith'd:**
trusted.   **[I should]** Q.   *should I* F.   73. **[ay]** *I* Q.   Om. F.   75. **practice:** conspiracy.   78. **[spurs]** Q.   *spirits* F.   79.
fast'ned: hardened.   80. **[I . . . him]** Q.   *said he?* F.   s.d. *Tucket:* flourish on a trumpet.   81. **[why]** Q.   *wher* F.   87. **capa-**
ble: able to inherit.   89. **[strange news]** Q.   *strangeness* F.   102. **expense and waste:** power of spending and wasting.   108.
child-like: filial.   109. **bewray:** reveal.   114. **strength:** authority.   122. **[poise]** Q: weight.   *prize* F.   126. **from:** away from.

Kent. I' th' mire.   5

Osw. Prithee, if thou lov'st me, tell me.

Kent. I love thee not.

Osw. Why, then, I care not for thee.

Kent. If I had thee in Lipsbury pinfold, I would make thee care for me.   10

Osw. Why dost thou use me thus? I know thee not.

Kent. Fellow, I know thee.

Osw. What dost thou know me for?   14

Kent. A knave; a rascal; an eater of broken meats; a base, proud, shallow, beggarly, three-suited, hundred-pound, filthy, worsted-stocking knave; a lily-livered, action-taking, whoreson, glass-gazing, superserviceable, finical rogue; one-trunk-inheriting slave; one that wouldst be a 20 bawd in way of good service, and art nothing but the composition of a knave, beggar, coward, pandar, and the son and heir of a mongrel bitch; one whom I will beat into clamorous whining, if thou deni'st the least syllable of thy addition.   26

Osw. Why, what a monstrous fellow art thou, thus to rail on one that is neither known of thee nor knows thee!   29

Kent. What a brazen-fac'd varlet art thou, to deny thou knowest me! Is it two days since I tripp'd up thy heels, and beat thee before the King? Draw, you rogue; for, though it be night, yet the moon shines. I'll make a sop o' th' moonshine of you, you whoreson cullionly barber-monger! Draw!   [*Drawing his sword.*] 36

Osw. Away! I have nothing to do with thee.

Kent. Draw, you rascal! You come with letters against the King; and take Vanity the puppet's part against the royalty of her father. Draw, you rogue, or I'll so carbonado your shanks, — draw, you rascal! Come your ways.   42

Osw. Help, ho! murder! help!

Kent. Strike, you slave! Stand, rogue, stand! You neat slave, strike.   [*Beating him.*]

Osw. Help, ho! murder! murder!   46

Enter Bastard [EDMUND] *with his rapier drawn,* CORNWALL, REGAN, GLOUCESTER, *and* Servants.

Edm. How now! What's the matter? Part.

Kent. With you, goodman boy, if you please. Come, I'll flesh ye; come on, young master.

Glou. Weapons! arms! What's the matter here?

Corn. Keep peace, upon your lives!   52 He dies that strikes again. What is the matter?

Reg. The messengers from our sister and the King.   55

Corn. What is your difference? Speak.

Osw. I am scarce in breath, my lord.

Kent. No marvel, you have so bestirr'd your valour. You cowardly rascal, Nature disclaims in thee. A tailor made thee.   60

Corn. Thou art a strange fellow. A tailor make a man?

Kent. A tailor, sir. A stone-cutter or a painter could not have made him so ill, though they had been but two years o' th' trade.   65

Corn. Speak yet, how grew your quarrel?

Osw. This ancient ruffian, sir, whose life I have spar'd at suit of his grey beard, —   68

Kent. Thou whoreson zed! thou unnecessary letter! My lord, if you will give me leave, I will tread this unbolted villain into mortar, and daub the wall of a jakes with him. Spare my grey beard, you wagtail?

Corn. Peace, sirrah! You beastly knave, know you no reverence?   75

Kent. Yes, sir; but anger hath a privilege.

Corn. Why art thou angry?

Kent. That such a slave as this should wear a sword, Who wears no honesty. Such smiling rogues as these, Like rats, oft bite the holy cords a-twain   80 Which are too intrinse t' unloose; smooth every passion That in the natures of their lords rebel; [Bring] oil to fire, snow to their colder moods; [Renege,] affirm, and turn their halcyon beaks With every gale and vary of their masters,   85 Knowing nought, like dogs, but following. A plague upon your epileptic visage! Smile you my speeches, as I were a fool? Goose, if I had you upon Sarum Plain, I'd drive ye cackling home to Camelot.   90

Corn. What, art thou mad, old fellow?

Glou. How fell you out? Say that.

Kent. No contraries hold more antipathy Than I and such a knave.

Corn. Why dost thou call him knave? What is his fault?   95

Kent. His countenance likes me not.

Corn. No more, perchance, does mine, nor his, nor hers.

Kent. Sir, 'tis my occupation to be plain;

Sc. ii, 9. **Lipsbury pinfold**: my teeth (?). 18. **lily-livered**: cowardly. **action-taking**: preferring going to law to fighting. 19. **glass-gazing**: vain. **superserviceable**: officious. 22. **composition**: combination. 26. **thy addition**: the titles I have given you. 35. **cullionly**: rascally. **barber-monger**: frequenter of barber-shops. 41. **carbonado**: slash. 45. **neat**: foppish. 59. **disclaims in**: renounces. 69. **zed**: Z, often omitted in old dictionaries. 71. **unbolted**: coarse. 72. **jakes**: privy. 80. **holy cords**: i.e., of natural affection. 81. **intrinse**: intricate. **smooth**: humor. 83. [Bring] Q. *Being* F. 84. [Renege] F$_2$: deny. *Revenge* F$_1$. **halcyon**: kingfisher, which, if hung up, was believed always to turn with its bill to the wind. 89. **Sarum**: Salisbury. 90. **Camelot**: Winchester. 96. **likes**: pleases.

I have seen better faces in my time
Than stands on any shoulder that I see   100
Before me at this instant.
    Corn.   This is some fellow
Who, having been prais'd for bluntness, doth affect
A saucy roughness, and constrains the garb
Quite from his nature. He cannot flatter, he;
An honest mind and plain, he must speak truth!
An they will take it, so; if not, he's plain.   106
These kind of knaves I know, which in this plain-
    ness
Harbour more craft and more corrupter ends
Than twenty silly ducking observants
That stretch their duties nicely.   110
    Kent. Sir, in good sooth, in sincere verity,
Under the allowance of your great aspect,
Whose influence, like the wreath of radiant fire
On [flickering] Phœbus' front, —
    Corn.   What mean'st by this?   114
    Kent. To go out of my dialect, which you dis-
commend so much. I know, sir, I am no flatterer.
He that beguil'd you in a plain accent was a plain
knave; which for my part I will not be, though I
should win your displeasure to entreat me to't.   120
    Corn. What was th' offence you gave him?
    Osw. I never gave him any.
It pleas'd the King his master very late
To strike at me, upon his misconstruction;
When he, compact, and flattering his displeasure,
Tripp'd me behind; being down, insulted, rail'd,   126
And put upon him such a deal of man
[That't] worthied him, got praises of the King
For him attempting who was self-subdued;
And, in the fleshment of this [dread] exploit,   130
Drew on me here again.
    Kent.   None of these rogues and cowards
But Ajax is their fool.
    Corn.   Fetch forth the stocks!
You stubborn ancient knave, you reverend brag-
    gart,
We'll teach you —
    Kent.   Sir, I am too old to learn.
Call not your stocks for me; I serve the King,   135
On whose employment I was sent to you.
You shall do small respects, show too bold malice
Against the grace and person of my master,
Stocking his messenger.
    Corn. Fetch forth the stocks! As I have life and
    honour,   140
There shall he sit till noon.

    Reg. Till noon! Till night, my lord; and all night
    too.
    Kent. Why, madam, if I were your father's dog,
You should not use me so.
    Reg.   Sir, being his knave, I will.
                     [*Stocks brought out.*
    Corn. This is a fellow of the self-same colour   145
Our sister speaks of. Come, bring away the stocks!
    Glou. Let me beseech your Grace not to do so.
[His fault is much, and the good King his master
Will check him for't. Your purpos'd low correc-
    tion
Is such as basest and contemned'st wretches   150
For pilferings and most common trespasses
Are punish'd with.] The King must take it ill
That he, so slightly valued in his messenger,
Should have him thus restrain'd.
    Corn.   I'll answer that.
    Reg. My sister may receive it much more worse
To have her gentleman abus'd, assaulted,   156
[For following her affairs. Put in his legs.]
             [*Kent is put in the stocks.*]
[Come, my good] lord, away.
          [*Exeunt [all but Gloucester and Kent*].
    Glou. I am sorry for thee, friend; 'tis the Duke's
    pleasure,
Whose disposition, all the world well knows,   160
Will not be rubb'd nor stopp'd. I'll entreat for
    thee.
    Kent. Pray, do not, sir. I have watch'd and
    travell'd hard;
Some time I shall sleep out, the rest I'll whistle.
A good man's fortune may grow out at heels.
Give you good morrow!   165
    Glou. The Duke's to blame in this; 'twill be ill
    taken.   [*Exit.*
    Kent. Good King, that must approve the com-
    mon saw,
Thou out of heaven's benediction com'st
To the warm sun!
Approach, thou beacon to this under globe,   170
That by thy comfortable beams I may
Peruse this letter! Nothing almost sees miracles
But misery. I know 'tis from Cordelia,
Who hath most fortunately been inform'd
Of my obscured course; [*reads*] " — and shall find
    time   175
From this enormous state — seeking to give
Losses their remedies." — All weary and o'er-
    watch'd,

---

103. **constrains the garb:** forces the manner.   109. **observants:** obsequious attendants.   110. **nicely:** punctiliously.   114. **[flickering]** Q. *flicking* F.   125. **compact:** taking his side.   127. **put...man:** took such a heroic attitude.   128. **[That 't]** (Anon.) *That* F. *That* Q.   129. **attempting:** attacking.   130. **fleshment:** excitement from first success.   **[dread]** Q. *dead* F.   132. **But...fool:** but pick on a plain blunt fellow like Ajax (?).   148–152. **[His...with]** Q. Om. F.   150. **contemned'st** (Capell). *temnest* or *contened* Q.   152. **King** Q. *King his master needs* F.   157. **[For...legs]** Q. Om. F.   158. **[Come, my good]** Q. *Corn. Come my* F.   162. **watch'd:** been awake long. Cf. l. 177.   167. **approve...saw:** prove the proverb true. 168–169. **out...sun:** from better to worse.

Take vantage, heavy eyes, not to behold
This shameful lodging.
Fortune, good-night! Smile once more; turn thy
   wheel!   [*Sleeps.*] 180

[SCENE III. *The same.*]

Enter EDGAR.

  Edg. I heard myself proclaim'd;
And by the happy hollow of a tree
Escap'd the hunt. No port is free; no place
That guard and most unusual vigilance
Does not attend my taking. Whiles I may scape 5
I will preserve myself, and am bethought
To take the basest and most poorest shape
That ever penury, in contempt of man,
Brought near to beast. My face I'll grime with
   filth,
Blanket my loins, elf all my hairs in knots, 10
And with presented nakedness out-face
The winds and persecutions of thy sky.
The country gives me proof and precedent
Of Bedlam beggars, who, with roaring voices,
Strike in their numb'd and mortified arms 15
Pins, wooden pricks, nails, sprigs of rosemary;
And with this horrible object, from low farms,
Poor pelting villages, sheep-cotes, and mills,
Sometimes with lunatic bans, sometimes with
   prayers, 19
Enforce their charity. Poor Turlygod! poor Tom!
That's something yet. Edgar I nothing am.
                       [*Exit.*

[SCENE IV. *The same.*]

Enter LEAR, FOOL, *and* GENTLEMAN. [KENT
in the stocks.]

  Lear. 'Tis strange that they should so depart
   from home,
And not send back my messengers.
  Gent.   As I learn'd,
The night before there was no purpose in them
Of this remove.
  Kent.   Hail to thee, noble master!
  Lear. Ha!   5
Mak'st thou this shame thy pastime?
  Kent.   No, my lord.
  Fool. Ha, ha! he wears cruel garters. Horses are
tied by the heads, dogs and bears by th' neck, mon-
keys by th' loins, and men by th' legs. When a
man's over-lusty at legs, then he wears wooden
nether-stocks.   11

  Lear. What's he that hath so much thy place
   mistook
To set thee here?
  Kent.   It is both he and she;
Your son and daughter.
  Lear. No.   15
  Kent. Yes.
  Lear. No, I say.
  Kent. I say, yea.
  [*Lear.* No, no, they would not.
  Kent. Yes, they have.]   20
  Lear. By Jupiter, I swear, no.
  Kent. By Juno, I swear, ay.
  Lear.   They durst not do't;
They could not, would not do't. 'Tis worse than
   murder
To do upon respect such violent outrage.
Resolve me with all modest haste which way 25
Thou mightst deserve, or they impose, this usage,
Coming from us.
  Kent.   My lord, when at their home
I did commend your Highness' letters to them,
Ere I was risen from the place that show'd
My duty kneeling, came there a reeking post, 30
Stew'd in his haste, half breathless, panting forth
From Goneril his mistress salutations;
Deliver'd letters, spite of intermission,
Which presently they read. On those contents,
They summon'd up their meiny, straight took
   horse;
Commanded me to follow, and attend 36
The leisure of their answer; gave me cold looks:
And meeting here the other messenger,
Whose welcome, I perceiv'd, had poison'd mine, —
Being the very fellow which of late 40
Display'd so saucily against your Highness, —
Having more man than wit about me, drew.
He rais'd the house with loud and coward cries.
Your son and daughter found this trespass worth
The shame which here it suffers.   45
  Fool. Winter's not gone yet, if the wild geese fly
that way.
    "Fathers that wear rags
      Do make their children blind;
    But fathers that bear bags   50
      Shall see their children kind.
    Fortune, that arrant whore,
    Ne'er turns the key to th' poor."
But, for all this, thou shalt have as many dolours
for thy daughters as thou canst tell in a year. 55
  Lear. O, how this mother swells up toward my
   heart!

180. **Smile...wheel.** Q attaches *once more* to *turn* rather than *smile.*
  Sc. iii, 5. **attend my taking:** wait to capture me. 10. **elf:** tangle as in elf-locks. 11. **presented:** exposed. 17. **object:** aspect. 18. **pelting:** petty. 19. **bans:** curses. 21. **Edgar...am:** of Edgar nothing will remain.
  Sc. iv, 11. **nether-stocks:** stockings. 19–20. [*Lear ... have*] Q. Om. F. 24. **upon respect:** deliberately. 25. **Resolve:** inform. 33. **spite of intermission:** careless of interrupting. 35. **meiny:** retinue. 41. **Display'd:** showed himself. 54. **dolours:** with a pun on *dollars.* 55. **tell:** count. 56. **mother:** hysteria.

Hysterica passio, down, thou climbing sorrow,
Thy element's below! — Where is this daughter?
  Kent. With the Earl, sir, here within.
  Lear.   Follow me not;
Stay here.   [*Exit*. 60
  Gent. Made you no more offence but what you
speak of?
  Kent. None.
How chance the King comes with so small a number?
  Fool. An thou hadst been set i' th' stocks for that
question, thou'dst well deserv'd it.   66
  Kent. Why, Fool?
  Fool. We'll set thee to school to an ant, to teach
thee there's no labouring i' th' winter. All that
follow their noses are led by their eyes but 70
blind men; and there's not a nose among twenty
but can smell him that's stinking. Let go thy hold
when a great wheel runs down a hill, lest it break
thy neck with following; but the great one that
goes upward, let him draw thee after. When a 75
wise man gives thee better counsel, give me mine
again; I would have none but knaves follow it,
since a fool gives it.

"That sir which serves and seeks for gain,
    And follows but for form,   80
Will pack when it begins to rain,
    And leave thee in the storm.
But I will tarry; the Fool will stay,
    And let the wise man fly.
The knave turns fool that runs away;   85
    The Fool no knave, perdy."

Re-enter LEAR *and* GLOUCESTER.

  Kent. Where learn'd you this, Fool?
  Fool. Not i' th' stocks, fool.
  Lear. Deny to speak with me? They are sick?
They are weary?
They have travell'd all the night? Mere fetches; 90
The images of revolt and flying off.
Fetch me a better answer.
  Glou.   My dear lord,
You know the fiery quality of the Duke;
How unremovable and fix'd he is
In his own course.   95
  Lear. Vengeance! plague! death! confusion!
"Fiery"? What "quality"? Why, Gloucester,
Gloucester,
I'd speak with the Duke of Cornwall and his
wife.
  Glou. Well, my good lord, I have inform'd them
so.
  Lear. "Inform'd" them! Dost thou under-
stand me, man?   100
  Glou. Ay, my good lord.

  Lear. The King would speak with Cornwall; the
dear father
Would with his daughter speak, commands [her]
service.
Are they "inform'd" of this? My breath and
blood!
"Fiery"? The fiery duke? Tell the hot duke
that —   105
No, but not yet; may be he is not well.
Infirmity doth still neglect all office
Whereto our health is bound; we are not ourselves
When nature, being oppress'd, commands the mind
To suffer with the body. I'll forbear;   110
And am fallen out with my more headier will,
To take the indispos'd and sickly fit
For the sound man. — Death on my state! where-
fore   [*Looking on Kent*.]
Should he sit here? This act persuades me
That this remotion of the Duke and her   115
Is practice only. Give me my servant forth.
Go tell the Duke and 's wife I'd speak with them,
Now, presently. Bid them come forth and hear me,
Or at their chamber-door I'll beat the drum
Till it cry sleep to death.   120
  Glou. I would have all well betwixt you. [*Exit*.
  Lear. O me, my heart, my rising heart! But,
down!
  Fool. Cry to it, nuncle, as the cockney did to the
eels when she put 'em i' th' paste alive; she knapp'd
'em o' th' coxcombs with a stick, and cried, "Down,
wantons, down!" 'Twas her brother that, in pure
kindness to his horse, buttered his hay.   128

Enter CORNWALL, REGAN, GLOUCESTER, *and*
Servants.

  Lear. Good morrow to you both.
  Corn.   Hail to your Grace!
                     [*Kent is set at liberty*.
  Reg. I am glad to see your Highness.
  Lear. Regan, I think you are; I know what rea-
son
I have to think so. If thou shouldst not be glad, 132
I would divorce me from thy mother's tomb,
Sepulchring an adulteress. [*To Kent*.] O, are you
free?
Some other time for that. Beloved Regan,
Thy sister's naught. O Regan, she hath tied
Sharp-tooth'd unkindness, like a vulture, here.
                [*Points to his heart*.]
I can scarce speak to thee; thou'lt not believe
With how deprav'd a quality — O Regan!   139
  Reg. I pray you, sir, take patience. I have hope
You less know how to value her desert
Than she to scant her duty.

90. fetches: tricks. 91. images: signs. flying off: deserting. 103. [her] Q. tends F. 107. office: duty. 111. headier: impetuous. 115. remotion: removal. 116. practice: trickery. 120. cry...to death: murder. 136. naught: wicked. 139. quality: manner.

Lear.   Say, how is that?
Reg. I cannot think my sister in the least
Would fail her obligation. If, sir, perchance
She have restrain'd the riots of your followers,   145
'Tis on such ground and to such wholesome end
As clears her from all blame.
   Lear. My curses on her!
   Reg.   O, sir, you are old;
Nature in you stands on the very verge
Of her confine. You should be rul'd and led   150
By some discretion that discerns your state
Better than you yourself. Therefore, I pray you,
That to our sister you do make return;
Say you have wrong'd her, sir.
   Lear.   Ask her forgiveness?
Do you but mark how this becomes the house: 155
"Dear daughter, I confess that I am old;
                    [*Kneeling.*]
Age is unnecessary. On my knees I beg
That you'll vouchsafe me raiment, bed, and food."
   Reg. Good sir, no more; these are unsightly tricks.
Return you to my sister.
   Lear.   [*Rising.*] Never, Regan: 160
She hath abated me of half my train;
Look'd black upon me; struck me with her tongue,
Most serpent-like, upon the very heart.
All the stor'd vengeances of heaven fall
On her ingrateful top! Strike her young bones,   165
You taking airs, with lameness!
   Corn.   Fie, sir, fie!
   Lear. You nimble lightnings, dart your blinding
      flames
Into her scornful eyes! Infect her beauty,
You fen-suck'd fogs, drawn by the powerful sun,
To fall and [blast her pride!]   170
   Reg. O the blest gods! so will you wish on me,
When the rash mood is on.
   Lear. No, Regan, thou shalt never have my
      curse.
Thy tender-hefted nature shall not give
Thee o'er to harshness. Her eyes are fierce; but
      thine   175
Do comfort and not burn. 'Tis not in thee
To grudge my pleasures, to cut off my train,
To bandy hasty words, to scant my sizes,
And in conclusion to oppose the bolt
Against my coming in. Thou better know'st   180
The offices of nature, bond of childhood,
Effects of courtesy, dues of gratitude.
Thy half o' th' kingdom hast thou not forgot,
Wherein I thee endow'd.
   Reg.   Good sir, to th' purpose.
                    [*Tucket within.*

Lear. Who put my man i' th' stocks?

                    Enter Steward [OSWALD].
   Corn.   What trumpet 's that?
   Reg. I know 't; my sister's. This approves her
      letter,   186
That she would soon be here. [*To Oswald.*] Is
      your lady come?
   Lear. This is a slave whose easy-borrowed pride
Dwells in the [fickle] grace of her he follows.
Out, varlet, from my sight!
   Corn.   What means your Grace?   190

                    Enter GONERIL.
   Lear. Who stock'd my servant? Regan, I have
      good hope
Thou didst not know on't. — Who comes here?
      O heavens,
If you do love old men, if your sweet sway
Allow obedience, if you yourselves are old,
Make it your cause; send down, and take my
      part!   195
[*To Gon.*] Art not asham'd to look upon this beard?
O Regan, will you take her by the hand?
   Gon. Why not by th' hand, sir? How have I
      offended?
All's not offence that indiscretion finds   199
And dotage terms so.
   Lear.   O sides, you are too tough;
Will you yet hold? How came my man i' th' stocks?
   Corn. I set him there, sir; but his own disorders
Deserv'd much less advancement.
   Lear.   You! did you?
   Reg. I pray you, father, being weak, seem so.
If, till the expiration of your month,   205
You will return and sojourn with my sister,
Dismissing half your train, come then to me.
I am now from home, and out of that provision
Which shall be needful for your entertainment.
   Lear. Return to her, and fifty men dismiss'd!   210
No, rather I abjure all roofs, and choose
To wage against the enmity o' th' air;
To be a comrade with the wolf and owl, —
Necessity's sharp pinch. Return with her?
Why, the hot-blooded France, that dowerless took
Our youngest born, I could as well be brought   216
To knee his throne, and, squire-like, pension beg
To keep base life afoot. Return with her?
Persuade me rather to be slave and sumpter
To this detested groom. [*Pointing at Oswald.*]
   Gon.   At your choice, sir.   220
   Lear. I prithee, daughter, do not make me mad;
I will not trouble thee, my child; farewell!

155. **house:** royal family.   157. **Age is unnecessary:** old people are useless.   165. **top:** head.   **young bones:** bones of her unborn child.   166. **taking:** infectious.   170. **fall:** humble.   [blast her pride] Q.   *blister* F.   174. **tender-hefted:** gentle.   178. **sizes:** allowances.   182. **Effects:** manifestations.   188. **easy-borrowed:** not justified by his own qualities, but on the reflection of his mistress's position.   189. [fickle] Q.   *sickly* F.   194. **Allow:** approve.   212. **wage:** contend.   219. **sumpter:** pack-horse.

We'll no more meet, no more see one another.
But yet thou art my flesh, my blood, my daughter;
Or rather a disease that's in my flesh,   225
Which I must needs call mine; thou art a boil,
A plague-sore, an embossed carbuncle,
In my corrupted blood. But I'll not chide thee;
Let shame come when it will, I do not call it.
I do not bid the thunder-bearer shoot,   230
Nor tell tales of thee to high-judging Jove.
Mend when thou canst; be better at thy leisure.
I can be patient; I can stay with Regan,
I and my hundred knights.
   Reg.   Not altogether so;
I look'd not for you yet, nor am provided   235
For your fit welcome. Give ear, sir, to my sister;
For those that mingle reason with your passion
Must be content to think you old, and so —
But she knows what she does.
   Lear.   Is this well spoken?
   Reg. I dare avouch it, sir. What, fifty follow-
    ers!   240
Is it not well? What should you need of more?
Yea, or so many, sith that both charge and danger
Speak 'gainst so great a number? How, in one house,
Should many people under two commands
Hold amity? 'Tis hard; almost impossible.   245
   Gon. Why might not you, my lord, receive at-
    tendance
From those that she calls servants or from mine?
   Reg. Why not, my lord? If then they chanc'd to
    slack ye,
We could control them. If you will come to me, —
For now I spy a danger — I entreat you   250
To bring but five and twenty; to no more
Will I give place or notice.
   Lear. I gave you all.
   Reg.   And in good time you gave it.
   Lear. Made you my guardians, my depositaries,
But kept a reservation to be followed   255
With such a number. What, must I come to you
With five and twenty, Regan? Said you so?
   Reg. And speak 't again, my lord; no more with
    me.
   Lear. Those wicked creatures yet do look well-
    favour'd
When others are more wicked; not being the worst
Stands in some rank of praise. [*To Gon.*] I'll go
    with thee.   261
Thy fifty yet doth double five and twenty,
And thou art twice her love.
   Gon.   Hear me, my lord:
What need you five and twenty, ten, or five,
To follow in a house where twice so many   265
Have a command to tend you?

   Reg.   What need one?
   Lear. O, reason not the need! Our basest beggars
Are in the poorest thing superfluous.
Allow not nature more than nature needs,
Man's life is cheap as beast's. Thou art a lady;   270
If only to go warm were gorgeous,
Why, nature needs not what thou gorgeous wear'st,
Which scarcely keeps thee warm. But, for true
    need, —
You heavens, give me that patience, patience I
    need!
You see me here, you gods, a poor old man,   275
As full of grief as age; wretched in both!
If it be you that stirs these daughters' hearts
Against their father, fool me not so much
To bear it tamely; touch me with noble anger,
And let not women's weapons, water-drops,   280
Stain my man's cheeks! No, you unnatural hags,
I will have such revenges on you both
That all the world shall — I will do such things, —
What they are, yet I know not; but they shall be
The terrors of the earth. You think I'll weep: 285
No, I'll not weep.
I have full cause of weeping; but this heart
             (*Storm and tempest.*)
Shall break into a hundred thousand flaws,
Or ere I'll weep. O, Fool! I shall go mad!
    [*Exeunt Lear, Gloucester, Kent, and Fool.*
   Corn. Let us withdraw; 'twill be a storm.   290
   Reg. This house is little; the old man and 's peo-
    ple
Cannot be well bestow'd.
   Gon. 'Tis his own blame; hath put himself from
    rest,
And must needs taste his folly.
   Reg. For his particular, I'll receive him gladly,
But not one follower.
   Gon.   So am I purpos'd.   296
Where is my Lord of Gloucester?

        Re-enter GLOUCESTER.

   Corn. Follow'd the old man forth. He is re-
    turn'd.
   Glou. The King is in high rage.
   Corn.   Whither is he going?
   Glou. He calls to horse; but will I know not
    whither.   300
   Corn. 'Tis best to give him way; he leads him-
    self.
   Gon. My lord, entreat him by no means to stay.
   Glou. Alack, the night comes on, and the high
    winds
Do sorely ruffle; for many miles about
There 's scarce a bush.

---

   227. embossed: swollen.   **242. charge:** expense.   **248. slack:** be lacking in their services.   **268. Are ... superfluous:** have at the worst more than bare necessities.   **288. flaws:** fragments.   **295. For his particular:** as far as he himself is concerned.   **304. ruffle:** bluster.

Reg.   O, sir, to wilful men,   305
The injuries that they themselves procure
Must be their schoolmasters.   Shut up your doors.
He is attended with a desperate train,
And what they may incense him to, being apt
To have his ear abus'd, wisdom bids fear.   310
Corn.   Shut up your doors, my lord; 'tis a wild
night:
My Regan counsels well.   Come out o' th' storm.
                                                [Exeunt.

ACT III

SCENE I.   [*The open country near Gloucester's
castle.*]

Storm still.   Enter KENT *and a* GENTLEMAN,
severally.

Kent.   Who's there, besides foul weather?
Gent.   One minded like the weather, most un-
quietly.
Kent.   I know you.   Where's the King?
Gent.   Contending with the fretful elements;
Bids the wind blow the earth into the sea,   5
Or swell the curled waters 'bove the main,
That things might change or cease; [tears his white
hair,
Which the impetuous blasts with eyeless rage
Catch in their fury, and make nothing of;
Strives in his little world of man to out-scorn   10
The to-and-fro-conflicting wind and rain.
This night, wherein the cub-drawn bear would couch,
The lion and the belly-pinched wolf
Keep their fur dry, unbonneted he runs,
And bids what will take all.]
Kent.   But who is with him?
Gent.   None but the Fool, who labours to out-
jest   16
His heart-struck injuries.
Kent.   Sir, I do know you,
And dare upon the warrant of my note
Commend a dear thing to you.   There is division,
Although as yet the face of it is cover'd   20
With mutual cunning, 'twixt Albany and Cornwall;
Who have — as who have not, that their great stars
Thron'd and set high? — servants, who seem no
less,
Which are to France the spies and speculations
Intelligent of our state.   What hath been seen,   25
Either in snuffs and packings of the Dukes,

Or the hard rein which both of them have borne
Against the old kind king, or something deeper,
Whereof perchance these are but furnishings —
[But, true it is, from France there comes a power   30
Into this scattered kingdom; who already,
Wise in our negligence, have secret feet
In some of our best ports, and are at point
To show their open banner.   Now to you:
If on my credit you dare build so far   35
To make your speed to Dover, you shall find
Some that will thank you, making just report
Of how unnatural and bemadding sorrow
The King hath cause to plain.
I am a gentleman of blood and breeding;   40
And, from some knowledge and assurance, offer
This office to you.]
Gent.   I will talk further with you.
Kent.   No, do not.
For confirmation that I am much more
Than my out-wall, open this purse and take   45
What it contains.   If you shall see Cordelia, —
As fear not but you shall, — show her this ring,
And she will tell you who that fellow is
That yet you do not know.   Fie on this storm!
I will go seek the King.   50
Gent.   Give me your hand.   Have you no more
to say?
Kent.   Few words, but, to effect, more than all
yet;
That, when we have found the King, — in which
your pain
That way, I'll this, — he that first lights on him
Holla the other.   *[Exeunt [severally].*   55

SCENE II.   [*The same.*]   *Storm still.*

Enter LEAR *and* FOOL.

Lear.   Blow, winds, and crack your cheeks! Rage!
Blow!
You cataracts and hurricanoes, spout
Till you have drench'd our steeples, drown'd the
cocks!
You sulph'rous and thought-executing fires,
Vaunt-couriers of oak-cleaving thunderbolts,   5
Singe my white head!   And thou, all-shaking thun-
der,
Strike flat the thick rotundity o' th' world!
Crack nature's moulds, all germens spill at once
That makes ingrateful man!   9
Fool.   O nuncle, court holy-water in a dry house

310. **abus'd:** misled.

Act III, sc. i, 6. **main:** mainland.   7–15. [tears . . . all] Q.   Om. F.   12. **cub-drawn:** sucked dry.   18. **note:** knowledge
(of you).   19. **dear:** important.   24. **speculations:** observers.   25. **Intelligent:** giving information.   26. **snuffs:** resent-
ments.   **packings:** plots.   30–42. [But . . . you] Q.   Om. F.   30. **power:** armed force.   31. **scattered:** divided.   33. **at
point:** ready.   39. **plain:** complain.   45. **out-wall:** exterior.   52. **to effect:** in effect, in importance.
Sc. ii, 3. **cocks:** weathercocks.   5. **Vaunt-couriers:** forerunners.   8. **germens:** germs, seeds.   10. **court holy-water:**
flattery.

is better than this rain water out o' door. Good
nuncle, in; ask thy daughters' blessing. Here's a
night pities neither wise men nor fools.

Lear. Rumble thy bellyful! Spit, fire! Spout,
     rain!
Nor rain, wind, thunder, fire are my daughters.   15
I tax not you, you elements, with unkindness;
I never gave you kingdom, call'd you children;
You owe me no subscription. Then let fall
Your horrible pleasure. Here I stand your slave,
A poor, infirm, weak, and despis'd old man;   20
But yet I call you servile ministers,
That will with two pernicious daughters join
Your high-engender'd battles 'gainst a head
So old and white as this. Oh! Oh! 'tis foul!

Fool. He that has a house to put 's head in has a
good head-piece.

     "The cod-piece that will house
        Before the head has any,
        The head and he shall louse;
        So beggars marry many.   30
     The man that makes his toe
        What he his heart should make
        Shall of a corn cry woe,
        And turn his sleep to wake."
For there was never yet fair woman but she made
mouths in a glass.   36

       Enter KENT.

Lear. No, I will be the pattern of all patience; I
will say nothing.

Kent. Who's there?

Fool. Marry, here's grace and a cod-piece; that's
a wise man and a fool.   41

Kent. Alas, sir, are you here? Things that love
     night
Love not such nights as these; the wrathful skies
Gallow the very wanderers of the dark,
And make them keep their caves. Since I was
     man,   45
Such sheets of fire, such bursts of horrid thunder,
Such groans of roaring wind and rain, I never
Remember to have heard. Man's nature cannot
     carry
Th' affliction nor the fear.

Lear.   Let the great gods,
That keep this dreadful pudder o'er our heads,   50
Find out their enemies now. Tremble, thou
     wretch
That hast within thee undivulged crimes,
Unwhipp'd of justice! Hide thee, thou bloody hand;
Thou perjur'd, and thou simular of virtue
That art incestuous! Caitiff, to pieces shake,   55

That under covert and convenient seeming
Has practis'd on man's life! Close pent-up guilts,
Rive your concealing continents, and cry
These dreadful summoners grace. I am a man
More sinn'd against than sinning.

Kent.   Alack, bare-headed!
Gracious my lord, hard by here is a hovel;   61
Some friendship will it lend you 'gainst the tempest.
Repose you there, while I to this hard house —
More harder than the stones whereof 'tis rais'd,
Which even but now, demanding after you,   65
Deni'd me to come in — return, and force
Their scanted courtesy.

Lear.   My wits begin to turn.
Come on, my boy. How dost, my boy? Art cold?
I am cold myself. Where is this straw, my fellow?
The art of our necessities is strange   70
And can make vile things precious. Come, your
     hovel.
Poor Fool and knave, I have one part in my heart
That's sorry yet for thee.

Fool. [*Singing.*]
"He that has and a little tiny wit, —
     With heigh-ho, the wind and the rain, —   75
Must make content with his fortunes fit,
     For the rain it raineth every day."

Lear. True, boy. Come, bring us to this hovel.
           [*Exeunt [Lear and Kent*].

Fool. This is a brave night to cool a courtezan.
I'll speak a prophecy ere I go: 80
     When priests are more in word than matter;
     When brewers mar their malt with water;
     When nobles are their tailors' tutors;
     No heretics burn'd, but wenches' suitors;
     When every case in law is right;   85
     No squire in debt, nor no poor knight;
     When slanders do not live in tongues;
     Nor cutpurses come not to throngs;
     When usurers tell their gold i' th' field;
     And bawds and whores do churches build;   90
Then shall the realm of Albion
Come to great confusion.
Then comes the time, who lives to see 't,
That going shall be us'd with feet.
This prophecy Merlin shall make; for I live before
     his time.   [*Exit.* 95

      SCENE III. [*Gloucester's castle.*]

     Enter GLOUCESTER *and* EDMUND.

Glou. Alack, alack, Edmund, I like not this unnatural dealing. When I desired their leave that
I might pity him, they took from me the use of

---

    18. **subscription:** allegiance.   23. **high-engender'd:** produced in the heavens.   44. **Gallow:** frighten.   50. **pudder:** turmoil.   54. **simular of:** pretender to.   58. **continents:** disguises.   58–59. **cry...grace:** ask mercy.   66. **Deni'd...in:** refused to admit me.   70. **art of:** skill created by.   80–95. This prophecy is influenced by a so-called "Chaucer's Prophecy," and is probably not by Shakespeare.

mine own house; charg'd me on pain of perpetual
displeasure neither to speak of him, entreat for him,
or any way sustain him.   6

Edm. Most savage and unnatural!

Glou. Go to; say you nothing. There is division
between the Dukes, and a worse matter than that.
I have received a letter this night; 'tis danger-   10
ous to be spoken; I have lock'd the letter in my
closet. These injuries the King now bears will be
revenged home; there is part of a power already
footed. We must incline to the King. I will look
him and privily relieve him. Go you and main-   15
tain talk with the Duke that my charity be not of
him perceived. If he ask for me, I am ill and gone
to bed. If I die for it, as no less is threat'ned me,
the King my old master must be relieved. There
is strange things toward, Edmund; pray you, be
careful.   [*Exit.* 21

Edm. This courtesy, forbid thee, shall the Duke
Instantly know; and of that letter too.
This seems a fair deserving, and must draw me
That which my father loses; no less than all.   25
The younger rises when the old doth fall.   [*Exit.*

SCENE IV. [*The open country. Before a hovel.*]

Enter LEAR, KENT, *and* FOOL.

Kent. Here is the place, my lord; good my lord,
     enter.
The tyranny of the open night 's too rough
For nature to endure.   [*Storm still.*

Lear.   Let me alone.

Kent. Good my lord, enter here.

Lear.   Wilt break my heart?

Kent. I had rather break mine own. Good
     my lord, enter.   5

Lear. Thou think'st 'tis much that this conten-
     tious storm
Invades us to the skin; so 'tis to thee;
But where the greater malady is fix'd,
The lesser is scarce felt. Thou'dst shun a bear;
But if thy flight lay toward the roaring sea,   10
Thou'dst meet the bear i' th' mouth. When the
     mind 's free,
The body 's delicate; the tempest in my mind
Doth from my senses take all feeling else
Save what beats there. Filial ingratitude!
Is it not as this mouth should tear this hand   15
For lifting food to't? But I will punish home.
No, I will weep no more. In such a night
To shut me out! Pour on! I will endure.
In such a night as this! O Regan, Goneril!
Your old kind father, whose frank heart gave all, —

O, that way madness lies; let me shun that;   21
No more of that.

Kent.   Good my lord, enter here.

Lear. Prithee, go in thyself; seek thine own ease.
This tempest will not give me leave to ponder
On things would hurt me more. But I'll go in.   25
[*To the Fool.*] In, boy; go first. You houseless
     poverty, —
Nay, get thee in. I'll pray, and then I'll sleep.
                            [*Exit* [*Fool*].
Poor naked wretches, wheresoe'er you are,
That bide the pelting of this pitiless storm,
How shall your houseless heads and unfed sides,   30
Your loop'd and window'd raggedness, defend you
From seasons such as these? O, I have ta'en
Too little care of this! Take physic, pomp;
Expose thyself to feel what wretches feel,
That thou mayst shake the superflux to them,   35
And show the heavens more just.

Edg. [*Within.*] Fathom and half, fathom and
     half! Poor Tom!
            [*The Fool runs out from the hovel.*]

Fool. Come not in here, nuncle, here's a spirit.
Help me, help me!   40

Kent. Give me thy hand. Who's there?

Fool. A spirit, a spirit! He says his name 's poor
Tom.

Kent. What art thou that dost grumble there i'
th' straw? Come forth.   45

[*Enter* EDGAR, *disguised as a madman.*]

Edg. Away! the foul fiend follows me!
"Through the sharp hawthorn blow the winds."
Hum! go to thy bed, and warm thee.

Lear. Did'st thou give all to thy daughters, and
art thou come to this?   50

Edg. Who gives anything to poor Tom? whom
the foul fiend hath led through fire and through
flame, and through [ford] and whirlpool, o'er bog
and quagmire; that hath laid knives under his pillow, and halters in his pew; set ratsbane by his   55
porridge; made him proud of heart, to ride on a bay
trotting-horse over four-inch'd bridges, to course
his own shadow for a traitor. Bless thy five wits!
Tom's a-cold, — O, do de, do de, do de. Bless thee
from whirlwinds, star-blasting, and taking!   60
Do poor Tom some charity, whom the foul fiend
vexes. There could I have him now, — and there,
— and there again, and there.   [*Storm still.*

Lear. Has his daughters brought him to this
     pass?   65
Couldst thou save nothing? Wouldst thou give
     'em all?

Sc. iii, 14. **footed:** landed.   22. **forbid thee:** which you are forbidden to render.   24. **deserving:** action by which I shall
acquire merit.

Sc. iv, 12. **delicate:** sensitive.   31. **loop'd and window'd:** full of holes.   53. **[ford]** *foord* Q.   *Sword* F.   57. **course:** chase.
60. **taking:** infection.

Fool. Nay, he reserv'd a blanket, else we had been all sham'd.

Lear. Now, all the plagues that in the pendulous air Hang fated o'er men's faults light on thy daughters! 70

Kent. He hath no daughters, sir.

Lear. Death, traitor! nothing could have subdu'd nature
To such a lowness but his unkind daughters.
Is it the fashion, that discarded fathers
Should have thus little mercy on their flesh? 75
Judicious punishment! 'Twas this flesh begot
Those pelican daughters.

Edg. "Pillicock sat on Pillicock-hill."
Alow, alow, loo, loo!

Fool. This cold night will turn us all to fools and madmen. 81

Edg. Take heed o' th' foul fiend. Obey thy parents; keep thy [word justly]; swear not; commit not with man's sworn spouse; set not thy sweet heart on proud array. Tom 's a-cold.

Lear. What hast thou been? 86

Edg. A serving-man, proud in heart and mind; that curl'd my hair; wore gloves in my cap; serv'd the lust of my mistress' heart and did the act of darkness with her; swore as many oaths as I 90 spake words, and broke them in the sweet face of heaven: one that slept in the contriving of lust, and wak'd to do it. Wine lov'd I dearly, dice dearly; and in woman out-paramour'd the Turk: false of heart, light of ear, bloody of hand; hog in 95 sloth, fox in stealth, wolf in greediness, dog in madness, lion in prey. Let not the creaking of shoes nor the rustling of silks betray thy poor heart to woman. Keep thy foot out of brothels, thy hand out of plackets, thy pen from lenders' books, and defy the foul fiend. 101
"Still through the hawthorn blows the cold wind."
Says suum, mun, nonny. Dolphin my boy, boy, sessa! let him trot by. [*Storm still.*

Lear. Thou wert better in a grave than to 105 answer with thy uncover'd body this extremity of the skies. Is man no more than this? Consider him well. Thou ow'st the worm no silk, the beast no hide, the sheep no wool, the cat no perfume. Ha! here 's three on 's are sophisticated! Thou 110 art the thing itself; unaccommodated man is no more but such a poor, bare, forked animal as thou art. Off, off, you lendings! come, unbutton here. 114
[*Tearing off his clothes.*]

Enter GLOUCESTER, *with a torch.*

Fool. Prithee, nuncle, be contented; 'tis a naughty night to swim in. Now a little fire in a wild field were like an old lecher's heart; a small spark, all the rest on 's body cold. Look, here comes a walking fire. 119

Edg. This is the foul [fiend] Flibbertigibbet; he begins at curfew, and walks [till the] first cock; he gives the web and the pin, squints the eye, and makes the hare-lip; mildews the white wheat, and hurts the poor creature of earth.
"St. Withold footed thrice the 'old; 125
He met the night-mare and her ninefold;
Bid her alight,
And her troth plight,
And, aroint thee, witch, aroint thee!"

Kent. How fares your Grace? 130

Lear. What's he?

Kent. Who's there? What is't you seek?

Glou. What are you there? Your names?

Edg. Poor Tom, that eats the swimming frog, the toad, the tadpole, the wall-newt, and the 135 water; that in the fury of his heart, when the foul fiend rages, eats cow-dung for salads; swallows the old rat and the ditch-dog; drinks the green mantle of the standing pool; who is whipp'd from tithing to tithing, and stock'd, punish'd, and im- 140 prison'd; who hath three suits to his back, six shirts to his body.
Horse to ride, and weapon to wear;
But mice and rats, and such small deer,
Have been Tom's food for seven long year.
Beware my follower. Peace, Smulkin; peace, thou fiend! 146

Glou. What, hath your Grace no better company?

Edg. The prince of darkness is a gentleman. Modo he's call'd, and Mahu.

Glou. Our flesh and blood, my lord, is grown so vile 150
That it doth hate what gets it.

Edg. Poor Tom 's a-cold.

Glou. Go in with me; my duty cannot suffer To obey in all your daughters' hard commands. Though their injunction be to bar my doors 155 And let this tyrannous night take hold upon you, Yet have I ventur'd to come seek you out, And bring you where both fire and food is ready.

Lear. First let me talk with this philosopher.

69. **pendulous:** suspended. 77. **pelican.** Young pelicans were believed to feed on their mother's blood. 83. [**word justly**] (Pope). *words justice* F; *words justly* Q. 88. **gloves,** as his mistress's favors. 94. **Turk:** Sultan. 95. **light of ear:** credulous. 100. **placket:** opening in a petticoat. 109. **cat:** civet cat. 111. **unaccommodated:** naked. 114. **lendings:** things not really belonging to one, clothes. 120. [**fiend**] Q. Om. F. Flibbertigibbet. See Introduction. 121. [**till the**] Q. *at* F. 122. **web...pin:** cataract. 125. **St. Withold** (Theobald) is supposed to be St. Vitalis. *Swithold* F. **'old:** wold. 126. **ninefold:** nine foals (?), imps (?). 129. **aroint thee:** begone. 136. **water:** water-newt, a lizard. 140. **tithing:** district. 151. **gets:** begets.

What is the cause of thunder?   160

Kent. Good my lord, take his offer; go into th'
house.

Lear. I'll talk a word with this same learned
Theban.

What is your study?

Edg. How to prevent the fiend, and to kill ver-
min.

Lear. Let me ask you one word in private. 165

Kent. Importune him once more to go, my lord;
His wits begin t' unsettle.

Glou.   Canst thou blame him?

                                 [Storm still.

His daughters seek his death. Ah, that good Kent!
He said it would be thus, poor banish'd man!
Thou say'st the King grows mad; I'll tell thee,
friend,   170

I am almost mad myself. I had a son,
Now outlaw'd from my blood; he sought my life,
But lately, very late. I lov'd him, friend,
No father his son dearer; true to tell thee,
The grief hath craz'd my wits. What a night 's
this!   175

I do beseech your Grace, —

Lear.   O, cry you mercy, sir.
Noble philosopher, your company.

Edg. Tom 's a-cold.

Glou. In, fellow, there, into th' hovel; keep thee
warm.

Lear. Come, let's in all.

Kent.   This way, my lord.

Lear.   With him;
I will keep still with my philosopher.   181

Kent. Good my lord, soothe him; let him take
the fellow.

Glou. Take him you on.

Kent. Sirrah, come on; go along with us.

Lear. Come, good Athenian.   185

Glou. No words, no words: hush.

Edg. "Child Rowland to the dark tower came;
His word was still, 'Fie, foh, and fum,
I smell the blood of a British man.'"

                                [Exeunt.

SCENE V. *[Gloucester's castle.]*

Enter CORNWALL *and* EDMUND.

Corn. I will have my revenge ere I depart his
house.

Edm. How, my lord, I may be censured that
nature thus gives way to loyalty, something fears
me to think of.   5

Corn. I now perceive, it was not altogether your
brother's evil disposition made him seek his death;
but a provoking merit, set a-work by a reproveable
badness in himself.   9

Edm. How malicious is my fortune, that I must
repent to be just! This is the letter which he spoke
of, which approves him an intelligent party to the
advantages of France. O heavens! that this treason
were not, or not I the detector!   14

Corn. Go with me to the Duchess.

Edm. If the matter of this paper be certain, you
have mighty business in hand.

Corn. True or false, it hath made thee Earl of
Gloucester. Seek out where thy father is, that he
may be ready for our apprehension.   20

Edm. [*Aside.*] If I find him comforting the King,
it will stuff his suspicion more fully. — I will per-
severe in my course of loyalty, though the conflict
be sore between that and my blood.   24

Corn. I will lay trust upon thee; and thou shalt
find a [dearer] father in my love.   *[Exeunt.*

SCENE VI. *[A building attached to Gloucester's castle.]*

Enter KENT *and* GLOUCESTER.

Glou. Here is better than the open air; take it
thankfully. I will piece out the comfort with what
addition I can. I will not be long from you. *[Exit.*

Kent. All the power of his wits have given way to
his impatience. The gods reward your kindness! 6

Enter LEAR, EDGAR, *and* FOOL.

Edg. Fraretto calls me; and tells me Nero is
an angler in the lake of darkness. Pray, innocent,
and beware of the foul fiend.

Fool. Prithee, nuncle, tell me whether a madman
be a gentleman or a yeoman?   11

Lear. A king, a king!

Fool. No, he's a yeoman that has a gentleman to
his son; for he's a mad yeoman that sees his son a
gentleman before him.   15

Lear. To have a thousand with red burning spits
Come hissing in upon 'em, —

[*Edg.* The foul fiend bites my back.

Fool. He's mad that trusts in the tameness of a
wolf, a horse's health, a boy's love, or a whore's
oath.   21

Lear. It shall be done; I will arraign them
straight.

[*To Edgar.*] Come, sit thou here, most learned
justicer;

[*To the Fool.*] Thou, sapient sir, sit here. Now,
you she foxes!

Edg. Look, where he stands and glares!   25

---

164. **prevent**: anticipate.

Sc. v, 3. **censured**: judged. 7. **his**: Gloucester's. 8. **provoking merit**: a good quality that incited him. 12. **intelligent**: informed. 22. **stuff**: strengthen. 26. [**dearer**] Q. *deere* F.

Sc. vi, 18–59. [*Edg....scape?*] Q. Om. F. 23. **justicer**: Theobald's correction of *Justice* Q.

Wantest thou eyes at trial, madam?
"Come o'er the bourn, Bessy, to me," —
Fool. "Her boat hath a leak,
    And she must not speak
    Why she dares not come over to thee."   30
Edg. The foul fiend haunts poor Tom in the
voice of a nightingale. Hopdance cries in Tom's
belly for two white herring. Croak not, black
angel; I have no food for thee.
Kent. How do you, sir? Stand you not so
    amaz'd: 35
Will you lie down and rest upon the cushions?
Lear. I'll see their trial first. Bring in their
    evidence.
[*To Edgar.*] Thou robed man of justice, take thy
    place;
[*To the Fool.*] And thou, his yoke-fellow of equity,
Bench by his side. [*To Kent.*] You are o' th' com-
    mission,   40
Sit you too.
Edg. Let us deal justly.
"Sleepest or wakest thou, jolly shepherd?
    Thy sheep be in the corn;
    And for one blast of thy minikin mouth,   45
    Thy sheep shall take no harm."
Purr! the cat is grey.
Lear. Arraign her first; 'tis Goneril. I here take
my oath before this honourable assembly, she kick'd
the poor king her father.   50
Fool. Come hither, mistress. Is your name
Goneril?
Lear. She cannot deny it.
Fool. Cry you mercy, I took you for a joint-
stool.   55
Lear. And here's another, whose warp'd looks
    proclaim
What store her heart is made on. Stop her there!
Arms, arms, sword, fire! Corruption in the place!
False justicer, why hast thou let her scape?]
Edg. Bless thy five wits!   60
Kent. O pity! Sir, where is the patience now
That you so oft have boasted to retain?
Edg. [*Aside.*] My tears begin to take his part so
    much,
They mar my counterfeiting.
Lear. The little dogs and all,   65
Tray, Blanch, and Sweetheart, see, they bark at me.
Edg. Tom will throw his head at them. Avaunt,
you curs!
    Be thy mouth or black or white,
    Tooth that poisons if it bite;   70
    Mastiff, greyhound, mongrel grim,
    Hound or spaniel, brach or [lym],

    Or bobtail [tike] or trundle-tail,
    Tom will make him weep and wail;
    For, with throwing thus my head,   75
    Dogs leapt the hatch, and all are fled.
Do de, de, de. Sessa! Come, march to wakes
and fairs and market-towns. Poor Tom, thy horn
is dry.   79
Lear. Then let them anatomize Regan; see
what breeds about her heart. Is there any cause
in nature that make these hard hearts? [*To Edg.*]
You, sir, I entertain for one of my hundred;
only I do not like the fashion of your garments.
You will say they are Persian, but let them be
chang'd.   86

Re-enter GLOUCESTER.

Kent. Now, good my lord, lie here and rest a
while.
Lear. Make no noise, make no noise; draw the
curtains; so, so, so. We'll go to supper i' th' morn-
ing.   91
Fool. And I'll go to bed at noon.
Glou. Come hither, friend; where is the King my
master?
Kent. Here, sir; but trouble him not, his wits are
gone.
Glou. Good friend, I prithee, take him in thy
    arms;   95
I have o'erheard a plot of death upon him.
There is a litter ready; lay him in't,
And drive toward Dover, friend, where thou shalt
    meet
Both welcome and protection. Take up thy mas-
    ter.
If thou shouldst dally half an hour, his life,   100
With thine and all that offer to defend him
Stand in assured loss. Take up, take up;
And follow me, that will to some provision
Give thee quick conduct.
Kent.   [*Oppressed nature sleeps.*
This rest might yet have balm'd thy broken sinews,
Which, if convenience will not allow,   106
Stand in hard cure. (*To the Fool.*) Come, help to
    bear thy master;
Thou must not stay behind.]
Glou.   Come, come, away.
    [*Exeunt [all but Edgar].*
[*Edg.* When we our betters see bearing our woes,
We scarcely think our miseries our foes.   110
Who alone suffers, suffers most i' th' mind,
Leaving free things and happy shows behind;
But then the mind much sufferance doth o'erskip,
When grief hath mates, and bearing fellowship.

27. **bourn:** burn, brook. 45. **minikin:** dainty. 57. **store:** material. 72. **[lym]** (Hanmer): bloodhound. *Hym* F. 73.
[tike] Q: cur. *tight* F. **trundle-tail:** curled tail. 76. **hatch:** lower half of a divided door. 83. **entertain:** engage. 104–
108. **[Oppressed ... behind]** Q. Om. F. 105. **sinews:** nerves. 109–122. **[Edg....lurk]** Q. Om. F. 114. **bearing:**
suffering.

How light and portable my pain seems now,   115
When that which makes me bend makes the King bow,
He childed as I fathered!   Tom, away!
Mark the high noises; and thyself bewray
When false opinion, whose wrong thoughts defile thee,
In thy just proof repeals and reconciles thee.   120
What will hap more to-night, safe scape the King!
Lurk, lurk.]   [*Exit.*]

SCENE VII.   [*Gloucester's castle.*]

Enter CORNWALL, REGAN, GONERIL, *Bastard*
[EDMUND], *and* SERVANTS.

Corn. [*To Gon.*]   Post speedily to my lord your
husband; show him this letter.   The army of France
is landed. — Seek out the traitor Gloucester.
                      [*Exeunt some of the Servants.*]
Reg. Hang him instantly.
Gon. Pluck out his eyes.   5
Corn. Leave him to my displeasure. — Edmund,
keep you our sister company; the revenges we are
bound to take upon your traitorous father are not
fit for your beholding.   Advise the Duke, where
you are going, to a most festinate preparation; we
are bound to the like.   Our posts shall be swift
and intelligent betwixt us.   Farewell, dear sister;
farewell, my Lord of Gloucester.   13

Enter Steward [OSWALD].

How now! where's the King?
Osw. My Lord of Gloucester hath convey'd him
hence.   15
Some five or six and thirty of his knights,
Hot questrists after him, met him at gate,
Who, with some other of the lord's dependants,
Are gone with him toward Dover, where they boast
To have well-armed friends.
Corn.   Get horses for your mistress.
Gon. Farewell, sweet lord, and sister.   21
Corn. Edmund, farewell.
        [*Exeunt* [*Goneril, Edmund, and Oswald*].
                Go seek the traitor Gloucester,
Pinion him like a thief, bring him before us.
                      [*Exeunt other Servants.*]
Though well we may not pass upon his life
Without the form of justice, yet our power   25
Shall do a court'sy to our wrath, which men
May blame, but not control.

Enter GLOUCESTER *and* SERVANTS.
                Who's there?   The traitor?
Reg. Ingrateful fox! 'tis he.

Corn. Bind fast his corky arms.
Glou. What means your Graces?   Good my
friends, consider   30
You are my guests.   Do me no foul play, friends.
Corn. Bind him, I say.   [*Servants bind him.*]
Reg.   Hard, hard.   O filthy traitor!
Glou. Unmerciful lady as you are, I'm none.
Corn. To this chair bind him.   Villain, thou
shalt find —   [*Regan plucks his beard.*]
Glou. By the kind gods, 'tis most ignobly done
To pluck me by the beard.   36
Reg. So white, and such a traitor!
Glou.   Naughty lady,
These hairs, which thou dost ravish from my chin,
Will quicken, and accuse thee.   I am your host:
With robber's hands my hospitable favours   40
You should not ruffle thus.   What will you do?
Corn. Come, sir, what letters had you late from
France?
Reg. Be simple-answer'd, for we know the truth.
Corn. And what confederacy have you with the traitors
Late footed in the kingdom?   45
Reg. To whose hands you have sent the lunatic king,
Speak.
Glou. I have a letter guessingly set down,
Which came from one that's of a neutral heart,
And not from one oppos'd.
Corn.   Cunning.
Reg.   And false.
Corn. Where hast thou sent the King?   50
Glou. To Dover.
Reg. Wherefore to Dover?   Wast thou not
charg'd at peril —
Corn. Wherefore to Dover?   Let him answer that.
Glou. I am tied to th' stake, and I must stand the course.
Reg. Wherefore to Dover?   55
Glou. Because I would not see thy cruel nails
Pluck out his poor old eyes; nor thy fierce sister
In his anointed flesh stick boarish fangs.
The sea, with such a storm as his bare head
In hell-black night endur'd, would have buoy'd up   60
And quench'd the stelled fires;
Yet, poor old heart, he holp the heavens to rain.
If wolves had at thy gate howl'd that stern time,
Thou shouldst have said, "Good porter, turn the key."
All cruels else subscribe; but I shall see   65
The winged vengeance overtake such children.

---

115. **portable:** bearable.   118. **bewray:** disclose.   120. **repeals:** recalls.   121. **What:** whatever.
Sc. vii, 10. **festinate:** speedy.   17. **questrists:** searchers.   29. **corky:** withered.   39. **quicken:** become alive.   40. **favours:** features.   41. **ruffle:** outrage.   54. **course:** attack of the dogs (bear-baiting).   61. **stelled fires:** stars.   65. **All ...** **subscribe.** Not satisfactorily explained.   All other cruelties yield to this (?).

Corn. See 't shalt thou never.   Fellows, hold the
  chair.
Upon these eyes of thine I'll set my foot.
  Glou. He that will think to live till he be old,
Give me some help! — O cruel!   O you gods!   70
  Reg. One side will mock another; th' other
  too.
  Corn. If you see vengeance, —
  [*1.*] *Serv.*   Hold your hand, my lord!
I have serv'd you ever since I was a child;
But better service have I never done you
Than now to bid you hold.
  Reg.   •   How now, you dog!
  [*1.*] *Serv.* If you did wear a beard upon your
  chin,   76
I'd shake it on this quarrel.   What do you mean?
  Corn. My villain!   [*They draw and fight.*]
  [*1.*] *Serv.* Nay, then, come on, and take the
  chance of anger.
  Reg. Give me thy sword.   A peasant stand up
  thus?   80
       [*Takes a sword, and runs at him behind.*
  [*1.*] *Serv.* Oh, I am slain!   My lord, you have
  one eye left
To see some mischief on him.   Oh!   [*Dies.*]
  Corn. Lest it see more, prevent it.   Out, vile
  jelly!
Where is thy lustre now?
  Glou. All dark and comfortless.   Where's my son
  Edmund?   85
Edmund, enkindle all the sparks of nature,
To quit this horrid act.
  Reg.   Out, treacherous villain!
Thou call'st on him that hates thee.   It was he
That made the overture of thy treasons to us,
Who is too good to pity thee.   90
  Glou. O my follies! then Edgar was abus'd.
Kind gods, forgive me that, and prosper him!
  Reg. Go thrust him out at gates, and let him
  smell
His way to Dover.   (*Exit [one] with Gloucester.*)
       How is't, my lord?   How look you?
  Corn. I have received a hurt; follow me, lady.   95
Turn out that eyeless villain; throw this slave
Upon the dunghill.   Regan, I bleed apace;
Untimely comes this hurt.   Give me your arm.
       [*Exit Cornwall, led by Regan.*]
  [*2. Serv.* I'll never care what wickedness I do,
If this man come to good.
  3. Serv.   If she live long,   100
And in the end meet the old course of death,
Women will all turn monsters.

  2. Serv. Let's follow the old earl, and get the Bedlam
To lead him where he would: his roguish madness
Allows itself to anything.   105
  3. Serv. Go thou; I'll fetch some flax and whites
  of eggs
To apply to his bleeding face.   Now, Heaven help
  him!]   [*Exeunt [severally].*

ACT IV

SCENE I.   [*The open country near Gloucester's
  castle.*]

Enter EDGAR.

  Edg. Yet better thus, and known to be con-
  temn'd,
Than, still contemn'd and flatter'd, to be worst.
The lowest and most dejected thing of fortune
Stands still in esperance, lives not in fear.
The lamentable change is from the best;   5
The worst returns to laughter.   Welcome, then,
Thou unsubstantial air that I embrace!
The wretch that thou hast blown unto the worst
Owes nothing to thy blasts.

Enter GLOUCESTER, *led by an* OLD MAN.

                    But who comes here?
My father, poorly led?   World, world, O world!   10
But that thy strange mutations make us hate thee,
Life would not yield to age.
  Old Man. O, my good lord, I have been your
tenant, and your father's tenant, these fourscore
years.   15
  Glou. Away, get thee away!   Good friend, be
  gone;
Thy comforts can do me no good at all;
Thee they may hurt.
  Old Man.   You cannot see your way.
  Glou. I have no way, and therefore want no
  eyes;
I stumbled when I saw.   Full oft 'tis seen,   21
Our means secure us, and our mere defects
Prove our commodities.   O dear son Edgar,
The food of thy abused father's wrath!
Might I but live to see thee in my touch   25
I'd say I had eyes again!
  Old Man.   How now!   Who's there?
  Edg. [*Aside.*] O gods!   Who is't can say, "I am
  at the worst"?
I am worse than e'er I was.
  Old Man.   'Tis poor mad Tom.

---

77. **What ... mean?** Probably this should be given to Cornwall or Regan.   89. **made the overture:** disclosed.   91.
abus'd: wronged.   99–107. [*2. Serv. . . . him*] Q.   Om. F.   101. **old:** usual.
  Act IV, sc. i, 1. **contemn'd:** despised.   4. **esperance:** hope.   6. **The worst ... laughter:** any change from the worst must
be for the better.   9. **Owes nothing:** cannot be called on to pay anything more.   12. **Life ... age:** we should never live to
be old.   22. **secure:** make careless.   23. **commodities:** advantages.   24. **food:** object.   **abused:** deceived.

Edg. [*Aside.*] And worse I may be yet; the worst
    is not
So long as we can say, "This is the worst."   30
    Old Man. Fellow, where goest?
    Glou.   Is it a beggar-man?
    Old Man. Madman and beggar too.
    Glou. He has some reason, else he could not beg.
I' th' last night's storm I such a fellow saw,
Which made me think a man a worm. My son
Came then into my mind, and yet my mind   36
Was then scarce friends with him. I have heard
    more since.
As flies to wanton boys, are we to th' gods,
They kill us for their sport.
    Edg.   [*Aside.*] How should this be?
Bad is the trade that must play fool to sorrow,   40
Ang'ring itself and others. — Bless thee, master!
    Glou. Is that the naked fellow?
    Old Man.   Ay, my lord.
    Glou. [Then, prithee,] get thee away. If, for
    my sake,
Thou wilt o'ertake us hence a mile or twain
I' th' way toward Dover, do it for ancient love;   45
And bring some covering for this naked soul,
Which I'll entreat to lead me.
    Old Man.   Alack, sir, he is mad.
    Glou. 'Tis the time's plague, when madmen lead
    the blind.
Do as I bid thee, or rather do thy pleasure;
Above the rest, be gone.   50
    Old Man. I'll bring him the best 'parel that I
    have,
Come on't what will.   [*Exit.*
    Glou. Sirrah, naked fellow, —
    Edg. Poor Tom 's a-cold. [*Aside.*] I cannot daub
    it further.
    Glou. Come hither, fellow.   55
    Edg. [*Aside.*] And yet I must. — Bless thy sweet
    eyes, they bleed.
    Glou. Know'st thou the way to Dover?
    Edg. Both stile and gate, horse-way and foot-
path. Poor Tom hath been scar'd out of his good
wits. Bless thee, good man's son, from the foul   60
fiend! [Five fiends have been in poor Tom at once;
of lust, as Obidicut; Hobbididence, prince of dumbness; Mahu, of stealing; Modo, of murder; Flibber-
t'gibbet, of mopping and mowing, who since possesses chambermaids and waiting-women. So, bless
thee, master!]   66
    Glou. Here, take this purse, thou whom the
    heavens' plagues
Have humbled to all strokes. That I am wretched

Makes thee the happier; heavens, deal so still!
Let the superfluous and lust-dieted man,   70
That slaves your ordinance, that will not see
Because he does not feel, feel your power quickly;
So distribution should undo excess,
And each man have enough. Dost thou know
    Dover?
    Edg. Ay, master.   75
    Glou. There is a cliff, whose high and bending
    head
Looks fearfully in the confined deep.
Bring me but to the very brim of it,
And I'll repair the misery thou dost bear
With something rich about me. From that place   80
I shall no leading need.
    Edg.   Give me thy arm;
Poor Tom shall lead thee.   [*Exeunt.*

SCENE II.   [*Before the Duke of Albany's
               palace.*]

Enter GONERIL, *Bastard* [EDMUND], *and Stew-
            ard* [OSWALD].

    Gon. Welcome, my lord! I marvel our mild hus-
    band
Not met us on the way. — Now, where's your mas-
    ter?
    Osw. Madam, within; but never man so chang'd.
I told him of the army that was landed;
He smil'd at it. I told him you were coming;   5
His answer was, "The worse." Of Gloucester's
    treachery,
And of the loyal service of his son,
When I inform'd him, then he call'd me sot,
And told me I had turn'd the wrong side out.
What most he should dislike seems pleasant to him;
What like, offensive.   10
    Gon. [*To Edm.*] Then shall you go no further.
It is the cowish terror of his spirit,
That dares not undertake; he'll not feel wrongs
Which tie him to an answer. Our wishes on the
    way
May prove effects. Back, Edmund, to my brother;
Hasten his musters and conduct his powers.   16
I must change [arms] at home, and give the distaff
Into my husband's hands. This trusty servant
Shall pass between us. Ere long you are like to
    hear,
If you dare venture in your own behalf,   20
A mistress's command. Wear this; spare speech;
Decline your head. This kiss, if it durst speak,
Would stretch thy spirits up into the air.

43. [Then, prithee] Q. Om. F.   54. daub: dissemble.   61–66. [Five...master!] Q. Om. F.   64. mopping and mowing: making faces.   70. superfluous: having too much.   71. slaves your ordinance: makes your laws subordinate to his
desires.   76. bending: overhanging.
    Sc. ii, 8. sot: fool.   12. cowish: cowardly.   15. prove effects: be realized.   17. [arms] Q.   names F. Goneril will take the
sword.

Conceive, and fare thee well.

Edm. Yours in the ranks of death.   [*Exit.*

Gon.   My most dear Gloucester!

O, the difference of man and man!   26
To thee a woman's services are due;
My Fool usurps my body.

Osw.   Madam, here comes my lord.

                                       [*Exit.*

Enter the DUKE OF ALBANY.

Gon. I have been worth the whistle.

Alb.   O Goneril!
You are not worth the dust which the rude wind 30
Blows in your face. [I fear your disposition.
That nature which contemns its origin
Cannot be bordered certain in itself.
She that herself will sliver and disbranch
From her material sap, perforce must wither   35
And come to deadly use.

Gon. No more; the text is foolish.

Alb. Wisdom and goodness to the vile seem vile;
Filths savour but themselves. What have you done?
Tigers, not daughters, what have you perform'd? 40
A father, and a gracious aged man,
Whose reverence even the head-lugg'd bear would
     lick,
Most barbarous, most degenerate! have you madded.
Could my good brother suffer you to do it?
A man, a prince, by him so benefited!   45
If that the heavens do not their visible spirits
Send quickly down to tame these vile offences,
It will come,
Humanity must perforce prey on itself,
Like monsters of the deep.]

Gon.   Milk-liver'd man!   50
That bear'st a cheek for blows, a head for wrongs,
Who hast not in thy brows an eye discerning
Thine honour from thy suffering, [that not know'st
Fools do those villains pity who are punish'd
Ere they have done their mischief, where's thy
     drum?   55
France spreads his banners in our noiseless land,
With plumed helm thy state begins to threat;
Whiles thou, a moral fool, sits still, and criest,
"Alack, why does he so?"]

Alb.   See thyself, devil!
Proper deformity seems not in the fiend   60
So horrid as in woman.

Gon.   O vain fool!

[*Alb.* Thou changed and self-cover'd thing, for
     shame!
Be-monster not thy feature. Were't my fitness
To let these hands obey my blood,

They are apt enough to dislocate and tear   65
Thy flesh and bones. Howe'er thou art a fiend,
A woman's shape doth shield thee.

Gon. Marry, your manhood — Mew!

Enter a MESSENGER.

Alb. What news?]

Mess. O, my good lord, the Duke of Cornwall 's
     dead;   70
Slain by his servant, going to put out
The other eye of Gloucester.

Alb.   Gloucester's eyes!

Mess. A servant that he bred, thrill'd with re-
     morse,
Oppos'd against the act, bending his sword
To his great master; who, thereat enrag'd,   75
Flew on him, and amongst them fell'd him dead;
But not without that harmful stroke which since
Hath pluck'd him after.

Alb.   This shows you are above,
You [justicers,] that these our nether crimes
So speedily can venge! But, O poor Gloucester!
Lost he his other eye?

Mess.   Both, both, my lord.   81
This letter, madam, craves a speedy answer.
'Tis from your sister.

Gon. [*Aside.*] One way I like this well;
But being widow, and my Gloucester with her,   85
May all the building in my fancy pluck
Upon my hateful life. Another way,
The news is not so tart. — I'll read, and answer.
                                   [*Exit.*

Alb. Where was his son when they did take his
     eyes?

Mess. Come with my lady hither.

Alb.   He is not here.

Mess. No, my good lord; I met him back again. 91

Alb. Knows he the wickedness?

Mess. Ay, my good lord; 'twas he inform'd against
     him;
And quit the house on purpose that their punish-
     ment
Might have the freer course.

Alb.   Gloucester, I live   95
To thank thee for the love thou show'dst the King,
And to revenge thine eyes. Come hither, friend;
Tell me what more thou know'st.   [*Exeunt.*

[SCENE III. *The French camp near Dover.*

Enter KENT *and a* GENTLEMAN.

Kent. Why the King of France is so suddenly
gone back, know you no reason?

31–50. [I fear . . . deep] Q. Om. F.   33. **bordered certain:** kept within bounds.   35. **material:** essential to life.   53–
59. [that . . . so?] Q. Om. F.   56. **noiseless:** peaceful.   60. **Proper:** that belongs to him.   62–69. [Alb. . . . news?] Q. Om.
F.   62. **self-cover'd:** whose real self is hidden.   63. **Were't my fitness:** were it suitable for me.   64. **blood:** impulse.   73.
remorse: pity.   79. [justicers] Q. *justices* F.   **nether:** committed here below.   86. **pluck:** pull down.

Gent. Something he left imperfect in the state,
which since his coming forth is thought of; which
imports to the kingdom so much fear and danger
that his personal return was most required and
necessary.   7
  Kent. Who hath he left behind him General?
  Gent. The Marshal of France, Monsieur La Far.
  Kent. Did your letters pierce the Queen to any
demonstration of grief?   12
  Gent. [Ay, sir]; she took them, read them in my
    presence;
And now and then an ample tear trill'd down
Her delicate cheek.   It seem'd she was a queen 15
Over her passion, who, most rebel-like,
Sought to be king o'er her.
  Kent.   O, then it mov'd her.
  Gent. Not to a rage; patience and sorrow [strove]
Who should express her goodliest.   You have seen
Sunshine and rain at once: her smiles and tears 20
Were like a better way; those happy smilets
That play'd on her ripe lip seem'd not to know
What guests were in her eyes, which, parted thence,
As pearls from diamonds dropp'd.   In brief,
Sorrow would be a rarity most beloved,   25
If all could so become it.
  Kent.   Made she no verbal question?
  Gent. Faith, once or twice she heav'd the name
    of "father"
Pantingly forth, as if it press'd her heart;
Cried, "Sisters! sisters!   Shame of ladies! sisters!
Kent! father! sisters!   What, i' th' storm?   i' th'
    night?   30
Let pity not be believ'd!"   There she shook
The holy water from her heavenly eyes;
And clamour moistened; then away she started
To deal with grief alone.
  Kent.   It is the stars,
The stars above us, govern our conditions;   35
Else one self mate and make could not beget
Such different issues.   You spoke not with her
    since?
  Gent. No.
  Kent. Was this before the King return'd?
  Gent.   No, since.
  Kent. Well, sir, the poor distressed Lear 's i' th'
    town;   40
Who sometime, in his better tune, remembers
What we are come about, and by no means
Will yield to see his daughter.
  Gent.   Why, good sir?

  Kent. A sovereign shame so elbows him.   His
    own unkindness,
That stripp'd her from his benediction, turn'd her 45
To foreign casualties, gave her dear rights
To his dog-hearted daughters, — these things sting
His mind so venomously, that burning shame
Detains him from Cordelia.
  Gent.   Alack, poor gentleman!
  Kent. Of Albany's and Cornwall's powers you
    heard not?   50
  Gent. 'Tis so, they are afoot.
  Kent. Well, sir, I'll bring you to our master Lear,
And leave you to attend him.   Some dear cause
Will in concealment wrap me up a while;
When I am known aright, you shall not grieve   55
Lending me this acquaintance.   I pray you, go
Along with me.]   [*Exeunt.*

SCENE [IV. *The same.   A tent.*]

Enter, with drum and colours, CORDELIA, [DOC-
    TOR], *and* Soldiers.

  Cor. Alack, 'tis he!   Why, he was met even now
As mad as the vex'd sea, singing aloud,
Crown'd with rank fumiter and furrow-weeds,
With hardocks, hemlock, nettles, cuckoo-flowers,
Darnel, and all the idle weeds that grow   5
In our sustaining corn.   A century send forth;
Search every acre in the high-grown field,
And bring him to our eye. [*Exit an Officer.*]   What
    can man's wisdom
In the restoring his bereaved sense?
He that helps him take all my outward worth.   10
  [*Doct.*] There is means, madam.
Our foster-nurse of nature is repose,
The which he lacks; that to provoke in him,
Are many simples operative, whose power
Will close the eye of anguish.
  Cor.   All blest secrets, 15
All you unpublish'd virtues of the earth,
Spring with my tears! be aidant and remediate
In the good man's [distress]!   Seek, seek for him,
Lest his ungovern'd rage dissolve the life
That wants the means to lead it.

Enter a MESSENGER.

  Mess.   News, madam!
The British powers are marching hitherward.   21
  Cor. 'Tis known before; our preparation stands
In expectation of them.   O dear father,

Sc. iii, Q. F omits scene. 13. **[Ay, sir]** (Johnson). *I say* Q. 18. **[strove]** (Pope). *streme* Q. 21. **like a better way:**
more beautiful than "sunshine and rain at once." 25. **rarity:** something precious. 33. **clamour moistened.** Q adds *her.*
The passage is probably corrupt.   Tears followed her outcry (?). 36. **self mate and make:** same husband and wife. 43.
yield: consent. 44. **sovereign:** over-mastering. **elbows:** holds him aloof (?). 46. **casualties:** risks. 53. **dear:** important.
  Sc. iv, S.D. [DOCTOR] Q. *Gentlemen* F. 3. **fumiter:** fumitory. 4. **hardocks:** perhaps for *burdocks* or *harlock*, wild mustard.
5. **Darnel:** a general term for weed; sometimes specifically rye-grass. 6. **century:** body of 100 men. *Centery* F. *centurie* Q.
11. **[Doct.]** Q. *Gent.* F. 14. **simples:** medicinal herbs. 17. **aidant:** helpful. **remediate:** healing. 18. **[distress]** Q. *desires* F.

It is thy business that I go about;
Therefore great France   25
My mourning and importun'd tears hath pitied.
No blown ambition doth our arms incite,
But love, dear love, and our ag'd father's right.
Soon may I hear and see him!   [*Exeunt.*

SCENE [V. *Gloucester's castle.*]

Enter REGAN *and* Steward [OSWALD].

Reg. But are my brother's powers set forth?
Osw.   Ay, madam.
Reg. Himself in person there?
Osw.   Madam, with much ado.
Your sister is the better soldier.
Reg. Lord Edmund spake not with your lord at
          home?
Osw. No, madam.   5
Reg. What might import my sister's letter to
          him?
Osw. I know not, lady.
Reg. Faith, he is posted hence on serious matter.
It was great ignorance, Gloucester's eyes being out,
To let him live; where he arrives he moves   10
All hearts against us.   Edmund, I think, is gone,
In pity of his misery, to dispatch
His nighted life; moreover, to descry
The strength o' th' enemy.
Osw. I must needs after him, madam, with my
          letter.   15
Reg. Our troops set forth to-morrow, stay with
          us;
The ways are dangerous.
Osw.   I may not, madam;
My lady charg'd my duty in this business.
Reg. Why should she write to Edmund?   Might
          not you
Transport her purposes by word?   Belike   20
Some things — I know not what.   I'll love thee
          much —
Let me unseal the letter.
Osw.   Madam, I had rather —
Reg. I know your lady does not love her husband;
I am sure of that; and at her late being here   24
She gave strange œillades and most speaking looks
To noble Edmund.   I know you are of her bosom.
Osw. I, madam?
Reg. I speak in understanding; y' are, I know 't.
Therefore I do advise you, take this note:
My lord is dead; Edmund and I have talk'd;   30
And more convenient is he for my hand
Than for your lady's.   You may gather more.
If you do find him, pray you, give him this;

And when your mistress hears thus much from you,
I pray, desire her call her wisdom to her.   35
So, fare you well.
If you do chance to hear of that blind traitor,
Preferment falls on him that cuts him off.
Osw. Would I could meet him, madam!   I should
          show
What party I do follow.
Reg.   Fare thee well.   40
                                              [*Exeunt.*

SCENE [VI.   *Fields near Dover.*]

Enter GLOUCESTER *and* EDGAR [*dressed like a
                    peasant*].

Glou. When shall I come to th' top of that same
          hill?
Edg. You do climb up it now; look, how we la-
          bour.
Glou. Methinks the ground is even.
Edg.   Horrible steep.
Hark, do you hear the sea?
Glou.   No, truly.
Edg. Why, then, your other senses grow im-
          perfect   5
By your eyes' anguish.
Glou.   So may it be, indeed.
Methinks thy voice is alter'd, and thou speak'st
In better phrase and matter than thou didst.
Edg. You're much deceiv'd.   In nothing am I
          chang'd
But in my garments.
Glou.   Methinks you're better spoken.
Edg. Come on, sir, here's the place; stand still.
          How fearful   11
And dizzy 'tis, to cast one's eyes so low!
The crows and choughs that wing the midway air
Show scarce so gross as beetles.   Half way down
Hangs one that gathers samphire, dreadful trade! 15
Methinks he seems no bigger than his head.
The fishermen, that walk upon the beach,
Appear like mice; and yond tall anchoring bark,
Diminish'd to her cock; her cock, a buoy
Almost too small for sight.   The murmuring surge,
That on th' unnumb'red idle pebbles chafes,   21
Cannot be heard so high.   I'll look no more,
Lest my brain turn, and the deficient sight
Topple down headlong.
Glou.   Set me where you stand.
Edg. Give me your hand; you are now within a
          foot   25
Of th' extreme verge.   For all beneath the moon
Would I not leap upright.

26. **importun'd**: importunate, urgent.   *important* Q.   27. **blown**: puffed up.
    Sc. v, 2. with much ado: persuaded with difficulty.   13. **nighted**: blinded.   25. **œillades**: amorous glances.   26. **of her
bosom**: in her confidence.   29. **take this note**: note this.
    Sc. vi, 13. choughs: jackdaws.   14. **gross**: big.   15. **samphire**: sea-fennel, used for pickling.   19. **cock**: cock-boat.

Glou.   Let go my hand.
Here, friend, 's another purse; in it a jewel
Well worth a poor man's taking.   Fairies and gods
Prosper it with thee!   Go thou further off;   30
Bid me farewell, and let me hear thee going.
    Edg.   Now fare ye well, good sir.
    Glou.   With all my heart.
    Edg.   Why I do trifle thus with his despair
Is done to cure it.
    Glou. [*Kneeling.*]   O you mighty gods!
This world I do renounce, and in your sights   35
Shake patiently my great affliction off.
If I could bear it longer, and not fall
To quarrel with your great opposeless wills,
My snuff and loathed part of nature should
Burn itself out.   If Edgar live, O bless him!   40
Now, fellow, fare thee well.   [*He falls.*
    Edg.   Gone, sir; farewell!
— And yet I know not how conceit may rob
The treasury of life, when life itself
Yields to the theft.   Had he been where he thought,
By this had thought been past.   Alive or dead? —
Ho, you sir! friend!   Hear you, sir! speak! —   46
Thus might he pass indeed; yet he revives. —
What are you, sir?
    Glou.   Away, and let me die.
    Edg.   Hadst thou been aught but gossamer, feath-
ers, air,
So many fathom down precipitating,   50
Thou 'dst shiver'd like an egg: but thou dost
breathe;
Hast heavy substance; bleed'st not; speak'st; art
sound.
Ten masts at each make not the altitude
Which thou hast perpendicularly fell.
Thy life's a miracle.   Speak yet again.   55
    Glou.   But have I fall'n, or no?
    Edg.   From the dread summit of this chalky
bourn.
Look up a-height; the shrill-gorg'd lark so far
Cannot be seen or heard.   Do but look up.
    Glou.   Alack, I have no eyes.   60
Is wretchedness depriv'd that benefit,
To end itself by death?   'Twas yet some comfort,
When misery could beguile the tyrant's rage,
And frustrate his proud will.
    Edg.   Give me your arm.
Up: so.   How is't?   Feel you your legs?   You
    stand.   65
    Glou.   Too well, too well.
    Edg.   This is above all strangeness.
Upon the crown o' th' cliff, what thing was that

Which parted from you?
    Glou.   A poor unfortunate beggar.
    Edg.   As I stood here below, methought his eyes
Were two full moons; he had a thousand noses,   70
Horns whelk'd and waved like the [enridged] sea.
It was some fiend; therefore, thou happy father,
Think that the clearest gods, who make them hon-
ours
Of men's impossibilities, have preserv'd thee.
    Glou.   I do remember now.   Henceforth I'll bear
Affliction till it do cry out itself   76
"Enough, enough," and die.   That thing you speak
of,
I took it for a man; often 't would say,
"The fiend, the fiend!"   He led me to that place.
    Edg.   Bear free and patient thoughts.

Enter LEAR [*fantastically dressed with wild
flowers*].

                    But who comes here?
The safer sense will ne'er accommodate   81
His master thus.
    Lear.   No, they cannot touch me for [coining];
I am the King himself.
    Edg.   O thou side-piercing sight!   85
    Lear.   Nature's above art in that respect.   There's
your press-money.   That fellow handles his bow
like a crow-keeper; draw me a clothier's yard.
Look, look, a mouse!   Peace, peace; this piece of
toasted cheese will do't.   There's my gauntlet; I'll
prove it on a giant.   Bring up the brown bills.   O,
well flown, bird!   I' th' clout, i' th' clout!   Hewgh!
Give the word.   93
    Edg.   Sweet marjoram.
    Lear.   Pass.
    Glou.   I know that voice.   96
    Lear.   Ha!   Goneril, with a white beard!   They
flatter'd me like a dog, and told me I had the white
hairs in my beard ere the black ones were there.
To say "ay" and "no" to everything that I said!
"Ay" and "no" too was no good divinity.   101
When the rain came to wet me once, and the wind
to make me chatter; when the thunder would not
peace at my bidding; there I found 'em, there I
smelt 'em out.   Go to, they are not men o' their
words: they told me I was everything; 'tis a lie, I
am not ague-proof.   107
    Glou.   The trick of that voice I do well remember.
Is't not the King?
    Lear.   Ay, every inch a king!
When I do stare, see how the subject quakes.   110
I pardon that man's life.   What was thy cause?

Adultery?
Thou shalt not die. Die for adultery! No:
The wren goes to't, and the small gilded fly
Does lecher in my sight.   115
Let copulation thrive; for Gloucester's bastard son
Was kinder to his father than my daughters
Got 'tween the lawful sheets.
To't, luxury, pell-mell! for I lack soldiers.
Behold yond simp'ring dame,   120
Whose face between her forks presages snow,
That minces virtue, and does shake the head
To hear of pleasure's name, —
The fitchew nor the soiled horse goes to't
With a more riotous appetite.   125
Down from the waist they are Centaurs,
Though women all above;
But to the girdle do the gods inherit,
Beneath is all the fiends';
There's hell, there's darkness, there's the sulphurous
     pit,   130
Burning, scalding, stench, consumption; fie, fie, fie!
pah, pah! Give me an ounce of civet; good apothe-
cary, sweeten my imagination. There's money
for thee.
    Glou. O, let me kiss that hand!   135
    Lear. Let me wipe it first; it smells of mortality.
    Glou. O ruin'd piece of nature! This great world
Shall so wear out to nought. Dost thou know me?
    Lear. I remember thine eyes well enough. Dost
thou squiny at me? No, do thy worst, blind
Cupid; I'll not love. Read thou this challenge; mark
but the penning of it.   142
    Glou. Were all thy letters suns, I could not see.
    Edg. [*Aside.*] I would not take this from report.
    It is;
And my heart breaks at it.   145
    Lear. Read.
    Glou. What, with the case of eyes?
    Lear. O, ho, are you there with me? No eyes
in your head, nor no money in your purse? Your
eyes are in a heavy case, your purse in a light; yet
you see how this world goes.
    Glou. I see it feelingly.   152
    Lear. What, art mad? A man may see how this
world goes with no eyes. Look with thine ears; see
how yond justice rails upon yond simple thief.
Hark, in thine ear: change places, and, handy-
dandy, which is the justice, which is the thief?
Thou hast seen a farmer's dog bark at a beggar? 159
    Glou. Ay, sir.
    Lear. And the creature run from the cur? There
thou mightst behold the great image of authority:
a dog's obey'd in office.

Thou rascal beadle, hold thy bloody hand!
Why dost thou lash that whore? Strip thy own
     back;   165
Thou hotly lusts to use her in that kind
For which thou whip'st her. The usurer hangs the
     cozener.
Through tatter'd clothes great vices do appear;
Robes and furr'd gowns hide all. [Plate] sins with
     gold,
And the strong lance of justice hurtless breaks; 170
Arm it in rags, a pigmy's straw does pierce it.
None does offend, none, I say, none; I'll able 'em.
Take that of me, my friend, who have the power
To seal th' accuser's lips. Get thee glass eyes,
And, like a scurvy politician, seem   175
To see the things thou dost not. Now, now, now,
     now.
Pull off my boots; harder, harder: so.
    Edg. O, matter and impertinency mix'd!
Reason in madness!
    Lear. If thou wilt weep my fortunes, take my
     eyes.   180
I know thee well enough; thy name is Gloucester.
Thou must be patient; we came crying hither.
Thou know'st, the first time that we smell the
     air,
We wawl and cry. I will preach to thee; mark.
    Glou. Alack, alack the day!   185
    Lear. When we are born, we cry that we are come
To this great stage of fools. — This' a good block.
It were a delicate stratagem, to shoe
A troop of horse with felt. I'll put 't in proof;
And when I have stol'n upon these son-in-laws, 190
Then, kill, kill, kill, kill, kill, kill!

      Enter a GENTLEMAN [*with Attendants*].

    Gent. O, here he is! Lay hand upon him. Sir,
Your most dear daughter —
    Lear. No rescue? What, a prisoner? I am even
The natural fool of fortune. Use me well;   195
You shall have ransom. Let me have surgeons;
I am cut to th' brains.
    Gent.   You shall have anything.
    Lear. No seconds? All myself?
Why, this would make a man a man of salt,
To use his eyes for garden water-pots,   200
[Ay, and laying autumn's dust.
    Gent.   Good sir, —]
    Lear. I will die bravely, like a smug bridegroom.
What!
I will be jovial. Come, come; I am a king,
My masters, know you that?
    Gent. You are a royal one, and we obey you. 205

---

119. **luxury:** lust.   121. **forks:** part of the head-dress.   **snow:** coldness, chastity.   122. **minces:** affects coyly.   124. **fitchew:** pole-cat.   **soiled:** richly fed.   128. **inherit:** possess.   140. **squiny:** squint.   147. **case:** sockets.   167. **cozener:** petty cheat.   169. **[Plate]** (Theobald).   *Place* F.   The reference is to plate armor.   172. **able:** warrant.   178. **impertinency:** irrelevance.   187. **block:** hat.   198. **seconds:** supporters.   199. **salt:** tears.   201. **[Ay ... sir]** Q. Om. F.

Lear. Then there's life in't. Come, an you get it, you shall get it by running. Sa, sa, sa, sa.

           [Exit [running; attendants follow].

  Gent. A sight most pitiful in the meanest wretch, Past speaking of in a king! Thou hast [one] daughter

Who redeems Nature from the general curse   210
Which twain have brought her to.

  Edg. Hail, gentle sir.

  Gent.   Sir, speed you: what's your will?

  Edg. Do you hear aught, sir, of a battle toward?

  Gent. Most sure and vulgar; every one hears that, Which can distinguish sound.

  Edg.   But, by your favour,   215
How near's the other army?

  Gent. Near and on speedy foot; the main descry Stands on the hourly thought.

  Edg.   I thank you, sir; that's all.

  Gent. Though that the Queen on special cause is here,

Her army is mov'd on.   *[Exit.*

  Edg.   I thank you, sir.   220

  Glou. You ever-gentle gods, take my breath from me;

Let not my worser spirit tempt me again
To die before you please!

  Edg.   Well pray you, father.

  Glou. Now, good sir, what are you?

  Edg. A most poor man, made tame to fortune's blows;   225

Who, by the art of known and feeling sorrows,
Am pregnant to good pity. Give me your hand,
I'll lead you to some biding.

  Glou.   Hearty thanks;
The bounty and the benison of Heaven
To boot, and boot!

Enter Steward [OSWALD].

  Osw. A proclaim'd prize! Most happy!   230
That eyeless head of thine was first fram'd flesh
To raise my fortunes. Thou old unhappy traitor,
Briefly thyself remember; the sword is out
That must destroy thee.

  Glou.   Now let thy friendly hand
Put strength enough to't.   *[Edgar interposes.]*

  Osw.   Wherefore, bold peasant,   235
Dar'st thou support a publish'd traitor? Hence;
Lest that the infection of his fortune take
Like hold on thee. Let go his arm.

  Edg. 'Chill not let go, zir, without vurther 'casion.

  Osw. Let go, slave, or thou diest!   241

  Edg. Good gentleman, go your gait, and let poor volk pass. An 'chud ha' bin zwagger'd out of my life, 'twould not ha' bin zo long as 'tis by a vortnight. Nay, come not near th' old man; keep out, 'che vor ye, or Ise try whether your costard or my ballow be the harder. 'Chill be plain with you.   248

  Osw. Out, dunghill!

  Edg. 'Chill pick your teeth, zir. Come, no matter vor your foins.   251

     [They fight, and Edgar knocks him down.]

  Osw. Slave, thou hast slain me. Villain, take my purse.

If ever thou wilt thrive, bury my body;
And give the letters which thou find'st about me   254
To Edmund Earl of Gloucester; seek him out
Upon the English party. O, untimely death!
Death!   *[Dies.*

  Edg. I know thee well; a serviceable villain,
As duteous to the vices of thy mistress
As badness would desire.

  Glou.   What, is he dead?

  Edg. Sit you down, father; rest you.   260
Let's see these pockets; the letters that he speaks of
May be my friends. He's dead; I am only sorry
He had no other death's-man. Let us see.
Leave, gentle wax; and, manners, blame us not.
To know our enemies' minds, we rip their hearts;
Their papers, is more lawful.   266

  (*Reads the letter.*) "Let our reciprocal vows be remem'red. You have many opportunities to cut him off; if your will want not, time and place will be fruitfully offer'd. There is nothing done, if he return the conqueror; then am I the prisoner, and his bed my gaol; from the loathed warmth whereof deliver me, and supply the place for your labour.   274

"Your — wife, so I would say —

        "Affectionate servant,

           "GONERIL."

O indistinguish'd space of woman's will!
A plot upon her virtuous husband's life;
And the exchange my brother! Here, in the sands,   280

Thee I'll rake up, the post unsanctified
Of murderous lechers; and in the mature time
With this ungracious paper strike the sight
Of the death-practis'd duke. For him 'tis well
That of thy death and business I can tell.   285

  Glou. The King is mad; how stiff is my vile sense
That I stand up and have ingenious feeling
Of my huge sorrows! Better I were distract;

---

209. [one] Q. *a* F.   213. **toward:** imminent.   214. **vulgar:** of common knowledge.   217-218. **the main ... thought:** every hour we expect to catch sight of the main body.   226. **art:** experience.   227. **pregnant:** ready.   228. **biding:** dwelling. 233. **thyself remember:** think on your soul's welfare.   239. **'Chill:** I will. Edgar takes the part of a peasant and uses Southern dialect.   243. **An 'chud:** if I could.   246. **'che vor:** I warn. **Ise:** I shall. **costard:** head.   248. **ballow:** cudgel.   251. **foins:** thrusts.   264. **Leave:** by your leave.   276. **servant:** lover.   278. **indistinguish'd space:** unlimited range. **will:** lust.   281. **rake:** cover.   284. **death-practis'd:** whose death is plotted.   287. **ingenious:** conscious.

So should my thoughts be sever'd from my griefs,
                       [*Drum afar off.*
And woes by wrong imaginations lose   290
The knowledge of themselves.
   Edg.   Give me your hand.
Far off, methinks, I hear the beaten drum.
Come, father, I'll bestow you with a friend.
                             [*Exeunt.*

Scene VII. [*A tent in the French camp.*]

Enter Cordelia, Kent, *and* [Doctor].

   Cor. O thou good Kent, how shall I live and work
To match thy goodness? My life will be too short,
And every measure fail me.
   Kent. To be acknowledg'd, madam, is o'erpaid.
All my reports go with the modest truth;   5
Nor more nor clipp'd, but so.
   Cor.   Be better suited;
These weeds are memories of those worser hours.
I prithee, put them off.
   Kent.   Pardon, dear madam;
Yet to be known shortens my made intent.
My boon I make it, that you know me not   10
Till time and I think meet.
   Cor. Then be't so, my good lord. [*To the Doctor.*]
     How does the King?
   [*Doct.*] Madam, sleeps still.
   Cor. O you kind gods,
Cure this great breach in his abused nature!   15
Th' untun'd and jarring senses, O, wind up
Of this child-changed father!
   [*Doct.*]   So please your Majesty
That we may wake the King? He hath slept long.
   Cor. Be govern'd by your knowledge, and proceed
I' th' sway of your own will.

Enter Lear *in a chair carried by* Servants.
    [Gentleman *in attendance.*]
                      Is he array'd?   20
   Gent. Ay, madam; in the heaviness of sleep
We put fresh garments on him.
   [*Doct.*] Be by, good madam, when we do awake
     him;
I doubt [not] of his temperance.
   [*Cor.*]   Very well.
   Doct. Please you, draw near. — Louder the
     music there!]   25
   Cor. O my dear father! Restoration hang
Thy medicine on my lips; and let this kiss

Repair those violent harms that my two sisters
Have in thy reverence made!
   Kent.   Kind and dear princess!
   Cor. Had you not been their father, these white
     flakes   30
Did challenge pity of them. Was this a face
To be oppos'd against the [warring] winds?
[To stand against the deep dread-bolted thunder?
In the most terrible and nimble stroke
Of quick, cross lightning? to watch — poor perdu! —
With this thin helm?] Mine enemy's dog,   36
Though he had bit me, should have stood that night
Against my fire; and wast thou fain, poor father,
To hovel thee with swine and rogues forlorn
In short and musty straw? Alack, alack!   40
'Tis wonder that thy life and wits at once
Had not concluded all. He wakes; speak to him.
   Doct. Madam, do you; 'tis fittest.
   Cor. How does my royal lord? How fares your
     Majesty?
   Lear. You do me wrong to take me out o' th'
     grave.   45
Thou art a soul in bliss; but I am bound
Upon a wheel of fire, that mine own tears
Do scald like molten lead.
   Cor.   Sir, do you know me?
   Lear. You are a spirit, I know; where did you die?
   Cor. Still, still, far wide!   50
   Doct. He's scarce awake; let him alone a while.
   Lear. Where have I been? Where am I? Fair
     daylight?
I am mightily abus'd. I should ev'n die with pity,
To see another thus. I know not what to say.
I will not swear these are my hands. Let's see;   55
I feel this pin prick. Would I were assur'd
Of my condition!
   Cor.   O, look upon me, sir,
And hold your hand in benediction o'er me.
[No, sir,] you must not kneel.
   Lear.   Pray, do not mock me.
I am a very foolish fond old man,   60
Fourscore and upward, not an hour more nor less;
And, to deal plainly,
I fear I am not in my perfect mind.
Methinks I should know you, and know this man;
Yet I am doubtful; for I am mainly ignorant   65
What place this is, and all the skill I have
Remembers not these garments; nor I know not
Where I did lodge last night. Do not laugh at me;
For, as I am a man, I think this lady
To be my child Cordelia.

---

293. **bestow:** lodge.
Sc. vii, s.d. [Doctor] Q. *Gentlemen* F. 9. **shortens:** interferes with. **made:** prearranged. 13, 17, 23. [*Doct.*] Q. *Gent.*
F. 16. **wind up.** The figure is of a stringed instrument. 17. **child-changed:** changed by his children's conduct. 24. [not]
Q. Om. F. **temperance:** sanity. 24–25. [*Cor.* . . . there] Q. Om. F. 32. [warring] Q. *iarring* F. 33–36. [To . . .
helm?] Q. Om. F. 35. **cross:** zigzag. **perdu:** a sentinel placed in a dangerous station. 36. **helm:** covering (of hair).
42. **all:** altogether. 50. **wide:** astray. 59. [No, sir] Q. Om. F. 65. **mainly:** completely.

Cor.   And so I am, I am.   70
Lear. Be your tears wet? Yes, faith. I pray,
     weep not.
If you have poison for me, I will drink it.
I know you do not love me; for your sisters
Have, as I do remember, done me wrong: 74
You have some cause, they have not.
     Cor.   No cause, no cause.
Lear. Am I in France?
Kent.   In your own kingdom, sir.
Lear. Do not abuse me.
Doct. Be comforted, good madam; the great rage,
You see, is kill'd in him: [and yet it is danger
To make him even o'er the time he has lost.]   80
Desire him to go in; trouble him no more
Till further settling.
     Cor. Will't please your Highness walk?
     Lear.   You must bear with me.
Pray you now, forget and forgive; I am old and
     foolish.
        [*Exeunt [all but Kent and Gentleman*].
[*Gent.* Holds it true, sir, that the Duke of Corn-
wall was so slain?   86
Kent. Most certain, sir.
Gent. Who is conductor of his people?
Kent. As 'tis said, the bastard son of Gloucester.
Gent. They say Edgar, his banish'd son, is with
the Earl of Kent in Germany.   91
Kent. Report is changeable. 'Tis time to look
about; the powers of the kingdom approach apace.
Gent. The arbitrement is like to be bloody.
Fare you well, sir.   [*Exit.*] 96
Kent. My point and period will be throughly
     wrought,
Or well or ill, as this day's battle's fought.] [*Exit.*

ACT V

Scene I. [*The British camp, near Dover.*]

Enter, with drum and colours, Edmund, Regan,
     Gentlemen, *and* Soldiers.

Edm. Know of the Duke if his last purpose hold,
Or whether since he is advis'd by aught
To change the course. He's full of alteration
And self-reproving; bring his constant pleasure.
        [*To a Gentleman, who goes out.*]
Reg. Our sister's man is certainly miscarried. 5
Edm. 'Tis to be doubted, madam.
Reg.   Now, sweet lord,
You know the goodness I intend upon you.

Tell me — but truly — but then speak the truth,
Do you not love my sister?
     Edm.   In honour'd love.
     Reg. But have you never found my brother's
     way   10
To the forfended place?
     [*Edm.*   That thought abuses you.
     Reg. I am doubtful that you have been conjunct
And bosom'd with her, — as far as we call hers.]
Edm. No, by mine honour, madam.
     Reg. I never shall endure her. Dear my lord,
Be not familiar with her.
     Edm.   Fear me not.   16
She and the Duke her husband!

Enter, with drum and colours, Albany, Goneril,
        and Soldiers.

     [*Gon.* [*Aside.*] I had rather lose the battle than
     that sister
Should loosen him and me.]
     Alb. Our very loving sister, well be-met.   20
Sir, this I heard: the King is come to his daughter,
With others whom the rigour of our state
Forc'd to cry out. [Where I could not be honest,
I never yet was valiant. For this business,
It toucheth us, as France invades our land,   25
Not bolds the King, with others, whom, I fear,
Most just and heavy causes make oppose.
     Edm. Sir, you speak nobly.]
     Reg.   Why is this reason'd?
     Gon. Combine together 'gainst the enemy;
For these domestic and particular broils   30
Are not the question here.
     Alb.   Let's then determine
With the ancient of war on our proceeding.
     [*Edm.* I shall attend you presently at your tent.]
     Reg. Sister, you'll go with us?
     Gon. No.   35
     Reg. 'Tis most convenient; pray you, go with us.
     Gon. [*Aside.*] O, ho, I know the riddle. — I will
     go.   [*Exeunt both the armies.*

[*As they are going out,*] *enter* Edgar [*disguised.*
        Albany remains].

Edg. If e'er your Grace had speech with man so
     poor,
Hear me one word.
     Alb.   I'll overtake you. — Speak.
     Edg. Before you fight the battle, ope this letter.
If you have victory, let the trumpet sound   41
For him that brought it. Wretched though I seem,

79–80. [and . . . lost] Q. Om. F.   85–98. [Gent. . . . fought] Q. Om. F.   97. **My . . . period**: the question of my end.
Act V, sc. i, 4. constant pleasure: fixed decision.   5. **is . . . miscarried**: has met disaster.   6. **doubted**: feared. Cf. l. 12,
doubtful.   11. **forfended**: forbidden. **abuses**: deceives.   11–13. [Edm. . . . hers] Q. Om. F.   13. **bosom'd**: intimate. **as
. . . hers**: to the utmost limit.   18–19. [Gon. . . . me] Q. Om. F.   23–28. [Where . . . nobly] Q. Om. F.   26. **Not bolds**:
not as it encourages.   28. **reason'd**: discussed.   32. **ancient**: veterans.   33. [Edm. . . . tent] Q. Om. F.   36. **convenient**:
suitable.

I can produce a champion that will prove
What is avouched there. If you miscarry,
Your business of the world hath so an end,   45
And machination ceases. Fortune love you!
    Alb. Stay till I have read the letter.
    Edg.   I was forbid it.
When time shall serve, let but the herald cry,
And I'll appear again.   [*Exit.*
    Alb. Why, fare thee well; I will o'erlook thy
    paper.   50

          Re-enter EDMUND.

    Edm. The enemy's in view; draw up your powers.
Here is the guess of their true strength and forces
By diligent discovery; but your haste
Is now urg'd on you.
    Alb.   We will greet the time.
                           [*Exit.*
    Edm. To both these sisters have I sworn my
    love;   55
Each jealous of the other as the stung
Are of the adder. Which of them shall I take?
Both? one? or neither? Neither can be enjoy'd,
If both remain alive. To take the widow
Exasperates, makes mad her sister Goneril;   60
And hardly shall I carry out my side,
Her husband being alive. Now then we'll use
His countenance for the battle; which being done,
Let her who would be rid of him devise
His speedy taking off. As for the mercy   65
Which he intends to Lear and to Cordelia,
The battle done, and they within our power,
Shall never see his pardon; for my state
Stands on me to defend, not to debate.   [*Exit.*

    SCENE II. [*A field between the two camps.*]

*Alarum within.   Enter, with drum and colours,
   Lear, Cordelia, and Soldiers, over the stage; and
   exeunt.*

       Enter EDGAR *and* GLOUCESTER.

    Edg. Here, father, take the shadow of this tree
For your good host; pray that the right may thrive.
If ever I return to you again,
I'll bring you comfort.
    Glou.   Grace go with you, sir!
                          [*Exit* [*Edgar*].

    Alarum and retreat within.   Re-enter EDGAR.

    Edg. Away, old man; give me thy hand; away!   5
King Lear hath lost, he and his daughter ta'en.

Give me thy hand; come on.
    Glou. No further, sir; a man may rot even here.
    Edg. What, in ill thoughts again? Men must
    endure
Their going hence even as their coming hither;   10
Ripeness is all. Come on.
    Glou.   And that's true too.
                         [*Exeunt.*

    SCENE III. [*The British camp near Dover.*]
Enter, in conquest, with drum and colours, EDMUND;
   LEAR *and* CORDELIA *as prisoners:* CAPTAIN,
   Soldiers, *etc.*

    Edm. Some officers take them away. Good
    guard,
Until their greater pleasures first be known
That are to censure them.
    Cor.   We are not the first
Who with best meaning have incurr'd the worst.
For thee, oppressed king, I am cast down;   5
Myself could else out-frown false Fortune's frown.
Shall we not see these daughters and these sis-
    ters?
    Lear. No, no, no, no! Come, let's away to
    prison.
We two alone will sing like birds i' th' cage.
When thou dost ask me blessing, I'll kneel down   10
And ask of thee forgiveness. So we'll live,
And pray, and sing, and tell old tales, and laugh
At gilded butterflies, and hear poor rogues
Talk of court news; and we'll talk with them too,
Who loses and who wins; who's in, who's out;   15
And take upon 's the mystery of things
As if we were God's spies; and we'll wear out,
In a wall'd prison, packs and sects of great ones,
That ebb and flow by th' moon.
    Edm.   Take them away.
    Lear. Upon such sacrifices, my Cordelia,   20
The gods themselves throw incense. Have I
    caught thee?
He that parts us shall bring a brand from heaven,
And fire us hence like foxes. Wipe thine eyes;
The good-years shall devour them, flesh and fell,
Ere they shall make us weep. We'll see 'em
    starv'd first.   25
Come.   [*Exeunt* [*Lear and Cordelia, guarded*].
    Edm. Come hither, captain; hark.
Take thou this note [*giving a paper*]; go follow them
    to prison.
One step I have advanc'd thee; if thou dost
As this instructs thee, thou dost make thy way
To noble fortunes. Know thou this, that men   30

---

53. **discovery:** scouting. 54. **greet the time:** meet the occasion. 69. **Stands on:** requires.
Sc. ii, 2. **host:** shelterer.
Sc. iii, 2. **their greater pleasures:** the desires of those greater persons. 3. **censure:** judge. 17. **God's spies:** spies on
God's ways. 23. **foxes.** Foxes were driven from their holes by fire and smoke. 24. **good-years:** an expression for some
vague evil influence. **fell:** skin.

Are as the time is; to be tender-minded
Does not become a sword.   Thy great employment
Will not bear question; either say thou'lt do't,
Or thrive by other means.
    Capt.   I'll do't, my lord.
    Edm. About it; and write happy when thou'st
       done.   35
Mark, I say instantly; and carry it so
As I have set it down.
    [*Capt.* I cannot draw a cart, nor eat dried oats;
If it be man's work, I'll do't.]   [*Exit.*

    Flourish. Enter ALBANY, GONERIL, REGAN,
         [*another* CAPTAIN] *and* Soldiers.

    Alb. Sir, you have show'd to-day your valiant
       strain,   40
And fortune led you well.   You have the captives
Who were the opposites of this day's strife;
I do require them of you, so to use them
As we shall find their merits and our safety
May equally determine.
    Edm.   Sir, I thought it fit   45
To send the old and miserable king
To some retention [and appointed guard];
Whose age had charms in it, whose title more,
To pluck the common bosom on his side,
And turn our impress'd lances in our eyes   50
Which do command them.   With him I sent the
       Queen,
My reason all the same; and they are ready
To-morrow, or at further space, t' appear
Where you shall hold your session.   [At this time
We sweat and bleed: the friend hath lost his friend;
And the best quarrels, in the heat, are curs'd   56
By those that feel their sharpness:
The question of Cordelia and her father
Requires a fitter place.]
    Alb.   Sir, by your patience,
I hold you but a subject of this war,   60
Not as a brother.
    Reg.   That's as we list to grace him.
Methinks our pleasure might have been demanded,
Ere you had spoke so far.   He led our powers,
Bore the commission of my place and person;
The which immediacy may well stand up,   65
And call itself your brother.
    Gon.   Not so hot.
In his own grace he doth exalt himself,
More than in your addition.
    Reg.   In my rights,
By me invested, he compeers the best.

    Alb. That were the most, if he should husband
       you.   70
    Reg. Jesters do oft prove prophets.
    Gon.   Holla, holla!
That eye that told you so look'd but a-squint.
    Reg. Lady, I am not well; else I should answer
From a full-flowing stomach.   General,
Take thou my soldiers, prisoners, patrimony;   75
Dispose of them, of me; the walls are thine.
Witness the world, that I create thee here
My lord and master.
    Gon.   Mean you to enjoy him?
    Alb. The let-alone lies not in your good will.
    Edm. Nor in thine, lord.
    Alb.   Half-blooded fellow, yes.   80
    Reg. [*To Edmund.*] Let the drum strike, and
       prove my title thine.
    Alb. Stay yet; hear reason.   Edmund, I arrest thee
On capital treason; and, in thy arrest,
This gilded serpent. [*Pointing to Gon.*]   For your
       claim, fair sister,
I bar it in the interest of my wife.   85
'Tis she is sub-contracted to this lord,
And I, her husband, contradict your bans.
If you will marry, make your loves to me,
My lady is bespoke.
    Gon.   An interlude!
    Alb. Thou art arm'd, Gloucester; let the trumpet
       sound.   90
If none appear to prove upon thy person
Thy heinous, manifest, and many treasons,
There is my pledge [*throwing down a glove*].   I'll
       [*prove*] it on thy heart,
Ere I taste bread, thou art in nothing less
Than I have here proclaim'd thee.
    Reg.   Sick, O, sick! 95
    Gon. [*Aside.*] If not, I'll ne'er trust medicine.
    Edm. There's my exchange [*throwing down a
       glove*].   What in the world he is
That names me traitor, villain-like he lies.
Call by the trumpet; — he that dares approach,
On him, on you, who not?   I will maintain   100
My truth and honour firmly.
    Alb. A herald, ho!
    [*Edm.*   A herald, ho, a herald!]
    Alb. Trust to thy single virtue; for thy soldiers,
All levied in my name, have in my name   104
Took their discharge.
    Reg.   My sickness grows upon me.
    Alb. She is not well; convey her to my tent.
                                   [*Exit Regan, led.*]

Enter a HERALD.

Come hither, herald, — Let the trumpet sound —
And read out this.
    [*Capt.* Sound, trumpet!]   109
                       [*A trumpet sounds.*

Her. (*Reads.*) "If any man of quality or degree
within the lists of the army will maintain upon
Edmund, supposed Earl of Goucester, that he is a
manifold traitor, let him appear by the third sound
of the trumpet. He is bold in his defence."   114
    [*Edm.* Sound!]   [*First trumpet.*
Her. Again!   [*Second trumpet.*
Her. Again!   [*Third trumpet.*
           [*Trumpet answers within.*

Enter EDGAR, *at the third sound, armed, with
a trumpet before him.*

Alb. Ask him his purposes, why he appears
Upon this call o' th' trumpet.
    Her.   What are you?
Your name, your quality? and why you answer   120
This present summons?
    Edg.   Know, my name is lost,
By treason's tooth bare-gnawn and canker-bit,
Yet am I noble as the adversary
I come to cope.
    Alb.   Which is that adversary?
    Edg. What's he that speaks for Edmund Earl of
         Gloucester?   125
    Edm. Himself; what say'st thou to him?
    Edg.   Draw thy sword.
That, if my speech offend a noble heart,
Thy arm may do thee justice; here is mine.
Behold, it is the privilege of mine honours,
My oath, and my profession. I protest,   130
Maugre thy strength, place, youth, and eminence,
Despite thy victor-sword and fire-new fortune,
Thy valour, and thy heart, thou art a traitor;
False to thy gods, thy brother, and thy father;
Conspirant 'gainst this high illustrious prince;   135
And, from th' extremest upward of thy head
To the descent and dust below thy foot,
A most toad-spotted traitor. Say thou "No,"
This sword, this arm, and my best spirits are bent
To prove upon thy heart, whereto I speak,   140
Thou liest.
    Edm.   In wisdom I should ask thy name;
But, since thy outside looks so fair and warlike,
And that thy tongue some 'say of breeding breathes,
What safe and nicely I might well delay
By rule of knighthood, I disdain and spurn.   145
Back do I toss these treasons to thy head;

With the hell-hated lie o'erwhelm thy heart;
Which, for they yet glance by and scarcely bruise,
This sword of mine shall give them instant way
Where they shall rest for ever. Trumpets, speak!
      [*Alarums. They fight.* [*Edmund falls.*]
    Alb. Save him, save him!   151
    Gon.   This is [mere] practice, Gloucester.
By th' law of war thou wast not bound to answer
An unknown opposite. Thou art not vanquish'd,
But cozen'd and beguil'd.
    Alb.   Shut your mouth, dame,
Or with this paper shall I stop it. Hold, sir. —   155
Thou worse than any name, read thine own evil.
No tearing, lady; I perceive you know it.
    Gon. Say, if I do, the laws are mine, not thine.
Who can arraign me for't?   [*Exit.*]
    Alb.   Most monstrous! oh! —
Know'st thou this paper?
    Edm.   Ask me not what I know.   160
    Alb. Go after her; she's desperate; govern her.
    Edm. What you have charg'd me with, that have
        I done;
And more, much more; the time will bring it out.
'Tis past, and so am I. But what art thou
That hast this fortune on me? If thou'rt noble,   165
I do forgive thee.
    Edg.   Let's exchange charity.
I am no less in blood than thou art, Edmund;
If more, the more thou'st wrong'd me.
My name is Edgar, and thy father's son.
The gods are just, and of our pleasant vices,   170
Make instruments to plague us.
The dark and vicious place where thee he got
Cost him his eyes.
    Edm.   Thou'st spoken right, 'tis true.
The wheel is come full circle; I am here.
    Alb. Methought thy very gait did prophesy   175
A royal nobleness. I must embrace thee.
Let sorrow split my heart, if ever I
Did hate thee or thy father!
    Edg.   Worthy prince, I know't.
    Alb. Where have you hid yourself?
How have you known the miseries of your father?
    Edg. By nursing them, my lord. List a brief
        tale;   181
And when 'tis told, oh, that my heart would burst!
The bloody proclamation to escape,
That follow'd me so near, — oh, our lives' sweetness!
That we the pain of death would hourly die   185
Rather than die at once! — taught me to shift
Into a madman's rags, t' assume a semblance
That very dogs disdain'd; and in this habit
Met I my father with his bleeding rings,   189

---

109. [*Capt.... trumpet*!] Q. Om. F.   112. **supposed:** pretended.   115. [*Edm.* Sound!] Q. Om. F.   122. **canker-bit:** worm-eaten.   129. **the privilege** (Pope). *my privilege, The* F. **honours:** rank.   131. **Maugre:** in spite of.   132. **fire-new:** brand-new.   137. **descent:** lowest part.   143. **'say:** trace.   144. **safe and nicely:** safely and with technical correctness.   151. [**mere**] Q. Om. F.   161. **govern:** restrain.

Their precious stones new lost; became his guide,
Led him, begg'd for him, sav'd him from despair;
Never, — O fault! — reveal'd myself unto him,
Until some half-hour past, when I was arm'd.
Not sure, though hoping, of this good success,
I ask'd his blessing, and from first to last   195
Told him our pilgrimage; but his flaw'd heart,
Alack, too weak the conflict to support!
'Twixt two extremes of passion, joy and grief,
Burst smilingly.
    Edm.   This speech of yours hath mov'd me,
And shall perchance do good. But speak you on;
You look as you had something more to say.   201
    Alb. If there be more, more woeful, hold it in;
For I am almost ready to dissolve,
Hearing of this.
    [*Edg.*   This would have seem'd a period
To such as love not sorrow; but another,   205
To amplify too much, would make much more,
And top extremity.
Whilst I was big in clamour came there in a man,
Who, having seen me in my worst estate,
Shunn'd my abhorr'd society; but then, finding   210
Who 'twas that so endur'd, with his strong arms
He fastened on my neck, and bellowed out
As he'd burst heaven; threw him on my father;
Told the most piteous tale of Lear and him
That ever ear receiv'd; which in recounting,   215
His grief grew puissant, and the strings of life
Began to crack. Twice then the trumpets sounded,
And there I left him tranc'd.
    Alb.   But who was this?
    Edg. Kent, sir, the banish'd Kent; who in disguise
Follow'd his enemy king, and did him service   220
Improper for a slave.]

Enter a GENTLEMAN *with a bloody knife.*

    Gent. Help, help, O, help!
    Edg.   What kind of help?
    Alb.   Speak, man.
    Edg. What means this bloody knife?
    Gent.   'Tis hot, it smokes;
It came even from the heart of — O, she's dead!
    Alb. Who dead? Speak, man.   225
    Gent. Your lady, sir, your lady; and her sister
By her is poison'd; she confesses it.
    Edm. I was contracted to them both. All three
Now marry in an instant.
    Edg.   Here comes Kent.

Enter KENT.

    Alb. Produce the bodies, be they alive or dead.
This judgement of the heavens, that makes us
    tremble,   231

Touches us not with pity.   [*Exit Gentleman.*]
     — O, is this he?
The time will not allow the compliment
Which very manners urges.
    Kent.   I am come
To bid my king and master aye good-night.   235
Is he not here?
    Alb.   Great thing of us forgot!
Speak, Edmund, where's the King? and where's
    Cordelia?
    [*The bodies of Goneril and Regan are
        brought in.*]
See'st thou this object, Kent?
    Kent. Alack, why thus?
    Edm.   Yet Edmund was belov'd!
The one the other poison'd for my sake,   240
And after slew herself.
    Alb. Even so. Cover their faces.
    Edm. I pant for life. Some good I mean to do,
Despite of mine own nature. Quickly send,
Be brief in it, to th' castle; for my writ   245
Is on the life of Lear and on Cordelia.
Nay, send in time.
    Alb.   Run, run, O, run!
    Edg. To who, my lord? Who has the office?
    Send
Thy token of reprieve.
    Edm. Well thought on. Take my sword,   250
Give it the captain.
    Edg.   Haste thee, for thy life.
                [*Exit Gentleman.*]
    Edm. He hath commission from thy wife and me
To hang Cordelia in the prison, and
To lay the blame upon her own despair,
That she fordid herself.   255
    Alb. The gods defend her! Bear him hence a
    while.   [*Edmund is borne off.*]

Re-enter LEAR *with Cordelia in his arms*
    [GENTLEMAN *following*].

    Lear. Howl, howl, howl! O, you are men of
    stones!
Had I your tongues and eyes, I'd use them so
That heaven's vault should crack. She's gone
    for ever!
I know when one is dead, and when one lives;   260
She's dead as earth. Lend me a looking-glass;
If that her breath will mist or stain the stone,
Why, then she lives.
    Kent.   Is this the promis'd end?
    Edg. Or image of that horror?
    Alb.   Fall, and cease!
    Lear. This feather stirs; she lives! If it be so,
It is a chance which does redeem all sorrows   266

196. **flaw'd:** cracked. 204–221. [***Edg.... slave***] Q. Om. F. 205–207. **but... extremity:** one more such circumstance, amplifying what is already too much, would increase it and pass all limits. 208. **big in clamour:** loud in grief. 213. **him** (Theobald). *me* Q. 218. **tranc'd:** unconscious. 255. **fordid:** destroyed. 262. **stone:** polished crystal, mirror. 263. **promis'd end:** Last Judgment.

That ever I have felt.

Kent. [*Kneeling.*] O my good master!

Lear. Prithee, away.

Edg.   'Tis noble Kent, your friend.

Lear. A plague upon you, murderers, traitors all!
I might have sav'd her; now she's gone for ever! 270
Cordelia, Cordelia! stay a little. Ha!
What is't thou say'st? Her voice was ever soft,
Gentle, and low; an excellent thing in woman.
I kill'd the slave that was a-hanging thee.

Gent. 'Tis true, my lords, he did.

Lear.   Did I not, fellow? 275
I have seen the day, with my good biting falchion
I would have made him skip. I am old now,
And these same crosses spoil me. Who are you?
Mine eyes are not o' th' best. I'll tell you straight.

Kent. If Fortune brag of two she lov'd and
    hated,   280
One of them we behold.

Lear. This is a dull sight. Are you not Kent?

Kent.   The same,
Your servant Kent. Where is your servant Caius?

Lear. He's a good fellow, I can tell you that;
He'll strike, and quickly too. He's dead and rotten.

Kent. No, my good lord; I am the very man, —

Lear. I'll see that straight.   287

Kent. — That, from your first of difference and
    decay,
Have follow'd your sad steps —

Lear.   You are welcome hither.

Kent. Nor no man else; All's cheerless, dark,
    and deadly.   290
Your eldest daughters have fordone themselves,
And desperately are dead.

Lear.   Ay, so I think.

Alb. He knows not what he says; and vain is it
That we present us to him.

Enter a MESSENGER.

Edg.   Very bootless.

Mess. Edmund is dead, my lord.

Alb.   That's but a trifle here. — 295
You lords and noble friends, know our intent.
What comfort to this great decay may come
Shall be appli'd. For us, we will resign,
During the life of this old majesty,
To him our absolute power; [*to Edgar and Kent*]
    you, to your rights,   300
With boot, and such addition as your honours
Have more than merited. All friends shall taste
The wages of their virtue, and all foes
The cup of their deservings. O, see, see!

Lear. And my poor fool is hang'd! No, no, no
    life!   305
Why should a dog, a horse, a rat, have life,
And thou no breath at all? Thou'lt come no more,
Never, never, never, never, never!
Pray you, undo this button. Thank you, sir.
Do you see this? Look on her, look, her lips, 310
Look there, look there!   [*Dies.*

Edg.   He faints! My lord, my lord!

Kent. Break, heart; I prithee, break!

Edg.   Look up, my lord.

Kent. Vex not his ghost; O, let him pass! He
    hates him
That would upon the rack of this tough world
Stretch him out longer.

Edg.   He is gone, indeed. 315

Kent. The wonder is he hath endur'd so long;
He but usurp'd his life.

Alb. Bear them from hence. Our present
    business
Is general woe. [*To Kent and Edgar.*] Friends of
    my soul, you twain
Rule in this realm, and the gor'd state sustain. 320

Kent. I have a journey, sir, shortly to go.
My master calls me; I must not say no.

Edg. The weight of this sad time we must obey;
Speak what we feel, not what we ought to say.
The oldest hath borne most; we that are young 325
Shall never see so much, nor live so long.

            [*Exeunt, with a dead march.*

---

278. **crosses:** sufferings. 288. **first...decay:** beginning of the change and decay of your fortunes. 305. **poor fool:** Cordelia. 320. **gor'd:** wounded. 323. **Edg.** F. *Duke* Q.

The Tragedy of Macbeth

MACBETH, NEXT TO *The Comedy of Errors,* Shakespeare's shortest play, was first published in the Folio of 1623, which consequently becomes the basis for all modern texts. The nature of the stage directions suggests that a theatrical manuscript, probably a transcript of the original with revisions, served as copy. The play's exceptional brevity, along with an abnormal number of broken lines, occasionally abrupt transitions, considerable mislineation, and mangling of metre, points to abridgment. On the other hand, such hints of cutting are offset by evidence of additions, and it is unlikely that the play was ever significantly longer than the surviving version. In particular, III.v. and IV.i.39–43, introducing the superfluous character of Hecate, whose speeches differ from the rest of the play in tone and metre, are manifest intrusions. Stage directions at III.v.34 and IV.i.43 call for songs which are to be found in full in *The Witch* by Thomas Middleton (c. 1614), and these, together with the appearance of Hecate as a conspicuous character in that play, strongly suggest Middleton as the interpolator. The genuineness of other portions has also been doubted (e.g., I.ii., I.iii.1–37, II.iii.1–23, III.vi., IV. iii.140–59, V.vi., and V.viii). These passages cannot all be discussed, but the authenticity of most of them can be reasonably vindicated. For example, the second scene of the play, though perhaps not memorable, provides imperative exposition quite adequately. The soliloquy of the Porter (II.iii), with its rare blend of low humor and high irony, ought never to have failed of appreciation. Act III, scene vi, presents another expository colloquy not unworthy of Shakespeare; the irony of Lennox should not be missed, and the fact that his interlocutor is an anonymous Lord need disturb nobody.

Several matters bear upon the date of the play, though none is conclusive. When King James visited Oxford on August 27, 1605, his advent was celebrated by a little drama enacted at the gates. Three students, dressed as Sibyls, recited Latin verses (by Dr. Matthew Gwinne) based upon the prophesies of the weird sisters to Banquo, the fabled head of James's royal line, and hailed the King in sequence as ruler of Scotland, England, and Ireland, and again as sovereign of Great Britain, Ireland, and France (cf. IV.i.121–22). It is entirely plausible that Shakespeare was moved by a report of this episode, which greatly pleased the King, to turn again to his favorite Holinshed, where he knew the story of Banquo was to be found, and that, doing so, he became inspired to write a play, not around Banquo, concerning whom dramatic material was insufficient, but around his more vivid associate, Macbeth. Though Banquo could not serve for protagonist, Shakespeare (was he not one of the King's men?) found other ways of gratifying James. Naturally he stresses the integrity of Banquo in contrast to the criminality of Macbeth (which involves, incidentally, a diplomatic departure from his source, for Holinshed represents Banquo as Macbeth's accomplice) and emphasizes the prophecy respecting Banquo's descendants. He alludes deferentially to the healing of scrofula by royal touch (IV.iii.146 ff.), a practice in which James had been ceremoniously indulging since the winter of 1604. If, as is conceivable, the Porter's treasonable equivocator (II.iii. 9–12) glances at the Jesuit Superior, Henry Garnet, who in his trial (1606) for complicity in the Gunpowder Plot defended the doctrine of equivocation, James must have been duly appreciative. All in all, it seems likely that *Macbeth* was composed near the middle or end of 1606, and a recollection of Banquo's Ghost in *The Knight of the Burning Pestle* (Beaumont and Fletcher, 1607) confirms the probability. It has been conjectured that Shakespeare prepared *Macbeth* with special reference to a performance at Court and that when his company gave three plays (unnamed in the Revels Account) for the entertainment of "his Maiestie and the kinge of Denmarke" in the summer of 1606, *Macbeth* was offered as new.

As already noted, the source for *Macbeth* is the *Chronicles* of Holinshed. Most of the substance is taken from the account of the reigns of Duncan and Macbeth (A.D. 1034–1057), but Shakespeare has made the rebellion of Macdonwald and the invasion by the Norwegian Sueno, though originally independent activities, sequential episodes of the same campaign, and has enriched dramatic effect by details drawn from other parts of the *Chronicles*. Thus, whereas the *Chronicles* record the assassination of Duncan in the single statement that Macbeth slew him at Inverness, Shakespeare appropriates the drugging of the grooms and the portents described in II.iv from the account of the murder of Duncan's ancestor Duffe (A.D. 972); and the voice that cried "Sleep no more!" to the troubled conscience of Duffe's brother Kenneth (who had poisoned a nephew) is assigned to harry the mind of Macbeth.

Of the witches Holinshed writes: " ... the common opinion was, that these women were either the weird sisters, that is (as ye would say) the goddesses of destinie, or else some nymphs or feiries, indued with knowledge of prophesie by their necromanticall science, bicause everie thing came to passe as they had spoken." It may be that from this somewhat non-committal statement Shakespeare's imagination apprehended these creatures unequivocally as powers of destiny, the Norns of Scandinavian mythology, but it cannot be proved that he knew about the Norns. Furthermore, as Shakespeare pursued the story in Holinshed, he found the influence of these figures upon Macbeth superseded by that of others. It was "certeine wizzards, in whose words he put great confidence," who told him "how that he ought to take heed of Makduffe," and the prediction that "he should never be slaine with man borne of anie woman, nor vanquished till the wood of Bernane came to the castell of Dunsinane" was made by "a certeine witch, whome hee had in great trust" (cf. IV.i.71–72, 92–94). The several oracular agents in Holinshed were fused by Shakespeare into the prophetic "instruments of darkness" of his play. Though the text consistently names them "weird sisters" (or an equivalent), in the stage directions they are called simply "witches"; and the figures they cut upon the stage and the language they speak are in accord with this conception. Shakespeare's audiences must have viewed these "secret, black, and midnight hags" in the light of current witch lore, but they may also have felt that they were no common witches, since Shakespeare has raised them to a fresh level of imagination, giving them an unearthly air and a spiritual significance in relation to the character of Macbeth.

To Shakespeare's Macbeth crime is at the outset neither natural nor congenial. Unlike the Macbeth of Holinshed, who is described as "somewhat cruel of nature," he is, when the play opens, a man of unblemished record. He is a gentleman of honor and a superlative soldier, and the "golden opinions" lately won "from all sorts of people" through his heroic achievements in the field bear no shadow of reservation. To these testimonies is added the private judgment of his wife, who stresses his probity and his humanity, in what is unquestionably a candid and true evaluation of him (I.v.17–26). Macbeth is "not without ambition," but ambition is proper to a man of his station, and Macbeth, she says, would not "play false" in the pursuit of it. Left to himself, Macbeth would not have fallen to crime, but a unique combination of temptation and circumstance coerce his will. Macbeth has no justification for killing Duncan, and every reason for not, as he knows only too well, and when he says (I.vii. 25–27) that he has no incitement but ambition he is honest with himself. The native ambition to which his wife has referred becomes perverted; one must therefore inquire what that ambition may earlier have amounted to.

On that point evidence is reasonably clear, but it must be interpreted carefully. Macbeth's excitement, perceptible to Banquo, upon the witches' prophetic salutation (I.iii.48–50) and the readiness with which he imagines murder as, after the immediate confirmation respecting Cawdor, he ponders the "supernatural solicitings," suggest that the witches have quickened a thought that is not new in Macbeth's mind. One may legitimately suppose that Macbeth had wished for the kingship, the monarchy in Scotland being elective (cf. I.iv.37–50; II.iv.29–32); but that he had heretofore seriously entertained criminal means of getting it is not a necessary consequence. The image of murder that rises in his mind (I.iii.130 ff.) betrays no contemplated purpose or antecedent temptation; rather it is the way in which his abnormally sensitive imagination develops the inevitable thought that unless he should murder Duncan, the prophecy of his future kingship must be long in fulfillment. The horror inspired by the notion argues that he has not made it familiar, and the natural conclusion for the moment comes in his words, "If chance will have me King, why, chance may crown me without my stir." The utterances of the witches, nevertheless, are calculated to rouse an ambitious man, and the thought of murder as the nearest way of realizing the "greatest" of them, repellent though he finds it, will not out of Macbeth's mind; so that when he reaches home, his wife reads in his face what he has been thinking (I. v.63 ff.). She too has been thinking about murder, and with her, thoughts are purposes. Though neither of them utters the word, Macbeth understands that she has resolved upon murder as the course to take, and he ends their talk with a determination to "speak further." It is during this further conversation, which we must think of as taking place between this action and the beginning of scene vii, that Macbeth makes up his mind, for when we hear him then in soliloquy, he has fixed his intent. At least, so he believes. When shortly Lady Macbeth taunts him in an effort to screw his failing courage to the sticking point, she refers to matters in their off-stage talk (I.vii.35 ff.). And it is her slurs upon his courage that finally rivet his resolve. Thus swiftly does evil suggestion corrupt honest ambition, making harmless desire appear as manifest destiny. To the fateful promptings of supernatural agency are added exceptional opportunity and irresistible urging. Events may move more rapidly than in actual life, but Shakespeare has obtained illusion of reality complete for dramatic purposes. He makes it clear that in murdering Duncan Macbeth murders his better nature. His heart is not in the deed; he repents it as soon as it is done, and a Nemesis of fear dogs him afterwards and drives him to more hideous crime and ultimate destruction.

The most memorable passages in this tragedy have, therefore, distinctive psychological interest. Macbeth is endowed with an imagination of appalling, indeed pathological, intensity. Though he is essentially an extrovert, his mind renders palpable and alive its plainest ideas and impressions. Thus the idea that he might murder the King becomes instantly the terrifying picture of himself doing it; thus, when in fact he is about to do it, his heated brain conjures a dagger, the handle toward his hand, pointing the way that he is going; thus, when the deed is done, he thinks he hears a voice cry "Sleep no more," and pictures his bloody hands coloring the oceans red. As time goes on, imagination tortures him less in this precise fashion, but harries him nonetheless with insecurity and fear. We hear of the terrible dreams which shake him nightly, and of his envy of Duncan, who after life's fitful fever sleeps well, while his murderer's mind is "full of scorpions." So Macbeth wades forward in blood, to make assurance double sure and take a bond of the fate that he but brings closer with every step.

Banquo's Ghost has for Macbeth a peculiar horror and presents a special problem. By many critics the Ghost is regarded as merely an hallucination, because Macbeth's mind has already conjured other figments, because it is seen by nobody but Macbeth, because it does not speak, because Lady Macbeth scouts it, and because, when the fit is passed, Macbeth refers it to his "strange and self-abuse." None of these facts, however, militates against its objectivity. In Elizabethan ghost lore it was understood that spectres could be visible to as many or as few in a company as they should choose, and unless their mission required it, as is not the case with Banquo's Ghost, they did not necessarily speak. Lady Macbeth, who sees nothing, naturally ridicules the apparition, and Macbeth, once it has vanished and he is himself again, quite as naturally begins to doubt

what he has seen. Under the circumstances his doubt is merely human. For the Elizabethans, on the other hand, familiar with ghosts in drama, the reality of this one would be clinched by its actual appearance on the stage, and that Shakespeare intended its introduction is attested by the stage direction (III.iv.37) describing its entrance and its usurping of Macbeth's place at the banquet. The effectiveness of this highly dramatic business is enhanced by its implications. For Macbeth, ironically, has bidden Banquo not to fail his feast, and the Ghost, with finer irony, keeps the date.

Lady Macbeth is Shakespeare's own remarkable creation. Holinshed merely mentions her as "verie ambitious, burning in unquenchable desire to beare the name of a queene." This yearning Shakespeare redirects. In the play Lady Macbeth wishes greatness only for her husband; otherwise, though she speaks of herself and of their "great business," she appears self-abnegating. In Macbeth's interests she is passionate and unswerving. She is a woman of supreme will and nerve, supplying both where he wavers. In these respects (and these dominate) she is masculine; but she is also distinctly feminine. She plays the hostess consummately. Apparently Shakespeare conceived her as physically slight (III. ii.45; V.i.57), as women of nervous intensity generally are. There are limits to this reserve of energy and control, however, as her need of a stimulant (II.ii.1–2), her swoon (II.iii.124), and her ultimate mental collapse show. In her single-mindedness, in her courage, and especially in the steadiness she exhibits during her husband's crisis in the banquet scene she is superb. And as if meeting that crisis had taxed her resources to the breaking point, we hear no more of her until we come to witness her tragic change. Her breakdown has its own peculiar irony. For it is not the susceptible, haunted mind of Macbeth that snaps, but hers, which, in contrast, had shown itself ever literal, practical, prosaic, and had spurned the visionary tendencies of his. In the sleep-walking scene (V.i) Lady Macbeth relives salient moments of the dreadful past, and the recapitulation, in chronological disorder, is pitiful. After the murder of Duncan, when Macbeth had stared in agony at the blood upon his hands, she had confidently proclaimed, "A little water clears us of this deed"; now she strives perpetually to wash the imagined blood from her own hands, which "all the perfumes of Arabia will not sweeten." Before the murder of Banquo, seeking to quell her husband's gloomy fears, she had scornfully asserted, "What's done is done"; now she cries in desperation, "What's done cannot be undone." It is somehow meet, though inglorious, that she who had been so masterful should take her own life.

When the news that his lady is dead is brought

to Macbeth, he accepts it without emotion, expressing in words of mournfullest cadence not personal grief, but the vanity and emptiness of life (V.v.17 ff.). Not that he has not loved her; she lived for him, and he knows it. They shared together fully, but they staked their happiness on evil and lost it. For each the end is bitter disillusionment. But the disillusionment of Macbeth is the greater, for he had once foreseen, though he had willfully ignored, that the assassination might not trammel up the consequence and that their bloody instructions might return to plague them. Now that evenhanded justice has taken off his wife and is closing in on him, Macbeth is careless. Life to him now is but "a walking shadow," a "tale told by an idiot." The speech embracing that thought is Macbeth's elegy for his wife and a confession of their common

failure. In spirit it expresses the negation of all that he was and might have been, the blasting of those golden opinions which he had deliberately sacrificed and upon the loss of which he reflects in unforgettable lines (V.iii.22–28). Though Macbeth rouses himself to meet his enemies and to die fighting with his old valor, he knows where he stands. He acknowledges the moral isolation he has brought upon himself, and the words, "I have lived long enough," revealing his weariness not alone with life but with himself, inform us that the death which he defies will be welcome to him. Macbeth proved a desperately wicked man, but as we observe him at the end we are reassured that he was more than the butcher the avenging Malcolm not unnaturally calls him.

THE TRAGEDY OF MACBETH

[DRAMATIS PERSONÆ

DUNCAN, *King of Scotland.*

MALCOLM, } *his sons.*
DONALBAIN,

MACBETH, } *generals of the King's army.*
BANQUO,

MACDUFF, ⎫
LENNOX, ⎪
ROSS, ⎪
MENTEITH, ⎬ *noblemen of Scotland.*
ANGUS, ⎪
CAITHNESS, ⎭

FLEANCE, *son to Banquo.*

SIWARD, *earl of Northumberland, commanding the English forces.*

Young SIWARD, *his son.*

SEYTON, *an officer attending on Macbeth.*
Boy, *son to Macduff.*
An English Doctor.
A Scotch Doctor.
A Captain.
A Porter.
An Old Man.

LADY MACBETH.
LADY MACDUFF.
Gentlewoman attending on Lady Macbeth.

HECATE.
Three Witches.
Apparitions.

Lords, Gentlemen, Officers, Soldiers, Murderers, Attendants, and Messengers.

SCENE: *Scotland; England.*]

ACT I

SCENE I. [*A heath.*]

Thunder and lightning. Enter three WITCHES.

1. Witch. When shall we three meet again
In thunder, lightning, or in rain?
2. Witch. When the hurlyburly's done,
When the battle's lost and won.
3. Witch. That will be ere the set of sun. 5
1. Witch. Where the place?
2. Witch.   Upon the heath.
3. Witch. There to meet with Macbeth.
1. Witch. I come, Graymalkin!
[*2. Witch.*] Paddock calls:—[*3. Witch.*] Anon! 10
All. Fair is foul, and foul is fair;
Hover through the fog and filthy air.   [*Exeunt.*

SCENE II. [*A camp near Forres.*]

Alarum within. Enter DUNCAN, MALCOLM, Donalbain, LENNOX, *with* Attendants, *meeting a bleeding* CAPTAIN.

Dun. What bloody man is that? He can report,
As seemeth by his plight, of the revolt
The newest state.
Mal.   This is the sergeant
Who like a good and hardy soldier fought
'Gainst my captivity. Hail, brave friend! 5
Say to the King the knowledge of the broil
As thou didst leave it.
Cap.   Doubtful it stood,
As two spent swimmers that do cling together
And choke their art. The merciless Macdonwald —
Worthy to be a rebel, for to that 10

Act I, sc. i, 9–10. Graymalkin (little gray cat) and **Paddock** (toad) are the names of the spirits serving the Witches. The third Witch answers without calling her spirit by name, but at IV.i.3 the name appears to be *Harpier* (derived, apparently, from "Harpy"). **10–12.** The distribution of speeches follows a suggestion of Hunter's adopted by Singer. F assigns to *All.*

Sc. ii, 1. The speeches of Duncan are all headed *King* in F. **3. sergeant.** Called "Captain" in the S.D. by F, which heads his speeches *Cap.* Some editors alter one title or the other to obtain consistency. **6. broil:** battle. **10. that:** i.e., that
nd.

The multiplying villanies of nature
Do swarm upon him — from the Western Isles
Of kerns and gallowglasses is suppli'd;
And Fortune, on his damned [quarrel] smiling,
Show'd like a rebel's whore. But all's too weak; 15
For brave Macbeth — well he deserves that
     name —
Disdaining Fortune, with his brandish'd steel,
Which smok'd with bloody execution,
Like Valour's minion carv'd out his passage
Till he fac'd the slave;   20
Which ne'er shook hands, nor bade farewell to him,
Till he unseam'd him from the nave to th' chaps,
And fix'd his head upon our battlements.
     Dun. O valiant cousin! worthy gentleman!
     Cap. As whence the sun gins his reflection 25
Shipwrecking storms and direful thunders [break],
So from that spring whence comfort seem'd to come
Discomfort swells.   Mark, King of Scotland, mark!
No sooner justice had, with valour arm'd,
Compell'd these skipping kerns to trust their heels,
But the Norweyan lord, surveying vantage,   31
With furbish'd arms and new supplies of men
Began a fresh assault.
     Dun.   Dismay'd not this
Our captains, Macbeth and Banquo?
     Cap.   Yes;
As sparrows eagles, or the hare the lion.   35
If I say sooth, I must report they were
As cannons overcharg'd with double cracks; so they
Doubly redoubled strokes upon the foe.
Except they meant to bathe in reeking wounds,
Or memorize another Golgotha,   40
I cannot tell.
But I am faint, my gashes cry for help.
     Dun. So well thy words become thee as thy
     wounds;
They smack of honour both.   Go get him surgeons.
                    [*Exit Captain, attended.*]

               Enter Ross *and* Angus.

Who comes here?
     Mal.   The worthy thane of Ross. 45
     Len. What a haste looks through his eyes! So
     should he look
That seems to speak things strange.
     Ross.   God save the King!
     Dun. Whence cam'st thou, worthy thane?

     Ross.   From Fife, great king;
Where the Norweyan banners flout the sky
And fan our people cold. Norway himself,   50
With terrible numbers,
Assisted by that most disloyal traitor,
The thane of Cawdor, began a dismal conflict;
Till that Bellona's bridegroom, lapp'd in proof,
Confronted him with self-comparisons,   55
Point against point, rebellious arm 'gainst arm,
Curbing his lavish spirit; and, to conclude,
The victory fell on us; —
     Dun.   Great happiness!
     Ross.   That now
Sweno, the Norways' king, craves composition;
Nor would we deign him burial of his men   60
Till he disbursed at Saint Colme's inch
Ten thousand dollars to our general use.
     Dun. No more that thane of Cawdor shall de-
     ceive
Our bosom interest.   Go pronounce his present
     death,
And with his former title greet Macbeth.   65
     Ross. I'll see it done.
     Dun. What he hath lost, noble Macbeth hath
     won.   [*Exeunt.*

SCENE III. [*A heath near Forres.*]

     Thunder.   Enter the three WITCHES.

     1. Witch. Where hast thou been, sister?
     2. Witch. Killing swine.
     3. Witch. Sister, where thou?
     1. Witch. A sailor's wife had chestnuts in her lap,
And munch'd, and munch'd, and munch'd. "Give
me!" quoth I.   5
"Aroint thee, witch!" the rump-fed ronyon cries.
Her husband's to Aleppo gone, master o' th' Tiger;
But in a sieve I'll thither sail,
And, like a rat without a tail,
I'll do, I'll do, and I'll do.   10
     2. Witch. I'll give thee a wind.
     1. Witch. Thou'rt kind.
     3. Witch. And I another.
     1. Witch. I myself have all the other,
And the very ports they blow,   15
All the quarters that they know
I' th' shipman's card.
I'll drain him dry as hay.

---

13. Of: with. **kerns and gallowglasses:** Irish foot soldiers. 14. [quarrel] (Hanmer). *quarry* F. 19. **minion:** darling.
22. **nave:** navel. **chaps:** jaws. 26. [break] (Pope). Om. F. 31. **surveying vantage:** seeing opportunity. 37.
cracks: charges. 39. **Except:** unless. 40. **memorize . . . Golgotha:** make the field memorable as another Golgotha, i.e.,
Calvary, "the place of skulls." 47. **to:** about to. 49. **flout:** mock. 54. **Bellona's bridegroom:** i.e., Macbeth. Bellona was
the goddess of war. **lapp'd in proof:** clad in armor. 55. **self-comparisons:** deeds the equal of his own. 57. **lavish:** uncontrolled. 59. **composition:** terms of peace. 61. **Saint . . . inch:** St. Columba's island, Inchcolm. 64. **bosom interest:** close
affection.
     Sc. iii, 6. **Aroint:** be gone. **rump-fed:** fed on refuse, or, perhaps, pampered. **ronyon:** scabby person. 9. **like:** in the shape
of. 15. **blow:** blow toward. 17. **card:** compass.

Sleep shall neither night nor day
Hang upon his pent-house lid;   20
He shall live a man forbid.
Weary sev'nights nine times nine
Shall he dwindle, peak, and pine.
Though his bark cannot be lost,
Yet it shall be tempest-tost.   25
Look what I have.
     2. Witch. Show me, show me.
     1. Witch. Here I have a pilot's thumb,
Wreck'd as homeward he did come.   [*Drum within.*
     3. Witch. A drum, a drum!   30
Macbeth doth come.
     All. The [weird] sisters, hand in hand,
Posters of the sea and land,
Thus do go about, about;
Thrice to thine, and thrice to mine,   35
And thrice again, to make up nine.
Peace! the charm's wound up.

         Enter MACBETH *and* BANQUO.

     Macb. So foul and fair a day I have not seen.
     Ban. How far is't call'd to [Forres]?   What are
     these
So wither'd and so wild in their attire,   40
That look not like th' inhabitants o' th' earth,
And yet are on't?   Live you? or are you aught
That man may question?   You seem to understand
     me,
By each at once her choppy finger laying
Upon her skinny lips.   You should be women,   45
And yet your beards forbid me to interpret
That you are so.
     Macb. Speak, if you can.   What are you?
     1. Witch. All hail, Macbeth! hail to thee, thane
     of Glamis!
     2. Witch. All hail, Macbeth! hail to thee, thane
     of Cawdor!
     3. Witch. All hail, Macbeth, that shalt be King
     hereafter!   50
     Ban. Good sir, why do you start, and seem to
     fear
Things that do sound so fair?   [*To the Witches.*] I'
     th' name of truth,
Are ye fantastical, or that indeed
Which outwardly ye show?   My noble partner
You greet with present grace and great prediction
Of noble having and of royal hope,   56
That he seems rapt withal; to me you speak not.
If you can look into the seeds of time,
And say which grain will grow and which will not,

Speak then to me, who neither beg nor fear   60
Your favours nor your hate.
     1. Witch. Hail!
     2. Witch. Hail!
     3. Witch. Hail!
     1. Witch. Lesser than Macbeth, and greater.   65
     2. Witch. Not so happy, yet much happier.
     3. Witch. Thou shalt get kings, though thou be
     none;
So all hail, Macbeth and Banquo!
     1. Witch. Banquo and Macbeth, all hail!
     Macb. Stay, you imperfect speakers, tell me
     more.   70
By Sinel's death I know I am thane of Glamis;
But how of Cawdor?   The thane of Cawdor lives,
A prosperous gentleman; and to be king
Stands not within the prospect of belief
No more than to be Cawdor.   Say from whence   75
You owe this strange intelligence, or why
Upon this blasted heath you stop our way
With such prophetic greeting.   Speak, I charge you.
                        [*Witches vanish.*
     Ban. The earth hath bubbles, as the water has,
And these are of them.   Whither are they van-
     ish'd?   80
     Macb. Into the air; and what seem'd corporal
     melted
As breath into the wind.   Would they had stay'd!
     Ban. Were such things here as we do speak about,
Or have we eaten on the insane root
That takes the reason prisoner?   85
     Macb. Your children shall be kings.
     Ban.   You shall be King.
     Macb. And thane of Cawdor too; went it not so?
     Ban. To the self-same tune and words.   Who's
     here?

         Enter ROSS *and* ANGUS.

     Ross. The King hath happily receiv'd, Macbeth,
The news of thy success; and when he reads   90
Thy personal venture in the rebels' fight,
His wonders and his praises do contend
Which should be thine or his.   Silenc'd with that,
In viewing o'er the rest o' th' self-same day,
He finds thee in the stout Norweyan ranks,   95
Nothing afeard of what thyself didst make,
Strange images of death.   As thick as [hail]
[Came] post with post; and every one did bear
Thy praises in his kingdom's great defence,
And pour'd them down before him.
     Ang.   We are sent

---

20. **pent-house:** sloping like the roof of a lean-to.   21. **forbid:** accursed.   32. [weird] (Theobald). *weyward* F. (and elsewhere, sometimes as *weyard*). For the weird sisters, see Introduction.   33. **Posters of:** swift travellers over.   39. [Forres] (Pope). *Soris* F.   43. **question:** talk to.   44. **choppy:** chapped.   53. **fantastical:** imaginary.   56. **having:** possessions.   57. **rapt:** carried out of himself.   67. **get:** beget.   71. **Sinel's:** Macbeth's father.   76. **owe:** have.   84. **insane:** causing insanity.   97. [hail] (Rowe). *tale* F.   98. [Came] (Rowe). *Can* F.   **post with post:** one messenger after another.

To give thee from our royal master thanks;   101
Only to herald thee into his sight,
Not pay thee.
   Ross. And for an earnest of a greater honour,
He bade me, from him, call thee thane of Cawdor;
In which addition, hail, most worthy thane!   106
For it is thine.
   Ban. [*Aside.*] What, can the devil speak true?
   Macb. The thane of Cawdor lives; why do you
       dress me
In borrowed robes?
   Ang.   Who was the thane lives yet;
But under heavy judgement bears that life   110
Which he deserves to lose. Whether he was com-
bin'd
With those of Norway, or did line the rebel
With hidden help and vantage, or that with both
He labour'd in his country's wreck, I know not;
But treasons capital, confess'd and prov'd,   115
Have overthrown him.
   Macb. [*Aside.*] Glamis, and thane of Cawdor!
The greatest is behind. [*To Ross and Angus.*]
       Thanks for your pains.
[*To Ban.*] Do you not hope your children shall be
       kings,
When those that gave the thane of Cawdor to me
Promis'd no less to them?
   Ban. [*Aside to Macbeth.*] That, trusted home,
Might yet enkindle you unto the crown,   121
Besides the thane of Cawdor. But 'tis strange;
And oftentimes, to win us to our harm,
The instruments of darkness tell us truths,
Win us with honest trifles, to betray 's   125
In deepest consequence.
Cousins, a word, I pray you.
   Macb.   [*Aside.*] Two truths are told,
As happy prologues to the swelling act
Of the imperial theme. — I thank you, gentlemen.
[*Aside.*] This supernatural soliciting   130
Cannot be ill, cannot be good. If ill,
Why hath it given me earnest of success,
Commencing in a truth? I'm thane of Cawdor.
If good, why do I yield to that suggestion
Whose horrid image doth unfix my hair   135
And make my seated heart knock at my ribs,
Against the use of nature? Present fears
Are less than horrible imaginings.
My thought, whose murder yet is but fantastical,
Shakes so my single state of man that function
Is smother'd in surmise, and nothing is   141
But what is not.

   Ban.   Look, how our partner's rapt.
   Macb. [*Aside.*] If chance will have me King,
       why, chance may crown me
Without my stir.
   Ban.   New honours come upon him,
Like our strange garments, cleave not to their
       mould   145
But with the aid of use.
   Macb.   [*Aside.*] Come what come may,
Time and the hour runs through the roughest day.
   Ban. Worthy Macbeth, we stay upon your lei-
sure.
   Macb. Give me your favour; my dull brain was
       wrought
With things forgotten. Kind gentlemen, your
       pains   150
Are regist'red where every day I turn
The leaf to read them. Let us toward the King.
[*To Ban.*] Think upon what hath chanc'd, and,
       at more time,
The interim having weigh'd it, let us speak   154
Our free hearts each to other.
   Ban.   Very gladly.
   Macb. Till then, enough. Come, friends.
                      [*Exeunt.*

SCENE IV. [*Forres. The palace.*]

Flourish. Enter [DUNCAN], MALCOLM, Donal-
       bain, Lennox, *and* Attendants.

   Dun. Is execution done on Cawdor? [Are] not
Those in commission yet return'd?
   Mal.   My liege,
They are not yet come back. But I have spoke
With one that saw him die; who did report
That very frankly he confess'd his treasons,   5
Implor'd your Highness' pardon, and set forth
A deep repentance. Nothing in his life
Became him like the leaving it. He died
As one that had been studied in his death
To throw away the dearest thing he ow'd,   10
As 'twere a careless trifle.
   Dun.   There's no art
To find the mind's construction in the face.
He was a gentleman on whom I built
An absolute trust.

   Enter MACBETH, BANQUO, ROSS, *and* ANGUS.
            O worthiest cousin!
The sin of my ingratitude even now   15
Was heavy on me. Thou art so far before

---

106. **addition:** title. 112. **line:** support. 120. **home:** fully. 122. **thane:** thanedom. 126. **deepest consequence:** very important matters. 130. **soliciting:** incitement. 139. **whose:** in which. 140. **single:** weak. 140–42. **function…not:** my faculties are overwhelmed by imagination and nothing exists for me but the unrealized future. 144. **stir:** making an effort. 145. **strange:** new. **their mould:** i.e., our shape. 155. **free hearts:** hearts freely.

  Sc. iv, 1. [Are] F₂. *Or* F₁. 2. **in commission:** delegated to the task. 10. **dearest…ow'd:** i.e., his life. 11. **careless:** worthless. 12. **construction:** interpretation.

That swiftest wing of recompense is slow
To overtake thee. Would thou hadst less deserv'd,
That the proportion both of thanks and payment
Might have been mine! Only I have left to say, 20
More is thy due than more than all can pay.
    Macb. The service and the loyalty I owe,
In doing it, pays itself. Your Highness' part
Is to receive our duties; and our duties
Are to your throne and state children and servants,
Which do but what they should, by doing every-
        thing 26
Safe toward your love and honour.
    Dun.   Welcome hither!
I have begun to plant thee, and will labour
To make thee full of growing. Noble Banquo,
That hast no less deserv'd, nor must be known 30
No less to have done so, let me infold thee
And hold thee to my heart.
    Ban.   There if I grow,
The harvest is your own.
    Dun.   My plenteous joys,
Wanton in fulness, seek to hide themselves
In drops of sorrow. Sons, kinsmen, thanes, 35
And you whose places are the nearest, know
We will establish our estate upon
Our eldest, Malcolm, whom we name hereafter
The Prince of Cumberland; which honour must
Not unaccompanied invest him only, 40
But signs of nobleness, like stars, shall shine
On all deservers. From hence to Inverness,
And bind us further to you.
    Macb. The rest is labour, which is not us'd for you.
I'll be myself the [harbinger] and make joyful 45
The hearing of my wife with your approach;
So humbly take my leave.
    Dun.   My worthy Cawdor!
    Macb. [*Aside.*] The Prince of Cumberland!
        That is a step
On which I must fall down, or else o'erleap,
For in my way it lies. Stars, hide your fires; 50
Let not light see my black and deep desires;
The eye wink at the hand; yet let that be
Which the eye fears, when it is done, to see. [*Exit.*
    Dun. True, worthy Banquo; he is full so valiant,
And in his commendations I am fed; 55
It is a banquet to me. Let's after him,
Whose care is gone before to bid us welcome.
It is a peerless kinsman.   [*Flourish. Exeunt.*

    SCENE V. [*Inverness. Macbeth's castle.*]

Enter MACBETH'S WIFE, *alone, with a letter.*

    Lady M. [*Reads.*] "They met me in the day of

success; and I have learn'd by the perfect'st report, they have more in them than mortal knowledge. When I burn'd in desire to question them
further, they made themselves air, into which they
vanish'd. Whiles I stood rapt in the wonder of it, 5
came missives from the King, who all-hail'd me
'Thane of Cawdor'; by which title, before, these
weird sisters saluted me, and referr'd me to the coming on of time with 'Hail, King that shalt be!' 10
This have I thought good to deliver thee, my dearest
partner of greatness, that thou mightst not lose the
dues of rejoicing by being ignorant of what greatness
is promis'd thee. Lay it to thy heart, and farewell."
Glamis thou art, and Cawdor; and shalt be 16
What thou art promis'd. Yet do I fear thy nature;
It is too full o' th' milk of human kindness
To catch the nearest way. Thou wouldst be great,
Art not without ambition, but without 20
The illness should attend it. What thou wouldst
        highly,
That wouldst thou holily; wouldst not play false,
And yet wouldst wrongly win. Thou'dst have,
        great Glamis,
That which cries, "Thus thou must do, if thou
        have it";
And that which rather thou dost fear to do 25
Than wishest should be undone. Hie thee hither
That I may pour my spirits in thine ear,
And chastise with the valour of my tongue
All that impedes thee from the golden round
Which fate and metaphysical aid doth seem 30
To have thee crown'd withal.

    Enter a MESSENGER.

                  What is your tidings?
    Mess. The King comes here to-night.
    Lady M.   Thou'rt mad to say it!
Is not thy master with him? who, were 't so,
Would have inform'd for preparation.
    Mess. So please you, it is true; our thane is com-
        ing. 35
One of my fellows had the speed of him,
Who, almost dead for breath, had scarcely more
Than would make up his message.
    Lady M.   Give him tending;
He brings great news.   [*Exit Messenger.*
                The raven himself is hoarse
That croaks the fatal entrance of Duncan 40
Under my battlements. Come, you spirits
That tend on mortal thoughts, unsex me here,
And fill me from the crown to the toe top-full
Of direst cruelty! Make thick my blood;
Stop up th' access and passage to remorse, 45

19–20. **the proportion . . . mine:** I might thank and pay you in proportion to your deserts. 27. **Safe toward:** to secure. 34. **Wanton:** profuse. 39. **Prince of Cumberland:** the title of the heir apparent. 45. **[harbinger]** (Rowe): officer sent ahead to provide lodging. *Herbenger* F. 52. **wink at:** fail to see.
    Sc. v, 1. Lady M. Here and throughout the play F heads the speeches of Lady Macbeth simply *Lady.* **6. missives:** messengers. **21. illness:** evil (cruelty). **29. round:** crown. **30. metaphysical:** supernatural. **42. mortal:** murderous.

That no compunctious visitings of nature
Shake my fell purpose, nor keep peace between
Th' effect and [it]! Come to my woman's breasts
And take my milk for gall, you murd'ring ministers,
Wherever in your sightless substances   50
You wait on nature's mischief! Come, thick night,
And pall thee in the dunnest smoke of hell,
That my keen knife see not the wound it makes,
Nor heaven peep through the blanket of the dark
To cry, "Hold, hold!"

         Enter MACBETH.

            Great Glamis! worthy Cawdor!
Greater than both, by the all-hail hereafter!   56
Thy letters have transported me beyond
This ignorant present, and I feel now
The future in the instant.
     Macb.   My dearest love,   59
Duncan comes here to-night.
     Lady M.   And when goes hence?
     Macb. To-morrow, as he purposes.
     Lady M.   O, never
Shall sun that morrow see!
Your face, my thane, is as a book where men
May read strange matters. To beguile the time,
Look like the time; bear welcome in your eye,   65
Your hand, your tongue; look like the innocent
        flower,
But be the serpent under 't. He that's coming
Must be provided for; and you shall put
This night's great business into my dispatch,
Which shall to all our nights and days to come   70
Give solely sovereign sway and masterdom.
     Macb. We will speak further.
     Lady M.   Only look up clear;
To alter favour ever is to fear.
Leave all the rest to me.   [*Exeunt.*

     SCENE VI. [*Before Macbeth's castle.*]

Hautboys and torches. Enter [DUNCAN], Malcolm,
Donalbain, BANQUO, Lennox, Macduff, Ross,
Angus, *and* Attendants.

     Dun. This castle hath a pleasant seat; the air
Nimbly and sweetly recommends itself
Unto our gentle senses.
     Ban.   This guest of summer,
The temple-haunting [martlet] does approve,

By his loved [mansionry], that the heaven's breath   5
Smells wooingly here; no jutty, frieze,
Buttress, nor coign of vantage, but this bird
Hath made his pendent bed and procreant cradle.
Where they [most] breed and haunt, I have observ'd
The air is delicate.

        Enter LADY [MACBETH].

     Dun.   See, see, our honour'd hostess!
The love that follows us sometime is our trouble,   11
Which still we thank as love. Herein I teach you
How you shall bid God 'ield us for your pains,
And thank us for your trouble.
     Lady M.   All our service
In every point twice done and then done double   15
Were poor and single business to contend
Against those honours deep and broad wherewith
Your Majesty loads our house. For those of old,
And the late dignities heap'd up to them,   19
We rest your hermits.
     Dun.   Where's the thane of Cawdor?
We cours'd him at the heels, and had a purpose
To be his purveyor; but he rides well,
And his great love, sharp as his spur, hath holp him
To his home before us. Fair and noble hostess,
We are your guest to-night.
     Lady M.   Your servants ever
Have theirs, themselves, and what is theirs, in
      compt,   26
To make their audit at your Highness' pleasure,
Still to return your own.
     Dun.   Give me your hand;
Conduct me to mine host. We love him highly,
And shall continue our graces towards him.   30
By your leave, hostess.   [*Exeunt.*

     SCENE VII. [*Within Macbeth's castle.*]

Hautboys and torches. Enter a Sewer, *and divers*
Servants *with dishes and service, over the stage.*
Then enter MACBETH.

     Macb. If it were done when 'tis done, then 'twere
      well
It were done quickly. If the assassination
Could trammel up the consequence, and catch
With his surcease success; that but this blow
Might be the be-all and the end-all here,   5
But here, upon this bank and [shoal] of time,

---

46. **compunctious visitings:** conscientious scruples. 47. **fell:** cruel. 47-48. **keep ... [it]:** i.e., keep purpose and accomplishment apart. [*it*] F3. *hit* F1. 49. **for:** in exchange for. 50. **sightless:** invisible. 52. **pall:** cover. **dunnest:** darkest. 64. **beguile:** delude. 72. **clear:** serene. 73. **favour:** expression. **to fear:** a sign of fear.

Sc. vi, S.D. **Hautboys:** wind instruments (oboes). 4. [**martlet**] (Rowe): martin. *Barlet* F. **approve:** prove. 5. [**mansionry**] (Theobald): nest building. *mansonry* F. 6. **jutty:** projection. 7. **coign of vantage:** convenient corner. 9. [**most**] (Rowe). *must* F. 11. **our trouble:** troublesome. 13. **bid ... pains:** pray God to reward ('ield) me for the trouble I give. 16. **single:** feeble. **contend:** match. 20. **rest ... hermits:** i.e., will gratefully pray for you. 22. **purveyor:** one who precedes to secure food and lodging. 26. **in compt:** in trust. 27. **audit:** rendering, account. 28. **Still:** always.

Sc. vii, S.D. **Sewer:** butler. 3. **trammel up:** entangle (as in a net). 4. **his surcease:** the stoppage of the consequence. 6. [**shoal**] (Theobald). *Schoole* F.

We'd jump the life to come. But in these cases
We still have judgement here, that we but teach
Bloody instructions, which, being taught, return
To plague th' inventor. This even-handed justice
Commends th' ingredients of our poison'd chalice 11
To our own lips. He's here in double trust:
First, as I am his kinsman and his subject,
Strong both against the deed; then, as his host,
Who should against his murderer shut the door,
Not bear the knife myself. Besides, this Duncan 16
Hath borne his faculties so meek, hath been
So clear in his great office, that his virtues
Will plead like angels, trumpet-tongu'd, against
The deep damnation of his taking-off; 20
And pity, like a naked new-born babe
Striding the blast, or heaven's cherubin hors'd
Upon the sightless couriers of the air,
Shall blow the horrid deed in every eye,
That tears shall drown the wind. I have no spur 25
To prick the sides of my intent, but only
Vaulting ambition, which o'erleaps itself
And falls on th' other —

    Enter LADY MACBETH
        How now! what news?
 Lady M. He has almost supp'd. Why have you
  left the chamber?
 Macb. Hath he ask'd for me?
 Lady M.   Know you not he has?
 Macb. We will proceed no further in this business.
He hath honour'd me of late; and I have bought
Golden opinions from all sorts of people,
Which would be worn now in their newest gloss,
Not cast aside so soon.
 Lady M.   Was the hope drunk 35
Wherein you dress'd yourself? Hath it slept since?
And wakes it now, to look so green and pale
At what it did so freely? From this time
Such I account thy love. Art thou afeard
To be the same in thine own act and valour 40
As thou art in desire? Wouldst thou have that
Which thou esteem'st the ornament of life,
And live a coward in thine own esteem,
Letting "I dare not" wait upon "I would,"
Like the poor cat i' th' adage?
 Macb.   Prithee, peace! 45
I dare do all that may become a man;
Who dares [do] more is none.
 Lady M.   What beast was 't, then,
That made you break this enterprise to me?
When you durst do it, then you were a man;
And, to be more than what you were, you would 50
Be so much more the man. Nor time nor place

Did then adhere, and yet you would make both.
They have made themselves, and that their fitness
 now
Does unmake you. I have given suck, and know
How tender 'tis to love the babe that milks me; 55
I would, while it was smiling in my face,
Have pluck'd my nipple from his boneless gums
And dash'd the brains out, had I so sworn as you
Have done to this.
 Macb.   If we should fail?
 Lady M.   We fail?
But screw your courage to the sticking-place, 60
And we'll not fail. When Duncan is asleep —
Whereto the rather shall his day's hard journey
Soundly invite him — his two chamberlains
Will I with wine and wassail so convince
That memory, the warder of the brain, 65
Shall be a fume, and the receipt of reason
A limbeck only. When in swinish sleep
Their drenched natures lie as in a death,
What cannot you and I perform upon
Th' unguarded Duncan? what not put upon 70
His spongy officers, who shall bear the guilt
Of our great quell?
 Macb.   Bring forth men-children only;
For thy undaunted mettle should compose
Nothing but males. Will it not be receiv'd,
When we have mark'd with blood those sleepy two
Of his own chamber and us'd their very daggers, 76
That they have done 't?
 Lady M.   Who dares receive it other,
As we shall make our griefs and clamour roar
Upon his death?
 Macb.   I am settled, and bend up
Each corporal agent to this terrible feat. 80
Away, and mock the time with fairest show;
False face must hide what the false heart doth know.
            [*Exeunt.*

ACT II

SCENE I. [*Within Macbeth's castle.*]

Enter BANQUO, *and* FLEANCE *with a torch before*
        him.

 Ban. How goest the night, boy?
 Fle. The moon is down; I have not heard the
  clock.
 Ban. And she goes down at twelve.
 Fle.   I take 't, 'tis later, sir.
 Ban. Hold, take my sword. There's husbandry
  in heaven;
Their candles are all out. Take thee that too. 5
A heavy summons lies like lead upon me,

---

 7. **jump:** risk. 17. **faculties:** powers. 18. **clear:** blameless. 37. **green:** sickly. 45. **th' adage.** "The cat would eat fish, and would not wet her feet." 47. **[do]** (Rowe). *no* F. 48. **break:** disclose. 52. **adhere:** agree. 60. **But:** only. 64. **wassail:** carousal. **convince:** overpower. 67. **limbeck:** retort, still. 71. **spongy:** drunken. 72. **quell:** killing.
  Act II, sc. i, 4. husbandry: economy. 5. **that:** his dagger.

And yet I would not sleep. Merciful powers,
Restrain in me the cursed thoughts that nature
Gives way to in repose!

Enter MACBETH, *and a* Servant *with a torch.*
              Give me my sword.
Who's there?   10
   Macb. A friend.
   Ban. What, sir, not yet at rest? The King's
a-bed.
He hath been in unusual pleasure, and
Sent forth great largess to your offices.
This diamond he greets your wife withal,   15
By the name of most kind hostess; and shut up
In measureless content.
   Macb.   Being unprepar'd,
Our will became the servant to defect;
Which else should free have wrought.
   Ban.   All's well.
I dreamt last night of the three weird sisters: 20
To you they have show'd some truth.
   Macb.   I think not of them;
Yet when we can entreat an hour to serve,
We would spend it in some words upon that busi-
     ness,
If you would grant the time.
   Ban.   At your kind'st leisure.
   Macb. If you shall cleave to my consent, when
'tis,   25
It shall make honour for you.
   Ban.   So I lose none
In seeking to augment it, but still keep
My bosom franchis'd and allegiance clear,
I shall be counsell'd.
   Macb.   Good repose the while!
   Ban. Thanks, sir; the like to you!   30
               [Exeunt Banquo [and Fleance].
   Macb. Go bid thy mistress, when my drink is
     ready,
She strike upon the bell. Get thee to bed.
                       [Exit [Servant].
Is this a dagger which I see before me,
The handle toward my hand? Come, let me clutch
thee.
I have thee not, and yet I see thee still.   35
Art thou not, fatal vision, sensible
To feeling as to sight? or art thou but
A dagger of the mind, a false creation,
Proceeding from the heat-oppressed brain?
I see thee yet, in form as palpable   40
As this which now I draw.

Thou marshall'st me the way that I was going,
And such an instrument I was to use.
Mine eyes are made the fools o' th' other senses,
Or else worth all the rest. I see thee still,   45
And on thy blade and dudgeon gouts of blood,
Which was not so before. There's no such thing.
It is the bloody business which informs
Thus to mine eyes. Now o'er the one half-world
Nature seems dead, and wicked dreams abuse   50
The curtain'd sleep. Witchcraft celebrates
Pale Hecate's offerings, and wither'd Murder,
Alarum'd by his sentinel, the wolf,
Whose howl's his watch, thus with his stealthy pace,
With Tarquin's ravishing [strides], towards his de-
     sign   55
Moves like a ghost. Thou [sure] and firm set earth,
Hear not my steps, which [way they] walk, for fear
The very stones prate of my whereabout
And take the present horror from the time,   59
Which now suits with it. Whiles I threat, he lives:
Words to the heat of deeds too cold breath gives.
                         [A bell rings.
I go, and it is done; the bell invites me.
Hear it not, Duncan; for it is a knell
That summons thee to heaven or to hell.   *[Exit.*

SCENE II. *[The same.]*

Enter LADY [MACBETH].

   Lady M. That which hath made them drunk hath
     made me bold;
What hath quench'd them hath given me fire.
     Hark! Peace!
It was the owl that shriek'd the fatal bellman
Which gives the stern'st good-night. He is about it.
The doors are open, and the surfeited grooms   5
Do mock their charge with snores. I have drugg'd
     their possets,
That death and nature do contend about them
Whether they live or die.

Enter MACBETH.

   Macb. Who's there? What, ho!
   Lady M. Alack, I am afraid they have awak'd,   10
And 'tis not done. Th' attempt and not the deed
Confounds us. Hark! I laid their daggers ready;
He could not miss 'em. Had he not resembled
My father as he slept, I had done 't. — My husband!
   Macb. I have done the deed. Didst thou not hear
     a noise?   15

14. largess: gifts. offices: servants' quarters. 16. shut up: concluded. 18. defect: deficiency. 19. free: bountifully.
25. consent: party, interests. when 'tis: when the time comes. 28. franchis'd: free from guilt. 36. sensible: perceptible. 46. dudgeon: handle. gouts: drops. 48. informs: speaks. 50. abuse: deceive. 52. Hecate: goddess of night
and of witchcraft. 55. [strides] (Pope). *sides* F. 56. [sure] (Pope conj.). *sowre* F. 57. [way they] (Rowe). *they may* F.
Sc. ii, 3. bellman. The night watchman customarily visited prisoners the night before their execution. 5. grooms:
king's body servants. 6. possets: drink made of wine, hot milk, etc.

Lady M. I heard the owl scream and the crickets cry.
Did not you speak?
    Macb.   When?
    Lady M.   Now.
    Macb.   As I descended?
    Lady M. Ay.
    Macb. Hark!
Who lies i' th' second chamber?
    Lady M.   Donalbain.   20
    Macb. This is a sorry sight.
                        [*Looking on his hands.*]
    Lady M. A foolish thought, to say a sorry sight.
    Macb. There's one did laugh in 's sleep, and one cried, "Murder!"
That they did wake each other. I stood and heard them;
But they did say their prayers, and address'd them
Again to sleep.
    Lady M.   There are two lodg'd together.   26
    Macb. One cried, "God bless us!" and "Amen" the other,
As they had seen me with these hangman's hands.
List'ning their fear. I could not say "Amen"
When they did say "God bless us!"
    Lady M.   Consider it not so deeply.
    Macb. But wherefore could not I pronounce "Amen"?   31
I had most need of blessing, and "Amen"
Stuck in my throat.
    Lady M. These deeds must not be thought
After these ways; so, it will make us mad.
    Macb. Methought I heard a voice cry, "Sleep no more!   35
Macbeth does murder sleep." — the innocent sleep,
Sleep that knits up the ravell'd sleave of care,
The death of each day's life, sore labour's bath,
Balm of hurt minds, great nature's second course,
Chief nourisher in life's feast.
    Lady M.   What do you mean?
    Macb. Still it cried, "Sleep no more!" to all the house;   41
"Glamis hath murder'd sleep, and therefore Cawdor
Shall sleep no more; Macbeth shall sleep no more."
    Lady M. Who was it that thus cried? Why, worthy thane,
You do unbend your noble strength, to think   45
So brainsickly of things. Go get some water,
And wash this filthy witness from your hand.
Why did you bring these daggers from the place?
They must lie there. Go carry them; and smear
The sleepy grooms with blood.
    Macb.   I'll go no more.   50

I am afraid to think what I have done;
Look on't again I dare not.
    Lady M.   Infirm of purpose!
Give me the daggers. The sleeping and the dead
Are but as pictures; 'tis the eye of childhood
That fears a painted devil. If he do bleed,   55
I'll gild the faces of the grooms withal;
For it must seem their guilt.
                   [*Exit. Knocking within.*
    Macb.   Whence is that knocking?
How is't with me, when every noise appalls me?
What hands are here? Ha! they pluck out mine eyes.
Will all great Neptune's ocean wash this blood   60
Clean from my hand? No, this my hand will rather
The multitudinous seas incarnadine,
Making the green one red.

        Re-enter LADY [MACBETH].

    Lady M. My hands are of your colour; but I shame
To wear a heart so white. (*Knocking.*) I hear a knocking   65
At the south entry. Retire we to our chamber.
A little water clears us of this deed;
How easy is it, then! Your constancy
Hath left you unattended. (*Knocking.*) Hark! more knocking.
Get on your nightgown, lest occasion call us   70
And show us to be watchers. Be not lost
So poorly in your thoughts.
    Macb. To know my deed, 'twere best not know myself.   [*Knocking.*
Wake Duncan with thy knocking! I would thou couldst!   [*Exeunt.*

      SCENE III. [*The same.*]

    Enter a PORTER. *Knocking within.*

    Porter. Here's a knocking indeed! If a man were porter of hell-gate, he should have old turning the key. (*Knocking.*) Knock, knock, knock! Who's there, i' th' name of Beelzebub? Here's a farmer, that hang'd himself on th' expectation   5 of plenty. Come in time; have napkins enow about you; here you'll sweat for't. (*Knocking.*) Knock, knock! Who's there, in th' other devil's name? Faith, here's an equivocator, that could swear in both the scales against either scale; who com-   10 mitted treason enough for God's sake, yet could not equivocate to heaven. O, come in, equivocator. (*Knocking.*) Knock, knock, knock! Who's there? Faith, here's an English tailor come hither for steal-

---

37. **ravell'd**: tangled. **sleave**: skein. 62. **incarnadine**: turn blood-red. 68-69. **constancy...unattended**: firmness has quit you. 70. **nightgown**: dressing-gown.
    Sc. iii, 2. **old**: a grand old time. 5-6. **farmer...plenty**. The farmer, having hoarded grain to sell at high prices, foresaw his ruin when crops proved plentiful. 6. **napkins**: handkerchiefs. 9-10. **swear...scale**: swear to an ambiguity.

ing out of a French hose. Come in, tailor; here 15
you may roast your goose. (*Knocking.*) Knock,
knock; never at quiet! What are you? But this
place is too cold for hell. I'll devil-porter it no
further. I had thought to have let in some of 20
all professions that go the primrose way to th' everlasting bonfire. (*Knocking.*) Anon, anon. I pray
you, remember the porter.   [*Opens the gate.*]

Enter MACDUFF *and* LENNOX.

Macd. Was it so late, friend, ere you went to bed,
That you do lie so late?   25
Port. Faith, sir, we were carousing till the second
cock; and drink, sir, is a great provoker of three
things.
Macd. What three things does drink especially
provoke?   30
Port. Marry, sir, nose-painting, sleep, and urine.
Lechery, sir, it provokes, and unprovokes; it provokes the desire, but it takes away the performance;
therefore, much drink may be said to be an equivocator with lechery: it makes him, and it mars 35
him; it sets him on, and it takes him off; it persuades
him, and disheartens him; makes him stand to, and
not stand to; in conclusion, equivocates him in a
sleep, and, giving him the lie, leaves him.   40
Macd. I believe drink gave thee the lie last night.
Port. That it did, sir, i' the very throat on me.
But I requited him for his lie; and, I think, being too
strong for him, though he took up my legs sometime,
yet I made a shift to cast him.   46

Enter MACBETH.

Macd. Is thy master stirring?
Our knocking has awak'd him; here he comes.
Len. Good morrow, noble sir.
Macb.   Good morrow, both.
Macd. Is the King stirring, worthy thane?
Macb.   Not yet.
Macd. He did command me to call timely on
him.   51
I have almost slipp'd the hour.
Macb.   I'll bring you to him.
Macd. I know this is a joyful trouble to you;
But yet 'tis one.
Macb. The labour we delight in physics pain.
This is the door.
Macd.   I'll make so bold to call,   56
For 'tis my limited service.   [*Exit.*
Len. Goes the King hence to-day?
Macb.   He does; — he did appoint so.
Len. The night has been unruly. Where we lay,
Our chimneys were blown down; and, as they say,

Lamentings heard i' th' air; strange screams of
death,   61
And prophesying with accents terrible
Of dire combustion and confus'd events
New hatch'd to th' woeful time. The obscure bird
Clamour'd the livelong night; some say, the earth 65
Was feverous and did shake.
Macb.   'Twas a rough night.
Len. My young remembrance cannot parallel
A fellow to it.

Re-enter MACDUFF.

Macd. O horror, horror, horror! Tongue nor
heart
Cannot conceive nor name thee!
Macb. }
Len. }   What's the matter?
Macd. Confusion now hath made his master-
piece!   71
Most sacrilegious murder hath broke ope
The Lord's anointed temple, and stole thence
The life o' th' building!
Macb.   What is 't you say? The life?
Len. Mean you his Majesty?   75
Macd. Approach the chamber, and destroy your
sight
With a new Gorgon. Do not bid me speak;
See, and then speak yourselves.
          [*Exeunt Macbeth and Lennox.*
          Awake, awake!
Ring the alarum-bell. Murder and treason!
Banquo and Donalbain! Malcolm! awake!   80
Shake off this downy sleep, death's counterfeit,
And look on death itself! Up, up, and see
The great doom's image! Malcolm! Banquo!
As from your graves rise up, and walk like sprites,
To countenance this horror! Ring the bell.   85
          [*Bell rings.*

Enter LADY MACBETH.

Lady M. What's the business,
That such a hideous trumpet calls to parley
The sleepers of the house? Speak, speak!
Macd.   O gentle lady,
'Tis not for you to hear what I can speak;
The repetition in a woman's ear   90
Would murder as it fell.

Enter BANQUO.

          O Banquo, Banquo,
Our royal master's murder'd!
Lady M.   Woe, alas!
What, in our house?

15–16. **French hose.** A tight-fitting kind, in the making of which it would be hard for tailors to steal any cloth. 16.
goose: pressing iron. 26–27. **the second cock:** 3 A.M. 41. **gave thee the lie:** (1) floored thee, (2) lied to thee. 46. **cast:** (1)
throw, (2) vomit. 51. **timely:** early. 55. **physics:** cures. 57. **limited:** appointed. 63. **combustion:** tumult. 64. **obscure bird:** owl. 71. **Confusion:** destruction. 77. **Gorgon.** The Gorgon Medusa turned to stone anyone who looked in
her face. 83. **doom's image:** image of Doomsday. 85. **countenance:** be in keeping with.

Ban.   Too cruel anywhere.
Dear Duff, I prithee, contradict thyself,
And say it is not so.   95

Re-enter MACBETH *and* LENNOX, *with* ROSS.

Macb. Had I but died an hour before this chance,
I had liv'd a blessed time; for, from this instant,
There's nothing serious in mortality.
All is but toys; renown and grace is dead;
The wine of life is drawn, and the mere lees   100
Is left this vault to brag of.

Enter MALCOLM *and* DONALBAIN.

Don. What is amiss?
Macb.   You are, and do not know 't.
The spring, the head, the fountain of your blood
Is stopp'd; the very source of it is stopp'd.
Macd. Your royal father's murder'd.
Mal.   O, by whom?
Len. Those of his chamber, as it seem'd, had
     done 't.   106
Their hands and faces were all badg'd with blood;
So were their daggers, which unwip'd we found
Upon their pillows.
They star'd, and were distracted; no man's life   110
Was to be trusted with them.
Macb. O, yet I do repent me of my fury,
That I did kill them.
Macd.   Wherefore did you so?
Macb. Who can be wise, amaz'd, temp'rate and
     furious,
Loyal and neutral, in a moment? No man.   115
The expedition of my violent love
Outrun the pauser, reason. Here lay Duncan,
His silver skin lac'd with his golden blood,   118
And his gash'd stabs look'd like a breach in nature
For ruin's wasteful entrance; there, the murderers,
Steep'd in the colours of their trade, their daggers
Unmannerly breech'd with gore. Who could refrain,
That had a heart to love, and in that heart
Courage to make 's love known?
Lady M.   Help me hence, ho!
Macd. Look to the lady.
Mal. [*Aside to Don.*] Why do we hold our
     tongues,   125
That most may claim this argument for ours?
Don. [*Aside to Mal.*] What should be spoken
     here, where our fate,
Hid in an auger-hole, may rush and seize us?
Let's away;
Our tears are not yet brew'd.

Mal. [*Aside to Don.*] Nor our strong sorrow
Upon the foot of motion.
Ban.   Look to the lady;   131
                              [*Lady Macbeth is carried out.*]
And when we have our naked frailties hid,
That suffer in exposure, let us meet
And question this most bloody piece of work,
To know it further. Fears and scruples shake us.
In the great hand of God I stand, and thence   136
Against the undivulg'd pretence I fight
Of treasonous malice.
Macd.   And so do I.
All.   So all.
Macb. Let's briefly put on manly readiness,
And meet i' th' hall together.
All.   Well contented.   140
     [*Exeunt* [*all but Malcolm and Donalbain*].
Mal. What will you do? Let's not consort with
     them;
To show an unfelt sorrow is an office
Which the false man does easy. I'll to England.
Don. To Ireland, I; our separated fortune
Shall keep us both the safer. Where we are,   145
There's daggers in men's smiles; the near in blood,
The nearer bloody.
Mal.   This murderous shaft that's shot
Hath not yet lighted, and our safest way
Is to avoid the aim. Therefore, to horse;
And let us not be dainty of leave-taking,   150
But shift away. There's warrant in that theft
Which steals itself, when there's no mercy left.
                                                   [*Exeunt.*

SCENE IV. [*Outside Macbeth's castle.*]

Enter ROSS *and an* OLD MAN.

Old M. Threescore and ten I can remember well;
Within the volume of which time I have seen
Hours dreadful and things strange; but this sore
     night
Hath trifled former knowings.
Ross.   Ah, good father,
Thou seest the heavens, as troubled with man's act,
Threatens his bloody stage. By th' clock 'tis day, 6
And yet dark night strangles the travelling lamp.
Is't night's predominance or the day's shame
That darkness does the face of earth entomb,
When living light should kiss it?
Old M.   'Tis unnatural, 10
Even like the deed that's done. On Tuesday last,
A falcon, tow'ring in her pride of place,

---

98. **mortality:** human life. 99. **toys:** trifles. 103. **head:** source. 107. **badg'd:** marked. 114. **amaz'd:** confused.
116. **expedition:** haste. 122. **breech'd:** covered. 126. **argument:** subject. 128. **auger-hole:** obscure spot. 131.
Upon...motion: ready to act. 132. **our...hid:** clothed ourselves. 135. **scruples:** suspicions. 139. **briefly:** quickly.
readiness: dress. 146-47. **the near...bloody:** i.e., the closer the blood ties, the greater the danger (**near:** nearer). 150.
dainty of: particular about.
Sc. iv, 3. **sore:** dreadful. 4. **trifled:** made trivial. 12. **tow'ring...place:** mounting proudly to the summit of her flight.

Was by a mousing owl hawk'd at and kill'd.

Ross. And Duncan's horses — a thing most
   strange and certain —
Beauteous and swift, the minions of their race,   15
Turn'd wild in nature, broke their stalls, flung out,
Contending 'gainst obedience, as they would make
War with mankind.

Old M.   'Tis said they eat each other.

Ross. They did so, to th' amazement of mine eyes
That look'd upon't.

          Enter MACDUFF.

          Here comes the good Macduff.   20
How goes the world, sir, now?

Macd.   Why, see you not?

Ross. Is't known who did this more than bloody
   deed?

Macd. Those that Macbeth hath slain.

Ross.   Alas, the day!
What good could they pretend?

Macd.   They were suborn'd.
Malcolm and Donalbain, the King's two sons,   25
Are stol'n away and fled; which puts upon them
Suspicion of the deed.

Ross.   'Gainst nature still!
Thriftless ambition, that will ravin up
Thine own life's means! Then 'tis most like
The sovereignty will fall upon Macbeth.   30

Macd. He is already nam'd, and gone to Scone
To be invested.

Ross.   Where is Duncan's body?

Macd. Carried to Colmekill,
The sacred storehouse of his predecessors   34
And guardian of their bones.

Ross.   Will you to Scone?

Macd. No, cousin, I'll to Fife.

Ross.   Well, I will thither.

Macd. Well, may you see things well done there,
   — adieu! —
Lest our old robes sit easier than our new!

Ross. Farewell, father.

Old M. God's benison go with you; and with
   those   40
That would make good of bad, and friends of foes!
                   [*Exeunt.*

ACT III

SCENE I. [*Forres. The palace.*]

         Enter BANQUO.

Ban. Thou hast it now: King, Cawdor, Glamis,
   all,
As the weird women promis'd, and, I fear,

Thou play'dst most foully for't; yet it was said
It should not stand in thy posterity,
But that myself should be the root and father   5
Of many kings. If there come truth from them —
As upon thee, Macbeth, their speeches shine —
Why, by the verities on thee made good,
May they not be my oracles as well,
And set me up in hope? But hush! no more.   10

Sennet sounded. Enter MACBETH, *as King,* LADY
  [MACBETH, *as Queen*], Lennox, Ross, Lords,
  [Ladies,] *and* SERVANTS.

Macb. Here's our chief guest.

Lady M.   If he had been forgotten,
It had been as a gap in our great feast,
And all-thing unbecoming.

Macb. To-night we hold a solemn supper, sir,
And I'll request your presence.

Ban.   Let your Highness
Command upon me; to the which my duties   16
Are with a most indissoluble tie
For ever knit.

Macb. Ride you this afternoon?

Ban. Ay, my good lord.   20

Macb. We should have else desir'd your good ad-
   vice,
Which still hath been both grave and prosperous,
In this day's council; but we'll take to-morrow.
Is't far you ride?

Ban. As far, my lord, as will fill up the time   25
'Twixt this and supper. Go not my horse the
   better,
I must become a borrower of the night
For a dark hour or twain.

Macb.   Fail not our feast.

Ban. My lord, I will not.   29

Macb. We hear our bloody cousins are bestow'd
In England and in Ireland, not confessing
Their cruel parricide, filling their hearers
With strange invention. But of that to-morrow,
When therewithal we shall have cause of state
Craving us jointly. Hie you to horse; adieu,   35
Till you return at night. Goes Fleance with you?

Ban. Ay, my good lord. Our time does call
   upon 's.

Macb. I wish your horses swift and sure of foot;
And so I do commend you to their backs.
Farewell.   [*Exit Banquo.*   40
Let every man be master of his time
Till seven at night. To make society
The sweeter welcome, we will keep ourself
Till supper-time alone; while then, God be with you!
      [*Exeunt* [*all but Macbeth, and a Servant*].

---

24. **pretend:** intend. **suborn'd:** criminally incited. 28. **ravin:** devour ravenously. 31. **Scone.** Where Scottish kings were
always crowned. 33. **Colmekill:** Iona (Columba's cell), then the burial place of Scottish royalty. 40. **benison:** blessing.
    Act III, sc. i, 7. **shine:** i.e., in fulfillment. 10. s.d. *Sennet:* trumpet call. 14. **solemn:** formal. 22. **still:** ever. 30. **are
bestow'd:** have taken refuge. 35. **Craving us jointly:** requiring our joint attention. 44. **while:** until.

Sirrah, a word with you. Attend those men   45
Our pleasure?
   Serv. They are, my lord, without the palace gate.
   Macb. Bring them before us.   [*Exit Servant.*
                    To be thus is nothing,
But to be safely thus. Our fears in Banquo
Stick deep; and in his royalty of nature   50
Reigns that which would be fear'd. 'Tis much he
    dares;
And, to that dauntless temper of his mind,
He hath a wisdom that doth guide his valour
To act in safety. There is none but he
Whose being I do fear; and, under him,   55
My Genius is rebuk'd, as, it is said,
Mark Antony's was by Cæsar. He chid the sisters
When first they put the name of king upon me,
And bade them speak to him; then prophet-like
They hail'd him father to a line of kings.   60
Upon my head they plac'd a fruitless crown,
And put a barren sceptre in my gripe,
Thence to be wrench'd with an unlineal hand,
No son of mine succeeding. If 't be so,
For Banquo's issue have I fil'd my mind;   65
For them the gracious Duncan have I murder'd;
Put rancours in the vessel of my peace
Only for them; and mine eternal jewel
Given to the common enemy of man,
To make them kings, the [seed] of Banquo kings!   70
Rather than so, come fate into the list,
And champion me to th' utterance! Who's there?

   Re-enter Servant, *with two* MURDERERS.

Now go to the door, and stay there till we call.
                        [*Exit Servant.*
Was it not yesterday we spoke together?
   [*1.*] *Mur.* It was, so please your Highness.
   Macb.   Well then, now
Have you consider'd of my speeches? Know   76
That it was he in the times past which held you
So under fortune, which you thought had been
Our innocent self. This I made good to you
In our last conference, pass'd in probation with you
How you were borne in hand, how cross'd, the in-
    struments,   81
Who wrought with them, and all things else that
    might
To half a soul and to a notion craz'd
Say, "Thus did Banquo."
   1. Mur.   You made it known to us.
   Macb. I did so, and went further, which is now   85
Our point of second meeting. Do you find

Your patience so predominant in your nature
That you can let this go? Are you so gospell'd
To pray for this good man and for his issue,   89
Whose heavy hand hath bow'd you to the grave
And beggar'd yours for ever?
   1. Mur.   We are men, my liege.
   Macb. Ay, in the catalogue ye go for men,
As hounds and greyhounds, mongrels, spaniels,
    curs,
Shoughs, water-rugs, and demi-wolves are clept
All by the name of dogs; the valued file   95
Distinguishes the swift, the slow, the subtle,
The housekeeper, the hunter, every one,
According to the gift which bounteous nature
Hath in him clos'd; whereby he does receive
Particular addition, from the bill   100
That writes them all alike; and so of men.
Now, if you have a station in the file,
Not i' th' worst rank of manhood, say 't;
And I will put that business in your bosoms,
Whose execution takes your enemy off,   105
Grapples you to the heart and love of us,
Who wear our health but sickly in his life,
Which in his death were perfect.
   2. Mur.   I am one, my liege,
Whom the vile blows and buffets of the world
Hath so incens'd that I am reckless what   110
I do to spite the world.
   1. Mur.   And I another
So weary with disasters, tugg'd with fortune,
That I would set my life on any chance,
To mend it or be rid on't.
   Macb.   Both of you
Know Banquo was your enemy.
   [*Both*] *Mur.*   True, my lord.   115
   Macb. So is he mine; and in such bloody distance,
That every minute of his being thrusts
Against my near'st of life; and though I could
With barefac'd power sweep him from my sight
And bid my will avouch it, yet I must not,   120
For certain friends that are both his and mine,
Whose loves I may not drop, but wail his fall
Who I myself struck down; and thence it is,
That I to your assistance do make love,
Masking the business from the common eye   125
For sundry weighty reasons.
   2. Mur.   We shall, my lord,
Perform what you command us.
   1. Mur.   Though our lives—
   Macb. Your spirits shine through you. Within
    this hour at most

---

48. **thus:** i.e., king.   51. **would:** must.   52. **to:** added to.   57. **Cæsar:** Octavius Cæsar.   62. **gripe:** grasp.   65. **fil'd:** defiled.   68–69. **mine...man:** given my soul to the devil.   70. **[seed]** (Pope). *Seedes* F.   71. **list:** arena of combat. 72. **th' utterance:** the death.   77. **he:** Banquo.   80. **pass'd in probation:** reviewed and proved.   81. **borne in hand:** deceived.   **cross'd:** thwarted.   83. **notion:** mind.   88. **gospell'd:** filled with the gospel.   92. **go:** pass.   94. **Shoughs:** shaggy dogs.   **water-rugs:** water-dogs.   **clept:** called.   95. **valued file:** list which specifies values.   97. **housekeeper:** watchdog.   100. **addition:** title.   101. **writes...alike:** enters them indiscriminately.   112. **tugg'd with:** pulled about by.   116. **distance:** enmity.   118. **near'st of life:** most vital spot.   120. **avouch:** justify.

I will advise you where to plant yourselves,   129
Acquaint you with the perfect spy o' th' time,
The moment on't; for't must be done to-night,
And something from the palace; always thought
That I require a clearness: and with him —
To leave no rubs nor botches in the work —
Fleance his son, that keeps him company,   135
Whose absence is no less material to me
Than is his father's, must embrace the fate
Of that dark hour.   Resolve yourselves apart;
I'll come to you anon.
    [*Both*] *Mur.*   We are resolv'd, my lord.
    Macb. I'll call upon you straight; abide within.
                   [*Exeunt Murderers.*]
It is concluded.   Banquo, thy soul's flight,   141
If it find heaven, must find it out to-night.   [*Exit.*

SCENE II. [*The same.*]

Enter LADY MACBETH *and a* SERVANT.

    Lady M. Is Banquo gone from court?
    Serv. Ay, madam, but returns again to-night.
    Lady M. Say to the King, I would attend his
      leisure
For a few words.
    Serv.   Madam, I will.   [*Exit.*
    Lady M.   Nought's had, all's spent,
Where our desire is got without content.   5
'Tis safer to be that which we destroy
Than by destruction dwell in doubtful joy.

Enter MACBETH.

How now, my lord! why do you keep alone,
Of sorriest fancies your companions making,
Using those thoughts which should indeed have
    died   10
With them they think on?   Things without all
    remedy
Should be without regard; what's done is done.
    Macb. We have [scotch'd] the snake, not kill'd it;
She'll close and be herself, whilst our poor malice
Remains in danger of her former tooth.   15
But let the frame of things disjoint, both the worlds
    suffer,
Ere we will eat our meal in fear and sleep
In the affliction of these terrible dreams
That shake us nightly.   Better be with the dead
Whom we, to gain our peace, have sent to peace,   20
Than on the torture of the mind to lie
In restless ecstasy.   Duncan is in his grave;

After life's fitful fever he sleeps well.
Treason has done his worst; nor steel, nor poison,
Malice domestic, foreign levy, nothing,   25
Can touch him further.
    Lady M.   Come on,
Gentle my lord, sleek o'er your rugged looks;
Be bright and jovial among your guests to-night.
    Macb. So shall I, love; and so, I pray, be you.
Let your remembrance apply to Banquo;   30
Present him eminence both with eye and tongue.
Unsafe the while that we
Must lave our honours in these flattering streams,
And make our faces vizards to our hearts,
Disguising what they are.
    Lady M.   You must leave this.   35
    Macb. O, full of scorpions is my mind, dear wife!
Thou know'st that Banquo and his Fleance lives.
    Lady M. But in them nature's copy's not eterne.
    Macb. There's comfort yet; they are assailable.
Then be thou jocund; ere the bat hath flown   40
His cloister'd flight, ere to black Hecate's summons
The shard-borne beetle with his drowsy hums
Hath rung night's yawning peal, there shall be done
A deed of dreadful note.
    Lady M.   What's to be done?
    Macb. Be innocent of the knowledge, dearest
    chuck,   45
Till thou applaud the deed.   Come, seeling night,
Scarf up the tender eye of pitiful day,
And with thy bloody and invisible hand
Cancel and tear to pieces that great bond
Which keeps me pale!   Light thickens, and the
    crow   50
Makes wing to th' rooky wood;
Good things of day begin to droop and drowse,
Whiles night's black agents to their preys do rouse.
Thou marvell'st at my words, but hold thee still;
Things bad begun make strong themselves by ill.
So, prithee, go with me.   [*Exeunt.* 56

SCENE III. [*A park near the palace.*]

Enter three MURDERERS.

    1. Mur. But who did bid thee join with us?
    3. Mur.   Macbeth.
    2. Mur. He needs not our mistrust, since he de-
    livers
Our offices and what we have to do
To the direction just.
    1. Mur.   Then stand with us;

---

130. **perfect...time**: exact time.   132. **something**: some distance.   133. **I...clearness**: I must not be suspected.
134. **rubs**: slips.   138. **Resolve yourselves**: make up your minds.
Sc. ii, 5. **content**: contentment.   10. **Using**: keeping company with.   13. **[scotch'd]** (Theobald): gashed. *scorch'd* F.
14. **close**: reunite.   22. **ecstasy**: frenzy.   27. **sleek**: smooth.   31. **eminence**: special favor.   34. **vizards**: masks.   38. **in
...eterne**: their lease (copy) of life is not eternal.   42. **shard-borne**: borne on hard wings.   46. **seeling**: blinding.   The
eyes of falcons were sewed up (seeled) in order to tame them.   49. **bond**: Banquo's life.   51. **rooky**: haunted by rooks.
    Sc. iii, 1. The speeches of the murderers are headed by numbers alone in F.   3. **offices**: duties.   4. **To...just**: precisely
according to his directions.

The west yet glimmers with some streaks of day. 5
Now spurs the lated traveller apace
To gain the timely inn; and near approaches
The subject of our watch.
    3. Mur.   Hark! I hear horses.
    Ban. (Within.) Give us a light there, ho!
    2. Mur.   Then 'tis he; the rest
That are within the note of expectation   10
Already are i' th' court.
    1. Mur.   His horses go about.
    3. Mur. Almost a mile; but he does usually,
So all men do, from hence to th' palace gate
Make it their walk.

      Enter BANQUO, *and* FLEANCE *with a torch.*

    2. Mur.   A light, a light!
    3. Mur.   'Tis he.
    1. Mur. Stand to't.   15
    Ban. It will be rain to-night.
    1. Mur.   Let it come down.
                    [They set upon Banquo.]
    Ban. O, treachery! Fly, good Fleance, fly, fly, fly!
Thou mayst revenge. O slave!
               [Dies. Fleance escapes.]
    3. Mur. Who did strike out the light?
    1. Mur.   Was 't not the way?
    3. Mur. There's but one down; the son is fled.
    2. Mur.   We have lost   20
Best half of our affair.
    1. Mur. Well, let's away, and say how much is
      done.   *[Exeunt.*

    SCENE IV. *[Hall in the palace.]*

A banquet prepared. Enter MACBETH, LADY
[MACBETH], ROSS, LENNOX, Lords, *and* Attendants.

    Macb. You know your own degrees; sit down.
    At first
And last, the hearty welcome.
    Lords.   Thanks to your Majesty.
    Macb. Ourself will mingle with society
And play the humble host.
Our hostess keeps her state, but in best time   5
We will require her welcome.
    Lady M. Pronounce it for me, sir, to all our
      friends,
For my heart speaks they are welcome.

    First MURDERER *[appears at the door].*

    Macb. See, they encounter thee with their hearts'
      thanks.   9
Both sides are even; here I'll sit i' th' midst.

Be large in mirth; anon we'll drink a measure
The table round. *[Approaching the door.]* — There's
    blood upon thy face.
    Mur. 'Tis Banquo's then.
    Macb. 'Tis better thee without than he within.
Is he dispatch'd?   15
    Mur. My lord, his throat is cut; that I did for
    him.
    Macb. Thou art the best o' th' cut-throats; yet
    he's good
That did the like for Fleance. If thou didst it,
Thou art the nonpareil.
    Mur.   Most royal sir,
Fleance is scap'd.   20
    Macb. Then comes my fit again. I had else been
    perfect,
Whole as the marble, founded as the rock,
As broad and general as the casing air;
But now I am cabin'd, cribb'd, confin'd, bound in
To saucy doubts and fears. But Banquo's safe?
    Mur. Ay, my good lord; safe in a ditch he bides,
With twenty trenched gashes on his head,   27
The least a death to nature.
    Macb.   Thanks for that;
There the grown serpent lies. The worm that's
    fled
Hath nature that in time will venom breed,   30
No teeth for th' present. Get thee gone; to-morrow
We'll hear ourselves again.   *[Exit Murderer.*
    Lady M.   My royal lord,
You do not give the cheer. The feast is sold
That is not often vouch'd, while 'tis a-making,
'Tis given with welcome. To feed were best at
    home;   35
From thence, the sauce to meat is ceremony;
Meeting were bare without it.

    Enter the Ghost *of Banquo, and sits in*
                Macbeth's place.

    Macb.   Sweet remembrancer!
Now, good digestion wait on appetite,
And health on both!
    Len.   May 't please your Highness sit.
    Macb. Here had we now our country's honour
    roof'd,   40
Were the grac'd person of our Banquo present,
Who may I rather challenge for unkindness
Than pity for mischance.
    Ross.   His absence, sir,
Lays blame upon his promise. Please 't your High-
    ness
To grace us with your royal company?   45
    Macb. The table's full.

---

    6. **lated:** belated. 10. **within... expectation:** on the list of expected guests.
    Sc. iv, 1. **degrees:** ranks (hence, order of seating). 1–2. **At... last:** once for all. 5. **state:** chair of state. 11. **large:**
liberal. **measure:** bumper. 14. **thee... within:** outside thee than inside him. 23. **general:** unconfined. **casing:** surrounding. 29. **worm:** serpent. 32. **hear ourselves:** confer. 33. **give the cheer:** play the host. 40. **roof'd:** under one roof.

Len.   Here is a place reserv'd, sir.
Macb. Where?
Len. Here, my good lord. What is't that
    moves your Highness?
Macb. Which of you have done this?
Lords.   What, my good lord?
Macb. Thou canst not say I did it; never shake 50
Thy gory locks at me.
Ross. Gentlemen, rise: his Highness is not well.
Lady M. Sit, worthy friends; my lord is often
    thus,
And hath been from his youth. Pray you, keep
    seat;
The fit is momentary; upon a thought   55
He will again be well. If much you note him,
You shall offend him and extend his passion.
Feed, and regard him not. Are you a man?
Macb. Ay, and a bold one, that dare look on that
Which might appall the devil.
Lady M.   O proper stuff! 60
This is the very painting of your fear;
This is the air-drawn dagger which, you said,
Led you to Duncan. O, these flaws and starts,
Impostors to true fear, would well become
A woman's story at a winter's fire,   65
Authoriz'd by her grandam. Shame itself!
Why do you make such faces? When all's done,
You look but on a stool.
Macb. Prithee, see there! behold! look! lo! how
    say you?
Why, what care I? If thou canst nod, speak too. 70
If charnel-houses and our graves must send
Those that we bury back, our monuments
Shall be the maws of kites.   [*Ghost vanishes.*]
Lady M.   What, quite unmann'd in folly?
Macb. If I stand here, I saw him.
Lady M.   Fie, for shame!
Macb. Blood hath been shed ere now, i' th'
    olden time,   75
Ere humane statute purg'd the gentle weal;
Ay, and since too, murders have been perform'd
Too terrible for the ear. The [time] has been,
That, when the brains were out, the man would die,
And there an end; but now they rise again.   80
With twenty mortal murders on their crowns,
And push us from our stools. This is more strange
Than such a murder is.
Lady M.   My worthy lord,
Your noble friends do lack you.
Macb.   I do forget.
Do not muse at me, my most worthy friends; 85

I have a strange infirmity, which is nothing
To those that know me. Come, love and health
    to all;
Then I'll sit down. Give me some wine; fill full.

              Re-enter Ghost.

I drink to th' general joy o' th' whole table,
And to our dear friend Banquo, whom we miss;
Would he were here! to all and him we thirst, 91
And all to all.
Lords.   Our duties, and the pledge.
Macb. Avaunt! and quit my sight! let the earth
    hide thee!
Thy bones are marrowless, thy blood is cold;
Thou hast no speculation in those eyes   95
Which thou dost glare with!
Lady M.   Think of this, good peers,
But as a thing of custom; 'tis no other.
Only it spoils the pleasure of the time.
Macb. What man dare, I dare.
Approach thou like the rugged Russian bear, 100
The arm'd rhinoceros, or th' Hyrcan tiger;
Take any shape but that, and my firm nerves
Shall never tremble. Or be alive again,
And dare me to the desert with thy sword;
If trembling I inhabit then, protest me   105
The baby of a girl. Hence, horrible shadow!
Unreal mock'ry, hence!   [*Ghost vanishes.*]
               Why, so; being gone,
I am a man again. Pray you, sit still.
Lady M. You have displac'd the mirth, broke
    the good meeting,
With most admir'd disorder.
Macb.   Can such things be,
And overcome us like a summer's cloud,   111
Without our special wonder? You make me
    strange
Even to the disposition that I owe,
When now I think you can behold such sights,
And keep the natural ruby of your cheeks,   115
When mine is blanch'd with fear.
Ross.   What sights, my lord?
Lady M. I pray you, speak not; he grows worse
    and worse;
Question enrages him. At once, good-night.
Stand not upon the order of your going,   119
But go at once.
Len.   Good-night; and better health
Attend his Majesty!
Lady M.   A kind good-night to all!
                       [*Exeunt Lords.*

---

55. **upon a thought:** in a moment. 57. **offend:** make worse. **extend his passion:** prolong his attack. 60. **proper stuff:** fine business! 63. **flaws:** outbursts. 64. **Impostors to:** (mere) frauds compared with. 66. **Authoriz'd:** vouched for. 73. **Shall ... kites:** had better be the stomachs of hawks (i.e., we should leave our dead unburied to be devoured). 76. **purg'd ... weal:** cleansed the state of violence, making it gentle. 78. **[time] has** (Grant White). *times has* F. *times have* F₂. 81. **mortal murders:** deadly wounds. 84. **lack:** miss. 85. **muse:** wonder. 91. **thirst:** i.e., eagerly drink. 95. **speculation:** comprehending sight. 101. **Hyrcan:** of Hyrcania, near the Caspian Sea. 105. **inhabit:** i.e., continue. Perhaps corrupt. 106. **baby:** doll. 110. **admir'd:** amazing. 111. **like ... cloud:** i.e., suddenly. 112-13. **make ... owe:** make me wonder if I have the courage I supposed.

Macb. It will have blood, they say; blood will
   have blood.
Stones have been known to move and trees to
   speak;
Augures and understood relations have
By maggot-pies and choughs and rooks brought
   forth   125
The secret'st man of blood. What is the night?
   Lady M. Almost at odds with morning, which is
   which.
   Macb. How say'st thou that Macduff denies his
   person
At our great bidding?
   Lady M.   Did you send to him, sir?
   Macb. I hear it by the way; but I will send. 130
There's not a one of them but in his house
I keep a servant fee'd. I will to-morrow,
And betimes I will, to the weird sisters.
More shall they speak; for now I am bent to know,
By the worst means, the worst. For mine own
   good   135
All causes shall give way. I am in blood
Stepp'd in so far that, should I wade no more,
Returning were as tedious as go o'er.
Strange things I have in head, that will to hand,
Which must be acted ere they may be scann'd. 140
   Lady M. You lack the season of all natures, sleep.
   Macb. Come, we'll to sleep. My strange and
   self-abuse
Is the initiate fear that wants hard use;
We are yet but young in deed.   [*Exeunt.*

SCENE V. [*A heath.*]

Thunder. Enter the three WITCHES, *meeting*
HECATE.

   1. Witch. Why, how now, Hecate! you look an-
   gerly.
   Hec. Have I not reason, beldams as you are,
Saucy and overbold? How did you dare
To trade and traffic with Macbeth
In riddles and affairs of death;   5
And I, the mistress of your charms,
The close contriver of all harms,
Was never call'd to bear my part,
Or show the glory of our art?
And, which is worse, all you have done   10
Hath been but for a wayward son,
Spiteful and wrathful, who, as others do,
Loves for his own ends, not for you.
But make amends now; get you gone,

And at the pit of Acheron   15
Meet me i' th' morning; thither he
Will come to know his destiny.
Your vessels and your spells provide,
Your charms and everything beside.
I am for th' air; this night I'll spend   20
Unto a dismal and a fatal end;
Great business must be wrought ere noon.
Upon the corner of the moon
There hangs a vap'rous drop profound;
I'll catch it ere it come to ground;   25
And that, distill'd by magic sleights,
Shall raise such artificial sprites
As by the strength of their illusion
Shall draw him on to his confusion.
He shall spurn fate, scorn death, and bear   30
His hopes 'bove wisdom, grace, and fear;
And, you all know, security
Is mortals' chiefest enemy.   [*Music, and a song.*
Hark! I am call'd; my little spirit, see,
Sits in a foggy cloud, and stays for me.   [*Exit.*]
   [*Sing within:* "Come away, come away,"
   etc.
   1. Witch. Come, let's make haste; she'll soon be
   back again.   [*Exeunt.* 36

SCENE VI. [*Forres. The palace.*]

Enter LENNOX *and another* LORD.

   Len. My former speeches have but hit your
   thoughts,
Which can interpret farther; only, I say,
Things have been strangely borne. The gracious
   Duncan
Was pitied of Macbeth; marry, he was dead.
And the right-valiant Banquo walk'd too late;   5
Whom, you may say, if 't please you, Fleance
   kill'd,
For Fleance fled; men must not walk too late.
Who cannot want the thought how monstrous
It was for Malcolm and for Donalbain
To kill their gracious father? Damned fact!   10
How it did grieve Macbeth! Did he not straight
In pious rage the two delinquents tear,
That were the slaves of drink and thralls of
   sleep?
Was not that nobly done? Ay, and wisely too;
For 'twould have anger'd any heart alive   15
To hear the men deny 't. So that, I say,
He has borne all things well; and I do think
That, had he Duncan's sons under his key —

---

124. **Augures...relations**: omens and significances rightly comprehended. 125. **By**: by means of. **maggot-pies**:
magpies. **choughs**: jackdaws. 136. **causes**: considerations. 141. **season**: preservative. 142. **strange and self-abuse**:
strange self-delusion. 143. **initiate...use**: fear felt by the novice unhardened (in crime).
  Sc. v, 2. **beldams**: hags. 7. **close**: secret. 24. **profound**: having deep potency. 29. **confusion**: ruin. 32. **security**:
over-confidence.
  Sc. vi, 3. **borne**: managed. 10. **fact**: crime.

As, an't please Heaven, he shall not — they should find
What 'twere to kill a father; so should Fleance.   20
But, peace! for from broad words, and 'cause he fail'd
His presence at the tyrant's feast, I hear
Macduff lives in disgrace. Sir, can you tell
Where he bestows himself?
    Lord.   The son of Duncan,
From whom this tyrant holds the due of birth,   25
Lives in the English court, and is receiv'd
Of the most pious Edward with such grace
That the malevolence of Fortune nothing
Takes from his high respect. Thither Macduff
Is gone to pray the holy king, upon his aid   30
To wake Northumberland and warlike Siward;
That by the help of these — with Him above
To ratify the work — we may again
Give to our tables meat, sleep to our nights,
Free from our feasts and banquets bloody knives, 35
Do faithful homage and receive free honours;
All which we pine for now: and this report
Hath so exasperate [the] King that he
Prepares for some attempt of war.
    Len.   Sent he to Macduff?
    Lord. He did; and with an absolute "Sir, not
    I,"   40
The cloudy messenger turns me his back,
And hums, as who should say, "You'll rue the time
That clogs me with this answer."
    Len.   And that well might
Advise him to a caution, t' hold what distance
His wisdom can provide. Some holy angel   45
Fly to the court of England and unfold
His message ere he come, that a swift blessing
May soon return to this our suffering country
Under a hand accurs'd!
    Lord.   I'll send my prayers with him.
                                     [*Exeunt.*

ACT IV

SCENE I. [*A cavern. In the middle, a boiling
              cauldron.*]

    Thunder. Enter the three WITCHES.

    1. Witch. Thrice the brinded cat hath mew'd.
    2. Witch. Thrice, and once the hedge-pig whin'd.
    3. Witch. Harpier cries; 'tis time, 'tis time.
    1. Witch. Round about the cauldron go;
In the poison'd entrails throw.   5
Toad, that under cold stone
Days and nights has thirty-one

Swelt'red venom sleeping got,
Boil thou first i' th' charmed pot.
    All. Double, double, toil and trouble;   10
Fire burn and cauldron bubble.
    2. Witch. Fillet of a fenny snake,
In the cauldron boil and bake;
Eye of newt and toe of frog,
Wool of bat and tongue of dog,   15
Adder's fork and blind-worm's sting,
Lizard's leg and howlet's wing,
For a charm of pow'rful trouble,
Like a hell-broth boil and bubble.
    All. Double, double, toil and trouble;   20
Fire burn and cauldron bubble.
    3. Witch. Scale of dragon, tooth of wolf,
Witches' mummy, maw and gulf
Of the ravin'd salt-sea shark,
Root of hemlock digg'd i' th' dark,   25
Liver of blaspheming Jew,
Gall of goat, and slips of yew
Sliver'd in the moon's eclipse,
Nose of Turk and Tartar's lips,
Finger of birth-strangled babe   30
Ditch-deliver'd by a drab,
Make the gruel thick and slab.
Add thereto a tiger's chaudron,
For th' ingredients of our cauldron.
    All. Double, double, toil and trouble;   35
Fire burn and cauldron bubble.
    2. Witch. Cool it with a baboon's blood,
Then the charm is firm and good.

    Enter HECATE *to the other three Witches.*

    Hec. O, well done! I commend your pains;
And every one shall share i' th' gains.   40
And now about the cauldron sing,
Like elves and fairies in a ring,
Enchanting all that you put in.
         [*Music and a song:* "Black spirits," etc.
                            [*Hecate retires.*]
    2. [*Witch*]. By the pricking of my thumbs,
Something wicked this way comes.   45
        Open, locks,
        Whoever knocks!

    Enter MACBETH.

    Macb. How now, you secret, black, and midnight
    hags!
What is't you do?
    All.   A deed without a name.
    Macb. I conjure you by that which you profess, 50
Howe'er you come to know it, answer me!
Though you untie the winds and let them fight

---

25. **holds**: withholds. 27. **Edward**: Edward the Confessor. 30. **upon**: for. 38. [**the**] (Hanmer). *their* F. 41. **cloudy**: sullen.
Act IV, sc. i, 8. Swelt'red: in sweaty drops. 12. **Fillet**: slice. **fenny**: swamp-dwelling. 16. **fork**: forked tongue. 17.
howlet's: owl's. 23. **mummy**: medicinal substance made from a mummy. **gulf**: gullet. 32. **slab**: sticky. 33. **chaudron**:
entrails.

Against the churches; though the yesty waves
Confound and swallow navigation up;
Though bladed corn be lodg'd and trees blown
   down;   55
Though castles topple on their warders' heads;
Though palaces and pyramids do slope
Their heads to their foundations; though the treas-
   ure
Of nature's [germens] tumble all together,
Even till destruction sicken; answer me   60
To what I ask you.
  1. Witch.   Speak.
  2. Witch.   Demand.
  3. Witch.   We'll answer.
  1. Witch. Say, if th' hadst rather hear it from our
    mouths,
Or from our masters'?
  Macb.   Call 'em; let me see 'em.
  1. Witch. Pour in sow's blood, that hath eaten
Her nine farrow; grease that's sweaten   65
From the murderer's gibbet throw
Into the flame.
  All.   Come, high or low;
Thyself and office deftly show!

   Thunder. First APPARITION, *an armed Head.*
  Macb. Tell me, thou unknown power, —
  1. Witch.   He knows thy thought.
Hear his speech, but say thou nought.   70
  1. App. Macbeth! Macbeth! Macbeth! beware
    Macduff;
Beware the thane of Fife. Dismiss me. Enough.
                    [Descends.
  Macb. Whate'er thou art, for thy good caution,
    thanks;
Thou hast harp'd my fear aright. But one word
    more, —
  1. Witch. He will not be commanded. Here's
    another,   75
More potent than the first.

   Thunder. Second APPARITION, *a bloody Child.*
  2. App. Macbeth! Macbeth! Macbeth!
  Macb. Had I three ears, I'd hear thee.
  2. App. Be bloody, bold, and resolute; laugh to
    scorn
The pow'r of man; for none of woman born   80
Shall harm Macbeth.   *[Descends.*
  Macb. Then live, Macduff: what need I fear of
    thee?
But yet I'll make assurance double sure

And take a bond of fate. Thou shalt not live;
That I may tell pale-hearted fear it lies,   85
And sleep in spite of thunder.

   Thunder. Third APPARITION, *a Child crowned,*
        with a tree in his hand.
                  What is this
That rises like the issue of a king,
And wears upon his baby-brow the round
And top of sovereignty?
  All.   Listen, but speak not to't.
  3. App. Be lion-mettled, proud, and take no
    care   90
Who chafes, who frets, or where conspirers are.
Macbeth shall never vanquish'd be until
Great Birnam wood to high Dunsinane hill
Shall come against him.   *[Descends.*
  Macb.   That will never be.
Who can impress the forest, bid the tree   95
Unfix his earth-bound root? Sweet bodements!
    good!
[Rebellion's head], rise never till the wood
Of Birnam rise, and our high-plac'd Macbeth
Shall live the lease of nature, pay his breath
To time and mortal custom. Yet my heart   100
Throbs to know one thing: tell me, if your art
Can tell so much, shall Banquo's issue ever
Reign in this kingdom?
  All.   Seek to know no more.
  Macb. I will be satisfied! Deny me this,
And an eternal curse fall on you! Let me know. 105
Why sinks that cauldron? And what noise is this?
                    [Hautboys.
  1. Witch. Show!
  2. Witch. Show!
  3. Witch. Show!
  All. Show his eyes, and grieve his heart;   110
Come like shadows, so depart!

  A show of Eight Kings, *[the last] with a glass in his*
      hand; [Banquo's Ghost following].
  Macb. Thou art too like the spirit of Banquo;
    down!
Thy crown does sear mine eye-balls. And thy hair,
Thou other gold-bound brow, is like the first.
A third is like the former. Filthy hags!   115
Why do you show me this? A fourth! Start, eyes!
What, will the line stretch out to th' crack of doom?
Another yet! A seventh! I'll see no more.
And yet the eighth appears, who bears a glass
Which shows me many more; and some I see   120

53. yesty: foamy. 55. lodg'd: beaten down. 59. [germens] (Camb. edd.): seeds. *Germaine* F. 65. farrow: litter. 69. S.D. armed Head. Perhaps signifying Macduff's rebellion. 77. S.D. a bloody Child. Signifying Macduff (see V.viii.15–16). 86. S.D. a Child crowned. Signifying Malcolm. tree. Foreshadowing the action of the soldiers of Malcolm in V.iv.4 ff. 89. top: crown. 95. impress: force into service. 96. bodements: prophecies. 97. [Rebellion's head] (Theobald conj.). *Rebellious dead* F. 112. S.D. F reads "A shew of eight Kings, and Banquo last, with a glasse in his hand." glass: mirror.

That twofold balls and treble sceptres carry.
Horrible sight! Now, I see, 'tis true;
For the blood-bolter'd Banquo smiles upon me,
And points at them for his.   [*Apparitions vanish.*]
    What, is this so?
  1. [*Witch*].   Ay, sir, all this is so; but why   125
Stands Macbeth thus amazedly?
Come, sisters, cheer we up his sprites,
And show the best of our delights.
I'll charm the air to give a sound,
While you perform your antic round;   130
That this great king may kindly say
Our duties did his welcome pay.
     [*Music.   The Witches dance, and vanish*
        [*with Hecate*].
  Macb.   Where are they?   Gone?   Let this per-
    nicious hour
Stand aye accursed in the calendar!   134
Come in, without there!

         Enter LENNOX.

  Len.   What's your Grace's will?
  Macb. Saw you the weird sisters?
  Len.   No, my lord.
  Macb. Came they not by you?
  Len.   No, indeed, my lord.
  Macb. Infected be the air whereon they ride,
And damn'd all those that trust them!   I did
    hear
The galloping of horse; who was 't came by?   140
  Len. 'Tis two or three, my lord, that bring you
    word
Macduff is fled to England.
  Macb.   Fled to England!
  Len. Ay, my good lord.
  Macb. [*Aside.*] Time, thou anticipat'st my dread
    exploits:
The flighty purpose never is o'ertook   145
Unless the deed go with it.   From this moment
The very firstlings of my heart shall be
The firstlings of my hand.   And even now,
To crown my thoughts with acts, be it thought and
    done.
The castle of Macduff I will surprise;   150
Seize upon Fife; give to the edge o' th' sword
His wife, his babes, and all unfortunate souls
That trace him in his line.   No boasting like a fool;
This deed I'll do before this purpose cool.
But no more sights! — Where are these gentlemen?
Come, bring me where they are.   [*Exeunt.*   156

SCENE II.   [*Fife, Macduff's castle.*]

  Enter LADY [MACDUFF], *her* SON, *and* ROSS.

  L. Macd.   What had he done, to make him fly
    the land?
  Ross.   You must have patience, madam.
  L. Macd.   He had none;
His flight was madness.   When our actions do not,
Our fears do make us traitors.
  Ross.   You know not
Whether it was his wisdom or his fear.   5
  L. Macd.   Wisdom! to leave his wife, to leave his
    babes,
His mansion and his titles, in a place
From whence himself does fly?   He loves us not,
He wants the natural touch; for the poor wren,
The most diminutive of birds, will fight,   10
Her young ones in her nest, against the owl.
All is the fear and nothing is the love;
As little is the wisdom, where the flight
So runs against all reason.
  Ross.   My dearest coz,
I pray you school yourself; but for your husband,
He is noble, wise, judicious, and best knows   16
The fits o' th' season.   I dare not speak much fur-
    ther;
But cruel are the times when we are traitors
And do not know ourselves; when we hold rumour
From what we fear, yet know not what we fear, 20
But float upon a wild and violent sea
Each way and move.   I take my leave of you;
Shall not be long but I'll be here again.
Things at the worst will cease, or else climb up-
    ward
To what they were before.   My pretty cousin,   25
Blessing upon you!
  L. Macd.   Father'd he is, and yet he's fatherless.
  Ross.   I am so much a fool, should I stay longer,
It would be my disgrace and your discomfort.
I take my leave at once.   [*Exit.*
  L. Macd.   Sirrah, your father's dead;
And what will you do now?   How will you live?   31
  Son.   As birds do, mother.
  L. Macd.   What, with worms and flies?
  Son.   With what I get, I mean; and so do they.
  L. Macd.   Poor bird! thou'dst never fear the net
    nor lime,
The pitfall nor the gin.   35
  Son.   Why should I, mother?   Poor birds they
    are not set for.
My father is not dead, for all your saying.

---

121. **twofold ... sceptres.** Referring respectively to England and Scotland, and to King James's taking the title "King of Great Britain, France and Ireland." Banquo was the mythical ancestor of James.   123. **blood-bolter'd**: with hair matted with blood.   126. **amazedly**: as in a trance.   130. **antic round**: fantastic circular dance.   145. **flighty**: fleeting. 147. **firstlings**: first-born.   153. **trace**: follow.
Sc. ii, 1. *L. Macd.* The speeches of Lady Macduff are headed *Wife* in F.   7. **titles**: title deeds, hence estates.   17. **fits ... season**: emergencies of the time.   19. **hold**: judge.   20. **From**: because of.   22. **move.** Perhaps corrupt. Camb. edd. read *none.*   29. **It ... discomfort**: i.e., I should weep.   35. **gin**: snare.

L. Macd. Yes, he is dead.　How wilt thou do for
　a father?
Son. Nay, how will you do for a husband?
L. Macd. Why, I can buy me twenty at any mar-
　ket.　　　　　　　　　　　　　　　　　40
Son. Then you'll buy 'em to sell again.
L. Macd. Thou speak'st with all thy wit; and yet,
　i' faith,
With wit enough for thee.
Son. Was my father a traitor, mother?
L. Macd. Ay, that he was.　　　　　　　45
Son. What is a traitor?
L. Macd. Why, one that swears and lies.
Son. And be all traitors that do so?
L. Macd. Every one that does so is a traitor, and
must be hang'd.　　　　　　　　　　　50
Son. And must they all be hang'd that swear and
lie?
L. Macd. Every one.
Son. Who must hang them?
L. Macd. Why, the honest men.　　　　55
Son. Then the liars and swearers are fools; for
there are liars and swearers enow to beat the honest
men and hang up them.
L. Macd. Now, God help thee, poor monkey!
But how wilt thou do for a father!　　　　60
Son. If he were dead, you'd weep for him; if you
would not, it were a good sign that I should quickly
have a new father.
L. Macd. Poor prattler, how thou talk'st!

Enter a MESSENGER.

Mess. Bless you, fair dame!　I am not to you
　known.　　　　　　　　　　　　　　65
Though in your state of honour I am perfect.
I doubt some danger does approach you nearly.
If you will take a homely man's advice,
Be not found here; hence, with your little
　ones.
To fright you thus, methinks, I am too savage;　70
To do worse to you were fell cruelty,
Which is too nigh your person.　Heaven preserve
　you!
I dare abide no longer.　　　　　　　[*Exit.*
　L. Macd.　　　　　　Whither should I fly?
I have done no harm.　But I remember now
I am in this earthly world, where to do harm　75
Is often laudable, to do good sometime
Accounted dangerous folly.　Why then, alas,
Do I put up that womanly defence,
To say I have done no harm?

Enter MURDERERS.

　　　　　　　What are these faces?
[*1.*] *Mur.* Where is your husband?　　　80
L. Macd. I hope, in no place so unsanctified
Where such as thou mayst find him.
[*1.*] *Mur.*　　　　　　He's a traitor.
Son. Thou liest, thou shag-ear'd villain!
[*1.*] *Mur.*　　　　　　What, you egg!
　　　　　　　[*Stabbing him.*]
Young fry of treachery!
Son.　　　　　　He has kill'd me, mother:
Run away, I pray you!　　　　　[*Dies.*]　85
　　[*Exit* [*Lady Macduff*] *crying* "Murder!"
　　[*Exeunt Murderers, following her.*]

SCENE III.　[*England.　Before the King's
　　palace.*]

Enter MALCOLM *and* MACDUFF.

Mal. Let us seek out some desolate shade, and
　there
Weep our sad bosoms empty.
　Macd.　　　　　　Let us rather
Hold fast the mortal sword, and like good men
Bestride our down-fall'n birthdom.　Each new
　morn
New widows howl, new orphans cry, new sorrows　5
Strike heaven on the face, that it resounds
As if it felt with Scotland, and yell'd out
Like syllable of dolour.
　Mal.　　　　　What I believe I'll wail,
What know believe, and what I can redress,
As I shall find the time to friend, I will.　　10
What you have spoke, it may be so perchance.
This tyrant, whose sole name blisters our tongues,
Was once thought honest; you have lov'd him well.
He hath not touch'd you yet.　I am young; but
　something
You may [deserve] of him through me, and wis-
　dom　　　　　　　　　　　　　15
To offer up a weak poor innocent lamb
T' appease an angry god.
　Macd. I am not treacherous.
　Mal.　　　　　　But Macbeth is.
A good and virtuous nature may recoil
In an imperial charge.　But I shall crave your par-
　don;　　　　　　　　　　　　　20
That which you are my thoughts cannot transpose.
Angels are bright still, though the brightest fell.
Though all things foul would wear the brows of
　grace,
Yet grace must still look so.

47. **swears and lies:** takes an oath and breaks it.　66. **in... perfect:** I know your rank.　67. **doubt:** fear.　68. **homely:**
plain.　71. **fell:** fierce.　83. **shag-ear'd:** with ears like a shaggy dog's.
　Sc. iii, 8. **Like... dolour:** similar cry of pain.　10. **to friend:** favorable.　12. **sole:** mere.　15. **[deserve]** (Theobald):
win.　*discerne* F.　**wisdom:** it were wise.　19-20. **recoil... charge:** give way under a king's command.　21. **transpose:**
change.

Macd.   I have lost my hopes.
Mal. Perchance even there where I did find my
   doubts.   25
Why in that rawness left you wife and child,
Those precious motives, those strong knots of love,
Without leave-taking? I pray you,
Let not my jealousies be your dishonours,   29
But mine own safeties. You may be rightly just,
Whatever I shall think.
   Macd.   Bleed, bleed, poor country!
Great tyranny! lay thou thy basis sure,
For goodness dare not check thee; wear thou thy
   wrongs;
The title is [affeer'd]! Fare thee well, lord:
I would not be the villain that thou think'st   35
For the whole space that's in the tyrant's grasp,
And the rich East to boot.
   Mal.   Be not offended;
I speak not as in absolute fear of you.
I think our country sinks beneath the yoke;
It weeps, it bleeds; and each new day a gash   40
Is added to her wounds. I think withal
There would be hands uplifted in my right;
And here from gracious England have I offer
Of goodly thousands. But, for all this,
When I shall tread upon the tyrant's head,   45
Or wear it on my sword, yet my poor country
Shall have more vices than it had before,
More suffer and more sundry ways than ever,
By him that shall succeed.
   Macd.   What should he be?
   Mal. It is myself I mean; in whom I know   50
All the particulars of vice so grafted
That, when they shall be open'd, black Macbeth
Will seem as pure as snow, and the poor state
Esteem him as a lamb, being compar'd
With my confineless harms.
   Macd.   Not in the legions 55
Of horrid hell can come a devil more damn'd
In evils to top Macbeth.
   Mal.   I grant him bloody,
Luxurious, avaricious, false, deceitful,
Sudden, malicious, smacking of every sin
That has a name; but there's no bottom, none,   60
In my voluptuousness. Your wives, your daughters,
Your matrons, and your maids could not fill up
The cistern of my lust, and my desire
All continent impediments would o'erbear
That did oppose my will. Better Macbeth   65
Than such an one to reign.
   Macd.   Boundless intemperance

In nature is a tyranny; it hath been
Th' untimely emptying of the happy throne
And fall of many kings. But fear not yet
To take upon you what is yours. You may   70
Convey your pleasures in a spacious plenty,
And yet seem cold; the time you may so hoodwink.
We have willing dames enough; there cannot be
That vulture in you to devour so many
As will to greatness dedicate themselves,   75
Finding it so inclin'd.
   Mal.   With this there grows
In my most ill-compos'd affection such
A stanchless avarice that, were I King,
I should cut off the nobles for their lands,
Desire his jewels and this other's house;   80
And my more-having would be as a sauce
To make me hunger more, that I should forge
Quarrels unjust against the good and loyal,
Destroying them for wealth.
   Macd.   This avarice
Sticks deeper, grows with more pernicious root 85
Than summer-seeming lust, and it hath been
The sword of our slain kings. Yet do not fear;
Scotland hath foisons to fill up your will,
Of your mere own. All these are portable,
With other graces weigh'd.   90
   Mal. But I have none. The king-becoming
   graces,
As justice, verity, temp'rance, stableness,
Bounty, perseverance, mercy, lowliness,
Devotion, patience, courage, fortitude,
I have no relish of them, but abound   95
In the division of each several crime,
Acting it many ways. Nay, had I power, I should
Pour the sweet milk of concord into hell,
Uproar the universal peace, confound
All unity on earth.
   Macd.   O Scotland, Scotland!   100
   Mal. If such an one be fit to govern, speak.
I am as I have spoken.
   Macd.   Fit to govern!
No, not to live. O nation miserable,
With an untitled tyrant bloody-scept'red,
When shalt thou see thy wholesome days again,
Since that the truest issue of thy throne   106
By his own interdiction stands accurs'd
And does blaspheme his breed? Thy royal father
Was a most sainted king; the queen that bore thee,
Oftener upon her knees than on her feet,   110
Died every day she liv'd. Fare thee well!
These evils thou repeat'st upon thyself

---

24. **hopes:** i.e., of Malcolm's cooperation. 25. **doubts:** i.e., of Macduff's honor. 26. **rawness:** haste, unpreparedness.
28. **jealousies:** suspicions. 33. **wrongs:** things wrongly gained. 34. **[affeer'd]** (Hanmer): confirmed (legal term). *affear'd*
F. 57. **top:** surpass. 58. **Luxurious:** lecherous. 59. **Sudden:** violent. 64. **continent:** restraining. 69. **yet:** nevertheless.
71. **Convey:** manage secretly. 72. **cold:** chaste. 77. **affection:** character. 78. **stanchless:** insatiable. 86. **summer-
seeming:** typical only of early age. 88. **foisons:** abundance. 89. **portable:** bearable. 90. **weigh'd:** balanced. 95. **relish:**
trace. 99. **Uproar:** make tumultuous. 108. **blaspheme:** slander. 111. **Died:** i.e., to the world.

Hath banish'd me from Scotland. O my breast,
Thy hope ends here!
  Mal.   Macduff, this noble passion,
Child of integrity, hath from my soul   115
Wip'd the black scruples, reconcil'd my thoughts
To thy good truth and honour. Devilish Macbeth
By many of these trains hath sought to win me
Into his power, and modest wisdom plucks me
From over-credulous haste. But God above 120
Deal between thee and me! for even now
I put myself to thy direction, and
Unspeak mine own detraction; here abjure
The taints and blames I laid upon myself,
For strangers to my nature. I am yet   125
Unknown to woman, never was forsworn,
Scarcely have coveted what was mine own,
At no time broke my faith, would not betray
The devil to his fellow, and delight
No less in truth than life; my first false speaking 130
Was this upon myself. What I am truly,
Is thine and my poor country's to command;
Whither indeed, before thy here-approach,
Old Siward, with ten thousand warlike men,
Already at a point, was setting forth.   135
Now we'll together; and the chance of goodness
Be like our warranted quarrel! Why are you
    silent?
  Macd. Such welcome and unwelcome things at
    once
'Tis hard to reconcile.

Enter a DOCTOR.

  Mal. Well; more anon. — Comes the King forth,
  I pray you?   140
  Doct. Ay, sir; there are a crew of wretched souls
That stay his cure. Their malady convinces
The great assay of art; but at his touch —
Such sanctity hath Heaven given his hand —
They presently amend.
  Mal.   I thank you, doctor. 145
                       [Exit Doctor.
  Macd. What's the disease he means?
  Mal.   'Tis call'd the evil:
A most miraculous work in this good king;
Which often, since my here-remain in England,
I have seen him do. How he solicits Heaven,
Himself best knows; but strangely-visited people,
All swoll'n and ulcerous, pitiful to the eye, 151
The mere despair of surgery, he cures,
Hanging a golden stamp about their necks,
Put on with holy prayers; and 'tis spoken,
To the succeeding royalty he leaves   155

The healing benediction. With this strange virtue,
He hath a heavenly gift of prophecy,
And sundry blessings hang about his throne
That speak him full of grace.

Enter ROSS.

  Macd.   See, who comes here?
  Mal. My countryman; but yet I know him not.
  Macd. My ever-gentle cousin, welcome hither. 161
  Mal. I know him now. Good God, betimes re-
    move
The means that makes us strangers!
  Ross.   Sir, amen.
  Macd. Stand Scotland where it did?
  Ross.   Alas, poor country!
Almost afraid to know itself. It cannot   165
Be call'd our mother, but our grave; where nothing,
But who knows nothing, is once seen to smile;
Where sighs and groans and shrieks that rend the
    air
Are made, not mark'd; where violent sorrow seems
A modern ecstasy. The dead man's knell 170
Is there scarce ask'd for who; and good men's lives
Expire before the flowers in their caps,
Dying or ere they sicken.
  Macd.   O, relation
Too nice, and yet too true!
  Mal.   What's the newest grief?
  Ross. That of an hour's age doth hiss the speaker;
Each minute teems a new one.
  Macd.   How does my wife? 176
  Ross. Why, well.
  Macd.   And all my children?
  Ross.   Well too.
  Macd. The tyrant has not batter'd at their
    peace?
  Ross. No; they were well at peace when I did
    leave 'em.
  Macd. Be not a niggard of your speech; how
    goes 't?   180
  Ross. When I came hither to transport the tid-
    ings,
Which I have heavily borne, there ran a rumour
Of many worthy fellows that were out;
Which was to my belief witness'd the rather,
For that I saw the tyrant's power afoot. 185
Now is the time of help; your eye in Scotland
Would create soldiers, make our women fight,
To doff their dire distresses.
  Mal.   Be 't their comfort
We're coming thither. Gracious England hath
Lent us good Siward and ten thousand men; 190

---

118. **trains:** devices. 135. **at a point:** fully prepared. 136. **goodness:** success. 137. **like...quarrel:** as good as our just cause. 142. **convinces:** defeats. 143. **great...art:** best medical skill. 147. **evil:** scrofula ("the king's evil," supposedly healed by royal touch). 150. **strangely-visited:** strangely afflicted. 152. **mere:** utter. 153. **stamp:** coin. 156. **virtue:** power. 160. **know:** recognize. 170. **modern ecstasy:** commonplace emotion. 174. **nice:** precise. 175. **hiss... speaker:** cause the speaker to be hissed (for telling old stuff). 176. **teems:** brings forth. 182. **heavily:** sorrowfully. 183. **out:** in arms.

An older and a better soldier none
That Christendom gives out.
　　Ross.　　　　　　　Would I could answer
This comfort with the like! But I have words
That would be howl'd out in the desert air,
Where hearing should not latch them.
　　Macd.　　　　　　What concern they?
The general cause? Or is it a fee-grief　　196
Due to some single breast?
　　Ross.　　　　　　No mind that's honest
But in it shares some woe, though the main part
Pertains to you alone.
　　Macd.　　　　　If it be mine,
Keep it not from me, quickly let me have it.　200
　　Ross. Let not your ears despise my tongue for
　　ever,
Which shall possess them with the heaviest sound
That ever yet they heard.
　　Macd.　　　　　Hum! I guess at it.
　　Ross. Your castle is surpris'd; your wife and
　　babes
Savagely slaughter'd. To relate the manner,　205
Were, on the quarry of these murder'd deer,
To add the death of you.
　　Mal.　　　　　Merciful heaven!
What, man! ne'er pull your hat upon your brows;
Give sorrow words. The grief that does not
　speak
Whispers the o'er-fraught heart and bids it break.
　　Macd. My children too?
　　Ross.　　　　Wife, children, servants, all　211
That could be found.
　　Macd.　　　　And I must be from thence!
My wife kill'd too?
　　Ross.　　　　I have said.
　　Mal.　　　　　Be comforted.
Let's make us med'cines of our great revenge
To cure this deadly grief.　　　　　　215
　　Macd. He has no children. — All my pretty
　　ones?
Did you say all? O hell-kite! All?
What, all my pretty chickens and their dam
At one fell swoop?
　　Mal. Dispute it like a man.
　　Macd.　　　　　I shall do so;　220
But I must also feel it as a man.
I cannot but remember such things were,
That were most precious to me. Did heaven look
　on,
And would not take their part? Sinful Macduff,
They were all struck for thee! naught that I am,　225
Not for their own demerits, but for mine,

Fell slaughter on their souls. Heaven rest them
　now!
　　Mal. Be this the whetstone of your sword; let
　grief
Convert to anger; blunt not the heart, enrage it.
　　Macd. O, I could play the woman with mine
　eyes　　　　　　　　　　　230
And braggart with my tongue! But, gentle heav-
　ens,
Cut short all intermission. Front to front
Bring thou this fiend of Scotland and myself;
Within my sword's length set him; if he scape,
Heaven forgive him too!
　　Mal.　　　　This [tune] goes manly.　235
Come, go we to the King; our power is ready;
Our lack is nothing but our leave. Macbeth
Is ripe for shaking, and the powers above
Put on their instruments. Receive what cheer you
　may;
The night is long that never finds the day.　240
　　　　　　　　　　　　　　[*Exeunt.*

ACT V

Scene I. [*Dunsinane. Ante-room in the castle.*]

Enter a Doctor *of Physic and a* Waiting Gen-
　　　　　tlewoman.

　Doct. I have two nights watch'd with you, but
can perceive no truth in your report. When was it
she last walk'd?　　　　　　　　　3
　Gent. Since his Majesty went into the field, I
have seen her rise from her bed, throw her night-
gown upon her, unlock her closet, take forth paper,
fold it, write upon 't, read it, afterwards seal it, and
again return to bed; yet all this while in a most
fast sleep.　　　　　　　　　9
　Doct. A great perturbation in nature, to receive
at once the benefit of sleep and do the effects of
watching! In this slumb'ry agitation, besides her
walking and other actual performances, what, at
any time, have you heard her say?　　15
　Gent. That, sir, which I will not report after her.
　Doct. You may to me: and 'tis most meet you
should.
　Gent. Neither to you nor any one; having no
witness to confirm my speech.　　　21

Enter Lady [Macbeth], *with a taper.*

Lo, you, here she comes! This is her very guise;
and, upon my life, fast asleep. Observe her; stand
close.

---

195. **latch:** catch. 196. **fee-grief:** private woe. 206. **quarry:** slaughtered heap. 210. **o'er-fraught:** over-burdened.
220. **Dispute:** fight. 225. **naught:** wicked. 235. **[tune]** (Rowe). *time* F. 237. **Our...leave:** we need only to take
leave (of King Edward). 239. **Put...instruments:** urge on their agents (us).
　Act V, sc. i, 11–12. **do...watching:** act as if awake. 12. **agitation:** activity. 22. **her very guise:** exactly what she has
been doing. 24. **close:** out of sight.

Doct. How came she by that light?   25

Gent. Why, it stood by her. She has light by her continually: 'tis her command.

Doct. You see her eyes are open.

Gent. Ay, but their sense are shut.

Doct. What is it she does now? Look how she rubs her hands.   31

Gent. It is an accustom'd action with her, to seem thus washing her hands. I have known her continue in this a quarter of an hour.

Lady M. Yet here's a spot.   35

Doct. Hark! she speaks. I will set down what comes from her, to satisfy my remembrance the more strongly.   38

Lady M. Out, damned spot! out, I say! — One: two: why, then 'tis time to do't. — Hell is murky! — Fie, my lord, fie! a soldier, and afeard? What need we fear who knows it, when none can call our pow'r to account? — Yet who would have thought the old man to have had so much blood in him?   45

Doct. Do you mark that?

Lady M. The thane of Fife had a wife; where is she now? — What, will these hands ne'er be clean? — No more o' that, my lord, no more o' that; you mar all with this starting.   50

Doct. Go to, go to; you have known what you should not.

Gent. She has spoke what she should not, I am sure of that; Heaven knows what she has known. 55

Lady M. Here's the smell of the blood still; all the perfumes of Arabia will not sweeten this little hand. Oh, oh, oh!

Doct. What a sigh is there! The heart is sorely charg'd.   60

Gent. I would not have such a heart in my bosom for the dignity of the whole body.

Doct. Well, well, well, —

Gent. Pray God it be, sir.   64

Doct. This disease is beyond my practice; yet I have known those which have walk'd in their sleep who have died holily in their beds.

Lady M. Wash your hands, put on your night-gown; look not so pale. — I tell you yet again, Banquo's buried; he cannot come out on 's grave.   71

Doct. Even so?

Lady M. To bed, to bed! there's knocking at the gate. Come, come, come, come, give me your hand. What's done cannot be undone. — To bed, to bed, to bed!   [*Exit.* 76

Doct. Will she go now to bed?

Gent. Directly.

Doct. Foul whisp'rings are abroad; unnatural deeds

Do breed unnatural troubles; infected minds   80
To their deaf pillows will discharge their secrets.
More needs she the divine than the physician.
God, God, forgive us all! Look after her;
Remove from her the means of all annoyance,
And still keep eyes upon her. So, good-night!   85
My mind she has mated, and amaz'd my sight.
I think, but dare not speak.

Gent.   Good-night, good doctor.

                                   [*Exeunt.*

Scene II. [*The country near Dunsinane.*]

Drum and colours. Enter Menteith, Caithness, Angus, Lennox, *and* Soldiers.

Ment. The English pow'r is near, led on by Malcolm,
His uncle Siward, and the good Macduff.
Revenges burn in them; for their dear causes
Would to the bleeding and the grim alarm
Excite the mortified man.

Ang.   Near Birnam wood   5
Shall we well meet them; that way are they coming.

Caith. Who knows if Donalbain be with his brother?

Len. For certain, sir, he is not; I have a file
Of all the gentry. There is Siward's son,
And many unrough youths that even now   10
Protest their first of manhood.

Ment.   What does the tyrant?

Caith. Great Dunsinane he strongly fortifies.
Some say he's mad, others that lesser hate him
Do call it valiant fury; but, for certain,
He cannot buckle his distemper'd cause   15
Within the belt of rule.

Ang.   Now does he feel
His secret murders sticking on his hands;
Now minutely revolts upbraid his faith-breach;
Those he commands move only in command,
Nothing in love. Now does he feel his title   20
Hang loose about him, like a giant's robe
Upon a dwarfish thief.

Ment.   Who then shall blame
His pester'd senses to recoil and start,
When all that is within him does condemn
Itself for being there?

Caith.   Well, march we on   25
To give obedience where 'tis truly ow'd.
Meet we the med'cine of the sickly weal,
And with him pour we in our country's purge
Each drop of us.

Len.   Or so much as it needs

---

37. **satisfy:** assure.   60. **charg'd:** burdened.   84. **annoyance:** self-harm.   86. **mated:** bewildered.
Sc. ii, 3. **dear:** deeply felt.   4. **bleeding ... alarm:** grim and bloody battle.   5. **mortified:** weakened, sickly.   6. **well:** probably.   10. **unrough:** beardless.   11. **Protest:** assert.   15–16. **buckle ... rule:** uphold his evil cause by controlled measures.   18. **minutely:** every minute.   27. **med'cine:** i.e., Malcolm.   **weal:** state.

To dew the sovereign flower and drown the weeds.
Make we our march towards Birnam.   31
                    [*Exeunt, marching.*

SCENE III. [*Dunsinane. A room in the castle.*]

Enter MACBETH, DOCTOR, *and* Attendants.

Macb. Bring me no more reports; let them fly all;
Till Birnam wood remove to Dunsinane
I cannot taint with fear. What's the boy Malcolm?
Was he not born of woman? The spirits that know
All mortal consequences have pronounc'd me thus:
"Fear not, Macbeth; no man that's born of wo-
          man   6
Shall e'er have power upon thee." Then fly, false
          thanes,
And mingle with the English epicures!
The mind I sway by and the heart I bear
Shall never sag with doubt nor shake with fear. 10

Enter a SERVANT.

The devil damn thee black, thou cream-fac'd loon!
Where got'st thou that goose look?
Serv. There is ten thousand —
Macb.   Geese, villain?
Serv.   Soldiers, sir.
Macb. Go prick thy face, and over-red thy fear,
Thou lily-liver'd boy. What soldiers, patch?   15
Death of thy soul! those linen cheeks of thine
Are counsellors to fear. What soldiers, whey-face?
Serv. The English force, so please you.
Macb. Take thy face hence.   *Exit Servant.*]
                    Seyton! — I am sick at heart
When I behold — Seyton, I say! — This push   20
Will cheer me ever, or [disseat] me now.
I have liv'd long enough. My way of life
Is fallen into the sear, the yellow leaf;
And that which should accompany old age,
As honour, love, obedience, troops of friends,   25
I must not look to have; but, in their stead,
Curses, not loud but deep, mouth-honour, breath
Which the poor heart would fain deny, and dare not.
Seyton!

Enter SEYTON.

Sey. What's your gracious pleasure?
Macb.   What news more?
Sey. All is confirm'd, my lord, which was re-
          ported.   31
Macb. I'll fight till from my bones my flesh be
          hack'd.
Give me my armour.

Sey.   'Tis not needed yet.
Macb. I'll put it on.
Send out moe horses; skirr the country round;   35
Hang those that talk of fear. Give me mine
          armour.
How does your patient, doctor?
Doct.   Not so sick, my lord,
As she is troubled with thick-coming fancies
That keep her from her rest.
Macb.   Cure her of that.
Canst thou not minister to a mind diseas'd,   40
Pluck from the memory a rooted sorrow,
Raze out the written troubles of the brain,
And with some sweet oblivious antidote
Cleanse the stuff'd bosom of that perilous stuff
Which weighs upon the heart?
Doct.   Therein the patient
Must minister to himself.   46
Macb. Throw physic to the dogs; I'll none of it.
Come, put mine armour on; give me my staff.
Seyton, send out. Doctor, the thanes fly from me.
Come, sir, dispatch. If thou couldst, doctor, cast
The water of my land, find her disease,   51
And purge it to a sound and pristine health,
I would applaud thee to the very echo,
That should applaud again. — Pull 't off, I say. —
What rhubarb, [senna], or what purgative drug,
Would scour these English hence? Hear'st thou of
          them?   56
Doct. Ay, my good lord; your royal preparation
Makes us hear something.
Macb.   Bring it after me.
I will not be afraid of death and bane,
Till Birnam forest come to Dunsinane.   60
Doct. [*Aside.*] Were I from Dunsinane away and
          clear,
Profit again should hardly draw me here. [*Exeunt.*

SCENE IV. [*Country near Birnam wood.*]

Drum and colours.   Enter MALCOLM, *old* SIWARD
and his Son, MACDUFF, MENTEITH, Caithness,
Angus, [Lennox, Ross,] *and* SOLDIERS, *marching.*

Mal. Cousins, I hope the days are near at hand
That chambers will be safe.
Ment.   We doubt it nothing.
Siw. What wood is this before us?
Ment.   The wood of Birnam.
Mal. Let every soldier hew him down a bough
And bear 't before him; thereby shall we shadow   5
The numbers of our host and make discovery
Err in report of us.

Sc. iii, 3. **taint:** be infected.   5. **mortal consequences:** human fortunes.   9. **sway:** act.   15. **patch:** fool.   17. **Are...to:** inspire.   20. **push:** crisis.   21. **cheer.** Many edd. read *chair.*   [**disseat**] (Steevens): dethrone.   *dis-eate* F₁: disease F₂₋₄.
35. **skirr:** scour.   42. **Raze:** blot.   43. **oblivious:** causing forgetfulness.   48. **staff:** lance.   50. **cast:** analyze.   51. **water:** urine.   52. **pristine:** perfect (as in former times).   55. [**senna**] F₄.   *Cyme* F₁.   58. **it:** the armor.
Sc. iv, 2. **chambers.** Alluding to Duncan's murder.   6. **discovery:** Macbeth's scouts.

Soldiers.   It shall be done.

Siw. We learn no other but the confident tyrant
Keeps still in Dunsinane, and will endure
Our setting down before 't.

Mal.   'Tis his main hope;   10
For where there is advantage to be given,
Both more and less have given him the revolt,
And none serve with him but constrained things,
Whose hearts are absent too.

Macd.   Let our just censures
Attend the true event, and put we on   15
Industrious soldiership.

Siw.   The time approaches
That will with due decision make us know
What we shall say we have and what we owe.
Thoughts speculative their unsure hopes relate,
But certain issue strokes must arbitrate;   20
Towards which advance the war.

                        [*Exeunt, marching.*

SCENE V. [*Dunsinane. Within the castle.*]

Enter MACBETH, SEYTON, *and* Soldiers, *with
drum and colours.*

Macb. Hang out our banners on the outward
    walls;
The cry is still, "They come!" Our castle's
    strength
Will laugh a siege to scorn; here let them lie
Till famine and the ague eat them up.
Were they not forc'd with those that should be
    ours,   5
We might have met them dareful, beard to beard,
And beat them backward home.

                    [*A cry of women within.*
                        What is that noise?

Sey. It is the cry of women, my good lord.
                                    [*Exit.*

Macb. I have almost forgot the taste of fears.
The time has been, my senses would have cool'd
To hear a night-shriek, and my fell of hair   11
Would at a dismal treatise rouse and stir
As life were in 't. I have supp'd full with horrors;
Direness, familiar to my slaughterous thoughts,
Cannot once start me.

[*Re-enter* SEYTON.]

                    Wherefore was that cry?

Sey. The Queen, my lord, is dead.   16

Macb. She should have died hereafter;
There would have been a time for such a word.
To-morrow, and to-morrow, and to-morrow
Creeps in this petty pace from day to day   20

To the last syllable of recorded time;
And all our yesterdays have lighted fools
The way to dusty death.   Out, out, brief candle!
Life's but a walking shadow, a poor player
That struts and frets his hour upon the stage   25
And then is heard no more.   It is a tale
Told by an idiot, full of sound and fury,
Signifying nothing.

Enter a MESSENGER.

Thou com'st to use thy tongue; thy story quickly.

Mess. Gracious my lord,   30
I should report that which I say I saw,
But know not how to do it.

Macb.   Well, say, sir.

Mess. As I did stand my watch upon the hill,
I look'd toward Birnam, and anon, methought,
The wood began to move.

Macb.   Liar and slave!   35

Mess. Let me endure your wrath, if 't be not so.
Within this three mile may you see it coming;
I say, a moving grove.

Macb.   If thou speak'st false,
Upon the next tree shalt thou hang alive,
Till famine cling thee; if thy speech be sooth,   40
I care not if thou dost for me as much.
I pull in resolution, and begin
To doubt th' equivocation of the fiend
That lies like truth. "Fear not, till Birnam wood
Do come to Dunsinane;" and now a wood   45
Comes toward Dunsinane.   Arm, arm, and out!
If this which he avouches does appear,
There is nor flying hence nor tarrying here.
I gin to be aweary of the sun,   49
And wish th' estate o' th' world were now undone.
Ring the alarum-bell! Blow, wind! come, wrack!
At least we'll die with harness on our back.
                                    [*Exeunt.*

SCENE VI. [*Dunsinane. Before the castle.*]

Drum and colours. Enter MALCOLM, *old* SIWARD,
MACDUFF, *and their* Army, *with boughs.*

Mal. Now near enough; your leavy screens throw
    down,
And show like those you are. You, worthy uncle,
Shall, with my cousin, your right noble son,
Lead our first battle. Worthy Macduff and we
Shall take upon 's what else remains to do,   5
According to our order.

Siw.   Fare you well.
Do we but find the tyrant's power to-night,
Let us be beaten if we cannot fight.

10. **setting down:** laying siege. 11. **advantage:** chance. 14. **censures:** judgments. 15. **Attend...event:** await the outcome.
Sc. v, 5. **forc'd:** reinforced. 10. **cool'd:** i.e., with terror. 11. **fell of hair:** head of hair. 12. **treatise:** story. 17. **should ...died:** was bound to die. 40. **cling:** shrivel. 42. **pull:** rein, draw. 51. **wrack:** ruin.
Sc. vi, 4. **battle:** battalion.

Macd. Make all our trumpets speak; give them
    all breath,   9
Those clamorous harbingers of blood and death.
                [*Exeunt. Alarums continued.*

SCENE VII. [*Another part of the field.*]

Enter MACBETH.

Macb. They have tied me to a stake; I cannot fly,
But, bear-like, I must fight the course.   What's he
That was not born of woman?   Such a one
Am I to fear, or none.

Enter young SIWARD.

Y. Siw. What is thy name?
Macb.   Thou'lt be afraid to hear it.
Y. Siw. No; though thou call'st thyself a hotter
    name   6
Than any is in hell.
Macb.   My name's Macbeth.
Y. Siw. The devil himself could not pronounce
    a title
More hateful to mine ear.
Macb.   No, nor more fearful.
Y. Siw. Thou liest, abhorred tyrant; with my
    sword   10
I'll prove the lie thou speak'st.
        [*They fight and young Siward is slain.*
Macb.   Thou wast born of woman.
But swords I smile at, weapons laugh to scorn,
Brandish'd by man that's of a woman born.   [*Exit.*

Alarums.   Enter MACDUFF.

Macd. That way the noise is.   Tyrant, show thy
    face!
If thou be'st slain and with no stroke of mine,   15
My wife and children's ghosts will haunt me still.
I cannot strike at wretched kerns, whose arms
Are hir'd to bear their staves; either thou, Macbeth,
Or else my sword with an unbattered edge
I sheathe again undeeded.   There thou shouldst
    be;   20
By this great clatter one of greatest note
Seems bruited.   Let me find him, Fortune!
And more I beg not.   [*Exit. Alarums.*

Enter MALCOLM *and old* SIWARD.

Siw. This way, my lord; the castle's gently
    rend'red:
The tyrant's people on both sides do fight;   25
The noble thanes do bravely in the war;

The day almost itself professes yours,
And little is to do.
Mal.   We have met with foes
That strike beside us.
Siw.   Enter, sir, the castle.
                  [*Exeunt. Alarums.*

[SCENE VIII.   *Another part of the field.*]

Enter MACBETH.

Macb. Why should I play the Roman fool, and
    die
On mine own sword?   Whiles I see lives, the gashes
Do better upon them.

Enter MACDUFF.

Macd.   Turn, hell-hound, turn!
Macb. Of all men else I have avoided thee.
But get thee back; my soul is too much charg'd   5
With blood of thine already.
Macd.   I have no words;
My voice is in my sword, thou bloodier villain
Than terms can give thee out!
               [*They fight. Alarum.*
Macb.   Thou losest labour.
As easy mayst thou the intrenchant air
With thy keen sword impress as make me bleed.   10
Let fall thy blade on vulnerable crests;
I bear a charmed life, which must not yield
To one of woman born.
Macd.   Despair thy charm;
And let the angel whom thou still hast serv'd
Tell thee, Macduff was from his mother's womb
Untimely ripp'd.   16
Macb. Accursed be that tongue that tells me so,
For it hath cow'd my better part of man!
And be these juggling fiends no more believ'd
That palter with us in a double sense,   20
That keep the word of promise to our ear,
And break it to our hope.   I'll not fight with thee.
Macd. Then yield thee, coward,
And live to be the show and gaze o' th' time!
We'll have thee, as our rarer monsters are,   25
Painted upon a pole, and underwrit,
"Here may you see the tyrant."
Macb.   I will not yield,
To kiss the ground before young Malcolm's feet
And to be baited with the rabble's curse.
Though Birnam wood be come to Dunsinane,   30
And thou oppos'd, being of no woman born,
Yet I will try the last.   Before my body

Sc. vii, 2. **course**: a round of bear-baiting.   18. **staves**: spears.   22. **bruited**: proclaimed.   24. **gently rend'red**: tamely
surrendered.   29. **strike...us**: only pretend to strike us, or fight on our side.
   Sc. viii. F begins no new scene at this point.   8. **terms...out**: words can describe.   9. **intrenchant**: that cannot be cut.
14. **angel**: evil genius.   18. **better...man**: i.e., courage.   26. **Painted...pole**: i.e., with your picture carried on a pole.
32. **the last**: i.e., my last hope, viz., to fight.

I throw my warlike shield. Lay on, Macduff,
And damn'd be him that first cries, "Hold,
    enough!"   *[Exeunt, fighting. Alarums.*

Retreat. Flourish. Enter, with drum and colours,
MALCOLM, *old* SIWARD, ROSS, *the other* Thanes,
and Soldiers.

Mal. I would the friends we miss were safe
    arriv'd.   35
Siw. Some must go off; and yet, by these I see,
So great a day as this is cheaply bought.
Mal. Macduff is missing, and your noble son.
Ross. Your son, my lord, has paid a soldier's debt.
He only liv'd but till he was a man;   40
The which no sooner had his prowess confirm'd
In the unshrinking station where he fought,
But like a man he died.
Siw.   Then he is dead?
Ross. Ay, and brought off the field. Your cause
    of sorrow
Must not be measur'd by his worth, for then   45
It hath no end.
Siw.   Had he his hurts before?
Ross. Ay, on the front.
Siw.   Why then, God's soldier be he!
Had I as many sons as I have hairs,
I would not wish them to a fairer death.   49
And so, his knell is knoll'd.
Mal.   He's worth more sorrow,
And that I'll spend for him.
Siw.   He's worth no more.

They say he parted well, and paid his score;
And so, God be with him! Here comes newer com-
    fort.

Re-enter MACDUFF, *with Macbeth's head.*
Macd. Hail, king! for so thou art. Behold where
    stands
Th' usurper's cursed head. The time is free.   55
I see thee compass'd with thy kingdom's pearl,
That speak my salutation in their minds;
Whose voices I desire aloud with mine:
Hail, King of Scotland!
All.   Hail, King of Scotland!
          [Flourish.
Mal. We shall not spend a large expense of time
Before we reckon with your several loves   61
And make us even with you. My thanes and kins-
    men,
Henceforth be earls, the first that ever Scotland
In such an honour nam'd. What's more to do,
Which would be planted newly with the time,   65
As calling home our exil'd friends abroad
That fled the snares of watchful tyranny;
Producing forth the cruel ministers
Of this dead butcher and his fiend-like queen,
Who, as 'tis thought, by self and violent hands
Took off her life; this, and what needful else   71
That calls upon us, by the grace of Grace
We will perform in measure, time, and place.
So, thanks to all at once and to each one,
Whom we invite to see us crown'd at Scone.   75
        [Flourish. Exeunt.

34. S.D. **Alarums.** F adds *Enter Fighting, and Macbeth slaine.* 36. **go off:** die. 50. **knoll'd:** tolled. 55. **time:** i.e., country, nation. 56. **compass'd ... pearl:** surrounded by the finest in your realm. 61. **reckon with:** i.e., reward.

The Life of Timon of Athens

THERE IS NO REASON to believe that *Timon of Athens* was either played or printed during the lifetime of Shakespeare. The first edition, and the basis of all later texts, is that in the First Folio (1623). The printing, especially in the matter of metre, is uncommonly bad; and it is often difficult to know whether a passage is meant by the writer to be prose or verse. Marginal insertions in the copy could account for some of the confusion. The present metrical arrangement is the result of the experiments of a long succession of editors.

The play is in a defective state in other respects. Though the dramatic relationship of Timon and Alcibiades as victims of Athenian ingratitude is clear enough, their respective stories are not adequately joined. The passage introducing Apemantus and the Fool (II.ii.47–131) seems to be a clumsy diversion thrust in to fill up the time required for the steward Flavius to inform Timon of the details of his bankruptcy. At IV.iii.356 Apemantus announces to Timon the approach of a Poet and a Painter, but nobody in fact enters for a space of forty-two lines, when Banditti suddenly arrive, the Poet and the Painter being side-tracked until the opening of Act V. Timon's epitaph (V.iv.70–73) consists of contradictory couplets. This state of affairs leads naturally to doubts about the complete authenticity of the play. Two theories have prevailed: that *Timon* is an adaptation by Shakespeare of a lost play; or, that it is an unfinished play of Shakespeare's completed by another hand. But the upholders of these theories have differed widely among themselves both as to the identity of the original dramatist or the reviser of Shakespeare, and as to the extent of the non-Shakespearean parts. Another view is now gaining acceptance, namely, that the play as it survives is a Shakespearean torso, a play which Shakespeare hewed out in the rough and abandoned. Such a view might explain the structural weakness and some of the metrical anarchy. Though it hardly accords with the facility in composition with which Heminge and Condell credit Shakespeare, it gains some countenance through the manner in which

Timon seems to have been admitted into the Folio. It is printed there between *Romeo and Juliet* and *Julius Cæsar*, but a gap of eight pages falls between it and *Julius Cæsar* in the pagination. The space between *Romeo and Juliet* and *Julius Cæsar* would, however, exactly fit *Troilus and Cressida*, which is actually inserted, with special signatures, between the Histories and the Tragedies, and is not listed at all in the table of contents. That *Troilus and Cressida* was at first intended to follow *Romeo and Juliet* is attested by the existence of two copies of the Folio with a cancelled sheet, on whose recto side the latter play concludes, and on whose verso the former begins. When *Troilus and Cressida* was removed from among the Tragedies (perhaps because of its ambiguous nature, perhaps because of difficulty over copyright), *Timon* was substituted. It is at least a respectable conjecture that the printing of *Timon* had not originally been planned, because, as suggested above, Shakespeare had not finished it and because it had not been acted.

Leaving aside all question of a lost play, we find the primary source of the present drama in an incidental account of Timon in Plutarch's *Life of Marcus Antonius*. This work Shakespeare read in Sir Thomas North's translation (1579, 1595, 1603), and he may well have noted Timon's story as far back as 1599 when he was reading Plutarch for *Julius Cæsar;* or he may have been struck by it when he was reading with an eye to *Antony and Cleopatra*. Although Plutarch gives the outlines of Timon's story, he supplies nothing for the part of the action preceding Timon's poverty, except the suggestion contained in the remark that his misanthropy was owing to "the unthankfulness of those he had done good vnto, and whom he tooke to be his friends." But in Lucian's dialogue of *Timon, or the Misanthrope*, Shakespeare found other details, such as the saving of a man from a debtors' prison, the gift of a dowry, the crowd of flatterers, the discovery of gold in the fields, the visit of a poet on the rumor of Timon's restoration to wealth, and the delegation from the Senate to plead for Timon's return; indeed, Shakespeare's conception of Timon's character is much more definitely foreshadowed in Lucian than in Plutarch. Lucian had not been translated into English in the time of Shakespeare, but there were versions in Latin, Italian, and French. The incident of finding the gold appears also in a play on Timon printed in 1842 from a manuscript of about 1600. This anonymous production seems to have been academic in origin, and there is no evidence to show that it was ever acted in London; so that on external grounds it would seem unlikely that it was known to Shakespeare. Yet it alone of the pre-Shakespearean accounts of the misanthrope contains a mock banquet and a faithful steward; and it is possible that it is the direct or indirect source of these features in the present play. Details concerning Alcibiades Shakespeare obtained from Plutarch's *Life of Alcibiades*, but the notion of joining his experiences with those of Timon appears to have been suggested to him by a passage in the *Life of Antonius*. There it is stated that Timon shunned "all other men's companies but the company of Alcibiades, a bold and insolent youth, whom he would gladly feast and make much of"; an indulgence which Timon explains, saying, "I doe it because I know that one day he shall doe great mischief vnto the Athenians." The character of Apemantus is created by Shakespeare from a hint in the *Life of Antonius*. As a caustic commentator he is kin to Thersites, but with an imagination less debased.

Evidence for the date of the play is internal and inconclusive. Metrical tests, which are less significant than usual on account of the wretched printing of the verse, point to a date between 1605 and 1608. Aesthetic and other characteristics agree with this. Some striking resemblances between the cursing of Timon and the maledictions of Lear, and the repeated comparisons in their respective dramas between the natures of man and of beast, suggest a date not long after that of *King Lear*; so that 1607 may be regarded as a fair approximation.

This thematic affiliation of *Timon* with *King Lear* is not supported by a corresponding kinship in greatness. The tragedy of the misanthrope has neither the dramatic vitality nor the human significance which inspires the tragedy of the misguided old king. Timon is not one in whom we can fully believe or about whom we can greatly care. His personality, so far as we are made aware of it, is too narrow, too artificial. His prodigal bounty and his blindness concerning the true character of the recipients are hardly credible. But that is not the point. Other plays of Shakespeare harbor notorious improbabilities, among which, for example, the initial situation in *King Lear* is eminent; yet Shakespeare is able to over-ride these, making his characters convincingly human and their experiences entirely plausible. In *Timon*, however, his magic fails him; the illusion of reality is not achieved. The structural defects of the play may be recalled in this connection. There are faults of proportion, too; and a consequent monotony of tone. Timon is deceived, not in one friend, or a few, but in many. His dominant trait of generosity is his only one, until it is supplanted by a wholesale misanthropy. He has one faithful servant, but no faithful friend; except, perhaps, Alcibiades, who is another malcontent (though of a different temper). The churlish Apemantus, who with his avowed cynicism would add gall to Timon's hate, is in reality a friend to no man. In his change of fortune Timon has no one to assuage his suffering, as Lear has Kent (and, for a space, Cordelia), and as Gloucester has Edgar. Flavius would console him if Timon would let him, but Timon has hardened his heart against everything human. In so doing he forfeits most of the sympathy which might otherwise be accorded him. There is no exaltation in the tragedy of Timon; he is in no way magnified through suffering, is in no manner redeemed. There is, on the contrary, only degeneration. In the second half of the play Timon becomes, abruptly, the complete reverse of his former self, and so he remains. His last words are a curse. He has cursed too much, and well before he has composed his epitaph and has crawled into his cave to die, we have wearied of him; so that when, in conclusion, Alcibiades speaks of the death of "noble Timon" and of his "faults forgiven," our acquiescence is reluctant.

THE LIFE OF TIMON OF ATHENS

[DRAMATIS PERSONÆ]

TIMON of Athens.

LUCIUS,
LUCULLUS, } flattering lords.
SEMPRONIUS,

VENTIDIUS, one of Timon's false friends.
ALCIBIADES, an Athenian captain.
APEMANTUS, a churlish philosopher.
[FLAVIUS, steward to Timon.]

FLAMINIUS,
SERVILIUS, } servants to Timon.
[LUCILIUS,]

PHILOTUS, TITUS, LUCIUS, HORTENSIUS, servants to usurers.
CAPHIS, servant [to a senator].
[Servants to Varro and Isidore.]
Poet, Painter, Jeweller, and Merchant.
[An old Athenian.
Three Strangers.
A Page.   A Fool.

PHRYNIA,
TIMANDRA, } mistresses to Alcibiades.]

Cupid [and Amazons in the Masque.]

[Lords,] Senators, [Officers, Soldiers, Banditti,] and Attendants.

[SCENE: Athens, and the neighbouring woods.]

purpose of this scene

ACT I

SCENE I. [Athens. A hall in Timon's house.]

Enter POET, PAINTER, JEWELLER, MERCHANT, *and [others] at several doors.*

Poet. Good day, sir.
Pain.   I am glad you're well.
Poet. I have not seen you long. How goes the
world?
Pain. It wears, sir, as it grows.
Poet.   Ay, that's well known;
But what particular rarity? What strange,
Which manifold record not matches? See,   5
Magic of bounty! all these spirits thy power
Hath conjur'd to attend. I know the merchant.
Pain. I know them both; th' other's a jeweller.
Mer. O, 'tis a worthy lord.

Jew.   Nay, that's most fix'd.
Mer. A most incomparable man, breath'd, as
it were,   10
To an untirable and continuate goodness;
He passes.
Jew.   I have a jewel here —
Mer. O, pray, let's see 't. For the Lord Timon,
sir?
Jew. If he will touch the estimate; but, for that —
Poet. [Reading from his poem.]
"When we for recompense have prais'd the vile, 15
It stains the glory in that happy verse
Which aptly sings the good."
Mer. [Looking at the jewel.] 'Tis a good form.
Jew. And rich. Here is a water, look ye.
Pain. You are rapt, sir, in some work, some
dedication
To the great lord.

Act I, sc. i, s.d. [others] (Malone). *Mercer* F. **2. long:** for a long time. **3. wears:** wears away. **grows:** grows older.
6. Magic of bounty: i.e., Timon's. **10. breath'd:** trained. **12. passes:** excels. **14. touch the estimate:** meet the price.
18. water: lustre. **19. rapt:** engrossed.

Poet.   A thing slipp'd idly from me. 20
Our poesy is as a [gum], which [oozes]
From whence 'tis nourish'd. The fire i' th' flint
Shows not till it be struck; our gentle flame
Provokes itself and, like the current, flies
Each bound it [chafes]. What have you there? 25
  Pain. A picture, sir. When comes your book
    forth?
  Poet. Upon the heels of my presentment, sir.
Let's see your piece.
  Pain.   'Tis a good piece.
  Poet. So 'tis. This comes off well and excellent.
  Pain. Indifferent.
  Poet.   Admirable! How this grace 30
Speaks his own standing! What a mental power
This eye shoots forth! How big imagination
Moves in this lip! To th' dumbness of the gesture
One might interpret.
  Pain. It is a pretty mocking of the life. 35
Here is a touch; is't good?
  Poet.   I will say of it,
It tutors nature. Artificial strife
Lives in these touches, livelier than life.

          Enter certain Senators [*and pass over*].

  Pain. How this lord is followed!
  Poet. The senators of Athens: happy [man]! 40
  Pain. Look, moe!
  Poet. You see this confluence, this great flood of
    visitors.
I have, in this rough work, shap'd out a man
Whom this beneath world doth embrace and hug
With amplest entertainment. My free drift 45
Halts not particularly, but moves itself
In a wide sea of wax. No levell'd malice
Infects one comma in the course I hold;
But flies an eagle flight, bold and forth on,
Leaving no tract behind. 50
  Pain. How shall I understand you?
  Poet.   I will unbolt to you.
You see how all conditions, how all minds,
As well of glib and slipp'ry creatures as
Of grave and austere quality, tender down
Their services to Lord Timon. His large for-
    tune, 55
Upon his good and gracious nature hanging,
Subdues and properties to his love and tendance
All sorts of hearts; yea, from the glass-fac'd flatterer
To Apemantus, that few things loves better
Than to abhor himself; even he drops down 60

The knee before him and returns in peace
Most rich in Timon's nod.
  Pain.   I saw them speak together.
  Poet. Sir, I have upon a high and pleasant hill
Feign'd Fortune to be thron'd. The base o' th'
    mount
Is rank'd with all deserts, all kind of natures, 65
That labour on the bosom of this sphere
To propagate their states. Amongst them all,
Whose eyes are on this sovereign lady fix'd,
One do I personate of Lord Timon's frame,
Whom Fortune with her ivory hand wafts to her; 70
Whose present grace to present slaves and servants
Translates his rivals.
  Pain.   'Tis conceiv'd to scope.
This throne, this Fortune, and this hill, methinks,
With one man beckon'd from the rest below,
Bowing his head against the steepy mount 75
To climb his happiness, would be well express'd
In our condition.
  Poet.   Nay, sir, but hear me on.
All those which were his fellows but of late,
Some better than his value, on the moment
Follow his strides, his lobbies fill with tendance, 80
Rain sacrificial whisperings in his ear,
Make sacred even his stirrup, and through him
Drink the free air.
  Pain.   Ay, marry, what of these?
  Poet. When Fortune in her shift and change of
    mood
Spurns down her late beloved, all his dependants 85
Which labour'd after him to the mountain's top
Even on their knees and hands, let him [slip] down,
Not one accompanying his declining foot.
  Pain. 'Tis common.
A thousand moral paintings I can show 90
That shall demonstrate these quick blows of For-
    tune's
More pregnantly than words. Yet you do well
To show Lord Timon that mean eyes have seen
The foot above the head.

Trumpets sound. Enter LORD TIMON, *addressing
    himself courteously to every suitor* [*a Messenger
    from* VENTIDIUS *talking with him;* LUCILIUS *and
    other servants following*].

  Tim.   Imprison'd is he, say you?
  Mess. Ay, my good lord; five talents is his
    debt, 95
His means most short, his creditors most strait.

---

21. **[gum]** (Pope). *gowne* F. **[oozes]** (Johnson). *uses* F. 25. **bound:** bank. **[chafes]** (Theobald). *chases* F. 27.
presentment: presentation (to Timon). 31. **standing:** posture. 34. **interpret:** supply words. 37. **Artificial strife:** the
vying of art with nature. 40. **[man]** (Theobald). *men* F. 45. **drift:** aim. 46. **particularly:** at any individual. 46–47.
moves . . . wax: i.e., idealizes. "Wax" has not been satisfactorily explained. 48. **comma:** detail. 49. **flies:** i.e., my course
is. 50. **tract:** trace, track. 57. **properties:** makes his own. 65. **rank'd . . . deserts:** lined with men of all degrees of merit.
67. **states:** fortunes. 71. **Whose:** i.e., Fortune's. **to present:** immediately to. 72. **Translates:** transforms. **to scope:**
adequately, fitly. 77. **condition:** profession, i.e., in painting. 81. **sacrificial:** making offerings. 87. **[slip]** (Rowe). *sit*
F. 90. **moral:** allegorical. 92. **pregnantly:** cogently. 93. **mean:** lowly. Theobald conj. *men's.* 95. **talents.** A talent
was worth about $1200. 96. **strait:** exacting.

Your honourable letter he desires
To those have shut him up; which failing,
Periods his comfort.
   Tim.   Noble Ventidius! Well;
I am not of that feather to shake off   100
My friend when he must need me. I do know him
A gentleman that well deserves a help,
Which he shall have. I'll pay the debt and free
   him.
   Mess. Your lordship ever binds him.
   Tim. Commend me to him. I will send his
   ransom;   105
And being enfranchis'd, bid him come to me.
'Tis not enough to help the feeble up,
But to support him after. Fare you well.
   Mess. All happiness to your honour!   [*Exit.*

Enter an OLD ATHENIAN.

   Old Ath. Lord Timon, hear me speak.
   Tim.   Freely, good father.   110
   Old Ath. Thou hast a servant named Lucilius.
   Tim. I have so. What of him?
   Old Ath. Most noble Timon, call the man before
   thee.
   Tim. Attends he here, or no? Lucilius!
   Luc. Here, at your lordship's service.   115
   Old Ath. This fellow here, Lord Timon, this thy
   creature,
By night frequents my house. I am a man
That from my first have been inclin'd to thrift;
And my estate deserves an heir more rais'd   119
Than one which holds a trencher.
   Tim.   Well; what further?
   Old Ath. One only daughter have I, no kin else,
On whom I may confer what I have got.
The maid is fair, o' th' youngest for a bride,
And I have bred her at my dearest cost
In qualities of the best. This man of thine   125
Attempts her love. I prithee, noble lord,
Join with me to forbid him her resort;
Myself have spoke in vain.
   Tim.   The man is honest.
   Old Ath. Therefore he will be, Timon.
His honesty rewards him in itself;   130
It must not bear my daughter.
   Tim.   Does she love him?
   Old Ath. She is young and apt.
Our own precedent passions do instruct us
What levity's in youth.
   Tim.   [*To Lucilius.*] Love you the maid?
   Luc. Ay, my good lord, and she accepts of it.   135
   Old Ath. If in her marriage my consent be miss-
   ing,
I call the gods to witness, I will choose

Mine heir from forth the beggars of the world,
And dispossess her all.
   Tim.   How shall she be endow'd,
If she be mated with an equal husband?   140
   Old Ath. Three talents on the present; in future,
   all.
   Tim. This gentleman of mine hath serv'd me
   long;
To build his fortune I will strain a little,
For 'tis a bond in men. Give him thy daughter;
What you bestow, in him I'll counterpoise,   145
And make him weigh with her.
   Old Ath.   Most noble lord,
Pawn me to this your honour, she is his.
   Tim. My hand to thee; mine honour on my
   promise.
   Luc. Humbly I thank your lordship. Never
   may
That state or fortune fall into my keeping,   150
Which is not ow'd to you!
            [*Exeunt [Lucilius and Old Athenian].*
   Poet. Vouchsafe my labour, and long live your
   lordship!
   Tim. I thank you; you shall hear from me anon.
Go not away. What have you there, my friend?
   Pain. A piece of painting, which I do beseech   155
Your lordship to accept.
   Tim.   Painting is welcome.
The painting is almost the natural man;
For since dishonour traffics with man's nature,
He is but outside: these pencill'd figures are
Even such as they give out. I like your work,   160
And you shall find I like it. Wait attendance
Till you hear further from me.
   Pain.   The gods preserve ye!
   Tim. Well fare you, gentleman; give me your
   hand.
We must needs dine together. — Sir, your jewel
Hath suffered under praise.
   Jew.   What, my lord! dispraise?   165
   Tim. A mere satiety of commendations.
If I should pay you for't as 'tis extoll'd,
It would unclew me quite.
   Jew.   My lord, 'tis rated
As those which sell would give; but you well know,
Things of like value differing in the owners   170
Are prized by their masters. Believe't, dear lord,
You mend the jewel by the wearing it.
   Tim. Well mock'd.

Enter APEMANTUS.

   Mer. No, my good lord; he speaks the common
   tongue
Which all men speak with him.   175

---

99. Periods: ends.   **120. holds a trencher:** is a waiter.   **125. qualities:** accomplishments.   **129. be:** i.e., continue to
be.   **131. bear:** win.   **132. apt:** impressionable.   **144. bond in:** duty of friendship among.   **152. Vouchsafe:** deign to
accept.   **159. but outside:** only what he lets appear.   **168. unclew:** undo.   **171. by:** according to.

Tim. Look who comes here; will you be chid?

Jew. We'll bear, with your lordship.

Mer.   He'll spare none.

Tim. Good morrow to thee, gentle Apemantus!

Apem. Till I be gentle, stay thou for thy good
     morrow;

When thou art Timon's dog, and these knaves
     honest.   180

Tim. Why dost thou call them knaves? Thou
     know'st them not.

Apem. Are they not Athenians?

Tim. Yes.

Apem. Then I repent not.

Jew. You know me, Apemantus?   185

Apem. Thou know'st I do; I call'd thee by thy
name.

Tim. Thou art proud, Apemantus.

Apem. Of nothing so much as that I am not like
Timon.   190

Tim. Whither art going?

Apem. To knock out an honest Athenian's
brains.

Tim. That's a deed thou'lt die for.

Apem. Right, if doing nothing be death by
th' law.   196

Tim. How lik'st thou this picture, Apemantus?

Apem. The best, for the innocence.

Tim. Wrought he not well that painted it?   200

Apem. He wrought better that made the painter;
and yet he's but a filthy piece of work.

Pain. You're a dog.

Apem. Thy mother 's of my generation; what's
she, if I be a dog?   205

Tim. Wilt dine with me, Apemantus?

Apem. No; I eat not lords.

Tim. An thou shouldst, thou'dst anger ladies.

Apem. O, they eat lords; so they come by great
bellies.   210

Tim. That's a lascivious apprehension.

Apem. So thou apprehend'st it. Take it for
thy labour.

Tim. How dost thou like this jewel, Apemantus?   215

Apem. Not so well as plain-dealing, which will
not cost a man a doit.

Tim. What dost thou think 'tis worth?

Apem. Not worth my thinking. How now,
poet!   220

Poet. How now, philosopher!

Apem. Thou liest.

Poet. Art not one?

Apem. Yes.

Poet. Then I lie not.   225

Apem. Art not a poet?

Poet. Yes.

Apem. Then thou liest. Look in thy last work,
where thou hast feign'd him a worthy fellow.

Poet. That's not feign'd; he is so.   230

Apem. Yes, he is worthy of thee, and to pay thee
for thy labour. He that loves to be flattered is
worthy o' th' flatterer. Heavens, that I were a
lord!

Tim. What wouldst do then, Apemantus?   235

Apem. E'en as Apemantus does now; hate a
lord with my heart.

Tim. What, thyself?

Apem. Ay.

Tim. Wherefore?   240

Apem. That I had [my] angry [will] to be a lord.
Art not thou a merchant?

Mer. Ay, Apemantus.

Apem. Traffic confound thee, if the gods will
not!   245

Mer. If traffic do it, the gods do it.

Apem. Traffic's thy god; and thy god confound
thee!

          Trumpet sounds. Enter a MESSENGER.

Tim. What trumpet's that?

Mess. 'Tis Alcibiades, and some twenty horse,
All of companionship.   251

Tim. Pray, entertain them; give them guide
     to us.   [*Exeunt some Attendants.*]
You must needs dine with me; go not you hence
Till I have thank'd you. When dinner's done,
Show me this piece. I am joyful of your sights. 255

          Enter ALCIBIADES, *with the rest.*

Most welcome, sir!

Apem.   So, so, [there!]
Aches contract and starve your supple joints!
That there should be small love 'mongst these sweet
     knaves,
And all this courtesy! The strain of man's bred out
Into baboon and monkey.   260

Alcib. Sir, you have sav'd my longing, and I feed
Most hungerly on your sight.

Tim.   Right welcome, sir!
Ere we depart, we'll share a bounteous time
In different pleasures. Pray you, let us in.
          [*Exeunt [all but Apemantus].*]

          Enter two LORDS.

1. Lord. What time o' day is't, Apemantus? 265

Apem. Time to be honest.

1. Lord. That time serves still.

Apem. The [more] accursed thou, that still
omitt'st it.

2. Lord. Thou art going to Lord Timon's feast?

199. innocence: silliness.   204. generation: species.   217. doit: half a farthing.   241. [my] ... [will] (Deighton).
no ... wit F.   251. companionship: one party.   256-57. [there!] Aches (Capell). *their Aches* F.   257. starve: paralyze.
259. bred out: degenerated.   267. still: always.   268. [more] (Hanmer). *most* F.   269. it: i.e., to be honest.

long scenes

Apem. Ay, to see meat fill knaves, and wine
heat fools.   271
2. Lord. Fare thee well, fare thee well.
Apem. Thou art a fool to bid me farewell twice.
2. Lord. Why, Apemantus?
Apem. Shouldst have kept one to thyself, for
I mean to give thee none.   276
1. Lord. Hang thyself!
Apem. No, I will do nothing at thy bidding;
make thy requests to thy friend.
2. Lord. Away, unpeaceable dog, or I'll spurn
thee hence!   281
Apem. I will fly, like a dog, the heels o' th' ass.
                              [*Exit.*
1. Lord. He's opposite to humanity. Come,
     shall we in
And taste Lord Timon's bounty? He outgoes   285
The very heart of kindness.
2. Lord. He pours it out: Plutus, the god of gold,
Is but his steward. No meed but he repays
Sevenfold above itself; no gift to him
But breeds the giver a return exceeding   290
All use of quittance.
1. Lord.   The noblest mind he carries
That ever govern'd man.
2. Lord. Long may he live in fortunes! Shall
     we in?
1. Lord. I'll keep you company.   [*Exeunt.*

[SCENE II. *A banqueting-room in Timon's house.*]

*Hautboys playing loud music. A great banquet
serv'd in;* [FLAVIUS *and others attending;*] *then
enter* LORD TIMON, *the* States, *the* Athenian
LORDS, [ALCIBIADES,] *and* VENTIDIUS. *Then
comes, dropping after all,* APEMANTUS, *discontent-
edly, like himself.*

Ven. Most honoured Timon,
It hath pleas'd the gods to remember my father's
     age,
And call him to long peace.
He is gone happy, and has left me rich.
Then, as in grateful virtue I am bound   5
To your free heart, I do return those talents,
Doubled with thanks and service, from whose help
I deriv'd liberty.
Tim.   O, by no means,
Honest Ventidius. You mistake my love;
I gave it freely ever; and there's none   10
Can truly say he gives if he receives.
If our betters play at that game, we must not dare
To imitate them; faults that are rich are fair.

Ven. A noble spirit!
Tim.   Nay, my lords,
     [*They all stand ceremoniously looking on
     Timon.*]
Ceremony was but devis'd at first   15
To set a gloss on faint deeds, hollow welcomes,
Recanting goodness, sorry ere 'tis shown;
But where there is true friendship, there needs none.
Pray, sit; more welcome are ye to my fortunes
Than my fortunes to me.   [*They sit.*]   20
1. Lord. My lord, we always have confess'd it.
Apem. Ho, ho, confess'd it! Hang'd it, have
     you not?
Tim. O, Apemantus, you are welcome.
Apem.   No;
You shall not make me welcome.
I come to have thee thrust me out of doors.   25
Tim. Fie, thou'rt a churl. Ye've got a humour
     there
Does not become a man; 'tis much to blame. They
say, my lords, "*Ira furor brevis est;*" but yond man
is [ever] angry. Go, let him have a table by him-
self, for he does neither affect company, nor is he
fit for't, indeed.   31
Apem. Let me stay at thine apperil, Timon.
I come to observe; I give thee warning on't.
Tim. I take no heed of thee; thou'rt an Athenian,
therefore welcome. I myself would have no power;
prithee, let my meat make thee silent.   37
Apem. I scorn thy meat; 'twould choke me,
for I should ne'er flatter thee. O you gods, what
a number of men eats Timon, and he sees 'em not!
It grieves me to see so many dip their meat in one
man's blood; and all the madness is, he cheers
them up too.   43
I wonder men dare trust themselves with men.
Methinks they should invite them without knives;
Good for their meat, and safer for their lives.   46
There's much example for 't: the fellow that sits
next him now, parts bread with him, pledges the
breath of him in a divided draught, is the readiest
man to kill him; 't has been proved. If I were a
huge man, I should fear to drink at meals   51
Lest they should spy my windpipe's dangerous
     notes.
Great men should drink with harness on their
     throats.
Tim. My lord, in heart; and let the health go
     round.
2. Lord. Let it flow this way, my good lord.   55
Apem. Flow this way! A brave fellow! he keeps
his tides well. Those healths will make thee and

283. **opposite:** hostile. 288. **meed:** gift. 291. **use of quittance:** customary requital.
Sc. ii, S.D. **Hautboys:** wind instruments. **States:** princes. 13. **faults . . . rich:** faults in the rich. 22. **confess'd . . . not.**
Echo of the proverb, "Confess and be hanged." 26. **humour:** disposition. 28. "***Ira . . . est***": wrath is a brief madness. 29.
[ever] (Rowe). *verie* F. 30. **affect:** like. 32. **apperil:** risk. 42–43. **cheers . . . up:** encourages them. 45. **knives.** In
Shakespeare's day guests brought their own knives. 49. **divided:** shared. 51. **huge:** great. 54. **in heart:** heartily.

purpose of ladies?

thy state look ill, Timon. Here's that which is
too weak to be a sinner, honest water, which ne'er
left man i' th' mire.   60
This and my food are equals; there's no odds.
Feasts are too proud to give thanks to the gods.

Apemantus' grace.

Immortal gods, I crave no pelf;
I pray for no man but myself.
Grant I may never prove so fond   65
To trust man on his oath or bond;
Or a harlot for her weeping;
Or a dog that seems a-sleeping;
Or a keeper with my freedom;
Or my friends, if I should need 'em.   70
Amen. So fall to't.
Rich men sin, and I eat root.
                              [*Eats and drinks.*]
Much good dich thy good heart, Apemantus!
  Tim. Captain Alcibiades, your heart's in the
field now.   75
  Alcib. My heart is ever at your service, my lord.
  Tim. You had rather be at a breakfast of enemies
than a dinner of friends.   79
  Alcib. So they were bleeding-new, my lord,
there's no meat like 'em. I could wish my best
friend at such a feast.
  Apem. Would all those flatterers were thine
enemies then, that then thou mightst kill 'em and
bid me to 'em!   85
  1. Lord. Might we but have that happiness,
my lord, that you would once use our hearts,
whereby we might express some part of our zeals,
we should think ourselves for ever perfect.   90
  Tim. O, no doubt, my good friends, but the gods
themselves have provided that I shall have much
help from you. How had you been my friends else?
Why have you that charitable title from thousands,
did not you chiefly belong to my heart? I have 95
told more of you to myself than you can with
modesty speak in your own behalf; and thus far I
confirm you. O you gods, think I, what need we
have any friends, if we should ne'er have need of
'em? They were the most needless creatures   100
living, should we ne'er have use for 'em, and would
most resemble sweet instruments hung up in cases
that keep their sounds to themselves. Why, I have
often wish'd myself poorer, that I might come
nearer to you. We are born to do benefits; and 105
what better or properer can we call our own than
the riches of our friends? O, what a precious
comfort 'tis to have so many, like brothers, commanding one another's fortunes! O joy, e'en made

away ere't can be born! Mine eyes cannot   110
hold out water, methinks; to forget their faults,
I drink to you.
  Apem. Thou weep'st to make them drink,
Timon.
  2. Lord. Joy had the like conception in our eyes,
And at that instant like a babe sprung up.   116
  Apem. Ho, ho! I laugh to think that babe a
    bastard.
  3. Lord. I promise you, my lord, you mov'd me
    much.
  Apem. Much!   [*Tucket, within.*
  Tim. What means that trump?

Enter a SERVANT.

                              How now? 120
  Serv. Please you, my lord, there are certain
ladies most desirous of admittance.
  Tim. Ladies! what are their wills?
  Serv. There comes with them a forerunner, my
lord, which bears that office to signify their pleas-
ures.   126
  Tim. I pray, let them be admitted.

Enter CUPID.

  Cup. Hail to thee, worthy Timon, and to all
That of his bounties taste! The five best senses
Acknowledge thee their patron, and come freely
To gratulate thy plenteous bosom. [Th' ear]. 131
Taste, touch, [and smell], pleas'd from thy table
    rise;
They only now come but to feast thine eyes.
  Tim. They're welcome all; let 'em have kind
    admittance:
Music, make their welcome!   [*Exit Cupid.*] 135
  1. Lord. You see, my lord, how ample you're
    belov'd.

[*Music. Re-enter* Cupid, *with a mask of* LADIES,
as] Amazons, *with lutes in their hands, dancing
and playing.*

  Apem. Hoy-day, what a sweep of vanity comes
    this way!
They dance! they are mad women.
Like madness is the glory of this life,
As this pomp shows to a little oil and root.   140
We make ourselves fools to disport ourselves,
And spend our flatteries to drink those men
Upon whose age we void it up again
With poisonous spite and envy.
Who lives that's not depraved or depraves?   145
Who dies that bears not one spurn to their graves
Of their friends' gift?

62. **Feasts:** feasters.   65. **fond:** foolish.   73. **dich:** may it do.   94. **from:** apart from.   98. **confirm you:** confirm
your protestations.   109. **made away:** dissolved (in tears).   110. **born:** expressed.   119. s.d. *Tucket:* trumpet call.
F here reads: *Sound Tucket. Enter the Maskers of Amazons, with* (etc. as at l. 137).   128. s.d. **Enter** CUPID.   F reads
Enter Cupid with the Maske of Ladies.   131. [**Th' ear**] (Warburton conj.).   *There* F.   132. [**and smell**] (Deighton).   *all* F.
139. **Like:** just such.   142. **drink:** drink healths to.   143. **age:** old age.   146. **spurn:** blow.   147. **gift:** giving.

I should fear those that dance before me now
Would one day stamp upon me; 't has been done;
Men shut their doors against a setting sun.   150

The Lords rise from table, with much adoring of
Timon; and to show their loves, each singles out an
Amazon, and all dance, men with women, a lofty
strain or two to the hautboys, and cease.

Tim. You have done our pleasures much grace,
   fair ladies,
Set a fair fashion on our entertainment,
Which was not half so beautiful and kind.
You have added worth unto 't and lustre,
And entertain'd me with mine own device;   155
I am to thank you for 't.
   1. [*Lady*]. My lord, you take us even at the best.
Apem. Faith, for the worst is filthy, and would
not hold taking, I doubt me.
   Tim. Ladies, there is an idle banquet attends
   you;   160
Please you to dispose yourselves.
   All Ladies. Most thankfully, my lord.
                  [*Exeunt* [*Cupid and Ladies*].
   Tim. Flavius.
   Flav. My lord?
   Tim.   The little casket bring me hither.
   Flav. Yes, my lord. — More jewels yet!   165
                       [*Aside.*]
There is no crossing him in 's humour;
Else I should tell him well (i' faith, I should),
When all's spent, he'd be cross'd then, an he could.
'Tis pity bounty had not eyes behind,
That man might ne'er be wretched for his mind.
                       [*Exit.*
   1. Lord. Where be our men?   171
   Serv. Here, my lord, in readiness.
   2. Lord. Our horses!

     [*Re-enter* FLAVIUS, *with the casket.*]

   Tim.   O my friends,
I have one word to say to you. Look you, my good
   lord,
I must entreat you honour me so much   175
As to advance this jewel. Accept it and wear it,
Kind my lord.
   1. Lord. I am so far already in your gifts, —
   All. So are we all.

         Enter a SERVANT.

   Serv. My lord, there are certain nobles of the
   Senate   180
Newly alighted, and come to visit you.
   Tim. They are fairly welcome.   [*Exit Serv.*]
   Flav.   I beseech your honour,

Vouchsafe me a word; it does concern you near.
   Tim. Near! why then, another time I'll hear thee.
I prithee, let's be provided to show them entertain-
   ment.   185
   Flav. [*Aside.*] I scarce know how.

       Enter a second SERVANT.

   [*2.*] *Serv.* May it please your honour, Lord
   Lucius,
Out of his free love, hath presented to you
Four milk-white horses, trapp'd in silver.
   Tim. I shall accept them fairly; let the presents
Be worthily entertain'd.   [*Exit Serv.*]   190

       Enter a third SERVANT.
                 How now! what news?
   3. Serv. Please you, my lord, that honourable
gentleman, Lord Lucullus, entreats your company
to-morrow to hunt with him, and has sent your
honour two brace of greyhounds.   195
   Tim. I'll hunt with him; and let them be re-
   ceiv'd,
Not without fair reward.   [*Exit Serv.*]
   Flav.   [*Aside.*] What will this come to?
He commands us to provide, and give great gifts,
And all out of an empty coffer;
Nor will he know his purse, or yield me this,   200
To show him what a beggar his heart is,
Being of no power to make his wishes good.
His promises fly so beyond his state
That what he speaks is all in debt; he owes
For ev'ry word. He is so kind that he now   205
Pays interest for 't; his land's put to their books.
Well, would I were gently put out of office
Before I were forc'd out!
Happier is he that has no friend to feed
Than such that do e'en enemies exceed.   210
I bleed inwardly for my lord.   [*Exit.*
   Tim.   You do yourselves
Much wrong; you bate too much of your own merits.
Here, my lord, a trifle of our love.
   2. Lord. With more than common thanks I will
   receive it.
   3. Lord. O, he's the very soul of bounty!   215
   Tim. And now I remember, my lord, you gave
Good words the other day of a bay courser
I rode on. 'Tis yours, because you lik'd it.
   [*3*] *Lord.* O, I beseech you, pardon, me, my lord,
   in that.
   Tim. You may take my word, my lord; I know,
   no man   220
Can justly praise but what he does affect.
I weigh my friend's affection with mine own;

---

157. [**Lady**] (Steevens). *Lord* F.   160. **idle**: trifling.   168. **be cross'd**: have his debts crossed out.   170. **for his mind**: because of his generosity.   176. **advance**: honor (by accepting).   190. **entertain'd**: looked after.   203. **state**: estate.   210. **such ... exceed**: such friends as do him more harm than enemies.   219. [*3*] *Lord* (Capell conj.).   *1. Lord* F.

I'll tell you true.   I'll call to you.
All Lords.   O, none so welcome.
Tim. I take all and your several visitations
So kind to heart, 'tis not enough to give;   225
Methinks, I could deal kingdoms to my friends,
And ne'er be weary.   Alcibiades,
Thou art a soldier, therefore seldom rich.
It comes in charity to thee; for all thy living
Is 'mongst the dead, and all the lands thou hast   230
Lie in a pitch'd field.
Alcib.   Ay, defil'd land, my lord.
1. Lord. We are so virtuously bound —
Tim.   And so
Am I to you.
2. Lord.   So infinitely endear'd —
Tim. All to you.   Lights, more lights!
1. Lord.   The best of happiness,   234
Honour, and fortunes, keep with you, Lord Timon!
Tim. Ready for his friends.
            [*Exeunt* [*all but Apemantus and Timon*].
Apem.   What a coil's here!
Serving of becks and jutting-out of bums!
I doubt whether their legs be worth the sums
That are given for 'em.   Friendship's full of
                dregs;
Methinks, false hearts should never have sound
                legs.   240
Thus honest fools lay out their wealth on curtsies.
Tim. Now, Apemantus, if thou wert not sullen,
I would be good to thee.   243
Apem. No, I'll nothing; for if I should be brib'd
too, there would be none left to rail upon thee, and
then thou wouldst sin the faster.   Thou giv'st so
long, Timon, I fear me thou wilt give away thyself
in paper shortly.   What needs these feasts, pomps,
and vain-glories?   249
Tim. Nay, an you begin to rail on society once,
I am sworn not to give regard to you.   Farewell;
and come with better music.   [*Exit.*
Apem. So;
Thou wilt not hear me now.   Thou shalt not, then;
I'll lock thy heaven from thee.   255
O, that men's ears should be
To counsel deaf, but not to flattery!   [*Exit.*

[ACT II]

[SCENE I.   *A Senator's house.*]

Enter SENATOR [*with papers in his hand*].

Sen. And late, five thousand; to Varro and to
    Isidore

He owes nine thousand; besides my former sum,
Which makes it five and twenty.   Still in motion
Of raging waste?   It cannot hold; it will not.
If I want gold, steal but a beggar's dog   5
And give it Timon; why, the dog coins gold.
If I would sell my horse and buy twenty more
Better than he, why, give my horse to Timon,
Ask nothing, give it him, it foals me straight,
And able horses.   No porter at his gate,   10
But rather one that smiles and still invites
All that pass by.   It cannot hold; no reason
Can [found] his state in safety.   Caphis, ho!
Caphis, I say!

Enter CAPHIS.

Caph.   Here, sir; what is your pleasure?
Sen. Get on your cloak and haste you to Lord
    Timon.   15
Importune him for my moneys; be not ceas'd
With slight denial, nor then silenc'd when
"Commend me to your master," and the cap
Plays in the right hand, thus; but tell him
My uses cry to me, I must serve my turn   20
Out of mine own.   His days and times are past,
And my reliances on his fracted dates
Have smit my credit.   I love and honour him,
But must not break my back to heal his finger.
Immediate are my needs, and my relief   25
Must not be toss'd and turn'd to me in words,
But find supply immediate.   Get you gone.
Put on a most importunate aspect,
A visage of demand; for I do fear,
When every feather sticks in his own wing,   30
Lord Timon will be left a naked gull,
Which flashes now a phœnix.   Get you gone.
Caph. I go, sir.
Sen. Take the bonds along with you,
And have the dates [in compt].
Caph.   I will, sir.
Sen.   Go.   35
                                    [*Exeunt.*

[SCENE II.   *The same.   A hall in Timon's house.*]

Enter Steward [FLAVIUS], *with many bills in his hand.*

Flav. No care, no stop! so senseless of expense,
That he will neither know how to maintain it,
Nor cease his flow of riot; takes no account
How things go from him, nor [resumes] no care
Of what is to continue; never mind   5
Was to be so unwise to be so kind.

223. **to you:** at your house.   229. **It ... thee:** to give to you is charity.   231. **defil'd:** with a quibble on *pitch'd*.   236.
coil: fuss.   237. **Serving of becks:** bowing.   238. **legs:** (1) limbs, (2) bows.
    Act II, sc. i, 1. **late:** lately.   13. **[found]** (Hanmer).   *sound* F.   **[found] ... state:** can regard his state as founded.   22.
fracted: broken.   30. **feather ... wing:** i.e., creditor has recovered his due.   31. **gull:** (1) unfledged bird, (2) dupe.   34.
Take. Before *take* Ff insert *I go sir?*, a pointless repetition.   35. **[in compt]** (Theobald).   *in.   Come* F.   **compt:** reckoning.
Sc. ii, 1. **Flav.** F heads the speeches of Flavius *Stew.*   4. **[resumes]** (Rowe): takes.   *resume* F.

What shall be done? He will not hear, till feel.
I must be round with him, now he comes from
    hunting.
Fie, fie, fie, fie!

Enter CAPHIS [*and the* Servants *of*] ISIDORE *and*
    VARRO.

Caph.   Good even, Varro. What, 9
You come for money?
  Var. [*Serv.*]   Is't not your business too?
  Caph. It is; and yours too, Isidore?
  Isid. [*Serv.*]   It is so.
  Caph. Would we were all discharg'd!
  Var. [*Serv.*]   I fear it.
  Caph. Here comes the lord.

    Enter TIMON *and his train* [*with* Alcibiades].

  Tim. So soon as dinner's done, we'll forth again,
My Alcibiades. — With me what is your will? 15
  Caph. My lord, here is a note of certain dues.
  Tim. Dues! Whence are you?
  Caph.   Of Athens here, my lord.
  Tim. Go to my steward.
  Caph. Please it your lordship, he hath put me off
To the succession of new days this month. 20
My master is awak'd by great occasion
To call upon his own, and humbly prays you
That with your other noble parts you'll suit
In giving him his right.
  Tim.   Mine honest friend,
I prithee, but repair to me next morning. 25
  Caph. Nay, good my lord, —
  Tim.   Contain thyself, good friend.
  Var. [*Serv.*] One Varro's servant, my good lord, —
  Isid. [*Serv.*] From Isidore.
He humbly prays your speedy payment.
  Caph. If you did know, my lord, my master's
    wants —
  Var. [*Serv.*] 'Twas due on forfeiture, my lord,
    six weeks 30
And past.
  Isid. [*Serv.*] Your steward puts me off, my lord,
And I am sent expressly to your lordship.
  Tim. Give me breath.
I do beseech you, good my lords, keep on; 35
I'll wait upon you instantly.
                [*Exeunt Alcibiades and Lords.*]
        [*To Flav.*] Come hither. Pray you,
How goes the world, that I am thus encount'red
With clamorous demands of [date-broke] bonds,
And the detention of long-since-due debts,
Against my honour?
  [*Flav.*]   Please you, gentlemen, 40
The time is unagreeable to this business.

Your importunacy cease till after dinner,
That I may make his lordship understand
Wherefore you are not paid.
  Tim. Do so, my friends. See them well en-
    tertain'd.   [*Exit.*] 45
  Flav. Pray, draw near.   [*Exit.*

    Enter APEMANTUS *and* FOOL.

  Caph. Stay, stay, here comes the Fool with
Apemantus; let's ha' some sport with 'em.
  Var. [*Serv.*] Hang him, he'll abuse us.
  Isid. [*Serv.*] A plague upon him, dog! 50
  Var. [*Serv.*] How dost, Fool?
  Apem. Dost dialogue with thy shadow?
  Var. [*Serv.*] I speak not to thee.
  Apem. No, 'tis to thyself. [*To the Fool.*] Come
away. 55
  Isid. [*Serv.*] [*to Var. Serv.*] There's the Fool hangs
on your back already.
  Apem. No, thou stand'st single; thou'rt not on
    him yet.
  Caph. Where's the Fool now? 59
  Apem. He last ask'd the question. Poor rogues,
and usurers' men! bawds between gold and want!
  All [*Serv.*]. What are we, Apemantus?
  Apem. Asses.
  All [*Serv.*]. Why? 65
  Apem. That you ask me what you are, and do
not know yourselves. Speak to 'em, Fool.
  Fool. How do you, gentlemen?
  All [*Serv.*]. Gramercies, good Fool; how does
your mistress? 70
  Fool. She's e'en setting on water to scald such
chickens as you are. Would we could see you at
Corinth!
  Apem. Good! gramercy.

    Enter PAGE.

  Fool. Look you, here comes my [mistress's]
page. 75
  Page. [*To the Fool.*] Why, how now, captain!
what do you in this wise company? How dost
thou, Apemantus?
  Apem. Would I had a rod in my mouth, that I
might answer thee profitably. 80
  Page. Prithee, Apemantus, read me the superscription of these letters; I know not which is which.
  Apem. Canst not read?
  Page. No. 85
  Apem. There will little learning die, then, that
day thou art hang'd. This is to Lord Timon; this
to Alcibiades. Go; thou wast born a bastard, and
thou'lt die a bawd. 89
  Page. Thou wast whelp'd a dog, and thou shalt

---

7. **feel:** (he) suffers. 8. **round:** blunt. 10. **Var.** [**Serv.**]. F heads the speeches of the servants by their masters' names.
23. **suit:** be consistent. 38. [**date-broke**] (Steevens): overdue. *debt, broken* F. 69. **Gramercies:** many thanks. 73.
Corinth: cant term for brothel. 75, 107. [**mistress's**] (Theobald). *Masters* F.

famish a dog's death.   Answer not; I am gone.
[*Exit.*
Apem. E'en so thou outrunn'st grace.   Fool,
I will go with you to Lord Timon's.
Fool. Will you leave me there?   95
Apem. If Timon stay at home.   You three serve
three usurers?
All [Serv.]. Ay; would they serv'd us!
Apem. So would I, — as good a trick as ever
hangman serv'd thief.   100
Fool. Are you three usurers' men?
All [Serv.]. Ay, Fool.
Fool. I think no usurer but has a fool to his
servant; my mistress is one, and I am her fool.
When men come to borrow of your masters, they
approach sadly and go away merry; but they enter
my [mistress's] house merrily, and go away sadly.
The reason of this?   108
Var. [Serv.] I could render one.
Apem. Do it then, that we may account thee a
whoremaster and a knave; which notwithstanding,
thou shalt be no less esteemed.
Var. [Serv.] What is a whoremaster, Fool?   113
Fool. A fool in good clothes, and something like
thee.   'Tis a spirit; sometime 't appears like a lord,
sometime like a lawyer, sometime like a philosopher,
with two stones moe than 's artificial one.   He is
very often like a knight; and, generally, in all shapes
that man goes up and down in from fourscore to
thirteen, this spirit walks in.   121
Var. [Serv.] Thou art not altogether a fool.
Fool. Nor thou altogether a wise man.   As much
foolery as I have, so much wit thou lack'st.
Apem. That answer might have become Apemantus.   126
All [Serv.]. Aside, aside; here comes Lord Timon.

Re-enter TIMON *and Steward* [FLAVIUS].

Apem. Come with me, Fool, come.
Fool. I do not always follow lover, elder brother,
and woman; sometime the philosopher.   131
[*Exeunt Apemantus and Fool.*]
Flav. Pray you, walk near; I'll speak with you
anon.   [*Exeunt [Servants].*]
Tim. You make me marvel.   Wherefore ere this
time
Had you not fully laid my state before me,
That I might so have rated my expense   135
As I had leave of means?
Flav.   You would not hear me,
At many leisures I propos'd.
Tim.   Go to!

Perchance some single vantages you took,
When my indisposition put you back,
And that unaptness made your minister   146
Thus to excuse yourself.
Flav.   O my good lord,
At many times I brought in my accounts,
Laid them before you; you would throw them off
And say you found them in mine honesty.
When, for some trifling present, you have bid me   145
Return so much, I have shook my head and wept;
Yea, 'gainst th' authority of manners, pray'd you
To hold your hand more close.   I did endure
Not seldom, nor no slight checks, when I have
Prompted you in the ebb of your estate   150
And your great flow of debts.   My lov'd lord,
Though you hear now, too late, — yet now's a
time, —
The greatest of your having lacks a half
To pay your present debts.
Tim.   Let all my land be sold.
Flav. 'Tis all engag'd, some forfeited and gone;
And what remains will hardly stop the mouth   156
Of present dues.   The future comes apace;
What shall defend the interim? and at length
How goes our reck'ning?
Tim. To Lacedæmon did my land extend.   160
Flav. O my good lord, the world is but a word;
Were it all yours to give it in a breath,
How quickly were it gone!
Tim.   You tell me true.
Flav. If you suspect my husbandry, or falsehood,
Call me before th' exactest auditors   165
And set me on the proof.   So the gods bless me,
When all our offices have been oppress'd
With riotous feeders, when our vaults have wept
With drunken spilth of wine, when every room
Hath blaz'd with lights and bray'd with min-
strelsy,   170
I have retir'd me to a wasteful cock
And set mine eyes at flow.
Tim.   Prithee, no more.
Flav. Heavens, have I said, the bounty of this
lord!
How many prodigal bits have slaves and peasants
This night englutted!   Who is not Timon's?   175
What heart, head, sword, force, means, but is Lord
Timon's?
Great Timon! noble, worthy, royal Timon!
Ah, when the means are gone that buy this praise,
The breath is gone whereof this praise is made.   179
Feast-won, fast-lost; one cloud of winter showers,
These flies are couch'd.
Tim.   Come, sermon me no further.

---

117. **artificial one:** the philosopher's stone.   129. **elder brother.** The elder brother, by custom of inheritance, would have more money.   150. **in:** in the matter of.   152. **time:** time at least to tell you.   153. **having:** possessions.   164. **husbandry:** management.   167. **offices:** larders.   169. **spilth:** spilling.   171. **cock:** spout, i.e., weeping.   181. **are couch'd:** go into hiding.

No villanous bounty yet hath pass'd my heart;
Unwisely, not ignobly, have I given.
Why dost thou weep? Canst thou the conscience lack
To think I shall lack friends? Secure thy heart; 185
If I would broach the vessels of my love,
And try the argument of hearts by borrowing,
Men and men's fortunes could I frankly use
As I can bid thee speak.
Flav.   Assurance bless your thoughts!
Tim. And, in some sort, these wants of mine
     are crown'd,   190
That I account them blessings; for by these
Shall I try friends. You shall perceive how you
Mistake my fortunes; I am wealthy in my friends.
Within there! [Flaminius!] Servilius!

Enter three SERVANTS [FLAMINIUS, Servilius, *and*
another].

Servants. My lord? my lord?   195
Tim. I will dispatch you severally; you to Lord
Lucius; to Lord Lucullus you, I hunted with his
honour to-day; you to Sempronius. Commend me
to their loves, and, I am proud, say, that my oc-
casions have found time to use 'em toward a supply
of money. Let the request be fifty talents.   202
Flam. As you have said, my lord.
Flav. [*Aside.*] Lord Lucius and Lucullus! Hum!
Tim. Go you, sir, to the senators —   205
Of whom, even to the state's best health, I have
Deserv'd this hearing — bid 'em send o' th' instant
A thousand talents to me.
Flav.   I have been bold —
For that I knew it the most general way —
To them to use your signet and your name;   210
But they do shake their heads, and I am here
No richer in return.
Tim.   Is't true? Can't be?
Flav. They answer, in a joint and corporate voice,
That now they are at fall, want treasure, cannot
Do what they would; are sorry — you are hon-
     ourable, —   215
But yet they could have wish'd — they know not —
Something hath been amiss — a noble nature
May catch a wrench — would all were well —
     'tis pity; —
And so, intending other serious matters,
After distasteful looks and these hard fractions, 220
With certain half-caps and cold-moving nods
They froze me into silence.
Tim.   You gods, reward them!
Prithee, man, look cheerly. These old fellows
Have their ingratitude in them hereditary.
Their blood is cak'd, 'tis cold, it seldom flows; 225

'Tis lack of kindly warmth they are not kind;
And nature, as it grows again toward earth,
Is fashion'd for the journey, dull and heavy.
[*To a Serv.*] Go to Ventidius. [*To Flav.*] Prithee,
     be not sad;
Thou art true and honest. Ingeniously I speak, 230
No blame belongs to thee. [*To Ser.*] Ventidius lately
Buried his father, by whose death he's stepp'd
Into a great estate. When he was poor,
Imprison'd, and in scarcity of friends,
I clear'd him with five talents. Greet him from
     me;   235
Bid him suppose some good necessity
Touches his friend, which craves to be rememb'red
With those five talents. [*Exit Ser.*] [*To Flav.*]
     That had, give 't these fellows
To whom 'tis instant due. Never speak or think
That Timon's fortunes 'mong his friends can sink.
Flav. I would I could not think it! That thought
     is bounty's foe;   241
Being free itself, it thinks all others so.   [*Exeunt.*

[ACT III]

[SCENE I. *A room in Lucullus' house.*]

FLAMINIUS *waiting to speak with a Lord from his
master. Enter a* SERVANT *to him.*

Serv. I have told my lord of you; he is coming
     down to you.
Flam. I thank you, sir.

Enter LUCULLUS.

Serv. Here's my lord.   3
Lucul. [*Aside.*] One of Lord Timon's men?
A gift, I warrant. Why, this hits right; I dreamt of
a silver basin and ewer to-night. — Flaminius,
honest Flaminius; you are very respectively welcome, sir. Fill me some wine. [*Exit Servant.*]
And how does that honourable, complete, free-
hearted gentleman of Athens, thy very bountiful
good lord and master?   11
Flam. His health is well, sir.
Lucul. I am right glad that his health is well,
sir; and what hast thou there under thy cloak,
pretty Flaminius?   15
Flam. Faith, nothing but an empty box, sir,
which, in my lord's behalf, I come to entreat your
honour to supply; who, having great and instant
occasions to use fifty talents, hath sent to your
lordship to furnish him, nothing doubting your
present assistance therein.   21
Lucul. La, la, la, la! "nothing doubting," says

184. **conscience:** intelligence. 185. **Secure:** set at ease. 186. **broach:** tap. 187. **argument of hearts:** professions of love. 189. **Assurance:** i.e., confirmation. 194. [Flaminius] (Rowe). *Flavius* F. 206. **to ... health:** to the extent of the state's utmost resources. 209. **general:** usual. 214. **at fall:** hard up. 220. **fractions:** fragments of discourse. 221. **half-caps:** grudging salutes. 226. **kindly:** natural. 230. **Ingeniously:** ingenuously, sincerely. 242. **free:** liberal.
Act III. sc. i. 7. **respectively:** particularly.

he? Alas, good lord! a noble gentleman 'tis, if he would not keep so good a house. Many a time and often I ha' din'd with him, and told him on't, and come again to supper to him of purpose to have 26 him spend less, and yet he would embrace no counsel, take no warning by my coming. Every man has his fault, and honesty is his. I ha' told him on't, but I could ne'er get him from 't. 30

Re-enter SERVANT, *with wine.*

Serv. Please your lordship, here is the wine.

Lucul. Flaminius, I have noted thee always wise. Here's to thee.

Flam. Your lordship speaks your pleasure. 35

Lucul. I have observed thee always for a to-wardly prompt spirit — give thee thy due — and one that knows what belongs to reason, and canst use the time well, if the time use thee well; good parts in thee. [*To Serv.*] Get you gone, sirrah. 40 [*Exit Serv.*] Draw nearer, honest Flaminius. Thy lord's a bountiful gentleman; but thou art wise, and thou know'st well enough, although thou com'st to me, that this is no time to lend money, especially upon bare friendship, without security. Here's 45 three solidares for thee; good boy, wink at me and say thou saw'st me not. Fare thee well.

Flam. Is't possible the world should so much differ,
And we alive that lived? Fly, damned baseness,
To him that worships thee! 51

                [*Throwing the money back.*]

Lucul. Ha! now I see thou art a fool, and fit for thy master.   [*Exit.*

Flam. May these add to the number that may scald thee!
Let molten coin be thy damnation, 55
Thou disease of a friend, and not himself!
Has friendship such a faint and milky heart,
It turns in less than two nights? O you gods,
I feel my master's passion! This slave,
Unto his honour, has my lord's meat in him; 60
Why should it thrive and turn to nutriment
When he is turn'd to poison?
O, may diseases only work upon't!
And, when he's sick to death, let not that part of nature
Which my lord paid for, be of any power 65
To expel sickness, but prolong his hour! [*Exit.*

[SCENE II. *A public place.*]

Enter LUCIUS, *with three* STRANGERS.

Luc. Who, the Lord Timon? He is my very good friend, and an honourable gentleman.

1. Stran. We know him for no less, though we are but strangers to him. But I can tell you one thing, my lord, and which I hear from common rumours: now Lord Timon's happy hours are done and past, and his estate shrinks from him. 8

Luc. Fie, no, do not believe it; he cannot want for money.

2. Stran. But believe you this, my lord, that not long ago one of his men was with the Lord Lucullus to borrow so many talents nay, urg'd extremely for't and showed what necessity belong'd to't, and yet was deni'd. 15

Luc. How!

2. Stran. I tell you, deni'd, my lord.

Luc. What a strange case was that! Now, before the gods, I am asham'd on't. Denied that honourable man! There was very little honour 20 show'd in't. For my own part, I must needs confess, I have received some small kindnesses from him, as money, plate, jewels, and such-like trifles, nothing comparing to his; yet, had he mistook him and sent to me, I should ne'er have denied his occasion so many talents. 26

Enter SERVILIUS.

Ser. See, by good hap, yonder's my lord; I have sweat to see his honour. My honour'd lord, —
                      [*To Lucius.*]

Luc. Servilius! you are kindly met, sir. Fare thee well; commend me to thy honourable virtuous lord, my very exquisite friend. 32

Ser. May it please your honour, my lord hath sent —

Luc. Ha! what has he sent? I am so much endeared to that lord; he's ever sending. How shall I thank him, think'st thou? And what has he sent now? 38

Ser. Has only sent his present occasion now, my lord, requesting your lordship to supply his instant use with so many talents. 41

Luc. I know his lordship is but merry with me;
He cannot want fifty-five hundred talents.

Ser. But in the meantime he wants less, my lord.
If his occasion were not virtuous, 45
I should not urge it half so faithfully.

Luc. Dost thou speak seriously, Servilius?

Ser. Upon my soul, 'tis true, sir.

Luc. What a wicked beast was I to disfurnish myself against such a good time, when I might ha' 50 shown myself honourable! How unluckily it happ'ned that I should purchase the day before for a little part, and undo a great deal of honour! Servilius, now, before the gods, I am not able to do, — the more beast, I say! — I was sending to use 55

Lord Timon myself, these gentlemen can witness;
but I would not, for the wealth of Athens, I had
done't now.   Commend me bountifully to his good
lordship; and I hope his honour will conceive the fairest of me, because I have no power to be kind.   60
And tell him this from me, I count it one of my
greatest afflictions, say, that I cannot pleasure such
an honourable gentleman.   Good Servilius, will you
befriend me so far as to use mine own words to him?
Ser. Yes, sir, I shall.   66
Luc. I'll look you out a good turn, Servilius.
                                    [*Exit Servilius.*
True, as you said, Timon is shrunk indeed;
And he that's once deni'd will hardly speed. [*Exit.*
    1. Stran. Do you observe this, Hostilius?
    2. Stran.   Ay, too well.
    1. Stran. Why, this is the world's soul; and just
        of the same piece   71
Is every flatterer's spirit.   Who can call him
His friend that dips in the same dish? for, in
My knowing, Timon has been this lord's father,
And kept his credit with his purse,   75
Supported his estate; nay, Timon's money
Has paid his men their wages.   He ne'er drinks
But Timon's silver treads upon his lip;
And yet — O, see the monstrousness of man
When he looks out in an ungrateful shape! —   80
He does deny him, in respect of his,
What charitable men afford to beggars.
    3. Stran. Religion groans at it.
    1. Stran.   For mine own part,
I never tasted Timon in my life,
Nor came any of his bounties over me   85
To mark me for his friend; yet, I protest,
For his right noble mind, illustrious virtue,
And honourable carriage,
Had his necessity made use of me,
I would have put my wealth into donation,   90
And the best half should have return'd to him,
So much I love his heart.   But I perceive
Men must learn now with pity to dispense,
For policy sits above conscience.   [*Exeunt.*

[SCENE III. *A room in Sempronius' house.*]

Enter a third SERVANT *with* SEMPRONIUS, *an-
        other of Timon's friends.*

Sem. Must he needs trouble me in't, — hum!
        — 'bove all others?
He might have tried Lord Lucius or Lucullus;
And now Ventidius is wealthy too,
Whom he redeem'd from prison.   All these
Owe their estates unto him.

Serv.   My lord, they   5
Have all been touch'd and found base metal, for
They have all denied him.
    Sem.   How! Have they deni'd him?
Has Ventidius and Lucullus deni'd him,
And does he send to me?   Three?   hum!
It shows but little love or judgement in him.   10
Must I be his last refuge?   His friends, like physi-
        cians,
[Thrice] give him over; must I take th' cure upon
        me?
Has much disgrac'd me in't; I'm angry at him,
That might have known my place.   I see no sense
        for't,
But his occasions might have wooed me first;   15
For, in my conscience, I was the first man
That e'er received gift from him;
And does he think so backwardly of me now,
That I'll requite it last?   No!
So [I] may prove an argument of laughter   20
To th' rest, and [amongst] lords be thought a fool.
I'd rather than the worth of thrice the sum,
Had sent to me first, but for my mind's sake;
I'd such a courage to do him good.   But now return,
And with their faint reply this answer join: 25
Who bates mine honour shall not know my coin.
                                    [*Exit.*
    Serv. Excellent!   Your lordship's a goodly villain.
The devil knew not what he did when he made man
politic; he crossed himself by 't; and I cannot think
but, in the end, the villanies of man will set him   30
clear.   How fairly this lord strives to appear foul!
takes virtuous copies to be wicked, like those that
under hot ardent zeal would set whole realms on fire;
Of such a nature is his politic love.   35
This was my lord's best hope; now all are fled,
Save only the gods.   Now his friends are dead,
Doors, that were ne'er acquainted with their wards
Many a bounteous year, must be employ'd
Now to guard sure their master.   40
And this is all a liberal course allows;
Who cannot keep his wealth must keep his house.
                                    [*Exit.*

[SCENE IV.   *The same.   A hall in Timon's house.*]

Enter VARRO'S MEN, *meeting* [TITUS *and*] *others, all
    [servants of] Timon's creditors, to wait for his
    coming out.   Then enter* LUCIUS *and* HORTENSIUS.

    [*1.*] *Var.* [*Serv.*] Well met; good morrow, Titus and
        Hortensius.
    Tit. The like to you, kind Varro.
    Hor.   Lucius!

69. **speed:** prosper.   81. **in respect of his:** in proportion to his resources.
Sc. iii, 6. **touch'd:** tested (as with a touchstone).   12. **[Thrice]** (Johnson).   *Thrive* F.   18. **backwardly:** late and unworthily.   20. **[I]** (Staunton conj.).   *it* F.   **argument:** theme.   21. **[amongst]** (Edd.).   *'mong'st* F.   **be** F₁.   *I be* F₂₋₄.   24. **courage:**
heart.   29. **crossed:** thwarted.   30-31. **set ... clear:** make him (the devil) look innocent.   38. **wards:** locks.   42. **must keep:**
must guard.
Sc. iv, 1. [*1.*] *Var.* [*Serv.*]   F reads *Var. men.*

What, do we meet together?

Luc.   Ay, and I think
One business does command us all; for mine
Is money.   5

Tit. So is theirs and ours.

Enter PHILOTUS.

Luc.   And Sir Philotus too!

Phi. Good day at once.

Luc.   Welcome, good brother.
What do you think the hour?

Phi.   Labouring for nine.

Luc. So much?

Phi.   Is not my lord seen yet?

Luc.   Not yet.

Phi. I wonder on't; he was wont to shine at
seven.   10

Luc. Ay, but the days are wax'd shorter with
him.
You must consider that a prodigal course
Is like the sun's; but not, like his, recoverable.
I fear 'tis deepest winter in Lord Timon's purse;
That is, one may reach deep enough and yet   15
Find little.

Phi.   I am of your fear for that.

Tit. I'll show you how t' observe a strange event.
Your lord sends now for money.

Hor.   Most true, he does.

Tit. And he wears jewels now of Timon's gift,
For which I wait for money.   20

Hor. It is against my heart.

Luc.   Mark, how strange it shows
Timon in this should pay more than he owes;
And e'en as if your lord should wear rich jewels
And send for money for 'em.

Hor. I'm weary of this charge, the gods can
witness.   25
I know my lord hath spent of Timon's wealth,
And now ingratitude makes it worse than stealth.

[I.] Var. [Serv.] Yes, mine's three thousand
crowns; what's yours?

Luc. Five thousand mine.

[I.] Var. [Serv.] 'Tis much deep: and it should
seem by th' sum   30
Your master's confidence was above mine;
Else surely his had equall'd.

Enter FLAMINIUS.

Tit. One of Lord Timon's men.

Luc. Flaminius! Sir, a word. Pray, is my lord
ready to come forth?   35

Flam. No, indeed, he is not.

Tit. We attend his lordship; pray, signify so
much.

Flam. I need not tell him that; he knows you are
too diligent.   [*Exit.*   40

Enter Steward [FLAVIUS] in a cloak, muffled.

Luc. Ha! is not that his steward muffled so?
He goes away in a cloud; call him, call him.

Tit. Do you hear, sir?

2. Var. [Serv.] By your leave, sir, —

[Flav.] What do ye ask of me, my friend?   45

Tit. We wait for certain money here, sir.

[Flav.]   Ay,
If money were as certain as your waiting,
'Twere sure enough.
Why then preferr'd you not your sums and bills
When your false masters eat of my lord's meat? 50
Then they could smile and fawn upon his debts,
And take down th' interest into their glutt'nous
maws.
You do yourselves but wrong to stir me up;
Let me pass quietly.
Believe 't, my lord and I have made an end;   55
I have no more to reckon, he to spend.

Luc. Ay, but this answer will not serve.

[Flav.] If 'twill not serve, 'tis not so base as you;
For you serve knaves.   [*Exit.*

1. Var. [Serv.] How! what does his cashier'd worship mutter?   61

2. Var. [Serv.] No matter what; he's poor, and
that's revenge enough. Who can speak broader
than he that has no house to put his head in? Such
may rail against great buildings.   65

Enter SERVILIUS.

Tit. O, here's Servilius; now we shall know some
answer.

Ser. If I might beseech you, gentlemen, to repair
some other hour, I should derive much from 't; for,
take 't of my soul, my lord leans wondrously to discontent. His comfortable temper has forsook him;
he's much out of health and keeps his chamber. 73

Luc. Many do keep their chambers are not sick;
And, if it be so far beyond his health,
Methinks he should the sooner pay his debts,
And make a clear way to the gods.

Ser.   Good gods!

Tit. We cannot take this for answer, sir.

Flam. (Within.) Servilius, help! My lord! my
lord!

Enter TIMON, in a rage [FLAMINIUS following].

Tim. What, are my doors oppos'd against my
passage?   80
Have I been ever free, and must my house
Be my retentive enemy, my gaol?
The place which I have feasted, does it now,

---

13. **recoverable:** retraceable.   25. **charge:** commission.   27. **stealth:** theft.   32. **his:** my master's loan.   63. **broader:**
more freely.   75. **it ... health:** his health is so far gone.   77. **the gods:** i.e., heaven.

Like all mankind, show me an iron heart?

Luc. Put in now, Titus.   85

Tit. My lord, here is my bill.

Luc. Here's mine.

[*Hor.*] And mine, my lord.

2. Var. [*Serv.*] And ours, my lord.

Phi. All our bills.   90

Tim. Knock me down with 'em; cleave me to the
girdle!

Luc. Alas, my lord, —

Tim. Cut my heart in sums.

Tit. Mine, fifty talents.

Tim. Tell out my blood.   95

Luc. Five thousand crowns, my lord.

Tim. Five thousand drops pays that.   What
yours? and yours?

1. Var. [*Serv.*] My lord, —

2. Var. [*Serv.*] My lord, —

Tim. Tear me, take me, and the gods fall upon
you!   [*Exit.* 100

Hor. Faith, I perceive our masters may throw
their caps at their money.   These debts may well
be call'd desperate ones, for a madman owes 'em.
[*Exeunt.*

Re-enter TIMON [*and* FLAVIUS].

Tim. They have e'en put my breath from me,
the slaves.

Creditors? Devils!   105

[*Flav.*] My dear lord, —

Tim. What if it should be so?

[*Flav.*] My lord, —

Tim. I'll have it so.   My steward!

[*Flav.*] Here, my lord.   110

Tim. So fitly?   Go, bid all my friends again,
Lucius, Lucullus, and Sempronius;
[Ventidius,] all:
I'll once more feast the rascals.

[*Flav.*]   O my lord,
You only speak from your distracted soul.   115
There is not so much left to furnish out
A moderate table.

Tim.   Be it not in thy care; go,
I charge thee, invite them all.   Let in the tide
Of knaves once more; my cook and I'll provide.
[*Exeunt.*

[SCENE V.   *The same.   The senate-house.*]

Enter three SENATORS *at one door,* ALCIBIADES
meeting them, with Attendants.

1. Sen. My lord, you have my voice to it; the
fault's

Bloody; 'tis necessary he should die.
Nothing emboldens sin so much as mercy.

2. Sen. Most true; the law shall bruise him.

Alcib. Honour, health, and compassion to the
Senate!   5

1. Sen. Now, captain?

Alcib. I am an humble suitor to your virtues,
For pity is the virtue of the law,
And none but tyrants use it cruelly.
It pleases time and fortune to lie heavy   10
Upon a friend of mine, who, in hot blood,
Hath stepp'd into the law, which is past depth
To those that, without heed, do plunge into 't.
He is a man, setting his [fault] aside,
Of comely virtues;   15
Nor did he soil the fact with cowardice —
An honour in him which buys out his fault —
But with a noble fury and fair spirit,
Seeing his reputation touch'd to death,
He did oppose his foe;   20
And with such sober and unnoted passion
He did [behave] his anger, ere 'twas spent,
As if he had but prov'd an argument.

1. Sen. You undergo too strict a paradox,
Striving to make an ugly deed look fair.   25
Your words have took such pains as if they labour'd
To bring manslaughter into form, and set quarrel-
ling
Upon the head of valour; which indeed
Is valour misbegot and came into the world
When sects and factions were newly born.   30
He's truly valiant that can wisely suffer
The worst that man can breathe, and make his
wrongs
His outsides, to wear them like his raiment, care-
lessly,
And ne'er prefer his injuries to his heart,
To bring it into danger.   35
If wrongs be evils and enforce us kill,
What folly 'tis to hazard life for ill!

Alcib. My lord, —

1. Sen.   You cannot make gross sins
look clear;
To revenge is no valour, but to bear.

Alcib. My lords, then, under favour, pardon
me   40
If I speak like a captain.
Why do fond men expose themselves to battle,
And not endure all threats, sleep upon 't,
And let the foes quietly cut their throats
Without repugnancy?   If there be   45
Such valour in the bearing, what make we
Abroad?   Why then, women are more valiant

88. [*Hor.*] (Capell).   *1. Var.* F.   91. **Knock... 'em.** A quibble on *bills:* (1) notes, (2) watchmen's clubs.   107. **What...
so?**: i.e., suppose I do it?   Timon has just conceived the idea of the banquet.   113. [**Ventidius**] (Grant White).   *VIIorxa* F.
Sc. v, 14. [**fault**] (Warburton conj.).   *fate* F.   16. **fact:** deed.   17. **buys out:** redeems.   21. **unnoted:** suppressed.   22.
[**behave**] (Rowe): control.   *behoove* F.   24. **undergo:** undertake.   27. **form:** good form.   **set:** i.e., as a crest.   34. **prefer:**
advance.

That stay at home, if bearing carry it;
And the ass more captain than the lion, the [felon]
Loaden with irons wiser than the judge,   50
If wisdom be in suffering. O my lords,
As you are great, be pitifully good.
Who cannot condemn rashness in cold blood?
To kill, I grant, is sin's extremest gust;
But, in defence, by mercy, 'tis most just.   55
To be in anger is impiety;
But who is man that is not angry?
Weigh but the crime with this.
    2. Sen. You breathe in vain.
    Alcib.   In vain! his service done
At Lacedæmon and Byzantium   60
Were a sufficient briber for his life.
    1. Sen. What's that?
    Alcib. [I] say, my lords, he has done fair service,
And slain in fight many of your enemies.
How full of valour did he bear himself   65
In the last conflict, and made plenteous wounds!
    2. Sen. He has made too much plenty with 'em.
He's a sworn rioter; he has a sin that often
Drowns him and takes his valour prisoner;
If there were no foes, that were enough   70
To overcome him. In that beastly fury
He has been known to commit outrages
And cherish factions. 'Tis inferr'd to us,
His days are foul and his drink dangerous.
    1. Sen. He dies.
    Alcib.   Hard fate! he might have died
        in war.   75
My lords, if not for any parts in him —
Though his right arm might purchase his own time
And be in debt to none — yet, more to move you,
Take my deserts to his, and join 'em both;
And, for I know your reverend ages love   80
Security, I'll pawn my victories, all
My honour to you, upon his good returns.
If by this crime he owes the law his life,
Why, let the war receive 't in valiant gore;
For law is strict, and war is nothing more.   85
    1. Sen. We are for law. He dies; urge it no more
On height of our displeasure. Friend or brother,
He forfeits his own blood that spills another.
    Alcib. Must it be so? It must not be. My
        lords,
I do beseech you, know me.   90
    2. Sen. How?
    Alcib. Call me to your remembrances.
    3. Sen.   What?
    Alcib. I cannot think but your age has forgot me;
It could not else be I should prove so base

To sue, and be deni'd such common grace.   95
My wounds ache at you.
    1. Sen.   Do you dare our anger?
'Tis in few words, but spacious in effect;
We banish thee for ever.
    Alcib.   Banish me!
Banish your dotage! Banish usury,
That makes the Senate ugly!   100
    1. Sen. If after two days' shine Athens contain
        thee,
Attend our weightier judgement. And, not to swell
        our spirit,
He shall be executed presently. [*Exeunt [Senators].*
    Alcib. Now the gods keep you old enough that
        you may live
Only in bone, that none may look on you!   105
I'm worse than mad. I have kept back their foes,
While they have told their money and let out
Their coin upon large interest, I myself
Rich only in large hurts. All those for this?
Is this the balsam that the usuring Senate   110
Pours into captains' wounds? Banishment!
It comes not ill; I hate not to be banish'd;
It is a cause worthy my spleen and fury,
That I may strike at Athens. I'll cheer up
My discontented troops, and lay for hearts.   115
'Tis honour with most lands to be at odds;
Soldiers should brook as little wrongs as gods.
                                          [*Exit.*

[SCENE VI. *The same. A banqueting-room in
        Timon's house.*]

[*Music. Tables set out:* Servants *attending.*] *Enter
divers friends* [LUCIUS, LUCULLUS, SEMPRONIUS,
VENTIDIUS, *and other* LORDS, Senators *and others,*]
at several doors.

    1. Lord. The good time of day to you, sir.
    2. Lord. I also wish it to you. I think this hon-
ourable lord did but try us this other day.
    1. Lord. Upon that were my thoughts tiring
when we encount'red. I hope it is not so low with
him as he made it seem in the trial of his several
friends.   7
    2. Lord. It should not be, by the persuasion of
his new feasting.
    1. Lord. I should think so. He hath sent me an
earnest inviting, which many my near occasions did
urge me to put off; but he hath conjur'd me beyond
them, and I must needs appear.   14
    2. Lord. In like manner was I in debt to my im-
portunate business, but he would not hear my ex-

---

48. **carry it:** i.e., gets the palm, is the thing. 49. **[felon]** (Johnson). *fellow* F. 54. **gust:** indulgence. 55. **mercy:** merciful judgment. 61. **briber:** pleader. 63. **[I]** (Pope). *Why* F. 73. **inferr'd:** alleged. 77. **his own time:** the right to the natural term of his life. 102. **Attend:** expect. **spirit:** anger. 105. **Only in bone:** mere skeletons. 107. **told:** counted. 115. **lay for hearts:** gain their loyalty.
    Sc. vi, 4. **tiring:** working. 11. **near:** important. 12. **put off:** decline.

cuse. I am sorry, when he sent to borrow of me, that my provision was out.

1. Lord. I am sick of that grief too, as I understand how all things go.   20

2. Lord. Every man here's so. What would he have borrowed of you?

1. Lord. A thousand pieces.

2. Lord. A thousand pieces!

1. Lord. What of you?   25

2. Lord. He sent to me, sir, — Here he comes.

Enter TIMON *and* Attendants.

Tim. With all my heart, gentlemen both; and how fare you?

1. Lord. Ever at the best, hearing well of your lordship.   30

2. Lord. The swallow follows not summer more willing than we your lordship.

Tim. [*Aside.*] Nor more willingly leaves winter; such summer birds are men. — Gentlemen, our dinner will not recompense this long stay; feast 35 your ears with the music a while, if they will fare so harshly. O, th' trumpet's sound; we shall to't presently.

1. Lord. I hope it remains not unkindly with your lordship that I return'd you an empty messenger.   41

Tim. O, sir, let it not trouble you.

2. Lord. My noble lord, —

Tim. Ah, my good friend, what cheer?   44
[*The banquet brought in.*

2. Lord. My most honourable lord, I am e'en sick of shame that, when your lordship this other day sent to me, I was so unfortunate a beggar.

Tim. Think not on't, sir.   49

2. Lord. If you had sent but two hours before, —

Tim. Let it not cumber your better remembrance. — Come, bring in all together!

2. Lord. All cover'd dishes!   55

1. Lord. Royal cheer, I warrant you.

3. Lord. Doubt not that, if money and the season can yield it.

1. Lord. How do you? What's the news?

3. Lord. Alcibiades is banish'd: hear you of it? 61

1. and 2. Lord. Alcibiades banish'd!

3. Lord. 'Tis so, be sure of it.

1. Lord. How! how!

2. Lord. I pray you, upon what?   65

Tim. My worthy friends, will you draw near?

3. Lord. I'll tell you more anon. Here's a noble feast toward.

2. Lord. This is the old man still.

3. Lord. Will 't hold? Will 't hold?   70

2. Lord. It does; but time will — and so —

3. Lord. I do conceive.

Tim. Each man to his stool, with that spur as he would to the lip of his mistress; your diet shall be in all places alike. Make not a city feast 75 of it, to let the meat cool ere we can agree upon the first place; sit, sit. The gods require our thanks.

You great benefactors, sprinkle our society with thankfulness. For your own gifts make your- 80 selves prais'd; but reserve still to give, lest your deities be despised. Lend to each man enough, that one need not lend to another; for, were your godheads to borrow of men, men would forsake the gods. Make the meat be beloved more than 85 the man that gives it. Let no assembly of twenty be without a score of villains; if there sit twelve women at the table, let a dozen of them be — as they are. The rest of your [foes], O gods — the senators of Athens, together with the common 90 [lag] of people — what is amiss in them, you gods, make suitable for destruction. For these my present friends, as they are to me nothing, so in nothing bless them, and to nothing are they welcome.

Uncover, dogs, and lap!   95
[*The dishes are uncovered and seen to be full of warm water.*]

Some speak. What does his lordship mean?

Some other. I know not.

Tim. May you a better feast never behold, You knot of mouth-friends! Smoke and lukewarm water
Is your perfection. This is Timon's last;   100
Who, stuck and spangled [with your] flatteries, Washes it off, and sprinkles in your faces Your reeking villainy.
[*Throwing the water in their faces.*]
Live loath'd and long.
Most smiling, smooth, detested parasites,   104
Courteous destroyers, affable wolves, meek bears, You fools of fortune, trencher-friends, time's flies, Cap-and-knee slaves, vapours, and minute-jacks! Of man and beast the infinite malady Crust you quite o'er! What, dost thou go? Soft! take thy physic first — thou too — and thou;
Stay, I will lend thee money, borrow none.   111
[*Throws the dishes at them, and drives them out.*]
What, all in motion? Henceforth be no feast Whereat a villain's not a welcome guest. Burn, house! sink, Athens! henceforth hated be Of Timon man and all humanity!   [*Exit.* 115

68. toward: at hand.   77. the … place: i.e., the order of seating.   89. [foes] (Hanmer). *fees* F.   90. [lag] (Rowe): dregs. *legge* F.   99. Smoke: steam.   101. [with your] (Warburton conj.).   *you with* F.   106. time's flies: fair-weather flies (cf. II.ii.180–81).   107. minute-jacks: time-servers.   108. the infinite: i.e., each and every.

Re-enter the SENATORS, *with other* LORDS.

1. Lord. How now, my lords!

2. Lord. Know you the quality of Lord Timon's fury?

3. Lord. Push! did you see my cap?

4. Lord. I have lost my gown.   120

1. Lord. He's but a mad lord, and nought but humours sways him. He gave me a jewel th' other day, and now he has beat it out of my hat. Did you see my jewel?

[*3.*] *Lord.* Did you see my cap?   125

[*2.*] *Lord.* Here 'tis.

4. Lord. Here lies my gown.

1. Lord. Let's make no stay.

2. Lord. Lord Timon's mad.

3. Lord. I feel 't upon my bones.   130

4. Lord. One day he gives us diamonds, next
    day stones.   [*Exeunt.*

[ACT IV]

[SCENE I. *Without the walls of Athens.*]

Enter TIMON.

Tim. Let me look back upon thee. O thou wall
That girdles in those wolves, dive in the earth
And fence not Athens! Matrons, turn incontinent!
Obedience fail in children! Slaves and fools,
Pluck the grave wrinkled Senate from the bench   5
And minister in their [steads]! To general filths
Convert o' th' instant green virginity!
Do 't in your parents' eyes! Bankrupts, hold fast;
Rather than render back, out with your knives
And cut your trusters' throats! Bound servants,
    steal!   10
Large-handed robbers your grave masters are
And pill by law. Maid, to thy master's bed;
Thy mistress is o' th' brothel! Son of sixteen,
Pluck the lin'd crutch from thy old limping sire;
With it beat out his brains! Piety, and fear,   15
Religion to the gods, peace, justice, truth,
Domestic awe, night-rest, and neighbourhood,
Instruction, manners, mysteries, and trades,
Degrees, observances, customs, and laws,
Decline to your confounding contraries,   20
And [let] confusion live! Plagues incident to men,
Your potent and infectious fevers heap
On Athens, ripe for stroke! Thou cold sciatica,
Cripple our senators, that their limbs may halt
As lamely as their manners! Lust and liberty   25
Creep in the minds and marrows of our youth,
That 'gainst the stream of virtue they may strive,

And drown themselves in riot! Itches, blains,
Sow all th' Athenian bosoms; and their crop
Be general leprosy! Breath infect breath,   30
That their society, as their friendship, may
Be merely poison! Nothing I'll bear from thee
But nakedness, thou detestable town!
Take thou that too, with multiplying bans!
Timon will to the woods, where he shall find   35
Th' unkindest beast more kinder than mankind.
The gods confound — hear me, you good gods all,—
Th' Athenians both within and out that wall!
And grant, as Timon grows, his hate may grow
To the whole race of mankind, high and low!   40
Amen.   [*Exit.*

[SCENE II. *Athens. A room in Timon's house.*]

Enter Steward [FLAVIUS,] *with two or three*
SERVANTS.

1. Serv. Hear you, master steward, where's our
    master?
Are we undone? cast off? nothing remaining?

Flav. Alack, my fellows, what should I say to
    you?
Let me be recorded by the righteous gods,
I am as poor as you.

1. Serv.   Such a house broke!   5
So noble a master fall'n! All gone! and not
One friend to take his fortune by the arm
And go along with him!

2. Serv.   As we do turn our backs
From our companion thrown into his grave,
So his familiars to his buried fortunes   10
Slink all away, leave their false vows with him,
Like empty purses pick'd; and his poor self,
A dedicated beggar to the air,
With his disease of all-shunn'd poverty,   14
Walks, like contempt, alone. More of our fellows.

Enter other SERVANTS.

Flav. All broken implements of a ruin'd house.

3. Serv. Yet do our hearts wear Timon's livery;
That see I by our faces; we are fellows still,
Serving alike in sorrow. Leak'd is our bark,
And we, poor mates, stand on the dying deck,   20
Hearing the surges threat. We must all part
Into this sea of air.

Flav.   Good fellows all,
The latest of my wealth I'll share amongst you.
Wherever we shall meet, for Timon's sake
Let's yet be fellows; let's shake our heads and say,
As 'twere a knell unto our master's fortunes,   26

---

119. **Push:** pshaw.   122. **humours:** caprices.

Act IV, sc. i, 6. **[steads]** (Theobald conj.). *steeds* F. **filths:** strumpets.   12. **pill:** pillage.   14. **lin'd:** padded.   17. **Domestic awe:** respect for parents. **neighbourhood:** neighborly feeling.   18. **mysteries:** crafts.   21. **[let]** (Hanmer). *yet* F. 25. **liberty:** license.   28. **blains:** swellings.   32. **merely:** entirely.   34. **bans:** curses.

Sc. ii, 10. **his ... fortunes:** those friends who were so close to his fortunes now lost.

"We have seen better days." Let each take some;
Nay, put out all your hands. Not one word more!
Thus we part rich in sorrow, parting poor.
        [*Servants embrace, and part several ways.*
O, the fierce wretchedness that glory brings us! 30
Who would not wish to be from wealth exempt,
Since riches point to misery and contempt?
Who'd be so mock'd with glory, or to live
But in a dream of friendship?
To have his pomp and all what state compounds 35
But only painted, like his varnish'd friends?
Poor honest lord, brought low by his own heart,
Undone by goodness! Strange, unusual blood,
When man's worst sin is he does too much good!
Who then dares to be half so kind again?   40
For bounty, that makes gods, does still mar men.
My dearest lord, bless'd to be most accurs'd,
Rich only to be wretched, thy great fortunes
Are made thy chief afflictions. Alas, kind lord!
He's flung in rage from this ingrateful seat   45
Of monstrous friends, nor has he with him to
Supply his life, or that which can command it.
I'll follow and inquire him out.
I'll ever serve his mind with my best will;
Whilst I have gold, I'll be his steward still.   50
        [*Exit.*

[SCENE III.]   *Woods [and cave, near the sea-shore.]*

Enter TIMON [*from the cave*].

Tim. O blessed breeding sun, draw from the earth
Rotten humidity; below thy sister's orb
Infect the air! Twinn'd brothers of one womb,
Whose procreation, residence, and birth
Scarce is dividant, touch them with several fortunes,
The greater scorns the lesser; not nature,   6
To whom all sores lay siege, can bear great fortune
But by contempt of nature.
Raise me this beggar, and deny 't that lord;
The senator shall bear contempt hereditary,   10
The beggar native honour.
It is the pasture lards the [rother's] sides,
The want that makes him [lean]. Who dares, who dares,
In purity of manhood stand upright
And say, "This man's a flatterer"? If one be, 15
So are they all; for every grise of fortune

Is smooth'd by that below. The learned pate
Ducks to the golden fool; all [is oblique];
There's nothing level in our cursed natures
But direct villainy. Therefore, be abhorr'd   20
All feasts, societies, and throngs of men!
His semblable, yea, himself, Timon disdains.
Destruction fang mankind! Earth, yield me roots!
        [*Digging.*]
Who seeks for better of thee, sauce his palate
With thy most operant poison! What is here? 25
Gold? Yellow, glittering, precious gold! No, gods,
I am no idle votarist; roots, you clear heavens!
Thus much of this will make black white, foul fair,
Wrong right, base noble, old young, coward valiant.
Ha, you gods! why this? What, this, you gods?
      Why, this   30
Will lug your priests and servants from your sides,
Pluck stout men's pillows from below their heads.
This yellow slave
Will knit and break religions, bless th' accurs'd,
Make the hoar leprosy ador'd, place thieves 35
And give them title, knee, and approbation
With senators on the bench. This is it
That makes the wappen'd widow wed again;
She, whom the spital-house and ulcerous sores
Would cast the gorge at, this embalms and spices 40
To th' April day again. Come, damn'd earth,
Thou common whore of mankind, that puts odds
Among the rout of nations, I will make thee
Do thy right nature. (*March afar off.*) Ha! a
      drum? Thou'rt quick,
But yet I'll bury thee; thou'lt go, strong thief, 45
When gouty keepers of thee cannot stand.
Nay, stay thou out for earnest.
        [*Keeping some gold.*]

Enter ALCIBIADES, *with drum and fife, in war-like manner;* PHRYNIA *and* TIMANDRA.

Alcib. What art thou there? Speak.
Tim. A beast, as thou art. The canker gnaw
    thy heart,
For showing me again the eyes of man!   50
    Alcib. What is thy name? Is man so hateful to
    thee
That art thyself a man?
    Tim. I am Misanthropos, and hate mankind.
For thy part, I do wish thou wert a dog,   54
That I might love thee something.
    Alcib.   I know thee well;
But in thy fortunes am unlearn'd and strange.

---

35. **what ... compounds**: that makes up dignity. 38. **blood**: nature.
Sc. iii, 5. dividant: divisible. **touch**: test. 6–8. **not ... nature**: human nature, subject to all kinds of evils, cannot bear prosperity without outraging natural affection. 11. **native honour**: honor as if born to it. 12. **lards**: fattens. [**rother's**] (Singer): ox's. *Brothers* F. 13. [**lean**] (Singer). *leave* F. 16. **grise**: step. 17. **smooth'd**: flattered. 18. **all [is oblique]** (Pope). *All's obliquie* F. 22. **semblable**: likeness. 23. **fang**: seize. 25. **operant**: active, potent. 27. **idle**: insincere. 38. **wappen'd**: worn. 39–40. **spital-house ... at**: hospital patients and sufferers from running sores would loathe. 42–43. **puts ... nations**: creates inequalities among all populations. 44. **Do ... nature**: i.e., corrupt people. **quick**: alive. 45. **go**: walk.

Tim. I know thee too; and more than that I
　know thee
I not desire to know.　Follow thy drum;
With man's blood paint the ground, gules, gules.
Religious canons, civil laws are cruel;　　　　59
Then what should war be?　This fell whore of
　thine
Hath in her more destruction than thy sword,
For all her cherubin look.
　　Phry.　　　　　　　　　Thy lips rot off!
　　Tim. I will not kiss thee; then the rot returns
To thine own lips again.　　　　　　　　65
　　Alcib. How came the noble Timon to this
　change?
　　Tim. As the moon does, by wanting light to
　give:
But then renew I could not, like the moon;
There were no suns to borrow of.
　　Alcib.　　　　　　　　　Noble Timon,
What friendship may I do thee?
　　Tim.　　　　　　　None, but to　70
Maintain my opinion.
　　Alcib.　　　　　　　What is it, Timon?
　　Tim. Promise me friendship, but perform none.
If thou wilt not promise, the gods plague thee, for
thou art a man!　If thou dost perform, confound
thee, for thou art a man!　　　　　　　75
　　Alcib. I have heard in some sort of thy miseries.
　　Tim. Thou saw'st them, when I had prosperity.
　　Alcib. I see them now; then was a blessed time.
　　Tim. As thine is now, held with a brace of harlots.
　　Timan. Is this th' Athenian minion, whom the
　world　　　　　　　　　　　　　80
Voic'd so regardfully?
　　Tim.　　　　　　Art thou Timandra?
　　Timan. Yes.
　　Tim. Be a whore still.　They love thee not that
　use thee;
Give them diseases, leaving with thee their lust.
Make use of thy salt hours; season the slaves
For tubs and baths; bring down rose-cheek'd
　youth　　　　　　　　　　　　　86
To the tub-fast and the diet.
　　Timan.　　　　　　　Hang thee, monster!
　　Alcib. Pardon him, sweet Timandra; for his wits
Are drown'd and lost in his calamities.
I have but little gold of late, brave Timon,　　90
The want whereof doth daily make revolt
In my penurious band.　I have heard, and griev'd,
How cursed Athens, mindless of thy worth,　93
Forgetting thy great deeds when neighbour states,
But for thy sword and fortune, trod upon them, —

Tim. I prithee, beat thy drum and get thee gone.
Alcib. I am thy friend and pity thee, dear Timon.
Tim. How dost thou pity him whom thou dost
　trouble?
I had rather be alone.
　Alcib.　　　　　　Why, fare thee well:
Here is some gold for thee.
　Tim.　　　　　　Keep it, I cannot eat it.
Alcib. When I have laid proud Athens on a
　heap, —　　　　　　　　　　　　101
Tim. Warr'st thou 'gainst Athens?
Alcib.　　　　　　Ay, Timon, and have cause.
Tim. The gods confound them all in thy con-
　quest;
And thee after, when thou hast conquer'd!
Alcib. Why me, Timon?
　Tim.　　　　　That, by killing of villains,
Thou wast born to conquer my country.　　106
Put up thy gold!　Go on, — here's gold, — go on;
Be as a planetary plague when Jove
Will o'er some high-vic'd city hang his poison
In the sick air.　Let not thy sword skip one.　110
Pity not honour'd Age for his white beard;
He is an usurer.　Strike me the counterfeit matron;
It is her habit only that is honest,
Herself's a bawd.　Let not the virgin's cheek
Make soft thy trenchant sword; for those milk-
　paps,　　　　　　　　　　　　115
That through the window [bars] bore at men's eyes,
Are not within the leaf of pity writ,
But set them down horrible traitors.　Spare not the
　babe,
Whose dimpled smiles from fools exhaust their
　mercy;
Think it a bastard, whom the oracle　　　120
Hath doubtfully pronounc'd thy throat shall cut,
And mince it sans remorse.　Swear against objects;
Put armour on thine ears and on thine eyes;
Whose proof nor yells of mothers, maids, nor babes,
Nor sight of priests in holy vestments bleeding,　125
Shall pierce a jot.　There's gold to pay thy soldiers,
Make large confusion; and, thy fury spent,
Confounded be thyself!　Speak not, be gone.
　Alcib. Hast thou gold yet?　I'll take the gold
　thou givest me;
Not all thy counsel.　　　　　　　　130
　Tim. Dost thou, or dost thou not, Heaven's
　curse upon thee!
　Phr. and Timan. Give us some gold, good Ti-
　mon; hast thou more?
　Tim. Enough to make a whore forswear her trade,
And to make whores, a bawd.　Hold up, you sluts,

---

59. **gules:** red (heraldic term).　61. **fell:** deadly.　80. **minion:** darling.　81. **Voic'd:** acclaimed.　85. **salt:** lascivious.
86–87. **tubs...diet.**　Allusions to the sweating cure for venereal diseases.　92. **penurious:** poverty-stricken.　108. **planetary:** induced by a malignant planet.　113. **habit:** demeanor.　116. **window [bars]:** lattice-work of the bodice.　[bars]
(Johnson).　*Barne* F.　119. **exhaust:** draw out.　121. **doubtfully:** ambiguously.　122. **sans:** without.　**objects:** objects
demanding pity.　124. **proof:** impenetrability.　127. **confusion:** ruin.　134. **to...bawd:** to make a bawd cease making
whores.

Your aprons mountant.   You are not oathable, —
Although, I know, you'll swear, terribly swear   136
Into strong shudders and to heavenly agues
Th' immortal gods that hear you, — spare your
          oaths;
I'll trust to your conditions.   Be whores still;
And he whose pious breath seeks to convert you, 140
Be strong in whore, allure him, burn him up;
Let your close fire predominate his smoke,
And be no turncoats; yet may your pains, six
          months,
Be quite contrary: and thatch your poor thin roofs
With burdens of the dead — some that were hang'd,
No matter; — wear them, betray with them.   Whore
          still;   146
Paint till a horse may mire upon your face;
A pox of wrinkles!
    Phr. and Timan.   Well, more gold; what then?
Believe 't, that we'll do anything for gold.   150
    Tim.   Consumptions sow
In hollow bones of man; strike their sharp shins,
And mar men's spurring.   Crack the lawyer's
          voice,
That he may never more false title plead,
Nor sound his quillets shrilly; hoar the flamen,
That scolds against the quality of flesh   156
And not believes himself.   Down with the nose,
Down with it flat; take the bridge quite away
Of him that, his particular to foresee,
Smells from the general weal.   Make curl'd-pate
          ruffians bald;   160
And let the unscarr'd braggarts of the war
Derive some pain from you.   Plague all,
That your activity may defeat and quell
The source of all erection.   There's more gold;
Do you damn others, and let this damn you,   165
And ditches grave you all!
    Phr. and Timan.   More counsel with more money,
          bounteous Timon.
    Tim.   More whore, more mischief first; I have
          given you earnest.
    Alcib.   Strike up the drum toward Athens!   Fare-
          well, Timon!
If I thrive well, I'll visit thee again.   170
    Tim.   If I hope well, I'll never see thee more.
    Alcib.   I never did thee harm.
    Tim.   Yes, thou spok'st well of me.
    Alcib.   Call'st thou that harm?
    Tim.   Men daily find it.   Get thee away, and
          take
Thy beagles with thee.

    Alcib.   We but offend him.   Strike!
          [*Drum beats.*]   *Exeunt* [*Alcibiades, Phry-
          nia, and Timandra*].
    Tim.   That nature, being sick of man's unkind-
          ness,   176
Should yet be hungry!   Common mother, thou
                                        [*Digging.*
Whose womb unmeasurable and infinite breast
Teems and feeds all; whose self-same mettle,   179
Whereof thy proud child, arrogant man, is puff'd,
Engenders the black toad and adder blue,
The gilded newt and eyeless venom'd worm,
With all the abhorred births below crisp heaven
Whereon Hyperion's quick'ning fire doth shine;
Yield him who all thy human sons [doth] hate, 185
From forth thy plenteous bosom, one poor root!
Ensear thy fertile and conceptious womb;
Let it no more bring out ingrateful man!
Go great with tigers, dragons, wolves, and bears;
Teem with new monsters, whom thy upward face 190
Hath to the marbled mansion all above
Never presented! — O, a root: dear thanks! —
Dry up thy marrows, vines, and plough-torn leas;
Whereof ingrateful man, with liquorish draughts
And morsels unctuous, greases his pure mind,   195
That from it all consideration slips!

          Enter APEMANTUS.
More man?   Plague, plague!
    Apem.   I was directed hither.   Men report
Thou dost affect my manners, and dost use them.
    Tim.   'Tis, then, because thou dost not keep a dog,
Whom I would imitate.   Consumption catch thee!
    Apem.   This is in thee a nature but infected;   202
A poor unmanly melancholy sprung
From change of fortune.   Why this spade? this
          place?
This slave-like habit? and these looks of care? 205
Thy flatterers yet wear silk, drink wine, lie soft;
Hug their diseas'd perfumes, and have forgot
That ever Timon was.   Shame not these woods
By putting on the cunning of a carper.
Be thou a flatterer now, and seek to thrive   210
By that which has undone thee; hinge thy knee,
And let his very breath, whom thou'lt observe,
Blow off thy cap; praise his most vicious strain,
And call it excellent.   Thou wast told thus;
Thou gav'st thine ears, like tapsters that bade
          welcome,   215
To knaves and all approachers.   'Tis most just
That thou turn rascal; hadst thou wealth again,

---

135. **oathable**: to be believed on oath.   139. **conditions**: characters.   143. **pains...months.** Probably corrupt.   144.
roofs: heads.   145. **burdens...dead**: i.e., false hair taken from dead bodies.   155. **quillets**: quibbles.   **hoar the**
flamen: make the priest mouldy.   156. **quality of flesh**: i.e., of the sacrifices.   159. **particular**: private gain.   160. **Smells**
from: loses scent of.   166. **grave**: entomb.   171. **If...well**: if my hope is granted.   183. **crisp**: curly (with clouds).   184.
Hyperion's: i.e., the sun's.   185. [**doth**] (Capell).   *do* F.   187. **Ensear**: dry up.   194. **liquorish**: appetizing.   196. **consider-**
ation: regard for others.   207. **perfumes**: perfumed mistresses.   209. **cunning**: profession.   **carper**: censurer, cynic.   212.
observe: court.

Rascals should have't. Do not assume my likeness.

Tim. Were I like thee, I'd throw away myself.

Apem. Thou hast cast away thyself, being like
    thyself;   220
A madman so long, now a fool. What, think'st
That the bleak air, thy boisterous chamberlain,
Will put thy shirt on warm? Will these [moss'd]
    trees,
That have outliv'd the eagle, page thy heels
And skip when thou point'st out? Will the cold
    brook,   225
Candied with ice, caudle thy morning taste
To cure thy o'er-night's surfeit? Call the creatures
Whose naked natures live in all the spite
Of wreakful heaven, whose bare unhoused trunks,
To the conflicting elements expos'd,   230
Answer mere nature; bid them flatter thee.
O, thou shalt find —

    Tim.   A fool of thee. Depart.

Apem. I love thee better now than ere I did.

Tim. I hate thee worse.

Apem.   Why?

Tim.   Thou flatter'st misery.

Apem. I flatter not, but say thou art a caitiff.

Tim. Why doest thou seek me out?

Apem.   To vex thee.   236

Tim. Always a villain's office or a fool's.
Dost please thyself in't?

    Apem.   Ay.

    Tim.   What! a knave too?

Apem. If thou didst put this sour cold habit on
To castigate thy pride, 'twere well; but thou   240
Dost it enforcedly; thou'dst courtier be again,
Wert thou not beggar. Willing misery
Outlives uncertain pomp, is crown'd before;
The one is filling still, never complete;
The other, at high wish. Best state, contentless,
Hath a distracted and most wretched being,   246
Worse than the worst, content.
Thou shouldst desire to die, being miserable.

    Tim. Not by his breath that is more miserable.
Thou art a slave, whom Fortune's tender arm   250
With favour never clasp'd, but bred a dog.
Hadst thou, like us from our first swath, proceeded
The sweet degrees that this brief world affords
To such as may the passive drugs of it
Freely command, thou wouldst have plung'd thyself
In general riot; melted down thy youth   256
In different beds of lust; and never learn'd
The icy precepts of respect, but followed
The sug'red game before thee. But myself,
Who had the world as my confectionary,   260

The mouths, the tongues, the eyes, and hearts of
    men
At duty, more than I could frame employment,
That numberless upon me stuck as leaves
Do on the oak, have with one winter's brush
Fell from their boughs and left me open, bare   265
For every storm that blows; I to bear this,
That never knew but better, is some burden.
Thy nature did commence in sufferance, time
Hath made thee hard in't. Why shouldst thou
    hate men?
They never flatter'd thee. What hast thou given?
If thou wilt curse, thy father, that poor rag,   271
Must be thy subject, who in spite put stuff
To some she-beggar and compounded thee
Poor rogue hereditary. Hence, be gone!
If thou hadst not been born the worst of men,   275
Thou hadst been a knave and flatterer.

    Apem.   Art thou proud yet?

    Tim. Ay, that I am not thee.

    Apem.   I, that I was
No prodigal.

    Tim.   I, that I am one now.
Were all the wealth I have shut up in thee,
I'd give thee leave to hang it. Get thee gone.   280
That the whole life of Athens were in this!
Thus would I eat it.   [*Eating a root.*]

    Apem.   Here; I will mend thy feast.
                     [*Offering him a root.*]

    Tim. First mend my company; take away thy-
    self.

    Apem. So I shall mend mine own, by th' lack of
    thine.   284

    Tim. 'Tis not well mended, so it is but botch'd;
If not, I would it were.

    Apem. What wouldst thou have to Athens?

    Tim. Thee thither in a whirlwind. If thou wilt,
Tell them there I have gold; look, so I have.

    Apem. Here is no use for gold.

    Tim.   The best and truest;
For here it sleeps, and does no hired harm.   291

    Apem. Where liest o' nights, Timon?

    Tim.   Under that's above me.
Where feed'st thou o' days, Apemantus?

    Apem. Where my stomach finds meat; or, rather,
where I eat it.   295

    Tim. Would poison were obedient and knew my
mind!

    Apem. Where wouldst thou send it?

    Tim. To sauce thy dishes.   299

    Apem. The middle of humanity thou never knew-
est, but the extremity of both ends. When thou

223. [moss'd] (Hanmer). *moyst* F. 226. Candied: frozen. caudle: serve a warm drink to. 229. wreakful: vengeful.
231. Answer...nature: contend with stark nature. 247. Worse...content: worse than the meanest state when con-
tentedly accepted. 249. breath: voice, advice. 252. swath: swaddling clothes. proceeded: passed through (university
term) 254. drugs: drudges. 260. confectionary: place where sweetmeats are made. 262. frame: provide with. 264.
have: i.e., and that have. 265. Fell: fallen. 268. sufferance: suffering. 285. it...botch'd: i.e., because you are still
in the company of yourself.

wast in thy gilt and thy perfume, they mock'd thee for too much curiosity; in thy rags thou know'st none, but art despis'd for the contrary. There's a medlar for thee, eat it.   305

Tim. On what I hate I feed not.

Apem. Dost hate a medlar?

Tim. Ay, though it look like thee.

Apem. An thou 'dst hated meddlers sooner, thou shouldst have loved thyself better now. What man didst thou ever know unthrift that was beloved after his means?   312

Tim. Who, without those means thou talk'st of, didst thou ever know belov'd?

Apem. Myself.

Tim. I understand thee; thou hadst some means to keep a dog.

Apem. What things in the world canst thou nearest compare to thy flatterers?   319

Tim. Women nearest; but men, men are the things themselves. What wouldst thou do with the world, Apemantus, if it lay in thy power?

Apem. Give it the beasts, to be rid of the men. 324

Tim. Wouldst thou have thyself fall in the confusion of men, and remain a beast with the beasts?

Apem. Ay, Timon.   328

Tim. A beastly ambition, which the gods grant thee t' attain to! If thou wert the lion, the fox would beguile thee. If thou wert the lamb, the fox would eat thee. If thou were the fox, the lion would suspect thee, when peradventure thou wert accus'd by the ass. If thou wert the ass, thy dulness would torment thee, and still thou liv'dst but as a 335 breakfast to the wolf. If thou wert the wolf, thy greediness would afflict thee, and oft thou shouldst hazard thy life for thy dinner. Wert thou the unicorn, pride and wrath would confound thee and make thine own self the conquest of thy fury.   340 Wert thou a bear, thou wouldst be kill'd by the horse. Wert thou a horse, thou wouldst be seiz'd by the leopard. Wert thou a leopard, thou wert germane to the lion, and the spots of thy kindred were jurors on thy life; all thy safety were remo- 345 tion and thy defence absence. What beast couldst thou be, that were not subject to a beast? And what a beast art thou already, that seest not thy loss in transformation!   349

Apem. If thou couldst please me with speaking to me, thou mightest have hit upon it here. The commonwealth of Athens is become a forest of beasts.

Tim. How has the ass broke the wall, that thou art out of the city?   355

Apem. Yonder comes a poet and a painter; the plague of company light upon thee! I will fear to catch it, and give way. When I know not what else to do, I'll see thee again.   359

Tim. When there is nothing living but thee, thou shalt be welcome. I had rather be a beggar's dog than Apemantus.

Apem. Thou art the cap of all the fools alive.

Tim. Would thou wert clean enough to spit upon!

Apem. A plague on thee! thou art too bad to
      curse.   365

Tim. All villains that do stand by thee are pure.

Apem. There is no leprosy but what thou speak'st.

Tim. If I name thee.
I'll beat thee, but I should infect my hands.

Apem. I would my tongue could rot them off!

Tim. Away, thou issue of a mangy dog!   371
Choler does kill me that thou art alive;
I swound to see thee.

Apem.   Would thou wouldst burst!

Tim.   Away,
Thou tedious rogue! I am sorry I shall lose   374
A stone by thee.   [*Throws a stone at him.*]

Apem.   Beast!

Tim.   Slave!

Apem.   Toad!

Tim.   Rogue, rogue, rogue!
I am sick of this false world, and will love nought
But even the mere necessities upon 't.
Then, Timon, presently prepare thy grave;
Lie where the light foam of the sea may beat
Thy grave-stone daily; make thine epitaph   380
That death in me at others' lives may laugh.
[*To the gold.*] O thou sweet king-killer, and dear
      divorce
'Twixt natural [son and sire]! thou bright defiler
Of Hymen's purest bed! thou valiant Mars!
Thou ever young, fresh, lov'd, and delicate wooer,
Whose blush doth thaw the consecrated snow   386
That lies on Dian's lap! thou visible god,
That sold'rest close impossibilities,
And makest them kiss! that speak'st with every
      tongue
To every purpose! O thou touch of hearts!   390
Think, thy slave man rebels, and by thy virtue
Set them into confounding odds, that beasts
May have the world in empire!

Apem.   Would 'twere so!
But not till I am dead. I'll say th' hast gold;
Thou wilt be throng'd to shortly.

Tim.   Throng'd to!

Apem.   Ay. 395

303. **curiosity:** fastidiousness.   305. **medlar:** a small fruit, eaten in a decaying state.   312. **after . . . means:** i.e., after his means were exhausted.   338. **unicorn.** It was fabled that a unicorn, infuriated by an enemy, would rush blindly, strike its horn against a tree, get stuck there, and be killed.   344. **germane:** akin.   345. **were . . . life:** would cause thy death.   **remotion:** retreat.   356. **Yonder . . . painter.** See Introduction.   363. **cap:** top, chief.   378. **presently:** at once. 383. **[son and sire]** (Rowe).   *Sunne and fire* F.   388. **close:** tightly.   390. **touch:** touchstone.   392. **them:** men.

Tim. Thy back, I prithee.

Apem.   Live, and love thy misery.

Tim. Long live so, and so die. I am quit.
Moe things like men! Eat, Timon, and abhor
[them].   [*Exit Apemantus.*

Enter BANDITTI.

1. Ban. Where should he have this gold? It is
some poor fragment, some slender ort of his   400
remainder. The mere want of gold, and the falling-
from of his friends, drove him into this melancholy.

2. Ban. It is nois'd he hath a mass of treasure.

3. Ban. Let us make the assay upon him. If   406
he care not for't, he will supply us easily; if he
covetously reserve it, how shall 's get it?

2. Ban. True; for he bears it not about him, 'tis
hid.

1. Ban. Is not this he?   410

Banditti. Where?

2. Ban. 'Tis his description.

3. Ban. He; I know him.

Banditti. Save thee, Timon.

Tim. Now, thieves?   415

Banditti. Soldiers, not thieves.

Tim. Both too; and women's sons.

Banditti. We are not thieves, but men that much
do want.

Tim. Your greatest want is, you want much of
meat.
Why should you want? Behold, the earth hath
roots;   420
Within this mile break forth a hundred springs;
The oaks bear mast, the briers scarlet hips;
The bounteous housewife, Nature, on each bush
Lays her full mess before you. Want! why want?

1. Ban. We cannot live on grass, on berries, water,
As beasts and birds and fishes.   426

Tim. Nor on the beasts themselves, the birds and
fishes;
You must eat men. Yet thanks I must you con
That you are thieves profess'd, that you work not
In holier shapes; for there is boundless theft   430
In limited professions. Rascal thieves,
Here's gold. Go, suck the subtle blood o' the grape
Till the high fever seethe your blood to froth,
And so scape hanging. Trust not the physician;
His antidotes are poison, and he slays   435
Moe than you rob. Take wealth and lives together;
Do [villany], do, since you protest to do't,

Like workmen. I'll example you with thievery:
The sun's a thief, and with his great attraction
Robs the vast sea; the moon's an arrant thief,   440
And her pale fire she snatches from the sun;
The sea's a thief, whose liquid surge resolves
The moon into salt tears; the earth's a thief,
That feeds and breeds by a composture stol'n
From gen'ral excrement; each thing's a thief;   445
The laws, your curb and whip, in their rough power
Has uncheck'd theft. Love not yourselves; away,
Rob one another. There's more gold. Cut throats;
All that you meet are thieves. To Athens go,
Break open shops; nothing can you steal,   450
But thieves do lose it. Steal [no] less for this
I give you; and gold confound you howso'er!
Amen.

3. Ban. Has almost charm'd me from my profession, by persuading me to it.   455

1. Ban. 'Tis in the malice of mankind that he thus
advises us; not to have us thrive in our mystery.

2. Ban. I'll believe him as an enemy, and give
over my trade.   460

1. Ban. Let us first see peace in Athens. There
is no time so miserable but a man may be true.
           [*Exeunt Banditti.*

Enter the Steward [FLAVIUS, *who remains at a
distance*].

Flav. O you gods!
Is yond despis'd and ruinous man my lord?   465
Full of decay and failing? O monument
And wonder of good deeds evilly bestow'd!
What an alteration of honour
Has desp'rate want made!
What viler thing upon the earth than friends   470
Who can bring noblest minds to basest ends!
How rarely does it meet with this time's guise,
When man was wish'd to love his enemies!
Grant I may ever love, and rather woo
Those that would mischief me than those that
do!
Has caught me in his eye. I will present   476
My honest grief unto him; and, as my lord,
Still serve him with my life. [*Coming forward.*] My
dearest master!

Tim. Away! what art thou?

Flav.   Have you forgot me, sir?

Tim. Why dost ask that? I have forgot all men;
Then, if thou grant'st thou'rt a man, I have forgot
thee.   481

397. **quit:** rid of you.   398. **Moe . . . [them].** F gives this line to *Apem.* Corrected by Hanmer. **[them]** (Rowe).   *then* F.   400. **ort:** scrap.   406. **assay:** trial.   408. **shall 's:** shall we.   415. **Now:** how now.   422. **mast:** acorns (lit., fruit). **hips:** fruit of the wild rose.   424. **mess:** dish.   428. **thanks . . . con:** I must be grateful.   431. **limited:** restricted.   434. **scape hanging:** i.e., by dying of fever.   437. **[villany]** (Rowe). *villaine* F. **protest:** profess.   438. **example:** furnish instances.   442. **resolves:** melts. Alluding to the moon's influence on the tides.   444. **composture:** manure.   446. **rough power:** unjust regulations.   451. **[no]** (Collier). Om. F.   459. **believe . . . enemy:** i.e., not take his advice.   462. **true:** honest.   472–73. **How . . . enemies:** how finely the command to love our enemies fits the spirit of the time!   475. **those that do:** i.e., those who do so in fact (though pretending kindness).

Flav. An honest poor servant of yours.

Tim. Then I know thee not.
I never had honest man about me, I; ail
I kept were knaves, to serve in meat to villains.   485

Flav. The gods are witness,
Nev'r did poor steward wear a truer grief
For his undone lord than mine eyes for you.

Tim. What, dost thou weep?   Come nearer.
Then I love thee,
Because thou art a woman and disclaim'st   490
Flinty mankind, whose eyes do never give
But thorough lust and laughter.   Pity's sleeping:
Strange times, that weep with laughing, not with
     weeping!

Flav. I beg of you to know me, good my lord,
T' accept my grief, and whilst this poor wealth lasts
To entertain me as your steward still.   496

Tim. Had I a steward
So true, so just, and now so comfortable?
It almost turns my dangerous nature [mild].
Let me behold thy face.   Surely, this man   500
Was born of woman.
Forgive my general and exceptless rashness,
You perpetual-sober gods! I do proclaim
One honest man — mistake me not — but one;
No more, I pray, — and he's a steward.   505
How fain would I have hated all mankind,
And thou redeem'st thyself; but all, save thee,
I fell with curses.
Methinks thou art more honest now than wise;
For, by oppressing and betraying me,   510
Thou mightst have sooner got another service;
For many so arrive at second masters,
Upon their first lord's neck.   But tell me true —
For I must ever doubt, though ne'er so sure —
Is not thy kindness subtle, covetous,   515
If not a usuring kindness, and, as rich men deal
     gifts,
Expecting in return twenty for one?

Flav. No, my most worthy master, in whose
     breast
Doubt and suspect, alas, are plac'd too late;
You should have fear'd false times when you did
     feast.   520
Suspect still comes where an estate is least.
That which I show, Heaven knows, is merely love,
Duty, and zeal to your unmatched mind,
Care of your food and living; and, believe it,
My most honour'd lord,   525
For any benefit that points to me,
Either in hope or present, I'd exchange
For this one wish, that you had power and wealth
To requite me by making rich yourself.

Tim. Look thee, 'tis so!   Thou singly honest
     man,   530
Here, take; the gods out of my misery
Ha' sent thee treasure.   Go, live rich and happy;
But thus condition'd: thou shalt build from men;
Hate all, curse all, show charity to none,
But let the famish'd flesh slide from the bone   535
Ere thou relieve the beggar; give to dogs
What thou deniest to men.   Let prisons swallow
     'em,
Debts wither 'em to nothing; be men like blasted
     woods,
And may diseases lick up their false bloods!
And so farewell and thrive.

Flav.   O, let me stay,   540
And comfort you, my master.

Tim.   If thou hat'st curses,
Stay not; fly, whilst thou art blest and free.
Ne'er see thou man, and let me ne'er see thee.

     [*Exit* [*Flavius.   Timon retires to his cave*].

[ACT V]

[SCENE I.   *The woods.   Before Timon's cave.*]

Enter POET *and* PAINTER.

Pain. As I took note of the place, it cannot be far
where he abides.

Poet. What's to be thought of him?   Does the
rumour hold for true that he's so full of gold?   4

Pain. Certain.   Alcibiades reports it; Phrynia
and Timandra had gold of him.   He likewise en'
rich'd poor straggling soldiers with great quantity.
'Tis said he gave unto his steward a mighty sum.

Poet. Then this breaking of his has been but a try
for his friends.   11

Pain. Nothing else.   You shall see him a palm
in Athens again, and flourish with the highest.
Therefore 'tis not amiss we tender our loves to him
in this suppos'd distress of his.   It will show honestly in us, and is very likely to load our purposes
with what they travail for, if it be a just and true
report that goes of his having.   18

Poet. What have you now to present unto him?

Pain. Nothing at this time but my visitation;
only I will promise him an excellent piece.

Poet. I must serve him so too, tell him of an intent
that's coming toward him.   23

Pain. Good as the best.   Promising is the very
air o' th' time; it opens the eyes of expectation.
Performance is ever the duller for his act; and, but
in the plainer and simpler kind of people, the deed of
saying is quite out of use.   To promise is most

---

485. **knaves:** (1) servants, (2) rascals.   491. **give:** yield tears.   492. **thorough:** through.   498. **comfortable:** comforting.
499. **[mild]** (Thirlby conj.).   *wilde* F.   502. **exceptless:** making no exception.   533. **thus condition'd:** on these conditions
from: remote from.
     Act V, sc. i, 10. **try:** test.   16. **load:** reward.   27-28. **deed of saying:** fulfillment of promise.

courtly and fashionable; performance is a kind of
will or testament which argues a great sickness in his
judgement that makes it.   31

Enter TIMON *from his cave.*

Tim. [*Aside.*] Excellent workman! thou canst
not paint a man so bad as is thyself.

Poet. I am thinking what I shall say I have provided for him. It must be a personating of himself;
a satire against the softness of prosperity, with a discovery of the infinite flatteries that follow youth and
opulency.   38

Tim. [*Aside.*] Must thou needs stand for a villain
in thine own work? Wilt thou whip thine own
faults in other men? Do so, I have gold for thee.

Poet. Nay, let's seek him.   43
Then do we sin against our own estate
When we may profit meet and come too late.

Pain. True;
When the day serves, before black-corner'd night,
Find what thou want'st by free and offer'd light.
Come.   49

Tim. [*Aside.*] I'll meet you at the turn. What a
   god's gold
That he is worshipp'd in a baser temple
Than where swine feed!
'Tis thou that rigg'st the bark and plough'st the
   foam,
Settlest admired reverence in a slave.
To thee be [worship], and thy saints for aye   55
Be crown'd with plagues, that thee alone obey!
Fit I meet them.   [*Coming forward.*]

Poet. Hail, worthy Timon!

Pain.   Our late noble master!

Tim. Have I once liv'd to see two honest men?

Poet. Sir,   60
Having often of your open bounty tasted,
Hearing you were retir'd, your friends fall'n off,
Whose thankless natures — O abhorred spirits!
Not all the whips of heaven are large enough —
What! to you,   65
Whose star-like nobleness gave life and influence
To their whole being! I am rapt and cannot cover
The monstrous bulk of this ingratitude
With any size of words.

Tim. Let it go naked, men may see 't the better.
You that are honest, by being what you are   71
Make them best seen and known.

Pain.   He and myself
Have travail'd in the great show'r of your gifts,
And sweetly felt it.

Tim.   Ay, you are honest men.

Pain. We are hither come to offer you our
   service.

Tim. Most honest men! Why, how shall I requite you?   76
Can you eat roots and drink cold water? No?

Both. What we can do, we'll do, to do you
   service.

Tim. Ye're honest men; ye've heard that I have
   gold;   79
I am sure you have. Speak truth; ye're honest men.

Pain. So it is said, my noble lord; but therefore
Came not my friend nor I.

Tim. Good honest men! Thou draw'st a coun-
   terfeit
Best in all Athens; thou'rt, indeed, the best;
Thou counterfeit'st most lively.

Pain.   So so, my lord.

Tim. E'en so, sir, as I say. — And, for thy
   fiction,   86
Why, thy verse swells with stuff so fine and smooth
That thou art even natural in thine art.
But, for all this, my honest-natur'd friends,
I must needs say you have a little fault.   90
Marry, 'tis not monstrous in you; neither wish I
You take much pains to mend.

Both.   Beseech your honour
To make it known to us.

Tim.   You'll take it ill.

Both. Most thankfully, my lord.

Tim.   Will you, indeed?

Both. Doubt it not, worthy lord.   95

Tim. There's never a one of you but trusts a
   knave
That mightily deceives you.

Both.   Do we, my lord?

Tim. Ay, and you hear him cog, see him dis-
   semble,
Know his gross patchery, love him, feed him,
Keep in your bosom; yet remain assur'd   100
That he's a made-up villain.

Pain. I know none such, my lord.

Poet.   Nor I.

Tim. Look you, I love you well; I'll give you gold.
Rid me these villains from your companies;   104
Hang them or stab them, drown them in a draught,
Confound them by some course, and come to me,
I'll give you gold enough.

Both. Name them, my lord, let's know them.

Tim. You that way and you this, but two in
   company,
Each man apart, all single and alone,   110
Yet an arch-villain keeps him company.
If where thou art two villains shall not be, [*To one.*]
Come not near him. — If thou wouldst not reside
But where one villain is, then him abandon. —
                                          [*To the other.*]

35. **himself:** i.e., his case.   37. **discovery:** exposure.   47. **black-corner'd:** obscuring things as in dark corners.   50.
turn: i.e., of the path.   54. **admired:** admiring.   55. **[worship]** (Rowe).   *worshipt* F.   88. **natural:** your natural self
i.e., hypocritical.   98. **cog:** cheat.   99. **patchery:** knavery   101. **made-up:** complete.   105. **draught:** privy.

Hence, pack! there's gold; you came for gold, ye
    slaves.   115
    [*To Painter.*] You have work for me; there's pay-
    ment for you; hence!
    [*To Poet.*] You are an alchemist; make gold of
    that.
Out, rascal dogs!
        [*Beats them out, and then retires to his cave.*]

    Enter Steward [FLAVIUS] *and two* SENATORS.

  Flav. It is in vain that you would speak with
    Timon;
For he is set so only to himself   120
That nothing but himself which looks like man
Is friendly with him.
  1. Sen.   Bring us to his cave;
It is our part and promise to th' Athenians
To speak with Timon.
  2. Sen.   At all times alike
Men are not still the same. 'Twas time and griefs   125
That fram'd him thus; time, with his fairer hand
Offering the fortunes of his former days,
The former man may make him. Bring us to him,
And chance it as it may.
  Flav.   Here is his cave.   129
Peace and content be here! Lord Timon! Timon!
Look out and speak to friends. Th' Athenians,
By two of their most reverend Senate, greet thee.
Speak to them, noble Timon.

    Enter TIMON *out of his cave.*

  Tim. Thou sun that comforts, burn! Speak and
    be hang'd.
For each true word, a blister! and each false   135
Be as a [cauterizing] to the root o' th' tongue,
Consuming it with speaking!
  1. Sen.   Worthy Timon, —
  Tim. Of none but such as you, and you of Timon.
  1. Sen. The senators of Athens greet thee, Timon.
  Tim. I thank them; and would send them back
    the plague,   140
Could I but catch it for them.
  1. Sen.   O, forget
What we are sorry for ourselves in thee.
The senators with one consent of love
Entreat thee back to Athens; who have thought
On special dignities, which vacant lie,   145
For thy best use and wearing.
  2. Sen.   They confess
Toward thee forgetfulness too general, gross;
Which now the public body, which doth seldom
Play the recanter, feeling in itself
A lack of Timon's aid, hath [sense] withal   150

Of it own [fail], restraining aid to Timon;
And send forth us to make their sorrowed render,
Together with a recompense more fruitful
Than their offence can weigh down by the dram;
Ay, even such heaps and sums of love and wealth
As shall to thee blot out what wrongs were theirs,
And write in thee the figures of their love,   157
Ever to read them thine.
  Tim.   You witch me in it,
Surprise me to the very brink of tears.
Lend me a fool's heart and a woman's eyes,   160
And I'll beweep these comforts, worthy senators.
  1. Sen. Therefore, so please thee to return with us,
And of our Athens, thine and ours, to take
The captainship, thou shalt be met with thanks,
Allow'd with absolute power, and thy good name 165
Live with authority; so soon we shall drive back
Of Alcibiades th' approaches wild,
Who, like a boar too savage, doth root up
His country's peace.
  2. Sen.   And shakes his threat'ning sword
Against the walls of Athens.
  1. Sen.   Therefore, Timon, —   170
  Tim. Well, sir, I will; therefore, I will, sir; thus:
If Alcibiades kill my countrymen,
Let Alcibiades know this of Timon,
That Timon cares not. But if he sack fair Athens,
And take our goodly aged men by th' beards,   175
Giving our holy virgins to the stain
Of contumelious, beastly, mad-brain'd war,
Then let him know, and tell him Timon speaks it,
In pity of our aged and our youth,
I cannot choose but tell him that I care not,   180
And let him take 't at worst; for their knives care
    not,
While you have throats to answer. For myself,
There's not a whittle in th' unruly camp
But I do prize it at my love before
The reverend'st throat in Athens. So I leave you
To the protection of the prosperous gods,   186
As thieves to keepers.
  Flav.   Stay not, all's in vain.
  Tim. Why, I was writing of my epitaph;
It will be seen to-morrow. My long sickness
Of health and living now begins to mend,   190
And nothing brings me all things. Go, live still;
Be Alcibiades your plague, you his,
And last so long enough!
  1. Sen.   We speak in vain.
  Tim. But yet I love my country, and am not
One that rejoices in the common wreck,   195
As common bruit doth put it.
  1. Sen.   That's well spoke.

---

115. **pack:** be off.   120. **set...to:** wrapped up in.   123. **part and promise:** promised part.   136. [cauterizing]
(Rowe). *Cantherizing* F.   150. [sense] (Rowe). *since* F.   151. **it:** its.   [fail] (Capell). *fall* F.   152. **sorrowed render:**
confession of sorrow.   165. **Allow'd:** approved.   183. **whittle:** clasp-knife.   186. **prosperous:** propitious.   191. **nothing:**
death.   196. **bruit:** rumor.

Tim. Commend me to my loving countrymen, —
1. Sen. These words become your lips as they pass
     through them.
2. Sen. And enter in our ears like great triumphers
In their applauding gates.
Tim.   Commend me to them,
And tell them that, to ease them of their griefs,   201
Their fears of hostile strokes, their aches, losses,
Their pangs of love, with other incident throes
That nature's fragile vessel doth sustain
In life's uncertain voyage, I will some kindness do
     them: 205
I'll teach them to prevent wild Alcibiades' wrath.
1. Sen. I like this well; he will return again.
Tim. I have a tree, which grows here in my close,
That mine own use invites me to cut down,
And shortly must I fell it.   Tell my friends,   210
Tell Athens, in the sequence of degree
From high to low throughout, that whoso please
To stop affliction, let him take his haste,
Come hither, ere my tree hath felt the axe,
And hang himself.   I pray you, do my greeting.   215
Flav. Trouble him no further; thus you still shall
     find him.
Tim. Come not to me again; but say to Athens,
Timon hath made his everlasting mansion
Upon the beached verge of the salt flood,
Who once a day with his embossed froth   220
The turbulent surge shall cover; thither come,
And let my grave-stone be your oracle.
Lips, let [sour] words go by and language end!
What is amiss plague and infection mend!   224
Graves only be men's works, and death their gain!
Sun, hide thy beams!   Timon hath done his reign.
                                             [*Exit.*
1. Sen. His discontents are unremoveably
Coupled to nature.
2. Sen. Our hope in him is dead.   Let us return,
And strain what other means is left unto us   230
In our dear peril.
1. Sen.   It requires swift foot.   [*Exeunt.*

[SCENE II.   *Before the walls of Athens.*]

Enter two other SENATORS *and a* MESSENGER.

1. Sen. Thou hast painfully discover'd.   Are his
     files
As full as thy report?
Mess.   I have spoke the least;
Besides, his expedition promises
Present approach.
2. Sen. We stand much hazard if they bring not
     Timon.   5

Mess. I met a courier, one mine ancient friend;
Whom, though in general part we were oppos'd,
Yet our old love made a particular force
And made us speak like friends.   This man was rid-
     ing
From Alcibiades to Timon's cave   10
With letters of entreaty, which imported
His fellowship i' th' cause against your city,
In part for his sake mov'd.

Enter the other SENATORS.

1. Sen.   Here comes our brothers.
3. Sen. No talk of Timon, nothing of him expect.
The enemies' drum is heard, and fearful scouring   15
Doth choke the air with dust.   In, and prepare;
Ours is the fall, I fear; our foes' the snare. [*Exeunt.*

[SCENE III.]   *The woods [near the sea.   Timon's
cave, and a rude tomb seen].*

Enter a SOLDIER, *seeking Timon.*

Sold. By all description this should be the place.
Who's here? speak, ho!   No answer!   What is this?
Timon is dead, who hath outstretch'd his span.
Some beast read this; there does not live a man.
Dead, sure; and this his grave.   What's on this tomb
I cannot read; the character I'll take with wax;   6
Our captain hath in every figure skill,
An ag'd interpreter, though young in days.
Before proud Athens he's set down by this,
Whose fall the mark of his ambition is.   [*Exit.*   10

[SCENE IV.]   *Before Athens.*

Trumpets sound.   Enter ALCIBIADES *with his
powers.*

Alcib. Sound to this coward and lascivious town
Our terrible approach.   [*A parley sounded.*

The SENATORS *appear upon the walls.*

Till now you have gone on and fill'd the time
With all licentious measure, making your wills
The scope of justice; till now myself and such   5
As slept within the shadow of your power
Have wander'd with our travers'd arms and
     breath'd
Our sufferance vainly.   Now the time is flush,
When crouching marrow in the bearer strong
Cries of itself, "No more!"   Now breathless Wrong
Shall sit and pant in your great chairs of ease,   11
And pursy Insolence shall break his wind
With fear and horrid flight.
1. Sen.   Noble and young,

202. **aches.** Pronounce *aitches.* 206. **prevent:** frustrate. 208. **close:** enclosure. 220. **embossed:** foaming. 223.
[**sour**] (Rowe). *foure* F. 231. **dear:** extreme.
  Sc. ii, 1. **Thou ... discover'd:** what you reveal is distressing. **files:** ranks. 7. **Whom:** respecting whom. **in ... part:** in
public matters. 15. **scouring:** hurrying.
  Sc. iii, 3. **outstretch'd:** passed. 3–4. Some edd. take these two lines as an inscription. 4. **read** F. *rear'd* Theobald.
  Sc. iv, 7. **travers'd:** folded. 8. **flush:** lusty. 9. **marrow:** strength. 12. **pursy:** short-winded. 13. **horrid:** quaking.

When thy first griefs were but a mere conceit,
Ere thou hadst power or we had cause of fear,   15
We sent to thee to give thy rages balm,
To wipe out our ingratitude with loves
Above their quantity.
 2. Sen.   So did we woo
Transformed Timon to our city's love
By humble message and by promis'd means.   20
We were not all unkind, nor all deserve
The common stroke of war.
 1. Sen.   These walls of ours
Were not erected by their hands from whom
You have receiv'd your [griefs]; nor are they
 such
That these great towers, trophies, and schools should
 fall   25
For private faults in them.
 2. Sen.   Nor are they living
Who were the motives that you first went out;
Shame, that they wanted cunning, in excess
Hath broke their hearts. March, noble lord,
Into our city with thy banners spread.   30
By decimation, and a tithed death —
If thy revenges hunger for that food
Which nature loathes — take thou the destin'd
 tenth,
And by the hazard of the spotted die
Let die the spotted.
 1. Sen.   All have not offended;   35
For those that were, it is not square to take
On those that are, revenge; crimes, like lands,
Are not inherited. Then, dear countryman,
Bring in thy ranks, but leave without thy rage;
Spare thy Athenian cradle and those kin   40
Which in the bluster of thy wrath must fall
With those that have offended; like a shepherd,
Approach the fold and cull th' infected forth,
But kill not all together.
 2. Sen.   What thou wilt,
Thou rather shalt enforce it with thy smile   45
Than hew to't with thy sword.
 1. Sen.   Set but thy foot
Against our rampir'd gates and they shall ope;
So thou wilt send thy gentle heart before,
To say thou'lt enter friendly.
 2. Sen.   Throw thy glove,

Or any token of thine honour else,   50
That thou wilt use the wars as thy redress
And not as our confusion, all thy powers
Shall make their harbour in our town till we
Have seal'd thy full desire.
 Alcib.   Then there's my glove;
[Descend], and open your uncharged ports.   55
Those enemies of Timon's and mine own
Whom you yourselves shall set out for reproof
Fall, and no more; and, to atone your fears
With my more noble meaning, not a man
Shall pass his quarter, or offend the stream   60
Of regular justice in your city's bounds,
But shall be [render'd] to your public laws
At heaviest answer.
 Both.   'Tis most nobly spoken.
 Alcib. Descend, and keep your words.
   [*The Senators descend, and open the gates.*]

    Enter [SOLDIER].
 Sold. My noble general, Timon is dead,   65
Entomb'd upon the very hem o' th' sea;
And on his grave-stone this insculpture, which
With wax I brought away, whose soft impression
Interprets for my poor ignorance.
 Alcib. (*Reads the epitaph.*) "*Here lies a wretched
  corse, of wretched soul bereft.*   70
*Seek not my name: a plague consume you wicked
  caitiffs left!*
Here lie I, Timon; who, alive, all living men did hate.
*Pass by and curse thy fill, but pass and stay not
  here thy gait.*"
These well express in thee thy latter spirits:
Though thou abhorr'dst in us our human griefs,   75
Scorn'dst our brain's flow and those our droplets
 which
From niggard nature fall, yet rich conceit
Taught thee to make vast Neptune weep for aye
On thy low grave, on faults forgiven. Dead
Is noble Timon, of whose memory   80
Hereafter more. Bring me into your city,
And I will use the olive with my sword,
Make war breed peace, make peace stint war, make
 each
Prescribe to other as each other's leech.
Let our drums strike.   [*Exeunt.*   85

14. conceit: fancy. 24. [griefs] (Theobald). *greefe* F. they: i.e., griefs. 27. motives...out: cause of your banishment. 28. Shame...in excess: excessive shame. 31. tithed death: killing of a tenth. 39. without: outside. 46. hew: cut thy way. 47. rampir'd: barricaded. 48. So: if only. 55. [Descend] F₂. *Defend* F₁. uncharged ports: unassailed gates. 60. quarter: lodging. 62. [render'd] (Chadworth conj.). *remedied* F. 63. At...answer: to pay fullest penalty. 70–73. On the contradiction in this epitaph, see Introduction. 75. griefs: faults. 76. brain's flow: tears. 83. stint: stop. 84. leech: physician.

The Tragedy of Antony and Cleopatra

ON MAY 20, 1608, Edward Blount entered in the Stationers' Register "a booke Called Anthony and Cleopatra," which does not seem to have been actually issued. Blount was one of the publishers of the First Folio, and in spite of the fact that Shakespeare's drama, first appearing there, was registered in 1623 along with the other plays "not formerly entered to any man," it is generally conceded that the entry of 1608 refers to it. Upon this evidence one may reasonably conjecture 1607 as the date of composition. A time very early in that year, or late in 1606, may be indicated by revisions in Samuel Daniel's *Cleopatra* (originally published in 1594 and newly printed in 1607), which may possibly have been inspired by Shakespeare's play. The First Folio, which, despite numerous misprints and some faulty lining, preserves a sound text, is the basis for all other editions.

Cleopatra had frequently been made the subject of dramatic treatment in the sixteenth century, but none of these earlier plays seems to have influenced Shakespeare. His sole source was Plutarch's *Life of Marcus Antonius*, in the translation from Amyot's French version by Sir Thomas North. This he followed with remarkable fidelity. Not only are practically all the incidents of the plot found in the biography, and in almost the same order, but there are numerous passages in the play — and these among the most brilliant — which follow the very diction of North as closely as verse can follow prose. Yet no play of Shakespeare's is less prosaic in style, and in none is the splendor of his imagination more superbly exhibited in the presentation of human character.

In Plutarch, then, who was an artist in the selection of detail and had an intense appreciation of greatness, Shakespeare found much of his work done for him. Yet between the *Life* and the tragedy there are contrasts of greatest significance. In the treatment of the whole action, which in reality covered ten years (from the death of Fulvia, in 40 B.C., to the deaths of Antony and Cleopatra in 30 B.C.), Shakespeare discarded long series of events,

like Antony's campaigns against the Parthians, which are described at length by Plutarch but which had no bearing on the tragic theme; and he relegated to the background important figures such as Cæsar and Octavia. Thus he makes no reference to the children of Antony and Octavia, he suppresses the fact that Octavia won Antony away from Cleopatra for a number of years, and he reduces Antony's protracted stay in Rome to a short visit. Similarly he compresses into a matter of days the months between the battle of Actium (September, 31 B.C.) and the deaths of Antony and Cleopatra, which, in their turn, were actually several days apart. Shakespeare has added something, too, to the great panorama. The vivid impressions of oriental luxury in the Alexandrian scenes are due in part to Shakespeare's imagination, in part to Plutarch; the orgy on Pompey's galley is developed from Plutarch's simple statement that Pompey gave a banquet there; the portraits of Iras and Charmian are elaborated from meagre sketches; the incident of Cleopatra's chastisement of the messenger is Shakespeare's invention; the character of Enobarbus is his creation.

Antony and Cleopatra is in effect a sequel to *Julius Cæsar*, though separated from it by some eight years. The infatuated protagonist of this play is the man whose oratory doomed the conspirators and who, joined with Octavius, now his rival, defeated Brutus and Cassius at Philippi. The tragedy in *Julius Cæsar* is the spiritual tragedy of Brutus, and the great tragedies intervening are signalized by a struggle within the hero. But here, although the crowning interest is the tragic passion of Antony, which is the cause of his ruin, the structure of the play is determined by the external and political struggle between the forces of Octavius and the forces of Antony. It is Rome against Egypt, and the love affair of Antony which precipitates the contest and determines its conclusion is at first subordinate to the larger issue. It is not until the outcome of the martial conflict is clear and Antony's ruin is imminent that the lovers' tragedy gains primary ascendancy. Then all the resources of a splendid orchestration give it immortal beauty. Then and not before does Shakespeare begin to dwell upon tragic emotion and strife in the mind of the hero. Earlier there is little of this. There is a mild struggle as Antony rouses himself to break his "strong Egyptian fetters"; he is pained and embarrassed taking leave of Cleopatra (I.iii.); but there is no upheaval in the mind now possessed by "Roman thoughts." The agitation is Cleopatra's, and it is not yet of tragic cast. In Rome Antony proceeds with the same assurance to make his peace with Cæsar, and with cool diplomacy to make his marriage of convenience. Yet in all of this we are not deceived, for Enobarbus declares that Antony will again to Egypt, and his prophecy is only hours old when Antony himself confirms it. The readiness with which he resolves to return to Cleopatra pointedly indicates that his heart has never been elsewhere. The words of the Soothsayer (II. iii.10 ff.) serve to rationalize the heart's desire. Though Antony's obedience to his sense of duty in shaking off his "dotage" may have been sincere enough under the impact of Fulvia's death and "the business she hath broached in the state," it could not endure. Of that fact there is sufficient intimation, for in the opening scene we witness the fullness of Antony's surrender to his eastern pleasures, and we soon learn on further testimony the range and potent magnetism of Cleopatra's charms. Indeed, in the scene of parting, Cleopatra, honest, yet "cunning past man's thought," caps her protests with amorous benediction, and Antony proclaims that in separation they are not divided (I.iii.86–105). Shakespeare's reason for minimizing emotional conflict in his hero during the early part of the action now emerges. Cleopatra must appear essentially irresistible; she must have no really credible rival in Antony's mind and heart.

To Plutarch, the love of Antony for Cleopatra was merely a baneful spell which stirred up the evil elements in his character and quenched what was left of good; and Cleopatra herself was a sensual coquette, full of trickery and deceit, whose grief for Antony at the end was genuine enough, but was disfigured by petulance, fear, and vacillation. Shakespeare ignores the more vulgar libertine elements in Antony's character, and presents him as a man with a genius for friendship, a splendid practical capacity, and a highly sensuous temperament, who is subdued by a passion which, however unworthy in some aspects, is redeemed from meanness by its magnificent intensity. The picture of the Egyptian queen is equally skillful and even more subtle. Shakespeare preserves nearly all the characteristics of selfishness

and guile that are found in Plutarch's sketch, and, save that he condenses and omits some ugly physical details, spares us nothing of the weakness and falsehood that are constantly appearing almost to the last. But he alternates these with amazing flashes of a magical fascination that render the creation unique; and he closes with a scene which, without any inconsistency with previous revelations of character, lifts both her and her Herculean Roman into the sphere of loftiest tragedy.

Enobarbus is remarkable among Shakespeare's minor characters. A caustic observer of Antony's gradual downfall, he serves as a kind of Chorus. But he is much more than this. As Antony's truest friend, he magnifies the tragic hero through his affection. Even his desertion, when Antony's fortunes are at lowest ebb, helps to raise the sunken hero in our eyes. For it prompts Antony to an act of splendid magnanimity (IV.v.12–17), and the remorse of Enobarbus, who dies broken-hearted, is a supreme expression of loyalty (IV.vi.30–39, IV.ix. 12–23). Similarly, the loyalty of Scarus and of Eros assist in reviving our esteem for Antony. And of Enobarbus one may remark that it is he who gives the magnificent description of Cleopatra in her barge (II.ii.195 ff.), a rich transmutation of the prose of North, where the account is given by Antony. One would not, perhaps, expect these raptures from the mocking realist, but Shakespeare's letting Enobarbus bear witness to the glory of Cleopatra adds important conviction; for Antony would be a prejudiced reporter.

When early in his career Shakespeare wrote a tragedy of love he gave us *Romeo and Juliet*, idealizing the pure passion of youth. When at the height of that career he turns to write a tragedy of love he gives us *Antony and Cleopatra*, celebrating a passion as mature, experienced, and artful as the other was artless and unabashed. Each, one may believe, would have been impossible in the other's place; for at the time of writing the first Shakespeare had not lived long enough to write the second, yet when he wrote the second he had lived too long to write the first. What taught Shakespeare to understand the infatuation of an Antony, the temperament of a Cleopatra, the greatness of a passion that exalts what it destroys, we cannot hope to know. But it could hardly have been insight alone. In the lyric impulse of *Romeo and Juliet* one acknowledges an affinity with Shakespeare's Sonnets. If the richer music of *Antony and Cleopatra* does not invite recollection of the Sonnets, the amorous theme does, and it is conceivable that through his enigmatic Dark Lady, Shakespeare was assisted in imagining what Antony's Cleopatra was like.

THE TRAGEDY OF
ANTONY AND CLEOPATRA

[DRAMATIS PERSONÆ

MARK ANTONY,
OCTAVIUS CÆSAR, } *triumvirs.*
M. ÆMILIUS LEPIDUS,
SEXTUS POMPEIUS.
DOMITIUS ENOBARBUS,
VENTIDIUS,
EROS,
SCARUS, } *friends to Antony.*
DERCETAS,
DEMETRIUS,
PHILO,
CANIDIUS, *lieutenant-general to Antony.*
MÆCENAS,
AGRIPPA,
DOLABELLA, } *friends to Cæsar.*
PROCULEIUS,
THYREUS,
GALLUS,

TAURUS, *lieutenant-general to Cæsar.*
MENAS,
MENECRATES, } *friends to Pompey.*
VARRIUS,
SILIUS, *an officer in Ventidius's army.*
EUPHRONIUS, *an ambassador from Antony to Cæsar.*
ALEXAS,
MARDIAN, *a eunuch,* } *attendants on Cleopatra.*
SELEUCUS,
DIOMEDES,
A Soothsayer.
A Clown.

CLEOPATRA, *Queen of Egypt.*
OCTAVIA, *sister to Cæsar and wife to Antony.*
CHARMIAN, } *attendants on Cleopatra.*
IRAS,

Officers, Soldiers, Messengers, and other Attendants.

SCENE: *In several parts of the Roman Empire.*]

ACT I

SCENE I. [*Alexandria. A room in Cleopatra's palace.*]

Enter DEMETRIUS *and* PHILO.

Phi. Nay, but this dotage of our general's
O'erflows the measure. Those his goodly eyes,
That o'er the files and musters of the war
Have glow'd like plated Mars, now bend, now turn
The office and devotion of their view   5
Upon a tawny front; his captain's heart,
Which in the scuffles of great fights hath burst

The buckles on his breast, reneges all temper,
And is become the bellows and the fan   9
To cool a gipsy's lust.

Flourish. Enter ANTONY, CLEOPATRA, *her Ladies, the train, with Eunuchs fanning her.*

                          Look, where they come!
Take but good note, and you shall see in him
The triple pillar of the world transform'd
Into a strumpet's fool. Behold and see.
   Cleo. If it be love indeed, tell me how much.
   Ant. There's beggary in the love that can be reckon'd.   15

Act I, sc. i, 4. **plated:** in armor. 5. **office:** service. 8. **reneges:** renounces. **temper:** discipline. 12. **triple pillar.** Antony as one of the triumvirs.

Cleo. I'll set a bourn how far to be belov'd.
Ant. Then must thou needs find out new heaven,
    new earth.

            Enter a MESSENGER.

Mess. News, my good lord, from Rome.
Ant.   Grates me: the sum.
Cleo. Nay, hear them, Antony.
Fulvia perchance is angry; or, who knows   20
If the scarce-bearded Cæsar have not sent
His powerful mandate to you: "Do this, or this;
Take in that kingdom, and enfranchise that;
Perform 't, or else we damn thee."
Ant.   How, my love!
Cleo. Perchance? Nay, and most like.   25
You must not stay here longer; your dismission
Is come from Cæsar; therefore hear it, Antony.
Where's Fulvia's process? — Cæsar's, I would say.
    Both?
Call in the messengers. As I am Egypt's queen,
Thou blushest, Antony, and that blood of thine   30
Is Cæsar's homager; else so thy cheek pays shame
When shrill-tongu'd Fulvia scolds. The messen-
    gers!
Ant. Let Rome in Tiber melt, and the wide
    arch
Of the rang'd empire fall! Here is my space.
Kingdoms are clay; our dungy earth alike   35
Feeds beast as man; the nobleness of life
Is to do thus, when such a mutual pair
                    [*Embracing.*]
And such a twain can do't, in which I bind,
On pain of punishment, the world to weet
We stand up peerless.
Cleo.   Excellent falsehood!   40
Why did he marry Fulvia, and not love her?
                      [*Aside.*]
I'll seem the fool I am not. — Antony
Will be himself.
Ant.   But stirr'd by Cleopatra.
Now, for the love of Love and her soft hours,
Let's not confound the time with conference
    harsh.   45
There's not a minute of our lives should stretch
Without some pleasure now. What sport to-
    night?
Cleo. Hear the ambassadors.
Ant.   Fie, wrangling queen!
Whom everything becomes — to chide, to laugh,
To weep; [whose] every passion fully strives   50
To make itself, in thee, fair and admir'd!
No messenger but thine; and all alone

To-night we'll wander through the streets and note
The qualities of people. Come, my queen;   54
Last night you did desire it. — Speak not to us.
       [*Exeunt* [*Ant. and Cleo.*] *with their train.*
Dem. Is Cæsar with Antonius priz'd so slight?
Phi. Sir, sometimes, when he is not Antony,
He comes too short of that great property
Which still should go with Antony.
Dem.   I am full sorry
That he approves the common liar, who   60
Thus speaks of him at Rome; but I will hope
Of better deeds to-morrow. Rest you happy!
                     [*Exeunt.*

    [SCENE II. *The same. Another room.*]

Enter ENOBARBUS, Lamprius, *a* SOOTHSAYER, Ran-
    nius, Lucilius, CHARMIAN, IRAS, Mardian *the*
    Eunuch, and ALEXAS.

Char. [Lord] Alexas, sweet Alexas, most any-
thing Alexas, almost most absolute Alexas, where's
the soothsayer that you prais'd so to th' Queen?
O, that I knew this husband, which, you say, must
[charge] his horns with garlands!   5
Alex. Soothsayer!
Sooth. Your will?
Char. Is this the man? Is't you, sir, that know
    things?
Sooth. In nature's infinite book of secrecy
A little I can read.
Alex.   Show him your hand.   10
Eno. Bring in the banquet quickly; wine enough
Cleopatra's health to drink.
Char. Good sir, give me good fortune.
Sooth. I make not, but foresee.
Char. Pray, then, foresee me one.   15
Sooth. You shall be yet far fairer than you are.
Char. He means in flesh.
Iras. No, you shall paint when you are old.
Char. Wrinkles forbid!
Alex. Vex not his prescience; be attentive.   20
Char. Hush!
Sooth. You shall be more beloving than beloved.
Char. I had rather heat my liver with drinking.
Alex. Nay, hear him.   24
Char. Good now, some excellent fortune! Let
me be married to three kings in a forenoon and
widow them all. Let me have a child at fifty, to
whom Herod of Jewry may do homage. Find me
to marry me with Octavius Cæsar, and companion
me with my mistress.   30
Sooth. You shall outlive the lady whom you serve.

---

16. **bourn:** limit.   18. **Grates:** it vexes.   **the sum:** be brief.   28. **process:** summons.   31. **homager:** vassal.   34.
rang'd: ordered.   39. **weet:** know.   43. **stirr'd:** inspired.   45. **confound:** spoil.   50. **[whose]** F$_2$. *who* F$_1$.   54. **quali-**
ties: characters.   58. **property:** quality.   60. **approves:** confirms.
    Sc. ii, 1. **[Lord]** (Johnson). *L.* F.   5. **[charge]** (Theobald). *change* F. **with garlands:** i.e., like a sacrificial beast. The
reference is to the imaginary horns of the cuckold.   23. **drinking:** i.e., as opposed to loving (l. 22).

Char. O excellent! I love long life better than
figs.

Sooth. You have seen and proved a fairer former
fortune

Than that which is to approach. 34

Char. Then belike my children shall have no
names. Prithee, how many boys and wenches
must I have?

Sooth. If every of your wishes had a womb,
And [fertile] every wish, a million.

Char. Out, fool! I forgive thee for a witch. 40

Alex. You think none but your sheets are privy
to your wishes.

Char. Nay, come, tell Iras hers.

Alex. We'll know all our fortunes.

Eno. Mine, and most of our fortunes to-night,
shall be — drunk to bed. 46

Iras. There's a palm presages chastity, if nothing
else.

Char. E'en as the o'erflowing Nilus presageth
famine. 50

Iras. Go, you wild bedfellow, you cannot sooth-
say.

Char. Nay, if an oily palm be not a fruitful
prognostication, I cannot scratch mine ear Prithee,
tell her but a worky-day fortune. 55

Sooth. Your fortunes are alike.

Iras. But how, but how? Give me particulars.

Sooth. I have said.

Iras. Am I not an inch of fortune better than
she? 60

Char. Well, if you were but an inch of fortune
better than I, where would you choose it?

Iras. Not in my husband's nose.

Char. Our worser thoughts heavens mend!
Alexas, — come, his fortune, his fortune! O let 65
him marry a woman that cannot go, sweet Isis, I
beseech thee! and let her die too, and give him a
worse! and let worse follow worse, till the worst of
all follow him laughing to his grave, fifty-fold a
cuckold! Good Isis, hear me this prayer, though
thou deny me a matter of more weight; good Isis, I
beseech thee! 72

Iras. Amen. Dear goddess, hear that prayer of
the people! for, as it is a heart-breaking to see a
handsome man loose-wiv'd, so it is a deadly sorrow
to behold a foul knave uncuckolded; therefore, dear
Isis, keep decorum, and fortune him accordingly! 78

Char. Amen.

Alex. Lo, now, if it lay in their hands to make
me a cuckold, they would make themselves whores
but they'd do't!

Enter CLEOPATRA.

Eno. Hush! here comes Antony.

Char. Not he; the Queen. 83

Cleo. [Saw] you my lord?

Eno. No, lady.

Cleo. Was he not here?

Char. No, madam.

Cleo. He was dispos'd to mirth, but on the
sudden 86
A Roman thought hath struck him. Enobarbus!

Eno. Madam?

Cleo. Seek him, and bring him hither.
Where 's Alexas?

Alex. Here, at your service. My lord approaches. 90

Enter ANTONY *with a* MESSENGER [*and* AT-
TENDANTS].

Cleo. We will not look upon him. Go with us.
[*Exeunt* [*Cleo. and train*].

Mess. Fulvia thy wife first came into the field.

Ant. Against my brother Lucius?

Mess. Ay; 94
But soon that war had end, and the time's state
Made friends of them, jointing their force 'gainst
Cæsar;
Whose better issue in the war from Italy,
Upon the first encounter, drave them.

Ant. Well, what worst?

Mess. The nature of bad news infects the teller.

Ant. When it concerns the fool or coward. On:
Things that are past are done with me. 'Tis thus:
Who tells me true, though in his tale lie death, 102
I hear him as he flatter'd.

Mess. Labienus —
This is stiff news — hath with his Parthian force
Extended Asia from Euphrates, 105
His conquering banner shook from Syria
To Lydia and to Ionia,
Whilst —

Ant. Antony, thou wouldst say, —

Mess. O, my lord!

Ant. Speak to me home; mince not the general
tongue.
Name Cleopatra as she is call'd in Rome; 110
Rail thou in Fulvia's phrase, and taunt my faults
With such full license as both truth and malice
Have power to utter. O, then we bring forth weeds
When our quick [minds] lie still; and our ills told us
Is as our earing. Fare thee well a while. 115

Mess. At your noble pleasure. [*Exit.*

Ant. From Sicyon, [ho], the news! Speak there!

39. [fertile] (Theobald). *foretell* F. 40. **witch:** wizard. 53. **oily.** A moist palm indicated licentiousness. 55.
worky-day: ordinary. 64. **Alexas** (Theobald). *Alexas.* F (as speech-heading). 66. **go:** walk. 84. [Saw] F₂. *Save* F₁.
105. **Extended:** seized. 109. **home:** plainly. **general tongue:** common talk. 114. **quick:** fertile. [minds] (Hanmer).
windes F. 115. **as our earing:** as beneficial to us as plowing (earing) to weedy soil. 117. [ho] (Dyce). *how* F

1. [*Att.*] The man from Sicyon, — is there such
 an one?
2. [*Att.*] He stays upon your will.
Ant.   Let him appear.
These strong Egyptian fetters I must break,   120
Or lose myself in dotage.

Enter another MESSENGER *with a letter.*
                          What are you?
[*2.*] *Mess.* Fulvia thy wife is dead.
Ant.   Where died she?
[*2.*] *Mess.* In Sicyon:
Her length of sickness, with what else more
 serious
Importeth thee to know, this bears.
                              [*Gives a letter.*]
Ant.   Forbear me.
                              [*Exit 2. Messenger.*]
There's a great spirit gone! Thus did I desire it.
What our contempts doth often hurl from us,   127
We wish it ours again; the present pleasure,
By revolution low'ring, does become
The opposite of itself.   She's good, being gone;
The hand could pluck her back that shov'd
 her on.
I must from this enchanting queen break off;   132
Ten thousand harms, more than the ills I know,
My idleness doth hatch.

Re-enter ENOBARBUS.
                    How now! Enobarbus!
Eno. What's your pleasure, sir?   135
Ant. I must with haste from hence.
Eno. Why, then, we kill all our women. We see
how mortal an unkindness is to them; if they suffer
our departure, death's the word.
Ant. I must be gone.   140
Eno. Under a compelling occasion, let women
die. It were pity to cast them away for nothing;
though, between them and a great cause, they
should be esteemed nothing. Cleopatra, catching
but the least noise of this, dies instantly; I   145
have seen her die twenty times upon far poorer
moment. I do think there is mettle in Death,
which commits some loving act upon her, she hath
such a celerity in dying.
Ant. She is cunning past man's thought.   150
Eno. Alack, sir, no; her passions are made of
nothing but the finest part of pure love. We cannot call her winds and waters sighs and tears; they

are greater storms and tempests than almanacs can
report. This cannot be cunning in her; if it be, she
makes a shower of rain as well as Jove.   157
Ant. Would I had never seen her!
Eno. O, sir, you had then left unseen a won-
derful piece of work; which not to have been blest
withal would have discredited your travel.
Ant. Fulvia is dead.   162
Eno. Sir?
Ant. Fulvia is dead.
Eno. Fulvia!
Ant. Dead.   166
Eno. Why, sir, give the gods a thankful sacrifice.
When it pleaseth their deities to take the wife of a
man from him, it shows to man the tailors of the
earth; comforting therein, that when old robes   170
are worn out, there are members to make new. If
there were no more women but Fulvia, then had
you indeed a cut, and the case to be lamented.
This grief is crown'd with consolation; your old
smock brings forth a new petticoat; and indeed the
tears live in an onion that should water this sorrow.   177
Ant. The business she hath broached in the state
Cannot endure my absence.
Eno. And the business you have broach'd here
cannot be without you; especially that of Cleo-
patra's, which wholly depends on your abode.   182
Ant. No more light answers. Let our officers
Have notice what we purpose. I shall break
The cause of our expedience to the Queen   185
And get her [leave] to part.   For not alone
The death of Fulvia, with more urgent touches,
Do strongly speak to us, but the letters too
Of many our contriving friends in Rome
Petition us at home.   Sextus Pompeius   190
[Hath] given the dare to Cæsar, and commands
The empire of the sea.   Our slippery people,
Whose love is never link'd to the deserver
Till his deserts are past, begin to throw
Pompey the Great and all his dignities   195
Upon his son; who, high in name and power,
Higher than both in blood and life, stands up
For the main soldier; whose quality, going on,
The sides o' th' world may danger.   Much is breed-
 ing
Which, like the courser's hair, hath yet but life, 200
And not a serpent's poison.   Say, our pleasure,
To such whose [place is] under us, [requires]
Our quick remove from hence.
Eno. I shall do't.   [*Exeunt.*]

118, 119. **[Att.]** (Capell). *Mes.* F. 122. **[2.].** 3. F. 123. **[2.].** Om. F. 125. **Forbear:** leave. 129. **By ... low'ring:**
growing worse through change. 131. **could:** would gladly. 169. **tailors ... earth:** i.e., those who can provide a new wife as
easily as tailors can make a new garment. 173. **cut:** bad luck. 178. **broached:** set going. 182. **abode:** staying. 185.
expedience: haste. 186. **[leave]** (Pope). *love* F. 187. **touches:** motives. 191. **[Hath]** F₂. *Have* F₁. 194. **throw:** bestow.
198. **main:** leading. 199. **sides:** frame. 200. **courser's hair.** Allusion to the belief that a horse's hair, put into water,
would become a snake. 202. **[place is] ... [requires]** F₂. *places ... require* F₁.

[SCENE III. *The same. Another room.*]

Enter CLEOPATRA, CHARMIAN, IRAS, *and* Alexas.

Cleo. Where is he?

Char.   I did not see him since.

Cleo. See where he is, who's with him, what he does.
I did not send you. If you find him sad,
Say I am dancing; if in mirth, report
That I am sudden sick. Quick, and return.   5
                       [*Exit Alexas.*]

Char. Madam, methinks, if you did love him dearly,
You do not hold the method to enforce
The like from him.

Cleo.   What should I do, I do not?

Char. In each thing give him way, cross him in nothing.

Cleo. Thou teachest like a fool: the way to lose him.   10

Char. Tempt him not so too far; I wish, forbear.
In time we hate that which we often fear.

Enter ANTONY.

But here comes Antony.

Cleo.   I am sick and sullen.

Ant. I am sorry to give breathing to my purpose, —

Cleo. Help me away, dear Charmian; I shall fall.
It cannot be thus long, the sides of nature   16
Will not sustain it.

Ant.   Now, my dearest queen, —

Cleo. Pray you, stand farther from me.

Ant.   What's the matter?

Cleo. I know, by that same eye, there's some good news.
What says the married woman? You may go.   20
Would she had never given you leave to come!
Let her not say 'tis I that keep you here;
I have no power upon you; hers you are.

Ant. The gods best know, —

Cleo.   O, never was there queen
So mightily betray'd! Yet at the first   25
I saw the treasons planted.

Ant.   Cleopatra, —

Cleo. Why should I think you can be mine and true,
Though you in swearing shake the throned gods,
Who have been false to Fulvia? Riotous madness,
To be entangled with those mouth-made vows,   30
Which break themselves in swearing!

Ant.   Most sweet queen, —

Cleo. Nay, pray you, seek no colour for your going,

But bid farewell and go. When you sued staying,
Then was the time for words; no going then;
Eternity was in our lips and eyes,   35
Bliss in our brows' bent; none our parts so poor
But was a race of heaven. They are so still,
Or thou, the greatest soldier of the world,
Art turn'd the greatest liar.

Ant.   How now, lady!

Cleo. I would I had thy inches; thou shouldst know   40
There were a heart in Egypt.

Ant.   Hear me, Queen.
The strong necessity of time commands
Our services a while; but my full heart
Remains in use with you. Our Italy
Shines o'er with civil swords; Sextus Pompeius   45
Makes his approaches to the port of Rome;
Equality of two domestic powers
Breed scrupulous faction; the hated, grown to strength,
Are newly grown to love; the condemn'd Pompey,
Rich in his father's honour, creeps apace   50
Into the hearts of such as have not thrived
Upon the present state, whose numbers threaten;
And quietness, grown sick of rest, would purge
By any desperate change. My more particular,
And that which most with you should safe my going,   55
Is Fulvia's death.

Cleo. Though age from folly could not give me freedom,
It does from childishness. Can Fulvia die?

Ant. She's dead, my queen.
Look here, and at thy sovereign leisure read   60
The garboils she awak'd: at the last, best;
See when and where she died.

Cleo.   O most false love!
Where be the sacred vials thou shouldst fill
With sorrowful water? Now I see, I see,
In Fulvia's death, how mine receiv'd shall be.   65

Ant. Quarrel no more, but be prepar'd to know
The purposes I bear; which are, or cease,
As you shall give the advice. By the fire
That quickens Nilus' slime, I go from hence
Thy soldier, servant; making peace or war   70
As thou [affect'st].

Cleo.   Cut my lace, Charmian, come!
But let it be; I am quickly ill and well,
So Antony loves.

Ant.   My precious queen, forbear;
And give true evidence to his love, which stands
An honourable trial.

Cleo.   So Fulvia told me.   75

Sc. iii, 11. **forbear:** i.e., that you would forbear.   32. **colour:** pretext.   33. **sued staying:** begged to stay.   37. **a . . . heaven:** of divine origin.   45. **civil:** of civil war.   48. **scrupulous faction:** carping dissension.   53. **purge:** i.e., seek cure. 54. **particular:** personal concern.   55. **safe:** make safe.   61. **garboils:** turmoils.   63. **sacred vials.** The small vials sometimes buried by the Romans with their dead were supposed to be for tears.   71. **[affect'st]** F₂: pleasest. *affects* F₁.

I prithee, turn aside and weep for her;
Then bid adieu to me, and say the tears
Belong to Egypt.　Good now, play one scene
Of excellent dissembling; and let it look
Like perfect honour.
　　Ant.　　　　　　You'll heat my blood.　No more.
　　Cleo. You can do better yet; but this is meetly. 81
　　Ant. Now, by [my] sword, —
　　Cleo.　　　　　　And target. — Still he mends;
But this is not the best.　Look, prithee, Charmian,
How this Herculean Roman does become
The carriage of his chafe.　　　　　　　　　85
　　Ant. I'll leave you, lady.
　　Cleo.　　　　　　Courteous lord, one word.
Sir, you and I must part, but that's not it;
Sir, you and I have lov'd, but there's not it;
That you know well.　Something it is I would, —
O, my oblivion is a very Antony,　　　　　90
And I am all forgotten.
　　Ant.　　　　　　But that your royalty
Holds idleness your subject, I should take you
For idleness itself.
　　Cleo.　　　　　　'Tis sweating labour
To bear such idleness so near the heart
As Cleopatra this.　But, sir, forgive me,　　95
Since my becomings kill me when they do not
Eye well to you.　Your honour calls you hence;
Therefore be deaf to my unpitied folly,
And all the gods go with you!　Upon your sword
Sit laurell'd victory, and smooth success　　100
Be strew'd before your feet!
　　Ant.　　　　　　Let us go. — Come;
Our separation so abides and flies,
That thou, residing here, [goest] yet with me,
And I, hence fleeting, here remain with thee.
Away!　　　　　　　　　　[*Exeunt.* 105

[SCENE IV.　*Rome.　Cæsar's house.*]

Enter OCTAVIUS [CÆSAR], *reading a letter,* LEPIDUS,
and their train.

　　Cæs. You may see, Lepidus, and henceforth
　　　　know,
It is not Cæsar's natural vice to hate
[Our] great competitor.　From Alexandria
This is the news: he fishes, drinks, and wastes
The lamps of night in revel; is not more manlike 5
Than Cleopatra, nor the queen of Ptolemy
More womanly than he; hardly gave audience, or

Vouchsaf'd to think he had partners.　You shall
　　　find there
A man who is the abstract of all faults
That all men follow.
　　Lep.　　　　　　I must not think there are
Evils enow to darken all his goodness.　　11
His faults, in him, seem as the spots of heaven,
More fiery by night's blackness; hereditary,
Rather than purchas'd; what he cannot change,
Than what he chooses.　　　　　　　　15
　　Cæs. You are too indulgent.　Let's grant it is not
Amiss to tumble on the bed of Ptolemy;
To give a kingdom for a mirth; to sit
And keep the turn of tippling with a slave;
To reel the streets at noon, and stand the buffet 20
With knaves that smell of sweat: say this becomes
　　　him, —
As his composure must be rare indeed
Whom these things cannot blemish, — yet must
　　　Antony
No way excuse his foils, when we do bear
So great weight in his lightness.　If he fill'd　25
His vacancy with his voluptuousness,
Full surfeits and the dryness of his bones
Call on him for't; but to confound such time
That drums him from his sport and speaks as loud
As his own state and ours, 'tis to be chid　　30
As we rate boys who, being mature in knowledge,
Pawn their experience to their present pleasure,
And so rebel to judgement.

Enter a MESSENGER.

　　Lep.　　　　　　Here's more news.
　　Mess. Thy biddings have been done, and every
　　　hour,
Most noble Cæsar, shalt thou have report　35
How 'tis abroad.　Pompey is strong at sea,
And it appears he is belov'd of those
That only have fear'd Cæsar.　To the ports
The discontents repair, and men's reports　39
Give him much wrong'd.
　　Cæs.　　　　　　I should have known no less.
It hath been taught us from the primal state,
That he which is was wish'd until he were;
And the ebb'd man, ne'er loved till ne'er worth love,
Comes [dear'd] by being lack'd.　This common
　　　body,
Like to a vagabond flag upon the stream,　45
Goes to and back, [lackeying] the varying tide,
To rot itself with motion.

Mess.   Cæsar, I bring thee word
Menecrates and Menas, famous pirates,
Makes the sea serve them, which they ear and wound
With keels of every kind. Many hot inroads   50
They make in Italy; the borders maritime
Lack blood to think on't, and flush youth revolt.
No vessel can peep forth but 'tis as soon
Taken as seen; for Pompey's name strikes more
Than could his war resisted.
Cæs.   Antony,   55
Leave thy lascivious [wassails]. When thou once
Was beaten from Modena, where thou slew'st
Hirtius and Pansa, consuls, at thy heel
Did famine follow; whom thou fought'st against,
Though daintily brought up, with patience more
Than savages could suffer. Thou didst drink   61
The stale of horses and the gilded puddle
Which beasts would cough at; thy palate then did
    deign
The roughest berry on the rudest hedge;
Yea, like the stag, when snow the pasture sheets,   65
The barks of trees thou [browsed'st]; on the Alps
It is reported thou didst eat strange flesh,
Which some did die to look on; and all this —
It wounds thine honour that I speak it now —
Was borne so like a soldier, that thy cheek   70
So much as lank'd not.
Lep.   'Tis pity of him.
Cæs. Let his shames quickly
Drive him to Rome. 'Tis time we twain
Did show ourselves i' th' field, and to that end
Assemble we immediate council. Pompey   75
Thrives in our idleness.
Lep.   To-morrow, Cæsar,
I shall be furnish'd to inform you rightly
Both what by sea and land I can be able
To front this present time.
Cæs.   Till which encounter,
It is my business too. Farewell.   80
Lep. Farewell, my lord. What you shall know
    meantime
Of stirs abroad, I shall beseech you, sir,
To let me be partaker.
Cæs.   Doubt not, sir;
I knew it for my bond.   [*Exeunt.*

[SCENE V. *Alexandria. Cleopatra's palace.*]

Enter CLEOPATRA, CHARMIAN, IRAS, *and*
MARDIAN.

Cleo. Charmian!
Char. Madam?

Cleo. Ha, ha!
Give me to drink mandragora.
Char.   Why, madam?
Cleo. That I might sleep out this great gap of
    time   5
My Antony is away.
Char.   You think of him too much.
Cleo. O, 'tis treason!
Char.   Madam, I trust not so.
Cleo. Thou, eunuch Mardian!
Mar.   What's your Highness' pleasure?
Cleo. Not now to hear thee sing; I take no pleas-
    ure
In aught an eunuch has. 'Tis well for thee,   10
That, being unseminar'd, thy freer thoughts
May not fly forth of Egypt. Hast thou affections?
Mar. Yes, gracious madam.
Cleo. Indeed!
Mar. Not in deed, madam, for I can do nothing
But what indeed is honest to be done;   16
Yet have I fierce affections, and think
What Venus did with Mars.
Cleo.   O Charmian,
Where think'st thou he is now? Stands he, or sits
    he?
Or does he walk? Or is he on his horse?   20
O happy horse, to bear the weight of Antony!
Do bravely, horse! for wot'st thou whom thou
    mov'st?
The demi-Atlas of this earth, the arm
And burgonet of men. He's speaking now,
Or murmuring, "Where's my serpent of old Nile?"
For so he calls me. Now I feed myself   26
With most delicious poison. Think on me,
That am with Phœbus' amorous pinches black,
And wrinkled deep in time? Broad-fronted Cæsar,
When thou wast here above the ground, I was   30
A morsel for a monarch; and great Pompey
Would stand and make his eyes grow in my brow;
There would he anchor his aspect and die
With looking on his life.

Enter ALEXAS.

Alex.   Sovereign of Egypt, hail!
Cleo. How much unlike art thou Mark Antony!
Yet, coming from him, that great med'cine hath   36
With his tinct gilded thee.
How goes it with my brave Mark Antony?
Alex. Last thing he did, dear queen,
He kiss'd, — the last of many doubled kisses, —   40
This orient pearl. His speech sticks in my heart.
Cleo. Mine ear must pluck it thence.

---

49. **ear:** plow.   52. **Lack blood:** grow pale. **flush:** lusty.   54. **strikes:** accomplishes.   55. **resisted:** if it were resisted. 56. [**wassails**] (Pope).   *Vassailes* F.   62. **stale:** urine.   **gilded:** covered with yellow slime.   66. [**browsed'st**] F₂.   *brows'd* F₁.   71. **lank'd not:** did not grow thin.   84. **bond:** duty.

    Sc. v, 4. **mandragora:** juice of the mandrake (a soporific).   11. **unseminar'd:** castrated.   12. **affections:** sexual passion. 23. **demi-Atlas:** supporter of half the world.   24. **burgonet:** helmet, i.e., defender.   28. **black:** swarthy.   29. **Broad-fronted:** with broad forehead.   **Cæsar:** Julius Cæsar.   33. **aspect:** gaze.   34. s.D. *Enter* ALEXAS. F adds *from Cæsar.* 37. **tinct:** tincture.

Alex.   "Good friend," quoth he,
"Say the firm Roman to great Egypt sends
This treasure of an oyster; at whose foot,
To mend the petty present, I will piece   45
Her opulent throne with kingdoms. All the East,
Say thou, shall call her mistress." So he nodded,
And soberly did mount an arm-gaunt steed,
Who neigh'd so high that what I would have spoke
Was beastly [dumb'd] by him.
   Cleo.   What, was he sad or merry?
   Alex. Like to the time o' th' year between the
         extremes   51
Of hot and cold, he was nor sad nor merry.
   Cleo. O well-divided disposition! Note him,
Note him, good Charmian, 'tis the man; but note him:
He was not sad, for he would shine on those   55
That make their looks by his; he was not merry,
Which seem'd to tell them his remembrance lay
In Egypt with his joy; but between both.
O heavenly mingle! Be'st thou sad or merry,
The violence of either thee becomes,   60
So does it no man else. Met'st thou my posts?
   Alex. Ay, madam, twenty several messengers.
Why do you send so thick?
   Cleo.   Who's born that day
When I forget to send to Antony,
Shall die a beggar. Ink and paper, Charmian.   65
Welcome, my good Alexas. Did I, Charmian,
Ever love Cæsar so?
   Char.   O that brave Cæsar!
   Cleo. Be chok'd with such another emphasis!
Say "the brave Antony."
   Char.   The valiant Cæsar!
   Cleo. By Isis, I will give thee bloody teeth,   70
If thou with Cæsar paragon again
My man of men.
   Char.   By your most gracious pardon,
I sing but after you.
   Cleo. My salad days,
When I was green in judgement, cold in blood,
To say as I said then! But, come, away;   75
Get me ink and paper.
He shall have every day a several greeting,
Or I'll unpeople Egypt.   [*Exeunt.*

[ACT II]

[Scene I. *Messina. Pompey's house.*]

Enter Pompey, Menecrates, *and* Menas, *in
warlike manner.*

Pom. If the great gods be just, they shall assist
The deeds of justest men.

   Mene.   Know, worthy Pompey,
That what they do delay, they not deny.
   Pom. Whiles we are suitors to their throne,
      decays
The thing we sue for.
   Mene.   We, ignorant of ourselves,
Beg often our own harms, which the wise powers 6
Deny us for our good; so find we profit
By losing of our prayers.
   Pom.   I shall do well.
The people love me, and the sea is mine;
My powers are crescent, and my auguring hope 10
Says it will come to th' full. Mark Antony
In Egypt sits at dinner, and will make
No wars without-doors. Cæsar gets money where
He loses hearts. Lepidus flatters both,
Of both is flatter'd; but he neither loves,   15
Nor either cares for him.
   Mene.   Cæsar and Lepidus
Are in the field; a mighty strength they carry.
   Pom. Where have you this? 'Tis false.
   Mene.   From Silvius, sir.
   Pom. He dreams. I know they are in Rome
      together,
Looking for Antony. But all the charms of love, 20
Salt Cleopatra, soften thy [wan'd] lip!
Let witchcraft join with beauty, lust with both!
Tie up the libertine in a field of feasts,
Keep his brain fuming; Epicurean cooks
Sharpen with cloyless sauce his appetite,   25
That sleep and feeding may prorogue his honour
Even till a Lethe'd dulness!

Enter Varrius.

                      How now, Varrius!
   Var. This is most certain that I shall deliver:
Mark Antony is every hour in Rome
Expected; since he went from Egypt 'tis   30
A space for farther travel.
   Pom.   I could have given less matter
A better ear. Menas, I did not think
This amorous surfeiter would have donn'd his helm
For such a petty war. His soldiership
Is twice the other twain; but let us rear   35
The higher our opinion, that our stirring
Can from the lap of Egypt's widow pluck
The [ne'er] lust-wearied Antony.
   [*Menas.*]   I cannot hope
Cæsar and Antony shall well greet together.
His wife that's dead did trespasses to Cæsar;   40
His brother [warr'd] upon him, although, I think,
Not mov'd by Antony.

---

48. **arm-gaunt:** gaunt with carrying armed warriors.   50. [**dumb'd**] (Theobald): made inaudible. *dumbe* F.   62.
several: separate. 71. **paragon:** match. 73. **salad days:** days of inexperience.

   Act II, sc. i, 10. **crescent:** increasing. 21. **Salt:** wanton. [**wan'd**] (Percy conj.): faded. *wand* F. 26. **prorogue:** suspend
(from action). 27. **Lethe'd:** oblivious. 31. **space:** interval long enough. 36. **opinion:** i.e., of ourselves. 37. **widow.**
Cleopatra had been married to Ptolemy, her brother. 38. [**ne'er**] (Pope). *neere* F. [**Menas**] (Malone). *Mene.* F. 30
greet. Furness suggests *gree.* 41. [**warr'd**] F₂. *wan'd* F.

Pom.   I know not, Menas,
How lesser enmities may give way to greater.
Were't not that we stand up against them all,
'Twere pregnant they should square between them-
     selves,   45
For they have entertained cause enough
To draw their swords; but how the fear of us
May cement their divisions and bind up
The petty difference, we yet not know.
Be't as our gods will have't! It only stands   50
Our lives upon to use our strongest hands.
Come, Menas.   [*Exeunt.*

[SCENE II. *Rome. The house of Lepidus.*]

Enter ENOBARBUS *and* LEPIDUS.

Lep. Good Enobarbus, 'tis a worthy deed,
And shall become you well, to entreat your captain
To soft and gentle speech.
Eno.   I shall entreat him
To answer like himself. If Cæsar move him,
Let Antony look over Cæsar's head   5
And speak as loud as Mars. By Jupiter,
Were I the wearer of Antonius' beard,
I would not shave't to-day.
Lep.   'Tis not a time
For private stomaching.
Eno.   Every time
Serves for the matter that is then [born] in't.   10
Lep. But small to greater matters must give way.
Eno. Not if the small come first.
Lep.   Your speech is passion;
But, pray you, stir no embers up. Here comes
The noble Antony.

Enter ANTONY *and* Ventidius.

Eno.   And yonder, Cæsar.

Enter CÆSAR, MÆCENAS, *and* AGRIPPA.

Ant. If we compose well here, to Parthia!   15
Hark, Ventidius.
Cæs.   I do not know,
Mæcenas; ask Agrippa.
Lep.   Noble friends,
That which combin'd us was most great, and let not
A leaner action rend us. What's amiss,
May it be gently heard; when we debate   20
Our trivial difference loud, we do commit
Murder in healing wounds; then, noble partners,
The rather, for I earnestly beseech,
Touch you the sourest points with sweetest terms,

Nor curstness grow to th' matter.
Ant.   'Tis spoken well.
Were we before our armies, and to fight,   26
I should do thus.   [*Flourish*
Cæs. Welcome to Rome.
Ant.   Thank you.
Cæs.   Sit.
Ant.   Sit, sir.
Cæs.   Nay, then.
Ant. I learn you take things ill which are not so,
Or being, concern you not.
Cæs.   I must be laugh'd at
If, or for nothing or a little, I   31
Should say myself offended, and with you
Chiefly i' th' world; more laugh'd at that I should
Once name you derogately, when to sound your
     name
It not concern'd me.
Ant.   My being in Egypt, Cæsar,
What was't to you?   36
Cæs. No more than my residing here at Rome
Might be to you in Egypt; yet, if you there
Did practise on my state, your being in Egypt
Might be my question.
Ant.   How intend you, practis'd?   40
Cæs. You may be pleas'd to catch at mine intent
By what did here befall me. Your wife and brother
Made wars upon me, and their contestation
Was theme for you; you were the word of war.
Ant. You do mistake your business; my brother
     never   45
Did urge me in his act. I did inquire it,
And have my learning from some true reports
That drew their swords with you. Did he not
     rather
Discredit my authority with yours,
And make the wars alike, against my stomach,   50
Having alike your cause? Of this my letters
Before did satisfy you. If you'll patch a quarrel,
As matter whole you have [not] to make it with,
It must not be with this.
Cæs.   You praise yourself
By laying defects of judgement to me; but   55
You patch'd up your excuses.
Ant.   Not so, not so.
I know you could not lack, I am certain on't,
Very necessity of this thought, that I,
Your partner in the cause 'gainst which he fought,
Could not with graceful eyes attend those wars   60
Which fronted mine own peace. As for my wife,
I would you had her spirit in such another.

45. **pregnant:** most probable. **square:** fight. 50-51. **It . . . upon:** it is imperative for us.
   Sc. ii, 4. move: anger. 8. **shave't:** i.e., to avoid having it plucked as a challenge. 9. **stomaching:** resentment. 10.
[born] F₃. *borne* F₁. 15. **compose:** agree. 25. **Nor . . . grow:** nor let scolding be added. 34. **derogately:** disparagingly.
39. **practise on:** plot against. 40. **question:** business. 44. **theme for you:** your business. 46. **urge me:** use my name.
50. **stomach:** desire. 51. **Having:** i.e., I having. 52. **patch a quarrel:** make a quarrel from a shred. 53. [not] (Rowe).
Om. F. 60. **graceful:** i.e., approving. 61. **fronted:** opposed.

The third o' th' world is yours, which with a snaffle
You may pace easy, but not such a wife.
  Eno. Would we had all such wives, that the men
might go to wars with the women!   66
  Ant. So much uncurable her garboils, Cæsar,
Made out of her impatience, which not wanted
Shrewdness of policy too, I grieving grant
Did you too much disquiet. For that you must
But say, I could not help it.
  Cæs.   I wrote to you   71
When rioting in Alexandria; you
Did pocket up my letters, and with taunts
Did gibe my missive out of audience.
  Ant.   Sir,
He fell upon me ere admitted. Then   75
Three kings I had newly feasted, and did want
Of what I was i' th' morning; but next day
I told him of myself, which was as much
As to have ask'd him pardon. Let this fellow
Be nothing of our strife; if we contend,   80
Out of our question wipe him.
  Cæs.   You have broken
The article of your oath; which you shall never
Have tongue to charge me with.
  Lep.   Soft, Cæsar!
  Ant.   No,
Lepidus, let him speak.
The honour is sacred which he talks on now,   85
Supposing that I lack'd it. But, on, Cæsar:
The article of my oath.
  Cæs. To lend me arms and aid when I requir'd
    them;
The which you both denied.
  Ant.   Neglected, rather;
And then when poisoned hours had bound me up 90
From mine own knowledge. As nearly as I may,
I'll play the penitent to you; but mine honesty
Shall not make poor my greatness, nor my power
Work without it. Truth is, that Fulvia,
To have me out of Egypt, made wars here;   95
For which myself, the ignorant motive, do
So far ask pardon as befits mine honour
To stoop in such a case.
  Lep.   'Tis noble spoken.
  Mæc. If it might please you, to enforce no further
The griefs between ye: to forget them quite   100
Were to remember that the present need
Speaks to atone you.
  Lep.   Worthily spoken, Mæcenas.
  Eno. Or, if you borrow one another's love for
the instant, you may, when you hear no more
words of Pompey, return it again. You shall
have time to wrangle in when you have nothing
else to do.   107

  Ant. Thou art a soldier only; speak no more.
  Eno. That truth should be silent I had almost
forgot.
  Ant. You wrong this presence; therefore speak
    no more.   111
  Eno. Go to, then; your considerate stone.
  Cæs. I do not much dislike the matter, but
The manner of his speech; for't cannot be
We shall remain in friendship, our conditions   115
So diff'ring in their acts. Yet, if I knew
What hoop should hold us stanch, from edge to edge
O' th' world I would pursue it.
  Agr.   Give me leave, Cæsar, —
  Cæs. Speak, Agrippa.
  Agr. Thou hast a sister by the mother's side, 120
Admir'd Octavia. Great Mark Antony
Is now a widower.
  Cæs.   Say not [so] Agrippa.
If Cleopatra heard you, your [reproof]
Were well deserved of rashness.
  Ant. I am not married, Cæsar; let me hear
Agrippa further speak.   126
  Agr. To hold you in perpetual amity,
To make you brothers, and to knit your hearts
With an unslipping knot, take Antony
Octavia to his wife; whose beauty claims   130
No worse a husband than the best of men;
Whose virtue and whose general graces speak
That which none else can utter. By this marriage,
All little jealousies, which now seem great,   134
And all great fears, which now import their dangers,
Would then be nothing. Truths would be tales,
Where now half-tales be truths. Her love to both
Would each to other and all loves to both
Draw after her. Pardon what I have spoke;
For 'tis a studied, not a present thought,   140
By duty ruminated.
  Ant.   Will Cæsar speak?
  Cæs. Not till he hears how Antony is touch'd
With what is spoke already.
  Ant.   What power is in Agrippa,
If I would say, "Agrippa, be it so,"
To make this good?
  Cæs.   The power of Cæsar, and 145
His power unto Octavia.
  Ant.   May I never
To this good purpose, that so fairly shows,
Dream of impediment! Let me have thy hand.
Further this act of grace; and from this hour
The heart of brothers govern in our loves   150
And sway our great designs!
  Cæs.   There's my hand.
A sister I bequeath you, whom no brother
Did ever love so dearly. Let her live

---

67. **garboils:** broils.   74. **missive:** messenger.   94. **it:** i.e., his greatness (position in the state), or, perhaps, honesty.
102. **atone:** reconcile.   112. **considerate:** reflective.   115. **conditions:** dispositions.   122. **[so]** (Rowe). *say* F.   123. **[reproof]** (Warburton conj.). *proofe* F.   135. **import:** carry with them.

To join our kingdoms and our hearts; and never
Fly off our loves again!
    Lep.   Happily, amen!   155
    Ant. I did not think to draw my sword 'gainst
        Pompey;
For he hath laid strange courtesies and great
Of late upon me. I must thank him only,
Lest my remembrance suffer ill report;
At heel of that, defy him.
    Lep.   Time calls upon 's. 160
Of us must Pompey presently be sought,
Or else he seeks out us.
    Ant.   Where lies he?
    Cæs. About the mount Misenum.
    Ant. What is his strength by land?
    Cæs. Great and increasing; but by sea 165
He is an absolute master.
    Ant.   So is the fame.
Would we had spoke together! Haste we for it;
Yet, ere we put ourselves in arms, dispatch we
The business we have talk'd of.
    Cæs.   With most gladness;
And do invite you to my sister's view, 170
Whither straight I'll lead you.
    Ant.   Let us, Lepidus,
Not lack your company.
    Lep.   Noble Antony,
Not sickness should detain me.
        [*Flourish. Exeunt Cæsar, Antony, Lepidus,*
         and Ventidius.
    Mæc. Welcome from Egypt, sir.   174
    Eno. Half the heart of Cæsar, worthy Mæcenas!
My honourable friend, Agrippa!
    Agr. Good Enobarbus!
    Mæc. We have cause to be glad that matters
are so well digested. You stay'd well by 't in
Egypt.   180
    Eno. Ay, sir; we did sleep day out of counte-
nance, and made the night light with drinking.
    Mæc. Eight wild boars roasted whole at a
breakfast, and but twelve persons there; is this
true?   185
    Eno. This was but as a fly by an eagle. We had
much more monstrous matter of feast, which
worthily deserved noting.
    Mæc. She's a most triumphant lady, if report
be square to her.   190
    Eno. When she first met Mark Antony, she
purs'd up his heart, upon the river of Cydnus.
    Agr. There she appear'd indeed, or my reporter
devis'd well for her.
    Eno. I will tell you.   195
The barge she sat in, like a burnish'd throne,
Burn'd on the water. The poop was beaten gold;

Purple the sails, and so perfumed that
The winds were love-sick with them. The oars
  were silver,
Which to the tune of flutes kept stroke, and made
The water which they beat to follow faster, 201
As amorous of their strokes. For her own person,
It beggar'd all description: she did lie
In her pavilion — cloth-of-gold of tissue —
O'er-picturing that Venus where we see 205
The fancy outwork nature. On each side her
Stood pretty dimpled boys, like smiling Cupids,
With divers-colour'd fans, whose wind did seem
To [glow] the delicate cheeks which they did cool,
And what they undid did.
    Agr.   O, rare for Antony!
    Eno. Her gentlewomen, like the Nereides, 211
So many mermaids, tended her i' th' eyes,
And made their bends adornings. At the helm
A seeming mermaid steers; the silken tackle
Swell with the touches of those flower-soft hands 215
That yarely frame the office. From the barge
A strange invisible perfume hits the sense
Of the adjacent wharfs. The city cast
Her people out upon her; and Antony
Enthron'd i' th' market-place, did sit alone, 220
Whistling to th' air, which, but for vacancy,
Had gone to gaze on Cleopatra too
And made a gap in nature.
    Agr.   Rare Egyptian!
    Eno. Upon her landing, Antony sent to her,
Invited her to supper. She replied, 225
It should be better he became her guest;
Which she entreated. Our courteous Antony,
Whom ne'er the word of "No" woman heard
  speak,
Being barber'd ten times o'er, goes to the feast,
And for his ordinary pays his heart 230
For what his eyes eat only.
    Agr.   Royal wench!
She made great Cæsar lay his sword to bed.
He plough'd her, and she cropp'd.
    Eno.   I saw her once
Hop forty paces through the public street;
And having lost her breath, she spoke, and
  panted,
That she did make defect perfection 236
And, breathless, power breathe forth.
    Mæc. Now Antony must leave her utterly.
    Eno. Never; he will not.
Age cannot wither her, nor custom stale 240
Her infinite variety. Other women cloy
The appetites they feed, but she makes hungry
Where most she satisfies; for vilest things
Become themselves in her, that the holy priests

---

166. **fame:** rumor. 167. **spoke:** i.e., to thank him (ll. 157–58). 204. **cloth ... tissue:** cloth woven of gold and silver threads.
209. **[glow]** (Rowe): make glow. *glove* F. 213. **bends:** bows. 216. **yarely frame:** nimbly do. 218. **wharfs:** banks. 221.
vacancy: i.e., causing a vacuum. 230. **ordinary:** meal. 237. **power:** i.e., charm. 244. **Become themselves:** are becoming.

Bless her when she is riggish. 245
Mæc. If beauty, wisdom, modesty, can settle
The heart of Antony, Octavia is
A blessed lottery to him.
Agr.   Let us go.
Good Enobarbus, make yourself my guest
Whilst you abide here.
Eno.   Humbly, sir, I thank you. 250
                    [Exeunt.

[SCENE III.   *Rome. Cæsar's house.*]

Enter ANTONY, CÆSAR, OCTAVIA *between them*
        [and Attendants].

Ant. The world and my great office will some-
      times
Divide me from your bosom.
Octa.   All which time
Before the gods my knee shall bow my prayers
To them for you.
Ant.   Good-night, sir. My Octavia,
Read not my blemishes in the world's report. 5
I have not kept my square; but that to come
Shall all be done by th' rule. Good-night, dear
      lady.
Good-night, sir.
Cæs. Good-night. *[Exeunt [Cæsar and Octavia].*

Enter SOOTHSAYER.

Ant. Now, sirrah, you do wish yourself in Egypt?
Sooth. Would I had never come from thence, nor
      you   11
Thither!
Ant. If you can, your reason?
Sooth.   I see it in
My motion, have it not in my tongue; but yet
Hie you to Egypt again.
Ant.   Say to me, 15
Whose fortunes shall rise higher, Cæsar's or mine?
Sooth. Cæsar's.
Therefore, O Antony, stay not by his side.
Thy demon, that thy spirit which keeps thee, is
Noble, courageous, high, unmatchable, 20
Where Cæsar's is not; but, near him, thy angel
Becomes a fear, as being o'erpower'd: therefore
Make space between you.
Ant.   Speak this no more.
Sooth. To none but thee; no more, but when to
      thee.
If thou dost play with him at any game, 25
Thou art sure to lose; and, of that natural luck,
He beats thee 'gainst the odds. Thy lustre thickens
When he shines by. I say again, thy spirit

Is all afraid to govern thee near him;
But, he [away], 'tis noble.
Ant.   Get thee gone. — 30
Say to Ventidius I would speak with him;
            [Exit [Soothsayer].
He shall to Parthia. — Be it art or hap,
He hath spoken true. The very dice obey him,
And in our sports my better cunning faints
Under his chance. If we draw lots, he speeds; 35
His cocks do win the battle still of mine,
When it is all to nought; and his quails ever
Beat mine, inhoop'd, at odds. I will to Egypt;
And though I make this marriage for my peace,
I' th' East my pleasure lies.

Enter Ventidius.

              O, come, Ventidius,
You must to Parthia. Your commission 's ready,
Follow me and receive 't.   *[Exeunt.*

[SCENE IV.   *Rome. A street.*]

Enter LEPIDUS, MÆCENAS, *and* AGRIPPA.

Lep. Trouble yourselves no further; pray you,
      hasten
Your generals after.
Agr.   Sir, Mark Antony
Will e'en but kiss Octavia, and we'll follow.
Lep. Till I shall see you in your soldier's dress,
Which will become you both, farewell.
Mæc.   We shall,
As I conceive the journey, be at [th'] Mount 6
Before you, Lepidus.
Lep.   Your way is shorter;
My purposes do draw me much about.
You'll win two days upon me.
Both.   Sir, good success!
Lep. Farewell.   *[Exeunt.* 10

[SCENE V.   *Alexandria. Cleopatra's palace.*]

Enter CLEOPATRA, CHARMIAN, IRAS, *and*
        Alexas.

Cleo. Give me some music; music, moody food
Of us that trade in love.
All.   The music, ho!

Enter MARDIAN *the Eunuch.*

Cleo. Let it alone; let's to billiards. Come,
      Charmian.
Char. My arm is sore; best play with Mardian.
Cleo. As well a woman with an eunuch play'd 5
As with a woman. Come, you'll play with me, sir?
Mar. As well as I can, madam.

Cleo. And when good will is showed, though 't
　　come too short,
The actor may plead pardon. I'll none now.
Give me mine angle, we'll to th' river; there,　　10
My music playing far off, I will betray
[Tawny-finn'd] fishes; my bended hook shall pierce
Their slimy jaws; and, as I draw them up,
I'll think them every one an Antony,
And say, "Ah, ha! you're caught."
　　Char.　　　　　　　　　　'Twas merry when
You wager'd on your angling; when your diver　16
Did hang a salt-fish on his hook, which he
With fervency drew up.
　　Cleo.　　　　　　That time, — O times! —
I laugh'd him out of patience; and that night
I laugh'd him into patience; and next morn,　　20
Ere the ninth hour, I drunk him to his bed;
Then put my tires and mantles on him, whilst
I wore his sword Philippan.

　　　　　Enter a MESSENGER.

　　　　　　　　　　　　　O, from Italy!
Ram thou thy fruitful tidings in mine ears,
That long time have been barren.
　　Mess.　　　　　　　　Madam, madam, —
　　Cleo. Antonio's dead! — If thou say so, villain,　26
Thou kill'st thy mistress; but well and free,
If thou so yield him, there is gold, and here
My bluest veins to kiss; a hand that kings
Have lipp'd, and trembled kissing.　　　　　30
　　Mess. First, madam, he is well.
　　Cleo.　　　　　　Why, there's more gold.
But, sirrah, mark, we use
To say the dead are well. Bring it to that,
The gold I give thee will I melt and pour
Down thy ill-uttering throat.　　　　　　　35
　　Mess. Good madam, hear me.
　　Cleo.　　　　　　　Well, go to, I will.
But there's no goodness in thy face; if Antony
Be free and healthful, [why] so tart a favour
To trumpet such good tidings? If not well,
Thou shouldst come like a Fury crown'd with
　　snakes,　　　　　　　　　　　　　40
Not like a formal man.
　　Mess.　　　　　　Will 't please you hear me?
　　Cleo. I have a mind to strike thee ere thou
　　speak'st;
Yet, if thou say Antony lives, [is] well,
Or friends with Cæsar, or not captive to him,
I'll set thee in a shower of gold, and hail　　45
Rich pearls upon thee.
　　Mess.　　　　　　Madam, he's well.
　　Cleo.　　　　　　　　　　Well said.
　　Mess. And friends with Cæsar.

　　Cleo.　　　　　　　Thou'rt an honest man.
　　Mess. Cæsar and he are greater friends than ever.
　　Cleo. Make thee a fortune from me.
　　Mess.　　　　　　　But yet, madam, —
　　Cleo. I do not like "But yet," it does allay　　50
The good precedence; fie upon "But yet"!
"But yet" is as a gaoler to bring forth
Some monstrous malefactor. Prithee, friend,
Pour out the pack of matter to mine ear,
The good and bad together. He's friends with
　　Cæsar;　　　　　　　　　　　　　55
In state of health thou say'st; and thou say'st free.
　　Mess. Free, madam? No; I made no such report.
He's bound unto Octavia.
　　Cleo.　　　　　　For what good turn?
　　Mess. For the best turn i' th' bed.
　　Cleo.　　　　　　　I am pale, Charmian.
　　Mess. Madam, he's married to Octavia.　　60
　　Cleo. The most infectious pestilence upon thee!
　　　　　　　　　　　　[*Strikes him down.*
　　Mess. Good madam, patience.
　　Cleo.　　　　　　　What say you? Hence,
　　　　　　　　　　　　[*Strikes him again.*
Horrible villain! or I'll spurn thine eyes
Like balls before me; I'll unhair thy head.
　　　　　　　　　[*She hales him up and down.*
Thou shalt be whipp'd with wire, and stew'd in
　　brine,　　　　　　　　　　　　　65
Smarting in ling'ring pickle.
　　Mess.　　　　　　Gracious madam,
I that do bring the news made not the match.
　　Cleo. Say 'tis not so, a province I will give thee,
And make thy fortunes proud; the blow thou
　　hadst
Shall make thy peace for moving me to rage;　70
And I will boot thee with what gift beside
Thy modesty can beg.
　　Mess.　　　　　　He's married, madam.
　　Cleo. Rogue, thou hast liv'd too long.
　　　　　　　　　　　　　[*Draws a knife.*
　　Mess.　　　　　　Nay, then I'll run.
What mean you, madam? I have made no fault.
　　　　　　　　　　　　　　　[*Exit.*
　　Char. Good madam, keep yourself within your-
　　self:　　　　　　　　　　　　　75
The man is innocent.
　　Cleo. Some innocents scape not the thunderbolt.
Melt Egypt into Nile! and kindly creatures
Turn all to serpents! Call the slave again.
Though I am mad, I will not bite him; call.　80
　　Char. He is afeard to come.
　　Cleo.　　　　　　I will not hurt him.
　　　　　　　　　　　　[*Exit Charmian.*]
These hands do lack nobility that they strike

Sc. v, 10. **angle:** rod and line. 12. **[Tawny-finn'd]** (Theobald). *Tawny fine* F. 22. **tires:** head-dresses. 38. **[why]**
(Rowe). Om. F. **tart a favour:** sour a face. 41. **formal:** ordinary. 43. **[is]** (Tyrwhitt conj.). *'tis* F. 50. **allay:** qualify
51. **precedence:** news which preceded (it). 63. **spurn:** kick. 71. **boot thee with:** give thee also.

A meaner than myself, since I myself
Have given myself the cause.

Re-enter [CHARMIAN *and*] MESSENGER.

Come hither, sir.
Though it be honest, it is never good   85
To bring bad news.   Give to a gracious message
An host of tongues, but let ill tidings tell
Themselves when they be felt.
  Mess.   I have done my duty.
  Cleo. Is he married?
I cannot hate thee worser than I do,   90
If thou again say yes.
  Mess.   He's married, madam.
  Cleo. The gods confound thee!   Dost thou hold
    there still?
  Mess. Should I lie, madam?
  Cleo.   O, I would thou didst,
So half my Egypt were submerg'd and made
A cistern for scal'd snakes!   Go, get thee hence! 95
Hadst thou Narcissus in thy face, to me
Thou wouldst appear most ugly.   He is married?
  Mess. I crave your Highness' pardon.
  Cleo.   He is married?
  Mess. Take no offence that I would not offend
    you.
To punish me for what you make me do   100
Seems much unequal.   He's married to Octavia.
  Cleo. O, that his fault should make a knave of
    thee,
That art not what thou'rt sure of.   Get thee hence;
The merchandise which thou hast brought from
    Rome   104
Are all too dear for me.   Lie they upon thy hand,
And be undone by 'em!   [*Exit Messenger.*]
  Char.   Good your Highness, patience.
  Cleo. In praising Antony I have disprais'd Cæsar.
  Char. Many times, madam.
  Cleo.   I am paid for't now.
Lead me from hence;
I faint, O Iras, Charmian!   'Tis no matter.   110
Go to the fellow, good Alexas; bid him
Report the feature of Octavia, her years,
Her inclination; let him not leave out
The colour of her hair.   Bring me word quickly.
                              [*Exit Alexas.*]
Let him for ever go; — let him not — Charmian,
Though he be painted one way like a Gorgon, 116
The other [way 's] a Mars.   Bid you Alexas
                              [*To Mardian.*]
Bring me word how tall she is.   Pity me, Charmian,

But do not speak to me.   Lead me to my chamber.
                              [*Exeunt.*

[SCENE VI.   *Near Misenum.*]

Flourish.   Enter POMPEY *and* MENAS *at one door,
  with drum and trumpet: at another,* CÆSAR, AN-
  TONY, LEPIDUS, ENOBARBUS, Mæcenas, Agrippa,
  with* Soldiers *marching.*

  Pom. Your hostages I have, so have you mine;
And we shall talk before we fight.
  Cæs.   Most meet
That first we come to words, and therefore have we
Our written purposes before us sent;
Which, if thou hast considered, let us know   5
If 'twill tie up thy discontented sword,
And carry back to Sicily much tall youth
That else must perish here.
  Pom.   To you all three,
The senators alone of this great world,
Chief factors for the gods, I do not know   10
Wherefore my father should revengers want,
Having a son and friends; since Julius Cæsar,
Who at Philippi the good Brutus ghosted,
There saw you labouring for him.   What was't
That mov'd pale Cassius to conspire; and what   15
Made [the] all-honour'd, honest Roman, Brutus,
With the arm'd rest, courtiers of beauteous freedom,
To drench the Capitol, but that they would
Have one man but a man?   And that is it
Hath made me rig my navy, at whose burden   20
The anger'd ocean foams; with which I meant
To scourge th' ingratitude that despiteful Rome
Cast on my noble father.
  Cæs.   Take your time.
  Ant. Thou canst not fear us, Pompey, with thy
    sails;   24
We'll speak with thee at sea.   At land, thou know'st
How much we do o'er-count thee.
  Pom.   At land, indeed,
Thou dost o'er-count me of my father's house;
But since the cuckoo builds not for himself,
Remain in't as thou mayst.
  Lep.   Be pleas'd to tell us —
For this is from the present — how you take   30
The offers we have sent you.
  Cæs.   There's the point.
  Ant. Which do not be entreated to, but weigh
What it is worth embrac'd.
  Cæs.   And what may follow,
To try a larger fortune.
  Pom.   You have made me offer

---

94. **So**: even if.   96. **Narcissus**: a mythical figure famous for his beauty.   103. **what...of**: i.e., the hateful news.
112. **feature**: shape, appearance.   113. **inclination**: disposition.   117. **[way 's]** F₄: way he is.   *wayes* F₁. The reference is
to "perspectives," pictures which showed different objects, according to the angle of view.
  Sc. vi, 7. tall: valiant.   13. **ghosted**: haunted.   16. **[the]** F₂. Om. F₁.   24. **fear**: frighten.   26. **o'er-count**: outnumber.
27. **o'er-count**: cheat. Plutarch writes that Antony, having bought the elder Pompey's house, refused to pay for it.   30.
present: i.e., present business.

Of Sicily, Sardinia; and I must　　　　　　35
Rid all the sea of pirates; then, to send
Measures of wheat to Rome. This 'greed upon,
To part with unhack'd edges and bear back
Our targes undinted.
　　All. That's our offer.
　　Pom. 　　　　　　　　Know, then,
I came before you here a man prepar'd　　41
To take this offer; but Mark Antony
Put me to some impatience. — Though I lose
The praise of it by telling, you must know,
When Cæsar and your brother were at blows, 45
Your mother came to Sicily and did find
Her welcome friendly.
　　Ant. 　　　　　I have heard it, Pompey,
And am well studied for a liberal thanks
Which I do owe you.
　　Pom. 　　　　　Let me have your hand.
I did not think, sir, to have met you here.　50
　　Ant. The beds i' th' East are soft; and thanks to
　　　　you,
That call'd me timelier than my purpose hither.
For I have gain'd by 't.
　　Cæs. 　　　　　Since I saw you last,
There is a change upon you.
　　Pom. 　　　　　Well, I know not
What counts harsh Fortune casts upon my face; 55
But in my bosom shall she never come,
To make my heart her vassal.
　　Lep. 　　　　　Well met here.
　　Pom. I hope so, Lepidus. Thus we are agreed.
I crave our composition may be written,
And seal'd between us.
　　Cæs. 　　　　　That's the next to do.
　　Pom. We'll feast each other ere we part; and
　　　　let's 　　　　　　　　　　　　　　61
Draw lots who shall begin.
　　Ant. 　　　　　That will I, Pompey.
　　Pom. No, Antony, take the lot; but, first
Or last, your fine Egyptian cookery
Shall have the fame. I have heard that Julius
　　　　Cæsar 　　　　　　　　　　　　65
Grew fat with feasting there.
　　Ant. 　　　　　You have heard much.
　　Pom. I have fair [meanings], sir.
　　Ant. 　　　　　And fair words to them.
　　Pom. Then so much have I heard;
And I have heard, Apollodorus carried —
　　Eno. No more [of] that; he did so.
　　Pom. 　　　　　What, I pray you?
　　Eno. A certain queen to Cæsar in a mattress. 71
　　Pom. I know thee now. How far'st thou, sol-
　　　　dier?
　　Eno Well;
And well am like to do, for, I perceive,

Four feasts are toward.
　　Pom. 　　　　　Let me shake thy hand; 75
I never hated thee. I have seen thee fight,
When I have envied thy behaviour.
　　Eno. 　　　　　　　　　Sir,
I never lov'd you much; but I ha' prais'd ye
When you have well deserv'd ten times as much
As I have said you did.
　　Pom. 　　　　　Enjoy thy plainness; 80
It nothing ill becomes thee.
Aboard my galley I invite you all:
Will you lead, lords?
　　All. 　　　　　Show [us] the way, sir.
　　Pom. 　　　　　　　　　Come.
　　　[Exeunt all but Menas and Enobarbus.
　　Men. [*Aside.*] Thy father, Pompey, would ne'er
have made this treaty. — You and I have known,
sir. 　　　　　　　　　　　　　　86
　　Eno. At sea, I think.
　　Men. We have, sir.
　　Eno. You have done well by water.
　　Men. And you by land.　　　　　　90
　　Eno. I will praise any man that will praise me;
though it cannot be denied what I have done by
land.
　　Men. Nor what I have done by water.　94
　　Eno. Yes, something you can deny for your own
safety. You have been a great thief by sea.
　　Men. And you by land.
　　Eno. There I deny my land service. But give me
your hand, Menas. If our eyes had authority, here
they might take two thieves kissing.　101
　　Men. All men's faces are true, whatsome'er their
hands are.
　　Eno. But there is never a fair woman has a true
face.　　　　　　　　　　　　105
　　Men. No slander; they steal hearts.
　　Eno. We came hither to fight with you.
　　Men. For my part, I am sorry it is turn'd to a
drinking. Pompey doth this day laugh away his
fortune.　　　　　　　　　　110
　　Eno. If he do, sure, he cannot weep 't back
again.
　　Men. You've said, sir. We look'd not for Mark
Antony here. Pray you, is he married to Cleo-
patra?　　　　　　　　　　　115
　　Eno. Cæsar's sister is called Octavia.
　　Men. True, sir; she was the wife of Caius
Marcellus.
　　Eno. But she is now the wife of Marcus Antonius.
　　Men. Pray ye, sir?　　　　　　120
　　Eno. 'Tis true.
　　Men. Then is Cæsar and he for ever knit together.
　　Eno. If I were bound to divine of this unity, I
would not prophesy so.　　　　　125

38. **edges:** swords.　55. **counts:** accounts.　59. **composition:** agreement.　67. **[meanings]** (Heath conj.).　*meaning* F.
70. **[of]** F₃. Om. F₁.　75. **toward:** being prepared.　85. **known:** been acquainted.

Men. I think the policy of that purpose made
more in the marriage than the love of the parties.

Eno. I think so too. But you shall find the band
that seems to tie their friendship together will be
the very strangler of their amity. Octavia is of a
holy, cold, and still conversation. 131

Men. Who would not have his wife so?

Eno. Not he that himself is not so; which is Mark
Antony. He will to his Egyptian dish again. Then
shall the sighs of Octavia blow the fire up in 135
Cæsar; and, as I said before, that which is the
strength of their amity shall prove the immediate
author of their variance. Antony will use his affection where it is; he married but his occasion here. 140

Men. And thus it may be. Come, sir, will you
aboard? I have a health for you.

Eno. I shall take it, sir; we have us'd our throats
in Egypt.

Men. Come, let's away.   [*Exeunt.* 145

[SCENE VII. *On board Pompey's galley, off
Misenum.*]

Music plays.   *Enter two or three* SERVANTS *with
a banquet.*

1. [*Serv.*] Here they'll be, man. Some o' their
plants are ill-rooted already; the least wind i' th'
world will blow them down.

2. Serv. Lepidus is [high-colour'd].

1. Serv. They have made him drink alms-drink. 6

2. Serv. As they pinch one another by the disposition, he cries out, "No more"; reconciles them
to his entreaty, and himself to th' drink.

1. Serv. But it raises the greater war between
him and his discretion. 11

2. Serv. Why, this it is to have a name in great
men's fellowship. I had as lief have a reed that
will do me no service as a partisan I could not
heave. 15

1. Serv. To be called into a huge sphere, and
not to be seen to move in't, are the holes where
eyes should be, which pitifully disaster the cheeks.

A sennet sounded. Enter CÆSAR, ANTONY, LEPIDUS,
POMPEY, Agrippa, Mæcenas, ENOBARBUS, MENAS,
with other captains.

Ant. [*To Cæsar.*] Thus do they, sir: they take
the flow o' th' Nile 20
By certain scales i' th' pyramid; they know,
By th' height, the lowness, or the mean, if dearth
Or foison follow. The higher Nilus swells,
The more it promises; as it ebbs, the seedsman
Upon the slime and ooze scatters his grain, 25
And shortly comes to harvest.

Lep. You've strange serpents there?

Ant. Ay, Lepidus.

Lep. Your serpent of Egypt is bred now of your
mud by the operation of your sun. So is your
crocodile. 31

Ant. They are so.

Pom. Sit, — and some wine! A health to Lepidus!

Lep. I am not so well as I should be, but I'll
ne'er out. 36

Eno. Not till you have slept; I fear me you'll be
in till then.

Lep. Nay, certainly, I have heard the Ptolemies'
pyramises are very goodly things; without contradiction, I have heard that. 41

Men. [*Aside to Pom.*] Pompey, a word.

Pom. [*Aside to Men.*] Say in mine ear: what is't?

Men. [*Aside to Pom.*] Forsake thy seat, I do beseech thee, captain,
And hear me speak a word.

Pom. (*Whispers in's ear.*) Forbear me till anon.—
This wine for Lepidus! 45

Lep. What manner o' thing is your crocodile?

Ant. It is shap'd, sir, like itself; and it is as
broad as it hath breadth. It is just so high as it
is, and moves with it own organs. It lives by
that which nourisheth it; and the elements once
out of it, it transmigrates. 51

Lep. What colour is it of?

Ant. Of it own colour too.

Lep. 'Tis a strange serpent.

Ant. 'Tis so. And the tears of it are wet. 55

Cæs. Will this description satisfy him?

Ant. With the health that Pompey gives him,
else he is a very epicure.

Pom. [*Aside to Men.*] Go hang, sir, hang! Tell
me of that? Away!
Do as I bid you. — Where's this cup I call'd for? 60

Men. [*Aside to Pom.*] If for the sake of merit
thou wilt hear me,
Rise from thy stool.

Pom. [*Aside to Men.*] I think thou'rt mad. The
matter?   [*Rises, and walks aside.*]

Men. I have ever held my cap off to thy fortunes.

Pom. Thou hast serv'd me with much faith.
What's else to say? —
Be jolly, lords.

Ant.   These quick-sands, Lepidus, 65
Keep off them, for you sink.

Men. Wilt thou be lord of all the world?

Pom.   What say'st thou?

Men. Wilt thou be lord of the whole world?
That's twice.

---

131. **conversation:** deportment.   140. **occasion:** expediency.
Sc. vii, *1*, etc. [*Serv.*] (Rowe). F designates the servants *1* and *2*. 2. **plants:** soles (of the feet). 4. [**high-colour'd**] F₂:
intoxicated. *high Conlord* F₁. 5. **alms-drink:** i.e., in addition to his own share. 6–7. **pinch...disposition:** fall to quarreling.
14. **partisan:** long-handled spear with double blade. 18. **disaster:** disfigure. 23. **foison:** plenty. 36. **out:** fail to drink my
share. 38. **in:** in drink. 63. **held...off:** been respectful.

Pom. How should that be?

Men.   But entertain it,
And, though thou think me poor, I am the man   70
Will give thee all the world.

Pom.   Hast thou drunk well?

Men. No, Pompey, I have kept me from the cup.
Thou art, if thou dar'st be, the earthly Jove.
Whate'er the ocean pales, or sky inclips,
Is thine, if thou wilt ha't.

Pom.   Show me which way.

Men. These three world-sharers, these competi-
     tors,   76
Are in thy vessel: let me cut the cable;
And, when we are put off, fall to their throats.
All there is thine.

Pom.   Ah, this thou shouldst have done,
And not have spoke on't! In me 'tis villany;   80
In thee 't had been good service. Thou must know,
'Tis not my profit that does lead mine honour;
Mine honour, it. Repent that e'er thy tongue
Hath so betray'd thine act. Being done unknown,
I should have found it afterwards well done   85
But must condemn it now. Desist, and drink.

Men. [*Aside.*] For this,
I'll never follow thy pall'd fortunes more.
Who seeks, and will not take when once 'tis offer'd,
Shall never find it more.

Pom.   This health to Lepidus!

Ant. Bear him ashore. I'll pledge it for him,
     Pompey.   91

Eno. Here's to thee, Menas!

Men.   Enobarbus, welcome!

Pom. Fill till the cup be hid.

Eno. There's a strong fellow, Menas.

     [*Pointing to the Attendant who carries off
     Lepidus.*]

Men. Why?   95

Eno. 'A bears the third part of the world, man;
see'st not?

Men. The third part, then, is drunk. Would it
     were all,
That it might go on wheels!

Eno. Drink thou; increase the reels.   100

Men. Come.

Pom. This is not yet an Alexandrian feast.

Ant. It ripens towards it. Strike the vessels, ho!
Here's to Cæsar!

Cæs.   I could well forbear 't.
It's monstrous labour when I wash my brain   105
And it [grows] fouler.

Ant.   Be a child o' th' time.

Cæs. Possess it, I'll make answer.

But I had rather fast from all, four days,
Than drink so much in one.   109

Eno. Ha, my brave emperor!   [*To Antony.*
Shall we dance now the Egyptian Bacchanals
And celebrate our drink?

Pom.   Let's ha't, good soldier.

Ant. Come, let's all take hands
Till that the conquering wine hath steep'd our sense
In soft and delicate Lethe.

Eno.   All take hands.
Make battery to our ears with the loud music; 116
The while I'll place you; then the boy shall sing.
The holding every man shall [bear] as loud
As his strong sides can volley.

     [*Music plays. Enobarbus places them hand
     in hand.*

THE SONG.

Come, thou monarch of the vine,   120
Plumpy Bacchus with pink eyne!
In thy fats our cares be drown'd,
With thy grapes our hairs be crown'd!
Cup us till the world go round,
Cup us till the world go round!   125

Cæs. What would you more? Pompey, good-
     night. Good brother,
Let me request you [off]; our graver business
Frowns at this levity. Gentle lords, let's part;
You see we have burnt our cheeks. Strong Enobarb
Is weaker than the wine, and mine own tongue 130
Splits what it speaks; the wild disguise hath almost
Antick'd us all. What needs more words? Good-
     night.
Good Antony, your hand.

Pom.   I'll try you on the shore.

Ant. And shall, sir; give 's your hand.

Pom.   O Antony,
You have my father's house, — But, what? we are
     friends.   135
Come, down into the boat.

Eno.   Take heed you fall not.

     [*Exeunt all but Enobarbus and Menas.*]
Menas, I'll not on shore.

[Men.]   No, to my cabin.
These drums! these trumpets, flutes! what!
Let Neptune hear we bid a loud farewell
To these great fellows. Sound and be hang'd,
     sound out!   [*Sound a flourish, with drums.*

Eno. Ho! says 'a. There's my cap.   141

Men. Ho! Noble captain, come.

     [*Exeunt.*

74. **pales:** fences in. **inclips:** embraces. 88. **pall'd:** waned. 99. **go on wheels:** run smoothly (proverbial). 103. **Strike the vessels:** clink the cups. 106. **[grows]** F$_2$; *grow* F$_1$. 107. **Possess it:** have your way, go ahead. 118. **holding:** refrain. **[bear]** (Theobald). *beate* F. 121. **pink:** small. 122. **fats:** vats. 127. **[off]** (Rowe and Hanmer): i.e., to excuse me. *of* F. 131. **disguise:** drunkenness. 132. **Antick'd:** made buffoons of. 133. **try you:** test your drinking powers. 138. **[Men.]** (Capell). Om. F.

[ACT III]

[SCENE I. *A plain in Syria.*]

Enter VENTIDIUS *as it were in triumph* [*with* SILIUS, *and other* Romans, Officers, *and* Soldiers;] *the dead body of Pacorus borne before him.*

Ven. Now, darting Parthia, art thou struck; and now
Pleas'd Fortune does of Marcus Crassus' death
Make me revenger. Bear the King's son's body
Before our army. Thy Pacorus, Orodes,   4
Pays this for Marcus Crassus.
[*Sil.*]   Noble Ventidius,
Whilst yet with Parthian blood thy sword is warm,
The fugitive Parthians follow. Spur through Media,
Mesopotamia, and the shelters whither
The routed fly; so thy grand captain, Antony,
Shall set thee on triumphant chariots and   10
Put garlands on thy head.
Ven.   O Silius, Silius,
I have done enough; a lower place, note well,
May make too great an act. For learn this, Silius:
Better to leave undone, than by our deed   14
Acquire too high a fame when him we serve 's away.
Cæsar and Antony have ever won
More in their officer than person. Sossius,
One of my place in Syria, his lieutenant,
For quick accumulation of renown,   19
Which he achiev'd by th' minute, lost his favour.
Who does i' th' wars more than his captain can
Becomes his captain's captain; and ambition,
The soldier's virtue, rather makes choice of loss,
Than gain which darkens him.
I could do more to do Antonius good,   25
But 'twould offend him; and in his offence
Should my performance perish.
[*Sil.*]   Thou hast, Ventidius, that
Without the which a soldier and his sword
Grants scarce distinction. Thou wilt write to Antony?
Ven. I'll humbly signify what in his name, 30
That magical word of war, we have effected;
How, with his banners and his well-paid ranks,
The ne'er-yet-beaten horse of Parthia
We have jaded out o' th' field.
[*Sil.*]   Where is he now?
Ven. He purposeth to Athens; whither, with what haste   35
The weight we must convey with 's will permit,

We shall appear before him. On, there; pass along!
[*Exeunt.*

[SCENE II. *Rome. An Ante-chamber in Cæsar's house.*]

Enter AGRIPPA *at one door,* ENOBARBUS *at another.*

Agr. What, are the brothers parted?
Eno. They have dispatch'd with Pompey, he is gone;
The other three are sealing. Octavia weeps
To part from Rome; Cæsar is sad; and Lepidus,
Since Pompey's feast, as Menas says, is troubled 5
With the green sickness.
Agr.   'Tis a noble Lepidus.
Eno. A very fine one. O, how he loves Cæsar!
Agr. Nay, but how dearly he adores Mark Antony!
Eno. Cæsar? Why, he's the Jupiter of men.
Agr. What's Antony? The god of Jupiter.   10
Eno. Spake you of Cæsar? How! the nonpareil!
Agr. O Antony! O thou Arabian bird!
Eno. Would you praise Cæsar, say "Cæsar"; go no further.
Agr. Indeed, he plied them both with excellent praises.
Eno. But he loves Cæsar best; yet he loves Antony.   15
Ho! hearts, tongues, figures, scribes, bards, poets, cannot
Think, speak, cast, write, sing, number, ho!
His love to Antony. But as for Cæsar,
Kneel down, kneel down, and wonder.
Agr.   Both he loves.
Eno. They are his shards, and he their beetle.
[*Trumpets within.*] So;   20
This is to horse. Adieu, noble Agrippa.
Agr. Good fortune, worthy soldier; and farewell.

Enter CÆSAR, ANTONY, LEPIDUS, *and* OCTAVIA.

Ant. No further, sir.
Cæs. You take from me a great part of myself;
Use me well in't. Sister, prove such a wife   25
As my thoughts make thee, and as my farthest band
Shall pass on thy approof. Most noble Antony,
Let not the piece of virtue which is set
Betwixt us as the cement of our love,
To keep it builded, be the ram to batter   30

Act III, sc. i, 1. **darting.** The Parthians were famous for their skill in throwing darts, especially to cover retreats. 5, 27, 34. [*Sil.*] (Theobald). *Romaine* or *Rom.* F. 12. **lower place:** subordinate. 29. **Grants...distinction:** are hardly distinguishable. 34. **jaded:** driven.
Sc. ii, 3. **sealing:** i.e., their agreement. 6. **green sickness:** usually anemia; here, effects of his debauch. 12. **Arabian bird:** Phoenix, a fabulous bird, only one of which was said to exist at a time. 20. **shards:** wing cases. 26. **band:** pledge. 27. **pass...approof:** certify thou shalt prove to be.

The fortress of it; for better might we
Have lov'd without this mean, if on both parts
This be not cherish'd.
Ant.   Make me not offended
In your distrust.
    Cæs.   I have said.
    Ant.   You shall not find,
Though you be therein curious, the least cause   35
For what you seem to fear. So, the gods keep
        you,
And make the hearts of Romans serve your ends!
We will here part.
    Cæs. Farewell, my dearest sister, fare thee well!
The elements be kind to thee, and make   40
Thy spirits all of comfort! Fare thee well!
    Oct. My noble brother!
    Ant. The April's in her eyes; it is love's spring,
And these the showers to bring it on. Be cheerful.
    Oct. Sir, look well to my husband's house; and —
    Cæs.   What,   45
Octavia?
    Oct.   I'll tell you in your ear.
    Ant. Her tongue will not obey her heart, nor can
Her heart inform her tongue, — the swan's down-
        feather,
That stands upon the swell at full of th' tide
And neither way inclines.
    Eno. [*Aside to Agr.*] Will Cæsar weep?   50
    Agr. [*Aside to Eno.*] He has a cloud in 's face.
    Eno. [*Aside to Agr.*] He were the worse for that,
        were he a horse;
So is he, being a man.
    Agr. [*Aside to Eno.*] Why, Enobarbus,
When Antony found Julius Cæsar dead,
He cried almost to roaring; and he wept   55
When at Philippi he found Brutus slain.
    Eno. [*Aside to Agr.*] That year, indeed, he was
        troubled with a rheum;
What willingly he did confound he wail'd,
Believe 't, till I [wept] too.
    Cæs.   No, sweet Octavia,
You shall hear from me still; the time shall not   60
Out-go my thinking on you.
    Ant.   Come, sir, come;
I'll wrestle with you in my strength of love.
Look, here I have you; thus I let you go,
And give you to the gods.
    Cæs.   Adieu; be happy!   64
    Lep. Let all the number of the stars give light
To thy fair way!
    Cæs.   Farewell, farewell!
                    [*Kisses Octavia.*
    Ant.   Farewell!
            [*Trumpets sound. Exeunt.*

[SCENE III. *Alexandria. Cleopatra's palace.*]

Enter CLEOPATRA, CHARMIAN, Iras, *and* ALEXAS.
    Cleo. Where is the fellow?
    Alex.   Half afeard to come.
    Cleo. Go to, go to. Come hither, sir.

            Enter the MESSENGER *as before.*
    Alex.   Good Majesty,
Herod of Jewry dare not look upon you
But when you are well pleas'd.
    Cleo.   That Herod's head
I'll have; but how, when Antony is gone,   5
Through whom I might command it? Come thou
        near.
    Mess. Most gracious Majesty, —
    Cleo. Didst thou behold Octavia?
    Mess. Ay, dread queen.
    Cleo. Where?   10
    Mess. Madam, in Rome;
I look'd her in the face, and saw her led
Between her brother and Mark Antony.
    Cleo. Is she as tall as me?
    Mess.   She is not, madam.
    Cleo. Didst hear her speak? Is she shrill-tongu'd
        or low?   15
    Mess. Madam, I heard her speak; she is low-
        voic'd.
    Cleo. That's not so good. He cannot like her long?
    Char. Like her! O Isis! 'tis impossible.
    Cleo. I think so, Charmian. Dull of tongue,
        and dwarfish!
What majesty is in her gait? Remember,   20
If e'er thou [look'dst] on majesty.
    Mess.   She creeps;
Her motion and her station are as one;
She shows a body rather than a life,
A statue than a breather.
    Cleo.   Is this certain?   24
    Mess. Or I have no observance.
    Char.   Three in Egypt
Cannot make better note.
    Cleo.   He's very knowing;
I do perceive 't. There's nothing in her yet.
The fellow has good judgement.
    Char.   Excellent.
    Cleo. Guess at her years, I prithee.
    Mess.   Madam,
She was a widow, —
    Cleo.   Widow! Charmian, hark.
    Mess. And I do think she's thirty.   31
    Cleo. Bear'st thou her face in mind? Is't long
        or round?
    Mess. Round even to faultiness.

---

35. **curious:** meticulous.   40. **elements:** weather.   51. **cloud:** dark spot.   57. **rheum:** cold, causing watery eyes.   58.
confound: destroy. **wail'd:** bewailed. 59. **[wept]** (Theobald). *weepe* F.
    Sc. iii, 21. **[look'dst]** (Pope). *look'st* F. 22. **station:** standing.

Cleo. For the most part, too, they are foolish
  that are so.
Her hair, what colour?   35
  Mess. Brown, madam; and her forehead
As low as she would wish it.
  Cleo.   There's gold for thee.
Thou must not take my former sharpness ill.
I will employ thee back again; I find thee
Most fit for business. Go make thee ready;   40
Our letters are prepar'd.   [*Exit Messenger.*]
  Char.   A proper man.
  Cleo. Indeed, he is so; I repent me much
That so I harried him. Why, methinks, by him,
This creature's no such thing.
  Char.   Nothing, madam.
  Cleo. The man hath seen some majesty, and
  should know.   45
  Char. Hath he seen majesty? Isis else defend,
And serving you so long!
  Cleo. I have one thing more to ask him yet,
  good Charmian:
But 'tis no matter; thou shalt bring him to me
Where I will write. All may be well enough.   50
  Char. I warrant you, madam.   [*Exeunt.*

[SCENE IV. *Athens. A room in Antony's house.*]

Enter ANTONY *and* OCTAVIA.

  Ant. Nay, nay, Octavia, not only that, —
That were excusable, that, and thousands more
Of semblable import, — but he hath wag'd
New wars 'gainst Pompey; made his will, and read it
To public ear;   5
Spoke scantly of me; when perforce he could not
But pay me terms of honour, cold and sickly
He vented them; most narrow measure lent me,
When the best hint was given him, he not [took 't],
Or did it from his teeth.
  Oct.   O my good lord,   10
Believe not all; or, if you must believe,
Stomach not all. A more unhappy lady,
If this division chance, ne'er stood between,
Praying for both parts.
The good gods will mock me presently,   15
When I shall pray "O, bless my lord and husband!"
Undo that prayer, by crying out as loud,
"O, bless my brother!" Husband win, win brother,
Prays, and destroys the prayer; no midway
'Twixt these extremes at all.
  Ant.   Gentle Octavia,   20
Let your best love draw to that point which seeks

Best to preserve it. If I lose mine honour,
I lose myself; better I were not yours
Than yours so branchless. But, as you requested,
Yourself shall go between 's. The meantime, lady,
I'll raise the preparation of a war   26
Shall stain your brother. Make your soonest haste;
So your desires are yours.
  Oct.   Thanks to my lord.
The Jove of power make me most weak, most weak,
Your reconciler! Wars 'twixt you twain would be
As if the world should cleave, and that slain men 31
Should solder up the rift.
  Ant. When it appears to you where this begins,
Turn your displeasure that way, for our faults
Can never be so equal that your love   35
Can equally move with them. Provide your going;
Choose your own company, and command what cost
Your heart has mind to.   [*Exeunt.*

[SCENE V. *The same. Another room.*]

Enter ENOBARBUS *and* EROS [*meeting*].

  Eno. How now, friend Eros!
  Eros. There's strange news come, sir.
  Eno. What, man?
  Eros. Cæsar and Lepidus have made wars upon
Pompey.
  Eno. This is old; what is the success?   6
  Eros. Cæsar, having made use of him in the
wars 'gainst Pompey, presently denied him rivality,
would not let him partake in the glory of the
action; and not resting here, accuses him of letters
he had formerly wrote to Pompey; upon his own
appeal, seizes him. So the poor third is up, till
death enlarge his confine.   13
  Eno. Then, [world], thou [hast] a pair of chaps,
  no more;
And throw between them all the food thou hast,
They'll grind [the one] the other. Where's Antony?
  Eros. He's walking in the garden — thus; and
  spurns
The rush that lies before him; cries, "Fool Lepidus!"
And threats the throat of that his officer   19
That murd'red Pompey.
  Eno.   Our great navy's rigg'd.
  Eros. For Italy and Cæsar. More, Domitius;
My lord desires you presently; my news
I might have told hereafter.
  Eno.   'Twill be nought:
But let it be. Bring me to Antony.
  Eros. Come, sir.   [*Exeunt.* 25

---

37. **she . . . it:** i.e., as could be.   41. **proper:** fine.   44. **such:** great.
  Sc. iv, 3. **semblable:** like.   6. **scantly:** grudgingly.   9. **hint:** opportunity.   **[took 't]** (Thirlby conj.).   *look't* F.   10. **from
his teeth:** i.e., not from his heart.   12. **Stomach:** resent.   27. **stain:** eclipse.
  Sc. v, 6. **success:** outcome.   8. **rivality:** equal rights as partner.   11–12. **his own appeal:** Cæsar's own accusation.
14. **[world] . . . [hast]** (Hanmer).   *would . . . hadst* F.   **chaps:** jaws.   16. **[the one]** (Johnson conj.).   Om. F.   22. **presently:**
at once.

[SCENE VI. *Rome. Cæsar's house.*]

Enter CÆSAR, AGRIPPA, *and* MÆCENAS.

Cæs. Contemning Rome, he has done all this
and more
In Alexandria.   Here's the manner of 't:
I' th' market-place, on a tribunal silver'd,
Cleopatra and himself in chairs of gold
Were publicly enthron'd.   At the feet sat   5
Cæsarion, whom they call my father's son,
And all the unlawful issue that their lust
Since then hath made between them.   Unto her
He gave the stablishment of Egypt; made her
Of lower Syria, Cyprus, Lydia,   10
Absolute queen.
     Mæc.   This in the public eye?
     Cæs. I' th' common show-place, where they
          exercise.
His sons [he there] proclaim'd the kings of kings:
Great Media, Parthia, and Armenia
He gave to Alexander; to Ptolemy he assign'd   15
Syria, Cilicia, and Phœnicia.   She
In th' habiliments of the goddess Isis
That day appear'd; and oft before gave audience,
As 'tis reported, so.
     Mæc.   Let Rome be thus
Inform'd.
     Agr. Who, queasy with his insolence   20
Already, will their good thoughts call from him.
     Cæs. The people knows it; and have now receiv'd
His accusations.
     Agr.   Who does he accuse?
     Cæs. Cæsar; and that, having in Sicily
Sextus Pompeius spoil'd, we had not rated him   25
His part o' th' isle.   Then does he say he lent me
Some shipping unrestor'd.   Lastly, he frets
That Lepidus of the triumvirate
Should be depos'd; and, being, that we detain
All his revenue.
     Agr.   Sir, this should be answer'd.   30
     Cæs. 'Tis done already, and the messenger gone.
I have told him Lepidus was grown too cruel;
That he his high authority abus'd,
And did deserve his change.   For what I have con-
          quer'd,
I grant him part; but then, in his Armenia   35
And other of his conquer'd kingdoms, I
Demand the like.
     Mæc.   He'll never yield to that.
     Cæs. Nor must not then be yielded to in this.

Enter OCTAVIA *with her train.*

     Oct. Hail, Cæsar, and my lord! Hail, most dear
          Cæsar!
     Cæs. That ever I should call thee castaway!   40

     Oct. You have not call'd me so, nor have you
          cause.
     Cæs. Why have you stolen upon us thus? **You**
          come not
Like Cæsar's sister.   The wife of Antony
Should have an army for an usher, and
The neighs of horse to tell of her approach   45
Long ere she did appear; the trees by th' way
Should have borne men, and expectation fainted,
Longing for what it had not; nay, the dust
Should have ascended to the roof of heaven,   49
Rais'd by your populous troops.   But you are come
A market-maid to Rome, and have prevented
The ostentation of our love, which, left unshown,
Is often left unlov'd.   We should have met you
By sea and land, supplying every stage
With an augmented greeting.
     Oct.   Good my lord,   55
To come thus was I not constrain'd, but did
On my free will.   My lord, Mark Antony,
Hearing that you prepar'd for war, acquainted
My grieved ear withal; whereon, I begg'd
His pardon for return.
     Cæs.   Which soon he granted,
Being an [obstruct] 'tween his lust and him.   61
     Oct. Do not say so, my lord.
     Cæs.   I have eyes upon him,
And his affairs come to me on the wind.
Where is he now?
     Oct.   My lord, in Athens.
     Cæs. No, my most wronged sister; Cleopatra   65
Hath nodded him to her.   He hath given his empire
Up to a whore; who now are levying
The kings o' th' earth for war.   He hath assembled
Bocchus, the King of Libya; Archelaus,
Of Cappadocia; Philadelphos, King   70
Of Paphlagonia; the Thracian king, Adallas;
King Malchus of Arabia; King of Pont;
Herod of Jewry; Mithridates, King
Of Comagene; Polemon and Amyntas,
The Kings of Mede and Lycaonia,   75
With a more larger list of sceptres.
     Oct.   Ay me, most wretched,
That have my heart parted betwixt two friends
That do afflict each other!
     Cæs.   Welcome hither!
Your letters did withhold our breaking forth,
Till we perceiv'd both how you were wrong led   80
And we in negligent danger.   Cheer your heart.
Be you not troubled with the time, which drives
O'er your content these strong necessities;
But let determin'd things to destiny
Hold unbewail'd their way.   Welcome to Rome;   85
Nothing more dear to me.   You are abus'd
Beyond the mark of thought; and the high gods,

Sc. vi, 3. **tribunal:** platform.   13. **[he there]** (Johnson).   *hither* F.   20. **queasy:** disgusted.   25. **spoil'd:** plundered.   **rated:** allotted.   61. **[obstruct]** (Theobald): obstruction.   *abstract* F.   81. **negligent:** unheeded.

To do you justice, [make them] ministers
Of us and those that love you.   Best of comfort,
And ever welcome to us.
    Agr.   Welcome, lady.   90
    Mæc. Welcome, dear madam.
Each heart in Rome does love and pity you;
Only th' adulterous Antony, most large
In his abominations, turns you off,
And gives his potent regiment to a trull.   95
That noises it against us.
    Oct.   Is it so, sir?
    Cæs. Most certain.   Sister, welcome.   Pray you,
Be ever known to patience.   My dear'st sister!
                                        [*Exeunt.*

[SCENE VII.   *Near Actium.   Antony's camp.*]

        Enter CLEOPATRA *and* ENOBARBUS.

Cleo. I will be even with thee, doubt it not.
Eno. But why, why, why?
Cleo. Thou hast forspoke my being in these wars,
And say'st it is not fit.
    Eno.   Well, is it, is it?
Cleo. [Is't] not denounc'd against us?   Why
        should not we   5
Be there in person?
    Eno.   Well, I could reply:
If we should serve with horse and mares together,
The horse were merely lost; the mares would bear
A soldier and his horse.
    Cleo.   What is't you say?   10
Eno. Your presence needs must puzzle Antony;
Take from his heart, take from his brain, from 's
        time,
What should not then be spar'd.   He is already
Traduc'd for levity; and 'tis said in Rome
That Photinus an eunuch and your maids   15
Manage this war.
    Cleo.   Sink Rome, and their tongues rot
That speak against us!   A charge we bear i' th' war,
And, as the president of my kingdom, will
Appear there for a man.   Speak not against it;
I will not stay behind.

        Enter ANTONY *and* CANIDIUS.

Eno.   Nay, I have done.   20
Here comes the Emperor.
    Ant.   Is it not strange, Canidius,
That from Tarentum and Brundusium
He could so quickly cut the Ionian Sea,
And take in Toryne?   You have heard on't, sweet?
    Cleo. Celerity is never more admir'd   25
Than by the negligent.

    Ant.   A good rebuke,
Which might have well becom'd the best of men,
To taunt at slackness.   Canidius, we
Will fight with him by sea.
    Cleo.   By sea! what else?   29
Can. Why will my lord do so?
Ant.   For that he dares us to't.
Eno. So hath my lord dar'd him to single fight.
Can. Ay, and to wage this battle at Pharsalia,
Where Cæsar fought with Pompey; but these offers,
Which serve not for his vantage, he shakes off;
And so should you.
    Eno.   Your ships are not well mann'd;
Your mariners are [muleters], reapers, people   36
Ingross'd by swift impress.   In Cæsar's fleet
Are those that often have 'gainst Pompey fought.
Their ships are yare; yours, heavy.   No disgrace
Shall fall you for refusing him at sea,   40
Being prepar'd for land.
    Ant.   By sea, by sea.
Eno. Most worthy sir, you therein throw away
The absolute soldiership you have by land;
Distract your army, which doth most consist
Of war-mark'd footmen; leave unexecuted   45
Your own renowned knowledge; quite forgo
The way which promises assurance; and
Give up yourself merely to chance and hazard,
From firm security.
    Ant.   I'll fight at sea.
Cleo. I have sixty sails, Cæsar none better.   50
Ant. Our overplus of shipping will we burn;
And, with the rest full-mann'd, from th' head of
        Actium
Beat the approaching Cæsar.   But if we fail,
We then can do't at land.

        Enter a MESSENGER.

                        Thy business?
Mess. The news is true, my lord; he is descried;
Cæsar has taken Toryne.   56
    Ant. Can he be there in person?   'Tis impossible;
Strange that his power should be.   Canidius,
Our nineteen legions thou shalt hold by land,
And our twelve thousand horse.   We'll to our ship;
Away, my Thetis!

        Enter a SOLDIER.

                How now, worthy soldier!   61
    Sold. O noble emperor, do not fight by sea;
Trust not to rotten planks!   Do you misdoubt
This sword and these my wounds?   Let the Egyp-
        tians
And the Phœnicians go a-ducking; we   65

88. [**make them**] (Capell).   *makes his* F.   95. **regiment**: government.   96. **noises it**: is clamorous.
Sc. vii, 3. **forspoke**: spoken against.   5. [**Is't**] (Tyrwhitt conj.).   *If* F.   **denounc'd**: declared.   9. **merely**: utterly.   11.
puzzle: confuse.   36. [**muleters**] F₂. (*Muliters*).   *Militers* F₁.   37. **Ingross'd**: enrolled.   **impress**: forced levy.   39. **yare**:
easily managed.   61. **Thetis**: a sea goddess.

Have us'd to conquer, standing on the earth,
And fighting foot to foot.
 Ant.   Well, well: away!
 [*Exeunt Antony, Cleopatra, and Enobarbus.*
 Sold. By Hercules, I think I am i' th' right.
 Can. Soldier, thou art; but his whole action grows
Not in the power on't.   So our [leader's led],   70
And we are women's men.
 Sold.   You keep by land
The legions and the horse whole, do you not?
 [*Can.*] Marcus Octavius, Marcus Justeius,
Publicola, and Cælius, are for sea;   74
But we keep whole by land.   This speed of Cæsar's
Carries beyond belief.
 Sold.   While he was yet in Rome,
His power went out in such distractions as
Beguil'd all spies.
 Can.   Who's his lieutenant, hear you?
 Sold. They say, one Taurus.
 Can.   Well I know the man.

     Enter a MESSENGER.

 Mess. The Emperor calls Canidius.   80
 Can. With news the time's with labour, and
     throes forth
Each minute some.   [*Exeunt.*

     [SCENE VIII.   *A plain near Actium.*]

     Enter CÆSAR [*and* TAURUS], *with his army,*
               marching.

 Cæs. Taurus!
 Taur. My lord?
 Cæs. Strike not by land; keep whole; provoke
     not battle
Till we have done at sea.   Do not exceed
The prescript of this scroll.   Our fortune lies   5
Upon this jump.   [*Exeunt.*

     [SCENE IX.   *Another part of the plain.*]

     Enter ANTONY *and* Enobarbus.

 Ant. Set we our squadrons on yond side o' th'
     hill,
In eye of Cæsar's battle; from which place
We may the number of the ships behold,
And so proceed accordingly.   [*Exeunt.*

     [SCENE X.   *Another part of the plain.*]
 Canidius marcheth with his land army one way over
     the stage; and Taurus, the lieutenant of Cæsar, the
     other way.   After their going in, is heard the noise
     of a sea-fight.

     Alarum.   Enter ENOBARBUS.

 Eno. Nought, nought, all nought!   I can behold
     no longer.
Th' Antoniad, the Egyptian admiral,
With all their sixty, fly and turn the rudder.
To see 't mine eyes are blasted.

     Enter SCARUS.

 Scar.   Gods and goddesses,
All the whole synod of them!
 Eno.   What's thy passion?   5
 Scar. The greater cantle of the world is lost
With very ignorance; we have kiss'd away
Kingdoms and provinces.
 Eno.   How appears the fight?
 Scar. On our side like the token'd pestilence,
Where death is sure.   Yon ribaldried nag of
     Egypt, —   10
Whom leprosy o'ertake! — i' th' midst o' th' fight,
When vantage like a pair of twins appear'd,
Both as the same, or rather ours the elder,
The breese upon her, like a cow in June,
Hoists sails and flies.   15
 Eno. That I beheld.
Mine eyes did sicken at the sight and could not
Endure a further view.
 Scar.   She once being loof'd,
The noble ruin of her magic, Antony,
Claps on his sea-wing, and, like a doting mallard,   20
Leaving the fight in height, flies after her.
I never saw an action of such shame;
Experience, manhood, honour, ne'er before
Did violate so itself.
 Eno.   Alack, alack!   24

     Enter CANIDIUS.

 Can. Our fortune on the sea is out of breath
And sinks most lamentably.   Had our general
Been what he knew himself, it had gone well.
O, [he] has given example for our flight,
Most grossly, by his own!
 Eno.   Ay, are you thereabouts?

69–70. **his ... on't:** his (purposed) conduct is not based on his true source of power.   70. **[leader's led]** (Theobald). *Leaders leade* F.   73. **[Can.]** (Pope).   *Ven.* F.   77. **distractions:** (small) detachments.   81. **throes:** brings painfully (forth).
 Sc. viii, 5. **prescript:** direction.   6. **jump:** hazard.
 Sc. ix, 2. **battle:** army.
 Sc. x, 2. **Antoniad:** the flag-ship.   5. **synod:** assembly.   6. **cantle:** corner, i.e., part.   9. **token'd:** spotted.   10. **Yon ribaldried:** yon lewd.   *Yon rebaudred* F$_{1-3}$.   *Your ribauldred* F$_4$.   12–13. **When ... same:** when chances were evenly balanced.   14. **breese:** gadfly.   18. **being loof'd:** having sailed away.   20. **mallard:** drake.   28. **[he]** F$_2$.   *His* F$_1$.   29. **thereabouts:** of that mind.

Why, then, good-night indeed.   30
  Can. Toward Peloponnesus are they fled.
  Scar. 'Tis easy to't; and there I will attend
What further comes.
  Can.   To Cæsar will I render
My legions and my horse. Six kings already
Show me the way of yielding.
  Eno.   I'll yet follow   35
The wounded chance of Antony, though my reason
Sits in the wind against me.   [*Exeunt.*]

[SCENE XI. *Alexandria. Cleopatra's palace.*]

Enter ANTONY *with* ATTENDANTS.

  Ant. Hark! the land bids me tread no more upon
    't;
It is asham'd to bear me! Friends, come hither.
I am so lated in the world, that I
Have lost my way for ever. I have a ship
Laden with gold; take that, divide it; fly,   5
And make your peace with Cæsar.
  All.   Fly! not we.
  Ant. I have fled myself, and have instructed
    cowards
To run and show their shoulders. Friends, be gone;
I have myself resolv'd upon a course
Which has no need of you; be gone.   10
My treasure's in the harbour; take it. O,
I follow'd that I blush to look upon.
My very hairs do mutiny; for the white
Reprove the brown for rashness, and they them
For fear and doting. Friends, be gone; you shall
Have letters from me to some friends that will   16
Sweep your way for you. Pray you, look not sad,
Nor make replies of loathness. Take the hint
Which my despair proclaims; let [that] be left
Which leaves itself. To the sea-side straightway;
I will possess you of that ship and treasure.   21
Leave me, I pray, a little; pray you now.
Nay, do so; for, indeed, I have lost command,
Therefore I pray you. I'll see you by and by.
                   [*Sits down.*

Enter CLEOPATRA, *led by* CHARMIAN *and* [IRAS;]
EROS [*following*].

  Eros. Nay, gentle madam, to him; comfort him.
  Iras. Do, most dear queen.   26
  Char. Do! Why, what else?
  Cleo. Let me sit down. O Juno!
  Ant. No, no, no, no, no.
  Eros. See you here, sir?   30
  Ant. O fie, fie, fie!

  Char. Madam!
  Iras. Madam, O good empress!
  Eros. Sir, sir, —
  Ant. Yes, my lord, yes; he at Philippi kept   35
His sword e'en like a dancer, while I struck
The lean and wrinkled Cassius; and 'twas I
That the mad Brutus ended. He alone
Dealt on lieutenantry and no practice had
In the brave squares of war; yet now — No matter.
  Cleo. Ah, stand by.   41
  Eros. The Queen, my lord, the Queen.
  Iras. Go to him, madam, speak to him;
He is unqualitied with very shame.
  Cleo. Well then, sustain me. Oh!   45
  Eros. Most noble sir, arise; the Queen ap-
    proaches.
Her head's declin'd, and death will [seize] her, but
Your comfort makes the rescue.
  Ant. I have offended reputation,
A most unnoble swerving.
  Eros.   Sir, the Queen.   50
  Ant. O, whither hast thou led me, Egypt? See
How I convey my shame out of thine eyes
By looking back what I have left behind
'Stroy'd in dishonour.
  Cleo.   O my lord, my lord,
Forgive my fearful sails! I little thought   55
You would have followed.
  Ant.   Egypt, thou knew'st too well
My heart was to thy rudder tied by th' strings,
And thou shouldst [tow] me after. O'er my spirit
[Thy] full supremacy thou knew'st, and that
Thy beck might from the bidding of the gods   60
Command me
  Cleo.   O, my pardon!
  Ant.   Now I must
To the young man send humble treaties, dodge
And palter in the shifts of lowness, who
With half the bulk o' th' world play'd as I pleas'd,
Making and marring fortunes. You did know   65
How much you were my conqueror, and that
My sword, made weak by my affection, would
Obey it on all cause.
  Cleo.   Pardon, pardon!
  Ant. Fall not a tear, I say; one of them rates
All that is won and lost. Give me a kiss.   70
Even this repays me. We sent our schoolmaster;
Is 'a come back? Love, I am full of lead.
Some wine, within there, and our viands! Fortune
    knows
We scorn her most when most she offers blows.
                   [*Exeunt.*

37. **Sits...against:** opposes.
  Sc. xi, 3. **lated:** benighted.   19. **[that]** (Capell). *them* F.   35. **kept:** i.e., in its sheath.   39. **Dealt on lieutenantry:** fought through subordinates.   40. **squares:** squadrons.   44. **unqualitied:** without his natural qualities.   47. **[seize]** F₂. *cease* F₁.   53. **what:** upon what.   58. **[tow]** (Rowe). *stowe* F.   59. **[Thy]** (Theobald). *the* F.   62. **treaties:** proposals.   63. **palter...lowness:** haggle by mean trickery.   69. **rates:** is worth.

[SCENE XII. *Egypt. Cæsar's camp.*]

Enter CÆSAR, Agrippa, DOLABELLA, [THYREUS,]
with others.

Cæs. Let him appear that's come from Antony.
Know you him?
Dol.   Cæsar, 'tis his schoolmaster;
An argument that he is pluck'd, when hither
He sends so poor a pinion of his wing,
Which had superfluous kings for messengers   5
Not many moons gone by.

Enter [EUPHRONIUS,] *ambassador from Antony.*

Cæs.   Approach and speak.
[*Euph.*] Such as I am, I come from Antony.
I was of late as petty to his ends
As is the morn-dew on the myrtle-leaf
To his grand sea.
Cæs.   Be't so: declare thine office.   10
[*Euph.*] Lord of his fortunes he salutes thee, and
Requires to live in Egypt; which not granted,
He [lessens] his requests and to thee sues
To let him breathe between the heavens and earth,
A private man in Athens. This for him.   15
Next, Cleopatra does confess thy greatness,
Submits her to thy might; and of thee craves
The circle of the Ptolemies for her heirs,
Now hazarded to thy grace.
Cæs.   For Antony,
I have no ears to his request. The Queen   20
Of audience nor desire shall fail, so she
From Egypt drive her all-disgraced friend,
Or take his life there. This if she perform,
She shall not sue unheard. So to them both.
[*Euph.*] Fortune pursue thee!
Cæs.   Bring him through the bands.
                    [*Exit Euphronius.*]
[*To Thyreus.*] To try thy eloquence, now 'tis time;
dispatch.   26
From Antony win Cleopatra; promise,
And in our name, what she requires; add more,
From thine invention, offers. Women are not
In their best fortunes strong, but want will perjure
The ne'er-touch'd vestal. Try thy cunning,
[Thyreus];   31
Make thine own edict for thy pains, which we
Will answer as a law.
Thyr.   Cæsar, I go.
Cæs. Observe how Antony becomes his flaw,
And what thou think'st his very action speaks   35

In every power that moves.
Thyr.   Cæsar, I shall.
                    [*Exeunt.*]

[SCENE XIII. *Alexandria. Cleopatra's palace.*]

Enter CLEOPATRA, ENOBARBUS, Charmian, *and*
Iras.

Cleo. What shall we do, Enobarbus?
Eno.   Think, and die.
Cleo. Is Antony or we in fault for this?
Eno. Antony only, that would make his will
Lord of his reason. What though you fled
From that great face of war, whose several ranges   5
Frighted each other? Why should he follow?
The itch of his affection should not then
Have nick'd his captainship, at such a point,
When half to half the world oppos'd, he being
The mered question. 'Twas a shame no less   10
Than was his loss, to course your flying flags,
And leave his navy gazing.
Cleo.   Prithee, peace.

Enter ANTONY *with* [EUPHRONIUS,] *the Am-*
bassador.

Ant. Is that his answer?
[*Euph.*] Ay, my lord.
Ant. The Queen shall then have courtesy, so she
Will yield us up.
[*Euph.*]   He says so.
Ant.   Let her know't.   16
To the boy Cæsar send this grizzled head,
And he will fill thy wishes to the brim
With principalities.
Cleo.   That head, my lord?
Ant. To him again. Tell him he wears the rose
Of youth upon him, from which the world should
note   21
Something particular. His coin, ships, legions,
May be a coward's; whose ministers would prevail
Under the service of a child as soon
As i' th' command of Cæsar. I dare him therefore
To lay his gay comparisons apart   26
And answer me declin'd, sword against sword,
Ourselves alone. I'll write it. Follow me.
                    [*Exeunt Antony and Euphronius.*]
Eno. [*Aside.*] Yes, like enough high-battl'd
Cæsar will
Unstate his happiness and be stag'd to th' show   30
Against a sworder! I see men's judgements are

Sc. xii, 7. [*Euph.*] (Capell). *Amb.* F. (throughout). 8. to: compared to. 12. Requires: requests. 13. [lessens] F₂.
Lessons F₁. 18. circle: crown. 31. [Thyreus] (Theobald). *Thidias* F (throughout; *Thid.* in speech-headings). 32. Make
. . . edict: name . . . reward. 34. becomes his flaw: bears his disaster. 35. speaks: signifies. 36. power that moves: i.e.,
gesture.

Sc. xiii, 1. Think: take thought. 3. will: desire. 8. nick'd: impaired. 10. mered question: sole point at issue. 11.
course: chase. 26. comparisons: superior advantages. 27. declin'd: i.e., in fortunes and in years. 30. Unstate: strip of
dignity. stag'd . . . show: exhibited publicly. 31. sworder: gladiator.

A parcel of their fortunes, and things outward,
Do draw the inward quality after them,
To suffer all alike. That he should dream,
Knowing all measures, the full Cæsar will   35
Answer his emptiness! Cæsar, thou hast subdu'd
His judgement too.

Enter a SERVANT.

Serv.   A messenger from Cæsar.
Cleo. What, no more ceremony? See, my wo-
men!
Against the blown rose may they stop their nose
That kneel'd unto the buds. Admit him, sir.   40
                              [*Exit Servant.*]
Eno. [*Aside.*] Mine honesty and I begin to
square.
The loyalty well held to fools does make
Our faith mere folly; yet he that can endure
To follow with allegiance a fall'n lord
Does conquer him that did his master conquer,   45
And earns a place i' th' story.

Enter [THYREUS].

Cleo.   Cæsar's will?
[*Thyr.*] Hear it apart.
Cleo.   None but friends: say boldly.
[*Thyr.*] So, haply, are they friends to Antony.
Eno. He needs as many, sir, as Cæsar has,
Or needs not us. If Cæsar please, our master   50
Will leap to be his friend; for us, you know
Whose he is we are, and that is Cæsar's.
[*Thyr.*]   So.
Thus then, thou most renown'd: Cæsar entreats
Not to consider in what case thou stand'st
Further than he is [Cæsar].
Cleo.   Go on: right royal.   55
[*Thyr.*] He knows that you embrace not Antony
As you did love, but as you fear'd him.
Cleo.   Oh!
[*Thyr.*] The scars upon your honour, therefore,
he
Does pity, as constrained blemishes,
Not as deserv'd.
Cleo.   He is a god and knows   60
What is most right. Mine honour was not yielded,
But conquer'd merely.
Eno.   [*Aside.*] To be sure of that,
I will ask Antony. Sir, sir, thou art so leaky
That we must leave thee to thy sinking, for
Thy dearest quit thee.   [*Exit.*
[*Thyr.*]   Shall I say to Cæsar   65
What you require of him? for he partly begs
To be desir'd to give. It much would please him
That of his fortunes you should make a staff

To lean upon; but it would warm his spirits
To hear from me you had left Antony   70
And put yourself under his shroud,
The universal landlord.
Cleo.   What's your name?
[*Thyr.*] My name is [Thyreus].
Cleo.   Most kind messenger,
Say to great Cæsar this: in [deputation]   74
I kiss his conqu'ring hand. Tell him, I am prompt
To lay my crown at 's feet, and there to kneel.
Tell him, from his all-obeying breath I hear
The doom of Egypt.
[*Thyr.*]   'Tis your noblest course.
Wisdom and fortune combating together,
If that the former dare but what it can,   80
No chance may shake it. Give me grace to lay
My duty on your hand.
Cleo.   Your Cæsar's father oft,
When he hath mus'd of taking kingdoms in,
Bestow'd his lips on that unworthy place,   84
As it rain'd kisses.

Re-enter ANTONY *and* ENOBARBUS.

Ant.   Favours, by Jove that thunders!
What art thou, fellow?
[*Thyr.*]   One that but performs
The bidding of the fullest man, and worthiest
To have command obey'd.
Eno.   [*Aside.*] You will be whipp'd.
Ant. Approach there! Ah, you kite! Now, gods
and devils!
Authority melts from me. Of late, when I cried
"Ho!"   90
Like boys unto a muss, kings would start forth
And cry, "Your will?" Have you no ears? I am
Antony yet.

Enter a SERVANT.

                  Take hence this Jack and whip him.
Eno. [*Aside.*] 'Tis better playing with a lion's
whelp
Than with an old one dying.
Ant.   Moon and stars! 95
Whip him! Were 't twenty of the greatest tribu-
taries
That do acknowledge Cæsar, should I find them
So saucy with the hand of she here, — what's her
name,
Since she was Cleopatra? Whip him, fellows,
Till, like a boy, you see him cringe his face   100
And whine aloud for mercy. Take him hence.
[*Thyr.*] Mark Antony, —
Ant.   Tug him away. Being whipp'd,
Bring him again; [this] Jack of Cæsar's shall

---

32. **A parcel of:** of a piece with.   41. **honesty:** honor.   **square:** quarrel.   55. **[Cæsar]** F₂: i.e., himself, a magnanimous victor. **Cæsars** F₁.   71. **shroud:** i.e., protection.   74. **in [deputation]** (Theobald): by deputy. *in disputation* F.   77. **all-obeying:** obeyed by all.   89. **kite:** harlot.   91. **muss:** scramble.   103. **[this]** (Pope). *the* F.

Bear us an errand to him. —

                  [Exit Servant with [Thyreus].

You were half blasted ere I knew you; ha!   105

Have I my pillow left unpress'd in Rome,

Forborne the getting of a lawful race,

And by a gem of women, to be abus'd

By one that looks on feeders?

  Cleo.   Good my lord, —

  Ant. You have been a boggler ever: 110

And when we in our viciousness grow hard —

O misery on't! — the wise gods seel our eyes;

In our own filth drop our clear judgements; make us

Adore our errors; laugh at 's while we strut

To our confusion.

  Cleo.   O, is't come to this?   115

  Ant. I found you as a morsel cold upon

Dead Cæsar's trencher; nay, you were a fragment

Of Cneius Pompey's; besides what hotter hours,

Unregist'red in vulgar fame, you have

Luxuriously pick'd out; for, I am sure,   120

Though you can guess what temperance should be,

You know not what it is.

  Cleo.   Wherefore is this?

  Ant. To let a fellow that will take rewards

And say "God quit you!" be familiar with

My playfellow, your hand, this kingly seal   125

And plighter of high hearts! O, that I were

Upon the hill of Basan, to outroar

The horned herd! For I have savage cause;

And to proclaim it civilly were like

A halter'd neck which does the hangman thank

For being yare about him.

        Re-enter SERVANT *with* [Thyreus.]

                 Is he whipp'd?   131

  Serv. Soundly, my lord.

  Ant.   Cried he? and begg'd a pardon?

  Serv. He did ask favour.

  Ant. If that thy father live, let him repent

Thou wast not made his daughter; and be thou

    sorry   135

To follow Cæsar in his triumph, since

Thou hast been whipp'd for following him. Henceforth

The white hand of a lady fever thee;

Shake thou to look on't. Get thee back to Cæsar;

Tell him thy entertainment. Look thou say   140

He makes me angry with him; for he seems

Proud and disdainful, harping on what I am,

Not what he knew I was. He makes me angry;

And at this time most easy 'tis to do't,

When my good stars, that were my former guides,

Have empty left their orbs and shot their fires   146

Into th' abysm of hell. If he mislike

My speech and what is done, tell him he has

Hipparchus, my enfranched bondman, whom

He may at pleasure whip, or hang, or torture,   150

As he shall like, to quit me. Urge it thou.

Hence with thy stripes, begone!   *[Exit [Thyreus].*

  Cleo. Have you done yet?

  Ant.   Alack, our terrene moon

Is now eclips'd, and it portends alone

The fall of Antony!

  Cleo.   I must stay his time.   155

  Ant. To flatter Cæsar, would you mingle eyes

With one that ties his points?

  Cleo.   Not know me yet?

  Ant. Cold-hearted toward me?

  Cleo.   Ah, dear, if I be so,

From my cold heart let heaven engender hail

And poison it in the source, and the first stone

Drop in my neck; as it determines, so   161

Dissolve my life! The next Cæsarion [smite]!

Till by degrees the memory of my womb,

Together with my brave Egyptians all,

By the [discandying] of this pelleted storm,   165

Lie graveless, till the flies and gnats of Nile

Have buried them for prey!

  Ant.   I am satisfied.

Cæsar [sits] down in Alexandria, where

I will oppose his fate. Our force by land

Hath nobly held; our sever'd navy too   170

Have knit again, and fleet, threat'ning most sealike.

Where hast thou been, my heart? Dost thou hear,

    lady?

If from the field I shall return once more

To kiss these lips, I will appear in blood;

I and my sword will earn our chronicle.   175

There's hope in't yet.

  Cleo. That's my brave lord!

  Ant. I will be treble-sinew'd, hearted, breath'd,

And fight maliciously; for when mine hours

Were nice and lucky, men did ransom lives   180

Of me for jests; but now I'll set my teeth

And send to darkness all that stop me. Come,

Let's have one other gaudy night. Call to me

All my sad captains; fill our bowls once more;

Let's mock the midnight bell.

  Cleo.   It is my birthday.

I had thought t' have held it poor; but, since my

    lord   186

Is Antony again, I will be Cleopatra.

  Ant. We will yet do well.

  Cleo. Call all his noble captains to my lord.

---

109. **feeders:** servants. 110. **boggler:** shifty one. 112. **seel:** sew up. 120. **luxuriously:** lustfully. 124. **quit:** requite. 127. **Basan.** See *Psalms,* 22.12 and 68.15. 128. **horned herd:** (1) bulls, (2) cuckolds. 131. **yare:** quick. 146. **orbs:** spheres. 149. **enfranched:** freed. Hipparchus had deserted Antony. 153. **terrene:** earthly. 157. **points:** laces (of clothing). 161. **determines:** melts. 162. [smite] (Rowe). *smile* F. 163. **memory:** memorials. 165. [discandying] (Thirlby conj.): thawing. *discandering* F. 168. [sits] (Johnson). *sets* F. 171. **fleet:** float. 180. **nice:** favorable.

Ant. Do so, we'll speak to them; and tonight I'll force   190
The wine peep through their scars. Come on, my queen;
There's sap in't yet. The next time I do fight,
I'll make Death love me; for I will contend
Even with his pestilent scythe.
                           [*Exeunt [all but Enobarbus].*
Eno. Now he'll outstare the lightning. To be furious,   195
Is to be frighted out of fear; and in that mood
The dove will peck the estridge; and I see still
A diminution in our captain's brain
Restores his heart. When valour [preys on] reason,
It eats the sword it fights with. I will seek   200
Some way to leave him.   [*Exit.*

[ACT IV]

[SCENE I. *Before Alexandria. Cæsar's camp.*]

Enter CÆSAR, Agrippa, *and* MÆCENAS, *with his Army; Cæsar reading a letter.*

Cæs. He calls me boy, and chides as he had power
To beat me out of Egypt. My messenger
He hath whipp'd with rods; dares me to personal combat,
Cæsar to Antony. Let the old ruffian know
I have many other ways to die; meantime   5
Laugh at his challenge.
Mæc.   Cæsar must think,
When one so great begins to rage, he's hunted
Even to falling. Give him no breath, but now
Make boot of his distraction. Never anger
Made good guard for itself.
Cæs.   Let our best heads   10
Know that to-morrow the last of many battles
We mean to fight. Within our files there are,
Of those that serv'd Mark Antony but late,
Enough to fetch him in. See it done,
And feast the army; we have store to do't,   15
And they have earn'd the waste. Poor Antony!
                                        [*Exeunt.*

[SCENE II. *Alexandria. Cleopatra's palace.*]

Enter ANTONY, CLEOPATRA, ENOBARBUS, Charmian, Iras, Alexas, *with others.*

Ant. He will not fight with me, Domitius.
Eno.   No?
Ant. Why should he not?
Eno. He thinks, being twenty times of better fortune,
He is twenty men to one.

Ant.   To-morrow, soldier,   5
By sea and land I'll fight; or I will live,
Or bathe my dying honour in the blood
Shall make it live again. Woo 't thou fight well?
Eno. I'll strike, and cry, "Take all!"
Ant.   Well said; come on.
Call forth my household servants; let's tonight
Be bounteous at our meal.

Enter three or four SERVITORS.

                            Give me thy hand,   10
Thou hast been rightly honest; — so hast thou; —
Thou, — and thou, — and thou. You have serv'd me well,
And kings have been your fellows.
Cleo.   [*Aside to Eno.*] What means this?
Eno. [*Aside to Cleo.*] 'Tis one of those odd tricks
                          which sorrow shoots
Out of the mind.
Ant.   And thou art honest too.   15
I wish I could be made so many men,
And all of you clapp'd up together in
An Antony, that I might do you service
So good as you have done.
All.   The gods forbid!
Ant. Well, my good fellows, wait on me tonight.
Scant not my cups; and make as much of me   21
As when mine empire was your fellow too,
And suffer'd my command.
Cleo. [*Aside to Eno.*] What does he mean?
Eno. [*Aside to Cleo.*] To make his followers weep.
Ant.   Tend me tonight;
May be it is the period of your duty: 25
Haply you shall not see me more; or if,
A mangled shadow. Perchance to-morrow
You'll serve another master. I look on you
As one that takes his leave. Mine honest friends,
I turn you not away; but, like a master   30
Married to your good service, stay till death.
Tend me to-night two hours, I ask no more,
And the gods yield you for't!
Eno.   What mean you, sir,
To give them this discomfort? Look, they weep;
And I, an ass, am onion-ey'd. For shame,   35
Transform us not to women.
Ant.   Ho, ho, ho!
Now the witch take me, if I meant it thus!
Grace grow where those drops fall! My hearty friends,
You take me in too dolorous a sense;   39
For I spake to you for your comfort, did desire you
To burn this night with torches. Know, my hearts,
I hope well of to-morrow, and will lead you
Where rather I'll expect victorious life

---

193. **contend**: compete. 197. **estridge**: falcon. 199. **[preys on]** (Rowe). *prayes in* F.
Act IV, sc. i, 9. boot: profit. 14. **fetch him in**: capture him. 16. **waste**: cost.
Sc. ii, 8. "Take all!": i.e., winner take everything. 33. **yield**: reward.

Than death and honour. Let's to supper, come,
And drown consideration.   [*Exeunt.* 45

[SCENE III. *The same. Before the palace.*]

Enter a Company of SOLDIERS.

1. Sold. Brother, good-night; to-morrow is the
day.
2. Sold. It will determine one way; fare you
well.
Heard you of nothing strange about the streets?
1. Sold. Nothing. What news?
2. Sold. Belike 'tis but a rumour. Good-night
to you.   5
1. Sold. Well, sir, good-night.

They meet other SOLDIERS.

2. Sold. Soldiers, have careful watch.
[*3.*] *Sold.* And you. Good-night, good-night.
     [*They place themselves in every corner of
the stage.*
[*4.*] *Sold.* Here we. And if to-morrow
Our navy thrive, I have an absolute hope   10
Our landmen will stand up.
[*3.*] *Sold.*   'Tis a brave army,
And full of purpose.
     [*Music of the hautboys is under the stage.*
2. Sold.   Peace! what noise?
1. Sold.   List, list!
2. Sold. Hark!
1. Sold.   Music i' th' air.
3. Sold.   Under the earth.
4. Sold. It signs well, does it not?
3. Sold.   No.
1. Sold.   Peace, I say.
What should this mean?   15
2. Sold. 'Tis the god Hercules, whom Antony
lov'd,
Now leaves him.
1. Sold. Walk; let's see if other watchmen
Do hear what we do.
     [*They advance to another post.*
2. Sold.   How now, masters!
     [*Speak together.*
All.   How now!
How now! do you hear this?
1. Sold.   Ay; is't not strange?
3. Sold. Do you hear, masters? Do you hear? 21
1. Sold. Follow the noise so far as we have quarter;
Let's see how it will give off.
All.   Content. 'Tis strange.
     [*Exeunt.*

[SCENE IV. *The same. A room in the palace.*]

Enter ANTONY *and* CLEOPATRA, [CHARMIAN,]
and others [*attending*].

Ant. Eros! mine armour, Eros!
Cleo.   Sleep a little.
Ant. No, my chuck. Eros, come; mine armour,
Eros!

Enter EROS [*with armour*].

Come, good fellow, put [mine] iron on.
If Fortune be not ours to-day, it is   4
Because we brave her. Come.
Cleo.   Nay, I'll help too.
What's this for?
[*Ant.*]   Ah, let be, let be! thou art
The armourer of my heart. False, false; this, this.
Cleo. Sooth, la, I'll help. Thus it must be.
Ant.   Well, well;
We shall thrive now. Seest thou, my good fellow?
Go put on thy defences.
Eros.   Briefly, sir.   10
Cleo. Is not this buckled well?
Ant.   Rarely, rarely:
He that unbuckles this, till we do please
To daff 't for our repose, shall hear a storm.
Thou fumblest, Eros, and my queen's a squire   14
More tight at this than thou. Dispatch. O love,
That thou couldst see my wars to-day, and knew'st
The royal occupation! Thou shouldst see
A workman in't.

Enter an armed SOLDIER.

     Good-morrow to thee; welcome.
Thou look'st like him that knows a warlike charge.
To business that we love we rise betime   20
And go to't with delight.
Sold.   A thousand, sir,
Early though 't be, have on their riveted trim,
And at the port expect you.
     [*Shout. Trumpets flourish.*

Enter CAPTAINS *and* SOLDIERS.

[*Capt.*] The morn is fair. Good-morrow, general.
All. Good-morrow, general.
Ant.   'Tis well blown, lads.
This morning, like the spirit of a youth   26
That means to be of note, begins betimes.
So, so; come, give me that. This way; well said.
Fare thee well, dame, whate'er becomes of me.
This is a soldier's kiss; rebukeable   30
And worthy shameful check it were, to stand

Sc. iii, 8, 9, 12. [*3.*], [*4.*], [*3.*] (Capell). F assigns to *1, 2,* and *1* respectively. 14. **signs well:** is a good omen. 22. **quarter:**
beat. 23. **give off:** end.
     Sc. iv, 3. [mine] (Hanmer). *thine* F. 5. **brave:** defy. 6. [*Ant.*] (Malone). F continues to *Cleo.* 7. **False:** wrong.
10. **Briefly:** quickly. 15. **tight:** deft. 23. **port:** gate. 24. [*Capt.*] (Rowe). *Alex.* F. 25. **blown.** See S.D. l. 24. 28.
said: done. 31. **check:** rebuke.

On more mechanic compliment.   I'll leave thee
Now, like a man of steel.   You that will fight,
Follow me close; I'll bring you to't.   Adieu.   34
    [*Exeunt [Antony, Eros, Captains, and Sol-
        diers*].
Char. Please you, retire to your chamber.
Cleo.   Lead me.
He goes forth gallantly.   That he and Cæsar might
Determine this great war in single fight!
Then, Antony, — but now — Well, on.   [*Exeunt.*

[SCENE V.   *Alexandria.   Antony's camp.*]

Trumpets sound.   Enter ANTONY *and* EROS.
    [*A* SOLDIER *meets them.*]

[*Sold.*] The gods make this a happy day to
    Antony!
Ant. Would thou and those thy scars had once
    prevail'd
To make me fight at land!
    [*Sold.*]   Hadst thou done so,
The kings that have revolted, and the soldier
That has this morning left thee, would have still   5
Followed thy heels.
Ant.   Who's gone this morning?
[*Sold.*]   Who!
One ever near thee.   Call for Enobarbus,
He shall not hear thee, or from Cæsar's camp
Say "I am none of thine."
Ant.   What sayest thou?
Sold.   Sir,
He is with Cæsar.
Eros.   Sir, his chests and treasure   10
He has not with him.
Ant.   Is he gone?
Sold.   Most certain.
Ant. Go, Eros, send his treasure after; do it;
Detain no jot, I charge thee.   Write to him —
I will subscribe — gentle adieus and greetings;
Say that I wish he never find more cause   15
To change a master.   O, my fortunes have
Corrupted honest men!   Dispatch. — Enobarbus!
                            [*Exeunt.*

[SCENE VI.   *Alexandria.   Cæsar's camp.*]

Flourish.   Enter CÆSAR, AGRIPPA, *with* ENOBARBUS,
    and Dolabella.

Cæs. Go forth, Agrippa, and begin the fight.
Our will is Antony be took alive;
Make it so known.
Agr. Cæsar, I shall.   [*Exit.*

Cæs. The time of universal peace is near.   5
Prove this a prosperous day, the three-nook'd world
Shall bear the olive freely.

Enter a MESSENGER.

Mess.   Antony
Is come into the field.
Cæs.   Go charge Agrippa
Plant those that have revolted in the van,
That Antony may seem to spend his fury   10
Upon himself.   [*Exeunt [all but Enobarbus*].
Eno. Alexas did revolt and went to Jewry on
Affairs of Antony; there did [persuade]
Great Herod to incline himself to Cæsar
And leave his master Antony; for this pains   15
Cæsar hath hang'd him.   Canidius and the rest
That fell away have entertainment, but
No honourable trust.   I have done ill;
Of which I do accuse myself so sorely
That I will joy no more.

Enter a SOLDIER *of Cæsar's.*

Sold.   Enobarbus, Antony   20
Hath after thee sent all thy treasure, with
His bounty overplus.   The messenger
Came on my guard, and at thy tent is now
Unloading of his mules.
Eno.   I give it you.
Sold. Mock not, Enobarbus;   25
I tell you true.   Best you saf'd the bringer
Out of the host; I must attend mine office,
Or would have done 't myself.   Your emperor
Continues still a Jove.   [*Exit.*
Eno. I am alone the villain of the earth,   30
And feel I am so most.   O Antony,
Thou mine of bounty, how wouldst thou have paid
My better service, when my turpitude
Thou dost so crown with gold! This blows my heart.
If swift thought break it not, a swifter means   35
Shall outstrike thought; but thought will do't, I
    feel.
I fight against thee!   No!   I will go seek
Some ditch wherein to die; the foul'st best fits
My latter part of life.   [*Exit.*

[SCENE VII.   *Field of battle between the camps.*]

Alarum.   Drums and trumpets.   Enter AGRIPPA
    [*and others*].

Agr. Retire, we have engag'd ourselves too far.
Cæsar himself has work, and our oppression
Exceeds what we expected.   [*Exeunt.*

Sc. v, 1. [*Sold.*] (Thirlby conj.).   *Eros.* F.   3, 7. [*Sold.*] (Capell).   *Eros.* F.   14. **subscribe:** sign.
Sc. vi, 6. **three-nook'd:** three-cornered.   13. [persuade] (Rowe).   *disswade* F.   17. **entertainment:** employment.   26.
saf'd: convoyed.   34. **blows:** swells.
Sc. vii, 2. **oppression:** opposition.

Alarums. Enter ANTONY, *and* SCARUS *wounded.*

Scar. O my brave emperor, this is fought indeed!
Had we done so at first, we had droven them home 5
With clouts about their heads.

Ant. Thou bleed'st apace,

Scar. I had a wound here that was like a T,
But now 'tis made an H.

Ant. They do retire.

Scar. We'll beat 'em into bench-holes. I have yet
Room for six scotches more. 10

Enter EROS.

Eros. They are beaten, sir; and our advantage serves
For a fair victory.

Scar. Let us score their backs,
And snatch 'em up, as we take hares, behind.
'Tis sport to maul a runner.

Ant. I will reward thee
Once for thy sprightly comfort, and tenfold 15
For thy good valour. Come thee on.

Scar. I'll halt after.
[*Exeunt.*

[SCENE VIII. *Under the walls of Alexandria.*]

Alarum. Enter ANTONY, *in a march;* Scarus,
with others.

Ant. We have beat him to his camp. Run one before,
And let the Queen know of our [gests]. To-morrow,
Before the sun shall see 's, we'll spill the blood
That has to-day escap'd. I thank you all;
For doughty-handed are you, and have fought 5
Not as you serv'd the cause, but as 't had been
Each man's like mine; you have shown all Hectors.
Enter the city, clip your wives, your friends,
Tell them your feats; whilst they with joyful tears
Wash the congealment from your wounds, and kiss
The honour'd gashes whole.

Enter CLEOPATRA [*attended*].

[*To Scarus.*] Give me thy hand; 11
To this great fairy I'll commend thy acts,
Make her thanks bless thee. [*To Cleo.*] O thou
day o' th' world,
Chain mine arm'd neck; leap thou, attire and all,
Through proof of harness to my heart, and there 15
Ride on the pants triumphing!

Cleo. Lord of lords!
O infinite virtue, com'st thou smiling from

The world's great snare uncaught?

Ant. My nightingale,
We have beat them to their beds. What, girl!
though grey
Do something mingle with our younger brown, yet
ha' we 20
A brain that nourishes our nerves, and can
Get goal for goal of youth. Behold this man;
Commend unto his lips thy [favouring] hand.
Kiss it, my warrior; he hath fought to-day
As if a god, in hate of mankind, had 25
Destroyed in such a shape.

Cleo. I'll give thee, friend,
An armour all of gold; it was a king's.

Ant. He has deserv'd it, were it carbuncled
Like holy Phœbus' car. Give me thy hand.
Through Alexandria make a jolly march; 30
Bear our hack'd targets like the men that owe them.
Had our great palace the capacity
To camp this host, we all would sup together
And drink carouses to the next day's fate,
Which promises royal peril. Trumpeters, 35
With brazen din blast you the city's ear;
Make mingle with our rattling tabourines,
That heaven and earth may strike their sounds
together,
Applauding our approach. [*Exeunt.*

[SCENE IX. *Cæsar's camp.*]

Enter a SENTRY, *and his* COMPANY. ENOBARBUS
follows.

Sent. If we be not reliev'd within this hour,
We must return to th' court of guard. The night
Is shiny, and they say we shall embattle
By the second hour i' th' morn.

1. [*Sold.*] This last day was
A shrewd one to 's.

Eno. O, bear me witness, night, — 5

2. Sold. What man is this?

1. Sold. Stand close, and list him.

Eno. Be witness to me, O thou blessed moon,
When men revolted shall upon record
Bear hateful memory, poor Enobarbus did
Before thy face repent!

Sent. Enobarbus!

2. Sold. Peace! 10
Hark further.

Eno. O sovereign mistress of true melancholy,
The poisonous damp of night disponge upon me,
That life, a very rebel to my will,
May hang no longer on me. Throw my heart 15

---

6. **clouts:** bandages. 10. **scotches:** cuts.

Sc. viii, 2. [gests] (Theobald): deeds. *guests* F. 8. **clip:** embrace. 15. **proof of harness:** tested armor. 17. **virtue:** valor. 23. [favouring] (Theobald). *savouring* F. 31. **owe:** own. 37. **tabourines:** drums.

Sc. ix, 4. [*Sold.*] (Malone). *Watch* F. Elsewhere in this scene the speeches of the soldiers are designated *1* or *2* by F.
5. **shrewd:** ill. 13. **disponge:** drop as from a squeezed sponge.

Against the flint and hardness of my fault;
Which, being dried with grief, will break to powder,
And finish all foul thoughts. O Antony,
Nobler than my revolt is infamous,
Forgive me in thine own particular;   20
But let the world rank me in register
A master-leaver and a fugitive.
O Antony! O Antony!   [*Dies.*]
    1. Sold.   Let's speak
To him.
    Sent. Let's hear him, for the things he speaks 25
May concern Cæsar.
    2. Sold.   Let's do so. But he sleeps.
    Sent. Swoons rather; for so bad a prayer as his
Was never yet for sleep.
    1. Sold.   Go we to him.
    2. Sold. Awake, sir, awake; speak to us.
    1. Sold.   Hear you, sir?
    Sent. The hand of death hath raught him.
        (*Drums afar off.*) Hark! the drums   30
Demurely wake the sleepers. Let us bear him
To th' court of guard; he is of note. Our hour
Is fully out.
    2. Sold.   Come on, then;
He may recover yet.   [*Exeunt [with the body].*

[SCENE X.   *Between the two camps.*]

Enter ANTONY *and* SCARUS, *with their Army.*

    Ant. Their preparation is to-day by sea;
We please them not by land.
    Scar.   For both, my lord.
    Ant. I would they'd fight i' th' fire or i' th' air;
We'd fight there too. But this it is: our foot
Upon the hills adjoining to the city   5
Shall stay with us. Order for sea is given;
They have put forth the haven. [Go we up]
Where their appointment we may best discover
And look on their endeavour.   [*Exeunt.*

[SCENE XI.   *Another part of the same.*]

Enter CÆSAR, *and his Army.*

    Cæs. But being charg'd, we will be still by land,
Which, as I take 't, we shall; for his best force
Is forth to man his galleys. To the vales,
And hold our best advantage.   [*Exeunt.*

[SCENE XII.   *Another part of the same.*]

Enter ANTONY *and* SCARUS.

    Ant. Yet they are not join'd. Where yond pine
does stand

I shall discover all; I'll bring thee word
Straight how 'tis like to go.   [*Exit.*
    Scar.   Swallows have built
In Cleopatra's sails their nests. The [augurers]
Say they know not, they cannot tell; look grimly, 5
And dare not speak their knowledge. Antony
Is valiant, and dejected; and, by starts,
His fretted fortunes give him hope and fear,
Of what he has and has not.
        [*Alarum afar off, as at a sea-fight.*

Re-enter ANTONY.

    Ant.   All is lost!
This foul Egyptian hath betrayed me.   10
My fleet hath yielded to the foe, and yonder
They cast their caps up and carouse together
Like friends long lost. Triple-turn'd whore! 'tis
        thou
Hast sold me to this novice, and my heart
Makes only wars on thee. Bid them all fly;   15
For when I am reveng'd upon my charm,
I have done all. Bid them all fly; begone.
        [*Exit Scarus.*]
O sun, thy uprise shall I see no more:
Fortune and Antony part here; even here
Do we shake hands. All come to this? The hearts
That [spaniel'd] me at heels, to whom I gave   21
Their wishes, do discandy, melt their sweets
On blossoming Cæsar; and this pine is bark'd,
That overtopp'd them all. Betray'd I am.
O this false soul of Egypt! this grave charm, —   25
Whose eye beck'd forth my wars and call'd them
        home,
Whose bosom was my crownet, my chief end, —
Like a right gipsy, hath at fast and loose
Beguil'd me to the very heart of loss.
What, Eros, Eros!

Enter CLEOPATRA.

                    Ah, thou spell! Avaunt!   30
    Cleo. Why is my lord enrag'd against his love?
    Ant. Vanish, or I shall give thee thy deserving
And blemish Cæsar's triumph. Let him take thee
And hoist thee up to the shouting plebeians!
Follow his chariot, like the greatest spot   35
Of all thy sex; most monster-like, be shown
For poor'st diminutives, for dolts; and let
Patient Octavia plough thy visage up
With her prepared nails.   [*Exit Cleopatra.*
'T is well thou'rt gone,

20. **in ... particular:** for yourself. 29. **raught:** reached. 31. **Demurely:** quietly.
Sc. **x**, 7. [Go we up] (Grant White). Om. F.
Sc. **xi**, 1. But being: unless we are.
Sc. **xii**, 4. sails: ships. [augurers] (Capell). *Auguries* F. 9. s.d. *Alarum* etc. Between sc. xi and xii in F. 13. **Triple-**
turn'd: thrice faithless. 16. **charm:** charmer. 21. [spaniel'd] (Hanmer). *pannelled* F. 27. **crownet:** coronet. 28. **fast**
and loose: a cheating game. 37. **diminutives ... dolts:** contemptuous terms for the crowd. Many edd. read *doits* and explain both as small coins charged for admission.

If it be well to live; but better 'twere   40
Thou fell'st into my fury, for one death
Might have prevented many.   Eros, ho!
The shirt of Nessus is upon me.   Teach me,
Alcides, thou mine ancestor, thy rage.
Let me lodge Lichas on the horns o' th' moon;   45
And with those hands, that grasp'd the heaviest
     club,
Subdue my worthiest self.   The witch shall die.
To the young Roman boy she hath sold me, and I
     fall
Under this plot.   She dies for't.   Eros, ho!   [Exit.

[SCENE XIII.   *Alexandria.   Cleopatra's
     palace.*]

Enter CLEOPATRA, CHARMIAN, Iras, *and* Mardian.

Cleo. Help me, my women!   O, he is more mad
Than Telamon for his shield; the boar of Thessaly
Was never so emboss'd.
Char.   To th' monument!
There lock yourself, and send him word you are
     dead.
The soul and body rive not more in parting   5
Than greatness going off.
Cleo.   To th' monument!
Mardian, go tell him I have slain myself;
Say that the last I spoke was "Antony,"
And word it, prithee, piteously.   Hence, Mardian,
And bring me how he takes my death.   To th'
     monument!   [*Exeunt.* 10

[SCENE XIV.   *The same.   Another room.*]

Enter ANTONY *and* EROS.

Ant. Eros, thou yet behold'st me?
Eros.   Ay, noble lord.
Ant. Sometime we see a cloud that's dragonish;
A vapour sometime like a bear or lion,
A tower'd citadel, a pendent rock,
A forked mountain, or blue promontory   5
With trees upon 't that nod unto the world
And mock our eyes with air.   Thou hast seen these
     signs;
They are black vesper's pageants.
Eros.   Ay, my lord.
Ant. That which is now a horse, even with a
     thought
The rack [dislimns], and makes it indistinct   10
As water is in water.
Eros.   It does, my lord.

Ant. My good knave Eros, now thy captain is
Even such a body.   Here I am Antony;
Yet cannot hold this visible shape, my knave.
I made these wars for Egypt; and the Queen, —   15
Whose heart I thought I had, for she had mine,
Which whilst it was mine had annex'd unto 't
A million moe, now lost, — she, Eros, has
Pack'd cards with Cæsar, and false-play'd my glory
Unto an enemy's triumph.   20
Nay, weep not, gentle Eros; there is left us
Ourselves to end ourselves.

Enter MARDIAN.

                         O, thy vile lady!
She has robb'd me of my sword.
Mar.   No, Antony;
My mistress lov'd thee, and her fortunes mingled
With thine entirely.
Ant.   Hence, saucy eunuch; peace!
She hath betray'd me and shall die the death.   26
Mar. Death of one person can be paid but once,
And that she has discharg'd.   What thou wouldst
     do
Is done unto thy hand; the last she spake
Was "Antony! most noble Antony!"   30
Then in the midst a tearing groan did break
The name of Antony; it was divided
Between her heart and lips.   She rend'red life,
Thy name so buried in her.
Ant.   Dead, then?
Mar.   Dead.
Ant. Unarm, Eros; the long day's task is done,   35
And we must sleep.   [*To Mar.*]   That thou de-
     part'st hence safe
Does pay thy labour richly; go.   [*Exit Mardian.*
                         Off, pluck off!
The seven-fold shield of Ajax cannot keep
The battery from my heart.   O, cleave, my sides!
Heart, once be stronger than thy continent,   40
Crack thy frail case!   Apace, Eros, apace.
No more a soldier.   Bruised pieces, go;
You have been nobly borne. — From me a while.
                         [*Exit Eros.*
I will o'ertake thee, Cleopatra, and
Weep for my pardon.   So it must be, for now   45
All length is torture; since the torch is out,
Lie down, and stray no farther.   Now all labour
Mars what it does; yea, very force entangles
Itself with strength.   Seal then, and all is done.
Eros! — I come, my queen! — Eros! — Stay for
     me!   50

43–45. **shirt . . . Lichas.** Deianeira, wife of Hercules (Alcides), innocently sent him, as a love charm, a shirt which had been dipped in the poisoned blood of the Centaur Nessus. In his pain Hercules hurled Lichas, who had brought it to him, into the sea.
   Sc. xiii, 2. **Telamon.** Ajax Telamon went mad and killed himself when, after the Trojan war, the armor of Achilles was given to Ulysses instead of to him.   **boar of Thessaly,** sent by Diana to ravage Calydon.   3. **emboss'd:** foaming.
   Sc. xiv, 10. **rack:** cloud.   **[dislimns]** (Theobald): effaces.   *dislimes* F.   12. **knave:** boy.   19. **Pack'd:** stacked.   40. **thy continent:** what contains thee.   49. **Seal:** conclude (the business).

Where souls do couch on flowers, we'll hand in hand,
And with our sprightly port make the ghosts gaze.
Dido and her Æneas shall want troops,
And all the haunt be ours. Come, Eros, Eros!

Re-enter EROS.

Eros. What would my lord?
 Ant.   Since Cleopatra died
I have liv'd in such dishonour that the gods   56
Detest my baseness. I, that with my sword
Quarter'd the world, and o'er green Neptune's back
With ships made cities, condemn myself to lack
The courage of a woman; less noble mind   60
Than she which by her death our Cæsar tells,
"I am conqueror of myself." Thou art sworn, Eros,
That, when the exigent should come, which now
Is come indeed, when I should see behind me
The inevitable prosecution of   65
Disgrace and horror, that, on my command,
Thou then wouldst kill me. Do't; the time is come.
Thou strik'st not me, 'tis Cæsar thou defeat'st.
Put colour in thy cheek.
 Eros.   The gods withhold me!
Shall I do that which all the Parthian darts,   70
Though enemy, lost aim and could not?
 Ant.   Eros,
Wouldst thou be window'd in great Rome and
  see
Thy master thus with pleach'd arms, bending down
His corrigible neck, his face subdu'd
To penetrative shame, whilst the wheel'd seat   75
Of fortunate Cæsar, drawn before him, branded
His baseness that ensued?
 Eros.   I would not see 't.
 Ant. Come, then; for with a wound I must be
  cur'd.
Draw that thy honest sword, which thou hast worn
Most useful for thy country.
 Eros.   O, sir, pardon me!
 Ant. When I did make thee free, swor'st thou not
  then   81
To do this when I bade thee? Do it at once;
Or thy precedent services are all
But accidents unpurpos'd. Draw, and come.
 Eros. Turn from me, then, that noble coun-
  tenance,   85
Wherein the worship of the whole world lies.
 Ant. Lo thee!   [*Turning from him.*]
 Eros. My sword is drawn.
 Ant.   Then let it do at once
The thing why thou hast drawn it.
 Eros.   My dear master,
My captain, and my emperor, let me say,   90
Before I strike this bloody stroke, farewell.

 Ant. 'Tis said, man; and farewell.
 Eros. Farewell, great chief. Shall I strike now?
 Ant.   Now, Eros.
 Eros. Why, there then. (*Kills himself.*) Thus
  I do escape the sorrow
Of Antony's death.
 Ant.   Thrice-nobler than myself!   95
Thou teachest me, O valiant Eros, what
I should, and thou couldst not. My queen and Eros
Have by their brave instruction got upon me
A nobleness in record; but I will be
A bridegroom in my death, and run into 't   100
As to a lover's bed. Come, then; and, Eros,
Thy master dies thy scholar: to do thus
      [*Falling on his sword.*]
I learn'd of thee. How! not dead? not dead?
The guard, ho! O, dispatch me!

Enter [DERCETAS *and*] GUARD.

 1. Guard.   What's the noise?
 Ant. I have done my work ill, friends. O, make
  an end   105
Of what I have begun.
 2. Guard.   The star is fall'n.
 1. Guard. And time is at his period.
 All.   Alas, and woe!
 Ant. Let him that loves me strike me dead.
 1. Guard.   Not I.
 2. Guard. Nor I.
 3. Guard. Nor any one.   [*Exeunt Guard.* 110
 Der. Thy death and fortunes bid thy followers
  fly.
This sword but shown to Cæsar, with this tidings,
Shall enter me with him.

Enter DIOMEDES.

 Dio. Where's Antony?
 Der.   There, Diomed, there.
 Dio.   Lives he?
Wilt thou not answer, man?   [*Exit Dercetas.* 115
 Ant. Art thou there, Diomed? Draw thy sword,
  and give me
Sufficing strokes for death.
 Dio.   Most absolute lord,
My mistress Cleopatra sent me to thee.
 Ant. When did she send thee?
 Dio.   Now, my lord.
 Ant.   Where is she?
 Dio. Lock'd in her monument. She had a pro-
  phesying fear   120
Of what hath come to pass; for when she saw —
Which never shall be found — you did suspect
She had dispos'd with Cæsar, and that your rage

---

52. **port:** bearing. 54. **haunt:** society, company. 63. **exigent:** emergency. 73. **pleach'd:** folded. 74. **corrigible:** submissive. 77. **ensued:** followed. 98. **got upon me:** gained over me. 113. **enter me:** bring me to favor. 120. **monument**
the tomb she had prepared for herself. 123. **dispos'd:** made terms.

Would not be purg'd, she sent you word she was
    dead;
But, fearing since how it might work, hath sent
Me to proclaim the truth; and I am come,   126
I dread, too late.
    Ant. Too late, good Diomed.   Call my guard, I
      prithee.
    Dio. What, ho, the Emperor's guard!   The
      guard, what, ho!
Come, your lord calls!   130

    Enter four or five of the GUARD *of Antony.*

    Ant. Bear me, good friends, where Cleopatra
      bides;
'Tis the last service that I shall command you.
    1. Guard. Woe, woe are we, sir, you may not live
      to wear
All your true followers out.
    All.   Most heavy day!
    Ant. Nay, good my fellows, do not please sharp
      fate   135
To grace it with your sorrows; bid that welcome
Which comes to punish us, and we punish it
Seeming to bear it lightly.   Take me up.
I have led you oft; carry me now, good friends,
And have my thanks for all.   140
              [*Exeunt, bearing Antony.*

    [SCENE XV.   *The same.   A monument.*]

    Enter CLEOPATRA, *and her maids aloft, with*
            CHARMIAN *and* IRAS.

    Cleo. O Charmian, I will never go from hence.
    Char. Be comforted, dear madam.
    Cleo.   No, I will not.
All strange and terrible events are welcome,
But comforts we despise; our size of sorrow,
Proportion'd to our cause, must be as great   5
As that which makes it.

    Enter [*below*] DIOMEDES.

            How now! is he dead?
    Dio. His death's upon him, but not dead.
Look out o' th' other side your monument;
His guard have brought him thither.

    Enter [*below*] ANTONY, *borne by the* Guard.

    Cleo.   O sun,
Burn the great sphere thou mov'st in!   Darkling
      stand   10
The varying shore o' th' world.   O Antony,
Antony, Antony!   Help, Charmian, help, Iras, help;
Help, friends below; let's draw him hither.
    Ant.   Peace!

Not Cæsar's valour hath o'erthrown Antony,
But Antony's hath triumph'd on itself.   15
    Cleo. So it should be, that none but Antony
Should conquer Antony; but woe 'tis so!
    Ant. I am dying, Egypt, dying; only
I here importune death a while, until
Of many thousand kisses the poor last   20
I lay upon thy lips.
    Cleo.   I dare not, dear, —
Dear my lord, pardon, — I dare not,
Lest I be taken.   Not th' imperious show
Of the full-fortun'd Cæsar ever shall
Be brooch'd with me; if knife, drugs, serpents,
      have
Edge, sting, or operation, I am safe.   26
Your wife Octavia, with her modest eyes
And still conclusion, shall acquire no honour
Demuring upon me.   But come, come, Antony, —
Help me, my women, — we must draw thee up.
Assist, good friends.
    Ant.   O, quick, or I am gone.   31
    Cleo. Here's sport indeed!   How heavy weighs
      my lord!
Our strength is all gone into heaviness,
That makes the weight.   Had I great Juno's power,
The strong-wing'd Mercury should fetch thee up   35
And set thee by Jove's side.   Yet come a little, —
Wishers were ever fools, — O, come, come, come;
         [*They heave Antony aloft to Cleopatra.*
And welcome, welcome!   Die [where] thou hast
      liv'd;
Quicken with kissing.   Had my lips that power,
Thus would I wear them out.
    All.   A heavy sight!   40
    Ant. I am dying, Egypt, dying.
Give me some wine, and let me speak a little.
    Cleo. No, let me speak; and let me rail so high,
That the false housewife Fortune break her wheel,
Provok'd by my offence.
    Ant.   One word, sweet queen:
Of Cæsar seek your honour, with your safety.   O! 46
    Cleo. They do not go together.
    Ant.   Gentle, hear me:
None about Cæsar trust but Proculeius.
    Cleo. My resolution and my hands I'll trust;
None about Cæsar.   50
    Ant. The miserable change now at my end
Lament nor sorrow at; but please your thoughts
In feeding them with those my former fortunes
Wherein I liv'd, the greatest prince o' th' world,
The noblest; and do now not basely die,   55
Not cowardly put off my helmet to
My countryman, — a Roman by a Roman
Valiantly vanquish'd.   Now my spirit is going;
I can no more.

Sc. xv, 10. **Darkling:** in darkness.   21. **dare not:** i.e., come down from the monument.   25. **brooch'd:** adorned.   28. **still conclusion:** silent judgment.   33. **heaviness:** (1) grief, (2) weight.   38. **[where]** (Pope). *when* F.   39. **Quicken:** revive.

Cleo.   Noblest of men, woo 't die?
Hast thou no care of me? Shall I abide   60
In this dull world, which in thy absence is
No better than a sty? O, see, my women.
                                        [*Antony dies.*]
The crown o' th' earth doth melt. My lord!
O, wither'd is the garland of the war,
The soldier's pole is fall'n! Young boys and girls
Are level now with men; the odds is gone,   66
And there is nothing left remarkable
Beneath the visiting moon.   [*Faints.*]
    Char.   O, quietness, lady!
    Iras. She is dead too, our sovereign.
    Char.   Lady!
    Iras.   Madam!
    Char. O madam, madam, madam!
    Iras.   Royal Egypt,
Empress!   71
    Char. Peace, peace, Iras!
    Cleo. No more but [e'en] a woman, and com-
          manded
By such poor passion as the maid that milks
And does the meanest chares. It were for me   75
To throw my sceptre at the injurious gods,
To tell them that this world did equal theirs
Till they had stol'n our jewel. All's but nought;
Patience is sottish, and impatience does
Become a dog that's mad: then is it sin   80
To rush into the secret house of death
Ere death dare come to us? How do you, women?
What, what! good cheer! Why, how now, Char-
          mian!
My noble girls! Ah, women, women, look,
Our lamp is spent, it's out! Good sirs, take heart.
We'll bury him; and then, what's brave, what's
          noble,   86
Let's do it after the high Roman fashion,
And make Death proud to take us. Come, away;
This case of that huge spirit now is cold.
Ah, women, women! come; we have no friend   90
But resolution and the briefest end.
        [*Exeunt; [those above] bearing off Antony's
          body.*]

[ACT V]

[SCENE I. *Alexandria. Cæsar's camp.*]

Enter CÆSAR, AGRIPPA, DOLABELLA, [MÆCENAS,
GALLUS, PROCULEIUS, *and others,*] *his council of
war.*

    Cæs. Go to him, Dolabella, bid him yield;
Being so frustrate, tell him he mocks
The pauses that he makes.
    Dol.   Cæsar, I shall. [*Exit.*]

Enter DERCETAS *with the sword of Antony.*

    Cæs. Wherefore is that? and what art thou that
          dar'st
Appear thus to us?
    Der.   I am call'd Dercetas;   5
Mark Antony I serv'd, who best was worthy
Best to be serv'd. Whilst he stood up and spoke,
He was my master; and I wore my life
To spend upon his haters. If thou please
To take me to thee, as I was to him   10
I'll be to Cæsar; if thou pleasest not,
I yield thee up my life.
    Cæs.   What is't thou say'st?
    Der. I say, O Cæsar, Antony is dead.
    Cæs. The breaking of so great a thing should make
A greater crack. The round world   15
Should have shook lions into civil streets,
And citizens to their dens. The death of Antony
Is not a single doom; in the name lay
A moiety of the world.
    Der.   He is dead, Cæsar;
Not by a public minister of justice,   20
Nor by a hired knife; but that self hand
Which writ his honour in the acts it did
Hath, with the courage which the heart did lend it,
Splitted the heart. This is his sword;
I robb'd his wound of it; behold it stain'd   25
With his most noble blood.
    Cæs.   Look you sad, friends?
The gods rebuke me, but it is tidings
To wash the eyes of kings.
    [*Agr.*]   And strange it is
That nature must compel us to lament
Our most persisted deeds.
    Mæc.   His taints and honours
Wag'd equal with him.
    [*Agr.*]   A rarer spirit never   31
Did steer humanity; but you gods will give us
Some faults to make us men. Cæsar is touch'd.
    Mæc. When such a spacious mirror 's set before
          him,
He needs must see himself.
    Cæs.   O Antony!   35
I have followed thee to this; but we do lance
Diseases in our bodies. I must perforce
Have shown to thee such a declining day,
Or look on thine; we could not stall together
In the whole world: but yet let me lament,   40
With tears as sovereign as the blood of hearts,
That thou, my brother, my competitor
In top of all design, my mate in empire,
Friend and companion in the front of war,
The arm of mine own body, and the heart   45
Where mine his thoughts did kindle,—that our stars,

---

65. **pole:** standard. 73. [e'en] (Johnson). *in* F. 75. **chares:** chores. **were:** i.e., would be proper.
Act V, sc. i, 2-3. **he…makes:** his delays are ridiculous. 19. **moiety:** half. 28, 31. [*Agr.*] (Theobald). *Dol.* F. 39.
stall: dwell.

Unreconciliable, should divide
Our equalness to this. Hear me, good friends, —
But I will tell you at some meeter season.

Enter an EGYPTIAN.

The business of this man looks out of him;   50
We'll hear him what he says, — Whence are you?
  Egyp. A poor Egyptian yet. The Queen my
    mistress,
Confin'd in all she has, her monument,
Of thy intents desires instruction,
That she preparedly may frame herself   55
To th' way she's forc'd to.
  Cæs.   Bid her have good heart.
She soon shall know of us, by some of ours,
How honourable and how kindly we
Determine for her; for Cæsar cannot [live]
To be ungentle.
  Egyp.   So the gods preserve thee! 60
                       [Exit.
  Cæs. Come hither, Proculeius. Go and say
We purpose her no shame. Give her what com-
    forts
The quality of her passion shall require,
Lest, in her greatness, by some mortal stroke
She do defeat us; for her life in Rome   65
Would be eternal in our triumph. Go,
And with your speediest bring us what she says,
And how you find of her.
  Pro.   Cæsar, I shall. *[Exit.*
  Cæs. Gallus, go you along. *[Exit Gallus.]*
    Where's Dolabella,
To second Proculeius?
  All.   Dolabella!   70
  Cæs. Let him alone, for I remember now
How he's employ'd; he shall in time be ready.
Go with me to my tent, where you shall see
How hardly I was drawn into this war,
How calm and gentle I proceeded still   75
In all my writings. Go with me, and see
What I can show in this.   *[Exeunt.*

[SCENE II. *Alexandria. A room in the monument.]*
Enter CLEOPATRA, CHARMIAN, IRAS, *and* Mardian.

  Cleo. My desolation does begin to make
A better life. 'Tis paltry to be Cæsar;
Not being Fortune, he's but Fortune's knave,
A minister of her will: and it is great
To do that thing that ends all other deeds;   5
Which shackles accidents and bolts up change;
Which sleeps, and never palates more the dung,
The beggar's nurse and Cæsar's.

Enter [*to the gates of the monument*] PROCULEIUS
      [GALLUS *and* Soldiers].

  Pro. Cæsar sends greeting to the Queen of Egypt,
And bids thee study on what fair demands   10
Thou mean'st to have him grant thee.
  Cleo.   What's thy name?
  Pro. My name is Proculeius.
  Cleo.   Antony
Did tell me of you, bade me trust you; but
I do not greatly care to be deceiv'd,
That have no use for trusting. If your master 15
Would have a queen his beggar, you must tell him
That majesty, to keep decorum, must
No less beg than a kingdom. If he please
To give me conquer'd Egypt for my son,
He gives me so much of mine own as I   20
Will kneel to him with thanks.
  Pro.   Be of good cheer.
You're fallen into a princely hand; fear nothing.
Make your full reference freely to my lord,
Who is so full of grace that it flows over
On all that need. Let me report to him   25
Your sweet dependency, and you shall find
A conqueror that will pray in aid for kindness
Where he for grace is kneel'd to.
  Cleo.   Pray you, tell him
I am his fortune's vassal, and I send him
The greatness he has got. I hourly learn   30
A doctrine of obedience, and would gladly
Look him i' th' face.
  Pro.   This I'll report, dear lady.
Have comfort, for I know your plight is pitied
Of him that caus'd it.
  [*Gall.*] You see how easily she may be surpris'd. 35
    [*Here Proculeius and two of the Guard enter
      the monument by a ladder to a window and
      come down behind Cleopatra.*]
Guard her till Cæsar come.   *[Exit.*
  Iras. Royal queen!
  Char. O Cleopatra! thou art taken, Queen.
  Cleo. Quick, quick, good hands.
                  [Drawing a dagger.]
  Pro.   Hold, worthy lady, hold!
              [Seizes and disarms her.]
Do not yourself such wrong, who are in this   40
Reliev'd, but not betray'd.
  Cleo.   What, of death too,
That rids our dogs of languish?
  Pro.   Cleopatra,
Do not abuse my master's bounty by
Th' undoing of yourself. Let the world see
His nobleness well acted, which your death   45
Will never let come forth.
  Cleo.   Where art thou, Death?

59. [live] (Rowe). *leave* F. 66. eternal: eternally glorious.
Sc. ii, 3. knave: servant. 7. never ... dung: no longer tastes (the) base food. 8. nurse: nourisher. 14. to be: i.e., if I
am. 23. reference: appeal. 27. pray in aid: summon assistance (legal term). 29. send him: i.e., acknowledge in him.
35. The introduction of Gallus (l. 8) and the S.D. here are based on Plutarch. 42. languish: lingering disease.

Come hither, come!   Come, come, and take a queen
Worth many babes and beggars!
   Pro.   O, temperance, lady!
   Cleo. Sir, I will eat no meat; I'll not drink, sir;
If idle talk will once be necessary,   50
I'll not sleep neither; this mortal house I'll ruin,
Do Cæsar what he can.   Know, sir, that I
Will not wait pinion'd at your master's court;
Nor once be chastis'd with the sober eye
Of dull Octavia.   Shall they hoist me up   55
And show me to the shouting varletry
Of censuring Rome?   Rather a ditch in Egypt
Be gentle grave unto me!   Rather on Nilus' mud
Lay me stark nak'd, and let the water-flies
Blow me into abhorring!   Rather make   60
My country's high pyramides my gibbet,
And hang me up in chains!
   Pro.   You do extend
These thoughts of horror further than you shall
Find cause in Cæsar.

Enter DOLABELLA.

   Dol.   Proculeius,
What thou hast done thy master Cæsar knows,
And he hath sent for thee.   For the Queen,   66
I'll take her to my guard.
   Pro.   So, Dolabella,
It shall content me best.   Be gentle to her.
[*To Cleo.*] To Cæsar I will speak what you shall
   please,
If you'll employ me to him.
   Cleo.   Say, I would die.   70
           [*Exeunt Proculeius [and Soldiers].*
   Dol. Most noble empress, you have heard of me?
   Cleo. I cannot tell.
   Dol.   Assuredly you know me.
   Cleo. No matter, sir, what I have heard or known.
You laugh when boys or women tell their dreams;
Is't not your trick?
   Dol.   I understand not, madam.   75
   Cleo. I dream'd there was an Emperor Antony.
O, such another sleep, that I might see
But such another man?
   Dol.   If it might please ye, —
   Cleo. His face was as the heavens; and therein
   stuck   79
A sun and moon, which kept their course and lighted
The little O, the earth.
   Dol.   Most sovereign creature, —
   Cleo. His legs bestrid the ocean; his rear'd arm
Crested the world; his voice was propertied
As all the tuned spheres, and that to friends;
But when he meant to quail and shake the orb,
He was as rattling thunder.   For his bounty,   86

There was no winter in't; [an autumn 'twas]
That grew the more by reaping.   His delights
Were dolphin-like: they show'd his back above
The element they liv'd in.   In his livery   90
Walk'd crowns and crownets; realms and islands
   were
As plates dropp'd from his pocket.
   Dol.   Cleopatra!
   Cleo. Think you there was or might be such a man
As this I dream'd of?
   Dol.   Gentle madam, no.
   Cleo. You lie, up to the hearing of the gods!   95
But, if there be [or] ever were one such,
It's past the size of dreaming.   Nature wants stuff
To vie strange forms with fancy; yet, t' imagine
An Antony were nature's piece 'gainst fancy,
Condemning shadows quite.
   Dol.   Hear me, good madam.   100
Your loss is as yourself, great; and you bear it
As answering to the weight.   Would I might never
O'ertake pursu'd success, but I do feel,
By the rebound of yours, a grief that [smites]
My very heart at root.
   Cleo.   I thank you, sir.   105
Know you what Cæsar means to do with me?
   Dol. I am loath to tell you what I would you
   knew.
   Cleo. Nay, pray you, sir, —
   Dol.   Though he be honourable, —
   Cleo. He'll lead me, then, in triumph?
   Dol. Madam, he will; I know 't.   110
             [*Flourish.*

Enter CÆSAR, Gallus, PROCULEIUS, Mæcenas,
   [SELEUCUS,] *and others of his train.*

   All. Make way there!   Cæsar!
   Cæs. Which is the Queen of Egypt?
   Dol. It is the Emperor, madam.
             [*Cleopatra kneels.*
   Cæs. Arise, you shall not kneel.
I pray you, rise; rise, Egypt.
   Cleo.   Sir, the gods   115
Will have it thus; my master and my lord
I must obey.
   Cæs.   Take to you no hard thoughts.
The record of what injuries you did us,
Though written in our flesh, we shall remember
As things but done by chance.
   Cleo.   Sole sir o' th' world,
I cannot project mine own cause so well   121
To make it clear; but do confess I have
Been laden with like frailties which before
Have often sham'd our sex.
   Cæs.   Cleopatra, know

---

50. **If ... necessary:** i.e., to keep awake. 56. **varletry:** rabble. 83–84. **was ... spheres:** had the music of the spheres in it.
87. **[an autumn 'twas]** (Thirlby conj.). *Anthony it was* F. 92. **plates:** coins. 96. **[or]** F₃. *nor* F₁. 97. **size:** capacity. 98.
vie: compete in. 99. **piece 'gainst:** masterpiece in the competition with. 103. **but:** unless. 104. **[smites]** (Capell). *suites* F

We will extenuate rather than enforce.   125
If you apply yourself to our intents,
Which towards you are most gentle, you shall find
A benefit in this change; but if you seek
To lay on me a cruelty, by taking
Antony's course, you shall bereave yourself   130
Of my good purposes, and put your children
To that destruction which I'll guard them from
If thereon you rely.   I 'll take my leave.
    Cleo. And may, through all the world; 't is yours;
        and we,
Your scutcheons and your signs of conquest, shall
Hang in what place you please.   Here, my good
        lord.   136
    Cæs. You shall advise me in all for Cleopatra.
    Cleo. This is the brief of money, plate, and jewels
I am possess'd of.   'Tis exactly valued,
Not petty things admitted.   Where's Seleucus?
    Sel. Here, madam.   141
    Cleo. This is my treasurer; let him speak, my lord,
Upon his peril, that I have reserv'd
To myself nothing.   Speak the truth, Seleucus.
    Sel. Madam,   145
I had rather seal my lips than to my peril
Speak that which is not.
    Cleo.   What have I kept back?
    Sel. Enough to purchase what you have made
        known.
    Cæs. Nay, blush not, Cleopatra; I approve   149
Your wisdom in the deed.
    Cleo.   See, Cæsar! O, behold,
How pomp is followed!   Mine will now be yours;
And, should we shift estates, yours would be mine.
Th' ingratitude of this Seleucus does
Even make me wild.   O slave, of no more trust
Than love that's hir'd!   What, goest thou back?
        Thou shalt   155
Go back, I warrant thee; but I'll catch thine eyes,
Though they had wings.   Slave, soulless villain, dog!
O rarely base!
    Cæs.   Good queen, let us entreat you.
    Cleo. O Cæsar, what a wounding shame is this,
That thou, vouchsafing here to visit me,   160
Doing the honour of thy lordliness
To one so meek, that mine own servant should
Parcel the sum of my disgraces by
Addition of his envy!   Say, good Cæsar,
That I some lady trifles have reserv'd,   165
Immoment toys, things of such dignity
As we greet modern friends withal: and say,
Some nobler token I have kept apart
For Livia and Octavia, to induce
Their mediation; must I be unfolded   170

With one that I have bred?   The gods! it smites me
Beneath the fall I have.   [*To Seleucus.*]   Prithee,
    go hence;
Or I shall show the cinders of my spirits
Through th' ashes of my chance.   Wert thou a man,
Thou wouldst have mercy on me.
    Cæs.   Forbear, Seleucus.
        [*Exit Seleucus.*]
    Cleo. Be it known that we, the greatest, are mis-
        thought   176
For things that others do; and, when we fall,
We answer others' merits in our name,
Are therefore to be pitied.
    Cæs.   Cleopatra,
Not what you have reserv'd, nor what acknowl-
        edg'd,   180
Put we i' th' roll of conquest.   Still be 't yours,
Bestow it at your pleasure; and believe,
Cæsar 's no merchant, to make prize with you
Of things that merchants sold.   Therefore be cheer'd;
Make not your thoughts your prisons; no, dear
        queen;   185
For we intend so to dispose you as
Yourself shall give us counsel.   Feed, and sleep.
Our care and pity is so much upon you,
That we remain your friend; and so, adieu.   189
    Cleo. My master, and my lord!
    Cæs.   Not so.   Adieu.
    [*Flourish.   Exeunt Cæsar and his train.*
    Cleo. He words me, girls, he words me, that I
        should not
Be noble to myself; but, hark thee, Charmian.
        [*Whispers Charmian.*]
    Iras. Finish, good lady; the bright day is done,
And we are for the dark.
    Cleo.   Hie thee again.
I have spoke already, and it is provided;   195
Go put it to the haste.
    Char.   Madam, I will.

        Re-enter DOLABELLA.

    Dol. Where is the Queen?
    Char.   Behold, sir.   [*Exit.*]
    Cleo.   Dolabella!
    Dol. Madam, as thereto sworn by your command,
Which my love makes religion to obey,
I tell you this: Cæsar through Syria   200
Intends his journey, and within three days
You with your children will he send before.
Make your best use of this.   I have perform'd
Your pleasure and my promise.
    Cleo.   Dolabella,
I shall remain your debtor.

---

125. **enforce:** stress. 163. **Parcel:** increase. 164. **envy:** malice. 166. **Immoment toys:** insignificant trifles. 167. **modern:** ordinary. 169. **Livia:** Cæsar's wife. 170–71. **unfolded With:** exposed by. 173. **spirits:** i.e., anger. 174. **chance:** misfortune. 175. **Forbear:** withdraw. 176. **misthought:** misjudged. 178. **merits:** demerits. 185. **Make...prisons:** do not regard yourself a prisoner. 193. **Finish:** die. 195. **it:** i.e.. the asp.

Dol.   I your servant.   205
Adieu, good queen; I must attend on Cæsar.
                                        [*Exit.*
Cleo. Farewell, and thanks!   Now, Iras, what
    think'st thou?
Thou, an Egyptian puppet, shall be shown
In Rome as well as I.   Mechanic slaves
With greasy aprons, rules, and hammers, shall   210
Uplift us to the view; in their thick breaths,
Rank of gross diet, shall we be enclouded,
And forc'd to drink their vapour.
Iras.   The gods forbid!
Cleo. Nay, 'tis most certain, Iras.   Saucy lictors
Will catch at us like strumpets, and scald rhymers
Ballad us out o' tune.   The quick comedians   216
Extemporally will stage us, and present
Our Alexandrian revels; Antony
Shall be brought drunken forth, and I shall see
Some squeaking Cleopatra boy my greatness   220
I' th' posture of a whore.
Iras.   O the good gods!
Cleo. Nay, that's certain.
Iras. I'll never see 't; for, I am sure, [my] nails
Are stronger than mine eyes.
Cleo.   Why, that's the way
To fool their preparation, and to conquer   225
Their most absurd intents.

                  Re-enter CHARMIAN.

                        Now, Charmian!
Show me, my women, like a queen.   Go fetch
My best attires; I am again for Cydnus
To meet Mark Antony.   Sirrah Iras, go.
Now, noble Charmian, we'll dispatch indeed;   230
And, when thou hast done this chare, I'll give thee
    leave
To play till doomsday.   Bring our crown and all.
Wherefore's this noise?
            [*Exit Iras.*]   *A noise within.*

            Enter a GUARDSMAN.

Guard.   Here is a rural fellow
That will not be deni'd your Highness' presence.
He brings you figs.   235
Cleo. Let him come in.   [*Exit Guardsman.*
                   What poor an instrument
May do a noble deed!   He brings me liberty.
My resolution 's plac'd, and I have nothing
Of woman in me; now from head to foot
I am marble-constant; now the fleeting moon   240
No planet is of mine.

Re-enter GUARDSMAN, *with* CLOWN [*bringing in a
            basket*].

Guard.   This is the man.

Cleo. Avoid, and leave him.   [*Exit Guardsman.*
Hast thou the pretty worm of Nilus there,
That kills and pains not?   244
Clown. Truly, I have him; but I would not be
the party that should desire you to touch him, for
his biting is immortal; those that do die of it do
seldom or never recover.
Cleo. Remember'st thou any that have died
    on't?   249
Clown. Very many, men and women too.   I
heard of one of them no longer than yesterday; a
very honest woman, but something given to lie, as
a woman should not do but in the way of honesty;
how she died of the biting of it, what pain she felt;
truly, she makes a very good report o' th' worm.   255
But he that will believe all that they say, shall never
be saved by half that they do.   But this is most
falliable, the worm 's an odd worm.
Cleo. Get thee hence; farewell.   260
Clown. I wish you all joy of the worm.
                        [*Setting down his basket.*]
Cleo. Farewell.
Clown. You must think this, look you, that the
worm will do his kind.
Cleo. Ay, ay; farewell.   265
Clown. Look you, the worm is not to be trusted
but in the keeping of wise people; for, indeed, there
is no goodness in the worm.
Cleo. Take thou no care; it shall be heeded.
Clown. Very good.   Give it nothing, I pray you,
for it is not worth the feeding.   271
Cleo. Will it eat me?
Clown. You must not think I am so simple but
I know the devil himself will not eat a woman.   I
know that a woman is a dish for the gods, if the   275
devil dress her not.   But, truly, these same whoreson
devils do the gods great harm in their women; for
in every ten that they make, the devils mar five.
Cleo. Well, get thee gone; farewell.   280
Clown. Yes, forsooth; I wish you joy o' th' worm.
                                        [*Exit.*

[*Re-enter* IRAS *with a robe, crown, etc.*]

Cleo. Give me my robe, put on my crown; I have
Immortal longings in me.   Now no more
The juice of Egypt's grape shall moist this lip.   285
Yare, yare, good Iras; quick.   Methinks I hear
Antony call; I see him rouse himself
To praise my noble act; I hear him mock
The luck of Cæsar, which the gods give men
To excuse their after wrath.   Husband, I come!
Now to that name my courage prove my title!   291
I am fire and air; my other elements
I give to baser life.   So; have you done?
Come then, and take the last warmth of my lips.

215. **scald:** scurvy.   216. **quick:** lively.   220. **boy.**   Referring to the playing of female rôles by boys on the Elizabethan
stage.   223. [**my**] *mine* F.   231. **chare:** task.   240. **fleeting:** changeable.   242. **Avoid:** depart.   243. **worm:** serpent.
264. **his kind:** what his nature dictates.   292. **other elements:** earth and water.

Farewell, kind Charmian; Iras, long farewell.   295
        [*Kisses them. Iras falls and dies.*]
Have I the aspic in my lips? Dost fall?
If thou and nature can so gently part,
The stroke of death is as a lover's pinch,
Which hurts, and is desir'd. Dost thou lie still?
If thus thou vanishest, thou tell'st the world   300
It is not worth leave-taking.
    Char. Dissolve, thick cloud, and rain; that I may say
The gods themselves do weep!
    Cleo.   This proves me base.
If she first meet the curled Antony,
He'll make demand of her, and spend that kiss   305
Which is my heaven to have. Come, thou mortal wretch,
      [*To an asp, which she applies to her breast.*]
With thy sharp teeth this knot intrinsicate
Of life at once untie. Poor venomous fool,
Be angry, and dispatch. O, couldst thou speak,
That I might hear thee call great Cæsar ass   310
Unpolicied!
    Char. O eastern star!
    Cleo.   Peace, peace!
Dost thou not see my baby at my breast,
That sucks the nurse asleep?
    Char.   O, break! O, break!
    Cleo. As sweet as balm, as soft as air, as gentle, —
O Antony! — Nay, I will take thee too: 315
      [*Applying another asp to her arm.*]
What should I stay —   [*Dies.*
    Char. In this vile world? So, fare thee well!
Now boast thee, death, in thy possession lies
A lass unparallel'd. Downy windows, close;
And golden Phœbus never be beheld   320
Of eyes again so royal! Your crown 's [awry];
I'll mend it, and then play —

        Enter the GUARD, *rushing in.*

    1. Guard. Where's the Queen?
    Char.   Speak softly, wake her not.
    1. Guard. Cæsar hath sent —
    Char.   Too slow a messenger.
                      [*Applies an asp.*]
O, come apace, dispatch! I partly feel thee.   325
    1. Guard. Approach, ho! All 's not well; Cæsar 's beguil'd.
    2. Guard. There 's Dolabella sent from Cæsar; call him.
    1. Guard. What work is here! Charmian, is this well done?
    Char. It is well done, and fitting for a princess
Descended of so many royal kings.   330
Ah, soldier!   [*Dies.*

          Re-enter DOLABELLA.

    Dol. How goes it here?
    2. Guard.   All dead.
    Dol.   Cæsar, thy thoughts
Touch their effects in this; thyself art coming
To see perform'd the dreaded act which thou
So sought'st to hinder.   335

     Re-enter CÆSAR *and all his train, marching.*

    All. A way there, a way for Cæsar!
    Dol. O sir, you are too sure an augurer;
That you did fear is done.
    Cæs.   Bravest at the last,
She levell'd at our purposes, and, being royal,
Took her own way. The manner of their deaths?
I do not see them bleed.   340
    Dol.   Who was last with them?
    1. Guard. A simple countryman, that brought her figs.
This was his basket.
    Cæs.   Poison'd, then.
    1. Guard.   O Cæsar,
This Charmian liv'd but now; she stood and spake.
I found her trimming up the diadem   343
On her dead mistress. Tremblingly she stood
And on the sudden dropp'd.
    Cæs.   O noble weakness!
If they had swallow'd poison, 'twould appear
By external swelling; but she looks like sleep,
As she would catch another Antony   350
In her strong toil of grace.
    Dol.   Here, on her breast,
There is a vent of blood and something blown.
The like is on her arm.
    1. Guard. This is an aspic's trail; and these fig-leaves
Have slime upon them, such as the aspic leaves   355
Upon the caves of Nile.
    Cæs.   Most probable
That so she died; for her physician tells me
She hath pursu'd conclusions infinite
Of easy ways to die. Take up her bed;
And bear her women from the monument.   360
She shall be buried by her Antony;
No grave upon the earth shall clip in it
A pair so famous. High events as these
Strike those that make them; and their story is
No less in pity than his glory which   365
Brought them to be lamented. Our army shall
In solemn show attend this funeral;
And then to Rome. Come, Dolabella, see
High order in this great solemnity.
                 [*Exeunt omnes.*

---

296. **aspic:** asp.   305. **make ... her:** ask her about me.   307. **intrinsicate:** intricate.   321. **[awry]** (Rowe). *away* F.   333. **Touch ... effects:** are realized.   339. **levell'd at:** guessed.   352. **blown:** swollen.   358. **conclusions:** experiments.   362. **clip:** enclose.

The Tragedy of Coriolanus

FOR THE TEXT of *Coriolanus* the First Folio (1623) is the sole authority. This is marred by considerable misprinting and mislineation, but unusually full stage-directions establish the authenticity of the copy and suggest Shakespeare's hand.

Evidence for the date is quite inconclusive. It is conceivable but unlikely that the simile of the "coal of fire upon the ice" (I.i.177) was reminiscent of the ice upon the Thames, which in January of 1608 froze over the first time since 1565; Shakespeare might have seen fires upon frozen streams more than once. A line in Ben Jonson's *Epicoene* (1609), "You have lurch'd your friends of the better halfe of the garland" (V.iv.227), which bears so close a likeness to "He lurch'd all swords of the garland" in II.ii.105, may be one of those gibing allusions of which Jonson was fond; but the expression was perhaps a current one. Another possible reference appears in the Preface to Robert Armin's poem *The Italian Tailor and His Boy* (1609), where the striking image of throwing up one's cap at the horns of the moon may have been plucked from I.i.216–17 of the present play. Armin was one of "the Principall Actors" of Shakespeare's company at the time his poem was printed. The foregoing evidence, for what it is worth, combines with that from style and metre to indicate a time late in 1608 or early in 1609 as the period of composition.

The source of the plot is Plutarch's *Life of Coriolanus*, which Shakespeare knew in the translation of Sir Thomas North. As in the case of *Julius Cæsar* and *Antony and Cleopatra*, which are also based on Plutarch, he followed his authority closely. Whole passages of some of the most notable speeches, such as the fable related by Menenius (I.i.99 ff.), the speech of Coriolanus presenting himself to Aufidius (IV.v.71 ff.), and the appeal of Volumnia to her son on behalf of Rome (V.iii.94 ff.), are couched almost in the words of the biography. The main lines of the characters are also followed faithfully, though many of the more subtle points are introduced by Shakespeare. For example, the episode in which Coriolanus begs of Cominius freedom for his Vol-

scian host is in Plutarch, but the finely characteristic touch by which he is represented as having forgotten the man's name is Shakespeare's (I.ix.79–90). The demagogic tribunes, Brutus and Sicinius, are virtually Shakespeare's creations, for in Plutarch their personalities are barely suggested. The portrait of Menenius is greatly elaborated in the play. Plutarch assigns to him merely the part of a dignified patrician who makes a single attempt to pacify the rebellious plebeians; Shakespeare conceives him as a genial and self-important old gentleman, who takes a touching pride in his intimacy with the hero, who is appreciated, even by the people, for his civic virtue, and who, with his command of salty, homely language and his skill in repartee, is responsible for most of the humor which helps to relieve the prevailing somberness of the tragedy. The dialogues of the citizens and such scenes as those with the servants of Aufidius are wholly invented; while as a basis for the actual language in which Coriolanus expresses his haughty and contemptuous nature, Shakespeare had merely Plutarch's statement that he was rough and insolent in conversation and undisciplined in temper. Although what is most attractive in Volumnia is provided by Plutarch, the harshness in her character is the addition of Shakespeare. In the biography, it is Valeria who induces the wife and mother of Coriolanus to go to plead with him, and her share in the action is treated with considerable fullness. This is represented in the play merely by her presence in the deputation; but Shakespeare supplies from his own imagination the admirable scene (I.iii) where she calls on Volumnia and Virgilia and finds them sewing. Virgilia is little more than a name in the source, and the skill with which in the play she is drawn in some half dozen lines is all Shakespeare's.

The facts of the political situation in which the action takes place Shakespeare has deliberately altered. The dignified secession of the *plebs*, which in Plutarch is a measure of passive resistance to severe economic oppression, he represents as the rioting of a hungry mob shouting for cheap corn; and the picture of the common crowd in this play, as elsewhere, is unflattering. It is wrong, however, to suppose that Shakespeare conceived this play primarily as a political document. One cannot recall too often that Shakespeare was a dramatist, not an essayist, and that therefore dramatic considerations always govern. In the present play class conflict is a postulate inherited from the source, and in making the narrative dramatic Shakespeare underlines the elements of opposition. Like most of his articulate contemporaries, Shakespeare viewed the established social order as part or counterpart of the rational order of the universe, in which all classes had their place and function. Therefore, although no champion of the masses, Shakespeare was, on the other hand, not their enemy. In *Coriolanus*, one should observe, the true source of danger is not in the nature of the people but in the pride of the leading aristocrat. Had Coriolanus had a modicum of charity or humility, even, one might say, of common sense, disaster might have been avoided. But he is a patrician bigot, identifying his own class with the State, ready in his fanatical scorn to take from the people even their traditional privileges. With such an attitude Shakespeare, of course, had no sympathy. It is useful to note, furthermore, that although the citizens are muddle-headed, fickle, and stupidly pliable, they have good instincts and honest intentions. When they cry, "That we did, we did for the best," they speak the truth (IV.vi.143). Until he has spurned their good will irretrievably, Coriolanus never lacks advocates among them. In the first scene when the crowd is out to kill him, a voice is raised recalling his services and warning against holding "what he cannot help in his nature" as a vice in him (I.i.42). When at the election Coriolanus demands of a citizen the price of the consulship, he is told that "the price is to ask it kindly" (II.iii.81). He does not ask it kindly, yet these citizens elect him just the same. Coriolanus could have their devotion if he would show them a decent respect.

The vocation of Coriolanus is war, and in that he is great. From his youth he has been dedicated to fighting, and he won distinction early (I.iii.1 ff.; II.ii.91 ff.). Success has not turned his head, and although he is haughty to excess with those whom he disdains, he is not vainglorious because of his victories. He is embarrassed by praise, and it is interesting to note that his indifference to it is a touch invented by Shakespeare. Not that he does not covet distinction; he does, and his deprecation of his exploits and his exaggerated impatience with eulogy look like a negative expression of his pride. His honesty, though too often tactless, is essentially to his credit. "What his breast forges, that his tongue must vent" (III.i.258). He knows the necessity for strategy in war, but of pacific diplomacy he is totally incapable. His pride wears no mask, and the people know what he thinks of them. He has done much for Rome which only he could do, and the idea most hideous to his imagination is that of traitor. When Sicinius calls him one he is enraged (III.i.162–72; III.iii.63–74), and it is a mighty irony that with this abhorrence of the crime, he should ever stoop to treason.

The capitulation of Coriolanus to the entreaties of his mother is highly revealing with respect to both his character and hers. This stalwart woman, one of Shakespeare's truly remarkable creations, is in a real sense responsible for the destiny of her son. He is bone of her bone and flesh of her flesh; she has directed his spirit and shaped his ideals, and she cherishes him as a projection of herself. "Thou art my warrior; I holp to frame thee," are the first words she speaks after he has raised her from her knees in Corioli (V.iii.62). His wounds incurred for Rome have ever been glorious in her eyes. In the victory which makes him "Coriolanus," her dreams for him — "my very wishes and the buildings of my fancy" — are realized, except for the consulship, which she is confident Rome will now bestow upon him (II.i.214–218). Though she despises the populace as much as he, she would have him dissimulate, and it is her rebuke of that pride which she has done so much to foster in him that moves him to his ill-fated effort (III.ii.128–30). But more than family and more than class, she loves her country, and when her son has shamed them all, she can abase her spirit in a last effort to save Rome. In her pleading with her son it is to his honor, not his pity, that she appeals; her personal feelings are consumed in her country's peril. It is not for Rome's sake, however, or for honor, that Coriolanus yields; it is because his family kneels and his mother begs. He had sworn that he would never be "such a gosling" as to obey instinct, and that he would deny his kin (V.iii.34 ff.). But that is the one thing he cannot do. Nature sways where no arguments avail, and when he tells his mother what she must but too well have divined, that his submission may prove most mortal to him, her feelings are too deep for words.

THE TRAGEDY OF CORIOLANUS

[DRAMATIS PERSONÆ

CAIUS MARCIUS, *afterwards* CAIUS MARCIUS CORIOLANUS.
TITUS LARTIUS, } *generals against the Volscians.*
COMINIUS,
MENENIUS AGRIPPA, *friend to Coriolanus.*
SICINIUS VELUTUS, } *tribunes of the people.*
JUNIUS BRUTUS,
Young MARCIUS, *son to Coriolanus.*
A Roman Herald.
TULLUS AUFIDIUS, *general of the Volscians.*

Lieutenant to Aufidius.
Conspirators with Aufidius.
A Citizen of Antium.
Two Volscian Guards.

VOLUMNIA, *mother to Coriolanus.*
VIRGILIA, *wife to Coriolanus.*
VALERIA, *friend to Virgilia.*
Gentlewoman, *attending on Virgilia.*

Roman and Volscian Senators, Patricians, Ædiles, Lictors, Soldiers, Citizens, Messengers, Servants to Aufidius, and other Attendants.

SCENE: *Rome and the neighbourhood; Corioli and the neighbourhood; Antium.*]

imagery of need for nourishment

ACT I

SCENE I. [*Rome. A street.*]

Enter a company of mutinous CITIZENS, *with staves, clubs, and other weapons.*

1. Cit. Before we proceed any further, hear me speak.

All. Speak, speak.

1. Cit. You are all resolv'd rather to die than to famish? 5

All. Resolv'd, resolv'd.

1. Cit. First, you know Caius Marcius is chief enemy to the people.

All. We know 't, we know 't. 9

1. Cit. Let us kill him, and we'll have corn at our own price. Is 't a verdict?

All. No more talking on 't; let it be done. Away, away!

2. Cit. One word, good citizens. 15

1. Cit. We are accounted poor citizens, the patricians good. What authority surfeits on would relieve us; if they would yield us but the superfluity while it were wholesome, we might guess they relieved us humanely; but they think we are too dear. The leanness that afflicts us, the 20 object of our misery, is as an inventory to particularize their abundance; our sufferance is a gain to them. Let us revenge this with our pikes ere we become rakes; for the gods know I speak this in hunger for bread, not in thirst for revenge. 25

2. Cit. Would you proceed especially against Caius Marcius?

All. Against him first; he's a very dog to the commonalty. 29

2. Cit. Consider you what services he has done for his country?

1. Cit. Very well; and could be content to give him good report for 't, but that he pays himself with being proud.

[*2. Cit.*] Nay, but speak not maliciously. 35

1. Cit. I say unto you, what he hath done famously, he did it to that end. Though soft-conscienc'd men can be content to say it was for his country, he did it to please his mother, and to be partly proud; which he is, even to the altitude of his virtue. 41

2. Cit. What he cannot help in his nature, you

Act I, sc. i, 21. object: sight. 22 sufferance: suffering. 24. rakes: i.e., thin. 35. [*2. Cit.*] (Malone). *All* F.

account a vice in him. You must in no way say he
is covetous.   44
    1. Cit. If I must not, I need not be barren of ac-
cusations; he hath faults, with surplus, to tire in
repetition. (*Shouts within.*) What shouts are
these? The other side o' th' city is risen; why stay
we prating here? To th' Capitol!
    All. Come, come.   50
    1. Cit. Soft! who comes here?

           Enter MENENIUS AGRIPPA.

    2. Cit. Worthy Menenius Agrippa, one that hath
always lov'd the people.
    1. Cit. He's one honest enough; would all the rest
were so!   55
    Men. What work 's, my countrymen, in hand?
        Where go you
With bats and clubs? The matter? Speak, I pray
    you.
    2. Cit. Our business is not unknown to th' Senate.
They have had inkling this fortnight what we intend
to do, which now we'll show 'em in deeds. They
say poor suitors have strong breaths; they shall
know we have strong arms too.   62
    Men. Why, masters, my good friends, mine
        honest neighbours,
Will you undo yourselves?
    2. Cit. We cannot, sir, we are undone already.
    Men. I tell you, friends, most charitable care
Have the patricians of you. For your wants,
Your suffering in this dearth, you may as well
Strike at the heaven with your staves as lift them   70
Against the Roman state, whose course will on
The way it takes, cracking ten thousand curbs
Of more strong link asunder than can ever
Appear in your impediment. For the dearth,
The gods, not the patricians, make it, and   75
Your knees to them, not arms, must help. Alack,
You are transported by calamity
Thither where more attends you, and you slander
The helms o' th' state, who care for you like fathers
When you curse them as enemies.   80
    2. Cit. Care for us! True, indeed! They ne'er
car'd for us yet: suffer us to famish, and their store-
houses cramm'd with grain; make edicts for usury,
to support usurers; repeal daily any wholesome act
established against the rich, and provide more   85
piercing statutes daily, to chain up and restrain the
poor. If the wars eat us not up, they will; and
there's all the love they bear us.
    Men. Either you must   90
Confess yourselves wondrous malicious,

Or be accus'd of folly. I shall tell you
A pretty tale. It may be you have heard it;
But, since it serves my purpose, I will venture
To [stale 't] a little more.   95
    2. Cit. Well, I'll hear it, sir; yet you must not
think to fob off our disgrace with a tale. But, an't
please you, deliver.
    Men. There was a time when all the body's
        members
Rebell'd against the belly, thus accus'd it: 100
That only like a gulf it did remain
I' th' midst o' th' body, idle and unactive,
Still cupboarding the viand, never bearing
Like labour with the rest, where th' other instru-
    ments
Did see and hear, devise, instruct, walk, feel   105
And, mutually participate, did minister
Unto the appetite and affection common
Of the whole body. The belly answer'd —
    2. Cit. Well, sir, what answer made the belly?   110
    Men. Sir, I shall tell you. With a kind of smile,
Which ne'er came from the lungs, but even thus —
For, look you, I may make the belly smile
As well as speak — it [tauntingly] replied
To th' discontented members, the mutinous parts
That envied his receipt; even so most fitly   116
As you malign our senators for that
They are not such as you.
    2. Cit.   Your belly's answer? What?
The kingly-crowned head, the vigilant eye,
The counsellor heart, the arm our soldier,   120
Our steed the leg, the tongue our trumpeter,
With other muniments and petty helps
In this our fabric, if that they —
    Men.   What then?
'Fore me, this fellow speaks! What then? what
        then?
    2. Cit. Should by the cormorant belly be re-
        strain'd.   125
Who is the sink o' th' body, —
    Men.   Well, what then?
    2. Cit. The former agents, if they did complain,
What could the belly answer?
    Men.   I will tell you.
If you'll bestow a small — of what you have little —
Patience a while, you'st hear the belly's answer.   130
    2. Cit. Ye're long about it.
    Men.   Note me this, good friend;
Your most grave belly was deliberate,
Not rash like his accusers, and thus answered:
"True is it, my incorporate friends," quoth he,
"That I receive the general food at first   135

---

58. *2. Cit.* Many edd. change to *1. Cit.* here and throughout the rest of the scene.   79. **helms:** pilots.   95. [stale 't]
(Theobald). *scale 't* F.   97. **fob . . . disgrace:** cajole us from our feeling of injury.   101. **gulf:** whirlpool.   106. **participate:**
cooperating.   107. **affection:** desire.   112. **ne'er . . . lungs:** i.e., was not a laugh.   113. [tauntingly] F₄. *taintingly* F₁.
116. **receipt:** what he received.   122. **muniments:** furnishings.   130. **you'st:** you shall.   134. **incorporate:** united in
one body.

Which you do live upon; and fit it is,
Because I am the store-house and the shop
Of the whole body. But, if you do remember,
I send it through the rivers of your blood,
Even to the court, the heart, to th' seat o' th' brain;
And, through the cranks and offices of man,   141
The strongest nerves and small inferior veins
From me receive that natural competency
Whereby they live. And though that all at once,
You, my good friends," — this says the belly, mark
me, —   145
   2. Cit. Ay, sir; well, well.
   Men.   "Though all at once cannot
See what I do deliver out to each,
Yet I can make my audit up, that all
From me do back receive the flour of all,   149
And leave me but the bran." What say you to 't?
   2. Cit. It was an answer. How apply you this?
   Men. The senators of Rome are this good belly,
And you the mutinous members; for examine
Their counsels and their cares, digest things rightly
Touching the weal o' th' common, you shall find
No public benefit which you receive   156
But it proceeds or comes from them to you
And no way from yourselves. What do you think,
You, the great toe of this assembly?
   2. Cit. I the great toe! Why the great toe?   160
   Men. For that, being one o' th' lowest, basest,
     poorest,
Of this most wise rebellion, thou goest foremost;
Thou rascal, that art worst in blood to run,
Lead'st first to win some vantage.
But make you ready your stiff bats and clubs;   165
Rome and her rats are at the point of battle,
The one side must have bale.

Enter CAIUS MARCIUS.

               Hail, noble Marcius!
   Mar. Thanks. What's the matter, you dissen-
     tious rogues,
That, rubbing the poor itch of your opinion,   169
Make yourselves scabs?
   2. Cit.   We have ever your good word.
   Mar. He that will give good words to thee will
     flatter
Beneath abhorring. What would you have, you
     curs,
That like nor peace nor war? The one affrights you,
The other makes you proud. He that trusts to you,
Where he should find you lions, finds you hares;   175
Where foxes, geese. You are no surer, no,
Than is the coal of fire upon the ice,

Or hailstone in the sun. Your virtue is
To make him worthy whose offence subdues him,
And curse that justice did it. Who deserves great-
     ness   180
Deserves your hate; and your affections are
A sick man's appetite, who desires most that
Which would increase his evil. He that depends
Upon your favours swims with fins of lead
And hews down oaks with rushes. Hang ye! Trust
     ye?   185
With every minute you do change a mind,
And call him noble that was now your hate,
Him vile that was your garland. What's the mat-
     ter,
That in these several places of the city
You cry against the noble Senate, who,   190
Under the gods, keep you in awe, which else
Would feed on one another? What's their seeking?
   Men. For corn at their own rates; whereof, they
     say,
The city is well stor'd.
   Mar.   Hang 'em! They say!
They'll sit by th' fire, and presume to know   195
What's done i' th' Capitol; who's like to rise,
Who thrives, and who declines; side factions, and
     give out
Conjectural marriages; making parties strong,
And feebling such as stand not in their liking
Below their cobbled shoes. They say there's grain
     enough!   200
Would the nobility lay aside their ruth
And let me use my sword, I'd make a quarry
With thousands of these quarter'd slaves as high
As I could pick my lance.
   Men. Nay, these are almost thoroughly per-
     suaded;   205
For though abundantly they lack discretion,
Yet are they passing cowardly. But, I beseech you,
What says the other troop?
   Mar.   They are dissolv'd, hang 'em!
They said they were an-hungry; sigh'd forth prov-
     erbs;
That hunger broke stone walls, that dogs must eat,
That meat was made for mouths, that the gods sent
     not   211
Corn for the rich men only. With these shreds
They vented their complainings; which being
     answer'd,
And a petition granted them, — a strange one
To break the heart of generosity,   215
And make bold power look pale, — they threw their
     caps
As they would hang them on the horns o' th' moon,

---

141. **cranks:** winding passages. **offices:** service rooms.   163. **rascal:** lean deer (therefore not worth hunting). **blood:** condition.   167. **bale:** disaster.   170. **scabs:** (1) sores, (2) scurvy rascals.   179. **whose ... him:** whose own fault has ruined him.   180. **that ... it:** the justice that punished him.   197. **side:** take sides with.   198. **marriages:** i.e., political alliances. **strong:** i.e., in report.   202. **quarry:** heap of dead.   203. **quarter'd:** slaughtered.   204. **pick:** pitch.   215. **generosity:** the gentry.

Shouting their emulation.

Men.   What is granted them?

Mar. Five tribunes to defend their vulgar wisdoms,

Of their own choice. One's Junius Brutus,   220

Sicinius Velutus, and I know not — 'Sdeath!

The rabble should have first unroof'd the city

Ere so prevail'd with me. It will in time

Win upon power and throw forth greater themes

For insurrection's arguing.

Men.   This is strange.   225

Mar. Go, get you home, you fragments!

Enter a MESSENGER, *hastily.*

Mess. Where's Caius Marcius?

Mar.   Here. What's the matter?

Mess. The news is, sir, the Volsces are in arms.

Mar. I am glad on't. Then we shall ha' means to vent

Our musty superfluity. See, our best elders.   230

Enter COMINIUS, TITUS LARTIUS, *and other* SENATORS; JUNIUS BRUTUS *and* SICINIUS VELUTUS.

1. Sen. Marcius, 'tis true that you have lately told us;

The Volsces are in arms.

Mar.   They have a leader

Tullus Aufidius, that will put you to't.

I sin in envying his nobility,

And were I anything but what I am,   235

I would wish me only he.

Com.   You have fought together?

Mar. Were half to half the world by th' ears and he

Upon my party, I'd revolt, to make

Only my wars with him. He is a lion

That I am proud to hunt.

1. Sen.   Then, worthy Marcius,

Attend upon Cominius to these wars.   241

Com. It is your former promise.

Mar.   Sir, it is;

And I am constant. Titus [Lartius], thou

Shalt see me once more strike at Tullus' face.

What, art thou stiff? Stand'st out?

Lart.   No, Caius Marcius;

I'll lean upon one crutch and fight with t'other   246

Ere stay behind this business.

Men.   O, true-bred!

[1.] Sen. Your company to th' Capitol; where, I know,

Our greatest friends attend us.

Lart.   *[To Com.]* Lead you on.

[To Mar.] Follow Cominius; we must follow you;

Right worthy you priority.

Com.   Noble Marcius!   251

[1.] Sen. *[To the Citizens.]* Hence to your homes; begone!

Mar.   Nay, let them follow.

The Volsces have much corn; take these rats thither

To gnaw their garners. Worshipful mutiners,

Your valour puts well forth; pray, follow.   255

     [Citizens steal away. Exeunt all but Sicinius and Brutus.

Sic. Was ever man so proud as is this Marcius?

Bru. He has no equal.

Sic. When we were chosen tribunes for the people, —

Bru. Mark'd you his lip and eyes?

Sic.   Nay, but his taunts.

Bru. Being mov'd, he will not spare to gird the gods.   260

Sic. Be-mock the modest moon.

Bru. The present wars devour him! He is grown

Too proud to be so valiant.

Sic.   Such a nature,

Tickled with good success, disdains the shadow

Which he treads on at noon. But I do wonder   265

His insolence can brook to be commanded

Under Cominius.

Bru.   Fame, at the which he aims,

In whom already he's well grac'd, cannot

Better be held nor more attain'd than by

A place below the first; for what miscarries   270

Shall be the general's fault, though he perform

To th' utmost of a man, and giddy censure

Will then cry out of Marcius, "O, if he

Had borne the business!"

Sic.   Besides, if things go well,

Opinion that so sticks on Marcius shall   275

Of his demerits rob Cominius.

Bru.   Come.

Half all Cominius' honours are to Marcius,

Though Marcius earn'd them not, and all his faults

To Marcius shall be honours, though indeed

In aught he merit not.

Sic.   Let's hence, and hear   280

How the dispatch is made, and in what fashion,

More than his singularity, he goes

Upon this present action.

Bru.   Let's along.   *[Exeunt.*

[SCENE II. *Corioli. The Senate-house.*]

Enter TULLUS AUFIDIUS *with* SENATORS *of Corioli.*

1. Sen. So, your opinion is, Aufidius,

That they of Rome are ent'red in our counsels

---

218. **emulation:** factiousness. 229. **vent:** get rid of. 233. **put you to't:** keep you busy. 243. **[Lartius]** (Rowe). *Lucius* F (as elsewhere). 248, 252. **[1.]** (Rowe). Om. F. 255. **puts well forth:** shows up well. 260. **gird:** scoff at. 276. **demerits:** deserts. 282. **More ... singularity:** apart from his individual peculiarities.

And know how we proceed.

Auf.   Is it not yours?
What ever have been thought on in this state,
That could be brought to bodily act ere Rome   5
Had circumvention? 'Tis not four days gone
Since I heard thence; these are the words: — I think
I have the letter here; yes, here it is: —
[*Reads.*] "They have press'd a power, but it is not
          known
Whether for east or west. The dearth is great;   10
The people mutinous; and it is rumour'd,
Cominius, Marcius your old enemy,
Who is of Rome worse hated than of you,
And Titus Lartius, a most valiant Roman,
These three lead on this preparation   15
Whither 'tis bent. Most likely 'tis for you;
Consider of it."

1. Sen.   Our army's in the field.
We never yet made doubt but Rome was ready
To answer us.

Auf.   Nor did you think it folly
To keep your great pretences veil'd till when   20
They needs must show themselves; which in the
          hatching,
It seem'd, appear'd to Rome. By the discovery
We shall be short'ned in our aim, which was
To take in many towns ere almost Rome
Should know we were afoot.

2. Sen.   Noble Aufidius,   25
Take your commission; hie you to your bands;
Let us alone to guard Corioli.
If they set down before 's, for the remove
Bring up your army; but, I think, you'll find
They've not prepar'd for us.

Auf.   O, doubt not that; 30
I speak from certainties. Nay, more;
Some parcels of their power are forth already,
And only hitherward. I leave your honours.
If we and Caius Marcius chance to meet,
'Tis sworn between us we shall ever strike   35
Till one can do no more.

All.   The gods assist you!
Auf. And keep your honours safe!
1. Sen.   Farewell.
2. Sen.   Farewell.
All. Farewell.   [*Exeunt.*

[SCENE III. *Rome. A room in Marcius' house.*]

Enter VOLUMNIA *and* VIRGILIA: *they set them
          down on two low stools, and sew.*

Vol. I pray you, daughter, sing; or express yourself in a more comfortable sort. If my son were my
husband, I should freelier rejoice in that absence
wherein he won honour than in the embracements
of his bed where he would show most love. When 5
yet he was but tender-bodied and the only son of my
womb, when youth with comeliness pluck'd all gaze
his way, when for a day of kings' entreaties a mother
should not sell him an hour from her beholding, I,
considering how honour would become such a 10
person, that it was no better than picture-like to
hang by th' wall, if renown made it not stir, was
pleas'd to let him seek danger where he was like to
find fame. To a cruel war I sent him; from whence
he return'd, his brows bound with oak. I tell 15
thee, daughter, I sprang not more in joy at first
hearing he was a man-child than now in first seeing
he had proved himself a man.   19

Vir. But had he died in the business, madam,
how then?

Vol. Then his good report should have been my
son; I therein would have found issue. Hear me
profess sincerely: had I a dozen sons, each in my love
alike and none less dear than thine and my good 25
Marcius, I had rather had eleven die nobly for their
country than one voluptuously surfeit out of action.

Enter a GENTLEWOMAN.

Gent. Madam, the Lady Valeria is come to visit
          you.
Vir. Beseech you, give me leave to retire myself.
Vol. Indeed, you shall not.   31
Methinks I hear hither your husband's drum;
See him pluck Aufidius down by the hair;
As children from a bear, the Volsces shunning him.
Methinks I see him stamp thus, and call thus: 35
"Come on, you cowards! you were got in fear,
Though you were born in Rome." His bloody brow
With his mail'd hand then wiping, forth he goes,
Like to a harvest-man that's task'd to mow
Or all or lose his hire.   40
Vir. His bloody brow! O Jupiter, no blood!
Vol. Away, you fool! it more becomes a man
Than gilt his trophy. The breasts of Hecuba,
When she did suckle Hector, look'd not lovelier
Than Hector's forehead when it spit forth blood 45
At Grecian sword, [contemning. Tell] Valeria,
We are fit to bid her welcome.   [*Exit Gent.*
Vir. Heavens bless my lord from fell Aufidius!
Vol. He'll beat Aufidius' head below his knee
And tread upon his neck.   50

Enter VALERIA, *with an* Usher *and* Gentlewoman.

Val. My ladies both, good day to you.
Vol. Sweet madam.

Sc. ii, 6. **circumvention**: means to circumvent. 9. **press'd a power**: conscripted troops. 20. **pretences**: designs. 28.
for the remove: to raise the siege.
Sc. iii, 11. **person**: comely figure. 39. **task'd**: committed. 43. **trophy**: monument. 46. [**contemning. Tell**] (Collier
conj.). *Contenning tell* F.

Vir. I am glad to see your ladyship.

Val. How do you both? You are manifest house-keepers. What are you sewing here? A fine spot, in good faith. How does your little son? 57

Vir. I thank your ladyship; well, good madam.

Vol. He had rather see the swords and hear a drum than look upon his schoolmaster. 61

Val. O' my word, the father's son. I'll swear, 'tis a very pretty boy. O' my troth, I look'd upon him o' Wednesday half an hour together; has such a confirm'd countenance. I saw him run after a 65 gilded butterfly; and when he caught it, he let it go again; and after it again; and over and over he comes, and up again; catch'd it again; or whether his fall enrag'd him, or how 'twas, he did so set his teeth and tear it. O, I warrant, how he mammock'd it! 71

Vol. One on 's father's moods.

Val. Indeed, la, 'tis a noble child.

Vir. A crack, madam. 74

Val. Come, lay aside your stitchery; I must have you play the idle housewife with me this afternoon.

Vir. No, good madam; I will not out of doors.

Val. Not out of doors!

Vol. She shall, she shall. 80

Vir. Indeed, no, by your patience; I'll not over the threshold till my lord return from the wars.

Val. Fie, you confine yourself most unreasonably. Come, you must go visit the good lady that lies in. 86

Vir. I will wish her speedy strength, and visit her with my prayers; but I cannot go thither.

Vol. Why, I pray you?

Vir. 'Tis not to save labour, nor that I want love. 91

Val. You would be another Penelope: yet, they say, all the yarn she spun in Ulysses' absence did but fill Ithaca full of moths. Come; I would your cambric were sensible as your finger, that you might leave pricking it for pity. Come, you shall go with us. 97

Vir. No, good madam, pardon me; indeed, I will not forth.

Val. In truth, la, go with me; and I'll tell you excellent news of your husband. 101

Vir. O, good madam, there can be none yet.

Val. Verily, I do not jest with you; there came news from him last night.

Vir. Indeed, madam? 105

Val. In earnest, it's true; I heard a senator speak it. Thus it is: the Volsces have an army forth; against whom Cominius the general is gone, with one part of our Roman power. Your lord and Titus Lartius are set down before their city Corioli; 110

they nothing doubt prevailing and to make it brief wars. This is true, on mine honour; and so, I pray, go with us.

Vir. Give me excuse, good madam; I will obey you in everything hereafter. 115

Vol. Let her alone, lady. As she is now, she will but disease our better mirth.

Val. In troth, I think she would. Fare you well, then. Come, good sweet lady. Prithee, Virgilia, turn thy solemness out o' door, and go along with us. 121

Vir. No, at a word, madam; indeed, I must not. I wish you much mirth.

Val. Well, then, farewell.   [*Exeunt.*

[SCENE IV.]   *Before Corioli.*

Enter, with drum and colours, MARCIUS, TITUS LARTIUS, *Captains and* Soldiers. *To them a* MESSENGER.

Mar. Yonder comes news. A wager they have met.

Lart. My horse to yours, no.

Mar.   'Tis done.

Lart.   Agreed.

Mar. Say, has our general met the enemy?

Mess. They lie in view; but have not spoke as yet.

Lart. So, the good horse is mine.

Mar.   I'll buy him of you.

Lart. No, I'll nor sell nor give him; lend you him I will 6

For half a hundred years. Summon the town.

Mar. How far off lie these armies?

Mess.   Within this mile and half.

Mar. Then shall we hear their 'larum, and they ours.

Now, Mars, I prithee, make us quick in work, 10

That we with smoking swords may march from hence

To help our fielded friends! Come, blow thy blast.

They sound a parley. Enter two SENATORS *with others on the walls.*

Tullus Aufidius, is he within your walls?

1. Sen. No, nor a man that fears you less than he,

That's lesser than a little. [*Drum afar off.*] Hark! our drums 15

Are bringing forth our youth. We'll break our walls,

Rather than they shall pound us up. Our gates,

Which yet seem shut, we have but pinn'd with rushes;

They'll open of themselves. [*Alarum afar off.*] Hark you, far off!

---

56. **spot**: pattern.   65. **confirm'd**: resolute.   71. **mammock'd**: tore to pieces.   72. **on's**: of his.   74. **crack**: rascal.
95. **sensible**: sensitive.   117. **disease**: disturb.   122. **at a word**: absolutely.
Sc. iv, 4. **spoke**: engaged in fight.   14. **less**. Apparently a slip for *more*.   17. **pound**: impound, shut.

There is Aufidius; list, what work he makes   20
Amongst your cloven army.
Mar.   O, they are at it!
Lart. Their noise be our instruction. Ladders, ho!

Enter the army of the Volsces.

Mar. They fear us not, but issue forth their city.
Now put your shields before your hearts, and fight
With hearts more proof than shields. Advance,
     brave Titus!   25
They do disdain us much beyond our thoughts,
Which makes me sweat with wrath. Come on, my
     fellows!
He that retires, I'll take him for a Volsce,
And he shall feel mine edge.   [*Exit.*]

*Alarum. The Romans are beat back to their trenches.
Re-enter* MARCIUS, *cursing.*

Mar. All the contagion of the south light on you,
You shames of Rome! you herd of — Boils and
     plagues   31
Plaster you o'er, that you may be abhorr'd
Further than seen, and one infect another
Against the wind a mile! You souls of geese,
That bear the shapes of men, how have you run   35
From slaves that apes would beat! Pluto and hell!
All hurt behind! Backs red, and faces pale
With flight and agued fear! Mend and charge
     home,
Or, by the fires of heaven, I'll leave the foe   39
And make my wars on you. Look to't; come on!
If you'll stand fast, we'll beat them to their wives,
As they us to our trenches followed.

Another alarum. [The Volsces fly,] and MAR-
CIUS *follows them to the gates.*

So, now the gates are ope; now prove good seconds.
'Tis for the followers fortune widens them,
Not for the fliers. Mark me, and do the like.   45
                   [*Enters the gates.*
1. Sol. Fool-hardiness; not I.
2. Sol.   Nor I.
                [*Marcius is shut in.*
1. Sol. See, they have shut him in.
                [*Alarum continues.*
All.   To th' pot, I warrant him.

Re-enter TITUS LARTIUS.

Lart. What is become of Marcius?
All.   Slain, sir, doubtless.
1. Sol. Following the fliers at the very heels,
With them he enters; who, upon the sudden,   50
Clapp'd to their gates. He is himself alone,
To answer all the city.

Lart.   O noble fellow!
Who sensibly outdares his senseless sword
And, when it bows, stand'st up. Thou art left,
     Marcius;
A carbuncle entire, as big as thou art,   55
Were not so rich a jewel. Thou wast a soldier
Even to [Cato's] wish, not fierce and terrible
Only in strokes; but, with thy grim looks and
The thunder-like percussion of thy sounds,
Thou mad'st thine enemies shake, as if the world   60
Were feverous and did tremble.

Re-enter MARCIUS, *bleeding, assaulted by the enemy.*

1. Sol.   Look, sir.
Lart.   O, 'tis Marcius!
Let's fetch him off, or make remain alike.
         [*They fight, and all enter the city.*

[SCENE V. *Corioli. A street.*]

Enter certain ROMANS, *with spoils.*

1. Rom. This will I carry to Rome.
2. Rom. And I this.
3. Rom. A murrain on't! I took this for silver.
     [*Exeunt. Alarum continues still afar off.*

Enter MARCIUS *and* TITUS [LARTIUS] *with a
Trumpet.*

Mar. See here these movers that do prize their
     hours   5
At a crack'd drachma! Cushions, leaden spoons,
Irons of a doit, doublets that hangmen would
Bury with those that wore them, these base slaves,
Ere yet the fight be done, pack up. Down with
     them!
And hark, what noise the general makes! To him!
There is the man of my soul's hate, Aufidius,   11
Piercing our Romans; then, valiant Titus, take
Convenient numbers to make good the city;
Whilst I, with those that have the spirit, will haste
To help Cominius.
Lart.   Worthy sir, thou bleed'st.   15
Thy exercise hath been too violent for
A second course of fight.
Mar.   Sir, praise me not;
My work hath yet not warm'd me; fare you well.
The blood I drop is rather physical
Than dangerous to me. To Aufidius thus   20
I will appear, and fight.
Lart.   Now the fair goddess, Fortune,
Fall deep in love with thee; and her great charms
Misguide thy opposers' swords! Bold gentleman,
Prosperity be thy page!
Mar.   Thy friend no less

---

25. **proof:** stout.   30. **south:** south wind (pestilential).   38. **Mend:** reform your lines.   43. **seconds:** helpers.   47. **th'
pot:** i.e., destruction.   57. **[Cato's]** (Theobald). *Calves* F.   62. **make . . . alike:** stay to share his fate.
Sc. v, 5. **movers:** looters.   6. **drachma:** Greek coin.   7. **of a doit:** worth a doit (small coin).   19. **physical:** healthful.

Than those she placeth highest! So, farewell. 25
  Lart. Thou worthiest Marcius! [*Exit Marcius.*]
Go sound thy trumpet in the market-place;
Call thither all the officers o' th' town,
Where they shall know our mind. Away! [*Exeunt.*]

[SCENE VI. *Near the camp of Cominius.*]

Enter COMINIUS, *as it were in retire, with soldiers.*

  Com. Breathe you, my friends; well fought. We
    are come off
Like Romans, neither foolish in our stands
Nor cowardly in retire. Believe me, sirs,
We shall be charg'd again. Whiles we have struck,
By interims and conveying gusts we have heard 5
The charges of our friends. [Ye] Roman gods!
Lead their successes as we wish our own,
That both our powers, with smiling fronts en-
    count'ring,
May give you thankful sacrifice.

Enter a MESSENGER.

                                Thy news?
  Mess. The citizens of Corioli have issued 10
And given to Lartius and to Marcius battle.
I saw our party to their trenches driven,
And then I came away.
  Com.   Though thou speak'st truth,
Methinks thou speak'st not well. How long is't
    since?
  Mess. Above an hour, my lord. 15
  Com. 'Tis not a mile; briefly we heard their
    drums.
How couldst thou in a mile confound an hour
And bring thy news so late?
  Mess.   Spies of the Volsces
Held me in chase, that I was forc'd to wheel
Three or four miles about, else had I, sir, 20
Half an hour since brought my report.

Enter MARCIUS.

  Com.   Who's yonder,
That does appear as he were flay'd? O gods!
He has the stamp of Marcius; and I have
Before-time seen him thus.
  Mar.   Come I too late?
  Com. The shepherd knows not thunder from a
    tabor 25
More than I know the sound of Marcius' tongue
From every meaner man.
  Mar.   Come I too late?
  Com. Ay, if you come not in the blood of others,
But mantled in your own.
  Mar.   O, let me clip ye

In arms as sound as when I woo'd, in heart 30
As merry as when our nuptial day was done
And tapers burn'd to bedward!
  Com.   Flower of warriors,
How is't with Titus Lartius?
  Mar. As with a man busied about decrees:
Condemning some to death, and some to exile; 35
Ransoming him, or pitying, threat'ning th' other;
Holding Corioli in the name of Rome,
Even like a fawning greyhound in the leash,
To let him slip at will.
  Com.   Where is that slave
Which told me they had beat you to your trenches?
Where is he? Call him hither.
  Mar.   Let him alone; 41
He did inform the truth. But for our gentlemen, —
The common file — a plague! tribunes for them! —
The mouse ne'er shunn'd the cat as they did budge
From rascals worse than they.
  Com.   But how prevail'd you? 45
  Mar. Will the time serve to tell? I do not think.
Where is the enemy? Are you lords o' th' field?
If not, why cease you till you are so?
  Com.   Marcius,
We have at disadvantage fought, and did
Retire to win our purpose. 50
  Mar. How lies their battle? Know you on which
    side
They have plac'd their men of trust?
  Com.   As I guess, Marcius,
Their bands i' th' vaward are the [Antiates],
Of their best trust; o'er them Aufidius,
Their very heart of hope.
  Mar.   I do beseech you, 55
By all the battles wherein we have fought,
By th' blood we have shed together, by the vows
We have made to endure friends, that you directly
Set me against Aufidius and his Antiates;
And that you not delay the present, but, 60
Filling the air with swords advanc'd and darts,
We prove this very hour.
  Com.   Though I could wish
You were conducted to a gentle bath
And balms applied to you, yet dare I never
Deny your asking. Take your choice of those 65
That best can aid your action.
  Mar.   Those are they
That most are willing. If any such be here —
As it were sin to doubt — that love this painting
Wherein you see me smear'd; if any fear
[Lesser] his person than an ill report; 70
If any think brave death outweighs bad life,
And that his country's dearer than himself;
Let him alone, or so many so minded,

Sc. vi, 5. **By...gusts:** at intervals, by gusts of wind. 6. **[Ye]** (Hanmer). *The* F. 16. **briefly:** a short time ago. 17. **confound:** waste. 25. **tabor:** small drum. 29. **clip:** embrace. 53. **vaward:** vanguard. **[Antiates]** (Pope). *Antients* F. 60. **present:** i.e., affair. 62. **prove:** try out. 70. **[Lesser]** F₃: less. *Lessen* F₁. **person:** personal harm.

Wave thus, to express his disposition
And follow Marcius.   75
   [*They all shout and wave their swords,
   take him up in their arms, and cast up
   their caps.*
O, me alone, make you a sword of me?
If these shows be not outward, which of you
But is four Volsces?   None of you but is
Able to bear against the great Aufidius
A shield as hard as his.   A certain number,   80
Though thanks to all, must I select from all; the rest
Shall bear the business in some other fight,
As cause will be obey'd.   Please you to march;
And four shall quickly draw out my command,
Which men are best inclin'd.
 Com.   March on, my fellows!   85
Make good this ostentation, and you shall
Divide in all with us.   [*Exeunt.*

[SCENE VII.   *The gates of Corioli.*]

TITUS LARTIUS, *having set a guard upon Corioli,*
going with drum and trumpet toward Cominius and
Caius Marcius, enters with a LIEUTENANT, *other*
Soldiers, and a Scout.

 Lart. So, let the ports be guarded; keep your
  duties,
As I have set them down.   If I do send, dispatch
Those centuries to our aid; the rest will serve
For a short holding.   If we lose the field,
We cannot keep the town.
 Lieu.   Fear not our care, sir.
 Lart. Hence, and shut your gates upon 's.   6
Our guider, come; to th' Roman camp conduct us.
         [*Exeunt.*

[SCENE VIII.   *A field of battle.*]

Alarum as in battle.   Enter MARCIUS *and* AU-
  FIDIUS *at several doors.*

 Mar. I'll fight with none but thee, for I do hate
  thee
Worse than a promise-breaker.
 Auf.   We hate alike.
Not Afric owns a serpent I abhor
More than thy fame and envy.   Fix thy foot.
 Mar. Let the first budger die the other's slave,   5
And the gods doom him after!
 Auf.   If I fly, Marcius,
Holloa me like a hare.
 Mar.   Within these three hours, Tullus,
Alone I fought in your Corioli walls

And made what work I pleas'd.   'Tis not my blood
Wherein thou seest me mask'd; for thy revenge   10
Wrench up thy power to th' highest.
 Auf.   Wert thou the Hector
That was the whip of your bragg'd progeny,
Thou shouldst not scape me here.
   [*Here they fight, and certain Volsces come in*
   the aid of Aufidius.   Marcius fights till
   they be driven in breathless.
Officious, and not valiant, you have sham'd me
In your condemned seconds. [*Exeunt.*] 15

[SCENE IX.   *The Roman camp.*]

Flourish.   Alarum.   A retreat is sounded.   Enter,
 at one door, COMINIUS *with the* Romans; *at another*
 door, MARCIUS, *with his arm in a scarf.*

 Com. If I should tell thee o'er this thy day's work,
Thou'lt not believe thy deeds; but I'll report it
Where senators shall mingle tears with smiles,
Where great patricians shall attend and shrug,
I' th' end admire, where ladies shall be frighted   5
And, gladly quak'd, hear more; where the dull
  tribunes,
That with the fusty plebeians hate thine honours,
Shall say against their hearts, "We thank the gods
Our Rome hath such a soldier."
Yet cam'st thou to a morsel of this feast,   10
Having fully din'd before.

 Enter TITUS [LARTIUS], *with his power, from the*
   pursuit.

 Lart.   O General,
Here is the steed, we the caparison.
Hadst thou beheld —
 Mar.   Pray now, no more.   My mother,
Who has a charter to extol her blood,   14
When she does praise me grieves me.   I have
  done
As you have done, that's what I can; induc'd
As you have been, that's for my country.
He that has but effected his good will
Hath overta'en mine act.
 Com.   You shall not be   19
The grave of your deserving; Rome must know
The value of her own.   'Twere a concealment
Worse than a theft, no less than a traducement,
To hide your doings and to silence that
Which, to the spire and top of praises vouch'd,
Would seem but modest; therefore, I beseech you —
In sign of what you are, not to reward   26
What you have done — before our army hear me.

---

83. **cause:** occasion.
Sc. vii, 1. **ports:** gates. 3. **centuries:** companies.
Sc. viii, 12. **of ... progeny:** possessed by your boasted ancestry (the Trojans).   15. **seconds:** support.
 Sc. ix, 4. **attend and shrug:** listen incredulously.   5. **admire:** be amazed.   6. **quak'd:** trembling.   7. **fusty:** mouldy.
12. **caparison:** trappings.   22. **traducement:** calumny.

Mar. I have some wounds upon me, and they
    smart
To hear themselves rememb'red.
    Com.   Should they not,
Well might they fester 'gainst ingratitude,   30
And tent themselves with death. Of all the horses,
Whereof we have ta'en good and good store, of all
The treasure in this field achiev'd and city,
We render you the tenth, to be ta'en forth,
Before the common distribution, at   35
Your only choice.
    Mar.   I thank you, General;
But cannot make my heart consent to take
A bribe to pay my sword. I do refuse it,
And stand upon my common part with those
That have beheld the doing.   40
        [*A long flourish. They all cry, "Marcius!*
        Marcius!" *cast up their caps and lances.*
        Cominius and Lartius stand bare.
May these same instruments, which you profane,
Never sound more! When drums and trumpets
    shall
I' th' field prove flatterers, let courts and cities be
Made all of false-fac'd soothing!
When steel grows soft as the parasite's silk,   45
Let him be made [a coverture] for th' wars!
No more, I say! For that I have not wash'd
My nose that bled, or foil'd some debile wretch, —
Which, without note, here's many else have done, —
You [shout] me forth   50
In acclamations hyperbolical,
As if I lov'd my little should be dieted
In praises sauc'd with lies.
    Com.   Too modest are you;
More cruel to your good report than grateful
To us that give you truly. By your patience,   55
If 'gainst yourself you be incens'd, we'll put you,
Like one that means his proper harm, in manacles,
Then reason safely with you. Therefore be it
    known,
As to us, to all the world, that Caius Marcius
Wears this war's garland; in token of the which,   60
My noble steed, known to the camp, I give him
With all his trim belonging; and from this time,
For what he did before Corioli, call him,
With all th' applause and clamour of the host,
[Caius Marcius] Coriolanus! Bear   65
Th' addition nobly ever!
        [*Flourish. Trumpets sound, and drums.*
    All. [Caius Marcius] Coriolanus!
    Cor. I will go wash;

And when my face is fair, you shall perceive
Whether I blush or no; howbeit, I thank you.   70
I mean to stride your steed, and at all times
To undercrest your good addition
To th' fairness of my power.
    Com.   So, to our tent;
Where, ere we do repose us, we will write
To Rome of our success. You, Titus Lartius,   75
Must to Corioli back, send us to Rome
The best. with whom we may articulate
For their own good and ours.
    Lart.   I shall, my lord.
    Cor. The gods begin to mock me. I, that now
Refus'd most princely gifts, am bound to beg   80
Of my Lord General.
    Com.   Take't; 'tis yours. What is't?
    Cor. I sometime lay here in Corioli
At a poor man's house; he us'd me kindly.
He cried to me, — I saw him prisoner, —
But then Aufidius was within my view,   85
And wrath o'erwhelm'd my pity. I request you
To give my poor host freedom.
    Com.   O well begg'd!
Were he the butcher of my son, he should
Be free as is the wind. Deliver him, Titus.
    Lart. Marcius, his name?
    Cor.   By Jupiter! forgot.
I am weary; yea, my memory is tir'd.   91
Have we no wine here?
    Com.   Go we to our tent.
The blood upon your visage dries; 'tis time
It should be look'd to. Come.   [*Exeunt.*

[Scene X. *The camp of the Volsces.*]

A flourish. Cornets. Enter Tullus Aufidius,
    bloody, with two or three Soldiers.

    Auf. The town is ta'en!
    [*1.*] *Sol.* 'Twill be deliver'd back on good condi-
    tion.
    Auf. Condition!
I would I were a Roman; for I cannot,
Being a Volsce, be that I am. Condition!   5
What good condition can a treaty find
I' th' part that is at mercy? Five times, Marcius,
I have fought with thee; so often hast thou beat me,
And wouldst do so, I think, should we encounter
As often as we eat. By th' elements,   10
If e'er again I meet him beard to beard,
He's mine, or I am his. Mine emulation

---

31. **tent:** cure. 32. **good store:** plenty. 44. **soothing:** flattery. 44–51. Some edd. rearrange, beginning the lines with *Made, Soft, A, For, Or, Here's, In.* 46. **him:** perhaps *it*, but the passage is probably corrupt. [a coverture] (Tyrwhitt). *an Overture* F. 48. **foil'd:** defeated. **debile:** weak. 55. **give:** report. 57. **proper:** own. 65, 67. [Caius Marcius] (Rowe). *Marcus Caius* F (also II.i.181). 72. **undercrest:** wear as a crest. **addition:** title. 73. **fairness . . . power:** best of my ability. 77. **articulate:** discuss terms.
Sc. x, 2, etc. [*1.*] *Sol.* (Capell). *Sol.* F. **condition:** terms. 7. **part . . . mercy:** conquered side. 12. **emulation:** rivalry.

Hath not that honour in't it had; for where
I thought to crush him in an equal force,
True sword to sword, I'll potch at him some way; 15
Or wrath or craft may get him.

[1.] *Sol.* He's the devil.

Auf. Bolder, though not so subtle. My valour's
  poison'd
With only suff'ring stain by him; for him
Shall fly out of itself. Nor sleep nor sanctuary,
Being naked, sick, nor fane nor Capitol, 20
The prayers of priests nor times of sacrifice,
Embargements all of fury, shall lift up
Their rotten privilege and custom 'gainst
My hate to Marcius. Where I find him, were
  it
At home, upon my brother's guard, even there, 25
Against the hospitable canon, would I
Wash my fierce hand in 's heart. Go you to th'
  city;
Learn how 'tis held, and what they are that must
Be hostages for Rome.

[1.] *Sol.* Will not you go?

Auf. I am attended at the cypress grove. I
  pray you — 30
'Tis south the city mills — bring me word thither
How the world goes, that to the pace of it
I may spur on my journey.

[1.] *Sol.* I shall, sir.

                               [*Exeunt.*]

ACT II

[SCENE I. *Rome. A public place.*]

Enter MENENIUS, *with the two Tribunes of the people,*
  SICINIUS *and* BRUTUS.

Men. The augurer tells me we shall have news
to-night.

Bru. Good or bad?

Men. Not according to the prayer of the people,
for they love not Marcius. 5

Sic. Nature teaches beasts to know their friends.

Men. Pray you, who does the wolf love?

Sic. The lamb.

Men. Ay, to devour him; as the hungry plebeians
would the noble Marcius. 11

Bru. He's a lamb indeed, that baes like a
bear.

Men. He's a bear indeed, that lives like a
lamb. You two are old men: tell me one thing that
I shall ask you. 16

Both. Well, sir.

Men. In what enormity is Marcius poor in, that
you two have not in abundance?

Bru. He's poor in no one fault, but stor'd with
all. 21

Sic. Especially in pride.

Bru. And topping all others in boasting.

Men. This is strange now. Do you two know
how you are censured here in the city, I mean of
us o' th' right-hand file? Do you? 26

Both. Why, how are we censur'd?

Men. Because you talk of pride now, — will you
not be angry?

Both. Well, well, sir, well. 30

Men. Why, 'tis no great matter; for a very little
thief of occasion will rob you of a great deal of
patience. Give your dispositions the reins and be
angry at your pleasures; at the least, if you take it
as a pleasure to you in being so. You blame
Marcius for being proud? 36

Bru. We do it not alone, sir.

Men. I know you can do very little alone, for
your helps are many, or else your actions would
grow wondrous single; your abilities are too 40
infant-like for doing much alone. You talk of pride:
O that you could turn your eyes toward the napes
of your necks and make but an interior survey of
your good selves! O that you could!

Both. What then, sir? 45

Men. Why, then you should discover a brace of
unmeriting, proud, violent, testy magistrates, alias
fools, as any in Rome.

Sic. Menenius, you are known well enough
too. 50

Men. I am known to be a humorous patrician,
and one that loves a cup of hot wine with not a drop
of allaying Tiber in't; said to be something imperfect in favouring the first complaint; hasty and
tinder-like upon too trivial motion; one that con- 55
verses more with the buttock of the night than with
the forehead of the morning. What I think, I utter,
and spend my malice in my breath. Meeting two
such wealsmen as you are — I cannot call you
Lycurguses — if the drink you give me touch 60
my palate adversely, I make a crooked face at it.
I [can't] say your worships have deliver'd the matter
well, when I find the ass in compound with the major
part of your syllables; and though I must be content
to bear with those that say you are reverend 65
grave men, yet they lie deadly that tell you have
good faces. If you see this in the map of my
microcosm, follows it that I am known well enough

---

15. **potch:** stab. 19. **fly out of itself:** change its nature. 20. **fane:** temple. 22. **Embargements:** impediments. 25. **up,
on:** under. 26. **hospitable canon:** law of hospitality. 30. **attended:** awaited.

Act II, sc. i, 25. **censured:** estimated. 26. **right-hand file:** upper class. 40. **single:** feeble. 51. **humorous:** whimsical.
53. **allaying Tiber:** i.e., diluting water. 54. **in . . . complaint:** i.e., without hearing the other side. 55. **tinder-like:** inflam-
mable. 55. **motion:** cause. 59. **wealsmen:** statesmen. 60. **Lycurguses.** Lycurgus was a famous Spartan law-giver.
62. **[can't]** (Theobald). *çan* F. 67-68. **map . . . microcosm:** my face.

too? What harm can your [bisson] conspectuities glean out of this character, if I be known well enough too? 72

Bru. Come, sir, come, we know you well enough.

Men. You know neither me, yourselves, nor anything. You are ambitious for poor knaves' caps and legs. You wear out a good wholesome forenoon in hearing a cause between an orange-wife and a faucet-seller and then rejourn the controversy of three pence to a second day of audience. When 80 you are hearing a matter between party and party, if you chance to be pinch'd with the colic, you make faces like mummers, set up the bloody flag against all patience, and, in roaring for a chamber-pot, dismiss the controversy bleeding, the more entan- 85 gled by your hearing. All the peace you make in their cause is calling both the parties knaves. You are a pair of strange ones. 89

Bru. Come, come, you are well understood to be a perfecter giber for the table than a necessary bencher in the Capitol.

Men. Our very priests must become mockers if they shall encounter such ridiculous subjects as 94 you are. When you speak best unto the purpose, it is not worth the wagging of your beards; and your beards deserve not so honourable a grave as to stuff a botcher's cushion, or to be entomb'd in an ass's pack-saddle. Yet you must be saying Marcius is proud; who, in a cheap estimation, is 100 worth all your predecessors since Deucalion, though peradventure some of the best of 'em were hereditary hangmen. God-den to your worships! More of your conversation would infect my brain, being the herdsmen of the beastly plebeians. I will be bold to take my leave of you. 105

[*Brutus and Sicinius go aside.*]

Enter VOLUMNIA, VIRGILIA, *and* VALERIA.

How now, my as fair as noble ladies — and the moon, were she earthly, no nobler — whither do you follow your eyes so fast? 109

Vol. Honourable Menenius, my boy Marcius approaches. For the love of Juno, let's go.

Men. Ha! Marcius coming home?

Vol. Ay, worthy Menenius; and with most prosperous approbation.

Men. Take my cap, Jupiter, [*tosses it up*] and I thank thee. Hoo! Marcius coming home! 116

2 Ladies. Nay, 'tis true.

Vol. Look, here's a letter from him; the state hath another, his wife another, and, I think, there's one at home for you. 120

Men. I will make my very house reel to-night. A letter for me!

Vir. Yes, certain, there's a letter for you; I saw 't. 124

Men. A letter for me! it gives me an estate of seven years' health, in which time I will make a lip at the physician. The most sovereign prescription in Galen is but empiricutic and, to this preservative, of no better report than a horse-drench. Is he not wounded? He was wont to come home wounded.

Vir. O, no, no, no. 132

Vol. O, he is wounded; I thank the gods for't.

Men. So do I too, if it be not too much. Brings 'a victory in his pocket? The wounds become him. 136

Vol. On 's brows. Menenius, he comes the third time home with the oaken garland.

Men. Has he disciplin'd Aufidius soundly?

Vol. Titus Lartius writes they fought together, but Aufidius got off. 141

Men. And 'twas time for him too, I'll warrant him that. An he had stay'd by him, I would not have been so fidius'd for all the chests in Corioli, and the gold that's in them. Is the Senate possess'd of this? 146

Vol. Good ladies, let's go. — Yes, yes, yes; the Senate has letters from the General, wherein he gives my son the whole name of the war. He hath in this action outdone his former deeds doubly. 151

Val. In troth, there's wondrous things spoke of him.

Men. Wondrous! ay, I warrant you, and not without his true purchasing. 155

Vir. The gods grant them true!

Vol. True! pow, wow.

Men. True! I'll be sworn they are true. Where is he wounded? [*To the Tribunes.*] God save your good worships! Marcius is coming home; he has more cause to be proud. — Where is he wounded? 162

Vol. I' th' shoulder and i' th' left arm. There will be large cicatrices to show the people, when he shall stand for his place. He received in the repulse of Tarquin seven hurts i' th' body. 166

Men. One i' th' neck, and two i' th' thigh, — there's nine that I know.

Vol. He had, before this last expedition, twenty-five wounds upon him. 170

Men. Now it's twenty-seven; every gash was an enemy's grave. Hark! the trumpets.

[*A shout and flourish.*]

Vol. These are the ushers of Marcius; before him

70. [bisson] (Theobald): blind. *beesome* F. conspectuities: vision. 75–76. caps and legs: bowings and scrapings. 79. rejourn: adjourn. 83. mummers: masked players. bloody flag: banner of war. 92. bencher: senator. 98. botcher: mender of old clothes. 101. Deucalion: the classical Noah. 103. God-den: good evening. 114. most...approbation: greatest triumph. 126. lip: grimace. 128. Galen: famous Greek physician (2d cent. A.D.). empiricutic: quackish. 144. fidius'd: in Aufidius's place. 149. name: honor. 164. cicatrices: scars.

he carries noise, and behind him he leaves tears. 176
Death, that dark spirit, in 's nervy arm doth lie,
Which, being advanc'd, declines, and then men die.

A sennet. Trumpets sound. Enter COMINIUS *the
General, and* TITUS LARTIUS; *between them,* CORIO-
LANUS, *crown'd with an oaken garland; with Cap-
tains and Soldiers, and a* HERALD.

Her. Know, Rome, that all alone Marcius did
fight
Within Corioli gates; where he hath won, 180
With fame, a name to [Caius Marcius]; these
In honour follows Coriolanus.
Welcome to Rome, renowned Coriolanus!
[*Flourish.*
All. Welcome to Rome, renowned Coriolanus!
Cor. No more of this; it does offend my heart.
Pray now, no more.
Com.   Look, sir, your mother!
Cor.   O, 186
You have, I know, petition'd all the gods
For my prosperity!   [*Kneels.*
Vol.   Nay, my good soldier, up;
My gentle Marcius, worthy Caius, and
By deed-achieving honour newly nam'd, — 190
What is it? — Coriolanus must I call thee? —
But, O, thy wife!
Cor.   My gracious silence, hail!
Wouldst thou have laugh'd had I come coffin'd
home,
That weep'st to see me triumph? Ah, my dear,
Such eyes the widows in Corioli wear, 195
And mothers that lack sons.
Men.   Now, the gods crown thee!
[*Cor.*] And live you yet? [*To Valeria.*] O my
sweet lady, pardon.
Vol. I know not where to turn. O, welcome
home;
And welcome, General; and you're welcome all.
Men. A hundred thousand welcomes! I could
weep 200
And I could laugh; I am light and heavy. Welcome!
A curse begin at very root on 's heart,
That is not glad to see thee! You are three
That Rome should dote on; yet, by the faith of men,
We have some old crab-trees here at home that will
not 205
Be grafted to your relish. Yet welcome, warriors;
We call a nettle but a nettle and
The faults of fools but folly.
Com.   Ever right.

Cor. Menenius ever, ever.
Her. Give way there, and go on!
Cor. [*To Volumnia and Virgilia.*] Your hand,
and yours. 210
Ere in our own house I do shade my head,
The good patricians must be visited;
From whom I have receiv'd not only greetings,
But with them change of honours.
Vol.   I have liv'd
To see inherited my very wishes 215
And the buildings of my fancy; only
There's one thing wanting, which I doubt not but
Our Rome will cast upon thee.
Cor.   Know, good mother,
I had rather be their servant in my way
Than sway with them in theirs.
Com.   On, to the Capitol!
[*Flourish. Cornets. Exeunt in state, as
before. Brutus and Sicinius [come for-
ward].*
Bru. All tongues speak of him, and the bleared
sights 221
Are spectacled to see him. Your prattling nurse
Into a rapture lets her baby cry
While she chats him; the kitchen Malkin pins
Her richest lockram 'bout her reechy neck, 225
Clamb'ring the walls to eye him; stalls, bulks,
windows,
Are smother'd up, leads fill'd, and ridges hors'd
With variable complexions, all agreeing
In earnestness to see him. Seld-shown flamens
Do press among the popular throngs and puff 230
To win a vulgar station; our veil'd dames
Commit the war of white and damask in
Their nicely-gawded cheeks to th' wanton spoil
Of Phœbus' burning kisses; — such a pother
As if that whatsoever god who leads him 235
Were slily crept into his human powers
And gave him graceful posture.
Sic.   On the sudden,
I warrant him consul.
Bru.   Then our office may,
During his power, go sleep.
Sic. He cannot temp'rately transport his honours
From where he should begin and end, but will 241
Lose those he hath won.
Bru.   In that there's comfort.
Sic.   Doubt not
The commoners, for whom we stand, but they
Upon their ancient malice will forget 244
With the least cause these his new honours, which

177. **nervy:** sinewy. 178. **advanc'd:** raised. **declines:** descends. 179. S.D. *sennet:* trumpet signal. 197. [*Cor.*] *Com.* F. 201. **light and heavy:** merry and sad. 214. **change of honours:** fresh honors. 215. **inherited:** realized. 220. **sway:** rule. 223. **rapture:** fit. 224. **chats:** chats about. **Malkin:** slattern. 225. **lockram:** linen. **reechy:** filthy. 226. **bulks:** stalls. 227. **leads:** leaded roofs. **hors'd:** bestridden. 228. **variable complexions:** all sorts of people. 229. **flamens:** priests. 230. **popular:** vulgar. 233. **nicely-gawded:** daintily decorated. 234. **Phœbus'...kisses:** the blazing sun. 245. **which:** which cause.

That he will give them make I as little question
As he is proud to do't.
   Bru.   I heard him swear,
Were he to stand for consul, never would he
Appear i' th' market-place, nor on him put
The napless vesture of humility,   250
Nor, showing, as the manner is, his wounds
To th' people, beg their stinking breaths.
   Sic.   'Tis right.
   Bru. It was his word. O, he would miss it rather
Than carry it but by the suit of the gentry to him
And the desire of the nobles.
   Sic.   I wish no better 255
Than have him hold that purpose and to put it
In execution.
   Bru.   'Tis most like he will.
   Sic. It shall be to him then as our good wills,
A sure destruction.
   Bru.   So it must fall out
To him or our authorities for an end.   260
We must suggest the people in what hatred
He still hath held them; that to 's power he would
Have made them mules, silenc'd their pleaders, and
Dispropertied their freedoms, holding them,
In human action and capacity,   265
Of no more soul nor fitness for the world
Than camels in [the] war, who have their provand
Only for bearing burdens, and sore blows
For sinking under them.
   Sic.   This, as you say, suggested
At some time when his soaring insolence   270
Shall [touch] the people — which time shall not
    want,
If he be put upon 't; and that's as easy
As to set dogs on sheep — will be his fire
To kindle their dry stubble; and their blaze
Shall darken him for ever.

Enter a MESSENGER.

   Bru.   What's the matter?
   Mess. You are sent for to the Capitol. 'Tis
    thought   276
That Marcius shall be consul.
I have seen the dumb men throng to see him, and
The blind to hear him speak. Matrons flung gloves,
Ladies and maids their scarfs and handkerchers 280
Upon him as he pass'd; the nobles bended,
As to Jove's statue, and the commons made
A shower and thunder with their caps and shouts.
I never saw the like.
   Bru.   Let's to the Capitol;
And carry with us ears and eyes for th' time,

But hearts for the event.
   Sic.   Have with you. 286
                       [*Exeunt.*

[SCENE II. *The same.*] *The Capitol.*

Enter two OFFICERS, *to lay cushions.*

   1. Off. Come, come, they are almost here. How
many stand for consulships?
   2. Off. Three, they say; but 'tis thought of every
one Coriolanus will carry it.   4
   1. Off. That's a brave fellow; but he's vengeance
proud, and loves not the common people.
   2. Off. Faith, there hath been many great men
that have flatter'd the people, who ne'er loved
them; and there be many that they have loved, 10
they know not wherefore; so that, if they love they
know not why, they hate upon no better a ground.
Therefore, for Coriolanus neither to care whether
they love or hate him manifests the true knowledge
he has in their disposition, and out of his noble carelessness lets them plainly see 't.   17
   1. Off. If he did not care whether he had their
love or no, he waved indifferently 'twixt doing them
neither good nor harm; but he seeks their hate with
greater devotion than they can render it him, 21
and leaves nothing undone that may fully discover
him their opposite. Now, to seem to affect the
malice and displeasure of the people is as bad as
that which he dislikes, to flatter them for their love.
   2. Off. He hath deserved worthily of his country;
and his ascent is not by such easy degrees as those
who, having been supple and courteous to the
people, bonneted, without any further deed to have
them at all into their estimation and report. 31
But he hath so planted his honours in their eyes
and his actions in their hearts that for their tongues
to be silent and not confess so much were a kind
of ingrateful injury; to report otherwise were a 35
malice that, giving itself the lie, would pluck reproof
and rebuke from every ear that heard it.
   1. Off. No more of him; he's a worthy man.
Make way, they are coming.   40

A sennet. Enter, with Lictors before them, COMINIUS
the consul, MENENIUS, CORIOLANUS, SENATORS,
SICINIUS *and* BRUTUS. *The Senators take their
places; the Tribunes take their places by themselves.
Coriolanus stands.*

   Men. Having determin'd of the Volsces and
To send for Titus Lartius, it remains,
As the main point of this our after-meeting,

---

250. **napless:** threadbare. 258. **as...wills:** as we desire. 260. **for an end:** ultimately. 262. **still:** ever. 264. **Dis-propertied:** robbed them of. 267. **[the]** (Hanmer). *their* F. **provand:** provender. 271. **[touch]** (Hanmer). *teach* F. **want:** be lacking. 286. **event:** outcome.
   Sc. ii, 5. **vengeance:** desperately. 8. **who:** i.e., the people. 19. **waved:** wavered. 22. **discover:** show. 23. **opposite:** adversary. **affect:** desire. 30. **bonneted:** doffed their caps,

To gratify his noble service that
Hath thus stood for his country; therefore, please
    you,   45
Most reverend and grave elders, to desire
The present consul and last general
In our well-found successes, to report
A little of that worthy work perform'd
By [Caius Marcius] Coriolanus, whom   50
We met here both to thank and to remember
With honours like himself.   [*Coriolanus sits.*]
   1. Sen.   Speak, good Cominius:
Leave nothing out for length, and make us think
Rather our state's defective for requital
Than we to stretch it out.   [*To the Tribunes.*]
        Masters o' th' people,   55
We do request your kindest ears, and after,
Your loving motion toward the common body
To yield what passes here.
   Sic.   We are convented
Upon a pleasing treaty, and have hearts
Inclinable to honour and advance   60
The theme of our assembly.
   Bru.   Which the rather
We shall be blest to do, if he remember
A kinder value of the people than
He hath hereto priz'd them at.
   Men.   That's off, that's off;
I would you rather had been silent. Please you   65
To hear Cominius speak?
   Bru.   Most willingly;
But yet my caution was more pertinent
Than the rebuke you give it.
   Men.   He loves your people;
But tie him not to be their bedfellow.
Worthy Cominius, speak.   (*Coriolanus rises and
    offers to go away.*) Nay, keep your place.   70
   [*1.*] *Sen.* Sit, Coriolanus; never shame to hear
What you have nobly done.
   Cor.   Your honours' pardon;
I had rather have my wounds to heal again
Than hear say how I got them.
   Bru.   Sir, I hope
My words disbench'd you not.
   Cor.   No, sir; yet oft,   75
When blows have made me stay, I fled from words.
You sooth'd not, therefore hurt not; but your people,
I love them as they weigh.
   Men.   Pray now, sit down.
   Cor. I had rather have one scratch my head i'
    th' sun

When the alarum were struck, than idly sit   80
To hear my nothings monster'd.   [*Exit.*
   Men.   Masters of the people,
Your multiplying spawn how can he flatter —
That's thousand to one good one — when you now
    see
He had rather venture all his limbs for honour
Than [one on 's] ears to hear it? Proceed, Co-
    minius.   85
   Com. I shall lack voice; the deeds of Coriolanus
Should not be utter'd feebly. It is held
That valour is the chiefest virtue and
Most dignifies the haver; if it be,
The man I speak of cannot in the world   90
Be singly counterpois'd. At sixteen years,
When Tarquin made a head for Rome, he fought
Beyond the mark of others. Our then dictator,
Whom with all praise I point at, saw him fight,
When with his Amazonian [chin] he drove   95
The bristled lips before him. He bestrid
An o'er-press'd Roman, and i' th' consul's view
Slew three opposers. Tarquin's self he met,
And struck him on his knee. In that day's feats,
When he might act the woman in the scene,   100
He prov'd best man i' th' field, and for his meed
Was brow-bound with the oak. His pupil age
Man-ent'red thus, he waxed like a sea,
And in the brunt of seventeen battles since
He lurch'd all swords of the garland. For this
    last,   105
Before and in Corioli, let me say,
I cannot speak him home. He stopp'd the fliers,
And by his rare example made the coward
Turn terror into sport; as weeds before
A vessel under sail, so men obey'd   110
And fell below his stem. His sword, death's stamp,
Where it did mark, it took; from face to foot
He was a thing of blood, whose every motion
Was tim'd with dying cries. Alone he ent'red
The mortal gate of th' city, which he painted   115
With shunless destiny; aidless came off,
And with a sudden reinforcement struck
Corioli like a planet; now all's his.
When, by and by, the din of war 'gan pierce
His ready sense, then straight his doubled spirit
Re-quick'ned what in flesh was fatigate,   121
And to the battle came he, where he did
Run reeking o'er the lives of men, as if
'Twere a perpetual spoil; and till we call'd
Both field and city ours, he never stood   125

---

44. **gratify:** reward.   47. **last:** late.   52. **like himself:** appropriate.   54–55. **Rather ... out:** our state lacks means to reward him rather than we willingness to stretch those means.   58. **yield:** report.   **convented:** convened.   59. **treaty:** proposal.   62. **blest:** most happy.   64. **off:** amiss.   71. [*1.*] (Rowe). Om. F.   77. **sooth'd:** flattered.   78. **weigh:** are worthy.   85. [**one on 's**] F$_3$: one of his. *on ones* F$_1$.   91. **singly counterpois'd:** equalled by any one.   92. **made ... for:** raised a force to attack.   95. **Amazonian:** i.e., beardless. [**chin**] F$_3$. *Shinne* F$_1$.   99. **on:** to.   100. **in the scene:** on the stage; alluding to the playing of female parts by boys.   105. **lurch'd:** robbed.   107. **speak him home:** praise him duly. 116. **shunless destiny:** the blood of the unavoidably doomed.   118. **planet.** A reference to the supposed malign influence of planets.   121. **fatigate:** fatigued.   124. **spoil:** slaughter.

To ease his breast with panting.

Men.   Worthy man!

[*1.*] *Sen.* He cannot but with measure fit the
    honours
Which we devise him.

Com.   Our spoils he kick'd at,
And look'd upon things precious as they were
The common muck of the world. He covets less 130
Than misery itself would give, rewards
His deeds with doing them, and is content
To spend the time to end it.

Men.   He's right noble.
Let him be call'd for.

[*1.*] *Sen.*   Call Coriolanus.

Off. He doth appear.   135

Re-enter CORIOLANUS.

Men. The Senate, Coriolanus, are well pleas'd
To make thee consul.

Cor.   I do owe them still
My life and services.

Men.   It then remains
That you do speak to the people.

Cor.   I do beseech you,
Let me o'erleap that custom; for I cannot   140
Put on the gown, stand naked and entreat them
For my wounds' sake to give their suffrage. Please
    you
That I may pass this doing.

Sic.   Sir, the people
Must have their voices; neither will they bate
One jot of ceremony.

Men.   Put them not to't.   145
Pray you, go fit you to the custom and
Take to you, as your predecessors have,
Your honour with your form.

Cor.   It is a part
That I shall blush in acting, and might well
Be taken from the people.

Bru.   Mark you that?   150

Cor. To brag unto them, "Thus I did, and thus";
Show them th' unaching scars which I should
    hide,
As if I had receiv'd them for the hire
Of their breath only!

Men.   Do not stand upon 't.   154
We recommend to you, tribunes of the people,
Our purpose to them; and to our noble consul
Wish we all joy and honour.

Senators. To Coriolanus come all joy and honour!

    [*Flourish of cornets. Exeunt all but Sicinius
       and Brutus.*

Bru. You see how he intends to use the people.

Sic. May they perceive 's intent! He will require
    them   160
As if he did contemn what he requested
Should be in them to give.

Bru.   Come, we'll inform them
Of our proceedings here. On th' market-place,
I know, they do attend us.

                                   [*Exeunt.*

[SCENE III.   *The same.   The Forum.*]

Enter seven or eight CITIZENS.

1. Cit. Once if he do require our voices, we ought
not to deny him.

2. Cit. We may, sir, if we will.

3. Cit. We have power in ourselves to do it, but
it is a power that we have no power to do; for   5
if he show us his wounds and tell us his deeds, we
are to put our tongues into those wounds and speak
for them; so, if he tell us his noble deeds, we must
also tell him our noble acceptance of them. Ingratitude is monstrous, and for the multitude to   10
be ingrateful were to make a monster of the multitude; of the which we being members, should bring
ourselves to be monstrous members.   14

1. Cit. And to make us no better thought of, a
little help will serve; for once we stood up about
the corn, he himself stuck not to call us the many-
headed multitude.   18

3. Cit. We have been called so of many; not that
our heads are some brown, some black, some auburn,
some bald, but that our wits are so diversely colour'd;
and truly I think if all our wits were to issue out
of one skull, they would fly east, west, north, south,
and their consent of one direct way should be at
once to all the points o' th' compass.   26

2. Cit. Think you so? Which way do you judge
my wit would fly?

3. Cit. Nay, your wit will not so soon out as
another man's will, 'tis strongly wedg'd up in a
block-head; but if it were at liberty, 'twould, sure,
southward.   32

2. Cit. Why that way?

3. Cit. To lose itself in a fog, where being three
parts melted away with rotten dews, the fourth
would return for conscience' sake to help to get
thee a wife.

2. Cit. You are never without your tricks; you
may, you may.   39

3. Cit. Are you all resolv'd to give your voices?
But that's no matter, the greater part carries it.
I say, if he would incline to the people, there was
never a worthier man.

127, 134. [*1.*] (Rowe). Om. F.   127. **with measure:** becomingly.   133. **to end it:** to pass the time.   143. **pass:** omit.   144. **voices:** votes.   148. **your form:** the usual formality.   154. **breath:** i.e., votes. **Do ... upon't:** don't insist. 155. **recommend:** entrust.   160. **require:** solicit.
    Sc. iii, 17. **stuck:** hesitated.   25. **consent of:** agreement about.   42. **incline to:** favor.

Enter CORIOLANUS *in a gown of humility, with* MENENIUS.

Here he comes, and in the gown of humility; mark
his behaviour. We are not to stay all together,   45
but to come by him where he stands, by ones, by
twos, and by threes. He's to make his requests by
particulars, wherein every one of us has a single
honour, in giving him our own voices with our own
tongues; therefore follow me, and I'll direct you how
you shall go by him.   52
   All. Content, content.   [*Exeunt citizens.*]
   Men. O sir, you are not right. Have you not
known
The worthiest men have done 't?
   Cor.   What must I say?
"I pray, sir," — Plague upon 't! I cannot bring   56
My tongue to such a pace, — "look, sir, my wounds!
I got them in my country's service, when
Some certain of your brethren roar'd and ran
From the noise of our own drums."
   Men.   O me, the gods!
You must not speak of that. You must desire them 61
To think upon you.
   Cor.   Think upon me! Hang 'em!
I would they would forget me, like the virtues
Which our divines lose by 'em.
   Men.   You'll mar all.
I'll leave you. Pray you, speak to 'em, I pray you,
In wholesome manner.   [*Exit.* 66

Re-enter three of the CITIZENS.

   Cor.   Bid them wash their faces
And keep their teeth clean. So, here comes a brace.—
You know the cause, sir, of my standing here.
   3. Cit. We do, sir; tell us what hath brought you
to 't.   70
   Cor. Mine own desert.
   2. Cit. Your own desert!
   Cor. Ay, [not] mine own desire.
   3. Cit. How not your own desire?
   Cor. No, sir, 'twas never my desire yet to trouble
the poor with begging.   76
   3. Cit. You must think, if we give you anything,
we hope to gain by you.
   Cor. Well then, I pray, your price o' th' consul
ship?   80
   1. Cit. The price is to ask it kindly.
   Cor. Kindly, sir, I pray, let me ha't. I have
wounds to show you, which shall be yours in private.
Your good voice, sir; what say you?
   2. Cit. You shall ha' it, worthy sir.   85
   Cor. A match, sir. There's in all two worthy
voices begg'd. I have your alms; adieu.

   3. Cit. But this is something odd.
   2. Cit. An't were to give again, — but 'tis no
matter.   [*Exeunt* [*the three Citizens*].   90

Re-enter two other CITIZENS.

   Cor. Pray you now, if it may stand with the tune
of your voices that I may be consul, I have here the
customary gown.
   [*4.*] *Cit.* You have deserved nobly of your country, and you have not deserved nobly.   95
   Cor. Your enigma?
   [*4.*] *Cit.* You have been a scourge to her enemies,
you have been a rod to her friends; you have not
indeed loved the common people.   99
   Cor. You should account me the more virtuous
that I have not been common in my love. I will,
sir, flatter my sworn brother, the people, to earn a
dearer estimation of them; 'tis a condition they
account gentle. And since the wisdom of their
choice is rather to have my hat than my heart,   105
I will practise the insinuating nod and be off to
them most counterfeitly; that is, sir, I will counterfeit the bewitchment of some popular man and give
it bountiful to the desirers. Therefore, beseech you,
I may be consul.   110
   [*5.*] *Cit.* We hope to find you our friend; and
therefore give you our voices heartily.
   [*4.*] *Cit.* You have received many wounds for
your country.   114
   Cor. I will not seal your knowledge with showing
them. I will make much of your voices, and so
trouble you no further.
   Both Cit. The gods give you joy, sir, heartily!
                                          [*Exeunt.*]

   Cor. Most sweet voices!
Better it is to die, better to starve,   120
Than crave the hire which first we do deserve.
Why in this [woolless toge] should I stand here
To beg of Hob and Dick, that [do] appear,
Their needless vouches? Custom calls me to't.
What custom wills, in all things should we do't,
The dust on antique time would lie unswept,   126
And mountainous error be too highly heapt
For truth to o'er-peer. Rather than fool it so,
Let the high office and the honour go
To one that would do thus. — I am half through; 130
The one part suffer'd, th' other will I do.

Re-enter three CITIZENS *more.*

Here come moe voices. —
Your voices! For your voices I have fought;
Watch'd for your voices; for your voices bear

48. **by particulars:** to each in turn.   64. **lose by 'em:** lose their time preaching to them (because they neglect to practise
them).   73. [not] F₃.   *but* F₁.   91. **stand:** accord.   94, 97, 113. [*4.*] (Camb. edd.).   *1.* F.   106. **be off:** doff my hat.
107. **counterfeitly:** hypocritically.   111. [*5.*] (Camb. edd.).   2. F.   122. [**woolless**] (Collier).   Cf. *napless* II.i.250.   *Wool-
vish* F.   [**toge**] (Steevens): toga.   *tongue* F₁.   *gowne* F₂₋₄.   123. [do] F₄.   *does* F₁.   128. **fool it:** play the fool.   134. **Watch'd:**
kept guard.

Of wounds two dozen odd; battles thrice six   135
I have seen and heard of; for your voices have
Done many things, some less, some more.   Your
    voices.
Indeed, I would be consul.
    [6.] *Cit.* He has done nobly, and cannot go with-
out any honest man's voice.   140
    [7.] *Cit.* Therefore let him be consul.   The gods
give him joy, and make him good friend to the
people!
    All Cit. Amen, amen.   God save thee, noble
    consul!   ˹*Exeunt.*]
    Cor. Worthy voices!   145

Re-enter MENENIUS, *with* BRUTUS *and* SICINIUS.
    Men. You have stood your limitation, and the
    tribunes
Endue you with the people's voice.   Remains
That, in th' official marks invested, you
Anon do meet the Senate.
    Cor.   Is this done?
    Sic. The custom of request you have discharg'd.
The people do admit you, and are summon'd   151
To meet anon upon your approbation.
    Cor. Where?   At the Senate-house?
    Sic.   There, Coriolanus.
    Cor. May I change these garments?
    Sic.   You may, sir.
    Cor. That I'll straight do, and, knowing myself
    again,   155
Repair to th' Senate-house.
    Men. I'll keep you company.   Will you along?
    Bru. We stay here for the people.
    Sic.   Fare you well.
                [Exeunt Coriolanus and Menenius.
He has it now, and by his looks methinks
'Tis warm at 's heart.   160
    Bru. With a proud heart he wore his humble
    weeds.
Will you dismiss the people?

Enter the PLEBEIANS.
    Sic. How now, my masters! have you chose this
    man?
    1. Cit. He has our voices, sir.
    Bru. We pray the gods he may deserve your
    loves.   165
    2. Cit. Amen, sir.   To my poor unworthy notice,
He mock'd us when he begg'd our voices.
    3. Cit.   Certainly
He flouted us downright.
    1. Cit. No, 'tis his kind of speech; he did not
    mock us.

    2. Cit. Not one amongst us, save yourself, but
    says   170
He us'd us scornfully.   He should have show'd us
His marks of merit, wounds receiv'd for 's country.
    Sic. Why, so he did, I am sure.
    All.   No, no; no man saw 'em.
    3. Cit. He said he had wounds, which he could
    show in private;
And with his hat, thus waving it in scorn,   175
"I would be consul," says he; "aged custom,
But by your voices, will not so permit me;
Your voices therefore."   When we granted that,
Here was "I thank you for your voices; thank you;
Your most sweet voices.   Now you have left your
    voices,   180
I have no further with you."   Was not this mockery?
    Sic. Why either were you ignorant to see 't,
Or, seeing it, of such childish friendliness
To yield your voices?
    Bru.   Could you not have told him
As you were lesson'd: when he had no power,   185
But was a petty servant to the state,
He was your enemy, ever spake against
Your liberties and the charters that you bear
I' th' body of the weal; and now, arriving
A place of potency and sway o' th' state,   190
If he should still malignantly remain
Fast foe to th' *plebeii*, your voices might
Be curses to yourselves?   You should have said
That as his worthy deeds did claim no less
Than what he stood for, so his gracious nature
Would think upon you for your voices and   196
Translate his malice towards you into love,
Standing your friendly lord.
    Sic.   Thus to have said,
As you were fore-advis'd, had touch'd his spirit
And tried his inclination; from him pluck'd   200
Either his gracious promise, which you might,
As cause had call'd you up, have held him to;
Or else it would have gall'd his surly nature,
Which easily endures not article
Tying him to aught; so putting him to rage,   205
You should have ta'en th' advantage of his choler
And pass'd him unelected.
    Bru.   Did you perceive
He did solicit you in free contempt
When he did need your loves, and do you think
That his contempt shall not be bruising to you   210
When he hath power to crush?   Why, had your
    bodies
No heart among you?   Or had you tongues to cry
Against the rectorship of judgement?
    Sic.   Have you
Ere now deni'd the asker, and now again

139, 141. [6.], [7.] (Camb. edd.).   *1, 2* F.   146. **limitation:** prescribed time.   148. **official marks:** insignia of office.
152. **upon ... approbation:** to confirm your election.   182. **ignorant:** too dull.   189. **weal:** commonwealth.   199. **touch'd:**
tested.   204. **article:** stipulation.   212. **heart:** courage.   213. **rectorship:** rule.

Of him that did not ask but mock, bestow   215
Your sued-for tongues?
  3. Cit. He's not confirm'd; we may deny him yet.
  2. Cit. And will deny him.
I'll have five hundred voices of that sound.
  1. Cit. I twice five hundred and their friends to
    piece 'em.   220
  Bru. Get you hence instantly, and tell those
    friends
They have chose a consul that will from them take
Their liberties, make them of no more voice
Than dogs, that are as often beat for barking
As therefore kept to do so.
  Sic.   Let them assemble,
And on a safer judgement all revoke   226
Your ignorant election.   Enforce his pride
And his old hate unto you; besides, forget not
With what contempt he wore the humble weed,
How in his suit he scorn'd you; but your loves,   230
Thinking upon his services, took from you
The apprehension of his present portance,
Which most gibingly, ungravely, he did fashion
After th' inveterate hate he bears you.
  Bru.   Lay
A fault on us, your tribunes, that we labour'd,   235
No impediment between, but that you must
Cast your election on him.
  Sic.   Say you chose him
More after our commandment than as guided
By your own true affections, and that your minds,
Pre-occupi'd with what you rather must do   240
Than what you should, made you against the grain
To voice him consul.   Lay the fault on us.
  Bru. Ay, spare us not.   Say we read lectures to
    you,
How youngly he began to serve his country,   244
How long continued, and what stock he springs of,—
The noble house o' th' Marcians, from whence came
That Ancus Marcius, Numa's daughter's son,
Who, after great Hostilius, here was king;
Of the same house Publius and Quintus were,
That our best water brought by conduits hither;
[And Censorinus, nobly named so,   251
Twice being by the people chosen censor,]
Was his great ancestor.
  Sic.   One thus descended,
That hath beside well in his person wrought
To be set high in place, we did commend   255
To your remembrances; but you have found,
Scaling his present bearing with his past,
That he's your fixed enemy, and revoke
Your sudden approbation.
  Bru.   Say, you ne'er had done 't —

Harp on that still — but by our putting on;   260
And presently, when you have drawn your number,
Repair to t' Capitol.
  All.   We will so.   Almost all
Repent in their election.   *[Exeunt Citizens.*
  Bru.   Let them go on;
This mutiny were better put in hazard
Than stay, past doubt, for greater.   265
If, as his nature is, he fall in rage
With their refusal, both observe and answer
The vantage of his anger.
  Sic.   To th' Capitol, come.
We will be there before the stream o' th' people;
And this shall seem, as partly 'tis, their own,   270
Which we have goaded onward.   *[Exeunt.*

ACT III

[SCENE I. *Rome.   A street.*]

Cornets.   *Enter* CORIOLANUS, MENENIUS, *all the*
  Gentry, COMINIUS, TITUS LARTIUS, *and other*
  SENATORS.

  Cor. Tullus Aufidius then had made new head?
  Lart. He had, my lord; and that it was which
    caus'd
Our swifter composition.
  Cor. So then the Volsces stand but as at first,   4
Ready, when time shall prompt them, to make road
Upon 's again.
  Com.   They are worn, Lord Consul, so
That we shall hardly in our ages see
Their banners wave again.
  Cor.   Saw you Aufidius?
  Lart. On safe-guard he came to me, and did curse
Against the Volsces for they had so vilely   10
Yielded the town.   He is retired to Antium.
  Cor. Spoke he of me?
  Lart.   He did, my lord.
  Cor.   How?   What?
  Lart. How often he had met you, sword to sword;
That of all things upon the earth he hated
Your person most; that he would pawn his fortunes
To hopeless restitution, so he might   16
Be call'd your vanquisher.
  Cor.   At Antium lives he?
  Lart. At Antium.
  Cor. I wish I had a cause to seek him there,
To oppose his hatred fully.   Welcome home.   20

    Enter SICINIUS *and* BRUTUS.

Behold, these are the tribunes of the people,
The tongues o' th' common mouth.   I do despise them

215. Of: on.   220. piece: increase.   227. Enforce: stress.   232. portance: demeanor.   233. ungravely: frivolously.
251–52. [And . . . censor] (Camb. edd.).   *And Nobly nam'd, so twice being Censor* F.   257. Scaling: weighing.   260. putting
on: urging.   265. stay: (to) wait.   267–68. answer . . . vantage: take advantage of.
  Act III, sc. i, 1. made new head: raised a new force.   3. composition: coming to terms.   16. To . . . restitution: beyond
hope of recovery.

For they do prank them in authority,
Against all noble sufferance.
  Sic.   Pass no further.
  Cor. Ha! what is that?   25
  Bru. It will be dangerous to go on. No further.
  Cor. What makes this change?
  Men. The matter?
  Com. Hath he not pass'd the noble and the
    common?
  Bru. Cominius, no.
  Cor.   Have I had children's voices?
  [*1.*] *Sen.* Tribunes, give way; he shall to the
    market-place.   31
  Bru. The people are incens'd against him.
  Sic.   Stop,
Or all will fall in broil.
  Cor.   Are these your herd?
Must these have voices, that can yield them now
And straight disclaim their tongues? What are
    your offices?   35
You being their mouths, why rule you not their
    teeth?
Have you not set them on?
  Men.   Be calm, be calm.
  Cor. It is a purpos'd thing, and grows by plot,
To curb the will of the nobility.
Suffer 't, and live with such as cannot rule 40
Nor ever will be rul'd.
  Bru.   Call 't not a plot.
The people cry you mock'd them, and of late,
When corn was given them gratis, you repin'd,
Scandal'd the suppliants for the people, call'd them
Time-pleasers, flatterers, foes to nobleness. 45
  Cor. Why, this was known before.
  Bru.   Not to them all.
  Cor. Have you inform'd them sithence?
  Bru.   How! I inform them!
  Com. You are like to do such business.
  Bru.   Not unlike,
Each way, to better yours.
  Cor. Why, then, should I be consul? By yond
    clouds,   50
Let me deserve so ill as you, and make me
Your fellow tribune.
  Sic.   You show too much of that
For which the people stir. If you will pass
To where you are bound, you must inquire your
    way,
Which you are out of, with a gentler spirit, 55
Or never be so noble as a consul,
Nor yoke with him for tribune.
  Men.   Let's be calm.

  Com. The people are abus'd; set on. This
    palt'ring
Becomes not Rome, nor has Coriolanus
Deserv'd this so dishonour'd rub, laid falsely 60
I' th' plain way of his merit.
  Cor.   Tell me of corn!
This was my speech, and I will speak 't again —
  Men. Not now, not now.
  [*1.*] *Sen.*   Not in this heat, sir, now.
  Cor. Now, as I live, I will. My nobler friends,
I crave their pardons;   65
For the mutable, rank-scented [many], let them
Regard me as I do not flatter, and
Therein behold themselves. I say again,
In soothing them we nourish 'gainst our Senate
The cockle of rebellion, insolence, sedition, 70
Which we ourselves have plough'd for, sow'd, and
    scatter'd,
By mingling them with us, the honour'd number,
Who lack not virtue, no, nor power, but that
Which they have giv'n to beggars.
  Men.   Well, no more.
  [*1.*] *Sen.* No more words, we beseech you.
  Cor.   How! no more!
As for my country I have shed my blood, 76
Not fearing outward force, so shall my lungs
Coin words till their decay against those measles,
Which we disdain should tetter us, yet sought
The very way to catch them.
  Bru.   You speak o' th' people
As if you were a god to punish, not 81
A man of their infirmity.
  Sic.   'Twere well
We let the people know 't.
  Men.   What, what? his choler?
  Cor. Choler!
Were I as patient as the midnight sleep, 85
By Jove, 'twould be my mind!
  Sic.   It is a mind
That shall remain a poison where it is,
Not poison any further.
  Cor.   Shall remain!
Hear you this Triton of the minnows? Mark you
His absolute "shall"?
  Com.   'Twas from the canon.
  Cor.   "Shall"!
O [good] but most unwise patricians! why, 91
You grave but [reckless] senators, have you thus
Given Hydra here to choose an officer,
That with his peremptory "shall," being but
The horn and noise o' th' monster's, wants not
    spirit   95

24. **Against...sufferance:** beyond the toleration of the nobility. 30, 63, 75. [*1.*] (Capell). Om. F. 47. **sithence:** since. 58. **abus'd:** deceived. 60. **rub:** impediment. 66. [many] F₄. *Meynie* F₁. 70. **cockle:** weed. 78. **measles:** leprosy. 79. **tetter:** infect. 89. **Triton:** a sea god. 90. **from the canon:** against the law. 91. [good] (Theobald). *God* F. 92. [reckless] (Hanmer). *wreaklesse* F. 93. **Hydra:** many-headed beast, i.e., the multitude. 95. **horn and noise:** noisy horn. *Horn* may refer back to Triton, *noise* to Hydra.

To say he'll turn your current in a ditch,
And make your channel his? If he have power,
Then [vail] your ignorance; if none, awake
Your dangerous lenity. If you are learn'd,
Be not as common fools; if you are not,   100
Let them have cushions by you. You are plebeians,
If they be senators; and they are no less,
When, both your voices blended, the great'st taste
Most palates theirs. They choose their magistrate,
And such a one as he, who puts his "shall,"   105
His popular "shall," against a graver bench
Than ever frown'd in Greece. By Jove himself!
It makes the consuls base; and my soul aches
To know, when two authorities are up,
Neither supreme, how soon confusion   110
May enter 'twixt the gap of both and take
The one by th' other.
    Com.   Well, on to th' market-place.
    Cor. Whoever gave that counsel, to give forth
The corn o' th' storehouse gratis, as 'twas us'd
Sometime in Greece, —
    Men.   Well, well, no more of that.
    Cor. Though there the people had more absolute
    power,   116
I say, they nourish'd disobedience, fed
The ruin of the state.
    Bru.   Why, shall the people give
One that speaks thus their voice?
    Cor.   I'll give my reasons,
More worthier than their voices. They know the
    corn   120
Was not our recompense, resting well assur'd
That ne'er did service for't; being press'd to th'
    war,
Even when the navel of the state was touch'd,
They would not thread the gates. This kind of
    service   124
Did not deserve corn gratis. Being i' th' war,
Their mutinies and revolts, wherein they show'd
Most valour, spoke not for them. Th' accusation
Which they have often made against the Senate,
All cause unborn, could never be the [motive]
Of our so frank donation. Well, what then?   130
How shall this bosom-multiplied digest
The Senate's courtesy? Let deeds express
What's like to be their words: "We did request it;
We are the greater poll, and in true fear   124
They gave us our demands." Thus we debase
The nature of our seats and make the rabble
Call our cares fears; which will in time
Break ope the locks o' th' Senate and bring in

The crows to peck the eagles.
    Men.   Come, enough.
    Bru. Enough, with over-measure.
    Cor.   No, take more!
What may be sworn by, both divine and human,   141
Seal what I end withal! This double worship,
Where one part does disdain with cause, the other
Insult without all reason; where gentry, title,
    wisdom,
Cannot conclude but by the yea and no   145
Of general ignorance, — it must omit
Real necessities and give way the while
To unstable slightness; purpose so barr'd, it follows
Nothing is done to purpose. Therefore, beseech
    you, —
You that will be less fearful than discreet,   150
That love the fundamental part of state
More than you doubt the change on't, that prefer
A noble life before a long, and wish
To jump a body with a dangerous physic
That's sure of death without it, at once pluck out
The multitudinous tongue; let them not lick   156
The sweet which is their poison. Your dishonour
Mangles true judgement and bereaves the state
Of that integrity which should become 't,   159
Not having the power to do the good it would,
For th' ill which doth control 't.
    Bru.   Has said enough.
    Sic. Has spoken like a traitor, and shall answer
As traitors do.
    Cor. Thou wretch, despite o'erwhelm thee!
What should the people do with these bald tribunes?
On whom depending, their obedience fails   166
To the greater bench. In a rebellion,
When what's not meet, but what must be, was law,
Then were they chosen; in a better hour,
Let what is meet be said it must be meet,   170
And throw their power i' th' dust.
    Bru. Manifest treason!
    Sic.   This a consul? No!
    Bru. The ædiles, ho!

            Enter an Ædile.
            — Let him be apprehended.
    Sic. Go, call the people; [*Exit Ædile*] in whose
    name myself
Attach thee as a traitorous innovator,   175
A foe to th' public weal. Obey, I charge thee,
And follow to thine answer.
    Cor.   Hence, old goat!

---

98. **[vail] your ignorance:** submit yourselves in your ignorance. **[vail]** F₄. *vale* F₁. 101. **cushions:** i.e., seats in the Senate. 103–104. **the ... theirs:** the dominant flavor comes from them, i.e., their votes decide. 111. **take:** overthrow. 121. **recompense:** payment for service. 124. **thread:** go through. 129. **[motive]** (Johnson conj.). *native* F. 131. **bosom-multiplied:** multitudinous bosom (cf. l. 156 below and II.iii.18), the common herd. Many edd. emend to *bisson* (blind) *multitude*. 142. **Seal:** confirm. 144. **Insult:** exult. **without:** beyond. 145. **conclude:** make a decision, decree. 152. **doubt:** fear. 154. **jump:** risk. 167. **greater bench:** senate. 173. **ædiles:** officers attached to the Tribunes. 175. **Attach:** arrest.

[*Senators, etc.*] We'll surety him.
Com.   Ag'd sir, hands off.
Cor. Hence, rotten thing! or I shall shake thy
        bones
Out of thy garments.
        Sic.   Help, ye citizens!   180

Enter a rabble of PLEBEIANS, *with the* ÆDILES.

Men. On both sides more respect.
Sic. Here's he that would take from you all
        your power.
Bru. Seize him, ædiles!
[*Citizens.*] Down with him! down with him!
2. Sen. Weapons, weapons, weapons!   185
        [*They all bustle about Coriolanus* [*crying,*]
Tribunes! Patricians! Citizens! What, ho!
Sicinius! Brutus! Coriolanus! Citizens!
        All. Peace, peace, peace! Stay, hold, peace!
        Men. What is about to be? I am out of breath;
Confusion's near; I cannot speak. You, tribunes
To the people! Coriolanus, patience!   191
Speak, good Sicinius.
        Sic.   Hear me, people; peace!
[*Citizens.*] Let's hear our tribune; peace! Speak,
        speak, speak!
Sic. You are at point to lose your liberties.
Marcius would have all from you; Marcius,   195
Whom late you have nam'd for consul.
        Men.   Fie, fie, fie!
This is the way to kindle, not to quench.
        [*1.*] *Sen.* To unbuild the city and to lay all flat.
        Sic. What is the city but the people?
[*Citizens.*]   True,
The people are the city.   200
        Bru. By the consent of all, we were establish'd
The people's magistrates.
[*Citizens.*]   You so remain.
        Men. And so are like to do.
        Com. That is the way to lay the city flat,
To bring the roof to the foundation   205
And bury all, which yet distinctly ranges,
In heaps and piles of ruin.
        Sic.   This deserves death.
        Bru. Or let us stand to our authority,
Or let us lose it. We do here pronounce,
Upon the part o' th' people, in whose power   210
We were elected theirs, Marcius is worthy
Of present death.
        Sic.   Therefore lay hold of him;
Bear him to th' rock Tarpeian, and from thence
Into destruction cast him.
        Bru.   Ædiles, seize him!
[*Citizens.*] Yield, Marcius, yield!

Men.   Hear me one word;
Beseech you, tribunes, hear me but a word.   216
Æd. Peace, peace!
Men. [*To Brutus.*] Be that you seem, truly your
        country's friend,
And temp'rately proceed to what you would
Thus violently redress.
        Bru.   Sir, those cold ways   220
That seem like prudent helps are very poisonous
Where the disease is violent. — Lay hands upon
        him
And bear him to the rock.
        Cor.   No, I'll die here.
                    [*Drawing his sword.*
There's some among you have beheld me fighting;
Come, try upon yourselves what you have seen me.
        Men. Down with that sword! Tribunes, with-
        draw a while.   226
        Bru. Lay hands upon him.
        Com.   Help Marcius, help;
You that be noble, help him, young and old!
[*Citizens.*] Down with him, down with him!
        [*In this mutiny, the Tribunes, the Ædiles,
                and the People, are beat in.*
Men. [*to Cor.*] Go, get you to [your] house;
        begone, away!   230
All will be naught else.
        2. Sen.   Get you gone.
        Com.   Stand fast;
We have as many friends as enemies.
        Men. Shall it be put to that?
        [*1.*] *Sen.*   The gods forbid!
I prithee, noble friend, home to thy house;
Leave us to cure this cause.
        Men.   For 'tis a sore upon us   235
You cannot tent yourself. Begone, beseech you.
[*Com.*] Come, sir, along with us.
[*Cor.*] I would they were barbarians — as they
        are,
Though in Rome litter'd — not Romans — as they
        are not,
Though calv'd i' th' porch o' th' Capitol!
        [*Men.*]   Begone!
Put not your worthy rage into your tongue;   241
One time will owe another.
        Cor.   On fair ground
I could beat forty of them.
        Men.   I could myself
Take up a brace o' th' best of them; yea, the two
        tribunes.
        Com. But now 'tis odds beyond arithmetic;   245
And manhood is call'd foolery when it stands
Against a falling fabric. Will you hence

---

178. [*Senators, etc.*] *All* F.   184, etc. [*Citizens*] (Capell).   *All* F. (and elsewhere).   186. s.d. [*crying*] (Camb. edd.).
Om. F.   206. **distinctly ranges**: has an independent setting.   213. **rock Tarpeian**: from which criminals were hurled.   230.
[**your**] (Rowe).   *our* F.   237. [**Com.**] F₂.   *Corio.* F₁.   238. [**Cor.**] (Tyrwhitt conj.).   *Mene.* F.   240. [**Men.**] Om. F.
242. **One ... another**: i.e., a good time will come.   247. **fabric**: structure.

Before the tag return, whose rage doth rend
Like interrupted waters, and o'erbear
What they are us'd to bear?
   Men.   Pray you, begone.
I'll try whether my old wit be in request   251
With those that have but little. This must be
    patch'd
With cloth of any colour.
   Com.   Nay, come away.
    [*Exeunt Coriolanus, Cominius* [*and others*].
   A Patrician. This man has marr'd his fortune.
   Men. His nature is too noble for the world;   255
He would not flatter Neptune for his trident,
Or Jove for 's power to thunder. His heart's his
    mouth;
What his breast forges, that his tongue must vent;
And, being angry, does forget that ever   259
He heard the name of death.   [*A noise within.*
Here's goodly work!
   A Patrician.   I would they were a-bed!
   Men. I would they were in Tiber! What the
    vengeance!
Could he not speak 'em fair?

   Re-enter BRUTUS *and* SICINIUS, *with the rabble.*

   Sic.   Where is this viper
That would depopulate the city and   264
Be every man himself?
   Men.   You worthy tribunes, —
   Sic. He shall be thrown down the Tarpeian rock
With rigorous hands. He hath resisted law,
And therefore law shall scorn him further trial
Than the severity of the public power
Which he so sets at nought.
   1. Cit.   He shall well know
The noble tribunes are the people's mouths,   271
And we their hands.
   [*Citizens.*] He shall, sure on't.
   Men.   Sir, sir, —
   Sic. Peace!
   Men. Do not cry havoc where you should but
    hunt   275
With modest warrant.
   Sic.   Sir, how comes 't that you
Have holp to make this rescue?
   Men.   Hear me speak.
As I do know the consul's worthiness,
So can I name his faults, —
   Sic.   Consul! what consul?
   Men. The consul Coriolanus.
   Bru.   He consul!   280
   [*Citizens.*] No, no, no, no, no.
   Men. If, by the tribunes' leave, and yours, good
    people,

I may be heard, I would crave a word or two;
The which shall turn you to no further harm
Than so much loss of time.
   Sic.   Speak briefly then;
For we are peremptory to dispatch   286
This viperous traitor. To eject him hence
Were but one danger, and to keep him here
[Our] certain death; therefore it is decreed
He dies to-night.
   Men.   Now the good gods forbid   290
That our renowned Rome, whose gratitude
Towards her deserved children is enroll'd
In Jove's own book, like an unnatural dam
Should now eat up her own!
   Sic. He's a disease that must be cut away.   295
   Men. O, he's a limb that has but a disease;
Mortal, to cut it off; to cure it, easy.
What has he done to Rome that's worthy death?
Killing our enemies, the blood he hath lost —
Which I dare vouch, is more than that he hath,   300
By many an ounce — he dropp'd it for his country;
And what is left, to lose it by his country
Were to us all that do't and suffer it
A brand to th' end o' th' world.
   Sic.   This is clean kam.
   Bru. Merely awry. When he did love his
    country,   305
It honour'd him.
   Men.   The service of the foot
Being once gangren'd, is not then respected
For what before it was, —
   Bru.   We'll hear no more.
Pursue him to his house and pluck him thence,
Lest his infection, being of catching nature,   310
Spread further.
   Men.   One word more, one word.
This tiger-footed rage, when it shall find
The harm of unscann'd swiftness, will too late
Tie leaden pounds to 's heels. Proceed by process,
Lest parties, as he is belov'd, break out   315
And sack great Rome with Romans.
   Bru.   If it were so, —
   Sic. What do ye talk?
Have we not had a taste of his obedience?
Our ædiles smote? ourselves resisted? Come.
   Men. Consider this: he has been bred i' th' wars
Since 'a could draw a sword, and is ill school'd   321
In bolted language; meal and bran together
He throws without distinction. Give me leave;
I'll go to him, and undertake to bring him
Where he shall answer, by a lawful form,   325
In peace, to his utmost peril.
   1. Sen.   Noble tribunes,
It is the humane way. The other course

248. **tag:** rabble.   275. **cry havoc:** give the signal for general slaughter.   289. [**Our**] (Theobald). *One* F.   292. **deserved:** deserving.   304. **clean kam:** all wrong.   305. **Merely:** entirely.   313. **unscann'd:** inconsiderate.   314. **process:** legal means.   315. **parties:** factions.   322. **bolted:** refined.   324. **bring him** (Pope). *bring him in peace* F.

Will prove too bloody, and the end of it
Unknown to the beginning.
 Sic.   Noble Menenius,
Be you then as the people's officer.   330
Masters, lay down your weapons.
 Bru.   Go not home.
 Sic. Meet on the market-place. We'll attend
  you there;
Where, if you bring not Marcius, we'll proceed
In our first way.
 Men.   I'll bring him to you.
[*To the Senators.*] Let me desire your company. He
  must come,   335
Or what is worst will follow.
 [*1.*] *Sen.*   Pray you, let's to him.
          [*Exeunt.*

[SCENE II. *A room in Coriolanus's house.*]

   Enter CORIOLANUS, *with* NOBLES.

 Cor. Let them pull all about mine ears, present
  me
Death on the wheel or at wild horses' heels,
Or pile ten hills on the Tarpeian rock,
That the precipitation might down stretch
Below the beam of sight, yet will I still 5
Be thus to them.

    Enter VOLUMNIA.

 Noble.   You do the nobler.
 Cor. I muse my mother
Does not approve me further, who was wont
To call them woollen vassals, things created 9
To buy and sell with groats, to show bare heads
In congregations, to yawn, be still and wonder
When one but of my ordinance stood up
To speak of peace or war. — I talk of you.
         [*To Vol.*]
Why did you wish me milder? Would you have me
False to my nature? Rather say I play 15
The man I am.
 Vol.   O, sir, sir, sir,
I would have had you put your power well on,
Before you had worn it out.
 Cor.   Let go.
 Vol. You might have been enough the man you
  are,
With striving less to be so. Lesser had been 20
The [thwartings] of your dispositions, if
You had not show'd them how ye were dispos'd,
Ere they lack'd power to cross you.
 Cor.   Let them hang!
 Vol. [*Aside.*] Ay, and burn too.

  Enter MENENIUS *with the* SENATORS.

 Men. Come, come, you have been too rough,
  something too rough;   25
You must return and mend it.
 [*1.*] *Sen.*   There's no remedy;
Unless, by not so doing, our good city
Cleave in the midst and perish.
 Vol.   Pray, be counsell'd.
I have a heart as little apt as yours.
But yet a brain that leads my use of anger 30
To better vantage.
 Men.   Well said, noble woman!
Before he should thus stoop to the [herd], but that
The violent fit o' th' time craves it as physic
For the whole state, I would put mine armour on, 34
Which I can scarcely bear.
 Cor.   What must I do?
 Men. Return to th' tribunes.
 Cor.   Well, what then? what then?
 Men. Repent what you have spoke.
 Cor. For them! I cannot do it to the gods;
Must I then do't to them?
 Vol.   You are too absolute;
Though therein you can never be too noble, 40
But when extremities speak. I have heard you say
Honour and policy, like unsever'd friends,
I' th' war do grow together. Grant that, and tell
  me
In peace what each of them by th' other lose
That they combine not there.
 Cor.   Tush, tush!
 Men.   A good demand.
 Vol. If it be honour in your wars to seem 46
The same you are not, which, for your best ends,
You adopt your policy, how is it less or worse
That it shall hold companionship in peace
With honour, as in war, since that to both 50
It stands in like request?
 Cor.   Why force you this?
 Vol. Because that now it lies you on to speak
To th' people; not by your own instruction,
Nor by the matter which your heart prompts you,
But with such words that are but roted in 55
Your tongue, though but bastards and syllables
Of no allowance to your bosom's truth.
Now, this no more dishonours you at all
Than to take in a town with gentle words,
Which else would put you to your fortune and 60
The hazard of much blood.
I would dissemble with my nature where
My fortunes and my friends at stake requir'd
I should do so in honour. I am in this
Your wife, your son, these senators, the nobles;

Sc. ii, 4. **precipitation:** steepness. 5. **beam:** i.e., reach. 7. **muse:** marvel. 10. **groats:** fourpenny coins. 12. **ordinance:** rank. 18. **Let go:** enough. 21. **[thwartings]** (Theobald). *things* F. 29. **apt:** docile. 32. **[herd]** (Warburton). *heart* F. 48. **adopt:** adopt as. 51. **It...request:** it is equally necessary. **force:** urge. 55. **roted:** learned by rote, memorized. 57. **Of...to:** unacknowledged by. 59. **take in:** capture. 64. **I am:** I am speaking for.

And you will rather show our general louts   66
How you can frown, than spend a fawn upon 'em
For the inheritance of their loves and safeguard
Of what that want might ruin.
    Men.   Noble lady!
Come, go with us; speak fair. You may salve so,
Not what is dangerous present, but the loss   71
Of what is past.
    Vol.   I prithee now, my son,
Go to them, with this bonnet in thy hand;
And thus far having stretch'd it — here be with
    them —   74
Thy knee bussing the stones — for in such business
Action is eloquence, and the eyes of th' ignorant
More learned than the ears — waving thy head,
Which often, thus, correcting thy stout heart,
Now humble as the ripest mulberry
That will not hold the handling — or say to them,
Thou art their soldier, and, being bred in broils,   81
Hast not the soft way which, thou dost confess,
Were fit for thee to use as they to claim,
In asking their good loves; but thou wilt frame
Thyself, forsooth, hereafter theirs, so far   85
As thou hast power and person.
    Men.   This but done,
Even as she speaks, why, their hearts were yours;
For they have pardons, being ask'd, as free
As words to little purpose.
    Vol.   Prithee now,
Go, and be rul'd; although I know thou hadst rather
Follow thine enemy in a fiery gulf   91
Than flatter him in a bower.

            Enter COMINIUS.
               Here is Cominius.
    Com. I have been i' th' market-place; and, sir,
    'tis fit
You make strong party, or defend yourself
By calmness or by absence. All's in anger.   95
    Men. Only fair speech.
    Com.   I think 'twill serve, if he
Can thereto frame his spirit.
    Vol.   He must, and will.
Prithee now, say you will, and go about it.
    Cor. Must I go show them my unbarb'd sconce?
    Must I
With my base tongue give to my noble heart   100
A lie that it must bear? Well, I will do't;
Yet, were there but this single plot to lose,
This mould of Marcius, they to dust should grind it
And throw 't against the wind. To th' market-
    place!   104
You have put me now to such a part which never
I shall discharge to th' life.

    Com.   Come, come, we'll prompt you.
    Vol. I prithee now, sweet son, as thou hast said
My praises made thee first a soldier, so,
To have my praise for this, perform a part
Thou hast not done before.
    Cor.   Well, I must do't. 110
Away, my disposition, and possess me
Some harlot's spirit! My throat of war be turn'd,
Which choir'd with my drum, into a pipe
Small as an eunuch's, or the virgin voice
That babies lull asleep! The smiles of knaves 115
Tent in my cheeks, and schoolboys' tears take up
The glasses of my sight! A beggar's tongue
Make motion through my lips, and my arm'd knees,
Who bow'd but in my stirrup, bend like his
That hath receiv'd an alms! — I will not do't, 120
Lest I surcease to honour mine own truth
And by my body's action teach my mind
A most inherent baseness.
    Vol.   At thy choice, then.
To beg of thee, it is my more dishonour
Than thou of them. Come all to ruin! Let 125
Thy mother rather feel thy pride than fear
Thy dangerous stoutness; for I mock at death
With as big heart as thou. Do as thou list.
Thy valiantness was mine, thou suck'st it from me,
But owe thy pride thyself.
    Cor.   Pray, be content. 130
Mother, I am going to the market-place;
Chide me no more. I'll mountebank their loves,
Cog their hearts from them, and come home belov'd
Of all the trades in Rome. Look, I am going;
Commend me to my wife. I'll return consul, 135
Or never trust to what my tongue can do
I' th' way of flattery further.
    Vol.   Do your will. [*Exit.*
    Com. Away! the tribunes do attend you. Arm
    yourself
To answer mildly; for they are prepar'd
With accusations, as I hear, more strong   140
Than are upon you yet.
    Cor. The word is "mildly." Pray you, let us go.
Let them accuse me by invention, I
Will answer in mine honour.
    Men.   Ay, but mildly.
    Cor. Well, mildly be it then. Mildly!   145
                              [*Exeunt.*

    [SCENE III. *The same. The Forum.*]

       Enter SICINIUS *and* BRUTUS.
    Bru. In this point charge him home, that he
    affects
Tyrannical power. If he evade us there,

---

    69. **want:** lack of their loves. 70. **salve:** remedy. 71. **Not:** not only. 74. **here ... them:** i.e., this is the way to win them. 75. **bussing:** kissing. 77. **waving:** bowing. 80. **hold:** bear. 83. **they:** for them. 99. **unbarb'd sconce:** bare head. 102. **this ... plot:** only this body. 103. **mould:** form. 121. **surcease:** cease. 130. **owe:** own. 132. **mountebank:** win by quackery. 133. **Cog:** cheat. 138. **Arm:** prepare. 143. **invention:** fraud.
    Sc. iii, 1. **affects:** wants.

Enforce him with his envy to the people,
And that the spoil got on the Antiates
Was ne'er distributed.

Enter an ÆDILE.

                What, will he come?   5
Æd. He's coming.
Bru.   How accompanied?
Æd. With old Menenius and those senators
That always favour'd him.
Sic.   Have you a catalogue
Of all the voices that we have procur'd
Set down by th' poll?
Æd.   I have; 'tis ready.   10
Sic. Have you collected them by tribes?
Æd.   I have.
Sic. Assemble presently the people hither;
And when they hear me say, "It shall be so
I' th' right and strength o' th' commons," be it
     either
For death, for fine, or banishment, then let them, 15
If I say fine, cry "Fine!" if death, cry "Death!"
Insisting on the old prerogative
And power i' th' truth o' th' cause.
Æd.   I shall inform them.
Bru. And when such time they have begun to
     cry,
Let them not cease, but with a din confus'd   20
Enforce the present execution
Of what we chance to sentence.
Æd.   Very well.
Sic. Make them be strong and ready for this hint
When we shall hap to give 't them.
Bru.   Go about it.
                     [Exit Ædile.]
Put him to choler straight. He hath been us'd
Ever to conquer, and to have his worth   26
Of contradiction. Being once chaf'd, he cannot
Be rein'd again to temperance; then he speaks
What's in his heart, and that is there which looks
With us to break his neck.

Enter CORIOLANUS, MENENIUS, *and* COMINIUS,
     with others [SENATORS *and* Patricians].

Sic.   Well, here he comes.
Men. Calmly, I do beseech you.   31
Cor. Ay, as an ostler, that [for the] poorest piece
Will bear the knave by th' volume. Th' honour'd
     gods
Keep Rome in safety, and the chairs of justice
Supplied with worthy men! plant love among 's! 35
[Throng] our large temples with the shows of peace,

And not our streets with war!
1. Sen.   Amen, amen.
Men. A noble wish.

Re-enter ÆDILE, *with* CITIZENS.

Sic. Draw near, ye people.
Æd. List to your tribunes. Audience! peace, I
     say!   40
Cor. First, hear me speak.
Both Tri.   Well, say. Peace, ho!
Cor. Shall I be charg'd no further than this
     present?
Must all determine here?
Sic.   I do demand
If you submit you to the people's voices,
Allow their officers, and are content   45
To suffer lawful censure for such faults
As shall be prov'd upon you?
Cor.   I am content.
Men. Lo, citizens, he says he is content.
The warlike service he has done, consider; think
Upon the wounds his body bears, which show   50
Like graves i' th' holy churchyard.
Cor.   Scratches with briers,
Scars to move laughter only.
Men.   Consider further,
That when he speaks not like a citizen,
You find him like a soldier. Do not take
His rougher [accents] for malicious sounds,   55
But, as I say, such as become a soldier
Rather than envy you.
Com.   Well, well, no more.
Cor. What is the matter
That being pass'd for consul with full voice,
I am so dishonour'd that the very hour   60
You take it off again?
Sic.   Answer to us.
Cor. Say, then; 'tis true, I ought so.
Sic. We charge you, that you have contriv'd to
     take
From Rome all season'd office and to wind
Yourself into a power tyrannical;   65
For which you are a traitor to the people.
Cor. How! traitor!
Men.   Nay, temperately; your promise.
Cor. The fires i' th' lowest hell fold in the people!
Call me their traitor! Thou injurious tribune!
Within thine eyes sat twenty thousand deaths,   70
In thy hands clutch'd as many millions, in
Thy lying tongue both numbers, I would say
"Thou liest" unto thee with a voice as free
As I do pray the gods.
Sic.   Mark you this, people?

---

   3. **envy:** malice.   12. **presently:** straightway.   21. **present:** immediate.   26. **worth:** fill.   29. **looks:** promises.   32.
[for the] F₃. *fourth* F₁. **piece:** coin.   33. **Will ... volume:** will swallow quantities of insults.   36. **[Throng]** (Theobald).
Through F.   45. **Allow:** acknowledge.   55. **[accents]** (Theobald). *Actions* F.   57. **envy you:** as malice toward you.   63.
contriv'd: plotted.   64. **season'd:** established.   69. **injurious:** insulting.

[*Citizens.*] To th' rock, to th' rock with him!
Sic.   Peace!
We need not put new matter to his charge.   76
What you have seen him do and heard him speak,
Beating your officers, cursing yourselves,
Opposing laws with strokes and here defying
Those whose great power must try him; even
    this
So criminal and in such capital kind,   81
Deserves th' extremest death.
    Bru.   But since he hath
Serv'd well for Rome, —
    Cor.   What do you prate of service?
    Bru. I talk of that, that know it.
    Cor. You?   85
    Men. Is this the promise that you made your
        mother?
    Com. Know, I pray you, —
    Cor.   I'll know no further.
Let them pronounce the steep Tarpeian death,
Vagabond exile, flaying, pent to linger
But with a grain a day, I would not buy   90
Their mercy at the price of one fair word;
Nor check my courage for what they can give,
To have 't with saying "Good morrow."
    Sic.   For that he has,
As much as in him lies, from time to time
Envi'd against the people, seeking means   95
To pluck away their power, as now at last
Given hostile strokes, and that not in the presence
Of dreaded justice, but on the ministers
That [do] distribute it; in the name o' th' people
And in the power of us the tribunes, we,   100
Even from this instant, banish him our city,
In peril of precipitation
From off the rock Tarpeian never more
To enter our Rome gates. I' th' people's name,
I say it shall be so.   105
    [*Citizens.*] It shall be so, it shall be so. Let him
        away!
He's banish'd, and it shall be so.
    Com. Hear me, my masters, and my common
        friends, —
    Sic. He's sentenc'd; no more hearing.
    Com.   Let me speak.
I have been consul, and can show [for] Rome   110
Her enemies' marks upon me. I do love
My country's good with a respect more tender,
More holy and profound, than mine own life,
My dear wife's estimate, her womb's increase
And treasure of my loins; then if I would   115
Speak that, —
    Sic.   We know your drift; speak what?

Bru. There's no more to be said, but he is
    banish'd
As enemy to the people and his country.
It shall be so.
    [*Citizens.*] It shall be so, it shall be so.
    Cor. You common cry of curs! whose breath I
        hate   120
As reek o' th' rotten fens, whose loves I prize
As the dead carcasses of unburied men
That do corrupt my air, I banish you!
And here remain with your uncertainty!
Let every feeble rumour shake your hearts!   125
Your enemies, with nodding of their plumes,
Fan you into despair! Have the power still
To banish your defenders, till at length
Your ignorance, which finds not till it feels,
Making [not] reservation of yourselves,   130
Still your own foes, deliver you as most
Abated captives to some nation
That won you without blows! Despising,
For you, the city, thus I turn my back;
There is a world elsewhere.   135
    [*Exeunt Coriolanus, Cominius [Menenius,
        Senators, and Patricians]. They all
        shout, and throw up their caps.*
Æd. The people's enemy is gone, is gone!
    [*Citizens.*] Our enemy is banish'd! he is gone!
        Hoo! hoo!
Sic. Go, see him out at gates, and follow him,
As he hath follow'd you, with all despite;
Give him deserv'd vexation. Let a guard   140
Attend us through the city.
    [*Citizens.*] Come, come; let's see him out at gates;
        come.
The gods preserve our noble tribunes! Come.
                                        [*Exeunt.*

ACT IV

[SCENE I. *Rome. Before a gate of the city.*]

Enter CORIOLANUS, VOLUMNIA, VIRGILIA, MENE-
NIUS, COMINIUS, *with the young Nobility of Rome.*

    Cor. Come, leave your tears: a brief farewell. The
        beast
With many heads butts me away. Nay, mother,
Where is your ancient courage? You were us'd
To say extremity was the trier of spirits;
That common chances common men could bear;
That when the sea was calm all boats alike   6
Show'd mastership in floating; fortune's blows,
When most struck home, being gentle, wounded,
    craves

89. **pent:** imprisoned.   97. **not:** not merely.   99. **[do]** F$_3$.   *doth* F$_1$.   110. **[for]** (Theobald). *from* F.   114. **estimate:** reputation.   120. **cry:** pack.   124. **uncertainty:** fickleness.   129. **finds:** learns. **feels:** suffers.   130. **Making...of:** sparing not even. **[not]** (Capell). *but* F.   132. **Abated:** humiliated.

Act IV, sc. i, 7–9. fortune's...cunning: when Fortune's blows are heaviest, to behave like a gentleman, if wounded, takes a noble mind.

A noble cunning. You were us'd to load me
With precepts that would make invincible   10
The heart that conn'd them.
  Vir. O heavens! O heavens!
  Cor.   Nay, I prithee, woman, —
  Vol. Now the red pestilence strike all trades in
    Rome,
And occupations perish!
  Cor.   What, what, what!
I shall be lov'd when I am lack'd. Nay, mother,
Resume that spirit when you were wont to say,   16
If you had been the wife of Hercules,
Six of his labours you'd have done, and sav'd
Your husband so much sweat. Cominius,   19
Droop not; adieu. Farewell, my wife, my mother;
I'll do well yet. Thou old and true Menenius,
Thy tears are salter than a younger man's,
And venomous to thine eyes. My sometime
    General,
I have seen thee stern, and thou hast oft beheld
Heart-hard'ning spectacles; tell these sad women   25
'Tis fond to wail inevitable strokes,
As 'tis to laugh at 'em. My mother, you wot well
My hazards still have been your solace; and
Believe 't not lightly — though I go alone,
Like to a lonely dragon, that his fen   30
Makes fear'd and talk'd of more than seen — your
    son
Will or exceed the common or be caught
With cautelous baits and practice.
  Vol.   My first son,
[Whither wilt] thou go? Take good Cominius
With thee a while; determine on some course,   35
More than a wild exposture to each chance
That starts i' th' way before thee.
  Cor.   O the gods!
  Com. I'll follow thee a month, devise with thee
Where thou shalt rest, that thou mayst hear of us
And we of thee; so if the time thrust forth   40
A cause for thy repeal, we shall not send
O'er the vast world to seek a single man
And lose advantage, which doth ever cool
I' th' absence of the needer.
  Cor.   Fare ye well!
Thou hast years upon thee, and thou art too full
Of the wars' surfeits to go rove with one   46
That's yet unbruis'd. Bring me but out at gate.
Come, my sweet wife, my dearest mother, and
My friends of noble touch; when I am forth,
Bid me farewell, and smile. I pray you, come.
While I remain above the ground, you shall   51
Hear from me still, and never of me aught
But what is like me formerly.
  Men.   That's worthily

As any ear can hear. Come, let's not weep.
If I could shake off but one seven years   55
From these old arms and legs, by the good gods,
I'd with thee every foot.
  Cor.   Give me thy hand:
Come.   [*Exeunt.*

[SCENE II. *The same. A street near the gate.*]

  Enter SICINIUS, BRUTUS, *and an* Ædile.

  Sic. Bid them all home; he's gone, and we'll no
    further.
The nobility are vexed, whom we see have sided
In his behalf.
  Bru.   Now we have shown our power,
Let us seem humbler after it is done
Than when it was a-doing.
  Sic.   Bid them home.   5
Say their great enemy is gone, and they
Stand in their ancient strength.
  Bru.   Dismiss them home.
        [*Exit Ædile.*]
Here comes his mother.

  Enter VOLUMNIA, VIRGILIA, *and* MENENIUS.

  Sic.   Let's not meet her.
  Bru.   Why?
  Sic. They say she's mad.
  Bru. They have ta'en note of us; keep on your
    way.   10
  Vol. O, you're well met. The hoarded plague o'
    th' gods
Requite your love!
  Men.   Peace, peace; be not so loud.
  Vol. If that I could for weeping, you should
    hear, —
Nay, and you shall hear some. [*To Brutus.*] Will
    you be gone?
  Vir. [*To Sicinius.*] You shall stay too. I would
    I had the power   15
To say so to my husband.
  Sic.   Are you mankind?
  Vol. Ay, fool; is that a shame? Note but this,
    fool.
Was not a man my father? Hadst thou foxship
To banish him that struck more blows for Rome   19
Than thou hast spoken words?
  Sic.   O blessed heavens
  Vol. Moe noble blows than ever thou wise words,
And for Rome's good. I'll tell thee what: — yet
    go.
Nay, but thou shalt stay too: — I would my son
Were in Arabia and thy tribe before him,
His good sword in his hand.

26. **fond**: foolish. 27. **wot**: know. 33. **cautelous**: crafty. **practice**: treachery. 34. [**Whither wilt**] (Capell). *Whether will* F. 36. **exposture**: exposure. 49. **noble touch**: proved nobleness.
  Sc. ii, 16. **mankind**: human. 18. **foxship**: craft.

Sic.   What then?
Vir.   What then!
He'd make an end of thy posterity.   26
    Vol. Bastards and all!
Good man, the wounds that he does bear for Rome!
    Men. Come, come, peace.
    Sic. I would he had continued to his country   30
As he began, and not unknit himself
The noble knot he made.
    Bru.   I would he had.
    Vol. "I would he had"! 'Twas you incens'd the
       rabble;
Cats, that can judge as fitly of his worth
As I can of those mysteries which heaven   35
Will not have earth to know.
    Bru.   Pray, let's go.
    Vol. Now, pray, sir, get you gone;
You have done a brave deed. Ere you go, hear
       this:
As far as doth the Capitol exceed
The meanest house in Rome, so far my son —   40
This lady's husband here, this, do you see? —
Whom you have banish'd, does exceed you all.
    Bru. Well, well, we'll leave you.
    Sic.   Why stay we to be baited
With one that wants her wits?
                 [*Exeunt Tribunes.*
    Vol.   Take my prayers with you.
I would the gods had nothing else to do   45
But to confirm my curses! Could I meet 'em
But once a-day, it would unclog my heart
Of what lies heavy to't.
    Men.   You have told them home;
And, by my troth, you have cause. You'll sup
       with me?
    Vol. Anger's my meat; I sup upon myself,   50
And so shall starve with feeding. Come, let's go.
[*To Virgilia.*] Leave this faint puling, and lament
       as I do,
In anger, Juno-like. Come, come, come. [*Exeunt.*
    Men. Fie, fie, fie!   [*Exit.*

[SCENE III. *A highway between Rome and Antium.*]

    Enter a ROMAN *and a* VOLSCE [*meeting*].

    Rom. I know you well, sir, and you know me.
Your name, I think, is Adrian.
    Vols. It is so, sir. Truly, I have forgot you.
    Rom. I am a Roman; and my services are, as
you are, against 'em. Know you me yet?   5
    Vols. Nicanor? No?
    Rom. The same, sir.
    Vols. You had more beard when I last saw you;
but your favour is well appear'd by your tongue.
What's the news in Rome? I have a note from

the Volscian state, to find you out there. You
have well saved me a day's journey.   12
    Rom. There hath been in Rome strange insur-
rections; the people against the senators, patricians,
and nobles.
    Vols. Hath been! Is it ended, then? Our
state thinks not so. They are in a most warlike
preparation and hope to come upon them in the
heat of their division.   19
    Rom. The main blaze of it is past, but a small
thing would make it flame again; for the nobles
receive so to heart the banishment of that worthy
Coriolanus, that they are in a ripe aptness to
take all power from the people and to pluck from
them their tribunes for ever. This lies glowing,
I can tell you, and is almost mature for the violent
breaking out.   27
    Vols. Coriolanus banish'd!
    Rom. Banish'd, sir.
    Vols. You will be welcome with this intelligence,
Nicanor.   31
    Rom. The day serves well for them now. I have
heard it said, the fittest time to corrupt a man's wife
is when she's fallen out with her husband. Your
noble Tullus Aufidius will appear well in these wars,
his great opposer, Coriolanus, being now in no request of his country.   38
    Vols. He cannot choose. I am most fortunate
thus accidentally to encounter you. You have
ended my business, and I will merrily accompany
you home.   42
    Rom. I shall, between this and supper, tell you
most strange things from Rome; all tending to the
good of their adversaries. Have you an army ready,
say you?   46
    Vols. A most royal one; the centurions and their
charges, distinctly billeted, already in th' entertainment, and to be on foot at an hour's warning.   50
    Rom. I am joyful to hear of their readiness, and
am the man, I think, that shall set them in present
action. So, sir, heartily well met, and most glad of
your company.   54
    Vols. You take my part from me, sir; I have the
most cause to be glad of yours.
    Rom. Well, let us go together.   [*Exeunt.*

[SCENE IV. *Antium. Before Aufidius's house.*]

    Enter CORIOLANUS, *in mean apparel, disguis'd*
           and muffled.

    Cor. A goodly city is this Antium. City,
'Tis I that made thy widows; many an heir
Of these fair edifices 'fore my wars
Have I heard groan and drop. Then know me
       not,

Sc. iii, 9. **favour:** face. **appear'd:** manifested. 48. **distinctly:** separately. **in th' entertainment:** enlisted.
Sc. iv, 3. **wars:** attacks.

Lest that thy wives with spits and boys with stones
In puny battle slay me.

Enter a CITIZEN.

                    Save you, sir.   6
Cit. And you.
Cor.   Direct me, if it be your will,
Where great Aufidius lies. Is he in Antium?
Cit. He is, and feasts the nobles of the state
At his house this night.
Cor.   Which is his house, beseech you? 10
Cit. This, here before you.
Cor.   Thank you, sir: farewell.
                                  [*Exit Citizen.*
O world, thy slippery turns! Friends now fast
      sworn,
Whose double bosoms seem to wear one heart,
Whose hours, whose bed, whose meal and exercise
Are still together, who twin, as 'twere, in love 15
Unseparable, shall within this hour,
On a dissension of a doit, break out
To bitterest enmity; so, fellest foes,
Whose passions and whose plots have broke their
      sleep
To take the one the other, by some chance,   20
Some trick not worth an egg, shall grow dear friends
And interjoin their issues. So with me;
My birthplace [hate] I, and my love's upon
This enemy town. I'll enter. If he slay me,
He does fair justice; if he give me way,   25
I'll do his country service.   [*Exit.*

[SCENE V. *The same. A hall in Aufidius's house.*]

Music within. Enter a SERVINGMAN.

1. Serv. Wine, wine, wine! What service is here!
I think our fellows are asleep.   [*Exit.*

Enter a second SERVINGMAN.

2. Serv. Where's Cotus? my [master] calls for him.
Cotus!   [*Exit.*

Enter CORIOLANUS.

Cor. A goodly house! The feast smells well but I
Appear not like a guest.   6

Re-enter the first SERVINGMAN.

1. Serv. What would you have, friend? Whence
are you? Here's no place for you; pray, go to the
door.   [*Exit.*
Cor. I have deserv'd no better entertainment 10
In being Coriolanus.

Re-enter second SERVINGMAN.

2. Serv. Whence are you, sir? Has the porter his

eyes in his head, that he gives entrance to such companions? Pray, get you out.
Cor. Away!   15
2. Serv. Away! get you away.
Cor. Now thou'rt troublesome.
2. Serv. Are you so brave? I'll have you talk'd
with anon.

Enter a third SERVINGMAN. *The first meets him.*

3. Serv. What fellow's this?   20
1. Serv. A strange one as ever I look'd on; I
cannot get him out o' th' house. Prithee, call my
master to him.   [*Retires.*]
3. Serv. What have you to do here, fellow? Pray
you, avoid the house.   25
Cor. Let me but stand; I will not hurt your hearth-
3. Serv. What are you?
Cor. A gentleman.
3. Serv. A marv'llous poor one.   30
Cor. True, so I am.
3. Serv. Pray you, poor gentleman, take up some
other station; here's no place for you. Pray you,
avoid. Come.   34
Cor. Follow your function, go and batten on cold
bits.   [*Pushes him away from him.*
3. Serv. What, you will not? Prithee, tell my
master what a strange guest he has here.
2. Serv. And I shall.   [*Exit.*
3. Serv. Where dwell'st thou?   40
Cor. Under the canopy.
3. Serv. Under the canopy?
Cor. Ay.
3. Serv. Where's that?
Cor. I' th' city of kites and crows.   45
3. Serv. I' th' city of kites and crows! What an
ass it is! Then thou dwell'st with daws too?
Cor. No, I serve not thy master.
3. Serv. How, sir! do you meddle with my
master?   51
Cor. Ay; 'tis an honester service than to meddle
with thy mistress.
Thou prat'st and prat'st; serve with thy trencher,
      hence!
          [*Beats him away. [Exit third Servingman.*]

Enter AUFIDIUS *with the* [*second*] SERVINGMAN.

Auf. Where is this fellow?   55
2. Serv. Here, sir. I'd have beaten him like a dog,
but for disturbing the lords within.   [*Retires.*]
Auf. Whence com'st thou? What wouldst thou?
      Thy name?
Why speak'st not? Speak, man: what's thy name?
Cor. If, Tullus [*unmuffling*], not yet thou 60
know'st me, and, seeing me, dost not think me for

17. **doit:** small coin. 22. **interjoin . . . issues:** intermarry their children. 23. **[hate]** (Capell). *have* F.
Sc. v, 3. **[master]** F4. M. F1. 14. **companions:** scurvy fellows. 18. **brave:** saucy. 25. **avoid:** quit. 35. **Follow . . .
function:** attend to your job. **batten:** fatten. 41. **canopy:** sky. 47. **daws:** jackdaws (foolish birds).

the man I am, necessity commands me name myself.

Auf. What is thy name?

Cor. A name unmusical to the Volscians' ears,
And harsh in sound to thine.

Auf.   Say, what's thy name?
Thou hast a grim appearance, and thy face   66
Bears a command in't; though thy tackle's torn,
Thou show'st a noble vessel.   What's thy name?

Cor. Prepare thy brow to frown.   Know'st thou
      me yet?

Auf. I know thee not.   Thy name?   70

Cor. My name is Caius Marcius, who hath done
To thee particularly and to all the Volsces
Great hurt and mischief; thereto witness may
My surname, Coriolanus.   The painful service,
The extreme dangers, and the drops of blood   75
Shed for my thankless country are requited
But with that surname; a good memory
And witness of the malice and displeasure
Which thou shouldst bear me.   Only that name re-
      mains.
The cruelty and envy of the people,   80
Permitted by our dastard nobles, who
Have all forsook me, hath devour'd the rest
And suffer'd me by th' voice of slaves to be
Whoop'd out of Rome.   Now this extremity
Hath brought me to thy hearth; not out of hope —
Mistake me not — to save my life, for if   86
I had fear'd death, of all the men i' th' world
I would have 'voided thee, but in mere spite,
To be full quit of those my banishers,
Stand I before thee here.   Then if thou hast   90
A heart of wreak in thee, that wilt revenge
Thine own particular wrongs and stop those maims
Of shame seen through thy country, speed thee
      straight
And make my misery serve thy turn.   So use it
That my revengeful services may prove   95
As benefits to thee, for I will fight
Against my cank'red country with the spleen
Of all the under fiends.   But if so be
Thou dar'st not this, and that to prove more for-
      tunes
Thou'rt tired, then, in a word, I also am   100
Longer to live most weary, and present
My throat to thee and to thy ancient malice;
Which not to cut would show thee but a fool,
Since I have ever followed thee with hate,
Drawn tuns of blood out of thy country's breast, 105
And cannot live but to thy shame, unless
It be to do thee service.

Auf.   O Marcius, Marcius!
Each word thou hast spoke hath weeded from my
      heart

A root of ancient envy.   If Jupiter
Should from yond cloud speak divine things,   110
And say "'Tis true," I'd not believe them more
Than thee, all noble Marcius.   Let me twine
Mine arms about that body, whereagainst
My grained ash an hundred times hath broke
And scarr'd the moon with splinters.   Here I clip
The anvil of my sword, and do contest   116
As hotly and as nobly with thy love
As ever in ambitious strength I did
Contend against thy valour.   Know thou first,
I lov'd the maid I married; never man   120
Sigh'd truer breath; but that I see thee here,
Thou noble thing, more dances my rapt heart
Than when I first my wedded mistress saw
Bestride my threshold.   Why, thou Mars, I tell
      thee,
We have a power on foot; and I had purpose   125
Once more to hew thy target from thy brawn,
Or lose mine arm for't.   Thou hast beat me out
Twelve several times, and I have nightly since
Dreamt of encounters 'twixt thyself and me;
We have been down together in my sleep,   130
Unbuckling helms, fisting each other's throat,
And wak'd half dead with nothing.   Worthy Mar-
      cius,
Had we no quarrel else to Rome but that
Thou art thence banish'd, we would muster all
From twelve to seventy, and pouring war   135
Into the bowels of ungrateful Rome,
Like a bold flood o'er-beat.   O, come, go in,
And take our friendly senators by th' hands;
Who now are here, taking their leaves of me,
Who am prepar'd against your territories,   140
Though not for Rome itself.

Cor.   You bless me, gods!

Auf. Therefore, most absolute sir, if thou wilt
      have
The leading of thine own revenges, take
Th' one half of my commission; and set down —
As best thou art experienc'd, since thou know'st 145
Thy country's strength and weakness, — thine own
      ways;
Whether to knock against the gates of Rome,
Or rudely visit them in parts remote,
To fright them ere destroy.   But come in;
Let me commend thee first to those that shall   150
Say yea to thy desires.   A thousand welcomes!
And more a friend than e'er an enemy;
Yet, Marcius, that was much.   Your hand; most
      welcome!

      [*Exeunt Coriolanus and Aufidius.   The two
      Servingmen* [*come forward*].

1. Serv. Here's a strange alteration!   154

---

77. **memory**: reminder. 91. **wreak**: vengeance. 92-93. **maims Of shame**: shameful injuries. 99. **prove**: try. 114.
grained ash: spear. 116. **anvil**: i.e., Coriolanus. 133. **quarrel** F₃. *other quarrel* F₁. 137. **o'er-beat**: beat (all) down. 142.
absolute: perfect.

2. Serv. By my hand, I had thought to have strucken him with a cudgel; and yet my mind gave me his clothes made a false report of him.

1. Serv. What an arm he has! He turn'd me about with his finger and his thumb as one would set up a top.   161

2. Serv. Nay, I knew by his face that there was something in him. He had, sir, a kind of face, methought, — I cannot tell how to term it.

1. Serv. He had so; looking as it were — would I were hang'd, but I thought there was more in him than I could think.   167

2. Serv. So did I, I'll be sworn. He is simply the rarest man i' th' world.

1. Serv. I think he is; but a greater soldier than he you wot one.   171

2. Serv. Who? My master?

1. Serv. Nay, it's no matter for that.

2. Serv. Worth six on him.

1. Serv. Nay, not so neither; but I take him to be the greater soldier.   176

2. Serv. Faith, look you, one cannot tell how to say that. For the defence of a town, our general is excellent.

1. Serv. Ay, and for an assault too.   180

Re-enter third SERVINGMAN.

3. Serv. O slaves, I can tell you news, — news, you rascals!

1. and 2. Serv. What, what, what? Let's partake.

3. Serv. I would not be a Roman, of all nations; I had as lieve be a condemn'd man.   186

1. and 2. Serv. Wherefore? wherefore?

3. Serv. Why, here's he that was wont to thwack our general, Caius Marcius.

1. Serv. Why do you say, "thwack our general"?   191

3. Serv. I do not say, "thwack our general"; but he was always good enough for him.

2. Serv. Come, we are fellows and friends; he was ever too hard for him; I have heard him say so himself.   196

1. Serv. He was too hard for him directly, to say the troth on't. Before Corioli he scotch'd him and notch'd him like a carbonado.

2. Serv. An he had been cannibally given, he might have boil'd and eaten him too.   201

1. Serv. But more of thy news.

3. Serv. Why, he is so made on here within as if he were son and heir to Mars; set at upper end o' th' table; no question ask'd him by any of the   205 senators but they stand bald before him. Our general himself makes a mistress of him; sanctifies

himself with 's hand and turns up the white o' th' eye to his discourse. But the bottom of the news is, our general is cut i' th' middle and but one   210 half of what he was yesterday; for the other has half by the entreaty and grant of the whole table. He'll go, he says, and sowl the porter of Rome gates by th' ears. He will mow all down before him, and leave his passage poll'd.   215

2. Serv. And he's as like to do't as any man I can imagine.

3. Serv. Do't! he will do't; for, look you, sir, he has as many friends as enemies; which friends, sir, as it were, durst not, look you, sir, show themselves, as we term it, his friends whilst he's in directitude.   222

1. Serv. Directitude! What's that?

3. Serv. But when they shall see, sir, his crest up again and the man in blood, they will out of their burrows like conies after rain, and revel all with him.   227

1. Serv. But when goes this forward?

3. Serv. To-morrow; to-day; presently; you shall have the drum struck up this afternoon. 'Tis, as it were, a parcel of their feast, and to be executed ere they wipe their lips.   232

2. Serv. Why, then we shall have a stirring world again. This peace is nothing but to rust iron, increase tailors, and breed ballad-makers.   235

1. Serv. Let me have war, say I; it exceeds peace as far as day does night; it's spritely, [waking], audible, and full of vent. Peace is a very apoplexy, lethargy; mull'd, deaf, sleepy, insensible; a getter of more bastard children than war's a destroyer of men.   241

2. Serv. 'Tis so; and as wars, in some sort, may be said to be a ravisher, so it cannot be denied but peace is a great maker of cuckolds.

1. Serv. Ay, and it makes men hate one another.   246

3. Serv. Reason; because they then less need one another. The wars for my money! I hope to see Romans as cheap as Volscians. — They are rising, they are rising.   250

1. and 2. Serv. In, in, in, in!   [*Exeunt.*

[SCENE VI. *Rome. A public place.*]

Enter SICINIUS *and* BRUTUS.

Sic. We hear not of him, neither need we fear him;

His remedies are tame. The present peace
And quietness of the people, which before
Were in wild hurry here, do make his friends

---

157. **gave:** told.   161. **set up:** spin.   197. **directly:** plainly.   198. **scotch'd:** slashed.   199. **carbonado:** meat cut for broiling.   213. **sowl:** drag.   215. **poll'd:** cleared.   222. **directitude:** blunder for *discredit.*   226. **conies:** rabbits.   237. **[waking]** (Pope): wide awake.   *walking* F.   238. **audible:** sharp-eared.   **vent:** activity (lit. outlet).   239. **mull'd:** drowsy.
   Sc. vi, 2. remedies: powers of redress.   4. **do** (Hanmer).   *do we* F.

Blush that the world goes well, who rather had,　5
Though they themselves did suffer by 't, behold
Dissentious numbers pest'ring streets than see
Our tradesmen singing in their shops and going
About their functions friendly.

Enter MENENIUS.

Bru. We stood to't in good time. Is this
Menenius?　　　　　　　　　　　　　　　10
Sic. 'Tis he, 'tis he. O, he is grown most kind of
late.
Hail, sir!
Men. Hail to you both!
Sic.　　　　　　　　　Your Coriolanus
Is not much miss'd but with his friends.
The commonwealth doth stand, and so would
do,
Were he more angry at it.　　　　　　　15
Men. All's well; and might have been much
better, if
He could have temporiz'd.
Sic.　　　　　　　Where is he, hear you?
Men. Nay, I hear nothing; his mother and his
wife
Hear nothing from him.

Enter three or four CITIZENS.

[*Citizens.*] The gods preserve you both!
Sic.　　　　　　　God-den, our neighbours,　20
Bru. God-den to you all, god-den to you all.
I. Cit. Ourselves, our wives, and children, on our
knees,
Are bound to pray for you both.
Sic.　　　　　　　　　　Live, and thrive!
Bru. Farewell, kind neighbours! We wish'd
Coriolanus　　　　　　　　　　　　24
Had lov'd you as we did.
[*Citizens.*]　　　　　　Now the gods keep you!
Both Tri. Farewell, farewell. [*Exeunt Citizens.*
Sic. This is a happier and more comely time
Than when these fellows ran about the streets,
Crying confusion.
Bru.　　　　　　Caius Marcius was
A worthy officer i' th' war, but insolent,　　30
O'ercome with pride, ambitious past all thinking,
Self-loving, —
Sic.　　　　　And affecting one sole throne,
Without assistance.
Men.　　　　I think not so.
Sic. We should by this, to all our lamentation,
If he had gone forth consul, found it so.　　35
Bru. The gods have well prevented it, and
Rome
Sits safe and still without him.

Enter an ÆDILE.

Æd.　　　　　　　　　Worthy tribunes,
There is a slave, whom we have put in prison,
Reports the Volsces with two several powers
Are ent'red in the Roman territories,　　　40
And with the deepest malice of the war
Destroy what lies before 'em.
Men.　　　　　　　　'Tis Aufidius,
Who, hearing of our Marcius' banishment,
Thrusts forth his horns again into the world;
Which were inshell'd when Marcius stood for
Rome,　　　　　　　　　　　　　45
And durst not once peep out.
Sic.　　　　　　Come, what talk you
Of Marcius?
Bru. Go see this rumourer whipp'd. It cannot
be
The Volsces dare break with us.
Men.　　　　　　　　Cannot be!
We have record that very well it can;
And three examples of the like hath been　　50
Within my age. But reason with the fellow,
Before you punish him, where he heard this,
Lest you shall chance to whip your information
And beat the messenger who bids beware
Of what is to be dreaded.
Sic.　　　　　　Tell not me!　　55
I know this cannot be.
Bru.　　　　　　Not possible.

Enter a MESSENGER.

Mess. The nobles in great earnestness are
going
All to the Senate-house; some news is [come]
That turns their countenances.
Sic.　　　　　　　'Tis this slave, —
Go whip him 'fore the people's eyes, — his raising;
Nothing but his report.
Mess.　　　　Yes, worthy sir,　　61
The slave's report is seconded; and more,
More fearful, is deliver'd.
Sic.　　　　　What more fearful?
Mess. It is spoke freely out of many mouths —
How probable I do not know — that Marcius,　65
Join'd with Aufidius, leads a power 'gainst Rome,
And vows revenge as spacious as between
The young'st and oldest thing.
Sic.　　　　　This is most likely!
Bru. Rais'd only that the weaker sort may wish
Good Marcius home again.
Sic.　　　　　The very trick on 't.　70
Men. This is unlikely.
He and Aufidius can no more atone
Than violent'st contrariety.

---

7. **pest'ring:** blocking. 19, etc. [*Citizens*] (Capell). *All* F. 51. **reason:** talk. 58. [**come**] (Rowe). *comming* F. 67.
between: i.e., to embrace. 69. **Rais'd:** made up. 72. **atone:** be reconciled.

Enter [a second] MESSENGER.

[*2.*] *Mess.* You are sent for to the Senate.
A fearful army, led by Caius Marcius   75
Associated with Aufidius, rages
Upon our territories; and have already
O'erborne their way, consum'd with fire, and took
What lay before them.

Enter COMINIUS.

Com. O, you have made good work!
Men.   What news? what news?
Com. You have holp to ravish your own daughters
and   81
To melt the city leads upon your pates,
To see your wives dishonour'd to your noses, —
Men. What's the news? what's the news?
Com. Your temples burned in their cement, and
Your franchises, whereon you stood, confin'd   86
Into an auger's bore.
Men.   Pray now, your news? —
You have made fair work, I fear me. — Pray, your
news?
If Marcius should be join'd with Volscians, —
Com.   If!
He is their god. He leads them like a thing   90
Made by some other deity than Nature,
That shapes man better; and they follow him
Against us brats with no less confidence
Than boys pursuing summer butterflies,   94
Or butchers killing flies.
Men.   You have made good work,
You and your apron-men; you that stood so much
Upon the voice of occupation and
The breath of garlic-eaters!
Com.   He will shake
Your Rome about your ears.
Men.   As Hercules
Did shake down mellow fruit. You have made fair
work!   100
Bru. But is this true, sir?
Com.   Ay; and you'll look pale
Before you find it other. All the regions
Do smilingly revolt; and who resists
Are mock'd for valiant ignorance
And perish constant fools. Who is't can blame
him?   105
Your enemies and his find something in him.
Men. We are all undone, unless
The noble man have mercy.
Com.   Who shall ask it?
The tribunes cannot do't for shame; the people
Deserve such pity of him as the wolf   110
Does of the shepherds. For his best friends, if they

Should say, "Be good to Rome," they charg'd him
even
As those should do that had deserv'd his hate,
And therein show'd like enemies.
Men.   'Tis true.
If he were putting to my house the brand   115
That should consume it, I have not the face
To say, "Beseech you, cease." You have made
fair hands,
You and your crafts! You have crafted fair!
Com.   You have brought
A trembling upon Rome, such as was never
S' incapable of help.
[*Both*] *Tri.*   Say not we brought it.   120
Men. How! Was 't we? We lov'd him; but,
like beasts,
[The] cowardly nobles gave way unto your clusters,
Who did hoot him out o' th' city.
Com.   But I fear
They'll roar him in again. Tullus Aufidius,
The second name of men, obeys his points   125
As if he were his officer. Desperation
Is all the policy, strength, and defence
That Rome can make against them.

Enter a troop of CITIZENS.

Men.   Here come the clusters.
And is Aufidius with him? You are they
That made the air unwholesome, when you cast 130
Your stinking greasy caps in hooting at
Coriolanus' exile. Now he's coming;
And not a hair upon a soldier's head
Which will not prove a whip. As many coxcombs
As you threw caps up will he tumble down,   135
And pay you for your voices. 'Tis no matter;
If he could burn us all into one coal,
We have deserv'd it.
[*Citizens.*] Faith, we hear fearful news.
1. Cit.   For mine own part,
When I said banish him, I said 'twas pity.   140
2. Cit. And so did I.
3. Cit. And so did I; and, to say the truth, so did
very many of us. That we did, we did for the best;
and though we willingly consented to his banish-
ment, yet it was against our will.   146
Com. You're goodly things, you voices!
Men.   You have made
Good work, you and your cry! Shall 's to the Capi-
tol?
Com. O, ay, what else?
                  [*Exeunt Cominius and Menenius.*
Sic. Go, masters, get you home; be not dismay'd.
These are a side that would be glad to have   151

---

74. [*2.*] (Hanmer). Om. F.   78. **O'erborne:** surged over.   86. **stood:** insisted. **confin'd:** shrunk.   96. **apron-men:**
artisans.   97. **occupation:** workingmen.   105. **constant:** steadfast.   112. **charg'd:** would be beseeching.   114. **show'd:**
would look.   117. **made . . . hands:** done fine work.   120. [*Both*] (Dyce). Om. F.   122. [The] (Gould conj.).   *And* F.
clusters: mobs.   125. **points:** directions.   134. **coxcombs:** fool's heads.

This true which they so seem to fear. Go home,
And show no sign of fear.
   1. Cit. The gods be good to us! Come, masters,
let's home. I ever said we were i' th' wrong when
we banish'd him.   156
   2. Cit. So did we all. But, come, let's home.
                         [Exeunt Citizens.
   Bru. I do not like this news.
   Sic. Nor I.   159
   Bru. Let's to the Capitol. Would half my wealth
Would buy this for a lie!
   Sic.   Pray, let's go.   *[Exeunt.*

[SCENE VII. *A camp, at a small distance from*
Rome.]

Enter AUFIDIUS *with his* LIEUTENANT.

   Auf. Do they still fly to th' Roman?
   Lieu. I do not know what witchcraft's in him, but
Your soldiers use him as the grace 'fore meat,
Their talk at table, and their thanks at end;
And you are dark'ned in this action, sir,   5
Even by your own.
   Auf.   I cannot help it now,
Unless, by using means, I lame the foot
Of our design. He bears himself more proudlier,
Even to my person, than I thought he would
When first I did embrace him; yet his nature   10
In that's no changeling, and I must excuse
What cannot be amended.
   Lieu.   Yet I wish, sir, —
I mean for your particular, — you had not
Join'd in commission with him; but either
[Had] borne the action of yourself, or else   15
To him had left it solely.
   Auf. I understand thee well; and be thou sure,
When he shall come to his account, he knows not
What I can urge against him. Although it seems,
And so he thinks, and is no less apparent   20
To th' vulgar eye, that he bears all things fairly,
And shows good husbandry for the Volscian state,
Fights dragon-like, and does achieve as soon
As draw his sword; yet he hath left undone
That which shall break his neck or hazard mine   25
Whene'er we come to our account.
   Lieu. Sir, I beseech you, think you he'll carry
    Rome?
   Auf. All places yield to him ere he sits down,
And the nobility of Rome are his.
The senators and patricians love him too;   30
The tribunes are no soldiers, and their people

Will be as rash in the repeal as hasty
To expel him thence. I think he'll be to Rome
As is the osprey to the fish, who takes it
By sovereignty of nature. First he was   35
A noble servant to them, but he could not
Carry his honours even. Whether 'twas pride,
Which out of daily fortune ever taints
The happy man; whether [defect] of judgement,
To fail in the disposing of those chances   40
Which he was lord of; or whether nature,
Not to be other than one thing, not moving
From th' casque to th' cushion, but commanding
    peace
Even with the same austerity and garb
As he controll'd the war; but one of these, —   45
As he hath spices of them all — not all, —
For I dare so far free him, — made him fear'd;
So, hated; and so, banish'd; but he has a merit
To choke it in the utt'rance. So our virtues
Lie in th' interpretation of the time;   50
And power, unto itself most commendable,
Hath not a tomb so evident as a chair
T' extol what it hath done.
One fire drives out one fire; one nail, one nail;
Rights by rights [falter], strengths by strengths do
    fail.   55
Come, let's away. When, Caius, Rome is thine,
Thou art poor'st of all; ther shortly art thou mine.
                               [Exeunt.

ACT V

[SCENE I. *Rome. A public place.*]

Enter MENENIUS, COMINIUS, SICINIUS, BRUTUS,
with others.

   Men. No, I'll not go. You hear what he hath
    said
Which was sometime his general who lov'd him
In a most dear particular. He call'd me father;
But what o' that? Go, you that banish'd him;
A mile before his tent fall down, and knee   5
The way into his mercy. Nay, if he coy'd
To hear Cominius speak, I'll keep at home.
   Com. He would not seem to know me.
   Men.   Do you hear?
   Com. Yet one time he did call me by my name.
I urg'd our old acquaintance, and the drops   10
That we have bled together. Coriolanus
He would not answer to; forbade all names;
He was a kind of nothing, titleless,

Sc. vii, 13. **particular:** personal good. 14. **commission:** command. 15. **[Had]** (Pope). *Have* F. **of:** by. 22. **husbandry:** economy. 28. **sits down:** lays siege. 34. **osprey:** fish hawk. 39. **happy:** lucky. **[defect]** F₂. *detect* F₁. 41. **nature:** i.e., it was his nature. 42. **moving:** i.e., changing his behavior when moving. 43. **casque:** helmet, i.e., battlefield. **cushion:** i.e., senate-house. 49. **it:** i.e., the enmity. 52–53. **Hath ... done:** is never so near its end as when it proclaims its own deserts. 55. **[falter]** (Dyce). *fouler* F. Other emendations are *founder, suffer.*
  Act V, sc. i, 3. particular: personal way. 6. **coy'd:** was reluctant.

Till he had forg'd himself a name o' th' fire
Of burning Rome.
   Men. Why, so; you have made good work! 15
A pair of tribunes that have wrack'd [fair] Rome
To make coals cheap! A noble memory!
   Com. I minded him how royal 'twas to pardon
When it was less expected; he replied,
It was a bare petition of a state 20
To one whom they had punish'd.
   Men.   Very well;
Could he say less?
   Com. I offered to awaken his regard
For 's private friends; his answer to me was,
He could not stay to pick them in a pile 25
Of noisome musty chaff. He said 'twas folly,
For one poor grain or two, to leave unburnt
And still to nose th' offence.
   Men.   For one poor grain or two!
I am one of those; his mother, wife, his child,
And this brave fellow too, we are the grains. 30
You are the musty chaff, and you are smelt
Above the moon; we must be burnt for you.
   Sic. Nay, pray, be patient. If you refuse your
    aid
In this so never-needed help, yet do not
Upbraid 's with our distress. But, sure, if you 35
Would be your country's pleader, your good tongue,
More than the instant army we can make,
Might stop our countryman.
   Men.   No, I'll not meddle.
   Sic. Pray you, go to him.
   Men.   What should I do?
   Bru. Only make trial what your love can do 40
For Rome, towards Marcius.
   Men.   Well, and say that Marcius
Return me, as Cominius is return'd,
Unheard; what then?
But as a discontented friend, grief-shot
With his unkindness? Say 't be so?
   Sic.   Yet your good will
Must have that thanks from Rome, after the
    measure 46
As you intended well.
   Men.   I'll undertake 't.
I think he'll hear me. Yet, to bite his lip
And hum at good Cominius much unhearts me.
He was not taken well; he had not din'd. 50
The veins unfill'd, our blood is cold, and then
We pout upon the morning, are unapt
To give or to forgive; but when we have stuff'd
These pipes and these conveyances of our blood
With wine and feeding, we have suppler souls 55
Than in our priest-like fasts: therefore I'll watch
    him

Till he be dieted to my request,
And then I'll set upon him.
   Bru. You know the very road into his kindness,
And cannot lose your way.
   Men.   Good faith, I'll prove him,
Speed how it will. I shall ere long have know-
    ledge 61
Of my success.   [*Exit.*
   Com.   He'll never hear him.
   Sic.   Not?
   Com. I tell you, he does sit in gold, his eye
Red as 'twould burn Rome; and his injury
The gaoler to his pity. I kneel'd before him; 65
'Twas very faintly he said, "Rise"; dismiss'd me
Thus, with his speechless hand. What he would
    do
He sent in writing after me; what he would not,
Bound with an oath to yield to his conditions;
So that all hope is vain, 70
Unless [in 's] noble mother and his wife,
Who, as I hear, mean to solicit him
For mercy to his country. Therefore, let's hence,
And with our fair entreaties haste them on.
                        [*Exeunt.*

[SCENE II. *Entrance of the Volscian camp before
    Rome.*] *The* WATCH *on guard.*

       Enter to them, MENENIUS.

   1. Watch. Stay! Whence are you?
   2. Watch.   Stand, and go back.
   Men. You guard like men; 'tis well; but, by your
    leave,
I am an officer of state, and come
To speak with Coriolanus.
   1. Watch.   From whence?
   Men.   From Rome.
   1. Watch. You may not pass, you must return;
    our general 5
Will no more hear from thence.
   2. Watch. You'll see your Rome embrac'd with
    fire before
You'll speak with Coriolanus.
   Men.   Good my friends,
If you have heard your general talk of Rome
And of his friends there, it is lots to blanks 10
My name hath touch'd your ears; it is Menenius.
   1. Watch. Be it so; go back. The virtue of your
    name
Is not here passable.
   Men.   I tell thee, fellow,
Thy general is my lover. I have been
The book of his good acts, whence men have read 15
His fame unparallel'd haply amplified;

---

    16. [fair] (Hanmer). *for* F. 20. **bare**: mere. 23. **offered**: tried. 37. **instant**: improvised. 50. **taken well**: ap-
proached at a good time. 63. **in gold**: on a throne of gold. 69. **Bound**: i.e., binding us. 71. [**in 's**] *his* F
    Sc. ii, 10. **lots to blanks**: certain (terms from lottery). 13. **passable**: current.

For I have ever verified my friends,
Of whom he's chief, with all the size that verity
Would without lapsing suffer; nay, sometimes,
Like to a bowl upon a subtle ground,   20
I have tumbled past the throw; and in his praise
Have almost stamp'd the leasing. Therefore, fellow,
I must have leave to pass.

1. Watch. Faith, sir, if you had told as many lies
in his behalf as you have uttered words in your
own, you should not pass here; no, though it were
as virtuous to lie as to live chastely. Therefore, go
back.   28

Men. Prithee, fellow, remember my name is
Menenius, always factionary on the party of your
general.   31

2. Watch. Howsoever you have been his liar, as
you say you have, I am one that, telling true under
him, must say you cannot pass. Therefore, go
back.   35

Men. Has he din'd, canst thou tell? for I would
not speak with him till after dinner.

1. Watch. You are a Roman, are you?

Men. I am, as thy general is.   39

1. Watch. Then you should hate Rome, as he
does. Can you, when you have push'd out your
gates the very defender of them, and, in a violent
popular ignorance, given your enemy your shield,
think to front his revenges with the easy groans of
old women, the virginal palms of your daughters,   45
or with the palsied intercession of such a decay'd
dotant as you seem to be? Can you think to blow
out the intended fire your city is ready to flame in,
with such weak breath as this? No, you are de-   50
ceiv'd; therefore, back to Rome, and prepare for
your execution. You are condemn'd; our general
has sworn you out of reprieve and pardon.   54

Men. Sirrah, if thy captain knew I were here,
he would use me with estimation.

1. Watch. Come, my captain knows you not.

Men. I mean, thy general.   58

1. Watch. My general cares not for you. Back,
I say, go; lest I let forth your half-pint of blood.
Back, that's the utmost of your having; back!

Men. Nay, but, fellow, fellow, —

Enter CORIOLANUS *with* AUFIDIUS.

Cor. What's the matter?   64

Men. Now, you companion, I'll say an errand
for you. You shall know now that I am in estimation; you shall perceive that a Jack guardant cannot
office me from my son Coriolanus. Guess but [by]

my entertainment with him if thou stand'st not i'
th' state of hanging, or of some death more long   70
in spectatorship and crueller in suffering; behold
now presently, and swoon for what's to come upon
thee. [*To Cor.*] The glorious gods sit in hourly
synod about thy particular prosperity, and love thee
no worse than thy old father Menenius does! O   75
my son, my son! thou art preparing fire for us; look
thee, here's water to quench it. I was hardly moved
to come to thee; but being assured none but myself
could move thee, I have been blown out of our   80
gates with sighs, and conjure thee to pardon Rome
and thy petitionary countrymen. The good gods
assuage thy wrath, and turn the dregs of it upon
this varlet here, — this, who, like a block, hath
denied my access to thee.   85

Cor. Away!

Men. How! away!

Cor. Wife, mother, child I know not. My affairs
Are servanted to others; though I owe
My revenge properly, my remission lies   90
In Volscian breasts. That we have been familiar,
Ingrate forgetfulness shall poison rather
Than pity note how much. Therefore, begone.
Mine ears against your suits are stronger than
Your gates against my force. Yet, for I loved thee,   95
Take this along. I writ it for thy sake,
          [*Gives a letter.*]
And would have sent it. Another word, Menenius,
I will not hear thee speak. This man, Aufidius,
Was my belov'd in Rome; yet thou behold'st!

Auf. You keep a constant temper.   100
          [*Exeunt [Coriolanus and Aufidius].*]

1. Watch. Now, sir, is your name Menenius?

2. Watch. 'Tis a spell, you see, of much power.
You know the way home again.

1. Watch. Do you hear how we are shent for keeping your greatness back?   105

2. Watch. What cause do you think I have to
swoon?

Men. I neither care for th' world nor your general; for such things as you, I can scarce think
there's any, you're so slight. He that hath a   110
will to die by himself fears it not from another.
Let your general do his worst. For you, be that
you are, long; and your misery increase with your
age! I say to you, as I was said to, "Away!" [*Exit.*

1. Watch. A noble fellow, I warrant him.   115

2. Watch. The worthy fellow is our general. He's
the rock, the oak not to be wind-shaken. [*Exeunt.*

---

17. **verified:** credited. Many emendations have been proposed, as *magnified, glorified, amplified.* 20. **subtle:** deceptive.
21. **throw:** mark. 22. **stamp'd the leasing:** certified a falsehood. 30. **factionary on:** adhering to. 47. **dotant:** dotard.
65. **say an errand:** deliver a message. 67. **Jack guardant:** ill-mannered guard. 68. **[by]** (Malone). *my* F. 77.
hardly: with difficulty. 84. **block:** blockhead. 89. **servanted:** subjected. 90. **properly:** to myself. **remission:** mercy.
104. **shent:** scolded. 111. **himself:** his own hand.

[SCENE III. *The tent of Coriolanus.*]

Enter CORIOLANUS, AUFIDIUS [*and others*].

Cor. We will before the walls of Rome to-morrow
Set down our host. My partner in this action,
You must report to th' Volscian lords, how plainly
I have borne this business.
Auf.   Only their ends
You have respected; stopp'd your ears against   5
The general suit of Rome; never admitted
A private whisper, no, not with such friends
That thought them sure of you.
Cor.   This last old man,
Whom with a crack'd heart I have sent to Rome,
Lov'd me above the measure of a father;   10
Nay, godded me, indeed. Their latest refuge
Was to send him; for whose old love I have,
Though I show'd sourly to him, once more offer'd
The first conditions, which they did refuse
And cannot now accept. To grace him only   15
That thought he could do more, a very little
I have yielded to. Fresh embassies and suits,
Nor from the state nor private friends, hereafter
Will I lend ear to. Ha! what shout is this?
                              [*Shout within.*
Shall I be tempted to infringe my vow   20
In the same time 'tis made? I will not.

Enter [*in mourning habits*] VIRGILIA, VOLUMNIA
[*leading*] *young* MARCIUS, Valeria, *with Attendants.*

My wife comes foremost; then the honour'd mould
Wherein this trunk was fram'd, and in her hand
The grandchild to her blood. But out, affection!
All bond and privilege of nature, break!   25
Let it be virtuous to be obstinate.
What is that curtsy worth? or those doves' eyes,
Which can make gods forsworn? I melt, and am
    not
Of stronger earth than others. My mother bows,
As if Olympus to a molehill should   30
In supplication nod; and my young boy
Hath an aspect of intercession which
Great nature cries, "Deny not." Let the Volsces
Plough Rome and harrow Italy, I'll never
Be such a gosling to obey instinct, but stand   35
As if a man were author of himself
And knew no other kin.
Vir.   My lord and husband!
Cor. These eyes are not the same I wore in Rome.
Vir. The sorrow that delivers us thus chang'd
Makes you think so.
Cor.   Like a dull actor now   40
I have forgot my part, and I am out,

Even to a full disgrace. Best of my flesh,
Forgive my tyranny; but do not say
For that, "Forgive our Romans." O, a kiss
Long as my exile, sweet as my revenge!   45
Now, by the jealous queen of heaven, that kiss
I carried from thee, dear; and my true lip
Hath virgin'd it e'er since. You gods! I [prate],
And the most noble mother of the world
Leave unsaluted. Sink, my knee, i' th' earth;
                              [*Kneels.*
Of thy deep duty more impression show   51
Than that of common sons.
Vol.   O, stand up bless'd!
Whilst, with no softer cushion than the flint,
I kneel before thee, and unproperly
Show duty, as mistaken all this while   55
Between the child and parent.   [*Kneels.*]
Cor. [*Instantly raising her.*] What's this?
Your knees to me? to your corrected son?
Then let the pebbles on the hungry beach
Fillip the stars; then let the mutinous winds
Strike the proud cedars 'gainst the fiery sun,   60
Murd'ring impossibility, to make
What cannot be, slight work.
Vol.   Thou art my warrior;
I holp to frame thee. Do you know this lady?
Cor. The noble sister of Publicola,
The moon of Rome, chaste as the icicle   65
That's curded by the frost from purest snow
And hangs on Dian's temple. Dear Valeria!
Vol. This is a poor epitome of yours,
Which by th' interpretation of full time
May show like all yourself.
Cor.   The god of soldiers,
With the consent of supreme Jove, inform   71
Thy thoughts with nobleness; that thou mayst prove
To shame unvulnerable, and stick i' th' wars
Like a great sea-mark, standing every flaw
And saving those that eye thee!
Vol.   Your knee, sirrah.
Cor. That's my brave boy!   76
Vol. Even he, your wife, this lady, and myself,
Are suitors to you.
Cor.   I beseech you, peace;
Or, if you'd ask, remember this before:
The thing I have forsworn to grant may never
Be held by you denials. Do not bid me   81
Dismiss my soldiers, or capitulate
Again with Rome's mechanics; tell me not
Wherein I seem unnatural; desire not
To allay my rages and revenges with   85
Your colder reasons.
Vol.   O, no more, no more!

Sc. iii, 3. **plainly:** honestly. 4. **borne:** conducted. 13. **show'd:** acted. 43. **tyranny:** cruelty. 48. **[prate]** (Theobald). *pray* F. 51. **duty:** reverence. 54. **unproperly:** unnaturally. 58. **hungry:** barren. 59. **Fillip:** strike at. 66. **curded:** congealed. 71. **inform:** inspire. 73. **stick:** stand out. 74. **standing:** withstanding. **flaw:** squall. 82. **capitulate:** come to terms.

You have said you will not grant us anything,
For we have nothing else to ask but that
Which you deny already.   Yet we will ask,
That, if you fail in our request, the blame   90
May hang upon your hardness; therefore hear us.
    Cor. Aufidius, and you Volsces, mark; for we'll
Hear nought from Rome in private.   Your request?
    Vol. Should we be silent and not speak, our
          raiment
And state of bodies would bewray what life   95
We have led since thy exile.   Think with thyself
How more unfortunate than all living women
Are we come hither; since that thy sight, which
          should
Make our eyes flow with joy, hearts dance with
          comforts,
Constrains them weep and shake with fear and
          sorrow;   100
Making the mother, wife, and child to see
The son, the husband, and the father tearing
His country's bowels out.   And to poor we
Thine enmity's most capital.   Thou barr'st us
Our prayers to the gods, which is a comfort   105
That all but we enjoy; for how can we,
Alas, how can we for our country pray,
Whereto we are bound, together with thy victory,
Whereto we are bound?   Alack, or we must lose
The country, our dear nurse, or else thy person, 110
Our comfort in the country.   We must find
An evident calamity, though we had
Our wish, which side should win; for either thou
Must, as a foreign recreant, be led
With manacles through our streets, or else   115
Triumphantly tread on thy country's ruin
And bear the palm for having bravely shed
Thy wife and children's blood.   For myself, son,
I purpose not to wait on fortune till
These wars determine.   If I cannot persuade thee
Rather to show a noble grace to both parts   121
Than seek the end of one, thou shalt no sooner
March to assault thy country than to tread —
Trust to't, thou shalt not — on thy mother's womb
That brought thee to this world.
    Vir.   Ay, and on mine,
That brought you forth this boy, to keep your
          name   126
Living to time.
    Young Mar. 'A shall not tread on me.
I'll run away till I am bigger, but then I'll fight.
    Cor. Not of a woman's tenderness to be,
Requires nor child nor woman's face to see.   130
I have sat too long.   [*Rising.*]
    Vol.   Nay, go not from us thus.

If it were so that our request did tend
To save the Romans, thereby to destroy
The Volsces whom you serve, you might condemn
          us,
As poisonous of your honour.   No; our suit   135
Is that you reconcile them: while the Volsces
May say, "This mercy we have show'd"; the
          Romans,
"This we receiv'd"; and each in either side
Give the all-hail to thee and cry, "Be blest
For making up this peace!"   Thou know'st, great
          son,   140
The end of war 's uncertain, but this certain,
That, if thou conquer Rome, the benefit
Which thou shalt thereby reap is such a name
Whose repetition will be dogg'd with curses,
Whose chronicle thus writ: "The man was noble,
But with his last attempt he wip'd it out,   146
Destroy'd his country, and his name remains
To th' ensuing age abhorr'd."   Speak to me, son.
Thou hast affected the [fine] strains of honour,
To imitate the graces of the gods;   150
To tear with thunder the wide cheeks o' th' air,
And yet to [charge] thy sulphur with a bolt
That should but rive an oak.   Why dost not speak?
Think'st thou it honourable for a noble man
Still to remember wrongs?   Daughter, speak you;
He cares not for your weeping.   Speak thou, boy; 156
Perhaps thy childishness will move him more
Than can our reasons.   There's no man in the world
More bound to 's mother; yet here he lets me prate
Like one i' th' stocks. — Thou hast never in thy
          life   160
Show'd thy dear mother any courtesy,
When she, poor hen, fond of no second brood,
Has cluck'd thee to the wars and safely home,
Loaden with honour.   Say my request 's unjust,
And spurn me back; but if it be not so,   165
Thou art not honest; and the gods will plague thee
That thou restrain'st from me the duty which
To a mother's part belongs. — He turns away.
Down, ladies; let us shame him with our knees.
To his surname Coriolanus longs more pride   170
Than pity to our prayers.   Down! an end;
This is the last.   So we will home to Rome,
And die among our neighbours. — Nay, behold 's!
This boy, that cannot tell what he would have,
But kneels and holds up hands for fellowship,   175
Does reason our petition with more strength
Than thou hast to deny 't. — Come, let us go.
This fellow had a Volscian to his mother;
His wife is in Corioli, and his child
Like him by chance. — Yet give us our dispatch. 180

---

90. **fail in:** refuse.   95. **bewray:** reveal.   114. **recreant:** traitor.   120. **determine:** end.   124. **Trust...not.**   In sense, this parenthesis follows "sooner," l. 122.   146. **attempt:** enterprise.   149. **[fine]** (Johnson).   *five* F.   152. **[charge]** (Warburton).   *change* F.   **sulphur:** the supposed source of lightning.   153. **rive an oak:** i.e., do little real harm.   167. **restrain'st:** withholdest.   170. **longs:** belongs.   176. **reason:** argue.   180. **dispatch:** dismissal.

I am hush'd until our city be a-fire,
And then I'll speak a little.

         [*He holds her by the hand, silent.*
   Cor.   O mother, mother!
What have you done?   Behold, the heavens do ope,
The gods look down, and this unnatural scene
They laugh at.   O my mother, mother!   O!   185
You have won a happy victory to Rome;
But, for your son, — believe it, O believe it —,
Most dangerously you have with him prevail'd,
If not most mortal to him.   But, let it come.
Aufidius, though I cannot make true wars,   190
I'll frame convenient peace.   Now, good Aufidius,
Were you in my [stead], would you have heard
A mother less, or granted less, Aufidius?

   Auf.   I was mov'd withal.

   Cor.   I dare be sworn you were;
And, sir, it is no little thing to make   195
Mine eyes to sweat compassion.   But, good sir,
What peace you'll make, advise me.   For my part,
I'll not to Rome, I'll back with you; and pray you,
Stand to me in this cause. — O mother! wife!

         [*Speaks apart with them.*
   Auf. [*Aside.*] I am glad thou hast set thy mercy
      and thy honour   200
At difference in thee.   Out of that I'll work
Myself a former fortune.

   Cor. [*To Volumnia, Virgilia, etc.*]   Ay, by and by;
But we will drink together; and you shall bear
A better witness back than words, which we,
On like conditions, will have counter-seal'd.   205
Come, enter with us.   Ladies, you deserve
To have a temple built you.   All the swords
In Italy, and her confederate arms,
Could not have made this peace.   [*Exeunt.*

     [SCENE IV.   *Rome.*   *A public place.*]

     Enter MENENIUS *and* SICINIUS.

   Men.   See you yond coign o' th' Capitol, yond
corner-stone?

   Sic.   Why, what of that?

   Men.   If it be possible for you to displace it with
your little finger, there is some hope the ladies of   5
Rome, especially his mother, may prevail with him.
But I say there is no hope in 't; our throats are
sentenc'd and stay upon execution.

   Sic.   Is't possible that so short a time can alter
the condition of a man?   10

   Men.   There is difference between a grub and a
butterfly; yet your butterfly was a grub.   This
Marcius is grown from man to dragon; he has wings;
he's more than a creeping thing.

   Sic.   He lov'd his mother dearly.   15

   Men.   So did he me; and he no more remembers
his mother now than an eight-year-old horse.
The tartness of his face sours ripe grapes; when he
walks, he moves like an engine, and the ground
shrinks before his treading.   He is able to pierce   20
a corslet with his eye; talks like a knell, and his
hum is a battery.   He sits in his state, as a thing
made for Alexander.   What he bids be done is
finish'd with his bidding.   He wants nothing of a
god but eternity and a heaven to throne in.   26

   Sic.   Yes, mercy, if you report him truly.

   Men.   I paint him in the character.   Mark what
mercy his mother shall bring from him.   There is
no more mercy in him than there is milk in a male
tiger; that shall our poor city find: and all this is
long of you.   32

   Sic.   The gods be good unto us!

   Men.   No, in such a case the gods will not be good
unto us.   When we banish'd him, we respected not
them; and, he returning to break our necks, they
respect not us.   37

     Enter a MESSENGER.

   Mess.   Sir, if you'd save your life, fly to your
     house.
The plebeians have got your fellow-tribune
And hale him up and down, all swearing, if   40
The Roman ladies bring not comfort home,
They'll give him death by inches.

     Enter a second MESSENGER.

   Sic.   What's the news?

   [*2.*] *Mess.*   Good news, good news!   The ladies
     have prevail'd,
The Volscians are dislodg'd, and Marcius gone.
A merrier day did never yet greet Rome,   45
No, not th' expulsion of the Tarquins.

   Sic.   Friend,
Art thou certain this is true?   Is't most certain?

   [*2.*] *Mess.*   As certain as I know the sun is fire.
Where have you lurk'd, that you make doubt of it?
Ne'er through an arch so hurried the blown tide,   50
As the recomforted through th' gates.   Why, hark
     you!

         [*Trumpets; hautboys; drums beat; all to-*
         gether.
The trumpets, sackbuts, psalteries, and fifes,
Tabors and cymbals and the shouting Romans,
Make the sun dance.   Hark you!

         [*A shout within.*
   Men.   This is good news;
I will go meet the ladies.   This Volumnia   55

---

192. [stead] F₄.   *steed* F₁.   199. **Stand to:** support.   201–202. **work . . . fortune:** retrieve my former fortune.
   Sc. iv, 1. coign: corner.   8. **stay upon:** await.   10. **condition:** nature.   19. **engine:** instrument of war.   22. **state:** chair
of state.   32. **long:** because.   35. **respected:** considered.   44. **dislodg'd:** decamped.   52. s.d. *hautboys:* oboes.   **sackbuts:**
trombones.   **psalteries:** stringed instruments.

Is worth of consuls, senators, patricians,
A city full; of tribunes, such as you,
A sea and land full. You have pray'd well to-day.
This morning for ten thousand of your throats
I'd not have given a doit. Hark, how they joy!

    [*Sound still, with the shouts.*

  Sic. First, the gods bless you for your tidings;
    next,   61
Accept my thankfulness.
  [2.] *Mess.*   Sir, we have all
Great cause to give great thanks.
  Sic.   They are near the city?
  [2.] *Mess.* Almost at point to enter.
  Sic.   We will meet them,
And help the joy.   [*Exeunt.* 65

[SCENE V. *The same. A street near the gate.*]

Enter two SENATORS *with Ladies* [Volumnia, Virgilia, Valeria, etc.], *passing over the stage, with other Lords.*

  [1.] *Sen.* Behold our patroness, the life of Rome!
Call all your tribes together, praise the gods,
And make triumphant fires! Strew flowers before
    them!
Unshout the noise that banish'd Marcius!
Repeal him with the welcome of his mother;   5
Cry, "Welcome, ladies, welcome!"
  All.   Welcome, ladies,
Welcome!   [*A flourish with drums and trumpets.*
                            [*Exeunt.*]

[SCENE VI. *Corioli. A public place.*]

Enter TULLUS AUFIDIUS, *with* Attendants.

  Auf. Go tell the lords o' th' city I am here;
Deliver them this paper. Having read it,
Bid them repair to th' market-place, where I,
Even in theirs and in the commons' ears,
Will vouch the truth of it. Him I accuse   5
The city ports by this hath enter'd, and
Intends to appear before the people, hoping
To purge himself with words. Dispatch.
                [*Exeunt Attendants.*]

Enter three or four CONSPIRATORS *of Aufidius' faction.*

Most welcome!
  1. *Con.* How is it with our general?
  Auf.   Even so   10
As with a man by his own alms empoison'd,
And with his charity slain.
  2. *Con.*   Most noble sir,
If you do hold the same intent wherein
You wish'd us parties, we'll deliver you

Of your great danger.
  Auf.   Sir, I cannot tell.   15
We must proceed as we do find the people.
  3. *Con.* The people will remain uncertain whilst
'Twixt you there's difference; but the fall of either
Makes the survivor heir of all.
  Auf.   I know it;
And my pretext to strike at him admits   20
A good construction. I rais'd him, and I pawn'd
Mine honour for his truth; who being so heighten'd,
He watered his new plants with dews of flattery,
Seducing so my friends; and, to this end,
He bow'd his nature, never known before   25
But to be rough, unswayable, and free.
  3. *Con.*   Sir, his stoutness
When he did stand for consul, which he lost
By lack of stooping, —
  Auf.   That I would have spoke of.   29
Being banish'd for't, he came unto my hearth,
Presented to my knife his throat. I took him;
Made him joint-servant with me; gave him way
In all his own desires; nay, let him choose
Out of my files, his projects to accomplish,
My best and freshest men; serv'd his designments
In mine own person; holp to reap the fame   36
Which he did end all his, and took some pride
To do myself this wrong; till, at the last,
I seem'd his follower, not partner, and
He wag'd me with his countenance as if   40
I had been mercenary.
  1. *Con.*   So he did, my lord.
The army marvell'd at it, and, in the last,
When he had carried Rome and that we look'd
For no less spoil than glory, —
  Auf.   There was it,
For which my sinews shall be stretch'd upon him.
At a few drops of women's rheum, which are   46
As cheap as lies, he sold the blood and labour
Of our great action. Therefore shall he die,
And I'll renew me in his fall. But, hark!
    [*Drums and trumpets sound, with great shouts of the People.*
  1. *Con.* Your native town you enter'd like a post,
And had no welcomes home; but he returns,   51
Splitting the air with noise.
  2. *Con.*   And patient fools,
Whose children he hath slain, their base throats tear
With giving him glory.
  3. *Con.*   Therefore, at your vantage,
Ere he express himself or move the people   55
With what he would say, let him feel your sword,
Which we will second. When he lies along,
After your way his tale pronounc'd shall bury
His reasons with his body.
  Auf.   Say no more.
Here come the lords.   60

Sc. vi, 40. **wag'd ... countenance:** paid me with his favor, patronized me. 45. **upon:** against. 46. **rheum:** tears. 50. **post:** messenger. 57. **along:** prostrate, dead. 58. **After ... pronounc'd:** your version of the story.

Enter the LORDS *of the city.*

All the Lords. You are most welcome home.

Auf.   I have not deserv'd it.
But, worthy lords, have you with heed perused
What I have written to you?

Lords.   We have.

1. Lord.   And grieve to hear 't.
What faults he made before the last, I think
Might have found easy fines; but there to end   65
Where he was to begin, and give away
The benefit of our levies, answering us
With our own charge, making a treaty where
There was a yielding, — this admits no excuse.

Auf. He approaches; you shall hear him.   70

Enter CORIOLANUS, *marching with drum and
colours;* Commoners *being with him.*

Cor. Hail, lords! I am return'd your soldier,
No more infected with my country's love
Than when I parted hence, but still subsisting
Under your great command. You are to know
That prosperously I have attempted and   75
With bloody passage led your wars even to
The gates of Rome. Our spoils we have brought home
Doth more than counterpoise a full third part
The charges of the action. We have made peace
With no less honour to the Antiates   80
Than shame to th' Romans; and we here deliver,
Subscrib'd by th' consuls and patricians,
Together with the seal o' th' Senate, what
We have compounded on.

Auf.   Read it not, noble lords;
But tell the traitor, in the highest degree   85
He hath abus'd your powers.

Cor. "Traitor!" How now!

Auf.   Ay, traitor, Marcius!

Cor.   "Marcius!"

Auf. Ay, Marcius, Caius Marcius! Dost thou
think
I'll grace thee with that robbery, thy stol'n name,
Coriolanus, in Corioli?   90
You lords and heads o' th' state, perfidiously
He has betray'd your business, and given up,
For certain drops of salt, your city Rome,
I say "your city," to his wife and mother;
Breaking his oath and resolution like   95
A twist of rotten silk; never admitting
Counsel o' th' war; but at his nurse's tears
He whin'd and roar'd away your victory,
That pages blush'd at him and men of heart
Look'd wond'ring each at others.

Cor.   Hear'st thou, Mars?   100

Auf. Name not the god, thou boy of tears!

Cor.   Ha!

Auf. No more.

Cor. Measureless liar, thou hast made my heart
Too great for what contains it. "Boy!" O slave!
Pardon me, lords, 'tis the first time that ever   105
I was forc'd to scold. Your judgements, my grave
lords,
Must give this cur the lie; and his own notion —
Who wears my stripes impress'd upon him, that
Must bear my beating to his grave — shall join
To thrust the lie unto him.   110

1. Lord. Peace, both, and hear me speak.

Cor. Cut me to pieces, Volsces; men and lads,
Stain all your edges on me. "Boy!" False hound!
If you have writ your annals true, 'tis there
That, like an eagle in a dove-cote, I   115
[Flutter'd] your Volscians in Corioli;
Alone I did it. "Boy!"

Auf.   Why, noble lords,
Will you be put in mind of his blind fortune,
Which was your shame, by this unholy braggart,
'Fore your own eyes and ears?

All Consp.   Let him die for't.   120

All the people. Tear him to pieces! Do it
presently! —He kill'd my son! — My daughter! —
He kill'd my cousin Marcus! — He kill'd my father!

2. Lord. Peace, ho! no outrage: peace!   125
The man is noble and his fame folds in
This orb o' th' earth. His last offences to us
Shall have judicious hearing. Stand, Aufidius,
And trouble not the peace.

Cor.   O that I had him,
With six Aufidiuses, or more, his tribe,   130
To use my lawful sword!

Auf.   Insolent villain!

All Consp. Kill, kill, kill, kill, kill him!

          [*Both the Conspirators draw, and kill
          Coriolanus, who falls: Aufidius stands
          on him.*

Lords.   Hold, hold, hold, hold!

Auf. My noble masters, hear me speak.

1. Lord.   O Tullus!

2. Lord. Thou hast done a deed whereat valour
          will weep.

3. Lord. Tread not upon him. Masters all, be
          quiet;   135
Put up your swords.

Auf. My lords, when you shall know — as in
          this rage,
Provok'd by him, you cannot — the great danger
Which this man's life did owe you, you'll rejoice
That he is thus cut off. Please it your Honours
To call me to your Senate, I'll deliver   141
Myself your loyal servant, or endure
Your heaviest censure.

1. Lord.   Bear from hence his body;

65. **easy fines:** light penalties. 67–68. **answering . . . charge:** only repaying us the cost of our war (cf. ll. 177–79). 84. **compounded:** agreed. 107. **notion:** sense. 116. **[Flutter'd]** F₃. *Flatter'd* F₁. 139. **did owe:** had in store for. 141. **deliver:** prove.

And mourn you for him.   Let him be regarded
As the most noble corse that ever herald   145
Did follow to his urn.
    2. Lord.   His own impatience
Takes from Aufidius a great part of blame.
Let's make the best of it.
    Auf.   My rage is gone,
And I am struck with sorrow.   Take him up.
Help, three o' th' chiefest soldiers; I'll be one.   150

Beat thou the drum, that it speak mournfully.
Trail your steel pikes.   Though in this city he
Hath widow'd and unchilded many a one,
Which to this hour bewail the injury,
Yet he shall have a noble memory.   155
Assist.
    [*Exeunt, bearing the body of Coriolanus.
    A dead march sounded.*

Venus and Adonis

THIS POEM, the first product of Shakespeare's pen to issue from the press, was printed in 1593 by his fellow-townsman, Richard Field. It seems to have become popular at once; and by the middle of the seventeenth century at least twelve editions had appeared. The dedication indicates that it was published with Shakespeare's consent, and it is to be presumed that it was printed from the author's manuscript, and, from the excellence of the text, that he read the proofs himself. The first edition is the sole authority for the text.

Of the date of composition the only additional evidence lies in the words of the dedication, "the first heir of my invention." Since, according to the accepted chronology, Shakespeare had by this time written several plays, it is necessary to suppose either that he used this phrase in a sense which excluded drama, or that the poem had at least been sketched some years before the date of publication, or that he means merely that it was his first publication. Modern opinion tends to place the composition in the winter of 1592–93.

Venus and Adonis belongs to a somewhat large class of Elizabethen poems in which classical legends were re-told with the luxuriant decoration characteristic of the spirit of the Renaissance. Ovid was the most frequent source of these themes, and in the present instance we find borrowings from several of the poems of the *Metamorphoses:* the reluctance of the hero from the legend of Hermaphroditus in Book iv; the boar from that of Meleager in Book viii; and other details from the account of Adonis in Book x. A large number of poetical treatments of the myth, going back to Theocritus as well as to Ovid, are found in the works of sixteenth-century poets in Italy, France, and Spain; and traces of their influence are supposed to be discernible in the present poem. The essential feature of the reluctance of Adonis, however, is not explicitly stated in any of the Continental versions, classical or Renaissance. It is present in incidental treatments of the theme by Greene and Marlowe; and Thomas Lodge, in his ornate re-telling of the Ovidian tale of *Glaucus and Scilla* (1589), had described a situation similar to that in Shakespeare's poem, by reversing, probably under the influence of Ovid's *Salmacis and Hermaphroditus*, the parts played by the hero and heroine. Lodge also treated in passing the story of Adonis; and the verse-form he employed is that used by Shakespeare. These indications, corroborated by the presence of numerous similarities in detail, point to Lodge's poem as the most important immediate suggestion for Shakespeare's poem.

Though Shakespeare's achievement in the field of drama has long eclipsed the fame he won from this poem and *Lucrece*, it should be kept in mind that it was *Venus and Adonis* that laid the foundation of his literary reputation in his own day. The drama was not yet regarded as literature, and the young Shakespeare made his bid for recognition as a poet in the genre which was most to the taste of the sophisticated readers of the latter part of Elizabeth's reign. The relation between the dates of Marlowe's *Hero and Leander* and the present poem cannot be fixed, but Marlowe's was not printed till 1598, so that at one bound Shakespeare took first place among the poets who were re-telling in the Renaissance manner the myths and legends of antiquity. Although his verse has not yet the flexibility and variety it later attained, *Venus and Adonis* is full of great music, and no contemporary had approached it in the vividness and actuality of its descriptions. Especially notable is the abundance of passages from nature, passages so fresh from first-hand observation of the Warwickshire country-side that earlier critics concluded that the poem had been written while he was still in Stratford. But the same kind of detail can be found in his plays, especially the earlier ones, and exact description of field and flower characterizes his writing to the end, and shows that his early delight in natural sights and sounds never left him.

VENUS AND ADONIS

Vilia miretur vulgus: mihi flavus Apollo
Pocula Castalia plena ministret aqua.

TO THE

RIGHT HONOURABLE HENRY WRIOTHESLEY,

EARL OF SOUTHAMPTON AND BARON OF TITCHFIELD.

RIGHT HONOURABLE, I know not how I shall offend in dedicating my unpolish'd lines to your Lordship, nor how the world will censure me for choosing so strong a prop to support so weak a burden; only if your Honour seem but pleased, I account myself highly praised, and vow to take advantage of all idle hours till I have honoured you with some graver labour. But if the first heir of my invention prove deformed, I shall be sorry it had so noble a godfather; and never after ear so barren a land, for fear it yield me still so bad a harvest. I leave it to your honourable survey, and your Honour to your heart's content, which I wish may always answer your own wish and the world's hopeful expectation.

Your Honour's in all duty,
WILLIAM SHAKESPEARE.

Even as the sun with purple-colour'd face
Had ta'en his last leave of the weeping morn,
Rose-cheek'd Adonis hied him to the chase;
Hunting he lov'd, but love he laugh'd to scorn.
  Sick-thoughted Venus makes amain unto him,
  And like a bold-fac'd suitor gins to woo him.   6

"Thrice fairer than myself," thus she began,
"The field's chief flower, sweet above compare,
Stain to all nymphs, more lovely than a man,
More white and red than doves or roses are;   10
  Nature that made thee with herself at strife,
  Saith that the world hath ending with thy life.

"Vouchsafe, thou wonder, to alight thy steed,
And rein his proud head to the saddle-bow;
If thou wilt deign this favour, for thy meed   15
A thousand honey secrets shalt thou know.
  Here come and sit, where never serpent hisses,
  And being set, I'll smother thee with kisses;

"And yet not cloy thy lips with loath'd satiety,
But rather famish them amid their plenty,   20
Making them red and pale with fresh variety,
Ten kisses short as one, one long as twenty.
  A summer's day will seem an hour but short,
  Being wasted in such time-beguiling sport."

With this she seizeth on his sweating palm,   25
The precedent of pith and livelihood,
And, trembling in her passion, calls it balm,
Earth's sovereign salve to do a goddess good.
  Being so enrag'd, desire doth lend her force
  Courageously to pluck him from his horse.   30

Over one arm the lusty courser's rein,
Under her other was the tender boy,
Who blush'd and pouted in a dull disdain,
With leaden appetite, unapt to toy;
  She red and hot as coals of glowing fire,   35
  He red for shame, but frosty in desire.

---

  5. **Sick-thoughted:** love-sick. 9. **Stain to:** surpassing in beauty. 11. **that...strife:** that strove to surpass herself in making thee. 24. **wasted:** spent. 26. **precedent:** evidence. **livelihood:** vigor.

The studded bridle on a ragged bough
Nimbly she fastens: — O, how quick is love! —
The steed is stalled up, and even now
To tie the rider she begins to prove.   40
    Backward she push'd him, as she would be thrust,
    And govern'd him in strength, though not in lust.

So soon was she along as he was down,
Each leaning on their elbows and their hips.
Now doth she stroke his cheek, now doth he frown
And gins to chide, but soon she stops his lips,   46
    And kissing speaks, with lustful language broken,
    "If thou wilt chide, thy lips shall never open."

He burns with bashful shame; she with her tears
Doth quench the maiden burning of his cheeks;   50
Then with her windy sighs and golden hairs
To fan and blow them dry again she seeks.
    He saith she is immodest, blames her miss:
    What follows more she murders with a kiss.

Even as an empty eagle, sharp by fast,   55
Tires with her beak on feathers, flesh, and bone,
Shaking her wings, devouring all in haste,
Till either gorge be stuff'd or prey be gone;
    Even so she kiss'd his brow, his cheek, his chin,
    And where she ends she doth anew begin.   60

Forc'd to content, but never to obey,
Panting he lies and breatheth in her face.
She feedeth on the steam as on a prey,
And calls it heavenly moisture, air of grace;
    Wishing her cheeks were gardens full of flowers, 65
    So they were dew'd with such distilling showers.

Look how a bird lies tangled in a net,
So fast'ned in her arms Adonis lies;
Pure shame and aw'd resistance made him fret,
Which bred more beauty in his angry eyes.   70
    Rain added to a river that is rank
    Perforce will force it overflow the bank.

Still she entreats, and prettily entreats,
For to a pretty ear she tunes her tale;
Still is he sullen, still he lours and frets,   75
'Twixt crimson shame and anger ashy-pale.
    Being red, she loves him best; and being white,
    Her best is better'd with a more delight.

Look how he can, she cannot choose but love;
And by her fair immortal hand she swears   80
From his soft bosom never to remove
Till he take truce with her contending tears,
    Which long have rain'd, making her cheeks all wet;
    And one sweet kiss shall pay this countless debt.

Upon this promise did he raise his chin,   85
Like a dive-dapper peering through a wave,
Who, being look'd on, ducks as quickly in;
So offers he to give what she did crave;
    But when her lips were ready for his pay,
    He winks, and turns his lips another way.   90

Never did passenger in summer's heat
More thirst for drink than she for this good turn.
Her help she sees, but help she cannot get;
She bathes in water, yet her fire must burn.
    "O, pity," gan she cry, "flint-hearted boy!   95
    'Tis but a kiss I beg; why art thou coy?

"I have been woo'd, as I entreat thee now,
Even by the stern and direful god of war,
Whose sinewy neck in battle ne'er did bow,
Who conquers where he comes in every jar;   100
    Yet hath he been my captive and my slave,
    And begg'd for that which thou unask'd shalt have.

"Over my altars hath he hung his lance,
His batt'red shield, his uncontrolled crest,
And for my sake hath learn'd to sport and dance,
To toy, to wanton, dally, smile, and jest,   106
    Scorning his churlish drum and ensign red,
    Making my arms his field, his tent my bed.

"Thus he that overrul'd I overswayed,
Leading him prisoner in a red-rose chain;   110
Strong-temper'd steel his stronger strength obeyed,
Yet was he servile to my coy disdain.
    O, be not proud, nor brag not of thy might,
    For mast'ring her that foil'd the god of fight!

"Touch but my lips with those fair lips of thine, —
Though mine be not so fair, yet are they red, —   116
The kiss shall be thine own as well as mine.
What seest thou in the ground?   Hold up thy head;
    Look in mine eye-balls, there thy beauty lies;
    Then why not lips on lips, since eyes in eyes?   120

"Art thou asham'd to kiss?   Then wink again,
And I will wink; so shall the day seem night;
Love keeps his revels where there are but twain;
Be bold to play, our sport is not in sight;
    These blue-vein'd violets whereon we lean   125
    Never can blab, nor know not what we mean.

"The tender spring upon thy tempting lip
Shows thee unripe; yet mayst thou well be tasted.
Make use of time, let not advantage slip;
Beauty within itself should not be wasted.   130
    Fair flowers that are not gath'red in their prime
    Rot and consume themselves in little time.

---

40. **prove:** try. 53. **miss:** misbehavior. 55. **sharp:** hungry. 56. **Tires:** tears and feeds ravenously. 71. **rank:** full.
82. **take truce:** come to terms. 86. **dive-dapper:** dabchick or little grebe. 90. **winks:** closes his eyes. 91. **passenger:** traveler.

"Were I hard-favour'd, foul, or wrinkled-old,
Ill-nurtur'd, crooked, churlish, harsh in voice,
O'erworn, despised, rheumatic, and cold,   135
Thick-sighted, barren, lean, and lacking juice,
   Then mightst thou pause, for then I were not for
     thee;
   But having no defects, why dost abhor me?

"Thou canst not see one wrinkle in my brow;
Mine eyes are grey and bright and quick in turning;
My beauty as the spring doth yearly grow,   141
My flesh is soft and plump, my marrow burning;
   My smooth moist hand, were it with thy hand
     felt,
   Would in thy palm dissolve, or seem to melt.

"Bid me discourse, I will enchant thine ear,   145
Or, like a fairy, trip upon the green,
Or, like a nymph, with long dishevelled hair,
Dance on the sands, and yet no footing seen.
   Love is a spirit all compact of fire,
   Not gross to sink, but light, and will aspire.   150

"Witness this primrose bank whereon I lie;
These forceless flowers like sturdy trees support me;
Two strengthless doves will draw me through the
   sky
From morn till night, even where I list to sport me.
   Is love so light, sweet boy, and may it be   155
   That thou should think it heavy unto thee?

"Is thine own heart to thine own face affected?
Can thy right hand seize love upon thy left?
Then woo thyself, be of thyself rejected,
Steal thine own freedom and complain on theft.
   Narcissus so himself himself forsook,   161
   And died to kiss his shadow in the brook.

"Torches are made to light, jewels to wear,
Dainties to taste, fresh beauty for the use,
Herbs for their smell, and sappy plants to bear;   165
Things growing to themselves are growth's abuse.
   Seeds spring from seeds and beauty breedeth
     beauty;
   Thou wast begot; to get it is thy duty.

"Upon the earth's increase why shouldst thou feed,
Unless the earth with thy increase be fed?   170
By law of nature thou art bound to breed,
That thine may live when thou thyself art dead;
   And so, in spite of death, thou dost survive,
   In that thy likeness still is left alive."

By this the love-sick queen began to sweat,   175
For where they lay the shadow had forsook them,

And Titan, tired in the mid-day heat,
With burning eye did hotly overlook them;
   Wishing Adonis had his team to guide,
   So he were like him and by Venus' side.   180

And now Adonis, with a lazy sprite,
And with a heavy, dark, disliking eye,
His louring brows o'erwhelming his fair sight,
Like misty vapours when they blot the sky,
   Souring his cheeks, cries, "Fie, no more of love!
   The sun doth burn my face; I must remove."   186

"Ay me," quoth Venus, "young, and so unkind?
What bare excuses mak'st thou to be gone!
I'll sigh celestial breath, whose gentle wind
Shall cool the heat of this descending sun: 190
   I'll make a shadow for thee of my hairs;
   If they burn too, I'll quench them with my tears.

"The sun that shines from heaven shines but warm,
And, lo, I lie between that sun and thee;
The heat I have from thence doth little harm,   195
Thine eye darts forth the fire that burneth me;
   And were I not immortal, life were done
   Between this heavenly and earthly sun.

"Art thou obdurate, flinty, hard as steel?
Nay, more than flint, for stone at rain relenteth.   200
Art thou a woman's son, and canst not feel
What 'tis to love? how want of love tormenteth?
   O, had thy mother borne so hard a mind,
   She had not brought forth thee, but died unkind.

"What am I, that thou shouldst contemn me this?
Or what great danger dwells upon my suit?   206
What were thy lips the worse for one poor kiss?
Speak, fair; but speak fair words, or else be mute.
   Give me one kiss, I'll give it thee again,
   And one for interest, if thou wilt have twain.   210

"Fie, lifeless picture, cold and senseless stone,
Well-painted idol, image dull and dead,
Statue contenting but the eye alone,
Thing like a man, but of no woman bred!
   Thou art no man, though of a man's complexion,
   For men will kiss even by their own direc-
     tion."   216

This said, impatience chokes her pleading tongue,
And swelling passion doth provoke a pause.
Red cheeks and fiery eyes blaze forth her wrong;
Being judge in love, she cannot right her cause;   220
   And now she weeps, and now she fain would
     speak,
   And now her sobs do her intendments break.

---

150. **aspire:** ascend.   157. **affected:** in love.   185. **Souring his cheeks:** scowling.   200. **relenteth:** softens.   204. **unkind:** without yielding to love.   205. **this:** thus.   220. **Being:** though she is.   222. **intendments:** intended speech.

Sometimes she shakes her head and then his hand,
Now gazeth she on him, now on the ground;
Sometimes her arms infold him like a band: 225
She would, he will not in her arms be bound;
   And when from thence he struggles to be gone,
   She locks her lily fingers one in one.

"Fondling," she saith, "since I have hemm'd thee
    here
Within the circuit of this ivory pale,   230
I'll be a park, and thou shalt be my deer:
Feed where thou wilt, on mountain or in dale;
   Graze on my lips; and if those hills be dry,
   Stray lower, where the pleasant fountains lie.

"Within this limit is relief enough,   235
Sweet bottom-grass and high delightful plain,
Round rising hillocks, brakes obscure and rough,
To shelter thee from tempest and from rain:
   Then be my deer, since I am such a park;   239
   No dog shall rouse thee, though a thousand bark."

At this Adonis smiles as in disdain,
That in each cheek appears a pretty dimple.
Love made those hollows, if himself were slain,
He might be buried in a tomb so simple;
   Foreknowing well, if there he came to lie,   245
   Why, there Love liv'd and there he could not die.

These lovely caves, these round enchanting pits,
Open'd their mouths to swallow Venus' liking.
Being mad before, how doth she now for wits?
Struck dead at first, what needs a second striking?
   Poor Queen of love, in thine own law forlorn,   251
   To love a cheek that smiles at thee in scorn!

Now which way shall she turn? What shall she say?
Her words are done, her woes the more increasing;
The time is spent, her object will away,   255
And from her twining arms doth urge releasing.
   "Pity," she cries, "some favour, some remorse!"
   Away he springs and hasteth to his horse.

But, lo, from forth a copse that neighbours by,
A breeding jennet, lusty, young, and proud,   260
Adonis' trampling courser doth espy,
And forth she rushes, snorts and neighs aloud.
   The strong-neck'd steed, being tied unto a tree,
   Breaketh his rein, and to her straight goes he.

Imperiously he leaps, he neighs, he bounds,   265
And now his woven girths he breaks asunder;
The bearing earth with his hard hoof he wounds,
Whose hollow womb resounds like heaven's thunder;

The iron bit he crusheth 'tween his teeth,
Controlling what he was controlled with.   270

His ears up-prick'd; his braided hanging mane
Upon his compass'd crest now stand on end;
His nostrils drink the air, and forth again,
As from a furnace, vapours doth he send;
   His eye, which scornfully glisters like fire,   275
   Shows his hot courage and his high desire.

Sometime he trots, as if he told the steps,
With gentle majesty and modest pride;
Anon he rears upright, curvets, and leaps,
As who should say, "Lo, thus my strength is tried,
   And this I do to captivate the eye   281
   Of the fair breeder that is standing by."

What recketh he his rider's angry stir,
His flattering "Holla," or his "Stand, I say"?
What cares he now for curb or pricking spur?   285
For rich caparisons or trappings gay?
   He sees his love, and nothing else he sees,
   For nothing else with his proud sight agrees.

Look, when a painter would surpass the life
In limning out a well-proportioned steed,   290
His art with nature's workmanship at strife,
As if the dead the living should exceed;
   So did this horse excel a common one
   In shape, in courage, colour, pace, and bone.

Round-hoof'd, short-jointed, fetlocks shag and long,
Broad breast, full eye, small head, and nostril
    wide,   296
High crest, short ears, straight legs and passing
    strong,
Thin mane, thick tail, broad buttock, tender hide:
   Look, what a horse should have he did not lack,
   Save a proud rider on so proud a back.   300

Sometime he sends far off and there he stares;
Anon he starts at stirring of a feather;
To bid the wind a base he now prepares,
And whe'er he run or fly they know not whether;
   For through his mane and tail the high wind
    sings,   305
   Fanning the hairs, who wave like feath'red wings.

He looks upon his love and neighs unto her;
She answers him as if she knew his mind;
Being proud, as females are, to see him woo her,
She puts on outward strangeness, seems unkind,   310
   Spurns at his love, and scorns the heat he feels,
   Beating his kind embracements with her heels.

---

257. **remorse:** pity.   260. **breeding jennet:** small Spanish mare.   272. **compass'd:** arched.   276. **courage:** desire.
277. **told:** counted.   279. **curvets:** prances.   290. **limning:** painting.   295. **shag:** shaggy.   303. **bid ... base:** challenge
the wind for speed.

Then, like a melancholy malcontent,
He vails his tail that, like a falling plume,
Cool shadow to his melting buttock lent;   315
He stamps and bites the poor flies in his fume.
  His love, perceiving how he was enrag'd,
  Grew kinder, and his fury was assuag'd.

His testy master goeth about to take him;
When, lo, the unback'd breeder, full of fear,   320
Jealous of catching, swiftly doth forsake him,
With her the horse, and left Adonis there.
  As they were mad, unto the wood they hie them,
  Out-stripping crows that strive to over-fly them.

All swoln with chafing, down Adonis sits,   325
Banning his boist'rous and unruly beast;
And now the happy season once more fits
That love-sick Love by pleading may be blest;
  For lovers say, the heart hath treble wrong
  When it is barr'd the aidance of the tongue.   330

An oven that is stopp'd, or river stay'd,
Burneth more hotly, swelleth with more rage;
So of concealed sorrow may be said,
Free vent of words love's fire doth assuage,
  But when the heart's attorney once is mute,   335
  The client breaks, as desperate in his suit.

He sees her coming, and begins to glow,
Even as a dying coal revives with wind,
And with his bonnet hides his angry brow;
Looks on the dull earth with disturbed mind,   340
  Taking no notice that she is so nigh,
  For all askance he holds her in his eye.

O, what a sight it was, wistly to view
How she came stealing to the wayward boy!
To note the fighting conflict of her hue,   345
How white and red each other did destroy!
  But now her cheek was pale, and by and by
  It flash'd forth fire, as lightning from the sky.

Now was she just before him as he sat,
And like a lowly lover down she kneels;   350
With one fair hand she heaveth up his hat,
Her other tender hand his fair cheek feels:
  His tenderer cheek receives her soft hand's print
  As apt as new-fallen snow takes any dint.

O, what a war of looks was then between them!   355
Her eyes petitioners to his eyes suing;
His eyes saw her eyes as they had not seen them;
Her eyes woo'd still, his eyes disdain'd the wooing:

And all this dumb play had his acts made plain
With tears, which, chorus-like, her eyes did rain.

Full gently now she takes him by the hand,   361
A lily prison'd in a gaol of snow,
Or ivory in an alabaster band;
So white a friend engirts so white a foe.
  This beauteous combat, wilful and unwilling,   365
  Show'd like two silver doves that sit a-billing.

Once more the engine of her thoughts began:
"O fairest mover on this mortal round,
Would thou wert as I am, and I a man,
My heart all whole as thine, thy heart my wound;
  For one sweet look thy help I would assure
    thee,   371
  Though nothing but my body's bane would cure
    thee."

"Give me my hand," saith he, "why dost thou feel
    it?"
"Give me my heart," saith she, "and thou shalt
    have it;
O, give it me, lest thy hard heart do steel it,   375
And being steel'd, soft sighs can never grave it:
  Then love's deep groans I never shall regard,
  Because Adonis' heart hath made mine hard."

"For shame," he cries, "let go, and let me go;
My day's delight is past, my horse is gone,   380
And 'tis your fault I am bereft him so.
I pray you hence, and leave me here alone;
  For all my mind, my thought, my busy care,
  Is how to get my palfrey from the mare."

Thus she replies: "Thy palfrey, as he should,   385
Welcomes the warm approach of sweet desire;
Affection is a coal that must be cool'd,
Else, suffer'd, it will set the heart on fire.
  The sea hath bounds, but deep desire hath none;
  Therefore no marvel though thy horse be gone.

"How like a jade he stood, tied to the tree,   391
Servilely master'd with a leathern rein!
But when he saw his love, his youth's fair fee,
He held such petty bondage in disdain;
  Throwing the base thong from his bending crest,
  Enfranchising his mouth, his back, his breast.   396

"Who sees his true-love in her naked bed,
Teaching the sheets a whiter hue than white,
But, when his glutton eye so full hath fed,
His other agents aim at like delight?   400

314. vails: lowers. 319. goeth about: tries. 326. Banning: cursing. 335. heart's attorney: tongue. 336. The client: the heart. breaks: goes into bankruptcy. 343. wistly: attentively. 359. his: its. 360. chorus-like: i.e., explaining. 367. engine ...thoughts: tongue. 372. bane: death. 391. jade: nag. 397. her naked bed: i.e., where she lay naked. 400. agents: senses. Cf. ll. 433-447.

Who is so faint that dare not be so bold
To touch the fire, the weather being cold?

"Let me excuse thy courser, gentle boy;
And learn of him, I heartily beseech thee,
To take advantage on presented joy;   405
Though I were dumb, yet his proceedings teach thee.
O, learn to love; the lesson is but plain,
And once made perfect, never lost again."

"I know not love," quoth he, "nor will not know it,
Unless it be a boar, and then I chase it;   410
'Tis much to borrow, and I will not owe it;
My love to love is love but to disgrace it;
For I have heard it is a life in death,
That laughs and weeps, and all but with a breath.

"Who wears a garment shapeless and unfinish'd? 415
Who plucks the bud before one leaf put forth?
If springing things be any jot diminish'd,
They wither in their prime, prove nothing worth.
The colt that's back'd and burden'd being young,
Loseth his pride and never waxeth strong.   420

"You hurt my hand with wringing; let us part,
And leave this idle theme, this bootless chat;
Remove your siege from my unyielding heart;
To love's alarms it will not ope the gate;
Dismiss your vows, your feigned tears, your flat-
t'ry;   425
For where a heart is hard they make no batt'ry."

"What! canst thou talk?" quoth she, "hast thou a
tongue?
O, would thou hadst not, or I had no hearing!
Thy mermaid's voice hath done me double wrong;
I had my load before, now press'd with bearing: 430
Melodious discord, heavenly tune harsh sounding,
Ear's deep sweet music, and heart's deep sore
wounding.

"Had I no eyes but ears, my ears would love
That inward beauty and invisible;
Or were I deaf, thy outward parts would move   435
Each part in me that were but sensible:
Though neither eyes nor ears to hear nor see,
Yet should I be in love by touching thee.

"Say, that the sense of feeling were bereft me,
And that I could not see, nor hear, nor touch,   440
And nothing but the very smell were left me,
Yet would my love to thee be still as much;
For from the stillitory of thy face excelling
Comes breath perfum'd that breedeth love by
smelling.

"But, O, what banquet wert thou to the taste,   445
Being nurse and feeder of the other four!
Would they not wish the feast might ever last,
And bid Suspicion double-lock the door,
Lest Jealousy, that sour unwelcome guest,
Should, by his stealing in, disturb the feast?"   450

Once more the ruby-colour'd portal open'd,
Which to his speech did honey passage yield;
Like a red morn, that ever yet betoken'd
Wreck to the seaman, tempest to the field,
Sorrow to shepherds, woe unto the birds,   455
Gusts and foul flaws to herdmen and to herds.

This ill presage advisedly she marketh:
Even as the wind is hush'd before it raineth,
Or as the wolf doth grin before he barketh,
Or as the berry breaks before it staineth,   460
Or like the deadly bullet of a gun,
His meaning struck her ere his words begun.

And at his look she flatly falleth down,
For looks kill love and love by looks reviveth;
A smile recures the wounding of a frown;   465
But blessed bankrupt, that by love so thriveth!
The silly boy, believing she is dead,
Claps her pale cheek, till clapping makes it red;

And all amaz'd brake off his late intent,
For sharply he did think to reprehend her,   470
Which cunning love did wittily prevent:
Fair fall the wit that can so well defend her!
For on the grass she lies as she were slain,
Till his breath breatheth life in her again.

He wrings her nose, he strikes her on the cheeks, 475
He bends her fingers, holds her pulses hard,
He chafes her lips; a thousand ways he seeks
To mend the hurt that his unkindness marr'd:
He kisses her; and she by her good will
Will never rise, so he will kiss her still.   480

The night of sorrow now is turn'd to day:
Her two blue windows faintly she up-heaveth,
Like the fair sun, when in his fresh array
He cheers the morn and all the earth relieveth;
And as the bright sun glorifies the sky,   485
So is her face illumin'd with her eye;

Whose beams upon his hairless face are fix'd,
As if from thence they borrowed all their shine.
Were never four such lamps together mix'd,
Had not his clouded with his brow's repine;   490
But hers, which through the crystal tears gave light,
Shone like the moon in water seen by night.

424. alarms: attacks.   426. batt'ry: forced entrance.   443. stillitory: still.   456. flaws: blasts.   457. advisedly: attentively.   465. recures: heals.   471. wittily: cleverly.   490. repine: discontent.

"O, where am I?" quoth she; "in earth or heaven,
Or in the ocean drench'd, or in the fire?
What hour is this? or morn or weary even? 495
Do I delight to die, or life desire?
But now I liv'd, and life was death's annoy;
But now I died, and death was lively joy.

"O, thou didst kill me; kill me once again.
Thy eyes' shrewd tutor, that hard heart of thine, 500
Hath taught them scornful tricks and such disdain
That they have murd'red this poor heart of mine;
And these mine eyes, true leaders to their queen,
But for thy piteous lips no more had seen.

"Long may they kiss each other, for this cure! 505
O, never let their crimson liveries wear!
And as they last, their verdure still endure
To drive infection from the dangerous year!
That the star-gazers, having writ on death,
May say the plague is banish'd by thy breath. 510

"Pure lips, sweet seals in my soft lips imprinted,
What bargains may I make, still to be sealing?
To sell myself I can be well contented,
So thou wilt buy and pay and use good dealing;
Which purchase if thou make, for fear of slips 515
Set thy seal-manual on my wax-red lips.

"A thousand kisses buys my heart from me;
And pay them at thy lesiure, one by one.
What is ten hundred touches unto thee?
Are they not quickly told and quickly gone? 520
Say, for non-payment that the debt should double
Is twenty hundred kisses such a trouble?"

"Fair queen," quoth he, "if any love you owe me,
Measure my strangeness with my unripe years;
Before I know myself, seek not to know me: 525
No fisher but the ungrown fry forbears;
The mellow plum doth fall, the green sticks fast,
Or being early pluck'd is sour to taste.

"Look, the world's comforter with weary gait
His day's hot task hath ended in the west; 530
The owl, night's herald, shrieks; 'tis very late;
The sheep are gone to fold, birds to their nest;
And coal-black clouds that shadow heaven's light
Do summon us to part and bid good-night.

"Now let me say 'Good-night,' and so say you;
If you will say so, you shall have a kiss." 536
"Good-night," quoth she, and, ere he says "Adieu,"
The honey fee of parting tend'red is:

Her arms do lend his neck a sweet embrace;
Incorporate then they seem; face grows to face;

Till, breathless, he disjoin'd, and backward drew 541
The heavenly moisture, that sweet coral mouth,
Whose precious taste her thirsty lips well knew,
Whereon they surfeit, yet complain on drouth.
He with her plenty press'd, she faint with dearth,
Their lips together glued, fall to the earth. 546

Now quick desire hath caught the yielding prey,
And glutton-like she feeds, yet never filleth;
Her lips are conquerors, his lips obey,
Paying what ransom the insulter willeth; 550
Whose vulture thought doth pitch the price so
high
That she will draw his lips' rich treasure dry.

And having felt the sweetness of the spoil,
With blindfold fury she begins to forage;
Her face doth reek and smoke, her blood doth boil,
And careless lust stirs up a desperate courage; 556
Planting oblivion, beating reason back,
Forgetting shame's pure blush and honour's
wrack.

Hot, faint, and weary, with her hard embracing,
Like a wild bird being tam'd with too much
handling, 560
Or as the fleet-foot roe that's tir'd with chasing,
Or like the froward infant still'd with dandling,
He now obeys, and now no more resisteth,
While she takes all she can, not all she listeth.

What wax so frozen but dissolves with temp'ring,
And yields at last to every light impression? 566
Things out of hope are compass'd oft with vent'ring,
Chiefly in love, whose leave exceeds commission:
Affection faints not like a pale-fac'd coward,
But then wooes best when most his choice is
froward. 570

When he did frown, O, had she then gave over,
Such nectar from his lips she had not suck'd.
Foul words and frowns must not repel a lover;
What though the rose have prickles, yet 'tis pluck'd.
Were beauty under twenty locks kept fast, 575
Yet love breaks through and picks them all at last.

For pity now she can no more detain him;
The poor fool prays her that he may depart:
She is resolv'd no longer to restrain him;
Bids him farewell, and look well to her heart, 580

---

494. **drench'd**: immersed.   497. **annoy**: suffering.   506. **wear**: wear out.   507. **verdure**: odor.   508–510. **dangerous year... plague.** Probably an allusion to the year 1592, when the plague closed the theaters.   515. **slips**: counterfeit coins. 524. **Measure... with**: regard my coldness as due to.   545. **press'd**: oppressed.   557. **Planting**: causing.   568. **whose... commission**: which allows itself more than is warranted.

The which, by Cupid's bow she doth protest,
He carries thence incaged in his breast.

"Sweet boy," she says, "this night I'll waste in
        sorrow,
For my sick heart commands mine eyes to watch.
Tell me, Love's master, shall we meet to-morrow?
Say, shall we? shall we?   Wilt thou make the
        match?"   586
    He tells her, no; to-morrow he intends
    To hunt the boar with certain of his friends.

"The boar!" quoth she; whereat a sudden pale,
Like lawn being spread upon the blushing rose,   590
Usurps her cheek; she trembles at his tale,
And on his neck her yoking arms she throws:
    She sinketh down, still hanging by his neck,
    He on her belly falls, she on her back.

Now is she in the very lists of love,   595
Her champion mounted for the hot encounter:
All is imaginary she doth prove,
He will not manage her, although he mount her;
    That worse than Tantalus' is her annoy,
    To clip Elysium and to lack her joy.   600

Even so poor birds, deceiv'd with painted grapes,
Do surfeit by the eye and pine the maw;
Even so she languisheth in her mishaps,
As those poor birds that helpless berries saw.
    The warm effects which she in him finds missing
    She seeks to kindle with continual kissing. 606

But all in vain; good queen, it will not be.
She hath assay'd as much as may be prov'd;
Her pleading hath deserv'd a greater fee;
She's Love, she loves, and yet she is not lov'd. 610
    "Fie, fie," he says, "you crush me; let me go;
    You have no reason to withhold me so."

"Thou hadst been gone," quoth she, "sweet boy,
        ere this,
But that thou told'st me thou wouldst hunt the
        boar.
O, be advis'd! thou know'st not what it is   615
With javelin's point a churlish swine to gore,
    Whose tushes never sheath'd he whetteth still,
    Like to a mortal butcher bent to kill.

"On his bow-back he hath a battle set
Of bristly pikes, that ever threat his foes;   620
His eyes, like glow-worms, shine when he doth fret;
His snout digs sepulchres where'er he goes;

Being mov'd, he strikes whate'er is in his way,
And whom he strikes his crooked tushes slay.

"His brawny sides, with hairy bristles armed,   625
Are better proof than thy spear's point can enter;
His short thick neck cannot be easily harmed;
Being ireful, on the lion he will venture.
    The thorny brambles and embracing bushes,
    As fearful of him, part, through whom he rushes.

"Alas, he nought esteems that face of thine,   631
To which Love's eyes pays tributary gazes;
Nor thy soft hands, sweet lips, and crystal eyne,
Whose full perfection all the world amazes;   634
    But having thee at vantage, — wondrous dread! —
    Would root these beauties as he roots the mead.

"O, let him keep his loathsome cabin still;
Beauty hath nought to do with such foul fiends.
Come not within his danger by thy will;   639
They that thrive well take counsel of their friends.
    When thou didst name the boar, not to dissemble,
    I fear'd thy fortune, and my joints did tremble.

"Didst thou not mark my face?   Was it not white?
Saw'st thou not signs of fear lurk in mine eye?
Grew I not faint? and fell I not downright?   645
Within my bosom, whereon thou dost lie,
    My boding heart pants, beats, and takes no rest,
    But, like an earthquake, shakes thee on my breast.

"For where Love reigns, disturbing Jealousy
Doth call himself Affection's sentinel;   650
Gives false alarms, suggesteth mutiny,
And in a peaceful hour doth cry, 'Kill, kill!'
    Distemp'ring gentle Love in his desire,
    As air and water do abate the fire.

"This sour informer, this bate-breeding spy,   655
This canker that eats up Love's tender spring,
This carry-tale, dissentious Jealousy,
That sometime true news, sometime false doth
        bring,
    Knocks at my heart and whispers in mine ear
    That if I love thee, I thy death should fear:

"And more than so, presenteth to mine eye   661
The picture of an angry chafing boar,
Under whose sharp fangs on his back doth lie
An image like thyself, all stain'd with gore;
    Whose blood upon the fresh flowers being shed
    Doth make them droop with grief and hang the
        head.   666

584. watch: remain awake. 597. she ... prove: which she experiences. 600. clip: embrace. 602. pine the maw: starve
the stomach. 608. prov'd: experienced. 617. tushes: tusks. 619. battle: battalion. 626. proof: armor. 636. root:
uproot. 637. cabin: den. 653. Distemp'ring: quenching. 655. bate-breeding: strife-causing. 656. canker: canker-
worm. spring: young shoots.

"What should I do, seeing thee so indeed,
That tremble at th' imagination?
The thought of it doth make my faint heart bleed,
And fear doth teach it divination: 670
　I prophesy thy death, my living sorrow,
　If thou encounter with the boar to-morrow.

"But if thou needs wilt hunt, be rul'd by me;
Uncouple at the timorous flying hare,
Or at the fox which lives by subtlety, 675
Or at the roe which no encounter dare:
　Pursue these fearful creatures o'er the downs,
　And on thy well-breath'd horse keep with thy
　　hounds.

"And when thou hast on foot the purblind hare, 679
Mark the poor wretch, to overshoot his troubles
How he outruns the wind, and with what care
He cranks and crosses with a thousand doubles.
　The many musets through the which he goes
　Are like a labyrinth to amaze his foes.

"Sometime he runs among a flock of sheep, 685
To make the cunning hounds mistake their smell,
And sometime where earth-delving conies keep,
To stop the loud pursuers in their yell,
　And sometime sorteth with a herd of deer; —
　Danger deviseth shifts; wit waits on fear; —

"For there his smell with others being mingled, 691
The hot scent-snuffing hounds are driven to doubt,
Ceasing their clamorous cry till they have singled
With much ado the cold fault cleanly out;
　Then do they spend their mouths: Echo replies,
　As if another chase were in the skies. 696

"By this, poor Wat, far off upon a hill,
Stands on his hinder legs with list'ning ear,
To hearken if his foes pursue him still.
Anon their loud alarums he doth hear; 700
　And now his grief may be compared well
　To one sore sick that hears the passing-bell.

"Then shalt thou see the dew-bedabbled wretch
Turn, and return, indenting with the way;
Each envious brier his weary legs do scratch, 705
Each shadow makes him stop, each murmur stay:
　For misery is trodden on by many,
　And, being low, never reliev'd by any.

"Lie quietly, and hear a little more;
Nay, do not struggle, for thou shalt not rise. 710
To make thee hate the hunting of the boar,
Unlike myself thou hear'st me moralize,

Applying this to that, and so to so;
For love can comment upon every woe.

"Where did I leave?" "No matter where," quoth
　he; 715
"Leave me, and then the story aptly ends;
The night is spent." "Why, what of that?" quoth
　she.
"I am," quoth he, "expected of my friends;
　And now 'tis dark, and going I shall fall."
　"In night," quoth she, "desire sees best of all. 720

"But if thou fall, O, then imagine this,
The earth, in love with thee, thy footing trips,
And all is but to rob thee of a kiss.
Rich preys make true men thieves; so do thy lips
　Make modest Dian cloudy and forlorn, 725
　Lest she should steal a kiss and die forsworn.

"Now of this dark night I perceive the reason:
Cynthia for shame obscures her silver shine,
Till forging Nature be condemn'd of treason
For stealing moulds from heaven that were divine;
　Wherein she fram'd thee in high heaven's de-
　　spite, 731
　To shame the sun by day and her by night.

"And therefore hath she brib'd the Destinies
To cross the curious workmanship of Nature,
To mingle beauty with infirmities, 735
And pure perfection with impure defeature,
　Making it subject to the tyranny
　Of mad mischances and much misery;

"As burning fevers, agues pale and faint,
Life-poisoning pestilence and frenzies wood, 740
The marrow-eating sickness, whose attaint
Disorder breeds by heating of the blood;
　Surfeits, imposthumes, grief, and damn'd despair
　Swear Nature's death for framing thee so fair.

"And not the least of all these maladies 745
But in one minute's fight brings beauty under;
Both favour, savour, hue, and qualities,
Whereat th' impartial gazer late did wonder,
　Are on the sudden wasted, thaw'd, and done,
　As mountain-snow melts with the midday sun.

"Therefore, despite of fruitless chastity, 751
Love-lacking vestals and self-loving nuns,
That on the earth would breed a scarcity
And barren dearth of daughters and of sons,
　Be prodigal: the lamp that burns by night 755
　Dries up his oil to lend the world his light.

674. **Uncouple:** unleash the hounds. 677. **fearful:** timid. 683. **musets:** gaps. 687. **keep:** dwell. 689. **sorteth:** keeps company. 694. **cold fault:** lost scent. 697. **Wat:** Walter, familiar name for the hare. 702. **passing-bell:** a bell rung for prayers for the dying. 704. **indenting:** zigzagging. 705. **envious:** malicious. 736. **defeature:** disfigurement. 740. **wood:** mad. 741. **attaint:** infection. 743. **imposthumes:** abscesses.

"What is thy body but a swallowing grave,
Seeming to bury that posterity
Which by the rights of time thou needs must have,
If thou destroy them not in dark obscurity?   760
    If so, the world will hold thee in disdain,
    Sith in thy pride so fair a hope is slain.

"So in thyself thyself art made away;
A mischief worse than civil home-bred strife,
Or theirs whose desperate hands themselves do slay,
Or butcher-sire that reaves his son of life.   766
    Foul-cank'ring rust the hidden treasure frets,
    But gold that's put to use more gold begets."

"Nay, then," quoth Adon, "you will fall again
Into your idle over-handled theme.   770
The kiss I gave you is bestow'd in vain,
And all in vain you strive against the stream;
    For, by this black-fac'd Night, Desire's foul nurse,
    Your treatise makes me like you worse and worse.

"If love have lent you twenty thousand tongues, 775
And every tongue more moving than your own,
Bewitching like the wanton mermaid's songs,
Yet from mine ear the tempting tune is blown;
    For know, my heart stands armed in mine ear,
    And will not let a false sound enter there,   780

"Lest the deceiving harmony should run
Into the quiet closure of my breast;
And then my little heart were quite undone,
In his bedchamber to be barr'd of rest.
    No, lady, no; my heart longs not to groan,   785
    But soundly sleeps while now it sleeps alone.

"What have you urg'd that I cannot reprove?
The path is smooth that leadeth on to danger.
I hate not love, but your device in love,
That lends embracements unto every stranger.
    You do it for increase: O strange excuse,   791
    When reason is the bawd to lust's abuse!

"Call it not love, for Love to heaven is fled,
Since sweating Lust on earth usurp'd his name;
Under whose simple semblance he hath fed   795
Upon fresh beauty, blotting it with blame;
    Which the hot tyrant stains and soon bereaves,
    As caterpillars do the tender leaves.

"Love comforteth like sunshine after rain,
But Lust's effect is tempest after sun;   800
Love's gentle spring doth always fresh remain,
Lust's winter comes ere summer half be done;
    Love surfeits not, Lust like a glutton dies;
    Love is all truth, Lust full of forged lies.

"More I could tell, but more I dare not say;   805
The text is old, the orator too green.
Therefore, in sadness, now I will away;
My face is full of shame, my heart of teen;
    Mine ears, that to your wanton talk attended,
    Do burn themselves for having so offended."

With this, he breaketh from the sweet embrace   811
Of those fair arms which bound him to her breast,
And homeward through the dark laund runs apace;
Leaves Love upon her back deeply distress'd.
    Look, how a bright star shooteth from the sky,
    So glides he in the night from Venus' eye;   816

Which after him she darts, as one on shore
Gazing upon a late-embarked friend,
Till the wild waves will have him seen no more,
Whose ridges with the meeting clouds contend;   820
    So did the merciless and pitchy night
    Fold in the object that did feed her sight.

Whereat amaz'd, as one that unaware
Hath dropp'd a precious jewel in the flood,
Or stonish'd as night-wand'rers often are,   825
Their light blown out in some mistrustful wood,
    Even so confounded in the dark she lay,
    Having lost the fair discovery of her way.

And now she beats her heart, whereat it groans,
That all the neighbour caves, as seeming troubled,
Make verbal repetition of her moans;   831
Passion on passion deeply is redoubled:
    "Ay me!" she cries, and twenty times, "Woe, woe!"
    And twenty echoes twenty times cry so.

She marking them begins a wailing note   835
And sings extemporally a woeful ditty;
How love makes young men thrall and old men dote;
How love is wise in folly, foolish-witty.
    Her heavy anthem still concludes in woe,
    And still the choir of echoes answer so.   840

Her song was tedious and outwore the night,
For lovers' hours are long, though seeming short;
If pleas'd themselves, others, they think, delight
In such-like circumstance, with such-like sport:
    Their copious stories oftentimes begun   845
    End without audience and are never done.

For who hath she to spend the night withal
But idle sounds resembling parasits,
Like shrill-tongu'd tapsters answering every call,
Soothing the humour of fantastic wits?   850

766. reaves: deprives.   767. frets: eats away.   774. treatise: discussion.   782. closure: enclosure.   787. reprove: refute.   789. device: behavior.   807. in sadness: seriously.   808. teen: sorrow.   813. laund: clear space in woods.

She says, "'Tis so:" they answer all, "'Tis so;"
And would say after her if she said "No."

Lo, here the gentle lark, weary of rest,
From his moist cabinet mounts up on high
And wakes the morning, from whose silver breast
The sun ariseth in his majesty;   856
  Who doth the world so glorious behold
  That cedar-tops and hills seem burnish'd gold.

Venus salutes him with this fair good-morrow:
"O thou clear god, and patron of all light,   860
From whom each lamp and shining star doth borrow
The beauteous influence that makes him bright,
  There lives a son that suck'd an earthly mother,
  May lend thee light, as thou dost lend to other."

This said, she hasteth to a myrtle grove,   865
Musing the morning is so much o'erworn,
And yet she hears no tidings of her love.
She hearkens for his hounds and for his horn;
  Anon she hears them chant it lustily,
  And all in haste she coasteth to the cry.   870

And as she runs, the bushes in the way
Some catch her by the neck, some kiss her face,
Some [twine] about her thigh to make her stay.
She wildly breaketh from their strict embrace,
  Like a milch doe, whose swelling dugs do ache, 875
  Hasting to feed her fawn hid in some brake.

By this, she hears the hounds are at a bay;
Whereat she starts, like one that spies an adder
Wreath'd up in fatal folds just in his way,
The fear whereof doth make him shake and shudder;
  Even so the timorous yelping of the hounds   881
  Appalls her senses and her spirit confounds.

For now she knows it is no gentle chase,
But the blunt boar, rough bear, or lion proud,
Because the cry remaineth in one place,   885
Where fearfully the dogs exclaim aloud.
  Finding their enemy to be so curst,
  They all strain court'sy who shall cope him first.

This dismal cry rings sadly in her ear,
Through which it enters to surprise her heart;   890
Who, overcome by doubt and bloodless fear,
With cold-pale weakness numbs each feeling part.
  Like soldiers, when their captain once doth yield,
  They basely fly and dare not stay the field.

Thus stands she in a trembling ecstasy;   895
Till, cheering up her senses all dismay'd,

She tells them 'tis a causeless fantasy
And childish error that they are afraid;
  Bids them leave quaking, bids them fear no
    more: —
  And with that word she spied the hunted boar, 900

Whose frothy mouth, bepainted all with red,
Like milk and blood being mingled both together,
A second fear through all her sinews spread,
Which madly hurries her she knows not whither:
  This way she runs, and now she will no further,
  But back retires to rate the boar for murther. 906

A thousand spleens bear her a thousand ways;
She treads the path that she untreads again;
Her more than haste is mated with delays,
Like the proceedings of a drunken brain,   910
  Full of respects, yet nought at all respecting;
  In hand with all things, nought at all effecting.

Here kennell'd in a brake she finds a hound,
And asks the weary caitiff for his master,
And there another licking of his wound,   915
'Gainst venom'd sores the only sovereign plaster;
  And here she meets another sadly scowling,
  To whom she speaks, and he replies with howling.

When he hath ceas'd his ill-resounding noise,
Another flap-mouth'd mourner, black and grim, 920
Against the welkin volleys out his voice;
Another and another answer him,
  Clapping their proud tails to the ground below,
  Shaking their scratch'd ears, bleeding as they
    go.

Look, how the world's poor people are amazed
At apparitions, signs, and prodigies,   926
Whereon with fearful eyes they long have gazed,
Infusing them with dreadful prophecies;
  So she at these sad signs draws up her breath,
  And sighing it again, exclaims on Death.   930

"Hard-favour'd tyrant, ugly, meagre, lean,
Hateful divorce of love," — thus chides she Death,—
"Grim-grinning ghost, earth's worm, what dost
    thou mean
To stifle beauty and to steal his breath,
  Who when he liv'd, his breath and beauty set   935
  Gloss on the rose, smell to the violet?

"If he be dead, — O no, it cannot be,
Seeing his beauty, thou should'st strike at it:
O yes, it may; thou hast no eyes to see,
But hatefully at random dost thou hit.   940

854. **cabinet:** nest.   870. **coasteth:** hastens.   873. [twine]. *twin'd* Q.   877. **at a bay:** surrounding the boar.   887. **curst:** vicious.   888. **cope:** encounter.   907. **spleens:** impulses.   909. **mated:** frustrated.   911. **respects:** considerations.   933. **worm:** serpent.

Thy mark is feeble age, but thy false dart
Mistakes that aim and cleaves an infant's heart.

"Hadst thou but bid beware, then he had spoke,
And, hearing him, thy power had lost his power.
The Destinies will curse thee for this stroke;   945
They bid thee crop a weed, thou pluck'st a flower.
　　Love's golden arrow at him should have fled,
　　And not Death's ebon dart, to strike him dead.

"Dost thou drink tears, that thou provok'st such
　　weeping?
What may a heavy groan advantage thee?   950
Why hast thou cast into eternal sleeping
Those eyes that taught all other eyes to see?
　　Now Nature cares not for thy mortal vigour,
　　Since her best work is ruin'd with thy rigour."

Here overcome, as one full of despair,   955
She vail'd her eyelids, who, like sluices, stopt
The crystal tide that from her two cheeks fair
In the sweet channel of her bosom dropt;
　　But through the flood-gates breaks the silver rain,
　　And with his strong course opens them again.   960

O, how her eyes and tears did lend and borrow!
Her eye seen in the tears, tears in her eye;
Both crystals, where they view'd each other's sor-
　　row,
Sorrow that friendly sighs sought still to dry;
　　But like a stormy day, now wind, now rain,   965
　　Sighs dry her cheeks, tears make them wet again.

Variable passions throng her constant woe,
As striving who should best become her grief;
All entertain'd, each passion labours so,
That every present sorrow seemeth chief,   970
　　But none is best: then join they all together,
　　Like many clouds consulting for foul weather.

By this, far off she hears some huntsman hallo;
A nurse's song ne'er pleas'd her babe so well.
The dire imagination she did follow   975
This sound of hope doth labour to expel;
　　For now reviving joy bids her rejoice,
　　And flatters her it is Adonis' voice.

Whereat her tears began to turn their tide,
Being prison'd in her eye like pearls in glass;   980
Yet sometimes falls an orient drop beside,
Which her cheek melts, as scorning it should pass
　　To wash the foul face of the sluttish ground,
　　Who is but drunken when she seemeth drown'd.

O hard-believing love, how strange it seems   985
Not to believe, and yet too credulous!

Thy weal and woe are both of them extremes;
Despair and hope makes thee ridiculous:
　　The one doth flatter thee in thoughts unlikely,
　　In likely thoughts the other kills thee quickly.   990

Now she unweaves the web that she hath wrought;
Adonis lives, and Death is not to blame;
It was not she that call'd him all to nought:
Now she adds honours to his hateful name;
　　She clepes him king of graves and grave for kings,
　　Imperious supreme of all mortal things.   996

"No, no," quoth she, "sweet Death, I did but jest;
Yet pardon me I felt a kind of fear
Whenas I met the boar, that bloody beast,
Which knows no pity, but is still severe;   1000
　　Then, gentle shadow, — truth I must confess, —
　　I rail'd on thee, fearing my love's decease.

"'Tis not my fault; the boar provok'd my tongue;
Be wreak'd on him, invisible commander;
'Tis he, foul creature, that hath done thee wrong;
I did but act, he's author of thy slander.   1006
　　Grief hath two tongues, and never woman yet
　　Could rule them both without ten women's wit."

Thus hoping that Adonis is alive,
Her rash suspect she doth extenuate;   1010
And that his beauty may the better thrive,
With Death she humbly doth insinuate;
　　Tells him of trophies, statues, tombs, and stories
　　His victories, his triumphs, and his glories.

"O Jove," quoth she, "how much a fool was I
To be of such a weak and silly mind   1016
To wail his death who lives and must not die
Till mutual overthrow of mortal kind!
　　For he being dead, with him is beauty slain,
　　And, beauty dead, black chaos come again.   1020

"Fie, fie, fond love, thou art as full of fear
As one with treasure laden, hemm'd with thieves;
Trifles, unwitnessed with eye or ear,
Thy coward heart with false bethinking grieves."
　　Even at this word she hears a merry horn,   1025
　　Whereat she leaps that was but late forlorn.

As falcons to the lure, away she flies;
The grass stoops not, she treads on it so light;
And in her haste unfortunately spies
The foul boar's conquest on her fair delight;   1030
　　Which seen, her eyes, [as] murd'red with the view,
　　Like stars asham'd of day, themselves withdrew;

Or, as the snail, whose tender horns being hit,
Shrinks backward in his shelly cave with pain,

---

981. **orient**: brilliant.　993. **all to nought**: worthless.　995. **clepes**: calls.　1000. **still severe**: always merciless.　1010. **suspect**: suspicion.　1012. **insinuate**: curry favor.　1013. **stories**. *stories*, Q.　1018. **mutual**: general.　1031. **[as]** Q₃. *are* Q₁,₂.

And there, all smoth'red up, in shade doth sit,   1035
Long after fearing to creep forth again;
  So, at his bloody view, her eyes are fled
  Into the deep-dark cabins of her head;

Where they resign their office and their light
To the disposing of her troubled brain;   1040
Who bids them still consort with ugly night,
And never wound the heart with looks again;
  Who, like a king perplexed in his throne,
  By their suggestion gives a deadly groan,

Whereat each tributary subject quakes;   1045
As when the wind, imprison'd in the ground,
Struggling for passage, earth's foundation shakes,
Which with cold terror doth men's minds confound.
  This mutiny each part doth so surprise
  That from their dark beds once more leap her
    eyes;   1050

And, being open'd, threw unwilling light
Upon the wide wound that the boar had trench'd
In his soft flank; whose wonted lily white
With purple tears, that his wound wept, [was]
    drench'd.
  No flow'r was nigh, no grass, herb, leaf, or
    weed,   1055
  But stole his blood and seem'd with him to bleed.

This solemn sympathy poor Venus noteth;
Over one shoulder doth she hang her head;
Dumbly she passions, franticly she doteth;
She thinks he could not die, he is not dead.   1060
  Her voice is stopt, her joints forget to bow;
  Her eyes are mad that they have wept till now.

Upon his hurt she looks so steadfastly,
That her sight dazzling makes the wound seem
    three;
And then she reprehends her mangling eye,   1065
That makes more gashes where no breach should be.
  His face seems twain, each several limb is doubled;
  For oft the eye mistakes, the brain being troubled.

"My tongue cannot express my grief for one,
And yet," quoth she, "behold two Adons dead!   1070
My sighs are blown away, my salt tears gone,
Mine eyes are turn'd to fire, my heart to lead:
  Heavy heart's lead, melt at mine eyes' red fire!
  So shall I die by drops of hot desire.

"Alas, poor world, what treasure hast thou lost!   1075
What face remains alive that's worth the viewing?
Whose tongue is music now?   What canst thou boast

Of things long since, or anything ensuing?
  The flowers are sweet, their colours fresh and trim;
  But true sweet beauty liv'd and died with him.

"Bonnet nor veil henceforth no creature wear!   1081
Nor sun nor wind will ever strive to kiss you:
Having no fair to lose, you need not fear;
The sun doth scorn you and the wind doth hiss you:
  But when Adonis liv'd, sun and sharp air   1085
  Lurk'd like two thieves, to rob him of his fair.

"And therefore would he put his bonnet on,
Under whose brim the gaudy sun would peep;
The wind would blow it off and, being gone,
Play with his locks: then would Adonis weep;
  And straight, in pity of his tender years,   1091
  They both would strive who first should dry his
    tears.

"To see his face the lion walk'd along
Behind some hedge, because he would not fear him;
To recreate himself, when he hath song,   1095
The tiger would be tame and gently hear him;
  If he had spoke, the wolf would leave his prey
  And never fright the silly lamb that day.

"When he beheld his shadow in the brook,
The fishes spread on it their golden gills;   1100
When he was by, the birds such pleasure took,
That some would sing, some other in their bills
  Would bring him mulberries and ripe-red cherries;
  He fed them with his sight, they him with
    berries.   1104

"But this foul, grim, and urchin-snouted boar,
Whose downward eye still looketh for a grave,
Ne'er saw the beauteous livery that he wore;
Witness the entertainment that he gave.
  If he did see his face, why then I know   1109
  He thought to kiss him, and hath kill'd him so.

"'Tis true, 'tis true; thus was Adonis slain;
He ran upon the boar with his sharp spear,
Who did not whet his teeth at him again,
But by a kiss thought to persuade him there;
  And nuzzling in his flank, the loving swine   1115
  Sheath'd unaware the tusk in his soft groin.

"Had I been tooth'd like him, I must confess,
With kissing him I should have kill'd him first;
But he is dead, and never did he bless
My youth with his; the more am I accurst."   1120
  With this, she falleth in the place she stood,
  And stains her face with his congealed blood.

1054. [was] Q₇ *had* Q₁. 1083. **fair**: beauty. 1094. **fear**: frighten. 1098. **silly**: innocent. 1105. **urchin**: hedgehog. 1114.
there: to stay there.

She looks upon his lips, and they are pale;
She takes him by the hand, and that is cold;
She whispers in his ears a heavy tale,   1125
As if they heard the woeful words she told;
    She lifts the coffer-lids that close his eyes,
    Where, lo, two lamps, burnt out, in darkness lies;

Two glasses, where herself herself beheld
A thousand times, and now no more reflect;   1130
Their virtue lost, wherein they late excell'd,
And every beauty robb'd of his effect.
    "Wonder of time," quoth she, "this is my spite,
    That, thou being dead, the day should yet be
      light.

"Since thou art dead, lo, here I prophesy: 1135
Sorrow on love hereafter shall attend;
It shall be waited on with jealousy,
Find sweet beginning, but unsavoury end,
    Ne'er settled equally, but high or low,
    That all love's pleasure shall not match his woe.

"It shall be fickle, false, and full of fraud,   1141
Bud and be blasted in a breathing-while;
The bottom poison, and the top o'erstraw'd
With sweets that shall the truest sight beguile.
    The strongest body shall it make most weak,   1145
    Strike the wise dumb and teach the fool to speak.

"It shall be sparing and too full of riot,
Teaching decrepit age to tread the measures;
The staring ruffian shall it keep in quiet,   1149
Pluck down the rich, enrich the poor with treasures:
    It shall be raging-mad and silly-mild,
    Make the young old, the old become a child.

"It shall suspect where is no cause of fear;
It shall not fear where it should most mistrust;
It shall be merciful and too severe,   1155
And most deceiving when it seems most just;
    Perverse it shall be where it shows most toward,
    Put fear to valour, courage to the coward.

"It shall be cause of war and dire events,
And set dissension 'twixt the son and sire;   1160
Subject and servile to all discontents,
As dry combustious matter is to fire.
    Sith in his prime Death doth my love destroy,
    They that love best their loves shall not enjoy."

By this, the boy that by her side lay kill'd   1165
Was melted like a vapour from her sight,
And in his blood that on the ground lay spill'd,
A purple flower sprung up, check'red with white,
    Resembling well his pale cheeks and the blood
    Which in round drops upon their whiteness stood

She bows her head, the new-sprung flower to smell,
Comparing it to her Adonis' breath,   1172
And says, within her bosom it shall dwell,
Since he himself is reft from her by death.
    She crops the stalk, and in the breach appears 1175
    Green-dropping sap, which she compares to tears.

"Poor flower," quoth she, "this was thy father's
      guise —
Sweet issue of a more sweet-smelling sire —
For every little grief to wet his eyes:
To grow unto himself was his desire,   1180
    And so 'tis thine; but know, it is as good
    To wither in my breast as in his blood.

"Here was thy father's bed, here in my breast;
Thou art the next of blood, and 'tis thy right.
Lo, in this hollow cradle take thy rest,   1185
My throbbing heart shall rock thee day and night;
    There shall not be one minute in an hour
    Wherein I will not kiss my sweet love's flower."

Thus weary of the world, away she hies,
And yokes her silver doves; by whose swift aid   1190
Their mistress, mounted, through the empty skies
In her light chariot quickly is convey'd;
    Holding their course to Paphos, where their queen
    Means to immure herself and not be seen.

1133. **spite:** grievance. 1148. **tread the measures:** dance. 1157. **toward:** willing. 1177. **guise:** way. 1193. **Paphos:** a city of Cyprus, chief seat of the worship of Venus.

The Rape of Lucrece

THE FIRST EDITION of *Lucrece*, the source of all succeeding texts, was printed in 1594 for John Harrison by Richard Field, the original publisher of *Venus and Adonis*. If it is assumed that it represents the "graver labour" promised in the dedication of the earlier poem, the date of composition must have been 1593–94. Eight editions are known to have been issued by 1655.

The story of Lucrece was so widely familiar, and had been so often the theme of various kinds of artistic effort, that it is impossible to state accurately and exhaustively the sources from which Shakespeare drew his knowledge of it. The versions of Ovid and Livy, either in the original or in the translations of Golding and Painter, and that of Chaucer in *The Legend of Good Women*, seem certainly to have been known to him; and for the ornaments and digressions he seems to have laid under contribution many of his contemporaries. The apostrophe to Time is a commonplace, of which that to Opportunity is a Shakespearean variation. The description of the painting of the fall of Troy derives many details from Virgil's *Æneid*, Books i and ii.

Daniel's *Complaint of Rosamond* (1592) seems to bear to *Lucrece* somewhat the same relation as Lodge's *Glaucus and Scilla* does to *Venus and Adonis*. It is written in the seven-lined stanza used here, and in the remorse of Rosamond it treats a theme closely parallel in tone and method to the laments of Lucrece.

In some manuscript notes which have survived, Gabriel Harvey remarks that "the younger sort takes much delight in Shakespeare's Venus and Adonis; but his Lucrece and his tragedie of Hamlet, Prince of Denmark, have it in them to please the wiser sort." *Lucrece*, indeed, with its picture of ancient Roman virtue, seems clearly to have been intended as an antithesis to the amoral paganism of *Venus and Adonis*. It is "graver," more deeply felt, less purely decorative. But it also has abundance of set pieces, wrought with elaborate rhetoric, which delay the action; and however their skill in description, their felicity of phrasing, their eloquence, and their epigrammatic quality may evoke our admiration, we are never for long carried away by sympathy.

THE RAPE OF LUCRECE

TO THE

RIGHT HONOURABLE HENRY WRIOTHESLEY,

EARL OF SOUTHAMPTON AND BARON OF TITCHFIELD.

The love I dedicate to your Lordship is without end; whereof this pamphlet, without beginning, is but a superfluous moiety. The warrant I have of your honourable disposition, not the
worth of my untutor'd lines, makes it assured of acceptance. What I have done is yours;
what I have to do is yours; being part in all I have, devoted yours. Were my worth greater,
my duty would show greater; meantime, as it is, it is bound to your Lordship, to whom I wish
long life, still length'ned with all happiness.   Your Lordship's in all duty,
                                                        WILLIAM SHAKESPEARE.

THE ARGUMENT

Lucius Tarquinius, for his excessive pride surnamed Superbus, after he had caused his own
father-in-law Servius Tullius to be cruelly murd'red,
and, contrary to the Roman laws and customs,
not requiring or staying for the people's suffrages,
had possessed himself of the kingdom, went, accompanied with his sons and other noblemen of Rome,
to besiege Ardea: during which siege the principal
men of the army meeting one evening at the tent of
Sextus Tarquinius, the king's son, in their discourses
after supper every one commended the virtues of
his own wife; among whom Collatinus extolled the
incomparable chastity of his wife Lucretia. In that
pleasant humour they all posted to Rome; and intending, by their secret and sudden arrival, to make
trial of that which every one had before avouched,
only Collatinus finds his wife, though it were late
in the night, spinning amongst her maids: the other
ladies were all found dancing and revelling, or in
several disports. Whereupon the noblemen yielded
Collatinus the victory, and his wife the fame. At
that time Sextus Tarquinius being inflamed with
Lucrece' beauty, yet smothering his passions for
the present, departed with the rest back to the
camp; from whence he shortly after privily withdrew
himself, and was, according to his estate, royally
entertained and lodged by Lucrece at Collatium.
The same night he treacherously stealeth into her
chamber, violently ravish'd her, and early in the
morning speedeth away. Lucrece, in this lamentable plight, hastily dispatcheth messengers, one to
Rome for her father, another to the camp for Collatine. They came, the one accompanied with
Junius Brutus, the other with Publius Valerius; and
finding Lucrece attired in mourning habit, demanded the cause of her sorrow. She, first taking
an oath of them for her revenge, revealed the actor,
and whole manner of his dealing, and withal suddenly stabbed herself. Which done, with one consent they all vowed to root out the whole hated
family of the Tarquins; and bearing the dead body
to Rome, Brutus acquainted the people with the
doer and manner of the vile deed, with a bitter in-
vective against the tyranny of the king; wherewith
the people were so moved, that with one consent
and a general acclamation the Tarquins were all
exiled, and the state government changed from kings
to consuls.

From the besieged Ardea all in post,
Borne by the trustless wings of false desire,
Lust-breathed Tarquin leaves the Roman host,
And to Collatium bears the lightless fire

Which, in pale embers hid, lurks to aspire   5
    And girdle with embracing flames the waist
    Of Collatine's fair love, Lucrece the chaste.
                5. **aspire:** ascend.

Haply that name of "chaste" unhap'ly set
This bateless edge on his keen appetite;
When Collatine unwisely did not let   10
To praise the clear unmatched red and white
Which triumph'd in that sky of his delight,
    Where mortal stars, as bright as heaven's beauties,
    With pure aspects did him peculiar duties.

For he the night before, in Tarquin's tent,   15
Unlock'd the treasure of his happy state;
What priceless wealth the heavens had him lent
In the possession of his beauteous mate;
Reck'ning his fortune at such high proud rate
    That kings might be espoused to more fame,   20
    But king nor peer to such a peerless dame.

O happiness enjoy'd but of a few!
And, if possess'd, as soon decay'd and done
As is the morning's silver melting dew
Against the golden splendour of the sun!   25
An expir'd date, cancell'd ere well begun:
    Honour and beauty, in the owner's arms,
    Are weakly fortress'd from a world of harms.

Beauty itself doth of itself persuade
The eyes of men without an orator;   30
What needeth then apologies be made
To set forth that which is so singular?
Or why is Collatine the publisher
    Of that rich jewel he should keep unknown
    From thievish ears, because it is his own?   35

Perchance his boast of Lucrece' sovereignty
Suggested this proud issue of a king,
For by our ears our hearts oft tainted be;
Perchance that envy of so rich a thing,
Braving compare, disdainfully did sting   40
    His high-pitch'd thoughts, that meaner men should vaunt
    That golden hap which their superiors want.

But some untimely thought did instigate
His all too timeless speed, if none of those.
His honour, his affairs, his friends, his state, 45
Neglected all, with swift intent he goes
To quench the coal which in his liver glows.
    O rash false heat, wrapp'd in repentant cold,
    Thy hasty spring still blasts, and ne'er grows old!

When at Collatia this false lord arrived,   50
Well was he welcom'd by the Roman dame,
Within whose face beauty and virtue strived
Which of them both should underprop her fame.
When virtue bragg'd, beauty would blush for shame;
    When beauty boasted blushes, in despite   55
    Virtue would stain that [o'er] with silver white.

But beauty, in that white intituled
From Venus' doves, doth challenge that fair field;
Then virtue claims from beauty beauty's red,
Which virtue gave the golden age to gild   60
Their silver cheeks, and call'd it then their shield;
    Teaching them thus to use it in the fight,
    When shame assail'd, the red should fence the white.

This heraldry in Lucrece's face was seen,
Argu'd by beauty's red and virtue's white;   65
Of either's colour was the other queen,
Proving from world's minority their right:
Yet their ambition makes them still to fight,
    The sovereignty of either being so great
    That oft they interchange each other's seat. 70

Their silent war of lilies and of roses
Which Tarquin view'd in her fair face's field,
In their pure ranks his traitor eye encloses;
Where, lest between them both it should be kill'd,
The coward captive vanquished doth yield   75
    To those two armies that would let him go
    Rather than triumph in so false a foe.

Now thinks he that her husband's shallow tongue,—
The niggard prodigal that prais'd her so, —
In that high task hath done her beauty wrong,   80
Which far exceeds his barren skill to show;
Therefore that praise which Collatine doth owe
    Enchanted Tarquin answers with surmise,
    In silent wonder of still-gazing eyes.

This earthly saint, adored by this devil,   85
Little suspecteth the false worshipper;
For unstain'd thoughts do seldom dream on evil;
Birds never lim'd no secret bushes fear:
So guiltless she securely gives good cheer
    And reverent welcome to her princely guest, 90
    Whose inward ill no outward harm express'd:

For that he colour'd with his high estate,
Hiding base sin in pleats of majesty;

9. **bateless:** not to be blunted. 10. **let:** refrain. 12. **that sky:** Lucrece's face. 31. **apologies:** eulogies. 37. **Suggested:** tempted. 42. **want:** lack. 47. **liver:** supposed the seat of desire. 49. **blasts:** is blighted. 56. **that:** those blushes. **[o'er]** (Gildon). *ore* Q. *or* (= gold) Malone. 57. **intituled:** having a right to. 58. **field.** Used in the heraldic sense as well as for battlefield. 60. **golden age:** when the world was young and innocent. Virtue gave the people of that time red to blush with. 63. **fence:** defend. 65. **Argu'd:** shown. 67. **world's minority:** the golden age of l. 60. 75. **coward captive:** Tarquin's eye. 82. **owe.** Because his praise was inadequate. 83. **answers:** pays, compensates for. 88. **lim'd:** caught by bird-lime. 89. **securely:** fearlessly.

That nothing in him seem'd inordinate,
Save sometime too much wonder of his eye,   95
Which, having all, all could not satisfy;
  But, poorly rich, so wanteth in his store,
  That, cloy'd with much, he pineth still for more.

But she, that never cop'd with stranger eyes,
Could pick no meaning from their parling looks,   100
Nor read the subtle shining secrecies
Writ in the glassy margents of such books.
She touch'd no unknown baits, nor fear'd no hooks;
  Nor could she moralize his wanton sight,
  More than his eyes were open'd to the light.   105

He stories to her ears her husband's fame,
Won in the fields of fruitful Italy;
And decks with praises Collatine's high name,
Made glorious by his manly chivalry,
With bruised arms and wreaths of victory.   110
  Her joy with heav'd-up hand she doth express,
  And, wordless, so greets Heaven for his success.

Far from the purpose of his coming thither,
He makes excuses for his being there.
No cloudy show of stormy blust'ring weather   115
Doth yet in his fair welkin once appear,
Till sable Night, mother of Dread and Fear,
  Upon the world dim darkness doth display,
  And in her vaulty prison stows the Day.

For then is Tarquin brought unto his bed,   120
Intending weariness with heavy sprite;
For, after supper, long he questioned
With modest Lucrece, and wore out the night.
Now leaden slumber with life's strength doth fight;
  And every one to rest themselves betake,   125
  Save thieves, and cares, and troubled minds, that
    wake.

As one of which doth Tarquin lie revolving
The sundry dangers of his will's obtaining;
Yet ever to obtain his will resolving,
Though weak-built hopes persuade him to abstain-
    ing.   130
Despair to gain doth traffic oft for gaining;
  And when great treasure is the meed proposed,
  Though death be adjunct, there's no death sup-
    posed.

Those that much covet are with gain so fond
That what they have not, that which they possess,
They scatter and unloose it from their bond,   136
And so, by hoping more, they have but less;
Or, gaining more, the profit of excess

Is but to surfeit, and such griefs sustain
That they prove bankrupt in this poor-rich gain.

The aim of all is but to nurse the life   141
With honour, wealth, and ease, in waning age;
And in this aim there is such thwarting strife
That one for all, or all for one, we gage,
As life for honour in fell battle's rage,   145
  Honour for wealth; and oft that wealth doth cost
  The death of all, and all together lost.

So that in vent'ring ill we leave to be
The things we are for that which we expect;
And this ambitious foul infirmity,   150
In having much, torments us with defect
Of that we have: so then we do neglect
  The thing we have; and, all for want of wit,
  Make something nothing by augmenting it.

Such hazard now must doting Tarquin make,   155
Pawning his honour to obtain his lust;
And for himself himself he must forsake:
Then where is truth, if there be no self-trust?
When shall he think to find a stranger just
  When he himself himself confounds, betrays   160
  To sland'rous tongues and wretched hateful days?

Now stole upon the time the dead of night,
When heavy sleep had clos'd up mortal eyes.
No comfortable star did lend his light,
No noise but owls' and wolves' death-boding cries;
Now serves the season that they may surprise   166
  The silly lambs.   Pure thoughts are dead and
    still,
  While lust and murder wakes to stain and kill.

And now this lustful lord leap'd from his bed,
Throwing his mantle rudely o'er his arm;   170
Is madly toss'd between desire and dread;
Th' one sweetly flatters, th' other feareth harm;
But honest fear, bewitch'd with lust's foul charm,
  Doth too too oft betake him to retire,
  Beaten away by brain-sick rude desire.   175

His falchion on a flint he softly smiteth,
That from the cold stone sparks of fire do fly;
Whereat a waxen torch forthwith he lighteth,
Which must be lode-star to his lustful eye;
And to the flame thus speaks advisedly: 180
  "As from this cold flint I enforc'd this fire,
  So Lucrece must I force to my desire."

Here pale with fear he doth premeditate
The dangers of his loathsome enterprise,

---

99. **cop'd:** encountered.   100. **parling:** speaking.   104. **moralize:** interpret.   121. **Intending:** professing.   122. **questioned:** discussed.   131. Despair and hope of gaining his end constantly alternate.   135. **That what.** *That oft* Q5. *For what* Capell MS.   144. **gage:** stake.   151-52. **defect Of:** the sense of lacking.   180. **advisedly:** deliberately.

And in his inward mind he doth debate 185
What following sorrow may on this arise.
Then looking scornfully, he doth despise
His naked armour of still slaughtered lust,
And justly thus controls his thoughts unjust:

"Fair torch, burn out thy light, and lend it not 190
To darken her whose light excelleth thine;
And die, unhallow'd thoughts, before you blot
With your uncleanness that which is divine;
Offer pure incense to so pure a shrine:
    Let fair humanity abhor the deed 195
    That spots and stains love's modest snow-white
        weed.

"O shame to knighthood and to shining arms!
O foul dishonour to my household's grave!
O impious act, including all foul harms!
A martial man to be soft fancy's slave! 200
True valour still a true respect should have;
    Then my digression is so vile, so base,
    That it will live engraven in my face.

"Yea, though I die, the scandal will survive,
And be an eye-sore in my golden coat; 205
Some loathsome dash the herald will contrive,
To cipher me how fondly I did dote;
That my posterity, sham'd with the note,
    Shall curse my bones, and hold it for no sin
    To wish that I their father had not been. 210

"What win I, if I gain the thing I seek?
A dream, a breath, a froth of fleeting joy.
Who buys a minute's mirth to wail a week,
Or sells eternity to get a toy?
For one sweet grape who will the vine destroy? 215
    Or what fond beggar, but to touch the crown,
    Would with the sceptre straight be strucken down?

"If Collatinus dream of my intent,
Will he not wake, and in a desp'rate rage
Post hither, this vile purpose to prevent? 220
This siege that hath engirt his marriage,
This blur to youth, this sorrow to the sage,
    This dying virtue, this surviving shame,
    Whose crime will bear an ever-during blame?

"O, what excuse can my invention make 225
When thou shalt charge me with so black a deed?
Will not my tongue be mute, my frail joints shake,
Mine eyes forgo their light, my false heart bleed?
The guilt being great, the fear doth still exceed;
    And extreme fear can neither fight nor fly, 230
    But coward-like with trembling terror die.

"Had Collatinus kill'd my son or sire,
Or lain in ambush to betray my life,
Or were he not my dear friend, this desire
Might have excuse to work upon his wife, 235
As in revenge or quittal of such strife;
    But as he is my kinsman, my dear friend,
    The shame and fault finds no excuse nor end.

"Shameful it is: ay, if the fact be known.
Hateful it is: there is no hate in loving. 240
I'll beg her love: but she is not her own.
The worst is but denial and reproving.
My will is strong, past reason's weak removing.
    Who fears a sentence or an old man's saw
    Shall by a painted cloth be kept in awe." 245

Thus, graceless, holds he disputation
'Tween frozen conscience and hot burning will,
And with good thoughts makes dispensation,
Urging the worser sense for vantage still;
Which in a moment doth confound and kill 250
    All pure effects, and doth so far proceed
    That what is vile shows like a virtuous deed.

Quoth he, "She took me kindly by the hand,
And gaz'd for tidings in my eager eyes,
Fearing some hard news from the warlike band 255
Where her beloved Collatinus lies.
O, how her fear did make her colour rise!
    First red as roses that on lawn we lay,
    Then white as lawn, the roses took away.

"And how her hand, in my hand being lock'd, 260
Forc'd it to tremble with her loyal fear!
Which struck her sad, and then it faster rock'd,
Until her husband's welfare she did hear;
Whereat she smiled with so sweet a cheer
    That, had Narcissus seen her as she stood, 265
    Self-love had never drown'd him in the flood.

"Why hunt I then for colour or excuses?
All orators are dumb when beauty pleadeth;
Poor wretches have remorse in poor abuses,
Love thrives not in the heart that shadows dreadeth;
Affection is my captain, and he leadeth; 271
    And when his gaudy banner is display'd,
    The coward fights, and will not be dismay'd.

"Then, childish fear, avaunt! debating, die!
Respect and reason, wait on wrinkled age! 275
My heart shall never countermand mine eye.
Sad pause and deep regard beseem the sage;
My part is youth, and beats these from the stage.
    Desire my pilot is, beauty my prize; 279
    Then who fears sinking where such treasure lies?"

188. **His... lust:** the weakness of lust's defence, which is always killed by its own fulfillment. 200. **fancy's:** love's. 207. **cipher:** decipher, express. 229. **exceed:** be extreme. 243. **will:** desire, lust. Cf. l. 247. 245. **painted cloth:** motto in a painted cloth (substitute for tapestry). 248. **makes dispensation:** dispenses. 267. **colour:** pretext.

As corn o'ergrown by weeds, so heedful fear
Is almost chok'd by unresisted lust.
Away he steals with open list'ning ear,
Full of foul hope and full of fond mistrust;
Both which, as servitors to the unjust,   285
    So cross him with their opposite persuasion,
    That now he vows a league, and now invasion.

Within his thought her heavenly image sits,
And in the self-same seat sits Collatine.
That eye which looks on her confounds his wits;   290
That eye which him beholds, as more divine,
Unto a view so false will not incline;
    But with a pure appeal seeks to the heart,
    Which once corrupted takes the worser part;

And therein heartens up his servile powers,   295
Who, flatt'red by their leader's jocund show,
Stuff up his lust, as minutes fill up hours;
And as their captain, so their pride doth grow,
Paying more slavish tribute than they owe.
    By reprobate desire thus madly led,   300
    The Roman lord marcheth to Lucrece' bed.

The locks between her chamber and his will,
Each one by him enforc'd, retires his ward;
But, as they open, they all rate his ill,
Which drives the creeping thief to some regard.   305
The threshold grates the door to have him heard:
    Night-wand'ring weasels shriek to see him there;
    They fright him, yet he still pursues his fear.

As each unwilling portal yields him way,
Through little vents and crannies of the place   310
The wind wars with his torch to make him stay,
And blows the smoke of it into his face,
Extinguishing his conduct in this case;
    But his hot heart, which fond desire doth scorch,
    Puffs forth another wind that fires the torch.   315

And being lighted, by the light he spies
Lucretia's glove, wherein her needle sticks.
He takes it from the rushes where it lies,
And griping it, the needle his finger pricks;
As who should say, "This glove to wanton tricks   320
    Is not inur'd; return again in haste;
    Thou see'st our mistress' ornaments are chaste."

But all these poor forbiddings could not stay him;
He in the worst sense construes their denial:
The doors, the wind, the glove that did delay him,
He takes for accidental things of trial;   326
Or as those bars which stop the hourly dial,

Who with a ling'ring stay his course doth let,
Till every minute pays the hour his debt.

"So, so," quoth he, "these lets attend the time,   330
Like little frosts that sometime threat the spring
To add a more rejoicing to the prime
And give the sneaped birds more cause to sing.
Pain pays the income of each precious thing;
    Huge rocks, high winds, strong pirates, shelves
        and sands,   335
    The merchant fears, ere rich at home he lands."

Now is he come unto the chamber-door
That shuts him from the heaven of his thought,
Which with a yielding latch, and with no more,
Hath barr'd him from the blessed thing he sought.
So from himself impiety hath wrought,   341
    That for his prey to pray he doth begin,
    As if the heavens should countenance his sin.

But in the midst of his unfruitful prayer,
Having solicited th' eternal power   345
That his foul thoughts might compass his fair fair,
And they would stand auspicious to the hour,
Even there he starts: quoth he, "I must deflower:
    The powers to whom I pray abhor this fact,
    How can they then assist me in the act?   350

"Then Love and Fortune be my gods, my guide!
My will is back'd with resolution.
Thoughts are but dreams till their effects be tried:
The blackest sin is clear'd with absolution;
Against love's fire fear's frost hath dissolution.   355
    The eye of heaven is out, and misty night
    Covers the shame that follows sweet delight."

This said, his guilty hand pluck'd up the latch,
And with his knee the door he opens wide.
The dove sleeps fast that this night-owl will catch;
Thus treason works ere traitors be espi'd.   361
Who sees the lurking serpent steps aside;
    But she, sound sleeping, fearing no such thing,
    Lies at the mercy of his mortal sting.

Into the chamber wickedly he stalks,   365
And gazeth on her yet unstained bed.
The curtains being close, about he walks,
Rolling his greedy eyeballs in his head.
By their high treason is his heart misled;
    Which gives the watch-word to his hand full soon
    To draw the cloud that hides the silver moon.   371

Look, as the fair and fiery-pointed sun,
Rushing from forth a cloud, bereaves our sight;

303. **retires his ward**: withdraws the ridge of metal which fits the notch in a key.   304. **rate**: scold.   313. **conduct**: guide (the torch).   327. **dial**: clock, or watch.   328. **let**: hinder.   330. **attend**: naturally accompany.   332. **prime**: spring. 333. **sneaped**: pinched with cold.   347. **they**: i.e., power(s), l. 345.   349. **fact**: deed.

Even so. the curtain drawn, his eyes begun
To wink, being blinded with a greater light: 375
Whether it is that she reflects so bright
    That dazzleth them, or else some shame supposed,
    ·But blind they are, and keep themselves enclosed.

O, had they in that darksome prison died,
Then had they seen the period of their ill!   380
Then Collatine again, by Lucrece' side,
In his clear bed might have reposed still!
But they must ope, this blessed league to kill;
    And holy-thoughted Lucrece to their sight
    Must sell her joy, her life, her world's delight.   385

Her lily hand her rosy cheek lies under,
Coz'ning the pillow of a lawful kiss;
Who, therefore angry, seems to part in sunder,
Swelling on either side to want his bliss;
Between whose hills her head entombed is;   390
    Where, like a virtuous monument, she lies,
    To be admir'd of lewd unhallow'd eyes.

Without the bed her other fair hand was,
On the green coverlet; whose perfect white
Show'd like an April daisy on the grass,   395
With pearly sweat, resembling dew of night.
Her eyes, like marigolds, had sheath'd their light,
    And canopi'd in darkness sweetly lay,
    Till they might open to adorn the day.

Her hair, like golden threads, play'd with her
    breath;   400
O modest wantons! wanton modesty!
Showing life's triumph in the map of death,
And death's dim look in life's mortality.
Each in her sleep themselves so beautify,
    As if between them twain there were no strife,   405
    But that life liv'd in death, and death in life.

Her breasts, like ivory globes circled with blue,
A pair of maiden worlds unconquered,
Save of their lord no bearing yoke they knew,
And him by oath they truly honoured: 410
These worlds in Tarquin new ambition bred;
    Who, like a foul usurper, went about
    From this fair throne to heave the owner out.

What could he see but mightily he noted?
What did he note but strongly he desired?   415
What he beheld, on that he firmly doted,
And in his will his wilful eye he tired.
With more than admiration he admired
    Her azure veins, her alabaster skin,
    Her coral lips, her snow-white dimpled chin.   420

As the grim lion fawneth o'er his prey,
Sharp hunger by the conquest satisfied,
So o'er this sleeping soul doth Tarquin stay,
His rage of lust by gazing qualified;
Slack'd, not suppress'd: for standing by her side,   425
    His eye, which late this mutiny restrains,
    Unto a greater uproar tempts his veins.

And they, like straggling slaves for pillage fighting,
Obdurate vassals fell exploits effecting,
In bloody death and ravishment delighting,   430
Nor children's tears nor mothers' groans respecting,
Swell in their pride, the onset still expecting.
    Anon his beating heart, alarum striking,
    Gives the hot charge and bids them do their liking.

His drumming heart cheers up his burning eye,   435
His eye commends the leading to his hand;
His hand, as proud of such a dignity,
Smoking with pride, march'd on to make his stand
On her bare breast, the heart of all her land;
    Whose ranks of blue veins, as his hand did scale,
    Left their round turrets destitute and pale.   441

They, must'ring to the quiet cabinet
Where their dear governess and lady lies,
Do tell her she is dreadfully beset,
And fright her with confusion of their cries.   445
She, much amaz'd, breaks ope her lock'd-up eyes,
    Who, peeping forth this tumult to behold,
    Are by his flaming torch dimm'd and controll'd.

Imagine her as one in dead of night
From forth dull sleep by dreadful fancy waking,   450
That thinks she hath beheld some ghastly sprite,
Whose grim aspect sets every joint a-shaking;
What terror 'tis! but she in worser taking,
    From sleep disturbed, heedfully doth view
    The sight which makes supposed terror true.   455

Wrapp'd and confounded in a thousand fears,
Like to a new-kill'd bird she trembling lies;
She dares not look; yet, winking, there appears
Quick-shifting antics, ugly in her eyes.
Such shadows are the weak brain's forgeries,   460
    Who, angry that the eyes fly from their lights,
    In darkness daunts them with more dreadful
    sights.

His hand, that yet remains upon her breast, —
Rude ram, to batter such an ivory wall! —
May feel her heart — poor citizen! — distress'd,
Wounding itself to death, rise up and fall,   466
Beating her bulk, that his hand shakes withal.

375. wink: close.   387. Coz'ning: cheating.   389. to want: because deprived of.   391. monument: reclining statue.
402. map: picture.   417. tired: devoured.   424. qualified: moderated.   442. cabinet: dwelling.   453. taking: agitation.
459. antics: grotesque figures.

This moves in him more rage and lesser pity
To make the breach and enter this sweet city.

First, like a trumpet, doth his tongue begin   470
To sound a parley to his heartless foe;
Who o'er the white sheet peers her whiter chin,
The reason of this rash alarm to know,
Which he by dumb demeanour seeks to show;
  But she with vehement prayers urgeth still   475
  Under what colour he commits this ill.

Thus he replies: "The colour in thy face,
That even for anger makes the lily pale
And the red rose blush at her own disgrace,
Shall plead for me and tell my loving tale.   480
Under that colour am I come to scale
  Thy never-conquered fort.   The fault is thine,
  For those thine eyes betray thee unto mine.

"Thus I forestall thee, if thou mean to chide:
Thy beauty hath ensnar'd thee to this night,   485
Where thou with patience must my will abide —
My will that marks thee for my earth's delight,
Which I to conquer sought with all my might;
  But as reproof and reason beat it dead,
  By thy bright beauty was it newly bred.   490

"I see what crosses my attempt will bring;
I know what thorns the growing rose defends:
I think the honey guarded with a sting:
All this beforehand counsel comprehends;
But Will is deaf and hears no heedful friends;   495
  Only he hath an eye to gaze on beauty,
  And dotes on what he looks, 'gainst law or duty.

"I have debated, even in my soul,
What wrong, what shame, what sorrow I shall breed;
But nothing can affection's course control,   500
Or stop the headlong fury of his speed.
I know repentant tears ensue the deed,
  Reproach, disdain, and deadly enmity;
  Yet strive I to embrace mine infamy."

This said, he shakes aloft his Roman blade,   505
Which, like a falcon tow'ring in the skies,
Coucheth the fowl below with his wings' shade,
Whose crooked beak threats, if he mount, he dies:
So under his insulting falchion lies
  Harmless Lucretia, marking what he tells   510
  With trembling fear, as fowl hear falcon's bells.

"Lucrece," quoth he, "this night I must enjoy thee.
If thou deny, then force must work my way,

For in thy bed I purpose to destroy thee;
That done, some worthless slave of thine I'll slay,
To kill thine honour with thy life's decay;   516
  And in thy dead arms do I mean to place him,
  Swearing I slew him, seeing thee embrace him.

"So thy surviving husband shall remain
The scornful mark of every open eye;   520
Thy kinsmen hang their heads at this disdain,
Thy issue blurr'd with nameless bastardy;
And thou, the author of their obloquy,
  Shalt have thy trespass cited up in rhymes,
  And sung by children in succeeding times.   525

"But if thou yield, I rest thy secret friend:
The fault unknown is as a thought unacted;
A little harm done to a great good end
For lawful policy remains enacted.
The poisonous simple sometime is compacted   530
  In a pure compound; being so applied,
  His venom in effect is purified.

"Then, for thy husband and thy children's sake,
Tender my suit; bequeath not to their lot
The shame that from them no device can take,   535
The blemish that will never be forgot,
Worse than a slavish wipe or birth-hour's blot;
  For marks descri'd in men's nativity
  Are nature's faults, not their own infamy."

Here with a cockatrice' dead-killing eye   540
He rouseth up himself and makes a pause;
While she, the picture of pure piety,
Like a white hind under the gripe's sharp claws,
Pleads, in a wilderness where are no laws,
  To the rough beast that knows no gentle right,
  Nor aught obeys but his foul appetite.   546

But when a black-fac'd cloud the world doth threat,
In his dim mist th' aspiring mountains hiding,
From earth's dark womb some gentle gust doth
  get,
Which blow these pitchy vapours from their
  biding,   550
Hind'ring their present fall by this dividing;
  So his unhallow'd haste her words delays,
  And moody Pluto winks while Orpheus plays.

Yet, foul night-waking cat, he doth but dally,
While in his hold-fast foot the weak mouse panteth.
Her sad behaviour feeds his vulture folly,   556
A swallowing gulf that even in plenty wanteth.
His ear her prayers admits, but his heart granteth

No penetrable entrance to her plaining;
Tears harden lust, though marble wear with raining. 561

Her pity-pleading eyes are sadly fixed
In the remorseless wrinkles of his face;
Her modest eloquence with sighs is mixed,
Which to her oratory adds more grace.
She puts the period often from his place; 565
  And midst the sentence so her accent breaks,
  That twice she doth begin ere once she speaks.

She conjures him by high almighty Jove,
By knighthood, gentry, and sweet ,friendship's
    oath;
By her untimely tears, her husband's love, 570
By holy human law, and common troth,
By heaven and earth, and all the power of both,
  That to his borrowed bed he make retire,
  And stoop to honour, not to foul desire.

Quoth she, "Reward not hospitality 575
With such black payment as thou hast pretended;
Mud not the fountain that gave drink to thee;
Mar not the thing that cannot be amended;
End thy ill aim before thy shoot be ended;
  He is no woodman that doth bend his bow 580
  To strike a poor unseasonable doe.

"My husband is thy friend; for his sake spare me:
Thyself art mighty; for thine own sake leave me:
Myself a weakling; do not then ensnare me:
Thou look'st not like deceit; do not deceive me. 585
My sighs, like whirlwinds, labour hence to heave
    thee.
  If ever man were mov'd with woman's moans,
  Be moved with my tears, my sighs, my groans:

"All which together, like a troubled ocean,
Beat at thy rocky and wreck-threat'ning heart,
To soften it with their continual motion; 591
For stones dissolv'd to water do convert.
O, if no harder than a stone thou art,
  Melt at my tears, and be compassionate!
  Soft pity enters at an iron gate. 595

"In Tarquin's likeness I did entertain thee:
Hast thou put on his shape to do him shame?
To all the host of heaven I complain me,
Thou wrong'st his honour, wound'st his princely
    name. 599
Thou art not what thou seem'st; and if the same,
  Thou seem'st not what thou art, a god, a king;
  For kings like gods should govern everything.

"How will thy shame be seeded in thine age,
When thus thy vices bud before thy spring?
If in thy hope thou dar'st do such outrage, 605
What dar'st thou not when once thou art a king?
O, be rememb'red, no outrageous thing
  From vassal actors can be wip'd away;
  Then kings' misdeeds cannot be hid in clay.

"This deed will make thee only lov'd for fear; 610
But happy monarchs still are fear'd for love:
With foul offenders thou perforce must bear
When they in thee the like offences prove.
If but for fear of this, thy will remove;
  For princes are the glass, the school, the book, 615
  Where subjects' eyes do learn, do read, do look.

"And wilt thou be the school where Lust shall
    learn?
Must he in thee read lectures of such shame?
Wilt thou be glass wherein it shall discern
Authority for sin, warrant for blame, 620
To privilege dishonour in thy name?
  Thou back'st reproach against long-living laud,
  And mak'st fair reputation but a bawd.

"Hast thou command? By him that gave it thee,
From a pure heart command thy rebel will; 625
Draw not thy sword to guard iniquity,
For it was lent thee all that brood to kill.
Thy princely office how canst thou fulfil,
  When, pattern'd by thy fault, foul sin may say
  He learn'd to sin, and thou didst teach the way!

"Think but how vile a spectacle it were 631
To view thy present trespass in another.
Men's faults do seldom to themselves appear;
Their own transgressions partially they smother:
This guilt would seem death-worthy in thy brother.
  O, how are they wrapt in with infamies 636
  That from their own misdeeds askance their eyes!

"To thee, to thee, my heav'd-up hands appeal,
Not to seducing lust, thy rash relier:
I sue for exil'd majesty's repeal; 640
Let him return, and flatt'ring thoughts retire:
His true respect will prison false desire,
  And wipe the dim mist from thy doting eyne,
  That thou shalt see thy state and pity mine."

"Have done," quoth he; "my uncontrolled tide
Turns not, but swells the higher by this let. 646
Small lights are soon blown out, huge fires abide,
And with the wind in greater fury fret.
The petty streams that pay a daily debt

569. gentry: noble breeding. 576. pretended: planned. 580. woodman: sportsman. 592. convert: change. 615.
glass: mirror. 634. partially: showing partiality. 637. askance: turn aside. 639. thy rash relier: the impulse to which
you are rashly trusting.

To their salt sovereign, with their fresh falls' haste
Add to his flow, but alter not his taste."   651

"Thou art," quoth she, "a sea, a sovereign king;
And, lo, there falls into thy boundless flood
Black lust, dishonour, shame, misgoverning,
Who seek to stain the ocean of thy blood.   655
If all these petty ills shall change thy good,
  Thy sea within a puddle's womb is hearsed,
  And not the puddle in thy sea dispersed.

"So shall these slaves be king, and thou their slave;
Thou nobly base, they basely dignifi'd;   660
Thou their fair life, and they thy fouler grave;
Thou loathed in their shame, they in thy pride.
The lesser thing should not the greater hide;
  The cedar stoops not to the base shrub's foot,
  But low shrubs wither at the cedar's root.   665

"So let thy thoughts, low vassals to thy state," —
"No more," quoth he; "by heaven, I will not hear
      thee.
Yield to my love; if not, enforced hate,
Instead of love's coy touch, shall rudely tear thee;
That done, despitefully I mean to bear thee   670
  Unto the base bed of some rascal groom,
  To be thy partner in this shameful doom."

This said, he sets his foot upon the light,
For light and lust are deadly enemies;
Shame folded up in blind concealing night,   675
When most unseen, then most doth tyrannize.
The wolf hath seiz'd his prey, the poor lamb cries;
  Till with her own white fleece her voice controll'd
  Entombs her outcry in her lips' sweet fold.

For with the nightly linen that she wears   680
He pens her piteous clamours in her head;
Cooling his hot face in the chastest tears
That ever modest eyes with sorrow shed.
O, that prone lust should stain so pure a bed!
  The spots whereof could weeping purify,   685
  Her tears should drop on them perpetually.

But she hath lost a dearer thing than life,
And he hath won what he would lose again;
This forced league doth force a further strife,
This momentary joy breeds months of pain,   690
This hot desire converts to cold disdain;
  Pure Chastity is rifled of her store,
  And Lust, the thief, far poorer than before.

Look, as the full-fed hound or gorged hawk,
Unapt for tender smell or speedy flight,   695
Make slow pursuit, or altogether balk

The prey wherein by nature they delight;
So surfeit-taking Tarquin fares this night:
  His taste delicious, in digestion souring,
  Devours his will, that liv'd by foul devouring.   700

O, deeper sin than bottomless conceit
Can comprehend in still imagination!
Drunken Desire must vomit his receipt,
Ere he can see his own abomination.
While Lust is in his pride, no exclamation   705
  Can curb his heat or rein his rash desire,
  Till, like a jade, Self-will himself doth tire.

And then with lank and lean discolour'd cheek,
With heavy eye, knit brow, and strengthless pace,
Feeble Desire, all recreant, poor, and meek,   710
Like to a bankrupt beggar wails his case.
The flesh being proud, Desire doth fight with
      Grace,
  For there it revels; and when that decays,
  The guilty rebel for remission prays.

So fares it with this faultful lord of Rome,   715
Who this accomplishment so hotly chased;
For now against himself he sounds this doom,
That through the length of times he stands dis-
      graced:
Besides, his soul's fair temple is defaced;
  To whose weak ruins muster troops of cares,   720
  To ask the spotted princess how she fares.

She says, her subjects with foul insurrection
Have batter'd down her consecrated wall,
And by their mortal fault brought in subjection
Her immortality, and made her thrall   725
To living death and pain perpetual;
  Which in her prescience she controlled still,
  But her foresight could not forestall their will.

Even in this thought through the dark night he
      stealeth,
A captive victor that hath lost in gain;   730
Bearing away the wound that nothing healeth,
The scar that will, despite of cure, remain;
Leaving his spoil perplex'd in greater pain.
  She bears the load of lust he left behind,
  And he the burden of a guilty mind.   735

He like a thievish dog creeps sadly thence;
She like a wearied lamb lies panting there;
He scowls and hates himself for his offence;
She, desperate, with her nails her flesh doth tear;
He faintly flies, sweating with guilty fear;   740
  She stays, exclaiming on the direful night;
  He runs, and chides his vanish'd, loath'd delight.

  657. **hearsed:** coffined. 684. **prone:** headlong. Q₃ reads *proud*. 696. **balk:** turn aside from. 703. **receipt:** what he had swallowed. 721. **the spotted princess:** Tarquin's defiled soul.

He thence departs a heavy convertite;
She there remains a hopeless castaway;
He in his speed looks for the morning light; 745
She prays she never may behold the day,
"For day," quoth she, "night's scapes doth open lay,
   And my true eyes have never practis'd how
   To cloak offences with a cunning brow.

"They think not but that every eye can see 750
The same disgrace which they themselves behold;
And therefore would they still in darkness be,
To have their unseen sin remain untold;
For they their guilt with weeping will unfold,
   And grave, like water that doth eat in steel, 755
   Upon my cheeks what helpless shame I feel."

Here she exclaims against repose and rest,
And bids her eyes hereafter still be blind.
She wakes her heart by beating on her breast,
And bids it leap from thence, where it may find 760
Some purer chest to close so pure a mind.
   Frantic with grief thus breathes she forth her spite
   Against the unseen secrecy of night:

"O comfort-killing Night, image of hell!
Dim register and notary of shame! 765
Black stage for tragedies and murders fell!
Vast sin-concealing chaos! nurse of blame!
Blind muffled bawd! dark harbour for defame!
   Grim cave of death! whisp'ring conspirator
   With close-tongu'd Treason and the ravisher! 770

"O hateful, vaporous, and foggy Night!
Since thou art guilty of my cureless crime,
Muster thy mists to meet the eastern light,
Make war against proportion'd course of time;
Or if thou will permit the sun to climb 775
   His wonted height, yet ere he go to bed,
   Knit poisonous clouds about his golden head.

"With rotten damps ravish the morning air;
Let their exhal'd unwholesome breaths make sick
The life of purity, the supreme fair, 780
Ere he arrive his weary noon-tide prick;
And let thy musty vapours march so thick
   That in their smoky ranks his smoth'red light
   May set at noon and make perpetual night.

"Were Tarquin Night, as he is but Night's child, 785
The silver-shining queen he would distain;
Her twinkling handmaids too, by him defil'd,
Through Night's black bosom should not peep again:
So should I have co-partners in my pain;

And fellowship in woe doth woe assuage, 790
As palmers' chat makes short their pilgrimage:

"Where now I have no one to blush with me,
To cross their arms and hang their heads with mine,
To mask their brows and hide their infamy;
But I alone, alone must sit and pine, 795
Seasoning the earth with showers of silver brine,
   Mingling my talk with tears, my grief with groans,
   Poor wasting monuments of lasting moans.

"O Night, thou furnace of foul reeking smoke,
Let not the jealous Day behold that face 800
Which underneath thy black all-hiding cloak
Immodestly lies martyr'd with disgrace!
Keep still possession of thy gloomy place,
   That all the faults which in thy reign are made
   May likewise be sepulcher'd in thy shade! 805

"Make me not object to the tell-tale Day!
The light will show, character'd in my brow,
The story of sweet chastity's decay,
The impious breach of holy wedlock vow;
Yea, the illiterate, that know not how 810
   To cipher what is writ in learned books,
   Will quote my loathsome trespass in my looks.

"The nurse, to still her child, will tell my story,
And fright her crying babe with Tarquin's name;
The orator, to deck his oratory, 815
Will couple my reproach to Tarquin's shame;
Feast-finding minstrels, tuning my defame,
   Will tie the hearers to attend each line,
   How Tarquin wronged me, I Collatine.

"Let my good name, that senseless reputation, 820
For Collatine's dear love be kept unspotted:
If that be made a theme for disputation,
The branches of another root are rotted,
And undeserv'd reproach to him allotted
   That is as clear from this attaint of mine 825
   As I, ere this, was pure to Collatine.

"O unseen shame! invisible disgrace!
O unfelt sore! crest-wounding, private scar!
Reproach is stamp'd in Collatinus' face,
And Tarquin's eye may read the mot afar, 830
How he in peace is wounded, not in war.
   Alas, how many bear such shameful blows,
   Which not themselves, but he that gives them knows!

"If, Collatine, thine honour lay in me,
From me by strong assault it is bereft. 835

---

743. **convertite**: penitent. 747. **scapes**: misdeeds. 761. **close**: enclose. 768. **defame**: disgrace. 774. **proportion'd**: regular. 781. **prick**: point (of time). 786. **distain**: defile. 787. **handmaids**: the stars. 792. **Where**: whereas. 807. **character'd**: written. 812. **quote**: note. 820. **senseless**: free from sensuality. 825. **attaint**: dishonor. 830. **mot**: motto, device.

My honey lost, and I, a drone-like bee,
Have no perfection of my summer left,
But robb'd and ransack'd by injurious theft.
  In thy weak hive a wand'ring wasp hath crept,
  And suck'd the honey which thy chaste bee
      kept.   840

"Yet am I guilty of thy honour's wrack;
Yet for thy honour did I entertain him;
Coming from thee, I could not put him back,
For it had been dishonour to disdain him.
Besides, of weariness he did complain him,   845
  And talk'd of virtue: O unlook'd-for evil,
  When virtue is profan'd in such a devil!

"Why should the worm intrude the maiden bud?
Or hateful cuckoos hatch in sparrows' nests?
Or toads infect fair founts with venom mud?   850
Or tyrant folly lurk in gentle breasts?
Or kings be breakers of their own behests?
  But no perfection is so absolute,
  That some impurity doth not pollute.

"The aged man that coffers-up his gold   855
Is plagu'd with cramps and gouts and painful
      fits,
And scarce hath eyes his treasure to behold,
But like still-pining Tantalus he sits
And useless barns the harvest of his wits;
  Having no other pleasure of his gain   860
  But torment that it cannot cure his pain.

"So then he hath it when he cannot use it,
And leaves it to be mast'red by his young,
Who in their pride do presently abuse it.
Their father was too weak and they too strong 865
To hold their cursed-blessed fortune long.
  The sweets we wish for turn to loathed sours
  Even in the moment that we call them ours.

"Unruly blasts wait on the tender spring;
Unwholesome weeds take root with precious flow'rs;
The adder hisses where the sweet birds sing;   871
What virtue breeds, iniquity devours.
We have no good that we can say is ours,
  But ill-annexed Opportunity
  Or kills his life or else his quality.   875

"O Opportunity, thy guilt is great!
'Tis thou that execut'st the traitor's treason.
Thou sets the wolf where he the lamb may get;
Whoever plots the sin, thou 'point'st the season;
'Tis thou that spurn'st at right, at law, at reason; 880
  And in thy shady cell, where none may spy him,
  Sits Sin, to seize the souls that wander by him.

"Thou mak'st the vestal violate her oath;
Thou blow'st the fire when temperance is thaw'd;
Thou smother'st honesty, thou murd'rest troth; 885
Thou foul abettor! thou notorious bawd!
Thou plantest scandal and displacest laud.
  Thou ravisher, thou traitor, thou false thief,
  Thy honey turns to gall, thy joy to grief!

"Thy secret pleasure turns to open shame,   890
Thy private feasting to a public fast,
Thy smoothing titles to a ragged name,
Thy sug'red tongue to bitter wormwood taste;
Thy violent vanities can never last.
  How comes it then, vile Opportunity,   895
  Being so bad, such numbers seek for thee?

"When wilt thou be the humble suppliant's friend
And bring him where his suit may be obtained?
When wilt thou sort an hour great strifes to end?
Or free that soul which wretchedness hath chained?
Give physic to the sick, ease to the pained?   901
  The poor, lame, blind, halt, creep, cry out for thee;
  But they ne'er meet with Opportunity.

"The patient dies while the physician sleeps;
The orphan pines while the oppressor feeds;   905
Justice is feasting while the widow weeps;
Advice is sporting while infection breeds.
Thou grant'st no time for charitable deeds:
  Wrath, envy, treason, rape, and murder's rages,
  Thy heinous hours wait on them as their pages. 910

"When Truth and Virtue have to do with thee,
A thousand crosses keep them from thy aid:
They buy thy help; but Sin ne'er gives a fee,
He gratis comes; and thou art well appaid
As well to hear as grant what he hath said.   915
  My Collatine would else have come to me
  When Tarquin did, but he was stay'd by thee.

"Guilty thou art of murder and of theft,
Guilty of perjury and subornation,
Guilty of treason, forgery, and shift,   920
Guilty of incest, that abomination;
An accessary by thine inclination
  To all sins past, and all that are to come,
  From the creation to the general doom.

"Mis-shapen Time, copesmate of ugly Night,   925
Swift subtle post, carrier of grisly care,
Eater of youth, false slave to false delight,
Base watch of woes, sin's pack-horse, virtue's snare;
Thou nursest all and murd'rest all that are.
  O, hear me then, injurious, shifting Time!   930
  Be guilty of my death, since of my crime.

875. his: its, referring to "good." 892. smoothing: flattering. 899. sort: arrange. 914. appaid: pleased. 925.
copesmate: companion.

"Why hath thy servant, Opportunity,
Betray'd the hours thou gav'st me to repose?
Cancell'd my fortunes, and enchained me
To endless date of never-ending woes?   935
Time's office is to fine the hate of foes,
  To eat up errors by opinion bred,
  Not spend the dowry of a lawful bed.

"Time's glory is to calm contending kings,
To unmask falsehood and bring truth to light, 940
To stamp the seal of time in aged things,
To wake the morn and sentinel the night,
To wrong the wronger till he render right,
  To ruinate proud buildings with thy hours,
  And smear with dust their glitt'ring golden tow'rs;

"To fill with worm-holes stately monuments,   946
To feed oblivion with decay of things,
To blot old books and alter their contents,
To pluck the quills from ancient ravens' wings,
To dry the old oak's sap and cherish springs,   950
  To spoil antiquities of hammer'd steel,
  And turn the giddy round of Fortune's wheel;

"To show the beldam daughters of her daughter,
To make the child a man, the man a child,
To slay the tiger that doth live by slaughter,   955
To tame the unicorn and lion wild,
To mock the subtle in themselves beguil'd,
  To cheer the ploughman with increaseful crops,
  And waste huge stones with little water-drops.

"Why work'st thou mischief in thy pilgrimage,   960
Unless thou couldst return to make amends?
One poor retiring minute in an age
Would purchase thee a thousand thousand friends,
Lending him wit that to bad debtors lends:
  O, this dread night, wouldst thou one hour come
    back,   965
  I could prevent this storm and shun thy wrack!

"Thou ceaseless lackey to eternity,
With some mischance cross Tarquin in his flight.
Devise extremes beyond extremity,   969
To make him curse this cursed crimeful night.
Let ghastly shadows his lewd eyes affright;
  And the dire thought of his committed evil
  Shape every bush a hideous shapeless devil.

"Disturb his hours of rest with restless trances,
Afflict him in his bed with bedrid groans;   975
Let there bechance him pitiful mischances
To make him moan, but pity not his moans;
Stone him with hard'ned hearts, harder than stones;
  And let mild women to him lose their mildness,
  Wilder to him than tigers in their wildness.   980

"Let him have time to tear his curled hair,
Let him have time against himself to rave,
Let him have time of Time's help to despair,
Let him have time to live a loathed slave,
Let him have time a beggar's orts to crave,   985
  And time to see one that by alms doth live
  Disdain to him disdained scraps to give.

"Let him have time to see his friends his foes,
And merry fools to mock at him resort;
Let him have time to mark how slow time goes
In time of sorrow, and how swift and short   99i
His time of folly and his time of sport;
  And ever let his unrecalling crime
  Have time to wail th' abusing of his time.

"O Time, thou tutor both to good and bad,   995
Teach me to curse him that thou taught'st this ill!
At his own shadow let the thief run mad,
Himself himself seek every hour to kill!
Such wretched hands such wretched blood should
    spill;   1000
  For who so base would such an office have
  As slanderous deathsman to so base a slave?

"The baser is he, coming from a king,
To shame his hope with deeds degenerate.
The mightier man, the mightier is the thing
That makes him honour'd, or begets him hate;   1005
For greatest scandal waits on greatest state.
  The moon being clouded presently is miss'd,
  But little stars may hide them when they list.

"The crow may bathe his coal-black wings in mire
And unperceiv'd fly with the filth away;   1010
But if the like the snow-white swan desire,
The stain upon his silver down will stay.
Poor grooms are sightless night, kings glorious day.
  Gnats are unnoted wheresoe'er they fly,
  But eagles gaz'd upon with every eye.   1015

"Out, idle words, servants to shallow fools!
Unprofitable sounds, weak arbitrators!
Busy yourselves in skill-contending schools;
Debate where leisure serves with dull debaters;
To trembling clients be you mediators.   1020
  For me, I force not argument a straw,
  Since that my case is past the help of law.

"In vain I rail at Opportunity,
At Time, at Tarquin, and uncheerful Night;
In vain I cavil with mine infamy,   1025
In vain I spurn at my confirm'd despite:
This helpless smoke of words doth me no right.
  The remedy indeed to do me good
  Is to let forth my foul defiled blood.

936. fine: end. 953. beldam: grandmother. 962. retiring: returning. 985. orts: fragments (of food). 993. unrecalling: irrevocable. 1001. slanderous: despicable. 1013. sightless: invisible. 1021. force: esteem.

"Poor hand, why quiver'st thou at this decree?   1030
Honour thyself to rid me of this shame;
For if I die, my honour lives in thee;
But if I live, thou liv'st in my defame.
Since thou couldst not defend thy loyal dame,
    And wast afeard to scratch her wicked foe,   1035
    Kill both thyself and her for yielding so."

This said, from her be-tumbled couch she starteth
To find some desperate instrument of death:
But this no slaughterhouse no tool imparteth
To make more vent for passage of her breath;   1040
Which, thronging through her lips, so vanisheth
    As smoke from Ætna, that in air consumes,
    Or that which from discharged cannon fumes.

"In vain," quoth she, "I live, and seek in vain
Some happy mean to end a hapless life.   1045
I fear'd by Tarquin's falchion to be slain,
Yet for the self-same purpose seek a knife;
But when I fear'd, I was a loyal wife:
    So am I now: O no, that cannot be;
    Of that true type hath Tarquin rifled me.   1050

"O, that is gone for which I sought to live,
And therefore now I need not fear to die.
To clear this spot by death, at least I give
A badge of fame to slander's livery,
A dying life to living infamy.   1055
    Poor helpless help, the treasure stolen away,
    To burn the guiltless casket where it lay!

"Well, well, dear Collatine, thou shalt not know
The stained taste of violated troth;
I will not wrong thy true affection so,   1060
To flatter thee with an infringed oath;
This bastard graff shall never come to growth.
    He shall not boast who did thy stock pollute
    That thou art doting father of his fruit.

"Nor shall he smile at thee in secret thought,   1065
Nor laugh with his companions at thy state;
But thou shalt know thy interest was not bought
Basely with gold, but stolen from forth thy gate.
For me, I am the mistress of my fate,
    And with my trespass never will dispense,   1070
    Till life to death acquit my forc'd offence.

"I will not poison thee with my attaint,
Nor fold my fault in cleanly-coin'd excuses;
My sable ground of sin I will not paint
To hide the truth of this false night's abuses.   1075
My tongue shall utter all; mine eyes, like sluices,
    As from a mountain-spring that feeds a dale,
    Shall gush pure streams to purge my impure tale."

By this, lamenting Philomel had ended
The well-tun'd warble of her nightly sorrow,   1080
And solemn night with slow sad gait descended
To ugly hell; when, lo, the blushing morrow
Lends light to all fair eyes that light will borrow;
    But cloudy Lucrece shames herself to see,
    And therefore still in night would cloist'red be.

Revealing day through every cranny spies,   1086
And seems to point her out where she sits weeping;
To whom she sobbing speaks: "O eye of eyes,
Why pry'st thou through my window?   Leave thy
        peeping;
Mock with thy tickling beams eyes that are sleep-
        ing;   1090
    Brand not my forehead with thy piercing light,
    For day hath nought to do what's done by night."

Thus cavils she with everything she sees.
True grief is fond and testy as a child,
Who wayward once, his mood with nought agrees.
Old woes, not infant sorrows, bear them mild;   1096
Continuance tames the one; the other wild,
    Like an unpractis'd swimmer plunging still,
    With too much labour drowns for want of skill.

So she, deep-drenched in a sea of care,   1100
Holds disputation with each thing she views,
And to herself all sorrow doth compare;
No object but her passion's strength renews;
And as one shifts, another straight ensues.
    Sometime her grief is dumb and hath no words;
    Sometime 'tis mad and too much talk affords.   1106

The little birds that tune their morning's joy
Make her moans mad with their sweet melody;
For mirth doth search the bottom of annoy,
Sad souls are slain in merry company;   1110
Grief best is pleas'd with grief's society;
    True sorrow then is feelingly suffic'd
    When with like semblance it is sympathiz'd.

'Tis double death to drown in ken of shore;
He ten times pines that pines beholding food;   1115
To see the salve doth make the wound ache more;
Great grief grieves most at that would do it good;
Deep woes roll forward like a gentle flood,
    Who, being stopp'd, the bounding banks o'erflows;
    Grief dallied with nor law nor limit knows.   1120

"You mocking birds," quoth she, "your tunes entomb
Within your hollow-swelling feathered breasts,
And in my hearing be you mute and dumb;
My restless discord loves no stops nor rests;
A woeful hostess brooks not merry guests.   1125

1054. **badge**: the arms of the master worn on a servant's livery.   1062. **graff**: graft.   1070. **with ... dispense**: pardon.
1092. **to do**: to do with.   1112–13. **True ... sympathiz'd.**   "Misery loves company."   1124. **stops ... rests**: musical terms.

Relish your nimble notes to pleasing ears;
Distress likes dumps when time is kept with tears.

"Come, Philomel, that sing'st of ravishment,
Make thy sad grove in my dishevell'd hair:
As the dank earth weeps at thy languishment,
So I at each sad strain will strain a tear, 1131
And with deep groans the diapason bear;
    For burden-wise I'll hum on Tarquin still,
    While thou on Tereus descants better skill.

"And whiles against a thorn thou bear'st thy part
To keep thy sharp woes waking, wretched I, 1136
To imitate thee well, against my heart
Will fix a sharp knife to affright mine eye;
Who, if it wink, shall thereon fall and die.
    These means, as frets upon an instrument, 1140
    Shall tune our heart-strings to true languishment.

"And for, poor bird, thou sing'st not in the day,
As shaming any eye should thee behold,
Some dark deep desert, seated from the way,
That knows not parching heat nor freezing cold,
Will we find out; and there we will unfold 1146
    To creatures stern, sad tunes to change their kinds;
    Since men prove beasts, let beasts bear gentle
        minds."

As the poor frighted deer, that stands at gaze
Wildly determining which way to fly, 1150
Or one encompass'd with a winding maze,
That cannot tread the way out readily;
So with herself is she in mutiny,
    To live or die which of the twain were better, 1154
    When life is sham'd, and death reproach's debtor.

"To kill myself," quoth she, "alack, what were it,
But with my body my poor soul's pollution?
They that lose half with greater patience bear it
Than they whose whole is swallowed in confusion.
That mother tries a merciless conclusion 1160
    Who, having two sweet babes, when death takes
        one,
    Will slay the other and be nurse to none.

"My body or my soul, which was the dearer,
When the one pure, the other made divine?
Whose love of either to myself was nearer, 1165
When both were kept for Heaven and Collatine?
Ay me! the bark peel'd from the lofty pine,
    His leaves will wither and his sap decay;
    So must my soul, her bark being peel'd away.

"Her house is sack'd, her quiet interrupted, 1170
Her mansion batter'd by the enemy;
Her sacred temple spotted, spoil'd, corrupted,
Grossly engirt with daring infamy:
Then let it not be call'd impiety,
    If in this blemish'd fort I make some hole 1175
    Through which I may convey this troubled soul.

"Yet die I will not till my Collatine
Have heard the cause of my untimely death;
That he may vow, in that sad hour of mine,
Revenge on him that made me stop my breath. 1180
My stained blood to Tarquin I'll bequeath,
    Which by him tainted shall for him be spent,
    And as his due writ in my testament.

"My honour I'll bequeath unto the knife
That wounds my body so dishonoured. 1185
'Tis honour to deprive dishonour'd life;
The one will live, the other being dead:
So of shame's ashes shall my fame be bred;
    For in my death I murder shameful scorn:
    My shame so dead, mine honour is new-born. 1190

"Dear lord of that dear jewel I have lost,
What legacy shall I bequeath to thee?
My resolution, love, shall be thy boast,
By whose example thou reveng'd mayst be.
How Tarquin must be us'd, read it in me: 1195
    Myself, thy friend, will kill myself, thy foe,
    And for my sake serve thou false Tarquin so.

"This brief abridgement of my will I make:
My soul and body to the skies and ground;
My resolution, husband, do thou take; 1200
Mine honour be the knife's that makes my wound;
My shame be his that did my fame confound;
    And all my fame that lives disbursed be
    To those that live, and think no shame of me.

"Thou, Collatine, shalt oversee this will; 1205
How was I overseen that thou shalt see it!
My blood shall wash the slander of mine ill;
My life's foul deed, my life's fair end shall free it.
Faint not, faint heart, but stoutly say, 'So be
    it:' 1209
    Yield to my hand; my hand shall conquer thee:
    Thou dead, both die, and both shall victors be."

This plot of death when sadly she had laid,
And wip'd the brinish pearl from her bright eyes,
With untun'd tongue she hoarsely calls her maid,

1126. **Relish:** make pleasing. 1127. **dumps:** sad songs. 1132. **diapason:** concord. 1133. **burden-wise:** the bass accompaniment of the melody. 1134. **descants:** singest the melody. 1139. **Who ... it:** my heart ... my eye. 1140. **frets:** ridges placed on the fingerboard of a stringed instrument to guide the fingers. 1144. **seated from:** situated away from. 1155. **death ... debtor:** death (by my own hand) would incur reproach. 1157. **But ... body:** but to add the sin of my body to. 1160. **conclusion:** experiment. 1206. **overseen:** deceived.

Whose swift obedience to her mistress hies;   1215
For fleet-wing'd duty with thought's feathers flies.
  Poor Lucrece' cheeks unto her maid seem so
  As winter meads when sun doth melt their snow.

Her mistress she doth give demure good-morrow,
With soft slow tongue, true mark of modesty,   1220
And sorts a sad look to her lady's sorrow,
For-why her face wore sorrow's livery;
But durst not ask of her audaciously
  Why her two suns were cloud-eclipsed so,   1224
  Nor why her fair cheeks over-wash'd with woe:

But as the earth doth weep, the sun being set,
Each flower moist'ned like a melting eye;
Even so the maid with swelling drops gan wet
Her circled eyne, enforc'd by sympathy
Of those fair suns set in her mistress' sky,   1230
  Who in a salt-wav'd ocean quench their light,
  Which makes the maid weep like the dewy night.

A pretty while these pretty creatures stand,
Like ivory conduits coral cisterns filling:
One justly weeps; the other takes in hand   1235
No cause, but company, of her drops spilling.
Their gentle sex to weep are often willing,
  Grieving themselves to guess at others' smarts,
  And then they drown their eyes or break their
    hearts.

For men have marble, women waxen, minds,   1240
And therefore are they form'd as marble will;
The weak oppress'd, the impression of strange kinds
Is form'd in them by force, by fraud, or skill.
Then call them not the authors of their ill,
  No more than wax shall be accounted evil   1245
  Wherein is stamp'd the semblance of a devil.

Their smoothness, like a goodly champaign plain,
Lays open all the little worms that creep;
In men, as in a rough-grown grove, remain
Cave-keeping evils that obscurely sleep.   1250
Through crystal walls each little mote will peep;
  Though men can cover crimes with bold stern
    looks,
  Poor women's faces are their own faults' books.

No man inveigh against the withered flow'r,   1254
But chide rough winter that the flower hath kill'd;
Not that devour'd, but that which doth devour,
Is worthy blame.   O, let it not be hild
Poor women's faults that they are so fulfill'd
  With men's abuses: those proud lords, to blame,
  Make weak-made women tenants to their shame.

The precedent whereof in Lucrece view,   1261
Assail'd by night with circumstances strong
Of present death, and shame that might ensue
By that her death, to do her husband wrong.
Such danger to resistance did belong   1265
  That dying fear through all her body spread;
  And who cannot abuse a body dead?

By this, mild patience bid fair Lucrece speak
To the poor counterfeit of her complaining:
"My girl," quoth she, "on what occasion break   1270
Those tears from thee, that down thy cheeks are
    raining?
If thou dost weep for grief of my sustaining,
  Know, gentle wench, it small avails my mood;
  If tears could help, mine own would do me good.

"But tell me, girl, when went" — and there she
    stay'd   1275
Till after a deep groan — "Tarquin from hence?"
"Madam, ere I was up," repli'd the maid,
"The more to blame my sluggard negligence.
Yet with the fault I thus far can dispense;
  Myself was stirring ere the break of day,   1280
  And, ere I rose, was Tarquin gone away.

"But, lady, if your maid may be so bold,
She would request to know your heaviness."
"O, peace!" quoth Lucrece: "if it should be told,
The repetition cannot make it less;   1285
For more it is than I can well express,
  And that deep torture may be call'd a hell
  When more is felt than one hath power to tell.

"Go, get me hither paper, ink, and pen;
Yet save that labour, for I have them here. —   1290
What should I say? — One of my husband's men
Bid thou be ready, by and by, to bear
A letter to my lord, my love, my dear.
  Bid him with speed prepare to carry it;
  The cause craves haste, and it will soon be
    writ."

Her maid is gone, and she prepares to write,   1296
First hovering o'er the paper with her quill.
Conceit and grief an eager combat fight;
What wit sets down is blotted straight with will;
This is too curious-good, this blunt and ill: 1304
  Much like a press of people at a door,
  Throng her inventions, which shall go before.

At last she thus begins: "Thou worthy lord
Of that unworthy wife that greeteth thee,
Health to thy person!   Next vouchsafe t' afford —

1221. **sorts:** fits.   1227. **flower.**   Q spells *floure.*   The meter requires two syllables.   1235. **takes in hand:** entertains.
1242. **strange kinds:** other natures.   1247. **champaign:** level.   1257. **hild:** held.   1258. **fulfill'd:** completely filled.   1261.
precedent: evidence, example.   1292. **by and by:** at once.

If ever, love, thy Lucrece thou wilt see —   1306
Some present speed to come and visit me.
   So, I commend me from our house in grief;
   My woes are tedious, though my words are brief."

Here folds she up the tenour of her woe,   1310
Her certain sorrow writ uncertainly.
By this short schedule Collatine may know
Her grief, but not her grief's true quality.
She dares not thereof make discovery,
   Lest he should hold it her own gross abuse,   1315
   Ere she with blood had stain'd her stain'd excuse.

Besides, the life and feeling of her passion
She hoards, to spend when he is by to hear her;
When sighs and groans and tears may grace the
    fashion
Of her disgrace, the better so to clear her   1320
From that suspicion which the world might bear her.
   To shun this blot, she would not blot the letter
   With words, till action might become them better.

To see sad sights moves more than hear them told;
For then the eye interprets to the ear   1325
The heavy motion that it doth behold,
When every part a part of woe doth bear.
'Tis but a part of sorrow that we hear;
   Deep sounds make lesser noise than shallow fords,
   And sorrow ebbs, being blown with wind of words.

Her letter now is seal'd, and on it writ,   1331
"At Ardea to my lord with more than haste."
The post attends, and she delivers it,
Charging the sour-fac'd groom to hie as fast
As lagging fowls before the northern blast.   1335
   Speed more than speed but dull and slow she
    deems:
   Extremity still urgeth such extremes.

The homely villain curtsies to her low;
And, blushing on her, with a steadfast eye
Receives the scroll without or yea or no,   1340
And forth with bashful innocence doth hie.
But they whose guilt within their bosoms lie
   Imagine every eye beholds their blame;
   For Lucrece thought he blush'd to see her shame,

When, silly groom! God wot, it was defect   1345
Of spirit, life, and bold audacity.
Such harmless creatures have a true respect
To talk in deeds, while others saucily
Promise more speed, but do it leisurely;
   Even so this pattern of the worn-out age   1350
   Pawn'd honest looks, but laid no words to gage.

His kindled duty kindled her mistrust
That two red fires in both their faces blazed;
She thought he blush'd, as knowing Tarquin's lust,
And, blushing with him, wistly on him gazed;   1355
Her earnest eye did make him more amazed.
   The more she saw the blood his cheeks replenish,
   The more she thought he spied in her some
    blemish.

But long she thinks till he return again,
And yet the duteous vassal scarce is gone.   1360
The weary time she cannot entertain,
For now 'tis stale to sigh, to weep, and groan.
So woe hath wearied woe, moan tired moan,
   That she her plaints a little while doth stay,
   Pausing for means to mourn some newer way.   1365

At last she calls to mind where hangs a piece
Of skilful painting, made for Priam's Troy;
Before the which is drawn the power of Greece
For Helen's rape the city to destroy,
Threat'ning cloud-kissing Ilion with annoy;   1370
   Which the conceited painter drew so proud,
   As heaven, it seem'd, to kiss the turrets bow'd.

A thousand lamentable objects there,
In scorn of nature, art gave lifeless life:
Many a dry drop seem'd a weeping tear,   1375
Shed for the slaught'red husband by the wife;
The red blood reek'd, to show the painter's strife;
   And dying eyes gleam'd forth their ashy lights,
   Like dying coals burnt out in tedious nights.

There might you see the labouring pioner   1380
Begrim'd with sweat, and smeared all with dust;
And from the towers of Troy there would appear
The very eyes of men through loop-holes thrust,
Gazing upon the Greeks with little lust.
   Such sweet observance in this work was had,   1385
   That one might see those far-off eyes look sad.

In great commanders grace and majesty
You might behold, triumphing in their faces;
In youth, quick bearing and dexterity;
And here and there the painter interlaces   1390
Pale cowards, marching on with trembling paces;
   Which heartless peasants did so well resemble,
   That one would swear he saw them quake and
    tremble.

In Ajax and Ulysses, O, what art
Of physiognomy might one behold!   1395
The face of either cipher'd either's heart;
Their face their manners most expressly told:
In Ajax' eyes blunt rage and rigour roll'd;

1312. **schedule:** document. 1329. **sounds:** straits, passages. 1338. **villain:** servant. 1345. **silly:** simple. 1351. **to gage:** in pledge. 1355. **wistly:** intently. 1368. **drawn:** arrayed. 1371. **conceited:** imaginative. 1377. **strife:** effort. 1380. **pioner:** soldier who digs trenches, etc. 1384. **lust:** pleasure.

But the mild glance that sly Ulysses lent
Showed deep regard and smiling government. 1400

There pleading might you see grave Nestor stand,
As 'twere encouraging the Greeks to fight;
Making such sober action with his hand,
That it beguil'd attention, charm'd the sight.
In speech, it seem'd, his beard, all silver white, 1405
    Wagg'd up and down, and from his lips did fly
    Thin winding breath, which purl'd up to the sky.

About him were a press of gaping faces,
Which seem'd to swallow up his sound advice,
All jointly list'ning, but with several graces, 1410
As if some mermaid did their ears entice,
Some high, some low, the painter was so nice;
    The scalps of many, almost hid behind,
    To jump up higher seem'd, to mock the mind.

Here one man's hand lean'd on another's head, 1415
His nose being shadowed by his neighbour's ear;
Here one being throng'd bears back, all boll'n and red;
Another, smother'd, seems to pelt and swear;
And in their rage such signs of rage they bear,
    As, but for loss of Nestor's golden words, 1420
    It seem'd they would debate with angry swords.

For much imaginary work was there;
Conceit deceitful, so compact, so kind,
That for Achilles' image stood his spear,
Gripp'd in an armed hand; himself, behind, 1425
Was left unseen, save to the eye of mind.
    A hand, a foot, a face, a leg, a head,
    Stood for the whole to be imagined.

And from the walls of strong-besieged Troy
When their brave hope, bold Hector, march'd to field, 1430
Stood many Troyan mothers, sharing joy
To see their youthful sons bright weapons wield;
And to their hope they such odd action yield,
    That through their light joy seemed to appear,
    Like bright things stain'd, a kind of heavy fear. 1435

And from the strand of Dardan, where they fought,
To Simois' reedy banks the red blood ran,
Whose waves to imitate the battle sought
With swelling ridges; and their ranks began
To break upon the galled shore, and than 1440
    Retire again, till, meeting greater ranks,
    They join and shoot their foam at Simois' banks.

To this well-painted piece is Lucrece come,
To find a face where all distress is stel'd. 1444
Many she sees where cares have carved some,
But none where all distress and dolour dwell'd
Till she despairing Hecuba beheld,
    Staring on Priam's wounds with her old eyes,
    Which bleeding under Pyrrhus' proud foot lies.

In her the painter had anatomiz'd 1450
Time's ruin, beauty's wreck, and grim care's reign.
Her cheeks with chaps and wrinkles were disguis'd;
Of what she was, no semblance did remain.
Her blue blood chang'd to black in every vein,
    Wanting the spring that those shrunk pipes had fed, 1455
    Show'd life imprison'd in a body dead.

On this sad shadow Lucrece spends her eyes,
And shapes her sorrow to the beldam's woes,
Who nothing wants to answer her but cries,
And bitter words to ban her cruel foes; 1460
The painter was no god to lend her those,
    And therefore Lucrece swears he did her wrong,
    To give her so much grief and not a tongue.

"Poor instrument," quoth she, "without a sound,
I'll tune thy woes with my lamenting tongue; 1465
And drop sweet balm in Priam's painted wound,
And rail on Pyrrhus that hath done him wrong;
And with my tears quench Troy that burns so long;
    And with my knife scratch out the angry eyes
    Of all the Greeks that are thine enemies. 1470

"Show me the strumpet that began this stir,
That with my nails her beauty I may tear.
Thy heat of lust, fond Paris, did incur
This load of wrath that burning Troy doth bear;
Thy eye kindled the fire that burneth here; 1475
    And here in Troy, for trespass of thine eye,
    The sire, the son, the dame, and daughter die.

"Why should the private pleasure of some one
Become the public plague of many moe?
Let sin, alone committed, light alone 1480
Upon his head that hath transgressed so;
Let guiltless souls be freed from guilty woe:
    For one's offence why should so many fall,
    To plague a private sin in general?

"Lo, here weeps Hecuba, here Priam dies, 1485
Here manly Hector faints, here Troilus swounds,
Here friend by friend in bloody channel lies,
And friend to friend gives unadvised wounds,
And one man's lust these many lives confounds.

1400. **government:** self-control. 1407. **purl'd:** curled. 1412. **nice:** subtle. 1417. **boll'n:** puffed, swollen. 1418. **pelt:** rage. 1423. **kind:** natural. 1436. **Dardan:** Troy. 1440. **galled:** chafed. **than:** then. 1444. **stel'd:** engraved (?), fixed (?). 1450. **anatomiz'd:** dissected, shown in detail. 1488. **unadvised:** unintentional.

Had doting Priam check'd his son's desire, 1490
Troy had been bright with fame and not with fire."

Here feelingly she weeps Troy's painted woes;
For sorrow, like a heavy-hanging bell,
Once set on ringing, with his own weight goes;
Then little strength rings out the doleful knell: 1495
So Lucrece, set a-work, sad tales doth tell
To pencill'd pensiveness and colour'd sorrow;
She lends them words, and she their looks doth
borrow.

She throws her eyes about the painting round,
And who she finds forlorn she doth lament. 1500
At last she sees a wretched image bound,
That piteous looks to Phrygian shepherds lent:
His face, though full of cares, yet show'd content;
Onward to Troy with the blunt swains he goes,
So mild that Patience seem'd to scorn his
woes. 1505

In him the painter labour'd with his skill
To hide deceit, and give the harmless show
An humble gait, calm looks, eyes wailing still,
A brow unbent, that seem'd to welcome woe;
Cheeks neither red nor pale, but mingled so 1510
That blushing red no guilty instance gave,
Nor ashy pale the fear that false hearts have.

But, like a constant and confirmed devil,
He entertain'd a show so seeming-just,
And therein so ensconc'd his secret evil, 1515
That jealousy itself could not mistrust
False creeping craft and perjury should thrust
Into so bright a day such black-fac'd storms,
Or blot with hell-born sin such saint-like forms.

The well-skill'd workman this mild image drew 1520
For perjur'd Sinon, whose enchanting story
The credulous old Priam after slew;
Whose words like wildfire burnt the shining glory
Of rich-built Ilion, that the skies were sorry,
And little stars shot from their fixed places, 1525
When their glass fell wherein they view'd their
faces.

This picture she advisedly perus'd,
And chid the painter for his wondrous skill,
Saying, some shape in Sinon's was abus'd;
So fair a form lodg'd not a mind so ill. 1530
And still on him she gaz'd; and gazing still,
Such signs of truth in his plain face she spied,
That she concludes the picture was belied.

"It cannot be," quoth she, "that so much guile" —
She would have said, "can lurk in such a look;" 1535
But Tarquin's shape came in her mind the while,
And from her tongue "can lurk" from "cannot"
took:
"It cannot be" she in that sense forsook,
And turn'd it thus, "It cannot be, I find,
But such a face should bear a wicked mind: 1540

"For even as subtle Sinon here is painted,
So sober-sad, so weary, and so mild,
As if with grief or travail he had fainted,
To me came Tarquin armed to begild
With outward honesty, but yet defil'd 1545
With inward vice. As Priam him did cherish,
So did I Tarquin; so my Troy did perish.

"Look, look, how list'ning Priam wets his eyes,
To see those borrowed tears that Sinon sheds!
Priam, why art thou old and yet not wise? 1550
For every tear he falls a Troyan bleeds;
His eye drops fire, no water thence proceeds;
Those round clear pearls of his, that move thy pity,
Are balls of quenchless fire to burn thy city.

"Such devils steal effects from lightless hell; 1555
For Sinon in his fire doth quake with cold,
And in that cold, hot-burning fire doth dwell;
These contraries such unity do hold
Only to flatter fools and make them bold: 1559
So Priam's trust false Sinon's tears doth flatter,
That he finds means to burn his Troy with water."

Here, all enrag'd, such passion her assails
That patience is quite beaten from her breast.
She tears the senseless Sinon with her nails,
Comparing him to that unhappy guest 1565
Whose deed hath made herself herself detest.
At last she smilingly with this gives o'er;
"Fool, fool!" quoth she, "his wounds will not be
sore."

Thus ebbs and flows the current of her sorrow, 1569
And time doth weary time with her complaining.
She looks for night, and then she longs for morrow,
And both she thinks too long with her remaining.
Short time seems long in sorrow's sharp sustaining;
Though woe be heavy, yet it seldom sleeps; 1574
And they that watch see time how slow it creeps:

Which all this time hath overslipp'd her thought
That she with painted images hath spent;
Being from the feeling of her own grief brought

1502. lent: caused to give. 1511. instance: evidence. 1516. jealousy: suspicion. 1526. glass: Troy, whose brilliance reproduced their own. 1527. advisedly: intently. 1529. abus'd: insulted. 1533. belied: deceptive. 1544-45. armed to be-gild With: prepared to give the impression of. Qq spell beguild. Malone emended to armed; so beguiled, explaining beguiled as beguiling. 1551. falls: lets fall.

By deep surmise of others' detriment,
Losing her woes in shows of discontent.   1580
  It easeth some, though none it ever cured,
  To think their dolour others have endured.

But now the mindful messenger, come back,
Brings home his lord and other company,
Who finds his Lucrece clad in mourning black;   1585
And round about her tear-distainèd eye
Blue circles stream'd, like rainbows in the sky.
  These water-galls in her dim element
  Foretell new storms to those already spent:

Which when her sad-beholding husband saw,   1590
Amazedly in her sad face he stares:
Her eyes, though sod in tears, look'd red and raw,
Her lively colour kill'd with deadly cares.
He hath no power to ask her how she fares.
  Both stood, like old acquaintance in a trance, 1595
  Met far from home, wond'ring each other's chance.

At last he takes her by the bloodless hand,
And thus begins: "What uncouth ill event
Hath thee befall'n, that thou dost trembling stand?
Sweet love, what spite hath thy fair colour spent?
Why art thou thus attir'd in discontent?   1601
  Unmask, dear dear, this moody heaviness,
  And tell thy grief, that we may give redress."

Three times with sighs she gives her sorrow fire
Ere once she can discharge one word of woe.   1605
At length address'd to answer his desire,
She modestly prepares to let them know
Her honour is ta'en prisoner by the foe;
  While Collatine and his consorted lords
  With sad attention long to hear her words.   1610

And now this pale swan in her wat'ry nest
Begins the sad dirge of her certain ending;
"Few words," quoth she, "shall fit the trespass best,
Where no excuse can give the fault amending.
In me moe woes than words are now depending;   1615
  And my laments would be drawn out too long
  To tell them all with one poor tired tongue.

"Then be this all the task it hath to say:
Dear husband, in the interest of thy bed
A stranger came, and on that pillow lay   1620
Where thou wast wont to rest thy weary head;
And what wrong else may be imagined
  By foul enforcement might be done to me,
  From that, alas, thy Lucrece is not free.

"For in the dreadful dead of dark midnight,   1625
With shining falchion in my chamber came
A creeping creature, with a flaming light,

And softly cried, 'Awake, thou Roman dame,
And entertain my love; else lasting shame
  On thee and thine this night I will inflict,   1630
  If thou my love's desire do contradict.

"'For some hard-favour'd groom of thine,' quoth
      he,
'Unless thou yoke thy liking to my will,
I'll murder straight, and then I'll slaughter thee
And swear I found you where you did fulfil   1635
The loathsome act of lust, and so did kill
  The lechers in their deed.   This act will be
  My fame and thy perpetual infamy.'

"With this, I did begin to start and cry;
And then against my heart he set his sword,   1640
Swearing, unless I took all patiently,
I should not live to speak another word;
So should my shame still rest upon record,
  And never be forgot in mighty Rome
  The adulterate death of Lucrece and her groom.

"Mine enemy was strong, my poor self weak,   1646
And far the weaker with so strong a fear.
My bloody judge forbade my tongue to speak;
No rightful plea might plead for justice there.
His scarlet lust came evidence to swear   1650
  That my poor beauty had purloin'd his eyes;
  And when the judge is robb'd, the prisoner dies.

"O, teach me how to make mine own excuse!
Or at the least this refuge let me find;
Though my gross blood be stain'd with this abuse,
Immaculate and spotless is my mind;   1656
That was not forc'd; that never was inclin'd
  To accessary yieldings, but still pure
  Doth in her poison'd closet yet endure."

Lo, here, the hopeless merchant of this loss,   1660
With head declin'd, and voice damm'd up with woe,
With sad set eyes, and wretched arms across,
From lips new waxen pale begins to blow
The grief away that stops his answer so:
  But, wretched as he is, he strives in vain;   1665
  What he breathes out his breath drinks up again.

As through an arch the violent roaring tide
Outruns the eye that doth behold his haste,
Yet in the eddy boundeth in his pride
Back to the strait that forc'd him on so fast;   1670
In rage sent out, recall'd in rage, being past:
  Even so his sighs, his sorrows, make a saw,
  To push grief on and back the same grief draw.

Which speechless woe of his poor she attendeth,
And his untimely frenzy thus awaketh: 1675

1588. **water-galls**: a rainbow fragment indicating rain. 1592. **sod**: sodden, p.p. of seethe. 1615. **depending**: impending.
1619. **in the interest of**: seeking.

"Dear lord, thy sorrow to my sorrow lendeth
Another power; no flood by raining slaketh.
My woe too sensible thy passion maketh
  More feeling-painful: let it then suffice
  To drown [one] woe, one pair of weeping eyes. 1680

"And for my sake when I might charm thee so,
For she that was thy Lucrece, now attend me:
Be suddenly revenged on my foe,
Thine, mine, his own: suppose thou dost defend me
From what is past: the help that thou shalt lend me
  Comes all too late, yet let the traitor die, 1686
  For sparing justice feeds iniquity.

"But ere I name him, you fair lords," quoth she,
Speaking to those that came with Collatine,
"Shall plight your honourable faiths to me 1690
With swift pursuit to venge this wrong of mine;
For 'tis a meritorious fair design
  To chase injustice with revengeful arms.
  Knights, by their oaths, should right poor ladies'
    harms."

At this request, with noble disposition 1695
Each present lord began to promise aid,
As bound in knighthood to her imposition,
Longing to hear the hateful foe bewray'd.
But she, that yet her sad task hath not said, 1699
  The protestation stops. "O, speak," quoth she,
  "How may this forced stain be wip'd from me?

"What is the quality of mine offence,
Being constrain'd with dreadful circumstance?
May my pure mind with the foul act dispense,
My low-declined honour to advance? 1705
May any terms acquit me from this chance?
  The poisoned fountain clears itself again;
  And why not I from this compelled stain?"

With this, they all at once began to say,
Her body's stain her mind untainted clears; 1710
While with a joyless smile she turns away
The face, that map which deep impression bears
Of hard misfortune, carv'd [in it] with tears.
  "No, no," quoth she, "no dame, hereafter living,
  By my excuse shall claim excuse's giving." 1715

Here with a sigh, as if her heart would break,
She throws forth Tarquin's name: "He, he," she
  says,
But more than "he" her poor tongue could not
  speak;
Till after many accents and delays,
Untimely breathings, sick and short assays, 1720

She utters this, "He, he, fair lords, 'tis he,
That guides this hand to give this wound to
  me."

Even here she sheathed in her harmless breast
A harmful knife that thence her soul unsheathed.
That blow did bail it from the deep unrest 1725
Of that polluted prison where it breathed.
Her contrite sighs unto the clouds bequeathed
  Her winged sprite, and through her wounds doth
    fly
  Life's lasting date from cancell'd destiny.

Stone-still, astonish'd with this deadly deed, 1730
Stood Collatine and all his lordly crew;
Till Lucrece' father, that beholds her bleed,
Himself on her self-slaught'red body threw;
And from the purple fountain Brutus drew
  The murd'rous knife, and, as it left the place, 1735
  Her blood, in poor revenge, held it in chase;

And bubbling from her breast, it doth divide
In two slow rivers, that the crimson blood
Circles her body in on every side,
Who, like a late-sack'd island, vastly stood 1740
Bare and unpeopled in this fearful flood.
  Some of her blood still pure and red remain'd,
  And some look'd black, and that false Tarquin
    stain'd.

About the mourning and congealed face
Of that black blood a watery rigol goes, 1745
Which seems to weep upon the tainted place:
And ever since, as pitying Lucrece' woes,
Corrupted blood some watery token shows;
  And blood untainted still doth red abide,
  Blushing at that which is so putrifi'd. 1750

"Daughter, dear daughter," old Lucretius cries,
"That life was mine which thou hast here de-
  prived.
If in the child the father's image lies,
Where shall I live now Lucrece is unlived?
Thou wast not to this end from me derived. 1755
  If children pre-decease progenitors,
  We are their offspring, and they none of ours.

"Poor broken glass, I often did behold
In thy sweet semblance my old age new born;
But now that fair fresh mirror, dim and old, 1760
Shows me a bare-bon'd death by time outworn.
O, from thy cheeks my image thou hast torn,
  And shiver'd all the beauty of my glass,
  That I no more can see what once I was!

1680. [one] Q₃. on Q₁. 1682. she: her. 1697. imposition: demand. 1698. bewray'd: revealed. 1713. [in it] (Capell MS.) it in Q. 1729. from ... destiny: thus escaping from the fate that is thereby cancelled. 1730. astonish'd: dumb-founded. 1740. vastly: like a waste, deserted. 1745. rigol: circle.

"O Time, cease thou thy course and last no longer,
If they surcease to be that should survive.   1766
Shall rotten Death make conquest of the stronger
And leave the falt'ring feeble souls alive?
The old bees die, the young possess their hive:
    Then live, sweet Lucrece, live again and see   1770
    Thy father die, and not thy father thee!"

By this, starts Collatine as from a dream,
And bids Lucretius give his sorrow place;
And then in key-cold Lucrece' bleeding stream
He falls, and bathes the pale fear in his face,   1775
And counterfeits to die with her a space;
    Till manly shame bids him possess his breath
    And live to be revenged on her death.

The deep vexation of his inward soul
Hath serv'd a dumb arrest upon his tongue;   1780
Who, mad that sorrow should his use control
Or keep him from heart-easing words so long,
Begins to talk; but through his lips do throng
    Weak words, so thick come in his poor heart's aid,
    That no man could distinguish what he said. 1785

Yet sometime "Tarquin" was pronounced plain,
But through his teeth, as if the name he tore.
This windy tempest, till it blow up rain,
Held back his sorrow's tide, to make it more;
At last it rains, and busy winds give o'er: 1790
    Then son and father weep with equal strife
    Who should weep most, for daughter or for wife.

The one doth call her his, the other his,
Yet neither may possess the claim they lay.
The father says, "She's mine." "O, mine she is,"
Replies her husband: "do not take away   1796
My sorrow's interest; let no mourner say
    He weeps for her, for she was only mine,
    And only must be wail'd by Collatine."

"O," quoth Lucretius, "I did give that life   1800
Which she too early and too late hath spill'd."
"Woe, woe," quoth Collatine, "she was my wife,
I ow'd her, and 'tis mine that she hath kill'd."
"My daughter!" and "My wife!" with clamours
    fill'd
    The dispers'd air, who, holding Lucrece' life, 1805
    Answer'd their cries, "My daughter!" and "My
    wife!"

Brutus, who pluck'd the knife from Lucrece' side,
Seeing such emulation in their woe,
Began to clothe his wit in state and pride,

Burying in Lucrece' wound his folly's show.   1810
He with the Romans was esteemed so
    As silly jeering idiots are with kings,
    For sportive words and utt'ring foolish things.

But now he throws that shallow habit by
Wherein deep policy did him disguise;   1815
And arm'd his long-hid wits advisedly
To check the tears in Collatinus' eyes.
"Thou wronged lord of Rome," quoth he, "arise.
    Let my unsounded self, suppos'd a fool,
    Now set thy long-experienc'd wit to school. 1820

"Why, Collatine, is woe the cure for woe?
Do wounds help wounds, or grief help grievous deeds?
Is it revenge to give thyself a blow
For his foul act by whom thy fair wife bleeds?
Such childish humour from weak minds proceeds;
    Thy wretched wife mistook the matter so,   1826
    To slay herself, that should have slain her foe.

"Courageous Roman, do not steep thy heart
In such relenting dew of lamentations;
But kneel with me and help to bear thy part, 1830
To rouse our Roman gods with invocations
That they will suffer these abominations
    (Since Rome herself in them doth stand disgraced)
    By our strong arms from forth her fair streets
    chased.

"Now, by the Capitol that we adore,   1835
And by this chaste blood so unjustly stained,
By heaven's fair sun that breeds the fat earth's store,
By all our country rights in Rome maintained,
And by chaste Lucrece' soul that late complained
    Her wrongs to us, and by this bloody knife,   1840
    We will revenge the death of this true wife."

This said, he struck his hand upon his breast,
And kiss'd the fatal knife, to end his vow:
And to his protestation urg'd the rest,
Who, wond'ring at him, did his words allow. 1845
Then jointly to the ground their knees they bow;
    And that deep vow, which Brutus made before,
    He doth again repeat, and that they swore.

When they had sworn to this advised doom,
They did conclude to bear dead Lucrece thence;
To show her bleeding body thorough Rome,   1851
And so to publish Tarquin's foul offence:
Which being done with speedy diligence,
    The Romans plausibly did give consent
    To Tarquin's everlasting banishment.   1855

1797. interest: right, claim.   1819. unsounded: unfathomed.   1829. relenting: softening.   1845. allow: approve.
1854. plausibly: approvingly.

Sonnets

THE FIRST COLLECTIVE EDITION of Shakespeare's Sonnets was published in 1609 by Thomas Thorpe, who registered the book on May 20th of that year. It is manifest that the copy was surreptitiously obtained, and the volume issued without the author's consent. The printing was very careless, but the text cannot be called a bad one. The Sonnets were not again printed till they appeared with much miscellaneous matter in an edition published in 1640. Thorpe's edition is the basis of the present text.

The date of composition is a matter of dispute. The chief external evidence is the reference by Meres in his *Palladis Tamia* (1598) to Shakespeare's "sugred Sonnets among his priuate friends," a phrase which clearly implies that some were then circulating privately in manuscript. This conclusion is strengthened by the printing of Sonnets 138 and 144 in *The Passionate Pilgrim* (1599). There can be no doubt that Shakespeare's sonneteering covered several years (Sonnet 104 mentions an interval of three), but which years one cannot say. That the majority of these poems, however, were written between 1593 and 1596 is now a widely accepted conjecture, for obvious parallels between the Sonnets and *Venus and Adonis* and *Lucrece*, and plays with romantic interest and conspicuous lyric quality, such as *Love's Labour's Lost, A Midsummer-Night's Dream*, and *Romeo and Juliet*, suggest some degree of chronological relationship among all these. Despite the danger of arguing in a circle, these manifest affinities, in conjunction with other matters, must be allowed some significance in dating both the plays mentioned and the Sonnets. The knowledge of the precise date of the narrative poems is in this connection a great advantage, and it is also relevant that the Elizabethan vogue of sonneteering, of which Shakespeare's work is the crown, tapered off conspicuously after 1596. On the other hand, although most of Shakespeare's Sonnets may plausibly be supposed to have been written within the period suggested, there is nothing to preclude Shakespeare's having added to the number up to 1599, or, for that matter, up to 1609.

Interpretation of these poems has its own peculiar difficulties, for added to the uncertainty of date is uncertainty about the sequence. There is nothing but internal evidence to tell us whether the order in which Thorpe printed the Sonnets is that in which the poet wrote them. A certain amount of reason in the present arrangement is not to be denied, but it is far from perfect. The series appears to fall into two main divisions: Sonnets 1 to 126, dominated by the fair young man, who is the poet's dear friend and patron; and Sonnets 127–154, dominated by the "dark lady," who is for a time his mistress. But within both groups coherence is occasionally obscured or broken. The mistress of the second series appears momentarily in the first, stealing the affection of the friend. A rival poet competes for a time for the favor of the friend. It is by no means certain that the Sonnets of the first group were all addressed to the same person. Indeed, many in both divisions give no indication of the sex of the one addressed, and not a few appear to be generalized utterances addressed to no one in particular.

Viewed in the light of the vast contemporary sonnet literature, many of these poems merely adhere to well-recognized literary conventions. The pleading with a beautiful youth to marry, the adulation of a noble patron, the power of verse to bestow immortality, the analysis of amorous emotion, the vituperation of the lady — these and other themes belong to the traditions of the form, which were well established before Shakespeare essayed it. But after this is recognized, the question remains whether, in re-working these ideas with unexampled brilliance and intensity, Shakespeare was prompted by mere professional emulation, or by actual experiences for which the current conventions gave a suitable form of expression, or by such an imaginative impulse as lies behind the living utterances of his dramatic creations. Some of the sonnets, it must be admitted, are so artificial as to make plausible for them the first explanation; many more, however, have such beauty and power of language that the authenticity of their emotion cannot reasonably be doubted; and some, especially those expressing the uncommon situation in which his friend wins his lady away from him while the poet retains his affection for both, and those referring to the indignity of the actor's profession, seem peculiarly personal.

The temptation is strong, therefore, to regard Shakespeare's Sonnets as autobiographical and to seek in them a detailed and coherent story. The temptation is increased by the natural desire to augment through so enticing a source of revelation our all too meagre knowledge of the poet's life. But efforts to read the Sonnets as personal history are doomed by the very deficiency which they are called upon to repair; for one cannot unlock their secrets without more circumstantial knowledge of Shakespeare's life than external sources have yielded. Nothing, moreover, could alter the fact that the splendor of the poems is mainly due to the same cause that gave supreme distinction to his dramatic productions — the intensity of the imaginative fervor of an essentially poetic mind. From this point of view it will be seen that attempts to decide the question of "sincerity" by historical identifications are bound to be futile and misleading, implying as they do a misconception of the nature of artistic emotion.

This consideration is not enough, however, to stop the theorizing. The fair youth addressed in the main body of the poems has been identified with William Herbert, the Earl of Pembroke, and with Henry Wriothesley, the Earl of Southampton. The adherents of both interpretations find confirmation in the "Mr. W. H." to whom Thorpe dedicated the volume. In either case the title has been suppressed, and if Southampton was the recipient, his initials have been reversed, a somewhat surprising though not incredible procedure. It is possible, though perhaps not likely, that the "onlie begetter" was merely the publisher's friend who procured for him the manuscript of the Sonnets. The most disconcerting feature of Thorpe's dedication, if it is supposed that either Southampton or Pembroke was the poet's friend, is the "Mr. [i.e., Master] W. H.," which is difficult to reconcile with nobility; and one cannot readily imagine some of the sonnets as being addressed to an Earl. Baffled as one comes to feel by these mysteries, it is permissible to surmise that more than one man was addressed by Shakespeare in the sonnets that Thorpe published. As to the rival poet, or poets, alluded to in Sonnets 78–86, Chapman, Daniel, Drayton, Spenser, Jonson, Barnes, and others have been proposed, but on this point we are not likely ever to obtain anything approaching assurance. The "dark lady" cannot be identified.

A concern with the problems which have occupied the scholars is not essential to an appreciation of Shakespeare's sonnets. These poems give consummate expression to many familiar thoughts and emotions and moods, and it is not necessary to know precisely what inspired these in Shakespeare in order to respond intelligently to his artistic communication of feeling. Behind many of the sonnets authentic and specific experiences do unquestionably lie, but in the best of them Shakespeare has so universalized the emotional content that anyone can appropriate it for himself.

SONNETS

TO . THE . ONLIE . BEGETTER . OF .
THESE . INSUING . SONNETS .
MR. W. H. ALL . HAPPINESSE .
AND . THAT . ETERNITIE .
PROMISED .
BY .
OUR . EVER-LIVING . POET .
WISHETH .
THE . WELL-WISHING
ADVENTURER . IN .
SETTING .
FORTH .

T. T.

1

From fairest creatures we desire increase,
That thereby beauty's rose might never die,
But as the riper should by time decease,
His tender heir might bear his memory:
But thou, contracted to thine own bright eyes,   5
Feed'st thy light's flame with self-substantial fuel,
Making a famine where abundance lies,
Thyself thy foe, to thy sweet self too cruel.
Thou that art now the world's fresh ornament
And only herald to the gaudy spring,   10
Within thine own bud buriest thy content
And, tender churl, mak'st waste in niggarding.
  Pity the world, or else this glutton be,
  To eat the world's due, by the grave and thee.

2

When forty winters shall besiege thy brow
And dig deep trenches in thy beauty's field,
Thy youth's proud livery, so gaz'd on now,
Will be a tatter'd weed, of small worth held.

Then being ask'd where all thy beauty lies,   5
Where all the treasure of thy lusty days,
To say within thine own deep-sunken eyes,
Were an all-eating shame and thriftless praise.
How much more praise deserv'd thy beauty's use
If thou couldst answer, "This fair child of mine   10
Shall sum my count and make my old excuse,"
Proving his beauty by succession thine!
  This were to be new made when thou art old,
  And see thy blood warm when thou feel'st it cold.

3

Look in thy glass, and tell the face thou viewest
Now is the time that face should form another;
Whose fresh repair if now thou not renewest,
Thou dost beguile the world, unless some mother.
For where is she so fair whose unear'd womb   5
Disdains the tillage of thy husbandry?
Or who is he so fond will be the tomb
Of his self-love, to stop posterity?

The Dedication may be paraphrased as follows: T. T. [i.e., Thomas Thorpe], the friendly publisher, wishes to the sole inspirer of the following sonnets, Mr. W. H. [identity unknown], all happiness and that eternity which our immortal poet promises him. Many critics, however, interpret *begetter* as the one who procured for Thorpe the manuscript of the sonnets.

1, 5. contracted: betrothed. **6. self-substantial fuel:** fuel of the substance of that flame. **11. thy content:** what you contain, i.e., potential fatherhood. **12. in niggarding:** by being niggardly. **14. To...thee:** i.e., to cheat the world of its due by your refusal to propagate your beauty before you die. **2, 4. weed:** garment. **9. use:** (1) usage, (2) profit. **11. sum ... excuse:** make my reckoning and my excuse when I am old. **3, 5. unear'd:** unploughed. **7. fond:** foolish.

Thou art thy mother's glass, and she in thee
Calls back the lovely April of her prime;   10
So thou through windows of thine age shalt see,
Despite of wrinkles, this thy golden time.
    But if thou live rememb'red not to be,
    Die single, and thine image dies with thee.

4

Unthrifty loveliness, why dost thou spend
Upon thyself thy beauty's legacy?
Nature's bequest gives nothing, but doth lend,
And, being frank, she lends to those are free.
Then, beauteous niggard, why dost thou abuse   5
The bounteous largess given thee to give?
Profitless usurer, why dost thou use
So great a sum of sums, yet canst not live?
For, having traffic with thyself alone,
Thou of thyself thy sweet self dost deceive.   10
Then how, when Nature calls thee to be gone,
What acceptable audit canst thou leave?
    Thy unus'd beauty must be tomb'd with thee,
    Which, used, lives th' executor to be.

5

Those hours, that with gentle work did frame
The lovely gaze where every eye doth dwell,
Will play the tyrants to the very same
And that unfair which fairly doth excel;
For never-resting time leads summer on   5
To hideous winter and confounds him there,
Sap check'd with frost and lusty leaves quite gone,
Beauty o'ersnow'd and bareness everywhere;
Then, were not summer's distillation left,
A liquid prisoner pent in walls of glass,   10
Beauty's effect with beauty were bereft,
Nor it nor no remembrance what it was:
    But flowers distill'd, though they with winter
        meet,
    Leese but their show; their substance still lives
        sweet.

6

Then let not winter's ragged hand deface
In thee thy summer ere thou be distill'd:
Make sweet some vial; treasure thou some place
With beauty's treasure, ere it be self-kill'd.
That use is not forbidden usury   5
Which happies those that pay the willing loan;
That's for thyself to breed another thee,
Or ten times happier, be it ten for one.
Ten times thyself were happier than thou art,
If ten of thine ten times refigur'd thee.   10
Then what could death do, if thou shouldst depart,
Leaving thee living in posterity?

Be not self-will'd, for thou art much too fair
To be death's conquest and make worms thine
    heir.

7

Lo! in the orient when the gracious light
Lifts up his burning head, each under eye
Doth homage to his new-appearing sight,
Serving with looks his sacred majesty;
And having climb'd the steep-up heavenly hill,   5
Resembling strong youth in his middle age,
Yet mortal looks adore his beauty still,
Attending on his golden pilgrimage;
But when from highmost pitch, with weary car,
Like feeble age he reeleth from the day,   10
The eyes, 'fore duteous, now converted are
From his low tract and look another way:
    So thou, thyself out-going in thy noon,
    Unlook'd on diest, unless thou get a son.

8

Music to hear, why hear'st thou music sadly?
Sweets with sweets war not, joy delights in joy.
Why lov'st thou that which thou receiv'st not
    gladly,
Or else receiv'st with pleasure thine annoy?
If the true concord of well-tuned sounds,   5
By unions married, do offend thine ear,
They do but sweetly chide thee, who confounds
In singleness the parts that thou shouldst bear.
Mark how one string, sweet husband to another,
Strikes each in each by mutual ordering,   10
Resembling sire and child and happy mother,
Who all in one, one pleasing note do sing;
    Whose speechless song, being many, seeming one,
    Sings this to thee: "Thou single wilt prove
        none."

9

Is it for fear to wet a widow's eye
That thou consum'st thyself in single life?
Ah! if thou issueless shalt hap to die,
The world will wail thee like a makeless wife;
The world will be thy widow and still weep   5
That thou no form of thee hast left behind,
When every private widow well may keep
By children's eyes her husband's shape in mind.
Look, what an unthrift in the world doth spend
Shifts but his place, for still the world enjoys it;   10
But beauty's waste hath in the world an end,
And kept unus'd, the user so destroys it.
    No love toward others in that bosom sits
    That on himself such murd'rous shame commits.

---

13. rememb'red . . . be: only to be forgotten.   4, 4. frank: liberal.   free: liberal.   5, 2. gaze: object.   4. unfair:
make unbeautiful.   fairly: in beauty.   6. confounds: destroys.   11. effect: product.   bereft: lost.   6, 1. ragged:
rough.   3. treasure: enrich.   8, 1. Music to hear: you, whom to hear is music.   7. confounds: destroyest.   9, 4.
makeless: mateless, widowed.   5. still: ever.   10. his: its.

10

For shame! deny that thou bear'st love to any,
Who for thyself art so unprovident.
Grant, if thou wilt, thou art belov'd of many,
But that thou none lov'st is most evident;
For thou art so possess'd with murd'rous hate   5
That 'gainst thyself thou stick'st not to conspire,
Seeking that beauteous roof to ruinate
Which to repair should be thy chief desire.
O, change thy thought, that I may change my
      mind!
Shall hate be fairer lodg'd than gentle love?   10
Be, as thy presence is, gracious and kind,
Or to thyself at least kind-hearted prove:
      Make thee another self for love of me,
      That beauty still may live in thine or thee.

11

As fast as thou shalt wane, so fast thou grow'st,
In one of thine, from that which thou departest;
And that fresh blood which youngly thou bestow'st
Thou mayst call thine when thou from youth
      convertest.
Herein lives wisdom, beauty, and increase;   5
Without this, folly, age, and cold decay.
If all were minded so, the times should cease
And threescore year would make the world away.
Let those whom Nature hath not made for store,
Harsh, featureless, and rude, barrenly perish: 10
Look, whom she best endow'd she gave the more;
Which bounteous gift thou shouldst in bounty
      cherisb.
      She carv'd thee for her seal, and meant thereby
      Thou shouldst print more, not let that copy die.

12

When I do count the clock that tells the time,
And see the brave day sunk in hideous night;
When I behold the violet past prime,
And sable curls [all] silver'd o'er with white;
When lofty trees I see barren of leaves   5
Which erst from heat did canopy the herd,
And summer's green all girded up in sheaves
Borne on the bier with white and bristly beard;
Then of thy beauty do I question make
That thou among the wastes of time must go,   10
Since sweets and beauties do themselves forsake
And die as fast as they see others grow;
      And nothing 'gainst Time's scythe can make de-
            fence
      Save breed, to brave him when he takes thee
            hence.

13

O that you were yourself! but, love, you are
No longer yours than you yourself here live:
Against this coming end you should prepare,
And your sweet semblance to some other give.
So should that beauty which you hold in lease   5
Find no determination; then you were
Yourself again after yourself's decease,
When your sweet issue your sweet form should bear.
Who lets so fair a house fall to decay,
Which husbandry in honour might uphold   10
Against the stormy gusts of winter's day
And barren rage of death's eternal cold?
      O, none but unthrifts!   Dear my love, you know
      You had a father: let your son say so.

14

Not from the stars do I my judgement pluck,
And yet methinks I have astronomy;
But not to tell of good or evil luck,
Of plagues, of dearths, or seasons' quality;
Nor can I fortune to brief minutes tell,   5
'Pointing to each his thunder, rain, and wind,
Or say with princes if it shall go well,
By oft predict that I in heaven find:
But from thine eyes my knowledge I derive,
And, constant stars, in them I read such art   10
As "Truth and beauty shall together thrive,
If from thyself to store thou wouldst convert;"
      Or else of thee this I prognosticate:
      "Thy end is truth's and beauty's doom and date."

15

When I consider everything that grows
Holds in perfection but a little moment,
That this huge stage presenteth nought but shows
Whereon the stars in secret influence comment;
When I perceive that men as plants increase,   5
Cheered and check'd even by the self-same sky,
Vaunt in their youthful sap, at height decrease,
And wear their brave state out of memory;
Then the conceit of this inconstant stay
Sets you most rich in youth before my sight,   10
Where wasteful Time debateth with Decay
To change your day of youth to sullied night;
      And all in war with Time for love of you,
      As he takes from you, I engraft you new.

16

But wherefore do not you a mightier way
Make war upon this bloody tyrant, Time?
And fortify yourself in your decay
With means more blessed than my barren rhyme?

10, 7. **roof:** i.e., body.   **11,** 2. **departest:** bestowest (i.e., the "fresh blood" of l. 3).   4. **convertest:** changest.
7. **times:** generations.   9. **store:** fertility, supply.   **12,** 2. **brave:** bright.   4. **[all]** (Malone). *or* Q. 9. **question make:**
consider.   14. **breed:** children.   **brave:** defy.   **13,** 6. **determination:** end.   **14,** 2. **astronomy:** astrology.   8. **oft**
predict: frequent portents.   10. **art:** knowledge.   12. **store ... convert:** produce offspring.   Cf. 11:9.   **15,** 7. **Vaunt:**
exult.   9. **conceit:** thought.   11. **debateth with:** strives in company with.   14. **engraft:** i.e., in my verse.

Now stand you on the top of happy hours,   5
And many maiden gardens, yet unset,
With virtuous wish would bear your living flowers,
Much liker than your painted counterfeit:
So should the lines of life that life repair,
Which this time's pencil or my pupil pen,   10
Neither in inward worth nor outward fair,
Can make you live yourself in eyes of men.
     To give away yourself keeps yourself still,
     And you must live, drawn by your own sweet skill.

17

Who will believe my verse in time to come
If it were fill'd with your most high deserts?
Though yet, heaven knows, it is but as a tomb
Which hides your life and shows not half your parts.
If I could write the beauty of your eyes   5
And in fresh numbers number all your graces,
The age to come would say, "This poet lies;
Such heavenly touches ne'er touch'd earthly faces."
So should my papers, yellowed with their age,
Be scorn'd like old men of less truth than tongue,   10
And your true rights be term'd a poet's rage
And stretched [metre] of an antique song:
     But were some child of yours alive that time,
     You should live twice, in it and in my rhyme.

18

Shall I compare thee to a summer's day?
Thou art more lovely and more temperate:
Rough winds do shake the darling buds of May,
And summer's lease hath all too short a date;
Sometime too hot the eye of heaven shines,   5
And often is his gold complexion dimm'd;
And every fair from fair sometime declines,
By chance or nature's changing course untrimm'd:
But thy eternal summer shall not fade
Nor lose possession of that fair thou ow'st;   10
Nor shall Death brag thou wand'rest in his shade,
When in eternal lines to time thou grow'st;
     So long as men can breathe or eyes can see,
     So long lives this, and this gives life to thee.

19

Devouring Time, blunt thou the lion's paws,
And make the earth devour her own sweet brood;
Pluck the keen teeth from the fierce tiger's jaws,
And burn the long-liv'd phœnix in her blood;
Make glad and sorry seasons as thou [fleets],   5
And do whate'er thou wilt, swift-footed Time,
To the wide world and all her fading sweets;
But I forbid thee one most heinous crime:

O, carve not with thy hours my love's fair brow,
Nor draw no lines there with thine antique pen;   10
Him in thy course untainted do allow
For beauty's pattern to succeeding men.
     Yet do thy worst, old Time.   Despite thy wrong,
     My love shall in my verse ever live young.

20

A woman's face with Nature's own hand painted
Hast thou, the master-mistress of my passion;
A woman's gentle heart, but not acquainted
With shifting change, as is false women's fashion;
An eye more bright than theirs, less false in rolling,
Gilding the object whereupon it gazeth;   6
A man in hue all hues in his controlling,
Which steals men's eyes and women's souls amazeth.
And for a woman wert thou first created;
Till Nature, as she wrought thee, fell a-doting,   10
And by addition me of thee defeated
By adding one thing to my purpose nothing.
     But since she prick'd thee out for women's pleasure,
     Mine be thy love, and thy love's use their treasure.

21

So is it not with me as with that Muse
Stirr'd by a painted beauty to his verse,
Who heaven itself for ornament doth use
And every fair with his fair doth rehearse,
Making a couplement of proud compare   5
With sun and moon, with earth and sea's rich gems,
With April's first-born flowers, and all things rare
That heaven's air in this huge rondure hems.
O let me, true in love, but truly write,
And then believe me, my love is as fair   10
As any mother's child, though not so bright
As those gold candles fix'd in heaven's air:
     Let them say more that like of hearsay well;
     I will not praise that purpose not to sell.

22

My glass shall not persuade me I am old
So long as youth and thou are of one date;
But when in thee time's [furrows] I behold,
Then look I death my days should expiate.
For all that beauty that doth cover thee   5
Is but the seemly raiment of my heart,
Which in thy breast doth live, as thine in me.
How can I then be elder than thou art?
O, therefore, love, be of thyself so wary
As I, not for myself, but for thee will,   10

16, 9. **lines of life:** living lines, i.e., children. 10. **this . . . pencil:** i.e., the painters of today. **this . . . pen** (Massey conj.). *this* (*Times pensel or my pupill pen*) Q. 11. **fair:** beauty. **17,** 4. **parts:** qualities. 6. **numbers:** verses. 11. **rage:** exuberance. 12. **stretched [metre]:** poetic license. **[metre]** (Gildon). *miter* Q. **18,** 8. **untrimm'd:** stripped of beauty. 10. **ow'st:** ownest. **19,** 5. **[fleets]** (Dyce). *fleet'st* Q. **20,** 2. **passion:** love. 7. **A . . . controlling:** a man whose complexion is all-excelling. **man in.** Mackail suggests that this is an error for *native*. 11. **defeated:** deprived. **21,** 1. **Muse:** poet. 8. **rondure:** circle, i.e., world. 13. **like . . . well:** i.e., rely on mere report. **22,** 3. **[furrows]** (Malone). *forrwes* Q. 4. **expiate:** end.

Bearing thy heart, which I will keep so chary
As tender nurse her babe from faring ill.
  Presume not on thy heart when mine is slain;
  Thou gav'st me thine, not to give back again.

23

As an unperfect actor on the stage
Who with his fear is put besides his part,
Or some fierce thing replete with too much rage,
Whose strength's abundance weakens his own heart,
So I, for fear of trust, forget to say   5
The perfect ceremony of love's [rite],
And in mine own love's strength seem to decay,
O'ercharg'd with burden of mine own love's might.
O, let my books be then the eloquence
And dumb presagers of my speaking breast,   10
Who plead for love and look for recompense
More than that tongue that more hath more
    express'd.
  O, learn to read what silent love hath writ:
  To hear with eyes belongs to love's fine wit.

24

Mine eye hath play'd the painter and hath [stell'd]
Thy beauty's form in table of my heart;
My body is the frame wherein 'tis held,
And perspective it is best painter's art.
For through the painter must you see his skill   5
To find where your true image pictur'd lies;
Which in my bosom's shop is hanging still,
That hath his windows glazed with thine eyes.
Now see what good turns eyes for eyes have done:
Mine eyes have drawn thy shape, and thine for me
Are windows to my breast, wherethrough the sun 11
Delights to peep, to gaze therein on thee.
  Yet eyes this cunning want to grace their art:
  They draw but what they see, know not the heart.

25

Let those who are in favour with their stars
Of public honour and proud titles boast,
Whilst I, whom fortune of such triumph bars,
Unlook'd for joy in that I honour most.
Great princes' favourites their fair leaves spread 5
But as the marigold at the sun's eye,
And in themselves their pride lies buried,
For at a frown they in their glory die.

The painful warrior famoused for [fight],
After a thousand victories once foil'd,   10
Is from the book of honour razed quite,
And all the rest forgot for which he toil'd.
  Then happy I, that love and am beloved
  Where I may not remove nor be removed

26

Lord of my love, to whom in vassalage
Thy merit hath my duty strongly knit,
To thee I send this written ambassage,
To witness duty, not to show my wit;
Duty so great, which wit so poor as mine   5
May make seem bare, in wanting words to show it,
But that I hope some good conceit of thine
In thy soul's thought, all naked, will bestow it;
Till whatsoever star that guides my moving
Points on me graciously with fair aspect,   10
And puts apparel on my tattered loving,
To show me worthy of [thy] sweet respect.
  Then may I dare to boast how I do love thee;
  Till then not show my head where thou mayst
    prove me.

27

Weary with toil, I haste me to my bed,
The dear repose for limbs with [travel] tired;
But then begins a journey in my head,
To work my mind when body's work's expired;
For then my thoughts, from far where I abide, 5
Intend a zealous pilgrimage to thee,
And keep my drooping eyelids open wide,
Looking on darkness which the blind do see;
Save that my soul's imaginary sight
Presents [thy] shadow to my sightless view,   10
Which, like a jewel hung in ghastly night,
Makes black night beauteous and her old face new.
  Lo, thus, by day my limbs, by night my mind,
  For thee and for myself no quiet find.

28

How can I then return in happy plight,
That am debarr'd the benefit of rest?
When day's oppression is not eas'd by night,
But day by night, and night by day, oppress'd,
And each, though enemies to either's reign,   5
Do in consent shake hands to torture me;

---

11. **Bearing:** because I bear. 13. **Presume not:** do not think to regain. **23,** 5. **for … trust:** lacking self-confidence. 6. [rite] (Malone). *right* Q. 9. **books.** Frequently emended to *looks.* 10. **presagers:** indicators (like the actors in a dumb show). 12. **that more … express'd:** that has more adequately expressed (1) love, (2) your perfections. **24,** 1. [stell'd] (Dyce): placed. *steeld* Q. 4. **And … art.** I.e., And perspective, which the frame (l. 3) helps to give the picture, is a feature of the best pictorial art. 5–6. **you … your:** one … one's (not the friend's). **25,** 4. **Unlook'd for:** beyond expectation. 9. **painful:** toiling. [fight] (Theobald conj.). *worth* Q. **26,** 7. **good conceit:** happy thought. 8. **all naked.** Refers to his expression of his "duty." **bestow:** lodge. 9. **moving:** i.e., life. 10. **aspect:** astrological influence. 12. [thy] (Capell MS.). *their* Q. This error is frequently repeated by Q and has been similarly corrected where it occurs. Later instances are noted only in the text. **27,** 2. [travel] (Ewing). *travail* Q. 6. **Intend:** direct. 10. **shadow:** image. 14. **For:** because of.

The one by toil, the other to complain
How far I toil, still farther off from thee?
I tell the day, to please him, thou art bright   9
And dost him grace when clouds do blot the heaven;
So flatter I the swart-complexion'd night,
When sparkling stars twire not, thou [gild'st] the
even:
    But day doth daily draw my sorrows longer,
    And night doth nightly make grief's [strength]
    seem stronger.

29

When, in disgrace with Fortune and men's eyes,
I all alone beweep my outcast state,
And trouble deaf heaven with my bootless cries,
And look upon myself and curse my fate,
Wishing me like to one more rich in hope,   5
Featur'd like him, like him with friends possess'd,
Desiring this man's art, and that man's scope,
With what I most enjoy contented least;
Yet in these thoughts myself almost despising,
Haply I think on thee; and then my state,   10
Like to the lark at break of day arising
From sullen earth, sings hymns at heaven's gate;
    For thy sweet love remem'bred such wealth brings
    That then I scorn to change my state with
    kings.

30

When to the sessions of sweet silent thought
I summon up remembrance of things past,
I sigh the lack of many a thing I sought,
And with old woes new wail my dear time's waste.
Then can I drown an eye, unus'd to flow,   5
For precious friends hid in death's dateless night,
And weep afresh love's long since cancell'd woe,
And moan th' expense of many a vanish'd sight.
Then can I grieve at grievances foregone,
And heavily from woe to woe tell o'er   10
The sad account of fore-bemoaned moan,
Which I new pay as if not paid before.
    But if the while I think on thee, dear friend,
    All losses are restor'd and sorrows end.

31

Thy bosom is endeared with all hearts
Which I by lacking have supposed dead;
And there reigns love and all love's loving parts,
And all those friends which I thought buried.
How many a holy and obsequious tear   5
Hath dear religious love stol'n from mine eye

As interest of the dead, which now appear
But things remov'd that hidden in [thee] lie!
Thou art the grave where buried love doth live,
Hung with the trophies of my lovers gone,   10
Who all their parts of me to thee did give:
That due of many now is thine alone.
    Their images I lov'd I view in thee,
    And thou, all they, hast all the all of me.

32

If thou survive my well-contented day,
When that churl Death my bones with dust shall
    cover,
And shalt by fortune once more re-survey
These poor rude lines of thy deceased lover,
Compare them with the bett'ring of the time,   5
And though they be outstripp'd by every pen,
Reserve them for my love, not for their rhyme,
Exceeded by the height of happier men.
O, then vouchsafe me but this loving thought:
"Had my friend's Muse grown with this growing
    age,   10
A dearer birth than this his love had brought,
To march in ranks of better equipage;
    But since he died and poets better prove,
    Theirs for their style I'll read, his for his love."

33

Full many a glorious morning have I seen
Flatter the mountain tops with sovereign eye,
Kissing with golden face the meadows green,
Gilding pale streams with heavenly alchemy;
Anon permit the basest clouds to ride   5
With ugly rack on his celestial face,
And from the forlorn world his visage hide,
Stealing unseen to west with this disgrace:
Even so my sun one early morn did shine
With all-triumphant splendour on my brow;   10
But out, alack! he was but one hour mine,
The region-cloud hath mask'd him from me now.
    Yet him for this my love no whit disdaineth;
    Suns of the world may stain when heaven's sun
    staineth.

34

Why didst thou promise such a beauteous day
And make me travel forth without my cloak,
To let base clouds o'ertake me in my way,
Hiding thy brav'ry in their rotten smoke?
'Tis not enough that through the cloud thou break
To dry the rain on my storm-beaten face,   6

28, 7. to complain: by making me complain. 12. twire: peep. [gild'st] (Sewell). *guil'st* Q. 14. [strength] (Capell). *length* Q. 29, 6. him: another. 8. what... enjoy. Perhaps "my best powers." Shakespeare may be referring (ll. 7–8) to his poetry. 30, 4. my...waste: time I wasted in seeking what I did not find. 8. expense: cost. 31, 1. endeared. Perhaps also with the sense of *enriched*. 5. obsequious: funereal. 7. interest of: due to. which: who. 8. [thee] (Gildon). *there* Q. 33, 6. rack: clouds. 12. region-cloud: high clouds (*region* signifies the upper air). 14. stain: grow dim, be obscured. 34, 4. brav'ry: splendor. rotten smoke: pestilential damps.

For no man well of such a salve can speak
That heals the wound and cures not the disgrace.
Nor can thy shame give physic to my grief;
Though thou repent, yet I have still the loss: 10
Th' offender's sorrow lends but weak relief
To him that bears the strong offence's [cross],
   Ah! but those tears are pearl which thy love sheds,
   And they are rich, and ransom all ill deeds.

35

No more be griev'd at that which thou hast done:
Roses have thorns, and silver fountains mud;
Clouds and eclipses stain both moon and sun,
And loathsome canker lives in sweetest bud.
All men make faults, and even I in this,   5
Authorizing thy trespass with compare,
Myself corrupting, salving thy amiss,
Excusing [thy] sins more than [thy] sins are;
For to thy sensual fault I bring in sense —
Thy adverse party is thy advocate —   10
And 'gainst myself a lawful plea commence.
Such civil war is in my love and hate
   That I an accessary needs must be
   To that sweet thief which sourly robs from me.

36

Let me confess that we two must be twain,
Although our undivided loves are one:
So shall those blots that do with me remain,
Without thy help by me be borne alone.
In our two loves there is but one respect,   5
Though in our lives a separable spite,
Which though it alter not love's sole effect,
Yet doth it steal sweet hours from love's delight.
I may not evermore acknowledge thee,
Lest my bewailed guilt should do thee shame,   10
Nor thou with public kindness honour me,
Unless thou take that honour from thy name.
   But do not so; I love thee in such sort
   As, thou being mine, mine is thy good report.

37

As a decrepit father takes delight
To see his active child do deeds of youth,
So I, made lame by Fortune's dearest spite,
Take all my comfort of thy worth and truth.
For whether beauty, birth, or wealth, or wit,   5
Or any of these all, or all, or more,

Entitled in [thy] parts do crowned sit,
I make my love engrafted to this store:
So then I am not lame, poor, not despis'd,
Whilst that this shadow doth such substance give
That I in thy abundance am suffic'd   11
And by a part of all thy glory live.
   Look, what is best, that best, I wish in thee:
   This wish I have; then ten times happy me!

38

How can my Muse want subject to invent
While thou dost breathe, that pour'st into my verse
Thine own sweet argument, too excellent
For every vulgar paper to rehearse?
O, give thyself the thanks if aught in me   5
Worthy perusal stand against thy sight;
For who's so dumb that cannot write to thee,
When thou thyself dost give invention light?
Be thou the tenth Muse, ten times more in worth
Than those old nine which rhymers invocate;   10
And he that calls on thee, let him bring forth
Eternal numbers to outlive long date.
   If my slight Muse do please these curious days,
   The pain be mine, but thine shall be the praise.

39

O, how thy worth with manners may I sing,
When thou art all the better part of me?
What can mine own praise to mine own self bring?
And what is't but mine own when I praise thee?
Even for this let us divided live,   5
And our dear love lose name of single one,
That by this separation I may give
That due to thee which thou deserv'st alone.
O absence, what a torment wouldst thou prove
Were it not thy sour leisure gave sweet leave   10
To entertain the time with thoughts of love,
Which time and thoughts so sweetly [do] deceive,
   And that thou teachest how to make one twain,
   By praising him here who doth hence remain!

40

Take all my loves, my love; yea, take them all.
What hast thou then more than thou hadst before?
No love, my love, that thou mayst true love call;
All mine was thine before thou hadst this more.
Then, if for my love thou my love receivest,   5
I cannot blame thee for my love thou usest;

12. [cross] (Malone). _losse_ Q.   **35, 4. canker:** canker-worm.   **6. compare:** i.e., the comparisons of ll. 2–4.   **8. are:** i.e., amount to.   **9. sense:** reason.   **36, 5. respect:** consideration, i.e., our forced separation.   **6. separable spite:** i.e., vexing separation.   **7. sole effect:** i.e., devotion.   **9–12. I…name.** Cf. 26:9–14.   **37, 3. dearest:** direst.   **7. Entitled …sit:** are rightfully sovereign among thy excellences.   **10. shadow:** i.e., imaginary possession.   **38, 3. argument:** subject.   **5. in me:** that I have written.   **12. numbers:** verses.   **13. curious:** fastidious.   **39, 1. with manners:** fittingly.   **12. [do]** (Capell). _dost_ Q. The subject is _which_, referring to _thoughts_, l. 11.   **deceive:** beguile.   **13. one twain:** two persons of one, one being actually absent, the other being present in imagination.   **40, 5. for…receivest:** for love of me you receive her whom I love.   **6. for:** because.

But yet be blam'd, if thou [thyself] deceivest
By wilful taste of what thyself refusest.
I do forgive thy robb'ry, gentle thief,
Although thou steal thee all my poverty;   10
And yet, love knows, it is a greater grief
To bear love's wrong than hate's known injury.
  Lascivious grace, in whom all ill well shows,
  Kill me with spites; yet we must not be foes.

41

Those pretty wrongs that liberty commits
When I am sometime absent from thy heart,
Thy beauty and thy years full well befits,
For still temptation follows where thou art.
Gentle thou art and therefore to be won;   5
Beauteous thou art, therefore to be assailed;
And when a woman woos, what woman's son
Will sourly leave her till [she] have prevailed?
Ay me! but yet thou mightst my seat forbear,
And chide thy beauty and thy straying youth,   10
Who lead thee in their riot even there
Where thou art forc'd to break a twofold truth:
  Hers, by thy beauty tempting her to thee,
  Thine, by thy beauty being false to me.

42

That thou hast her, it is not all my grief,
And yet it may be said I lov'd her dearly;
That she hath thee, is of my wailing chief,
A loss in love that touches me more nearly.
Loving offenders, thus I will excuse ye: 5
Thou dost love her because thou know'st I love her,
And for my sake even so doth she abuse me,
Suff'ring my friend for my sake to approve her.
If I lose thee, my loss is my love's gain,
And losing her, my friend hath found that loss; 10
Both find each other, and I lose both twain,
And both for my sake lay on me this cross.
  But here's the joy: my friend and I are one;
  Sweet flattery! then she loves but me alone.

43

When most I wink, then do mine eyes best see,
For all the day they view things unrespected;
But when I sleep, in dreams they look on thee,
And, darkly bright, are bright in dark directed.
Then thou, whose shadow shadows doth make
    bright,   5
How would thy shadow's form form happy show

To the clear day with thy much clearer light,
When to unseeing eyes thy shade shines so!
How would, I say, mine eyes be blessed made
By looking on thee in the living day,   10
When in dead night [thy] fair imperfect shade
Through heavy sleep on sightless eyes doth stay!
  All days are nights to see till I see thee,
  And nights bright days when dreams do show
      thee me.

44

If the dull substance of my flesh were thought,
Injurious distance should not stop my way;
For then, despite of space, I would be brought,
From limits far remote, where thou dost stay.
No matter then although my foot did stand   5
Upon the farthest earth remov'd from thee;
For nimble thought can jump both sea and land
As soon as think the place where he would be.
But, ah! thought kills me that I am not thought,
To leap large lengths of miles when thou art gone, 10
But that, so much of earth and water wrought,
I must attend time's leisure with my moan,
  Receiving [naught] by elements so slow
  But heavy tears, badges of either's woe.

45

The other two, slight air and purging fire,
Are both with thee, wherever I abide;
The first my thought, the other my desire,
These present-absent with swift motion slide.
For when these quicker elements are gone   5
In tender embassy of love to thee,
My life, being made of four, with two alone
Sinks down to death, oppress'd with melancholy;
Until life's composition be recured
By those swift messengers return'd from thee, 10
Who even but now come back again, assured
Of [thy] fair health, recounting it to me.
  This told, I joy; but then no longer glad,
  I send them back again and straight grow sad.

46

Mine eye and heart are at a mortal war
How to divide the conquest of thy sight;
Mine eye my heart [thy] picture's sight would bar,
My heart mine eye the freedom of that right.
My heart doth plead that thou in him dost lie, —
A closet never pierc'd with crystal eyes —   6

7. **[thyself]** (Gildon). *this selfe* Q. 8. **what ... refusest:** legitimate wedlock (?). 14. **spites:** injuries. **41,** 8. **[she]** (Malone). *he* Q. 12. **truth:** constancy. **42,** 3. **chief:** chief cause. 8. **approve:** test. 9. **love's:** i.e., mistress's. **43,** 1. **wink:** i.e., sleep. 2. **unrespected:** unheeded. 4. **darkly ... directed:** (they) seeing, though closed, are clearly guided in the dark. 5. **shadow:** image. **shadows:** shades of night. 6. **thy ... form:** i.e., the shadow cast by thy body. 11. **imperfect:** i.e., because only a shadow of the friend, who is perfect. **44,** 4. **where:** to the place where. 11. **wrought:** compounded. 13. **[naught]** (Gildon). *naughts* Q. 14. **either's woe:** i.e., earth's, because it is heavy and hence sluggish; water's, because it is wet, as with tears. **45,** 4. **present-absent:** now here, now gone again. 9. **recured:** restored. **46,** 1. **mortal:** deadly. 2. **conquest ... sight:** the right to gaze on your image. The reference may be to an actual portrait. Cf. Sonnet 24, where the picture is clearly imaginary.

But the defendant doth that plea deny
And says in him [thy] fair appearance lies.
To ['cide] this title is impanneled
A quest of thoughts, all tenants to the heart,   10
And by their verdict is determined
The clear eye's moiety and the dear heart's part;
    As thus: mine eye's due is [thy] outward part,
    And my heart's right [thy] inward love of heart.

47

Betwixt mine eye and heart a league is took,
And each doth good turns now unto the other.
When that mine eye is famish'd for a look,
Or heart in love with sighs himself doth smother,
With my love's picture then my eye doth feast   5
And to the painted banquet bids my heart.
Another time mine eye is my heart's guest
And in his thoughts of love doth share a part.
So, either by thy picture or my love,
Thyself away [art] present still with me;   10
For thou [no] farther than my thoughts canst move,
And I am still with them and they with thee;
    Or, if they sleep, thy picture in my sight
    Awakes my heart to heart's and eye's delight.

48

How careful was I, when I took my way,
Each trifle under truest bars to thrust,
That to my use it might unused stay
From hands of falsehood, in sure wards of trust!
But thou, to whom my jewels trifles are,   5
Most worthy comfort, now my greatest grief,
Thou, best of dearest and mine only care,
Art left the prey of every vulgar thief.
Thee have I not lock'd up in any chest,
Save where thou art not, though I feel thou art,   10
Within the gentle closure of my breast,
From whence at pleasure thou mayst come and part;
    And even thence thou wilt be stol'n, I fear,
    For truth proves thievish for a prize so dear.

49

Against that time, if ever that time come,
When I shall see thee frown on my defects,
Whenas thy love hath cast his utmost sum,
Call'd to that audit by advis'd respects;
Against that time when thou shalt strangely pass   5
And scarcely greet me with that sun, thine eye,
When love, converted from the thing it was,
Shall reasons find of settled gravity, —
Against that time do I ensconce me here
Within the knowledge of mine own desert,   10

And this my hand against myself uprear,
To guard the lawful reasons on thy part:
    To leave poor me thou hast the strength of laws,
    Since why to love I can allege no cause.

50

How heavy do I journey on the way
When what I seek, my weary travel's end,
Doth teach that ease and that repose to say,
"Thus far the miles are measur'd from thy friend!"
The beast that bears me, tired with my woe,   5
Plods dully on, to bear that weight in me,
As if by some instinct the wretch did know
His rider lov'd not speed, being made from thee.
The bloody spur cannot provoke him on
That sometimes anger thrusts into his hide;   10
Which heavily he answers with a groan,
More sharp to me than spurring to his side;
    For that same groan doth put this in my mind:
    My grief lies onward and my joy behind.

51

Thus can my love excuse the slow offence
Of my dull bearer when from thee I speed:
From where thou art why should I haste me thence?
Till I return, of posting is no need.
O, what excuse will my poor beast then find,   5
When swift extremity can seem but slow?
Then should I spur, though mounted on the wind,
In winged speed no motion shall I know.
Then can no horse with my desire keep pace;
Therefore desire, of [perfect'st] love being made, 10
Shall neigh — no dull flesh — in his fiery race;
But love, for love, thus shall excuse my jade:
    Since from thee going he went wilful-slow,
    Towards thee I'll run, and give him leave to go.

52

So am I as the rich whose blessed key
Can bring him to his sweet up-locked treasure,
The which he will not ev'ry hour survey,
For blunting the fine point of seldom pleasure.
Therefore are feasts so solemn and so rare,   5
Since, seldom coming, in the long year set,
Like stones of worth they thinly placed are,
Or captain jewels in the carcanet.
So is the time that keeps you as my chest,
Or as the wardrobe which the robe doth hide,   10
To make some special instant special blest
By new unfolding his imprison'd pride.
    Blessed are you, whose worthiness gives scope,
    Being had, to triumph, being lack'd, to hope.

9. ['cide] (Gildon): decide. *side* Q. 10. **quest:** jury. 12. **moiety:** share. **47,** 10. [art] (Capell MS.). *are* Q. 11. [no] (Capell MS.). *nor* Q. **48,** 5. **to:** compared to. 6. **grief:** i.e., because absent. 8. **vulgar:** common. 14. **truth:** honesty, honor. **49,** 3. **cast . . . sum:** reckoned his final sum, closed his accounts. 4. **advis'd respects:** considered reasons. 8. **reasons:** i.e., for the change. 10. **desert:** small merit. **51,** 1. **slow offence:** offense of slowness. 6. **swift extremity:** extreme speed. 7. **should I:** if I should. 10. [perfect'st] (Knight). *perfects* Q. 14. **go:** walk. **52,** 4. **For:** for fear of. 8. **captain:** principal. **carcanet:** necklace.

53

What is your substance, whereof are you made,
That millions of strange shadows on you tend?
Since every one hath, every one, one shade,
And you, but one, can every shadow lend.
Describe Adonis, and the counterfeit   5
Is poorly imitated after you;
On Helen's cheek all art of beauty set,
And you in Grecian tires are painted new.
Speak of the spring and foison of the year:
The one doth shadow of your beauty show,   10
The other as your bounty doth appear;
And you in every blessed shape we know.
　　In all external grace you have some part,
　　But you like none, none you, for constant heart.

54

O, how much more doth beauty beauteous seem
By that sweet ornament which truth doth give!
The rose looks fair, but fairer we it deem
For that sweet odour which doth in it live.
The canker-blooms have full as deep a dye   5
As the perfumed tincture of the roses,
Hang on such thorns, and play as wantonly
When summer's breath their masked buds discloses;
But, for their virtue only is their show,
They live unwoo'd and unrespected fade,   10
Die to themselves.　Sweet roses do not so;
Of their sweet deaths are sweetest odours made.
　　And so of you, beauteous and lovely youth,
　　When that shall fade, [my] verse distills your truth.

55

Not marble nor the gilded monuments
Of princes shall outlive this pow'rful rhyme;
But you shall shine more bright in these contents
Than unswept stone besmear'd with sluttish time.
When wasteful war shall statues overturn,   5
And broils root out the work of masonry,
Nor Mars his sword nor war's quick fire shall burn
The living record of your memory.
'Gainst death and all-oblivious enmity
Shall you pace forth; your praise shall still find room
Even in the eyes of all posterity   11
That wear this world out to the ending doom.
　　So, till the Judgement that yourself arise,
　　You live in this, and dwell in lovers' eyes.

56

Sweet love, renew thy force; be it not said
Thy edge should blunter be than appetite,

Which but to-day by feeding is allay'd,
To-morrow sharp'ned in his former might.
So, love, be thou; although to-day thou fill   5
Thy hungry eyes even till they wink with fullness,
To-morrow see again, and do not kill
The spirit of love with a perpetual dullness.
Let this sad int'rim like the ocean be
Which parts the shore, where two contracted new   10
Come daily to the banks, that, when they see
Return of love, more blest may be the view;
　　[Or] call it winter, which being full of care,
　　Makes summer's welcome thrice more wish'd,
　　more rare.

57

Being your slave, what should I do but tend
Upon the hours and times of your desire?
I have no precious time at all to spend,
Nor services to do, till you require.
Nor dare I chide the world-without-end hour   5
Whilst I, my sovereign, watch the clock for you,
Nor think the bitterness of absence sour
When you have bid your servant once adieu.
Nor dare I question with my jealous thought
Where you may be, or your affairs suppose,   10
But, like a sad slave, stay and think of nought
Save where you are how happy you make those.
　　So true a fool is love that in your will,
　　Though you do anything, he thinks no ill.

58

That god forbid, that made me first your slave,
I should in thought control your times of pleasure,
Or at your hand th' account of hours to crave,
Being your vassal, bound to stay your leisure!
O, let me suffer, being at your beck,   5
Th' imprison'd absence of your liberty;
And patience, tame to sufferance, bide each check
Without accusing you of injury.
Be where you list, your charter is so strong
That you yourself may privilege your time   10
To what you will; to you it doth belong
Yourself to pardon of self-doing crime.
　　I am to wait, though waiting so be hell;
　　Not blame your pleasure, be it ill or well.

59

If there be nothing new, but that which is
Hath been before, how are our brains beguil'd,
Which, labouring for invention, bear amiss
The second burden of a former child!

O, that record could with a backward look,   5
Even of five hundred courses of the sun,
Show me your image in some antique book,
Since mind at first in character was done!
That I might see what the old world could say
To this composed wonder of your frame;   10
Whe'er we are mended, or whe'er better they,
Or whether revolution be the same.
　　O, sure I am, the wits of former days
　　To subjects worse have given admiring praise.

60

Like as the waves make towards the pebbled shore,
So do our minutes hasten to their end;
Each changing place with that which goes before,
In sequent toil all forwards do contend.
Nativity, once in the main of light,   5
Crawls to maturity, wherewith being crown'd,
Crooked eclipses 'gainst his glory fight,
And Time that gave doth now his gift confound.
Time doth transfix the flourish set on youth
And delves the parallels in beauty's brow,   10
Feeds on the rarities of nature's truth,
And nothing stands but for his scythe to mow;
　　And yet to times in hope my verse shall stand,
　　Praising thy worth, despite his cruel hand.

Time important in Romeo & Juliet and Mid. Dream too

61

Is it thy will thy image should keep open
My heavy eyelids to the weary night?
Dost thou desire my slumbers should be broken
While shadows like to thee do mock my sight?
Is it thy spirit that thou send'st from thee   5
So far from home into my deeds to pry,
To find out shames and idle hours in me,
The scope and [tenour] of thy jealousy?
O, no! thy love, though much, is not so great;
It is my love that keeps mine eye awake;   10
Mine own true love that doth my rest defeat,
To play the watchman ever for thy sake.
　　For thee watch I whilst thou dost wake elsewhere,
　　From me far off, with others all too near.

62

Sin of self-love possesseth all mine eye
And all my soul and all my every part;
And for this sin there is no remedy,
It is so grounded inward in my heart.
Methinks no face so gracious is as mine,   5
No shape so true, no truth of such account;
And for myself mine own worth do define,
As I all other in all worth surmount.

But when my glass shows me myself indeed,
Beated and chopp'd with tann'd antiquity,   10
Mine own self-love quite contrary I read;
Self so self-loving were iniquity.
　　'Tis thee, myself, that for myself I praise,
　　Painting my age with beauty of thy days.

63

Against my love shall be, as I am now,
With Time's injurious hand crush'd and o'erworn;
When hours have drain'd his blood and fill'd his brow
With lines and wrinkles; when his youthful morn
Hath travell'd on to age's steepy night,   5
And all those beauties whereof now he's king
Are vanishing or vanish'd out of sight,
Stealing away the treasure of his spring;
For such a time do I now fortify
Against confounding age's cruel knife,   10
That he shall never cut from memory
My sweet love's beauty, though my lover's life:
　　His beauty shall in these black lines be seen,
　　And they shall live, and he in them still green.

64

When I have seen by Time's fell hand defaced
The rich proud cost of outworn buried age;
When sometime lofty towers I see down-rased,
And brass eternal slave to mortal rage;
When I have seen the hungry ocean gain   5
Advantage on the kingdom of the shore,
And the firm soil win of the wat'ry main,
Increasing store with loss and loss with store;
When I have seen such interchange of state,
Or state itself confounded to decay;   10
Ruin hath taught me thus to ruminate,
That Time will come and take my love away.
　　This thought is as a death, which cannot choose
　　But weep to have that which it fears to lose.

65

Since brass, nor stone, nor earth, nor boundless
　　　sea,
But sad mortality o'er-sways their power,
How with this rage shall beauty hold a plea,
Whose action is no stronger than a flower?
O, how shall summer's honey breath hold out   5
Against the wreckful siege of batt'ring days,
When rocks impregnable are not so stout,
Nor gates of steel so strong, but Time decays?
O fearful meditation! Where, alack,
Shall Time's best jewel from Time's chest lie hid? 10

---

8. **character:** writing. **done:** expressed. 10. **composed wonder:** wonderful composition. 12. **revolution:** i.e., the new cycle.　**60,** 5. **main:** immensity. 8. **confound:** destroy. 11. **truth:** genuineness (as opposed to artificiality). 13. **times in hope:** future times.　**61,** 8. **scope:** aim. [tenour] (Capell MS.): purport. *tenure* Q. 12. **play the watchman:** keep awake.　**62,** 7. **do:** I do. 8. **As:** so that.　**63,** 1. **Against:** in anticipation of the time when. 10. **confounding:** destroying.　**64,** 9–10. **state...state:** condition...greatness.　**65,** 1. **Since:** since there is neither.

Or what strong hand can hold his swift foot back?
Or who his spoil [of] beauty can forbid?
  O, none, unless this miracle have might,
  That in black ink my love may still shine bright.

66

Tir'd with all these, for restful death I cry:
As, to behold desert a beggar born,
And needy nothing trimm'd in jollity,
And purest faith unhappily forsworn,
And gilded honour shamefully misplace'd,   5
And maiden virtue rudely strumpeted,
And right perfection wrongfully disgrac'd,
And strength by limping sway disabled,
And art made tongue-tied by authority,
And folly, doctor-like, controlling skill,   10
And simple truth miscall'd simplicity,
And captive good attending captain ill:
  Tir'd with all these, from these would I be gone,
  Save that, to die, I leave my love alone.

67

Ah! wherefore with infection should he live
And with his presence grace impiety,
That sin by him advantage should achieve
And lace itself with his society?
Why should false painting imitate his cheek   5
And steal dead seeing of his living hue?
Why should poor beauty indirectly seek
Roses of shadow, since his rose is true?
Why should he live, now Nature bankrupt is,
Beggar'd of blood to blush through lively veins? 10
For she hath no exchequer now but his,
And, proud of many, lives upon his gains.
  Oh, him she stores, to show what wealth she had
  In days long since, before these last so bad.

68

Thus is his cheek the map of days outworn,
When beauty liv'd and died as flowers do now,
Before these bastard signs of fair were born,
Or durst inhabit on a living brow;
Before the golden tresses of the dead,   5
The right of sepulchres, were shorn away
To live a second life on second head;
Ere beauty's dead fleece made another gay.
In him those holy antique hours are seen,
Without all ornament, itself and true,   10
Making no summer of another's green,
Robbing no old to dress his beauty new;

And him as for a map doth Nature store,
To show false Art what beauty was of yore.

69

Those parts of thee that the world's eye doth view
Want nothing that the thought of hearts can mend;
All tongues, the voice of souls, give thee that [due],
Utt'ring bare truth, even so as foes commend.   4
[Thy] outward thus with outward praise is crown'd;
But those same tongues that give thee so thine own
In other accents do this praise confound
By seeing farther than the eye hath shown.
They look into the beauty of thy mind,
And that, in guess, they measure by thy deeds; 10
Then, churls, their thoughts, although their eyes
    were kind,
To thy fair flower add the rank smell of weeds.
  But why thy odour matcheth not thy show,
  The [soil] is this, that thou dost common grow.

70

That thou [art] blam'd shall not be thy defect
For slander's mark was ever yet the fair;
The ornament of beauty is suspect,
A crow that flies in heaven's sweetest air.
So thou be good, slander doth but approve   5
[Thy] worth the greater, being woo'd of Time;
For canker vice the sweetest buds doth love,
And thou present'st a pure unstained prime.
Thou hast pass'd by the ambush of young days,
Either not assail'd, or victor being charg'd; 10
Yet this thy praise cannot be so thy praise,
To tie up envy evermore enlarg'd:
  If some suspect of ill mask'd not thy show,
  Then thou alone kingdoms of hearts shouldst owe.

71

No longer mourn for me when I am dead
Than you shall hear the surly sullen bell
Give warning to the world that I am fled
From this vile world, with vilest worms to dwell.
Nay, if you read this line, remember not   5
The hand that writ it; for I love you so
That I in your sweet thoughts would be forgot
If thinking on me then should make you woe.
O, if, I say, you look upon this verse
When I perhaps compounded am with clay, 10
Do not so much as my poor name rehearse,
But let your love even with my life decay,
  Lest the wise world should look into your moan
  And mock you with me after I am gone.

---

12. **spoil**: plundering. **[of]** (Malone). *or* Q.   **66**, 3. **needy nothing**: i.e., the worthless, unmeriting (lit., barren nothingness) as compared with *desert* (l. 2). 4. **unhappily**: wickedly. 10. **doctor-like**: with learned air. 11. **simplicity**: stupidity. **67**, 1. **with infection**: in a corrupt age. 4. **lace**: embellish. 6. **seeing**: appearance. 7. **indirectly**: artificially. 8. **of shadow**: imitation. 12. **gains**: what he can provide her. **68**, 3. **fair**: beauty. 10. **itself**: undefiled. **69**, 3. **the … souls**: candidly. **[due]** (Capell MS.). *end* Q. 4. **even … commend**: i.e., without exaggeration. 6. **thine own**: your due. 11-12. **their thoughts … weeds**. I.e., although approving what they saw, they disparage you in their thoughts. 14. **[soil]** (Capell MS.): ground, explanation. *solye* Q. **70**, 1. **[art]** (ed. 1640). *are* Q. 3. **suspect**: suspicion. 5. **So**: if only. **approve**: prove. 6. **of Time**: by the world(?). 11-12. **cannot … enlarg'd**: is not sufficient to stop calumny (envy) which is ever active. 14. **owe**: own.

72

O, lest the world should task you to recite
What merit liv'd in me, that you should love
After my death, dear love, forget me quite,
For you in me can nothing worthy prove;
Unless you would devise some virtuous lie   5
To do more for me than mine own desert,
And hang more praise upon deceased I
Than niggard truth would willingly impart:
O, lest your true love may seem false in this,
That you for love speak well of me untrue,   10
My name be buried where my body is,
And live no more, to shame nor me nor you.
    For I am sham'd by that which I bring forth,
    And so should you, to love things nothing
        worth.

73 *Time again*

That time of year thou mayst in me behold
When yellow leaves, or none, or few, do hang
Upon those boughs which shake against the cold,
Bare [ruin'd] choirs where late the sweet birds
    sang.
In me thou see'st the twilight of such day   5
As after sunset fadeth in the west,
Which by and by black night doth take away,
Death's second self, that seals up all in rest.
In me thou see'st the glowing of such fire
That on the ashes of his youth doth lie,   10
As the death-bed whereon it must expire,
Consum'd with that which it was nourish'd by.
    This thou perceiv'st, which makes thy love more
        strong,
    To love that well which thou must leave ere
        long.

74

But be contented: when that fell arrest
Without all bail shall carry me away,
My life hath in this line some interest,
Which for memorial still with thee shall stay.
When thou reviewest this, thou dost review   5
The very part was consecrate to thee:
The earth can have but earth, which is his due;
My spirit is thine, the better part of me.
So then thou hast but lost the dregs of life,
The prey of worms, my body being dead,   10
The coward conquest of a wretch's knife,
Too base of thee to be remembered.
    The worth of that is that which it contains,
    And that is this, and this with thee remains.

75

So are you to my thoughts as food to life,
Or as sweet-season'd showers are to the ground;
And for the peace of you I hold such strife
As 'twixt a miser and his wealth is found:
Now proud as an enjoyer, and anon   5
Doubting the filching age will steal his treasure;
Now counting best to be with you alone,
Then better'd that the world may see my pleasure;
Sometime all full with feasting on your sight,
And by and by clean starved for a look;   10
Possessing or pursuing no delight
Save what is had or must from you be took.
    Thus do I pine and surfeit day by day,
    Or gluttoning on all, or all away.

76

Why is my verse so barren of new pride,
So far from variation or quick change?
Why with the time do I not glance aside
To new-found methods and to compounds strange?
Why write I still all one, ever the same,   5
And keep invention in a noted weed,
That every word doth almost [tell] my name,
Showing their birth and where they did proceed?
O, know, sweet love, I always write of you,
And you and love are still my argument;   10
So all my best is dressing old words new,
Spending again what is already spent:
    For as the sun is daily new and old,
    So is my love still telling what is told.

77

Thy glass will show thee how thy beauties wear,
Thy dial how thy precious minutes waste;
The vacant leaves thy mind's imprint will bear,
And of this book this learning mayst thou taste.
The wrinkles which thy glass will truly show   5
Of mouthed graves will give thee memory;
Thou by thy dial's shady stealth mayst know
Time's thievish progress to eternity.
Look, what thy memory cannot contain
Commit to these waste [blanks], and thou shalt find
Those children nurs'd, deliver'd from thy brain,   11
To take a new acquaintance of thy mind.
    These offices, so oft as thou wilt look,
    Shall profit thee and much enrich thy book.

78

So oft have I invok'd thee for my Muse
And found such fair assistance in my verse

72, 10. **untrue:** untruly.   **73,** 4. **[ruin'd]** (ed. 1640). *rn'wd* Q.   **74,** 13-14. **The ... this:** i.e., the worth of my body is my spirit, and that is my poetry.   **75,** 3. **of you:** to be found in you.   6. **Doubting:** fearing.   8. **better'd that:** made happier because.   14. **all:** i.e., all delights. **all away:** having no joy at all.   **76,** 3. **time:** fashion.   6. **noted weed:** well-known style.   7. **[tell]** (Capell MS.). *fel* Q.   10. **argument:** theme.   **77,** 3. **vacant leaves:** blank pages of the notebook which, apparently, Shakespeare is sending to his friend.   6. **mouthed:** gaping.   7. **shady stealth:** stealing shadow.   10. **[blanks]** (Theobald conj.). *blacks* Q.   11. **nurs'd:** cared for. **deliver'd:** which have been delivered.   13. **offices:** practices.

As every alien pen hath got my use
And under thee their poesy disperse.
Thine eyes, that taught the dumb on high to sing   5
And heavy ignorance aloft to fly,
Have added feathers to the learned's wing
And given grace a double majesty.
Yet be most proud of that which I compile,
Whose influence is thine and born of thee: 10
In others' works thou dost but mend the style,
And arts with thy sweet graces graced be;
    But thou art all my art, and dost advance
    As high as learning my rude ignorance.

79

Whilst I alone did call upon thy aid
My verse alone had all thy gentle grace,
But now my gracious numbers are decay'd
And my sick Muse doth give another place.
I grant, sweet love, thy lovely argument   5
Deserves the travail of a worthier pen,
Yet what of thee thy poet doth invent
He robs thee of and pays it thee again.
He lends thee virtue, and he stole that word
From thy behaviour; beauty doth he give,   10
And found it in thy cheek; he can afford
No praise to thee but what in thee doth live.
    Then thank him not for that which he doth
       say,
    Since what he owes thee thou thyself dost pay.

80

O, how I faint when I of you do write,
Knowing a better spirit doth use your name,
And in the praise thereof spends all his might
To make me tongue-tied, speaking of your fame!
But since your worth, wide as the ocean is,   5
The humble as the proudest sail doth bear,
My saucy bark, inferior far to his,
On your broad main doth wilfully appear.
Your shallowest help will hold me up afloat,
Whilst he upon your soundless deep doth ride;   10
Or, being wreck'd, I am a worthless boat,
He of tall building and of goodly pride.
    Then if he thrive and I be cast away,
    The worst was this: my love was my decay.

81

Or I shall live your epitaph to make,
Or you survive when I in earth am rotten;
From hence your memory death cannot take,
Although in me each part will be forgotten.

Your name from hence immortal life shall have,   5
Though I, once gone, to all the world must die:
The earth can yield me but a common grave,
When you entombed in men's eyes shall lie.
Your monument shall be my gentle verse,
Which eyes not yet created shall o'er-read,   10
And tongues to be your being shall rehearse
When all the breathers of this world are dead;
    You still shall live — such virtue hath my pen —
    Where breath most breathes, even in the mouths
      of men.

82

I grant thou wert not married to my Muse,
And therefore mayst without attaint o'erlook
The dedicated words which writers use
Of their fair subject, blessing every book.
Thou art as fair in knowledge as in hue,   5
Finding thy worth a limit past my praise,
And therefore art enforc'd to seek anew
Some fresher stamp of the time-bettering days.
And do so, love; yet when they have devis'd
What strained touches rhetoric can lend,   10
Thou, truly fair, wert truly sympathiz'd
In true plain words by thy true-telling friend;
    And their gross painting might be better us'd
    Where cheeks need blood; in thee it is abus'd.

83

I never saw that you did painting need,
And therefore to your fair no painting set;
I found, or thought I found, you did exceed
The barren tender of a poet's debt,
And therefore have I slept in your report,   5
That you yourself, being extant, well might show
How far a modern quill doth come too short,
Speaking of worth, what worth in you doth grow.
This silence for my sin you did impute,
Which shall be most my glory, being dumb;   10
For I impair not beauty being mute,
When others would give life and bring a tomb.
    There lives more life in one of your fair eyes
    Than both your poets can in praise devise.

84

Who is it that says most, which can say more
Than this rich praise: that you alone are you,
In whose confine immured is the store
Which should example where your equal grew?
Lean penury within that pen doth dwell   5
That to his subject lends not some small glory;

78, 3. **As:** that. **use:** habit.   4. **thee:** i.e., thy patronage.   **79,** 3. **gracious:** pleasing.   4. **give ... place:** give place to another.   5. **thy ... argument:** theme of thy beauty.   **80,** 2. **better spirit:** greater genius.   10. **soundless:** unfathomed.   14. **decay:** ruin.   **81,** 3, 5. **hence:** i.e., my poetry.   4. **part:** trait.   12. **world:** age.   **82,** 2. **attaint:** disgrace.   **o'erlook:** read.   5. **hue:** beauty.   11. **sympathiz'd:** matched.   **83,** 4. **tender:** offering.   5. **slept ... report:** neglected to praise you.   6. **That:** because.   7. **modern:** ordinary.   **84,** 1. **which:** who.   3. **store:** i.e., of beauty.   4. **example:** give example of, bear witness

But he that writes of you, if he can tell
That you are you, so dignifies his story.
Let him but copy what in you is writ,
Not making worse what nature made so clear,   10
And such a counterpart shall fame his wit,
Making his style admired everywhere.
   You to your beauteous blessings add a curse,
   Being fond on praise, which makes your praises
      worse.

85

My tongue-tied Muse in manners holds her still,
While comments of your praise, richly compil'd,
Reserve their character with golden quill
And precious phrase by all the Muses fil'd.
I think good thoughts whilst other write good words,
And, like unlettered clerk, still cry "Amen"   6
To every hymn that able spirit affords
In polish'd form of well-refined pen.
Hearing you prais'd, I say, "'Tis so, 'tis true,"
And to the most of praise add something more;   10
But that is in my thought, whose love to you,
Though words come hindmost, holds his rank
   before.
   Then others for the breath of words respect;
   Me for my dumb thoughts, speaking in effect.

86

Was it the proud full sail of his great verse,
Bound for the prize of all-too-precious you,
That did my ripe thoughts in my brain inhearse,
Making their tomb the womb wherein they grew?
Was it his spirit, by spirits taught to write   5
Above a mortal pitch, that struck me dead?
No, neither he, nor his compeers by night
Giving him aid, my verse astonished.
He, nor that affable familiar ghost
Which nightly gulls him with intelligence,   10
As victors of my silence cannot boast;
I was not sick of any fear from thence:
   But when your countenance fill'd up his line,
   Then lack'd I matter; that enfeebled mine.

87

Farewell! thou art too dear for my possessing,
And like enough thou know'st thy estimate.
The charter of thy worth gives thee releasing;
My bonds in thee are all determinate.
For how do I hold thee but by thy granting,   5
And for that riches where is my deserving?

The cause of this fair gift in me is wanting,
And so my patent back again is swerving.
Thyself thou gav'st, thy own worth then not knowing,
Or me, to whom thou gav'st it, else mistaking;   10
So thy great gift, upon misprision growing,
Comes home again, on better judgement making.
   Thus have I had thee as a dream doth flatter —
   In sleep a king, but waking no such matter.

88

When thou shalt be dispos'd to set me light
And place my merit in the eye of scorn,
Upon thy side against myself I'll fight
And prove thee virtuous, though thou art forsworn.
With mine own weakness being best acquainted,   5
Upon thy part I can set down a story
Of faults conceal'd, wherein I am attainted,
That thou in losing me shall win much glory.
And I by this will be a gainer too;
For, bending all my loving thoughts on thee,   10
The injuries that to myself I do,
Doing thee vantage, double-vantage me.
   Such is my love, to thee I so belong,
   That for thy right myself will bear all wrong.

89

Say that thou didst forsake me for some fault,
And I will comment upon that offence;
Speak of my lameness, and I straight will halt,
Against thy reasons making no defence.
Thou canst not, love, disgrace me half so ill,   5
To set a form upon desired change,
As I'll myself disgrace, knowing thy will.
I will acquaintance strangle and look strange,
Be absent from thy walks, and in my tongue
Thy sweet beloved name no more shall dwell,   10
Lest I, too much profane, should do it wrong
And haply of our old acquaintance tell.
   For thee against myself I'll vow debate,
   For I must ne'er love him whom thou dost hate.

90

Then hate me when thou wilt! if ever, now;
Now, while the world is bent my deeds to cross,
Join with the spite of fortune, make me bow,
And do not drop in for an after-loss.
Ah, do not, when my heart hath scap'd this sorrow,
Come in the rearward of a conquer'd woe;   6
Give not a windy night a rainy morrow,
To linger out a purpos'd overthrow.

---

10. **clear:** glorious.   11. **counterpart:** copy.   14. **Being fond:** doting.   **worse.** I.e., because the poets strain for effects. **85,** 1. **in manners:** modestly.   2. **compil'd:** composed.   3. **Reserve:** dignify. There may be an error; the sense of the line appears to be, "refine their writing (character) with eloquent pen."   4. **fil'd:** polished.   11. **But...thought:** i.e., but I do it silently.   12. **holds...before:** surpasses others' love.   14. **speaking in effect:** expressed in (my) actions.   **86,** 3. **in- hearse:** bury.   8. **astonished:** dismayed.   10. **gulls:** cheats.   **87,** 2. **estimate:** worth.   4. **determinate:** expired. 8. **patent:** privilege, title   11. **upon...growing:** originating in an error.   **88,** 1. **set me light:** esteem me little. 14. **right:** i.e., good, welfare.   **89,** 2. **comment:** expatiate.   4. **reasons:** assertions.   6. **form:** suitable appearance **& strange:** like a stranger.   13. **debate:** warfare.   **90,** 2. **cross:** thwart.   8. **linger out:** protract.

If thou wilt leave me, do not leave me last,
When other petty griefs have done their spite, 10
But in the onset come. So shall I taste
At first the very worst of fortune's might;
    And other strains of woe, which now seem woe,
    Compar'd with loss of thee will not seem so.

91

Some glory in their birth, some in their skill,
Some in their wealth, some in their bodies' force,
Some in their garments, though new-fangled ill,
Some in their hawks and hounds, some in their
    horse;
And every humour hath his adjunct pleasure, 5
Wherein it finds a joy above the rest:
But these particulars are not my measure;
All these I better in one general best.
Thy love is [better] than high birth to me,
Richer than wealth, prouder than garments'
    cost, 10
Of more delight than hawks or horses be;
And having thee, of all men's pride I boast;
    Wretched in this alone, that thou mayst take
    All this away and me most wretched make.

92

But do thy worst to steal thyself away,
For term of life thou art assured mine,
And life no longer than thy love will stay,
For it depends upon that love of thine.
Then need I not to fear the worst of wrongs, 5
When in the least of them my life hath end.
I see a better state to me belongs
Than that which on thy humour doth depend;
Thou canst not vex me with inconstant mind,
Since that my life on thy revolt doth lie. 10
O, what a happy title do I find,
Happy to have thy love, happy to die!
    But what's so blessed-fair that fears no blot?
    Thou mayst be false, and yet I know it not.

93

So shall I live, supposing thou art true,
Like a deceived husband; so love's face
May still seem love to me, though alter'd new —
Thy looks with me, thy heart in other place.
For there can live no hatred in thine eye; 5
Therefore in that I cannot know thy change.
In many's looks the false heart's history
Is writ in moods and frowns and wrinkles strange;
But heaven in thy creation did decree
That in thy face sweet love should ever dwell; 10

Whate'er thy thoughts or thy heart's workings be,
Thy looks should nothing thence but sweetness tell.
    How like Eve's apple doth thy beauty grow,
    If thy sweet virtue answer not thy show!

94

They that have pow'r to hurt and will do none,
That do not do the thing they most do show,
Who, moving others, are themselves as stone,
Unmoved, cold, and to temptation slow,
They rightly do inherit heaven's graces 5
And husband nature's riches from expense;
They are the lords and owners of their faces,
Others but stewards of their excellence.
The summer's flow'r is to the summer sweet
Though to itself it only live and die, 10
But if that flow'r with base infection meet,
The basest weed outbraves his dignity:
    For sweetest things turn sourest by their deeds;
    Lilies that fester smell far worse than weeds.

95

How sweet and lovely dost thou make the shame
Which, like a canker in the fragrant rose,
Doth spot the beauty of thy budding name!
O, in what sweets dost thou thy sins enclose!
That tongue that tells the story of thy days, 5
Making lascivious comments on thy sport,
Cannot dispraise but in a kind of praise;
Naming thy name blesses an ill report.
O, what a mansion have those vices got
Which for their habitation chose out thee, 10
Where beauty's veil doth cover every blot
And all things turns to fair that eyes can see!
    Take heed, dear heart, of this large privilege;
    The hardest knife ill-us'd doth lose his edge.

96

Some say thy fault is youth, some wantonness;
Some say thy grace is youth and gentle sport;
Both grace and faults are lov'd of more and less;
Thou mak'st faults graces that to thee resort.
As on the finger of a throned queen 5
The basest jewel will be well esteem'd,
So are those errors that in thee are seen
To truths translated and for true things deem'd.
How many lambs might the stern wolf betray
If like a lamb he could his looks translate! 10
How many gazers mightst thou lead away
If thou wouldst use the strength of all thy state!
    But do not so; I love thee in such sort
    As, thou being mine, mine is thy good report.

97

How like a winter hath my absence been
From thee, the pleasure of the fleeting year!
What freezings have I felt, what dark days seen!
What old December's bareness everywhere!
And yet this time remov'd was summer's time, 5
The teeming autumn, big with rich increase,
Bearing the wanton burden of the prime,
Like widowed wombs after their lords' decease.
Yet this abundant issue seem'd to me
But hope of orphans and unfathered fruit; 10
For summer and his pleasures wait on thee.
And, thou away, the very birds are mute;
    Or, if they sing, 'tis with so dull a cheer
    That leaves look pale, dreading the winter 's near.

98

From you have I been absent in the spring,
When proud-pied April, dress'd in all his trim,
Hath put a spirit of youth in everything,
That heavy Saturn laugh'd and leap'd with him.
Yet nor the lays of birds, nor the sweet smell 5
Of different flowers in odour and in hue,
Could make me any summer's story tell,
Or from their proud lap pluck them where they grew;
Nor did I wonder at the lily's white,
Nor praise the deep vermilion in the rose; 10
They were but sweet, but figures of delight
Drawn after you, you pattern of all those.
    Yet seem'd it winter still, and, you away,
    As with your shadow I with these did play.

99

The forward violet thus did I chide:
Sweet thief, whence didst thou steal thy sweet that
    smells,
If not from my love's breath? The purple pride
Which on thy soft cheek for complexion dwells
In my love's veins thou hast too grossly dy'd. 5
The lily I condemned for thy hand,
And buds of marjoram had stol'n thy hair:
The roses fearfully on thorns did stand,
[One] blushing shame, another white despair;
A third, nor red nor white, had stol'n of both 10
And to his robbery had annex'd thy breath;
But, for his theft, in pride of all his growth
A vengeful canker eat him up to death.
    More flowers I noted, yet I none could see
    But sweet or colour it had stol'n from thee.

100

Where art thou, Muse, that thou forget'st so long
To speak of that which gives thee all thy might?
Spend'st thou thy fury on some worthless song,
Dark'ning thy power to lend base subjects light?
Return, forgetful Muse, and straight redeem 5
In gentle numbers time so idly spent;
Sing to the ear that doth thy lays esteem
And gives thy pen both skill and argument.
Rise, resty Muse, my love's sweet face survey
If Time have any wrinkle graven there; 10
If any, be a satire to decay,
And make Time's spoils despised everywhere.
    Give my love fame faster than Time wastes life;
    So thou prevent'st his scythe and crooked knife.

101

O truant Muse, what shall be thy amends
For thy neglect of truth in beauty dy'd?
Both truth and beauty on my love depends;
So dost thou too, and therein dignifi'd.
Make answer, Muse: wilt thou not haply say, 5
"Truth needs no colour with his colour fix'd;
Beauty no pencil, beauty's truth to lay;
But best is best if never intermix'd"?
Because he needs no praise, wilt thou be dumb?
Excuse not silence so; for 't lies in thee 10
To make him much outlive a gilded tomb
And to be prais'd of ages yet to be.
    Then do thy office, Muse; I teach thee how
    To make him seem long hence as he shows now.

102

My love is strength'ned, though more weak in
    seeming;
I love not less, though less the show appear;
That love is merchandiz'd whose rich esteeming
The owner's tongue doth publish everywhere.
Our love was new and then but in the spring 5
When I was wont to greet it with my lays,
As Philomel in summer's front doth sing
And stops [her] pipe in growth of riper days:
Not that the summer is less pleasant now
Than when her mournful hymns did hush the night, 10
But that wild music burdens every bough
And sweets grown common lose their dear de-
    light.
    Therefore, like her, I sometime hold my tongue,
    Because I would not dull you with my song.

103

Alack, what poverty my Muse brings forth,
That having such a scope to show her pride,
The argument all bare is of more worth
Than when it hath my added praise beside!

97, 5. **remov'd:** of absence. 7. **prime:** Spring. 10. **hope of orphans:** expectation of posthumous children. **98,** 2. **proud-pied:** brilliantly multi-colored. 4. **Saturn:** an austere, gloomy god. **99.** This is Shakespeare's only fifteen-line sonnet. 1. **forward:** early. 6. **for:** i.e., for stealing (its whiteness from). 9. **[One]** (Sewell). *Our* Q. **100,** 6. **numbers:** verses. 8. **argument:** theme. 9. **resty:** sluggish. 11. **be ... to:** satirize. **101,** 4. **dignifi'd:** art dignified. 8. **intermix'd:** i.e., with praise. **102,** 3. **merchandiz'd:** commercialized. 7. **Philomel:** the nightingale. **front:** beginning. 8. **[her]** (ed. 1640). *his* Q.

O, blame me not, if I no more can write!   5
Look in your glass, and there appears a face
That over-goes my blunt invention quite,
Dulling my lines and doing me disgrace.
Were it not sinful then, striving to mend,
To mar the subject that before was well?   10
For to no other pass my verses tend
Than of your graces and your gifts to tell;
    And more, much more, than in my verse can sit
    Your own glass shows you when you look in it.

104

To me, fair friend, you never can be old,
For as you were when first your eye I ey'd,
Such seems your beauty still.   Three winters cold
Have from the forests shook three summers' pride,
Three beauteous springs to yellow autumn turn'd   5
In process of the seasons have I seen,
Three April perfumes in three hot Junes burn'd,
Since first I saw you fresh, which yet are green.
Ah! yet doth beauty, like a dial-hand,
Steal from his figure, and no pace perceiv'd;   10
So your sweet hue, which methinks still doth stand,
Hath motion, and mine eye may be deceiv'd;
    For fear of which, hear this, thou age unbred:
    Ere you were born was beauty's summer dead.

105

Let not my love be call'd idolatry,
Nor my beloved as an idol show,
Since all alike my songs and praises be
To one, of one, still such, and ever so.
Kind is my love to-day, to-morrow kind,   5
Still constant in a wondrous excellence;
Therefore my verse, to constancy confin'd,
One thing expressing, leaves out difference.
"Fair, kind, and true" is all my argument,
"Fair, kind, and true" varying to other words;
And in this change is my invention spent,   11
Three themes in one, which wondrous scope affords.
    "Fair, kind, and true" have often liv'd alone,
    Which three till now never kept seat in one.

106

When in the chronicle of wasted time
I see descriptions of the fairest wights,
And beauty making beautiful old rhyme
In praise of ladies dead and lovely knights;
Then, in the blazon of sweet beauty's best,   5
Of hand, of foot, of lip, of eye, of brow,
I see their antique pen would have express'd
Even such a beauty as you master now.

So all their praises are but prophecies
Of this our time, all you prefiguring;   10
And, for they look'd but with divining eyes,
They had not [skill] enough your worth to sing:
    For we, which now behold these present days,
    Have eyes to wonder, but lack tongues to praise.

107

Not mine own fears, nor the prophetic soul
Of the wide world, dreaming on things to come,
Can yet the lease of my true love control,
Suppos'd as forfeit to a confin'd doom.
The mortal moon hath her eclipse endur'd,   5
And the sad augurs mock their own presage;
Incertainties now crown themselves assur'd,
And peace proclaims olives of endless age.
Now with the drops of this most balmy time
My love looks fresh, and Death to me subscribes,   10
Since, spite of him, I'll live in this poor rhyme,
While he insults o'er dull and speechless tribes:
    And thou in this shalt find thy monument,
    When tyrants' crests and tombs of brass are spent.

108

What's in the brain that ink may character
Which hath not figur'd to thee my true spirit?
What's new to speak, what [new] to register,
That may express my love or thy dear merit?
Nothing, sweet boy; but yet, like prayers divine,   5
I must each day say o'er the very same,
Counting no old thing old, thou mine, I thine,
Even as when first I hallow'd thy fair name.
So that eternal love in love's fresh case
Weighs not the dust and injury of age,   10
Nor gives to necessary wrinkles place,
But makes antiquity for aye his page,
    Finding the first conceit of love there bred
    Where time and outward form would show it
    dead.

109

O, never say that I was false of heart,
Though absence seem'd my flame to qualify!
As easy might I from myself depart
As from my soul, which in thy breast doth lie.
That is my home of love; if I have rang'd,   5
Like him that travels I return again,
Just to the time, not with the time exchang'd,
So that myself bring water for my stain.
Never believe, though in my nature reign'd
All frailties that besiege all kinds of blood,   10

103, 7. over-goes: exceeds. 11. pass: end.   **104**, 14. summer: crown, perfection.   **105**, 8. difference: variety.
106, 1. wasted: by-gone. 2. wights: persons. 5. blazon: celebration. 8. master: possess. 11. divining: prophetic,
therefore distant. 12. [skill] (Tyrwhitt conj.). *still* Q.   **107**, 4. confin'd: early. 5. mortal moon. Generally
believed to refer to Queen Elizabeth, but there is no agreement as to the interpretation of the allusions in ll. 5–8. 10.
subscribes: submits. 12. speechless: inarticulate.   **108**, 1. character: write. 3. what [new] (Malone). *what now*
Q. 9. fresh case: perpetual vitality. 12. antiquity: old age. 13. conceit: conception, i.e., bloom.   **109**, 2. qualify:
moderate. 7. Just...time: punctually. exchang'd: altered. 10. blood: temperament.

That it could so preposterously be stain'd,
To leave for nothing all thy sum of good;
  For nothing this wide universe I call,
  Save thou, my rose; in it thou art my all.

110

Alas, 'tis true I have gone here and there
And made myself a motley to the view,
Gor'd mine own thoughts, sold cheap what is most
    dear,
Made old offences of affections new;
Most true it is that I have look'd on truth   5
Askance and strangely; but, by all above,
These blenches gave my heart another youth,
And worse essays prov'd thee my best of love.
Now all is done, have what shall have no end!
Mine appetite I never more will grind   10
On newer proof, to try an older friend,
A god in love, to whom I am confin'd.
  Then give me welcome, next my heaven the best,
  Even to thy pure and most most loving breast.

111

O, for my sake do you [with] Fortune chide,
The guilty goddess of my harmful deeds,
That did not better for my life provide
Than public means which public manners breeds.
Thence comes it that my name receives a brand,
And almost thence my nature is subdu'd   6
To what it works in, like the dyer's hand.
Pity me then and wish I were renew'd,
Whilst, like a willing patient, I will drink
Potions of eisel 'gainst my strong infection;   10
No bitterness that I will bitter think,
Nor double penance, to correct correction.
  Pity me then, dear friend, and I assure ye
  Even that your pity is enough to cure me.

112

Your love and pity doth th' impression fill
Which vulgar scandal stamp'd upon my brow·
For what care I who calls me well or ill,
So you o'er-green my bad, my good allow?
You are my all the world, and I must strive   5
To know my shames and praises from your tongue;
None else to me, nor I to none alive,
That my steel'd sense or changes right or wrong.

In so profound abysm I throw all care
Of others' voices, that my adder's sense   10
To critic and to flatterer stopped are.
Mark how with my neglect I do dispense:
  You are so strongly in my purpose bred
  That all the world besides, methinks, [are] dead.

113

Since I left you, mine eye is in my mind;
And that which governs me to go about
Doth part his function and is partly blind,
Seems seeing, but effectually is out;
For it no form delivers to the heart   5
Of bird, of flow'r, or shape, which it doth [latch].
Of his quick objects hath the mind no part,
Nor his own vision holds what it doth catch;
For if it see the rud'st or gentlest sight,
The most sweet favour or deformed'st creature,
The mountain or the sea, the day or night,   11
The crow or dove, it shapes them to your feature.
  Incapable of more, replete with you,
  My most true mind thus mak'th mine [eye] un-
    true.

114

Or whether doth my mind, being crown'd with you,
Drink up the monarch's plague, this flattery?
Or whether shall I say mine eye saith true,
And that your love taught it this alchemy,
To make of monsters and things indigest   5
Such cherubins as your sweet self resemble,
Creating every bad a perfect best,
As fast as objects to his beams assemble?
O, 'tis the first; 'tis flatt'ry in my seeing,
And my great mind most kingly drinks it up.   10
Mine eye well knows what with his gust is 'greeing
And to his palate doth prepare the cup.
  If it be poison'd, 'tis the lesser sin
  That mine eye loves it and doth first begin.

115

Those lines that I before have writ do lie,
Even those that said I could not love you dearer;
Yet then my judgement knew no reason why
My most full flame should afterwards burn clearer.
But reckoning Time, whose million'd accidents   5
Creep in 'twixt vows and change decrees of kings,

110, 2. a ... view: a public jester. 3. what ... dear: i.e., my emotions. 4. old ... new: new ties, offending old friends. 7. blenches: glances aside. 9. what ... end: i.e., my constant love. 11. proof: experiment. 111, 1. [with] (Gildon). *wish* Q. 4. public means: subsistence through pleasing the public. public manners: vulgar manners. 8. renew'd: cured. 10. eisel: vinegar. 12. Nor ... correction: nor will I refuse double penance, doubly to reform me. 112, 1. th' impression fill: efface the scar. 4. o'er-green: cover (as with grass). allow: approve. 7–8. None ... wrong: (for me) there is no one alive but us, and you alone can change my fixed opinions, right or wrong. 10. adder's sense. The adder was supposedly deaf. 12. with ... dispense: excuse my neglect. 14. [are] (Steevens). *y'are* Q. 113, 1. mine ... mind: what I see is your image. 3. part: divide. 4. effectually: really. 6. [latch] (Capell MS.): lay hold of. *lack* Q. 7. quick: rapidly presented. 14. [eye] (Capell MS.). Om. Q. 114, 1, 3. Or whether. A phrase used to introduce two alternatives. 1. crown'd with: intoxicated with thoughts of. 2. flattery: illusion (cf. 5–7, and 113:9–12). 5. indigest: formless. 11. gust: taste. 115, 5. reckoning: reckoning with.

Tan sacred beauty, blunt the sharp'st intents,
Divert strong minds to th' course of alt'ring
   things —
Alas, why, fearing of Time's tyranny,
Might I not then say, "Now I love you best."
When I was certain o'er incertainty,   11
Crowning the present, doubting of the rest?
  Love is a babe; then might I not say so,
  To give full growth to that which still doth grow

116

Let me not to the marriage of true minds
Admit impediments. Love is not love
Which alters when it alteration finds,
Or bends with the remover to remove. *Petrarchan*
O, no! it is an ever-fixèd mark   *likin to norm*   5
That looks on tempests and is never shaken;
It is the star to every wand'ring bark,
Whose worth's unknown, although his height be
  taken.
Love's not Time's fool, though rosy lips and cheeks
Within his bending sickle's compass come;   10
Love alters not with his brief hours and weeks,
But bears it out even to the edge of doom.
  If this be error and upon me proved,
  I never writ, nor no man ever loved.

117

Accuse me thus: that I have scanted all
Wherein I should your great deserts repay;
Forgot upon your dearest love to call,
Whereto all bonds do tie me day by day;
That I have frequent been with unknown minds,   5
And given to time your own dear-purchas'd right;
That I have hoisted sail to all the winds
Which should transport me farthest from your sight.
Book both my wilfulness and errors down,
And on just proof surmise accumulate;   10
Bring me within the level of your frown,
But shoot not at me in your wakened hate,
  Since my appeal says I did strive to prove
  The constancy and virtue of your love.

118

Like as, to make our appetites more keen,
With eager compounds we our palate urge;
As, to prevent our maladies unseen,
We sicken to shun sickness when we purge;
Even so, being full of your ne'er-cloying sweetness,
To bitter sauces did I frame my feeding,   6

And, sick of welfare, found a kind of meetness
To be diseas'd ere that there was true needing.
Thus policy in love, t' anticipate
The ills that were not, grew to faults assured,   10
And brought to medicine a healthful state
Which, rank of goodness, would by ill be cured;
  But thence I learn, and find the lesson true,
  Drugs poison him that so fell sick of you.

119

What potions have I drunk of Siren tears,
Distill'd from limbecks foul as hell within,
Applying fears to hopes and hopes to fears,
Still losing when I saw myself to win!
What wretched errors hath my heart committed,   5
Whilst it hath thought itself so blessed never!
How have mine eyes out of their spheres been fitted
In the distraction of this madding fever!
O benefit of ill! Now I find true
That better is by evil still made better;   10
And ruin'd love, when it is built anew,
Grows fairer than at first, more strong, far greater.
  So I return rebuk'd to my content,
  And gain by ills thrice more than I have spent.

120

That you were once unkind befriends me now,
And for that sorrow which I then did feel
Needs must I under my transgression bow,
Unless my nerves were brass or hammered steel.
For if you were by my unkindness shaken   5
As I by yours, you've pass'd a hell of time,
And I, a tyrant, have no leisure taken
To weigh how once I suffered in your crime.
O, that our night of woe might have rememb'red
My deepest sense, how hard true sorrow hits,   10
And soon to you, as you to me, then tend'red
The humble salve which wounded bosoms fits!
  But that your trespass now becomes a fee;
  Mine ransoms yours, and yours must ransom me.

121

'Tis better to be vile than vile esteemed
When not to be receives reproach of being,
And the just pleasure lost which is so deemed
Not by our feeling but by others' seeing.
For why should others' false adulterate eyes   5
Give salutation to my sportive blood?
Or on my frailties why are frailer spies,
Which in their wills count bad what I think good?

---

13. **then:** at that time (i.e., when "Love [was] a babe," as Cupid is represented). **might...so:** I ought not to have said so.   **116,** 4. **remover:** i.e., the inconstant one.   8. **Whose.** The antecedent is *star*.   12. **doom:** Doomsday. **117,** 5. **unknown minds:** nonentities.   6. **time:** the world.   9. **Book:** write, reckon.   10. **on...accumulate:** to what you can prove add what you suspect.   **118,** 2. **eager:** bitter.   7. **sick of welfare:** gorged with happiness.   11. **brought to medicine:** prescribed drugs for.   12. **rank:** too full.   **119,** 2. **limbecks:** alembics, stills.   7. **fitted:** convulsed. **120,** 2. **for...feel:** i.e., knowing how I suffered then, when *you* offended.   8. **weigh:** consider.   **crime:** offense against me.   9. **woe:** i.e., estrangement.   **rememb'red:** reminded.   **121,** 3. **so:** vile.   4. **seeing:** judgment.   6. **Give salutation to:** treat as akin (to their baseness).

No, I am that I am, and they that level
At my abuses reckon up their own;   10
I may be straight, though they themselves be bevel;
By their rank thoughts my deeds must not be
      shown, —
   Unless this general evil they maintain:
   All men are bad, and in their badness reign.

122

Thy gift, thy tables, are within my brain
Full character'd with lasting memory,
Which shall above that idle rank remain
Beyond all date, even to eternity;
Or, at the least, so long as brain and heart   5
Have faculty by nature to subsist.
Till each to raz'd oblivion yield his part
Of thee, thy record never can be miss'd.
That poor retention could not so much hold,
Nor need I tallies thy dear love to score;   10
Therefore to give them from me was I bold,
To trust those tables that receive thee more.
   To keep an adjunct to remember thee
   Were to import forgetfulness in me.

123

No, Time, thou shalt not boast that I do change.
Thy pyramids built up with newer might
To me are nothing novel, nothing strange;
They are but dressings of a former sight.
Our dates are brief, and therefore we admire   5
What thou dost foist upon us that is old,
And rather make them born to our desire
Than think that we before have heard them told.
Thy registers and thee I both defy,
Not wond'ring at the present nor the past,   10
For thy records and what we see doth lie,
Made more or less by thy continual haste.
   This I do vow and this shall ever be;
   I will be true, despite thy scythe and thee.

124

If my dear love were but the child of state,
It might for Fortune's bastard be unfather'd,
As subject to Time's love or to Time's hate,
Weeds among weeds, or flowers with flowers gath-
      er'd.
No, it was builded far from accident;   5
It suffers not in smiling pomp, nor falls

Under the blow of thralled discontent,
Whereto th' inviting time our fashion calls;
It fears not policy, that heretic,
Which works on leases of short-numb'red hours,   10
But all alone stands hugely politic,
That it nor grows with heat nor drowns with show-
      ers.
   To this I witness call the fools of Time,
   Which die for goodness, who have liv'd for crime.

125

Were 't aught to me I bore the canopy,
With my extern the outward honouring,
Or laid great bases for eternity,
Which proves more short than waste or ruining?
Have I not seen dwellers on form and favour   5
Lose all, and more, by paying too much rent
For compound sweet; forgoing simple savour,
Pitiful thrivers, in their gazing spent?
No, let me be obsequious in thy heart,
And take thou my oblation, poor but free,   10
Which is not mix'd with seconds, knows no art,
But mutual render, only me for thee.
   Hence, thou suborn'd informer! A true soul
   When most impeach'd stands least in thy control.

126

O thou, my lovely boy, who in thy power
Dost hold Time's fickle glass, his sickle, hour;
Who hast by waning grown, and therein show'st
Thy lovers withering as thy sweet self grow'st;
If Nature, sovereign mistress over wrack,   5
As thou goest onwards, still will pluck thee back,
She keeps thee to this purpose, that her skill
May Time disgrace and wretched [minutes] kill.
Yet fear her, O thou minion of her pleasure!
She may detain, but not still keep, her treasure;   10
Her audit, though delay'd, answer'd must be,
And her quietus is to render thee.

127

In the old age black was not counted fair,
Or if it were, it bore not beauty's name;
But now is black beauty's successive heir,
And beauty slander'd with a bastard shame:
For since each hand hath put on Nature's power, 5
Fairing the foul with Art's false borrow'd face,

9. **level:** aim. 11. **bevel:** slanting. 13. **general:** universal. **maintain:** prove. 14. **reign:** prosper (?).   **122,** 1. **tables:** notebooks. 2. **character'd:** lettered. 3. **idle rank:** useless series of pages. 9. **retention:** retainer. 12. **more:** more cap- ably. 13. **adjunct:** something outside myself. 14. **import:** imply.   **123,** 7. **make:** think. 11. **doth:** do. 12. **Made ... less:** magnified or dwarfed.   **124,** 1. **state:** circumstance. 2. **for ... unfather'd:** be branded as the fatherless son of Fortune. 8. **fashion:** fashionable life. 13. **fools of Time:** time-servers.   **125,** 1. **bore the canopy:** i.e., rendered homage. 2. **extern:** exterior. 7. **simple savour:** pure happiness. 11. **seconds:** baser matter. 13. **suborn'd:** false.   **126.** This poem of six couplets is omitted from the ed. of 1640. 2. **glass:** mirror. **hour:** hour-glass. 3. **by ... grown:** grown in beauty with becoming older. 8. **[minutes]** (Capell MS.). *minute* Q. 10. **still:** always. 12. **quietus:** discharge. **127,** 3. **successive:** by order of succession. 4. **beauty:** i.e., blonde beauty. 5. **put:** taken.

1 -

Sweet beauty hath no name, no holy bower,
But is profan'd, if not lives in disgrace.
Therefore my mistress' [brows] are raven black,
Her eyes so suited, and they mourners seem   10
At such who, not born fair, no beauty lack,
Sland'ring creation with a false esteem:
    Yet so they mourn, becoming of their woe,
    That every tongue says beauty should look so.

128

How oft, when thou, my music, music play'st,
Upon that blessed wood whose motion sounds
With thy sweet fingers, when thou gently sway'st
The wiry concord that mine ear confounds,
Do I envy those jacks that nimble leap   5
To kiss the tender inward of thy hand,
Whilst my poor lips, which should that harvest reap,
At the wood's boldness by thee blushing stand!
To be so tickl'd, they would change their state
And situation with those dancing chips,   10
O'er whom [thy] fingers walk with gentle gait,
Making dead wood more blest than living lips.
    Since saucy jacks so happy are in this,
    Give them [thy] fingers, me thy lips to kiss.

129

Th' expense of spirit in a waste of shame
Is lust in action; and till action, lust
Is perjur'd, murd'rous, bloody, full of blame,
Savage, extreme, rude, cruel, not to trust;
Enjoy'd no sooner but despised straight,   5
Past reason hunted, and no sooner had
Past reason hated, as a swallow'd bait
On purpose laid to make the taker mad;
[Mad] in pursuit and in possession so;
Had, having, and in quest to have, extreme;   10
A bliss in proof, and [prov'd, a] very woe;
Before, a joy propos'd; behind, a dream.
    All this the world well knows; yet none knows well
    To shun the heaven that leads men to this hell.

130

My mistress' eyes are nothing like the sun;
Coral is far more red than her lips' red;
If snow be white, why then her breasts are dun;
If hairs be wires, black wires grow on her head.
I have seen roses damask'd, red and white,   5
But no such roses see I in her cheeks;
And in some perfumes is there more delight
Than in the breath that from my mistress reeks.

I love to hear her speak, yet well I know
That music hath a far more pleasing sound;   10
I grant I never saw a goddess go;
My mistress, when she walks, treads on the ground:
    And yet, by heaven, I think my love as rare
    As any she beli'd with false compare.

131

Thou art as tyrannous, so as thou art,
As those whose beauties proudly make them cruel;
For well thou know'st to my dear doting heart
Thou art the fairest and most precious jewel.
Yet, in good faith, some say that thee behold   5
Thy face hath not the power to make love groan;
To say they err I dare not be so bold,
Although I swear it to myself alone.
And to be sure that is not false I swear,
A thousand groans, but thinking on thy face,   10
One on another's neck, do witness bear
Thy black is fairest in my judgement's place.
    In nothing art thou black save in thy deeds,
    And thence this slander, as I think, proceeds.

132

Thine eyes I love, and they, as pitying me,
Knowing thy heart torments me with disdain,
Have put on black and loving mourners be,
Looking with pretty ruth upon my pain.
And truly not the morning sun of heaven   5
Better becomes the grey cheeks of the east,
Nor that full star that ushers in the even
Doth half that glory to the sober west,
As those two mourning eyes become thy face.
O, let it then as well beseem thy heart   10
To mourn for me, since mourning doth thee grace,
And suit thy pity like in every part.
    Then will I swear beauty herself is black
    And all they foul that thy complexion lack.

133

Beshrew that heart that makes my heart to groan
For that deep wound it gives my friend and me!
Is 't not enough to torture me alone,
But slave to slavery my sweet'st friend must be?
Me from myself thy cruel eye hath taken,   5
And my next self thou harder hast engrossed:
Of him, myself, and thee, I am forsaken;
A torment thrice threefold thus to be crossed.
Prison my heart in thy steel bosom's ward,
But then my friend's heart let my poor heart bail;   10

7. **name**: repute. 8. **profan'd**: desecrated. 9. **[brows]** (Staunton conj.). *eyes* Q. 10. **suited**: matching. 11. **no ...lack**: i.e., because they use cosmetics. 13. **becoming of**: adorned by. **128,** 2. **wood**: the keys of the spinet or virginal. 5. **jacks**: (here) keys. **129,** 1. **spirit**: vital energy. 9. **[Mad]** (Gildon). *Made* Q. 10. **extreme**: violent. 11. **[prov'd, a]** (Capell MS.). *proud and* Q. **130,** 5. **damask'd**: mingled red and white. **131,** 1. **so...art**: just as you are (dark and not beautiful). 8. **alone**: privately. 10. **but...on**: when I but think of. 11. **One...neck**: in quick succession. **132,** 12. **suit thy pity**: let thy pity wear similar mourning. **133,** 4. **slave to slavery**: doubly enslaved. 6. **next**: second. 10. **bail**: liberate, go bail for.

Whoe'er keeps me, let my heart be his guard.
Thou canst not then use rigour in my gaol;
    And yet thou wilt, for I, being pent in thee,
    Perforce am thine, and all that is in me.

134

So, now I have confess'd that he is thine
And I myself am mortgag'd to thy will,
Myself I'll forfeit, so that other mine
Thou wilt restore, to be my comfort still.
But thou wilt not, nor he will not be free,   5
For thou art covetous and he is kind;
He learn'd but surety-like to write for me
Under that bond that him as fast doth bind.
The statute of thy beauty thou wilt take,
Thou usurer, that put'st forth all to use,   10
And sue a friend came debtor for my sake;
So him I lose through my unkind abuse.
    Him have I lost; thou hast both him and
        me:
    He pays the whole, and yet am I not free.

135

Whoever hath her wish, thou hast thy *Will*,
And *Will* to boot, and *Will* in overplus;
More than enough am I that vex thee still,
To thy sweet will making addition thus.
Wilt thou, whose will is large and spacious,   5
Not once vouchsafe to hide my will in thine?
Shall will in others seem right gracious,
And in my will no fair acceptance shine?
The sea, all water, yet receives rain still
And in abundance addeth to his store;   10
So thou, being rich in *Will*, add to thy *Will*
One will of mine, to make thy large *Will* more.
    Let no unkind, no fair beseechers kill;
    Think all but one, and me in that one *Will*.

136

If thy soul check thee that I come so near,
Swear to thy blind soul that I was thy *Will*,
And will, thy soul knows, is admitted there;
Thus far for love my love-suit, sweet, fulfil.
Will will fulfil the treasure of thy love,   5
Ay, fill it full with wills, and my will one.
In things of great receipt with ease we prove
Among a number one is reckon'd none:
Then in the number let me pass untold,
Though in thy store's account I one must be;   10

For nothing hold me, so it please thee hold
That nothing me, a something sweet to thee.
    Make but my name thy love and love that still,
    And then thou lov'st me, for my name is *Will*.

137

Thou blind fool, Love, what dost thou to mine eyes
That they behold, and see not what they see?
They know what beauty is, see where it lies,
Yet what the best is take the worst to be.
If eyes, corrupt by over-partial looks,   5
Be anchor'd in the bay where all men ride,
Why of eyes' falsehood hast thou forged hooks,
Whereto the judgement of my heart is tied?
Why should my heart think that a several plot
Which my heart knows the wide world's common
        place?   10
Or mine eyes seeing this, say this is not,
To put fair truth upon so foul a face?
    In things right true my heart and eyes have erred,
    And to this false plague are they now transferred.

138

When my love swears that she is made of truth,
I do believe her, though I know she lies,
That she might think me some untutor'd youth,
Unlearned in the world's false subtleties.
Thus vainly thinking that she thinks me young,   5
Although she knows my days are past the best,
Simply I credit her false-speaking tongue:
On both sides thus is simple truth suppress'd.
But wherefore says she not she is unjust?
And wherefore say not I that I am old?   10
O, love's best habit is in seeming trust,
And age in love loves not to have years told:
    Therefore I lie with her and she with me,
    And in our faults by lies we flattered be.

139

O, call not me to justify the wrong
That thy unkindness lays upon my heart;
Wound me not with thine eye but with thy tongue,
Use power with power and slay me not by art.
Tell me thou lov'st elsewhere, but in my sight,   5
Dear heart, forbear to glance thine eye aside;
What need'st thou wound with cunning when thy
        might
Is more than my o'er-press'd defence can bide?
Let me excuse thee: ah! my love well knows
Her pretty looks have been mine enemies,   10

134, 3. **other mine:** my other self.   7. **surety-like:** as a guarantor.   **write:** endorse (my bond)   9. **statute:** security.
10. **to use:** at interest.   11. **came:** who became.   12. **my . . . abuse:** the unkind mistreatment of me.   **135**, 1. *Will:*
carnal desire.   2. *Will* **to boot:** another *Will* also (the friend).   *Will:* Shakespeare.   In this sonnet and in 136 and 143,
the capitalization and italics are from Q.   **136**, 1. **check:** upbraid.   7. **receipt:** capacity.   9. **untold:** uncounted.
13. **my name:** i.e., your own will.   **137**, 4. **what . . . be:** take the worst for the best.   7. **eyes' falsehood:** my
eyes' false admiration.   9. **several:** private.   14. **this . . . plague:** the penalty of (always) judging falsely.   **138,**
7. **Simply:** foolishly.   9. **unjust:** untrue.   11. **habit:** behavior.   **seeming:** simulated.   **139**, 4. **with power:**
energetically.

And therefore from my face she turns my foes,
That they elsewhere might dart their injuries.
  Yet do not so; but since I am near slain,
  Kill me outright with looks and rid my pain.

140

Be wise as thou art cruel; do not press
My tongue-tied patience with too much disdain,
Lest sorrow lend me words, and words express
The manner of my pity-wanting pain.
If I might teach thee wit, better it were,   5
Though not to love, yet, love, to tell me so;
As testy sick men, when their deaths be near,
No news but health from their physicians know;
For if I should despair, I should grow mad,
And in my madness might speak ill of thee;   10
Now this ill-wresting world is grown so bad,
Mad slanderers by mad ears believed be.
  That I may not be so, nor thou beli'd,
  Bear thine eyes straight, though thy proud heart
    go wide.

141

In faith, I do not love thee with mine eyes,
For they in thee a thousand errors note;
But 'tis my heart that loves what they despise,
Who, in despite of views, is pleas'd to dote.
Nor are mine ears with thy tongue's tune delighted;
Nor tender feeling, to base touches prone,   6
Nor taste, nor smell, desire to be invited
To any sensual feast with thee alone;
But my five wits nor my five senses can
Dissuade one foolish heart from serving thee,   10
Who leaves unsway'd the likeness of a man,
Thy proud heart's slave and vassal wretch to be.
  Only my plague thus far I count my gain,
  That she that makes me sin awards me pain.

142

Love is my sin, and thy dear virtue hate,
Hate of my sin, grounded on sinful loving:
O, but with mine compare thou thine own state,
And thou shalt find it merits not reproving;
Or, if it do, not from those lips of thine,   5
That have profan'd their scarlet ornaments
And seal'd false bonds of love as oft as mine,
Robb'd others' beds' revenues of their rents.
Be it lawful I love thee, as thou lov'st those
Whom thine eyes woo as mine importune thee.   10
Root pity in thy heart, that, when it grows,
Thy pity may deserve to pitied be.
  If thou dost seek to have what thou dost hide,
  By self-example mayst thou be deni'd!

143

Lo! as a careful housewife runs to catch
One of her feathered creatures broke away,
Sets down her babe and makes all swift dispatch
In pursuit of the thing she would have stay,
Whilst her neglected child holds her in chase,   5
Cries to catch her whose busy care is bent
To follow that which flies before her face,
Not prizing her poor infant's discontent;
So runn'st thou after that which flies from thee,
Whilst I, thy babe, chase thee afar behind;   10
But if thou catch thy hope, turn back to me,
And play the mother's part, kiss me, be kind:
  So will I pray that thou mayst have thy *Will*,
  If thou turn back and my loud crying still.

144

Two loves I have of comfort and despair,
Which like two spirits do suggest me still:
The better angel is a man right fair,
The worser spirit a woman colour'd ill.
To win me soon to hell, my female evil   5
Tempteth my better angel from my [side],
And would corrupt my saint to be a devil,
Wooing his purity with her foul pride.
And whether that my angel be turn'd fiend
Suspect I may, yet not directly tell;   10
But being both from me, both to each friend,
I guess one angel in another's hell.
  Yet this shall I ne'er know, but live in doubt,
  Till my bad angel fire my good one out.

145

Those lips that Love's own hand did make
Breath'd forth the sound that said "I hate"
To me that languish'd for her sake;
But when she saw my woeful state,
Straight in her heart did mercy come,   5
Chiding that tongue that, ever sweet,
Was us'd in giving gentle doom,
And taught it thus anew to greet:
"I hate" she alter'd with an end
That follow'd it as gentle day   10
Doth follow night, who like a fiend
From heaven to hell is flown away;
  "I hate" from hate away she threw,
  And saved my life, saying "not you."

146

Poor soul, the centre of my sinful earth,
[...] these rebel powers that thee array!
Why dost thou pine within and suffer dearth,
Painting thy outward walls so costly gay?

140, 4. **pity-wanting:** unpitied. 6. **Though ... love:** even if you don't love me. **so:** that you do. 11. **ill-wresting:** that puts a bad construction on everything.   **141,** 11. **Who ... man:** which (my heart) leaves me ungoverned and merely the semblance of a man.   **142,** 2. **grounded ... loving:** i.e., which (sin) is illicit love. 13. **hide:** refuse.
143, 8. **prizing:** regarding.   **144,** 2. **suggest:** tempt. 6. **[side]** (ed. 1640). *sight* Q. 11. **each friend:** each other friendly.
145, 13. **from hate:** from hateful meaning.   **146,** 1. **earth:** body. 2. **[...]** *My sinfull earth* Q. Numberless suggestions have been made from Malone's *Fool'd by* to Pooler's *Rebuke*. **rebel:** contrary to your welfare.

Why so large cost, having so short a lease,   5
Dost thou upon thy fading mansion spend?
Shall worms, inheritors of this excess,
Eat up thy charge?   Is this thy body's end?
Then, soul, live thou upon thy servant's loss,
And let that pine to aggravate thy store;   10
Buy terms divine in selling hours of dross:
Within be fed, without be rich no more.
   So shalt thou feed on Death that feeds on men,
   And Death once dead, there's no more dying then.

147

My love is as a fever, longing still
For that which longer nurseth the disease,
Feeding on that which doth preserve the ill,
Th' uncertain sickly appetite to please.
My reason, the physician to my love,   5
Angry that his prescriptions are not kept,
Hath left me, and I desperate now approve
Desire is death, which physic did except.
Past cure I am, now reason is past care,
And frantic-mad with evermore unrest;   10
My thoughts and my discourse as madmen's are,
At random from the truth vainly express'd;
   For I have sworn thee fair and thought thee bright,
   Who art as black as hell, as dark as night.

148

O me, what eyes hath Love put in my head,
Which have no correspondence with true sight!
Or, if they have, where is my judgement fled,
That censures falsely what they see aright?
If that be fair whereon my false eyes dote,   5
What means the world to say it is not so?
If it be not, then love doth well denote
Love's eye is not so true as all men's: no,
How can it?   O, how can Love's eye be true,
That is so vex'd with watching and with tears?   10
No marvel then, though I mistake my view;
The sun itself sees not till heaven clears.
   O cunning Love! with tears thou keep'st me
      blind,
   Lest eyes well-seeing thy foul faults should find.

149

Canst thou, O cruel! say I love thee not,
When I against myself with thee partake?
Do I not think on thee, when I forgot
Am of myself, all tyrant, for thy sake?
Who hateth thee that I do call my friend?   5
On whom frown'st thou that I do fawn upon?

Nay, if thou lour'st on me, do I not spend
Revenge upon myself with present moan?
What merit do I in myself respect,
That is so proud thy service to despise,   10
When all my best doth worship thy defect,
Commanded by the motion of thine eyes?
   But, love, hate on, for now I know thy mind;
   Those that can see thou lov'st, and I am blind.

150

O, from what power hast thou this powerful might
With insufficiency my heart to sway?
To make me give the lie to my true sight,
And swear that brightness doth not grace the day?
Whence hast thou this becoming of things ill,   5
That in the very refuse of thy deeds
There is such strength and warrantise of skill
That, in my mind, thy worst all best exceeds?
Who taught thee how to make me love thee more
The more I hear and see just cause of hate?   10
O, though I love what others do abhor,
With others thou shouldst not abhor my state:
   If thy unworthiness rais'd love in me,
   More worthy I to be belov'd of thee.

151

Love is too young to know what conscience is;
Yet who knows not conscience is born of love?
Then, gentle cheater, urge not my amiss,
Lest guilty of my faults thy sweet self prove:
For, thou betraying me, I do betray   5
My nobler part to my gross body's treason;
My soul doth tell my body that he may
Triumph in love; flesh stays no farther reason,
But, rising at thy name, doth point out thee
As his triumphant prize.   Proud of this pride,   10
He is contented thy poor drudge to be,
To stand in thy affairs, fall by thy side.
   No want of conscience holds it that I call
   Her "love" for whose dear love I rise and fall.

152

In loving thee thou know'st I am forsworn,
But thou art twice forsworn, to me love swearing;
In act thy bed-vow broke, and new faith torn
In vowing new hate after new love bearing.
But why of two oaths' breach do I accuse thee,   5
When I break twenty?   I am perjur'd most;
For all my vows are oaths but to misuse thee,
And all my honest faith in thee is lost;

   8. **charge:** expense.   9. **thy servant's:** the body's.   10. **aggravate:** increase.   11. **terms divine:** eternity.   **147,** 1.
still: ever.   7–8. **I...except:** I, now despairing, find by experience that desire (love), rejecting the medicine of reason,
brings death.   9. **care:** caring (for me).   **148,** 4. **censures:** judges.   10. **watching:** wakefulness.   11. **my view:** what
I see.   **149,** 2. **partake:** take sides.   4. **all tyrant:** thou complete tyrant.   9. **respect:** value.   11. **defect:** insufficiency
(cf. 150:2).   **150,** 2. **With:** i.e., despite your.   7. **warrantise:** pledge, surety.   14. **More worthy I:** i.e., because of
my unworthiness.   **151,** 3. **urge:** stress.   **amiss:** fault.   10. **Proud of:** swelling with.   **152,** 7. **are...thee:** i.e., have
misrepresented thee, who art false.

For I have sworn deep oaths of thy deep kind-
    ness,
Oaths of thy love, thy truth, thy constancy,   10
And, to enlighten thee, gave eyes to blindness,
Or made them swear against the thing they see;
    For I have sworn thee fair; more perjur'd I,
    To swear against the truth so foul a lie!

153

Cupid laid by his brand and fell asleep.
A maid of Dian's this advantage found.
And his love-kindling fire did quickly steep
In a cold valley-fountain of that ground;
Which borrow'd from this holy fire of Love   5
A dateless lively heat, still to endure,
And grew a seething bath, which yet men prove
Against strange maladies a sovereign cure.
But at my mistress' eye Love's brand new-fired,
The boy for trial needs would touch my breast;

I, sick withal, the help of bath desired,   11
And thither hied, a sad distemper'd guest,
    But found no cure: the bath for my help lies
    Where Cupid got new fire — my mistress' [eyes].

154

The little Love-god lying once asleep
Laid by his side his heart-inflaming brand,
Whilst many nymphs that vow'd chaste life to keep
Came tripping by; but in her maiden hand
The fairest votary took up that fire   5
Which many legions of true hearts had warm'd;
And so the general of hot desire
Was, sleeping, by a virgin hand disarm'd.
This brand she quenched in a cool well by,
Which from Love's fire took heat perpetual,   10
Growing a bath and healthful remedy
For men diseas'd; but I, my mistress' thrall,
    Came there for cure, and this by that I prove:
    Love's fire heats water, water cools not love.

153, 7. prove: find by experience.   14. [eyes] (ed. 1640).   *eye* Q.

A Lover's Complaint

THIS POEM is appended to the *Sonnets* in the edition of 1609, and is there ascribed to Shakespeare. No external evidence of the date of composition exists, and no contemporary allusion confirms the ascription of authorship. The pastoralism and some of the diction are reminiscent of Spenser, but the poem surely cannot be his. A tortuous and often clumsy compression, which occasional beauty cannot redeem, mars the style.

Chapman has been proclaimed the author, and his title denied, with equal confidence. If the poem is by Shakespeare — and his claim is as good as anybody's — a plausible conjecture is that he wrote it at a period not far removed from the date of his *Venus and Adonis*. And in this connection it is perhaps significant that the stanza used in *Lucrece* is here employed.

From off a hill whose concave womb re-worded
A plaintful story from a sist'ring vale,
My spirits t' attend this double voice accorded,
And down I laid to list the sad-tun'd tale;
Ere long espied a fickle maid full pale,   5
Tearing of papers, breaking rings a-twain,
Storming her world with sorrow's wind and rain.

Upon her head a platted hive of straw,
Which fortified her visage from the sun,
Whereon the thought might think sometime it
    saw   10
The carcass of a beauty spent and done.
Time had not [scythed] all that youth begun,
Nor youth all quit; but, spite of heaven's fell rage,
Some beauty peep'd through lattice of sear'd age.

Oft did she heave her napkin to her eyne,   15
Which on it had conceited characters,
Laund'ring the silken figures in the brine
That seasoned woe had pelleted in tears,
And often reading what contents it bears;
As often shrieking undistinguish'd woe   20
In clamours of all size, both high and low.

Sometimes her levell'd eyes their carriage ride,
As they did batt'ry to the spheres intend;
Sometimes diverted their poor balls are tied
To th' orbed earth; sometimes they do extend   25
Their view right on; anon their gazes lend
To every place at once, and, nowhere fix'd,
The mind and sight distractedly commix'd.

Her hair, nor loose nor tied in formal plat,
Proclaim'd in her a careless hand of pride;   30
For some, untuck'd, descended her sheav'd hat,
Hanging her pale and pined cheek beside;
Some in her threaden fillet still did bide
And, true to bondage, would not break from
    thence,
Though slackly braided in loose negligence.   35

A thousand favours from a maund she drew,
Of amber, crystal, and of [beaded] jet,
Which one by one she in a river threw,
Upon whose weeping margent she was set,
Like usury, applying wet to wet,   40
Or monarch's hands that lets not bounty fall
Where want cries some but where excess begs all.

1. **re-worded**: repeated, echoed. 2. **sist'ring**: neighboring. 3. **accorded**: consented. 5. **fickle**: agitated. 7. **storming her world**: creating a storm in herself. 8. **hive**: head-covering (cf. *sheav'd hat*, l. 31). 10. **thought**: mind. 11. **done**: decayed. 12. **[scythed]** (Ewing). *sithed* Q. 13. **Nor . . . quit**: nor had youthfulness all disappeared. **fell**: cruel. 14. **sear'd**: withered. 15. **napkin**: handkerchief. **eyne**: eyes. 16. **conceited characters**: fanciful markings. 18. **pelleted in tears**: made into round tears. 20. **undistinguish'd**: inarticulate. 22. **levell'd**: aimed. This word and others in this passage are from gunnery. 24. **diverted**: turned (downward). 30. **a . . . pride**: a calculated carelessness. 31. **sheav'd**: made of straw. 33. **threaden**: woven of threads. 36. **maund**: basket. 37. **[beaded]** (Sewell). *bedded* Q. 39. **weeping margent**: bank wet with her tears. 42. **cries**: calls out for.

Of folded schedules had she many a one,
Which she perus'd, sigh'd, tore, and gave the flood;
Crack'd many a ring of posied gold and bone, 45
Bidding them find their sepulchres in mud;
Found yet moe letters sadly penn'd in blood,
With sleided silk feat and affectedly
Enswath'd, and seal'd to curious secrecy.

These often bath'd she in her fluxive eyes, 50
And often kiss'd, and often [gan] to tear;
Cried, "O false blood, thou register of lies,
What unapproved witness dost thou bear!
Ink would have seem'd more black and damned
        here!"
This said, in top of rage the lines she rents, 55
Big discontent so breaking their contents.

A reverend man that graz'd his cattle nigh —
Sometime a blusterer that the ruffle knew
Of court, of city, and had let go by
The swiftest hours, observed as they flew — 60
Towards this afflicted fancy fastly drew,
And, privileg'd by age, desires to know
In brief the grounds and motives of her woe.

So slides he down upon his grained bat,
And comely-distant sits he by her side; 65
When he again desires her, being sat,
Her grievance with his hearing to divide:
If that from him there may be aught appli'd
Which may her suffering ecstasy assuage,
'Tis promis'd in the charity of age. 70

"Father," she says, "though in me you behold
The injury of many a blasting hour,
Let it not tell your judgement I am old;
Not age, but sorrow, over me hath power.
I might as yet have been a spreading flower, 75
Fresh to myself, if I had self-appli'd
Love to myself and to no love beside.

"But woe is me! too early I attended
A youthful suit — it was to gain my grace —
[Of one] by nature's outwards so commended 80
That maidens' eyes stuck over all his face.
Love lack'd a dwelling and made him her place;

And when in his fair parts she did abide,
She was new lodg'd and newly deifi'd.

"His browny locks did hang in crooked curls, 85
And every light occasion of the wind
Upon his lips their silken parcels hurls.
What's sweet to do, to do will aptly find.
Each eye that saw him did enchant the mind,
For on his visage was in little drawn 90
What largeness thinks in Paradise was sawn.

"Small show of man was yet upon his chin;
His phœnix down began but to appear
Like unshorn velvet on that termless skin,
Whose bare out-bragg'd the web it seem'd to wear;
Yet show'd his visage by that cost more dear, 96
And nice affections wavering stood in doubt
If best were as it was, or best without.

"His qualities were beauteous as his form,
For maiden-tongu'd he was, and thereof free; 100
Yet, if men mov'd him, was he such a storm
As oft 'twixt May and April is to see,
When winds breathe sweet, unruly though they be.
His rudeness so with his authoriz'd youth
Did livery falseness in a pride of truth. 105

"Well could he ride, and often men would say,
'That horse his mettle from his rider takes,
Proud of subjection, noble by the sway,
What rounds, what bounds, what course, what stop
        he makes!'
And controversy hence a question takes, 110
Whether the horse by him became his deed,
Or he his manage by th' well-doing steed.

"But quickly on this side the verdict went:
His real habitude gave life and grace
To appertainings and to ornament, 115
Accomplish'd in himself, not in his case;
All aids, themselves made fairer by their place,
[Came] for additions; yet their purpos'd trim
Piec'd not his grace, but were all grac'd by him.

"So on the tip of his subduing tongue 120
All kind of arguments and question deep,

43. **schedules:** slips of paper with writing. 45. **posied:** inscribed with mottoes (*posies*). 48. **sleided:** divided into threads. **feat:** neatly. **affectedly:** lovingly. 49. **curious:** careful. 50. **fluxive:** flowing (with tears). 51. **[gan]** (Malone). *gaue* Q. 53. **unapproved:** unsupported (by action). 58. **ruffle:** bustling life. 60. **observed:** i.e., though learning from them. 61. **fancy:** love-sick lady (lit., *love*). 64. **grained bat:** staff with the grain of the wood visible. 67. **divide:** share. 69. **her ...ecstasy:** the madness of her sorrow. 78. **attended:** heeded. 80. **[Of one]** (Tyrwhitt conj.). *done* Q. 81. **stuck... all:** were riveted to. 88. **to...find:** i.e., will readily find people to do it. 91. **What...sawn:** i.e., the beauty that a large imagination would think was to be seen in Eden. 93. **phœnix:** of this peerless creature. 94. **termless:** indescribable. 95. **bare out-bragg'd:** bareness excelled. **web:** i.e., covering. 96. **cost:** ornament. 101. **mov'd:** angered. 104-105. **His ...truth:** his youth, excusing his roughness, arrayed his falseness in the proud dress of truth. 108. **by the sway:** because of his control. 110-112. **And...steed:** and thus it was debated whether his steed performed so well because of his horsemanship, or whether he managed so well because he had a well-trained steed. 114. **habitude:** personality. 116. **case:** situation, i.e., having so good a horse. 118. **[Came]** (Sewell): counted. *Can* Q. **trim:** adornment. 119. **Piec'd:** made up. 121. **question:** talk.

All replication prompt and reason strong,
For his advantage still did wake and sleep.
To make the weeper laugh, the laugher weep,
He had the dialect and different skill, 125
Catching all passions in his craft of will,

"That he did in the general bosom reign
Of young, of old; and sexes both enchanted
To dwell with him in thoughts, or to remain
In personal duty, following where he haunted. 130
Consents bewitch'd, ere he desire, have granted;
And dialogu'd for him what he would say,
Ask'd their own wills, and made their wills obey.

"Many there were that did his picture get
To serve their eyes, and in it put their mind; 135
Like fools that in th' imagination set
The goodly objects which abroad they find
Of lands and mansions, theirs in thought assign'd,
And labouring in moe pleasures to bestow them
Than the true gouty landlord which doth owe
    them. 140

"So many have, that never touch'd his hand,
Sweetly suppos'd them mistress of his heart.
My woeful self, that did in freedom stand
And was my own fee-simple, not in part,
What with his art in youth and youth in art, 145
Threw my affections in his charmed power,
Reserv'd the stalk and gave him all my flower.

"Yet did I not, as some my equals did,
Demand of him, nor being desired yielded;
Finding myself in honour so forbid, 150
With safest distance I mine honour shielded.
Experience for me many bulwarks builded
Of proofs new-bleeding, which remain'd the foil
Of this false jewel, and his amorous spoil.

"But, ah, who ever shunn'd by precedent 155
The destin'd ill she must herself assay?
Or forc'd examples, 'gainst her own content,
To put the by-past perils in her way?
Counsel may stop awhile what will not stay;
For when we rage, advice is often seen, 160
By blunting us, to make our wits more keen.

"Nor gives it satisfaction to our blood
That we must curb it upon others' proof,

To be forbod the sweets that seem so good
For fear of harms that preach in our behoof. 165
O appetite, from judgement stand aloof!
The one a palate hath that needs will taste,
Though Reason weep and cry, 'It is thy last.'

"For further I could say, 'This man's untrue,'
And knew the patterns of his foul beguiling; 170
Heard where his plants in others' orchards grew;
Saw how deceits were gilded in his smiling;
Knew vows were ever brokers to defiling;
Thought characters and words merely but art,
And bastards of his foul adulterate heart. 175

"And long upon these terms I held my city,
Till thus he gan besiege me: 'Gentle maid,
Have of my suffering youth some feeling pity,
And be not of my holy vows afraid.
That's to ye sworn to none was ever said; 180
For feasts of love I have been call'd unto,
Till now did ne'er invite, nor never [woo].

"'All my offences that abroad you see
Are errors of the blood, none of the mind;
Love made them not; with acture they may be 185
Where neither party is nor true nor kind.
They sought their shame that so their shame did
    find;
And so much less of shame in me remains
By how much of me their reproach contains.

"'Among the many that mine eyes have seen, 190
Not one whose flame my heart so much as warmed,
Or my affection put to th' smallest teen,
Or any of my leisures ever charmed.
Harm have I done to them, but ne'er was harmed;
Kept hearts in liveries, but mine own was free
And reign'd, commanding in his monarchy. 196

"'Look here, what tributes wounded fancies sent
    me,
Of pallid pearls and rubies red as blood,
Figuring that they their passions likewise lent
    me
Of grief and blushes, aptly understood 200
In bloodless white and the encrimson'd mood;
Effects of terror and dear modesty,
Encamp'd in hearts, but fighting outwardly.

---

122. replication: repartee. 125. different: diverse. 126. craft of will: powerful influence. 127. That: so that. 130. duty: attendance. haunted: went, frequented. 131. Consents: consenting persons. 132. dialogu'd: expressed, imagined. 138. theirs...assign'd: pretending that they own them. 140. owe: own. 144. was...part: had complete, not divided, power over myself. 148. my equals: i.e., girls of my own age. 149. being desired: i.e., at his first request. 153. proofs: examples. 157. forc'd: urged. content: desires. 158. put...way: set the past dangers (of others) as deterrents in her own way. 159. stay: be prevented altogether. 161. blunting: opposing. 162. blood: passions. 164. forbod: forbidden. 173. brokers: agents, go-betweens. 174. characters: letters. 182. [woo] (Capell MS.). vow Q. 185. with...be: they may be enacted. 188–189. And...contains: i.e., the greater the blame they put on me, the less my shame. 192. teen: sorrow. 195. liveries: i.e., servitude. 200. understood: symbolized.

"'And, lo, behold these talents of their hair,
With twisted metal amorously impleach'd,   205
I have receiv'd from many a several fair,
Their kind acceptance weepingly beseech'd,
With the annexions of fair gems enrich'd,
And deep-brain'd sonnets that did amplify
Each stone's dear nature, worth, and quality.   210

"'The diamond — why, 'twas beautiful and hard,
Whereto his invis'd properties did tend;
The deep-green em'rald, in whose fresh regard
Weak sights their sickly radiance do amend;
The heaven-hu'd sapphire and the opal blend   215
With objects manifold: each several stone,
With wit well blazon'd, smil'd or made some moan.

"'Lo, all these trophies of affections hot,
Of pensiv'd and subdu'd desires the tender,
Nature hath charg'd me that I hoard them not,
But yield them up where I myself must render,   221
That is, to you, my origin and ender;
For these, of force, must your oblations be,
Since I their altar, you enpatron me.   224

"'O, then, advance of yours that phraseless hand,
Whose white weighs down the airy scale of praise;
Take all these similes to your own command,
[Hallowed] with sighs that burning lungs did raise;
What me, your minister, for you obeys,
Works under you; and to your audit comes   230
Their distract parcels in combined sums.

"'Lo, this device was sent me from a nun,
Or sister sanctified, of holiest note,
Which late her noble suit in court did shun,
Whose rarest havings made the blossoms dote;   235
For she was sought by spirits of richest coat,
But kept cold distance, and did thence remove
To spend her living in eternal love.

"'But, O my sweet, what labour is 't to leave
The thing we have not, mast'ring what not strives,
Playing the place which did no form receive,   241
Playing patient sports in unconstrained gyves?
She that her fame so to herself contrives,
The scars of battle scapeth by the flight,
And makes her absence valiant, not her might.   245

"'O, pardon me, in that my boast is true:
The accident which brought me to her eye
Upon the moment did her force subdue,
And now she would the caged cloister fly.
Religious love put out Religion's eye.   250
Not to be tempted would she be immur'd,
And now, to tempt, all liberty procur'd.

"'How mighty then you are, O, hear me tell!
The broken bosoms that to me belong
Have emptied all their fountains in my well,   255
And mine I pour your ocean all among.
I strong o'er them, and you o'er me being strong,
Must for your victory us all congest,
As compound love to physic your cold breast.

"'My parts had pow'r to charm a sacred [nun],
Who, disciplin'd, ay, dieted in grace,   261
Believ'd her eyes when they t' assail begun,
All vows and consecrations giving place.
O most potential love! vow, bond, nor space,
In thee hath neither sting, knot, nor confine;   265
For thou art all, and all things else are thine.

"'When thou impressest, what are precepts worth
Of stale example? When thou wilt inflame,
How coldly those impediments stand forth
Of wealth, of filial fear, law, kindred, fame!   270
Love's arms are peace, 'gainst rule, 'gainst sense,
        'gainst shame,
And sweetens, in the suff'ring pangs it bears,
The aloes of all forces, shocks, and fears.

"'Now all these hearts that do on mine depend,
Feeling it break, with bleeding groans they pine;
And supplicant their sighs to you extend   276
To leave the batt'ry that you make 'gainst mine,
Lending soft audience to my sweet design,
And credent soul to that strong-bonded oath
That shall prefer and undertake my troth.'   280

"This said, his wat'ry eyes he did dismount,
Whose sights till then were levell'd on my face;
Each cheek a river running from a fount
With brinish current downward flow'd apace.
O, how the channel to the stream gave grace!   285

---

204. **talents:** treasures, precious cuttings.   205. **impleach'd:** entwined.   209. **amplify:** fully interpret.   212. **invis'd:** unseen.   215–216. **blend With:** i.e., accompanied.   217. **blazon'd:** interpreted, i.e., in the "deep-brain'd sonnets" (l. 209).   219. **pensiv'd:** sad.   **tender:** offerings.   224. **I . . . me:** I am the altar on which they were offered up, and you are my patron saint.   225. **phraseless:** indescribable (cf. *termless*, l. 94).   226. **airy:** verbal.   227. **similes:** i.e., the symbolical gems and the explanatory poems.   228. **[Hallowed]** (Sewell).   *Hollowed* Q.   229–230. **What . . . you:** whatever, instead of serving *you*, serves *me*, who am your servant, is really at *your* service; i.e., things given to me are really yours.   231. **distract:** separate, individual.   234. **suit:** suitors.   235. **havings:** endowments.   **blossoms:** i.e., courtiers.   236. **richest coat:** highest rank (*coat* = coat of arms).   240. **not strives:** involves no struggle.   241. **Playing . . . receive.** Corrupt. By the emendation *Paling*, Malone obtained a forced sense: "securing within the pale of a cloister that heart which had never received the impression of love."   242. **unconstrained gyves:** voluntary fetters.   243. **contrives:** i.e., reserves, secures.   258. **congest:** collect.   260. **[nun]** (Malone conj.).   *Sunne* Q.   271. **are peace:** i.e., secure a peaceful mind (for lovers). But Malone's conjecture, *are proof* is very plausible.   **'gainst:** in spite of.   273. **aloes:** bitterness.   275. **bleeding groans.** A sigh was thought to cost the heart a drop of blood.   280. **prefer:** put forth.   **undertake:** guarantee.

Who glaz'd with crystal gate the glowing roses
That flame through water which their hue encloses.

"O father, what a hell of witchcraft lies
In the small orb of one particular tear!
But with the inundation of the eyes   290
What rocky heart to water will not wear?
What breast so cold that is not warmed here?
O cleft effect! cold modesty, hot wrath,
Both fire from hence and chill extincture hath.

"For, lo, his passion, but an art of craft,   295
Even there resolv'd my reason into tears;
There my white stole of chastity I daff'd,
Shook off my sober guards and civil fears;
Appear to him, as he to me appears,
All melting; though our drops this diff'rence bore:
His poison'd me, and mine did him restore.   301

"In him a plentitude of subtle matter,
Applied to cautels, all strange forms receives,
Of burning blushes, or of weeping water,
Or [swooning] paleness; and he takes and leaves,
In either's aptness, as it best deceives,   306
To blush at speeches rank, to weep at woes,
Or to turn white and swoon at tragic shows;

"That not a heart which in his level came
Could scape the hail of his all-hurting aim,   310
Showing fair nature is both kind and tame;
And, veil'd in them, did win whom he would
    maim.
Against the thing he sought he would exclaim;
When he most burn'd in heart-wish'd luxury,
He preach'd pure maid, and prais'd cold chastity.

"Thus merely with the garment of a Grace   316
The naked and concealed fiend he cover'd;
That th' unexperient gave the tempter place,
Which like a cherubin above them hover'd.
Who, young and simple, would not be so
    lover'd?   320
Ay me! I fell; and yet do question make
What I should do again for such a sake.

"O, that infected moisture of his eye,
O, that false fire which in his cheek so glow'd,
O, that forc'd thunder from his heart did fly,   325
O, that sad breath his spongy lungs bestow'd,
O, all that borrowed motion seeming ow'd,
Would yet again betray the fore-betray'd
And new pervert a reconciled maid!"   329

286. **Who.** The antecedent is *stream*, and the sense is that his tears made his cheeks look like roses seen through glass. 293. **cleft:** twofold. 296. **resolv'd:** melted. 298. **civil:** grave. 302. **matter:** i.e., craft, cunning. 303. **cautels:** deceits. 305. **[swooning]** (Sewell). *sounding* Q. 305–306. **he...deceives:** according as each (of these tricks) served his deceitful purpose, he used it or omitted it. 307. **rank:** gross. 309. **level:** range. 312. **them:** the *strange forms* of l. 303. 314. **luxury:** lust. 316. **merely:** completely. 318. **unexperient:** inexperienced. 320. **so lover'd:** provided with such a lover. 323. **infected:** false. 327. **borrowed:** feigned. **ow'd:** owned, i.e., natural. 329. **reconciled:** repentant; one whose sin has been absolved and expiated.

The Passionate Pilgrim

THE VOLUME entitled "*The Passionate Pilgrim.* By William Shakespeare" is a small piratical octavo printed for William Jaggard in 1599. Of the second edition no copy is known for certain to have survived, although a unique fragment of what may be the second edition is bound up with a copy of the first now in the Folger Library. A third edition, also ascribed to Shakespeare, appeared in 1612, with unacknowledged additions from Thomas Heywood. Heywood, claiming to speak for Shakespeare as well as himself, protested against the theft, and a new title page was printed without Shakespeare's name. In 1640 the contents were again reprinted, along with Shakespeare's Sonnets and other miscellaneous poems.

The whole of the first edition is here reprinted, although of its twenty poems only five are indisputably Shakespeare's. Of these, Nos. I and II appeared later as Sonnets 138 and 144 in the edition of 1609, with slight differences which may illustrate what happens to the texts of poems when they are circulated in manuscript, as Meres tells us that Shakespeare's Sonnets had been. Nos. III, V, and XVI are from *Love's Labour's Lost* (IV.iii.60–73; IV.ii.109–122; and IV.iii.101–120 respectively), with variations which suggest that they too were printed from copies in private circulation rather than from the Quarto of the play. Nos. IV, VI, IX, and XI, being variations on the theme of Venus and Adonis, are thus affiliated with Shakespeare's narrative poem. Although they are somewhat flat, there is nothing in their style to preclude Shakespeare's authorship, and one might regard them as preliminary sketches for the longer work if it were not for the fact that No. XI appears as the third sonnet in Bartholomew Griffin's *Fidessa* (1596), which raises the more plausible belief that they were all from the latter's hand. But Shakespeare may, of course, have been responsible for one or more of them. Nos. VIII and XX are by Richard Barnefield, printed among his *Poems: In diuers humors* (1598), and No. XVII has frequently been assigned to him. No. XIX is by Marlowe, and its last stanza, "Love's Answer," is the first in a poem ascribed by Walton to Raleigh. Of the authorship of the remaining poems (Nos. VII, X, XII, XIII, XIV, XV, and XVIII) nothing is known; in the consensus of recent opinion the likelihood that Shakespeare wrote any of them is exceedingly small. "Sonnets to Sundry Notes of Music" is merely the title of the second part of *The Passionate Pilgrim.*

THE PASSIONATE PILGRIM

I

When my love swears that she is made of truth,
I do believe her, though I know she lies,
That she might think me some untutor'd youth,
Unskilful in the world's false forgeries.
Thus vainly thinking that she thinks me young,
Although I know my years be past the best, 6
I, smiling, credit her false-speaking tongue,
Outfacing faults in love with love's ill rest.
But wherefore says my love that she is young?
And wherefore say not I that I am old? 10
O, love's best habit is a soothing tongue,
And age, in love, loves not to have years told.
    Therefore I'll lie with love, and love with me,
    Since that our faults in love thus smother'd
    be.

II

Two loves I have, of comfort and despair, 15
That like two spirits do suggest me still;
My better angel is a man right fair,
My worser spirit a woman colour'd ill.
To win me soon to hell, my female evil
Tempteth my better angel from my side, 20
And would corrupt my saint to be a devil,
Wooing his purity with her fair pride.
And whether that my angel be turn'd fiend,
Suspect I may, yet not directly tell;
For being both to me, both to each friend, 25
I guess one angel in another's hell.
    The truth I shall not know, but live in doubt,
    Till my bad angel fire my good one out.

III

Did not the heavenly rhetoric of thine eye,
'Gainst whom the world could not hold argument,
Persuade my heart to this false perjury? 31
Vows for thee broke deserve not punishment.

A woman I forswore; but I will prove,
Thou being a goddess, I forswore not thee:
My vow was earthly, thou a heavenly love; 35
Thy grace being gain'd cures all disgrace in me.
My vow was breath, and breath a vapour is;
Then, thou fair sun, that on this earth doth shine,
Exhale this vapour vow; in thee it is:
If broken then, it is no fault of mine; 40
    If by me broke, what fool is not so wise
    To break an oath to win a paradise?

IV

Sweet Cytherea, sitting by a brook
With young Adonis, lovely, fresh, and green,
Did court the lad with many a lovely look, 45
Such looks as none could look but beauty's queen.
She told him stories to delight his [ear];
She show'd him favours to allure his eye;
To win his heart she touch'd him here and there —
Touches so soft still conquer chastity. 50
But whether unripe years did want conceit,
Or he refus'd to take her figured proffer,
The tender nibbler would not touch the bait,
But smile and jest at every gentle offer.
    Then fell she on her back, fair queen, and toward:
    He rose and ran away; ah, fool too froward! 56

V

If love make me forsworn, how shall I swear to love?
O never faith could hold, if not to beauty vowed:
Though to myself forsworn, to thee I'll constant
    prove;
Those thoughts, to me like oaks, to thee like osiers
    bowed. 60
Study his bias leaves and makes his book thine
    eyes,
Where all those pleasures live that art can com-
    prehend.

---

4. **forgeries:** deceits. 8. **with:** along with. **rest:** remainder(?) 11. **habit:** behavior. **soothing:** flattering. 12. **told:** counted. 16. **suggest:** tempt. 24. **directly:** precisely. 25. **being ... friend:** since they are friends to me and friendly to each other. 26. **in ... hell:** i.e., in a hell prepared by the other. 39. **Exhale:** draw up. 44. **green:** young. 45. **lovely:** amorous. 47. **[ear]** (Malone). *eares.* Octavo₁. 51. **conceit:** power of imagination. 52. **figured:** i.e., indirect. 55. **toward:** willing. 61. **Study:** i.e., the student. **bias:** bent, i.e., chosen study. 62. **art:** learning.

If knowledge be the mark, to know thee shall suf-
fice;
Well learned is that tongue that well can thee com-
mend;
All ignorant that soul that sees thee without won-
der; 65
Which is to me some praise, that I thy parts admire.
Thine eye Jove's lightning seems, thy voice his
dreadful thunder,
Which, not to anger bent, is music and sweet fire.
　Celestial as thou art, O do not love that wrong,
　To sing heaven's praise with such an earthly
　　tongue. 70

VI

Scarce had the sun dried up the dewy morn,
And scarce the herd gone to the hedge for shade,
When Cytherea, all in love forlorn,
A longing tarriance for Adonis made
Under an osier growing by a brook, 75
A brook where Adon us'd to cool his spleen.
Hot was the day; she hotter that did look
For his approach that often there had been.
Anon he comes, and throws his mantle by,
And stood stark naked on the brook's green brim. 80
The sun look'd on the world with glorious eye,
Yet not so wistly as this queen on him.
　He, spying her, bounc'd in whereas he stood.
　"O Jove," quoth she, "why was not I a flood?"

VII

Fair is my love, but not so fair as fickle; 85
Mild as a dove, but neither true nor trusty;
Brighter than glass, and yet, as glass is, brittle;
Softer than wax, and yet, as iron, rusty:
　A lily pale, with damask dye to grace her;
　None fairer, nor none falser to deface her. 90

Her lips to mine how often hath she joined,
Between each kiss her oaths of true love swearing!
How many tales to please me hath she coined,
Dreading my love, the loss whereof still fearing!
　Yet in the midst of all her pure protestings, 95
　Her faith, her oaths, her tears, and all were jest-
　　ings.

She burn'd with love, as straw with fire flameth;
She burn'd out love, as soon as straw out-burneth;
She fram'd the love, and yet she foil'd the framing;
She bade love last, and yet she fell a-turning. 100
　Was this a lover, or a lecher whether?
　Bad in the best, though excellent in neither.

[VIII]

If music and sweet poetry agree,
As they must needs, the sister and the brother,
Then must the love be great 'twixt thee and me, 105
Because thou lov'st the one, and I the other.
Dowland to thee is dear, whose heavenly touch
Upon the lute doth ravish human sense;
Spenser to me, whose deep conceit is such
As, passing all conceit, needs no defence. 110
Thou lov'st to hear the sweet melodious sound
That Phœbus' lute, the queen of music, makes;
And I in deep delight am chiefly drown'd
Whenas himself to singing he betakes.
　One god is god of both, as poets feign; 115
　One knight loves both, and both in thee remain.

IX

Fair was the morn when the fair queen of love,

. 　 . 　 . 　 . 　 . 　 . 　 . 　 . 　 .

Paler for sorrow than her milk-white dove,
For Adon's sake, a youngster proud and wild, 120
Her stand she takes upon a steep-up hill.
Anon Adonis comes with horn and hounds;
She, silly queen, with more than love's good will,
Forbade the boy he should not pass those grounds.
"Once," quoth she, "did I see a fair sweet youth 125
Here in these brakes deep-wounded with a boar,
Deep in the thigh, a spectacle of ruth!
See, in my thigh," quoth she, "here was the sore."
　She showed hers: he saw more wounds than one,
　And blushing fled and left her all alone. 130

X

Sweet rose, fair flower, untimely pluck'd, soon
　faded;
Pluck'd in the bud, and faded in the spring!
Bright orient pearl, alack, too timely shaded!
Fair creature, kill'd too soon by death's sharp sting!
　Like a green plum that hangs upon a tree, 135
　And falls through wind before the fall should
　　be.

I weep for thee, and yet no cause I have,
For why thou [left'st] me nothing in thy will;
And yet thou [left'st] me more than I did crave,
For why I craved nothing of thee still. 140
　O yes, dear friend, I pardon crave of thee,
　Thy discontent thou didst bequeath to me.

[XI]

Venus, with young Adonis sitting by her
Under a myrtle shade, began to woo him.

---

82. **wistly**: intently. 83. **whereas**: where. 89. **damask**: pale red. 90. **to . . . her**: i.e., to her disgrace. 101. **whether**:
which one? 105. **thee**. Barnefield addressed this poem to R. L. (probably Richard Linch), a minor poet, whose Sonnets
were printed in 1596. 107. **Dowland**: a famous composer and lutanist. 109, 110. **conceit . . . conceit**: imagination . . .
conception. 116. **knight**. Sir George Carey has been suggested. 133. **timely**: early. 138, 140. **For why**: because.
138, 139. **[left'st]** (Malone). *lefts* Octavo₁.

She told the youngling how god Mars did try
her,   145
And as he fell to her, [so fell she] to him.
"Even thus," quoth she, "the warlike god em-
brac'd me,"
And then she clipp'd Adonis in her arms;
"Even thus," quoth she, "the warlike god unlac'd
me,"
As if the boy should use like loving charms;   150
"Even thus," quoth she, "he seized on my lips,"
And with her lips on his did act the seizure:
And as she fetched breath, away he skips,
And would not take her meaning nor her pleasure.
   Ah, that I had my lady at this bay,   155
   To kiss and clip me till I run away!

XII

Crabbed age and youth cannot live together:
Youth is full of pleasance, age is full of care;
Youth like summer morn, age like winter weather;
Youth like summer brave, age like winter bare.
Youth is full of sport, age's breath is short; 161
   Youth is nimble, age is lame;
Youth is hot and bold, age is weak and cold;
   Youth is wild, and age is tame.
Age, I do abhor thee; youth, I do adore thee;   165
   O, my love, my love is young!
Age, I do defy thee: O, sweet shepherd, hie thee,
   For methinks thou [stay'st] too long.

XIII

Beauty is but a vain and doubtful good;
A shining gloss that fadeth suddenly;   170
A flower that dies when first it gins to bud;
A brittle glass that's broken presently:
   A doubtful good, a gloss, a glass, a flower,
   Lost, faded, broken, dead within an hour.

And as goods lost are seld or never found,   175
As faded gloss no rubbing will refresh,
As flowers dead lie withered on the ground,
As broken glass no [cement] can redress,

So beauty blemish'd once for ever lost,
In spite of physic, painting, pain, and cost.   180

XIV

Good-night, good rest. Ah, neither be my share!
She bade good-night that kept my rest away;
And daff'd me to a cabin hang'd with care,
To descant on the doubts of my decay.
   "Farewell," quoth she, "and come again to-
      morrow."   185
Fare well I could not, for I supp'd with sorrow.

Yet at my parting sweetly did she smile,
In scorn or friendship, nill I construe whether.
'T may be, she joy'd to jest at my exile,
'T may be, again to make me wander thither: 190
   "Wander," a word for shadows like myself,
   As take the pain but cannot pluck the pelf.

Lord, how mine eyes throw gazes to the east!
My heart doth charge the watch; the morning rise
Doth cite each moving sense from idle rest.   195
Not daring trust the office of mine eyes,
   While Philomela sits and sings, I sit and mark,
   And wish her lays were tuned like the lark;

For she doth welcome daylight with her ditty,
And drives away dark dreaming night.   200
The night so pack'd, I post unto my pretty;
Heart hath his hope, and eyes their wished sight:
   Sorrow chang'd to solace, and solace mix'd with
      sorrow;
   For why, she sigh'd and bade me come to-morrow.

Were I with her, the night would post too soon; 205
But now are minutes added to the hours;
To spite me now, each minute seems [a moon];
Yet not for me, shine sun to succour flowers!
   Pack night, peep day; good day, of night now
      borrow:
   Short, night, to-night; and length thyself, to-
      morrow.   210

SONNETS TO SUNDRY NOTES OF MUSIC

[xv]

It was a lording's daughter, the fairest one of three,
That liked of her master as well as well might be,
Till looking on an Englishman, the fair'st that eye
   could see,
   Her fancy fell a-turning.

Long was the combat doubtful that love with love
   did fight,   215
To leave the master loveless, or kill the gallant
   knight:
To put in practice either, alas, it was a spite
   Unto the silly damsel!

146. **he:** Mars. **him:** Adonis. **[so fell she]** (Griffin). *she fell* Octavo₁. 155. **bay:** close quarters. 168. **[stay'st]** (Ewing): delayest. *staies* Octavo₁. 172. **presently:** instantly. 178. **[cement]** (Sewell). *symant* Octavo₁. 183. **daff'd:** sent off. 184. **descant:** comment. 192. **As:** who. 194. **charge the watch:** bid the watchman to announce the dawn. 195. **cite:** summon. 197. **Philomela:** the nightingale. **sits and.** Clark and Wright suggest the omission of these words. 199. **she:** the lark. 201. **pack'd:** departed (cf. *pack*, l. 209). 207. **[a moon]** (Steevens conj.). *an houre* Octavo₁. 210. **short:** be short. 212. **master:** tutor.

But one must be refused; more mickle was the
  pain
That nothing could be used to turn them both to
  gain,   220
For of the two the trusty knight was wounded with
  disdain:
  Alas, she could not help it!
Thus art with arms contending was victor of the
  day,
Which by a gift of learning did bear the maid away,
Then, lullaby, the learned man hath got the lady
  gay;   225
  For now my song is ended.

XVI

On a day, alack the day!
Love, whose month was ever May,
Spied a blossom passing fair,
Playing in the wanton air.   230
Through the velvet leaves the wind,
All unseen, gan passage find;
That the lover, sick to death,
Wish'd himself the heaven's breath.
"Air," quoth he, "thy cheeks may blow;   235
Air, would I might triumph so!
But, alas! my hand hath sworn
Ne'er to pluck thee from thy [thorn];
Vow, alack! for youth unmeet,
Youth, so apt to pluck a sweet.   240
Thou for whom Jove would swear
Juno but an Ethiope were;
And deny himself for Jove,
Turning mortal for thy love."

[XVII]

My flocks feed not,   245
My ewes breed not,
My rams speed not,
  All is amiss;
Love is dying,
Faith's defying,   250
Heart's [renying],
  Causer of this.
All my merry jigs are quite forgot,
All my lady's love is lost, God wot.
Where her faith was firmly fix'd in love,   255
There a nay is plac'd without remove.
One silly cross
Wrought all my loss;
  O frowning Fortune, cursed, fickle dame!
For now I see   260
Inconstancy
  More in women than in men remain.

In black mourn I,
All fears scorn I,
Love hath forlorn me,   265
  Living in thrall;
Heart is bleeding,
All help needing,
O cruel speeding,
  Fraughted with gall.   270
My shepherd's pipe can sound no deal;
My wether's bell rings doleful knell;
My curtal dog, that wont to have play'd,
Plays not at all, but seems afraid;
With sighs so deep   275
Procures to weep,
  In howling wise, to see my doleful plight.
How sighs resound
Through heartless ground,
  Like a thousand vanquish'd men in bloody
  fight!   280

Clear wells spring not,
Sweet birds sing not,
Green plants bring not
  Forth their dye;
Herds stand weeping,   285
Flocks all sleeping.
Nymphs [back] peeping
  Fearfully.
All our pleasure known to us poor swains,
All our merry meetings on the plains,   290
All our evening sport from us is fled,
All our love is lost, for Love is dead.
Farewell, sweet [lass],
Thy like ne'er was
  For a sweet content, the cause of all my [moan].
Poor Corydon   296
Must live alone;
  Other help for him I see that there is none.

XVIII

Whenas thine eye hath chose the dame,
And stall'd the deer that thou shouldst strike,   300
Let reason rule things worthy blame,
As well as fancy, [partial like].
  Take counsel of some wiser head,
  Neither too young nor yet unwed.

And when thou com'st thy tale to tell,   305
Smooth not thy tongue with filed talk,
Lest she some subtle practice smell, —
A cripple soon can find a halt; —
  But plainly say thou lov'st her well,
  And set thy person forth to sell.   310

---

238. [thorn] (Malone). *throne* Octavo₁. 251. [renying] (Malone): disowning. *nenying* Octavo₁. 265. **forlorn**: forsaken. 270. **fraughted**: loaded. 271. **no deal**: not at all. 273. **curtal**: with a docked tail. 276. **Procures**: contrives. 287. [back] (Malone). *blacke* Octavo₁. 293. [lass] (Malone). *loue* Octavo₁. 295. [moan] (Malone). *woe* Octavo₁. 300. **stall'd**: come within range of. 302. **fancy**: love. [partial like] (MS. owned by Samuel Lysons, quoted by Malone). *party all might* Octavo₁. 306. **filed**: polished. 310. **to sell**: i.e., advantageously.

What though her frowning brows be bent,
Her cloudy looks will calm ere night;
And then too late she will repent
That thus dissembled her delight;
    And twice desire, [ere] it be day,   315
    That which with scorn she put away.

What though she strive to try her strength,
And ban and brawl, and say thee nay,
Her feeble force will yield at length,
When craft hath taught her thus to say: 320
    "Had women been so strong as men,
    In faith, you had not had it then."

And to her will frame all thy ways;
Spare not to spend, and chiefly there
Where thy desert may merit praise,   325
By ringing in thy lady's ear.
    The strongest castle, tower, and town,
    The golden bullet beats it down.

Serve always with assured trust,
And in thy suit be humble true;   330
Unless thy lady prove unjust,
Press never thou to choose a new.
    When time shall serve, be thou not slack
    To proffer, though she put thee back.

The wiles and guiles that women work,   335
Dissembled with an outward show,
The tricks and toys that in them lurk,
The cock that treads them shall not know.
    Have you not heard it said full oft,
    A woman's nay doth stand for nought?   340

Think women seek to strive with men
To sin, and never for to saint:
[Here] is no heaven; [they] holy then
{Begin, when age doth] them attaint.
    Were kisses all the joys in bed,   345
    One woman would another wed.

But, soft! enough — too much, I fear —
Lest that my mistress hear my song;
She will not stick to [wring my ear],
To teach my tongue to be so long.   350
    Yet will she blush, here be it said,
    To hear her secrets so bewray'd.

XIX

Live with me, and be my love,
And we will all the pleasures prove

That hills and valleys, dales and fields,   355
And all the craggy mountains yields.

There will we sit upon the rocks,
And see the shepherds feed their flocks
By shallow rivers, by whose falls
Melodious birds sing madrigals.   360

There will I make thee a bed of roses,
With a thousand fragrant posies;
A cap of flowers, and a kirtle
Embroidered all with leaves of myrtle;

A belt of straw and ivy buds,   365
With coral clasps and amber studs;
And if these pleasures may thee move,
Then live with me and be my love.

LOVE'S ANSWER

If that the world and love were young,
And truth in every shepherd's tongue,   370
These pretty pleasures might me move
To live with thee and be thy love.

XX

As it fell upon a day
In the merry month of May,
Sitting in a pleasant shade   375
Which a grove of myrtles made,
Beasts did leap and birds did sing,
Trees did grow and plants did spring;
Every thing did banish moan,
Save the nightingale alone.   380
She, poor bird, as all forlorn,
Lean'd her breast up-till a thorn,
And there sung the dolefull'st ditty,
That to hear it was great pity.
"Fie, fie, fie," now would she cry;   385
"Tereu, tereu!" by and by;
That to hear her so complain,
Scarce I could from tears refrain;
For her griefs, so lively shown,
Made me think upon mine own.   390
Ah, thought I, thou mourn'st in vain!
None takes pity on thy pain.
Senseless trees they cannot hear thee;
Ruthless beasts, they will not cheer thee.
King Pandion he is dead;   395
All thy friends are lapp'd in lead;
All thy fellow birds do sing,
Careless of thy sorrowing.

314. **That**: that she. 315. **[ere]** (Ed. 1640). *yer* Octavo₁. 318. **ban**: curse. 337. **toys**: whims. 343. **[Here]** ... **[they]** (Lysons MS.). *There ... by* Octavo₁. 344. **[Begin ... doth]** (Lysons MS.). *When time with age shall* Octavo₁. 349. **[wring my ear]** (Halliwell-Phillipps): box my ear. *round me on the ear* Octavo₁. 382. **up-till**: against. 395. **Pandion**: the father of Philomela, who died prematurely from grief over the ravishing of his daughter. 396. **lapp'd**: entombed. 398. After this line, a version in *England's Helicon* (1600) inserts *Even so, poor bird, like thee, None alive will pity me.*

Whilst as fickle Fortune smil'd,
Thou and I were both beguil'd.   400
Every one that flatters thee
Is no friend in misery.
Words are easy, like the wind;
Faithful friends are hard to find:
Every man will be thy friend   405
Whilst thou hast wherewith to spend;
But if store of crowns be scant,
No man will supply thy want.
If that one be prodigal,
Bountiful they will him call,   410
And with such-like flattering,
"Pity but he were a king!"
If he be addict to vice,

Quickly him they will entice;
If to women he be bent,   415
They have at commandement;
But if Fortune once do frown,
Then farewell his great renown;
They that fawn'd on him before
Use his company no more.   420
He that is thy friend indeed,
He will help thee in thy need:
If thou sorrow, he will weep;
If thou wake, he cannot sleep;
Thus of every grief in heart   425
He with thee doth bear a part.
These are certain signs to know
Faithful friend from flatt'ring foe.

The Phœnix and the Turtle

THIS POEM, with Shakespeare's name attached, appeared in Robert Chester's *Loves Martyr: Or, Rosalins Complaint. Allegorically shadowing the truth of Loue, in the constant Fate of the Phœnix and Turtle.* Besides Chester's own work, the volume contained verses on the Phœnix and the Turtle attributed to Shakespeare, Marston, Chapman, Jonson, and "Ignoto." The ascription to Shakespeare is generally, though not universally, accepted, such scepticism as exists being usually based upon the absence among his acknowledged works of anything with precisely the same characteristics. The poem exhibits the influence of a number of literary conventions, such as the congress of birds, the metaphysical quibbling on unity in duality, Platonic affection, the debate between Love and Reason, and the emblematic signification of the Phœnix and the Turtle-dove as typifying Rarity and Constancy, or Beauty and Truth. There is no difficulty in conceiving Shakespeare as joining with a group of his fellows to exercise his ingenuity on such themes. If the poem has any purpose beyond this, it would appear to celebrate a marriage that was not only childless but virginal. On the other hand, although it may contain more than meets the eye, no evidence exists for establishing an historical or personal reference.

Let the bird of loudest lay,
On the sole Arabian tree,
Herald sad and trumpet be,
To whose sound chaste wings obey.

But thou shrieking harbinger, 5
Foul precurrer of the fiend,
Augur of the fever's end,
To this troop come thou not near!

From this session interdict
Every fowl of tyrant wing, 10
Save the eagle, feath'red king;
Keep the obsequy so strict!

Let the priest in surplice white,
That defunctive music can,
Be the death-divining swan, 15
Lest the requiem lack his right.

And thou treble-dated crow,
That thy sable gender mak'st
With the breath thou giv'st and tak'st,
'Mongst our mourners shalt thou go. 20

Here the anthem doth commence:
Love and Constancy is dead;
Phœnix and the turtle fled
In a mutual flame from hence.

So they lov'd as love in twain 25
Had the essence but in one;
Two distincts, division none:
Number there in love was slain.

Hearts remote, yet not asunder;
Distance, and no space was seen 30
'Twixt this turtle and his queen:
But in them it were a wonder.

1. **bird of loudest lay.** The identity of the bird is not clear. 3. **sad:** serious, dignified. **trumpet:** trumpeter. 4. **chaste wings.** The reference is to the birds which are to be summoned. 5. **harbinger:** i.e., the screech-owl, believed to herald death. Hence "foul precurrer" (forerunner) in l. 6. 9. **interdict:** be debarred. 14. **defunctive:** funereal. **can:** knows, is skilled in. 15. **death-divining.** The swan was supposed to sing at the approach of its death. 16. **his right:** its due. 17. **treble-dated:** long-lived. 18. **gender:** race. **mak'st:** dost propagate. There was a curious notion that crows propagated their kind "at the bill." 23. **turtle:** turtle-dove. 24. **flame:** passion, love. 25–26. **as . . . one:** that their love made them in effect only one. The idea is expanded in ll. 27–28 and developed with variations throughout the poem. 32. **But in them:** in any but them.

So between them love did shine,
That the turtle saw his right
Flaming in the phœnix' sight;   35
Either was the other's mine.

Property was thus appalled,
That the self was not the same;
Single nature's double name
Neither two nor one was called.   40

Reason, in itself confounded,
Saw division grow together,
To themselves yet either neither;
Simple were so well compounded

That it cried, "How true a twain   45
Seemeth this concordant one!
Love hath reason, Reason none,
If what parts can so remain."

Whereupon it made this threne
To the phœnix and the dove,   50

Co-supremes and stars of love,
As chorus to their tragic scene.

THRENOS

Beauty, Truth, and Rarity,
Grace in all simplicity,
Here enclos'd, in cinders lie.   55

Death is now the phœnix' nest;
And the turtle's loyal breast
To eternity doth rest,

Leaving no posterity:
'Twas not their infirmity,   60
It was married chastity.

Truth may seem, but cannot be;
Beauty brag, but 'tis not she;
Truth and Beauty buried be.

To this urn let those repair   65
That are either true or fair;
For these dead birds sigh a prayer.

34. **his right**: i.e., the love due him. 35. **sight**: i.e., eyes. 36. **mine**: treasure. 37. **Property**. This word is a personified abstraction of the idea of individuality, what is peculiar to a person. 38. **That...same**: that single personality was lost in the fusing of identities. 42. **division**: separate things. 44. **Simple**: i.e., single elements. 45. **it**: Reason. 47–48. **Love...remain**: i.e., Love is right and Reason is wrong (has always been misguided), since distinct elements can attain such perfect union. 49. **threne**: lament, dirge.

INDEX TO THE CHARACTERS IN
SHAKESPEARE'S PLAYS

This Index records the act and scene in which each character first speaks, not necessarily the same as that in which he first appears. Only persons who speak are included, except a few marked with asterisk.

Aaron. TA. II. i.
Abbess, Lady. CofE. V. i.
Abergavenny, Lord. H8. I. i.
Abhorson. Meas. IV. ii.
Abraham. R&J. I. i.
Achilles. T&C. II. i.
Adam. AYLI. I. i.
Adrian. Tmp. II. i.
Adriana. CofE. II. i.
Ædile, an. Cor. III. i.
Ægeon. CofE. I. i.
Æmilia. CofE. V. i.
Æmilius. TA. IV. iv.
Æneas. T&C. I. i.
Agamemnon. T&C. I. iii.
Agrippa. A&C. II. ii.
Aguecheek, Sir Andrew. TwN. I. ii.
Ajax. T&C. II. i.
Alarbus. TA.*
Albany, Duke of. Lear I. i.
Alcibiades. Tim. I. i.
Alençon, Duke of. 1H6. I. ii.
Alexander. T&C. I. ii.
Alexas. A&C. I. ii.
Alice. H5. III. iv.
Alonso. Tmp. I. i.
Ambassadors. Hml. V. ii; H5. I. ii; 1H6. V. i.
Amiens. AYLI. II. i. v.
Andromache. T&C. V. iii.
Andronicus. *See* Titus, Marcus.
Angelo. CofE. III. i.
Angelo. Meas. I. i.
Angus. Mcb. I. ii.
Anne Bullen, Queen. H8. I. iv.
Anne, Lady. R3. I. ii.
Anne Page. MWW. I. i.
Antigonus. WT. II. i.
Antiochus, King of Antioch. Per. I. i.

Antipholus of Ephesus. CofE. III. i.
Antipholus of Syracuse. CofE. I. ii.
Antonio. Merch. I. i.
Antonio. MAdo. I. ii.
Antonio. Tmp. I. i.
Antonio. TGV. I. iii.
Antonio. TwN. II. i.
Antony. JC. I. ii; A&C. I. i.
Apemantus. Tim. I. i.
Apothecary. R&J. V. i.
Apparitions. Mcb. IV. i.
Archbishop. *See* York, Canterbury.
Archidamus. WT. I. i.
Ariel. Tmp. I. ii.
Armado, Don. LLL. I. ii.
Arragon, Prince of. Merch. II. ix.
Artemidorus. JC. II. iii.
Arthur, Duke of Bretagne. John II. i.
Arviragus. Cym. III. iii.
Astringer, Gentle. AWEW. V. i.
Attendants. A&C. I. ii; Hml. IV. vi. *See* Servants.
Audrey. AYLI. III. iii.
Aufidius, Tullus. Cor. I. ii.
Aumerle, Duke of. R2. I. iii.
Austria, Archduke of. John II. i. *See* Lymoges.
Autolycus. WT. IV. iii.
Auvergne, Countess of. 1H6. II. iii.

Bagot. R2. II. ii.
Balthasar. MAdo. II. iii.
Balthazar. CofE. III. i.
Balthazar. Merch. III. iv.
Balthazar. R&J. I. i.
Banditti. Tim. IV. iii.
Banquo. Mcb. I. iii.
Baptista. TofS. I. i.
Bardolph. 1H4. II. ii; 2H4. II. i; H5. II. i; MWW. I. i.

Venice, Duke of. Merch. IV. i.
Venice, Duke of. Oth. I. iii.
Ventidius. A&C. III. i.
Ventidius. Tim. I. ii.
Verges. MAdo. III. iii.
Vernon. 1H6. II. iv.
Vernon, Sir Richard. 1H4. IV. i.
Vincentio. TofS. IV. v.
Vincentio, Duke. Meas. I. i.
Vintner. 1H4. II. iv.
Viola. TwN. I. ii.
Violenta. AWEW. III. v.
Virgilia. Cor. I. iii.
Volsce, a. Cor. IV. iii.
Voltimand. Hml. I. ii.
Volumnia. Cor. I. iii.
Volumnius. JC. V. v.

Wall. MND. V. i.
Warders. 1H6. I. iii.
Wart. 2H4. III. ii.
Warwick (Beauchamp), Earl of. 2H4. III. i; H5.
    IV. viii; 1H6. II. iv.
Warwick (Nevil), Earl of. 2H6. I. i; 3H6. I. i.
Watchmen. Cor. V. ii; 3H6. IV. iii; MAdo. III.
    iii; R&J. V. iii.

Westminster, Abbot of. R2. IV. i.
Westmoreland, Earl of. 1H4. I. i; 2H4. IV. i; H5.
    I. ii.
Westmoreland, Earl of. 3H6. I. i.
Whitmore, Walter. 2H6. IV. i.
Widow. TofS. V. ii.
Widow, of Florence. AWEW. III. v.
William. AYLI. V. i.
Williams. H5. IV. i.
Willoughby, Lord. R2. II. i.
Winchester, Bishop of. 1H6. I. i; 2H6. I. i.
Winchester (Gardiner), Bishop of. H8. V. i.
Witches. Mcb. I. i.
Wolsey, Cardinal. H8. I. i.
Woodville. 1H6. I. iii.
Worcester, Earl of. 1H4. I. iii.

York, Archbishop of. See Rotherham and Scroop.
York, Duchess of. R2. V. ii.
York, Duchess of. R3. II. ii.
York, Duke of. H5. IV. iii.
York, Duke of. See Richard.
York, Duke of. See Richard, son of Edward
    IV.
York, Edmund Langley, Duke of. R2. II. i.
Young Marcius. Cor. V. iii.